International Dictionary of Films and Filmmakers - 2

DIRECTORS

International Dictionary of Films and Filmmakers

International Dictionary of Films and Filmmakers - 2

DIRECTORS

SECOND EDITION

EDITOR
NICHOLAS THOMAS

PICTURE EDITOR
LEANDA SHRIMPTON

St J

St James Press

Chicago and London

Front cover — Michael Powell

British Library Cataloguing in Publication Data
Directors. — 2nd ed.
 I. Thomas, Nicholas, *1965-*
 II. [The international dictionary of films
 and filmmakers]
 791.43

 ISBN 1-55862-038-9

Library of Congress Catalog Card Number: 90-64265

First edition published 1984;
second edition 1991.

CONTENTS

EDITOR'S NOTE

This is a revised edition of the second volume of the *International Dictionary of Films and Filmmakers.* The second edition of Volume 1, *Films,* was published in 1990, while new editions of Volume 3, *Actors and Actresses,* Volume 4, *Writers and Production Artists,* and Volume 5, a *Title Index* for the whole series, will follow.

The book comprises some 480 entries, each consisting of a brief biography, a complete filmography, a selected bibliography of works on and by the entrant, and an expository essay by a specialist in the field. Most of the entries from the previous edition have been retained here, although all have been thoroughly updated. There are, however, some 80 entrants new to this edition. (It should be noted that directors primarily associated with animation, many of whom appeared in the first edition of this volume, will now appear in the revised edition of Volume 4.) For the new edition, the format has been adapted and expanded for greater clarity, and, since film is primarily a visual medium, the majority of entries are illustrated, either by a portrait or by a representative still from the entrant's *oeuvre.*

The selection of entrants is once again based on the recommendations of the advisers listed on page xi. It was not thought necessary to propose criteria for selection: the book is intended to represent the wide range of interests within North American, British, and West European film scholarship and criticism. The eclecticism in both the list of entrants and the critical stances of the different writers emphasises the multifarious notions of the cinema, and indeed of the director's role within it. On the vexed question of authorship in the cinema, it is to be hoped that this volume is properly seen in the context of a series which also focusses on the contribution to the cinema of actors and actresses (Volume 3), along with screenwriters, cameramen, editors, animators, composers and other (Volume 4), as well as the individual films themselves (Volume 1).

Thanks are due to the following: the staff of the British Film Institute Library, where much of the research for this edition was carried out; Michael Moulds at the International Federation of Film Archives; all the advisers and contributors for their cooperation; and finally, my predecessors on this series, especially Jim Vinson, whose achievements I am proud and fortunate to build on.

A NOTE ON THE ENTRIES

Non-English language film titles are ordinarily given in the original language or a transliteration of it. Alternate release titles in the original language(s) are found within parentheses, in italic, and are followed by release titles in English (American then British if there is a difference). Titles have been placed within brackets if they are known to be literal translations not used as release titles.

In the list of films in each entry, information within parentheses following each film modifies, if necessary, then adds to the subject's principal function(s). The commonest abbreviations used are: "pr" — producer; "d" — director; "sc" — scenarist or scriptwriter; "ph" — cinematographer or director of photography; "ed" — editor; "assoc" — associate; "asst" — assistant; and "ro" — role. "co-" preceding a function indicates collaboration with one or more persons. A name in parentheses following a film title is that of the director.

ACKNOWLEDGEMENTS

We are grateful to the following for supplying photographs, and granting permission to reproduce them in this volume.

Artificial Eye Film Company Ltd (Bertrand Blier, Werner Herzog, Jim Jarmusch)

British Film Institute, Department of Stills, Posters and Designs

Cinemateca de Cuba (Santiago Alvarez, Sara Gómez, Humberto Solas)

Cinemateca do Museu de Arte Moderna, Rio de Janeiro (Humberto Mauro)

Cinepromotion, Berlin (Margarethe von Trotta)

Columbia Pictures Industries Inc. (Budd Boetticher, Peter Bogdanovich, Richard Brooks, John Cassavetes, Richard Fleischer, Jan Kadár, Elia Kazan, Fritz Lang, Anatole Litvak, Sidney Lumet, Anthony Mann, Sam Peckinpah, Bob Rafelson, Alan Rudolph, Claude Sautet, Franklin J. Schaffner, Steven Spielberg, Charles Vidor)

Curzon Film Distributors Ltd (Carlos Saura)

Daiei Co. Ltd., Tokyo (Teinosuke Kinugasa)

Enterprise Pictures Ltd (Pedro Almodóvar)

Film Polski, Warsaw (Jerzy Kawalerowicz, Andrzej Munk)

Les Films du Losange, Paris (Jacques Rivette)

Hulton-Deutsch Collection (Edward Dmytryk, Allan Dwan, Alexander Korda, Sergio Leone, Jerry Lewis, Walter Ruttman, Mack Sennett, John M. Stahl, George Stevens, Sergei Vasiliev, King Vidor, Erich von Stroheim, Harry Watt, James Whale, Fred Zinnemann)

Hungarofilm (Márta Mészáros)

The Kobal Collection (Hal Ashby, Bernardo Bertolucci, John Boorman, Mel Brooks, Luis Buñuel, George Cukor, Michael Curtiz, Delmer Daves, Brian De Palma, John Ford, Bill Forsyth, Henry Hathaway, George Lucas, Rouben Mamoulian, George Miller, Alan J. Pakula, Ken Russell)

Andrew Hamilton Lane (Costa-Gavras, Terence Davies, Stephen Frears, Derek Jarman, Neil Jordan)

Roger Mayne (Lindsay Anderson)

National Film Archive of India (Mehboob Khan, Bimal Roy)

Nikkatsu Corporation, Tokyo (Shohei Imamura)

Orion Pictures Corporation (Susan Seidelman)

Rank Film Distributors (John Carpenter)

The Samuel Goldwyn Company, © **1937** (Henry King)

Osvald Schorm (Evald Schorm)

Tazio Secchiaroli (Federico Fellini)

ADVISERS

Joseph Anderson
Dudley Andrew
Roy Armes
Dimitar Bardasky
Erik Barnouw
DeWitt Bodeen
Rui Santana Brito
Robert Burgoyne
Michel Ciment
David A. Cook
Robert Dunbar
Jack C. Ellis
William K. Everson
Greg S. Faller
Louis D. Giannetti
John Gillett
Douglas Gomery
E. Ann Kaplan

Ephraim Katz
Dave Kehr
Philip Kemp
Satti Khanna
Richard Dyer MacCann
Gerald Mast
Ib Monty
John Mraz
Liam O'Leary
Richard Peña
Lauren Rabinovitz
Maria Racheva
P. Adams Sitney
Anthony Slide
Frances Thorpe
Ravi Vasudevan
Robin Wood

CONTRIBUTORS

Charles Affron
Mirella Jona Affron
Anthony Ambrogio
Dudley Andrew
Roy Armes
José Arroyo
Jeanine Basinger
John Baxter
Audie Bock
DeWitt Bodeen
David Bordwell
Ronald Bowers
Stephen E. Bowles
Geoff Brown
Robert Burgoyne
Julianne Burton
Fred Camper
Michel Ciment
Tom Conley
Samantha Cook
R.F. Cousins
Tony D'Arpino
Charles Derry
Wheeler Winston Dixon
Susan M. Doll
Robert Dunbar
Raymond Durgnat
Rob Edelman
Robert Edmonds
Jack C. Ellis
Gretchen Elsner-Sommer
Patricia Erens
Mark W. Estrin
Quentin Falk
Greg S. Faller
Rodney Farnsworth
Howard Feinstein
Leslie Felperin

Lilie Ferrari
Theresa Fitzgerald
M.S. Fonseca
Alexa Foreman
Saul Frampton
John Gillett
Verina Glaessner
Douglas Gomery
Joseph Gomez
Patricia King Hanson
Steve Hanson
Ann Harris
Louise Heck-Rabi
Kyoko Hirano
Deborah Holdstein
Vivian Huang
Peter Hutchings
Stuart M. Kaminsky
Joel Kanoff
Dave Kehr
Philip Kemp
Satti Khanna
Katherine Singer Kovács
Joseph Lanza
James L. Limbacher
Richard Lippe
Kimball Lockhart
Janet E. Lorenz
Ed Lowry
G.C. Macnab
Elaine Mancini
Roger Manvell
Gina Marchetti
Gerald Mast
Vacláv Merhaut
Russell Merritt
Lloyd Michaels
Joseph Milicia

Norman Miller
Ib Monty
James Morrison
John Mraz
William T. Murphy
Ray Narducy
Dennis Nastav
Kim Newman
Bill Nichols
Clea H. Notar
Linda J. Obalil
Daniel O'Brien
John O'Kane
Liam O'Leary
Vladimir Opela
R. Barton Palmer
Richard Peña
Julian Petley
Duncan J. Petrie
Gene D. Phillips
Zuzana Mirjam Pick
Dana B. Polan
Richard Porton
Lauren Rabinovitz
Maria Racheva
Herbert Reynolds
E. Rubinstein
Marie Saeli
W. Curtis Schade
Lillian Schiff
H. Wayne Schuth

Michael Selig
David Shipman
Ulrike Sieglohr
Charles L.P. Silet
Scott Simmon
P. Adams Sitney
Josef Skvorecký
Anthony Slide
Edward S. Small
Eric Smoodin
Cecile Starr
Karel Tabery
Richard Taylor
J.P. Telotte
Nicholas Thomas
Doug Tomlinson
Andrew Tudor
Blažená Urgošíková
Ravi Vasudevan
Dorothee Verdaasdonk
Ginette Vincendeau
Mark Walker
Herman Weinberg
James M. Welsh
Dennis West
M.B. White
Colin Williams
Bill Wine
Rob Winning
Jessica R. Wolff
Robin Wood

International Dictionary of Films and Filmmakers-2
DIRECTORS

CONTENTS A-Z

Bert Haanstra
Robert Hamer
Susumu Hani
Henry Hathaway
Howard Hawks
Josef Heifitz
Astrid and Bjarne Henning-Jensen
Cecil Hepworth
Jaime Humberto Hermosillo
Werner Herzog
George Roy Hill
Walter Hill
Alfred Hitchcock
Holger-Madsen
Med Hondo
Hou Hsiao-Hsien
William K. Howard
John Hughes
John Huston

Kon Ichikawa
Tadashi Imai
Shohei Imamura
Rex Ingram
Otar Ioseliani
Juzo Itami
Joris Ivens
James Ivory

Miklos Jancsó
Derek Jarman
Jim Jarmusch
Humphrey Jennings
Norman Jewison
Jaromil Jireš
Neil Jordan
Claude Jutra

Karel Kachyna
Ján Kadár
Raj Kapoor
Lawrence Kasdan
Mani Kaul
Helmut Käutner
Jerzy Kawalerowicz
Elia Kazan
Buster Keaton
Krzysztof Kieślowski
Henry King
King Hu
Keisuke Kinoshita
Teinosuke Kinugasa
Elem Klimov
Alexander Kluge
Masaki Kobayashi
Alexander Korda
Andras Kovács
Grigori Kozintsev
Robert Kramer
Stanley Kubrick
Lev Kuleshov
Akira Kurosawa

Gregory La Cava
John Landis
Fritz Lang
Alberto Lattuada

Frank Launder and Sidney Gilliat
Richard Leacock
David Lean
Paul Leduc
Spike Lee
Roger Leenhardt
Jean-Pierre Lefebvre
Malcolm Le Grice
Mitchell Leisen
Claude Lelouch
Paul Leni
Sergio Leone
Mervyn Leroy
Richard Lester
Barry Levinson
Jerry Lewis
Joseph H. Lewis
Marcel L'Herbier
Miguel Littin
Anatole Litvak
Ken Loach
Pare Lorentz
Joseph Losey
Ernst Lubitsch
George Lucas
Sidney Lumet
Louis Lumière
David Lynch

Alexander Mackendrick
Dusan Makavejev
Terrence Malick
Louis Malle
Rouben Mamoulian
Joseph L. Mankiewicz
Anthony Mann
Chris Marker
Gregory Markopoulos
Humberto Mauro
Albert and David Maysles
Paul Mazursky
Leo McCarey
Norman Z. McLeod
Mehboob Khan
Jonas Mekas
Georges Méliès
Jean-Pierre Melville
Jirí Menzel
Márta Mészáros
Oscar Micheaux
Andrei Mikhalkov-Konchalovsky
Lewis Milestone
Claude Miller
George Miller
Vincente Minnelli
Kenji Mizoguchi
Gutaf Molander
Mario Monicelli
Robert Mulligan
Andrzej Munk
F.W. Murnau

Mikio Naruse
Jean Negulesco
Marshall Neilan
Jan Nemec
Fred Niblo

Mike Nichols

Sidney Olcott
Manoel de Oliveira
Ermanno Olmi
Marcel Ophuls
Max Ophüls
Nagisa Oshima
Ulrike Ottinger
Yasujiro Ozu

G.W. Pabst
Marcel Pagnol
Alan J. Pakula
Gleb Panfilov
Sergei Paradzhanov
Alan Parker
Pier Paolo Pasolini
Ivan Passer
Giovanni Pastrone
George Pearson
Sam Peckinpah
Arthur Penn
Nelson Pereira dos Santos
Lester James Peries
Pierre Perrault
Elio Petri
Dadasaheb Phalke
Maurice Pialat
Lupu Pick
Roman Polanski
Sydney Pollack
Abraham Polonsky
Gillo Pontecorvo
Edwin S. Porter
Michael Powell and Emeric Pressburger
Otto Preminger
Yakov Protazanov
Vsevolod Pudovkin

Bob Rafelson
Yvonne Rainer
Nicholas Ray
Satyajit Ray
Carol Reed
Michael Reeves
Karel Reisz
Jean Renoir
Alain Resnais
Tony Richardson
Hans Richter
Leni Riefenstahl
Dino Risi
Martin Ritt
Jacques Rivette
Glauber Rocha
Nicolas Roeg
Eric Rohmer
George A. Romero
Jørgen Roos
Francesco Rosi
Roberto Rossellini
Robert Rossen
Paul Rotha
Jean Rouch
Bimal Roy
Alan Rudolph

Raúl Ruiz
Ken Russell
Walter Ruttman

Jorge Sanjinés
Carlos Saura
Claude Sautet
Victor Saville
John Sayles
Franklin J. Schaffner
Fred Schepisi
John Schlesinger
Volker Schlöndorff
Ernest B. Schoedsack
Evald Schorm
Paul Schrader
Werner Schroeter
Ettore Scola
Martin Scorsese
Ridley Scott
Susan Seidelman
Ousmane Sembene
Mrinal Sen
Mack Sennett
Kaneto Shindo
Masahiro Shinoda
Esther Shub
Don Siegel
Joan Micklin Silver
Robert Siodmak
Douglas Sirk
Alf Sjöberg
Victor Sjöström
Jerzy Skolimowski
Michael Snow
Fernando E. Solanas and Octavio Getino
Humberto Solás
Steven Spielberg
John M. Stahl

Wolfgang Staudte
George Stevens
Robert Stevenson
Mauritz Stiller
Oliver Stone
Henri Storck
Jean-Marie Straub and Danièle Huillet
John Sturges
Preston Sturges
Arne Sucksdorff
Hans-Jurgen Syberberg
István Szabó

Alain Tanner
Andrei Tarkovsky
Frank Tashlin
Jacques Tati
Bertrand Tavernier
Paolo and Vittorio Taviani
Leopoldo Torre Nilsson
Jacques Tourneur
Maurice Tourneur
François Truffaut

Edgar Ulmer

Roger Vadim
Stan Vanderbeek
Willard Van Dyke
Agnès Varda
Sergei and Georgi Vasiliev
Dziga Vertov
Charles Vidor
King Vidor
Jean Vigo
Luchino Visconti
Alexander Volkov
Josef von Sternberg
Erich von Stroheim

Margarethe von Trotta

Andrzej Wajda
Raoul Walsh
Charles Walters
Andy Warhol
John Waters
Peter Watkins
Harry Watt
Lois Weber
Peter Weir
Jiri Weiss
Orson Welles
William Wellman
Wim Wenders
Lina Wertmüller
James Whale
Joyce Wieland
Robert Wiene
Herbert Wilcox
Billy Wilder
Robert Wise
Frederick Wiseman
Sam Wood
Basil Wright
William Wyler

Xie Jin

Peter Yates
Kozabura Yoshimura

Krzysztof Zanussi
Franco Zeffirelli
Robert Zemeckis
Mai Zetterling
Fred Zinnemann

A

AKERMAN, Chantal.

Belgian. Born in Brussels, June 1950. Educated at INSAS film school, Brussels, 1967–68; studied at Université Internationale du Théâtre, Paris, 1968–69. Career: *Saute ma vie* entered in Oberhausen festival, 1971; lived in New York, 1972; returned to France, 1973.

Films as Director:

1968   *Saute ma vie*
1971   *L'Enfant aimé*
1972   *Hotel Monterey*; *La Chambre*
1973   *Le 15/18* (co-d); *Hanging Out Yonkers* (unfinished)
1974   *Je tu il elle*
1975   ***Jeanne Dielman, 23 Quai du Commerce, 1080 Bruxelles***
1977   *News from Home*
1978   *Les Rendez-vous d'Anna*
1980   *Dis-moi*
1982   *Toute une nuit* (*All Night Long*)
1983   *Les Années 80* (*The Golden Eighties*) (co-sc); *Un Jour pina a demandé*
1984   *L'Homme à la valise*; *J'ai faim, j'ai froid* (episode in *Paris vu par . . . 20 ans après*); *Family Business*; *New York, New York Bis*
1989   *Histoires d'Amérique: Food, Family and Philosophy/American Stories*

Publications:

By AKERMAN: book—

Les Rendez-vous d'Anna, Paris, 1978.

By AKERMAN: articles—

Interview with C. Alemann and H. Hurst, in *Frauen und Film* (Berlin), March 1976.
Interview with Danièle Dubroux, and others, in *Cahiers du Cinéma* (Paris), July 1977.
Interview with P. Carcassone and L. Cugny, in *Cinématographe* (Paris), November 1978.
Interview in *Stills* (London), December 1984-January 1985.
Interview in *Inter/View* (New York), February 1985.
Interview in *Cinéma* (Paris), 25 June 1986.
Interview in *Nouvel Observateur* (Paris), 28 September 1989.

On AKERMAN: articles—

Bertolina, G., "Chantal Akerman: il cinema puro," in *Filmcritica* (Rome), March 1976.
Creveling, C., "Women Working," in *Camera Obscura* (Berkeley), Fall 1976.
Mairesse, E., "A propos des films de Chantal Akerman: Un temps atmosphere," in *Cahiers du Cinéma* (Paris), October 1977.
Bergstrom, Janet, in *Camera Obscura* (Berkeley), Fall 1978.
Martin, Angela, "Chantal Akerman's Films," in *Feminist Review*, no. 3, 1979.
Seni, N., in *Frauen und Film* (Berlin), September 1979.

Perlmutter, Ruth, "Visible Narrative, Visible Woman," in *Millenium* (New York), Spring 1980.
Delavaud, G., "Les chemins de Chantal Akerman," in *Cahiers du Cinéma* (Paris), April 1981.
Philippon, A., "Fragments bruxellois/Nuit torride," in *Cahiers du Cinéma* (Paris), November 1982.
Dossier on Akerman, in *Versus* (Nijmegen), no. 1, 1985.
Barrowclough, S., "Chantal Akerman: Adventures in perception," in *Monthly Film Bulletin* (London), April 1984.
Squire, C., "Toute une heure," in *Screen* (London), November–December 1984.
Castiel, E., in *24 Images* (Montreal), nos. 34/35, 1987.
Paskin, Sylvia, "Waiting for the next shot," in *Monthly Film Bulletin* (London), March 1990.

*   *   *

At 15 Chantal Akerman saw Godard's *Pierrot le fou* and realized that filmmaking could be experimental and personal. She dropped in and out of film school and has since created short and feature films for viewers who appreciate the chance to think about sounds and images. Her films are often shot in real time, and in space that is part of the characters' identity.

During a self-administered apprenticeship in New York (1972–74) shooting short films on very low budgets, Akerman learned much, she has said, from the work of innovators Michael Snow and Stan Brakhage. She was encouraged to explore organic techniques for her personal subject matter. In her deliberately paced films there are long takes, scenes shot with stationary camera, and a play of light in relation to subjects and their space. (In *Jeanne Dielman, 23 Quai du Commerce, 1080 Bruxelles*, as Jeanne rides up or down in the elevator, diagonals of light from each floor cut across her face in a regular rhythm.) There are vistas down long corridors, acting with characters' backs to the camera, and scenes concluded with several seconds of darkness. In Akerman films there are hotels and journeys, little conversation. Windows are opened and sounds let in, doors opened and closed; we hear a doorbell, a radio, voices on the telephone answering machine, footsteps, city noises. Each frame is carefully composed, each gesture the precise result of Akerman's direction. A frequent collaborator is her sensitive cameraperson Babette Mangolte who has worked with Akerman on *Jeanne Dielman, 23 Quai du Commerce, 1080 Bruxelles, News from Home* and *Toute une nuit*. Mangolte has also worked with avant gardists Yvonne Rainer, Marcel Hanoun and Michael Snow.

In Akerman films plot is minimal, or non-existent. Old welfare clients come and go amid the impressive architecture of a once splendid hotel on New York's Upper West Side in *Hotel Monterey*. New York City plays its busy, noisy self for the camera as Akerman's voice on the sound track reads concerned letters from her mother in Belgium in *News from Home*. A young filmmaker travels to Germany to appear at a screening of her latest film, meets people who distress her, and her mother who delights her, and returns home in *Les Rendez-vous d'Anna.* Jeanne Dielman, super-efficient housewife, earns money as a prostitute to support herself and her son. Her routine breaks down by chance, and she murders one of her customers.

The films (some semi-autobiographical) are not dramatic in the conventional sense, nor are they glamorized or eroticized; the excitement is inside the characters. In a film Akerman calls a love letter to her mother, Jeanne Dielman is seen facing the steady camera as members of a cooking class might see her, and she prepares a meatloaf—in real time. Later she gives herself a thorough scrubbing in the bathtub; only her head and the motion of her arms are visible. Her straightening and arranging and smoothing are seen as a child would see and remember them.

In *Toute une nuit* Akerman continues her precision and control as she stages the separate, audience-involving adventures of a huge cast of all ages that wanders out into Brussels byways one hot, stormy night. In this film, reminiscent of Wim Wenders and his wanderers and Marguerite Duras with her inventive sound tracks, choreography and sense of place, Akerman continues to explore her medium using no conventional plot, few spoken words, many sounds, people leaving the frame to a lingering camera, and appealing images. A little girl asks a man to dance with her, and he does. The filmmaker's feeling for the child and the child's independence can't be mistaken.

—Lillian Schiff

ALDRICH, Robert.

American. Born in Cranston, Rhode Island, 9 August 1918. Educated at Moses Brown School, Providence, and University of Virginia, graduated (law and economics) 1941. Married Harriet Foster, 1941 (divorced 1965); children: Adell, William, Alida, and Kelly; married fashion model Sibylle Siegfried, 1966. Worked for RKO studios, 1941–1944; under contract to Enterprise studios, 1945–1948; TV director, from 1952; founded "Associates and Aldrich Company," 1955; signed contract for Columbia Pictures, then fired after refusing to "soften" script of *The Garment Jungle*; after five year period working abroad, returned to Hollywood, 1962; after *The Dirty Dozen*, established Aldrich Studios, 1967, but forced to sell up, 1973; elected President of the Directors Guild, 1975; "Aldrich Company" reorganised, 1976. Recipient: Silver Prize, Venice Festival, for *The Big Knife*, 1955; Silver Bear Award for Best Direction, Berlin Festival, for *Autumn Leaves*, 1956; Italian Critics Award, Venice Festival, for *Attack!*, 1956. *Died in Los Angeles, of kidney failure, 5 December 1983.*

Films as Director:

1953   *The Big Leaguer*
1954   *World for Ransom* (+co-pr); *Apache*; *Vera Cruz*
1955   *Kiss Me Deadly* (+pr); *The Big Knife* (+pr)
1956   *Autumn Leaves*; *Attack!* (+pr)
1957   *The Garment Jungle* (un-credited)
1959   *The Angry Hills*; *Ten Seconds to Hell* (+co-sc)
1961   *The Last Sunset*
1962   *Sodoma e Gomorra* (*Sodom and Gomorrah*); *Whatever Happened to Baby Jane?* (+pr)
1963   *Four for Texas* (+co-pr, co-sc)
1964   *Hush . . . Hush, Sweet Charlotte* (+pr)
1966   *Flight of the Phoenix* (+pr)

1967   *The Dirty Dozen*
1968   *The Legend of Lylah Clare* (+pr); *The Killing of Sister George* (+pr)
1969   *Too Late the Hero* (+pr, co-sc)
1971   *The Grissom Gang* (+pr)
1972   *Ulzana's Raid*
1973   *Emperor of the North* (*The Emperor of the North Pole*)
1974   *The Longest Yard* (*The Mean Machine*)
1975   *Hustle* (+co-pr)
1977   *Twilight's Last Gleaming*; *The Choirboys*
1979   *The Frisco Kid*
1981   *All the Marbles* (*California Dolls*)

Other Films:

1945   ***The Southerner*** (Renoir) (1st asst-d)
1946   *The Story of G.I. Joe* (Wellman) (1st asst-d); *Pardon My Past* (Fenton) (1st asst-d); *The Strange Love of Martha Ivers* (Milestone) (1st asst-d)
1947   *The Private Affairs of Bel Ami* (Lewin) (1st asst-d); *Body and Soul* (Rossen) (1st asst-d)
1948   *Arch of Triumph* (Milestone) (1st asst-d); *So This is New York* (Fleischer) (1st asst-d); *No Minor Vices* (Milestone) (1st asst-d)
1949   *Force of Evil* (Polonsky) (1st asst-d); *The Red Pony* (Milestone) (1st asst-d); *A Kiss for Corliss* (Wallace) (1st asst-d)
1950   *The White Tower* (Tetzlaff) (1st asst-d); *Teresa* (Zinnemann) (pre-production work)
1951   *The Prowler* (Losey) (1st asst-d); *M* (Losey) (1st asst-d); *Of Men and Music* (Reis) (1st asst-d); *New Mexico* (Reis) (1st asst-d)
1952   *Abbott and Costello Meet Captain Kidd* (Lamont) (1st asst-d); ***Limelight*** (Chaplin) (1st asst-d); *The Trio: Rubinstein, Heifetz and Piatigorsky* (*Million Dollar Trio*) (Dassin) (1st asst-d); *The Steel Trap* (Stone) (pr supervision)
1957   *The Ride Back* (pr)
1969   *Whatever Happened to Aunt Alice?* (pr)

Publications:

By ALDRICH: articles—

Interview with George Fenin, in *Film Culture* (New York), July/August 1956.
Interviews with François Truffaut, in *Cahiers du Cinéma* (Paris), November 1956 and April 1958.
"High Price of Independence," in *Films and Filming* (London), June 1958.
"Learning from My Mistakes," in *Films and Filming* (London), June 1960.
"Hollywood . . . Still an Empty Tomb," in *Cinema* (Beverly Hills), May/June 1963.
"What Ever Happened to American Movies?," in *Sight and Sound* (London), Winter 1963/64.
Interview with Joel Greenburg, in *Sight and Sound* (London), Winter 1968/69.
"Why I Bought My Own Studio," in *Action* (Los Angeles), January/February 1969.
"Impressions of Russia," in *Action* (Los Angeles), July/August 1971.
"Dialogue," with Bernardo Bertolucci, in *Action* (Los Angeles), March/April 1974.
"Up to Date with Robert Aldrich," interview with Harry Ringel, in *Sight and Sound* (London), Summer 1974.
"Aldrich Interview," with Pierre Sauvage, in *Movie* (London), Winter 1976/77.
"Dialogue on Film: Robert Aldrich," in *American Film* (Washington, D.C.), November 1978.

On ALDRICH: books—

Micha, Rene, *Robert Aldrich*, Brussels, 1957.
Higham, Charles, *The Celluloid Muse: Hollywood Directors Speak*, London, 1969.

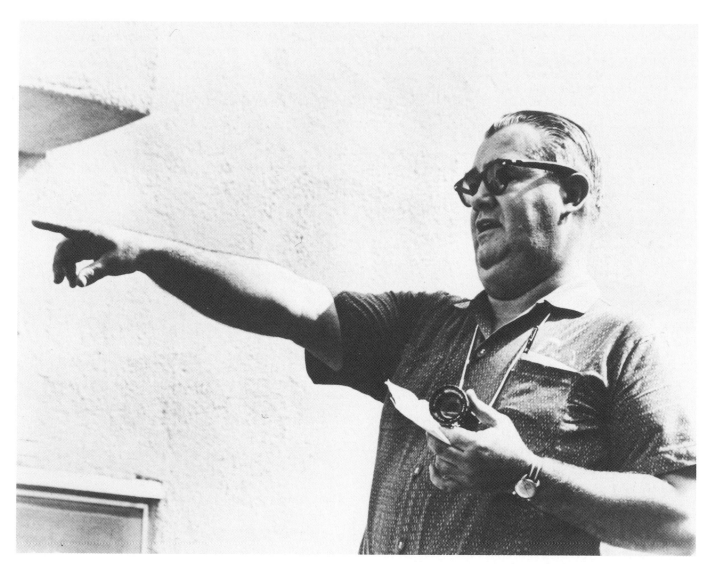

Robert Aldrich

Silver, Alain, and Elizabeth Ward, *Robert Aldrich: A Guide to References and Resources*, Boston, 1979.
Salizzato, Claver, *Robert Aldrich*, Florence, 1983.
Piton, Jean-Pierre, *Robert Aldrich*, Paris, 1985.
Arnold, Edwin T., and Eugene L. Miller, *The Films and Career of Robert Aldrich*, Knoxville, Tennessee, 1986.
Maheo, Michel, *Robert Aldrich*, Paris, 1987.

On ALDRICH: articles—

Rivette, Jacques, "On Revolution," in *Cahiers du Cinéma* (Paris), no. 54, 1955.
Jarvie, Ian, "Hysteria and Authoritarianism in the Films of Robert Aldrich," in *Film Culture* (New York), Summer 1961.
Cameron, Ian, and Mark Shivas, "Interview and Filmography," in *Movie* (London), April 1963.
Bitsch, Charles, and Bertrand Tavernier, "La Fonction de Producer," and Claude Chabrol, "Directed By:," in *Cahiers du Cinéma* (Paris), December/January 1964/65.
Silke, James, editor, "Robert Aldrich," in *Dialogue on Film* (Washington, D.C.), no. 2, 1972.
Silver, Alain, "Mr Film Noir Stays at the Table," in *Film Comment* (New York), Spring 1972.
Beaupre, Lee, "Bob Aldrich: Candid Maverick," in *Variety* (New York), 27 June 1973.
Ringel, Harry, "Robert Aldrich: The Director as Phoenix," in *Take One* (Montreal), September 1974.

Silver, Alain, "*Kiss Me Deadly*: Evidence of a Style," in *Film Comment* (New York), March/April 1975.
Combs, Richard, "Worlds Apart: Aldrich Since *The Dirty Dozen*," in *Sight and Sound* (London), Spring 1976.
Duval, B., "Aldrich le rebelle," in *Image et Son* (Paris), May 1976.
Legrand, Gerard, "Robert Aldrich et l'incompletude du nihilism," in *Positif* (Paris), June 1976.
Gazano, R., and M. Cusso, "L'Homme d'Aldrich," in *Cinéma* (Paris), June 1980.
McCarthy, T., obituary of Aldrich in *Variety* (New York), 7 December 1983.
"Aldrich Section" of *Cinéma* (Paris), February 1984.
"Robert Aldrich," in *Film Dope* (London), March 1985, and March 1988.
Lang, Robert, "Looking for the 'Great Whatzit': *Kiss Me Deadly* and Film Noir," in *Cinema Journal* (Champaign, Illinois), Spring 1988.

*   *   *

Despite a commercially respectable career both within the studio system and as an independent producer-director, Robert Aldrich remains an ill-appreciated, if not entirely bothersome presence for most American critics. Andrew Sarris did praise Aldrich in 1968 as "one of the most strikingly personal directors of the past two decades"; yet, for the most part, it has remained to the French and the English to attempt to unravel the defiant quirkiness of Aldrich's career. Only the other-worldly *Kiss Me Deadly*, which Paul Schrader unequivocally dubbed "the masterpiece of film noir," has received anything like the attention it deserves on this side of the Atlantic; yet the film is quite indicative of the bitter ironies, bizarre stylistics and scathing nihilism characteristic of most of Aldrich's work.

In bringing Mickey Spillane's neo-fascist hero Mike Hammer to the screen, *Kiss Me Deadly* plays havoc with the conventions of the hardboiled detective, turning the existential avenger into a narcissistic materialist who exploits those around him for the benefit of his plush lifestyle. In an outrageous alteration of the novel's plot, Hammer becomes a modern neanderthal whose individualism is revealed as insanity when it causes him to botch a case involving a box of pure nuclear energy and thus the fate of the world. The result is a final shot of a mushroom cloud rising from a California beachhouse, consuming both Hammer and the bad guys. Only at this extreme and this distance in time has Aldrich's acute sense of irony impressed itself upon a liberal critical establishment whose repugnance to the surfaces of his films has usually served as an excuse for ignoring their savage, multi-layered critiques of Hollywood genres and American ideology.

The extremity of Aldrich's re-interpretations of the Western in *Ulzana's Raid*, of the war movie in *Attack!*, of the cop film in *The Choirboys*, and of the women's melodrama in *Autumn Leaves* betrays a cynicism so bitter that it could only arise from a liberal sensibility utterly disillusioned by an age in which morality has become a cruel joke. In fact, the shattering of illusions is central to Aldrich's work, and it is a powerfully self-destructive process, given the sweetness of the illusions and the anger of his iconoclasm. In *Whatever Happened to Baby Jane?*, a gothic horror film whose terms are explicitly the hideous realities hidden beneath the sugar-coating of the entertainment industry, Aldrich virtually defines the genre of camp, offering derisive laughter as the only alternative to an unbearably absurd cosmos. This sense of black comedy (which Aldrich shares with, and developed at the same time as, Hollywood contemporary Stanley Kubrick) has frequently been responsible for the volatile relationship his films have had with popular audiences. Given the context of a life-and-death prison football game in *The Longest Yard*, Aldrich was able to enlist the audience in the hero's bitter laughter in the face of a triumphant totalitarian authority. But when he adopted the same black humor toward the scandalous chicanery of the marginally psychotic cops in *The Choirboys*, he angered almost everybody, not the least of whom was the novel's author Joseph Wambaugh.

Turned in an introspective direction, Aldrich's acid sensibility resulted in an intensely discomforting, stylistically alienated version of Clifford Odets's Hollywood-hating *The Big Knife* and the madly ambitious *The Legend of Lylah Clare*, an *8½* cum *Vertigo* far too complex by any Hollywood standard. When turned outward toward the world at large, that same sensibility was responsible for a downbeat, disheartening masterpiece like the much-maligned *Hustle*, a film which succeeds better than almost any other in summing up the moral displacement and emotional anguish of the whole decade of the 1970's.

At his most skillful, Aldrich could juggle ideologically volatile issues so well that his most popular film *The Dirty Dozen*, made during the politically turbulent period of the Vietnam war, played equally well to hawks and doves. Its story of death row prisoners exploited by the military bureaucracy into participation in a suicide raid, where they are to attack a chateau, slaughtering both German officers and civilians, seemed explicitly antiwar in its equation of heroism and criminality and its critique of the body-count mentality of a morally corrupt system. Yet, *The Dirty Dozen* still managed to emerge as a gung-ho war movie in the best Hollywood tradition. The multiple contradictions of the film's stance are nowhere clearer than in its climactic scene, where Aldrich has black athlete Jim Brown re-create one of his famous touchdown runs in order to set off an underground holocaust explicitly parallelled to Auschwitz.

In a far less popular film, the revisionist western *Ulzana's Raid*, Aldrich does confront the horrors of Vietnam with a nearly intolerable accuracy via the properly bloody metaphor of a cavalry company using West Point tactics to fight a band of Apache guerilla warriors. The film relentlessly refuses to diminish the brutality of the red man; even as it demonstrates the poverty of the white man's Christian idealism. The result is perhaps the first western ever to cast America's doctrine of Manifest Destiny in explicitly colonial terms.

More than any other mainstream director, Aldrich insisted on presenting the radical contradictions of American ideology. If we adopt a stance not nearly as cynical as his own in most of his films, we might observe that his capacity to do so has frequently resulted in sizable profits. Yet it is also important to remember that, while Stanley Kubrick (whose 1950's films bear striking stylistic and thematic similarities to those of Aldrich) found it necessary to retreat to England, reducing his output to two or three films a decade, Aldrich chose to fight it out in Hollywood, where his capacity for money-making allowed him the space to vent his own personal anger at the compromises we all must make.

—Ed Lowry

ALEA, Tomas Gutiérrez. *See* **GUTIÉRREZ ALEA, Tomas.**

ALLÉGRET, Yves.

French. Born in Paris, 13 October 1907. Married actress Simone Signoret, 1944 (divorced 1949), one daughter. Introduced to film industry by brother Marc Allégret, 1929; worked as assistant director, 1931; directed short films, 1932–1939; first worked with writer Jacques Sigurd (on *Dédée d'Anvers*, starring Signoret), 1948. Awarded (posthumous) César for Career Achievement, 1987. *Died in Paris, 31 January 1987.*

Films as Director:

1932   *Ténériffe* (short)
1934   *Prix et profits* (short)
1935   *Le Gagnant* (short)
1938   *Jeunes Filles de France* (*The Girls of France*) (doc short)
1939   *L'Émigrante* (co-d, +co-sc)
1941   *La Roue tourne* (unfinished); *Tobie est un ange* (unreleased, destroyed)
1942   *Les Deux Timides* (*Jeunes Timides*) (under pseudonym Yves Champlain, +sc)
1943   *La Boîte aux rêves* (begun by Jean Choux) (+co-sc)
1946   *Les Démons de l'aube*
1948   *Dédée d'Anvers* (*Dédée*) (+co-sc)
1949   *Une si jolie petite plage* (Riptide)
1950   *Manèges* (*The Cheat*, *Riding for a Fall*)

Yves Allegret: Marcel Dalio and Simone Signoret in *Dédée d'Anvers*

1951 *Les Miracles n'ont lieu qu'une fois*
1952 *Nez de cuir* (+adapt); "La Luxure (Lust)" episode of *Les Sept Péchés capitaux* (*The Seven Deadly Sins*); *La Jeune Folle* (*Desperate Decision*)
1953 *Les Orgueilleux* (*The Proud and the Beautiful*) (+co-sc)
1954 *Mam'zelle Nitouche* (+co-sc)
1955 *Oasis*
1956 *La Meilleure Part* (+co-sc)
1957 *Quand la femme s'en mêle*; *Méfiez-vous fillettes* (*Young Girls Beware*)
1958 *La Fille de Hambourg* (*Port of Desire*) (+co-sc)
1959 *L'Ambitieuse*
1961 *La Chien de pique* (+co-sc)
1962 *Terreur sur la savane* (*Konga-Yo*) (+co-sc; doc)
1963 *Germinal*
1966 *Johnny Banco* (+co-sc)
1970 *L'Invasion*
1975 *Orzowei*
1976 *Mords pas—on t'aime* (+co-sc)

Other Films:

1931 *Les Amants de minuit* (Genina and Marc Allégret) (asst-d); *Mam'zelle Nitouche* (Marc Allégret) (asst-d); *L'Amour à l'americaine* (Fejos and Heymann) (asst-d); *La Chienne* (Renoir) (asst-d); *Fantômas* (Fejos) (asst-d)
1933 *Ciboulette* (Autant-Lara) (co-costume des)
1934 *Lac-aux-Dames* (Marc Allégret) (asst-d)
1936 *Vous n'avez rien à déclarer?* (Joannon) (asst-d)

1937 *Forfaiture* (L'Herbier) (tech advisor)

Publications:

On ALLÉGRET: articles—

Truffaut, François, "Une certaine tendance du cinéma française," in *Cahiers du Cinéma* (Paris), January 1954.
Image et Son (Paris), February 1954.
Films and Filming (London), October 1955.
"Yves Allégret," in *Film Dope* (London), December 1972 and March 1988.
Obituary in *Cinéma* (Paris), 4 February 1987.
Obituary in *Variety* (New York), 4 February 1987.
Adair, Gilbert, in *Independent* (London), 9 February 1987.
Revue du Cinéma (Paris), May 1987.

*   *   *

Yves Allégret followed his older brother Marc into the cinema in 1929. A friend from the outset of Cavalcanti, Renoir, and the producer Diamant-Berger, he was destined to find a place in the burgeoning Paris film industry at the birth of the sound era.

Displaying a sharp technical aptitude, he was hired by Pierre Braunberger to oversee the installation of sound in his suburban Billancourt studios. One of Braunberger's first productions was to be Renoir's *La Chienne* and Allégret was kept on to serve as assistant.

His apprenticeship was exemplary for he moved both in cinematic and theatrical circles (assisting his brother on the wonderful *Lac-aux-Dames* and Autant-Lara on *Ciboulette*) while helping the October Group put on their guerrilla theater sketches around Paris. He became a trusted resource and was even asked by Renoir to finish *A Day in the Country* when the master was forced to leave that little film to supervise *La Marseillaise*.

But *A Day in the Country* was shelved by Braunberger, initiating an excruciating series of unfinished and censored projects that dogged Allégret's career right through to the Liberation. It was not until 1948, nearly twenty years after he had entered the field, that Allégret made a notable film. The success of *Dédée d'Anvers* has been attributed by many to its scriptwriter Jacques Sigurd. In truth Sigurd and Allégret, working together for the first time here, discovered a theme and a style that would carry them through several other successes. This approach, termed "psychological realism," was a product of script, direction, and acting alike.

All this sounds like a return to "poetic realism," and undoubtedly Allégret was hoping to repeat the Carné-Prévert pre-war successes. But the times had changed and his style was much more analytic just as Sigurd's scripts were far more bitter.

Dédée d'Anvers is the story of smalltime gangsters. Simone Signoret, Marcel Dalio, and Bernard Blier live lives of jealousy and distrust in the bistros and along the docks of Anvers. As their petty crimes move toward murder a film noir style is invoked, only the component of suspense is deliberately downplayed in favor of atmosphere and acting.

Both this film and its successor *Une si jolie petite place*, undoubtedly Allégret's greatest work, expend all their effort in depicting an atmosphere of despair that drives the hero of the latter, Gérard Philipe, to a Gabin-like suicide at the end. But Allégret doesn't share his hero's dreams the way Carné seemed to. Instead he observes, almost sadistically, the debilitating effect of small town life on a character whose past haunts him. The incessant rain, the grotesque visitors in the hotel, and the back-alley sex give him no reprieve from his past and drive him to his death.

In *Manèges* Sigurd and Allégret go further in taking apart the hypocritical lives of their characters. This time Simone Signoret is an undisguised cynic as she seduces a wealthy bourgeois and then robs him blind while consorting with lovers from her own lower class. The filmmakers' cynicism is as great as that of their heroine. While still wielding a powerfully evocative style in painting this atmosphere of upper-class hypocrisy and lower-class sex, Allégret's utter misanthropy begins to turn the film toward satire. With no respect for his characters and with a Darwinian view of private and social behavior, a patronizing tone results.

Of his many later films, only *Les Orgueilleux* compares in stature to the 1948–50 trilogy. Adapted from a novel by Sartre, Allégret's penchant for nasty details and intolerable living conditions comes out in this existentialist (non)morality play. The excessive wearing down of the characters that is part of his psychological realism this time was in tune with the film's philosophic theme.

Yves Allégret is not a likable director. His long career produced only four powerful films, all of which dwell excessively on human meanness. Yet his genius for making us feel this meanness and his audacious effort to make everything including plot serve the unveiling of human motivation make him perhaps the key filmmaker of the immediate post-war period.

—Dudley Andrew

_____

ALLEN, Woody.

American. Born Allen Stewart Konigsberg in Brooklyn, 1 December 1935. Educated at Midwood High School, Brooklyn, at New York University, and at City College of New York. Married Harlene Rosen, 1954 (divorced); Louise Lasser, 1966 (divorced); one son and one daughter by actress Mia Farrow. Joined staff of Sid Caesar Show, 1952; became stand-up comedian, 1961; hired by producer Charles Feldman to write *What's New, Pussycat?*, 1964; production of his play *Don't Drink the Water* opened on Broadway, 1966; starred in Broadway run of *Play It Again, Sam*, 1969–1970; began collaboration with writer Marshall Brickman, 1976. Recipient: Oscar for Best Direction, *Annie Hall*, 1976, and for Best Screenplay, *Annie Hall* (co-recipient), 1976, and *Hannah and Her Sisters*, 1986. Address: c/o Rollins and Joffe, 130 W. 57th Street, New York, NY 10019.

Films as Director, Scriptwriter, and Actor:

1969 *Take the Money and Run*
1971 *Bananas* (co-sc)
1972 *Everything You Always Wanted to Know About Sex But Were Afraid to Ask*
1973 *Sleeper*
1975 *Love and Death*
1977 **Annie Hall** (co-sc)
1978 *Interiors* (d, sc only)
1979 **Manhattan** (co-sc)
1980 *Stardust Memories*
1982 *A Midsummer Night's Sex Comedy*
1983 **Zelig**
1984 *Broadway Danny Rose*
1985 *The Purple Rose of Cairo* (d, sc only); *Hannah and her Sisters*
1986 *Radio Days* (role as narrator)
1987 *September* (d, sc only)
1988 *Another Woman* (d, sc only)
1989 "Oedipus Wrecks" episode in *New York Stories*
1990 *Crimes and Misdemeanors*

Other Films:

1965 *What's New, Pussycat?* (sc, ro)
1966 *What's Up, Tiger Lily?* (co-sc, +assoc.pr, ro as host/narrator); *Don't Drink the Water* (play basis)
1967 *Casino Royale* (Huston and others) (ro)
1972 *Play It Again, Sam* (Ross) (sc, ro)
1976 *The Front* (Ritt) (ro)
1990 *Scenes from a Mall* (Mazursky) (ro)

Publications:

By ALLEN: books—

Getting Even, New York, 1971.
Without Feathers, New York, 1976.
The Floating Lightbulb, New York, 1982.
Four Films of Woody Allen (Annie Hall, Interiors, Manhattan, Stardust Memories), New York, 1983.
Hannah and Her Sisters, New York, 1987.
Three Films of Woody Allen (Zelig, Broadway Danny Rose, The Purple Rose of Cairo), New York, 1987.

By ALLEN: articles—

"Woody Allen Interview," with Robert Mundy and Stephen Mamber, in *Cinema* (Beverly Hills), Winter 1972/73.
"The Art of Comedy: Woody Allen and *Sleeper*," interview with J. Trotsky, in *Filmmakers Newsletter* (Ward Hill, Mass.), Summer 1974.
"A Conversation with the Real Woody Allen (or Someone Just Like Him)," with K. Kelley, in *Rolling Stone* (New York), 1 July 1976.

Woody Allen

"Woody Allen is Feeling Better," interview with B. Drew, in *American Film* (Washington, D.C.), May 1977.

"Comedy Directors: Interviews with Woody Allen," with M. Karman, in *Millimeter* (New York), October 1977.

"Scenes from a Mind," interview with I. Halberstadt, in *Take One* (Montreal), November 1978.

"Vous avez dit Woody?," interview with Robert Benayoun, in *Positif* (Paris), May 1984.

"The Kobal Tapes: Woody Allen," interview with John Kobal, in *Films and Filming* (London), December 1985.

"Fears of a Clown," an interview with Tom Shales, and "Killing Joke," an interview with Roger Ebert, in *Time Out* (London), 1 November 1989.

Interview with Silvio Bizio, in *Empire* (London), August 1990.

On ALLEN: books—

Lax, Eric, *On Being Funny: Woody Allen and Comedy*, New York, 1975.

Jacobs, Diane, . . . *But We Need the Eggs: The Magic of Woody Allen*, New York, 1982.

Brode, Douglas, *Woody Allen: His Films and Career*, London, 1985.

Benayoun, Robert, *Woody Allen: Beyond Words*, London, 1987; as *The Films of Woody Allen*, New York, 1987.

Bendazzi, Giannalberto, *The Films of Woody Allen*, Florence, 1987.

de Navacelle, Thierry, *Woody Allen on Location*, London, 1987.

Pogel, Nancy, *Woody Allen*, Boston 1987.

Sinyard, Neil, *The Films of Woody Allen*, London, 1987.

McCann, Graham, *Woody Allen: New Yorker*, New York, 1990.

On ALLEN: articles—

"Woody, Woody Everywhere," in *Time* (New York), 14 April 1967.

"Woody Allen Issue," of *Cinema* (Beverly Hills), Winter 1972/73.

Wasserman, Harry, "Woody Allen: Stumbling Through the Looking Glass," in *Velvet Light Trap* (Madison), Winter 1972/73.

Maltin, Leonard, "Take Woody Allen—Please!," in *Film Comment* (New York), March–April 1974.

Remond, A., "*Annie Hall*," in *Avant-Scène du Cinéma* (Paris), 15 December 1977.

Yacowar, Maurice, "Forms of Coherence in the Woody Allen Comedies," in *Wide Angle* (Athens, Ohio), no.2, 1979.

Canby, Vincent, "Film View: Notes on Woody Allen and American Comedy," in *New York Times*, 13 May 1979.

Dempsey, M., "The Autobiography of Woody Allen," in *Film Comment* (New York), May/June 1979.

Teitelbaum, D., "Producing Woody: an Interview with Charles H. Joffe," in *Cinema Papers* (Melbourne), April/May 1980.

Combs, Richard, "Chameleon Days: Reflections on non-being," in *Monthly Film Bulletin* (London), November 1983.

Lahr, John, in *Automatic Vaudeville: Essays on Star Turns*, New York, 1984.

Liebman, R.L., "Rabbis or rakes, schlemiels or supermen? Jewish identity in Charles Chaplin, Jerry Lewis and Woody Allen," in *Literature/Film Quarterly* (Salisbury, Maryland), July 1984.

"Woody Allen Section," of *Film Comment* (New York), May–June 1986.

Combs, Richard, "A trajectory built for two," in *Monthly Film Bulletin* (London), July 1986.

Morris, Christopher, "Woody Allen's Comic Irony," in *Literature/Film Quarterly* (Salisbury, Maryland), vol. 15, no. 3, 1987.

Yacowar, Maurice, "Beyond Parody: Woody Allen in the 80's," in *Post Script* (Jacksonville, Florida), Winter 1987.

Dunne, Michael, "*Stardust Memories, The Purple Rose of Cairo*, and the tradition of metafiction," in *Film Criticism* (Meadville, Pennsylvania), Fall 1987.

Preussner, Arnold W., "Woody Allen's *The Purple Rose of Cairo* and the Genres of Comedy," and Paul Salmon and Helen Bragg, "Woody Allen's Economy of Means: An Introduction to *Hannah and Her Sisters*," in *Literature/Film Quarterly* (Salisbury, Maryland), vol. 16, no. 1, 1988.

"Woody Allen," in *Film Dope* (London), March 1988.

Downing, Crystal, "Broadway Roses: Woody Allen's Romantic Inheritance," and Ronald D. LeBlanc, "*Love and Death* and Food: Woody Allen's Comic Use of Gastronomy," in *Literature/Film Quarterly* (Salisbury, Maryland), vol. 17, no. 1, 1989.

On ALLEN: film—

Woody Allen: An American Comedy (Harold Mantell), 1978.

*   *   *

Woody Allen's roots in American popular culture are broad and laced with a variety of European literary and filmic influences, some of them paid explicit homage within his films (Ingmar Bergman and Dostoevsky, for example), others more subtly woven into the fabric of his work from a wide range of earlier comic traditions. Allen's genuinely original voice in the cinema recalls writer-directors like Buster Keaton, Charlie Chaplin, and Preston Sturges, who dissect their portions of the American landscape primarily through comedy. In his creative virtuosity Allen also resembles Orson Welles, whose visual and verbal wit, though contained in seemingly non-comic genres, in fact exposes the American character to satirical scrutiny.

Allen generally appears in his own films, resembling the great silent screen clowns who created, then developed an ongoing screen presence. However, Allen's film persona depends upon *heard* dialogue and especially thrives as an updated, urbanly hip, explicitly Jewish amalgam of personality traits and delivery methods associated with comic artists who reached their pinnacle in radio and film in the 1930's and 1940's. The key figures Allen plays in his own films puncture the dangerous absurdities of their universe and guard themselves against them by maintaining a cynical, even misogynistic verbal offense in the manner of Groucho Marx and W.C. Fields, but alternating it with incessant displays of self-deprecation, in the manner of the cowardly, unhandsome persona established by Bob Hope in, for example, his *Road* series.

Allen's early films emerge logically from the sharp, pointedly exaggerated jokes and sketches he wrote for others, then delivered himself as a stand-up comic in clubs and on television. Like the early films of Buster Keaton, most of these early films depend upon explicit parody of recognizable film genres. Even the films of this pre-*Annie Hall* period which do not formally rely upon a particular film genre incorporate references to various films and directors as commentary on the specific targets of social, political, or literary satire: political turbulence of the 1960's via television news coverage in *Bana-*nas; the pursuit by intellectuals of large religious and philosophical questions via the methods of Tolstoy and Dostoevsky in *Love and Death*; American sexual repression via the self-discovery guarantees offered by sex manuals in *Everything You Always Wanted to Know About Sex*.

All these issues will reappear in Allen's later, increasingly mature work—and they will persist in revealing an anomaly: Allen's comedy is cerebral in nature, dependent even in its occasional sophomoric moments upon an educated audience that responds to his brand of self-reflexive, literary, political and sexual humor. But Allen distrusts and satirizes formal education and institutionalized discourse, which in his films lead repeatedly to humorless intellectual preening. "Those who can't, do teach, and those who can't teach, teach gym," declares Alvy Singer in *Annie Hall*. No character in that film is treated with greater disdain than the Columbia professor who smugly pontificates on Fellini while standing in line waiting to see *The Sorrow and the Pity*; Allen inflicts swift, cinematically appropriate justice. Yale, a university professor of English, bears the brunt of *Manhattan*'s moral condemnation as a self-rationalizing cheat who is far "too easy" on himself.

In *Annie Hall*, his Oscar-winning breakthrough film, Allen the writer (with Marshall Brickman) recapitulates and expands emerging Allen topics but removes them from the highly exaggerated apparatus of his earlier parodies. Alvy Singer (Allen) and Annie Hall (Diane Keaton in her most important of several roles in Allen's films) enact an urban-neurotic variation on the mismatched lovers of screwball comedy, now oriented away from farce and toward character analysis set against a realistic New York City *mise-en-scène*.

Annie Hall makes indelible the Woody Allen onscreen persona—a figure somehow involved in show business or the arts and obsessive about women, his parents, his childhood, his values, his terror of illness and death; perpetually and hilariously taking the mental temperature of himself and everyone around him. Part whiner, part *nebbish*, part hypochondriac, this figure is also brilliantly astute and consciously funny, miraculously irresistible to women—for a while—particularly (as in *Annie Hall* and *Manhattan*) when he can serve as their teacher. This developing figure in Allen's work is both comic victim and witty victimizer, a moral voice in an amoral age who repeatedly discovers that the only true gods in a Godless universe are cultural and artistic—movies, music, art, architecture—a perception pleasurably reenforced visually and aurally throughout his best films. With rare exception—*Hannah* is a notable one—this figure at the film's fadeout appears destined to remain alone, by implication enabling him to continue to function as a sardonically detached observer of human imperfection, including his own. In *Annie Hall*, this characterization, despite its suffusion in *angst*, remains purely comic but Allen becomes progressively darker—and harder on himself—as variants of this figure emerge in the later films.

Comedy, even comedy that aims for a laughter of recognition based on credibility of character and situation, depends heavily upon exaggeration. In *Zelig*, the tallest of Woody Allen's cinematic tall tales, the film's central figure is a human chameleon who satisfies his overwhelming desire for conformity by physically transforming himself into the people he meets. Zelig's bizarre behavior is made even more visually believable by stunning shots that appear to place the character of Leonard Zelig (Allen) alongside famous historical figures within actual newsreel footage of the 1920's and 1930's.

Shot in Panavision and velvety black-and-white, and featuring a Gershwin score dominated by "Rhapsody in Blue," *Manhattan* reiterates key concerns of *Annie Hall* but enlarges the circle of participants in a sexual *la ronde* that increases Allen's ambivalence toward the moral terrain occupied by his characters—especially by Ike Davis (Allen), a forty-two year old man justifying a relationship with a seventeen-year-old girl. By film's end she has become an eighteen-year-old woman who has outgrown him, just as Annie Hall outgrew Alvy Singer. The film (like *Hannah and Her Sisters* later) is, above all, a celebration of New York City which Ike, like Allen, "idolize[s] all out of proportion."

In the Pirandellian *Purple Rose of Cairo*, the fourth Allen film to star Mia Farrow, a character in a black-and-white film within the color film leaps literally out of the frame into the heroine's local movie theatre. Here film itself—in this case the movies of the 1930's—both distorts reality (by setting dangerously high, incongruous expectations) and makes it more bearable (by permitting Cecilia, Allen's heroine, to escape from her dismal Depression existence). Like *Manhattan* before it, and *Hannah and Her Sisters* and *Radio Days* after it, *Purple Rose of Cairo* examines the healing power of popular art.

Arguably Allen's finest film to date, *Hannah and Her Sisters* shifts his own figure further away from the center of the story than he has ever been before, treating him as one of nine prominent characters in the action. Allen's screenplay weaves an ingenious tapestry around three sisters, their parents, assorted mates, lovers, and friends (including Allen as Hannah's ex-husband Mickey Sachs). A Chekhovian exploration of the upper middle-class world of a group of New Yorkers a decade after *Annie Hall*, Hannah is deliberately episodic in structure, its sequences separated by Brechtian title cards that suggest thematic elements of each succeeding segment. Yet it is an extraordinarily seamless film, unified by the family at its center; three Thanksgiving dinner scenes at key intervals; an exquisite color celebration of an idyllic New York City; and music by Cole Porter, Rodgers and Hart, and Puccini (among others) that italicizes the genuinely romantic nature of the film's tone. The most optimistic of Allen's major films, *Hannah* restores its inhabitants to a world of pure comedy, their futures epitomized by the fate of Mickey Sachs. For once, the Allen figure is a man who will live happily ever after, a man formerly sterile, now apparently fertile, as is comedy's magical way.

Crimes and Misdemeanors further marginalizes—and significantly darkens—the figure Woody Allen invites audiences to confuse with his offscreen self. The self-reflexive plight of filmmaker Cliff Stern (Allen) alternates with the central dilemma confronted by ophthalmologist Judah Rosenthal, a medical pillar of society who bears primary, if indirect, responsibility for the murder of his mistress. Religious and philosophical issues present in Allen's films since *Love and Death* achieve a new and serious resonance, particularly through the additional presence of a faith-retaining rabbi gradually (in one of numerous Oedipal references in Allen's work) losing his sight, and a Holocaust survivor-philosopher who preaches the gospel of endurance—then commits suicide by (as his note prosaically puts it) "going out the window." In its pessimism diametrically opposed to the joyous *Hannah and Her Sisters*, *Crimes and Misdemeanors* posits a universe utterly devoid of poetic justice. The picture's genuinely comic sequences, usually involving Cliff and his fatuous producer brother-in-law ("Comedy is tragedy plus time!") do not contradict the fact that it is Allen's most somber major film, a family comedy-melodrama that in its final sequence crosses the brink to the level of domestic tragedy. Here, the Allen figure is not only alone, as he has been in the past, but alone and *in despair*.

—Mark W. Estrin

ALLIO, René.

French. Born in Marseilles, 1924. Educated in literature. Worked as set and costume designer in Parisian avant-garde theatre, 1950's, then for Comedie Française, Paris Opera, and in London and Milan; began theatrical collaboration with Roger Planchon, 1957; designed animation film for Planchon's production of *Dead Souls*, 1960; directed first film, *La Meule*, 1963; helped to found production organization "Unité de production cinématographique" at Vitrolles, near Marseilles, 1976.

Films as Director and Scriptwriter:

1963　*La Meule* (*The Haystack*)
1965　*La Vieille Dame indigne* (*The Shameless Old Lady*)
1967　*L'Une et l'autre* (*The Other One*)
1968　*Pierre et Paul*
1970　*Les Camisards*
1973　*Rude Journée pour la reine* (co-sc)
1976　*Moi, Pierre Rivière, ayant égorgé ma mère, ma soeur et mon frère*
1980　*Retour à Marseille*
1982　*L'heure exquise*
1984　*Le matelot 512*
1988　*Un médécin des lumières*

Publications:

By ALLIO: articles—

Interview with André Zavriew, in *Film* (London), Spring 1969.
"*Les Camisards*," in *Avant-Scène du Cinéma* (Paris), no. 122, 1972.
"René Allio et *Les Camisards*," interview with A.J. Gili and M. Martin, in *Ecran* (Paris), February 1972.
Interview with B. Cohn and C. Gauteur, in *Positif* (Paris), May 1972.
Interview with S. Le Peron and others, in *Cahiers du Cinéma* (Paris), November 1976.
"Le Retour de Pierre Rivière," interview with G. Gauthier, in *Image et Son* (Paris), December 1976.
"L'Histoire au cinéma," discussion with Marc Ferro and others, in *Positif* (Paris), January 1977.
Interview with J.-P. Gatlato, in *Cinéma* (Paris), May 1977.
"La Place de l'artiste dans la cinéma politique," interview with B. Nave, in *Jeune Cinéma* (Paris), December/January 1979/80.
"3 cinéastes en quête de l'histoire," interview with J.-P. Bertin-Maghit, in *Image et Son* (Paris), July/August 1980.

On ALLIO: articles—

"Pasolini-Varda-Allio-Sarris-Michelson," in *Film Culture* (New York), Fall 1966.
Godard, Jean-Luc, and Michel Delahaye, "Two Arts in One: René Allio and Antoine Bourseiller," in *Cahiers du Cinéma in English* (New York), December 1966.
"Le réalisateur: René Allio," in *Avant-Scène du Cinéma* (Paris), February 1972.
"*Rude journée* Issue" of *Avant-Scène du Cinéma* (Paris), January/February 1974.
Delavaud, G., "Le retour à Marseille de René Allio," in *Cahiers du Cinéma* (Paris), February 1980.
Joliet, Bruno, "Les lumières de la verité," in *Cinéma* (Paris), 20 January 1988.
"René Allio," in *Film Dope* (London), March 1988.

*　　*　　*

René Allio was in his early forties and had already established his name and reputation as a stage director when he began his feature filmmaking career with two remarkable studies of characters who deliberately change their identity—to the consternation of those closest to them. *La Vieille Dame indigne* was adapted from a Brecht story and relocated in Allio's native Marseilles. It offered the veteran actress Sylvie one of her finest roles as an old woman who, on the verge of death, suddenly decides to spend the little money she has on herself rather than leave it to her heirs. *L'Une et l'autre*, which followed two years later, has an explicitly theatrical setting but shows the same mastery in the capturing of everyday detail and the tiny gestures by which people relate. The heroine is an actress who, realising that her life has become meaningless, takes on the identity of her sister as a prelude to finding the ability to express to the man she lives with her need to live an independent life.

The same blend of realism and theatricality together with an intense sympathy for ordinary people, capturing the banality of their existence and also their dreams, characterises his subsequent three films, despite their striking differences in subject matter. Pierre, the hero of *Pierre et Paul*, has an ordered existence on which he depends far more than he realises. When his father's death destroys his peace of mind and plunges him into debt, he cannot cope and is driven to a mad outburst of violence. In contrast, *Les Camisards* is a historical study made without stars or even star roles, which traces the failed revolt of the Protestants of the Ceyennes against the oppression of Louis XIV at the beginning of the 18th century. Just as the careful naturalistic detail of *Pierre et Paul* does not exclude comment on wider aspects of the consumer society, so here the historical costumes and period reconstruction do not prevent the issues of freedom and struggle, which have a quite contemporary relevance, from coming to the fore. *Rude Journée pour la reine* in 1973 is another new departure, which traces with precision and an involving rhythm the interaction of dream and reality in the head of an ordinary, aging housewife, played with characteristic forcefulness by Simone Signoret.

Allio was unable subsequently to maintain this rhythm of a film every two years or so, and only two films follow in the next ten years. *Moi, Pierre Rivière, ayant égorgé ma mère, ma soeur et mon frère* is a remarkable work. Based on a 50 page confessional text discovered and published by Michel Foucault, the film combines exemplary naturalism of detail (the actual locations of the crime, real peasants, precise period reconstruction) with a refusal to dramatise events. These are simply presented for our attention, to engage our emotions but at the same time to give rise to thought about the shaping impact of social conditions. *Retour à Marseilles*, a fictional account of a man's return to Marseilles, which is also the filmmaker's own return to his native city, did not have the same impact. But Allio's career over fifteen years is a striking and important one. To a French cinema which is still essentially Parisian, he gives an authentic provincial voice; in a cinema which tends to avoid social comment, he locates his characters precisely in period and class. His sense of realist detail is sure, but is balanced by a theatrical awareness of staging and creating dramatic involvement. As a result the figures Allio puts before us engage our sympathies and provoke our thought in a way which is both personal and original.

—Roy Armes

ALMODÓVAR, Pedro.

Spanish. Born in Calzada de Clatrava, La Mancha, Spain, 1951 (some sources give 1947). Moved to Madrid and worked for National Telephone Company, 1967; wrote comic strips and articles for underground magazines; joined independent

Pedro Almodóvar

theatre group *Los Goliardos* and started making Super-8 films with them, 1974; first feature, *Pepi*, released, 1980. Also a rock musician, has written music for his own films. Recipient: Glauber Rocha Award for Best Director, Rio Film Festival, and LA Film Critics Association "New Generation" Award, 1987.

Films as Director:

1974 *Dos Futas, or, Historia de Amor que termina en boda* (*Two Whores, or, A Love Story which Ends in Marriage*) (Super-8); *La Caida de Sodoma* (*The Fall of Sodom*) (Super-8)
1975 *Homenaje* (*Homage*) (Super-8)
1976 *La Estrella* (*The Stars*) (Super-8)
1977 *Sexo va: Sexo Vienne* (*Sex Comes and Goes*) (Super-8); *Complementos* (shorts)
1978 *Folle, Folle, Folleme, Tim* (*Fuck Me, Fuck Me, Fuck Me, Tim*) (Super-8, full-length); *Salome* (16mm)
1980 *Pepi, Luci, Bom y otras chicas de montón* (*Pepi, Luci, Bom and lots of other girls*)
1982 *Laberinto de pasiones* (*Labyrinth of Passions*)
1983 *Entre Tinieblas* (*Into the Dark*; *The Sisters of Darkness*)
1984 *Qué me hecho yo para merecer esto?* (*What Have I Done to Deserve This?*)
1986 *Matador*; *La Ley del Deseo* (*Law of Desire*)
1987 *Mujeres al Borde de un Ataque de Nervios* (*Women on the Verge of a Nervous Breakdown*)
1990 *Atame!* (*Tie Me Up, Tie Me Down!*)

Publications:

By ALMODÓVAR: books—

El Sueno de la Razon (short stories), Madrid, 1980.
Fuego en las Entranas (*Fire Deep Inside*) (novel), Madrid, 1982.

By ALMODÓVAR: articles—

Interview in *Contracampo* (Madrid), September 1981.
Interview with J.C. Rentero, in *Casablanca* (Madrid), May 1984.
"Pleasure and the new Spanish Mentality," an interview with Marsha Kinder, in *Film Quarterly* (Berkeley), Fall 1987.

Interview in *Time Out* (London), 2 November 1988.
Interview in *Film Comment* (New York), November–December 1988.
Interview in *Films and Filming* (London), June 1989.
Interview in *Inter/View* (New York), January 1990.
Interview in *City Limits* (London), 5 July 1990.
Regular column (as "Patty Diphusa") in *La Luna* (Madrid)

On ALMODÓVAR: articles—

Sanchez Valdès, J., "Pedro Almodóvar: *Laberinto de pasiones*," in *Casablanca* (Madrid), April 1982.
Paranagua, P.-A., "Pedro Almodóvar. En deuxième vitesse," in *Positif* (Paris), June 1986.
Fernandez, Enrique, "The Lawyer of Desire," in *Village Voice* (New York), 7 April 1987.
Film Quarterly (Los Angeles), Fall 1987.
Kael, Pauline, "Red on Red," in *New Yorker*, 16 May 1988.
"Spain's Pedro Almodóvar on the Verge of Global Fame," in *Variety* (New York), 24 August 1988.
Kael, Pauline, "Unreal," in *New Yorker*, 14 November 1988.
Filmbiography, in *Monthly Film Bulletin* (London), January 1989.
Films in Review (New York), January 1989.
Bennett, Annie, "Tour de Farce," in *20/20* (London), January 1990.
Corliss, Richard, "Almodóvar à la Mode," in *Time* (New York), 30 January 1989.
"Pedro Almodóvar," in *National Film Theatre Booklet* (London), July 1990.

*   *   *

Pedro Almodóvar is more than the most successful Spanish film export since Carlos Saura. At home, the production of Almodóvar's films, their premieres, and the works themselves are surrounded by scandal, and the Spanish popular press examines what the director eats, the qualities he looks for in a lover and his weight fluctuations in a fashion normally reserved for movie stars and European royalty. Abroad, the films have surprised those with set notions of what Spanish camera is or should be; Almodóvar's uncompromising incorporation of elements specific to a gay culture into mainstream forms with wide crossover appeal has been held up as a model for other gay directors to emulate. The films and Almodóvar's creation of a carefully cultivated persona in the press have meshed into "Almodóvar," a singular trademark. "Almodóvar" makes the man and the movies interchangeable even as it overshadows both. The term now embodies, and waves the flag for, the "New Spain" as it would like to see itself: democratic, permissive, prosperous, international, irreverent and totally different from what it was in the Franco years.

Almodóvar's career can be usefully divided into three stages: a marginal underground period in the 1970's in which he personally funded and controlled every aspect of the shoe-string-budgeted, generally short films and which culminated in *Pepi, Luci, Bom y Otras Chicas del Monton*, his feature film debut; the early to mid-1980's in which he was still writing and directing his increasingly costly though still low-budget films but for other producers and with varying degrees of state subsidization; and, from *The Law of Desire* in 1986, a period in which he reverted to producing his own films which now benefitted from substantial budgets (by Spanish standards), top technicians and maximum state subsidies. Though critical reaction to his work has varied, each of his films has enjoyed increasing financial success until *Women on the Verge of a Nervous Breakdown*, which became 1989's highest grossing foreign film in North America and, up to the present, the most successful Spanish film ever in Spain.

The titles of Almodóvar's shorts foreshadow elements of his style that can be detected throughout his films: a camp sensibility, the fetishization of the pop-icon, the forefronting of taboo. All of them were mixed into *Pepi*, a corrosive urban cartoon, episodic in structure and anarchic in sensibility. The film is free of technique and overeager to shock, to test the boundaries of post-Franco Spain's much vaunted permissiveness. But, like the subsequent *Labyrinth of Passion*, the film is also eager to please. The protagonists have no depth, they are sketched-in cartoon characters in a freewheeling and irreverent search for pleasure. The operatic emotions that Almodóvar would later delineate both sharply and subtly to invoke either laughter (*Women . . .*) or tears (*The Law*) are, in his early features, used as quick and superficial points of reference to parody romantic conventions.

Almodóvar's oeuvre makes a good argument for the auteur theory. One can trace to his first films themes and strategies that he would explore in different forms, with varying degrees of success, but with increasing technical expertise, throughout the rest of his career. Almodóvar's films posit the absolute autonomy of the individual. From *Pepi* to *Tie Me Up! Tie Me Down!* the central characters in his films (mostly women) either act as if there are no social restrictions, or are conscious of the price of transgression but willing to pay it if such actions lead to, or contain, pleasure.

In Almodóvar's films, the various paths to pleasure lead to a destination and fulfillment (*Matador*), a dead end and disappointment (*Dark Hideout, Women . . .*) or an endlessly winding path and continuous displacement (*The Law of Desire*) but never in resignation. To explore these varied roads Almodóvar has over the years accumulated a rep company of actors (Carmen Maura, Antonio Banderas, Eusebio Poncela, Julieta Serrano, Chus Lampreave). They appear in most of his movies, whether in leads or supporting roles. Even Maura, whom Almodóvar has called his muse and who starred in *Pepi, What Have I Done . . ., The Law*, and *Women . . .*, has also played supporting roles in *Dark Hideout* and *Matador*. When in an Almodóvar film, no matter how absurd the situation their characters might find themselves in, all the actors are directed to a style that relies on understatement and has often been called "naturalist" or "realist." For example, when in *The Law of Desire*, Tina tells her brother that "she" had previously been a "he" and had run off to Morocco to have a love affair with their father, Carmen Maura acts it in a style considerably subtler than that used by, for example, June Allyson to tell us she really shouldn't have broken that date with Peter Lawford. This style of acting is partly what enables Almodóvar's often outrageous characters to be so emotionally compelling.

Almodóvar borrows indiscriminately from film history. A case in point is *What Have I Done to Deserve This?* which contains direct reference to, or echoes of, neo-realism, the caper film, *Carrie*, Buñuel, Wilder, Warhol and Waters. Moreover, by his second period, beginning with *Dark Hideout*, it became clear that Almodóvar's preferred mode of cinema was the melodramatic. It is a mode that cuts across genre, equally capable of conveying the tragic and the comic, eminently emotional, adept at arousing intense audience identification and capable of communicating complex psychological processes no matter what the character's gender or sexual orientation.

Almodóvar's signature, and a unique contribution to the movies, is the synthesis of the melodramatic mode with a clash of quotations. This combination allows Almodóvar both a quasi-classical Hollywood narrative structure (which facilitates audience identification) and a very self-conscious narration (which normally produces an alienation effect). This results in dialectical moments in which the absurd is embued with emotional resonance (the mother selling her son to the dentist in *What Have I Done . . .?*); the emotional can be checked with cheek without disrupting identification (superimposing a character's crying eyes with the wheels of a car in *The Law*); and camp can be imbued with depth without losing its wit (the transference of emotions that occurs when we see Pepa dubbing Joan Crawford's dialogue from *Johnny Guitar* in *Women . . .*). At his best (*What Have I Done to Deserve This?*, *The Law of Desire*, *Women on the Verge of a Nervous Breakdown*), Almodóvar drills a heart into the postmodern and fills it with an operatic range of feeling.

—José Arroyo

ALTMAN, Robert.

American. Born in Kansas City, Missouri, 20 February 1925. Attended University of Missouri, Columbia. Married Kathryn Reed (3rd marriage), two sons; one daughter and two sons from previous marriages. Bomber pilot, U.S. Air Force, 1943–47. Directed industrial films for Calvin Company, Kansas City, 1947; wrote, produced, and directed first feature, *The Delinquents*, 1955; TV director, 1957–63; co-founder of TV production company, 1963; founder, Lion's Gate production company (named after his own 8-track sound system), 1970, Westwood Editorial Services, 1974, and Sandcastle 5 Productions; made *Tanner '88* for TV during American Presidential Campaign, 1988. Recipient: Palme d'Or, Cannes Festival, for *M*A*S*H*, 1970; New York Critics' Film Circle Award for Best Director, for *Nashville,* 1975; Golden Bear, Berlin Festival, for *Buffalo Bill and the Indians*, 1976. Agent: International Creative Management, 40 W.57th St., New York, NY 10019, U.S.A.

Films as Director:

1954   *The Builders* (medium length publicity film)
1955   *The Delinquents* (+pr, sc)
1957   *The James Dean Story* (co-d, +co-pr, co-ed)
1964   *The Party* (short)
1965   *Pot au Feu* (short); *The Katherine Reed Story* (short)
1967   *Countdown* (moon-landing sequence d uncred by William Conrad)
1969   *That Cold Day in the Park*
1970   *M*A*S*H*; *Brewster McCloud* (+pr)
1971   *McCabe and Mrs. Miller* (+co-sc)
1972   *Images* (+pr,sc)
1973   *The Long Goodbye*
1974   *Thieves Like Us* (+co-sc); *California Split* (+co-pr)
1975   *Nashville* (+co-pr, co-songwriter: "The Day I Looked Jesus in the Eye")
1976   *Buffalo Bill and the Indians, or Sitting Bull's History Lesson* (+pr, co-sc)
1978   *A Wedding* (+pr, co-sc)
1979   *Quintet* (+pr, co-sc); *A Perfect Couple* (+pr, co-sc)
1979   *Health* (+pr, sc)
1980   *Popeye*
1981   *The Easter Egg Hunt*
1982   *Come Back to the Five and Dime, Jimmy Dean, Jimmy Dean*
1983   *Streamers* (+pr); *The Diviners*
1984   *Secret Honor* (*Secret Honor: The Political Testament of Richard M. Nixon. Secret Honor: A Political Myth*) (+pr)
1985   *Fool for Love*; *O.C. and Stiggs* (+pr)
1987   "Les Boreades" in *Aria*; *Beyond Therapy*
1989   *The Room*; *The Dumb Waiter*
1990   *Vincent and Theo*

Other Films:

1976   *Welcome to L.A.* (pr)
1977   *The Late Show* (pr)
1978   *Remember My Name* (pr)
1979   *Rich Kids* (pr)

Publications:

By ALTMAN: book—

Buffalo Bill and the Indians, or Sitting Bull's History Lesson, with Alan Rudolph, New York, 1976.

By ALTMAN: articles—

Interview with S. Rosenthal, in *Focus on Film* (London), Spring 1972.
Interview with Russell Auwerter, in *Directors in Action*, edited by Bob Thomas, New York, 1973.
Interview with Michel Ciment and Bertrand Tavernier, in *Positif* (Paris), February 1973.
"Robert Altman Speaking," interview with J. Dawson, in *Film Comment* (New York), March/April 1974.
"An Altman Sampler," interview with B.J. Demby, in *Filmmakers Newsletter* (Ward Hill, Massachusetts), October 1974.
Robert Altman Seminar, in *Dialogue on Film* (Beverly Hills), February 1975.
"The Artist and the Multitude Are Natural Enemies," interview with F.A. Macklin, in *Film Heritage* (Dayton, Ohio), Winter 1976/77.
Interview with Jean-André Fieschi, in *Cinématographe* (Paris), June 1977.
Interview with Jonathan Rosenbaum and Charles Michener, in *Film Comment* (New York), September/October 1978.
Interview and article by J.-P. Le Pavec and others, in *Cinéma* (Paris), November 1978.
"Jumping Off the Cliff," in *Monthly Film Bulletin* (London), December 1978.
Interview with Michel Ciment and M. Henry, in *Positif* (Paris), March 1979.
"Robert Altman: Backgammon and Spinach," interview with Tom Milne and Richard Combs, in *Sight and Sound* (London), Summer 1981.
"Peripheral Vision," interview with A. Stuart, in *Films* (London), July 1981.
Interview with Leo Braudy and Robert Phillip Kolker, in *Post Script* (Jacksonville, Florida), Fall 1981 and Winter 1982.
"'A Foolish Optimist': Interview with Robert Altman," by H. Kloman, Lloyd Michaels, and Virginia Wright Wexman, in *Film Criticism* (Meadville, Pennsylvania), Spring 1983.
Interview with Michel Ciment, in *Positif* (Paris), June 1984.
Stills (London), November 1984.
Interview with Richard Combs, in *Monthly Film Bulletin* (London), January 1985.
"On the Road with Robert Altman," an interview with Nick Roddick, in *Cinema Papers* (Melbourne), September 1986.
"Mrs. Miller's Tale," an interview with Sheila Johnston, in the *Independent* (London), 6 April 1990.
"How the Western Was Lost," an interview with Derek Malcolm, in the *Guardian* (London), 11 April 1990.
Interview with Richard Combs in *Monthly Film Bulletin* (London), July 1990.

On ALTMAN: film—

"Robert Altman," for *South Bank Show*, London Weekend Television, April 1990.

On ALTMAN: books—

Hardin, Nancy, editor, *On Making a Movie: Brewster McCloud*, New York, 1971.
Feineman, Neil, *Persistence of Vision: The Films of Robert Altman*, New York, 1976.
Kass, Judith M., *Robert Altman: American Innovator*, New York, 1978.
Karp, Alan, *The Films of Robert Altman*, Metuchen, New Jersey, 1981.
Kolker, Robert Phillip, *A Cinema of Loneliness: Penn, Kubrick, Coppola, Scorsese, Altman*, Oxford, 1980, revised edition, 1988.
Bourget, Jean-Loup, *Robert Altman*, Paris, 1981.
Karp, Alan, *The Films of Robert Altman*, Metuchen, New Jersey, 1981.

Robert Altman

Kagan, Norman, *American Skeptic: Robert Altman's Genre-Commentary Films*, Ann Arbor, Michigan, 1982.

Micciche, Lino, *L'incubo americano: Il cinema di Robert Altman*, Venice, 1984.

Wexman, Virginia Wright, and Gretchen Bisplinghoff, *Robert Altman: A Guide to References and Resources*, Boston, 1984.

Plecki, Gerard, *Robert Altman*, Boston, 1985.

Weis, Elisabeth, and John Belton, editors, *Film Sound: Theory and Practice*, New York, 1985.

Wood, Robin, *Hollywood from Vietnam to Reagan*, New York, 1986.

McGilligan, Patrick, *Robert Altman: Jumping off the Cliff: A biography of the Great American Director*, New York, 1989.

On ALTMAN: articles—

Cutts, John, "*MASH, McCloud*, and *McCabe*," in *Films and Filming* (London), November 1971.

Dawson, J., "Altman's Images," in *Sight and Sound* (London), Spring 1972.

Engle, Gary, "*McCabe and Mrs. Miller*: Robert Altman's Anti-Western," in *Journal of Popular Film* (Bowling Green, Ohio), Fall 1972.

Baker, C.A., "The Theme of Structure in the Films of Robert Altman," in *Journal of Popular Film* (Bowling Green), Summer 1973.

Brackett, Leigh, "From *The Big Sleep* to the *The Long Goodbye* and More or Less How We Got There," in *Take One* (Montreal), January 1974.

Stewart, Garrett, "*The Long Goodbye* from *Chinatown*," in *Film Quarterly* (Berkeley), Winter 1974/75.

Rosenbaum, Jonathan, "Improvisations and Interactions in Altmanville," in *Sight and Sound* (London), Spring 1975.

Oliver, Bill, "*The Long Goodbye* and *Chinatown*: Debunking the Private Eye Tradition," in *Literature/Film Quarterly* (Salisbury, Maryland), Summer 1975.

"Altman Issue" of *Film Heritage* (Dayton, Ohio), Fall 1975.

Wood, Robin, "Smart-ass and Cutie-pie: Notes Toward an Evaluation of Altman," in *Movie*, Fall 1975.

Benayoun, Robert, "Altman, U.S.A.," in *Positif* (Paris), December 1975.

Byrne, Connie and William O. Lopez, "*Nashville* (An Interview Documentary)," in *Film Quarterly* (Berkeley), Winter 1975/76.

Self, Robert, "Invention and Death: The Commodities of Media in Robert Altman's *Nashville*," in *Journal of Popular Film* (Bowling Green, Ohio), no. 5, 1976.

Levine, R., "R. Altman & Co.," in *Film Comment* (New York), January/February 1977.

Canby, Vincent, "Film View: Altman—A Daring Filmmaker Falters," in *The New York Times*, 18 February 1979.

"Playing the Game, or Robert Altman and the Indians," in *Sight and Sound* (London), Summer 1979.

Bonnet, J.-C., and others, "Dossier: Robert Altman," in *Cinématographe* (Paris), January 1980.

Yacowar, Maurice, "Actors as Conventions in the Films of Robert

Altman," in *Cinema Journal* (Evanston), Fall 1980.

Eyman, S., "Against Altman," in *Focus on Film* (London), October 1980.

Altman, D., "Building Sand Castles," in *Cinema Papers* (Melbourne), July/August 1981.

Self, Robert, "The Art Cinema and Robert Altman," in *Velvet Light Trap* (Madison, Wisconsin), no. 19, 1982.

Durgnat, Raymond, "Popeye pops up," in *Films* (London), April and May 1982.

Self, Robert, "The Perfect Couple: 'Two are Halves of One,' in the Films of Robert Altman," in *Wide Angle* (Athens, Georgia), vol. 5, no. 4, 1983.

Edgerton, G., "Capra and Altman: Mythmaker and Mythologist," in *Literature/Film Quarterly* (Salisbury, Maryland), January 1983.

Jaehne, K., and P. Auderfeide, "Secret honor," in *Cineaste* (New York), vol. 14, no. 2, 1985.

Farber, Stephen, "Five horsemen after the apocalypse," in *Film Comment* (New York), July–August 1985.

Self, Robert, "Robert Altman and the Theory of Authorship," in *Cinema Journal* (Champaign, Illinois), Fall 1985.

"Altman Section" of *Positif* (Paris), January 1986.

White, A., "Play Time," in *Film Comment* (New York), January–February 1986.

Self, Robert, and Leland Poague, "Dialogue," in *Cinema Journal* (Champaign, Illinois), Spring 1986.

Combs, Richard, "A trajectory built for two," in *Monthly Film Bulletin* (London), July 1986.

"Robert Altman," in *Film Dope* (London), March 1988.

Film Comment (New York), September/October 1989.

See p. 4. *Sight and Sound* (London), Spring 1990.

*   *   *

The American 1970's may have been dominated by a "New Wave" of younger, auteurist-inspired filmmakers including George Lucas, Peter Bogdanovich, Steven Spielberg, Martin Scorsese, and Francis Ford Coppola, all contemporaries as well as sometime colleagues. It is, however, an outsider to this group, the older Robert Altman, perhaps that decade's most consistent chronicler of human behavior, who could be characterized as the artistic rebel most committed to an unswerving personal vision. If the generation of whiz kids tends to admire the American cinema as well as its structures of production, Altman tends to regard the American cinema critically and to view the production establishment more as an adversary to be cunningly exploited on the way to an almost European ambiguity.

Although Altman has worked consistently within American genres, his work can instructively be seen as anti-genre: *McCabe and Mrs. Miller* is a kind of anti-western, exposing the myth of the heroic westerner (as described by Robert Warshow and executed by John Wayne and John Ford) and replacing it with an almost Marxist view of the Westerner as financier, spreading capitalism and corruption, with opportunism and good cheer. *The Long Goodbye* sets itself in opposition to certain aspects of the hard-boiled detective genre, as Elliott Gould's Philip Marlowe reflects a moral stance decidedly more ambiguous than that of Raymond Chandler's conventional lonely moralist. Similarly, *Countdown* can be seen in relationship to the science-fiction film; *Thieves Like Us* (based on *They Live by Night*) in relationship to the bandit-gangster film; *That Cold Day in the Park* in relationship to the psychological horror film inaugurated by Alfred Hitchcock's *Psycho*; and *California Split* in relationship to that generic phenomenon so common to the 1970's, the "buddy film." Even *Nashville*, Altman's complex bicentennial musical released in 1975, can be seen in relationship to a generic tradition with roots in *Grand Hotel* and branches in *Earthquake*, a kind of disaster film about the American dream.

Aside from his generic preoccupations, Altman seems especially interested in people. His films characteristically contain perceptive observations, telling exchanges, moments of crystal clear revelation of human folly, most persuasively in relationship to a grand social organization: that of the upper classes and *nouveaux riches* in *A Wedding*; health faddists and, metaphorically, the American political process, in *Health*; and so forth. Certainly Altman's films offer a continuous critique of American society: people are constantly using and exploiting others, though often with the tacit permission of those being exploited. One thinks of the country-western singers' exploitation by the politician's p.r. man in *Nashville*, for instance; or the spinster in *That Cold Day in the Park*. Violence is often the climax of an Altman film—almost as if the tensions among the characters must ultimately explode. Notable examples include the fiery deaths and subsequent "surprise ending" in *A Wedding*, or the climactic assassination in *Nashville*.

Another recurring interest for Altman in his preoccupation with the psychopathology of women: one thinks of the subtly encroaching madness of Sandy Dennis's sexually repressed spinster in *That Cold Day in the Park*, an underrated, early Altman film; the disturbing instability of Ronee Blakley in *Nashville*; the relationships among the unbalanced subjects of *Three Women*, based on one of Altman's own dreams; and the real/surreal visions of Susannah York in the virtual horror film, *Images*. Because almost all of Altman's characters tend to be hypocritical, psychotic, weak, or morally flawed in some way, with very few coming to a happy end, Altman has often been attacked for a kind of trendy cynicism. However, this cynicism seems not a mannerism of the director as much as his genuine attempt to avoid the conventional myth-making of the American cinema by imbuing as many of his characters as possible with that sloppy imperfection associated with human beings as they are, with life as it is lived.

Performers enjoy working with Altman in part because of the freedom he allows them to develop their characters and often alter the script through improvisation and collaboration. Like Bergman, Altman has worked often with a stock company of performers who appear in one role after another, among them Elliott Gould, Sally Kellerman, Rene Auberjonois, Keith Carradine, Shelley Duvall, Michael Murphy, Bert Remsen, and Henry Gibson.

Altman's distinctive style transforms whatever subject he approaches. He often takes advantage of widescreen compositions in which the frame is filled with a number of subjects and details competing for the spectator's attention. Working with cinematographer Vilmos Zsigmond, he has achieved films that are visually distinguished and tend toward the atmospheric. Especially notable are the use of the zoom lens in the smoky cinematography of *McCabe and Mrs. Miller*; the reds, whites, and blues of *Nashville*; the constantly mobile camera, specially mounted, of *The Long Goodbye*, which so effortlessly reflects the hazy moral center of the world the film presents; and the pastel prettiness of *A Wedding*, particularly the first appearance of that icon of the American cinema, Lillian Gish, whose subsequent filmic death propels the narrative.

Altman's use of multi-track sound is also incredibly complex: sounds are layered upon one another, often emanating from different speakers in such a way that the audience member must also decide what to listen for. Indeed, watching and listening to an Altman film inevitably requires an active participant: events unroll with a Bazinian ambiguity. Altman's Korean War comedy *M*A*S*H* was the director's first public success with this kind of soundtrack. One of his more extreme uses of this technique can be found in *McCabe and Mrs. Miller*, generally thought to be among the director's finest achievements.

Nashville, Altman's most universally acclaimed work, is a

panoramic view of the American experience and society, following the interrelated experiences of 24 characters in the country-western capital. In its almost three-hour length, *Nashville* accumulates a power of the whole even greater than the vivid individual parts which themselves resonate in the memory: the incredibly controlled debut performance of Lily Tomlin and the sensitive performances of at least a dozen others; the lesson on sexual politics Altman delivers when he photographs several women listening to a song by Keith Carradine; the vulnerability of Ronee Blakley who suffers a painful breakdown in front of her surprisingly fickle fans; the expressions on the faces of the men who watch Gwen Welles's painfully humiliating striptease; the final cathartic song of Barbara Harris, as Altman suddenly reveals the conventional "Star is Born" myth in his apparent anti-musical like a magician stunning us with an unexpected trick.

Overall, Altman's career itself has been rather weird. His output since the 1971 *M*A*S*H* has been prodigious indeed, especially in light of the fact that a great number of his films have been financial and/or critical failures. In fact, several of his films, among them *A Perfect Couple* and *Quintet* (with Paul Newman) barely got a national release; and *Health* (which starred Glenda Jackson, Carol Burnett, James Garner, and Lauren Bacall) languished on the shelf for years before achieving even a limited release in New York City. The most amazing thing about Altman's *Popeye*, which was relatively successful with critics and the public, was that Altman managed to secure the assignment at all, not that the film emerged as one of the most cynical and ultimately disturbing of children's films, in line with Altman's consistent vision of human beings and social organization.

The most recent period of Altman's career has been dominated by a number of film adaptations of theatre pieces, including *Come Back to the Five & Dime, Jimmy Dean, Jimmy Dean*; *Streamers*; *The Laundromat*; *Secret Honor*; *Beyond Therapy*; and *Fool for Love*. Although many of these works are fascinating and contain incredibly modulated performances and surprisingly evocative cinematography (particularly *Jimmy Dean*), these films have been neither influential, financially successful, nor critically popular. As such, Robert Altman now finds himself increasingly marginalized from both the industry and art he had previously invigorated.

—Charles Derry

ALVAREZ, Santiago.

Cuban. Born in Havana, 1919. Educated at University of Havana; Columbia University, New York. After revolution, served as Vice-President of newly formed Instituto Cubano del Arte e Industria Cinematograficas (ICAIC), 1959; director of the Latin American ICAIC newsreel, from 1960.

Films as Director:

1960   *Un año de libertad* (co-d)
1961   *Escambray*; *Muerte al invasor* (co-d)
1962   *Forjadores de la paz*; *Cumplimos*; *Crisis en el Caribe*
1963   *Ciclon*; *El Barbaro del Ritmo*; *Fidel en la URSS*
1964   *Via libre a la zafra del '64*; *Primeros Juegos Deportivos Militares*
1965   *Solidaridad Cuba y Vietnam*; *Cuba dos de enero*; *Pedales sobra Cuba*; *Now*; *Segunda Declaracion de la Habana*; *La escalada del chantaje*

1966   *Abril de Giron*; *Cerro Pelado*; *Año Siete*; *Ocho años de Revolucion*
1967   *La guerra olvidados* (*Laos, the Forgotten War*); *Hasta la victoria siempre* (*Till Victory Always*); *Golpeando en la selva*; *Hanoi, martes 13*
1968   *Amarrando el Cordon*; *L.B.J.*
1969   *Despegue a la 18.00*; *79 Primaveras* (*79 Springtimes of Ho Chi Minh*)
1970   *Once por cero*; *Piedra sobre piedra*; *El sueño del Pongo*; *Yanapanacuna*
1971   *Quemando tradiciones*; *Como, por qué y para qué asesina a un general?*; *La estampida*; *El pájaro del faro*
1972   *De America soy hijo . . . y a ella me debo*
1973   *Y el cielo fue tomado por asalto*; *El tigre salto y mato . . . pero morira . . . morira* (*The Tiger Leaped and Killed, But He Will Die, He Will Die*)
1974   *60 Minutos con el primer mundial de boxeo amateur*; *Rescate*; *Los cuatro puentes*
1975   *Abril de Vietnam en el año del gato*; *El primer delegado*
1976   *El Tiempo es el viento*; *El sol no se puede tapar con un dedo*; *Luanda ya no es de San Pablo*; *Morir por la patria es vivir*; *Maputo*; *Meridiano Novo*; *Los Dragones de Ha-Long*
1977   *Mi Hermano Fidel*; *El Octubre de todos*
1978   *Sobre el problema fronterizo entre Kampuchea y Vietnam*; *. . . y la noche se hizo arcoiris*
1979   *El Gran salto al vacio*; *Tengo fe en ti*; *La cumbre que nos une*; *El desafio*
1980   *Celia, imagen del pueblo*; *Marcha del pueblo combatiente*; *El mayo de las tres banderas*; *Un Amazonus de pueblo embravecido*; *Lo que el viento se llevó*; *La guerra necessaria*
1981   *La importancia universal del hueco*; *Tiempo libre a la roca*; *Comenzo a retumbar el Momtombo*; *26 es también 19*; *Mazazo macizo*; *Contrapunto*
1982   *Nova sinfonia*; *A galope sobre la historia*; *Operación abril del Caribe*
1983   *Los refugiados de la Cueva del Muertro*; *Biografía de un carnaval*; *Las campanas tambien pueden doblar mañana*
1984   *Gracias Santiago*; *Dos rostros y una sola imagen*; *El soñador del Kremlin*; *Por primera vez elecciones libres*
1985   *Taller de la vida*; *La soledad de los dioses*; *Reencuentro*
1986   *Las antípodas de la victoria*; *Aires de renovación en el meridiano 37*; *Memorias de un reencuentro*

Publications:

By ALVAREZ: book—

Santiago Alvarez: Cronista del tercer mundo, edited by Edmundo Aray, Caracas, 1983.

By ALVAREZ: articles—

"Santiago Alvarez habla de su cine," in *Hablemos de Cine* (Lima), July/August 1970.
Interview in *Cineaste* (New York), vol. 6, no. 4, 1975.
"El Periodismo cinematografico," in *Cine Cubano* (Havana), no. 94, 1979.
"Cinema and Revolution: Talking with Santiago Alvarez," in *Issues: A Monthly Review of International Affairs* (London), May 1980.
Interview with M. Pereira, in *Cine Cubano* (Havana), no. 104, 1983.
Interview with C. Galiano and R. Chavez, in *Cine Cubano* (Havana), no. 107, 1984.
"Now," in *Cine Cubano* (Havana), no. 110, 1984.
"Hablar de estas fotos: Conversación con Santiago Alvarez," in *Revolución y Cultura* (Havana), November 1986.

On ALVAREZ: books—

Nelson, L., *Cuba: The Measure of a Revolution*, Minneapolis, 1972.
Myerson, Michael, *Memories of Underdevelopment: The Revolutionary Films of Cuba*, New York, 1973.
Chanan, Michael, editor, *Santiago Alvarez*, London, 1982.
Waugh, Thomas, editor, *"Show Us Life": Toward a History and Aesthetics of the Committed Documentary*, Metuchen, New Jersey, 1984.
Chanan, Michael, *The Cuban Image: Cinema and Cultural Politics in Cuba*, London, 1985.

Santiago Alvarez

On ALVAREZ: articles—

Sutherland, Elizabeth, "Cinema of Revolution – 90 Miles From Home," in *Film Quarterly* (Berkeley), Winter 1961/62.
Douglas, M.E., "The Cuban Cinema," in *Take One* (Montreal), July/August 1968.
Adler, Renata, in *New York Times*, 10, 11, and 12 February 1969.
Engel, Andi, "Solidarity and Violence," in *Sight and Sound* (London), Autumn 1969.
Rubenstein, Lenny, "*79 Springtimes of Ho Chi Minh*," in *Cineaste* (New York), Winter 1970/71.
Sauvage, P., "Cine Cubano," in *Film Comment* (New York), Spring 1972.
Chávez, R., "El internaciolalismo en el obra de Santiago Alvarez," in *Cine Cubano* (Havana), March 1978.
Burton, Julianne, "Introduction to Revolutionary Cuban Cinema," in *Jump Cut* (Chicago), December 1978.
Hood, Stuart, "Murder on the Way: Santiago Alvarez Season at NFT," in *New Statesman* (London), April 1980.
Mraz, John, "Santiago Alvarez: From Dramatic Form to Direct Cinema," in *Documentary Strategies: Society/Ideology/History in Latin American Documentary, 1950–1985*, Pittsburgh, 1990.

*   *   *

Predominantly associated with the educational or the exotic in the United States, the documentary film occupies a very different place in the cinema of revolutionary Cuba. 90–95% of the films produced under the revolution have been documentaries, and the man most responsible for the international stature of Cuban documentary cinema is Santiago Alvarez.

As the director of the weekly "Latin American Newsreel" produced by the Cuban Film Institute (ICAIC), Alvarez has directed an enormous number of newsreels as well as many other short and feature-length documentaries. Never having formally studied cinema, he became a filmmaker by "handling millions of feet of film." Alvarez feels himself to be a journalist, but believes that cinematic journalism should have a permanence beyond simple reportage. To achieve such transcendency, Alvarez's newsreels are typically monothematic and integrated, with the result that they appear more like individual documentary films than the sort of generalized news reporting normally associated with newsreels.

The dominant characteristic of Alvarez's style is the extraordinarily rhythmic blend of visual and audio forms. Alvarez utilizes everything at hand to convey his message: live and historical documentary footage, still photos, bits from TV programs and fiction films, animation, and an incredible range of audio accompaniment. Believing that "50% of the value of a film is in the soundtrack," Alvarez mixes rock, classical, and tropical music, sound effects, participant narration—even silence—to the furious pace of his visual images. For Alvarez, cinema has its own language, different from that of television or of radio, and the essence of this language is montage.

Alvarez's documentaries focus on both national and international themes. For example, *Ciclon* is an early newsreel on the effects of hurricane Flora in Cuba. Although it lacks the elaborate visual montage for which Alvarez later became famous, the film shows great skill in the use of sound. There is no verbal narration, and the track is limited to the source sound of trucks and helicopters, and the organ music which eerily punctuates the scenes of caring for the wounded and burying the dead.

Now, a short dealing with racism in the U.S. and edited to the rhythm of Lena Horne's song, shows the master at his best in working with still photographs. Particularly effective is a sequence in which Alvarez cuts between the chained hands of arrested blacks and the linked hands of protestors to suggest a dynamic of collective struggle in which people are seen not only as products of their circumstances, but as historical actors capable of changing their circumstances. Here, Alvarez fuses ideology and art by making graphic the third of Marx's "Theses on Feuerbach." Alvarez's tribute to Che Guevara, *Hasta la victoria siempre*, deals with much the same concept. He begins with a series of beautifully shot stills of poverty in the Altiplano. Then, following footage of Che speaking in the Sierra Maestra of Cuba, he dissolves a still of Che into a still of a Gulf Oil Co. camp in Bolivia. Through this technique he links the earlier struggle in Cuba with the later guerrilla war in the Andes.

One of the finest examples of Alvarez's work is *79 Springtimes*, a beautifully controlled montage on Ho Chi Minh's life and death. He opens the short by ironically mixing elapsed-time photography of flowers opening with slow-motion footage of bombs falling from U.S. planes. He goes on to cut between scenes of U.S. atrocities in Viet Nam and protest marches in the U.S., visually depicting the position that the real enemy is not the people of the U.S., but the ruling class and its mercenaries. In the final sequence, Alvarez uses what seems to be every available visual effect—torn and burned strips of film, film frames, bits of paper—to create an incredible animated montage. The sound track underscores the visual dynamic with music and poems by Ho Chi Minh and Jose Martí.

Alvarez continues to be thought of as one of the foremost documentary filmmakers in Latin America, although some consider his earlier short films to be superior to the later and longer works. This may result from the fact that in the earlier films the line between heroes (Che, Ho Chi Minh) and villains (U.S. imperialism and racism) was more clearly drawn, while the later works reflect the international compromises with the Soviet Union and reformist Latin American governments that have been required of the Cuban revolution. Nonetheless, Alvarez persists in his indefatigable quest for an "audacious and constantly renewed optic."

—John Mraz

ANDERSON, Lindsay.

British. Born Lindsay Gordon Anderson in Bangalore, South India, 17 April 1923. Educated at Cheltenham College and at Wadham College, Oxford. Member of Army Intelligence Corps during WWII. Editor, *Sequence* magazine, 1947–52; helped organize first Free Cinema program, National Film Theatre, 1956; directed first feature, *This Sporting Life*, 1963; Associate Artistic Director, Royal Court Theatre, 1971–75; has also directed TV plays and commercials. Recipient: Oscar for Best Short Subject, for *Thursday's Children*, 1955; Palme d'Or, Cannes Festival, for *If . . .* , 1969. Address: 9 Stirling Mansions, Canfield Gardens, London NW6 3JT.

Films as Director:

1948	*Meet the Pioneers* (+sc, co-ed, narration)
1949	*Idlers That Work* (+sc, narration)
1952	*Three Installations* (+sc, narration); *Trunk Conveyor* (+sc, narration); *Wakefield Express* (+sc)
1953	*Thursday's Children* (co-d, +co-sc); *O Dreamland* (+sc)
1955	*Green and Pleasant Land* (+sc); *Henry* (+sc,ro); *The Children Upstairs* (+sc); *A Hundred Thousand Children* (+sc); *£20 a Ton* (+sc); *Energy First* (+sc); *Foot and Mouth* (+sc, narration)
1957	*Every Day Except Christmas* (+sc)
1963	*This Sporting Life*
1967	*The White Bus*; *Raz, dwa, trzy (The Singing Lesson)* (+sc)
1969	*If . . .* (+pr)
1972	*O Lucky Man!* (+co-pr)
1974	*In Celebration*
1982	*Britannia Hospital*
1986	*The Whales of August*
1988	*Glory! Glory!*

Other Films:

1949	*Out of Season* (Brendon) (narrator)
1952	*The Pleasure Garden* (Broughton) (pr, ro)
1956	*Together* (Mazzetti) (supervising ed)
1958	*March to Aldermaston* (supervising ed)
1960	*Let My People Go* (Krish) (sponsor)
1962	*The Story of Private Pooley* (Alsen—English language version of *Der Schwur des Soldaten Pooley*) (narrator)
1965	*The Threatening Sky* (Ivens—English language version of *Le Ciel, la terre*) (narrator)
1966	*Mucednici Iásky (Martyrs of Love)* (Němec) (ro)
1967	*About 'The White Bus'* (Fletcher) (ro as himself)
1968	*Abel Gance—The Charm of Dynamite* (Brownlow) (for TV) (narrator); *Inadmissable Evidence* (Page) (ro)
1969	*The Parachute* (Page) (for TV) (ro)
1970	*Hetty King—Performer* (Robinson) (narrator)
1971	*A Mirror from India* (Sarabhai) (narrator)
1981	*Chariots of Fire* (Hudson) (ro as schoolmaster)

Publications:

By ANDERSON: books—

Making a Film: The Story of "Secret People", London, 1952.
If . . . : A Film by Lindsay Anderson, with David Sherwin, New York, 1969.
O Lucky Man!, with David Sherwin, New York, 1973.

By ANDERSON: articles—

"Angles of Approach," in *Sequence* (London), Winter 1947.
"The Need for Competence," in *Sequence* (London), Spring 1948.
"What Goes On," in *Sequence* (London), Summer 1948.
"Creative Elements," in *Sequence* (London), Autumn 1948.
"British Cinema: The Descending Spiral," in *Sequence* (London), Spring 1949.
"The Film Front," in *Sequence* (London), Summer 1949.
"Films of Alfred Hitchcock," in *Sequence* (London), Autumn 1949.
"Notes at Cannes," in *Sequence* (London), New Year issue 1950.
"The Director's Cinema?," in *Sequence* (London), Autumn 1950.
"Retrospective Review: *Wagonmaster* and *Two Flags West*," in *Sight and Sound* (London), December 1950.
"Goldwyn at Claridges," in *Sequence* (London), New Year issue 1951.
"John Ford," in *Films in Review* (New York), February 1951.
"Minnelli, Kelly and *An American in Paris*," in *Sequence* (London), New Year Issue 1952.
"As the Critics Like It: Some Personal Choices," in *Sight and Sound* (London), October/December 1952.
"Only Connect: Some Aspects of the Work of Humphrey Jennings," in *Sight and Sound* (London), April/June 1953; reprinted in *The Documentary Tradition*, edited by Lewis Jacobs, New York, 1974.
"Encounter with Prévert," in *Sight and Sound* (London), July/September 1953.

Lindsay Anderson, 1960   © **Roger Mayne**

"French Critical Writing," in *Sight and Sound* (London), October/December 1954.

"Stand Up! Stand Up!," in *Sight and Sound* (London), Autumn 1956.

"Notes from Sherwood," in *Sight and Sound* (London), Winter 1956.

"Ten Feet Tall," in *Sight and Sound* (London), Summer 1957.

"The Critical Issue: A Discussion Between Paul Rotha, Basil Wright, Lindsay Anderson, Penelope Houston," in *Sight and Sound* (London), Autumn 1957.

"Two Inches Off the Ground," in *Sight and Sound* (London), Winter 1957.

"Get Out and Push!," in *Declaration*, edited by Tom Maschler, London, 1958.

"Sport, Life and Art," in *Films and Filming* (London), February 1963.

"An Interview with Lindsay Anderson," with Peter Cowie, in *Film Quarterly* (Berkeley), Summer 1964.

"The Film Maker and the Audience," in *Film Makers on Film Making*, edited by Harry Geduld, Bloomington, Indiana, 1967.

Interview, in *Documentary Explorations: 15 Interviews with Filmmakers*, by G. Roy Levin, New York, 1971.

"Stripping the Veils Away," interview with David Robinson, in the *Times* (London), 21 April 1973.

"From Theater to Film . . . Lindsay Anderson," interview with M. Carducci, in *Millimeter* (New York), January 1975.

"Revolution is the opium of the intellectuals;" an interview with E. Rampell, in *Cineaste* (New York), vol. 12, no. 4, 1983.

"Lindsay Anderson, unfashionable humanist, in conversation," interview with Gerald Pratley, in *Cinema Canada* (Montreal), June 1985.

Interview in *American Cinematographer* (Los Angeles), October 1987.

Interview with John Russell Taylor, in *Films and Filming* (London), March 1988.

On ANDERSON: books—

Manvell, Roger, *New Cinema in Britain*, New York, 1969.

Sussex, Elizabeth, *Lindsay Anderson*, New York, 1969.

Barsam, Richard, *Nonfiction Film*, New York, 1973.

Silet, Charles L. P., *Lindsay Anderson: A Guide to References and Resources*, Boston, 1979.

Graham, Allison, *Lindsay Anderson*, Boston, 1981.

On ANDERSON: articles—

Berger, John, "Look at Britain!," in *Sight and Sound* (London), Summer 1957.

Milne, Tom, "*This Sporting Life*," in *Sight and Sound* (London), Summer 1962.

Robinson, David, "Anderson Shooting *If . . .*," in *Sight and Sound* (London), Summer 1968.

Gladwell, David, "Editing Anderson's *If . . .*," in *Screen* (London), January/February 1969.

Lovell, Alan, and Jim Hillier, "Free Cinema," in *Studies in Documentary*, New York, 1972.

Lovell, Alan, "The Unknown Cinema of Britain," in *Cinema Journal* (Evanston), Spring 1972.

Wilson, D., "*O Lucky Man!*," in *Sight and Sound* (London), Summer 1973.

Taylor, John, "Lindsay Anderson," in *Directors and Directions*, London, 1975.

Lovell, Alan, "Brecht in Britain–Lindsay Anderson," in *Screen* (London), Winter 1975.

Durgnat, Raymond, "Britannia Waives the Rules," in *Film Comment* (New York), July/August 1976.

Lefèvre, Raymond, "Lindsay Anderson, ou la fidelité au Free Cinema," in *Image et Son* (Paris), October 1982.

Schickel, Richard, "Ford Galaxy," in *Film Comment* (New York), March–April 1984.

Houston, Penelope, "Parker, Attenborough, Anderson," in *Sight and Sound* (London), Summer 1986.

*   *   *

In a 1958 essay entitled "Get Out and Push," Lindsay Anderson expressed his approach to working in the cinema. The way Anderson, the individual, approaches working in the cinema, the system of film production, parallels the world view he puts forth in his feature films: the individual must examine the basis of the system within which he finds himself, "the motives that sustain it and the interests that it serves." It is the responsibility of the individual to actively seek a new self-definition beyond the confines of the established system; the individual cannot look for change to come from or through any outside authority—political, social, or spiritual. This theme is consistently present in Anderson's feature films.

In *This Sporting Life*, Anderson approaches the repression of a traditionally structured society through the personal, subjective story of Frank Machin and Margaret Hammond. The setting of *This Sporting Life*, an industrial northern city, is an environment divided into economic classes, a division which serves to emphasize the central problem of the film—the division within Frank Machin. Machin finds himself limited to the realm of the physical, and constantly attempts to connect with others on an emotional level. Despite his attempts, he is only seen in terms of his physical qualities; he is valued only when he is participating in the physical act of playing rugby.

Frank Machin is aware of his limitations but does not know how to change; he lacks direction. He tries to make others responsible for his happiness: Margaret Hammond, the rugby team, and even the elites of society who populate the world of Mr. and Mrs. Weaver, owners of the rugby team. Machin constantly attempts to break into the established system, seemingly unaware that it is this same system which controls and restrains him.

Mick Travis, the protagonist of Anderson's second feature film *If . . .*, struggles instead to break out of the established system. Mick takes on the responsibility of action, and although his revolution is not complete, he does not remain trapped like Frank.

The environment in *If . . .*, the English public school system, is a metaphor for, as Elizabeth Sussex states, the "separation of intellect from imagination." The environment of College House does not allow for the creative development of the individual; it encourages separation and fragmentation of the self. The students of College House are told to, "Work, play, but don't mix the two."

Film technique in *If . . .* also serves to reveal the narrative theme of the division of the self. The chapter headings physically divide the film into rigidly ordered sections, reflecting the separation of intellect and imagination encouraged by the nature of the tradition of College House. These chapter headings, along with the alternation between black and white and color film, function as distancing devices, making the viewer more aware of the medium.

A narrative technique which Anderson uses to illustrate the process that leads to Mick's eventual break from the system is the establishment of verbal language as an essential part of the structure of College House. When Mick expresses his disdain for College House through words, they are simply absorbed by the system. There is no change in Mick's situation until he initiates action by bayoneting the college chaplain. After this point, Mick no longer recites revolutionary rhetoric; in fact, he rarely speaks. He is no longer existing within the structure of College House. Totally free of the system, Mick launches into the destruction of the established order. Mick is no longer acted upon but is the creator of action; in this respect, he triumphs where Frank Machin fails.

In *O Lucky Man!*, the thematic sequel to *If . . .*, the medium of film itself becomes one of the narrative themes, and self-reflexive film techniques serve to reveal not only the narrative theme of self-definition, but also the process of filmmaking. The titles used in *O Lucky Man!* announce different sections of the film but do not impose order; on the contrary, their abrupt appearance and brevity tend to interrupt the order of the narrative. It is as if the medium of film itself breaks through to remind the viewer of its existence. Indeed the medium, specifically the energy the medium generates, is one of the themes of *O Lucky Man!* The process of creation in the medium far exceeds anything Mick accomplishes in the narrative until the two meet in the final sequence.

Mick Travis, the character, confronts Lindsay Anderson, the director, at an audition for the film *O Lucky Man!* Mick obediently projects the different emotions Anderson demands of him until he is asked to smile. It is at this point that Mick finally takes action and rejects a direct order: "What is there to smile about?" he asks. Mick is looking outside himself for motivation, as he has done throughout the film, before he will take action. Anderson, exasperated, strikes Mick with a script. After receiving the blow, Mick is able to smile. He soon finds that he is one of the actors in the film; he too is capable of creating action.

Britannia Hospital, the final work in the series begun by *If . . .*, presents a much darker vision than Anderson's two previous films. As in *If . . .*, the physical environment of the film, the hospital, is a metaphor for a static, repressive system. Unlike *If . . .*, this film contains little hope for change or progress, not for the individual and certainly not within the system itself.

Mick Travis appears in this film as an investigative reporter who has achieved success by selling "something the people want," a reference to his former position in *O Lucky Man!* and a description of his motives as a news reporter. He is attempting to expose the questionable experiments of Britannia Hospital staff member Dr. Millar, the same unethical researcher from *O Lucky Man!* Although Mick puts up a fight, the system finally overwhelms him in this film.

Glory! Glory!, a Home Box Office production, is somewhat of a synthesis of Anderson's previous work in both theme and technique. The institution that stands as metaphor in this case is one peculiar to the United States, a television evangelism empire—The Church of the Companions of Christ. Like the school in *If . . .*, this institution has a verbal language essential to its structure, the use of which sanctions just about any action. Throughout the film people have "revelations" or "visions" in which God makes key decisions for them, removing all personal responsibility. Any action is justifiable—deception, fraud, blackmail—as long as it is done in "a holy cause" or "for the church."

The film techniques Anderson uses in *Glory! Glory!* are related to his earlier works. The medium is present throughout the narrative in the form of chapter headings and blackouts between chapters and between some scenes within chapters. Music is important to this narrative as it is in *O Lucky Man!*, but in the later film it is integrated into the narrative structure rather than used as a distancing device.

The theme of personal responsibility for self-definition is clearly seen in the character of Ruth. She struggles throughout the film with the idea of who she wants to be and with the identities others want to impose on her. She reaches a key point in her personal progression when she admits that she has always needed some kind of crutch—sex, drugs, God. Not long after realizing that she has been looking outside herself for an identity, Ruth reveals that she finally understands God. In essence, she has created her own god, her own mythology. Ruth remains within the system, but for the first time actually believes in what she's "selling" because she has defined for herself the "authority" and the basis for the system.

Anderson's feature films have been generally well received critically; *Britannia Hospital* did not do well in Britain, but was praised by critics elsewhere. Anderson's other features, *In*

Celebration and *The Whales of August*, contain more subjective narratives but still explore the theme of the individual's responsibility for self-definition.

—Marie Saeli

ANGELOPOULOS, Theodoros.

(Surname also spelled "Anghelopoulos") Greek. Born in Athens, 27 April 1935. Studied in Athens 1953–59, Sorbonne, Paris, 1961–64, and at IDHEC, Paris, 1962–63. Military Service, 1959–60. Film critic for left-wing journal *Dimoktatiki Allaghi* until its suppression in 1967 coup; worked as lawyer until 1969; began association with cinematographer Giorgios Arvanitis on *Reconstruction*, 1970; taught at Stavrakou Film School in 1970's. Recipient: Georges Sadoul Award, 1971; FIPRESCI Grand Prix, 1975; Golden Lion Award, Venice, 1980. Lives in Athens.

Films as Director and Scriptwriter:

1968   *Ekpombi (The Broadcast, L'Emission)*
1970   *Anaparastassi (Reconstruction, Reconstitution) (+ro)*
1972   *Mères tou 36 (Days of '36, Jours de 36)*
1975   *O Thaissos (The Travelling Players, Le Voyage des comédiens)*
1977   *I Kynighi (The Hunters) (+co-pr)*
1980   *O Megalexandros (Alexander the Great) (+pr)*
1982   *Athens (doc)*
1984   *Taxidi sta Kithira (Voyage to Cythera)*
1986   *O Melissokomos (The Beekeeper)*
1988   *Topio stia Omichli (Landscape in the Mist)*

Role:

1968   in *Kieron* (Theos)

Publications:

By ANGELOPOULOS: articles—

"Mes films sont des appels à la discussion . . . ," interview with N. Ghali, in *Cinéma* (Paris), September/October 1975.
"*Le Voyage des comédiens*," interview with J.-P. Brossard and others, in *Image et Son* (Paris), November 1975.
Interview with Michel Ciment, in *Positif* (Paris), June 1977.
Interview with D. Rabourdin, in *Cinéma* (Paris), August/September 1977.
"Les Chasseurs," interview with O. Barrot and M. Demopoulos, in *Ecran* (Paris), November 1977.
"Animating Dead Space and Dead Time," interview and article with T. Mitchell, in *Sight and Sound* (London), Winter 1980/81.
Interviews with Michel Ciment, in *Positif* (Paris), February 1985 and May 1987.
Interview with G. Merat, in *Revue du Cinéma* (Paris), November 1988.

On ANGELOPOULOS: books—

Schuster, Mel, *The Contemporary Greek Cinema*, Metuchen, New Jersey, 1979.
Orati, Daniela, *Thodoros Anghelopoulos*, Venice, 1982.
Estève, Michel, *Theo Angelopoulos*, Paris, 1985.
Ciment, Michel, and Hélène Tiarchent, *Theo Angelopoulos*, Paris, 1989.
Kolovos, Nikos, *Theo Angelopoulos*, Athens, 1990.
O'Grady, Gerald, editor, *Theo Angelopoulos (MOMA Exhibition Catalogue)*, New York, 1990.

On ANGELOPOULOS: Articles—

Cineforum (Bergamo), September 1975.
Positif (Paris), October 1975.
Avant-Scène du Cinéma (Paris), December 1975.
Giacci, V., in *Cineforum* (Bergamo), September 1976.
Horton, Andrew, "Theodoros Angelopoulos and the New Greek Cinema," in *Film Criticism* (Meadville, Pennsylvania), Fall 1981.
Dossier on Angelopoulos, in *Cinéma* (Paris), November 1982.
"Angelopoulos Section" of *Revue du Cinéma/Image et Son* (Paris), January 1985.
Amengual, Barthélémy, "Une esthetique 'théatrale' de la realité: sur Theo Angelopoulos," in *Positif* (Paris), February 1985.
"Angelopoulos Issue" of *Revue Belge du Cinéma* (Brussels), Spring 1985.
Sight and Sound (London), Winter 1988 and Autumn 1989.
Brown, Georgia, in *Village Voice* (New York), 20 February 1990.

*   *   *

Angelopoulos's considerable achievements in the 1970's and 1980's have made him not only the most important Greek filmmaker to date, but one of the truly creative and original artists of his time. In 1970 he convinced a young producer, George Papalios, to finance his first film, *Anaparastassi*. The story follows the pattern of a crime tale à la James Cain. A Greek peasant is killed by his wife and her lover on his return from Germany where he had gone to find work. A judge tries to reconstruct the circumstances of the murder but finds himself unable to communicate with the accused who belong to a totally different culture. To shoot this Pirandellian story of misunderstanding, Angelopoulos adopted an austere style with long camera movements that show a bleak and desolate Greek landscape, far from the tourist leaflets. Very much like Visconti's *Ossessione*, this is a film noir that opens the way to more daring aesthetic ventures.

His trilogy, *Days of 36, The Travelling Players* and *The Hunters* can be seen as an exploration of contemporary Greek history. If his style shows some influences—particularly Jancsó's with his use of the one reel-one take and Antonioni's for its slow, meditative mood—Angelopoulos has nevertheless created an authentic epic cinema akin to Brecht's theatre where aesthetic emotion is counterbalanced by a reflexive approach that questions the surfaces of reality. The audience is neither allowed to identify with a central character, nor to follow a dramatic development, or given a reassuring morality. The director boldly goes from the present to the past within the same shot and in *The Hunters* broadens his investigation by including the fantasies of his characters. The sweep of a movie like *Travelling Players*, which includes songs and dances, is breathtaking and its length (four hours) transforms it into the earth odyssey of an actors group circulating through Greece from 1939 to 1952 performing a pastoral play. Angelopoulos's masterpiece had been preceded by the haunting *Days of 36*, a political thriller about a murder in a prison which was a prelude to events of national importance. It is the director's most radical use of off-screen space and off-screen sound, of the dialectic between the seen and the unseen. With its closed doors, whispering voices in corridors, and silhouettes running to and fro, it evokes the mystery that surrounds the exercise of power.

Angelopoulos's fifth film, *Alexander the Great* breaks new ground: it deals with myth and develops the exploration of the popular unconscious already present in *Travelling Players* and *The Hunters*. At the turn of the 20th century, a bandit is seen as the reincarnation of the Macedonian king. He kidnaps some English residents in Greece, leads them to the mountains, tries to blackmail the British government and ends by killing his hostages. Angelopoulos opposes several groups: the foreigners, the outlaws, some Italian anarchists who have taken refuge in Greece, and village people who try to establish a uto-pian community. The director's indictment of hero-worshipping and his portrayal of diverse forms of political failure reveal a growing pessimism in his works. But his style is as masterly as ever, reaching a kind of austere grandeur reminiscent of Byzantine mosaics. Few have blended so satisfyingly a political investigation with a search for new forms of expression.

—Michel Ciment

————

ANGER, Kenneth.

American. Born in Santa Monica, California, 1930. Played changeling in Max Reinhardt's film of *A Midsummer Night's Dream*, 1934; studied tap-dancing in class including Shirley Temple, 1935; completed first film, 1941; after moving to Europe, first edition of *Hollywood Babylon* published in France, 1959; returned to U.S., 1962; following destruction of his film *Lucifer Rising*, placed an ad in *Variety* "In Memoriam Kenneth Anger 1947–1967," and returned to Europe, 1967; completed second version of *Lucifer Rising*, 1974 (released 1980). Address: c/o American Federation of Arts Film Program, 41 E. 65th St., New York, NY 10021, U.S.A.

Films (Conception, Direction, Photography and Editing):

1941   *Who Has Been Rocking My Dream Boat*
1941/42   *Tinsel Tree*
1942   *Prisoner of Mars*
1943   *The Nest*
1944   *Escape Episode*
1945   *Drastic Demise*
1946   *Escape Episode* (sound version)
1947   *Fireworks** (+ro as The Dreamer)
1948   *Puce Women* (unfinished)
1949   *Puce Moment**; *The Love That Whirls* (unfinished)
1950   *La Lune des Lapins* (*Rabbit's Moon*)* (conception, d and ed only, +prod.design)
1951/52   *Maldoror* (unfinished)
1953   *Eaux d'artifice** (+costume design); *Le Jeune Homme et la mort*
1954   *Inauguration of the Pleasure Dome** (+ro as Hecate)
1955   *Thelema Abbey* (conception, d and ed only)
1962/63   *Scorpio Rising**
1965   *Kustom Kar Kommandos**
1969   *Invocation of My Demon Brother**
1971   *Rabbit's Moon*
1974   *Lucifer Rising**
1980   *Lucifer Rising** (second version)
1989   *Mouse Heaven*

Note:*indicates films contained and distributed in Anger's definitive portfolio "The Magick Lantern Cycle".

Publications:

By ANGER: books—

Hollywood Babylon, Phoenix, Arizona, 1965; reprinted San Francisco, 1975.
Magick Lantern Cycle: A Special Presentation in Celebration of the Equinox Spring 1966, New York, 1966.
Hollywood Babylon II, New York, 1984.

By ANGER: articles—

Interview in *Spider Magazine*, v.1, no. 13, 1965.
Interview in *Film Culture* (New York), Spring 1966.
Article in *Film Makers on Filmmaking*, edited by Harry Geduld, Bloomington, Indiana, 1967.

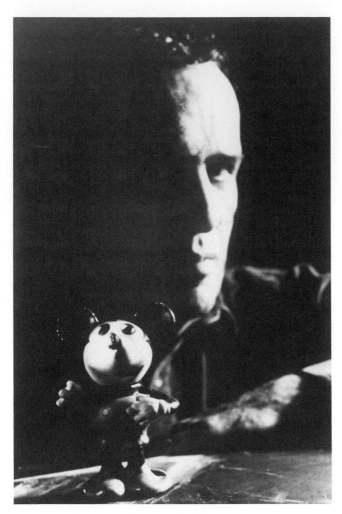

Kenneth Anger with the star of *Mouse Heaven*

Interview with Bruce Martin and Joe Medjuck, in *Take One* (Montreal), August 1967.
Interview with Lenny Lipton, in *Filmmakers Newsletter* (Ward Hill, Mass.), November 1967.
Correspondence between Kenneth Anger and Paul Johnston, in *Film Culture* (New York), nos. 70–71, 1983.
Interview with J. English, in *On Film* (Los Angeles), Summer 1983.
Interview in *City Limits* (London), 7 February 1986.

On ANGER: books—

Battcock, Gregory, editor, *The New American Cinema*, New York, 1967.
Youngblood, Gene, *Expanded Cinema*, New York, 1970.
Sitney, P. Adams, *Visionary Film*, New York, 1974.
Hanhardt, John, and others, *A History of the American Avant-Garde Cinema*, New York, 1976
Haller, Robert A., *Kenneth Anger*, St. Paul, Minnesota, 1980.
Burchfield, John, *Kenneth Anger: The Shape of His Achievements*, New York, n.d.
O'Pray, Michael, and Jayne Pilling, *Into the Pleasure Dome: The Films of Kenneth Anger*, London, 1990.

On ANGER: articles—

"Filmography of Kenneth Anger," in *Film Culture* (New York), no. 31, 1963/64.
Kelman, Kenneth, "Thanatos in Chrome," and P. Adams Sitney, "Imagism in Four Avant-Garde Films," in *Film Culture* (New York), Winter 1963/64.
Micha, Rene, "Le Nouveau Cinéma," in *Les Temps modernes* (Paris), no. 214, 1964.
Kelman, Kenneth, "Appendix to Thanatos in Chrome," in *Film Culture* (New York), Spring 1964.
Alexander, Thomas, "San Francisco's Hipster Cinema," in *Film Culture* (New York), no. 44, 1967.
Cornwall, Regina, "On Kenneth Anger," in *December* (New York), no. 1, 1968.
Rayns, Tony, "*Lucifer*: A Kenneth Anger Kompendium," in *Cinema* (Cambridge), October 1969.
Sitney, P. Adams, "The Avant-Garde: Kenneth Anger and George Landow," in *Afterimage* (Rochester, New York), no. 2, 1970.
Mekas, Jonas, Richard Whitehall, and P. Adams Sitney, "Three Notes on *Invocation of My Demon Brother*," in *Film Culture* (New York), Winter/Spring 1970.
Magny, Joel, "Collectif jeune cinéma: 3e nuit blanche," in *Cinéma* (Paris), April 1972.
"Anger at Work," in *Cinema Rising*, April 1972.
Rowe, C., "Illuminating Lucifer," in *Film Quarterly* (Berkeley), Summer 1974.
Saslow, James, "Kenneth Anger: Holding a Magick Lantern Up to the Future," in *Advocate*, 23 July 1981.
Hardy, Robin, "Kenneth Anger: Master in Hell," and Michael Wade, "Kenneth Anger: Personal Traditions and Satanic Pride," in *Body Politic*, April 1982.
Hoberman, J., "Sympathy for the devil," in *American Film* (Washington, D.C.), March 1981.
Wees, W.C., "Before *Lucifer*: Preternatural light in the films of Kenneth Anger," in *Cine-Tracts* (Montreal), Summer-Fall 1982.
Rayns, Tony, "The Elusive Lucifer," in *Monthly Film Bulletin* (London), September 1982.
"Kenneth Anger," in *Film Dope* (London), March 1988.

*   *   *

One of the key figures of the postwar American avant-garde, Kenneth Anger represents a fiercely original talent, relatively free of the independent circles and movements which his own work managed to anticipate in almost every case. Creator of an oeuvre and a persona defined by their dialectical relationship to dominant representational, ideological, industrial, sexual and aesthetic practices, Anger embodies the "radical otherness" of the avant-garde filmmaker, casting himself not only outside the mainstream, but as its negative image. While other experimentalists were exploring "ways of seeing" through cinematic abstraction, Anger remained committed to a search for meanings, even as his films pursued a variety of aesthetic paths. Anger's meanings emerge from his subversive reworkings of sources already charged with significance: the iconography of American popular culture (movie stars, comic strips, car clubs), the conventional rhetoric of narrative forms (from the commedia dell'arte to the lyrics of rock songs), the imagery of classic cinema (Cocteau, Eisenstein, DeMille), and the symbolism of various mythologies (Egyptian, Greek, astrological, alchemical, centered by the cosmology of master "magickian" Aleister Crowley.

Anger gained international prominence and notoriety at the age of 17 with his film *Fireworks*, in which he appeared as the protagonist of a homoerotic fantasy in the oneiric tradition of Cocteau and Maya Deren, shot through with the romantic sadism of the American film noir. Three years later, he made *Rabbit's Moon*, a delicately humorous, Méliès-like fantasy involving a Pierrot character and a magic lantern, shot in Cocteau's own studio in Paris. Another three years found Anger in Italy, where he choreographed an elaborately baroque game of hide-and-seek through Tivoli's water gardens in *Eaux d'artifice*. Focusing at intervals on the visual patterns of water flowing from the fountains, this film experiments with the textures of an abstract filmic image a full two years before Brakhage's *Wonder Ring*. Yet, characteristically, the multiple superimpositions of Anger's colorful mass/masquerade *Inauguration of the Pleasure Dome* have less to do with abstraction than with an effort to achieve a magical condensation of mythological imagery. *Scorpio Rising*, however, remains Anger's most influential and original work. A tour-de-force collage of pop imagery, it is a paean to the American motorcyclist, a revelation of the violent, homoerotic undercurrent of American culture, and a celebration of the forces of chaos in the universe.

Anger spent most of the mid- to late-1960's on two abortive projects. His *Kustom Kar Kommandos* was cut short by the death of the young man playing its protagonist, although one sensual sequence, involving the dusting of a custom hot rod with a powder puff, has survived. Far more ambitious, however, was a master opus entitled *Lucifer Rising*, a project cut tragically short when, at a 1967 San Francisco screening of the work-in-progress, the single print of the film was stolen by one of the film's actors, Manson cultist Bobby Beausoleil, and was supposedly buried somewhere in Death Valley, never to be recovered. This event was followed by Anger's self-imposed retirement, interrupted in 1969 by the appearance of an 11-minute structural black mass constructed largely of *Lucifer's* outtakes, backed by a maddeningly monotonous soundtrack by Mick Jagger, and entitled *Invocation of my Demon Brother*.

By 1974, however, Anger had completed another version of *Lucifer Rising*, a dense meditative work shot mostly in Egypt, imbued with Crowleian mysticism and most memorable for the thoroughly uncanny image of a pinkish flying saucer hovering above the pyramids. The far more complete version finally released by Anger in 1980 marks a quantum leap in terms of *Lucifer Rising's* complexity, and remains the *chef-d'oeuvre* of Anger's career.

—Ed Lowry

———————

ANTONIONI, Michelangelo.

Italian. Born in Ferrara, Italy, 29 September 1912. Studied at University of Bologna, 1931–35, and at Centro Sperimentale di Cinematografica, Rome, 1940–41. Journalist and bank teller, 1935–39; moved to Rome, 1939; film critic for *Cinema* (Rome) and others, 1940–49; assistant director on *I due Foscari* (Fulchignoni), 1942; wrote screenplays for Rossellini, Fellini, and others, 1942–52; directed first film, *Gente del Po*, 1943 (released 1947). Recipient: Special Jury Prize, Cannes Festival for *L'avventura*, 1960, and *L'eclisse*, 1962; FIPRESCI Award from Venice Festival, for *Il deserto Rosso*, 1964; Best Director Award, National Society of Film Critics, for *Blow-Up*, 1966; Palme d'Or, Cannes Festival, for *Blow-Up*, 1967. Address: Via Vicenzo Tiberio 18, Rome, Italy.

Films as Director:

1950   *Cronaca di un amore (Story of a Love Affair)* (+co-sc)
1952   *I Vinti (I nostri figli, The Vanquished)* (+co-sc)
1953   *La signora senza camelie (Camille Without Camelias)* (+co-sc); "Tentato suicidio" episode of *L'Amore in città* (+sc)
1955   *Le amiche (The Girlfriends)* (+co-sc)
1957   *Il grido (The Outcry)* (+co-sc)
1959   *L'avventura* (+co-sc)
1960   *La notte (The Night)* (+co-sc)
1962   *L'eclisse (The Eclipse)* (+co-sc)
1964   *Deserto rosso (Red Desert)* (+co-sc)
1965   "Prefizione" episode of *Tre Volti* (+sc)
1966   *Blow-Up* (+co-sc)

1970   *Zabriskie Point* (+co-sc)
1972   *Chung Kuo (La cina)* (+sc)
1975   **Professione: Reporter (The Passenger)** (+co-sc)
1979   *Il mistero di Oberwald (The Oberwald Mystery)* (+sc)
1982   *Identificazione di una donna* (+sc)

Short Films as Director and Scriptwriter:

1947   *Gente del Po*
1948   *N.U. (Nettezza urbana)*; *Roma—Montevideo*; *Oltre l'oblio*
1949   *L'amorosa menzogna*; *Bomarzo*; *Superstizione*; *Ragazze in bianco*
1950   *Sette canne e un vestito*; *La villa dei mostri*; *La funivia del Faloria*; *Uomini in piú*

Publications:

By ANTONIONI: books—

La Nuit: La Notte, with Tonino Guerra and E. Flaiano, Paris, 1961.
L'eclisse, with Tonino Guerra and E. Bartolini, Capelli, 1962.
Screenplays by Michelangelo Antonioni, New York, 1963.
Michelangelo Antonioni, Rome, 1964.
Blow-Up, with Tonino Guerra, Turin, 1968; New York, 1971.
L'Avventura, with E. Bartolini, New York, 1969; New Brunswick, New Jersey, 1989.
Il Primo Antonioni (screenplays or working scripts for early Antonioni documentaries and films), edited by Carlo di Carlo, Bologna, 1973.
Il mistero di Oberwald, Turin, 1980.
That Bowling Alley on the Tiber: Tales of a Director, Oxford, 1986.

By ANTONIONI: articles—

"Brevario del cinema," in *Cinema* (Rome), no 11, 16, 20, 37, 41, 1949.
"Le allegre ragazze del '24," in *Cinema Nuovo* (Turin), 1956.
"There Must be a Reason for Every Film," in *Films and Filming* (London), April 1959.
Interview with M. Manceaux and Richard Roud, in *Sight and Sound* (London), Winter 1960/61.
Interview with André Labarthe, in *New York Film Bulletin*, no. 8, 1961.
"Reflections on a Film Career," in *Film Culture* (New York), no. 22–23, 1961.
"Eroticism—The Disease of Our Age," in *Films and Filming* (London), January 1961.
"La malattia dei sentimenti," in *Bianco e Nero* (Rome), February–March 1961.
"Making a Film is My Way of Life," in *Film Culture* (New York), Spring 1962.
"The Event and the Image," in *Sight and Sound* (London), Winter 1963/64.
"What Directors are Saying," in *Action* (Los Angeles), September/October 1969.
"Conversazione con Michelangelo Antonioni," in *Filmcritica* (Rome), March 1975.
"Antonioni after China: Art versus Science," interview with Gideon Bachmann, in *Film Quarterly* (Berkeley), Summer 1975.
"Antonioni Speaks . . . and Listens," interview with R. Epstein, in *Film Comment* (New York), July/August 1975.
"Antonioni and the Two-Headed Monster," interview with J.F. Lane, in *Sight and Sound* (London), Winter 1979/80.
Antonioni, Michelangelo, "Il 'big bang' della nascita di un film," in *Cinema Nuovo* (Bari), December 1981.
Interview with Gideon Bachman, in *Film Quarterly* (Berkeley), Summer 1983.
Interview with F. Tomasulo, in *On Film* (Los Angeles), Fall 1984.
"Michelangelo critico cinematografico (1935–1949)," edited by Aldo Tassone, in *Bianco e Nero* (Rome), July–September 1985.
"Quel big-bang con cui esplose lo spazio," in *Cinema Nuovo* (Bari), January/February 1987.

On ANTONIONI: books—

Carpi, Fabio, *Michelangelo Antonioni*, Parma, 1958.
Cowie, Peter, *Antonioni, Bergman, Resnais*, New York, 1963.

Michelangelo Antonioni

Leprohon, Pierre, *Michelangelo Antonioni: An Introduction*, New York, 1963.

Taylor, John Russell, *Cinema Eye, Cinema Ear*, New York, 1964.

Strick, Philip, *Antonioni*, London, 1965.

Sarris, Andrew, *Interviews with Film Directors*, New York, 1967.

Cameron, Ian, and Robin Wood, *Antonioni*, New York, 1969.

Huss, Roy, editor, *Focus on 'Blow-Up'*, Englewood Cliffs, New Jersey, 1971.

Samuels, Charles Thomas, *Encountering Directors*, New York, 1972.

Rifkin, Ned, *Antonioni's Visual Language*, Ann Arbor, Michigan, 1982.

Barthes, Roland, and others, *Michelangelo Antonioni*, Munich, 1984.

Biarese, Cesare, and Aldo Tassone, *I film di Michelangelo Antonioni*, Rome, 1985.

Chatman, Seymour, *Antonioni; or, The Surface of the World*, Berkeley, 1985.

Dervin, Daniel, *Through a Freudian Lens deeply: A Psychoanalysis of Cinema*, Hillsdale, New Jersey, 1985.

Mancini, Michele, and Giuseppe Perrella, *Michelangelo: Architecture in Vision*, Rome, 1986.

Perry, Ted, and René Prieto, *Michelangelo Antonioni: A Guide to References and Resources*, Boston, 1986.

Rohdie, Sam, *Antonioni*, London, 1990.

On ANTONIONI articles—

Bollero, Marcello, "Il documentario: Michelangelo Antonioni," in *Sequenze* (Italy), December 1949.

Cavallaro, Giambattista, "Michelangelo Antonioni, simbolo di una generazione," in *Bianco e Nero* (Rome), September 1957.

Renzi, Renzo, "Cronache del l'angoscia in Michelangelo Antonioni," in *Cinema Nuovo* (Turin), May/June 1959.

Roud, Richard, "Michelangelo Antonioni: Five Films," in *Sight and Sound* (London), Winter 1960/61.

Kauffmann, Stanley, "Arrival of an Artist," in the *New Republic* (New York), 10 April 1961.

Pepper, C.F., "Rebirth in Italy: Three Great Movie Directors," in *Newsweek* (New York), 10 July 1961.

Special Issue of *Film Quarterly* (Berkeley), Fall 1962.

"Antonioni issue" of *Seventh Art* (New York), Spring 1963.

Barthelme, Donald, "L'lapse," in the *New Yorker*, 2 March 1963.

Gerard, L.N., "Antonioni," in *Films in Review* (New York), April 1963.

"Michelangelo Antonioni: l'homme et l'objet," in *Etudes Cinématographiques* (Paris), no. 36–37, 1964.

Houston, Penelope, "Keeping up with the Antonionis," in *Sight and Sound* (London), Autumn 1964.

Garis, R., "Watching Antonioni," in *Commentary* (New York), April 1967.

Kinder, Marsha, "Antonioni in Transit," in *Sight and Sound* (London), Summer 1967.

Simon, J., and others, "Antonioni: What's the Point," in *Film Heritage* (Dayton, Ohio), Spring 1970.

Gow, Gordon, "Antonioni Men," in *Films and Filming* (London), June 1970.

Hernacki, T., "Michelangelo Antonioni and the Imagery of Disintegration," in *Film Heritage* (Dayton, Ohio), Fall 1970.

Lane, J. F., "Antonioni Discovers China," in *Sight and Sound* (London), Spring 1973.

Strick, Philip, "Antonioni Report," in *Sight and Sound* (London), Winter 1973/74.

Renzi, Renzo, "Antonioni nelle vesti del drago bianco," in *Cinema Nuovo* (Turin), May/June 1974.

Bachmann, Gideon, "Antonioni Down Under," in *Sight and Sound* (London), no. 4, 1976.

Burke, F., "The Natural Enmity of Words and Moving Images: Language, *La notte*, and the Death of the Light," in *Literature/Film Quarterly* (Salisbury, Maryland), no. 1, 1979.

Barthes, Roland, "Lettre à Antonioni," in *Cahiers du Cinéma* (Paris), May 1980.

Special Issue of *Camera/Stylo* (Paris), November 1982.

"Antonioni Section" of *Cahiers du Cinéma* (Paris), December 1982.

"Antonioni Section" of *Positif* (Paris), January 1983.

Ranvaud, Don, "Chronicle of a Career: Michelangelo Antonioni in Context," in *Monthly Film Bulletin* (London), March 1983.

Aristarco, G., "Notes on Michelangelo Antonioni," and A. Graham, "The Phantom Self," in *Film Criticism* (Meadville, Pennsylvania), Fall 1984.

Casetti, Francesco, "Antonioni and Hitchcock: Two Strategies of Narrative Investment," *SubStance* (Madison, Wisconsin), vol. 15, no. 3, 1986.

"Michelangelo Antonioni," in *Film Dope* (London), March 1988.

Lev, Peter, "*Blow Up*, Swinging London, and the Film generation," in *Literature/Film Quarterly* (Salisbury, Maryland), vol. 17, no. 2, 1989.

*   *   *

Antonioni's cinema is one of non-identification and displacement. In almost all of his films shots can be found whose striking emphasis on visual structure works in opposition to the spectator's desire to identify, as in classical Hollywood cinema, with either a protagonist's existential situation or with anything like a seamless narrative continuity—the "impression of reality" so often evoked in conjunction with the effect of fiction films on the spectator.

Since his first feature, *Cronaca di un amore*, Antonioni's introduction of utterly autonomous, graphically stunning shots into the film's narrative flow has gradually expanded to the point where, in *Professione: Reporter*, but even more emphatically in *Il mistero di Oberwald* and *Identificazione di una donna*, the unsettling effect of these discrete moments in the narrative continuity of the earlier work has taken over entirely. If these graphically autonomous shots of Antonioni's films of the fifties and sixties functioned as striking "figures" which unsettled the "ground" of narrative continuity, his latest films undo altogether this opposition between form and content, technique and substance, in order to spread the strangeness of the previously isolated figure across the entirety of the film which will thus emphatically establish itself as a "text."

That which might at first seem to mark a simple inversion of this opposition—where narrative substance would take a back seat to formal technique—instead works to question, in a broad manner, the ways in which films establish themselves as fictions. Antonioni's cinema strains the traditional conventions defining fiction films to the breaking point where, beginning at least as early as *Professione: Reporter*, those aspects always presumed to define what is "given" or "specific" or "proper" to film (which are commonly grouped together under the general heading of "technique") find themselves explicitly incorporated into the overall fabric of the film's narration; technique finds itself drawn into that which it supposedly presents neutrally, namely, the film's fictional universe. One might name this strategy the fictionalization of technique.

Such a strategy, however, is anything but self-reflexive, nor does it bear upon the thematics of Antonioni's films. In even those films where the protagonist has something to do with producing images, narratives, or other works of art (the filmmaker of *La signora senza camelie*, the architect of *L'av-*

ventura, the novelist of *La notte*, the photographer of *Blow-up*, the television reporter of *Professione: Reporter*, the poet of *Il mistero di Oberwald*, and the film director of *Identificazione di una donna*), their professions remain important only on the level of the film's drama, never in terms of its technique. It is as though the image of the artist were trapped in a world where self-reflection is impossible. Indeed, one common strand linking the thematics of all of Antonioni's films—the impossibility for men to communicate with women—might be seen to illustrate, on the level of drama, the kind of communicational impasse to be found on the level of "technique" in his cinema. Though his films are far from "experimental" in the sense of the work of Hollis Frampton, Michael Snow or Andy Warhol, Antonioni's fictional narratives always feel flattened or, to borrow a term from Roland Barthes, they seem curiously *mat*, as if the spectator's ability to gain immediate access to the fiction were being impeded by something.

Antonioni's films, then, are not simply "about" the cinema, but rather, in attempting to make films which always side-step the commonplace or the conventional (modes responsible for spectatorial identification and the "impression of reality"), they call into question what is taken to be a "language" of cinema by constructing a kind of textual idiolect which defies comparison with any other film, even Antonioni's other films. This may at least in part account for the formidable strangeness and difficulty of Antonioni's work, not just for general audiences but for mainstream critics as well. One constantly has the impression that the complexity of his films requires years in the cellar of critical speculation before it is ready to be understood; a film that is initially described as sour and flat ends up ten years later, as in the case of *L'avventura*, being proclaimed one of the ten best films of all time ("International Critics Poll," *Sight and Sound*). To judge from the reception in the United States of his most recent work, it appears that we are still at least ten years behind Antonioni.

As Antonioni has himself stressed repeatedly, the dramatic or the narrative aspect of his films—telling a story in the manner of literary narrative—comes to be of less and less importance; frequently, this is manifested by an absurd and complete absence of dramatic plausibility (*Zabriskie Point, Professione: Reporter, Il mistero di Oberwald*). The non-verbal logic of what remain narrative films depends, Antonioni says, upon neither a conceptual, nor emotional organization: "Some people believe I make films with my head; a few others think they come from the heart; for my part, I feel as though I make them with my stomach."

—Kimball Lockhart

———

ARMSTRONG, Gillian.

Australian. Born Melbourne, 18 December 1950. Educated at Swinburne College, studied Filmmaking at Melbourne and Australian Film and Television School, Sydney. Married, one daughter. Worked as production assistant, editor, art director, and assistant designer, and directed several short films; wrote and directed *The Singer and the Dancer*, which won best short fiction film award at Sydney Festival, 1976; directed first feature, *My Brilliant Career*, 1979; also director of documentaries and commercials. Agent: Judy Scott-Fox, William Morris Agency, 151 El Camino Drive, Beverly Hills, CA 90212.

Gillian Armstrong

Films as Director:

1970 *Old Man and Dog* (short)
1971 *Roof Needs Mowing* (short)
1973 *Gretel*; *Satdee Night*; *One Hundred a Day* (shorts)
1975 *Smokes and Lollies* (doc)
1976 *The Singer and the Dancer* (+pr, sc)
1979 **My Brilliant Career**
1980 *Fourteen's Good, Eighteen's Better* (doc) (+pr); *Touch Wood* (doc)
1982 *Starstruck*
1983 *Having a Go* (doc)
1984 *Mrs. Soffel*
1987 *High Tide*
1988 *Bingo, Bridesmaids and Braces* (+pr)

Publications:

By ARMSTRONG: articles—

Interviews in *Cinema Papers* (Melbourne), January 1974 and March–April 1979.
Films in Review (New York), June–July 1983.
Interview in *Encore* (Manly, New South Wales), 31 January 1985.
"Gillian Armstrong Returns to Eden," an interview with A. Grieve, in *Cinema Papers* (Melbourne), May 1987.
Interview in *Encore* (Manly, New South Wales), 29 September 1988.

On ARMSTRONG: books—

Tulloch, John, *Australian Cinema: Industry, Narrative, and Meaning*, Sydney and London, 1982.

McFarlane, Brian, *Words and Images: Australian Novels into Films*, Richmond, Victoria, 1983.
Mathews, Sue, *35mm Dreams: Conversations with Five Australian Directors*, Ringwood, Victoria, 1984.
Hall, Sandra, *Critical Business: The New Australian Cinema in Review*, Adelaide, 1985.
Moran, Albert, and Tom O'Regan, editors, *An Australian Film Reader*, Sydney, 1985.
McFarlane, Brian, *Australian Cinema 1970–85*, London, 1987.

On ARMSTRONG: articles—

"Profile," in *Time Out* (London), 24 January 1980.
Rickey, C., "Where the Girls Are," in *American Film* (Washington, D.C.), January–February 1985.
Enker, D., "Coming in from the Cold," in *Cinema Papers* (Melbourne), July 1985.
Mordue, Mark, "Homeward Bound: a profile of Gillian Armstrong," in *Sight and Sound* (London), Autumn 1989.

*   *   *

While women directors in film industries around the world are still seen as anomalous (if mainstream) or are marginalized as avant garde, the Antipodes have been home to an impressive cadre of female filmmakers who negotiate and transcend such notions.

Before the promising debuts of Ann Turner (*Celia*) and Jane Campion (*Sweetie*), Gillian Armstrong blazed a bush trail with *My Brilliant Career*, launching a brilliant career of her own as an international director. Like Turner and Campion, Armstrong's films resist easy categorization as either "women's films" or Australian ones, and as much as her male compatriots like Peter Weir, Bruce Beresford, or Paul Cox, her films mix and intermingle genres in ways which, if not openly subvert, undermine and illuminate afresh filmic conventions. Formally, however, the pleasures of her films are traditional ones, such as sensitive and delicate cinematography (often by Russell Boyd), fluid editing, an evocative feel for setting and costume, and most importantly, a commitment to solid character development and acting. All in all, her work reminds one of the best of classical Hollywood cinema, and the question of whether her aim is parody or homage is often left pleasingly ambiguous.

Although she has often spoken in interviews about her discomfort at being confined to the category of woman filmmaker of women's films, and has articulated her desire to reach an audience of both genders and all nationalities, Armstrong's work continually addresses sexual politics and family tensions. Thematically, escape from and struggle with traditional sex roles and the pitfalls and triumphs therein are frequently addressed in her films, from *One Hundred a Day*, her final year project at the Australian Film and Television School, through *My Brilliant Career*, her first and best known feature, to *High Tide*. Even one of her earliest films at Swinburne College, the short *Roof Needs Mowing*, obliquely tackled this theme, using a typical student filmmaker's pastiche of advertising and surrealism. Like most maturing filmmakers with an eye on wider distribution, Armstrong dropped the "sur" from surrealism in her later work, so that by *One Hundred a Day*, an adaptation of an Alan Marshall story about a shoe-factory employee getting a back street abortion in the 1930's, she had developed a more naturalistic handling of material, while her use of soundtrack and fast editing remained highly stylized and effective.

Made on a tiny budget and heavily subsidized by the Australian Film Commission, the award winning *The Singer and the Dancer* was a precocious study of the toll men take on women's lives and marked the onset of Armstrong's mature style. On the strength of this and *One Hundred a Day*, producer Margaret Fink offered her the direction of *My Brilliant Career*. Daunted at first by the scale of the project and lack of confidence in her own abilities, she accepted because she "thought it could be bungled by a lot of men."

While *The Singer and the Dancer* had been chastised by feminist critics for its downbeat ending, the heroine returning to her philandering lover after a half-hearted escape attempt, *My Brilliant Career* was widely celebrated for its feminist fairy tale story as well as its employment of women crew members. Adapted from Miles Franklin's semi-autobiographical novel, *My Brilliant Career*, with its turn of the century setting in the Australian outback, works like *Jane Eyre* in reverse (reader, she doesn't marry him), while retaining the romantic allure of such a story and all the glossy production values of a period setting that Australian cinema had been known for up until then. Distinguished by an astonishing central performance from the then unknown Judy Davis (fresh from playing Juliet to Mel Gibson's Romeo on the drama school stage), the film managed to present a positive model of feminine independence without belying the time in which it was set. Like Armstrong's later *Mrs. Soffel*, *My Brilliant Career* potently evokes smothered sensuality and conveys sexual tension by small telling details, as in the boating scene.

Sadly none of Armstrong's later films has been awarded commensurate critical praise or has been as widely successful, possibly because of her refusal to conform to expectations and churn out more upbeat costume dramas. Her next feature, *Starstruck*, although it too features a spunky ambitious heroine, was a rock musical set in the present and displaying a veritable rattle bag of influences, including Judy Garland-

Mickey Rooney "lets-put-on-a-show" films, Richard Lester editing techniques, new wave pop videos, and even Sternberg's *Blond Venus*, when the heroine sheds her kangeroo suit to sing her "torch song" à la Marlene Dietrich. Despite a witty script and fine bit characters, the music is somewhat monotonous, and the film was only mildly successful.

Armstrong's first and so far only film to be financed and filmed in America was *Mrs. Soffel*. Based on a true story and set at the turn of the century, it delineated the tragic story of the eponymous warder's wife who falls in love with a convict, helps him escape and finally runs off with him. The bleak, monochrome cinematography is powerfully atmospheric but was not to all reviewers' tastes, especially in America. For Armstrong, the restricted palette was quite deliberate so that the penultimate images of blood on snow would be all the more striking and effective. A sadly under-rated film, it features some unexpectedly fine performances from Diane Keaton in the title role and Mel Gibson as her paramour (a fair impersonation of young Henry Fonda) and the young Matthew Modine as his kid brother. At its best, it recalls, if not *MacCabe and Mrs. Miller*, then at least *Bonnie and Clyde*.

High Tide returns to Australia for its setting in a coastal caravan park, and comes up trumps as an unabashedly sentimental weepie, and none the worse for it. It features three generations of women: Lilli (Judy Davis again), back up singer to an Elvis impersonator and drifter, the pubescent Ally (Claudia Karvan), the daughter she left behind, and mother-in-law Bet (Jan Adele), who views with Lilli for Ally's affections. In terms of camera work, it is Armstrong's most restless film, utilizing nervous zip pans, fast tracking, and boomshots and then resting for quiet, intense close-ups on surfboards, legs being shaved, and shower nozzles, all highly motivated by the characters' perspectives. Like *Mrs. Soffel*, *High Tide* uses colours symbolically to contrast the gentle tones of the seaside's natural landscape with the garish buildings of the town called Eden.

Armstrong wears her feminist credentials lightly, never on her sleeve, but like her documentaries, which have followed three women from the ages of 14 to 25, her fiction films can be seen as charting over the years the trajectory of the women's movement: *My Brilliant Career* in the 1970's celebrated women's independence as Sybylla rejects the roles of wife and mother; *Mrs. Soffel* in the mid 1980's reopens negotiations with men (with tragic results); and finally *High Tide* returns to the literally and diegetically rejected motherhood role, with all its attendant joys and anxieties.

—Leslie Felperin

———

ARZNER, Dorothy.

American. Born in San Francisco, 3 January 1900. Studied medicine at University of Southern California. Ambulance Driver in World War I, 1917–18; typist for William C. De Mille, at Famous Players-Lasky (Paramount), 1919; editor for "Realart," a subsidiary of Paramount, 1922; wrote and edited *Old Ironsides* (Cruze), 1925; directed Paramount's first sound film, *Wild Party*, 1929; retired from directing, 1943. Honored at 1st International Festival of Women's Films, New York, 1972, and by Director's Guild of America, 1975. *Died 1 October 1979.*

Dorothy Arzner

Films as Director:

1927 *Fashions for Women*; *Get Your Man*; *10 Modern Commandments*
1928 *Manhattan Cocktail*
1929 *The Wild Party*
1930 *Sarah and Son*; "The Gallows Song—Nichavo" sequence in *Paramount on Parade*; *Anybody's Woman*; *Behind the Makeup* (co-d); *Charming Sinners* (co-d, uncredited)
1931 *Honor Among Lovers*; *Working Girls*
1932 *Merrily We Go to Hell*
1933 **Christopher Strong**
1934 *Nana (Lady of the Boulevard)*
1936 *Craig's Wife*
1937 *The Bride Wore Red*; *The Last of Mrs. Cheyney* (co-d, uncredited)
1940 **Dance, Girl, Dance**
1943 *First Comes Courage*

Other Films:

1922 *Blood and Sand* (ed)
1923 *The Covered Wagon* (ed)
1924 *Inez from Hollywood* (ed, sc); *The Bread of the Border* (sc); *The No-Gun Man* (sc)
1925 *Red Kimono* (sc); *When Husbands Flirt* (sc)
1926 *Old Ironsides* (ed, sc)

Publications:

By ARZNER: article—

Interview with Gerald Peary, in *Cinema* (Beverly Hills), no. 34, 1974.

On ARZNER: books—

Brownlow, Kevin, *The Parade's Gone By*, New York, 1968.
Johnston, Claire, *Notes on Women's Cinema*, London, 1973.
Pratt, George, *Spellbound in Darkness: A History of Silent Film*, Greenwich, Connecticut, 1973.
Rosen, Marjorie, *Popcorn Venus: Women, Movies, and the American Dream*, New York, 1973.
Haskell, Molly, *From Reverence to Rape: The Treatment of Women in the Movies*, New York, 1974.
Smith, Sharon, *Women Who Make Movies*, New York, 1975.
Johnston, Claire, editor, *The Work of Dorothy Arzner: Towards a Feminist Cinema*, London, 1975.
Slide, Anthony, *Early Women Directors*, South Brunswick, New Jersey, 1977.
Heck-Rabi, Louise, *Women Filmmakers: A Critical Reception*, Metuchen, New Jersey, 1984.
Penley, Constance, editor, *Feminism and Film Theory*, London, 1988.

On ARZNER: articles—

"Hollywood Notes," in *Close-Up* (London), April 1928.
Cruikshank, H., "Sketch," in *Motion Picture Classic* (Brooklyn), September 1929.
Potamkin, H.A., "The Woman as Film Director," in *American Cinematographer* (Los Angeles), January 1932.
St. John, Adela Rogers, "Get Me Dorothy Arzner," in *Silver Screen* (New York), December 1933.
"They Stand Out from the Crowd," in *Literary Digest* (New York), 3 November 1934.
Feldman, J. and H., "Women Directors," in *Films in Review* (New York), November 1950.
Pyros, J., "Notes on Women Directors," in *Take One* (Montreal), November/December 1970.
Henshaw, Richard, "Women Directors," in *Film Comment* (New York), November 1972.
Parker, F., "Approaching the Art of Arzner," in *Action* (Los Angeles), July/August 1973.
Slide, Anthony, "Forgotten Early Women Directors," in *Films in Review*, March 1974.
Castle, W., "Tribute to Dorothy Arzner," in *Action* (Los Angeles), March/April 1975.

Kaplan, E. Ann, "Aspects of British Feminist Film Theory," in *Jump Cut* (Berkeley), no. 12–13, 1976.
Johnston, Claire, in *Jump Cut* (Berkeley), 30 December 1976.
Bergstrom, J., "Rereading the work of Claire Johnston," in *Camera Obscura* (Berkeley), Summer 1979.
Obituary in the *New York Times*, 12 October 1979.
Houston, Beverle, "Missing in Action: Notes on Dorothy Arzner," in *Wide Angle* (Athens, Georgia), vol. 6, no. 3, 1984.
Forster, A., "*Dance, Girl, Dance*," in *Skrien* (Amsterdam), September–October 1984.

*   *   *

Dorothy Arzner's career as a commercial Hollywood director covered little more than a decade, but she had prepared for it by extensive editing and script writing work. Ill health forced her to abandon a career that might eventually have led to the recognition she deserved from her contemporaries. One of only a handful of women operating within the structure of Hollywood's post-silent boom, Arzner has been the subject of feminist critical attention, with film retrospectives of her work both in the US and UK in the 1970's, when her work was "rediscovered."

Most feminists would recognise that the mere re-insertion of women into a dominant version of film history is a dubious activity, even while asserting that women's contributions to cinema have been excluded from most historical accounts. Recognition of the work of a "popular" director like Arzner and an evaluation of her contribution to Hollywood cinema must be set against an awareness of her place in the dominant patriarchal ideology of classic Hollywood cinema. Arzner's work is particularly interesting in that it was produced *within* the Hollywood system with all its inherent constraints (time, budget, traditional content requirements of particular genres, etc.).

While Arzner directed "women's pictures"—classic Hollywood fare—she differed from other directors of the genre in that in place of a narrative seen simply from a female point of view, she actually succeeded in challenging the orthodoxy of Hollywood from within, offering perspectives that questioned the dominant order.

The films often depict women seeking independence through career—a burlesque queen and an aspiring ballerina (*Dance, Girl, Dance*), a world champion aviatrix (*Christopher Strong*). Alternatively, the escape route can be through exit from accepted female positions in the hierarchy—a rich daughter "escaping" into marriage with a poverty-stricken drunk (*Merrily We Go to Hell*). Even excess can be a way of asserting independence, as with the obsessive housekeeper rejecting family relationships in favour of a passion for domesticity and the home (*Craig's Wife*).

The films frequently play with notions of female stereotyping (most notably in *Dance, Girl, Dance*, with its two central female types of Nice Girl and Vamp). Arzner's "nice girls" are likely to have desires which conflict with male desires, while narrative requirements will demand that they still please the male. While these tensions are not always resolved, Arzner's strategies in underlining these opposing desires are almost gleeful at times.

In addition Arzner's films offer contradictions which disturb the spectator's accepted relationship with what is on screen, most notably in *Dance, Girl, Dance*, when dancer Judy O'Brien turns on her Burlesque (male) audience and berates them for their voyeurism. This scene has been the focus for much debate about the role of the spectator in relation to the woman as spectacle (notably in the work of Laura Mulvey).

Although the conventions of plot and development are present in Arzner's films, Claire Johnston sees these elements as subverted by a "women's discourse": the films may offer us the kinds of narrative closure we expect from the classic Holly-wood text—the "happy" or the "tragic" ending—but Arzner's insistence on this female discourse gives the films an exciting and unsettling quality. In Arzner's work, she argues, it is the male universe which invites scrutiny and which is "rendered strange."

Dorothy Arzner's position inside the studio system has made her a unique subject for debate. As the Women's Movement set about reassessing the role of women in history, so feminist film theorists began not only to re-examine the role of women as a creative force in cinema, but also to consider the implications behind the notion of women as spectacle. The work of Dorothy Arzner has proved a rich area for investigation into both these questions.

—Lilie Ferrari

_____

ASHBY, Hal.

American. Born in Ogden, Utah, 1932. Attended Utah State University. Mimeographer in Universal script department, Los Angeles, 1950–51; worked at Republic studios, becoming assistant editor, 1950's; became full editor, 1963; directed first feature, *The Landlord*, 1970. Recipient: Oscar for Best Editing, for *In the Heat of the Night*, 1967. *Died in Los Angeles, 27 December 1988.*

Films as Director:

1970   *The Landlord*
1971   *Harold and Maude*
1973   *The Last Detail*
1975   *Shampoo*
1976   *Bound for Glory*
1978   *Coming Home*
1979   *Being There* (+ed)
1981   *Second Hand Hearts* (+ed)
1982   *Lookin' to Get Out* (+co-ed); *Let's Spend the Night Together*
1983   *Time is On Our Side* (+ed)
1984   *The Slugger's Wife*
1985   *Eight Million Ways to Die*

Other Films:

1958   *The Big Country* (Wyler) (asst ed); *The Diary of Anne Frank* (Stevens) (asst ed)
1961   *The Young Doctors* (Karlson) (asst ed)
1962   *The Children's Hour* (*The Loudest Whisper*) (Wyler) (asst ed)
1964   *The Best Man* (Schaffner) (asst ed)
1965   *The Greatest Story Ever Told* (Stevens) (asst ed); *The Loved One* (co-ed); *The Cincinnati Kid* (Jewison) (ed); *The Russians Are Coming, the Russians Are Coming* (Jewison) (ed)
1967   *In the Heat of the Night* (Jewison) (ed)
1968   *The Thomas Crown Affair* (Jewison) (assoc pr, supervising ed)
1969   *Gaily, Gaily* (Jewison) (assoc pr)

Publications:

By ASHBY: articles—

"Breaking Out of the Cutting Room," in *Action* (Los Angeles), September/October 1970.

Interview with L. Salvato and D. Schaefer, in *Millimeter* (New York), October 1976.
"David Carradine and Hal Ashby on *Bound for Glory*," interview with C. Amata, in *Focus on Film* (London), no. 27, 1977.
"Positive Thinking: Hal Ashby," interview with R. Appelbaum, in *Films and Filming* (London), July 1978.
"Dialogue on Film: Hal Ashby," in *American Film* (Washington, D.C.), May 1980.

On ASHBY: book—

Tuska, Jon, editor, *Close-Up: The Contemporary Director*, Metuchen, New Jersey, 1981.

On ASHBY: articles—

Jørgensen, U., "Hal Ashby—en auteur?," in *Kosmorama* (Copenhagen), September 1974.
Harmetz, A., "Gambling on a Film About the Great Depression," in *New York Times*, 5 December 1976.
Jacobs, Diane, "Hal Ashby," in *Hollywood Renaissance*, New York, 1977.
Pollock, Dale, "Whatever Happened to Hal Ashby?," in the *Los Angeles Times*, 17 October 1982.
"Hal Ashby," in *Film Dope* (London), March 1988.
Obituary in *Ciné Revue* (Paris), 5 January 1989.
Obituary in *Screen International* (London), 7 January 1989.

*   *   *

Hal Ashby has a reputation for showing a light touch as a director; he stated that he preferred to let the actors develop their characters. During the filming of *Coming Home*, for example, he threw out a script when Jon Voight saw one of the major characters differently than the screenwriter. The people in his films generally face choices in situations that reflect major social concerns. In *The Landlord* characters have to make decisions involving the issue of race; in *Shampoo* they must decide which side they are on in a complex political and sexual skirmish set in the turbulent summer of 1968; and in *Coming Home*, the effects of the Viet Nam War force both characters involved directly with the war as well as those at home to deal with unexpected changes in their lives. The solutions to these decisions when faced by the characters are never facile. In *Harold and Maude*, Harold gains some degree of maturity but loses the love of his life, Maude; the military police of *The Last Detail* have given the prisoner a way to face life, but have also delivered him to prison; while George, in *Shampoo*, realizes how empty his life is and appears to want to change it, but at the same time has lost what chances he had for happiness.

Ashby's experience as an editor is evident; he employed a wide variety of editing effects in his films. His use of both dissolves and rapid cutting to show the passage of time in *The Last Detail* serves as an example. His predilection for varying editing techniques could explain in part, what Ashby himself admitted, that he had not shown a distinctive style, but rather attempted to adapt his style to the type and subject of each film.

Though he has been called a "maverick director," Ashby's career garnered him a good deal of respect from the critics, and his films have done well at the box office. *Shampoo, Coming Home*, and *Being There* represent his major financial successes, while the reputation of *Harold and Maude* was made in a slightly different manner. After an initial panning and a short general release, the film caught on in the Midwest, running in several theaters for over a year. The film has since become a cult favorite and has received positive critical response.

—Ray Narducy

_____

Hal Ashby

ASQUITH, Anthony.

British. Born in London, 9 November 1902; commonly known by childhood name "Puffin." Son of the Liberal Prime Minister H.H. Asquith. Educated at Winchester, and at Balliol College, Oxford 1921–25. Founder member of London Film Society, 1925; visited Hollywood as guest of Douglas Fairbanks and Mary Pickford, 1926; joined British Instructional Films, 1926; directed (sometimes uncredited or credited as co-director) first feature, *Shooting Stars*, from his own screenplay, 1927; signed to Gainsborough Films, 1932; President of Association of Cinematographic Technicians, 1937–68; began association with writer Terence Rattigan, 1939; produced *Carmen* for Covent Garden, 1953; directs ballets for TV, mid-1950's. Recipient: Fellow, British Film Institute, Commander of the Order of Al Merito della Republica, Italy. *Died in London, 21 February 1968.*

Films as Director:

1927   *Shooting Stars* (+sc)
1928   *Underground* (+sc); *The Runaway Princess (Princess Priscilla's Fortnight)* (+sc)
1929   *A Cottage on Dartmoor (Escape From Dartmoor)* (+sc)
1931   *Tell England (Battle of Gallipoli)* (co-d, co-sc); *Dance, Pretty Lady* (+sc, adapt)
1933   *The Lucky Number*
1934   *Unfinished Symphony* (co-d for English version only)
1935   *Moscow Nights (I Stand Condemned)* (+co-sc)
1938   *Pygmalion* (co-d, co-sc)
1939   *French Without Tears*
1940   *Freedom Radio (The Voice in the Night)*; *Quiet Wedding*; *Channel Incident* (doc) (+pr)
1941   *Rush Hour* (doc); *Cottage to Let (Bombsight Stolen)*
1942   *Uncensored*
1943   *We Dive at Dawn*; *The Demi-Paradise (Adventure for Two)*; *Welcome to Britain* (doc)
1944   *Fanny By Gaslight (Man of Evil)*; *Two Fathers* (doc)
1945   *The Way to the Stars (Johnny in the Clouds)*
1947   *While the Sun Shines*
1948   *The Winslow Boy*
1950   *The Woman in Question (Five Angles on Murder)*; *The Browning Version*
1951   *The Importance of Being Earnest* (+sc)
1952   *The Net (Project M7)*; *The Final Test*
1954   *The Young Lovers (Chance Meeting)*
1955   *On Such a Night*
1956   *Carrington VC (Court Martial)*
1958   *Orders to Kill*; *The Doctor's Dilemma*
1959   *Libel!*
1960   *The Millionairess*; *Zero*
1961   *Two Living, One Dead*
1962   *Guns of Darkness*
1963   *The VIPs*; *An Evening with the Royal Ballet* (doc) (co-d)
1964   *The Yellow Rolls-Royce*

Other Films:

1927   *Boadicea* (Hill) (asst-d)
1932   *Marry Me* (Thiele) (sc)
1933   *Letting in the Sunshine* (Lane) (sc)

Publications:

By ASQUITH: articles—

"Anthony Asquith and His Art," in *Film Weekly* (London), 26 November 1928.
"Anthony Asquith's Defence," in *Film Weekly* (London), 7 November 1931.

"The Secrets of Screen Success," in *Picturegoer* (London), 20 May 1933.
"The Director and the Actor," in *Picturegoer* (London), 9 November 1935.
"Wanted—A Genius," in *Sight and Sound* (London), Spring 1938.
"Ten Years of Technique," in *Film Weekly* (London), 22 October 1938.
"I Decide to be a Film Director," in *Listener* (London), 11 June 1942.
"The Tenth Muse Climbs Parnassus," in *Penguin Film Review* (London), no. 1, 1946.
"A Style in Film Direction," in *Cine-Technician* (London), July–August 1951.
"The Directorial Touch," in *Cine-Technician* (London), September–October 1951.
"Days with Chaplin: Hollywood Memories of the 1920's," in *Cine Technician* (London), November/December 1952.
"The Importance of Being Faithful," in *Theatre Arts* (London), April 1953.
"Note on Americanization," in *Film* (London), September/October 1955.
"The Play's the Thing," in *Films and Filming* (London), February 1959.

On ASQUITH: books—

Noble, Peter, *Anthony Asquith*, London, 1951.
Elvin, George, and others, editors, *Anthony Asquith: A Tribute*, London, 1968.
Durgnat, Raymond, *A Mirror for England*, London, 1970.
Minney, R.J., *"Puffin" Asquith: A Biography of the Hon. Anthony Asquith, Aesthete, Aristocrat, Prime Minister's Son and Film Maker*, London, 1973; as *The Films of Anthony Asquith*, New York, 1976.
Armes, Roy, *A Critical History of the British Cinema*, London, 1978.
Association of Cinematograph, Television and Allied Technicians, *ACTION! Fifty Years in the Life of a Union*, London, 1983.
Richards, Jeffrey, and Tony Aldgate, *Britain Can Take It: The British Cinema and the Second World War*, London, 1983.

On ASQUITH: articles—

Benedict, William, "Limelight on Anthony Asquith," in *Picturegoer* (London), 21 March 1942.
Woodhouse, Bruce, "Asquith the Enthusiastic," in *Picturegoer* (London), 14 August 1948.
Massie, Paul, "What Asquith Did For Me," in *Films and Filming* (London), February 1958.
Cowie, Peter, "This England," in *Films and Filming* (London), October 1963.
de Grunwald, Anatole, "The Champagne Set," in *Films and Filming* (London), February 1965.
Balcon, Michael, "Anthony Asquith, 1902–1968," in *Sight and Sound* (London), April 1968.
Kalish, Robert, "Filmed Theatre: The Importance of Being Asquith," in *Thousand Eyes Magazine* (New York), November 1975.
"Anthony Asquith," in *Film Dope* (London), March 1988.

*   *   *

Anthony Asquith was a competent, occasionally brilliant director whose career in the British Film industry spanned an unbroken period of over 40 years. Yet while, as a by-product of the critical rehabilitation of the British cinema undertaken over the last 15 or so years, several of his peers and contemporaries have been lauded and rediscovered, Asquith's place in the pantheon of Great British Filmmakers is far from established. Perhaps it is that with the anglophobia endemic in the history of British film criticism (despite the contribution to world cinema of Chaplin, Grierson, Hitchcock, Lean, and Powell, among others), the *auteurs* of British cinema tend to be seen as working outside a mainstream which, though dismissed, is never clearly defined. Asquith "fails" as an *auteur* because, despite attempts to categorise him as a director of "mere" literary adaptations, his *oeuvre* contains a wide range of generic styles and influences, making an authorial, individuated presence difficult to detect. Yet in this very "failure" he

Anthony Asquith

may be said to represent, to a greater degree than any other director, the diverse and often contradictory nature of British cinema's mainstream.

Given his privileged background as the Oxford-educated son of the Prime Minister, his membership of the London Film Society in the 1920s, and his early eagerness to incorporate techniques from German, Swedish, Soviet and French cinema into his own films, Asquith might have fitted more easily into the stereotype of the documentary filmmaker. Yet, although invited to join the Empire Marketing Board by John Grierson in the early 1930s, he chose to remain in the far-from-respectable popular field. His background had enabled him to visit Hollywood in 1926 and stay as a guest at Pickfair, while observing Lubitsch and Chaplin at work, but on his return he began in a humble role with Harry Bruce Woolfe's British Instructional Films. Within a year he was allowed to develop his own original script, and with the veteran director A.V. Bramble nominally in charge, *Shooting Stars* was made. With its cinematic wit, its audacious self-reflexivity, and its stylistic bravura, the film is clearly Asquith's.

Yet his career, despite the promise of *Shooting Stars* and films such as *A Cottage on Dartmoor*, compared at the time to Hitchcock not only for its lower-middle class murder milieu, floundered somewhat in the early 1930s. The presence of a soundtrack suddenly made Asquith's characters seem unappealingly fey in contrast to the apparently classless stars of the

American cinema. Despite being contracted to Alexander Korda and Michael Balcon, the two foremost producers of the period, Asquith (like the British Cinema as a whole) made little of note during the mid-1930s.

The turning point came with *Pygmalion*, where, ironically, the very issues of class and accent, so problematic for Asquith's career and for the British cinema, are central to the film. *Pygmalion*, rarely, was especially popular in America, and the inventiveness and fluidity with which Shaw's wordy (though Oscar-winning) screenplay is treated by Asquith and his editor, David Lean, make this, far from being a "stagey" adaptation, a film which bears comparison with the masterpieces of the French cinema of the time, whose roots were often similarly theatrical. From this success Asquith went on, during the war, to a run of films which perhaps represent the peak of his filmmaking career.

The Way to the Stars is perhaps his finest film. An evocation of the lives of British and American Airmen on a war-time air base, the film, with its opening shots of a deserted base and its notable absence of any gung-ho jerry-bashing, struck a deep chord with audiences in 1945. In its understated, reserved tone, however, it seems a long way from the less "serious" Gainsborough melodrama *Fanny by Gaslight*, made the year before, a film nevertheless richly enjoyable. The narrative tension aboard the stranded submarine in *We Dive at Dawn* parallels the struggle between the documentary mode employed and Asquith's more dramatic concerns, while the film itself features, like so many of the director's, an outstanding acting performance, here by the brooding Eric Portman. The pictures of Englishness—towards which Asquith's direction displays a curious ambivalence—in the documentary *A Welcome to Britain* (aimed at American Servicemen), and in the intriguingly bizarre *The Demi-Paradise* (uniquely, a pro-Soviet film), together with the polished comedy of *Quiet Wedding* and the spy thriller-comedy of *A Cottage to Let* (in which the apparently redoubtable John Mills plays a Nazi spy), complete a body of work which, in its generic diversity as much as its concentration of purpose, might stand for many of the achievements of the British cinema as a whole during the Second World War.

Equally important in Asquith's contribution to British film culture—the environment in which films are made, seen and discussed—was his work in helping to establish, then lead, the unionisation of the British film industry. As President of the Association of Cine-Technicians from its beginnings in the late 1930s to his death, he played a key role, especially during the Second World War, in fighting for continuity of film production in Britain, gaining powerful enemies in the process. His motivation, unlike that of many of his colleagues in the ACTT, did not spring from a radical political position so much as from an indefatigable commitment to the British cinema. This, together with his appreciation of his fellow technicians' role in the filmmaking process, was reflected also in his theoretical discussions of cinema which, in the 1930s especially, appeared in the popular film magazines of the day. That he wrote for *Picturegoer* and not its highbrow equivalents typified his belief in an intelligent but ultimately popular British cinema.

In the immediate post-war years, when the British cinema underwent a genuine revival, Asquith, despite his earlier successes, did not play such a prominent role. His collaborations with the playwright Terence Rattigan (characterised by Raymond Durgnat as "Rattigasquith") were, with their upper-middle class world view, representative of a certain form of "quality" cinema. Though dismissed subsequently as stuffy and irredeemably bourgeois, the films occasionally transcend the class-bound world they inhabit: *The Browning Version*, for instance, rather than being a repressed film, may be seen now as a moving and beautifully pointed study of repression.

Although, throughout the 1950s, Asquith regularly directed films, to generally favourable reviews, most have been overlooked. Several from this period, made before the better-known but embarrassingly banal star-studded efforts of the early 1960s, are worth re-assessing. In *Orders to Kill*, Asquith uses music, always a notable element in his work, to chilling effect: the murder scene should be compulsory viewing for those who dismiss him as a "cosy" or "safe" director. *Libel*, in which Dirk Bogarde portrays three apparently identical characters—one a nobleman, one a charlatan, and one a shambling wreck—perhaps offers a comment on the director's own personal struggles. Where the earlier *Fanny by Gaslight*, in the context of a jolly costume romp, worked through the all-important questions of class and respectability (questions from which this Honorable son of the Prime Minister, despite regulation on-set attire of a boiler suit, never managed to escape), *Libel*, thanks to Bogarde's performance, transcends the realms of the courtroom drama to offer a fascinating study of lost identity, a problem shared by the British cinema and Asquith (exacerbated in his case by a struggle against alcoholism).

Yet by the end of the decade, the new generation who came out of Oxford to take the world of cinema by storm saw in Asquith's work much of what they perceived to be wrong with British cinema, and turned their cameras towards the rugged working classes. The angry young men were cruelly dismissive of their predecessor, a blow from which his reputation has yet to recover, despite the ironic similarities between "Puffin" Asquith and, for instance, the ever-irascible Lindsay Anderson. For his directing, his union activities, but above all for his attempts, while working in the mainstream, to transcend the binary oppositions endemic in British cinema—documentary/melodrama, union/management, popular/avant-garde, upper class/working class, literary/cinematic—Asquith should now be seen as one of the key figures in its reconstructed history.

—Nicholas Thomas

ASTRUC, Alexandre.

French. Born in Paris, 13 July 1923. Educated at Saint-Germain-en-Laye, and at Polytechnique. Literary and Film critic, mid-1940's; publishes novel *Les Vacances*, 1945; assistant to Marcel Achard and Marc Allegret, 1946–47; makes two short films, 1948–49; begins series of six feature-length films with *Mauvaises rencontres*, 1955.

Films as Director:

1948   *Aller et retour (Aller-retour)* (+sc)
1949   *Ulysse ou Les Mauvaises rencontres* (+sc)
1953   *Le Rideau cramoisi (The Crimson Curtain)* (+sc)
1955   *Les Mauvaises rencontres* (+co-sc)
1958   *Une Vie (End of Desire)* (+co-sc)
1960   *La Proie pour l'ombre* (+co-sc)
1962   *L'Education sentimentale* (+sc)
1963   *Le Puits et le pendule (The Pit and the Pendulum)* (for TV) (+sc)
1965   *Evariste Galois* (+sc)
1966   *La Longue Marche* (+co-sc)
1968   *Flammes sur l'Adriatique* (+co-sc)
1976   *Sartre par lui-même* (co-d)

Other Films:

1948   *Jean de la Lune* (Achard) (co-sc)
1949   *La P . . . respecteuse* (Pagliero) (co-sc); *La Valse de Paris* (Achard) (role)
1950   *L'Affaire Manet* (Aurel) (commentary)
1954   *Le Vicomte de Bragelonne* (Cerchio) (co-sc)
1964   *Bassae* (Pollet) (sc)

Publications:

By ASTRUC: book—

Sartre, Paris, 1977.

By ASTRUC: articles—

"Le Feu et la glace," in *Cahiers du Cinéma* (Paris), December 1952; as "Fire and Ice," in *Cahiers du Cinéma in English* (New York), January 1966.
Interview in *Film Français* (Paris), 6 March 1987.

On ASTRUC: articles—

Eisner, Lotte, "Venice Film Festival," in *Film Culture* (New York), vol. 2, no. 1, 1956.
Weber, Eugene, "An Escapist Realism," in *Film Quarterly* (Berkeley), Winter 1959.

"Sur une émission de télévision," in *Cahiers du Cinéma* (Paris), February/March 1974.

Beylie, Claude, "Quatre de la forfanterie," in *Ecran* (Paris), October 1975.

"Alexandre Astruc," in *Film Dope* (London), March 1988.

* * *

Alexandre Astruc was the embodiment of the revolutionary hopes of a renewed cinema after the war. True, Clément, Bresson, and Melville were already making films in a new way, but making them in the age old industry. Astruc represented a new, arrogant sensibility. He had grown up on the ideas of Sartre and was one of the youthful literati surrounding the philosopher in the St. Germain-des-Prés cafes. There he talked of a new French culture being born, one that demanded new representations in fiction and film.

His personal aspirations were great and grew even greater when his novel *Les Vacances* was published by the prestigious N.R.F., almost winning an important prize. While writing essays on art and culture for *Combat* and *L'Ecran français* he became convinced that the cinema must replace the novel.

But first the cinema must become more like the novel. In his crucial essay "Le Caméra stylo," written the same year as Sartre's "Situation of the Writer in 1948," he called for an end to institutional cinema and for a new style that would be both personal and malleable. He wanted cinema to be able to treat diverse ideas and a range of expressions. He, like Sartre, wanted to become ethical.

This was the first loud clarion cry of the New Wave and it provoked attention in its own day. Astruc found himself linked with Bazin, Cocteau, Marker, and Tacchella against the Stalinists at *L'Ecran français* led by Louis Daquin. Banding together to form "Objectif 48," these men created a new atmosphere for cinema, attracting the young Truffaut and Godard to their screenings.

Everyone looked to Astruc to begin turning out short films, but his 16mm efforts ran aground. Soon he began writing scripts for acceptable standard directors like Marc Allégret. Finally in 1952 he was able to make *Le Rideau cramoisi* in his own way. It was a remarkable way: this 19th century mystery tale was reduced to a set of unforgettable images and a soundtrack that contained no dialogue whatsoever. Pushing the voice-over discoveries of Bresson and Melville to the limit, Astruc's narrational device places the film somewhere between dream and memory. This coincides perfectly with the haunting night photography and Anouk Aimée's inscrutably romantic performance.

There followed more adaptations, not because Astruc had joined the industry's penchant for such quality material, but because he always believed in the overriding import of style, seeing plots as pretexts only. The color photography in *Une Vie*, for example, explores the painterly concerns of the impressionists. But since the plot comes from a Maupassant tale written in the same era, the result is unpretentious.

In his older age Astruc has renounced this obsession with style. The themes that possess him now, crises in marriage and love, can actually be seen in all his earlier work as well. Now he can explore these issues in television, the medium that seems perfectly suited to his early ideas. Only now his ideas have changed and so has his following. Alexandre Astruc must always be mentioned in any chronicle of modern French cinema, but his career can only be thought of as disappointing.

—Dudley Andrew

———

AUTANT-LARA, Claude.

French. Born in Luzarches (Seine-et-Oize), 5 August 1903. Educated at Lycée Janson-de-Sailly, Paris, at Ecole nationale supérieure des arts décoratifs, at Ecole des Beaux Arts, and at Mill Hill School, London. Married Ghislain Auboin. Art director on L'Herbier's *Le Carnaval des vérités*, 1925; made several avant-garde films, and worked as assistant to René Clair, 1923–25; made French versions of American films in Hollywood, 1930–32; returned to France and directed first feature, 1933; President of Syndicat des techniciens du cinéma, 1948–55; President of Fédération nationale du spectacle, 1957–63. Recipient: Grand prix du Cinema français, 1954; Prix Europa, Rome, 1974; Chevalier de la Légion d'honneur; Commandeur des Arts et des Lettres. Address: 66 rue Lepic, 75018 Paris, France.

Films as Director:

1923   *Faits divers*
1926   *Construire un feu*; *Vittel*
1930   *Buster se marie* (d of French version of American film *Parlor, Bedroom and Bath* (Sedgwick))
1931   *Le Plumbier amoureux* (d of French version of American film *The Passionate Plumber* (Sedgwick)); *Le Fils du Rajah* (d of French version of American film *Son of India* (Feyder)); *La Pente* (d of French version of American film); *Pur Sang* (d of French version of American film)
1932   *L'Athlète incomplet* (d of French version of American film); *Le Gendarme est sans pitié*; *Un Client sérieux*; *Monsieur le Duc*; *La Peur des coups*; *Invite Monsieur à dîner*
1933   *Ciboulette* (+co-sc, co-costume des)
1936   *My Partner Mr. Davis* (*The Mysterious Mr. Davis*) (+co-sc)
1937   *L'Affaire du courrier de Lyon* (*The Courier of Lyon*) (co-d)
1938   *Le Ruisseau* (co-d)
1939   *Fric-Frac* (co-d)
1942   *Le Mariage de Chiffon*; *Lettres d'amour*
1943   *Douce* (*Love Story*)
1944   *Sylvie et le fantôme* (*Sylvie and the Phantom*)
1947   ***Le Diable au corps (Devil in the Flesh)***
1949   *Occupe-toi d'Amélie* (*Oh Amelia!*)
1951   *L'Auberge rouge* (*The Red Inn*) (+co-sc)
1952   "L'Orgueil" (Pride) episode of *Les 7 Péchés capitaux* (*The Seven Deadly Sins*) (+co-sc)
1953   *Le Bon Dieu sans confession* (+co-sc); *Le Blé en herbe* (*The Game of Love*) (+co-sc)
1954   *Le Rouge et le noir*
1956   *Marguerite de la nuit*; *La Traversée de Paris* (*Four Bags Full*)
1958   *En Cas de malheur* (*Love Is My Profession*); *Le Joueur*
1959   *La Jument verte* (*The Green Mare*) (+pr)
1960   *Les Régates de San Francisco*; *Le Bois des amants*
1961   *Tu ne tueras point* (*Non uccidere, Thou Shalt Not Kill*) (+co-pr); *Le Comte de Monte Cristo* (*The Story of the Count of Monte Cristo*)
1962   *Vive Henri IV . . . Vive l'amour!*
1963   *Le Meurtrier* (*Enough Rope*)
1964   *Le Magot de Joséfa* (+co-sc); "La Fourmi" episode of *Humour noir*
1965   *Le Journal d'une femme en blanc* (*A Woman in White*)
1966   *Le Nouveau Journal d'une femme en blanc* (*Une Femme en blanc se révolte*)
1967   "Aujourd'hui" (Paris Today) episode of *Le Plus Vieux Métier du monde* (*The Oldest Profession*); *Le Franciscain de Bourges*
1969   *Les Patates* (+co-sc)
1971   *Le Rouge et le blanc*
1973   *Lucien Leuwen* (for TV)
1977   *Gloria* (+co-sc)

Other Films:

1919 *Le Carnaval des vérités* (L'Herbier) (art d, costume des);
     L'Ex-voto (L'Herbier) (art d, costume des)
1920 *L'Homme du large* (L'Herbier) (art d, costume des)
1921 *Villa Destin* (L'Herbier) (art d, costume des); *Eldorado*
     (L'Herbier) (co-art d, costume des)
1922 *Don Juan et Faust* (L'Herbier) (art d, costume des)
1923 *L'Inhumaine* (L'Herbier) (co-art d, costume des); *Le
     Marchand de plaisir* (Catelain) (co-art d, costume des);
     Nana (Renoir) (co-art d, co-costume des)
1927 *Le Diable au coeur* (L'Herbier) (art d, costume des)

Publications:

By AUTANT-LARA: books—

La Rage dans le couer: Chronique cinématographique du 20ème siècle,
Paris, 1984.
*Hollywood Cake-walk (1930–1932): Chronique cinématographique du
20ème siècle*, Paris, 1985.

By AUTANT-LARA: articles—

"Styles du cinéma français," in *La Livre d'or du Cinéma Français
1947–48*, edited by René Jeanne and Charles Ford, Paris, 1948.
Numerous polemical articles on state of French cinema, studios, and
attacking government policies, in *La Technicien du Film* (Paris), *Les
Lettres Françaises* (Paris), and other French periodicals, early to
mid-1950's.
"*La Traversée de Paris* est un film insolité," interview with Martine
Monod, in *Les Lettres Françaises* (Paris), 4 October 1956.
"Les Etrennes du cinéma françaises," in *Les Lettres Françaises*
(Paris), 3 January 1957.
"Attention, notre métier n'est pas un métier d'hurluberlus," in *La
Technicien du Film* (Paris), May 1958.
"La Parole est à Claude Autant-Lara," interview with Marcel Oms, in
Cahiers de la Cinématheque (Paris), Summer 1973.
Interview with J.-C. Bonnet and others, in *Cinématographe* (Paris),
April 1978.
"Lausanne (Autant-Lara)," in *Positif* (Paris), December 1981.
Interview in *Cahiers du Cinéma* (Paris), Summer 1983.
Interview in *Film Français* (Paris), 6 March 1987.

On AUTANT-LARA: books—

Buache, Freddy, *Claude Autant-Lara*, Lausanne, 1982.
L'Institut Lumière présente Claude Autant-Lara en 33 films, Lyons,
1983.

On AUTANT-LARA: articles—

de la Roche, Catherine, "The Fighter," in *Films and Filming* (London), January 1955.
Durgnat, Raymond, "The Rebel with Kid Gloves," in *Films and Filming* (London), October and November 1960.
Biofilmography in *Film Dope* (London), no. 2, 1973.
Special issue of *Cahiers de la Cinématheque* (Paris), Spring 1973.
"*L'Auberge rouge* Dossier," in *Cinéma* (Paris), July–August 1982.
Carbonnier, A., and Joel Magny, in *Cinéma* (Paris), September 1982.
"Claude Autant-Lara," in *Film Dope* (London), March 1988.
Joffre, Laurent, "La tache brune: De l'affaire du Carmel aux propos
d'Autant-Lara," in *Nouvel Observateur* (Paris), 14 September 1989.
Bergan, Ronald, "Out of Sight, Out of Mind," in *Guardian* (London),
28 September 1989.

* * *

Claude Autant-Lara is best known for his post-World War II
films in the French "tradition of quality." His earliest work in
the industry was more closely related to the avant-garde movements of the 1920's than to the mainstream commercial cinema
with which he was later identified. He began as a set designer in
the 1920's, serving as art director for several of Marcel L'Herbier's films, including *L'Inhumaine* and for Jean Renoir's
Nana; and assisted René Clair on a number of his early shorts.

After directing several films, he worked on an early widescreen experiment. *Construire un feu* using the Hypergonar
system designed by Henri Chretien. On the basis of his work in
this format, he was brought to Hollywood and ended up directing French language versions of American films for several
years. He returned to France, and directed his first feature of
note, *Ciboulette*, in 1933.

During the war Autant-Lara exercised greater control in his
choice of projects, and started working with scenarists Jean
Aurenche and Pierre Bost who would continue to be among his
most consistent collaborators. He also started assembling a
basic crew that worked with him through the 1960's: composer
René Cloerec, designer Max Douy, editor Madeleine Gug,
and cameraman Jacques Natteau. Autant-Lara rapidly established his reputation as a studio director in the tradition of
quality. For many, the names Aurenche, Bost, and Autant-
Lara are synonymous with this movement. Their films are characterized by an emphasis on scripting and dialogue, a high
proportion of literary adaptations, a solemn "academic" visual
style, and general theatricality (due largely to the emphasis on
dialogue and its careful delivery to create a cinematic world
determined by psychological realism). They frequently attack
or ridicule social groups and institutions.

Autant-Lara's first major post-war film, *Le Diable au corps*,
was adapted from a novel by Raymond Radiguet. Set during
World War I, it tells the story of an adolescent's affair with a
young married woman whose husband is away at war. While
the film was considered scandalous by many for its valorization
of adultery and tacit condemnation of war, it was also seen to
express the cynical mood of post-war youth. Autant-Lara's
films seem to revel in irreverent depictions of established authority and institutions. *L'Auberge rouge* is a black comedy
involving murderous innkeepers, a group of insipid travellers
(representing a cross-section of classes), and a monk trapped
by the vows of confession.

Throughout the 1950's Autant-Lara was extremely active.
His successes of the period include *Le Rouge et le noir*, adapted
from Stendhal; *La Traversée de Paris*, a comedy about black
market trading in occupied France; and *En cas de malheur*, a
melodrama involving a middle-aged lawyer, his young client,
and her student lover. At the same time Autant-Lara was an
active spokesman for the French film industry. As head of several film trade unions and other groups promoting French film,
he criticized (often harshly) the CNC (Centre National du
cinéma française) for its inadequate support of the industry;
the American film industry for its stultifying presence in the
French market; and government censorship policies for limiting freedom of expression.

Autant-Lara's prominence was effectively eclipsed with the
emergence of the French New Wave, although he continued
directing films. In the 1950's he, along with Aurenche and
Bost, had been subject to frequent critical attacks, most notably by François Truffaut. In the wake of the success of the new
generation of directors, Autant-Lara's work is often seen as no
more than the "stale" French cinema of the 1950's which was
successfully displaced by the more vital films of the New Wave.
Yet in spite of, indeed owing to, their "armchair" criticism of
authority, bleak representation of human nature, and slow-
paced academic style, they possess a peculiarly appealing,
insolent sensibility.

—M.B. White

BABENCO, Hector.

Argentinian. Born in Buenos Aires, 7 February 1946. Travelled to Europe, 1963; worked as bible salesman and as extra for Cinecitta, Rome; moved to Sao Paolo, Brazil, 1971; made first feature, *Rei da noite*, 1976; made first English language film, *Kiss of the Spider Woman*, 1983.

Films as Director:

1975   *Rei da noite* (*King of the Night*)
1978   *Lucio Flavio*
1981   *Pixote*
1985   *Kiss of the Spider Woman*
1988   *Ironweed*; *The Second Killing of the Dog*
1990   *My Foolish Heart*

Publications:

By BABENCO: articles—

"Individual Solutions," an interview with G. Csicsery, in *Film Quarterly* (Los Angeles), Fall 1982.
Interview with B. Kawin, in *Film Quarterly* (Los Angeles), February 1986.
"Dialogue on Film: Hector Babenco," in *American Film* (Washington, D.C.), April 1986.
"Hector Babenco: Bear-faced Brilliance," an interview with D. Nicholson, in *Films and Filming* (London), May 1988.
Interview in *Time Out* (London), 18 May 1988.

On BABENCO: articles—

Yakir, Dan, "Braziliant," in *Film Comment* (New York), May–June 1984.
Stone, J., "On the edge," in *American Film* (Washington, D.C.), October 1984.
Chaillet, Jean Paul, "Hector Babenco: Le franc-tireur," in *Première* (Paris), June 1985.

*   *   *

Hector Babenco, an Argentinian who has so far filmed only in Brazil and the United States, is one of the current cinema's most consistent miners of marginality. If his burrowing has not always hit gold, it has resulted in a relatively small number of films that, as a body of work, represent a penetrating and richly variegated portrait of marginality in the americas. His debut film's very title, *King of the Night*, is telling. In the film, a bourgeois man's hypocritical and cowardly rejection of a prostitute's love is the catalyst for a descent into promiscuity, alcoholism, murder and jail. The film ends with him drunk, alone and out on the street. Night conjures up crime, sex, deviance and dreams, and a materialist but poetic rendering of its conjurations is the fabric of Babenco's *oeuvre*.

Outsiders are at the centre of Babenco's work. The eponymous hero of *Lúcio Flávio* is a bandit; the gang of delinquents in *Pixote* are escapees from juvenile prison who make a living selling drugs, stealing, pimping and killing; the two cellmates in *The Kiss of the Spiderwoman* are a political prisoner and a homosexual; and lastly, the romantic lovers in *Ironweed* are a pair of Bowery bums.

Babenco's outsiders differ from those of many other directors in that their alienation is not merely internal. As *Pixote* clearly exemplifies, it has its origins outside the psyche and is the result of social, political and/or economic exclusion. Even in *Ironweed*, though Francis (Jack Nicholson) decides to leave his family when he drops his baby, that fatal accident is the culmination of a powerlessness brought to an increasingly unbearable pitch by low wages, strike-breaking, and unemployment. On the rare occasion that Babenco's characters choose to opt out of society (Frank, Valentin in *Kiss*) their decision is also rooted in the social. More often, they are kicked out (Molina in *Kiss*) or prevented from entering it (the children in *Pixote*).

Marginalization, however, does have psychological repercussions and Babenco does not ignore them. By the standards of middle-class morality, his characters are warped. They lie, steal, and sometimes even kill. And they perceive these acts as bordering on the banal. The extraordinary power of *Pixote* is due partly to its graphic depictions of the facility with which children can perform the most grisly actions, incorporate them into their quotidian, yet still retain a childish innocence.

The social and psychological alienation experienced by Babenco's characters is not, as is often the case in American films, accompanied by emotional retardation. On the contrary, love, desire, want or need, are articulately expressed through either word or gesture then spontaneously gratified or denied. In Babenco's films only the bourgeois (Valentin in *Kiss*, for example) are scared of, or stingy with their emotions. The rest are free with their feelings. However, the expression of emotion is not an end in itself for Babenco: his characters can be changed by it (some, like Molina, for the better, others, like the King of the Night, for the worst). Love can keep one going. But it is often unreliable and impermanent and, more importantly, it doesn't get one a meal, better living conditions, or out of jail. Life has made Babenco's characters hard. They are cynical about institutions and experience has taught that justice exists only for others. Yet in each other they continue to hope and trust; to each other they often become family.

Babenco's characters can escape the material world only in fantasy. Sometimes the dream sequence is really a nightmare, as when Lúcio Flávio dreams first of his girlfriend's murder and then, near the end of the film, of his own. Sometimes the fantasies are only verbalised: in *Pixote*, the children *tell* each other their hopes of being rich, owning a car and living on the beach. Yet the dream sequence we are shown is Pixote's nightmare of running nude through the night attempting to escape a flashing car. Fantasy, of course is the very heart of *Kiss*—it is what makes Molina and Valentin's life bearable.

Hector Babenco directing William Hurt in *Kiss of the Spider Woman*

Babenco makes no great distinction between the real and the imaginary. Dreams inform life, are part of life. In some instances, the films' movement from external to internal world is motivated (Pixote sniffs glue, Molina begins to weave his story). But Babenco has the facility of shifting from the real to the imaginary with a cut. Indeed his talent for transporting the viewer in and out of people's heads is Tolstoyan. In *Ironweed*, for example, Francis' past, the ghosts that haunt him, and Helen's fantasy of herself as a singer share equal billing with their external reality. The film changes point-of-view without heavy symbolism or visible strain.

In spite of the dream or fantasy elements, Babenco's films are various attempts at representations of realism. *Lúcio Flávio* was based on a life of a real outlaw who collaborated with the police. *Pixote* began as a documentary and was turned into a fiction film only when the authorities refused Babenco permission to shoot in the juvenile detention centres. Both *Lúcio* and *Pixote* were marketed as *exposés*. Babenco himself is on camera in front of a slum at the beginning of *Pixote* introducing the film and simultaneously testifying to the authenticity of the problem that is about to be dramatized. The Brazilian films were received as realist; at home, audience and author share in the cultural negotiations of such definitions. In North America and Western Europe, on-location shootings, non-professional actors, and themes of poverty and deprivation are commonly

accepted as the signifiers that best communicate Latin America.

It is Babenco's American films, however, which reveal the extent to which a text is understood in light of its context. The cultural specificity of the notion of realism is made manifest in *Kiss of the Spiderwoman*, Babenco's first American film. The film tries to make a distinction between the artifices of the black and white fantasy movie-within-the-movie and the supposedly stark steely-hued realism of the protagonists' life in jail, but it doesn't quite succeed. Realism is the style that most successfully hides its artifices from its audience. The sets, the social setting, and the acting of William Hurt and Raul Julia (as Molina and Valentin respectively) seemed forced. Likewise, one could argue that *Ironweed* is too dreamy and too verbose for a big-budget American star vehicle, however Bowery the setting. In transplanting his style to a different context, Babenco's work seems transformed. Aesthetic strategies such as on-location shooting, the combination of professional and non-professional actors, relatively lengthy shots, and dream sequences had made his Brazilian films seem the height of gritty realism. Similar strategies make his American films seem slow and self-consciously poetic.

Babenco's work makes great raw material for investigations of the limits of cross-cultural communication. But the reason why one returns to see his films again is because Babenco makes us understand and identify with his derelicts. That identification creates a complicity with the characters' actions and is therefore the catalyst for an existential dilemma that most of us would not normally face. The audience is confronted with the possibility that given certain options, they too might choose to sell their bodies, steal or kill, and that this might not necessarily make them evil. Babenco's greatest gift is how in all of his films he extracts and highlights a moral dimension from the conventionally immoral.

—José Arroyo

BACON, Lloyd.

American. Born in San José, California, 16 January 1890. Educated in California public schools and at Santa Clara College. Married Margaret Balach. Member David Belasco's Los Angeles stock company, 1911; stage actor in Lloyd Hamilton comedies, 1913; worked in Chaplin comedies, 1916; served in Photo dept., U.S. Navy, 1917; actor at Mutual, 1918, and at Triangle, 1919; director for Mack Sennett and Lloyd Hamilton, 1921; moved to Warners and directed first feature, *Broken Hearts of Hollywood*, 1926; moved to 20th Century-Fox, 1944; finished career with two films at Universal and two at RKO, 1953. *Died in Burbank, California, 15 November 1955.*

Films as Director:

1926   *Broken Hearts of Hollywood*; *Private Izzy Murphy*
1927   *Finger Prints*; *White Flannels*; *The Heart of Maryland*; *A Sailor's Sweetheart*; *Brass Knuckles*
1928   *Pay as You Enter*; *The Lion and the Mouse*; *Women They Talk About*; *The Singing Fool*
1929   *Stark Mad*; *No Defense*; *Honky Tonk*; *Say It with Songs*; *So Long Letty*
1930   *The Other Tomorrow*; *She Couldn't Say No*; *A Notorious Affair*; *Moby Dick*; *The Office Wife*
1931   *Sit Tight*; *Kept Husbands*; *Fifty Million Frenchmen*; *Gold Dust Gertie*; *Honor of the Family*
1932   *Manhattan Parade*; *Fireman Save My Child*; *Alias the Doctor*; *The Famous Ferguson Case*; *Miss Pinkerton*; *Crooner*; *You Said a Mouthful*
1933   ***42nd Street***; *Picture Snatcher*; *Mary Stevens M.D.*; *Footlight Parade*; *Son of a Sailor*
1934   *Wonder Bar*; *A Very Honorable Guy*; *He Was Her Man*; *Here Comes the Navy*; *Six-Day Bike Rider*
1935   *Devil Dogs of the Air*; *In Caliente*; *Broadway Gondolier*; *The Irish in Us*; *Frisco Kid*
1936   *Sons o' Guns*; *Cain and Mabel*; *Gold Diggers of 1937*
1937   *Marked Woman*; *Ever Since Eve*; *San Quentin*; *Submarine D-1*
1938   *A Slight Case of Murder*; *Cowboy from Brooklyn*; *Rocket Busters*; *Boy Meets Girl*
1939   *Wings of the Navy*; *The Oklahoma Kid*; *Indianapolis Speedway*; *Espionage Agent*
1940   *A Child Is Born*; *Invisible Stripes*; *Three Cheers for the Irish*; *Brother Orchid*; *Knute Rockne—All American*
1941   *Honeymoon for Three*; *Footsteps in the Dark*; *Affectionately Yours*; *Navy Blues*
1942   *Larceny, Inc.*; *Wings for the Eagle*; *Silver Queen*
1943   *Action in the North Atlantic*
1944   *Sunday Dinner for a Soldier*
1945   *Captain Eddie*
1946   *Home Sweet Homicide*; *Wake Up and Dream*
1947   *I Wonder Who's Kissing Her Now*
1948   *You Were Meant For Me*; *Give My Regards to Broadway*; *Don't Trust Your Husband (An Innocent Affair)*
1949   *Mother Is a Freshman*; *It Happens Every Spring*; *Miss Grant Takes Richmond*
1950   *Kill the Umpire*; *The Good Humor Man*; *The Fuller Brush Girl*
1951   *Call Me Mister*; *The Frogmen*; *Golden Girl*
1953   *The I Don't Care Girl*; *The Great Sioux Uprising*; *Walking My Baby Back Home*
1954   *The French Line*; *She Couldn't Say No*

Other Films:

1915   *The Champion* (Chaplin) (role); *In the Park* (Chaplin) (role); *The Jitney Elopement* (Chaplin) (role); *The Bank* (Chaplin) (role); *The Tramp* (Chaplin) (role)
1916   *The Floorwalker* (Chaplin) (role); *The Vagabond* (Chaplin) (role); *Behind the Screen* (Chaplin) (role); *The Rink* (Chaplin) (role); *The Fireman* (Chaplin) (role)
1919/20   Roles for Mutual and Triangle studios

Publications:

On BACON: books—

Meyer, William, *Warner Brothers Directors*, New York, 1978.
Fuments, Rocco, editor *42nd Street*, Madison, Wisconsin, 1980.
Feuer, Jane, *The Hollywood Musical*, London, 1982.
Roddick, Nick, *A New Deal in Entertainment: Warner Brothers in the 1930's*, London, 1983.
Altman, Rick, *The American Film Musical*, Bloomington, Indiana and London, 1989.

On BACON: articles—

"Lloyd Bacon . . . Warner Brothers' Ace," in *Cue* (New York), 6 April 1935.
Parsons, Louella, "Cosmopolitan's Citation for the Best Direction of the Month," in *Cosmopolitan* (New York), May 1949.

*   *   *

Lloyd Bacon is probably best known for his director's credit on such classic Warner Bros. films as *42nd Street*, *Footlight Parade*, *Knute Rockne—All American*, and *Action in the North Atlantic*. But others are more remembered for these films: choreographer Busby Berkeley for the musicals, and actors Pat O'Brien, Ronald Reagan, and Humphrey Bogart in the 1940's films. Today Bacon is lost in the literature about Warner Bros. and is not even ranked by Andrew Sarris in his *American Directors* book.

In his day Lloyd Bacon was recognized as a consummate Hollywood professional. One cannot help standing in some awe of Bacon's directorial output in the era from the coming of sound to the Second World War. During these 14 years he directed an average of five films per annum for Warner Bros. (Seven were released in 1932 alone.) Bacon's *42nd Street* and *Wonder Bar* were among the industry's top-grossing films of the decade. For a time he was considered Warners' top musicals specialist. The corporation paid him accordingly, some $200,000 per year, making him one of its highest paid contract directors of the 1930's.

Bacon's status declined during the 1940's. His craftsmanship remained solid for he knew the classical Hollywood system of production as well as anyone on the Warners lot. But Bacon never seemed to find his special niche, skipping from one genre to another. He seemed to evolve into Warners' handyman director. His greatest success came with war films. For example, *Wings of the Navy* had a million dollar budget, and helped kick off Warners' string of successful World War II films. Probably Bacon's best-remembered film of the 1940's is *Action in the North Atlantic*, a tribute to the U.S. Merchant Marine. (This also was Bacon's last film at Warners.)

In 1944 Bacon moved to Twentieth Century-Fox to work for his former boss, Darryl F. Zanuck. There he re-established

Lloyd Bacon directing Monte Blue in *No Defense*

himself in musicals as well as films of comedy and family romance, but still seemed unable to locate a long-term specialty. He finished at Fox with an early 1950's series of Lucille Ball comedies, and ended his directorial career in somewhat ignominious fashion, helping Howard Hughes create a 3-D Jane Russell spectacle, *The French Line*.

Bacon's most significant contribution to film history probably came during his early days at Warners as that studio pioneered new sound technology in the late 1920's. Bacon presided over several significant transitional films, none more important than *The Singing Fool*. Although *The Jazz Singer* usually gets credit as the first (and most important) transitional talkie, *The Singing Fool* should receive far more credit because for more than a decade, this film stood as the highest grossing feature in Hollywood annals. As its director, Bacon was honored by the trade publication *Film Daily* as one of the top ten directors of the 1928–29 season. As a consequence of this and other films, Bacon established his reputation as a director who helped thrust Hollywood into an era of movies with sound.

—Douglas Gomery

BADHAM, John.

American. Born in Luton, England, 25 August 1943. Moved to U.S. 1945, naturalized 1950. Educated at Yale University, B.A., 1963, M.F.A., 1965. U.S. Army, 1963–64. Married Bonnie Sue Hughes, 1967 (divorced 1979), one daughter. Worked in mailroom, as casting director, then trailer director for Universal Studios, Hollywood; TV director, early 1970's; directed first feature, *Bingo Long . . .*, 1976; formed Great American Picture Show Co., and signed to Warners as producer-director, 1984. Address: c/o Adams, Ray, and Rosenberg, 9200 Sunset Blvd., Los Angeles, CA 90069, U.S.A.

Films as Director:

1976 *The Bingo Long Traveling All Stars and Motor Kings*
1977 *Saturday Night Fever*
1979 *Dracula*
1981 *Whose Life Is It Anyway?*
1983 *Blue Thunder*; *Wargames*
1985 *American Flyers*
1986 *Short Circuit*
1987 *Stakeout*
1989 *Bird on a Wire*

Publications:

By BADHAM: articles—

Interview in *Cineaste* (New York), Winter 1978–79.
Interview in *American Cinematographer* (Los Angeles), June 1979.
Interview in *Films in Review* (New York), December 1981.
Interview with N. Glauberman, in *American Film* (Washington, D.C.), May 1983.
Interview in *L'Ecran Fantastique* (Paris), December 1984 and August 1986.
Interview with Philip Strick, in *Films and Filming* (London), December 1986.
Interview in *Time Out* (London), 24 February 1988.

On BADHAM: articles—

Screen International (London), 20 January 1979.
Lash, G., "John Badham's *Whose Life is it Anyway*," in *Millimeter* (New York), December 1981.
Schmidt, K., in *Kosmorama* (Copenhagen), December 1983.
Revue du Cinéma/Image et Son (Paris), May 1990.

*   *   *

Although there has been a critical tendency to dismiss John Badham as a lower-case Lumet or as a Keystone Kubrick at various points of his career, examination of his body of films belies this approach. His work, varied and sure, falls into three chronological stages: the first and most diverse lot shows interest in adaptations, the second in human interaction with machines, and the third in the workings of screwball action-comedies. While these stages are more distinct than similar, certain similarities persist throughout. All Badham's movies present a balanced liberal leaning; nearly all evidence a warm sense of humor; and all show great interest in character.

The adaptations include *Bingo Long's Traveling All-Stars and Motor Kings*, from the novel; *Saturday Night Fever*, from a *New York* magazine article; *Dracula*, from a play based on the novel; and *Whose Life Is It Anyway?*, from the play. In *Bingo Long* Badham's liberal stance clearly emerges, especially in the scene where the black baseball players triumph over an audience of bigots. While they may lose the game, they win the audience, and baseball bridges the races, at least while the game goes on. Badham's liberalism here is both multi-faceted and wistful; things are gained as things are given up. James Earl Jones rebels against acting like a clown to appease white audiences, and when a black player crosses over to the white leagues, Jones and Billy Dee Williams know it means the end of black baseball.

John Travolta's almost magical conversion to liberalism and away from his homeboys at the end of *Saturday Night Fever* also fits into this trend. While Travolta rejects their small-mindedness and racism, he also turns away from the violent warmth displayed throughout the film, by them and especially by Travolta's family. *Whose Life Is It Anyway?* presents a similar conflict, but elevated to one of life-or-death. Richard Dreyfuss battles the conservative John Cassavetes for his right to die after becoming a quadriplegic. While Dreyfuss wins his case, Cassavetes emerges as extremely sympathetic, urging his patient to remain in the hospital to ensure that he will not suffer as well as to give him a chance to change his mind.

Badham's move away from adaptations towards original scripts coincides with his exploration of man's interaction with machines. In this latter sense Badham fits into a line of filmmakers including Kubrick and early De Palma, although Badham's films are generally much more good-natured than others of this type. *Blue Thunder, Wargames,* and *Short Circuit* all pit small groups against monolithic right-wing counterparts. (This same pattern also emerges, to a lesser extent, in *American Flyers*.) In each of these cases David uses Goliath's own high-tech wizardry against him.

The human element predominates: a man flips a helicopter in a way that is "technically impossible" and defeats his enemy, a teenager teaches Joshua the computer to think and staves off nuclear war, and a robot becomes alive and eludes the would-be "disassemblers" of Nova Laboratories (which sports, ironically enough, a replica of Leonardo's "Canon of proportions/measure of man" drawing as its corporate logo). These middle films, too, are notable for sharp character work by Daniel Stern, Warren Oates, and Malcolm McDowell in *Blue Thunder*, by the two computer nerds who "can get a little nervous" in *Wargames*, and by Fisher Stevens in *Short Circuit*. These films also show an increasing tendency towards a Bergsonian mechanical-encrusted-upon-the-living sense of humor, culminating in the character of the crowd-pleasing robot, Johnny Five.

Stakeout and *Bird on a Wire* continue Badham's movement toward comedy. These two pictures feature strong romantic leads, madcap chases involving vehicles of all descriptions, climactic shootouts in colorful places, and strong embrace at closure. *Stakeout*, the more successful of the two, picks up many of the threads of Badham's earlier work. Richard Dreyfuss, a local policeman at odds with the FBI, struggles to find a vicious bank robber. The sparkling scene in which Dreyfuss calms down a drunk recalls the warmth of *Saturday Night Fever* or *American Flyers*. Here, though, the love interest moves more to the foreground than in most of Badham's work. Similarly, *Bird on a Wire* puts at center stage the romance between Mel Gibson and Goldie Hawn. The narrative line that has Gibson battling corrupt Drug Enforcement agents and an FBI man as well as the bureaucracy they control occupies equal footing at best. *Disorganized Crime*, a film to which Badham contributed but did not direct, contains many of these same elements, but lacks his sure hand. And a sure hand it is, as Badham has guided a number of diverse projects with a high degree of artistry and a remarkably consistent degree of box office success.

—Mark Walker

––––––––––

BAILLIE, Bruce.

American. Born in Aberdeen, South Dakota, 24 September 1931. Educated at University of Minnesota, B.A. 1955; University of California at Berkeley, 1956–58; London School of Film Technique, 1959. Served in Korean War. Worked under Will Hindle for Marvin Becker Films, San Francisco, and began first film, *On Sundays*, 1960; started Canyon Cinema, San Francisco, 1961; taught film at Rice University, Houston, 1970 (later taught at Bard and Evergreen Colleges). Recipient: Creative Arts Award for Filmmaking, Brandeis University, 1970. Address: 669 W. 1050 South, Camano Island, WA 98292, U.S.A.

Films:

1960/61   *On Sundays*
1961   *David Lynn's Sculpture*; *Mr Hayashi*; *The Gymnasts*
1962   *Friend Fleeing* (unfinished); *Everyman*; *News No. 3*; *Have You Thought of Talking to the Director?*; *Here I Am*
1962/63   *A Hurrah for Soldiers*
1963   *To Parsifal*
1964   *Mass for the Dakota Sioux*; *The Brookfield Recreation Center*
1964/65   *Quixote* (revised 1967)

1965   *Yellow Horse*
1966   *Tung*; *Castro Street*; *All My Life*; *Still Life*; *Termination*; *Port Chicago*; *Show Leader*
1967   *Valentin De Las Sierras*
1970   *Quick Billy*
1971–present   *Roslyn Romance* (multi-part film in progress)
1981–present   *The Cardinal's Visit* (final section of *Roslyn Romance*)

Publications:

By BAILLIE: articles—

Frequent poems and letters, in *Canyon Cinema News* (San Francisco)
"Letters: San Francisco Film Scene," in *Film Culture* (New York), Summer 1963.
Interview with Richard Whitehall, in *Film Culture* (New York), Summer 1969.
Interview in *Film Culture* (New York), Spring 1971.
"Bruce Baillie," in *Film Comment* (New York), Spring 1971.
"Dr. Bish," in *Downtown Review*, Fall/Winter 1979/80, Spring 1980, Fall 1980.

On BAILLIE: books—

Hanhardt, John, and others, *A History of the American Avant-Garde Cinema*, New York, 1976.
Callenbach, Ernest, *Bruce Baillie*, St. Paul, Minnesota, 1979.

On BAILLIE: articles—

Callenbach, Ernest, "Bruce Baillie," in *Film Quarterly* (Berkeley), Fall 1964.
Polt, Harriet, "The Films of Bruce Baillie," in *Film Comment* (New York), Fall 1964.
Kent, Thomas, "San Francisco's Hipster Cinema," in *Film Culture* (New York), Spring 1967.
"Baillie Issue" of *Harbinger* (Houston), July 1967.
"Baillie Section" of *Film Culture* (New York), no. 67–69, 1979.

*   *   *

The career of Bruce Baillie has two central aspects, which are also features of the whole American avant-garde film movement. First, his films are generally intensely poetic, lyrical evocations of persons and places in which the subject matter is transformed by the subjective methods used to photograph it. Second, many of his films display a strong social awareness, describing attitudes critical towards, and alienated from, mainstream American society. In many cases, Baillie fuses these concerns within single films.

Stylistically, Baillie's films are characterized by images of haunting, evanescent beauty. An object will appear with spectacular clarity, only to dissolve away an instant later. Light itself often becomes a subject, shining across the frame or reflected from objects, suggesting a level of poetry in the subject matter that lies beyond easy interpretation. Baillie combines images with other images, and images with sound, in dense, collage-like structures. Thus, many of his films cut frequently between scenes, or superimpose objects on each other. One is constantly aware of a restlessness, an instability, which seems to result from his images' appearance and flow. It is significant, too, that many of Baillie's films contain, or are structured as, journeys.

The effect of Baillie's films is to make the viewer feel that any moment of the viewing, any single image he is looking at is a mere illusion that will soon vanish. The sensuousness of the light and colors only heighten one's awareness of their unreality. It is as if there is a void, a nothingness, that lies behind all things. It is not irrelevant in this regard that Baillie has evidenced strong interest, over the years, in Eastern religious thought.

Some degree of social comment is present in most of Baillie's films, but in widely varying degrees. *Mr. Hayashi* places the poetic and the social in a very precise balance. The imagery consists of evocative, sun-drenched images forming a short, haiku-like portrait of a man. On the soundtrack, we hear the man speak of his life, and his difficulty in finding work. *Mass* and *Quixote* indict American society as overly aggressive, toward its citizens, toward Native Americans, and toward nature; as impersonal and dehumanizing; as lacking physical or moral roots. For *Quixote*, Baillie uses an extremely dense, collage-like form, in which images and fragments of images are intercut with and superimposed on others, with a similarly complex soundtrack. At times, the film's multiple themes seem to blur into each other, as if the filmmaker is acknowledging that he is as "lost" as the society he is depicting.

Castro Street, *Tung*, and *Valentin de las Sierras* are, by contrast, apparently simpler portraits of people and places. By keeping his camera very close to things, Baillie renders their details ever more stunning, while his collage editing and soundtrack again create an instability leading to "nothingness". *Castro Street*, which depicts an industrialized area, is extraordinary for its combination of diverse photographic representations—black and white, color, positive and negative—in editing and superimposition. *Quick Billy* contains thematic and stylistic elements of most of Baillie's previous films; its motifs include autobiography, "portrait"-like representation of people and events, and an underlying theme, made explicit in the film's final section, of Western man's aggressiveness toward his surroundings.

—Fred Camper

_____

BARDEM, Juan Antonio.

Spanish. Born Juan Antonio Bardem-Munoz in Madrid, 2 July 1922. Educated in agriculture, and at Instituto de Investigaciones Cinematograficas, 1947–48. Worked for Spanish Ministry of Agriculture, assigned to Cinema section, 1946; wrote for film periodicals, and on scripts with Luis Berlanga, from 1947; began film magazine *Objectivo*, 1953 (banned by government, 1955); arrested for political reasons, 1956 and later; produced through Uninci company, 1958–61; head of Spanish directors' guild, 1970's; directed Bulgarian/U.S.S.R./East German production of *The Warning*, 1981.

Films as Director:

1949   *Paseo sobre una guerra antigua* (co-d, co-sc) (silent short incorporated by Luis Escobar into feature *La honradez de la cerradura*)
1950   *Barajas, aeropuerto internacional* (short) (+sc)
1951   *Esa pareja feliz* (*That Happy Pair*) (co-d, co-sc)
1954   *Cómicos* (*Comedians*) (+sc); *Felices Pascuas* (+co-sc)
1955   **Muerte de un ciclista** (**Death of a Cyclist, Age of Infidelity**) (+sc)
1956   *Calle Mayor* (*Grand Rue, The Lovemaker*) (+sc)
1957   *La muerte de Pio Baroja* (unreleased) (+sc); *La venganza* (*The Vengeance*) (+sc)
1959   *Sonatas* (+pr, sc)
1960   *A las cinco de la tarde* (+pr, co-sc)
1962   *Los inocentes* (+sc)
1963   *Nunca pasa nada* (+co-sc)
1965   *Los pianos mécanicos* (*Les Pianos méchaniques, The Uninhibited*) (+sc)
1969   *El ultimo dia de la guerra* (*The Last Day of the War*) (+co-sc)
1971   *Varietes* (+sc)

Juan Antonio Bardem

1973 Four versions of *The Mysterious Island*: 1. *La isla misteriosa* (for Spanish and Latin American distribution), 2. *L'isola misteriosa e il Capitano Nemo* (for Italian distribution, incorporates material directed by Henri Colpi), 3. *L'ile mystérieuse* and *The Mysterious Island* (French, English and international version, co-d with Colpi), 4. six-hour TV version for international distribution; *La corrupción de Chris Miller* (*The Corruption of Chris Miller*) (+ role); *Behind the Shutters*
1976 *El podor del deseo*; *Foul Play*
1977 *The Dog*; *El puente*
1979 *7 Dias de enero* (*Seven Days in January*) (+sc)
1982 *The Warning*

Other films:

1952 *Bienvenido, Mr. Marshall!* (*Welcome, Mr. Marshall!*) (Berlanga) (co-sc)
1953 *Novio a la vista* (Berlanga) (co-sc)
1954 *El torero* (Wheeler) (Spanish version of *Châteaux en Espagne*)) (co-dialogue)
1955 *Playa prohibida* (*El esconocido*) (Soler) (sc)
1956 *El amór de Don Juan* (*Don Juan*) (Berry) (co-sc); *Carte a Sara* (Manzanos and Bercovici) (sc)
1958 *L'uomo dai calzoni corti* (*Tal vez mañana*) (Pellegrini) (pr)
1961 **Viridiana** (Buñuel) (pr)

Publications:

By BARDEM: articles—

"Spanish Highway," in *Films and Filming* (London), June 1957.
Film Makers on Filmmaking, edited by Harry Geduld, Bloomington, Indiana, 1967.
"Cara a cara . . . Bardem-Berlanga," in *Cinema 2002* (Madrid), July/August 1980.
Interview with P. Farinas, in *Cine Cubano* (Havana), no. 103, 1983.

On BARDEM: books—

Oms, Marcel, *J.A. Bardem*, Lyons (Premier Plan no. 21).
Scwartz, Ronald, *Spanish Film Directors* (*1950–85*)*: 21 Profiles*, Metuchen, New Jersey, 1986.
Hopewell, John, *Out of the Past: Spanish Cinema After Franco*, London, 1987.
Higginbotham, Virginia, *Spanish Film Under Franco*, Austin, Texas, 1988.

On BARDEM: articles—

"The Arrest," in *Sight and Sound* (London), Spring 1956.
Aranda, J.F., "Bardem: Une Méthode de travail," in *Cinéma* (Paris), no. 33, 1959.
Durand, Philippe, "Juan Antonio Bardem, homme d'Espagne," in *Image et Son* (Paris), October 1959.
Carril, M. Martinex, "Despues de 27 años, Bardem se revitaliza," in *Cinemateca Revista* (Andes), July 1980.
Biofilmography, in *Cahiers de la Cinémathèque* (Perpignan), Winter 1984.

* * *

A pioneer figure in Spanish film, Juan Antonio Bardem is also one of Spain's most consistently political filmmakers. In his early movies co-directed with Luis Garcia Berlanga, *Esa pareja feliz* and *Bienvenido Mr. Marshall*, he broke with prevailing Francoist film traditions which emphasized militarism, folklore, literary adaptations and costume dramas. Bardem and Berlanga chose instead to present scenes of contemporary Spanish life and used humor to describe and criticize aspects of Spanish society. With *Bienvenido Mr. Marshall* the two directors were recognized as leading filmmakers and along with others of their generation, they set about to revitalize the Spanish film industry and to rescue Spanish films from mediocrity. At a meeting held in Salamanca in 1955, they drafted a statement of principles in which Bardem wrote: "After 60 years, Spanish cinema is politically futile, socially false, intellectually worthless, esthetically valueless and industrially paralytic." Bardem went on to note that Spanish cinema "had turned its back on reality . . . (and was) totally removed from Spanish realistic traditions [as found] in paintings and novels."

Bardem and other filmmakers who attended the meeting at Salamanca also deplored the lack of general film culture in Spain, noting that it was not possible to see 95% of movies made abroad. Bardem felt that it was important for Spaniards to keep abreast of worldwide trends in filmmaking and especially to become familiar with Italian neo-realism. This was the single most important influence in the development of his own cinematic style. Both in his movies and in his writings he remained faithful to the tenets of neo-realism. In order to foster a film culture in Spain, Bardem founded *Objetivo*, a cinema journal that was eventually banned by the government. During its brief existence, it nevertheless became a rallying point for Spanish cineastes, raised the level of film criticism in Spain and informed readers about prohibited films. Several years later in yet another effort to ensure the autonomy and integrity of Spanish film, Bardem joined with Berlanga, Carlos Saura, and other directors and founded a production company, UNINCI, which operated until 1962, when it was closed down for co-producing Luis Buñuel's *Viridiana*.

Because of these endeavors as well as his political outspokenness, Bardem was arrested seven times during the Franco years. He nevertheless persisted in his efforts to make political films in Spain. In spite of his lack of favor at home, he won many prizes at film festivals around the world and directed co-productions in Italy, France, Argentina, and Bulgaria.

The movies with which he is most closely associated are those that chronicle the negative effects of Francoism on the psyche of Spaniards of different classes, regions and social milieus. In several films he dramatizes the alienation fostered by Francoism by focusing upon a single individual who often bears his own name of Juan. This Spanish everyman feels frustrated and stifled in a closed society. He attempts to find outlets through hobbies, intrigues, even through radio contests but all means prove to be unsatisfactory. In the course of his efforts, Juan is led to re-evaluate himself and the world around him in order to find new options. The spectator judges the choices that each Juan makes, becoming increasingly critical of individuals who act selfishly, cowardly, or who refuse to take a stand. These general themes continue in the movies he has made since the death of Franco.

—Katherine Singer Kovács

———

BARNET, Boris.

Russian. Born in Moscow, 1902, grandson of an English settler. Studied at School of Art and Architecture, Moscow. Joined Red Army, 1919, later PT instructor for Army then professional boxer. Joined Lev Kuleshov's "Eccentric Workshop," 1924; directed first film, 1926. Retrospectives at La Rochelle Festival, 1982, and Locarno Festival, 1985. *Died (suicide), 8 January 1965.*

Films as Director:

1926 *Miss Mend* (serial) (co-d, co-sc, role)

Boris Barnet: *Okraina*

1927 *Devushka s korobkoi* (*The Girl with the Hat Box*); *Moskva v oktyabre* (*Moscow in October*) (+role)
1928 *Dom na Trubnoi* (*House on Trubnaya*)
1929 *Zhivye dela* (*Living Things*) (short) (+co-sc)
1930 *Proizvodstvo muzykal'nykh instrumentov* (*The Manufacture of Musical Instruments*) (short)
1931 *Ledolom* (*The Thaw*)
1933 *Okraina* (*Outskirts. Patriots*) (+co-sc)
1935 *U samogo sinego morya* (*By the Deep Blue Sea*)
1939 *Noch' v sentyabre* (*One September Night*) (+role)
1940 *Staryi nayezdnik* (*The Old Jockey*) (released 1959)
1941 "Muzhestvo" ("Courage") episode of *Boyevoy kinosbornik no. 3* (*Fighting Film Album no. 3*)
1942 "Bestsennaya golova" ("A Priceless Head") episode of *Boyevoy kinosbornik no. 10* (*Fighting Film Album no. 10*)
1943 *Novgorodtsy* (*Men of Novgorod*) (not released)
1945 *Odnazhdy noch'yu* (*Once One Night*) (+role)
1947 *Podvig razvedchika* (*The Exploits of an Intelligence Agent*) (+role)
1948 *Stranitsy zhizni* (*Pages from a Life*) (co-d)
1950 *Schedroe leto* (*A Bounteous Summer*)
1952 *Kontsert masterov ukrainskogo iskusstva* (*Masters of Ukrainian Art in Concert*) (+sc)

1955 *Lyana* (+co-sc)
1957 *Poet* (*The Poet*); *Borets i kloun* (*The Wrestler and the Clown*) (co-d)
1959 *Annushka*
1961 *Alyonka*
1963 *Polustanok* (*The Whistle-Stop*) (+ co-sc)

Films as Actor only:

1924 ***Neobychainiye priklucheniya Mistera Vesta v stranye Bolshevikov* (*The Adventures of Mr. West in the Land of the Bolsheviks*)** (Kuleshov)
1925 *Shakhmatnaya goryachka* (*Chess fever*) (Pudovkin) (short); *Na vernom sledu* (*On the Right Track*) (A. Dmitriyev)
1926 *Protsess o trekh millionakh* (*The Three Millions Trial*) (Protazanov)
1928 ***Potomok Chingis-khana* (*The Heir to Genghis Khan. Storm Over Asia*)** (Pudovkin)
1929 *Zhivoi trup* (*The Living Corpse*) (Otsep)
1936 *Lyubov' i nenavist'* (*Love and Hate*) (A. Endelstein)
1946 *Sinegoriya* (*The Blue Mountains*) (Garin and Lokshina)

Publications:

On BARNET: books—

Kushnirov, M., *Zhizn' i fil'my Boris Barneta* [The Life and Films of Boris Barnet], Moscow, 1977.
Albera, F., and R. Cosandey, editors, *Boris Barnet: Ecrits, Documents, Etudes, Filmographie*, Locarno, 1985.

On BARNET: articles—

Obituary in *Kino* (Warsaw), no. 2, 1965.
Obituary in *Cinéma* (Paris), no. 96, 1965.
"Boris Barnet," in *Film Culture* (New York), Fall 1965.
Kuzmina, "A Tribute to Boris Barnet," in *Film Comment* (New York), Fall 1968.
"Boris Barnet," in *Film Dope* (London), March 1973.
Gillett, John, in *National Film Theatre Booklet* (London), July 1980.
Gillett, John, in *Sight and Sound* (London), Autumn 1980.
Cahiers du Cinéma (Paris), November 1982.
Revue du Cinéma (Paris), October 1983.
Jeune Cinéma (Paris), November 1984.
Cahiers du Cinéma (Paris), October 1985.
Eisenschitz, B., "A Fickle Man, or Portrait of Boris Barnet as a Soviet Director," in *Inside the Film Factory: New Approaches to Russian and Soviet Cinema*, edited by Richard Taylor and Ian Christie, London and New York, 1991.

*   *   *

Boris Barnet's career as a director has been much under-rated in the West, yet it spanned almost forty years of Soviet film-making. After a brief period as a PT instructor in the Red Army and then as a professional boxer, he joined Kuleshov's workshop as an actor and handyman. In 1924 Barnet played the part of Cowboy Jeddy, a grotesque caricature of an American, in Kuleshov's eccentric comedy *The Extraordinary Adventures of Mr West in the Land of the Bolsheviks*. He frequently appeared later in his own films, often in cameo roles.

Like Kuleshov, Barnet went to work for the Mezhrabpom-Rus studio, where experimentation was combined with the production of films that were commercially successful. Barnet collaborated with Fyodor Otsep on the serial thriller *Miss Mend* and then made his first two feature films *The Girl with the Hatbox* and *The House on Trubnaya*. Both films involved actors from the Kuleshov workshop and both were light-hearted comedies, satirising the excesses of the New Economic Policy and the social and economic tensions associated with it. The first centred on a lost lottery ticket and the second on the arrival of a country girl in Moscow, but Barnet managed very gently to broaden their frame of reference, so that they marked him out by the end of the 1920's as a director of originality and distinction.

The advent of sound seems to have caused Barnet fewer problems than it did other directors: he made two sound shorts about musical instruments in 1930, neither of which has been preserved, and his first sound feature film, *Okraina* in 1933. This was a remarkably powerful, and in some ways almost Chekhovian, portrayal of life in a provincial Russian town during the First World War and the start of the Revolution. The lives of the characters are almost imperceptibly intertwined with the historical events unfolding far away. The relationship between individuals and events was however too subtle for many of Barnet's contemporaries and, like so many other Soviet film-makers of the time, he was attacked for ideological obscurantism. Hence it was that Barnet later remarked that he was not merely a "film director" but a "Soviet film director."

The reception for Barnet's next film, *By the Deep Blue Sea*, was even more hostile. On one level the film was a light-hearted love intrigue set on a collective farm on the banks of the Caspian Sea. On another it can be read as an allegorical tale of the eternal struggle between dream and reality, with the collective farm itself as a latterday utopia, emphasised by the somewhat ironic title—a dangerous comparison in 1936. Given the atmosphere of the time, it is perhaps not altogether surprising that Barnet's next film, *One September Night*, was devoted to a more conventional account of the birth of the Stakhanovite movement, with the secret police as heroes, defending the Soviet Union against sabotage. But *The Old Jockey*, made the year after, fell foul of the authorities and was not released until 1959.

The Second World War dominated Barnet's output for the next few years and his efforts were rewarded with the Stalin Prize in 1948. He returned to his true métier, comedy, in 1950, with his first colour film, *A Bounteous Summer*, made in the Ukraine, and *Lyana*, made in Moldavia five years later. Barnet's last completed film, *The Whistle-Stop*, was also a comedy but other films that he made during the last decade of his life are more properly characterised as dramas. But to say that is to underestimate Barnet, because his films cannot be easily pigeon-holed.

Barnet's career in Soviet cinema spanned four decades. He belonged to the generation of lesser known film-makers who in fact constituted the backbone of that cinema, while taking a back seat in the theoretical polemics that attracted international curiosity and focused attention on the avant-garde. His films displayed a mastery of visual technique and a disciplined economy of style. He was a mainstream director but a subversive artist, whose work, tinged with warmth, humour and humanity, constantly attracted Soviet audiences. He took his own life in 1965.

—Richard Taylor

———

BAUER, Evgeni.

Russian. Born Evgeni Frantsevich Bauer, 1865, son of a zither player. Educated at the Moscow College of Painting, Sculpture and Architecture. Married Lina Anvharova, a dancer and later actress in his films. Worked as a magazine caricaturist, newspaper satirist, theatre impresario and set designer; started directing films in 1913, working for Pathé, Drankov and Taldykin; joined Khanzhonkov's company, becoming one of the main shareholders, late 1913. *Died of pneumonia, 9th June 1917.*

Films as Director:

1913   *Sumerki Zhenskoi Dushi* (*The Twilight of a Woman's Soul*) (+art dir)
1914   *Ditya Bol'shogo Goroda* (*Child of the Big City*) [*Devushka s Ulitsy* (*The Girl from the Street*)] (art dir); *Ee Geroiski Podvig* (*Her Heroic Feat*); *Lyulya Bek*; *Slava Nam—Smert' Vagram* (*Glory to Us, Death to the Enemy*); *Tol'ko Raz v Godu* (*Only Once a Year*) [*Doroga v ad* (*The Road to Hell*)]; *Kholodnye Dushi* (*Cold Showers. Frigid Souls*)
1915   *Grezy* (*Daydreams*) [*Obmanutye Mechty* (*Deceived Dreams*)]; *Deti Veka* (*Children of the Age*); *Zhemchuzhnoe Ozherel'e* (*The Pearl Necklace*); *Leon Drey* [*Pokoritel' Zhenskikh Serdets* (*The Lady-Killer*)] (+art dir); *Pervaya Lyubov'* (*First Love*); *Schast'e Vechnoi Nochi* (*The Happiness of Eternal Night*); *Tysyacha Vtoraya Khitrost* (*The Thousand and Second Ruse*); *Yuri Nagornyi* [*Obol'stitel* (*The Seducer*)]
1916   *Zhizn' za Zhizn'* (*A Life for a Life*) [*Za Kazhduyu slezu po Kable Krovi* (*A Tear for Every Drop of Blood*)/*Sestry-*

Evgeni Bauer: *Deti Veka*

Sopernitsy (*The Rival Sisters*)*]* (+sc); *Nelly Raintseva*;
PriklyuchenieLiny v Sochi (*Lina's Adventure in Sochi*)
1917   *Umirayushchii Lebed'* (*The Dying Swan*); *Za Schast'em* (*For Luck*); *Korol' Parizha* (*The King of Paris*) (+co-sc); *Lina Pod Ekspertizoi ili Buinyi Pokoinik* (*Lina Under Examination; or, The Turbulent Corpse*); *Nabat* (*The Alarm*) (+sc); *Revolyutsioner* (*The Revolutionary*)
Note: These are the only films which remain from the 82 with which he has been credited.

Publications:

On BAUER: book—

Tsivian, Yuri, and others, *Silent Witnesses: Russian Films 1908–1919*, (in English and Italian), London and Pordenone, 1989.

On BAUER: articles—

Revue Internationale d'Histoire du Cinéma (Paris), no. 1, 1975.
Robinson, David, "Evgeni Bauer and the Cinema of Nikolai II," in *Sight and Sound* (London), Winter 1989–90.

*   *   *

When, in 1989, the Russians released a hoard of movies of the Czarist era, few of which had been seen in the West, we discovered a new "great" director. Evgeni Bauer was found to tower over all his contemporaries, including Victor Sjöström: for while Bauer's films could be as emotionally complex as those of Sjöström, he was a marvel at something which did not motivate the Swedish master—the mechanics of cinema. Bauer understood the language of the cinema better than any of his contemporaries, and in that Silent era, he exploited silence as no one else did until Keaton. The Hollywood of Keaton's time, ten years later, was still only groping towards some of Bauer's techniques—the travelling or roving camera, the sudden or unexpected close-up, the zoom-in (if used in a primitive way), angle-shots from above, the masked screen, the use of movement and editing (e.g. in a frenzied dance) to build to a climax, the split screen, vivid composition. Visually then, his films are exciting, and furthermore he uses locations tellingly to enhance his dramatic material, as we may expect from a former art director. These elements, when added to natural playing, with generally above-average stories, which invariably include a biting, if implicit, commentary on bourgeois society, make up a body of work unparalleled in early cinema. And who else at this time could take his narrative from A to D, without plodding through B and C?

Bauer entered the cinema as set designer for Drankov, but when, in that capacity, he moved over to Khanzhonov he was given an entirely free hand, directing as well for him—and his first film as such, *Twilight of a Woman's Soul* (1913), still survives. Like most Russian film-makers of this period, Bauer gave audiences the doom and gloom they craved, often with a last-reel suicide—but he did it with a sophistication matched only by Yakov Protazanov. For instance, in *Child of the Big*

City a working-girl is wooed by a rich man, attracted to women outside his own class; after marriage he bores her and she seduces a valet before deciding to use her husband's friends to become a courtesan, because she does not wish to give up a life of luxury. He, ruined, seeks her out, only to find her no less contemptuous than she was when their marriage ended.

The *Silent Witnesses* of the title are the servants of Moscow's sybaritic high society, but they have an independent life of their own, caring and principled. When one young maid has a mind to the advantages of being a rich man's lady, and, after a half-hearted refusal, acquiesces, she finds her position too insecure to protest against his continuing infidelities. In all of Bauer's films drunken parties and sexual licence are the prerogatives of the rich, who are also vindictive, cruel and without moral values: but they are also dangerously attractive. In *Children of the Age* a loving young wife allows an aged roué to seduce her and remains with him even after he has reduced her husband to penury by having him sacked. Her options are open, and furthermore she remains sympathetic, though the peasant audiences of Czarist Russia might well have thought that this brutally unequal society ought to be destroyed forthwith. It would be an overstatement to describe Bauer as subversive, but the society he depicts is wholly unadmirable, mortally sick.

There is abnormal psychology—perhaps specifically of the Russian variety—at the heart of both *Daydreams* and *After Death*. In the first a man becomes a recluse after his wife's death, only to become obsessed by an actress who resembles her; and she, while perhaps still loving him, fatally mocks his passion for his dead wife. In the second a man, inconsolable after the death of his mother, drives to suicide the actress who has aspired to be the new woman in his life, then kills himself after reading her diaries to discover her motives. *Happiness of Eternal Night* marks a firm return to Bauer's central theme, the rottenness of society, but the plot is a silly thing about a wealthy blind girl who marries a rake, persuaded by his brother who, because of his love for her, had trained to be an eye-surgeon in order to cure her.

Because Bauer was his leading director, Khanzonkov offered him a choice of subjects when he decided to make a super-production to rival Yermoliev's *Queen of Spades*. Bauer chose a now-forgotten French novel, which emerged as *A Life for a Life*, a complex melange of high society gambols, infidelity, and debts. Since all the characters are well-off and one of them, a wealthy widow, does an exemplary job in running a factory, the film (unlike any of the others of Bauer's still extant), lacks any immediate revolutionary portents. *Yuri Nagorni* was designed to tell its story without intertitles, thus pushing us willy-nilly into an incomprehensible plot about an adulterous wife who makes a play for a libidinous opera-singer, the eponymous Yuri: she leaves him, at the end of the first half to die in a fire, but the second part, in flashback, contains all that we need to know. Bauer was fascinated by the underside of life, the past and dreams, and both feature in a return to the subject of death, in *The Dying Swan*, in which an artist fantasises about a ballerina as she expires. *To Happiness* holds to this theme as a widow encourages her long-time admirer to court her adolescent daughter, whose fatal illness is halted when she conceives a passion for him. This was Bauer's last-completed film, and the dialectic is less "true" than the first of his movies, but he atones for the deficiencies of the plot by setting it lovingly in the shimmering Crimean sun, with distant vistas of the sea. It also shows, rarely for its time, two mature people genuinely in love with each other.

Bauer died in the Crimea, after sustaining an accident while scouting locations for his next film, *The King of Paris* (1917), completed after the February revolution by Olga Rakh-manova, who had acted in several of his pictures. The intertitles have not survived, so the plot is not easy to follow, but it is only clear, in this tale of intrigue and blackmail, that the two leading characters are homosexual: the sequence in which the older man takes home a young stranger, having impulsively paid his gambling debts, is quite extraordinary, as the two of them look guiltily about them.

Bauer's films, with their predatory, managing women and their weak, hedonistic men, suggest a homosexual sensitivity, but he is too modern in outlook to be categorised. With Sjöström, he is the only director of the teens of this century whose work can still be watched with satisfaction and enjoyment. Sjöström's studies of rural life in the last century are valuable, but Bauer's portrait of Czarist Russia in its last days are even more so, because he was actually there. We have to wait for Lamprecht's Berlin and Ozu's Tokyo before we have any other filmed record of a contemporary society, and Ozu is far less pungent, perhaps because, unlike Bauer and Lamprecht, he did not see that as his aim. Bauer made over 80 films, of which only one third have survived. Sjöström made 45 films in Sweden, of which only 13 were known to be extant: but two turned up in the 1980's. May we dare hope that there are still some Bauers to come to light?

—David Shipman

————

BAXTER, John.

British. Born in Kent, 1896. Worked as Theatre Manager, until 1932; theatrical agent, and casting director for Sound City, 1930's; directed first feature, *Doss House*, 1933; producer/director for British National, during World War II; managing director, Group 3 Films, 1951. *Died February 1975.*

Films as Director:

1933 *Doss House*; *Song of the Plough*; *Taking Ways*
1934 *Lest We Forget*; *Say It With Flowers*; *Music Hall*; *Floodtide*; *Kentucky Minstrels*
1935 *A Real Bloke*; *Jimmy Boy*; *The Small Man*; *Birds of a Feather*
1936 *Men of Yesterday*; *Hearts of Humanity*
1937 *The Academy Decides*; *Talking Feet*; *Song of the Road*
1938 *Stepping Toes*
1939 *What Would You Do Chums?*; *Secret Journey* (*Among Human Wolves*)
1940 *Old Mother Riley in Society*; *Laugh It Off*; *Crook's Tour*; *Old Mother Riley in Business*
1941 *Love on the Dole*; *The Common Touch*
1942 *Let the People Sing*; *We'll Smile Again*
1943 *Theatre Royal*; *The Shipbuilders*; *When We Are Married*
1944 *Dreaming*
1945 *Here Comes the Sun*
1946 *Grand Escapade*
1947 *Fortune Lane*; *When You Come Home*
1948 *Nothing Ventured*; *The Last Load*
1950 *The Dragon of Pendragon Castle*; *The Second Mate*; *Judgment Deferred*
1956 *Ramsbottom Rides Again*

Publications:

On BAXTER: books—

Richards, Jeffrey, *The Age of the Dream Palace: Cinema and Society in Britain 1930–39*, London, 1984.
Brown, Geoff, and Tony Aldgate, *The Common Touch: The Films of John Baxter*, London, 1989.

John Baxter: *Love on the Dole*

On BAXTER: articles—

"A Guide to British Film Production," in *Sight and Sound* (London), Autumn 1958.
Obituaries in *The Stage* (London), 27 February and 6 March 1975.
MacCann, Richard Dyer, "Subsidy for the Screen: Grierson and Group 3, 1951–57," in *Sight and Sound* (London), Summer 1977.
Richards, Jeffrey, "A Filmmaker with the Common Touch," in *Daily Telegraph* (London), 22 February 1989.
National Film Theatre Booklet (London), March 1989.

*   *   *

On the whole, working-class people have received a rough deal from British fiction films, especially during the 1930's, when their lot in real life was particularly hard. To most directors, they occasionally proved useful as comic relief, but their problems paled beside the glitter of dapper young things doing the rounds of Mayfair. John Baxter stood out from the crowd: not, to be sure, through any huge cinematic gift—the technical level of his films rarely exceeds the competent—but through a deeply-felt concern for society's lower depths. The ordinary blokes, the small traders, the market stall holders, the down-and-outs: these were his preferred heroes.

Baxter's best-known film, *Love on the Dole* (1941), an impassioned portrait of a Lancashire family struggling through the Depression, owes much of its strength to Walter Greenwood's original novel; but one can trace the same sympathetic feeling for life's hard knocks through most of his best work, beginning with *Doss House*, his remarkable debut in 1933—a

short, no-frills feature exploring the characters gathered one night in a London lodgings house. *Say It With Flowers* told the atmospheric tale of market traders rallying to help a flower-seller down on her luck; *A Real Bloke* championed the pride of a navvy thrown out of work; other films considered the plight of old soldiers facing hard times. Baxter developed many of these "human subjects", as he liked to call them, while working near the bottom rung of the British industry's ladder. It was a remarkable achievement: in the budget-conscious, conveyor-belt film factories of the mid-1930's, sensitive subject-matter generally came last on the priority list.

Unlike some of his documentary colleagues, Baxter's class feelings were never channelled into a political ideology. The films follow the conformist trends of the time by avoiding any call to arms: characters may air their grievances, often pungently, but at the end of the day they accept their lot, and the cap is still doffed to the paternalistic guv'nor. Baxter was a Christian Scientist, and it is the tradition of Christian compassion, rather than Karl Marx, that ripples through *Doss House* and its successors.

There is another key ingredient: music-hall. Baxter's early years as a stage singer and producer left him with an unquenchable love of music-hall and variety artistes, and he wove them constantly into his films. Sometimes—as in *Say It With Flowers*—the plot embraced them with ease; at other times, they seemed dragged in by the heels to pad out the reels. Baxter's intuitive feeling for the music-hall brand of exuberant, sentimental comedy stood him in good stead in the 1940's, when he balanced ambitious films like *Love on the Dole* and *The Shipbuilders* with a run of comedies securely aimed at the box-office. Those featuring Old Mother Riley remain an acquired taste; but the warmth and exuberance of Flanagan and Allen vehicles like *Theatre Royal, Dreaming*, and *Here Comes the Sun* survive the years well.

During the Second World War, Baxter's career reached its peak. He had moved out of the "quota quickie" twilight into the world of medium-budget respectability at British National. The war context made his sense of community spirit and concern for the working man particularly pertinent; for a few years, he chimed with the times. *The Common Touch* provided an elaborate variation on the "doss house" theme and looked to a post-war future where ordinary people would be given their just desserts; *The Shipbuilders*, based on George Blake's novel about the Clydeside during the Depression, placed the focus on the loyalty and pride of the working man, and the misery and waste of unemployment.

After the war, Baxter's approach began to look naive and old-fashioned. He toiled away at children's films, and worked behind the scenes as a production controller for Group 3, a short-lived experiment to promote new talent in modest second features. But by the time the kitchen sink brigade marched into British features from theatre and television, trumpeting a new concern for the working class, Baxter, quite unfairly, had become one of his own characters: a forgotten figure, one of yesterday's men.

—Geoff Brown

BECKER, Jacques.

French. Born in Paris, 15 September 1906. Educated at Lycée Condorcet, and at Schola Cantorum, Paris. Married actress Françoise Fabian, son Jean and daughter. Became assistant to Jean Renoir, 1932; made first short film, *Le Commissaire . . .*, 1935; German prisoner of war, 1941–42; directed first feature, *Le Dernier Atout*, 1942; son and assistant Jean Becker completed *Le Trou* following death. *Died 1960.*

Films as Director:

1935   *Le Commissaire est bon enfant, le gendarme est sans pitie* (co-d, co-sc with Pierre Prevert); *Tête de turc* (*Une Tête qui rapporte*) (+co-sc)
1938   short documentary on Communist Party Congress at Arles
1939   *L'Or du Cristobal* (co-d, uncredited)
1942   *Le Dernier Atout* (+co-pr, co-sc)
1943   *Goupi Mains rouges* (*It Happened at the Inn*) (+co-sc)
1945   *Falbalas* (*Paris Frills*) (+co-sc)
1947   *Antoine et Antoinette* (+co-sc)
1949   *Rendez-vous de Juillet* (+co-sc)
1951   *Édouard et Caroline* (+co-sc)
1952   *Casque d'Or* (+co-sc)
1953   *Rue de l'Estrapade*
1954   *Touchez pas au Grisbi* (*Grisbi*) (+co-sc); *Ali Baba et les quarante voleurs* (*Ali Baba*) (+co-sc)
1956   *Les Aventures d'Arsène Lupin* (*The Adventures of Arsène Lupin*) (+co-sc)
1957   *Montparnasse 19* (*Modigliani of Montparnasse*) (+co-sc)
1960   *Le Trou* (*The Night Watch, The Hole*) (co-d, +co-sc)

Other Films:

1929   *Le Bled* (Renoir) (role); *Le Rendez-vous de Cannes* (Petrossian – documentary) (appearance)
1932   ***Boudu sauvé des eaux*** (Renoir) (asst, role); *La Nuit du carrefour* (Renoir) (asst)
1933   *Chotard & Compagnie* (Renoir) (asst)
1934   *Madame Bovary* (uncredited, asst)
1935   ***Le Crime de Monsieur Lange*** (Renoir) (asst); *Toni* (Renoir) (asst)
1936   *Les Bas-Fonds* (Renoir) (asst, role); ***Une Partie de campagne*** (Renoir) (asst, role); *La Vie est à nous* (Renoir) (asst, role)
1938   ***La Grande Illusion*** (Renoir) (asst, role); *La Marseillaise* (Renoir) (asst); ***La Bête humaine*** (Renoir) (asst)
1939   ***Le Règle du jeu*** (Renoir) (asst); *L'Héritier des Montdésir* (Valentin) (asst)

Publications:

On BECKER: book—

Armes, Roy, *French Cinema Since 1946: Vol. 1—The Great Tradition*, New York, 1970.

On BECKER: articles—

De la Roche, Catherine, "The Stylist," in *Films and Filming* (London), March 1955.
Lisbona, Joseph, "Microscope Director," in *Films and Filming* (London), December 1956.
Baxter, Brian, "Jacques Becker and Montparnasse 19," in *Film* (London), September/October 1958.
"Becker," in *Sight and Sound* (London), Spring 1960.
Guillermo, Gilberto Perez, "Jacques Becker: Two Films," in *Sight and Sound* (London), Summer 1969.
Lederlé, J.-L., "Un Couple sans histoire," in *Cinématographe* (Paris), May 1977.
Aubert, F., "Françoise Fabian parle de Becker," and Rene Predal, "Jacques Becker," in *Cinéma* (Paris), 11 December 1985.
Chevrie, Marc, "Un Pur Cinéaste," in *Cahiers du Cinéma* (Paris), December 1985.

On BECKER: film—

Viallet, Pierre, and Marcel L'Herbier, *Portraits filmés . . . Jacques Becker*, 1954.

*   *   *

Next to Jean Grémillon, Jacques Becker is surely the most neglected of France's great directors. Known in France for *Goupi Mains rouges* and *Antoine et Antoinette*, his only film to reach an international critical audience was *Casque d'Or*. But from 1942 to 1959 Becker fashioned 13 films, none of which could be called a failure and each of which merits respect and attention.

Tied to Jean Renoir through a youthful friendship (their families were both close to the Cézannes), Becker began assisting Renoir in 1932. For eight years he helped put together some of the greatest films ever made, allowing the generous genius of Renoir to roam unconcerned over the details he had already prearranged. Becker gave Renoir the kind of grounding and order which kept his films from flying into thin air. His fastidiousness and precision made him the perfect assistant and many of his friends doubted that such a sensibility could ever command the energy needed to finish a film.

Nevertheless nearly from the first this was his ambition. It was he who developed the idea for *Le Crime de M. Lang* and when the producer insisted that Renoir take over, it cost them their friendship for a time. Soon Becker was directing a cheap anarchist subject *Le Commissaire est bon enfant* with the Octobre groupe company of actors. He wasn't to be held back.

Like so many others he was given his chance with the Occupation. The producer who had financed the 1936 short let him try a detective comedy *Le Dernier Atout* which he brought in under budget and to a good box office response. This opened

Jacques Becker with Claire Maffei on the set of *Antoine et Antoinette*

his career, permitting him to film the unforgettable *Goupi*. Georges Sadoul claims that after the war an American firm bought up the film and had it destroyed so that it wouldn't compete with American products as *Open City* had done. Whether this is true or not, the film remains today impressive in the clarity of its partly cynical, partly mysterious tone; and it shows Becker to be a brilliant director of actors.

The sureness of touch in each of his films derives from a precision some link to craftsmanship; but Becker was striving for far more than competence, veneer, or "quality." He was first and always interested in rhythm. A musician, he was obsessed with jazz and ragtime. No other standard director spent so much time collaborating with his editor (who was Marguerite Renoir).

Goupi is only the first of a host of films whose subjects are difficult to define. Becker seems to have gone out of his way to set himself problems. Many of his films are about groups of characters, most notably his final work *Le Trou*. Others are about milieux: *Antoine et Antoinette* captures the working class quarters of Paris; *Rendez-vous de Juillet* must be the first film anywhere to explicitly bring out the youth culture of postwar Europe; *Falbalas* evokes the world of high fashion as only someone raised in such a world could know it; and of course, *Casque d'Or* makes the turn-of-the century Parisian underworld come to life with a kind of grim romanticism.

Becker stated that his fastidious attention to milieu was the only way he could approach his characters. Bazin goes further, claiming that only through the exactitude of social particularity

could the universality of his characters and their situations come to life. For Bazin, *Edouard et Caroline* is, if not his greatest film, at least his most revealing one. This brilliant farce in the style of Marivaux is virtually plotless. Becker was able, via the minuteness of his *découpage* and the sympathy he had for his actors to build a serious moral comedy from literally nothing. *Edouard et Caroline*, along with *Le Trou*, shows him working at his best, working without plots and without the luxury of breadth. Both films take place in prison cells, *Le Trou* in an actual prison, *Edouard et Caroline* in the dingy apartment they share and the more menacing jail of her uncle's mansion.

Becker has been called "the mechanic" of cinema, for he took a delight in its workings and he went about his own job with such order and method. This separates him further from such "quality" directors as Autant-Lara, Cayatte, and Delannoy, whose themes may seem grander. Becker was interested in what the cinema could do just as he was interested in what men and women do. Never searching for the extraordinary, he would go to endless lengths to bring out not some abstract rhythm in the lives of people (as René Clair did) but the true style and rhythm of their sensibilities.

In 1956 Max Ophuls bequeathed to Becker his project on the life of Modigliani. While the resultant film *Montparnasse 19* is one of his least successful, its style is illustrative. Within weeks after taking over the project, both the scriptwriter (Henri Jeanson) and the set designer (Annenkov) left in outrage, for Becker refused to let them show off with words and drapery. His was always a reduced idea of cinema even when, as in *Fal-*

balas, his subject was fashion. Nor did he ever choose name actors, except perhaps Gérard Philipe as Modigliani. He had a sureness of taste, backed up by scrupulous reflection. Filmmaking for him was an endless series of choices each of which could founder the project.

Truffaut once claimed that Becker had his own pace of living; he would linger over meals, but race his car. He would spend hours of film over minor incidents in the lives of his characters, while whipping through the core of the intrigue which brought those characters together. Perhaps this is why *Le Trou* is a fitting finale to his career. For here the intrigue is given in advance and in a sense is without interest: five men struggling to escape from jail. For two and a half hours we observe the minutiae of their efforts and the silent camaraderie that develops among them. This is for Becker the state of life on earth: despite the ingenuity we bring to our struggle for freedom, we are doomed to failure; but in the effort we come upon another value, greater even than liberty, an awareness that our struggle is shared and the friendship and respect that confers. If *Casque d'Or* is destined to remain his most popular and most acclaimed film (it was his personal favorite), it will not betray these sentiments, for Manda gives up not only liberty, but life with Marie-Casque d'Or in order to be true to his friend. The stunning scene at the guillotine which ends that film evokes a set of emotions as contradictory as life itself. Jacques Becker was uniquely able to express such contradictions.

—Dudley Andrew

BEINEIX, Jean-Jacques.

Born 1946. Educated in medicine in Paris. Left medical school and became assistant director, 1968; worked under Becker, Berri, Clement, and Jerry Lewis, until *Diva*, 1981. Director of TV advertisements and an AIDS information film for French Ministry of Health.

Films as Director:

1977 *Le Chien de Monsieur Michel* (short)
1981 *Diva* (+sc)
1983 *La Lune dans le caniveau* (*The Moon in the Gutter*)
1986 *37.2 degrés le matin* (*Betty Blue*)
1989 *Roselyne et les Lions* (*Roselyne and the Lions*)

Publications:

By BEINEIX: articles—

Interview in *Ecran Fantastique* (Paris), May 1983.
Interview with Dan Yakir, in *Film Comment* (New York), July-August 1983.
Interview with M. Buckley, in *Films in Review* (New York), January 1984.
Interview in *Films* (London), February 1984.
Interview with A. Caron and S. Gendron, in *Séquences* (Montreal), April 1987.
Interview in *Revue du Cinéma/Image et Son* (Paris), April 1989.
Interview in *Nouvel Observateur* (Paris), 6 April 1989.
Interview in *Time Out* (London), 6 December 1989.
Interview in *American Film* (Washington, D.C.), January 1990.

On BEINEIX: articles

Auty, C., "Diva's encore," in *American Film* (Washington, D.C.), March 1981. *Time Out* (London), 27 August 1982.
Ross, P., and C. de Bechade, "Jean-Jacques Beineix," in *Revue du Cinéma* (Paris), July-August 1983.

Assayas, Olivier, "La publicité, point aveugle du cinéma français," in *Cahiers du Cinéma* (Paris), September 1983.
Production Report in *Première* (Paris), December 1985.
Booth, C., "Blue Jean," in *Films and Filming* (London), October 1986.
Combs, Richard, "Universal Mariner," in *Monthly Film Bulletin* (London), October 1986.
Pally, M., "Beineix Blue," in *Film Comment* (New York), January–February 1987.
Russell, David, "Two or three things we know about Beineix," in *Sight and Sound* (London), Winter 1989–90.

*   *   *

Beineix's early award-winning short, *Le Chien de M. Michel*, is revealing. A macabre parody of a nonsense rhyme, it tells of a hungry man who invents a pet dog to get meat from his sympathetic butcher. To sustain the deception he imitates barking, and when his neighbours complain, he makes great play of reluctantly doing away with his fictitious pet. Guilt-ridden, the neighbours buy him a real dog which promptly devours not only the butcher's scraps but M. Michel as well.

Reworked narratives concerned with reality and illusion, deception and integrity, performance and sincerity, characterize Beineix's feature films. With the exception of *Roselyne et les lions*, all are drawn from fiction: *Diva*, *La Lune dans le caniveau* and *37.2 degrés le matin* from novels by Delacorta, Goodis and Djian respectively. Not that Beineix believes in faithful adaptations: as a self-professed *auteur* increasingly committed to exercising total control of his films, he treats written sources as no more than raw material awaiting his transformation.

A childhood addiction to the cinema which led Beineix to "experience life through films rather than through reality" was transformed into practical experience in TV, with Jean Becker, and in film production as an assistant to such diverse directors as René Clément, Claude Zidi, Nadine and Jean-Louis Trintignant, Marc Simenon, Claude Berri and, from America, Willard Huyck and Jerry Lewis. This eclectic training was further broadened by work on numerous publicity shorts. Not surprisingly this diversity is reflected in his own richly textured and allusive style of filmmaking.

A Beineix film is often a teasing amalgam of traditional genres, may lurch disconcertingly between modes of realism and fantasy, juxtapose high art with popular culture, portray ordinary individuals alongside comic strip characters, and contain frequent references to other directors. *Diva*, for example, draws not only on the tradition of countless French gangster films but alludes in passing to both *The French Connection* and *Some Like It Hot*. These playful manipulations of an extensive cinema culture serve to draw attention to the medium itself: the images on the screen, Beineix contends, "are not so much a representation of reality but a representation of representation." In exploring this concept he has been accused of exploiting a modish surface brilliance at the expense of any form of reflective substance.

For Beineix the modern world is dominated by the stylised images and myths created by advertising and the make-believe of film. The contemporary consciousness is determined by the visual rhetoric of the video/TV/film age to such a degree that dreams, ambitions or emotions are constructed accordingly. Publicity has imbued brand names with potent associations through which individuals communicate: a Rolex watch, a Rolls Royce, a Naga tape recorder express perfection in *Diva*. Accordingly, decor becomes an expressive mental landscape in *La Lune* or *37.2 degrés*, with the hoarding opposite Gérard's slum dwelling in *La Lune*, for example, constantly inviting him, and the viewer, to look beyond a prosaic reality, "to try another world." Beineix's literary reference points are, not surprisingly, the symbolic, suggestive worlds of Baudelaire and Mallarmé.

Jean-Jacques Beineix: *Diva*

People caught up in the media projection of relationships have learned to relate to each other through these models. In *La Lune* Beineix attempted, unsuccessfully, to undercut established romantic clichés by making the sea and the cathedral overblown fakes, and to challenge the accepted stylisation of reality in *film noir* as outmoded and meaningless. Both in *Diva* and *La Lune*, the atmospheric qualities were inspired by the hallucinatory, tonal sets of Hilton McConnico and by Philippe Rousset's evocatively-lit camera-work.

Decidedly of their era, Beineix's youthful, free-wheeling characters seem apolitical individuals guided by a self-determined sense of morality. They invariably strive to satisfy a personal goal, often pursuing a particular image of perfection: a post boy seeks to possess the unrivalled but unrecorded voice of an opera singer (*Diva*); a docker is driven by an obsession to understand the true circumstances of his sister's suicide (*La Lune*); Betty struggles to create a new reality for the unpublished author Zorg (*37.2 degrés*); in *Roselyne et les lions*, the lion tamers (here standing for all creative artists) risk their lives to achieve the ultimate performance. These characters find their task far from easy: the worlds in which they operate are debased by commercial interests, corrupt individuals, and intimidating social systems. Images of corruption, of material and spiritual prostitution punctuate Beineix's work.

The director's neo-baroque insistence on delighting the senses through luxurious colour and sound is reflected in self-conscious images of performance (the opera house, the circus ring). As playful as the surrealists (the Mona Lisa smiles upon the copulating Zorg and Betty), Beineix provocatively mixes the mundane with the exquisite, hi-tech with tradition, conventional genre stylisations with innovative re-workings in films which glide oneirically between the banal and the surreal. The critical response to these stylish experiments has been decidedly mixed.

—R.F. Cousins

BELLOCCHIO, Marco.

Italian. Born in Piacenza, 9 November 1939. Educated in Milan, at Centro Sperimentale di Cinematografica, Rome, and at Slade School of Fine Arts, London (on scholarship), 1959–63. Directed first feature, *I pugni in tasca*, 1965; joined cooperative dedicated to militant cinema, 1968; co-directed 5-part series for TV, *La macchina cinema*, 1977–78.

Films as Director:

1965   *I pugni in tasca (**Fists in the Pocket**)* (+sc)
1967   *La Cina è vicina (**China is Near**)* (+co-sc)
1969   "Discutiamo discutiamo" episode of *Amore e rabbia* (*Vangelo '70*) (+co-sc, role)
1971   *Nel nome del padre (**In the Name of the Father**)* (+sc)
1972   *Sbatti il mostro in prima pagina (**Strike the Monster on Page One**)* (co-d uncredited, co-sc)
1974   *Nessuno o tutti—Matti da slegare* (co-d, co-sc)
1976   *Marcia trionfale* (+co-sc)

Marco Bellochio: *I pugni in tasca*

1977   *Il gabbiano* (+co-sc)
1979   *Salto nel vuoto* (+sc)
1980   *Leap into the Void* (+sc)
1981   *Vacanze in Valtrebbia*
1982   *Gli occhi, la bocca* (*The Eyes, the Mouth*)
1983   *Enrico IV* (*Henry IV*)
1986   *Devil in the Flesh*
1987   *La visionè del sabba* (*The Visions of Sabbath*)

Other films:

1958   *La colpa e la pena, Abbasso lo zio* (as student at Centro
        Sperimentale); *Ginepro fatto uomo* (diploma film at Centro
        Sperimentale)

Publications:

By BELLOCCHIO: books—

La Cina è vicina, Bologna, 1967; as *China is Near*, New York, 1969.
I pugni in tasca, Milan, 1967.

By BELLOCCHIO: articles—

Interview in *Film Society Review* (New York), January 1972.
"La Place de la politique," an interview with G. Fofi, in *Positif* (Paris),
    April 1972.
Interview with N. Zalaffi, in *Sight and Sound* (London), Autumn 1973.
"Marco Bellochio on Victory March," interview with R. Schar, in
    Cinema Papers (Melbourne), September/October 1976.

"Marco Bellocchio – l'alibi du grand public n'est qu'une justification
    hypocrite," interview with D. Rabourdin, in *Cinéma* (Paris), March
    1977.
Interview with Dan Yakir, in *Film Comment* (New York),
    March–April 1983.
Interview with J.-C. Bonnet, in *Cinématographe* (Paris), June 1986.
Interview in *Filmcritica* (Florence), April–May 1988.

On BELLOCCHIO: books—

Wlaschin, Ken, *Italian Cinema Since the War*, Cranbury, New Jersey,
    1971.
Leprohon, Pierre, *The Italian Cinema*, New York, 1972.
Tassone, Aldo, *Le Cinema italien parle*, Paris, 1982.
Michalczyk, John J., *The Italian Political Filmmakers*, Cranbury, New
    Jersey, 1986.

On BELLOCCHIO: articles—

Tessier, Max, "Au nom du père et de la politique," in *Ecran* (Paris),
    February 1973.
Comuzio, E., "Marco Bellocchio au miroir de Tchekhov," in *Jeune
    Cinéma* (Paris), April/May 1979.
Croyden, Margaret, "A Fresh Cinematic Voice from Italy," in *New
    York Times*, 11 December 1983.
Martin, Marcel, "*Les yeux, la bouche*" in *Revue du Cinéma/Image et
    Son* (Paris), November 1984, +filmo.
Stefanutto-Rosa, S., "Il diavola nel subconscio dello psicoanalista sel-
    vaggio," in *Cinema Nuovo* (Bari), March–April 1986.

*   *   *

One of the healthiest aspects of the ever-more impressive cinematic output of the 1960's was the greater respect accorded to different, even opposing, approaches to political filmmaking. Thus, a Godard or a Straub could comfortably accept being called a political filmmaker while their work analyzed the process of creating meaning in cinema. One of Italy's most gifted directors to have emerged since the war, Marco Bellocchio chose to delve into his own roots, and scrutinize those primary agents of socialization—the classroom, the church, and most crucially for him, the family. Besides serving to reproduce selected values and ideas about the world, these structures are depicted by Bellocchio to be perfect, if miniature, reflections of society at large.

Bellocchio's films are black comedies centered around the threat of impending chaos. Typically, Bellocchio's protagonists are outsiders who, after learning the rules by which societal structures remain intact, set about circumventing or ignoring them. Through their actions, they expose the fragility of the social order by exposing the fragility of all presumed truths. The judge, in *Leap into the Void*, for example, devises a bizarre plot to have his sister killed, in order not to suffer the embarrassment of sending her to a mental institution.

The nuclear family, as an incarnation of the social order, represents a system of clearly understood, if unexpressed, power relationships within a fixed hierarchy. These power relationships are expressed in familial terms: Bellocchio's women, for example, are usually defined as mothers or sisters. Even the radical political beliefs which some of his characters profess must be judged with regard to their application in the family sphere: shocked to discover that his sister is no longer a virgin, Vittorio in *China Is Near* admits "You can be a Marxist-Leninist but still insist that your sister doesn't screw around."

Along with his countryman Bernardo Bertolucci, Bellocchio is a primary example of the first European generation of film-school-educated directors. Often, these directors—under the influence of *la politique des auteurs* perhaps—tended to exhibit an extreme self-conciousness in their films. While watching a Bellocchio film, one is struck at how little or nothing is left open to interpretation—everything seems achingly precise and intentional. Yet what saves his films from seeming airless or hopelessly "arty" is that they're often outrageously funny. The havoc which his characters wreak on all those around them is ironically counterpointed to the controlled precision of the direction. There is a kind of mordant delight in discovering just how far Bellocchio's characters will go in carrying out their eerie intrigues. The sense of shrewd critical intelligence orchestrating comic pandemonium into lucid political analyses is one of the most pleasurable aspects of his cinema.

—Richard Peña

———

BEMBERG, Maria Luisa.

Argentinian. Born in Buenos Aires, 1925. Wrote first screenplay, *Cronica de una Senora* (*Chronicle of a Woman*), 1971; attended Strasberg Institute, New York, 1980; directed first feature, *Momentos*, 1981.

Films as Director and Scriptwriter:

1981   *Momentos* (*Moments*)
1982   *Señora de Nadie* (*Nobody's Woman*)

1984   *Camila*
1987   *Miss Mary*
1990   *Yo, la peor de todas* (*I, the Worst of All*)

Films as Scriptwriter Only:

1971   *Cronica de una Señora* (*Chronicle of a Woman*)
1972   *El Mundo de la Mujer* (short)
1975   *Triangulo de Cuatro* (Ayala)
1978   *Juguetes* (short)

Publications:

By BEMBERG: articles—

"Maria Luisa Bemberg: El rescate de la mujer en el cine Argentino," an interview with J.C. Huayhuaca, and others, in *Hablemos de Cine* (Lima), March 1984.
Interview with K. Jaehne and G. Crowdus, in *Cineaste* (New York), vol. 14, no. 3, 1986.
Interview with Sheila Whitaker, in *Monthly Film Bulletin* (London), October 1987.

On BEMBERG: book—

King, John, and Nissa Torrents, *The Garden of Forking Paths: Argentine Cinema*, London, 1988.

On BEMBERG: article—

Maeckley, Monika, "Machismo Takes a Knock," in *Guardian* (London), 10 December 1982.

*   *   *

After an "asphyxiating and uneventful" life (her own words), born into one of the wealthiest families in Buenos Aires and only entering the film industry aged 46 after her children had grown and she had obtained a divorce, Maria Luisa Bemberg is now one of the most subversive and popular Argentinian directors. In addition, she has been acclaimed in Europe and the States.

Her first (semi-autobiographical) screenplay, *Cronica de una Señora*, gained acclaim as a contemporary domestic drama, focusing on a regressive political system as it affected the female protagonist. Wishing to exert more control over her screenplays, but with no formal training, she spent three months as an actress at the Lee Strasberg Institute in New York and returned to Argentina to direct. In 1982 she caused a stir with *Senora de Nadie*, which featured a friendship between a gay man and a separated woman, challenging in one swoop the sacred notions of marriage, family and the Church. Released on the day that Argentina invaded the Malvinas, the film's impact was overshadowed somewhat by political events, but the crumbling state of the military regime (that had exerted so much censorship and control over the film industry that by the late 1970's only 12 films were being produced per year) ultimately helped the film succeed. Hugely popular with female audiences, it made a powerful and overtly feminist intervention into a culture crippled by its own repression and machismo.

After the overthrow of the military regime, and the humiliation of defeat in the Falklands War, Bemberg still saw much to come to terms with and much to struggle against in her national identity. She saw her role as a filmmaker, and as a woman in a fiercely patriarchal society, to explore political oppression as a backdrop and context for intense personal conflict. Her films dwell anxiously on Argentina's troubled past, and suggest that only by coming to terms with it can the nation—and the individual—put it to rest.

In 1984, Bemberg directed *Camila*, the first Argentinian film ever to break into the American market. Receiving an Oscar nomination for best foreign language film, it is all the more remarkable in that many other directors, attempting to film this true story of illicit love between a priest and a young woman in 1847, had previously been prevented from doing so by the government. By casting the Priest as a beautiful object of desire and Camila (historically portrayed as the innocent victim) as the temptress, Bemberg created a passionate melodrama; consciously moving away from her earlier, hard-bitten domestic dramas into a more emotional, lyrical sphere. The historical basis of *Camila* offers a mythical arena in which to explore her very real contemporary political concerns.

Miss Mary continues to focus on these concerns, exploring English influence over the Argentinian upper class through the crucial figure of the nanny in the years before World War II. Politics and history are expressed through family structures, sexuality and human behaviour. Female characters, even the repressed and unsympathetic nanny (played by Julie Christie), are portrayed with understanding—although Miss Mary is a reactionary agent of oppression, the film works to explore *why* she is so—in an attempt to study the forces that could create both she and the sick family for which she works.

Bemberg's strong sense of the melancholy is an integral part of her work, causing an uneasy tension in all her films: while they all indict the reactionary political system, they are also impregnated with a tragic sensibility that presents events as somehow out of the protagonists' control. However, although the bleak endings (in which transgressors are punished and traditional structures remain apparently intact) seem pessimistic, the very expression of transgression, the tentative exploration of the disruptions that inevitably threaten an apparently monolithic system, by an individual who could so easily be a victim of that system (female, bourgeois, divorced), is not merely laudable, but remarkable.

—Samantha Cook

BENEGAL, Shyam.

Indian. Born in Alwal, near Hyderabad, 14 December 1934. Educated at Osmania University. Advertising copywriter and director (over 620 advertising shorts) for Lintas Agency, Bombay, 1960–66; received Bhabha fellowship and worked in U.S.; returned to India and became independent producer, 1970; directed first feature in Hindi, *Ankur (The Seedling)*, 1974; director of the Indian National Film Development Corporation, 1980's; made TV mini-series *The Discovery of India*, 1989.

Films as Director:

1967 *A Child of the Streets* (doc short)
1968 *Close to Nature* (doc short); *Indian Youth—An Exploration* (doc short); *Sinhasta or The Path to Immortality* (doc short)
1969 *Poovanam (The Flower Path)* (doc short)
1970 *Horoscope for a Child* (doc short)
1971 *Pulsating Giant* (doc short); *Steel: A Whole New Way of Life* (doc short); *Raga and the Emotions* (doc short)
1972 *Tala and Rhythm* (doc short); *The Shruti and Graces of Indian Music* (doc short); *The Raag Yaman Kalyan* (doc short); *Notes on a Green Revolution* (doc short); *Power to the People* (doc short); *Foundations of Progress* (doc short)
1974 *Ankur (The Seedling)* (+sc)
1974/5 *Learning Modules for Rural Children* (doc)
1975 *Nishant (Night's End)*; *Charandas Chor (Charandas the Thief)*
1975 *A Quiet Revolution* (doc)

1976 *Manthan (The Churning)*; *Tomorrow Begins Today*; *Industrial Research* (short); *Epilepsy* (short)
1977 *Bhumika (The Role)* (+co-sc); *Kondura/Anugrahan (Telugu version) (The Boon)* (+co-sc); *New Horizons in Steel* (doc)
1978 *Junoon (The Obsession)*
1980 *Hari Hondal Bargadar (Share Cropper)* (+sc)
1981 *Kalyug (The Machine Age)*
1982 *Arohan (Ascending Scale)*
1983 *Mandi (The Market Place)*
1985 *Jawaharlal Nehru* (doc); *Satyajit Ray* (doc); *Trikaal (Past, Present, and Future)*
1986 *Susman (The Essence)*

Publications:

By BENEGAL: book—

The Churning, with Vijay Tendulkar, Calcutta, 1984.

By BENEGAL: articles—

Interview with Behroze Gandhy, in *Framework* (Norwich), no. 12, 1980.
Interview with F. El Guedj, in *Cinématographe* (Paris), September–October 1983.
Interview in *Screen International* (London), 13 December 1986.

On BENEGAL: books—

da Cunha, Uma, editor, *Film India: The New Generation 1960–1980*, New Delhi, 1981.
Willemen, Paul, and Behroze Gandhy, *Indian Cinema*, London, 1982.
Pfleiderer, Beatrix, and Lothar Lutze, *The Hindi Film: Agent and Re-Agent of Cultural Change*, New Delhi, 1985.
Ramachandran, T.M., *70 Years of Indian Cinema (1913–1983)*, Bombay, 1985.
Armes, Roy, *Third World Filmmaking and the West*, Berkeley, 1987.

On BENEGAL: articles—

"Shyam Benegal," article and interview in *Cinéma* (Paris), September/October 1975.
Dharker, Anil, "Shyam Benegal," in *International Film Guide 1979*, London, 1978.
Posthumus, P., and T. Custers, "Film in India: interview—achtergrondon—Shyam Benegal," in *Skrien* (Amsterdam), Winter 1980/81.
Tesson, C., "La Route des Indes," in *Cahiers du Cinéma* (Paris), September 1983.
Gillett, John, "Style and Passion: The Films of Shyam Benegal," in *National Film Theatre Programme* (London), May 1988.

*   *   *

The career of Shyam Benegal, which began with a first feature in 1974, has some similarity in terms of both approach and tenacity to that of Satyajit Ray 20 years earlier. Among shared aspects one may note: a background in the film society movement, a strong western influence, commercial work in an advertising agency, and direction of work for children (in Benegal's case the feature length *Charandas the Thief*, made in 1975 for the Children's Film Society). But Benegal was 40 by the time he made his first feature and had already directed a large number of sponsored documentaries and commercials. Moreover, virtually all his filmmaking has been in Hindi, the language of the commercial "all-India" movie, not in a regional dialect.

Benegal's personal style is already apparent and fully formed in the loose trilogy of studies of rural oppression made between 1974 and 1976: *The Seedling, Night's End* and *The Churning*, the latter financed collectively—at two rupees apiece—by the farmers of Gujarat state. In each case the interaction of the rural populace and often well-meaning outsiders ends disastrously, but the note of revolt is very muted. Though Benegal's social commitment is unquestionable he does not offer any clear way out for his characters. In *The Seedling* the

Shyam Benegal: *Arohan*

seduction and abandoning of the servant girl is followed by the savage beating of her deaf-mute husband, but the only answer is the stone thrown at the landlord's house by a small boy in the film's final sequence. This is the "seedling," but Benegal offers no indication as to how it can be nurtured. In *Night's End* a schoolmaster's efforts lead to violence when his wife is kidnapped by the landlord's family who are accustomed to exploiting and brutalizing the peasants at will. But the final peasant revolt stirred up by the middle class hero gets totally and blindly out of hand, and one knows that it will be put down—no doubt savagely—by the authorities and passivity will resume. *The Churning* is more optimistic, but even here the advocates of change are eventually defeated, though their efforts may some day bear fruit. Typical of Benegal's approach is the way in which women—so often a personification of new values in third world films—are depicted as passive suffering figures in these films. Always Benegal's style is solidly realistic, with stress on a carefully worked out narrative line and well-drawn characters. The pace is generally slow and measured, but enlivened by excellent observation and fine choice of significant detail.

In the late 1970's Benegal retained this somewhat austere style with a total professionalism but without ever slipping into the extravagance or melodrama of the conventional Hindi film. *The Role*, one of his richest films, tells of a more dynamic woman, a film star who tries desperately to live her own life, but is cruelly exploited by men from childhood onwards. The film, essentially a problem picture of a kind familiar in the West, has a muted, open ending and is enlivened by vigorously recreated extracts from the films in which the actress is purported to star. Subsequently Benegal continued the widening of his chosen area of subject matter with *The Boon*, a film shot in two language versions and known as *Kondura* in Hindi and *Anugrahan* in Telegu. A study of the tragic effect of a young man's belief that he has been granted supernatural powers, it was followed by *The Obsession*, a tale of inter-racial love set at the time of the Indian Mutiny, and *The Machine Age*, a story of bitter rivalry between industrialists which is also an archetypal tale of conflict based on an ancient Hindi epic. But *Ascending Scale*, which depicts a peasant family destroyed as it is pitted against the reactionary forces of rural India, shows Benegal's fidelity to the themes with which he had begun his career. Working aside from the dominant Hindi traditions, the director offers a striking example of integrity and commitment to an unrelenting vision.

—Roy Armes

———

BENTON, Robert.

American. Born Robert Douglas Benton in Waxahachie, Texas, 29 September 1932. Educated at University of Texas, and at Columbia University, New York City. Served in U.S. Army, 1954–56. Married Sally Rendigs, 1964, one son. Art Director of *Esquire* magazine, New York, 1957–61 (consulting editor, 1962-); began screenwriting partnership with David Newman, on *Bonnie and Clyde*, 1967; directed first feature, *Bad Company*, 1972. Recipient: National Society of Film critics Award, and Writers Guild Award, for *Bonnie and Clyde*, 1967; Oscars for Best Screenplay and Best Director, *Kramer vs Kramer*, 1979. Address: c/o Sam Cohn, International Creative Management, 40 W. 57th Street, New York, NY 10019, U.S.A.

Films as Director and Co-Scriptwriter:

1972 *Bad Company*
1976 *The Late Show* (sc)
1979 *Kramer vs Kramer*
1982 *Still of the Night*
1984 *Places in the Heart* (*The Texas Project*)
1987 *Nadine*

Films as Scriptwriter Only (with David Newman except as indicated):

1967 *Bonnie and Clyde* (Penn)
1970 *There Was a Crooked Man* (J. Mankiewicz)
1972 *What's Up Doc?* (Bogdanovich) (co-sc with Newman and Buck Henry)
1978 *Superman* (Donner) (co-sc with David Newman, Mario Puzo and Leslie Newman)

Publications:

By BENTON: books—

The In and Out Book, with Harvey Schmidt, New York, 1959.
Little Brother, No More, New York, 1960.
The Worry Book, with Harvey Schmidt, New York, 1962.
Extremism: A Non-Book, with David Newman, New York, 1964.
Don't Ever Wish for a Seven Foot Bear, with Sally Rendigs, New York, 1972.

By BENTON: articles—

Interviews in *Film Comment* (New York), March/April 1973, January/February 1977, and July/August 1978.
Interview in *American Film* (Washington, D.C.), July/August 1979.
Interview in *Image et Son* (Paris), April 1980.
Interview with Leslie Bennetts, in *New York Times*, 7 October 1984.
Interview in *Time Out* (London), 28 February 1985.
Interview with Sheila Johnston, in *Stills* (London), March 1985.

On BENTON: articles—

"Robert Benton," in *Film Dope* (London), August 1973.
Sight and Sound (London), Autumn 1973.
Millimeter (New York), October 1976.
Sarris, Andrew, "A Low-Rent Romance," in *Village Voice* (New York), 11 August 1987.
Almendros, Nestor, in *American Cinematographer* (Los Angeles), September 1987.

*   *   *

There were many ways to make it as a bigtime Hollywood director in the 1970's. Robert Benton's experience provides a common mode: a successful screenwriter turned director. Benton teamed with another aspiring author, David Newman, to pen the script of Arthur Penn's wildly successful, highly influential *Bonnie and Clyde* (1967), a film that showed Hollywood how to meld comedy, melodrama, and social com-

mentary. The story of how Benton and Newman came to write *Bonnie and Clyde* is the stuff of Hollywood legend. In 1964 they were working for *Esquire* magazine developing the magazine's annual college issue, crafting the infamous Dubious Achievement Awards. Caught up with the art cinema of Ingmar Bergman, Federico Fellini, and Akira Kurosawa, they sought to do an American version of Jean-Luc Godard's *Breathless* through the story of two desperados of the 1930's, Bonnie Parker and Clyde Barrow.

Benton and Newman wrote a seventy page treatment, trying to make their film feel like an Hitchcock thriller, but with the comic violent tone of François Truffaut's *Shoot the Piano Player*. First they sent the "Bonnie and Clyde" script to Truffaut who passed on it, as did Jean-Luc Godard. Warren Beatty rescued the project, agreed to produce it, and Arthur Penn became the director. Here were the first members of the film generation of the 1960's making what in some ways came to represent the most influential film of the decade, capturing the restlessness of an age, the era's ethical ambiguity. *Bonnie and Clyde* at once demonstrated that Hollywood films could successfully incorporate the stylistic flourishes of the French New Wave into Classic Hollywood genre material.

The *Bonnie and Clyde* script won numerous awards, and the duo went on to co-script *There Was a Crooked Man* (1970), *What's Up Doc?* (1972), and *Superman* (1978). The latter two proved Benton and Newman were able to make movies that made money. *What's Up Doc?* finished in the top ten earners for 1971; *Superman* generated more than 100 million dollars worldwide. But Benton aspired to be his own director, and thus through the 1970's, worked single-mindedly at that goal. Success came with *Kramer vs. Kramer* (1979) on the third try. Based on his screenplay, *Kramer vs. Kramer* won the Oscar for Best Picture, Best Actor [Dustin Hoffman], Best Screenplay, Best Director, and Supporting Actress [Meryl Streep], a sweep rarely accomplished in Hollywood history. More importantly for Benton's future, *Kramer vs. Kramer* finished atop the domestic box-office rankings for the year. Robert Benton had reached his goal; he was as hot a property as there was in Hollywood as the 1980's opened.

But thereafter his filmmaking successes were limited. Benton did reach another peak in 1984 with *Places in the Heart* where he directed and wrote the award-winning screenplay. Here was one man's affectionate look at life in his hometown of Waxahachie, Texas during the hard days of the great depression. On the other hand Benton's *Nadine* (1987) was also set in Texas, but this comedy failed to capture either the fancy of the critics or the public.

As we move in to the 1990's Benton carefully selects projects and surely, given the success of *Kramer vs. Kramer* and *Places in the Heart*, will be able to continue to make movies in Hollywood. Many see Benton as the principle case of the power of the screenwriter as auteur. Perhaps this is so, but continuing success at the top, a Hollywood prerequisite if one wants to control one's movies, seems to have sucked the life from Benton's story-telling ability. It seems difficult for a filmmaker who has crafted stories of characters who are outsiders, from Bonnie Parker to the aging detective of the *Late Show*, to function as a member of the Hollywood establishment.

—Douglas Gomery

BERESFORD, Bruce.

Australian. Born in 1940. Educated at Sydney University. Married, 3 children. Worked in advertising and for ABC TV, late 1950's; moved to London, 1961, and taught at girl's school, Willesden; film editor, East Nigerian Film Unit, 1964–66; head of British Film Institute Production Board, 1966–70: produced 86 films, notably short documentaries; moved to Australia, 1971; directed first feature, *The Adventures of Barry MacKenzie*, 1972; moved to U.S., 1981. Recipient: Best Director, Australian Film Awards, for *Don's Party*, 1976, and *Breaker Morant*, 1980; Best Director, American Film Institute Awards, for *Don's Party*, 1977.

Films as Director:

1972   *The Adventures of Barry MacKenzie* (+sc)
1974   *Barry MacKenzie Holds His Own* (+co-sc)
1975   *Don's Party*
1977   *The Getting of Wisdom*
1978   *Money Movers* (+sc)
1980   *Breaker Morant* (+sc)
1981   *The Club*
1982   *Puberty Blues*
1983   *Tender Mercies*
1985   *King David; Fringe Dwellers*
1986   *Crimes of the Heart*
1987   episode in *Aria*
1989   *Driving Miss Daisy*
1990   *Her Alibi*

Publications:

By BERESFORD: articles—

"An Aussie in Hollywood," an interview with G. Crowdus and U. Gupta, in *Cineaste* (New York), vol. 12, no. 4, 1983.
Interview in *Screen International* (London), 21 May 1983.
"The Paramount *King David*," an interview with Brent Lewis, in *Films* (London), December 1984–January 1985.
"Tender Crimes," an interview with Margy Rochlin, in *American Film* (Washington, D.C.), January–February 1987.

On BERESFORD: books—

Tulloch, John, *Australian Cinema: Industry, Narrative, and Meaning*, Sydney and London, 1982.
Bruce Beresford: An Annotated Bibliography, Melbourne, 1985.
Hall, Sandra, *Critical Business: The New Australian Cinema in Review*, Adelaide, 1985.
Moran, Albert, and Tom O'Regan, editors, *An Australian Film Reader*, Sydney, 1985.
McFarlane, Brian, *Australian Cinema 1970–85*, London, 1987.

On BERESFORD: articles—

Connelly, Keith, "The Films of Bruce Beresford," in *Cinema Papers* (Melbourne), August–September 1980.
Robinson, David, "Bruce Beresford's New Australian Cinema," in the *Times* (London), 23 October 1980.
Lewis, Brent, "A Deft Talent," in *Films* (London), February 1985.
"Bruce Beresford is Home," in *Encore* (Manly, New South Wales), 7 November 1985.
Pym, John, "*Mister Johnson*," in *Sight and Sound* (London), Spring 1990.

*   *   *

Bruce Beresford's career has been described as both interesting and uneven but uneven in interesting ways. Certainly since his debut as a maker of feature films in 1972 with the broad comedy *The Adventures of Barry MacKenzie*, Beresford has made a wide variety of movies. But there is unity in this variety. If his Australian films such as *The Getting of Wisdom* and *Breaker Morant* seem more hard-edged and political than *Tender Mercies, Crimes of the Heart*, or *Driving Miss Daisy*, his latest American films nevertheless carry a social comment, if ever so quietly.

Beresford showed an interest in making films from an early age but moved to England when he saw little chance of being able to direct in Australia. After holding a number of jobs abroad, including working for the British Film Institute, he returned home when government subsidies offered the possibilities for an expanded local production schedule. His first film *The Adventures of Barry MacKenzie* was deliberately commercial and pitched at a popular level since he felt at the time that what Australian films needed most was to prove their marketability. The success of this film and his next "ocker" epic *Barry MacKenzie Holds His Own* gave him the leverage within the industry to be able to do a different kind of work.

The more serious social comment of *Don's Party* which was set against the failure of the Labor Party in the national elections of 1969 offered a clear-eyed look at Australian society of the 1960's and pursued in a more serious way the contradictions in the Australian character. *Don's Party* is a small movie based on David Williamson's play and was filmed largely within the confines of a suburban house. Its intense probing of character and at times claustrophobic atmosphere surfaced in the director's later, better-known films.

Beresford next turned to a project he had wanted to do for some time, *The Getting of Wisdom* based on the autobiographical novel by H. H. Richardson tracing the adventures of a young woman who arrives from the outback to receive a proper education at a city girl's school. The film is a period piece but provides a devastating look at the overly genteel pretensions of the class-bound, nineteenth-century Australian society. Not yet secure in its own identity this society still copied the Victorian social arrangements of the motherland. A stunningly beautiful film, *The Getting of Wisdom* established Beresford as a maker of serious and thoughtful films in the European Art film tradition.

After shooting a caper film, *The Money Movers*, Beresford made *Breaker Morant*, which both returned to Australia's past and explored the colonial relationship with Great Britain against the background of the Boer War. The film confirmed Beresford's international reputation and opened the way for him to make films outside the rather limited resources of the Australian cinema. *Breaker Morant* contains a savage look at British attitudes towards its former colony and examines the exploitation and condescension such attitudes produce. Although the film's leading character was played by an Englishman, the movie was also a showcase for Australian acting talent.

With *The Club* and *Puberty Blues*, Beresford returned to contemporary Australia. *The Club*, adapted from another of Bruce Williamson's plays, is a satire on the inner workings of an Australian football club with its financial woes, moral tensions, and labor disputes. *Puberty Blues* dealt with a pair of would-be "surfer-girls" growing up along the southern beachside suburbs of Sydney and deftly explores the macho world of Australian surfers while offering up an unflattering picture of how young women in this world are exploited and abused.

In part because of his growing international reputation, Beresford moved to the United States to direct his next film, *Tender Mercies* from a Horton Foote script about a down and out country singer who finds love and solace with a small town Texan widow and her son. On first glance this seems an unusual subject for Beresford to film but *Tender Mercies* contains much of the same social commentary and the visual beauty of his earlier films. The acting is notable as is the evocation of locale, which is not unlike the arid spaces of the Australian outback. It is a quiet, small film, the kind of movie Beresford was used to making, and it set the pattern for the other successful

Bruce Beresford: *Breaker Morant*

American films that followed. Only when venturing into the mega-epic with *King David* did the Beresford touch falter.

Returning to Australia Beresford made *The Fringe Dwellers* about a family of aborigines who are trying to integrate themselves into white Australian society, and how they fail, causing a split between the generations and a dissolution of the family itself. Long a touchy subject in Australia, much as the same topic in the States, Beresford handled the integration issue with sensitivity, tracing the sad divisions between the races. *King David* came next and although fraught with high expectations the film was a critical and box-office disaster, experiences, however, that Beresford had shared before. He recouped whatever damage the fiasco might have done to his career by turning to *Crimes of the Heart*, an adaptation of Beth Henley's play about three eccentric sisters who have come together as a result of a family crisis. Once again the ambience of the small Southern town was captured with gentleness and affection. The three sisters, all played by major Hollywood stars who worked remarkably well together under Beresford's direction, come off as a loving but strange by-product of regional gentility and repression. Underlying the film is a steady and unblinking look at the place of women in this traditional society.

It is not without notice that Beresford's next film rated a large spread in the financial section of the *New York Times*.

Driving Miss Daisy cleaned up at the box-office as well as at the Oscars, and has made Beresford's name a known quantity among film audiences around the world. A quiet film about the relationship between a Black man and his elderly Jewish female employer is set once again in the South and provides a tour de force acting opportunity for both of the principal stars. For the most part the film does not deal with racial or social problems, but prejudice hovers around the edges of the world of the film and subtly affects its tone. It is another of Beresford's small films of intense concentration, which is focused on a microcosm of the modern world and which, in its unfolding, explores broad human as well as social issues.

Although Bruce Beresford has become in some ways a Hollywood director, liking the larger budgets and what he can do with them, his films remain really quite consistent. Preferring ensemble acting to star vehicles, smaller films to epics (even though *Breaker Morant* was favorably compared to a David Lean epic by the critics, the film is still basically a courtroom drama) and always infusing his films with an insistent social examination, Beresford has fashioned a remarkably consistent career for all of its seeming disparity.

—Charles L. P. Silet

BERGMAN, Ingmar.

Swedish. Born Ernst Ingmar Bergman in Uppsala, Sweden, 14 July 1918. Educated at Palmgrens School, Stockholm, and Stockholm University, 1938–40. Married 1) Else Fisher, 1943 (divorced 1945), one daughter; 2) Ellen Lundström, 1945 (divorced 1950), two sons, two daughters; 3) Gun Grut, 1951, one son; 4) Käbi Laretei, 1959 (separated 1965), one son; 5) Ingrid von Rosen, 1971. Also one daughter by actress Liv Ullmann. Joined Svensk Filmindustri as scriptwriter, 1943; director of Helsingborg City Theatre, 1944; directed first film, *Kris*, 1946; began association with producer Lorens Marmstedt, and with Gothenburg Civic Theatre, 1946; began association with cinematographer Gunnar Fischer, 1948; director, Municipal Theatre, Malmo, 1952–58; began associations with Bibi Andersson and Max von Sydow, 1955; began association with cinematographer Sven Nykvist, 1959; became artistic advisor at Svensk Filmindustri, 1961; head of Royal Dramatic Theatre, Stockholm, 1963–66; settled on island of Faro, 1966; established Cinematograph production company, 1968; moved to Munich, following arrest on alleged tax offences and subsequent breakdown, 1976; formed Personafilm production company, 1977; director at Munich Residenzteater, 1977–82; returned to Sweden, 1978; announced retirement from filmmaking, following *Fanny and Alexander*, 1982; directed *These Blessed Two* for Swedish TV, 1985. Recipient: Golden Bear, Berlin Festival, for *Wild Strawberries*, 1958; Gold Plaque, Swedish Film Academy, 1958; Oscars for Best Foreign Language Film, *The Virgin Spring*, 1961, and *Through a Glass Darkly*, 1962; Erasmus Prize (shared with Charles Chaplin), Netherlands, 1965; honorary doctorate of philosophy, Stockholm University, 1975.

Films as Director:

1946   *Kris* (*Crisis*) (+sc); *Det regnar på vår kärlek* (*It Rains on Our Love, The Man with an Umbrella*) (+co-sc)
1947   *Skepp till Indialand* (*A Ship Bound for India, The Land of Desire*) (+sc)
1948   *Musik i mörker* (*Music in Darkness, Night Is My Future*); *Hamnstad* (*Port of Call*) (+co-sc)
1949   *Fängelse* (*Prison, The Devil's Wanton*) (+sc); *Törst* (*Thirst, Three Strange Loves*)
1950   *Till glädje* (*To Joy*) (+sc); *Sånt händer inte här* (*High Tension, This Doesn't Happen Here*)
1951   *Sommarlek* (*Summer Interlude, Illicit Interlude*) (+co-sc)
1952   *Kvinnors väntan* (*Secrets of Women, Waiting Women*) (+sc)
1953   *Sommaren med Monika* (*Monika, Summer with Monika*) (+co-sc); ***Gycklarnas afton* (*The Naked Night, Sawdust and Tinsel*)** (+sc)
1954   *En lektion i kärlek* (*A Lesson in Love*) (+sc)
1955   *Kvinnodröm* (*Dreams, Journey into Autumn*) (+sc); ***Sommarnattens leende* (*Smiles of a Summer Night*)** (+sc)
1957   ***Det sjunde inseglet* (*The Seventh Seal*)** (+sc); ***Smultronstället* (*Wild Strawberries*)** (+sc)
1958   *Nära livet* (*Brink of Life, So Close to Life*) (+co-sc); *Ansiktet* (*The Magician, The Face*) (+sc)
1960   *Jungfrukällen* (*The Virgin Spring*); *Djävulens öga* (*The Devil's Eye*) (+sc)
1961   *Såsom i en spegel* (*Through a Glass Darkly*) (+sc)
1963   *Nattvardsgästerna* (*Winter Light*) (+sc); ***Tystnaden* (*The Silence*)** (+sc)
1964   *För att inte tala om alla dessa kvinnor* (*All These Women, Now About These Women*) (+co-sc under pseudonym "Buntel Eriksson")
1966   ***Persona*** (+sc)
1967   "Daniel" episode of *Stimulantia* (+sc, ph)
1968   *Vargtimmen* (*Hour of the Wolf*) (+sc); *Skammen* (*Shame, The Shame*) (+sc)
1969   *Riten* (*The Ritual, The Rite*) (+sc); *En passion* (*The Passion of Anna, A Passion*) (+sc); *Fårö-dokument* (*The Fårö Document*) (+sc)
1971   *Beröringen* (*The Touch*) (+sc)
1973   ***Viskningar och rop* (*Cries and Whispers*)** (+sc); *Scener ur ett äktenskap* (*Scenes from a Marriage*) (+sc, +narration, voice of the photographer) in 6 episodes: "Oskuld och panik (Innocence and Panic)"; "Kunsten att sopa unter mattan (The Art of Papering Over Cracks)"; "Paula"; "Tåredalen (The Vale of Tears)"; "Analfabeterna (The Illiterates)"; "Mitt i natten i ett mörkt hus någonstans i världen (In the Middle of the Night in a Dark House Somewhere in the World)" (shown theatrically in shortened version of 168 minutes)
1977   *Das Schlangenei* (*The Serpent's Egg, Ormens ägg*) (+sc)
1978   *Herbstsonate* (*Autumn Sonata, Höstsonaten*) (+sc)
1979   *Fårö-dokument 1979* (*Fårö 1979*) (+sc, narration)
1980   *Aus dem Leben der Marionetten* (*From the Life of the Marionettes*) (+sc)
1982   ***Fanny och Alexander* (*Fanny and Alexander*)** (+sc)

Other Films:

1944   *Hets* (*Torment, Frenzy*) (Sjöberg) (sc)
1947   *Kvinna utan ansikte* (*Woman Without a Face*) (Molander) (sc)
1948   *Eva* (Molander) (co-sc)
1950   *Medan staden sover* (*While the City Sleeps*) (Kjellgren) (synopsis)
1951   *Frånskild* (*Divorced*) (Molander) (sc)
1956   *Sista paret ut* (*Last Couple Out*) (Sjöberg) (sc)
1961   *Lustgården* (*The Pleasure Garden*) (Kjellin) (co-sc under pseudonym "Buntel Eriksson")
1974   *Kallelsen* (*The Vocation*) (Nykvist) (pr)
1975   *Trollflöjten* (*The Magic Flute*) (for TV) (+sc)
1976   *Ansikte mot ansikte* (*Face to Face*) (+co-pr, sc) (for TV, originally broadcast in serial form); *Paradistorg* (*Summer Paradise*) (Lindblom) (pr)
1977   *A Look at Liv* (Kaplan) (role as interviewee)

Publications:

By BERGMAN: books—

Four Screenplays of Ingmar Bergman, New York, 1960.
The Virgin Spring, New York, 1960.
A Film Trilogy (*Through a Glass Darkly, Winter Light*, and *The Silence*), New York, 1967.
Persona and Shame, New York, 1972.
Bergman on Bergman, edited by Stig Björkman and others, New York, 1973.
Scenes from a Marriage, New York, 1974.
Face to Face, New York, 1976.
Four Stories by Ingmar Bergman, New York, 1977.
The Serpent's Egg, New York, 1978.
Autumn Sonata, New York, 1979.
From the Life of the Marionettes, New York, 1980.
Fanny and Alexander, New York, 1982; London, 1989.
Talking with Ingmar Bergman, edited by G. William Jones, Dallas, Texas, 1983.
The Marriage Scenarios: Scenes From a Marriage; *Face to Face*; *Autumn Sonata*, New York, 1983.
The Seventh Seal, New York, 1984.
Bergman, Ingmar, *Laterna Magica*, Stockholm, 1987; as *The Magic Lantern: An Autobiography*, London, 1988.

By BERGMAN: articles—

"Self-Analysis of a Film-Maker," in *Films and Filming* (London), September 1956.
"Dreams and Shadows," in *Films and Filming* (London), October 1956.
Interview with Jean Béranger, in *Cahiers du Cinéma* (Paris), October 1958.
"Each Film is My Last," in *Films and Filming* (London), July 1959.
"Bergman on Victor Sjöstrom," in *Sight and Sound* (London), Spring 1960.

Ingmar Bergman

"The Snakeskin," in *Sight and Sound* (London), August 1965.

"Schizophrenic Interview with a Nervous Film Director," by 'Ernest Riffe' (pseudonym), in *Film in Sweden* (Stockholm), no.3, 1968, and in *Take One* (Montreal), January/February 1969.

"Moment of Agony," interview with Lars-Olof Löthwall, in *Films and Filming* (London), February 1969.

"Conversations avec Ingmar Bergman," with Jan Aghed, in *Positif* (Paris), November 1970.

Interview with William Wolf, in *New York*, 27 October 1980.

"The Making of *Fanny and Alexander*," an interview with L.-L., and F.J. Marker, in *Films and Filming* (London), February 1983.

Interview with Peter Cowie, in *Monthly Film Bulletin* (London), April 1983.

"Goodbye to all that. Ingmar Bergman's farewell to film," an interview with F. van der Linden and B.J. Bertina, in *Cinema Canada* (Montreal), February 1984.

On BERGMAN: books—

Béranger, Jean, *Ingmar Bergman et ses films*, Paris, 1959.

Donner, Jörn, *The Personal Vision of Ingmar Bergman*, Bloomington, Indiana, 1964.

Maisetti, Massimo, *La Crisi spiritulai dell'uomo moderno nei film di Ingmar Bergman*, Varese, 1964.

Nelson, David, *Ingmar Bergman: The Search for God*, Boston, 1964.

Steene, Birgitta, *Ingmar Bergman*, New York, 1968.

Gibson, Arthur, *The Silence of God:Creative Response to the Films of Ingmar Bergman*, New York, 1969.

Wood, Robin, *Ingmar Bergman*, New York, 1969.

Sjögren, Henrik, *Regi: Ingmar Bergman*, Stockholm, 1970.

Young, Vernon, *Cinema Borealis: Ingmar Bergman and the Swedish Ethos*, New York, 1971.

Simon, John, *Ingmar Bergman Directs*, New York, 1972.

Kaminsky, Stuart, editor, *Ingmar Bergman: Essays in Criticism*, New York, 1975.

Bergom-Larsson, Maria, *Ingmar Bergman and Society*, San Diego, 1978.

Kawin, Bruce, *Mindscreen: Bergman, Godard and the First-Person Film*, Princeton, 1978.

Sjöman, Vilgot, *L. 136. Diary with Ingmar Bergman*, Ann Arbor, Michigan, 1978.

Manvell, Roger, *Ingmar Bergman: An Appreciation*, New York, 1980.

Mosley, Philip, *Ingmar Bergman: The Cinema as Mistress*, Boston, 1981.

Petrić, Vlada, editor, *Film and Dreams: An Approach to Ingmar Bergman*, South Salem, New York, 1981.

Cowie, Peter, *Ingmar Bergman: A Critical Biography*, New York, 1982.

Livingston, Paisley, *Ingmar Bergman and the Ritual of Art*, Ithaca, New York, 1982.

Steene, Birgitta, *A Reference Guide to Ingmar Bergman*, Boston, 1982.

Jones, William G., editor, *Talking with Ingmar Bergman*, Dallas, Texas, 1983.

Lefèvre, Raymond, *Ingmar Bergman*, Paris, 1983.

Dervin, Daniel, *Through a Freudian Lens Deeply: A Psychoanalysis of Cinema*, Hillsdale, New Jersey, 1985.

Gado, Frank, *The Passion of Ingmar Bergman*, Durham, North Carolina, 1986.

Ketcham, Charles B., *The Influence of Existentialism on Ingmar Bergman: An Analysis of the Theological Ideas Shaping a Filmmaker's Art*, Lewiston, New York, 1986.

On BERGMAN: articles—

Ulrichsen, Erik, "Ingmar Bergman and the Devil," in *Sight and Sound* (London), Summer 1958.

Godard, Jean-Luc, "Bergmanorama," in *Cahiers du Cinéma* (Paris), July 1958.

Archer, Eugene, "The Rack of Life," in *Film Quarterly* (Berkeley), Summer 1959.

Alpert, Hollis, "Bergman as Writer," in *Saturday Review* (New York), 27 August 1960.

Alpert, Hollis, "Style Is the Director," in *Saturday Review* (New York), 23 December 1961.

Nykvist, Sven, "Photographing the Films of Ingmar Bergman," in *American Cinematographer* (Los Angeles), October 1962.

Persson, Göran, "Bergmans trilogi," in *Chaplin* (Stockholm), no.40, 1964.

Fleisher, Frederic, "Ants in a Snakeskin," in *Sight and Sound* (London), Autumn 1965.

Lefèvre, Raymond, "Ingmar Bergman," in *Image et Son* (Paris), March 1969.

Sammern-Frankenegg, Fritz, "Learning 'A Few Words in the Foreign Language': Ingmar Bergman's 'Secret Message' in the Imagery of Hand and Face," in *Scandinavian Studies*, Summer 1977.

Sorel, Edith, "Ingmar Bergman: I Confect Dreams and Anguish," in *New York Times*, 22 January 1978.

Kinder, Marsha, "*From the Life of the Marionettes* to *The Devil's Wanton*," in *Film Quarterly* (Berkeley), Spring 1981.

Lundell, T., and A. Mulac, "Husbands and Wives in Bergman films: A close analysis based on empirical data," in *Journal of University Film association* (Carbondale, Illinois), Winter 1981.

Nave, B., and H. Welsh, "Retour de Bergman: Au ciné-club et au stage de Boulouris," in *Jeune Cinéma* (Paris), April–May 1982.

Cowie, Peter, "Bergman at Home," in *Sight and Sound* (London), Summer 1982.

Corliss, Richard, and W. Wolf, "God, Sex, and Ingmar Bergman," in *Film Comment* (New York), May–June 1983.

McLean, T., "Knocking on Heaven's door," in *American Film* (Washington, D.C.), June 1983.

Boyd, D., "*Persona* and the cinema of representation," in *Film Quarterly* (Los Angeles), Winter 1983–84.

Tornqvist, E., "August StrindBERGman Ingmar," in *Skrien* (Amsterdam), Winter 1983–84.

Koskinen, M., "The typically Swedish in Ingmar Bergman," in 25th Anniversary issue of *Chaplin* (Stockholm), 1984.

Ingemanson, B., "The screenplays of Ingmar Bergman: Personification and olfactory detail," and J.F. Maxfield, "Bergman's *Shame*: A dream of punishment," in *Literature/Film Quarterly* (Salisbury, Maryland), January 1984.

"Dialogue on Film: Sven Nykvist," in *American Film* (Washington, D.C.), March 1984.

"Ingmar Bergman Section" of *Positif* (Paris), March 1985.

Barr, Alan P., "The Unraveling of Character in Bergman's *Persona*," in *Literature/Film Quarterly* (Salisbury, Maryland), vol. 15, no. 2, 1987.

American Film (Washington, D.C.), October 1988.

Corliss, Richard, "The Glass Eye," in *Film Comment* (New York), November–December 1988.

On BERGMAN: film—

Greenblatt, Nat, producer, *The Directors*, 1963 (appearance).

Donner, Jörn, director, *Tre scener med Ingmar Bergman* (*Three Scenes with Ingmar Bergman*) (for Finnish TV), 1975.

Donner, Jörn, director, *The Bergman File*, 1978.

*   *   *

Bergman's unique international status as a filmmaker would seem assured on many grounds: his prolific output of largely notable work (40 features 1946–82); the profoundly personal nature of his best films since the 1950's; the innovative nature of his technique combined with its essential simplicity even when employing surrealistic and dream-like treatments (as, for example, in *Wild Strawberries* and *Persona*); his creative sensitivity in relation to his players; and his extraordinary capacity to evoke distinguished acting from his regular interpreters, notably Gunnar Björnstrand, Max von Sydow, Bibi Andersson, Ingrid Thulin and Liv Ullmann.

After an initial period of derivative, melodramatic filmmaking largely concerned with bitter man-woman relationships ("I just grabbed helplessly at any form that might save me, because I hadn't any of my own," he confesses in *Bergman on Bergman*), Bergman reached an initial maturity of style in *Summer Interlude* and *Summer with Monika*, romantic studies of adolescent love and subsequent disillusionment. In *The Naked Night* he used a derelict travelling circus—its proprietor with a faithless young mistress and its clown with a faithless middle-aged wife—as a symbol of human suffering through misplaced love and the ultimate loneliness of the human condition, a theme common to much of his work. Not that Bergman's films are all gloom and disillusionment. He has a recurrent, if veiled, sense of humour. His comedies, *A Lesson in Love* and *Smiles of a Summer Night* are ironically effective ("You're a gynaecologist who knows nothing about women," says the man's mistress in *A Lesson in Love*), and even in *Wild Strawberries* the aged professor's relations with his housekeeper offer comic relief. Bergman's later comedies, the Shavian *The Devil's Eye* and *Now About All These Women* are both sharp and fantastic.

"To me, religious problems are continuously alive . . . not . . . on the emotional level, but on an intellectual one," wrote Bergman at the time of *Wild Strawberries*. *The Seventh Seal, The Virgin Spring, Through a Glass Darkly, Winter Light*, and *The Silence* lead progressively through to the rejection of religious belief, leaving only the conviction that human life is haunted by "a virulent, active evil." The crusading knight of *The Seventh Seal* who cannot face death once his faith is lost survives only to witness the cruelty of religious persecution. Faith belongs to the simple-minded and innocent. *The Virgin Spring* exposes the violence of vengeance in a period of primitive Christianity. Bergman no longer likes these films, considering them "bogus"; nevertheless, they are excellently made in his highly professional style. Disillusionment with Lutheran denial of love is deep in *Winter Light*, and the mad girl in *Through a Glass Darkly* perceives God as a spider. "In *Winter Light* I swept my house clean," Bergman has said, and the ailing sister in *The Silence* faces death with the loneliness that passes all understanding as a result of the frigid silence of God in the face of her sufferings. However, in *The Face* Bergman takes sardonic delight in letting the rationalistic miracle-man in the end suspect that his bogus miracles are in fact genuine.

With *Wild Strawberries* Bergman turned increasingly to psychological dilemmas and ethical issues in human and social relations once religion has proved a failure. Above all else love, understanding and common humanity seem lacking. The aged medical professor in *Wild Strawberries* comes through a succession of dreams to realize the truth about his cold and loveless nature. In *Persona*, the most psychologically puzzling, controversial, yet significant of all Bergman's films, with its Brechtian alienation technique and surreal treatment of dual personality, the self-imposed silence of the actress stems from her failure in love for husband and son, though she responds with horror to the self-destructive violence in the world around her. This latter theme is carried still further in *The Shame* in which an egocentric musician attempts non-involvement in his country's war only to collapse into irrational acts of violence himself through sheer panic. *The Shame* and *Hour of the Wolf* are concerned with artists who are too self-centered to care about the larger issues of the society in which they live.

"It wasn't until *A Passion* that I really got to grips with the man-woman relationship," says Bergman; this film deals with "the dark, destructive forces" in human nature which sexual urges can inspire. Bergman's later films reflect, he claims, his "ceaseless fascination with the whole race of women," adding that "the film . . . should communicate psychic states." The love and understanding needed by women is too often denied them, witness the case of the various women about to give birth in *Brink of Life* and the fearful, haunted, loveless family relationships in *Cries and Whispers*. The latter, with *The Shame* and *The Serpent's Egg*, is surely among the most terrifying of Bergman's films, though photographed in exquisite color by his principal cinematographer, Sven Nykvist.

Man-woman relationships are successively and uncompromisingly examined in *The Touch*, showing a married woman driven out of her emotional depth in an extra-marital affair; in *Face to Face*, one of Bergman's most moving films, concerning the nervous breakdown of a cold-natured woman analyst and the hallucinations she suffers; and in his film made in series for television, but reissued more effectively in a shortened, re-edited form for the cinema, *Scenes from A Marriage*, about the troubled, long-term love of a professional couple who are divorced but unable to endure separation. Supreme performances were given by Bibi Andersson in *Persona* and *The Touch*, and by Liv Ullmann in *Cries and Whispers, Scenes from a Marriage* and *Face to Face*.

Bergman's latest films, made in Sweden or during his period of self-imposed exile, are more miscellaneous. *The Magic Flute* is one of the best, most delightful of opera-films, *The Serpent's Egg* a savage study in the sadistic origins of Nazism, and *Autumn Sonata* the case of a mother who cannot love. Bergman has declared his filmmaking at an end with his brilliant, German-made misanthropic study of a fatal marriage, *From the Life of the Marionettes*, and the semi-autobiographical television series *Fanny and Alexander*, Swedish produced, and with a re-edited version for the cinema.

—Roger Manvell

BERKELEY, Busby.

American. Born Busby Berkeley William Enos in Los Angeles, 29 November 1895. Educated Mohegan Military Academy, Peekshill, New York, 1907–1914. Married six times. Organized marching drills and later touring stage shows for U.S. and French armies, 1917–19; actor, stage manager, and choreographer, 1919–27; director of *A Night in Venice* on Broadway, 1928; director of dance numbers in *Whoopee* for Samuel Goldwyn, 1930; worked for Warners, 1933–39; hired as dance advisor and director by MGM, 1939; returned to Warners, 1943; released from Warners contract, returned to Broadway, 1944; directed last film, *Take Me Out to the Ball Game*, 1949. *Died 14 March 1976.*

Films as Director:

1933   *She Had to Say Yes* (+co-d, ch)
1935   *Gold Diggers of 1935* (+ch); *Bright Lights* (+ch); *I Live for Love* (+ch)
1936   *Stage Struck* (+ch)
1937   *The Go-Getter* (+ch); *Hollywood Hotel* (+ch)
1938   *Men Are Such Fools* (+ch); *Garden of the Moon* (+ch); *Comet Over Broadway* (+ch)
1939   *They Made Me a Criminal* (+ch); *Babes in Arms* (+ch); *Fast and Furious* (+ch)
1940   *Strike Up the Band* (+ch); *Forty Little Mothers* (+ch)
1941   *Blonde Inspiration* (+ch); *Babes on Broadway* (+ch)
1942   *For Me and My Gal* (+ch)
1943   *The Gang's All Here* (+ch)
1946   *Cinderella Jones* (+ch)
1949   *Take Me Out to the Ball Game* (+ch)

Other Films:

1930   *Whoopee* (ch)
1931   *Palmy Days* (ch); *Flying High* (ch)

1932   *Night World* (ch); *Bird of Paradise* (ch); *The Kid from Spain*
       (ch)
1933   ***42nd Street*** (ch); ***Gold Diggers of 1933*** (ch); *Footlight Parade*
       (ch); *Roman Scandals* (ch)
1934   *Wonder Bar* (ch); *Fashions of 1934* (ch); *Dames* (ch)
1935   *Go Into Your Dance* (ch); *In Caliente* (ch); *Stars Over*
       Broadway (ch)
1937   *Gold Diggers of 1937* (ch); *The Singing Marine* (ch); *Varsity*
       Show (ch)
1938   *Gold Diggers in Paris* (ch)
1939   *Broadway Serenade* (ch)
1941   *Ziegfield Girl* (ch); *Lady Be Good* (ch); *Born to Sing* (ch)
1943   *Girl Crazy* (ch)
1950   *Two Weeks with Love* (ch)
1951   *Call Me Mister* (ch); *Two Tickets to Broadway* (ch)
1952   *Million Dollar Mermaid* (ch)
1953   *Small Town Girl* (ch); *Easy to Love* (ch)
1954   *Rose Marie* (ch)
1962   *Jumbo* (ch)
1970   *The Phynx* (role in cameo appearance)

Publications:

By BERKELEY: book—

The Busby Berkeley Book, with Tony Thomas and Jim Terry, New
   York, 1973.

By BERKELEY: articles—

Interview with John Gruen, in *Close-Up*, New York, 1968.
Interview with P. Brion and R. Gilson, in *Contracampo* (Madrid),
   September 1981.

On BERKELEY: books—

Dunn, Bob, *The Making of "No, No, Nanette"*, New York, 1972.
Pike, Bob, and Dave Martin, *The Genius of Busby Berkeley*, Reseda,
   California, 1973.
Meyer, William, *Warner Brothers Directors*, New York, 1978.
Hirschhorn, Clive, *The Warner Bros. Story*, New York, 1979.
Delamater, Jerome, *Dance in the Hollywood Musical*, Ann Arbor,
   Michigan, 1981.
Feuer, Jane, *The Hollywood Musical*, London, 1982.
Morsiani, Alberto, *Il Grande Busby: Il Cinema di Busby Berkeley*,
   Modena, 1983.
Roddick, Nick, *A New Deal in Entertainment: Warner Brothers in the*
   1930's, London, 1983.
Altman, Rick, *The American Film Musical*, Bloomington, Indiana,
   and London, 1989.

On BERKELEY: articles—

Sarris, Andrew, "Likable but Elusive," in *Film Culture* (New York),
   Spring 1963.
Comolli, Jean-Louis, "Dancing Images," and Patrick Brion and René
   Gilson, "A Style of Spectacle," in *Cahiers du Cinema in English*
   (New York), no. 2, 1966.
Jenkinson, Philip, "The Great Busby," in *Film* (London), Spring
   1966.
Thomas, John, "The Machineries of Joy," in *Film Society Review*
   (New York), February 1967.
Bevis, D.L., "A Berkeley Evening," in *Films in Review* (New York),
   June/July 1967.
Roman, R.C., "Busby Berkeley," in *Dance* (New York), February
   1968.
Sidney, George, "The Three Ages of the Musical," in *Films and Film-*
   ing (London), June 1968.
"What Directors are Saying," in *Action* (Los Angeles), May/June
   1970.
Gorton, D., "Busby and Ruby," in *Newsweek* (New York), 3 August
   1970.
Knight, Arthur, "Busby Berkeley," in *Action* (Los Angeles), May/
   June 1974.
Roth, M., "Some Warners Musicals and the Spirit of the New Deal,"
   in *Velvet Light Trap* (Madison), Winter 1977.
Tessier, Max, "Busby Berkeley 1895–1976," in *Avant-Scène du*
   Cinéma (Paris), 15 April 1978.

Delamater, Jerome, "Busby Berkeley: an American Surrealist," in
   Wide Angle (Athens, Ohio), vol. 1, no. 1, 1979.
Telotte, J.P., "A Gold Digger Aesthetic: The depression Musical and
   its Audience," in *Post Script* (Jacksonville, Florida), Fall 1981.
Durgnat, Raymond, "Busby Berkeley: Filmed theatre and pure
   theatre," in *Films* (London), January 1982.

*   *   *

No American film director explored the possibilities of the
mobile camera more fully or ingeniously than Busby Berkeley.
He was the Méliès of the musical, the corollary of Vertov in the
exploration of the possibilities of cinematic movement. His
influence has since been felt from movie musicals to television
commercials.

Certain aspects of Berkeley's personal history are obvious in
their importance to a discussion of his cinematic work, most
specifically his World War I service and his work in the theatre.
Born to a theatrical family, Berkeley learned early of the
demands of the theatrical profession: when his father died, his
mother refused to take the night off, instilling in Busby the
work ethic of "the show must go on." Throughout most of his
career, Gertrude Berkeley and her ethic reigned, no wife
successfully displacing her as spiritual guide and confidante
until after her death in 1948, while Berkeley drove himself at
the expense of his many marriages.

Berkeley's World War I service was significant for the images he created in his musical sequences. He designed parade
drills for both the French and U.S. armies and his later service
as an aerial observer with the Air Corps formed the basis of an
aesthetic which incorporated images of order and symmetry
often seen from the peculiar vantage of an overhead position.
In addition, that training developed his approach to economical direction which included storyboarding to effect his editing-
in-the-camera approach, and the blackboard instruction of
chorines by which he illustrated the formations they were to
achieve.

Returning from war, Berkeley found work as a stage actor,
his first role directed by John Cromwell with Gertrude serving
as his dramatic coach. He soon graduated to direction and
choreography, in 1929 becoming the first man on Broadway to
direct a musical for which he also staged the dance numbers,
setting a precedent for such talents as Jerome Robbins, Gower
Champion, Bob Fosse and Tommy Tune. When Samuel Goldwyn invited him to Hollywood in 1930 as a dance director, that
Broadway division of labor was in effect and Berkeley had to
wait until *Golddiggers of* 1935 before being allowed to do both
jobs on the same film.

From 1933 through 1939 Berkeley worked for Warner Bros.
where he created a series of dance numbers which individually
and collectively represent much of the best Hollywood product
of the period. An examination of his work in this period in relation to the Production Code and the developing conventions of
the musical genre illustrates his unique contribution to cinema.

Boy/girl romance and the success story were standard narrative ingredients of 1930's musicals, and Berkeley's work contributed significantly to the formulation of these conventions.
Where he was unique was in his visualization of the onstage as
opposed to the backstage segments of these dramas. Relying
on his war service, he began to fashion onstage spectacles
which had been impossible on the Broadway stage. In his films
he was able to explode any notion of the limitations of a proscenium and the relationship of the theatre spectator to it: the
fixed perspective of that audience was abandoned for one
which lacked defined spatial or temporal coordinates. His camera was regularly mounted on a crane (or on the monorail he
invented) and swooped over and around or toward and away
from performers in a style of choreography for camera which
was more elaborate than that mapped out for the dancers.

Busby Berkeley

Amusingly, in his direction of non-musical scenes, he generally reversed this procedure, making the backstage dramas appear confined within a stage space and bound to the traditions of theatrical staging and dialogue.

As he created the illusion of theatre in his musical numbers, so too he created the illusion of dance. Having never studied dance, he rarely relied on trained dancers, preferring to create movement through cinematic rather than choreographic means. Occasionally when he would include sophisticated dance routines, such as in the Lullaby of Broadway number from *Golddiggers of 1935*, he would highlight the dancers' virtuosity in a series of shots which preserved the integrity of their movement without infringing on the stylistics of his camerawork.

The virtuosity of his camera movement remains important not only for a discussion of aesthetics, but also for the meaning Berkeley brought to the depiction of sexual fantasy and spectacle in a period of Hollywood history when the Production Code Administration was keeping close watch over screen morality. Throughout the 1930's, Berkeley's camera caressed as if involved in foreplay, penetrated space as if seeking sexual gratification, and soared in an approximation of sexual ecstasy. Whether tracking through the legs of a line of chorus girls in *42nd Street*, swooping over an undulating vagina-shaped construction of pianos in *Golddiggers of 1935*, or caressing gigantic bananas manipulated by scantily clad chorines in *The Gang's All Here*, his sexual innuendos were titillating in both their obviousness and seeming naiveté. Berkeley's ability to inject such visual excitement meant that he was often called upon to rescue a troubled picture by adding one or more extravagantly staged musical numbers.

After leaving Warner Bros. in 1939, he returned to MGM where, although generally less innovative, his work set precedents for the genre: he directed the first Judy Garland/Mickey Rooney musical, the first Garland/Gene Kelly film, and with his last effort as a director, introduced the team of Gene Kelly and Stanley Donen. Undoubtedly the master director of American musicals in the first decade of sound film and a huge influence on many of the musical talents of succeeding decades, Berkeley worked only occasionally through the 1950's, staging musical numbers for various studios, his last being in the 1962 MGM film, *Jumbo*.

With the nostalgia craze of the late 1960's, Berkeley's aesthetic was resurrected and in 1971 he triumphantly returned to the Broadway stage where he directed a revival of the 1920's hit *No, No, Nanette*, starring his leading lady of the 1930's, Ruby Keeler, herself in retirement for 30 years. That moment was surely the fulfillment of all the success stories he had directed over his long career.

—Doug Tomlinson

BERLANGA, Luis García. *See* **GARCÍA BERLANGA, Luis.**

BERTOLUCCI, Bernardo.

Italian. Born in Parma, Italy, 16 March 1940. Attended University of Rome, 1960–62. Married Clare Peptoe. Assistant director on *Accattone* (Pasolini), 1961; directed first feature, *La commare secca*, 1962; joined Italian Communist Party (PCI), late 1960's. Recipient: Special Award, Cannes Festival, for *Prima della revoluzione*, 1964; Best Director Award, National Society of Film Critics, for *Il conformista*, 1971; Oscars for Best Director and Best Screenplay, and Directors Guild of America Award for Outstanding Feature Film Achievement, for *The Last Emperor*, 1987. Address: lives in London.

Films as Director:

1962   *La commare secca (The Grim Reaper)* (+sc)
1964   *Prima della rivoluzione (Before the Revolution)* (+co-sc)
1965/66   *La vie del Petrolio* (+sc); *Il canale* (+sc)
1966/67   *Ballata de un milliardo* (+co-sc)
1967   "Il fico infruttuoso" episode of *Amore e rabbia (Vangelo '70, Love and Anger)* (+sc)
1968   *Partner* (+co-sc)
1969   *La strategia del ragno (The Spider's Strategem)* (+co-sc)
1970   *Il conformista (The Conformist)* (+sc)
1971   *La saluta e malato o I poveri muorioro prima (La Sante est malade ou Les Pauvres meurent les premiers)* (+sc); *L'inchiesa* (+co-sc)
1972   ***Ultimo tango a Parigi (Le Dernier Tango à Paris, Last Tango in Paris)*** (+co-sc)
1976   ***1900 (Novecento)*** (presented in two parts in Italy: *Novecento atto I* and *Novecento atto II*) (+co-sc)
1979   *La luna* (+co-sc)
1981   *La tragedia di un uomo ridicolo (La Tragedie d'un homme ridicule)* (+sc)
1987   ***The Last Emperor***
1989   *The Sheltering Sky*

Other Films:

1961   *Accattone* (Pasolini) (asst-d)
1967   ***C'era una volta il West (Once Upon a Time in the West)*** (Leone) (co-sc)

Publications:

By BERTOLUCCI: books—

In cerca del mistero, Milan, 1962.
Bertolucci by Bertolucci, interviewed by Don Ranvaud and Enzo Ungari, London, 1987.

By BERTOLUCCI: articles—

Interview with Jacques Bontemps and Louis Marcorelles, in *Cahiers du Cinéma* (Paris), March 1965.
"A Conversation with Bernardo Bertolucci," with John Bragin, in *Film Quarterly* (Berkeley), Fall 1966.
"Versus Godard," in *Cahiers du Cinéma* (Paris), January 1967; also in *Cahiers du Cinéma in English* (New York), May 1967.
"Prima della rivoluzione," in *Avant-Scène du Cinéma* (Paris), June 1968.
"Bertolucci on *The Conformist*," with Marilyn Goldin, in *Sight and Sound* (London), Spring 1971.
Interview with Amos Vogel, in *Film Comment* (New York), Fall 1971.
"A Conversation with Bernardo Bertolucci," by Joan Mellen, in *Cinéaste* (New York), vol. 5, no.4, 1973.
"Every Sexual Relationship is Condemned: Interview," with Gideon Bachmann, in *Film Quarterly* (Berkeley), Spring 1973.
"Dialogue: Bertolucci and Aldrich," in *Action* (Los Angeles), March/April 1974.
"Dialogue on Film," in *American Film* (Washington, D.C.), April 1974.
"Films Are Animal Events," interview with Gideon Bachmann, in *Film Quarterly* (Berkeley), Autumn 1975.
"Propos de Bernardo Bertolucci," interview with Guy Braucourt, in *Ecran* (Paris), October 1976.
Interview with D. Buckley and others, in *Cineaste* (New York), Winter 1976/77.

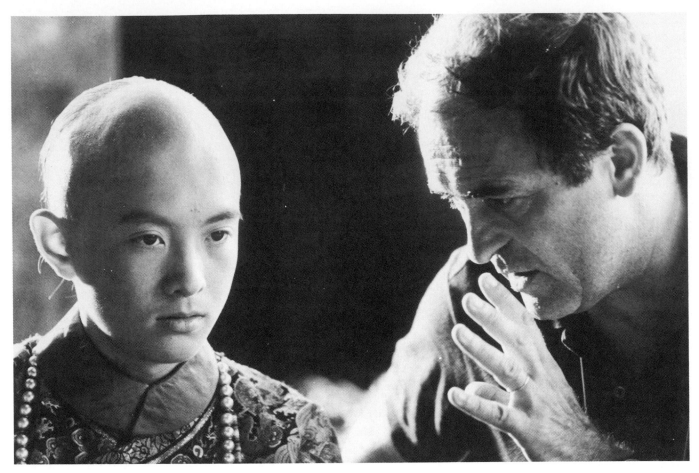

Bernardo Bertolucci directing *The Last Emperor*

Interview with D. O'Grady, in *Cinema Papers* (Melbourne), July 1977.

"History Lessons," interview with D. Young, in *Film Comment* (New York), November/December 1977.

Interview with Gordon Gow, in *Films and Filming* (London), June 1978.

"Bertolucci on *La Luna*," an interview with Richard Roud, in *Sight and Sound* (London), no.4, 1979.

"Bernardo Bertolucci on *Luna*," interview with M. Sclauzero, in *Interview* (New York), October 1979.

Interview with Michel Ciment and Gerard Legrand, in *Positif* (Paris), November 1979.

"*Luna* and the Critics," interview with G. Crowdus and D. Georgakas, in *Cineaste* (New York), Winter 1979/80.

"Dialogue on Film: Bernardo Bertolucci," in *American Film* (Washington, D.C.), January/February 1980.

Interview with M. Magill, in *Films in Review* (New York), April 1982.

Interview with G. Graziani, in *Filmcritica* (Florence), February–March 1983.

"After the revolution? A conversation with Bernardo Bertolucci," by D. Lavin, in *Literature/Film Quarterly* (Salisbury, Maryland), January 1984.

Interview about Pasolini, in *Cinema e Cinema* (Rome), May/August 1985.

Interview with A. Philippon and S. Toubiana, in *Cahiers du Cinéma* (Paris), November 1987.

Film Comment (New York), November/December 1987.

Interview in *Films in Review* (New York), March 1988.

On BERTOLUCCI: books—

Leprohon, Pierre, *Le Cinéma italien*, Paris, 1966.

Gelmis, Joseph, *The Film Director as Superstar*, Garden City, New York, 1970.

Mellen, Joan, *Women and Sexuality in the New Film*, New York, 1973.

Casetti, F., *Bertolucci*, Florence, 1975.

Ungari, Enzo, *Bertolucci*, Milan, 1982.

Kolker, Robert Phillip, *Bernardo Bertolucci*, London, 1985.

Kline, T. Jefferson, *Bertolucci's Dream Loom: A Psychoanalytical Study of the Cinema*, Amherst, Massachusetts, 1987.

On BERTOLUCCI: articles—

Kael, Pauline, "Starburst by a Gifted 22-Year Old," in *Life* (New York), 13 August 1965.

Beck, Julian, "Tourner avec Bertolucci," in *Cahiers du Cinéma* (Paris), October 1967.

Tailleur, Roger, "Les Vacances rouges," in *Positif* (Paris), May 1968.

Purdon, N., "Bernardo Bertolucci," in *Cinema* (London), no.8, 1971.

Kreitzman, R., "Bernardo Bertolucci, an Italian young master," in *Film* (London), Spring 1971.

Roud, Richard, "Fathers and Sons," in *Sight and Sound* (London), Spring 1971.

"*Le Dernier Tango à Paris*," in *Avant-Scène du Cinéma* (Paris), February 1973.

Kinder, Marsha, and Beverle Houston, "Bertolucci and the Dance of Danger," in *Sight and Sound* (London), Autumn 1973.

Lopez, D., "The Father Figure in *The Conformist* and in *Last Tango in Paris*," in *Film Heritage* (New York), Summer 1976.

Aitken, W., "Bertolucci's Gay Images," in *Jump Cut* (Berkeley), November 1977.

Schwartzman, P., "Embarrass me more!," in *Film Comment* (New York), November/December 1979.

Horton, A., "History as Myth and Myth as History in Bertolucci's *1900*," in *Film and History* (Newark, New Jersey), February 1980.

"*La Luna* Issue" of *Avant-Scène du Cinéma* (Paris), 15 November 1980.

Magny, Joel, "Biofilmographie commentée de Bernardo Bertolucci," in *Cinéma* (Paris), October 1981.

Gentry, R., "Bertolucci directs Tragedy of a ridiculous man," in *Millimeter* (New York), December 1981.

Ranvaud, Don, "After the revolution," in *American Film* (Washington, D.C.), October 1986.

"*Last Emperor* Section" of *Cinéma* (Paris), 25 November 1987.

Film Comment (New York), July/August 1989.

*   *   *

At the age of 21, Bernardo Bertolucci established himself as a major artist in two distinct art forms, winning a prestigious award in poetry and receiving high critical acclaim for his initial film, *La commare secca*. This combination of talents is evident in all of his films, which have a lyric but exceptionally concrete style. His father, Attilio Bertolucci, was famous in his own right as a critic, professor, and poet, and in 1961 introduced Bernardo to Pier Paolo Pasolini, an esteemed literary figure. This friendship led both writers, ironically, away from poetry and into the cinema. Serving as the assistant director on Pasolini's inaugural film, *Accattone*, Bertolucci was very quickly entrusted with the full direction of Pasolini's next project, *La commare secca*, based on a story by the writer.

La commare secca is an auspicious debut; as both screenwriter and director, Bertolucci found at once the high visual style and narrative complexity which distinguish his later films. The sex murder of a prostitute is its central narrative event; as the probable witnesses and suspects are brought in for questioning, a series of lives are unraveled, with each sad story winding toward the city park where the murder occurred. Formally, the film is an ambitious amalgam of a film noir atmosphere and narrative style with a neorealist concentration on behavioral detail and realistic settings.

In *Before the Revolution*, Bertolucci first presents the theme which will become foremost in his work: the conflict between freedom and conformity. Fabrizio, the leading character, is obliged to decide between radical political commitment and an alluring marriage into the bourgeoisie. In this reworking of Stendhal's *The Charterhouse of Parma*, Bertolucci expressly delineates the connection between politics and sexuality. The film also establishes the Freudian theme of the totemic father, which will recur throughout Bertolucci's work, here emblematized in the figure of Fabrizio's communist mentor, whom Fabrizio must renounce as a precondition to his entry into moneyed society.

Bertolucci diverged from the style of his first two critically successful films with *The Partner*, a complex, experimental work based on Dostoevski's *The Double*. Heavily influenced by the films of Godard and the events of May '68, it eschews narrative exposition, developing instead a critique of literary consumerism, academic pacifism, and the student left, through a series of polemical debates between a bookish student and his radical double. For the most part *The Partner* is an anomalous film, which conveys very little of the heightened lyricism of his major works.

With *The Spider's Strategem*, originally made for television in 1969, and *The Conformist*, Bertolucci combines an experimental narrative technique with lavish visual design, achieving in *The Conformist* an unprecedented commercial and critical triumph. Sexuality is here explicitly posited as the motor of political allegiance, as Marcello, the lead character in *The Conformist*, becomes a Fascist in order to suppress his growing recognition of his homosexuality. The character performs an outlandishly deviant act—killing his former professor, now a member of the Resistance, in order to declare his own conventionality and membership in the Fascist order. Conformity and rebellion are thus folded together, not only in the psyche of

Marcello, but in the culture as a whole, as Bertolucci examines the interpenetrating structures, the twin pathologies, of family and politics. Bertolucci here unveils the full range of stylistic features—the elaborate tracking shots, the opulent color photography (realized by the virtuoso cinematographer Vittorio Storara), the odd, surrealistic visual incongruities—that give his work such a distinctive surface. It is here, also, that Bertolucci connects most directly with the general evolution of the postwar Italian cinema. Beginning with Visconti, and continuing with Antonioni and Bellocchio, an increasing emphasis is placed on the psychology of transgression, a motif which links politics and the libido. The inner life of the alienated protagonist becomes the lens displaying the spectrum of social forces, as the politics of the state are viewed in the mimetic behavior of disturbed individuals.

Last Tango in Paris depicts the last week in the life of Paul, played by Marlon Brando, as a man who is both geographically and spiritually in exile. His orbit crosses that of "the girl," played by Maria Schneider. The raw sexual encounters which ensue serve as a kind of purgation for the Brando character, who retaliates against the hypocrisy of cultural institutions such as family, church and state through the medium of Jeanne's body. Sex is used as a weapon and symbolic cure, as the libidinal rage of the character is focused on the entire apparatus of social constraints. The outsized human passion Bertolucci depicts, chiefly through the threatening figure of Marlon Brando, seems to literalize the filmmaker's comment that "films are animal events." In addition to the players, the music by Gatto Barbieri and the cinematography of Vittorio Storaro contribute to the febrile intensity of the work.

The world acclaim brought by *Last Tango* assured Bertolucci of the financial resources to complete the long-planned Marxian epic, *1900*. Setting the film in the rural areas of Parma, a few miles from his childhood home, Bertolucci set out to compose a paean to a way of life that was passing—the "culture of the land" of the peasant farmers, seen as a native and pure form of communism. The film depicts the cruel historical awakening of the farmers of the region, part of an entire class that has been regularly brutalized, first by aristocratic landowners, and then by the Fascist regime. Bertolucci localizes this conflict in the twin destinies of two characters born on the same day in *1900*—Olmo, who becomes a peasant leader, and Alfredo, the scion of the feudal estate in which the film takes place.

The controversial work was released in a six-hour form in Europe, and shortened to three hours for American release. Bertolucci had complete control of the cutting of the film, and considers the shorter version a more finished work. The epic sweep remains, as do the contradictions—for the film amalgamates the most divergent elements: a Marxian epic, it is furnished with an international star cast; a portrait of the indigenous peasantry, its principle language is English. Intentionally fashioned for wide commercial appeal, it nonetheless broaches untried subject matter. The film keeps these elements in suspension, never dissolving these differences into an ideological portrait of life "after the revolution." The film's ending seems instead to return to the customary balance and tension between historical forces and class interests.

In *Luna*, Bertolucci turns to a much more intimate subject: the relation between mother and son. The work has a diminutive scale but a passionate focus, a quality crystallized in the opera scenes in which the mother, Caterina, performs. The reconciliation of mother, son and father occurs during a rehearsal in which the mother reveals, through song, the identity of father and son. This cathartic and bravura scene plays in high relief the characteristic patterns of Bertolucci's cinema, in which the family drama is played against the backdrop of a ritualized art form, opera in this case, dance in *Last Tango*, and theater (the *Macbeth* scene in *Before the Revolution*).

With *Tragedy of a Ridiculous Man*, Bertolucci continues his inquiry into the relations between politics and family life, here framing the ambivalent bond between father and son with the correlative conflict between capitalism and political terror.

Bertolucci returned to the wide canvas of the historical film with *The Last Emperor* in 1987. Frustrated by his inability to acquire financing for a film of the Dashiell Hammett story *Red Harvest*, and unhappy with the state of filmmaking in Italy, the director turned to the autobiography of Pu Yi, China's last Emperor, and had the privilege not only of filming in China but also of filming in the Forbidden City in Beijing, the first time such access had been allowed.

The story of Pu Yi illustrates a striking change in the political focus of Bertolucci's filmmaking. The relationship between individual psychology and the political and historical forces that mold it remains, as before, the central subject of the film, linking it to works such as *Before the Revolution, The Conformist*, and *1900*. But the resolution of the film seems to take place outside the political and historical context. The transformation of Pu Yi, in Bertolucci's words, from "a dragon to a butterfly," occurs only in the context of individual friendship. In depicting the rise and fall of imperialism, republicanism, and fascism, and ending the film with a portrayal of the harsh excesses of the Cultural Revolution, Bertolucci depicts a sequence of destructive political "solutions" that somehow clear the way for the journey of the main character from "darkness to light."

—Robert Burgoyne

BIRRI, Fernando.

Argentinian. Born 13 March 1925. Educated at Universidad Nacional del Litoral, Santa Fe, Argentina, 1942–47, and at Centro Sperimentale di Cinematografia, Rome, 1950–52. Married. Assistant to Vittorio De Sica on *Il tetto*, 1954; returned to Argentina to found Instituto de Cinematografia, later La Escuela Documental de Santa Fe, 1956; left Argentina for political reasons, 1963; moved to Italy, 1964; attended 1st International Festival of the New Latin American Cinema, Havana, 1979; taught at Universidad Nacional Autonoma de Mexico, 1980, and at Film School of Universidad de Los Andes, Merida, Venezuela, 1980–83. Director of International School of Cinema and TV of San Antonio de Los Banos, 1983–. Recipient: Grand Prize, SODRE Festival, Montevideo, for *Tire Die*, 1960; Golden Lion, Venice Festival, for *Los Inundados*, 1962; Honored at Festivals in Benalmadena, Spain, 1979, and Pesaro, Italy, 1981.

Films as Director:

1951   *Selinunte* (short); *Alfabeto notturno* (short)
1952   *Immagini Populari Siciliane Sacre*; *Immagini Populari Siciliane Profane*
1959   *La primera fundacion de Buenos Aires* (animation)
1960   *Tire die (Toss Me a Dime)* (co-sc, co-d, co-ph); *Buenos dias, Buenos Aires* (short)
1961   *Los inundados (Flooded Out)*
1962   *Che, Buenos Aires* (comprising two previous films); *La pampa gringa* (doc)
1966   *Castagnino, diario romano* (short)
1979   *Org* (co-d)

1983   *Rafael Alberti, un retrato del poeta por Fernando Birri*
1984   *Rte.: Nicaragua (carta al mundo)* (short film)
1985   *Mi hijo, el Che*

Other Films:

1955   *Gli sbanditi* (Maselli) (role)
1982   *La Rose des vents* (P. Guzman) (role)

Publications:

By BIRRI: book—

La Escuela Documental de Santa Fe, Santa Fe, Argentina, 1964.

By BIRRI: articles—

"Cine y subdesarrollo," in *Cine Cubano* (Havana), May/July 1967.
"Revolución en la revolución del nuevo cine latinoamericano," in *Cine Cubano* (Havana), August/December 1968.
"Fernando Birri y las raices del huevo cine latinoamericano," an interview with Francisco Lombardi, in *Hablemos de Cine* (Lima), March 1984.
"For a nationalist, realist, critical and popular cinema," in *Screen* (London), May–August 1985.

On BIRRI: books—

Mahieu, Jose Agustin, *Breve historia del cine argentino*, Buenos Aires, 1966.
Micciche, Lino, editor, *Fernando Birri e la Escuela Documental de Santa Fe*, Pesaro, Italy, 1981.
Burton, Julianne, *The New Latin American Cinema: An Annotated Bibliography of Sources in English, Spanish, and Portuguese*, New York, 1983.
Burton, Julianne, editor, *Cinema and Social Change in Latin America: Conversations with Filmmakers*, Austin, Texas, 1986.
King, John, and Nissa Torrents, *The Garden of Forking Paths: Argentine Cinema*, London, 1986.

On BIRRI: articles—

Pussi, Dolly, "Breve historia del documental en la Argentina," in *Cine Cubano* (Havana), October 1973.
Burton, Julianne, "The Camera as Gun: Two Decades of Film Culture and Resistance in Latin America," in *Latin American Perspectives*, Austin, Texas, 1978.
"Fernando Birri Section" of *Cine Cubano* (Havana), no. 100, 1981.
Mahieu, A., "Revision critica del cine argentino," in *Cine Cubano* (Havana), no. 107, 1984.
Martinez Carril, M., "Fernando Birri, un mito, una obra," in *Cinemateca Revista* (Montevideo), February 1986.

*   *   *

Because he was more interested in creating filmmakers than in creating films; because he attempted to offer a sustained and systematic counter-example to existing industrial modes of filmmaking and to the ideological assumptions which limited both the process and the product; because he developed a concrete theoretical-practical approach and founded the first school of documentary filmmaking in Latin America in order to teach that methodology; and finally because his students fanned out across the continent putting his ideas into practice, Fernando Birri is a key figure in the history of the New Latin American Cinema.

Born in the provincial capital of Santa Fe, Birri was a poet and puppeteer before turning to the cinema in search of a broad popular audience. Unable to break into the tightly controlled national film industry, Birri travelled to Italy to study at Rome's Centro Sperimentale di Cinematografia during the early 1950's, when the neo-realist movement was still at its height. Profoundly influenced by the ideology, aesthetics and methodology of this first anti-industrial, anti-Hollywood model for a national cinema, Birri returned to Argentina in

1956 hoping to found a national film school. Rejecting the closed commercialism of the Buenos Aires-based film industry, one of the three largest in Latin America at the time, Birri returned to Santa Fe.

Birri recalls, "Fresh from Europe, what I had in mind was a film school modeled on the Centro Sperimentale, a fictional film school which would train actors, directors, cinematographers, set designers, etc. But when I confronted the actual conditions in Argentina and in Santa Fe, I realized that my plan was premature. What was needed was something else: a school which would not only provide apprenticeship in filmmaking, but also in sociology, and even in Argentine history, geography and politics, because the most essential quest is the quest for national identity, in order to recover and rediscover what had been alienated, distorted and destroyed by centuries of cultural penetration. This search for a national identity is what led me to pose the problem in strictly *documentary* terms, because I believe that the first step for any national cinema is to document its own reality."

La Escuela Documental de Santa Fe grew out of the *Instituto de Cinematografía*, which was in turn an outgrowth of a 4-day seminar on filmmaking led by Birri. Birri's goal was to lay the foundations for a regional film industry whose films would be "national, realist, and popular": national in that they would address the most pressing problems of national life; realist (documentary) in approach in contrast to the highly artificial style and milieux of the "official" film industry; popular in their focus on and appeal to the less privileged classes. Birri emphasized process over product, viewing each film project as the opportunity for practical apprenticeship on the part of the largest possible number of students, in keeping with his determination to integrate theory and practice. He was the first of the Latin American filmmakers to posit technical imperfection as a positive attribute, preferring *un sentido imperfecto a una perfeccion sin sentido* (an imperfect/sincere meaning to a meaningless perfection).

Birri's best-known films are the 33-minute documentary *Tire die* (*Toss Me a Dime*) and *Los inundados* (*Flooded Out*), a picaresque feature in the neorealist style about the adventures of a squatter family displaced by seasonal floods. Both played to huge and enthusiastic audiences at their local premieres but could not achieve broad national exhibition even after winning important prizes in international festivals.

An inhospitable political climate compelled Birri to leave Argentina in 1963. Subsequent months in São Paulo catalyzed an important documentary movement there, but Birri himself returned to Italy and, until recently, relative obscurity. His presence at the First International Festival of the New Latin American Cinema in Havana in 1979 signaled renewed activity and recognition. Since then, Birri has taught at Mexico's national university and at the University of Los Andes in Venezuela. The Benalmadena and Pesaro Festivals (Spain, 1979 and Italy, 1981) organized special programs honoring his work.

—Julianne Burton

BLACHÉ, Alice. *See* **GUY, Alice.**

BLACKTON, J. Stuart.

American. Born James Stuart Blackton in Sheffield, England, 5 January 1875. Educated at City College, New York. Married four times. Moved to U.S., 1885; as journalist-illustrator for *New York World*, met Edison, who, using his Kinematograph camera, made *Blackton, the Evening World Cartoonist*, 1895; formed Vitagraph Company with Albert E. Smith and William T. Rock, 1897; president of Vitagraph, 1900–1915; formed Vitagraph stock of actors, 1905; built glass-enclosed studios in Flatbush, Brooklyn, 1905–6; made series of animated films, pioneering single-frame animation techniques, 1906–10; organized and became president of Motion Picture Board of Trade (later Association of Motion Picture Producers and Distributors of America), also publisher and editor, *Motion Picture Magazine*, 1915; independent producer, from 1917; directed in England, and experimented with color film, early 1920's; Vitagraph sold to Warner Bros. for $1 000 000; retired from filmmaking, 1925; bankrupt, 1931; went on relief, directed Federal work relief movie project, 1935; director of production for Anglo-American Film Company, late 1930's. *Died in Hollywood following auto accident, 13 August 1941.*

Films as Director:

(Partial listing as no director's credit given on Vitagraph's early films)
1898   *Burglar on the Roof* (+role)
1899   *A Visit to the Spiritualist*
1900   "Happy Hooligan" series (+role); *The Enchanted Drawing*
1905   *Monsieur Beaucaire* (+role); *The Automobile Thieves* (+role); *Raffles, the Amateur Cracksman*
1906   *Humorous Phases of Funny Faces*; *100 to 1 Shot*
1907   *The Haunted Hotel*
1909   *The Magic Fountain Pen*; *Princess Nicotine*
1909/10   *The Life of Moses*
1917   *The Message of the Mouse*; "Country Life" series; *The Judgment House* (+sc, pr)
1918   *World for Sale* (+pr); *Missing* (+pr, co-sc); *The Common Cause* (+pr); *Safe for Democracy* (+pr)
1919   *The Moonshine Trail* (+pr, co-sc); *My Husband's Other Wife* (+pr); *A House Divided* (+pr); *Dawn* (+pr)
1920   *Respectable By Proxy* (+pr); *The Blood Barrier* (+pr); *Passers-By* (+pr); *The House of the Tolling Bell* (+pr); *Forbidden Valley* (+pr)
1922   *The Glorious Adventure* (+pr); *The Gypsy Cavalier* (+pr)
1923   *The Virgin Queen* (+pr); *On the Banks of the Wabash* (+pr)
1924   *Let Not Man Put Asunder* (+pr); *Between Friends* (+pr); *Behold This Woman* (+pr); *The Clean Heart* (+pr); *The Beloved Brute* (+pr)
1925   *The Redeeming Sin* (+pr); *Tides of Passion* (+pr); *The Happy Warrior* (+pr)
1926   *Bride of the Storm* (+pr); *The Gilded Highway* (+pr); *Hell-Bent for Heaven* (+pr); *The Passionate Quest* (+pr)
1933   *The Film Parade* (*March of the Movies, Cavalcade of the Movies*) (+pr) (compilation film with some footage "recreated" by Blackton)

Publications:

By BLACKTON: book—

Marine Studies, undated.

By BLACKTON: articles—

Interview, in *The Moving Picture World*, 19 December 1908.
Introduction to *The Photodrama* by Henry Phillips, 1914.
"Awake America!," in *The Theatre* (New York), September 1915.
"The Battle Cry of Peace," in *Motion Picture* (New York), September 1915/January 1916.
"Yesterdays of Vitagraph," in *Photoplay* (New York), July 1919.
"The Movies Are Growing Up," in *Motion Picture* (New York), February 1925.

J. Stuart Blackton (holding script) directing *The Gypsy Cavalier*

On BLACKTON: books—

Orman, Felix, *The Pioneer of the Photoplay*, pamphlet n.d. (ca. 1921).
Slide, Anthony, *The Big V: A History of the Vitagraph Company*, 1976.
Trimble, Marian Blackton, *J. Stuart Blackton: A Personal Biography*, Metuchen, New Jersey, 1984.

On BLACKTON: articles—

Haskins, H., article in *Motion Picture Classic* (Brooklyn), September 1918.
Sketch in *Current Biography*, New York, 1941.
Obituary in the *New York Times*, 14 August 1941.
Slide, Anthony, "Films on 8 & 16," in *Films in Review* (New York), February 1978.
Desmond, Kevin, "Props from Spools: The story of J. Stuart Blackton," in *Eyepiece* (London), Christmas 1986.

*   *   *

J. Stuart Blackton was both a pioneering producer/director and a pioneering animator. The American film industry may well be said to have its origins in the founding by Blackton and Albert E. Smith of the Vitagraph Company, and most historians agree that animation originates with Blackton's 1907 production of *The Haunted Hotel*.

The Haunted Hotel combined animation, live action and special effects and had its origins in the fantasies of Georges Méliès. In France the film certainly influenced the work of Emile Cohl. Of course, Blackton had experimented with a form of animation long before *The Haunted Hotel*, notably with the undated *Cohen and Coon*, in which Blackton writes those two words on a blackboard and proceeds to translate each word into the appropriate stereotype, and with *Humorous Phases of Funny Faces*, which again had Blackton creating comic faces on blackboards.

As a pioneering producer, J. Stuart Blackton was required to serve as producer and director, as well as occasional cameraman and actor on the films released by Vitagraph through 1909. With his recreation of *The Battle of Manila Bay*, Blackton introduced a form of special effects to the cinema. The same film demonstrated the patriotic and propaganda value of the motion picture, which Blackton was later to exploit to its fullest with *The Battle Cry of Peace*, which he co-directed and conceived of in partnership with Theodore Roosevelt as a message for preparedness in the United States at a time when many were advocating U.S. noninvolvement in the First World War.

Albert E. Smith was the business head of Vitagraph, as well

as the company's first cameraman, while J. Stuart Blackton took responsibility for the production end of the company, which with an artistic genius such as Blackton meant an influx of considerable creativity and ingenuity. Thanks to Blackton, the films of the Vitagraph Company through the mid-teens were and are considered some of the best produced in the United States.

However, Blackton failed to keep abreast of changes in the industry, as indicated by the poor quality and equally poor reception of the independent features he directed after leaving Vitagraph in 1917. Yet he remained an innovator, as evidenced by *The Glorious Adventure*, shot in Prizma Color in England, an impressive if dull attempt at historical spectacle. Blackton continued to direct through 1926, but his films received little attention, and those that have survived appear unimpressive.

A social climber who amassed and lost great sums of money during his career, Blackton was also a fun-loving filmmaker, and nowhere is this more evident than in his last fling, a highly personal history of the cinema, *The Film Parade* (also known as *The March of the Movies*), which Blackton made in association with his former director William P.S. Earle in the early 1930's. Blackton blithely recreated his own early films and even donned blackface to impersonate Al Jolson in *The Jazz Singer*. *The Film Parade* is no masterpiece, but it is a fitting tribute to a major, and much underrated, figure in American film history.

—Anthony Slide

BLASETTI, Alessandro.

Italian. Born in Rome, 3 July 1900. Doctor of Law. Gave up law practice, 1924; founded *Il mondo dello schermo* (*Screen World*), 1926; joined Alessandro, Barbaro, and others in film-making cooperative Augustus; founded *Cinematografo* and *Lo spettacolo d'Italia*, 1928; directed and produced first film, *Sole*, 1929; director of first Italian film school at music academy S. Cecile, Rome. *Died in Rome, 2 February 1987.*

Films as Director:

1929   *Sole* (+ed, co-sc, pr)
1930   *Nerone* (+co-sc, co-ed)
1931   *Resurrectio* (+co-sc, co-ed); *Terra madre* (+co-sc, co-ed);
1932   *Palio* (+co-sc, co-ed); *La tavola dei poveri* (+co-sc, co-ed)
1933   *Il caso Haller* (+co-sc, co-ed)
1934   *1860* (*Gesuzza la sposa Garibaldina*) (+co-sc, co-ed); *L'impiegata di papa* (+co-sc, co-ed); *Vecchia guardia* (+co-sc, co-ed)
1935   *Aldebaran* (+co-sc, role)
1937   *La contessa di Parma* (+co-sc, co-ed)
1938   *Ettore Fieramosca* (+co-sc, co-ed); *Caccia alla volpe* (+co-sc, co-ed)
1939   *Retroscena* (+co-sc, co-ed)
1940   *Un'avventura di Salvator Rosa* (+co-sc, co-ed); *Napoli e le terre d'oltremare* (unfinished) (+co-sc, co-ed)
1941   *La corona di ferro* (*The Iron Crown*) (+co-sc); *La cena delle beffe* (+co-sc)
1942   *Quattro passi fra le nuvole* (*Four Steps in the Clouds*) (+co-sc, role)
1943   *Nessuno torna indietro* (+co-sc)
1946   *Un giorno nella vita* (+co-sc); *La gemma orientale di Papi* (+co-sc); *Il Duomo di Milano* (+co-sc); *Castel Sant'Angelo* (+co-sc)

1948   *Fabiola* (+co-sc)
1950   *Prima comunione* (*Father's Dilemma*) (+co-sc); *Ippodromi all'Alba* (+co-sc)
1952   *Altri tempi* (*Times Gone By*) (+co-sc); *La fiammata* (+co-sc)
1953   *Tempi nostri* (*Anatomy of Love*) (+co-sc)
1954   *Peccato che sia una canaglia* (*Too Bad She's Bad*) (+co-sc)
1955   *La fortuna di essere donna* (*Lucky to Be a Woman*) (+co-sc)
1957   *Amore e chiacchiere* (+co-sc)
1959   *Europa di notte* (*European Nights*)
1961   *Io amo, tu ami* (*I Love—You Love*) (+co-sc)
1963   "La lepre e la tartaruga" episode of *Le quattro verita* (+co-sc)
1964   *Liolà*
1966   *Io, io, io . . . e gli altri* (+co-sc)
1967   *La ragazza del bersagliere* (+co-sc)
1969   *Simon Bolivar* (+co-sc)
1982   *Venezia, una Mostra per il cinema* (documentary) (+co-sc)

Publications:

By BLASETTI: books—

Come nasce un film, Rome, 1932.
Scritti sul cinema, edited by Adriano Apra, Venice, 1982.
Il cinema che ho vissuto, Bari, 1982.
Sole, with Alberto Boero and Aldo Vergano, Rome, 1985.

By BLASETTI: articles—

"Alessandro Blasetti/ogni volta da capo," interview in *Bianco e nero* (Rome), September/December 1975.
"La storia dei miei stivali de Sole per tufta la mia vita," in *Cinema Nuovo* (Bari), May–June 1978.
"Andai a Mosca per incontrare Nikolaj Ekk," in *Cinema Nuovo* (Bari), August 1980.
"Quel folle amore dinanzi allo specchio," in *Cinema Nuovo* (Bari), December 1980.
"Sur le seuil de ma vie," in *Positif* (Paris), March 1981.
Interview and article with F. Cuel and B. Villien, in *Cinématographe* (Paris), November 1981.

On BLASETTI: books—

Gori, Gianfranco, *Alessandro Blasetti*, Florence, 1984.
Salizzato, Claver, and Vito Zagarrio, editors, *La corona di ferro: Un modo di produzione italiano*, Rome, 1985.

On BLASETTI: articles—

"The Big Screen," in *Sight and Sound* (London), Spring 1955.
Jeancolas, J.-P., "Ni chemises noires, ni telephones blancs: cinema italien 1923–1943 (Pesaro)," and P. Mereghetti, "Blasetti, le fascisme et la virilité . . . ," in *Positif* (Paris), October 1976.
"Blasetti Issue" of *Bianco e Nero* (Rome), April–June 1985.
Stuart, J., obituary, in *Variety* (New York), 4 February 1987.
Obituary in *Film Français* (Paris), 13 February 1987.

*   *   *

After a period as both lawyer and film critic, Alessandro Blasetti collaborated with several other young film enthusiasts in forming a film-making co-operative called Augustus. His first film as director, *Sole*, exists only as a fragment, but it contains powerful imagery clearly influenced by the Soviet school of the 1920's. His first really important work was *La Tavola dei poveri*, a remarkable precursor of later "neo-realism" in that its plot (a group of aristocrats banding together to feed the poor) bears a close resemblance to De Sica's *Miracle in Milan*. Blasetti's treatment has much formal ingenuity as he uses a very mobile camera style somewhat akin to Max Ophüls' work at this time. Another film in a "neo-realist" vein was *1860*, about Garibaldi's conquest of Sicily. This was contrasted with the controversial *Vecchia Guardia* which, although seemingly siding with the Blackshirts, told its family story with a good deal of genuine warmth and observation.

After this, Blasetti embarked on a series of lavish costume dramas which established him as a technically fluent dramatic director: *La Contessa di Parma, Ettore Fieramosca* and

Alessandro Blasetti

particularly *Un Avventura di Salvator Rosa* and *La Corona di ferro*. In these films, Blasetti created a kind of swashbuckling historical/fantasy world with elaborate settings and costumes, well-staged action scenes and a sense of romance not without its tongue-in-cheek elements. His dashing heroes and hapless heroines belong to a long tradition of romantic adventures (both European and American) which can be traced right up to Indiana Jones and his companions.

Alongside these spectaculars, Blasetti made several more intimate local comedies featuring working-class characters and the trappings of "neo-realism." Two of the best were *Four Steps in the Clouds* and *Prima Comunione*, which received much much wider world distribution than his more substantial dramas and historical films.

If Mario Camerini was the leading director of comedies and light social dramas in the Italian 1930's and 1940's, Blasetti must be regarded as the leading exponent of period pieces and more politically motivated dramas. It is curious that after their many successes in this period, the post-war work of both directors saw a serious falling-off. Blasetti made a few more rather empty spectacles like *Fabiola* and a series of raucous comedies and episode films (in colour and 'Scope) often starring Sophia Loren which, despite some lively moments, were distressingly similar to the commercial fodder being turned out by many other directors. His career virtually ended with a large-scale South American epic *Simon Bolivar*, which was hardly shown anywhere.

All in all, it is a curiously uneven and ambiguous career, with its flirtation with Fascism in the 1930's and then a period when he turned his back on the contemporary scene in favour of period escapism. He will probably be best remembered for these vigorous, sometimes outrageous, historical romps which still give much pleasure today.

Of his several acting appearances, the most notable is his Cinecittá film director in Visconti's *Bellissima* with Anna Magnani.

—John Gillett.

BLIER, Bertrand.

French. Born in Paris, 11 March 1939. Assistant director on films of Lautner, Christian-Jaque, Delannoy, and others, 1960–63; directed first feature, *Hitler? Connais pas!*, 1963. Recipient: Oscar for Best Foreign Language Film, for *Preparez vos mouchoirs*, 1978.

Films as Director:

1963 *Hitler? Connais pas!* (+sc)
1966 *La Grimace* (+sc)
1967 *Si j'etais un espion* (*Breakdown, If I Were a Spy*) (+co-sc)
1973 *Les Valseuses* (*Going Places*) (+sc)
1975 *Calmos* (*Femmes Fatales*) (+co-sc)
1977 *Preparez vos mouchoirs* (*Get Out Your Handkerchiefs*) (+sc)
1979 *Buffet froid* (+sc)
1981 *Beau-père* (+sc)
1982 *La Femme de mon pote* (*My Best Friend's Girl*)
1984 *Notre Histoire* (*Our Story*)
1986 *Tenue de soirée* (*Menage*)
1989 *Trop belle pour toi*

Other Films:

1970 *Laisse aller, c'est une valse* (Lautner) (sc)

Publications:

By BLIER: books—

Les Valseuses, Paris, 1972.
Beau-père, Paris, 1980.

By BLIER: articles—

"*Les Valseuses* de Bertrand Blier: le nuvité du cinéma français," interview with R. Gay, in *Cinéma Québec* (Montreal), v. 3., no. 8, 1974.
Interview with B. Villien and P. Carcassonne, in *Cinématographe* (Paris), January 1980.
"*Beau-père*: Entretien avec Bertrand Blier," with C. de Béchade and H. Descrues, in *Image et Son* (Paris), September 1981.
"A la recherche de l'histoire," an interview with Marc Chevrie and D. Dubroux, in *Cahiers du Cinéma* (Paris), May 1985.
Interview with Sheila Johnston, in *Stills* (London), May 1985.
Interview with P. Le Guay, in *Cinématographe* (Paris), May 1986.
Interview in *Première* (Paris), May 1989.
Interview in *Time Out* (London), 14 February 1990.

On BLIER: articles—

Buckley, T., "The Truth About Making a Movie in Singapore," in *New York Times*, 2 February 1979.
Alion, Yves, "*Buffet froid* Issue" of *Avant-Scène du Cinéma* (Paris), 15 March 1980.
"Blier Section," in *Cinéma* (Paris), July–August 1981.
Rickey, C., "Lolita Française," in *American Film* (Washington D.C.), October 1981.
Toubiana, Serge, and Pierre Bonitzer, "Le cauchemar d'Antoine. Les mots et les choses," in *Cahiers du Cinéma* (Paris), April 1986.
Blier Section of *Revue du Cinéma* (Paris), June 1986.
Yakir, Dan, "Manhandler," in *Film Comment* (New York), September–October 1986.

*   *   *

Bertrand Blier directs erotic buddy movies featuring men who are exasperated by the opposite sex, who perceive of themselves as macho but are incapable of satisfying the women in their lives. Really, his heroes are terrified of feminism, of the "new woman" who demands her right to experience and enjoy orgasm. But Blier's females are in no way villainesses. They are just elusive—and so alienated that they can only find fulfillment from oddballs, or young boys.

Going Places (*Les Valseuses*, which in French is slang for testicles), based on Blier's best-selling novel, was a box office smash in France. Gérard Depardieu and Patrick Dewaere both achieved stardom as a couple of outsiders, adult juvenile delinquents; chronicled are their sexual and sadistic adventures as they travel across France. They are both unable to bring to orgasm a young beautician (played by Miou-Miou) they pick up and take on as a sexual partner. They then attempt to please an older woman (Jeanne Moreau), who has just spent ten years in prison. After a night together, she commits suicide by shooting herself in the vagina. Eventually, Miou-Miou is satisfied by a crazy, physically unattractive ex-con.

In *Femmes Fatales*, middle-aged Jean-Pierre Marielle and Jean Rochefort, one a gynaecologist and the other a pimp, decide to abandon wives and mistresses for the countryside, but end up pursued by an army of women intent on enslaving them as studs. Again, men cannot escape women's sexual demands: here, the latter come after the former with tanks and guns. And, in *Get Out Your Handkerchiefs*, driving instructor Depardieu is so anxious to please bored, depressed wife Carol Laure that he finds her a lover, a total stranger, playground instructor Dewaere. Both men feel that she will be happy if she can only have a child. She in her own way does this, finding a substitute for them in a precocious young boy barely into his

Bertrand Blier directing Gérard Depardieu and Carole Bouquet in *Trop belle pour toi*

teens. *Handkerchiefs* is a prelude of sorts to *Beau-Père*, which features only one male lead (as does the later *Trop Belle Pour Toi*, in which Depardieu is at the centre of a love triangle). Here, a struggling pianist, played by Dewaere, is seduced by the refreshingly self-confident 14-year-old daughter of his recently deceased lover. The teenager's feelings are deep and pure, while the "adult" is immature, too self-conscious and self-absorbed to accept her.

In Blier's films, men do not understand women. "Maybe one day I'll do *Camille*," the filmmaker says. "But I won't do *An Unmarried Woman*, because I don't feel I have the right to do it. I don't know what goes on in a woman's head. I believe I know what certain men think, but not women." As a result, in Blier's movies, the sexual barriers between the sexes seem irrevocable. His men are more at ease talking among themselves about women than with actually being with wives or lovers; their relationships with each other are for them more meaningful than their contacts with the opposite sex. There are alternatives to women: become homosexual (the characters in *Going Places* sleep with each other when they are lonely or celibate which, in *Femmes Fatales*, they are denied).

Another Blier film, *Buffet Froid*, is also about male bonding: Depardieu, as a psychopathic killer, becomes involved with a mass murderer (Jean Carmet) and a homicidal cop (the director's father, the distinguished character actor Bernard Blier). However, *Buffet Froid* is mostly a study of alienation in urban society, and the acceptance of random, irrational violence. It is thematically more closely related to, for example, Jules Feiff-er's *Little Murders* than *Going Places* or *Get Out Your Handkerchiefs*.

Bertrand Blier best explains what he attempts to communicate in his films: "The relations between men and women are constantly evolving and it's interesting to show people leading the lifestyle of tomorrow."

—Rob Edelman

BLOM, August.

Danish. Born 26 December 1869. Married 1) Agnete von Prangen, 1908; 2) Johanne Fritz-Petersen. Actor at Folketeatret, Copenhagen, from 1893; actor at Nordisk Films Kompagni, 1908; director for Nordisk Films Kompagni, 1910–24; manager of Copenhagen cinema, 1934–47. *Died 10 January 1947.*

Films as Director:

1910   *Livets Storme* (*Storms of Life*); *Robinson Crusoe*; *Den hvide Slavehandel I* (*The White Slave*); *Spinonen fra Tokio* (*The Red Light*); *Den skaebnesvangre Opfindelse* (*Dr. Jekyll and*

Mr. Hyde); *Jagten paa Gentlemanrøveren*; *Singaree*;
Hamlet; *Spøgelset i Gravkaelderen* (*The Ghost of the
Variety*); *Den dø des Halsbaand* (*The Necklace of the Dead*)

1911   *Den hvide Slavehandel II* (*In the Hands of Impostors*); *Den
farlige Alder* (*The Price of Beauty*); *Ved Faengslets Port*
(*Temptations of a Great City*); *Vildledt Elskov* (*The Bank
Book*); *Potifars Hustru* (*The Victim of a Character*);
Politimesteren (*Convicts No. 10 and No. 13*); *Den blaa
Natviol* (*The Daughter of the Fortune Teller*); *Damernes
Blad* (*The Ladies' Journal*); *Balletdanserinden* (*The Ballet
Dancer*); *Jernbanens Datter* (*The Daughter of the Railway*);
Den naadige Frøken (*Lady Mary's Love*); *En Lektion*
(*Aviatikeren og Journalistens Hustru, The Aviator and the
Journalist's Wife*); *Ekspeditricen* (*Ungdom og Letsind, In
the Prime of Life*); *Desdemona*; *En Opfinders Skaebne* (*The
Aeroplane Inventor*); *Fader og Søn* (*Onkel og Nevø, A
Poisonous Love*); *Dødsdrømmen* (*A Dream of Death*); *Min
første Monocle* (*Herr Storms første Monocle, His First
Monocle*); *Fru Potifar* (*Den skaebnesvangre Løgn, A Fatal
Lie*); *Kaerlighedens Styrke* (*The Power of Love*);
Mormonens Offer (*The Victims of the Mormon*); *Haevnet*
(*Det bødes der for, Vengeance*); *Det mørke Punkt* (*Mamie
Rose, Annie Bell*); *Eventyr paa Fodrejsen* (*Den udbrudte
Slave, The Two Convicts*); *Ungdommens Ret* (*The Right of
Youth*); *Tropisk Kaerlighed* (*Love in the Tropics*);
Vampyrdanserinden (*The Vampire Dancer*); *Det gamle
Købmandshus* (*Midsommer, Midsummer-Time*); *Dødens
Brud* (*A Bride of Death*) *Gadeoriginalen*

1912   *Brillantstjernen* (*For Her Sister's Sake*); *Guvernørens Datter*
(*The Governor's Daughter*); *Kaerlighed gør blind* (*Love is
Blind*); *Dyrekøbt Venskab* (*Dearly Purchased Friendship*);
Den sorte Kansler (*The Black Chancellor*); *Hjertets Guld* (*Et
Hjerte af Guld, Faithful Unto Death*); *Direktørens Datter*
(*Caught in His Own Trap*); *Det første Honorar* (*Hans første
Honorar, His First Patient*); *Elskovs Magt* (*Gøgleren, Man's
Great Adversary*); *Historien om en Moder* (*En Moders
Kaerlighed, The Life of a Mother*); *De tre Kammerater* (*The
Three Comrades*); *Operabranden* (*Bedstemoders Vuggevise,
The Song Which Grandmother Sang*); *Den første Kaerlighed*
(*Her First Love Affair*); *Hjerternes Kamp* (*A High Stake*);
Hans vanskeligste Rolle (*His Most Difficult Part*); *Den tredie
Magt* (*The Secret Treaty*); *Fodselsdagsgaven* (*Gaven, The
Birthday Gift*); *En Hofintrige* (*A Court Intrigue*); *Den sande
Kaerlighed* (*Flugten gennem Skyerne, The Fugitives*); *Hvem
var Forbryderen?* (*Samvittighedsnag, At the Eleventh Hour*);
Alt paa ét Kort (*Guldmønten, Gold from the Gutter*)

1913   *Pressens Magt* (*Et Bankrun, A Harvest of Tears*); *Troløs*
(*Gøglerblod, Artists*); *Højt Spil* (*Et forfejlet Spring, A Dash
for Liberty*); *Naar Fruen gaar paa Eventyr*
(*Pompadourtasken, The Lost Bag*); *Bristet Lykke* (*A
Paradise Lost*); *Fem Kopier* (*Five Copies*); *Atlantis*; *En
farlig Forbryder* (*Knivstikkeren, A Modern Jack the
Ripper*); *Af Elskovs Naade* (*Acquitted*); *Elskovsleg* (*Love's
Devotee*); *Vasens Hemmelighed* (*Den kinesiske Vase, The
Chinese Vase*)

1914   *Sønnen* (*Her Son*); *Den store Middag* (*The Guestless Dinner
Party*); *Tugthusfange No.97* (*En Gaest fra en anden Verden,
The Outcast's Return*); *Faedrenes Synd* (*Nemesis*);
Aegteskab og Pigesjov (*Mr. King paa Eventyr, A Surprise
Packet*); *Aeventyrersken* (*Exiled*); *En ensom Kvinde* (*Hvem
er han?, The Doctor's Legacy*); *Revolutionsbryllup* (*A
Revolution Marriage*); *Et Laereaar* (*The Reformation*); *Den
lille Chauffør* (*The Little Chauffeur*); *Den største Kaerlighed*
(*En Moders Kaerlighed, "Escaped the Law, But . . ."*); *Pro
Patria*; *Kaerligheds-Vaeddemaalet* (*The Wager*)

1915   *Du skal elske din Naeste* (*For de Andre, The Samaritan*);
Giftpilen (*The Poisonous Arrow*); *Hjertestorme*;
Kaerligheds Laengsel (*Den Pukkelryggede, The Cripple
Girl*); *Lotteriseddel No.22152* (*Den blinde Skaebne, Blind
Fate*); *Rovedderkoppen* (*Den røde Enke*); *Syndens Datter*
(*Den, der sejrer, Nobody's Daughter*); *Syndig Kaerlighed*
(*Eremitten, The Hermit*); *Truet Lykke* (*Et Skud i Mørket,
The Evil Genius*); *Verdens Undergang* (*Flammesvaerdet,
The Flaming Sword*); *For sit Lands Aere* (*Hendes Aere, For
His Country's Honor*)

1916   *Den mystiske Selskabsdame* (*The Mysterious Companion*);
Gillekop
1918   *Grevindens Aere* (*Kniplinger, Lace*); *Maharadjaens
Yndlingshustru II*, (*The Favorite Wife of the Maharaja II, A
Daughter of Brahma*); *Via Crucis*
1919   *Prometheus I-II* (*Bonds of Hate*)
1920   *Hans gode Genius* (*Mod Stjernerne, His Guardian Angel*);
Praesten i Vejlby (*The Vicar of Vejlby, The Land of Fate*)
1924   *Det store Hjerte* (*Lights from Circus Life, Side Lights of the
Sawdust Ring*); *Den store Magt*
1925   *Hendes Naade*; *Dragonen*

Other Films:

1909   *Droske 519* (*Cab No. 519*) (role); *En Kvinde af Folket* (*A
Woman of the People*) (role): *Dr. Nicola I* (*Den skjulte Skat*)
(role); *Dr. Nicola* (*Hvorledes Dr. Nicola erhvervede den
kinesiske Stok, How Dr. Nicola Procured the Chinese Cane*)
(role); *Barnet* (*A Child's Love*) (role); *Madame Sans Gène*
(role); *Faderen* (*A Father's Grief*) (role); *Museumsmysteriet*
(*The Mystery of the Museum*) (role); *Dr. Nicola III* (*Dr.
Nicola in Tibet*) (role); *Et Budskab til Napoleon paa Elba* (*A
Message to Napoleon*) (role); *Revolutionsbryllup* (*A
Wedding During the French Revolution*) (role)
1910   *Sølvdaasen med Juvelerne* (*The Jewel Case*) (role); *Tyven* (*A
Society Sinner*) (role); *To Tjenestepiger* (*The Rival Servants*)
(role); *Kean* (role); *Medbejlerens Haevn* (*Caught in His
Own Net*) (role); *Forraederen* (*A Traitor to His Country*)
(role)

*   *   *

When August Blom came to Nordisk Films Kompagni in 1909
it was the major film production company in Denmark, having
been founded in 1906 by Ole Olsen. Nordisk dominated the so-
called "belle époque" (from 1910 to 1914) in Danish filmmaking, and August Blom was the leading force in this period.
From 1911 Blom was head of production, besides being a
director. He was in charge of scripts and actors, and he
launched the career of Valdemar Psilander, who showed a
natural talent for understated and realistic film acting and
became an immensely popular star in Denmark and Europe
until his premature death in 1917. In 1911 Blom directed 16 of
Psilander's 17 films.

In 1910 Blom made *Ved Faengslets Port* (released 1911)
which, with Urban Gad's *Afgrunden*, introduced the erotic
melodrama, a genre refined by Blom in the following years.
Ved Faengslets Port is typical of the kind of films which made
Nordisk famous all over the world. The story is about a young
aristocrat who is in the grip of a moneylender and at the same
time loves the moneylender's daughter. Although Blom tried
to introduce contemporary themes in his films, the stories were
always the weak part of his and most other Danish films in this
period. The compensation for the banal magazine stories was
found in the way Blom told these stories. His films are often
about contrasts, social and sexual. The films are passionate and
reveal the many faces of love with great imagination. As a
former actor Blom put great weight on the acting and he had a
fine feeling for the direction of actresses. His portraits of
women are quite often subtle and daring.

Blom put immense care into the making of his films. The sets
were used in a dramatic way, playing an important role in the
story as a means of characterizing the people. His narrative
technique made use of cross-cutting and, assisted by his favourite cameraman Johan Ankerstjerne, he was an innovator in
lighting. One of his stylistic devices, used to great and surprising effect, was mirrors as a means of expanding the dramatic content of a scene.

Blom must be considered as one of the important pioneers in
the early silent film. It was quite natural that Blom was com-

August Blom: *Atlantis*

missioned to direct the greatest and most ambitious film of the period, a film which introduced a literary era in the Danish film. This was *Atlantis*, based on Gerhart Hauptmann's novel of 1912. It was an attempt to transpose a modern novel with a complicated plot and interesting characters to film. Blom's direction is astonishingly mature, confident and imaginative, and in many ways *Atlantis* is ahead of its time. Johan Ankerstjerne's camera work points forward to the expressionist-inspired German films. Another fine film by Blom was *Verdens Undergang*.

Bloom made 78 of his approximately 100 films in the years 1910–14, but he was a company man, and he stayed with Nordisk in the years of decline. He left filming in 1924. During the golden age of the Danish cinema Blom was the great stylist, a gifted and civilized director.

—Ib Monty

BOETTICHER, Budd.

American. Born Oscar Boetticher, Jr., in Chicago, 29 July 1916. Educated at Ohio State University. Football star at Ohio State, early 1930's; after recuperating from football injury in Mexico, became professional matador, 1940; technical advisor on Mamoulian's *Blood and Sand*, 1940; messenger boy at Hal Roach studios, 1941–1943; assistant to William Seiter, George Stevens, and Charles Vidor, 1943–44; military service, made propaganda films, 1946–47; made cycle of Westerns for Ranown production company, 1956–60; left Hollywood to make documentary on matador Carlos Arruza, 1960; after many setbacks, returned to Hollywood, 1967.

Films as Director:

(as Oscar Boetticher)

1944   *One Mysterious Night*; *The Missing Juror*; *Youth on Trial*
1945   *A Guy, a Gal and a Pal*; *Escape on the Fog*
1946   *The Fleet That Came to Stay* (and other propaganda films)
1948   *Assigned to Danger*; *Behind Locked Doors*
1949   *Black Midnight*; *Wolf Hunters*
1950   *Killer Shark*

(as Budd Boetticher)

1951   *The Bullfighter and the Lady* (+co-story); *The Sword of D'Artagnan*; *The Cimarron Kid*
1952   *Bronco Buster*; *Red Ball Express*; *Horizons West*
1953   *City Beneath the Sea*; *Seminole*; *The Man from the Alamo*; *Wings of the Hawk*; *East of Sumatra*
1955   *The Magnificent Matador* (+story); *The Killer is Loose*

1956 *Seven Men from Now*
1957 *The Tall T*; *Decision at Sundown*
1958 *Buchanan Rides Alone*
1959 *Ride Lonesome* (+pr); *Westbound*
1960 *Comanche Station*; *The Rise and Fall of Legs Diamond*
1971 *Arruza* (+pr, co-sc; production completed 1968); *A Time for Dying* (+sc; production completed 1969)

Other Films:

1970 *Two Mules for Sister Sara* (Siegel) (sc)

Publications:

By BOETTICHER: book—
When in Disgrace, New York, 1971.

By BOETTICHER: articles—

Interview with Bertrand Tavernier, in *Cahiers du Cinéma* (Paris), July 1964.
Interviews with Michel Ciment and others, in *Positif* (Paris), November 1969.
Interview, in *The Director's Event* by Eric Sherman and Martin Rubin, New York, 1970.
Interview with O. Assayas and B. Krohn, in *Cahiers du Cinéma* (Paris), April 1982.
"The Bullfighter and the Director," in *American Film* (Washington, D.C.), October 1985.

On BOETTICHER: books—

Kitses, Jim, *Horizons West*, Bloomington, Indiana, 1969.

Kitses, Jim, editor, *Budd Boetticher: The Western*, London, 1969.
Buscombe, Ed, editor, *BFI Companion to the Western*, London, 1988.
Budd Boetticher, Madrid (La Filmoteca Espanola), n.d.

On BOETTICHER: articles—

"The Director and the Public: a Symposium," in *Film Culture* (New York), March/April 1955.
"Un Western exemplaire," in *Qu'est-ce que le cinéma* by André Bazin, Paris, 1961.
Sarris, Andrew, "Esoterica," in *Film Culture* (New York), Spring 1963.
Schmidt, Eckhart, "B.B. wie Budd Boetticher," in *Film* (Germany), October/November 1964.
Russell, Lee, "Budd Boetticher," in *New Left Review*, July/August 1965.
Coonradt, P., "Boetticher Returns," in *Cinema* (Los Angeles), December 1968.
Wicking, Christopher, "Budd Boetticher," in *Screen* (London), July/October 1969.
Sequin, Louis, "Deu Westerns d'Oscar 'Budd' Boetticher," in *Positif* (Paris), November 1969.
Schrader, Paul, "Budd Boetticher: A Case Study in Criticism," in *Cinema* (Los Angeles), Fall 1970.
Millar, Gavin, "Boetticher's Westerns," in *Listener* (London), 6 October 1983.
Hollywood Reporter, 2 July 1984.
Krohn, B., "Le retour de Budd Boetticher," in *Cahiers du Cinéma* (Paris), November 1987.

*   *   *

Budd Boetticher: *The Tall T*

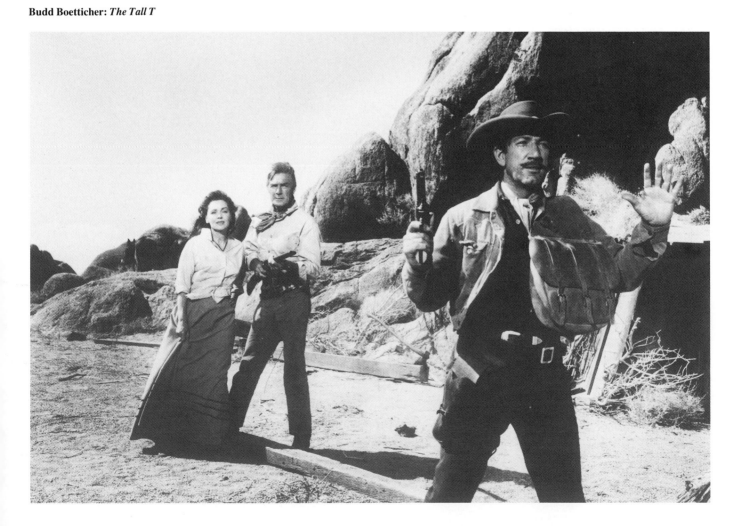

Budd Boetticher will be remembered as a director of Westerns, although his bullfight films have their fervent admirers, as does his *Scarface*-variant, *The Rise and Fall of Legs Diamond*, notwithstanding its chilly and distanced title performance. Since Boetticher's Westerns are so variable in quality, it's tempting to overcredit Burt Kennedy, the scriptwriter for all of the finest. But Kennedy's own efforts as director (*Return of the Seven, Hannie Caulder, The War Wagon*, etc.) are tediously paced dramas or failed comedies. Clearly the Boetticher/Kennedy team clicked to make Westerns significantly superior to what either could create on their own. Indeed, *The Tall T, Seven Men from Now*, and (on a slightly lower level) *Ride Lonesome* look now like the finest work in the genre during the 1950's, less pretentious and more tightly controlled than even that of Anthony Mann or John Ford.

Jim Kitses's still-essential *Horizons West* rightly locates Boetticher's significant Westerns in the "Ranown" cycle (a production company name taken from producer Harry Joe Brown and his partner Randolph Scott). But the non-Kennedy entries in the cycle have, despite Scott's key presence, only passing interest. One might have attributed the black comedy in the series to Kennedy without the burlesque *Buchanan Rides Alone*, which wanders into an episodic narrative opposite to the taut, unified action of the others; *Decision at Sundown* is notable only for its remarkably bitter finale and a morally pointless showdown, as if it were a cynic's answer to *High Noon*.

The Tall T's narrative is typical of the best Boetticher/Kennedy: it moves from a humanizing comedy so rare in the genre into a harsh and convincing savagery. Boetticher's villains are relentlessly cruel, yet morally shaded. In *The Tall T*, he toys with the redeemable qualities of Richard Boone, while deftly characterizing the other two (Henry Silva asks, "I've never shot me a woman, have I Frank?") Equally memorable are Lee Marvin (in *Seven Men from Now*) and Lee Van Cleef (*Ride Lonesome*).

Randolph Scott is the third essential collaborator in the cycle. He's generally presented by Boetticher as a loner not by principle or habit but by an obscure terror in his past (often a wife murdered). Thus he's not the asexual cowpoke so much as one who, temporarily at least, is beyond fears and yearnings. There's a Pinteresque sexual confrontation in *Seven Men from Now* among Scott, a pioneer couple, and an insinuating Lee Marvin when the four are confined in a wagon. And indeed the typical Boetticher landscape—smooth, rounded, and yet impassible boulders—match Scott's deceptively complex character as much as the majestic Monument Valley towers match Wayne in Ford's Westerns, or the harsh cliffs match James Stewart's in Mann's.

Clearly the Westerns of the sixties and seventies owe more to Boetticher than Ford. Even such very minor works as *Horizons West, The Wings of the Hawk*, and *The Man from the Alamo* have the tensions of Spaghetti Westerns (without the iciness), as well as the Peckinpah fantasy of American expertise combining with Mexican peasant vitality. If Peckinpah and Leone are the masters of the post-"classic" Western, then it's worth noting how *The Wings of the Hawk* anticipates *The Wild Bunch*, and how *Once Upon a Time in the West* opens like *Seven Men from Now* and closes like *Ride Lonesome*. Boetticher's films are the final great achievement of the traditional Western, before the explosion of the genre.

—Scott Simmon

BOGDANOVICH, Peter.

American. Born in Kingston, New York, 30 July 1939. Educated at Collegiate School, New York; studied acting at Stella Adler's Theatre Studio. Married 1) Polly Platt, 1962 (divorced 1970), two daughters; 2) Louise Stratten (Hoogstraten), 1988, sister of murdered former lover Dorothy Stratten. Actor in American and New York Shakespeare Festivals, 1956–58; first play as producer, *The Big Knife*, off-Broadway, 1959; film critic for *Esquire, New York Times*, and *Cahiers du Cinéma*, among others, from 1961; moved to Hollywood, 1964; 2nd unit director on *The Wild Angels* (Corman), 1966; directed first film, *Targets* (produced by Corman), 1968; Paramount formed and financed The Directors Company, independent unit partnership of Bogdanovich, Francis Ford Coppola and William Friedkin, 1973; formed Copa de Oro production company, 1975; owner, Crescent Moon productions, Inc., from 1986. Recipient: New York Film Critics Award and British Academy Award for Best Screenplay, for *The Last Picture Show*, 1971; Writer's Guild of America Award for Best Screenplay, for *What's Up, Doc?*, 1972; Critics Prize, Venice Festival, for *Saint Jack*, 1979. Address: c/o William Peiffer, 2040 Avenue of the Stars, Century City, CA 90067, U.S.A.

Films as Director:

1967   *Targets* (+co-sc, pr, ed, role as Sammy Michaels)
1971   *Directed by John Ford* (+sc); **The Last Picture Show** (+co-sc)
1972   *What's Up, Doc?* (+pr, co-sc)
1973   *Paper Moon* (+pr)
1974   *Daisy Miller* (+pr)
1975   *At Long Last Love* (+pr, sc, co-songwriter: "Poor Young Millionaire")
1976   *Nickelodeon* (+co-sc)
1979   *Saint Jack* (+co-sc, role as Eddie Schuman)
1983   *They All Laughed* (+sc)
1984   *Mask*
1987   *Illegally Yours*
1990   *Texasville*

Other Films:

1966   *The Wild Angels* (Corman) (co-sc, 2nd unit d, all uncredited, +bit role, voice); *Voyage to the Planet of the Prehistoric Women (Gill-Women of Venus)* (from Russian science fiction film by Pavel Klushantsev *Planeta Burg (Cosmonauts on Venus, Storm Clouds of Venus)* dubbed and re-edited for American Int'l Pictures) (supervising ed, na, d of add'l scenes under pseudonym Derek Thomas and/or Peter Stewart)
1967   *The Trip* (Corman) (role)
1969   *Lion's Love* (Varda) (guest star role)
1970   *The Other Side of the Wind* (Welles, unreleased) (role as Higgam
1973   *F for Fake* (Welles) (voice-over)
1975   *Diaries, Notes & Sketches—Volume 1, reels 1–6: Lost Lost Lost* (Jonas Mekas) (appearance in reel 3); *The Gentleman Tramp* (Patterson) ("special thanks" credit for supervising scenes shot at Charles Chaplin's home in Switzerland)
1978   *Opening Night* (Cassavetes) (guest star role)

Publications:

By BOGDANOVICH: books—

The Cinema of Orson Welles, New York, 1961.
The Cinema of Howard Hawks, New York, 1962.
The Cinema of Alfred Hitchcock, New York, 1963.
Fritz Lang in America, New York, 1967; revised edition, 1981.
John Ford, Berkeley, California, 1968; revised edition, 1978.

Peter Bogdanovich

Alan Dwan: The Last Pioneer, New York, 1971; rev. ed. 1981.
Pieces of Time, New York, 1973; revised, as *Pieces of Time: Peter Bogdanovich on The Movies 1961–85*, New York, 1985.
The Killing of the Unicorn: Dorothy Stratten (1960–1980), New York, 1984.

By BOGDANOVICH: articles—

"Bogie in Excelsis," in *Esquire* (New York), September 1964.
"Go-Go and Hurry: It's Later Than You Think," in *Esquire* (New York), February 1965.
"Th'Respawnsibility of Bein' J . . . Jimmy Stewart. Gosh!," in *Esquire* (New York), July 1966.
"Godard in Hollywood," in *Take One* (Montreal), June 1968.
"*Targets*," in *Sight and Sound* (London), Winter 1969/70.
"Inter/View with Peter Bogdanovich," with G. O'Brien and R. Feiden, in *Inter/View* (New York), March 1972.
"Without a Dinosaur," interview with Gordon Gow, in *Films and Filming* (London), June 1972.
"Peter Bogdanovich on *Paper Moon*," interview with D. Lyons and others, in *Interview* (New York), July 1973.
"Cybill and Peter," interview with Andy Warhol and others, in *Inter/View* (New York), June 1974.
"Polly Platt: Sets the Style," interview with M. McAndrew, in *Cinema* (Beverly Hills), no.35, 1976.
"Dialogue on Film: Peter Bogdanovich," in *American Film* (Washington, D.C.), December/January 1978/79.
Interview with O. Assayas and B. Krohn, in *Cahiers du Cinéma* (Paris), April 1982.
Interview with Thomas J. Harris, in *Literature/Film Quarterly* (Salisbury, Maryland), vol. 16, no. 4, 1988.

On BOGDANOVICH: books—

Sherman, Eric, and Martin Rubin, *The Director's Event*, New York, 1970.
Giacci, V., *Bogdanovich*, Florence, 1975.
Tuska, Jon, editor, *Close-Up: The Contemporary Director*, Metuchen, New Jersey, 1981.

On BOGDANOVICH: articles—

Houston, Penelope, "Hitchcockery," in *Sight and Sound* (London), Autumn 1968.
Patterson, R., "*Directed by John Ford*: Producing a Compilation Documentary," in *American Cinematographer* (Los Angeles), November 1971.
Rainer, P., "Bogged Down: a Twitch in the Auteur Niche," in *Film Critic* (New York), September/October 1972.
Kasindorf, Martin, "Peter Bogdanovich," in *Action* (Los Angeles), July/August 1973.
Starr, Cecile, "Peter Bogdanovich Remembered and Assessed," in *Filmmakers Newsletter* (Ward Hill, Massachusetts), September 1973.
Dawson, Jan, "The Continental Divide," in *Sight and Sound* (London), Winter 1973/74.
Fieschi, J., "Dossier: Hollywood 79: Peter Bogdanovich," in *Cinématographe* (Paris), March 1979.
Buckley, T., "How Bogdanovich Learned to Think Small Again," in *New York Times*, 20 April 1979.
Le Fanu, Mark, "Peter Bogdanovich," in *Films and Filming* (London), August 1984.
de Waal, F., "In memoriam Peter Bogdanovich," in *Skoop* (Amsterdam), May 1985.

"Dialogue on Film: Peter Bogdanovich," in *American Film* (Washington, D.C.), June 1986.

*   *   *

Of all trades ancillary to the cinema, few offer worse preparation for a directing career than criticism. Bogdanovich's background as Hollywood historian and profiler of its legendary figures inevitably invited comparisons between his movies and those of directors like Ford, Hawks and Dwan whom he had deified. That he should have occasionally created films which deserve such comparison argues for his skill and resilience.

He first attracted attention with *Targets*, a flashy exercise with an ailing Karloff playing straight man to Bogdanovich's filmbuff director and a psychotic sniper menacing the audience at a drive-in cinema. The documentary *Directed by John Ford* likewise exploited Hollywood history, but with uncertain scholarship and even less certain taste. Yet in his first major fiction feature, based on Larry McMurtry's rural nocturne *The Last Picture Show*, Bogdanovich created a precise and moving chronicle of small-town values eroded by selfishness and disloyalty. He also showed a flair for casting in his choice of underrated veterans and fresh newcomers. Ben Johnson, Cloris Leachman and Ellen Burstyn earned new respect, while Timothy Bottoms, Jeff Bridges and Cybill Shepherd received boosts to nascent careers—though Shepherd, via her relationship with the director, was to prove a troublesome protégée.

What's Up Doc? and *Paper Moon* are among the shapeliest comedies of the seventies, trading on nostalgia but undercutting it with sly character playing and dead pan wit. Ryan and Tatum O'Neal achieve a stylish ensemble performance in the latter as 1930's con-man and unwanted orphan auxiliary; in the former, O'Neal makes a creditable attempt at playing Cary Grant to Barbra Streisand's Hepburn, backed up by a typically rich character cast, notably Austin Pendleton, Kenneth Mars and the ululating Madeline Kahn.

Daisy Miller, a period vehicle for Shepherd more redolent of Henry King than Henry James, inaugurated Bogdanovich's decline. An attempt at a thirties Cole Porter musical, *At Long Last Love* likewise flopped, as did *Nickelodeon*, an unexpectedly leaden tribute to pioneer moviemaking. He returned to form with a low-budget adaptation of Paul Theroux's *Saint Jack*, dignified by Ben Gazzara's performance as the ironic man of honor coping with Occidental venality and Asian corruption. And the Manhattan comedy *They All Laughed*, though widely disliked, showed a truer synthesis of screwball humour and sentimentality than other equivalent films, and marked a return by Bogdanovich to the spirit of the classical directors he admires.

Bogdanovich worked little in the 1980's, apparently traumatised by the murder of lover Dorothy Stratten shortly after her acting debut in *They All Laughed*. At decade's end, in a twin return to his roots that offered some hope for his future, he married Stratten's sister and directed *Texasville*, a *Last Picture Show* sequel with many of the original cast.

—John Baxter

———

BOORMAN, John.

British. Born in Shepperton, Middlesex, 18 January 1933. Educated Salesian College. Married Christel Kruse, 1957, one son (actor Charley Boorman), three daughters. Sergeant in British Army, 1951–53. Film critic for BBC Radio and for *Manchester Guardian*, 1950–54; film editor, Independent Television News, 1955–58; head of documentaries, BBC Television, 1960–64; directed first feature, *Catch Us If You Can*, 1965; moved to U.S. to make *Point Blank*, 1967; chairor, National Film Studios of Ireland, 1975–85; governor, British Film institute, from 1985. Recipient: Best Director Award, Cannes Festival, for *Leo the Last*, 1970; Chevalier de l'Ordre des Arts et Lettres, 1985; New York Film Critics Circle Awards for Best Director and Best Screenplay, for *Hope and Glory*, 1987. Agent: Edgar Gross, International Business Management, 1801 Century Park E., Suite 1132, Los Angeles, CA 90067, U.S.A.. Address: The Glebe, Annamoe, County Wicklow, Ireland.

Films as Director:

1965	*Catch Us If You Can (Having a Wild Weekend)*
1967	*Point Blank*
1968	*Hell in the Pacific*
1970	*Leo the Last*
1972	*Deliverance*
1973	*Zardoz*
1977	*The Exorcist II: The Heretic*
1980	*Merlin and the Knights of King Arthur*
1981	*Excalibur* (+pr, co-sc)
1985	*The Emerald Forest* (+pr)
1987	*Hope and Glory* (+pr, sc)
1990	*Where the Heart Is*

As Producer only:

1984	*Dream One*

Publications:

By BOORMAN: books—

Zardoz, London, 1983.
Money Into Light: The Emerald Forest: A Diary, London, 1985.
Hope and Glory, London, 1987.

By BOORMAN: articles—

"Playboy in a Monastery," interview with Gordon Gow, in *Films and Filming* (London), February 1972.
"Conversation with John Boorman," with L. Strawn, in *Action* (Los Angeles), November/December 1972.
"Zardoz," interview with Philip Strick, in *Sight and Sound* (London), Spring 1974.
Interviews with Michel Ciment, in *Positif* (Paris), March 1974 and February 1978.
"Director John Boorman Talks About His Work," in *American Cinematographer* (Los Angeles), March 1975.
Interview with J.-P. Le Pavec and D. Rabourdin, in *Cinéma* (Paris), March 1978.
"The Sorcerer: John Boorman Interviewed," by D. Yakir, in *Film Comment* (New York), May/June 1981.
"The Technology of Style," interview with J. Verniere, in *Filmmakers Monthly* (Ward Hill, Massachusetts), June 1981.
"The world of King Arthur according to John Boorman," an interview with H. Kennedy, in *American Film* (Washington, D.C.), March 1981.
"Jungle John," an interview with G. Fuller, in *Stills* (London), November 1985.
"John Boorman en quête de mythologie," an interview with C. Blanchet, in *Cinéma* (Paris), 19 February 1986.
"Christopher Isherwood: Stranger in Paradise," in *American Film* (Washington, D.C.), October 1986.
Interview in *Positif* (Paris), November 1987.
"Worshipping at the Shrine: Los Angeles in the Season of the Oscars," in *Sight and Sound* (London), Summer 1988.

John Boorman directing *Hope and Glory*

"Gardening and Parking," in *Sight and Sound* (London), Autumn 1988.

"Bohemian Rhapsody," an interview with Brian Case, in *Time Out* (London), 1 August 1990.

On BOORMAN: books—

Piccardi, Adriano, *John Boorman*, Florence, 1982.
Ciment, Michel, *John Boorman*, Paris, 1985; London, 1986.

On BOORMAN: articles—

Farber, Stephen, "The Writer in American Films," in *Film Quarterly* (Berkeley), Summer 1968.

Brown, John, "Islands of the Mind," in *Sight and Sound* (London), Winter 1969/70.

McGillivray, D., "John Boorman," in *Focus on Film* (London), Autumn 1972.

Dempsy, M., "*Deliverance*/Boorman: Dickey in the Woods," in *Cinema* (Beverly Hills), Spring 1973.

Legrand, Gérard, "Hommage à Boorman," in *Positif* (Paris), March 1974.

Stair, Bill, "En travaillant avec Boorman," in *Positif* (Paris), March 1974.

McCarthy, T., "The Exorcism of *The Heretic*," in *Film Comment* (New York), September/October 1977.

"*Exorcist II* Issue" of *Avant-Scène du Cinéma* (Paris), 1 February 1978.

Sineux, M., "Un Héraut de notre temps," in *Positif* (Paris), October 1981.

"John Boorman Section" of *Positif* (Paris), July–August 1985.

Comiskey, R., "Man, myth, and magic," in *Cinema Papers* (Melbourne), November 1985.

Camy, G., "John Boorman, l'enchanteur moraliste," in *Jeune Cinéma* (Paris), November–December 1985.

"John Boorman Section" of *Positif* (Paris), November 1987.

* * *

"Film making is the process of turning money into light and then back into money again." John Boorman's neat epigram will probably haunt him for the rest of his film-making days. Not simply because it is so tidy a formulation, but because the tensions it articulates have played such a prominent part in Boorman's own career.

He has always been much concerned with the look of his films. In both *Deliverance* and *Point Blank* (shot, incidentally, in exquisite 'scope) he went to unusual lengths to control colour tones; *Zardoz* and *Exorcist II: The Heretic* are remarkable for their pictorial inventiveness; the images of the Irish countryside in *Excalibur* and of the Brazilian rain-forest in *The Emerald Forest* are carefully imbued with a luminous, almost magical quality; and the extraordinary street of housing built for *Hope and Glory* (one of the largest sets constructed in Britain since the heyday of the studio system) speaks volumes for Boorman's commitment to a cinema of distinctively visual qualities.

He can certainly turn money into light. Turning it back into money, however, has not always proved so easy, and the commercial weakness of *Zardoz* and the near total box-office disaster of *Exorcist II* were no help to him in trying to develop his ambitious projects of the eighties. After all, an Irish-based adaptation of Malory's *Morte d'Arthur*, a "green" allegory scheduled for location filming in South America, and an autobiographical evocation of his wartime childhood, are hardly the most obviously marketable ideas, even from a thoroughly bankable director. Yet sell them he did, and if *The Emerald Forest* doesn't come off as well as either *Excalibur* or *Hope and Glory*, two out of three is no mean record for an independent-minded film-maker with a taste for startling visuals and unusual stories.

Boorman's is a high risk approach. When it goes wrong, it goes wrong with a vengeance, and both *Exorcist II* and *The Emerald Forest* sacrifice narrative conviction in the cause of pictorial splendour and some risible metaphysics. But when it goes right it is more than enough to justify his reputation as one of the most courageous and imaginative film-makers still working in the commercial mainstream.

At its best (in *Point Blank, Deliverance, Excalibur* and *Hope and Glory*) Boorman's cinema is rich and subtle, his fascination with images matched by taut story-telling and a nice sense of the opacity of people's motives, his characters constantly made aware of the complex and unanticipated consequences of their actions. In many of his films, strong-willed individualists find themselves embroiled in a clash between established order and disorder, a context within which they appear as representative figures caught up in near mythical confrontations. In *Hell in the Pacific*, for instance, Lee Marvin and Toshiro Mifune play two enemy soldiers stranded on an island. As they continue to conduct the war their roles become emblematic, and they play out the tensions between conditioned aggression and common humanity.

In *Point Blank*, perhaps Boorman's most elegantly realised film, the force for disorder is Walker (Lee Marvin), a man obsessed by what he considers to be his just desserts. Double-crossed in a robbery, he wants only his share of the spoils, a goal he pursues step by step up the hierarchy of a criminal syndicate. The film leaves us little choice but to identify with Walker who is, like Sean Connery in *Zardoz*, an absolute individualist, a man who cannot be restrained by the hierarchical order on which he impinges so forcefully.

Yet *Point Blank* somehow transcends the conventional morality of assertive individualism. Walker is ruthless and violent, certainly, but it is his symbolic force to which we respond. The movie creates a paradox in which this unlovely figure comes to represent a more human spirit than that embodied in the syndicate's bureaucratic order. As ever, Boorman provides no easy solutions. After much death and violence it emerges that Walker, too, has been manipulated, and, sharing his perspective as we do, we are left with a pervasive sense of impotence in the face of larger impersonal forces.

Deliverance, too, shows us order and certainty revealed as precarious fabrications, with its four men on a canoe trip through the wilderness forced to recognise that their ideas about morality and their belief in the social niceties are ineffectual constructs in the face of adverse and unintelligible circumstances. Having killed a man who buggers one of their party at gunpoint, they find that action leading them to yet more lies and more death. "There's no end to it," one character observes, close to despair. And *Excalibur*, perhaps inevitably given its source in Arthurian myth, tells of the imposition of order onto chaos and of the terrible price to be paid when that order isn't firmly based. Human frailty destroys Camelot when Arthur finds Guinevere and Lancelot asleep in the forest, and, in another of Boorman's inspired cinematic images, plunges Excalibur into the ground between them. The despairing Guinevere is left curled naked around the sword while the land falls into pestilence and war.

In these three films Boorman ensures that we appreciate how difficult to make are judgments of good and evil, how tangled the threads of motivation. But he does so not only as a pessimistic observer of human failings; he also has hope. There is a lovely scene in *Hope and Glory*, his most romantic of films, when young Bill (Boorman himself, for the film is autobiographical) has the "googly" explained to him by his father. When he realises what it involves (bowling a cricket ball so that it turns one way but with a bowling action which suggests that it will turn in the opposite direction) he is both horrified and fascinated. "That's like telling fibs," he says, in a children's term for lying which is as accurate to the period as it is precise in its childish evocation of acceptable untruth. In Bill's (and Boorman's) world people are forever telling fibs; like the googly, things are not always what they seem. But, also like the googly, that complexity can be a matter as much for celebration as for concern.

—Andrew Tudor

BOROWCZYK, Walerian.

Polish. Born in Kwilcz, Poland, 2 October 1923 (some sources give 2 February). Studied at Cracow Academy of Fine Art, 1946–51. Married Ligia Branice. Lithographer and poster designer, 1951–56; made first film (as animator), *Glowa*, 1953; made series of films with Jan Lenica, 1957–58; moved to France, 1959; member of Cinéastes Associés group, Paris, from 1963; first live-action feature, *Goto, l'ile d'amour*, 1966.

Films as Animator:

1953 *Glowa*
1954 *Photographies Vivantes; Atelier de Fernard Léger*
1955 *Jesien*
1957 *Byl sobie raz (Once upon a Time)* (co); *Nagrodzone uczucia (Love Required)* (co); *Strip-Tease* (co); *Sztandar mlodych (Banner of Youth)*
1958 *Szkola (The School); Dom (The House)*
1959 *Monsieur Tête (Mr. Head)* (co); *Les Astronautes (The Astronauts)* (co); *Terra incognita*
1962 *Concert*
1963 *Holy Smoke; Renaissance; Les Strogoscopes (Magasins du XIXe siècle); Les Bibliothèques; Les Ecoles; La Fille sage; L'Ecriture; Gancia; Les Félins (Joy House)* (Clément) (titles only)
1964 *Les Jeux des anges; Le Petit Poucet; Le Musée*
1965 *Le Dictionnaire de Joachim; Théâtre de Monsieur et Madame Kabal* (compilation); *La Vie de château* (Rappeneau) (titles only)

Films as Director (Live-Action):

1966 *Rosalie*
1967 *Diptyque; Gavotte*
1968 *Goto, l'ile d'amour*
1969 *Le Phonographe*
1970 *Blanche*
1973 *Une Collection particulière; Contes immoreaux*
1975 *La Bête; Dzieje grzechu (Story of a Sin)*
1976 *La Marge*
1977 *Interno di un convento*
1978 *Les Héroines du mal;* "L'Armoire" episode of *Collections privées*
1980 *Lulu*

Walerian Borowczyk: *Blanche*

1981   *Docteur Jekyll et les femmes*
1983   *L'Art d'aimer (Ars Amandi)*
1987   *Emmanuelle 5*

Publications:

By BOROWCZYK: articles—

Etudes Cinématographes (Paris), nos. 40–42, 1965.
Hubert Arnault in *Image et Son* (Paris), nos. 215 and 222, 1968.
Interview in *Cahiers du Cinéma* (Paris), no. 209, 1969.
Interview in *Cinéma* (Paris), March 1972.
Kino (Warsaw), April 1975.
Interview with Max Tessier in *Ecran* (Paris), September 1975.
Film Comment (New York), January–February 1976.
Cinématographe (Paris), October–November 1976.
Luis Rebolledo Boceta in *Dirigido por . . .* (Barcelona), April 1977.
Image et Son (Paris), no. 207, 1978.
Interview with Silvana Dini in *Filmcritica* (Rome), February 1978.
Ecran Fantastique (Paris), no. 18, 1981.
"Enticements to Voyeurism," an interview with S. Adler, in *Cinema Papers* (Melbourne), February–March 1985.

On BOROWCZYK: books—

Borowczyk, cinéaste onirique, Paris, 1981.
Horodniceanu, Emanuele, *Walerian Borowczyk*, Venice, 1982.

On BOROWCZYK: articles—

Czartoryska, Urszula, in *Fotografia* (Warsaw), no. 1, 1961.
Porebski, M., in *Kwartalnik Filmowy* (Warsaw), no. 4, 1964.
Benayoun, Robert, in *Cinéma* (Paris), no. 98, 1965.
Graham, Peter, in *Film Quarterly* (Berkeley, California), Winter 1965–66.
Wibom, A.L., in *Chaplin* (Stockholm), no. 63, 1966.
Strick, Philip, in *Sight and Sound* (London), Autumn 1969.
Chaplin (Stockholm), 1970.
Filmowy Serwis Prasowy (Warsaw), 1–15 April 1975.
Cornand, André and Mérigeau, Pascal, in *Image et Son* (Paris), November 1977; additions, June 1978.
Banc-Titre (Paris), nos. 1–2, 1978.
Alemanno, R., "Esoterismo e liturgia del cinema panico," in *Cinema Nuovo* (Bari), December 1979.
Avant-Scène (Paris), December 1983.
Roudevitch, M., "Les iles du Dr. Boro," in *Positif* (Paris), June 1987.

*   *   *

Even while he was a student in Cracow, Walerian Borowczyk began to make small films in reduced format. After a trip to France in 1954, moreover, he was so affected by the studio of the painter Léger that he produced two short films, *Photographies vivantes* and *Atelier de Fernand Léger*. In fact, the actual form of painting would be of particular use to him in his later films. While making cinema posters, he met Jan Lenica, and they undertook the production of animated designs resembling nothing yet seen. Using original ideas and much fantasy, the two artists were the first to introduce to Poland methods which would overthrow the traditional criteria and habits of animated film. They refused to see the future of the genre in the perfection of line and silhouette multiplied mechanically (the style of Disney). And their first film was not made in an animation studio. This first film, *Once upon a Time*, was executed according to a new cinema technique, that of cut-outs using simple graphic elements formed from colored paper and images taken from old magazines. In a kind of play, the collages offer unusual and incongruous encounters with a rhythm that recalls musical structures. The film was called "experimental," but was very successful, winning several festival awards. In *The House* in the following year Borowczyk and Lenica introduced real images into the animated ones, creating a poetic style full of metaphors and symbols, recalling in certain respects avant-garde films made in France in the 1920's. The two filmmakers went their separate ways after two years, though their role as innovators has always been recognized.

In his first solo films, Borowczyk used animated photographs, and in a collaboration with Chris Marker, *Les Astronautes*, utilized the various combinations he had earlier devised, in this case animated prints with real backgrounds. After moving to France permanently, he made *Renaissance*, where objects displaced in space and time create mysterious and nostalgic outlines, and *Les Jeux des anges*, an evocation of concentration camps with an omnipresent atmosphere of fear and death. His first feature-length film, *Théâtre de Monsieur et Madame Kabal*, uses black humor and dadaist gags which become cruel and sadistic. He also designed the title sequences for two fiction films.

Little by little, Borowczyk has abandoned animation for fiction films. His first feature-length fiction film, *Goto, l'île d'amour*, introduces an unusual world, entirely imaginary but suggesting the reality of an implacable, cruel, and absurd dictatorship; the mixture of objects and persons reveals his personal style. *Blanche* is a modern story transposed into medieval France. But with *Contes immoraux* Borowczyk achieved notoriety because of the perverted eroticism of the subject matter (four sketches based on historical characters). His masterpiece among his fiction films is undoubtedly *Story of a Sin*, an excellent adaptation of the novel by Stefan Zeromski. His later "versions" of *Lulu* and *Doctor Jekyll et les femmes* have a certain breathlessness. His early willingness to confront taboos, even sexual ones, seems to have given way to a complaisance that is not controlled by his earlier standards.

—Karel Tabery

BORZAGE, Frank.

American. Born in Salt Lake City, Utah, 23 April 1893. Married 1) Rena Rogers (divorced 1945); 2) Edna Marie Stillwell, 1945 (divorced 1949); 3) Juanita Borzage. Joined theatrical touring company as prop boy, 1906; moved to California, 1912; actor in many Ince Westerns and Mutual Comedies, 1913–15; began directing for Universal, 1916; signed to MGM, 1935–42; joined Republic Pictures as producer-director, 1945. Recipient: Oscars for Best Director, for *Seventh Heaven*, 1927/28, and *Bad Girls*, 1931/32. *Died of cancer in Los Angeles, 19 June 1962.*

Films as Director:

1916   *That Gal of Burke's* (+role); *Mammy's Rose* (co-d, role); *Life's Harmony* (co-d, role); *The Silken Spider* (+role); *The Code of Honor* (+role); *Nell Dale's Men Folks* (+role); *The Forgotten Prayer* (+role); *The Courtin' of Calliope Clew* (+role); *Nugget Jim's Pardner* (+role); *The Demon of Fear* (+role); *Land o' Lizards* (*Silent Shelby*) (+role); *Immediate Lee* (*Hair Trigger Casey*) (+role); *Enchantment* (+sc, role); *The Pride and the Man* (+sc, role); *Dollars of Dross* (+sc)
1917   *Wee Lady Betty* (co-d, role); *Flying Colors*; *Until They Get Me*
1918   *The Atom* (role); *The Gun Woman* (+role); *Shoes That Danced*; *Innocent's Progress*; *An Honest Man*; *Society for Sale*; *Who Is to Blame?*; *The Ghost Flower*; *The Curse of Iku* (+role)
1919   *Toton*; *Prudence of Broadway*; *Whom the Gods Destroy*; *Ashes of Desire*

1920   *Humoresque*
1921   *The Duke of Chimney Butte*; *Get-Rich-Quick Wallingford*
1922   *Back Pay*; *Billy Jim*; *The Good Provider*; *Hair Trigger Casey* (re-ed version); *Silent Shelby* (reissue of *Land o' Lizards*); *The Valley of Silent Men*; *The Pride of Palomar*
1923   *The Nth Commandment*; *Children of the Dust*; *Age of Desire*
1924   *Secrets*
1925   *The Lady*; *Daddy's Gone A-Hunting*; *Lazybones*; *Wages for Wives*; *The Circle*
1926   *The First Year*; *The Dixie Merchant*; *Early to Wed*; *Marriage License?*
1927   ***Seventh Heaven***
1928   *Street Angel*
1929   *The River*; *Lucky Star*; *They Had to See Paris*
1930   *Son o' My Heart*; *Liliom*
1931   *Doctors' Wives*; *Young as You Feel*; *Bad Girl*
1932   *After Tomorrow*; *Young America*; *A Farewell to Arms*
1933   *Secrets* (remake of 1924 film); *Man's Castle*
1934   *No Greater Glory*; *Little Man What Now?* (+pr); *Flirtation Walk* (+pr)
1935   *Living on Velvet*; *Stranded*; *Shipmates Forever*
1936   *Desire*; *Hearts Divided*
1937   *Green Light*; *History Is Made at Night*; *Big City*
1938   *Mannequin*; *Three Comrades*; *The Shining Hour*
1939   *Disputed Passage* (+co-pr)
1940   *Strange Cargo*; *The Mortal Storm* (+co-pr)
1941   *Flight Command*; *Smilin' Through*
1942   *The Vanishing Virginian*; *Seven Sweethearts*
1943   *Stage Door Canteen*; *His Butler's Sister* (+co-pr)
1944   *Till We Meet Again* (+pr)
1945   *The Spanish Main*
1946   *I've Always Loved You* (+pr); *Magnificent Doll*
1947   *That's My Man* (+pr)
1948   *Moonrise*
1958   *China Doll* (+pr)
1959   *The Big Fisherman*

Publications:

By BORZAGE: articles—

Article in *Motion Picture Directing: The Facts and Theories of the Newest Art*, by Peter Milne, New York, 1922.
Interview with V. Tully, in *Vanity Fair* (New York), February 1927.
"What's Wrong with the Movies?," in *Motion Picture* (New York), September 1933.

On BORZAGE: books—

Kyrou, Ado, *Amour, éroticisme et cinéma*, Paris, 1957.
Belton, John, *The Hollywood Professionals vol.3*, New York, 1974.
Lamster, Frederick, *Souls made Great through Love and Adversity: The Film Work of Frank Borzage*, Metuchen, New Jersey, 1981.
Belton, John, *Cinema Stylists*, Metuchen, New Jersey, 1983.

On BORZAGE: articles—

Agel, Henri, "Frank Borzage," in *New York Film Bulletin*, no.12–14, 1961.
Obituary in *New York Times*, 20 June 1962.
Sarris, Andrew, "Second Line," in *Film Culture* (New York), Spring 1963.
Belton, John, "Souls Made Great By Love and Adversity: Frank Borzage," in *Monogram* (London), no. 4, 1972.
Beylie, Claude, "Sur cinq films de Frank Borzage," in *Ecran* (Paris), September 1976.
Camper, Fred, "Disputed Passage," in *Cinema* (London), v.9, no. 10.
Toulet, E., and Michel Ciment, "Avignon 1986: Panoramique du cinéma 1915–1920. Ford et Borzage," in *Positif* (Paris), September 1987.

*   *   *

Frank Borzage had a rare gift of taking characters, even those who were children of violence, and fashioning a treatment of them abundant with lyrical romanticism and tenderness, even a spirituality that reformed them and their story.

He arrived in Hollywood in 1913, and Thomas H. Ince gave him his first small roles as a film actor, gradually promoting him to leads, and also to directing. He usually played the romantic lead in Westerns and romantic melodrama with such Triangle players as Sessue Hayakawa (*The Typhoon and Wrath of the Gods*, both 1914) and Olive Thomas (*Toton*, 1919). The first really important feature he directed was *Humoresque*, written by Frances Marion from a Fannie Hurst story. It had all the elements which were later to stamp a picture as a Borzage film—hope, love, and faith in himself and others in a world that was poverty-stricken and could be cruel. It won *Photoplay Magazine*'s award as Best Picture of the year.

He insisted that "Real art is simple, but simplicity requires the greatest art," adding that "Naturalness is the primary requisite of good acting. I like my players to perform as though there were no camera on the set."

He did exceedingly well at Paramount's Cosmopolitan and at First National, where he directed two Norma Talmadge favorites, *Secrets* and *The Lady*. Then he moved over to Fox and in 1927 with *Seventh Heaven* he established himself as one of the best in the business. He directed two others with Janet Gaynor and Charles Farrell, *Street Angel* and *Lucky Star*. His *The River* of 1928, starring Farrell, is a virtual cinematic poem. In 1929 he directed his first all-talking feature, *They Had to See Paris*, starring Will Rogers, Fox's number one box-office star.

The year 1933 was probably his finest as a director, for he made three films which still rate as superb examples of the romantic cinema: *A Farewell to Arms*, from the Hemingway novel, with Gary Cooper and Helen Hayes; Mary Pickford's final and her very best, a re-make of *Secrets* in which Norma Talmadge had starred in the silent era; and *Man's Castle* with Spencer Tracy and Loretta Young, a very moving romance. There was a lasting tenderness about Borzage's treatment of a love story, and during the days of the Depression and the rise of Fascism, his pictures were ennobling melodramas about the power of love to create a heaven on earth. He made four with Margaret Sullavan that clearly indicated that she was the quintessential heroine for Borzage films: *Little Man, What Now?*, a study of love in the midst of deprivation and the growing terror in Germany; *Three Comrades*, in which Sullavan played an ill-fated tubercular wife; *The Shining Hour* featuring her as a self-sacrificing woman; and *The Mortal Storm*, a moving film of the imminent battle with the Nazi forces. No director since Griffith had made love seem so timeless and eternal.

Also, he had directed three others during this time of stress that were extraordinary departures for him: *Desire*, a sleek romance in the Lubitsch tradition, starring Marlene Dietrich and Gary Cooper; *Mannequin*, co-starring Joan Crawford with Spencer Tracy, one of their best; and a drama that combined romance with effective disaster, *History Is Made at Night*, with Jean Arthur and Charles Boyer as lovers trapped in a Titanic-like explosion of violence. It is true that in the case of *Desire* Ernst Lubitsch was producer, but the picture has touches that are just as indicative of Borzage as they are of Lubitsch, for both were masters of cinematic subtlety.

In the post-war period, it began to be clear that Borzage's career was on the wane. His best picture was *Moonrise*. Penelope Gilliatt has remarked that "He had a tenderness rare in melodrama and absolute pitch about period. He understood adversity." Outside of Griffith, there has never been another director in the business who could so effectively triumph over sentimentality, using true sentiment with an honest touch.

—DeWitt Bodeen

BOULTING, Roy and John.

British. Born twins in Bray, Berkshire, 21 November 1913. Educated at McGill University, Toronto. Roy married six times, including actress Hayley Mills, 1971 (divorced). John entered film industry as office boy, worked as salesman, publicity writer, and editor, mid-1930's; introduced by John, Roy began as assistant director; they founded Charter Films, 1937; John served in Film Unit of Royal Air Force, Roy in British Army Film Unit, 1940–45; obtained leave at same time to make *Thunder Rock*, 1942; began series of comedies with *Seagulls Over Sorrento*, 1954; both joined board of British Lion Film Corp. *John died, in Sunningdale, Berkshire, 17 June 1985*.

Films with Roy as Director, John as Producer (though functions overlap):

1938   *The Landlady*; *Ripe Earth*; *Seeing Stars*; *Consider Your Verdict*
1939   *Trunk Crime*
1940   *Inquest*; *Pastor Hall*
1941   *Dawn Guard*
1942   *Thunder Rock*; *They Serve Abroad*
1943   *Desert Victory*
1944   *Tunisian Victory* (co-d)
1945   *Burma Victory*; *Journey Together* (John as d, Roy pr)
1947   *Fame Is the Spur*; *Brighton Rock* (*Young Scarface*) (John d and Roy pr)
1948   *The Guinea Pig* (*The Outsider*) (+co-sc)
1950   *Seven Days to Noon* (John d and Roy pr)
1951   *Singlehanded* (*Sailor of the King*); *High Treason* (+co-sc); *The Magic Box* (John d and Roy pr)
1954   *Seagulls Over Sorrento* (*Crest of the Wave*) (Roy and John co-d and co-pr, sc)
1955   *Josephine and Men*
1956   *Run for the Sun* (+co-sc); *Private's Progress* (John d and Roy pr, co-sc)
1957   *Brothers in Law* (+co-sc); *Happy Is the Bride* (+co-sc); *Lucky Jim* (John d and Roy pr)
1959   *Carlton-Browne of the F.O.* (*Man in a Cocked Hat*) (co-d, co-sc); *I'm All Right Jack* (John d and Roy pr, co-sc)
1960   *A French Mistress* (+co-sc); *Suspect* (*The Risk*) (Roy and John co-d and co-pr)
1963   *Heavens Above!* (John d and Roy pr, co-sc)
1965   *Rotten to the Core* (John d and Roy pr)
1966   *The Family Way* (+co-adaptation)
1968   *Twisted Nerve* (+co-sc)
1970   *There's a Girl in My Soup*
1974   *Soft Beds and Hard Battles* (*Undercovers Hero*) (+co-sc)
1979   *The Number*

Publications:

By the BOULTINGS: articles—

"Bewitched, Bothered and Bewildered," in *Kine Weekly* (London), 9 November 1950.
"What Makes the British Laugh?," an interview with John, in *Films and Filming* (London), February 1959.
Interviews with John in *Today's Cinema* (London), 21 April and 5 December 1969.
"Who Dictates the Price of a Film," by John in *Today's Cinema* (London), 1 December 1970.
"Getting it Together," by Roy, in *Films and Filming* (London), February 1974.
Interview with Roy in *Photoplay Film Monthly* (London), March 1974.
"Flour Power," by both in *The Month in Yorkshire*, March 1981.
Letter signed by both in the *Times* (London), 10 April 1981.

On the BOULTINGS: books—

Durgnat, Raymond, *A Mirror for England*, London, 1970.

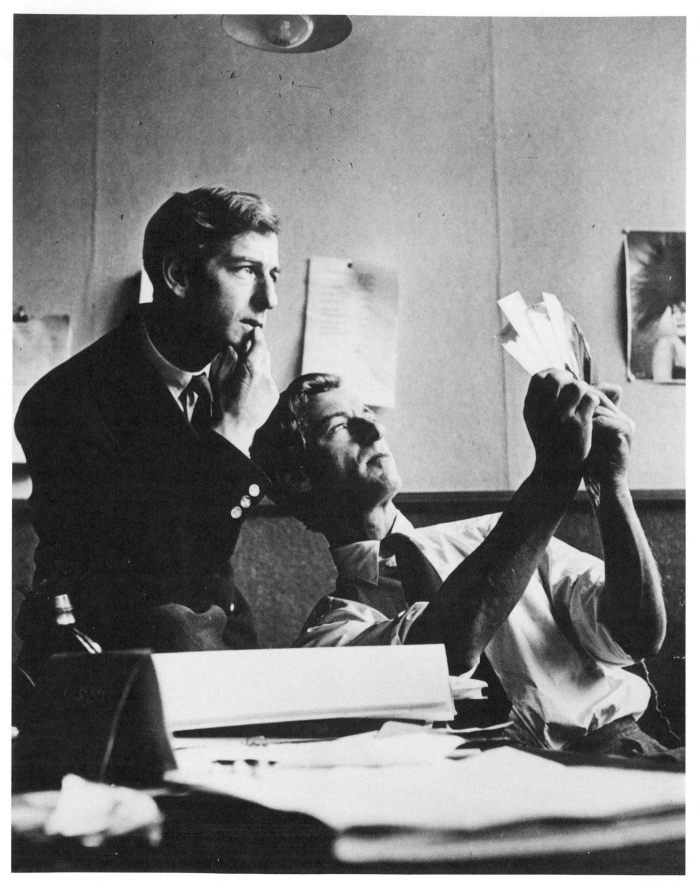

John and Roy Boulting

Hill, John, *Sex, Class, and Realism: British Cinema 1956–63*, London, 1986.

Murphy, Robert, *Realism and Tinsel*, London, 1989.

On the BOULTINGS: articles—

Watts, S., "The Boulting Twins," in *Films in Review* (New York), February 1960.

Sheed, W., "Pitfalls of Pratfalls: Boulting Brothers Comedies," in *Commonweal* (New York), 5 July 1963.

Film and TV Technician (London), March 1964.

Lewin, David, "Why the Boultings Can Be Bastards," in *Today's Cinema* (London), 24 November 1970.

Norman, Barry, "The Boultings: Fun at 60" in the *Times* (London), 26 January 1974.

"The Boulting Brothers," in *Film Dope* (London), March 1974.

Millar, Gavin, in *Listener* (London), 17 March 1983.

"John Boulting," in *St. James Press Annual Obituary 1985*, London, 1985.

McCarthy, T., obituary of John Boulting, in *Variety* (New York), 26 June 1985.

Tribute to John in *Screen International* (London), 29 June 1985.

"A Celebration for the Life of John Boulting," in *National Film Theatre Booklet* (London), September/October 1985.

TV Times (London), 16 November 1985.

*   *   *

The Boultings' *auteurial* films (interspersed by potboilers, usually comic) outline a "pilgrim's progress," or regress, from a moral earnestness and puritan conscience, to a sort of hilarious gloom about The State of England.

Their first feature, *Pastor Hall*, was inspired by Martin Niemoller, the Nazi-defying German clergyman, via a play by ex-Expressionist Ernst Toller. With commentary by Eleanor Roosevelt added, it created a furore in isolationist America. *Thunder Rock* adapted Robert Ardrey's pro-interventionist dream-play, still remarkable for its didactic strategies, more persuasive than Brecht's, and its self-reflexivity à la Pirandello. After these calls to conscience, came their war documentaries. *Desert Victory*, a compilation of newsreel footage, with its famous "gunflash montage" of British artillery bombarding by night, won 10,000 bookings in US theatres; its realism redirected US propaganda strategies. *Tunisian Victory* was delayed by US services' haggling over duly proportionate representation and by Churchill's wish to sit beside the moviola deciding the exact re-editing of its last shots.

The Boultings' next phase reflects the hopes, strains and glooms of Austerity and the "Welfare Revolution". *Fame Is the Spur* adapted Howard Spring's best-seller, inspired by Ramsay MacDonald's evolution from Socialist firebrand to the Labour Party's "Colonel Blimp." *The Guinea Pig* depicted a working-class scholarship boy's tribulations in an upper-crust school. The Boultings then switched moral target, from left-idealism becoming sluggish to left-idealism becoming fanatical. In *Seven Days To Noon* an atomic scientist vows to destroy London unless Britain unilaterally disarms. In *High Treason* a motley array of ultra-leftists sabotage British power-stations prior to invasion "from the East." Conversely, the noble hero of *Pastor Hall* finds his "antithesis" in *Brighton Rock*, from Grahame Greene's gangster novel. The Boy is petty, vile and doomed less through social environment than through *natural* evil, and/or *spiritual* deprivation. *Vis-a-vis* atomic scientist and gangster alike, the Boultings' spokespersons for ordinary humanity are blowsy aging blondes, no better than they ought to be; as if to emblemise lowered expectations of human nature.

The Magic Box, a tribute to British film pioneer Friese-Greene, was the British film industry's "official" contribution to the Festival of Britain, and, like *Single-Handed*, a (dullish) tribute to old-fashioned British pluck. The mid-1950s' deepen-ing anxieties about declining efficiency and social morality provoked the Boultings to satirical comedies; their sarcasms began where Ealing's left off. Typically, an earnest innocent (often Ian Carmichael) struggles against the general moral grubbiness, before giving up and joining it. The humour oscillates between tolerant and fraught, puritan and populist, realistic and farcical. *Private's Progress* targeted the army, *Brothers-in-Law* the law, *Carleton-Brown of the F.O* government. *Lucky Jim* (targeting Oxbridge) is a stodgy version of the Kingsley Amis novel, but *I'm All Right Jack* (industrial relations) is arguably *the* crucial movie about post-war Britain, Peter Sellers infusing with warmth and pathos a bloody-minded shop-steward. *Heaven's Above* (about the Anglican Church), from an idea by the Socialist-turned-Anglican Malcolm Muggeridge, intriguingly mixes *Carry On* buffoonery with Evelyn Waugh-type satire.

The Boultings' bouts of *Carry On*-type ribaldry aren't moral cop-out, but a deliberate moral position, an affectionate enjoyment of humanity despite its moral mediocrity, and without the guilt of stereotypical puritanism. This mellowness keys their last serious films. In *The Family Way*, a working-class newly-wed's various troubles make him temporarily impotent; and his trusting father never realises that his best friend was the boy's real father. *The Twisted Nerve*, about a mongoloid's brother given to homicide, offended the mental health lobby, but sought to brood seriously on human nature, irreducible evil, and the everyday.

The overt discussion of moral fibre, choice, and consequence in *Thunder Rock* is the key to the Boultings' films. Contemplating the characters from outside, they ask moral questions, rather than giving psychological data from the inside; and they stress the erosion of idealism, by puzzlement, weariness, or its paradoxical conflicts with decency. *Brighton Rock* focuses less on Pinky's mind, or the criminal *milieu*, than on the (a) moral tropisms of the more hesitant characters. Such emphasis on "moral intuition" is central to the British character, and the Boultings' steady popularity evinces a profound, not a glib, affinity with audiences. The switch from very earnest to very satirical forms is another facet of their moralism.

Wherever possible they operated as a semi-independent unit, often called Charter Films, but on becoming Directors of British Lion in 1963, were crucial in its renaissance, albeit embroiled in the controversial decisions preceding its dissolution.

—Raymond Durgnat

———

BRAKHAGE, Stan.

American. Born in Kansas City, Missouri, 14 January 1933. Educated at Dartmouth College, 1951, attended Institute of Fine Arts, San Francisco, 1953. Married 1) Jane Collum, 1957 (divorced 1987), five children; 2) Marilyn Jull, 1989, one child. Performed as boy soprano on live radio and recordings, 1937–46; dropped out of college, ran small theatre in Central City, Colorado, began making films, 1952; studies with Edgar Varese, New York, 1954; shot film for Joseph Cornell, 1955; worked for Raymond Rohauer in Los Angeles, 1956; made TV commercials and industrial films, 1956–64; moved to Denver, 1957; began lecturing on film, from 1960; completes major works *The Art of Vision* and *Dog Star Man*, 1964; lectured in film history and aesthetics, Colorado University, 1969; taught at School of the Art Institute, Chicago, from 1970; began

Stan Brakhage

working in super-8mm, 1976; teacher at Colorado, from 1981. Recipient: James Ryan Morris Award, 1979; Telluride Film Festival Medallion, 1981; Maya Deren Award for Independent Film and Video Artists, 1986; MacDowell Medal, 1989. Agent: Film-Makers' Cooperative, 175 Lexington Ave., New York, NY 10016, U.S.A. Address: c/o Film Studies, Hunter 102, Campus Box 316, University of Colorado, Boulder, CO 80309, U.S.A.

Films as Director:

1952 *Interim*
1953 *Unglassed Windows Cast a Terrible Reflection*; *The Boy and the Sea*
1954 *Desistfilm*; *The Extraordinary Child*; *The Way to Shadow Garden*
1955 *In Between*; *Reflections on Black*; *The Wonder Ring* (with Joseph Cornell); "Tower House" (photographed for Joseph Cornell under working titles "Bolts of Melody" and "Portrait of Julie", finally became Cornell's *Centuries of June*); *Untitled Film of Geoffrey Holder's Wedding* (collaboration with Larry Jordan)
1956 *Zone Moment*; *Flesh of Morning*; *Nightcats*
1957 *Daybreak and Whiteye*; *Loving*; *Martin Missil Quarterly Reports* (commercial work)
1958 *Anticipation of the Night*; "Opening" for *G.E. Television Theatre* (commercial work)
1959 *Wedlock House: An Intercourse*; *Window Water Baby Moving*; *Cat's Cradle*; *Sirius Remembered*; *Untitled Film on Pittsburgh* (commercial work)
1960 *The Dead*
1961 *Thigh Line Lyre Triangular*; *Films By Stan Brakhage: An Avant-Garde Home Movie*; *The Colorado Legend and the Ballad of the Colorado Ute* (commercial work)

1962 *Blue Moses*; *Silent Sound Sense Stars Subotnick and Sender*; *Mr Tomkins Inside Himself* (commercial work)
1963/5 Film on Mt. Rushmore, photographed for Charles Nauman's Part II film on Korczak Ziolkowski; film on Chief Sitting Bull.
1963 *Oh Life—A Woe Story—The A Test News*; "Meat Jewel" (incorporated into *Dog Star Man: Part II*); *Mothlight*
1964 **Dog Star Man (in prelude and four parts dated as follows: Prelude, 1962; Part I, 1963; Part II, 1964; Part III, 1964; Part IV, 1964)**
1965 *The Art of Vision* (derived from *Dog Star Man*); *Three Films* (includes *Blue White, Blood's Tone, Vein*); *Fire of Waters*; *Pasht*; *Two: Creeley/McClure* (also incorporated in *Fifteen Song Traits*); *Black Vision*
1968 *Lovemaking*; *The Horseman, The Woman and The Moth*
1969 *Songs* (dated as follows: *Songs 1 to 8*, 1964; *Songs 9 to 14*, 1965; *15 Song Traits*, 1965; *Songs 16 to 22*, 1965; *23rd Psalm Branch: Part I*, 1966 and *Part II* and *Coda*, 1967; *Songs 24 and 25*, 1967; *Song 26*, 1968; *My Mountain Song 27*, 1968; *Song 27 (Part II) Rivers*, 1969; *Songs 28 and 29*, 1969; *American 30's Song*, 1969; *Window Suite of Children's Songs*, 1969)
1970 *Scenes from Under Childhood* (dated as follows: *Section No.1*, 1967; *Section No.2*, 1969; *Section No.3*, 1969; *Section No.4*, 1970); *The Weir-Falcon Saga*; *The Machine of Eden*; *The Animals of Eden and After*
1971 "*The Pittsburgh Documents*" (*Eyes*; *Deus Ex*; *The Act of Seeing with One's Own Eyes*); *Foxfire Childwatch*; *Angels' Door*; *Western History*; *The Trip to Door*; *The Peaceable Kingdom*
1972 *Eye Myth* (begun in 1968 as sketch for *The Horseman, The Woman and The Moth*) (16mm version); *Sexual Meditations* (titled and dated as follows: *Sexual Meditation No. 1: Motel*, 1970; *Sexual Meditation: Room with View*, 1971; *Sexual Meditation: Faun's Room Yale*, 1972; *Sexual Meditation: Office Suite*, 1972; *Sexual Meditation: Open Field*, 1972; *Sexual Meditation: Hotel*, 1972); *The Process*; *The Riddle of Lumen*; *The Shores of Phos: A Fable*; *The Presence*; *The Wold Shadow*
1973 *Gift*; *Sincerity*; *The Women*
1974 *Skein*; *Aquarien*; *Hymn to Her*; *Star Garden*; *Flight*; *Dominion*; *he was born, he suffered, he died*; *Clancy*; *The Text of Light*; *The Stars Are Beautiful*; *Sol*
1975 *Sincerity II*; *Short Films: 1975* (divided into Parts I-X)
1976 *Gadflies*; *Sketches*; *Airs*; *Window*; *Trio*; *Desert*; *Rembrandt, Etc. and Jane*; *Short Films: 1976*; *Tragoedia*; *Highs*; *The Dream, NYC, The Return, The Flower*; *Absence*
1977 *Soldiers and Other Cosmic Objects*; *The Governor*; *The Domain of the Moment*
1978 *Sincerity III*; *Nightmare Series*; *Duplicity*; *Duplicity II*; *Purity and After*; *Centre*; *Bird*; *Thot Fal'n*; *Burial Path*; *Sluice*
1979 *Creation*
1980 *Sincerity IV*; *Sincerity V*; *Duplicity III*; *Salome*; *Other*; *Made Manifest*; *Aftermath*; *Murder Psalm*
1981 *Eye Myth* (original 35 mm version); *Roman Numeral Series* (dated and titled as follows: *I and II*, 1979; *III, IV, V, VI, VII*, 1980; *VIII and IX*, 1981); *Nodes*; *RR*; *The Garden of Earthly Delights*; *Hell Spit Flexion*
1982 *Arabics* (dated and titled as follows: *I, 2 and 3*, 1980; *4, 5, 6, 7, 8, 9, 0+10, 11, 12, 13*, 1981; *14, 15, 16, 17, 18, 19*, 1982); *Unconscious London Strata*
1984 *Egyptian Series*; *Tortured Dust*
1986 *Jane*; *Caswallan Trilogy* (*The Aerodyne, Dance Shadows by Danielle Helander, Fireloop*); *The Loop*; *Nightmusic*; *Confession*
1987 *FaustFilm: An Opera*; *Loud Visual Noises*; *The Dante Quartet*; *Kindering*
1988 *Faust's Other: An Idyll*; *Faust 3: Candida Albacore*; *Matins*; *I . . . Dreaming*; *Marilyn's Window*; *Rage Net*
1989 *Faust 4*; *Visions in Meditation #1*; *Babylon Series*
1990 *Babylon Series #2*; *City Streaming*; *The Thatch of Night*; *Glaze of Cathexis*; *Visions in Meditation #2*

Note: beginning 1978, many films first issued in 8mm or Super-8mm reissued in 16mm.

Publications:

By BRAKHAGE: books—
Metaphors on Vision, New York, 1963.
A Motion Picture Giving and Taking Book, West Newbury, Massachusetts, 1971.
The Brakhage Lectures, Chicago, 1972.
Stan Brakhage, Ed Emshwiller, edited by Rochelle Reed, Washington, D.C., 1973.
Seen, San Francisco, 1975.
Film Biographies, Berkeley, California, 1977.
Brakhage Scrapbook: Collected Writings 1964–1980, edited by Robert A. Haller, New York, 1982.
I . . . Sleeping (Being a Dream Journal and Parenthetical Explication), New York, 1989.
Film at Wit's End—Eight Avant-Garde Filmmakers, New York, 1989.

By BRAKHAGE: articles—
"The Silent Sound Sense," in *Film Culture* (New York), Summer 1960.
"Province-and-Providential Letters," in *Film Culture* (New York), Spring 1962.
"Excerpts from Letters," in *Film Culture* (New York), Summer 1962.
"Sound and Cinema," (exchange of letters with James Tenney and Gregory Markopoulos), in *Film Culture* (New York), no.29, 1963.
"Metaphors on Vision," in *Film Culture* (New York), no.30, 1963.
Interview with P. Adams Sitney, in *Film Culture* (New York), Fall 1963.
"Letter to Gregory Markopoulos," in *Film Culture* (New York), Winter 1963/64.
"Letter from Brakhage: On Splicing," in *Film Culture* (New York), Winter 1964/65.
"Letter to Yves Kovacs," in *Yale Literary Magazine* (New Haven), March 1965.
"Stan Brakhage Letters," in *Film Culture* (New York), Spring 1966.
"A Moving Picture Giving and Taking Book," in *Film Culture* (New York), Summer 1966.
"On Dance and Film," in *Dance Perspectives*, Summer 1967.
"Letter to Jonas Mekas, September 1967," in *Filmmakers Newsletter* (Ward Hill, Massachusetts), December 1967.
"Transcription of Some Remarks . . . ," in *Take One* (Montreal), September/October 1970.
"In Defense of the Amateur Filmmaker," in *Filmmakers Newsletter* (Ward Hill, Massachusetts), Summer 1971.
"Stan and Jane Brakhage Talking," with Hollis Frampton, in *Artforum* (New York), January 1973.
"On Filming Light," with Forrest Williams in *The Structurist* (Saskatoon), no. 13/14, 1973–74.
Various writings, in *Film Culture* (New York), no.67–69, 1979.
"The Swiftly Perceived Blur," in *Rolling Stock* (Boulder, Colorado), no. 1, Summer 1980.
"Stan Brakhage Reviews the 15th Telluride Film Festival," in *Rolling Stock* (Boulder, Colorado), Winter 1989.

On BRAKHAGE: books—

Clark, Dan, *Brakhage*, New York, 1966.
Richie, Donald, *Stan Brakhage—A Retrospective*, New York, 1970.
Mekas, Jonas, *Movie Journal, The Rise of a New American Cinema, 1959–1971*, New York, 1972.
Camper, Fred, *Stan Brakhage*, Los Angeles, 1976.
Hanhardt, John, and others, *A History of the American Avant-Garde Cinema*, New York, 1976.
Nesthus, Marie, *Stan Brakhage*, Minneapolis/St. Paul, 1979.
Sitney, P. Adams, *Visionary Film*, New York, 1979.
Camper, Fred, *By Brakhage: Three Decades of Personal Cinema*, catalogue, New York, 1981.
Barrett, Gerald R., and Wendy Brabner, *Stan Brakhage: A Guide to References and Resources*, Boston, 1983.
McBride, Joseph, editor, *Filmmakers on Filmmakers 2*, Los Angeles, 1983.
Keller, Marjorie, *The Untutored Eye: Childhood in the Films of Cocteau, Cornell and Brakhage*, Cranbury, New Jersey, 1986.
Elder, R. Bruce, *The Body in Film*, Toronto, Ontario, 1989.
James, David, E., *Allegories of Cinema: American Film in the Sixties*, Princeton, New Jersey, 1989.

On BRAKHAGE: articles—
Tyler, Parker, "Stan Brakhage," in *Film Culture* (New York), No.18, 1958.
"Brakhage Issue" of *Filmwise*, no.1, 1961.
Callenbach, Ernest, "Films of Stan Brakhage," in *Film Quarterly* (Berkeley), Spring 1961.
Sitney, P. Adams, "*Anticipation of the Night* and *Prelude*," in *Film Culture* (New York), no.26, 1962.
Brakhage, Jane, "The Birth Film," in *Film Culture* (New York), Winter 1963/64.
Hill, Jerome, "Brakhage and Rilke," in *Film Culture* (New York), no.37, 1965.
Hill, Jerome, and Guy Davenport, "Two Essays on Brakhage and His Songs," in *Film Culture* (New York), Spring 1966.
Kroll, K. "Up from the Underground," in *Newsweek* (New York), 13 February 1967.
Camper, Fred, "*The Art of Vision*, a Film by Stan Brakhage," and "*23rd Psalm Branch (Song XXIII)*, a Film by Stan Brakhage," in *Film Culture* (New York), Autumn 1967.
Camper, Fred, "My Mtn. Song 27," in *Film Culture* (New York), Summer 1969.
Creeley, Robert, "Mehr Light . . . ," in *Film Culture* (New York), Summer 1969.
Sitney, P. Adams, "Avant Garde Film," in *Afterimage* (Rochester), Autumn 1970.
Hill, Jerome, "Brakhage's Eyes," in *Film Culture* (New York), Spring 1971.
Camper, Fred, "*Sexual Meditation No.1: Motel*, a Film by Stan Brakhage," and P. Adams Sitney, "The Idea of Morphology," in *Film Culture* (New York), Spring 1972.
"Brakhage Issue" of *Artforum* (New York), January 1973.
Levoff, Daniel, "Brakhage's *The Act of Seeing with One's Own Eyes*," in *Film Culture* (New York), Spring 1973.
Barr, William, "Brakhage: Artistic Development in Two Childbirth Films," in *Film Quarterly* (Berkeley), Spring 1976.
Kelman, Ken, "Animal Cinema," in *Film Culture* (New York), no.63–64, 1977.
Nesthus, Marie, "The Influence of Olivier Messiaen on the Visual Art of Stan Brakhage in *Scenes from under Childhood*, Part I," in *Film Culture* (New York), no.63–64, 1977.
Sitney, P. Adams, "Autobiography in Avant-Garde Film," in *Millenium* (New York), Winter 1977/78.
Cohen, Phoebe, "Brakhage's *Sincerity III*," in *Millenium Film Journal* (New York), no.4–5, 1979.
Jenkins, Bruce, and Noel Carroll, "*Text of Light*," in *Film Culture* (New York), no.67–69, 1979.
Sharrett, Christopher, "Brakhage's Dreamscape," in *Millenium Film Journal* (New York), Spring 1980.
Cohen, Phoebe, "Brakhage's *I, II, III*," in *Millenium Film Journal* (New York), no.7–8–9, 1980/81.
Hoberman, J., "Duplicitously Ours: Brakhage in New York," in *Village Voice* (New York), 8 April 1981.
James, D., "The filmmaker as romantic poet: Brakhage and Olson," in *Film Quarterly* (Los Angeles), Spring 1982.
Sharrett, Christopher, "Brakhage's Scrapbook," in *Millenium* (New York), Fall–Winter 1984–85.
"Brakhage Sections" of *Monthly Film Bulletin* (London), February and March 1986.
Sharrett, Christopher, "Brakhage's dreamscape," in *Millenium* (New York), Spring 1986.
Wees, William C., "Words and Images in Stan Brakhage's 23rd Psalm Branch," in *Cinema Journal* (Champaigne, Illinois), Winter 1988.
Camper, Fred, "Stan Brakhage's New Vision," in *Chicago Reader*, 27 January 1989.

*   *   *

Brakhage has been the most prolific and consistent of avant-garde filmmakers. Perhaps Andy Warhol made more films, or more hours of film, between 1963 and 1968, and James Broughton, Harry Smith, and Kenneth Anger have been making films for more years than Brakhage, but the outpouring of films he has created since he began in 1952 constitutes one of the most astounding achievements of any filmmaker. It is difficult to number Brakhage's films because so many of them are short and gathered into series under a collective title, e.g., thirty different *Songs* (some of which have subdivisions) or ten different *Short Films: 1975*. A conservative tally would list over a 100 titles. Only ten of them have soundtracks; and of those seven were made in his first five years, before his mature style emerged.

In his often obscure and poetic theoretical texts, Brakhage has at times held the position that sound has been an aesthetic error for the cinema. Yet generally he invokes the Emersonian argument of "necessity" to define his own production as not needing sound (in the sense of requiring it for clarity or effect) and of himself not needing to make sound films (in the sense of hieratic inspiration, beyond his personal and rational decisions). The heart of Brakhage's theory (as forcefully represented in *Metaphors on Vision* and *Brakhage Scrapbook: Collected Writings* is the notion of cinema as the imitation of the act of seeing, which includes simultaneously the perpetually scanning eyes, the visual imagination and memory, and the phosphenes which are most distinct when the eyes are closed. For him, the act of making a film intensifies and makes conscious this perpetual process of vision. Any dramatic representation whatsoever is anathematized by him.

As a consequence of this thinking, the films of his maturity (since 1958) describe his daily life. The birth of his five children, his travels as a lecturer, visits to a hospital, morgue, grammar school, cemetery, a few days with the governor of Colorado, etc., are examples of the more thematically unified and conventionally intense experiences he has translated onto film. Yet more often the montage of glimpses from his daily life constructs a fabric of memory, fantasy, or dream, in which visual association plays a dominant role. No filmmaker, not even the great Soviet masters, can challenge the skill and diversity of Brakhage's editing. No major filmmaker has been as fanatical about performing all the operations of filmmaking himself.

Brakhage began to make films in 1952, in his native Colorado after dropping out of Dartmouth College as a freshman. He quickly met and fell under the influence of the chief figures of the avant-garde of the 1940's: Maya Deren, Willard Maas, Kenneth Anger, and Sidney Peterson. But it was the encounter with the very personal, and less expressionistic films of Marie Menken that seems to have had the most lasting influence, along with a passionate and prolonged reading of Gertrude Stein. There are hints of his turn from the acted psychodramas of his first period in the film Joseph Cornell commissioned about the soon-to-be-destroyed Third Avenue El, *Wonder Ring*, in his study of cats, *Nightcats*, and his portrait of friends necking, *Loving*. However, with his 42-minute long *Anticipation of the Night*, a melancholy meditation on suicide and the loss of innocent vision, he succeeded for the first time in making a film which described the act of seeing as well as the hopes and disappointments which attended his quest for a visionary experience.

In extreme poverty during the first years of his marriage, Brakhage had to conserve film materials penuriously, yet he managed to make a dozen films between 1959 and 1964 which established his reputation as the leading American avant-garde filmmaker. In this period of great intensity and invention, which includes his four part cosmological "epic" *Dog Star Man*, he wrote most of *Metaphors on Vision*. It was at that time that he actually sandwiched bits of flowers and mothwings between layers of mylar splicing tape to create the remarkable *Mothlight* because he could not afford film, but could not stop working. The complex achievements of this early period continue to define Brakhage's cinematic project: the representation

of a lyrical self through camera movements, shifting light values, hand-painting over film, and above all associative editing, in response to the imagistic material presented on the screen.

The ineluctable need to keep making films led Brakhage to concentrate on 8mm filmmaking between 1964 and 1969. His complex series *Songs* began as an alternative to the painstaking editing of his 16mm films (and as an economic necessity when his equipment was stolen in 1964), but eventually they became even more painstaking and expensive as when he made the *23rd Psalm Branch*, his intricate, seven-part response to the Vietnam War.

The late sixties and seventies were dominated by a vast autobiographical film, still in progress, which contains the series *Scenes from Under Childhood* in four parts, *The Weir-Falcon Saga* in three, *Sincerity* in five, and *Duplicity* in three. In the same period he completed six *Sexual Meditations*, three "Pittsburgh Documents" consisting of *Eyes*, shot in a police car, *Deus Ex* in a surgery room, and the grisly *The Act of Seeing with One's Own Eyes* at an autopsy. In 1975 he began a series of films shot in Super-8mm and blown up to 16mm to enhance their grainy texture, and later, after a plethora of short films, he completed two series of purely abstract works, *Roman Numeral Series I-X* and *Arabics 1-0+10*.

—P. Adams Sitney

BRENON, Herbert.

American. Born in Dublin, 13 January 1880; became U.S. citizen, 1918. Educated at St. Paul's School, and at King's College, London. Married Helen Oberg, 1904, one son. Emigrated to U.S. and settled in New York, 1896; director, Dick Ferris stock company, Minneapolis, 1903; headed stock company in Johnstown, Pennsylvania, 1908–10; scenario editor for Carl Laemmle's IMP co., 1911; directed first one-reeler, 1912; formed independent production company, Tiffany Film Corp., 1914; directed *The Kreutzer Sonata* for William Fox, 1915; left Fox, formed production company in Hudson Heights, New Jersey, and made first film for Lewis J. Selznick Alliance, *War Brides*, 1916; dissolve production company, 1918; directed for Select Film Company, London, and for Unione Cinematografica Italiana, Rome, 1918–20; returned to U.S., 1920; under contract to Famous players-Lasky (Paramount), 1923–27; signed to independent producer I.E. Chadwick, releasing through Monogram, 1932; directed in Britain, 1935–40. *Died 21 June 1958.*

Films as Director:

(listing incomplete before 1921)
1912   *All for Her* (+sc, role); *The Clown's Triumph*; *Leah the Forsaken* (+sc)
1913   *Ivanhoe* (+sc, role as Isaac of York); *Time Is Money* (+role); *Kathleen Mavourneen* (+sc); *The Angel of Death*; *The Anarchist*; *Time Is Money*
1914   *Absinthe*; *Neptune's Daughter* (co-d, role); *The Secret of the Air*; *Across the Atlantic* (+role as Japanese spy) (completed 1913)
1915   *The Heart of Maryland* (+pr); *The Kreutzer Sonata* (+sc); *The Two Orphans* (+sc, role as Pierre, the scissors-grinder); *The Clemenceau Case* (+sc); *Sin* (+sc); *The Soul of Broadway* (+sc)

Herbert Brenon

1916   *A Daughter of the Gods* (d uncredited, sc); *War Brides*; *Whom the Gods Destroy*; *Marble Heart* (+sc); *The Ruling Passion*
1917   *The Eternal Sin*; *The Lone Wolf*; *The Fall of the Romanoffs*; *Empty Pockets*; *Kismet*
1918   *The Passing of the Third Floor Back*; *Victory and Peace*
1919   *Twelve: Ten* (+pr); *Princess Impudence*; *A Sinless Sinner*
1920   *Sister Against Sister* (U.S. release 1922); *Chains of Evidence*
1921   *The Passion Flower* (+co-sc); *The Sign on the Door* (+co-sc); *The Wonderful Thing* (+co-sc)
1922   *Any Wife*; *A Stage Romance*; *Shackles of Gold*; *Moonshine Valley* (+co-sc); *A Kiss for Cinderella*
1923   *The Custard Cup*; *The Rustle of Silk*; *The Woman with Four Faces*; *The Spanish Dancer* (+ pr)
1924   *Shadows of Paris*; *The Side Show of Life* (+pr); *The Alaskan*; *Peter Pan*; *The Breaking Point*
1925   *The Little French Girl*; *The Street of Forgotten Men*
1926   *Dancing Mothers*; *Beau Geste*; *The Great Gatsby*; *God Gave Me Twenty Cents*; *The Song and Dance Man*
1927   *Sorrell and Son* (+sc); *The Telephone Girl* (+pr)
1928   *Laugh Clown Laugh*
1929   *The Rescue*
1930   *Lummox*; *The Case of Sergeant Grischa*
1931   *Beau Ideal*
1932   *Transgression*; *Girl of the Rio*
1933   *Wine, Women and Song*
1935   *Royal Cavalcade* (*Regal Cavalcade*); *Honours Easy*
1936   *Living Dangerously*; *Someone at the Door*
1937   *The Dominant Sex*; *Spring Handicap*; *The Live Wire*
1938   *The Housemaster*; *Yellow Sands*
1939   *Black Eyes*
1940   *The Flying Squadron* (*The Flying Squad*)

Other Films:

1933   *Oliver Twist* (pr spvr)
1934   *Sorrell and Son* (pr; remake of 1927 film) (Raymond)

Publications:

By BRENON: article—

Interview in *The Picture Show* (London), 2 August 1919.

On BRENON: articles—

Pictures and Picturegoer (London), 12 October 1918.
Picturegoer (London), November 1923.
Films in Review (New York), March 1955.
Obituary in the *Times* (London), 24 June 1958.
Obituary in *Variety* (New York), 25 June 1958.

*   *   *

Dublin-born Herbert Brenon brought to the cinema an Irish temperament and a versatility which made him equally at ease with historical drama, fantasy and melodrama. After a year of learning his craft with Carl Laemmle's IMP Company, Brenon came to prominence as the director of *Ivanhoe*, a curtailed if respectable film version of Sir Walter Scott's novel, shot on location in England and starring the IMP Company's best-known leading man, King Baggot. *Ivanhoe* typified many of Brenon's productions; it was well-received critically and publicly, it offered spectacle and yet it was a somewhat static creation, lacking in zest.

In the mid-teens, Brenon directed Australian swimming star Annette Kellermann (who had become a vaudeville sensation thanks to her one-piece swimming costume) in *Neptune's Daughter* and *A Daughter of the Gods*. Both films were highly regarded, thanks in no small part to their star's "nude" sequences. Brenon's credit was removed from the latter film because its producer, William Fox, felt the director had spent an inordinate amount of time—nine months—on the production. The director sued Fox unsuccessfully, but his action did lead to Brenon's colleagues insisting on contracts granting them screen credit. Melodramas with Theda Bara (*The Kreutzer Sonata*) and about the Russian Revolution (*The Fall of the Romanoffs*) followed, and Brenon was even able to get a passable performance out of stage actor Sir Johnston Forbes-Robertson in *The Passing of the Third Floor Back*, but it was not until 1923 and the signing of a long-term contract with Famous Players-Lasky that Brenon again achieved the prominence he had held in the teens.

Brenon's Irish background should never be overlooked for assuredly it helped him bring just the right amount of whimsy to *Peter Pan* and *A Kiss for Cinderella*, which made a star of Betty Bronson. Its fantastical charm has seldom been equalled in the cinema. Whatever Brenon turned his directorial hand to, it seemed he could do no wrong in the 1920's, be it the flapper revolution in *Dancing Mothers*, a foreign legion melodrama such as *Beau Geste*, or the first screen version of F. Scott Fitzgerald's *The Great Gatsby*. He seemed ill at ease with his first talkie, a stagey, depressing Fannie Hurst melodrama, *Lummox*. Brenon ended his career directing from 1935 through 1940 in England, where he was responsible for one minor masterpiece, *The Housemaster*, adapted from the Ian Hay play and a far more satisfactory study of public school life than, say, *Goodbye Mr. Chips*.

Herbert Brenon was not apparently an easy man to work with. He was a fierce taskmaster who was prone to fits of anger toward anyone who failed to measure up to his demands. Nevertheless, he was a reliable technician who could rise to spectacular heights, as with *A Daughter of the Gods* and *Peter Pan*, and handle romantic melodrama, such as *Sorrell and Son*, without descending to the maudlin.

—Anthony Slide

BRESSON, Robert.

French. Born in Bromont-Lamothe (Put-de-Dome), France, 25 September 1907. Educated at Lycée Lakanal à Sceaux, Paris. Married Leidia van der Zee, 1926. Attempted career as painter, to 1933; directed first film, *Les Affaires publique*, 1934; assistant director to René Clair on *Air pur* (unfinished), 1939; German prisoner of war, 1940–41; directed first major film, *Les Anges du péché*, 1943; elected President d'honneur de la Société des realisateurs de films, 1968. Recipient: International Prize, Venice Film Festival, for *Le Journal d'un curé campagne*, 1951; Best Director Award, Cannes Festival, for *Un Condamné a mort s'est échappé*, 1957; Special Jury Prize, Cannes Festival, for *Le Procès de Jeanne d'Arc*, 1962; Grand Prix national des Arts et des Lettres (Cinéma), France, 1978; Officier de la Légion d'honneur. Address: 49 Quai de Bourbon, 75004 Paris, France.

Films as Director:

1934   *Les Affaires publiques* (no known copies exist) (+sc)
1943   *Les Anges du péché* (*Angels of the Streets*) (+co-sc)
1945   **Les Dames du Bois de Boulogne** (***The Ladies of the Bois de Boulogne***) (+co sc)
1950   *Journal d'un curé de campagne* (*Diary of a Country Priest*) (+sc)
1956   **Un Condamné a mort s'est échappé** (***Le Vent souffle où il veut, A Condemned Man Escapes***) (+sc)
1959   **Pickpocket** (+sc)
1962   *Le Procès de Jeanne d'Arc* (*The Trial of Joan of Arc*) (+sc)

Robert Bresson directing *Le Procès de Jeanne d'Arc*

1966   *Au hasard Balthazar* (*Balthazar*) (+sc)
1967   *Mouchette* (+sc)
1969   *Une Femme douce* (+sc)
1971   *Quatre Nuits d'un rêveur* (*Four Nights of a Dreamer*) (+sc)
1974   *Lancelot du Luc* (*Le Graal, Lancelot of the Lake*) (+sc)
1977   *Le Diable probablement* (+sc)
1983   *L'Argent* (+sc)

Other Films:

1933   *C'était un musicien* (Zelnick and Gleize) (dialogue)
1936   *Les Jumeaux de Brighton* (Heymann) (co-sc); *Courrier Sud* (Billon) (co-adaptation)

Publications:

By BRESSON: book—

Notes sur le cinématographe, Paris, 1975; as *Notes on the Cinema*, New York, 1977, and London, 1986.

By BRESSON: articles—

"Bresson on Location: Interview," with Jean Douchet, in *Sequence* (London), no. 13, 1951.
Interview with Ian Cameron, in *Movie* (London), February 1963.
Interview with Jean-Luc Godard and M. Delahaye, in *Cahiers du Cinema in English* (New York), February 1967.
"Four Nights of a Dreamer," an interview with Carlos Clarens, in *Sight and Sound* (London), Winter 1971/72.
"Deux Nuits d'un rêveur," an interview with Claude Beylie, in *Ecran* (Paris), April 1972.
"*Lancelot du Lac*," in *Avant-Scène du Cinéma* (Paris), February 1975.
Interview, in *Sight and Sound* (London), Winter 1976/77.
Interview with J. Fieschi, in *Cinématographe* (Paris), July/August 1977.
"Robert Bresson, Possibly," interview with Paul Schrader, in *Film Comment* (New York), September/October 1977.
"The Poetry of Precision," an interview with Michel Ciment, in *American Film* (Washington, D.C.), October 1983.
"Bresson et lumiere," an interview with David Thompson, in *Time Out* (London), 2 September 1987.

On BRESSON: books—

Sarris, Andrew, editor, *The Film*, Indianapolis, Indiana, 1968.
The Films of Robert Bresson, by five reviewers, New York, 1969.
Armes, Roy, *French Cinema Since 1946, Vol. 1*, New York, 1970.
Cameron, Ian, *The Films of Robert Bresson*, London, 1970.
Bazin, André, and others, *La Politique des auteurs: Entretiens avec Jean Renoir etc*, Paris, 1972; revised edition, 1989.
Schrader, Paul, *Transcendental Style on Film: Ozu, Bresson, Dreyer*, Los Angeles, 1972.
Sloan, Jane, *Robert Bresson: A Guide to References and Resources*, Boston, 1983.
Esteve, Michel, *La Passion du cinématographe*, Paris, 1985.
Hanlon, Lindley, *Fragments: Bresson's Film Style*, Cranbury, New Jersey, 1986.

On BRESSON: articles—

Lambert, Gavin, "Notes on Robert Bresson," in *Sight and Sound* (London), Summer 1953.
Monod, Roland, "Working with Bresson," in *Sight and Sound* (London), Summer 1957.
Gow, Gordon, "The Quest for Realism," in *Films and Filming* (London), December 1957.
Baxter, Brian, "Robert Bresson," in *Film* (London), September/October 1958.
Roud, Richard, "The Early Work of Robert Bresson," in *Film Culture* (New York), no. 20, 1959.
Ford, Charles, "Robert Bresson," in *Films in Review* (New York), February 1959.
Green, Marjorie, "Robert Bresson," in *Film Quarterly* (Berkeley), Spring 1960.
Roud, Richard, "French Outsider with the Inside Look," in *Films and Filming* (London), April 1960.

Sontag, Susan, "Spiritual Style in the Films of Robert Bresson," in *Seventh Art* (New York), Summer 1964.
Sarris, Andrew, "Robert Bresson," in *Interviews with Film Directors*, New York, 1967.
Skoller, S. Donald, "Praxis as a Cinematic Principle in the Films of Robert Bresson," in *Cinema Journal* (Evanston, Illinois), Fall 1969.
Rhode, Eric, "Dostoevsky and Bresson," in *Sight and Sound* (London), Spring 1970.
Zeman, Marvin, "The Suicide of Robert Bresson," in *Cinema* (Los Angeles), Spring 1971.
Prokosch, M., "Bresson's Stylistics Revisited," in *Film Quarterly* (Berkeley), v.15, no.1, 1972.
Samuels, Charles, "Robert Bresson," in *Encountering Directors*, New York, 1972.
Polhemus, H.M., "Matter and Spirit in the Films of Robert Bresson," in *Film Heritage* (Dayton, Ohio), Spring 1974.
Westerbeck, Jr., Colin, "Robert Bresson's Austere Vision," in *Artforum* (New York), November 1976.
Nogueira, R., "Burel and Bresson," in *Sight and Sound* (London), Winter 1976/77.
Dempsey, M., "Despair abounding: The recent films of Robert Bresson," in *Film Quarterly* (Los Angeles), Fall 1980.
Hourigan, J., "On two deaths and three births: The cinematography of Robert Bresson," in *Stills* (London), Autumn 1981.
Latille Dactec, M., "Bresson, Dostoievski," in *Cinématographe* (Paris), December 1981.
Dossier on Robert Bresson, in *Cinéma* (Paris), June 1983.
Bergala, Alain, and others, "*L'Argent* de Robert Bresson," in *Cahiers du Cinéma* (Paris), June–July 1983.
"Bresson Issue," of *Camera/Stylo* (Paris), January 1985.
Affron, Mirella Jona, "Bresson and Pascal: Rhetorical affinities," in *Quarterly Review of Film Studies* (New York), Spring 1985.
Milne, Tom, in *Sight and Sound* (London), Summer 1987.
Adair, "Lost and Found: Beby re-inaugurates," in *Sight and Sound* (London), Autumn 1987.
Baxter, Brian, "Robert Bresson," in *Films and Filming* (London), September 1987.

On BRESSON: films—

Weyergans, Francois, *Robert Bresson*, 1965.
Kotulla, Theodor, *Zum Beispiel Bresson*, 1967.

*   *   *

Robert Bresson began and quickly gave up a career as a painter, turning to cinema in 1934. The short film he made that year, *Les Affaires publiques*, is never shown. His next work, *Les Anges du péché* was his first feature film, followed by *Les Dames du Bois du Boulogne* and *Le Journal d'un curé de campagne* which firmly established his reputation as one of the world's most rigorous and demanding filmmakers. In the next 15 years he made only four films: *Un Condamné à mort s'est échappé, Pickpocket, Le Procès de Jeanne d'Arc* and *Au hasard Balthazar*, each a work of masterful originality and unlike the others. Since then he has made films with more frequency and somewhat less intensity. In 1975 Gallimard published his gnomic *Notes sur le cinématographe*.

As a whole Bresson's oeuvre constitutes a crucial investigation of the nature of cinematic narration. All three films of the 1950's are variations on the notion of a written diary transposed to a voice-over commentary on the visualized action. More indirectly, *Le Procès de Jeanne d'Arc* proposes yet another variant through the medium of the written transcript of the trial; *Une Femme douce* is told through the voice of the husband as he keeps a vigil for his suicidal wife; and in *Quatre nuits d'un rêveur* both of the principle characters narrate their previous histories to each other. In all of these instances Bresson allows the tension between the continuity of written and spoken language and the fragmentation of shots in a film to become an important thematic concern. His narrators tell themselves (and us) stories in order to find meaning in what has happened to them. The elusiveness of that meaning is reflected in the elliptical style of Bresson's editing.

For the most part, Bresson employs only amateur actors. He avoids histrionics and seldom permits his "models" (as he calls them, drawing a metaphor from painting) to give a traditional performance. The emotional tensions of the films derive from the elaborate interchange of glances, subtle camera movements, offscreen sounds, carefully placed bits of baroque and classical music, and rhythmical editing.

The Bressonian hero is often defined by what he or she sees. We come to understand the sexual tensions of Ambricourt from a few shots seen from the country priest's perspective; the fierce desire to escape helps the condemned man to see the most ordinary objects as tools for his purpose; the risk the pickpocket initially takes to prove his moral superiority to himself leads him to see thefts where we might only notice people jostling one another: the film initiates its viewers into his privileged perspective. Only at the end does he realize that this obsessive mode of seeing has blinded him to a love which he ecstatically embraces.

Conversely, Mouchette kills herself suddenly when she sees the death of a hare (with which she identified herself); the heroine of *Une Femme douce* kills herself because she can see no value in things, while her pawnbroker husband sees nothing but the monetary worth of everything he handles. The most elaborate form this concentration on seeing takes in Bresson's cinema is the structure of *Au hasard Balthazar*, where the range of human vices is seen through the eyes of a donkey as he passes through a series of owners.

The intricate shot-countershot of Bresson's films reinforces his emphasis on seeing, as does his careful use of camera movement. Often he reframes within a shot to bring together two different objects of attention. The cumulative effect of this meticulous and often obsessive concentration on details is the sense of a transcendent and fateful presence guiding the actions of characters who come to see only at the end, if at all, the pattern and goal of their lives.

Only in *Un Condamné*, *Pickpocket*, and *Quatre Nuits* does the protagonist survive the end of the film. A dominant theme of his cinema is dying with grace. In *Mouchette*, *Une Femme douce*, and *Le Diable probablement* the protagonists commit suicide. In *Les Anges* and *L'Argent* they give themselves up as murderers. Clearly Bresson, who is the most prominent of Catholic filmmakers, does not reflect the Church's condemnation of suicide. Death, as he represents it, comes as the acceptance of one's fate. The three suicides emphasize the enigma of human will; they seem insufficiently motivated, but are pure acts of accepting death.

—P. Adams Sitney

BROCA, Philippe de.

French. Born in Paris, 15 March 1933. Educated at Ecole Technique de Photographie et du Cinema, Paris. Military service as cameraman in North Africa, 1950's; assistant director to Chabrol and Truffaut, 1958–59; directed first feature, *Les Jeux de l'amour* (produced by Chabrol), 1960; formed Fildebroc production company, 1965.

Films as Director:

1954   *Salon nautique* (doc short) (+ph)

1955   *Opération Gas-oil* (doc short) (+ph); *Sous un autre soleil* (doc short) (+ph)
1960   *Les Jeux de l'amour* (*The Love Game*) (+co-sc)
1961   *Le Farceur* (*The Joker*) (+co-sc); *L'Amant de cinq jours* (*The Five Day Lovers*) (+co-sc)
1962   "La Gourmandise (Gluttony)" episode of *Les Sept Péchés capitaux* (*The Seven Deadly Sins*); *Cartouche* (+co-sc, bit role); "La Vedette" episode of *Les Veinards* (+co-sc)
1963   *L'Homme de Rio* (*That Man from Rio*) (+co-sc)
1964   *Un Monsieur de compagnie* (*Male Companion*) (-co-sc, co-adapt)
1965   *Les Tribulations d'un chinois en Chine* (*Up to His Ears*) (+co-sc)
1966   *Le Roi de coeur* (*King of Hearts*) (+pr)
1967   "Mademoiselle Mimi" episode of *Le Plus Vieux Métier du monde* (*The Oldest Profession*)
1968   *Le Diable par la queue* (*The Devil by the Tail*) (+co-sc)
1969   *Les Caprices de Marie* (*Give Her the Moon*) (+co-sc)
1971   *La Poudre d'escampette* (*Touch and Go*) (+co-sc)
1972   *Chère Louise* (+co-sc)
1973   *Le Magnifique* (*Comment détruire la reputation du plus célèbre agent secret du monde*, *How to Destroy the Reputation of the Greatest Secret Agent*) (+role)
1975   *L'Incorrigible* (+co-sc)
1977   *Julie Pot de Colle*; *Tendre Poulet* (*Dear Inspector, Dear Detective*) (+co-sc)
1978   *Le Cavaleur* (*Practice Makes Perfect*) (+co-sc)
1980   *On a vole la cuisse de Jupiter* (*Somebody's Stolen the Thigh of Jupiter*) (+sc)
1983   *L'Africain* (*The African*) (+co-sc)
1988   *Chouans!*

Other Films:

1957   *Tous peuvent me tuer* (Decoin) (asst d, credit as 'stagiaire'); *Charmants garcons* (Decoin) (2nd asst d); *La Cargaison blanche* (Lacombe) (2nd asst d)
1958   *Ramuntcho* (Schoendoerffer) (asst d); ***Les Quatre Cents Coups (The Four Hundred Blows)*** (Truffaut) (asst d); *Le Beau Serge* (Chabrol) (asst d, role)
1959   *Les Cousins* (Chabrol) (asst d); *A Double Tour* (Chabrol) (asst d); ***A bout de souffle (Breathless)*** (Godard) (bit role)
1964   *Les Pieds-Nickelés* (Chambon) (role)
1967   *Ne jouez pas avec les Martiens* (Lanoë) (co-sc, pr); *O salto* (*Le Voyage du silence, Le Saut*) (de Chalonge) (pr)
1970   *Le Cinéma de papa* (Berri) (role)

Publications:

By BROCA: articles—

Interview in *Cinéma* (Paris), no. 111, 1966.
Interview in *Revue du Cinéma* (Paris), January 1971.
"What Directors Are Saying," in *Action* (Los Angeles), March/April 1975.
Interview in *Film Français* (Paris), 27 June 1975.
Cinéma Français (Paris), May and December 1980.
Interview in *Film Français* (Paris), 18 February 1983.
Interview in *Première* (Paris), April 1988.

On BROCA: articles—

Film (Frankfurt), no. 2, 1966.
"Philippe de Broca," in *Film Dope* (London), July 1974 and April 1980.
Curran, T., "Philippe de Broca," in *Films in review* (New York), November 1980.
Duval, B., "De bric-a-brac baroque et de Broca," in *Revue du Cinéma* (Paris), March 1983.

* * *

The most successful films of Philippe de Broca are honest, sincere comedies which stress illusion over reality. His characters are nonconformists who celebrate life and the joy of personal liberation. Structurally, de Broca's works are highly visual, more concerned with expression, with communication by images, than any specifics in the scenario. And these images are generally picturesque. The filmmaker acknowledges his desire to give pleasure to the esthetic sense and, as such, he is a popular artist. His films may not be as rich as those of Truffaut (with whom he worked as assistant director on *The 400 Blows*) or as cinematic as those of Chabrol (he was this filmmaker's assistant on *Beau Serge* and *Les Cousins*) but he is still a solid stylist with his share of worthy credits.

De Broca's films are non-tragic, with humorous treatments of characters and their situations. One of his favorite themes is the relationship between the sexes, explored in his earliest films *Les Jeux de l'Amour*, *Le Farceur* and *L'Amant de Cinq Jours*, all featuring Jean-Pierre Cassel as lighthearted lovers; this character ages 20 years in *Le Cavaleur*, with Jean Rochefort as a bored, self-centered womanizer. But his most popular features include *Cartouche*, a flavorful comedy-swashbuckler chronicling the exploits of kind-hearted criminals in 18th century Paris; *That Man from Rio*, a charming James Bond spoof about a soldier (Jean-Paul Belmondo, also toplined in *Cartouche*) on leave who is led to a stunningly photographed Brazil on a chase for treasure; and *King of Hearts*, featuring a town during World War I that has been abandoned by all except for the residents of its insane asylum. The last, de Broca's most renowned effort, is a staple on the cult film circuit. It ran for six-and-a-half years alone at a Cambridge, Massachusetts, moviehouse.

King of Hearts is de Broca's idea of an anti-war film. Typically, he does not focus on the calamity of a youthful hero who is robbed of his life (as in *All Quiet on the Western Front*), or soldiers needlessly and maddeningly put to death by a military bureaucracy (*Paths of Glory, Breaker Morant*), or the bloody slaughter of his protagonists (any of a score of films). Instead, he gently, satirically celebrates individual freedom: his inmates are more sane than the society which has labelled them mad while intent on blowing itself to smithereens. Deaths and tragedies in a de Broca feature are usually obscured by humorous situations.

De Broca is more concerned with good than evil. He began his career as a newsreel cameraman in Algeria, but switched to narrative filmmaking because he "decided the real world was just too ugly." The work in his first decade as filmmaker is generally more satisfying than his more recent efforts. But, at his best, de Broca deals with possibilities—for peace, beauty, hope, love.

While Philippe de Broca's scenarios may be a screenwriter's fantasy, their essence is emotionally genuine.

—Rob Edelman

BROCKA, Lino.

Filipino. Born Lino Ortiz Brocka in San José, Nuevo Ecija, Philippines, 1940. Educated at University of Philippines. Worked as Mormon missionary, and as actor/director for the theatre, to 1965; script supervisor on *Flight to Fury* (Hellman and Romero), 1965; became head of Philippine Educational Theatre Association, late 1960's; co-founded Cinemanila production company; Cinemanila closed, Brocka took over debts of company, spent next decade paying off backers, 1977; directed for TV, Film, and theatre, 1977–80; Elected president of Directors Guild of the Philippines, 1980; member of "Con-

cerned artists of the Philippines," and noted critic of the Marcos regime; arrested in Manila, and held for 19 days on suspicion of sedition, 1985. Recipient: Best Director Award, Filipino Academy of Movie Arts and Sciences, for *Tubog Sa Ginto*, 1971, for *Tinimbang Ka't Ngu nit Kulang*, 1975, and for *Maynila sa Kuko nig Liwanag*, 1976; British Film Institute Award for *Bayan Ko*, London Film Festival, 1984.

Films as Director:

1970   *Wanted*; *Perfect Mother*; *Santiago*
1971/3   *Tubog Sa Ginto*; *Now*; *Lumuha Pati Mga Anghel*; *Cadena de Amor*; *Cherry Blossoms*; *Villa Miranda*; *Stardoom*
1974   *Tinimbang ka Nguni't Kulang* (*You Are Weighed in the Balance But Are Found Lacking*); *Talto, Dalawa, Isa*
1975   *Maynila sa Kuko nig Liwanag* (*Manila in the Claws of Light*)
1976   *Lunes, Martes, Myerkoles . . .* ; *Insiang*
1977   *Tahan Na Empy, Tahan*; *Inay*
1978   *Mananayan* (*The Dancer*); *Ang Tatay Kong Manay* (*My Mother is My Father*); *In This Corner*; *Gumising Ka, Maruja* (*Wake Up, Maruja*); *Hayop sa Hayop* (*Beast to Beast*); *Init* (*Heat*); *Rubia Servos*
1979   *Ina, Kapatid, Anak* (*Mother, Sister, Daughter*); *Jaguar*; *Ina Ka ng Anak Mo* (*A Whore of a Mother*)
1980   *Nakaw na Pag-Ibig* (*Stolen Love*); *Angela Markado*; *Bona*
1981   *Kontrobersyal* (*Controversial*); *Burgis* (*Bourgeois*); *Hello, Young Lovers*; *Binata si Mister, Dalaga si Misis* (*My Husband is a Bachelor, My Wife is Unmarried*); *Palipat-Lipat, Paplit Palit* (*Changing Apartments, Changing Lovers*); *Caught in the Act*; *PX*
1982   *Mother Dear*; *Cain at Abel* (*Cain and Abel*)
1983   *Hot Property*; *Adultery*; *Your Body is Mine*
1984   *Bayan Ko—Kapit sa Patilim* (*My Own Country—Hanging on a Knife Edge*)
1988   *Macho Dancer*

Publications:

By BROCKA: articles—

"Salut aux Philippines," interview and article with A. Garsault and A. Sotto, in *Positif* (Paris), June 1978.
Interview with Michel Ciment, in *Positif* (Paris), June 1980.
"Philippine Cinema: Hollywood of the Pacific," interview and article with I. Stocks, in *Cinema Papers* (Melbourne), October/November 1980.
Interview with O. Assayas and C. Tesson, in *Cahiers du Cinéma* (Paris), September 1981.
"Lino Brocka, un amor impossible," an interview with M. Grosso, in *Casablanca* (Madrid), June 1982.
Interview with Marc Chevrie, in *Cahiers du Cinéma* (Paris), December 1984.
"Lino Brocka: De Marcos a Aquino," an interview with M. Neubourg, in *Cinématographe* (Paris), June 1986.
"Film and revolution," in *Cinema Papers* (Melbourne), September 1986.

On BROCKA: book—

Estève, Michel, *Le Pouvoir en question: Essai sur le dignité de l'homme a l'ecran*, Paris, 1984.

On BROCKA: articles—

Dossier on Lino Brocka, in *Positif* (Paris), January 1982.
Tesson, C., "Deux cinéastes philippins," in *Cahiers du Cinéma* (Paris), March 1982.
Dossier on Lino Brocka, in *Cinématographe* (Paris), April 1982.
Tessier, Max, "Le Cinéma philippin, ou les miroirs de Manille," in *Im age et Son* (Paris), September 1982.
Valot, J., "Du desir comme moteur du cinéma," in *Revue du Cinéma* (Paris), April 1983.
Rayns, Tony, "Lino Brocka," in *Sight and Sound* (London), Spring 1985.

Malcolm, Derek, "Lone Ranger in the Tondo," in *Guardian* (London), 2 April 1987.

Rayns, Tony, "Easterners: Manila," in *Sight and Sound* (London), Summer 1988.

Stanbrook, Alan, "Crackdown in the Philippines," in *Films and Filming* (London), June 1988.

*   *   *

Lino Ortiz Brocka is undoubtedly the most important Filipino filmmaker to date. Unknown outside of his own country until he was discovered by the French critics and revealed at the 1978 Cannes Film Festival with the presentation of *Insiang*, he has since become a focus of attention and the flagbearer of a new wave of filmmakers which includes Mike De Leon who had produced and photographed one of Brocka's films, *Manila in the Claws of Light*. There were forerunners, of course, like Lamberto Avellana and Gerardo De Leon, but it was Brocka who showed for the first time a consistent attempt at creating a body of work distinct from the crassly commercial and superficial entertainment produced by a national industry releasing some 200 films a year. In little more than a decade he shot over 40 films and many of these are not distinguishable from the run-of-the-mill. They were made to pay his debts, to fund his other artistic activities or just to survive till the censor would accept one of his projects.

The son of a fisherman and a schoolteacher, he has always shown a concern for the poor and the lower middle class. He shoots films, he says, "to make people angry." His first film, *Wanted: Perfect Mother* uses the Filipino comic strips as a source of inspiration and reaches the audience by a clever use of popular culture. In his second venture *Santiago*, a war drama, he made use of actors he had worked with in theater. But it is with *You Are Weighed In The Balance But Are Found Lacking* that he makes his real breakthrough, mocking the shortcomings, the inhumanity, and the hypocrisy of a society in a brilliant ironical tale.

The ruthless social films of Brocka, often set in the slums or the poor districts of Manila, borrow from several sources: Italian neorealism, the Spanish melodrama and the American film noir of Kazan and Dassin. *Manila in the Claws of Light* shows the slow degradation of youths arriving from the country to face urban corruption and vice. In his trilogy, *Insiang, Jaguar* and *Bona*, he shows characters who are totally subservient, accepting the weight of societal pressures till they revolt in a final act, suddenly conscious of their alienation. In Brocka's films the social and human relationships are closely intertwined and the realistic approach is enhanced by a larger-than-life theatricality. Brutality is accompanied by sudden outbursts of lyricism (*Jaguar* is reminiscent of *You Only Live Once* or *They Live By Night*), the tragic and the comic alternating in a style that is at once feverish and precise.

—Michel Ciment

BROOKS, Mel.

American. Born Melvin Kaminsky in Brooklyn, New York, 28 June 1926. Attended Virginia Military Institute, 1944, and Brooklyn College. Married 1) Florence Baum (divorced), one son, two daughters; 2) actress Anne Bancroft, one son. Combat engineer, U.S. Army, 1944–46. Jazz drummer, stand-up comedian, and social director, Grossinger's resorts, late 1940's; writer and occasional performer for Sid Caesar's TV show, 1950–58; conceived, wrote, and narrated cartoon short *The Critic*, 1963; co-creator (with Buck Henry) of *Get Smart* TV show, 1965–69; directed first feature, *The Producers*, 1968; founder, Brooksfilms, 1980. Recipient: Oscar for Best Short Subject, for *The Critic*, 1963; Oscar for Best Story and Screenplay, and Writers Guild Award for Best Written Screenplay, for *The Producers*, 1969. Address: Brooksfilms, Ltd., Twentieth Century-Fox Studios, P.O. Box 900, Beverly Hills, CA 90213, U.S.A.

Films as Director:

1963	*The Critic* (cartoon) (+sc)
1968	*The Producers* (+sc)
1970	*The Twelve Chairs* (+sc, mus, role)
1974	*Blazing Saddles* (+co-sc, mus, role); *Young Frankenstein* (+co-sc)
1976	*Silent Movie* (+co-sc, role)
1977	*High Anxiety* (+pr, co-sc, mus, role)
1981	*The History of the World, Part I* (+pr, co-sc, mus, role)
1983	*To Be or Not to Be* (+pr, co-sc)
1987	*Spaceballs* (+pr, ro, co-sc)

Films as Executive Producer:

1980	*The Elephant Man*
1985	*The Doctor and the Devils*
1986	**The Fly**; *Solarbabies*
1987	*84 Charing Cross Road*

Publications:

By BROOKS: books—

Silent Movie, New York, 1976.
The History of the World, Part I, New York, 1981.

By BROOKS: articles—

"Confessions of an Auteur," in *Action* (Los Angeles), November/December 1971.

Interview with James Atlas, in *Film Comment* (New York), March/April 1975.

"Fond Salutes and Naked Hate," interview with Gordon Gow, in *Films and Filming* (London), July 1975.

Interview with A. Remond, in *Ecran* (Paris), November 1976.

"Comedy Directors: Interview with Mel Brooks," with R. Rivlin, in *Millimeter* (New York), October and December 1977.

Interview with Alan Yentob, in *Listener* (London), 8 October 1981.

Interview in *Time Out* (London), 16 February 1984.

Interview in *Screen International*, 3 March 1984.

Interview in *Hollywood Reporter*, 27 October 1986.

On BROOKS: books—

Bendazzi, G., *Mel Brooks: l'ultima follia di Hollywood*, Milan, 1977.

Allen, Steve, *Funny People*, New York, 1981.

Yacowar, Maurice, *Method in Madness: The Comic Art of Mel Brooks*, New York, 1981.

Smurthwaite, Nick, and Paul Gelder, *Mel Brooks and the Spoof Movie*, London, 1982.

Squire, Jason, E., *The Movie Business Book*, Englewood Cliffs, New Jersey, 1983.

On BROOKS: articles—

"Two Thousand Year Old Man," in *Newsweek* (New York), 4 October 1965.

Diehl, D., "Mel Brooks," in *Action* (Los Angeles), January/February 1975.

Lees, G., "The Mel Brooks Memos," in *American Film* (Washington, D.C.), October 1977.

Carcassonne, P., "Dossier: Hollywood 79: Mel Brooks," in *Cinématographe* (Paris), March 1979.

Karoubi, N., "Mel Brooks follies," in *Cinéma* (Paris), February 1982.

Mel Brooks directing *High Anxiety*

"Mel Brooks," in *Dictionary of Literary Biography, vol. 26: American Screenwriters*, Detroit, 1984.

*   *   *

Brooks's central concern (with *High Anxiety* and *To Be or Not to Be* as possible exceptions) is the pragmatic, absurd union of two males, starting with the more experienced member trying to take advantage of the other, and ending in a strong friendship and paternal relationship. The dominant member of the duo, confident but ill-fated, is Zero Mostel in *The Producers*, Frank Langella in *The 12 Chairs*, and Gene Wilder in *Blazing Saddles* and *Young Frankenstein*.

The second member of the duo, usually physically weak and openly neurotic, represents the victim who wins, who learns from his experience and finds friendship to sustain him. These "Jewish weakling" characters include Wilder in *The Producers*, Ron Moody, and Cleavon Little. Though this character, as in the case of Little, need not literally be Jewish, he displays the typical characteristics.

Women in Brooks's films are grotesque figures, sex objects ridiculed and rejected. They are either very old or sexually gross and simple. The love of a friend is obviously worth more than such an object. The secondary male characters, befitting the intentional infantilism of the films, are men-babies given to crying easily. They are set up as examples of what the weak protagonist might become without the paternal care of his reluctant friend. In particular, Brooks sees people who hide behind costumes—cowboy suits, Nazi uniforms, clerical garb, homosexual affectations—as silly children to be made fun of.

The plots of Brooks's films deal with the experienced and inexperienced man searching for a way to triumph in society. They seek a generic solution or are pushed into one. Yet there is no escape into generic fantasy in the Brooks films, since the films take place totally within the fantasy. There is no regard, as in Woody Allen's films, for the pathetic nature of the protagonist in reality. In fact, the Brooks films reverse the Allen films' endings as the protagonists move into a comic fantasy of friendship. (A further contrast with Allen is in the nature of the jokes and gags. Allen's humor is basically adult embarrassment; Brooks's is infantile taboo-breaking.)

In *The Producers* the partners try to manipulate show business and wind up in jail, planning another scheme because they enjoy it. In *The 12 Chairs* they try to cheat the government; at the end Langella and Moody continue working together though they no longer have the quest for the chairs in common. In *Blazing Saddles* Little and Wilder try to take a town; it ends with the actors supposedly playing themselves, getting into a studio car and going off together as pals into the sunset. In these films it is two men alone against a corrupt and childish society. Though their schemes fall apart—or are literally exploded as in *The Producers* and *The 12 Chairs*—they still have each other.

Young Frankenstein departs from the pattern with each of the partners, monster and doctor, sexually committed to women, and while the basic pattern of male buddies continued when Brooks began to act in his own films, he also winds up with the woman when he is the hero star (*High Anxiety, Silent Movie, The History of the World, To Be or Not to Be*). It is interesting that Brooks always tries to distance himself from the homosexual implications of his central theme by including scenes in which overtly homosexual characters are ridiculed. It is particularly striking that these characters are, in *The Producers, Blazing Saddles*, and *The 12 Chairs*, stage or film directors.

—Stuart M. Kaminsky

———

BROOKS, Richard.

American. Born in Philadelphia, 8 May 1912. Educated at Temple University, Philadelphia. Married actress Jean Simmons, 1961. Served in U.S. Marine Corps., 1943–45. Sports reporter for *Atlantic City Press Union*, then *World Telegram*, 1934–36; worked for radio station WNEW, then for NBC, 1936; director for Mild Pond Theatre, New York, 1940; wrote daily radio program from Hollywood, also collaborated on film scripts. 1941; after working with producer Mark Hellinger, signed for MGM, 1946; directed first feature, *Crisis*, 1950; became independent producer, 1965; formed production co., Crime Inc. Pictures, with actor Robert Culp, 1987. Recipient: Oscar for Best Screenplay, and Writers Guild Award for Best-Written Drama, for *Elmer Gantry*, 1960; Laurel Award for Achievement, Writers Guild, 1966.

Films as Director:

1950 *Crisis* (+sc)
1951 *The Light Touch* (+sc)
1952 *Deadline USA* (+sc)
1953 *Battle Circus* (+sc); *Take the High Ground*
1954 *The Flame and the Flesh*; *The Last Time I Saw Paris* (+co-sc)
1955 *The Blackboard Jungle* (+sc)
1956 *The Last Hunt* (+sc); *The Catered Affair*
1957 *Something of Value* (+sc)
1958 *The Brothers Karamazov* (+co-sc); *Cat on a Hot Tin Roof* (+co-sc)
1960 *Elmer Gantry* (+sc)
1961 *Sweet Bird of Youth* (+sc)
1965 *Lord Jim* (+sc)
1966 *The Professionals* (+sc)
1967 *In Cold Blood* (+sc)
1969 *The Happy Ending* (+sc)
1971 *Dollars* (+co-sc)
1975 *Bite the Bullet* (+sc)
1977 *Looking for Mr. Goodbar* (+sc)
1982 *Wrong is Right* (*The Man with the Deadly Lens*)
1985 *The Fever*

Other Films:

1942 *Sin Town* (Enright) (co-sc); *Men of Texas* (co-sc)
1943 *The White Savage* (Lubin) (co-sc); *Cobra Woman* (Siodmak) (co-sc); *My Best Gal* (Anthony Mann) (co-sc); *Don Winslow of the Coast Guard* (co-sc)
1946 *Swell Guy* (Tuttle) (co-sc); *The Killers* (Siodmak) (co-sc)
1947 *Brute Force* (Dassin) (co-sc)
1948 *To the Victor* (Daves) (co-sc); *Key Largo* (Huston) (co-sc); *The Naked City* (Dassin) (co-sc)
1949 *Storm Warning* (Heisler) (co-sc); *Any Number Can Play* (John Sturges) (co-sc)
1950 *Mystery Street* (John Sturges) (co-sc)

Publications:

By BROOKS: books—

The Brick Foxhole, New York, 1946.
The Boiling Point, New York, 1948.
The Producer, New York, 1951.

By BROOKS: articles—

"A Novel Isn't a Movie," in *Films in Review* (New York), February 1952.
"Two Story Conferences," with King Vidor, in *Sight and Sound* (London), October/December 1952.
"On Filming Karamazov," in *Films in Review* (New York), February 1958.
"Dostoievsky, Love and American Cinema," in *Films in Review* (New York), April 1958.
Interview with Charles Bitsch, in *Cahiers du Cinéma* (Paris), February 1959.
"Richard Brooks and *Lord Jim*," interview with Paul Joyce, in *Film* (London), Winter 1964.
"*Lord Jim* Interview," in *Cinema* (Beverly Hills), March/April 1965.
"In Cold Blood," interview in *Cahiers du Cinema in English* (New York), no.5, 1966.
"Richard Brooks Directs *Looking for Mr. Goodbar*," interview with J. Mariani, in *Millimeter* (New York), July/August 1977.
"Richard Brooks Seminar" in *American Film* (Washington, D.C.), October 1977.
Interview with J. Hurley, in *Films in Review* (New York), May 1982.
Interview with D. Rabourdin, in *Cinéma* (Paris), April 1983.

On BROOKS: book—

Brion, Patrick, *Richard Brooks*, Paris, 1986.

On BROOKS: articles—

"Personality of the Month," in *Films in Review* (New York), May 1956.
"Brooks Section" of *Positif* (Paris), July 1956.
Johnson, A., "Richard Brooks," in *Sight and Sound* (London), Autumn 1960.
Godard, Jean-Luc, "Note sur Richard Brooks," in *Cahiers du Cinéma* (Paris), December 1963.
"Brooks Section" of *Movie* (London), Spring 1965.
"Brooks Section" of *Image et Son* (Paris), May 1972.
Thomas, B., "The Secret Scripts of Richard Brooks," in *Action* (Los Angeles), September/October 1975.
Le Pavec, J.-P., and others, "Dossier auteur Richard Brooks," in *Cinéma* (Paris), December 1980.
Interim, L., "Le message de Richard Brooks," in *Cahiers du Cinéma* (Paris), November 1981.
Sinyard, Neil, "Directors of the decade: Richard Brooks," in *Films and Filming* (London), August 1983.

*   *   *

Richard Brooks had his literary education in the hard school of radio and the program picture, where "licking the story" and "getting out the pages" marked progress to an acceptable screenplay. In the tradition of such writers, he won critical acceptance with his bottom-drawer novel, *The Brick Foxhole*, later filmed (and traduced) as *Crossfire*. Projects of an increasing sophistication followed, until he reached his goal of writing

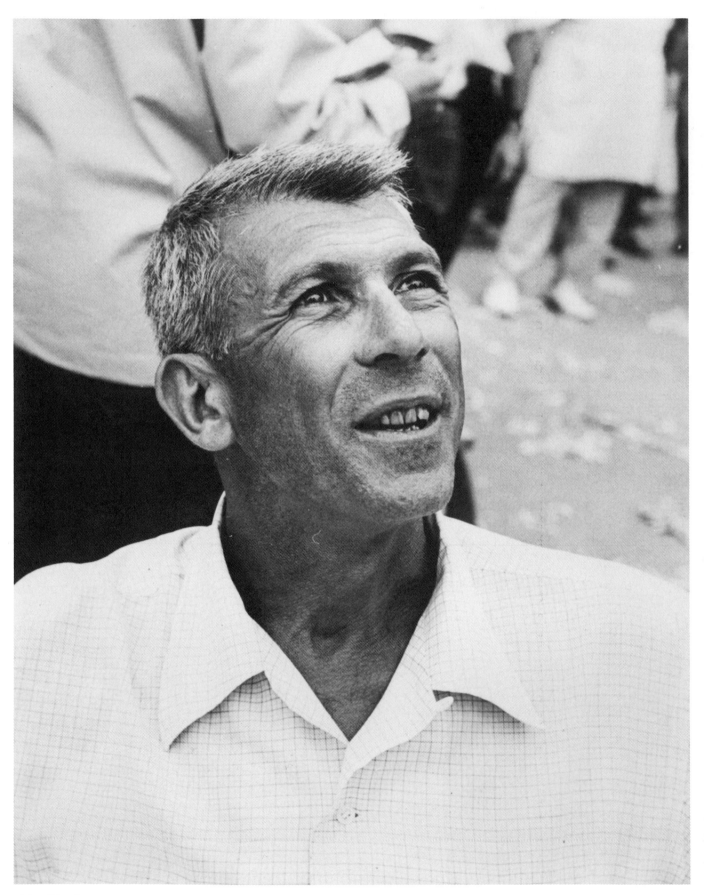

Richard Brooks

and directing serious, "significant" films, only to find the cinema moving away from such material towards a self-regarding personal style he was ill-fitted to pursue.

What won Brooks his commercial success, and will continue to sustain him where films like *The Brothers Karamazov, Lord Jim, In Cold Blood* and *Looking For Mr. Goodbar* may not, are his films of action, for which he displayed a notable skill in his program days, and on which he capitalized in a series of polished and thoughtful westerns. *The Last Hunt, Bite the Bullet* and particularly *The Professionals* all deal effectively with arresting by-ways of the frontier experience. Brooks is interested in the interface between old and new ways, old and new men; the buffalo hunters of *The Last Hunt* represent the conflicting forces of ruthless slaughter and environmental protection, and the long-distance horse racers of *Bite the Bullet* a set of rival motives in which an attitude to horses arises frequently as a symbol. The least overtly significant of them all, *The Professionals* is also the most entertaining, a stylish and character-rich variation on *The Magnificent Seven* which repays frequent re-viewing.

Brooks's literary adaptations are sustained by their bravura performances and little more. He coaxed high passion from Elizabeth Taylor in *Cat on a Hot Tin Roof*, and banked down the same fires in Burt Lancaster to make *Elmer Gantry* one of his best works. But in "licking" essentially unfilmable books like *Lord Jim, The Brothers Karamazov* and *In Cold Blood* he turned first-rate literature into second-rate film. It may be that one of his most tawdry creations, the earliest of the teen exploitation films, *The Blackboard Jungle*, will be the production for which he is best remembered.

—John Baxter

BROWN, Clarence.

American. Born in Clinton, Massachusetts, 10 May 1890. Educated in engineering at University of Tennessee, 1910. Married 1) actress Mona Maris; 2) actress Alice Joyce; 3) former secretary Marian Ruth Spies. Served as Aviator, World War I, 1918. Worked for Moline Automobile Co. and Stephen Duryea Co., then founded Brown Motor Car Company, Birmingham, Alabama, 1911–12; became assistant to Maurice Tourneur, 1915; joined MGM, 1925; helped found Clarence Brown Theatre for the Performing Arts, University of Tennessee, Knoxville, 1971. *Died 17 August 1987.*

Films as Director:

1920   *The Great Redeemer* (co-d with Maurice Tourneur); *The Last of the Mohicans* (co-d with Maurice Tourneur)
1921   *The Foolish Matrons* (co-d with Maurice Tourneur)
1922   *The Light in the Dark*
1923   *Don't Marry for Money*; *The Acquittal*
1924   *The Signal Tower*; *Butterfly*; *Smouldering Fires*
1925   *The Goose Woman*; *The Eagle*
1926   *Kiki*
1927   *The Flesh and the Devil*
1928   *A Woman of Affairs*
1929   *The Trail of '98*; *Wonder of Women*; *Navy Blues*
1930   *Anna Christie*; *Romance*
1931   *Inspiration*; *A Free Soul*; *Possessed*
1932   *Emma*; *Letty Lynton*; *The Son-Daughter*
1933   *Looking Forward*; *Night Flight*

1934   *Sadie McKee*; *Chained*
1935   *Anna Karenina*; *Ah Wilderness*
1936   *Wife Versus Secretary*; *The Gorgeous Hussy*
1937   *Conquest*
1938   *Of Human Hearts*
1939   *Idiot's Delight*; *The Rains Came*
1940   *Edison the Man*
1941   *Come Live with Me*; *They Met in Bombay*
1943   *The Human Comedy*
1944   *The White Cliffs of Dover*; *National Velvet*
1946   *The Yearling*
1947   *Song of Love* (+pr)
1949   *Intruder in the Dust* (+pr)
1950   *To Please a Lady* (+pr)
1951   *Angels in the Outfield* (+pr); episode of *It's a Big Country* (+pr)
1952   *When in Rome* (+pr); *Plymouth Adventure* (+pr)

Other Films:

1949   *The Secret Garden* (Ardrey) (pr)
1953   *Never Let Me Go* (Daves) (pr)

Publications:

By BROWN: articles—

"Bringing Saroyan to the Screen," in *Lion's Roar* (Hollywood), April 1943.
"The Producer Must Be Boss," in *Films in Review* (New York), February 1951.

On BROWN: books—

Brownlow, Kevin, *The Parade's Gone*, London and New York, 1968.
Estrin, Allen, *Capra, Cukor, Brown*, New York, 1980.

On BROWN: articles—

Manners, D., sketch in *Motion Picture Classic* (Brooklyn), April 1928.
Tully, J., "Estimate," in *Vanity Fair* (New York), April 1928.
Brion, P., "Clarence Brown: un grand cinéaste intimiste," in *Cinéma* (Paris), February 1979.
Cebe, G., and others, "Redecouvrir Clarence Brown," in *Ecran* (Paris), 15 June 1979.
Viviani, C., "Inspiration et romance chez Clarence Brown," in *Positif* (Paris), March 1980.
Hollywood Reporter, 19 and 21 August 1987.
McCarthy, T., obituary, in *Variety* (New York), 26 August 1987.
Obituary in *Revue du Cinéma* (Paris), November 1987.

*   *   *

It was in 1915 that Clarence Brown saw a movie being filmed at Fort Lee, New Jersey, and he was so fascinated that he sold his business as head of the Brown Motor Company, and apprenticed himself to Maurice Tourneur, who was about to direct Clara Kimball Young in a film version of *Trilby*. He was then 25 years old, and spent the next five years as assistant to Tourneur, whom he freely acknowledged as his god.

"I owe it all to him," he once said. "Before he got into filmmaking, he was a painter. He used the screen like a canvas. Everything I know about lighting and composition and arrangement I learned from him."

During the making of *The Last of the Mohicans*, Tourneur was injured, and Clarence Brown finished the picture for him; they share the directorial credit. Tourneur and Brown collaborated once again on directing another feature, *The Foolish Matrons*, and Tourneur then told him that he was ready to direct a feature on his own. Brown signed with Universal, then under the management of Carl Laemmle, where he found that he was happiest working with female stars like Pauline Frederick and Laura La Plante in *Smouldering Fires* and Louise Dresser in *The Goose Woman*. Joseph Schenck admired his

Clarence Brown

work, and signed him to direct two for him at United Artists—*The Eagle*, one of the few really good pictures that Rudolph Valentino made, and *Kiki*, which starred Schenck's wife, Norma Talmadge.

Brown signed then with MGM, where he remained the rest of his career until 1952, save for only one loan-out to 20th Century-Fox for *The Rains Came*, a picture he wanted to make. Louis B. Mayer always held him in high regard; in fact, he is the only director at MGM with whom Mayer did not at some time or another quarrel.

The important thing was that MGM had a veritable galaxy of female stars, and it was the woman star with whom Brown felt most compatible. His range as a director at MGM was enviable; he was never typed. He moved from his first picture there, *Flesh and the Devil*, which made Garbo an important star, to an American epic like his last, *Plymouth Adventure*. In between he directed, among others, seven films for Garbo, five for Crawford, and two for Shearer. In spite of that record, he will probably be known best for his cinematic adventures in Americana like *Ah, Wilderness, Of Human Hearts, The Human Comedy, The Yearling*, and *Intruder in the Dust*.

—DeWitt Bodeen

BROWNING, Tod.

American. Born Charles Albert Browning in Louisville, Kentucky, 12 July 1880. Attended school in Churchill Downs. Married Alice Houghton (actress Alice Wilson), 1918. Ran away from home to join a carnival, 1898; worked carnival circuit, then Vaudeville and Burlesque shows; joined Biograph film studio as comedic actor, 1913; directed first film, *The Lucky Transfer*, 1915; joined Universal Studios, began association with Lon Chaney, 1919; signed by MGM, 1925. Recipient: Honorary Life Membership, Directors Guild of America. *Died 6 October 1962.*

Films as Director:

1915 *The Lucky Transfer; The Slave Girl; The Highbinders; The Living Death; The Burned Hand; The Woman from Warren's; Little Marie; The Story of a Story; The Spell of the Poppy; The Electric Alarm*
1916 *Puppets; Everybody's Doing It; The Deadly Glass of Beer (The Fatal Glass of Beer)*
1917 *Jim Bludso* (co-d, co-sc); *Peggy, The Will o' th' Wisp; The Jury of Fate; A Love Sublime* (co-d); *Hands Up!* (co-d)
1918 *The Eyes of Mystery; The Legion of Death; Revenge; Which Woman; The Deciding Kiss; The Brazen Beauty; Set Free* (+sc)
1919 *The Wicked Darling; The Exquisite Thief; The Unpainted Woman; A Petal on the Current; Bonnie, Bonnie Lassie* (+sc)
1920 *The Virgin of Stamboul* (+sc)
1921 *Outside the Law* (+co-sc); *No Woman Knows* (+co-sc)
1922 *The Wise Kid; Under Two Flags* (+co-sc); *Man Under Cover*
1923 *Drifting* (+co-sc); *White Tiger* (+co-sc); *Day of Faith*
1924 *The Dangerous Flirt; Silk Stocking Girl (Silk Stocking Sal)*
1925 *The Unholy Three* (+co-sc); *The Mystic* (+co-sc); *Dollar Down*
1926 *The Black Bird* (+co-sc); *The Road to Mandalay* (+co-sc)
1927 *London After Midnight* (+co-sc); *The Show; The Unknown* (+co-sc)
1928 *The Big City* (+co-sc); *West of Zanzibar*

1929 *Where East is East* (+co-sc); *The Thirteenth Chair*
1930 *Outside the Law* (+co-sc)
1931 **Dracula** (+co-sc); *The Iron Man*
1932 **Freaks**
1933 *Fast Workers*
1935 *Mark of the Vampire* (+sc)
1936 *The Devil-Doll* (+co-sc)
1939 *Miracles for Sale*

Other Films:

1913 *Scenting a Terrible Crime* (for Biograph) (role); *A Fallen Hero* (for Biograph) (role)
1914 *A Race for a Bride* (for Komic) (role); *The Man in the Couch* (for Komic) (role); *An Exciting Courtship* (for Komic) (role); *The Last Drink of Whiskey* (for Komic) (role); *Hubby to the Rescue* (for Komic) (role); *The Deceivers* (for Komic) (role); *The White Slave Catchers* (for Komic) (role); *Wrong All Around* (for Komic) (role); *Leave It to Smiley* (for Komic) (role); *The Wild Girl* (for Komic) (role); *Ethel's Teacher* (for Komic) (role); *A Physical Culture Romance* (for Komic) (role); *The Mascot* (for Komic) (role); *Foiled Again* (for Komic) (role); *The Million Dollar Bride* (for Komic) (role); *Dizzy Joe's Career* (for Komic) (role); *Casey's Vendetta* (for Komic) (role); *Out Again—In Again* (for Komic) (role); *A Corner in Hats* (for Komic) (role); *The Housebreakers* (for Komic) (role); *The Record Breakers* (for Komic) (role)
1914/5 Mr. Hadley in "Bill" series through no. 17 *Ethel Gets Consent* (for Komic) (role)
1915 *The Queen of the Band* (Myers) (story); *Cupid and the Pest* (for Komic) (role); *Music Hath Its Charms* (for Komic) (role); *A Costly Exchange* (for Komic) (role)
1916 *Sunshine Dad* (Dillon) (co-story); *The Mystery of the Leaping Fish* (Emerson) (story); *Atta Boy's Last Race* (Seligmann) (sc); **Intolerance** (Griffith) (role, asst d for crowd scenes)
1919 *The Pointing Finger* (Kull) (supervisor)
1921 *Society Secrets* (McCarey) (supervisor)
1928 *Old Age Handicap* (Mattison) (story under pseudonym Tod Underwood)
1946 *Inside Job* (Yarborough) (story)

Publications:

By BROWNING: articles—

"A Maker of Mystery," interview with Joan Dickey, in *Motion Picture Classic* (Brooklyn), March 1928.

On BROWNING: articles—

Geltzer, George, "Tod Browning," in *Films in Review* (New York), October 1953.
Romer, Jean-Claude, "Tod Browning," in *Bizarre* (Paris), no. 3, 1962.
Obituary in *New York Times*, 10 October 1962.
Guy, Rory, "The Browning Version," in *Cinema* (Beverly Hills), June/July 1963.
Savada, Eli, "Tod Browning," in *Photon* (New York), no. 23, 1973.
Rosenthal, Stuart, "Tod Browning," in *The Hollywood Professionals* vol. 4, London, 1975.
"*Freaks* Issue" of *Avant-Scène du Cinéma* (Paris), July/September 1975.
Garsault, A., "Tod Browning: à la recherche de la réalité," in *Positif* (Paris), July/August 1978.
Hoberman, James, "Tod Browning's Side Show," in the *Village Voice* (New York), 17 September 1979.

*   *   *

It was not through any comparison of his films to the poetry of his namesake Robert Browning that Tod Browning became recognized as a major Hollywood cult director, but rather to the works of Edgar Allen Poe. However, unlike Poe, Tod Browning was, by all accounts, a quiet and gentle man who

Tod Browning

could rise to sarcasm and sardonics when necessary to bring out the best from his players or to ward off interference from the front office.

Browning came to Hollywood as an actor, after working circus and vaudeville, a background obviously supplying elements in many of his films, notably *The Unholy Three, The Show* and *Freaks*. He worked initially in the film industry as an actor until D.W. Griffith (for whom Browning had worked on *Intolerance* as both a performer and assistant director) gave him the chance to direct at the Fine Arts Company. Browning directed a few films for Metro, but came to fame at Universal with a series of features starring Priscilla Dean. It was *The Virgin of Stamboul* which critics particularly admired, but it was his next film, *Outside the Law*, which has more historical significance, marking the first time that Browning was to direct Lon Chaney. (Browning remade the feature as a talkie.)

These Universal productions were little more than pretentious romantic melodramas, but they paved the way for a series of classic M-G-M horror films starring Lon Chaney, from *The Unholy Three* in 1925 through *Where East Is East* in 1929. They were notable for the range of Chaney's performances—a little old lady, a cripple, an armless circus performer, a gangster, and so on—and for Browning's penchant for the macabre. All were stylish productions, well directed, but all left the viewer with a sense of disappointment, of unfulfilled climaxes. Aside from directing, Tod Browning also wrote most of his films, and once explained that the plots were secondary to the characterizations, which perhaps explains the dismal, unexciting endings to many of his features.

Tod Browning made an easy transition to sound films, although surprisingly he did not direct the 1930 remake of *The Unholy Three*. Instead he directed the atmospheric *Dracula*, which made a legend of Bela Lugosi and skillfully blended elements of both comedy and horror. A year later, Browning directed another classic horror talkie, *Freaks*, a realistic and at times offensive melodrama about the physically deformed members of a circus troupe, one of whom, midget Harry Earles marries a trapeze artiste (Olga Baclanova).

Browning ended his career with *The Mark of the Vampire*, a remake of the Chaney feature *London After Midnight*; *The Devil Doll*, in which Lionel Barrymore appears as an old lady, a similar disguise to that adopted by Chaney in *The Unholy Three*; and *Miracles for Sale*, a mystery drama involving professional magicians. Tod Browning will, of course, be best remembered for his horror films, but it should also be recalled that during the first half of his directorial career he stuck almost exclusively to romantic melodrama.

—Anthony Slide

BUÑUEL, Luis.

Spanish. Born in Calanda, province of Teruel, Spain, 22 February 1900. Educated at Jesuit schools in Zaragosa, 1906–15, at Residencia de Estudiantes, Madrid, 1917–20, and at University of Madrid, graduated 1924. Married Jeanne Rucar, 1933, two sons. Assistant to Jean Epstein in Paris, 1925; joined Surrealist group, and directed first film, *Un Chien andalou*, 1929; worked for Paramount in Paris, 1933; Executive Producer for Filmofono, Madrid, 1935; served Republican

government in Spain, 1936–39; worked at Museum of Modern Art, New York, 1939–42; produced Spanish versions of Warners films, Hollywood, 1944; moved to Mexico, 1946; returned to Spain to make *Viridiana*, 1961 (film suppressed). Recipient: Best Director Award and International Critics Prize, Cannes festival, for *Los olvidados*, 1951; Gold Medal, Cannes Festival, for *Nazarin*, 1959, and *Viridiana*, 1961; Golden Lion, Venice festival, for *Belle de jour*, 1967. *Died in Mexico City, 29 July 1983.*

Films as Director:

1929   *Un Chien andalou* (+pr, co-sc, ed, role as Man with razor)
1930   *L'Age d'or* (+co-sc, ed, mu)
1932   *Las Hurdes—Tierra sin pan* (*Land Without Bread*) (+sc, ed)
1935   *Don Quintin el amargao* (Marquina) (co-d uncredited, +pr, co-sc); *La hija de Juan Simón* (Sáenz de Heredia) (co-d uncredited, +pr, co-sc)
1936   *Centinela alerta!* (Grémillon) (co-d uncredited, +pr, co-sc)
1940   *El Vaticano de Pio XII* (*The History of the Vatican*) (short, special issue of *March of Time* series)
1947   *Gran Casino* (*Tampico*)
1949   *El gran calavera*
1950   *Los olvidados* (*The Forgotten, The Young and the Damned*) (+co-sc); *Susana* (*Demonio y carne*) (+co-sc)
1951   *La hija del engaño* (*Don Quintín el amargao*); *Cuando los hijos nos juzgan* (*Una mujer sin amor*); *Subida al cielo* (+sc)
1952   *El Bruto* (+co-sc); *Las aventuras de Robinson Crusoe* (*Adventures of Robinson Crusoe*) (+co-sc); *El* (+co-sc)
1953   *Abismos de pasión* (*Cumbres borrascoses*) (+co-sc); *La ilusión viaja en tranvía* (+co-sc)
1954   *El rio y la muerte* (+co-sc)
1955   *Ensayo de un crimen* (*La Vida Criminal de Archibaldo de La Cruz, The Criminal Life of Archibaldo de la Cruz*) (+co-sc); *Cela s'appelle l'Aurore* (+co-sc)
1956   *La Mort en ce jardin* (*La muerte en este jardin*) (+co-sc)
1958   *Nazarín* (+co-sc)
1959   *La Fièvre monte à El Pao* (*Los Ambiciosos*) (+co-sc)
1960   *The Young One* (*La Joven, La Jeune Fille*) (+co-sc)
1961   *Viridiana* (+co-sc, story)
1962   *El ángel exterminador* (*The Exterminating Angel*) (+co-sc, story)
1963   *Le Journal d'une femme de chambre* (+co-sc)
1965   *Simón del desierto* (+co-sc)
1966   *Belle de jour* (+co-sc)
1969   *La Voie lactée* (*The Milky Way, La via lattea*) (+co-sc, mu)
1970   *Tristana* (+co-sc)
1972   *Le Charme discret de la bourgeoisie* (*The Discreet Charm of the Bourgeoisie*) (+co-sc)
1974   *Le Fantôme de la liberté* (*The Phantom of Liberty*) (+sc, sound effects)
1977   *Cet obscur objet du desir* (*That Obsure Object of Desire*) (+co-sc)

Other Films:

1926   *Mauprat* (Epstein) (asst d, role as monk)
1927   *La Sirène des tropiques* (Etiévant and Nalpas) (asst d)
1928   *La Chute de la maison Usher* (Epstein) (asst d)
1936   *Quién me quiere a mi?* (Sáenz de Heredia) (pr, co-sc, ed)
1937   *Espagne 1937/España leal en armas!* (compilation, ed)
1940   *Triumph of Will* (supervising editor, commentary, edited compilation of Riefenstahl's *Triumph des Willens* and Hans Bertram's *Feuertaufe*)
1950   *Si usted no puede, yo sí* (Soler) (co-story)
1964   *Llanto por un bandido* (*Lament for a Bandit*) (Saura) (role as the executioner; tech advisor on arms and munitions); *En este pueblo no hay ladrones* (Isaac) (role)
1972   *Le Moine* (Kyrou) (co-sc)
1973   *La Chute d'un corps* (Polac) (role)

Publications:

By BUÑUEL: books—

Viridiana, Paris, 1962; Mexico City, 1963.
El ángel exterminador, Barcelona, 1964.
L'Age d'or and Une Chien andalou, London, 1968.
Three Screenplays: Viridiana, The Exterminating Angel, Simon of the Desert, New York, 1969.
Belle de Jour, London, 1971.
Tristana, London, 1971.
The Exterminating Angel/Nazarín/Los Olvidados, London, 1972.
My Last Breath, New York, 1983.

By BUÑUEL: articles—

Interview with Jacques Doniol-Valcroze and André Bazin, in *Cahiers du Cinéma* (Paris), June 1954.
Interview with Daniel Aubry and Jean Lacor, in *Film Quarterly* (Berkeley), Winter 1958.
"Poésie et cinéma," in *Cinéma* (Paris), June 1959.
"Luis Buñuel—A Statement," in *Film Culture* (New York), Summer 1960.
"The Cinema: An Instrument of Poetry," in *New York Film Bulletin*, February 1961.
Interview with Kenji Kanesaka, in *Film Culture* (New York), Spring 1962.
"Illisible, fils de flûte: synopsis d'un scénario non réalisé," with Jean Larrea, in *Positif* (Paris), March 1963.
"Luis Buñuel: voix off," an interview with Manuel Michel, in *Cinéma* (Paris), March 1965.
"Buñuel contre son mythe," an interview with Manuel Michel, in *Cinéma* (Paris), April 1966.
"Luis Buñuel," in *Interviews with Film Directors*, edited by Andrew Sarris, New York, 1967.
Interview with J. Cobos and G. S. de Erice, in *Cahiers du Cinéma* (Paris), June 1967.
"Buñuel Scenes," an interview with Carlos Fuentes, in *Movietone News* (Seattle), February 1975.
"Aragón, Madrid, Paris . . . Entrevista con Luis Buñuel," with J. de la Colina and T. Pérez, in *Contracampo* (Madrid), October/November 1980.
Interview with Aldo Tassone, in *Chaplin* (Stockholm), vol. 24, no. 3, 1982.
"Dali intervista Buñuel," in *Cinema Nuovo* (Bari), December 1983.

On BUÑUEL: books—

Kyrou, Ado, *Luis Buñuel*, Paris, 1962.
Estève, Michel, editor, *Luis Buñuel*, Paris, 1962/63.
Durgnat, Raymond, *Luis Buñuel*, Berkeley, California, 1968.
Luis Buñuel: Biografia Critica, Madrid, 1969.
Buache, Freddy, *Luis Buñuel*, Lausanne, 1970; as *The Cinema of Luis Buñuel*, London, 1973.
Matthews, J. H., *Surrealism and Film*, Ann Arbor, Michigan, 1971.
Alcalá, Manuel, *Buñuel (Cine e ideologia)*, Madrid, 1973.
Aranda, José Francisco, *Luis Buñuel: A Critical Biography*, New York, 1975
Cesarman, Fernando, *El ojo de Buñuel*, Barcelona, 1976.
Drouzy, M., *Luis Buñuel, architecte du rêve*, Paris, 1978.
Mellen, Joan, editor, *The World of Luis Buñuel*, New York, 1978.
Cameron, Ian, *Luis Buñuel*, Berkeley, California, 1979.
Higginbotham, Virginia, *Luis Buñuel*, Boston, 1979.
Bazin, André, *The Cinema of Cruelty: From Buñuel to Hitchcock*, New York, 1982.
Cesarman, Fernando, *L'Oeil de Buñuel*, Paris, 1982.
Edwards, Gwynne, *The Discreet Art of Luis Buñuel: A Reading of His Films*, London, 1982.
Rees, Margaret A., *Luis Buñuel: A Symposium*, Leeds, 1983.
Lefèvre, Raymond, *Luis Buñuel*, Paris, 1984.
Vidal, Agustin Sanchez, *Luis Buñuel: Obra Cinematografica*, Madrid, 1984.
Aub, Max, *Conversaciones con Buñuel: Seguidas de 45 Entrevistas con Familiares, Amigos y Colaboradores del Cineasta Aragones*, Madrid, 1985.
Bertelli, Pino, *Buñuel: L'Arma dello Scandalo: L'Anarchia nel Cinema di Luis Buñuel*, Turin, 1985.

Oms, Marcel, *Luis Buñuel*, Paris, 1985.
De la Colina, José, and Tomas Perez Turrent, *Luis Buñuel: Prohibido Asomarse al Interior*, Mexico, 1986.
Sandro, Paul, *Diversions of Pleasure: Luis Buñuel and the Crises of Desire*, Columbus, Ohio, 1987.

On BUÑUEL: articles—

Demeure, Jacques, "Luis Buñuel: poète de la cruaute," in *Positif* (Paris), no.10, 1954.
Richardson, Tony, "The Films of Luis Buñuel," in *Sight and Sound* (London), January/March 1954.
Robles, Emmanuel, "A Mexico avec Luis Buñuel," in *Cahiers du Cinéma* (Paris), October 1956.
Riera, Emilio, "The Eternal Rebellion of Luis Buñuel," in *Film Culture* (New York), Summer 1960.
Bazin, André, "Los Olvidados," in *Qu'est ce que le cinéma* vol.3, Paris, 1961.
Aranda, José Francisco, "Surrealist and Spanish Giant," in *Films and Filming* (London), October 1961.
Aranda, José Francisco, "Back from the Wilderness," in *Films and Filming* (London), November 1961.
"Buñuel Issue" of *Positif* (Paris), November 1961.
Prouse, Derek, "Interviewing Buñuel," in *Sight and Sound* (London), Summer 1962.
Almendros, Nestor, "Luis Buñuel: Cinéaste hispanique," in *Objectif* (Paris), July 1963.
Lovell, Alan, "Luis Buñuel," in *Anarchist Cinema*, London, 1964.
Hammond, Robert, "Luis Alcoriza and the Films of Luis Buñuel," in *Film Heritage* (Dayton, Ohio), Autumn 1965.
Milne, Tom, "The Mexican Buñuel," in *Sight and Sound* (London), Winter 1965/66.
Kanesaka, Kenji, "A Visit to Luis Buñuel," in *Film Culture* (New York), Summer 1966.
Harcourt, Peter, "Luis Buñuel: Spaniard and Surrealist," in *Film Quarterly* (Berkeley), Spring 1967.
Torres, Augusto, "Luis Buñuel/Glauber Rocha: échos d'une conversation," in *Cinéma* (Paris), February 1968.
"Buñuel Issue" of *Jeune Cinéma* (Paris), April 1969.
Pechter, William, "Buñuel," in *24 Times a Second*, New York, 1971.
"Buñuel Issue" of *Image et Son* (Paris), May 1971.
"Buñuel Issue" of *Cine Cubano*, no.78/80, 1973.
Lyon, E.H., "Luis Buñuel: The Process of Dissociation in Three Films," in *Cinema Journal* (Evanston, Illinois), Fall 1973.
Fuentes, Carlos, "Spain, Catholicism, Surrealism and Anarchism: The Discreet Charm of Luis Buñuel," in *New York Times Magazine*, 11 March 1973.
Murray, S., "Erotic Moments in the Films of Luis Buñuel," in *Cinema Papers* (Melbourne), July 1974.
"*Le Fantôme de la liberté* Issue" of *Avant-Scène du Cinéma* (Paris), October 1974.
George, G.L., "The Discreet Charm of Luis Buñuel," in *Action* (Los Angeles), November/December 1974.
Mortimore, R., "Buñuel, Sáenz de Heredia and Filmófono," in *Sight and Sound* (London), Summer 1975.
Conrad, Randall, "The Minister of the Interior is on the Telephone: The Early Films of Luis Buñuel," in *Cineaste* (New York), no. 7, 1976.
Conrad, Randall, "A Magnificent and Dangerous Weapon: The Politics of Luis Buñuel's Later Films," in *Cineaste* (New York), no.8, 1976.
Yutkevich, S., "Ein Realist—streng und mitleidlos," in *Film und Fernsehen* (Berlin), February 1980.
Wood, M., "The discreet charm of Luis Buñuel," in *American Film* (Washington, D.C.), September 1982.
Perez, G., "The Thread of the disconcerting," in *Sight and Sound* (London), Winter 1982–83.
Rubinstein, E., "Visit to a familiar planet: Buñuel among the Hurdanos," in *Cinema Journal* (Chicago), Summer 1983.
McCarthy, T., obituary in *Variety* (New York), 3 August 1983.
Millar, Gavin, "Buñuel—the careful entomologist," in *Listener* (London), 11 August 1983.
Mayersberg, P., "The happy ending of Luis Buñuel," in *Sight and Sound* (London), Autumn 1983.

Luis Buñuel

"Buñuel Section" of *Cinématographe* (Paris), September–October 1983.

Yakir, Dan, and others, "Luis Buñuel, 1900–1983," in *Film Comment* (New York), September–October 1983.

"Buñuel Section" of *Positif* (Paris), October 1983.

Greenbaum, R., obituary in *Films in Review* (New York), October 1983.

"Buñuel Issue" of *Avant-Scène du Cinéma* (Paris), November 1983.

"Buñuel Issue," of *Bianco e Nero* (Rome), July–September 1984.

"Luis Buñuel," in *Film Dope* (London), March 1985.

Carrière, Jean-Claude, "Les aventures du sujet," in *Cahiers du Cinéma* (Paris), May 1985.

"*Cet objet obscur de desir* Issue" of *Avant-Scène du Cinéma* (Paris), November 1985.

Poplein, Michael, "Wuthering Heights and Its 'Spirit'," in *Literature/ Film Quarterly* (Salisbury, Maryland), vol. 15, no. 2, 1987.

Taves, B., "Whose hand? Correcting a Buñuel Myth," in *Sight and Sound* (London), Summer 1987.

On BUÑEL: films—

Bazin, Jeanine, and André Labarthe, *Cinéastes de notre temps*, for TV, 1967.

Labarthe, André, *Luis Buñuel*, with interview with Georges Sadoul, Paris, 1967.

*   *   *

For all the critical attention (and furious critical controversy) his work occasioned over half a century, Luis Buñuel resisted our best taxonomical efforts. To begin with, while no artist of this century strikes one as more quintessentially Spanish than Buñuel, how can one apply the term "Spanish filmmaker" to a man whose *oeuvre* is far more nearly identified with France and Mexico than with the land of his birth? By the same token, can one speak of any film as "typical" of the man who made both *L'Age d'or* and *Nazarín*, both *Los olvidados* and *Belle de jour*, both *Land Without Bread* and *Le Charme discret de la bourgeoisie?* Nonetheless, from *Un Chien andalou* to *Cet obscur objet du désir*, a Buñuel film is always (albeit, as in many of the Mexican pieces of the 1940's and 1950's, only sporadically), a Buñuel film.

Perhaps the easiest way to deal with Buñuel's career is to suggest that certain avatars of Luis Buñuel may be identified at different (if sometimes slightly overlapping) historical periods. The first Luis Buñuel is the Surrealist: the man who slit eyeballs (*Un Chien andalou*), the man to whom blasphemy was less a matter of specific utterances and gestures than a controlling style out of which might emerge new modes of feeling and of expression (*L'Age d'or*), the man who documentarized the unimaginable (*Land Without Bread*) and finally, the man who demonstrated more clearly than any other that surrealist perspectives demanded cinematographic realism. The second Luis Buñuel (and the saddest, and much the least identifiable, now as then) is the all-but-anonymous journeyman film professional: the collaborator, often unbilled and almost always unremarked, on Spanish films which to this day remain unknown to any but the most dogged researchers; the archivist and adapter and functionary in New York and Hollywood; the long-term absentee from the world's attention. The third is the Mexican director, the man who achieved a few works that at the time attracted varying degrees of notice outside the sphere of Latin American commercial distribution (*Los olvidados, Él, Archibaldo de la Cruz, Robinson Crusoe*) but also of others that at the time attracted no notice at all. The fourth is the Luis Buñuel who gradually made his way back to Europe by way of a few French films made in alternation with films in Mexico; and who then, with *Viridiana*, returned to appall, and so to reclaim, his native land; and who thenceforth, and no matter where or under what conditions he operated, persuasively reasserted himself as a figure of unmistakable moment in world cinema. The last Luis Buñuel, following his emergence in the mid-1960's, was the past master, at once awesome and beloved, as serene in his command of his medium as he was cheerfully intrepid in his pursuit of whatever of value might be mined from the depths of the previously unexplored.

Each of the Buñuels of the preceding catalogue, except for the obscure and essentially uncreative second one, is manifest, or at least implicit, in the others. Even in his Mexican work, including some otherwise less than exalted assignments (and Buñuel himself, unlike certain of his more indiscriminate adulators, was perfectly willing to acknowledge that much of his Mexican work was shoddy or aborted or simply dull), the scion of surrealism showed his hand. There are several astonishing dream sequences, of course: the vision of slabs of raw meat hanging from the racks of a Mexico City streetcar (*La ilusión viaja en tranvía*), the incongruous verticality of the skeletal skyscrapers rising from the Mexico City slums (*Los olvidados*), and the necrophiliac ragings at the end of the Buñuel version of *Wuthering Heights* (*Abismos de pasión*). At the same time, it was in his Mexican studio movies, with their often absurdly brief shooting schedules, that Buñuel developed the unobtrusive but sovereign sway over narrative continuity and visual construction that so exhilarates admirers of such later works as *Le Journal d'une femme de chambre* or *Cet obscur objet du*

désir. (According to Francisco Aranda, Alfred Hitchcock in 1972 called Buñuel "the best director in the world.")

Similarly, one may recognize in *Tristana* that same merciless anatomy of a specific social milieu, and in *The Exterminating Angel* that same theme of inexplicable entrapment, that one first encountered in *Land Without Bread*. And when, in *El rio y la muerte*, we watch a man, all of him save his head imprisoned in an iron lung, submitting to a round of face-slapping, and when we recognize in the image (and in the gasp of laughter it provokes) something of the merciless attack on our pieties of Buñuel's early Surrealist works and something of the more offhand wicked humor of, say, *Le Charme discret*, then we know that the variety of styles and accents in which Buñuel addressed us over the years is almost irrelevant. The political and social (or anti-social) canons of early surrealism could not contain him, nor could the foolish melodramatic conventions of some of his Mexican films stifle his humor, nor could the elegant actors and luxurious color cinematography of some of the later French films finally seduce him. Against all odds, his vision sufficed to transcend any and all stylistic diversions.

"Vision," perhaps the most exhausted word in the critical vocabulary, struggles back to life when applied to Buñuel and his camera. In the consistent clarity of its perception, in its refusal to distinguish between something called "reality" and something called "hallucination," Buñuel's camera always acts in the service of a fundamental surrealist principle, one of the few principles of any kind that Buñuel was never tempted to call into question. Whether focused on the tragic earthly destiny of an inept wouldbe saint (*Nazarín*) or on the bizarre obsessions of an inept wouldbe sinner (the uncle in *Viridiana*, among a good many others), Buñuel's camera is the instrument of the most rigorous denotation, invoking nothing beyond that which it so plainly and patiently registers. The uncertainties and ambivalences we may feel as we watch a Buñuel film arise not from the camera's capacity to mediate but from the camera's capacity to record: our responses are inherent in the subjects Buñuel selects, in those extremes of human experiences that we recognize as his special domain.

—E. Rubinstein

C

CACOYANNIS, Michael.

Greek. Born in Limassol, Cyprus, 11 June 1927. Educated at
Greek Gymnasium; Gray's Inn Law School, London, called to
the Bar, 1948; Central School of Speech and Drama, London;
Stage Directing course, Old Vic School, London. Radio Producer for BBC, and actor in London, early 1950's; returned to
Greece and directed first film, *Windfall in Athens*, 1953; later
directed stage productions in London and on Broadway. Lives
in Greece.

Films as Director:

1953   *Windfall in Athens*
1955   *Stella*
1957   *A Girl in Black*
1958   *The Final Lie* (*A Matter of Dignity*)
1959   *Our Last Spring*
1960   *The Wastrel*
1962   *Electra*
1964   *Zorba the Greek*
1967   *The Day the Fish Came Out*
1971   *The Trojan Women* (*Women of Troy*)
1975   *Atilla 74* (doc)
1977   *Iphigenia*
1987   *Sweet Country*

Publications:

By CACOYANNIS: articles—

Interview with Pierre Billard, in *Cinéma* (Paris), February 1957.
Interview in *Films and Filming* (London), January 1960.
Films and Filming (London), June 1963.
Interview in *Screen International* (London), 13 May 1978.
Interview with James Potts, in *Educational Broadcasting Internation-
    al*, September 1978.

On CACOYANNIS: book—

Schuster, Mel, *The Contemporary Greek Cinema*, Metuchen, New
    Jersey, 1979.

On CACOYANNIS: articles—

Stanbrook, Alan, "Rebel with a Cause," in *Film* (London), no. 24,
    1960.
Bianco e Nero (Rome), December 1963.
"Michael Cacoyannis," in *Film Dope* (London), November 1974.
"Michael Cacoyannis," in *International Film Guide 1976*, edited by
    Peter Cowie, London, 1976.
National Film Theatre Booklet (London), April 1978.
Rivista del Cinematografo, May 1981.

*   *   *

A man between two worlds—this is how the life and work of
Michael Cacoyannis could be characterized. The first world is
one which draws on classical drama, his background in the
modern theatre, and modern European cinema. The second
world incorporates a mixture of the cultural knowledge acquired during his training in England with an inborn sense of
the Greek tradition. This is the background from which
Cacoyannis creates an original cinematographic depiction of
contemporary life.

At the beginning of his career, Cacoyannis's inspiration
came from the film classics as much as from his theatrical background; for his debut *Kyriakatiko ksypnéma*, it is René Clair
who appears to be his spiritual tutor. Cacoyannis's creative
path then led from comedy to drama, to an analysis of the fragile nature of human relations. His stories, of Stella the singer,
of the "girl in black" on the island of Hydros, or the story of the
lost hopes of a broken family, are attempts to interpret the contemporary Greek reality in a very raw way. The films capture
the archaic rigidity of social relations and the feelings of loneliness. The random tragic moments in which the city intellectuals, as well as the ordinary village people, find themselves are

Michael Cacoyannis (left) on the set of *Our Last Spring*

milestones along their path to happiness. City streets, forgotten villages on lonely islands, and scorched foothills provide a suitably poignant backdrop for the fates of Cacoyannis's characters. It is said—with good reason—that early Cacoyannis films carry the spiritual heritage of Italian neo-realism.

These efforts culminated, through directly drawing upon literature, in the creation of the full-blooded renaissance figure, in *Zorba the Greek*, of Alexis Zorba—a portait of a man who lives (and loves) life to the full. The friendship of this "Man of Nature" with the young writer as shown by the director in a confrontation of dramatically realistic (but also poetic) pictures, is the victory of the human spirit over convention. Also here in "sotto voce" is the pathos of sights and thoughts, a ghost-like echo of ancient Greek tragedy.

This mainstream of the contemporary dramas is also expanded to incorporate elements of classical Greek traditions. Using Greek locations, under a blazing sun, Cacoyannis reworks not only the story of Elektra, but from mythology picks the story of the Trojans in *The Trojan Women*, while in the grand scenery of Olive groves he lets the figure of Euripides talk about the Princess in *Iphigenia*. Cacoyannis does all this in order to address, for a contemporary audience, the eternal question of crime and punishment, to show that evil among people ultimately produces only more evil. For him the ancient myths encapsulate eternal conflicts of the human soul. Thus is Michael Cacoyannis a poet of the modern Greek cinema.

—Vacláv Merhaut

CAMERINI, Mario.

Italian. Born in Rome, 6 February 1895. Studied Law. Served in Italian Army, World War I, imprisoned as German prisoner-of-war. Joined cousin Augusto Genina in film industry, as writer and assistant, 1920; left Genina, 1922, and directed first film, *Jolly*, 1923; first used actor Vittorio De Sica, in *Gli uomine, che mascalzoni!*, 1932. Died 6 February 1981.

Films as Director and Co-Scriptwriter:

1923 *Jolly—Clown da circo*
1924 *La Casa dei Pulcini*
1925 *Maciste contro lo Sceicco*; *Voglio Tradire mio Marito*
1926 *Saetta—Principe per un Giorno*
1927 *Kiff Tebbi* (*As You Please*)
1929 *Rotaie* (*Railway Tracks*)
1930 *La Riva dei Bruti* (*The Banks of the Brutes*)
1931 *Figaro e la sua Gran Giornato* (*Figaro and His Great Day*)
1932 *L'Ultima Avventura* (*The Last Adventure*); *Gli Uomine che Mascalzoni!* (*Men, What Scoundrels!*)
1933 *Cento di questi Giorno*; *Giallo*; *T'Amerò sempre* (*I Will Always Love You*)
1934 *Il Capello a tre Punte* (*The Three-Cornered Hat*); *Come le Foglie* (*As the Leaves*)
1936 *Darò un milione* (*I Will Give You a Million*); *Il grande appello* (*The Great Appeal. The Last Roll-Call*); *Ma non é una Cosa seria* (*It Isn't a Serious Thing*) (German version, *Der Mann der nicht nein sagen kann*, released 1938)
1937 *Il Signor Max* (*Mr. Max*)
1938 *Batticuore* (*Heartbeat*)
1939 *Il Documento Fatale*; *I Grandi Magazzini* (*Department Store*)
1940 *Centomila Dollari*; *Una Romantica Avventura*
1941 *I Promessi Sposi* (*The Spirit and the Flesh. The Betrothed*)
1942 *Una Storia d'Amore* (*A Love Story*)
1943 *T'Amerò sempre*
1945 *Due Lettere Anonime* (*Two Anonymous Letters*)
1946 *L'Angelo e il Diavolo*
1947 *La Figlia del Capitano* (*The Captain's Daughter*)
1948 *Molti Sogni per le Strade* (*Woman Trouble. Many Dreams along the Streets*)
1949 *Due Mogli sono Troppe* (*Honeymoon Deferred. Two Wives are Too Many*)
1950 *Il Brigante Musolini* (*Mussolini the Bandit*)
1951 *Moglie per una notte* (*Wife for One Night*)
1952 *Gli Eroi della Domenica* (*Sunday Heroes*)
1954 *Ulisse* (*Ulysses*)
1955 *La Bella Mugnaiai!* (*The Miller's Beautiful Wife*)
1956 *Suor Letizia* (*The Awakening. When Angels Don't Fly*)
1957 *Vacanze a Ischia* (*Holiday Island*)
1958 *Primo Amore*
1960 *Via Margutta* (*Run With the Devil*); *Crimen* (*And Suddenly It's Murder*)
1961 *I Briganti Italiani* (*Seduction of the South*)
1963 *Kali Yug—La Dea della Vendetta*; *Il Mistero del Tempio Indiano*
1966 *Delitto quasi Perfetto*
1971 *Io non vedo tu non parli lui non sente*
1972 *Don Camillo e i Giovanni d'Oggi*

Film as Scriptwriter Only:

1956 *War and Peace* (King Vidor)

Publications:

By CAMERINI: articles—

Interview in *Rivista del Cinematografo*, January/February 1980.

On CAMERINI: book—

Leprohon, Pierre, *The Italian Cinema*, New York, 1972.

On CAMERINI: articles—

Cinema (Rome), 1 February 1952.
Positif (Paris), October 1976.
Obituary in *Variety* (New York), 11 February 1981.
Obituary in the *Times* (London), 26 February 1981.
Obituary in *Image et Son* (Paris), April 1981.
Rivista del cinematografo, August and November 1981.
Dossier on Camerini, in *Positif* (Paris), March 1986.

*   *   *

Mario Camerini was directing movies for five decades but is notable only for his work in the 1930s, when he made some fresh comedies featuring workers of humble origin. He entered the film industry in 1920, as assistant to his cousin, Augusto Genina, who had been directing since 1913. Camerini was given the chance to direct in 1923, but was not prolific, partly because the Italian industry was in a parlous state at this point, virtually ruined, reeling under competition, principally from Germany and the U.S. The few Italian films still extant from this time are surprisingly amateurish, given the technical polish of the "diva" movies which preceded them. Camerini's one surviving Silent film is no exception, *Voglio Tradire Mio Marito!* (1925), which may be said to be a comedy in the Lubitsch manner, of marital misunderstandings. It trades much on the sins promised in the title, with the male cast either overweight or over-age, and all dreary performers. Only Linda Pini, as a wife tempted to desert her philandering husband, has any sparkle.

Camerini's *Kiff Tebbi*, filmed on location in Africa, was reckoned to be one of the better Italian films of the period, and certainly his *Gli Uomini che Mascalzoni!* is one of the best Italian films of the early Sound period. Like *Kiff Tebbi* it was almost wholly photographed on location, which would seem natural in a sunny country like Italy. The Italian neo-realists have been wrongly credited with discovering *plein air*: Italian painting of this period was much concerned with outdoor subjects and the working classes. Camerini's film further confounds the propagandists of the neo-realists by being aggressively concerned with ordinary people, as a shopgirl (Lia Franca) and a chauffeur (Vittorio De Sica) fall in love. It is not technically accomplished, but it is affectionate, confident and charming on the ways of human behaviour.

The same qualities are evident in *T'Amerò Sempre* (1933), which starts with the disadvantage of being in the tradition of peasant drama, with a poor girl (Elsa de Giorgo) being seduced and abandoned by a Count. Yet the irony implied in the title—he told her he would always love her—is immediately apparent, and the piece is gently funny, mainly at the expense of the bourgeoisie. *Il Cappello a Tre Punti* was a pretty, noisy and accomplished version of the Spanish tale that we know best as the ballet with music by Manuel de Falla, in this case used as a vehicle for the De Filipo brothers. Unlike his earlier work, this gives no hint of Camerini as social satirist, which was his declared aim with both *Darò un Milione* and *Il Signor Max*, his most outstanding films of the period. Both were vehicles for De Sica, who had become the country's leading matinee idol; in the first he is a millionaire who, out of boredom, exchanges clothes with a hobo, and in the second an ambitious young ne'er-do-well in pursuit of a wealthy wife but unable to refrain from flirting with the maid when his target is not in view. Several jokes misfire and a general desperation points back to *Voglio Tradire Mio Marito!*, but there is a geniality and a sense that Italian society had some strange values. Cesare Zavattini and Mario Soldati respectively wrote the screenplays with Camerini.

It was Zavattini's first credited work in films, but Soldati had been a screenwriter since 1931. He turned director in 1938, and in 1941 enjoyed a success with a literary adaptation, *Piccolo Mondo Antico*. The restrictions imposed by the War and Mussolini's government resulted in a plethora of similar adaptations, known as the "calligraphic" school, from the meticulous way in which they were made. Camerini attempted an expensive version of Manzoni's novel *I Promessi Sposi*, but it was pedestrian and not well served by Dina Sassoli in the leading-role. In 1943 he remade *T'Amerò Sempre*, and when the War was over alternated between comedies and literary adaptations of no great distinction. Meanwhile, De Sica had turned director and with Zavattini as writer was making some of the greatest pictures of the neo-realist movement, notably *Ladri di Biciclette*, which was acclaimed the world over. But not in Italy, which meant that there was no pressing need for Camerini to abandon the increasingly commercial films he was making. In the 1960's he was directing crime thrillers and jungle adventures of no individuality, but there is a slight, wayward charm to some of his films of the previous decade, especially *La Bella Mugnaia* a remake of *Il Cappello a Tre Punti* with De Sica and Sophia Loren. He may also be remembered as the director in charge of the first of the many Italian attempts to make movies for the international market, *Ulysses*, which should have deterred others from trying.

—David Shipman

CAPRA, Frank.

American. Born in Bisaquino, Sicily, 18 May 1897; emigrated with family to Los Angeles, 1903. Educated at Manual Arts High School, Los Angeles; studied chemical engineering at California Institute of Technology, Pasadena, graduated 1918. Married 1) Helen Howell, 1924 (divorced 1938); 2) Lucille Reyburn, 1932, two sons, one daughter, Ballistics teacher, U.S. Army, 1918–19. Lab assistant for Walter Bell, 1922–23; prop man, editor for Bob Eddy, writer for Hal Roach and Mack Sennett, 1923–25; hired by Columbia Pictures, 1928; began to work with Robert Riskin, 1931; elected President of Academy, 1935; elected President of Screen Directors' Guild, 1938; formed Frank Capra Productions with writer Robert Riskin, 1939; Major in Signal Corps, 1942–45; formed Liberty Films with Sam Briskin, William Wyler, and George Stevens, 1945 (sold to Paramount, 1948). Recipient: Oscar for Best Director, for *It Happened One Night*, 1934, for *Mr. Deeds Goes to Town*, 1936, and *You Can't Take It With You*, 1938; Distinguished Service Medal, U.S. Armed Forces, 1945; D.W. Griffith Award, Directors Guild of America, 1958; Honorary Doctorates, Temple University, Philadelphia, 1971, and Carthage College, Wisconsin, 1972. Address: P.O. Box 980, La Quinta, CA 92253, U.S.A.

Films as Director:

1922	*Fultah Fisher's Boarding House*
1926	*The Strong Man* (+co-sc)
1927	*Long Pants*; *For the Love of Mike*
1928	*That Certain Thing*; *So This is Love*; *The Matinee Idol*; *The Way of the Strong*; *Say It With Sables* (+co-story); *Submarine*; *The Power of the Press*; *The Swim Princess*; *The Burglar (Smith's Burglar)*
1929	*The Younger Generation*; *The Donovan Affair*; *Flight* (+dialogue)
1930	*Ladies of Leisure*; *Rain or Shine*
1931	*Dirigible*; *The Miracle Woman*; *Platinum Blonde*
1932	*Forbidden* (+sc); *American Madness*
1933	*The Bitter Tea of General Yen* (+pr); *Lady for a Day*
1934	*It Happened One Night*; *Broadway Bill*
1936	*Mr. Deeds Goes to Town* (+pr)
1937	*Lost Horizon* (+pr)
1938	*You Can't Take It With You* (+pr)
1939	*Mr. Smith Goes to Washington* (+pr)
1941	*Meet John Doe* (+pr)
1942	*Why We Fight (Part 1): Prelude to War* (+pr)
1943	*Why We Fight (Part 2): The Nazis Strike* (co-d, pr); *Why We Fight (Part 3): Divide and Conquer* (co-d, pr)
1944	*Why We Fight (Part 6): The Battle of China* (co-d, pr); *Tunisian Victory* (co-d, pr); *Arsenic and Old Lace* (+pr) (filmed in 1942)
1945	*Know Your Enemy: Japan* (co-d, pr); *Two Down, One to Go* (+pr)
1946	*It's a Wonderful Life* (+pr, co-sc)
1948	*State of the Union* (+pr)
1950	*Riding High* (+pr)
1951	*Here Comes the Groom* (+pr)
1956	*Our Mr. Sun* (+pr, sc) (Bell System Science Series Numbers 1 to 4)
1957	*Hemo the Magnificent* (+pr, sc); *The Strange Case of the Cosmic Rays* (+pr, co-sc)
1958	*The Unchained Goddess* (+pr, co-sc)
1959	*A Hole in the Head* (+pr)
1961	*Pocketful of Miracles* (+pr)

Other Films:

1924	(as co-sc with Arthur Ripley on films featuring Harry

Frank Capra

Longdon): *Picking Peaches*; *Smile Please*; *Shanghaied Lovers*; *Flickering Youth*; *The Cat's Meow*; *His New Mama*; *The First Hundred Years*; *The Luck o' the Foolish*; *The Hansom Cabman*; *All Night Long*; *Feet of Mud*

1925 (as co-sc with Arthur Ripley on films featuring Harry Langdon): *The Sea Squawk*; *Boobs in the Woods*; *His Marriage Wow*; *Plain Clothes*; *Remember When?*; *Horace Greeley, Jr.*; *The White Wing's Bride*; *Lucky Stars*; *There He Goes*; *Saturday Afternoon*

1926 (as co-sc with Arthur Ripley on films featuring Harry Langdon): *Fiddlesticks*; *The Soldier Man*; *Tramp, Tramp, Tramp*

1943 *Why We Fight (Part 4): The Battle of Britain* (pr)

1944 *The Negro Soldier* (pr); *Why We Fight (Part 5): The Battle of Russia* (pr); *Know Your Ally: Britain* (pr)

1945 *Why We Fight (Part 7): War Comes to America* (pr); *Know Your Enemy: Germany* (pr)

1950 *Westward the Women* (story)

Publications:

By CAPRA: books—

The Name Above the Title, New York, 1971.

It's a Wonderful Life, with Frances Goodrich and Albert Hackett, New York, 1986.

By CAPRA: articles—

"The Gag Man," in *Breaking Into Movies*, edited by Charles Jones, New York, 1927.

"Sacred Cows to the Slaughter," in *Stage* (New York), 13 July 1936.

"We Should All Be Actors," in *Silver Screen* (New York), September 1946.

"Do I Make You Laugh?," in *Films and Filming* (London), September 1962.

"Capra Today," with James Childs, in *Film Comment* (New York), vol.8, no.4, 1972.

"Mr. Capra Goes to College," with Arthur Bressan and Michael Moran, in *Interview* (New York), June 1972.

"Why We (Should Not) Fight," interview with G. Bailey, in *Take One* (Montreal), September 1975.

"'Trends Change Because Trends Stink'—An Outspoken Talk with Legendary Producer/Director Frank Capra," with Nancy Anderson, in *Photoplay* (New York), November 1975.

Interview with J. Mariani, in *Focus on Film* (London), no.27, 1977.

"Dialogue on Film," in *American Film* (Washington, D.C.), October 1978.

Interview with H.A. Hargreave, in *Literature/Film Quarterly* (Salisbury, Maryland), vol. 9, no. 3, 1981.

On CAPRA: books—

Griffith, Richard, *Frank Capra*, London, 1951.

Silke, James, *Frank Capra: One Man—One Film*, Washington, D.C., 1971.

Bergman, Andrew, *We're in the Money: Depression America and Its Films*, New York, 1972.

Willis, Donald, *The Films of Frank Capra*, Metuchen, New Jersey, 1974.

Glatzer, Richard, and John Raeburn, editors, *Frank Capra: The Man and His Films*, Ann Arbor, 1975.

Poague, Leland, *The Cinema of Frank Capra: An Approach to Film Comedy*, South Brunswick, New Jersey, 1975.

Bohn, Thomas, *An Historical and Descriptive Analysis of the 'Why We Fight' Series*, New York, 1977.

Maland, Charles, *American Visions: The Films of Chaplin, Ford, Capra and Welles, 1936–1941*, New York, 1977.

Scherle, Victor, and William Levy, *The Films of Frank Capra*, Secaucus, New Jersey, 1977.

Bohnenkamp, Dennis, and Sam Grogg, editors, *Frank Capra Study Guide*, Washington, D.C., 1979.

Maland, Charles, *Frank Capra*, Boston, 1980.

Giannetti, Louis, *Masters of the American Cinema*, Englewood Cliffs, New Jersey, 1981.

Zagarrio, Vito, *Frank Capra*, Florence 1985.

Carney, Raymond, *American Vision: The Films of Frank Capra*, Cambridge, 1986.

Lazere, Donald, editor, *American Media and Mass Culture: Left Perspectives*, Berkeley, 1987.

Wolfe, Charles, *Frank Capra: A Guide to References and Resources*, Boston, 1987

On CAPRA: articles—

"How Frank Capra Makes a Hit Picture," in *Life* (New York), 19 September 1938.

Hellman, Geoffrey, "Thinker in Hollywood," in *New Yorker*, 5 February 1940.

Ferguson, Otis, "Democracy at the Box Office," in *New Republic* (New York), 24 March 1941.

Salemson, Harold, "Mr. Capra's Short Cuts to Utopia," in *Penguin Film Review* no.7, London, 1948.

Deming, Barbara, "Non-Heroic Heroes," in *Films in Review* (New York), April 1951.

"Capra Issue" of *Positif* (Paris), December 1971.

Richards, Jeffrey, "Frank Capra: The Classic Populist," in *Visions of Yesterday*, London, 1973.

Nelson, J., "Mr. Smith Goes to Washington: Capra, Populism and Comic-Strip Art," in *Journal of Popular Film* (Bowling Green, Ohio), Summer 1974.

Badder, D.J., "Frank Capra," in *Film Dope* (London), November 1974 and October 1975.

"Capra Issue" of *Film Comment* (New York), vol.8, no.4, 1972.

Sklar, Robert, "The Making of Cultural Myths: Walt Disney and Frank Capra," in *Movie-Made America*, New York, 1975.

"Lost and Found: The Films of Frank Capra," in *Film* (London), June 1975.

Rose, B., "It's a Wonderful Life: The Stand of the Capra Hero," in *Journal of Popular Film* (Bowling Green, Ohio), v.6, no.2, 1977.

Quart, Leonard, "Frank Capra and the Popular Front," in *Cineaste* (New York), Summer 1977.

Gehring, Wes, "McCarey vs. Capra: A Guide to American Film Comedy of the '30s," in *Journal of Popular Film and Television* (Bowling Green, Ohio), vol.7, no.1, 1978.

Dickstein, M., "It's a Wonderful Life, But . . . ," in *American Film* (Washington, D.C.), May 1980.

Jameson, R.T., "Stanwyck and Capra," in *Film Comment* (New York), March/April 1981.

"Capra Issue" of *Film Criticism* (Edinboro, Pennsylvania), Winter 1981.

Basinger, Jeanine, "America's love affair with Frank Capra," in *American Film* (Washington, D.C.), March 1982.

Edgerton, G., "Capra and Altman: Mythmaker and mythologist," in *Literature/Film Quarterly* (Salisbury, Maryland), January 1983.

Dossier on Capra, in *Positif* (Paris), July–August 1987.

American Film (Washington, D.C.), December 1987.

Gottlieb, Sidney, "From Heroine to Brat: Frank Capra's Adaptation of "Night Bus" (*It Happened One Night*)," in *Literature/Film Quarterly* (Salisbury, Maryland), vol. 16, no. 2, 1988.

* * *

The critical stock of Frank Capra has fluctuated perhaps more wildly than that of any other major director. During his peak years, the 1930's, he was adored by the press, by the industry and, of course, by audiences. In 1934 *It Happened One Night* won nearly all the Oscars in sight, and through the rest of the decade a film of Frank Capra was either the winner or the strong contender for that honor. Long before the formulation of the *auteur* theory, the Capra signature on a film was recognized. But after World War II his career went into serious decline. His first post-war film, *It's a Wonderful Life*, was not received with the enthusiasm he thought it deserved (although it has gone on to become one of his most-revived films). Of his last five films, two are remakes of material he treated in the thirties. Many contemporary critics are repelled by what they deem indigestible Capracorn and have even less tolerance for an ideology characterized as dangerously simplistic in its populism, its patriotism, its celebration of all-American values.

Indeed, many of Capra's most famous films can be read as excessively sentimental and politically naive. These readings, however, tend to neglect the bases for Capra's success—his skill as a director of actors, the complexity of his staging configurations, his narrative economy and energy, and most of all, his understanding of the importance of the spoken word in sound film. Capra captured the American voice in cinematic space. The words often serve the cause of apple pie, mom, the little man and other greeting card clichés (indeed, the hero of *Mr. Deeds Goes to Town* writes verse for greeting cards). But often, in the sound of the voice we hear uncertainties about those very clichés.

Capra's career began in the pre-talkie era, when he directed silent comic Harry Langdon in two successful films. His action films of the early thirties are not characteristic of his later work, yet already, in the films he made with Barbara Stanwyck, his individual gift can be discerned. The narrative pretext of *The Miracle Woman* is the urgency of Stanwyck's voice, its ability to move an audience, to persuade listeners of its sincerity. Capra exploited the raw energy of Stanwyck in this and other roles, where her qualities of fervor and near-hysterical conviction are just as essential to her persona as her hard-as-nails implacability would be in the forties. Stanwyck's voice is theatricalized, spatialized in her revivalist circus-tent in *The Miracle Woman* and on the hero's suicide tower in *Meet John Doe*, where her feverish pleadings are the only possible tenor for the film's unresolved ambiguities about society and the individual.

John Doe is portrayed by Gary Cooper, another American voice with particular resonance in the films of Capra. A star who seems to have invented the "strong, silent" type, Cooper first plays Mr. Deeds, whose platitudinous doggerel comes from a simple, do-gooder heart, but who enacts a crisis of communication in his long silence at the film's climax, a sanity hearing. When Mr. Deeds finally speaks it is a sign that the community (if not sanity) is restored—the usual resolution of a Capra film. As John Doe, Cooper is given words to voice by reporter Stanwyck, and he delivers them with such conviction that the whole nation listens. The vocal/dramatic center of the film is located in a rain-drenched ball park filled with John Doe's "people." The hero's effort to speak the truth, to reveal his own imposture and expose the fascistic intentions of his sponsor, is stymied when the lines of communication are literally cut between microphone and loudspeaker. The Capra narrative so often hinges on the protagonist's ability to speak and be heard, on the drama of sound and audition.

The bank run in *American Madness* is initiated by a montage of telephone voices and images, of mouths spreading a rumor. The panic is quelled by the speech of the bank president (Walter Huston), a situation repeated in more modest physical surroundings in *It's a Wonderful Life*. The most extended speech in the films of Capra occurs in *Mr. Smith Goes to Washington*. The whole film is a test of the hero's voice, and it culminates in a filibuster, a speech that, by definition, cannot be interrupted. The climax of *State of the Union* involves a different kind of audience and audition. There, the hero confesses his political dishonesty and his love for his wife on television.

The visual contexts, both simple and complex, never detract from the sound of Capra's films. They enhance it. The director's most elaborately designed film, *The Bitter Tea of General Yen* (recalling the style of Josef von Sternberg in its chiaroscuro lighting and its exoticism) expresses the opposition of cultural values in its visual elements, to be sure, but also in the voices of Stanwyck and Nils Asther, a Swedish actor who impersonates a Chinese war lord. Less unusual but not less significant harmonies are sounded in *It Happened One Night*, where a society girl (Claudette Colbert) learns "real" American speech from a fast-talking reporter (Clark Gable). The love scenes in *Mr. Deeds* are for Gary Cooper and Jean Arthur, another quintessential Capra heroine, whose vocal personality is at least as memorable as her physical one. In James Stewart Capra finds his most disquieting voice, ranging in *Mr. Smith* from ingenuousness to hysterical desperation, and in *It's a Wonderful Life*, to an even higher pitch of hysteria when the hero loses his identity.

The sounds and sights of Capra's films bear the authority of a director whose autobiography is called *The Name above the Title*. With that authority comes an unsettling belief in authorial power, the power dramatized in his major films, the persuasiveness exercised in political and social contexts. That persuasion reflects back on the director's own power to engage the viewer in his fiction, to call upon a degree of belief in the fiction—even when we reject the meaning of the fable.

—Charles Affron

CARNÉ, Marcel.

French. Born in Batignolles, Paris, 18 August 1909. Worked as insurance clerk, mid-1920's; assistant to cameraman Georges Périnal on *Les Nouveaux Messieurs*, 1928; worked as film critic, and made short film, 1929; assistant to René Clair on *Sous les toits de Paris*, 1930; editor-in-chief, *Hebdo-Films* journal, and member, "October" group, early 1930's; assistant to Jacques Feyder, 1933–35; directed first feature, *Jenny*, 1936. Recipient: Special Mention, Venice Festival, for *Quai des brumes*, 1938.

Films as Director:

1929　*Nogent, Eldorado du dimanche*
1936　*Jenny*
1937　*Drôle de drame (Bizarre Bizarre)*
1938　**Quai des brumes (Port of Shadows)**; *Hôtel du Nord*
1939　**Le Jour se lève (Daybreak)**; *École communale* (abandoned due to war)
1942　*Les Visiteurs du soir (The Devil's Envoys)*
1945　**Les Enfants du paradis (Children of Paradise)**
1946　*Les Portes de la nuit (Gates of the Night)*
1947　*La Fleur de l'âge* (not completed)
1949　*La Marie du port* (+co-sc)
1951　*Juliette ou la Clé des songes* (+co-sc)
1953　*Thérèse Raquin (The Adulteress)* (+co-sc)
1954　*L'Air de Paris* (+co-sc)
1956　*Le Pays d'où je viens* (+co-sc)
1958　*Les Tricheurs (The Cheaters)*
1960　*Terrain vague* (+co-sc)
1962　*Du mouron pour les petits oiseaux* (+co-sc)
1965　*Trois Chambres à Manhattan* (+co-sc)
1967　*Les Jeunes Loups (The Young Wolves)*
1971　*Les Assassins de l'ordre* (+co-sc)
1974　*La Merveilleuse Visite* (+co-sc)
1976　*La Bible* (feature doc for TV and theatrical release)

Publications:

By CARNÉ: book—

Les Enfants du Paradis, with Jacques Prevert, London, 1988.

By CARNÉ: articles—

Interview, with F. Cuel and others, in *Cinématographe* (Paris), May 1978.

Marcel Carné

"Comment est ne *Le Quai des brumes*," in *Avant-Scène du Cinéma* (Paris), 15 October 1979.
"Marcel Carné sous la coupole," in *Avant-Scène du Cinéma* (Paris), 1 July 1980.
Interview in *Avant-Scène du Cinéma* (Paris), October 1988.

On CARNÉ: books—

Béranger, Jean-Louis, *Marcel Carné*, Paris, 1945.
Landrey, Bernard, *Marcel Carné, sa vie, ses films*, Paris,
Quéval, Jean, *Marcel Carné*, Paris, 1952.
Prévert, Jacques, *Children of Paradise*, New York, 1968.
Armes, Roy, *French Film Since 1946: The Great Tradition*, New York, 1970.
Prévert, Jacques, *Le Jour se lève*, New York, 1970.
Perez, Michel, *Les films de Carné*, Paris, 1986.
Turk, Edward Baron, *Child of Paradise: Marcel Carné and the Golden Age of Cinema*, Cambridge, Massachusetts, 1989.

On CARNÉ: articles—

Manvell, Roger, "Marcel Carné," in *Sight and Sound* (London), Spring 1946.
Lodge, J.F., "The Cinema of Marcel Carné," in *Sequence* (London), December 1946.
Lambert, Gavin, "Marcel Carné," in *Sequence* (London), Spring 1948.
Michel, J., "Carné ou la Clé des songes," in *Cinéma* (Paris), no.12, 1956.
Sadoul, Georges, "Les Films de Marcel Carné, expression de notre époque," in *Les Lettres Françaises* (Paris), 1 March 1956.
Stanbrook, Alan, "The Carné Bubble," in *Film* (London), November/December 1959.
"Carné Issue" of *Cahiers de la Cinémathèque* (Perpignan), Winter 1972.
Turk, Edward Baron, "The Birth of Children of Paradise," in *American Film* (Washington, D.C.), July/August 1979.

"*Le Quai des brumes* Issue" of *Avant-Scène du Cinéma* (Paris), 15 October 1979.

Gillett, John, "Salute to a French Master," in *Radio Times* (London), 2 March 1985.

Virmaux, A., and O. Virmaux, "La malediction: Le film inachève de Carné et Prevert," in *Cinématographe* (Paris), October 1986.

Thoraval, Yves, "Marcel Carné: Un Parisian à Toulouse," in *Cinéma* (Paris), 14 January 1987.

Kolker, Robert Phillip, "Carné's *Les Portes de la nuit* and the Sleep of French Cinema," in *Post Script* (Jacksonville, Florida), Fall 1987.

*   *   *

At a time when film schools were non-existent and training in filmmaking was acquired through assistantship, no one could have been better prepared for a brilliant career than Marcel Carné. He worked as assistant to Clair on the first important French sound film, *Sous les toits de Paris*, and to Feyder on the latter's three great films of 1934–35. Though he had also made a successful personal documentary, *Nogent, Eldorado du dimanche*, and a number of publicity shorts, it was only thanks to the support of Feyder and his wife, the actress Françoise Rosay, that Carné was able to make his debut as a feature film-maker with *Jenny* in 1936. If this was a routine melodrama, Carné was able in the next three years to establish himself as one of Europe's leading film directors.

During the period up to the outbreak of war in 1939 Carné established what was to be a ten-year collaboration with the poet and screenwriter Jacques Prévert, and gradually built up a team of collaborators—including the designer Alexandre Trauner and composer Maurice Jaubert—which was unsurpassed at this period. In quick succession Carné made the comedy *Drôle de drame*, which owes more to Prévert's taste for systematic absurdity and surreal gags than to the director's professionalism, and a trio of fatalistic romantic melodramas, *Quai des brumes*, *Hôtel du nord* and *Le Jour se lève*.

These are perfect examples of the mode of French filmmaking which had been established by Jacques Feyder: a concern with visual style and a studio-created realism, a reliance on detailed scripts with structure and dialogue separately elaborated, and a foregrounding of star performers to whom all elements of decor and photography are subordinate. Though the forces shaping a character's destiny may be outside his or her control, the story focuses on social behavior and the script offers set-piece scenes and confrontations and witty or trenchant dialogue which enables the stars to display their particular talents to the full.

The various advocates of either Prévert or Carné have sought to make exclusive claims as to which brought the poetry to the nebulous and ill-defined "poetic realism" which these films are said to exemplify. In retrospect, however, these arguments seem over-personalized, since the pair seem remarkably well-matched. The actual differences seem less in artistic approach than in attitude to production. From the first, Carné, heir to a particular mode of quality filmmaking, was concerned with an industry, a technique, a career. Prévert, by contrast, though he is a perfect example of the archetypal 1930's screenwriter, able to create striking star roles and write dazzling and memorable dialogue, is not limited to this role and has a quite separate identity as surrealist, humorist and poet.

The pair share a certain fantastic conception of realism, with film seen as a studio construct in which fidelity to life is balanced by attention to a certain poetic atmosphere. Carné's coldly formal command of technique is matched by Prévert's sense of the logic of a tightly woven narrative. If it is Prévert's imagination that allows him to conceive both the *amour fou* which unites the lovers and the grotesque villains who threaten it, it is Carné's masterly direction of actors which turns Jean

Gabin and Michèle Morgan into the 1930's ideal couple and draws such memorable performances from Michel Simon, Jules Berry and Arletty.

The collaboration of Prévert and Carné was sustained during the very different circumstances of the German Occupation, when they together made two films which rank among the most significant of the period. Since all the films of the 1930's poetic realism were now banned, it is hardly surprising that they should have found the need to adopt a radically new style. Remaining within the concept of the studio-made film, but leaving behind the contemporary urban gloom of *Le Jour se lève*, they opted for a style of elaborate and theatrical period spectacle. The medieval fable of *Les Visiteurs du soir* was an enormous contemporary success but it has not worn well. Working with very limited resources the filmmakers—assisted clandestinely by Trauner and the composer Joseph Kosma—succeeded in making an obvious prestige film, a work in which Frenchmen could take pride at a dark moment of history. But despite the presence of such players as Arletty and Jules Berry, the overall effect is ponderous and stilted.

Prévert and Carné's masterpiece is *Les Enfants du paradis*, shot during the war years but released only after the Liberation. Running for over three hours and comprising two parts, each of which is of full feature length, *Les Enfants du paradis* is one of the most ambitious films ever undertaken in France. Set in the twin worlds of theatre and crime in nineteenth century Paris, this all-star film is both a theatrical spectacle in its own right and a reflection on the nature of spectacle. The script is one of Prévert's richest, abounding in wit and aphorism, and Carné's handling of both stars and crowd scenes is masterly. The sustained vitality and dynamism of the work as it moves seemingly effortlessly from farce to tragedy, from delicate love scenes to outrageous buffoonery is exemplary and its impact is undimmed by the years.

Marcel Carné was still only 36 and at the height of his fame when the war ended. Younger than most of those who now came to the fore, he had already made masterly films in two quite different contexts and it seemed inevitable that he would continue to be a dominant force in French cinema despite the changed circumstances of the postwar era. But in fact the first post-war Carné-Prévert film, *Les Portes de la nuit*, was an expensive flop and when a subsequent film, *La Fleur de l'âge*, was abandoned shortly after production had begun, one of the most fruitful partnerships in French cinema came to an end. Carné directed a dozen more films from *La Marie du port* in 1950 to *La Merveilleuse Visite* in 1973, but he was no longer a major force in French filmmaking.

Marcel Carné was an unfashionable figure long before his directing career came to an end. Scorned by a new generation of filmmakers, Carné grew more and more out of touch with contemporary developments, despite an eagerness to explore new subjects and use young performers. His failure is a measure of the gulf which separates 1950's and 1960's conceptions of cinema from the studio era of the war and immediate prewar years. He was, however, the epitome of this French studio style, its unquestioned master even if—unlike Renoir—he was unable to transcend its limitations. While future critics are unlikely to find much to salvage from the latter part of his career, films like *Drôle de drame* and *Quai des brumes*, *Le Jour se lève* and *Les Enfants du paradis* remain rich and complex monuments to a decade of filmmaking which will reward fresh and unbiased critical attention.

—Roy Armes

CARPENTER, John.

American. Born in Carthage, New York, 16 January 1948. Studied filmmaking at University of Southern California, graduated 1972. Married actress Adrienne Barbeau, 1979. Made first feature, *Dark Star*, 1974. Recipient: Oscar for Best Short Subject, for *The Resurrection of Bronco Billy*, 1970. Agent: c/o The Gersh Agency, 222 N. Canon Drive, Beverly Hills, CA 90210, U.S.A.

Films as Director:

1970	*The Resurrection of Bronco Billy* (short) (+ed, mus)
1974	*Dark Star* (+pr, co-sc)
1977	*Assault on Precinct 13* (+sc, mus)
1978	*Halloween* (+co-sc)
1980	*The Fog* (+sc, mus)
1981	*Escape from New York* (+co-sc, co-pr)
1982	*The Thing*
1983	*Christine*
1984	*Starman*
1986	*Big Trouble in Little China*
1987	*Prince of Darkness*; *Armed and Dangerous*
1988	*They Live* (+co-mus)

Other Films

1962–70	(short films, as director): *Revenge of the Colossal Beasts*; *Gorgon versus Godzilla*; *Terror from Space*; *Sorcerer from Outer Space*; *Warrior and the Demon*; *Gorgon, the Space Monster*
1978	*The Eyes of Laura Mars* (Kershner) (sc)
1981	*Halloween II* (Rosenthal) (pr, co-sc)
1983	*Halloween III: Season of the Witch* (Wallace) (mus)
1984	*The Philadelphia Experiment* (Raffill) (sc)
1986	*Black Moon Rising* (Cokliss) (co-sc)

Publications:

By CARPENTER: articles—

"The Man in the Cyrogenic Freezer," an interview with Tom Milne and Richard Combs, in *Sight and Sound* (London), Spring 1978.
"Trick and Treat," an interview with T. McCarthy, in *Film Comment* (New York), January/February 1980.
"New Fright Master: John Carpenter," an interview with J. Wells, in *Films in Review* (New York), April 1980.
Interview in *Starburst* (London), nos. 36 and 37, 1981.
Interview in *Cahiers du Cinéma* (Paris), September 1982.
Interview in *Films* (London), May 1985.
Interview in *American Cinematographer* (Los Angeles), September 1988.
"Cheap Thrills and Dark Glasses," an interview with Sheila Johnston, in *The Independent* (London), 22 June 1989.

On CARPENTER: books—

Meyers, Richard, *For One Week Only: The World of Exploitation Films*, Piscataway, New Jersey, 1983.
Newman, Kim, *Nightmare Movies: A Critical History of the Horror Movie from 1968*, London, 1988.

On CARPENTER: articles—

Appelbaum, R., "From Cult Homage to Creative Control," in *Films and Filming* (London), June 1979.
Scanlon, P., "*The Fog*: A Spook Ride on Film," in *Rolling Stone* (New York), 28 June 1979.
Stevenson, James, "Profiles: People Start Running," in *New Yorker*, 28 January 1980.
Ross, P., "John Carpenter: Les rhythmes de l'angoisse," in *Revue du Cinéma* (Paris), February 1984.
"John Carpenter," in *Casablanca* (Madrid), November 1984.

* * *

While his career has been neither as erratic as Wes Craven's nor as disaster-littered as that of Tobe Hooper, John Carpenter currently stands as an out-of-time B specialist who has not so much failed to live up to the promise of his earliest films as been unable to match their perfect achievements. His first three movies are marvellously economical, deftly exciting, genuinely distinctive and slyly amusing, and cover a wide range of generic bases. *Dark Star*, made as a student in collaboration with Dan O'Bannon, is one of the miracles of the 1970's, an intelligent and approachable science fiction film made in the wake of *2001* but fresh and lively, with a satiric bite carried over from the *written* s-f of the 1950's—its surfing punchline is an apt borrowing from Ray Bradbury—and a near-absurdist sense of humour, as the crew of the spaceship Dark Star plunge into their own isolation-fuelled insanity as their twenty-year mission to demolish useless planets with sentient bombs drags on and on, that repays many repeat viewings. And *Assault on Precinct 13*, an urban Western rooted in *Rio Bravo* and *Night of the Living Dead*, is at once a lean generic action machine, as a nightmarish street gang besiege and lay waste to an isolated police station, and a witty transposition of the certainties of a Hawksian ensemble piece into the racially and sexually tense 1970's. In these films, Carpenter demonstrated that suspense and humour could be combined, and that he was a skilled handler of unfamiliar actors, concentrating unusually on nuances of character in forms where spectacle and effects often take precedence, and also a talented composer of driving, minimalist, synthesiser themes.

Halloween is every bit as good as the first few films, but seems less fresh because it has been so influential. Itself a psycho suspense horror movie in the vein of *The Spiral Staircase* or *Black Christmas* (and Carpenter's lady-stalking 1978 TV movie *Someone's Watching Me*), *Halloween* single-handedly revived the drive-in horror movie in the late 1970's, inspiring such nasty pieces of work as *Friday the 13th* and literally hundreds of blatant imitations, not to mention a series of sequels which find the intriguing Nigel Kneale-scripted box office failure *Halloween III: Season of the Witch* bracketed by the Carpenter-produced *Halloween II* and a couple of films he had nothing to do with, *Halloweens* 4 and 5. With Jamie Lee Curtis pursued by an unkillable, masked madman and Donald Pleasence as a hammy shrink on the killer's trail, the film establishes its own world of horror, as enclosed and unreal as the Transylvanian backlots of the Universal or Hammer series, located in a mythic American small town teenage milieu, where Halloween is a magical evocation of terror and delight and baby-sitting, trick-or-treating and blind-dating hold possibilities of joy and/or terror. With its absolute mastery of the hand-through-the-window shock moment and cunning use of the Panavision shape and a shivery theme tune, *Halloween* is a slender but masterly confection, and should not be blamed for the floodgates it opened.

However, Carpenter has seemed in his subsequent career to be unlearning many of the skills his first films exhibited and, although there are pleasures to be found in most of his works, he has never quite recaptured the confidence and streamlined form of the early pictures. *The Fog*, a maritime ghost story, and *Escape From New York*, a science fiction action picture, are enjoyable, entertaining movies that straggle through illogical plots, but nevertheless find performers—particularly Carpenter's then-wife Adrienne Barbeau, but also regulars Kurt Russell, Donald Pleasence, Tom Atkins, Nancy Loomis and Chuck Cyphers—doing nice little things with characters, and individual scare or suspense sequences overriding the general messiness of the stories. The same bitty feel can be found in films made by others from scripts he wrote in this period, Stewart Raffill's *The Philadelphia Experiment* and Harley Cokliss'

John Carpenter: *The Fog*

Black Moon Rising, not to mention the 1990 TV Western *El Diabolo*. Stepping up onto the big studio league, Carpenter was then given a chance to remake Hawks' and Nyby's *The Thing From Another World* (1950) and came through with *The Thing*, a controversially downbeat but genuinely effective movie in which an Arctic base is undermined by the presence of a shape-changing alien and the edgy, paranoid playing of a well-chosen cast of flabby, unreliable types is frequently punctured by incredible bursts of special effects activity. *The Thing* handles its set-pieces—severed heads sprouting spiderlegs, a stomach opening up into a toothy mouth, a dog exploding into tentacular gloopiness—remarkably well, but Carpenter is also in control of the funny, tense, questioning passages in between.

Nevertheless, the commercial failure of *The Thing*, which arrived on Earth just as the box office was embracing *E.T.* and evil aliens were temporarily unfashionable, appears to have disconcerted Carpenter enough to force him into a succession of blighted big studio movies: *Christine* is the regulation Stephen King adaptation, loud and watchable but essentially empty and ordinary; *Starman* is an uncomfortable and impersonal hybrid of *It Happened One Night* and *The Man Who Fell to Earth*; and *Big Trouble in Little China* is a whacky kung fu-monster-comedy-musical-action-adventure-horror-fantasy that features Kurt Russell's funniest Carpenter hero role (he had first joined up with the director for the TV *Elvis* in 1978) and some weird and wayward sequences, but never quite catches the magic of the Hong Kong films upon which it is obviously based. Subsequently, Carpenter deserted the big studios and handled a pair of smaller projects, in an attempt to get back to the basics of his best work, yielding *Prince of Darkness*, a labyrinthine and diffuse horror movie with a nuclear physics subplot, and *They Live*, a funny and pointed update of *Invasion of the Body Snatchers* in which the aliens have invaded earth to exploit it economically. These two films display traces of Carpenter's old flair, even if they both open a great deal better than they close, and *They Live*, in particular, is as interesting and offbeat a movie as *The Fog* or *Escape From New York*. But, for the moment, Carpenter is still a wayward, drifting talent, not yet settled into the rut that Tobe Hooper has dug for himself, but not yet achieving the generic apotheosis of a George Romero or a David Cronenberg either.

—Kim Newman

CASSAVETES, John.

American. Born in New York City, 9 December 1929. Educated at Mohawk College, Colgate University, and New York Academy of Dramatic Arts, graduated 1950. Married actress Gena Rowlands, 1958, two sons, one daughter. Title character in TV series *Johnny Staccato*, 1959–60; directed first film, *Shadows*, 1960; hired by Paramount, then by Stanley Kramer, 1961; worked as independent filmmaker, from 1964. Recipient: Critics Award, Venice Festival, for *Shadows*, 1960; Best Screenplay, National Society of Film Critics, and Five Awards from Venice Festival, for *Faces*, 1968; Golden Lion, Venice Festival, for *Gloria*, 1980; Golden Bear, Berlin Festival, for *Love Streams*, 1984; Los Angeles Film Critics Career Achievement Award, 1986. *Died of cirrhosis of the liver, in Los Angeles, 3 February 1989.*

Films as Director:

1960   *Shadows* (+sc)
1961   *Too Late Blues* (+sc, pr)
1962   *A Child is Waiting*
1968   *Faces* (+sc)
1970   **Husbands** (+sc, role as Gus)
1971   *Minnie and Moskowitz* (+sc, role as Husband)
1974   *A Woman Under the Influence* (+sc)
1976   *The Killing of a Chinese Bookie* (+sc)
1977/78   *Opening Night* (+sc)
1980   *Gloria*
1984   *Love Streams*
1986   *Big Trouble*

Other Films:

1951   *Fourteen Hours* (Hathaway) (role as extra)
1953   *Taxi* (Ratoff) (role)
1955   *The Night Holds Terror* (Stone) (role)
1956   *Crime in the Streets* (Siegel) (role)
1957   *Edge of the City* (Ritt) (role)
1958   *Saddle the Wind* (Parrish) (role); *Virgin Island* (P. Jackson) (role)
1962   *The Webster Boy* (Chaffey) (role)
1964   *The Killers* (Siegel) (role as Johnny North)
1967   *The Dirty Dozen* (Aldrich) (role as Victor Franko); *Devil's Angels* (Haller) (role)
1968   **Rosemary's Baby** (Polanski) (role as Rosemary's Husband); *Gli Intoccabili* (*Machine Gun McCain*) (Montaldo) (role)
1969   *Roma coma Chicago* (*Bandits in Rome*) (De Martino) (role); *If It's Tuesday, This Must Be Belgium* (M. Stuart) (cameo role)
1976   *Two-Minute Warning* (Pearce) (role)
1978   *The Fury* (De Palma) (role)
1982   *The Tempest* (Mazursky) (role)

Publications:

By CASSAVETES: books—

Faces, New York, 1970.
John Cassavetes, Peter Falk, edited by Bruce Henstell, Washington, D.C., 1972.

By CASSAVETES: articles—

"What's Wrong with Hollywood," in *Film Culture* (New York), April 1959.
". . . and the Pursuit of Happiness," in *Films and Filming* (London), February 1961.
"Incoming Tide: Interview," in *Cinema* (Beverly Hills), no.1, 1962.
"Faces: Interview," in *Cinema* (Beverly Hills), Spring 1968.
"Masks and Faces: Interview," with David Austen, in *Films and Filming* (London), September 1968.
"The Faces of the Husbands," in *New Yorker*, 15 March 1969.
Interview with Jonas Mekas, in the *Village Voice* (New York), 23 December 1971.
Interview with L. Gross, in *Millimeter* (New York), April 1975.
"*Shadows* Issue" of *Avant-Scène du Cinéma* (Paris), 1 December 1977.
"Cassavetes on Cassavetes," in *Monthly Film Bulletin* (London), June 1978.
"Le Bal des vauriens. Entretien avec John Cassavetes," with Y. Lardeau and L. Marcorelles, in *Cahiers du Cinéma* (Paris), June 1978.
"Crucial Culture," interview with R. Appelbaum, in *Films* (London), January 1981.
"Retracting the stream of love," an interview with Richard Combs, in *Monthly Film Bulletin* (London), April 1984.
Interview with Brian Case, in *Stills* (London), June–July 1984.
Interview in *Film Comment* (New York), July–August 1988.

On CASSAVETES: books—

Loeb, Anthony, editor, *Filmmakers in Conversation*, Chicago, 1982.
Alexander, Georg, and others, *John Cassavetes*, Munich, 1983.

John Cassavetes (left) with Peter Falk and Ben Gazzara in *Husbands*

Carney, Raymond, *American Dreaming: The Films of John Cassavetes and the American Experience*, Berkeley, 1985.
Gavron, Laurence, and Denis Lenoir, *John Cassavetes*, Paris, 1986.

On CASSAVETES: articles—

Taylor, John Russell, "Cassavetes in London," in *Sight and Sound* (London), Autumn 1960.
Mekas, Jonas, "Cassavetes, the Improvisation," in *Film Culture* (New York), Spring 1962.
Sarris, Andrew, "Oddities and One-Shots," in *Film Culture* (New York), Spring 1963.
Guerin, A., "After Faces, a Film to Keep the Man-Child Alive," in *Life* (New York), 9 May 1969.
"Robert Aldrich on John Cassavetes," in *Dialogue on Film* (Washington, D.C.), no.2, 1972.
Benoit, C., and A. Tournes, "Femmes et maris dans l'oeuvre de Cassavetes," in *Jeune Cinéma* (Paris), September/October 1976.
Simsolo, Noel, "Notes sur le cinéma de John Cassavetes," in *Cahiers du Cinéma* (Paris), May 1978.
Courant, G., and J. Farren, "John Cassavetes," in *Cinéma* (Paris), October 1979.
Stevenson, J., "John Cassavetes: Film's Bad Boy," in *American Film* (Washington, D.C.), January/February 1980.
Landy, M., and S. Shostack, "The Cinema of John Cassavetes," in *Ciné-Tracts* (Montreal), Winter 1980.
Prades, J., "La méthode de Cassavetes," in *Cinématographe* (Paris), April 1982.
"John Cassavetes Section" of *Positif* (Paris), January 1985.

Obituary in *Variety* (New York), 8 February 1989.
Obituary in *Time Out* (London), 15 February 1989.

*   *   *

As perhaps the most influential of the independently produced feature films of its era (1958–1967), *Shadows* came to be seen as a virtual breakthrough for American alternative cinema. The film and its fledgling writer-director had put a group of young, independent filmmakers on the movie map, together with their more intellectual, less technically polished, decidedly less commercial, low-budget alternatives to Hollywood features.

Beginning as an improvisational exercise in the method-acting workshop actor Cassavetes was teaching, and partly financed by his earnings from the *Johnny Staccato* television series, *Shadows* was a loosely plotted, heavily improvised work of cinema verité immediacy which explored human relationships and racial identity against the background of the beat atmosphere of the late 1950's, given coherence by the jazz score of Charles Mingus.

The origins and style of *Shadows* were to characterize John Cassavetes's work throughout his directorial career, once he got the studio-financed production bug out of his system—and his system out of theirs.

The five prizes garnered by *Shadows*, including the prestigious Critics Award at the 1950 Venice Film Festival, led to Cassavetes's unhappy and resentful experience directing two studio-molded productions (*Too Late Blues*, *A Child is Waiting*), both of which failed critically and commercially. Thereafter, he returned to independent filmmaking, acting in mainstream movies such as *The Dirty Dozen*, *Rosemary's Baby*, and *Two Minute Warning*, in between directing feature films in his characteristic, controversial style.

That style centers around a freedom afforded his actors to share in the creative process. Cassavetes's scripts serve as sketchy blueprints for the performers' introspective explorations and emotional embellishments. Consequently, camera movements, at the command of the actors' intuitive behavior, are of necessity spontaneous.

The amalgam of improvisational acting, hand-held camera work, grainy stock, loose editing, and thread-bare plot give his films a texture of recreated rather than heightened reality, often imbuing them with a feeling of astonishing psychodramatic intensity as characters confront each other and lay bare their souls. Detractors, however, see Cassavetes as too dedicated to the performers' art, too trusting of the actor's self-discipline, with the result being a mild form of aesthetic anarchy.

At worst Cassavetes's films are admittedly formless and self-indulgent. Scenes are stretched excruciatingly far beyond their climactic moments, lines are delivered falteringly, dialogue is repetitious. But, paradoxically, these same blemishes seem to make possible the several lucid, provocative, and moving moments of transcendent human revelation that a Cassavetes film almost inevitably delivers.

As his career progressed, Cassavetes changed his thematic concerns, upgraded his technical production values, and, not surprisingly, attracted a wider audience—but without overhauling his actor-as-auteur approach.

Faces represented Cassavetes's return to his favored semi-documentary style, complete with the seemingly obligatory excesses and gaffes, but also containing moments of truth and exemplary acting. Not only did this highly charged drama about the disintegration of a middle-class marriage in affluent Southern California find favor with the critical and filmmaking communities, it broke through as one of the first independent films to find a sizable audience among the general moviegoing public.

In *Husbands*, Cassavetes continued his exploration of marital manners, morals and sexual identity by focusing on a trio of middle-class husbands—played by Cassavetes, Ben Gazzara, and Peter Falk—who confront their own mortality when a friend dies. Director Cassavetes's doubled-edged trademark—brilliant moments of intense acting amid the banal debris of over-indulgence—had never been in bolder relief.

Minnie and Moskowitz was Cassavetes's demonstration of a lighter touch, an amusing and touching interlude prior to his most ambitious and commercially successful film. Starring Gena Rowlands (Cassavetes's wife) and Seymour Cassel as a pair of dissimilar but similarly lonely people ensnared in a manic romance, it was Cassavetes again examining miscommunication but in a much more playful vein.

By far his most polished, accessible, gripping, and technically proficient film was *A Woman Under the Influence*, for which Cassavetes departed from his accustomed style of working by writing a fully detailed script during pre-production. Starring Gena Rowlands in a magnificent performance as a lower-middle class housewife coming apart at the seams, and the reliable Peter Falk as the hardhat husband who is ill-equipped to deal with his wife's mental breakdown, *Woman* offered a more palatable balance of Cassavetes's strengths and weaknesses. The over-long scenes and overindulgent acting jags are there, but in lesser doses, while the privileged moments and bursts of virtuoso screen acting seem more abundant than usual.

Financed by Falk and Cassavetes, its crew and cast (including many family members) working on deferred salaries; promoted via a tour undertaken by the nucleus of the virtual repertory company (Cassavetes, Rowland, Falk); and booked without a major distributor, *Woman* collected generally ecstatic reviews, Academy Award nominations for Cassavetes and Rowlands, and impressive box office returns.

Cassavetes's next two films (*The Killing of a Chinese Bookie*, *Opening Night*) feature a return to his earlier structure (or lack thereof)—inaccessible, interminable, and insufferable for all but diehard buffs. However, *Gloria*, showcasing Rowlands as a former gangster's moll, while uneven in tone and erratic in pace, represented a concession by Cassavetes to film-goers seeking heightened cinematic energy and narrative momentum.

"People who are making films today are too concerned with mechanics—technical things instead of feeling," Cassavetes told an interviewer in 1980. "Execution is about eight percent to me. The technical quality of a film doesn't have much to do with whether it's a good film."

—Bill Wine

CASTELLANI, Renato.

Italian. Born in Finale Ligure (Savona), 4 September 1913. Educated in Argentina to 1925, then in Geneva; studied architecture in Milan. Journalist, then scriptwriter for Camerini, Genina, Soldati, and Blasetti, 1930's; assistant to Blasetti, 1940; directed first film, *Un Colpo di pistola*, 1941. Recipient: Best Film, Venice Festival, for *Sotto il sole di Roma*, 1948; Best Film, Cannes Festival, for *Due Soldi di speranza*, 1952; Golden Lion, Venice Festival, for *Giulietta e Romeo*, 1954. *Died 28 December 1985.*

Films as Director:

1941 *Un Colpo di pistola* (+co-sc)
1942 *Zaza* (+sc)
1943 *La Donna del Montagna* (+sc)
1946 *Mio Figlio Professore* (*Professor My Son*) (+co-sc)
1948 *Sotto il sole di Roma* (*Under the Sun of Rome*) (+sc)
1949 *E'primavera* (*It's Forever Springtime*) (+co-sc)
1952 *Due Soldi di speranza* (*Two Cents Worth of Hope*) (+sc)
1954 *Giulietta e Romeo* (*Romeo and Juliet*) (+sc)
1957 *I sogni nel cassetto* (+sc)
1959 *Nella città l'inferno* (*And the Wild, Wild Women*) (+co-sc)
1961 *Il Brigante* (+sc)
1962 *Mare Matto* (+co-sc)
1964 "La Vedova" episode of *Tre notti di amore* (*Three Nights of Love*) (+co-sc): "Una Donna d'Afari" episode of *Controsesso* (+co-sc)
1967 *Questi fantasmi* (*Ghosts Italian Style*) (+co-sc)
1969 *Una breve stagione* (+co-sc)
1972 *Leonardo da Vinci* (condensed from 5-part TV series) (+co-sc)

Other Films:

1938 *L'oròlogio a Cucu* (Mastrocinque) (co-sc); *Batticuore* (Camerini) (co-sc); *Castelli in aria* (Camerini) (co-sc)

1939 *Grandi magazzini* (Camerini) (co-sc, asst d); *Il documento* (Camerini) (co-sc); *Un'avventura di Salvator Rosa* (Blasetti) (co-sc, asst d); *Due milioni per un sorriso* (Borghesio and Soldati) (co-sc)
1940 *Centomila dollari* (Camerini) (asst d); *Una romantica avventura* (Camerini) (co-sc); *La corona di ferro* (Blasetti) (co-sc, asst d)
1941 *La cena della beffe* (Blasetti) (co-sc)
1942 *Malombra* (Soldati) (co-sc)
1944 *Quartieri alti* (Soldati) (co-sc)
1945 *Malia* (Amato) (co-sc); *Notte di tempesta* (Franciolini) (sc)
1958 *Resurrezione* (*Auferstehung*) (Hansen) (co-sc)
1962 *Venere imperiale* (Delannoy) (idea only – begun by Castellani in 1958, discontinued due to dispute with producers and star Gina Lollobrigida)
1964 *Matrimonio all'italiana* (de Sica) (co-sc)

Publications:

By CASTELLANI: article—

"Putting Gloss on Prison," in *Films and Filming* (London), April 1959.

On CASTELLANI: books—

Ames, Roy, *Patterns of Realism: A Study of Italian Neo-Realist Cinema*, New York, 1971.
Leprohon, Pierre, *The Italian Cinema*, New York, 1972.
Atti del Convegno della X mostra internazionale del nuovo cinema, Venice, 1975.
Verdone, Mario, *Cinema neo-realista da Rossellini a Pasolini*, Palermo, 1977.
Gili, Jean A., *Le Cinéma italien II*, Paris, 1982.
Trasatti, Sergio, *Renato Castellani*, Florence, 1984

On CASTELLANI: articles—

Frosali, S., "Renato Castellani: Regista 'inattuale'?" in *Bianco e Nero* (Rome), January–March 1984.
Obituary in *Variety* (New York), 1 January 1986.
Pintus, Pietro, "Renato Castellani viaggiatore instancabile," in *Bianco e Nero* (Rome), April–June 1986.

*   *   *

Poggioli, Lattuada, Chiarini, Soldati—the "calligraphers": with these directors, novelists, and critics Castellani is associated at the beginning of his film career (1940–1948). The "calligraphers" are interested in form above all, strongly attached to the narrative tradition of the nineteenth century, committed to an essentially bourgeois cinema, refined, cultivated, intellectual. Their aesthetic is articulated in theory and in practice, and resistant, even antithetical, to the demands of the new realism voiced by De Santis and others in *Cinema*, and by Visconti in *Ossessione*. *Un colpo di pistola*, *Zaza* (a comedy in the French manner set during the "belle époque"), and *La donna della montagna* are films of escape. Through them Castellani managed his own flight: from the reality of the present, to be sure, but also from fascist propaganda and fascist censorship.

The opposition between "calligraphy" and neorealism must be treated cautiously, as Roy Armes points out in *Patterns of Realism*. Not only did the two tendencies share a number of temptations (to historicism, for example), but individual artists, Castellani among them, passed with apparent ease from one to the other. "Calligrapher" as late as 1946, Castellani joined the neo-realists with *Sotto il sole di Roma*, announcing his new allegiance in the very first frame with this intertitle: "This film was inspired by events that actually took place. It was performed by non-professional actors, and shot entirely in Rome, in the neighborhoods depicted in the film." While the presence of Alberto Sordi undermines the claim of a non-professional cast, his performance as a shoe salesman (recalling, in comic mode, the shoes of *Paisà* and *Shoe Shine*), the music of Nino Rota, the theme of black marketeering, the Roman locales and dialect, the events of early summer 1943 to the end of summer of 1944 (from the invasion of Sicily to the liberation of Rome), cast the film firmly in the honored mold of Rossellini and De Sica. The chronology of *Sotto il sole di Roma* is that of *Paisà*; it is the story of the coming of age of a group of adolescent boys, matured by destruction and death. At its conclusion, unlike the children of *Open City*, *Bicycle Thief*, and *Shoe Shine*, they face the future with confidence—in themselves and in the society of which they are a part.

Two films follow in the wake of *Sotto il sole di Roma* to shape a trilogy on youth and young love: *E primavera* and *Two Cents Worth of Hope*. To their scripts are linked the names of Suso Cecchi d'Amico, Cesare Zavattini, and Titina de Filippo, names in turn allied with Visconti, De Sica, and the master family of Italian comedy. Shot on location from one end of the peninsula to the other, the burning questions of the day—the *mezzogiorno*, unemployment, Communist vs. Christian Democrat—are cloaked in humor, more importantly in an optimism that, as Leprohon notes in *The Italian Cinema*, official Italy found reassuring. Threatened by the bleak view of Italy exported by the post-war Italian cinema, the government reacted by passing the Andreotti Law (1948) in the same year Castellani launched what came to be known as "rosy neorealism."

The trilogy was followed by *Giulietta e Romeo*. This story of young love thwarted by parents and convention had already found expression in the contemporary working class settings of the three previous films, and was drawn from two Renaissance versions: Shakespeare's and Luigi Da Porto's. Professional and non-professional actors, including a Juliet chosen from an avalanche of responses to a talent search conducted in the neorealist style, combined to create a tension of text and performance that elicited considerable critical controversy. Once again, Castellani had adapted neorealism to his own uses. This time it was a literary neorealism, redefined to suit his inspiration, and dependent as always on the rejection of mimicry and doctrine.

—Mirella Jona Affron

CAVALCANTI, Alberto.

Brazilian. Born Alberto de Almeida Cavalcanti in Rio de Janeiro, 6 February 1897. Educated at law school, Brazil, and at Geneva Fine Art School, Switzerland. Art director in Paris, early 1920's; directed first film, *Rien que les heures*, 1926; directed French language versions of American films for Paramount, Joinsville, 1929–30; joined General Post Office (GPO) Film Unit, London, 1937 (Head of Unit, 1937); joined Ealing Studios as feature director, 1940; Head of Production, Vera Cruz group, Brazil, and co-founder, Brazilian Film Institute, 1949–50; settled in Europe, 1955; director, British and French TV, 1950's–68; teacher, film course, U.C.L.A., 1963–65. Recipient: American States Medal for Superior Artistic Achievement, 1972. *Died in Paris, 23 August 1982.*

Films as Director:

1925 *Le Train sans yeux* (+sc, ed)
1926 ***Rien que les heures*** (*Only the Hours*) (+pr, sc, ed)
1927 *Yvette* (+sc, ed); *En rade* (*Sea Fever*) (+co-sc, ed); *La P'tite Lilie* (+sc, ed supervisor)
1928 *La Jalousie du barbouillé* (+sc, ed, art d); *Le Capitaine Fracasse* (+co-sc, ed)

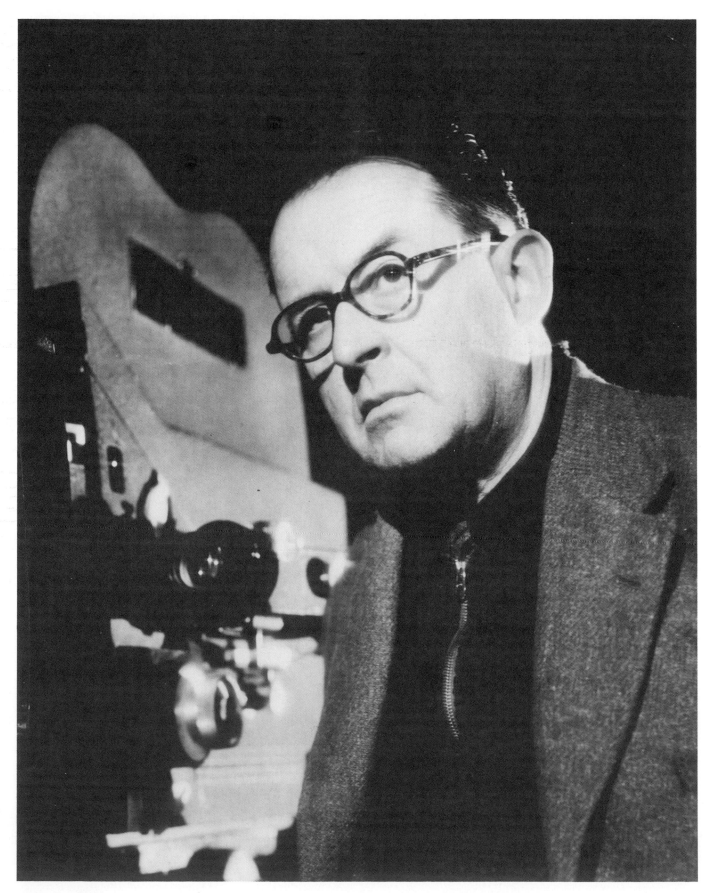

Alberto Cavalcanti

1929   *Le Petit Chaperon rouge* (+sc, ed, art d); *Vous verrez la semaine prochaine* (+sc, ed); *A michemin du ciel* (French language version of George Abbott's *Half-Way to Heaven*)
1930   *Toute sa vie* (French language version of Dorothy Arzner's *Sarah and Son*); *A canção do berço* (Portuguese version of Arzner's *Sarah and Son*); *Les Vacances du diable* (French language version of Edmund Goulding's *The Devil's Holiday*); *Dans une île perdue* (French language version of William Wellman's *Dangerous Paradise*)
1932   *En lisant le journal*; *Le Jour du frotteur* (+sc, ed); *Revue Montmartroise* (+sc); *Nous ne ferons jamais de cinéma*; *Le Truc du brésilien*; *Le Mari garçon* (*Le Garçon divorcé*)
1933   *Plaisirs défendus*; *Tour de chant* (+sc); *Coralie et Cie* (+sc)
1934   *Pett and Pott* (+sound supervisor, bit role); *New Rates*
1935   *Coalface* (+sound supervisor)
1936   *Message from Geneva*
1937   *We Live in Two Worlds* (+pr); *The Line to Tschierva Hut* (+pr); *Who Writes to Switzerland* (+pr)
1938   *Four Barriers* (+pr); *The Chiltern Country* (+pr)
1939   *Alice in Switzerland* (+pr); *Midsummer Day's Work* (+pr, sc)
1940   *La Cause commune* (+pr) (made in Britain for showing in France); *Factory Front* (+pr) (British version of preceding film); *Yellow Caesar* (*The Heel of Italy*) (+pr)
1941   *Young Veteran* (+pr); *Mastery of the Sea* (+pr)
1942   *Went the Day Well?* (*48 Hours*)
1943   *Watertight* (*Ship Safety*)
1944   *Champagne Charlie*; *Trois Chansons de la résistance* (*Trois Chants pour la France*)
1945   "*The Ventriloquist's Dummy (The Christmas Party)*" episode of **Dead of Night**
1947   *The Life and Adventures of Nicholas Nickleby*; *They Made Me a Fugitive* (*I Became a Criminal*)
1948   *The First Gentleman* (*Affairs of a Rogue*)
1949   *For Them That Trespass*
1952   *Simão o caolho* (*Simon the One-Eyed*) (+pr)
1953   *O canto do mar* (*The Song of the Sea*) (+pr, co-sc) (remake of *En rade*)
1954   *Mulher de verdade* (*A Real Woman*) (+pr)
1955   *Herr Puntila und sein Knecht Matti* (+co-sc)
1956   *Die Windrose* (d prologue only, collective film co-supervised with Joris Ivens)
1958   *La Prima notte* (*Les Noces vénitiennes*)
1960   *The Monster of Highgate Ponds*
1967   *Thus Spake Theodor Herzl* (*The Story of Israel*) (+sc)

Other Films:

1923   *L'Inhumaine* (L'Herbier) (co-art d)
1924   *L'Inondation* (Delluc) (art d); *La Galerie des monstres* (Catelain) (asst d, art d); **Feu Mathias Pascal** (L'Herbier) (art d)
1926   *The Little People* (Pearson) (art d)
1931   *Au pays du scalp* (de Wavrin) (ed)
1934   *Windmill in Barbados* (Wright) (sound supervisor); *Granton Trawler* (Anstey) (sound supervisor); **Song of Ceylon** (Wright) (sound supervisor)
1935   *Book Bargain* (McLaren) (pr); *Big Money* (Watt) (pr)
1936   *Rainbow Dance* (Lye) (pr); **Night Mail** (Wright and Watt) (pr, sound supervisor); *Calendar of the Year* (Spice) (pr)
1937   *The Saving of Bill Blewitt* (Watt) (pr); *Roadways* (Coldstream and Legg) (pr)
1938   *North or Northwest* (Lye) (pr); *North Sea* (Watt) (pr, sound supervisor); *Distress Call* (Watt) (pr) (shortened silent version of preceding title); *Many a Pickle* (McLaren) (pr); *Happy in the Morning* (Jackson) (pr)
1939   *The City* (Elton) (pr); *Men in Danger* (Jackson) (pr); *Spare Time* (Jennings) (pr); *Health of a Nation* (*Health for the Nation, Forty Million People*) (Monck) (pr); *Speaking from America* (Jennings) (pr); *Spring Offensive* (*An Unrecorded Victory*) (Jennings) (pr); *The First Days* (Watt, Jennings, and Jackson) (pr)
1940   *Men of the Lightship* (Macdonald) (pr); *Squadron 992* (Watt) (pr); *Sea Fort* (Dalrymple) (pr); *Salvage with a Smile* (Brunel) (pr)

1941   *Guests of Honour* (Pitt) (pr); *The Big Blockade* (Frend) (assoc pr); *Merchant Seamen* (*Merchant Convoy*) (Holmes) (pr); *The Foreman Went to France* (*Somewhere in France*) (Frend) (assoc pr); *Find, Fix and Strike* (Bennett) (pr)
1942   *Greek Testament* (*The Shrine of Victory*) (Hasse) (pr)
1944   *The Halfway House* (Dearden) (assoc pr)
1950   *Caicara* (Loafer) (Celi) (pr, supervisor)
1951   *Terra sempere terra* (*Land Is Forever Land*) (Payne) (pr); *Painel* (*Panel*) (Barreto) (pr); *Santuario* (*Sanctuary*) (Barreto) (pr)
1952   *Volta redonda* (*Round Trip*) (Waterhouse) (pr); *Film and Reality* (selection and compilation)
1969   *Lettres de Stalingrad* (Katz) (role)

Publications:

By CAVALCANTI: book—

Film and Reality, London, 1942; as *Film e realidade*, Rio de Janeiro, 1952.

By CAVALCANTI: articles—

"Sound in Films," in *Film* (London), November 1939.
"Cavalcanti in Brazil," in *Sight and Sound* (London), April/June 1953.
Interview with J. Hillier and others, in *Screen* (London), Summer 1972.
Cavalcanti, Alberto, in *Filme Cultura* (Rio de Janeiro), January–April 1984.

On CAVALCANTI: books—

Klaue, Wolfgang, and others, *Cavalcanti*, Berlin, 1952.
Hardy, Forsyth, editor, *Grierson on Documentary*, revised edition, London, 1966.
Lovell, Alan, and Jim Hillier, *Studies in Documentary*, New York, 1972.
Barsam, Richard, *The Non-Fiction Film*, New York, 1973.
Rotha, Paul, *Documentary Diary*, London, 1973.
Sussex, Elizabeth, *The Rise and Fall of British Documentary: The Story of the Film Movement Founded by John Grierson*, Berkeley, 1975.
Ellis, Jack C., *The Documentary Idea*, Englewood Cliffs, New Jersey, 1989.

On CAVALCANTI: articles—

De La Roche, Catherine, "Cavalcanti in Brazil," in *Sight and Sound* (London), January/March 1955.
Monegal, Emir Rodriguez, "Alberto Cavalcanti," in *Quarterly of Film, Radio, and Television* (Berkeley), Summer 1955.
Minish, Geoffrey, "Cavalcanti in Paris," in *Sight and Sound* (London), Summer 1970.
Taylor, J.R., "Surrealist Admen," in *Sight and Sound* (London), Autumn 1971.
Beylie, Claude, and others, "Alberto Cavalcanti," in *Ecran* (Paris), November 1974.
Sussex, E., "Cavalcanti in England," in *Sight and Sound* (London), August 1975.
Zapiola, G., "Medio siglo de cine en la obra del eurobrasileño Alberto Cavalcanti," in *Cinemateca Revista* (Montevideo), September 1982.
Courcier, J., obituary in *Cinéma* (Paris), October 1982.
Obituary in *Films and Filming* (London), November 1982.
Pilard, P., "Cavalcanti à Londres. Quinze ans de cinéma brittanique," in *Revue du Cinéma* (Paris), November 1983.

*   *   *

Cavalcanti was multi-national to a remarkable extent. Brazilian by birth, he worked in French commercial and avant-garde cinema of the 1920's, in British documentary of the 1930's and features of the 1940's, returned briefly to Brazil in an effort to revitalize its production, lived in Paris during his last years but visited and made films elsewhere. In the long view, however, Cavalcanti may be most closely associated with British film, especially with British documentary.

Even his early years in France led to that subsequent connection. Following work as a set designer, most notably for Marcel

L'Herbier, he made the seminal *Rien que les heures* in 1926. Though part of the avant-garde experimentation of the 1920's, *Rien* inaugurated the "city symphonies," one of the lines picked up by John Grierson as he was molding the British documentary of the 1930's. (The other lines came from the work of Flaherty, and of the Soviets, notably Vertov, Eisenstein, and Turin.)

Before being invited to join the General Post Office Film Unit by Grierson, Cavalcanti had experience in the early sound film of the French studios. In British documentary he would distinguish himself especially through his work with sound in relation to image. *Granton Trawler, The Song of Ceylon, Coal Face, Night Mail*, and *North Sea* offer evidence of his contributions. It might be argued that these films contain more sophisticated multi-layered sound and edited images—what Eisenstein called vertical montage—than that evident in narrative fiction films of the time. Cavalcanti's personal creativity became the basis for teaching other, younger members of the documentary group. Harry Watt, Basil Wright, and others have attested to Cavalcanti's significance as teacher of conception and technique.

Though Grierson always acknowledged Cavalcanti's importance to the artistry of British documentary, there developed a split between the Grierson faction (dedicated to making films to bring about social change) and the Cavalcanti faction (more concerned with ways in which realist film technique and style could be brought to the larger audiences of the theatres). In fact, an anthology surveying the documentary film, *The Film and Reality*, co-produced by Cavalcanti and Ernest Lindgren in 1942, created a furor behind the scenes on its release. It represents essentially an aesthetic history of documentary (Cavalcanti selected the excerpts), ending on feature fiction films embodying some of the characteristics of documentary. The Grierson group were reputedly outraged that no attention was paid to the dominant purpose of British documentary, which was a sort of citizenship education—communication by the government to the citizenry. For his part, Cavalcanti said late in life that he always thought he and Grierson were up to the same thing essentially—that of course he had a social sense, as surely as did Grierson. The real trouble was that he hadn't received adequate screen credits for the work he had done for the GPO Film Unit during Grierson's regime. (Grierson favored the idea of anonymous collective rather than individual auteurs.)

When Cavalcanti returned to entertainment filmmaking early in the war he was missed by the documentary bunch. At the same time it must be said that Cavalcanti (like Watt, who followed him shortly) brought with him a documentary influence to Ealing Studios that extended into the wartime fiction film; it can be seen in, for example, *The Foreman Went to France*, which he produced, and *Went the Day Well?*, which he directed. On the other hand, Cavalcanti's finest achievement as fictional producer/director may well be *Dead of Night*, the surrealist elements of which—the mingling of fantasy and actuality—recall the French avant-garde.

In summary it can be said that Cavalcanti seemed always to be the artist, personal creator and, especially, consummate technician, who applied himself to the basic modes of film art—narrative fiction, avant-garde, documentary—in a full range of capacities—set designer, sound recordist, producer, director. A charming journeyman artist, cosmopolitan, urban and tasteful, he taught and influenced a lot of other filmmakers and was responsible for noteworthy innovation and experimentation in many of the films with which he was associated.

—Jack C. Ellis

CAYATTE, André.

French. Born in Carcassonne, 3 February 1909. Journalist and lawyer, to mid 1930's; became scenarist in collaboration with Henri Jeanson, then Charles Spaak, directed first feature, *La Fausse Maîtresse*, 1942. Recipient: Lion of St. Mark, Venice Festival, for *Justice est faite*, 1950, and *Le Passage du Rhin*, 1960; Special Jury Prize, Cannes Festival, for *Nous sommes tous les assassins*, 1952. Died of a heart attack, 6 February 1989.

Films as Director and Scriptwriter:

1942   *La Fausse Maîtresse*
1943   *Au bonheur des dames (Shop-Girls of Paris)*; *Pierre et Jean*
1946   *Le Dernier Soul* (completed 1944); *Sérénade aux nuages*; *Roger-la-Honte*; *La Revanche de Roger-la-honte*
1947   *Le Chanteur inconnu*
1948   *Le Dessous des cartes*
1949   *Les Amants de Vérone (The Lovers of Verona)*; "Tante Emma" episode of *Retour à la vie*
1950   *Justice est faite (Justice Is Done)*
1952   *Nous sommes tous des assassins (We Are All Murderers)*
1954   *Avant le déluge*
1955   *Le Dossier noir*
1957   *Œil pour œil (An Eye for an Eye)*
1958   *Le Miroir à deux faces (The Mirror Has Two Faces)*
1960   *Le Passage du Rhin (Tomorrow Is My Turn)*
1963   *Le Glaive et la balance (Two Are Guilty)*
1964   *La Vie conjugale (Anatomy of a Marriage)* (composed of two films: *Françoise (My Nights with Françoise)* and *Jean-Marc (My Days with Jean Marc)*
1965   *Piège pour Cendrillon (A Trap for Cinderella)*
1967   *Les Risques du métier*
1969   *Les Chemins de Katmandou*
1970   *Mourir d'aimer (To Die of Love)*
1973   *Il n'y a pas de fumée sans feu (Where There's Smoke)*
1975   *Le Testament (The Verdict)*
1977   *A chacun son enfer*
1978   *La Raison d'état*; *Justices*; *L'Amour en question*

Other Films:

1938   *Entrée des artistes* (Allegret) (co-sc)
1939   *Tempête sur Paris* (Bernard-Deschamps) (sc)
1941   *Remorques* (Grémillon) (co-sc); *Le Club des soupirants* (Gleize) (co-sc); *Montmartre sur Seine* (Lacombe) (co-sc); *Caprices* (Joannon) (co-sc)
1942   *Le Camion blanc* (Joannon) (co-sc)
1945   *Farandole* (Zwoboda) (co-sc)
1946   *La Couple idéal* (Roland) (synopsis)

Publications:

By CAYATTE: books—

Mesures pour rien (poems), Paris, 1927.
La Peau des autres (novel), Paris, 1936.
Le Traquenard, Paris, 1939.

By CAYATTE: articles—

Interview in *Unifrance* (Paris), December/January 1954/55.
"My Friend Bourvil," in *Unifrance* (Paris), October 1958.
"La Cybernétique d'André Cayatte," in *Qu'est-ce que le cinéma?*, with André Bazin, Paris, 1961.
"André Cayatte accuse les critiques," interview with André Parinaud, in *Arts* (Paris), 20 February 1963.

On CAYATTE: book—

Braucourt, Guy, *André Cayatte*, Paris, 1969.

André Cayatte

On CAYATTE: articles—

Audibert, Jacques, article in *Comœdia* (Paris), 22 August 1941 and 31 July 1943.
"A French Winner at Venice," in *Films in Review* (New York), October 1950.
Ciment, Michel, in *Positif* (Paris), April 1971.
Obituary in *Ciné Revue* (Paris), 16 February 1989.

On CAYATTE: film—

Viallet, Pierre, and Marcel L'Herbier, *Portraits filmées . . . André Cayatte*, for TV, 1953.

*   *   *

Andre Cayatte was surely one of the most satisfied directors in history. He knew continual success and made the kinds of films he felt it was his destiny to make. Moreover, these films in his eyes, and in the eyes of a great many others, were of the highest social value. The fact that they have done well at the box office is a final indication of a long and happy career.

Cayatte chose the cinema because it was in his view the most powerful and efficient communications medium in the modern world. He was not drawn to its glamour, nor to its artistic potential. Rather it seemed to him the logical tool for anyone interested in formulating and conveying important ideas. As a young lawyer schooled in the humanities, Cayatte was full of ideas. At first he published stories and novels, winning an important prize in 1934. But the slowness of writing discouraged him, as did its oblique relation to a tangible public and to the themes he was devoted to.

The cinema, on the other hand, put one in contact with an audience. Its materials were not airy words but hard technology directed at actual social situations. Even if these situations were generally fabricated on sound stages, the confrontation of ideas, actors, settings, and points of view appeared authentic. Besides, he was certain he could dramatize situations on screen quickly, never being interested in refined subtlety. After writing several scripts, Cayatte had little trouble finding a directorial assignment, particularly in view of the paucity of directors after the Nazi takeover.

To learn the art, Cayatte became a specialist in literary adaptation. Balzac, Zola, and Maupassant served him in his first three ventures. As thin as these films seem today, they exhibit a clarity of purpose and rhetoric that would serve him later on. *Au bonheur des dames* from Zola is a genuinely interesting socio-economic melodrama concerned with the birth of the first department store in Paris and the demise of the small shops. Virtually the same theme guides *The Magnificent Ambersons* made the same year. But where Welles's *mise en scene* is deep, Cayatte's is two-dimensional, as if he were fascinated by the glittery surface of his tale, not its consequences.

In 1949 Cayatte made the film that gave him carte blanche in the industry, *The Lovers of Verona*. The script by Jacques Prévert flattered Cayatte's intellectual pretensions, while justifying his thin studio style, for this was a retelling of the Romeo and Juliet story, or rather a double retelling, as the actors playing the tragic roles find themselves condemned to live out those roles in real life.

From 1950 on Cayatte and his writer Charles Spaak turned out over a dozen problem films dealing with such issues as euthanasia (*Justice est faite*), capital punishment (*Nous sommes tous des assassins*), delinquency (*Avant le déluge*) and marriage. Even his more recent *To Die of Love* achieved international success in exposing prejudice against the sexual independence of an admirable schoolteacher (Annie Girardot).

But Cayatte's more standard films like *Passage du Rhin* display the shallowness of characterization that Bazin early on claimed was the ruin of his fabricated *"films à thèse."* There is little ambiguity in his point of view. This directness is both his best and most damaging trait.

—Dudley Andrew

CHABROL, Claude.

French. Born in Paris, 24 June 1930. Educated at University of Paris. Married 1) Agnes Goute, 1952 (divorced), two sons; 2) actress Stephane Audran, 1964, one son. Film critic for *Arts* and for *Cahiers du Cinéma*, Paris, 1953–57 (under own name and as "Charles Eitel" and "Jean-Yves Goute"); Head of Production company AJYM, 1956–61; directed first film, *Le Beau Serge*, 1958; director, *Macbeth*, Théâtre Recamier, Paris, 1967; director, French TV, 1970's. Recipient: Golden Bear, Berlin Festival, for *Les Cousins*, 1959.

Films as Director:

1958 *Le Beau Serge (Bitter Reunion)* (+pr, sc, bit role)
1959 *Les Cousins (The Cousins)* (+pr, sc); *A double tour (Web of Passion, Leda)* (+bit role)
1960 *Les Bonnes Femmes* (+adapt, bit role)
1961 *Les Godelureaux* (+co-adapt, bit role); "L'Avarice" episode of *Les Sept Péchés capitaux (The Seven Deadly Sins)* (+bit role)
1962 *L'Œil du malin (The Third Lover)* (+sc); *Ophélia* (+co-sc)
1963 *Landru (Bluebeard)* (+co-sc)
1964 "L'Homme qui vendit la tour Eiffel" episode of *Les Plus Belles Escroqueries du monde (The Beautiful Swindlers)*; *Le Tigre aime la chair fraîche (The Tiger Likes Fresh Blood)*; *La Chance et l'amour* (Tavernier, Schlumberger, Bitsch and Berry) (d linking sequences only)
1965 "La Muette" episode of *Paris vu par . . . (Six in Paris)* (+sc, role); *Marie-Chantal contre le Docteur Kha* (+co-sc, bit role); *Le Tigre se parfume à la dynamite (An Orchid for the Tiger)* (+bit role)
1966 *La Ligne de démarcation (Line of Demarcation)* (+co-sc)
1967 *Le Scandale (The Champagne Murders)*; *La Route de Corinthe (Who's Got the Black Box?, The Road to Corinth)* (+role)
1968 *Les Biches (The Does, The Girlfriends)* (+co-sc, role)
1969 ***La Femme infidèle (Unfaithful Wife)*** (+co-sc): *Que la bête meure (This Man Must Die, Killer!)*
1970 *Le Boucher* (+sc); *La Rupture (Le Jour des parques, The Breakup)* (+sc, bit role)
1971 *Juste avant la nuit (Just Before Nightfall)* (+sc)
1972 *La Décade prodigieuse (Ten Days' Wonder)* (+co-sc); *Docteur Popaul* (+co-song)
1973 *Les Noces rouges (Wedding in Blood)* (+sc)
1974 *Nada (The NADA Gang)*; *Histoires insolites* (series of 4 TV films)
1975 *Une Partie de plaisir (A Piece of Pleasure, Pleasure Party)*; *Les Innocents aux mains sales (Dirty Hands, Innocents with Dirty Hands)* (+sc); *Les Magiciens (Initiation à la mort, Profezia di un delitto)*
1976 *Folies bourgeoises (The Twist)* (+co-sc)
1977 *Alice ou La Dernière Fugue (Alice or the Last Escapade)* (+sc)
1978 *Blood Relatives (Les Liens de sang)* (+co-sc): *Violette Nozière (Violette)*
1982 *Les Fantômes du chapelier (The Hatmaker)*
1983 *Le Sang des autres (The Blood of Others)*
1984 *Poulet au vinaigre (Cop au Vin)*
1985 *Inspecteur Lavardin*
1986 *Masques*
1987 *Le cri du hibou*

Claude Chabrol (in checked shirt) with François Truffaut, at Cannes

1989 *Une Affaire des femmes* (*Story of Women*)
1990 *Quiet Days in Clichy*; *Docteur M*

Other Films:

1956 *Le Coup de berger* (Rivette) (co-sc, uncred co-mu, role)
1959 *A bout de souffle* (Godard) (tech adv); *Les Jeux de l'amour* (de Broca) (role)
1960 *Paris nour appartient* (Rivette) (role); *Saint-Tropez blues* (Moussy) (role); *Les Distractions* (Dupont) (role)
1961 *Ples v dezju* (*Dance in the Rain*) (Hladnik) (supervisor); *Les Menteurs* (Greville) (role)
1964 *Les Durs à cuire* (Pinoteau) (role)
1965 *Brigitte et Brigitte* (Moullet) (role)
1966 *Happening* (Bokanowski) (tech adv); *Zoe bonne* (Deval) (role)
1968 *La Femme ecarlate* (Valere) (role)
1969 *Et crac!* (Douchet) (role); *Version latine* (Detre) (role); *Le Travail* (Detre) (role)
1970 *Sortie de secours* (Kahane) (role)
1971 *Eglantine* (Brialy) (tech adv); *Aussi loin que l'amour* (Rossif) (role)
1972 *Piège à pucelles* (Leroi) (tech adv); *Un Meurtre est un meurtre* (Périer) (role)
1973 *Le Flipping* (Volatron) (role as interviewee)

Publications:

By CHABROL: books—

Hitchcock, with Eric Rohmer, Paris, 1957.
Les Noces rouges, Paris, 1973.
Et pourtant, je tourne . . . , Paris, 1976.

By CHABROL: articles—

Note: regular contributor to *Cahiers du Cinéma* (Paris), under pseudonyms 'Charles Eitel' and 'Jean-Yves Goute,' 1950's.
"Tout ce qu'il faut savoir pour mettre en scène s'apprend en quatre heures," an interview with François Truffaut, in *Arts* (Paris), 19 February 1958.
"Vers un néo-romanticisme au cinéma," in *Lettres Françaises* (Paris), March 1959.
"Big Subjects, Little Subjects," in *Movie* (London), June 1962.
Interview with Gilles Jacob, in *Cinéma* (Paris), September/October 1966.
"Claude Chabrol," in *Interviews with Film Directors*, edited by Andrew Sarris, New York, 1967.
Articles anthologized in *The New Wave*, edited by Peter Graham, New York, 1968.
"La Femme Infidèle," and "La Muette," in *Avant-Scène du Cinéma* (Paris), no.42, 1969.
Interview with Michel Ciment and others, in *Positif* (Paris), April 1970.
Interview with Noah James, in *Take One* (Montreal), September/October 1970.
Interview with Rui Nogueira, in *Sight and Sound* (London), Winter 1970/71.
Interview with M. Rosier and D. Serceau, in *Cinéma* (Paris), September/October 1973.
Interviews with G. Braucourt, in *Ecran* (Paris), May 1975 and February 1977.
"Chabrol's Game of Mirrors," an interview with D. Overbey, in *Sight and Sound* (London), Spring 1977.
"The Magical Mystery World of Claude Chabrol," an interview with Dan Yakir, in *Film Quarterly* (Berkeley), no.3, 1979.
"I Fell in Love with Violette Nozière," in *Monthly Film Bulletin* (London), April 1979.
Interview with D. Simmons, in *Film Directions* (Belfast), vol. 5, no. 18, 1983.
Conversation with Georges Simenon, in *Filmkritik* (Munich), February 1983.
Interview with Jill Forbes, in *Stills* (London), June–July 1984.
"Jeu de massacre: Attention les yeux," an interview with Pierre Bonitzer and others, in *Cahiers du Cinéma* (Paris), March 1986.

On CHABROL: books—

Armes, Roy, *French Cinema Since 1946: Vol.2—The Personal Style*, New York, 1966.
Wood, Robin, and Michael Walker, *Claude Chabrol*, London, 1970.
Braucourt, Guy, *Claude Chabrol*, Paris, 1971.
Monaco, James, *The New Wave*, New York, 1976.
Magny, Joel, *Claude Chabrol*, Paris, 1987.

On CHABROL: articles—

"New Wave" issue of *Cinéma* (Paris), February 1960.
"Chabrol Issue" of *Movie* (London), June 1963.
Gow, Gordon, "The Films of Claude Chabrol," in *Films and Filming* (London), March 1967.
Baxter, Brian, "Claude Chabrol," in *Film* (London), Spring 1969.
"Chabrol Issue" of *L'Avant-scène du Cinéma* (Paris), May 1969.
Wood, Robin, "Chabrol and Truffaut," in *Movie* (London), Winter 1969/70.
Allen, Don, "Claude Chabrol," in *Screen* (London), February 1970.
Milne, Tom, "Chabrol's Schizophrenic Spider," in *Sight and Sound* (London), Spring 1970.
Haskell, Molly, "The Films of Chabrol—A Priest among Clowns," in *Village Voice* (New York), 12 November 1970.
Milne, Tom, "Songs of Innocence," in *Sight and Sound* (London), Winter 1970/71.
Bucher, F., and Peter Cowie, "Welles and Chabrol," in *Sight and Sound* (London), Autumn 1971.
"Chabrol Issue" of *Filmcritica* (Rome), April/May 1972.
Cornand, A., "*Les Noces rouges*, Chabrol et la censure," in *Image et Son* (Paris), April 1973.
Appel, A. Jr., "The Eyehole of Knowledge," in *Film Comment* (New York), May/June 1973.
"Chabrol Issue" of *Image et Son* (Paris), December 1973.
Dawson, Jan, "The Continental Divide," in *Sight and Sound* (London), Winter 1973/74.
Le Fanu, Mark, "The Cinema of Irony: Chabrol, Truffaut in the 1970s," in *Monogram* (London), no.5, 1974.
Walker, M., "Claude Chabrol into the 70s," in *Movie* (London), Spring 1975.
Fassbinder, Rainer Werner, "Insects in a Glass Case: Random Thoughts on Claude Chabrol," in *Sight and Sound* (London), no.4, 1976.
Harcourt, P., "Middle Chabrol," in *Film Comment* (New York), November/December 1976.
Poague, Leland, "The Great God Orson: Chabrol's '10 Days' Wonder," in *Film Criticism* (Edinboro, Pennsylvania), no.3, 1979.
Jenkins, Steve, "And the Chabrol we haven't seen . . . ," in *Monthly Film Bulletin* (London), July 1982.
Dossier on Chabrol, in *Cinématographe* (Paris), September 1982.
Bergan, Ronald, "Directors of the Decade—Claude Chabrol," in *Films and Filming* (London), December 1983.
"Chabrol Section" of *Revue du Cinéma* (Paris), May 1985.
Monthly Film Bulletin (London), August 1987.
Auld, Deborah, "I, Claude," in *Village Voice* (New York), 8 August 1989.

On CHABROL: film—

Yentob, Alan, *Getting Away with Murder or The Childhood of Claude Chabrol*, for BBC TV, London, 1978.

* * *

If Jean-Luc Godard appeals to critics because of his extreme interest in politics and film theory, if François Truffaut appeals to the popular audience because of his humanism and sentimentality, it is Claude Chabrol—film critic, filmmaker, philosopher—whose work consistently offers the opportunity for the most balanced appeal. His partisans find especially notable the subtle tone of Chabrol's cinema: his films are apparently cold and objective portraits of profoundly psychological situations; and yet that coldness never approaches the kind of fashionable cynicism, say, of a Stanley Kubrick, but suggests, rather, something closer to the viewpoint of a god who, with compassion but without sentiment, observes the follies of his creations.

Chabrol's work can perhaps best be seen as a cross between the unassuming and popular genre film and the pretentious and elitist art film: Chabrol's films tend to be thrillers with an incredibly self-conscious, self-assured style—that is, pretentious melodrama, aware of its importance. For some, however, the hybrid character of Chabrol's work is itself a problem: indeed, just as elitist critics sometimes find Chabrol's subject matter beneath them, so too do popular audiences sometimes find Chabrol's style and incredibly slow pace alienating.

Chabrol's films are filled with allusions and references to myth (as in *La Rupture*, which begins with an epigraph from Racine's *Phaedra*: "What an utter darkness suddenly surrounds me!"). The narratives of his films are developed through a sensuousness of decor, a gradual accumulation of psychological insight, an absolute mastery of camera movement, and the inclusion of objects and images—beautiful and evocative, like the river in *Le Boucher* or the lighthouse in *Dirty Hands*—which are imbued with symbolic intensity. Like Balzac whom he admires, Chabrol attempts, within a popular form, to present a portrait of his society in microcosm.

Chabrol began his career as a critic for *Cahiers du cinéma*. With Eric Rohmer, he wrote a groundbreaking book-length study of Alfred Hitchcock, and, with his friends (Truffaut, Godard, Rohmer, Jacques Rivette, and others) attempted to turn topsy-turvy the entire cinematic value system. That their theories of authorship remain today a basic (albeit modified and continuously examined) premise certainly indicates the success of their endeavor. Before long, Chabrol found himself functioning as financial consultant and producer for a variety of films inaugurating the directorial careers of his fellow critics who, like himself, were no longer content merely to theorize.

Chabrol's career can perhaps be divided into four semi-discrete periods: 1) the early personal films, beginning with *Le Beau Serge* in 1958 and continuing through *Landru* in 1962; 2) the commercial assignments, beginning with *The Tiger Likes Fresh Blood* in 1964 and continuing through *The Road to Corinth* in 1967; 3) the mature cycle of masterpieces, beginning with *Les Biches* in 1968 and continuing through *Wedding in Blood* in 1973, almost all starring his wife, Stéphane Audran; and 4) the more diverse (and uneven) accumulation of films from 1974 to the present, which have tended neither to garner automatic international release nor to feature Audran in any central role.

If Hitchcock's *Shadow of a Doubt*, as analyzed by Chabrol and Rohmer, is constructed upon an exchange of guilt, Chabrol's first film, *Le Beau Serge*, modeled after it, is constructed upon an exchange of redemption. Chabrol followed *Le Beau Serge*, in which a city-dweller visits a country friend, with *Les Cousins*, in which a country-dweller visits a city friend. Most notably, *Les Cousins* offers Chabrol's first "Charles" and "Paul," the names Chabrol would continue to use throughout much of his career, Charles to represent the more serious bourgeois man, Paul the more hedonistic id-figure. *A double tour*, Chabrol's first color film, is especially notable for its striking cinematography, its complex narrative structure, and exhuberance of its flamboyant style; it represents Chabrol's first studied attempt to examine and criticize the moral values of the bourgeoisie as well as to dissect the sociopsychological causes of the violence which inevitably erupts as the social and family structures prove inadequate. Perhaps the most wholly successful film of this period is the infrequently screened *L'Œil du malin*, which presents the most typical Chabrol situation: a triangle consisting of a bourgeois married couple—Hélène and her stolid husband—and the outsider whose involvement with the couple ultimately leads to violence and tragedy. Here can be found Chabrol's first "Hélène," the recurring beautiful and slightly aloof woman, generally played by Stéphane Audran.

When these and other personal films failed to ignite the box-office, despite often positive critical responses, Chabrol embarked on a series of primarily commercial assignments (such as *Marie-Chantal contre le Docteur Kha*), during which his career went into a considerable critical eclipse. Today, however, even these fairly inconsequential films seem to reflect a fetching style and some typically quirky Chabrolian concerns.

Chabrol's breakthrough occurred in 1968 with the release of *Les Biches*, an elegant thriller in which an outsider, Paul, disrupts the lesbian relationship between two women. All of Chabrol's films in this period are slow psychological thrillers which tend basically to represent variations upon the same theme: an outsider affecting a central relationship until violence results. In *La Femme infidèle*, one of Chabrol's most self-assured films, the marriage of Hélène and Charles is disrupted when Charles kills Hélène's lover. In the Jansenist *Que la bête meure*, Charles tracks down the unremittingly evil hit-and-run killer of his young son, and while doing so disrupts the relationship between the killer, Paul, and his sister-in-law Hélène. In *Le Boucher*, the butcher Popaul, who is perhaps a homicidal killer, attempts a relationship with a cool and frigid schoolteacher, Hélène, who has displaced her sexual energies onto her teaching of her young pupils, particularly onto one who is conspicuously given the name Charles.

In the extravagantly expressive *La Rupture*, the outsider Paul attempts a plot against Hélène in order to secure a better divorce settlement desired by the rich parents of her husband Charles, who has turned to drug addiction to escape his repressive bourgeois existence. In *Juste avant la nuit*, it is Charles who has taken a lover, and Charles's wife Hélène who must ultimately resort to an act of calculated violence in order to keep the bourgeois surface intact. In the detective variation *Ten Days' Wonder*, the relationship between Charles and Hélène is disrupted by the intervention of a character named Théo (*Theos*, representing God), whose false image must be unmasked by the outsider Paul. And in *Wedding in Blood*, based on factual material, it is the wife and her lover who team together to plot against her husband.

Jean Renoir said that all great directors make the same film over and over; perhaps no one has taken this dictum as seriously as Chabrol; indeed, all these films represent a kind of formal geometry as Charles, Hélène, and Paul play out their fated roles in a universe strongly influenced by Fritz Lang, the structures of their bourgeois existence unable to contain their previously repressed passions. Noteworthy too is the consistency of collaboration on these films: usually with Stéphane Audran, Michel Bouquet, and Jean Yanne as performers; Jean Rabier as cinematographer; Paul Gégauff as co-scriptwriter; André Génovès as producer; Guy Littaye as art director; Pierre Jansen as composer; Jacques Gaillard as editor; Guy Chichignoud on sound.

In the late 1970's and 1980's, Chabrol has increasingly explored different kinds of financing, making television films as well as international co-productions. Meanwhile, without his regular collaborators, most notably Stéphane Audran, Chabrol has had to establish a new "team." Yet while films like *Poulet au vinaigre*, *Les Fantômes du Chapelier*, and *Masques* are worthy of note, they do not measure up to the films with Audran, suggesting that her contribution to the director's earlier career may have been underestimated. Perhaps it is that a director of such style and cool control as Chabrol requires a strong, central female presence as performer.

Certainly *Une affaire des femmes*, starring Isabelle Huppert (who had previously starred in *Violet Nozière*) seems the most notable of the post—Audran films. The story of a woman abortionist who ends up the last female guillotined in France (by the Vichy government), *Une Affaire des femmes* did, unlike other recent Chabrol films, receive international distribution, and also won a variety of awards. Produced in association with Martin Karmitz, it may prove an important development, perhaps ushering in another cycle of major works.

Chabrol's most surprising film of the 1980's, though, was *Le Cheval d'Orgueil*, an ethnographic drama chronicling the simplicity and terrible harshness of Peasant life in Brittany prior to World War I with a straight-forwardness and lack of sentimentality which is often riveting. Indeed the film seems so different from much of Chabrol's work that it forces a kind of re-evaluation of his career. Less an emulator of Hitchcock or Lang, Chabrol seems now much more an emulator of Balzac, attempting to create his own *Comédie humaine*, offering a panoramic account of the society about him.

—Charles Derry

————

CHAHINE, Youssef.

Egyptian. (Name also spelled "Shahin"). Born in Alexandria, 25 January 1926. Educated at Victoria College, and Alexandria University; studied acting at Pasadena Playhouse, California, 1946–48. Returned to Egypt, worked with Italian documentarist Gianni Vernuccio, 1948; introduced to film production by Alvisi Orfanelli, "pioneer of the Egyptian cinema," directed first film, *Baba Amine*, 1950; introduced actor Omar Sharif, in *Sera'a fil Wadi*, 1953; voluntary exile in Libya, 1965–67. Recipient: Special Jury Prize, Berlin Festival, for *Alexandria . . . Why?*, 1979.

Films as Director:

1950 *Baba Amine (Father Amine)*
1951 *Ibn el Nil (The Nile's Son)*; *El Muharraj el Kabir (The Great Clown)*
1952 *Sayidet el Kitar (The Lady in the Train)*; *Nessa bala Rejal (Women without Men)*
1953 *Sera'a fil Wadi (Struggle in the Valley)*
1954 *Shaitan el Sahara (Devil of the Desert)*
1955 *Sera'a fil Mina (Struggle on the Pier)*
1956 *Inta Habibi (You Are My Love)*
1957 *Wadaat Hobak (Farewell to Your Love)*
1958 *Bab el Haded (Iron Gate, Cairo Station, Gare centrale)* (+role as Kennawi); *Gamila Bohraid (Djamila)*
1959 *Hub illal Abad (Forever Yours)*
1960 *Bayn Ideak (Between Your Hands)*
1961 *Nedaa el Ochak (Lover's Call)*; *Rajol fi Hayati (A Man in My Life)*
1963 *El Naser Salah el Dine (Saladin)*
1964 *Fajr Yum Jadid (Dawn of a New Day)*
1965 *Baya el Khawatim (The Ring Seller)*
1966 *Rimal min Zahab (Sand of Gold)*
1968 *El Nas wal Nil (People and the Nile)*
1969 *El Ard (The Land)*
1970 *Al Ekhtiar (The Choice)*
1973 *Al Asfour (The Sparrow)*
1976 *Awdat al Ibn al Dal (Return of the Prodigal Son)*
1978 *Iskindria . . . Leh? (Alexandria . . . Why?)* (+sc)
1982 *Hadota Misreya (An Egyptian Story, La Memoire)* (+sc)
1984 *Al Wedaa ya Bonaparte (Adieu Bonaparte)*

Publications:

By CHAHINE: articles—

Interview with C.M. Cluny, in *Cinéma* (Paris), September/October 1973.
"Entretien avec Youssef Chahine (Le moineau)," by G. Gauthier, in *Image et Son* (Paris), December 1974.
"Youssef Chahine: Aller aussi loin qu'un peut," interview with N. Ghali, in *Jeune Cinéma* (Paris), December 1974/January 1975.
"Youssef Chahine: La memoire," an interview with Marcel Martin, in *Revue du Cinéma* (Paris), July–August 1983.
"La verité de personnages," an interview with C. Tesson, in *Cahiers du Cinéma* (Paris), June 1985.
Interview in *Cinématographe* (Paris), December 1986.

On CHAHINE: books—

Richter, Erika, *Realistischer Film in Agypten*, Berlin, 1974.
Armes, Roy, *Third World Filmmaking and the West*, Berkeley, 1987.

On CHAHINE: articles—

Arnaud, C., "Youssef Chahine," in *Image et Son* (Paris), January 1978.
Tournes, A., "Chahine, le nationalisme demystifie: 'Alexandrie pourquoi?'," in *Jeune Cinéma* (Paris), no.3, 1979.
Armes, Roy, "Youssef Chahine and Egyptian Cinema," in *Framework* (Norwich), Spring 1981.
Joseph, I., and C. Jages, "Le Cinéma, l'Egypte et l'histoire," in *Cahiers du Cinéma* (Paris), September 1982.
Nave, B., A. Tournes, and M. Martin, "Un film bilan: La memoire de Chahine," in *Jeune Cinéma* (Paris), April 1983.
Toubiana, Serge, "Chahine a la conque te de Bonaparte," in *Cahiers du Cinéma* (Paris), October 1984.
Dossier on Chahine, in *Revue du Cinéma* (Paris), December 1984.
Chaillet, Jean-Paul, "Soleil d'Egypte," in *Première* (Paris), May 1985.
Kieffer, A., "Youssef Chahine: Un homme de dialogue," in *Jeune Cinéma* (Paris), July–August 1985.
Tesson, C., "La Descente du Nil," in *Cahiers du Cinéma* (Paris), July–August 1986.

*   *   *

Youssef Chahine is one of the most forceful and complex of Egyptian filmmakers, whose progress over the 40 years or so since his debut at the age of 24 offers remarkable insight into the evolution of Egyptian society. A series of sharply critical social studies—of which *The Sparrow* in 1975 is undoubtedly the most successful—was interrupted by a heart attack while the director was still in his early fifties. This led him to question his own personal stance and development in a manner unique in Arab cinema and the result was the splendidly fluent autobiography, *Alexandria . . . Why?* in 1978, which was followed four years later by a second installment entitled *An Egyptian Story*, shot in a style best characterized as an amalgam of Fellini and Bob Fosse's *All That Jazz*.

As such references indicate, Chahine is an eclectic filmmaker, whose cosmopolitan attitudes can be traced back to his origins. He was born in Alexandria in 1926 of middle-class parents. His father, a supporter of the nationalist Wafd party, was a scrupulous but financially unsuccessful lawyer, and Chahine was brought up as a Christian, educated first at religious school and then at the prestigious Victoria College, where the language of tuition was English. After a year at Alexandria University he persuaded his parents to allow him to study drama for two years at Pasadena Playhouse, near Los Angeles, and on his return to Egypt plunged into the film industry, then enjoying a period of boom in the last years of King Farouk's reign.

Alexandria . . . Why? presents a vividly drawn picture of this vanished world: Alexandria in 1942, awaiting the arrival of Rommel's troops who, it is hoped, will finally drive out the British. The film is peopled with English soldiers and Egyptian patriots, aristocrats and struggling bourgeoises, the enthusias-

Youssef Chahine: *Iskindria . . . Leh?*

tic young and their disillusioned or corrupt elders. Chahine mocks the excesses of the nationalists (his terrorist patriots are mostly caricatures), leaves condemnation of Zionism to Jew, and tells love stories that cross the neatly drawn barriers separating Muslim and Jew, Egyptian aristocrat and English Tommy. The revelation of Chahine's own background and a few of his personal obsessions (as with the crucified Christ) seems to have released fresh creative powers in the director. His technique of intercutting the action with scenes from Hollywood musicals and newsreel footage from the Imperial War Museum in London is as successful as it is audacious, and the transitions of mood are brilliantly handled.

Youssef Chahine is a key figure in Third World Cinema. Unlike some of the other major filmmakers who also emerged in the 1950's—such as Satyajit Ray or Lester James Peries—he has not turned his back on commercial cinema. He has always shown a keen desire to reach a wide audience and *Alexandria . . . Why?*, though personal, is by no means an inaccessible or difficult work. Chahine's strength as a filmmaker lies indeed in his ability to combine mainstream production techniques with a very individual style and approach. Though intensely patriotic, he has shown a readiness to criticize government policies with which he does not agree, such as those of the late President Sadat. It is ironic therefore that the appearance of *Alex-*

andria . . . Why? should have coincided with the Camp David agreements between Egypt and Israel. As a result, Chahine's very personal statement of his belief in a tolerant society came to be widely criticized in the Arab world as an opportunistic political statement and a justification of Sadat's policies.

—Roy Armes

CHAPLIN, Charles.

British. Born Charles Spencer Chaplin in London, 16 April 1889. Married 1) Mildred Harris, 1918 (divorced 1920); 2) Lita Grey, 1924 (divorced 1927), two sons; 3) Paulette Goddard, 1936 (divorced 1941); Oona O'Neill, 1943, eight children. Music-Hall Performer, in London, and in provincial theatres, from 1898; engaged by Fred Karno troupe, 1907; toured U.S. with Karno, 1910 and 1912; signed to Keystone and moved to Hollywood, 1913; after acting in 11 Keystone comedies, began directing (35 films for Keystone), 1914; signed with Essanay (14 films), 1915; signed with Mutual (11 films), 1916; signed with First National (9 films), 1917; joint-founder, with Griffith, Pickford, and Fairbanks, United Artists, 1919; left U.S. to visit London, reentry permit rescinded en route, 1952; moved to Vevey, on Lake Geneva, Switzerland, 1953. Recipient: Best Actor, New York Film Critics, for *The Great Dictator*, 1940 (award refused); Honorary Oscar, "for the incalculable effect he has had in making motion pictures the art form of the country," 1971; Medallion Award, Writers Guild of America, 1971; Oscar for Best Original Dramatic Score Academy Award (shared), for *Limelight*, 1972. Knighted 1975. *Died in Vevey, 25 December 1977.*

Films as Director, Actor and Scriptwriter:

1914 *Caught in a Cabaret (Jazz Waiter, Faking with Society)* (co-d, co-sc); *Caught in the Rain (Who Got Stung?, At It Again)*; *A Busy Day (Lady Charlie, Militant Suffragette)*; *The Fatal Mallet (The Pile Driver, The Rival Suitors, Hit Him Again)* (co-d, co-sc); *Her Friend the Bandit (Mabel's Flirtation, A Thief Catcher)* (co-d, co-sc); *Mabel's Busy Day (Charlie and the Sausages, Love and Lunch, Hot Dogs)* (co-d, co-sc); *Mabel's Married Life (When You're Married, The Squarehead)* (co-d, co-sc); *Laughing Gas (Tuning His Ivories, The Dentist)*; *The Property Man (Getting His Goat, The Roustabout, Vamping Venus)*; *The Face on the Bar-Room Floor (The Ham Artist)*; *Recreation (Spring Fever)*; *The Masquerader (Putting One Over, The Female Impersonator)*; *His New Profession (The Good-for-Nothing, Helping Himself)*; *The Rounders (Two of a Kind, Oh, What a Night!, The Love Thief)*; *The New Janitor (The Porter, The Blundering Boob)*; *Those Love Pangs (The Rival Mashers, Busted Hearts)*; *Dough and Dynamite (The Doughnut Designer, The Cook)*; *Gentlemen of Nerve (Some Nerve, Charlie at the Races)*; *His Musical Career (The Piano Movers, Musical Tramps)*; *His Trysting Place (Family Home)*; *Getting Acquainted (A Fair Exchange, Hullo Everybody)*; *His Prehistoric Past (A Dream, King Charlie, The Caveman)*
1915 (for Essanay): *His New Job*; *A Night Out (Champagne Charlie)*; *The Champion (Battling Charlie)*; *In the Park (Charlie on the Spree)*; *A Jitney Elopement (Married in Haste)*; *The Tramp (Charlie the Hobo)*; *By the Sea (Charlie's Day Out)*; *Work (The Paper Hanger, The Plumber)*; *A Woman (The Perfect Lady)*; *The Bank*; *Shanghaied (Charlie the Sailor, Charlie on the Ocean)*; *A Night in the Show*
1916 (for Essanay): *Carmen (Charlie Chaplin's Burlesque on Carmen)*; *Police! (Charlie the Burglar)*; (for Mutual): *The Floorwalker (The Store)*; *The Fireman*; *The Vagabond*; *One A.M.*; *The Count*; *The Pawnshop*; *Behind the Screen*; *The Rink*
1917 (for Mutual): **Easy Street**; *The Cure*; *The Immigrant*; *The Adventurer*
1918 (for First National): *A Dog's Life*; (for Liberty Loan Committee): *The Bond*; *Triple Trouble* (compiled from 1915 footage plus additional non-Chaplin film by Essanay after he left); (for First National): *Shoulder Arms*
1919 (for First National): *Sunnyside*; *A Day's Pleasure*
1921 **The Kid**; (+pr); *The Idle Class* (+pr)
1922 *Pay Day* (+pr); *Nice and Friendly* (+pr) (made privately and unreleased)
1923 *The Pilgrim* (+pr); *A Woman of Paris* (+pr)
1925 **The Gold Rush** (+pr, narration, mus for sound reissue)
1926 *A Woman of the Sea (The Sea Gull)* (von Sternberg) (unreleased) (pr, d additional scenes)
1927 *The Circus* (+pr, mus, song for sound reissue)
1931 *City Lights* (+pr, mus)
1936 **Modern Times** (+pr, mus)
1940 **The Great Dictator** (+pr, mus)
1947 **Monsieur Verdoux** (+pr, mus); **Limelight** (+pr, mus, co-choreographer)
1957 *A King in New York* (+pr, mus)

1959 *The Chaplin Revue* (+pr, mus) (comprising *A Dog's Life, Shoulder Arms,* and *The Pilgrim,* with commentary and music)
1967 *A Countess from Hong Kong* (+ mus)

Other Films:

1914 *Making a Living (A Busted Johnny, Troubles, Doing His Best)* (Lehrman) (role as reporter); *Kid Auto Races at Venice (The Kid Auto Race)* (Lehrman) (role as Charlie); *Mabel's Strange Predicament (Hotel Mixup)* (Lehrman and Sennett) (role as Charlie); *Between Showers (The Flirts, Charlie and the Umbrella, In Wrong)* (Lehrman) (role as Charlie); *A Film Johnnie (Movie Nut, Million Dollar Job, Charlie at the Studio)* (Sennett) (role as Charlie); *Tango Tangles (Charlie's Recreation, Music Hall)* (Sennett) (role as Charlie); *His Favorite Pastime (The Bonehead, His Reckless Fling)* (Nichols) (role as Charlie); *Cruel, Cruel Love* (Sennett) (role as Charlie); *The Star Boarder (The Hash-House Hero)* (Sennett) (role as Charlie); *Mabel at the Wheel (His Daredevil Queen, Hot Finish)* (Normand and Sennett) (role as Charlie); *Twenty Minutes of Love (He Loved Her So, Cops and Watches)* (Sennett) (role as Charlie, +sc); *The Knock Out (Counted Out, The Pugilist)* (Arbuckle) (role as Charlie); *Tillie's Punctured Romance (Tillie's Nightmare, For the Love of Tillie, Marie's Millions)* (Sennett) (role as Charlie); *His Regeneration* (Anderson) (guest appearance)
1921 *The Nut* (Reed) (guest appearance)
1923 *Souls for Sale* (Hughes) (guest appearance)
1928 *Show People* (King Vidor) (guest appearance)

Publications:

By CHAPLIN: books—

Charlie Chaplin's Own Story, Indianapolis, 1916.
My Trip Abroad, New York, 1922.
My Autobiography, London, 1964.
My Life in Pictures, London, 1974.

By CHAPLIN: articles—

Interview with Margaret Hinxman, in *Sight and Sound* (London), Autumn 1957.
Interview with Richard Merryman, in *Life* (New York), 10 March 1967.
"Charles Chaplin parle," interviews excerpted by C. Gauteur, in *Image et Son* (Paris), November 1972.
"Chaplin est mort, vive Charlot!," interview with Philippe Soupault, text by Chaplin from 1921, and round-table discussion, in *Ecran* (Paris), March 1978.
"The INS interview with Chaplin," edited by Charles J. Maland, in *Cineaste* (New York), vol. 14, no. 4, 1986.

On CHAPLIN: books—

Delluc, Louis, *Charlot*, Paris, 1921.
Tyler, Parker, *Chaplin, Last of the Clowns*, New York, 1947.
Huff, Theodore, *Charlie Chaplin*, New York, 1951.
Bessy, Maurice, and Robert Florey, *Monsieur Chaplin ou le rire dans la nuit*, Paris, 1952.
Payne, Robert, *The Great God Pan: A Biography of the Tramp Played by Charlie Chaplin*, New York, 1952.
Sadoul, Georges, *Vie de Charlot*, Paris, 1952; as *Vie de Charlot: Charles Spencer Chaplin, ses films et son temps*, Paris, 1978.
Mitry, Jean, *Charlot et la "fabulation" chaplinesque*, Paris, 1957.
McDonald, Gerald, and others, *The Films of Charlie Chaplin*, Secaucus, New Jersey, 1965.
Martin, Marcel, *Charlie Chaplin*, Paris, 1966; 3rd edition, Paris, 1983.
Brownlow, Kevin, *The Parade's Gone By*, London, 1968.
McCaffrey, Donald, *Four Great Comedians: Chaplin, Lloyd, Keaton, Langdon*, London, 1968.
Quigly, Isabel, *Charlie Chaplin: Early Comedies*, London, 1968.
Leprohon, Pierre, *Charles Chaplin*, Paris, 1970.
McCaffrey, Donald, editor, *Focus on Chaplin*, Englewood Cliffs, New Jersey, 1971.

Charles Chaplin

Mitry, Jean, *Tout Chaplin: Tous les films, par le texte, par le gag et par l'image*, Paris, 1972.

Mast, Gerald, *The Comic Mind*, New York, 1973.

Manvell, Roger, *Chaplin*, Boston, 1974.

Lyons, T.J., compiler, *Charles Chaplin—a Guide to References and Resources*, Boston, 1977.

Sobel, Raoul, and David Francis, *Chaplin, Genesis of a Clown*, London, 1977.

McCabe, John, *Charlie Chaplin*, New York, 1978.

Nysenholc, Adolphe, *L'Age d'or du comique: sémiologie de Charlot*, Brussels, 1979.

Eisenstein, Sergei, *Film Essays and a Lecture*, edited by Jay Leyda, Princeton, New Jersey, 1982.

Gehring, Wes D., *Charlie Chaplin: A Bio-Bibliography*, Westport, Connecticut, 1983.

Robinson, David, *Chaplin: The Mirror of Opinion*, London, 1983.

Kamin, Dan, *Charlie Chaplin's One-Man Show*, Metuchen, New Jersey, 1984.

Smith, Julian, *Chaplin*, Boston, 1984.

Geduld, Harry M., *Charlie Chaplin's Own Story*, Bloomington, Indiana, 1985.

Robinson, David, *Chaplin: His Life and Art*, London, 1985.

Geduld, Harry M., *Chapliniana 1: The Keystone Films*, Bloomington, Indiana, 1987.

Mitry, Jean, *Tout Chaplin: L'Oeuvre complète presentée par le texte et par l'image*, Paris, 1987.

Saint-Martin, Catherine, *Charlot/Chaplin; ou, La Conscience du mythe*, Paris, 1987.

Epstein, Jerry, *Remembering Charlie: The Story of a Friendship*, London, 1988.

Schickel, Richard, *Schickel on Film: Encounters—critical and personal—with movie immortals*, New York, 1989.

On CHAPLIN: articles—

Churchill, Winston, "Everybody's Language," in *Collier's* (New York), 26 October 1935.

Eisenstein, Sergei, "Charlie the Kid," and "Charlie the Grown Up," in *Sight and Sound* (London), Spring and Summer 1946.

Huff, Theodore, "Chaplin as Composer," in *Films in Review* (New York), September 1950.

Hickey, Terry, "Accusations Against Charles Chaplin for Political and Moral Offenses," in *Film Comment* (New York), Winter 1969.

Lyons, T.J., "Roland H. Totheroh Interviewed: Chaplin Films," in *Film Culture* (New York), Spring 1972.

"Chaplin Issue" of *Film Comment* (New York), September/October 1972.

"Chaplin Issue" of *Positif* (Paris), July/August 1973.

Cott, J., "The Limits of Silent Film Comedy," in *Literature/Film Quarterly* (Salisbury, Maryland), Spring 1975.

Adorno, Theodor, "Quel giorno che Chaplin mi fece l'imitazione," in *Cinema Nuovo* (Bari), July–August 1976.

"Chaplin Issue" of *Film und Fernsehen* (Berlin), March 1978.

Corliss, Richard, "Chaplin," in *Film Comment* (New York), March/April 1978.

"Pour saluter Charlot," in *Avant-Scène du Cinéma* (Paris), 1 May 1978.

"Chaplin Issue" of *University Film Association Journal* (Houston), no.1, 1979.

Sato, Tadao, "The Comedy of Ozu and Chaplin—a Study in Contrast," in *Wide Angle* (Athens, Ohio), no.2, 1979.

"Dossier: Charles Chaplin et l'opinion publique," in *Cinématographe* (Paris), January 1981.

Ingrao, P., "Chaplin: The antagonism of the comic hero," in *Film Quarterly* (Los Angeles), Fall 1981.

Everson, William K., "Rediscovery: 'New' Chaplin Films," in *Films in Review* (New York), November 1981.

Manning, H., and T.J. Lyons, "Charlie Chaplin's early life: Fact and fiction," in *Historical Journal of Film, Radio, and Television* (Abingdon, Oxon), March 1983.

Balio, Tino, "Charles Chaplin, homme d'affaires: Un artiste associé," in *Filméchange* (Paris), Spring 1983.

Millar, Gavin, "The unknown Chaplin," in *Sight and Sound* (London), Spring 1983.

Classic Images (Muscatine, Iowa), nos. 98–106, August 1983–April 1984.

Slide, Anthony, "The American Press and Public v Charles Spencer Chaplin," in *Cineaste* (New York), vol. 13, no. 4, 1984.

Maland, Charles J., "The Millionaire Tramp," in *Post Script* (Jacksonville, Florida), Spring–Summer 1984.

Jaffe, I.S., "Chaplin's labor of Performance: the circus and *Limelight*," and R.L. Liebman, "Rabbis or rakes, schlemiels or supermen? Jewish identity in Charles Chaplin, Jerry Lewis and Woody Allen," in *Literature/Film Quarterly* (Salisbury, Maryland), July 1984.

"Chaplin Section" of *American Film* (Washington, D.C.), September 1984.

Naremore, J., "Film and the Performance Frame," in *Film Quarterly* (Los Angeles), Winter 1984–85.

Maland, Charles J., "A Documentary Note on Charlie Chaplin's Politics," in *Historical Journal of Film, Radio, and Television* (Abingdon, Oxon), vol. 5, no.2, 1985.

Heurtebise, "On first looking into Chaplin's humor," in *Sight and Sound* (London), Spring 1985.

Davis, D. William, "A Tale of Two Movies: Charlie Chaplin, United Artists, and the Red Scare," in *Cinema Journal* (Champaigne, Illinois), Fall 1987.

Florey, Robert, with Brian Naves, "Charlie Dearest," in *Film Comment* (New York), March–April 1988.

On CHAPLIN: films—

Carlson, Wallace, *Introducing Charlie Chaplin*, 1915.

Abramson, Hans, "Upptäckten (Discovery)" episode of *Stimulantia*, Sweden, 1967.

Becker, Vernon, *The Funniest Man in the World*, 1967.

Hurwitz, Harry, *Chaplinesque, My Life and Hard Times* (*The Eternal Tramp*), for TV, 1967.

*   *   *

Charles Chaplin was the first and the greatest international star of the American silent comic cinema. He was also the twentieth century's first media "superstar," the first artistic creator and popularized creature of our global culture, whose face, onscreen antics, and offscreen scandals were disseminated around the globe by new media which knew no geographical or linguistic boundaries. But more than this, Chaplin was the first acknowledged artistic genius of the cinema, recognized as such by a young generation of writers and artists whose number included George Bernard Shaw, H.G. Wells, Bertolt Brecht, Pablo Picasso, James Joyce, Samuel Beckett, and the surrealist painters and poets of both Paris and Berlin. Chaplin may be the one cinema artist who might truly be called a seminal figure of the century—if only because of his influence on virtually every other recognized seminal figure of the century.

Born in London into a theatrical family, his mother and father alternated between periods of separation and union, activities onstage and difficulties offstage (his father's alcoholism, his mother's insanity). The young Chaplin spent his life on the London streets and in a London workhouse, until he started earning his living on the stage at the age of eight. Like Buster Keaton and Stan Laurel, Chaplin's career indicates that physical comedians develop their bodies as children (like concert pianists and ballet dancers) or never really develop them at all. By the time he was 20 Chaplin had become the star attraction of the Fred Karno Pantomime Troupe, an internationally acclaimed English music-hall act, and it was on his second tour of America that a representative of the Keystone comedy film company (either Mack Sennett himself, Mabel Normand, the Sennett comedienne, or Charles Bauman, co-owner of the company) saw Chaplin and, in 1913, offered him a job at Keystone. Chaplin went to work at the Keystone lot in Burbank, California, in January of 1914.

To some extent, the story of Chaplin's popular success and artistic evolution can be told with a series of numbers. In 1914 at Keystone, Chaplin appeared in 35 one- and two-reel films (with the exception of the six-reeler, *Tillie's Punctured Romance*), about half of which he directed himself, for the yearly salary of $7,800. In 1915, Chaplin made 14 one- and two-reel films for the Essanay Film Company—all of which he wrote and directed himself—for a salary of $67,000. In 1916–17, Chaplin wrote, directed and starred in 12 two-reel films for the Mutual Film company, and then signed a contract with First National Corporation for an even million dollars—to write, direct, produce, and star in 12 more two-reel films. The contract allowed him to build his own studio, which he alone used until 1952 (it is now the studio for A&M Records), but his developing artistic consciousness kept him from completing the contract until 1923 with nine films of lengths ranging from two to six reels. Finally, in 1919, Chaplin became one of the founders of his own film company, United Artists (along with Mary Pickford, Douglas Fairbanks, and D.W. Griffith), through which Chaplin released eight feature films, made between 1923 and 1952, after which he sold his interest in the company.

In his early one- and two-reel films Chaplin evolved the comic tools and means that would lead to his future success. His character of the Tramp, the "little fellow," with derby, cane, floppy shoes, baggy pants, and tight jacket debuted in his second Keystone film, *Kid Auto Races at Venice*. Because the tramp was a little guy, he made an easy target for the obviously larger and tougher, but his quick thinking, agile body, and surprising ingenuity in converting ordinary objects into extraordinary physical allies, helped him more than hold his own in a big, mean world. Although he was capable of lechery (*The Masquerader, Dough and Dynamite*) he could also selflessly aid the innocent woman under attack (*The New Janitor, The Tramp, The Bank*). Although he deserved her affection as a reward, he was frequently rejected for his social or sexual inadequacies (*The Tramp, The Bank, The Vagabond, The Adventurer*). Many of his early films combined his dexterous games with physical objects with deliberate attempts at emotional pathos (*The Tramp, The Vagabond, The Pawnshop*) or with social commentary on the corruption of the police, the brutality of the slums, or the selfishness of the rich (*Police, Easy Street, The Adventurer*). Before Chaplin, no one had demonstrated that physical comedy could be simultaneously hilariously funny, emotionally passionate, and pointedly intellectual. While his cinema technique tended to be invisible—emphasizing the actor and his actions—he gradually evolved a principle of cinema based on framing: finding the exact way to frame a shot to reveal its motion and meaning completely without the necessity of making a disturbing cut.

Chaplin's later films evolved more complicated or ironic situations in which to explore the Tramp's character and the moral paradoxes of his existence. His friend and ally is a mongrel dog in *A Dog's Life*; he becomes a doughboy in *Shoulder*

Arms; acquires a child in *The Kid*; becomes a preacher in *The Pilgrim*; and explores the decadent Parisian high life in *A Woman of Paris*, a comedy-melodrama of subtle visual techniques in which the Tramp does not appear. Chaplin's four feature films between 1925 and 1936 might be called his "marriage group," in which he explores the circumstances by which the tramp might acquire a sexual-romantic mate. In *The Gold Rush* the Tramp succeeds in winning the dance-hall gal who previously rejected him, because she now appreciates his kindness and he is loaded with new-found wealth. The happy ending is as improbable as the Tramp's sudden riches—perhaps a comment that kindness helps but money gets the girl. But in *The Circus* Charlie turns his beloved over to the romantic high-wire daredevil, Rex, since the girl rejects him not because of Charlie's kindness or poverty but because he cannot fulfill the woman's image of male sexual attractiveness. *City Lights* builds upon this problem as it rises to a final question it leaves deliberately and poignantly unanswered: can the blind flower seller, whose vision has been restored by Charlie's kindness, love him for his kindness alone since her vision now reveals him to look so painfully different from the rich and handsome man she imagined and expected? And in *Modern Times* Charlie successfully finds a mate, a social outcast and child of nature like himself; unfortunately, their marriage can find no sanctification or existence within contemporary industrial society. So the two of them take to the road together, walking away from society toward who knows where—the Tramp's final departure from the Chaplin world.

Although both *City Lights* and *Modern Times* used orchestral music and cleverly comic sound effects (especially *Modern Times*), Chaplin's final three American films were talking films—*The Great Dictator*, in which Chaplin burlesques Hitler and Nazism, *Monsieur Verdoux*, in which Chaplin portrays a dapper mass murderer, and *Limelight*, Chaplin's nostalgic farewell to the silent art of pantomime which nurtured him. In this film, in which Buster Keaton also plays a major role, Chaplin bids farewell not only to a dead movie tradition—silent comedy—but to a 200 year tradition of physical comedy on both stage and screen, the tradition out of which both Keaton and Chaplin came, which would produce no clowns of the future.

Chaplin's later years were scarred by personal and political difficulties produced by his many marriages and divorces, his supposed sexual philanderings, his difficulties with the Internal Revenue Service, his outspoken defence of liberal political causes, and his refusal to become an American citizen. Although never called to testify before the House Un-American Activities Committee, Chaplin's films were picketed and boycotted by right-wing activist groups. When Chaplin left for a trip abroad in 1952, the State Department summarily revoked his automatic re-entry permit. Chaplin sent his young wife, Oona O'Neill, daughter of the playwright, Eugene O'Neill, back to America to settle their business affairs. He established his family in Switzerland and conveyed his outrage against his former country by not returning to America for 20 years, by refusing to let any of his films circulate in America for two decades, and by making in 1957 a very uneven, often embarrassing satire of American democracy, *A King in New York*. This film, like *A Countess from Hong Kong*, made ten years later, was a commercial and artistic disappointment, perhaps partially because Chaplin was cut off from the familiar studio, the experienced production team, and the painstakingly slow production methods he had been using for over three decades.

—Gerald Mast

CHEN KAIGE.

Chinese. Born in Beijing, 12 August 1952, son of film director Chen Huai'ai. Sent to work in Rubber plantation in Yunnan province to "Learn from the people," as part of Cultural Revolution, 1967. Served in Army. Worked in film processing lab, Beijing, 1975–78, then studied at Beijing Film Academy, 1978–82; assigned to Beijing Film Studio, assistant to Huang Jianzhong; transferred (with Zhang Yimou and He Qun) to Guangxi Film Studios, and directed first feature, *Huang Tudi*, 1984.

Films as Director:

1984   *Huang Tudi' (Yellow Earth)*; *Qiangxing Qifei (Forced Take-Off)* (for TV)
1985   *Da Yuebing (The Big Parade)* (released in 1987)
1987   *Haizi Wang (King of the Children)*

Publications:

By CHEN: articles—

Interview with Tony Rayns, in *Time Out* (London), 6 August 1986.
Interview in *Film Comment* (New York), July/August 1988.
Interview in *Films and Filming* (London), August 1988.
Interview with Don Ranvaud in the *Guardian* (London), 11 August 1988.
Interview in *Time Out* (London), 17 August 1988.
Interview with Jonathan Mirsky, in *New Statesman and Society* (London), 19 August 1988.
Interview in *Monthly Film Bulletin* (London), September 1988.

On CHEN: books—

Berry, Chris, editor, *Perspectives on Chinese Cinema*, New York, 1985.
Quiquemelle, Marie-Claire, and Jean-Loup Passek, *Le Cinema chinois*, Paris, 1985.
Armes, Roy, *Third World Filmmaking and the West*, Berkeley, 1987.
Clark, Paul, *Chinese Cinema: Culture and Politics Since 1949*, Cambridge, 1987.
Semsel, George Stephen, editor, *Chinese Film: The State of the Art in the Chinese Republic*, New York, 1987.
Berry, Chris, editor, *Perspectives on Chinese Cinema*, London, 1991.

*   *   *

Chen Kaige is the leading voice among the "fifth generation" of Chinese film makers, the first group of students to have graduated following the re-opening of the Beijing Film Academy in 1978, after the depredations of the Cultural Revolution. As both participant in (he was a Red Guard) and a victim of the Cultural Revolution (his secondary education was curtailed and, like the protagonist of *King of the Children* he was sent to the country to "learn from the peasants") Chen is particularly well-placed to voice the concerns of his generation and at the same time to begin to map a new path for Chinese cinema.

His three films so far constitute an intelligent and powerfully felt meditation on recent Chinese history. Chen in interview has stressed their complementary nature, although stylistically they appear very different. *Yellow Earth* examines the relationship of "man and the land," *The Big Parade* looks at "the individual and the group," and *King of the Children* considers "man and culture." *Yellow Earth* seems to adopt the structure of the folk ballads that provide a focus for its narrative, with its long held shots and almost lapidary editing. *The Big Parade* alternates static parade ground shots with the chaos of barrack room life while the third film mobilises a more rhetorical style of poetic realism. Together the films act as a triple rebuttal of any heroic reading of Maoism and the revolution, precisely by taking up subjects much used in propagandist art—the arrival of the People's Liberation Army in a village, the training of new recruits, the fate of the teacher sent to the country—and by refuting their simplifications and obfuscations, shot for shot, with quite trenchant deliberation. Attention in *Yellow Earth* is focused not on the Communist Army whose soldier arrives at the village collecting songs, but on the barren plateau from which the peasantry attempts to wring a meagre existence. In the process the account of Yenan which sees it as the birthplace of Communism is marginalised. *King of the Children* banishes the bright-eyed pupils and spotless classrooms of propaganda in favour of a run-down school-room graffitti-ed and in disrepair, from which the social fabric seems to have fallen away. Likewise *The Big Parade* banishes heroics and exemplary characters in favour of a clear-eyed look at the cost of moulding the individual into the collective.

In Chen's films what is unsaid is as important as that which is said; indeed the act of silence becomes a potent force. The voiceless appear everywhere, the almost mute brother in *Yellow Earth*, the girl's unspoken fears for her marriage ("voiced" in song), the mute cowherd in *King of the Children*. In *Yellow Earth* the girl's voice is silenced by the force of nature as she drowns singing an anthem about the Communist Party. It is almost better, Chen implies, not to speak at all than, as he suggests in *King of the Children*, to copy, to repeat to "shout to make it right." In that film he encourages his star pupil to speak not for his father, but for himself. Likewise what is not shown is also important. The famous original last shot of *The Big Parade* (the film was altered at the PLA's behest) ran the sounds of the eponymous "big parade" in Tianenmen Square over a shot of an empty square. In *King of the Children* he avoids naturalism by a poetic use of shots of the landscape, either richly varied or subject to the seemingly pointless desecration.

Of the three films it is *Yellow Earth* that seems the most fully achieved and, ironically, considering that it became the key film in an anti-elitism in cinema policy when it was criticised for its "incomprehensibility," the most Chinese.

—Verina Glaessner

CHRISTENSEN, Benjamin.

Danish. Born in Viborg, Denmark, 28 September 1879. Educated in medicine; entered dramatic school of the Royal Theatre, Copenhagen, 1901. Married 1) Ellen Arctander, 1904; 2) Sigrid Stahl, 1922; 3) Kamma Winther, 1927. Actor in Aarhus Theatre (Jutland), then Folketeatret, Copenhagen, to 1907; left stage, became agent for French champagne firm Lanson, 1907; began as film actor, 1912; directed first film, 1913; went to Germany, worked for Erich Pommer, 1923; worked in U.S., 1926–34. *Died 2 April 1959.*

Films as Director:

1913 *Det hemmelighedsfulde X (The Mysterious X)* (+role)
1915 *Haevnens Nat (Blind Justice)* (+role)
1922 **Häxan (Witchcraft Through the Ages)** (+sc, role as Devil and doctor)
1923 *Seine Frau, die Unbekannte (His Mysterious Adventure)*
1924 *Die Frau mit dem schlechten Ruf (The Woman Who Did)* (not completed)

1926 *The Devil's Circus*
1927 *Mockery*
1928 *Hawk's Nest; The Haunted House; House of Horror*
1929 *Seven Footprints to Satan*
1939 *Skilsmissens Børn*
1940 *Barnet*
1941 *Gaa med mig hjem*
1942 *Damen med de lyse handsker*

Other Films:

1912 *Skaebnebaeltet* (role)
1913 *Gidslet* (role); *Scenens Børn* (role); *Store Klaus og Lille Klaus* (role); *Rumaensk Blod or Søstrene Corrodi* (role); *Vingeskudt* (role)
1924 *Michael* (role)

Publications:

By CHRISTENSEN: book—

Hollywood Skaebner (short stories), 1945.

On CHRISTENSEN: book—

Ernst, John, *Benjamin Christensen*, Copenhagen, 1967.

On CHRISTENSEN: articles—

Gillett, John, "The Mysterious X," in *Sight and Sound* (London), Spring 1966.
Higham, Charles, "Christensen Continued," in *Sight and Sound* (London), Autumn 1966.
Tessier, Max, "La Sorcellerie à travers les âges," in *Cinéma* (Paris), no.130, 1968.
Routt, W.D., "Buried Directors," in *Focus on Film* (London), Spring 1972.

*   *   *

Benjamin Christensen's first film was one of the most amazing directorial debuts in the history of the film. *Det hemmelighedsfulde X* is a spy melodrama about a lieutenant accused of betraying his country who is saved at the last minute. If the story is conventional, the handling of it shows a natural instinct for film that is way ahead of its time. It is completely free from literary clichés in its narrative style, being told in often very imaginatively composed pictures, and Christensen demonstrates an ability to transform the psychology of his characters into physical action. The camerawork (by Emil Dinesen) is full of significant contrasts, the cutting is dynamic and gives the film a marvelous drive. The film was received with admiration; everybody was stunned by its remarkable visual style, and Christensen was immediately recognized as the individualist and the experimenter of the Danish film of his day. His next film, *Haevnens Nat*, was a social melodrama, burdened by a pathetic story, but also distinguished by an inventive camera style. Christensen played lead roles in both these films.

Benjamin Christensen provoked his contemporaries and set himself in opposition to the filmmaking practices of his time. He had a strong belief in himself and worked consciously with film as a new art form. He considered the director as the author of the film and stated that "like any other artist he should reveal his own individuality in his own work." Thus Christensen can be regarded as one of the first auteurs of the cinema. Carl Th. Dreyer has characterized Christensen as "a man who knew exactly what he wanted and who pursued his goal with uncompromising stubbornness."

Christensen's main work is *Häxan*, an ambitious and unique film and a pioneer achievement in both the documentary and the fiction film. In this film Christensen combined his rationalistic ideas with his passionate temperament.

Christensen was always an isolated director in the Danish

Benjamin Christensen

film, and after *Häxan* he left Denmark. He made an insignificant film in Germany and was seen in Dreyer's *Michael* as the master. He got an offer from Hollywood and made six films there. He used his talent for the strange and the peculiar in *Seven Foot-prints to Satan*, a witty horror comedy.

Christensen returned to Denmark in the thirties and in 1939 he was hired by Nordisk Films Kompagni. Again Christensen showed himself a controversial filmmaker. He wanted to break the trivial pattern of Danish cinema at that time, and he made three films which dealt with topical problems, arising from conflicts between generations. One is about children from divorce-ridden homes, another about abortion. Christensen's last film was a spy thriller in international settings. It was a total failure, and Christensen left film production. For the rest of his life he lived in splendid isolation as manager of a small and insignificant cinema in the suburbs of Copenhagen.

—Ib Monty

CHRISTIAN-JAQUE.

French. Born Christian Maudet in Paris, 4 September 1904.

Educated at Ecole des beaux-arts, and Ecole des arts décoratifs, Paris. Married five times, including actresses Simone Renant, 1938; Renée Faure, 1945; Martine Carol, 1952. Film poster designer, 1926; film critic for *Cinegraf*, and art director and assistant director to Duvivier, Roussel, and Hugon, 1927–30; directed first film, *Bidon d'or*, 1931. Recipient: Best Director, Cannes Festival, for *Fanfan la Tulipe*, 1952.

Films as Director:

1931 *Bidon d'or*
1932 *Le Tendron d'Achile*; *Adhémar Lampiot*
1933 *Ça colle*; *Le Boeuf sur la langue*; *La Montre*
1934 *Atroce menace*; *Vilaine histoire*; *Le Père Lampion*; *Compartiment pour dames seules*
1935 *La Sonnette d'alarme*; *Voyage d'agrément*; *La Famille Pont-Biquet*; *Sacré Léonce*; *Sous la griffe*
1936 *On ne roule pas Antoinette*; *L'École des journalistes*; *Un de la Légion*; *Rigolboche*; *Monsieur Personne*; *Josette*; *La Maison d'en face*
1937 *Les Dégourdis de la onzième*; *Les Perles de la couronne* (*The Pearls of the Crown*) (co-d); *A Venise, une nuit*; *Les Pirates du rail*; *François Ier* (*Francis the First*)
1938 *Les Disparus de St. Agil* (*Boys School*); *Ernest le Rebelle* (*C'était moi*); *Raphaël le Tatoué*
1939 *Le Grand Élan*; *L'Enfer des anges*; *Tourelle III* (unfinished)
1941 *L'Assassinat du Père Noël* (*Who Killed Santa Claus?*); *Premier Bal*; *La Symphonie fantastique*

Christian-Jaque

1943   *Carmen*; *Voyage sans espoir*
1944   *Sortilèges (The Bellman)* (+co-sc)
1945   *Boule de Suif (Angel and Sinner)* (+co-sc)
1946   *Un Revenant (A Lover's Return)* (+co-sc)
1947   *La Chartreuse de Parma (La certosa di Parma)* (+co-sc)
1948   *D'homme à hommes (Man to Men)* (+co-sc)
1949   *Singoalla (The Wind Is My Lover, The Mask and the Sword)* (+co-sc); *Barrières* (+co-sc) (short)
1950   *Souvenirs perdus* (+co-sc)
1951   *Barbe-Bleue (Blaubart, Bluebeard)* (+adapt); *Fanfan la Tulipe (Fanfan the Tulip)* (+co-sc)
1952   *Adorables Créatures (Adorable Creatures)* (+co-sc); *Lucrèce Borgia (Lucrezia Borgia, Sins of the Borgias)* (+co-sc); "Lysistrata" episode of *Destinées (Daughters of Destiny)* (+co-sc)
1954   *Madame Du Barry* (+co-sc); *Nana* (+co-sc)
1955   *Si tous les gars du monde (If All the Guys in the World)* (+co-sc)
1957   *Nathalie (The Foxiest Girl in Paris)* (+pr, co-sc)
1958   *La Loi . . . c'est la loi (The Law Is the Law)* (+co-sc)
1959   *Babette s'en va-t-en guerre (Babette Goes to War)*
1960   "Divorce" episode of *La Française et l'amour (Love and the Frenchwoman)* (+co-sc)
1961   *Madame Sans-Gêne (Madame)* (+co-sc)
1962   *Marco Polo (L'Échiquier de Dieu)* (+co-sc) (unfinished)
1963   *Les Bonnes Causes (Don't Tempt the Devil)* (+co-sc); *La Tulipe noire (The Black Tulip)* (+co-sc)
1964   *Le Gentleman de Cocody (Man from Cocody)* (+co-sc); *Le Repas des fauves* (+co-sc)
1965   *La Guerre secrète (The Dirty Game, La guerra segreta, Spione unter sich)* (co-d, co-sc)
1966   *La Seconde Vérité* (+co-sc); *Le Saint prend l'affût* (+co-sc)
1967   *Leux Billets pour Mexico (Dead Run)* (+co-sc)
1968   *Lady Hamilton (Les Amours de Lady Hamilton, Emma Hamilton, The Making of a Lady)* (+co-sc)
1970   *Don Camillo et les contestataires* (+co-sc) (unfinished due to Fernandel's death)
1971   *Les Pétroleuses (The Legend of Frenchy King)*
1975   *Dr. Justice*

Other Films:

1927   *Une Java* (Roussel) (art d)
1928   *La Marche nuptiale* (Hugon) (art d); *La Vie miraculeuse de Thérèse Martin* (Duvivier) (art d)
1929   *Au Bonheur des Dames* (Duvivier) (co-art d); *Maman Colibri* (Duvivier) (art d); *La Grande Passion* (Hugon) (art d); *Les Trois Masques* (Hugon) (art d)
1930   *La Femme et le rossignol* (Hugon) (art d); *Lévy et Cie* (Hugon) (art d)
1931   *La Tendresse* (Hugon) (art d); *Le Marchande de sable* (Hugon) (art d); *La Croix du Sud* (Hugon) (art d); *Les Galeries Lévy et Cie* (Hugon) (art d)
1952   *Koenigsmark* (Térac) (supervisor)

Publications:

By CHRISTIAN-JAQUE: articles—

"Making It International," in *Films and Filming* (London), October 1960.
Interview with G. Cebe, J. Fieschi, and J.-C. Sabria, in *Cinématographe* (Paris), January 1982.

On CHRISTIAN-JAQUE: articles—

Biofilmography, in *Film Dope* (London), April 1975.
Christian-Jaque Issue of *Avant-Scène du Cinéma* (Paris), April 1988.

On CHRISTIAN-JAQUE: film—

Viallet, Pierre, and Marcel L'Herbier, *Portraits filmées . . . Christian-Jaque*, France, 1954.

*   *   *

Of all France's important filmmakers, Christian-Jaque has unquestionably been the most prolific. Director of more than 50 films in virtually all genres, his facility has been a mark against him in the eyes of most critics. Nevertheless, no one denies the lusty dynamism of his action scenes nor the technical ingenuity he loves to display in even his most run-of-the-mill efforts. For a time between 1937 and 1950 he had to be reckoned as one of the leading men in French cinema, not only as regards box-office where he has always had success, but in terms of the possibilities of the art of the cinema.

Born Christian Maudet, he took on the name with which he and a collaborator signed the film ads they designed in the 1920's, "Christian-Jaque." When the coming of sound made Paris the center of European film production, his peripheral relation to the movies and his training as an architect helped him secure a job with Paramount in Joinville. Always eager to please, and a favorite director for actors to work with, he found his first efforts well received. The steady production of cheap vehicles for Fernandel wore down his spirits but did give him immense technical training and the film industry's confidence.

At last he made use of that confidence, selling an idea for a film about a boy's school to an independent producer. *Les Disparus de St. Agil* was an enormous success. Its delicate romanticism, stemming largely from Pierre Very's novel as put into dialogue by Jacques Prévert, was set off against the truly disturbing role played by Erich von Stroheim. This film put Christian-Jaque in a position of power during the Occupation and no one made more films than he in this era.

He specialized in two genres, both very popular during the war, the romantic mystery tale and the transcription on film of past cultural monuments. Representative of the former are *Sortilèges* and *L'Assassinat du Père Noël*. Both films are rich in evocative images such as a wild horse galloping through town at midnight, its mane blowing behind it. Both feature clever intrigues about mysterious personalities and occurrences. Both are delightfully satisfying, if overly cute. The other genre contains films of music and musicians on the one side and literary adaptations on the other. His life of Berlioz, *La Symphonie fantastique*, goes beyond all limits in insisting on the grandeur of musical genius. Jean-Louis Barrault throws himself at women, converses in cafes with Balzac and Delacroix, and pounds out the composition after which the film is titled in a fever compounded by wild lighting and compositions. The later *Carmen* is equally unrestrained, as though the fame of the original gave license to the filmmaker to go beyond all realistic bounds. As for literary adaptations, his *Boule de suif* from Maupassant and *La Chartreuse de Parme* from Stendhal are vehicles for France's most ostentatious actors to dress up as their favorite characters. The latter film has genuine moments of visual excitement and some of the brash tone of the original, but both films remain at best on the surface.

Concerned with decoration, Christian-Jaque is finally a frothy director. When dealing with a star (and he married three of his leading ladies, Martine Carol being the most famous) or with a light action picture such as *Fanfan la Tulipe* he is delightful, but aside from the short period surrounding World War II, little of his work merits a second look. That period, though, culminating with *Un Revenant* captures the dreamy romanticism to which much of the culture escaped in its most difficult moment.

—Dudley Andrew

Vera Chytilova: *Sedmikrásky*

CHYTILOVÁ, Věra.

Czech. Born in Ostrava, 2 February 1929. Studied architecture at Charles University; Film Academy (FAMU), Prague, 1957–62. Married cinematographer Jaroslav Kucera. Assistant director on *3 Men Missing* (Ztracenci), 1956; directed first film, *Strop*, 1962; forbidden to direct or work for foreign producers, 1969–76. Address: c/o Barrandov Studios, Prague, Czechoslovakia.

Films as Director:

1962   *Strop* (*The Ceiling*) (+sc); *Pytel blech* (*A Bag of Fleas*) (+sc)
1963   *O něčem jiném* (*Something Different, Something Else, Another Way of Life*) (+sc)
1965   "Automat Svět" ("The World Cafe") segment of *Perličky na dně* (*Pearls of the Deep*) (+co-sc)
1966   *Sedmikrásky* (*Daisies*) (+co-sc)
1969   *Ovoce stromů rajských jíme* (*The Fruit of Paradise, The Fruit of the Trees of Paradise*) (+co-sc)
1977   (*The Apple Game*) (+sc)
1979   *Panelstory* (*Prefab Story*) (+co-sc)
1980   *Kalamita* (*Calamity*) (+co-sc)
1983   *Faunovo prilis pozdni odpoledne* (*The Very Late Afternoon of a Faun*)

1985   *Praha, neklidne srace Europy* (*Prague, the Restless Heart of Europe*) (short)
1986   *Vlci bouda* (*Wolf's hole*)
1987   *Sasek a kralovna* (*The Jester and the Queen*)

Other Films:

1958   *Konec jasnovidce* (*End of a Clairvoyant*) (role as girl in bikini)

Publications:

By CHYTILOVÁ: articles—

"Neznám opravdový čin, který by nebyl riskantní," [I Don't Know Any Action that Would Not Be Risky], interview with Galina Kopaněvová, in *Film a doba* (Prague), no.1, 1963.
"Režijní explikace k filmu *O něčem jiném*," [The Director's Comments on *Something Different*], in *Film a Doba* (Prague), no.1, 1964.
"*Sedmikrásky*: režijní explikace," [*Daisies*: the Directress Comments], in *Film a Doba* (Prague), no.4, 1966.
Interview in *New York Times*, 12 March 1978.
"A Film Should Be a Little Flashlight," interview with H. Polt, in *Take One* (Montreal), November 1978.
Interview with H. Heberle and others, in *Frauen & Film* (Berlin), December 1978.
Interview with B. Eriksson-Vodakova, in *Chaplin* (Stockholm), vol. 27, no. 6, 1985.

On CHYTILOVÁ: books—

Boček, Jaroslav, *Modern Czechoslovak Film 1945–1965*, Prague, 1965.
Janoušek, Jiri, *3 Í*, Prague, 1965.
Skvorecký, Josef, *All the Bright Young Men and Women*, Toronto, 1971.
Dewey, Langdon, *Outline of Czechoslovakian Cinema*, London, 1971.
Liehm, Antonin, *Closely Watched Films*, White Plains, New York, 1974.
Liehm, Mira and Antonin, *The Most Important Art: East European Film After 1945*, Berkeley, 1977.
Habova, Milada, and Jitka Vysekalova, editors, *Czechoslovak Cinema*, Prague, 1982.
Hames, Peter, *The Czechoslovak New Wave*, Berkeley, 1985.

On CHYTILOVÁ: articles—

Boček, Jaroslav, "Podobenství Věry Chytilové," [The Parable of Věra Chytilová], in *Film a Doba* (Prague), no.11, 1966.
Hames, P., "The Return of Vera Chytilova," in *Sight and Sound* (London), no.3, 1979.
Martinek, Karel, "Filmový svět Véry Chytilové," [The Film World of Věra Chytilová], in *Film a Doba* (Prague), no.3, 1982.
Zůna, Miroslav, and Vladimir Solecký, in *Film a Doba* (Prague), no.5, 1982.
Benoit, O., "Dans la grisaille tcheque: Vera Chytilova," in *Cinéma* (Paris), May 1984.
Waller, E., in *Skrien* (Amsterdam), September–October 1984.
Manceau, Jean-Louis, "Vera Chytilova a Creteil," in *Cinéma* (Paris), 18 March 1987.

*   *   *

So far the only important woman director of the Czech cinema is Věra Chytilová, its most innovative and probably most controversial personality. She is the only contemporary Czech filmmaker to work in the Eisensteinian tradition. She combines didacticism with often daring experimentation, based in essence on montage. Disregarding chronology and illustrative realism, she stresses the symbolic nature of images as well as visual and conceptual shock. Influenced to some extent also by cinema verité, particularly by its female representatives, and militantly feminist in her attitudes, she nevertheless made excellent use of the art of her husband, the cameraman Jaroslav Kučera in her boldest venture to date, *Daisies*. This film, Chytilová's best known, is a dazzling display of montage, tinting, visual deformation, film trickery, color processing etc.; a multifaceted tour de force which, among other things, is also a tribute to the classics of the cinema, from the Lumière Brothers to Chaplin and Abel Gance. It contains shots, scenes and sequences that utilize the most characteristic techniques and motives of the masters. *Daisies* is Chytilová at her most formalist. In her later films, there is a noticeable shift towards realism. However, all the principles mentioned above still dominate the more narrative approach, and a combination of unusual camera angles, shots, etc., together with a bitterly sarcastic vision, lead to hardly less provocative shock effects.

The didactical content of these highly sophisticated and subtly formalist works of filmic art, as in Eisenstein, is naive and crude: young women should prefer "useful" vocations to "useless" ones (*The Ceiling*); extremes of being active and being inactive both result in frustration (*Something Different*); irresponsibility and recklessness lead to a bad end (*Daisies*); a sexual relationship is something serious, not just irresponsible amusement (*The Apple Game*); people should help each other (*Panel Story, The Calamity*). Given the fact that Chytilová has worked mostly under the conditions of an enforced and harshly repressive establishment, a natural explanation of this seeming incongruity offers itself: the "moral messages" of her films are simply libations that enable her, and her friends among the critics, to defend the unashamedly formalist films and the harshly satirical presentation of social reality they contain. This is corroborated by Chytilová's many clashes with the political authorities in Czechoslovakia: from an interpellation in the Parliament calling for a ban of *Daisies* because so much food—"the fruit of the work of our toiling farmers"—is destroyed in the film, to her being fired from the Barrandov studios after the Soviet invasion in 1968, to her open letter to President Husák printed in Western newspapers. In each instance she won her case by a combination of publicly stated kosher ideological arguments, stressing the alleged "messages" of her works, and of backstage manipulation, not excluding the use of her considerable feminine charm. Consequently, she is the only one from among the new wave of directors from the 1960's who, for a long time, had been able to continue making films in Czechoslovakia without compromising her aesthetic creed and her vision of society, as so many others had to do in order to remain in business (e.g. Jaromil Jireš, Hynek Bočan, Jaroslav Papoušek, and to some extent Jiří Menzel).

Panel Story and *Calamity*, earned her hateful attacks from establishment critics, and intrigues by her second-rate colleagues who are thriving on the absence of competition from such exiled or banned directors as Miloš Forman, Ivan Passer, Jan Němec, Evald Schorm, and Vojtěch Jasný. The two films were practically withdrawn from circulation and can be occasionally seen only in suburban theatres. The only critical film periodical *Film a doba* published, in 1982, a series of three articles which, in veiled terms and using what playwright Václav Havel calls "dialectical metaphysics" ("on the one hand it is bad, but on the other hand it is also good"), defended the director and her right to remain herself. In her integrity, artistic boldness and originality, and in her ability to survive the most destructive social and political catastrophes, Chytilová was a unique phenomenon in post-invasion Czech cinema. Unfortunately, during the last years of Communist rule in Czechoslovakia, she seems to have lost something of her touch, and her latest films—such as *The Very Late Afternoon of a Faun* or *The Jester and the Queen*—are clearly not on the level of *Daisies* or *Panel Story*.

—Josef Skvorecký

———

CIMINO, Michael.

American. Born in New York, 1940. Educated at Yale University, M.F.A., painting, 1963. Moved to New York, 1963; studied acting and ballet, directed documentaries, industrial films, and TV commercials, 1963–71; moved to Hollywood, worked as scriptwriter, 1971; directed first film, *Thunderbolt and Lightfoot*, 1974. Recipient: Oscar for Best Director, and Best Director Award, Directors Guild, for *The Deer Hunter*, 1979.

Films as Director:

1974   *Thunderbolt and Lightfoot* (+sc)
1978   **The Deer Hunter** (+co-sc, co-pr)
1980   **Heaven's Gate** (+sc)
1985   *Year of the Dragon* (co-sc)
1987   *The Sicilian*
1988   *Santa Anna Winds*

Other Films:

1972 *Silent Running* (Trumbull) (co-sc)
1973 *Magnum Force* (Post) (co-sc)

Publications:

By CIMINO: articles—

"Stalking the Deer Hunter: An interview with Michael Cimino," with M. Carducci, in *Millimeter* (New York), March 1978.
Interview with Herb Lightman, in *American Cinematographer* (Los Angeles), November 1980.
Interview with B. Krohn, in *Cahiers du Cinéma* (Paris), June 1982.
Interview with Jean Narboni, and others, in *Cahiers du Cinéma* (Paris), November 1985.
"*L'année du dragon*: un film ambigu," an interview with G. Camy and C. Vivian, in *Jeune Cinéma* (Paris), December 1985–January 1986.

On CIMINO: books—

Bach, Steven, *The Final Cut: Dream and Disaster in the making of "Heaven's Gate"*, New York, 1985.
Bliss, Michael, *Martin Scorsese and Michael Cimino*, Metuchen, New Jersey, 1985.
Wood, Robin, *Hollywood from Vietnam to Reagan*, New York, 1986.
Adair, Gilbert, *Hollywood's Vietnam*, London, 1989.

On CIMINO: articles—

Valley, J., "Michael Cimino's Battle to Make a Great Movie," in *Esquire* (New York), 2 January 1979.
Harmetz, A., "Oscar-winning *Deer Hunter* is Under attack as Racist film," in *New York Times*, 26 April 1979.
"*Heaven's Gate* Issue" of *American Cinematographer* (Los Angeles), November 1980.
"*Deer Hunter* Section" of *Literature/Film Quarterly* (Salisbury, Maryland), January 1983.
Greene, N., "Coppola, Cimino: The operatics of history," in *Film Quarterly* (Los Angeles), Winter 1984–85.
Films and Filming (London), February 1988.

*   *   *

Erratic as his achievement has been, Michael Cimino is, with Martin Scorsese, one of the two most important filmmakers to have emerged in the Hollywood cinema of the 1970's. His reputation must rest, so far, essentially on two enormously ambitious and controversial films, *The Deer Hunter* and *Heaven's Gate*, and his stature will only receive due recognition when the latter is re-released (in its "original" 3½-hour version) and revalued. One can confidently prophesy that it will come as a major revelation.

In one respect, Scorsese and Cimino appear opposites of each other. Scorsese (prior, at least, to *The Last Temptation of Christ*) characteristically starts from a small, precise, concrete subject and radically explores it until it reveals strains, tensions, and contradictions central to our culture; Cimino begins with a vague and grandiose 'vision' and proceeds to map in its salient features and attempt to render it concrete by developing its detail. That Scorsese's method is by far the more conducive to assured artistic success is obvious, and Cimino has yet to produce work as secure in its aim and tone as *Raging Bull* or *King of Comedy*.

We may start with *Heaven's Gate* and its critical reception: the peak of Cimino's achievement to date (it remains, for me, the greatest Hollywood film of the past fifteen years), it was almost universally savaged by the American press. The pervasive complaint was that Cimino "can't tell a story," despite the fact that he had already managed to do so very successfully, as the screenwriter of *Silent Running* and the director of *Thunderbolt and Lightfoot*; that he might wish to attempt something rather different was not considered as a possibility. Much critical and theoretical work has now been done attacking the overwhelming dominance in Hollywood cinema of the rules of classical narrative, centred on individual psychology and scene-by-scene causality: the dominance, to adopt Barthesian terminology, of the proairetic and hermeneutic codes. These form the basis of the kind of cinema to which Hollywood has so long accustomed us, but there is no reason why custom should be institutionalized as an unchallengeable and absolute system of construction, permitting no divergence.

The structure of *Heaven's Gate* is quite other, the best analogy being with architecture. Each scene or segment can be viewed as a building block enacting (though not in any obviously didactic or explicit way) a "history lesson" in the Brechtian sense of the term. Within obvious limits (the film *does* have a discernible narrative, with a beginning, middle and end in that order), these blocks relate to each other freely *across the entire film*, rather than forming a causal a, b, c . . . progression; they gradually add up to a complex structure of thematic interrelatedness. It is significant that when Cimino, after the disastrous North American premières, himself edited a 2½-hour version for general release, he produced not just a *shorter* version but a different film: not only does he use perceptibly different takes of certain shots, but whole narrative segments are transposed to different parts of the film, and one brief incident is included which he cut from the original version. This also explains why the film, in whatever version, always appears unfinished: the addition, removal or transposition of the "blocks" could be an interminable process, the structure (freed from the strictures of narrative causality) being logically incompletable (there was once, according to Steven Bach, a 5½-hour version). It is also significant that one of the film's finest set-pieces, the magnificent roller-skating sequence, has no narrative necessity whatever, neither developing character nor furthering the plot, though it is crucial to the film's "grand design." There are no precedents in Hollywood cinema for this type of formal strategy; to find them, one must go further afield, to the Kurosawa of *High and Low* and *Ikiru*, or to the Pasolini of *Medea*.

Another initial critical objection was to the film's "Marxist content." By denying the viewer the traditional narrative pleasures of causality and close identification, Cimino transfers attention from individuals to movements, and the film's overall movement is toward the destruction of a genuinely multicultural, non-sexist, and *potentially* socialist America by the capitalist greed for wealth and power. In view of this, it is ironic that *The Deer Hunter* has been widely perceived as a right-wing movie. In fact, the two films are generally consistent. More intuitive than theoretical, more emotional than rational, Cimino does not have a completely consistent ideological position which the films dramatize: they seem, on the contrary, often ideologically incoherent, insufficiently *thought* (particularly the case with *Year of the Dragon*, which disintegrates under the strain of its own internal contradictions).

Though less formally radical than *Heaven's Gate*, *The Deer Hunter* is also characterized by great architectural strength. It is composed of five "blocks," two set in Vietnam alternating with three set in Clairton, Pennsylvania; in both sets, each block is substantially shorter than its predecessor, enacting on the formal level the theme of "dwindling" on which the action of the film is constructed. The controversial ending, in which the survivors sing "God bless America," is neither affirmative (i.e. right wing) nor ironic (i.e. leftist): the singing is characterized by an extreme tentativeness, a failure of confidence in both an available "America" that might be blessed or a God to bless it. As in *Heaven's Gate* (and the point relates back interestingly to the work of John Ford and the whole complex American tradition for which it speaks), the "America" that might be affirmed, represented by social outsiders (in Cimino's case immigrant ethnic groups), is felt to be irredeemably lost,

Michael Cimino directing Robert De Niro in *The Deer Hunter*

overwhelmed by the Nixonite/Reaganite America of corporate capitalism.

Cimino's career since *Heaven's Gate* has been as disappointing as Scorsese's since *King of Comedy*. There is perhaps a common cause: the sheer difficulty of setting up intelligent, personal, original or challenging work in the era of endless mindless sequels and "packages," in a Hollywood dominated by precisely the kind of capitalist concern that *Heaven's Gate* assaults, more concerned with "business" than with cinema. In Cimino's case there is a more specific cause: the general distrust generated by the now almost proverbial financial catastrophe of *Heaven's Gate*. For all that, *Year of the Dragon* and *The Sicilian* though neither can be counted an artistic success, seem far more *interesting* than *The Color of Money* or *The Last Temptation of Christ*. The former contains scenes of stunning brilliance and virtuosity, but is centrally flawed by its inability to construct a coherent attitude toward its protagonist (Mickey Rourke). The film's three most sympathetic characters—his young Chinese assistant, his wife, his mistress—are all given speeches denouncing him; he is indirectly responsible for the deaths of the first two and the gang-rape of the third. Yet Cimino also clearly wishes to affirm the character, an impulse culminating in a conclusion which even Mahler cannot save. *The Sicilian*, like *Heaven's Gate*, is an epic that precludes identification: with the possible exception of Giuliano's fiancée

(a relatively minor and somewhat stereotypical role), every position dramatized in the film (including that of the hero) is shown to be severely compromised and untenable. Unlike *Heaven's Gate*, however, the detail of the film only intermittently comes alive, and then only in the supporting roles (Joss Ackland, John Turturro). Cimino seems seriously hampered by the doubtless mandatory fidelity to Mario Puzo's elephantine and cliché-ridden novel, and by the casting of Christopher Lambert, who totally lacks the charisma that alone would make Giuliano plausible. More importantly, perhaps, Cimino has shown himself in all his previous films intensely concerned with "America" (the ideological image more than the appalling reality), and relates rather distantly to a foreign environment.

At time of writing we await *The Desperate Hours*, a remake of William Wyler's 1955 thriller: a surprisingly modest project for one of Hollywood's great overreachers, but one that offers the potential of grappling with American values at their core. In purely practical terms, there is little hope of another *Heaven's Gate* in the foreseeable future.

—Robin Wood.

CLAIR, René.

French. Born René Chomette in Paris, 11 November 1898. Educated at Lycée Montaigne, and Lycée Louis-le-Grand, Paris, 1913–17. Married Bronya Perlmutter, 1926, one son. Served in Ambulance corps, 1917; retired to Dominican monastery, 1918; began acting at Gaumont studios, 1920; as René Clair, became film editor of *Le Théâtre et comoedia illustré*, Paris, 1922; directed first film, *Paris qui dort*, 1923; directed for Alexander Korda in Britain, 1935–38; emigrated to U.S. and signed to Universal, 1940; returned to Paris, 1946. Recipient: honorary doctorate, Cambridge University, 1956; elected to Academie Française, 1960; Doctor *Honoris Causa*, Royal College of Arts, London, 1967; Commander of the Legion of Honour; Commander of Arts and Letters; Commander of the Italian Order of Merit. *Died in Neuilly, France, 15 March 1981.*

Films as Director:

1923   *Paris qui dort* (+sc, ed)
1924   *Entr'acte*; *Le Fantôme du Moulin Rouge* (+sc)
1925   *Le Voyage imaginaire* (+sc)
1926   *La Proie du vent* (+sc)
1927   *Un Chapeau de paille d'Italie* (+sc)
1928   *La Tour* (+sc); *Les Deux Timides* (+sc)
1930   *Sous les toits de Paris* (+sc)
1931   *Le Million* (+sc); *A Nous la liberté* (+sc)
1932   *Quatorze Juillet* (+sc)
1934   *Le Dernier Milliardaire* (+sc)
1935   *The Ghost Goes West* (+co-sc)
1937   *Break the News* (+co-sc)
1939   *Air pur* (+sc) (uncompleted)
1940   *The Flame of New Orleans* (+co-sc)
1942   Sketch featuring Ida Lupino in *Forever and a Day* (Lloyd) (+sc); *I Married a Witch* (+co-sc, pr)
1943   *It Happened Tomorrow* (+co-sc)
1945   *And Then There Were None* (+co-sc, pr)
1947   *Le Silence est d'or* (+pr, sc)
1949   *La Beauté du diable* (+co-sc, pr)
1952   *Les Belles-de-nuit* (+sc, pr)
1955   *Les Grandes Manoeuvres* (+co-sc, pr)
1957   *Porte des Lilas* (+co-sc, pr)
1960   "Le Mariage" episode of *La Française et l'amour* (+sc)
1961   *Tout l'or du monde* (+co-sc, pr)
1962   "Les Deux Pigeons" episode of *Les Quatres vérités* (+sc)
1965   *Les Fêtes galantes* (+pr, sc)

Other Films:

1920   *Le Lys de la Vie* (Fuller) (role); *Les Deux Gamines* (Feuillade—serial) (role)
1921   *Le Sens de la mort* (Protozanoff) (role); *L'Orpheline* (Feuillade) (role); *Parisette* (Feuillade—serial) (role)
1922   *Parisette* (Feuillade) (role)
1930   *Prix de beauté* (*Miss Europe*) (Genina) (sc contribution)
1939   *Un Village dans Paris* (co-pr)
1959   *La Grande Époque* (French version of Robert Youngson's *The Golden Age of Comedy*) (narrator)

Publications:

By CLAIR: books—

De fil en aiguille, Paris, 1951.
La Princesse de Chine, Paris, 1951.
Réflexion faite, Paris, 1951.
Reflections on the Cinema, London, 1953.
Comédies et commentaires, Paris, 1959.
Tout l'or du monde, Paris, 1962.
"À nous la liberté" and "Entr'acte," New York, 1970.

Four Screenplays, New York, 1970.
Cinema Yesterday and Today, New York, 1972.
Jeux d'hasard, Paris, 1976.

By CLAIR: articles—

"A Conversation with René Clair," with Bernard Causton, in *Sight and Sound* (London), Winter 1933.
"It Happened Tomorrow," with Dudley Nichols, in *Theatre Arts* (New York), June 1944.
"Television and Cinema," in *Sight and Sound* (London), January 1951.
"René Clair in Moscow," in *Sight and Sound* (London), Winter 1955/56.
"Nothing is more artificial than Neo-realism," in *Films and Filming* (London), June 1957.
"Picabia, Satie et la première d'*Entr'acte*," in *L'Avant-Scène du Cinéma* (Paris), November 1968.
"René Clair in Hollywood," an interview with R.C. Dale, in *Film Quarterly* (Berkeley), Winter 1970/71.
Interview in *Encountering Directors* by Charles Samuels, New York, 1972.
"A Conversation with René Clair," with John Baxter and John Gillett, in *Focus on Film* (London), Winter 1972.
"René Clair," interviews with Patrick McGilligan and Debra Weiner, in *Take One* (Montreal), January/February 1973 and May 1974.
"René Clair at 80," an interview with G. Mason, in *Literature/Film Quarterly* (Salisbury, Maryland), vol. 10, no. 2, 1982.
Interview in *Avant-Scène du Cinéma* (Paris), March 1988.

On CLAIR: books—

Viazzi, G., *René Clair*, Milan, 1946.
Bourgeois, J., *René Clair*, Geneva, 1949.
Charensol, Georges, and Roger Régent, *Un Maître du cinéma: René Clair*, Paris, 1952.
Charensol, George, *René Clair et Les Belles de nuit*, Paris, 1953.
De La Roche, Catherine, *René Clair, an Index*, London, 1958.
Mitry, Jean, *René Clair*, Paris, 1960.
Amengual, Barthélemy, *René Clair*, Paris, 1969.
Barrot, Olivier, *René Clair; ou, Le Temps mesuré*, Renens, 1985.
Greene, Naomi, *René Clair: A Guide to References and Resources*, Boston, 1985.
Dale, R.C., *The Films of René Clair*, 2 vols, Metuchen, New Jersey, 1986.

On CLAIR: articles—

Potamkin, Harry, "René Clair and Film Humor," in *Hound and Horn* (New York), October/December 1932.
Jacobs, Louis, "The Films of René Clair," in *New Theatre* (New York), February 1936.
Lambert, Gavin, "The Films of René Clair," in *Sequence* (London), no. 6, 1949.
"Clair Issue" of *Bianco e Nero* (Rome), August/September 1951.
Gauteur, Claude, "René Clair, hélas . . . !," in *Image et Son* (Paris), June 1963.
Beylie, Claude, "*Entr'acte*, le film sans maître," in *Cinéma* (Paris), February 1969.
Fraenkel, Helene, "*It Happened Tomorrow*," in *Films in Review* (New York), August/September 1974.
Fischer, Lucy, "René Clair, *Le Million*, and the Coming of Sound," in *Cinema Journal* (Evanston, Illinois), Spring 1977.
Carroll, Noel, "*Entr'acte*, Paris and Dada," in *Millenium Film Journal* (New York), Winter 1977/78.
Haustrate, Gaston, "René Clair: était-il un grand cinéaste?," in *Cinéma* (Paris), April 1981.
Adair, Gilbert, "Utopia Ltd., the Cinema of René Clair," in *Sight and Sound* (London), Summer 1981.
"*Sous les toits de Paris* Issue" of *Avant-Scène du Cinéma* (Paris), 1 February 1982.
Kramer, S.P., "René Clair: Situation and Sensibility in *A nous la liberté*," in *Literature/Film Quarterly* (Salisbury, Maryland), April 1984.
Vittorini, E., "Nella poetica di Clair una lezione di linguaggio," in *Cinema Nuovo* (Bari), March-April 1986.

René Clair

On CLAIR: film—

Knapp, Hubert, and Igor Barrère, *Le Rouge est mis*, documentary on making of *Les Belles de nuit*, 1952.

*   *   *

During the 1930's, when the French cinema reigned intellectually pre-eminent, René Clair ranked with Renoir and Carné as one of its greatest directors—perhaps the most archetypally French of them all. His reputation has since fallen (as has Carné's), and comparison with Renoir may suggest why. Clair's work, though witty, stylish, charming and technically accomplished, seems beside Renoir's to lack a dimension; there is a certain over-simplification, a fastidious turning away from the messier, more complex aspects of life. (Throughout nearly the whole of his career, Clair rejected location shooting, preferring the controllable artifice of the studio.) Critics have alleged superficiality, and emotional detachment. Yet, at their best, Clair's films have much of the quality of champagne—given so much sparkle and exhilaration, it would seem churlish to demand nourishment as well.

At the outset of his career, Clair directed one of the classic documents of surrealist cinema, *Entr'acte*, and this grounding in surrealism underlies much of his comedy. The Surrealists' love of sight gags (Magritte's cloud-baguettes, Duchamp's urinal) and mocking contempt for bourgeois respectability can be detected in the satiric farce of *Un Chapeau de paille d'Italie*, Clair's masterpiece of the silent era. Dream imagery, another surrealist preoccupation, recurs constantly throughout his career, from *Le Voyage imaginaire* to *Les Belles-de-nuit*, often transmuted into fantasy—touchingly poetic at its best, though in weaker moments declining into fey whimsicality.

The key films in Clair's early career, and those which made him internationally famous, were his first four sound pictures: *Sous les toits de Paris, Le Million, A Nous la liberté* and *Quatorze Juillet*. Initially sceptical of the value of sound—"an unnatural creation"—he rapidly changed his opinion on realizing the creative, non-realistic possibilities which the soundtrack offered. Sound effects, music, even dialogue could be used imaginatively, to counterpoint and comment on the image, or to suggest a new perspective on the action. Words and pictures, Clair showed, need not, and in fact should not, be tied together clumsily duplicating information. Dialogue need not always be audible; and even in a sound picture, silence could claim a validity of its own.

In these four films, Clair created a wholly individual cinematic world, a distinctive blend of fantasy, romance, social satire and operetta. Song and dance are introduced into the action with no pretence at literal realism, characters are drawn largely from stock, and the elaborate sets are explored with an effortless fluidity of camera movement which would be impossible in real locations. These qualities, together with the pioneering use of sound, and Clair's knack for effective pacing and brilliant visual gags, resulted in films of exceptional appeal, full of charm, gaiety and an ironic wit which at times—notably in the satire on mechanised greed in *A Nous la liberté*—darkened towards an underlying pessimism.

As always, Clair wrote his own scripts, working closely on all four films with the designer Lazare Meerson and cinematographer Georges Périnal. Of the four, *Le Million* most effectively integrated its various elements, and is generally rated Clair's finest film. But all were successful, especially outside France, and highly influential: both Chaplin (*Modern Times*) and the Marx Brothers (*A Night at the Opera*) borrowed from them. In some quarters, though, Clair was criticized for lack of social relevance. Ill-advisedly, he attempted to respond to such criticisms; *Le Dernier Milliardaire* proved a resounding flop,

and led to Clair's long exile. For 13 years he made no films in France, apart from the abortive *Air pur*, and his six English-language pictures—two in Britain, four in America—have an uneasy feel about them, the fantasy strained and unconvincing. By the time Clair finally returned to France in 1946, both he and the world had changed.

The films that Clair made after the war rarely recapture the lighthearted gaiety of his early work. In its place, the best of them display a new-found maturity and emotional depth, while preserving the characteristic elegance and wit. The prevailing mood is an autumnal melancholy that at times, as in the elegiac close of *Les Grandes Manoeuvres*, comes near to tragedy. Characters are no longer the stock puppets of the pre-war satires, but rounded individuals, capable of feeling and suffering. More serious subjects are confronted, their edges only slightly softened by their context: *Porte des Lilas* ends with a murder, *La Beauté du diable* with a vision of the atomic holocaust. Nearest in mood to the earlier films is the erotic fantasy of *Les Belles-de-nuit*, but even this is darkly underscored with intimations of suicide.

In the late 1950's Clair came under attack from the writers of *Cahiers du cinéma*, François Truffaut in particular, who regarded him as the embodiment of the "Old Guard," the ossified *cinéma de papa* against which they were in revolt. To what he saw as Clair's emotionless, studio-bound artifice, Truffaut opposed an alternative, more "truly French" cinematic tradition, the lyrical freedom of Renoir and Jean Vigo. Clair's reputation never fully recovered from these onslaughts, nor from the lukewarm reception which met his last two films, *Tout l'or du monde* and *Les Fêtes galantes*.

But although Clair no longer commands a place among the very first rank of directors, he remains undoubtedly one of the most original and distinctive stylists of the cinema. His explorations of sound, movement and narrative technique, liberating at the time, still appear fresh and inventive. For all his limitations, which he readily acknowledged—"a director's intelligence," he once wrote, "can be judged partly by his renunciations"—Clair succeeded in creating a uniquely personal vision of the world, which in his best films still retains the power to exhilarate and delight.

—Philip Kemp

————

CLARKE, Shirley.

American. Born Shirley Brimberg in New York City, 1925. Educated at Stephens College, John Hopkins University, Bennington College, and University of North Carolina. Married lithographer Burt Clarke, one daughter. Dancer with Martha Graham and Doris Humphrey, also chairwoman, National Dance Foundation, 1946–53; made first film, *A Dance in the Sun*, 1954; co-founder, with Jonas Mekas, Filmmakers Cooperative, 1962; worked with Public Broadcast Lab, late 1960's (fired 1969); Professor of Film and Video at U.C.L.A, 1975–85. Lives in New York City.

Films as Director:

1954 *A Dance in the Sun* (+pr, ph, ed, co-choreo); *In Paris Parks* (+pr, ph, ed, co-choreo)
1955 *Bullfight* (+pr, co-ph, ed, co-choreo)
1957 *A Moment in Love* (+pr, co-ph, ed, co-choreo)

1958 *The Skyscraper* (pr, co-d only); *Brussels "Loops"* (12 film
loops made for Brussels Exposition, destroyed) (+pr,
co-ph, ed)
1959 *Bridges-Go-Round* (+pr, co-ph, ed)
1960 *A Scary Time* (+co-sc, ph)
1961 *The Connection* (+co-pr, ed)
1963 *The Cool World* (+co-sc, ed); *Robert Frost: A Lover's Quarrel
with the World* (co-d)
1967 *Portrait of Jason* (+pr, ed, voice); *Man in Polar Regions*
(11-screen film for Expo '67)
1978 *Trans; One Two Three; Mysterium; Initiation* (all video)
1981 *Savage/Love* (video)
1982 *Tongues* (video/theatre collaboration with Sam Shepard)
1985 *Ornette, Made in America*

Other Films:

1959 *Opening in Moscow* (Pennebaker) (co-ed)
1969 *Lion's Love* (Varda) (role as herself)

Publications:

By CLARKE: articles—

"The Expensive Art," in *Film Quarterly* (Berkeley), Summer 1960.
"*The Cool World*," in *Films and Filming* (London), December 1963.
Interview with Harriet Polt, in *Film Comment* (New York), no. 2,
1964.
Interview with Axel Madsen, in *Cahiers du Cinéma* (Paris), March
1964.
Interview with James Blue, in *Objectif* (Paris), February/March 1965.
Interview with Gretchen Berg, in *Film Culture* (New York), Spring
1967.
"A Statement on Dance and Film," in *Dance Perspectives* (New
York), Summer 1967.
"A Conversation—Shirley Clarke and Storm DeHirsch," in *Film Cul-
ture* (New York), Autumn 1967 and October 1968.
"Entretiens—Le Depart pour Mars," an interview with Michel Dela-
haye, in *Cahiers du Cinéma* (Paris), October 1968.
"Shirley Clarke: Image and Ideas," an interview with S. Rice, in *Take
One* (Montreal), February 1972.
"What Directors Are Saying," in *Action* (Los Angeles), March/April
1975.

On CLARKE: books—

Hanhardt, John, and others, editors, *A History of the American Avant-
Garde Cinema*, New York, 1976.
Kowalski, Rosemary A.R., *A Vision of One's Own: Four Women Film
directors*, Ann Arbor, Michigan, 1980.
Heck-Rabi, Louise, *Women Filmmakers: A Critical reception*, Metu-
chen, New Jersey, 1984.

On CLARKE: articles—

Breitrose, Henry, "Films of Shirley Clarke," in *Film Quarterly* (Ber-
keley), Summer 1960.
Archer, Eugene, "Woman Director Makes the Scene," in *New York
Times Magazine*, 26 August 1962.
Pyros, J., "Notes on Woman Directors," in *Take One* (Montreal),
November/December 1970.
Mekas, Jonas, in *Village Voice* (New York), 20 May 1971.
Cooper, K., "Shirley Clarke," in *Filmmakers Newsletter* (Ward Hill,
Massachusetts), June 1972.
Bebb, Bruce, "The many media of Shirley Clarke," in *Journal of Uni-
versity Film Association* (Carbondale, Illinois), Spring 1982.
American Film (Washington, D.C.), June 1982.

*   *   *

Shirley Clarke was a leader and major filmmaker in the New
York film community in the 1950's and 1960's. Her films, which
exemplify the artistic directions of the independent movement, are classic examples of the best work of American independent filmmaking. Clarke began her professional career as a
dancer, and participated in the late 1940's in the avant-garde

dance community centered around New York City's Young
Men's-Young Women's Hebrew Association's (YM-YWHA)
performance stage and Hanya Holm's classes for young choreographers. In 1953, Clarke adapted dancer-choreographer
Daniel Nagrin's *Dance in the Sun* to film. In her first dance film,
Clarke relied on editing concepts to choreograph a new cinematic space and rhythm. She then applied her cinematic choreography to a non-dance subject in *In Paris Parks*, and further
explored the cinematic possibilities for formal choreography in
her dance films, *Bullfight* and *A Moment in Love*.

Clarke, during this time period, studied filmmaking with
Hans Richter at City College of New York and participated in
informal filmmaking classes with director and cinematographer Peter Glushanok. In 1955, she became an active member of Independent Filmmakers of America (IFA), a
short-lived New York organization that tried to improve promotion and distribution for independent films. Through the
IFA, Clarke became part of the Greenwich Village artistic circle that included avant-garde filmmakers Maya Deren, Stan
Brakhage, and Jonas Mekas. It also introduced her to the importance of an economic structure for the growth of avant-
garde film, a cause she championed throughout the 1960's.

Clarke worked with filmmakers Willard Van Dyke, Donn
Alan Pennebaker, Ricky Leacock, and Wheaton Galentine on
a series of film loops on American life for the United States
Pavilion at the 1958 World's Fair in Brussels. With the leftover
footage of New York City bridges, she then made her experimental film masterpiece, *Bridges-Go-Round* utilizing editing
strategies, camera choreography, and color tints to turn naturalistic objects into a poem of dancing abstract elements. It is
one of the best and most widely seen examples of a cinematic
Abstract Expressionism in the 1950's.

Clarke made the documentary film *Skyscraper* in 1958 with
Van Dyke, Pennebaker, Leacock, and Galentine, followed by
A Scary Time (1960), a film commissioned by the United
Nations International Children's Emergency Fund (UNI-
CEF). Clarke also began work on a public television film on
Robert Frost, *A Lover's Quarrel With the World*, but due to
artistic disagreements and other commitments, she left the
project before the film's completion still retaining a credit as
co-director.

Influenced by the developing cinema-verité style in documentary films by Leacock and Pennebaker, Clarke adapted
cinema verité to two feature-length dramatic films, *The Connection* and *The Cool World*. *The Connection* was a landmark
for the emergence of a New York independent feature film
movement. It heralded a new style that employed a greater
cinematic realism and addressed relevant social issues in black-
and-white low budget films. It was also important because
Clarke made the film the first test case in the courts in a successful fight to abolish New York State's censorship rules. Her next
feature film, *The Cool World*, was the first movie to dramatize
a story on black street gangs without relying upon Hollywood-
style moralizing, and it was the first commercial film to be shot
on location in Harlem. In 1967, Clarke directed a 90-minute
cinema verité interview with a black homosexual. *Portrait of
Jason* is an insightful exploration of one person's character
while it simultaneously addresses the range and limitations of
cinema verité style. Although Clarke's features had only mod-
erate commercial runs and nominal success in the United
States, they have won film festival awards and critical praise in
Europe making Clarke one of the most highly regarded American independent filmmakers among European film audiences.

In the 1960's, Clarke also worked for the advancement of the
New York independent film movement. She was one of the 24
filmmakers and producers who wrote and signed the 1961
manifesto, "Statement for a New American Cinema" which

called for an economic, artistic, and political alternative to Hollywood moviemaking. With Jonas Mekas in 1962, she co-founded Film-Makers Cooperative, a non-profit distribution company for independent films. Later, Clarke, Mekas and filmmaker Louis Brigante co-founded Film-Makers Distribution Center, a company for distributing independent features to commercial movie theatres. Throughout the 1960's, Clarke lectured on independent film in universities and museums in the United States and Europe, and in 1969 she turned to video as her major medium in which to work.

—Lauren Rabinovitz

CLAYTON, Jack.

British. Born in Brighton, Sussex, 1 March 1921. Married 1) actress Christine Norden; 2) Kathleen Kath; 3) Haya Hara-neet. Trained as racing ice skater. Third assistant director, assistant director, then editor, London Films, 1935–40; served in Royal Air Force Film Unit, finally Commanding Officer, 1940–46; associate producer, Romulus Films, 1950's; directed first feature, *Room at the Top*, 1958. Recipient: Special Prize, Venice Festival, for *The Bespoke Overcoat*, 1956; Best Director Award, British Academy, for *Room at the Top*, 1959. Address: Heron's Flight, Highfield Park, Marlow, Bucks., England.

Films as Director:

1944 *Naples Is a Battlefield* (+sc, co-ph—uncredited)
1955 *The Bespoke Overcoat* (+pr)
1958 ***Room at the Top***
1961 *The Innocents* (+pr)
1964 *The Pumpkin Eater*
1967 *Our Mother's House*
1974 *The Great Gatsby*
1983 *Something Wicked this Way Comes*
1988 *The Lonely Passion of Judith Hearne*

Other Films:

1948 *Bond Street* (Parry) (2nd unit d); *An Ideal Husband* (A. Korda) (pr mgr); *The Queen of Spades* (Dickinson) (assoc pr)
1951 *Flesh and Blood* (Kimmins) (assoc pr)
1952 *Moulin Rouge* (Huston) (assoc pr)
1953 *Beat the Devil* (Huston) (assoc pr)
1954 *The Good Die Young* (Gilbert) (assoc pr)
1955 *I Am a Camera* (Cornelius) (assoc pr)
1956 *Sailor Beware!* (*Panic in the Parlor*) (Parry) (pr); *Dry Rot* (Elvey) (pr); *Three Men in a Boat* (Annakin) (pr)
1957 *The Story of Esther Costello* (Miller) (assoc pr, 2nd unit d)
1958 *The Whole Truth* (Guillermin) (pr)

Publications:

By CLAYTON: articles—

"Challenge from Short Story Films," in *Films and Filming* (London), February 1956.
"The Way Things Are," an interview with Gordon Gow, in *Films and Filming* (London), April 1974.
"I'm proud of that film," an interview with M. Rosen, in *Film Comment* (New York), July/August 1974.

"Feats of Clayton," an interview with Nick Roddick, in *Stills* (London), November–December 1983.
Interview in *American Film* (Washington, D.C.), December 1987.

On CLAYTON: book—

Craston, George M.A., *Jack Clayton: A Guide to References and Resources*, Boston, 1981.

On CLAYTON: articles—

Cowie, Peter, "Clayton's Progress," in *Motion* (London), Spring 1962.
McVay, Douglas, "The House that Jack Built," in *Films and Filming* (London), October 1967.
Houston, Penelope, "West Egg at Pinewood," in *Sight and Sound* (London), Autumn 1973.
Gregory, C.T., "There'll Always Be Room at the Top for Nothing But the Best," in *Journal of Popular Film* (Bowling Green, Ohio), Winter 1973.
Houston, Penelope, "*Gatsby*," in *Sight and Sound* (London), Spring 1974.
"Gatsby le magnìfique," in *Avant-Scène du Cinéma* (Paris), January 1975.
Rebello, Stephen, "Jack Clayton's *The Innocents*," in *Cinefantastique* (Oak Park, Illinois), June–July 1983.
Sinyard, Neil, "Directors of the Decade: Jack Clayton," in *Films and Filming* (London), September 1983.

*   *   *

Though nearly forty before directing his first feature, Clayton had a solid professional grounding as Associate Producer. His credits, though few, have been mostly major productions; though he disclaims consciously *auteurial* choices, his films evince a heavily recognisable temperament. True, his approach is national-generational, insofar as his heavy, faintly expressionistic, blocking-in of a basic mood perpetuates the lyrical emphasis conspicuous in such "quality" films of the 1940's as *Brief Encounter, Odd Man Out* and *Dead of Night*; as does his penchant for themes of melancholy, frustration, obsession, hallucination, and hauntings.

Clayton attracted much critical praise, and an Oscar, with *The Bespoke Overcoat*, a "long short" brought in for £5000; writer Wolf Mankowitz adapted Gogol's tale of a haunted tailor to London's East End. His first feature was *Room at the Top*, from John Braine's novel. Laurence Harvey played the ambitious young Northerner who sacrifices his true love, Simone Signoret, to a cynical career-move, impregnating an industrialist's innocent daughter. Its sexual frankness (as the first "quality" film to carry the new X certificate) and its class-consciousness (its use of brand-names being as snobbery-conscious as James Bond's—though lower-class) elicited powerful audience self-recognition. It marked a major breakthrough for British cinema, opening it to other "angry young men," with their "kitchen-sink realism" and social indignation (though politically more disparate than legend has it).

Clayton kept his distance from such trends, turning down both *Saturday Night and Sunday Morning* and *The L-Shaped Room*, to select a very "literary," Victorian, ghost story, *The Innocents*, from Henry James's *The Turn of the Screw*. Deborah Kerr played the children's governess who sees ghosts by sunlight while battling to save her charges from possession by the souls of two evil, and very sexual, servants. Is the lonely governess imagining everything, or projecting her own evil? *The Pumpkin-Eater* adapted Penelope Mortimer's novel about a mother of eight (Anne Bancroft) whose new husband, a film scriptwriter, bullies her into having a hysterectomy. In *Our Mother's House*, a family of children conceal their mother's death from the authorities to continue living as a family—until their scapegrace father (Dirk Bogarde) returns and takes over,

Jack Clayton

introducing, not so much "reality," as *his*, disreputable, reality.

The three films are all but a trilogy, brooding with "haunted realism" over the psychic chaos obtaining between parental—especially mother—figures and children caught in half-knowledge of sexuality, death, and individuality. Atmospheres sluggish or turbulent, strained or cavernous, envelop women or child-women enmeshed in tangles of family closeness and loneliness. If *The Innocents* arraigns Victorian fears of childhood sexuality, it acknowledges also the evil in children. *The Pumpkin Eater* balances assumptions of "excessive" maternal instinct being a neurotic defence by raising the question of whether modern superficiality is brutally intolerant of maternal desire. *Our Mother's House* concerns a "lost tribe" of children, caught between the modern, "small-family" world, infantile over-severity (with dangers of a *Lord of the Flies* situation) and adult dissipation (with Dirk Bogarde somewhat reminiscent of *The Servant*). Its echoes of other films may do it injustice.

Several years and aborted projects later came *The Great Gatsby*, an ultra-lavish version of Scott Fitzgerald's tale of the lost love of a bootlegger turned socialite. It's a 1920's yuppie story, but its glitzy surfaces, and characters even wispier than their originals, acquire an icy, sarcophagal air. Almost as expensive, *Something Wicked This Way Comes*, from Ray Bradbury, about an eerie carnival touring lonely prairie towns to snare unsatisfied souls, evokes children's storybook illustrations, but proved a heavy commercial failure. *The Lonely Passion of Judith Hearne* reverted to more intimate and lacerating material, Brian Moore's novel of a genteel but alcoholic spinster (Maggie Smith) courted by an opportunist (Bob Hoskins) for the money he mistakenly thinks she has.

Clayton's "family trilogy" achieves a strange osmosis of 1940's "lyrical realism" and a more "calligraphic" sensitivity, of strong material and complicated interactions between profoundly different people. The resultant tensions between a central subjectivity and "the others," emphasise the dark, confused, painful gaps between minds. If the films border on the "absurdist" experience (Pinter adapted the Mortimer), they retain the richness of "traditional" themes and forms. Critics (and collaborators) keenly discussed shifts between Mortimer's first person narration and the camera as third person, and the relegation of Fitzgerald's narrator to onlooker status. Even in the lesser films, "shifting emphases" (between gloss and core in *Gatsby*, space and emotion in *Wicked*) repay re-seeing, and Clayton's combinations of fine literary material with a troubling temperament, make powerful testimony to their time and to abiding human problems.

—Raymond Durgnat

CLÉMENT, René.

French. Born in Bordeaux, 18 March 1913. Educated in architecture at Ecole des Beaux-Arts. Made animated film, *Cesar chez les Gaulois*, while a student, early 1930's; directed first live-action film, *Soigne ton gauche* (with Jacques Tati), 1936; made documentaries in Arabia and North Africa, 1936–39; technical consultant on Cocteau's *La Belle et la bête*, 1946. Recipient: Best Director Award, Cannes festival, for *La Bataille du rail*, 1946, and *Au-dela des grilles*, 1949.

Films as Director:

1936	*Soigne ton gauche* (short)
1937	*L'Arabie interdite* (short)
1938	*La Grande Chartreuse* (short)
1939	*La Bièvre, fille perdue* (short)
1940	*Le Triage* (short)
1942	*Ceux du rail* (short)
1943	*La Grande Pastorale* (short)
1944	*Chefs de demain* (short)
1945	**La Bataille du rail (Battle of the Rails)** (+sc)
1946	*Le Père tranquille* (Mr. Orchid)
1947	*Les Maudits* (The Damned) (+co-adapt)
1948	*Au-delà des grilles* (Le Mura di Malapaga, The Walls of Malapaga)
1950	*Le Chateau de verre* (+co-sc)
1951	**Les Jeux interdits (Forbidden Games)** (+co-sc)
1954	*Monsieur Ripois* (Knave of Hearts; Lovers, Happy Lovers) (+co-sc)
1956	*Gervais*
1958	*Barrage contre le Pacifique* (La Diga sul Pacifico; This Angry Age; The Sea Wall) (+co-sc)
1959	*Plein soleil* (Purple Noon; Lust for Evil) (+co-sc)
1961	*Che gioia vivere* (Quelle joie de vivre) (+co-sc)
1962	*Le Jour et l'heure* (The Day and the Hour) (+co-sc)
1964	*Les Félins* (Joy House; The Love Cage) (+co-sc)
1966	*Paris brûle-t-il?* (Is Paris Burning?)
1969	*Le Passager de la pluie* (Rider on the Rain)
1971	*La Maison sous les arbres* (The Deadly Trap)
1972	*La Course du lièvre à travers les champs* (And Hope To Die)
1975	*La Baby-Sitter*

Publications:

By CLÉMENT: articles—

Interview with Francis Koval, in *Sight and Sound* (London), June 1950.
"On Being a Creator," in *Films and Filming* (London), October 1960.

On CLÉMENT: books—

Siclier, Jacques, *René Clément*, Brussels, 1956.
Farwagi, André, *René Clément*, Paris, 1967.
Armes, Roy, *French Cinema Since 1946: Vol.1—The Great Tradition*, New York, 1970.

On CLÉMENT: articles—

Queval, Jean, in *L'Écran Français* (Paris), 16 October 1946.
Régent, Roger, in *L'Écran Français* (Paris), 14 October 1947.
Eisner, Lotte, "Style of René Clément," in *Film Culture* (New York), nos. 12 and no. 13, 1957.
Riffaud, Madeleine, in *Lettres Françaises* (Paris), 14 November 1957.
Gilson, René, in *Cinéma* (Paris), no.44, 1960.
Mardore, Michel, in *Cinéma* (Paris), no.62, 1962.
Bellour, Raymond, in *Lettres Françaises* (Paris), 11 June 1964.
McVay, Douglas, "The Darker Side of Life," in *Films and Filming* (London), December 1966.
"*Plein soleil* Issue" of *Avant-Scène du Cinéma* (Paris), 1 February 1981.
Dossier on *La bataille du rail*, in *Cinéma* (Paris), July–August 1982.
Oliva, L., "René Clement kdysi—a potom," in *Film a Doba* (Prague), November 1983.

*   *   *

René Clément was the most promising filmmaker to emerge in France at the end of World War II. He became the most technically adroit and interesting of the makers of "quality" films during the 1950's only to see his career begin to disappoint the critics. In the years of the New Wave it was Clément, above all, who tied the older generation to the younger, especially through a film like *Purple Noon*. In a more recent phase he was associated with grand-scale dramas (*Is Paris Burning?*) and with small, personal, lyric films (*Rider on the Rain*).

Clément began his career auspiciously, helping Cocteau

René Clément

with *Beauty and the Beast*, and directing France's only great resistance film, *La Bataille du rail*. These films showed the world his wide range. The first is a classic of fantasy while the second exhibits what can only be termed a "neo-realist" style. Because *La Bataille du rail* was shot on location with non-actors, and because its episodic story was drawn from the chronicle of everyday life, Clément, at the end of the war, was championed as France's answer to the powerful Italian school of the liberation.

For a time Clément seemed anxious to live up to this reputation. He associated himself with the progressive journal *L'Ecran francais*, and sought other realist topics for his films. In *Les Maudits* he observed the plight of a group of Germans and refugees aboard a submarine. Evidently more concerned with the technical problems of filming in small spaces than with the moral dimensions of his plot, this film was not a great success. But with *The Walls of Malapaga* Clément recovered his audience. This film, which won the Academy Award for best foreign film, was in fact a Franco-Italian co-production and brought together on the screen the most popular star of each country: Jean Gabin and Isa Miranda. The plot and style returned Clément to the poetic-realist films of pre-war France and continued to exhibit that tension of realism and abstraction that characterized all his work.

Unquestionably he was, along with Claude Autant-Lara, the most important figure in the French film industry during the 1950's. His *Forbidden Games* remains a classic today and is notable both for the ingenuous performances of his child actors against a natural location and for the moral incisiveness of its witty plot and dialogue, scripted by the team Aurenche and Bost. Doubtless because he had begun working with these writers, Truffaut condemned Clément in his notorious 1954 essay, "A Certain Tendency in French Cinema," but Bazin, commenting on this essay, found Truffaut to have been too harsh in Clément's case. Indeed Bazin lobbied to have the Cannes Film Festival award its Golden Palm to Clément's next feature, *Monsieur Ripois*. Starring Gérard Philipe, this film makes extensive use of subjective camera and voice over. Shot on location in London, it is clearly an experimental project.

But Clément's experiments are always limited. Technical problems continue to interest him, but he has never relinquished his belief that a film must be well-crafted in the traditional sense of that term. This is what must always distinguish him from the New Wave filmmakers with whom he otherwise has something in common. His all-knowing pessimism, and his literary good taste, finally put him in the camp of the "quality" directors.

Clément, then, must be thought of as consummately French. His technical mastery sits well with his advanced political and moral ideas. He is cultured and trained. He makes excellent films both on a grand scale and on a smaller more personal one. But finally there is something impersonal about even these small films, for, before representing himself, René Clément represents the institution of filmmaking in France. He is a good representative, perhaps the best it had after the war right up through the New Wave.

—Dudley Andrew

CLOUZOT, Henri-Georges.

French. Born in Niort, 20 November 1907. Educated at Ecole Navale, Brest. Married Vera Amado Gibson, 1950 (died 1960). As reporter for *Paris-Midi*, offered job in film industry while interviewing Adolphe Osso, 1930; assistant to Carmine Gallone, Anatole Litvak, and others, 1930–34; contracted pleurisy, confined to sanatoriums, 1934–38; reentered film industry as writer, 1938; directed first film, *L'Assassin habite au 21*, 1942. Recipient: Best Director, Venice Festival, for *Quai des Orfèvres*, 1947; Grand Prix, Cannes Festival, for *Le Salaire de la peur*, 1953; Prix Louis Delluc, for *Les Diaboliques*, 1955; Jury Prize, Cannes Festival, for *Le Mystère Picasso*, 1955; Oscar for Best Foreign Film, for *La Verité*, 1960. *Died 12 January 1977.*

Films as Director:

1931 *La Terreur des Batignolles* (short)
1942 *L'Assassin habite au vingt-et-un* (+co-sc)
1943 *Le Corbeau* (+co-sc)
1947 *Quai des Orfèvres* (+co-sc)
1948 *Manon* (+co-sc)
1949 "Le Retour de Jean" in *Retour à la vie* (+co-sc); *Miquette et sa mère* (+co-sc)
1952 *Le Salaire de la peur* (+sc)
1954 *Les Diaboliques* (+co-sc)
1955 *Les Espions* (+co-sc)
1960 *La Verite* (+sc)
1968 *La Prisonnière* (+sc)

Other Films:

1931 *Ma Cousine de Varsovie* (Gallone) (co-sc); *Un Soir de Rafle* (Gallone) (adaptation); *Je serai seule après minuit* (de Baroncelli) (co-sc): *Le Chanteur inconnu* (Tourjansky) (co-adapt)
1932 *Le Roi des palaces* (Gallone) (co-sc); *Le Dernier Choc* (de Baroncelli) (co-sc); *La Chanson d'une nuit* (French language version of Anatole Litvak's *Das Lied einer Nacht*) (co-adapt + dialogue); *Faut-il les marier?* (French version of Carl Lamac's *Die grausame Freundin*, co-d with Pierre Billon) (adapt + dialogue)
1933 *Caprice de princesse* (French version of Karl Hartl's *Ihre Durchlacht, die Verkäuferin*) (adapt, assoc d, ed, sc); *Chateau de rêve* (French version of Geza von Bolvary's *Das Schloss im Süden*) (sc, adapt, assoc d, ed); *Tout pour l'amour* (French version of Joe May's *Ein Lied für dich*) (sc, adapt, co-dialogue, lyrics, assoc d)
1934 *Itto d'Afrique* (Benoit-Lévy) (lyrics)
1938 *Le Révolté* (Mathot) (co-sc, lyrics + dialogue)
1939 *Le Duel* (Fresnay) (co-sc, lyrics + dialogue); *Le Monde tremblera* (*La Révolté des vivants*) (Pottier) (co-sc, lyrics + dialogue)
1941 *Le Dernier des six* (Lacombe) (lyrics + dialogue); *Les Inconnus dans la maison* (Decoin) (co-adapt, lyrics + dialogue)
1955 *Si tous les gars du monde . . .* (Christian-Jaque) (co-adapt)

Publications:

By CLOUZOT: books—

Le Corbeau, with Louis Chavance, Paris, 1948.
Retour à la vie, with others, Paris, 1949.
Le Cheval des dieux, Paris, 1951.

By CLOUZOT: articles—

"*Le Salaire de la peur*," in *Avant-Scène du Cinéma* (Paris), no.17, 1962.
"*Quai des Orfèvres*," in *Avant-Scène du Cinéma* (Paris), no.29, 1963.
"Voix off: Clouzot," interview with Claire Clouzot, in *Cinéma* (Paris), May 1965.
"An Interview with Henri-Georges Clouzot," with Paul Schrader, in *Cinema* (Beverly Hills), no.4, 1969.

Henri-Georges Clouzot

On CLOUZOT: books—

Chalais, François, *H.G. Clouzot*, Paris, 1950.
Lacassin, Francis, and others, *Le Procès Clouzot*, Paris, 1964.
Pilard, Philippe, *H.G. Clouzot*, Paris, 1969.
Armes, Roy, *French Cinema Since 1946: Vol.1—The Great Tradition*, New York, 1970.

On CLOUZOT: articles—

Tennant, Sylvia, "Henri-Georges Clouzot," in *Film* (London), March/April 1956.
Bianchi, Pietro, "Henri-Georges Clouzot," in *Yale French Studies* (New Haven, Connecticut), Summer 1956.
Marilen, Jacques, "Dangers et vertus de l'orfèvrerie," in *Positif* (Paris), November 1956.
Berger, John, "Clouzot as Delilah," in *Sight and Sound* (London), Spring 1958.
Sety, Gerard, "Clouzot: He Plans Everything from Script to Screen," in *Films and Filming* (London), December 1958.
Fontaine, A., "Clouzot sort de sa légende," in *Lettres Françaises* (Paris), July 1960.

Beylie, Claude, obituary in *Ecran* (Paris), February 1977.
Lacourbe, R., "Henri-Georges Clouzot, 1907–1977," in *Avant-Scène du Cinéma* (Paris), 15 April 1977.
Yakir, Dan, "Clouzot: the Wages of Film," in *Film Comment* (New York), November/December 1981.
Listener (London), 15 October 1987.
Ciné Revue (Paris), 29 October 1987.

*   *   *

In a country like France where good taste is so admired, Henri-Georges Clouzot has been a shocking director. A film critic during the age of surrealism, Clouzot was always eager to assault his audience with his style and concerns.

Like so many others, he found his chance to move from scriptwriting to directing during the Occupation when there was a paucity of directors in France. His first effort *L'Assassin habite au 21* was a safe film since its script followed two similar films he had written which had been well-received by audiences. These witty police dramas are exercises in style and cleverness, befitting the epoch. *Le Corbeau*, made the next year, was in contrast a shattering film, unquestionably hitting hard at the society of the war years. Retaining all the conventions of the thriller, Clouzot systematically exposed the physical and psychological grotesqueries of every character in the film. A grim picture of small-town mores, *Le Corbeau* was condemned by the Nazis and French patriots alike.

When the war ended Clouzot found himself barred from the industry for two years by the "purification committee," an industry-appointed watchdog group that self-righteously judged complicity with the Germans. Clouzot's crime was to have made films for a German-financed company, though he was officially arraigned on charges of having maligned the French character and having demoralized the country during its dark hours. But even at this time many critics claimed that *Le Corbeau* was the only authentically engaged film made during the entire Occupation.

When he did resume his career, Clouzot's grim view of life had not improved. Both *Quai des Orfèvres* and his 1948 adaptation of *Manon* emulate American film noir with their lowlife settings. Both are extremely well acted, but ultimately small works.

Clouzot's fame in the United States came in the mid-1950's when *The Wages of Fear* and *Diabolique* gave him a reputation as a French Hitchcock, interested in the mechanics of suspense. But in France these films, especially *Diabolique*, were seen as only well-made studio products. His 1960 *La Vérité*, starring Brigitte Bardot, was designed to win him favor in the youth culture obsessed by New Wave Life and movies. While the film outgrossed its New Wave competition, a cloyingly paternalistic style shows how far Clouzot is from the spontaneity of the New Wave. The cafe scenes are insincere and the inevitable indictment of society rings false.

All of Clouzot's films even up to the 1968 *La Prisonnière* were financial successes, but in the end he ceased being the instrumental force in the film industry he had been 20 years earlier.

—Dudley Andrew

COCTEAU, Jean.

French. Born in Maisons-Lafitte, near Paris, 5 July 1889. Educated at Lycée Condorcet and Fenelon, Paris. Actor, playwright, poet, librettist, novelist, painter and graphic artist in 1920's and throughout career. Directed first film, *Le Sang d'un poète*, 1930; became manager of boxer Al Brown, 1937; remained in Paris during the Occupation, 1940. Recipient: Chevalier de la Légion d'honneur, 1949; member, Academie Royale de Belgique, 1955; member, Academie Française, 1955; honorary doctorate, Oxford University, 1956. *Died in Milly-la-Foret, France, 11 October 1963.*

Films as Director:

1925　*Jean Cocteau fait du cinéma* (+sc) (neg lost?)
1930　**Le Sang d'un poète** (originally **La Vie d'un poète**) (+ed, sc, voice-over)
1946　**La Belle et la bête** (+sc)
1947　**L'Aigle à deux têtes** (+sc)
1948　*Les Parent terribles* (+sc, voice-over)

1950　***Orphée*** (+sc); *Coriolan* (+sc, role); a 1914 "dramatic scene" by Cocteau included in *Ce siècle a cinquante ans* (Tual) (+sc)
1952　*La Villa Santo-Sospir* (+sc)
1960　*Le Testament d'Orphée (Ne me demandez pas pourquoi)* (+sc, role as le poète)

Other Films:

1940　*La Comedie du bonheur* (L'Herbier) (co-sc)
1942　*Le Baron fantôme* (de Poligny) (sc, role as Le Baron)
1943　*L'Eternel Retour* (Delannoy) (sc); *La Malibran* (Guitry) (narration + role as Alfred de Musset)
1945　**Les Dames du Bois de Boulogne** (Bresson) (co-sc)
1946　*L'Amitie noire* (Villiers and Krull) (role and narration)
1947　*Ruy Blas* (Billon) (sc)
1948　*La Voix humaine* (Rossellini, from Cocteau's play); *Les Noces de sable* (Zvoboda) (sc, voice-over); *La Légende de Sainte Ursule* (Emmer) (role and narration)
1949　*Tennis* (Martin) (role + narration)
1950　*Les Enfants terribles* (Melville) (sc); *Colette* (Bellon) (role + narration); *Venise et ses amants* (Emmer and Gras) (role + narration)
1951　*Desordre* (Baratier) (role + narration)
1952　*La Couronne noire* (Saslavski) (co-sc); *8 × 8* (Richter) (role + narration)
1953　*Le Rouge est mis* (Barrère and Knapp) (role + narration)
1956　*A l'aube d'un monde* (Lucot) (role + narration); *Pantomimes* (Lucot) (role + narration)
1957　*Le Bel indifferent* (Demy, from Cocteau's play)
1958　*Django Reinhardt* (Paviot) (role + narration); *Le Musée Grevin* (Demy and Masson) (role + narration)
1959　*Charlotte et son Jules* (Godard, from same play as Demy 1957 film)
1961　*La Princesse de Cleves* (Delannoy) (co-sc)
1963　*Anna la bonne* (Jutra, from song by Cocteau)
1965　*Thomas l'imposteur* (Franju) (co-sc)
1970　*La Voix humaine* (Delouche, from Poulenc and Cocteau opera)

Publications:

By COCTEAU: books—

L'Aigle à deux têtes, Paris, 1946.
Diary of a Film [La Belle et la bête], New York, 1950.
Cocteau on the Film, New York, 1954.
Jean Cocteau par lui-même, edited by André Fraigneau, Paris, 1957.
Le Sang d'un poète, with drawings, Monaco, 1957.
Le Testament d'Orphée (filmscript), Paris, 1961.
The Eagle with Two Heads, London, 1962.
The Journals of Jean Cocteau, edited by Wallace Fowlie, Bloomington, Indiana, 1964.
The Difficulty of Being, London, 1966.
Two Screenplays [The Blood of a Poet and The Testament of Orpheus], New York, 1968.
Beauty and the Beast, edited by Robert Hammond, New York, 1970.
Professional Secrets: An Autobiography of Jean Cocteau, edited by Robert Phelps, New York, 1970.
Cocteau on the Film, New York, 1972.
Jean Cocteau: Three Screenplays [The Eternal Return, Beauty and the Beast and Orpheus], New York, 1972.
Le Testament d'Orphée; Le Sang d'un poète, Monaco, 1983.
Past Tense, Volume 1: Diaries, London, 1987.

By COCTEAU: articles—

Interview with Francis Koval, in *Sight and Sound* (London), August 1950.
"Conversation," in *Sight and Sound* (London), July/September 1952.
"Cocteau," in *Film* (London), March 1955.
Interview in *Film Makers on Filmmaking*, edited by Harry Geduld, Bloomington, Indiana, 1967.
"Four Letters by Jean Cocteau to Leni Riefenstahl," in *Film Culture* (New York), Spring 1973.

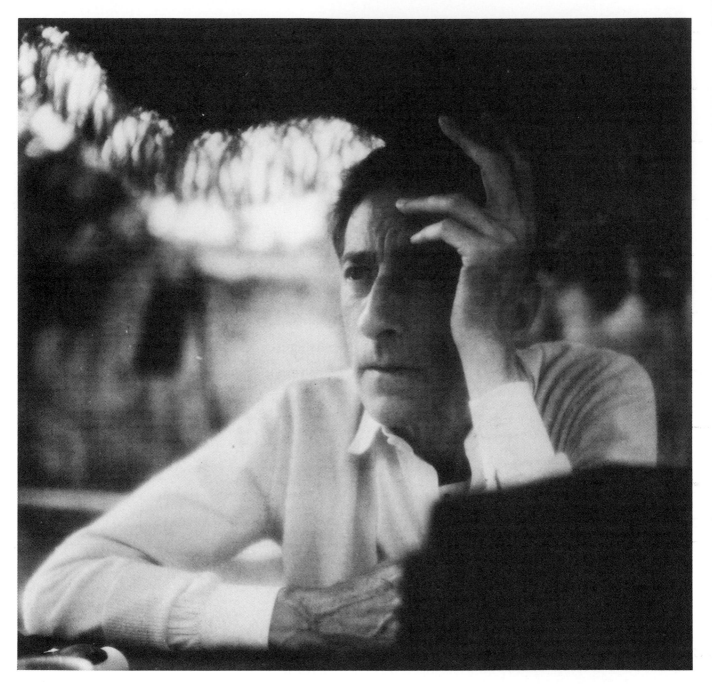

Jean Cocteau

"Aphorismes cinématographiques," and "Cocteau face a La Belle et la bête," in *Avant-Scène du Cinéma* (Paris), July/September 1973.

On COCTEAU: books—

Crosland, Margaret, *Jean Cocteau*, London, 1955.
Dauven, Jean, *Jean Cocteau chez les Sirènes*, Paris, 1956.
Pillaudin, Roger, *Jean Cocteau tourne son dernier film*, Paris, 1960.
Fraigneau, André, *Cocteau*, New York, 1961.
Fowlie, Wallace, *Jean Cocteau: The History of a Poet's Age*, Bloomington, Indiana, 1968.
Lannes, Roger, *Jean Cocteau*, Paris, 1968.
Sprigge, Elizabeth, and Jean-Jacques Kihm, *Jean Cocteau: The Man and the Mirror*, New York, 1968.
Gilson, René, *Cocteau*, New York, 1969.
Armes, Roy, *French Cinema Since 1946: Vol. 1—The Great Tradition*, New York, 1970.

Steegmuller, Francis, *Cocteau*, Boston, 1970.
Evans, Arthur, *Jean Cocteau and His Films of Orphic Identity*, Philadelphia, 1977.
Anderson, Alexandra, and Carol Saltus, editors, *Jean Cocteau and the French Scene*, New York, 1984.
de Miomandre, Philippe, *Moi, Jean Cocteau*, Paris, 1985.
Keller, Marjorie, *The Untutored Eye: Childhood in the Films of Cocteau, Cornell and Brakhage*, Cranbury, New Jersey, 1986.
Peters, Arthur King, *Jean Cocteau and his World: An Illustrated Biography*, London, 1987.

On COCTEAU: articles—

Lambert, Gavin, "Cocteau and Orpheus," in *Sequence* (London), Autumn 1950.
Oxenhandler, Neal, "On Cocteau," in *Film Quarterly* (Berkeley), Fall 1964.

Durgnat, Raymond, "Images of the Mind—Part 13: Time and Time-lessness," in *Films and Filming* (London), July 1969.

Amberg, G., "The Testament of Jean Cocteau," in *Film Comment* (New York), Winter 1971/72.

"Cocteau Issue" of *Image et Son* (Paris), June/July 1972.

"Cocteau Issue" of *Avant-Scène du Cinéma* (Paris), July/September 1973.

Renaud, T., "Retrospective: Jean Cocteau. Un cineaste? Peut-etre. Un auteur? Certainement.," in *Cinéma* (Paris), December 1973.

Gow, Gordon, "Astonishments: Magic Film from Jean Cocteau," and "The Mirrors of Life," in *Films and Filming* (London), January and February 1978.

"Cocteau Issue" of *Avant-Scène du Cinéma* (Paris), 1 May 1983.

"Cocteau Supplement," in *Cinéma* (Paris), May 1983.

Milani, R., "Cocteau dell'immaginario," in *Filmcritica* (Florence), June 1984.

Combs, Richard, "Dream work," in *Listener* (London), 29 May 1986.

* * *

Jean Cocteau's contribution to cinema is as eclectic as one would expect from a man who fulfilled on occasion the roles of poet and novelist, dramatist and graphic artist, and dabbled in such diverse media as ballet and sculpture. As well as directing his own films, Cocteau also wrote scripts and dialogue, made acting appearances and realized amateur films. His work in other media has inspired adaptations by a number of filmmakers ranging from Rossellini to Franju and Demy, and he himself published several collections of eclectic and stimulating thoughts on the film medium. Though he took his first real steps as a filmmaker at the very beginning of the sound era, his period of greatest involvement was in the 1940's, when he contributed to the scripts of a half-dozen films, at times dominating his director, as in *L'Eternel Retour*, at others submitting to the discipline of contributing to another's vision as in his dialogue for Bresson's *Les Dames du Bois de Boulogne*. In addition he directed his own adaptations of such diverse works as the fairy tale *La Belle et la bête*, his own period melodrama *L'Aigle à deux têtes* and his intense domestic drama, *Les Parents terribles*.

But Cocteau's essential work in cinema is contained in just three wholly original films in which he explores his personal myth of the poet as Orpheus: *Le Sang d'un poète*, *Orphée* and *Le Testament d'Orphée*. Though made over a period of 30 years, these three works have a remarkable unity of inspiration. They are works of fascination in a double sense. They convey Cocteau's fascination with poetry and his own creative processes, and at the same time his openness to all the ways of fascinating an audience by the use of stars and trickery, found material and sheer fantasy. The tone is characterized by a unique mixture of reality and dream and his definition of *Le Sang d'un pòete* as "a realistic documentary of unreal events" can stand for all his finest work. Crucial to the lasting quality of Cocteau's work, which at times seems so light and fragile, is the combination of artistic seriousness and persistent, but unemphatic, self-mockery. For this reason his enclosed universe with its curiously idyllic preoccupation with death is never oppressive or constricting, allowing the spectator a freedom rare in mainstream cinema of the 1930's and 1940's. In technical terms there is a similar ability to cope with the contributions of totally professional collaborators, while still retaining a disarming air of ingenuousness, which has sometimes been wrongly characterized as amateurism.

Reviled by the Surrealists as a literary poseur in the 1920's and 1930's and distrusted as an amateur in the 1940's, Cocteau nonetheless produced films of lasting quality. In retrospect he is to be admired for the freedom with which he expressed a wholly personal vision and for his indifference to the given rules of a certain period of French "quality" filmmaking. He was one of the few French filmmakers of the past to whom the directors of the New Wave could turn for inspiration, and it is totally fitting that Cocteau's farewell to cinema, *Le Testament d'Orphée*, should have been produced by one of the most talented of these newcomers, François Truffaut.

—Roy Armes

————

COHEN, Larry.

American. Born in New York City, 1938. Educated at City College Film Institute, New York. Actor and Stage Director, then began writing for TV, 1958; Creator and scriptwriter of the following TV series (from the late 1950's): *Coronet Blue, Branded, The Invaders, The Blue Light, Griff, Custer, Cool Million*, and *Sparrow*. "Murder Consultant" on *Columbo*, and scriptwriter for other TV shows, including *87th Precinct, Kraft Television Theatre, Espionage, The Defenders, Branded*, and *The Nurses*, from 1959; set up film production company, Larco, 1965; wrote and directed stage plays [*Nature of the Crime* (1970), *Motive* (1976), and *Trick* (1979)] performed in London and New York; TV director, from 1980.

Films as Director, Scriptwriter, and Producer:

1972　*Bone* (*Beverly Hills Nightmare. Dial Rat for Terror*)
1973　*Black Caesar* (*Godfather of Harlem*); *Hell Up in Harlem*
1974　*It's Alive*
1977　*God Told Me To* (*Demon*); *The Private Files of J. Edgar Hoover*
1978　*It Lives Again*
1981　*Full Moon High*
1982　*Q* (*Q—The Winged Serpent. The Winged Serpent*)
1985　*Perfect Strangers* (*Blind Alley*); *Special Effects*
1986　*The Stuff*
1987　*Island of the Alive: It's Alive III*; *A Return to Salem's Lot*; *Deadly Illusion* (*Love You to Death*) (co-d)
1989　*Apparatus*; *Wicked Stepmother*
1990　*Ambulance*; *Into Thin Air*

Other Films:

1966　*I Deal in Danger* (Grauman) (sc); *Return of the Seven* (Kennedy) (sc)
1969　*Daddy's Gone A-Hunting* (Robson) (co-sc)
1970　*El Condor* (Guillermin) (co-sc)
1979　*The American Success Story* (*American Success. Success*) (Richert) (co-sc)
1981　*I, The Jury* (Heffron) (sc)
1985　*Spies Like Us* (Landis) (role as Ace Tomato Agent)
1988　*Maniac Cop* (pr, sc)

Publications:

By COHEN: articles—

Interview in *Ecran Fantastique* (Paris), January 1983.

Interview in *Sight and Sound* (London), Winter 1983/4.

Interview in *Starburst* (London), July 1985.

Interview with Paul Taylor, in *Monthly Film Bulletin* (London), April 1986.

Interview in *Movie* (London), Winter 1986.

On COHEN: books—

Meyers, Richard, *For One Week Only: The World of Exploitation Films*, Piscataway, New Jersey, 1983.

Wood, Robin, *Hollywood from Vietnam to Reagan*, New York, 1986.
Newman, Kim, *Nightmare Movies: A Critical History of the Horror Film from 1968*, London, 1988.

On COHEN: articles—

Wood, Robin, in *Film Comment* (New York), September–October 1978.
"Checklist: Larry Cohen," in *Monthly Film Bulletin* (London), April 1979 and March 1983.
Time Out (London), 18 May 1979.
City Limits (London), 3 April 1986.
Hoberman, J., "God Told Him To," in *Village Voice* (New York), 5 August 1986.
Camper, Fred, "Reel Life: The Low-Budget Genius of American Film," in *Chicago Reader*, 12 June 1987.
Hollywood Reporter, 23 May 1988.

*   *   *

Larry Cohen is that rare breed, a director who works outside the commercial mainstream of mega-budgets and mega-hits, but whose oeuvre does not fall into one or two genres. He has made horror films (*It's Alive!* and *Q*), a gangster-melodrama (*Perfect Strangers*), a "blaxploitation" film (*Black Caesar*), and a pseudo-documentary so odd that it falls into no established tradition (*The Private Files of J. Edgar Hoover*). Yet underlying all this work is a single energetic, and eccentric, sensibility.

What American narrative cinema is about first of all is rhythm. When its sense of history, or (less often) of character, falters, it is sustained by a rhythmic drive in which one shot follows another with a feeling of intuitive, inevitable rightness. When an inspired director like Cohen uses rhythm for higher ends, the result is often extraordinary. Witness, for example, the opening of *God Told Me To*, depicting the terror unleashed by a sniper in Manhattan: the already somewhat chaotic rhythms of Manhattan streets are shattered by the intrusion of gunshots.

That Cohen presents the sniping as the disruption of one rhythmic system by another, and that it is further possible to see in the street life before the sniping begins not smooth balletic movement of the "city symphony" film but a series of small disruptions of which the gunshots prove a massive echo, are both keys to Cohen's cinema as a whole. His is an art based on the audacious juxtaposition of multiple, and apparently contradictory perspectives, which, in his subtlest films, are also seen as being partial reflections of each other.

Cohen's camera enlivens his horror films by giving us point-of-view shots through the eyes of the monster-baby in *It's Alive!* or the giant bird in *Q*. The prismatic, handheld images as seen by the crawling baby in *It's Alive!* not only build our sympathy for it; they also remind us that the very different and more conventional views of its adult pursuers that make up the bulk of the film are themselves representative of only one particular way of seeing. Similarly, as we sweep down toward apartment building roof-tops to attack unsuspecting victims with the *Q*-bird, the feeling of excitement engendered by flight incriminates us into the monster's evil.

Cohen's cinema owes much of its richness to the fact that rather than simply organizing his films around multiple perspectives which are presented as mutually exclusive viewpoints, he, like Hitchcock and Fuller before him, mixes it up by having each apparently disparate perspective echoed in its ostensible opposite. Thus, in *Special Effects*, a detective investigating a murder involving a movie director who has confused reality with cinematic illusion once too often is soon himself trying to break into the industry; near the film's end this detective gives a press conference that is the formal echo of the press conference with the director that begins the film.

Perfect Strangers is perhaps Cohen's most complex film. There are four separate characters, each living in a separate universe: a young mother, her son, her ex-husband, and a mob hit-man. Their lives cross, and they speak with each other, but none can truly communicate; each works at cross-purposes and through multiple misunderstandings. The hit-man courts the mother and young son for his own dark purposes, but also grows to genuinely like them. While the moral uneasiness we feel in this unpleasant situation is standard fare in recent cinema, the cinematic translation of that unease into moral equivocation is characteristically Cohen's. In the film's climactic image, the mother, thinking the mobster has harmed her son, shoots him when he appears in her doorway. We view him head on, from her and her gun's perspective, as he falls, revealing her unharmed son behind. The viewer, whose sympathy had been with the mother, and who was thus comfortable assuming her perspective, suddenly finds his moral universe turned upside-down, and his sympathy now with the dying man on the floor.

Cohen's cinema, then, is one of contradictions, collisions, and violent reversals, and in this sense he is an authentic Fuller heir: the moral flip that occurs at the end of *Perfect Strangers* is also found in most of Fuller's work. Cohen's audacious mixture of hand-held and static shots, his combining of multiple rhythms and multiple perspectives, makes him one of the few authentic artists working in Hollywood today.

—Fred Camper

————

COMENCINI, Luigi.

Italian. Born in Salo, Brescia, 8 June 1916. Educated in architecture at Politecnico, Milan, 1934–39. Began private cinema club with Alberto Lattuada and Mario Ferrari, mid-1930's; made first short, *La Novelletta*, 1937; film critic of *Corrente* and assistant director on several films, early 1940's; directed first feature, *Proibito rubare* (for producer Carlo Ponti), 1948; co-founder, with Lattuada, of Cineteca Italiana film archives, Milan, 1949. Recipient: Golden Lion Award for Career Achievements, Venice Festival, 1987.

Films as Director:

1937   *La Novelletta* (short)
1946   *Bambini in città* (short)
1948   *Il museo dei sogni* (short); *L'ospedale del delitto* (short); *Proibito rubare* (*Guaglio*) (+co-sc)
1949   *L'imperatore di Capri* (+co-sc)
1951   *Persiane chiuse* (*Behind Closed Shutters*)
1952   *La tratta della bianche* (*Girls Marked Danger*) (+co-sc); *Heidi*
1953   *Pane, amore e fantasia* (*Bread, Love and Dreams*) (+co-sc); *La valigia dei sogni* (+co-sc)
1954   *Pane, amore e gelosia* (*Frisky*) (+co-sc)
1955   *La bella di Roma* (+co-sc)
1956   *La finestra sul Luna Park* (+co-sc)
1957   *Mariti in città* (+co-sc)
1958   *Mogli pericolose* (+co-sc)
1959   *Und das am Montagmorgen* (+co-sc); *La sorprese dell'amore* (+co-sc)
1960   *Tutti a casa* (*Everybody Go Home!*) (+co-sc)
1961   *A cavallo della tigre* (+co-sc)
1962   *Il commissario*

Luigi Comencini

1963 *La ragazza di Bube* (*Bebo's Girl*) (+co-sc)
1964 "Fatebenefratelli" episode of *Tre notti d'amore* (*Three Nights of Love*) (+co-sc); "Eritrea" episode of *La mia signora* (+co-sc); "Il trattato di eugenetica" ["Treatise in Eugenics"] episode of *Le bambole* (*The Dolls*); *Il compagno Don Camillo*
1965 *La bugiarda* (*Six Days a Week*) (+co-adaptation)
1967 *Incompreso* (*Vita col figlio*) (+co-sc)
1968 *Italian Secret Service* (+co-sc)
1969 *Senza sapere niente di lei* (+co-sc); *Infanzia, vocazione e prime esperienze di Giacomo Casanova veneziano* (+co-sc)
1971 *Le avventure di Pinocchio* (+co-sc)
1972 *Lo scopone scientifico*
1974 *Delitto d'amore* (+co-sc); *Mio Dio, come sono caduta in basso!* (+co-sc): *Educazione civica* (short)
1975 *La donna della domenica* (*The Sunday Woman*)
1976 2 episodes of *Signore e signori, buona-notte* (co-d); "L'equivoco" episode of *Basta che non si sappia in giro*; "L'ascensore" episode of *Quelle strane occasioni*
1977 *Il gatto*
1979 *L'ingorgo, una storia impossibile* (+co-sc)
1980 *Voltati Eugenio* (+sc)
1982 *Cercasi Gesù*
1984 *Cuore*
1986 *La Storia*
1987 *Un ragazzo di Calabria.* (*A Child of Calabria*); *Run, Boy, Run*
1989 *La Boheme*

Publications:

By COMENCINI: articles—

"En guise d'autoportrait," in *Positif* (Paris), February 1974.
"Un vrai crime d'amour," an interview with J.-A. Gili, in *Ecran* (Paris), January 1975.
Interview in *Bianco e Nero* (Rome), September/December 1975.
"L'Idée de la mort," in *Positif* (Paris), December/January 1977/78
"Les Paradoxes de Luigi Comencini," interview with D. Rabourdin and J. Roy, in *Cinéma* (Paris), May and June 1978.
"Conversation avec Luigi Comencini," with L. Codelli, in *Positif* (Paris), May 1979.
"En revoyant les notes de travail d'Eugenio," in *Positif* (Paris), January 1981.
Interview with Jean A. Gili, in *Positif* (Paris), February 1983.
Comencini, Luigi, in *Positif* (Paris), January 1984 and September 1985.
"*Cuore* Issue" of *Avant-Scène du Cinéma* (Paris), no. 345, 1985.
Interview in *Positif* (Paris), April 1987.

On COMENCINI: books—

Gili, Jean A., *Luigi Comencini*, Paris, 1981.
Tassone, Aldo, *Le Cinéma italien*, Paris, 1983.

On COMENCINI: articles—

Codelli, L., and others, "Luigi Comencini," in *Positif* (Paris), March 1974.

Tournès, A., "Comencini: le rire et les larmes," in *Jeune Cinéma* (Paris), September/October 1974.

"Comencini Issue" of *Avant-Scène du Cinéma* (Paris), 1 May 1978.

Kane, P., "Minorités impudiques," in *Cahiers du Cinéma* (Paris), May 1978.

Lefèvre, R., "Comencini pontissalien," in *Image et Son* (Paris), October 1979.

"Comencini Section" of *Cineforum* (Bergamo), June 1982.

Biofilmography in *Avant-Scène du Cinéma* (Paris), December 1985.

*　　*　　*

With more than 30 feature films, several TV documentaries and a few shorts, Luigi Comencini's work is considerable, but has only attracted critical attention in the 1970's though he has always enjoyed popular success in his own country. It is this very popularity which has probably worked against his artistic status. Working within traditional genres (comedy, thrillers, melodramas), dependent on his scripts and the whims of producers, Comencini has been accused, together with his contemporaries Mario Monicelli and Dino Risi, of having betrayed the heritage of neo-realism by using it as a background adjunct to conventional story-telling.

Squeezed between the great authors (Rossellini, Fellini, Antonioni, Visconti, De Sica, Zavattini) with their obvious stylistic preoccupations and the directors of the Italian renaissance of the early 1960's (Rosi, Olmi, Pasolini, the Tavianis), Comencini has been neglected much like some of his Hollywood colleagues. Starting as a documentary filmmaker, a photographer, a movie critic for the socialist paper *Avanti* and the co-founder of the Italian Film Archives, Comencini has had a checkered career but has finally been recognized, particularly in France, as an important artist. His work owes much to the neorealist movement, being firmly grounded in a social context, showing humanitarian preoccupations, and displaying interest in all strata of society.

The enormous success in his early career of a picturesque and charming comedy about a *carabiniere* and a beautiful country girl, *Pane, amore e fantasia* and its sequel *Pane, amore e gelosia*, starring Vittorio De Sica and Gina Lollobrigida, have given a false image of Comencini as a specialist in folksy escapism. Much more revealing is his first film *Proibito rubare* about the relationship between a priest and street kids in postwar Naples. The sentimentality is accompanied by a firm stand on social iniquities. The theme of children proves itself a fruitful one for Comencini, allowing him to oppose innocence and experience and to show the dryness and hypocrisy of the adult world. Some of the best and most personal of his films thus deal with children: *La finestra sul Luna Park*; *Incompreso*, remade in 1983 by Jerry Schatzberg under the same title; *Infanzia, vocazione e prime esperienze di Giacomo Casanova Veneziano* using the first five chapters of Casanova's memoirs to evoke the life of Venice in the 18th century through the eyes of a child who later becomes a rake; *Pinocchio*, a masterful adaptation of Collodi's book; and *Voltati Eugenio* in which a young boy severely judges his parents who had themselves been rebellious youths in the 1960's.

Like many Italians, Comencini has turned to World War II as a key experience in his country's history. *Tutti a casa* is one of the best films on this period, an epic comedy about a soldier, Schweik (Alberto Sordi), slowly becoming a resistance fighter. *La ragazze di Bube*, which tells about the love of a country girl (Claudia Cardinale) for a communist partisan who killed a fascist after the war, is also a sensitive portrait of the Mussolini period's aftermath.

Comencini displays a clarity of vision, a satiric sense and a taste for fables and allegories as in *A cavallo della tigre*, *La scopone scientifico*, *L'ingorgo, una storia impossibile* and *Cercasi Gesù*. Comencini thus reveals himself as rational and reform-ist, but ultimately a sceptic with a philosophy close to that of the Enlightenment. However his ironical tone does not exclude at times an emotional inspiration which leads him to melodramatic subjects set for example in the world of prostitution (*Pagine chiuse*) or factory work (*Delitto d'amore*). Rich in human details, varied in inspiration, and served by some of the best Italian actors, his work deserves the re-evaluation which is underway.

—Michel Ciment

CONNER, Bruce.

American. Born in McPherson, Kansas, 18 November 1933. Studied at University of Wichita and at University of Nebraska, B.F.A. Active as artist, making assemblage works, sculpture, painting and drawing, 1950's-present; moved to San Francisco, 1957; made first film, *A Movie*, to accompany exhibition of his sculpture, 1958. Recipient: Ford Foundation Fellowship Grant, 1964; National Endowment for the Arts Fellowship Grant, 1973; American Film Institute Grant, 1974; Guggenheim Fellowship, 1975; Citation in Film, Brandeis University Creative Awards, 1979.

Films as Director: (in 16mm):

1958	*A Movie*
1960-62	*Cosmic Ray*
1961-67	*Looking for Mushrooms*
1963-67	*Report*
1964	*Leader*
1964/65	*Vivian*
1965	*Ten Second Film*
1966	*Breakaway*
1967	*The White Rose*; *Liberty Crown*
1969	*Permian Strata*
1969-73	*Marilyn Times Five*
1976	*Crossroads*; *Take the 5:10 to Dreamland*
1977	*Valse Triste*
1978	*Mongoloid*
1982	*America Is Waiting*

Publications:

By CONNER: articles—

Interview with Robert Brown, in *Film Culture* (New York), no. 33, 1964.

"Bruce Conner Makes a Sandwich," in *Artforum* (New York), September 1967.

"'I Was Obsessed . . .'," in *Film Library Quarterly* (New York), Summer 1969.

"Excerpts from an Interview with Bruce Conner Conducted in July of 1971," with R. Haller, in *Film Culture* (New York), no.67-69, 1979.

"Amos Vogel and Bruce Conner: Two Views of the Money Crunch," in *Film Comment* (New York), September/October 1981.

On CONNER: books—

Curtis, David, *Experimental Cinema: A Fifty Year Evaluation*, New York, 1971.

Johnson, Lincoln, *Film: Space Time Light & Sound*, New York, 1974.

Sitney, P Adams, *Visionary Film*, New York, 1974.

Hanhardt, John, and others, *A History of the American Avant-Garde Cinema*, New York, 1976.

On CONNER: articles—

O'Doherty, Brian, "Bruce Conner and His Films," in *The New American Cinema*, edited by Gregory Battcock, New York, 1967.

Belz, Carl, "Three Films by Bruce Conner," in *Film Culture* (New York), Spring 1967.
"Bruce Conner," in *Film Comment* (New York), Winter 1969.
Kelman, Ken, "The Anti-Information Film (Conner's *Report*)," in *The Essential Cinema: Essays on the Films in the Collection of Anthology Film Archives* vol.1, New York, 1975.
Fischer, Lucy, "Countdown: Some Thoughts on Bruce Conner," in *University Film Study Center Newsletter* (Cambridge, Massachusetts), no.2, 1976.
Moritz, W., and B. O'Neill, "Fallout: Some Notes on the Films of Bruce Conner," in *Film Quarterly* (Berkeley), Summer 1978.
Cook, Scott, "*Valse Triste* and *Mongoloid*," in *Millenium Film Journal* (New York), Fall/Winter 1980/81.
Bass, William, "The past restructured: Bruce Conner and others," in *Journal of University Film Association* (Carbondale, Illinois), Spring 1981.
Grindon, L., "Significance reexamined: A report on Bruce Conner," in *Post Script* (Jacksonville, Florida), Winter 1985.
Wide Angle (Athens, Ohio), vol. 8, nos. 3–4, 1986.
Monthly Film Bulletin (London), October and November 1987.

*   *   *

After graduating from the University of Nebraska, Bruce Conner moved to San Francisco to begin an exceptionally successful and still very productive career as an experimental filmmaker. Conner's production over the past thirty years manifests certain salient characteristics typical in the works of this genre. His films tend to be brief (the shortest being his 1965 *Ten Second Film*; the longest, his 1975 *Crossroads*, running 36 minutes). Beyond grant subsidy, his production is financially independent, allowing him total freedom in creativity and distribution. And his works are essentially a-collaborative, being in essence solely under Conner's control from conception through all phases of construction. However, since Conner is particularly known for the techno-structural resource of "compilation" (i.e., the use of extant or "found" footage shot by other filmmakers for various purposes), this a-collaborative characteristic deserves special qualification.

While not all of Conner's films manifest compilation (e.g. each of the brief shots that form the hectic, three-minute montage of *Looking for Mushrooms* was the result of Conner's cinematography), compilation is clearly his hallmark and the intrinsic reflexivity of compilation probably accounts for the continued success of Conner's early and later films today. "Reflexivity" is indeed that contemporary preoccupation—both inside and outside the experimental film genre—with grasping and expressing the special materiality that distinguishes film from other forms such as written literature, theatre, music, etc. Since montage or editing has classically been regarded as essential to "film as film," Conner's work can best be experienced as an ongoing exploration of montage's quintessential qualities.

Early works like Conner's *A Movie* or *Cosmic Ray* easily exemplify this thesis. Constructed from bits and pieces of such things as old newsreels, animated cartoons, Hollywood features, war documentaries, academy ("count-down") leader, home movies, and 1950's pornography, the actual cinematography is at once very varied and very anonymous. Indeed, such disparate footage is largely cut together with no attempt to disguise or mitigate abrupt changes in tonality, grain, cinematographic style, or subject matter. Conner's clear exhibition of the "joints" of his montage is in contradistinction to more commercial use of library or file footage in fictive features or television news, where such visibility would prove a liability. Instead, Conner always reminds his audience that they are watching "a movie," an artifact whose very essence is bound to the extraordinary power and sometimes subtle imitations of montage.

Conner's earlier works like *Report*, a 1967 review of sounds and images from the day of John F. Kennedy's shocking assassination, tend—stylistically—more to abrupt junctures enhanced by frenzied editing rates. Also the earlier films are marked more by humor and biting ironies. Later compilation pieces such as *Crossroads* (built totally from declassified film records of early atomic bomb tests) manifest much slower pacing and more wistful moods. Comparably, *Take the 5:10 to Dreamland* employs sepia print stock to homogenize tonality, and its bittersweet representation of the past constitutes a distinct, more mature sensibility than Conner's earlier works. Still, all his production remains remarkably fresh, and remarkably appealing even to popular audiences who might otherwise find experimental production arcane or bizarre. He is doubtless one of the finest American experimental filmmakers working today.

—Edward Small

COPPOLA, Francis Ford.

American. Born in Detroit, Michigan, 7 April 1939. Educated at Hofstra University, B.A., 1959; University of California, Los Angeles, M.F.A. in cinema, 1967. Married Eleanor Neil, 1963; children: Sophia, Giancarlo (died 1987), Roman. Worked in various capacities for Roger Corman at American International, 1962–64; director for Seven Arts, 1964–68; founder, American Zoetrope production organization, San Francisco, 1969; director for American Conservatory Theatre and San Francisco Opera Company, 1971–72; founder, with Peter Bogdanovich and William Friedkin, Directors Company, 1972; publisher, *City* magazine, 1975–76; opened Zoetrope Studios, San Francisco, 1980. Recipient: Oscar for Best Screenplay, for *Patton* (with Edmund H. North), 1970; Oscar for Best Screenplay (with Mario Puzo), and Best Director Award, Directors Guild of America, for *The Godfather*, 1973; Palme d'or, Cannes Festival, for *The Conversation*, 1974; Oscars for Best Director and Best Screenplay (with Puzo) for *The Godfather II*, 1975; Palme d'or and FIPRESCI Prize, Cannes Festival, 1979, for *Apocalypse Now*, 1979. Address: Office: Zoetrope Studios, 916 Kearny Street, San Francisco, CA 94133, U.S.A.

Films as Director and Scriptwriter:

1962   *The Playgirls and the Bellboy* (co-d, co-sc); *Tonight for Sure* (+pr);
1963   *The Terror* (*Lady of the Shadows*) (assoc-pr, co-d); *Dementia 13* (*The Haunted and the Hunted*) (co-sc)
1966   *You're a Big Boy Now*
1968   *Finian's Rainbow* (d only)
1969   *The Rain People*
1972   **The Godfather** (co-sc)
1974   **The Conversation** (+pr); **The Godfather, Part II** (co-sc, +co-pr)
1979   **Apocalypse Now** (co-sc, +pr, role, co-mus)
1982   *One From the Heart* (co-sc, +pr)
1983   *The Outsiders* (+pr); *Rumble Fish* (co-sc, +pr)
1984   *The Cotton Club* (co-sc)
1986   *Peggy Sue Got Married* (+pr)
1987   *Gardens of Stone* (+pr)
1988   *Tucker: The Man and His Dream* (+pr)
1989   episode in *New York Stories*
1991   *The Godfather, Part III*

Francis Ford Coppola

Other Films:

1962   *The Premature Burial* (Corman) (asst-d); *Tower of London* (dialogue d); *The Magic Voyage of Sinbad* (adaptor)
1963   *The Young Racers* (Corman) (sound, 2nd unit ph—uncredited); *Battle Beyond the Sun* (Corman) (sc)
1966   *This Property is Condemned* (Pollack) (co-sc); *Is Paris Burning?* (*Paris brûle-t-il?*) (Clément) (co-sc)
1967   *Reflections in a Golden Eye* (Huston) (sc)
1970   *Patton* (Schaffner) (co-sc)
1971   *THX 1138* (Lucas) (exec pr)
1973   **American Graffiti** (Lucas) (exec pr)
1974   *The Great Gatsby* (Clayton) (sc)
1979   *The Black Stallion* (Ballard) (exec pr)
1982   *Hammett* (Wenders) (exec pr); *The Escape Artist* (Deschanel) (exec pr)
1983   *The Black Stallion Returns* (Dalva) (exec pr)
1985   *Mishima: A Life in Four Chapters* (Schrader) (exec pr)
1987   *Tough Guys Don't Dance* (Mailer) (exec pr)

Publications:

By COPPOLA: book—

The Cotton Club, with William Kennedy, New York, 1986.

By COPPOLA: articles—

"The Youth of Francis Ford Coppola," an interview with R. Koszarski, in *Films in Review* (New York), November 1968.
"The Dangerous Age," an interview with John Cutts, in *Films and Filming* (London), May 1969.
"The Making of *The Conversation*," an interview with Brian De Palma, in *Filmmakers Newsletter* (Ward Hill, Massachusetts), May 1974.
Interview with Marjorie Rosen, in *Film Comment* (New York), August 1974.
"Journey Up the River," an interview with Greil Marcus, in *Rolling Stone* (New York), 1 November 1979.
Interview with O. Assayas, and others, in *Cahiers du Cinéma* (Paris), April 1982.
Coppola, Francis Ford, "Je me considere comme un compositeur de films," in *Cinéma* (Paris), April 1983.
"Ten years of a dreamer," interview with Gideon Bachmann, in *Stills* (London), September–October 1983.
"Idols of the king," an interview with D. Thomson and L. Gray, in *Film Comment* (New York), September-October 1983.
Interview in *American Film* (Washington, D. C.), June 1988.
Interview with Ric Gentry, in *Post Script* (Jacksonville, Florida), Spring-Summer 1987 and Fall 1988.
Interview in *Time Out* (London), 2 November 1988.

On COPPOLA: books—

Johnson, Robert, *Francis Ford Coppola*, Boston, 1977.
Coppola, Eleanor, *Notes*, New York, 1979.
Pye, Michael, and Lynda Myles, *The Movie Brats: How the Film Generation took over Hollywood*, London, 1979.
Kolker, Robert Phillip, *A Cinema of Loneliness: Penn, Kubrick, Coppola, Scorsese, Altman*, Oxford, 1980, revised edition, 1988.
Chaillet, Jean-Paul, and Elizabeth Vincent, *Francis Ford Coppola*, Paris, 1984.
Zuker, Joel S., *Francis Ford Coppola*, Paris, 1984.
Frundt, Bodo, and others, *Francis Ford Coppola*, Munich, 1985.
Chown, Jeffrey, *Hollywood Auteur: Francis Coppola*, New York, 1987.
Cowie, Peter, *Coppola*, London, 1989.
Goodwin, Michael, and Naomi Wise, *On the Edge: The Life and Times of Francis Coppola*, New York, 1989.

On COPPOLA: articles—

Taylor, John Russell, "Francis Ford Coppola," in *Sight and Sound* (London), Winter 1968/69.
McGillivray, D., "Francis Ford Coppola," in *Focus on Film* (London), Autumn 1972.
Pearce, Christopher, "San Francisco's Own American Zoetrope," in *American Cinematographer* (Los Angeles), October 1972.

Braudy, Susan, "Francis Ford Coppola: A Profile," in *Atlantic Monthly* (Boston), August 1976.
Bock, Audie, "Zoetrope and *Apocalypse Now*," in *American Film* (Washington, D.C.), September 1979.
McGilligan, Patrick, "Coppola on the Beat," in *Films and Filming* (London), December 1981.
Bygrave, M., and J. Goodman, "Meet me in Las Vegas," in *American Film* (Washington, D.C.), October 1981.
Myles, Lynda, "The Zoetrope saga," in *Sight and Sound* (London), Spring 1982.
Benayoun, Robert, and others, "Le chat et la pendule," in *Positif* (Paris), April 1984.
Krohn, B., "Coppola des studios Zoetrope aux studios Astorias," in *Cahiers du Cinema* (Paris), December 1984.
Greene, N., "Coppola, Cimino: The Operatics of History," in *Film Quarterly* (Los Angeles), Winter 1984–85.
"Coppola Section," in *Positif* (Paris), February 1985.
"The backdrop is only an inch away," in *Monthly Film Bulletin* (London), June 1985.
Turnquist, K., "Grape Expectations," in *American Film* (Washington, D.C.), November 1985.
Braudy, Leo, "The Sacraments of Genre: Coppola, De Palma, Scorsese," in *Film Quarterly* (Los Angeles), Spring 1986.
Post Script (Jacksonville, Florida), Spring–Summer 1987.

* * *

Francis Ford Coppola became the first major American film director to emerge from a university degree program in film making. He received his Master of Cinema degree from UCLA in 1968, after submitting his first film of consequence, *You're a Big Boy Now* (1967), a free-wheeling comedy about a young man on the brink of manhood, to the university as his master's thesis.

The Rain People (1969), based on an original scenario of his own, followed in due course. The plot of this tragic drama concerns a depressed housewife who impulsively decides to walk out on her family one rainy morning to make a cross-country trek in her station wagon, in the hope of getting some perspective on her life. For the first time Coppola's overriding theme, which centers on the importance of the role of a family spirit in people's lives, is clearly delineated in one of his films.

Coppola's preoccupation with the importance of family in modern society is brought into relief in his *Godfather* films, which depict an American family over a period of more than seventy years. Indeed, the thing that most attracted him to the project in the first place was the fact that the best-selling book on which the films are based is really the story of a family. It is about "this father and his sons," he says, "and questions of power and succession." In essence, *The Godfather* (1972) offers a chilling depiction of the way in which young Michael Corleone's loyalty to his flesh-and-blood family gradually turns into an allegiance to the larger Mafia family to which they in turn belong—a devotion that in the end renders him a cruel and ruthless mass murderer. With this film Coppola definitely hit his stride as a film maker, and the picture was an enormous critical and popular success.

The Godfather II (1974) treats events that happened before and after the action covered in the first film. The second Godfather movie not only chronicles Michael's subsequent career as head of the "family business," but also presents, in flashback, the early life of his father in Sicily, as well as his rise to power in the Mafia in New York City's Little Italy. *The Godfather II*, like *The Godfather*, was a success both with the critics and the public, and Coppola won Oscars for directing the film, co-authoring the screenplay, and co-producing the best picture of the year. In 1990 he made his third *Godfather* film. This trilogy of movies, taken together, represents one of the supreme achievements of the cinematic art.

In contrast to epic films like the *Godfather* series, *The Out-*

siders was conceived on a smaller scale; it revolves around a gang of underprivileged teenage boys growing up in Tulsa, Oklahoma in the 1960's. *The Outsiders* was a box-office hit, as was *Peggy Sue Got Married*, a remarkable fantasy. The title character is a woman approaching middle age who passes out at a high school reunion, and wakes up back in high school in 1960. But she brings with her on her trip down memory lane a 42-year-old mind, and hence views things from a more mature perspective than she possessed the first time around.

Coppola has made two films about the Viet Nam War. *Apocalypse Now*, the first major motion picture about the war, is a king-sized epic shot on location in the Philippines; and it contains some of the most extraordinary combat footage ever filmed. But there are no such stunning battle sequences in its companion film, *Gardens of Stone*, since it takes place stateside, and is concerned with the homefront during the same period.

His next subject was a biographical film about Preston Tucker, a maverick automobile designer, entitled *Tucker: The Man and His Dream*. Coppola contends that Tucker developed plans for a car that was way ahead of its time in terms of engineering; yet the auto industry at large stubbornly resisted his ideas. Unfortunately, Coppola comments, creative people do not always get a chance to exercise their creativity.

Francis Coppola is one creative person who has continued to exercise his considerable talent throughout his career. Admittedly, he has had his occasional failure, such as the off-center teen movie, *Rumble Fish* (1983). But the majority of the films he has directed over the years have demonstrated that he is one of the most gifted directors to come across the Hollywood horizon since Stanley Kubrick.

Coppola himself observes that he looks upon the movies he has directed in the past as providing him with the sort of experience that will help him to make better films in the future. So the only thing for a film maker to do, he concludes, is to just keep going.

—Gene D. Phillips

———

CORMAN, Roger.

American. Born Roger William Corman in Detroit, Michigan, 5 April 1926. Attended Beverly Hills High Schools; Stanford University, California, engineering degree; Oxford University, one term, 1950. Married Julie Halloran, 1969, one daughter, two sons. Served in United States Navy during World War II. Messenger boy, 20th Century-Fox, then television stagehand and literary agent, Hollywood, early 1950's; scriptwriter and producer, then director and producer, mainly for American International Pictures, from 1953; directed first film, *Guns West*, 1954; founder and director of production and distribution company New World Pictures, 1970–83; founded production company New World Pictures, 1983, and distribution company Concorde, 1985; set up Brentwood TV company, 1990. Address: c/o New Horizons Production Company, 11600 San Vicente Boulevard, Los Angeles, California 90049, U.S.A.

Films as Producer and Director:

1954   *Guns West*
1955   *Apache Woman*; *Day the World Ended*

1956   *The Oklahoma Woman*; *It Conquered the World*; *Gunslinger*; *Swamp Woman*; *The Undead*
1957   *She-Gods of Shark Reef* (*Shark Reef*); *Naked Paradise*; *Not of This Earth*; *Rock All Night*; *Attack of the Crab Monsters*; *Carnival Rock*; *Teenage Doll*; *Sorority Girl* (*The Bad One*); *The Saga of the Viking Women and Their Voyage to the Waters of the Great Sea Serpent* (*Viking Women and the Sea Serpent*; *Viking Women*)
1958   *War of the Satellites* (+ role); *Machine Gun Kelly*; *Teenage Caveman* (*Out of the Darkness*); *I, Mobster* (*The Mobster*); *Last Woman on Earth* (+ role)
1959   *The Wasp Woman* (+ role); *A Bucket of Blood*
1960   *Ski Troop Attack* (+ role); *The Fall of the House of Usher* (*House of Usher*); *The Little Shop of Horrors* (+ role); *Creature from the Haunted Sea* (+ role); *Atlas*
1961   *Pit and the Pendulum*; *The Intruder* (*I Hate Your Guts*)
1962   *The Premature Burial*; *Tales of Terror*; *Tower of London*
1963   *The Raven*; *The Young Racers* (+ role); *The Haunted Palace*; *The Terror*; *X* (*The Man with the X-Ray Eyes*)
1964   *The Secret Invasion*; **The Masque of the Red Death**; *The Tomb of Ligeia*
1966   *The Wild Angels*
1967   *The St. Valentine's Day Massacre*
1970   *Gass-s-s-s, or It Became Necessary to Destroy the World in Order to Save it*
1971   *Von Richthofen and Brown* (*The Red Baron*)
1989   *Frankenstein Unbound*

Films as Producer or Executive Producer:

1954   *Highway Dragnet* (Juran) (+ co-sc); *Monster from the Ocean Floor* (Ordung); *The Fast and the Furious* (Ireland and Sampson)
1955   *Beast with 1,000,000 Eyes* (Kramarsky)
1958   *Stake Out on Dope Street* (Kershner); *The Cry Baby* (Addiss); *Monster from Galaxy 27* (Kowalski); *Hot Car Girl* (Kowalski); *Night of the Blood Beast* (Kowalski); *The Brain Eaters* (Ve Sota); *Paratroop Command* (Witney); *The Wild Ride* (Berman)
1959   *Tank Commando* (*Tank Commandos*) (Topper); *Crime and Punishment U.S.A.* (Sanders); *High School Big Shot* (*The Young Sinners*) (Rapp); *Attack of the Giant Leeches* (*Demons of the Swamp*) (Kowalski); *Beast from a Haunted Cave* (Hellman); *T-Bird Gang* (*The Pay-Off*) (Harbinger); *Battle of Blood Island* (Rapp)
1961   *Night Tide* (Harrington); *The Mermaids of Tiburon* (*Aquasex*) (Lamb)
1962   *The Magic Voyage of Sinbad* (Posco—re-edited version of Ptuschko's 1952 film *Sadko*); *Battle Beyond the Sun* (Colchart—re-edited version of Kozyr and Karyukov's 1960 film *Nebo zovet/The Heavens Call*)
1963   *Dementia* (*The Haunted and the Hunted*) (Coppola)
1965   *The Girls on the Beach* (Witney); *Sky Party* (Rafkin); *Beach Ball* (Weinrib); *The Shooting* (Hellman); *Ride in the Whirlwind* (Hellman); *Blood Bath* (Hill and Rothman)
1966   *Queen of Blood* (Harrington)
1967   *Targets* (Bogdanovich); *Devil's Angels* (Haller)
1969   *The Dunwich Horror* (Haller); *Naked Angels* (Clark); *Pit Stop* (Hill); *Paddy* (Haller)
1970   *Student Nurses* (Rothman); *Angels Die Hard!* (Compton)
1971   *Angels Hard as They Come* (Viola); *Women in Cages* (de Leon); *Private Duty Nurses* (Armitage); *The Big Doll House* (Hill); *The Velvet Vampire* (Rothman)
1972   *The Final Comedown* (Williams); *Boxcar Bertha* (Scorsese); *The Big Bird Cage* (Hill); *The Unholy Rollers* (Zimmerman); *Night Call Nurses* (Kaplan), *Fly Me* (Santiago); *The Young Nurses* (Kimbro); *The Hot Box* (Viola); *Night of the Cobra Woman* (Meyer)
1973   *I Escaped from Devil's Island* (Meyer); *The Arena* (Carver); *The Student Teachers* (Kaplan); *Tender Loving Care* (*Naughty Nurses*) (Edmonds)
1974   *Cheap* (Swenson); *Candy Stripe Nurses* (Holleb); *Cockfighter* (*Born to Kill*) (Hellman); *Big Bad Mama* (Carver); *Caged*

Roger Corman: *The Intruder*

Heat (Demme); *TNT Jackson* (Santiago); *Street Girls* (Miller); *The Woman Hunt* (Romero)

1975 *Capone* (Carver); *Death Race 2000* (Bartel); *Crazy Mama* (Demme); *Summer School Teachers* (Peeters); *Dark Town Strutters* (Witney); *Cover Girl Models* (Santiago)

1976 *Hollywood Boulevard* (Arkush and Dante); *Fighting Mad* (Demme); *Cannonball* (*Carquake*) (Bartel); *Jackson County Jail* (Miller); *Nashville Girl* (*New Girl in Town*) (Trikonis); *Moving Violation* (Dubin); *God Told Me To* (*Demon*) (Cohen); *Dynamite Women* (*The Great Texas Dynamite Chase*) (Pressman); *Eat My Dust!* (Wilson)

1977 *Black Oak Conspiracy* (Kelljan); *Grand Theft Auto* (Howard); *I Never Promised You a Rose Garden* (Page); *Thunder and Lightning* (Allen); *Andy Warhol's Bad* (Johnson); *Moonshine County Express* (Trikonis); *Dirty Duck* (Swenson); *Maniac* (*Assault on Paradise*) (Compton); *A Hero Ain't Nothin' But a Sandwich* (Nelson)

1978 *Deathsport* (Suso and Arkush); *Piranha* (Dante); *Avalanche* (Allen); *Outside Chance* (Miller); *The Bees* (Zacharias)

1981 *Smokey Bites the Dust* (Griffith); *Galaxy of Terror* (Clark)

1982 *Forbidden World* (Holzman)

1983 *Star Child* (Cohne)

1984 *Love Letters* (Jones)

1985 *Barbarian Queen* (Oliveira); *Streetwalkin'* (Freeman)

1986 *Cocaine Wars* (Oliveira), *Big Bad Mama II* (Wynorski)

1987 *Munchies* (Hirsch); *Stripped to Kill* (Ruben); *The Lawless Land* (Hess)

1988 *The Drifter* (Brand); *Daddy's Boys* (Minion); *Half Life* (Ruben); *Saturday the 14th Strikes Back* (Howard Cohen)

Other Films:

1967 *A Time for Killing* (*The Long Ride Home*) (Karlson) (uncredited co-dir); *Wild Racers* (Haller) (uncredited 2nd unit dir)

1969 *De Sade* (Enfield) (uncredited co-dir)

1974 ***The Godfather, Part II*** (Coppola) (role)

1980 *The Howling* (Dante) (role)

1983 *Der Stand der Dinge* (*The State of Things*) (Wenders) (role)

Publications:

By CORMAN: book—

How I Made a Hundred Movies in Hollywood and Never Lost a Dime, with Jim Jerome, New York, 1990.

By CORMAN: articles—

Sight and Sound (London), Summer 1963.
Midi-Minuit Fantastique (Paris), no. 10–11, 1965.

Image et Son (Paris), March 1967.

"A Letter from Roger Corman," *Take One* (Montreal), July–August 1968.

Interview in *The Film Director as Superstar* by Joseph Gelmis, New York, 1970.

Interview with Joe Medjuck, in *Take One* (Montreal), July–August 1970.

Interview with Philip Strick, in *Sight and Sound* (London), Autumn 1970.

Interview with Charles Goldman, in *Film Comment* (New York), Fall 1971.

Séquences (Montreal), October 1974.

Millimeter (New York), December 1975.

Interview with Bill Davidson, in *New York Times Magazine*, 28 December 1975.

Interview in *Journal of Popular Film* (Washington, D.C.), vol. 5, no. 3–4, 1976.

Interview in *Cahiers du Cinéma* (Paris), January 1979.

Interviews in *Ecran Fantastique* (Paris), no. 18, 1981, and May 1984.

Interview in *Films and Filming* (London), November 1984.

Interview with Robin Wood and Richard Lippe, in *Movie* (London), Winter 1986.

Interview in *Film Comment* (New York), July/August 1988.

On CORMAN: books—

Will, David and others, *Roger Corman: The Millenic Vision*, Edinburgh, 1970.

McCarthy, Todd and Flynn, Charles, eds., *King of the Bs*, New York, 1975.

Turroni, Guiseppe, *Roger Corman*, Florence, 1976.

di Franco, J. Philip, *The Movie World of Roger Corman*, New York, 1979.

Hillier, Jim and Lipstadt, Aaron, *Roger Corman's New World*, London, 1981.

Naha, Ed, *The Films of Roger Corman*, New York, 1982.

Bourgoin, Stéphane, *Roger Corman*, Paris, 1983.

McGee, Mark Thomas, *The Story of American International Pictures*, Jefferson, North Carolina, 1984.

Morris, Gary, *Roger Corman*, Boston, 1985.

McGee, Mark Thomas, *Roger Corman: The Best of the Cheap Acts*, Jefferson, North Carolina, 1988.

On CORMAN: articles—

Monthly Film Bulletin (London), vol. 31, 1964.

Positif (Paris), March 1964.

Dyer, Peter John, "Z Films" in *Sight and Sound* (London), Autumn 1964.

Midi-Minuit Fantastique (Paris), no. 1, 1965.

Film (London), no. 43, 1965.

French, Philip, "Incitement Against Violence" in *Sight and Sound* (London), Winter 1967–68.

Wallace, Eric in *Screen Education* (London), July–August 1968.

Jeune Cinéma (Paris), February 1969.

Action (Los Angeles), July–August 1969.

Montage (London), April 1970.

Diehl, Digby in *Show* (New York), May 1970.

Ecran Fantastique (Paris), December 1970.

Koszarski, Richard, in *Film Comment* (New York), Fall 1971.

Ciné Revue (Paris), 5 February 1976.

National Film Theatre booklets (London), December 1976 and January 1977.

Avant-Scène (Paris), 15 May 1980.

National Film Theatre booklet (London), February 1981.

Chute, David, in *Film Comment* (New York), March–April 1982.

"Corman Issue" of *Cinema Nuovo* (Turin), January–February 1984.

Goldstein, Patrick in *American Film* (Washington, D.C.) January–February 1985.

Newman, Kim, "The Roger Corman Alumni Association," in *Monthly Film Bulletin* (London), November and December 1985.

Strick, Philip, "The Return of Roger Corman," in *Films and Filming* (London), March 1986.

Hillier, Jim, and Aaron Lipstadt, "The Economics of Independence: Roger Corman and New World Pictures 1970–80," in *Movie* (London), Winter 1986.

Hollywood Reporter, 26 March 1987.

Exline, P., "King of the B's," in *American Film* (Washington, D.C.), September 1987.

* * *

Grand master and patron saint of the American exploitation film, Roger Corman has forged a reputation for creative filmmaking on means so minimal as to seem absurd. He began his career in the mid-1950's producing and directing westerns, gangster movies, mythological "spectacles," teen pictures, and sci-fi/horror films distinguished largely by their five-digit budgets and shooting schedules as short as three days. By the early 1960's his business savvy and understanding of the developing "youth" market had made him the most valuable commodity at American International Pictures, and his shrewd innovations in production and distribution contributed substantially to that company's pre-eminence in the exploitation market.

Backhandedly dubbed by critics "the King of Schlock" and "the Orson Welles of Z-Pictures," Corman has become a symbol of the creativity available to those willing to accept the economic limitations of working outside the mainstream. As a producer, he was able to provide decisive career breaks for a number of actors (Jack Nicholson, Ellen Burstyn, Robert De Niro, Cindy Williams), screenwriters (Robert Towne), and directors (Francis Ford Coppola, Peter Bogdanovich, Martin Scorsese, Jonathan Demme) who were to rise toward the upper echelons of the New Hollywood. Meanwhile, Corman insisted on maintaining his own kingdom on the fringes. When AIP's growing budgets and pretenses began to tighten studio control over individual projects, Corman left and, in 1970, established his own studio, New World Pictures, which quickly usurped AIP's place in the exploitation field. Corman did not direct at New World, but instead exerted a decisive influence as producer, cultivating the drive-in/inner city audience by developing specialized sub-genres (women's prison pictures; soft-core nurse/teacher films; hard-core action and horror movies) and a strict formula, requiring given amounts of violence, nudity, humor, and social commentary. The social element not only reflected Corman's own attitudes (a self-characterized "liberal to radical" politically, he independently financed his anti-racist *The Intruder* when no studio would put up the money), but also an understanding of the politically disfranchised groups which comprised the New World audience. At the same time, Corman used the company to provide some of the first intelligent American marketing of foreign "art films," accruing respectable successes with Bergman's *Cries and Whispers*, Fellini's *Amarcord*, Truffaut's *Adele H.* and Kurosawa's *Dersu Uzala*.

Yet it would not be quite fair to dismiss Corman, as Andrew Sarris did in 1968, as a producer "miscast" as a director. Admittedly, at that time Corman's most accomplished, complex, and disturbing film, *Bloody Mama*, was still to be made. But Corman had his first artistic stride in the early 1960's with a series of seven flamboyantly artificial color horror films, loosely based on Poe and ranging in tone from slightly tongue-in-cheek to openly parodic. The cycle peaked with *Masque of the Red Death*, which made ingenious use of imagery borrowed from Bergman's *Seventh Seal*, to the disbelief of American critics and the delight of the Europeans, who have always seemed willing to take Corman fairly seriously. Indeed, even in the 1950's Corman had learned to make artistic virtue of low-budget tawdriness, which contributed greatly to the existential bleakness of such tortured morality plays as *Teenage Doll* and *Sorority Girl*, and to the essential minimalism of the definitive black comedies, *Bucket of Blood* and *Little Shop of Horrors*. Yet, even if one is unwilling to recognize the philosophical despair of the moralist struggling against nihilism which underlies the straight-faced lunacy of *It Conquered the World*, the visionary metaphysics of *X—The Man with the X-Ray Eyes*, and even the Urbiker picture of the 1960's *The Wild Angels*, Corman's audacious independence has at least earned him the right to symbolize the myriad contradictions between artistic ambition and fiscal responsibility which seem inherent to commercial filmmaking.

—Ed Lowry

COSTA-GAVRAS, Constantin.

French. Born Konstantinos Gavras in Athens, 1933 (naturalized French citizen, 1956). Educated at the Sorbonne, Paris, and I.D. Hautes Etudes Cinématographiques. Married Michèle Ray, 1968, one son, one daughter. Ballet dancer in Greece, then moved to Paris, 1952; assistant to Yves Allegret, René Clair, René Clément, Henri Verneuil, and Jacques Demy, 1958–65; directed first film, *Compartiment tueurs*, 1966. Recipient: Best Director, New York Film Critics Award, and Jury Prize, Cannes Festival, for *Z*, 1970; Best Director Award, Cannes Festival, for *Special Section*, 1975; Palme d'or, Cannes Festival, 1982, and Oscar for Best Screenplay (with Donald Stewart), for *Missing*, 1983. Agent: John Ptak, William Morris Agency, 151 El Camino Drive, Beverly Hills, CA 90212, U.S.A.

Films as Director and Scriptwriter:

1966   *Compartiment tueurs* (*The Sleeping Car Murder*)
1968   *Un Homme de trop* (*Shock Troops*)
1969   *Z* (co-sc)
1970   *L'Aveu* (*The Confession*)
1973   *Etat de siège* (*State of Siege*) (co-sc)
1975   *Section speciale* (*Special Section*) (co-sc)
1979   *Clair de femme* (*Womanlight*)
1982   *Missing* (co-sc)
1983   *Hanna K* (co-sc, +pr)
1985   *Family Business*
1988   *Summer Lightning* (*Sundown*); *Betrayed* (d only)
1990   *Music Box* (d only)

Other Films:

1977   *La Vie devant soi* (*Madame Rosa*) (Mizrahi) (role as Ramon)
1985   *Spies Like Us* (Landis) (role as Tadzhik); *Thé au harem d'Archimede* (*Tea in the Harem*) (sc)

Publications:

By COSTA-GAVRAS: articles—

"Costa-Gavras Talks," an interview with Dan Georgakas and Gary Crowdus, in *Take One* (Montreal), July/August 1969.
Interview with David Austen, in *Films and Filming* (London), June 1970.
"A film is like a match: You can make a big fire or nothing at all," an interview with H. Kalishman and Gary Crowdus, in *Cineaste* (New York), vol. 6, no. 1, 1973.
Interview with F. Guerif and S. Levy-Klein, in *Cahiers de la Cinémathèque* (Perpignan), Spring/Summer 1978.
Interview with John Pilger, in *Time Out* (London), 8 December 1983.
Interview in *Cineaste* (New York), vol. 16, no. 4, 1988.
Interview in *Film Comment* (New York), July–August 1988.

"Black and White Movies," an interview with Sheila Johnston, in *Independent* (London), 31 May 1990

On COSTA-GAVRAS: books—

Solinas, Franco, *State of Siege*, (includes articles), New York, 1973.
Michalczyk, John J., *Costa-Gavras: The Political Fiction Film*, Philadelphia, 1984.

On COSTA-GAVRAS: articles—

Sauvaget, D., and others, "A propos de Costa-Gavras," in *Image et Son* (Paris), December 1977.
Crowdus, G., and L. Rubenstein, "The 'Missing' Dossier," in *Cineaste* (New York), vol. 12, no. 1, 1982.
Wood, M., "In search of the Missing," in *American Film* (Washington, D.C.), March 1982.
Yakir, Dan, "*Missing* in action," in *Film Comment* (New York), March/April 1982.
Camy, G., "Costa-Gavras: Pour un certain cinéma politique," in *Jeune Cinéma* (Paris), November 1983.
Johnston, Sheila, "Costa-Gavras," in *Sight and Sound* (London), Summer 1984.

*   *   *

The films of Costa-Gavras are exciting, enthralling, superior examples of dramatic moviemaking, but the filmmaker is far from being solely concerned with keeping the viewer in suspense. A Greek exile when he made *Z*, set in the country of his birth, Costa-Gavras is most interested in the motivations and misuses of power: politically, he may be best described as an anti-fascist, a humanist. As such, his films are as overtly political as any above-ground, internationally popular and respected filmmaker in history.

Costa-Gavras's scenarios are often based on actual events in which citizens are deprived of human rights, and which expose the hypocrisies of governments to both the left and right of center. In *Z*, Greek pacifist leader Yves Montand is killed by a speeding truck, a death ruled accidental by the police. Journalist Jean-Louis Trintignant's investigation leads to a right-wing reign of terror against witnesses and friends of the deceased, and to revelations of a government scandal. *The Confession* is the story of a Communist bureaucrat (Montand) who is unjustifiably tortured and coerced into giving false testimony against other guiltless comrades. *State of Siege* is based on the political kidnapping of a United States official in Latin America (Montand); the revolutionaries slowly discover the discreetly hidden function of this "special advisor"—to train native police in the intricacies of torture. In *Special Section*, a quartet of young Frenchmen are tried and condemned by an opportunistic Vichy government for the killing of a German naval officer in occupied Paris. In *Missing*, an idealistic young American writer (John Shea) is arrested, tortured, and killed in a fascist takeover of a Latin American country. His father, salt-of-the-earth businessman Jack Lemmon, first feels it's all a simple misunderstanding. After he realizes that he has been manipulated and lied to by the American embassy, he applies enough pressure and embarrasses enough people so that he can finally bring home the body of his son.

Despite these sobering, decidedly non-commercial storylines, Costa-Gavras has received popular as well as critical success, particularly with *Z* and *Missing*, because the filmmaker does not bore his audience by structuring his films in a manner that will appeal only to intellectuals. Instead, he casts actors who are popular—international stars with box office appeal. Apart from a collective message, that fascism and corruption may occur in any society anywhere in the world, Costa-Gavras's films also work as mysteries and thrillers. He has realized that he must first entertain in order to bring his point of view to a wider, more diversified audience, as well as exist and even thrive within the boundaries of motion picture economics

Costa-Gavras   © **Andrew Hamilton Lane**

in the Western world. As Pauline Kael so aptly noted, *Z* is "something very unusual in European films—a political film with a purpose and, at the same time, a thoroughly commercial film." Costa-Gavras, however, is not without controversy: *State of Siege* caused a furor when it was cancelled for political reasons from the opening program of the American Film Institute theater in Washington.

Not all of Costa-Gavras's features are "political": *The Sleeping Car Murders* is a well-made, atmospheric murder mystery, while *Clair de femme* is the dreary tale of a widower and a woman scarred by the death of her young daughter. Both, again, star Yves Montand. But while Costa-Gavras's most characteristic works, do indeed condemn governments that control other governments, or suppress human rights, his concerns as a filmmaker have perhaps shifted towards the more personal. The two features made with scriptwriter Joe Eszterhaus, *Betrayed* and *Music Box*, have won acclaim while focusing on the relationship between the central female character and a man (a lover in *Betrayed*, a father in *Music Box*) who is subsequently revealed as a fascist.

—Rob Edelman

CRAVEN, Wes.

Born Wesley Earl Craven in Cleveland, Ohio, 2 August 1939. Educated at Wheaton College, B.A.; John Hopkins University, M.A. Married, one son, one daughter. College Humanities Professor, left to work as a messenger in a film production house, New York City; assistant editor for Sean Cunningham, from 1970; directed first feature, *Last House on the Left*, 1972, for $90 000 (it made $20 million); also TV director, from 1985. Recipient: Best Director Award, Madrid Festival, 1988. Address: c/o Alive Films, 8271 Melrose Avenue, Los Angeles, CA 90046, U.S.A.; Agent: Andrea Eastman, International Creative Management, 8899 Beverly Boulevard, Los Angeles, CA 90048, U.S.A.

Films as Director and Scriptwriter:

1973   *Last House on the Left* (+ed)
1977   *The Hills Have Eyes* (+ed)
1981   *Deadly Blessing*
1982   *Swamp Thing*
1983   *The Hills Have Eyes, Part II*
1984   *A Nightmare on Elm Street*
1986   *Deadly Friend*
1988   *Serpent and the Rainbow*
1989   *Shocker*

Other Films:

1971   *Together (Sensual Paradise)* (Cunningham) (asst-pr)
1972   *It Happened in Hollywood* (Cunningham) (ed); *You've Got to Walk It Like You Talk It or You'll Lose That Beat* (Cunningham) (ed)
1986   *A Nightmare on Elm Street 3: Dream Warriors* (co-sc, exec pr)
1987   *Flowers in the Attic* (co-sc)

Publications:

By CRAVEN: articles—

Interview with T. Williams, in *Journal of Popular Film* (Washington, D.C.), Fall 1980.
Interviews in *Ecran Fantastique* (Paris), no. 24, 1982, and March 1985.
Interview in *Starburst* (London), April 1982.
Interview with Paul Taylor, in *Monthly Film Bulletin* (London), August 1982.
"Fairy Tales for the Apocalypse," an interview with C. Sharrett, in *Literature/Film Quarterly* (Salisbury, Maryland), vol. 13, no. 3, 1985.
Interview with E. Caron-Lowins, in *Revue du Cinéma* (Paris), April 1985.
Interview in *Cinefantastique* (Oak Park, Illinois), July 1985.
Interview in *Time Out* (London), 29 August 1985.
Interviews in *Hollywood Reporter*, 5 February and 26 August 1988.
Interview with A. Martin, in *Cinema Papers* (Melbourne), November 1988.

On CRAVEN: books—

Meyers, Richard, *For One Week Only: The World of Exploitation Films*, Piscataway, New Jersey, 1983.
Newman, Kim, *Nightmare Movies: A Critical History of the Horror Film from 1968*, London, 1988.

On CRAVEN: articles—

"Wes Craven," in *Image et Son* (Paris), May 1981.
Starburst (London), April and July 1985, and April 1986.
National Film Theatre Booklet (London), June 1988.
Time Out (London), 1 June 1988.

*   *   *

Of all the horror specialists who came to prominence during the 1970's, Wes Craven has had the least settled career. While Tobe Hooper and John Carpenter have had major creative slumps, George Romero and Larry Cohen have carved out their own areas of independent endeavour and David Cronenberg and Brian De Palma have, with various levels of success, graduated to major studio projects, Craven has been bouncing between successes (*The Hills Have Eyes, A Nightmare on Elm Street*) and failures (*Swamp Thing, Deadly Friend*) with a manic energy, forced occasionally to take work on television to keep going. While his best work exhibits a canny grasp of genre and a disturbing understanding of the place of violence within society, and *Elm Street*—after a long and difficult gestation period—emerged as one of the most influential horror movies of the 1980's, his worst films literally flounder in the wake of his successes, frequently (as in *The Hills Have Eyes, Part 2* and *Shocker*) resorting to self-plagiarism to tie together blatantly misconceived projects, suggesting a desperate intellect which too often tries to find a short cut.

Craven's first movie, *Last House on the Left*, a hard-gore remake of Bergman's *The Virgin Spring*, was an ultra-low-budget sleeper that hit the drive-ins well before *The Texas Chain Saw Massacre* and served to drag the genre away from the then-tired mists of Hammer-style gothic towards the more fruitful modern fields of grotty psychosis and social unrest. As with the early films of Romero, Hooper and Cohen, the focus of *Last House* is on the destructive potential of the family, as a group of homicidal maniacs torture a pair of innocent girls and are themselves slaughtered by the martyr heroine's "normal" parents. Filmed with a raw style and a sense of fascinated revulsion, *Last House*—still banned in the United Kingdom—is one of the strongest of horror pictures, and remains so tough that most audiences can't take it, either when the maniacs are disembowelling their victims or the parents are fighting back. *The Hills Have Eyes* is a more expansive, more fantastically horrid re-run of the first movie, stirring in some black humour and an EC Comics-style set of inbred mutants as it replays the wagon train Western scenario out in the desert as a vacationing family of normals clash with their degenerate mirror image. Although it tackles the same thematic territory as *Last House*, *The Hills Have Eyes* is a more approachable work, and shows off Craven's especial skills with simple action, even daring to turn the heroes' dog into a modern movie hero who relates to Rin-Tin-Tin much as Dirty Harry relates to George Dixon.

Despite these two powerful pictures, which at once demonstrated Craven's competence as a director and his flair for the intriguingly horrific, he then fell into a career hole of botched projects, including TV work and an interesting attempt to film David Morell's *First Blood*. *Deadly Blessing* a hotch-potch of psychotic and demonology themes, is alarmingly inconsistent, featuring some of the best and the worst of Craven as it deals with a series of murders in a cleverly-evoked Hittite community, but *Swamp Thing*, an adaption of the DC comic, is a misconceived and childish superhero picture dragged under by ridiculous monster suits and an underdeveloped screenplay, although it has one memorably unchildish scene when Adrienne Barbeau takes a nude swim in the swamp. After this, it is easy to see how Craven could resort to making *The Hills Have Eyes, Part 2*, which contains an inordinate amount of flashback footage from the first film simply because the budget ran out before the movie was actually completed. Although *Deadly Friend* and *Shocker* are more expensively bad, *Hills 2* stands as Craven's worst film.

However, Craven then turned his career round, dashing off the unexceptional but acceptable *Invitation to Hell* and *Chiller* and several pretty good *Twilight Zone* segments—including "Shatterday," a Harlan Ellison story with Bruce Willis, and the disorienting "Word Play"—before finally getting the green light on *A Nightmare on Elm Street*. *Last House* and *Deadly Blessing* had experimented with surreal, disorienting dream sequences—a bit of nightmare dentistry, and a spider-falling-into-mouth shock—but *Elm Street* is built around such moments, and features a dreamstalking bogeyman, Freddy Krueger (Robert Englund), who somehow became a cult hero through the course of four sequels—only one of which, *A Nightmare on Elm Street, Part 3: Dream Warriors*, did Craven have anything to do with, as a writer—and a TV series. The first *Elm Street* is a seamless stalk-and-scare horror movie which fully deserved its success for its clever reassembly of the elements of the school of teenage horror established by Carpenter with *Halloween* and Stephen King in *Carrie* and *Christine*. However, it is a less rigorous, less satisfying movie than Craven's best early films, reducing their ambiguous culture clash to a simple conflict between an innocent heroine (Heather Langenkamp) and an unredeemable monster villain. Part of the disturbing quality of *Last House* and *Hills* comes from their occasionally sympathetic approaches to their villains, and in the way the heroes' violent revenge is seen to degrade them to the level of the monsters, while Langenkamp's guerilla-style assault on Freddy is simply a cheerable demonstration of American resourcefulness.

Leaving the *Elm Street* sequels, which had been set up by a fairly annoying last-minute logical lapse at the end of the first film, to other hands, Craven departed the independent sector for a pair of big studio projects—the execrable *Deadly Friend*,

Wes Craven: *A Nightmare on Elm Street*

a cute-robot-cum-teen-zombie movie adapted from Diana Henstell's novel *Friend*, and *The Serpent and the Rainbow*, an interesting and seductive voodoo picture adapted from Wade Davis' non-fiction novel. Both films carry over the dream theme from *Elm Street*, in the first case to beef up a badly sagging storyline and, in the second, as part of a bizarre and affecting cultural travelogue that develops the old Craven's fascination with magical and monstrous societies as opposed to individuals. However, following that experience, Craven returned to the independents, like John Carpenter before him, and produced another carbon copy of his own most successful work in *Shocker*, which is nothing but an identikit of *A Nightmare on Elm Street* with more ideas than it can handle and severe lapses of script, characterisation and tone to pull it down between its undeniably brilliant sequences (a grand guignol electrocution, a final chase through "television land"). Craven's entire career has been like *Shocker*, with moments of startling inspiration and genre craftsmanship let down by hurried scripts and just plain wrong decisions.

—Kim Newman

CRICHTON, Charles.

British. Born in Wallasey, England, 6 August 1910. Educated at Oundle School and Oxford University. Began as cutter for London Film Productions, 1931; editor on major Korda productions, 1935–40; joined Ealing Studios, 1940; directed first film, *For Those in Peril*, 1944; TV director, from 1960's.

Films as Director:

1944　*For Those in Peril*
1945　*Painted Boats* (*The Girl on the Canal*); "The Golfing Story"
　　　episode of **Dead of Night**
1946　*Hue and Cry*
1948　*Against the Wind; Another Shore*
1949　"The Orchestra Conductor" episode of *Train of Events*
1950　*Dance Hall*
1951　**The Lavender Hill Mob**; *Hunted* (*The Stranger in Between*)
1952　*The Titfield Thunderbolt*
1953　*The Love Lottery*
1954　*The Divided Heart*
1956　*The Man in the Sky* (*Decision Against Time*)
1958　*Law and Disorder; Floods of Fear* (+sc)
1959　*The Battle of the Sexes*
1960　*The Boy Who Stole a Million* (+co-sc)
1964　*The Third Secret*
1965　*He Who Rides a Tiger*
1968　*Tomorrow's Island* (+sc)
1988　*A Fish Called Wanda*, (+ co-sc)

Other Films:

1932　*Men of Tomorrow* (Sagan) (asst ed)
1933　*Cash* (*For Love or Money*) (Z. Korda) (asst ed); **The Private
　　　Life of Henry VIII** (A. Korda) (asst ed); *The Girl from
　　　Maxim's* (A. Korda) (asst ed)
1935　*Sanders of the River* (Z. Korda) (ed); **Things to Come**
　　　(Menzies) (co-assoc ed)
1937　*Elephant Boy* (Flaherty and Z. Korda) (ed); *Twenty-One
　　　Days* (*The First and the Last, Twenty-One Days Together*)
　　　(Dean) (ed)

1938　*Prison without Bars* (Hurst) (ed)
1940　*Old Bill and Son* (Dalrymple) (ed); *The Thief of Bagdad*
　　　(Berger, Powell, Whelan) (ed); *Yellow Caesar* (*The Heel of
　　　Italy*) (Cavalcanti) (ed)
1941　*The Big Blockade* (Frend) (co-ed); *Guests of Honour* (Pitt)
　　　(ed); *Young Veteran* (Cavalcanti) (ed); *Find, Fix and Strike*
　　　(Bennett) (ed, assoc pr)
1942　*Nine Men* (Watt) (ed, assoc pr); *Greek Testament* (*The Shrine
　　　of Victory*) (Hasse) (assoc pr)

Publications:

By CRICHTON: book—

A Fish Called Wanda, with John Cleese, London, 1988.

By CRICHTON: article—

Interview in *Directing Motion Pictures*, edited by Terence Marner,
　New York, 1972.

On CRICHTON: books—

Balcon, Michael, *A Lifetime of Films*, London, 1969.
Barr, Charles, *Ealing Studios*, London, 1977.
Perry, George, *Forever Ealing*, London, 1981.

On CRICHTON: articles—

Tynan, Kenneth, "Ealing: The Studio in Suburbia," in *Films and Film-
　ing* (London), November and December 1955.
Barr, Charles, "Projecting Britain and the British Character: Ealing
　Studios," in *Screen* (London), Summer 1974.
Green, Ian, "Ealing: In the Comedy Frame," in *British Cinema His-
　tory*, edited by James Curran and Vincent Porter, London, 1983.
Barr, Charles, "Charles Crichton," in *Edinburgh Film Festival Book-
　let*, 1988.
Falk, Quentin, "*Wanda*: Cleese, Crichton, and Man-Management,"
　in *Sight and Sound* (London), Spring 1988.
Listener (London), 13 October 1988.

*　　　*　　　*

The demise of Ealing Studios seemed to cast a blight on the careers of those who worked there. Within ten years of the final Ealing release virtually all the studio's leading directors—Mackendrick, Hamer, Harry Watt, Charles Frend—had shot their last film; only Basil Dearden was still active. And until recently the career of Charles Crichton appeared to have followed the same dispiriting pattern. His triumphant comeback at the age of 78, with the huge international success of *A Fish Called Wanda*, was as heartening as it was wholly unexpected.

Wanda kicks off with a jewel heist sequence notable for the wit and precision of its editing. Like several of his Ealing colleagues Crichton started out in the cutting room, working for Korda on *Things to Come* and *The Thief of Bagdad*, and was said to be one of the finest editors in the British film industry. (Among his uncredited achievements is the rescue of Mackendrick's *Whisky Galore*, which he recut after it had been botched by its original editor.) A sense of pace and timing, the skilled editor's stock-in-trade, distinguishes all his best work.

Comedy has always been seen as Crichton's forte. His reputation, prior to *Wanda*, rested on the three comedies he directed at Ealing to scripts by T E B Clarke: *Hue and Cry*, *The Lavender Hill Mob*, and *The Titfield Thunderbolt*. If all three seem to belong more to the writer's oeuvre than to the director's, this may be because Crichton has always been dependent in his comedies on the quality of the script. *Lavender Hill Mob*, perhaps the archetypal comedy of the Ealing mainstream, gains enormously from his supple comic timing; but given stodgy material, as in *The Love Lottery* or *Another Shore*, his lightness of touch deserts him. Even *Titfield*, with Clarke writing some way below his best, feels sluggish and under-directed beside its two predecessors.

Charles Crichton directing *The Divided Heart*

Though the serious side of Crichton's output, the dramas and thrillers, has attracted little attention, he often seems here less at the mercy of his script, able to make something personal even of flawed material. His one non-comedy with Clarke, the Resistance drama *Against the Wind*, has a downbeat realism, a refusal of easy heroics, that recalls Thorold Dickinson's *Next of Kin* (and probably ensured its failure at the post-war box-office). *Hunted*, a killer-on-the-run thriller, builds up a complex tension, as well as offering Dirk Bogarde a rare intelligent role amid the dross of his early career. And Crichton's cool, unemphatic handling of the central conflict in *The Divided Heart* deftly avoids emotional overkill—though nothing, perhaps, could have prevented the film's final slide into sententiousness.

After Ealing, projects attuned to his talents became increasingly rare. Given the darker aspects of his work, black comedy was clearly well within his range, and *The Battle of the Sexes*, with Peter Sellers as the Scots clerk trying to bump off efficiency expert Constance Cummings, would have been ideal—were it not for a script that junked the quiet implacability of the original (Thurber's caustic tour-de-force *The Catbird Seat*) for cautious whimsy and a vapid happy ending. After a couple of interestingly off-beat thrillers—*The Third*

Secret and *He Who Rides a Tiger*—both marred by clumsy writing and uncertainty of tone, Crichton cut his losses and retreated into television.

From there, directing corporate videos must have seemed like a further downhill step. But the company involved was John Cleese's Video Arts, and it was Cleese's enthusiastic backing—and his status as a bankable star—that enabled Crichton, after more than twenty years, to return to the cinema. *A Fish Called Wanda*, with its four ill-assorted crooks, its central portrait of respectability undermined by larcenous urges, and its running theme of internecine treachery, crosses *The Lavender Hill Mob* with *The Ladykillers*—and adds a degree of sex and violence that would certainly have alarmed Michael Balcon. But had Ealing comedy survived Balcon's death and lived on into the late 1980's *Wanda* is most likely what it would have looked like—and its bite and vitality only inspire regret for the films left unmade during Crichton's years in the wilderness.

—Philip Kemp

CROMWELL, John.

American. Born Elwood Dager in Toledo, Ohio, 23 December 1887. Educated at Howe High School, Howe, Indiana, 1901–05. Married 1) Alice Indahl; 2) Marie Goff; 3) Kay Johnson; 4) Ruth Nelson; one son. Actor on Broadway, from 1910; theatre director for William Brady, from 1913; actor and stage director, New York Repertory Theatre, 1915–1919 (military service 1917–18); stage actor-producer to 1928; hired by Paramount as dialogue director, 1928; directed first film, *Close Harmony*, 1929; hired by RKO, 1933; President, Screen Actors' Guild, 1944–45; returns to Broadway, 1951, and to repertory theatre, 1960's. *Died in Santa Barbara, California, 26 September 1979.*

Films as Director:

1929	*Close Harmony* (co-d); *The Dance of Life* (co-d with Sutherland, role as doorkeeper); *The Mighty* (+ role as Mr. Jamieson)
1930	*The Street of Chance* (+ role as Imbrie); *The Texan*; *Seven Days Leave* (*Medals*); *For the Defense*; *Tom Sawyer*
1931	*Scandal Sheet*; *Unfaithful*; *Vice Squad*; *Rich Man's Folly*
1932	*The World and the Flesh*
1933	*Sweepings*; *The Silver Cord*
1934	*Of Human Bondage*; *The Fountain*; *Jalna*; *I Dream Too Much*
1936	*Little Lord Fauntleroy*; *To Mary with Love*; *Banjo on My Knee*
1937	*The Prisoner of Zenda*
1938	*Algiers*
1939	*Made for Each Other*; *In Name Only*
1940	*Abe Lincoln in Illinois* (*Spirit of the People*) (+role as John Brown); *Victory*
1941	*So Ends Our Night*
1942	*Son of Fury*
1944	*Since You Went Away*
1945	*The Enchanted Cottage*
1946	*Anna and the King of Siam*
1947	*Dead Reckoning*; *Night Song*
1950	*Caged*
1951	*The Company She Keeps*; *The Racket*
1958	*The Goddess*
1959	*The Scavengers*
1960	*De Sista Stegen* (*A Matter of Morals*)

Other Films:

1929	*The Dummy* (R. Milton) (role as Walter Babbing)
1957	*Top Secret Affair* (*Their Secret Affair*) (H.C. Potter) (role as General Grimshaw)
1977	*Three Women* (Altman) (role)
1978	*A Wedding* (Altman) (role as cardinal)

Publications:

By CROMWELL: articles—

Interview with D. Lyons, in *Interview* (New York), February 1972.
Interview with Leonard Maltin, in *Action* (Los Angeles), May/June 1973.

On CROMWELL: articles—

G.D., "*The Goddess*," in *Films in Review* (New York), May 1958.
Rotha, Paul, in *Films and Filming* (London), August 1958.
Prouse, Derek, in *Sight and Sound* (London), Autumn 1958.
Sarris, Andrew, "Likable But Elusive," in *Film Culture* (New York), Spring 1963.
Cutts, John, "The Finest Zenda of Them All," in *Cinema* (Beverly Hills), Spring 1968.
Frey, R., "John Cromwell," in *Sight and Sound* (London), Autumn 1972.

Canham, Kingsley, "John Cromwell: Memories of Love, Elegance, and Style," in *The Hollywood Professionals*, Vol.5, London, 1976.
Bleys, J.-P., "John Cromwell ou la mélodie du mélodrame," in *Cahiers de la Cinémathèque* (Perpignan), no.28, 1979.
"Cromwell Section," in *Positif* (Paris), March 1979.
Obituary in *New York Times*, 28 September 1979.
Obituary in *Cinéma* (Paris), March 1980.

*   *   *

John Cromwell was a very fine New York actor, and had a distinguished list of credits when he was hired by Paramount in 1928. Talking films were a new medium then, and Cromwell was eminently qualified to direct dialogue. He started in collaboration with Edward Sutherland on *Close Harmony* and *The Dance of Life* (from the play, *Broadway*), and then Paramount promoted him to solo status, on such films as *The Street of Chance* with William Powell, and *The Texan* and *Seven Days Leave*, both with Gary Cooper.

Once established as an ace director, he went over to the new RKO studios where in 1933 he directed such movies as *The Silver Cord* (from Sidney Howard's play), starring Irene Dunne with Joel McCrea; and the adaptation of Maugham's novel *Of Human Bondage* with Leslie Howard and Bette Davis. He met David O. Selznick at this time, and subsequently directed such Selznick films as *Little Lord Fauntleroy, The Prisoner of Zenda, Made for Each Other*, and *Since You Went Away*.

Meanwhile, he continued as director for such RKO successes as *In Name Only*, with Cary Grant, Carole Lombard, and Kay Francis; and Robert Sherwood's *Abe Lincoln in Illinois* starring Raymond Massey. He also directed Hedy Lamarr's American film debut with Charles Boyer in *Algiers, Victory*, from the Joseph Conrad novel, and *So Ends Our Night*, a remarkably tense melodrama of World War, with Fredric March, Margaret Sullavan, Glenn Ford, Frances Dee, and Erich von Stroheim.

In 1944 Harriet Parsons at RKO signed him as director for *The Enchanted Cottage*, a sensitive drama of a plain girl (Dorothy McGuire) and a scarred, crippled war veteran (Robert Young) who begin to see one another as straight and beautiful through the power of love. By this time, Cromwell was a thorough craftsman. He believed in full rehearsals with camera before any shooting took place. "For every day of full rehearsal you give me," he was fond of saying, "I'll knock off a day on the shooting schedule." At RKO they gave him three days for rehearsal, and he obligingly came in three days early. *The Enchanted Cottage* was a tricky assignment; the love story was so sensitive that it could easily slip into sentimentality, but it never did. He treated it realistically, and as he said, "It's the only way to treat a fantasy. It always works."

Cromwell directed Irene Dunne and Rex Harrison in *Anna and the King of Siam*, a film of great pictorial beauty. His best subsequently were a woman's prison story, *Caged*, and *The Goddess*, a realistic story about a film star.

Cromwell was falsely accused by Howard Hughes of being a Communist during the McCarthy era. "I was never anything that suggested a Red," he said, "and there never was the slightest evidence with which to accuse me of being one." He was black-listed, however, and the assignments ceased coming his way. He simply returned to the theatre as an actor, and was brilliant as Henry Fonda's father in the stage play of John Marquand's, *Point of No Return*.

—DeWitt Bodeen

CRONENBERG, David.

Canadian. Born in Toronto, 15 May 1943. Studied at University of Toronto, B.A. 1967. After making two short films, made first feature, *Stereo*, 1969; travelled to France, directed filler material for French and Canadian TV, 1971. Address: David Cronenberg Productions, 217 Avenue Road, Toronto M5R 2J3, Canada. Agent: Michael Narcus, Creative Artists Agency, 1888 Century Park E., Suite 1400, Los Angeles, CA 90067, U.S.A.

Films as Director and Scriptwriter:

1966   *Transfer* (short) (+ph, ed)
1967   *From the Drain* (short) (+ph, ed)
1969   *Stereo* (+pr, ph, ed)
1970   *Crimes of the Future* (+pr, ph)
1975   *Shivers (They Came from Within. The Parasite Murders. Frissons)*
1976   *Rabid (Rage)*
1978   *Fast Company; The Brood*
1979   *Scanners*
1982   *Videodrome*
1983   *The Dead Zone* (d only)
1986   ***The Fly*** (+role as gynaecologist)
1988   *Dead Ringers (Twins)*

Other Films:

1985   *Into the Night* (Landis) (role)
1989   *Nightbreed* (Barker) (role)

Publications:

By CRONENBERG: articles—

Interview in *Ecran Fantastique* (Paris), no. 2, 1977.
Interview in *Time Out* (London), 6 January 1978.
Interview in *Cinema Canada* (Montreal), September/October 1978.
Interview in *Starburst* (London), nos. 36/37, 1981.
Interview in *Films* (London), June 1981.
Interviews in *Ecran Fantastique* (Paris), June and November 1983.
Interview with S. Ayscough, in *Cinema Canada* (Montreal), December 1983.
Interview in *Starburst* (London), May 1984.
Interview with C. Tesson and T. Cazals, in *Cahiers du Cinéma* (Paris), January 1987.
Interview with Brent Lewis, in *Films and Filming* (London), February 1987.
Interview in *Film Comment* (New York), September/October 1988.
Interview in *American Film* (Washington, D.C.), October 1988.
Interview in *Cinefex* (Riverside, California), November 1988.
Interview with Derek Malcolm, in the *Guardian* (London), 29 December 1989.

On CRONENBERG: books—

McCarty, John, *Splatter Movies: Breaking the Last Taboo*, New York, 1981.
Handling, Piers, editor, *The Shape of Rage: The Films of David Cronenberg*, Toronto, 1983.
Drew, Wayne, editor, *David Cronenberg*, London, 1984.
Newman, Kim, *Nightmare Movies: A Critical History of the Horror Film from 1968*, London, 1988.

On CRONENBERG: articles—

Film Comment (New York), March/April 1980.
"Cronenberg Section" of *Cinema Canada* (Montreal), March 1981.
"Cronenberg Section" of *Cinefantastique* (Oak Park, Illinois), Spring 1981.
Sutton, M., "Schlock! Horror! The Films of David Cronenberg," in *Films and Filming* (London), October 1982.

Harkness, J., "The Word, the flesh, and the Films of David Cronenberg," in *Cinema Canada* (Montreal), June 1983.
Sharrett, C., "Myth and Ritual in the Post-Industrial Landscape: The Films of David Cronenberg," in *Persistence of Vision* (Maspeth, New York), Summer 1986.
Edelstein, R., "Lord of the Fly," in *Village Voice* (New York), 19 August 1986.
Lucas, Tim, in *American Cinematographer* (Los Angeles), September 1986.
"*The Fly* Issue" of *Starburst* (London), January 1987.
"*The Fly* Issue" of *Ecran Fantastique* (Paris), January 1987.
Newman, Kim, "King in a Small Field," in *Monthly Film Bulletin* (London), February 1987.
Time Out (London), 11 February 1987.
Revue du Cinéma (Paris), May 1987.

*   *   *

David Cronenberg's breakthrough movie, *Shivers*, carries over the Burroughsian mind-and-body-bending themes of his underground pictures—*Stereo* and *Crimes of the Future*—but also benefits from the influence of Romero's *Night of the Living Dead* and Siegel's *Invasion of the Body Snatchers* in its horror movie imagery, relentless pacing and general vision of a society falling apart, locating Cronenberg at the centre of the thriving 1970's horror movement that produced such figures as Romero, Larry Cohen, John Carpenter, Wes Craven and Tobe Hooper. As a mad scientist's creations, a horde of creeping parasites that look like phallic turds, infect people with a combination of venereal disease and aphrodisiac, a chilly, luxurious, modernist skyscraper apartment building becomes a Boschian nightmare of blood and carnality. An undisciplined film, *Shivers* gains from its scattershot approach. Cronenberg has since proved himself capable of more control but, in a movie about the encroachment of chaos upon order, it's appropriate that the narrative itself should break down. While strong enough in its mix of sex and violence to give fuel to critics who view Cronenberg as a reactionary moralist, it is clear that his approach is ambiguous, and that he is as concerned with the anomie of the normality disrupted as he is with the nature of the outbreak. The orgiastic solution of the blood parasites may be too extreme, but the soulless routine they replace suggests the straight world deserves to be eaten away from within.

His follow-up movies, *Rabid*, *The Brood*, and *Scanners*, develop the themes of *Shivers*—although his odd-man-out film, the drag-racing drama *Fast Company* comes from this period also—and gradually struggle away from impersonal nihilism. *Rabid* is a plague story, with Marilyn Chambers quite affecting as the Typhoid Mary, while *The Brood* is an intense family melodrama about child abuse triggered by Nola (Samantha Eggar), a mad mother who can manifest her anger as murderous malformed children, and *Scanners* concerns itself with the feuds of a race of telepaths who co-exist with humanity and are unsure whether to conquer or save the world. With its exploding heads and car chases, *Scanners* is a progression away from the venereal apocalypse of the earlier films and is almost an upbeat movie after the icy down-ness of *The Brood*. *Scanners* has the typical early Cronenberg construction: it crams in more ideas than it can possibly deal with and tears through its overly-complex plot so quickly that the holes only become apparent when it's all over. The unrelenting action of *Shivers* and *Rabid* show a society tearing itself apart; and, given the breakup of Nola's family, the incestuous cruelty of *The Brood* is inevitable; but *Scanners* follows a purposeful conflict between opposing, highly-motivated sides, out of which a new world will emerge. If *The Brood* finds a balance between mind and body, *Scanners* finally achieves a hard-won harmony. *Crimes of the Future*, *Shivers*, *Rabid* and *The Brood* all end with the persistent disease threatening to spread. In

David Cronenberg directing Jeremy Irons in *Dead Ringers*

Scanners, for the first time in a David Cronenberg film, the Good Guys win.

Cronenberg closed this phase of his career with *Videodrome*, which summed up his work to date. Structurally reminiscent of *Shivers*, the film follows Max Renn (James Woods), a cable TV hustler whose justification for his channel's output of "softcore pornography and hardcore violence" is "better on television than in the streets." Renn is trying to track down a pirate station that's transmitting *Videodrome*, "a show that's just torture and murder. No plot. No characters. Very realistic," because he thinks "it's the coming thing." Underneath the stimulating images of sex and violence is a signal which causes a tumor in Renn's brain that makes him subject to hallucinations which increasingly take over the flow of the film, completely fracturing reality with disturbing developments of Cronenberg's by-now familiar bodily evolutions. A television set pulses with life and Renn buries his head in its mammary screen as he kisses the image of his fantasy lover (Deborah Harry). A vaginal slot grows from a rash on his stomach and the villains plunge living videocassettes into it which program him as an assassin. His hand and gun grow together to create a sickening biomechanical synthesis. Once Renn has been exposed to *Videodrome*, the film cannot hope to sustain its storyline, and, as Paul Taylor wrote in *Monthly Film Bulletin*, "becomes most akin to sitting before a TV screen while someone else switches channels at random."

After travelling so far into his own personal—and uncommercial—nightmare, Cronenberg felt the need to ease off by tackling an uncomplicated project. *The Dead Zone*, a bland but efficient adaption of Stephen King's novel, is the only film he has directed without having been involved in the writing. Having proved that he could work in the mainstream, Cronenberg turned to more personal projects that still somehow pass as commercial cinema, keeping up a miraculous balancing act that has put him, in a career sense, on a much more solid footing than Romero, Hooper, Cohen, Carpenter or Craven, all of whom he has outstripped. *The Fly*, a major studio remake of the 1958 monster movie, is despite its budget and lavish special effects a quintessentially Cronenbergian movie, pruning away the expected melodrama to concentrate on a single relationship, between Seth Brundle (Jeff Goldblum), a gawky scientist whose teleportation device has set in motion a metamorphosis that turns him into an insect, and his horrified but compassionate lover (Geena Davis). *The Fly* is an even more concentrated, intimate movie than *The Brood*, with only three main characters and one major setting. Like Rabid Rose and Max Renn, Brundle remains himself as he changes, tossing away nervous remarks about his collection of dropped-off body parts, giving an amusingly disgusting TV-chef-style demonstration of the flylike manner in which the new creature eats a doughnut, humming "I know an old lady who swallowed a fly," and treating his mutation as a voyage of discovery.

Based on a true-life *National Enquirer* headline ("Twin Docs Found Dead in Posh Pad"), *Dead Ringers* follows the lives of Beverly and Elliot Mantle, identical twins (Jeremy Irons) who develop a precocious interest in the problems of sex and the female anatomy and grow up to be a world-beating team of gynaecologists, and find their intense relationship, when unbalanced by the presence of a third party (Genevieve Bujold), eventually leads to their destruction. The film takes fear of surgery about as far as it can go when Beverly, increasingly infuriated that women's bodies don't conform to his textbooks, brings in a Giger-ish surrealist metalworker to create a set of "Gynaecological Instruments for Operating on Mutant Women." In the theatre, Beverly is kitted up in scarlet robes more suited to a mass and horrifyingly blunders through a supposedly simple operation, wielding these bizarre and distorted implements. The home stretch is profoundly depressing, and yet deeply moving, as the twins come to resemble each other more and more in their degradation; the calculating Elliot following Beverly into drug addiction on the theory that only if the Mantle brothers really become identical can the two inadequate personalities separate from each other and get back to some kind of functioning normality. Too often genre publications sneer at film-makers who achieve success with horror but then claim they want to move on, but notions of genre are inherently limiting, and Cronenberg is entirely justified in leaving behind the warmed-over science fiction elements of his earlier films and concentrating on a more intellectual, character-based mode. For the first time, he is able to present the inhuman condition without recourse (one slightly too blatant dream sequence apart, as in *The Fly*) to slimy special effects, borrowings from earlier horror films and the trappings of conventional melodrama. This is not the work of someone trying for the commercial high ground, and it certainly isn't by any stretch of the imagination a mainstream movie. *Dead Ringers* isn't a horror film. It's a David Cronenberg film, and entering the 1990's, that put it at the cutting edge of the nightmare cinema.

—Kim Newman

———

CRUZE, James.

American. Born Jens Cruz Bosen in Five Points, near Ogden, Utah, 27 March 1884. Studied at "Colonel" F. Cooke Caldwell dramatic school, 1900–03. Married 1) actress Marguerite Snow, 1913 (divorced 1924); 2) actress Betty Compson, 1924 (divorced 1930). Left home, went to San Francisco, 1900; barker (selling snake-bite cure) for Billy Banks Travelling Stock Co., then organized own troupe, 1903; member of Belasco company, New York, 1906; joined Thanhouser Film Company as featured player, 1911; joined Lasky company, 1916, began directing, 1918; began production company James Cruze Inc., 1927 (James Cruze Productions Inc., 1929). *Died 3 August 1942.*

Films as Director:

1918 *Too Many Millions*; *The Dub*
1919 *Alias Mike Moran*; *The Roaring Road*; *You're Fired*; *The Love Burglar*; *The Valley of the Giants*; *The Lottery Man*; *An Adventure in Hearts*; *Hawthorne of the U.S.A.*
1920 *Terror Island*; *Mrs. Temple's Telegram*; *The Sins of St. Anthony*; *What Happened to Jones*; *A Full House*; *Food for Scandal*; *Always Audacious*; *The Charm School*
1921 *The Dollar-a-Year Man*; *Crazy to Marry*; *Gasoline Gus*; *The Fast Freight* (*Freight Prepaid, Via Fast Freight*) (unreleased)
1922 *Leap Year* (*Skirt Shy*) (unreleased); *One Glorious Day*; *Is Matrimony a Failure?*; *The Dictator*; *The Old Homestead*; *Thirty Days*

1923 *The Covered Wagon*; *Hollywood*; *Ruggles of Red Gap*; *To the Ladies*
1924 *The Fighting Coward*; *The Enemy Sex*; *Merton of the Movies*; *The City That Never Sleeps*; *The Garden of Weeds*
1925 *Waking Up the Town* (+co-story); *The Goose Hangs High*; *Welcome Home*; *Marry Me*; *Beggar on Horseback*; *The Pony Express*
1926 *Mannequin*; *Old Ironsides* (*Sons of the Sea*); *The Waiter from the Ritz* (unreleased)
1927 *We're All Gamblers*; *The City Gone Wild*; *On to Reno*
1928 *The Mating Call*; *The Red Mark*; *Excess Baggage* (+pr)
1929 *A Man's Man* (+pr); *The Duke Steps Out* (+pr); *The Great Gabbo*
1930 *Once a Gentleman*; *She Got What She Wanted*
1931 *Salvation Nell*
1932 *Racetrack*; *Washington Merry-Go-Round* (*Invisible Power*); "The Condemned Man" episode (or, according to other sources, "The Streetwalker" and "The Old Ladies' Home" episodes) of *If I Had a Million*
1933 *Sailor Be Good*; *I Cover the Waterfront*; *Mr. Skitch*
1934 *David Harum*; *Their Big Moment* (*Afterwards*); *Helldorado*
1935 *Two-Fisted*
1936 *Sutter's Gold*
1937 *The Wrong Road*
1938 *Prison Nurse*; *Gangs of New York*; *Come On Leather-necks*

Other Films:

1911 *A Boy of the Revolution* (role); *The Higher Law* (Nicholls) (role); *She* (Nicholls) (role)
1912 *Dr. Jekyll and Mr. Hyde* (Henderson) (role); *The Arab's Bride* (Nicholls) (role); *On Probation* (role); *Flying to Fortune* (role); *For Sale—A Life* (role); *Into the Desert* (Nicholls) (role); *Rejuvenation* (role); *Miss Arabella Snaith* (role); *Love's Miracle* (role); *Jess* (Nicholls) (role); *The Ring of a Spanish Grandee* (role); *East Lynne* (Nicholls) (role); *Called Back* (Nicholls) (role); *Whom God Hath Joined* (Nicholls) (role); *Lucille* (role); *Undine* (role); *But the Greatest of These Is Charity* (role); *Put Yourself in His Place* (role); *Miss Robinson Crusoe* (role); *When Mercy Tempers Justice* (role); *The Thunderbolt* (role); *Cross Your Heart* (role); *The Other Half* (role); *A Militant Suffragette* (role); *The Cry of the Children* (role); *The Star of Bethlehem* (role)
1913 *The Dove in the Eagle's nest* (Marston) (role); *A Poor Relation* (role); *The Tiniest of Stars* (When the Studio Burned* (Marston) (role); *Good Morning, Judge* (role); *Napoleon's Lucky Stone* (role); *The Idol of the Hour* (role); *Her Gallant Knights* (role); *For Her Boy's Sake* (role); *Cymbeline* (role); *The Woman Who Did Not Care* (role); *The Marble Heart* (role); *Her Sister's Secret* (role); *The Snare of Fate* (role); *The Lost Combination* (role); *Tannhauser* (role); *Rosie's Revenge* (role); *The Ward of the King* (role); *The Message of Headquarters* (Heffron) (role); *Plot Against the Governor* (role); *A Girl Worth While* (role)
1914 *Joseph in the Land of Egypt* (Moore) (role); *Frou Frou* (role); *The Legend of Provence* (role); *Why Reginald Reformed* (role); *The Woman Pays* (role); *Cardinal Richelieu's Ward* (role); *A Leak in the Foreign Office* (role); *The Desert Tribesman* (role); *The Cat's Paw* (role); *The Million Dollar Mystery* (Hansel) (serial) (role); *A Debut in the Secret Service* (role); *A Mohammedan Conspiracy* (role); *From Wash to Washington* (role); *Zudora* (*The Zudora Mystery*) (Sullivan) (serial) (role)
1915 *The Twenty Million Dollar Mystery* (Hansel) (serial) (role); *The Heart of Princess Mitsari* (role); *The Patriot and the Spy* (role); *His Guardian Auto* (role); *Armstrong's Wife* (role)
1916 *The Snowbird* (Carewe) (role)
1917 *What Money Can't Buy* (Tellegen) (role); *The Call of the East* (Melford) (role); *Nan of Music Mountain* (Melford) (role)
1918 *Hidden Pearls* (Melford) (role); *Wild Youth* (Melford) (role); *Believe Me Xantippe* (Crisp) (role); *The Source* (Melford) (role); *Under the Top* (Crisp) (role)
1919 *Johnny Get Your Gun* (Crisp) (role)

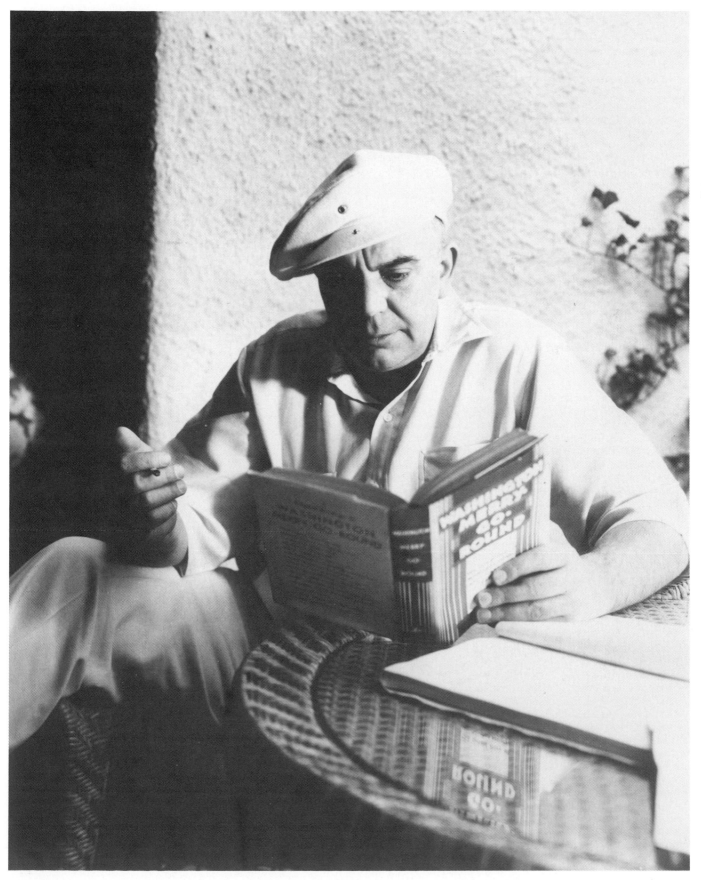

James Cruze

Publications:

By CRUZE: articles—

"Jimmie Cruze," an interview with Frank Condon, in *Photoplay* (New York), September 1914.
Interview in *Motion Picture Classic* (Brooklyn), November 1918.

On CRUZE: books—

Everson, William K., and George N. Fenin, *The Western: From Silents to Cinerama*, New York, 1962; revised edition, as *The Western: From Silents to the Seventies*, 1977.
Brownlow, Kevin, *The War, The West, and the Wilderness*, New York, 1979.
Buscombe, Ed, editor, *The BFI Companion to the Western*, London, 1989.

On CRUZE: articles—

Donnell, D., "Cruze, Trail-Breaker," in *Motion Picture Classic* (Brooklyn), September 1925.
Condon, Frank, "Cruze, Director," in *Collier's* (New York), 28 March 1936.
Obituary in *New York Times*, 5 August 1942.
Obituary in *Time* (New York), 17 August 1942.
Geltzer, George, "James Cruze," in *Films in Review* (New York), June/July 1954.
Cohen, J., "Cruze's Last Efforts," in *Films in Review* (New York), August/September 1954.
Starman, R., "James Cruze—Cinema's Forgotten Director," in *Films in Review* (New York), October 1985.
Brown, Karl, "James Cruze," in *Films in Review* (New York), April 1986.

*   *   *

James Cruze was selected in the "Film Daily" annual nationwide poll as one of the top-ten Hollywood directors in 1926 and 1928. During the year in between, he was the highest salaried one, earning an impressive $7,000 a week. Yet, today, Cruze is no more than a footnote in film history, long deceased and long forgotten. His career did survive the advent of sound but, unlike Ford and Lubitsch and others, he did not really thrive. Cruze was far from a great director: even at his peak, his films were awkwardly constructed, unimaginative and even monotonous. But they were extremely popular, and his career is not unworthy of reappraisal.

Cruze began working in Hollywood in front of the camera, playing leads at Pathé and Thanhouser; in the second decade of the century, he was Thanhouser's most popular male star. He first directed Wallace Reid in *Too Many Millions*, then guided the actor through romantic farces and melodramas. He also made Fatty Arbuckle comedies.

Cruze's great contribution to cinema history came in 1923, with *The Covered Wagon*. The film is stagily directed, and plays quite badly today, but it is the first of its kind: a large-scale, larger-than-life western drama of epic proportion, centering on the travails of a wagon train on its way west. Previously, westerns focused mostly on character interaction and drama; while these ingredients are noticably lacking in *The Covered Wagon*, Cruze in this film was the first to open up and explore the possibility of setting them in the wide open spaces of the Southwest. Additionally, the film was responsible for renewing audience interest in westerns, which despite the popularity of Tom Mix and a few others, had been in decline. Cruze later unsuccessfully tried to repeat *The Covered Wagon*'s popularity with *The Pony Express*, *Old Ironsides* and, during the 1930's, *Sutter's Gold*, the latter almost bankrupting Universal Pictures.

Cruze also directed two of the early satires detailing the frustrations of hopeful youngsters who trek from small towns to Hollywood in the hope of motion picture stardom: *Hollywood* and *Merton of the Movies*. In 1927, he organized his own independent production-distribution organization, and then made

The Great Gabbo, one of the earliest talkies. Erich von Stroheim starred in this bizarre drama of an egomaniacal, intolerant ventriloquist whose love for a dancer is communicated via the mouth of his dummy. There have subsequently been numerous variations on this theme, most memorably in the Cavalcanti classic, *Dead of Night*, and the atmospheric, underrated 1960's mystery, *Devil Doll*.

Cruze's sound films are not all potboilers. He made *Washington Merry Go Round*, a political drama, the May Robson sequence in *If I Had a Million*, Will Rogers' *David Harum* and a solid drama, *I Cover the Waterfront*. But his star rapidly dimmed and, like so many other silent era personalities, his decline was striking. His last credits before retiring in 1938 were such Republic "B" films as *Prison Nurse*, *Gangs of New York* and *Come On, Leathernecks*.

As the Associated Press reported, on his death in 1942, "James Cruze, former motion picture director and producer, once had a hilltop mansion and a million dollars, but when he died, Aug. 3, his estate was valued at only $1,000."

—Rob Edelman

CUKOR, George.

American. Born George Dewey Cukor in New York, 7 July 1899. Educated at DeWitt Clinton High School, New York. Served in U.S. armed forces, directed film for the Signal Corps., 1943. Stage manager on Broadway, 1919–24; manager, stock company in Rochester, New York, and director, New York City, 1924–26; stage director, New York, 1926–29; co-director for Paramount, Hollywood, 1929–32; joined RKO, began association with Katharine Hepburn, 1932; began association with writers Ruth Gordon and Garson Kanin, 1947. Recipient: Oscar for Best Director, and Directors Guild of America Award, for *My Fair Lady*, 1964; Honorary doctorates, University of Southern California, 1968, and Loyola University, Chicago, 1976; D.W. Griffith Award, Directors Guild of America, 1981; Golden Lion, Venice Festival, 1982. *Died 24 January 1983.*

Films as Director:

1930   *Grumpy* (co-d); *The Virtuous Sin* (co-d); *The Royal Family of Broadway* (co-d)
1931   *Tarnished Lady*; *Girls About Town*
1932   *What Price Hollywood?*; *A Bill of Divorcement*; *Rockabye*; *One Hour With You* (co-d with Lubitsch, uncredited, + dialogue director); *The Animal Kingdom* (co-d, uncredited)
1933   *Our Betters*; *Dinner at Eight*; *Little Women*; *David Copperfield* (*The Personal History, Adventures, Experience, and Observations of David Copperfield, the Younger*); *No More Ladies* (co-d, uncredited)
1936   *Sylvia Scarlett*; *Romeo and Juliet*
1937   **Camille**
1938   *Holiday*
1939   *Zaza*; *The Women*; **Gone With the Wind** (co-d, uncredited)
1940   *Susan and God*; **The Philadelphia Story**
1941   *A Woman's Face*; *Two-Faced Woman*
1942   *Her Cardboard Lover*
1943   *Keeper of the Flame*
1944   *Gaslight*; *Winged Victory*
1945   *I'll Be Seeing You* (co-d, uncredited)
1947   *A Double Life*; *Desire Me* (co-d, uncredited)
1949   *Edward My Son*; **Adam's Rib**
1950   *A Life of Her Own*; **Born Yesterday**

George Cukor

1951 *The Model and the Marriage Broker*
1952 *The Marrying Kind; Pat and Mike*
1953 *The Actress*
1954 *It Should Happen to You; A Star is Born*
1956 *Bhowani Junction*
1957 *Les Girls; Wild is the Wind*
1958 *Hot Spell* (co-d, uncredited)
1960 *Heller in Pink Tights; Let's Make Love; Song Without End*
    (co-d, uncredited)
1962 *The Chapman Report*
1964 *My Fair Lady*
1969 *Justine*
1972 *Travels With My Aunt*
1975 *Love Among the Ruins* (for TV)
1976 *The Bluebird*
1979 *The Corn is Green* (for TV)
1981 *Rich and Famous*

Other Films:

1929 *River of Romance* (Wallace) (dialogue d)
1930 **All Quiet on the Western Front** (Milestone) (dialogue d)

Publications:

By CUKOR: articles—

Interview with Eric Rohmer and Jean Domarchi, in *Cahiers du Cinéma* (Paris), January 1961.
"Conversation with George Cukor," with John Gillett and David Robinson, in *Sight and Sound* (London), Autumn 1964.
Interview with Richard Overstreet, in *Interviews with Film Directors* edited by Andrew Sarris, New York, 1969.
Interview, in *The Celluloid Muse* by Charles Higham and Joel Greenberg, New York, 1972.
Interview with Gene Phillips, in *Film Comment* (New York), Spring 1972.
"Cukor and Cukor," with J. Calendo, in *Interview* (New York), December 1973.
"The Director," in *Hollywood Directors: 1914–40* edited by Richard Koszarski, New York, 1976.
"Surviving," an interview with John Taylor, in *Sight and Sound* (London), Summer 1977.
"Dialogue on Film: George Cukor," edited by James Powers, in *American Film* (Washington, D.C.), February 1978.
"Carry On, Cukor," with J. McBride and T. McCarthy, in *Film Comment* (New York), September/October 1981.
Interview with Gene D. Phillips, in *Films and Filming* (London), January 1982.
Interview with J.-P. Le Pavec and D. Rabourdin, in *Cinéma* (Paris), March 1982.

On CUKOR: books—

Langlois, Henri, and others, *Hommage a George Cukor*, Paris, 1963.
Domarchi, Jean, *George Cukor*, Paris, 1965.
Carey, Gary, *Cukor and Company: The Films of George Cukor and His Collaborators*, New York, 1971.
Lambert, Gavin, *On Cukor*, New York, 1972.
Clarens, Carlos, *George Cukor*, London, 1976.
Phillips, Gene D., *George Cukor*, Boston, 1982.
Bernadoni, James, *George Cukor: A Critical Study and Filmography*, Jefferson, North Carolina, 1985.
Haver, Ronald, *A Star is Born: The Making of the 1954 Movie and its 1983 Restoration*, London, 1989.

On CUKOR: articles—

Houston, Penelope, "Cukor and the Kanins," in *Sight and Sound* (London), Spring 1955.
Tozzi, Romano, "George Cukor: His Success Directing Women Has Obscured His Other Directorial Virtues," in *Films in Review* (New York), February 1958.
Reid, John, "So He Became a Lady's Man," in *Films and Filming* (London), August 1960.
"Retrospective Cukor" issue of *Cahiers du Cinéma* (Paris), February 1964.

Buscombe, Ed, "On Cukor," in *Screen* (London), Autumn 1973.
Grisolia, M., "George Cukor, ou comment le desir vient aux femmes," in *Cinéma* (Paris), February 1974.
McBride, J., "George Cukor: The Blue Bird," in *Action* (Los Angeles), November/December 1975.
Friedman, A., "George Cukor: A Tribute," in *Cinema* (Beverly Hills), no.35, 1976.
Sarris, Andrew, "Cukor," in *Film Comment* (New York), March/April 1978.
Estrin, Allen, "George Cukor," in *The Hollywood Professionals*, London and New York, 1980.
Bodeen, De Witt, "George Cukor," in *Films in Review* (New York), November 1981.
Flint, Peter, obituary in *New York Times*, 26 January 1983.
Hollywood Reporter, 26 and 28 January 1983.
Kanin, Garson, "George Cukor's Loving Marriage to the Movies," in *New York Times*, 30 January 1983.
"Cukor Section" of *Casablanca* (Madrid), March 1983.
Magny, Joel, "George Cukor: Un homme qui s'affiche," in *Cinéma* (Paris), March 1983.
Taylor, John Russell, "Remembering George Cukor," in *Films and Filming* (London), March 1983.
Clarens, Carlos, "The Cukor touch," in *Film Comment* (New York), March–April 1983.
Ward, L.E., "The Films of George Cukor," in *Classic Images* (Muscatine, Iowa), December 1986.

*   *   *

George Cukor's films range from classics like Greta Garbo's *Camille*, through his films with Spencer Tracy and Katharine Hepburn such as *Adam's Rib*, to the Judy Garland musical *A Star is Born*. Throughout the years he managed to "weather the changes in public taste and the pressures of the Hollywood studio system without compromising his style, his taste, or his ethical standards," as his honorary degree from Loyola University of Chicago is inscribed. Indeed, Cukor informed each of the stories which he brought to the screen with his affectionately critical view of humanity. In film after film he sought to prod the mass audience to reconsider their cherished illusions in order to gain fresh insights into the problems that confront everyone. As Andrew Sarris has written, "When a director has provided tasteful entertainment of a high order consistently" (over a period of half a century indeed) "it is clear that he is much more than a mere entertainer, he is a genuine artist."

Although most of Cukor's films are adaptations of preexisting novels and plays, he has always chosen material that has been consistent with his view of reality. Most often he has explored the conflict between illusion and reality in peoples' lives. The chief characters in his films are frequently actors and actresses, for they, more than anyone, run the risk of allowing the world of illusion with which they are constantly involved to become their reality. This theme is obvious in many of Cukor's best films and appears in some of his earliest work including *The Royal Family of Broadway*, which he co-directed. In it he portrays a family of troupers, based on the Barrymores, who are wedded to their world of fantasy in a way that makes a shambles of their private lives.

The attempt of individuals to reconcile their cherished dreams with the sober realities of life continues in films as superficially different as *Dinner at Eight, The Philadelphia Story*, and *A Double Life*. Ronald Colman earned an Academy Award in the latter as an actor who becomes so identified with the parts he plays that, while enacting Othello, he develops a murderous streak of jealousy which eventually destroys him.

While it is true that Cukor was often drawn to stories about show people, his films also suggest that everyone leads a double life that moves between illusion and reality, and everyone must seek to sort out fantasy from fact if they are to cope realistically with their problems—something Cukor's characters frequently fail to do. *Les Girls* is the most explicit of all Cukor's films in treating this theme. Here the same events are told from four different points of view at a libel trial, each version differing markedly from the others. Because Cukor allows each narrator "equal time," he is sympathetic to the way each of them has subconsciously revised their common experiences in a manner that enables him or her to live with the past in the present. As Sarris remarks, Cukor does not imply that people necessarily are liars, but rather that they tell the truth in their own fashion.

Though Cukor must have harbored some degree of affection and sympathy for the world of romantic illusion, for there is always a hint of regret in his films when actuality inevitably asserts itself in the life of one of his dreamers, his movies nonetheless remain firmly rooted in, and committed to, the workaday world of reality.

Directing his last film, *Rich and Famous*, merited Cukor the distinction of being one of the oldest filmmakers ever to direct a major motion picture, and likewise marked him as enjoying the longest continuous career of any director in film or television. Some of the satisfaction which he derived from his long career was grounded in the fact that few directors have commanded such a large portion of the mass audience. "His movies," Richard Schickel has noted, "can be appreciated—no, liked—at one level or another by just about everyone."

For his part, Cukor once reflected that "I look upon every picture that I make as the first one I've ever done—and the last. I love each film I have directed, and I try to make each one as good as I possibly can. Mind you, making movies is no bed of roses. Every day isn't Christmas. It's been a hard life, but also a joyous one."

—Gene D. Phillips

CURTIZ, Michael.

Hungarian. (Also known as Michael Courtice.) Born Mihály Kertész in Budapest, 24 December 1888. Educated at Markoszy University and Royal Academy of Theatre and Art, Budapest. Married 1) actress Lucy Dorraine, 1915 (divorced 1923); 2) Bess Meredyth. Stage actor, 1906–12; directed first Hungarian feature film, *Az utolsó bohém*, 1912; studied filmmaking at Nordisk Studios in Denmark, 1912–14; served in Hungarian infantry, 1914–15; managing director, Phönix Studios, Hungary, 1917; left Hungary, worked in Swedish, French, and German film industries, 1918; director for Sascha Films, Austria, 1919; signed by Jack Warner, directed first Hollywood film, *The 3rd Degree*, 1926; Recipient: Oscar for Best Director, for *Casablanca*, 1943. *Died 11 April 1962.*

Films as Director:
(as Kertész Mihály)

1912 *Az utolsó bohém (The Last Bohemian)*; *Ma es holnap (Today and Tomorrow)* (+role)
1913 *Rablélek (Captive Soul)*; *Hazasodik az uram (My Husband Lies)*
1914 *A hercegnö Pongyolaban (Princess Pongyola)*; *Az éjszaka rabjai (Slaves of the Night)* (+role); *A Kölcsönkért csecsemök (Borrowed Babies)*; *Bánk bán*; *A tolonc (The Vagrant)*; *Aranyáso (The Golden Shovel)*
1915 *Akit ketten szeretnek (Loved By Two)* (+role)

1916 *Az ezust kecske (The Silver Goat)* (+co-sc); *A medikus (The Apothecary)*; *Doktor ur (The Doctor)*; *Farkas (The Wolf)*; *A fekete szivarvany (The Black Rainbow)*; *Makkhetes (Seven of Clubs)*; *Karthauzi (The Carthusian)*; *A Magyar föld ereje (The Strength of the Hungarian Soil)*
1917 *Arendás zsidó (John, the Tenant)*; *Az ezredes (The Colonel)*; *A föld embere (The Man of the Soil)*; *Halálcsengö (The Death Bell)*; *A kuruzslo (The Charlatan)*; *A Szentjóbi erdö titka (The Secret of St. Job Forest)*; *A senki fia (Nobody's Son)*; *Tavasz a télben (Spring in Wintertime)*; *Zoárd Mester (Master Zoard)*; *Tatárjárás (Invasion)*; *A béke ut ja (The Road to Peace)*; *A vörös Sámson (The Red Samson)*; *Az utolsó hajnal (The Last Dawn)*; *Egy krajcár története (The Story of a Penny)*
1918 *Kilencvenkilenc (99)*; *Judás*; *Lulu*; *Az ördög (The Devil)*; *A napraforgós hölgy (The Lady with Sunflowers)*; *Alraune* (co-d); *Vig özvegy (The Merry Widow)* (+sc); *Varázskeringö (Magic Waltz)*; *Lu, a kokott (Lu, the Cocotte)*; *A Wellingtoni rejtély (The Wellington Mystery)*; *Szamárbör (The Donkey Skin)*; *A csunya fiu (The Ugly Boy)*; *A skorpió (The Scorpion)*
1919 *Jön az öcsem (John the Younger Brother)*; *Liliom* (unfinished)

(in Austria, as Michael Kertesz):

1919 *Die Dame mit dem schwarzen Handschuh (The Lady with the Black Glove)*
1920 *Der Stern von Damaskus*; *Die Dame mit den Sonnenblum* (+sc); *Herzogin Satanella*; *Boccaccio* (+pr); *Die Gottesgeisel*
1921 *Cherchez la femme*; *Dorothys Bekenntnis (Frau Dorothys Bekenntnis)*; *Wege des Schreckens (Labyrinth des Grauens)*; *Miss Tutti Frutti*
1922 *Sodom und Gomorrah (Die Legende von Sünde und Strafe): Part 1. Die Sünde* (+co-sc)
1923 *Sodom und Gomorrah (Die Legende von Sünde und Strafe): Part II. Die Strafe* (+co-sc); *Samson und Dalila* (co-d); *Der Lawine (Avalanche)*; *Der junge Medardus*; *Namenlos (Der Scharlatan, Der falsche Arzt)*
1924 *Ein Spiel ums Leben*; *Harun al Raschid*; *Die Slavenkönigin (Moon of Israel)*
1925 *Celimene, Poupee de Montmartre (Das Spielzeug von Paris, Red Heels)*
1926 *Der goldene Schmetterling (The Road to Happiness)*; *Fiaker Nr. 13 (Einspänner Nr. 13)*
1938 *Gold is Where You Find It*; **The Adventures of Robin Hood** (co-d); *Four Daughters*; *Four's a Crowd*; *Angels with Dirty Faces*
1939 *Dodge City*; *Sons of Liberty*; *The Private Lives of Elizabeth and Essex*; *Four Wives*; *Daughters Courageous*
1940 *Virginia City*; *The Sea Hawk*; *Santa Fe Trail*
1941 *The Sea Wolf*; *Dive Bomber*
1942 *Captains of the Clouds*; **Yankee Doodle Dandy**; **Casablanca**
1943 *Mission to Moscow*; *This is the Army*
1944 *Passage to Marseille*; *Janie*
1945 *Roughly Speaking*; **Mildred Pierce**
1946 *Night and Day*
1947 *Life with Father*; *The Unsuspected*
1948 *Romance on the High Seas (It's Magic)*
1949 *My Dream is Yours* (+pr); *Flamingo Road* (+exec pr); *The Lady Takes a Sailor*
1950 *Young Man with a Horn (Young Man of Music)*; *Bright Leaf*; *Breaking Point*
1951 *Jim Thorpe—All American (Man of Bronze)*; *Force of Arms*
1952 *I'll See You in My Dreams*; *The Story of Will Rogers*
1953 *The Jazz Singer*; *Trouble Along the Way*
1954 *The Boy from Oklahoma*; *The Egyptian*; *White Christmas*
1955 *We're No Angels*
1956 *The Scarlet Hour* (+pr); *The Vagabond Kin*; *The Best Things in Life are Free*
1957 *The Helen Morgan Story (Both Ends of the Candle)*
1958 *The Proud Rebel*; *King Creole*
1959 *The Hangman*; *The Man in the Net*
1960 *The Adventures of Huckleberry Finn*; *A Breath of Scandal (Olympia)*

Michael Curtiz

1961 *Francis of Assisi*
1962 *The Comancheros*

Other Films:

1913 *Atlantis* (Blom) (asst d, role)

Publications:

By CURTIZ: article—

"Talent Shortage is Causing Two-Year Production Delay," in *Films and Filming* (London), June 1956.

On CURTIZ: books—

Martin, Pete, *Hollywood Without Makeup*, New York, 1948.
Anobile, Richard, editor, *Michael Curtiz's "Casablanca"*, New York, 1975.
Rosenzweig, Sidney, *"Casablanca" and other Major Films of Michael Curtiz*, Ann Arbor, Michigan, 1982.
Kinnard, Roy, and R.J. Vitone, *The American Films of Michael Curtiz*, Metuchen, New Jersey, 1986.
Mayne, Judith, *Private Novels, Public Films*, Athens, Georgia, 1988.

On CURTIZ: articles—

Martin, Pete, "Hollywood's Champion Language Assassin," in *Saturday Evening Post* (New York), 2 August 1947.
Sarris, Andrew, "Likable but Elusive," in *Film Culture* (New York), Spring 1963.
Dienstfrey, Harris, "Hitch Your Genre to a Star," in *Film Culture* (New York), Fall 1964.
Callenbach, Ernest, "Comparative Anatomy of Folk-Myth Films: *Robin Hood* and *Antonio das Mortes*," in *Film Quarterly* (Berkeley), Winter [1969]/70.
Nolan, Jack Edmund, "Michael Curtiz," in *Films in Review* (New York), No. 9, 1970.
Behlmer, R., and A. Pinto, "Letters," in *Films in Review* (New York), February 1971.
Davis, John, "*Captain Blood*," in *Velvet Light Trap* (Madison, Wisconsin), June 1971.
Davis, John, "*The Unsuspected*," in *Velvet Light Trap* (Madison, Wisconsin), Summer 1972.
Davis, John, "The Tragedy of *Mildred Pierce*," in *Velvet Light Trap* (Madison, Wisconsin), Fall 1972.
Canham, Kingsley, "Michael Curtiz," in *The Hollywood Professionals, Vol. 1*, London, 1973.
Shadoian, J., "Michael Curtiz' *Twenty Thousand Years in Sing Sing*," in *Journal of Popular Film* (Bowling Green, Ohio), Spring 1973.
Davis, John, "When Will They Ever Learn?," in *Velvet Light Trap* (Madison), Autumn 1975.
Berard, V.R., and P. Canniere, "Michael Curtiz: Maître du baroque," in *Image et Son* (Paris), February 1982.
Werner, G., "Fran Lidingon till *Casablanca*?" in *Chaplin* (Stockholm), vol. 26, no. 2, 1984.

*   *   *

The films of Michael Curtiz have come to symbolize Warner Brothers Studios of the 1930's and 1940's. Many favorites from that era were directed by this one man: *Captain Blood, The Charge of the Light Brigade, The Sea Hawk, Yankee Doodle Dandy, 20,000 Years in Sing Sing*, and *Mildred Pierce*. He helped guide Bette Davis as her popularity rose in the 1930's, and helped establish Errol Flynn as the symbol of the swashbuckling hero. James Cagney (*Yankee Doodle Dandy*) and Joan Crawford (*Mildred Pierce*) both won Oscars under Curtiz's direction. His long career and directorial strengths benefited from the constant work available in the studios of the 1930's and 1940's. Most observers note a precipitous decline in the quality of Curtiz's films after World War II.

Surely Curtiz's most famous creation for today's audience is his only Oscar-winning film for Best Director, *Casablanca*. This cult favorite now has achieved a life of its own, making Bogart and Bergman into modern folk heroes. Director Curtiz has been lost in the shuffle. The anti-auteurist argument seems to be that this particular film represents a happy "accident" of the studio system, and its popularity should not be credited to its director. What is lost in this analysis is the fact that *Casablanca* was a major hit of 1943 (finishing among the top grossing films of the year), won three Academy Awards (Best Picture, Director and Screenplay), and earned Curtiz several awards as the year's best director. Critics of the day recognized Curtiz's input. Certainly today we should give proper credit to the director of a film which was popular upon release, continues to be popular today, and has influenced countless other works.

Curtiz has been difficult for film historians to deal with because of the length and breadth of his career. Usually overlooked is the time he spent in Europe; Curtiz did not begin with Warners until he came to the United States at age 38. His career began in Hungary where he participated in the beginning of the Hungarian film industry, usually receiving credit for directing that country's first feature film. Curtiz remained active until the outbreak of the first World War. After the war, he moved to Vienna where he directed several important films, including the epic *Sodom and Gomorrah*. But this is about all scholars know about this part of this important director's career. Accounts of other activities lead only to contradictions; no wholly reliable list of credits exists. Sadly, historians have written off the first two decades of Curtiz's career. We know a great deal of the work of other emigrés, such as Fritz Lang and F.W. Murnau, but virtually nothing of Curtiz.

Not unexpectedly there exist several versions of why and how Warner Brothers' contacted Curtiz, and brought him to the United States. Regardless, from 1926 on Curtiz became intertwined with all the innovations of the Warner Brothers' studio. In the mid-1920's he was thrust into Warners' attempts to innovate sound. His *Tenderloin* and *Noah's Ark* were two-part talkies which achieved considerable popularity and millions in box-office revenues. In a key transitional year, 1930, Curtiz directed no less than six Warners' talkies. In that same year Warner Brothers tried to introduce color, but with none of the success associated with the studio's efforts with sound. Curtiz's *Mammy*, one of Jolson's follow-ups to *The Jazz Singer* and *The Singing Fool*, had color sequences. In 1933 he directed the well-regarded all-color horror film, *The Mystery of the Wax Museum*.

Curtiz's record during the transition to sound elevated him to the top echelon of contract directors at Warners. Unlike others, Curtiz seemed not to utilize this success to push for greater freedom and independence, but rather seemed content to take what was assigned, and execute it in a classic style. He produced crisp flowing narratives, seeking efficiency of method. He was a conservative director, adapting, borrowing and ultimately utilizing all the dominant codes of the Hollywood system. Stylistic innovations were left to others. Today critics praise the film noir look of *Mildred Pierce*, but in its day, this film was never thought of as one of the forerunners of that style. Curtiz could do film noir, and then move on to his next two projects, *Night and Day*, the fictionalized life of Cole Porter with Cary Grant, and *Life With Father*, a nostalgic, light family romance starring William Powell and Irene Dunne. Both of these latter features took in a great deal of money, and earned considerable critical praise, once again demonstrating how well Curtiz could operate when called upon by his employer.

If there is a way to get a handle on the enormous output of Curtiz's career, it is through genre analysis. In the early 1930's Curtiz stuck to formula melodramas. His limited participation in the Warners' social realism cycles came with films like *Black*

Fury which looked at strikebreaking. Curtiz seemed to hit his stride with the Warners' Errol Flynn pirate cycle of the late 1930's. *Captain Blood* and *The Sea Hawk* stand as symbols to Hollywood's ability to capture the sweep of romantic adventure. Warners also sent director Curtiz and star Flynn to the Old West in *Dodge City*, and *Virginia City*.

In the early 1940's the Warners studio returned to the musical, establishing its niche with the biographical film. Curtiz participated, directing *Yankee Doodle Dandy* (George M. Cohan's life), *This Is the Army* (Irving Berlin), and the aforementioned *Night and Day* (Cole Porter). *Yankee Doodle Dandy* demonstrated how well this European emigré had taken to the United States. Curtiz would continue to deal with Americana in his 1940's films. For example, he touched deep American ideological strains with *Casablanca*, while *Mildred Pierce* examined the dark side of the American family. Feminist critics have noted how this portrait of a strong woman mirrors the freedom women achieved during World War II—a freedom withdrawn after the war when the men returned home. The family in *Mildred Pierce* is constructed in an odd, bitter way, contrasting with Curtiz's affectionate portrait in *Life with Father*.

Genre analysis is helpful but in the end still tells us too little of what we want to know about this important director. As critics and historians continue to go through the films, and utilize the records now available at the University of Wisconsin, University of Southern California, and Princeton, more will come to light about Curtiz's participation in the Hollywood studio system. And always, Curtiz's films will live on for the fans with continual re-screenings of *Casablanca, Mildred Pierce*, and *The Adventures of Robin Hood*.

—Douglas Gomery

D

DANTE, Joe.

American. Born in Morristown, New Jersey, 1948. Raised in Parsippany, New Jersey. Educated at Philadelphia College of Art, graduated 1968. Made *The Movie Orgy*, a seven-hour collage of film clips, with fellow student Jon Davison, late 1960's; contributing editor to *Castle of Frankenstein* magazine, from 1962, also managing editor of *Film Bulletin*, 1968–74; trailer editor for Roger Corman's New World Pictures 1974–76; directed first feature, *Hollywood Boulevard*, 1976; director for *Police Squad, The Twilight Zone*, and *Amazing Stories* for TV, from 1982. Agent: David Gersh, The Gersh Agency, 222 N. Canon Drive, Suite 202, Beverly Hills, CA 90210, U.S.A.

Films as Director:

1976 *Hollywood Boulevard* (co-d, +co-ed)
1978 *Piranha* (+co-ed)
1980 *The Howling* (+co-ed)
1983 "It's a Good Life" episode of *Twilight Zone—The Movie*
1984 *Gremlins*
1985 *Explorers*
1986 *Innerspace*
1987 *Amazon Women on the Moon* (co-d)
1989 *The Burbs*
1990 *Gremlins 2: The New Batch*

Other Films:

1977 *Grand Theft Auto* (Howard) (ed)
1979 *Rock 'n' Roll High School* (Arkush) (story)

Publications:

By DANTE: articles—

Numerous articles in *Castle of Frankenstein*, 1962–75.
Cinefantastique (Oak Park, Illinois), Winter 1980.
Interviews in *Starburst* (London), nos. 36 and 37, 1981.
Interview with B. Krohn, in *Cahiers du Cinéma* (London), January 1983.
"Joe Dante's Guilty Pleasures," in *Film Comment* (New York), May–June 1983.
Interviews in *L'Ecran Fantastique* (Paris), January and December 1984, and December 1985.
Interview with D. Chute, in *Film Comment* (New York), May–June 1984.
"Joe Dante Section" of *Revue du Cinéma* (Paris), December 1984.
Interviews in *Starburst* (London), June 1984 and January 1985.
Interview in *Cinefantastique* (Oak Park, Illinois), January 1986.
Interview in *Time Out* (London), 17 December 1986.
"Films in the Blood," an interview with W.J. Weatherby, in the *Guardian* (London), 26 November 1987.

On DANTE: books—

Meyers, Richard, *For One Week Only: The World of Exploitation Films*, Piscataway, New Jersey, 1983.
Newman, Kim, *Nightmare Movies: A Critical History of the Horror Film from 1968*, London, 1988.

On DANTE: article—

Kawin, Bruce, in *Film Quarterly* (Los Angeles), Fall 1981.

*   *   *

Like French *auteurs* Truffaut and Godard (and their American counterpart, Bogdanovich), Joe Dante began his career as a film critic (significantly, of the horror/fantasy/s.f. genre in which he would later specialize). His first "sort-of" movie was a Warholian seven-hour compilation, *The Movie Orgy* (done with Jon Davison, later producer of Dante's first two features), made up of spliced-together scenes from 1950's B-pictures, an appropriate exercise for a genre *aficionado* who'd soon become an editor for Roger Corman's New World pictures.

At New World, Dante, Davison, and Allan Arkush had the unenviable task of making exciting trailers for tedious Filipino imports. This called for much "creative editing": "We used to have an exploding helicopter shot that we would put in almost every trailer which wasn't up to snuff. Whenever we needed a little action, we'd just cut to the exploding helicopter." His experience on these trailers proved invaluable when he obtained his first directorial assignment: Corman let him and Arkush make an *extremely* low-budget film. So they used a lot of stock footage from those Filipino war films, and created *Hollywood Boulevard*—a spoof on low-budget filmmaking.

Hollywood Boulevard, though not very good (Dante: "It's a moderately awful movie"), established many of Dante's trademarks:

1. A penchant for the fantastic. (*Hollywood Boulevard* boasts a mad slasher, a futuristic "Deathrace" movie, robots and aliens.)

2. A fondness for cinematic allusions. (Dante: "I feel more comfortable making movies that way. I have always liked movies that show a sense of film history.")

3. Cinematic/media self-reflexiveness. (While the heroine's movie-rape scene transpires on screen, the projectionist attacks her in his booth.)

4. The use of a dependable repertory group of performers, beginning with veteran Dick Miller here—who's been in every Dante film—and later including Kevin McCarthy, Kenneth Tobey, and newcomers like Robert Picardo and Belinda Belaski.

5. The post-end-credit sequence (as David Bartholomew remarks, "Dante has said he always likes to include something extra for the people who stay for the credits, as a reward")—a practice sadly curtailed on his big-budget films.

Dante's best films to date have been his collaborations with novelist/filmmaker John Sayles: *Piranha* and *The Howling*. Dante and Sayles make *Piranha*, conceived as a *Jaws* rip-off, something more. Their characters are refreshingly human (bucking the increasingly impersonal trend of 1980's horror); they are never "meat." Belinda Belaski's demise in both films is doubly wrenching because the viewer actively cares about her character.

Dante's crowning achievement is *The Howling* (the first and best of a spate of 1980's werewolf movies), which, like *Piranha*, he also co-edited with Mark Goldblatt. The first reel is brilliantly constructed, cross-cutting between events in a TV studio and the perambulations of a "wired" TV reporter on her way to a rendezvous with a serial killer, culminating in a police shootout in a peepshow booth. During the length of this sequence, Dante introduces and differentiates at least eight major characters, without letting the action slip a beat. Almost immediately, the picture shifts to the Colony, an Esalen-like retreat, where he smoothly introduces *another* half-dozen characters while keeping up the story's forward momentum.

Never has Dante's proclivity for filmic allusions been so thematically apt. Since the picture ultimately deals with reality, TV "reality," and the blurring of the two, the juxtaposition of clips from *The Wolfman* and big-bad-wolf cartoons and the naming of most characters after directors of werewolf movies is only fitting in *Howling*'s self-reflexive world, in which both participants and viewers are trapped.

Dante has yet to top *The Howling*, although, in box-office terms, his *Gremlins* dwarfed it. *Gremlins* single-handedly (with an assist from *Indiana Jones and the Temple of Doom*'s heart-ripper scene) caused the MPAA to institute the PG-13 rating to placate parents upset by its cartoon violence (even though most of the "gory" stuff—e.g., "blenderized" gremlin—was directed against the title creatures). *Gremlins*, although typically well made, is atypically mean-spirited for Dante, particularly Phoebe Cates's character's monologue about why she hates Christmas.

"Life imitating art" (film/video versus reality; film/video as reality) permeates Dante's work. His *Amazon Women on the Moon* segments include a *Sneak Previews*-like TV show, which "reviews" the life of the ordinary Joe who's watching the program (and gives it thumbs down). In "It's a Good Life," his *Twilight Zone* segment, Anthony's monstrous images and ideas come from the cartoons he watches on tv. In his box-office flop, *Explorers*, his preteen astronauts encounter aliens who speak in a non-stop stream-of-media-consciousness and who, through a montage of 1950's s.f.-film destruction-of-monsters scenes (perhaps left over from *The Movie Orgy*), show why they fear prolonged contact with earthlings.

Innerspace relies more on fantastic comedy and less on cinematic allusions (although the entire film is a variation on *Fantastic Voyage* by way of Woody Allen's parody of same in *Everything You Always Wanted to Know About Sex*. It's funny, but fails because, although Martin Short and Dennis Quaid's characters' unusual "male bonding" changes Short's hypochondria to self-reliance, there's no perceptible change in Quaid.

We'll never know if *The 'Burbs* could have been better; it was locked into a tight shooting schedule because of a looming IA union walkout, and the writers' strike prevented any script fixes before production began. (Dante: "Nobody was ever happy with the script the way it was.") Thus, this Reagan-era fable of suburban paranoia plays it both ways, making a statement about the extremes to which hysterical mistrust can lead and at the same time showing that such suspicion is ultimately justified.

Perhaps because of the relative failure of his last three projects, Dante agreed to make *Gremlins 2: The New Batch*, though it seems that he believed he could do something new with the concept. Dante has been anything but prolific, partly because he always makes effects films, with long shooting and pre- and post-production schedules, but mostly because he only makes the films he wishes to make. As he says, "The one thing I'd like to is to think I really *want* to do the picture, rather than just doing it to do it. That leads to another one you do just to do it, and finally you're making Michael Winner movies. If you can't care about the film, why should anyone else?"

—Anthony Ambrogio

D'ARRAST, Harry d'Abbadie.

American. Born in Argentina, 1897. Educated at Lycée Janson-de-Sailly, Paris, and at Bradford University, England. Married Eleanor Boardman, 1937. Served in French Army (wounded and decorated), World War I. Arrived in Hollywood, technical advisor to Chaplin, 1922; director for William Randolph Hearst's Cosmopolitan Pictures, 1925; signed to Paramount, 1927; signed to Fox, 1928; made *It Happened in Spain* for United Artists in Spain, 1934; returned to France, 1937; idle in Hollywood, 1940–46; returned to France, 1946. *Died 16 March 1968.*

Films as Director:

1927   *Service for Ladies*; *A Gentleman of Paris*; *Serenade*
1928   *The Magnificent Flirt* (+co-sc); *Dry Martini*
1929   *Laughter* (+co-sc)
1930   *Raffles* (co-d, uncredited)
1933   *Topaze*
1934   *It Happened in Spain* (*The Three-Cornered Hat*) (co-d); *La traviesa molinera* (*El sombrero de tres picos*) (co-d) (Spanish language version of *It Happened in Spain*); *La Meunière débauchée* (*Le Tricorne*) (French language version of *It Happened in Spain*)

Other Films:

1930   *Rive gauche* (co-story) (French language version of *Laughter*); *Die Männer um Lucie* (co-story) (German language version of *Laughter*); *Lo mejor es reir* (co-story) (Spanish language version of *Laughter* directed by Emerich Emo)

Note: according to Herman Weinberg, *Laughter* and *Topaze* are the only existing d'Arrast films.

Publications:

On D'ARRAST: book—

Weinberg, Herman, *Saint Cinema: Selected Writings (1929–1970)*, New York, 1970.

On D'ARRAST: articles—

Weinberg, Herman, "In Memoriam: H. D'Abbadie D'Arrast, 1897–1968," in *Film Comment* (New York), Fall 1969.
"Harry d'Abbadie d'Arrast," in *Film Dope* (London), April 1976.
McGillivray, David, "Now You Know," in *Films and Filming* (London), October 1982.

*   *   *

It is almost as if Harry d'Abbadie d'Arrast had never existed. Certainly he occupies no niche at all in the cinema pantheon, where he belongs. Of course, d'Arrast had a short career, hardly spanning seven years, from 1927 to 1934, during which

Harry d'Abbadie d'Arrast: Myrna Loy and John Barrymore in *Topaze*

he managed to make eight films. In a quantitative sense, this was, perhaps, not much, though by movie standards it was rather more than is usually the case with stubborn artists up against equally stubborn financial backers.

Qualitatively, however, these eight by Harry d'Arrast (as he was popularly known at the time of his florescence) were notable—eight quiet, witty comedies, sometimes edged with satire but always with elegance and charm, made by a civilized gentleman who thought that it was something to dedicate oneself to laughter as Chaplin and the "Sultan of Satire," Lubitsch, did, as René Clair did, and as others such as Malcolm St. Clair did.

Nor did d'Arrast eschew the niceties of film technique. He cloaked his urbanity in a silken sheen, his photography being so incandescent that it was said he could not photograph even a telephone in close-up without making it a thing of beauty. This is especially true of d'Arrast's quintet of silent films, where the physical aspect of the scenes was a part of what the films were about. A master of pace and cutting, with never a frame too much, he made the slightest gesture count and the human face—most important of all—reflect the joy of living.

His films were comedies of manners done in high comic style—as if the cinema were not a mass medium but a patrician one, an aristocratic and cerebral one. His films were like a string quartet, in which the subtlest effects are obtained in the least ostentatious manner, for an audience that brings to the work its own worldly wisdom, its own capacity for appreciation for what is being done, its own delight in meaningful nuances.

D'Arrast's first picture, which starred Adolphe Menjou, was *Service for Ladies*, and few directorial debuts have been more auspicious. From a delectable truffle by Ernest Vajda and Benjamin Glazer, d'Arrast had spun a completely winning tale of a *maître d'hôtel* who falls in love with a visiting American debutante.

The second film was *A Gentleman of Paris*, a sort of denatured *Affairs of Anatol* with a harsh touch of *Daybreak*—indeed, if Schnitzler could ever have compromised with Hollywood and lent his talents as a writer to the film capital, the result might have been something like *A Gentleman of Paris*, for though this, too, was a gay and scintillating comedy of a charming roué, eternally "on the make", it also had sombre glints when the "gentleman of Paris" is framed by his valet to appear as a card cheat and is faced with the only honorable way out—a gun. But the Hollywood of 1927 was not the pre-World War I of Vienna, and so an ironic twist at the end preserves the happy ending. His third picture, *Serenade*, was again derived from a gossamer fluff by Ernest Vajda and again starred Menjou, this time as an operetta composer in Vienna, while *The Magnificent Flirt*, the last of his incomparable quartet of silent comedies for Paramount, was a dream to watch.

D'Arrast's old friend, Monta Bell, was in 1929 a producer at Paramount's Long Island Studio. He sent for d'Arrast and asked him to make his first sound film. The result was *Laughter*, a wry comedy about an ex-chorus girl (Nancy Carroll) who marries a millionaire (Frank Morgan) only to find that she prefers one of her erstwhile "bohemian" friends, a struggling composer (Fredric March). Out of the smallest things d'Arrast made a delight; when Nancy Carroll puts out her hands to receive several diamond bracelets from her maid, she places her wrists together with a tired smile as if she were to be handcuffed, for that's what her jeweled bracelets are, handcuffs that keep her tied to her dull millionaire.

In 1933 an opportunity came at RKO to direct John Barrymore in *Topaze*, from the satirical comedy by Marcel Pagnol, in an adaptation by Ben Hecht. In 1934 d'Arrast went to Spain, and with a release contract with United Artists he made *The Three Cornered Hat*, based on the 19th century tale by Pedro de Alarcón that had already served Manuel de Falla so well for

his 1919 ballet. D'Arrast accomplished hardly a whit less. The film was made in three versions—English, French and Spanish, and it was released as *It Happened in Spain*. It did not do well at the box office.

The New York Times and *Variety* on March 17, 1968 briefly noted d'Arrast's death in Monte Carlo, where he had been living in seclusion for many years. Richard Watts Jr.—he alone of all the critics in America, and one of d'Arrast's early appreciators during the years when Watts was film reviewer of the *New York Herald Tribune*—paid him a tribute in the *New York Post*: "The late Harry d'Arrast was one of the distinguished directors from the great days of the silent cinema."

—Herman Weinberg

DASSIN, Jules.

American. Born in Middletown, Connecticut, 12 December 1911. Educated at Morris High School, the Bronx, New York. Married 1) Beatrice Launer, 1933 (divorced 1962), one son, two daughters; 2) actress Melina Mercouri, 1966. Member of Artef Players (Jewish socialist theatre collective), 1936; directed first Broadway production, *Medicine Show*, 1939; contracted to RKO (moved to MGM after eight months), Hollywood, 1940; left MGM and worked with producer Mark Hellinger, 1946; named by Edward Dmytryk and Frank Tuttle in HUAC testimony as member of Hollywood "Communist faction," 1951; subpoenaed by HUAC, 1952; moved to Europe, 1953. Recipient: Best Director Award (shared), Cannes Festival, for *Rififi*, 1955. Address: 25 Anagnostopoulou St., Athens, Greece.

Films as Director:

1941 *The Tell-Tale Heart* (short)
1942 *Nazi Agent; The Affairs of Martha* (*Once Upon a Thursday*);
       Reunion (*Reunion in France, Mademoiselle France*)
1943 *Young Ideas*
1944 *The Canterville Ghost*
1946 *A Letter for Evie; Two Smart People*
1947 *Brute Force*
1948 **The Naked City**
1949 *Thieves' Highway*
1950 *Night and the City*
1955 **Du Rififi chez les hommes (Rififi)** (+co-sc, role as jewel thief
       under pseudonym Perlo Vita)
1958 *Celui qui doit mourir* (*He Who Must Die*) (+co-sc)
1959 *La legge* (*La Loi*) (released in U.S. 1960 as *Where the Hot
       Winds Blow*) (+sc)
1960 *Pote tin kyriaki* (*Never on Sunday*) (+pr, sc, role)
1962 *Phaedra* (+pr, co-sc)
1964 *Topkapi* (+pr)
1966 *10:30 p.m. Summer* (+co-pr, sc, bit role)
1967 *Survival 67* (+co-pr, appearance) (documentary)
1968 *Uptight!* (+pr, co-sc)
1971 *La Promesse de l'aube* (*Promise at Dawn*) (+pr, sc, role as
       Ivan Mozhukhin under pseudonym Perlo Vita)
1974 *The Rehearsal* (+sc)
1978 *A Dream of Passion* (+pr, sc)
1980 *Circle of Two* (released in USA 1982)

Publications:

By DASSIN: articles—

Interview with Claude Chabrol and François Truffaut, in *Cahiers du Cinéma* (Paris), April and May 1955.

Jules Dassin: *The Naked City*

Interview with Cynthia Grenier, in *Sight and Sound* (London), Winter 1957/58.

Interview with George Bluestone, in *Film Culture* (New York), February 1958.

"I See Dassin Make The Law," interview with John Lane, in *Films and Filming* (London), September 1958.

"Style and Instinct," interview with Gordon Gow, in *Films and Filming* (London), February and March 1970.

"'A Dream of Passion': An Interview with Jules Dassin," with D. Georgakas and P. Anastasopoulos, in *Cinéaste* (New York), Fall 1978.

On DASSIN: books—

Ferrero, Adelio, *Jules Dassin*, Parma, 1961.

McArthur, Colin, *Underworld USA*, London, 1972.

Schuster, Mel, *The Contemporary Greek Cinema*, Metuchen, New Jersey, 1979.

Arnold, Frank, and Michael Esser, *Hommage fur Melina Mercouri und Jules Dassin*, Berlin, 1984.

Siclier, Fabrien, and Jacques Levy, *Jules Dassin*, Paris, 1986.

On DASSIN: articles—

Alpert, Hollis, "Greek Passion," in *Saturday Review* (New York), 20 December 1958.

Hammel, F., "A Director's Return," in *Cue* (New York), 10 March 1962.

"Jules Dassin," in *Film Dope* (London), April 1976.

Horton, A., "Jules Dassin: A Multi-national filmmaker considered," in *Film Criticism* (Meadville, Pennsylvania), Spring 1984.

*   *   *

Between the mid-1940's and the late 1950's, Jules Dassin directed some of the better realistic, hard-bitten, fast-paced crime dramas produced in America, before his blacklisting, and subsequent move to Europe. However, while he has made some very impressive films, his career as a whole is lacking in artistic cohesion.

Dassin's films are occasionally innovative: *The Naked City* is one of the first police dramas shot on location, on the streets of New York; *Rififi* is a forerunner of detailed jewelry heist dramas, highlighted by a 35-minute sequence chronicling the break-in, shot without a word of dialogue or note of music; *Never on Sunday*, starring his wife Melina Mercouri as a happy hooker, made the actress an international star, won her an Academy Award nomination and popularized in America the Greek *bouzouki* music. *The Naked City* and *Rififi* are particularly exciting, as well as trend-setting, while *Brute Force* remains a striking, naturalistic prison drama, with Burt Lancaster in one of his most memorable early performances and Hume Cronyn wonderfully despicable as a Hitlerish guard captain. *Thieves' Highway*, also shot on location is a vivid drama of truck driver Richard Conte taking on racketeer Lee J. Cobb. *Topkapi* is a *Rififi* remake, with a delightful touch of comedy.

Many of Dassin's later films, such as *Brute Force* and *Thieves' Highway*, attempt to observe human nature: they focus on the individual fighting his own demons while trying to survive within a chaotic society. For example, in *A Dream of Passion*, an up-dating of Sophocles' *Medea*, an American woman is jailed in Greece for the murder of her three children; *Up Tight*, the filmmaker's first American-made release after the McCarthy hysteria, is a remake of *The Informer* set in a black ghetto. Unfortunately, they are all generally flawed: with the exception of *Never on Sunday* and *Topkapi*, his collaborations with Melina Mercouri (from *He Who Must Die* to *A Dream of Passion*) are disappointing, while *Up Tight* pales beside the original. *Circle of Two*, with teen-ager Tatum O'Neal baring her breasts for aging Richard Burton, had a limited release. Dassin's early triumphs have been obscured by his more recent fiascos, and as a result his critical reputation is now irrevocably tarnished.

The villain in his career is the blacklist, which tragically clipped his wings just as he was starting to fly. Indeed, he could not find work in Europe for five years, as producers felt American distributors would automatically ban any film with his signature. When *Rififi* opened, critics wrote about Dassin as if he were European. The *New York Herald Tribune* reported in 1961, "At one ceremony, when the award to *Rififi* was announced, (Dassin) was called to the dais, and a French flag was raised above him. 'It should have been a moment of triumph but I feel awful. They were honoring my work and I'm an American. It should have been the American flag raised in honor.'" The blacklist thus denied Jules Dassin his roots. In 1958, it was announced that he was planning to adapt James T. Farrell's *Studs Lonigan*, a project that was eventually shelved. It is one more tragedy of the blacklist that Dassin was not allowed to follow up *Brute Force*, *The Naked City* and *Thieves' Highway* with *Studs Lonigan*.

—Rob Edelman

———

DAVES, Delmer.

American. Born in San Francisco, 24 July 1904. Educated in civil engineering, law degree at Stanford University. Married actress Mary Lou Lender. Lived for several months in Arizona desert among Hopi and Navajo, renounced law career, and joined Pasadena Playhouse, 1925; joined James Cruze production company as property boy, 1927; scriptwriter at Warner Bros., also actor, from 1929; directed first film, *Destination Tokyo*, 1944; formed Diamond-D productions, 1950's. *Died September 1977.*

Films as Director and Scriptwriter:

1944	*Destination Tokyo*; *The Very Thought of You*; *Hollywood Canteen*
1945	*Pride of the Marines* (*Forever in Love*, *Body and Soul*)
1947	*The Red House*; *Dark Passage*
1948	*To the Victor* (d only)
1949	*A Kiss in the Dark*; *Task Force*
1950	*Broken Arrow* (d only)
1951	*Bird of Paradise*
1952	*Return of the Texan* (d only)
1953	*Treasure of the Golden Condor*; *Never Let Me Go* (d only)
1954	*Demetrius and the Gladiators* (d only); *Drum Beat*
1956	*Jubal*; *The Last Wagon*
1957	*3:10 to Yuma* (d only)
1958	*Cowboy* (d only); *Kings Go Forth* (d only); *The Badlanders* (d only)
1959	*The Hanging Tree* (d only); *A Summer Place* (+pr)
1961	*Parrish* (+pr); *Susan Slade* (+pr)
1962	*Rome Adventure* (*Lovers Must Learn*) (+pr)
1963	*Spencer's Mountain* (+pr)
1964	*Youngblood Hawke* (+pr)
1965	*The Battle of the Villa Fiorita* (+pr)

Other Films:

1915	*Christmas Memories* (Leonard) (role)
1925	*Zander the Great* (Hill) (role)

1928 *The Night Flyer* (Lang) (role, prop man); *Three Sinners* (Lee)
       (role); *The Red Mark* (Cruze) (role, prop man); *Excess
       Baggage* (Cruze) (role, prop man)
1929 *So This Is College* (Wood) (co-sc, role); *A Man's Man* (Cruze)
       (bit role, prop man); *The Duke Steps Out* (Cruze) (role,
       tech adv)
1930 *The Bishop Murder Case* (Grinde and Burton) (role); *Good
       News* (Grinde and McGregor)
1931 *Shipmates* (Pollard) (co-adapt, co-dialogue, role, sc)
1932 *Divorce in the Family* (Riesner) (sc, role)
1933 *Clear All Wires* (Hill) (continuity)
1934 *No More Women* (Rogell) (co-sc, co-story); *Dames* (Enright)
       (sc); *Flirtation Walk* (Borzage) (sc)
1935 *Stranded* (Borzage) (co-sc); *Page Miss Glory* (LeRoy) (co-sc);
       Shipmates Forever (Borzage) (sc)
1936 *The Petrified Forest* (Mayo) (co-sc)
1937 *The Go Getter* (Berkeley) (sc); *Slim* (Enright) (co-sc,
       uncredited); *The Singing Marine* (Enright) (sc); *She
       Married an Artist* (Gering) (co-sc)
1938 *Professor Beware* (Nugent) (sc)
1939 *Love Affair* (McCarey) (co-sc); *Thousand Dollars a
       Touchdown* (Hogan) (sc)
1940 *The Farmer's Daughter* (Hogan) (story, sc); *Safari* (Edward
       Griffith) (sc); *Young America Flies* (Eason) (short) (sc)
1941 *The Night of January 16th* (Clemens) (co-sc); *Unexpected
       Uncle* (Godfrey) (co-sc)
1942 *You Were Never Lovelier* (Seiter) (co-sc)
1943 *Stage Door Canteen* (Borzage) (sc)
1955 *White Feather* (Webb) (co-sc)
1957 *An Affair to Remember* (McCarey) (co-sc) (remake of *Love
       Affair* 1939)
1972 *Seventy-Five Years of Cinema Museum* (Hershon and Guerra)
       (appearance)

Publications:

By DAVES: articles—

Interview with Christopher Wicking, in *Screen* (London), July/
October 1969.

On DAVES: book—

Pigenet, M., *Delmer Daves*, IDHEC, Paris, 1960.

On DAVES: articles—

Whitehall, Richard, "On the 3:10 to Yuma—Delmer Daves," in *Films
and Filming* (London), April and May 1963.
Wallington, Mike, "Auteur and Genre: The Westerns of Delmer
Daves," in *Cinema* (Cambridge), October 1969.
"Screenwriters Symposium," in *Film Comment* (New York), Winter
1970/71.
"Daves Issue" of *Filmkritik* (Munich), January 1975.
Rabourdin, D., "Delmer Daves ou le secreat perdu," in *Cinéma*
(Paris), October 1977.
Cebe, G., obituary in *Ecran* (Paris), October 1977.
Passek, J.-L., obituary in *Cinéma* (Paris), November 1977.
Ledieu, Christian, "Delmer Daves ou la raison du cœur," in *Etudes
Cinématographiques* (Paris), no.12–13,

On DAVES: film—

Wilkinson, Hazel, director, *The Critic and "3:10 to Yuma"*, Great Britain, 1961.

*   *   *

Delmer Daves is perhaps best remembered for the highly successful youth-oriented movies which he made for Warner
Brothers in the late 1950's and early 1960's. *A Summer Place*,
the definitive teenage love film, was the most financially successful of these. Yet it is unfair to relegate Daves to the realm
of glossy soap opera directors. When analyzed as a whole, the
body of his work reveals some fine moments. *Pride of the
Marines*, *Broken Arrow*, and *3:10 to Yuma* are all very different films, yet each is regarded by film historians as a classic.

After an early career in films as an actor, Daves turned to

Delmer Daves

screenwriting in the early 1930's and worked, often in collaboration with others, on a variety of films, the most prominent
of which were *The Petrified Forest* and *Love Affair*. When he
began directing he continued to write the screenplays for his
own films. His directorial debut was *Destination Tokyo*, not a
great film but at least a cut above the glut of wartime propaganda movies being made at the time. It was also noteworthy
as the only film which Cary Grant ever made with no romance,
or even any women in the plot.

Another war film, *Pride of the Marines*, was one of Hollywood's first attempts to dramatize the plight of the returning
G.I.'s. On a par with such other celebrated movies as *Bright
Victory* and *The Men*, *Pride of the Marines* simply and without
over-dramatizing, showed the anxieties and frustrations of war
veterans who were wounded both physically and psychologically by their experiences. It also dealt, albeit briefly, with
the sociological issue of minority soldiers who would return
home to a nation perhaps unaware of the value of their contributions to their country.

Some of Daves's most significant movies were westerns
which were both sympathetic to Indians and unglamorizing in
their approach to traditional western themes. *Broken Arrow* is
often cited as the first film to portray Indians without sterotyp-
ing them, even if most of the actors were white. *3:10 to Yuma*
was one of the earliest "anti-hero" westerns and is regarded as
a classic both in the United States and Europe. *Cowboy* was
another atypical western. Although ostensibly a comic western, *Cowboy* had an underlying anti-macho theme ahead of its
time. In the beginning of the film the main characters, played
by Glenn Ford and Jack Lemmon, are opposites: Ford a traditional "he-man" cowboy, and Lemmon a tenderfoot. By the
end of the film both characters become aware of the opposite
sides of their own natures. At least a decade before the theme
became popular, *Cowboy* showed that men's hard and soft

sides could co-exist and could make entertaining subject matter for a motion picture.

Daves's final film, *The Battle of Villa Fiorita*, is regarded by most critics as a run-of-the-mill soap opera, yet even that shows his ability to build a film around an important social theme before it became popular. In its story which, like *Cowboy* begins as a comedy and gradually becomes a drama, Daves's characters are faced by problems which are now such an issue of social concern: divorce, remarriage (or in this case cohabitation), and the rearing of step-children. In this film, like *A Summer Place* and his other well known "soap operas," Daves's writing and direction make the work much better than its subject matter would suggest. Like his contemporary Douglas Sirk, whose films have been criticized in terms similar to those directed at Daves, his films are actually richer than general critical opinion would seem to indicate.

—Patricia King Hanson

———

DAVIES, Terence.

British. Born in Liverpool, 1945. Studied at Drama School in Coventry, 1971–73, and at National Film School, Beaconsfield, late 1970's. Clerk and accountant in a shipping office, 1960–1971; directed first film, *Children*, 1974. Recipient: International Critics' Prize, Cannes Festival, for *Distant Voices, Still Lives*, 1988.

Films as Director and Scriptwriter:

1974   *Children*
1980   *Madonna and Child*
1983   *Death and Transfiguration*
1984   *Terence Davies Trilogy* (comprising three previous films)
1988   **Distant Voices, Still Lives**

Publications:

By DAVIES: articles—

"Voices from the Past," an interview with P. Wyeth, in *Stills* (London), March 1986.
Interview with D. Heinrich, in *Cinéma* (Paris), 1 June 1988.
Interview with Harlan Kennedy, in *Film Comment* (New York), September/October 1988.
Interview with Nigel Floyd, in *Monthly Film Bulletin* (London), October 1988.
Interview with Brian Baxter and A. Hunter, in *Films and Filming* (London), October 1988.
Interview in *Time Out* (London), 5 October 1988.

On DAVIES: articles—

Variety (New York), 21 March 1984.
Baxter, Brian, "A Film Trilogy by Terence Davies," in *Films and Filming* (London), October 1984.
Gibson, Ben, "*Death and Transfiguration*," in *Monthly Film Bulletin* (London), October 1984.
Baxter, Brian, in *Films and Filming* (London), January 1988.
Variety (New York), 18 May 1988.
Tixeront, A., in *Cinéma* (Paris), 25 May 1988.
Wilson, David, "Family Album," in *Sight and Sound* (London), Autumn 1988.
Barker, Adam, in *Monthly Film Bulletin* (London), October 1988.

*   *   *

"I make films to come to terms with my family history . . . If there had been no suffering, there would have been no films."

Hardly the most unusual of artistic subjects, but for Terence Davies it has been the source of perhaps the most emotionally and technically distinctive films in recent British film history. *The Terence Davies Trilogy* and *Distant Voices, Still Lives* chart what some might think unremarkable territory—working class life in northern England after the war—but do so with an artistic seriousness more usually seen as the exclusive preserve of "European" cinema.

Born in Liverpool in 1945, the youngest of ten children (seven of whom survived infancy), Davies's early life was overshadowed by the mute malevolence and tyrannical violence of his father, for whom he still feels undiminished hatred. In a house where domesticity would cut violently to the most extreme brutality, Davies developed a sensitivity to mood and detail that was to prove intrinsic to his later filmmaking. "I have a very retentive memory, and can remember things, even atmospheres on particular days. And I think it's these details, particularly about people's behaviour that reveal the greater truth. As a child, up to the point when my father died, because you had to gauge whether he was in a good mood or not, all my nerve endings were exposed. And when you're a child, you're like an animal, you smell things, so that now that instinct is absolutely there." His father died when he was eight, of a stomach cancer perhaps accelerated by drinking disinfectant to avoid being called-up. And the next few years, until his secondary school, were relatively happy, particularly through his discovery of American Musicals. Davies left school at the age of 15 and began working as a clerk in a shipping office and an accountant, spending his spare moments writing for the stage and radio. By the age of 26 he had a script, but was rejected by all the TV companies he sent it to. It was after leaving Drama school in Coventry that he applied for and received a grant from the British Film Institute Production Board to direct. *Children* received critical acclaim, including the bronze Hugo at the Chicago film festival. But again he had to be saved from accountancy, this time by winning a place, second time round, at the National Film School where he began his second film.

The Trilogy of films *Children, Madonna and Child*, and *Death and Transfiguration* took ten years to complete, requiring three different sources of funding including the Greater London Arts Association. But it was a period in which his critical reputation began to accrue. Showing the three stages in the life of Robert Tucker—from being bullied at school through a loveless middle age of masochistic homosexual fantasy to death—it constituted an expiation of sexual and religious guilt. "Not having come to terms with being gay, I had prayed for forgiveness until my knees were literally raw, and I just thought, that's it. I was so angry, it seemed that even if there was a God he was just inhumane. . . . Although I had rejected Catholicism before I made the films, in the making of the trilogy I worked out my precise reasons for doing so." The autobiographical base, however, opened onto a startling emotional maturity, looking into the bleak potential future of Davies's life—a lonely death (and transfiguration) in a geriatric ward on Christmas Day. But the subject matter was not to everyone's taste. Religious groups in America protested at its sexual content. And according to one critic, "It makes Ingmar Bergman look like Jerry Lewis." But its thoughtful handling of non-linear narrative and "spare and beautiful" black and white photography picked up an array of prizes.

Distant Voices, Still Lives, again made in parts with a variety of funds, was the confirmation of this critical reputation, dealing this time with his family's history rather than his own. Moreover, it achieved a deepened emotional range and presented considerable technical innovation, winning major prizes at Cannes, Locarno and Toronto. The desperate groping for critical terms with which critics responded suggests the originality of his achievement. "If you can readily imagine a

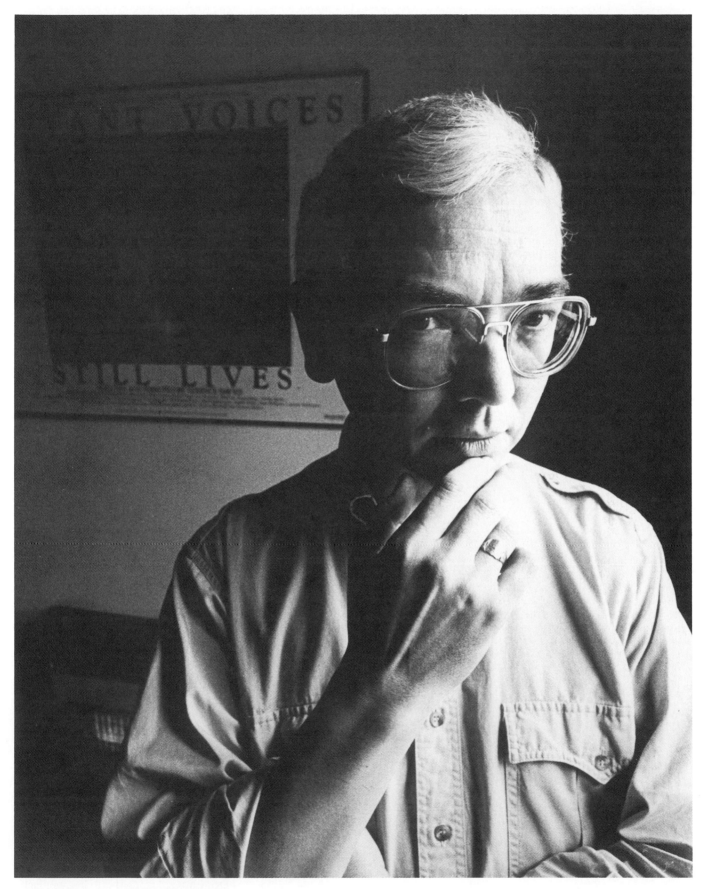

Terence Davies © **Andrew Hamilton Lane**

musical version of *Coronation Street* directed by Robert Bresson, with additional dialogue by Sigmund Freud and Tommy Handley, you might know what to expect from Terence Davies;" "A proletarian Proust;" "A musical, albeit a brutal, Proustian one." Whilst 1950's revivals were not uncommon at this time, this was unmistakably something new. As Davies put it, "I remember the 1950's which have now become very fashionable and unreal, with films like *Absolute Beginners* and all those television commercials. . . . It was not romantic, and that's why I chose to shoot the film in that particular shade of brown, because I didn't want it to look like 'The Good Old Days.'" This colouring was achieved through a "Bleach By-Pass" operation in the laboratory, and careful suppression of primary colours on the set, apart from the red of lipstick and nail-varnish. The effect is stunning. In set pieces that look like tinted photographs it captures the romance and sterility of a culture bound in working-class patriarchy, but glazed with Hollywood escapism. The father's brutality—cutting from him gently filling the children's Christmas stockings, to demolishing the dinner table—is contrasted by the love songs tripping off the girls' lips, and ironised by a soundtrack of songs such as "Taking A Chance On Love." Scenes are overlapped through the music, and static holds are animated by sound (the incantationary Home Service Shipping Forecast in the opening shot).

Such qualities have marked Davies as the most promising director in British cinema. It's a reputation he's likely to expand with a projected film about the brief period of happiness in his childhood. He shows a passionate concern with film *craft*, lamenting what he sees as the British instinct to use film as a medium for recorded theatre; primarily verbal, sentimental, and in the tight bodice of traditional narrative. His films are remarkable in disturbing so strong a collective memory—and myth—of British cultural life with such cinematic ingenuity.

—Saul Frampton

DE ANTONIO, Emile.

American. Born in Scranton, Pennsylvania, 1920. Educated at Harvard, and at Columbia University, New York. Served in World War II. Teacher of Philosophy, Longshoreman, and Editor, 1940's and 1950's; formed G-String productions, 1958; began making compilation documentaries with *Point of Order*, 1963. *Died December 1989.*

Films as Director:

1963   *Point of Order* (+co-pr)
1965   *That's Where the Action Is* (for TV) (+pr)
1966   *Rush to Judgment* (+co-pr)
1968   *In the Year of the Pig* (+pr)
1969   *America Is Hard to See* (+co-pr)
1971   *Millhouse: A White House Comedy* (*Millhouse: A White Comedy*) (+pr)
1972   *Painters Painting* (+pr)
1976   *Underground* (co-d, pr)
1983   *In the King of Prussia*
1989   *Mr. Hoover and I*

Other Films:

1961   *Sunday* (Drasin) (pr)

1965   *Drunk* (Warhol) (role)

Publications:

By DE ANTONIO: articles—

Interview with Jonas Mekas, in *Village Voice* (New York), 13 November 1969.
"Radical Scavenging: An Interview with Emile de Antonio," with Bernard Weiner, in *Film Quarterly* (Berkeley), Fall 1971.
Interview with G. O'Brien, in *Inter/View* (New York), February 1972.
"Rencontre avec Emile de Antonio," with L. Marcorelles, in *Cahiers du Cinéma* (Paris), December 1976.
"Filmer de que ne montre pas l'histoire 'officielle'," an interview with M. Euvrard, in *Cinéma Quebec* (Montreal), v.5, no.19, 1977.
Interview with A. Rosenthal, in *Film Quarterly* (Berkeley), Fall 1978.
Interview in *Cineaste* (New York), v.12, no.2, 1982.
"History is the theme of all my films," an interview with Gary Crowdus and Dan Georgakas, in *Cineaste* (New York), vol. 12, no. 2, 1982.
"De Antonio and the Plowshares Eight," an interview with D. Segal, in *Sight and Sound* (London), Summer 1982.
"Emile De Antonio interviews himself," in *Film Quarterly* (Los Angeles), Fall 1982.
"My brush with painting," in *American Film* (Washington, D.C.), March 1984.
"Quotations from Chairman 'Dee': Decodifying de Antonio," in *Cinema Canada* (Montreal), July–August 1984.

On DE ANTONIO: articles—

Bazelon, David, "Background of *Point of Order*," in *Film Comment* (New York), Winter 1964.
Westerbeck, Colin, Jr., "Some Out-Takes from Radical Film Making: Emile de Antonio," in *Sight and Sound* (London), Summer 1970.
Hess, J., "Political Filmmaking: Feds Harrass Film Crew," in *Jump Cut* (Berkeley), September 1975.
Linfield, Susan, "De Antonio's Day in Court," in *Village Voice* (New York), 8 February 1983.
Obituary in *Variety* (New York), 27 December 1989.

*   *   *

A Communist with impeccable Ivy League credentials, Emile De Antonio came to filmmaking relatively late in his career. Leaving Harvard in the 1930's, he had first flexed his muscles as a longshoreman on Baltimore Docks. After World War II, he had returned to academia, attending graduate school at Columbia University, and then teaching a stint at William and Mary College, Virginia.

The late 1950's found him in New York, engaged in get-rich-quick schemes. (With a friend, he set up "Sailor's Surplus," a mail order business.) More significantly, he was making acquaintances in the New York art world. He went drinking with Rauschenberg and Jasper Johns, and organized "galas" for the minimalist composer John Cage and the dancer Merce Cunningham. As far as his future filmmaking was concerned, this period was crucial: he was encountering the wealthy liberal arts patrons whose backing would later be so important to him.

De Antonio was a member of "The Group," a "free open organization of American cinema," set up in the summer of 1961, and with the avowed aim of rejecting censorship and exploding the "myth of budget," and comprising of such luminaries of the New York avant garde film scene as Jonas Mekas and Shirley Clarke. However, it was as a film producer/distributor, not as a filmmaker, that he was associated with this organization. In 1958, he had formed G String Productions to distribute the celebrated underground classic, *Pull My Daisy*.

In the early 1960's, De Antonio was given access to 188 hours worth of kinetoscopes of the McCarthy hearings. He managed to raise $75,000 from his friend, the Standard Oil heir, Eliot Pratt, and set to work editing.

It took him more than two years, and he went broke in the process, but in 1964 De Antonio emerged with his first documentary, *Point of Order*. Paul Newman offered to do a narration. De Antonio turned him down. He had already evolved his film philosophy, and it held no place for narrators:

"... the narrator on TV becomes a super figure who has to explain to you what you've seen, or what you haven't been allowed to see. It's not the same as the jackboot of the nazis, but it is a kind of fascism of the mind."

In a sense, De Antonio was the great precursor of scratch video and sampling. He described his own method as "radical scavenging:" what it entailed was expropriating footage from the TV networks, and editing the footage together to make a scathing critique of some aspect of American society. He was looking for the parapraxes, the out-takes, those moments never broadcast, but consigned to the deepest vaults of the network archives.

The 1960's were a good period for him. Although *Point of Order* was slammed by the New York Times, it was successful with students, who were beginning to be politicized by the Vietnam War. Pressed as to why he did not shoot his own footage, De Antonio would ask critics what chance an independent filmmaker had against the all powerful TV stations, "the ruling class of America," as he described them. An independent filmmaker would not have been allowed to get near Kennedy on that fateful day in Dallas.

Kennedy's assassination, indeed, was the subject for De Antonio's second film, *Rush to Judgment*. Sponsored in the UK by Woodfall Films, Tony Richardson's production company, this project did not endear him to the establishment. Although officially shunned, he was privately helped by "insiders" who gave him access to sensitive material. Nonetheless, the networks had an annoying tendency of destroying the most valuable, and most incriminating, footage.

His Vietnam film, *In the Year of the Pig*, was again eccentrically financed. Mrs Orville Schell, a wealthy New York socialite, gave dinner parties at which the production money was raised, and she is credited as the film's executive producer. De Antonio managed to find an interview with the US General, George Patton, in which Patton described the young Americans in Vietnam as "a bloody good bunch of killers." His 1976 effort, *Underground*, in which he managed to track down and interview the infamous Weather Underground, exasperated the authorities, who hadn't been able to get near the group. The FBI therefore tried to subpoena the film and crew.

Not long before his death, Emile De Antonio discovered that J. Edgar Hoover and the FBI had been keeping files on him for nearly 30 years. Appalled by American "secret society," he could not help but be amused at the same time. There was something pathetic and comic about this sinister man, Hoover, and his pet organization. De Antonio, in *Mr. Hoover and I*, took great pleasure in FBI minutiae: the way that Hoover made all his employees wear felt hats; his admiration for the Jewish star of the TV series about the FBI, an admiration which took no account of his own notorious anti-semitism; Hoover's insistence on his driver never taking a left turn because once the FBI chief had been injured in a car accident when a left turn had been taken; all appealed to De Antonio's sense of irony. ("I am as much Dada as I am a Marxist," he said in an interview he conducted with himself for *Film Quarterly*.)

A strange mixture of Thomas Paine and Huckleberry Finn, Emile De Antonio was a devout patriot, who defined his role as "artist" in constructively negative terms. As far as he was concerned, art was necessarily adversary, and he was determinedly critical and anarchistic. He saw it as his duty.

—G.C. Macnab

DEARDEN, Basil.

British. Born Basil Dear in Westcliffe-on-Sea, England, 1 January 1911. Married actress Melissa Stribling, 1947, two sons (including scriptwriter James). Actor in repertory, toured U.S. with Ben Greet Company, late 1920's; general stage manager for Basil Dean (changed name to avoid confusion), 1931–36; production manager, associate producer and scriptwriter at Ealing studios, 1936–40; co-directed several Will Hay comedies, 1941–43; directed first film, *The Bells Go Down*, 1943; worked with producer Michael Relph, 1949–71 (TV director, 1960's). Recipient: British Film Academy Awards, with Michael Relph, for *The Blue Lamp*, 1950, and *Sapphire*, 1960. *Died in auto accident, 23 March 1971.*

Films as Director:

1941   *The Black Sheep of Whitehall* (co-d)
1942   *The Goose Steps Out* (co-d)
1943   *The Bells Go Down*; *My Learned Friend* (co-d)
1944   *The Halfway House*; *They Came to a City*
1945   "The Hearse Driver" episode and linking story of **Dead of Night**
1946   *The Captive Heart*
1947   *Frieda*
1948   *Saraband for Dead Lovers* (*Saraband*)
1949   "The Actor" and "The Prisoner of War" episodes of *Train of Events* (+co-sc, Michael Relph producer); **The Blue Lamp**
1950   *Cage of Gold*; *Pool of London*
1951   *I Believe in You* (co-d + co-pr with Michael Relph, co-sc)
1952   *The Gentle Gunman* (co-d + co-pr with Michael Relph)
1953   *The Square Ring* (co-d + co-pr with Michael Relph)
1954   *The Rainbow Jacket* (co-d + co-pr with Michael Relph); *Out of the Clouds* (co-d + co-pr with Michael Relph)
1955   *The Ship That Died of Shame* (co-d + co-pr with Michael Relph, co-sc); *Who Done It?* (co-d + co-pr with Michael Relph)
1957   *The Smallest Show on Earth*
1958   *Violent Playground*
1959   *Sapphire*; *The League of Gentlemen*
1960   *Man in the Moon*; *The Secret Partner*
1961   **Victim**; *All Night Long* (co-d, co-pr with Relph)
1962   *Life for Ruth* (*Walk in the Shadow*)
1963   *The Mind Benders*; *A Place to Go*
1964   *Woman of Straw*; *Masquerade*
1966   *Khartoum*
1968   *Only When I Larf*; *The Assassination Bureau*
1970   *The Man Who Haunted Himself* (+co-sc)

Other Films:

1938   *It's in the Air* (Kimmins) (asst d); *Penny Paradise* (Reed) (asst d); *This Man Is News* (MacDonald) (co-sc)
1939   *Come On, George!* (Kimmins) (asst d)
1940   *Let George Do It* (Varnel) (co-sc); *Spare a Copper* (Carstairs) (assoc pr)
1941   *Young Veteran* (Cavalcanti) (asst d)
1941   *Turned Out Nice Again* (Varnel) (assoc pr)
1956   *The Green Man* (Day) (supervisor, uncredited)
1957   *Davy* (Relph) (pr)
1958   *Rockets Galore* (*Mad Little Island*) (Relph) (pr)
1959   *Desert Mice* (Relph) (pr)

Publications:

On DEARDEN: books—

Balcon, Michael, *A Lifetime of Films*, London, 1969.
Barr, Charles, *Ealing Studios*, London, 1977.
Perry, George, *Forever Ealing*, London, 1981.
Hill, John, *Sex, Class, and Realism: British Cinema 1956–63*, London, 1986.

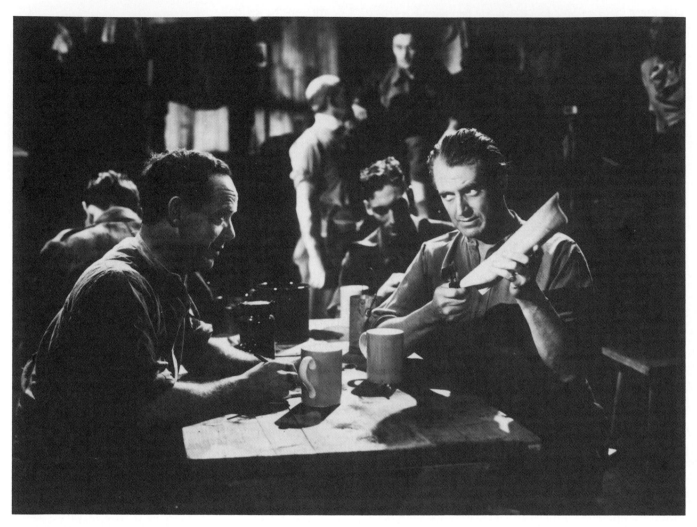

Basil Dearden: *The Captive Heart*

On DEARDEN: articles—

Tynan, Kenneth, "Ealing: The Studio in Suburbia," in *Films and Filming* (London), November and December 1955.
"Dearden and Relph: Two on a Tandem," in *Films and Filming* (London), July 1966.
Barr, Charles, "Projecting Britain and the British Character: Ealing Studios," in *Screen* (London), Summer 1974.
Ellis, John, "Made in Ealing," in *Screen* (London), Spring 1975.

*   *   *

Basil Dearden is, par excellence, the journeyman-director of British cinema, standing in much the same relation to Ealing (the studio for which he directed the greater part of his output) as, say, Michael Curtiz did to Warner Brothers. More than any other director, Dearden personified the spirit of Ealing films: concerned, conscientious, socially aware, but hampered by a certain innately British caution. Dearden was the complete professional, unfailingly competent and meticulous; his films were never less than thoroughly well-constructed, and he enjoyed a reputation in the industry for total reliability, invariably bringing in assignments on schedule and under budget.

Such careful craftsmanship, though, should not be equated with dullness. Dearden's films may often have been safe, but they were rarely dull (despite the allegations of some critics). His work shows a natural flair for pace and effective action: narrative lines are clear and uncluttered, and although in many ways they have dated, his films remain eminently watchable and entertaining. In the moral climate of the time, too, his choice of subjects showed considerable boldness. Dearden tackled such edgy topics as race (*Sapphire*), homosexuality (*Victim*), sectarian bigotry (*Life for Ruth*), and post-war anti-German prejudice (*Frieda*), always arguing for tolerance and understanding. It was perhaps inevitable, given his background and the ethos of the studio, that these "social problem" movies tended towards overly reasonable solutions. "Dearden's films," Charles Barr has pointed out in his definitive study *Ealing Studios*, "insistently *generalize* their moral lessons."

For most of his directing career Dearden worked closely with Michael Relph, who produced nearly all his films, collaborated with him on the scripts, and occasionally co-directed; after the demise of Ealing, the two men formed their own production company. Their joint output covered a wide variety of genre, including costume drama (*Saraband for Dead Lovers*) and comedy (*The Smallest Show on Earth*), as well as large scale epic (*Khartoum*). Dearden's flair for action was effectively exploited in the classic "heist" movie, *The League of Gentlemen*, and in *The Blue Lamp*, a seminal police drama and one of the first Ealing films shot almost entirely on location. Early in his career, Dearden also evinced a weakness for slightly stagey allegories such as *Halfway House*, and *They Came To A City*, in which groups of disparate individuals are brought to a change of heart through supernatural intervention.

There can also be detected in Dearden's films, perhaps slightly unexpectedly, a muted but poetic vision of an idealized community—seen most clearly in his first film with Relph, *The Captive Heart*, a sympathetic study of prisoners-of-war. "The community" Charles Barr has noted "is presented as part of a wider society involving all of us—and encompassing England." In his strengths and in his weaknesses—the restraint verging on inhibition, the competent versatility tending towards lack of directorial character—Dearden was in many ways an archetypally "British" director. Anyone wishing to understand the success and limitations of post-war British cinema, and indeed of post-war British society, could do far worse than study the films of Basil Dearden.

—Theresa FitzGerald

DE BROCA, Philippe, *see* BROCA, Philippe de

DE FUENTES, Fernando.

Mexican. Born in Veracruz, 13 December 1894. Film editor and assistant director, 1920's; first Mexican offered opportunity to direct by Compañia Nacional Productora de Peliculas, 1932; producer and director for newly formed Grovas production company, 1942; co-founder, Diana Films, 1945. *Died 4 July 1958.*

Films as Director:

1932 *El anonimo*
1933 *El prisionero trece*; *La calandria*; *El tigre de Yautepec*; *El compadre Mendoza*
1934 *El fantasma del convento*; *Cruz diablo*
1935 *Vamonos con Pancho Villa*; *La familia Dressel*
1936 *Las mujeres mandan*; *Alla en el rancho grande*
1937 *Bajo el cielo de Mexico*; *La Zandunga*
1938 *La casa del ogro*
1939 *Papacito lindo*
1940 *Alla en el tropico*; *El jefe maximo*; *Creo en Dios*
1941 *La gallina clueca*
1942 *Asi se quiere en Jalisco*
1943 *Dona Barbara*; *La mujer sin alma*
1944 *El rey se divierte*
1945 *Hasta que perdio Jalisco*; *La selva de fuego*
1946 *La devoradora*
1948 *Alla en el Rancho Grande*; *Jalisco canta en Sevilla*
1949 *Hipolito el de Santa*
1950 *Por la puerta falsa*; *Crimen y castigo*
1952 *Los hijos de Maria Morales*; *Cancion de cuna*
1953 *Tres citas con el destino*

Publications:

On DE FUENTES: books—

Riera, Emilio Garcia, *Historia documental del cine mexicano*, vol. 1–6, Mexico City 1969/74.
Blanco, Jorge Ayala, *La aventura del cine mexicano*, Mexico City, 1979.

Mora, Carl, *Mexican Cinema: Reflections of a Society, 1896–1980*, Berkeley, 1982.
Riera, Emilio Garcia, *Fernando de Fuentes (1894–1958)*, Mexico City, 1984.
De los Reyes, Aurelio, *Medio siglo de cine mexicano (1896–1947)*, Mexico City, 1987.

On DE FUENTES: articles—

De la Vega, Eduardo, "Fernando de Fuentes: La mirada critica sobre la Revolucion Mexicana," in *Filmoteca* (Mexico City), no. 1, 1979.
Paranagua, P.A., "Cannes 82: Homanaje a dos maestros del cine latinoamericano," in *Contracampo* (Madrid), August-September 1982.

*   *   *

The first Mexican cineaste of note, Fernando De Fuentes is still considered the director whose interpretations of the revolution and whose contributions to typical Mexican genres have not been surpassed. Early sound film production in Mexico was dominated by foreigners: Russians who accompanied Eisenstein in the making of *Que Viva México*, Spaniards who passed through Hollywood, Cubans and U.S. citizens who somehow ended up there. De Fuentes was one of the first Mexicans to be given a chance to direct sound films in his country.

After several false starts with "grey and theatrical melodramas," De Fuentes indicated first in *Prisionero trece* that his métier was the "revolutionary tragedy." During 1910–17, Mexico passed through a cataclysmic social revolution whose cultural expression resounded principally in the extraordinary murals of Diego Rivera, David Siquieros, and José Orozco. Fiction films did not examine this watershed event seriously until 1933 when De Fuentes made *El compadre Mendoza*. Far from the epic monumentality of revolutionary transformation painted on the walls by Rivera or Siquieros, *El compadre Mendoza* recreates the revolution from a perspective similar to Orozco's vision of individual tragedies and private pain.

Rosalio Mendoza is the owner of a large hacienda which is constantly threatened by the conflict's warring factions. In order to appease them, Mendoza pretends to support whichever group is currently visiting him—something he accomplishes by wining and dining his guests in a room conspicuously decorated with a portrait of the appropriate leader. Eventually, Mendoza and General Nieto (a follower of Emiliano Zapata's agrarian revolt) become close friends. Mendoza names his son after Nieto and asks him to be the *compadre* (godfather). But after Mendoza is ruined economically, he betrays Nieto in order to flee to Mexico City. The emphasis on fraternal bloodletting, the corruption of ideals, and the disillusion in the aftermath of the revolution is powerfully conveyed in both *El compadre Mendoza* and *Vámonos con Pancho Villa*. They remain even today the best cinematic treatments of the Mexican revolution.

De Fuentes's work in traditional Mexican genres is also important. *Allá en el Rancho Grande* is the progenitor of the *charro* genre, the Mexican singing cowboy having received his cinematic introduction to Mexico and the rest of Latin America in this immensely popular film. The attraction of such nostalgia for a never-existent Arcadia can be seen in the fact that the year following the release of *Rancho Grande* more than half of the Mexican films produced were similar pastoral fantasies, and these have continued to be a staple of Mexican cinema. The *charro* genre's domination of Mexican cinema is almost matched by films about the Mexican mother. De Fuentes directed perhaps the most palatable of such works, *La gallina clueca* starring Sara García, the character actress who is the national paradigm of the sainted, long-suffering, self-sacrificing mother. In De Fuentes's hands the overworked Oedipal melodrama is denied its usual histrionics and becomes

Fernando De Fuentes

an interesting work as well as the definitive film of this sub-genre.

His better films demonstrate De Fuentes's strong narrative style, noted for its consistency and humor. They do not seem particularly dated, and De Fuentes utilizes visual techniques such as the rack focus or the dissolve particularly effectively and unobtrusively. He also makes telling use of overlay montages, à la Eisenstein or Vertov, to convey moods or concepts. In regard to singing—one of the banes of Mexican cinema—De Fuentes has been uneven. For example, in the 2 films on the revolution, restraint is shown and songs function well in relation to the story line. Unfortunately, *Allá en el Rancho Grande* and its various sequels are characteristically glutted with songs.

De Fuentes's career as a director went from the sublime to the ridiculous. In one year he plummeted from the heights of *Vámonos con Pancho Villa* to the depths of *Allá en el Rancho Grande*, whose enormous commercial success throughout Latin America sealed De Fuentes's fate. It was popular because De Fuentes is a talented director; but the commercial rewards for those talents came at a high price. After *Vámonos con Pancho Villa*, De Fuentes settled into the repetition of mediocre and conventional formula films.

—John Mraz

DELANNOY, Jean.

French. Born in Noisy-le-Sec, 8 August 1908. Educated at Lille University, and Paris University. Began as film actor while at University (sister is actress Henriette Delannoy), late 1920's; in Service Cinématographique des Armées, then chief editor, Paramount Studios, Joinville, 1930–32; feature director, from 1935; became President of Institut des Hautes Etudes Cinématographiques (IDHEC), Paris, 1975. Recipient: Best Film, Cannes festival, for *La Symphonie Pastorale*, 1946; International Prize, Venice Festival, for *Dieu a besoin des hommes*, 1950.

Films as Director and Co-Scriptwriter or Co-Adaptor:

1933   *Franches lippées* (short)
1934   *Une Vocation irrésistible* (short); *L'École des detectives* (short)
1935   *Paris-Deauville*
1936   *La Moule* (medium-length)
1937   *Ne tuez pas Dolly!* (medium-length)
1938   *La Vénus de l'or*
1939   *Macao, l'enfer du jeu*; *Le Diamánt noir*
1941   *Fièvres*
1942   *L'Assassin a peur la nuit*; *Pontcarral, Colonel d'Empire*
1943   *Macao, l'enfer du jeu* (partially re-shot version with Pierre Renoir in role played by Erich von Stroheim who was forbidden by German authorities; original version of *Macao* re-released after war); *L'Éternel Retour* (*The Eternal Return*)
1944   *Le Bossu*
1945   *La Part de l'ombre* (*Blind Desire*)
1946   *La Symphonie pastorale*
1947   *Les Jeux sont faits* (*The Chips Are Down*)
1948   *Aux yeux du souvenir* (*Souvenir*)
1949   *Le Secret de Mayerling*
1950   *Dieu a besoin des hommes* (*God Needs Men*)
1951   *Le Garçon sauvage* (*Savage Triangle*)
1952   *La Minute de vérité* (*L'ora della verità, The Moment of Truth*) (+co-sc); "Jeanne (Joan of Arc)" episode of *Destinées* (*Daughters of Destiny*)
1953   *La Route Napoléon*; "Le Lit de la Pompadour" episode of *Secrets d'alcôve*
1954   *Obsession*
1955   *Chiens perdus sans collier*; *Marie-Antoinette*
1956   *Notre-Dame de Paris* (*The Hunchback of Notre Dame*)
1957   *Maigret tend un piège* (*Inspector Maigret*)
1958   *Guinguette*; *Maigret et l'affaire Saint-Fiacre*
1959   *Le Baron de l'Ecluse*
1960   "L'Adolescence" episode of *La Française et l'amour* (*Love and the Frenchwoman*); *La Princesse de Clèves*
1962   *Le Rendez-vous*; *Venere imperiale* (*Vénus impériale*)
1964   *Les Amitiés particulières* (*This Special Friendship*); *Le Majordôme*
1965   "Le Berceau" and "La Répétition" episodes of *Le Lit à deux places* (*The Double Bed*); *Les Sultans*
1967   *Le Soleil des voyous* (*Action Man*)
1969   *La Peau de Torpedo*
1972   *Pas folle la guêpe*

Other Films: (partial list)

1926   *Miss Helyett* (Monca and Keroul) (role)
1927   *Casanova* (Volkoff) (role)
1929   *La Grande Passion* (Hugon) (role)
1932   *La Belle Marinière* (Lachman) (ed); *Une Étoile disparaît* (Villers) (ed); *Le Fils improvisé* (Guissart) (ed)
1933   *Le Père prématuré* (Guissart) (ed); *Les Aventures du roi Pausole* (Granowsky) (ed)
1934   *Le Roi des Champs-Elysées* (Nosseck) (ed)
1935   *Michel Strogoff* (de Baroncelli and Eichberg) (ed); *Tovaritch* (Deval) (co-ed)

1936 *Club de femmes* (Deval) (tech adv, co-ed); *Nitchevo* (de
       Baroncelli) (ed)
1937 *Tamara la complaisante* (Gandera) (tech adv, co-sc
       uncredited); *Feu!* (de Baroncelli) (ed)
1938 *Le Paradis de Satan* (Gandera) (tech adv)

Publications:

By DELANNOY: articles—

"Le Réalisateur," in *Le Cinéma par ceux qui le font*, Paris, 1949.

On DELANNOY: book—

Guiget, Claude, Emmanuel Papillon, and Jacques Pinturault, *Jean Delannoy: Filmographie, props, temoignanes*, Aulnay-sur-Bois, 1985.

On DELANNOY: articles—

"Jean Delannoy," in *Film Dope* (London), September 1976.
Tribute to Delannoy in *Film Francais* (Paris), 21 February 1986.

On DELANNOY: films—

Knapp, Hubert, and Igor Barrère, *Echos de plateau* (on making of *La Minute de vérité*), 1952.

*   *   *

Critics have not been kind to Jean Delannoy although the public certainly has, for nearly all his films were solid box-office hits. But Delannoy, both by personal pretention and by the subject matter of his major films, demanded more serious attention. Just as André Cayatte is France's director of social problem films, so Delannoy may be considered its moral philosopher. *La Symphonie pastorale* and *God Needs Man*, made just after the war, brought him this reputation and remain his best known work, along with *Les Jeux sont faits* made in collaboration with Sartre. But more than a score of films surround this core, few of which measure up to the ambition and values for which they stand.

Delannoy flirted with the cinema in the 1920's while working at a bank. Godard would later recall these beginnings in his caricature of Delannoy "going into the Billancourt studios briefcase in hand; you would have sworn he was going into an insurance office." His initial training as an editor provided him with a sense of dramatic economy that may be at the origin of his popular success and critical failure. A Protestant, his calculated distance, even coolness, alienated many critics, most notably the passionate New Wave cinephiles at *Cahiers*.

No one would have paid Delannoy any attention had he not turned away from the competent studio dramas he first directed to stronger material. *Fontcarral* was his first remarkable effort, bringing him fame as a man of conviction when this Napoleonic adventure tale was interpreted as a direct call to resistance against the Nazi occupation forces.

He was then chosen to help Jean Cocteau bring to the screen *L'Eternel Retour*. Whether, as some suspect, Cocteau pushed him far beyond his usually cautious methods, or because the legendary tragedy of this Tristan and Isolde update was perfect material for the frigidity of his style, the film was a striking success, haunting in its bizarre imagery and in the mysterious implications of its plot and dialogue.

Just after the war came the films already mentioned as central to Delannoy as an auteur. Evidently Gide, Sartre, and Queffelec inspired him to render great moral and philosophical issues in a dramatically rigorous way. Today these films seem overly cautious and pretty, even prettified. But in their day they garnered worldwide respect, the first winning the Grand Prize at Cannes in 1946 and the last the Grand Prize at Venice in 1950. The cinematic ingenuity they display, particularly in the use of geography as a moral arena (a snowy alpine village, a destitute seacoast village), and in the taut editing,

Jean Delannoy: *La Symphonie pastorale*

gives some, though not sufficient, justification for the staginess of the weighty dialogue.

Delannoy became perhaps the director most maligned by *Cahiers du cinéma* because of the battle he fought with Bresson over rights to *Diary of a Country Priest* (which Bresson won) and *La Princesse de Clèves* (which Delannoy won). Their accusations of his inauthenticity were borne out in the many hack productions he directed in the 1950's, including a superproduction of *Notre Dame de Paris*. While none of these films is without some merit, the 1960 *Princesse de Clèves* being full of tasteful production values, his style more and more represented the most deprecated face of the "cinema of quality."

—Dudley Andrew

DELLUC, Louis.

French, Born Louis Jean René Delluc in Cadouin, Dordogne, 14 October 1890. Educated at Lycée Henri IV, Paris, until 1909. Married actress Eve Francis, 1919. Editor-in-chief of *Film* magazine, 1917; began column in *Paris-Midi*, 1918; directed first film, *Fumée noire*, and co-founded *Journal de ciné-club*, 1920; helped start *Cinema* magazine and "Matinées de Cinéma," 1921. From 1937, Prix Louis Delluc awarded annually (except during war years) to an outstanding French feature film. *Died of tuberculosis in Paris, 22 March 1924.*

Films as Director:

1920 *Fumée noire* (co-d, sc); *Le Silence* (+sc)

Louis Delluc: *La Femme de nulle part*

1921 *Fièvre* (+sc); *Le Chemin d'Ernoa* (*L'Américain*) (+sc); *Le Tonnerre* (*Évangeline et la tonnerre*) (+sc)
1922 *La Femme de nulle part* (+sc)
1923 *L'Inondation* (+sc)

Other Films:

1919 *La Fête espagnole* (Dulac) (sc)
1921 *Prométhée banquier* (L'Herbier) (role)

Publications:

By DELLUC: books—

Cinéma et Cie, Paris, 1919.
Photogénie, Paris, 1920.
Charlot, Paris, 1921; as *Charlie Chaplin*, London, 1922.
La Jungle du cinéma, Paris, 1921.
Drames de cinéma (including *La Fête espagnole, Le Silence, Fièvre* and *La Femme de nulle part*), Paris, 1923.
Ecrits cinématographique, edited by Pierre Lherminier, Paris, 2 vols., 1985–86.

On DELLUC: books—

Amiguet, Philippe, *Cinéma! Cinéma!*, Lausanne, 1923.
Gance, Abel, *Prisme*, Paris, 1930.
Francis, Eve, *Temps héroïques*, Paris, 1949.
Tariol, Marcel, *Louis Delluc*, Paris, 1965.

On DELLUC: articles—

"Delluc Issue" of *Ciné-club* (Paris), March 1949.
Francis, Eve, and others, *Lettres Françaises* (Paris), 19 March 1964.
McCreary, E.C., "Louis Delluc, Film Theorist, Critic and Prophet," in *Cinema Journal* (Evanston, Illinois), Fall 1976.

McCreary, Eugene, "Film criticism and the historian," in *Film and History* (Newark, New Jersey), February 1981.
Régent, R., "'Le Delluc': un prix de copains," in *Avant-Scène du Cinéma* (Paris), 15 April 1981.
McCreary, Eugene, "Louis Delluc et le cinema americain," in *Cahiers de la Cinémathèque* (Perpignan), Autumn 1982.

* * *

Louis Delluc was one of the key figures in the renewal of French cinema after the collapse of the industry's world dominance in the years before World War I. Though in no sense the leader of a unified movement or faction, Delluc has considerable importance as both critic and filmmaker. His impact was crucial during the years after 1919, though he died in 1924 before the full flowering of the French film renaissance to which he had made such a contribution.

Like so many of his contemporaries, Delluc initially had literary ambitions. Abandoning his studies for a career in journalism, he wrote poetry, plays, novels and dramatic criticism. He continued to write even after he had turned to filmmaking and published—despite his early death—over a dozen literary works of various kinds, in addition to three collections of film criticism. He was also one of the few filmmakers of the early 1920's to publish a collection of his screenplays, under the title *Drames de cinéma*, in 1923. The work which opened Delluc's eyes to the potential of film as an artistic medium was Cecil B. DeMille's *The Cheat*, distributed in France under the title *Forfaiture*. Though Delluc's writings show his clear awareness of the specific limitations of this particular work, which became a cult film for the cinematically-inclined French intellectuals of the period, he was very responsive to the form of cinema which it represented. This was the narrative continuity cinema which had developed during the previous five years or so in the United States and from which French filmmakers had been shielded by the economic power of the French commercial giants, Pathé and Gaumont.

Like André Bazin some thirty years later, Delluc developed his ideas in relation to specific films—attacking the Feuillade of *La Nouvelle Mission de Judex*, while offering a keen appreciation of American and Swedish cinema and the films of French contemporaries such as Antoine, L'Herbier and Gance. Delluc does not offer a worked-out theory of cinema, but a number of key ideas recur: the importance of cinema as a popular art, the crucial significance of rhythm and pacing in a form now based on sequences of shots instead of the long-held *plan séquences*, the importance of expressive, poetic imagery and the choice of concrete realistic detail, together with the need for restraint in acting. He sought a cinema which would be truly the expression of its author and put stress on the inner life of its characters.

Between 1919 and 1923 Delluc scripted one film, *La Fête espagnol*, and directed eight others, from *Fumée noire* in 1920 to *L'Inondation* in 1923. With one exception, all of these were from original scripts, conceived directly for the screen. Though Delluc drew inspiration from American movies and advocated a popular cinema, he placed little emphasis on physical action. These films concentrate on the ramifications of a single incident and depict the intense interaction of a handful of characters. For none of this work did Delluc enjoy adequate resources and he was denied the popular success which would have given him bigger budgets. Moreover, unlike Gance and L'Herbier, he did not have an instinctive flair for images, and the interest of his films lies more in their construction than their realization. Almost all contain some noteworthy stylistic exploration: the atmosphere of a single set in *Fièvre*, the use of landscape in *Le Chemin d'Ernoa*, or the interaction of past and present in *Le Silence* and his generally recognised masterpiece, *La Femme de nulle part*. The fact that he died at the age of 34, while his contemporaries Gance and L'Herbier survived into their nineties, makes Delluc something of a figure apart, but his place among the formative influences on French cinema is assured.

—Roy Armes

DELVAUX, André.

Belgian. Born in Héverlé, near Louvain, Belgium, 21 March 1926. Studied at the Free University of Brussels, 1945–52; piano and composition at Royal Conservatory of Brussels. Piano accompanist at the Belgian Cinémathèque, from 1950; head of a programme of film education for Belgian teachers, then lecturer at National Superior Institute of the Entertainment arts (INSAS), from 1963; made first series of films as TV director, on Federico Fellini, 1960; directed first feature, *L'Homme au crane rasé*, 1966. Recipient: Prix Louis Delluc, for *Rendez-vous à Bray*, 1972.

Films as Director and Scriptwriter:

1962   *Le Temps des ecoliers* (short)
1966   *L'Homme au crane rasé (Die Man die zijn Haar kort liet knippen. The Man Who Had His Hair Cut Short)* (co-sc)

1968   *Un Soir un train*
1971   *Rendez-vous à Bray*
1973   *Belle*
1975   *Dirk Bouts (Dieric Bouts)*
1979   *Femme entre chien et loup (Een Vrouw tussen hon en wolf. Woman in a Twilight Garden)*
1981   *To Woody Allen, From Europe With Love*
1983   *Benvenuta*
1985   *Babel Opera, ou la répétition de Don Juan*
1988   *L'oeuvre au noir (The Abyss)*

Publications:

By DELVAUX: articles—

Interview in *Image et Son* (Paris), September 1973.
Interview in *Ecran* (Paris), November 1973.
Interview in *The Thousand Eyes Magazine* (New York), December 1976.
Interview in *Sight and Sound* (London), Spring 1977.
Interviews in *Revue Belge du Cinéma* (Brussels), October and December 1977.
Interview in *Cinéma* (Paris), July/August 1979.
Interview in *A.I.P. & Co.* (London), July/August 1980.
Interview in *Revue Belge du Cinéma* (Brussels), no. 20, 1981.
Interview with D. Michiels, in *Film en Televisie* (Brussels), October 1983.
Interview with T. Louis, in *Séquences* (Montreal), August 1987.
"André Delvaux Section" of *Avant-Scene du Cinéma* (Paris), May 1988.
Interview in *Revue du Cinéma* (Paris), June 1988.

On DELVAUX: books—

Pacquet, André, editor, *Le Cinéma en Belgique*, Quebec, Montreal, 1972.
Ellero, Roberto, *André Delvaux*, Venice, 1981.
Nysenholc, Adolphe, editor, *André Delvaux, ou les visages de l'imaginaire*, Brussels, 1985.

On DELVAUX: articles—

Cinéma (Switzerland), no. 4, 1974.
"Andre Delvaux," in *Film Dope* (London), September 1976.
Milne, Tom, "Countries of the Mind," in *Sight and Sound* (London), Spring 1972.
National Film Theatre Booklet (London), May 1980.
Variety (New York), September 4, 1985.
Helfgoot, H., "Andre Delvaux à pied d'oeuvre," in *Séquences* (Montréal), March 1988.
Variety (New York), 18 May 1988.

*   *   *

André Delvaux's growing body of cinema until now can be called one of tone, mood, and impression. A harbinger of French symbolist writers of the late nineteenth and early twentieth century, for whom esthetic effects are sustained independently of narrative design, Delvaux writes and directs films that disperse synchronies of sound and image. Contact seems to be established with the spectator exactly when the thread of his stories is untied. Music and dialogue appear ungrounded or else alternately joined to and detached from their origins in either dialogue or visual composition. Quite often human figures seem to disappear in misty landscapes that are marked as much by sparse musical notes as physical contour. His films script effects of the dissolution of language. They are crafted through labor of collaboration with and quotation from other works of writing and art, notably Marguerite Yourcenar (*L'oeuvre au noir*) and Julien Gracq (*Le roi Copheta* inspiring *Rendez-vous à Bray*). He portrays Northern and Baroque traditions of painting that include Dirk Bouts and Caravaggio, while his affiliation with Surrealists—Ernst and others—are obvious in the graphic resemblance of the aptly entitled *Femme entre chien et loup* with Buñuel/Dali's *Un chien anda-*

André Delvaux directing *Belle*

lou. Through fugacious and passing shapes the director articulates space "between" fantasm and reality.

If the films are inspired by the epoch of the *nouvelle vague*, in which a literary cinema is proposed as an alternative to the industrial heritage of entertainment in Hollywood, their signature is nonetheless of a Belgian, metaphysical style. They lead to thought that erases boundaries usually demarcating real from imaginary worlds. He creates mental landscapes that recall the musical sense of language that had been the stuff first of Mallarmé, and later, especially, of Maeterlinck's theater. It is effective when displaced into the more immediate realm of cinema.

Perhaps the keenest impressions of his films can be felt in evanesence of sound and image. Loss of discernable forms paradoxically traces the memory of paintings and poetry that interfere with dialogue and music. Through slow montage Delvaux allows the spectator to expand the narrative field that is being viewed. In, for instance, *Rendez-vous à Bray*, soldiers of the 1870's sport uniforms with decorous colors on their epaulettes and chevrons. Set against grey mist, they set tones that immediately recall the both dreamy and lucid view of timeless death and beauty that Rimbaud—another writer of Northern French inspiration—offers in his famous sonnet, "Le dormeur du val." Film and poetry coalesce to leave fleeting sensations that concretize a moment of European history and of style, at the moment just prior to the beginnings of cinema.

Delvaux is not everyone's director. He asks his viewer to *read* hieroglyphs fashioned from music, painting, and literature that reach into collective memory and, no less, emerge from oblivion. His work merits extensive study for its range of sources and its meditation on the origins and the freedom of film form.

—Tom Conley

DE MILLE, Cecil B.

American. Born Cecil Blount De Mille in Ashfield, Massachusetts, 12 August 1881. Educated at Pennsylvania Military Academy, Chester, 1896–98, and at American Academy of Dramatic Arts, New York, 1898–1900. Married Constance Adams, 16 August 1902, two sons, two daughters. Actor, playwright, stage producer, and associate with mother in De Mille Play Co. (theatrical agency), to 1913; co-founder, then Director-General, Jesse L. Lasky Feature Play Co., 1913 (becomes Paramount Pictures Corp. on merger, 1918); directed first film, *The Squaw Man*, 1914; founder, Mercury Aviation Co., 1919; established De Mille Pictures Corp., 1924; joined MGM as producer-director, 1928; co-founder, Screen Directors Guild, 1931; independent producer for Paramount, 1932; producer, Lux Radio Theatre of the Air, 1936–45. Recipient:

Outstanding Service Award, War Agencies of the Government of the U.S.; Special Oscar "for 37 years of brilliant showmanship," 1949; Irving Thalberg Award, Academy, 1952; Milestone Award, Screen Producers' Guild, 1956; Chevalier de Légion d'honneur, France; Honorary doctorate, University of Southern California. *Died 21 January 1959.*

Films as Director:

1914   *The Squaw Man (The White Man)* (co-d, sc, bit role); *The Call of the North* (+sc, introductory appearance); *The Virginian* (+sc, co-ed); *What's His Name* (+sc, ed): *The Man from Home* (+sc, ed); *Rose of the Rancho* (+sc, ed): *Brewster's Millions* (co-d, uncredited, sc); *The Master Mind* (co-d, uncredited, sc); *The Man on the Box* (co-d, uncredited, sc); *The Only Son* (co-d, uncredited, sc); *The Ghost Breaker* (co-d, uncredited, co-sc)

1915   *The Girl of the Golden West* (+sc, ed); *The Warrens of Virginia* (+sc, ed); *The Unafraid* (+sc, ed); *The Captive* (+co-sc, ed); *The Wild Goose Chase* (+co-sc, ed); *The Arab* (+co-sc, ed); *Chimmie Fadden* (+co-sc, ed): *Kindling* (+sc, ed); *Carmen* (+sc, ed); *Chimmie Fadden Out West* (+co-sc, ed); *The Cheat* (+sc, ed); *The Golden Chance* (+co-sc, ed); *The Goose Girl* (co-d with Thompson, uncredited, co-sc)

1916   *Temptation* (+co-story, ed); *The Trail of the Lonesome Pine* (+sc, ed); *The Heart of Nora Flynn* (+ed); *Maria Rosa* (+ed); *The Dream Girl* (+ed)

1917   *Joan the Woman* (+ed); *A Romance of the Redwoods* (+co-sc, ed); *The Little American* (+co-sc, ed); *The Woman God Forgot* (+ed); *The Devil Stone* (+ed); *Nan of Music Mountain* (co-d with Melford, uncredited); *Lost and Won*

1918   *The Whispering Chorus* (+ed); *Old Wives for New* (+ed); *We Can't Have Everything* (+co-ed); *Till I Come Back to You*; *The Squaw Man*

1919   *Don't Change Your Husband*; *For Better, For Worse*; *Male and Female (The Admirable Crichton)*

1920   *Why Change Your Wife?*; *Something to Think About*

1921   *Forbidden Fruit* (+pr); *The Affairs of Anatol (A Prodigal Knight)*; *Fool's Paradise*

1922   *Saturday Night*; *Manslaughter*; *Don't Tell Everything* (co-d with Wood, uncredited) (incorporates two reel unused *The Affairs of Anatol* footage)

1923   *Adam's Rib*; *The Ten Commandments*

1924   *Triumph* (+pr); *Feet of Clay*

1925   *The Golden Bed*; *The Road to Yesterday*

1926   *The Volga Boatman*

1927   *The King of Kings*

1929   *The Godless Girl*; *Dynamite* (+pr)

1930   *Madame Satan* (+pr)

1931   *The Squaw Man* (+pr)

1932   *The Sign of the Cross* (+pr) (re-released 1944 with add'l footage)

1933   *This Day and Age* (+pr)

1934   *Four Frightened People* (+pr); *Cleopatra* (+pr)

1935   *The Crusades* (+pr)

1937   *The Plainsman* (+pr)

1938   *The Buccaneer* (+pr)

1939   *Union Pacific* (+pr)

1940   *North West Mounted Police* (+pr, prologue narration)

1942   *Reap the Wild Wind* (+pr, prologue narration)

1944   *The Story of Dr. Wassell* (+pr)

1947   *Unconquered* (+pr)

1949   *Samson and Delilah* (+pr, prologue narration)

1952   *The Greatest Show on Earth* (+pr, narration, introductory appearance)

1956   *The Ten Commandments* (+pr, prologue narration)

Other Films:

1914   *Ready Money* (Apfel) (co-sc); *The Circus Man* (Apfel) (co-sc); *Cameo Kirby* (Apfel) (co-sc)

1915   *The Country Boy* (Thompson) (co-sc); *A Gentleman of Leisure* (Melford) (sc); *The Governor's Lady* (Melford) (co-sc); *Snobs* (Apfel) (co-sc)

1916   *The Love Mask* (Reicher) (co-sc)

1917   *Betty to the Rescue* (Reicher) (co-sc, supervisor)

1923   *Hollywood* (Cruze) (guest appearance)

1930   *Free and Easy* (Sedgwick) (guest appearance)

1935   *The Hollywood You Never See* (short) (seen directing *Cleopatra*); *Hollywood Extra Girl* (Moulton) (seen directing *The Crusades*)

1942   *Star Spangled Rhythm* (Marshall) (guest appearance)

1947   *Variety Girl* (Marshall) (guest appearance); *Jens Mansson i Amerika (Jens Mansson in America)* (Janzon) (guest appearance); *Aid to the Nation* (short) (appearance)

1950   ***Sunset Boulevard*** (Wilder) (role as himself)

1952   *Son of Paleface* (Tashlin) (guest appearance)

1956   *The Buster Keaton Story* (Sheldon) (guest appearance)

1957   *The Heart of Show Business* (Staub) (narrator)

1958   *The Buccaneer* (pr, supervisor, introductory appearance)

Publications:

By DE MILLE: book—

The Autobiography of Cecil B. De Mille, Englewood Cliffs, New Jersey, 1959.

By DE MILLE: articles—

"After Seventy Pictures," in *Films in Review* (New York), March 1956.
"De Mille Answers His Critics," in *Films and Filming* (London), March 1958.

By DE MILLE: plays—

The Royal Mounted (1899)
The Return of Peter Grimm, with David Belasco

On DE MILLE: books—

De Mille, William, *Hollywood Saga*, New York, 1939.
De Mille, Agnes, *Dance to the Piper*, New York, 1951.
Crowther, Bosley, *The Lion's Share*, New York, 1957.
Koury, Phil, *Yes, Mr. De Mille*, New York, 1959.
Wagenknecht, Edward, *The Movies in the Age of Innocence*, Oklahoma, 1962.
Mourlet, Michel, *Cecil B. De Mille*, Paris, 1968.
Ringgold, Gene, and De Witt Bodeen, *The Films of Cecil B. De Mille*, New York, 1969.
Essoe, Gabe, and Raymond Lee, *De Mille: The Man and His Pictures*, New York, 1970.
Higham, Charles, *Cecil B. De Mille*, New York, 1973.
Higashi, Sumiko, *Cecil B. De Mille: A Guide to References and Resources*, Boston, 1985.
Norman, Barry, *The Film Greats*, London, 1985.
Edwards, Anne, *The De Milles: An American Family*, New York, 1988.

On DE MILLE: articles—

Lardner, Ring Jr., "The Sign of the Boss," in *Screen Writer*, November 1945.
Feldman, Joseph and Harry, "Cecil B. De Mille's Virtues," in *Films in Review* (New York), December 1950.
Harcourt-Smith, Simon "The Siegfried of Sex," in *Sight and Sound* (London), February 1951.
Johnson, Albert, "The Tenth Muse in San Francisco," in *Sight and Sound* (London), January/March 1955.
Baker, Peter, "Showman for the Millions," in *Films and Filming* (London), October 1956.
Card, James, "The Greatest Showman on Earth," in *Image* (Rochester, New York), November 1956.
Arthur, Art, "C.B. De Mille's Human Side," in *Films in Review* (New York), April 1967.
"DeMille Issue" of *Présence du Cinéma* (Paris), Autumn 1967.
Ford, Charles, "Cecil B. De Mille," in *Anthologie du Cinéma* vol.3, Paris, 1968.
Bodeen, Dewitt, "Cecil B. De Mille," in *Films in Review* (New York), August/September 1981.

Cecil B. De Mille

Mandell, P.R., "Parting the Red Sea (and other miracles)," in *American Cinematographer* (Los Angeles), April 1983.
D'Arc, J.V., "'So let it be written . . . ,'" in *Literature/Film Quarterly* (Salisbury, Maryland), January 1986.

*   *   *

For much of his 40-year career, the public and the critics associated Cecil B. DeMille with a single kind of film, the epic. He certainly made a great many of them: *The Sign of the Cross, The Crusades, King of Kings*, two versions of *The Ten Commandments, The Greatest Show on Earth*, and others. As a result, DeMille became a symbol of Hollywood during its "Golden Age." He represented that which was larger than life, often too elaborate, but always entertaining. By having such a strong public personality, however, DeMille came to be neglected as a director, even though many of his films, and not just the epics, stand out as extraordinary.

Although he made films until 1956, DeMille's masterpiece may well have come in 1915 with *The Cheat*. Even this early in his career, we can locate some of the motifs that turn up again and again in DeMille's work: a faltering upper-class marriage, the allure and exoticism of the Far East, and sexual attraction equated with hypnotic control. He also made a major aesthetic advancement in the use of editing in *The Cheat* that soon became a part of the repertoire of most filmmakers.

For the cinema's first 20 years, editing was based primarily on following action. During a chase, when actors exited screen right, the next shot had them entering screen left; or, a director might cut from a person being chased to those characters doing the chasing. In either case, the logic of the action controls the editing, which in turn gives us a sense of the physical space of a scene. But in *The Cheat*, through his editing, DeMille created a sense of psychological space. Richard Hardy, a wealthy businessman, confronts his wife with her extravagant bills, but Mrs. Hardy can think only of her lover, Haka, who is equally obsessed with her. DeMille provides a shot/counter-shot here, but the scene does not cut from Mr. Hardy to his wife, even though the logic of the action and the dialogue seems to indicate that it should. Instead, the shots alternate between Mrs. Hardy and Haka, even though the two lovers are miles apart. This sort of editing, which follows thoughts rather than actions, may seem routine today, but in 1915 it was a major development in the method of constructing a sequence.

As a visual stylist, however, De Mille became known more for his wit than for his editing innovations. At the beginning of *The Affairs of Anatol*, for instance, our first view of the title character, Anatol DeWitt Spencer, is of his feet. He taps them nervously while he waits for his wife to make breakfast. Our first view of Mrs. Spencer is also of her feet—a maid gives them a pedicure. In just seconds, and with only two shots, DeMille lets us know that this couple is in trouble. Mrs. Spencer's toenails must dry before Anatol can eat. Also from these opening shots, the viewers realize that they have been placed firmly within the realm of romantic comedy. These closeups of feet have no place within a melodrama.

One normally does not think of DeMille in terms of pairs of shots. Instead, one thinks on a large scale, and remembers the crowd scenes (the lions versus Christians extravaganza in *The Sign of the Cross*), the huge upper-crust social functions (the charity gala in *The Cheat*), the orgiastic parties (one of which takes place in a dirigible in *Dynamite*), and the bathrooms that DeMille turns into colossal marble shrines.

DeMille began directing in the grand style quite early in his career. In 1915, with opera star Geraldine Farrar in the lead role, he made one of the best film versions of *Carmen*, and two years later, again with Farrar, he directed *Joan the Woman*. Again and again, DeMille would refer to history as a foundation for the believability of his stories, as if his most obvious excesses could be justified if they were at least remotely based on real-life incidents. Just a quick look at his filmography shows many films based on historical events (often so far back in the past that accuracy hardly becomes an issue): *The Sign of the Cross, The Crusades, Union Pacific, Northwest Mounted Police*, and others. When history was inconvenient, DeMille made use of a literary text to give his films a high gloss of acceptability and veracity. In the opening credits of *The Affairs of Anatol*, for instance, DeMille stresses that the story derives from the play by Schnitzler.

In both his silent and sound films, DeMille mixes Victorian morality with sizable doses of sex and violence. The intertitles of *Why Change Your Wife?*, for example, rail against divorce as strongly as any nineteenth century marital tract, but the rest of the film deals openly with sexual obsession, and shows two women in actual physical combat over one man. Similarly, all of the religious epics extol the Christian virtues while at the same time revelling in scenes depicting all of the deadly sins. Though it is tension between extremes that makes DeMille's films so intriguing, critics have often made this aspect of his work seem laughable. Even today DeMille has barely received the serious recognition and study that he deserves.

—Eric Smoodin

———

DEMME, Jonathan.

American. Born in Baldwin, New York, 1944. Educated at University of Miami. Married director Evelyn Purcell. U.S. Air Force, 1966. Publicity writer for United Artists, Avco Embassy and Pathe Contemporary Films, early 1960's; writer on *Film Daily*, 1968–69; worked in London, 1969; unit publicist, then writer for Roger Corman, 1970; directed first film, *Caged Heat*, 1974; also director of TV films, commercials, and promo videos, including *Perfect Kiss* for New Order. Office: c/o Lee Winkler, Global Business Management, 9000 Sunset Boulevard, Suite 1115, Beverly Hills, CA 90069, U.S.A.

Films as Director:

1974   *Caged Heat* (+sc)
1975   *Crazy Mama*
1976   *Fighting Mad* (+sc)
1977   *Citizen's Band* (*Handle With Care*)
1979   *Murder in Aspic*
1980   *Melvin and Howard*
1983   *Swing Shift* (co-d)
1984   *Stop Making Sense*
1986   *Something Wild*
1987   *Swimming to Cambodia*
1988   *Married to the Mob*; *Famous All Over Town*

Other Films:

1970   *Sudden Terror* (*Eyewitness*) (Irwin Allen) (music coordinator)
1972   *Angels Hard as They Come* (Viola) (pr, co-sc); *The Hot Box* (Viola) (pr, co-sc)

Publications:

By DEMME: articles—

"Demme Monde," an interview with Carlos Clarens, in *Film Comment* (New York), "Demme Monde," an interview with Carlos Clarens, in *Film Comment* (New York), September/October 1980.

Jonathan Demme: *Stop Making Sense*

Interview with M. Stragow, in *American Film* (Washington, D.C.), January–February 1984.
Interview in *Time Out* (London), 1 July 1987.
Interview with Quentin Curtis in *Independent* (London), 15 June 1989.

On DEMME: articles—

Goodwin, Michael, "Velvet Vampires and Hot Mamas: Why Exploitation Films Get to Us," in *Village Voice* (New York), 7 July 1975.
Kehr, Dave, in *Film Comment* (New York), September/October 1977.
Baumgarten, Marjorie, and others, "*Caged Heat*," in *Cinema Texas Program Notes* (Austin), Spring 1978.
Maslin, Janet, in *New York Times*, 13 May 1979.
Black, Louis, "*Crazy Mama*," in *Cinema Texas Program Notes* (Austin), Spring 1978.
Schruers, Fred, "Jonathan Demme: A Study in Character," in *Rolling Stone* (New York), 19 May 1988.

*   *   *

Jonathan Demme has proved himself one of the more acute observers of the inner life of America in a directorial career that began in the early-1970's as just another protégé of the Roger Corman apprentice school of film-making. Demme's concern with character—focused particularly through the observation of telling eccentricities—is perhaps his trademark, combined with a vitality and willingness to use the frameworks of various genres to the full. A film such as *Something Wild*, for example, combines a tale of character and relationship development in an exhilarating movie which successfully mixes classic screwball comedy (you could imagine Hepburn and Tracy in the leads) with a very real menace in the closing stages that extends earlier comic confusion into the deadlier paranoia of the thriller.

Perhaps inspired by the "anything goes" aura of his Corman days, Demme has never been afraid to experiment with mood and subject matter in his films: Hitchcockian suspense in *The Last Embrace*, the possibilities of monologue in *Swimming To Cambodia*, romantic comedy in *Swing Shift* and gangster conventions in *Married To The Mob*.

Even his earliest films—*Caged Heat* and *Fighting Mad* (which he also wrote)—showed Demme exploiting the possibilities offered by the sex-and-violence format (rampaging girl-gangs in the first, rampaging rednecks in the second) for original and highly distinctive exploration of subjects and style.

Caged Heat also gave early signs of Demme's concern with those struggling to take control of their lives—particularly, but not exclusively, women—which has remained a theme throughout his work, and even earned him a reputation as a champion of feminism, from the women prisoners of *Caged Heat* and munitions worker (Goldie Hawn) in *Swing Shift* to the central characters in *Something Wild* (Melanie Griffiths) and *Married To The Mob* (Michelle Pfeiffer). Their struggle to establish themselves against patriarchal attitudes epitomises, for Demme, the struggles of the underdog which he has called "heroic." This real concern for his characters is clear in the (usually affectionate) intensity with which they—and their lives—are portrayed, and Demme recently described his films as "a little old-fashioned, at the same time as we try to make them modern."

Demme is concerned to entertain a mass audience and it is probably unwise to consider the low-key mood of the earlier critically-adored films *Citizen's Band* (a blackly-comic reflection of lack of communication based on a small town's obsession with CB-radio) and *Melvin And Howard* (an offbeat comedy based on a true story of a working-class man giving a lift to a hobo Howard Hughes in the Nevada desert) as being necessarily closest to his own heart. Both films, however good they may be, were also conscious reactions to the over-the-top nature of earlier Corman-inspired work.

Misjudgement of his concerns is nothing new for Demme. His much-noted focus on the everyday kitsch of Americana, for example, is driven more by an understanding of its importance as a yardstick with which consumerist America measures itself ("it's our kind of fetishism") than with being "hip." For Demme, observing kitsch is simply a form of realism in a country where the bizarre is often real.

Though much concerned with achieving an honest view of character, Demme is not uncaring about stylish direction. A sequence such as the series of out-takes for the final credits of *Married To The Mob* is one mark of a freewheeling approach to film-making which has roots in the knowing wit of the French New Wave (Demme cites Truffaut as an early influence), while his pared-down vision of a Talking Heads concert in *Stop Making Sense* is a distinctive, classy example of the rock film which pointedly eschews the tacky visual trappings too often associated with the genre.

Ultimately, though, his concern is with character rather than style—content over form. Demme is more into exploring humanity than proving himself an auteur for film critics. His own description of *Married To The Mob* offers an excellent insight into what he has sought after in his work. "It was intelligent fun, it didn't patronise the characters or the audience, it was good-hearted. Those are tough commodities to come by."

—Norman Miller

DEMY, Jacques.

French. Born in Pontchâteau (Loire-Atlantique), 5 June 1931. Educated at Ecole des Beaux-Arts, Nantes and at Ecole Technique de Photographie et de Cinématographiques, Paris. Married director Agnes Varda, 1962. Assistant to animator Paul Grimault, 1952; assistant to Georges Rouquier, 1954; made first short film, *Le Sabotier du Val de Loire*, began association with editor Anne-Marie Cotret, 1955; directed first feature, *Lola*, 1961.

Films as Director and Scriptwriter:

1956   *Le Sabotier du Val de Loire*
1957   *Le Bel Indifférent*
1958   *Le Musée Grévin*
1959   *La Mère et l'infant* (co-d); *Ars*
1961   *Lola*
1962   "La Luxure (Lust)" episode of *Les Sept Péchés capitaux* (*Seven Deadly Sins*)
1963   *La Baie des Anges* (*Bay of the Angels*)
1964   **Les Parapluies de Cherbourg (The Umbrellas of Cherbourg)**
1967   *Les Demoiselles de Rochefort* (*The Young Girls of Rochefort*)
1969   *The Model Shop* (+pr)
1971   *Peau d'ane* (*Donkey Skin*)
1972   *The Pied Piper of Hamelin* (*The Pied Piper*)
1973   *L'Évènement le plus important depuis que l'homme a marché sur la lune* (*A Slightly Pregnant Man*)
1978   *Lady Oscar*
1982   *Une Chambre en ville* (*A Room in Town*)
1985   *Parking*

Other Films:

1954   *Lourdes et ses miracles* (Rouquier) (asst d)
1955   *Arthur Honegger* (Rouquier) (asst d)
1956   *S.O.S. Noronha* (Rouquier) (asst d)
1959   **Les Quatre Cents Coups** (Truffaut) (role as policeman)
1960   *Paris nous appartient* (Rivette) (role as guest at party)

Publications:

By DEMY: articles—

"I Prefer the Sun to the Rain," in *Film Comment* (New York), Spring 1965.
Interview with Marsha Kinder, in *Film Heritage* (Dayton, Ohio), Spring 1967.
"Frenchman in Hollywood," an interview with Philip Scheuer, in *Action* (Los Angeles), November/December 1968.
"Lola in Los Angeles," in *Films and Filming* (London), April 1970.
"Cinéastes et musiciens," round table including Demy, in *Ecran* (Paris), September 1975.
Interview and biofilmography, in *Film Dope* (London), September 1976.
Interview with G. Haustrate, in *Cinéma* (Paris), July/August 1981.
Interview with Serge Daney, Jean Narboni, and Serge Toubiana, in *Cahiers du Cinéma* (Paris), November 1982.

On DEMY: book—

Berthome, Pierre, *Jacques Demy: Les Racines du reve*, Nantes, 1982.

On DEMY: articles—

Roud, Richard, "Rondo Galant," in *Sight and Sound* (London), Summer 1964.
Billard, Ginette, "Jacques Demy and His Other World," in *Film Quarterly* (Berkeley), Fall 1964.
Strick, Philip, "Demy Calls the Tune," in *Sight and Sound* (London), Autumn 1971.
Petrie, G., "Jacques Demy," in *Film Comment* (New York), Winter 1971/72.
"Journals: Gilbert Adair from Paris," in *Film Comment* (New York), March/April 1979.
"Demy Issue" of *Cinéma* (Paris), July/August 1981.
Dossier on Jacques Demy, in *Cinématographe* (Paris), October 1982.
Haustrate, Gaston, "Grand prix national du cinéma à Jacques Demy et Jean-Luc Godard," in *Cinéma* (Paris), February 1983.
Biofilmography in *Première* (Paris), November 1988.

On DEMY: film—

Delvaux, André, *Derrière l'écran*, 1966.

*   *   *

Demy's first feature film, *Lola*, is among the early distinguished products of the New Wave and is dedicated to Max Ophüls: two facts that in conjunction define its particular character. It proved to be the first in a series of loosely interlinked films (the intertextuality is rather more than a charming gimmick, relating as it does to certain thematic preoccupations already established in *Lola* itself); arguably, it remains the richest and most satisfying work so far in Demy's erratic, frustrating, but also somewhat underrated career.

The name and character of Lola (Anouk Aimée) herself relate to two previous celebrated female protagonists: the Lola Montès of Max Ophüls's film of that name, and the Lola-Lola (Marlene Dietrich) of von Sternberg's *The Blue Angel*, to which Demy pays homage in a number performed by Aimée in a top hat. The explicit philosophy of Lola Montès ("For me, life is movement") is enacted in Demy's film by the constant comings and goings, arrivals and departures, and intricate intercrossings of the characters. Ophüls's work has often been linked to concepts of fate; at the same time the auteurs of the early New Wave were preoccupied with establishing Freedom—as a metaphysical principle, to be enacted in their pro-

Jacques Demy directing Jeanne Moreau in *La Baie des Anges*

fessional methodology. The tension between fate and freedom is there throughout Demy's work. *Lola's* credit sequence alternates the improvisatory freedom of jazz with the slow movement of Beethoven's 7th Symphony which is explicitly associated with destiny in the form of the huge white American car that brings back Michel, Lola's lover and father of her child, who, like his predecessors in innumerable folk songs, has left her for seven years to make his fortune. No film is more intricately and obsessively patterned, with all the characters interlinked: the middle-aged woman used to be Lola (or someone like her), her teenage daughter may become Lola (or someone like her). Yet neither resembles Lola as she is in the film: everyone is different, yet everyone is interchangeable.

Two subsequent Demy films relate closely to *Lola*: in the all-sung *Les Parapluies de Cherbourg* Roland, Lola's rejected lover, recounts his brief liaison with Lola, to the visual accompaniment of a flashback to the arcade that was one of their meeting-places; and Lola herself re-appears in *The Model Shop*. Two other films are bound in to the series, *Les Demoiselles de Rochefort* by means of a certain cheating—Lola has been found murdered and dismembered in a laundry basket, but it's a different Lola. Especially poignant, as the series continues, is the treatment of the abrupt, unpredictable, seemingly fortuitous happy ending. At the end of *Lola*, Lola drives off with Michel and their child (as Roland of *Parapluies*, discarded and embittered, departs on his diamond-smuggling trip to South Africa); at the end of *Le Baie des Anges*—a film that, at the time, revealed no connection with *Lola*—Jackie (Jeanne Moreau), a compulsive gambler, manages to leave the casino to follow her lover *before* she knows the result of her bet: two happy endings which are exhilarating precisely because they are so arbitrary. Then, several films later, in *Model Shop*, Lola recounts how her great love Michel abandoned her to run off with a compulsive gambler called Jackie: both happy endings reversed in a single blow. Yet it is not so much that Demy doesn't believe in happy endings: he simply doesn't believe in *permanent* ones (as "life is movement"). The ambivalent, bittersweet "feel" of Demy is perhaps best summed up in the end of *Les Parapluies de Cherbourg*, where the lovers, now both married to others, accidentally meet, implicitly acknowledge their love, and return with acceptance to the relationships to which they are committed.

Outside the *Lola* series, Demy's touch has been uncertain. His two fairy-tale films, *Peau d'ane* and *The Pied Piper*, unfortunately tend to confirm the common judgment that he is more a decorator than a creator. But he should not be discounted. *A Room in Town*, a return to the *Lola* mode if not to the *Lola* characters, was favorably received.

—Robin Wood

DE PALMA, Brian.

American. Born in Newark, New Jersey, 11 September 1940. Educated at Columbia University, New York, and at Sarah Lawrence College (writing fellowship), 1963–64. Married actress Nancy Allen, 1979 (divorced 1984). Directed first feature, *Murder a la Mod*, 1967. Also film teacher and instructor. Recipient: Rosenthal Foundation award for *Woton's Wake*, 1963; Silver Bear Award, Berlin Festival, for *Greetings*, 1969. Address: c/o Fetch Productions, 1600 Broadway, New York, NY 10003, U.S.A.

Films as Director:

1961	*Icarus* (short); *660214, the Story of an IBM Card* (short)
1963	*Woton's Wake* (short)
1964	*Jennifer* (short)
1965	*Bridge that Gap* (short)
1966	*Show Me a Strong Town and I'll Show You a Strong Bank* (short); *The Responsive Eye* (doc)
1967	*Murder a la Mod* (+sc, ed)
1968	*Greetings* (+co-sc, ed)
1969	*The Wedding Party* (+pr, ed, co-sc; release delayed from 1966)
1970	*Dionysus in '69* (co-d, co-ph, co-ed; completed 1968); *Hi, Mom!* (+co-sc)
1972	*Get to Know Your Rabbit*
1973	*Sisters (Blood Sisters)* (+co-sc)
1974	*Phantom of the Paradise* (+sc)
1976	*Obsession* (+co-sc); *Carrie*
1978	*The Fury*
1979	*Home Movies*
1980	*Dressed to Kill* (+sc)
1981	*Blow Out* (+sc)
1983	*Scarface*
1984	*Body Double* (+pr, sc)
1986	*Wise Guys*
1987	*The Untouchables*
1989	*Casualties of War*

Publications:

By DE PALMA: articles—

Interview, in *The Film Director as Superstar* by Joseph Gelmis, Garden City, New York, 1970.
Interview with E. Margulies, in *Action* (Los Angeles), September/October 1974.
"Phantoms and Fantasies," interview with A. Stuart, in *Films and Filming* (London), December 1976.
"Things That Go Bump in the Night," interview with S. Swires, in *Films in Review* (New York), August/September 1978.
Interview with Serge Daney and Jonathan Rosenbaum, in *Cahiers du Cinéma* (Paris), April 1982.
"Double Trouble," an interview with Marcia Pally, in *Film Comment* (New York), September–October 1984.
"Brian De Palma's Guilty Pleasures," in *Film Comment* (New York), May–June 1987.

On DE PALMA: books—

Nepoti, Roberto, *Brian De Palma*, Florence, 1982.
Bliss, Michael, *Brian de Palma*, Metuchen, New Jersey, 1983.
Dworkin, Susan, *Double De Palma: A Film Study with Brian De Palma*, New York, 1984.
Wood, Robin, *Hollywood from Vietnam to Reagan*, New York, 1986.
Bouzereau, Laurent, *The De Palma Cut: The Films of America's Most Controversial Director*, New York, 1988.
Dworkin, Susan, *Double De Palma*, New York, 1990.
MacKinnon, Kenneth, *Misogyny in the Movies: The De Palma Question*, New York, 1990.

On DE PALMA: articles—

Rubinstein, R., "The Making of *Sisters*," in *Filmmakers Newsletter* (Ward Hill, Massachusetts), September 1973.
Henry, M., "L'Oeil du malin (à propos de Brian de Palma)," in *Positif* (Paris), May 1977.
Brown, R.S., "Considering de Palma," in *American Film* (Washington, D.C.), July/August 1977.
Matusa, P., "Corruption and Catastrophe: De Palma's *Carrie*," in *Film Quarterly* (Berkeley), Fall 1977.
Garel, A., "Brian de Palma," in *Image et Son* (Paris), December 1977.
Byron, Stuart, "Rules of the Game," in *Village Voice* (New York), 5 November 1979.
Jameson, R.T., "Style vs. 'Style'," in *Film Comment* (New York), March/April 1980.
Button, S., "Visceral poetry," in *Films* (London), November 1982.
Eisen, K., "The young misogynists of American cinema," in *Cineaste* (New York), vol. 8, no. 1, 1983.

Brian De Palma

Brown, G.A., "Obsession," in *American Film* (Washington, D.C.), December 1983.

Rafferty, T., "De Palma's American Dreams," in *Sight and Sound* (London), Spring 1984.

Fisher, W., "Re: Writing: Film History: From Hitchcock to De Palma," in *Persistence of Vision* (Maspeth, New York), Summer 1984.

Denby, David, and others, "Pornography: Love or Death?" in *Film Comment* (New York), November–December 1984.

Braudy, Leo, "The Sacraments of Genre: Coppola, De Palma, Scorsese," in *Film Quarterly* (Los Angeles), Spring 1986.

Hugo, Chris, "Three Films of Brian De Palma," in *Movie* (London), Winter 1989.

*   *   *

The conventional dismissal of De Palma—that he is a mere "Hitchcock imitator"—though certainly unjust, provides a useful starting-point, the relation being far more complex than such a description suggests. It seems more appropriate to talk of symbiosis than of imitation: if De Palma borrows Hitchcock's plot-structures, the impulse is rooted in an authentic identification with the Hitchcock thematic that results in (at De Palma's admittedly infrequent best) valid variations that have their own indisputable originality. *Sisters* and *Dressed to Kill* are modelled on *Psycho*, *Obsession* and *Body Double* on *Vertigo*; *Body Double* also borrows from *Rear Window*, as does *Blow Out*. The debt is of course enormous, but—at least in the cases of *Sisters*, *Obsession* and *Blow Out*, De Palma's three most satisfying films to date—the power and coherence of the films testifies to the genuineness of the creativity.

Central to the work of both directors are the tensions and contradictions arising out of the way in which gender has been traditionally constructed in a male-dominated culture. According to Freud, the human infant, while biologically male or female, is not innately "masculine" or "feminine": in order to construct the socially correct man and woman of patriarchy, the little girl's masculinity and the little boy's femininity must be repressed. This repression tends to be particularly rigorous and particularly damaging in the male, where it is compounded by the pervasive association of "femininity" with castration (on both the literal and symbolic levels). The significance of De Palma's best work (and, more powerfully and consistently, that of Hitchcock before him) lies in its eloquent evidence of what happens when the repression is partially unsuccessful. The misogyny of which both directors have been accused, expressing itself in the films' often extreme outbursts of violence against women (both physical and psychological), must be read as the result of their equally extreme identification with the "feminine" and the inevitable dread that such an identification brings with it.

Sisters is concerned single-mindedly with castration: the symbolic castration of the woman within patriarchy, the answering literal castration that is the form of her revenge. The basic concept of female Siamese twins, one active and aggressive, one passive and submissive, is a brilliant inspiration, the action of the entire film arising out of the attempts by men to destroy the active aspect in order to construct the "feminine" woman who will accept her subordination. The aggressive sister Dominique (dead, but still alive as Danielle's unconscious) is paralleled by Grace Collier (Jennifer Salt), the assertive young reporter who usurps the accoutrements of "masculinity" and eventually assumes Dominique's place in the extraordinary climactic hallucination sequence in which the woman's castration is horrifyingly reasserted. *Sisters*, although weakened by De Palma's inability to take Grace seriously enough or give the character the substance the allegory demands, remains his closest to a completely satisfying film: the monstrousness of woman's oppression under patriarchy and its appalling consequences for both sexes have never been rendered more vividly. *Blow Out* rivals it in coherence and surpasses it in sensitivity: one would describe it as De Palma's masterpiece were it not for one unpardonable and unfortunately extended lapse, the entirely gratuitous sequence depicting the murder of the prostitute in the railway station, which one can account for only in terms of a fear that the film wasn't "spicy" enough for the box office (it failed anyway). It can stand as a fitting counterpart to *Sisters*, a rigorous dissection of the egoism fostered in the male by the culture's obsession with "masculinity." It is clear that Travolta's obsession with establishing the reality of his perceptions has little to do with an impersonal concern for truth and everything to do with his need to establish and assert the symbolic phallus at whatever cost—the cost involving, crucially, the manipulation and exploitation of a woman, eventually precipitating her death.

Since *Body Double*—a tawdry ragbag of a film that might be seen as De Palma's gift to his detractors—De Palma seems to have abandoned the Hitchcock connection, and it is not yet clear that he has found a strong thematic with which to replace it. *The Untouchables* seems a work of empty efficiency; it is perhaps significant that one remains uncertain whether to take the patriarchal idyll of Elliott Ness's domestic life straight or as parody. *Casualties of War* is more interesting, though severely undermined by the casting of the two leads: one grasps the kind of contrast De Palma had in mind, but it is not successfully realized in that between Sean Penn's shameless mugging and Michael J. Fox's intractable blandness. Like most Hollywood movies on Vietnam, the film suffers from the inability to see Asians in terms other than an undifferentiated "otherness": it is symptomatic that the two Vietnamese girls, past and present, are played by the same actress. His return to the film of political protest (and specifically to the Vietnam war) brings De Palma's career to date full circle: his early work in an independent avant-garde (*Greetings, Hi, Mom!*) is too often overlooked. But nothing in *Casualties of War*, for all the strenuousness of its desire to disturb, achieves the genuinely disorienting force of the remarkable "Be Black, Baby" sections of *Hi, Mom!*.

—Robin Wood

DEREN, Maya.

Russian/American. Born in Kiev, 1917, became U.S. citizen. Educated at League of Nations School, Geneva, Switzerland; studied journalism at University of Syracuse, New York; New York University, B.A.; Smith College, M.A. Married (second time) Alexander Hackenschmied (Hamid), 1942 (divorced; later married Teijo Ito. Family emigrated to America, 1922; made first film *Meshes of the Afternoon*, 1943; travelled to Haiti, 1946; secretary for Creative Film Foundation, 1960. Recipient: Guggenheim Fellowship for work in creative film, 1946. *Died of a cerebral hemorrhage in Queen's, New York, 13 October 1961.*

Films as Director:

1943 ***Meshes of the Afternoon*** (with Alexander Hammid) (+role); *The Witches' Cradle* (unfinished)
1944 *At Land* (+role)
1945 *A Study in Choreography for Camera*; *The Private Life of a Cat* (home movie, with Hammid)

Maya Deren in *Meshes of the Afternoon*

1946   *Ritual in Transfigured Time* (+role)
1948   *Meditation on Violence*
1959   *The Very Eye of Night*

Publications:

By DEREN: books—

An Anagram of Ideas on Art, Form and the Film, New York, 1946.
The Divine Horseman: The Living Gods of Haiti, New York, 1953.
Divine Horsemen: Voodoo Gods of Haiti, New York, 1970.

By DEREN: articles—

"Choreography of Camera," in *Dance* (New York), October 1943.
"Cinema as an Art Form," in *Introduction to the Art of the Movies* edited by Lewis Jacobs, New York, 1960.
"Cinematography: The Creative Use of Reality," in *Daedalus: The Visual Arts Today*, 1960.
"Movie Journal," in the *Village Voice* (New York), 25 August 1960.
"A Statement of Principles," in *Film Culture* (New York), Summer 1961.
"Movie Journal," in the *Village Voice* (New York), 1 June 1961.
"A Lecture . . . ," in *Film Culture* (New York), Summer 1963.
"Notes, Essays, Letters," in *Film Culture* (New York), Winter 1965.
"A Statement on Dance and Film," in *Dance Perspectives*, no.30, 1967.

"Tempo and Tension," in *The Movies as Medium* edited by Lewis Jacobs, New York, 1970.

On DEREN: books—

Hanhardt, John, and others, *A History of the American Avant-Garde Cinema*, New York, 1976.
Sitney, P. Adams, *Visionary Film*, second edition, New York, 1979.
Clark, Veve A., Millicent Hodson, and Catrina Neimans, *The Legend of Maya Deren: A Documentary Biography and Collected Works: Vol. 1, Pt. 1, Signatures (1917–1942)*, New York, 1984.
Heck-Rabi, Louise, *Women Filmmakers: A Critical Reception*, Metuchen, New Jersey, 1984.

On DEREN: articles—

Farber, Manny, "Maya Deren's Films," in the *New Republic* (New York), 28 October 1946.
"Deren Issue" of *Filmwise*, no.2, 1961.
Obituary in *New York Times*, 14 October 1961.
Tallmer, Jerry, "For Maya Deren," in the *Village Voice* (New York), 19 October 1961.
Arnheim, Rudolf, "To Maya Deren," in *Film Culture* (New York), no.24, 1962.
Sitney, P. Adams, "The Idea of Morphology," in *Film Culture* (New York), No. 53, 54, and 55, 1971.
Cornwell, Regina, "Maya Deren and Germaine Dulac: Activists of

the Avant-Garde," in *Film Library Quarterly* (New York), Winter 1971/72.

Bronstein, M., and S. Grossmann, "Zu Maya Derens Filmarbeit," in *Frauen und Film* (Berlin), December 1976.

Camera Obscura Collective, The, "Excerpts from an interview with 'The Legend of Maya Deren' Project," in *Camera Obscura* (Berkeley), Summer 1979.

Mayer, T., "The Legend of Maya Deren: Champion of American Independent Film," in *Film News* (New York), September/October 1979.

"Kamera Arbeit: Der schopferische umgang mit der realitat," in *Frauen und Film* (Berlin), October 1984.

"Maya Deren Issue," of *Film Culture* (New York), 72–75, 1985.

Millsapps, J.L., "Maya Deren, Imagist," in *Literature/Film Quarterly* (Salisbury, Maryland), January 1986.

Monthly Film Bulletin (London), June and July 1988.

*   *   *

Maya Deren was the best-known independent, experimental filmmaker in the United States during and after World War II. She developed two types of short, subjective films: the psychodrama and the ciné-dance film. She initiated a national nontheatrical network to show her six independently-made works, which have been referred to as visual lyric poems, or dreamlike trance films. She also lectured and wrote extensively on film as an art form. Her films remain as provocative as ever; her contributions to cinematic art indisputable.

Intending to write a book on dance, Deren toured with Katherine Dunham's dance group as a secretary. Dunham introduced Deren to Alexander Hammid, and the following year the couple made *Meshes of the Afternoon*. Considered a milestone in the chronology of independent film in the United States, it is famous for its four-stride sequence (from beach to grass to mud to pavement to rug). Deren acted the role of a girl driven to suicide. Continuous action is maintained while time-space unities are severed, establishing a trance-like mood by the use of slow motion, swish-pan camera movements, and well executed point-of-view shots.

In her next film, *At Land*, a woman (Deren) runs along a beach and becomes involved in a chess game. P. Adams Sitney refers to this work as a "pure American trance film." The telescoping of time occurs as each scene blends with the next in unbroken sequence, a result of pre-planned editing. *At Land* is also studded with camera shots of astounding virtuosity.

Other films include her first ciné-dance film, the three-minute *A Study in Choreography for Camera*. Filmed in slow motion, a male ballet dancer, partnered by the camera, moves through a variety of locales. Continuity of camera movement is maintained as the dancer's foot changes location, and space is compressed, time expanded. According to Sitney, the film's importance resides in two fresh observations: space and time in film are *created* space and time, and the camera's optimal use is as a dancer itself. *Ritual in Transfigured Time*, another dance-on-film, portrays psycho-dramatic ritual by use of freeze frames, repeated shots, shifting character identities, body movements, and locales. *Meditation on Violence* explores Woo (or Wu) Tang boxing with the camera as sparring partner, panning and zooming to simulate human response. *The Very Eye of Night* employed Metropolitan Ballet School members to create a celestial ciné-ballet of night. Shown in its negative state, Deren's handheld camera captured white figures on a total black background. Deren evolved, in her four dance-films, a viable form of ciné-choreography which was adapted and adjusted to commercial feature films later, meritoriously exampled in *West Side Story*.

Deren traced the evolution of her six films in "A letter to James Card," dated April 19, 1955. *Meshes* was her "point of departure" and "almost expressionist;" *At Land* depicted dormant energies in mutable nature, and *Choreography* distilled the essence of this natural changing. In *Ritual* she defined the processes of changing while *Meditation* extends the study of metamorphosis. In *The Very Eye* she expressed her love of life and its living. "Each film was built as a chamber and became a corridor, like a chain reaction."

In 1946, Deren published *An Anagram of Ideas on Art, Form, and the Film*, a monograph declaring two major statements: the rejection of symbolism in film, and a strong support for independent film after an analysis of industrial and independent filmmaking activities in the United States.

Although *Meshes* remains the most widely-seen film of its type, with several of its effects unsurpassed by filmmakers, Deren had been forgotten until recently. Her reputation now enjoys a renaissance well-deserved by the filmmaker whom Rudolf Arnheim eulogized as one of the film's "most delicate magicians".

—Louise Heck-Rabi

————

DE SANTIS, Giuseppe.

Italian. Born in Fondi, Latina, 11 February 1917. Educated at University of Rome and at Centro Sperimentale di Cinematografia, Rome. Married Giovanna Valeri, 1943. Writer for *Cinema* magazine, Rome, 1941–43; directed first feature, *Caccia tragica*, 1947. Recipient: Golden Globe Award, Los Angeles Film Critics, for *La Strada lunga un anno*, 1958. Address: Piazza Faleri, 1, Fiano Romano, Italy.

Films as Director and Co-Scriptwriter:

1945   episode of *Giorni di gloria*
1947   *Caccia tragica* (*Tragic Hunt*)
1948   *Riso amaro* (*Bitter Rice*)
1949   *Non c'e pace tra gli ulivi* (*Under the Olive Tree*)
1952   *Roma ore undici* (*Rome 11 O'Clock*)
1953   *Un marito per Anna Zaccheo* (*A Husband for Anna*)
1954   *Giorni d'amore* (*Days of Love*)
1956   *Uomini e lupi* (*Men and Wolves*)
1957   *L'Uomo senza domenica*
1958   *Cesta duga godinu dana* (*La strada lunga un anno*)
1960   *La Garçonnière*
1964   *Italiani, brava gente*
1972   *Un Apprezzato professionista di sicuro avvenire*

Other Films:

1940   *Don Pasquale* (sc)
1942   ***Ossessione*** (Visconti) (co-sc, asst d)
1943   *Desiderio* (Rossellini and Paglièro) (co-sc, asst d to Rossellini)
1945   *Il sole sorge ancora* (co-sc, asst d, role uncredited)
1946   *Ultimo amore* (co-sc)
1953   *Donne proibite* (sc)
1964   *La visita* (co-sc)

Publications:

By DE SANTIS: books—

Riso amaro: un film diretto da Giuseppe de Santis, with C. Lizzani, Rome, 1978

Giuseppe De Santis verso il neorealismo, edited by Callisto Cosulich, Bologna, 1982.

Giuseppe De Santis

By DE SANTIS: articles—

Interview with Claude Souef, in *Lettres Françaises* (Paris), November 1952.
"Una lettera di De Santis," in *Cinema Nuovo* (Turin), 15 February 1957.
Interview with Michel Delahaye and Jean Wagner, in *Cinéma* (Paris), April 1959.
"E con 'Ossessione' osai il primo giro di manovella," in *Cinema Nuovo* (Bari), June and August–October 1984.
"De Santis, entre realisme, neorealisme et realisme socialiste," in *Jeune Cinéma* (Paris), March 1985.
Hollywood Reporter, 14 July 1987.

On DE SANTIS: books—

Farnassino, Alberto, *Giuseppe De Santis*, Milan, 1978.
Masi, Stefano, *Giuseppe De Santis*, Florence, 1981.
Pacisi, Antonio, *Il cinema di Giuseppe De Santis: Tra passione e ideologia*, Rome, 1983.

On DE SANTIS: articles—

Krier, Jacques, "Giuseppe De Santis est à Paris," in *L'Écran Français* (Paris), 29 May 1950.
Lane, John, "De Santis and Italian Neo-Realism," in *Sight and Sound* (London), August 1950.
"De Santis Issue" of *Positif* (Paris), no.5, undated.
Oms, Marcel, in *Positif* (Paris), no.23, 1957.
Martini, Andrea, and Marco Melani, "De Santis," in *Il neorealismo cinematografico italiano*, Venice, 1975.
Dossier on De Santis, in *Cinema e Cinema* (Rome), January–March 1982.

*   *   *

For a brief period of five years, Giuseppe De Santis's film career was the most often discussed, the most highly applauded and the most commercially successful of the Italian neorealist directors. In addition, his writings in the Italian magazine *Cinema* from 1941 until 1943 took an active, prescriptive, and radical stance previously unknown to film criticism.

Like the later generation of French critics-turned-directors, such as Jean-Luc Godard or François Truffaut, De Santis's first films showed new approaches while displaying a mastery of the medium, but also succeeded in capturing popular imagination. "Popular" is the key to appreciating De Santis's work. Despite rigorous theorizing, and a profound dedication to Marxist principles, De Santis's films never appeared aloof or difficult to understand to a mass audience. He proved that the popular world was no longer something to be considered as different, but was actually the norm. While his first features are concerned with Italy, they are most significant as studies of changes in cultures, and as commentaries upon filmmaking and other mass media as the modern international culture. De Santis was the first Italian director to truly appreciate the effects of the mass media which appear in their various forms—newspapers, radio, television, cinema, posters, pop music, magazines, photo novels, pin-ups, advertisements, dancing—throughout all of his films. Like many of his colleagues, he displayed an admiration of American literature and American cinema, but he perceived more clearly why those were popular—not merely in a commercial sense but because they were creating a new culture that international audiences found meaningful in their daily lives and habits.

Mass media, and cinema in particular, formed the modern means of education, cultural formation, and inspiration in addition to providing role models. Two aspects of this phenomenon were the star system and eroticism, joined together in Silvana Mangano's most famous performance—in *Bitter Rice*, a film nominated for an Academy Award in 1949. In this, her film debut, De Santis transformed Mangano into an instant star. The eroticism in the film liberated the human body from something to be leered at to something that could be celebrated and enjoyed, thus starting a trend in the Italian cinema which made stars of such women as Mangano, Gina Lollabrigida and Sophia Loren.

Ironically, the very director who freed Italian cinema from provincialism found it increasingly difficult to get his projects accepted and funded in his own country. His best works of the second half of his career were made only partially with Italian capital, and often outside the country. *La Strada lunga un anno*, about the building of a road, was filmed in and financed by Yugoslavia, and indicated the possibility of a socialist cinema by joyfully depicting the solidarity of unpaid workers. Much applauded in the United States, it received the Golden Globe from the Hollywood critics as well as an Academy Award nomination. *Italiani brava gente* was the first Italian-Soviet co-production, with some American financing. Successfully and convincingly, De Santis creates a gallery of characters at the Russian front during the war: a Roman, a Sicilian, a Pugliese, and Emilian played by a Soviet actor, a Milanese commandant played by Arthur Kennedy, and a Neapolitan of the medical corps played by Peter Falk! The circumstances of this production permitted De Santis to express one of his strongest beliefs: differences between people are no longer based on nationalities but on class and occupation.

—Elaine Mancini

DE SICA, Vittorio.

Italian/French. Born in Sora (near Rome), 7 July 1902, became French citizen (in order to marry 2nd wife), 1968. Educated at Institut Superieur de Commerce, Rome, and University of Rome. Married 1) Giuditta Rissone (divorced 1968); 2) Maria Mercader, 1968, two sons. Actor in Tatiana Pavlova's Stage Company, 1923; formed own stage company with actress-wife, late 1920's; leading film actor, from 1931; directed first film, *Rose scarlette*, 1940. *Died in Paris, 13 November 1974.*

Films as Director:

1940   *Rose scarlette* (co-d, role as The Engineer)
1941   *Maddelena zero in condotta* (+dialogue, role as Carlo Hartman); *Teresa Venerdi* (+co-sc, role)
1942   *Un garibaldino al convento* (+co-sc, role as Nino Bixio)
1943   *I bambini ci guardano* (+co-sc)
1946   *La porta del cielo* (+co-sc, completed 1944); **Sciuscia (Shoeshine)** (+co-sc)
1948   **Ladri di biciclette (The Bicycle Thief)** (+pr, co-sc)
1950   **Miracolo a Milano (Miracle in Milan)** (+co-sc)
1952   **Umberto D** (+pr, co-sc)
1953   *Stazione Termini (Indiscretion of an American Wife, Indiscretion)* (+co-pr)
1954   *L'oro di Napoli (Gold of Naples)* (+co-sc, role)
1956   *Il tetto (The Roof)* (+pr)
1960   *La ciociara (Two Women)*
1961   *Il giudizio universale* (+role)
1962   "La Riffa (The Raffle)" episode of *Boccaccio '70*; *I sequestrati di Altona (The Condemned of Altona)*
1963   *Il boom*; *Ieri, oggi, domani (Yesterday, Today and Tomorrow)*
1964   *Matrimonio all'italiana (Marriage, Italian Style)*
1965   *Un Monde nouveau (Un Monde jeune, Un mondo nuovo, A Young World)*

Vittorio De Sica

1966 *Caccia alla volpe (After the Fox)* (+guest role); "Un sera come le altre (A Night Like Any Other)" episode of *Le streghe (The Witches)*
1967 *Woman Times Seven (Sept fois femmes)*
1968 *Amanti (A Place for Lovers)* (+co-sc)
1970 *I girasoli (Sunflower);* **Il giardino dei Finzi Contini (The Garden of the Finzi-Continis)**; "Il leone" episode of *Le coppie (Les Couples)*
1972 *Lo chiameremo Andrea*
1973 *Una breve vacanza (A Brief Vacation)*
1974 *Il viaggio (The Journey, The Voyage)*

Other Films:

1918 *Il processo Clémenceau (L'Affaire Clemenceau)* (Bencivenga) (role)
1926 *La bellezza del mondo* (Almirante) (role)
1928 *La compagnia dei matti (La compagnie des fous)* (Almirante) (role)
1932 *La vecchia signora* (Palermi) (role); *La segretaria per tutti* (Palermi) (role); *Due cuori felici* (Negroni) (role); *Gli uomini . . . che mascalzoni* (Camerini) (role)
1933 *Un cattivo soggetto* (Bragaglia) (role); *Il signore desidera?* (Righelli) (role); *La canzone del sole* (German version: *Das Lied der Sonne*) (Neufeld) (role as The Secretary); *Lisetta* (Boese) (role)
1934 *Tempo massimo* (Mattoli) (role)

1935 *Darò un millione* (Camerini) (role as The Millionaire); *Amo te sola* (Mattòli) (role)
1936 *Lohengrin* (Malasomma) (role); *Ma non è una cosa seria!* (Camerini) (role); *Non ti conosco più* (Malasomma) (role); *L'uomo che sorride* (Mattoli) (role)
1937 *Hanno rapito un uomo* (Righelli) (role); *Il signor Max* (Camerini) (role); *Questi ragazzi* (Mattoli) (role)
1938 *Napoli d'altri tempi* (Palermi) (role); *L'orologio a cucù* (Mastrocinque) (role); *Partire* (Palermi) (role); *Ai vostri ordini, signora!* (Mattòli) (role); *La mazurka di papà* (Biancoli) (role); *Le due madri* (Palermi) (role); *Castelli in aria* (German version: *Ins blaue Leben*, 1939) (Genina) (role)
1939 *Grandi magazzini* (Camerini) (role); *Finisce sempre cosí* (Susini) (role); *Napoli che non muore* (Palermi) (role)
1940 *La peccatrice* (Palermi) (role); *Pazza di giola* (Bragaglia) (role); *Manon Lescaut* (Gallone) (role)
1941 *L'avventuriera del piano di sopra* (Matarazzo) (role)
1942 *Se io fossi onesto!* (Bragaglia) (role, co-sc); *La guardia del corpo* (Bragaglia) (role, co-sc)
1943 *I nostri sogni* (Cottafavi) (role, co-sc); *Non sono superstizioso, ma . . . !* (Bragaglia) (role, co-sc); *L'ippocampo* (Rosmino) (role, co-sc); *Diece minuti di vita* (Longanesi) (unfinished; another version made 1944 with different cast) (role); *Nessuno torna indietro* (Blasetti) (role)
1945 *Lo sbaglio di essere vivo* (Bragagalia) (role); *Il mondo vuole cosi* (Bianchi) (role)
1946 *Roma città libera* (co-sc); *Il marito povero* (Amara) (co-sc); *Abbasso la ricchezza!* (Righelli) (role, co-sc)

1947 *Sperduti nel buio* (Mastrocinque) (role as Nanzio, co-sc); *Natale al campo 119* (Francisci) (supervisor, role as The noble Neopolitan)

1948 *Lo sconosciuto di San Marino* (Waszinsky) (role as The Proprietor); *Cuore* (Coletti) (co-sc, role as The Landlord)

1950 *Domani è troppo tardi* (Moguy) (role as Professor Landi)

1951 *Cameriera bella presenza offresi* (Pastina) (role as The Actor); "Il processo di Frine" episode of *Altri tempi* (Blasetti) (role as the Barrister); *Gli uomini non guardano il cielo* (Scarpelli) (role)

1952 *Buongiorno elefante!* (*Sabú principle ladro*) (Franciolini) (co-sc, role as Garetti); "Scena all'aperto" (role as Count) and "Don Corradino" (role as Don Corradino) episodes of *Tempi nostri* (Blasetti)

1953 **Madame De . . .** (Ophuls) (role as Fabrizio Donati); *Pane, amore e fantasia* (Comencini) (role as Marshal Carotenuto); "Pendolin" episode of *Cento anni d'amore* (De Felice) (role); "Incidente a Villa Borghese" episode of *Villa Borghese* (Franciolini) (role); *Il matrimonio* (Petrucci) (role); "Il fine dicitore" episode of *Gran varietà* (Paolella) (role); "Le Divorce (Il divorzio)" episode of *Secrets d'alcôve* (*Il letto*) (Franciolini) (role)

1954 *Vergine moderna* (Pagliero) (role as The Banker); *L'Allegro Squadrone* (Moffa) (role as The General); *Pane, amore e gelosia* (Comencini) (role); *Peccato che sia una canaglia* (Blasetti) (role as Mr. Stroppiani)

1955 *Il segno di Venere* (Risi) (role as Alessio Spano, the Poet); *Gli ultimi cinque minuti* (*The Last Five Minutes*) (Amato) (role as Carlo); *La bella mugnaia* (Camerini) (role as The Governor); *Pane, amore e . . .* (Risi) (role as Carotenuto); *Racconti romani* (Franciolini) (role); *Il bigamo* (Emmer) (role as The Barrister)

1956 *Mio figlio Nerone* (*Nero's Weekend*) (Steno) (role as Sénèquel); *Tempo di villeggiatura* (Racioppi) (role as The Celebrity); *The Monte Carlo Story* (*Montecarlo*) (Taylor) (role as Count Dino Giocondo Della Fiaba); *I giorni più belli* (*I nostri anni più belli, Gli anni più belli*) (Mattòli) (role as The Banker); *Noi siamo le colonne* (D'Amico) (role as Celimontani)

1957 *Padri e figli* (Monicelli) (role as The tailor Corallo); *I colpevoli* (Vasile) (role as the barrister Vasari); *Souvenir d'Italie* (*It Happened in Rome*) (Pietrangeli) (role as The Count); *La donna che venne del mare* (De Robertis) (role as Bordigin); *Vacanze a Ischia* (Camerini) (role as Occhipinti); *I conte Max* (Bianchi) (role as Count Max Orsini Baraldo); *Amore e chiacchiere* (Blasetti) (role as Bonelli); *Il medico e lo stregone* (Monicelli) (role as Locoratolo); *Totò, Vittorio e la dottoressa* (Mastrocinque) (role as The sick nobleman); *Casino de Paris* (Hunebelle) (role as Alexandre Gordy)

1958 *A Farewell to Arms* (Vidor) (role as Count Alessandro Rinaldi); *Domenica è sempre domenica* (Mastrocinque) (role as Mr. Guastaldi); *Ballerina e buon Dio* (Leonviola) (roles as The policeman, the taxi driver, and the costume porter); *Kanonenserenade* (*Pezzo, capopezzo e capitano*) (Staudte) (role as Count Ernesto De Rossi); *Anna di Brooklyn* (Denham and Lastricati) (supervisor, co-music, role as Don Luigino); *La ragazza di Piazza S. Pietro* (Costa) (role as Armando Conforti); *Gli zitelloni* (Bianchi) (role as Professor Landi); *Pane, amore e Andulasia* (Setò) (role as Carotenuto); *La prima notte* (Cavalcanti) (role as Alfredo)

1959 *Nel blu dipinto di blu* (Volare) (Tellini) (role as Spartaco); *Il nemico di mia moglie* (Puccini) (role as The Husband); *Vacanze d'inverno* (Mastrocinque) (role as Manrizie); *Il moralista* (Bianchi) (role as The President); *Il Generale Della Rovere* (Rossellini) (role as Giovanni Bertone); *Il mondo dei miracoli* (Capuano) (role as Pietro Giordani); *Uomini e nobiluomini* (Bianchi) (role as Marquis Nicolas Peccoli); *Ferdinando I, re di Napoli* (Franciolini) (role as Ceccano); *Gastone* (Bonnard) (role as The Prince); *Les trois etc . . . du colonel* (*Le tre eccetera del colonnello*) (Boissol) (role as Colonel Belalcazar)

1960 *Il vigile* (Zampa) (role as The Trustee); *Le pillole di Ercole* (Salce) (role as Colonel Pietro Cuocolo); *Austerlitz* (Gance) (role as Pope Pius VII); *The Angel Wore Red* (*La sposa bella*) (Johnson) (role as General Clave); *The Millionairess* (Asquith) (role as Joe); *It Started in Naples* (Shavelson) (role as Mario Vitale; *Gli incensurati* (Giaculli) (role as comic actor); *Un amore a Roma* (Risi) (role)

1961 *Gli attendenti* (Bianchi) (role as Colonel Bitossi); *I due marescialli* (Corbucci) (role as Antonio Cotone); *Le meraviglie di Aladino* (*The Wonders of Aladdin*) (Bava and Levin) (role as The Genie); *L'onorata società* (Pazzaglia) (role as The Chef); *La Fayette* (*La Fayette, una spada per due bandiere*) (Dréville) (role as Bancroft)

1962 *Vive Henry IV, vive l'amour* (Autant-Lara) (role as Don Pedro)

1965 *The Amorous Adventures of Moll Flanders* (T. Young) (role as The Count)

1966 *Io, io, io . . . e gli altri* (Blasetti) (role as Count Trepossi)

1967 *Gli altri, gli altri e noi* (Arena) (role as man on pension); *Un italiano in America* (Sordi) (role as Giuseppe's Father); *The Biggest Bundle of Them All* (Annakin) (role as Cesare Celli); *Caroline Cherie* (de la Patelliere) (role as Count de Bièvres)

1968 *The Shoes of the Fisherman* (*Les Souliers de Saint-Pierre*) (M. Anderson) (role as Cardinal Rinaldi)

1969 *If It's Tuesday, This Must Be Belgium* (M. Stuart) (role as The Shoemaker); *Una su tredici* (*12 + 1*) (Gessner and Lucignani) (role as Di Seta)

1970 *Cose di Cosa Nostra* (Steno) (role as The Lawyer); *L'Odeur des fauves* (Balducci) (role as Milord)

1971 *Trastevere* (Tozzi) (role as Enrico Formichi); *Io non vedo, tu non parli, lui non sente* (Camerini) (role as Count at the Casino)

1972 *Pinocchio* (Comencini) (for TV) (role as The Judge); *Snow Job* (*The Ski Raiders*) (Englund) (role as Dolphi); *Ettore lo fusto* (Castellari) (role as Giove); *Siamo tutti in libertà provvisoria* (Scarpelli) (role)

1973 *Storia de fratelli e de cortelli* (Amendola) (role as The Marshal); *Il delitto Matteotti* (Vancini) (role as Mauro del Giudice)

1974 *Andy Warhol's Dracula* (*Dracula cerca sangue di vergine e . . . morì di sete!!, Blood for Dracula*) (Morrissey) (role as Marquis di Fiori); *C'eravamo tanto amati* (Scola) (role as himself); *Vittorio De Sica, il Regista, l'attore, l'uomo* (Gragadze) (role)

Publications:

By DE SICA: books—

Umberto D., with Cesare Zavattini, Rome, 1954.
The Bicycle Thief, with Cesare Zavattini, New York, 1968.
Miracle in Milan with Cesare Zavattini and others, New York, 1968.

By DE SICA: articles—

Interview with F. Koval, in *Sight and Sound* (London), April 1950.
"The Most Wonderful Years of My Life," in *Films and Filming* (London), December 1955.
"Money, the Public, and Umberto D," in *Films and Filming* (London), January 1956.
"Illiberal Censorship," in *Film* (London), January/February 1956.
"Hollywood Shocked Me," in *Films and Filming* (London), February 1956.
"I Must Act to Pay My Debts," in *Films and Filming* (London), March 1956.
"British Humor? It's the Same in Italy," in *Films and Filming* (London), April 1959.
"What's Right With Hollywood," in *Films and Filming* (London), November 1963.
Interview in *Encountering Directors*, edited by Charles Thomas Samuels, New York, 1972.
Interview with D. Lyons, in *Interview* (New York), February 1972.
"Le Jardin des Finzi-Contini," interview with G. Braucourt, in *Ecran* (Paris), February 1972.

On DE SICA: books—

Ferrara, Giuseppe, *Il nuovo cinema italiano*, Florence, 1957.

Agel, Henri, *Vittorio De Sica*, 2nd edition, Paris, 1964.
Leprohon, Pierre, *Vittorio De Sica*, Paris, 1966.
Bazin, André, *Qu'est-ce que le cinéma*, 2nd edition, Paris, 1975.
Mercader, Maria, *La mia vita con Vittorio De Sica*, Milan, Italy, 1978.
Anthologie du cinéma, vol.10, Paris, 1979.
Darreta, John, *Vittorio De Sica: A Guide to References and Resources*, Boston, 1983.
Bolzoni, Francesco, *Quando De Sica era Mister Brown*, Turin, 1984.

On DE SICA: articles—

Jacobson, H.L., "De Sica's *Bicycle Thieves* and Italian Humanism," in *Hollywood Quarterly*, Fall 1949.
Hawkins, R.F., "De Sica Dissected," in *Films in Review* (New York), May 1951.
Lambert, Gavin, "The Case of De Sica," in *Sight and Sound* (London), June 1951.
Sargeant, W., "Bread, Love, and Neo-Realism," in the *New Yorker*, 29 June and 6 July 1957.
Rhode, Eric, "Why Neo-Realism Failed," in *Sight and Sound* (London), Winter 1960/61.
Lane, J.F., "A Case of Artistic Inflation," in *Sight and Sound* (London), Summer 1963.
McVay, D., "Poet of Poverty," in *Films and Filming* (London), November 1964.
Comuzio, E., "De Sica o della doppia costante: il sorriso e il tarlo segreto," in *Cineforum* (Bergamo), January 1975.
Bachmann, Gideon, "Vittorio de Sica: Always a True Window," in *Sight and Sound* (London), Spring 1975.
"De Sica Issue" of *Bianco e Nero* (Rome), Fall 1975.
Passalacqua, J., "Vittorio de Sica," in *Films in Review* (New York), April 1978.
"Vittorio de Sicà Issue" of *Avant-Scène du Cinéma* (Paris), 15 October 1978.
Carcassonne, P., "Dossier: le neo-realisme: De Sica 'le menteur'," in *Cinématographe* (Paris), January 1979.
Shipman, David, "Directors of the Decade: Forties," in *Films and Filming* (London), June 1983.
"Vittorio De Sica," in *Cinema Nuovo* (Bari), February 1985.

On DE SICA: films—

De Reisner, Bika, *Meet De Sica*
Dragadze, Peter, *Vittorio De Sica: Il regista, l'attore, l'uomo*, for TV, 1974.

*   *   *

The films of Vittorio De Sica are among the most enduring of the Italian post-war period. His career suggests an openness to form and a versatility uncommon among Italian directors. De Sica began acting on stage as a teenager and played his first film role in 1918. In the 1920's, his handsome features and talent made him something of a matinee idol, and from the mid-1930's he appeared in a number of films by Mario Camerini including *Gliuomini, che mascalzoni, Daro un milione . . .* and *Grandi magazzine*. During his lifetime, he made over 100 films in Italy and abroad as actor, using this means to finance his own films. He specialized in breezy comic heroes, men of great self assurance or confidence men (as in Rossellini's *Generale della Rovere*). The influence of his tenure as actor cannot be overestimated in his directorial efforts, where the expressivity of the actor in carefully written roles was one of his foremost technical implements. In this vein De Sica has continually mentioned the influence on his work of Charlie Chaplin. The tensive continuity between tragic and comic, the deployment of a detailed yet poetic gestural language, and a humanist philosophy without recourse to the politically radical are all paralleled in the silent star's films.

De Sica's directorial debuts, *Rose scarlatte* and *Maddalena, zero in condotta*, are both attempts to bring theater pieces to the screen with suitable roles for himself. With his fourth film, *I bambini ci guardano*, De Sica teamed with Cesare Zavattini, who was to become his major collaborator for the next three decades, and together they began to demonstrate elements of the post-war realist aesthetic which, more than any other director except Visconti and Rossellini, De Sica helped shape and determine. Despite the overt melodrama of the misogynistic story (a young mother destroys her family by deserting them), the filmmaker has refused to narrow the perspective through an overwrought Hollywoodian mise-en-scène, preferring instead a refreshing simplicity of composition and a subdued editing style. Much of the film's original flavor can be traced to the clear, subjective mediation of a child as promised in the title.

De Sica's intense feeling for children's sensibilities led him to imagine how children viewed the failing adult reconstruction of society after the war. *Sciuscia*, a realistic look at the street and prison life of poor, abandoned children, was the result. It is the story of how the lasting friendship of two homeless boys, who make their living shining shoes for the American G.I.'s, is betrayed by their contact with adults. At the end one inadvertently causes the other's death. Although Zavattini insists that his creative role was minimal in this instance, the presence of his poetic imagination is evident in the beautiful white horse which cements the boys' mutual bond and their hope for a future. Though a miserable failure in Italy, *Sciuscia* marked De Sica's entry into international prominence winning a special Oscar in 1947.

For the balance of the neorealist period it was an uphill fight to finance his films through friends and acting salaries. *Ladri di biciclette* anchors searching social documentation in metaphor and a non-traditional but highly structured narrative. The workman Ricci's desperate search for his bicycle is an odyssey that enables us to witness a varied collection of characters and situations among the poor and working class of Rome. Each episode propels the narrative toward a sublimely Chaplinesque but insufficiently socially critical ending in which Ricci is defeated in his search and therefore in his attempts to provide for his family. Reduced to being a thief himself, he takes his son's hand and disappears into the crowd. Like De Sica's other neorealist films, *Ladri di biciclette* gives the impression of technical nonchalance only to the indiscriminate eye for De Sica planned his work with attention to minute details of characterization, mise-en-scène, and camera technique. During this period he preferred the non-professional actor for his or her ability to accept direction without the mediation of learned acting technique.

The story of Toto the Good in *Miracolo a Milano* remains one of the outstanding stylistic contradictions of the neorealist period (there are many) yet one which sheds an enormous amount of light on the intentions and future of the De Sica-Zavattini team. The cinematography and setting, markedly neorealist in this fable about the struggle to found a shanty town for the homeless, is undercut at every moment with unabashed clowning both in performance and in cinematic technique. Moreover, the film moves toward a problematic fairy tale ending in which the poor, no longer able to defend their happy, make-shift village now beleaguered by the voracious appetite of capitalist entrepreneurs, take to the skies on magic broomsticks. (The film has more special effects than anyone would ever associate with neorealism; could De Sica have left his mark on Steven Spielberg?) Still, Zavattini, who had wanted to make the film for a number of years, and De Sica defend it as the natural burlesque transformation of themes evident in their earlier work together.

By this time De Sica's films were the subject of a good deal of controversy in Italy, and generally the lines were drawn between Catholic and Communist critics. The latter had an especially acute fear (one which surfaced again with Fellini's *La Strada*) that the hard-won traits of neorealism had begun to backslide into those of the so-called "calligraphic" films of the Fascist era. These were based on an ahistorical, formal concern for aesthetic, compositional qualities and the nuances of clever storytelling. However their next film, *Umberto D*, comes closest to Zavattini's ideas on the absolute responsibility of the camera eye to observe life as it is lived without the traditional compromises of entertaining narratives. The sequence of the maid waking up and making the morning coffee has been praised many times for its day-in-the-life directness and simplicity. *Il Tetto*, about a curious attempt to erect a small house on municipal property, is generally recognized as the last neorealist film of this original period.

Continually wooed by Hollywood, De Sica finally acquiesced to make *Stazione termini* in 1953, produced by Selznick and filmed in Rome with Jennifer Jones and Montgomery Clift. Unfortunately, neorealist representation formed only an insignificant background to this typically American star vehicle. A similar style is employed in *La ciociara* from a Moravia story about the relationship of a mother and daughter uprooted by the war. De Sica attempted in it to reconstruct reality in the studio making use of a somewhat unsuccessful stylized lighting technique but, as usual, he obtains excellent performances in an engaging dramatic vehicle. (Sophia Loren won an Oscar.)

The filmmakers returned to comedic vehicles in 1954 in *L'oro di Napoli*. Human comedy emerges from the rich diversity and liveliness of Neapolitan life. Though still within the confines of realism, the film foreshadows the director's entrance into the popular Italian market for sexual satire and farce. The exactitude with which he sculpts his characters and his reluctance to reduce the scenario to a mere bunch of gags demonstrates his intention to fuse comedy and drama, putting De Sica at the top of his class in this respect—among Risi, Comencini, and Monicelli. Often with Zavattini but also with Eduardo De Filippo, Tonino Guerra, and even Neil Simon (*After the Fox*), De Sica turned out about eight such films for the lucrative international market between 1961 and 1968, the best of which are: *Il giudizio universale* with an all-star cast of international comedians; *Ieri, oggi, domani* and *Matrimonio all'Italiana* both with Loren and Mastroianni; and *Sette volte donna*.

Il giardino dei Finzi Contini from a Bassani novel about the incarceration of Italian Jews during the war shows a strong Viscontian influence in its lavish setting and thematics, dealing with the dissolution of the bourgeois family. *Una breve vacanza*, an examination of a woman who has managed to break out of the confines of an oppressive marriage during a sanitorium stay, reinstitutes the tensive relationship between comedy and tragedy of the earlier films. De Sica's last film, *Il viaggio*, is from a Pirandello novel.

—Joel Kanoff

DE TOTH, André.

Hungarian. Born Sásvrái Farkasfawi Tóthfalusi Tóth Endre Antai Mihaly in Mako, Hungary, 1910. Educated at the University of Budapest. Married Veronica Lake, 1944 (divorced 1952). Worked for Bavarisch Pictura Productions, Vienna, from 1929; scriptwriter, editor, 2nd unit director and actor in Hungarian films, 1930's; emigrated to England, signed to Alexander Korda's London Film Productions, 1939; moved to Hollywood, 1943; TV director, 1960's. Address: 3690 Barham Blvd., Los Angeles, CA 90068, U.S.A.

Films as Director:
(as Toth Endre in Hungary):

1939   *Öt óra 40* (*At 5:40*); *Két lány az utcán* (*Two Girls of the Street*); *Semmelweiss*; *Hat hét boldogság* (*Six Weeks of Happiness*); *Balalaika*; *Toprini nász* (*Wedding in Toprin*) (+co-sc)

(as André de Toth in U.S.):

1943   *Passport of Suez* (+story, uncredited)
1944   *None Shall Escape*; *Dark Waters*; *Guest in the House* (Brahm) (d of several scenes, co-sc, both uncredited)
1947   *Ramrod*; *The Other Love*
1948   *Pitfall*
1949   *Slattery's Hurricane*
1951   *Man in the Saddle* (*The Outcast*)
1952   *Carson City*; *Springfield Rifle*; *Last of the Comanches* (*The Sabre and the Arrow*)
1953   *House of Wax*; *Thunder Over the Plains*; *The Stranger Wore a Gun*
1954   *The Bounty Hunter*; *Tanganyika*; *Crime Wave* (*The City Is Dark*); *Riding Shotgun*
1955   *The Indian Fighter*
1957   *Monkey on My Back*; *Hidden Fear* (+co-sc)
1959   *The Two Headed Spy*; *Day of the Outlaw*
1960   *Man on a String* (*Confessions of a Counterspy*)
1961   *Morgan il pirata* (*Morgan the Pirate*) (co-d, co-sc); *I Mongoli* (*The Mongols*) (co-d)
1962   *Oro per i Cesari* (*Gold for the Caesars*) (co-d)
1968   *Play Dirty* (+exec pr)

Other Films:

1937   *Falu rossza* (*Evil Village*) (Pásztor) (story); *The Life of Emile Zola* (Dieterle) (co-sc uncredited)
1941   *Lydia* (Duvivier) (pr asst, co-sc both uncredited)
1946   *Young Widow* (Marin) (co-sc, uncredited)
1947   *Dishonored Lady* (Stevenson) (co-sc, uncredited)
1950   *The Gunfighter* (King) (co-story)
1956   *Westward Ho the Wagons!* (Beaudine) (co-sc uncredited)
1967   *Billion Dollar Brain* (Russell) (exec pr)
1970   *El Condor* (Guillermin) (pr)

Publications:

By DE TOTH: article—

Interview in *Films in Review* (New York), August–September 1987.

On DE TOTH: book—

Hayes, R.M., *3-D Movies*, Jefferson, North Carolina, 1989.

On DE TOTH: articles—

Bangs, B., "Problem Child with Good Intentions," in *Silver Screen* (New York), March 1945.
Howard, M., "The Amazing de Toths," in *Silver Screen* (New York), July 1947.
"André de Toth," in *Film Dope* (London), January 1977.

*   *   *

André De Toth is a superb visual stylist of remarkable control and intensity whose work is virtually unknown today except to a few scholars who see him as a true artist. His excellent body of work contains a unifying set of thematic and visual characteristics which add up to a strong personal cinema.

The films of André De Toth seem to begin in the middle of events which are already under way. Both the main characters and the viewers find themselves in an already determined chain of events in which one's position is not fully understood. The films use space, geography, location and setting to represent the inner psychology of the characters. In *Dark Waters*, the leading lady (Merle Oberon) has been psychologically damaged by a wartime experience in which the boat carrying her and her parents was torpedoed. The "dark waters" of her emotions, her confused memories of the resulting deaths of her parents, and her deep fears for her own safety are represented on screen by the swamp that surrounds the southern mansion she visits. Ultimately, she must save herself from the villains by entering the swamp and plunging into the dark waters to hide, confronting her fear.

The universe in which the characters in a De Toth film live is a treacherous one. It is a world in which safety falls away, and danger is objectively demonstrated through "deep waters," quicksands, and hostile terrain. In such circumstances, a hero frequently has to behave villainously in order to survive. In *Pitfall*, Dick Powell is supposedly safe inside his typical suburban home of the 1950's, but a killer stalks him there. Powell is forced to move outside and begins to stalk the killer. Thus the hero and the villain exchange places, a change which De Toth demonstrates skillfully through camera movement, point of view, and composition.

Whether working in the film noir tradition in such films as *Dark Waters* and *Pitfall* or in westerns such as *Ramrod, Day of the Outlaw*, and *Indian Fighter*, De Toth's films reflect common themes. Ordinary people are trapped in situations beyond their control and are forced to struggle for mastery. They are subject to betrayals by those they considered friends, and characters reverse themselves as to behavior patterns. A desire for escape or adventure can lead a character into a nightmare situation. Above all, the films reflect a cynical attitude toward human nature. Deception and treachery are everyday occurrences, and the ambiguous endings of the films seem to be happy, but upon reflection may not be. De Toth uses a moving camera to create tension, employing reverse pans against tracks to demonstrate the treacherous nature of events upon the screen.

The frequent reversals of character are ably demonstrated formally on the screen, as De Toth matches his manipulation of the tools of film technique to story events with great skill. In the opening sequence of *Play Dirty*, a German soldier is seen driving a jeep across the North African desert during World War II. The radio loudly plays "Lili Marlene." At a certain point, the soldier checks his map, calmly removes his German cap and jacket, and dons a British uniform, switching the radio to an English broadcast. This is the perfect statement of De Toth's world and his characters. The world is tricky and can change swiftly, because human beings are tricky and capable of being the opposite of what they seem. Furthermore, such behavior is necessary for survival.

André De Toth was never a popular director with critics, most of whom ignored his low-budget films. If he was known at all, it was as a former husband of the glamorous actress Veronica Lake, or perhaps as the one-eyed man who directed a 3-D smash hit of the 1950's, *House of Wax*, even though he could not perceive true depth. His cruel themes and deliberately visual form of story-telling did not create beloved, well-remembered films which pleased either audiences or critics. In the great reevaluation of film directors inspired by the first waves of American auteurism in the 1960's, he was more or less overlooked. His work, with its visual and thematic rewards, is yet to be fully discovered and analyzed.

—Jeanine Basinger

DÍAZ, Rolando.

Cuban. Born in Havana, 1947. Studied at University of Havana, 1965–70. Entered Instituto Cubano de Arte e Industria Cinematográfica (ICAIC) as sound assistant, 1967; director of military newsreel team in Angola, 1975–77; worked for ICAIC in the Latin American Newsreel, directed over 70 newsreels and 10 documentary shorts, from 1977; directed first feature, *Los pájaros tirándole a la escopeta*, 1984.

Films as Director:

1977   *Momentos del Cardín* (doc short)
1978   *45 días* (doc short); *Medellín '78* (doc short)
1979   *Redonda y viene en caja cuadrada* (doc short)
1983   *Contraversia* (doc short)
1984   *Los pájaros tirándole a la escopeta*
1985   *En tres y dos*
1988   *La vida en rosa*

Publications:

By DÍAZ: articles—

"Golpear la imagen en términos cinematograficos," an interview with Romualda Santos, in *Cine Cubano* (Havana), no. 99, 1981.
"Así es," in *Cine Cubano* (Havana), no. 100, 1981.
"Más vale pajaro en mano . . . ," an interview with Rebeca Chávez, in *Cine Cubano* (Havana), no. 110, 1984.

On DÍAZ: book—

Chanan, Michael, *The Cuban Image*, London, 1985.

On DÍAZ: articles—

Aufderheide, Pat, "Red Harvest," in *American Film* (Washington, D.C.), March 1984.
Macédon, Filipo, "Con una buena escopeta," in *Cine Cubano* (Havana), no. 111, 1985.

*   *   *

The most interesting and entertaining of the new Cuban directors, Rolando Díaz deals with problems of everyday life in innovative and exciting ways. Díaz followed the route of most post-revolutionary Cuban filmmakers, studying at the University of Havana and then entering the Cuban Film Institute (ICAIC) as an assistant. After serving as the director of a military newsreel team in Angola, he returned to ICAIC and worked on the Latin American Newsreel (Noticiero) for several years, while also making documentary films. The experience of directing documentaries is seen to be crucial to Cuban filmmakers, for it serves to bring them close to the reality of Latin America. Cineastes in Cuba and of the New Latin American Cinema have long decried the colonization of their nations' screens by Hollywood and European films, and called for the portrayal of Latin American problems, expressed in their own language. A product of the 30 years of efforts to create a new cinema, Díaz manifests those concerns in both thematic choice and filmic structure.

The themes of Díaz's films range from sport to marital discord. Making movies about sport would seem to have little transcendence, but Díaz was more interested in visual structures that could stand on their own than he was in glorifying athletes. Thus he breaks sharply with the traditional sports documentary and its didactic recounting of who won what. Instead, he told his camera operators to look for the unusual at sporting events; they did so, capturing the crowds, the referees, and the commentators as well as the athletes. Díaz, who asserts that what interests him most in filmmaking is the editing, then assembled these shots into extraordinarily funny and moving vignettes of sport. Although these films are universal in their immediate appeal, Díaz feels that they are also very Cuban in developing a language which expresses the natural joy of living and gaiety of the island culture.

If humor is the abiding element of Díaz's films, this does not mean that he uses it to ignore problems, and probably the most pointed of Díaz's criticism is leveled at Cuban machismo. In the documentary short, *Controversia*, Díaz films discussions between rural husbands and wives, which reveal unresolved tensions over domestic sex roles. As the conversations heat up, Díaz intercuts images of a macho on horseback whose mount becomes increasingly skittish—seemingly affected by the rising tone of the arguments—until horse and rider wheel about and run off. Attacks on machismo are not unknown in Cuban cinema, but Díaz took them to a new level with the social comedy, *Los pájaros tirándole a la escopeta* (Birds shooting at the shotgun, or The world turned upside down). Díaz calls the film "a history of everyday people," and its theme is relatively simple: two lovers are shocked when her father and his mother begin an affair. Concerned to get behind appearances, Díaz points out that while the young can often appear to be the most progressive, they are often the repository of unexamined reactionary ideas. In *Pájaros*, the attack on the machismo takes the form of criticizing in particular the attitudes of the young man who is scandalized by his mother's behavior. The eclectic style utilized by Díaz is an exciting mix of fiction, documentary, and television footage, which is characteristic of Cuban films. The combination of a timely theme, a stimulating film form, and Díaz's ironic wit resulted in one of the most popular Cuban movies ever, drawing an audience of two million in its first two months of exhibition.

In *En tres y dos* (Three Balls, Two Strikes), Díaz returned to the world of sports for inspiration. The film deals with the travails of a star athlete on the eve of retiring. As he passes through the various stages of learning to accept the inevitability of retirement, historical documentary footage of Cuban sports legends—the boxers Kid Chocolate and Teófilo Stevenson, and the runner Alberto Juantorena—are cut together with interviews in which they talk about the difficulties they faced in ending their careers. Díaz's deft hand in editing together fiction and documentary, his acute rendering of the crowds' ambience, and his constant downplaying of the importance of games make this one of the few films to utilize sport as a metaphor for larger issues. And, in this particular case the metaphor may have an immediate political target, being a veiled allusion to the necessarily impending retirement of Fidel Castro. Rolando Díaz has shown himself to be a filmmaker with an uncanny instinct for finding meaning in the apparently insignificant.

—John Mraz

DICKINSON, Thorold.

British. Born in Bristol, 16 November 1903. Educated at Clifton College and at Keble College, Oxford. Married architect Joanna Macfadyen, 1929. Interpreter for George Pearson in France, 1925; subsequently editor, director and scriptwriter; programme controller, the London Film Society, 1929–39; Vice-President, Association of Cine-Technicians, 1936–53; directed first film, *High Command*, 1937; organized Army Kinematograph Service Production Group, 1942–43; Chairman of the British Film Academy, 1950–53; film advisor in Israel, 1953–54; Chief of the Film Service, Office of Public Information, United Nations, 1956–60; President of the International Federation of Film Societies, 1958–66; lecturer in film studies at Slade School of Fine Art, 1960 (first Professor of Film in Britain, 1967). Recipient: Commander of the British Empire, 1973. *Died 14 April 1984.*

Films as Director:

1937   *The High Command*
1938   *Spanish ABC* (short) (co-d, co-ed); *Behind the Spanish Lines* (short) (co-d, co-ed)
1939   *The Arsenal Stadium Mystery* (+co-adapt); *The Mikado* (Schertzinger) (2nd unit d)
1940   *Gaslight* (*Angel Street*); (short films for Ministry of Information): *Westward Ho! 1940* (+pr, co-ed); *Yesterday Is Over Your Shoulder* (+pr, co-ed); *The Horseshoe Nail* (abandoned because of objections of Ministry of Aircraft Production)
1941   *The Prime Minister*
1942   *The Next of Kin* (+co-sc)
1946   *Men of Two Worlds* (*Kisenga, Man of Africa*) (+co-sc)
1948   *The Queen of Spades*
1951   *Secret People* (+story, co-sc)
1954   *Hakarka ha a dom* (*The Red Ground*) (short) (+co-sc, ed, bit role as man playing cards)
1955   *Hill Twenty-Four Doesn't Answer* (+co-pr, co-sc, co-ed)

Other Films:

1926   *The Little People* (Pearson) (asst d, co-sc)
1927   *Huntingtower* (Pearson) (asst d)
1928   *Love's Option* (Pearson) (co-ed, asst d)
1929   *Auld Lang Syne* (Pearson) (co-ed, synchronization of song sequences)
1930   *The School for Scandal* (Elvey) (ed)
1931   *The Sport of Kings* (Saville) (ed); *Contraband Love* (Morgan) (ed); *Other People's Sins* (Hill) (ed); *The Great Gay Road* (Hill) (ed); *Lloyd of the CID* (*Detective Lloyd*) (12 episode serial) (MacRae) (ed 8 episodes)
1932   *The First Mrs. Fraser* (Hill) (ed); *Karma* (Raid and Freer-Hunt) (ed); *Perfect Understanding* (Gardner) (ed)
1933   *Going Gay* (*Kiss Me Goodbye*) (Gallone, completed 1931) (ed); *For Love of You* (Gallone, completed 1931) (ed); *Loyalties* (Dean) (ed)
1934   *Java Head* (Ruben) (ed, completion of film after director fell ill); *Sing as We Go!* (Dean) (ed)
1935   *The Silent Passenger* (Denham) (ed); *Midshipman Easy* (*Men of the Sea*) (Reed) (ed, supervisor)
1936   *Whom the Gods Love* (*Mozart*) (Dean) (ed); *Calling the Tune* (Denham) (co-ed); *The House of the Spaniard* (Denham) (ed)
1942   (partial list for Army Kinematograph Service): *The New Lot* (Reed) (pr/spvr); *Tank Tactics* series (F.A. Young and others) (six 2-reelers) (pr/spvr); plus ten other titles
1957   *Question in Togoland* (Porter) (short for U.N.) (pr/spvr); *Out* (Rogosin) (short for U.N.) (pr/spvr); *Blue Vanguard* (McNeill) (for U.N.) (pr/spvr); *Three of Our Children* (Reed and Estelle) (short for U.N.) (pr/spvr)
1958   *Overture* (Polidoro and Singh) (short for U.N.) (pr/spvr); *Exposure* (Hughes and Singh) (short for U.N.) (pr/spvr); *Pablo Casals Breaks His Journey* (Sarma) (short for U.N.) (pr/spvr); *Big Day in Bogo* (N. Reed) (short for U.N.) (pr/spvr); *Power Among Men* (Hammid, Polidoro and Sarma) (short for U.N.) (pr/spvr, co-sc, ed)
1959   *In Our Hands* (Sarma) (short for U.N.) (pr/spvr); *A Scary Time* (Clarke) (short for U.N.) (pr/spvr); *Workshop for Peace* (Hammid, revised version of a 1955 film) (short for U.N.) (pr/spvr)
1960   *The Farmers of Fermathe* (Polidoro) (footage from *Power Among Men*, 1958) (short for U.N.) (pr/spvr)

Thorold Dickinson

Publications:

By DICKINSON: books—

Soviet Cinema, with Catherine de la Roche, London, 1948; reissued New York, 1972.
Screenplay of *Secret People*, in *Making a Film* by Lindsay Anderson, London, 1952.
Introduction to *The Technique of Film Editing* by Karel Reisz, London, 1952.
A Discovery of Cinema, London, 1971.

By DICKINSON: articles—

"Search for Music" and "Indian Spring," in *Penguin Film Review*, London, 1948.
"The Filmwright and the Audience," in *Sight and Sound* (London), March 1950.
"The Work of Sir Michael Balcon," in *The Year's Work in Film*, London, 1951.
"A Day in the Life of a Film," in *Sight and Sound* (London), August 1951.
"Griffith and the Development of the Silent Film," in *Sight and Sound* (London), October 1951.
"Secret People," in *Cinema* (London), 1952.
"Heaven Preserve Us from the Passive Audience!," in *Film* (London), September/October 1955.
"The Sponsoring of Films," in *Film* (London), March/April 1956.
"Conference in Paris," in *Sight and Sound* (London), Summer 1956.
"The Personal Style," in *Film* (London), March/April 1957.
"This Documentary Business," in *Film Culture* (New York), October 1957.
Interview in *Film Dope* (London), January 1977.
"Experiences in the Spanish Civil War, 1938," in *Historical Journal of Film, Radio, and Television* (Abingdon, Oxon), October 1984.

On DICKINSON: book—

Richards, Jeffrey, *Thorold Dickinson: The Man and His Films*, London, 1986.

On DICKINSON: articles—

Sainsbury, Frank, "Closeups," in *Cine-Technician* (London), August 1940.
Listener (London), 3 June 1982.
Anstey, Edgar, "Paul Rotha and Thorold Dickinson," in *Sight and Sound* (London), Summer 1984.
Obituary in *Hollywood Reporter*, 1 May 1984.
Obituary in *Revue du Cinéma* (Paris), July–August 1984.

On DICKINSON: film—

Manvell, Roger, *A Film Is Made* (BBC), 1948.

* * *

Though his work has received far less attention and acclaim than that of his contemporary Michael Powell, Thorold Dickinson has strong claims to be considered as one of British cinema's major artists. Like Powell, he belongs to the studio era of the 1940's and 1950's but marked out a highly individual path, rejecting both the literary adaptation style of Reed and Lean and the cosy conformities of Balcon's Ealing studios. Dickinson is the most English of feature directors. He learned his craft from the veteran George Pearson while still an undergraduate at Oxford and later as an editor in the mainstream of British commercial film production of the 1930's. His breakthrough to feature filmmaking came with *The High Command* in 1937 and his work soon began to show his interest in the psychological motivation of his characters and his concern to analyse British liberal values.

The 1940 *Gaslight*, his third feature film, is his first major work. A stylish period thriller, it is a version of the play later adapted in Hollywood by George Cukor. Though overshadowed by Cukor's version, this is a fine professional piece, which shows a characteristic Dickinson concern with the psychological state of the characters and their reactions under the intense pressure. In a very different vein, *The Next of Kin* began as a project for a military training film before being transformed by Dickinson and his producer Balcon into a feature-length fiction which achieved considerable commercial success. Though imbued with the patriotic spirit typical of its period, *The Next of Kin* avoids the rhetoric and self-glorification so common in the 1940's. Indeed its unsparing portrayal of a country ill-prepared for the war in which it is engaged caused it some initial problems with the film censors.

The early postwar years saw three further remarkably diverse features, all of enormous interest and power. *Men of Two Worlds* is one of the few British studies of the impact of colonialism on the educated African elite which remains viable in its analysis. In contrast to its highly constructed realism (it was researched in Tanganyika but shot in the studio), Dickinson's adaptation of Pushkin's *The Queen of Spades* has an elegant period style which shows the influence of Jean Cocteau and the German expressionists in its creation of atmosphere. Again the director's interest in the madness which stems from the failure to control passion is evident. *Secret People*, again produced by Balcon, but in no way an "Ealing film," probed another sensitive area for the liberal conscience: the use of violence for political ends, with the focus again on questions of identity and motivation. It proved to be Dickinson's last major film as a director, though he subsequently made a fictional feature in Israel, *Hill 24 Doesn't Answer*, worked as a producer for the United Nations, and became Britain's first professor of film at the Slade School of Fine Art, London.

Dickinson's work in the feature film has a restraint and subtlety akin to that displayed by Jennings in the documentary. It is exemplary in its use of the imaginative potential of the film studio and for the director's acute moral sense. The handful of films which Dickinson directed in the course of just a dozen or so years are among the most rewarding—as well as most neglected British films of their period.

—Roy Armes

DIEGUES, Carlos.

Brazilian. Born in Maceio, state of Alagoas, 19 May 1940. Educated in law, Catholic University of Rio de Janeiro. Married entertainer Nara Leao. Organizer of Metropolitan Union of students, also film critic and poet, early 1960's; directed first feature, *Ganga Zumba*, 1964; emigrated to France following Brazilian military takeover, late 1960's; directed *Séjour* for French TV, 1970; returned to Brazil, mid-1970's.

Films as Director:

1960 *Fuga* (short) (co-d)
1961 *Domingo* (short)
1962 "Escola de samba, alegria de viver" episode of *Cinco vêzes Favela*
1964 *Ganga Zumba* (+co-adapt)
1965 *A 8a. Bienal de São Paulo* (short)
1966 *A grande cidade* (*The Big City*) (+co-sc)
1967 *Oito Universitários* (short)
1969 *Os herdeiros* (*The Inheritors. The Heirs*)
1972 *Quando a Carnaval chegar* (*When Carnival Comes*)
1973 *Joanna Francesa* (*Jeanne la française*) (+sc)
1976 *Xica da Silva* (*Xica*)
1977 *Chuvas de verao* (*Summer Showers, A Summer Rain*) (+sc)

Carlos Diegues: *Bye Bye Brasil*

1978   *Os filhos do medo* (*Les Enfants de la peur*) (TV documentary)
1980   *Bye Bye Brasil* (+sc)
1984   *Quilombo*
1987   *Un tren para las estrellas*

Other Films:

1965   *O Circo* (Jabor) (ed)
1967   *Terra em transe* (*Land in Trance*) (Rocha) (assoc pr)
1968   *Capitu* (Saraceni) (assoc pr)
1980   *Prova de Fogo* (Altberg) (assoc pr)

Publications:

By DIEGUES: articles—

"Diegues fala de Moreau e 'Joana'," interview, in *Filme Cultura* (Rio de Janeiro), January/February 1973.
"Carlos Diegues: 'cette chose trés simple, aimer le peuple'," interview with J. Delmas, in *Jeune Cinéma* (Paris), July/August 1978.
Interview with Federico De Cardenas, in *Los años de la conmoción*, by Isaac León Frías, Mexico City, 1979.
"The Mind of Cinema Novo," interview with D. Yakir, in *Film Comment* (New York), September/October 1980.
"Le Cinéma nuovo dix ans aprés," an interview with G. Haustrate and D. Rabourdin, in *Cinéma* (Paris), November 1980.
"Adieu, cinema novo," an interview with P.A. Paranagua, in *Positif* (Paris), May 1981.
Interview with J.C. Rodrigues, in *Filme Cultura* (Rio de Janeiro), August–October 1982.
Interview with C. Espinosa Dominguez, in *Cine Cubano* (Havana), no. 104, 1983.

Interview with André Tournès, in *Jeune Cinéma* (Paris), July–August 1984.
"Cine: arte del presente," "Sobre el cinema novo," and "Diez años de cine nacional," in *Hojas de cine: Testimonios y Documentos del Nuevo Cine Latinoamericano 1*, Mexico City, 1986.
"Choosing between Legend and History," an interview with Coco Fusco, in *Cineaste* (New York), vol. 15, no. 1, 1986.

On DIEGUES: books—

Johnson, Randal, *Cinema Novo x5: Masters of Contemporary Brazilian Film*, Austin, Texas, 1984.
Burton, Julianne, editor, *Cinema and Social Change in Latin America: Conversations with Filmmakers*, Austin, Texas, 1986.
Johnson, Randal, and Robert Stam, editors, *Brazilian Cinema*, Austin, Texas, 1988.

On DIEGUES: articles—

Prédal, R., "Bio-filmographie: Carlos Diegues," in *Etudes Cinématographiques* (Paris), no.93–96, 1972.
Johnson, Randal, "*Xica de Silva*: Sex, Politics, and Culture," in *Jump Cut* (Berkeley), May 1980.
Trujillo, Marisol, "Tormento y pasión en *Los herederos* de Carlos Diegues," in *Cine Cubano* (Havana), no. 100, 1981.
Yakir, Dan, "Braziliant," in *Film Comment* (New York), May–June 1984.
Dossier on Carlos Diegues, in *Revue du Cinema* (Paris), November 1984.
Osiel, Mark, "Bye Bye Boredom: Brazilian Cinema Comes of Age," in *Cineaste* (New York), vol 15, no. 1, 1986.

*   *   *

One of the founders of *Cinema Novo*—the movement that transformed film in Brazil and was a pivotal influence in the New Latin American Cinema—Carlos Diegues is probably the most historically minded of its adherents. Like the other directors of *Cinema Novo*, Diegues is concerned to make films which are "culturally Brazilian, and impregnated with national and Latin American problems;" and his entrance into the national reality was, as with many other members of this group, through documentary films that put him in direct contact with social problems. Diegues also shares the interest in popular culture that is characteristic of *Cinema Novo*, although he tends to emphasize the contribution of black culture, which "gave us originality. It's the element that has completely modified Brazil, which otherwise would be a mere cultural colony of Portugal and Spain."

Perhaps that which most differentiates Diegues from his *Cinema Novo* colleagues is his historical orientation. On the one hand, this can be seen in his insistent recurrence to historical themes. But, on the other, Diegues' conception of history is complex: he feels that the most important element in cinema is its *adecuación* (fitness) to the time in which it is made. To the degree that a film speaks to the problems and possibilities of the epoch in which it appears, it allows for the sort of "political cinema" Diegues prefers, a cinema with which the audience can interact. It is this perspective that Diegues brings to his perception of his films as corresponding to particular historical contexts.

His first works, *Samba School* and *Ganga Zumba*, are products of what Diegues describes as a "fantastic, euphoric period" in which emerged new Brazilian cinema, music, and theater. *Samba School* was typical of the early works of *Cinema Novo*, focusing on the popular culture of the slums through an analysis of the alienation represented by the schools of samba. Diegues made the film on a barebones budget and worked at practically all the production tasks, including appearing as an actor. *Ganga Zumba* was Diegues' first feature. A reconstruction of the Palmares Republic of runaway slaves in Brazil during the 17th century, it corresponded to the search for identity in which many Brazilian artists were then engaged. It also represented the first *Cinema Novo* film to value Afro-Brazilian culture, as well as the beginning of Diegues' interest in bringing black history to the screen: "I tried to make a black film, not a film about blacks," he stated.

The military coup of 1964, and its increasingly repressive legislation during the 1960's, changed the cultural scene profoundly. In film, an "aesthetic of silence" reigned, and Diegues perceives this as his "sick period," during which he made *The Heirs* and *Joanna Francesa* as expressions of the depressing tableau presented by the "Dante-esque levels" military terrorism reached. *The Heirs* is a historical work on the period 1930–1964, which allegorically evokes the role of Getulio Vargas (a populist president-dictator who oscillated between fascism and socialism) through following the trajectory of a bourgeois family. Diegues says that his main intention was to "project a precise image of this strange, violent and sentimental, baroque and surrealist, sincere and subtle country called Brazil, whose passion torments me more than anything else in life." In *Joanna Francesa*, Diegues returned again to analyze the Revolution of 1930, this time in a film he considers a "lament" on the death of a culture and a civilization, which reflected the dolorous days through which Brazil was passing.

The liberalization of military rule led to what Diegues has described as the third phase of *Cinema Novo*, which he characterizes as "the aesthetic of life." Within this category, he places the two reconstructions, *Xica da Silva* and *Quilombo*, which continue the black history of colonial Brazil he began with *Ganga Zumba*, as well as the popular *Bye Bye Brazil*. Both *Xica da Silva* and *Quilombo* are more mythic than historic, for Diegues believes that "history is always written by the winners," and therefore a real history of blacks is either impossible or depressing. Thus, he focuses on the character of Francisca (Xica), a black slave whom a wealthy Portuguese freed and took as his lover. Little real information exists on this 18th-century woman because all mention of her was exorcised by the townspeople, but her love of freedom is an important myth of Brazilian popular culture.

Quilombo was made just two or three years before Brazil was liberated from military rule, and that context allowed Diegues to utilize the story of the runaway slave republic as a metaphor for the building of a utopia. With even less information available about *quilombos* than existed on Xica, Diegues allowed himself free rein; the result, as he intended, says more about the future than about the past. *Xica da Silva* was immensely popular in Brazil, but the film which has achieved the most international recognition is *Bye Bye Brazil*. In this exuberant film "dedicated to Brazilians in the 21st century," Diegues returns to *Cinema Novo*'s insistent concern with popular culture and concludes that the way in which culture is assimilated and re-elaborated is more important than its origin or alleged "purity." This is perhaps one of the more useful lessons Diegues has to teach his fellow filmmakers of *Cinema Novo*.

—John Mraz

DIETERLE, William.

German. Born Wilhelm Dieterle in Ludwigshafen, 15 July 1893; became U.S. citizen, late 1930's. Studied acting with Paul Tietsch, Mannheim. Married 1) comedienne and writer Charlotte Hagenbruch, 1921 (died 1965); 2) Elisabeth Dieterle. Actor in German theatre, from 1911; member of Max Reinhardt's company, Berlin, and film actor, 1920–23; directed first film, *Der Mensch am Wege*, 1923; began avant-garde Dramatisches Theater with Georg Kaiser and others, Berlin, 1924; founded Charha-Film production company, 1927; signed by Carl Laemmle to Deutsch Universal for five films, 1929; left, with wife, for U.S., 1930; signed seven-year contract with Warner Bros., 1931; left Warners for RKO, working as own producer: also, with Fritz Lang, financed emigration to U.S. of Brecht, Weill, and Helene Weigel, 1941; signed long-term contract with Hal Wallis, producing for Paramount, 1942; following McCarthyist attacks, passport confiscated, 1951 (and in 1953); returned to Germany, 1958; TV director, from 1961. *Died in Ottobrunn, 9 December 1972.*

Films as Director:

1923 *Der Mensch am Wege* (+sc, role as the angel); *Die grüne Manuela* (co-d with Dupont, role)
1924 *Das Wachsfigurenkabinett* (co-d with Leni, role)
1927 *Das Geheimnis des Abbé X* (*Der Mann, der nicht lieben darf*) (+pr, sc, role)
1928 *Die Heilige und ihr Narr* (*La Sainte et le fou*) (+pr, role as Harro, Count of Torstein); *Geschlecht in Fesseln—Die Sexualnot der Gefangenen* (*Chaînes, Les Sexes enchaînés*) (+role as Franz Sommer)
1929 *Ich liebe für dich* (*Le Triomphe de la vie*) (+role as Bergson); *Frühlingsrauschen* (*Tränen die ich dir geweint, Rêves de printemps, Nostalgie*) (+role as Friedrich); *Das Schweigen im Walde* (*Le Silence dans la forêt, La Nuit de la Saint-Jean*) (+role as Ettingen)

William Dieterle: *Geschlecht in Fesseln*

1930 *Ludwig der Zweite, König von Bayern* (+co-sc, role as Ludwig II of Bavaria); *Eine Stunde glück* (+co-sc, role as Eddy)

(Films made in U.S.):
1930 *Der Tanz geht weiter* (German version of William Beaudine's *Those Who Dance*) (+role as Fred Hogan); *Die Maske fällt* (German version of Frank Lloyd's *The Way of All Men*); *Kismet* (German version of Dillon film); *Dämon des Meeres* (co-d) (German version of Curtiz's *Moby Dick*)
1931 *Die Heilige Flamme* (co-d) (German version of Archie Mayo's *The Sacred Flame*); *The Last Flight*; *Her Majesty*; *Love*
1932 *Man Wanted*; *Jewel Robbery*; *Six Hours to Live!*; *The Crash*; *Scarlet Dawn*
1933 *Lawyer Man*; *Grand Slam*; *Adorable*; *The Devil's in Love*; *Female* (co-d); *From Headquarters*
1934 *Fashions of 1934* (co-d); *Madame du Barry*; *Fog Over Frisco*; *Doctor Monica* (co-d); *The Firebird*; *The Secret Bride*
1935 *A Midsummer Night's Dream* (co-d); *Dr. Socrates*
1936 *The Story of Louis Pasteur*; *The White Angel*; *Satan Met a Lady*
1937 *The Great O'Malley*; *Another Dawn*; *The Life of Emile Zola*
1938 *Blockade*
1939 *Juarez*; *The Hunchback of Notre Dame*
1940 *Dr. Ehrlich's Magic Bullet* (*The Story of Dr. Ehrlich's Magic Bullet, The Magic Bullet*); *A Dispatch from Reuter's* (*This Man Reuter*); *All That Money Can Buy* (*The Devil and Daniel Webster*) (+pr, co-sc)
1942 *Syncopation* (+pr, co-sc); *Tennessee Johnson* (*The Man on America's Conscience*)
1943 *Kismet*
1944 *I'll be Seeing You* (co-d)
1945 *This Love of Ours*; *Love Letters*
1946 **Duel in the Sun** (co-d); *The Searching Wind*

1948 *Paid in Full*; *The Accused*
1949 *Portrait of Jennie* (*Tidal Wave*) (production begun 1947); *Rope of Sand*; *Volcano*
1950 *September Affair*; *Dark City*
1952 *Red Mountain* (co-d, produced in 1950); *Boots Malone*; *The Turning Point*
1953 *Salome*
1954 *Elephant Walk*
1956 *Magic Fire* (+co-pr, shot in 1954); *One Against Many* (+co-sc, made for TV)
1957 *Peking Express* (produced in 1951); *The Loves of Omar Khayyam*

(after return to Germany):
1959 *Il Vendicatore* (*Dubrowsky, L'Aigle noir, Révolte sur la Volga*)
1960 *Herrin der Welt* (*Apocalisse sull fiume giallo, Les Mystères d'Angkor*) in two parts: "Herrin der Welt" and "Angkor-Vat" (co-d); *Die Fastnachtsbeichte*
1965 *The Confession* (*Quick, Let's Get Married, Seven Different Ways*)

Other Films:

1913 *Fiesko* (role)
1915 *Der Erbföster* (Oberläner) (role)
1921 *Die Geier-Wally* (Dupont) (role); *Die Hintertreppe* (Jessner and Leni) (role); *Fräulein Julie* (Basch) (role); *Die Silbermöwe* (Sauer) (role)
1922 *Frauenopfer* (Grüne) (role); *Es leuchtet meine Liebe* (Stein) (role); *Der Graf von Charolais* (Grune) (role); *Lukrezia*

Borgia (Oswald) (role); *Marie-Antoinette—Das Leben einer König*in (Meinert) (role)

1923 *Boheme—Künstlerliebe* (Righelli) (role); *Der zweite Schuss* (Krol) (role); *Die Pagode* (Fekete) (role); *Die Austreibung—Die Macht der zweiten Frau* (Murnau) (role)

1924 *Carlos und Elisabeth—Eine Herrschertragödie* (Oswald) (role); *Moderne Ehen* (Otto) (role); *Mutter und Kind* (Froehlich) (role)

1925 *Wetterleuchten* (Walther-Fein) (role); *Lena Warnstetten* (Eriksen) (role); *Die Blumenfrau von Potsdamer Platz* (Speyer) (role); *Sumpf und Moral* (Walther-Fein) (role); *Die vom Niederrhein* (Walther-Fein) (role); *Der Hahn im Korb* (Jacoby) (role); *Der Rosa Diamant* (Gliese) (role); *Die Dame aus Berlin* (von Kabdebo) (role); *Die Gesunkenen* (Walther-Fein) (role); *Gerechtigkeit* (role); *Der Traumkönig* (role)

1926 *Die Mühle von Sanssouci* (Philippini) (role); *Die Förster-christel* (Zelnik) (role); *Qualen der Nacht* (Bernhardt) (role); *Familie Schimeck* (*Wiener Herzen*) (Halm) (role); *Die Flucht in den Zirkus* (*Verurteilt nach Sibirien—Moskau 1912*) (Bonnard and Schamberg) (role); *Zopf und Schwert* (*Eine tolle Prinzessin*) (Janson) (role); *Faust—Eine Deutsche Volkssage* (Murnau) (role); *Hölle der Liebe—Erlebnisse aus einem Tanzpalais* (Rahn) (role); *Wie bliebe ich jung und schön* (*Ehegeheimnisse*) (Rahn) (role); *Der Jäger von Fall* (Seitz) (role); *Der Pfarrer von Kirchfeld* (Fleck) (role)

1927 *Unter Ausschluss der Öffentlichkeit* (Wiene) (role); *Der Zigeunerbaron* (*Sandor, Prince Vagabond*) (Zelnik) (role); *Violantha* (Froehlich) (role); *Die vom Schicksal verfolgten* (Kleinmann) (role); *Am Rande der Welt* (Grüne) (role); *Die Weber* (Zelnik) (role); *Ich habe im Mai von der Liebe geträumt* (Seits) (pr, role); *Liebesreigen* (Walther-Fein) (role); *Petronella* (Schwartz) (role); *Heimweh* (Righelli) (role); *Das Geheimnis des Abbe* (*Der Mann der nicht lieben darf, Behind the Altar*) (+pr, sc, role)

1928 *Frau Sorge* (Land) (role); *Apachenliebe* (*Die Apachen von Paris*) (Malikoff) (role); *Diebe* (Heuberger) (role); *Ritter der Nacht* (*Le Gentilhomme des bas-fonds, Les Chevaliers de la nuit*) (Reichmann) (role)

Publications:

By DIETERLE: book—

The Good Tidings, New York, 1950.

By DIETERLE: articles—

"The Great God Box-Office," in *Cinema Progress* (Los Angeles), February/March 1938.
"Hollywood and the European Crisis," in *Studies in Philosophy and Social Science* (New York), v.9, 1941.
"Do Films Have a Pedagogical Mission for the Masses?," in *Decision* (New York), March 1941.
Interview with Francis Koval, in *Sight and Sound* (London), May 1950.
"Directors in a Rut," in *Cine-Technician* (London), April 1954.
"Max Reinhardt in Hollywood," in *A Centennial Festschrift*, New York, 1973.
"William Dieterle: the Plutarch of Hollywood," an interview with T. Flinn, in *Velvet Light Trap* (Madison), Autumn 1975.

On DIETERLE: book—

Von Deutschland nach Hollywood: W. Dieterle, Berlin, 1973.

On DIETERLE: articles—

Lydo, Waldemar, "William Dieterle und der Filmschnitt," in *Reichs-filmblatt* (Berlin), 5 October 1929.
Luft, Herbert, "William Dieterle," in *Films in Review* (New York), April 1957 (see also Dieterle's response in May 1957, and Luft's response in June/July issue)
Pinto, Alfonso, and Francisco Rialp, "The Films of William Dieterle," in *Films in Review* (New York), October 1968.
Beylie, Claude, "William Dieterle l'heteroclite," in *Ecran* (Paris), February 1973.
"William Dieterle," in *Film Dope* (London), January 1977.

Dumont, Hervé, "William Dieterle 1893–1972," in *Avant-Scène du Cinéma* (Paris), 15 November 1977.
Wide Angle (Athens, Ohio), vol. 8, no. 2, 1986.

* * *

Dieterle came from that cradle of film talent, the theatre of Max Reinhardt. Although he appeared in a film *Fiesko* in 1913 it was in Dupont's *Die Geierwally* with Henny Porten that he established himself as a screen actor. He became much sought after and appeared with Asta Nielsen in *Fraulein Julie*, in Jessner's *Hintertreppe*, Oswald's *Lukretia Borgia* and *Carlos and Elizabeth*, Leni's *Waxworks*, Dupont's *Die grüne Manuela* and Murnau's *Die Austreibung* and *Faust*.

He ran his own theatre in Berlin in 1924 and had married the actress Charlotte Hagenbruch who was to be his close collaborator in both Europe and America. Already in 1915 he had directed *Der Erbförster*. In 1923 he directed Marlene Dietrich in a small part. By 1928 and 1929 he was directing many films two of which, *Die Heilige und ihr Narr* and *Geschlecht in Fesseln*, were outstanding. The latter, dealing with the sexual problems of prisoners, ran into censor trouble and was banned at one stage. He played in his own productions including *Ludwig der Zweite* with a script by his wife and design by Ernst Stern. In 1927 he appeared in Karl Grüne's unusual anti-war film *Am Rande der Welt* and Friedrich Zelnik's version of Hauptmann's *Die Weber*.

In 1930 he went to Hollywood to direct German versions of American films. Soon he was directing in English and was one of the most popular and successful of immigrant filmmakers. He directed Janet Gaynor in *Adorable* with a story by Billy Wilder. In 1934 he made two Bette Davis films, *Fashions of 1934* and *Fog Over Frisco*. He collaborated with his old master Reinhardt on *A Midsummer Night's Dream*. Then followed *The Story of Louis Pasteur* for which Paul Muni won an Academy Award as best actor, and the brilliant *Juarez*, with Muni, Davis, and Brian Aherne. Another biographical film, *Dr. Ehrlich's Magic Bullet*, starred Edward G. Robinson. *Blockade* proved controversial as it touched on the Spanish Civil War. Perhaps the best film he made in America was *All That Money Can Buy* based on Steven Vincent Benet's *The Devil and Daniel Webster*. This was a transposition of the Faust legend to a rural New England setting. The film was remarkable for its atmosphere and the fact that in it the supernatural really worked. It was visually very beautiful with impeccable acting from a distinguished cast including Edward Arnold as Webster and Walter Huston as Mr. Scratch, the homely and rogueish Mephistopheles of the story. He directed Charles Laughton in *The Hunchback of Notre Dame* in 1939 and made two distinguished films with Jennifer Jones, *Love Letters* and *Portrait of Jenny*. But his version of *Salome* with Rita Hayworth in 1953 added nothing to his reputation and a decline set in. He returned to Germany in 1955, directing a film on Richard Wagner, *Magic Fire*, and the Pushkin story *Dubrovsky*, which he made in Yugoslavia.

He had begun life as a carpenter in Ludwigshaven. He was a man of large stature and dynamic energy coupled with a cultured elegance which made his Hollywood home a salon where artists and writers met. In the studios he appeared with large hat and white gloves marking him out as *the director*. His skilled artistry enabled him to cover a wide range of subject matter and all his films carried an air of refinement of thought and feeling.

—Liam O'Leary

Edward Dmytryk

DMYTRYK, Edward.

American. Born in Grand Forks, British Columbia, Canada, 4 September 1908, became U.S. citizen, 1939. Studied at California Institute of Technology, 1926–27. Married second wife, actress Jean Porter, 1948, one son. Messenger and handy boy at Famous Players-Lasky, 1923, subsequently cutter, then editor; directed first film, *The Hawk*, 1935; directed series of films for Columbia, 1940–42, and for RKO, 1942–47; subpoenaed to appear before House Un-American Activities Committee as one of "Hollywood Ten," 1947; moved to England, 1948; forced to return to U.S., fined and given six months jail sentence for contempt of Congress, 1950; appeared as friendly witness before HUAC, and hired by producer Stanley Kramer, 1951; moved to England, 1971; taught at University of Texas, Austin, 1978; Professor of Filmmaking at University of Southern California, from 1981.

Films as Director:

1935   *The Hawk*
1939   *Television Spy*; *Emergency Squad*; *Million Dollar Legs* (co-d with Grinde, uncredited)
1940   *Golden Gloves*; *Mystery Sea Raider*; *Her First Romance*
1941   *The Devil Commands*; *Under Age*; *Sweetheart of the Campus* (*Broadway Ahead*); *The Blonde from Singapore* (*Hot Pearls*); *Secrets of the Lone Wolf* (*Secrets*); *Confessions of Boston Blackie* (*Confessions*)
1942   *Counter-Espionage*; *Seven Miles from Alcatraz*
1943   *Hitler's Children*; *The Falcon Strikes Back*; *Captive Wild Woman*; *Behind the Rising Sun*; *Tender Comrade*
1944   *Farewell, My Lovely* (*Murder My Sweet*)
1945   *Back to Bataan*; *Cornered*
1946   *Till the End of Time*
1947   **Crossfire**; *So Well Remembered*
1949   *Obsession* (*The Hidden Room*); *Gives Us This Day* (*Salt to the Devil*)
1952   *Mutiny*; *The Sniper*; *Eight Iron Men*
1953   *The Juggler*; *Three Lives* (short)
1954   *The Caine Mutiny*; *Broken Lance*; *The End of the Affair*
1955   *Soldier of Fortune*; *The Left Hand of God*; *Bing Presents Oreste* (short)
1956   *The Mountain* (+pr)
1957   *Raintree County*
1958   *The Young Lions*
1959   *Warlock* (+pr); *The Blue Angel*
1962   *The Reluctant Saint* (+pr); *Walk on the Wild Side*
1963   *The Carpetbaggers*
1964   *Where Love Has Gone*; *Mirage*
1966   *Alvarez Kelly*
1968   *Lo sbarco di Anzio* (*Anzio, The Battle for Anzio*); *Shalako*
1972   *Barbe-Bleue* (*Bluebeard*) (+co-sc)
1975   *The "Human" Factor*
1976   *He Is My Brother*

Other Films:

1930   *Only Saps Work* (Gardner and Knopf) (ed); *The Royal Family of Broadway* (Cukor and Gardner) (ed)
1932   *Million Dollar Legs* (Cline) (ed)
1934   *Belle of the Nineties* (McCarey) (co-ed, uncredited); *College Rhythm* (Taurog) (co-ed)
1935   *Ruggles of Red Gap* (McCarey) (ed)
1936   *Too Many Parents* (McGowan) (ed); *Three Cheers for Love* (Ray McCarey) (ed); *Three Married Men* (Buzzell) (ed); *Easy to Take* (Tryon) (ed)
1937   *Murder Goes to College* (Riesner) (ed); *Turn Off the Moon* (Seiler) (ed); *Double or Nothing* (Reed) (ed); *Hold 'em Navy* (*That Navy Spirit*) (Neumann) (ed)

1938   *Bulldog Drummond's Peril* (Hogan) (ed); *Prison Farm* (Louis King) (ed)
1939   *Zaza* (Cukor) (ed); *Love Affair* (McCarey) (co-ed); *Some Like It Hot* (Archainbaud) (ed)
1950   *The Hollywood Ten* (Berry) (co-sc, appearance)
1968   *Hamlet* (Wirth) (dubbing d)
1976   *Hollywood on Trial* (Helpern) (role as interviewee)

Publications:

By DMYTRYK: books—

It's a Hell of a Life But Not a Bad Living, New York, 1978.
On Screen Directing, London, 1984.
On Screen Acting, Boston, 1984.
On Filmmaking, Boston, 1986.
Cinema: Concept and Practice, Boston, 1988.

By DMYTRYK: articles—

"Reply to R. English," in *Nation* (New York), 26 May 1951.
"The Director-Cameraman Relationship," interview with Herb Lightman, in *American Cinematographer* (Los Angeles), May 1968.
"The Director and the Editor," in *Action* (Los Angeles), March/April 1969.
"Dmytryk On Film," in *Journal of University Film Association* (Carbondale, Illinois), Spring 1982.
"A very narrow path: The politics of Edward Dmytryk," an interview with L.D. Friedman, in *Literature/Film Quarterly* (Salisbury, Maryland), October 1984.
"Edward Dmytryk remembers," an interview with J. Bawden, in *Films in Review* (New York), December 1985.

On DMYTRYK: articles—

English, R., "What Makes a Hollywood Communist?," in the *Saturday Evening Post* (Philadelphia), 19 May 1951.
Tozzi, Romano, "Edward Dmytryk," in *Films in Review* (New York), February 1962.
"The Cinema of Edward Dmytryk," in *Films Illustrated* (London), October 1971.
"Edward Dmytryk," in *Film Dope* (London), June 1977.
McClure, L., "Edward Dmytryk: the Director as Professor," in *Filmmakers Monthly* (Ward Hill, Massachusetts), January 1979.

*   *   *

Edward Dmytryk rose through the Hollywood ranks, beginning as a projectionist in the 1920's working as an editor through most of the 1930's and directing low-budget films during the first half of the 1940's before making his first A-budget film, *Tender Comrade*, in 1943. He continued to make notable films like *Crossfire* and *Murder My Sweet* before being subpoenaed to testify before HUAC. Dmytryk subsequently became one of the Hollywood Ten and, after completing his jail sentence, the only member of the Ten to become a friendly witness and name names. After doing one film for the King brothers, *Mutiny*, in 1952, Stanley Kramer hired him to direct four features that culminated with *The Caine Mutiny*. He continued to direct films regularly through the 1950's and 1960's and later taught at U.S.C. in Los Angeles.

In many of his films Dmytryk displays much the same sensibility informing the work of Frank Capra: a faith in ordinary people, a belief in the virtues of working together, a deep reverence for traditional American ideals and heros, and a strongly utopian bent that tends to see evil as a localized aberration capable of correction. Characters often "see the light" (*Hitler's Children*, or *Salt to the Devil*,) find themselves transformed by the example or expectations of others (*The Left Hand of God* or *The Juggler*), or reveal a tender, committed side that is not immediately apparent (*Soldier of Fortune* and *Broken Lance*). Utopianism, then, instead of becoming a positive affirmation of values, becomes more an implicit trust in goodness that sometimes defuses dramatic conflict by rendering evil ineffectively or by side-stepping intense confrontations or issues.

(*Walk on the Wild Side*, for example, presents a more pollyannaish view of down-and-out Depression life in New Orleans, affirming the nobility of true love despite adversity, than the Nelson Algren novel it is based on.)

Dmytryk directs with an essentially serious tone that minimizes comedy and seldom romanticizes the agrarian or nonurban ethos so dear to Capra. He also tends to work with more interiorized states of personal feeling that run counter to Capra's tendency to play conflicts out in public among a diverse, somewhat stereotyped range of characters. But, like Capra, Dmytryk dwells upon the issue of faith—the need for it and the tests it is subjected to. *Salt to the Devil, Tender Comrade, Soldier of Fortune, Raintree County, The Juggler, Broken Lance, The Left Hand of God, The Caine Mutiny, Hitler's Children*, these and other films involve tests of faith and commitment for their central characters. Characters strive to find and affirm a sense of personal dignity, whatever the odds, and usually do so within a private setting that uses the broader social context as a dramatic backdrop, even in *Hitler's Children* or *The Young Lions*, two films dealing with Nazism. Some have argued that Dmytryk's work simply deteriorated after his testimony before HUAC; it may also be that recurring themes bridge this period and offer intriguing parallels between the political climate, Dmytryk's personal view of life, and his overall film accomplishments.

—Bill Nichols

DONEN, Stanley.

American. Born in Columbia, South Carolina, 13 April 1924. Studied dance at Town Theatre, Columbia, then University of South Carolina, until 1940. Married actress Yvette Mimieux, 1972. Broadway debut in *Pal Joey*, 1940; choreographer for MGM musicals, Hollywood, 1943–49; co-directed (with Gene Kelly) first film, *On the Town*, 1949. Business Manager: Edward Traubner, Traubner & Flynn, 2049 Century Park East, Suite 2500, Los Angeles, CA 90067, U.S.A.

Films as Director:

1949 ***On the Town*** (co-d, co-chor)
1951 *Royal Wedding* (*Wedding Bells*)
1952 ***Singin' in the Rain*** (co-d, co-chor); *Love Is Better Than Ever* (*The Light Fantastic*); *Fearless Fagan*
1953 *Give a Girl a Break* (+co-chor)
1954 *Seven Brides for Seven Brothers*; *Deep in My Heart* (+co-chor)
1955 *It's Always Fair Weather* (co-d, co-chor)
1957 *Funny Face*; *The Pajama Game* (co-d, co-pr); *Kiss Them For Me*
1958 *Indiscreet* (+pr); *Damn Yankees* (*What Lola Wants*) (co-d, co-pr)
1960 *Once More with Feeling* (+pr); *Surprise Package* (+pr); *The Grass Is Greener* (+pr)
1963 *Charade* (+pr)
1966 *Arabesque* (+pr)
1967 *Two For the Road* (+pr); *Bedazzled* (+pr)
1969 *Staircase* (+pr)
1974 *The Little Prince* (+pr)
1975 *Lucky Lady* (+pr)
1978 *Movie Movie* (+pr)
1980 *Saturn 3* (+pr)
1984 *Blame It On Rio*

Films as Choreographer or Co-Choreographer:

1943 *Best Foot Forward* (Buzzell)
1944 *Hey Rookie* (Barton); *Jam Session* (Barton); *Kansas City Kitty* (Lord); *Cover Girl* (Vidor)
1945 *Anchors Aweigh* (Sidney)
1946 *Holiday in Mexico* (Sidney); *No Leave, No Love* (Martin)
1947 *This Time for Keeps* (Thorpe); *Living in a Big Way* (La Cava); *Killer McCoy* (Rowland)
1948 *A Date with Judy* (Thorpe); *The Big City* (Taurog); *The Kissing Bandit* (Benedek)
1949 *Take Me Out to the Ball Game* (Berkeley) (+co-sc)

Publications:

By DONEN: articles—

"Giving Life an Up-Beat," in *Films and Filming* (London), July 1958.
"What to Do with Star Quality," in *Films and Filming* (London), August 1960.
Interview with Bertrand Tavernier and Gilbert Palas, in *Cahiers du Cinéma* (Paris), May 1963.
"Talking in the Sun," an interview with Colo and Bertrand Tavernier, in *Positif* (Paris), December 1969.
Interview with S. Harvey, in *Film Comment* (New York), July/August 1973.
Interview with Jim Hillier, in *Movie* (London), Spring 1977.

On DONEN: books—

Comden, Betty, and Adolph Green, *Singin' in the Rain* (script) New York, 1972.
Charness, Casey, *Hollywood Cine-Dance: A Description of the Interrelationship of Camerawork and Choreography in the Films of Stanley Donen and Gene Kelly*, Ann Arbor, Michigan, 1978.
Casper, Joseph Andrew, *Stanley Donen*, Metuchen, New Jersey, 1985.
Altman, Rick, *The American Film Musical*, Bloomington, Indiana, 1989.

On DONEN: articles—

Knight, Arthur, "From Dance to Film Director," in *Dance* (New York), August 1954.
Johnson, Albert, "The Tenth Muse in San Francisco," in *Sight and Sound* (London), Summer 1956.
Knight, Arthur, "Dance in the Movies," in *Dance* (New York), October 1958.
"Musical Comedy Issue" of *Cinéma* (Paris), August/September 1959.
McVay, Douglas, "Moanin' for Donen," in *New York Film Bulletin*, no.9, 1961.
Luft, Herbert, "Donen at Work," in *Films in Review* (New York), February 1961.
"Stanley Donen," in *Film Dope* (London), June 1977.
Telotte, J.P., "Ideology and the Kelly-Donen Musicals," in *Film Criticism* (Meadville, Pennsylvania), Spring 1984.
Sloman, Tony, "Feet First: Kelly and Donen," in *National Film Theatre Booklet*, London, May 1990.

*   *   *

Stanley Donen is most frequently remembered for his work as a musical director/choreographer at MGM under the "Arthur Freed Unit," a production team that Donen claims existed only in Arthur Freed's head (*Movie*, spring 1977). With Gene Kelly, he co-directed three of the musical genre's best films: *On the Town, Singin' in the Rain*, and *It's Always Fair Weather*. Kelly was, in a sense, responsible for giving Donen his start in Hollywood; their first collaboration being the "doppelganger" dance in *Cover Girl*. Donen followed a path typical of that time, from Broadway dancer to Hollywood dancer and choreographer to director. Directing solo, he won recognition for *Royal Wedding* (his first effort), *Seven Brides for Seven Brothers, Funny Face, The Pajama Game* and *Damn Yankees*.

Andrew Sarris believes that Donen always seems to function best as a "hyphenated director" or a "genial catalyst;" that any

Stanley Donen   © **Peter Smith**

personal style he may possess is usually submerged under that of the performer's (Kelly, Astaire, Fosse) or choreographer's (Michael Kidd, Eugene Loring, Bob Fosse) and hence is difficult to assess. This view may simply reflect that period of studio production (mid 1940's to late 1950's), when there was a constant melding of creative personnel. As Jerome Delamater explains: "Performers, choreographers, and directors worked together and in many instances one cannot discern the auteur, as it were, or—more accurately—there seem to be several auteurs." Donen credits Astaire for his inspiration and it comes as no surprise that he feels his musical work is an extension of the Astaire/Rogers format (which itself is derived from the films of Clair and Lubitsch). This format is not logically grounded in reality, but functions more or less in the realm of pure emotion. Such a world of spontaneous singing and dancing can most accurately be presented in visual terms through forms of surrealism.

Donen's oeuvre demonstrates a reaction against the presentation of musical numbers on the stage, choreographing them instead on the streets of everyday life. It is this combination of a visual "reality" and a performing "unreality" (a performing "reality" is some type of stage that is clearly delineated from normal, day to day activity), that creates the tension inherent in surrealism. What Donen did with the integrated musical was geared towards the unreal; our functional perception of the real world does not include singing and dancing as a means of normal interpersonal communication. As he said in an interview with Jim Hillier, "A musical . . . is anything but real." It possesses its own peculiar internal reality, not directly connected to everyday life. Leo Braudy points out that Donen's musical films explore communities and the reaction/interaction of the people that dwell within. Even though Donen left the musical genre after *Damn Yankees* (returning to it in 1973), he continued to explore the situation of the individual in a social community, and the absurd, occasionally surrealistic experiences that we all face, in such deft "comedies" as *Bedazzled, Two for the Road*, and *Charade* (the last in hommage to Hitchcock)

—Greg Faller

DONNER, Jörn.

Finnish. Born in Helsinki, Finland, 5 February 1933. Educated in political science and Swedish literature at Helsinki University. Married actress Harriet Andersson. Journalist, publisher and critic in Finland, 1950's; as conscientious objector spends 18 months as hospital orderly in Pori, 1959–61; film critic for *Dagens Ntheter* newspaper, Stockholm, 1961; directed first feature, *En Söndag i September*, 1963; returned to Finland, acquired majority interest in FJ-Filmi, merging it with Jörn Donner Productions, 1967; curator, Swedish Film Institute, 1972–75, then executive producer, 1975–77, and President, from 1978; made *Yhdeksan Tapaa Lahesta Helsinkia (Nine Ways to Approach Helsinki)* for TV, 1982.

Films as Director:

1954 *Aamua Kaupungissa (Morning in the City)* (+sc, ed) (short)
1955 *Näinä Päivinä (In These Days)* (short) (+sc, ed)
1956 *Porkala* (short) (+sc, ed)
1957 *Vettä (Water)* (short) (+sc, ed)

1962 *Vittnesbörd om Henne (Testimonies)* (short) (+sc, ed)
1963 *En Söndag i September (A Sunday in September)* (+sc)
1964 *Att Älska (To Love)* (+sc)
1965 *Här Börjar Äventyret (Adventure Starts Here)* (+sc)
1967 sequence in *Teenage Rebellion (Mondo Teeno)* (Herman) (+sc); "Han-Hon (He-She)", episode no.3 in *Stimulantia* (+sc); *Tvärbalk (Rooftree, Crossbeam)* (+sc, ed)
1968 *Mustaa Valkoisella (Black on White)* (+exec pr, sc, ed, role as Juha Holm)
1969 *Sixtynine* (+exec pr, sc, role as Timo)
1970 *Naisenkuvia (Portraits of Women)* (+exec pr, sc, ed, role as Pertti); *Anna* (+exec pr, co-sc)
1971 *Perkele! Kuvia Suomesta (Fuck Off! Images of Finland)* (doc) (+exec pr, sc)
1972 *Hellyys (Tenderness)* (+exec pr, sc)
1973 *Baksmälla (Hangover, Sexier Than Sex)* (rev. version of *Tenderness*) (+exec pr, sc)
1975 *The World of Ingmar Bergman* (doc) (+exec pr, sc)
1978 *Manrape (Man Cannot Be Raped)* (+exec pr, sc)

Other Films:

1968 *Asfalttilampaat (The Asphalt Lambs)* (Niskanen) (role)
1972 *Marja pieni! (Poor Marja!)* (Bergholm) (pr)
1973 *Laukaus Tehtaalla (Shot in the Factory)* (Kivikoski) (pr); *Mommilan Veriteot 1917 (The Mommilla Murders)* (Pennanen) (pr, ed)
1976 *Drömmen om Amerika (The American Dream)* (Abrahamsen) (exec pr); *Långt Borta och Nara (Near and Far Away)* (Ahrne) (pr)
1977 *Hemåt i Natten (Harri! Harri!, Homeward in the Night, Home and Refuge)* (Lindström) (pr); *Tabu (Taboo)* (Sjöman) (pr); *Elvis! Elvis!* (Pollak) (pr)
1978 *Bluff Stop* (exec pr)

Publications:

By DONNER: books—

Filmipulmamme [Our Film Problem] with Martti Savo, Helsinki, 1953.
The Personal Vision of Ingmar Bergman, Bloomington, Indiana, 1966.
The Films of Ingmar Bergman, New York, 1972.

By DONNER: articles—

"After Three Films," in *Sight and Sound* (London), Autumn 1966.
"After Six Films," in *Sight and Sound* (London), Spring 1970.
"Filminstitutet som idébank," an interview with B. Heurling and L. Åhlander, in *Chaplin* (Stockholm), v.20, no.4, 1978.
"Donner on Swedish Cinema," in *Variety* (New York), 19 September 1979.
Donner, Jörn, "Dagbook fran Svenska Filminstitutet 1978–1982," in *Chaplin* (Stockholm), vol. 24, no. 1, 1982.
Interview in *Filmihullu* (Helsinki???), no. 1, 1985.

On DONNER: articles—

"Jörn Donner: An Outsider at Home," in *Films and Filming* (London), December 1968.
Reyner, L., "Jörn Donner," in *Film* (London), Spring 1969.
"Director of the Year," in *International Film Guide*, London, 1972.
"Jörn Donner," in *Film Dope* (London), June 1977.

* * *

If we look closely at the work of Jörn Donner as an artist, as an organisation man, and as a social activist, it seems scarcely feasible that so many different things could be crammed into one human life. From even a limited list of his achievements the wide range of his interests and the great vitality of his personality become self-evident.

After studying political science and Swedish literature at the Helsinki University, he founded the journal *Arena* devoted to literary and political matters, then worked as a reporter,

Jörn Donner

undertaking a number of study trips to various countries, as well as being a literary and film critic. He has written over twenty books, including several novels as well as collections of comments, essays, studies, and short stories. In many of these he speaks about film work; indeed some of them are dedicated to filmmaking. Together with the films he has made (and the films made from his writing by other directors) he has been responsible for a unique body of outstanding and exuberant work linking two distinctive cultures—those of Finland and Sweden.

While he was in charge of Jörn Donner Productions as well as being Chairman of the FJ (Filmi Oy), both companies made an extraordinary contribution to the development of Finnish film and opened the way for a whole generation of young filmmakers. He was also the director of the Swedish Film Institute for over seven years. All this might give the impression that administrative activities took precedence over his film directing, but this is not the case.

Jörn Donner stood at the cradle of the Swedish film movement in the 1960s when he made several important films notable for both their form and subject matter (*En Söndag i september* was his first feature film). He showed himself to be a creator of social dramas from contemporary life, giving his undivided attention to portraits of girls and women. As a rule, his films, whether in the form of serious drama or situational comedy, are intimate studies of relations between young people, of the magic of love and the clashes of social conventions. Another subject matter of his work is the liberation of women from marital and conventional ties (*Att Älska*).

He also often worked in his mother country, Finland, frequently returning to the same theme. "I am a writer," he says, "with very limited imagination. That's why I often go back to the past like a crab." *Tvaärbalk*, *Mustaa velkoisella* and *Sixtynine* are different versions of the same story and display what might be seen as satirical traits. "Satire takes on many forms. I do not know whether it is the right word to apply to the kind my films represent. Some people view them more as social criticism or irony."

Jörn Donner is a filmmaker who usually does not work from a cast-iron screenplay: it is more or less a sketch of situations without dialogue, and all the scenes are improvised. He tries to "mix fantasy with reality," and has also acted leading roles in his own films. Yet an important part of his film work is formed by documentaries, whether they analyse contemporary Finland or Sweden or offer a sensitive depiction of the film world, as in *Tre scener med Ingmar Bergman*. While as a film director he sensitively analyses and comment on human relations in a developed society, we must not forget either his important work as a producer. In fact, when making a resumé of all his work in the film business, it is clear that Jörn Donner is one of the outstanding personalities of Scandinavian cinema.

—Vacláv Merhaut

DONSKOI, Mark.

Soviet. Born Mark Semyonovich Donskoi in Odessa, 6 March 1901. Educated in medicine and music, then law at University of Simferopol, to 1925; State Film School, under Eisenstein, 1926. Married scriptwriter Irina Sprink, 1936, two sons. Served in Red Army during civil war, 1919–21. Worked in Ukrainian police force, early 1920's; after Film School, joined Belgoskino studios, Leningrad, and directed first film, *Zhizn*,

1927; directed first sound film for Vostokkino, 1934; began at Soyuzdietfilm, Moscow (Children's Film Studios), 1940; worked at Kiev Studios, 1942–45; returned to Soyuzdietfilm (renamed Maxim Gorky Studios), 1946; assigned to Kiev Studios, 1949; returned to Gorky Studios, Moscow, late 1950's. Recipient: Stalin Prize, 1941, 1946, 1948; Order of Lenin, 1944, 1971; Silver Seal, Locarno Festival, 1960; People's Artist of the Soviet Union, 1966; Hero of Socialist Labor, 1971. *Died 24 March, 1981.*

Films as Director:

1927   *Zhizn* (*Life*) (co-d, co-sc); *V bolshom gorode* (*In the Big City*) (co-d, co-sc)
1928   *Tsena cheloveka* (*The Price of Man. Man's Value, The Lesson*) (co-d)
1929   *Pizhon* (*The Fop*)
1930   *Chuzoi bereg* (*The Other Shore*); *Ogon* (*Fire*)
1934   *Pesnya o shchastye* (*Song about Happiness*) (co-d)
1938   *Detstvo Gorkovo* (*Childhood of Gorky. The Childhood of Maxim Gorki*) (+co-sc)
1939   *Vlyudyakh* (*Among People. My Apprenticeship*) [*In the World*] (+co-sc)
1940   *Moi universiteti* (*My Universities*) (+co-sc)
1941   *Romantiki* (*Children of the Soviet Arctic*) (+co-sc)
1942   *Kak zakalyalas stal* (*How the Steel Was Tempered. Heroes Are Made*) (+sc); "Mayak (Beacon, The Signal Tower)" (d only), "Kvartal (Block 14)" (+spvr), "Sinie skali (Blue Crags)" (+spvr) segments of *Boevi kinosbornik* (*Fighting Film Album*) No.9
1944   *Raduga* (*The Rainbow*) (+co-sc)
1945   *Nepokorenniye* (*Semya tarassa. Unvanquished. Unconquered*) (+co-sc)
1947   *Selskaya uchitelnitsa* (*Varvara. An Emotional Education. Rural Institute. A Village School-teacher*)
1949   *Alitet ukhodit v gory* (*Zakoni Bolshoi zemli. Alitet Leaves for the Hills*) (+co-sc) (film banned, partially destroyed)
1950   *Sportivnaya slava* (*Nachi chempiony. Sporting Fame. Our Champions*) (short)
1956   *Mat* (*Mother*) (+co-sc)
1957   *Dorogoi tsenoi* (*At Great Cost. The Horse That Cried*)
1959   *Foma Gordeyev* (+co-sc)
1962   *Zdravstvuitye deti* (*Hello Children*) (+co-sc)
1966   *Serdtse materi* (*A Mother's Heart*)
1967   *Vernost materi* (*A Mother's Loyalty*)
1972   *Chaliapin*
1973   *Nadezhda*

Other Films:

1926   *Prostitutka* (*The Prostitute*) (Frelikh) (role as passerby)
1927   *Yevo prevosoditelstvo* (*His Excellency*) (Roshal) (ed)
1935   *Nevidimi chelovek* (*The Invisible Man*) (Whale) (spvr of dubbing and reediting)
1940   *Brat geroya* (*Brother of a Hero*) (Vasilchikov) (art d)

Publications:

By DONSKOI: articles—

"Ceux qui savent parler aux dieux . . . ," in *Cinéma* (Paris), November 1959.
"Mon Idéal c'est un humanisme combattant," in *Les Lettres Françaises* (Paris), 19 December 1963.
Interview with Robert Grelier, in *Cinéma* (Paris), December 1967.
"My—propagandisty partii," in *Iskusstvo Kino* (Moscow), November 1972.
"Tret'e izmerenie," in *Iskusstvo Kino* (Moscow), December 1974.

On DONSKOI: books—

Leyda, Jay, *Kino: A History of the Russian and Soviet Film*, London, 1960.

Cervoni, Albert, *Marc Donskoi*, Paris, 1966.
Liehm, Mira and Antonin, *The Most Important Art: Eastern European Film After 1945*, Berkeley, California, 1977.

On DONSKOI: articles—

de la Roche, Catherine, "Mark Donskoi," in *Sequence* (London), Autumn 1948.
Fox, Charles, "The Gorki Trilogy—The Poetry of Cinema," in *Film* (London), February 1955.
Marcorelles, Louis, in *Cahiers du Cinéma* (Paris), no.93, 1959.
Haudiquet, Philippe, "Mark Donskoi," in *Image et Son* (Paris), November 1964.
Gillett, John, "Mark Donskoi," in *Focus on Film* (London), March April 1970.
"Director of the Year," in *International Film Guide*, London, 1971.
"Mark Donskoi," in *Film Dope* (London), June 1977.
Fadeeva, Y, "Mark Donskoi: Irrepressible Youth," in *Soviet Film* (Moscow), no.3, 1979.
"Mark Donskoi," in *Avant-Scène du Cinéma* (Paris), 15 February 1979.
Zak, M., and others, "V kontekste istorii," in *Iskusstvo Kino* (Moscow), March 1981.
Cluny, C.M., "Hommage: Marc Donskoi," in *Cinéma* (Paris), May 1981.

*   *   *

Mark Donskoi may not be as familiar to western audiences as Eisenstein, Pudovkin or Dovzhenko; his films are in no way as readily recalled as *Battleship Potemkin*, *Mother* or *Earth*. Like other Soviet filmmakers, he does propagandize about the glories of the Bolshevik Revolution and highlight the life of Lenin. But Donskoi's great and unique contribution to Russian cinema is his adaption to the screen of Maxim Gorki's autobiographical trilogy: *The Childhood of Gorki*, *My Apprenticeship* and *My Universities*, all based on the early life of the famed writer and shot during the late 1930's. (Years later, Donskoi adapted two other Gorki works, *Mother*—the same story filmed by Pudovkin in 1926—and *Foma Gordeyev*.)

In the trilogy, Donskoi chronicles the life of Gorki from childhood on, focusing on the experiences which alter his view of the world. At their best, these films are original and pleasing: the first presents a comprehensive and richly detailed view of rural life in Russia during the 1870's. While delineating the dreams of 19th-century Russian youth, Donskoi lovingly recreates the era. The characters are presented in terms of their conventional ambitions and relationships within the family structure. They are not revolutionaries, but farmers and other provincials with plump bodies and commonplace faces. The result is a very special sense of familiarity, of fidelity to a time and place. Of course, villains in Gorki's childhood are not innately evil, but products of a repressive czarist society. They are thus compassionately viewed. Donskoi pictures the Russian countryside with imagination, and sometimes even with grandeur.

Donskoi's later noteworthy works include *How the Steel Was Tempered*, one of the first Russian films to deal with World War II. While based on a Civil War story, the filmmaker includes only the sequences pertaining to Ukrainian resistance to German invaders in 1918, paralleling that situation to the Nazi invasion. The story also recalls the Gorki trilogy in its presentation of a boy who is changed by his encounter with life's challenges.

The Rainbow, an appropriately angry drama shot at the height of World War II, details the struggles of life in a German-occupied village. Donskoi's message is that despite Nazi brutality, including the shooting of small boys, the spirit of the Soviet people will endure. This film is particularly inspirational; its approach may even have influenced Italian neorealism. *The Unvanquished*, about occupied Kiev, is a kind of sequel to *The Rainbow*. It graphically depicts the slaughter of Jews at Babi Yar.

The careers of few Russian filmmakers have outlasted that of Donskoi, who in his youth had fought in the Civil War and been imprisoned by the White Russians. His films span 50 years, though his Gorki trilogy alone would have assured him of a niche in cinema history.

—Rob Edelman

———

DOS SANTOS, Nelson Pereira *see* **PEREIRA DOS SANTOS, Nelson**

———

DOVZHENKO, Alexander.

Ukrainian. Born in Sosnytsia, Chernigov province of Ukraine, 12 September 1894. Educated at Hlukhiv Teachers' Institute, 1911–14; Kiev University, 1917–18; Academy of Fine Arts, Kiev, 1919. Married 1) Barbara Krylova, 1920 (divorced 1926); 2) Julia Solntseva, 1927. Teacher, 1914–19; military service, 1919–20; chargé d'affaires, Ukrainian embassy, Warsaw, 1921; attached to Ukrainian embassy, Berlin, studied painting with Erich Heckel, 1922; returned to Kiev, expelled from Communist Party, became cartoonist, 1923; co-founder, VAPLITE (Free Academy of Proletarian Literature), 1925; joined Odessa Film Studios, directed first film, *Vasya-reformator*, 1926; moved to Kiev Film Studios, 1928; Solntseva began as his assistant, 1929; lectured at State Cinema Institute (VGIK), Moscow, 1932; assigned to Mosfilm by Stalin, 1933; artistic supervisor, Kiev Studio, 1940; frontline correspondent for *Red Army* and *Izvestia* in the Ukraine, 1942–43; denounced as "bourgeois nationalist," transferred to Mosfilm, 1944; theatre director, 1945–47; settled in Kakhiva, 1952. Julia Solntseva directed five films based on Dovzhenko's writings, 1958–69. Recipient: Lenin Prize, 1935; Honored Art Worker of the Ukrainian SSR, 1939; 1st Degree Stalin Prize for *Schors*, 1941; Order of the Red Flag, 1943; Order of the Red Labor Flag, 1955. *Died in Moscow, 26 November 1956.*

Films as Director:

1926   *Vasya-reformator (Vasya the Reformer)* (co-d, sc); *Yahidka kokhannya (Love's Berry. Yagodko lyubvi)* (+sc)
1927   *Teka dypkuryera (The Diplomatic Pouch. Sumka dipkuryera)* (+revised sc, role)
1928   *Zvenyhora (Zvenigora)* (+revised sc)
1929   ***Arsenal (Arsenal: The January Uprising in Kiev in 1918)*** (+sc)
1930   ***Zemlya (Earth)*** (+sc)
1932   *Ivan* (+sc)
1935   *Aerograd (Air City, Frontier)* (+sc)
1939   *Shchors* (co-d, co-sc)
1940   *Osvobozhdenie (Liberation)* (co-d, ed, sc)
1945   *Pobeda na pravoberezhnoi Ukraine i izgnanie Nemetskikh zakhvatchikov za predeli Ukrainskikh Sovetskikh zemel (Victory in Right-Bank Ukraine and the Expulsion of the Germans from the Boundaries of the Ukrainian Soviet Earth)* (co-d, commentary)
1948   *Michurin* (co-d, pr, sc)

Alexander Dovzhenko

Other Films:

1940 *Bukovyna-Zemlya Ukrayinska (Bucovina-Ukrainian Land)* (Solntseva) (artistic spvr)
1941 *Bohdan Khmelnytsky* (Savchenko) (artistic spvr)
1942 *Alexander Parkhomenko* (Lukov) (artistic spvr)
1943 *Bytva za nashu Radyansku Ukrayinu (The Battle for Our Soviet Ukraine)* (Solntseva and Avdiyenko) (artistic spvr, narration)
1946 *Strana rodnaya (Native Land. Our Country)* (co-ed uncredited, narration)

(films directed by Julia Solntseva, prepared or written by Dovzhenko or based on his writings):
1958 *Poema o more (Poem of an Inland Sea)*
1961 *Povest plamennykh let (Story of the Turbulent Years. The Flaming Years. Chronicle of Flaming Years)*
1965 *Zacharovannaya Desna (The Enchanted Desna)*
1968 *Nezabivaemoe (The Unforgettable. Ukraine in Flames)*
1969 *Zolotye vorota (The Golden Gates)*

Publications:

By DOVZHENKO: books—

Izbrannoie, Moscow, 1957.
Tvori v triokh tomakh, Kiev, 1960.
Sobranie sotchinenyi (4 toma), izdatelstvo, Moscow, 1969.
Polum'iane zhyttia: spogadi pro Oleksandr a Dovzhenka, compiled by J. Solntseva, Kiev, 1973.

By DOVZHENKO: articles—

Interview with Georges Sadoul, in *Lettres Françaises* (Paris), 1956.
"Avtobiographia," in *Iskusstvo Kino* (Moscow), no.5, 1958.
"Iz zapisnykh knijek," in *Iskusstvo Kino* (Moscow), nos.1,2,4,5, 1963.
Dovzhenko, Alexander, "Pis'ma raznyh let," in *Iskusstvo Kino* (Moscow), April 1984.
"Listy Aleksandra Dowzenki do zony," (Letters to Julia Solnceva 1942–52), in *Kino* (Warsaw), May 1985.

On DOVZHENKO: books—

Yourenev, R., *Alexander Dovzhenko,* Moscow, 1958.
Schnitzer, Luda and Jean, *Dovjenko,* Paris, 1966.
Mariamov, Alexandr, *Dovjenko,* Moscow, 1968.
Oms, Marcel, *Alexandre Dovjenko,* Lyons, 1968.
Amengual, Barthélemy, *Alexandre Dovjenko,* Paris, 1970.
Carynnyk, Marco, editor, *Alexander Dovzhenko: The Poet as Filmmaker,* Cambridge, Massachusetts, 1973.
Marshall, Herbert, *Masters of the Soviet Cinema: Crippled Creative Biographies,* London, 1983.
Kepley, Vance, *In the Service of the State: The Cinema of Alexander Dovzhenko,* Madison, Wisconsin, 1986.

On DOVZHENKO: articles—

"Dovzhenko at Sixty," in *Sight and Sound* (London), Autumn 1955.
Obituary in *New York Times,* 27 November 1956.
Montagu, Ivor, "Dovzhenko—Poet of Life Eternal," in *Sight and Sound* (London), Summer 1957.
"Dovzhenko Issue" of *Film* (Venice), August 1957.
Shibuk, Charles, "The Films of Alexander Dovzhenko," in *New York Film Bulletin,* nos.11–14, 1961.
Robinson, David, "Dovzhenko," in *The Silent Picture* (London), Autumn 1970.
Carynnyk, Marco, "The Dovzhenko Papers," in *Film Comment* (New York), Fall 1971.
"Dovzhenko Issue" of *Iskusstvo Kino* (Moscow), September 1974.
Biofilmography in *Film Dope* (London), January 1978.
Trimbach, S., "Tvorchestvo A.P. Dovzhenko i narodnaia kul'tura," in *Iskusstvo Kino* (Moscow), no.10, 1979.
Kepley, Vance, Jr., "Strike him in the eye: *Aerograd* and the Stalinist terror," in *Post Script* (Jacksonville, Florida), Winter 1983.
Bondarchuk, Sergei, "Alexander Dovzhenko," in *Soviet Film* (Moscow), January 1984.
"Dovzhenko Sections," of *Iskusstvo Kino* (Moscow), September and October 1984.
Bernard, J., "Odzak dia a mysleni Alexandra Petrovice Dovzenka," in *Film a Doba* (Prague), September and October 1984.
Pisarevsky, D., "Radiant talent," in *Soviet Film* (Moscow), September 1984.
Navailh, F., "Dovjenko: 'L'or pur et la verite'," in *Cinema* (Paris), January 1985.
Amiel, Vincent, "Hommage a Dovjenko," in *Positif* (Paris), September 1986.

On DOVZHENKO: film—

Hyrhorovych, Yevheniya, (Evgeni Grigorovich), *Alexander Dovzhenko,* 1964.

*   *   *

Unlike many other Soviet filmmakers, whose works are boldly and aggressively didactic, Alexander Dovzhenko's cinema is personal, fervently private. His films are clearly political, yet at the same time he is the first Russian director whose art is so emotional, so vividly his own. His best films, *Arsenal, Earth* and *Ivan,* are all no less than poetry on celluloid. Their emotional and poetic expression, almost melancholy simplicity, and celebration of life ultimately obliterate any external event in their scenarios. His images—most specifically, farmers, animals, and crops drenched in sunlight—are penetratingly, delicately real. With Eisenstein and Pudovkin, Dovzhenko is one of the great inventors and masters of the Russian cinema.

As evidenced by his very early credits, Dovzhenko might have become a journeyman director and scenarist, an adequate technician at best: *Vasya the Reformer,* his first script, is a forgettable comedy about an overly-curious boy; *The Diplomatic Pouch* is a silly tale of secret agents and murder. But in *Zvenigora,* his fourth film, he includes scenes of life in rural Russia for the first time. This film is complex and confusing, but it is the forerunner of *Arsenal, Earth,* and *Ivan,* a trio of classics released within four years of each other, all of which honor the lives and struggles of peasants.

In *Arsenal,* set in the Ukraine in a period between the final year of World War I and the repression of a workers' rebellion in Kiev, Dovzhenko does not bombard the viewer with harsh, unrealistically visionary images. Despite the subject matter, the film is as lyrical as it is piercing and pointed; the filmmaker manages to transcend the time and place of his story. While he was not the first Soviet director to unite pieces of film with unrelated content to communicate a feeling, his *Arsenal* is the first feature in which the totality of its content rises to the height of pure poetry. In fact, according to John Howard Lawson, "No film artist has ever surpassed Dovzhenko in establishing an intimate human connection between images that have no plot relationship."

The storyline of *Earth,* Dovzhenko's next—and greatest—film, is deceptively simple: a peasant leader is killed by a landowner after the farmers in a small Ukrainian village band together and obtain a tractor. But these events serve as the framework for what is a tremendously moving panorama of rustic life and the almost tranquil admission of life's greatest inevitability: death. Without doubt, *Earth* is one of the cinema's few authentic masterpieces.

Finally, *Ivan* is an abundantly eloquent examination of man's connection to nature. Also set in the Ukraine, the film chronicles the story of an illiterate peasant boy whose political consciousness is raised during the building of the Dnieper River dam. This is Dovzhenko's initial sound film: he effectively utilizes his soundtrack to help convey a fascinating combination of contrasting states of mind.

None of Dovzhenko's subsequent films approach the greatness of *Arsenal, Earth* and *Ivan.* Stalin suggested that he direct *Shchors,* which he shot with his wife, Yulia Solntseva. Filmed over a three-year period, and under the ever-watchful eye of

Stalin and his deputies, the scenario details the revolutionary activity of a Ukrainian intellectual, Nikolai Shchors. The result, while unmistakably a Dovzhenko film, still suffers from rhetorical excess when compared to his earlier work.

Eventually, Dovzhenko headed the film studio at Kiev, wrote stories and made documentaries. His final credit, *Michurin*, about the life of a famed horticulturist, was based on the play he wrote during World War II. After *Muchurin*, the filmmaker spent several years putting together a trilogy set in the Ukraine, chronicling the development of a village from 1930 on. He was sent to commence shooting when he died, and Solntseva completed the projects.

It is unfortunate that Dovzhenko never got to direct these last features. He was back on familiar ground: perhaps he might have been able to recapture the beauty and poetry of his earlier work. Still, *Arsenal, Ivan* and especially *Earth* are more than ample accomplishments for any filmmaker's lifetime.

—Rob Edelman

DREYER, Carl Theodor.

Danish. Born in Copenhagen, 3 February 1889. Married Ebba Larsen, 1911, two sons. Journalist in Copenhagen, 1909–13; after writing scripts for Scandinavisk-Russiske Handelshus, joined Nordisk Films Kompagni, 1913; directed first film, *Praesidenten*, 1919; moved to Berlin, worked for Primusfilm, 1921; joined Ufa, 1924; returned to Copenhagen, 1925; hired by Société Generale de Films, Paris, 1926; left film industry, returned to journalism in Denmark, 1932; returned to filmmaking with documentary *Good Mothers*, 1942; awarded managership of a film theatre by Danish government, 1952; worked on film project on the life of Jesus, 1964–68. Recipient: Golden Lion Award, Venice Festival, for *Ordet*, 1955. *Died in Copenhagen, 20 March 1968.*

Films as Director:

1919   *Praesidenten* (*The President*) (+sc, co-art d)
1920   *Prästänkan* (*The Parson's Widow. The Witch Woman. The Fourth Marriage of Dame Margaret*) (+sc)
1921   *Blade af Satans Bog* (*Leaves from Satan's Book*) (+co-sc, co-art d) (shot in 1919)
1922   *Die Gezeichneten* (*The Stigmatized One, Love One Another*) (+sc); *Der Var Engang* (*Once Upon a Time*) (+co-sc, ed)
1924   *Michael* (+co-sc)
1925   *Du Skal Aere Din Hustru* (*Thou Shalt Honor Thy Wife, The Master of the House*) (+co-sc, art d)
1926   *Glomdalsbruden* (*The Bride of Glomdal*) (+sc, art d)
1928   **La Passion de Jeanne d'Arc** (+co-sc)
1932   **Vampyr** (**The Dream of David Gray**) (+co-sc, pr)
1942   *Mødrehjaelpen* (*Good Mothers*)
1943   **Vredens Dag** (**Day of Wrath**) (+co-sc)
1945   *Två Manniskor* (*Two People*) (+co-sc, ed)
1946   *Vandet Pa Låndet* (*Water from the Land*) (never finished) (+sc)
1947   *Landsbykirken* (*The Danish Village Church*) (+co-sc); *Kampen Mod Kraeften* (*The Struggle Against Cancer*) (+co-sc)
1948   *De Naaede Faergen* (*They Caught the Ferry*) (+sc)
1949   *Thorvaldsen* (+co-sc)
1950   *Storstrømsbroen* (*The Bridge of Storstrøm* (+sc)
1954   *Et Slot I Et Slot* (*Castle within a Castle*) (+sc)
1955   **Ordet** (**The Word**) (+sc)
1964   **Gertrud** (+sc)

Other Films:

1912   *Bryggerens Datter* (*The Brewer's Daughter*) (Ottesen) (co-sc)
1913   *Balloneksplosionen* (*The Balloon Explosion*) (sc); *Krigskorrespondenten* (*The War Correspondent*) (Glückstadt) (sc); *Hans og Grethe* (*Hans and Grethe*) (sc); *Elskovs Opfindsomhed* (*Inventive Love*) (Wolder) (sc); *Chatollets Hemmelighed, eller Det gamle chatol* (*The Secret of the Writing Desk. The Old Writing Desk*) (Davidsen) (sc)
1914   *Ned Med Vabnene* (*Lay Down Your Arms*) (Holger-Madsen) (sc)
1915   *Juvelerernes Skræk, eller Skelethaanden, eller Skelethaandens sidste bedrift* (*The Jeweller's Terror. The Skeleton's Hand. The Last Adventure of the Skeleton's Hand*) (Christian) (sc)
1916   *Penge* (*Money*) (Mantzius) (sc); *Den Hvide Djævel, eller Djævelens Protege* (*The White Devil. The Devil's Protegé*) (Holger-Madsen) (sc); *Den Skonne Evelyn* (*Evelyn the Beautiful*) (Sandberg) (sc); *Rovedderkoppen, eller Den røde Enke* (*The Robber Spider. The White Widow*) (Blom) (sc); *En Forbryders Liv og Levned, eller En Forbryders Memoirer* (*The Life and Times of a Criminal. The Memoirs of a Criminal*) (Christian) (sc); *Guldets Gift, eller Lerhjertet* (*The Poison of Gold. The Clay Heart*) (Holger-Madsen) (sc); *Pavillonens Hemmelighed* (*The Secret of the Pavilion*) (Mantzius) (sc)
1917   *Den Mystiske Selskabsdame, eller Legationens Gidsel* (*The Mysterious Lady's Companion. The Hostage of the Embassy*) (Blom) (sc); *Hans Rigtige Kone* (*His Real Wife*) (Holger-Madsen) (sc); *Fange Nr. 113* (*Prisoner No.113*) (Holger-Madsen) (sc); *Hotel Paradis* (*Hotel Paradiso*) (Dinesen) (sc)
1918   *Lydia* (Holger-Madsen) (sc); *Glaedens Dag, eller Miskendt* (*Day of Joy. Neglected*) (Christian) (sc)
1919   *Gillekop* (Blom) (sc); *Grevindens Aere* (*The Countess' Honor*) (Blom) (sc)
1947   *De Gamle* (*The Seventh Age*) (sc)
1949   *Radioens Barndom* (sc)
1950   *Shakespeare og Kronborg* (*Hamlet's Castle*) (Roos) (sc)
1954   *Rønnes og Nexøs Genopbygning* (*The Rebuilding of Ronne and Nexø*) (sc)

Publications:

By DREYER: books—

Om filmen, Copenhagen, 1959.
Five Film af Carl Th. Dreyer, edited by Ole Storm, Copenhagen, 1964.
Jesus fra Nazaret. Et filmmanuskript, Copenhagen, 1968; as *Jesus*, New York, 1972.
Four Screenplays, New York, 1970.
Oeuvres cinématographiques 1926–1934, edited by Maurice Drouzy and Charles Tesson, Paris, 1983.

By DREYER: articles—

"Lunch with Carl Dreyer," with Ragna Jackson, in *Penguin Film Review* (London), August 1947.
Interview with John Winge, in *Sight and Sound* (London), January 1950.
"Visit with Carl Th. Dreyer," with James Card, in *Image* (Rochester, New York), December 1953.
"Rencontre avec Carl Dreyer," with Lotte Eisner, in *Cahiers du Cinéma* (Paris), June 1955.
"Thoughts on My Craft," in *Sight and Sound* (London), no.3, 1955/56.
Interview with Herbert Luft, in *Films and Filming* (London), no.9, 1961.
"Dreyer Mosaik," in *Kosmorama* (Copenhagen), December 1963.
"Carl Dreyer nous dit: 'Le principal intérêt d'un homme: les autres hommes.'," an interview with Georges Sadoul, in *Lettres Françaises* (Paris), 24 December 1964.
Interview with Michel Delahaye, in *Cahiers du Cinéma* (Paris), no.170, 1965.
Interview with Børge Trolle, in *Film Culture* (New York), Summer 1966.
"My Way of Working is in Relation to the Future: A Conversation with Carl Dreyer," with Carl Lerner, in *Film Comment* (New York), Fall 1966.

Carl Theodor Dreyer: *La Passion de Jeanne d'Arc*

"Carl Dreyer: Utter Bore or Total Genius?," with Denis Duperley, in *Films and Filming* (London), February 1968.
Interview with Michel Delahaye, in *Interview with Film Directors*, edited by Andrew Sarris, New York, 1969.
"Metaphysic of Ordet," in *The Film Culture Reader*, edited by P. Adams Sitney, New York, 1970.

On DREYER: books—

Neergaard, Ebbe, *Carl Theodor Dreyer: A Film Director's Work*, London, 1950.
Trolle, Børge, *The Art of Carl Dreyer: An Analysis*, Copenhagen, 1955.
Sémolué, Jean, *Dreyer*, Paris, 1962.
Bowser, Eileen, *The Films of Carl Dreyer*, New York, 1964.
Monty, Ib, *Portrait of Carl Th. Dreyer*, Copenhagen, 1965.
Dyssegaard, Soren, editor, *Carl Th. Dreyer, Danish Film Director*, Copenhagen, 1968.
Milne, Tom, *The Cinema of Carl Dreyer*, New York, 1971.
Ernst, Helge, *Dreyer: Carl Th. Dreyer—en dansk filmskaber*, Copenhagen, 1972.
Schrader, Paul, *Transcendental Style in Film: Ozu, Bresson, Dreyer*, Los Angeles, 1972.
Bordwell, David, *Dreyer*, London, 1973.
Skoller, Donald, editor, *Dreyer in Double Reflection*, New York, 1973.
Nash, Mark, editor, *Dreyer*, London, 1977.
Bordwell, David, *The Films of Carl-Theodor Dreyer*, Berkeley, California, 1981.
Drouzy, M., *Carl Th. Dreyer, né Nilsson*, Paris, 1982.
Carney, Raymond, *Speaking the Language of Desire: The Films of Carl Dreyer*, Cambridge, 1989.

On DREYER: articles—

"Dreyer Issue" of *Ecran Français* (Paris), 11 November 1947.
Rowland, Richard, "Carl Dreyer's World," in *Hollywood Quarterly*, no.1, 1950.
Duca, Lo, "Trilogie mystique de Dreyer," in *Cahiers du Cinéma* (Paris), February 1952.
Rehben, Ernst, "Carl Dreyer, poète tragique du cinéma," in *Positif* (Paris), no.8, 1953.
Trolle, Børge, "The World of Carl Dreyer," in *Sight and Sound* (London), Winter 1955/56.
Luft, Herbert, "Carl Dreyer—A Master of His Craft," in *Quarterly of Film, Radio and Television* (Berkeley), no.2, 1956.
Eisner, Lotte, "Réalisme et irréel chez Dreyer," in *Cahiers du Cinéma* (Paris), December 1956.
Luft, Herbert, "Dreyer," in *Films and Filming* (London), June 1961.
Cowie, Peter, "Dreyer at Seventy-Five," in *Films and Filming* (London), no.6, 1964.
Kelman, Ken, "Dreyer," in *Film Culture* (New York), no.35, 1964/65.
Milne, Tom, "Darkness and Light," in *Sight and Sound* (London), no.4, 1965.
Téchiné, André, "L'Archaisme nordique de Dreyer," in *Cahiers du Cinéma* (Paris), no.170, 1965.
Bond, Kirk, "The World of Carl Dreyer," in *Film Quarterly* (Berkeley), Fall 1965.
"Dreyer Issue" of *Kosmorama*, (Copenhagen), June 1968.
"Dreyer Issue" of *Cahiers du Cinéma* (Paris), December 1968.
Amette, Jacques-Pierre, "Carl Th. Dreyer," in *Dossiers du cinéma: Cinéastes I*, Paris, 1971.
Bordwell, David, "Passion, Death and Testament: Carl Dreyer's Jesus Film," in *Film Comment* (New York), Summer 1972.

Wood, Robin, "Carl Dreyer," in *Film Comment* (New York), March/April 1974.

Vaughan, Dai, "Carl Dreyer and the Theme of Choice," in *Sight and Sound* (London), Summer 1974.

Petric, Vlada, "Dreyer's Concept of Abstraction," in *Sight and Sound* (London), Spring 1975.

De Benedictus, M., "Dreyer: La regola del pendolo," in *Bianco e Nero* (Rome), January–February 1979.

Schepelern, P., in *Kosmorama* (Copenhagen), December 1982.

Devilliers, M., "Dreyer, la chair et l'ombre," in *Cinématographe* (Paris), November 1983.

Lardeau, Yves, and C. Tesson, "Dreyer en images," in *Cahiers du Cinéma* (Paris), December 1983.

"*Gertrud* Issue" of *Avant-Scène du Cinéma* (Paris), December 1984.

"*La Passion de Jeanne d'Arc* Section," of *Skrien* (Amsterdam), November–December 1985.

Rosenbaum, Jonathan, "*Gertrud*: The Desire for the image," in *Sight and Sound* (London), Winter 1985–86.

"*Passion de Jeanne d'Arc* Issue," of *Avant-Scène du Cinéma* (Paris), January–February 1988.

Milne, Tom, "Carl Dreyer," in *Radio Times* (London), 25 February 1989.

*   *   *

Carl Th. Dreyer is the greatest filmmaker in the Danish cinema, in which he was always a solitary personality. But he is also among the few international directors who turned films into an art and made them a new means of expression for the artistic genius. Of Dreyer's feature films, seven were produced in Denmark, three in Germany, two in France, two in Sweden and one in Norway.

If one tries to understand the special nature of Dreyer's art, one can delve into his early life to find the roots of his never failing contempt for pretentions and his hatred of bourgeois respectability, of his preoccupation with suffering and martyrdom. In his biography of Dreyer, M. Drouzy has revealed the fate of Dreyer's biological mother, who died in the most cruel way following an attempted abortion. Dreyer, who was adopted by a Copenhagen family, learned about this when he was 18, and Drouzy's psychoanalytical study finds the victimized woman in all of Dreyer's films. But of what value is the biographical approach to the understanding of a great artist? The work of an artist need not be the illumination of his private life. This may afford some explanation when we are inquiring into the fundamental point of departure for an artist, but Dreyer's personality is expressed very clearly and graphically in his films. Therefore we can well admire the consistency which has always characterized his outlook on life.

Like many great artists, Dreyer is characterized by the relatively few themes that he constantly played upon. One of the keynotes in Dreyer's work is suffering, and his world is filled with martyrs. Yet suffering and martyrdom are surely not the fundamentals. They are merely manifestations, the results of something else. Suffering and martyrdom are the consequences of wickedness, and it is malice and its influence upon people that his films are concerned about. Already in his second film, *Leaves From Satan's Book*, Dreyer tackled this theme which he was never to let go: the power of evil over the human mind.

If the popular verdict is that Dreyer's films are heavy and gloomy, naturally the idea is suggested by the subjects which he handled. Dreyer never tried to make us believe that life is a bed of roses. There is much suffering, wickedness, death and torment in his films, but they often conclude in an optimistic conviction in the victory of spirit over matter. With death comes deliverance. It is beyond the reach of malice.

In his delineation of suffering man, devoid of any hope before the arrival of death, Dreyer was never philosophically abstract. Though his films were often enacted on a supersensible plane, and are concerned with religious problems, his method as an artist was one of psychological realism, and his object was always the individual. Dreyer's masterly depiction of milieu has always been greatly admired; his keen perception of the characteristic detail is simply dazzling. But this authenticity in settings has never been a means towards a meticulous naturalism. He always sought to transcend naturalism so as to reach a kind of purified, or classically simplified realism.

Though Dreyer occupied himself with the processes of the soul, he always preserved an impartiality when portraying them. One might say that he maintained a high degree of objectivity in his description of the subjective. It can be sensed in his films as a kind of presentation rather than forceful advocacy. Dreyer himself, when describing his method in *La Passion de Jeanne d'Arc*, once employed the expression "realized mysticism." It indicates quite precisely his endeavours to render understandable things that are difficult to comprehend, to make the irrational appear intelligible. The meaning behind life lies in just this recognition of the necessity to suffer in order to arrive at deliverance. The characters nearly always suffered defeat in the outward world because Dreyer considered defeat or victory in the human world to be of no significance. For him the triumph of the soul over life was what was most important.

There are those who wish to demonstrate a line of development in Dreyer's production, but there is no development in the customary sense. Quite early Dreyer's world seemed established, and his films merely changed in their way of viewing the world. There was a complete congruity between his ideas and his style, and it was typical of him to have said: "The soul is revealed in the style, which is the artist's expression of the way he regards his material." For Dreyer the image was always the important thing, so important that there is some justification in describing him as first and foremost the great artist of the silent film. On the other hand, his last great films were concerned with the effort to create a harmony between image and sound, and to that end he was constantly experimenting.

Dreyer's pictorial style has been characterized by his extensive and careful employment of the close-up. His films are filled with faces. In this way he was able to let his characters unfold themselves, because he was chiefly interested in the expression which is the result of spiritual conflicts. Emphasis has often been given to the slow lingering rhythm in Dreyer's films. It is obvious that this dilatoriness springs from the wish to endow the action with a stamp of monumentality, though it could lead dangerously close to empty solemnity, to the formalistic.

Dreyer quickly realized the inadequacy of the montage technique, which had been regarded as the foundation of film for so many years. His films became more and more based on long uncut sequences and by the end of his career his calm, elaborating style was quite in conformity with the newer trends in the cinema.

—Ib Monty

———

DULAC, Germaine.

French. Born Charlotte Elisabeth Germaine Saisset-Schneider in Amiens, 17 November 1882. Married Marie-Louis Albert Dulac, 1905 (divorced 1920). Writer and editor for feminist journal *La Francaise*, 1909–13; offered position as

Germaine Dulac

camerawoman on *Caligula* by actress friend Stacia de Napier-kowska, 1914; formed D.H. production company with husband and scenarist Irène Hillel-Erlanger; directed first film, *Les Soeurs enemies*, 1915; travelled to U.S. to observe production techniques, 1921; general secretary of Ciné-Club de France, from 1922; directed newsreels for Gaumont, 1930's. *Died in Paris, July 1942.*

Films as Director:

1915 *Les Soeurs enemies*
1916 *Geo le mysterieux*; *Venus Victrix*; *Dans l'ouragan de la vie*
1917 *Ames de fous* (+sc)
1918 *Le Bonheur des autres*
1919 *La Fête espagnole*; *La Cigarette* (+co-sc)
1920 *Malencontre*; *La Belle Dame sans merci*
1921 *La Mort du soleil*
1922 *Werther* (incomplete)
1923 *La Souriante Madame Beudet* (*The Smiling Madame Beudet*); *Gossette*
1924 *Le Diable dans la ville*
1925 *Ame d'artiste* (+co-sc); *La Folie des vaillants*
1926 *Antoinette Sabrier*
1927 *La Coquille et le clergyman* (*The Seashell and the Clergyman*); *L'Invitation au voyage*; *Le Cinéma au service de l'histoire*
1928 *La Princesse Mandane*; *Disque 927*; *Thèmes et variations*; *Germination d'un haricot*
1929 *Etude cinégraphique sur une arabesque*

Other Films:

1928 *Mon Paris* (Guyot) (supervision)
1932 *Le Picador* (Jacquelux) (supervision)

Publications:

By DULAC: articles—

"Un Article? Mais que faut-il prouver?," in *Le Film* (Paris), 16 October 1919.
"Aux amis du cinéma," address in *Cinémagazine* (Paris), 19 December 1924.
"L'Art des nuances spirituelles," in *Cinéa-Ciné pour tous* (Paris), January 1925.
"Du sentiment à la ligne," in *Schémas*, no.1, 1927.
"Les Esthètiques, les entraves, la cinégraphie intégrale," in *L'Art cinématographique*, Paris, 1927.
"Sur le cinéma visuel," in *Le Rouge et le noir* (Paris), July 1928.
"Jouer avec les bruits," in *Cinéa-Ciné pour tous* (Paris), 15 August 1929.
"Das Wesen des Films: Die visuelle idee," and "Das Kino der Avant-garde," in *Frauen und Film* (Berlin), October 1984.

On DULAC: book—

Heck-Rabi, Louise, *Women Filmmakers: A Critical Reception*, Metuchen, New Jersey, 1984.

On DULAC: articles—

Ford, Charles, biography in *Anthologie du cinéma* (Paris), no.31, January 1968.
Cornwell, Regina, "Maya Deren and Germaine Dulac: Activists of the Avant-Garde," in *Film Library Quarterly* (New York), Winter 1971/72.
Van Wert, W., "Germaine Dulac: First Feminist Filmmaker," in *Women and Film* (Santa Monica, California), vol.1, nos. 5–6, 1974.
Dozoretz, Wendy, "Dulac versus Artaud," in *Wide Angle* (Athens, Ohio), vol. 3, no.1, 1979.
Dozoretz, Wendy, and Sandy Flitterman, in *Wide Angle* (Athens, Ohio), vol. 5, no.3, 1983.
Flitterman, Sandy, "Theorizing the Feminine: Women as the Figure of desire in *The Seashell and the Clergyman*," in *Wide Angle* (Athens, Ohio), vol. 6., no.3, 1984.

Serra, R., "La prima scrittura femminile del cinema," in *Cinema Nuovo* (Bari), August–October 1984.
Tol, I., "Films van Germaine Dulac," in *Skrien* (Amsterdam), Winter 1985–86.

* * *

Before becoming a film director, Germaine Dulac had studied music, was interested in photography and had written for two feminist journals—all of which played a role in her development as a filmmaker. There were three phases to her filmmaking career: in commercial production, in the avant-garde, and in newsreels. In addition, filmmaking was only one phase of her film career; she also was prominent as a theorist and promoter of the avant-garde film, and as an organizer of the French film unions and the ciné-club movement. The French historian Charles Ford, in *Femmes Cinéastes*, writes that Dulac was the "heart" of the avant-garde in France, that without her there would have been no avant-garde. Her role in French film history has been compared to that of Maya Deren in the U.S., three decades later.

Dulac learned the rudiments of filmmaking by assisting a friend who was making a film in 1914. The following year she made her first film, *Les Soeurs enemies*, which was distributed by Pathé. It was the ideal time for a woman to enter commercial production, since many men had been called into the army. After directing several other conventional story films, Dulac became more and more drawn to the avant-garde cinema, which she defined in 1927 as—"Lines, surfaces, volumes, evolving directly without contrivance, in the logic of their forms, stripped of representational meaning, the better to aspire to abstraction and give more space to feelings and dreams—INTEGRAL CINEMA."

It is generally reported that Dulac became involved in the French film avant-garde movement through her friendship with Louis Delluc; but Ester Carla de Miro claims that it was in fact through her that he became involved in film. Delluc wrote that her first film was worth "more than a dozen of each of her colleagues . . . But the cinema is full of people . . . who cannot forgive her for being an educated woman . . . or for being a woman at all".

Dulac's best-known and most impressive film (of the few that have been seen outside France) is *The Smiling Madame Beudet*, based on a play by Andre Obey. It depicts the life and dreams of a housewife in a small town married to a coarse, if not repulsive, businessman and created a sensation in its day. Dulac succeeded with what was, at the time, signal originality in expressing by pictorial means the atmosphere and implications of this study of domestic conflicts.

Currently, showings of *The Seashell and the Clergyman*, based on an original screenplay by Antonin Artaud, have generally been accompanied by program notes indicating Artaud's outrage at Dulac's "feminized" direction. Yet, as P. Adams Sitney points out in his introduction to *The Avant-Garde Film*, Artaud in an essay entitled "Cinema et l'abstraction" praised the actors and thanked Dulac for her interest in his script. (Wendy Dozoretz has pointed out that the protest aimed against Dulac at the film's Paris opening in 1928 was based on a misunderstanding; at least one protester, Georges Sadoul, later said he had thought he was protesting against Artaud.)

At the other end of the cinema spectrum, Dulac began to use time-lapse cinematography to reveal the magical effects of tiny plants emerging from the soil with leaf after leaf unfolding and stretching to the sun. "Here comes Germaine Dulac and her lima bean," became a popular joke among film-club devotees, a joke that did not exclude admiration.

The last decade of Dulac's life was spent directing newsreels for Gaumont. She died in 1942, during the German occupation. Charles Ford, who has collected her articles, indicates that she expressed ideas in "clear and accessible language," which others often set forth "in hermetic formulas." One American writer, Stuart Liebman, sums up the opposing view: "Despite their undeniable importance for the film culture of the 1920's, the backward-looking character of Dulac's film theory, constituted by her nostalgia for the aesthetic discourse of the past, both defines and delimits our interest in her theoretical contributions today." The final assessment of Germaine Dulac's life and work as filmmaker and theorist still awaits the availability of a well-documented biography, of all her writings (some short pieces are now available in English translations), and all her existing films.

—Cecile Starr

———

DUPONT, E.A.

German. Born Ewald André Dupont in Seitz, Saxony, 25 December 1891. Educated at University of Berlin. Film critic for *BZ am Mittag*, Berlin, from 1911; story editor for Richard Oswald, 1916; directed first feature, *Das Geheimnis des Amerika-Docks*, 1917; director in Hollywood, 1926; signed for British-International Pictures, London, 1928; returned to Berlin, 1931; director for Universal, Hollywood, 1933–36; signed to Paramount, 1936–37; signed for Warners, 1938; dismissed from *Hell's Kitchen*, began editing *Hollywood Tribune*, 1939; formed talent agency, 1941; returned to directing, 1951. *Died of cancer in Los Angeles, 12 December 1956.*

Films as Director:

1917   *Das Geheimnis des Amerika-Docks* (*The Secret of the America Dock*) (+sc)
1918   *Es Werde Licht* (*Let There Be Light*) part 2 (co-d, co-sc); *Europa-Postlagernd* (*Post Office Europe*) (+sc); *Mitternacht* (+sc); *Der Schatten* (*Der lebender Schatten*) (+sc); *Der Teufel* (+sc); *Die Japanerin* (+sc)
1919   *Grand Hotel Babylon* (+sc); *Die Apachen* (*Paris Underworld*) (+sc); *Das Derby* (+sc); *Die Würger der Welt* (+sc); *Die Maske* (+sc); *Die Spione* (+sc)
1920   *Der Mord ohne Täter* (*Murder Without Cause*) (+co-sc); *Die weisse Pfau* (*The White Peacock*) (+co-sc); *Herztrumpf* (+sc); *Whitechapel* (+sc)
1921   *Der Geier-Wally* (*Ein Roman aus den Bergen. Geierwally. The Woman Who Killed a Vulture*) (+sc)
1922   *Kinder der Finsternis* (*Children of Darkness*) part 1—*Der Mann aus Neapel* (*The Man from Naples*) (+co-sc): *Kinder der Finsternis* part 2—*Kämpfende Welten* (*Worlds in Struggle*) (+co-sc); *Sie und die Drei* (*She and the Three*) (+sc)
1923   *Die grüne Manuela* (*The Green Manuela*); *Das alte Gesetz* (*Baruch. The Ancient Law*)
1925   *Der Demütige und die Sängerin* (*The Humble Man and the Singer, La Meurtrière*) (+co-sc); *Varieté* (*Variety. Vaudeville. Varietes*) (+co-sc)
1927   *Love Me and the World Is Mine* (*Implacable Destiny*) (+co-sc)
1928   *Moulin-Rouge* (+sc, pr); *Piccadilly* (sound version released 1929) (+pr)
1929   *Atlantic* (+pr); *Atlantik* (German version) (+pr, co-sc)
1930   *Atlantis* (French version) (co-d, pr); *Cape Forlorn* (*The Love Storm*) (+pr, co-sc); *Menschen im Käfig* (German version) (+pr); *Le Cap perdu* (French version) (+pr); *Two Worlds* (+pr, co-story); *Zwei Welten* (German version) (+pr); *Les Deux Mondes* (French version) (+pr)

1931   *Salto Mortale* (*The Circus of Sin*)
1932   *Peter Voss, der Millionendieb* (*Peter Voss, Who Stole Millions*) (+co-sc)
1933   *Der Läufer von Marathon* (*The Marathon Runner*)

(in U.S.):
1933   *Ladies Must Love*
1935   *The Bishop Misbehaves* (*The Bishop's Misadventures*)
1936   *A Son Comes Home*; *Forgotten Faces*
1937   *A Night of Mystery* (*The Greene Murder Case*); *On Such a Night*; *Love on Toast*
1939   *Hell's Kitchen* (co-d with Seiler, uncredited)
1951   *The Scarf* (The Dungeon) (+sc)
1953   *Problem Girls*; *The Neanderthal Man*; *The Steel Lady* (*Secret of the Sahara, The Treasure of Kalifa*)
1954   *Return to Treasure Island* (*Bandit Island of Karabei*); *Miss Robin Crusoe* (co-d, uncredited)

Other Films:

1917   *Rennfieber* (*Horse Race Fever*) (Oswald) (sc); *Der Onyxkopf* (May) (sc); *Sturmflut* (Zeyn) (sc); *Die sterbende Perlen* (Meinert) (sc); *Die Faust des Riesen* parts 1 and 2 (Biebrach) (sc)
1918   *Ferdinand Lassalle* (Meinert) (sc); *Der Saratoga-Koffer* (Meinert) (sc); *Die Buchhalterin* (von Woringen) (co-sc); *Nur um tausend Dollars* (Meinert) (sc)
1927   *Madame Pompadour* (Wilcox) (sc)
1956   *Magic Fire* (Dieterle) (sc)

Publications:

By DUPONT: articles—

Varieté, with Leo Birinski, in *Antologia di Bianco e nero*, Rome, 1943.
Interview with Ezra Goodman, in *Daily News* (Los Angeles), 10 April 1950.

On DUPONT: books—

Kracauer, Siegfried, *From Caligari to Hitler*, Princeton, 1947.
Eisner, Lotte, *The Haunted Screen*, Berkeley, 1968.
Luft, Herbert, *E.A. Dupont, Anthologie du Cinéma*, Paris

On DUPONT: articles—

Weinberg, Herman, in *Take One* (Montreal), January/February 1970.
Luft, Herbert, "E.A. Dupont 1891–1956," in *Films in Review* (New York), June/July 1977.
Pinto, A., letter in *Films in Review* (New York), October 1977.
"E.A. Dupont," in *Film Dope* (London), January 1978.
"E.A. Dupont—Der Augenmensch," in *Film und Fernsehen* (East Berlin), no. 11, 1983.

*   *   *

Some directors are able to maintain a steady flow of talent in all their work. Others, like E.A. Dupont are remembered for one outstanding moment in their career. *Varieté*, or *Vaudeville* as it is also known, was one of the most exciting films to come from Germany in the 1920's. He made many other good films but his career as a whole is a rather tragic one. This was partly due to personal deficiencies and partly due to circumstances over which he had no control. Some European directors flourished in Hollywood; Dupont was not one of them.

He had been a film critic and also wrote film scripts, before becoming Richard Oswald's story editor and contributing to the latter's sensational sex film *Es werde Licht*. In 1917 he began to direct thrillers like *Das Geheimnis des America Docks* and *Europa Postlagernd*. Recognition came with *Die Geierwally* in 1921. This Henny Porten film was distinguished by settings of Paul Leni, and camera work by Karl Freund. It also popularized Wilhelm Dieterle. Dupont had previously launched the careers of Paul Richter and Bernhardt Goetzke, later featured in the films of Fritz Lang. Freund photographed

E.A. Dupont: *Atlantic*

his next film, *Kinder der Finsternis*, which was in two parts with striking sets by Leni. 1923 was a bumper year for Dupont. His *Die grüne Manuela*, about a young dancer who falls in love with a smuggler whose brother gives his life to ensure their happiness, won international appreciation as did *Das alte Gesetz*, a story of a young Jew's flight from his orthodox home to seek fame in the Austrian theater. In the depiction of Jewish rituals and the life of the Austrian court and theatre, the film had a rich authenticity.

Dupont worked outside the then-current German expressionist style, being more human and realistic in his approach to filmmaking. This was evident in his tour de force *Variété*, a tale of jealousy and death amongst trapeze artists. Its powerful realism, its visual fluidity and daring techniques, coupled with the superb performances of Jannings, Lya de Putti and Warwick Ward, made it stand out in a year rich with achievement. The virtuoso camerawork of Karl Freund contributed not merely to the spatial and temporal aspects of the film but in the revelation of motive and thought. The uninhibited sensuality depicted by the film led to censorship problems in many countries. Inevitably Dupont went to Hollywood where he directed a not entirely successful *Love Me and the World Is Mine* for Universal. In 1928 he made two stylish films in England: *Moulin Rouge*, exploiting the sensual charms of Olga Tschechowa, and *Piccadilly* with Gilda Gray and Anna May

Wong and with Charles Laughton making his film debut in a small role.

With the coming of sound, *Atlantic*, made in German and English proved a considerable version of the Titanic story but the two British sound films that followed suffered from weak acting that belied the striking sets. With *Salto Mortale*, made in Germany in 1931 with Anna Sten and Adolph Wohlbruch, Dupont returned to the scene of his earlier *Variété*. Two more films were made in Germany before he found himself a Jewish refugee in Hollywood. Here his career was uneven. B pictures, factory produced, gave him no scope for his talents.

Being dismissed for slapping a Dead End Kid who was mocking his foreign accent was a humiliating experience which played havoc with his morose and withdrawn personality. He became a film publicist, a talent agent, wrote some scripts and returned in 1951 to direct *The Scarf*, a film of some merit for United Artists. He dabbled in television. He wrote the script for a film on Richard Wagner, directed by his former protege Wilhelm Dieterle in 1956. In December of the same year he died of cancer in Los Angeles. A sad case. Sad too to see the name of his great photographer Karl Freund on the credits of "I Love Lucy."

—Liam O'Leary

DURAS, Marguerite.

French. Born Marguerite Donnadieu in Giadinh, French Indo-China, 1914. Educated in mathematics, law and political science at the Sorbonne, Paris. Published first novel, *Les Impudents*, 1943; subsequently novelist, journalist and playwright; directed first film, *La Musica*, 1966. Recipient: Prix Goncourt for novel *L'Amant*, 1984, Ritz Paris Hemingway, Paris, 1986. Address: 5 Rue Saint-Benoît, 75006 Paris, France.

Films as Director:

1966 *La Musical* (co-d, sc)
1969 *Détruire, dit-elle* (*Destroy She Said*) (+sc)
1971 *Jaune de soleil* (+pr, co-ed, sc, from her novel *Abahn, Sabana, David*)
1972 *Nathalie Granger* (+sc, music)
1974 *La Femme du Ganges* (+sc)
1975 **India Song** (+sc, voice)
1976 *Des journées entières dans les arbres* (*Days in the Trees*) (+sc); *Son Nom de Venise dans Calcutta desert* (+sc)
1977 *Baxter, Vera Baxter* (+sc); *Le Camion* (+sc, role)
1978 *Le Navire Night* (+sc)
1978/79 *Aurelia Steiner* (4-film series): *Cesarée* (1978) (+sc); *Les Mains negatives* (1978) (+sc); *Aurelia Steiner—Melbourne* (1979) (+sc); *Aurelia Steiner—Vancouver* (1979) (+sc)
1981 *Agatha et les lectures illimitées* (*Agatha*) (+sc)
1985 *Les Enfants* (*The Children*)

Other Films:

1959 **Hiroshima mon amour** (Resnais) (sc)
1960 *Moderato cantabile* (Brook) (sc, co-adapt from her novel)
1961 *Une Aussi Longue Absence* (*The Long Absence*) (Colpi) (co-sc from her novel)
1964 *Nuit noire, Calcutta* (Karmitz) (short) (sc)
1965 "*Les Rideaux blancs*" (Franju) episode of *Der Augenblick des Friedens* (*Un Instant de la paix*) (for W.German TV) (sc)
1966 *10:30 P.M. Summer* (Dassin) (co-sc uncredited, from her novel *Dix Heures et demie du soir en été*); *La Voleuse* (Chapot) (sc, dialogue)

Publications:

By DURAS: screenplays—

Hiroshima mon amour, Paris, 1959.
Moderato Cantabile, with Gérard Jarlot and Peter Brook, 1960.
Une Aussi Longue Absence, with Gérard Jarlot, Paris, 1961.
10:30 P.M. Summer, with Jules Dassin, Paris, 1966.
La Musica, Paris, 1966.
Detruire, dit-elle, Paris, 1969; as *Destroy, She Said*, New York, 1970.
Les rideaux blancs, Paris, 1966.
Jaune le soleil, Paris, 1971
Nathalie Granger, suivi de La Femme du Gange, Paris, 1973.
India Song—texte—theatre—film, Paris, 1975; as *India Song*, New York, 1976.
Des journées entières dans les arbres, Paris, 1976.
Son Nom de Venises dans Calcutta desert, Paris, 1976.
Le Camion, Paris, 1977.
Le Navire Night, Les Mains négatives, Aurelia Steiner, Paris, 1979.
Vera Baxter; ou, Les Plages de l'Atlantique, Paris, 1980.
Agatha, Paris, 1981.
Les Enfants, Paris, 1985.

By DURAS: fiction—

Les Impudents, Paris, 1943.
La Vie tranquille, Paris, 1944.
Un Barrage contre le Pacifique, Paris, 1950; as *The Sea Wall*, New York, 1952; as *A Sea of Troubles*, London, 1953.

Le Marin de Gibraltar, Paris, 1952; as *The Sailor From Gibraltar*, London and New York, 1966.
Les Petits Chevaux de Tarquinia, Paris, 1953; as *The Little Horses of Tarquinia*, London, 1960.
Des journées entières dans les arbres, Paris, 1954; as *Whole Days in the Trees*, New York, 1981.
Le Square, Paris, 1955.
Moderato Cantabile, Paris, 1958, and New York, 1987.
Dix heures et demi du soir en été, Paris, 1960; as *Ten-Thirty on a Summer Night*, London, 1962.
L'Après-midi de Monsieur Andesmas, Paris, 1962; as *The Afternoon of Monsieur Andesmas*, London, 1964.
Le Ravissement de Lol V. Stein, Paris, 1964; as *The Ravishing of Lol V. Stein*, New York, 1967; as *The Rapture of Lol V. Stein*, London, 1967.
Le Vice-consul, Paris, 1966; as *The Vice-Consul*, London, 1968, New York, 1987.
L'Amante anglaise, Paris, 1967, New York, 1968.
Abahn Sabana David, Paris, 1970.
L'Amour, Paris, 1971.
Ah! Ernesto, with Bernard Bonhomme, Paris, 1971.
La Maladie de la mort, Paris, 1983; as *The Malady of Death*, New York, 1986.
L'Amant, Paris, 1984; as *The Lover*, New York, 1985.
Les Yeux bleus cheveux noirs, Paris, 1987; as *Blue Eyes, Black Hair*, London and New York, 1988.
Emily L., Paris, 1987, New York, 1989.

By DURAS: plays—

Théâtre 1 (includes *Les Eaux et fôrets, Le Square, La Musica*), Paris, 1965.
Théâtre 2 (includes *Susanna Andler; Yes, peut-être; Le Shaga; Des journées entières dans les arbres; Un Homme est venu me voir*), Paris, 1968.
L'Homme assis dans le couloir, Paris, 1980.
L'Homme Atlantique, Paris, 1982.
Savannah Bay, Paris, 1982.
The Square, Edinburgh, 1986.
Yes, peut-etre, Edinburgh, 1986.

By DURAS: other books—

Les Parleuses, with Xaviere Gauthier, Paris, 1974.
Étude sur l'oeuvre littéraire, théâtrale, et cinématographique, with Jacques Lacan and Maurice Blanchot, Paris, 1976.
Territoires du féminin, with Marcelle Marini, Paris, 1977.
Les Lieux de Duras, with Michelle Porte, Paris, 1978.
L'Été 80, Paris, 1980.
Outside: Papiers d'un jour, Paris, 1981, Boston 1986.
The War: A Memoir, New York, 1986.
The Physical Side, London, 1990.

By DURAS: articles—

"Conversation with Marguerite Duras," with Richard Roud, in *Sight and Sound* (London), Winter 1959/60.
"Marguerite Duras en toute liberté," interview with F. Dufour, in *Cinéma* (Paris), April 1972.
"Du livre au film," in *Image et Son* (Paris), April 1974.
"India Song, a Chant of Love and Death," interview with F. Dawson, in *Film Comment* (New York), November/December 1975.
"India Song and Marguerite Duras," interview with Carlos Clarens, in *Sight and Sound* (London), Winter 1975/76.
Interview with J.-C. Bonnet and J. Fieschi, in *Cinématographe* (Paris), November 1977.
"Les Yeux verts," special issue written and edited by Duras, of *Cahiers du Cinéma* (Paris), June 1980.
Interview with D. Fasoli, in *Filmcritica* (Florence), June 1981.
Interview with A. Grunert, in *Filmfaust* (Frankfurt), February–March 1982.
"The places of Marguerite Duras," an interview with M. Porte, in *Enclitic* (Minneapolis), Spring 1983.
Interview with P. Bonitzer, C. Tesson, and Serge Toubiana, in *Cahiers du Cinéma* (Paris), July–August 1985.
Interview with Jean-Luc Godard, in *Cinéma* (Paris), 30 December 1987.

Marguerite Duras: *Le Camion*, with **Gérard Depardieu**

On DURAS: books—

Bernheim, N.-L., *Marguerite Duras tourne un film*, Paris, 1976.
Ropars-Wuilleumier, Marie-Claire, *La Texte divisé*, Paris, 1981.
Trastulli, Daniela, *Dalla parola all imagine: Viaggio nel cinema di Marguerite Duras*, Geneva, 1982.
Borgomano, Madeleine, *L'Ecriture filmique de Marguerite Duras*, Paris, 1985.
Brossard, Jean-Pierre, editor, *Marguerite Duras: Cinéaste, écrivain*, La Chaux-de-Fonde, 1985.
Guers-Villate, Yvonne, *Continuité/discontinuité de l'oeuvre Durassienne*, Brussels, 1985.
Fernandes, Marie-Pierre, *Travailler avec Duras: La musica deuxième*, Paris, 1986.
Selous, Trista, *The Other Woman: Feminism and Femininity in the Work of Marguerite Duras*, New Haven, Connecticut, 1988.

On DURAS: articles—

Gollub, Judith, "French Writers Turned Film Makers," in *Film Heritage* (New York), Winter 1968/69.
"Reflections in a Broken Glass," in *Film Comment* (New York), November/December 1975.
Lakeland, M.J., "Marguerite Duras in 1977," in *Camera Obscura* (Berkeley), Fall 1977.
Van Wert, W.F., "The Cinema of Marguerite Duras: Sound and Voice in a Closed Room," in *Film Quarterly* (Berkeley), Fall 1979.
Seni, N., "Wahrnehungsformen von Zeit und Raum am Beispiel der Filme von Marguerite Duras und Chantal Akerman," in *Frauen und Film* (Berlin), September 1979.
"Marguerite Duras à l'action," in *Positif* (Paris), July/August 1980.
Andermatt, V., "Big mach (on the truck)," in *Enclitic* (Minneapolis), Spring 1980.
Lyon, E., "Marguerite Duras: Bibliography/Filmography," in *Camera Obscura* (Berkeley), Fall 1980.
Murphy, C.J., "The role of desire in the films of Marguerite Duras," in *Quarterly Review of Film Studies* (New York), Winter 1982.
Fedwik, P., "Marguerite Duras: Feminine Field of Nostalgia," in *Enclitic* (Minneapolis), Fall 1982.
Sarrut, B., "Marguerite Duras: Barrages against the Pacific," in *On Film* (Los Angeles), Summer 1983.
Murphy, C.J., "New narrative regions: The role of desire in the films and novels of Marguerite Duras," in *Literature/Film Quarterly* (Salisbury, Maryland), April 1984.
Le Masson, H., "La voix tatouee," in *Cahiers du Cinéma* (Paris), January 1985.
McWilliams, D., "Aesthetic tripling: Marguerite Duras's *Le navire Night*," in *Literature/Film Quarterly* (Salisbury, Maryland), January 1986.

*   *   *

As a writer, Duras's work is identified, along with that of such authors as Alain Robbe-Grillet and Jean Cayrol, with the tradition of the New Novel. Duras began working in film as a screenwriter, with an original script for Alain Resnais's first feature, *Hiroshima mon amour*. She subsequently wrote a number of film adaptations from her novels, and directed her first film, *La Musica*, in 1966. If *Hiroshima mon amour* remains her best known work in cinema, her later films have won widespread praise for the profound challenge they offer to conventional dramatic narrative.

The nature of narrative and the potential contained in a single text are major concerns of Duras's films. Many of her works have appeared in several forms, as novels, plays, and films. This not only involves adaptations of a particular work, but also extends to cross-referential networks that run through her texts. The film *Woman of the Ganges* combines elements from three novels—*The Ravishing of Lol V. Stein, The Vice-Consul,* and *L'Amour. India Song* was initially written as a play, taking characters from *The Vice-Consul* and elaborating on the structure of external voices developed in *Woman of the Ganges. India Song* was made as a film in 1975, and its verbal track was used to generate a second film, *Son Nom de Venises dans Calcutta Desert.*

This process of transformation suggests that all works are "in progress," inherently subject to being otherwise constructed. In part this is because Duras's works are more concerned with the quality or intensity of experience than with events *per se.* The films evoke narrative, rather than presenting a linear, unambiguous sequence of events. In *Le Camion* two characters, played by Gerard Depardieu and Duras, sit in a room as the woman describes a movie about a woman who hitches a ride with a truck driver and talks with him for an hour and twenty minutes. This conversation is intercut with scenes of a truck driving around Paris, picking up a female hitchhiker (with Depardieu as the driver, and Duras as the hitchhiker). Thus the verbal description of a potential film is juxtaposed by images of what that film might be.

An emphasis on the soundtrack is also a crucial aspect of Duras's films; her verbal texts are lyrical and are as important as the images. In *India Song,* sound and image function contrapuntally, and the audience must actively assess the relation between them, reading across the body of the film, noting continuities and disjunctions. The verbal text often refers in past tense to events and characters on screen, as the viewer is challenged to figure out the chronology of events described and depicted—which name on the soundtrack corresponds to which actor, whether the voices belong to on or off screen characters, and so forth. In this way the audience participates in the search for a story, constructing possible narratives.

As minimal as they are, Duras's narratives are partially derived from melodrama, focusing on relations between men and women, the nature or structure of desire, and colonialism and imperialism in both literal and metaphoric senses. In pursuing these issues through non-conventional narrative forms, and shifting the burden of discovering meaning to the audience, Duras's films provide an alternative to conventional ways of watching movies. Her work is seen as exemplifying a feminine writing practice that challenges the patriarchal domination of classical narrative cinema. In an interview Duras said, "I think the future belongs to women. Men have been completely dethroned. Their rhetoric is stale, used up. We must move on to the rhetoric of women, one that is anchored in the organism, in the body." It is this new rhetoric, a new way of communicating, that Duras strives for in her films.

—M.B. White

DUTT, Guru.

Indian. Born 9 July 1925. Educated in Calcutta; studied dancing in Uday Sankar's Art Academy, Almora, 1942–44. Joined Prabhat Film Co., Poona, 1944; directed first film, *Baazi*, 1951; founded Guru Dutt Films, 1954; directed first Indian film in Cinemascope, *Kaagaz ke Phool*, 1959. *Died (suicide) 10 October 1964.*

Films as Director:

1951   *Baazi (The Wager)*
1952   *Jaal (The Net)*
1953   *Baaz* (+role)
1954   *Aar Paar (Heads or Tails)* (+pr, role)
1955   *Mr. and Mrs. 55* (+pr, role)
1956   *Sailaab*
1957   *Pyaasa (The Thirsty One)* (+pr, role)
1959   *Kaagaz Ke Phool (Paper Flowers)* (+pr, role)

Other Films:

1945   *Lakharani* (Bedekar) (asst-d, role)
1946   *Hum ek Hain* (Santoshi) (asst-d)
1947   *Mohan* (A. Banerji) (asst-d)
1949   *Girls School* (Chakrabarty) (asst-d)
1950   *Sangram* (Gyan Mukherji) (asst-d)
1956   *C.I.D.* (pr)
1958   *12 O'Clock* (role)
1960   *Chaudhwin ka Chand* (pr, role)
1962   *Sahib, Bibi aur Ghulam (King, Queen, Slave)* (Abrar Alvi) (co-d, pr, role); *Sautela Bhai* (role)
1963   *Bahurani* (role); *Bharosa* (role)
1964   *Sanjh aur Savera* (role); *Suhagan* (role)

Note: Films Incomplete at the time of his death: *Professor; Raaz; Gouri; Ek Tuku Chhuua; Kaneez; Baharen Phir bhi Ayengi; Love and God* (Asif)

Publications:

On DUTT: books—

Khopkar, Arun, *Guru Dutt: A Three Act Tragedy*, Marathi, n.d.
Rangoonwala, Firoze, *Guru Dutt: A Monograph*, Poona, 1973.
Barnouw, Erik, and S. Krishnaswamy, *Indian Film*, 2nd edition, New York, 1980.
Gandhy, Behroze, and Paul Willemen, *Indian Cinema*, London, 1982.
Ramachandran, T.M., *70 Years of Indian Cinema (1913–1983)*, Bombay, 1985.

On DUTT: articles—

Micciollo, Henri, "Guru Dutt, 1925–64," in *Avant-Scène du Cinéma* (Paris), 1975 (also as *Anthologie du Cinéma*, no. 83).
Micciollo, Henri, "Guru Dutt le tendre," in *Cinéma* (Paris), May 1985.
Tournès, André, "Un cinéaste mis à mort: Guru Dutt," in *Jeune Cinéma* (Paris), September 1985.
Cooper, Darius, "The Hindi film song and Guru Dutt," in *East West Film Journal*, June 1988.

*   *   *

Guru Dutt's romanticism, as director and actor, has of recent years found an enthusiastic audience abroad. In India, some of his films, notably the great *Pyaasa (The Thirsty One)*, were successful in his lifetime, but others such as *Kaagaz Ke Phool (Paper Flowers)* and *Saheb, Bibi aur Ghulam (King, Queen, Slave*, co-directed by Abrar Alvi), found popularity long after his death in 1964.

In his early work, light thrillers such as *Baazi (The Wager), Jaal, (The Net),* and *Aar Paar (Heads or Tails)*, dispossessed

Guru Dutt, with Waheeda Rehman in *Pyaasa*

but happy-go-lucky heroes move in a squalid, realistic world. These films were generically tied to other crime films of the period, such as Raj Kapoor's *Awara* (*Vagabond*). Yet they also display a certain attitude to sexuality which dominates the later, more poetic work: the hero is repeatedly presented as object of the heroine's sensual desire. In *Mr and Mrs 55*, a chauvinist satire about modern women, the flighty, sensation seeking young heroine (Madhubala) is transformed into a woman who desperately yearns for the lover she believes has left her. In the last frames the hero, played by the director himself, emerges to bestow fulfilment on her.

This romantic enshrinement of the male hero is a major feature in *Pyaasa* and *Kaagaz Ke Phool*. These films, and Guru Dutt's screen personality as their protagonist, strongly refer to Devdas, a character of Indian literature and cinema who, thwarted in love by society's strictures, drinks his life away. *Pyaasa*, the story of Vijay, an unemployed poet, is a carefully conceived counter-cultural variation of *Devdas*. Vijay's romantic failure does not stem from social strictures, but because his beloved, Meena (Mala Sinha), finds him wanting by society's criteria of success. In contrast a prostitute, Gulab (Waheeda Rehman), enshrines him in her truly worshipful gaze. "Society" is portrayed as mercenary and debasing, and it is those marginal to it who retain their moral dignity.

The film is cinematically distinguished for its inventive usage of visual and aural registers of subjectivity. The poet's point of view repeatedly transfers present images of Meena into romantic flashbacks, at once covering over and drawing attention to the passage of time and the facts of separation. Strategies of subjectivity also invest present time with a reverie about personal loss. Vijay's grief at his mother's death flows into reflections on the death of female dignity through prostitution; the routine sounds of the red light area are abruptly arrested or appropriated to the hero's intoning of Sahir Ludhianavi's great poem on the subject.

The objects of this traumatic masculine reverie are the lost feminine figures of the mother and beloved. The film moves from phases of subjectivity into modes fixing Vijay in tableaux of humiliation which expose the malign forces at work. His masculine dignity and power are reasserted through Gulab's adoring look, but can only be realised in a space outside an irredeemable society.

In *Kaagaz Ke Phool* the story unravels as a long flashback from the point of view of an aged film director (Guru Dutt). Here it is the cinema itself—and the director's past glory—which has been lost and is longed for. As in *Pyaasa*, it is the denial of the hero's vision which is addressed. But in *Kaagaz Ke Phool* there is no compensation because the figures who could fulfil this need, a daughter (Baby Naaz) and an impossible love (Waheeda Rehman), are subordinated to the fascination with masculine vision itself. Here Guru Dutt works out an obsession with the idea of the sensitive male vision denied acknowledgement in society. The focus on male vision is more narcissistic, more closed in on itself than in *Pyaasa*. But it is also more uncompromising, for the conclusion suggests that the cinema finally offers the fantasy of male authority nothing but the vision of its own death.

Kaagaz Ke Phool signalled the end of a fixation. In his final directorial collaboration, *Sahib, Bibi aur Ghulam*, Guru Dutt was able to displace attention from himself and direct it towards a remote world of decadent excess and wilful female sensuality. The earlier Dutt heroes were spectators of a vision which they themselves had produced. In *Sahib . . .* , the point of view of the Dutt character, Bhootnath, structures perception, but his own story remains a subsidiary, lighter romance to offset the darker, more compelling story of Chhoti Bahu (Meena Kumari), the neglected wife of a rentier landlord (Rehman). Bhootnath watches in fascination and even abets Chhoti Bahu in her schemes to assume the sensual image which will entice her husband away from drunken whoring. She finally fails, but the image is always somewhat in excess of the objective, as her sensuality floats free into an auto-erotic register. Many years later, Bhootnath comes across her skeletal remains in the foundations of the old mansion as it is dug up. In this, his last film before his suicide in 1964, Guru Dutt no longer saw the cinema as a metaphor for an idealised male vision, but as the place in which a disturbing female sexuality had been interred.

—Ravi Vasudevan

DUVIVIER, Julien.

French. Born in Lille, 8 October 1896. Educated at Lille University; studied acting in Paris. Worked in André Antoine's Théâtre Libre, then assistant to Antoine as filmmaker, 1916; directed first film, *Haceldama ou Le Prix du Sang*, 1919; joined "Film d'Art" of Marcel Vandal and Charles Delac, 1925; made *The Great Waltz* for MGM, Hollywood, 1938; moved to U.S., 1940; returned to France, 1945. *Died in auto accident, 26 October 1967.*

Films as Director:

1919   *Haceldama ou Le Prix du Sang* (+sc)
1920   *La Réincarnation de Serge Renaudier* (negative destroyed by fire before film shown) (+sc)
1922   *Les Roquevillard* (+sc); *L'Ouragan sur la montagne* (+sc); *Der unheimliche Gast* (*Le Logis de l'horreur*) (+sc)
1923   *Le Reflet de Claude Mercoeur* (+sc)
1924   *Credo ou La Tragédie de Lourdes* (+sc); *Coeurs farouches* (+sc); *La Machine à refaire la vie* (co-d, re-released with sound 1933, sc); *L'Oeuvre immortelle* (+sc)
1925   *L'Abbé Constantin* (+sc); *Poil de carotte* (+co-sc)
1926   *L'Agonie de Jerusalem* (+sc); *L'Homme à l'Hispano*
1927   *Le Mariage de Mademoiselle Beulemans* (+sc); *Le Mystère de la Tour Eiffel* (+sc)
1928   *Le Tourbillon de Paris*
1929   *La Divine croisière* (+sc); *Maman Colibri* (+co-sc); *La Vie miraculeuse de Thérèse Martin* (+sc); *Au bonheur des dames* (+co-sc)
(Sound films):
1930   *David Golder* (+sc)
1931   *Les Cinq Gentlemen maudits* (+sc); *Allo Berlin? Ici Paris!* (*Hallo! Hallo! Hier spricht Berlin*) (+sc); *Die funf verfluchten Gentlemen* (German version) (+sc)
1932   *Poil de carotte* (remake) (+sc); *La Tête d'un homme* (+co-sc)

1933   *Le Petit Roi* (+sc); *Le Paquebot 'Tenacity'* (+co-sc)
1934   *Maria Chapdelaine* (+sc)
1935   *Golgotha* (+sc, adapt); *La Bandera* (+co-sc)
1936   *L'Homme du jour* (+co-sc); *Golem* (*Le Golem*) (+co-sc); *La Belle Équipe* (+co-sc)
1937   **Pépé-le-Moko** (+co-sc); *Un Carnet de bal* (+sc)
1938   *The Great Waltz* (*Toute la ville danse*) (+sc); *La Fin du jour* (+co-sc): *Marie Antoinette* (Van Dyke, d uncredited, sc)
1939   *La Charrette Fantôme* (+sc)
1940   *Untel père et fils* (+co-sc)
1941   *Lydia* (+sc, co-story)
1942   *Tales of Manhattan* (+co-sc)
1943   *Flesh and Fantasy* (+co-pr)
1944   *The Imposter* (+sc)
1946   *Panique* (+co-sc)
1948   *Anna Karenina* (+co-sc)
1949   *Au royaume des cieux* (+sc, pr)
1950   *Black Jack* (+co-sc, pr); *Sous le ciel de Paris* (+co-sc)
1951   *Le Petit Monde de Don Camillo* (*Il piccolo mondo di Don Camillo*) (+co-sc)
1952   *La Fête à Henriette* (+co-sc)
1953   *Le Retour de Don Camillo* (*Il ritorno di Don Camillo*) (+co-sc)
1954   *L'Affaire Maurizius* (+sc)
1955   *Marianne de ma jeunesse* (+sc)
1956   *Voice le temps des assassins* (+co-sc)
1957   *L'Homme à l'imperméable* (+co-sc); *Pot Bouille* (+co-sc)
1958   *La Femme et le pantin* (+sc, co-adapt)
1959   *Marie Octobre* (+co-sc)
1960   *Das kunstseidene Mädchen* (*La Grande Vie*) (+co-sc); *Boulevard* (+co-sc)
1962   *La Chambre ardente* (+co-sc); *Le Diable et les dix commandements* (+co-sc)
1963   *Chair de poule* (+co-sc)
1967   *Diaboliquement vôtre* (+sc, co-adapt)

Other Films:

1918   *Les Travailleurs de la mer* (Antoine) (asst d)
1920   *L'Agonie des aigles* (Bernard-Deschamps) (adaptation); *La Terre* (Antoine) (asst d)
1921   *Crépuscule d'épouvante* (Etiévant) (sc)
1922   *L'Arlésienne* (Antoine) (asst d)
1924   *La Nuit de la revanche* (Etievant) (story)
1946   *Collège swing* (*Amours, délices et orgues*) (Berthomieu) (co-sc)

Publications:

By DUVIVIER: articles—

"Un Réalisateur compare deux méthodes," interview with Pierre Leprohon, in *Cinémonde* (Paris), 6 May 1946.
"De la création à la mise en scène," in *Cinémonde* (Paris), Christmas 1946.
"Julien Duvivier: 'Pourquoi j'ai trahi Zola'," interview with Yvonne Baby, in *Lettres Françaises* (Paris), 31 October 1957.
Reminiscences in *Avant-Scène du Cinéma* (Paris), 1 February 1977.

On DUVIVIER: books—

Chirat, Raymond, *Julien Duvivier*, Lyon, 1968.
Leprohon, Pierre, "Julien Duvivier," in *Anthologie du cinéma* vol.4, Paris, 1969.

On DUVIVIER: articles—

Aubriant, Michel, "Julien Duvivier," in *Cinémonde* (Paris), 28 November 1952.
"Débat sur Duvivier," in *Arts* (Paris), 18 April 1956.
Epstein, Marie, "Comment ils travaillent? Julien Duvivier," in *Technique Cinématographique* (Paris), December 1958.
Marcabru, P., "Les Français à Hollywood," in *Arts* (Paris), 8 February 1961.
Obituary in *New York Times*, 30 October 1967.
Renoir, Jean, "Duvivier, le professionel," in *Le Figaro Littéraire* (Paris), 6 November 1967.

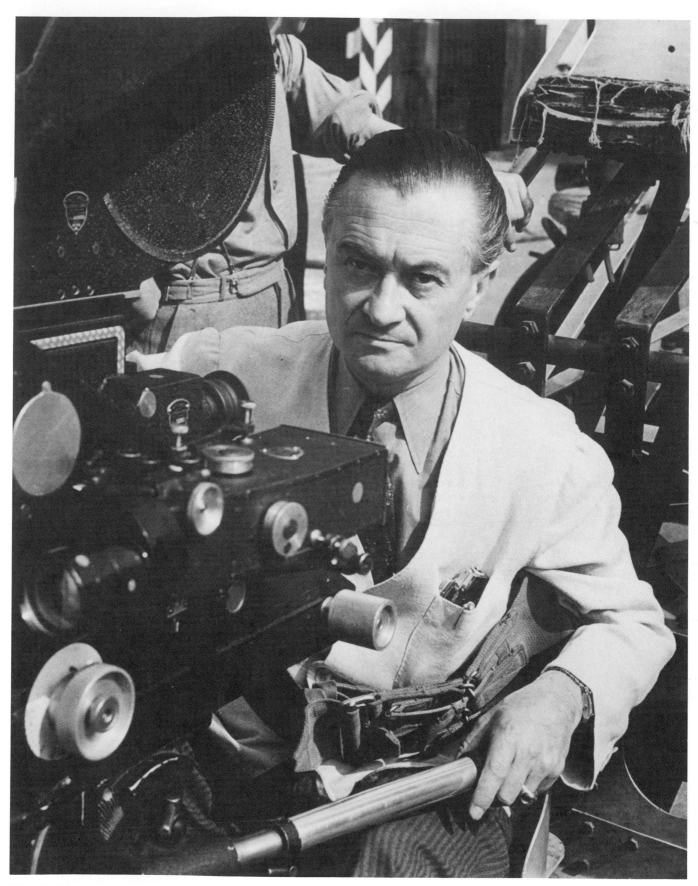

Julien Duvivier

Amengual, Barthélemy, "Défense de Duvivier," in *Cahiers de la Cinémathèque* (Perpignan), Spring 1975.
"*Pépé le Moko* Issue" of *Avant-Scène du Cinéma* (Paris), 1 June 1981.
Simsolo, Noel, "A propos de Julien Duvivier," in *Image et Son* (Paris), November 1981.
"Special Mac Orlan; La Bandera, Julian Duvivier," in *L'Avant-Scène du Cinéma* (Paris), April 1982.
Douin, Jean-Luc, "Duvivier, la mauvaise reputation," in *Télérama* (Paris), 25 January 1986.

On DUVIVIER: film—

Viallaet, Pierre, and Marcel l'Herbier, *Portraits filmées . . . Julien Duvivier*, for TV, 1953.

*   *   *

No one speaks of Julien Duvivier without apologizing. So many of his 50-odd films are embarrassing to watch that it is hard to believe he was ever in charge of his career in the way we like to imagine Renoir or Clair were in charge of theirs. But Duvivier had neither the luxury nor the contacts to direct his career. He began and remained a yeoman in the industry. A director at the Théâtre Antoine in the teens, he began his film career in 1922 and made over a score of silent films, mainly melodramas. From the first he separated himself from the experiments in narration and visual style that characterized much of that period.

His reputation as a reputable, efficient director jumped in the sound era when he made a string of small but successful films (*David Golder, Les Cinq Gentilhommes maudits, Allo Berlin? Ici Paris!, Poil de carotte, La Tête d'un homme*). Evidently his flair for the melodramatic and his ability to control powerful actors put him far ahead of the average French director trying to cope with the problems of sound. But in this era as always, Duvivier discriminated little among the subjects he filmed. This couldn't be more evident than in 1935. First came *Golgotha*, a throwback to the religious films he made in the silent era, and now completely outmoded. Duvivier struggles to energize the static tableaux the film settles into. He moves his camera wildly, but seldom reaches for a key closeup or for an authentic exchange among his actors. It is all picture postcards, or rather holy cards, set off to Jacques Ibert's operatic score.

This solemn, even bombastic, film could not be farther from the swiftness and authentic feeling of the romantic Foreign Legion film *La Bandera* made the same year. Where *Golgotha* is an official presentation of French cinema, *La Bandera* seems more intimate, more in the spirit of the times. Its success was only the first of a set of astounding films that include *La Belle Équipe, Pépé-le-Moko, Un Carnet de bal*, and *Le Fin du jour*.

It is tempting to surmise that cultural history and Julien Duvivier came for once into perfect coincidence in this age of poetic realism. Like Michael Curtiz and *Casablanca*, Duvivier's style and the actors who played out the roles of his dramas spoke for a whole generation. In France it was a better generation, vaguely hopeful with the popular front, but expecting the end of day.

Duvivier's contribution to these films lies in more than the direction of actors. Every film contains at least one scene of remarkable expressiveness, like the death of Regis in *Pépé-Le-Moko*, gunned down by his own victim with the jukebox blaring. Duvivier's sureness of pace in this era brought him a Hollywood contract even before the Nazi invasion forced him to leave France. Without the strong personality of Renoir or Clair, and with far more experience in genre pictures, Duvivier fitted in rather well with the American methods. He deplored the lack of personal control or even personal contribution in the industry, but he acquitted himself well until the Liberation.

Hoping to return to the glory years of poetic realism, his first postwar project in France, *Panique*, replicated the essence of its style: sparse sets, atmosphere dominating a reduced but significant murder drama, the evocative play of Michel Simon and Vivian Romance in an offbeat policier from Simenon. But the country had changed. The film failed, and Duvivier began what would become a lifelong search for the missing formula. With varying degrees of box office success he turned out contemporary and historical comedies and melodramas; the only one which put him in the spotlight was *Don Camillo* with Fernandel.

Believing far more in experience, planning, and hard work than in spontaneity and genius, he never relaxed. Every film taught him something and, by rights, he should have ended a better director than ever. But he will be remembered for those five years in the late 1930's when his every choice of script and direction was in tune with the romantically pessimistic sensibility of the country.

—Dudley Andrew

DWAN, Allan.

American. Born Joseph Aloysius Dwan in Toronto, Canada, 3 April 1885, family moved to U.S., 1893. Educated at North Division High School, Chicago; Notre Dame University, Indiana, degree in electrical engineering, 1907. Married 1) Pauline Bush, 1915 (divorced 1920); 2) Marie Shelton, early 1920's (died 1954). As illuminating engineer work on mercury vapor arc light led to association with Essanay film company, 1909; wrote stories while supervising lighting; American Film Company ("Flying A") formed by Essanay staff, Dwan joined as chief scenario editor, 1910; signed to Universal Pictures, 1913; signed with Famous Players Company, New York, 1914; joined Triangle Company under supervision of D.W. Griffith, 1915; worked in England, 1932–34; trained camera units for U.S. Armed Services photographic division, 1943; contracted to Republic Pictures, 1945–54. *Died in Woodland Hills, California, 21 December 1981.*

Films as Director:
(incomplete list; Dwan estimated 1850 films)

1911   *Branding a Bad Man* and *A Western Dreamer* (split reel) (+pr, sc); *A Daughter of Liberty* and *A Trouper's Heart* (split reel) (+pr, sc); *Rattlesnakes and Gunpowder* and *The Ranch Tenor* (split reel) (+pr, sc); *The Sheepman's Daughter* (+pr, sc); *The Sagebrush Phrenologist* and *The Elopements on Double L Ranch* (split reel) (+pr, sc); *$5,000 Reward—Dead or Alive* (+pr, sc); *The Witch of the Range* (+pr, sc); *The Cowboy's Ruse* and *Law and Order on Bar L Ranch* (split reel) (+pr, sc); *The Yiddisher Cowboy* and *The Broncho Buster's Bride* (split reel) (+pr, sc); *The Hermit's Gold* (+pr, sc); *The Actress and the Cowboys* and *The Sky Pilot's Intemperance* (split reel) (+pr, sc); *A Western Waif* (+pr, sc); *The Call of the Open Range* (+pr, sc); *The School Ma'am of Snake* and *The Ranch Chicken* (split reel) (+pr, sc); *Cupid in Chaps* (+pr, sc); *The Outlaw's Trail* (+pr, sc); *The Ranchman's Nerve* (+pr, sc); *When East Comes West* (+pr, sc); *The Cowboy's Deliverance* (+pr, sc); *The Cattle Thief's Brand* (+pr, sc); *The Parting Trails* (+pr, sc); *The Cattle Rustler's End* (+pr, sc); *Cattle, Gold and Oil* (+pr, sc); *The Ranch Girl* (+pr, sc); *The Poisoned Flume* (+pr, sc); *The Brand of Fear* (+pr, sc): *The Blotted Brand* (+pr, sc); *Auntie and the Cowboys* (+pr, sc); *The Western Doctor's Peril* (+pr, sc); *The Smuggler and the Girl* (+pr, sc); *The Cowboy and the Artist* (+pr, sc); *Three Million*

Dollars (+pr, sc); *The Stage Robbers of San Juan* (+pr, sc); *The Mother of the Ranch* (+pr, sc); *The Gunman* (+pr, sc); *The Claim Jumpers* (+pr, sc); *The Circular Fence* (+pr, sc); *The Rustler Sheriff* (+pr, sc); *The Love of the West* (+pr, sc); *The Trained Nurse at Bar Z* (+pr, sc); *The Miner's Wife* (+pr, sc); *The Land Thieves* (+pr, sc); *The Cowboy and the Outlaw* (+pr, sc); *Three Daughters of the West* and *Caves of La Jolla* (split reel) (+pr, sc); *The Lonely Range* (+pr, sc); *The Horse Thief's Bigamy* (+pr, sc): *The Trail of the Eucalyptus* (+pr, sc); *The Stronger Man* (+pr, sc); *The Water War* (+pr, sc); *The Three Shell Game* (+pr, sc); *The Mexican* (+pr, sc); *The Eastern Cowboy* (+pr, sc); *The Way of the West* (+pr, sc); *The Test* (+pr, sc); *The Master of the Vineyard* (+pr, sc); *Sloppy Bill of the Rollicking R* (+pr, sc); *The Sheriff's Sisters* (+pr, sc); *The Angel of Paradise Ranch* (+pr, sc); *The Smoke of the 45* (+pr, sc); *The Man Hunt* (+pr, sc); *Santa Catalina, Magic Isle of the Pacific* (+pr, sc); *The Last Notch* (+pr, sc); *The Gold Lust* (+pr, sc); *The Duel of the Candles* (+pr, sc); *Bonita of El Cajon* (+pr, sc); *The Lawful Holdup* (+pr, sc); *Battleships* (+pr, sc); *Dams and Waterways* (+pr, sc)

1912 *A Midwinter Trip to Los Angeles* (+pr, sc); *The Misadventures of a Claim Agent* and *Broncho Busting for Flying A Pictures* (split reel) (+pr, sc); *The Winning of La Mesa* (+pr, sc); *The Locket* (+pr, sc); *The Relentless Outlaw* (+pr, sc); *Justice of the Sage* (+pr, sc); *Objections Overruled* (+pr, sc); *The Mormon* (+pr, sc); *Love and Lemons* (+pr, sc); *The Best Policy* (+pr, sc); *The Real Estate Fraud* (+pr, sc); *The Grubstake Mortgage* (+pr, sc); *Where Broadway Meets the Mountains* (+pr, sc); *An Innocent Grafter* (+pr, sc); *Society and Chaps* (+pr, sc); *The Leap Year Cowboy* (+pr, sc); *The Land Baron of San Tee* (+pr sc): *An Assisted Elopement* (+pr, sc); *From the Four Hundred to the Herd* (+pr, sc); *The Broken Ties* (+pr, sc): *After School* (+pr, sc); *A Bad Investment* (+pr, sc); *The Full Value* (+pr, sc); *The Tramp's Gratitude* (+pr, sc); *Fidelity* (+pr, sc); *Winter Sports and Pastimes of Coronado Beach* (+pr, sc); *The Maid and the Man* (+pr, sc); *The Cowboy Socialist* (+pr, sc); *Checkmate* and *The Ranchman's Marathon* (split reel) (+pr, sc); *The Coward* (+pr, sc); *The Distant Relative* (+pr, sc); *The Ranch Detective* (+pr, sc); *Driftwood* (+pr, sc); *The Eastern Girl* (+pr, sc); *The Pensioners* (+pr, sc); *The End of the Feud* (+pr, sc); *The Wedding Dress* (+pr, sc); *Mystical Maid of Jamasha Pass* (+pr, sc); *The Other Wise Man* (+pr, sc); *The Haters* (+pr, sc); *The Thread of Life* (+pr, sc); *The Wandering Gypsy* (+pr, sc); *The Reward of Valor* (+pr, sc); *The Brand* (+pr, sc); *The Green Eyed Monster* (+pr, sc); *Cupid Through Padlocks* (+pr, sc); *For the Good of Her Men* (+pr, sc); *The Simple Love* (+pr, sc); *The Weaker Brother* and *Fifty Mile Auto Contest* (split reel) (+pr, sc); *The Wordless Message* (+pr, sc); *The Evil Inheritance* (+pr, sc); *The Marauders* (+pr, sc); *The Girl Back Home* (+pr, sc); *Under False Pretences* (+pr, sc); *Where There's a Heart* (+pr, sc); *The Vanishing Race* (+pr, sc); *The Fatal Mirror* and *Point Loma, Old Town* (split reel) (+pr, sc); *The Tell Tale Shells* (+pr, sc); *Indian Jealousy* and *San Diego* (split reel) (+pr, sc); *The Canyon Dweller* (+pr, sc); *It Pays to Wait* (+pr, sc); *A Life for a Kiss* (+pr, sc); *The Meddlers* (+pr, sc); *The Girl and the Gun* (+pr, sc); *The Battleground* (+pr, sc); *The Bad Man and the Ranger* (+pr, sc); *The Outlaw Colony* (+pr, sc); *The Land of Death* (+pr, sc); *The Bandit of Point Loma* (+pr, sc); *The Jealous Rage* (+pr, sc); *The Will of James Waldron* (+pr, sc); *The House that Jack Built* (+pr, sc); *Curtiss's School of Aviation* (+pr, sc); *The Stepmother* (+pr, sc); *The Odd Job Man* (+pr, sc); *The Liar* (+pr, sc); *The Greaser and the Weakling* (+pr, sc); *The Stranger at Coyote* (+pr, sc); *The Dawn of Passion* (+pr, sc); *The Vengeance that Failed* (+pr, sc); *The Fear* (+pr, sc); *The Foreclosure* (+pr, sc); *White Treachery* (+pr, sc); *Their Hero Son* (+pr, sc); *Calamity Anne's Ward* (+pr, sc); *Father's Favorite* (+pr, sc); *Jack of Diamonds* (+pr, sc); *The Reformation of Sierra Smith* (+pr, sc); *The Promise* (+pr, sc); *The New Cowpuncher* (+pr, sc); *The Best Man Wins* (+pr, sc); *The*

Wooers of Mountain Kate (+pr, sc); *One, Two, Three* (+pr, sc); *The Wanderer* (+pr, sc); *Maiden and Men* (+pr, sc); *God's Unfortunate* (+pr, sc); *Man's Calling* (+pr, sc); *The Intrusion at Lompoc* (+pr, sc); *The Thief's Wife* (+pr, sc); *The Would-Be Heir* (+pr, sc); *Jack's Word* (+pr, sc); *Her Own Country* (+pr, sc); *Pals* (+pr, sc); *The Animal Within* (+pr, sc); *The Law of God* (+pr, sc); *Nell of the Pampas* (+pr, sc); *The Daughters of Senor Lopez* (+pr, sc); *The Power of Love* (+pr, sc); *The Recognition* (+pr, sc); *Blackened Hills* (+pr, sc); *The Loneliness of Neglect* (+pr, sc); *Paid in Full* (+pr, sc); *Ranch Life on the Range* (+pr, sc); *The Man from the East* (+pr, sc); *The Horse Thief* (+pr, sc); *The Good Love and the Bad* (+pr, sc)

1913 *The Fraud that Failed* (+pr, sc); *Another Man's Wife* (+pr, sc); *Calamity Anne's Inheritance* (+pr, sc); *Their Masterpiece* (+pr, sc); *His Old-Fashioned Mother* (+pr, sc); *Where Destiny Guides* (+pr, sc); *The Silver-Plated Gun* (+pr, sc); *A Rose of Old Mexico* (+pr, sc); *Building the Great Los Angeles Aqueduct* (+pr, sc); *Women Left Alone* (+pr, sc); *Andrew Jackson* (+pr, sc); *Calamity Anne's Vanity* (+pr, sc); *The Fugitive* (+pr, sc); *The Romance* (+pr, sc); *The Finer Things* (+pr, sc); *Love is Blind* (+pr, sc); *Then the Light Fades* (+pr, sc); *High and Low* (+pr, sc); *The Greater Love* (+pr, sc); *The Jocular Winds* (+pr, sc); *The Transgression of Manuel* (+pr, sc); *Calamity Anne, Detective* (+pr, sc); *The Orphan's Mine* (+pr, sc); *When a Woman Won't* (+pr, sc); *An Eastern Flower* (+pr, sc); *Cupid Never Ages* (+pr, sc); *Calamity Anne's Beauty* (+pr, sc); *The Renegade's Heart* (+pr, sc); *Matches* (+pr, sc); *The Mute Witness* (+pr, sc); *Cupid Throws a Brick* (+pr, sc); *Woman's Honor* (+pr, sc); *Suspended Sentence* (+pr, sc); *In Another's Nest* (+pr, sc); *The Ways of Fate* (+pr, sc); *Boobs and Bricks* (+pr, sc); *Calamity Anne's Trust* (+pr, sc); *Oil on Troubled Waters* (+pr, sc); *The Road to Ruin* (+pr, sc); *The Brothers* (+pr, sc); *Human Kindness* (+pr, sc); *Youth and Jealousy* (+pr, sc); *Angel of the Canyons* (+pr, sc); *The Great Harmony* (+pr, sc); *Her Innocent Marriage* (+pr, sc); *Calamity Anne Parcel Post* (+pr, sc); *The Ashes of Three* (+pr, sc); *On the Border* (+pr, sc); *Her Big Story* (+pr, sc); *When Luck Changes* (+pr, sc); *The Wishing Seat* (+pr, sc); *Hearts and Horses* (+pr, sc); *The Reward of Courage* (+pr, sc); *The Soul of a Thief* (+pr, sc); *The Marine Law* (+pr, sc); *The Road to Success* (+pr, sc); *The Spirit of the Flag*; *The Call to Arms* (+sc); *Women and War*; *The Power Flash of Death* (+sc); *The Picket Guard*; *Mental Suicide*; *Man's Duty*; *The Animal* (+sc); *The Wall of Money*; *The Echo of a Song*; *Criminals*; *The Restless Spirit* (+sc); *Jewels of a Sacrifice*; *Back to Life*; *Red Margaret, Moonshiner*; *Bloodhounds of the North*; *He Called Her In* (+sc); *The Menace* (+sc); *The Chase*; *The Battle of Wills*

1914 *The Lie*; *The Honor of the Mounted*; *Remember Mary Magdalene* (+sc); *Discord and Harmony*; *The Menace to Carlotta*; *The Embezzler* (+sc); *The Lamb, the Woman, the Wolf* (+sc); *The End of the Feud*; *Tragedy of Whispering Creek*; *The Unlawful Trade*; *The Forbidden Room*; *The Hopes of Blind Alley*; *The Great Universal Mystery*; *Richelieu* (+sc); *Wildflower*; *The Country Chairman* (+sc); *The Small Town Girl*; *The Straight Road*; *The Conspiracy*; *The Unwelcome Mrs. Hatch*; *The Man on the Case*

1915 *The Dancing Girl*; *David Harum*; *The Love Route*; *The Commanding Officer*; *May Blossom*; *The Pretty Sister of Jose*; *A Girl of Yesterday*; *The Foundling*; *Jordan is a Hard Road* (+sc)

1916 *Betty of Greystone*; *The Habit of Happiness* (*Laugh and the World Laughs*) (+sc); *The Good Bad Man* (*Passing Through*); *An Innocent Magdalene*; *The Half-Breed*; *Manhattan Madness*; *Fifty-Fifty* (+sc)

1917 *Panthea* (+sc); *The Fighting Odds*; *A Modern Musketeer* (+sc)

1918 *Mr. Fix-It* (+sc); *Bound In Morocco* (+sc); *He Comes Up Smiling*

1919 *Cheating Cheaters*; *Getting Mary Married*; *The Dark Star*; *Soldiers of Fortune*

1920 *The Luck of the Irish*; *The Forbidden Thing* (+pr, co-sc)

Allan Dwan

1921	*A Perfect Crime* (+pr, sc); *A Broken Doll* (+pr, sc); *The Scoffer* (+pr); *The Sin of Martha Queed* (+pr, sc); *In the Heart of a Fool* (+pr)
1922	*The Hidden Woman* (+pr); *Superstition* (+pr); *Robin Hood*
1923	*The Glimpses of the Moon* (+pr); *Lawful Larceny* (+pr); *Zaza* (+pr); *Big Brother* (+pr)
1924	*A Society Scandal* (+pr); *Manhandled* (+pr); *Her Love Story* (+pr); *Wages of Virtue*; *Argentine Love* (+pr)
1925	*Night Life in New York* (+pr); *Coast of Folly* (+pr); *Stage Struck* (+pr)
1926	*Sea Horses* (+pr); *Padlocked* (+pr); *Tin Gods* (+pr); *Summer Bachelors* (+pr)
1927	*The Music Master* (+pr); *West Point* (+pr); *The Joy Girl* (+pr); *East Side, West Side* (+sc); *French Dressing* (+pr)

1928	*The Big Noise* (+pr)
1929	*The Iron Mask*; *Tide of Empire*; *The Far Call*; *Frozen Justice*; *South Sea Rose*
1930	*What a Widow!* (+pr); *Man to Man*
1931	*Chances*; *Wicked*
1932	*While Paris Sleeps*
1933	*Her First Affaire*; *Counsel's Opinion*
1934	*The Morning After* (*I Spy*); *Hollywood Party* (uncredited)
1935	*Black Sheep* (+sc); *Navy Wife*
1936	*Song and Dance Man*; *Human Cargo*; *High Tension*; *15 Maiden Lane*
1937	*Woman-Wise*; *That I May Live*; *One Mile from Heaven*; *Heidi*
1938	*Rebecca of Sunnybrook Farm*; *Josette*; *Suez*
1939	*The Three Musketeers*; *The Gorilla*; *Frontier Marshal*

1940 *Sailor's Lady*; *Young People*; *Trail of the Vigilantes*
1941 *Look Who's Laughing* (+pr); *Rise and Shine*
1942 *Friendly Enemies*; *Here We Go Again* (+pr)
1943 *Around the World* (+pr)
1944 *Up in Mabel's Room*; *Abroad with Two Yanks*
1945 *Brewster's Millions*; *Getting Gertie's Garter*
1946 *Rendezvous with Annie* (+co-pr)
1947 *Calendar Girl* (+co-pr); *Northwest Outpost* (+co-pr); *Driftwood*
1948 *The Inside Story* (+pr); *Angel in Exile*
1949 *Sands of Iwo Jima*
1950 *Surrender* (+co-pr)
1951 *Belle le Grand*; *The Wild Blue Yonder*
1952 *I Dream of Jeannie (With the Light Brown Hair)*; *Montana Belle*
1953 *Woman They Almost Lynched*; *Sweethearts on Parade* (+co-pr)
1954 *Flight Nurse*; *Silver Lode*; *Passion*; *Cattle Queen of Montana*
1955 *It's Always Sunday (for Screen Director's Playhouse TV series)*; *Escape to Burma*; *Pearl of the South Pacific*; *Tennessee's Partner*
1956 *Slightly Scarlet*; *Hold Back the Night*
1957 *The River's Edge*; *The Restless Breed*
1958 *Enchanted Island*
1961 *Most Dangerous Man Alive*

Publications:

By DWAN: articles—

Interview with F.T. Pope, in *Photoplay* (New York), September 1923.
"Must actors have temperament?," in *Motion Picture* (New York), February 1926.
"As It Was," in *Making Films* (New York), June 1971.
"What Directors Are Saying," in *Action* (Los Angeles), August 1971.
"Angel in Exile: Alan Dwan," interview with G. Morris and H. Mandelbaum, in *Bright Lights* (Los Angeles), no.4, 1979.

On DWAN: books—

Brownlow, Kevin, *The Parade's Gone By*, London and New York, 1968.
Bogdanovich, Peter, *Allan Dwan, the Last Pioneer*, New York, 1971.

On DWAN: articles—

Sarris, Andrew, "Esoterica," in *Film Culture* (New York), Spring 1963.
Smith, J.M., "Allan Dwan," in *Brighton Film Review*, February 1970.
Schickel, Richard, "Good Days, Good Years," in *Harper's* (New York), October 1970.
"Six Pioneers," in *Action* (Los Angeles), November/December 1972.
Dorr, J.H., "Allan Dwan: Master of the American Folk Art of Filmmaking," in *Take One* (Montreal), September 1973.
Dorr, J., "The Griffith Tradition," in *Film Comment* (New York), March/April 1974.
Biette, J.-C., "Allan Dwan, ou le cinéma nature," in *Cahiers du Cinéma* (Paris), February 1982.
McGillivray, D., obituary, in *Films and Filming* (London), March 1982.

*   *   *

Allan Dwan was a pioneer among pioneers, men like D.W. Griffith and Cecil B. DeMille, whose careers spanned the birth and the growth of the American motion picture industry. Active in the industry for over 50 years, he participated in creating at least 800 films—his own estimate was 1,850. Most of these were one-to-four-reel silents of which some two-thirds are lost, and for that reason his career remains one which has never been properly assessed. The artistic disparity of his 70-odd sound films fail to adequately represent this technically innovative, unpretentious, avid storyteller and his is surely a career which will undergo considerable re-evaulation as the study of film history progresses.

It was the scientific aspect of motion pictures which attracted Dwan to the medium and in 1909 he joined Essanay as a lighting man. He then joined the American Flying A Company as a writer but soon found himself directing short films, mostly Westerns. He moved next to Universal, then to Famous Players where in 1915 he introduced the dolly shot for *David Harum*, and directed Mary Pickford in *The Foundling*.

The same year he joined Fine Arts-Triangle where his films were supervised by D.W. Griffith. He directed many of Griffith's top stars including Dorothy Gish in *Betty of Greystone* and her sister Lillian in *An Innocent Magdalene* and he once stated how impressed he was with the "economy of gesture" of Griffith's players. He credits Griffith with developing his clean, spare visual style and Griffith frequently sought out Dwan for his technical knowledge. One such request resulted in Dwan's improvising an elevator on a moving track to film the massive sets of *Intolerance*. Also at Fine Arts-Triangle, Dwan established his association with Douglas Fairbanks, a professional relationship which resulted in 11 films including *The Half-Breed*, *A Modern Musketeer*, *Bound in Morocco* and the celebrated *Robin Hood*, described by Robert Sherwood as "the high-water mark of film production in the farthest step that the silent drama has ever taken along the high road to art."

In 1923, Dwan directed his favorite film *Big Brother*, about under-privileged boys, and then embarked on the first of eight buoyant comedies starring Gloria Swanson, the best of which were *Zaza* and *Manhandled*. With the arrival of sound, Dwan signed a long-term contract with Fox (1930–41) where he was unfortunately relegated to their B unit except for occasional reprieves—Shirley Temple's *Heidi* and *Rebecca of Sunnybrook Farm*, and *Suez*, much admired for its typhoon sequence. He then signed with producer Edward Small for whom he directed a delightful quartet of farces—*Up in Mabel's Room, Getting Gertie's Garter, Abroad with Two Yanks,* and *Brewster's Millions*. He then unwisely signed an exclusive deal with Republic Pictures where, except for *Sands of Iwo Jima*, his creativity was constricted by studio head Herbert Yates. Moving to RKO, he persevered despite the many obstacles of 1950s filmmaking, churning out entertaining actioners.

Dwan loved movie making and was described as the "last of the journeyman filmmakers" by Richard Roud. Of his self-imposed retirement in 1958, Dwan explained: "It was no longer a question of 'Let's get a bunch of people together and make a picture.' It's just a business that I stood as long as I could and I got out of it when I couldn't stand it any more."

—Ronald Bowers

EDWARDS, Blake.

American. Born William Blake McEdwards in Tulsa, Oklahoma, 26 July 1922. Served in the U.S. Coast Guard, 1944–45. Married 1) Patricia Walker, 1953, one son, one daughter; 2) actress Julie Andrews, 1969, two adopted daughters. Created NBC radio series, *Richard Diamond, Private Detective*, for Dick Powell, 1949; as writer/director for Columbia B-picture Unit, directed first feature *Bring Your Smile Along*, 1955; directed first A-picture, *Mister Cory*, 1957; creator, *Peter Gunn*, 1958, *Mr. Lucky*, 1959, and *Dante's Inferno*, 1960, for TV; after dispute over *The Carey Treatment*, moved to Europe; signed 3-picture deal with Orion, 1978, agreement terminated after *10*, 1979. Recipient: Oscars for Best Screenplays, for *Victor/Victoria*, 1982, and *The Man Who Loved Women*, (with Geoffrey Edwards), 1983. Lives in Gstaad, Switzerland. Address: c/o Blake Edwards Entertainment, 1888 Century Park E., Suite 1616, Los Angeles, CA 90067, U.S.A.

Films as Director:

1955   *Bring Your Smile Along* (+ sc)
1956   *He Laughed Last* (+ sc)
1958   *This Happy Feeling* (+ sc)
1959   *The Perfect Furlough* (+ sc); *Operation Petticoat* (+ sc)
1960   *High Time* (+ sc)
1961   *Breakfast at Tiffany's*
1962   *Experiment in Terror* (*The Grip of Fear*) (+ pr, sc); *Days of Wine and Roses*; *Walk on the Wild Side* (Dmytryk) (d add'l scenes, uncredited)
1964   *The Pink Panther* (+ co-sc); *A Shot in the Dark* (+ sc)
1965   *The Great Race* (+ sc, co-story, bit role as troublemaker); *What Did You Do in the War, Daddy?* (+ sc, co-story, pr)
1967   *Gunn* (+ co-sc)
1968   *The Party* (+ co-sc, pr)
1970   *Darling Lili* (+ co-sc, co-pr)
1971   *The Wild Rovers* (+ co-pr, sc)
1972   *The Carey Treatment* (*Emergency Ward*)
1974   *The Tamarind Seed* (+ sc); *The Return of the Pink Panther* (+ co-sc, pr)
1976   *The Pink Panther Strikes Again* (+ co-sc, pr)
1978   *Revenge of the Pink Panther* (+ co-sc, pr)
1979   *10* (+ sc, pr)
1981   *S.O.B.* (+ sc, pr)
1982   *Victor Victoria* (+ co-pr, sc); *Trail of the Pink Panther* (+ pr)
1983   *Curse of the Pink Panther* (+ pr, sc); *The Man Who Loved Women* (+ pr, co-sc)
1984   *Micki and Maude* (+ pr)
1986   *A Fine Mess* (*The Music Box*) (+ sc); *That's Life* (*Crisis*) (+ co-sc)
1987   *Blind Date*
1988   *Sunset*
1989   *Skin Deep*

Other Films:

1942   *Ten Gentlemen from West Point* (Hathaway) (role); *Lucky Legs* (Barton) (role)
1943   *A Guy Named Joe* (Fleming) (role)
1944   *In the Meantime, Darling* (Preminger) (role); *Marshal of Reno* (Grissell) (role); *See Here, Private Hargrove* (Ruggles) (role); *Ladies Courageous* (Rawlins) (role); *The Eve of St. Mark* (Stahl) (role); *Marine Raiders* (Schuster) (role); *Wing and a Prayer* (Hathaway) (role); *My Buddy* (Sekely) (role); *The Unwritten Code* (Rotsten) (role); *Thirty Seconds over Tokyo* (LeRoy) (role); *She's a Sweetheart* (Lord) (role)
1945   *This Man's Navy* (Wellman) (role); *A Guy, a Gal, and a Pal* (Boetticher) (role); *Gangs of the Waterfront* (Blair) (role); *What Next, Corporal Hargrove?* (Thorpe) (role); *They Were Expendable* (Ford) (role); *Tokyo Rose* (Landers) (role); *Strangler of the Swamp* (Wisbar) (major role)
1946   *The Strange Love of Martha Ivers* (Milestone) (role); *Till the End of Time* (Dmytryk) (role); *The Best Years of Our Lives* (Wyler) (role)
1947   *The Beginning or the End* (Taurog) (role); *Panhandle* (co-sc, co-pr, role)
1948   *Leather Gloves* (*Loser Take All*) (Quine and Asher) (sc, role)
1949   *Stampede* (Selander) (co-sc, pr)
1952   *Sound Off* (Quine) (sc); *Rainbow Round My Shoulder* (Quine) (sc)
1953   *All Ashore* (Quinc) (sc); *Cruisin' Down the River* (Quine) (sc)
1954   *Drive a Crooked Road* (Quine) (sc); *The Atomic Kid* (Martinson) (story, sc)
1955   *My Sister Eileen* (Quine) (sc)
1956   *Operation Mad Ball* (Quine) (co-sc)
1961   *The Couch* (Crump) (co-story)
1962   *The Notorious Landlady* (Quine) (co-sc)
1963   *Soldier in the Rain* (Nelson) (co-sc, pr)
1967   *Inspector Clouseau* (Yorkin) (sc)

Publications:

By EDWARDS: articles—

"Un Humour sérieux," in *Cahiers du Cinéma* (Paris), May/June 1965.
"Sophisticated Naturalism," interview with Jean-Francois Hauduroy, in *Cahiers du Cinéma in English* (New York), no. 3, 1966.
"Confessions of a Cult Figure," interview with Stuart Byron, in *Village Voice* (New York), 5 August 1971.
"Dans la tradition classique," interview with C. Viviani, in *Positif* (Paris), June 1973.
Interview with P. Stamelman, in *Millimeter* (New York), January 1977.
"Riding Herd on a Chinese Fire Drill," interview, in *American Cinematographer* (Los Angeles), July 1978.
"Too much to do, not enough time to do it," interview with P. Lehman and W. Luhr, in *Wide Angle* (Athens, Ohio), vol. 3, no. 3, 1980.
Interview in *Hollywood Reporter*, 56th Anniversary Edition, 1986.

On EDWARDS: books—

Lehman, Peter, and William Luhr, *Blake Edwards*, Athens, Ohio, 1980.

Lehman, Peter, and William Luhr, *Returning to the Scene: Blake Edwards, Volume 2*, Athens, Ohio, 1989.

On EDWARDS: articles—

Haller, Robert, "*Peter Gunn*: The Private Eye of Blake Edwards," in *Film Heritage* (New York), Summer 1968.
Lightman, Herb, "*Wild Rovers*: Case History of a Film," in *American Cinematographer* (Los Angeles), July 1971.
Benayoun, Robert, "Blake Edwards ou la sophistication de l'innocence," in *Positif* (Paris), June 1973.
Luhr, William, and Peter Lehman, "You'll Never Work in Hollywood Again," in *Wide Angle* (Athens, Ohio), vol. 1, no. 4, 1977; "The Case of the Missing Lead Pipe Cinch," in *Wide Angle* (Athens, Ohio), no. 1, 1979; and "Crime in the Bedroom," in *Wide Angle* (Athens, Ohio), no. 2, 1979.
Morris, G., "Blake Edwards Takes *10*," in *Film Comment* (New York), November/December 1979.
Kennedy, Harlan, "Blake Edwards: Life after *10*." in *American Film* (Washington, D.C.), July/August 1981.
"Lost in Gloss or Cineaste maudit. The Strange Case of Blake Edwards," in Monthly *Film Bulletin* (London), July 1984.
Tobin, Y., and A. Masson, in *Positif* (Paris), April 1985.
Ciné Revue (Paris), 16 June 1988.

On EDWARDS: Films—

Hindle, Will, *Experiment on "Experiment"*, for TV, 1962.
Anderson, Edward, *Gift of Laughter*, Great Britain, 1975.

*   *   *

Blake Edwards is one of the few filmmakers formed in the late classical period of American movies (the late 1940's and 1950's) to survive and prosper through the 1980's. If anything, Edwards's work has deepened with the passing decades, though it no longer bears much resemblance to the norms and styles of contemporary Hollywood. Edwards is an isolated figure, but a vital one.

His critical and box office reputation first peaked in the early 1960's with such films as *Operation Petticoat, Breakfast at Tiffany's, Days of Wine and Roses*, and *The Pink Panther*. But as the new, post-studio Hollywood moved away from his brand of classicism, Edwards had a string of commercial disappointments—*What Did You Do in the War, Daddy?, Gunn, The Party*—leading up to the total failure of the multi-million dollar musical *Darling Lili*. In the early 1970's, Edwards was barely visible, issuing occasional programmers—*The Wild Rovers, The Carey Treatment, The Tamarind Seed*—until his decision to revive the Inspector Clouseau character for *The Return of the Pink Panther*. The mordant slapstick of the Panther films was back in style, and Edwards rode the success of *Return* through three more sequels, with the promise (despite the death of Clouseau's interpreter, Peter Sellers) of more to come. The success of the Panther films allowed Edwards to capitalize more personal projects, one of which—the 1979 *10*—became a sleeper hit. In his sixties, he again became a brand name, with his own production company, Blake Edwards Entertainment, and a measure of security.

For all his artistic independence, Edwards has always chosen to work within well-defined, traditional genres—the musical, the melodrama, the slapstick farce, the thriller. There is little continuity in tone between a film like *The Tamarind Seed* (a transcendant love story) and *S.O.B.* (a frenzied black farce), yet there are the more important continuities of personality. Edwards has no particular commitment to any single genre (though his greatest successes have been comedies); he varies his choices as a painter varies the colors of his palette, to alter the tonal mix. The single stylistic constant has been Edwards's use of Panavision; with very few exceptions, his films have used the widescreen format as the basic unit of organization and expression.

At their most elemental level, Edwards's films are about

Blake Edwards

space—crossing it, filling it, transcending it. In the comedies, the widescreen space becomes a vortex fraught with perils—hidden traps, aggressive objects, spaces that abruptly open onto other, unexpected spaces. Edwards extends the principles of silent comedy into modern technology and modern absurdism; his comic heroes are isolated in the hostile widescreen space, unable to conquer it as Chaplin and Keaton could conquer the more manageable dimensions of the silent frame. (Though the Panther films employ this principle, Edwards's masterpiece in this vein is the relatively unknown 1968 film, *The Party*.)

Visually, Edwards's thrillers appear to be more dense, more furnished, more confining than his comedies (and two of the best of them, *Gunn* and *Experiment in Terror*, were photographed in the standard screen ratio); the threat comes not from empty space, but from the crowding of objects, colors, surfaces—the hard, cold *thingness* of things: a deathly solidity that gives way, when the surfaces dissolve, to a more deathly chaos. In the romances, that operative space is the space between the characters; it must be collapsed, transformed, overcome. In *Darling Lili*, a room full of red roses is an emblem of love; it is not the trite symbolism of the flowers that gives the image its power, but the complete filling in of the widescreen space, its emotional conquest. In *The Tamarind Seed*, the lovers' conquest of space entails, as it does in the sublime 1930's romances of Frank Borzage, a conquest of death.

With *10* and *Victor/Victoria*, Edwards managed to blend the styles and assumptions of his comedies and romances; the strict genre divisions that once ruled his work have broken down, and with their dissolution a new humanism appears. *10* uses its long lenses trained on Bo Derek's face (as perfect a blank, deathly surface as any in Edwards's films) to create looming, overlarge images of romantic fantasy. But when Dudley Moore finds his way back to Julie Andrews, Edwards shifts to balanced wide-screen compositions—two lovers occupying the same stable space—which become images of a realistic, responsible romanticism. *Victor/Victoria*, with its theatrical metaphors, builds small proscenium spaces for each of its role-playing characters; as the constricting roles are cast off, these isolating spaces give way to an overall openness and warmth. The widescreen space is no longer inherently hostile, but contains the promise of closeness and comfort.

—Dave Kehr

EISENSTEIN, Sergei.

Russian. Born Sergei Mikhailovich Eisenstein in Riga, Latvia, 23 January 1898. Educated in St. Petersburg and at gymnasium in Riga; Institute of Civil Engineering, St. Petersburg (studied architecture), 1914–17; studied Japanese at General Staff Academy, Moscow, 1920. Married Peta Attasheva. Sent for Officer training, 1917; poster artist on front at Minsk, then demobilized, 1920; scenic artist, then co-director of Proletkult Theatre, Moscow, 1920; designer for Vsevolod Meyerhold's "directors' workshop," 1922; directed *Stachka*, 1925; made professor at State Institute for Cinema, 1926; with Grigori Alexandrov and Edouard Tisse, travelled to Hollywood, 1929; signed for Paramount, but after work on various scripts, contract broken, 1930; refused a work permit by State Department, went to Mexico to work on *Que Viva Mexico!*; refused reentry permit to U.S., after financier Sinclair Lewis halts shooting and keeps uncut film; returned to U.S.S.R., 1932; began teaching at Moscow Film Institute, 1933; *Behzin Meadow* project denounced, production halted, 1937; worked on Pushkin film project, named Artistic Director of Mosfilm Studios, 1940; after finishing *Ivan the Terrible*, suffered heart attack, 1946; prepared a 3rd part to *Ivan*, to have been made in color, 1947. Recipient: Gold Medal, Exposition Internationale des Arts Décoratifs, Paris, for *Strike!*, 1925; Order of Lenin, 1939; Stalin Prize, 1st Class, for *Ivan the Terrible, Part I*, 1946. *Died in Moscow, 11 February, 1948.*

Films as Director:

1923   *Kinodnevik Glumova* (*Glumov's Film Diary*) (short film inserted in production of Ostrovsky's *Enough Simplicity in Every Wise Man*, Proletkult Theater, Moscow) (+ sc)
1925   **Stachka (The Strike)** (+ co-sc, ed); **Bronenosets Potemkin (The Battleship Potemkin)** (+ sc, ed)
1928   **Oktiabr (October, Ten Days That Shook the World)** (co-d, co-sc)
1929   *Staroe i novoe* (*Old and New*) [film produced as *Generalnaia linia* (*The General Line*), title changed before release] (co-d, co-sc)
1930   *Romance sentimentale* (co-d, sc)
1933   *Thunder Over Mexico* (unauthorized, produced by Sol Lesser from *Que Viva Mexico!* footage, seen by Eisenstein 1947 and disowned); *Death Day* and *Eisenstein in Mexico* (also unauthorized productions by Sol Lesser from *Que Viva Mexico!* footage)
1938   *Aleksandr Nevskii* (*Alexander Nevsky*) (+ co-sc, set des, costume des, ed)
1939   *Time in the Sun* (produced by Marie Seton from *Que Viva Mexico!* footage); *The Ferghana Canal* (short documentary out of footage from abandoned feature subject on same subject) (+ sc)
1941   shorts edited by William Kruse for Bell and Howell from *Que Viva Mexico!* footage: *Mexico Marches*; *Conquering Cross*; *Idol of Hope*; *Land and Freedom*; *Spaniard and Indian*; *Mexican Symphony* (feature combining previous 5 titles); *Zapotecan Village*
1944   *Ivan Groznyi* (*Ivan the Terrible, Part I*) (+ sc, set des, costume des, ed)
1958   *Ivan Groznyi II: Boyarskii zagovor* (*Ivan the Terrible, Part II: The Boyars' Plot*) (+ sc) (completed 1946); *Eisenstein's Mexican Project* (+ sc) (unedited sequences of *Que Viva Mexico!* assembled by Jay Leyda)
1966   *Bezhin Lug* (*Bezhin Meadow*) (+ sc) (25min montage of stills from original film assembled by Naum Kleiman, with music by Prokofiev)

Other Films:

1924   *Doktor Mabuze—Igrok* (co-ed) (Russian version of Lang's *Dr. Mabuse der Spieler*)
1929   *Everyday* (Hans Richter) (role as London policeman)

Publications:

By EISENSTEIN: books—

The Soviet Screen, Moscow, 1939.
The Film Sense, edited by Jay Leyda, New York, 1942.
Notes of a Film Director, Moscow, 1948.
Film Form, edited by Jay Leyda, New York, 1949.
Charlie Chaplin, Zurich, 1961.
Que Viva Mexico, London, 1951.
Drawings, Moscow, 1961.
Ivan the Terrible: A Screenplay, New York, 1962.
Sergei Eizenshtein, Izbrannye proizvedeniya (6 vols.), edited by P.M. Atasheva and others, Moscow, 1964–71.
Film Essays with a Lecture, edited by Jay Leyda, London, 1968.
Potemkin, New York, 1968.
The Battleship Potemkin, text by Andrew Sinclair, London, 1968.
Notes of a Film Director, New York, 1970.
Collected Works of Sergei Eisenstein, edited by Herbert Marshall, Cambridge, Massachusetts, 1971.
The Complete Works of Sergei M. Eisenstein, edited by Marcel Martin, Guy Lecouvette and Abraham Segal, New York, 1971.
Eisenstein: Three Films, edited by Jay Leyda, New York, 1974.
The Complete Films of Eisenstein, New York, 1974.
Immoral Memories: An Autobiography, translated by Herbert Marshall, Boston, 1983.
October and Alexander Nevsky, edited by Jay Leyda, New York, 1984.
Iz tvorcheskogo naslediya S.M. Eizenshteina, edited by L. Kozlov and N. Kleiman, Moscow, 1985.
Nonindifferent Nature, edited by Herbert Marshall, Cambridge, 1987.
Eisenstein: Selected Works, Volume 1: Writings 1922–1934, edited by Richard Taylor, London, 1988.
S.M. Eisenstein: The Psychology of Composition, edited by A.Y. Upchurch, London, 1988.
Eisenstein: Selected Works, Volume 2: Towards a Theory of Montage, edited by Richard Taylor and Michael Glenny, London, 1991.

By EISENSTEIN: articles—

"Mass Movies," in *Nation* (New York), 9 November 1927.
"Mexican Film and Marxian Theory," in *New Republic* (New York), 9 December 1931.
"The Cinematographic Principle and Japanese Culture," in *Experimental Cinema*, no. 3, 1932.
"Through Theatre to Cinema," in *Theatre Arts* (New York), September 1936.
"The Mistakes of *Bezhin Lug*," in *International Literature* (Moscow), no. 1, 1937.
"My Subject is Patriotism," in *International Literature* (Moscow), no. 2, 1939.

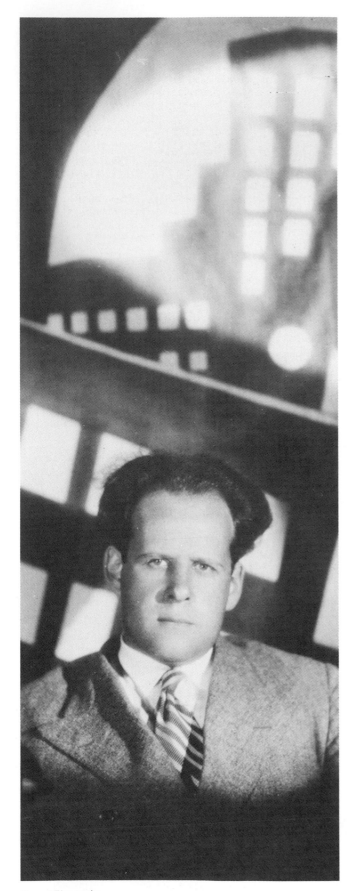

Sergei Eisenstein

"Charlie the Kid," in *Sight and Sound* (London), Spring 1946.
"Charlie the Grownup," in *Sight and Sound* (London), Summer 1946.
"The Birth of a Film," in *Hudson Review* (Nutley, New Jersey), no. 2, 1951.
"Sketches for Life," in *Films and Filming* (London), April 1958.
"One Path to Colour: An Autobiographical Fragment," in *Sight and Sound* (London), Spring 1961.
Interview, in *Interviews with Film Directors* edited by Andrew Sarris, New York, 1967.
"La Quatrième Dimension du cinéma," in *Cahiers du Cinéma* (Paris), September/October 1976.
"Sergei Eisenstein, Wilhelm Reich correspondence," edited by F. Albera, in *Screen* (London), vol. 22, no. 4, 1981.
"A Postcard and a letter from S.M. Eisenstein to Renaud De Jouvenel," in *Film Culture* (New York), nos. 70–71, 1983.

On EISENSTEIN: books—

Rotha, Paul, Ivor Montagu, and John Grierson, *Eisenstein 1898–1948*, London, 1948.
Arnheim, Rudolph, *Film as Art*, Berkeley, 1957.
Leyda, Jay, *Kino*, London, 1960.
Mitry, Jean, *S.M. Eisenstein*, Paris, 1961; revised edition, 1978.
Montagu, Ivor, *With Eisenstein in Hollywood*, New York, 1969.
Nizhny, Vladimir, *Lessons with Eisenstein*, New York, 1969.
Geduld, Harry, and Ronald Gottesman, *Sergei Eisenstein and Upton Sinclair: The Making and Unmaking of "Que Viva Mexico!"*, Bloomington, Indiana, 1970.
Moussinac, Léon, *Sergei Eisenstein*, New York, 1970.
Brakhage, Stan, *The Brakhage Lectures*, Chicago, 1972.
Mayer, D., *Eisenstein's Potemkin: A Shot-by-shot Presentation*, New York, 1972.
Barna, Yon, *Eisenstein*, Bloomington, Indiana, 1973.
Shlovskii, V., *Eizenshtein*, Moscow, 1973.
Fernandez, Dominique, *Eisenstein*, Paris, 1975.
Swallow, N., *Eisenstein: a Documentary Portrait*, London, 1976; New York, 1977.
Ropars-Wuilleumier, Marie-Claire, and others, *Octobre, Ecriture et idéologie*, Paris, 1976.
Barthes, Roland, *Image/Music/Text*, New York, 1977.
Marshall, Herbert, editor, *Sergei Eisenstein's "The Battleship Potemkin"*, New York, 1978.
Seton, Marie, *Sergei M. Eisenstein*, London, 1978.
Aumont, Jacques, *Montage Eisenstein*, Paris, 1979.
Ropars-Wuilleumier, Marie-Claire, and others, *La Révolution figurée*, Paris, 1979.
Thompson, Kristin, *Eisenstein's Ivan the Terrible, a Neoformalist Analysis*, Princeton, 1981.
Leyda, Jay, and Zina Vignow, *Eisenstein at Work*, New York, 1982.
Marshall, Herbert, *Masters of the Soviet Cinema: Crippled Creative Biographies*, London, 1983.
Polan, Dana B., *The Political Language of Film and the Avant-Garde*, Ann Arbor, Michigan, 1985.
Yurenev, R., *Sergei Eizenshtein, Zamysli, Fil'my, Metod, vol. 1: 1898–1929*, Moscow, 1985; *vol. 2: 1930–1945*, Moscow, 1988.
Aumont, Jacques, *Montage Eisenstein*, London, 1987.
Christie, Ian, and David Elliot, editors, *Eisenstein at 90*, London, 1988.
Christie, Ian, and Richard Taylor, editors, *Eisenstein Rediscovered*, London, 1991.

On EISENSTEIN: articles—

Wilson, Edmund, "Eisenstein in Hollywood," in *New Republic* (New York), 4 November 1931.
Montagu, Ivor, "Sergei Eisenstein," in *Penguin Film Review* (London), September 1948.
Seton, Marie, "Eisenstein's Images and Mexican Art," in *Sight and Sound* (London), September 1953.
Harrah, D., "Aesthetics of the Film: The Pudovkin-Arnheim-Eisenstein Theory," in *Journal of Aesthetics and Art Criticism*, December 1954.
Knight, Arthur, "Eisenstein and the Mass Epic," in *The Liveliest Art*, New York, 1957.
Sadoul, Georges, "Entretiens sur Eisenstein," in *Cinéma* (Paris), 1960.

Leyda, Jay, "Care of the Past," in *Sight and Sound* (London), Winter 1961/62.

Leyda, Jay, "Missing Reel," in *Sight and Sound* (London), Spring 1965.

Yourenev, Rostislav, "Eisenstein," in *Anthologie du Cinéma*, Paris, 1966.

Siegler, R., "Masquage, an Extrapolation of Eisenstein's Theory of Montage-as-Conflict to the Multi-image Film," in *Film Quarterly* (Berkeley), Spring 1968.

Wollen, Peter, "Eisenstein: Cinema and the Avant-Garde," in *Art International* (Lugano), November 1968.

Henderson, Brian, "Two Types of Film Theory," in *Film Quarterly* (Berkeley), Spring 1971.

Pleynet, M., "The 'Left' Front of Art: Eisenstein and the Old 'Young' Hegelians," in *Screen* (London), Spring 1972.

Kuleshov, Lev, "Kuleshov, Eisenstein, and the Others," in *Film Journal* (New York), Fall/Winter 1972.

Levaco, R., "The Eisenstein-Prokoviev Correspondence," in *Cinema Journal* (Evanston), Fall 1973.

Seydor, P., "Eisenstein's Aesthetics: A Dissenting View," in *Sight and Sound* (London), Winter 1973/74.

"Eisenstein Issue" of *Cine Cubano* (Havana), no. 89–90, 1974.

Barthes, Roland, "Diderot, Brecht, Eisenstein," in *Screen* (London), Summer 1974.

Bordwell, David, "Eisenstein's Epistemological Shift," in *Screen* (London), Winter 1974/75 (see also Bordwell letter in *Screen*, Spring 1975).

Perlmutter, R., "Le Gai Savoir: Godard and Eisenstein: Notions of Intellectual Cinema," in *Jump Cut* (Berkeley), May/July 1975.

"Eisenstein Issue" of *Cinema Journal* (Evanston), Fall 1977.

Gallez, D.W., "The Prokoviev-Eisenstein Collaboration," in *Cinema Journal* (Evanston), Spring 1978.

Goodwin, J., "Eisenstein: Ideology and Intellectual Cinema," and H. Marshall, "A Note on Eisenstein's Shot Montage . . . ," in *Quarterly Review of Film Studies* (Pleasantville, New York), Spring 1978.

Burch, Noel, "Film's Institutional Mode of Representation and the Soviet Response," in *October* (Cambridge, Massachusetts), Winter 1979.

Gutiérrez Alea, T., "Alienation and De-Alienation in Eisenstein and Brecht," in *Cinema Papers* (Melbourne), July/August 1981.

Goodwin, J., "Plusiers Eisenstein: Recent criticism," in *Quarterly Review of Film Studies* (New York), Fall 1981.

Selden, D.L., "Vision and Violence: The Rhetoric of Potemkin," in *Quarterly Review of Film Studies* (New York), Fall 1982.

"*Alexander Nevsky* Section" of *Film Culture* (New York), no. 70–71, 1983.

Perry, T., "Sergei Eisenstein: A Career in Pictures," in *American Film* (Washington, D.C.), January/February 1983.

Bordwell, David, "Narrative and Scenography in the Later Eisenstein," in *Millenium Film Journal* (New York), Fall 1983–Winter 1984.

Hogenkamp, Bert, "De russen komen! Poedowkin, Eisenstein en Wertow in Nederland," in *Skrien* (Amsterdam), November/December 1985.

Taylor, Richard, "Eisenstein: 1898–1948–1988," in *Historical Journal of Film, Radio, and TV* (Abingdon, Oxon), Summer 1988.

Christie, Ian, "Eisenstein at 90," in *Sight and Sound* (London), Summer 1988.

"Eisenstein Lives," in *National Film Theatre Booklet* (London), September, October, and December 1988.

On EISENSTEIN: films—

Aslem, Henk, *Eisenstein in Nederland* (*Eisenstein in Holland*), Holland, 1930.

Attasheva, Pera, (directed and scripted by), *In Memory of Eisenstein*, USSR

Seton, Marie, and John Minchinton, *Eisenstein Survey*, Great Britain, 1952.

Katanyan, V., *S.M. Eisenstein* (*Sergei Eisenstein Film Biography*), USSR, 1958.

Eisenstein Directs Ivan (derived from previous film), Great Britain, 1969.

Hudsmith, Philip, *Eisenstein in Mexico*, Canada, 1977.

*   *   *

Eisenstein is generally considered to be one of the most important figures—perhaps *the* most important figure—in the history of cinema. But he was not only the leading director and theorist of Soviet cinema in his own lifetime, he was also a theatre and opera director, scriptwriter, graphic artist, teacher and critic. His contemporaries called him quite simply "the Master."

Eisenstein's reputation as a film-maker rests on only seven completed feature films but among them *The Battleship Potemkin* has consistently been regarded as one of the greatest films ever made. The pivotal scene in the film—the massacre on the Odessa Steps—has become the most famous sequence in film history and a paradigm of the montage techniques that were central to Eisenstein's theories of film-making.

Like many early Soviet film-makers, Eisenstein came to cinema by a circuitous route. Born in Riga, then a largely German-speaking provincial city of the Russian Empire, he saw his first film on a visit to Paris with his parents when he was only eight: *Les 400 farces du diable* by Méliès. He was educated at a technical grammar school so that he would follow his father's career as an engineer. Despite, or perhaps because of, his artistic bent, he was consistently given low marks at school for his drawing, his best subject equally consistently being religious knowledge. In 1909 his parents separated and his mother went to live in St Petersburg. On various visits to her, Eisenstein was entranced by his first taste of the circus and intrigued by his clandestine reading of her copies of *Venus in Furs* by Sacher-Masoch and Mirabeau's *The Torture Garden*. Reflections of this can be detected in his later work.

In 1915 Eisenstein entered the Institute for Civil Engineering in Petrograd, where he saw his first Meyerhold productions in the theatre. After the Revolution he abandoned his courses and joined the Red Army. He was assigned to a theatrical troupe, where he worked as a director, designer and actor. In 1920 he was demobilised to Moscow and rapidly became head of design at the First Proletkult Workers Theatre. His first sets were for a production of *The Mexican*, by Lenin's favourite writer, Jack London. In 1921 he joined Meyerhold's theatre workshop (he was later to describe Meyerhold as his "spitirual father") and worked on designs for *Puss in Boots*.

Eisenstein's first stage production, a version of Ostrovsky's *Enough Simplicity for Every Wise Man* in 1923 included his first venture into cinema, *Glumov's Diary*. This was inspired by the use of a short film in the Kozintsev and Trauberg production of Gogol's *The Wedding*, which he had seen the year before. His production of Tretyakov's *Gas Masks* in 1924 staged in the Moscow gasworks was an attempt to bridge the gap between stage "realism" and the reality of everyday life. It failed and, as Eisenstein himself put it, he "fell into cinema."

He had already worked with Esfir Shub re-editing Fritz Lang's *Dr Mabuse* for Soviet audiences in 1923 but he made his first full-length film *The Strike*, set in 1905, in 1925. In this film he applied to cinema the theory of the "montage of attractions" that he had first developed in *Enough Simplicity for Every Wise Man*. Eisenstein was not the first to develop the notion of montage as the essence of cinema specificity: that honour belonged to Lev Kuleshov in 1917. Unlike Kuleshov, however, Eisenstein thought that montage depended on a *conflict* between different elements from which a new synthesis would arise. This notion developed partly from his study of Japanese ideograms and partly from his own partial understanding of the Marxist dialectic. It followed from the primacy accorded to montage in this theory that the actor's role was diminished while the director's was enhanced. Eisenstein's view of the primacy of the director was to cause him serious problems on both sides of the Atlantic.

In his silent films Eisenstein used amateur actors who were

the right physical types for the part and called this "typage": hence an unknown worker, Nikandrov, played the role of Lenin in *October*, released in 1927. Most of the parts in his second full-length film, *The Battleship Potemkin*, released in 1926, were played by amateurs. Even the local actors who appeared in the Odessa Steps sequence were chosen, not for their professional training but because they looked right for the parts. It was *Potemkin* that secured Eisenstein's reputation both at home and abroad, especially in Germany, where it was a spectacular commercial success and attracted far greater audiences than in the USSR itself. *Potemkin* put Soviet cinema on the world map.

After *Potemkin* Eisenstein started work on a film about collectivisation, *The General Line*, but broke off to make *October* for the tenth anniversary of the October Revolution. It was with this film that his serious problems with the authorities began. Critics were divided about the film. Some enthused about the birth of a new "intellectual cinema," based on "intellectual montage," which, like Brecht's "alienation effect," stimulated audiences to think rather than to react solely with their emotions. Other critics were troubled by what they saw as an overabundance of abstract symbolism that was, in the (officially inspired) catch-phrase of the times, "unintelligible to the millions."

When Eisenstein returned to *The General Line* and completed it in 1929, the Party's general line on agriculture had changed and Trotsky had fallen from grace: the film therefore had to be re-edited to reflect these developments and it was finally released under the title of *The Old and the New*. The political problems Eisenstein encountered with this project were to recur in all his subsequent film work in the Soviet Union.

In 1929 Eisenstein went abroad, with his assistants Alexandrov and Tisse, ostensibly to study the new medium of sound film. In his "Statement on Sound," published in the summer of 1928, he had warned against the dangers of purely illustrative sound, as in the "talkies," and argued for the application of the techniques of the montage of attractions to produce what he called "orchestral counterpoint." It was to be another ten years before he had the chance to put these ideas into effect.

Eisenstein first visited Western Europe and then travelled to Hollywood to work for Paramount. From the outset he was subjected to a hostile press campaign characterising him as a "red dog" and a Bolshevik. After rejecting several of his film projects, Paramount cancelled his contract. He went on to start filming *Que Viva Mexico!* with funds provided by the Socialist millionaire novelist Upton Sinclair. Eisenstein spent most of 1931 working on the film but Sinclair was not satisfied either with the pace of progress or the escalating cost. Material for three-quarters of the Mexican film had however been shot when the project collapsed in acrimonious exchanges and Eisenstein returned to the Soviet Union in May 1932. He had accepted assurances from Sinclair that the raw footage would be shipped to Moscow so that he could edit it, but this assurance was never honoured.

The Soviet Union that Eisenstein had returned to was significantly different from the country he had left three years earlier. The political and economic changes associated with the first Five-Year Plan had led to concomitant changes in Soviet cinema, which was now run by an Old Bolshevik, Boris Shumyatsky, determined to create a "cinema for the millions." After several abortive projects, including *Moscow*, a history of the capital, *The Black Consul*, which would have starred Paul Robeson, and a film version of Karl Marx's *Das Kapital*, Eisenstein began making his first sound feature, *Bezhin Meadow* in 1935. The film focused on the generational conflict engendered by the collectivisation programme but it too was dogged with

problems and was eventually stopped on the orders of Shumyatsky in March 1937. Eisenstein was forced to confess his alleged errors in public and this submission, together with the dismissal of Shumyatsky in January 1938, enabled him to start filming again.

The result was his most popular film, *Alexander Nevsky*, made in record time and released in 1938, but it was also the film that he regarded as his least successful. Nevertheless, it contains the best, and most famous, illustration of his technique of "orchestral counterpoint" in the sequence of the Battle on the Ice. On the other hand, *Nevsky* to some extent gave Eisenstein the reputation of "court film-maker," particularly after he was awarded the Order of Lenin. It was because of this that, after the signature of the Nazi-Soviet Pact—and the subsequent withdrawal of *Nevsky* from distribution—Eisenstein was asked to direct a new production of Wagner's *Die Walküre* at the Bolshoi Theatre.

When not filming, Eisenstein taught at the State Institute of Cinema, where he had been head of the directing department since his return to the Soviet Union and where he was made professor in January 1937, shortly before the final crisis with *Bezhin Meadow*. He also devoted an increasing amount of time and energy to his theoretical writings but his magnum opus on *Direction*, like his other works on *Mise-en-Scène* and the theory of montage remained unfinished at his death.

His last film, arguably his masterpiece of masterpieces, was also unfinished: filming of the first part of *Ivan the Terrible* was begun in 1943 in Alma-Ata, where the Moscow studios had been evacuated because of the war, and released in 1945, when it was an instant success and earned Eisenstein and his associates the Stalin Prize. While celebrating this award in February 1946, Eisenstein suffered a heart attack, which encouraged his premonitions of an early death at the age of fifty. He threw himself into a flurry of frenzied activity, completing his memoirs and Part 2 of *Ivan* and starting on Part 3. In Part 2, however, the historical parallels between Ivan and Stalin became too obvious and, although completed, the film was not shown until 1958.

Eisenstein died of a second, massive heart attack in February 1948, just past his fiftieth birthday. He died very much under a cloud in his own country, but has since been universally acknowledged as one of cinema's greatest creative geniuses and a towering figure in the culture of the twentieth century. Some of his most important theoretical texts are only now being properly assembled and published, both in the Soviet Union and abroad.

—Richard Taylor

EMSHWILLER, Ed.

American. Born in East Lansing, Michigan, 1925. Educated at University of Michigan, Bachelor of Design, 1949; studied graphics at Ecole des Beaux-Arts, Paris, 1949–50; Art Students League, New York, 1951. As "EMSH," active as painter and illustrator of books and magazines, 1951–64; collaborator on dance films with choreographer Alwin Nikolais, 1963–73; Member of Board of Trustees, American Film Institute, 1969–75; artist in residence, WNET-TV/Channel 13 TV lab, New York, 1972–79; Ford Foundation research fellow at Center for Music Research, University of California at San Diego, 1965; Dean of the School of Film and Video, California Institute of the Arts, Valencia, from 1979 (Provost 1981–85). Recipient: Special Award, Oberhausen Festival, for *Relativity*,

1967; Von Stroheim Prize for most original feature, Mannheim Festival, for *Image, Flesh and Voice*, 1970; INDY Award, Association of Independent Video and Filmmakers, 1976; American Film Institute Maya Deren Award for Independent Film and Video Makers, 1987. Film Distributor: Filmmakers Cooperative, 175 Lexington Ave., New York, NY 10016, U.S.A. Video Distributor: Electronic Arts Intermix, 84 5th Ave., New York, NY 10011, U.S.A. *Died July 1990.*

Films as Director:

1955/58 *Paintings by Ed Emshwiller*
1959 *Dance Chromatic; Transformation*
1960 *Lifelines*
1960/61 *Variable Studies*
1961 *Time of the Heathen* (collaboration with Peter Kass)
1962 *Thanatopsis*
1963 *Totem* (collaboration with Alwin Nikolais); *Scrambles*
1964 *George Dumpson's Place*
1965 *Dlugoszewski Concert; Faces of America*
1966 *Relativity; Art Scene USA*
1967 *Fusion* (collaboration with Alwin Nikolais)
1968 *Project Apollo*
1969 *Image, Flesh and Voice*
1970 *Carol; Film with Three Dancers; Branches*
1971 *Choice Chance Woman Dance; Images* (video)
1972 *Computer Graphics No. 1* (video); *Thermogenesis* (video—short version of *Computer Graphics No. 1*); *Woe Oh Ho No; The Chalk Line; Inside the Gelatin Factory; Scape-Mates* (video)
1973 *Chrysalis* (collaboration with Alwin Nikolais); *Positive Negative Electronic Faces* (video—collaboration with Tony Bannon); *Identities*
1974 *Pilobolus and Joan* (video); *Interrupted Solitude; Crossings and Meetings* (video)
1975 *Inside Edges* (video); *Family Focus* (video)
1976 *New England Visions Past and Future* (video—collaboration with William Thompson); *Short and Very Short Films* (video—compilation of films from 1952–76); *Collisions* (video); *Self Trio* (video)
1977 *Slivers* (video) (multi-monitor installation with partly masked screens); *Sur Faces* (video); *Face Off* (video)
1978 *Dubs* (video)
1979 *Sunstone* (video—computer animation)
1982 *Passes* (video) [4-monitor installation comprised of following videotapes: *Space Passes* (1981); *Vascular Passes* (1982); *Cut Passes* (1981); *Pan Passes* (1982); *Echo Passes* (1979–82)]
1984 *Skin-matrix* (computer graphics with live video)
1986 *Vertigo* (multi-monitor concert piece)
1987 *Hungers* (multi-screen computer graphics/video, collaboration with Morton Subotnick)
1989 *The Blue Wall* (interactive computer graphics and live video installation); *Versions/Stages* (multi-screen concert piece in collaboration with Roger Reynolds); *"2×4"* (multi-media computer animation, video and performance)

Other Films: (partial listing)

1961 *The American Way* (ph)
1963 *Hallelujah the Hills* (Mekas) (ph); *Film Magazine No. 1* (ph); *The Streets of Greenwood* (ph); *The Quiet Takeover* (ph)
1964 *The Opinion Makers* (ph); *The Existentialist* (ph)
1965 *Oysters* (ph)
1967 *Norman Jacobson* (ph)
1972 *Painters Painting* (de Antonio) (ph)

Publications:

By EMSHWILLER: book—

Stan Brakhage, Ed Emshwiller, edited by Rochelle Reed, Washington, D.C., 1973.

By EMSHWILLER: articles—

"A Statement," in *Film Culture* (New York), Summer 1963.
Interview with James Mullins, in *Film Culture* (New York), Fall 1966.
"Cine-dance," in *Dance Perspectives* (New York), Summer 1967.
"Movies," in *New Worlds*, no. 178, 1968.
"Images from the Underground," in *Dialogue*, vol. 4, no. 1, 1971.
"AFI Seminar," in *Dialogue on Film* (Washington, D.C.), January 1973.
Interview with Scott Hammon, in *Afterimage* (Rochester, New York), September 1974.
Article, in *Directing the Film: Film Directors on Their Art* by Eric Sherman, Washington, D.C., 1976.
"Image Maker Meets Video, or, Psyche to Physics and Back," in *The New Television* edited by Douglas Davis and Allison Simmons, Cambridge, Massachusetts, 1977.
Interview with G. Jamison, in *Filmmakers Newsletter* (Ward Hill, Massachusetts), November 1977.
Interview with Melanie Mitzner, in *Video Systems*, February 1983.
Interview with R. Allezaud, in *Cinéma* (Paris), March 1984.
Interview with Gene Youngblood, in *Send*, Spring 1985.

On EMSHWILLER: books—

Curtis, David, *Experimental Cinema*, New York, 1971.
Mekas, Jonas, *Movie Journal: The Rise of the New American Cinema, 1959–1971*, New York, 1972.
Staples, Don, editor, *The American Cinema*, New York, 1981.

On EMSHWILLER: articles—

Mancia, Adrienne, and Willard Van Dyke, "Four Artists as Filmmakers," in *Art in America* (New York), January/February 1967.
Whitehall, Richard, "The Films of Ed Emshwiller," in *Film Quarterly* (Berkeley), Spring 1967.
Whitehall, Richard, "Relativity Re-Affirms Emshwiller's Stature," in *Filmmakers Newsletter* (Ward Hill, Massachusetts), November 1967.
Mekas, Jonas, in the *Village Voice* (New York), 25 June 1970.
Eisenhauer, Letty Lou, "Ed Emshwiller: Beginnings," in *Art and Artists* (London), March 1974.
Belloir, Dominique, in *Cahiers du Cinéma* (Paris), no. 10, 1981.
Ancona, Victor, "Combining Inner and Outer Landscapes," in *Videography*, September 1983.

*   *   *

Ed Emshwiller's first major film was *Dance Chromatic* which, like *Transformations* and *Life Lines*, was an admixture of animated and live action images. By the early 1970's he had completed over 20 works, many of them very famous and—for the experimental film genre—very successful. His film *Relativity*, made under a Ford Grant, displays the fine craftsmanship and technical precision that helped assure an international appeal and repeated awards for his various productions. His concerns during this early period were diverse, ranging from animated graphics through dance films to live action experimental constructions—all characterized by compositional and cinematographic virtuosity that made them mainstays of the American underground film. During the same period he was active as cinematographer on other artists' shorts, features, and documentaries. Further, Emshwiller himself produced or collaborated on many mixed-media productions (e.g. *Split 5th*, with the Denver Symphony) which were quite innovative for the time.

From the early 1970's Emshwiller extended his skill in cinematographic construction to electronic image-making. His *Images 1971* Whitney Museum video exhibition was followed by over a dozen experimental video projects that augment his continued experimental film production. Such fluency with diverse technological resources has always marked Emshwiller's career. But because changes in technology are invariably structurally consequential, his more recent video productions—often predicated upon computer generated or synthesized graphics—resulted in essential differences from his earlier film work. The silent three-minute *Sunstone* of 1980, an eight-month endeavor employing a digital computer, is a case in point. With its post-structuralist attention to cathode-ray tube dimensionality and to movement and radiated color, *Sunstone* is so distinct from the limbo-lighting and cinematic superimpositions of *Dance Chromatic* that audiences might find difficulty in assigning both constructions to the same author.

Thus Emshwiller's personal evolution from painter's graphics, through film and mixed media, into video provides scholars with a fine microcosmic example of progressions marking the larger technostructural transformation of experimental film as a historical genre.

—Edward S. Small

EPSTEIN, Jean.

French. Born in Warsaw, 25 March 1897. Educated at Collège Francais, Villa Saint-Jean, Fribourg; Ecole Centrale, Lyons, degree in medicine, 1916. Met Auguste Lumière, 1916; founder of revue, *Le Promenoir*, 1920; hired as editor by Editions de la Sirène, 1921; directed first film, *Pasteur*, for Jean Benoit-Levy, 1922; signed to Pathé, 1923; joined Alexandre Kamenska's Films Albatros, 1924; set up Les Films Jean Epstein, 1926; with sister, scenarist Marie Epstein, captured by Gestapo, saved from deportation through intervention of friends and Red Cross, early 1940's; taught at IDHEC after the war. *Died of cerebral hemorrhage, in Paris, 3 April 1953.*

Films as Director:

1922   *Pasteur; Les Vendanges*
1923   *L'Auberge rouge* (+ sc); *Coeur fidèle* (+ sc); *La Montagne infidèle*; *La Belle Nivernaise* (+ sc)
1924   *Le Lion des Mogols* (+ adaptation); *L'Affiche*; *La Goutte de sang* (Mariaud, uncredited d)
1925   *Le Double Amour*; *Les Aventures de Robert Macaire*
1926   *Mauprat* (+ pr); *Au pays de George Sand* (+ pr)
1927   *Six et demi onze* (+ pr); *La Glace a trois faces* (+ pr)
1928   *La Chute de la maison Usher* (+ pr)
1929   *Finis terrae* (+ sc); *Sa Tête* (+ sc)
1930   *Le Pas de la mule* (+ pr)
1931   *Mor-Vran* (*La Mer des corbeaux*) (+ pr); *Notre-Dame de Paris* (+ pr); *La Chanson des peupliers* (+ pr); *Le Cor* (+ pr)
1932   *L'Or des mers* (+ sc); *Les Berceaux* (+ pr); *La Villanelle des Rubans* (+ pr); *Le Vieux Chaland* (+ pr)
1933   *L'Homme a l'Hispano* (+ sc, pr); *La Chatelaine du Liban* (+ sc, pr)
1934   *Chanson d'armor* (+ pr, adaptation); *La Vie d'un grand journal* (+ pr)
1936   *Coeur de Gueux* (+ pr, adaptation); *La Bretagne* (+ pr); *La Bourgogne* (+ pr)
1937   *Vive la vie* (+ pr); *La Femme du bout de monde* (+ pr, sc)
1938   *Les Batisseurs* (+ pr); *Eau vive* (+ pr, sc)
1939   *Arteres de France* (+ pr); *La Charrette fantôme* (Duvivier) (d superimpositions and special photographic effects)
1947   *Le Tempestaire* (+ pr, sc)
1948   *Les Feux de la mer* (+ pr); *La Bataille de l'eau lourde* (*Kampen om tungtvannet*) (Marin and Vibe-Muller; d prologue)

Other Film:

1921   *Le Tonnerre* (Delluc) (asst d)

Publications:

By EPSTEIN: books—

Bonjour cinéma, Paris, 1921.
La Poésie d'aujourd'hui—Un nouvel état d'intelligence, Paris, 1921.
La Lyrosophie, Paris, 1922.
Le Cinématographe vu de l'Etna, Paris, 1926.
L'Or des mers, Valois, 1932.
Les Recteurs et la sirène, Paris, 1934.
Photogénie de l'impondérable, Paris, 1935.
L'Intelligence d'une machine, Paris, 1946.
Le Cinéma du diable, Paris, 1947.
Esprit de cinéma, Paris, 1955.

By EPSTEIN: articles—

"Jean Epstein nous parle de ses projets et du film parlant," interview with Pierre Leprohon, in *Pour vous* (Paris), 17 October 1929.
Article in *Cahiers du Cinéma* (Paris), June 1953.

On EPSTEIN: books—

Gawrak, Zbigniew, *Jan Epstein*, Warsaw, 1962.
Leprohon, Pierre, *Jean Epstein*, Paris, 1964.

On EPSTEIN: articles—

Leprohon, Pierre, "Un Poète de l'image," in *Cinémonde* (Paris), 28 February 1929.
Wunscher, Catherine, "Jean Epstein," in *Sight and Sound* (London), October/December 1953.
"Epstein Issue" of *Cinemages* (New York), edited by Gideon Bachmann, vol. 2, 1955.
Toussenot, R., "Souvenirs en l'honneur de Jean Epstein," in *L'Age Nouveau* (Paris), October 1956.
Haudiquet, Philippe, "Epstein," in *Anthologie du Cinéma*, vol. 2, Paris, 1967.
"Jean Epstein," in *Film Dope* (London), March 1978.
"Jean Epstein," in *Travelling* (Lausanne), Summer 1979.
"Cinema Rising: Epstein in the Twenties," special section in *Afterimage* (Rochester), no.10, 1981.
"Cine-mystique," in *Millenium Film Journal* (New York), Fall 1981/Winter 1982.
"A propos de Jean Epstein," in *Avant-Scène du Cinéma* (Paris), October 1983.

*   *   *

Jean Epstein belongs to the generation of 1920's French filmmakers who were drawn to the cinema from early interest in literature by the impact of the Hollywood productions of Griffith, Chaplin, and Ince. Gifted with a precocious intelligence, Epstein had already published books on literature, philosophy, and the cinema when he made his debut as a filmmaker with a documentary on Pasteur in 1922 at the age of only 25. Three fictional features in the following year, including *Coeur fidèle* which contains virtuoso passages to rank with the work of Gance and L'Herbier, put him in the forefront of French avant-garde filmmaking.

The four films he made during 1925–26 for the Albatros company run by the Russian emigré Alexandre Kamenka include two, *L'Affiche* and *Le Double Amour*, from scripts by Jean's sister Marie Epstein. The spectacular *Le Lion des Mogols* from a preposterous script by its star, the great actor Ivan Mosjoukine, was followed by *Les Aventures de Robert Macaire*, an adaptation of the play parodied by Frédéric Lemaître in Carné's *Les Enfants du paradis*. None of these are generally considered to be among Epstein's best work, but they established him as a director after the controversies which had surrounded the showings of *Coeur fidèle*, and enabled him to set up his own production company in 1926.

The films which he both produced and directed are very varied. He began with two films in which his own artistic aspirations were balanced by the demands of commercial popularity: an adaption of George Sand's novel, *Mauprat*, which had

Jean Epstein: *La Chute de la maison Usher*

formed part of his childhood reading, and *Six et demi onze*, again from a script by his sister. But the last two films of Les Productions Jean Epstein were resolutely independent works. The short feature *La Glace à trois faces* is remarkable for its formal pattern which looks forward to experiments in narrative structure of a kind which were still striking to audiences 30 years later when Alain Resnais made *Hiroshima mon amour*. Even more accomplished in terms of acting and setting, and as intriguing in terms of narrative, is Epstein's atmospheric evocation of the dark world of Edgar Allan Poe, *La Chute de la maison Usher*. This tale of love, art, and madness is told in a marvellously controlled style which makes extensive use of slow motion and multiple superimposition. Just as the hero refuses to accept the division of life and death and, through the effort of will, summons back the woman he has killed through devotion to his art, so too Epstein's film creates a universe where castle and forest, interior and exterior interpenetrate.

After this masterly evocation of a world of Northern imagination, which can rank with Dreyer's *Vampyr* and is a reminder of Epstein's part-Polish ancestry, the director largely withdrew from the world of Parisian film production. With only occasional forays into commercial filmmaking, Epstein devoted much of his efforts over the 18 years that spread from the silent *Finis terrae* in 1929 to the short *Le Tempestaire* in 1947 to a masterly series of semi-documentary evocations of the Breton countryside and seascape.

Epstein is a complex and uncompromising figure whose filmmaking was accompanied by a constant theoretical concern with his chosen medium. If the central concept of his 1930's writing—*La photogénie*—remains not merely undefined but undefinable, and he makes recourse to notions of a magical or mystical essence of cinema unfortunately typical of the period, his theoretical work remains of great interest. The republication of his complete works, *Ecrits sur le Cinéma*, in 1974–75, demonstrated the modernity and continuing interest of his explorations of key aspects of the relationship between the spectator and the screen.

—Roy Armes

FÁBRI, Zoltan.

Hungarian. Born in Budapest, 1917. Educated at Academy of Fine Arts and Academy of Dramatic and Film Art, Budapest, diploma 1941. Stage designer, actor and director, interned as prisoner of war, 1941–45; at Artists Theatre, Budapest, 1945–49; artistic director of Hunnia Studios, 1949; made first feature, 1952; began collaboration with cameraman György Illés on *Húsz óra*, 1964. President of Union of Hungarian Cinema and Television Artists, and Professor at Academy of Dramatic and Cinema Arts, Budapest. Recipient: Special Jury Prize, Moscow Festival, for *141 perc a Befejezetlen mondatból*, 1975; Grand Prize, Moscow Festival, for *Az ötödik pecsét*, 1977.

Films as Director:

1951	*Gyarmat a föld alatt* [Colony Beneath the Earth] (co-d)
1952	*Vihar* (*Storm*)
1954	*Életjel* (*Vierzehn Menschenleben*) [Life Signs]
1955	*Körhinta* (*Merry-Go-Round, Karussell*) (+ co-sc, art d)
1956	*Hannibál tanár úr* (*Professor Hannibal*) (+ co-sc)
1957	*Bolond április* (*Summer Clouds*) [Crazy April]; *Édes Anna* (*Anna, Schuldig?*) (+ co-sc)
1959	*Duvad* (*The Brute, Das Scheusal*) (+ sc)
1961	*Két félidö a pokolban* (*The Last Goal*) (+ art d)
1963	*Nappali sötétség* (*Darkness in Daytime, Dunkel bei Tageslicht*) (+ sc, art d)
1964	*Húsz óra* (*Twenty Hours*)
1965	*Vizivárosi nyár* (*A Hard Summer*) (for TV)
1967	*Utószezon* (*Late Season*)
1968	*A Pál utcai fiúk* (*The Boys of Paul Street*) (+ co-sc)
1969	*Isten hozta, örnagy úr!* (*The Toth Family*) (+ co-sc)
1971	*Hangyaboly* (+ co-sc)
1973	*Plusz mínusz egy nap* (*One Day More, One Day Less*)
1974	*141 perc a Befejezetlen mondatból* (*141 Minutes from the Unfinished Sentence*) (+ co-sc)
1976	*Az ötödik pecsét* (*The Fifth Seal*) (+ sc)
1977	*Magyarok* (*The Hungarians*) (+ sc)
1979	*Fábián Bálint találkozása Istennel* (*Balint Fabian Meets God*) (+ sc)
1981	*Requiem*

Publications:

By FÁBRI: articles—

Interview with M. Ember in *Filmkultura* (Budapest), April 1975.
"Az emberi méltóság védelme foglalkoztat," in *Filmkultura* (Budapest), September/October 1977.
"Bálint Fábián's Encounter with God," in *Hungarofilm Bulletin* (Budapest), no. 4, 1979.

On FÁBRI: articles—

Biographical note, in *International Film Guide*, London, 1965.
Hanisch, Michael, "Zoltán Fábri," in *Regiestühle*, Berlin, 1972.

Biofilmography in *Film und Fernsehen* (Berlin), no. 3, 1976.
Nemes, K., "Egy életmü—a társadalom fejlödésében," in *Filmkultura* (Budapest), September/October 1977.
Revy, E., in *Filmkultura* (Budapest), March/April 1984.

On FÁBRI: films—

Nádassy, László, director, *Fábri portré*, 1980.

* * *

Having been a theatre director and designer, Zoltán Fábri began to work in films in 1950 and quickly discovered his true vocation. In 1952 he made his first film, *Vihar*, a drama about the collectivization of a village. *Körhinta*, presented at Cannes in 1956, was astonishing for the beauty of its images and feelings, and for the appearance of a young actress, Mari Töröcsik, whom he picked again two years later for his film *Édes Anna*.

Also in 1956 he made *Hannibál tanár úr*, the tragedy of a man broken by the pressure of his conformist milieu, with the outstanding Ernö Szabó in the main role. This film, honored at the Karlovy Vary Festival in 1957, raised the problem of the heritage of a fascist past and indirectly attacked the oppressive atmosphere of the Stalinist period. Following the political events which supervened in 1956, it was excluded from Hungarian screens.

In all of his work, nourished by Hungarian literature, Fábri deals with moral problems bound up with the history of his country, making use of a vigorous realism. Besides the meticulous composition of his narratives, and precise evocation of atmosphere and the milieu where they unfold, it's necessary to underline the importance given to his work with actors and his own participation in the creation of some set designs.

Following a drama showing the present-day problems of life in the countryside, *Dúvad*, Fábri continued with *Két félidö a pokolban*, set in a concentration camp. The moral behavior of men in times of crisis, the confrontation of ideas and of characters, of cowardice and heroism, totally absorb him and are at the heart of all his films. In *Húsz óra*, made in 1964, he uses an investigation undertaken by a journalist as the starting point for a brilliant reflection on the impact in Hungary of political events in the recent past, confirming anew his abilities as an analyst and director. For this film he was again able to engage György Illés as cameraman, and they have continued a constant collaboration since.

Having given the Hungarian cinema an international audience, Fábri in 1968 directed a Hungarian-American coproduction, *The Boys of Paul Street*, faithfully adapted from the popular novel by Ferenc Molnár, a touching story of childhood heroism. After *Hangyaboly*, a drama that unfolds behind the walls of a convent, with Mari Töröcsik, he made *141 perc a Befejezetlen mondatból*, then returned to a moral analysis of the wartime period with *Az ötödik pecsét*, a work of deep psychological insight, which received the Grand Prize at the

Zoltan Fábri: *Hannibál tanár úr*

Moscow Festival in 1977 and remains one of the director's best films. With *Magyarok*, and its sequel *Fábián Bálint találkozása Istennel*, he traces in epic style and more conventional form the fate of the peasants in the period between the wars. In *Requiem*, he sets against the drama of a young girl the tragic consequences of the postwar political dislocations. In attempting thus to renew his method, he succeeds once again in powerfully expressing the message of a great moralist.

Having received the Kossuth Prize three times, as well as being President of the Union of Hungarian Cinema and Television Artists, and professor at Budapest's Academy of Dramatic and Cinema Arts, Fábri is a key figure of the Hungarian cinema.

—Karel Tabery

FASSBINDER, Rainer Werner.

German. Born in Bad Wörishofen, Bavaria, 31 May 1946. Educated at the Rudolf Steiner School and Secondary schools in Augsburg and Munich until 1964; studied acting at Fridl-Leonhard Studio, Munich. Married Ingrid Caven, 1970 (divorced). Worked as decorator and in archives of *Süddeutsche Zeitung*, Munich, 1964–66; failed entrance exam to West Berlin Film and Television Academy, 1965; joined *action-theater*, Munich, with Hanna Schygulla, 1967; 1st original play produced (*Katzelmacher*), *action-theater* closed in May, co-founded *anti-theater*, 1968; began making films with members of *anti-theater*, 1969; worked in German theatre and radio, and as actor, 1969–82; founder, Tango Film, independent company, 1971; with Kurt Raab and Roland Petri, took over Theater am Turm (TAT), Frankfurt, 1974; TAT project failed, returned to Munich to concentrate on film work, 1975. Recipient: Golden Bear, Berlin Festival, for *Die Sehnsucht der Veronika Voss*, 1982. *Died, probably of overdose of sleeping pills and cocaine, in Munich, 10 June 1982.*

Films as Director:
(under pseudonym Franz Walsch):

1965   *Der Stadtstreicher* (*The City Tramp*) (+ sc, ed, uncredited pr, role)
1966   *Das kleine Chaos* (*The Little Chaos*) (+ sc, ed, role, uncredited pr)
1969   *Liebe ist kälter als der Tod* (*Love is Colder than Death*) (+ sc, ed, role as Franz, uncredited pr); *Katzelmacher* (+ sc, ed, art d, role as Jorgos, uncredited pr); *Götter der Pest* (*Gods of the Plague*) (+ sc, ed, role as Porno Buyer, uncredited pr); *Warum läuft Herr R amok?* (*Why Does Herr R Run Amok?*) (co-d, co-sc, co-ed, uncredited pr)
1970   *Rio das Mortes* (+ sc, role as Discotheque-goer); *Whity* (+ sc, co-ed, role as Guest in Saloon, uncredited pr); *Die Niklashauser Fahrt* (*The Niklashausen Journey*) (co-d, co-sc, co-ed, role as Black Monk, uncredited pr); *Der*

amerikanische Soldat (*The American Soldier*) (sc, song, role as Franz); *Warnung vor einer heiligen Nutte* (*Beware of a Holy Whore*) (+ co-ed, sc, role as Sascha, uncredited pr)

(under real name):

1971   *Pioniere in Ingolstadt* (*Pioneers in Ingolstadt*) (+ sc, uncredited pr); *Das Kaffeehaus* (*The Coffee House*) (for TV) (+ sc, uncredited pr); *Der Händler der vier Jahreszeiten* (*The Merchant of the Four Seasons*) (+ sc, role as Zucker, uncredited pr).

1972   *Die bitteren Tränen der Petra von Kant* (*The Bitter Tears of Petra von Kant*) (+ sc, des, uncredited pr); *Wildwechsel* (*Wild Game*) (+ sc, uncredited pr); *Acht Stunden sind kein Tag* (*Eight Hours Don't Make a Day*) (+ sc, uncredited pr) (shown on German television in 5 monthly segments, each between 88 and 101 min long); *Bremer Freiheit* ("*Bremen Freedom*") (for TV) (+ sc, uncredited pr)

1973   *Welt am Draht* (*World on a Wire*) (in 2 parts) (+ co-sc, uncredited pr); **Angst essen Seele auf (Fear Eats the Soul)** (+ sc, des, uncredited pr); *Martha* (+ sc, uncredited pr); *Nora Helmer* (for TV) (+ sc, uncredited pr)

1974   *Fontane Effi Briest* (*Effi Briest*) (+ sc, role as narrator, uncredited pr); *Faustrecht der Freiheit* (*Fox*) (+ co-sc, role as Franz Biberkopf—'Fox', uncredited pr); *Wie ein Vogel auf dem Draht* ("*Like a Bird on a Wire*") (for TV) (+ sc, uncredited pr)

1975   *Mutter Küsters Fahrt zum Himmel* (*Mother Küster's Trip to Heaven*) (+ co-sc, uncredited pr); *Angst vor der Angst* (*Fear of Fear*) (+ sc, uncredited pr)

1976   *Ich will doch nur, dass Ihr mich liebt* (*I Only Want You to Love Me*) (+ sc, uncredited pr); *Satansbraten* (*Satan's Brew*) (+ sc, uncredited pr); *Chinesisches Roulette* (*Chinese Roulette*) (+ sc, co-pr)

1977   *Bolwieser* (+ sc, uncredited pr); *Frauen in New York* (*Women in New York*); *Eine Reise ins Licht* (*Despair*)

1978   episode of *Deutschland im Herbst* (*Germany in Autumn*) (+ sc, role, uncredited pr); **Die Ehe der Maria Braun (The Marriage of Maria Braun)** (+ story); *In einem Jahr mit dreizehn Monden* (*In a Year with Thirteen Moons*) (+ sc, ph, uncredited pr)

1979   *Die dritte Generation* (*The Third Generation*) (+ sc, ph, uncredited pr)

1980   *Berlin Alexanderplatz* (for TV, in 13 episodes with epilogue) (+ sc, ph, role as himself in dream sequence, uncredited pr); *Lili Marleen* (+ sc, ph, uncredited pr)

1981   **Lola** (+ sc, ph, uncredited pr); *Theater in Trance* (TV documentary) (+ commentary)

1982   *Die Sehnsucht der Veronika Voss* (*Veronika Voss*) (+ sc, uncredited pr, ph); *Querelle* (+ sc, ph, uncredited pr)

Other Films:

1967   *Tony Freunde* (Vasil) (role as Mallard)
1968   *Der Bräutigam, die Komödiantin und der Zuhalter* (*The Bridegroom, the Comedienne and the Pimp*) (Straub) (role as the pimp)
1969   *Fernes Jamaica* (*Distant Jamaica*) (Moland) (sc); *Alarm* (Lemmel) (role as the man in uniform); *Al Capone im deutschen Wald* (Wirth) (role as Heini); *Baal* (Schlöndorff) (role as Baal); *Frei bis zum nächsten Mal* (Köberle) (role as the mechanic)
1970   *Matthias Kneissl* (Hauff) (role as Flecklbauer); *Der plötzliche Reichtum der armen Leute von Kombach* (Schlöndorff) (role as a peasant); *Supergirl* (Thome) (role as man who looks through window)
1973   *Zärtlichkeit der Wölfe* (Lommel) (role as Wittkowski)
1974   *1 Berlin-Harlem* (Lambert) (role as himself)
1976   *Schatten der Engel* (*Shadow of Angels*) (Schmid) (sc, role as Raoul, the pimp)
1978   *Bourbon Street Blues* (Sirk, Schonherr, and Tilman) (role)
1980   *Lili Marleen* (Weisenborn) (role)

Publications:

By FASSBINDER: books—

Antitheater, Frankfurt, 1973.
Antitheater 2, Frankfurt, 1974.
Stücke 3, Munich, 1978.
Querelle Filmbuch, Munich 1982.
Film Befreien den Kopf: Essays und Arbeitsnotizen, edited by Michael Toteburg, Frankfurt, 1984.
Die Anarchie der Phantasie: Gesprache und Interviews, edited by Michael Toteburg, Frankfurt, 1986.
The Marriage of Maria Braun, edited by Joyce Rheuban, New Brunswick, New Jersey, 1986.
Die Kinofilme 1, Munich, 1987.

By FASSBINDER: articles—

"*Liebe ist kälter als der Tod*," in *Film* (London), no. 8, 1969.
Interview in *Filmkritik* (Munich), August 1969.
"Imitation of Life: On the Films of Douglas Sirk," in *Douglas Sirk*, edited by Mulvey and Halliday, Edinburgh, 1972.
Interview in *Sight and Sound* (London), Winter 1974/75.
Interview in *Film Comment* (New York), November/December 1975.
"Insects in a Glass Case," in *Sight and Sound* (London), Autumn 1976.
Interview in *Cineaste* (New York), Autumn 1977.
"Ich bin das Gluck dieser Erde. Ach war' das schon wenn's so ware," an interview with B. Steinborn and R. von Naso, in *Filmfaust* (Frankfurt), April–May 1982.
Interview with P. Pawlikowski, in *Stills* (London), November/December 1982.

On FASSBINDER: books—

Limmer, Wolfgang, *Fassbinder*, Munich, 1973.
Jansen, Peter, and Wolfram Schütte, editors, *Reihe Film 2: Rainer Werner Fassbinder*, Munich, 1979.
Eckhardt, Bernd, *Rainer Werner Fassbinder: In 17 jahren 42 Filme—Stationen eines Leben fur den Deutschen Film*, Munich, 1982.
Iden, Peter, and others, *Rainer Werner Fassbinder*, Munich, 1982.
Raab, Kurt, and Karsten Peters, *Die Sehnsucht des Rainer Werner Fassbinder*, Munich, 1982.
Foss, Paul, editor, *Fassbinder in Review*, Sydney, 1983.
Hayman, Ronald, *Fassbinder: Filmmaker*, London, 1984.
Phillips, Klaus, *New German Filmmakers: From Oberhausen through the 1970's*, New York, 1984.
Katz, Robert, and Peter Berling, *Love is Colder than Death: The Life and Times of Rainer Werner Fassbinder*, London, 1987.
Elsaesser, Thomas, *New German Cinema: A History*, London, 1989.
Lardeau, Yann, *Rainer Werner Fassbinder*, Paris, 1990.

On FASSBINDER: articles—

Wilson, David, "Anti-Cinema: Rainer Werner Fassbinder," in *Sight and Sound* (London), no. 2, 1972.
"Fassbinder and Sirk," in *Film Comment* (New York), November/December 1975.
"Gay Men and Film Section," in *Jump Cut* (Berkeley), no. 16, 1977.
"Fassbinder Issue" of *October* (Cambridge, Massachusetts), Summer 1982.
Hoberman, J., "Explorations," in *American Film* (Washington, D.C.), September 1982.
Dossier on Fassbinder, in *Cinéma* (Paris), July–August 1982.
Roud, Richard, "Biter Bit," in *Sight and Sound* (London), Autumn 1982.
Riley, B., and H. Kennedy, obituaries, in *Film Comment* (New York), September/October 1982.
MacBean, J.R., "The Success and Failure of Rainer Werner Fassbinder," in *Sight and Sound* (London), Winter 1982/83.
MacBean, J.R., "The Cinema as Self Portrait: The Final Films of R.W. Fassbinder," in *Cineaste* (New York), vol. 12, no. 4, 1983.
Sirk, Douglas, "Obituary for Rainer Werner Fassbinder," in *Framework* (Norwich), no. 20, 1983.
Erffmeyer, T.E., "I only want you to love me: Fassbinder, melodrama and Brechtian form," in *Journal of University Film Association* (Carbondale, Illinois), Winter 1983.

Rainer Werner Fassbinder

Feinstein, Herbert, "BRD 1–2–3: Fassbinder's Postwar trilogy and the Spectacle," in *Cinema Journal* (Champaign, Illinois), Fall 1983.

Katz, Robert, "Fear Ate His Soul," in *American Film* (Washington, D.C.), July/August 1985.

Krasnova, G., "Über Rainer Werner Fassbinder," in *Beiträge zur Film und Fernsehwissenschaft* (Berlin), vol. 26, no. 2, 1985.

On FASSBINDER: films—

von Mengershausen, Joachim, *Ende einer Kommune*, West Germany, 1970.

Ballhaus, Michael, and Dietmar Buchmann, *Fassbinder produziert: Film Nr. 8*, West Germany, 1971.

Wiebel, Martin, and Ludwig Metzger, *Glashaus-TV Intern*, West Germany, 1973.

Plater, Edward M.V., "The Externalization of the Protagonist's Mind in Fassbinder's *Despair*," in *Film Criticism* (Meadville, Pennsylvania), vol. 11, no. 3, 1987.

* * *

Rainer Werner Fassbinder was the leading member of a group of second-generation, alternative filmmakers in West Germany, the first consisting of Alexander Kluge and others who in 1962 drafted the Oberhausen Manifesto, initiating what has come to be called the "New German Cinema." Fassbinder's most distinguishing trait within the tradition of "counter-cinema," aside from his reputation for rendering filmically fragments of the new left ideology of the 1960's, was his modification of the conventions of political cinema initiated in the 1920's and subsequently tailored to modern conditions of Hol-lywood cinema, to a greater degree than Godard, who is credited with using these principles as content for filmic essays on narrative.

In an interview in 1971 Fassbinder asserted what has come to represent his most convincing justification for his innovative attachment to story: "The American cinema is the only one I can take really seriously, because it's the only one that has really reached an audience. German cinema used to do so, before 1933, and of course there are individual directors in other countries who are in touch with their audiences. But American cinema has generally had the happiest relationship with its audience, and that is because it doesn't try to be 'art.' Its narrative style is not so complicated or artificial. Well, of course it's artificial, but not 'artistic.' "

This concern with narrative and popular expression (some of his productions recall the good storytelling habits of Renoir) was evident early in the theatrical beginnings of his career, when he forged an aesthetic that could safely be labeled a creative synthesis of Brecht and Artaud oriented toward the persuasion of larger audiences. This began with a turn to the stage in 1967, having finished his secondary school training in 1964 in Augsburg and Munich. He joined the Action-Theater in Munich, with Hanna Schygulla whom he had met in acting school. After producing his first original play in 1968, the Action-Theater was closed by the police in May of that year, whereupon he founded the "anti-teater," a venture loosely organized around the tenets of Brechtian theater translated into terms alluring for contemporary audiences. Though the 1969 *Liebe ist kälter als der Tod* marks the effective beginning of his feature film career (*Der Stadtsreicher* and *Das kleine Chaos* constituting minor efforts), he was to maintain an intermittent foothold in the theater all the way until his premature death, working in various productions throughout Germany as well as producing a number of radio plays in the early 1970's. The stint with "anti-teater" was followed by the assuming of directorial control, with Kurt Raab and Roland Petri, over the Theater am Turm (TAT) of Frankfurt in 1974, and the founding of Albatross Productions for coproductions in 1975.

When TAT failed, Fassbinder became less involved in the theater, but a trace of his interest always remained in the form of his frequent appearances in his own films. In fact, out of the more than forty feature films produced during his lifetime there have only been a handful or so where Fassbinder has not appeared in one way or another, and he has had a major role in at least ten of them.

Fassbinder's mixing together of Hollywood and avantgarde forms took a variety of turns throughout his brief career. In the films made during the time of the peak of 1960's activism in Germany—specifically *Katzelmacher, Liebe ist kälter als der Tod, Götter der Pest,* and *Warum läuft Herr R. Amok?*—theatrical conventions, principally those derived from his Brechtian training, join forces with a "minimalist" aesthetic and the indigenous energies of the *Heimatfilm* to portray such sensitive issues as the foreign worker problem, contradictions within supposedly revolutionary youth culture, and concerns of national identity. These early "filmed theater" pieces, inevitably conforming to a static, long-take style because of a dearth of funding, tended to resemble parables or fables in their brevity and moral, didactic structuring. As funding from the Government increased proportionate to his success, the popular forms associated with Hollywood became his models. His output from 1970 through the apocalyptic events of October 1977 (the culmination of a series of terrorists actions in Hans-Martin Schleyer's death, etc.) is an exploration of the forms of melodrama and the family romance as a way to place social issues within the frame of sexual politics. *Whity, Der Händler der vier Jahreszeiten, Die bitteren Tränen der Petra von Kant, Martha, Faustrecht der Freiheit,* and *Frauen in New York* are perhaps the most prominent examples. A self-reflexive pastiche of the gangster film is evident as well in *Der amerikanische Soldat.* This attention to the mediation of other forms ultimately began to assume the direction of a critique of the "art film": *Warnung vor einer heiligen Nutte,* an update of *8¹/₂*; *Satansbraten,* a comment on aesthetics and politics around the figure of Stephen George; and *Chinesisches Roulette,* a parody concerning an inbred aristocracy.

The concern with the continuation of fascism into the present day receives some attention in this period (specifically in *Wildwechsel, Despair,* and *Bolwieser*), but it becomes the dominant structuring motivation in the final period, 1977–82. Here there is a kind of epic recombination of all earlier innovations in service of an understanding of fascism and its implications for the immediate postwar generation. Fassbinder's segment in *Deutschland im Herbst* (a collective endeavor of many German intellectuals and filmmakers) inaugurates this period. It and *Die Ehe der Maria Braun, Lili Marleen, Lola,* and *Die Sehnsucht der Veronika Voss* may be seen as a portrayal of the consolidation of German society to conform to the "American Model" of social and economic development. *In einem Jahr mit 13 Monden, Berlin Alexanderplatz,* and *Querelle* are depictions of the crisis in sexual identity, and the criminal and counter-cultural worlds associated with that process, in relation to "capitalism in crisis." *Die dritte Generation* is a kind of cynical summation of the German new left in the wake of a decade of terrorist activities. This final phase, per-

haps Fassbinder's most brilliant cinematically, will be the one given the greatest critical attention in future years. It is the one which evinces the keenest awareness of the intellectual spaces traversed in Germany since the years of fascism (and especially since the mid-1960's), and the one as well which reveals the most effective assimilation of the heritage of forms associated with art and political cinema.

—John O'Kane

FEJÖS, Paul.

Hungarian. Born Pál Fejös in Budapest, 24 January 1897; became U.S. citizen, 1930. Educated at school in Veszprem and at Kecskemet; studied medicine. Served on Italian front, organized plays for soldiers, 1914–18; set designer for opera and for Orient-Film studios, 1918; director for Studio Mobil, from 1919; travelled across Europe, worked with Max Reinhardt and Fritz Lang, left for U.S.A., 1923; medical research assistant at Rockefeller Institute, moved to Hollywood, 1926; signed to Universal, 1928; with cameraman Hal Mohr, designed crane allowing great camera mobility, 1929; signed to MGM, 1930; invited to Paris by Pierre Braunberger, 1931; director for Films Osso in Hungary, broke MGM contract, 1932; signed to Nordisk Films, 1934; went to Madagascar, 1935–36; signed to Svensk Filmindustri, travelled to Indonesia and New Guinea, 1937; director of Viking Fund, New York, 1941; later director of Wenner-Gren Foundation for Anthropological Research. *Died in New York, 23 April 1963.*

Films as Director:
(in Hungary):

1920 *Pan; Lidércnyomás (Nightmare, Hallucination, Lord Arthur Saville's Crime)* (+ co-sc); *Ujraélök (Reincarnation); Jóslat (Prophecy)*
1921 *Fekete Kapitany (The Black Captain); Arsén Lupin utolsó kalandja (The Last Adventure of Arsène Lupin)*
1922 *Szenzáció (Sensation)*
1923 *Egri csillagok (The Stars of Eger)* (+ sc, incomplete)

(in U.S.):

1928 *The Last Moment (Le Dernier Moment)* (+ sc, ed); *Lonesome (Solitude)*
1929 *Broadway; The Last Performance* (working title: "Erik the Great")
1930 *Captain of the Guard (Marseillaise)* (co-d, uncredited); *Menschen hinter Gittern* (German version of George Hill's *The Big House*)

(in France):

1931 *Fantômas* (+ co-sc)

(in Hungary):

1932 *Tavaszi zápor (Marie, légende hongroise, Une Histoire d'amour)* (+ co-sc); *Itél a Balaton (Storm at Balaton)*

(in Austria):

1933 *Sonnenstrahl (Gardez le sourire)* (+ co-pr, co-sc); *Frühlingsstimmen (Les Voix du printemps)*

(in Denmark):

1934 *Flugten fra millionerne (Flight from the Millions, Les Millions en fuite)* (+ sc)
1935 *Fange nr. 1 (Prisoner No. 1)* (+ co-sc); *Det gyldne Smil (The Golden Smile, Le Sourire d'or)* (+ sc)

Paul Fejös: *The Last Moment*

(in Madagascar):

1935/36   *Svarta Horisonter* (*Horizons noirs*) series: 1. *Danstävlingen
i Esira* (*Dance Contest in Esira*); 2. *Skönhetsvård i djungeln*
(*Beauty Care in the Jungle*); 3. *Världens mest Användbara
Träd* (*The Most Useful Tree in the World*); 4. *Djungeldansen*
(*Jungle Dance*); 5. *Havets Djävul* (*The Sea Devil*); 6. *Våra
Faders Gravar* (*Tombs of Our Ancestors*)

(in Indonesia and New Guinea):

1937/38   *Stammen Lever an* (*The Tribe Lives On*); *Bambuå påldern
på Mentawei* (*The Age of Bamboo at Mentawei*);
Hövdingens Son är död (*The Chief's Son Is Dead*); *Draken
på Komodo* (*The Dragon of Komodo*); *Byn vid den
Trivsamma Brunnen* (*The Village Near the Pleasant
Fountain*); *Tambora*; *Att Segla är Nödvändigt* (*To Sail Is
Necessary*) (completed by Åke Leijonhufvud)

(in Thailand):

1938   *En Handfull Ris* (*A Handful of Rice*); *Man och Kvinna*
(*Homme et femme*) (co-d)

(in Peru):

1940/41   *Yagua* ("directed" by Yagua tribe shaman with Fejos
controlling camera)

Other Films:

1923   *Land of the Lawless* (Buckinham) (adapt)
1931   *L'Amour a l'américaine* (supervision)

Publications:

On FEJÖS: books—

Dodds, John, *The Several Lives of Paul Fejos*, New York, 1973.

On FEJÖS: articles—

Bréchignac, Jean-Vincent, "La Carrière de Paul Fejos," in *Pour Vous*
(Paris), 31 January 1929.
Doré, Claude, "Fantômas reparait," in *Ciné-Miroir* (Paris), 22 Janu-
ary 1932.
Wunscher, Catherine, "Paul Fejos," in *Films in Review* (New York),
March 1954.
Kraft, R., "Fejos's Broadway," letter in *Films in Review* (New York),
April 1954.
Molnar, Istvan, "Fejös Pal es a *Tavaszi Zapor*," in *Filmkultura*
(Budapest), October 1960.
Bidney, David, "Paul Fejos (1897–1963)," in *The American Anthro-
pologist* (New York), February 1964.
Balint, Lajos, "Fejös Pal—A Tavolbalato," in *Filmvilag* (Budapest),
15 July 1966.
Haudiquet, Philippe, "Paul Fejos 1897–1963," in *Anthologie du
Cinéma* (Paris), vol. 4, 1968.
Ban, Robert, in *Film, Szinhaz, Muzsika* (Budapest), 17 August 1968.
Petrie, Graham, "Fejos," in *Sight and Sound* (London), Summer
1978.
Petrie, Graham, "Paul Fejos in America," in *Film Quarterly* (Berke-
ley), no. 2, 1979.
"Fejos Issue" of *Filmkritik* (Munich), August 1979.

*   *   *

Few directors can have had such a curious and diverse career as that of Paul Fejos, who was equally at home behind a camera directing entertainment features and documentaries or on anthropological expeditions to South America and the Far East.

After an early career in his native Hungary which embraced medicine, painting and play production, Paul Fejos became a film director in the late teens. A trip to Paris persuaded him that he wanted to direct in the West, specifically the United States. In 1921 he arrived in the New World and started to work at the Rockefeller Institute. Eventually Fejos came to Hollywood—penniless—and made his first American film, *The Last Moment*, for $5,000, borrowed from Edward Spitz. An experimental drama in which a drowning man (Otto Matiesen) relives his life, *The Last Moment* was hailed by the Hollywood intelligentsia and landed Fejos a contract at Universal. The film also indicated that Fejos was to be no ordinary Hollywood-style producer. He was going to use every technical trick the cinema offered to put over his films be they melodramas about magicians (*The Last Performance*) or screen adaptations of popular Broadway productions (*Broadway*).

Paul Fejos's one genuine screen masterpiece (and the only one of his films which is readily available for appraisal today) is *Lonesome*, which uses cinéma vérité to provide a study of two lonely New Yorkers who spend a Saturday afternoon and evening at Coney Island. Not only are the visuals in *Lonesome* stunningly exciting, but the director manages to obtain realistic performances from his two stars, Barbara Kent and Glenn Tryon, neither of whom had previously shown much sign of histrionic greatness.

The director's Hollywood career ended as suddenly as it had begun. There were arguments over the direction of *All Quiet on the Western Front* (a project which he cherished) being assigned to Lewis Milestone, and Fejos returned to Hungary, where he directed *Marie*, generally considered the best pre-war production from that country. He also directed films in Austria and Denmark, and then embarked on a documentary filmmaking trip to the Far East, China and Japan, where he made *Black Horizons* and *A Handful of Rice*, among others. In 1941, he joined the Wenner-Gren Foundation in New York and spent the rest of his life directing anthropological research.

—Anthony Slide

FELLINI, Federico.

Italian. Born in Rimini, Italy, 20 January 1920. Educated at Catholic schools in Rimini, until 1938. Married Giulietta Masina in Rome, 30 October 1943, one son (died). Worked on *420* and *Avventuroso* magazines in Florence, 1938; caricature artist and writer in Rome, from 1939; through friend Aldo Fabrizi, worked as screenwriter, from 1941; worked on Rossellini's *Rome, Open City*, 1944; screenwriter and assistant director, 1946–52; formed Capitolium production company with Alberto Lattuada for *Variety Lights*, 1950; formed Federiz production company with Angelo Rizzoli (subsequently taken over by Clemente Fracazzi), 1961. Recipient: Grand Prize, Venice Festival, 1954, New York Film Critics Circle Award, 1956, Screen Directors Guild Award, 1956, and Oscar for Best Foreign Film, 1956, for *La strada*; Oscar for Best Foreign Film,

for *La notti di Cabiria*, 1957; Oscar for Best Foreign Film, 1960, Palme d'or, Cannes Festival, 1960, and New York Critics Circle Award, 1961, for *La dolce vita*; Oscar for Best Foreign Film, for *8¹/₂*, 1963; Oscar for Best Foreign Film, and New York Film Critics Circle Award, for *Amarcord*, 1974; Special Prize, Cannes Festival, 1987; Honorary Doctor of Humane Letters, Columbia University, New York, 1970. Address: Via Margutta 110, Rome, Italy.

Films as Director and Scriptwriter:

1950	*Luci del varieta* (co-d, + co-pr)
1951	*Lo Sceicco Bianco*
1953	*I Vitelloni*; "Un'agenzia matrimoniale" in *Amore in citta* (Zavattini)
1954	*La strada*
1955	*Il bidone*
1956	*La notti di Cabiria* (*Nights of Cabiria*)
1960	*La dolce vita*
1962	"Le tentazioni del dottor Antonio" in *Boccaccio '70* (Zavattini)
1963	*Otto e mezzo* (*8¹/₂*)
1965	*Giulietta degli spiriti* (*Juliet of the Spirits*)
1968	"Toby Dammit (Il ne faut jamais parier sa tête contre le diable)" in *Histoires extraordinaires/Tre passi nel delirio* (anthology film)
1969	*Block-notes di un regista* (*Fellini: A Director's Notebook*) (for TV) (+ narration, role); *Satyricon* (*Fellini Satyricon*)
1970	*I clowns* (*The Clowns*)
1972	*Roma* (*Fellini Roma*) (+ role)
1974	*Amarcord*
1976	*Casanova* (*Il Casanova di Federico Fellini*)
1978	*Prova d'orchestra* (*Orchestra Rehearsal*) (for TV)
1980	*La città delle donne* (*City of Women*)
1983	*E la nave va* (*And the Ship Sailed On*)
1986	*Ginger and Fred* (+ co-sc)
1987	*Intervista* (*The Interview*)
1990	*La voce della luna* (*The Voice of the Moon*)

Other Films:

1939	*Lo vedi come . . . lo vedi come sei?!* (Mattòli) (gagman)
1940	*Non me lo dire!* (Mattòli) (gagman); *Il pirata sono io!* (Mattòli) (gagman)
1941	*Documento Z3* (Guarini) (sc/co-sc, uncredited)
1942	*Avanti, c'e posto* (Bonnard) (sc/co-sc, uncredited); *Chi l'ha vistro?* (Alessandrini) (sc/co-sc); *Quarta pagina* (Manzari and Gambino) (sc/co-sc)
1943	*Apparizione* (de Limur) (sc/co-sc, uncredited); *Campo dei fiori* (Bonnard) (sc/co-sc); *Tutta la città canta* (Freda) (sc/co-sc); *L'ultima carrozzella* (Mattòli) (sc/co-sc)
1945	*Roma, città aperta* (Rossellini) (asst d, co-sc)
1946	*Paisà* (Rossellini) (asst d, co-sc)
1947	*Il delitto di Giovanni Episcopo* (Lattuada) (co-sc); *Il passatore* (Coletti) (co-sc); *La fumeria d'oppio* (*Ritorna Za-la-mort*) (Matarazzo) (co-sc); *L'ebreo errante* (Alessandrini) (co-sc)
1948	"Il miracolo" episode of *L'amore* (Rossellini) (asst d, co-sc, role as stranger mistaken for St. Joseph); *Il mulino del Po* (Lattuada) (co-sc); *In nome della legge* (Germi) (co-sc); *Senza pietà* (Lattuada) (co-sc); *La città dolente* (Bonnard) (co-sc)
1949	*Francesco, giullare di Dio* (Rossellini) (co-sc, asst d)
1950	*Il cammino della speranza* (Germi) (co-sc); *Persiane chiuse* (Comencini) (co-sc)
1951	*La città si difende* (Germi) (co-sc); *Cameriera bella presenza offresi* (Pastina) (co-sc)
1952	*Il brigante di Tacca del Lupo* (Germi) (co-sc); *Europa '51* (Rossellini) (co-sc, uncredited)
1958	*Fortunella* (De Filippo) (co-sc)
1970	*Alex in Wonderland* (Mazursky) (role as himself)
1974	*C'eravamo tanto amati* (Scola) (guest appearance)

Federico Fellini (left) with Marcello Mastroianni © **Tazio Secchiaroli**

Publications:

By FELLINI: books—

Il Bidone, with Ennio Flaiano and Tullio Pinelli, Paris, 1956.
Le notti di Cabiria di Federico Fellini, edited by Lino del Fra, Rocca San Casiano, Italy, 1957.
La dolce vita di Federico Fellini, edited by Tullio Kezich, Bologna, 1960; New York, 1961.
8½ di Federico Fellini, edited by Camilla Cederna, Rocca San Casciano, Italy, 1963.
Giulietta degli spiriti, edited by Tullio Kezich, Rocca San Casciano, Italy, 1965; as *Juliet of the Spirits*, New York, 1965.
La mia Rimini, Bologna, 1967.
Tre passi nel delirio, with Louis Malle and Roger Vadim, Bologna, 1968.
Fellini Satyricon di Federico Fellini, edited by Dario Zanelli, Bologna, 1969; as *Fellini Satyricon*, New York, 1970.
Il primo Fellini: Lo sceicco blanco, I vitelloni, La strada, Il bidone, edited by Renzo Renzi, Bologna, 1969.
Federico Fellini, Discussion no. 1, Beverly Hills, 1970.
I clowns, edited by Renzo Renzi, Bologna, 1970; 2nd edition, 1988.
Three Screenplays, New York, 1970.
Early Screenplays: Variety Lights, The White Sheik, New York, 1971.
Roma di Federico Fellini, Rocca San Casciano, Italy, 1972.
Amarcord, with Tonino Guerra, Milan, 1973; as *Amarcord: Portrait of a Town*, with Tonino Guerra, London, 1974.
Federcord: disegni per Amarcord di Federico Fellini, edited by L. Betti and O. Del Buono, Milan, 1974.
Il Casanova di Fellini: sceneggiatura originale, with Bernardino Zapponi, Turin, 1974.
4 film: I vitelloni, La dolce vita, 8½, Giulietta degli spiriti, Turin, 1974.
Fellini on Fellini, edited by Christian Strich, New York, 1976.
Fare un film, Turin, 1980.
Bottega Fellini. La città delle donne, with text by Raffaele Monti, Rome, 1981.
Federico Fellini: Intervista sul cinema, edited by Giovanni Grazzini, Rome, 1983; as *Federico Fellini: Comments on Film*, Fresno, California, 1988.
Ginger e Fred, with Tonino Guerra and Tullio Pinelli, Milan, 1986.
8½ (Otto e mezzo), edited by Charles Affron, New Brunswick, New Jersey, 1987.
La strada, New Brunswick, New Jersey, 1987.
Fellini's Cinecitta, London, 1989.

By FELLINI: articles—

"Strada sabarrata: via libera ai vitelloni," in *Cinema Nuovo* (Turin), 1 January 1953.
"Ogni margine è bruciato," in *Cinema* (Rome), 10 August 1954.
"Enquête sur Hollywood," in *Cahiers du Cinéma* (Paris), Christmas 1955.
"A Personal Statement," in *Film* (London), January/February 1957.
"Les Femmes libres de Magliano," in *Cahiers du Cinéma* (Paris), February 1957.
Interview with George Bluestone, in *Film Culture* (New York), October 1957.
"Crisi e neorealismo," in *Bianco e Nero* (Rome), July 1958.
"Témoignage à André Bazin," in *Cahiers du Cinéma* (Paris), January 1959.
"My Sweet Life," in *Films and Filming* (London), April 1959.
"Su *La dolce vita* la parola a Fellini," in *Bianco e Nero* (Rome), January/February 1960.
"The Bitter Life—of Money," in *Films and Filming* (London), January 1961.
Interview with Enzo Peri, in *Film Quarterly* (Berkeley), Fall 1961.
"The Screen Answers Back," in *Films and Filming* (London), May 1962.
Interview with Gideon Bachmann, in *Sight and Sound* (London), Spring 1964.
"'I Was Born for the Cinema': A Conversation with Federico Fellini," with Irving Levine, in *Film Comment* (New York), Fall 1966.
Interview with Pierre Kast, in *Interviews with Film Directors*, edited by Andrew Sarris, Indianapolis, 1967.
Interview with Roger Borderie and others, in *Cahiers du Cinéma* (Paris), May/June 1971.

Interview, in *Encountering Directors* by Charles Samuels, New York, 1972.
"Huit Entretiens autour du Casanova de Fellini," with O. Volta, in *Positif* (Paris), March 1977.
"The Cinema Seen as a Woman," an interview with Gideon Bachmann, in *Film Quarterly* (Berkeley), Winter 1980/81.
Interview with Gideon Bachmann, in *Film Comment* (New York), May/June 1985.
Interview with J.-A. Gili, in *Positif* (Paris), February 1986.
Interview in *Monthly Film Bulletin* (London), November 1986.

On FELLINI: books—

Bastide, François-Régis, Juliette Caputo, and Chris Marker, editors, *La Strada*, Paris, 1955.
Renzi, Renzo, *Federico Fellini*, Parma, 1956; Lyons, 1960.
Solmi, Angelo, *Storia di Federico Fellini*, Milan, 1962.
Rondi, Brunello, *Il Cinema di Fellini*, Rome, 1965.
Budgen, Suzanne, *Fellini*, London, 1966.
Solmi, Angelo, *Fellini*, New York, 1967.
Salachas, Gilbert, *Federico Fellini: An Investigation into his Films and Philosophy*, New York, 1969.
Novi, Mario, editor, *Fellini TV: I clowns*, Rome, 1970.
Hughes, Eileen, *On the Set of Fellini Satyricon: A Behind-the-Scenes Diary*, New York, 1971.
Pecori, Franco, *Federico Fellini*, Florence, 1974.
Ketcham, Charles, *Federico Fellini: The Search for a New Mythology*, New York, 1976.
Murray, Edward, *Fellini the Artist*, New York, 1976.
Rosenthal, Stuart, *The Cinema of Federico Fellini*, London, 1976.
Alpert, Hollis, *Fellini: A Life*, New York, 1981.
Fruttero, Carlo, and Franco Lucentini, *Je te trouve un peu pale: Recit d'été avec trente fantasmes feminins de Federico Fellini*, Paris, 1982.
Costello, Donald P., *Fellini's Road*, Notre Dame, Indiana, 1983.
Burke, Frank, *Federico Fellini: Variety Lights to La Dolce Vita*, Boston, 1984.
Fava, Claudio F., and Aldo Vigano, *The Films of Federico Fellini*, Secaucus, New Jersey, 1985.
Kezich, Tullio, *Fellini*, Milan, 1987.
Ciment, Michel, *Federico Fellini*, Paris, 1988.

On FELLINI: articles—

Autera, Leonardo, editor, "Fellini e la critica," in *Bianco e Nero* (Rome), June 1957.
Taylor, John, "Federico Fellini," in *Cinema Eye, Cinema Ear*, New York, 1964.
Ross, Lillian, "Profiles: 10½," in the *New Yorker*, 30 October 1965.
Harcourt, Peter, "The Secret Life of Federico Fellini," in *Film Quaterly* (Berkeley), Spring 1966.
Walter, Eugene, "The Wizardry of Fellini," in *Films and Filming* (London), June 1966.
Eason, Patrick, "Notes on Double Structure and the Films of Fellini," in *Cinema* (London), March 1969.
Cox, Harvey, Jr., "The Purpose of the Grotesque in Fellini's Films," in *Celluloid and Symbols*, edited by Cooper and Skrade, Philadelphia, 1970.
"Fellini Issue" of *L'Arc* (Aix-en-Provence, France), no. 45, 1971.
Julia, Jacques, "Psychanalyse de Fellini," in *Cinéma* (Paris), May 1971.
Chemasi, Antonio, "Fellini's *Casanova*: The Final Nights," in *American Film* (Washington, D.C.), September 1976.
Sarne, M., "Meeting Fellini," in *Films and Filming* (London), April 1978.
Comuzio, Ermanno, "Fellini/Rota: Un matrimonio concertato," in *Bianco e Nero* (Rome), July–August 1979.
Burke, F.M. "Reason and Unreason in Federico Fellini's *I vitelloni*," in *Literature/Film Quarterly* (Salisbury, Maryland), vol. 8, no. 2, 1980.
Fumento, R., "Maestro Fellini, studente Angelucci," in *Literature/Film Quarterly* (Salisbury, Maryland), October 1982.
Dossier on Fellini, in *Cinématographe* (Paris), January 1984.
Polan, Linda, "With Fellini," in *Sight and Sound* (London), Summer 1984.
Gilliatt, Penelope, "*La dolce vita*," in *American Film* (Washington, D.C.), November 1985.

"Fellini Section," of *Literature/Film Quarterly* (Salisbury, Maryland), vol. 15, no. 2, 1987.

Lavery, D., "'Major Man': Fellini as an Autobiographer," in *Post Script* (Jacksonville, Florida), Winter 1987.

"Fellini Section" of *Positif* (Paris), December 1987.

On FELLINI: films—

Goldbarb, Peter, *Fellini*, for TV, Canada, 1968.

Bachmann, Gideon, *Ciao, Federico!*, U.S., 1970.

*   *   *

Federico Fellini is one of the most controversial figures in the recent history of Italian cinema. Though his successes have been spectacular as in the cases of *La strada*, *La dolce vita* and *Otto e mezzo*, his failures have been equally flamboyant. This has caused considerable doubt in some quarters as to the validity of his ranking as a major force in contemporary cinema and has made it somewhat difficult for him to achieve sufficient financial backing in recent years to support his highly personalized film efforts. Certainly, few directors in any country can equal Fellini in his interest in the history of the cinema or share his certainty as to the appropriate place within its progression of films for the body of his work. Consequently, he has molded each of his film projects in such a way that any discussion of their individual merits is inseparable from the autobiographical details of his personal legend.

His first film, *La sceicco bianco* gave a clear indication of autobiographical nature of the works to follow by drawing upon his experience as a journalist and merging it with many of the conceits he had developed in his early motion picture career as a gag writer and script writer. However, he also had been an instrumental part of the development of the neorealistic film in the 1940's, writing parts of the screenplays of Roberto Rossellini's *Roma città aperta* and *Paisà*, and his reshaping of that tradition toward an autobiographical mode of expression in his first film troubled a number of his former collaborators. But, on his part, Fellini was seemingly just as critical of the brand of neorealism practiced by Rossellini with its penchant for overt melodrama.

In a succeeding film, *La strada*, he took his autobiographical parallels a step farther, even casting his wife, Giulietta Masina in the major female role. This highly symbolic work was variously interpreted as a manifesto on human rights or, at least, a treatise on women's liberation. In these contexts, however, it roused the ire of strict neorealists who regarded it as containing too much justification for political oppression. Yet, as a highly metaphorical personal parable about the relationship between a man and a woman it was a critical success and a confirmation of the validity of Fellini's autobiographical instincts. This gave him the confidence to indulge in a subtle criticism of the neorealistic style in his next film, *Il bidone* which became, in effect, a tongue-in-cheek criticism of the form's sentimental aspects.

In the films of his middle period, beginning in 1959 with *La dolce vita*, Fellini became increasingly preoccupied with his role as an international "auteur" and as a result, the autobiographical manifestations in his films became more introspective and extended to less tangible areas of his psyche than anything that he had previously brought to the screen. While *La dolce vita* is a relatively straightforward psychological extension of what might have become of Moraldo, the director's earlier biographical persona (*I vitelloni*) after forsaking his village for the decadence of Rome, its successors increasingly explored the areas of its creator's fears, nightmares and fantasies.

After establishing actor Marcello Mastroianni as his alter ego in *La dolce vita*, Fellini again employed him in his masterpiece, *Otto e mezzo* (*8½*) as a vehicle for his analysis of the complex nature of artistic inspiration. Then, in a sequel of sorts, he examined the other side of the coin. In *Giulietta degli spiriti* (*Juliet of the Spirits*), he casts his wife as the intaglio of the Guido figure in *8½*. Both films, therefore, explored the same problems from different sexual perspectives while, on the deeper, ever-present, autobiographical plane, the two characters became corresponding sides of Fellini's mythic ego.

Subsequent films have continued the rich, flamboyant imagery that has become a Fellini trademark, but with the exception of the imaginative fantasy *Fellini Satyricon*, they have, for the most part, returned to the vantage point of direct experience that characterized his earlier works. Finally, in 1980, with *La città delle donne*, again featuring Mastroianni, he returned to the larger than life examination of his psyche. In fact, a number of critics regarded it as the ultimate statement in an ideological trilogy, begun with *8½* and continued in *Juliet of the Spirits*, in which he finally attempts a rapprochement with his inner sexual and creative conflicts. Unfortunately, however, *City of Women* is too highly derivative of the earlier work and, consequently, does not resolve the issues raised in the earlier two films.

Several of his films are masterpieces by anyone's standards and yet in no other director's body of films does each work identifiably relate a specific image of himself that its creator wishes to present to the world and to posterity. Whether any of the films are truely autibiographical in any traditional sense is open to debate. They definitely do not interlock to provide a history of a man and yet each is a deliberately crafted building block in the construction of a larger than life Fellini legend which may eventually come to be regarded as the "journey of a psyche."

—Stephen L. Hanson

FERNÁNDEZ, Emilio.

Mexican. (Also known as "El Indio".) Born in Hondo, Coahuila, 26 March, 1904. Married 1) Gladys Fernández, 1941 (divorced), one daughter; 2) actress Columbia Domínguez (divorced), one daughter; 3) Gloria Cabiedes (divorced), one son; 4) Beatriz (divorced). Took part in the rebellion of Adolfo de la Huerta against the Mexican government, captured and sentenced to prison, but escaped to U.S.A., 1923; actor in California, returned to Mexico following amnesty, 1934; directed first film, 1941; served 6 months of 4½ year sentence for manslaughter, 1976. Recipient: Best Film, Cannes Festival, for *María Candelaria*, 1946. *Died in Mexico City, 6 August 1986.*

Films as Director and Co-Scriptwriter:

1941   *La isla de la pasión* (*Passion Island*)
1942   *Soypuro mexicano*
1943   *Flor silvestre* (+ role as Rogelio Torres); ***María Candelaria***
1944   *Las abandonadas*; *Bugambilia*
1945   *Pepita Jiménez*; *La perla* (*The Pearl*)
1946   *Enamorada*
1947   *Río Escondido* (*Hidden River*)
1948   *Maclovia*; *Salón México*; *Pueblerina*
1949   *La malquerida*; *Duelo en las montañas*; *Del odio nació el amor* (*The Torch. The Beloved*)
1950   *Undia de vida*; *Victimas del pecado*; *Islas Marías*; *Siempre Tuya*
1951   *La bien amada*; *Acapulco*; *El mar y tú*

Emilio Fernandez: *Maclovia*

1952   *Cuando levanta la niebla*
1953   *La red* (*The Net*); *Reportaje*; *El rapto*; *La rosa blanca*
1954   *La rebelión de los colgados*; *Nostros dos*
1955   *La Tierra de Fuego se apaga*
1956   *Una cita de amor*; *El imposter*
1961   *Pueblito*
1963   *Paloma herida*
1967   *Un dorado de Pancho Villa* (*A Loyal Soldier of Pancho Villa*)
1968   *El crepúscolo de un Dios*
1973   *La Choca*
1975   *Zona roja*
1977   *México norte*
1978   *Erótica*

Films as Actor:

1927   *The Gaucho* (Jones)
1933   *Flying Down to Rio* (Freeland) (as dancer)
1934   *Corazón bandolero* (Sevilla) (as Chacal); *Cruz Diablo* (De Fuentes) (as Toparca); *Tribu* (Contreras); *Janitzio* (Navarro) (as Zirahuén)
1935   *Mariá Elena* (Sevilla) (as dancer); *Celos* (Boytler)
1936   *Marijuana* (*El monstruo verde*) (Bohu) (as El Indio); *Las mujeres mandan* (De Fuentes) (as dancer); *Allá en el Rancho Grande* (De Fuentes) (as dancer); *El superloco* (Segura) (as Idúa); *El Impostor* (Kirkland)
1937   *Adiós Nicanor* (Portas) (as Nicanor); *Las cuatro milpas* (Pereda)

1938   *Aquí llego el valentón* (*El fanfarron*) (Rivero); *Juan sin miedo* (Segura) (as Valentín)
1939   *Con los dorados de Villa* (de Anda); *Los de abajo* (*Con la División del Norte*) (Urueta)
1940   *El Charro Negro* (de Anda); *Rancho alegre* (Aguila); *El zorro de Jalisco* (Benavides) (as Ernesto)
1958   *La Cucaracha* (I. Rodríguez) (as Coronel Antonia Zeta)
1961   *Los hermanos de Hierro* (I. Rodríguez) (as Pascual Velasco)
1962   *La Bandida* (R. Rodríguez) (as Epigmenio Gómez)
1963   *El revólver sangriento* (Delgado) (as Félix Gómez); *Night of the Iguana* (Huston) (as barman, also assoc d)
1964   *Los Hermanos Muerte* (Baledón) (as Marcos Zermeño); *Yo, el valiente* (Corona Blake) (as El Cuervo); *La recta final* (Taboada) (as Lucio); *Un callejón sin salida* (Baledón) (as Antonio)
1965   *Duelo de pistoleros* (Delgado) (as Pancho Gatillo Romero); *La conquista de El Dorado* (Portillo) (as Indio Romo); *Un tipo difícil de matar* (Portillo) (as Ringo); *Los malvados* (Corona Blake) (as Emilio); *The Reward* (Bourgignon); *Return of the Seven* (Kennedy)
1966   *El silencioso* (Mariscal) (as Emilio Segura); *The Appaloosa* (Furie); *The War Wagon* (Kennedy)
1967   *El caudillo* (Mariscal); *El jinete fantasma* (Zugsmith); *Cuando corre el alazán* (Mendoza)
1968   *El Yaqui* (Martínez)
1969   **The Wild Bunch** (Peckinpah)
1971   *Indio* (de Anda)
1972   *Derecho de asilo* (Zeceña); *El rincón de las Virgenes* (Isaac); *Pat Garrett and Billy the Kid* (Peckinpah)

1973 *Bring Me the Head of Alfredo Garcia* (Peckinpah)
1980 *Las cabareteras* (Cisneros); *Una gallina muy ponedora*
(Portillo); *Ahora mis pistolas hablan* (Orozco)
1983 *Mi abuelo, mi perro y yo* (Fernández); *Los amantes* (Vega);
Mercenarios (Cisneros); *Under the Volcano* (Huston); *El
tesoro del Amazonas* (Cardona); *Lola la trailera*
(Fernández)
1985 *Cuando corrió el alazán* (Perez)

Publications:

By FERNÁNDEZ: books—

En su propio espejo (*Entrevista con Emilio "El Indio" Fernández*),
edited by Julia Tuñon, Mexico City, 1988.

By FERNÁNDEZ: articles—

"After the revolution," in *Films and Filming* (London), June 1963.
Interview in *The Mexican Cinema: Interviews with 13 Directors*, by
Beatriz Reyes Navares, Albuquerque, New Mexico, 1976.

On FERNÁNDEZ: books—

Riera, Emilio García, *Historia documental del cine mexicano*, vol.
1–9, Mexico City, 1969.
Blanco, Jorge Ayala, *La aventura del cine mexicano*, Mexico City,
1979.
Mora, Carl, *Mexican Cinema: Reflections of a Society, 1896–1980*,
Berkeley, 1982.
de Luna, Andrés, *La batalla y su sombra* (*La revolución en el cine mex-
icano*), Mexico City, 1984.
Blanco, Jorge Ayala, *La condición del cine mexicano*, Mexico City,
1986.
Fernández, Adela, *El Indio Fernández: Vida y mito*, Mexico City,
1986.
Taibo, Paco Ignacio, *El Indio Fernández: El cine por mis pistolas*,
Mexico City, 1986.
de los Reyes, Aurelio, *Medio Siglo de cine mexicano* (*1896–1947*),
Mexico City, 1987.

On FERNÁNDEZ: articles—

"El Indio," in *Time* (New York), 11 November 1946.
Ellis, K., "Stranger than Fiction: Emilio Fernandez' Mexico," in *Jour-
nal of Popular Film* (Washington, D.C.), Spring 1982.
Cuel, F., and J.P. Royer, "Emilio Fernandez," in *Cinématographe*
(Paris), April 1982.
Tesson, C., "Portrait d'Emilio Fernandez en metteur en scène," in
Cahiers du Cinéma (Paris), May 1982.
Mraz, John, "Of *Churros* and *Charros*," in *Jump Cut* (Berkeley), no.
29, 1984.
Obituaries in *Hollywood Reporter*, 8 and 19 August 1986.
Obituary in *Variety* (New York), 13 August 1986.
Dávalos, Federico, "Por México: La leyenda del Indio Fernández," in
Pantalla (Mexico City), November 1986.
Rozado, Alejandro, "Lo trágico en el cine de Emilio Fernández," in
Dicine (Mexico City), November 1987.

*   *   *

If he did not already exist, it would be necessary to invent Emilio "El Indio" Fernández. His manneristic visual style, his folk-
loric themes and characters, and his distinctively Indian
physiognomy made him an integral element of Mexico's culture of nationalism, as well as the nation's best-known director. Fleeing Mexico with the defeat of his faction in the
rebellion of 1923, Fernández ended up digging ditches in Hollywood. As has been the case with so many Latin American
artists and intellectuals, Fernández discovered his fatherland
by leaving it: "I understood that it was possible to create a
Mexican cinema, with our own actors and our own stories. . . .
From then on the cinema became a passion with me, and I
began to dream of Mexican films." Making Mexican cinema
became Fernández's obsession and, as is so often true of cultural nationalism, a short-term gain was to turn into a long-term
dead end.

Perhaps that which most distinguishes Fernández's films is
their strikingly beautiful visual style. Fernández and Gabriel
Figueroa, the cinematographer, created the classical visual
form of Mexican cinema. Ironically, their expressive cinematic
patriotism was significantly inspired by foreign models—the
most important of which was that of Sergei Eisenstein and his
cameraman Eduard Tisse. Fernández evidently saw *Qué Viva
Mexico!* in Hollywood, and he later played the lead in *Janitzio*,
a film influenced by Eisenstein and the documentaries of Robert Flaherty and Willard Van Dyke and which he went on to
"re-make" twice as *Maria Candelaria* and *Maclovia*. Another
important antecedent was Paul Strand's photography in *Los
Redes*, which must itself have reflected Eisenstein's examples
as well as Strand's experiences in the Film and Photo League.

Foreign models were prominent at a formal level, but
nationalism was presumably communicated in the content of
the visual images. Fernández's and Figueroa's films are a celebration of Mexico's natural beauty: stony Indian faces set off
by dark rebozos and white shirts, *charros* and their stallions
riding through majestic cactus formations, fishermen and their
nets reflected in the swirling ocean tides, flower vendors in
Xochimilco's canals moving past long lines of tall poplar trees;
and over it all, the monumentally statuesque masses of rolling
clouds made impossibly luminous by photographic filters.

In the earlier films, the incredible beauty of the visual structures functioned as a protagonist, contexting the story and res-
onating with the characters' emotions. However, Fernández
and Figueroa apparently became victims of their own myths,
for their later films manifest a coldness and immobility which
indicate an emphasis on visual form at the expense of other
cinematic concerns. The dangers inherent in their "tourist's"
images of Mexico were ever-present, of course; but they
became increasingly obvious with the petrification of the style.

Fernández's stories have been summed up by Carlos Monsi-
vais, a leading Mexican critic, as "monothematic tragedies: the
couple is destroyed by the fate of social incomprehension,
Nature is the essence of the Motherland, beauty survives
crime, those who sacrifice themselves for others understand
the world." One is tempted to add: the Indian is a cretin, the
charro a blustering *macho*, women are long-suffering and self-
denying saints—and the revolution a confused tangle of meaningless atrocities.

Fernández's picturesque myths still retain vigor in the statist
nationalism which dominates ideological discourse in Mexico.
And, judging from the international attention that Fernández
received for his early works, they were evidently also what the
world expected from Mexican cinema. The pity is that Emilio
"El Indio" Fernández did not demand a little more from
himself.

—John Mraz

FERRERI, Marco.

Italian. Born in Milan, 11 May 1928. Educated in veterinary
medicine. Married Jacqueline (Ferreri). Dropped out of university, worked as liquor salesman and advertising agent, late
1940's; produced 2 issues of filmic "magazine" *Documento
mensile*, 1950–51; film actor and writer, 1952–53; optical
instrument salesman in Spain, 1954; directed first feature, *El
Pisito*, 1958. Recipient: International Critics Award, Venice
Festival, for *The Wheelchair*, 1960; International Critics
Award, Cannes Festival, for *La Grande Bouffe*, 1973.

Films as Director:

1958 *El Pisito* (+ co-sc)
1959 *Los chicos* (+ co-sc)
1960 *El cochecito* (*The Wheelchair, The Motorcart*) (+ co-sc); *Le Secret des hommes bleus* (*Caravan pour Zagora, El secreto de los hommes azules*) (d begun by Ferreri, completed by Edmon Agabra)
1961 "Gli adulteri (L'infidelità conjugale)" episode of *Le italiane e l'amore* (+ sc)
1963 *Una storia moderna: l'ape regina* (*The Conjugal Bed*) (+ co-sc)
1964 *La donna scimmia* (*The Ape Woman*) (+ co-sc); "Il professore" episode of *Controsesso* (+ co-sc)
1965 "L'uomo dei cinque palloncini (The Man with the Balloons)" episode of *Oggi, domani, dopodomani* (+ co-sc)
1966 *Marcia nuziale* (+ co-sc)
1967 *L'harem* (+ co-sc)
1968 *Dillinger è morto* (*Dillinger Is Dead*) (+ co-sc); *Break-Up* (revised version of episode from 1964 film *Oggi, domani, dopodomani*) (+ sc)
1969 *Il seme dell'uomo* (*The Seed of Man*) (+ co-sc)
1970 *Perché pagare per essere felici!* (documentary, for TV) (+ sc)
1971 *L'udienza* (+ co-sc)
1972 *Liza* (*La cagna*) (+ co-sc)
1973 *La grande abbuffata* (*La Grande Bouffe, Blow-Out*) (+ sc); *Non toccate la donna bianca* (*Touche pas la femme blanche*) (+ co-sc, role)
1976 *L'ultima donna* (*La Dernière Femme, The Last Woman*) (+ co-sc)
1978 *Bye Bye Monkey* (*Ciao maschio*) (+ co-sc)
1979 *Chiedo asilo* (*My Asylum*) (+ sc)
1981 *Tales of Ordinary Madness* (*Storie di ordinaria follia*) (+ co-sc)
1983 *Storia di Piera* (*Piera's Story*) (+ co-sc)
1986 *Ti amo* (*I Love You*)
1988 *Y'a bon les blancs* (*Um good, de white folks*)

Other Films:

1950 *Il principe ribelle* (Mercanti) (role)
1951 *Documento mensile* (2 "issues" or 3 according to other sources) (prod mgr); *Il cappotto* (Lattuada) (prod mgr)
1953 *Amore in città* (anthology film) (prod mgr); *La spiaggia* (Lattuada) (prod mgr, role)
1954 *Donne e soldati* (Malerba and Marchi) (prod mgr, co-sc, role)
1956 *Fiesta brava* (*Toro bravo*) (Cottafavi, unauthorized release) (prod mgr)
1962 *Mafioso* (Lattuada) (co-sc)
1964 *Casanova '70* (Monicelli) (role)
1967 *Il fischio al naso* (Tognazzi) (role)
1969 *Porcile* (Pasolini) (role); *Le vent d'est* (Godard) (role)
1970 *Ciao Gulliver* (Tuzii) (role); *Sortilegio* (Bonomi) (role)
1971 *Lui per lei* (Rispoli) (role)

Publications:

By FERRERI: articles—

"Je fais du cinéma commercial parce que je ne suis pas un héros," an interview with Noel Simsolo, in *Cinéma* (Paris), January 1973.
"Touche pas la femme blanche," interview with J.A. Gili and G. Braucourt, in *Ecran* (Paris), March 1974.
"Perché ho fatto un film fisiologico," interview edited by P. Mereghetti, in *Cineforum* (Bergamo), May 1974.
Interview with P. Bonitzer and others, in *Cahiers du Cinéma* (Paris), July/August 1976.
"Marco Ferreri on *L'ultima donna*," with R. Schar, in *Cinema Papers* (Melbourne), September/October 1976.
"Why? Why Not?," interview with P.-L. Thirard, in *Positif* (Paris), June 1978.
Interview with G. Buscaglia and others, in *Framework* (Norwich), no. 12, 1980.
Interview with Dan Yakir, in *Film Comment* (New York), March/April 1983.

Interview with O. Dazat, in *Cinématographe* (Paris), May 1986.
Interview with F. Sabouraud and Serge Toubiani, in *Cahiers du Cinéma* (Paris), January 1988.

On FERRERI: books—

Migliarini, Angelo, *Marco Ferreri: La distruzione dell'uomo storico*, Pisa, 1984.
Maheo, Michel, *Marco Ferreri*, Paris, 1986.
Borin, Fabrizio, editor, *Marco Ferreri*, Venice, 1988.

On FERRERI: articles—

Lane, J.F., "The Face of '63—Italy," in *Films and Filming* (London), April 1963.
"L'Audience," in *Avant-Scène du Cinéma* (Paris), March 1973.
Peruzzi, G., "Il Recupero del fantastico nell'opera di Marco Ferreri," in *Cinema Nuovo* (Turin), July/August 1973.
"La Grand Bouffe," in *Avant-Scène du Cinéma* (Paris), January/February 1974.
Depuyper, C., "Ferreri: un cinéma de moeurs-fiction," in *Cinéma* (Paris), September/October 1974.
"Marco Ferreri," in *Film Dope* (London), September 1978.
Martin, Marcel, and others, "Marco Ferreri," in *Revue du Cinéma* (Paris), July/August 1983.
"Ferreri Issue" of *Cinema Nuovo* (Bergamo), March/April 1984.
Maheo, M., "Un Corps a corps avec le mythe," in *Cinéma* (Paris), October 1984.
Première (Paris), July 1987.

*   *   *

Marco Ferreri's films are daringly excessive, outrageous, to some even obscene. But the filmmaker does not wish to shock or startle or offend the viewer solely for effect. Rather, he wants to jar his audience into pondering his themes: the break-up of the nuclear family, the redefinition of sex roles, the alienation inherent in modern city living. He is a social critic who captures in his images a contemporary world on the edge of social chaos. Ferreri is if anything a humanist—and a pessimist—so frustrated by his perceptions of society that his art can only border on the absurd.

Ferreri's early films center around the crumbling institution of marriage. In *The Conjugal Bed* (*L'Ape Regina*, the translation of which is *The Queen Bee*), a pleasant, fortyish bachelor (Ugo Tognazzi) cannot keep up with youthful wife Marina Vlady's sexual demands, becoming an invalid and dying before the final credits. The heavy, though, is not always the wife. *The Ape Woman*, played by Annie Girardot, has her body and face covered with hair. She is exploited by a two-bit showman (Tognazzi, again), who eventually must marry her to keep her from leaving his freak show. In the film's Italian-released print, the title character dies in childbirth and her husband has her stuffed, putting her on exhibit. *Dillinger Is Dead*, arguably Ferreri's masterpiece, sums up the first phase of his career. It is the surreal, ambiguous tale of an industrial designer (Michel Piccoli), disenchanted with his wife, job and home, who polishes and fixes an old revolver, kills his mate, and escapes to Tahiti. But, perhaps, all this might have occurred in his imagination, as he is driving home from work.

The filmmaker's scenarios during the 1970's expand beyond familial relationships. In *La Grande Bouffe*, a quartet of bored middle-aged men (a chef, airline pilot, judge, and television producer) eat themselves to death in an orgy of gluttony. In *Bye Bye Monkey*, Ferreri's first English language feature, Gerard Depardieu is gang-raped by several women and a rat colony that has overrun New York City devours a baby chimp. Ben Gazzara stars in *Tales of Ordinary Madness* as a rumpled, booze-loving beat poet who rambles through a maze of hookers, nymphomaniacs, neurotics and weirdos. *The Last Woman* is the story of a male chauvinist factory engineer (Depardieu), who appears throughout almost entirely in the nude. He has his consciousness raised by nursery school teacher Ornella

Muti and, at the finale, slices off his sex organ with an electric carving knife. In this last film, Ferreri's characters exist in an ambience of stark, impersonal, dehumanizing factories, high-rises, shopping centers, and superhighways.

Marco Ferreri's films range from the superb (*Dillinger Is Dead*) to the dreadful (*Tales of Ordinary Madness*). But they are unified in their despair for modern society. He offers no positive solutions: his characters gorge themselves to death, or deny themselves of the sexuality that is the essence of their lives. The filmmaker explains it best: " . . . society is finished. The values that once existed no longer exist. The family, the bourgeoisie—I'm talking about values, morals, economic relationships—they no longer serve a purpose. My films are reactions translated into images. The Roman Empire is over. We are entering the new Middle Ages. What interests me are moments when the world is dissolving and exploding."

—Rob Edelman

———

FEUILLADE, Louis.

French. Born in Lunel, France, 19 February 1873. Educated at the Institut de Brignac and at the Petit Séminaire, Carcassonne. Served with French Army, 1891–95, and 1915. Married Jeanne-Léontine Janjou, 1895 (daughter married to filmmaker Maurice Champreux). Worked in publishing in Paris, 1898; founder of satirical journal *La Tomate*, 1903; hired as writer by Alice Guy at Gaumont Studios, 1905; replaced Guy as Director of Gaumont Productions, 1907; began series of "ciné-romans" (serials) with *Judex*, 1916; first President of the Societé des Auteurs de Films, 1917–18; moved, with Gaumont, to Nice, 1918. *Died in Nice, 26 February 1925.*

Films as Director:

(Feuillade wrote and directed an estimated 800 films; this partial listing includes all series titles and known non-series titles)

1906   *Le billet de banque*; *C'est Papa qui prend la purge*; *Les deux Gosses*; *La Porteuse de pain*; *Mireille* (co-d); *N'te promène donc pas toute nue*

1907   *Un accident d'auto*; *La course des belles-mères*; *Un facteur trop ferré*; *L'homme aimanté*; *La légende de la fileuse*; *Un paquet embarrassant*; *La sirène*; *Le thé chez la concierge*; *Vive le sabotage*

1908   *Les agents tels qu'on nous les présente*; *Une dame vraiment bien*; *La grève des apaches*; *Nettoyage par le vide*; *Une nuit agitée*; *Prométhé*; *Le récit du colonel*; *Le roman de Sœur Louise*; *Un tic*

1909   *L'aveugle de Jerusalem*; *La chatte métamorphosée en femme*; *La cigale et la fourmi*; *Le collier de la reine*; *Les filles du cantonnier*; *Les heures*; *Histoire de puce*; *Le huguenot*; *Judith et Holopherne*; *Fra Vincenti*; *La légende des phares*; *La mère du moine*; *La mort de Mozart*; *La mort*; *La possession de l'enfant*; *Le savetier et le financier*; *Le printemps*; *Vainqueur de la course pédestre*;

1910   *Benvenuto Cellini*; *Le Christ en croix*; *Esther*; *L'Exode*; *Le festin de Balthazar*; *La fille de Jephté*; *Mil huit cent quatorze*; *Mater dolorosa*; *Maudite soit la guerre*; *Le pater*; *Le roi de Thulé*;

1910/11   "Le Film Esthétique" series: [1910: *Les sept péchés capitaux*, *La nativité*; 1911: *La vierge d'Argos*]

1910/13   "Bébé" series (74 films, from 88 to 321 meters length) [series begins with *Bébé fume* (1910); final title is *Bébé en vacances* (1913)]

1911   *L'aventurière, dame de compagnie*; *Aux lions les chrétiens*; *Dans la vie*; *Les doigts qui voient*; *Fidélité romaine*; *Le fils de la sunamité*; *Le fils de Locuste*; *Les petites apprenties*; *Quand les feuilles tombent*; *Sans le joug*; *Le trafiquant*

1911/13   "La vie telle qu'elle est" series: [1911: *Les vipères*, *Le mariage de l'aînée*, *Le roi Lear au village*, *En grève*, *Le bas de laine (Le Trésor)*, *La tare*, *Le poison*, *La souris blanche*, *Le trust (Les batailles de l'argent)*, *Le chef-lieu de Canton*, *Le destin des mères*, *Tant que vous serez heureux*; 1912: *L'accident*, *Les braves gens*, *Le nain*, *Le pont sur l'Abime*; 1913: *S'affranchir*]

1912   *Amour d'automne*; *Androclès*; *L'anneau fatal*; *L'attrait du bouge*; *Au pays des lions*; *L'Aventurière*; *La cassette de l'emigrée*; *Le chateau de la peur*; *Les cloches de Paques*; *Le cœur et l'argent*; *La course aux millions*; *Dans la brousse*; *La demoiselle du notaire*; *La fille du margrave*; *La hantise*; *Haut les mains!*; *L'homme de proie*; *La maison des lions*; *Le maléfice*; *Le mort vivant*; *Les noces siciliennes*; *Le Noël de Francesca*; *Préméditation*; *La prison sur le gouffre*; *Le témoin*; *Le tourment*; *Tyrtée*; *La vertu de Lucette*; *La vie ou la mort*; *Les yeux qui meurent*

1912/16   "Bout-de-Zan" series (53 films, from 79 to 425 meters length) [series begins with *Bout-de-Zan revient du cirque* (1912); final title is *Bout-de-Zan et la torpille* (1916)]

1912/13   "Le Détective Dervieux" series [1912: *Le Proscrit*, *L'oubliette*; 1913: *Le guet-apens*, *L'écrin du rajah*]

1913   *L'agonie de Byzance*; *L'angoisse*; *Les audaces du cœur*; *Bonne année*; *Le bon propriétaire*; *Le browning*; *Les chasseurs de lions*; *La conversion d'Irma*; *Un drame au pays basque*; *L'effroi*; *Erreur tragique*; *La gardienne du feu*; *Au gré des flots*; *L'intruse*; *La marche des rois*; *Le mariage de miss Nelly*; *Le ménestrel de la reine Anne*; *La mort de Lucrèce*; *La petite danseuse*; *Le revenant*; *La rose blanche*; *Un scandale au village*; *Le secret du forçat*; *La vengeance du sergent de ville*; *Les yeux ouverts*

1913/14   "Fantômas" series: [1913: **Fantômas, Juve contre Fantômas, La mort qui tue**; 1914: **Fantômas contre Fantômas, Le faux magistrat**]

1913/16   "La vie drôle" series (35 films of which 26 are preserved) [series begins with *Les millions de la bonne* (1913), and includes *L'Illustre Machefer* (1914), *Le colonel Bontemps* (1915), and *Lagourdette, gentleman cambrioleur* (1916)]

1914   *Le calvaire*; *Le coffret de Tolède*; *Le diamant du Sénéchal*; *L'enfant de la roulotte*; *L'épreuve*; *Les fiancés de 1914*; *Les fiancés de Séville*; *Le gendarme est sans culotte*; *La gitanella*; *L'hôtel de la gare*; *Les lettres*; *Manon de Montmartre*; *La neuvaine*; *Paques rouges*; *La petite Andalouse*; *La rencontre*; *Severo Torelli*

1915   *L'angoisse au foyer*; *La barrière*; *Le blason*; *Celui qui reste*; *Le collier de perles*; *Le coup du fakir*; *La course a l'abîme*; *Deux Françaises*; *L'escapade de Filoche*; *L'expiation*; *Le fer a cheval*; *Fifi tambour*; *Le furoncle*; *Les noces d'argent*; *Noël du poilu*; *Le sosie*; *Union sacrée*

1915/16   "Les vampires" series [1915: 1. **La tête coupée**; 2. **La bague qui tue**; 3. **Le cryptogramme rouge**; 1916: 4. **Le spectre**; 5. **L'évasion du mort**; 6. **Les yeux qui fascinent**; 7. **Satanas**; 8. **Le maître de la foudre**; 9. **L'homme des poisons**; 10. **Les noces sanglantes**]

1916   *L'aventure des millions*; *C'est le printemps*; *Le double jeu*; *Les fiançailles d'Agénor*; *Les fourberies de Pingouin*; *Le malheur qui passe*; *Un mariage de raison*; *Les mariés d'un jour*; *Notre pauvre cœur*; *Le poète et sa folle amante*; *La peine du talion*; *Le retour de Manivel*; *Si vous ne m'aimez pas*; *Judex* (serial in a prologue and 12 episodes)

1917   *L'autre*; *Le bandeau sur les yeux*; *Débrouille-toi*; *Déserteuse*; *La femme fatale*; *La fugue de Lily*; *Herr Doktor*; *Mon oncle*; *La nouvelle mission de Judex* (serial in 12 episodes); *Le passé de Monique*

1918   *Aide-toi*; *Les petites marionnettes*; *Tih Minh* (serial in 12 episodes); *Vendémiaire*

1919   *Barrabas* (serial in 12 episodes); *L'engrenage*; *L'énigme (Le mot de l')*; *L'homme sans visage*; *Le nocturne*

1920   *Les deux Gamines* (serial in 12 episodes)

1921   *L'Orpheline* (serial in 12 episodes); *Parisette* (serial in 12 episodes)

1921/22 *"Belle humeur"* series [1921: *Gustave est médium, Marjolin ou la fille manquée, Saturnin ou le bon allumeur, Séraphin ou les jambes nues, Zidore ou les métamorphoses*; 1922: *Gaétan ou le commis audacieux, Lahire ou le valet de cœur*]
1922 *Le fils du flibustier* (serial in 12 episodes)
1923 *Le gamin de Paris*; *La gosseline*; *L'orphelin de Paris* (serial in 6 episodes); *Vindicta* (film released in 5 parts)
1924 *La fille bien gardée*; *Lucette*; *Pierrot Pierrette*; *Le stigmate* (serial in 6 episodes)

Other Films:

1905 *Le coup de vent* (*Le chapeau*) (sc)
1906 *La course au potiron* (sc)

Publications:

By FEUILLADE: books—

Le Clos (play), with Etienne Arnaud, Paris, 1905.
Les Vampires, with George Meirs, Paris, 1916.
Judex, with Arthur Bernède, Paris, 1917 (and 1934).
La nouvelle Mission de Judex, with Arthur Bernède, Paris, 1919.
Tih Minh, with Georges Le Faure, Paris, 1919.
Barrabas, with Maurice Level, Paris, 1920.

By FEUILLADE: articles—

"Naundor, la genèse d'un crime historique," (under pseudonym P. Valergues), in *Revue mondiale* (Paris), 10 November 1904 through 25 October 1905.
Manifestos on the series "Le film esthétique" and "La vie telle qu'elle est", in *L'Anthologie du Cinéma* [*edited by Marcel Lapierre, Paris, 1946.*]

On FEUILLADE: books—

Delluc, Louis, *Cinéma et Compagnie*, Paris, 1919.
Védrès, Nicole, *Images du cinéma français*, Paris, 1945.
Lacassin, Francis, *Louis Feuillade*, Paris, 1964.
Prédal, René, *Le Cinéma muet à Nice*, Aix-en-Provence, 1964.
Florey, Robert, *La Lanterne magique*, Lausanne, 1966.

On FEUILLADE: articles—

Beylie, Claude, "Louis Feuillade," in *Ecrans de France* (Paris), 15 May 1959.
Lacassin, F., and R. Bellour, "En effeuillant la Marguerite," in *Cinéma* (Paris), March through June 1961.
Florey, Robert, "Une Saison dans la cage à mouches avec Feuillade," in *Cinéma* (Paris), June 1962.
Fieschi, Jean-André, "Feuillade (l'homme aimanté)," in *Cahiers du Cinéma* (Paris), November 1964.
Lacassin, Francis, "Louis Feuillade," in *Sight and Sound* (London), Winter 1964/65.
Lacassin, Francis, "Les lettres de Léon Gaumont à Louis Feuillade," in *Cinéma* (Paris), no. 95, 1965.
"Feuillade," in *Anthologie du Cinéma*, vol. 2, Paris, 1967.
Roud, Richard, "Maker of Melodrama," in *Film Comment* (New York), November/December 1976.
"Louis Feuillade," in *Film Dope* (London), September 1978.
Cartier, C., and M. Oms, "Quand Louis Feuillade cinématographiait à la cité de Carcassonne," in *Cahiers de la Cinémathèque* (Paris), Winter 1979.
"*Fantômas* Issue" of *Avant-Scène du Cinéma* (Paris), 1 July 1981.
You, D., "*Fantômas* et *Judex* au tribunal: Feuillade a-t-il cédé ses droits," in *Filméchange* (Paris), Winter 1983.
Lacassin, F., "Naissance d'un héros," in *Avant-Scène du Cinéma* (Paris), April 1984.
Pithon, R., "Retour à Feuillade," in *Positif* (Paris), February 1987.
Abel, R., "Before *Fantômas*: Louis Feuillade and the Development of Early French Cinema," in *Post Script* (Jacksonville, Florida), Fall 1987.

*   *   *

Louis Feuillade was one of the most solid and dependable talents in French cinema during the teens. He succeeded Alice Guy as head of production at Gaumont in 1906 and worked virtually without a break—aside from a period of war service—until his death in 1925, producing some 800 films of every conceivable kind: comedies and contemporary melodramas, biblical epics and historical dramas, sketches and series with numerous episodes adding up to many hours of running time. Though most of these films were made from his own scripts, Feuillade was not an innovator. The years of his apprenticeship in the craft of filmmaking were those in which French producers reigned supreme and he worked uncomplainingly in a context in which commercial criteria were paramount. For Feuillade—as for so many of his successors in the heyday of Hollywood—aesthetic strategies not rooted in sound commercial practices were inconceivable, and a filmmaker's only viable ambition was to reach the widest possible audience.

Most of Feuillade's output forms part of a series of some kind and he clearly saw films in generic terms rather than as individually sculpted works. Though not an originator in terms of the forms or styles he adopted, he made films which are among the finest examples of the various popular genres he successively explored. Before 1914 his work is enormously diverse: 30 comic films in the series of *La Vie drôle*, a group of seriously intended dramas in which a concern with the quality of the pictorial image is apparent, marketed under the banner of the *Film esthétique*, and a number of contemporary dramas, *La Vie telle qu'elle est*, with somewhat ambiguous claims to realism. In addition he made some 76 films with a four-year-old child star, Bébé, and a further 50 or so with the urchin Bout-de-Zan.

But the richest vein of Feuillade's work is the series of crime melodramas from *Fantômas* in 1913–14 to *Barrabas* in 1920. Starting with his celebration of Fantômas, master criminal and master of disguise, who triumphs effortlessly over the dogged ordinariness of his opponent Inspector Juve, Feuillade went on to make his wildest success with *Les Vampires*. Made to rival the imported American serials, this series reflects the chaotic wartime state of French production in its improvised stories refusing all logic, its bewildering changes of casting (necessary as actors were summoned to the war effort), its economical use of real locations and dazzling moments of total incongruity. *Les Vampires* reach a level Feuillade was never subsequently to achieve. *Judex* and especially *La Nouvelle Mission de Judex* are marked by a new tone of moralising, with the emphasis now on the caped avenger rather than the feckless criminals. If the later serials, *Tih Minh* and *Barrabas*, contain sequences able to rank with the director's best, Feuillade's subsequent work in the 1920's lacks the earlier forcefulness.

It was the supreme lack of logic, the disregard of hallowed bourgeois values—so appropriate at a time when the old social order of Europe was crumbling under the impact of World War I—which led the surrealists such as André Breton and Louis Aragon to hail *Fantômas* and *Les Vampires*, and most of Feuillade's subsequent advocates have similarly celebrated the films' anarchistic poetry. But this should not lead us to see Feuillade as any sort of frustrated artist or poet of cinema, suffocating in a world dominated by business decisions. On the contrary, the director was an archetypal middle class family man, who prided himself on the commercial success of his work and conducted his personal life in accord with strictly ordered bourgeois principles.

—Roy Armes

FEYDER, Jacques.

Belgian. Born Jacques Frédérix in Ixelles, Belgium, 21 July 1885, became French citizen, 1928. Educated at the Ecole régimentaire, Nivelles, 1905. Served in Belgian Army, 1917–19. Married Françoise Rosay, 1917, three sons. Worked in family's cannon foundry, 1906–7; theatre actor in Paris, 1911–13, and in Lyons, 1913–14; also film actor, from 1912; assistant to film director Gaston Ravel, 1914; directed first film, for Gaumont, 1916; *Les Nouveaux Messieurs* banned in France for insulting "the dignity of parliament and its ministers," accepted MGM offer and moved to Hollywood, 1928; MGM contract terminated, 1933; moved to Switzerland, 1942; producer in Paris, 1945. Recipient: Best Foreign Film Award, New York Film Critics, and Best Direction, Venice Festival, for *La Kermesse héroïque*, 1935. *Died in Prangins, Switzerland, 25 May 1948.*

Films as Director:

1915   *Monsieur Pinson, policier* (co-d)
1916   *Têtes de femmes, femmes de tête*; *Le Pied qui etreint* (4 episodes) (+ sc); *L'Homme au foulard à pois* (+ sc); *Le Bluff* (+ sc); *Un Conseil d'ami* (+ sc); *L'Homme de compagnie*; *Tiens, vous êtes à Poitiers?* (+ sc); *Le Frère de lait* (+ sc)
1917   *L'Instinct est maître*; *Le Billard cassé* (+ sc); *Abrégeons les formalités!* (+ sc); *La Trouvaille de Bûchu* (+ sc); *Le Pardessus de demi-saison*; *Les Vieilles Femmes de l'Hospice*
1919   *La Faute d'orthographe* (+ sc)
1921   *L'Atlantide* (*Missing Husbands*) (+ sc)
1922   *Crainquebille* (+ sc, art d)
1925   *Visages d'enfants* (*Faces of Children*) (+ sc, art d); *L'Image* (+ co-sc, role); *Gribiche* (*Mother of Mine*) (+ sc)
1926   *Carmen* (+ sc)
1927   *Au pays du Roi Lépreux* (documentary) (+ sc)
1928   *Thérèse Raquin* (*Du sollst nicht Ehe brechen, Shadows of Fear*) (+ co-sc); *Les Nouveaux Messieurs* (*The New Gentlemen*) (+ co-sc)
1929   *The Kiss* (+ co-sc); *Anna Christie* (German version of Clarence Brown film) (+ sc)
1930   *Le Spectre vert* (French version of Lionel Barrymore's *The Unholy Night*) (+ sc); *Si l'Empereur savait ça* (French version of *His Glorious Night*) (+ sc); *Olympia* (French version) (+ sc)
1931   *Daybreak*; *Son of India*
1934   *Le Grand Jeu* (+ co-sc)
1935   *Pension Mimosas* (+ co-sc); **La Kermesse héroïque (Carnival in Flanders)** (+ co-sc)
1936   *Die klugen Frauen* (German version of *La Kermesse héroïque*) (+ sc)
1937   *Knight without Armour*
1938   *Les Gens du voyage* (+ co-sc); *Fahrendes Volk* (German version of *Les Gens du voyage*) (+ sc)
1942   *La Loi du nord* (made 1939; during Occupation titled *La Piste du nord*) (+ co-sc); *Une Femme disparait* (*Portrait of a Woman*) (+ co-sc)

Jacques Feyder: *Thérèse Raquin*

Other Films:

1913 First episode of series *Protéa* (Jasset) (role)
1914 *Quand minuit sonna* (role)
1915 *Autour d'une bague* (Ravel) (role); *Les Vampires* (serial) (Feuillade) (bit role)
1925 *Poil de carotte* (Duvivier) (sc)
1928 *Gardiens de Phare* (Grémillon) (sc)
1943 *Maturareise* (*Jeunes filles d'aujourd'hui*) (Steiner) (tech + artistic supervision)
1946 *Macadam* (*Back Streets of Paris*) (Blistène) (art d)

Publications:

By FEYDER: book—

Le Cinéma, notre métier, with Françoise Rosay, Geneva, 1946.

By FEYDER: articles—

"Impressions de Hollywood, L'Ordre," in *Anthologie du Cinéma* edited by Marcel Lapierre, Paris, 1946.
"Transposition visuelle," in *Intelligence du cinématographe* edited by Marcel l'Herbier, Paris, 1946.
"Je crois au film parlant, Pour vous," in *L'Art du cinéma* edited by Pierre Lherminier, Paris, 1960.
"La Kermesse héroïque," in *Avant-Scène du Cinéma* (Paris), no. 26, 1965.

On FEYDER: books—

Jacques Feyder ou le Cinéma concret (anthology), Brussels, 1949.
Bachy, Victor, *Jacques Feyder*, Paris, 1966.
Ford, Charles, *Jacques Feyder*, Paris, 1973.
Abel, R.D., *French Cinema: The First Wave*, Princeton, New Jersey, 1984.

On FEYDER: articles—

Chaperot, Georges, "Souvenirs sur Jacques Feyder," in *Revue du Cinéma* (Paris), 1 July 1930.
Obituary in *New York Times*, 26 May 1948.
"Feyder Issue" of *L'Ecran Français* (Paris), 8 June 1948.
"Feyder Issue" of *Ciné-Club* (Paris), 2 November 1948.
"Jacques Feyder" in *Film Dope* (London), September 1978.
"Jacques Feyder," *National Film Theatre Booklet* (London), August 1983.
Dossier on Feyder, in *Cahiers de la Cinématheque* (Perpignan), Summer 1984.

On FEYDER: film—

Antoine, Raymond, and Charles Van Der Hagen, *Jacques Feyder et son chef d'oeuvre*, Belgium, 1974.

*　　　*　　　*

Underneath everything Jacques Feyder did was a great love and mastery of his medium, giving integrity and style to his work. As a young man he rejected the bourgeois background of his Belgian home and became an actor. He fell in love with the talented Françoise Rosay who became his partner for life. He acted in the cinema of Victorin Jasset, Feuillade, and Léon Gaumont, then became a scriptwriter, and finally began directing.

His individual approach to *La Faute d'orthographe* did not commend itself to Gaumont and Feyder raised the money to make the popular novel of Pierre Benois, *L'Atlantide*. This, in spite of an ill-chosen Napierkowska in the lead, was an international success. Its scenes shot in the Sahara under difficult conditions balanced the picturesque and exotic interiors, depicting an underground city.

Dining out in Montmartre he and Françoise discovered a boy playing in the street. This was little Jean Forest whom Feyder directed with consummate skill in three films, *Crainquebille*, *Visages d'enfants* and *Gribiche*. The first, based on the Anatole France story, added to Feyder's reputation while the second, shot with simplicity and sensitivity in the Haut

Valais, Switzerland, showed a remarkable skill in directing child actors. *Gribiche* was his first film for the Russian-inspired Albatros Company, and introduced the designer Lazare Meerson, working in the Art Deco style. It also featured Françoise Rosay in her first major role. Following a pictorially beautiful *Carmen*, with a recalcitrant Raquel Meller in the title role, came Feyder's masterpiece *Thérèse Raquin*, shot in a German studio with Gina Manes in her greatest part. Zola's sombre bourgeois tragedy was brought vividly to life. The details of the Raquin home, the human tensions, the unspoken words and the looming shadows created an unforgettable effect. At the end the old dumb and paralysed woman watches through those shadows the dead bodies of the murderous lovers lying on the floor in one of the great moments of cinema.

After an irreverent satire on French politics, *Les Nouveaux Messieurs* which succeeded in getting itself banned, Feyder set out for Hollywood where he directed Garbo in *The Kiss*, her last silent film and one of her most intelligent. Feyder now tackled the sound film with European versions of *Anna Christie*, *Le Spectre vert* and *Olympia*. In 1931 he directed Ramon Novarro in *Son of India* and *Day Break* before returning to France. Teaming up with his fellow countryman Charles Spaak he made in quick succession *Le Grand Jeu*, one of the best films of the Foreign Legion, *Pension Mimosas* with Rosay in a great tragic role, and the delightful, decorative and witty *La Kermesse héroïque*, a costume film that defies the ravages of time. The latter outraged the sensibilities of his fellow Belgians even as it delighted the rest of the world.

He directed *Knight without Armour* for Alexander Korda in London, Dietrich playing opposite Robert Donat. This story of the revolution in Russia saw an elegant Marlene moving through picturesque landscapes and great buildings designed by Lazare Meerson in one of his last assignments. Feyder then went to Germany to Germany to make *Les Gens du voyage* in two versions. After this story of circus life he returned to France and made his last important film *La Loi du nord* with Michele Morgan. The story of a Mounted Police search for a murderer in the Far North still showed the Feyder quality. It just managed to be completed by the time France was invaded. Feyder chose to live in Switzerland during the war, turning out a star vehicle for Françoise Rosay, *Une Femme disparait* in 1941. He died in Switzerland in 1948, a year which saw the passing of Eisenstein and Griffith. Feyder was in the company of his peers. But in 1970 René Clair could still say "Jacques Feyder does not occupy today the place his work and his example should have earned him."

—Liam O'Leary

────────

FISHER, Terence.

British. Born in London, 23 February 1904. Educated at Christ's Hospital, Horsham, Sussex. Apprenticeship aboard training ship H.M.S. Conway, 1926–28; junior officer for P & O Lines, 1929; window-dresser for London Department Store, 1930; clapper boy, runner, then assistant film editor, at Shepherd's Bush Studios, from 1930; editor, from 1936; directed first feature, for Rank, *A Song for Tomorrow*, 1948; joined Hammer Company, 1952; also TV director, on *Robin Hood* and others, from 1952. *Died 18 June 1980.*

Terence Fisher

Films as Director:

1948 *A Song for Tomorrow*; *Colonel Bogey*; *To the Public Danger*;
      Portrait from Life (*The Girl in the Painting*)
1949 *Marry Me*; *The Astonished Heart* (+ co-d)
1950 *So Long at the Fair* (co-d)
1951 *Home to Danger*
1952 *The Last Page* (*Manbait*); *Stolen Face*; *Wings of Danger* (*Dead
      on Course*); *Distant Trumpet*
1953 *Mantrap* (*Man in Hiding*) (+ co-sc); *Four Sided Triangle* (+
      co-sc); *Spaceways*; *Blood Orange*
1954 *Face the Music* (*The Black Glove*); *The Stranger Came Home*
      (*The Unholy Four*); *Final Appointment*; *Mask of Dust* (*Race
      for Life*); *Children Galore*
1955 *Murder by Proxy* (*Blackout*); *Stolen Assignment*; *The Flaw*
1956 *The Gelignite Gang*; *The Last Man to Hang?*
1957 *Kill Me Tomorrow*; *The Curse of Frankenstein*
1958 **Dracula (Horror of Dracula)**; *The Revenge of Frankenstein*
1959 *The Hound of the Baskervilles*; *The Man Who Could Cheat
      Death*; *The Mummy*; *The Stranglers of Bombay*
1960 *The Brides of Dracula*; *The Two Faces of Dr. Jekyll* (*House of
      Fright*); *Sword of Sherwood Forest*
1961 *The Curse of the Werewolf*
1962 *The Phantom of the Opera*; *Sherlock Holmes und der
      Halsband des Todes*; *Sherlock Holmes and the Deadly
      Necklace* (English version of the preceding)

1964 *The Horror of It All*; *The Earth Dies Screaming*; *The Gorgon*
1965 *Dracula—Prince of Darkness*
1966 *Island of Terror*; *Frankenstein Created Woman*
1967 *Night of the Big Heat* (*Island of the Burning Damned*)
1968 *The Devil Rides Out* (*The Devil's Bride*)
1969 *Frankenstein Must Be Destroyed*
1973 *Frankenstein and the Monster from Hell*

Other Films:

1935 *Brown on Resolution* (*Forever England, Born for Glory*)
      (Asquith) (asst ed)
1936 *Tudor Rose* (*Nine Days a Queen*) (Stevenson) (ed); *Jack of All
      Trades* (*The Two of Us*) (Stevenson and Hulbert) (ed);
      Where There's a Will (Beaudine) (ed); *Everybody Dance*
      (Reisner) (co-ed); *Windbag the Sailor* (Beaudine) (ed)
1938 *Mr. Satan* (Woods) (ed)
1939 *On the Night of the Fire* (*The Fugitive*) (Hurst) (ed)
1940 *George and Margaret* (King) (ed)
1941 *Atlantic Ferry* (*Sons of the Sea*) (Forde) (ed); *The Seventh
      Survivor* (Hiscott) (ed)
1942 *Flying Fortress* (Forde) (ed); *The Peterville Diamond* (Forde)
      (ed); *Tomorrow We Live* (*At Dawn We Die*) (King)
      (supervising ed); *The Night Invader* (Mason) (supervising
      ed)

1943 *The Dark Tower* (Harlow) (ed); *The Hundred Pound Window*
  (Hurst) (supervising ed); *Candlelight in Algeria* (King)
  (supervising ed)
1944 *One Exciting Night* (*You Can't Do Without Love*) (Forde)
  (ed); *Flight from Folly* (Mason) (supervising ed)
1945 *The Wicked Lady* (Arliss) (ed)
1947 *The Master of Bankdam* (Forde) (supervising ed)

Publications:

By FISHER: articles—

"Horror Is My Business," an interview with Raymond Durgnat and
  John Cutts, in *Films and Filming* (London), July 1964.
Interview with P. Bachmann, in *Positif* (Paris), January 1975.

On FISHER: books—

Pirie, David, *Heritage of Horror: The English Gothic Cinema
  1946–1972*, London, 1973.
Eyles, Allen, Robert Adkinson, and Nicholas Fry, *The House of Horror: The Story of Hammer Films*, London, 1973; revised edition,
  1981.
Bourgoin, Stéphane, *Terence Fisher*, Paris, 1984.

On FISHER: articles—

Ringel, H. "The Horrible Hammer Films of Terence Fisher," in *Take
  One* (Montreal), May 1973.
"*Le Cauchemar de Dracula*," in *Avant-Scène du Cinéma* (Paris), July/
  September 1975.
Carrère, E., "Prométhée délivré (sur les *Frankenstein* de Terence
  Fisher)," in *Positif* (Paris), July/August 1977.
"Terence Fisher," in *Film Dope* (London), February 1979.
Ross, P., "Terence Fisher, le prince des ténèbres," in *Image et Son*
  (Paris), September 1980.
"Terence Fisher Section" of *Avant-Scène du Cinéma* (Paris), 1
  November 1982.

*   *   *

Between 1957 and the mid-1960's Terence Fisher directed the
majority of the "classic" Hammer horror films. To a certain
extent, his work can be seen to have set the terms, stylistically
and thematically, for British horror in general, so that even
those later British horror films which attempted to be different
were largely defining themselves against the "norm" created in
part by Fisher at Hammer.

Before discussing Fisher's career as a filmmaker, it is worth
briefly considering his place in the critical pantheon of British
film directors. Some critics, most notably David Pirie, have
claimed that Fisher was an "auteur," someone whose work
expressed a distinctive aesthetic and moral vision. Other critics, perhaps the majority, have been less generous, seeing
Fisher as at best a "journeyman" filmmaker, a competent producer of horror potboilers.

Perhaps the truth about Fisher lies somewhere between
these two critical positions. Certainly when compared with
other British horror films from the period in which he was
working, Fisher's films for Hammer do exhibit distinctive and
recognisable features. In particular, one can point out as marks
of his authorship a pervasive compositional balance, smooth
tracks and precise, symmetrical editing patterns, with these in
turn linked with a moral certainty, whereby the forces of good
and evil within the films in question are implacably and unambiguously opposed.

At the same time Fisher's career does not offer itself as that
of an "auteur." Throughout the first half of the 1950's, he
made a number of films (some of them for Hammer, before its
rebirth as the horror factory) in a variety of genres. While some
of these contained elements of fantasy (*Stolen Face*, *The Four-
Sided Triangle* and *Spaceways*) or a period setting equivalent
to the later Hammer horrors (most notably, the film he co-
directed with Anthony Darnborough for Gainsborough Pic-

tures, *So Long At The Fair*), the majority were competently
made but essentially anonymous programme-fillers.

It is fair to say that when Fisher did eventually emerge as a
director with an identifiable signature from 1957 (and *The
Curse of Frankenstein*) onwards, it was as just one part, albeit
an important one, of the creative team at Hammer. This team
included producer-writer Anthony Hinds, producer Michael
Carreras, writer Jimmy Sangster, production designer Bernard Robinson, composer James Bernard and a number of
others, all of whom contributed extensively towards the distinctive Hammer horror "look." It is against the background
of this tightly-knit grouping that Fisher's prolific output at the
studio needs to be understood. This is not to downgrade Fisher's achievement, merely to contextualise it. (It is significant,
however, that the few films Fisher made for companies other
than Hammer in the 1960's contain few or none of the qualities
which one associates with the best of his work at Hammer.)

The almost paternal authority of Fisher's directorial
style—perhaps his main contribution to Hammer—enabled
him to represent effectively and sympathetically those father
figures (including Van Helsing in *Dracula* and *The Brides of
Dracula* and Sherlock Holmes in *The Hound of the Baskervilles*) around which many of Hammer's horror films revolved.
The orderliness of his *mise-en-scène* was also ideally suited for
his recreation of the ordered Victorian and Edwardian settings
in which most of the films took place.

Fisher's later work for Hammer—especially *Frankenstein
Created Woman*, *The Devil Rides Out* and *Frankenstein Must
Be Destroyed*—reveals a further maturing of his directorial
skills. These films, virtuoso variations upon and questionings
of basic Hammer horror assumptions about the nature of good
and evil, are dark and often despairing dramas. They show a
depth of response which perhaps had not been there before,
and Fisher's *mise-en-scène* has become even more precise and
magisterial. They stand as a further testament, if such is
needed, to Fisher's accomplishment as a director, an accomplishment which is still largely overshadowed by his association with horror, one of the most critically despised of all film
genres.

—Peter Hutchings

———

FLAHERTY, Robert.

American. Born Robert Joseph Flaherty in Iron Mountain,
Michigan, 16 February 1884. Educated at Upper Canada College, Toronto, and Michigan College of Mines. Married
Frances Hubbard, 1914. Explorer, Surveyor and Prospector
for Canadian Grand Trunk Railway and Canadian Mining
Syndicates, 1900's; worked for industrial entrepreneur William MacKenzie, searching for iron ore deposits along Hudson
Bay, 1910–16; made first travelogue film, 1915; made first feature, *Nanook of the North*, 1922; made *Moana* with backing of
Paramount (then Famous Players-Lasky), 1923–25; invited to
work for Irving Thalberg at MGM, quit and formed company
with F.W. Murnau to produce *Tabu*, 1928; made *Industrial
Britain* for John Grierson's Empire Marketing Board, 1931;
moved to Aran Islands and made *Man of Aran*, 1932–34, made
The Land for U.S. Government, 1939–41; hired by Frank
Capra to work in U.S. Army Orientation Film unit, 1942;
made *Louisiana Story*, sponsored by Standard Oil, 1946–48.
Robert Flaherty Foundation (later renamed International
Film Seminars Inc.) established, 1953. Recipient: Internation-

al Prize, Venice Festival, for *Louisiana Story*, 1948. *Died 23 July 1951.*

Films as Director:

1922   ***Nanook of the North*** (+ ph, ed, sc)
1925   *The Potterymaker* (*Story of a Potter*) (short) (+ ph, sc)
1926   *Moana* (*Moana: A Romance of the Golden Age. Moana: The Love Life of a South Sea Siren*) (+ co-sc, co-ph, co-ed)
1927   *The Twenty-Four-Dollar Island* (short) (+ sc, ph)
1931   *Tabu* (co-d, co-sc, uncredited co-ph)
1933   *Industrial Britain* (co-d, co-ph); *The English Potter* (short) (+ ph; edited by Marion Grierson from footage shot for *Industrial Britain*); *The Glassmakers of England* (short) (+ ph; edited from *Industrial Britain* footage); *Art of the English Craftsman* (short) (+ ph; from *Industrial Britain* footage)
1934   ***Man of Aran*** (+ sc, co-ph)
1937   *Elephant Boy* (co-d)
1942   ***The Land*** (+ sc, co-ph, narration)
1948   ***Louisiana Story*** (+ co-sc, co-ph, pr)
1949   *The Titan* (+ sc, ph)
1967   *Studies for Louisiana Story* (+ sc, ph) (15 hours of outtakes from *Louisiana Story* edited by Nick Cominos)

Other Films:

1945   *What's Happened to Sugar* (David Flaherty) (pr)
1949   *The Story of Michelangelo* (co-pr)
1950   *Green Mountain Land* (short) (David Flaherty) (pr)
1951   *St. Matthew's Passion* (ed, narration) (reedited version of Ernst Marischka's 1949 *Matthaus-Passion*)

Publications:

By FLAHERTY: books—

Anerca: Drawings by Enooesweetof, revised ed, Toronto, 1959.
Eskimo by Edmund Carpenter with Frederick Varley and Flaherty, Toronto, 1959.

By FLAHERTY: articles—

Article on *North Sea*, a film by Harry Watt, in *Sight and Sound* (London), Summer 1938.
Interview with Theodore Strauss, in the *New York Times*, 12 October 1941.
"How I Filmed *Nanook of the North*," in *Filmmakers on Filmmaking*, edited by Harry M. Geduld, Bloomington, Indiana, 1971.

On FLAHERTY: books—

Rotha, Paul, *The Film Till Now*, London, 1930.
Flaherty, Frances, *Elephant Dance*, New York, 1937.
Flaherty, Frances, *Sabu: The Elephant Boy*, New York, 1937.
Rotha, Paul, *Documentary Film*, New York, 1952.
Flaherty, Frances, *The Odyssey of a Film-Maker: Robert Flaherty's Story*, Urbana, Illinois, 1960.
Quintar, Fuad, *Robert Flaherty et le Documentaire Poetique: Etudes Cinématographique No. 5*, Paris, 1960.
Cuenca, Carlos Fernandez, *Robert Flaherty*, Madrid, 1963.
Klaue, Wolfgang, compiler, *Robert Flaherty*, Berlin, 1964.
Agel, Henri, *Robert J. Flaherty*, Paris, 1965.
Calder-Marshall, Arthur, *The Innocent Eye: The Life of Robert Flaherty*, London, 1970.
Griffith, Richard, *The World of Robert Flaherty*, New York, 1970.
Hardy, Forsyth, editor, *Grierson on Documentary*, revised ed, New York, 1971.
Levin, G. Roy, *Documentary Explorations: Fifteen Interviews with Filmmakers*, Garden City, New York, 1971.
Barsam, Richard, *Nonfiction Film: A Critical History*, New York, 1973.
Armes, Roy, *Film and Reality: An Historical Survey*, Baltimore, 1974.
Barnouw, Erik, *Documentary: A History of the Non-Fiction Film*, New York, 1974.

Napolitano, Antonio, *Robert J. Flaherty*, Florence, 1975.
Murphy, William T., *Robert Flaherty: A Guide to References and Resources*, Boston, 1978.
Williams, Christopher, *Realism and Cinema: A Reader*, London, 1980.
Rotha, Paul, *Robert J. Flaherty: A Biography*, Philadelphia, 1983.
Barsam, Richard, *The Vision of Robert Flaherty: The Artist as Myth and Filmmaker*, Bloomington, Indiana, 1988.

On FLAHERTY: articles—

Ramsaye, Terry, "Flaherty, Great Adventurer," in *Photoplay* (New York), May 1928.
Grierson, John, "Flaherty," in *Cinema Quarterly* (London), Autumn 1934.
Griffith, Richard, "Flaherty and the Future," in *New Movies* (New York), January 1943.
Rosenheimer, Arthur (Arthur Knight), "They Make Documentaries: No. 1—Robert Flaherty," in *Film News* (New York), April 1946.
Taylor, Robert Lewis, "Profile of Flaherty," in the *New Yorker*, 11, 18 and 25 June 1949.
Gray, Hugh, "Robert Flaherty and the Naturalist Documentary," in *Hollywood Quarterly*, Fall 1950.
Grierson, John, "Flaherty as Innovator," in *Sight and Sound* (London), October/November 1951.
"Flaherty in Review," in *Sight and Sound* (London), November/December 1951.
Huston, John, "Regarding Flaherty," in *Sequence* (London), no. 14, 1952.
George, George L., "The World of Robert Flaherty," in *Film News* (New York), no. 4, 1953.
Manvell, Roger, "Robert Flaherty, Geographer," in *The Geographical Magazine* (New York), February 1957.
Siepmann, Charles, "Robert Flaherty—The Man and the Filmmaker," in *Film Book I: The Audience and the Filmmaker* edited by Robert Hughes, New York, 1959.
Flaherty, Frances, "Flaherty's Quest for Life," in *Films and Filming* (London), January 1959.
Bachmann, Gideon, "Bob," in *Film* (London), September/October 1959.
Van Dongen, Helen, "Robert J. Flaherty, 1884–1951," in *Film Quarterly* (Berkeley), Summer 1965.
Barnouw, Erik, "Robert Flaherty," in *Film Culture* (New York), Spring 1972.
Corliss, Richard, "Robert Flaherty: The Man in the Iron Myth," in *Film Comment* (New York), November/December 1973.
Zinnemann, Fred, "Remembering Robert Flaherty," in *Action* (Los Angeles), May/June 1976.
"Robert Flaherty," in *Film Dope* (London), February 1979.
Lee, R., "Robert Flaherty: Free Spirit," in *American Cinematographer* (Los Angeles), January 1984.
Winston, B., "The White Man's Burden," in *Sight and Sound* (London), Winter 1984/85.
"The Innocent Eye: Robert Flaherty," in *National Film Theatre Booklet* (London), September 1984.
Barsam, Richard, "The Vision of Robert Flaherty," in *Sight and Sound* (London), Autumn 1988.

On FLAHERTY: films—

Romine, Charles, producer, *Odyssey: The World of Robert Flaherty*, for CBS-TV in cooperation with the Museum of Modern Art, broadcast 17 February 1957.
Stoney, George, *How the Myth Was Made: A Study of Robert Flaherty's Man of Aran*, for TV, 1978.

*   *   *

Robert Flaherty was already 36 years old when he set out to make a film, *Nanook of the North*, as his primary purpose. Before that he had established himself as a prospector, surveyor, and explorer, having made several expeditions to the sub-Arctic regions of the Hudson Bay. He had shot motion picture footage on two of these occasions, but before *Nanook*, filmmaking was only a sideline.

Yet these years in the wilderness were to have a profound

Robert Flaherty: *Man of Aran*

effect on his development as a filmmaker. First, the expeditions brought Flaherty into intimate contact with the Eskimo culture. Second, they enhanced his knowledge about the human condition in a natural setting. Third, the numerous evenings that he spent in isolation encouraged him to contemplate the day's events by writing in his diaries, from which he developed highly skilled powers of observation which sharpened his sense of photographic imagery and detail. Also a violinist and an accomplished storyteller, Flaherty had clearly cultivated an artistic sensibility before becoming a filmmaker. Filmmaking became a compelling mechanism for expressing this sensibility.

Flaherty turned to filmmaking not only as a means of creation but also to communicate to the outside world his rare, close look at Eskimo culture. He held a profound admiration for these people who lived close to nature and whose daily existence was an unrelenting struggle to survive. The struggle ennobled this proud race. Flaherty sought to portray their existence in a manner that would illustrate the purity and nobility of their lives, a purpose underlying each of his films.

Flaherty developed a method of working that was fairly consistent from film to film. The films about the people of Hudson Bay, Samoa, the Aran Islands, and the Louisiana Bayou demonstrate a more or less constant concern with people who live in natural settings. These geographical locations are incidental; others would have done just as well. Eskimo culture was the only one in which he was deeply versed. Nevertheless, the locations were chosen because they represented societies on the verge of change. Indeed, Flaherty has often been criticized for presenting his subjects as they existed years ago, not as he found them. But for Flaherty this meant the last opportunity to capture a way of life on film.

Another consistent feature of his technique was the selection of a "cast." Although he pioneered the use of real people to re-enact their own everyday lives before the camera lens, he deliberately chose ideal types on the basis of physical appearance and even created artificial families to act before the camera.

Flaherty worked without a plot or script, allowing for a maximum of improvisation. The Flaherty method entailed total immersion in these cultures in order to discover the basic patterns of life. *Nanook* represented the least difficulty because of his thorough familiarity with Eskimo culture. However, *Moana* and *Man of Aran* represented unfamiliar territory. Flaherty had to become steeped in strange cultures. His search for struggle and conflict in Savaii misled him and he later abandoned it. Struggle was more readily apparent in the Aran Islands, in terms of conflict between man and the sea; the hunt for the basking shark which he portrayed, abandoned in practice some years earlier, helps us to visualize this conflict.

Flaherty's technical facility also served him well. Generally he carried projectors and film printers and developing equipment to these far off places so that he could view his rushes on a daily basis. Flaherty, a perfectionist, shot enormous quantities of footage for his films; the lack of a script or scenario contributed to this. He went to great lengths to achieve photographic excellence, often shooting when shadows were longest. In *Moana* he used the new panchromatic film stock which was much more sensitive to color than orthochromatic film. He pioneered the use of long lenses for close-up work allowing an intimacy with his subjects that was novel for its time.

Flaherty's films were generally well received in the popular press and magazines as well as in the more serious critical literature. *Nanook* was praised for its authenticity and its documentary value as well as its pictorial qualities. John Grierson first used the term documentary as applying to a film in his review of *Moana*. Subsequently Grierson, through his film-making activities and writings, began to formulate a documentary aesthetic dealing with social problems and public policy, subjects that Flaherty (except for *The Land*) tried to avoid. Nevertheless, Grierson's writings, which were to influence the development of the modern sponsored film, had their foundations in Flaherty's work. Their purposes were ultimately quite different, but Grierson gave due credit to Flaherty for working with real people, shaping the story from the material, and bringing a sense of drama to the documentary film.

Man of Aran aroused the most critical responses to Flaherty's work. It was released at a time when the world was beset with enormous political, social, and economic problems, and many enthusiasts of documentary film believed it was irresponsible and archaic of Flaherty to produce a documentary making no reference to these problems or concealing them from public view. *Louisiana Story*, on the other hand, was greeted as the culminating work of a master filmmaker, and recognized for its skillful interweaving of sound and image, an audiovisual symphony as one critic described it. However, in today's world of pollution and oil spills it is much more difficult to accept the benign presence of the oil industry in the bayou.

Although Flaherty made a relatively small number of films in his long career, one would be hard pressed to find a more influential body of work. He always operated outside the mainstream of the documentary movement. Both he and Grierson, despite their contradictory purposes, can be credited with the development of a new genre and a documentary sensibility; Flaherty by his films, Grierson by his writing. Watching today's 16mm distribution prints and video cassettes it is often difficult to appreciate the photographic excellence of Flaherty's work. Nevertheless, the clean lines are there as well as an internal rhythm created by the deft editing touch of Helen Van Dongen. Although his films were improvised, the final product was never haphazard. It showed a point of view which he wished to share.

—William T. Murphy

FLEMING, Victor.

American. Born in Pasadena, California, 23 February 1883. Car-racing driver and chauffeur, then hired as assistant cameraman at American Film Company, 1910; began working with Allan Dwan, 1911; cameraman at Triangle, under D.W. Griffith, 1915; joined photographic section of U.S. Army Signal Corps, 1917; cameraman for Walter Wanger at Versailles Peace Conference, 1919; directed first feature, 1920; contract director for MGM, from 1932. Recipient: Oscar for Best Director, for *Gone With the Wind*, 1939. *Died in 1949.*

Films as Director:

1919   *When the Clouds Roll By* (co-d); private film, featuring
        Douglas Fairbanks, Sr., made for the Duke of Sutherland
1920   *The Mollycoddle*
1921   *Mamma's Affair*; *Woman's Place*
1922   *The Lane That Had No Turning*; *Red Hot Romance*; *Anna
        Ascends*
1923   *Dark Secrets*; *The Law of the Lawless*; *To the Last Man*; *The
        Call of the Canyon*
1924   *Code of the Sea*; *Empty Hands*

Victor Fleming (in straw hat) directing *Mantrap*

1925 *The Devil's Cargo*; *Adventure*; *A Son of His Father*; *Lord Jim*
1926 *The Blind Goddess*; *Mantrap*
1927 *The Rough Riders* (*The Trumpet Call*); *The Way of All Flesh*;
 Hula
1928 *The Awakening*
1929 *Abie's Irish Rose*; *Wolf Song*; *The Virginian*
1930 *Common Clay*; *Renegades*
1931 *Around the World With Douglas Fairbanks* (*Around the World
 in Eighty Minutes with Douglas Fairbanks*) (+ role)
1932 *The Wet Parade*; *Red Dust*
1933 *The White Sister*; *Bombshell* (*Blond Bombshell*)
1934 *Treasure Island*
1935 *Reckless*; *The Farmer Takes a Wife*
1937 *Captains Courageous*; *The Good Earth* (co-d with Franklin,
 uncredited); *A Star Is Born* (Wellman) (d add'l scenes)
1938 *Test Pilot*; *The Crowd Roars* (Thorpe) (d add'l scenes); *The
 Great Waltz* (co-d with Duvivier, uncredited)
1939 ***The Wizard of Oz***; ***Gone With the Wind***
1941 *Dr. Jekyll and Mr. Hyde* (+ pr)
1942 *Tortilla Flat*
1943 *A Guy Named Joe*
1945 *Adventure*
1948 *Joan of Arc*

Other Films: (incomplete listing)

1916 *His Picture in the Papers* (Emerson) (ph); *The Habit of
 Happiness* (*Luugh and the World Laughs*) (Dwan) (ph); *The
 Good Bad Man* (*Passing Through*) (Dwan) (ph); *Betty of
 Greystone* (Dwan) (ph); *Macbeth* (Emerson) (ph); *Little
 Meena's Romance* (Powell) (ph); *The Mystery of the
 Leaping Fish* (Emerson) (ph) (short); *The Half-breed*
 (Dwan) (ph); *An Innocent Magdalene* (Dwan) (ph); *A*

Social Secretary (Emerson) (ph); *Manhattan Madness*
(Dwan) (ph); *50–50* (Dwan) (ph); *American Aristocracy*
(Ingraham) (ph); *The Matrimaniac* (Powell) (ph); *The
Americano* (Emerson) (ph)
1917 *Down to Earth* (Emerson) (ph); *The Man from Painted Post*
 (Henabery) (ph); *Reaching for the Moon* (Emerson) (co-
 ph); *A Modern Musketeer* (Dwan) (ph)
1919 *His Majesty, the American* (*One of the Blood*) (Henabery)
 (ph)

Publications:

On FLEMING: books—

Thompson, Frank, *Between Action and Cut: 5 American Directors*,
 Metuchen, New Jersey, 1985.
Harmetz, Aljean, *The Making of The Wizard of Oz*, London, 1989.

On FLEMING: articles—

Obituary in *New York Times*, 7 January 1949.
Reid, John, "The Man Who Made *Gone With the Wind*," in *Films and
 Filming* (London), December 1967.
Reid, John, "Fleming: The Apprentice Years," in *Films and Filming*
 (London), January 1968.
"Checklist—Victor Fleming," in *Monthly Film Bulletin* (London),
 October 1977.
Brownlow, Kevin, "Victor Fleming," in *Film Dope* (London), Febru-
 ary 1979.
Gallagher, J., "Victor Fleming," in *Films In Review* (New York),
 March 1983.

*   *   *

In his day, Victor Fleming was a successful, respected director
of some of Metro-Goldwyn-Mayer's biggest and most cele-

brated films (*Red Dust, Captains Courageous, Test Pilot*) as well as two undisputed Hollywood classics by the standards of popular taste, *The Wizard of Oz* and *Gone with the Wind*. Ironically, it is probably the enormous continuing popularity of the latter two titles that has eclipsed Fleming's personal reputation. Correctly perceived as producer-dominated, studio-influenced cinema, both *Oz* and *Gone with the Wind*, are talked and written about extensively, but never as Victor Fleming films. They are classic examples of the complicated collaborations which took place under the old studio system. Although Fleming received directorial credit (and 1939's Oscar as Best Director) for *Gone with the Wind*, others made significant contributions to the final film, among them George Cukor.

Fleming served his film apprenticeship as a cinematographer, working with such pioneers as Allan Dwan at the Flying A company and D.W. Griffith at Triangle. He photographed several Douglas Fairbanks films, among them *The Americano, Wild and Woolly*, and *Down to Earth*. He developed a skillful sense of storytelling through the camera, as well as a good eye for lighting and composition during those years. After he became a director, his critical reputation became tied to the studio at which he made the majority of his films, Metro-Goldwyn-Mayer. Known unofficially as a "producer's studio," MGM concentrated on showcasing its well-known stable of stars in suitable vehicles.

At Metro, Fleming was frequently thought of as a counterpart to George Cukor; Cukor was labelled a "woman's director," Fleming a "man's director." Besides being a close personal friend and favorite director of Clark Gable, Fleming was responsible for directing the Oscar-winning performance of Spencer Tracy in *Captains Courageous*. His flair for getting along with male stars enabled him to create an impressive group of popular films that were loved by audiences, who saw them as "Gable films" or "Tracy films." Both Henry Fonda (whose screen debut was in Fleming's *The Farmer Takes a Wife*) and Gary Cooper (whose first big screen success was in *The Virginian*) owed much of their early recognition to Fleming's talent for directing actors. One of Fleming's chief characteristics was that of spotting potential stars and understanding the phenomenon of the star persona. In addition to his work with male actors, he also played a key role in the career development of Jean Harlow. Under Fleming's direction, she was encouraged to mix comedy with her sex appeal.

The Virginian, Fleming's first sound film, is an underrated movie which demonstrates a remarkable ability to overcome the problems of the early sound era, shooting both outdoors and indoors with equal fluidity and success. Fleming's use of naturalistic sound in this film did much to influence other early films. However, Fleming's work is not unified by a particular cinematic style, although it is coherent in thematic terms. His world is one of male camaraderie, joyous action, pride in professionalism, and lusty love for women who are not too ladylike to return the same sort of feelings. In this regard, his work is not unlike that of Howard Hawks, but Fleming lacks Hawks's ability to refine style and content into a unified vision.

Fleming's name is not well-known today. Although he received directorial credit for what is possibly the most famous movie ever made in Hollywood (*Gone with the Wind*), he is not remembered as its director. His work stands as an example of the best done by those directors who worked within the studio system, allowing the studio stamp to become the style of the film rather than creating a personal vision of their own.

—Jeanine Basinger

FLOREY, Robert.

French. Born in Paris, 14 September 1900. Educated in Switzerland. Actor/writer in Switzerland, 1918–19; writer for *Ciné-magazine* and *La Cinématographie française*, Paris, then for Feuillade's Studios, Nice, 1920; gagman, then director of foreign publicity for Douglas Fairbanks, Mary Pickford, and Rudolph Valentino, Hollywood, 1921–23; assistant director at MGM, 1924–26; left MGM to direct *One Hour of Love* for Tiffany, 1926; director for Paramount, 1928; returned to Europe, 1929, directed for UFA; returned to Hollywood, 1932; left filmmaking, became TV director, 1950. Recipient: French Legion d'Honneur, 1950. *Died 16 May 1979.*

Films as Director:

1919 *Heureuse Intervention* (+ sc); *Isidore sur le lac* (+ sc); *Isidore a la deveine* (+ sc)
1923 *Valentino en Angleterre* (+ sc); *50–50* (+ sc)
1926 *One Hour of Love*; *That Model from Paris* (co-d with Gasnier, uncredited, + sc);
1927 *The Romantic Age*; *The Cohens and the Kellys* (Beaudine) (2nd unit d); *Face Value*; *Life and Death of a Hollywood Extra* (*The Life and Death of 9413—A Hollywood Extra*) (+ sc); *Johann the Coffin Maker* (+ sc); *The Loves of Zero* (+ sc)
1928 series of 24 shorts for Paramount featuring New York stage stars; *Night Club*; *Skyscraper Symphony* (+ sc, ph); *The Pusher-in-the-Face*; *Bonjour, New York!* (+ sc); *The Hole in the Wall*
1929 *The Cocoanuts* (co-d); *The Battle of Paris* (*The Gay Lady*); *Eddie Cantor* (+ sc); *La Route est belle*
1930 *L'Amour chante* (also directed German version: *Komm' zu mir zum Rendezvous*, and Spanish: *Professor de mi Señora*); *Anna Christie* (Brown) (d New York exteriors, uncredited)
1932 *Le Blanc et le noir* (co-d); *The Murders in the Rue Morgue* (+ co-sc); *The Man Called Back*; *Those We Love*; *A Study in Scarlet* (+ sc); *The Blue Moon Murder Case*; *Girl Missing*; *Ex-lady*
1933 *The House on 56th Street*; *Bedside*; *Registered Nurse*; *Smarty* (*Hit Me Again*)
1934 *Oil for the Lamps of China* (LeRoy) (d exteriors); *Shanghai Orchid* (d exteriors); *I Sell Anything*; *I Am a Thief*; *The Woman in Red*
1935 *Go into Your Dance* (co-d with Mayo, uncredited); *The Florentine Dagger*; *Going Highbrow*; *Don't Bet on Blonds*; *The Payoff*; *Ship Cafe*; *The Rose of the Rancho* (Gering) (d add'l scenes, uncredited); *The Preview Murder Mystery*
1936 *Till We Meet Again*; *Hollywood Boulevard* (+ co-sc); *Outcast*
1937 *The King of the Gamblers*; *This Way Please*; *Mountain Music*; *Daughter of Shanghai* (*Daughter of the Orient*); *Disbarred*; *King of Alcatraz*
1938 *Dangerous to Know*; *Hotel Imperial*
1939 *The Magnificent Fraud*; *Parole Fixer*; *Death of a Champion*; *Women without Names*
1940 *Meet Boston Blackie*; *The Face Behind the Mask*
1941 *Two in a Taxi*; *Dangerously They Live*; *Lady Gangster*
1942 *The Desert Song* (+ co-sc)
1943 *Bomber's Moon* (co-d with Fuhr, uncredited); *Roger Touhy, Gangster* (*The Last Gangster*); *The Man from Frisco*
1944 *Escape in the Desert* (co-d with Blatt, uncredited); *God Is My Co-Pilot*
1945 *Danger Signal*; *The Beast with Five Fingers*
1947 *Tarzan and the Mermaids*
1948 *Rogue Regiment* (+ sc); *Outpost in Morocco*
1949 *The Crooked Way*; *Johnny One-Eye*
1950 *The Vicious Years* (*The Gangster We Made*)

Other Films:

1918 *Le Cirque de la mort* (Lindt) (role as le détective)

Robert Florey directing *One Hour of Love*

1921 *L'Orpheline* (serial in 12 episodes) (Feuillade) (asst d, role as un apache); *Saturnin* (*Le Bon Allumeur*) (Feuillade) (asst d, role as un gazier); *Monte Cristo* (Flynn) (historical advisor)
1922 *Robin Hood* (Dwan) (French sub-titles)
1923 *Wine* (Gasnier) (asst d)
1924 *Parisian Nights* (Santell) (asst d, tech advisor); *The Exquisite Sinner* (von Sternberg) (asst d); *Time the Comedian* (Leonard) (asst d)
1925 *The Masked Bride* (von Sternberg) (asst d); *La Boheme* (King Vidor) (asst d); *Escape* (Rosen) (asst d); *Paris* (*Shadows of Paris*) (Goulding) (asst d, tech advisor); *Dance Madness* (Leonard) (asst d); *Toto* (Stahl) (asst d)
1926 *Monte Carlo* (*Dreams of Monte Carlo*) (Cabanne) (asst d); *Bardelys the Magnificent* (King Vidor) (asst d)
1926 *The Magic Flame* (King) (asst d)
1927 *The Woman Disputed* (King) (asst d)
1932 **Frankenstein** (Whale) (sc)
1947 **Monsieur Verdoux** (Chaplin) (co-assoc d)
1948 *Adventures of Don Juan* (Sherman) (sc under pseudonym Florian Roberts)

Publications:

By FLOREY: books—

Filmland, Paris, 1923.

Deux ans dans les studios américains, Paris, 1924; revised edition, 1984.
Douglas Fairbanks, sa vie, ses films, ses aventures, Paris, 1926.
Pola Negri, Paris, 1926.
Adolphe Menjou, with André Tinchant, Paris, 1927.
Charlie Chaplin, Paris, 1927.
Ivan Mosjoukine, with Jean Arnoy, Paris, 1927.
Hollywood d'hier et d'aujourd'hui, Paris, 1948.
Monsieur Chaplin, or Le Rire dans la nuit, with Maurice Bessy, Paris, 1952.
La Lanterne magique, Lausanne, 1966.
Hollywood années zéro. La Préhistoire, l'invention, les pionniers, naissance des mythes, Paris, 1972.
Hollywood Village: Naissance des studiós de Californie, Paris, 1986.

By FLOREY: articles—

From 1921 to 1926: several hundred articles for *Cinémagazine* (Paris); numerous articles for Parisian publications including *Pour Vous, Saint Cinéma des Prés, Ciné-Club, Le Technicien du Film, La Cinématographie Française*, and *Cinéma*
Interview in *Film Comment* (New York), March/April 1988.

On FLOREY: books—

Bourgoin, Stéphane, *Robert Florey*, Paris, 1986.

Taves, Brian, *Robert Florey: The French Expressionist*, Metuchen, New Jersey, 1987.

On FLOREY: articles—

Spears, Jack, "Robert Florey," in *Films in Review* (New York), April 1960 (collected in his *Hollywood: The Golden Era*, New York, 1971)
Higham, Charles, "Visitors to Sydney," in *Sight and Sound* (London), Summer 1962.
Salmi, M., "Robert Florey," in *Film Dope* (London), February 1979.
Beylie, Claude, obituary in *Ecran* (Paris), 15 July 1979.
Luft, Herbert, "Robert Florey," in *Films in Review* (New York), August/September 1979.
American Cinematographer (Los Angeles), April 1987.

* * *

It is not easy to define Robert Florey's status in the history of the American film. As a list of his films quite clearly attests, he was not a major director, but he was certainly an interesting and intriguing one who seemed able to keep abreast with trends and changes in the methodology of filmmaking.

After working on a number of minor silent program features, Florey reached the peak of his artistic filmmaking career in the late 1920's with the production of four experimental shorts—*The Life and Death of 9413—A Hollywood Extra, The Loves of Zero, Johann the Coffin Maker*, and *Skyscraper Symphony*—which showed a skillful understanding of editing and the influence of German expressionist cinema. The best known of these shorts is *A Hollywood Extra*, which no longer appears to survive in its entirety, but which nonetheless illustrates Florey's grasp of montage and satire. Florey never again returned to this form of filmmaking, but thanks to these shorts he was invited to direct a number of early talkies at Paramount. Aside from *Cocoanuts*, which is more Marx Brothers than Florey, these Paramount features—notably *The Battle of Paris*—again demonstrate that the director was not only totally cognizant of developments in the sound film but also was able to bring ingenuity and fluidity to the medium.

A crucial point in Florey's career came in 1931 when he was asked to script and direct *Frankenstein*. Although some elements of the Florey screenplay are utilized, his script was basically scrapped and he was replaced as director by James Whale. Had Florey been allowed to keep the assignment, he would doubtless have become a major Hollywood director. Instead he was assigned *Murders in the Rue Morgue*, which certainly contains some nice atmospheric lighting effects as well as moments of surprising brutality, but has never achieved the cult popularity of *Frankenstein*. For the next 20 years Robert Florey toiled away as a reliable contract director, whose films were never more than pleasant and diverting entertainments. Even when he worked as co-director with Chaplin on *Monsieur Verdoux*, Florey saw his more daring directing ideas rejected by the comedian in favor of a static filmmaking style which Chaplin favored. Florey moved exclusively into television direction in 1950, and seemed very much at ease working on programs such as *The Loretta Young Show*, whose star and content suited his own conservative temperament.

Aside from his work as a director, Robert Florey deserves recognition as a commentator on and witness to the Hollywood scene. He *loved* cinema from his first involvement in his native France as an assistant to Louis Feuillade. That love led to his coming to Hollywood in the early 1920's as a correspondent for a French film magazine and to the writing of eight books on the history of the cinema, all of which are exemplary works of scholarship.

—Anthony Slide

FORD, John.

American. Born Sean Aloysius O'Feeney (or John Augustine Feeney) in Cape Elizabeth, Maine, 1 February 1895. Educated at Portland High School, Maine and at University of Maine, 1913 or 1914 (for 3 weeks). Married Mary McBryde Smith, 1920, one son, one daughter. Joined brother Francis (director for Universal) in Hollywood, 1914; actor, stuntman and special effects man for Universal, 1914–17; assumes name "Jack Ford," 1916; contract director for Universal, 1917–21; signed to Fox Film Corp., 1921; began collaboration with screenwriter Dudley Nichols on *Men without Women*, 1930; assembled film crew that became Field Photographic Branch of U.S. Office of Strategic Services, 1940; Lieutenant-Commander, U.S. Marine Corps, 1942–45 (wounded at Battle of Midway); in U.S. Naval Reserve, given rank of Admiral by President Nixon. Recipient: Oscar for Best Director, and Best Direction Award, New York Film Critics, for *The Informer*, 1935; Best Direction Award, New York Film Critics, for *Stagecoach*, 1939; Oscar for Best Director, for *Grapes of Wrath*, 1940; Oscar for Best Director and Best Direction Award, New York Film Critics, for *How Green Was My Valley*, 1941; Oscar for Best Documentary, for *Battle of Midway*, 1942; Legion of Merit and Purple Heart; Annual Award, Directors Guild of America, 1952; Grand Lion Award, Venice Festival, 1971; Lifetime Achievement Award, American Film Institute, 1973. *Died in Palm Desert, California, 31 August 1973.*

Films as Director:

1917 *The Tornado* (+ sc, role); *The Trail of Hate* (may have been directed by Francis Ford); *The Scrapper* (+ sc, role); *The Soul Herder*; *Cheyenne's Pal* (+ story); *Straight Shooting*; *The Secret Man*; *A Marked Man* (+ story); *Bucking Broadway*
1918 *The Phantom Riders*; *Wild Woman*; *Thieves' Gold*; *The Scarlet Drop* (+ story); *Hell Bent* (+ co-sc); *A Woman's Fool*; *Three Mounted Men*
1919 *Roped*; *The Fighting Brothers*; *A Fight for Love*; *By Indian Post*; *The Rustlers*; *Bare Fists*; *Gun Law*; *The Gun Packer* (*The Gun Pusher*); *Riders of Vengeance* (+ co-sc); *The Last Outlaw*; *The Outcasts of Poker Flat*; *The Ace of the Saddle*; *The Rider of the Law*; *A Gun Fightin' Gentleman* (+ co-story); *Marked Men*
1920 *The Prince of Avenue A*; *The Girl in Number 29*; *Hitchin' Posts*; *Just Pals*; *The Big Punch* (+ co-sc)
1921 *The Freeze Out*; *Desperate Trails*; *Action*; *Sure Fire*; *Jackie*
1922 *The Wallop*; *Little Miss Smiles*; *The Village Blacksmith*; *Silver Wings* (Carewe) (d prologue only)
1923 *The Face on the Barroom Floor*; *Three Jumps Ahead* (+ sc); *Cameo Kirby*; *North of Hudson Bay*; *Hoodman Blind*
1924 *The Iron Horse*; *Hearts of Oak*
1925 *Lightnin'*; *Kentucky Pride*; *The Fighting Heart*; *Thank You*
1926 *The Shamrock Handicap*; *Three Bad Men*; *The Blue Eagle*
1927 *Upstream*
1928 *Mother Machree*; *Four Sons*; *Hangman's House*; *Napoleon's Barber*; *Riley the Cop*
1929 *Strong Boy*; *Salute*; *The Black Watch*
1930 *Men Without Women* (+ co-story); *Born Reckless*; *Up the River* (+ co-sc, uncredited)
1931 *Seas Beneath*; *The Brat*; *Arrowsmith*; *Flesh*
1933 *Pilgrimage*; *Dr. Bull*
1934 *The Lost Patrol*; *The World Moves On*; *Judge Priest*
1935 *The Whole Town's Talking*; **The Informer**; *Steamboat Round the Bend*
1936 *The Prisoner of Shark Island*; *Mary of Scotland*; *The Plough and the Stars*
1937 *Wee Willie Winkie*; *The Hurricane*
1938 *Four Men and a Prayer*; *Submarine Patrol*
1939 **Stagecoach**; *Drums Along the Mohawk*; **Young Mr. Lincoln**
1940 **The Grapes of Wrath**; *The Long Voyage Home*

John Ford

1941   *Tobacco Road*; *Sex Hygiene*; *How Green Was My Valley*
1942   *The Battle of Midway* (+ co-ph); *Torpedo Squadron*
1943   *December Seventh* (co-d); *We Sail at Midnight*
1945   *They Were Expendable*
1946   **My Darling Clementine**
1947   *The Fugitive* (+ co-pr)
1948   *Fort Apache* (+ co-pr); *Three Godfathers* (+ co-pr)
1949   **She Wore a Yellow Ribbon** (+ co-pr)
1950   *When Willie Comes Marching Home*; *Wagonmaster* (+ co-pr);
        Rio Grande (+ co-pr)
1951   *This is Korea!*
1952   *What Price Glory*; **The Quiet Man** (+ co-pr)
1953   *The Sun Shines Bright*; *Mogambo*
1955   *The Long Gray Line*; *Mister Roberts* (co-d); *Rookie of the
        Year* (episode for *Screen Directors Playhouse* TV series);
        The Bamboo Cross (episode for *Fireside Theater* TV series)
1956   **The Searchers**
1957   *The Wings of Eagles*; *The Rising of the Moon*
1958   *The Last Hurrah*
1959   *Gideon of Scotland Yard* (*Gideon's Day*); *Korea*; *The Horse
        Soldiers*
1960   *The Colter Craven Story* (episode for *Wagon Train* TV series);
        Sergeant Rutledge
1961   *Two Rode Together*
1962   **The Man Who Shot Liberty Valance**; *Flashing Spikes* (episode
        for *Alcoa Premiere* TV series); *How the West Was Won*
        (directed "The Civil War" segment)
1963   *Donovan's Reef* (+ pr)
1964   *Cheyenne Autumn*
1965   *Young Cassidy* (+ co-d)
1966   *Seven Women*
1970   *Chesty: A Tribute to a Legend*

Other Films:

1914   *Lucille Love, the Girl of Mystery* (15 episode serial) (Francis
        Ford) (role); *The Mysterious Rose* (Francis Ford) (role)
1915   **The Birth of a Nation** (Griffith) (role); *Three Bad Men and a
        Girl* (Francis Ford) (role); *The Hidden City* (Francis Ford)
        (role); *The Doorway of Destruction* (Francis Ford) (asst d,
        role); *The Broken Coin* (22 episode serial) (Francis Ford)
        (role)
1916   *The Lumber Yard Gang* (Francis Ford) (role); *Peg o' the Ring*
        (15 episode serial) (Francis Ford and Jacques Jaccard)
        (role); *Chicken-Hearted Jim* (Francis Ford) (role); *The
        Bandit's Wager* (Francis Ford) (role)
1929   *Big Time* (Kenneth Hawks) (role as himself)
1971   *Vietnam! Vietnam!* (Beck, for USIA) (exec pr)

Publications:

By FORD: book—

John Ford's Stagecoach, edited by Richard Anobile, New York, 1975.
My Darling Clementine, edited by Robert Lyons, New Brunswick,
   New Jersey, 1984.

By FORD: articles—

Interview with Lindsay Anderson, in *Sequence* (London), New Year
   issue 1952.
"Rencontre avec John Ford," in *Cahiers du Cinéma* (Paris), March
   1955.
"Poet in an Iron Mask," interview with Michael Barkun, in *Films and
   Filming* (London), February 1958.
"Ford on Ford," in *Cinema* (Beverly Hills), July 1964.
"Rencontre avec John Ford," with Axel Madsen, in *Cahiers du
   Cinéma* (Paris), July 1965.
Interview with Jean Mitry, in *Interviews with Film Directors*, edited by
   Andrew Sarris, New York, 1967.
"Our Way West," interview with Burt Kennedy, in *Films and Filming*
   (London), October 1969.

On FORD: books—

Mitry, Jean, *John Ford*, Paris, 1954.
Haudiquet, Philippe, *John Ford*, Paris, 1966.
Kitses, Jim, *Horizons West*, London, 1969.
Baxter, John, *The Cinema of John Ford*, New York, 1971.

French, Warren, *Filmguide to The Grapes of Wrath*, Bloomington,
   Indiana, 1973.
McBride, Joseph, and Michael Wilmington, *John Ford*, London,
   1975.
Sarris, Andrew, *The John Ford Movie Mystery*, London, 1976.
Bogdanovich, Peter, *John Ford*, Berkeley, 1978.
Ford, Dan, *Pappy: The Life of John Ford*, Englewood Cliffs, New Jer-
   sey, 1979.
Sinclair, Andrew, *John Ford*, New York, 1979.
Anderson, Lindsay, *About John Ford*, London, 1981.
Caughie, John, editor, *Theories of Authorship: A Reader*, London,
   1981.
Schatz, Thomas, *Hollywood Genres: Formulas, Filmmaking and the
   Studio System*, New York, 1981.
Reed, Joseph W., *Three American Originals: John Ford, William
   Faulkner, Charles Ives*, Middletown, Connecticut, 1984.
Gallagher, Tag, *John Ford: The Man and His Films*, Berkeley, 1986.
Stowell, Peter, *John Ford*, Boston, 1986.
Buscombe, Ed, editor, *The BFI Companion to the Western*, London,
   1989.

On FORD: articles—

McVay, Douglas, "The Five Worlds of John Ford," in *Films and Film-
   ing* (London), November 1955.
Barkun, Michael, "Notes on the Art of John Ford," in *Film Culture*
   (New York), Summer 1962.
Bogdanovich, Peter, "Autumn of John Ford," in *Esquire* (New York),
   April 1964.
"John Ford Issue" of *Présence du Cinéma* (Paris), March 1965.
"John Ford Issue" of *Cahiers du Cinéma* (Paris), October 1966.
Tavernier, Bertrand, "John Ford à Paris," in *Positif* (Paris), March
   1967.
Beresford, Bruce, "Decline of a Master," in *Film* (London), Autumn
   1969.
Anderson, Lindsay, "John Ford," in *Cinema* (Beverly Hills), Spring
   1971.
"John Ford Issue" of *Focus on Film* (London), Spring 1971.
"John Ford Issue" of *Velvet Light Trap* (Madison, Wisconsin), August
   1971.
"Special Issue Devoted to John Ford and His Towering Achievement,
   Stagecoach," in *Action* (Los Angeles), September/October 1971.
"Ford's Stock Company Issue" of *Filmkritik* (Munich), January 1972.
Editors of *Cahiers du Cinéma*, "John Ford's *Young Mr. Lincoln*," in
   Screen (London), Autumn 1972.
McBride, J., "Drums Along the Mekong: I Love America, I Am
   Apolitical," in *Sight and Sound* (London), Autumn 1972.
McBride, J., "Bringing in the Sheaves," in *Sight and Sound* (London),
   Winter 1973/74.
Rubin, M., "Ford and Mr. Rogers," in *Film Comment* (New York),
   January/February 1974.
"John Ford (1895–1973) Issue" of *Anthologie du Cinéma* (Paris),
   March 1975.
Dempsey, M., "John Ford: A Reassessment," in *Film Quarterly* (Ber-
   keley), Summer 1975.
Gallagher, Tag, "John Ford: Midway. The War Documentaries," in
   Film Comment (New York), September/October 1975.
Belton, J.R., "Ceremonies of Innocence: Two Films by John Ford," in
   Velvet Light Trap (Madison), Winter 1975.
Budd, M., "A Home in the Wilderness: Visual Imagery in John Ford's
   Westerns," in *Cinema Journal* (Evanston), Fall 1976.
Roth, W., "Where Have You Gone, My Darling Clementine?," in
   Film Culture (New York), no. 63–64, 1977.
Stowell, H.P., "John Ford's Literary Sources: From Realism to
   Romance," in *Literature/Film Quarterly* (Salisbury, Maryland),
   Spring 1977.
"John Ford Issue" of *Wide Angle* (Athens, Ohio), vol. 2, no. 4, 1978.
McCarthy, T., "John Ford and Monument Valley," in *American Film*
   (Washington, D.C.), May 1978.
Ellis, K., "On the Warpath: John Ford and the Indians," in *Journal of
   Popular Film* (Washington, D.C.), vol. 8, no. 2, 1980.
Combs, Richard, "At Play in the Fields of John Ford," in *Sight and
   Sound* (London), Spring 1982.
"John Ford Section" of *Casablanca* (Madrid), January 1983.
Roth, L., "Ritual Brawls in John Ford's Films," in *Film Criticism*
   (Meadville, Pennsylvania), Spring 1983.

Bogdanovich, Peter, "Touch of Silence for Mr. Ford," in *New York*, October 1983.

Schickel, Richard, "Ford Galaxy," in *Film Comment* (New York), March/April 1984.

Stevens, G., Jr., and Robert Parrish, "Directors at War," in *American Film* (Washington, D.C.), July/August 1985.

Gallagher, Tag, "Acting for John Ford," in *American Film* (Washington, D.C.), March 1986.

Nolley, Ken, "Reconsidering Ford's Military Trilogy," in *Literature/Film Quarterly* (Salisbury, Maryland), April 1986.

Wood, Robin, "*Drums Along the Mohawk*," in *Cine Action!* (Toronto), no. 8, 1987.

Nolley, Ken, "Reconsidering *The Quiet Man*," in *Cine Action!* (Toronto), no. 9, 1987.

Bernstein, Matthew, "Hollywood's 'Arty Cinema': John Ford's *The Long Voyage Home*," in *Wide Angle* (Athens, Ohio), vol. 10, no. 1, 1988.

Card, James, "*The Searchers*: by Alan LeMay and John Ford," in *Literature/Film Quarterly* (Salisbury, Maryland), vol. 16, no. 1, 1988.

On FORD: films—

Haggard, Mark, *John Ford: Memorial Day 1970*, U.S., 1970.
Bogdanovich, Peter, *Directed by John Ford*, U.S., 1971.
Sanders, Denis, *The American West of John Ford*, U.K., 1971.

*　　　*　　　*

John Ford has no peers in the annals of cinema. This is not to place him above criticism, merely above comparison. His faults were unique, as was his art, which he pursued with a single-minded and single-hearted stubbornness for 60 years and 112 films. He grew up with the American cinema. That he should have begun his career as an extra in the Ku Klux Klan sequences of *The Birth of a Nation* and ended it supervising the documentary *Vietnam! Vietnam!* conveys the remarkable breadth of his contribution to film, and the narrowness of its concerns.

Ford's subject is his life and times. Immigrant, Catholic, Republican, he speaks for the generations that created the modern United States between the Civil and Great Wars. Like Walt Whitman, Ford chronicles the society of that half century, expansionist by design, mystical and religious by conviction, hierarchical by agreement; an association of equals within a structure of command, practical, patriotic and devout: the society Whitman celebrated as "something in the doings of man that corresponds with the broadcast doings of night and day."

Mythologizing the armed services and the church as paradigms of structural integrity, Ford adapts their rules to his private world. All may speak in Ford's films, but when divine order is invoked, the faithful fall silent, to fight and die as decreed by a general, a president or some other member of a God-anointed elite.

In Ford's hierarchy, Native and African Americans share the lowest rung, women the next. Businessmen, uniformly corrupt in his world, hover below the honest and unimaginative citizenry of the United States. Above them begins Ford's elite, within which members of the armed forces occupy a privileged position. In authority over them is an officer class of career military men and priests, culminating in a few near-saintly figures of which Abraham Lincoln is the most notable, while over all rules a retributory, partial and jealous God.

The consistency of Ford's work lies in his fidelity to the morality implicit in this structure. *Mary of Scotland*'s Mary Queen of Scots, the retiring Nathan Brittles in *She Wore a Yellow Ribbon* and outgoing mayor Frank Skeffington in *The Last Hurrah* all face the decline in their powers with a moral strength drawn from a belief in the essential order of their lives. Mary goes triumphant to the scaffold, affirming Catholicism and the divine right of kings. Duty to his companions of the 7th Cavalry transcending all, Brittles returns to rejoin them in danger. Skeffington prefers to lose rather than succumb to modern vote-getters like TV.

"I make westerns," Ford announced on one well-publicized occasion. Like most of his generalizations, it was untrue. Only a third of his films are westerns, and of those a number are rural comedies with perfunctory frontier settings: *Doctor Bull, Judge Priest, Steamboat Round the Bend, The Sun Shines Bright*. Many of his family films, like *Four Men and a Prayer* and *Pilgrimage*, belong with the stories of military life, of which he made a score. A disciple of the US Navy, from which he retired with the emeritus rank of Rear Admiral, Ford found in its command structure a perfect metaphor for moral order. In *They Were Expendable*, he chose to falsify every fact of the Pacific War to celebrate the moral superiority of men trained in its rigid disciplines—men who obey, affirm, keep faith.

Acts, not words, convey the truths of men's lives; public affirmations of this dictum dominate Ford's films. Dances and fights signify in their vigor a powerful sense of community; singing and eating and getting drunk together are the great acts of Fordian union. A film like *The Searchers*, perhaps his masterpiece, makes clear its care for family life and tradition in a series of significant actions that need no words. Ward Bond turns away from the revelation of a woman's love for her brother-in-law exposed in her reverent handling of his cloak—the instinctive act of a natural gentleman. Barred from the family life which his anger and independence make alien to his character, John Wayne clutches his arm in a gesture borrowed from Ford's first star, Harry Carey, and, in a memorable final image, the door closes on him, rejecting the eternal clanless wanderer.

Ford spent his filmmaking years in a cloud of critical misunderstanding, each new film compared unfavorably with earlier works. *The Iron Horse* established him as an epic westerner in the mold of Raoul Walsh, *The Informer* as a Langian master of expressionism, the cavalry pictures as Honest John Ford, a New England primitive whose work, in Lindsay Anderson's words, was "unsophisticated and direct." When, in his last decades of work, he returned to reexamine earlier films in a series of revealing remakes, the sceptical saw not a moving reiteration of values but a decline into self-plagiarism. Yet it is *The Man Who Shot Liberty Valance*, in which he deals with the issues raised in *Stagecoach*, showing his beloved populist west destroyed by law and literacy, that stands today among his most important films.

Belligerent, grandiose, deceitful and arrogant in real life, Ford seldom let these traits spill over into his films. They express at their best a guarded serenity, a sceptical satisfaction in the beauty of the American landscape, muted always by an understanding of the dangers implicit in the land, and a sense of the responsibility of all men to protect the common heritage. In every Ford film there is a gun behind the door, a conviction behind the joke, a challenge in every toast. Ford belongs in the tradition of American narrative art where telling a story and drawing a moral are twin aspects of public utterance. He saw that we live in history, and that history embodies lessons we must learn. When Fordian man speaks, the audience is meant to listen—and listen all the harder for the restraint and circumspection of the man who speaks. One hears the authentic Fordian voice nowhere more powerfully than in Ward Bond's preamble to the celebrating enlisted men in *They Were Expendable* as they toast the retirement of a comrade. "I'm not going to make a speech," he states. "I've just got something to say."

—John Baxter

FORMAN, Milos.

Czech. Born in Kaslov, Czechoslovakia, 18 February 1932, became U.S. citizen, 1977. Educated at Academy of Music and Dramatic Art, Prague, and at Film Academy (FAMU), Prague, 1951–56. Married 1) Jana Brejchová (divorced); 2) Vera Kresadlova (divorced). Collaborated on screenplay for Frič's *Leave It to Me*, 1956; theatre director for Laterna Magika, Prague, 1958–62; directed first feature, *Black Peter*, 1963; moved to New York, 1969; co-director of Columbia University Film Division, from 1975. Recipient: Czechoslovak Film Critics' Prize, for *Black Peter*, 1963; Czechoslovak State Prize, 1967; Oscar for Best Director, and Best Director Award, Directors Guild of America, for *One Flew Over the Cuckoo's Nest*, 1975; Oscar for Best Director, for *Amadeus*, 1984. Agent: Robert Lantz, 888 Seventh Ave., New York, NY 10106, U.S.A.

Films as Director:

1963 *Cerný Petr* (*Black Peter, Peter and Pavla*); (+ co-sc); *Konkurs* (*Talent Competition*) (+ co-sc)
1965 *Lásky jedné plavovlásky* (*Loves of a Blonde*) (+ co-sc); *Dobře placená procházka* (*A Well Paid Stroll*) (+ co-sc)
1967 *Hoří, má panenko* (*The Firemen's Ball*) (+ co-sc)
1970 *Taking Off* (+ co-sc)
1972 "Decathlon" segment of *Visions of Eight* (+ co-sc)
1975 *One Flew Over the Cuckoo's Nest*
1979 *Hair*
1981 *Ragtime*
1983 *Amadeus*
1989 *Valmont*

Other Films:

1955 *Nechte to na mně* (*Leave It to Me*) (Frič) (+ co-sc); *Dědeček automobil* (*Old Man Motorcar*) (Radok) (asst d, role)
1957 *Stěnata* (*The Puppies*) (+ co-sc)
1962 *Tam za lesem* (*Beyond the Forest*) (Blumenfeld) (asst d, role as the physician)
1968 *La Pine à ongles* (Carrière) (+ co-sc)
1975 *Le Mâle du siècle* (Berri) (story)

Publications:

By FORMAN: books—

Taking Off, with John Guare and others, New York, 1971.
Milos Forman, with others, London, 1972.

By FORMAN: articles—

"Closer to Things," in *Cahiers du Cinéma in English* (New York), January 1967.
Interview with Galina Kopaněvová, in *Film a Doba* (Prague), no. 8, 1968.
Interview, in *The Film Director as Superstar*, edited by Joseph Gelmis, New York, 1970.
"Getting the Great Ten Percent," an interview with Harriet Polt, in *Film Comment* (New York), Fall 1970.
"A Czech in New York," an interview with Gordon Gow, in *Films and Filming* (London), September 1971.
Interview in *American Cinematographer* (Los Angeles), November 1972.
Interview with L. Sturhahn, in *Filmmakers Newsletter* (Ward Hill, Massachusetts), December 1975.
Interview with T. McCarthy, in *Film Comment* (New York), March/April 1979.
Interview with Michel Ciment, in *Positif* (Paris), November 1984.
Interview in *Films* (London), March 1985.
Interview with T.J. Slater, in *Post Script* (Jacksonville, Florida), Spring/Summer and Fall 1985.
Interview in *Première* (Paris), July 1987.

On FORMAN: books—

Boček, Jaroslav, *Modern Czechoslovak Film 1945–1965*, Prague, 1965.
Skvorecký, Josef, *All the Bright Young Men and Women*, Toronto, 1971.
Henstell, Bruce, editor, *Milos Forman, Ingrid Thulin*, Washington, D.C., 1972.
Liehm, Antonín, *Closely Watched Films*, White Plains, New York, 1974.
Liehm, Antonín, *The Milos Forman Stories*, White Plains, New York, 1975.

On FORMAN: articles—

Dyer, Peter, "Star-Crossed in Prague," in *Sight and Sound* (London), Winter 1965/66.
Bor, Vladimír, "Formanovský film a některé předsudky" ["The Formanesque Film and Some Prejudices"], in *Film a Doba* (Prague), no. 1, 1967.
Effenberger, Vratislav, "Obraz člověka v českém film," ["The Portrayal of Man in the Czech Cinema"] in *Film a Doba* (Prague), no. 7, 1968.
"Director of the Year," in *International Film Guide*, London, 1969.
Combs, Richard, "Sentimental Journey," in *Sight and Sound* (London), Summer 1977.
Baker, B., "Milos Forman," in *Film Dope* (London), April 1979.
Cameron, J., "Milos Forman and *Hair*: Styling the Age of Aquarius," in *Rolling Stone* (New York), 19 April 1979.
Stein, H., "A Day in the Life: Milos Forman: Moment to Moment with the Director of *Hair*," in *Esquire* (New York), 8 May 1979.

On FORMAN: film—

Weingarten, Mira, *Meeting Milos Forman*, U.S., 1971.

*   *   *

In the context of Czechoslovak cinema in the early 1960's, Milos Forman's first films (*Black Peter* and *Competition*) amounted to a revolution. Influenced by Czech novelists who revolted against the establishment's aesthetic dogmas in the late 1950's rather than by Western cinema (thought the mark of late neorealism, in particular Ermanno Olmi, is visible), Forman, in these early films, introduced to the cinema after 1948 (the year of the Communist coup) portrayals of working-class life untainted by the formulae of socialist realism.

Though initially he was fiercely attacked by Stalinist reviewers, the more liberal faction of the Communist party, then in the ascendancy, appropriated Forman's movies as expressions of the new concept of "socialist" art. Together with great box office success and an excellent reputation gained at international festivals, these circumstances made Forman into the undisputed star of the Czech New Wave. His style was characterized by a sensitive use of non-actors (usually coupled with professionals); by refreshing, natural-sounding, semi-improvised dialogue which reflected Forman's intimate knowledge of the milieu he was capturing on the screen; and by an unerring ear for the nuances of Czech folk-rock and for music in general.

All these characteristic features of the two early films are even more prominent in *Loves of a Blonde*, and especially in *Firemen's Ball* which works equally well on the level of a realistic humorous story, and on the allegorical level that points to the aftermath of the party's decision to reveal some of the political crimes committed in the 1950's (the Slánský trial). In all these films—developed, except for *Black Peter*, from Forman's original ideas—he closely collaborated with his scriptwriters Ivan Passer and Jaroslav Papousek, who later became directors in their own right.

Shortly after the Soviet invasion of 1968, *Firemen's Ball* was banned and Forman decided to remain in the West, where he was during the events of August 1968. He was working on the script for what was to become the only film in which he would

Milos Forman: *Horí, má panenko*

apply the principles of his aesthetic method and vision to indigenous American material, *Taking Off*. It is also his only American movie developed from his original idea; the rest are adaptations. Traces of the pre-American Forman are easily recognizable in his most successful U.S. film, *One Flew Over the Cuckoo's Nest*, which radically changed Ken Kesey's story and—just as in the case of Papousek's novel *Black Peter*—brought it close to the director's own objective and comical vision. The work received an Oscar in 1975. In that year Forman became an American citizen. Unfortunately, the Forman touch is much less evident in his reworking of the musical *Hair*, and almost—though not entirely—absent from his version of Doctorow's novel *Ragtime*. The same is true of the box-office smash hit and multiple Oscar winner *Amadeus*, and his later adaptation, *Valmont*. Of marginal importance are the two remaining parts of Forman's oeuvre, *The Well-Paid Stroll*, a jazz opera adapted from the stage for Prague TV, and *Decathlon*, his contribution to the 1972 Olympic documentary *Visions of Eight*.

Forman is a merciless observer of the *comedie humaine* and, both in Czechoslovakia and in the West, has often been accused of cynicism. To such criticisms he answers with Chekhov, pointing out that what is cruel in the first place is life itself. But apart from such arguments, the rich texture of acutely observed life and the sensitive portrayal of and apparent sympathy for people as victims—often ridiculous—of circumstances over which they wield no power, render such critical statements null and void. Forman's vision is deeply rooted in the anti-ideological, realistic and humanist tradition of such "cynics" of Czech literature as Jaroslav Hasek (*The Good Soldier Svejk*), Bohumil Hrabal (*Closely Watched Trains*) or Josef Skvorecký (whose novel *The Cowards* Forman was prevented from filming by the invasion of 1968). Though the influence of his method may be felt even in some North American films, his lasting importance will, very probably, rest with his three Czech movies to which *Taking Off* should be added, a valiant attempt to show America to Americans through the eyes of a sensitive, if caustic, foreign observer. After the mixed reception of this film, Forman took off in the direction of adaptations of best sellers and stage hits. He remains an outstanding craftsman and a first-class actors' director; however, in the context of American cinema he does not represent the innovative force he was in Prague.

—Josef Skvorecký

FORSYTH, Bill.

Scottish. Born in Glasgow, 1947. Studied at National Film School, Beaconsfield, Bucks., for three months, 1971. Left school at 16 and worked for documentary filmmaker Stanley Russell; set up Tree Films with Charles Gormley, 1972; producer of documentaries, 1970's; began working with Glasgow Youth Theatre, 1977; directed first feature, *That Sinking Feeling*, 1979. Recipient: British Academy Award for Best Screenplay, for *Gregory's Girl*, 1981; Honorary Doctorate, University of Glasgow, 1983.

Films as Director and Scriptwriter:

1979   *That Sinking Feeling*
1980   **Gregory's Girl**
1983   *Local Hero*
1984   *Comfort and Joy*
1987   *Housekeeping* (*Sylvie's Ark*)
1989   *Breaking In*
1990   *Rebecca's Daughter*

Bill Forsyth

Publications:

By FORSYTH: articles—

Interview in *Sight and Sound* (London), Autumn 1981.
"A Suitable Job for a Scot," an interview with J. Brown, in *Sight and Sound* (London), Summer 1983.
Interview with A. Hunter, in *Films and Filming* (London), August 1984.
"The Forsyth Saga," an interview with E. Stein, in *American Film* (Washington, D.C.), November 1984.
Interview with Graham Fuller, in *Listener* (London), 19 November, 1987.
Interview in *Films and Filming* (London), December 1987.
Interview with L. Tanner, in *Films in Review* (New York), February 1988.

On FORSYTH: books—

Park, James, *Learning to Dream: The New British Cinema*, London, 1985.
Roddick, Nick, and Chris Auty, *British Cinema Now*, London, 1985.
Walker, Alexander, *National Heroes: British Cinema in the '70s and '80s*, London, 1985.
Dick, Eddie, editor, *From Limelight to Satellite: A Scottish Film Book*, London, 1990.
Hardy, Forsyth, *Scotland in Film*, Edinburgh, 1990.

On FORSYTH: articles—

Films Illustrated (London), August 1981.
Falk, Quentin, "Local heroes," in *Sight and Sound* (London), Autumn 1982.
Films (London), July 1983.
Nave, B., "Humour ecossais: *Local Hero*," in *Jeune Cinema* (Paris), April 1984.
Malcomson, S.L., "Modernism Comes to the Cabbage Patch," in *Film Quarterly* (Berkeley), Spring 1985.
Pym, John, "*Housekeeping*," in *Sight and Sound* (London), Winter 1987–88.

*   *   *

For a while during the early 1980's Scottish cinema was virtually synonymous with Bill Forsyth. Today his work remains among the most original and distinctive to have emerged not only from Scotland but from Britain as a whole. The Forsyth oeuvre is rooted in a gentle and extremely charming off-beat view of the world which has affinities with a variety of comic traditions including Ealing comedy, Frank Capra, Jacques Tati and Ermanno Olmi (*Il Posto* is practically a blueprint in tone and feel for *Gregory's Girl*), but which maintains its own individuality and character. Forsyth's choice of comedy as his mode of expression was partly dictated by the fact that his first two films were made on tiny budgets. In characteristically modest fashion he regarded comedy as more appropriate, being less self-indulgent and more fun to do for everyone involved. Crucially it gave these films a vitality which helped them transcend their budgetary limitations and, in the case of *Gregory's Girl*, find a sizeable audience outside Scotland.

Forsyth's charm lies in his attention to detail, particularly the various quirks and idiosyncrasies of his characters which are conveyed equally effectively through both image and dialogue. These characters are often marginalised individuals caught up in circumstances they are ill equipped to deal with. Forsyth finds a great deal of humour in their predicaments but he does so in a wry and generous manner which is never at the expense of the characters, his approach amounting rather to a celebration of the human spirit with all its foibles and shortcomings.

Forsyth's acute perception of human behaviour gives his films a depth which transcends their initial charm as quirky comedies. *Gregory's Girl*, for example, is populated by dreamers lost in their various obsessions. At the centre is the first stirrings of sexuality in rather awkward male adolescents. Gregory is obsessed with the enigmatic and ultimately unobtainable Dorothy (a situation repeated in *Local Hero* with Danny and McIntyre's unrequited love for Marina and Stella respectively). But Forsyth also uncovers a variety of obsessions ranging from a fascination with numbers to useless facts and cookery, which are an expression of the problems and confusions associated with adolescence: in essence a redirection of sexual energy.

Although equally obsessed with boys, the girls in the film are more knowing, more sophisticated (Gregory constantly seeks advice on matters of the heart from his eleven-year-old sister) and more in control of their own destinies—Dorothy overcomes the sexist opposition of the coach to earn a place in the football team, while Susan ingeniously uses her friends to divert Gregory's romantic attentions away from Dorothy and towards herself. Forsyth obviously has a great empathy with the female point of view, and it is no coincidence that his most mature and accomplished work *Housekeeping* concentrates totally on the relationship between two young girls and their rather eccentric aunt.

Despite the generally up-beat ambience, Forsyth's cinema has its darker side. There are poignant moments of irony in *That Sinking Feeling*, a film which despite its quirkiness and innocence features a group of teenagers attempting to cope with the problems of unemployment set against a bleak and crumbling urban landscape. *Local Hero* has a rather subdued ending, which compensates for the cosy and contrived resolution reached between beachcomber Ben Knox and Happer the oil tycoon, with McIntyre resuming a life in Texas which he has come to regard as shallow and meaningless. *Comfort and Joy* is darker than its predecessors not only in theme but in visual style. It concentrates on one solitary character and charts his development from morbid introspection when his girlfriend leaves him at Christmas, to a fascination with the absurdities of the world around him. Despite Forsyth's intention to make a gloomier film, *Comfort and Joy* appears rather whimsical when compared to the brutality of the real Glasgow "Ice Cream Wars" which occurred at about the same time.

But Forsyth's most serious effort by far is *Housekeeping*, his first adaptation and first film to be shot outside Scotland. In exploring the dilemma of whether to conform to social expectations or opt out altogether, it successfully mixes very real moments of tragedy and grief (it is the only Bill Forsyth film to provoke real anxiety and even tears), with lighter and more familiar Forsythian observations and character traits. *Housekeeping* marks a major development in Forsyth's career, demonstrating a greater emotional complexity and directorial assuredness. It opens out his cinema from its provincial Scottish roots while retaining the charm and warmth of his earlier work and suggests that we may not yet have seen the best of this major film-making talent.

—Duncan J. Petrie

FOSSE, Bob.

American. Born Robert Louis Fosse in Chicago, 23 June 1927. Educated at Amundsen High School, Chicago, graduated 1945; studied acting at American Theatre Wing, New York, 1947. Married 1) Mary Ann Niles (divorced); 2) Joan McCracken (divorced); 3) Gwen Verdon, 1960 (divorced). Formed dance team, "The Riff brothers," with Charles Grass, 1940; master of ceremonies in a night club, 1942; enlisted in U.S. Navy, 1945, assigned to entertainment units in Pacific; chorus dancer in touring companies, 1948–50; Broadway debut in *Dance Me a Song*, 1950; signed to MGM, Hollywood, 1953; Broadway debut as choreographer with *The Pajama Game*, 1954; directed first film, *Sweet Charity*, 1968. Recipient: Nine "Tony" Awards; Oscar for Best Director, and British Academy Award for Best Director, for *Cabaret*, 1972; also Emmy Award, for *Liza with a "Z"*, 1973. *Died of a heart attack, in Washington, D.C., 23 September 1987.*

Films as Director:

1968	*Sweet Charity* (+ chor)	
1972	*Cabaret* (+ chor)	
1974	*Lenny*	
1979	*All That Jazz* (+ chor)	
1983	*Star 80*	

Other Films:

1953 *The Affairs of Dobie Gillis* (Weis) (role); *Kiss Me Kate* (Sidney) (role); *Give a Girl a Break* (Donen) (role)

1955 *My Sister Eileen* (Quine) (chor, role)
1957 *The Pajama Game* (Donen and Abbott) (chor)
1958 *Damn Yankees* (*What Lola Wants*) (Donen and Abbott) (chor, dancer in "Who's Got the Pain" number)
1974 *The Little Prince* (Donen) (chor "Snake in the Grass" number, role)
1976 *Thieves* (Berry) (role)

Publications:

By FOSSE: articles—

"Inter/View with Bob Fosse," with L. Picard, in *Inter/View* (New York), March 1972.
"The Making of *Lenny*," interview with S. Hornstein, in *Filmmakers Newsletter* (Ward Hill, Massachusetts), February 1975.
Interview in *Cinématographe* (Paris), March 1984.

On FOSSE: books—

Altman, Rick, *The American Film Musical*, Bloomington, Indiana, 1989.
Grubb, Kevin Boyd, *Razzle Dazzle: The Life and Work of Bob Fosse*, New York, 1989.

On FOSSE: articles—

Vallance, T., "Bob Fosse," in *Focus on Film* (London), Summer 1972.
Gardner, P., "Bob Fosse," in *Action* (Los Angeles), May/June 1974.
Badder, D.J., "Bob Fosse," in *Film Dope* (London), April 1979.
Drew, B., "Life as a Long Rehearsal," in *American Film* (Washington, D.C.), November 1979.
Braun, E., "In Camera: The Perfectionist," in *Films and Filming* (London), January 1980.
Valot, J., P. Ross, and D. Parra, "Bob Fosse," in *Revue du Cinéma* (Paris), March 1984.
Mizejewski, Linda, "Women, Monsters, and the Masochistic Aesthetic in Fosse's *Cabaret*," in *Journal of Film and Video* (Boston), vol. 39, no. 4, 1987.
Wood, Robin, "Cloven Hoofer: Choreography as Autobiography in *All That Jazz*," in *Post Script* (Jacksonville, Florida), Winter 1987.
Obituary in *Variety* (New York), 24 September 1987.
Obituary in *Hollywood Reporter*, 25 September 1987.
Obituary in *Films and Filming* (London), November 1987.
Kemp, P., "Degrees of Radiance," in *Cinema Papers* (Melbourne), March 1988.

*   *   *

Rex Reed once said of Bob Fosse (in a review of his performance as The Snake in *The Little Prince*), "The man can do anything!" Somewhat effusive, Reed's comment nonetheless has more than a kernel of truth: Fosse won 8 Tonys, 1 Oscar, and 1 Emmy. In fact, he garnered four of the awards (the Oscar for *Cabaret*, the Emmy for *Liza with a Z*, and two Tonys for *Pippin*) in one year.

Fosse started his career as a dancer and choreographer on Broadway and divided his time almost equally between directing for the stage and for films. All of Fosse's films are musicals (with the exception of *Lenny*) and it is within this genre that he made significant contributions. The directorial choices employed by Fosse stemmed, not surprisingly, from his style of dancing and choreography: a type of eccentric jazz that isolates and exaggerates human motion, breaking it up into small components. It has been noted that there appears to be little difference between the dance material for Fosse's stage and film choreography. But the presentation of the dance is radically different. On the stage, only the performers could create the fragmentation of Fosse's choreography. In film, the use of multiple camera set-ups and editing allows an amplification of this fragmentation, essentially obliterating the dance material and the mise-en-scène.

This style can be seen as the complete opposite of Astaire's presentation which strives to preserve spatial and temporal integrity. "I love the camera," Fosse once said, "I love camera movement and camera angles. As a choreographer you see everything with a frame." Camera angle and camera image become more important choreographically than the dancing. The routine itself is non-essential, subordinated to a more complex system of integration and commentary, as Jerome Delameter has noted.

Fosse's notions of integration and commentary drastically altered the structure of the American musical film. Reacting against 30-odd years of the Arthur Freed musical, Fosse broke new ground in 1972 with *Cabaret*. No longer were the musical numbers "integrated" into the narrative with people singing to each other. All performance was logically grounded, occurring where it might be expected—on a stage for example (and never leaving that stage as Berkeley did)—and was distinctly separated from the narrative. The "integration" took place in the sense that each performance was a comment on the narrative action. In an interview with Glenn Loney for *After Dark*, Fosse sheds some light on his approach. "I don't think there is any such thing as a realistic musical. As soon as people start to sing to each other, you've already gone beyond realism in the usual sense. . .I have generally tried to make the musical more believable." (Not more realistic, just more plausible or more logical.) Fosse expounded on his concepts of "believability," "integrated commentary," and visual fragmentation of performance via camera angle and editing with *All That Jazz*, a film in which musical numbers are literal hallucinations, obviously separated from the narrative but still logically grounded within it.

—Greg Faller

———

FRAMPTON, Hollis.

American. Born in Wooster, Ohio, 11 March 1936. Educated at Western Reserve University, 1954–57. Moved to New York City, 1958; technician in film laboratories, 1961–69; primarily engaged in still photography, 1959–66; finished first released film, *Manual of Arms*, 1966; taught filmmaking at Free University of New York, 1966–7; Assistant Professor, Hunter College, New York, 1969–73; also lectured at School of Visual Arts and The Cooper Union, New York; Associate Professor, State University of New York at Buffalo, from 1973; co-designer and programmer of DEMON, an interpretative microcomputer language for audio-frequency data editing and control, 1979, and of IMAGO, a video master graphics computer language, 1980–81. *Died March 1984.*

Films: note: entire body of film preserved by Royal Film Archive of Belgium)

1962 *Clouds Like White Sheep* (destroyed)
1963 *A Running Man* (destroyed)
1964 *Ten Mile Poem* (destroyed)
1965 *Obelisk Ampersand Encounter* (lost)
1966 *Manual of Arms*; *Process Red*; *Information*; *A & B in Ontario* (abandoned)
1967 *States*; *Heterodyne*
1968 *Snowblind*; *Maxwell's Demon*; *Surface Tension*
1969 *Palindrome*; *Carrots and Peas*; *Lemon*; *Prince Ruperts Drops*; *Works and Days*; *Artificial Light*
1970 *Zorns Lemma*
1971 *Nostalgia*; *Travelling Matte*; *Critical Mass*
1972 *Special Effects*; *Poetic Justice*; *Ordinary Matter*; *Remote Control*; *Hapax Legomena*; *Apparatus Sum*; *Tiger Balm*; *Yellow Springs*

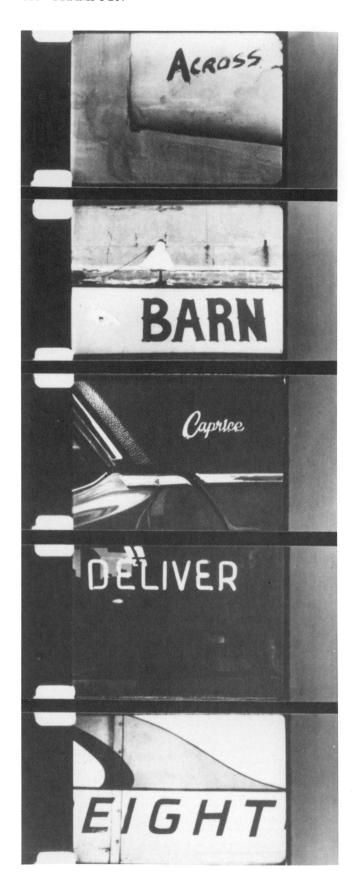

Hollis Frampton: *Zorn's Lemma*

1973   *Public Domain*; *Less*
1974   *Autumnal Equinox*; *Noctiluca*; *Winter Solstice*; *Banner*
1975   *Ingenium Nobis Ipsa Puella Fecit*; *Solariumagelani*; *Drum*; *Pas de Trois*
1976   *Magellan: At the Gates of Death*: Part I: *The Red Gate,* Part II: *The Green Gate*; *Otherwise Unexplained Fires*; *Not the First Time*; *For Georgia O'Keeffe*; *Quaternion*; *Tuba*; *Procession*
1979   *More than Meets the Eye*; *Gloria! The Birth of Magellan: Dreams of Magellan: Parts I–VI*
1980   *The Birth of Magellan: Mindfall: Parts I–VII*; *The Birth of Magellan: Fourteen Cadenzas*

Unfinished Projects:

1972–   *Magellan*
1973–   *Monsieur Phot*: *A Film by Joseph Cornell*
1980–   *R*

Publications:

By FRAMPTON: books—

Poetic Justice, Rochester, New York, 1973.
Fictcryptokrimsographs, Buffalo, New York, 1975.
Carl André—Hollis Frampton: 12 Dialogues 1962–1963, New York, 1980.
Circles of Confusion, Rochester, New York, 1983.

By FRAMPTON: articles—

Interview with Michael Snow, in *Film Culture* (New York), Winter/Spring 1970.
"For a Metahistory of Film: Commonplace Notes and Hypotheses," in *Artforum* (New York), September 1971.
"Nostalgia: Voice-Over Narration for a Film of that Name," in *Film Culture* (New York), Spring 1972.
Interview with Simon Field and Peter Sainsbury, in *Afterimage* (London), Fall 1972.
"Digressions on the Photographic Agony," in *Artforum* (New York), November 1972.
"Eadweard Muybridge: Fragments of a Tesseract," in *Artforum* (New York), March 1973.
"Incisions in History/Segments of Eternity," in *Artforum* (New York), October 1974.
Interview in *Structural Film Anthology*, edited by Peter Gidal, London, 1976.
"Notes on Composing in Film," in *October* (New York), Spring 1976.
Interview with Mitch Tuchmann, in *Film Comment* (New York), September/October 1977.
"Impromptus on Edward Weston: Everything in Its Place," in *October* (New York), Summer 1978.
"Talking about *Magellan*," an interview with Bill Simon, in *Millenium Film Journal* (New York), Fall/Winter 1980/81.
3 Talks by Frampton, in *Millenium Film Journal* (New York), Fall/Winter 1986/87.

On FRAMPTON: books—

The Films of Hollis Frampton, Minneapolis, 1972.
Sitney, P. Adams, editor, *The Avant-Garde film: A Reader of Theory and Criticism*, New York, 1979.
Sitney, P. Adams, *Visionary Film*, New York, 1980.
Jenkins, Bruce, and Susan Krane, *Hollis Frampton: Recollections/Recreations*, Cambridge, Massachusetts, 1984.
Macdonald, Scott, *A Critical Cinema: Interviews with Independent Filmmakers*, Berkeley, 1988.

On FRAMPTON: articles—

Field, Simon, "Alphabet as Ideogram," in *Art and Artists* (London), August 1972.
Mekas, Jonas, "Movie Journal," in *Village Voice* (New York), 4 and 11 April 1974.
Rayns, Tony, "Lines Describing an Impasse: Experimental Five," in *Sight and Sound* (London), Spring 1975.
Gunning, Tom, "The Participatory Film," in *American Film* (Washington, D.C.), October 1975.

Weinstein, Dave, "Hollis Frampton—Film as Symbol," in *Artweek* (Oakland, California), 8 May 1976.

Simon, Bill, "Reading *Zorn's Lemma*," in *Millenium Film Journal* (New York), Spring/Summer 1978.

Jenkins, Bruce, "Frampton Unstructured: Notes for a Metacritical History," in *Wide Angle* (Athens, Ohio), Fall 1978.

Fischer, Lucy, "Frampton and the Magellan Metaphor," in *American Film* (Washington, D.C.), May 1979.

Lindemann, Bernhard, "Experimental Film as Meta-Film: Frampton's *Zorn Lemma*," in *Enclitic* (Minneapolis), Fall 1979.

Tuchman, Mitch, "Frampton," in *Film Comment* (New York), July/August 1985.

Millenium Film Journal (New York), Fall/Winter 1984/85.

*   *   *

Hollis Frampton worked in poetry, painting, and photography before coming to filmmaking. In addition, he studied widely in a variety of disciplines outside of as well as within the arts. Much of the richness and complexity of his films results from influences culled from many diverse fields and fused within single works.

Many of Frampton's films exhibit complex, spectacularly strict structures. *Zorn's Lemma*, his best-known work, has a long central section in which alphabetized signs are gradually replaced with wordless images. This and similar devices involve the audience in an overtly participatory way. In (*nostalgia*), we hear still photographs described before seeing them, and are thus involved with constructing a mental image from the description, which generally is quite different from the actual photograph we then see. Many of Frampton's pre-*Magellan* films involve game-like activities of counting, reading, guessing. While carefully controlled structures and audience participation were common to other avant-garde films and other arts in the late 1960's, Frampton's films in this mode are characterized by a unique rigor. He seeks to bring to cinema some of the precision of the sciences, of mathematics.

True to the modernist tradition of which he is a part, Frampton devoted much of his cinema's energy to the act of investigating the medium itself. In a great number of early films made before *Zorn's Lemma*, he explored a vast range of cinematic possibilities, from the simplest use of black and white portrait imagery (*Manual of Arms*) to abstract shapes (*Palindrome*) to various modifications of photo imagery (*Artificial Light*). He said that film itself "is what all films are about," and much of his work can be taken as the proffering of possible alternative definitions of the medium. But by defining Frampton does not mean to delimit, so not only do different films offer different definitions: each film tries to be the most perfect example of its possibility that it can. These works are characterized by their frequently spectacular photographic qualities, and their absolute formal precision.

In seeking to investigate the properties of his medium, rather than placing primary emphasis on the idiosyncratic qualities of his own inner vision, Frampton set different goals for himself than those of Brakhage or Baillie. But an autobiographical element is often also present in Frampton's work, most strongly in his serial film *Hapax Legomena*, of which (*nostalgia*) is the first of seven parts. The sections that make up this work simultaneously display a range of possible interactions between film and other media (still photography, writing, video, spoken language), and tell an implied story of the birth of a filmmaker via an evolution through film-related media (photography, a film script) to cinema itself. The sequence's seventh and final section, *Special Effects*, completes this movement by presenting a moving white-outlined rectangle at the edge of a black frame, and is a meditation on one of cinema's essences, the frame itself. The evolution within *Hapax Lego-*

mena can also be seen to lead to Frampton's massive, multipart (uncompleted) *Magellan*.

Of Frampton's other areas of involvement, still photography seemed to have the strongest influence on his filmmaking. He saw in photographers like Weston the possibility that a photo image, in the sensuality of its tiniest modulations, can constitute an ineluctable mystery which is finally outside of language. The subject matter and photographic and editing styles of *Magellan*'s completed sections are many and various, but again and again the editing functions to return the viewer to a contemplation of the graphic qualities of the screen imagery, as if cinematically recreating the process of looking at a still photograph. The filmmaker's exhibition scheme for the completed film defied anything yet attempted in the medium; for instance, there was to be at least one different film for each day of the year. *Magellan*'s encyclopedic goal is perhaps best expressed by Frampton himself, as being an attempt to record, and render comprehensible, the sights and sounds of the visible world.

—Fred Camper

FRANJU, Georges.

French. Born in Fougères, Brittany, 12 April 1912. Educated at religious school in Fougères. Military service in Algeria, 1928–32. Set builder for Folies Bergères and the Casino de Paris, 1932–33; began Cercle du Cinéma programme with Henri Langlois, and directed *Le Metro*, 1934; co-founder, with Langlois, of Cinémathèque Française and *Cinématographe* magazine, 1937; Executive secretary of La Fédération Internationale des Archives du Film (FIAF), from 1938; Secretary-General of the Institut de Cinématographie Scientifique, 1945–54; founder, L'Academie du Cinéma, 1946; directed first feature-length film, 1958; director for French TV (including *Chroniques de France*), from 1965. Recipient: Chevalier de la Légion d'honneur; Officier de l'ordre national du Mérite et des Arts et des Lettres. *Died 5 November 1987.*

Films as Director:

1934   *Le Metro* (co-d, sc) (short)
1949   **Le Sang des bêtes** (+ sc) (short)
1950   *En passant par la Lorraine* (+ sc) (short)
1951   *Hôtel des Invalides* (+ sc) (short)
1952   *Le Grand Méliès* (+ sc) (short)
1953   *Monsieur et Madame Curie* (+ sc) (short)
1954   *Les Poussières* (+ sc) (short); *Navigation marchande (Marine marchande)* (+ sc) (short; disowned by Franju)
1955   *A propos d'une rivière (Le Saumon Atlantique)* (+ sc) (short); *Mon chien* (+ sc) (short)
1956   *Le Théâtre National Populaire (Le T.N.P.)* (+ sc) (short); *Sur le Pont d'Avignon* (+ sc)(short)
1957   *Notre Dame, cathédrale de Paris* (+ sc) (short)
1958   *La Première nuit* (+ sc) (short); *La Tête contre les murs (The Keepers)*
1959   **Les Yeuxs sans visage** (+ co-adapt)
1960   *Pleins feux sur l'assassin (Spotlight on Murder)*
1962   **Thérèse Desqueyroux** (+ co-sc)
1963   *Judex*
1964   *Thomas l'imposteur (Thomas the Imposter)* (+ co-sc)
1970   *La Faute de l'Abbé Mouret (The Demise of Father Mouret)* (+ co-sc)
1974   *Nuits rouges (L'Homme sans visage. Shadowman)* (+ co-mus)

Other Film:

1956 *Décembre, mois des enfants* (Storck) (co-sc)

Publications:

By FRANJU: book—

De Marey à Renoir, trésors de la Cinémathèque Française 1882–1939, Paris, 1981.

By FRANJU: articles—

Interview with Freddy Buache, in *Positif* (Paris), September 1957.
Interview with François Truffaut, in *Cahiers du Cinéma* (Paris), November 1959.
Interview with Jean-André Fieschi and André Labarthe, in *Cahiers du Cinéma* (Paris), November 1963.
"*Hôtel des Invalides*," in *Avant-Scène du Cinéma* (Paris), no. 38, 1964.
"*Le Sang des bêtes*," in *Avant-Scène du Cinéma* (Paris), no. 41, 1964.
"Réalisme et Surréalisme," in *Etudes Cinématographiques* (Paris), no. 41/42, 1965.
Interview with Tom Milne, in *Sight and Sound* (London), Spring 1975.
"*Les Yeuxs sans visage*," in *Avant-Scène du Cinéma* (Paris), June 1977.
"A propos du *Grand Méliès*," in *Positif* (Paris), December 1977/January 1978.
"Mystery and melodrama: A Conversation with Georges Franju," by R. Conrad, in *Film Quarterly* (Los Angeles), Winter 1981/82.
Interview with P. Hillairet, in *Cinématographe* (Paris), October 1986.

On FRANJU: books—

Agel, Henri, *Miroirs de l'insolité dans le cinéma français*, Paris, 1957.
Durgnat, Raymond, *Franju*, Berkeley, 1968.
Vialle, Gabriel, *Georges Franju*, Paris, 1968.

On FRANJU: articles—

Grenier, Cynthia, "Franju," in *Sight and Sound* (London), Spring 1957.
Godard, Jean-Luc, "Georges Franju," in *Cahiers du Cinéma* (Paris), December 1958.
"Franju Issue" of *Image et Son* (Paris), March 1966.
Milne, Tom, "Songs of Innocence," in *Sight and Sound* (London), Winter 1970/71.
MacLochlainn, A., "The Films of Luis Buñuel and Georges Franju," in *Film Journal* (New York), Summer 1971.
Gow, Gordon, "Franju," in *Films and Filming* (London), August 1971.
Wood, Robin, "Terrible Buildings: The World of Georges Franju," in *Film Comment* (New York), November/December 1973.
"*Nuits rouges* Issue" of *Avant-Scène du Cinéma* (Paris), January 1975.
Brown, R., "Georges Franju: Behind Closed Windows," in *Sight and Sound* (London), Autumn 1983.
"Georges Franju Issue" of *Avant-Scène du Cinéma* (Paris), April 1984.
"*La Tête contre les murs* Issue" of *Avant-Scène du Cinéma* (Paris), no. 353, 1986.
Monthly Film Bulletin (London), May 1987.
Obituary in *Variety* (New York), 11 November 1987.
Tribute in *Première* (Paris), December 1987.
Tribute in *Revue du Cinéma* (Paris), January 1988.

*   *   *

Franju's career falls clearly into two parts, marked by the format of the films: the early period of documentary shorts, and a subsequent period of fictional features. The parts are connected by many links of theme, imagery, attitude, and iconography. Critical attention has focused primarily on the shorts, and there is some justice in this. While it is difficult to accept Noel Burch's assertion that "the magic that is so much a part of his nonfiction work no longer survives in his fiction features," it is true that nothing in the later work surpasses *Le Sang des bêtes* and *Hôtel des Invalides*, and the intensity and poetic concentration of those early masterpieces are recaptured only in intermittent moments. It is necessary to define the *kind* of

documentary Franju made (it is highly idiosyncratic, and I can think of no close parallels; though Resnais's documentaries are often linked with his, the differences seem more important than the similarities). The traditional documentary has three main modes: the factual, the lyrical, and the politically tendentious. It is the peculiar distinction of Franju's documentaries that they correspond to none of these modes. The kind of organization that structures them is essentially poetic, built upon imagery, juxtaposition, rather than on overt statement or clear-cut symbolism. *Hôtel des Invalides* might well have been expected, from its genesis, to correspond to either the second or third type of documentary (or an amalgamation of the two, a quite common phenomenon). It was commissioned by an organization called *Forces et Voix de France*, and the intention was to celebrate a national monument-institution: the Musée de L'Armée, home of Napoleon's tomb, an edifice dedicated to the glory of France and of war. Franju seized upon and made central to his film the fact that the building also houses the *victims* of war and "glory": the veterans' hospital of the film's title, peopled with the shell-shocked, the crippled, the mutilated, who continue to carry military banners, wear their medals, and attend the religious ceremonies that constitute an aspect of their oppression. Beyond the skillful use of purely cinematic codes (lighting, camera movement, editing, etc.) and Maurice Jarre's music, Franju adds nothing extraneous to his raw material: the introductory commentary (spoken by Michel Simon), locating the museum in place and history, is rigorously factual and unemotional; once inside, we have only the "authentic" commentary of the museum guides. Yet the application of cinematic codes to this material transforms its meaning totally, producing a continuous irony that modulates back and forth between the violent and the subtle: the emblems of military glory and national pride become sinister, monstrous, terrifying.

A politically tendentious documentary after all, then? Certainly not in any simple or clear-cut way. Ultimately, *Hôtel des Invalides* is no more an anti-war movie than *Le Sang des bêtes* is an appeal for vegetarianism—though those meanings can and will be read by many viewers. The film's elements of rage and protest are finally subordinated to an overriding sense of irredeemable insanity, an intimation of a world and a species so fundamentally crazy that protest is almost superfluous. The supreme irony Franju produces out of his material involves the museum's very status as a national monument: here, at the heart of civilization, regarded with pride, admiration and wonderment, stands what amounts to a monument to pain, cruelty, ugliness, death—and no one notices.

The basic problem with Franju's feature films is that he does not seem greatly interested in narrative. He has usually relied on the support of a pre-existent literary work, whose structure, characters, and movement he recreates with a generally scrupulous fidelity, delicacy, and discretion, the changes being mainly of emphasis and omission. The curious feat of *Thérèse Desqueyroux* has often been noted: a faithful, almost literal translation of a novel by a famous Catholic writer (Mauriac) that never violates the integrity of Franju's atheism. Cocteau singled out Franju as the director to whom he would most confidently entrust his work, and Franju justified that confidence fully with his version of *Thomas l'imposteur*. Nonetheless, these films are discernibly Franju's: the directorial reticence should not be mistaken for abdication. The clearest way to demonstrate the continuity is to show how the Franjuesque iconography that is already fully developed in the documentaries recurs in the features, to produce those moments of poetic density and resonance that are the films' chief distinction.

If *Les Yeux sans visage* remains the finest of Franju's feature films, it is because it is the one that permits the greatest concentration of poetry created out of the association of these elements.

—Robin Wood

FRANKENHEIMER, John

American. Born in Malba, New York, 19 February 1930. Educated at La Salle Military Academy, graduated 1947; Williams College, B.A., 1951. Married 1) Carolyn Miller, 1954 (divorced), two daughters; 2) Evans Evans, 1964. Served in newly-formed Film Squadron, U.S. Air Force, 1951–53; assistant director, later director, CBS TV, New York, 1953; TV director, *Playhouse 90*, Hollywood, from 1955; directed first feature, *The Young Stranger*, 1957; formed John Frankenheimer Productions, 1963. Address: c/o John Frankenheimer Productions, 2800 Olympic Blvd., Suite 201, Santa Monica, CA 90404, U.S.A.

Films as Director:

1957 *The Young Stranger*
1961 *The Young Savages*
1962 **The Manchurian Candidate** (+ co-pr); *All Fall Down*; *Birdman of Alcatraz*
1963 *Seven Days in May*
1964 *The Train*
1966 *Grand Prix*; *Seconds*
1968 *The Extraordinary Seaman*; *The Fixer*
1969 *The Gypsy Moths*
1970 *I Walk the Line*; *The Horsemen*
1973 *L'Impossible Objet* (*Impossible Object*); *The Iceman Cometh*
1974 *99 44/100 Dead* (retitled *Call Harry Crown* for general release in U.K.)
1975 *French Connection II*
1976 *Black Sunday* (+ bit role as TV controller)
1979 *Prophecy*
1982 *The Challenge*
1985 *The Holcroft Covenant*
1986 *52 Pick Up*
1987 *Across the River and Into the Trees*
1989 *Dead Bang*; *The Fourth War*

Publications:

By FRANKENHEIMER: articles—

"Seven Ways with *Seven Days in May*," in *Films and Filming* (London), June 1964.
Interview, in *The Celluloid Muse* edited by Charles Higham and Joel Greenberg, London, 1969.
Interview with Russell Au Werter, in *Action* (Los Angeles), May/June 1970.
Interview with J. O'Brien, in *Inter/View* (New York), August 1971.
"Filming *The Iceman Cometh*," in *Action* (Los Angeles), January/February 1974.
Interview with L. Gross and R. Avrech, in *Millimeter* (New York), July/August 1975.
Interviews with R. Appelbaum, in *Films and Filming* (London), October and November 1979.
Interview with P. Broeske, in *Films in Review* (New York), February 1983.
Interview in *Films and Filming* (London), February 1985.

On FRANKENHEIMER: book—

Pratley, Gerald, *The Cinema of John Frankenheimer*, New York, 1969.

On FRANKENHEIMER: articles—

Mayersberg, Paul, "John Frankenheimer," in *Movie* (London), December 1962.
Thomas, John, "John Frankenheimer, the Smile on the Face of the Tiger," in *Film Quarterly* (Berkeley), Winter 1965/66.
Casty, Alan, "Realism and Beyond: The Films of John Frankenheimer," in *Film Heritage* (New York), Winter 1966/67.
Higham, Charles, "Frankenheimer," in *Sight and Sound* (London), Spring 1968.
Filmer, Paul, "Three Frankenheimer Films: A Sociological Approach," in *Screen* (London), July/October 1969.
Madsen, Axel, "*99 and 44/100 Dead*," in *Sight and Sound* (London), Winter 1973/74.
Drew, B., "John Frankenheimer: His Fall and Rise," in *American Film* (Washington, D.C.), March 1977.
Combs, Richard, "A Matter of Conviction," in *Sight and Sound* (London), no. 4, 1979.
Cook, B., "The War Between the Writers and the Directors: Part II: The Directors," in *American Film* (Washington, D.C.), June 1979.
"Directors of the Decade: John Frankenheimer," in *Films and Filming* (London), February 1984.
Scheinfeld, Michael, "*The Manchurian Candidate*," in *Films in Review* (New York), vol. 39, no. 11, 1988.

*   *   *

The seven features John Frankenheimer directed between 1961 and 1964 stand as a career foundation unique in American cinema. In a single talent, film had found a perfect bridge between television and Hollywood drama, between the old and new visual technologies, between the cinema of personality and that of the corporation and the computer.

Frankenheimer's delight in monochrome photography, his instinct for new light cameras, fast stocks and lens systems like Panavision informed *The Manchurian Candidate, Seven Days in May* and *Seconds* with a flashing technological intelligence. No less skillful with the interior drama he'd mastered as a director of live TV, he turned *All Fall Down* and *The Young Savages* into striking personal explorations of familial disquiet and social violence. He seemed unerring. Even *Birdman of Alcatraz* and *The Train*, troubled projects taken over at the last minute from Charles Crichton and Arthur Penn respectively, emerged with the stamp of his forceful technique.

His career began to sour with *Seconds*, arguably too self-conscious with its fish-eye sequences and rampant paranoia. *Grand Prix*, an impressive technical feat in Super Panavision, showed less virtuosity in the performances. His choices thereafter were erratic: heavy handed comedy, rural melodrama, a further unsuccessful attempt at spectacle in the Afghanistan-shot *The Horsemen*. Frankenheimer relocated in Europe, no doubt mortified that Penn, Lumet and Delbert Mann, lesser lights of live TV drama, had succeeded where he failed.

Despite a revival with the 1975 *French Connection II*, a sequel which equalled its model in force and skill, he has not since hit his stride. The choices remain variable in intelligence, though by staying within the area of violent melodrama he has at least ceased to dissipate his talent in the pursuit of production values. *Black Sunday* is a superior terrorist thriller, *Prophecy* a failed but worthy horror film with environmental overtones, and *The Challenge* a stylish Japanese romp in the style of *The Yakuza*. Unfortunately, new directors who grew up with the Frankenheimer work as benchmarks do such material better; he appears to have suffered the fate of bridges everywhere, and been passed over.

—John Baxter

FREARS, Stephen

British. Born in Leicester, 1941. Studied law at Cambridge University, 1960–63. Assistant at the Royal Court Theatre, 1964; assistant on films, from 1966; directed first film, 1967; director and producer for TV, from 1969, including *Me! I'm Afraid of Virginia Woolf* (series of plays by Alan Bennett, 1978) and *Walter* for Channel 4, 1982; also director of TV commercials.

Films as Director:

1967	*The Burning* (+ pr)
1971	*Gumshoe*
1984	*The Hit*
1985	*My Beautiful Laundrette*
1987	*Prick Up Your Ears*; *Sammy and Rosie Get Laid*
1988	*Dangerous Liaisons*
1990	*The Grifters*

Other Films:

1966	*Morgan, a Suitable Case for Treatment* (Reisz) (asstd)
1967	*Charlie Bubbles* (Finney) (asstd)
1968	*If . . .* (Anderson) (asstd)
1973	*O Lucky Man!* (Anderson) (asstd)
1978	*Long Shot* (Hatton) role

Publications:

By FREARS: articles—

Interview in *Time Out* (London), 10 November 1983.
Interview with P. Merigeau and F. Guerif, in *Revue du Cinema* (Paris), November 1984.
"Sheer Frears," an interview with J. Saynor, in *Stills* (London), November 1985.
Interview with Harlan Kennedy, in *Film Comment* (New York), March–April 1987.
Interview in *Inter/View* (New York), April 1987.
Interview with K.M. Chanko, in *Films in Review* (New York), October 1987.
American Film (Washington, D.C.), December 1988.

On FREARS: articles—

"Song of Experience – Stephen Frears," in *Monthly Film Bulletin* (London), May 1987.
"Stephen Frears Section" of *Positif* (Paris), November 1987.

*   *   *

Stephen Frears has had two major periods as a director of feature films; he first came to public theatrical notice as the creator of an oddly memorable crime thriller, laced with parodic, self-reflexive overtones, 1971's *Gumshoe*. This comedy/drama starred Albert Finney and Billie Whitelaw, and surprisingly, had a music score by the then comparatively unknown Andrew Lloyd Webber. It was a gentle, unassuming film, and had its adherents, but was soon forgotten.

Then, after a lapse of more than a decade, Frears directed a blistering series of features, which established him at a stroke as one the more important British directors of the late 1980's. The breakthrough film was *My Beautiful Laundrette*, a movie part-funded by Channel 4 TV that also launched Daniel Day Lewis as an actor, brought Shirley Anne Field back to the screen, and gave the screenwriter Hanif Kureishi his first substantial hit.

Frears had done some other work before *My Beautiful Laundrette* put him back on the map. In 1978, he made *Long Shot*, a film which mirrored his own personal and professional dilemma: how to raise the money to finance a film. Made on a shoestring, the film was positively received, but did not effectively revitalize Frears' career. His 1984 film *The Hit* had a great cast (John Hurt, Terence Stamp, and Fernando Rey), and told the story of a small-time hood Willie Parker (Stamp), who informs upon his partners-in-crime. Ten years later, Stamp has managed to evade his former associates, but suddenly finds that his hiding place has been discovered. Eric Clapton wrote the theme song for the film, but despite the favorable critical press, the film failed to catch on.

The Hit is tense, well-acted, and has an authentic air of despair and failure in its tightly constructed visuals, yet at the same time it manages to be quite funny, and oddly difficult to grasp. It reminds one of the Hammer psychological thrillers of the early 1960's, in which Jimmy Sangster's scripts kept the audience guessing throughout; it also stands up well against more contemporary works, such as *The Long Good Friday*. But it was *My Beautiful Laundrette* that really re-established Frears' career, taking him out of the grind of ordinary television production, and affording him a more luxurious canvas with which to work. Nevertheless, it is clear that his work in TV had prepared him for this moment: the fast pace of television production allowed Frears to wring every last value out of minimal funding.

A titillating, cheaply exotic and yet deeply romantic film, *Laundrette* is set firmly in the world of 1980's London, a barren, Thatcherite landscape of failing businesses, exploited workers, and simmering racial tension. The love affair between Johnny (Day Lewis) and the Asian Omar crosses the "barrier" of the heterosexual ruling faction, as well as being an "affront" to the rigid class and racial barriers of an England caught in the grip of a pervasive economic depression. The film's look is lush, multi-hued, and dreamy; it exists outside of time, as its protagonists most truly come to life outside the structures imposed upon them.

It was a surprise "art house" hit in the United States, and revived Frears' career as a director. With *Laundrette*, Frears, by aligning himself with a strong scenarist, who also sought to revitalize British cinema, and the iconic structures that had come to be taken as fixed points of reference in its landscape (Kureishi stated that one of his ambitions in writing the script for the film was to make a gay-themed British movie "without Dirk Bogarde"), overhauled his career, and was able to plunge into a group of new works that consolidated his second reputation.

Sammy and Rosie Get Laid, another Kureishi script, was perhaps less successful than *Laundrette*, but still did respectable business in the United States and Britain, and found several critical champions. *Sammy and Rosie* took the basic image of London in collapse posited in *Laundrette* several steps further. *Sammy and Rosie* is a clever re-interpretation of Godard's vision of the city-as-apocalypse, with a Buñuelian flair for surreal interruptions and the grimy look of 1960's British directors like Tony Richardson and Karel Reisz.

In the same year, Frears' *Prick Up Your Ears*, a life of the playwright Joe Orton, from an Alan Bennett screenplay, received substantial critical acclaim both in England and the United States.

Frears' most successful and popular film, *Dangerous Liaisons*, owes a considerable stylistic debt to Roger Vadim's 1960 *Les Liaisons Dangereuses*, a modern-dress version of the same text by Laclos. Vadim's film featured Jeanne Moreau and Gerard Philipe; Frears's film, from a screenplay by Christopher Hampton, is anchored by the brilliant performances of Glenn Close and John Malkovich, and succeeds because of the sense of period verisimilitude it creates. Frears' camera seems almost a recording angel within the context of the film's narra-

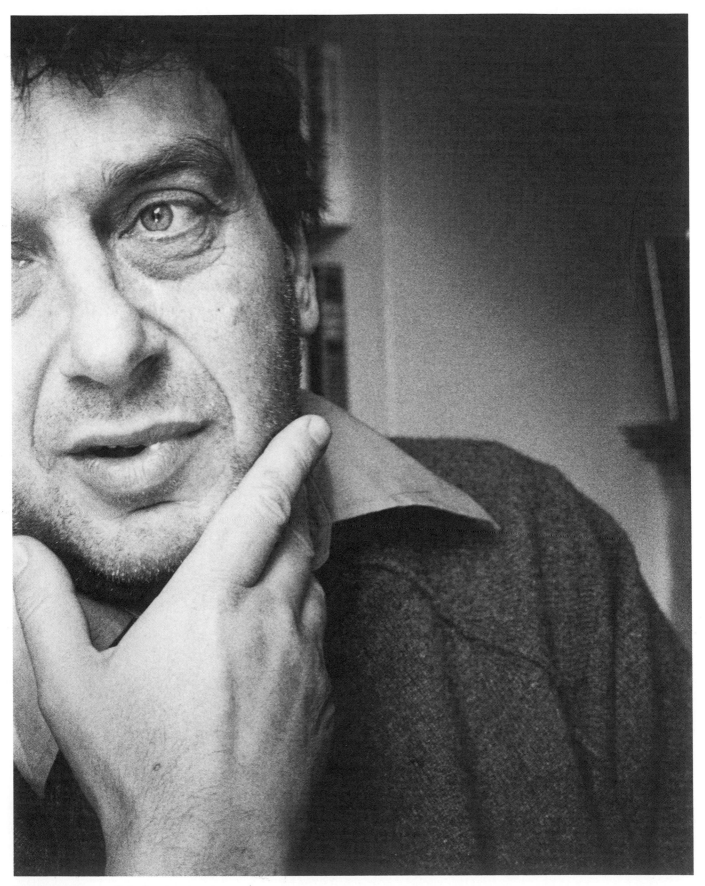

Stephen Frears   © **Andrew Hamilton Lane**

tive; it is omnipresent, but never oppressive, and maintains a discreet distance, except in the climactic duelling sequence.

Dangerous Liaisons does not strive to be sumptuous; rather, it plants the characters firmly within the context of the decor, and lets them do their work. Malkovich, in particular, has never appeared to better advantage, and the final shot of Glenn Close, having been scorned in public, wiping her evening's make-up off her face with brutal finality while regarding herself in her dressing room mirror, is one of the most despairingly triumphant moments in recent cinema history.

Interestingly, Frears completely eschews the aggressive visual style of *Laundrette* and *Sammy and Rosie* in *Dangerous Liaisons*; rather, his camera seems entirely at the service of the actors, and frames them in introductory wide-shots in the classical studio manner, before going in for intimate close-ups. In this, the film is a double period piece, recreating the British studio system, and its inherent dependence upon actors, as well as the 18th-century period in which the fictive text is set. Perhaps because of this double-classicism, the film has proven to be Frears's most accessible and popularly-praised work.

—Wheeler Winston Dixon

FRIČ, Martin

Czech. Born in Prague, 29 March 1902. Married actress Suzanne Marwille, 1932. Actor in Prague and Bratislava, 1918; lab man, cameraman, and designer, 1919–21; began film acting, scriptwriting, 1922; began collaboration with Karel Lamac, 1924; billed as Mac Frič on films made during occupation, 1940's; TV director, from 1961; 1st Chairman, Union of Czechoslovakian Film and Television Artists, 1965. Recipient: National Artist; Order of the Republic; Laureate; State Prize. *Died 22 August 1968.*

Films as Director (partial listing):

1928 *Páter Vojtěch (Father Vojtech)* (+ sc, role)
1929 *Varhaník v sv. Víta (The Organist at St. Vitus)* (+ co-sc); *Chudá holka (Poor Girl)* (+ sc)
1930 *Vše pro lásku (All for love)* (+ co-sc)
1931 *Der Zinker (The Informer)* (co-d); *On a jeho sestra (He and His Sister)* (co-d); *Dobrý voják Svejk (The Good Soldier Schweik)* (+ ed)
1932 *Kantor Ideál (Master Ideál)*; *Sestra Angelika (Sister Angelika)* (+ ed)
1933 *Revisor (The Inspector)* (+ ed); *U snědeného krámu (The Emptied-out Grocer's Shop)* (+ ed); *Pobočník Jeho Výsosti (Adjutant to His Highness)* (+ ed); *Zivot je pes (A Dog's Life)* (+ co-sc); *Dvanáct křesel (The Twelve Chairs)* (co-d); *S vyloučením veřejnosti (Closed Doors)*
1934 *Hej rup! (Heave-ho!)* (+ ed, co-sc); *Poslední muž (The Last Man)*; *Mazlíček (Darling)* (+ ed, co-sc)
1935 *Hrdina jedné noci (Hero for a Night)* (+ ed); *Jánošík* (ed, co-sc); *Jedenácté přikázání (The Eleventh Commandment)* (+ ed); *Ať žije nebožtik (Long Live the Deceased)* (+ ed, co-sc)
1936 *Pater Vojtěch (Father Vojtech)* (remake); *Svadlenka (The Seamstress)*; *Ulička v ráji (Paradise Road)*
1937 *Svět patří nám) (The World Is Ours)* (+ co-sc, role); *Hordubalové (The Hordubals)*; *Lidé na kře (People on a Glacier)*
1938 *Krok do tmy (Madman in the Dark)*; *Skola, základ života (School, the Basis of Life)*
1939 *Eva tropí hlouposti (The Escapades of Eva)*; *Kristián (Christian)* (+ co-sc); *Muž z neznáma (The Reluctant Millionaire)*

1940 *Muzikantská Liduška (Liduška of the Stage, Musicians' Girl)*; *Baron Prášil (Baron Munchhausen)*; *Katakomby (Catacombs)*; *Druhá směna (Second Tour)*
1941 *Těžký život dobrodruha (Hard is the Life of an Adventurer)*; *Hotel Modrá hvězda (The Hotel Blue Star)* (+ co-sc)
1942 *Barbora Hlavsová*
1943 *Experiment*; *Der zweite Schuss (The Second Shot)* (+ co-sc)
1944 *Počestné paní pardubické (The Virtuous Dames of Pardubice)*; *Prstýnek (The Wedding Ring)*
1945 *13. revír (Beat 13)*
1947 *Varuj! (Warning!)* (+ co-sc); *Capkovy povídky (Tales from Capek)* (+ co-sc)
1948 *Návrat domu (Lost in Prague)*; *Polibek ze stadionu (A Kiss from Stadium)* (+ co-sc)
1949 *Pětistovka (Motorcycles)*; *Pytlákova schovanka (The Kind Millionaire)*
1950 *Past (The Trap)*; *Zoceleni (Tempered Steel. Steel Town)*
1951 *Císařv pekař a Pekařuv pekař (The Emperor's Baker and the Baker's Emperor)* (+ co-sc); *Akce B (Action B)* (+ co-sc)
1953 *Tajemství krve (The Secret of Blood)* (+ co-sc)
1954 *Psohlavci (Dog-Heads)* (+ co-sc)
1955 *Nechte to na mně (Leave It to Me)* (+ co-sc)
1956 *Zaostřit, prosím (Watch the Birdie!)* (+ co-sc)
1958 *Povodeň (The Flood)*; *Dnes naposled (Today for the Last Time)*
1959 *Princezna se zlatou hvězdou (The Princess with the Golden Star)* (+ co-sc)
1960 *Dařbuján a Pandrhola (A Compact with Death)*; *Bilá spona (The White Slide)*
1963 *Krák Králu (King of Kings)*; *Tři zlaté vlasy děda Vševěda (The Three Golden Hairs of Old Man Know-All)*
1964 *Hvězda zvaná Pelyněk (A Star Named Wormwood)*
1966 *Lidé z maringotek (People on Wheels)* (+ co-sc)
1967 *Přísně tajné premiéry (Recipe for a Crime, Strictly Secret Previews)*
1968 *Nejlepší ženská mého života (The Best Woman of My Life)* (+ co-sc)

Publications:

By FRIČ: article—

Interview, in *Closely Watched Films* by Antonín Liehm, White Plains, New York, 1974.

On FRIČ: book—

Modern Czechoslovak film, Prague, 1965.

On FRIČ: articles—

Hrbas, J., "Martin Frič: Lidový vyprávěč," (in 4 parts) in *Film a Doba* (Prague), January through April 1972.
Dewey, L., "Czechoslovakia: Silence into Sound," in *Film* (London), no. 60.
Taussig, P., *Film a Doba* (Prague), December 1983 and April 1984.
Bartosek, L., "Scenes from the History of Czechoslovak Cinema," in *Czechoslovak Film* (Prague), Summer 1985.

*   *   *

Scion of a notable middle-class Prague family, Martin Frič left the road marked out by family tradition at the age of 16 to follow the uncertain path of a cabaret performer, actor, and filmmaker. In 1919 he designed a poster for Jan Stanislav Kolár's film *Dáma s malou nozkou (Lady With a Little Foot)*, and thus began his years of apprenticeship. He was by turns an actor, a scenarist, a film laboratory worker, a cameraman. Of crucial importance to the young Frič was his collaboration and friendship with the most influential director in Czech film, Karel Lamac, who taught him the film trade and enabled him to become familiar with the film studios of Berlin and Paris.

In 1928 he made his debut with the film *Páter Vojtěch (Father Vojtech)* and followed it immediately with his most important film of the silent era, *Varhaník u sv. Vita (The Organist at St.*

Martin Frič: *Jánosík*

Vitus), which dealt with the tragedy of a man suspected of murder. In the sound era Frič quickly gained a position of prominence, chiefly through his ability to work fast (making up to six films a year) and, no matter what, with surprising ease and dexterity. Comedy became his domain. His comedies, often produced in two language versions (German or French), featured popular comedians but also actors and actresses whose comic talent he recognized and helped to develop. First and foremost was Vlasta Burián in the situation comedies *On a jeho sestra* (*He and His Sister*) with Anny Ondráková, *Pobočník Jeho Výsosti* (*Adjutant to His Highness*), *Dvanáct křesel* (*The 12 Chairs*), *Katakomby* (*Catacombs*), and also in the film adaptation of Gogol's *Revisor* (*The Inspector*). Frič had much to do with shaping the film acting of Hugo Haas in such films as *Zivot je pes* (*A Dog's Life* – the first Czech screwball comedy with Adina Mandlová). *Ať žije nebožlík* (*Long Live the Deceased*), *Jedenácté přikázání* (*The Eleventh Commandment*), and *Ulička a ráji* (*Paradise Road*). Together with Voskovec and Werich he made the social comedy *Hej rup!* (*Heave-ho*) and the modern political satire *Svět patří nám* (*The World Is Ours*). Then came *Kristián* (*Christian*), a social comedy with Oldrich Nový that is undoubtedly Frič's best work.

But Frič also demonstrated his directorial abilities in infrequent excursions into other genres. His *Jánošík* (*Jánosík*), a poetic epic about a legendary highwayman, is one of the pinnacles of Czechoslovak cinematography. Frič showed sensitivity and an understanding of the atmosphere of the time in his film rendition of *U sněděného krámu* (*The Emptied-Out Grocer's Shop*), a story by the 19th-century Czech writer Ignát Hermann. He also made felicitous film versions of the dramas *Hordubalové* (*The Hordubals*), based on the novel by Karel Capek, *Lidé na kře* (*People on a Glacier*), and *Barbora Hlavsová*.

Following the nationalization of Czechoslovak filmmaking, Frič aided in the development of filmmaking in Slovakia with his film *Varuj...!* (*Warning!*). In 1949, in collaboration with Oldrich Nový, he fashioned his next masterpiece, *Pytlákova schovanka* (*The Kind Millionaire*), a parody of film kitsch. Following the successful costume comedy *Císařuv pekař a Pekařuv pekař* (*The Emperor's Baker and the Baker's Emperor*) with Jan Werich, and an excursion into the biographical genre with the film *Tajemství krve* (*The Secret of Blood*), Frič made a few films that were – for the first time, actually – neither a popular nor a critical success.

Frič's last creative surge came at the beginning of the 1960's. He made fine adaptations for Czechoslovak television and directed Chekhov's tales *Medved* (*The Bear*), *Slzy, které svě nevidi* (*Tears the World Can't See*), and *Námluvy* (*Courting*), and once more returned to the studios. The tragicomedy *Hvězda zvaná Pelyněk* (*A Star Named Wormwood*) and the comedy *Nejlepší ženská mého života* (*The Best Woman of My Life*), the premieres of which he did not live to see, close out his final period of creativity.

Frič's creation is the work of a solid and honest artist who demonstrated his talent in diverse genres from psychological drama to madcap comedy. He produced two masterful comedies, *Kristián* and *Pytlákova schovanka*, which can be numbered among the world's best of the period. The best proof of the quality and vitality of his creative work is the fact that almost a third of the films he made are still shown in the theaters of Czechoslovakia, where they bring pleasure to new generations of viewers.

—Vladimír Opela

FRIEDKIN, William.

American. Born in Chicago, 29 August 1939. Married 1) Jeanne Moreau, 1977 (divorced); 2) Lesley-Anne Down, 1982 (divorced), one son. Mailroom assistant, then studio floor manager, WGN-TV, Chicago, 1955; TV director, 1957–67; partner, with Francis Ford Coppola and Peter Bogdanovich, in The Directors Company, 1973 (withdrew, 1974); Recipient: Oscar for Best Director, for *The French Connection*, 1971. Agent: c/o Tony Fantozzi, William Morris Agency, 151 El Camino Drive, Beverly Hills, CA 90212, U.S.A.

Films as Director:

1967	*Good Times*
1968	*The Night They Raided Minsky's*; *The Birthday Party*
1970	*The Boys in the Band*
1971	*The French Connection*
1973	*The Exorcist*
1977	*Soceror* (*Wages of Fear*)
1978	*The Brink's Job*
1980	*Cruising* (+ sc)
1981	*Duet for One*
1983	*The Deal of the Century*
1985	*To Live and Die in L.A.* (+ sc); *Sea Trial*
1986	*Judgement Day*
1987	*Rampage*

Publications:

By FRIEDKIN: articles—

"Anatomy of a Chase," in *Take One* (Montreal), July/August 1971.
"Photographing *The French Connection*," with Herb Lightman, in *American Cinematographer* (Los Angeles), February 1972.
Interview with M. Shedlin, in *Film Quarterly* (Berkeley), Summer 1972.
"Dialogue on Film: William Friedkin," in *American Film* (Washington, D.C.), February/March 1974.
"Mervyn Leroy Talks with William Friedkin," in *Action* (Los Angeles), November/December 1974.
Interview with R. Appelbaum, in *Films and Filming* (London), March 1979.
Interview with R. Gentry, in *Post Script* (Jacksonville, Florida), Spring/Summer and Fall 1986.

On FRIEDKIN: book—

Segaloff, Nat, *Hurricane Billy: The Career of William Friedkin*, New York, 1989.

On FRIEDKIN: articles—

Maslin, Janet, "Friedkin Defends his *Cruising*," in *New York Times*, 18 September 1979.
"William Friedkin," in *Film Dope* (London), September 1979.
Gentry, R., "Louma Crane and William Friedkin," in *American Cinematographer* (Los Angeles), August 1985.

*   *   *

The success, both critical and commercial, of William Friedkin's films has been uneven since the release of his first feature in 1967. Although his works span several different genres, they share some common thematic and technical characteristics. His heroes are nontraditional and find themselves in unconventional situations or environments foreign to the average viewer. Technically, Friedkin often seems more concerned with creating mood and establishing atmosphere than with the progress of the narrative or character development. His great attention to detail and characteristic use of long establishing shot sequences do create mood and atmosphere but often do not contribute to the film as a whole.

In two of Friedkin's early films, *The Birthday Party* and *The*

William Friedkin

Boys in the Band (both based on stage productions), the use of establishing prologues works very well. *The Birthday Party* begins with an early morning shot of a deserted beach. Empty canvas beach chairs look out over an unnatural vastness of sameness – a seemingly endless grayish blue ocean that disappears into a grayish blue sky. This slightly unsettling visual sets the mood for Harold Pinter's play. To the beginning of *The Boys in the Band*, Friedkin adds a montage prologue that introduces all of the main characters. But these are the only personal interpretations evident in these two works.

In *The Night They Raided Minsky's*, Friedkin's attention to detail successfully establishes 1920's period authenticity and adds to a richness of character missing in his other works. The film was criticized, however, for having too broad a narrative told through overly long sequences that do not contribute to the story. This characteristic would prove to be a major flaw of several of Friedkin's subsequent films.

Friedkin's two most popular films, *The French Connection* and *The Exorcist*, have some aspects in common. In addition to nontraditional heroes in unusual situations, both films have broad narratives expressed through similar filmic techniques: minimal dialogue; long, detailed sequences; and documentary-style use of the camera.

The French Connection, Friedkin's most critically acclaimed work, maintains a precarious balance between becoming

tedious to watch and portraying the tedium and fatigue of Jimmy Doyle' and Buddy Russo's lives. Friedkin uses a long prologue to establish the drug operation in Marseilles. This sequence, filmed with little dialogue and great attention to detail, not only serves to introduce the drug operation but also to contrast the lifestyles of French narcotics dealer Alain Charnier and New York City cops Doyle and Russo. This very long sequence is followed by another that establishes the cops' personalities and beat. Consequently, it takes quite some time before the actual narrative begins.

Friedkin's ability to create atmosphere does work well in *The French Connection* because the environment itself, New York City, is one of the main characters. The city and its inhabitants are depicted in detail. The scenes, sometimes gritty, sometimes gory, sometimes dull, produce the urban reality, and at the same time reflect the reality of policework, which is also sometimes dull, but sometimes dangerous.

The Exorcist, a commercially successful film, is tedious throughout. The film plods along through an excessively long opening sequence (the significance of which is never made clear), a pseudo psychological explanation of the character Father Karras, countless close-ups of "meaningful" facial expressions, and predictable stages in both the possession and exorcism of Regan MacNeil. Friedkin does succeed at times in creating tension and suspense, but this mood is not sustained throughout the film. Apparently, the shock value of watching the disturbing physical transformation of Regan from young girl to hideous monster is enough to maintain viewer interest, since this continues to be a popular film.

Sorcerer did not follow the trend of commerical success begun by the two previous films. A remake of Clouzot's *The Wages of Fear, Sorcerer* is a good action adventure once the story finally gets under way. Like other Friedkin films, it is weighed down by several long introductory sequences. After these initial sequences, the use of documentary technique, including hand-held tracking shots, creates a reality of place that can almost be smelled and touched.

Friedkin's more recent films contain his characteristic cinematic techniques. His filmic representation of the sadomasochistic homosexual subculture in New York City in *Cruising* is too realistic and brutal for many reviewers. *Deal of the Century*, although not commerically or critically popular, is a fair satire on the profitable business of selling arms to third world nations, using an introductory sequence very effectively to set the tone. *The Guardian*, a horror film, was not well received either critically or at the box office.

—Marie Saeli

———

FUENTES, Carlos De *See* **DE FUENTES, Carlos.**

———

FULLER, Samuel.

American. Born Samuel Michael Fuller in Worcester, Massachusetts, 12 August 1911. Served in 16th regiment of U.S. Army 1st Division, 1942–45, awarded Bronze Star, Silver Star, and Purple Heart. Married actress Christa Lang, 1965. Copyboy and journalist, *New York Journal*, from 1924; crime reporter, from 1928; screenplay writer in Hollywood, from 1936; screenwriter at Warner Bros., 1946–48; directed first feature, 1948; signed to 20th Century-Fox, 1951–57; TV director, 1960's.

Films as Director:

1948   *I Shot Jesse James* (+ sc)
1950   *The Baron of Arizona* (+ sc); *The Steel Helmet* (+ sc, co-pr)
1951   *Fixed Bayonets* (+ sc)
1952   *Park Row* (+ sc, co-pr)
1953   *Pick Up on South Street* (+ sc) [remade in 1968 as *Cape Town Affair* (Webb)]
1954   *Hell and High Water* (+ co-sc)
1955   *The House of Bamboo* (+ co-sc, role as Japanese policeman)
1957   *Run of the Arrow* (+ pr, sc); *China Gate* (+ pr, sc); *Forty Guns* (+ pr, sc)
1958   *Verboten* (+ pr, sc)
1959   *The Crimson Kimono* (+ pr, sc)
1960   *Underworld USA* (+ pr, sc)
1962   *Merrill's Marauders* (+ co-sc)
1963   *Shock Corridor* (+ pr, sc); *The Naked Kiss* (+ co-pr, sc)
1967   *Caine* (+ sc)
1973   *Dead Pigeon on Beethoven Street* (+ sc, role as United States Senator)
1980   *The Big Red One* (+ sc)
1982   *White Dog*
1983   *Thieves After Dark*
1989   *Street of No Return* (+ co-sc)

Other Films:

1936   *Hats Off* (Petroff) (sc)
1937   *It Happened in Hollywood* (Lachman) (sc)
1938   *Gangs of New York* (Cruze) (remade in 1945 as *Gangs of the Waterfront*) (Blair) (sc); *Adventure in Sahara* (Lederman) (sc); *Federal Man-Hunt* (Grinde) (sc)
1940   *Bowery Boy* (Morgan) (sc)
1941   *Confirm or Deny* (Lang, Mayo) (sc)
1943   *Power of the Press* (Landers) (sc)
1948   *Shockproof* (Sirk) (sc)
1951   *The Tanks Are Coming* (Seiler) (sc)
1952   *Scandal Sheet* (Karlson) (sc)
1953   *The Command* (Butler) (sc)
1965   *Pierrot le fou* (Godard) (role as himself)
1966   *Brigitte et Brigitte* (Moullet) (role as himself)
1971   *The Last Movie* (Hopper) (role as himself)
1974   *The Klansman* (Young) (sc)
1976   ***Der Amerikanische Freund (The American Friend)*** (Wenders) (role as The American)
1979   *1941* (Spielberg) (small role)

Publications:

By FULLER: books—

Burn, Baby, Burn, New York, 1935.
Test Tube Baby, New York, 1936.
Make Up and Kiss, New York, 1938.
The Dark Page, New York, 1944 (published as *Murder Makes a Deadline*, New York, 1952).
The Naked Kiss, New York, 1964.
Crown of India, New York, 1966.
144 Piccadilly, New York, 1971.
Dead Pigeon on Beethoven Street, New York, 1973.
Fuller, Samuel, *Il etait un fois . . . Samuel Fuller: Histoires d'Ameriques*, edited by Jean Narboni and Noel Simsolo, Paris, 1986.

By FULLER: articles—

"What is Film?" in *Cinema* (Beverly Hills), July 1964.
"Samuel Fuller: Two Interviews," with Stig Björkman and Mark Shivas, in *Movie* (London), Winter 1969/70.
Interview in *The Director's Event* by Eric Sherman and Martin Rubin, New York, 1970.
Interview with Ian Christie and others, in *Cinema* (Cambridge), February 1970.
"Sam Fuller Returns," interview with Claude Beylie and J. Lourcelles, in *Ecran* (Paris), January 1975.
"War That's Fit to Shoot," in *American Film* (Washington, D.C.), November 1976.
"Three Times Sam: The Flavor of Ketchup," interview with R. Thompson, in *Film Comment* (New York), January/February 1977.
Interview with Russell Merritt and P. Lehman, in *Wide Angle* (Athens, Ohio), vol. 4, no. 1, 1980.
"Samuel Fuller—Survivor," an interview with T. Ryan, in *Cinema Papers* (Melbourne), December/January 1980/81.
"Fuller mis au défi par l'avocat du diable," in *Cahiers du Cinéma* (Paris), April 1982.
Interview with A. Hunter, in *Films and Filming* (London), November 1983.
Interview in *Monthly Film Bulletin* (London), March 1984.

On FULLER: books—

Will, David, and Peter Wollen, editors, *Samuel Fuller*, Edinburgh, 1969.
Hardy, Phil, *Samuel Fuller*, New York, 1970.
Garnham, Nicholas, *Samuel Fuller*, New York, 1971.
MacArthur, Colin, *Underworld U.S.A.*, London, 1972.
Amiel, Victor, *Samuel Fuller*, Paris, 1985.
Caprara, Valerio, *Samuel Fuller*, Florence, 1985.

Samuel Fuller directing *The Naked Kiss*

On FULLER: articles—

Lee, Russell, "Samuel Fuller," in *New Left Review*, January/February 1964.

Wollen, Peter, "Notes Toward a Structural Analysis of the Films of Samuel Fuller," in *Cinema* (Cambridge), December 1968.

Canham, Kingsley, "The World of Samuel Fuller," in *Film* (London), November/December 1969.

Canham, Kingsley, "Samuel Fuller's Action Films," in *Screen* (London), November/December 1969.

McArthur, Colin, "Samuel Fuller's Gangster Films," in *Screen* (London), November/December 1969.

Belton, John, "Are You Waving the Flag At Me: Samuel Fuller and Politics," in *Velvet Light Trap* (Madison, Wisconsin), Spring 1972.

McConnell, F., "*Pick up on South Street* and the Metamorphosis of the Thriller," in *Film Heritage* (New York), Spring 1973.

Cook, B., "Sam Fuller Lands with the Big One," in *American Film* (Washington, D.C.), June 1979.

Valot, J., "Love, Action, Death, Violence: Cinema Is Emotion (sur quelques films de Samuel Fuller)," in *Image et Son* (Paris), July/August 1980.

Milne, Tom, "Sam Fuller's War," in *Sight and Sound* (London), Autumn 1980.

"Fuller Section" of *Image et Son* (Paris), April 1981.

"Fuller Issue" of *Avant-Scène du Cinéma* (Paris), 1 November 1981.

Dossier on Fuller, in *Framework* (Norwich), no. 19, 1982.

Revue du Cinéma (Paris), April 1988.

*   *   *

Sam Fuller's narratives investigate the ways that belonging to a social group simultaneously functions to sustain and nurture individual identity and, conversely, to pose all sorts of emotional and ideological threats to that identity. Fuller's characters are caught between a solitude that is both liberating and debilitating, and a communality that is both supportive and oppressive. Unlike, say, Howard Hawks, whose films suggest the triumph of the group over egoism. Fuller is more cynical and shows that neither isolation nor group membership is without its hardships and tensions.

Many of the films touch upon a broad kind of belonging: membership in a nation specifically the United States (although *China Gate* comments on several other nationalities) as a driving idea and ideal, national identity becoming a reflection of personal identity. For example, in Fuller films about the building of the West, such as *Forty Guns*, *The Baron of Arizona*, or *Run of the Arrow*, the central characters initially understand their own quests as necessarily divergent from the quest of America for its own place in the world. Even though the course of the films suggests the moral and emotional losses that such divergence leads to, the films also imply that there is something inadequate in the American quest itself, in the ways such a quest undercuts its own purity by finding strength in a malevolent violence (the readiness of "ordinary" people in *The Baron of Arizona* to lynch at a moment's notice), in mistrust and prejudice (unbridled racism in *Run of the Arrow*), or in political corruption.

Similarly, in several films, such as *House of Bamboo*, *Underworld USA*, and *Pickup on South Street*, about criminal organizations infiltrated by revenging outsiders, the narrative trajectory will begin by suggesting the moral separation of good guys and bad guys, but will then continue to demonstrate their parallelism, their interweaving, even their blurring. For example, in *Underworld USA*, the criminals and crimefighters resemble each other in their methods, in their cold calculation and determination, and in their bureaucratic organization. Tolly, the film's central character, may agree to map his own desire for revenge onto the crimefighters' desire to eliminate a criminal element, but the film resolutely refuses to unambiguously propagandize the public good over personal motives.

At a narrower level of group concern. Fuller's films examine the family as a force that can be nurturing, but is often stifling and riddled with contradictions. Not accidentally, many of Fuller's films concentrate on childless or parentless figures: the family here is not given but something that one loses or that one has to grope towards. Often, the families that do exist are, for Fuller, like the nation-state initially presenting an aura of innocent respectability but ultimately revealing a corruption and rotted perversity. Indeed, *The Naked Kiss* connects questions of political value to family value in its story of a woman discovering that her fiancé, a town's benefactor, its model citizen, is actually a child molester. Similarly, *Verboten!* maps the story of postwar America's self-image as benefactor to the world onto an anti-love love story composed of a German woman initially marrying a G.I. for financial support and then finding she really does love him, only to discover that he no longer loves her.

Love, to be sure, is a redemptive promise in Fuller's films but it is run through by doubt, anger, mistrust, deception. Any reciprocity or sharing that Fuller's characters achieve comes at a great price ranging from mental and physical pain to death. For example, in *Underworld USA*, Tolly is able to drop his obsessional quest and give himself emotionally to the ex-gangster's moll, Cuddles, only when he is at a point of no return that will lead him to his death. Against the possibility of love (which, if it ever comes, comes so miraculously as to call its own efficacy into doubt), Fuller's films emphasize a world where everyone is potentially an outsider and therefore a mys-

tery and even a menace. No scene in Fuller's cinema encapsulates this better than the opening of *Pickup on South Street* where a filled subway car becomes the site of intrigued and intriguing glances as a group of strangers warily survey each other as potential victims and victimizers. Echoing the double-entendre of the title (the pickup is political—the passing on of a secret microfilm—as well as sexual), the opening scene shows a blending of sexual desire and aggression as a sexual come-on reveals itself to be a cover for theft, and passive passengers reveal themselves to be government agents.

In a world of distrust, where love can easily betray, the Fuller character survives either by fighting for the last vestiges of an honest, uncorrupted love (in the most optimistic of the films) or, in the more cynical cases, by displacing emotional attachment from people to ideas; to myths of masculine power in *Forty Guns*; to obsessions (for example, Johnny Barratt's desire in *Shock Corridor* to win the Pulitzer Prize even if that desire leads him to madness); to mercenary self-interest; to political or social ideals; and ultimately, to a professionalism that finally means doing nothing other than doing your job right without thinking about it. This is especially the case in Fuller's war films which show characters driven to survive for survival's sake, existence being defined in *Merrill's Marauders* as "put(ting) one foot in front of the other."

Fuller's style, too, is one based on tensions: a conflict of techniques that one can read as an enactment for the spectator of Fuller themes. Fuller is both a director of rapid, abrupt, shocking montage, as in the alternating close-ups of robber and victim in *I Shot Jesse James*, and a director who uses extremely long takes incorporating a complex mix of camera movement and character action. Fuller's style is the opposite of graceful; his style seems to suggest that in a world where grace provides little redemption, its utilization would be a kind of lie. Thus, a stereotypically beautiful shot like the balanced image of Mount Fujiyama in *House of Bamboo* might seem a textbook example of the well-composed nature shot but for the fact that the mountain is framed through the outstretched legs of a murdered soldier.

—Dana B. Polan

G

GAÁL, István.

Hungarian. Born in Salgótarján, 25 August 1933. Educated at Academy of Theatre and Film Art, Budapest, graduated 1959; studied at Centro Sperimentale, Rome, 1959–61. Director and cameraman for Hungarian Newsreel Dept, 1961; directed first feature, 1964; director for Hungarian TV, from 1977.

Films as Director:

1957 *Pályamunkások (Surfacemen)* [Railroaders] (+ sc, ed) (short)
1961 *Etude* (+ sc, ed) (short)
1962 *Tisza—öszi vázlatok (Tisza—Autumn Sketches)* (+ sc, ed) (short); *Oda—vissza (To and Fro)* (+ sc, ed) (short)
1964 *Sodrásban (The Stream. Current)* (+ sc, ed)
1965 *Zöldár (Green Flood. The Green Years)* (+ ed, co-sc)
1967 *Krónika (The Chronicle)* (+ sc, ed, ph) (short); *Keresztelö (Christening Party)* (+ sc, ed)
1969 *Tiz éves Kuba (Cuba's Ten Years)* (+ sc, ed, ph) (short)
1970 *Bartók Béla: az éjszaka zenéje (Béla Bartók: The Music of the Night, The Night Music)* (+ sc, ed) (short); *Magasiskola (The Falcons)* (+ sc, ed)
1971 *Holt vidék (The Dead Country)* (+ co-sc, ed)
1977 *Legato (Ties)* (+ co-sc, ed); *Naponta két vonat (Two Trains a Day)* (+ sc, ed) (for TV); *Vámhatár (Customs Frontier)* (+ ed) (for TV)
1981 *Cserepek (Buffer Zone)* (+ sc, ed)

Other Films:

1962 *Cigányok (Gypsies)* (Sára) (ed, ph) (short)
1964 *Férfiarckép (Portrait of a Man)* (Gyöngyössy) (co-ph) (short)
1967 *Vizkereszet (Twelfth Night)* (Sára) (co-sc) (short)

Publications:

By GAÁL: articles—

"Un Réalisateur hongrois," interview with J. Camerlain, in *Séquences* (Paris), January 1973.
Interview in *Cinema Canada* (Montreal), April/May 1973.
"Interviewing István Gaál," in *Hungarofilm Bulletin* (Budapest), no. 4, 1977.
"A Challenge and a Trial of Strength," an interview in *Hungarofilm Bulletin* (Budapest), no. 5, 1983.

On GAÁL: book—

Petrie, Graham, *History Must Answer to Man*, London, 1978.

On GAÁL: articles—

Petrie, Graham, "István Gaál and *The Falcons*," in *Film Quarterly* (Berkeley), Spring 1974.
Martin, M., and Y. Biro, "István Gaál, de *Remous à Paysage mort*: itinéraire d'un témoin," in *Ecran* (Paris), March 1974.
"Istvan Gaal," in *Film Dope* (London), September 1979.

Predal, René, "Istvan Gaal: les remous de la quarantaine," in *Jeune Cinéma* (Paris), October 1981.
Pörös, G., in *Filmkultura* (Budapest), May/June 1984.

* * *

The artistic personality of the film editor, cameraman, scriptwriter, and director István Gaál was formed by his study at the Higher School of Theatrical and Film Art in Budapest, where he arrived as a young electrical engineer determined to devote himself to the art of film. Here he shaped and precisely defined his artistic viewpoint in a classroom that is already legendary today as the meeting place of later notable personalities in Hungarian cinematography—Judit Elek, Pál Gábor, Imre Gyöngyössy, Zoltán Huszárik, Ferenc Kardos, Zsolt Kérdi-Kovács, János Rózsa, István Szabó, Sándor Sára, Ferenc Kósa, and others. He took his first, already conspicuous step in a creative workshop, the experimental studio of Béla Balázs. The artistic path he chose was a difficult one, because it was the specific, individual form of documentary. In the course of his creative career he returns constantly to this basic source, but at the same time he applies its elements in his not very extensive but masterfully suggestive artistic film work.

He is one of the founders of the Hungarian new wave of the mid-1960's, which he inaugurated with his deeply emotive debut *Sodrásban*. Not only did this work reflect the positive social events of the time, but the author also applied genuine elements of a subjectively motivated poetics. With every important subsequent film—and these are for the most part adaptions of his own literary work—Gaál reveals the strange world of the Hungarian countryside, a world of desolation and unromantically flat landscapes with scattered lonely settings where solitary tree trunks, well-beams, and the whitewashed walls of old buildings loom from time to time. In this microcosm he uncovers human community, relationships, and problems of morality. In intimate episodes he manages to take up and treat delicate problems of the past and generalize them in the form of a profound philosophical drama that reveals the roots of violence and evil and the dangerous elements of apathy and indifference, despair and loneliness. At the same time, his films, with their limited dialogue and almost totally graphic conception, are poetic pictures that have dramatic tension. However, István Gaál is not the romantic poet of the countryside he may appear to be. In a brief moment and in simple fashion he suggests the atmosphere and the relationships among characters, and he is equally adept at capturing the essence of a hunting lodge in the wilderness, a depopulated village, or the smell of a provincial town. For him the environment is merely a symbolic medium, because each of his works offers a kind of parallel between the world of nature and human society, a metaphor with deep ideological and moral significance.

There is a close union of all artistic components in films under his direction—a carefully constructed script, a poetic

313

István Gaál: *Sodrásban*

form of screen photography, simple non-illustrative music, and dramatically motivated editing, along with prodigious acting by the noted performers whom the director gets to "shed their theatrical skin," enabling them to achieve quite a remarkable degree of expression before the camera.

In the intervals between making his fictional film works, István Gaál constantly returns to the pure documentary, which is for him a starting point and perhaps also an experimental station. But he shapes his documentaries with the same fire and originality. Here again, there is an alteration between people and nature, and a struggle between the two.

In his most recent films, István Gaál turns more to the inner world of his contemporaries. His works delineate masterful psychological portraits in which there is more and more reflection of history on a general plane. His films are personal, poetically veiled confessions about present-day people, their problems and relations.

—Václav Merhaut

GAD, Urban.

Danish. Born in Korsør, 12 February 1879. Educated in Copenhagen until 1897; attended art school in Paris. Married 1) Asta Nielsen, 1912 (divorced 1918); 2) Esther Burgert Westenhagen, 1922. Artistic advisor and playwright, Copenhagen, then directed first film, 1910; worked in German film industry, 1911–22; manager of "Grand" film theatre, Copenhagen, 1922–47. *Died 26 December 1947.*

Films as Director:

1910   *Afgrunden (The Abyss)*
1911   *Den sorte Drøm; Hulda Rasmussen or Dyrekøbt Glimmer (When Passion Blinds Honesty); Aedel Daad or Den store Flyver (Generosity); Gennem Kamp til Sejr (Through Trials to Victory); Der fremde Vogel; Die Verräterin; Heisses Blut; In dem grossen Augenblick; Nachtfalter; Zigeunerblut (Gypsy Blood)*
1912   *Den hvide Slavehandel III or Det berygtede Hus (Nina, In the Hands of the Impostors); Das Mädchen ohne Vaterland; Der Totentanz; Die arme Jenny; Die Kinder des Generals; Die Macht des Goldes; Jugend und Tollheit; Komödianten; Wenn die Maske fällt; Zum Tode gehetz*
1913   *Der Tod in Sevilla; Die Filmprimadonna; Die Sünden der Vater; Die Suffragette; Engelein; S.I.*
1914   *Aschenbrödel; Das Feuer; Das Kind ruft; Die ewige Nacht; Die Tochter der Landstrasse; Engeleins Hochzeit; Vordertreppe und Hintertreppe; Weisse Rosen; Zapatas Bande*
1916   *Der rote Streifen*
1917   *Der breite Weg; Die Gespensterstunde; Die Vergangenheit rächt sich; Die verschlossene Tür; Klosterfriede*
1918   *Das sterbende Modell; Das verhängnisvolle Andenken; Der Schmuck des Rajah; Die Kleptomanin; Die neue Dalila; Vera Panina*

1919 *Das Spiel von Liebe und Tod*; *Mein Mann—der Nachtredakteur*
1920 *Der Abgrund der Seelen*; *Der Liebes-Korridor*; *So ein Mädel*; *Weltbrand*
1921 *Christian Wahnschaffe*; *Der vergiftete Brunnen*; *Die Insel der Verschollenen*
1922 *Hanneles Himmelfahrt*
1926 *Lykkehjulet* (*The Gay Huskies*)

Publications:

By GAD: book—

Filmen: Dens Midler og Maal, Copenhagen, 1919; as *Der Film: seine Mittel—seine Ziele*, 1921.

On GAD: article—

Wollenberg, H.H., obituary in *Penguin Film Review* (London), September 1948.

* * *

"The part he played in the early history of European film art can be compared with that of D.W. Griffith in America," wrote H.H. Wollenberg in his obituary of Urban Gad (in *Penguin Film Review*, September 1948). These kind words are—to put it mildly—an exaggeration of Urban Gad's importance in the history and development of the film. Considering his total output, Urban Gad might better be characterized as a cultivated craftsman, who was mainly occupied with the handling of actors. With his background, coming from a high-society milieu with a cultural leaning, and having worked as a dramatic consultant for Copenhagen theaters, this is quite natural. He was an intellectual with a great affection for and belief in the film as an artistic means of expression. His book *The Film: Its Means and Ends*, published in 1919 and two years later translated into German, was a very intelligent, open-minded and stimulating theoretical work, which was remarkable at a time when few intellectuals had any respect for film.

Gad's position in early film history is secured by one work, and this was his first, *Afgrunden*, which he wrote and directed, assisted by the experienced cameraman Alfred Lind. The story was about a young bourgeois girl, who is infatuated with a circus artist. She abandons her quiet and safe life, follows the performer, and in the end she murders him in a rage of jealousy. *Afgrunden* introduced the erotic melodrama, with a background of social contrast, which became in the next few years a Danish specialty, influencing the international film. Gad had written the role of the girl for Asta Nielsen. She made her

Urban Gad: Poul Reumert and Asta Nielsen in *Afgrunden*

screen debut in the film and was an instant sensation. Her sensuality and frankness shocked the audience and one scene, in which Nielsen performs a gaucho dance with Poul Reumert, the leading man, was a hitherto unseen demonstration of sexual provocation. Urban Gad had created the first European film star.

Gad was known for his meticulous care when filming and he had a reputation for being a very demanding director. In the next two films, made for Nordisk before he went to Germany, he used more sets than was customary. Gad left Denmark with Asta Nielsen and he wrote and directed 34 of her films until 1914, when they separated. Asta Nielsen rose to stardom; but Gad never played an important part in German film. After a couple of films in Denmark in the 1920's he left film production in 1926. For the rest of his life he was held in great esteem as the manager of one of Copenhagen's prestige cinemas.

—Ib Monty

GALLONE, Carmine.

Italian. Born in Taggia, 18 September 1886. Married Soava (Gallone), 1912. Playwright and poet, early 1900's; began working at Teatro Argentina, Rome, 1911; director and screenwriter at Cines studio, from 1913. *Died April 1973.*

Films as Director:

1913   *Il bacio di Cirano*; *La donna nuda*
1914   *Turbine d'odio*
1915   *Avatar*; *Redenzione*; *Fior di male*; *Marzia nuziale*; *Senza colpa*
1916   *La falena*; *Malombra*; *Fede*; *Tra i gorghi*; *La storia dei tredici*
1917   *Lo chiamavano Cosetta*; *Madonna Grazia*
1918   *Storia di un peccato*
1919   *Maman Popee*; *La figlie del mare*; *Il destino e il timoniere*; *Il mare di Napoli*
1920   *La Vie d'une femme*; *Il bacio di Cirano*; *Marcella*; *La Fanciulla, il poeta e la laguna*; *La figlia del tempesta* (+ sc); *Il Colonnello Chabert*; *La grande tormenta*; *Amleto e il suo clown*
1921   *Nemesis*; *L'ombra di un trono*
1922   *La madre folle* (+ pr); *Le braccia aperte*; *Il Reggimento Royal Cravate*; *Il segreto della grotta azzurra*; *La vedova scaltra*
1923   *Amore* (+ pr); *Tormenta* (*Nella tormenta*); *I volti dell'amore*
1924   *Il corsaro* (co-d); *La signorina madre di famiglia*; *Jerry*; *La fiammata*
1926   *Gli ultimi giorni di Pompeii* (*The Last Days of Pompeii*)
1927   *La cavalcata ardente*; *Celle qui domine* (co-d); *Die Stadt der tausend Freuden*; *Liebeshölle* (*L'inferno dell'amore, Pawns of Passion*); *Marter der Liebe*; *S.O.S.*
1929   *Das Land ohne Frauen* (*Terra senza donne, Bride 68*)
1930   *Die singende Stadt*
1931   *Un Soir de rafle*; *The City of Song* (*Farewell to Love*)
1932   *Le Chant du marin*; *Un Fils d'Amerique*; *Ma Cousine de Varsovie*; *Le Roi des palaces*
1933   *King of the Ritz* (American version of *Le Roi des palaces*); *Eine Nacht in Venedig*
1934   *Two Hearts in Waltz Time*; *Going Gay*; *For Love of You*
1935   *Wenn die Musik nicht wär*; *Im Sonnenschein* (*Opernring, Thank You Madame*); *Mein Herz ruft nach Dir* (*E lucean le stelle, My Heart Is Calling, Mon Coeur t'appelle*); *Casta Diva* (*The Divine Spark*); *Al sole*
1937   *Scipione l'Africano* (*Scipio Africanus*)
1938   *Solo per te*; *Manège* (*Un dramma al circo*); *Marionette* (*Dir gehört mein Herz*); *Giuseppe Verdi*

1939   *Das Abenteuer geht weiter*; *Il sogno di Butterfly*; *Manon Lescaut*
1940   *Oltre d'amore*; *Melodie eterne* (*Eternal Melodies*); *Marcella*; *Amami, Alfredo!*
1941   *L'amante segreta*; *Primo amore*; *La Regina di Navarra*
1942   *Le due orfanelle* (*The Two Orphans*); *Odessa in fiamme*; *Harlem*
1943   *Tristi amori*
1945   *Il canto della vita*
1946   *Biraghin*; *Devanti a lui tremava tutta Roma* (*Before Him All Rome Trembled, Tosca*)
1947   *Rigoletto*
1948   *La signora delle camelie* (*La traviata, The Lost One*)
1949   *La leggenda di Faust* (*Faust and the Devil*); *Il trovatore*
1950   *La forza del destino*; *Taxi di notte* (*Singing Taxi Driver*) (+ pr)
1951   *Addio Mimi* (*Her Wonderful Lie*) (completed 1947); *Messalina* (*The Affairs of Messalina*) (+ co-sc)
1953   *Puccini* (+ co-sc); *Cavalleria rusticana* (*Fatal Desire*) (+ co-sc); *Senza veli* (+ co-sc)
1954   *Casa Ricordi* (*House of Ricordi*)
1955   *Madama Butterfly* (+ co-sc); *Don Camillo e l'onorevole Peppone*; *Casta Diva*
1956   *Tosca*; *Michele Strogoff*
1958   *Polijuschka*
1959   *Cartagine in fiamme*
1961   *Don Camillo Monsignore ma non troppo*
1962   *La Monaca di Monza*; *Carmen di Trastavere*

Other Films:

1920   *Sterimator Vesevo* (sc)
1955   *La figlia di Mata Hari* (supervisor)

Publications:

By GALLONE: article—

"L'arte di inscenare," in *Bianco e Nero* (Rome), July/August 1952.

On GALLONE: articles—

"*Scipione l'Africano* Issue" of *Bianco e Nero* (Rome), no. 7–8, 1937.
Paolella, Roberto, in *Bianco e Nero* (Rome), no. 7–8, 1952.
Beylie, Claude, "Carmine Gallone le grandiloquent," in *Ecran* (Paris), May 1973.
Bianco e Nero (Rome), July/September 1986.

* * *

Gallone started his career in 1911 at the Teatro Argentina in Rome but was quickly attracted to the cinema, entering the Cines studio as scriptwriter in 1913. His directorial talent being immediately recognized, Cines gave him the project of adapting a version of *Cyrano de Bergerac*. From then on, most notably working with Lucio D'Ambra, Gallone became a leading director during the golden age of Italian silent cinema that lasted until the end of the First World War. He was largely responsible for the growth of an elaborate star system, wherein the films were tailored specifically to the stars' talents and personae. Such films dominated Italian production. Gallone's favorite players were Soava Gallone, a Polish actress, who married him in 1912 and starred in a dozen of his films, Lyda Borelli, Emilio Ghione, and Amleto Novelli. Even though Gallone could film in a realist style, for example in *Storia di un peccato*, he seemed more adept at torrid love stories, historical epics, and adaptations of famous literature. In a period governed by the artistic style and philosophy of Gabriele D'Annunzio, Gallone was perhaps the best at portraying the prevailing sensibility on a grand scale. Gallone placed great emphasis on composition, the pictorial elements of the image, and set decoration. He believed in visual orchestration whereby concepts are realized through the mise-en-scène itself. He insisted that actors work very closely with the set designer so

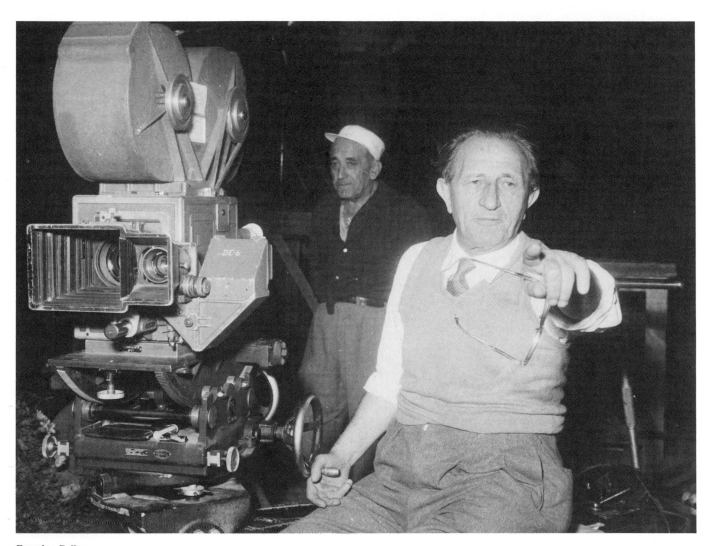

Carmine Gallone

that the design and performances would be consonant with each other. His films were enormously successful both in his native country and abroad, so much so that their popularity demanded remakes by Gallone, as in the cases of *Il Bacio di Cirano, La grande tormenta*, and *Casta Diva*.

During the years of extreme crisis in the Italian cinema in the late 1920's, Gallone, like many of his contemporaries, made films in other countries, and multiple-language versions of sound films for national markets. For a decade, he directed in Germany, Austria, France, and worked for the continental studios of British Gaumont. He had no difficulty making the transition to sound and, in fact, one of his first sound films, the French *Un soir de rafle*, starring Annabella and Albert Prejean (who made three films with Gallone) proved to be a huge success. Outside of Italy as well he worked with popular stars: Conrad Veidt, Martha Eggerth, Brigitte Helm. He was called back to Italy in 1936 for the colossal project in praise of the Roman empire, *Scipione l'Africano*, famous because it is one of the few outright pieces of propaganda produced by the film industry under Fascism, and for its immense scope: 20 principal actors, 32,848 extras, 50 elephants, 1,000 horses, and a shooting schedule of 232 days lasting from August 1936 until March 1937.

During the sound period, before and after the war, Gallone was best known as a director of musicals, lavishly produced, and filmed operas. Most of the films starring the tenor Beniamino Gigli just before the war were directed by Gallone. His 1946 Resistance film, which he co-scripted, was, in fact, an operatic depiction of Fascism starring Anna Magnani and Tito Gobbi.

—Elaine Mancini

GANCE, Abel.

French. Born in Paris, 25 October 1889. Educated at Collège de Chantilly; Collège Chaptal, Paris, baccalaureate 1906. Served with Service Cinématographique et Photographique de l'Armée, 1917. Married (second wife) actress Odette Vérité, 1933, daughter: Clarisse (Mme. Jacques Raynaud). Actor at Théâtre du Parc, Brussels, 1908–09; began selling screenplays to Gaumont, 1909; formed production company, Le Film Français, 1911; artistic director of Le Film d'Art, 1917; after death of first wife, travelled to U.S.A., 1921; patented widescreen "Polyvision" process, 1926; patented "Perspective Sonore," stereophonic sound process, 1929; directed *Marie*

Tudor for TV, 1965; lived in Nice, worked on screenplay for *Christophe Colomb* project, first begun in 1939, 1970's; reassembled *Napoléon* premiered in New York, 1981. Recipient: Gold Medal, Union Française des Inventeurs, and Cinérama Gold Medal, Société des Auteurs, 1952; Théâtre de l'Empire named for Gance, Paris, 1961; Grand prix national de Cinéma, 1974; César Award, 1980; Commandeur de la Légion d'honneur; Grand officier de l'ordre national du Merité, et des Arts et des Lettres. *Died in Paris, 10 November 1981.*

Films as Director:

1911   *La Digue, ou Pour sauver la Hollande* (+ sc)
1912   *Le Nègre blanc* (+ sc, role); *Il y a des pieds au plafond* (+ sc); *Le Masque d'horreur* (+ sc)
1915   *Un drame au Château d'Acre* (*Les Morts reviennent-ils?*) (+ sc); *Ecce Homo* (+ sc) (unfinished)
1916 *La Folie du Docteur Tube* (+ sc); *L'Enigme de dix heures* (+ sc); *Le Fleur des ruines* (+ sc); *L'Heroïsme de Paddy* (+ sc); *Fioritures* (*La Source de beauté*) (+ sc); *Le Fou de la falaise* (+ sc); *Ce que les flots racontent* (+ sc); *Le Périscope* (+ sc): *Barberousse* (+ sc); *Les Gaz mortels* (*Le Brouillard sur la ville*) (+ sc); *Strass et compagnie* (+ sc)
1917 *Le Droit à la vie* (+ sc): *La Zone de la mort* (+ sc); *Mater Dolorosa* (+ sc)
1918   *La Dixième Symphonie* (+ sc); *Le Soleil noir* (+ sc) (unfinished)
1919   *J'Accuse* (+ sc)
1923   *La Roué* (+ sc); *Au secours!* (+ sc)
1927   **Napoléon vu par Abel Gance** (+ sc)
1928   *Marines et Cristeaux* (+ sc) (experimental footage for "Polyvision")
1931   *La Fin du monde* (+ sc)
1932   *Mater Dolorosa* (+ sc)
1934   *Poliche* (+ sc); *La Dame aux Camélias* (+ sc); *Napoléon Bonaparte* (+ sc) (sound version, with additional footage)
1935   *Le Roman d'un jeune homme pauvre* (+ sc); *Lucrèce Borgia*
1936   *Un Grande Amour de Beethoven* (*The Life and Loves of Beethoven*) (+ sc); *Jérome Perreau, héro des barricades* (*The Queen and the Cardinal*); *Le Voleur de femmes* (+ sc)
1937   *J'accuse* (*That They May Live*) (+ sc)
1939   *Louise* (+ co-sc); *Le Paradis perdu* (*Four Flights to Love*) (+ co-sc)
1941   *La Vénus aveugle* (+ sc)
1942   *Le Capitaine Fracasse* (+ co-sc)
1944   *Manolete* (+ sc) (unfinished)
1954   *Quatorze Juillet* (+ sc); *La Tour de Nesle* (+ sc)
1956   *Magirama* (+ sc, co-pr; demonstration of "Polyvision" in color)
1960   *Austerlitz* (co-d, + co-sc)
1964   *Cyrano et d'Artagnan* (+ co-sc)
1971   *Bonaparte et la révolution* (+ sc, co-pr)

Other Films:

1909   *Le Portrait de Mireille* (Perret) (sc); *Le Glas du Père Césaire* (+ sc); *La Légende de l'arc-en-ciel* (sc); *Molière* (Perret) (role)
1909/10   Some Max Linder short comedies (role as Max's brother)
1910   *Paganini* (sc); *La Fin de Paganini* (sc); *Le Crime de Grand-père* (Perret) (sc); *Le Roi des parfums* (sc); *L'Aluminité* (sc); *L'Auberge rouge* (sc); *Le Tragique Amour de Mona Lisa* (Capellani) (sc)
1911   *Cyrano et D'Assoucy* (Capellani) (sc); *Un Clair de lune sous Richelieu* (Capellani) (sc); *L'Électrocuté* (Morlhon) (sc)
1912   *Une Vengeance d'Edgar Poe* (Capellani) (sc); *La Mort du Duc d'Enghien* (Capellani) (sc); *La Conspiration des drapeaux* (sc); *La Pierre philosophe* (sc)
1914   *L'Infirmière* (Pouctal) (sc)
1920   *L'Atre* (Boudrioz) (pr)
1929   *Napoléon auf St. Helena* (*Napoléon à Saint-Hélène*) (Pick) (sc)

1933   *Le Maître de forges* (Rivers) (sc, supervisor)
1953   *Lumière et l'invention du cinématographe* (*Louis Lumière*) (Paviot) (commentary, narration)
1954   *La Reine Margot* (Dréville) (sc)

Publications:

By GANCE: books—

J'Accuse, Paris, 1922.
Napoléon vu par Abel Gance, Paris, 1927.
La Roué, scénario original arrangé par Jean Arroy, Paris, 1930.
Prisme, Paris, 1930.
La Fin du Monde, scénario arrangé par Joachim Renez, Paris, 1931.
Mater Dolorosa, scénario original arrangé par Joachim Renez, Paris, 1932.
Napoléon, as seen by Abel Gance, edited by B. Ballard, London, 1990.

By GANCE: articles—

"Qu'est-ce que le cinématographe? Un sixième art," in *Intelligence du cinématographe* by Marcel L'Herbier, Paris, 1946.
"Les nouveaux chapitres de notre syntaxe," in *Cahiers du Cinéma* (Paris), October 1953.
"Départ vers la polyvision," in *Cahiers du Cinéma* (Paris), December 1954.
"Entretien avec Jacques Rivette et François Truffaut," in *Cahiers du Cinéma* (Paris), January 1955.
"*The Kingdom of the Earth*," in *Film Culture* (New York), December 1957.
"Film as Incantation: An Interview with Abel Gance," in *Film Comment* (New York), March/April 1974.

On GANCE: books—

Arroy, Jean, *En tournant "Napoléon" avec Abel Gance*, Paris, 1927.
Daria, Sophie, *Abel Gance, hier et demain*, Paris, 1959.
Icart, Roger, *Abel Gance*, Toulouse, 1960.
Brownlow, Kevin, *The Parade's Gone By*, New York, 1969.
Kramer, Steven, and James Welsh, *Abel Gance*, Boston, 1978.
Icart, Roger, *Abel Gance; ou, Le Promethée foudroyé*, Lausanne, 1983.
King, Norman, *Abel Gance: A Politics of Spectacle*, London, 1984.
Groppali, Enrico, *Abel Gance*, Florence, 1986.

On GANCE: articles—

Epstein, Jean, "Mon ami Gance," in *Cahiers du Cinéma* (Paris), August/September 1955.
"Gance Issue" of *L'Ecran* (Paris), April/May 1958.
Lenning, Arthur, "*Napoléon* and *La Roue*," in *The Persistence of Vision* edited by Joseph McBride, Madison, Wisconsin, 1968.
Brownlow, Kevin, "*Bonaparte et la révolution*," in *Sight and Sound* (London), Winter 1971/72.
Welsh, J.M., and S.P. Kramer, "Abel Gance's Accusation Against War," in *Cinema Journal* (Evanston), Spring 1975.
Gilliatt, Penelope, in the *New Yorker*, 6 September 1976.
Drew, W.M., "Abel Gance: Prometheus Bound," in *Take One* (Montreal), July 1978.
Nerguy, C., and Y. Alion, "*Un Grand Amour de Beethoven*," in *Avant-Scène du Cinéma* (Paris), 1 October 1978.
Brownlow, Kevin, "Abel Gance," in *Film Dope* (London), September 1979.
Allen, W., "*Napoléon* reconstructed," in *Stills* (London), Autumn 1981.
Obituary, in the *New York Times*, 11 November 1981.
Cluny, C.M., "Abel Gance: trop grand pour le cinéma?," in *Cinéma* (Paris), December 1981.
Lafaye, C., obituary, in *Cinéma* (Paris), January 1982.
Riley, B., obituary, in *Film Comment* (New York), January/February 1982.
Jeancolas, J.-P., "Abel Gance entre *Napoléon* et *Philippe Pétain*," in *Positif* (Paris), June 1982.
Icart, R., C. Lafaye, and L. Martin, "Tumultueux Abel Gance," in *Revue du Cinéma* (Paris), May 1983.
King, Norman, "The Sounds of Silents," in *Screen* (London), May/June 1984.
Virmaux, A. and O., "Deux amis," in *Cinématographe* (Paris), November 1986.

Abel Gance on the set of *Napoleon*

On GANCE: films—

Ford, Charles, and Jacques Guillon, *Les Éloquents*, France, 1956.

Kaplan, Nelly, *Abel Gance, hier et demain* (*Abel Gance, Yesterday and Tomorrow*), Paris, 1964.

Brownlow, Kevin, *Abel Gance—the Charm of Dynamite*, London, 1968.

*   *   *

Abel Gance's career as a director was long and flamboyant. He wrote his first scripts in 1909, turning to directing a couple of years later, and made his last feature, *Cyrano et d'Artagnan*, in 1964. As late as 1971 he re-edited a four hour version of his Napoleon footage to make *Bonaparte et la révolution*, and he lived long enough to see his work again reach wide audiences.

Gance's original aspirations were as a playwright and throughout his life he treasured the manuscript of his verse tragedy *La Victoire de Samothrace*, written for Sarah Bernhardt and on the brink of production when the war broke out in 1914. If Gance's beginnings in the film industry he then despised were unremarkable, he was already showing a characteristic audacity and urge for experiment with the unreleased *La Folie du Docteur Tube*, which made great use of distorting lenses, in 1916. Learning his craft in a dozen or more films during 1916–17, best remembered of which are *Les Gaz mortels*, *Barberousse*, and *Mater dolorosa*, he reached fresh heights with a somewhat pretentious and melodramatic study of a

great and suffering composer, *La Dixième Symphonie*, and especially his ambitious and eloquent antiwar drama, *J'Accuse*, released in 1919. These films estalished him as the leading French director of his generation and gave him a pre-eminence he was not to lose until the coming of sound.

The 1920's saw the release of just three Gance films. If *Au secours!*, a comedy starring his friend Max Linder, is something of a lighthearted interlude, the other two are towering landmarks of silent cinema. *La Roue* began as a simple melodramatic tale but in the course of six months scripting and a year's location shooting, the project took on quite a new dimension. In the central figure of Sisif, Gance seems to have struggled to create an amalgam of Oedipus, Sisyphus, and Lear, while the cut portions of the film also apparently developed a social satire of such ferocity that the railway unions demanded its excision. This was the most expensive film as yet made in France and its production was again delayed when the death of Gance's wife caused him to abandon work and take a five month trip to the U.S. Like his previous work, *La Roue* had been conceived and shot in the pre-1914 style of French cinema, which was based on a conception of film as a series of long takes, each containing a significant section of the action, rather than as a succession of scenes made up of intercut shots of different lengths, taken from varying distances. But in Hollywood, where he met D.W. Griffith, Gance came into contact with the new American style of editing and on his return to

France spent a whole year reediting his film. On its release in 1923 *La Roue* proved to be one of the stunning films of the decade, even in its shortened version comprising a prologue and four parts, with a combined running time of nearly eight hours.

Gance's imagination and energy at this period seemed limitless and almost immediately he plunged into an even vaster project whose title clearly reflects his personal approach, *Napoléon va par Abel Gance*. If *La Roue* was particularly remarkable for its editing, with certain sequences becoming classic moments of French 1920s avant-garde experiment, *Napoléon* attracted immediate attention for its incredibly mobile camerawork created by a team under the direction of Jules Kruger. *Napoléon* thus emerges as a key masterpiece of French cinema at a time when visual experimentation took precedence over narrative and the disorganization of production offered filmmakers the chance to produce extravagant and ambitious personal works within the heart of the commercial industry. Gance's conception of himself as visionary filmmaker and of Napoleon as a master of his destiny points to the roots of Gance's style in the 19th century and a very romantic view of the artist as hero. The scope of Gance's film, bursting into triple screen effects at the moment of Napoleon's climactic entry into Italy, remains staggering even today.

The 1920s in France were a period of considerable creative freedom and a widespread urge to experiment with the full potential of the medium. If the freedom came from the lack of a tightly controlled studio system, the desire to explore new forms of filmic expression can be traced to a reaction against the situation imposed by Pathé and Gaumont before 1914, when film was seen as a purely commercial product, underfinanced and devoid of artistic or personal expression. This had been the cinema in which Gance had made his debut, and he was one of those striving most forcefully in the 1920s both to increase the possibilities for personal expressiveness and to widen the technical scope of cinema. He pioneered new styles of cutting and camerawork, and also widescreen and multiscreen techniques. It's ironic, then, that the advent of the greatest technical innovation of the period should have left him stranded. The explanation for this lies less in the irrelevance of sound to his personal vision of the medium—he was pioneering a new stereophonic system with *La Fin du monde* as early as 1929—than in the new forms of tighter production control which came as a result of the greater costs involved in sound filmmaking.

The 1930s emerge as a sad era for a man accustomed to being in the forefront of the French film industry. Gance, whose mind had always teemed with new and original projects, was now reduced to remaking his old successes: sound versions of *Mater dolorosa* in 1932, *Napoléon Bonaparte* in 1934 and J'accuse in 1937. Otherwise the projects he was allowed to make were largely adaptations of fashionable stage dramas or popular novels: *Le Maître de forges, Poliche, La Dame aux camélias, Le Roman d'un jeune homme pauvre*. In the late 1930s he was able to treat subjects in which his taste for grandly heroic figures is again apparent: Savonarola in *Lucrèce Borgia*, or the great composer—played by Harry Baur—in *Un Grand Amour de Beethoven*, but by 1942, when he made *Le Capitaine Fracasse*, Gance's career seemed to have come to an end. Though a dozen years were to pass before he directed another feature film, he maintained his incredible level of energy and refusal to be beaten, continuing his experiments with "polyvision" which were to culminate in his *Magirama* spectacle, and eventually making three further features, all historical dramas in which his zest, if not the old towering imagination, is still apparent: *La Tour de Nesle, Austerlitz* and *Cyrano et d'Artagnan*.

The French 1920s cinema of which Gance is the major figure has consistently been undervalued by film historians, largely because its rich experimentation with visual style and expressiveness was not accompanied by an similar concern with the development of film narrative. Gance's roots are in the 19th century romantic tradition and despite his literary background, he, like his contemporaries, was willing to accept virtually any melodramatic story which would allow him to pursue his visual interests. For this reason French 1920s work has been marginalized in accounts of film history which see the growth of storytelling techniques as the central unifying factor. The rediscovery of Gance's *Napoléon* in the 1980s—thanks largely to 20 years of effort by Kevin Brownlow—has made clear to the most sceptical the force and mastery achieved in the years preceding the advent of sound, and restored Gance's reputation as a master of world cinema.

—Roy Armes

GARCÍA BERLANGA, Luis.

Spanish. Born Luis García-Berlanga Marti in Valencia, 12 July 1921. Studied at Jesuit school, Switzerland; Valencia University; IIEC (School of Cinema), Madrid, 1947–50. Served in División Azul (Blue Division) of Spanish volunteers with German forces on Russian front, early 1940's. Painter and poet, 1942–47; with Antonio Bardem, directed first film, 1951; several projects banned by censor, 1950's; began collaboration with writer Rafael Azcona on *Plácido*, 1961; Professor at IIEC, 1970's; President of Filmoteca Nacional, 1980's.

Films as Director:

1948/49   *Paseo sobre una guerra antigua* (as IIEC student); *Tres cantos* (IIEC student); *El circo* (+ sc, ed) (IIEC student)
1951   *Esa pareja feliz* (*That Happy Couple*) (co-d, ph, co-sc)
1952   *¡Bienvenido, Mr. Marshall!* (*Welcome, Mr. Marshall*) (+ co-sc)
1953   *Novio a la vista* (*Fiancé in sight*) (+ co-sc)
1956   *Calabuch* (+ co-sc)
1957   *Los jueves, milagro* (*Thursdays, Miracle*) (+ co-sc)
1961   *Plácido* (+ co-sc)
1962   "*La muerte y el leñador* (Death and the Woodcutter)" episode of *Las cuatro verdades* (+ co-sc)
1963   ***El verdugo (The Executioner, Not On Your Life)*** (+ co-sc)
1967   *Las pirañas* (+ co-sc)
1969   *Vivan los novios* (*Long Live the Bride and Groom*) (+ co-sc)
1973   *Tamaño natural* (*Life Size*) (+ co-sc)
1978   *La escopeta nacional* (*The National Rifle. The Spanish Shotgun*) (+ co-sc)
1979   *Cuentos eróticos* (*Erotic Tales*) (collectively directed)
1980   *Patrimonio nacional* (+ co-sc)

Other Films:

1953   *Sangre y luces* (Muñoz) (sc) (Spanish language version of Georges Rouquier's *Sang et lumières*)
1955   *Familia provisional* (Rovira Beleta) (co-sc)
1967   *No somos de piedra* (*We Are Not Made Out of Stone*) (Summers) (role)
1968   *Sharon vestida de rojo* (Lorente) (role)
1971   *Apunte sobre Ana* (*Memorandum on Ana*) (Galán) (role)

Luis Garcia Berlanga: *Placido*

Publications:

By GARCÍA BERLANGA: articles—

"The Day I Refused to Work," in *Films and Filming* (London), December 1961.
"Cara a cara . . . Bardem—Berlanga," in *Cinema 2002* (Madrid), July/August 1980.
"Berlanga Life Size," interview with Katherine Kovacs, in *The Quarterly Review of Film Studies* (Pleasantville, New York), Spring 1983.

On GARCÍA BERLANGA: books—

Santolaya, Ernesto, *Luis G. Berlanga*, Vitoria, 1979.
Perucha, Julio Pérez, *Sobre Luis G. Berlanga*, Valencia, 1981.
Higginbotham, Virginia, *Spanish Film Under Franco*, Austin, Texas, 1988.

On GARCÍA BERLANGA: articles—

Cobos, Juan, "Spanish Fighter," in *Films and Filming* (London), February 1958.
"*Grandeur nature*," in *Avant-Scène du Cinéma* (Paris), November 1974.
Les, J. Hernandez, "Luis Berlanga aujourd'hui et hier," in *Jeune Cinéma* (Paris), April/May 1979.
Acosta, J.L., "Berlanga—B. Wilder: Buscando un punto común," in *Cinema 2002* (Madrid), April 1980.

Marías, Miguel, "El Patrimonio de Berlanga," in *Casablanca* (Madrid), April 1981.
Guarner, José Luis, "Luis G. Berlanga," in *International Film Guide 1981*, London, 1982.
"Spanish Cinema Section" of *Cinéma* (Paris), June 1984.
Screen International (London), 25 June 1988.

*   *   *

For many years in Spain strict censorship guidelines inhibited the development of a vital and creative film industry. The first original *auteur* of the post-Civil War period was Luis García Berlanga. When he began to make movies in the early 1950's, Berlanga and fellow filmmaker Juan Antonio Bardem were referred to as the two palm trees in the desert of Spanish film. Since then, and in spite of the fact that he could make relatively few films under Franco, Berlanga has remained one of Spain's foremost talents.

In the early years, the most important influence on Berlanga's filmmaking was Italian neo-realism. At the Conversations of Salamanca (1955) Berlanga and other young directors enthusiastically supported it as an antidote to Francoist cinema, a way of making authentic films that dealt with the everyday problems of ordinary people. From his first movie, *Esa pareja feliz*, which he co-directed with Bardem in 1951, to his "trilogy" on the Spanish aristocracy, Berlanga has remained true to the spirit of Salamanca.

In many movies he has exposed the pitfalls of Spanish society and satirized those institutions or individuals who take themselves too seriously, often using black humor to deflate their pretensions. Berlanga's sympathies are with the underdogs of whatever social class, those who are victims of fate, institutions, or other forces which they cannot control. In a number of his films, we follow the efforts of an individual who wants to achieve something or attain some goal, struggles to do so, and in the end is defeated, ending up in the same or in a worse situation than before. This unfortunate outcome reflects Berlanga's pessimism about a society in which the individual is powerless and in danger of being devoured. There are no winners in Berlanga's movies; all of the victories are Pyrrhic ones. But never one to deliver messages or lessons, Berlanga expresses his pessimistic viewpoint with such verve, vitality and humor that audiences leave the theatre elated with the spontaneity and inventiveness of his films.

Berlanga prefers working with groups of characters rather than concentrating on the fate of a single protagonist. Rarely does one individual dominate the action. Usually we move from one person to the next so that our point of view on the action is constantly shifting. This approach is supported by Berlanga's distinctive camera style. He tends to use very long takes in which the camera surreptitiously follows the movement of the characters, the shot lasting as long as the sequence. (In *Patrimonio nacional* there are some takes that last six or seven minutes.) These sequences are not, however, the carefully arranged and choreographed efforts of a Jancsó. As Berlanga explains it, until he begins shooting he has no specific setup in mind: "What I do is organize the actors' movements and then tell the cameraman how to follow them. When we bump into some obstacle, we stop shooting." In shooting the often feverish activities of his characters in this way, Berlanga gives a fluid, spontaneous feeling to his films. His predilection for these shots expresses what Berlanga calls his "god complex"—his desire to be everywhere at once and to express the totality of any scene.

In his scrutiny of contemporary Spanish life, Berlanga is also attached to much older Spanish literary and cultural traditions, most notably to that of the picaresque novel, in which a *pícaro* or rogue is thrust out into the world and forced to fend for himself. At the bottom of the social heap, the *pícaro* is afforded "a worm's eye view" of society and learns to be tricky in order to survive. The *pícaro* keeps hoping and waiting for a miracle, a sudden change in fate that will change his or her fortune in one stroke. Berlanga's *pícaros*, whether they be naive like Plácido (*Plácido*) or noble like the Marquis of Leguineche (*Patrimonio nacional*) share the same hopes and tenacious desire to survive. These characters, like Berlanga himself, are deeply attached to Spanish cultural traditions. In fact, one might even consider Berlanga to be a sort of picaresque hero who managed to survive the vagaries of the Franco regime and its system of censorship. A popular director since *Welcome Mr. Marshall*, Berlanga has gone on to even greater success since Franco's death with *La escopeta nacional*, a satiric look at a hunting party of Spain's notables during the Franco regime. In this irreverent and amusing comedy and in its two sequels, Berlanga introduced himself and his vision of his country to a new generation of Spaniards.

—Katherine Singer Kovács

GARNETT, Tay.

American. Born in Los Angeles, 13 June 1894. Educated at Los Angeles High School. Joined Naval Air Service, 1917; studied at Massachusetts Institute of Technology and in Navy Schools, then instructor at San Diego Air Station. Married 1) actress Patsy Ruth Miller (divorced); 2) actress and writer Helga Moray (divorced); 3) actress Mari Aldon (divorced). Went to Hollywood, 1920; scriptwriter, gag man (for Hal Roach and Mack Sennett), and stunt man, early 1920's; scriptwriter on De Mille unit at Pathé, 1927; directed first film, *Celebrity*, 1928; formed Thor Productions with Bert Friedlob, 1949; director for TV, including *Wagon Train, Rawhide*, and *The Untouchables*, from late 1950's. Died in 1977.

Films as Director:

1928   *Celebrity* (+ co-sc); *The Spieler* (*The Spellbinder*) (+ co-adapt)
1929   *The Flying Fool* (+ co-sc); *Oh, Yeah!* (*No Brakes*) (co-d, adapt, co-lyrics)
1930   *Officer O'Brien*; *Her Man* (+ co-story)
1931   *Bad Company* (+ co-sc); *One Way Passage*
1932   *Prestige* (+ co-adapt); *Okay America* (*The Penalty of Fame*)
1933   *Destination Unknown*; *S.O.S. Iceberg* (English language version of Fanck's *S.O.S. Eisberg*; location footage shot by Fanck)
1935   *Professional Soldier*; *China Seas*; *She Couldn't Take It* (*Woman Tamer*)
1937   *Love Is News*; *Slave Ship*; *Stand-in*
1938   *Joy of Living*; *Trade Winds* (+ story)
1939   *Eternally Yours* (+ bit role as pilot)
1940   *Slightly Honorable*; *Seven Sinners*
1941   *Cheers for Miss Bishop*
1942   *My Favorite Spy*
1943   *Bataan*; *The Cross of Lorraine*
1944   *Mrs. Parkington*; *See Here, Private Hargrove* (co-d with Ruggles, uncredited)
1945   *The Valley of Decision*
1946   *The Postman Always Rings Twice*
1947   *Wild Harvest*
1948   *A Connecticut Yankee* (*A Yankee in King Arthur's Court*)
1950   *The Fireball* (+ co-sc); *Cause for Alarm!*
1951   *Soldiers Three*
1952   *One Minute to Zero*
1953   *Main Street to Broadway*
1954   *The Black Knight*
1955   *Seven Wonders of the World* (d Indian sequence only)
1960   *A Terrible Beauty* (*The Night Fighters*)
1963   *Cattle King* (*Guns of Wyoming*)
1970   *The Delta Factor* (+ pr, sc)
1975   *Challenge to be Free* (co-d, + role) (completed 1972); *Timber Tramps* (completed 1972)

Other Films:

1922   *Broken Chains* (Holubar) (co-sc, uncredited); *The Hottentot* (Horne) (co-sc)
1924   *Don't Park There!* (Wagner) (co-sc); *Off His Trolley* (Cline) (co-story); *Honeymoon Hardships* (Cedar) (co-story)
1925   *Somewhere in Wrong* (Pembroke) (titles); *The Snow Hawk* (Pembroke) (titles); *Half a Man* (Sweet) (titles); *Who's Your Friend* (Sheldon) (continuity)
1926   *That's My Baby* (Beaudine) (co-sc, uncredited); *Up in Mabel's Room* (Hopper) (co-sc); *The Strong Man* (Capra) (co-sc, uncredited); *There You Are!* (Sedgwick) (co-sc); *The Cruise of the Jasper B.* (Horne) (co-adapt)
1927   *Rubber Tires* (*10,000 Reward*) (Hale) (co-sc); *Getting Gertie's Garter* (Hopper) (co-sc, uncredited); *White Gold* (Howard) (co-sc); *Long Pants* (Capra) (co-sc, uncredited); *No Control* (Sidney) (co-sc); *The Wise Wife* (Hopper) (co-sc); *Turkish Delight* (Sloane) (sc)

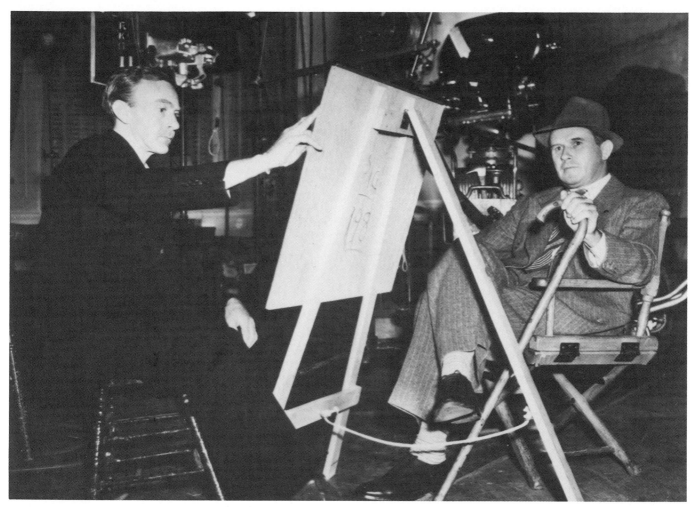

Tay Garnett (right)

1928 *Skyscraper* (Higgin) (co-sc); *The Cop* (Crisp) (sc); *Power*
(Higgin) (sc)
1941 *Unexpected Uncle* (Godfrey) (pr); *Weekend for Three* (Reis)
(pr)

Publications:

By GARNETT: books—

A Man Laughs Back, 1935.
Light Up Your Torches and Pull Up Your Tights, New Rochelle, New
York, 1973.

By GARNETT: articles—

"The Director's Problems," in *Photoplay* (New York), September
1939.
"Les 44 films de Tay Garnett," with Claude Beylie, in *Ecran* (Paris),
April and May 1977.
"Tay Garnett," with J.-L. Passek, in *Cinéma* (Paris), December 1977.
"Tay Garnett Speaking," an interview with R. Fernandez, in *Velvet
Light Trap* (Madison, Wisconsin), Spring 1978.

On GARNETT: articles—

Thomas, B., "Tay Garnett: A Man for All Films," in *Action* (Los
Angeles), September/October 1972.
Navacelle, T., "Hommage à Tay Garnett," in *Cinéma* (Paris), January
1978.
Salmi, M., "Tay Garnett," in *Film Dope* (London), September 1979.
Viviani, C., "Tay Garnett (1898–1977)," in *Avant-Scène du Cinéma*
(Paris), 1 April 1980.

Gallagher, J., "Tay Garnett," in *Films in Review* (New York), December 1981.
Classic Images (Muscatine, Iowa), November 1984.

* * *

Tay Garnett's career can best be described as chaotic. He has
directed comedies and dramas, war films and women's pictures, a couple of classics, more than a couple of solid entertainments, and one too many turkeys.

Garnett's career did not develop in a cohesive manner, one
that can be successfully charted. Most of his best films were
made during the early part of his career. *Her Man*, a Frankie
and Johnny story set in Cuba, is exceptional for its period ambience and smooth camerawork. *One Way Passage*, a sophisticated drama about a romance between terminally ill Kay
Francis and con man William Powell, remains a woman's picture of the highest caliber. *China Seas*, a melodrama with
Clark Gable, Jean Harlow and a stellar cast aboard a Hong
Kong-bound ship, is corny but exciting. *Stand-in* is a funny,
underrated satire of Hollywood.

Garnett's one outstanding post-1940 feature is *The Postman
Always Rings Twice* a sizzling drama of adultery and murder,
from the James M. Cain story, that is far superior to Bob Rafelson's recent remake. In fact, of all Garnett's credits, only *One
Way Passage* and *The Postman Always Rings Twice* approach
the level of greatness. The rest are all good examples of their
respective types, but are in no way linked by any artistic vision.

However, Garnett's films are generally evenly paced. Even in his less auspicious productions the narrative flows smoothly, and there is an effective union of background and storyline. Garnett was aware that a film was sometimes unevenly paced because it was too slow, rather than fast. He would often re-shoot scenes, attempting to trim them down by an all-important eight or ten seconds.

Garnett was also a keen observer of actors. When necessary, he could be stern as with Wallace Beery, a difficult star with a large ego. Yet he was particularly patient with a performer (for instance, Jean Harlow) who was not naturally gifted but still was willing to work and learn. As a result, he would accentuate the strengths of his actors. He insisted on casting Humphrey Bogart, then known solely for gangster roles, as a leading man in *Stand-in*.

Andrew Sarris wrote, in 1968, "Inconsistency is the hobgoblin of Tay Garnett's career, and inconsistency can never be defined satisfactorily. . . . For the moment, Garnett's ultimate reputation is still unusually elusive." From the late 1940s on, Garnett's films do become increasingly mediocre. At their best, however, they're likable as well as competently made, and Garnett deserves to be called an entertainer—not an uncomplimentary appellation.

—Rob Edelman

GERASIMOV, Sergei.

Soviet. Born Sergei Apollinarievich Gerasimov in Zlatoust, Ural region, 21 May 1906. Educated at Leningrad Art School; studied scenic design at State Institute of Dramatic Art, Leningrad, 1920–25. Joined FEKS group founded by Grigori Kozintsev and Leonid Trauberg, early 1920's; directed first film, 1930; Head of Acting and Directing Master Class, Lenfilm Studios, 1931–41; in charge of *Fighting Film Album No. 1*, Moscow, 1941; continued war work, in charge of official films of Yalta and Berlin conferences, 1942–44; Head of Central Newsreel and Documentary Studios, Moscow, 1944; Professor, Moscow Film School (VGIK), 1944–1970's; Artistic Supervisor, Gorki Film Studios, 1955; served as Deputy to the Supreme Soviet of the RSFSR, Secretary of Soviet Union of Cinematographers, and on editorial board of *Isskustvo Kino*, 1970's. Recipient: Red Banner of Labor, 1940 and 1950; Red Star, 1944; Peoples' Artist of USSR, 1948; State prizes, for *Uchitel*, 1941, *The Young Guard*, 1949, and for *Liberated China*, 1951. Died 27 November 1985.

Films as Director:

1930   *Twenty-Two Misfortunes* (co-d)
1931   *The Forest* (+ sc)
1932   *Solomon's Heart* (co-d, + sc)
1934   *Do I Love You?* (+ sc)
1936   *Semero smelykh* (*The Bold Seven*)
1938   *Komsomolsk* (+ co-sc)
1939   *Uchitel* (*Teacher*) (+ sc)
1941   *Masquerade* (+ sc, role as the stranger); *Meeting with Maxim* segment of *Fighting Film Album No. 1*; *The Old Guard*
1943   *The Invincible* (*The Unconquerable*) (co-d, + co-sc); *Film-Concert Dedicated to the Twenty-Fifth Anniversary of the Red Army* (*Cine-Concert . . .*) (co-d, + co-sc)
1944   *Great Land* (*The Mainland*) (+ sc)
1947   *Molodaya gvardiya* (*Young Guard*) (+ sc)

1950   *Liberated China* (+ sc)
1951   *Selskiy vrach* (*Country Doctor*)
1954   *Nadezhda* (+ sc)
1957/58   *Tikhy Don* (*And Quiet Flows the Don*) (+ sc)
1959   *Sputnik Speaking* (*The Sputnik Speaks*) (co-d, co-sc)
1962   *Men and Beasts* (+ sc)
1967   *Zhurnalist* (*The Journalist*) (+ sc)
1969   *U ozera* (*By the Lake*) (+ sc)
1972   *Lyubit cheloveka* (*For the Love of Man*) (+ sc)
1974   *Materi i docheri* (*Mothers and Daughters*)
1984   *Lev Tolstoj*

Other Films:

1925   *Michki protiv Youdenitsa* (*Mishka Against Yudenitch*) (Kozintsev and Trauberg) (role as the spy)
1926   *Chyortovo koleso* (*The Devil's Wheel*) (Kozintsev and Trauberg) (role as the conjuror); *Shinel* (*The Cloak*) (Kozintsev and Trauberg) (role as the card-shark); *Bratichka* (*Little Brother*) (Kozintsev and Trauberg) (role as the driver)
1927   *S.V.D.* (*The Club of the Big Deed*) (Kozintsev and Trauberg) (role as Medoks); *Someone Else's Jacket* (Boris Shpis) (role as Skalkovsky)
1929   *Novyi Vavilon* (**The New Babylon**) (Kozintsev and Trauberg) (asst d, role as the journalist Lutreau); *Oblomok imperii* (*Fragment of an Empire*) (Ermler) (role as the Menshevik)
1931   *Odna* (*Alone*) (Kozintsev and Trauberg) (asst d, role as the chairman of the village soviet)
1932   *Three Soldiers* (Ivanov) (role as Commander of the Iron Regiment)
1933   *Dezertir* (*Deserter*) (Pudovkin) (role as the bonze); *Razbudite Lenochky* (*Wake Up Lenochka*) (Kudryavtseva) (role)
1935   *The Frontier* (Dubson) (role as Yakov the Tailor)
1939   *Chapayev is with Us* (co-sc); *Vyborgskaya storona* (*New Horizons. The Vyborg Side*) (Kozintsev) (role as the Socialist-Revolutionary)
1944   *The Yalta Conference* (pr supervisor)
1945   *The Berlin Conference* (pr supervisor)
1955   *Damy* (Organisyan and Kulidzhanov) (artistic supervisor)
1956   *The Road of Truth* (Frid) (sc)
1958   *Memory of the Heart* (Lioznova) (sc)
1961   *Dimy Gorina* (*Career of Dima*) (Doblatyan and Mirski) (artistic supervisor)
1962   *U Krutovo Yara* (*On the Steep Cliff*) (K. and A. Morakov) (artistic supervisor)
1963   *Venski Les* (*Vienna Woods*) (Grigoriev) (artistic supervisor)
1964   *Sostyazanie* (*Controversy*) (Mansurev) (artistic supervisor)

Publications:

By GERASIMOV: book—

Vospitanie kinorezhisseva, Moscow, 1978.

By GERASIMOV: articles—

"Socialist Realism and the Soviet Cinema," in *Films and Filming* (London), December 1958.
"All Is Not Welles," in *Films and Filming* (London), September 1959.
"A Clash of Conscience," in *Films and Filming* (London), March 1961.
Interview with Roger Hudson, in *Film* (London), Spring 1969.
"V dobryi chas!," in *Iskusstvo Kino* (Moscow), no. 10, 1976.
"Soviet Cinema: Films, Personalities, Problems," with others, in *Soviet Film* (Moscow), no. 271, 1979.
"Akyual'nost' istorii," interview with G. Maslovskij, in *Iskusstvo Kino* (Moscow), September 1980.
Interview in *Isskustvo Kino* (Moscow), December 1982.
Interview in *Soviet Film* (Moscow), February 1984.
Film a Doba (Prague), May 1986.

On GERASIMOV: articles—

Vronskaya, J., "Recent Russian Cinema," in *Film* (London), Summer 1971.

"Sergei Gerasimov," in *Soviet Film* (Moscow), no. 261, 1979.
Obituary in *Variety* (New York), 4 December 1985.
Obituary in *Soviet Film* (Moscow), no. 6, 1987.

*   *   *

The brilliant, original, almost iconoclastic young Sergei Gera-simov became a successful survivor, whose very survival tended to obscure the importance of his earlier contributions to cinema. The somewhat stern image of a grim conservative headmaster he seemed to project to students at the Moscow Film School (VGIK) in the early 1970's was an antithesis of his prewar self.

His own career started in Leningrad when, after graduating as a theatrical designer he joined the "Factory of Eccentric Actors" (FEKS) and became one of the strongest and most original actors in Soviet silent cinema, much attracted to complex roles. Together with what he learned from Kozintsev and Trauberg, who directed most of the productions in which he appeared, his deep study of acting was an important part of Gerasimov's apprenticeship as a filmmaker.

He cut his directorial teeth on three silent productions in the early 1930's, but it was not until 1936, with his first sound film *Semero Smelykh* (*The Bold 7*) that Gerasimov came into his own as a major talent. In this and his next film (*Komsomolsk*) he broke new ground in his choice of subject and in his sincere and unusually successful attempt to portray ordinary young people as varied, breathing, living human beings rather than animated heroic sculptures. His sympathetic direction of his young cast, together with his romantic but naturalistic scripts (pitting teams of young people against the elements) achieved something approaching the elusive ideal of socialist realism.

Uchitel (*Teacher*) in 1939 completed his trio of lyrical but unpretentious evocations of the new Soviet generation in the Russian countryside, by far the most successful films of their genre during the 1930's. This tale of a young man who leaves the bright lights of the city to return to his native village as a schoolmaster, begins, perhaps, to show some signs of the stress imposed by the increasing rigidity of official dogma, not achieving the freshness of the previous two films. Yet, sadly, some seven years later Gerasimov castigated himself for not having adhered more strictly to the party line. "I loved the film," he wrote, "and I still love it, despite the fact that it is far too polished . . . and not a little too obsequious in its attitude to Art." By this time the war had intervened and Gerasimov (in 1944) had become a member of the Communist Party.

Besides his rural trilogy, his only other prewar feature, *Masquerade*, was a lavish version of Lermontov's verse tragedy which, although successful at the time, was also criticized by the director himself, a stern exponent of "socialist self-criticism". Admitting that the film had helped him "refine his art," he considered it "haphazard and unplanned" and lacking sufficient appreciation of Lermontov's particular genius. He had certainly set himself an uphill task in trying to combine his FEKS style with the tradition of stage drama and dialogue in verse, although his own performance as "The Stranger" was an echo of his old FEKS philosophy and the Leningrad setting was spectacular.

During the war, Gerasimov was put in charge of the documentary film studios, where he brought together the talents of feature directors and documentarists and once more proved his flair for encouraging good work from others. This led to his appointment in 1944 as head of the directing and acting workshops of the Moscow Film School (VGIK). Occupying this seminal position through the following 30 years, he has had an enormous influence on the whole present generation of Soviet filmmakers.

After the war his own work seems drastically to have swung from his self-effacing, sympathetic form of filmmaking to the grandiose style fashionable during Stalin's final phase. Fadeev's patriotic, lyrical novel *The Young Guard* would seem to have been ideal source material for a typical Gerasimov film, yet it turned out to be bombastic, pompous, and overblown. His other huge epic, *And Quiet Flows the Don*, shown in three full-length parts, unfortunately suffered from similar grandiosity. Apart from this foray into gigantism, and a documentary on China, much of Gerasimov's post-Stalin output saw a return to his themes of the 1930's. Though always a highly competent director, however, he never quite recaptured his freshness of approach and lightness of touch.

—Robert Dunbar

————

GERIMA, Haile.

Ethiopian. Born in Gonder, Ethiopia. Studied theatre at Goodman School of Drama, Chicago, from 1967; filmmaking at University of California, Los Angeles (UCLA), graduated 1975. Returned to Ethiopia to make *Harvest: 3000 Years*, 1974; set up production company Myphudeh Films ("Myphudeh" is a Ge'ez word meaning "Sacred Shield"); teacher of filmmaking at Howard University, Washington, D.C. Address: c/o School of Communications, Howard University, 2400 Sixth St NW, Washington, D.C. 20059, U.S.A.

Films as Director:

1972	*Child of Resistance*
1975	*Bush Mama*
1976	*Mirt sost shi amit* (*Harvest: 3000 Years*)
1978	*Wilmington 10, USA 10,000*
1982	*Ashes and Embers*
1985	*After Winter: Sterling Brown*

Publications:

By GERIMA: articles—

Interview in *Framework* (Norwich), no. 7, 1978.
Interview with Yves Lardeau, in *Cahiers du Cinéma* (Paris), October 1982.
Interview with T. Safford and W. Triplett, in *Journal of the University Film Association* (Carbondale, Illinois), Spring 1983.

On GERIMA: books—

Martin, Angela, *African Films: The Context of Production*, London, 1982.
Armes, Roy, *Third World Filmmaking and the West*, Berkeley, 1987.
Pfaff, Françoise, *25 Black African Filmmakers: A Critical Study*, Westport, Connecticut, 1988.

On GERIMA: articles—

"Gerima Section" of *Filmfaust* (Frankfurt), May/June 1984.
Howard, S., "A Cinema of Transformation: The Films of Haile Gerima," in *Cineaste* (New York), vol. 14, no. 1, 1985.
Pines, Jim, in *National Film Theatre Booklet* (London), August 1986.

*   *   *

Gerima's importance stems from his unique situation astride African and Black American cultures. The first twenty years of Gerima's life were spent in his native Ethiopa, to which he returned in 1974, on the eve of the Emperor Haile Selassie's downfall, to shoot his sole African film, *Harvest 3000 Years*

Haile Gerima: *Harvest: 3000 Years*

(*Mirt sost shi amit*). Gerima's father was a playwright with a travelling theatre group and it was to study drama that he initially went to the United States. Caught up in Black American politics at a peak moment of the late 1960's, he subsequently moved to California, where he developed a growing interest in cinema through study at UCLA. Though his first films were made within the structures of UCLA—and with university equipment and crews—Gerima showed himself from the first to be resolutely independent in his stylistic choices. Rejecting the aesthetics of mainstream entertainment cinema, Gerima has produced work which is both immensely personal and a highly articulate expression of many of the central concerns of contemporary Black American culture. The tone is set by the title of one of his early shorts: *Child of Resistance*.

Gerima's graduate film at UCLA, *Bush Mama* is centrally located within the struggles of urban American Blacks. It is set in a world of crippling violence, beginning with a failed bank-raid and ending with the shooting of a white rapist by the black victim's mother. But the film avoids a merely naturalistic depiction of lives destroyed by a pitiless environment and instead allows its characters an inner freedom and the possibility of growing self-awareness. *Harvest 3000 Years* is similarly less a realistic depiction of peasant life than an allegory of oppression, with characters, gestures and objects taking on a symbolic significance. While the film contains many of the ingredients of a western-style realist approach (slow rhythms, Amharic dialogue, use of real peasant players) its real significance is its use of narrative patterns derived from Ethiopian oral storytelling. The world of externally-observed reality in *Harvest 3000 Years* is constantly shot through with images of dream, fear and memory, and a wealth of visual manipulation is used to maintain a distance between spectator and text.

Wilmington 10, USA 10,000, a commissioned work of political polemic, contains several striking sequences, but lacks the obsessive personal involvement of Gerima's finest work and shows the director's limitations when confronted with the problem of creating a simple documentary record of reality. In *Ashes and Embers* Gerima returns to his central preoccupations and his highly personal style with a deeply felt study of a Black Vietnam veteran tortured by anguish and self-doubt. As is customary in the director's work, this exemplary drama, with its mass of political implications, is acted out in settings which, though observed with documentary fidelity, are transformed by the narrative into elements of a symbolic reality. Gerima's cinema offers no glib answers or neat solutions, but it raises

with rare force the issues of social rebellion and personal creativity, of the need for memory and the urge for commitment.

—Roy Armes

GERMI, Pietro.

Italian. Born in Genoa, 14 September 1914. Educated at Instituto Nautico; studied acting and directing at Centro Sperimentale di Cinematografia, Rome. Directed first film, *Il testimone*, 1946; retired from *Amici miei* project because of ill health, 1974. Recipient: Oscar for Best Story and Screenplay, with Alfredo Giannetti and Ennio de Concini, for *Divorce Italian Style*, 1962; Best Film (co-recipient), Cannes Festival, for *Signore e signori*, 1966. *Died in Rome, 5 December 1974.*

Films as Director:

1946   *Il testimone* (+ co-sc)
1947   *Gioventù perduta* (*Lost Youth*) (+ co-sc)
1949   *In nome della legge* (*Mafia*) (+ co-sc)
1950   *Il cammino della speranza* (*The Path of Hope*) (+ co-story, co-adapt)
1951   *La città si difende* (*Four Ways Out*) (+ co-sc)
1952   *La presidentessa* (*Mademoiselle Gobette*) (+ co-sc); *Il brigante di Tacca del Lupo* (+ co-sc)
1953   *Gelosia* (+ co-sc)
1954   "Guerra 1915–1918" episode of *Amori di mezzo secolo*
1956   *Il ferroviere* (*The Railroad Man. Man of Iron*) (+ co-sc, role)
1957   *L'uomo di paglia* (+ co-sc, role)
1962   *Divorzio all'italiana* (*Divorce Italian Style*) (+ co-sc)
1964   *Sedotta e abbandonata* (*Seduced and Abandoned*) (+ co-sc)
1965   *Signore e signori* (*The Birds, the Bees and the Italians*) (+ co-sc, co-pr)
1967   *L'immorale* (*The Climax. Too Much for One Man*) (+ co-sc)
1968   *Serafino* (+ co-sc, pr)
1970   *Le castagne sono buone* (*Till Divorce Do You Part*) (+ co-sc, pr)
1972   *Alfredo, Alfredo* (+ co-sc, pr)

Other Films:

1939   *Retroscena* (Blasetti) (asst d, co-sc)
1943   *Nessuno torna indietro* (Blasetti) (asst d)
1945   *I dieci comandamenti* (Chili) (co-sc)
1946   *Monte Cassino* (Gemmiti) (role)
1948   *Fuga in Francia* (Soldati) (role)
1959   *Jovanka e le altre* (*Five Branded Women*) (Ritt) (role)
1960   *Il rossetto* (Damiani) (role)
1961   *La viaccia* (Bolognini) (role); *Il sicario* (Damiani) (role)
1963   *The Directors* (pr: Greenblatt) (appearance)
1975   *Amici miei* (Monicelli) (co-sc, + credit "A Film by Pietro Germi")

Publications:

By GERMI: articles—

"Man Is Not Large Enough for Man," in *Films and Filming* (London), September 1966.

On GERMI: articles—

Passek, J.-L., "Pietro Germi," in *Cinéma* (Paris), February 1975.
Monicelli, M., "Pietro Germi, mon amour," in *Ecran* (Paris), September 1976.

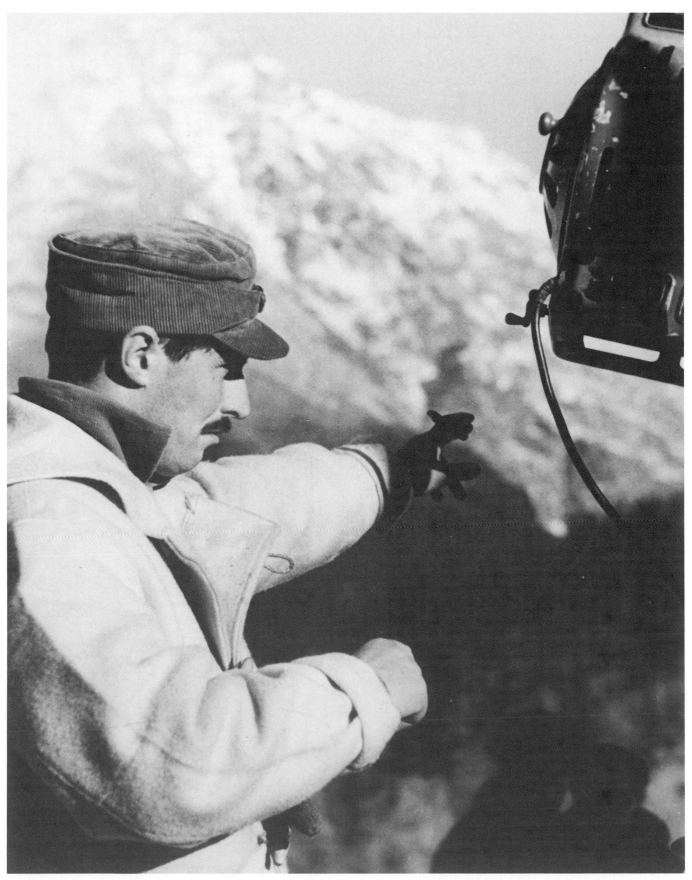

Pietro Germi

Pattison, B., "Pietro Germi," in *Film* (London), October 1976.
"Pietro Germi," in *Film Dope* (London), December 1979.
Filméchange (Paris), Autumn 1984.

*   *   *

Pietro Germi, though often regarded by scholars as fundamentally a neorealist director who made a transition in mid-career to social comedy, never actually considered himself to be an adherent to the style popularized by Roberto Rossellini. Like several other Italian directors achieving prominence in the late 1940s, notably Alberto Lattuada, Alberto De Santis and, of course, Vittorio DeSica, he produced films notable for breaking with prevailing themes that dealt with the immediate aftermath of World War II. His early works addressed themselves instead to the fundamental, even timeless, social issues affecting postwar Italy and in particular, those exemplified in the poverty of the island of Sicily.

His early films, notably *In nome della legge* and *Il cammino della speranza*, owe as much, if not more, to the influence of American director John Ford as they do to neorealism. Sicily easily replaces Ford's Monument Valley and the island's traditional knife duels supplant the American director's classic showdowns. In all other respects, however, the fundamental issues in Germi's first few films differ little from a typical John Ford production like *Stagecoach*. Indeed the themes of the aforementioned Germi films, consisting, in the first instance, of the clash between a young judge and the local Mafia over his attempts to enforce the law and, in the second, of the problem of illegal immigration, deal with problems not too far removed from those of the actual post-Civil War American west.

Interestingly, the fact that Germi dared to propose solutions to the problems that he examined in these and in succeeding films effectively removed him from the realm of pure neorealism which, as construed by Rossellini and his immediate followers, must limit itself merely to the exposition of a particular social condition. It cannot suggest solutions. Unfortunately, in a number of cases (*Il cammino della speranza* in particular), the director's solutions were overly romanticized, pat and simplistic.

During the latter part of the 1950s, Germi began to compress the scope of his social concerns to those affecting the individual and his relationship to the family unit albeit as components of the larger society. In *Il ferroviere* and *L'uomo di Paglia*, however, he continued to be plagued by his penchant for simplistic and overly contrived solutions as well as a tendency to let the films run on too long. They are redeemed to some extent by their realistic portrayals of working class characters which, though considered melodramatic by many reviewers at the time of their release, have come to be more highly regarded.

He corrected his problems in the 1960s by changing his narrative style to one dominated by satirical devices. Yet he did not compromise his family-centered social vision. *Divorzio all'italiana*, for which he won an Academy Award for best screenplay, *Sedotta e abbandonata,* and *Signori e signore* all magnify social questions all out of proportion to reality and thus, through the chaos that results, reduce the issues to absurdity.

Divorzio all'italiana, in particular, is a craftsmanlike portrayal of the internal upheavals within a family, set in the oppressive atmosphere of a small Sicilian village. It features the deft use of a moving camera that passes swiftly, almost intimately, through endless groups of gawking townspeople. Also, his use of actors, including Marcello Mastroianni and Daniella Rocca, as well as his own latent sense of humor, make the social commentary in this film quite possibly more penetrating than in his early neorealist films.

Though he shifted over the length of his career from social dramas to socio-moral satires, his social concerns and his favorite setting for them—Sicily—remained constant. As is not normally the case with many artists of his stature, his most polished and commercially successful efforts also turned out to be the critical equals of his earlier and more solemn ones.

—Stephen L. Hanson

———

GHATAK, Ritwik.

Indian. Born Ritwik Kumar Ghatak in Dhaka, East Bengal (now Bangladesh), 4 November 1925. Educated at schools in Pabna, Rajshahi, and Mymensingh; Krishna`Nath College, Baharampur, graduated in English Literature, 1948; Calcutta University, 1948–50. Married Surama (Ghatak), three children. Assistant to the filmmaker Manoj Bhattacharya, 1950; wrote and directed *Nagarik*, 1952 (released 1982); theatre actor, writer, director, and translator (of Brecht), also novelist and editor of journals *Abhidhara* and *Abhinoy Darpan*; Vice-Principal, and instructor in filmmaking, Film and Television Institute, Poona, 1965–66. Recipient: Padma Shri (awarded by the President of India), 1970. *Died in Calcutta, 7 February 1976.*

Films as Director and Scriptwriter:

1952   *Nagarik (The Citizen)* (released 1982)
1958   *Ajantrik (The Pathetic Fallacy)*
1959   *Bari Theke Palive (The Runway)*
1960   *Meghe Dhaka Tara (The Cloud-Capped Star)*
1961   *Komal Gandhar (E-Flat)*
1963   *Suvarna Rekha*
1973   *Titles Ekti Nadir Naam (A River Called Titas)*
1974   *Jukti, Takke Aar Gappo (Reason, Debate and a Tale)*

Films as Scriptwriter:

1955   *Madhumati*; *Musafir*; *Oraon* (doc)
1958   *Arjun Sardar*
1960   *Swaralipi*
1962   *Kumari Mon*; *Scissors* (doc)
1963   *Balidann*; *Aranyak*; *Alauddin Khan* (doc)
1965   *Fear* (doc); *Rendezvous* (doc)
1966   *Sansar Simante*
1968   *Scientists of Tomorrow* (doc)
1969   *Kumar Sambhaber Ashtam Swarga*
1970   *Chhou Dance of Puralia* (doc); *Amar Lenin* (doc); *The Question* (doc)
1971   *Durbargati Padma* (doc)
1975   *Ramkinkar*

Publications:

By GHATAK: books—

Cinema and I, Calcutta, 1987.
Ritwik Ghatak: Arguments/Stories, Bombay, 1987.

On GHATAK: books—

Banerjee, Shampa, editor, *Ritwik Ghatak: An Attempt to Explore His Cinematic Perception*, New Delhi, 1982.
Rajakhyaksha, Ashish, *Ritwik Ghatak: A Return to the Epic*, Bombay, 1982.
Banerjee, Haimanti, *Ritwik Kumar Ghatak*, Poona, 1985.

Ritwik Ghatak: *Ajantrik*

On GHATAK: articles—

Malcolm, Derek, "Tiger," in *Sight and Sound* (London), Summer 1982.
"By Popular Demand—Ritwik Ghatak," in *National Film Theatre booklet* (London), July and December 1982.
Tesson, C., "Découvrons Guru Dutt et Ritwik Ghatak," in *Cahiers du Cinéma* (Paris), January 1983.
Berthomé, J.-P., "Ritwik Ghatak, un cinéma de la déchirure," in *Positif* (Paris), April 1983.
"Indian Cinema Section" of *Jeune Cinéma* (Paris), September 1985.
Shahani, K., "Violence and Responsibility," in *Framework* (Norwich), no. 30–31, 1986.
Rajadhyaksha, A., "Neo-traditionalism," in *Framework* (Norwich), no. 32–33, 1986.
"Ritwik Ghatak Section" of *Positif* (Paris), November 1986.
Framework (Norwich), no. 34, 1987.

*   *   *

Ritwik Ghatak was enamoured of the stage as a means to Revolution but chose cinema instead to express his tormented self, because through it alone he could "reach and rouse" more people. Of no other Indian filmmaker can it be said that creativity through celluloid became more of a suicidal obsession. His was a feverish search for a truly cinematic form and a laconic style—"Dry without but juicy within."

His first two films, *Nagarik* and *Ajaantrik*, amply established his command over the neorealist style, developed by Zavattini and De Sica in the early 1940's. From this bold and innovative approach, he went on to look for, and emphasize, the archetypes of the Bengali mind through such highly moving and original films as *Meghe Dhaka Tara, Komal Gandhar*, and *Suvarna Rekha*. Dogged by want and depressed by repeated commercial failures of his feature films, but all the while consumed by a burning passion for "archetypal cinema" (and, of course, liquor), Ghatak became a schizophrenic in the early 1970's and was admitted to a Calcutta mental hospital wherefrom he fled to try another film. He gave up the well-paid job of Vice Principal in India's prestigious Film Institute of Poona (now FTTI) where he inspired a number of young students like Kumar Shahani and Mani Kaul to develop into *avant garde* filmmakers, because he could not adjust to its bureaucratic ethos.

His creative mind was obsessed with, and swung in between, his happy childhood days in East Bengal and his adult trauma caused by the Partition and surrender of his motherland to East Pakistan. In film after film, he peeled off these layers of his sensitivity, rather compulsively. His eight completed films, of which only six were released while he was alive, still move viewers to the depths of their being, even those who do not belong to, or are unfamiliar with, his milieu. In many respects he was more daring and original than Satyajit Ray who had great regard and affection for him. After seeing *Nagarik*, Ray told him that if it had been released in 1952, the year in which it was made, Ghatak, not he, would have been the pioneer of New Wave in India. Ghatak's films sweep the audience like emotional typhoons with very little left to reflect upon, unlike those of Ray, who found "a lack of humour" in Ghatak's film. With his early death, his single-minded search for archetypes of Bengali sensibility ended, leaving no follower.

—Bibekananda Ray

GILLIAM, Terry.

American. Born in Minneapolis, Minnesota, 22 November 1940. Studied at Occidental College, Los Angeles, graduated in Political Science. Associate editor, *HELP* magazine, and freelance illustrator, New York, from 1962; moved to London, 1967; illustrator and animator for *Marty, We Have Ways of Making You Laugh*, and *Do Not Adjust Your Set*, for TV, 1968; member of *Monty Python's Flying Circus*, from 1969; directed first solo project, *Jabberwocky*, 1977.

Films as Director:

1975 *Monty Python and the Holy Grail* (co-d)
1977 *Jabberwocky*
1981 *Time Bandits*
1985 **Brazil**
1988 *The Adventures of Baron Munchausen*

Other Films:

1971 *And Now for Something Completely Different* (co-sc, anim, role)
1979 *Monty Python's Life of Brian* (Jones) (co-sc, design)
1982 *Monty Python Live at the Hollywood Bowl* (role)
1983 *Monty Python's The Meaning of Life* (Jones) (co-sc, anim, d some sequences, role)

Publications:

By GILLIAM: books—

Time Bandits, with Michael Palin, London, 1981.
The Adventures of Baron Munchausen, with Charles McKeown, New York and London, 1989.

By GILLIAM: articles—

Interview in *Inter/View* (New York), vol. 7, no. 6, 1975.
Interview in *Film Comment* (New York), November/December 1981.
Interview with D. Rabourdin, in *Cinéma* (Paris), February 1985.
Interview with Nick Roddick, in *Stills* (London), February 1985.
Interview with B. Howell, in *Films and Filming* (London), March 1985.
Interview with M. Girard and A. Caron, in *Séquences* (Montreal), April 1986.
Interview with D. Morgan, in *Sight and Sound* (London), Autumn 1988.
Interview in *Starburst* (London), April 1989.

On GILLIAM: books—

Perry, George, *Life of Python*, London, 1983.

On GILLIAM: articles—

"*Brazil* Section" of *Revue du Cinéma* (Paris), March 1985.
"Gilliam Section" of *Positif* (Paris), March 1985.
American Film (Washington, D.C.), March 1989.
"Gilliam Issue" of *Cinefex* (Riverside, California), May 1989.

*   *   *

"A trilogy about the ages of Man and the subordination of magic to realism." So Terry Gilliam described the trio of films which stretched from *Time Bandits* through *Brazil* to *The Adventures Of Baron Munchausen*. Gilliam has worked resolutely in the space between the two elements of magic and reality in all his work, hardly surprising in a man whose beginnings were as the provider of brilliant, surreal animations to the *Monty Python* team in the late 1960s and early 1970s.

Gilliam is very much on the side of imagination in his films in both visual and narrative terms. Despite his often surreal vision, however, the products of the imagination do not necessarily have to be fantastic. Love, for example—often a triumph of emotional imagination over reality—has been an important arena in Gilliam's battle between magic and realism—comical and childlike in *Jabberwocky*, bittersweet and adult in *Brazil*.

For Gilliam the magical counterbalances what he perceives as the sterility of the rational, manifest in extreme form in the Orwellian nightmare world of *Brazil*. If love is perhaps the emotional expression of Gilliam's magic then visual and narrative fantasy is the conceptual. The fantastic has been an ever-present in Gilliam's work from his *Monty Python* days to the spectacles of *Baron Munchausen* (an island transformed into a giant fish, a ship gliding through a desert strewn with statues). His feature films often seem, in fact, semi-conscious attempts to recreate the world of his early animations in live-action.

Fellow director Alex Cox has described Gilliam as a "highly skilled visualist," a judgement which cannot really be disputed. (It is worth noting that Gilliam's cinematographer for the dazzling *Brazil* was Roger Pratt, later to give a similar gloss to the mega-buck *Batman*.)

Gilliam is often criticized, however, for opting for visual pyrotechnics at the expense of narrative solidity. The issue is clouded by Gilliam's constant return to the fairy-tale/fantasy format where the requirement of narrative sense or continuity is arguably less strict anyway: Arthurian legend in *Monty Python And The Holy Grail* (co-directed with Terry Jones); Lewis Carroll's nonsense world in *Jabberwocky*; time-travel in *Time Bandits*; an insane world in *Brazil*; and 18th-century tall tales in *Baron Munchausen*. Is Gilliam merely an escapist with a remarkably fertile imagination? In opting to undermine the bedrock of dull rationality does he fail to offer anything in return? It is, after all, perfectly possible to make films which are funny and surreal *and* which have bite—satire as opposed to escapism.

Gilliam's defense against such charges is *Brazil*. Without *Brazil*, Gilliam's output smacks a little too much of clownish entertainment. But with *Brazil* it is clear that the clown can also wear a sadder, darker face. For here, Gilliam opts to take on board the challenging burdens of rationality rather than trying merely to escape them. His vision has *weight*. If he escapes here it is through facing the deadening products of rationality and triumphing over them through a combination of acid ridicule and emotional willpower. The sights which influenced his perception of the story included a Los Angeles riot, and he has half-cryptically, half-menacingly described the setting of the film as "somewhere on the Los Angeles/Belfast border."

Brazil revealed depths to Gilliam's talent which had only been promises till then, most clearly hinted at in his blackly-comic *Monty Python* animations rather than his earlier fea-

Terry Gilliam

tures. *Baron Munchausen*, disappointingly, proved a regression back to escapism rather than a development of the inspired mood of *Brazil* (though the pressures of an ever-escalating budget cannot have helped). Perhaps the battle he had to fight with Warner Bros. over *Brazil*—first over a re-edit (read massacre), then over even releasing the film—had warned him from attempting anything with real edge.

Gilliam's vision is dazzling and often very funny. One wishes, however, that he would push towards its limits and make films which were meals rather than snacks. *Brazil* is the taste of what could have been, and it leaves one crying out for more.

—Norman Miller

———

GILLIAT, Sidney *See* **LAUNDER, Frank, and GILLIAT, Sidney**

———

GODARD, Jean-Luc.

French. Born in Paris, 3 December 1930, became citizen of Switzerland. Educated at Nyon, Switzerland; Lycée Buffon, Paris; Sorbonne, 1947–49, certificate in ethnology 1950. Married 1) Anna Karina, 1960 (divorced); 2) Anne Wiamzensky, 1967 (divorced). Delivery boy, cameraman, assistant editor for Zurich television, construction worker, and gossip columnist (for *Les Temps de Paris*), in Switzerland and Paris, 1949–56; founded short-lived *Gazette du cinéma*, writing as "Hans Lucas," 1950–51; critic for *Cahiers du cinéma*, from 1952; directed first film, *Opération Béton*, 1954; worked as film editor, 1956; worked in publicity department, 20th Century-Fox, Paris, with producer Georges de Beauregard, 1957; working for Beauregard, directed first feature, *A bout de souffle*, 1959; formed Anoucka films with Anna Karina, 1964; led protests over firing of Henri Langlois, director of Cinémathèque, instigated shut down of Cannes Festival, 1968; began collaboration with Jean-Pierre Gorin, editor of *Cahiers marxistes-léninistes*, 1969 (partnership terminated 1973); "reclaimed" work from 1969–72 as that of the Dziga Vertov group; established Sonimage film and video studio in Grenoble with Anne-Marie Miéville, 1974–75; directed jeans advertisement, 1987. Recipient: Best Direction Award, Berlin Festival, for *A bout de souffle*, 1960; Honorary César, 1986. Address: 15 rue du Nord, 1180 Roulle, Switzerland.

Films as Director:

1954　*Opération Béton* (+ pr, sc) (released 1958)
1955　*Une Femme coquette* (d as 'Hans Lucas', + sc pr, ph, bit role as man visiting prostitute)
1957　*Charlotte et Véronique ou Tous les garçons s'appellent Patrick* (+ sc)
1958　*Une Histoire d'eau* (co-d: actual shooting by Truffaut, + co-sc) (released 1961); *Charlotte et son Jules* (+ sc, dubbed voice of Jean-Paul Belmondo) (released 1961)
1959　**A bout de souffle (Breathless)** (+ sc, role as passerby who points out Belmondo to police)
1961　*Une Femme est une femme* (+ sc)

1962　"La Paresse" episode of *Les Sept Péchés capitaux* (+ sc; **Vivre sa vie (My Life to Live)** (+ sc, dubbed voice of Peter Kassowitz), "Il nuovo mondo (Le Nouveau Monde)" in *RoGoPaG (Laviamoci il cervello)* (+ sc, bit role)
1963　*Le Petit Soldat* (+ sc, bit role as man at railway station) (completed 1960); *Les Carabiniers* (+ sc); *Le Mépris* (+ sc, role)
1964　"Le Grand Escroc" in *Les Plus Belles Escroqueries du monde* (+ sc, narration, bit role as man wearing Moroccan chéchia); *Bande à part* (+ sc); *La Femme mariée (Une Femme mariée)* (+ sc); *Reportage sur Orly* (+ sc) (short)
1965　"Montparnasse—Levallois" in *Paris vu par . . .* (+ sc); **Alphaville** (+ sc); *Une Étrange aventure de Lemmy Caution* (+ sc); *Pierrot le fou* (+ sc)
1966　*Masculin-féminin (Masculin féminin: quinze faits précis)* (+ sc); *Made in U.S.A.* (+ sc, voice on tape recorder)
1967　*Deux ou trois choses que je sais d'elle* (+ sc); "Anticipation" episode of *Le Plus Vieux Métier du monde* (+ sc); *La Chinoise ou Plutôt à la chinoise* (+ sc); "Caméra-oeil" in *Loin du Viêt-Nam* (+ sc, appearance); **Le Weekend (Weekend)** (+ sc)
1968　*Le Gai Savoir* (+ sc); *Cinétracts* (+ sc) (series of untitled, creditless newsreels); *Un Film comme les autres* (+ sc, voice); *One Plus One (Sympathy for the Devil)* (+ sc, voice); *One A.M. (One American Movie)* (+ sc) (unfinished)
1969　*British Sounds (See You at Mao)* (co-d, co-sc); *Pravda* (+ sc) (collective credit to Groupe Dziga-Vertov); *Lotte in Italia (Luttes en Italie)* (+ sc) (collective credit to Groupe Dziga-Vertov); "L'amore" episode of *Amore e rabbia* (+ sc) (completed 1967: festival showings as "Andante e ritorno dei figli prodighi" episode of *Vangelo 70*)
1970　*Vent d'est* (co-d, co-sc); *Jusqu'à la victoire (Till Victory)* (co-d, + sc) (unfinished)
1971　*Vladimir et Rosa* (+ sc, collective credit to Groupe Dziga-Vertov, role as U.S. policeman, appearance, narration)
1972　*Tout va bien* (co-d, + co-sc, pr); *A Letter to Jane or Investigation About a Still (Lettre à Jane)* (co-d, + co-sc, co-pr, narration)
1975　*Numéro deux* (+ co-sc, co-pr, appearance)
1976　*Ici et ailleurs* (co-d, + co-sc) (includes footage from *Jusqu'à la victoire*); *Comment ça va* (co-d, + co-sc)
1977　*6 × 2: sur et sous la communication* (co-d, + co-sc) (for TV)
1980　*Sauve qui peut (La Vie)* (+ co-sc, co-ed)
1982　*Passion* (+ sc)
1983　*Prenom: Carmen (First Name: Carmen)*
1985　*Hail Mary*; *Detective*
1987　*Soigne ta droite*; episode in *Aria*; *King Lear*

Other Films:

1950　*Quadrille* (Rivette) (pr, role)
1951　*Présentation ou Charlotte et son steack* (Rohmer) (role)
1956　*Kreutzer Sonata* (Rohmer) (pr); *Le Coup du berger* (Rivette) (role)
1958　*Paris nous appartient* (Rivette) (Godard's silhouette)
1959　*Le Signe du lion* (Rohmer) (role)
1961　*Cléo de cinq à sept* (Varda) (role with Anna Karina in comic sequence); *Le Soleil dans l'oeil* (Bourdon) (role)
1963　*Schehérézade* (Gaspard-Huit) (role); *The Directors* (pr: Greenblatt) (appearance); *Paparazzi* (Rozier) (appearance); *Begegnung mit Fritz Lang* (Fleischmann) (appearance); *Petit Jour* (Pierre) (appearance)
1966　*L'Espion (The Defector)* (Levy) (role)
1970　*One P.M. (One Parallel Movie)* (Pennebaker) (includes footage from abandoned *One A.M.* and documentary footage of its making)

Publications:

By GODARD: books—

Jean-Luc Godard par Jean-Luc Godard: articles, essais, entretiens, edited by Jean Narboni, Paris, 1968; as *Godard on Godard: Critical Writings*, edited by Narboni and Tom Milne, New York, 1986.

Jean-Luc Godard

Weekend, New York, 1972.
A bout de souffle, Paris, 1974.
Jean-Luc Godard: Three Films—"A Woman is a Woman," "A Married Woman," "Two or Three Things I Know about Her", New York, 1975.
Introduction à une véritable histoire du cinéma, Paris, 1980.

By GODARD: articles—

Contributing editor of *La Gazette du Cinéma* (Paris), 1950; regular contributor to *Cahiers du Cinéma* (Paris), 1952 through 1968, and to *Arts* (Paris), 1957 through 1960.
"*Charlotte et son Jules*," in *Avant-Scène du Cinéma* (Paris), June 1961.
"*Une Histoire d'eau*," in *Avant-Scène du Cinéma* (Paris), September 1961.
"*Vivre sa vie*," in *Avant-Scène du Cinéma* (Paris), October 1962; also in *Film Culture* (New York), Winter 1962.
Interview with Tom Milne, in *Sight and Sound* (London), Winter 1962.
Interview with Herbert Feinstein, in *Film Quarterly* (Berkeley), Spring 1964.
"*La Femme mariée*," in *Avant-Scène du Cinéma* (Paris), March 1965.
"*Les Carabiniers*," in *Avant-Scène du Cinéma* (Paris), May 1965.
"*Deux ou trois choses que je sais d'elle*," in *Avant-Scène du Cinéma* (Paris), May 1967.
"*A bout de souffle*," in *Avant-Scène du Cinéma* (Paris), March 1968.
"Struggle on Two Fronts," an interview with Jacques Bontemps, in *Film Quarterly* (Berkeley), Winter 1968.
"*La Chinoise*," in *Avant-Scène du Cinéma* (Paris), May 1971.

"*Pierrot le fou*," in *Avant-Scène du Cinéma* (Paris), July/September 1976.
"Jean-Luc Godard . . . For Himself," in *Framework* (Norwich), Autumn 1980.
"En attendant *Passion*. Le chemin vers la parole," an interview with Alain Bergala, Serge Daney and Serge Toubiana, in *Cahiers du Cinéma* (Paris), May 1982.
Interview with Don Ranvaud and A. Farassino, in *Framework* (Norwich), Summer 1983.
"The Carrots are Cooked," an interview with Gideon Bachmann, in *Film Quarterly* (Berkeley), Spring 1984.
"Genesis of a Camera," with J.-P. Beauviala, in *Camera Obscura* (Berkeley), Spring/Summer 1985.
"Godard in His 'Fifth' Period," an interview with K. Dieckmann, in *Film Quarterly* (Berkeley), Winter 1985/86.
"*Colles et ciseaux*," in *Cahiers du Cinéma* (Paris), December 1987.
Interview with Alain Bergala and Serge Toubiana, in *Cahiers du Cinéma* (Paris), January 1988.

On GODARD: books—

Collet, Jean, *Jean-Luc Godard*, Paris, 1963; New York, 1970.
Roud, Richard, *Jean-Luc Godard*, New York, 1967.
Mussman, Toby, editor, *Jean-Luc Godard: A Critical Anthology*, New York, 1968.
Cameron, Ian, editor, *The Films of Jean-Luc Godard*, London, 1969.
Brown, Royal, editor, *Focus on Godard*, Englewood Cliffs, New Jersey, 1972.

Monaco, James, *The New Wave*, New York, 1976.

MacCabe, Colin, *Godard: Images, Sounds, Politics*, London, 1980.

Walsh, Martin, *The Brechtian Aspect of Radical Cinema*, London, 1981.

Lefevre, Raymond, *Jean-Luc Godard*, Paris, 1983.

Bordwell, David, *Narration in the Fiction Film*, London, 1985.

Weis, Elisabeth, and John Belton, *Film Sound: Theory and Practice*, New York, 1985.

Cerisuelo, Marc, *Jean-Luc Godard*, Paris, 1989.

Desbarats, Carole, and Jean-Paul Gorce, *L'Effet Godard*, Toulouse, 1989.

Douin, Jean-Luc, *Jean-Luc Godard*, Paris, 1989.

On GODARD: articles—

Moullet, Luc, "Jean-Luc Godard," in *Cahiers du Cinéma* (Paris), April 1960.

Fieschi, Jean-André, "Godard: Cut Sequence: *Vivre sa vie*," in *Movie* (London), January 1963.

Bellour, Raymond, "Godard or Not Godard," in *Les Lettres Françaises* (Paris), 14 May 1964.

Sarris, Andrew, and Andrew Blasi, "Waiting for Godard," in *Film Culture* (New York), Summer 1964.

Kael, Pauline, "Godard est Godard," in *New Yorker*, 9 October 1965.

Metz, Christian, "Le Cinéma moderne et la narrative," in *Cahiers du Cinéma* (Paris), December 1966.

Bertolucci, Bernardo, "Versus Godard," in *Cahiers du Cinéma* (Paris), January 1967.

"Godard Issue" of *Image et Son/Revue du Cinéma* (Paris), December 1967.

"Godard Issue" of *Film Heritage* (Dayton, Ohio), Spring 1968.

Schickel, Richard, "The Trying Genius of M. Godard," in *Life* (New York), 12 April 1968.

Clouzot, Claire, "Godard and the U.S.," in *Sight and Sound* (London), Summer 1968.

Farber, Manny, "The Films of Jean-Luc Godard," in *Artforum* (New York), October 1968.

MacBean, James, "Politics, Poetry, and the Language of Signs in Godard's *Made in U.S.A.*," in *Film Quarterly* (Berkeley), Spring 1969.

Sainsbury, Peter, "Jean-Luc Godard," in *Afterimage* (New York), April 1970.

Goodwin, Michael, and others, "The Dziga Vertov Group in America," in *Take One* (Montreal), March/April 1971.

MacBean, James, "Godard and the Dziga Vertov Group: Film and Dialectic," in *Film Quarterly* (Berkeley), Fall 1972.

Kolkeon, R.P., "Angle and Reality: Godard and Gorin in America," in *Sight and Sound* (London), Summer 1973.

Rayns, Tony, "The Godard Film Forum," in *Film* (London), January 1974.

MacCabe, Colin, "Realism and the Cinema: Notes on Some Brechtian Theses," in *Screen* (London), Summer 1974.

Lesage, Julia, "Visual Distancing in Godard," in *Wide Angle* (Athens, Ohio), no. 3, 1976.

Gilliatt, Penelope, "Profile," in *New Yorker*, 25 October 1976.

Lefèvre, Raymond, "La Lettre et la cinématographe: L'Ecrit dans les films de Godard," in *Image et Son* (Paris), May 1977.

Forbes, Jill, "Jean-Luc Godard: Two into Three," in *Sight and Sound* (London), Winter 1980/81.

"Godard Issue" of *Camera Obscura* (Berkeley), Fall 1982.

Burgoyne, Robert, "The Political Topology of Montage: The Conflict of Genres in the Films of Godard," in *Enclitic* (Minneapolis), Spring 1983.

Lovell, Alan, "Epic Theater and Counter Cinema," and Julia Lesage, "Godard' and Gorin's Left Politics," in *Jump Cut* (Berkeley), April 1983.

Dossier on Godard, in *Cinématographe* (Paris), December 1983.

"Godard Issue" of *Avant-Scène du Cinéma* (Paris), March 1984.

MacCabe, Colin, "Every Man for Himself," in *American Film* (Washington, D.C.), June 1984.

Gervais, M., "Jean-Luc Godard 1985—These are not the days," in *Sight and Sound* (London), Autumn 1985.

Durgnat, Raymond, "Jean-Luc Godard: His Crucifixion and Resurrection," in *Monthly Film Bulletin* (London), September 1985.

"Godard Issue" of *Revue Belge du Cinéma* (Brussels), Summer 1986.

Wide Angle (Athens, Ohio), vol. 9, no. 1, 1987.

"Godard Issue" of *Cinéma* (Paris), 30 December 1987.

Ciment, Michel, "Je vous salue Godard," in *Positif* (Paris), February 1988.

Monthly Film Bulletin (London), November 1989.

On GODARD: films—

Bazin, Janine, and others, *Jean-Luc Godard, ou le cinéma de défi*, for TV, 1964.

Doniol-Valcroze, Jacques, *Pour le plaisir*, for TV, 1965.

Thanhauser, Ralph, *Godard in America*, U.S.A., 1970.

Berckmans, Jean-Pierre, *La Longue Marche de Jean-Luc Godard*, Belgium, 1972.

Costard, Hellmuth, *Der kleine Godard*, West Germany, 1978.

*   *   *

If influence on the development of world cinema be the criterion, Godard is certainly the most important filmmaker of the past 30 years; he is also one of the most problematic.

His career so far fàlls roughly into three periods: the early works from *About de souffle* to *Weekend* (1959–1968), a period whose end is marked decisively by the latter film's final caption, "Fin de Cinéma"; the period of intense politicization, during which Godard collaborated (mainly though not exclusively) with Jean-Pierre Gorin and the Dziga Vertov group (1968–1972); and the subsequent work, divided between attempts to renew communication with a wider, more "mainstream" cinema audience and explorations of the potentialities of video (in collaboration with Anne-Marie Miéville). (One might separate the films from *Masculin-Féminin* to *Weekend* as representing a transitional phase from the first to the Dziga Vertov period; though in a sense all Godard's work is transitional.) What marks the middle period off from its neighbours is above all the difference in intended audience: the Dziga Vertov films were never meant to reach a general public, being aimed at already committed Marxist or leftist groups, campus student groups, and so on, to stimulate discussion of revolutionary politics and aesthetics, and, crucially, the relationship between the two.

Godard's importance lies in his development of an authentic modernist cinema in opposition to (though, during the early period, at the same time *within*) mainstream cinema; it is with his work that film becomes central to our century's major aesthetic debate, the controversy developed through such figures as Lukács, Brecht, Benjamin, and Adorno as to whether realism or modernism is the more progressive form. As ex-*Cahiers du cinéma* critic and New Wave filmmaker, Godard was initially linked with Truffaut and Chabrol in a kind of revolutionary triumvirate; it is easy, in retrospect, to see that Godard was from the start the truly radical figure, the "revolution" of his colleagues operating purely on the aesthetic level and easily assimilable into the mainstream. A simple way of demonstrating the essential thrust of Godard's work is to juxtapose his first feature, *Breathless*, with the excellent American remake. Jim McBride's film follows the original fairly closely, with the fundamental difference that in it all other elements are subordinated to the narrative and the characters. In Godard's film, on the contrary, this traditional relationship between signifier and signified shows a continuous tendency to come adrift, so that the *process of narration* (which mainstream cinema strives everywhere to conceal) becomes foregrounded; *A bout de souffle* is "about" a story and characters, certainly, but it is also about the cinema, about film techniques, about Jean Seberg, etc.

This foregrounding of the process—and the means—of narration is developed much further in subsequent films, in which Godard systematically breaks down the traditional barrier between fiction/documentary, actor/character, narrative film/experimental film to create freer, "open" forms. Persons appear as themselves in works of fiction, actors address the camera/audience in monologues or as if being interviewed, materiality of film is made explicit (the switches from positive to negative in *Une Femme mariée*, the turning on and off of the soundtrack in *Deux ou trois choses que je sais d'elle*, the showing of the clapper-board in *La Chinoise*). The initial motivation for this seems to have been the assertion of personal freedom: the filmmaker shatters the bonds of traditional realism in order to be able to say and do whatever he wants, creating films spontaneously. (*Pierrot le fou*—significantly, one of Godard's most popular films—is the most extreme expression of this impulse.) Gradually, however, a political motivation (connected especially with the influence of Brecht) takes over. There is a marked sociological interest in the early films (especially *Vivre sa vie* and *Une Femme mariée*), but the turning-point is *Masculin, féminin* with its two male protagonists, one seeking fulfilment through personal relations, the other a political activist. The former's suicide at the end of the film can be read as marking a decisive choice: from here on, Godard increasingly listens to the voice of revolutionary politics and eventually (in the Dziga Vertov films) adopts it as his own voice.

The films of the Dziga Vertov group (named after the great Russian documentarist who anticipated their work in making films that foreground the means of production and are continuously self-reflexive) were the direct consequence of the events of May, 1968. More than ever before the films are directly concerned with their own process, so that the ostensible subjects—the political scene in Czechoslovakia (*Pravda*) or Italy (*Lotte in Italia*), the trial of the Chicago Eight (*Vladimir and Rosa*)—become secondary to the urgent, actual subject: how does one make a revolutionary film? It was at this time that Godard distinguished between making political films (i.e. films on political subjects: Costa-Gavras's *Z* is a typical example) and making films politically, the basic assumption being that one cannot put radical content into traditional form without seriously compromising, perhaps negating, it. Hence the attack on realism initiated at the outset of Godard's career manifests its full political significance: realism is a bourgeois art form, the means whereby the bourgeoisie endlessly reassures itself, validating its own ideology as "true," "natural," "real"; its power must be destroyed. Of the films from this period, *Vent d'est* (the occasion for Peter Wollen's seminal essay on "Counter-Cinema" in *After Image*) most fully realized this aesthetic: the original pretext (the pastiche of a Western) recedes into the background, and the film becomes a discussion about itself—about the relationship between sound and image, the materiality of film, the destruction of bourgeois forms, the necessity for continuous self-criticism and self-awareness.

The assumption behind the Dziga Vertov films is clearly that the revolutionary impetus of May '68 would be sustained, and it has not been easy for Godard to adjust to its collapse. That difficulty is the subject of one of his finest works, *Tout va bien* (again in collaboration with Gorin), an attempt to return to commercial filmmaking without abandoning the principles (both aesthetic and political) of the preceding years. Beginning by foregrounding Godard's own problem (how does a radical make a film within the capitalist production system?) the film is strongest in its complex use of Yves Montand and Jane Fonda (simultaneously fictional characters/personalities/star images) and its exploration of the issues to which they are central: the relationship of intellectuals to the class struggle; the relationship between professional work, personal commitment, and political position; the problem of sustaining a radical impulse in a non-revolutionary age. *Tout va bien* is Godard's most authentically Brechtian film, achieving radical force and analytical clarity without sacrificing pleasure and a degree of emotional involvement.

Godard's relationship to Brecht has not always been so clearcut. While the justification for Brecht's distanciation principles was always the communication of clarity, Godard's films often leave the spectator in a state of confusion and frustration. He continues to seem by temperament more anarchist than Marxist. One is troubled by the continuity between the criminal drop-outs of the earlier films and the political activists of the later. The insistent intellectualism of the films is often offset by a wilful abeyance of systematic thinking, the abeyance, precisely, of that self-awareness and self-criticism the political works advocate. Even in *Tout va bien*, what emerges from the political analysis as the film's own position is an irresponsible and ultimately desperate belief in spontaneity. Desperation, indeed, is never far from the Godardian surface, and seems closely related to the treatment of heterosexual relations: even through the apparent feminist awareness of the recent work runs a strain of unwitting misogyny (most evident, perhaps, in *Sauve qui peut*). The central task of Godard criticism, in fact, is to sort out the remarkable and salutary nature of the positive achievement from the temperamental limitations that flaw it.

—Robin Wood

GÓMEZ, Manuel Octavio.

Cuban. Born in Havana, 14 November 1934. Married Idalia Anreus. Newspaper and television writer, film critic, and member of Vision cine-club, Havana, 1950's; after revolution, became part of National Board of Culture organized by Julio García Espinosa, 1959; Instituto Cubano del Arte e Industria Cinematograficos (ICAIC) also established by revolutionary government; assistant to Espinola and Gutiérrez Alea, also director of documentary shorts, from 1959; directed first feature, *El encuentro*, 1964. *Died of a heart attack, in Havana, 2 January 1988.*

Films as Director:

1959   *El tejedor de Yarey*; *El agua*; *Cooperativas agrícolas* (doc shorts)
1961   *Una escuela en el campo* (doc short); *Guacanayabo*
1962   *Historia de una batalla* (*History of a Battle*)
1963   *Cuentos de Alhambra*
1964   *El encuentro*
1965   *La salación*
1967   *Tulipa*
1968   *Nuevitas*
1969   ***La primera carga al machete* (*First Charge of the Machete*)**
1971   *Los días de agua* (*Days of Water*)
1974   *Ustedes tienen la palabara* (*Now It's Up to You*)
1977   *La tierra y el cielo*
1978   *Una mujer, un hombre, una ciudad* (*A Woman, A Man, A City*)
1982   *Patakin*
1983   *El Señor Presidente*
1987   *Gallego*

Publications:

By GÓMEZ: articles—

Interview with Mario Rodríguez Alemán, in *Cine Cubano* (Havana), no. 40, 1967.

Manuel Octavio Gómez: *La primera carga al machete*

Interview with Enrique I. Colina, in *Cine Cubano* (Havana), no. 56/57, 1969.

"Manuel Octavio Gómez Interviewed: Popular Culture, Perpetual Quest," with Julianne Burton, in *Jump Cut* (Chicago), May 1979.

Interview with F. Cárdenas and I. Léon Frías, in *Hablemos de Cine* (Lima), May 1982.

On GÓMEZ: books—

Nelson, L., *Cuba: The Measure of a Revolution*, Minneapolis, 1972.

Myerson, Michael, *Memories of Underdevelopment: The Revolutionary Films of Cuba*, New York, 1973.

Chanan, Michael, *The Cuban Image*, London, 1985.

On GÓMEZ: articles—

Douglas, M.E., "The Cuban Cinema," in *Take One* (Montreal), July/August 1968.

Adler, Renata, in *New York Times*, 10, 11 and 12 February 1969.

Engel, Andi, "Solidarity and Violence," in *Sight and Sound* (London), Autumn 1969.

Sauvage, P., "Cine Cubano," in *Film Comment* (New York), Spring 1972.

Crowdus, Gary, "The Spring 1972 Cuban Film Festival Bust," in *Film Society Review* (New York), March/May 1972.

Burton, Julianne, "Introduction to Revolutionary Cuban Cinema," in *Jump Cut* (Chicago), December 1978.

Hess, John, "*Now It's Up to You* and *A Woman, A Man, A City*: The Personal is Political in Cuba," in *Jump Cut* (Chicago), May 1979.

Obituary in *Variety* (New York), 16 March 1988.

Morales, Eduardo Lopez, "*La primera carga* . . . : A la luz del tiempo," in *Cine Cubano* (Havana), no. 122, 1988.

*   *   *

Perhaps best known for his capacity to rework traditional and popular film forms into exciting, innovative, and revolutionary cinema, Manuel Octavio Gómez was a member of the first generation of filmmakers trained in Cuba since the triumph of the revolution in January of 1959. Prior to that date, he worked as a film critic while informally studying film direction—even though "being a filmmaker seemed like an impossible dream in pre-revolutionary Cuba."

Gómez entered the Cuban Film Institute (ICAIC) upon its founding, and "learned to make films by making them." He began with documentaries, a characteristic path for ICAIC's directors, as it requires that they first immerse themselves in the material reality and national culture of Cuba. Among his better documentaries is *History of a Battle*, a fine encapsulation of the first years of the revolution, which juxtaposes the victory at the Bay of Pigs with the successes achieved in the Literacy Campaign. Gómez felt that this background in documentary film was an essential formative experience for Cuban cineastes, and argued that "The documentary medium constitutes one of the most efficient ways to understand and portray a problem—and to put the idea into practice that art shouldn't just reflect reality, but should be one of the conscious factors that assists in its transformation."

The first of the traditional genres receiving Gómez's attention was historical cinema, which he considered "unbearable." Although he viewed the distinction between "historical" and "contemporary" cinema as a mystification, he did feel that there exists "a national necessity—rather, one for the whole Third World—a necessity to rescue, to revise, to de-alienate our true history—a thousand times falsified, twisted, and hidden . . . in order to feel ourselves more deeply rooted in our nationality and with a greater consciousness of our present." To accomplish this, films must make history "more alive, more urgent."

To make contemporary the "100 years of anti-imperialist struggles that give Cuba a historical continuity," Gómez directed *First Charge of the Machete*. This film links past and present through several devices: the formal contrast of modern and archaic film styles; the centrality of the machete, tool of war and weapon in the economic struggles of 1968; and the implied relationship of Maximo Gómez (Dominican rebel leader in the 1868 uprising) to Che Guevara, both foreigners who joined Cubans in their liberation movements.

Manuel Octavio Gómez reinterpreted other traditional genres in his following films. *Days of Water* contains a sequence critical of the pre-revolutionary cabaret aesthetic, one example of the ways in which authentic forms of popular culture were distorted and commercialized. *Now It's Up to You* and *A Woman, a Man, a City* both penetrating analyses of contemporary problems in Cuba, rework the courtroom drama and detective genres, respectively, by inverting the traditional narrative structure we associate with these forms. Although they begin with the sort of individualist focus usual in bourgeois cinema, they open up into historical and political analyses rather than remain at the level of personal melodrama.

In his "perpetual quest," Gómez was guided through his early "confused and erroneous notions about personal expression and 'being or not being' an artist" by the concrete reality of Cuba's revolutionary transformation. He stated, "On top of this small, 'painful,' and individual conflict, a revolution was generating changes, inverting values, and engendering new social, ideological, and cultural duties." Among the duties of Gómez were the production of vigorous and critical films, worthy of his revolutionary commitment.

—John Mraz

GÓMEZ, Sara.

Cuban. Born in Havana, 1943. Educated at Conservatory of Music, Havana. Assistant director at Instituto Cubano del Arte e industria Cinematograficos (ICAIC), under Tomás Gutiérrez Alea, Jorge Fraga, and Agnes Varda, from 1961; directed first film, *Ire a Santiago*, 1964; shot and edited first feature, *De cierta manera*, 1974; original negative, damaged in processing, restored under supervision of Gutiérrez Alea and Rigoberto Lopez, 1974–76. *Died of acute asthma, 2 June 1974.*

Films as Director:

1964   *Ire a Santiago*
1965   *Excursion a Vueltabajo*
1967   *Y tenemos sabor*
1968   *En la otra isla*
1969   *Isla del tesero*
1970   *Poder local, poder popular*
1971   *Un documental a proposito del transito*
1972   *Atencion prenatal*; *Ano uno*
1973   *Sobre horas extras y trabajo voluntario*
1977   **De cierta manera (One Way or Another)**

Publications:

On GÓMEZ: book—

Chanan, Michael, *The Cuban Image*, London, 1985.

On GÓMEZ: articles—

Chijona, Geraldo, and Rigoberto López, in *Cine Cubano* (Havana), no. 93.
Burton, Julianne, "Individual Fulfillment and Collective Achievement," in *Cinéaste* (New York), January 1977.
Burton, Julianne, "Introduction to the Revolutionary Cuban Cinema," and Carlos Galiano, "*One Way or Another*: The Revolution in Action," in *Jump Cut* (Chicago), December 1978.
Lesage, Julia, "*One Way or Another*: Dialectical, Revolutionary, Feminist," in *Jump Cut* (Chicago), May 1979.

*   *   *

Sara Gómez

We shall never know all that Sara Gómez might have given to us. We have her one feature film, the marvelous *De cierta manera*, and a few short documentaries to indicate what might have been had she lived beyond the age of 31. But we will never really know all that this prodigiously talented black woman was capable of.

Sara Gómez could be seen as prototypical of the new Cuban directors. Entering the Cuban Film Institute (ICAIC) at an early age, she worked as assistant director for various cineastes, including Tomás Gutiérrez Alea, whose influence marked her work as it has so many of the young directors. During a ten-year period (1964–74) she fulfilled the usual apprenticeship among Cuban cineastes by directing documentary films. Documentaries are seen as an important training ground for Cuban directors because they force them to focus on the material reality of Cuba and thus emphasize the use of cinema as an expression of national culture. As Gutiérrez Alea noted, "The kind of cinema which adapts itself to our interests, fortunately, is a kind of light, agile cinema, one that is very directly founded upon our own reality." This is precisely the kind of cinema Sara Gómez went on to produce, beginning work on *De cierta manera* in 1974 and finishing the editing of the film shortly before her death of acute asthma.

Her early training in documentaries and the influence of Gutiérrez Alea is evident in *De cierta manera*. The film combines the documentary and fiction forms so inextricably that they are impossible to disentangle. Through this technique, she emphasized the material reality that is at the base of all creative endeavor and the necessity of bringing a critical perspective to all forms of film.

In choosing this style, which I call "dialectical resonance," Gómez appeared to follow Gutiérrez Alea's example in the superb *Memories of Underdevelopment*. But, there is a crucial difference between the two films—a difference that might be said to distinguish the generation of directors who came of age before the triumph of the revolution (e.g. Gutiérrez Alea) from those who have grown up within the revolution. In spite of its ultimate commitment to the revolutionary process, *Memories* remains in some ways the perspective of an "outsider" and might be characterized as "critical bourgeois realism." However, *De cierta manera* is a vision wholly from within the revolution, despite the fact that every position in the film is subjected to criticism—including that of the institutionalized revolution, which is presented in the form of an annoyingly pompous omniscient narration. Thus, the perspective of Gomez might be contrasted to that of *Memories* by calling it "critical socialist realism." The emphasis on dialectical criticism, struggle, and commitment, is equally great in both films, but the experience of having grown up within the revolution created a somewhat different perspective.

Despite its deceptively simple appearance—a result of being shot in 16mm on a very low budget—*De cierta manera* is the work of an extremely sophisticated filmmaker. Merely one example among many of Gómez's sophistication is the way in which she combined a broad range of modern distanciation techniques with the uniquely Cuban tropical beat to produce a film that is simultaneously rigorously analytic and powerfully sensuous—as well as perhaps the finest instance to date of a truly dialectical film. Although we are all a little richer for the existence of this work, we remain poorer for the fact that she will make no more films.

—John Mraz

GORETTA, Claude.

Swiss. Born in Geneva, 23 June 1929. Educated in law at Université de Genève. With Alain Tanner, moves to London, 1955; worked at British Film institute, 1956–57; TV director in Switzerland, from 1958; formed production company "Groupe de 5," with Tanner, Jean-Louis Roy, Claude Soutter, and Yves Yersin, 1968; directed first feature, *Le Fou*, 1970. Recipient: Ecumenical Prize, Cannes festival, for *La Dentellière*, 1977.

Films as Director and Scriptwriter:

1957 *Nice Time* (co-d, co-sc)
1970 *Le Fou* (*The Madman*) (+ co-pr)
1973 *L'Invitation* (*The Invitation*) (co-sc)
1975 *Pas si méchant que ça* (*Not as Wicked as That. The Wonderful Crook*) (co-sc)
1977 *La Dentellière* (*The Lacemaker*) (co-sc); *Jean Piaget* (*The Epistemology of Jean Piaget*)
1980 *La Provinciale*
1983 *La Mort de Mario Ricci* (*The Death of Mario Ricci*)
1985 *Orfeo*
1987 *Si le soleil ne revenais pas* (*If the Sun Never Returns*)

Publications:

By GORETTA: book—

La Dentellière, Paris, 1981.

By GORETTA: articles—

Interview with G. Langlois, in *Cinéma* (Paris), April 1973.
Interview with M. Boujut, in *Cinema* (Zurich), vol. 21, no. 1, 1975.
Interview with D. Maillet, in *Cinématographe* (Paris), June 1977.
Interview with Judith Kass, in *Movietone News* (Seattle), 14 August 1978.

On GORETTA: articles—

Delmas, J., "Tanner, Goretta, la Suisse et nous," in *Jeune Cinéma* (Paris), September/October 1973.
"Claude Goretta," in *Cinema* (Zurich), vol. 20, no. 1, 1974.
Milne, Tom, "Goretta's *Roads of Exile*," in *Sight and Sound* (London), no. 2, 1979.
Milne, Tom, "Claude Goretta," in *Film Dope* (London), April 1980.
"*La Dentellière* Issue" of *Avant-Scène du Cinéma* (Paris), 15 April 1981.
Buache Freddy, "Claude Goretta," in *Revue Belge du Cinéma* (Brussels), Winter 1985.

*   *   *

Claude Goretta's gentle comedies and sensitive depictions of provincial naifs have been among the most successful Swiss films of recent years. Although Goretta shares his countryman Alain Tanner's preoccupation with Renoiresque evocations of landscape and lovable eccentrics, there is a sharp disparity between these two idiosyncratic Swiss directors. As Goretta himself has observed, "Tanner's films always have a discourse, while mine do everything they can to avoid one."

Goretta's first film, an experimental short called *Nice Time*, was in fact made with the collaboration of Alain Tanner when both men were affiliated with the British Film Institute. This impressionistic view of Piccadilly Circus, one of the sleazier parts of central London, prefigures both directors' subsequent interest in whimsical vignettes with serious, and occasionally acerbic, sociological underpinnings. Like many contemporary directors of note, Goretta served his apprenticeship in television. Many of his early television films were literary adaptations, including an adaptation of four Chekhov stories, *Chekov ou le miroir des vies perdues*.

Goretta's first feature film, *Le Fou*, featured one of his favorite actors, the distinguished character player, François Simon. Despite a mixed critical reception, *Le Fou* was awarded a prize as the best Swiss film of 1970 by the Swiss Critics' Association. *L'Invitation* was the first of Goretta's films to receive widespread international recognition. This unpretentious comedy about the loss of inhibitions experienced by a group of office workers during a mildly uproarious party was ecstatically reviewed by British and American critics who casually invoked the names of both Buñuel and Renoir for the sake of comparison. *Pas si mechant que ça* fared less well with both the critics and public, although Gérard Depardieu's charming portrayal of a whimsical thief was widely praised.

Le Dentellière, an incisive character study of a guileless young beautician played flawlessly by Isabelle Huppert (in her first major role), received an even more rhapsodic critical reception than *L'Invitation*. Jean Boffety's pristine cinematography and Goretta's restrained direction were singled out for praise, although several feminist critics cogently observed that Goretta's reverence for the Huppert character's enigmatic passivity was a singularly insidious example of male condescension.

Les Chemins de l'exil marked Goretta's return to his roots in documentary filmmaking. This leisurely biographical portrait of Jean-Jacques Rousseau stars François Simon as the famed *philosophe* who remains one of the most celebrated figures in Swiss cultural history. *La Provinciale* was a somewhat muddled attempt to reiterate many of the themes first explored in *La Dentellière*, although Nathalie Baye's performance was suffused with integrity. *The Death of Mario Ricci* was favorably received at the 1983 Cannes film festival.

—Richard Porton

GOSHO, Heinosuke.

Japanese. Born in Tokyo, 1 February 1902. Educated at Keio Commerce School, graduated 1921. Married three times. Assistant to director Yasujiro Shimazu, Shochiku-Kamata studio, 1923; directed first film, *Nanto no haru*, 1925; moved to Daiei studio, 1941; returned to Shochiku-Ofuna, 1945, then to Toho until 1948; established Studio 8 Productions, affiliated with Shin-Toho, 1951; worked for several studios, from 1954; also writer for TV; President of the Japanese Association of Film Directors, 1964–75; also Director of the Japanese Haiku Art Association. Recipient: 11 films placed among Kinema Jumpo Best Films of the Year between 1927 and 1968; Mainichi Film Prize, Japan, for *One More Time*, 1947; Kun Yon-to Asahi Shoju sho Order of the Japanese Government, 1947; International Peace Prize, Berlin Festival, for *Where Chimneys Are Seen*, 1953. Died 1 May 1981.

Films as Director:

1925 *Nanto no haru* (*Spring of Southern Island*) (+ sc); *Sora wa haretari* (*No Clouds in the Sky*); *Otokogokoro* (*Man's Heart*) (+ sc); *Seishun* (*Youth*) (+ sc); *Tosei tamatebako* (*A Casket for Living*)

1926 *Machi no hitobito* (*Town People*); *Hatsukoi* (*First Love*) (+ sc); *Hahayo koishi* (*Mother, I Miss You. Mother's Love*); *Honryu* (*A Torrent*); *Musume* (*A Daughter*) (+ sc); *Kaeranu sasabue* (*Bamboo Leaf Flute of No Return. No Return*); *Itoshi no wagako* (*My Loving Child*) (+ sc); *Kanojo* (*She. Girl Friend*) (+ sc)

1927 *Sabishiki ranbomono* (*Lonely Hoodlum*); *Hazukashii yume* (*Shameful Dream*), *Karakuri musume* (*Fake Girl*) (+ co-sc); *Shojo no shi* (*Death of a Maiden*) (+ sc); *Okame* (*A Plain Woman*) (+ sc); *Tokyo koshinkyoku* (*Tokyo March*)

1928 *Sukinareba koso* (*Because I Love. If You Like It*) (+ co-sc); *Mura no hanayome* (*The Village Bride*); *Doraku shinan* (*Guidance to the Indulgent. Debauchery Is Wrong*) (+ co-sc); *Kami e no michi* (*Road to God*); *Hito no yo no sugata* (*Man's Worldly Appearance*); *Kaido no kishi* (*Knight of the Street*); *Haha yo, kimi no na o kegasu nakare* (*Mother, Do Not Shame Your Name*)

1929 *Yoru no mesuneko* (*Cat of the Night*); *Shin josei kagami* (*A New Kind of Woman*); *Oyaji to sono ko* (*Father and His Son*); *Ukiyo-buro* (*The Bath Harem*) (+ sc); *Netsujo no ichiya* (*A Night of Passion*) (+ co-sc)

1930 *Dokushinsha goyojin* (*Bachelors Beware*) (+ co-sc); *Dai-Tokyo bi ikkaku* (*A Corner of Great Tokyo*) (+ add'l dialogue); *Hohoemu jinsei* (*A Smiling Life*); *Onna yo, kini no na o kegasu nakare* (*Women, Do Not Shame Your Names*); *Shojo nyuyo* (*Virgin Wanted*); *Kinuyo monogatari* (*The Kinuyo Story*); *Aiyoku no ki* (*Record of Love and Desire*)

1931 *Jokyu aishi* (*Sad Story of a Barmaid*); *Yoru hiraku* (*Open at Night*); *Madamu to nyobo* (*Next Door Madame and My Wife. The Neighbor's Wife and Mine*); *Shima to ratai jiken* (*Island of Naked Scandal*) (+ add'l dialogue); *Gutei kenkei* (*Stupid Young Brother and Wise Old Brother*) (+ add'l dialogue); *Wakaki hi no kangeki* (*Memories of Young Days*)

1932 *Niisan no baka,* (*My Stupid Brother*); *Ginza no yanagi* (*Willows of Ginza*); *Tengoku ni musubu koi* (*Heaven Linked with Love*); *Satsueijo romansu: Renai annai* (*Romance at the Studio: Guidance to Love*); *Hototogisu* (*A Cuckoo*); *Koi no Tokyo* (*Love in Tokyo*)

1933 *Hanayome no negoto* (*The Bride Talks in Her Sleep*); *Izu no odoriko* (*Dancer of Izu*); *Jukyu-sai no haru* (*The Nineteenth Spring*); *Shojo yo sayonara* (*Virgin, Goodbye*); *Lamuru* (*L'Amour*)

1934 *Onna to umaretakaranya* (*Now That I Was Born a Woman*); *Sakura Ondo* (*Sakura Dance*); *Ikitoshi Ikerumono* (*Everything That Lives*)

1935 *Hanamuko no negoto* (*The Bridegroom Talks in His Sleep*); *Hidari uchiwa* (*A Life of Luxury*); *Fukeyo koikaze* (*Breezes of Love*); *Akogare* (*Yearning*); *Jinsei no onimotsu* (*Burden of Life*)

1936 *Oboro yo no onna* (*Woman of Pale Night*); *Shindo* (*New Way*) parts I and II; *Okusama shakuyosho* (*A Married Lady Borrows Money*)

1937 *Hanakago no uta* (*Song of the Flower Basket*) (+ adapt)

1940 *Mokuseki* (*Wood and Stone*)

1942 *Shinsetsu* (*New Snow*)

1944 *Goju-no to* (*The Five-storied Pagoda*)

1945 *Izu no musumetachi* (*Girls of Izu*)

1947 *Ima hitotabi no* (*One More Time*)

1948 *Omokage* (*A Vestige*)

1951 *Wakare-gumo* (*Drifting Clouds*) (+ co-sc)

1952 *Asa no hamon* (*Trouble in the Morning*)

1953 **Entotsu no mieru basho** (**Four Chimneys. Where Chimneys Are Seen**)

1954 *Osaka no yado* (*An Inn at Osaka* (+ co-sc); *Niwatori wa futatabi naku* (*The Cock Crows Twice*); *Ai to shi no tanima* (*The Valley Between Love and Death*)

1955 *Takekurabe* (*Growing Up*)

1956 *Aruyo futatabi* (*Again One Night*) (+ co-sc)

1957 *Kiiroi karasu* (*Yellow Crow. Behold Thy Son*); *Banka* (*Elegy of the North*)

1958 *Hotaru-bi* (*Firefly's Light*); *Yoku* (*Desire*); *Ari no Machi no Maria* (*Maria of the Street of Ants*)

1959 *Karatachi nikki* (*Journal of the Orange Flower*)

1960 *Waga ai* (*When a Woman Loves*); *Shiroi kiba* (*White Fangs*)

1961 *Ryoju* (*Hunting Rifle*); *Kumo ga chigireru toki* (*As the Clouds Scatter*) (+ co-pr); *Aijo no keifu* (*Record of Love*) (+ co-pr)

1962 *Kachan kekkon shiroyo* (*Mother, Get Married*) (+ co-sc)

1963 *Hyakumanin no musumetachi* (*A Million Girls*) (+ co-sc)

1964 *Osore-zan no onna* (*A Woman of the Osore Mountains. An Innocent Witch*)

Heinosuke Gosho: *Next Door Madame and My Wife*

1966   *Kachan to Juichi-nin no Kodomo* (*Mother and Eleven Children. Our Wonderful Years*)
1967   *Utage* (*Feast. Rebellion in Japan*)
1968   *Onna no misoshiru* (*Women and Miso Soup*); *Meiji haruaki* (*Seasons of Meiji*)

Publications:

On GOSHO: books—

Anderson, Joseph, and Donald Richie, *The Japanese Film*, New York, 1961; revised edition, 1982.
Mellen, Joan, *The Waves at Genji's Door*, New York, 1976.
Bock, Audie, *Japanese Film Directors*, New York, 1978; revised edition, Tokyo, 1985.

On GOSHO: articles—

Anderson, J.L., and Donald Richie, "The Films of Heinosuke Gosho," in *Sight and Sound* (London), Autumn 1956.
Gillett, John, "Coca-Cola and the Golden Pavilion," in *Sight and Sound* (London), Summer 1970.
Gillett, John, "Heinosuke Gosho," in *Film Dope* (London), April 1980.
Tessier, Max, "Heinosuke Gosho," in *Image et Son* (Paris), June 1981.
"Heinosuke Gosho: A Pattern of Living," in *National Film Theatre Booklet* (London), March 1986.
Le Fanu, Mark, "To love is to suffer," in *Sight and Sound* (London), Summer 1986.
Niogret, H., "Heinosuke Gosho et la maîtrise du découpage," in *Positif* (Paris), March 1987.

*   *   *

At the beginning of his career in 1925 as a disciple of Yasujiro Shimazu at Shochiku Studio, Gosho proved his skill at the genre of "shomin-geki," stories of the life of ordinary people, characteristic of his mentor's work at that studio. Gosho's early films were criticized as "unsound" because they often involved characters physically or mentally handicapped (*The Village Bride* and *Faked Daughter*). Gosho's intention, however, was to illustrate a kind of warm and sincere relationship born in pathos. Today, these films are highly esteemed for their critique of feudalistic village life. Gosho was affected by this early criticism, however, and made his next films about other subjects. This led him into a long creative slump, although he continued to make five to seven films annually.

His first film to attract attention was *Lonely Hoodlum* of 1927, a depiction of the bittersweet life of common people, Gosho's characteristic subject. In 1931, Shochiku gave him the challenge of making the first Japanese "talkie" (because many established directors had refused). The film, *Next Door Madame and My Wife*, was welcomed passionately by both audiences and critics. It is a light and clever comedy, using ambient sounds such as a baby's cries, an alarm clock, a street vendor's voice, and jazz music from next door. Because every sound had to be synchronized, Gosho explored many technical devices, and also used multiple cameras, different lenses, and frequent cuts to produce a truly "filmic" result.

Gosho preferred many cuts and close-up shots and he related it to his studying Lubitsch carefully in his youth.

Gosho's technique of creating a poetic atmosphere with editing is most successful in *Dancer of Izu*, in which he intentionally chose the silent film form after making several successful talkies.

Even after the success of these films, Gosho had to accept many projects which he did not want to do. He later reflected that only those films that he really wanted to do were well-made. For example, he found the subject of *The Living* most appealing—its protagonist tries to protest against social injustice but is unable to continue his struggle to the end.

Gosho is believed to be at his best making films depicting the human side of life in his native Tokyo (*Woman of Pale Night, Song of the Flower Basket, Where Chimneys Are Seen*, and *Comparison of Heights*). However, the director also worked in many other genres, including romantic melodrama, family drama, light comedy, and social drama. He further extended his range in such films as *An Elegy*, a contemporary love story, and *A Woman of Osore-zan*, which is unusual for its unfamiliar dark tones and its eccentricity. His experimental spirit is illustrated by his story of the treatment of a disturbed child with color-oriented visual therapy in *Yellow Crow*.

Throughout his career, Gosho expressed his basic belief in humanistic values. The warm, subtle, and sentimental depiction of likable people is characteristic both of Gosho's major studio productions and his own independent films.

—Kyoko Hirano

GOULDING, Edmund.

British. Born in London, 20 March 1891. Stage debut in London, 1903; writer, actor, and director, London theatre, until 1914; New York stage debut, 1915; served with British Army in France, 1915–18; returned to America, worked as writer, 1919; hired by MGM as director/scriptwriter, 1925. *Died in Los Angeles, 24 December 1959.*

Films as Director:

1925   *Sun-up* (+ sc); *Sally, Irene and Mary* (+ sc)
1926   *Paris* (*Shadows of Paris*) (+ sc)
1927   *Women Love Diamonds* (+ story); *Love* (*Anna Karenina*) (+ adapt, uncredited, pr, sc)
1930   "Dream Girl" episode of *Paramount on Parade* (+ role); *The Devil's Holiday* (+ sc, music, song) [foreign language versions: *Les Vacances du diable* (Cavalcanti); *La vacanza del diavolo* (Salvatori); *La fiesta del diablo* (Millar); *Sonntag des Lebens* (Mittler); *En kvinnas morgondag* (Bergman)]
1931   *Reaching for the Moon* (+ sc); *The Night Angel* (+ sc, song melodies)
1932   *Grand Hotel*; *Blondie of the Follies* (+ co-lyrics, bit role as Follies director)
1934   *Riptide*; *Hollywood Party* (co-d, uncredited)
1935   *The Flame Within* (+ sc)
1937   *That Certain Woman* (+ sc)
1938   *White Banners*; *The Dawn Patrol*
1939   *Dark Victory* (+ song); *The Old Maid*; *We Are Not Alone*
1940   *'Til We Meet Again*
1941   *The Great Lie*
1943   one episode of *Forever and a Day*; *The Constant Nymph*; *Claudia*
1946   *Of Human Bondage*; *The Razor's Edge*; *The Shocking Miss Pilgrim* (Seaton) (d several scenes while Seaton ill)
1947   *Nightmare Alley*
1949   *Everybody Does It*
1950   *Mr. Eight Hundred Eighty*
1952   *Down Among the Sheltering Palms*; *We're Not Married*
1956   *Teenage Rebel* (+ music for song *Dodie*)
1958   *Mardi Gras*

Other Films:

1911   *Henry VIII* (Parker) (role)
1914   *The Life of a London Shopgirl* (Raymond) (role)
1916   *Quest of Life* (sc, co-play basis)
1917   *The Silent Partner* (Neilan) (sc, story)
1918   *The Ordeal of Rosetta* (Chautard) (sc, story)
1919   *The Perfect Love* (Ralph Ince) (sc); *The Glorious Lady* (Irving) (sc, story); *A Regular Girl* (Young) (sc, co-story); *Sealed Hearts* (Ralph Ince) (sc, co-story); *The Imp* (Ellis) (sc, co-story)
1920   *A Daughter of Two Worlds* (Young) (sc); *The Sin That Was His* (Henley) (sc); *The Dangerous Paradise* (Earle) (sc, story); *The Devil* (Young) (sc)
1921   *Dangerous Toys* (*Don't Leave Your Husband*) (Bradley) (sc, story); *The Man of Stone* (Archainbaud) (sc, co-story); **Tol'able David** (King) (co-sc); *Peacock Alley* (Leonard) (sc)
1922   *The Seventh Day* (King) (sc); *Fascination* (Leonard) (sc); *Broadway Rose* (Leonard) (sc); *Till We Meet Again* (Cabanne) (sc); *Heroes of the Street* (Beaudine) (co-sc); *Fury* (King) (sc; d erroneously attributed to Goulding in Library of Congress Copyright Catalogue); *Three Little Ghosts* (Fitzmaurice) (role)
1923   *Dark Secrets* (Fleming) (sc); *Jazzmania* (Leonard) (sc); *The Bright Shawl* (Robertson) (sc); *Bright Lights of Broadway* (*Bright Lights and Shadows*) (Campbell) (sc); *Tiger Rose* (Franklin) (co-sc)
1924   *Dante's Inferno* (Otto) (sc); *The Man Who Came Back* (Flynn) (sc); *Gerald Cranston's Lady* (Flynn) (sc)
1925   *The Dancers* (Flynn) (sc); *The Scarlet Honeymoon* (Hale) (sc, story; some sources credit story to Fannie Davis); *The Fool* (Millarde) (sc); *Havoc* (Lee) (sc); *The Beautiful City* (Webb) (sc, story)
1926   *Dancing Mothers* (Brenon) (co-play basis)
1928   *Happiness Ahead* (Seiter) (story); *A Lady of Chance* (Leonard) (adapt)
1929   *The Broadway Melody* (Beaumont) (story)
1930   *The Grand Parade* (Newmeyer) (sc, pr, songs)
1932   *Flesh* (Ford) (story); *No Man of Her Own* (Ruggles) (co-story)
1940   *Two Girls on Broadway* (*Choose Your Partner*) (Simon) (remake of *The Broadway Melody*, 1929)
1944   *Flight from Folly* (Mason) (story basis)

Publications:

By GOULDING: book—

Fury, 1922.

By GOULDING: article—

"*The Razor's Edge*," in *Life* (New York), 12 August 1946.

On GOULDING: articles—

Time (New York), 19 May 1947.
Obituary, in the *New York Times*, 25 December 1959.
Sarris, Andrew, "Likable But Elusive," in *Film Culture* (New York), Spring 1963.
Brooks, Louise, "Why I Will Never Write My Memoirs," in *Film Culture* (New York), no. 67–69, 1979.
Walker, Michael, "Edmund Goulding," in *Film Dope* (London), April 1980.
Films and Filming (London), July 1983.
"Edmund Goulding: Love, Marriage, Infidelity," in *National Film Theatre Booklet* (London), January 1984.

*   *   *

Our sense of Edmund Goulding is, of course, skewed by his frequently revived *Grand Hotel* and *Dark Victory*. These films

Edmund Goulding

are viewed today not as examples of the director's art, but rather as star acting vehicles, the second also being seen as a prototypical "woman's film." It is generally assumed that such films were primarily authored by the studio and the stars. Yet, without suggesting that Goulding had a visual signature as distinctive as von Sternberg's or a thematic/ideological one as coherent as Capra's, we must recognize the director's personality in the care of the stagings and in the vitality of the performances complemented by those stagings.

Grand Hotel seems, at first, a product of MGM's collective enterprise rather than Goulding's particular imagination. The sleekness of the writing, photography and art direction are exemplary of the studio that defined cinematic luxury. The assembly of stars—Garbo, Crawford, Beery, John and Lionel Barrymore—in a "hotel" as grand as the studio itself would seem sufficient *direction* of the film. Yet we must give Goulding credit for the exceptionally involved choreography of faces, voices, and bodies in *Grand Hotel* when we look at the same stars in other movies of the period. The film's numerous two-shots are organized with a nuance that makes us as attentive to the shifting relationships between those starry faces as we are to the faces themselves. And we need only see Garbo as directed by Clarence Brown or George Fitzmaurice to appreciate the contribution of Edmund Goulding. He is exceptionally sensitive to the time it takes the actress to register thought through her mere act of presence.

That sensitivity is not diminished when Goulding directs Bette Davis, whose rhythm is totally dissimilar to Garbo's. In *Dark Victory* and *The Old Maid* the director presides over shots that permit us to perceive star and character simultaneously, a requisite of successful screen star performance. Goulding's strength is in characterization, in creating the kind of atmosphere in which actors explore the richest areas within themselves, and in creating the visual/aural contexts that put such exploration in relief for the viewer. This is certainly the case in *The Constant Nymph*. Its precious narrative conceit—a soulful adolescent girl (Joan Fontaine) inspires an excessively cerebral composer (Charles Boyer) to write music with emotion—both reflects the emotional qualities of Goulding's films and displays the actors at their most courageous.

For Goulding, the mature Joan Fontaine is able to sustain her impersonation of an impulsive, loving girl for the whole length of a film. And in *Nightmare Alley*, Tyrone Power is pushed to expose his own persona in the most unflattering light—the "handsome leading man" as charlatan. But that exposure, one of many in the films of Goulding, is also evidence of his affinity for the dilemma of the performing artist, vulnerable in the magnifying exposures of the cinematic medium and dependent on the director's empathy if that vulnerability is to become a meaningful cinematic sign.

—Charles Affron

GREENAWAY, Peter.

British. Born in London, 5 April 1942. Studied painting. First exhibition of paintings, London, 1964; worked as a film editor for Central Office of Information, 1965–76; made first film, *Train*, 1966; made first feature, *The Falls*, 1980; *A TV Dante* broadcast, 1990.

Films as Director:

1966   *Train*; *Tree*
1967   *Revolution*; *Five Postcards From Capital Cities*
1969   *Intervals*
1971   *Erosion*
1973   *H is for House*
1975   *Windows*; *Water*; *Water Wrackets*
1976   *Goole By Numbers*
1977   *Dear Phone*
1978   *1–100*; *A Walk Through H*; *Vertical Features Remake*
1980   *The Falls*
1981   *Act of God*; *Zandra Rhodes*
1982   ***The Draughtsman's Contract***
1983   *Four American Composers*
1984   *Making a Splash*; *A TV Dante—Canto 5*
1985   *Inside Rooms—The Bathroom*; *A Zed and Two Noughts*
1987   *The Belly of an Architect*
1988   *Drowning by Numbers*
1989   *The Cook, the Thief, His Wife and Her Lover*

Publications:

By GREENAWAY: books—

A Zed and Two Noughts, London, 1986.
The Belly of an Architect, London, 1988.
Drowning by Numbers, London, 1988.

By GREENAWAY: articles—

Interview with K. Jaehne, in *Cineaste* (New York), vol. 13, no. 2, 1984.
Interviews with Michel Ciment, in *Positif* (Paris), February 1984 and October 1987.
Interview with E. Decaux and B. Villien, in *Cinématographe* (Paris), March 1984.
Interview with Don Ranvaud, in *Sight and Sound* (London), Summer 1987.
"Architecture and Morality," an interview with J. Clarke, in *Films and Filming* (London), October 1987.
Interview in *Post Script* (Jacksonville, Florida), Winter 1989.
Interview in *Cinema Papers* (Melbourne), March 1990.
Interview in *Inter/View* (New York), March 1990.

On GREENAWAY: book—

Caux, Daniel, and others, *Peter Greenaway*, Paris, 1987.

On GREENAWAY: articles—

Simon, L., "Music and Film: An Interview with Michael Nyman," in *Millenium* (New York), Fall 1981/Winter 1982.
Kennedy, Harlan, "Peter Greenaway: His rise and *Falls*," in *Film Comment* (New York), January/February 1982.
Brown, R., "*The Draughtsman's Contract*: From a view to death," in *Monthly Film Bulletin* (London), November 1982.
Auty, Chris, "Greenaway's Games," in *Stills* (London), May/June 1983.
Rayns, Tony, "Peter Greenaway," in *American Cinematographer* (Los Angeles), September 1983.
"*The Draughtsman's Contract* Issue" of *Avant-Scène du Cinéma* (Paris), October 1984.
Rayns, Tony, "Of Natural History and Mythology Born," in *Monthly Film Bulletin* (London), December 1985.
"Peter Greenaway Section" of *Positif* (Paris), April 1986.
Elsaesser, Thomas, and Tony Rayns, "*Drowning By Numbers*: Games of Love and Death," in *Monthly Film Bulletin* (London), October 1988.

*   *   *

An ancient Chinese encyclopedia, according to Borges, divides animals into "(a) those that belong to the Emperor, (b) embalmed ones, (c) those that are trained, (d) suckling pigs, (e) mermaids, (f) fabulous ones, (g) stray dogs, (h) those that are included in this classification, (i) those that tremble as if they are mad, (j) innumerable ones, (k) those drawn with a very fine camel's hair brush, (l) others, (m) those that have just broken a flower vase, (n) those that resemble flies from a distance." One is tempted to add, (o) those featured in Peter

Peter Greenaway © **Peter Smith**

Greenaway's films. The inclusion would seem appropriate for a filmmaker who has constantly displayed a fascination for the organic and the classificatory, in a body of films that have themselves retained an art-house individuality within the broader criteria of popular success.

Greenaway's biography implies a deeper integration between life and his art than some critics might suggest. He grew up in in post-war Essex, his father was an ornithologist—perhaps the quintessential English hobby—and the petit-bourgeois world of public respectibility and private eccentricity seems to have left him with a taste for the contradictory that hallmarks his work ("The black humour, irony, distancing, a quality of being in control, an interest in landscape, treating the world as equal with an image, these are very English qualities. I can't imagine myself living abroad"). He trained as a painter rather than a filmmaker, but his first exhibition "Eisenstein at the Winter Palace" indicated an interest that led him into film editing at the Central Office of Information, the government department responsible for informing the public in the unique "home-counties" voice of domestic propaganda.

These years also saw Greenaway developing a crop of his own absurdist works—films, art, novels, illustrated books, drawings—with titles such as *Goole by Numbers* and *Dear Phone*, as well as directing (non-absurdist) Party Political Broadcasts for the Labour Party. They also saw the introduction of his fictional alter ego, Tulse Luper, archivist, cartographer, ornithologist extraordinaire ("He's me at about 65. A know-all, a Buckminster Fuller, a McLuhan, a John Cage, a pain"). Nomenclature means a lot to Greenaway, in determining where one would be filed in the unfortunate event of a stat-

istically (im)probable end. *The Falls* is a catalogue of victims of V.U.E. (Violent Unknown Event), with characters such as Mashanter Fallack, Carlos Fallanty, Raskado Fallcastle, and Hearty Fallparco. The epitomy of absurdity was perhaps reached in *Act of God*, a film based around interviews with people who'd been struck by lightning in an attempt to find out what led to such an unpredictable event.

But perhaps the most tickling piece of absurdity for Greenaway came in the commercial success of *The Draughtsman's Contract*, his first film made on a reasonable budget. It made an uncharacteristic concession to plot, characterization, and scenic coherence. A stylish, lavish and enigmatic puzzle revolving around murder in a seventeenth-century English stately home, it soon became the subject of a mythical French film conference that discussed its title for five days, and gained popular fame in being the film of which everyone asked what was it all about. But it made Greenaway's name, and briefly contested box office ratings with the likes of *E.T.* and *Gandhi*, although Greenaway's intended length was four hours—"one suspects it was originally closer to *Tristram Shandy* than *Murder at the Vicarage*," as one critic remarked.

Greenaway's ideas tend to work in twos. *A Zed and Two Noughts* took Siamese twins separated at birth and saw them coping with the grief at the death of their wives in a study in the decomposition of zoo animals. *Belly of an Architect* silhouetted the visceral mortality of Stourley Kracklite against his plans for an exhibition on an eighteenth-century visionary architect, Etiénne-Louis Boullée. But the dialectic seems more important than the ideas themselves, as Greenaway hints: "The important thing about Boullée—and this is where he's very like a filmmaker, who tends to spend much more time on uncompleted projects than completed ones—is that very few of his buildings were constructed. I've taken that up in Kracklite's fear of committal, being prepared to go half-way and no further, which is Kracklite's position and maybe my position as well."

In this position Greenaway's always been most successful when casting 'strong' leading actors: Brian Dennehy as Kracklite, and in arguably his most successful film *The Cook, The Thief, His Wife, and Her Lover*, Michael Gambon (the Thief) and Helen Mirren (his Wife). His ideas are always sufficiently ambiguous to resist trivialisation, but invariably involve death: Death and Landscape, Death and Animals, Death and Architecture, Death and Sex, Death and Food (cannibalism). But there are factors which make them more palatable. One of them is a taste for sumptuous painterly framing (helped by cinematographer Sacha Vierney), in which he envisages an aesthetic complexity similar to that of the golden age of Dutch art, "where those amazing manifestations of the real world that we find in Vermeer and Rembrandt are enriched by a fantastic metaphorical language." The other is his close collaboration with the composer Michael Nyman, whose insistent scores lend an inexorability to Greenaway's sometimes spatial fabric of ideas.

There are contradictions in his works, a fact that seems to openly provoke divided opinion. Some would suggest that the fecundity of his vision, his intellectual rigour, is the stuff of great cinema; whilst others, admitting his originality, would still look for evidence of a deeper engagement with film as a medium, rather than as a vehicle for ideas. Lauded in Europe, under-distributed in the United States, loved and reviled in his own country, Greenaway is, nevertheless, in an enviable position for a filmmaker.

—Saul Frampton

GRÉMILLON, Jean.

French. Born in Bayeux, Normandy, 3 October 1901. Educated at l'Ecole Communale de Saint-Lô, Lycée de Brest, and Ecole des Cordeliers, Dinan; Schola Cantorum, Paris (studied with Vincent d'Indy), 1920. Military service, 1920–22. Married Christiane (Grémillon). Film titler, editor, and director of short films, from 1923; worked in Spain and Germany, 1935–38; war cinematographer, from 1939; elected President of Cinémathèque Française, 1944; President of C.G.T., film technicians union, 1946–50. *Died 25 November 1959.*

Films as Director:

1923   *Chartres* (*Le Cathédrale de Chartres*) (+ ed); *Le Revêtement des routes* (+ ed)
1924   *La Fabrication du fil* (+ ed); *Du fil à l'aiguille* (+ ed); *La Fabrication du ciment artificiel* (+ ed); *La Bière* (+ ed); *Le Roulement à billes* (+ ed); *Les Parfums* (+ ed); *L'Étirage des ampoules électriques* (+ ed); *La Photogénie mécanique* (+ ed)
1925   *L'Education professionelle des conducteurs de tramway* (6 short films) (+ ed); *L'Electrification de la ligne Paris-Vierzon* (+ ed); *L'Auvergne* (+ ed); *La Naissance des cigognes* (+ ed); *Les Aciéries de la marine et d'Homécourt* (+ ed)
1926   *La Vie des travailleurs italiens en France* (+ ed); *La Croisière de L'Atalante* (+ ed); *Un Tour au large* (+ ed, sc, music—recorded on piano rolls)
1927   *Maldone* (+ ed, co-music); *Gratuités* (+ ed)
1928   *Bobs* (+ ed)
1929   *Gardiens de phare* (+ ed)
1930   *La Petite Lise* (+ ed)
1931   *Dainah la métisse* (+ ed) (disowned due to unauthorized reediting); *Pour un sou d'amour* (no d credit on film; + ed)
1932   *Le Petit Babouin* (+ ed, music)
1933   *Gonzague ou L'Accordeur* (+ sc)
1934   *La Dolorosa*
1935   *La Valse royale* (French version of Herbert Maisch's *Königswalzer*)
1936   *Centinella alerta!* (not completed by Grémillon); *Pattes de mouches* (+ co-sc)
1937   *Gueule d'amour*
1938   *L'Etrange Monsieur Victor*
1941   *Remorques*
1943   *Lumière d'été*
1944   *Le Ciel est à vous*
1945   *Le Six Juin à l'aube* (*Sixth of June at Dawn*) (+ sc, music)
1949   *Pattes blanches* (+ co-dialogue); *Les Charmes de l'existence* (co-d, co-sc, co-commentary, music advisor)
1951   *L'Etrange Madame X*
1952   *Astrologie ou Le Miroir de la vie* (+ sc, co-music); "Alchimie" episode of *L'Encyclopédie filmée—Alchimie, Azur, Absence* (+ sc)
1954   *L'Amour d'une femme* (+ sc, dubbed actor Paolo Stoppa); *Au cœur de l'Ile de France* (+ sc, co-music)
1955   *La Maison aux images* (+ sc, music)
1956   *Haute Lisse* (+ sc, music adapt)
1958   *André Masson et les quatre éléments* (+ sc, music)

Other Film:

1951   *Désastres de la guerre* (Kast) (commentary and co-music)

Publications:

By GRÉMILLON: books—

Hommage à Jacques Feyder, Paris, 1948.
Le Printemps de la Liberté, Paris, 1948.

By GRÉMILLON: articles—

"Propositions," in *Comoedia* (Paris), 27 November 1925.
"Le Cinema? Plus qu'un art . . . ," in *L'Ecran Français* (Paris), August 1947.
"Jacques Feyder, ce combattant," in *L'Ecran Français* (Paris), 8 June 1948.
"Conférences sur Flaherty," in *Cinéma* (Paris), no. 9–10, 1956.
"Ma rencontre avec André Masson," in *Les Lettres Françaises* (Paris), 24 November 1960.

On GRÉMILLON: books—

Jean Grémillon, Première Plan no. 5, Paris, 1960.
Agel, Henri, *Jean Grémillon*, in *Cinéma d'aujourd'hui* no. 58, Paris, 1969.
Sellier, Geneviève, *Jean Grémillon: Le Cinéma est à vous*, Paris, 1989.

On GREMILLON: articles—

Hackett, Hazel, "Jean Grémillon," in *Sight and Sound* (London), Summer 1947.
Kast, Pierre, "Exercice d'un tragique quotidien . . . ," in *Revue du Cinéma* (Paris), August 1948.
"Grémillon Issue" of *Ciné-Club* (Paris), January/February 1951.
Laurent, F., "Sur Jean Grémillon," in *Image et Son* (Paris), February 1955.
"Gremillon Issue" of *Lettres Françaises* (Paris), 3 December 1959.
Chevassu, François, "Dossier Jean Grémillon," in *Image et Son* (Paris), January 1960.
Mayoux, Michel, "Jean Grémillon, cinéaste de la réalité," in *Cahiers du Cinéma* (Paris), February 1960.
"Grémillon Issue" of *Cinéma* (Paris), March 1960.
Clair, René, "Jean Grémillon devant l'avenir," in *Lettres Françaises* (Paris), 24 November 1960.
Vivet, J.-P., "Hommage à Jean Grémillon," in *Avant-Scène du Cinéma* (Paris), 15 September 1962.
Billard, Pierre, "Jean Grémillon," in *Anthologie du Cinéma* vol.2, Paris, 1967.
Siclier, Jacques, "Portrait: Jean Grémillon," in *Radio-Télé-Cinéma* (Paris), 24 November 1969.
"Jean Grémillon," in *Dossier du Cinéma*, Paris, 1971.
Le Dantec, and M. Latil, "Jean Grémillon: le réalisme et le tragique," in *Cinématographe* (Paris), no. 40, 1978.
Le Dantec, and M. Latil, "Le Cinéma de Jean Grémillon," in *Cinématographe* (Paris), no. 41, 1978.
Biofilmography, in *Film Dope* (London), October 1980.
"Jean Grémillon Section" of *Cinéma* (Paris), November 1981.
"*Le Ciel est à vous* Issue" of *Avant-Scène du Cinéma* (Paris), 15 November 1981.
"Grémillon Issue" of *Filmkritik* (Munich), April 1983.
Detassis, P., "Jean Grémillon, 'l'uomotramite' tra due epoche del cinema francese," in *Bianco e Nero* (Rome), October/December 1983.
Kast, Pierre, in *Cinéma* (Paris), December 1984.

*   *   *

Jean Grémillon is finally beginning to enjoy the reputation most French film scholars always bestowed upon him. Although Americans have until recently been able to see only one or two of his dozen important works, he has generally been placed only slightly below Renoir, Clair, and Carné in the hierarchy of French classical cinema.

Evidently no one was more versatile than Grémillon. A musician, he composed many of his own scores and supervised all aspects of his productions scrupulously. Along with the search for a romantic unity of feeling and consistency of rhythm, his films also display an attention to details and locations that derives from his earliest documentaries. No one was more prepared than Grémillon for the poetic realist sensibility that dominated French cinema in the 1930s. Even in the silent period his *Maldone* and *Gardiens de phare* reveal a heightening of strange objects as they take on fatal proportions in these tense and dark melodramas. *La Petite Lise* displayed these same qualities with an incredibly imaginative and rigo-

Jean Grémillon: Mireille Balin and Jean Gabin in *Gueule d'amour*

rous use of sound. It should be called the first poetic realist film, anticipating Carné's work in particular. After a few years of obscurity, Grémillon re-emerged with *Gueule d'amour*, a Foreign Legion love story with Jean Gabin. Then came a series of truly wonderful films: *L'Étrange M. Victor, Remorques, Le Ciel est à vous*, and *Lumière d'été*. Spanning the period of French subjugation by the Nazis, these films capture the sensibility of the times with their wistful romanticism, the fatality of their conclusions, and their attention to social classes.

Le Ciel est à vous must be singled out as a key film of the Occupation. Enormously popular, this tale of a small town couple obsessed with aviation has been variously interpreted as promoting Vichy morality (family, small-town virtues, hard work) and as representing the indomitable French spirit ready to soar beyond the temporary political restraints of the Occupation. Charles Vanel and Madeleine Renaud give unforgettable performances.

Grémillon often sought mythic locations (mysterious villages in the Alps or Normandy, the evocative southern cities of Orange and Toulon) where his quiet heroes and heroines played out their destinies of passion and crime. Unique is the prominent place women hold in his dramas. From the wealthy femme fatale murdered by Gabin in *Gueule d'amour* to the independent professional woman refusing to give up her medical career even for love (*L'Amour d'une femme*), women are shown to be far more prepossessed than the passionate but childish men who pursue them.

It is perhaps the greatest tragedy of French cinema that Grémillon's career after World War II was derailed by the con-

ditions of the industry. His *Sixth of June at Dawn* shows how even a documentary project could in his hands take on poetic proportions and become a personal project. Yet the final years before his death in 1959 (when he was only 57) were spent in teaching and preparing unfinanced scripts. This is a sad end for the man some people claim to have been the most versatile cinematic genius ever to work in France.

—Dudley Andrew

GRIERSON, John.

Scottish. Born in Deanston, Scotland, 18 April 1898. Educated at Glasgow University, degree in philosophy, 1923. Served in Royal Navy, World War I. Married Margaret Taylor, 1930. Travelled to U.S. to study press, cinema, and other mass media, 1924–27; joined Empire Marketing Board (EMB) Film Unit under Stephen Tallents, London, 1927; produced and directed *Drifters*, 1928–29; became head of General Post Office (GPO) Film Unit when EMB dissolved and its Film unit transferred to GPO, 1933; resigned from GPO to form Film Centre with Arthur Elton, Stuart Legg, and J.P.R. Golightly, 1937; Film Advisor to Imperial Relations Trust, and to Canadian, Australian and New Zealand Governments, 1937–40; Film Commissioner of Canada, helped establish

National Film Board of Canada, 1939–45; Co-coordinator of Mass Media at UNESCO, 1947; Controller, Films Division of Central Office of Information, London, 1948–50; Joint Executive Producer of Group 3, established by National Finance Company to produce feature films, 1951–54; became member of Films on Scotland Committee, 1954; produced and presented *This Wonderful World* for Scottish TV, 1955–65. Recipient: Commander of the British Empire, 1948; Golden Thistle Award, Edinburgh Film Festival, 1968. *Died 19 February 1972.*

Films as Director:

1929   *Drifters* (+ sc)

Other Films:

1930   *Conquest* (pr, co-ed)
1931   *The Country Comes to Town* (Wright) (pr); *Shadow on the Mountain* (pr); *Upstream* (pr)
1931/32 *Industrial Britain* (Flaherty) (pr, co-ed)
1932   *King Log* (pr); *The New Generation* (pr); *The New Operator* (pr); *O'er Hill and Dale* (Wright) (pr); *The Voice of the World* (pr)
1933   *Aero-Engine* (pr); *Cargo from Jamaica* (Wright) (pr); *The Coming of the Dial* (pr); *Eskimo Village* (pr); *Line Cruising South* (Wright) (pr); *So This Is London* (pr); *Telephone Workers* (pr); *Uncharted Waters* (pr); *Windmill in Barbados* (Wright) (pr)
1934   *BBC: Droitwich* (Watt) (pr); *Granton Trawler* (Cavalcanti) (pr, ph); *Pett and Pott* (Cavalcanti) (pr); *Post Haste* (pr); *Six-Thirty Collection* (Watt) (pr); *Song of Ceylon* (Wright) (pr, co-sc); *Spring Comes to England* (co-pr); *Spring on the Farm* (pr); *Weather Forecast* (pr)
1935   *BBC: The Voice of Britain* (co-pr); *Coalface* (Cavalcanti) (pr); *Introducing the Dial* (pr)
1936   *Night Mail* (Watt and Wright) (pr, co-sc); *The Saving of Bill Blewett* (Watt) (pr); *Trade Tattoo* (pr)
1937   *Calender of the Year* (pr); *Children at School* (Wright) (co-pr); *Four Barriers* (pr); *Job in a Million* (pr); *Line to Tschierva Hut* (Cavalcanti) (pr); *The Smoke Menace* (co-pr); *We Live in Two Worlds* (pr)
1938   *The Face of Scotland* (Wright) (pr)
1939   *The Londoners* (co-pr)
1951   *Judgment Deferred* (exec pr); *Brandy for the Parson* (exec pr)
1952   *The Brave Don't Cry* (exec pr); *Laxdale Hall* (exec pr); *The Oracle* (exec pr); *Time Gentlemen Please* (exec pr); *You're Only Young Twice* (exec pr)
1953   *Man of Africa* (exec pr); *Orders are Orders* (exec pr)
1959   *Seawards the Great Ships* (treatment)
1961/62 *Heart of Scotland* (treatment)

Publications:

By GRIERSON: books—

Grierson on Documentary, edited by Forsyth Hardy, revised edition, London, 1966.

By GRIERSON: articles—

"Future for British Film," in *Spectator* (London), 14 May 1932.
"The Symphonic Film I," in *Cinema Quarterly* (London), Spring 1933.
"The Symphonic Film II," in *Cinema Quarterly* (London), Spring 1934.
"One Hundred Percent Cinema," in *Spectator* (London), 23 August 1935.
"Dramatising Housing Needs and City Planning," in *Films* (London), November 1939.
"Post-War Patterns," in *Hollywood Quarterly*, January 1946.
"Prospect for Documentary," in *Sight and Sound* (London), Summer 1948.
"Flaherty as Innovator," in *Sight and Sound* (London), October/December 1951.

"The Front Page," in *Sight and Sound* (London), April/June 1952.
"The BBC and All That," in *Quarterly of Film, Radio, Television* (Berkeley), Fall 1954.
"Making of *Man of Africa*," in *Films and Filming* (London), October 1954.
"The Prospect for Cultural Cinema," in *Film* (London), January/February 1956.
"I Derive My Authority from Moses," in *Take One* (Montreal), January/February 1970.
"The Golden Years of Grierson," interview with Elizabeth Sussex, in *Sight and Sound* (London), Summer 1972.
"Grierson on Documentary: Last Interview," with Elizabeth Sussex, in *Film Quarterly* (Berkeley), Fall 1972.

On GRIERSON: books—

Rotha, Paul, *Rotha on Film*, London, 1958.
Rotha, Paul, *Documentary Film*, 4th Edition, London, 1964.
Lovell, Alan, and Jim Hillier, *Studies in Documentary*, New York, 1972.
Sussex, Elizabeth, *The Rise and Fall of British Documentary: The Story of the Film Movement Founded by John Grierson*, Berkeley, 1975.
Beveridge, J.A., *John Grierson—Film Master*, New York, 1978.
Hardy, Forsyth, *John Grierson: A Documentary Biography*, London, 1979.
Evans, Gary, *John Grierson and the National Film Board: The Politics of Wartime Propaganda*, Toronto, 1984.
Ellis, Jack C., *John Grierson: A Guide to References and Resources*, Boston, 1986.
Nelson, Joyce, *The Colonized Eye: Rethinking the Grierson Legend*, Toronto, 1988.
Ellis, Jack C., *The Documentary Idea*, Englewood Cliffs, New Jersey, 1989.

On GRIERSON: articles—

Lambert, Gavin, "Who Wants True?," in *Sight and Sound* (London), April/June 1952.
Ellis, Jack C., "The Young Grierson in America," in *Cinema Journal* (Evanston, Illinois), Fall 1968.
Ellis, Jack C., "John Grierson's First Years at the National Film Board," in *Cinema Journal* (Evanston, Illinois), Fall 1970.
Sussex, Elizabeth, "John Grierson," in *Sight and Sound* (London), Spring 1972.
James, R., "Le Rêve de Grierson," in *Cinéma Québec* (Montreal), May 1972.
Ellis, Jack C., "Grierson at University," in *Cinema Journal* (Evanston), Spring 1973.
Dickinson, T., "The Rise and Fall of the British Documentary," in *Film Comment* (New York), January/February 1977.
Goetz, W., "The Canadian Wartime Documentary," in *Cinema Journal* (Evanston), Spring 1977.
MacGann, R.D., "Subsidy for the Screen: Grierson and Group Three/1951–55," in *Sight and Sound* (London), Summer 1977.
Herrick, D., "The Canadian Connection: John Grierson," in *Cinema Canada* (Montreal), September/October 1978.
Cox, K., "The Grierson Files," in *Cinema Canada* (Montreal), June/July 1979.
"John Grierson," in *Film Dope* (London), October 1980.
Ellis, Jack C., "Changing of the Guard: From the Grierson documentary to Free Cinema," in *Quarterly Review of Film Studies* (New York), Winter 1982.
Pratley, Gerald, "Only Grierson," in *Films and Filming* (London), March 1982.
Swann, P., "John Grierson and the G.P.O. Film Unit, 1933–39," in *Historical Journal of Film, Radio and TV* (Abindon, Oxon), March 1983.
Ellis, Jack C., "The Final Years of British Documentary as the Grierson Movement," in *Journal of Film and Video* (Boston), Fall 1984.
Tomaselli, K., "Grierson in South Africa: Culture, State and Nationalist Ideology in the South African Film Industry: 1940–41," in *Cinema Canada* (Montreal), September 1985.
"Grierson Issue" of *Historical Journal of Film, Radio and TV* (Abingdon, Oxon), vol. 9, no. 3, 1989.

*   *   *

John Grierson (right of camera) directing *Drifters*

More than any one other person, Grierson was responsible for the documentary film as it has developed in the English-speaking countries. He was the first to use the word *documentary* in relation to film, applying it to Robert Flaherty's *Moana* while Grierson was in the United States in the 1920s.

He took the term and his evolving conception of a new kind and use of film back to Britain with him in 1927. There he was hired by Stephen Tallents, Secretary of the Empire Marketing Board, a unique government public relations agency intended to promote the marketing of the products of the British Empire.

The first practical application of Grierson's ideas at the EMB was *Drifters* in 1929, a short feature about herring fishing in the North Sea. Following its success, Grierson established, with the full support of Tallents, the Empire Marketing Board Film Unit instead of pursuing a career as an individual filmmaker. He staffed the Film Unit with young people, mostly middle class and well educated (many from Cambridge University). Basil Wright, Arthur Elton, Edgar Anstey, and Paul Rotha were among the early recruits; Stuart Legg and Harry Watt came later, as did Humphrey Jennings. Alberto Cavalcanti joined the group, shortly after it had moved to the General Post Office, as a sort of co-producer and co-teacher with Grierson.

The training at the EMB Film Unit and subsequently the General Post Office Film Unit was ideological as well as technical and aesthetic. The young filmmakers exposed to it came to share Grierson's broad social purposes, and developed an extraordinary loyalty to him and to his goals. It was in this way that the British documentary movement was given shape and impetus.

What Grierson wanted documentary to do was to inform the public about their nation and involve them emotionally with the workings of their government. His assumptions were as follows: if people at work in one part of the Empire are shown to people in the other parts, and if a government service is presented to the population at large, an understanding and appreciation of the interrelatedness of the modern world, and of our dependency on each other, will develop and everyone will want to contribute his or her share to the better functioning of the whole. On these assumptions was based the first phase in Grierson's lifelong activity on behalf of citizenship education. Phase one included some of the most innovative, lovely, and lasting of the British documentaries: *Drifters, Industrial Britain, Granton Trawler, Song of Ceylon, Coal Face*, and *Night Mail*.

Phase two, which began in the mid-1930s, consisted of calling public attention to pressing problems faced by the nation, of insistence that these problems needed to be solved, of suggestions about their causes and possible solutions. Since these matters may have involved differing political positions and in any case did not relate directly to the concerns of the sponsoring General Post Office, Grierson stepped outside the GPO to enlist sponsorship from private industry. Big oil and gas concerns were especially responsive to his persuasion. The subjects dealt with in this new kind of documentary included unemployment (*Workers and Jobs*), slums (*Housing Problems*), malnutrition among the poor (*Enough to Eat?*), smog (*The Smoke Menace*), and education (*Children at School*). Unlike the earlier British documentaries, these films were journalistic rather than poetic, and seemed quite unartistic. Yet they incorporated formal and technical experiments. Most notable among these was the direct interview, with slum dwellers in *Housing Problems*, for example, presaging the much later cinéma vérité method, and a standard technique of television documentary today.

The use of institutional sponsorship, public and private, to pay for his kind of filmmaking, rather than dependence on returns from the box office, was a key Grierson innovation in the development of documentary. A second innovation, complementing the first, was nontheatrical distribution and exhibition: going outside the movie theaters to reach audiences in schools and factories, union halls and church basements.

During the ten years between *Drifters* and Grierson's departure for Canada, in 1939, the 60 or so filmmakers who comprised the British documentary movement made over 300 films. These films and the system they came out of became models for other countries. Paul Rotha, one of Grierson's principal lieutenants, went on a six month missionary expedition to the United States in 1937, and film people from America and other countries visited the documentary units in Britain. Grierson carried his ideas himself not only to Canada, where he drafted legislation for the National Film Board and became its first head, but to New Zealand, Australia, and later South Africa, all of which established national film boards.

The National Film Board of Canada stands as the largest and most impressive monument to Grierson's concepts and actions relating to the use of film by governments in communicating with their citizens. During his Canadian years he moved beyond national concerns to global ones. The Film Board's *The World in Action*, a monthly series for the theaters along *March of Time* lines, expressed some of these concerns. His ideas regarding the education of citizens required in a world at war, and a new world to follow, were expressed in major essays that have inspired many who have read them. "The Challenge of Peace," reprinted in *Grierson on Documentary*, is one of them.

It is for his many-faceted, innovative leadership in film and in education that Grierson is most to be valued. As a theoretician he articulated the basis of the documentary film, its form and function, its aesthetic and its ethic. As a teacher he trained and, through his writing and speaking, influenced many documentary filmmakers, not only in Britain and Canada but throughout the world. As a producer he was responsible to one extent or another for thousands of films and played a decisive creative role in some of the most important of them. And almost all of his life he was an adroit political figure and dedicated civil servant. Whether being paid by a government or not, his central concern was always with communicating to the people of a nation and of the world the information and attitudes that he thought would help them to lead more useful and productive, more satisfying and rewarding lives.

—Jack C. Ellis

GRIFFITH, D.W.

American. Born David Wark Griffith on Oldham County Farm, near Centerfield, Kentucky, 23 January 1875. Educated at district schools in Oldham County, Shelby County, and Louisville, Kentucky. Married 1) Linda Arvidson, 1906 (divorced 1936); 2) Evelyn Baldwin, 1936 (divorced 1947). As "Lawrence Griffith," "Alfred Lawrence," "Lawrence Brayington," and "Thomas Griffith," actor in regional stock companies, 1895–99; actor in New York and in touring companies, 1899–1906; actor for Edison Company and Biograph Pictures, also sold scenarios to Biograph and American Mutascope, 1907; director and scriptwriter for Biograph (approximately 485 one- and two-reelers), 1908–13; began association with cameraman G.W. (Billy) Bitzer, and with actress Mary Pickford, 1909; supervised Mack Sennett's first films, 1910; made first film with Lillian and Dorothy Gish, *An Unseen Enemy*, 1912; joined Reliance Majestic (affiliated with Mutual), 1913; became partner in Triangle Pictures, 1915; travelled to Britain to aid war effort, 1917; engaged by Paramount, 1918; with Pickford, Fairbanks and Chaplin, formed United Artists, 1919; built own studio at Mamaroneck, New York, 1920; directed three pictures for Paramount, 1925–26; returned to United Artists, 1927 (through 1931); directed his first talking picture, *Abraham Lincoln*, 1930; resigned as Head of his own production company, resigned from United Artists Board and sold UA stock, 1932–33; returned to Hollywood to work on *One Million B.C.*, 1939. Recipient: Director of the Year, 1931, and Special Award, 1936, from Academy of Motion Picture Arts and Sciences; Honorary Doctorate, University of Louisville, 1945. *Died in Los Angeles, 23 July 1948.*

Films as Director and Scriptwriter:
(at Biograph):

1908   *The Adventures of Dolly*; *The Redman and the Child*; *The Tavern Keeper's Daughter*; *The Bandit's Waterloo*; *A Calamitous Elopement*; *The Greaser's Gauntlet*; *The Man and the Woman*; *For Love of Gold*; *The Fatal Hour*; *For a Wife's Honor*; *Balked at the Altar*; *The Girl and the Outlaw*; *The Red Girl*; *Betrayed by a Hand Print*; *Monday Morning in a Coney Island Police Court*; *Behind the Scenes*; *The Heart of Oyama*; *Where the Breakers Roar*; *The Stolen Jewels*; *A Smoked Husband*; *The Zulu's Heart*; *The Vaquaro's Vow*; *Father Gets in the Game*; *The Barbarian, Ingomar*; *The Planter's Wife*; *The Devil*; *Romance of a Jewess*; *The Call of the Wild*; *After Many Years*; *Mr. Jones at the Ball*; *Concealing a Burglar*; *Taming of the Shrew*; *The Ingrate*; *A Woman's Way*; *The Pirate's Gold*; *The Guerrilla*; *The Curtain Pole*; *The Song of the Shirt*; *The Clubman and the Tramp*; *Money Mad*; *Mrs. Jones Entertains*; *The Feud and the Turkey*; *The Test of Friendship*; *The Reckoning*; *One Touch of Nature*; *An Awful Moment*; *The Helping Hand*; *The Maniac Cook*; *The Christmas Burglars*; *A Wreath in Time*; *The Honor of Thieves*; *The Criminal Hypnotist*; *The Sacrifice*; *The Welcome Burglar*; *A Rural Elopement*; *Mr. Jones Has a Card Party*; *The Hindoo Dagger*; *The Salvation Army Lass*; *Love Finds a Way*; *Tragic Love*; *The Girls and a Daddy*
1909   *Those Boys*; *The Cord of Life*; *Trying to Get Arrested*; *The Fascinating Mrs. Frances*; *Those Awful Hats*; *Jones and the Lady Book Agent*; *The Drive for Life*; *The Brahma Diamond*; *Politician's Love Story*; *The Jones Have Amateur Theatricals*; *Edgar Allen Poe*; *The Roué's Heart*; *His Wife's Mother*; *The Golden Louis*; *His Ward's Love*; *At the Altar*; *The Prussian Spy*; *The Medicine Bottle*; *The Deception*; *The Lure of the Gown*; *Lady Helen's Escapade*; *A Fool's Revenge*; *The Wooden Leg*; *I Did It, Mama*; *The Voice of the Violin*; *And a Little Child Shall Lead Them*; *The French Duel*; *Jones and His New Neighbors*; *A Drunkard's*

D.W. Griffith

Reformation; *The Winning Coat*; *A Rude Hostess*; *The Road to the Heart*; *The Eavesdropper*; *Schneider's Anti-Noise Crusade*; *Twin Brothers*; *Confidence*; *The Note in the Shoe*; *Lucky Jim*; *A Sound Sleeper*; *A Troublesome Satchel*; *Tis an Ill Wind That Blows No Good*; *The Suicide Club*; *Resurrection*; *One Busy Hour*; *A Baby's Shoe*; *Eloping with Auntie*; *The Cricket on the Hearth*; *The Jilt*; *Eradicating Auntie*; *What Drink Did*; *Her First Biscuits*; *The Violin Maker of Cremona*; *Two Memories*; *The Lonely Villa*; *The Peach Basket Hat*; *The Son's Return*; *His Duty*; *A New Trick*; *The Necklace*; *The Way of Man*; *The Faded Lilies*; *The Message*; *The Friend of the Family*; *Was Justice Served?*; *Mrs. Jones' Lover* or *"I Want My Hat!"*; *The Mexican Sweethearts*; *The Country Doctor*; *Jealousy and the Man*; *The Renunciation*; *The Cardinal's Conspiracy*; *The Seventh Day*; *Tender Hearts*; *A Convict's Sacrifice*; *A Strange Meeting*; *Sweet and Twenty*; *The Slave*; *They Would Elope*; *Mrs. Jones' Burglar*; *The Mended Lute*; *The Indian Runner's Romance*; *With Her Card*; *The Better Way*; *His Wife's Visitor*; *The Mills of the Gods*; *Franks*; *Oh, Uncle*; *The Sealed Room*; *1776* or *The Hessian Renegades*; *The Little Darling*; *In Old Kentucky*; *The Children's Friend*; *Comata, the Sioux*; *Getting Even*; *The Broken Locket*; *A Fair Exchange*; *The Awakening*; *Pippa Passes*; *Leather Stockings*; *Fools of Fate*; *Wanted, a Child*; *The Little Teacher*; *A Change of Heart*; *His Lost Love*; *Lines of White on the Sullen Sea*; *The Gibson Goddess*; *In the Watches of the Night*; *The Expiation*; *What's Your Hurry*; *The Restoration*; *Nursing a Viper*; *Two Women and a Man*; *The Light that Came*; *A Midnight Adventure*; *The Open Gate*; *Sweet Revenge*; *The Mountaineer's Honor*; *In the Window Recess*; *The Trick That Failed*; *The Death Disc*; *Through the Breakers*; *In a Hempen Bag*; *A Corner in Wheat*; *The Redman's View*; *The Test*; *A Trap for Santa Claus*; *In Little Italy*; *To Save Her Soul*; *Choosing a Husband*; *The Rocky Road*; *The Dancing Girl of Butte*; *Her Terrible Ordeal*; *The Call*; *The Honor of His Family*; *On the Reef*; *The Last Deal*; *One Night, and Then—*; *The Cloister's Touch*; *The Woman from Mellon's*; *The Duke's Plan*; *The Englishman and the Girl*

1910 *The Final Settlement*; *His Last Burglary*; *Taming a Husband*; *The Newlyweds*; *The Thread of Destiny*; *In Old California*; *The Man*; *The Converts*; *Faithful*; *The Twisted Trail*; *Gold is Not All*; *As It Is in Life*; *A Rich Revenge*; *A Romance of the Western Hills*; *Thou Shalt Not*; *The Way of the World*; *The Unchanging Sea*; *The Gold Seekers*; *Love Among the Roses*; *The Two Brothers*; *Unexpected Help*; *An Affair of Hearts*; *Romona*; *Over Silent Paths*; *The Implement*; *In the Season of Buds*; *A Child of the Ghetto*; *In the Border States*; *A Victim of Jealousy*; *The Face at the Window*; *A Child's Impulse*; *The Marked Time-table*; *Muggsy's First Sweetheart*; *The Purgation*; *A Midnight Cupid*; *What the Daisy Said*; *A Child's Faith*; *The Call to Arms*; *Serious Sixteen*; *A Flash of Light*; *As the Bells Rang Out*; *An Arcadian Maid*; *The House with the Closed Shutters*; *Her Father's Pride*; *A Salutary Lesson*; *The Usurer*; *The Sorrows*

of the Unfaithful; In Life's Cycle; Wilful Peggy; A Summer
Idyll; The Modern Prodigal; Rose o' Salem Town; Little
Angels of Luck; A Mohawk's Way; The Oath and the Man;
The Iconoclast; Examination Day at School; That Chink at
Golden Gulch; The Broken Doll; The Banker's Daughters;
The Message of the Violin; Two Little Waifs; Waiter No.
Five; The Fugitive; Simple Charity; The Song of the
Wildwood Flute; A Child's Strategem; Sunshine Sue; A Plain
Song; His Sister-in-law; The Golden Supper; The Lesson;
When a Man Loves; Winning Back His Love; His Trust; His
Trust Fulfilled; A Wreath of Orange Blossoms; The Italian
Barber; The Two Paths; Conscience; Three Sisters; A Decree
of Destiny; Fate's Turning; What Shall We Do with Our
Old?; The Diamond Star; The Lily of the Tenements; Heart
Beats of Long Ago;

1911   Fisher Folks; His Daughter; The Lonedale Operator; Was He a
Coward?; Teaching Dad to Like Her; The Spanish Gypsy;
The Broken Cross; The Chief's Daughter; A Knight of the
Road; Madame Rex; His Mother's Scarf; How She
Triumphed; In the Days of '49; The Two Sides; The New
Dress; Enoch Arden, Part I; Enoch Arden, Part II; The
White Rose of the Wilds; The Crooked Road; A Romany
Tragedy; A Smile of a Child; The Primal Call; The Jealous
Husband; The Indian Brothers; The Thief and the Girl; Her
Sacrifice; The Blind Princess and the Poet; Fighting Blood;
The Last Drop of Water; Robby the Coward; A Country
Cupid; The Ruling Passion; The Rose of Kentucky; The
Sorrowful Example; Swords and Hearts; The Stuff Heroes
Are Made Of; The Old Confectioner's Mistake; The
Unveiling; The Eternal Mother; Dan the Dandy; The Revue
Man and the Girl; The Squaw's Love; Italian Blood; The
Making of a Man; Her Awakening; The Adventures of Billy;
The Long Road; The Battle; Love in the Hills; The Trail of
the Books; Through Darkened Vales; Saved from Himself;
A Woman Scorned; The Miser's Heart; The Failure;
Sunshine Through the Dark; As in a Looking Glass; A
Terrible Discovery; A Tale of the Wilderness; The Voice of
the Child; The Baby and the Stork; The Old Bookkeeper; A
Sister's Love; For His Son; The Transformation of Mike; A
Blot on the 'Scutcheon; Billy's Strategem; The Sunbeam; A
String of Pearls; The Root of Evil;

1912   The Mender of the Nets; Under Burning Skies; A Siren of
Impulse; Iola's Promise; The Goddess of Sagebrush Gulch;
The Girl and Her Trust; The Punishment; Fate's
Interception; The Female of the Species; Just Like a Woman;
One is Business, the Other Crime; The Lesser Evil; The Old
Actor; A Lodging for the Night; His Lesson; When Kings
Were the Law; A Beast at Bay; An Outcast Among Outcasts;
Home Folks; A Temporary Truce; The Spirit Awakened;
Lena and the Geese; An Indian Summer; The Schoolteacher
and the Waif; Man's Lust for Gold; Man's Genesis; Heaven
Avenges; A Pueblo Legend; The Sands of Dee; Black Sheep;
The Narrow Road; A Child's Remorse; The Inner Circle; A
Change of Spirit; An Unseen Enemy; Two Daughters of Eve;
Friends; So Near, Yet So Far; A Feud in the Kentucky Hills;
In the Aisles of the Wild; The One She Loved; The Painted
Lady; The Musketeers of Pig Alley; Heredity; Gold and
Glitter; My Baby; The Informer; The Unwelcome Guest;
Pirate Gold; Brutality; The New York Hat; The Massacre;
My Hero; Oil and Water; The Burglar's Dilemma; A Cry for
Help; The God Within; Three Friends; The Telephone Girl
and the Lady; Fate; An Adventure in the Autumn Woods; A
Chance Deception; The Tender Hearted Boy; A
Misappropriated Turkey; Brothers; Drink's Lure; Love in
an Apartment Hotel

1913   Broken Ways; A Girl's Strategem; Near to Earth; A Welcome
Intruder; The Sheriff's Baby; The Hero of Little Italy; The
Perfidy of Mary; A Misunderstood Boy; The Little Tease;
The Lady and the Mouse; The Wanderer; The House of
Darkness; Olaf—An Atom; Just Gold; His Mother's Son;
The Yaqui Cur; The Ranchero's Revenge; A Timely
Interception; Death's Marathon; The Sorrowful Shore; The
Mistake; The Mothering Heart; Her Mother's Oath; During
the Round-up; The Coming of Angelo; An Indian's Loyalty;
Two Men of the Desert; The Reformers or The Lost Art of

Minding One's Business; The Battle at Elderbush Gulch
(released 1914); In Prehistoric Days (original title: Wars of
the Primal Tribes, and released as Brute Force); Judith of
Bethulia (+ sc) (released 1914)

Films as Director:
(after quitting Biograph):

1914   The Battle of the Sexes; The Escape; Home, Sweet Home; The
Avenging Conscience
1915   **The Birth of a Nation** (+ co-sc, co-music)
1916   **Intolerance** (+ co-music)
1918   Hearts of the World (+ sc under pseudonyms, co-music
arranger); The Great Love (+ co-sc); The Greatest Thing in
Life (+ co-sc)
1919   A Romance of Happy Valley (+ sc); The Girl Who Stayed at
Home; True-Heart Susie; Scarlet Days; **Broken Blossoms** (+
sc, co-music arranger); The Greatest Question
1920   The Idol Dancer; The Love Flower; **Way Down East**
1921   Dream Street (+ sc); Orphans of the Storm
1922   One Exciting Night (+ sc)
1923   The White Rose (+ sc)
1924   America: Isn't Life Wonderful (+ sc)
1925   Sally of the Sawdust
1926   That Royle Girl; The Sorrows of Satan
1928   Drums of Love; The Battle of the Sexes
1929   Lady of the Pavements
1930   Abraham Lincoln
1931   The Struggle (+ pr, co-music arranger)

Publications:

By GRIFFITH: books—

The Rise and Fall of Free Speech in America, Los Angeles, 1916;
reprinted, 1967.
The Man Who Invented Hollywood: The Autobiography of D.W. Griffith, edited by James Hart, Louisville, Kentucky, 1972.

By GRIFFITH: articles—

"What I Demand of Movie Stars," in Motion Picture Magazine (Los
Angeles), February 1917.
"The Motion Picture Today—and Tomorrow," in Theatre Magazine
(New York), October 1929.
"An Old Timer Advises Hollywood," in Liberty (New York), 17 June
1939.

On GRIFFITH: books—

Hastings, Charles, and Herman Holland, A Biography of David Wark
Griffith, New York, 1920.
Trauberg, Leonid, and Georg Ronen, David Griffith, Moscow, 1926.
Huff, Theodore, A Shot Analysis of D.W. Griffith's Birth of a Nation,
New York, 1961.
Barry, Iris, and Eileen Bowser, D.W. Griffith: American Film Master,
New York, 1965.
Mitry, Jean, Griffith, in Anthologie du Cinéma, Paris, 1966.
Brownlow, Kevin, The Parade's Gone By, New York and London,
1968.
Gish, Lillian, The Movies, Mr. Griffith, and Me, with Ann Pinchot,
Englewood Cliffs, New Jersey, 1969.
Henderson, Robert, D.W. Griffith: The Years at Biograph, New York,
1970.
O'Dell, Paul, Griffith and the Rise of Hollywood, New York, 1970.
Geduld, Harry, editor, Focus on D.W. Griffith, Englewood Cliffs,
New Jersey, 1971.
Lahue, Kalton, Dreams for Sale: The Rise and Fall of the Triangle Film
Corporation, New York, 1971.
Henderson, Robert, D.W. Griffith: His Life and Work, New York,
1972.
Bowser, Eileen, editor, The Biograph Bulletins 1908–1912, New
York, 1973.
Brown, Karl, Adventures with D.W. Griffith, New York, 1973.
Niver, Kemp, D.W. Griffith: His Biograph Films in Perspective, Los
Angeles, 1974.

Wagenknecht, Edward, and Anthony Slide, *The Films of D.W. Griffith*, New York, 1975.
Williams, Martin, *Griffith: First Artist of the Movies*, New York, 1980.
Brion, Patrick, editor, *D.W. Griffith*, Paris, 1982.
Brown, Karl, *Adventures with D.W. Griffith*, edited by Kevin Brownlow, London, 1983; revised edition, 1988.
Mottet, Jean, editor, *D.W. Griffith: Colloque International*, Paris, 1984.
Schickel, Richard, *D.W. Griffith: An American Life*, New York, 1984; as *D.W. Griffith and the Birth of Film*, London, 1984.
Graham, Cooper C., and others, *D.W. Griffith and the Biograph Company*, Metuchen, New Jersey, 1985.
Drew, William M., *D.W. Griffith's Intolerance: Its Genesis and Its Vision*, Jefferson, North Carolina, 1986.
Jesionowski, Joyce E., *Thinking in Pictures: Dramatic Structures in D.W. Griffith's Biograph Films*, Berkeley, 1987.
Lang, Robert, *American Film Melodrama: Griffith, Vidor, Minnelli*, New Jersey, 1989.
Elsaesser, Thomas, and Adam Barker, editors, *Early Cinema: Space-Frame-Narrative*, London, 1990.

On GRIFFITH: articles—

Gordon, Henry Stephen, "The Story of D.W. Griffith," in *Photoplay* (New York), June through November 1916.
Feldman, Joseph and Harry, "The D.W. Griffith Influence," in *Films in Review* (New York), July/August 1950.
Eisenstein, Sergei, "Dickens, Griffith and the Film Today," in *Film Form*, New York, 1949; also in *Sight and Sound* (London), June, July, and November 1950.
Stern, Seymour, "The Cold War Against D.W. Griffith," in *Films in Review* (New York), February 1956.
Pratt, George, "In the Nick of Time, D.W. Griffith and the Last-Minute Rescue," in *Image* (Rochester, New York), 2 May 1959.
"*Birth of a Nation* Issue" of *Film Culture* (New York), Summer 1965.
Batman, Richard, "D.W. Griffith: The Lean Years," in *California Historical Society Quarterly*, September 1965.
Silverstein, Norman, "D.W. Griffith and Anarchy in American Films," in *Salmagundi* (New York), Winter 1966.
Meyer, Richard, "The Films of David Wark Griffith: The Development of Themes and Techniques in 42 of His Films," in *Film Comment* (New York), Fall/Winter 1967.
Casty, Alan, "The Films of D.W. Griffith: A Style of the Times," in *Journal of Popular Film* (Bowling Green, Ohio), Spring 1972.
"Griffith Issues" of *Cahiers de la Cinémathèque* (Lyons), Spring 1972 and Christmas 1975.
"Griffith Issue" of *Ecran* (Paris), February 1973.
"Griffith Issue" of *Filmkritik* (Berlin), April 1975.
"Griffith Issue" of *Filmcritica* (Rome), May/June 1975.
"Griffith Issue" of *Films in Review* (New York), October 1975.
"Special Issues" of *Griffithiana* (Genoa), March/July 1980 and January 1982.
Merritt, Russell, "Rescued from a Perilous Nest: D.W. Griffith's Escape from Theatre into Film," in *Cinema Journal* (Evanston), Fall 1981.
Merritt, Russell, "D.W. Griffith Directs the Great War: The Making of *Hearts of the World*," in *Quarterly Review of Film Studies* (Salisbury, Maryland), Winter 1981.
"Griffith Issue" of *Avant-Scène du Cinéma* (Paris), 15 February 1983.
"Griffith Sections" of *Positif* (Paris), December 1982, March 1983 and April 1983.
Gunning, Thom, "The Movies, Mr. Griffith, and Us," in *American Film* (Washington, D.C.), June 1984.
Corliss, Richard, and Richard Schickel, "Writing in Silence," in *Film Comment* (New York), July/August 1985.
Neilan, Marshall, and R.S. Birchard, "Griffith—An Untold Chapter," in *American Cinematographer* (Los Angeles), January 1986.
Doty, Alexander, "D.W. Griffith's Poetics of Place and the Rural Ideal," in *Journal of Comparative Poetics*, Spring 1986.
Keil, Charles, "Transition through Tension: Stylistic Diversity in the Late Griffith Biographs," in *Cinema Journal* (Evanston), Spring 1989.
Literature/Film Quarterly (Salisbury, Maryland), vol. 18, no. 2, 1990.

* * *

Perhaps no other director has generated such a broad range of critical reaction as D.W. Griffith. For students of the motion picture, Griffith's is the most familiar name in film history. Generally acknowledged as America's most influential director (and certainly one of the most prolific), he is also perceived as being among the most limited. Praise for his mastery of film technique is matched by repeated indictments of his moral, artistic, and intellectual inadequacies. At one extreme, Kevin Brownlow has characterized him as "the only director in America creative enough to be called a genius." At the other, Paul Rotha calls his contribution to the advance of film "negligible" and Susan Sontag complains of his "supreme vulgarity and even inanity"; his work "reeks of a fervid moralizing about sexuality and violence" and his energy comes "from suppressed voluptuousness."

Griffith started his directing career in 1908, and in the following five years made some 485 films, almost all of which have been preserved. These films, one or two reels in length, have customarily been regarded as apprentice works, films in which, to quote Stephen Zito, "Griffith borrowed, invented, and perfected the forms and techniques that he later used to such memorable effect in *The Birth of a Nation, Intolerance, Broken Blossoms*, and *Way Down East*." These early "Biographs" (named after the studio at which Griffith worked) have usually been studied for their stylistic features, notably parallel editing, camera placement, and treatment of light and shadow. Their most famous structuring devices are the last-minute rescue and the cross-cut.

In recent years, however, the Biographs have assumed higher status in film history. Many historians and critics rank them with the most accomplished work in Griffith's career. Vlada Petric, for instance, calls them "masterpieces of early cinema, fascinating lyrical films which can still affect audiences today, conveying the content in a cinematic manner often more powerful than that of Griffith's later feature films."

Scholars have begun studying them for their characters, images, narrative patterns, themes, and ideological values, finding in them a distinctive signature based on Griffith's deep-seated faith in the values of the woman-centered home. Certain notable Biographs—*The Musketeers of Pig Alley, The Painted Lady, A Corner in Wheat, The Girl and Her Trust, The Battle of Elderbush Gulch, The Unseen Enemy*, and *A Feud in the Kentucky Hills*—have been singled out for individual study.

Griffith reached the peak of his popularity and influence in the five years between 1915 and 1920, when he released *The Birth of a Nation, Intolerance, Broken Blossoms*, and *Way Down East*. Each of these films is examined individually in volume 1, *Films*. He also directed *Hearts of the World* during this period, a First World War propaganda epic which, alone among his early spectacles, is ignored today. But in 1918 it was the most popular war film of its time, and rivalled *The Birth of a Nation* as the most profitable of all Griffith's features. Today, it is usually studied as an example of World War I hysteria or as a pioneering effort at government-sponsored mass entertainment which incorporates newsreel and faked documentary footage into an epic fictional narrative.

Although Griffith's epics are generally grouped together, Paul Goodman points out that his films are neither so ideologically uniform nor so consistent as recent writers have generally assumed. With equal fervor Griffith could argue white supremacy and make pleas for toleration, play the liberal crusader and the reactionary conservative, appear tradition-bound yet remain open to experimentation, saturate his work in Victorian codes while struggling against a Victorian morality. Frustrated by his inability to find consistent ideological threads in Griffith's work, Norman Silverstein has called

Griffith the father of anarchy in American films because his luminous movements in these epics never appear to sustain a unified whole.

Yet, as Robert Lang observes, the epics do share broad formal characteristics, using history as a chaotic background for a fictional drama that stresses separation and reunification. Whether set in the French Revolution (*Orphans of the Storm*), the American Revolution (*America*), the Civil War (*Birth of a Nation*), or in the various epochs of *Intolerance*, the Griffith epic is an action-centered spectacle that manipulates viewer curiosity with powerfully propulsive, intrinsically developmental scenes culminating in a sensational denouement.

Griffith made a much different sort of feature during these years which only recently has received serious critical attention—the pastoral romance. In these films stripped of spectacle and historical surroundings, the cast of principal characters does not exceed two or three, the action is confined in time and space, and the story is intimate. Here, in films like *Romance of Happy Valley*, *True-heart Susie*, and *The Greatest Question*, Griffith experiments with alternative narrative possibilities, whereby he extends the techniques of exposition to the length of a feature film. Strictly narrative scenes in these films are suspended or submerged to convey the illusion of near-plotlessness. The main figures, Griffith implied (usually played by Lillian Gish and Bobby Harron), would emerge independent of fable; atmosphere would dominate over story line.

From the start, critics and reviewers found the near absence of action sequences and overt physical struggle noteworthy in the Griffith pastorals, but differed widely in their evaluation of it. Most of the original commentators assumed they had found a critical shortcoming, and complained about the thinness of plot, padded exposition, and frequent repetition of shots. Even Kenneth MacGowan, who alone among his contemporaries preferred Griffith's pastorals to his epics, scored the empty storyline of *The Romance of Happy Valley* for its "loose ends and dangling characters." More recent critics, on the other hand—notably Jean Mitry, John Belton, and Rene Kerdyk—have found transcendental virtues in the forswearing of event-centered plots. Ascribing to Griffith's technique a liberating moral purpose, Mitry called *True-heart Susie* "a narrative which follows characters without entrapping them, allowing them complete freedom of action and event." For John Belton, *True-heart Susie* is one of Griffith's "purest and most immediate films" because, "lacking a 'great story' there is nothing between us and the characters." Equating absence of action sequences with the elimination of formal structure, Belton concludes that "it is through the characters not plot that Griffith expresses and defines the nature of the characters' separation."

If these judgments appear critically naive (plainly these films have plots and structures even if these are less complex than in *Intolerance* and *Birth*), they raise important questions Griffith scholars continue to debate: how does Griffith create the impression that characters exist independent of action, and, in a temporal medium, how does Griffith create the impression of narrative immobility?

By and large, Griffith's films of the mid-and late-1920s have not fared well critically, although they have their defenders. The customary view—that Griffith's work became dull and undistinguished when he lost his personal studio at Mamaroneck in 1924—continues to prevail, despite calls from John Dorr, Arthur Lennig, and Richard Roud for re-evaluation. The eight films he made as a contract director for Paramount and United Artists are usually studied (if at all) as examples of late 1920s studio style. What critics find startling about them—particularly the United Artists features—is not the lack of quality, but the absence of any identifiable Griffith traits. Only *Abraham Lincoln* and *The Struggle* (Griffith's two sound films) are recognizable as his work, and they are usually treated as early 1930s oddities.

—Russell Merritt

GUERRA, Ruy.

Mozambiquian. Born in Lourenço Marques, Mozambique, 22 August 1931. Educated in Mozambique and Portugal; attended I.D.H.E.C., Paris, 1952–54; Théâtre National Populaire, 1955. Assistant director in Paris, 1956–57; invited to direct *Joana* (unrealized), in Brazil, 1958; remained in Brazil until returning to Paris, 1967; following independence of Mozambique, returned to help plan film industry, late 1970's.

Films as Director:

1954   *Les Hommes et les autres* (+ sc) (short, IDHEC diploma work)
1960   *Oros* (+ sc) (short, unfinished)
1961   *O cavalo de Oxumaire* (*The Horse of Oxumaire*) (co-d, + co-sc, unfinished)
1962   *Os cafajestes* (*The Unscrupulous Ones*) (+ co-sc)
1964   *Os fuzis* (**The Guns**) (+ co-sc, co-ed)
1967   "Vocabulaire" episode of *Loin du Viêt-nam* (not included in released version) (+ sc)
1969   *Sweet Hunters* (+ co-sc)
1970   *Os deuses e os mortos* (*The Gods and the Dead*) (+ co-sc, co-ed)
1978   *A queda* (*The Fall*) (co-d, + co-sc, co-music, co-ed)
1979   *Mueda, memória e massacre* (*Mueda, Memory and Massacre*) (+ co-ph, ed)
1983   *Erendira* (+ sc)
1986   *Opera do Malandro*
1988   *Fábula de la bella palomera* (*Fable of the Beautiful Pigeon-Fancier*)

Other Films:

1955   *Souvenir de Paris* (Théocary) (asst d); *Chiens perdus, sans collier* (Delannoy) (asst d)
1957   *S.O.S. Noronha* (Rouquier) (asst d, role)
1958   *Le Tout pour le tout* (Dally) (asst d)
1963   *Os mendigos* (role)
1969   *Benito Cereno* (Roullet) (role)
1970   *Le Maître du temps* (Pollet) (role); *Le Mur* (Roullet) (role)
1971   *Les Soleils de l'Ile de Pâques* (Kast) (role); *O homem das estrelas* (*Man and the Stars*) (Barreto) (role)
1972   *Aguirre, der Zorn Göttes* (*Aguirre, the Wrath of God*) (Herzog) (role)

Publications:

By GUERRA: articles—

Interview with J.A. Fieschi and J. Narboni, in *Cahiers du Cinéma* (Paris), April 1967.
Interview with Thomas Elsaesser, in *Monogram* (London), no. 5, 1974.
Interview with Rui Nogueira, in *Image et Son* (Paris), December 1974.
"Filmen in Mozambique," interview with F. Sartor, in *Film en Televisie* (Brussels), May/June 1981.
Interview with Michel Ciment, in *Positif* (Paris), June 1983.
Interview with Serge Toubiana, in *Cahiers du Cinéma* (Paris), December 1983.
Interview with M. Buruiana, in *24 Images* (Montréal), Winter 1987.

Ruy Guerra: *Os deuses e os mortos*

On GUERRA: books—

Johnson, Randal, *Cinema Novo x 5: Masters of Contemporary Brazilian Film*, Austin, Texas, 1984.

On GUERRA: articles—

Mardore, Michel, "Diaphragme à quatre," in *Cahiers du Cinéma* (Paris), November 1964.
Ciment, Michel, "Le Dieu, le diable et les fusils," in *Positif* (Paris), May 1967.
Zele, Van, "*Os Fuzis*," in *Image et Son* (Paris), November 1969.
Demeure, Jacques, "Pour un réalisme magique," in *Positif* (Paris), January 1971.
"Le 'cinema nôvo' brésilien Issue" of *Études Cinématographiques* (Paris), no. 93–96, 1972.
"Ruy Guerra," in *Film Dope* (London), March 1981.

*   *   *

A truly cosmopolitan artist, Ruy Guerra was born in Mozambique of Portuguese settlers, got a higher education in Lisbon, and studied cinema at the the Paris I.D.H.E.C. He was one of the leaders of the Brazilian *cinema novo* with two films that broke new ground both ethical and aesthetic, *Os cafajestes* and *Os fuzis*. He shot *Sweet Hunters*, in French and in English, and went back to Mozambique after it became independent to organize the newly born cinema industry and to shoot a documentary, *Mueda, memória e massacre* before going to Mexico to adapt Gabriel García Marquez's *Erendira* in 1983. Besides writing his own scripts, Guerra is the author of lyrics for Latin American pop songs (sung in particular by Baden Powell), and an actor in his own right (he plays in Herzog's *Aguirre* and in Serge Roullet's adaptation of *Benito Cereno*).

The product of a cultural melting pot, Guerra's style is hard to define. Very classical in form (except in the extraordinary *Os deuses e os mortes*, the epitome of Brazilian tropicalist aesthetics with virtuoso camera movements and sequence shots), it shows none of the *external* signs of modernity such as non-chronological sequences, manipulation of the sound track, or elaborate framing. On the other hand, it displays a very unusual use of rhythm, and makes use of great variety of tempos akin to that found in some Japanese films such as those of Kurosawa.

Guerra is preoccupied, even obsessed with the theme of frustration and disappointed expectations. Guerra's interest in social issues is already evident in his first film, *Os cafajestes*, about penniless young loafers in Rio who blackmail a girl after having taken photos of her in the nude. *Os fuzis*, set in the northeast of Brazil, opposes a sergeant and four soldiers guarding a harvest destined for town (to profit the landowner mayor) and the covetous desires of hungry peasants. Thirteen years later Guerra shot a sequel, *A queda* (*The Fall*), with the same actors to show what happened to the characters after a decade spent in the big city.

Os deuses e os mortes presents in grand operatic manner a feud between two families of farmers. This film reveals another aspect of Guerra's personality: a taste for magic and dream, an interest in myths and surrealism. The economic and the psychic are bound together in this difficult and fascinating work. *Sweet Hunters*, Guerra's most poetic film (with Sterling Hayden, Susan Strasberg, and Stuart Whitman), is set on an island where the three characters act out their obsessions and frustrated desires. Allan, a keen ornithologist, is waiting for the migration of birds, his wife Clea for the arrival of a man who has escaped from a nearby prison, and his sister for her departure. Very logically, Guerra was picked to adapt García Marquez's novella *Erendira* set in an imaginary country where a mythical and monstrous grandmother (Irene Pappas) sells her granddaughter as a prostitute. A picaresque tale of economic exploitation, with ironical characters and nightmarish situations, it offers a good synthesis of Guerra's style even if the faithfulness of his adaptation does not allow him to give full vent to his ordinarily richer and more personal inspiration.

—Michel Ciment

GUITRY, Sacha.

French. Born Alexandre-Georges Pierre Guitry in St. Petersburg, Russia, 21 February 1885. Educated at Lycée Jeanson-de-Sailly, St. Petersburg, 1894, then at 12 different schools until 1902. Married 1) Charlotte Lysès, 1907 (divorced); 2) Yvonne Printemps, 1919 (divorced); 3) Jacqueline Delubac, 1935 (divorced); 4) Geneviève de Séréville, 1942 (divorced); 5) Lana Marconi, 1949. Debut as actor, with father Lucien Guitry, 1904; playwright and stage actor, through 1930's; directed first feature, *Bonne Chance*, 1935; arrested for collaborating with the Nazis, released after 2 months, 1944; officially cleared of charges, ban on work lifted, 1947. Recipient: Chevalier de la Légion d'Honneur, 1923; Commander of the Légion d'Honneur, 1936; elected to the Goncourt Academy, 1939; Grande Médaille d'Or de la Société des Auteurs, 1955. *Died in Paris, 24 July 1957.*

Films as Director:

1915   *Ceux de chez nous* (+ sc, ph)
1935   *Pasteur* (co-d, + sc, role as Pasteur); *Bonne chance* (+ sc, role as Claude)
1936   *Le Nouveau Testament* (+ sc, role as Jean Marcelin); *Le Roman d'un tricheur* (*The Story of a Cheat*) (+ sc, role as the cheat); *Mon Père avait raison* (+ sc, role as Charles Bellanger); *Faisons un rêve* (+ sc, role as He)
1937   *Le Mot de Cambronne* (+ sc, role as Cambronne); *Les Perles de la couronne* (*Pearls of the Crown*) (+ sc, role as François I, Barras, Napoleon III, Jean Martin); *Désiré* (+ sc, role as Désiré Tronchais)
1938   *Quadrille* (+ sc, role as Philippe de Moranes); *Remontons les Champs-Elysées* (+ sc, role as the teacher, Louis XV, Ludovic at 54 years of age, Jean-Louis at 54, Napoleon III)
1939   *Ils étaient neuf célibataires* (+ sc, role as Jea Lécuyer)
1942   *Le Destin fabuleux de Desirée Clary* (+ sc, role as Napoleon I)
1943   *Donne-moi tes yeux* (+ sc, role as François Bressoles)
1944   *La Malibran* (+ sc, role as M. Malibran)
1948   *Le Comédien* (+ sc, role as Lucien Guitry at 40)
1949   *Le Diable boiteux* (+ sc, role as Talleyrand); *Aux deux colombes* (+ sc, role as Jean-Pierre Walter); *Toâ* (+ sc, role as Michel Desnoyers)
1950   *Le Trésor de Cantenac* (+ sc, role as Baron de Cantenac); *Tu m'as sauvé la vie* (+ sc, role as Baron de Saint-Rambert)
1951   *Deburau* (+ sc, role as Jean-Gaspard Deburau); *La Poison* (+ sc)
1952   *Je l'ai été trois fois* (+ sc, role as Jean Renneval)
1953   *La Vie d'un honnête homme* (+ sc)
1954   *Si Versailles m'etait conté* (+ sc, role as Louis XIV)
1955   *Napoléon* (+ sc, role as Talleyrand)
1956   *Si Paris nous était conté* (+ sc)
1957   *Assassins et voleurs* (+ sc); *Les Trois font la paire* (+ sc)

Other Films:

1918   *Un Roman d'amour . . . et d'aventures* (Hervil and Mercanton) (role)
1931   *Le Blanc et le noir* (+ sc)
1935   *Les Deux coverts* (+ sc)
1938   *L'Accroche-coeur* (+ sc); *Bluebeard's Eighth Wife* (Lubitsch) (guest appearance as man leaving hotel with girl on arm)
1951   *Adhemar* or *Le Jouet de la fatalité* (+ sc)
1958   *La Vie à deux* (sc)

Publications:

By GUITRY: books—

Si j'ai bonne mémoire, Paris, 1934.
Mémoires d'un tricheur, Paris, 1935.
De Jeanne d'Arc à Philippe Pétain, Paris, 1944.
Toutes réflexions faites, Paris, 1947.
Le Comédien, Paris, 1948.
Et Versailles vous est conté, Paris, 1954.
Théâtre, je t'adore!, Paris, 1958.
Les Femmes et l'amour, Paris, 1959.
Théâtre, Volumes I–XIV, Paris, 1959/62.
Le Cinéma et moi, Paris, 1977.
Le Petit Carnet rouge et autres souvenirs inedits, Paris, 1979.
A bâtons rompus, Paris, 1981.

On GUITRY: books—

Madis, Alex, *Sacha*, Paris, 1950.
Prince, Stéphane, *Sacha Guitry hors sa légende*, Paris, 1959.
Lauwick, Hervé, *Sacha Guitry et les femmes*, Paris, 1965.
Sicilier, Jacques, *Sacha Guitry*, in *Anthologie du Cinéma II*, Paris, 1967.
Harding, James, *Sacha Guitry: The Last Boulevardier*, New York, 1968.
Lorcey, Jacques, *Sacha Guitry par les témoins de sa vie*, Paris, 1976.
Knapp, Bettina, *Sacha Guitry*, Boston, 1981.
Lorcey, Jacques, *Sacha Guitry: L'Homme et l'oeuvre*, Paris, 1982.
Lorcey, Jacques, *Sacha Guitry: Cent ans de théâtre et d'esprit*, Paris, 1985.
Simsolo, Nöel, *Sacha Guitry*, Paris, 1988.

On GUITRY: articles—

Obituary, in the *New York Times*, 24 July 1957.
Marcorelles, Louis, "Sacha Guitry," in *Sight and Sound* (London), Autumn 1957.
"Guitry Issue" of *Cahiers du Cinéma* (Paris), no. 173, 1965.
"Guitry Issue" of *Revue du Cinéma* (Paris), vol. 3, 1971.
Fieschi, J., "La Mise en pièce du film," in *Cinématographe* (Paris), no. 40, 1978.
Adair, Gilbert, "Sacha, an Introduction to Guitry," in *Sight and Sound* (London), Winter 1980/81.
Dossier on Guitry, in *Cinématographe* (Paris), February 1983.
Tesson, C., "Le Convive des dernières fates," in *Cahiers du Cinéma* (Paris), January 1984.
Viviani, C., "Sur quatre films de Sacha Guitry," in *Positif* (Paris), January 1984.
Gauteur, C., "Harry Baur/Sacha Guitry ou la croisée des destins," in *Cinéma* (Paris), May 1984.
"Sacha: An introduction to Guitry," in *National Film Theatre Booklet* (London), September/October 1985.

On GUITRY: films—

Prince, Stéphane, *Le Musée de Sacha Guitry* (short)
de Givray, Claude, *Cinéastes de notre temps: Sacha Guitry*, for TV, France, 1965.

*   *   *

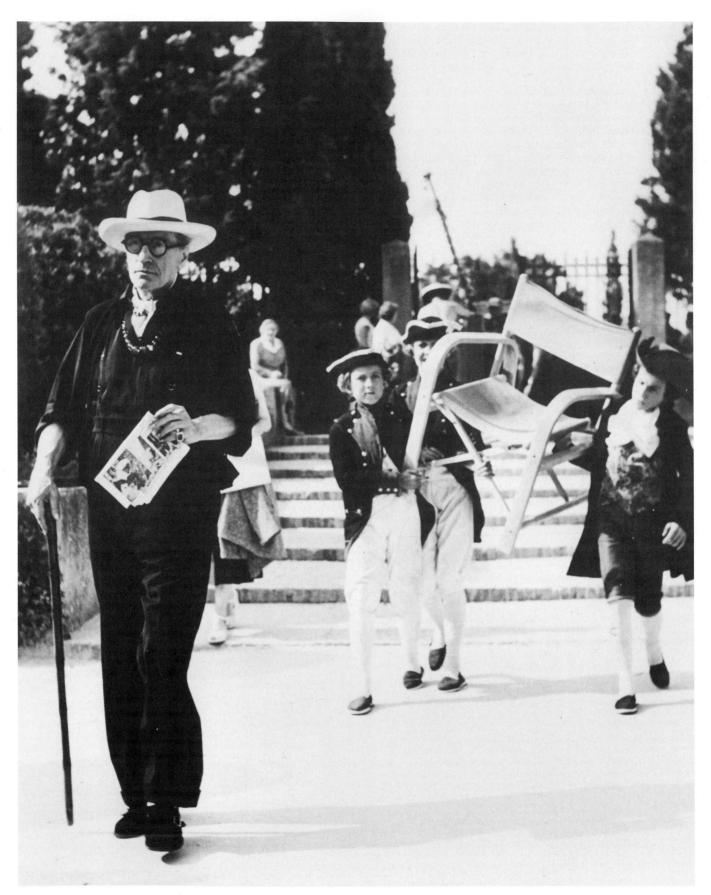

Sacha Guitry

Values change and time plays tricks on one's memory of how it really was. Back in the early 1930's, when talking pictures were gaining a foothold in this country and all foreign nations were exhibiting their product in America, it seemed as if there were nobody in films as charming, witty, and multi-talented as Sacha Guitry. His films made in France appeared at all the best art houses; he was a delightful actor, a director with a Lubitsch-like wit, and a writer of amusing sophisticated comedy. Seeing his films today in revival, they don't seem that funny; they are old-fashioned and often dull; and his preoccupation with sex is too often mere lechery. Only two films are still diamond-bright: one that he co-directed with Christian-Jaque, *Les Perles de la couronne*, and *Le Roman d'un tricheur*.

The first has a narrative device that enables Guitry to skip back and forth from one century to another and from one country to another, and still keep the story clear and funny; the second is a razor-sharp treatise on the rewards of dishonesty. It involves a hero who as a young boy is punished by being sent to bed without dinner because of a lie he has told. Because he does not eat the meal that has been prepared, he lives while all other members of his family perish, having consumed a dish prepared from toad-stools rather than fresh mushrooms. In *Les Perles de la couronne* Guitry plays tricks with actual events and people. The comedy has a nice bite, and Guitry pulls off a narrative resolution that is masterly in its irony.

Sacha Guitry was once the toast of Paris, where one season he had as many as three plays running simultaneously. When he turned his talents to talking pictures, the medium seemed to have been invented expressly for his convenience. His father, Lucien Guitry, was France's greatest actor, and in time his talented son wrote two plays that his father turned into pure gold—*Pasteur* and *Mon Père avait raison*. In all, Sacha Guitry wrote more than a hundred plays; his films were often adaptations of these. Most were boudoir farces, remarkable in that they always seemed to work thanks to skillful construction, though they were also generally feather light and too often highly forgettable.

He married five actresses who all rose to prominence in whatever he wrote before he divorced them. The one who became a star in her own right was Yvonne Printcmps, the second actress he married; she divorced him finally to marry her leading man, handsome Pierre Fresnay, while Guitry that same year married a new leading lady, the beautiful Jacqueline Delubac.

In World War Two Guitry was trapped in Paris, and he was not permitted by the Nazis to act on the Parisian stage. After four years, when the Germans were forced to quit Paris, Guitry was arrested by a ridiculous quirk of fate for having collaborated with the enemy; he was released after two months, exonerated, and freed to go on with his career.

—DeWitt Bodeen

_____

GÜNEY, Yilmaz.

Turkish. Born Yilmaz Putun in village near Adana in southern Turkey, 1937. Educated in law in Ankara; studied economics in Istanbul. Worked for film distribution company, 1952; began working with director Atif Yilmaz, 1958; sentenced to 18 months in prison and 6 months exile for publishing "communist" novel *Equations with 3 Strangers*, 1961; began career in commercial cinema, as writer and actor, known as "Cirkin kral" ("The Ugly King"), 1963; founded Güney-Filmcilik production company, 1968; arrested on charge of sheltering wanted anarchist students, imprisoned without trial for 26 months, 1972 (released under general amnesty, 1974); alleged to have shot judge in restaurant, sentenced to 24 years hard labor (later commuted to 18 years); while in prison, allowed to continue scripting films and overseeing productions, 1974–80; films banned following military takeover, 1980; escaped to France, 1981, stripped of Turkish citizenship. Recipient: Best Film (co-recipient), Cannes Festival, for *Yol*, 1982. *Died of cancer, in Paris, 9 September 1984.*

Films as Director:

1966   *At avrat silah (The Horse, the Woman, and the Gun)* (+ sc, role)
1967   *Bana kursun islemez (Bullets Cannot Pierce Me)* (+ sc, role); *Benim adim Kerim (My Name Is Kerim)* (+ sc, role)
1968   *Pire Nuri (Nuri the Flea)* (co-d, + sc, role); *Seyyit Han "Topragin Gelini" (Seyyit Khan, Bride of the Earth)* (+ sc, role as Seyyit Han)
1969   *Ac kurtlar (The Hungry Wolves)* (+ sc, role); *Bir cirkin adam (An Ugly Man)* (+ sc, role)
1970   *Umut (Hope)* (+ co-sc, role as Cabar); *Piyade Osman (Osman the Wanderer)* (co-d, + sc, role); *Yedi belalilar (The Seven No-goods)* (co-d, + sc, role)
1971   *Kacaklar (The Fugitives)* (+ sc, role); *Vurguncular (The Wrongdoers)* (+ sc, role); *Ibret (The Example)* (co-d, + sc, role); *Yarin son gündür (Tomorrow Is the Final Day)* (+ sc, role); *Umutsuzlar (The Hopeless Ones)* (+ sc, role); *Aci (Pain)* (+ sc, role); *Ağit (Elegy)* (+ sc, role as Copanoğlu); *Baba (The Father)* (+ sc, role as Cemal, the Boatman)
1974   *Arkadas (The Friend)* (+ sc, role as the friend); *Endise (Anxiety)* (co-d, + sc)
1975   *Zavallilar (The Poor Ones)* (co-d, + co-sc, role as Abu) (begun 1972)
1982   *Le Mur (The Wall)* (+ sc, role)

Other Films:

1958   *Alageyik (The Hind)* (Yilmaz) (co-sc, role); *Bu vatanin cocuklari (The Children of This Country)* (Yilmaz) (co-sc, role)
1959   *Karacaoğlanin kara sevdasi (Karacaoğlan's Mad Love)* (Yilmaz) (co-sc); *Tütün zamani (Arlburnu)* (role)
1960   *Clum perdesi (The Screen of Death)* (Yilmaz) (asst d)
1961   *Dolandiricilar (The King of Thieves)* (Yilmaz) (asst d) *Kizil vazo (The Red Vase)* (Yilmaz) (asst d); *Seni kaybederesen (If I Lose You)* (Yilmaz) (asst d); *Yaban gülü (The Desert Laughs)* (Utku) (co-sc); *Dolandiricilar sahi* (Yilmaz) (role); *Tatli-Bela* (Yilmaz) (role)
1963   *Ölüme yalniz gidilar (The Dead Only Perish)* (Yalinkilic) (sc); *Ikisi de cesurdu (Two Brave Men)* (co-sc, role)
1964   *Hergün ölmektense* (Ceylan) (sc, role); *Kamali zeybek (Hero with a Knife)* (Akinci) (sc, role); *Dağlarin kurdu Kocero (Kocero, Mountain Wolf)* (Utku) (sc, role); *Halimeden mektup var* (Doğan) (role); *Kocaoğlan* (Demirel) (role); *Kara sahin* (Akinci) (role); *Mor defter* (Ergün) (role); *10 Korkusuz adam* (Basaran) (role); *Prangasiz mahkumlar* (Ariburnu) (role); *Zimba gibi delikanli* (Jöntürk) (role)
1965   *Kasimpasali* (Akinci) (sc, role); *Kasimpasali recep* (Akinci) (sc, role); *Konyakci (The Drunkard)* (Basaran) (sc, role); *Kirallar kirali (King of Kings)* (Olgac) (sc, role); *Ben öldükce yasarim* (Sağiroğlu) (role); *Beyaz atli adam* (Jöntürk) (role); *Dağlarin oğlu* (Atadeniz) (role); *Davudo* (Kazankaya) (role); *Gönül kusu* (Gülnar) (role); *Sayili kabadayilar* (Kazankaya) (role); *Kan Gövdeyi götürdü* (Atadeniz) (role); *Kahreden kursun* (Atadeniz) (role); *Haracima dokunma* (Kazankaya) (role); *Kanli buğday* (Ceylan) (role); *Korkuszlar* (Evin) (role); *Silaha yeminliydim* (Inci) (role); *Sokakta kan vardi* (Turkali) (role); *Tehlikeli adam* (Kazankaya) (role); *Torpido Yilmaz* (Okcugil) (role); *Ücünüzü de mihlarim* (Olgac) (role); *Yarali kartal* (Dursun) (role)

Yilmaz Güney: *The Hungry Wolves*

1966 *Burcak tarlasi* (Utku) (sc); *Aslanlarin dönüsü* (*Return of the Heroes*) (Atadeniz) (sc, role); *Esrefpasali* (Tokatli) (sc, role); *Hudutlarin kanunu* (*The Law of Smuggling*) (Akad) (sc, role); *Yedi dağin aslani* (*Seven Wild Lions. The Mountain King*) (Atadeniz) (sc, role); *Tilki Selim* (*Crafty Selim*) (Hancer) (sc, role); *Aanasi yiğit doğurmus* (Kurthan) (role); *Cirkin kiral* (Atadeniz) (role); *Kovboy Ali* (Atadeniz) (role); *Silahlarin kanunu* (Atadeniz) (role); . . . *Veda silahlara veda* . . . (Jöntürk) (role); *Yiğit yarali olur* (Görec) (role)

1967 *At hirsizi banus* (Jöntürk) (sc, role); *Seytanin oğlu* (Aslan) (sc, role); *Balatli arif* (Yilmaz) (role); *Bomba Kemal* (Kurthan) (role); *Büyük cellatlar* (Duru) (role); *Cirkin kiral affetmez* (Atadeniz) (role); *Eskiya celladi* (Jöntürk) (role); *Ince cumali* (Duru) (role); *Kizilirmak-Karakoyun* (Akad) (role); *Kozanoğlu* (Yilmaz) (role); *Kuduz recep* (Sağirğlu) (role); *Kurbanlik katil* (Akad) (role)

1968 *Azrail benim* (*The Executioner*) (sc, role); *Kargaci Halil* (*Halil, the Crow-Man*) (Yalinkilic) (sc, role); *Aslan bey* (Yalinkilic) (role); *Beyoğlu canavari* (Görec) (role); *Canpazari* (Görec) (role); *Marmara hasan* (Aslan) (role); *Öldürmek hakkimdir* (Ergün) (role)

1969 *Belanin yedi türlüsü* (*Seven Kinds of Trouble*) (Ergün) (sc, role); *Bin defa ölürüm* (Aslan) (role); *Cifte tabancali kabadayi* (Aslan) (role); *Güney ölüm saciyor* (Aslan) (role); *Kan su gibi akacak* (Atadeniz) (role); *Kursunlarin kanunu* (Ergün) (role)

1970 *Imzam kanla yazilir* (*I Sign in Blood*) (Aslan) (sc, role); *Sevgili muhafizin* (*My Dear Bodyguard*) (Jöntürk) (sc, role); *Seytan kayaliklari* (*Devil Crag*) (Filmer) (sc, role); *Cifte yürekli* (Evin) (role); *Kanimin son damlasina kadar* (Figenli) (role); *Onu Allah affetsin* (Elmas) (role); *Son kizgin adam* (Davutoğlu) (role); *Zeyno* (Yilmaz) (role)

1971 *Cirkin ve cesur* (Ozer) (role); *Namus ve silah* (Görec) (role)

1972 *Sabte yar* (Görec) (role)

1975 *Izin* (Leave) (Gürsü) (sc); *Bir gün mutlaka* (*One Day Certainly*) (Olgac) (sc)

1978 *Sürü* (*The Herd*) (Ökten) (sc, pr supervision)

1979 *Düsman* (*The Enemy*) (Ökten) (sc, pr supervision)

1981 *Yol* (*The Way*) (sc, pr supervision, ed)

Publications:

By GÜNEY: articles—

"Entretien avec Yilmaz Güney (1977)," in *Positif* (Paris), April 1980.

Interview with Michel Ciment, in *Positif* (Paris), June 1982.

Interview with Marcel Martin, in *Image et Son* (Paris), July–August 1982.

"Güney's last journey," an interview with C. Gardner, in *Stills* (London), October 1984.

On GÜNEY: books—

Armes, Roy, *Third World Filmmaking and the West*, Berkeley, 1987.

On GÜNEY: articles—

Weales, G. "Istanbul Journal," in *Film Comment* (New York), January/February 1975.

Kazan, Elia, "The View from a Turkish Prison," in *New York Times Magazine*, 4 February 1979.

"Guney Issue" of *Positif* (Paris), April 1980.

Armes, Roy, "Yilmaz Guney: The Limits of Individual Action," in *Framework* (Norwich), Summer 1981.

Elley, Derek, "Yilmaz Güney," in *International Film Guide 1983*, London, 1982.

Giles, D., and H. Sahin, "Revolutionary Cinema in Turkey: Yilmaz Güney," in *Jump Cut* (Berkeley), July 1982.

Rayns, Tony, "From Isolation," in *Sight and Sound* (London), Spring 1983, Bassan, R., "*Le Mur*: L'Itinéraire escarpé de Yilmaz Güney," in *Revue du Cinéma* (Paris), June 1983.

Obituary in *Variety* (New York), 12 September 1984.

Finlayson, E., "Levantine Approaches: On First looking into Güney's Turkey," in *Monthly Film Bulletin* (London), October 1984.

Listener (London), 15 January 1987.

On GÜNEY: film—

Stempel, Hans, and Martin Ripken, *Besuch auf Imrali* (*Portrait of Yilmaz Güney*), 1979.

*   *   *

Yilmaz Güney's life was fully as dramatic as any of his films. The son of a rural worker, he supported himself through studies at university in Ankara and Istanbul. Though his career was interrupted by a series of arrests for political activities, he established himself as a scriptwriter and actor in the 1960s and developed a wide popular following. More than a film star in the conventional sense, he became something of a popular myth, a figure in whose sufferings and ruthless quest for vengeance the poor and oppressed could see their lives and aspirations reflected. When he turned to directing in the late 1960s, his first films were in the same commercial tradition as his early hits. But the early 1970s saw a fresh burst of creativity, brought to an end by a new prison sentence of two years. On his release he completed one of his most interesting films, *Arkadas*, (*The Friend*) in 1974, before finding himself back in prison, this time on a murder charge for which he received a sentence of 24 years imprisonment. But even this could not put a stop to his career. He maintained contact with the outside world and continued scripting films, some of which, like *Sürü* (*The Herd*), achieved international success. When he finally made his escape from Turkey in 1981 he was able to work on yet another film he had scripted, *Yol* (*The Way*), which won the Cannes Grand Prix in 1982.

Perhaps Güney's major achievement as an actor-director in the early 1970s was to make the transition from the heroic superman figure of the early films such as *Ac Kurtlar* (*The Hungry Wolves*), to the vulnerable individual of his later work. In the series of masterly films beginning with the ironically titled *Umut* (*Hope*) in 1970, the failure of the isolated individual acting alone becomes the uniting thread of Güney's work. Already in *The Hungry Wolves* the picture of Turkish society is most remarkable for what is lacking: no concerned government to maintain the law, no self-help for the terrorized peasants, no acceptable role for women, no vision beyond instinctive revolt on the part of the bandits. These factors continue to form the background for the series of defeated individuals in both rural settings (as in the bandit film, *Ağit* (*Elegy*) and the urban environment as in *Baba* (*The Father*) and *Zavallilar* (*The Poor Ones*). The one film which posits a set of positive values is his last completed work as a director before his arrest in 1974, *The Friend*. But even here the vision is a dark one, for the intellectual hero (played by Güney) confronts an erstwhile friend with his empty life and thereby drives him to suicide.

The next film he began, *Endise* (*Anxiety*), was completed by his friend and former assistant Serif Gören following Güney's arrest. He was to spend eight years in prison, but he continued to write film scripts indefatigably. Among his best films of this period are those which offer a vivid picture of the life of peasants in the still feudal world of his native district, Adana: *Anxiety* and *The Herd*, the latter directed by Zeki Ökten. Güney's final Turkish work, *Yol*, which he edited himself in exile, is even wider in its scope, offering an image of the whole breadth of Turkey through its intercut stories of five detainees released from prison for a week and travelling home to their families. Despite Güney's strong political commitment, his films are social studies rather than overtly political tracts. He himself never failed to make the distinction between his political activity, which is directed towards revolutionary change in society, and his filmmaking. For Güney, the fictional feature film remained first and foremost a popular form, a way of communicating with a mass audience, and, as *Yol* shows, he used in an exemplary way the possibilities it offers for stating and examining the contradictions that underlie modern Turkish society.

—Roy Armes

————

GUTIÉRREZ ALEA, Tomás.

Cuban. Born in Havana, 11 December 1928. Educated in law at the University of Havana; Centro Sperimentale, Rome, 1951–53; worked with Cine-Revista newsreel organisation, late 1950's; following establishment of Instituto Cubano del Arte e Industria Cinematograficos (ICAIC) by revolutionary government, began making documentaries, 1959; later collaborated with younger filmmakers, in keeping with ICAIC policy.

Films as Director:

1955   *El megano* (co-d)
1959   *Esta tierra nuestra*
1960   *Asemblea General*
1961   *Muerte al invasor* (co-d); *Historias de la revolucion*
1962   *Las doce sillas* (*The Twelve Chairs*)
1964   *Cumbite*
1966   *La muerte de un burócrata* (*The Death of a Bureaucrat*)
1968   **Memorias del subdessarrolo** (**Memories of Underdevelopment**)
1971   *Una pelea cubana contra los demonios* (*A Cuban Struggle Against the Demons*)
1974   *El arte del tobaco*
1976   *La última cena* (*The Last Supper*)
1979   *Los Sobrevivientes* (*Survivors*) (+ co-sc)
1983   *Hasta cierto punto* (*Up to a Point*)
1988   *Cartas del parque* (*Letters from the Park*)

Publications:

By GUTIÉRREZ ALEA: book—

Las doce sillas, Havana, 1963.

By GUTIÉRREZ ALEA: articles—

"Individual Fulfillment and Collective Achievement: An Interview with Tomás Gutiérrez Alea," with Julianne Burton, in *Cineaste* (New York), January 1977.
"Towards a Renewal of Cuban Revolutionary Cinema," an interview with Zuzana Mirjam Pick, in *Cine-Tracts* (Montreal), no. 3/4, 1978.
Interview with G. Chijona, in *Framework* (Norwich), Spring 1979.
Interview with M. Ansara, in *Cinema Papers* (Melbourne), May/June 1981.
"Dramaturgia (cinematografica) y realidad," in *Cine Cubano* (Havana), no. 105, 1983.
Interview with E. Colina, in *Cine Cubano* (Havana), no. 109, 1984.
"I Wasn't Always a Filmmaker," in *Cineaste* (New York), vol. 14, no. 1, 1985.
Interview with Gary Crowdus, in *Cineaste* (New York), vol. 14, no. 2, 1985.
Interview with J.R. MacBean, in *Film Quarterly* (Berkeley), Spring 1985.
"The Viewer's Dialectic," in *Reviewing Histories*, edited by Coco Fusco, Buffalo, New York, 1987.

On GUTIÉRREZ ALEA: books—

Nelson, L., *Cuba: The Measure of a Revolution*, Minneapolis, 1972.
Myerson, Michael, editor, *Memories of Underdevelopment: The Revolutionary Films of Cuba*, New York, 1973.

Chanan, Michael, *The Cuban Image*, London, 1985.
Burton, Julianne, editor, *Cinema and Social Change in Latin America: Conversations with Filmmakers*, Austin, Texas, 1986.
Fornet, Ambrosio, *Alea: Una retrospectiva critica*, Havana, 1987.

On GUTIÉRREZ ALEA: articles—

Sutherland, Elizabeth, "Cinema of Revolution—Ninety Miles From Home," in *Film Quarterly* (Berkeley), Winter 1961/62.
Adler, Renata, in *New York Times*, 10, 11 and 12 February 1969.
Engel, Andi, "Solidarity and Violence," in *Sight and Sound* (London), Autumn 1969.
Crowdus, Gary, "The Spring 1972 Cuban Film Festival Bust," in *Film Society Review* (New York), March/May 1972.
Lesage, Julia, "Images of Underdevelopment," in *Jump Cut* (Chicago), May/June 1974.
Kernan, Margot, "Cuban Cinema: Tomás Gutiérrez Alea," in *Film Quarterly* (Berkeley), Winter 1976.
Burton, Julianne, "Introduction to Revolutionary Cuban Cinema," in *Jump Cut* (Chicago), December 1978.
West, Dennis, "Slavery and Cinema in Cuba: The Case of Gutiérrez Alea's *The Last Supper*," in *The Western Journal of Black Studies*, Summer 1979.
Alexander, W., "Class, Film Language, and Popular Cinema," in *Jump Cut* (Berkeley), March 1985.
"Tomás Gutiérrez Alea," in *Film Dope* (London), March 1988.
Chanan, Michael, "Tomás Gutiérrez Alea: The Man in Havana," in *National Film Theatre Booklet* (London), October/November 1989.

*   *   *

The narrative and structural approaches and the style of Gutiérrez Alea's films have varied widely, but his best works show a significant thematic unity stemming from the director's position as a committed revolutionary filmmaker working within a film industry controlled by a socialist state. The director's greatest films all explore aspects of revolution. This central theme of revolution is announced in the neorealist-influenced *Historias de la revolución*, the first feature made by Gutiérrez Alea after the triumph of the Cuban revolution.

Gutiérrez Alea believes that bureaucracy is a part of revolutionary Cuba's bourgeois heritage. His *La muerte de un burócrata* is a polemical yet humorous feature on bureaucratization in a revolutionary socialist society. This masterful satire is outstanding for its dimension of playful inventiveness: credits which are typed in "bureaucratese," the humorous use of animated cartoons, and the many well-integrated parodies of renowned sequences from world cinema. *La muerte de un burócrata* demonstrates that socialist cinema need not resort to heavy-handed methods to express important themes.

Gutiérrez Alea's masterpiece, *Memorias del subdesarrollo*, is a critique of the colonized bourgeois mentality. The protagonist is a man without a future: a middle-aged bourgeois intellectual who refuses to flee to Miami but who is unable to integrate himself into the Cuban revolutionary process. Gutiérrez Alea successfully draws on historical motifs (speeches by Kennedy and Castro) and elements of other film genres (documentary and newsreel) in order to show this individual's place in the march of history.

A primary goal of Cuba's revolutionary filmmakers has been to decolonize the taste of the Cuban film-going public, which for decades had been subjected to standard Hollywood fare. In *Memorias del subdesarrollo*, Gutiérrez Alea contributes overtly to this effort by including a sequence in which clips from a pornographic film are shown in order to critique that genre. *Memorias del subdesarrollo* also features more subtle efforts at decolonization; the director subverts and questions conventional film techniques and strategies through self-conscious and self-reflective devices, as when the director appears as himself in the Instituto Cubano del Arte e Industria Cinematográficos (ICAIC) commenting on this very film, and when the author of the novel *Memorias del subdesarrollo* participates in a round table on literature and underdevelopment.

In *La última cena*, Gutiérrez Alea abandons self-conscious and self-reflective techniques in favor of a realist style and a conventional chronological treatment of the story line. He uses traditional Christian motifs associated with the Last Supper and the Resurrection in order to reveal the religious ideology of the white planter class—a dead-letter Christianity which reinforced the socio-economic status quo and reconciled black slaves to a life of bondage. One of the goals of ICAIC has been to contribute to the forging of an authentic national identity through the reassessment of Cuban history. *La última cena* re-examines the historical role of blacks by depicting a slave revolt which is based on an actual incident. Gutiérrez Alea and others at ICAIC supported this film project because Cuba's tradition of black resistance (to slavery and to Spanish colonial powers) was seen as a major contribution to today's socialist Cuba, whose proclaimed objectives include an end to the oppressive legacy of colonialism and to all forms of domination.

The films of Gutiérrez Alea have been well received by Cuban audiences and by critics of many nations. Gutiérrez Alea is one of the greatest Latin American filmmakers because of his ability to mold widely different structural and stylistic approaches to a variety of significant revolutionary themes. This achievement is particularly impressive for having been accomplished in a developing country with modest financial and technical resources.

—Dennis West

GUY, Alice.

French. Also known as Alice Guy-Blaché and Alice Blaché. Born in Saint-Mandé, 1 July 1873. Educated at convent du Sacré-Coeur, Viry, France 1879–85; religious school at Ferney, and brief term in Paris; studied stenography. Married Herbert Blaché-Bolton, 1907 (divorced 1922), two children. Secretary to Léon Gaumont, 1895; directed first film, *La Fée aux choux*, 1896 (some sources give 1900); director of Gaumont film production, 1897–1907; using Gaumont "chronophone," made 1st sound films, 1900; moved to U.S. with husband, who was to supervise Gaumont subsidiary, Solax, 1907; ceased independent production, lectured on filmmaking at Columbia University, 1917; assistant director to husband, 1919–20; returned to France, 1922; moved to U.S., 1964. Recipient: Legion of Honor, 1955. *Died in Mahwah, New Jersey, 24 March 1968.*

Films as Director and Scriptwriter:

1896   *La Fée aux choux* (*The Cabbage Fairy*)

1897   *Le Pêcheur dans le torrent*; *Leçon de danse*; *Baignade dans le torrent*; *Une nuit agitée*; *Coucher d'Yvette*; *Danse fleur de lotus*; *Ballet Libella*; *Le Planton du colonel*; *Idylle*; *L'Aveugle*

1897/98   *L'Arroseur arrosé*; *Au réfectoire*; *En classe*; *Les Cambrioleurs*; *Le Cocher de fiacre endormi*; *Idylle interrompue*; *Chez le magnétiseur*; *Les Farces de Jocko*; *Scène d'escamotage*; *Déménagement à la cloche de bois*; *Je vous y prrrends!*

1898/99   *Leçons de boxe*; *La Vie du Christ* (11 tableaux)

1899/1900   *Le Tondeur de chiens*; *Le Déjeuner des enfants*; *Au cabaret*; *La Mauvaise Soupe*; *Un Lunch*; *Erreur judiciaire*; *L'Aveugle*; *La Bonne Absinthe*; *Danse serpentine par Mme Bob Walter*; *Mésaventure d'un charbonnier*; *Monnaie de lapin*; *Les Dangers de l'acoolisme*; *Le Tonnelier*; *Transformations*; *Le Chiffonier*; *Retour des champs*; *Chez le Maréchal-Ferrant*; *Marché à la volaille*; *Courte échelle*; *L'Angélus*; *Bataille d'oreillers*; *Bataille de boules de neige*; *Le marchand de coco*

1900   *Avenue de l'Opéra*; *La petite magicienne*; *Leçon de danse*; *Chez le photographe*; *Sidney's Joujoux* series (9 titles); *Dans les coulisses*; *Au Bal de Flore* series (3 titles); *Ballet Japonais* series (3 titles); *Danse serpentine*; *Danse du pas des foulards par des almées*; *Danse de l'ivresse*; *Coucher d'une Parisienne*; *Les Fredaines de Pierrette* series (4 titles); *Vénus et Adonis* series (5 titles); *La Tarantelle*; *Danse des Saisons* series (4 titles); *La Source*; *Danse du papillon*; *La Concierge*; *Danses* series (3 titles); *Chirurgie fin de siècle*; *Une Rage de dents*; *Saut humidifié de M. Plick*

1900/01   *La Danse du ventre*; *Lavatory moderne*; *Lecture quotidienne*

1900/07   (Gaumont "Phonoscènes", i.e. films with synchronized sound recorded on a wax cylinder): *Carmen* (12 scenes); *Mireille* (5 scenes); *Les Dragons de Villars* (9 scenes); *Mignon* (7 scenes); *Faust* (22 scenes); *Polin* series (13 titles); *Mayol* series (13 titles); *Dranem* series of comic songs (12 titles); Series recorded in Spain (11 titles); *La Prière* by Gounod

1901   *Folies Masquées* series (3 titles); *Frivolité*; *Les Vagues*; *Danse basque*; *Hussards et grisettes*; *Charmant FrouFrou*; *Tel est pris qui croyait prendre*

1902   *La fiole enchantée*; *L'Equilibriste*; *En faction*; *La Première Gamelle*; *La Dent récalcitrante*; *Le Marchand de ballons*; *Les Chiens savants*; *Miss Lina Esbrard Danseuse Cosmopolite et Serpentine* series (4 titles); *Les Clowns*; *Sage-femme de première classe*; *Quadrille réaliste*; *Une Scène en cabinet particulier vue à travers le trou de la serrure*; *Farces de cuisinière*; *Danse mauresque*; *Le Lion savant*; *Le Pommier*; *La Cour des miracles*; *La Gavotte*; *Trompé mais content*; *Fruits de saison*; *Pour secourer la salade*

1903   *Potage indigeste*; *Illusioniste renversant*; *Le Fiancé ensorcelé*; *Les Apaches pas veinards*; *Les Aventures d'un voyageur trop pressé*; *Ne bougeons plus*; *Comment monsieur prend son bain*; *La Main du professeur Hamilton ou Le Roi des dollars*; *Service précipité*, *La Poule fantaisiste*; *Modelage express*; *Faust et Méphistophélès*; *Lutteurs américains*; *La Valise enchantée*; *Compagnons de voyage encombrants*; *Cake-Walk de la pendule*; *Répétition dans un cirque*; *Jocko musicien*; *Les Braconniers*; *La Liqueur du couvent*; *Le Voleur sacrilège*; *Enlèvement en automobile et mariage précipite*;

1903/04   *Secours aux naufragés*; *La Mouche*; *La Chasse au cambrioleur*; *Nos Bon Etudiants*; *Les Surprises de l'affichage*; *Comme on fait son lit on se couche*; *Le Pompon malencontreux 1*; *Comment on disperse les foules*; *Les Enfants du miracle*; *Pierrot assassin*; *Les Deux Rivaux*

1904   *L'Assassinat du Courrier de Lyon*; *Vieilles Estampes* series (4 titles); *Mauvais coeur puni*; *Magie noire*; *Rafle de chiens*; *Cambrioleur et agent*; *Scènes Directoire* series (3 titles); *Duel tragique*; *L'Attaque d'un diligence*; *Culture intensive ou Le Vieux Mari*; *Cible humaine*; *Transformations*; *Le Jour du terme*; *Robert Macaire et Bertrand*; *Electrocuté*; *Le Rêve du chasseur*; *Le Monolutteur*; *Les Petits Coupeurs de bois vert*; *Clown en sac*; *Triste Fin d'un vieux savant*; *Le Testament de Pierrot*; *Les Secrets de la prestidigitation dévoilés*; *La Faim . . . L' occasion . . . L'herbe tendre*; *Militaire et nourrice*; *La Première Cigarette*; *Départ pour les vacances*; *Tentative d'assassinat en chemin de fer*; *Paris la nuit ou Exploits d' apaches à Montamartre*; *Concours de bébés*; *Erreur de poivrot*; *Volée par les bohémiens (Rapt d' enfant par les romanichels)*; *Les Bienfaits du cinématographe*; *Pâtissier et ramoneur*; *Gage d'amour*; *L'Assassinat de la rue du Temple (Le Crime de la rue du Temple)*; *Le Réveil du jardinier*; *Les Cambrioleurs de Paris*

Alice Guy

1905   *Réhabilitation*; *Douaniers et contrebandiers* (*La Guérité*); *Le Bébé embarrassant*; *Comment on dort á Paris!*; *Le Lorgnon accusateur*; *La Charité du prestidigitateur*; *Une Noce au lac Saint-Fargeau*; *Le Képi*; *Le Pantalon coupé*; *Le Plateau*; *Roméo pris au piége*; *Chien jouant á la balle*; *La Fantassin Guignard*; *La Statue*; *Villa dévalisée*; *Mort de Robert Macaire et Bertrand*; *Le Pavé*; *Les Maçons*; *La Esmeralda*; *Peintre et ivrogne*; *On est poivrot, mais on a du cœur*; *Au Poulailler!*

1906   *La Fée au printemps*; *La Vie du marin*; *La Chaussette*; *La Messe de minuit*; *Pauvre pompier*; *Le Régiment moderne*; *Les Druides*; *Voyage en Espagne* series (15 titles); *La Vie de Christ* (25 tableaux); *Conscience de prêtre*; *L'Honneur du Corse*; *J'ai un hanneton dans mon pantalon*; *Le Fils du garde-chasse*; *Course de taureaux à Nîmes*; *La Pègre de Paris*; *Lèvres closes* (*Sealed Lips*); *La Crinoline*; *La Voiture cellulaire*; *La Marâtre*; *Le Matelas alcoolique*; *A la recherche d'un appartement*

1907   *La vérité sur l'homme-singe* (*Ballet de Singe*); *Déménagement à la cloche de bois*; *Les Gendarmes*; *Sur la barricade* (*L'enfant de la barricade*)

1910   *A Child's Sacrifice* (*The Doll*)

1911   *Rose of the Circus*; *Across the Mexican Line*; *Eclipse*; *A Daughter of the Navajos*; *The Silent Signal*; *The Girl and the Bronco Buster*; *The Mascot of Troop 'C'*; *An Enlisted Man's Honor*; *The Stampede*; *The Hold-Up*; *The Altered Message*; *His Sister's Sweetheart*; *His Better Self*; *A Revolutionary Romance*; *The Violin Maker of Nuremberg*

1912   *Mignon or The Child of Fate*; *A Terrible Lesson*; *His Lordship's White Feather*; *Falling Leaves*; *The Sewer*; *In the Year 2000*; *A Terrible Night*; *Mickey's Pal*; *Fra Diavolo*; *Hotel Honeymoon*; *The Equine Spy*; *Two Little Rangers*; *The Bloodstain*; *At the Phone*; *Flesh and Blood*; *The Paralytic*; *The Face at the Window*

1913   *The Beasts of the Jungle*; *Dick Whittington and His Cat*; *Kelly From the Emerald Isle*; *The Pit and the Pendulum*; *Western Love*; *Rogues of Paris*; *Blood and Water*; *Ben Bolt*; *The Shadows of the Moulin Rouge*; *The Eyes that Could Not Close*; *The Star of India*; *The Fortune Hunters*

1914   *Beneath the Czar*; *The Monster and the Girl*; *The Million Dollar Robbery*; *The Prisoner of the Harem*; *The Dream Woman*; *Hook and Hand*; *The Woman of Mystery*; *The Yellow Traffic*; *The Lure*; *Michael Strogoff or The Courier to the Czar*; *The Tigress*; *The Cricket on the Hearth*

1915   *The Heart of a Painted Woman*; *Greater Love Hath No Man*; *The Vampire*; *My Madonna*; *Barbara Frietchie* (co-d)

1916   *What Will People Say?*; *The Girl with the Green Eyes*; *The Ocean Waif*; *House of Cards*

1917   *The Empress*; *The Adventurer*; *A Man and the Woman*; *When You and I Were Young*; *Behind the Mask*

1918   *The Great Adventure*

1920   *Tarnished Reputation*

Other Films:

1919   *The Divorcee* (asst d); *The Brat* (asst d)
1920   *Stronger than Death* (asst d)

Publications:

By GUY: book—

Autobiographie d'une pionnière du cinéma 1873–1968, Paris, 1976; as *The Memoirs of Alice Guy-Blaché*, edited by Anthony Slide, Metuchen, New Jersey, 1986.

By GUY: articles—

"Woman's Place in Photoplay Production," in *The Moving Picture World* (New York), 11 July 1914.
Letter in *Films in Review* (New York), May 1964.
"La Naissance du cinéma," in *Image et Son* (Paris), April 1974.
"Tournez, mesdames . . . ," in *Ecran* (Paris), August/September 1974.

On GUY: books—

Slide, Anthony, *Early Women Directors*, New York, 1977.
Elsaesser, Thomas, and Adam Barker, editors, *Early Cinema: Space-Frame-Narrative*, London, 1990.

On GUY: articles—

Levine, H.Z., "Madame Alice Blaché," in *Photoplay* (New York), March 1912.
Ford, Charles, "The First Female Producer," in *Films in Review* (New York), March 1964.
Smith, F.L., "Alice Guy-Blaché," in *Films in Review* (New York), April 1964.
Lacassin, Francis, "Out of Oblivion: Alice Guy-Blaché," in *Sight and Sound* (London), Summer 1971.
Mitry, Jean, "A propos d'Alice Guy," in *Ecran* (Paris), July 1976.
Deslandes, J., "Sur Alice Guy: polémique," in *Ecran* (Paris), September 1976.
Peary, Gerald, "Czarina of the Silent Screen," in *Velvet Light Trap* (Madison, Wisconsin), Winter 1977.

*   *   *

Alice Guy was the first person, or among the first, to make a fictional film. The story-film was quite possibly "invented" by her in 1896 when she made *La Fée aux choux* (*The Cabbage Fairy*). Certain historians claim that films of Louis Lumière and Georges Méliès preceded Guy's first film. The question remains debatable; Guy claimed precedence, devoting much effort in her lifetime to correcting recorded errors attributing her films to her male colleagues, and trying to secure her earned niche in film history. There is no debate regarding Guy's position as the world's first woman filmmaker.

Between 1896 and 1901 she made films averaging just 75 feet in length; from 1902 to 1907 she made numerous films of all types and lengths using acrobats, clowns, and opera singers as well as large casts in ambitious productions based on fairy and folk tales, Biblical themes, paintings, and myths. The "tricks" she used—running film in reverse and the use of double exposure—were learned through trial-and-error. In this period she also produced "talking pictures," in which Gaumont's Chronophone synchronized a projector with sound recorded on a wax cylinder.

One of these sound films, *Mireille*, was made by Guy in 1906. Herbert Blaché-Bolton joined the film crew of *Mireille* to learn directing. Alice Guy and Herbert were married in early 1907, and moved to the U.S. where they eventually set up a studio in Flushing, N.Y. The Blachés then established the Solax Company, with a Manhattan office. In its four years of existence, Solax released 325 films including westerns, military movies, thrillers, and historical romances. Mme. Blaché's first picture in the U.S. was *A Child's Sacrifice* (in 1910) centering on a girl's attempts to earn money for her family. In her *Hotel Honeymoon* of 1912, the moon comes alive to smile at human lovers, while in *The Violin Maker of Nuremberg* two apprentices contend for the affections of their instructor's daughter.

The Blachés built their own studio at Fort Lee, N.J., with a daily printing capacity of 16,000 feet of positive film. For its inauguration, in February 1912, Mme. Blaché presented an evening of Solax films at Weber's Theatre on Broadway. In that year she filmed two movies based on operas: *Fra Diavolo* and *Mignon*, each 3-reelers, with orchestral accompaniment. Her boldest enterprises were films using animals and autos.

Cataclysmic changes in the film industry finally forced the Blachés out of business. They rented, and later sold, their studio, then directed films for others. In 1922, the Blachés divorced. Herbert directed films until 1930, but Alice could not find film work and never made another film. She returned to France but without prints of her films, she had no evidence of her accomplishments. She could not find work in the French film industry either. She returned to the U.S. in 1927 to search the Library of Congress and other film depositories for her films, but in vain: only a half-dozen of her one-reelers survive. In 1953, she returned to Paris, where, at 78, she was honored as the first woman filmmaker in the world. Her films, characterized by innovation and novelty, explored all genres, and successfully appealed to both French and American audiences. Today she is finally being recognized as a unique pioneer of the film industry.

—Louise Heck-Rabi

―――――

GUZMÁN, Patricio.

Chilean. Born in Santiago de Chile, 11 August 1941. Educated at Escuela oficial de cinematografia (EOC), Madrid, graduated 1969. After writing novels, joined Filmic Institute, Catholic University in Santiago, 1965; left for Spain, 1967; returned to Chile, joined Chile-Films (national film production company), heading Documentary Film Workshops, 1970; constituted Group of the Third Year to produce *The Battle of Chile*, imprisoned shortly after September coup d'etat, 1973; moved to Cuba, 1974, completed *The Battle of Chile*, 1977; moved to Spain, 1980.

Films as Director:

1965 *Viva la libertad* (*Hail to Freedom*) (short)
1966 *Artesania popular* (*Popular Crafts*) (short); *Electroshow* (short)
1967 *Cien Metros con Charlot* (*One Hundred Meters with Chaplin*); *Escuela de sordomudos* (*School for Deafmutes*)
1968 *La tortura* (*Torture*); *Imposibrante*
1969 *Opus seis* (*Opus Six*); *El Paraiso ortopedico* (*Orthopedic Paradise*)
1970 *Elecciones municipales* (*Municipal Elections*); *El primer año* (*The First Year*)
1972 *La respuesta de Octobre* (*The Response in October*); *Comandos comunales* (*Communal Organization*); *Manuel Rodriquez* (unfinished)
1974 **La batalla de Chile: La lucha de un pueblo sin armas (The Battle of Chile: The Struggle of an Unarmed People)** Part 1: **La insurrección de la burguesia (Insurrection of the Bourgeoisie)**
1976 Part 2: **El golpe de estado (Coup d'état)**
1979 Part 3: **El poder popular (The Popular Power)**
1983 *La rosa de los vientos* (*Rose of the Winds*)

Publications:

By GUZMÁN: books—

La insurrección de la burgesia, edited by Racinante, Caracas, 1975.
La batalla de Chile: La lucha de un pueblo sin armas, Madrid, 1977.
El cine contra el fascismo, with P. Sempere, edited by Fernando Torres, Valencia, 1977.

By GUZMÁN: articles—

"Le Cinéma dans la politique de l'Unité Populaire," in *Jeune Cinéma* (Paris), November 1974.
"La Bataille du Chili II," interview with Marcel Martin, in *Ecran* (Paris), January 1977.
"Politics and the Documentary in People's Chile," interview with Julianne Burton, in *Socialist Review*, October 1977.
"La batalla de Chile," interview with Carlos Galiano, in *Cine Cubano* (Havana), no. 91–92, 1978.

"Chile," 3: Guzmán," and "Chile," in *Framework* (Norwich), Spring and Autumn 1979.
Interview with Z.M. Pick, in *Ciné-Tracts* (Montreal), Winter 1980.

On GUZMÁN: books—

Burton, Julianne, editor, *Cinema and Social Change in Latin America: Conversations with Filmmakers*, Austin, Texas, 1986.
King, John, *Magical Realism: A History of Cinema in Latin America*, London, 1990.

On GUZMÁN: articles—

Gauthier, Guy, "Chili: la première année," in *Image et Son* (Paris), March 1973.
Gauthier, Guy, "*La Bataille du Chili*, première partie: *L'Insurrection de la bourgeoisie*," in *Image et Son* (Paris), January 1976.
Niogret, Hubert, "*La Batalla de Chile: el golpe de estado*," in *Positif* (Paris), July/August 1976.
Delmas, Jean, "*La Batalla de Chile*, deuxième partie: *Le Coup d'état*," in *Jeune Cinéma* (Paris), February 1977.
West, Dennis, "*The Battle of Chile*," in *Cineaste* (New York), vol. 11, no. 2, 1978.
West, Dennis, "Documenting the End of the Chilean Road to Socialism: *La Batalla de Chile*," in *The American Hispanist*, February 1978.
"*La Batalla de Chile* Section" of *Cine Cubano* (Havana), March 1978.
Angry Arts group, "*Battle of Chile* in Context," and V. Wallis, "*Battle of Chile*: Struggle of People without Arms," in *Jump Cut* (Chicago), November 1979.
Mouesca, J., "El cine chileño en el exilio (1973–1983)," in *Cine Cubano* (Havana), no. 109, 1984.

*　　*　　*

Chilean director Patricio Guzmán studied fiction filmmaking in Spain in the 1960s, but he eventually dropped plans to make fiction features when he returned to Chile during the presidency of the Marxist-socialist Salvador Allende (1970–73). Guzmán is above all a political filmmaker, and the intense everyday political activities in Allende's Chile stimulated Guzmán to take to the streets and factories in order to make documentary records of those fast-paced events. In all three of his documentaries on Allende's Chile—*El primer año, La respuesta de octubre*, and *La batalla de Chile*—the director rejected archival footage and the compilation approach in favor of immersing himself in significant political events in order to obtain actuality footage.

Guzmán's success in obtaining meaningful and abundant actuality footage is owing in large part to his (and his colleagues') marked ability to understand and foresee the flow of political events. Political savvy coupled with rigorous and disciplined production techniques allowed Guzmán and his production groups to overcome formidable obstacles, including financial and technical difficulties. To film the three feature-length parts of the masterwork *La batalla de Chile*, the director and his collective had access to one 16mm Eclair camera and one Nagra tape recorder; film stock, unavailable in Chile, had been sent from abroad by a European colleague.

During his stay in Allende's Chile, Guzmán successfully combined his personal political militancy with his concept of the role of the filmmaker. Guzmán, a committed Marxist, wished to make films that would help Allende's leftist Popular Unity coalition take power. Marx and Engels (*Manifesto of the Communist Party*) viewed classes as the protagonists of history, and conflict as an inherent dimension of class societies; Guzmán follows this Marxist conception in that classes are the protagonists of his films and events are framed in terms of class conflict. In accordance with the Marxist-Leninist revolutionary view that there can be no peaceful transition to socialism before the repressive machinery of the bourgeois state is broken up and replaced, the first two parts of *La batalla de Chile* follow the military's drift to the right as well as the anti-Allende activities of the opposition-dominated legislature. Both *La respuesta de octubre* and part three of *La batalla de Chile* center on workers organizing as a class in order to achieve self-emancipation and transform the world the bourgeoisie created.

The style of the journalistic *El primer año* is unexceptional, and it was only with *La batalla de Chile* that Guzmán found a distinctive documentary style. This style is characterized by the frequent use of the sequence shot, which the director prefers because it is a synthetic device allowing spectators to see events unfolding in front of their eyes without breaks in the flow of the images.

El primer año and *La respuesta de octubre* have not circulated widely outside of Allende's Chile. Inside Allende's Chile, these documentaries were well received by working-class audiences. *La respuesta de octubre* was particularly popular with workers who, heartened to see their efforts to create worker-controlled industrial zones documented on film, facilitated the documentary's distribution in the factories. Guzmán's international reputation as a documentary filmmaker has been secured by *La batalla de Chile*, hailed by both Marxist and non-Marxist critics in many countries as a landmark in the history of the political documentary.

—Dennis West

HAANSTRA, Bert.

Dutch. Born in Holten, Holland, 31 May 1916. Educated at
Academy of Arts, Amsterdam. Painter and press photographer, from late 1930's; joined Royal Dutch Shell Film Unit,
1952; producer and manager, Shell Film Unit, Venezuela,
1956; founded production company, Bert Haanstra Filmproductie, 1960. Recipient: Grand Prix (documentary), Cannes
Festival, for *Mirror of Holland*, 1951.

Films as Director:

1948 *De Muiderkring herleeft* (*The Muyder Circle Lives Again*) (+
    sc, ph, ed)
1950 *Spiegel van Holland* (*Mirror of Holland*) (+ sc, ph, ed)
1951 *Nederlandse beeldhouwkunst tijdens de late Middeleeuwen*
    (*Dutch Sculpture*) (+ co-ed); *Panta Rhei* (*All Things Flow*)
    (+ sc, ph, ed)
1952 *Dijkbouw* (*Dike Builders*) (+ sc, ed)
1954 *Ont staan en vergaan* (*The Changing Earth*) (+ sc); *De
    opsporing van aardolie* (*The Search for Oil*) (+ sc); *De
    verkenningsboring* (*The Wildcat*) (+ sc); *Het olieveld* (*The
    Oilfield*) (+ sc)
1955 *The Rival World* (*Strijd zonder einde*) (+ ed, sc); *God Shiva*
    (+ sc, pr, ed); *En de zee was niet meer* (*And There Was No
    More Sea*) (+ pr, sc, ed)
1957 *Rembrandt, schilder van de mens* (*Rembrandt, Painter of Man*)
    (+ pr, sc, ed)
1958 *Over glas gesproken* (*Speaking of Glass*) (+ pr, sc, ed); *Glas*
    (*Glass*) (+ co-ed, pr, sc); *Fanfare* (+ co-sc, co-ed)
1960 *De zaak M.P.* (*The M.P. Case*) (+ co-sc, co-ed, pr)
1962 *Zoo* (+ pr, sc, ed); *Delta Phase I* (+ pr, sc, ed)
1963 *Alleman* (*The Human Dutch*) (+ co-sc, narration for English
    and German versions)
1966 *De stem van het water* (*The Voice of the Water*) (+ co-sc, pr,
    ed)
1967 *Retour Madrid* (*Return Ticket to Madrid*) (+ co-pr, co-ph)
1972 *Bij de beesten af* (*Ape and Super Ape*) (+ pr, sc, ed, co-
    commentary, co-add'l ph, narration)
1975 *Dokter Pulder zaait papavers* (*Dr. Pulder Sows Poppies. When
    the Poppies Bloom Again*) (+ pr)
1978 *Nationale Parken . . . noodzaak* (*National Parks . . . a
    Necessity. National Parks in the Netherlands*) (+ pr, sc, ed)
1979 *Een pak slaag* (*Mr. Slotter's Jubilee*) (+ pr)
1983 *Vroeger kon je lachen* (*One Could Laugh in Former Days*) (+
    pr, sc); *Nederland* (*The Netherlands*) (+ pr, sc, ed)

Other Films:

1949 *Myrte en de demonen* (*Myrte and the Demons*) (Schreiber)
    (ph); *Boer Pietersen schiet in de roos* (*Bull's Eye for Farmer
    Pietersen*) (I◄ usse) (ph)
1955 *Belgian Grand Prix* (Hughes) (co-ph)
1957 *De gouden Ilsy* (*The Golden Ilsy*) (van der Linden) (ph); *Olie
    op reis* (*Pattern of Supply*) (Pendry) (pr)

1959 *Paleontologie* (*Schakel met het verleden. Story in the Rocks*)
    (van Gelder) (pr, tech advisor)
1960 *Lage landen* (*Hold Back the Sea*) (Sluizer) (tech advisor)
1962 *De overval* (*The Silent Raid*) (Rotha) (co-sc, uncredited)
1968 *Pas assez* (*Not Enough. Niet genoeg*) (van der Velde) (ed)
1970 *Trafic* (Tati) (collaborator); *Summer in the Fields* (van der
    Linden) (ed)
1972 *Grierson* (Blais) (role as interviewee)
1979 *Juliana in zeventig bewogen jaren* (*Juliana in Seventy
    Turbulent Years*) (Kohlhaas) (advisor)

Publications:

By HAANSTRA: articles—

"Gresprek met Bert Haanstra en prof. dr. G.P. Behrends," with R. du
Mèe and others, in *Skoop* (Amsterdam), v.8, no.6, 1972.
"Geen klachten over hoeveelheid aandacht voor Nederlandse film,"
in *Skoop* (Amsterdam), February 1976.

On HAANSTRA: book—

Verdaasdonk, Dorothee, editor, *Bert Haanstra*, Amsterdam, 1983.

On HAANSTRA: articles—

"Director of the Year," in *International Film Guide*, London, 1966.
Cowie, Peter, "Bert Haanstra," in *Focus on Film* (London), Spring
1972.
"Bert Haanstra," in *Film Dope* (London), March 1981.
Bertina, B.J., "Haanstra en het onverzorgde corpus van Dorothee
Verdaasdonk," in *Skoop* (Amsterdam), December 1983/January
1984.

*   *   *

Bert Haanstra is one of Holland's most renowned filmmakers.
The 28 films he has made from 1948 until the present day
belong to various genres. His first films were documentaries.
Typical of these, and a hallmark of Haanstra's personal style, is
the frequent use of "rhyming images" and of images blending
into each other. Critics responded warmly to the lyrical and
pictorial qualities of Haanstra's early work. In his films about
oil drilling, commissioned by Shell, Haanstra showed that
instructional films can be of artistic as well as informative
value.

Haanstra's first feature film, *Fanfare*, was a comedy and a
big hit at the box-office. The film, however, was also praised
for its artistic importance and considered by many as a turning
point in the situation of the Dutch film: "This film should set
the tone for the future production of Dutch feature-films,"
wrote a critic. His second feature film, *De zaak M. P.*, was very
coolly received, however, and Haanstra turned again to making documentaries.

Discussions in the 1960's about the establishment of a tradition of Dutch feature films—a tradition which was lacking at
that time—were heavily influenced by the views on film
expressed by the French *nouvelle vague* cineastes. Haanstra's
long documentaries, *Alleman, De stem van het water*, and *Bij*

Bert Haanstra: *Alleman*

de beesten af, show that the filmmaker is perfectly able to catch the peculiarities of human behavior, especially those of the Dutch. These three films still enjoy a firm reputation in Holland and also in other countries. *Alleman* and *Bij de beesten af* were nominated for Academy awards. Although the number of movie-goers in Holland has sharply decreased, Haanstra's public has remained large and loyal.

In 1975 Haanstra made his first novel-based film. *Dokter Pulder zaait papavers* gives a subtle and detailed analysis of a number of fundamental human problems: loss of love, social failure, aging, addiction to drugs and liquor. The film is psychologically convincing and full of tension. *Een pak slaag*, again based on a novel by Anton Koolhaas, failed to interest the public. In 1983 Haanstra brought out another feature film with Simon Carmiggelt as the main character listening to the tragicomical monologues of all kinds of ordinary people. Carmiggelt's art, as an author, in rendering this type of monologue had won a wide audience for his daily columns which have appeared since 1945 in a Dutch newspaper. The film, *Vroeger kon je lachen*, was well received.

By virtue of the diversity of genres to which his films belong, and of the great reputation they have won him with critics and the public, Haanstra has made an invaluable contribution to the establishment of a Dutch film tradition. He is a very important representative of the Dutch documentary school which grew to fame in the 1960s and won countless awards at international film festivals. Haanstra's own films have won over 70 prizes; he received an Oscar for *Glas*, a short documentary film. As a director of feature films he has convinced a large audience that Dutch films can (and should) be judged according to the same standards as important foreign films.

His films, and also his cooperation with Simon Carmiggelt and Anton Koolhaas, show that Haanstra's work is firmly rooted in Dutch culture which, however, he transcends by taking it as an example of more general aspects of human behavior. This is beautifully exemplified in *Bij de beesten af*. Although his films do not contain explicit political statements, Haanstra is anything but a "neutral observer." By the art of montage he gives his films a deeper meaning which not infrequently embodies a critical view of human society. His eye for humorous, often tragicomical, situations yields poignant scenes in which general values mark individual lives and make them seem typical.

—Dorothee Verdaasdonk

HAMER, Robert.

British. Born in Kidderminster, 31 March 1911. Educated at Rossall and at Corpus Christi College, Cambridge. Started as cutter for London Films, 1935; editor, from 1938, then associate producer, from 1943; directed episode of *Dead of Night*, 1945; directed first feature, *Pink String and Sealing Wax*, 1945. *Died 4 December 1963*.

Films as Director:

1944   *Fiddlers Three* (Watt) (d of add'l scenes, assoc-pr, co-lyrics)
1945   "The Haunted Mirror" episode of **Dead of Night**; *Pink String and Sealing Wax*
1947   **It Always Rains on Sunday** (+ co-sc); *The Loves of Joanna Godden* (Frend) (d some scenes while Frend ill)
1949   **Kind Hearts and Coronets** (+ co-sc); *The Spider and the Fly*
1951   *His Excellency* (+ sc)
1952   *The Long Memory* (+ co-sc)
1954   *Father Brown* (*The Detective*) (+ co-sc); *To Paris with Love*
1958   *The Scapegoat* (+ sc)
1959   *School for Scoundrels* (*How to Win without Actually Cheating*)

Other Films:

1938   *Vessel of Wrath* (*The Beachcomber*) (Pommer) (ed); *St. Martin's Lane WC2* (*Sidewalks of London*) (Whelan) (co-ed)
1939   *Jamaica Inn* (Hitchcock) (ed)
1940   *La Cause commune* (*Factory Front*) (Cavalcanti) (short) (ed); *French Communique* (Cavalcanti) (short) (ed)
1941   *Mastery of the Sea* (Cavalcanti) (short) (ed); *Turned Out Nice Again* (Varnel) (ed, uncredited); *Ships with Wings* (Nolbandov) (ed); *The Foreman Went to France* (*Somewhere in France*) (Frend) (ed)
1943   *My Learned Friend* (Dearden and Hay) (assoc-pr, uncredited); *San Demetrio London* (Frend) (assoc-pr, co-sc)
1955   *Rowlandson's England* (Hawkesworth) (short) (co-sc); *Molière* (Tildian and de Chessin) (short) (commentary for English-language version)
1962   *Fifty-Five Days at Peking* (Ray) (add'l dialogue)
1963   *A Jolly Bad Fellow* (*They All Died Laughing*) (Chaffey) (co-sc)

Publications:

By HAMER: book—

Kind Hearts and Coronets, London and New York, 1974.

Robert Hamer (in coat, standing) directing *It Always Rains on Sunday*

By HAMER: articles—

Interview with Freda Lockhart, in *Sight and Sound* (London), October/December 1951.
"A Free Hand," in *Sight and Sound* (London), Spring 1959.

On HAMER: books—

Slide, Anthony, editor, *Michael Balcon, Producer*, London, 1969.
Barr, Charles, *Ealing Studios*, London, 1977.
Perry, George, *Forever Ealing*, London, 1981.
Fluegel, Jane, editor, *Michael Balcon: The Pursuit of British Cinema*, New York, 1984.
Murphy, Robert, *Realism and Tinsel*, London, 1989.

On HAMER: articles—

Vincent, J., "Hamer's Potted Lifemanship," in *Films and Filming* (London), July 1959.
Barr, Charles, "Projecting Britain and the British Character: Ealing Studios," in *Screen* (London), Summer 1974.
"*It Always Rains on Sunday* Section" of *Framework* (Norwich), Winter 1978–79.
"Robert Hamer," in *Film Dope* (London), March 1981.

*   *   *

Rarely can a director's career have risen and declined quite so abruptly as that of Robert Hamer. (Only Preston Sturges, perhaps, furnishes a comparable example.) Within the space of 15 years, Hamer directed two films (plus an episode of *Dead of Night*) evincing increasing mastery and promise, achieved one outstanding masterpiece, then went into virtually instantaneous decline, and produced half a dozen disappointing pictures culminating with a dismal flop. Three years later he was dead, at the age of 52: in David Thomson's words, "the most serious miscarriage of talent in the post-war British cinema."

Something of the forces that contributed to Hamer's sadly blighted career can be inferred from his films—especially the later ones, which often center around lonely, unattached individuals, victims of emotional atrophy. (Four of his pictures starred Alec Guinness, whose remote, withdrawn quality as an actor clearly matched Hamer's requirements.) The protagonists of *The Scapegoat, The Long Memory*, and *The Spider and the Fly* are all isolated, at odds with society; and a similarly bleak despair pervades the Chestertonian humor of *Father Brown*, preventing laughter. Only once, in *Kind Hearts and Coronets*, did Hamer strike the ideal balance between comedy and the blackness of his vision.

From the first, Hamer's films evoked a dark, dangerous world lurking below the calm surface of everyday life. (This, in itself, is enough to set them apart from the commonsense mainstream of Ealing Studios, for whom all Hamer's early films were made.) In his *Haunted Mirror* episode from *Dead of Night*, a bland young man is drawn into a past filled with sexual jealousy and madness. The son in *Pink String and Sealing Wax* escapes from his stiflingly respectable Victorian family into a glittering night-world of drink, lust and, ultimately, murder. The exciting, threatening past, in the person of her convict ex-lover, returns to confront the heroine of *It Always Rains on Sunday*. In all these films, Hamer displays an exceptional flair for the vivid recreation of atmosphere and milieu, as sure with the lush Victoriana of *Pink String* as with the contemporary East End realism of *It Always Rains on Sunday*. The latter offers a rare example of the pre-war fatalism of Carné effectively transposed to a British context.

All these elements—the black humour, the concern with suppressed passion, the sense of atmosphere, as well as Hamer's savagely ambiguous view of family life—come together in his one masterpiece, *Kind Hearts and Coronets*. Undoubtedly the finest black comedy ever produced by the British cinema, *Kind Hearts* blends wit, elegance, and unfailingly apt visual effects into a stylish and consistently satisfying film. The

humour, both verbal and visual, is wickedly subversive, and complemented by superb performances—especially from Dennis Price, Joan Greenwood, and Alec Guinness in his famous eight-fold role.

From there on, it was all downhill. Neither *The Spider and the Fly* nor *Father Brown* could be dismissed as failures, but they never approach the sustained mastery of *Kind Hearts*, and the vitality of the early films is also lacking. Michael Balcon, the head of Ealing, felt that Hamer was "engaged on a process of self-destruction." In the light of the artistic deterioration of the later films, paralleled by the director's gradual descent into alcoholism, Balcon's verdict would, sadly, appear to be justified.

—Philip Kemp

————

HANI, Susumi.

Japanese. Born in Tokyo, 19 October 1926. Graduated from Jiyu Gakuen, Tokyo. Married actress Sachiko Hidari, 1960. Began working for Kyoto News Agency, 1945; joined Iwanami Eiga production company, initially as still photographer, 1950; directed first film, 1952; producer, writer and director for TV, from 1959; formed Hani productions, mid-1960's. Recipient: First Prize (educational short), Venice Festival, and First Prize (short film), Cannes Festival, for *Children Who Draw*, 1955; Special Jury Prize for Best Direction, Moscow festival, for *Children Hand in Hand*, 1965.

Films as Director:

1952 *Seikatsu to mizu (Water in Our Life)* (co-d, co-sc) *Yuki matsuri (Snow Festival)* (+ sc)
1953 *Machi to gesui (The Town and Its Drains)* (+ sc)
1954 *Anata no biru (Your Beer)* (+ sc); *Kyoshitsu no kodomotachi (Children in the Classroom)* (+ sc)
1955 *Eo kaku kodomotachi (Children Who Draw)* (+ sc)
1956 *Group no shido (Group Instruction)* (+ sc); *Soseiji gakkyu (Twin Sisters)* (+ sc); *Dobutsuen nikki (Zoo Story)* (feature) (+ sc)
1958 *Shiga Naoya* (+ sc); *Horyu-ji (Horyu Temple)* (+ sc); *Umi wa ikiteiru (The Living Sea)* (feature) (+ sc); *Nihon no buyo (Dances in Japan)* (+ sc): *Tokyo 1958* (co-d, co-sc, co-ed)
1960 *Furyo shonen (Bad Boys)*
1962 *Mitasareta seikatsu (A Full Life)* (+ co-sc): *Te o tsunagu kora (Children Hand in Hand)*
1963 *Kanojo to kare (She and He)* (+ co-sc)
1965 *Bwana Toshi no uta (The Song of Bwana Toshi)* (+ co-sc)
1966 *Andesu no hanayome (Bride of the Andes)* (+ sc)
1968 *Hatsuoki jig ok uhen (Inferno of First Love. Nanami: Inferno of First Love)* (+ co-sc)
1969 *Aido (Aido, Slave of Love)*
1970 *Mio* (+ sc, co-ed)
1972 *Gozenchu no jikanwari (Timetable. Morning Schedule)* (+ co-sc)
1981 *Afurika monogatari (A Tale of Africa)* (co-d)

Publications:

By HANI: books—

Engishinai shuyakutachi [The Leading Players Who Do Not Act, The Non-professional Actor], 1958.
Camera to maiku no ronri [Aesthetics of Camera and Microphone], 1960.

Susumu Hani

Afurika konnan ryoko [My Travels in Africa, Report About Film Making in Africa], 1965.
Andes ryoko [Travels in the Andes, Report About Film Making in the Andes], 1966.

By HANI: articles—

Interview with James Blue, in *Film Comment* (New York), Spring 1969.
"En préparant Mio," in *Ecran* (Paris), July/August 1972.
"Susumu Hani: a decouvrir avec *Bwana Toshi*," interview with A. Tournès, in *Jeune Cinéma* (Paris), April/May 1979.

On HANI: books—

Mellen, Joan, *Voices from the Japanese Cinema*, New York, 1975.
Sato, Tadao, *Currents in Japanese Cinema*, Tokyo, 1982.

On HANI: article—

"Susumu Hani," in *Film Dope* (London), September 1981.

*   *   *

Hani was born in Tokyo in 1928, the son of a famous liberal family. After schooling, he worked for a while as a journalist at Kyoto Press and entered filmmaking as a documentarist in 1950 when he joined Iwanami Productions. Most of his later dramatic features reflect his early documentary training, relying on authentic locations, amateur actors, hand-held camera techniques, and an emphasis upon contemporary social issues.

His film career comprises three areas: documentary films; narratives relating to social problems, especially among the young; and dramas focusing on the emerging woman. Of the 18 documentaries made between 1952 and 1960, the best known are *Children in the Classroom* and *Children Who Draw Pictures*. The latter won the 1957 Robert Flaherty Award.

Hani's first dramatic feature, *Bad Boys*, emanated from many of his previous concerns. The film, a loose series of situations about reform school, was re-enacted by former inmates who improvised dialogue. For Hani, truth emerges from the juxtaposition of fiction and fact. He also believes that all people have an innate capacity for acting.

Subsequent films which deal with the effect of post-war urban realities on the lives of the young include *Children Hand in Hand* and *Inferno of First Love*. The former depicts young children in a provincial town and especially one backward child who becomes the butt of the other children's malicious teasing and pranks; the latter is a story of two adolescents in modern Tokyo, each of whom has been exploited, who find with each other a short-lived refuge.

Like his earlier documentaries, these films explore the themes of broken homes, the alienation of modern society, the traumatic effects of childhood, the oppressiveness of a feudal value system, and the difficulty of escaping, even in an alternative social structure. To all these films Hani brings a deep psychological understanding of the workings of the human psyche. Finally, each of these films focuses on individual growth and self-awakening, although Hani is clear to indicate that the problems cannot be solved on a personal level. Both topics—growing self-awareness and a critique of the existing social order—connect these works with Hani's second major theme, the emergence of women.

Hani's first film on this subject was *A Full Life*, which deals with the efforts of a young wife, married to a self-involved older man, to forge a life of her own in the competitive world of modern Tokyo. After demeaning work and involvement in the student demonstrations of the early 1960s, the wife returns home, a changed woman.

Hani's other films on this theme are *She and He*, the depiction of a middle-class marriage in which the wife gains independence by her kindness to a local ragpicker, and *Bride of the Andes*, the story of a mail-order Japanese bride in Peru, who finds personal growth through her relationship with the South American Indians. As in *A Full Life*, none of these women are able to make a full break with their husbands. However, through personal growth (usually affected by contact with a group or person marginal to society), they are able to challenge the patriarchal values of Japanese society as represented by their husbands and to return to the relationship with new understanding and dignity. Both films starred Sachiko Hidari, who was then his wife.

Contact with non-Japanese society, a challenge to deep-seated Japanese xenophobia, is also the theme of Hani's *The Song of Bwana Toshi*, which was filmed in Kenya and deals with Toshi, an ordinary Japanese man living in Central Africa. Here he cooperates with the natives and thus rises above his isolation to establish brotherhood with foreigners.

Hani's subsequent work *Timetable* combines his interest in contemporary youth with his continued interest in modern women. The story deals with two high school girls who decide to take a trip together. The fiction feature, which is narrated, was filmed in 8mm and each of the major actors was allowed to shoot part of the film. Further, the audience is informed of who is shooting, thereby acknowledging the filmmaker within the context of the work. The use of 8mm is not new for Hani. More than half of his fourth film was originally shot in 8mm. Likewise, the use of a narrator dates back to *A Full Life*.

Throughout his career Hani has concerned himself with people who have difficulty in communicating with one another and he remains one of the foremost psychologists of the Japanese cinema.

—Patricia Erens

HATHAWAY, Henry.

American. Born Marquis Henri Leopold de Fiennes in Sacramento, California, 13 March 1898. Educated in California until 1912. Military Service, 1918–19. Entered film industry as child actor and protégée of Allan Dwan, 1908; prop boy for Universal studios, 1912; film actor, 1912–17; assistant director for Sam Goldwyn's studio, then for Paramount, 1919–32; directed first film, *Heritage of the Desert*, for Paramount, 1932. *Died in Hollywood, 11 February 1985.*

Films as Director:

1932   *Heritage of the Desert; Wild Horse Mesa*
1933   *Under the Tonto Rim; Sunset Pass; Man of the Forest; To the Last Man; The Thundering Herd*
1934   *The Last Round-Up; Come on Marines!; The Witching Hour; Now and Forever*
1935   *The Lives of a Bengal Lancer; Peter Ibbetson*
1936   *Trail of the Lonesome Pine; Go West, Young Man; I Loved a Soldier* (unfinished)
1937   *Souls at Sea; Lest We Forget*
1938   *Spawn of the North*
1939   *The Real Glory*
1940   *Johnny Apollo; Brigham Young (Brigham Young—Frontiersman); Sundown*
1941   *The Shepherd of the Hills*
1942   *Ten Gentlemen from West Point; China Girl*
1944   *Home in Indiana; Wing and a Prayer*
1945   *Nob Hill; The House on 92nd Street*
1946   *The Dark Corner; 13 Rue Madeleine*
1947   *Kiss of Death*

Henry Hathaway

1948 *Call Northside 777*
1949 *Down to the Sea in Ships*
1950 *The Black Rose*; *Rawhide*
1951 *You're in the Navy Now* (*U.S.S. Tea Kettle*); *Fourteen Hours*; *The Desert Fox* (*Rommel—Desert Fox. The Story of Rommel*)
1952 *Diplomatic Courier*; "The Clarion Call" episode of *O. Henry's Full House* (*Full House*) (d linking scenes, uncredited); *Red Skies of Montana* (co-d with Newman, uncredited)
1953 *Niagara*; *White Witch Doctor*; *The Coronation Parade*
1954 *Prince Valiant*; *Garden of Evil*
1955 *The Racers* (*Such Men Are Dangerous*)
1956 *The Bottom of the Bottle* (*Beyond the River*); *Twenty-three Paces to Baker Street*
1957 *Legend of the Lost* (+ co-pr)
1958 *From Hell to Texas* (*Manhunt*)
1959 *Woman Obsessed*
1960 *North to Alaska* (+ pr); *Seven Thieves*
1962 "The Rivers", "The Plains" and "The Outlaws" episodes of *How the West Was Won*
1963 *Rampage* (Karlson; d begun by Hathaway)
1964 *Circus World* (*The Magnificent Showman*); *Of Human Bondage* (Hughes; Hathaway began film and d add'l scenes)
1965 *The Sons of Katie Elder*
1966 *Nevada Smith* (+ pr)
1967 *The Last Safari* (+ pr)
1968 *Five Card Stud*
1969 *True Grit*
1970 *Airport* (some direction when George Seaton became ill)
1971 *Raid on Rommel*; *Shootout*
1974 *Hangup*

Other Films:

1917 *The Storm Boy* (Baldwin) (role)
1923 *The Spoilers* (Hillyer) (asst d); *To the Last Man* (Fleming) (asst d)
1924 *The Heritage of the Desert* (Willat) (asst d); *The Border Legion* (Howard) (asst d)
1925 *The Thundering Herd* (Howard) (asst d); *Wild Horse Mesa* (Seitz) (asst d)
1926 *Bachelor Brides* (*Bachelor's Brides*) (Howard) (asst d); *Mantrap* (Fleming) (asst d); *Man of the Forest* (Waters) (asst d)
1927 *Hula* (Fleming) (asst d); *The Rough Riders* (*The Trumpet Call*) (Fleming) (asst d); **Underworld** (*Paying the Penalty*) (von Sternberg) (asst d)
1928 *The Last Command* (von Sternberg) (asst d); *Under the Tonto Rim* (Raymaker) (asst d); *The Shopworn Angel* (Wallace) (asst d)
1929 *Sunset Pass* (Brower) (asst d); *Wolf Song* (Fleming) (asst d); *Thunderbolt* (von Sternberg) (asst d); *The Virginian* (Fleming) (asst d); *Redskin* (Schertzinger) (asst d)
1930 *Seven Days Leave* (*Medals*) (Wallace) (asst d); *The Texan* (Cromwell) (asst d); *Morocco* (von Sternberg) (asst d); *The Spoilers* (Carewe) (asst d)
1931 *Dishonored* (von Sternberg) (asst d)
1932 **Shanghai Express** (von Sternberg) (asst d)
1972 *Seventy-five Years of Cinema Museum* (Herson and Guerra) (appearance)

Publications:

By HATHAWAY: articles—

Interview with Rui Nogueira, in *Focus on Film* (Washington, D.C.) v.7.
Interview with Michel Ciment and Bertrand Tavernier, in *Positif* (Paris), March 1972.
Interview with E. Decaux and B. Villien, in *Cinématographe* (Paris), October 1983.

On HATHAWAY: articles—

Crichton, K., "Lives of a Hollywood Director," in *Collier's* (New York), 5 September 1936.
Reid, John Howard, "The Best Second Fiddle," in *Films and Filming* (London), November 1962.
Sarris, Andrew, "Likable but Elusive," in *Film Culture* (New York), Spring 1963.
Eyles, Allen, "Henry Hathaway: Filmography," in *Focus on Film* (London), January/February 1970.
Kerbel, Michael, in *Village Voice* (New York), 18 November 1971.
Tavernier, Bertrand, "Sur Henry Leopold de Fienne, dit Hathaway," in *Positif* (Paris), February 1972.
Canham, Kingsley, "An Appreciation of Henry Hathaway," in *The Hollywood Professionals, Vol.1*, London, 1973.
Kaminsky, Stuart, "Legend of the Lost," in *Velvet Light Trap* (Madison), Winter 1975.
"Henry Hathaway," in *Film Dope* (London), September 1981.
Bawden, J., "Henry Hathaway," in *Films in Review* (New York), March 1984.
Obituary in *Variety* (New York), 20 February 1985.
Obituary in *Revue du Cinéma* (Paris), April 1985.
Ciné Revue (Paris), 27 August 1987.

* * *

Henry Hathaway had a reputation for being difficult on actors, but efficient with film. Aside from strictly biographical information, very little is generally said or known about Hathaway, and to a large extent this neglect is due to film critics.

Hathaway's career can be seen in terms of four distinct periods, each period representing a change in his assignments, control and interests. His western period (1932–34) comprises nine films including *Wild Horse Mesa*, *To the Last Man*, and *Under the Tonto Rim*. "Commercial versatility" characterizes films from 1934–45 including such contract projects as *Lives of a Bengal Lancer*, *Peter Ibbetson*, *Souls at Sea*, *Johnny Apollo*, and *Sundown*. The noir and semi-documentary films of 1945–52 include *The House on 92nd Street*, *The Dark Corner*, *14 Hours*, *13 Rue Madeleine*, *Kiss of Death*, and *Call Northside 777*. It is the films of Hathaway's mature period, beginning with *Niagara*, in 1952, that have been most neglected by critics.

Hathaway is clearly interested in foreign or exotic locales. This has been true throughout his career, but most strikingly in his mature period when only four of his films have had a contemporary or American setting. He has tended to see all of his exotic settings—Africa, the Old West, Mexico—as primitive, mysterious, grotesque, and even comic, dominated by a visual unreality. It has generally been accepted that Hathaway's one major excursion into surrealism was *Peter Ibbetson*. The evidence of the film shows, however, that depiction of unreality, the conversion of supposedly "real" settings into personal, unreal visions, is a growing interest with Hathaway. Unreality frequently intrudes on Hathaway's films, most strikingly in his use of painted backdrops and optical effects.

Hathaway's heroes are always remarkably humble and humanly weak. They drink, wench, cheat, but always respect and believe in the unknown. They are, like John Wayne in *Legend of the Lost*, mystics in a strange landscape, god-fearing men who have either been through a terrible crisis which taught them humility, or are undergoing that crisis in the course of the film.

The films in the mature period are about specific, dangerous quests undertaken by small groups in hostile, barren lands (with this in mind, *Prince Valiant* is not an act of commercial pandering, but a quintessential Hathaway film). The quest, for the hero, is an act of communion with nature or he learns that it should be. If the protagonist-hero is a younger man, he transgresses intentionally or by accident and is shown the way back to righteousness by an older, paternal figure. Invariably, the young protagonist or the woman must face the crisis of a father or husband who proves to have been less than he should have been. The woman, young man, or even villain must have the strength to accept this Jobian lesson or be destroyed by it and by their own hatred.

As should be obvious by now, Hathaway's films are filled with striking mixtures of Christianity and paganism. Mystical omens and forebodings abound, and Hathaway characters frequently quote from the Old Testament to gain strength or understanding.

—Stuart M. Kaminsky

HAWKS, Howard.

American. Born Howard Winchester Hawks in Goshen, Indiana, 30 May 1896. Educated at Pasadena High School, California, 1908–13; Phillips Exeter Academy, New Hampshire, 1914–16; Cornell University, New York, degree in mechanical engineering, 1917. Served in U.S. Army Air Corps, 1917–19. Married 1) Athole (Hawks), 1924 (divorced 1941); 2) Nancy Raye Gross, 1941 (divorced), one daughter; 3) Mary (Dee) Hartford (divorced), two sons, two daughters. Worked in property dept. of Famous Players-Lasky during vacations, Hollywood, 1916–17; designer in airplane factory, 1919–22; worked in independent production as editor, writer, and assistant director, from 1922; in charge of story dept. at Paramount, 1924–25; signed as director for Fox, 1925–29; directed first feature, *Road to Glory*, 1926; formed Motion Picture Alliance for the Preservation of American Ideals, with Borden Chase, 1944. Recipient: Quarterly Award, Directors Guild of America, for *Red River*, 1948/49; Honorary Oscar for "A master American filmmaker whose creative efforts hold a distinguished place in world cinema," 1974. *Died in Palm Springs, California, 26 December 1977.*

Films as Director:

1926 *The Road to Glory* (+ story); *Fig Leaves* (+ story)
1927 *The Cradle Snatchers*; *Paid to Love*; *Fazil*
1928 *A Girl in Every Port* (+ co-sc); *The Air Circus* (co-d)
1929 *Trent's Last Case*
1930 *The Dawn Patrol*
1931 *The Criminal Code*
1932 *The Crowd Roars* (+ story); *Tiger Shark*; **Scarface: The Shame of a Nation** (+ pr, bit role as man on bed)
1933 *Today We Live*; *The Prizefighter and the Lady* (*Everywoman's Man*) (Van Dyke; d parts of film, claim disputed)
1934 *Viva Villa!* (Conway; d begun by Hawks); *Twentieth Century*
1935 *Barbary Coast*; *Ceiling Zero*
1936 *The Road to Glory*; *Come and Get It* (co-d)
1938 **Bringing Up Baby**
1939 *Only Angels Have Wings*
1940 **His Girl Friday**
1941 *The Outlaw* (Hughes; d begun by Hawks); *Sergeant York*; *Ball of Fire*
1943 *Air Force*
1944 **To Have and Have Not**
1946 **The Big Sleep**
1947 *A Song is Born* (remake of *Ball of Fire*)
1948 **Red River** (+ pr)
1949 *I Was a Male War Bride* (*You Can't Sleep Here*)
1952 *The Big Sky* (+ pr); "The Ransom of Red Chief" episode of *O. Henry's Full House* (episode cut from some copies) (+ pr); *Monkey Business*
1953 *Gentlemen Prefer Blondes*
1955 *Land of the Pharaohs* (+ pr)
1959 **Rio Bravo** (+ pr)
1962 *Hatari!* (+ pr)
1963 *Man's Favorite Sport* (+ pr)
1965 *Red Line 7000* (+ story, pr)
1966 *El Dorado* (+ pr)
1970 *Rio Lobo* (+ pr)

Other Films:

1917 *A Little Princess* (Neilan) (d some scenes, uncredited; prop boy)
1923 *Quicksands* (Conway) (story, sc, pr)
1924 *Tiger Love* (Melford) (sc)
1925 *The Dressmaker from Paris* (Bern) (co-story, sc)
1926 *Honesty—the Best Policy* (Bennett and Neill) (story, sc); **Underworld** (von Sternberg) (co-sc, uncredited)
1932 *Red Dust* (Fleming) (co-sc, uncredited)
1936 *Sutter's Gold* (Cruze) (co-sc, uncredited)
1937 *Captain Courageous* (Fleming) (co-sc, uncredited)
1938 *Test Pilot* (Fleming) (co-sc, uncredited)
1939 **Gone with the Wind** (Fleming) (add'l dialogue, uncredited); *Gunga Din* (Stevens) (co-sc, uncredited)
1943 *Corvette K-225* (*The Nelson Touch*) (Rosson) (pr)
1951 *The Thing* (*The Thing from Another World*) (Nyby) (pr)

Publications:

By HAWKS: book—

Hawks on Hawks, edited by Joseph McBride, Berkeley, 1982.

By HAWKS: articles—

Interview with Jacques Becker, Jacques Rivette, and Francois Truffaut, in *Cahiers du Cinéma* (Paris), February 1956.
Interview in *Movie* (London), 5 November 1962.
"Man's Favorite Director, Howard Hawks," interview in *Cinema* (Beverly Hills), November/December 1963.
Interview with James R. Silke, Serge Daney, and Jean-Louis Noames, in *Cahiers du Cinéma* (Paris), November 1964.
Interview, in *Interviews with Film Directors* by Andrew Sarris, New York, 1967.
Interview with Jean-Louis Comolli, Jean Narboni, and Bertrand Tavernier, in *Cahiers du Cinéma* (Paris), July/August 1967.
"Gunplay and Horses," with David Austen, in *Films and Filming* (London), October 1968.
"Do I Get to Play the Drunk this Time," an interview in *Sight and Sound* (London), Spring 1971.
Interviews with Naomi Wise and Michael Goodwin, in *Take One* (Montreal), November/December 1971 and March 1973.
"Hawks Talks," interview with J. McBride, in *Film Comment* (New York), May/June 1974.
"Hawks on Film, Politics, and Childrearing," interview with C. Penley and others, in *Jump Cut* (Berkeley), January/February 1975.
"You're goddam right I remember," interview with K. Murphy and R.T. Jameson, in *Movietone News* (Seattle), June 1977.

On HAWKS: books—

Bogdanovich, Peter, *The Cinema of Howard Hawks*, New York, 1962.
Missiaen, Jean-Claude, *Howard Hawks*, Paris, 1966.
Wood, Robin, *Howard Hawks*, London, 1968, revised 1981.
Gili, J.-A., *Howard Hawks*, Paris, 1971.
Willis, D.C., *The Films of Howard Hawks*, Metuchen, New Jersey, 1975.
Murphy, Kathleen A., *Howard Hawks: An American Auteur in the Hemingway Tradition*, Ann Arbor, Michigan, 1978.
Giannetti, Louis D., *Masters of the American Cinema*, Englewood Cliffs, New Jersey, 1981.
Mast, Gerald, *Howard Hawks, Storyteller*, New York, 1982.
Poague, Leland, *Howard Hawks*, Boston, 1982.
Belton, John, *Cinema Stylists*, Metuchen, New Jersey, 1983.
Simsolo, Noel, *Howard Hawks*, Paris, 1984.
Branson, Clark, *Howard Hawks: A Jungian Study*, Los Angeles, 1987.

Howard Hawks

On HAWKS: articles—

Rivette, Jacques, and François Truffaut, "Howard Hawks," in *Films in Review* (New York), November 1956.

Perez, Michel, "Howard Hawks et le western," in *Présence du Cinéma* (Paris), July/September 1959.

Dyer, John Peter, "Sling the Lamps Low," in *Sight and Sound* (London), Summer 1962.

Sarris, Andrew, "The World of Howard Hawks," in *Films and Filming* (London), July and August 1962.

"Hawks Issue" of *Cahiers du Cinéma* (Paris), January 1963.

"Hawks Issue" of *Movie* (London), 5 December 1962.

Comolli, Jean-Louis, "Howard Hawks ou l'ironique," in *Cahiers du Cinéma* (Paris), November 1964.

Brackett, Leigh, "A Comment on the Hawksian Woman," in *Take One* (Montreal), July/August 1971.

Wise, Naomi, "The Hawksian Woman," in *Take One* (Montreal), April 1972.

"Hawks Issue" of *Filmkritik* (Munich), May/June 1973.

Wood, Robin, "To Have (Written) and Have Not (Directed)," in *Film Comment* (New York), May/June 1973.

Haskell, Molly, "Howard Hawks: Masculine Feminine," in *Film Comment* (New York), March/April 1974.

Cohen, M., "Hawks in the Thirties," in *Take One* (Montreal), December 1975.

Richards, Jeffrey, "The Silent Films of Howard Hawks," in *Focus on Film* (London), Summer/Autumn 1976.

Durgnat, Raymond, "Hawks Isn't Good Enough," in *Film Comment* (New York), July/August 1977; see also February and March/April 1978.

"Hawks Section" of *Positif* (Paris), July/August 1977.

"Dossier: le cinéma de Howard Hawks," in *Cinématographe* (Paris), March 1978.

Rohmer, Eric, and others, "Hommage à Hawks," in *Cinema* (Paris), March 1978.

McBride, J., "Hawks," in *Film Comment* (New York), March/April 1978.

Burdick, D.M., "Danger of Death: The Hawksian Woman as Agent of Destruction," in *Post Script* (Jacksonville, Florida), Fall 1981.

McCarthy, T., "Phantom Hawks," in *Film Comment* (New York), September/October 1982.

Lev, P., "Elaborations on a Theme," in *Quarterly Review of Film Studies* (New York), Spring 1984.

Jewell, R.B., "How Howard Hawks Brought Baby Up," in *Journal of Popular Film* (Washington, D.C.), Winter 1984.

Walker, Michael, "Hawks and *Film Noir: The Big Sleep*," in *Cine-Action!* (Toronto), no. 13/14, 1988.

On HAWKS: films—

Bogdanovich, Peter, *The Great Professional—Howard Hawks*, for TV, Great Britain, 1967.

Schickel, Richard, *The Men Who Made the Movies: Howard Hawks*, for TV, U.S., 1973.

Blumenberg, Hans, *Ein verdammt gutes Leben* (*A Hell of a Good Life*), West Germany, 1978.

*   *   *

Howard Hawks was perhaps the greatest director of American genre films. Hawks made films in almost every American genre, and each of these films could well serve as one of the very best examples and artistic embodiments of the type: gangster (*Scarface*), private eye (*The Big Sleep*), western (*Red River, Rio Bravo*), screwball comedy (*Bringing Up Baby*), newspaper reporter (*His Girl Friday*), prison picture (*The Criminal Code*), science fiction (*The Thing*), musical (*Gentlemen Prefer Blondes*), race-car drivers (*The Crowd Roars, Red Line 7000*), air pilots (*Only Angels Have Wings*). But into each of these narratives of generic expectations Hawks infused his particular themes, motifs, and techniques. Born in the midwest at almost the same time that the movies themselves were born in America, Hawks migrated with his family to southern California when the movies did; he spent his formative years working on films, learning to fly, and studying engineering at Cornell University. His initial work in silent films as a writer and producer would serve him well in his later years as a director, when he would produce and, if not write, then control the writing of his films as well. Although Hawks's work has been consistently discussed as exemplary of the Hollywood studio style, Hawks himself did not work for a single studio on a long-term contract but was an independent producer who sold his projects to every Hollywood studio.

Whatever the genre of a Hawks film, it bore traits that made it unmistakably a Hawks film. The narrative was always elegantly, symmetrically structured and patterned, a sign of both Hawks's sharp sense of storytelling and his good sense to work closely with very talented writers: Ben Hecht, William Faulkner, and Jules Furthman being the most notable among them. Hawks's films were devoted to characters who were professionals with fervent vocational commitments, men who were good at what they did, whether flying the mail, driving race cars, driving cattle, or reporting the news. These vocational commitments were usually fulfilled by the union of two apparently opposite physical types who were spiritually one: either the union of the harder, tougher, older male and a softer, younger, prettier male (John Wayne and Montgomery Clift in *Red River*, Wayne and Ricky Nelson in *Rio Bravo*), or by a sharp, tough male and an equally sharp, tough female (Cary Grant and Rosalind Russell in *His Girl Friday*, Bogart and Bacall in *To Have and Have Not* and *The Big Sleep*, John Barrymore and Carole Lombard in *Twentieth Century*). This spiritual alliance of physical opposites revealed Hawks's unwillingness to accept the cultural stereotype that those who are able to accomplish difficult tasks are those who appear able to accomplish them.

This tension between appearance and ability, surface and essence in Hawks's films led to several other themes and techniques. Characters talk very tersely in Hawks films, refusing to put their thoughts and feelings into explicit speeches which would either sentimentalize or vulgarize those internal abstractions. Instead, Hawks's characters reveal their feelings in action, not in talk, showing what they mean by what they do, not what they say. Hawks deflects his portrayal of the inner life from explicit speeches to symbolic physical objects—concrete visual images of things that convey the intentions of the person who handles, uses, or controls the piece of physical matter. One of those things, the coin which George Raft nervously flips in *Scarface*, has become a mythic icon of American culture itself—symbolic in itself of American gangsters and American gangster movies (and used as such in both *Singin' in the Rain* and *Some Like It Hot*). Another of Hawks's favorite things, the lighting of cigarettes, became his subtextual way of showing who cares about whom without recourse to dialogue.

Consistent with his narratives, Hawks's visual style was one of dead-pan understatement, never proclaiming its trickiness or brilliance but effortlessly communicating the values of the stories and the characters. Hawks was a master of point-of-view, knowing precisely which camera perspective would convey the necessary psychological and moral information. That point of view could either confine us to the perceptions of a single character (Marlowe in *The Big Sleep*), ally us with the more vital of two competing life styles (with the vitality of Oscar Jaffe in *Twentieth Century*, Susan Vance in *Bringing Up Baby*, Walter Burns in *His Girl Friday*, or withdraw to a scientific detachment that allows the viewer to weigh the paradoxes and ironies of a love battle between two equals (between the two army partners in *I Was a Male War Bride*, the husband and wife in *Monkey Business*, or the older and younger cowboy in *Red River*). Hawks's films are also masterful in their atmospheric lighting, and the hanging electric or kerosene lamp that dangles into the top of a Hawks frame became almost as much his signature as the lighting of cigarettes.

Hawks's view of character in film narrative was that in movies actor and character were inseparable. As a result his films were very improvisatory, allowing actors to add, interpret, or alter lines as they wished, rather than forcing them to stick to the script. This trait not only led to the energetic spontaneity of many Hawks films but also to their helping to create or shape the human archetype that the star came to represent in our culture. John Barrymore, John Wayne, Humphrey Bogart, and Cary Grant all refined or established their essential personae under Hawks's direction, while many who would become stars were either discovered by Hawks or given their first chance to play a major role in one of his films. Among Hawks's most important discoveries were Paul Muni, George Raft, Carole Lombard, Angie Dickinson, Montgomery Clift, and his Galatea, Lauren Bacall.

Although Hawks continued to make films until he was almost 75, there is disagreement about the artistic energy and cinematic value of the films he made after 1950. For some, Hawks's artistic decline in the 1950s and 1960s was both a symptom and an effect of the overall decline of the movie industry and the studio system itself. For others, Hawks's later films—slower, longer, less energetically brilliant than his studio-era films—were more probing and personal explorations of the themes and genres he had charted for the three previous decades.

—Gerald Mast

HEIFITZ, Josef.

Russian. Born Josef Yefimovitch Heifitz (sometimes transliterated as Kheifits) in Minsk, Russia, 17 December 1905. Educated at Leningrad School of Screen Arts, graduated 1927. Married, two sons filmmakers Vladimir and Dmitri Svetozarov. Formed partnership with fellow student Alexander Zarkhi; they directed first film together, *A Song of Steel*, for Sovkino, 1928; joined Soyuzfilm, 1933, Lenfilm, 1935; ended partnership with Zarkhi, 1950. Recipient: Stalin Prize, for *Razgrom Japonii*, 1945.

Films as Director:

1928 *Pesn o metallye* (*A Song of Steel*) (co-d, + co-sc, co-ed)
1930 *Veter v litso* (*Facing the Wind*) (co-d)
1931 *Polden* (*Noon*) (co-d, + co-sc)
1933 *Moya rodina* (*My Fatherland. My Country*) (co-d, + co-sc)
1935 *Goryachie dyenechki* (*Hectic Days*) (co-d, + co-sc)
1936 *Deputat Baltiki* (*Baltic Deputy*) (co-d, + co-sc)
1940 *Chlen pravitelstva* (*The Great Beginning. Member of the Government*) (co-d, + co-sc)
1942 *Yevo zovut Sukhe-Bator* (*His Name is Sukhe-Bator*) (co-d, + co-sc)
1944 *Malakhov Kurgan* (co-d, + co-sc)
1945 *Razgrom Japonii* (*The Defeat of Japan*) (co-d, + co-sc, co-ed)
1946 *Vo imya zhizni* (*In the Name of Life*) (co-d, + co-sc)
1948 *Dragotsennye zerna* (*The Precious Grain*) (co-d)
1950 *Ogni Baku* (*Flames over Baku. Fires of Baku*) (co-d) (released 1958)
1953 *Vesna v Moskve* (*Spring in Moscow*) (co-d)
1954 *Bolshaya semya* (*The Big Family*)
1956 *Dyelo Rumyantseva* (*The Rumyantsev Case*) (+ co-sc)
1958 *Dorogoi moi chelovek* (*My Dear Fellow. My Dear Man*) (+ co-sc)
1960 *Dama s sobachkoi* (*The Lady with the Little Dog*) (+ sc)
1962 *Gorizont* (*Horizon*)
1964 *Dyen schastya* (*A Day of Happiness*) (+ co-sc)
1967 *V gorodye S* (*In the Town of S*) (+ sc)
1970 *Saliut, Maria!* (*Salute, Maria*) (+ co-sc)
1973 *Plokhoy khoroshyi chelovek* (*The Duel. The Bad Good Man*) (+ sc)
1976 *Edinstvennaia* (*The Only One. The One and Only*) (+ co-sc)
1977 *Asya* (*Love Should be Guarded*) (+ sc)
1979 *Vpervye zamuzhem* (*Married for the First Time*) (+ co-sc)
1982 *Shurochka*
1985 *Podsudimy* (*The Accused*) (+ co-sc)
1987 *Vspomnim, Tovarisc*

Other Films:

1928 *Luna sleva* (*The Moon is to the Left*) (Ivanov) (co-sc, asst-d)
1930 *Transport ognya* (*Transport of Fire*) (Ivanov) (co-sc, asst-d)

Publications:

By HEIFITZ: articles—

"Director's Notes," in *Iskusstvo Kino* (Moscow), no. 1, 1966.
Interview in *Iskusstvo Kino* (Moscow), no. 2, 1971.
Interview in *Soviet Film* (Moscow), no. 9, 1976.
Article in *Soviet Film* (Moscow), no. 11, 1978.

On HEIFITZ: books—

Christie, Ian, and Richard Taylor, editors, *The Film Factory: Russian and Soviet Cinema in Documents 1896–1939*, London, 1988.

On HEIFITZ: articles—

Soviet Film (Moscow), no. 2, 1967, and no. 2, 1971.
Panoráma, no. 4, 1976.
Lipkov, "Iosif Heifits," in *Soviet Film* (Moscow), February 1983.
"Iosif Kheifits," in *Film Dope* (London), September 1984.
Gillett, John, and Claire Kitson, "Chekhov and After: The Films of Iosif Heifits," in *National Film Theatre Booklet* (London), December 1986.
Dobrotvorsky, S., "Father and Sons," in *Soviet Film* (Moscow), April 1987.

*   *   *

It is impossible to discuss the career of Iosif Heifitz without also paying tribute to Alexander Zarkhi, with whom he worked for over 20 years after they both left the Leningrad Technicum of Cinema Art in 1927. The first film they made together was *A Head Wind* but their first collaboration to gain prominence was *Baltic Deputy*, a landmark film of "socialist" or "historic" realism which transcends the genre's usual limitations of bombastic propaganda, moral and political schematism, and impossibly perfect and idealised heroes and heroines. The story of an elderly professor who, despite the disapproval of his stuffy academic colleagues, joins the forces of revolution in 1917 and is eventually elected to the Petrograd Soviet by the sailors of the Baltic fleet, it contains both humour and humanity, and is particularly distinguished by an excellent central performance from Nikolai Cherkasov. Equally impressive, for the same reasons, is *Member of the Government* which, through the story of a young farm worker who, during the rural collectivisation period, rises to government level despite the opposition of her husband, deals with the improved status of women in the USSR after 1917 (similar concern with the position of women can be seen in his later *Married for the First Time*). Vera Maretskaya is superb throughout, the first of several memorable female leading roles in Heifitz's films.

Both Zarkhi and Heifitz benefited creatively from their split in 1950, although it is undoubtedly Heifitz who has become the

Josef Heifitz: *Dama s sobachkoi*

better known. His second film on his own, *The Big Family*, is an impressive piece of work and has come to be recognised as one of the first forerunners of the post-Stalin rejuvenation of the Soviet cinema. Focussing on the lives of a family of shipbuilders it has a feeling for everyday realities, a lively, detailed texture, is concerned with the problems of the individual as opposed to the masses, and generally tries to avoid producing neat, formulaic, ideologically "sound" solutions.

In 1960 Heifitz made the film for which he is probably best known, *The Lady with the Little Dog*, which turned out to be the first of a Chekhov trilogy comprising *In the Town of S* and *The Bad Good Man*. It is hardly surprising that the director should have been drawn to Chekhov, nor that his Chekhov adaptations are among his finest works, for both share an understanding of the complexity of human beings, a feeling for the minute, telling detail, and a remarkable ability to conjure an almost tangible sense of atmosphere. Indeed, in the trilogy some of the most "Chekhovian" moments are not in the original stories at all! Thus it is hardly surprising to find Heifitz admitting (in an interview in *Soviet Film*) that "much as I love Dostoevsky I regard Chekhov as my teacher." Stressing Chekhov's concern with the importance of clear and legible writing (in both senses of the word) he continues, "I try to apply the laws of Chekhovian prose, with due adjustments to suit our time, in my films about the present. I have always considered Chekhov to be among the most modern of writers, and have never treated him as a venerable, 'moth-eaten' classic. To me Chekhov has always been an example of a social-minded writer. . . . The hallmark of Chekhov's approach is that, while describing these small, weak people living in an atmosphere of triviality and inaction, he preserved his faith in a better future

and in the power of the human spirit. So he imparted to them an important quality—the capacity to make a critical judgment of the surrounding world and of oneself. This is the quality that I prize most highly."

Thus, in spite of his obvious relish for period feel in Chekhov (and Turgenev, in the beautiful *Asya*), Heifitz is obviously a great deal more than a "period" director. Claiming that modern Soviet film-makers are "heirs to the humanistic tradition of Russian literature" he has said that his films are "a panorama of the better part of a century." Looking at the remarkable gallery of characters which he has presented with his characteristic mix of everyday heroism and humanity, it is hard to disagree. No-one would claim that Heifitz is a stylistic innovator, but his films, whether set in the past or present, all exhibit an equally strong feeling for the minutiae of daily life and the humanity of their characters. In this last respect it should be pointed out that Heifitz is a masterly director of actors, and that he largely "discovered" Nikolai Cherkasov, Vera Maretskaya, Iya Savvina and Alexei Batalov, all of whom have given some of their finest performances in his films. As he himself characteristically put it, "many directors today strive for documentary realism and naturalness of tone. But in that case individuality disappears, and the human voice with its infinite inflections gives way to banality. . . . Directing in the cinema means above all directing the actor. The actor is the focal point of the director's efforts and experience."

—Julian Petley.

HENNING-JENSEN, Astrid and Bjarne.

Danish. Born in Frederiksberg, Denmark; Astrid (née Astrid Smahl), 10 December 1914, Bjarne: 6 October 1908. Married 6 October 1938. Bjarne actor at various theatres, Astrid actress at "Riddersalen," Copenhagen, 1931–38; Bjarne director at Nordisk Films Kompagni, 1940–50; Astrid assistant director, 1941, then director, at Nordisk, 1943; Astrid at Norsk Film A/S, Oslo, 1950–52; Bjarne and Astrid both worked as freelance writers and directors for film, theatre, radio and television, from early 1950's. Recipient: Astrid: Catholic Film Office Award, Cannes Festival, for *Paw*, 1960; Best Director, Berlin Festival, for *Winter Children*, 1979. Address: Astrid: Frederiksberg Allé 76, DK-1820 Copenhagen V, Denmark; Bjarne: Fasangården, Svennerup, DK-4683 Rønnede, Denmark.

Films as Directors:

1940 *Cykledrengene i Tørvegraven* (Bjarne only)
1941 *Hesten paa Kongens Nytorv* (Bjarne only); *Brunkul* (Bjarne only); *Arbejdet kalder* (Bjarne only); *Chr. IV som Bygherre* (*Christian IV: Master Builder*) (Bjarne only)
1942 *Sukker* (*Sugar*) (Bjarne only)
1943 *Korn* (*Corn*) (Bjarne only); *Hesten* (*Horses*) (Bjarne only); *Føllet* (Bjarne only); *Papir* (*Paper*) (Bjarne only); *Naar man kun er ung* (*To Be Young*) (Bjarne only); *S.O.S. Kindtand* (*S.O.S. Molars*)
1944 *De danske Sydhavsøer* (*Danish Island*) (Bjarne only)
1945 *Flyktingar finner en hamn* (*Fugitives Find Shelter*); *Dansk politi i Sverige* (Astrid only); *Folketingsvalg 1945*; *Brigaden i Sverige* (*Danish Brigade in Sweden*) (Bjarne only); *Frihedsfonden* (*Freedom Committee*) (Bjarne only)
1946 *Ditte Menneskebarn* (*Ditte: Child of Man*) (Bjarne only)
1947 *Stemning i April*; *De pokkers unger* (*Those Blasted Kids*); *Denmark Grows Up* (Astrid co-d only)
1948 *Kristinus Bergman*
1949 *Palle alene i Verden* (*Palle Alone in the World*) (Astrid only)
1950 *Vesterhavsdrenge* (*Boys from the West Coast*)
1951 *Kranes Konditori* (*Krane's Bakery Shop*) (Astrid only)
1952 *Ukjent mann* (*Unknown Man*) (Astrid only)
1953 *Solstik*
1954 *Tivoligarden spiller* (*Tivoli Garden Games*); *Ballettens børn* (*Ballet Girl*) (Astrid only)
1955 *Kaerlighed pa kredit* (*Love on Credit*) (Astrid only); *En saelfangst i Nordgrønland* (Bjarne only); *Hvor bjergene sejler* (*Where Mountains Float*) (Bjarne only)
1959 *Hest på sommerferie* (Astrid only); *Paw* (*Boy of Two Worlds. The Lure of the Jungle*) (Astrid only)
1961 *Een blandt mange* (Astrid only)
1962 *Kort är sommaren* (*Short Is the Summer*) (Bjarne only)
1965 *De blå undulater* (Astrid only)
1966 *Utro* (*Unfaithful*) (Astrid only)
1967 *Min bedstefar er en stok* (Astrid only)
1968 *Nille* (Astrid only)
1969 *Mig og dig* (*Me and You*) (Astrid only)
1974 *Skipper & Co.* (Bjarne only)
1978 *Vinterbørn* (*Winter Children*) (Astrid only, + sc, ed)
1980 *Øjeblikket* (*The Moment*) (Astrid only)
1986 *Barndommens gade* (*Street of Childhood*) (Astrid only)

Other Films:

1937 *Cocktail* (Astrid: role)
1938 *Kongen bød* (Bjarne: role)
1939 *Genboerne* (Bjarne: role)
1940 *Jens Langkniv* (Bjarne: role)
1942 *Damen med de lyse Handsker* (Christensen) (Bjarne: role)

*　　　*　　　*

Astrid and Bjarne Henning-Jensen started as stage actors, but shortly after they married in 1938 they began working in films. Bjarne Henning-Jensen directed several government documentaries beginning in 1940 and he was joined by Astrid in 1943. At that time the Danish documentary film, strongly influenced by the British documentary of the 1930s was blooming, and Bjarne Henning-Jensen played an important part in this. In 1943 he made his first feature film, Astrid serving as assistant director. *Naar man kun er ung* was a light, everyday comedy, striving for a relaxed and charming style, but it was too cute, and it was politely received. Their next film, *Ditte Menneskebarn*, was their breakthrough, and the two were instantly considered as the most promising directors in the postwar Danish cinema. The film was an adaptation of a neoclassical novel by Martin Andersen-Nexø. It was a realistic story of a young country girl and her tragic destiny as a victim of social conditions. The novel, published between 1917 and 1921, was in five volumes, but the Henning-Jensens used only parts of the novel. The sentimentality of the book was, happily, subdued in the film, and it is a sensitive study of a young girl in her milieu. The film was the first example of a more realistic and serious Danish film and it paralleled similar trends in contemporary European cinema, even if one would refrain from calling the film neorealistic. It was a tremendous success in Denmark and it also won a certain international recognition.

Astrid and Bjarne Henning-Jensen's film was a sincere attempt to introduce reality and authentic people to the Danish film. They continued this effort in their subsequent films, but a certain facile approach, a weakness for cute effects, and a sensibility on the verge of sentimentality, made their films less and less interesting. In the 1950s Bjarne Henning-Jensen returned to documentaries. In 1955 he made the pictorially beautiful *Hvor bjergene sejler*, about Greenland. He attempted a comeback to features in 1962 with a rather pedestrian adaptation of Knut Hamsun's novel *Pan* called *Kort är sommaren*. His last film, in 1974, was a failure. Astrid Henning-Jensen continued making films on her own. She made two carefully directed and attractive films in Norway, and in the 1960s she tried to keep up with the changing times in a couple of films. But it was not until the last few years that she regained her old position. In *Vinterbørn*, about women and their problems in a maternity ward, and in *Øjeblikket*, treating the problems of a young couple when it is discovered that the woman is dying of cancer, she worked competently within an old established genre in Danish films, the problem-oriented popular drama.

—Ib Monty

HEPWORTH, Cecil.

British. Born in Lambeth, London, 19 March 1874. Patented hand-feed lamp for optical lantern, 1895; assistant projectionist to Birt Acres, 1896; became cameraman for Charles Urban, 1898; formed Hepwix Films at Walton-on-Thames, worked as actor and director, and patented film developing system; formed Hepworth Manufacturing Company, 1904; patented Vivaphone "Talking Film" device and became first chairman, Kinematograph Manufacturer's Association, 1910; founded British Board of Film Censors, 1911; founded Hepworth Picture Plays, 1919 (company goes bankrupt, 1923); technical advisor and producer, National Screen Service, 1936. *Died in Greenford, Middlesex, 9 February 1953.*

Cecil Hepworth

Films as Director:

1898   *Oxford and Cambridge Boat Race* (short); *The Interrupted Picnic* (short); *Exchange Is No Robbery* (short); *The Immature Punter* (short); *The Quarrelsome Anglers* (short); *Two Fools in a Canoe* (short)
1899   *Express Train in a Railway Cutting* (short)
1900   *Wiping Something Off the Slate* (short); *The Conjurer and the Boer* (short); *The Punter's Mishap* (short); *The Gunpowder Plot* (short); *Explosion of a Motor Car* (short); *The Egg-Laying Man* (short); *Clown and Policeman* (short); *Leapfrog as Seen by the Frog* (short); *How It Feels to be Run Over* (short); *The Eccentric Dancer* (short); *The Bathers* (short); *The Sluggard's Surprise* (short); *The Electricity Cure* (short); *The Beggar's Deceit* (short); *The Burning Stable* (short); *Topsy Turvy Villa* (short); *The Kiss* (short)
1901   *How the Burglar Tricked the Bobby* (short); *The Indian Chief and the Seidlitz Powder* (short); *Comic Grimacer* (short); *Interior of a Railway Carriage* (short); *Funeral of Queen Victoria* (short); *Coronation of King Edward VII* (short); *The Glutton's Nightmare* (short)
1902   *The Call to Arms* (short); *How to Stop a Motor Car* (short)
1903   *The Absent-Minded Bootblack* (short); *Alice in Wonderland* (short); *Firemen to the Rescue* (short); *Saturday's Shopping* (short)
1904   *The Jonah Man* (short)
1905   *Rescued by Rover* (short); *Falsely Accused* (short); *The Alien's Invasion* (short); *A Den of Thieves* (short)
1907   *A Seaside Girl* (short)
1908   *John Gilpin's Ride* (short)
1909   *Tilly the Tomboy* (short)
1911   *Rachel's Sin* (short)
1914   *Blind Fate* (short); *Unfit or The Strength of the Weak* (short); *The Hills Are Calling* (short); *The Basilisk*; *His Country's Bidding* (short); *The Quarry Mystery* (short); *Time the Great Healer*; *Morphia the Death Drug* (short); *Oh My Aunt* (short)
1915   *The Canker of Jealousy*; *A Moment of Darkness* (short); *Court-Martialled*; *The Passing of a Soul* (short); *The Bottle*; *The Baby on the Barge*; *The Man Who Stayed at Home*; *Sweet Lavender*; *The Golden Pavement*; *The Outrage*; *Iris*
1916   *Trelawney of the Wells*; *A Fallen Star*; *Sowing the Wind*; *Annie Laurie*; *Comin' Thro' the Rye*; *The Marriage of William Ashe*; *Molly Bawn*; *The Cobweb*
1917   *The American Heiress*; *Nearer My God to Thee*
1918   *The Refugee*; *Tares*; *Broken in the Wars*; *The Blindness of Fortune*; *The Touch of a Child*; *Boundary House*
1919   *The Nature of the Beast*; *Sunken Rocks*; *Sheba*; *The Forest on the Hill*
1920   *Anna the Adventuress*; *Alf's Button*; *Helen of Four Gates*; *Mrs. Erricker's Reputation*
1921   *Tinted Venus*; *Narrow Valley*; *Wild Heather*; *Tansy*
1922   *The Pipes of Pan*; *Mist in the Valley*; *Strangling Threads*; *Comin' Thro' the Rye* (2nd version)
1927   *The House of Marney*
1929   *Royal Remembrances*

Publications:

By HEPWORTH: books—

Animated Photography, London, 1898.
Came the Dawn: Memories of a Film Pioneer, New York, 1951.

By HEPWORTH: articles—

"My Film Experiences," in *Pearson's Magazine* (London), 1920.
"Those Were the Days," in *Penguin Film Review* (London), no.6, 1948.

On HEPWORTH: books—

Barnes, John, *The Beginnings of Cinema in England*, London, 1976.
Barnes, John, *Pioneers of the British Film 1894–1901*, London, 1983.

On HEPWORTH: articles—

"Cecil Hepworth Comes Through," in *Era* (London), 3 May 1935.

"Hepworth: His Studios and Techniques," in *British Journal of Photography* (London), 15 and 22 January 1971.

*   *   *

The son of a famous magic lanternist and photographer named T.C. Hepworth (who authored an important early volume titled *The Book of the Lantern*), Cecil Hepworth was—along with Robert W. Paul—the best known and most important of early British film pioneers. In the first 20 years of British cinema, Hepworth's place is easy to determine. He was a major figure, who wrote the first British book on cinematography, *Animated Photography, the A.B.C. of the Cinematograph* (published in 1897) and who produced *Rescued by Rover*, which is to British cinema what D.W. Griffith's *The Adventures of Dollie* is to the American film industry. But as the industry grew, Cecil Hepworth failed to grow along with it, and as the English critic and historian Ernest Betts has written, "Although a craftsman and a man of warm sympathies, an examination of his career shows an extremely limited outlook compared with Americans or his contemporaries."

A cameraman before turning to production in the late 1890s, "Heppy," as he was known to his friends and colleagues, founded the first major British studio at Walton-on-Thames (which was later to become Nettlefold Studios). He experimented with sound films before 1910 and was also one of the few British pioneers to build up his own stable of stars, not borrowed from the stage, but brought to fame through the cinema. Alma Taylor, Chrissie White, Stewart Rome, and Violet Hopson were his best known "discoveries." So omnipotent was Hepworth in British cinema prior to the First World War that major American film-makers such as Larry Trimble and Florence Turner were eager to associate with him when they came over from the United States to produce films.

Hepworth's problem and the cause of his downfall was shared with many other pioneers. He did not move with the times. His films were always exquisitely photographed, beautiful to look at, but totally devoid of drama. The editing techniques which he had displayed in *Rescued by Rover* were forgotten by the teens. His productions were all too often like the magic lantern presentations of his father, lifeless creations, with slow dissolves from one sequence or even one bit of action to the next, when it was obvious to anyone that quick cuts were needed. Hepworth appeared to despise anything that would bring movement to his films, preferring that the camera linger on the pictorial beauty of the scene. Nowhere is this more apparent than in Hepworth's best-known feature, *Comin' thro' the Rye* (which he filmed twice, in 1916 and 1922). As Iris Barry was forced to admit, when writing of the latter version, it is "a most awful film."

Bankruptcy and a closed mind drove Cecil Hepworth from the industry which he had helped to create. He returned late in life to supervise the production of trailers for National Screen Service, and also served as Chairman of the History Research Committee of the British Film Institute, at which time he also wrote his autobiography, *Came the Dawn*.

—Anthony Slide

HERMOSILLO, Jaime Humberto.

Mexican. Born 22 January 1942 in Aguascalientes, Mexico. Studied at the Centro Universitario de Estudios Cinematográficos (CUEC). Accountant in Mexico City, from 1959;

Jaime Humberto Hermosillo: *La pasión segun Berenice*

collaborator on film magazine *Cine Avance*, 1960's; directed short films, *Homesick* and *S.S. Glencairn* while student at CUEC; directed first feature, *La verdadera vocación de Magdalena*, 1972; teacher of screenwriting, University of Guadalajara, from 1984. Address: c/o Centro de Investigación y Enseñanza Cinematográficas, Universidad de Guadalajara, Av. Vallarta 2182, Sector Juárez, Guadalajara, Jalisco, México.

Films as Director and Scriptwriter:

1970   *Los nuestros*
1971   *La verdadera vocación de Magdalena*
1972   *El Señor de Osanto*
1974   *El cumpleanos del Perro*
1976   *La pasión segun Berenice*; *Matinée*
1977   *Naufragio*; *Las apariencias enganan*
1978   *Amor libre*
1979   *María de mi corazón*
1982   *Confidencias*
1983   *El corazón de la noche*
1984   *Doña Herlinda y su hijo*

1987   *Clandestino destino*
1988   *El verano de la Señora Forbes*
1989   *Intimades en un cuarto de baño*
1990   *La tarea* (video)

Publications:

By HERMOSILLO: book—

La pasión segun Berenice, Mexico City, 1981.

By HERMOSILLO: article—

Interview with Francisco Lombardi, in *Hablemos de Cine* (Lima), May 1982.

On HERMOSILLO: books—

Blanco, Jorge Ayala, *La busqueda del cine Mexicano (1968–1972)*, 2nd edition, Mexico City, 1986.
Blanco, Jorge Ayala, *La condicion del cine Mexicano (1973–1985)*, Mexico City, 1986.
Costa, Paola, *La "Apetura" cinematografica: Mexico 1970–1976*, Puebla, Mexico, 1988.
Ponce, Miguel Barbachano, *Criticas*, Mexico City, 1988.
Mora, Carl J., *Mexican Cinema: Reflections of a Society*, revised edition, Berkeley, 1989.

Sánchez, Francisco, *Hermosillo: Pasión por la libertad*, Mexico City, 1989.

Sánchez, Francisco, *Cronica antisolemne del cine Mexicano*, Xalapa, Mexico, 1989.

On HERMOSILLO: articles—

García Márquez, Gabriel, "*María de mi corazón*," in *Cine Cubano* (Havana), no. 101, 1982.

Wood, Robin, "Notes for the Exploration of Hermosillo," in *Cine-Action* (Toronto), May 1986.

Stein, Elliot, "Don Hermosillo and the Sun," in *Film Comment* (New York), May/June 1986.

West, Dennis, "Mexico: From the Golden Age to the Present," in *World Cinema since 1945*, edited by William Luhr, New York, 1987.

*   *   *

Jaime Humberto Hermosillo is an exceptional figure in the history of Mexican cinema because he has produced a substantial body of very personal work while avoiding pedestrian directing assignments of little interest. Hermosillo has scripted or co-scripted most of his own features since he sees himself not just as a director, but as an *auteur* who endeavors to tell his own stories on film. Because of the economic difficulties of producing quality films in Mexico, Hermosillo has experimented with different modes of production ranging from the mainstream commercial industry to low-cost cooperative arrangements. His prize-winning *María de mi corazón* was shot in 16 mm on a shoestring by a cooperative that received modest financial backing from a university.

Like his confrère Luis Buñuel, Hermosillo is an iconoclast who brings a powerful artistic vision to his exploration of the conventions and values of contemporary society. Hermosillo's best films from the 1970s and 1980s—the drama *La pasión según Berenice*, the gay comedy *Doña Herlinda y su hijo*, and the childhood adventure-thriller *Matinée*—are landmarks in the history of Mexican cinema because they offer innovative and profound critiques of hitherto sacrosanct subjects, such as middle-class morality, myths, and values and the structure of the bourgeois family. Sexuality is Hermosillo's key theme; and his films upend traditional notions of male and female sexuality as they unabashedly explore homosexuality, sex role reversals, and repressed female eroticism.

Hermosillo's unusual treatment of sexual and other themes has produced a gallery of unforgettable characters headed by the protagonists of *La pasión según Berenice* and *Doña Herlinda y su hijo*. A frustrated and repressed Berenice shatters the stereotype of the modest and passive Mexican woman first when she sketches a huge phallus on the wall of a public restroom and later when she calmly torches her avaricious godmother. The scheming but nice Doña Herlinda unveils a new image of the Mexican mother when she arranges for her bisexual son, his wife, their baby, and the son's homosexual lover to live together—with the blessing of high society—as the happy family that she heads.

Hermosillo has successfully experimented with genre expectations and the mixing of genres in films such as *María de mi corazón* and *Matinée*. Although he is not a master stylist, most of the director's long takes and sequences shots show a carefully conceived mise-en-scène. His recent 60-minute video *La tarea* offers an in-depth examination of a heterosexual couple's relationship as recorded by a stationary camera in a single, long-duration shot. *La tarea* offers proof of Hermosillo's continuing commitment to artistic experimentation in spite of the unending difficulties of financing film production in Mexico.

—Dennis West

———

HERZOG, Werner

German. Born Werner Stipetič in Sachrang, 5 September 1942. Educated at classical Gymnasium, Munich, until 1961; University of Munich and Duquesne University, Pittsburgh, early 1960's. Married journalist Martje Grohmann, one son. Worked for U.S. National Aeronautics and Space Administration, also founded Werner Herzog Filmproduktion, 1966; walked from Munich to Paris to visit film historian Lotte Eisner, 1974. Recipient: Bundesfilmpreis, and Silver Bear, Berlinale, for *Signs of Life*, 1968; Bundespreis, and Special Jury Prize, Cannes Festival, for *Every Man for Himself and God Against All*, 1975; Best Director, Cannes Festival, for *Fitzcarraldo*, 1982. Address: Neureutherstr. 20, D-8000 München 13, Germany.

Films as Director:

(beginning 1966, films are produced or co-produced by Werner Herzog Filmproduktion)

1962	*Herakles* (+ pr, sc)
1964	*Spiel im Sand* [Playing in the Sand] (incomplete) (+ pr, sc)
1966	*Die beispiellose Verteidigung der Festung Deutschkreuz* [The Unparalleled Defense of the Fortress of Deutschkreuz] (+ pr, sc)
1968	*Lebenszeichen* (*Signs of Life*) (+ sc, pr); *Letzte Worte* [Last Words] (+ pr, sc)
1969	*Massnahmen gegen Fanatiker* [Measures Against Fanatics] (+ pr, sc)
1970	*Die fliegenden Ärzte von Ostafrika* (*The Flying Doctors of East Africa*) (+ pr, sc); *Auch Zwerge haben klein angefangen* (*Even Dwarfs Started Small*) (+ pr, sc, mu arrangements); *Behinderte Zukunft* (*Frustrated Future*) (+ pr, sc); *Fata Morgana* (+ sc, pr)
1971	*Land des Schweigens und der Dunkelheit* (*Land of Silence and Darkness*) (+ pr, sc)
1972	***Aguirre, der Zorn Göttes (Aguirre, the Wrath of God)*** (+ pr, sc)
1974	*Die grosse Ekstase des Bildschnitzers Steiner* (*The Great Ecstasy of the Sculptor Steiner*) (+ pr, sc); ***Jeder für sich und Gott gegen alle (Every Man for Himself and God Against All. The Enigma of Kaspar Hauser)*** (+ pr, sc)
1976	*How Much Wood Would a Woodchuck Chuck* (+ pr, sc); *Mit mir will keiner spielen* [No One Will Play with Me] (+ pr, sc); *Herz aus Glas* (*Heart of Glass*) (+ pr, co-sc, bit role as glass carrier)
1977	*La Soufrière* (+ pr, sc, narration, appearance); *Stroszek* (+ pr, sc)
1979	*Nosferatu—Phantom der Nacht* (*Nosferatu the Vampire*) (+ pr, sc, bit role as monk); *Woyzeck* (+ pr, sc)
1982	*Fitzcarraldo* (+ pr, sc)
1984	*Wo Die Grünen Ameisen Traümen* (*Where the Green Ants Dream*)
1985	*Ballade vom Kleinen Soldaten*
1987	*Cobra Verde* (+ sc)

Publications:

By HERZOG: books—

Werner Herzog: Drehbücher I, Munich, 1977.

Werner Herzog: Drehbücher II, Munich 1977.

Sur le chemin des glaces: Munich-Paris du. 23.11 au 14.12.1974, Paris, 1979.

Werner Herzog: Stroszek, Nosferatu: Zwei Filmerzählungen, Munich, 1979.

Cobra Verde, Munich, 1987.

By HERZOG: articles—

"Rebellen in Amerika," in *Filmstudio* (Frankfurt), May 1964.

"Neun Tage eines Jahres," in *Filmstudio* (Frankfurt), September 1964.

"Mit den Wölfen heulen," in *Filmkritik* (Munich), July 1968.

"Warum ist überhaupt Seiendes und nicht vielmehr Nichts?," in *Kino* (West Berlin), March/April 1974.

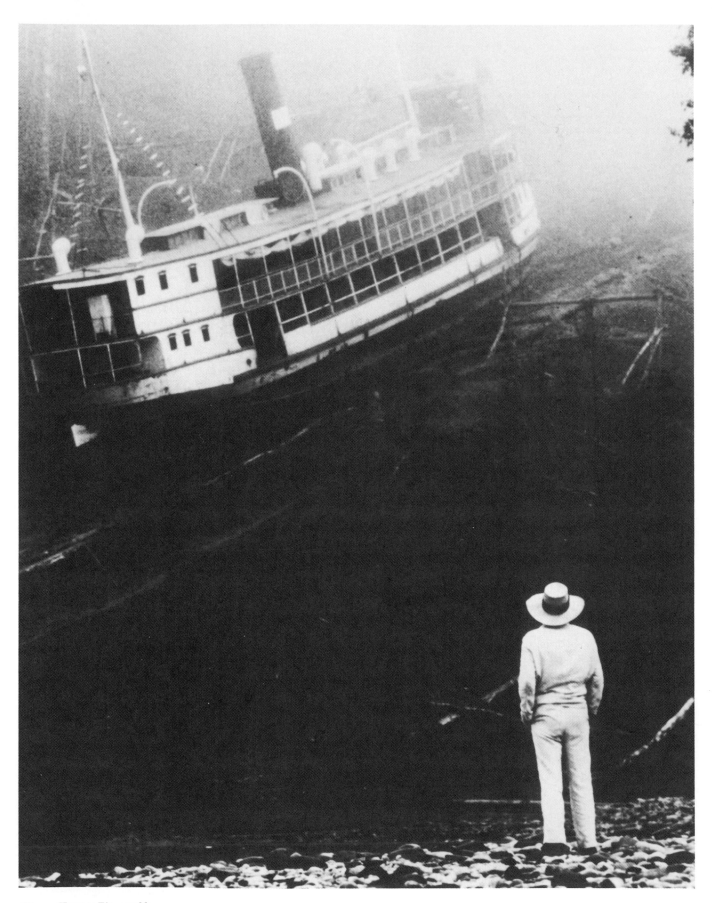

Werner Herzog: *Fitzcarraldo*

Interview with S. Murray, in *Cinema Papers* (Melbourne), December 1974.

"Every Man for Himself," interview with D.L. Overbey, in *Sight and Sound* (London), Spring 1975.

Interview with Michel Ciment, in *Positif* (Paris), May 1975.

L'énigme de Kaspar Hauser, cutting continuity and dialogue, in *Avant-Scène du Cinéma* (Paris), June 1976.

"Signs of Life: Werner Herzog," interview with Jonathan Cott, in *Rolling Stone* (New York), 18 November 1976.

Aguirre, la colère de Dieu, cutting continuity and dialogue, in *Avant-Scène du Cinéma* (Paris), 15 June 1978.

"I Feel That I'm Close to the Center of Things," interview with L. O'Toole, in *Film Comment* (New York), November/December 1979.

Interview with B. Steinborn and R. von Naso, in *Filmfaust* (Frankfurt), February/March 1982.

Interview with G. Bechtold and G. Griksch, in *Filmfaust* (Frankfurt), October/November 1984.

Interview in *Time Out* (London), 20 April 1988.

On HERZOG: books—

Greenberg, Alan, *Heart of Glass*, Munich, 1976.

Schütte, Wolfram, and others, *Herzog/Kluge/Straub*, Vienna, 1976.

Franklin, James, *New German Cinema: From Oberhausen to Hamburg*, Boston, 1983.

Phillips, Klaus, editor, *New German Filmmakers: From Oberhausen through the 1970's*, New York, 1984.

Corrigan, Timothy, *The Films of Werner Herzog: Between Mirage and History*, New York, 1986.

Elsaesser, Thomas, *New German Cinema: A History*, London, 1989.

On HERZOG: articles—

"Herzog Issue" of *Cinema* (Zurich), vol. 18, no. 1, 1972.

Wetzel, Kraft, "Werner Herzog," in *Kino* (West Berlin), April/May 1973.

Bachmann, Gideon, "The Man on the Volcano," in *Film Quarterly* (Berkeley), Autumn 1977.

Dorr, John, "The Enigma of Werner Herzog," in *Millimeter* (New York), October 1977.

Walker, B., "Werner Herzog's *Nosferatu*," in *Sight and Sound* (London), Autumn 1978.

Andrews, N., "Dracula in Delft," in *American Film* (Washington, D.C.), October 1978.

Morris, George, "Werner Herzog," in *International Film Guide 1979*, London, 1978.

Cleere, E., "Three Films by Werner Herzog," in *Wide Angle* (Athens, Ohio), vol. 3, no. 4, 1980.

Van Wert, W.F., "Hallowing the Ordinary, Embezzling the Everyday: Werner Herzog's Documentary Practice," in *Quarterly Review of Film Studies* (Pleasantville, New York), Spring 1980.

Davidson, D., "Borne Out of Darkness: the Documentaries of Werner Herzog," in *Film Criticism* (Edinboro, Pennsylvania), Fall 1980.

"Werner Herzog," in *Film Dope* (London), March 1982.

Goodwin, M., "Herzog the God of Wrath," in *American Film* (Washington, D.C.), June 1982.

Carroll, Noel, "Herzog, presence, and paradox," in *Persistence of Vision* (Maspeth, New York), Fall 1985.

Kennedy, Harlan, "Amazon grace," in *Film Comment* (New York), September/October 1986.

Davidson, David, "Borne Out of Darkness: The Documentaries of Werner Herzog," in *Film Criticism* (Meadville, Pennsylvania), no. 1/2, 1987.

Mouton, Jan, "Werner Herzog's *Stroszek*: A Fairy-Tale in an Age of Disenchantment," in *Literature/Film Quarterly* (Salisbury, Maryland), vol. 15, no. 2, 1987.

Caltvedt, Lester, "Herzog's *Fitzcarraldo* and the Rubber Era," in *Film and History* (New York), vol. 18, no. 4, 1988.

"Herzog Issue" of *Post Script* (Jacksonville, Florida), Summer 1988.

Elsaesser, Thomas, "Werner Herzog: Tarzan Meets Parsifal," in *Monthly Film Bulletin* (London), May 1988.

On HERZOG: films—

Weisenborn, Christian, and Erwin Keusch, *Was ich bin sind meine Filme*, Munich, 1978.

Blank, Les, *Werner Herzog Eats His Shoe*, U.S., 1980.

Blank, Les, *Burden of Dreams*, U.S., 1982.

*   *   *

The nature of Herzog's talents is hard to define because they are still evolving, and because his often contradictory qualities can only be encompassed within paradoxes. "Grotesque" presents itself as a useful term to define Herzog's work. His use of an actor like Klaus Kinski, whose singularly ugly face is sublimated by Herzog's camera, can best be described by such a term. Persons with physical defects like deafness and blindness, and dwarfs, are given a type of grandeur in Herzog's artistic vision. Herzog, as a contemporary German living in the shadow of remembered Nazi atrocities, demonstrates a penchant for probing the darker aspects of human behavior. His characters run the gamut from a harmlessly insane man (played by a mentally-ill actor) who is murdered for no apparent reason, to a Spanish conquistador lusting after gold, power, and blood. Herzog's vision renders the ugly and horrible sublime, while the beautiful is omitted or destroyed.

Closely related to the grotesque in Herzog's films is the influence of German expressionism on him. Two of Herzog's favorite actors, Klaus Kinski and Bruno S., have been compared to Conrad Veidt and Fritz Kortner, prototypical actors of German expressionistic dramas and films during the teens and 1920s. Herzog's actors make highly stylized, indeed often stock, gestures; in close-ups, their faces are set in exaggerated grimaces.

The characters of Herzog's films often seem deprived of free will, merely reacting to an absurd universe. Any exertion of free will in action leads ineluctably to destruction and death. He is a satirist who demonstrates what is wrong with the world but, as yet, seems unable or unwilling to articulate the ways to make it right; indeed, one is at a loss to find in his world view any hope, let alone prescription, for improvement.

Herzog's mode of presentation has been termed by some critics as romantic and by others as realistic. This seeming contradiction can be resolved by an approach that compares him with those Romantic artists who first articulated elements of the later realistic approach. The scientific objectivity with which Géricault renders his series of portraits treating inmates of an insane asylum offers an art-historical parallel to the style and content of Herzog's films. A similar disinterestedness coupled with abnormal subject matter in the novels of Balzac offers itself for comparison with Herzog's approach. Critics have found in the quasi-photographic paintings of Caspar David Friedrich an analogue for Herzog's super-realism. As with these artists, there is an aura of unreality in Herzog's realism. Everything is seen through a camera that rarely goes out of intense, hard focus. Often it is as if his camera is deprived of the normal range of human vision, able only to perceive part of the whole through a telescope or a microscope.

In this strange blend of romanticism and realism lies the paradoxical quality of Herzog's talent: he, unlike Godard, Resnais, or Altman, has not made great innovations in film language; if his style is to be defined at all it is as an eclectic one; and yet, his films do have a distinctive stylistic quality. He renders the surface reality of things with such an intensity that the viewer has an uncanny sense of seeing the essence beyond. *Aguirre*, for example, is unrelenting in its concentration on filth, disease, and brutality; and yet it is also an allegory which can be read on several levels: in terms of Germany under the Nazis, America in Vietnam, and more generally on the bestiality that lingers beneath the facade of civilized conventions. In one of Herzog's romantic tricks within his otherwise realistic vision, he shows a young Spanish noblewoman wearing an ever-pristine velvet dress amid mud and squalor; further, only she of all the rest is not shown dying through violence and is allowed to disappear almost mystically into the dense vegetation of the forest: clearly, she represents that transcendent quality in human nature that incorruptibly endures. This figure is dropped like a hint to remind us to look beyond mere surface.

Herzog's films have developed their own uncanny structures, like forms of rare hothouse plants. As he says himself, his films will only come to be appreciated "in the next fifty years." For the most part, he avoids making films in Germany; indeed, he delights in going to strange locations, like the South American rain forests of *Aguirre*. This film however demonstrates an important recent development in German cinema: it was a TV-cinema co-production.

—Rodney Farnsworth

HILL, George Roy.

American. Born in Minneapolis, Minnesota, 20 December 1921. Educated at Blake School, Hopkins, Minnesota; Yale University, B.A. (Music), 1943; Trinity College, Dublin, B. Litt., 1949. Served as U.S. Marine Corps transport pilot, 1943–45, and during Korean war. Married Louisa Horton, 1951, four children. Theatre actor, early 1950's; writer, producer, and director for US TV, 1954–57; director on and off Broadway, 1957–62; directed first film, *Period of Adjustment*, 1962; signed a 5-year contract with Universal, 1975; Recipient: Emmy Awards for *A Night to Remember*, 1954; Best Direction Award, British Academy, for *Butch Cassidy and the Sundance Kid*, 1970; Jury Prize, Cannes Festival, for *Slaughterhouse-Five*, 1972; Oscar for Best Director, and Director Award, Directors Guild of America, for *The Sting*, 1973. Business address: Pan Arts Productions, 75 Rockefeller Plaza, New York, NY 10019, U.S.A.

Films as Director:

1962   *Period of Adjustment*
1963   *Toys in the Attic*
1964   *The World of Henry Orient*
1966   *Hawaii*
1967   *Thoroughly Modern Millie*
1969   *Butch Cassidy and the Sundance Kid*
1972   *Slaughterhouse-Five*
1973   *The Sting*
1975   *The Great Waldo Pepper* (+ story)
1977   *Slap Shot*
1979   *A Little Romance*
1982   *The World According to Garp*
1984   *The Little Drummer Girl*
1988   *Funny Farm*

Other Films:

1952   *Walk East on Beacon* (*Crime of the Century*) (Werker) (role)

Publications:

By HILL: articles—

Interview with C. Flynn, in *Focus on Film* (London), Spring 1970.
Interview with J.-A. Gili and others, in *Ecran* (Paris), November 1972.
"Flying High: George Roy Hill," an interview with R. Appelbaum, in *Films and Filming* (London), August 1979.
Interview with B.L. Zito, in *Millimeter* (New York), October 1979.

"Butch and Millie," an interview in *Films* (London), March 1981.
Interview in *Film Comment* (New York), July/August 1988.

On HILL: books—

Goldman, William, *Adventures in the Screen Trade*, New York, 1983.
Shores, Edward, *George Roy Hill*, Boston, 1983.
Horton, Andrew, *The Films of George Roy Hill*, New York, 1984.

On HILL: articles—

"Stage to Film," in *Action* (Los Angeles), October 1968.
Thomas, B., "Award Winner," in *Action* (Los Angeles), May/June 1974.
"L'Arnaque," in *Avant-Scène du Cinéma* (Paris), June 1974.
Owen, Derek, "George Roy Hill," in *Film Dope* (London), March 1982.
"George Roy Hill Section" of *Revue du Cinéma* (Paris), April 1985.
Parshall, Peter F., "Meditations on the Philosophy of Tralfamadore: Kurt Vonnegut and George Roy Hill," in *Literature/Film Quarterly* (Salisbury, Maryland), vol. 15, no. 1, 1987.

On HILL: film—

Crawford, Robert, *The Making of Butch Cassidy and the Sundance Kid*, U.S.A., 1970.

*   *   *

George Roy Hill has found his greatest popular success when he works with actors Paul Newman and Robert Redford. Before the emergence of George Lucas and Steven Spielberg, Hill's two collaborations with the duo earned him the distinction of being the only director to have made two among the ten most financially successful films.

Butch Cassidy and the Sundance Kid is an examination of the western hero, the myth and the reality. Butch and Sundance are nearly Robin Hood characters of the Old West but they are also shown to be trapped in their criminal profession and in their own myths. Their violent deaths are inevitable as there is no way for heros or criminals to get old. Helped considerably by the screen charm of Newman and Redford, Hill makes the pair into lovable, wisecracking rogues. The freeze frame death scene seems to be Hill's acknowledgment that the western myth must be recognized as a viable entity even though most of the action preceding their end seems to undercut the myth.

Hill's second film with Newman and Redford was *The Sting*. Illusions abound as experienced con men set up an elaborate scheme to avenge a friend's death. Redford's character's first big successful con is actually a mistake that leads to his mentor's death. Newman's character seems to be a down and out drunk but soon proves his merit as an extremely competent con man and schemer. Hill's ultimate illusion in the film is the con game the film plays on the audience.

Hill again directed Redford in *The Great Waldo Pepper*, focusing on the myth and reality of the barnstorming early years of aviation. Redford's character finally achieves his goal of showing how good a pilot he is when he turns an illusion (a filmed aerial battle) into a real aerial battle. Newman's character in *Slap Shot* is similar. In this, the most underrated film of Hill's career (mostly criticized for the profane but accurately observed locker room talk), Hill shows the development of a minor league hockey coach Reg Dunlop. Reg, late in his career, recognizes that sport in America is just an illusionary entertainment and that a sport can be manipulated to please a blood-thirsty audience. His team wins the championship when his star player breaks down and strips, thus joining "the team" Reg has created.

Hill has not yet found great acceptance with the critics. Generally his films are regarded as superficial entertainment rather than serious works, in much the same way that Redford and Newman are regarded as "pretty faces" rather than actors. Critics do acknowledge Hill's ability to tell a narrative compellingly and completely. This ability coupled with charismatic stars certainly are at the base of the appeal of Hill's films. Audiences know that a Hill film will tell a story and allow the star to shine. Perhaps this might be labeled an old fashioned approach, but Hill has shown that this can work time and time again.

—Ray Narducy

Walter Hill

HILL, Walter.

American. Born in Long Beach, California, 10 January 1942. Educated at Michigan State University. Began in films as writer; directed first film, *Hard Times*, 1975; created *Dog and Cat* TV series, 1977. Address: c/o Lone Wolf Co., 8800 Sunset Boulevard, Suite 210, Los Angeles, CA 90069, U.S.A.

Films as Director:

1975   *Hard Times (The Streetfighter)* (+ co-sc)
1978   *The Driver* (+ sc)
1979   *The Warriors* (co-sc)
1980   *The Long Riders*
1981   *Southern Comfort* (co-sc)
1982   *48 HR.S* (+ sc)
1984   *Streets of Fire* (+ sc, pr)
1985   *Brewster's Millions*
1986   *Crossroads*
1987   *Extreme Prejudice*
1988   *Red Heat* (+ sc, pr)
1989   *Johnny Handsome*
1990   *Another 48 HR.S*

Other Films:

1968   *The Thomas Crown Affair* (Jewison) (2nd asst-d)
1969   *Take the Money and Run* (Allen) (asst-d)
1972   *Hickey and Boggs* (Culp) (sc); *The Getaway* (Peckinpah) (sc)
1973   *The Thief Who Came to Dinner* (Yorkin) (sc); *The Mackintosh Man* (Huston) (sc)
1975   *The Drowning Pool* (Rosenberg) (co-sc)
1979   *Alien* (Scott) (co-pr)
1986   *Aliens* (Cameron) (co-pr); *Blue City* (Manning) (co-sc, pr)

Publications:

By HILL: articles

Interview with A.J. Silver and E. Ward, in *Movie* (London), Winter 1978/79.
"Making *Alien*," an interview with M.P. Carducci, in *Cinefantastique* (Oak Park, Illinois), no. 1, 1979.
Interview with M. Greco, in *Film Comment* (New York), May/June 1980.
Interview with Pat Broeske, in *Films in Review* (New York), December 1981.
"Dead End Streets," an interview with D. Chute, in *Film Comment* (New York), July/August 1984.
Interview with A. Hunter, in *Films and Filming* (London), October 1984.

On HILL: articles—

"Walter Hill," in *Film Dope* (London), March 1982.
Sragow, M., "Don't Jesse James Me," in *Sight and Sound* (London), Summer 1982.

Rafferty, T., "The Paradoxes of Home: Three Films by Walter Hill," in *Film Quarterly* (Berkeley), Fall 1982.
Sragow, M., "Hill's Street Blues," in *American Film* (Washington, D.C.), June 1984.
Heuring, D., "*Red Heat*—Cross-Culture Cop Caper," in *American Cinematographer* (Los Angeles), June 1988.
Revue du Cinéma/Image et Son (Paris), June 1990.

*   *   *

Established in the early 1970s as a writer of action movies, Hill went almost unnoticed for his first two directorial ventures. Not so with his third. *The Warriors* reportedly occasioned gang fights in the U.S., while one British newspaper dubbed it "the film they mustn't show here." Replete with highly stylized violence, *The Warriors* has been described by Hill as "a comic book rock 'n' roll version of the Xenophon story." It is a precise description: the movie takes the *Anabasis* and adapts it to an appropriately mythical setting among the street gangs of modern New York. The stranded Warriors fight their way home through the subways and streets of an extraordinary fantasy city. This world, as so often in Hill's movies, is evacuated of any sense of the everyday, and is rendered with the use of the strong reds, yellows, and blues of comic book design. In its subway scenes especially, colors leap from the screen much as, say, a Roy Lichtenstein picture leaps from the canvas, its direct assault on our vision as basic as that of a comic strip.

The pleasure of the movie lies in that style, transforming its much maligned violence into a sort of ritual. You could as well accuse Hill of celebrating gang warfare as you could accuse Lichtenstein of condoning aerial combat in his painting *Whaam!*. Hill's cinema evokes and elaborates upon mythical worlds, in this case grounded in ancient Greece and in comics, though in his other movies more often based in the cinema itself. Thus *Driver* eliminates orthodox characterization in favor of thriller archetypes: the Driver, the Detective, and the Girl, as the credits list them. They revolve around each other in a world of formally defined roles, roles made archetypal by movies themselves. *The Long Riders*, in presenting a version of the Jesse James story, traps its characters in their own movie mythology so that they even seem to be aware that they are playing out a sort of destiny. *Southern Comfort* manipulates and undermines the war-movie ideology of the small military group, while *48 HR.S* pursues its unstoppable action in precisely the fashion of the Don Siegel cop-movie—*Madigan*, say, or *Dirty Harry*.

As he tours the popular genres Hill has emerged as the major action director of the contemporary cinema. He is highly skilled in the narrative use of chase and confrontation, adept at the montage techniques so central to the genre's tension, while offering us not a "reality" but a distillation of the rules of the genre game. In his films we witness the *enmything* of characters, if that neologism is not too pompous for so pleasurable an experience, a self-conscious evocation of genre but without the knowing wink which often attends such exercises. Hill manages to take the genre seriously *and* to reflect upon it.

Inevitably such immersion in popular genre conventions, however skilled, risks critical opprobrium. *The Warriors, Southern Comfort,* and *48 HR.S* have all been dismissed as shallow and morally suspect, lacking in the "seriousness" considered necessary to redeem their almost exclusive focus on action. This, however, is to miss the pleasures of Hill's cinema, its visual power, its narrative force, and its absorbing concern with myth-making and myth-breaking. These, too, are qualities to which the label "serious" properly may be applied.

—Andrew Tudor

HITCHCOCK, Alfred.

British. Born Alfred Joseph Hitchcock in Leytonstone, London, 13 August 1899, became U.S. citizen, 1955. Educated at Salesian College, Battersea, London, 1908; St. Ignatius College, Stamford Hill, London, 1908–13; School of Engineering and Navigation, 1914; attended drawing and design classes under E.J. Sullivan, London University, 1917. Married Alma Reville, 2 December 1926, daughter Patricia born 1928. Technical clerk, W.T. Henley Telegraph Co., 1914–19; title-card designer for Famous Players-Lasky at Islington studio, 1919; scriptwriter and assistant director, from 1922; directed 2 films for producer Michael Balcon in Germany, 1925; signed with British International Pictures as director, 1927; directed first British film to use synchronized sound, *Blackmail*, 1929; signed with Gaumont-British Studios, 1933; moved to America to direct *Rebecca* for Selznick International Studios, decided to remain, 1939; returned to Britain to make short films for Ministry of Information, 1944; directed first film in color, *Rope*, 1948; producer and host, *Alfred Hitchcock Presents*, (*The Alfred Hitchcock Hour*, from 1962), for TV, 1955–65. Recipient: Irving Thalberg Academy Award, 1968; Chevalier de la Légion d'Honneur, 1971; Commander of the Order of Arts and Letters, France, 1976; Life Achievement Award, American Film Institute, 1979; Honorary Doctorate, University of Southern California; Knight of the Legion of Honour of the Cinémathèque Français; knighted, 1980. *Died of kidney failure, in Los Angeles, 29 April 1980.*

Films as Director:

1922   *Number Thirteen* (or *Mrs. Peabody*) (uncompleted)
1923   *Always Tell Your Wife* (Croise; completed d)
1926   *The Pleasure Garden* (*Irrgarten der Leidenschaft*); *The Mountain Eagle* (*Der Bergadler. Fear o' God*); *The Lodger; A Story of the London Fog* (*The Case of Jonathan Drew*) (+ co-sc, bit role as man in newsroom, and onlooker during Novello's arrest)
1927   *Downhill* (*When Boys Leave Home*); *Easy Virtue; The Ring* (+ sc)
1928   *The Farmer's Wife* (+ sc); *Champagne* (+ adapt); *The Manxman*
1929   *Blackmail* (+ adapt, bit role as passenger on "tube") (silent version also made); *Juno and the Paycock* (*The Shame of Mary Boyle*) (+ co-sc)
1930   *Elstree Calling* (Brunel; d after Brunel dismissed, credit for "sketches and other interpolated items"); *Murder* (+ co-adapt, bit role as passerby) (1931 German version *Mary* (*Sir John greift ein!*)); *An Elastic Affair* (short)
1931   *The Skin Game* (+ co-sc)
1932   *Rich and Strange* (*East of Shanghai*) (+ co-sc): *Number Seventeen* (+ co-sc)
1933   *Waltzes from Vienna* (*Strauss's Great Waltz, The Great Waltz*)
1934   *The Man Who Knew Too Much*
1935   *The Thirty-Nine Steps* (+ bit role as passerby)
1936   *Secret Agent; Sabotage* (*The Woman Alone*)
1937   *Young and Innocent* (*The Girl Was Young*) (+ bit as photographer outside courthouse)
1938   *The Lady Vanishes* (+ bit role as man at railway station)
1939   *Jamaica Inn*
1940   *Rebecca* (+ bit role as man outside phone booth); *Foreign Correspondent* (+ bit role as man reading newspaper)
1941   *Mr. and Mrs. Smith* (+ bit role as passerby); *Suspicion*
1942   *Saboteur* (+ bit role as man by newsstand)
1943   *Shadow of a Doubt* (+ bit role as man playing cards on train)
1944   *Life Boat* (+ bit role as man in "Reduco" advertisement); *Bon Voyage* (short); *Aventure Malgache* (*The Malgache Adventure*) (short)
1945   *Spellbound* (+ bit role as man in elevator)
1946   *Notorious* (+ story, bit role as man drinking champagne)
1947   *The Paradine Case* (+ bit role as man with cello)
1948   *Rope* (+ bit role as man crossing street)
1949   *Under Capricorn; Stage Fright* (+ bit role as passerby)
1951   *Strangers on a Train* (+ bit role as man boarding train with cello)
1953   *I Confess* (+ bit role as man crossing top of flight of steps)
1954   *Dial M for Murder* (+ bit role as man in school reunion dinner photo); *Rear Window* (+ bit role as man winding clock); *To Catch a Thief* (+ bit role as man at back of bus); *The Trouble with Harry* (+ bit role as man walking past exhibition)
1955   *The Man Who Knew Too Much* (+ bit role as man watching acrobats);
1956   *The Wrong Man* (+ intro appearance)
1957   *Vertigo* (+ bit role as passerby)
1959   *North by Northwest* (+ bit role as man who misses bus)
1960   *Psycho* (+ bit role as man outside realtor's office)
1963   *The Birds* (+ bit role as man with two terriers)
1964   *Marnie* (+ bit role as man in hotel corridor)
1966   *Torn Curtain* (+ bit role as man in hotel lounge with infant)
1969   *Topaz* (+ bit role as man getting out of wheelchair)
1972   *Frenzy* (+ bit role as man in crowd listening to speech)
1976   *Family Plot* (+ bit role as silhouette on office window)

Alfred Hitchcock

Other Films:

1920 *The Great Day* (Ford) (inter-titles des); *The Call of Youth* (Ford) (inter-titles des)
1921 *The Princess of New York* (Crisp) (inter-titles des); *Appearances* (Crisp) (inter-titles des); *Dangerous Lies* (Powell) (inter-titles des); *The Mystery Road* (Powell) (inter-titles des); *Beside the Bonnie Brier Bush* (*The Bonnie Brier Bush*) (Crisp) (inter-titles des)
1922 *Three Live Ghosts* (Fitzmaurice) (inter-titles des); *Perpetua* (*Love's Boomerang*) (Robertson and Geraghty) (inter-titles des); *The Man from Home* (Fitzmaurice) (inter-titles des); *Spanish Jade* (Robertson and Geraghty) (inter-titles des); *Tell Your Children* (Crisp) (inter-titles des)
1923 *Woman to Woman* (Cutts) (co-sc, asst-d, art-d, ed); *The White Shadow* (*White Shadows*) (Cutts) (art-d, ed)
1924 *The Passionate Adventure* (Cutts) (co-sc, asst-d, art-d); *The Prude's Fall* (Cutts) (asst-d, art-d)
1925 *The Blackguard* (*Die Prinzessin und der Geiger*) (Cutts) (asst-d, art-d)
1932 *Lord Camber's Ladies* (Levy) (pr)
1940 *The House Across the Bay* (Mayo) (d add'l scenes); *Men of the Lightship* (MacDonald, short) (reediting, dubbing of US version)
1941 ***Target for Tonight*** (Watt) (supervised reediting of US version)
1960 *The Gazebo* (Marshall) (voice on telephone telling Glenn Ford how to dispose of corpse)
1963 *The Directors* (pr: Greenblatt) (appearance)
1970 *Makin' It* (Hartog) (documentary appearance from early thirties)
1977 *Once Upon a Time . . . Is Now* (Billington, for TV) (role as interviewee)

Publications:

By HITCHCOCK: book—

Le Cinéma selon Hitchcock, with François Truffaut, Paris, 1966; as *Hitchcock*, New York, 1985.

By HITCHCOCK: articles—

"My Own Methods," in *Sight and Sound* (London), Summer 1937.
"On Suspense and Other Matters," in *Films in Review* (New York), April 1950.
Interview with Claude Chabrol, in *Cahiers du Cinéma* (Paris), February 1955.
Interview with Catherine de la Roche, in *Sight and Sound* (London), Winter 1955/56.
"Rencontre avec Alfred Hitchcock," with François Truffaut, in *Cahiers du Cinéma* (Paris), September 1956.
"Alfred Hitchcock Talking," in *Films and Filming* (London), July 1959.
Interview with Ian Cameron and V.F. Perkins, in *Movie* (London), 6 January 1963.
"Hitchcock on Style," in *Cinema* (Beverly Hills), August/September 1963.
"Film Production," in *Encyclopaedia Brittanica*, London, 1968.
"*Rear Window*," in *Take One* (Montreal), November/December 1968.
"Alfred Hitchcock: The German Years," an interview with B. Thomas, in *Action* (Los Angeles), January/February 1973.
"Hitchcock," transcript of address to Film Society of Lincoln Center, 29 April 1974, in *Film Comment* (New York), July/August 1974.
"Hitchcock," an interview with Andy Warhol, in *Inter/View* (New York), September 1974.
"Surviving," an interview with John Taylor, in *Sight and Sound* (London), Summer 1977.

On HITCHCOCK: books—

Amengual, Barthélémy, and Raymond Borde, *Alfred Hitchcock*, Paris, 1957.
Rohmer, Eric, and Claude Chabrol, *Hitchcock*, Paris, 1957.
Bogdanovich, Peter, *The Cinema of Alfred Hitchcock*, New York, 1962.
Perry, George, *The Films of Alfred Hitchcock*, London, 1965.

Wood, Robin, *Hitchcock's Films*, London, 1965; as *Hitchcock's Films Revisited*, New York, 1989.
Douchet, Jean, *Alfred Hitchcock*, Paris, 1967.
Simsolo, Noel, *Alfred Hitchcock*, Paris, 1969.
Taylor, John Russell, *Hitch*, New York, 1978.
Bellour, Raymond, *L'Analyse du film*, Paris, 1979.
Fieschi, J.-A., and others, *Hitchcock*, Paris, 1981.
Hemmeter, Thomas M., *Hitchcock the Stylist*, Ann Arbor, Michigan, 1981.
Bazin, Andre, *The Cinema of Cruelty: From Bunuel to Hitchcock*, New York, 1982.
Narboni, Jean, editor, *Alfred Hitchcock*, Paris, 1982.
Rothman, William, *Hitchcock—The Murderous Gaze*, Cambridge, Massachusetts, 1982.
Spoto, Donald, *The Dark Side of Genius: The Life of Alfred Hitchcock*, New York, 1982.
Weis, Elisabeth, *The Silent Scream: Alfred Hitchcock's Sound Track*, Rutherford, New Jersey, 1982.
Belton, John, *Cinema Stylists*, Metuchen, New Jersey, 1983.
Phillips, Gene D., *Alfred Hitchcock*, Boston, 1984.
Douchet, Jean, *Alfred Hitchcock*, Paris, 1985.
Deutelbaum, Marshall, and Leland Poague, *A Hitchcock Reader*, Ames, Iowa, 1986.
Hogan, David J., *Dark Romance: Sexuality in the Horror Film*, Jefferson, North Carolina, 1986.
Humphries, Patrick, *The Films of Alfred Hitchcock*, Greenwich, Connecticut, 1986.
Kloppenburg, Josef, *Die Dramaturgische Funktion der Musik in Filmen Alfred Hitchcocks*, Munich, 1986.
Ryall, Tom, *Alfred Hitchcock and the British Cinema*, London, 1986.
Sinyard, Neil, *The Films of Alfred Hitchcock*, London, 1986.
Leff, Leonard J., *Hitchcock and Selznick: The Rich and Strange Collaboration of Alfred Hitchcock and David O. Selznick in Hollywood*, New York, 1987.
Modleski, Tania, *The Women Who Knew Too Much: Hitchcock and Feminist Theory*, New York, 1988.
Brill, Linda, *The Hitchcock Romance: Love and Irony in Hitchcock's Films*, Princeton, New Jersey, 1988.

On Hitchcock: articles—

Pratley, Gerald, "Alfred Hitchcock's Working Credo," in *Films in Review* (New York), December 1952.
"Hitchcock Issue" of *Cahiers du Cinéma* (Paris), October 1953.
May, Derwent, in *Sight and Sound* (London), October/December 1954.
Bazin, André, "Alfred Hitchcock," in *Radio, Cinéma, Télévision* (Paris), 23 January 1955.
Sarris, Andrew, "The Trouble with Hitchcock," in *Film Culture* (New York), Winter 1955.
"Hitchcock Issue" of *Cahiers du Cinéma* (Paris), August/September 1956.
Pett, John, "A Master of Suspense," in *Films and Filming* (London), November and December 1959.
Cameron, Ian, "Hitchcock and the Mechanics of Suspense," in *Movie* (London), October 1962.
Higham, Charles, "Hitchcock's World," in *Film Quarterly* (Berkeley), December/January 1962/63.
Houston, Penelope, "The Figure in the Carpet," in *Sight and Sound* (London), Autumn 1963.
Truffaut, François, "Skeleton Keys," in *Film Culture* (New York), Spring 1964.
Cameron, Ian, and Richard Jeffrey, "The Universal Hitchcock," in *Movie* (London), Spring 1965.
"An Alfred Hitchcock Index," in *Films in Review* (New York), April 1966.
Sonbert, Warren, "Alfred Hitchcock: Master of Morality," in *Film Culture* (New York), Summer 1966.
Lightman, Herb, "Hitchcock talk about Light, Camera, Action," in *American Cinematographer* (Hollywood), May 1967.
Braudy, Leo, "Hitchcock, Truffaut, and the Irresponsible Audience," in *Film Quarterly* (Berkeley), Summer 1968.
Houston, Penelope, "Hitchcockery," in *Sight and Sound* (London), Autumn 1968.
Millar, Gavin, "Hitchcock versus Truffaut," in *Sight and Sound* (London), Spring 1969.

Durgnat, Raymond, "The Strange Case of Alfred Hitchcock," in *Films and Filming* (London), February 1970 through November 1970.

Smith, J.M., "Conservative Individualism: A Selection of English Hitchcock," in *Screen* (London), Autumn 1972.

Kaplan, G., "Lost in the Wood," in *Film Comment* (New York), November/December 1972.

Poague, Lee, "The Detective in Hitchcock's *Frenzy*: His Ancestors and Significance," in *Journal of Popular Film* (Bowling Green, Ohio), Winter 1973.

Sarris, Andrew, "Alfred Hitchcock, Prankster of Paradox," in *Film Comment* (New York), March/April 1974.

Simer, D., "Hitchcock and the Well-Wrought Effect," in *Literature/Film Quarterly* (Salisbury, Maryland), Summer 1975.

Fisher, R., "The Hitchcock Camera 'I,'" in *Filmmakers Newsletter* (Ward Hill, Massachusetts), December 1975.

Silver, A.J., "Fragments of a Mirror: Uses of Landscape in Hitchcock," in *Wide Angle* (Athens, Ohio), v. 1, no. 3, 1976.

Bellour, Raymond, "Hitchcock, the Enunciator," in *Camera Obscura* (Berkeley), Fall 1977.

Lehman, Ernest, "He Who Gets Hitched," in *American Film* (Washington, D.C.), May 1978.

"Hitchcock Section" of *Wide Angle* (Athens, Ohio), vol. 4, no. 1, 1980.

Combs, Richard, "Perché Hitchcock?," and Ivor Montagu, "Working with Hitchcock," in *Sight and Sound* (London), Summer 1980.

"Hitchcock Issue" of *Cinématographe* (Paris), July/August 1980.

Lehman, Ernest, "Hitch," in *American Film* (Washington, D.C.), August 1980.

Wollen, P., "Hybrid Plots in *Psycho*," in *Framework* (Norwich, England), Autumn 1980.

Belton, John, "Alfred Hitchcock's *Under Capricorn*: Montage entranced by mise-en-scène," in *Quarterly Review of Film Studies* (New York), Fall 1981.

"Hitchcock Issue" of *Camera/Stylo* (Paris), November 1981.

Brown, R.S., "Herrmann, Hitchcock, and the Music of the Irrational," in *Cinema Journal* (Chicago), Spring 1982.

Rossi, J., "Hitchcock's *Foreign Correspondent*," in *Film and History* (Newark, New Jersey), May 1982.

"Hitchcock Issue" of *Avant-Scène du Cinéma* (Paris), 1 December 1982.

Wood, Robin, "Fear of Spying," in *American Film* (Washington, D.C.), November 1983.

Jenkins, Steve, and Richard Combs, "Hitchcock x 2. Refocussing the Spectator: Just Enough Rope . . . ," in *Monthly Film Bulletin* (London), February 1984.

Sussex, Elizabeth, "The Fate of F3080," in *Sight and Sound* (London), Spring 1984.

Kehr, Dave, "Hitch's Riddle," in *Film Comment* (New York), May/June 1984.

"Hitchcock Issues" of *Revue Belge du Cinéma* (Brussels), Autumn 1984 and Winter 1984/85.

Bannon, B.M., "Double, Double, Toil and Trouble," in *Literature/Film Quarterly* (Salisbury, Maryland), January 1985.

Allen, J. Thomas, "The Representation of Violence to Women: Hitchcock's *Frenzy*," in *Film Quarterly* (Berkeley), Spring 1985.

French, Philip, "Alfred Hitchcock—The Filmmaker as Englishman and Exile," in *Sight and Sound* (London), Spring 1985.

Kapsis, Robert E., "Alfred Hitchcock: Auteur or Hack?," in *Cineaste* (New York), vol. 14, no. 3, 1986.

Zirnite, D., "Hitchcock, On the Level: The Heights of Spatial Tension," in *Film Criticism* (Meadville, Pennsylvania), Spring 1986.

Miller, G., "Beyond the Frame: Hitchcock, Art, and the Ideal," in *Post Script* (Jacksonville, Florida), Winter 1986.

Abel, Richard, "*Stage Fright*: The Knowing Performance," in *Film Criticism* (Meadville, Pennsylvania), no. 1/2, 1987.

Anderegg, Michael, "Hitchcock's *The Paradine Case* and Filmic Unpleasure," in *Cinema Journal* (Chicago), vol. 26, no. 4, 1987.

Kapsis, Robert E., "Hollywood Filmmaking and Reputation Building: Hitchcock's *The Birds*," in *Journal of Popular Film and TV* (Washington, D.C.), Spring 1987.

Greig, Donald, "The Sexual Differentiation of the Hitchcock Text," in *Screen* (London), Winter 1987.

Lee, Sander H., "Escape and Commitment in Hitchcock's *Rear Window*," in *Post Script* (Jacksonville, Florida), vol. 7, no. 2, 1988.

Wood, Robin, "Symmetry, Closure, Disruption: The Ambiguity of *Blackmail*," in *CineAction!* (Toronto), no. 15, 1988.

American Cinematographer (Los Angeles), January 1990.

On HITCHCOCK: films—

Casson, Philip, *Interview with Alfred Hitchcock*, for TV, Great Britain, 1966.

Ya'acovolitz, M., and S. Melul, *Im Hitchcock bi Yerushalayin (With Hitchcock in Jerusalem)*, short, Israel 1967.

Schickel, Richard, *The Men Who Made the Movies: Alfred Hitchcock*, for TV, U.S., 1973.

*   *   *

In a career spanning just over 50 years (1925–1976), Hitchcock completed 53 feature films, 23 in the British period, 30 in the American. Through the early British films we can trace the evolution of his professional/artistic image, the development of both the Hitchcock style and the Hitchcock thematic. His third film (and first big commercial success), *The Lodger*, was crucial in establishing him as a maker of thrillers, but it was not until the mid-1930s that his name became consistently identified with that genre. Meanwhile, he had assimilated the two aesthetic influences that were major determinants in the formation of his mature style: German Expressionism and Soviet montage theory. The former, with its aim of expressing emotional states through a deformation of external reality, is discernible in his work from the beginning (not surprisingly, as he has acknowledged Lang's *Die müde Tod* as his first important cinematic experience, and as some of his earliest films were shot in German studios). Out of his later contact with the Soviet films of the 1920s evolved his elaborate editing techniques: he particularly acknowledged the significance for him of the Kuleshov experiment, from which he derived his fondness for the point-of-view shot and for building sequences by cross-cutting between person seeing/thing seen.

The extreme peculiarity of Hitchcock's art (if his films do not seem very odd it is only because they are so familiar) can be partly accounted for by the way in which these aesthetic influences from high art and revolutionary socialism were pressed into the service of British middle-class popular entertainment. Combined with Hitchcock's all-pervasive scepticism ("Everything's perverted in a different way, isn't it?"), this process resulted in an art that at once endorsed (superficially) and undermined (profoundly) the value system of the culture within which it was produced, be that culture British or American.

During the British period the characteristic plot structures that recur throughout Hitchcock's work are also established. I want here to single out three, not because they account for *all* of the films, but because they link the British to the American period, because their recurrence is particularly obstinate, and because they seem, taken in conjunction, central to the thematic complex of Hitchcock's total *oeuvre*.

1. The story about *the accused man*—This is already established in *The Lodger* (in which the male protagonist is suspected of being Jack the Ripper); it often takes the form of the "double chase," in which the hero is pursued by the police and in turn pursues (or seeks to unmask) the actual villains. Examples in the British period are *The 39 Steps* and *Young and Innocent*. In the American period it becomes the commonest of all Hitchcock plot structures: *Saboteur, Spellbound, Strangers on a Train, I Confess, To Catch a Thief, The Wrong Man, North by Northwest* and *Frenzy* are all based on it.

2. The story about *the guilty woman*—Although there are guilty women in earlier films, the structure is definitively established in *Blackmail*, Hitchcock's (and Britain's) first sound film. To it, in the British period, we may add *Sabotage*, but it is

in the American period that examples proliferate: *Rebecca* (Hitchcock's first Hollywood film), *Notorious, Under Capricorn, The Paradine Case, Vertigo, Psycho* (the first third), *The Birds* and *Marnie* are all variations on the original structure.

Before proceeding, it is necessary to add some notes on these two plot-structures and their relationship to each other. First, it is striking that the opposition of the two is almost complete; there are very few Hitchcock films in which the accused man turns out to be guilty after all (*Shadow of a Doubt* and *Stage Fright* are the obvious exceptions; *Suspicion* would have been a third if Hitchcock had been permitted to carry out his original intentions), and really none in which the accused woman turns out to be innocent (*Dial M for Murder* comes closest, but even there, although the heroine is innocent of murder, she is guilty of adultery). Second, it should be noticed that while the falsely accused man is usually (not quite always) the central consciousness of type 1, it is less habitually the case that the guilty woman is the central consciousness of type 2: frequently, she is the object of the male protagonist's investigation. Third, the outcome of the guilty woman films (and this may be dictated as much by the Motion Picture Production Code as by Hitchcock's personal morality) is dependent upon the *degree* of guilt: the woman can sometimes be "saved" by the male protagonist (*Blackmail, Notorious, Marnie*), but not if she is guilty of murder or an accomplice to it (*The Paradine Case, Vertigo*). Fourth, one should note the function of the opposite sex in the two types. The heroine of the falsely accused man films is, typically, hostile to the hero at first, believing him guilty; she subsequently learns to trust him, and takes his side in establishing his innocence. The function of the male protagonist of the guilty woman films is either to save the heroine or to be destroyed (at least morally and spiritually) by her. Fifth, it is important to recognize that the true nature of the guilt is always sexual, and that the falsely accused man is usually seen to be contaminated by this (though innocent of the specific crime, typically murder, of which he is accused). Richard Hannay in *The 39 Steps* can stand as the prototype of this: when he allows himself to be picked up by the woman in the music hall, it is in expectation of a sexual encounter, the notion of sexual disorder being displaced on to "espionage," and the film moves from this systematically towards the construction of the "good" (i.e. socially approved) couple. The very title of *Young and Innocent*, with its play on the connotations of the last word, exemplifies the same point, and it is noteworthy that in that film the hero's *sexual* innocence remains in doubt (we only have his own word for it that he was not the murdered woman's gigolo). Finally, the essential Hitchcockian dialectic can be read from the alternation, throughout his career, of these two series. On the whole, it is the guilty woman films that are the more disturbing, that leave the most jarring dissonances: here, the potentially threatening and subversive female sexuality, precariously contained within social norms in the falsely accused man films, erupts to demand recognition, is answered by an appalling violence (both emotional and physical), the cost of its destruction or containment leaving that "nasty taste" often noted as the dominant characteristic of Hitchcock's work.

3. It is within this context that the third plot structure takes on its full significance: the story about the *psychopath*—Frequently, this structure occurs in combination with the falsely accused man plot (see, for example, *Young and Innocent, Strangers on a Train, Frenzy,*) with a parallel established between the hero and his perverse and sinister adversary, who becomes a kind of shadowy alter ego. Only two Hitchcock films have the psychopath as their indisputably central figure, but they (*Shadow of a Doubt, Psycho*) are among his most famous and disturbing. The Hitchcock villain has a number of characteristics which are not necessarily common to all but unite in various combinations: a) Sexual "perversity" or ambiguity: a number are more or less explicitly coded as gay (the transvestite killer in *Murder!*, Philip in *Rope*, Bruno Anthony in *Strangers on a Train*); others have marked mother-fixations (Uncle Charlie in *Shadow of a Doubt*, Anthony Perkins in *Psycho*, Bob Rusk in *Frenzy*), seen as a source of their psychic disorder. (b) Fascist connotations: this becomes politically explicit in the U-boat commander of *Lifeboat*, but is plain enough in, for example, *Shadow of a Doubt* and *Rope*. (c) The subtle associations of the villain with the devil: Uncle Charlie and Smoke in *Shadow of a Doubt*, Bruno Anthony in the paddle-boat named Pluto in *Strangers on a Train*, Norman Bates remarking to Marion Crane that "No one ever comes here unless they've gotten off the main highway" in *Psycho*. (d) Closely connected with these characteristics is a striking and ambiguous fusion of power and impotence operating on both the sexual and non-sexual levels. What is crucially significant here is that this feature is by no means restricted to the villains. It is shared, strikingly, by the male protagonists of what are perhaps Hitchcock's two supreme masterpieces, *Rear Window* and *Vertigo*. It also relates closely to the obsession with control and fear of losing it that characterized Hitchcock's own methods of filmmaking: his preoccupation with a totally finalized and story-boarded shooting-script, his domination of actors and shooting conditions. (e) Finally, it's notable that the psychopath/villain is invariably the most fascinating and seductive character of the film, its chief source of energy, his inevitable destruction leaving behind an essentially empty world.

If one adds together all these factors, one readily sees why Hitchcock is so much more than the skilful entertainer and master-craftsman he was once taken for. His films overall represent an incomparable exposure of the sexual tensions and anxieties (especially *male* anxieties) that characterize a culture built upon repression, sexual inequality, and the drive to domination.

—Robin Wood

HOLGER-MADSEN

Danish. Born Holger Madsen, 11 April 1878, began spelling name with hyphen, 1911. Actor in Danish provinces, 1896–1904, and in Copenhagen, from 1904; actor in films, from 1907; directed first film, 1912; director for Nordisk Films Kompagni, 1913–20; worked in Germany, from 1920; returned to Denmark, 1930; manager of small Copenhagen cinema, 1938–43. *Died 30 November 1943.*

Films as Director:

1912 *Kun en Tigger* (+ role)
1913 *Under Savklingens Taender* (*The Usurer's Son*) (+ role);
       Under Mindernes Trae (*Dengamle Baenk. Left Alone*);
       Skaebnens Veje (*Under Kaerlighedens Aag. In the Bonds of Passion*); *Det mørke Punkt* (*Staalkongens Vilje. The Steel King's Last Wish*); *Mens Pesten raser* (*Laegens Hustru. During the Plague*); *Ballettens Datter* (*Danserinden. Unjustly Accused*); *Elskovsleg* (*Love's Devotee*); *Prinsesse Elena* (*The Princess's Dilemma*); *Den hvide Dame* (*The White Ghost*); *Fra Fyrste til Knejpevaert* (*The Gambler's Wife*); *Millionaerdrengen* (*The Adventures of a Millionaire's*

Holger-Madsen: *Himmelskibet*

Son); *Guldet og vort Hjerte* (*Et vanskeligt Valg. The Heart's Voice*)

1914   *Tempeldanserindens Elskov* (*Bajaderens Haevn. The Bayadere's Revenge*); *Børnevennerne* (*A Marriage of Convenience*); *En Opstandelse* (*Genopstandelsen. A Resurrection*); *Husassistenten* (*Naar Fruen skifter Pige. The New Cook*); *Søvngaengersken* (*The Somnambulist*); *Opiumsdrømmen* (*The Opium Smoker's Dream*); *Den mystiske Fremmede* (*A Deal with the Devil*); *Endelig Alene* (*Alone at Last*); *Min Ven Levy* (*My Friend Levy*); *Ned med Vaabnene* (*Lay Down Your Arms*); *Trold kan taemmes* (*The Taming of the Shrew*); *De Forviste* (*Uden Faedreland. Without a Country*); *Et Huskors* (*Lysten styret. Enough of It*); *Barnets Magt* (*The Child*); *Et Haremseventyr* (*An Adventure in a Harem*); *Evangeliemandens Liv* (*The Candle and the Moth*); *Kaerlighedens Triumf* (*Testamentet. The Romance of a Will*); *Krig og Kaerlighed* (*Love and War*); *Spiritisten* (*A Voice from the Past*): *Det stjaalne Ansigt* (*The Missing Admiralty Plans*); *En Aeresoprejsning* (*Misunderstood*); *Liykken draeber*

1915   *Cigaretpigen* (*The Cigarette Maker*); *Hvem er Gentlemantyven* (*Strakoff the Adventurer*); *En Ildprøve* (*A Terrible Ordeal*); *Danserindens Haevn* (*Circus Arrives. The Dancer's Revenge*); *Danserindens Kaerlighedsdrøm* (*Den Dødsdømte. A Dancer's Strange Dream. The Condemned*); *Den frelsende Film* (*The Woman Tempted Me*); *Grevinde Hjerteløs* (*The Beggar Princess*); *Guldets Gift* (*The Tempting of Mrs. Chestney*); *Den hvide Djaevel* (*Caught in the Toils. The Devil's Protege*); *Hvo som elsker sin Fader or Faklen* (*Who So Loveth His Father's Honor*); *I Livets Braending* (*The Crossroads of Life*); *Manden uden Fremtid* (*The Man without a Future*); *Den omstridte Jord* (*Jordens Haevn. The Earth's Revenge*); *Sjaeletyven* (*The Unwilling*

Sinner. His Innocent Dupe); *Det unge Blod* (*The Buried Secret*); *Krigens Fjende* (*Acostates første Offer. The Munition Conspiracy*); *En Kunstners Gennembrud* (*Den Dødes Sjael. The Soul of the Violin*)

1916   *For sin Faders Skyld* (*The Veiled Lady. False Evidence*); *Maaneprinsessen* (*Kamaeleonen. The Mysterious Lady. The May-Fly*); *Børnenes Synd* (*The Sins of the Children*); *Fange no. 113* (*Convict No. 113*); *Hans rigtige Kone* (*Which Is Which*); *Hendes Moders Løfte* (*Dødens Kontrakt. A Super Shylock*); *Hittebarnet* (*The Foundling of Fate*): *Hvor Sorgerne glemmes* (*Søster Cecilies Offer. Sister Cecilia*); *Livets Gøglespil* (*An Impossible Marriage*); *Manden uden Smil*; *Nattens Mysterium* (*Who Killed Barno O'Neal*); *Nattevandreren* (*Edison Maes Dagbog. Out of the Underworld*); *Pax Aeterna*; *Lydia* (*The Music Hall Star*); *Lykken* (*The Road to Happiness. Guiding Conscience*); *Praestens Datter*; *Testamentets Hemmelighed* (*Den Dødes Røst. The Voice of the Dead. Nancy Keith*); *Den Aereløse* (*The Infamous. The Prison Taint*); *Smil* (*Far's Sorg. Father Sorrow. The Beggar Man of Paris*)

1917   *Himmelskibet* (*A Trip to Mars*); *Retten sejrer* (*Justice Victorious*); *Hendes Helt* (*Vogt dig for dine Venner*)

1918   *Folkets Ven* (*A Friend of the People*); *Mod Lyset* (*Towards the Light*); *Manden, der sejrede* (*The Man Who Tamed the Victors. Fighting Instinct*)

1919   *Gudernes Yndling* (*Digterkongen. Trials of Celebrity. The Penalty of Fame*); *Har jeg Ret til at tage mit eget Liv* (*Flugten fra Livet. The Flight from Life. Beyond the Barricade*); *Det Største i Verden* (*Janes gode Ven. The Greatest in the World. The Love That Lives*)

1921   *Am Webstuhl der Zeit*; *Tobias Buntschuh* (+ role); *Den dvende Stad* (*Die sterbende Stadt*)

1922   *Pömperly's Kampf mit dem Schneeschuh* (co-d)

1923   *Das Evangelium; Zaida, die Tragödie eines Modells*
1924   *Der Mann um Mitternacht*
1925   *Ein Lebenskünstler*
1926   *Die seltsame Nacht; Die Sporck'schen Jäger; Spitzen*
1927   *Die heilige Lüge*
1928   *Freiwild; Die seltsame Nacht der Helga Wansen; Was ist los mit Nanette*
1934   *København, Kalundborg og—?* (co-d)
1936   *Sol over Danmark*

Films as Actor:

1907   *Den sorte Hertug*
1908   *Magdalene; En grov Spøg (A Practical Joke and a Sad End); Verdens Herkules (Hercules the Athlete); Karneval (The Bank Director. Carnival); Svend Dyrings Hus (The Stepmother); De smaa Landstrygere (Sold to Thieves); Smaeklaasen (The Spring Lock); Natten før Kristians Fødelsdag (The Night Before Christian's Birthday); Rulleskøjterne (On Roller Skates); Sherlock Holmes I; Sherlock Holmes III*
1909   *Den graa Dame (The Gray Dame)*
1911   *Det store Fald or Malstrømmen; Dødssejleren or Dynamitattentatet paa Fyrtaarnet; Den svarte doktorn*
1912   *Paa Livets Skyggeside*
1913   *Elskovs Mast*
1931   *Praesten i Vejlby; Krudt med Knald*
1933   *Fem raske Piger; Med tuld Musik*
1934   *Lynet; 7-9-13*
1935   *Kidnapped*

*   *   *

The two leading directors at Nordisk Films Kompagni in the Golden Age of the Danish cinema from 1910 to 1914 were August Blom and Holger-Madsen. They were similar in many respects. They both started as actors, but unlike Blom, Holger-Madsen began as a director with companies other than Nordisk. When he came to Nordisk he worked in almost all of the genres of the period—sensational films, comedies, farces, dramas, and tragedies. But little by little Holger-Madsen developed his own personality, both in content and style.

Holger-Madsen specialized in films with spiritual topics. His main film in this genre was *Evangeliemandens Liv*, in which Valdemar Psilander plays the leading part of a dissolute young man of good family who suddenly realizes how empty and pointless his life is. He becomes a Christian and starts working as a preacher among the poor and the social outcasts of the big city. He succeeds in rescuing a young man from the path of sin. There are several of the cliches of the period in this tale, but the characterization of the hero is largely free of sentimentality, and Holger-Madsen coached Psilander into playing the role with a mature, calm and genuine strength of feeling. Formally the film is exquisite. The sets, the camerawork, and the lighting are executed with great care, and the film is rich in striking pictorial compositions, which was the forte of Holger-Madsen. He had a predilection for extraordinary, often bizarre images and picturesque surroundings. With his cameraman, Marius Clausen, he emphasized the visual look of his films. His use of side light, inventive camera angles and close-ups, combined with unusual sets, made him an original stylist. He was not very effective in his cutting technique, but he could establish marvelously choreographed scenes, in which people are moving in elegant patterns within the frame.

Holger-Madsen's reputation as an idealistic director lead him to direct the big prestige films with pacifist themes which Ole Olsen, the head of Nordisk Films Kompagni, wanted to make in the naive hope that he could influence the fighting powers in the First World War. The films were often absurdly simple, but Holger-Madsen brought his artistic sense to the visual design of these sentimental stories. One of his most famous films is *Himmelskibet* from 1917 about a scientist who flies to Mars in a rocket ship. There he is confronted with a peaceful civilization. The film has obtained a position as one of the first science fiction films.

When the Danish cinema declined, Holger-Madsen went to Germany. Returning to Denmark after the 1920s, he was offered the opportunity of directing during the early sound film period, but his productions were insignificant. He was a silent film director; the image was his domain, and he was one of the craftsmen who molded and refined the visual language of film.

—Ib Monty

———

HONDO, Med.

Mauritanian. Born Abid Mohamed Medoun Hondo in Mauritania (formerly Mauretania), 4 May 1936. Trained as a chef at hotel management school, Rabat, Morocco, 1954–58. Moved to France, 1959; worked in restaurants and as Swiss cheese salesman in Paris; took drama classes, from 1965, then formed own theatre company "Shango" (named after Yoruba god of thunder); actor, then assistant director on films, from 1967; directed first feature, *Soleil O*, 1969, and set up production company Films Soleil O; helped found the African Committee of Filmmakers, 1982. Recipient: Golden Leopard, Locarno Festival, 1970, and International Critics Prize, Pan-African Festival, Ougadougou, 1971, for *Soleil O*.

Films as Director:

1969   *Balade aux sources (Ballad to the Sources)* (short); *Partout ou peut-être nulle part (Everywhere, Nowhere Maybe)* (short); *Soleil O (O Sun)*
1973   *Les Bicots-nègres, vos voisins (The Black-Wogs, Your Neighbours. Arabs and Niggers, Your Neighbours)*
1977   *Nous aurons toute la mort pour dormir (We Have All of Death for Sleeping. We'll Sleep When We Die)*
1979   *Polisario, un peuple en armes (Polisario, A People in Arms); West Indies, les nègres marrons de la liberté*
1986   *Sarraounia*

Other Films:

1967   *Shock Troops* (Costa-Gavras) (role)
1968   *Tante Zita* (Enrico) (role)
1969   *A Walk with Love and Death* (Huston) (role)

Publications:

By HONDO: articles—

Interview with Jean Delmas, in *Jeune Cinéma* (Paris), June/July 1970.
Interview with Michel Ciment and Paul-Louis Thirard, in *Positif* (Paris), September 1970.
"Je suis un immigré," an interview with Nourredine Ghali, in *Jeune Cinéma* (Paris), September/October 1974.
Interview in *Filmfaust* (Frankfurt), September/October 1977.
Interview with Don Ranvaud, in *Framework* (Norwich), Spring 1978.
"What is Cinema for Us?," in *Framework* (Norwich), Autumn 1979.
"Africa: Towards a National Cinema," an interview with Anne Head, in *Screen International* (London), 23 February 1985.
Interview with Mark Reid, in *Jump Cut* (Berkeley), March 1986.
Interview with J. Leahy, in *Monthly Film Bulletin* (London), January 1988.

On HONDO: books—

Martin, Angela, editor, *African Film: The Context of Production*, London, 1982.
Pfaff, Françoise, *25 Black African Filmmakers: A Critical Study*, Westport, Connecticut, 1988.

On HONDO: articles—

Ciment, Michel, "*Soleil O*," in *Positif* (Paris), September 1970.
"African Film Section" of *Jump Cut* (Berkeley), March 1986.
Mirmont, Roger, "Impressions d'Afrique," in *Première* (Paris), July 1986.

*   *   *

Med Hondo, born in Mauritania but living since 1959 in Paris, is one of the leading figures in African filmmaking. His theatrical background is very apparent in his first feature, *Soleil O*, which comprises a mixture of documentary observations and dramatic scenes and sketches, acted out by a small group of African and Antillean players who take on a variety of successive roles. The film explores the whole range of issues raised by the experiences of an African worker newly arrived in France, beginning with the hero's delusions ("Sweet France . . . I've come home") and ending with his anguish and alienation. *Soleil O* has all the qualities and some of the defects of a well-directed piece of agit-prop: some telling points, a few good jokes and the occasional passage of tedium. But its crucial importance is its assured manner of putting forward what had rarely been heard in cinema: an authentically African voice.

In *The Black-Wogs, Your Neighbours* (*Les bicots-nègres vos voisins*) there is the same potentially powerful collage of documentary and drama, but this time the *cinéma-vérité* elements predominate. As a result, the film raises a mass of interesting issues concerning exploitation, emigration and culture but has only a limited audience impact, since the argument emerges as too long and undisciplined. Some of the same weaknesses characterise Hondo's documentary in support of the Polisario Front, *We Have All of Death for Sleeping* (*Nous avons toute la mort pour dormir*). There can be little doubt about the sincerity of the filmmaker's commitment or the justice of his message. But the celebration of revolution is little more than lyrical rhetoric, a preaching to the already converted.

Fortunately Hondo's two subsequent fictional features have shown his dazzling skills as a director of drama. *West Indies* deals with some four centuries of colonial impact in the Antilles and a variety of forms of slavery and oppression. But instead of offering an alternative history as such (in terms of the names and dates of the oppressed), the film gives us visual, spatial enactments of revolt. Using the single stylised set of a slave ship (built in its entirety at a disused railway station), *West Indies* offers the celebratory anticipation of the dawn of liberation through the whirling colours and shapes of popular dance. The interweaving of music, sound effects, dance, declamation and song gives *West Indies* a forceful impact.

Set in the 1890's *Sarraounia* chronicles the exemplary resistance of the pagan queen of the Aznas to a powerful and well-armed French force which rampages across the country, threatening all who stand in its path. But the film is not the story of an individual princess and her prowess. Instead Hondo is concerned to spell out dramatically the unity of pagan and Moslem Africans against a violent force which disintegrates under the pressures wrought by the overweaning personal ambition of the French commander. The director's confident handling of his resources and masterly sense of pace and rhythm place him in the forefront of contemporary African film making.

—Roy Armes

_____

HOU HSIAO-HSIEN

Taiwanese. (Name is pseudonym of Hour, Shiaw-shyan; name in pinyin: Hou, Xiaoxian.) Born in Meixian, Kuangtung (Canton) province, 8 April 1947, moved to Hualien, Taiwan, 1948. Educated in the film program of the Taiwan National Academy of the Arts, 1969–72. Electronic calculator salesman, 1972–73; script boy, then assistant director, from 1974, also scriptwriter from 1975; directed first film, *Cute Girls*, 1979; sold house to finance *Growing Up*, 1982; actor in *When Husband Is out of Town*, for TV, and director of music video, 1985. Recipient: Best Director Award, Asian-Pacific Film Festival, for *A Summer at Grandpa's*, 1985; Golden Lion Award, Venice Festival, and Best Director, Golden Horse Awards, Taiwan, for *A City of Sadness*, 1989.

Films as Director:

1979   *Chiu Shih Liu Liu Tê T'a* (*Cute Girls*) (+ sc)
1980   *Feng Erh T'i T'a Ts'ai* (*Cheerful Wind*) (+ sc)
1982   *Tsai Nei Ho P'an Ch'ing Ts'ao Ch'ing* (*The Green, Green Grass of Home*) (+ sc)
1983   episode of *Erh Tzu Tê Ta Wan Ou* (*The Sandwich Man. Son's Big Doll*)
1984   *Fêng Kuei Lai Tê Jen* (*The Boys From Fengkuei*) (+ co-sc); *Tung Tung Te Chia Ch'i* (*A Summer at Grandpa's*)
1985   *T'ung Nein Wang Shih* (*A Time to Live and a Time to Die*)
1986   *Lien Lien Feng Ch'eng* (*Dust in the Wind*) (+ role)
1987   *Ni Luo Ho Nü Erh* (*Daughter of the Nile*) (+ role)
1989   *Pei Ch'ing Ch'êng Shih* (*A City of Sadness*) (+ role)

Other Films:

1974   *Yun shen Pu Chih Ch'u* (*Lost in the Deep Cloud*) (asst-d); *Chin shui Lou Tai* (*A Better Chance*) (asst-d)
1975   *Tao Hua Neu Tou Chao Kung* (*The Beauty and the Old Man*) (sc, asst-d); *Yeuh Hsia Lao Jen* (*The Matchmaker*) (sc, asst-d)
1976   *Ai Yu Ming T'ien* (*Love Has Tomorrow*) (asst-d); *Yen Shuio Han* (*The Glory of the Sunset*) (asst-d); *Nan Hai Yü Nü Hai Tê Chan Chêng* (*The War Between Boys and Girls*) (asst-d)
1977   *Ts'ui Hu Han* (*The Chilly Green Lake*) (asst-d); *Yen P'o Chiang Shang* (*On the Foggy River*) (sc, asst-d); *Tsao an Taipei* (*Good Morning, Taipei*) (sc); *Pei Chih Ch'iu* (*Sadness of Autumn*) (sc)
1978   *Tso Yeh Yü Hsiao Hsiao* (*The Rushing Rain of Last Night*) (sc, asst-d); *Wo T'a Laong Erh Lai* (*I Come with the Wave*) (sc, asst-d)
1979   *T'ien Liang Hao Kê Ch'iu* (*What a Cold but Wonderful Autumn*) (sc, asst-d); *Ch'iu Lien* (*Autumn Lotus*) (sc)
1980   *P'eng P'eng I Ch'uan Hsin* (*Pounding Hearts*) (sc, asst-d)
1981   *Ch'iao Ju Ts'ai Tieh Fei Fei Fei* (*A Butterfly Girl*) (sc, asst-d)
1982   *Hsiao Pi Te Ku Shih* (*Growing Up*) (co-pr, co-sc, asst-d)
1984   *Yu Ma Ts'ai Tzu* (*Ah Fei*) (co-sc); *Hsiao Pa Pa Te T'ien K'ung* (*Out of the Blue*) (co-sc); *Ch'ing Mei Chu Ma* (*Taipei Story*) (role); *Tsui Hsiang Nien Tê Chi Chieh* (sc)

Publications:

By HOU: articles—

Interview with Olivier Assayas, in *Cahiers du Cinéma* (Paris), December 1984.
Interview with Tony Rayns, in *Monthly Film Bulletin* (London), June 1988.
"Not the Best Possible Face," an interview with Tony Rayns, in *Monthly Film Bulletin* (London), June 1990.

On HOU: articles—

Huang, Vivian, "Taiwan's Social Realism," in *The Independent* (New York), January/February 1990.

Hou Hsiao-Hsien: *A City of Sadness*

Combs, Richard, "*Dust in the Wind*," in *Monthly Film Bulletin* (London), April 1990.

*　　*　　*

Hou Hsiao-hsien is the most internationally renowned of the filmmakers associated with Taiwan's "New Cinema" movement. The "New Cinema" was forged out of the country's aging industry in the early 1980s by a group of emerging filmmakers, most of whom were in their early thirties at the time. The members of this cohesive group helped each other make films, and were strongly supported in turn by a group of film critics belonging to the same generation. Their works diverged from mainstream films of the time both in style and in content; instead of the escapist romances and propaganda films in melodramatic form that dominated Taiwan's film market in the 1970s, this new wave of filmmakers used a realistic style to convey their socially concerned themes.

The experiences of life in Taiwan figure prominently in Hou's work, due to his personal background: Hou, who has lived in Taiwan for most of his life, was a year old in 1948 when he and his family, on a visit from the mainland, were forced to remain more or less permanently as a result of the Civil War. Unlike the previous generation of filmmakers, who were brought up and educated in mainland China and who hired professionals to dub all the dialogue with standard Mandarin, the official language of both Taiwan and mainland China, Hou began using large amounts of the Taiwanese dialect spoken by most of the island's inhabitants. Following *The Sandwich Man*, Hou also mixed in the dialect of the ancient Hakkas ethnic group, as well as Japanese. (Japan had occupied Taiwan for almost 50 years, previous to the Nationalist takeover.) While the previous generation of filmmakers identified with or bowed to the Nationalist strategy of mandating exclusive use of the Mandarin language to "Chinacize" the people of Taiwan, Hou and his peers, whether mainlander or islander, recognized the fact that Taiwan was not synonymous with China. Due to this break from the state-enforced ideology, the New Cinema practitioners were able to begin to face and examine the sources and manifestations of their society's problems.

Perhaps most dynamic in this rapidly industrializing country was the emotional as well as physical dislocation resulting from the urbanization of Taiwan's traditionally rural culture. The conflict between urban and rural values is a recurring theme in Hou's films. Hou, who grew up in the countryside and moved to Taipei at the beginning of his college studies, retains a strong attachment to traditional Taiwanese values. On the screen, he uses country living and sentiments in the idyllic scene structure of his films. In *A Summer At Grandpa's*, the protagonist Tung Tung, a young boy who grew up in Taipei but stayed at his Grandfather's in the country while his mother was hospitalized, gained "real" childhood experiences, playing in the river and exchanging his toy car with another child's live turtle, as well as more gritty life experiences, learning of the complexities of social relationships through the rape of an insane woman and her subsequent unsuccessful pregnancy. Contrasted with the positive influences one can gain from country life in most of Hou's films are the attractions of the city, with its opportunities for a living wage and concomitant confusion of an alien social structure and its dissimilar types of human relationships.

In *The Boys from Fengkuei*, when three young men arrive at Kaohsiung, they find that their friend's sister, who has moved to the city from their home town, has somehow become "morally corrupted." While they wander around on the streets of the city, a stranger on a motorcycle collects their money to see an underground porno film, sending them into an empty building still under construction. Instead of a movie screen, they view the city landscape from huge holes awaiting windows. A silent long take and a long shot shows the three naive boys staring at the city, the farce turning out to be their first taste of the bitterness of the city, without anger but with a deep sense of helplessness.

That the urban experience can prove damaging to one's physical as well as mental health is illustrated in *Dust in the Wind*. The protagonist Ah-Yuan is beaten up by his boss's wife for failing to deliver a lunch box to her son, and some friends of Ah-Yuan, including his girl friend, are injured during their work. While these country children are wounded by the city, they can always go back to their rural homes to recuperate from their mental and physical injuries. However, in *Daughter of the Nile*, when the teenaged girl Shao Yang and her brother Shao Fang settle in the city of Taipei, they become the orphans of the world. *Daughter of the Nile* is Hou's first and thus far only film that takes place entirely in Taipei. Hou's shots of the dark city illuminated by the colorful neon signs eerily illuminate the materialism that dislocates the youths, and finally takes Shao Fang's life.

The uneasiness and the difficulties of adjusting to social changes was the other theme in almost all of Hou's directorial works. In *The Sandwich Man*, Hou used a clown costume as the symbol of this discomfort. In *Dust In The Wind*, this discomfort is transformed into physical suffering when the rural teenagers are beaten and otherwise abused by their working environment. Death also played the main metaphoric role of the transition in *A Time To Live And A Time To Die*: The death of protagonist Ah-ha's father, mother and grandmother punctuate his stages of growing up as well as his ideological divergence from the Nationalist party between the years 1958 to 1966. Similarly, in *A City of Sadness*, each of the four brothers of the Lin family was killed either physically or mentally in differing political climates and social circumstances during the 1940s, their deaths indicating their failure in adjusting to the new eras.

Hou's achievement is not only in his cinematic sensitivities but also in his social consciousness. As much as he is a filmmaker, Hou is a historical and social commentator of the first order.

—Vivian Huang

HOWARD, William K.

American. Born William Kerrigan Howard in St. Mary's, Ohio, 16 June 1899. Educated in engineering and law, Ohio State University. Served with American Expeditionary Force, France, 1917–18. Worked for film distributor, Cincinatti, then Vitagraph sales manager, Minnesota, 1916–17; sales advisor for Universal, Hollywood, 1919; assistant director, 1920, then director, for Fox, 1921; signed with Famous Players-Lasky, 1924; joined Cecil B. de Mille's Producers Distributing Corps, 1926; under contract to Fox, 1928–33; made *A Guy Could Change* for Republic, 1946. *Died 21 February 1954.*

Films as Director:

1921   *Get Your Man* (co-d); *Play Square*; *What Love Will Do*
1922   *Extra! Extra!*; *Lucky Dan*; *Deserted at the Altar* (co-d); *Captain Fly-by-Night*
1923   *The Fourth Musketeer*; *Danger Ahead*; *Let's Go*
1924   *The Border Legion*; *East of Broadway*
1925   *The Thundering Herd*; *Code of the West*; *The Light of Western Stars*
1926   *Red Dice*; *Bachelor Brides* (*Bachelor's Brides*); *Volcano*; *Gigolo*
1927   *White Gold*; *The Main Event*
1928   *A Ship Comes in* (*His Country*); *The River Pirate*
1929   *Christina*; *The Valiant*; *Love, Live and Laugh* (dialogue scenes d by Henry Kolker)
1930   *Good Intentions* (+ co-sc, dialogue scenes d by Henry Kolker); *Scotland Yard* (*Detective Clive, Bart.*)
1931   *Don't Bet on Women* (*More than a Kiss*); *Transatlantic*; *Surrender*
1932   *The Trial of Vivienne Ware*; *The First Year*; *Sherlock Holmes*
1933   *The Power and the Glory* (*Power and Glory*); *The Cat and the Fiddle*
1934   *This Side of Heaven*; *Evelyn Prentice*
1935   *Vanessa, Her Love Story*; *Rendezvous*; *Mary Burns, Fugitive*
1936   *The Princess Comes Across*; *Fire over England*
1937   *The Squeaker* (*Murder on Diamond Row*); *Over the Moon* (Freeland; d uncredited)
1939   *Back Door to Heaven* (+ pr, story)
1940   *Money and the Woman*; *Knute Rockne—All American* (*A Modern Hero*) (Bacon; d begun by Howard)
1941   *Bullets for O'Hara*
1942   *Klondike Fury*
1943   *Johnny Come Lately* (*Johnny Vagabond*)
1944   *When the Lights Go on Again*
1946   *A Guy Could Change* (+ assoc pr)

Other Films:

1920   *The Skywayman* (Hogan) (asst d)
1921   *The One-Man Trail* (Durning) (sc)
1922   *Trooper O'Neill* (Dunlap and Wallace) (sc); *The Crusader* (Mitchell) (co-sc)
1929   *Sin Town* (co-sc)
1937   *The Green Cockatoo* (*Four Dark Hours, Race Gang*) (Menzies) ("A William K. Howard Production")

Publications:

On HOWARD: book—

Thompson, Frank, editor, *Between Action and Cut: Five American Directors*, Metuchen, New Jersey, 1985.

On HOWARD: articles—

Obituary, in *New York Times*, 22 February 1954.
Everson, William K., "William K. Howard," in *Films in Review* (New York), May 1954.
Rutherford, T.S., "William K. Howard," in *Film Dope* (London), November 1982.

*   *   *

For more than 20 years, William K. Howard was a reliable Hollywood director, able to turn his attention with ease to most types of features. He was not a major director, the majority of his films being no better than those turned out by his contemporaries, but Howard does deserve more than passing recognition for his work on *White Gold*, *Sherlock Holmes*, *The Power and the Glory*, and *Fire Over England*.

Howard's silent features were always well-made commercial successes, with the best-known titles being a version of Zane Grey's *The Thundering Herd*, starring Jack Holt and Tim McCoy, and a spectacular melodrama featuring Bebe Daniels, *Volcano*. Most historians agree that Howard's best silent film

William K. Howard directing Laurence Olivier and Vivien Leigh in *Fire Over England*

work is *White Gold*, which owes much to German expressionist cinema and which one historian, William K. Everson, has compared favorably to *The Last Laugh*. Certainly the film's star, Jetta Goudal, has never given a more impressive performance, one that is immediately reminiscent of Lillian Gish in *The Wind*. In the early 1940s Howard actively considered a remake of *White Gold*.

Curiously, William K. Howard seemed to establish far more of a visual style with his sound films than with his silent efforts. This is particularly apparent in *Sherlock Holmes* and, above all, in *The Power and the Glory*. The latter utilizes a series of flashbacks—rather like *Citizen Kane* some years later—to tell of a railroad executive's rise to power. Highly regarded at the time, the film's continuing appeal owes as much to Howard's direction as to its obviously brilliant script by Preston Sturges. For example, it is doubtful that a lesser team than Howard and Sturges could have created the sequence in which Spencer Tracy and Colleen Moore become engaged, told as the couple climb a steeper and steeper hill with no dialogue except for the commentary by Ralph Morgan.

From 1936 through 1938 Howard worked in England, notably on *Fire Over England*, based on the A.E.W. Mason historical romance set during the reign of Elizabeth I. Obviously Howard was aided by a cast which included Flora Robson (as Elizabeth), Laurence Olivier, Vivien Leigh, and Raymond Massey, not to mention the cinematography of James Wong Howe, but even so the director deserves credit for his capable handling of both sweeping historical spectacle and intimate drama.

With his return to the States, Howard settled down to directing routine melodramas. He did create something of a sensation in the film community in 1936 when he ordered his supervising producer off the set during the filming of *The Princess Comes Across*, the first time a director had enforced the policies of the fledgling Screen Directors Guild. Contemporaries of Howard have described him as both brilliant and cynical, and it is perhaps the latter trait which enabled the director to add a reasonable amount of artistry to films which might otherwise have been nothing more than mere box office successes.

—Anthony Slide

———

HUGHES, John.

American. Born in Detroit, 1937. Studied at University of Arizona. Gag writer for Rodney Dangerfield and others, also worked for Leo Burnett Advertising Agency; writer and editor, *National Lampoon* magazine, 1970s; wrote script for *National Lampoon's Class Reunion*, 1982; directed first feature, *Sixteen Candles*, 1984; set up John Hughes Production Company, 1985. Address: c/o John Hughes Production Company, Paramount Pictures, 5555 Melrose Avenue, Los Angeles, CA 90038, U.S.A.

Films as Director and Scriptwriter:

1984 *Sixteen Candles*
1985 *The Breakfast Club*; *Weird Science* (+ pr)
1986 *Ferris Bueller's Day Off* (+ co-pr)
1987 *Planes, Trains and Automobiles*
1988 *She's Having a Baby*
1989 *Uncle Buck*

Films as Scriptwriter:

1982 *National Lampoon's Class Reunion*
1983 *National Lampoon's Vacation*; *Nate and Hayes* (co-sc); *Mr. Mom*
1985 *National Lampoon's European Vacation*
1986 *Pretty in Pink* (Deutsch) (+ exec pr)
1987 *Some Kind of Wonderful* (Deutsch) (+ pr)

Publications:

By HUGHES: articles—

Interview with B. Mills, in *Stills* (London), June–July 1985.
Interview in *Inter/View* (New York), August 1985.
Interview in *L'Ecran Fantastique* (Paris), November 1985.

On HUGHES: articles—

Barth, J., "Kinks of Comedy," in *Film Comment* (New York), May/June 1984.
Revue du Cinéma/Image et Son (Paris), June 1990.

*   *   *

John Hughes is the Frank Capra of contemporary cinema, and

if *The Breakfast Club* and *Ferris Bueller's Day Off*—for all their admirable qualities—don't seem likely to last as well as *Mr Smith Goes to Washington* or *It's a Wonderful Life*, then perhaps that has more to do with the mindsets of their respective audiences and the changing nature of Hollywood studio production than any gap between the populist perception and perspective of their creators. Hughes' first films as a director, from *Sixteen Candles* through to *Ferris Bueller* and including his scripting of *Pretty in Pink*, established the modern "teen movie" as a genre, drawing from such precedents as the Andy Hardy films, the juvenile delinquency/rock 'n' roll movies of the 1950s, the AIP Beach Party films of the 1960s and such varied 1970s artefacts as *American Graffiti* and *Carrie* to create a self-contained generic world, with its own iconic presences (Molly Ringwald, Anthony Michael Hall, Emilio Estevez, Ally Sheedy, Matthew Broderick, Jennifer Grey), dialogue style (Hughes is especially smart in choosing to make up personalised slang rather than researching it, since that's exactly how teenagers create their own languages), recurrent references (fast cars, British rock music, sexual nerves) and comedy-romance-caper narrative structures.

In establishing the modern American high school and its teenage society as a generic venue to compete with the small towns of Capra Americana or the frontier communities of the Western, Hughes provided a cornerstone for any number of imitations—from lazy action pictures like *3:15* and *The Principal*, nerdy Hughes imitations like *Adventures in Babysitting*, *Can't Buy Me Love* and *She's Out of Control* and challenging, form-stretching works like Michael Lehmann's *Heathers*, Keith Gordon's *The Chocolate War*, Rob Reiner's *Stand By Me* and Tim Hunter's *River's Edge*, all of which need the exist-

John Hughes: *The Breakfast Club*

ence of the Hughes-created genre to react against or play games with. Coming to films from a succession of doggy screenplay assignments (the underrated *National Lampoon's Vacation* and the overrated *Mr Mom*) and an apprenticeship on *National Lampoon*, Hughes' *Sixteen Candles* seemed like a one-off miniature, making clever use of Molly Ringwald's gawky edge-of-unsympathetic charm, but *The Breakfast Club*, an artificial conceit about a cross-section of high school society confined in detention and talking through their lives and problems, is an eye-catching work. Acutely perceptive about the class distinctions that American cinema usually does not acknowledge, and still perfectly-crafted as a teenage entertainment, *The Breakfast Club*, like *Ferris Bueller*, is calculated to alienate parental figures, like most movie critics, and to mean something to its chosen audience that at once lends it an immediate appeal and makes it liable to age quickly.

Completing his "Shermer High" trilogy with *Weird Science*, a messy but rather endearing s-f spoof with Kelly LeBrock disorientatingly bizarre as a barbie doll Mary Poppins magically reshaping the lives of two high school nerds, Hughes graduated to *Ferris Bueller's Day Off*, a caper movie about "one man's tireless crusade to take it easy," which stretches the high school set about as far as it will bend, and forces the audience to make judgements about the fast-talking, manipulative hero that the film never does. While Broderick's Bueller, the coolest imaginable teen, is the centre of the film, the weight of the movie is with the background characters whose lives are affected by his strange crusade. Hughes, in evolving the teen movie from Frankie Avalon rather than James Dean, sometimes suggests the "I'm Okay—You're Okay" generation in his too-neat last-reel resolves, which never have the emotional catharsis of, say, George Bailey's Christmas regeneration in *It's a Wonderful Life*, but there are darker shadows in his films, in the suggestion that the teenage heroes are liable to repeat the errors demonstrated by their variously failed elders.

Leap-frogging the unfortunate *She's Having a Baby*, the first obvious attempt to deal with adulthood in Hughes work, he came up with the logical extension of *Ferris Bueller* in *Planes, Trains and Automobiles* and *Uncle Buck*, both of which feature John Candy as self-confident, defiantly sloppy, emotionally retarded adults who could well be Ferris Bueller twenty years later, his irresponsibility finally catching up with him. *Planes* is a demonstration of just how sharp Hughes' comedy skills are, with Candy and a cleverly-cast Steve Martin playing neatly off each other as the slob and the anal-retentive forced to travel across country together as Martin's frustration escalates and Candy's amiability slips into despair, while *Uncle Buck* turns the tables completely, by pitting the irresponsible, anarchic Buck against an uptight, materialistic, snobbish teenage princess (Jean Louisa Kelly), whose education parallels that of Bueller's overintense principal (Jeffrey Jones), while, as in *Planes*, a few odd little scenes between the uproarious fun suggest just how bleak and dangerous the Ferris Bueller lifestyle is when it gets to the end of the road. Lightweight but rarely negligible, Hughes may be the definitive late 1980s film-maker, representing where American movies are at as squarely as Capra, Altman or Spielberg did in their heyday, and it is easy, considering one's problematic reaction to the cinematic and actual world which he represents, to overlook his genuine skills as a director and writer of social comedy, in the construction of surprisingly neat plots, and in the reflection/creation of teenage fast-food culture.

—Kim Newman

———

HUSTON, John.

Irish/American. Born John Marcellus Huston, son of actor Walter, in Nevada, Missouri, 5 August 1906, became Irish citizen, 1964. Educated at boarding school in Los Angeles and at Lincoln High School, Los Angeles, 1923–24. Served in Signal Corps, Army Pictorial Service, discharged as Major, 1942–45. Married 1) Dorothy Jeanne Harvey, 1926 (divorced 1933); 2) Leslie Black, 1937 (divorced 1944); 3) Evelyn Keyes, 1946 (divorced 1950), one adopted son; 4) Ricki Soma, 1950 (died 1969), one son, two daughters including actress Anjelica; also son Daniel by Zoë Sallis; 5) Celeste Shane, 1972 (divorced 1977). Doctors in St. Paul, Minnesota, diagnose enlarged heart and kidney disease, taken to California for cure, 1916; boxer in California, 1920's; actor in New York, 1924; competition horseman, Mexico, 1927; journalist in New York, 1928–30; scriptwriter and actor in Hollywood, 1930; worked for Gaumont-British, London, 1932; moved to Paris, intending to study painting, 1933; returned to New York, editor *Midweek Pictorial*, 1934; stage actor, 1934; writer for Warner Bros., Hollywood, 1936; directed first film, *The Maltese Falcon*, 1941; with William Wyler and Philip Dunne, formed Committee for the 1st Amendment to counteract HUAC investigation, 1947; formed Horizon pictures with Sam Spiegel, 1948; formed John Huston Productions for unrealized project *Matador*, 1952; moved to Ireland, 1955; narrator for TV, from mid-1960's; moved to Mexico, 1972. Recipient: Legion of Merit, U.S. Armed Services, 1944; Oscar for Best Direction, for *Treasure of the Sierra Madre*, 1947. *Died of pneumonia, in Newport, Rhode Island, 28 August 1987.*

Films as Director:

1941   ***The Maltese Falcon*** (+ sc)
1942   *In This Our Life* (+ co-sc, uncredited); *Across the Pacific* (co-d)
1943   *Report from the Aleutians* (+ sc); *Tunisian Victory* (Capra and Boulting; d some replacement scenes when footage lost, + co-commentary)
1945   *San Pietro (The Battle of San Pietro)* (+ sc, co-ph, narration)
1946   *Let There Be Light* (unreleased) (+ co-sc, co-ph); *A Miracle Can Happen (On Our Merry Way)* (King Vidor and Fenton; d some Henry Fonda/James Stewart sequences, uncredited)
1948   ***The Treasure of the Sierra Madre*** (+ sc, bit role as man in white suit); *Key Largo* (+ co-sc)
1949   *We Were Strangers* (+ co-sc, bit role as bank clerk)
1950   ***The Asphalt Jungle*** (+ co-sc)
1951   *The Red Badge of Courage* (+ sc)
1952   ***The African Queen*** (+ co-sc)
1953   *Moulin Rouge* (+ pr, co-sc)
1954   *Beat the Devil* (+ co-pr, co-sc)
1956   *Moby Dick* (+ pr, co-sc)
1957   *Heaven Knows, Mr. Allison* (+ co-sc); *A Farewell to Arms* (Charles Vidor; d begun by Huston)
1958   *The Barbarian and the Geisha*; *The Roots of Heaven*
1960   *The Unforgiven*
1961   *The Misfits*
1963   *Freud (Freud: The Secret Passion)* (+ narration); *The List of Adrian Messenger* (+ bit role as Lord Ashton)
1964   *The Night of the Iguana* (+ co-pr, co-sc)
1965   *La bibbia (The Bible)* (+ role, narration)
1967   *Casino Royale* (co-d, role); *Reflections in a Golden Eye* (+ voice heard at film's beginning)
1969   *Sinful Davey*; *A Walk with Love and Death* (+ role); *De Sade* (Enfield; d uncredited) (+ role as the Abbe)
1970   *The Kremlin Letter* (+ co-sc, role)
1971   *The Last Run* (Fleischer; d begun by Huston)
1972   *Fat City* (+ co-pr); *The Life and Times of Judge Roy Bean* (+ role as Grizzly Adams)
1973   *The Mackintosh Man*

1975 *The Man Who Would Be King* (+ co-sc)
1976 *Independence* (short)
1979 *Wise Blood* (+ role)
1980 *Phobia*
1981 *Victory* (*Escape to Victory*)
1982 *Annie*
1984 *Under the Volcano*
1985 *Prizzi's Honor*
1987 *The Dead*

Other Films:

1929 *The Shakedown* (Wyler) (small role); *Hell's Heroes* (Wyler)
(small role)
1930 *The Storm* (Wyler) (small role)
1931 *A House Divided* (Wyler) (dialogue, sc)
1932 *Murders in the Rue Morgue* (Florey) (dialogue, sc)
1935 *It Started in Paris* (Robert Wyler) (co-adapt, sc); *Death Drives
Through* (Cahn) (co-story, sc)
1938 *Jezebel* (Wyler) (co-sc); *The Amazing Dr. Clitterhouse*
(Litvak) (co-sc)
1939 *Juarez* (Dieterle) (co-sc)
1940 *The Story of Dr. Ehrlich's Magic Bullet* (*Dr. Ehrlich's Magic
Bullet*) (Dieterle) (co-sc)
1941 **High Sierra** (Walsh) (co-sc); *Sergeant York* (Hawks) (co-sc)
1946 **The Killers** (Siodmak) (sc, uncredited); *The Stranger* (Welles)
(co-sc, uncredited); *Three Strangers* (Negulesco) (co-sc)
1951 *Quo Vadis* (LeRoy) (pre-production work)
1963 *The Cardinal* (Preminger) (role as Cardinal Glennon); *The
Directors* (pr: Greenblatt, short) (appearance)
1968 *Candy* (Marquand) (role as Dr. Dunlap); *The Rocky Road to
Dublin* (Lennon) (role as interviewee)
1970 *Myra Breckenridge* (Sarne) (role as Buck Loner)
1971 *The Bridge in the Jungle* (Kohner) (role as Sleigh); *The
Deserter* (Kennedy) (role as General Miles); *Man in the
Wilderness* (Sarafian) (role as Captain Henry)
1974 *Battle for the Planet of the Apes* (Thompson) (role as
Lawgiver); **Chinatown** (Polanski) (role as Noah Cross)
1975 *Breakout* (Gries) (role as Harris); *The Wind and the Lion*
(Milius) (role as John Hay)
1976 *Sherlock Holmes in New York* (Sagal) (role as Professor
Moriarty)
1977 *Tentacles* (Hellman) (role as Ned Turner); *Il grande attacco*
(*La battaglia di Mareth. The Biggest Battle*) (Lenzi) (role);
El triangulo diabolico de la Bermudas (*Triangle: The
Bermuda Mystery. The Mystery of the Bermuda Triangle*)
(Cardona) (role); *Angela* (Sagal) (role)
1978 *Il visitatore* (*The Visitor*) (Paradisi) (role)
1979 *Jaguar Lives* (Pintoff) (role); *Winter Kills* (Richert) (role)
1980 *Head On* (Grant) (role); *Agee* (Spears) (role as interviewee)
1981 *To the Western World* (Kinmonth) (narrator)
1982 *Cannery Row* (Ward) (narrator)
1983 *Lovesick* (Brickman) (role as psychiatrist)

Publications:

By HUSTON: books—

Frankie and Johnny, New York, 1930.
The Maltese Falcon, New York, 1974.
The Treasure of the Sierra Madre, edited by James Naremore, Madison, Wisconsin, 1979.
The Asphalt Jungle, with Ben Maddow, Carbondale, Illinois, 1980.
An Open Book, New York, 1980.
Juarez, with Aeneas Mackenzie and Wolfgang Reinhardt, Madison, Wisconsin, 1983.

By HUSTON: articles—

Interview with Karel Reisz, in *Sight and Sound* (London), January/
March 1952.
"How I Make Films," interview with Gideon Bachmann, in *Film
Quarterly* (Berkeley), Fall 1965.
"Huston!," interview with C. Taylor and G. O'Brien, in *Inter/View*
(New York), September 1972.

"Talk with John Huston," with D. Ford, in *Action* (Los Angeles),
September/October 1972.
"The Innocent Bystander," interview with D. Robinson, in *Sight and
Sound* (London), Winter 1972/73.
"Talking with John Huston," with Gene Phillips, in *Film Comment*
(New York), May/June 1973.
Interview with D. Brandes, in *Filmmakers Newsletter* (Ward Hill,
Massachusetts), July 1977.
Interview with P.S. Greenberg, in *Rolling Stone* (New York), June/
July 1981.
"Dialogue on Film: John Huston," in *American Film* (Washington,
D.C.), January/February 1984.
Interview with Michel Ciment and D. Allison, in *Positif* (Paris),
October 1987.

On HUSTON: books—

Davay, Paul, *John Huston*, Paris, 1957.
Allais, Jean-Claude, *John Huston*, Paris, 1960.
Agee, James, *Agee on Film: Five Film Scripts*, foreword by John Huston, Boston, 1965.
Nolan, William, *John Huston, King Rebel*, Los Angeles, 1965.
Benayoun, Robert, *John Huston*, Paris, 1966; revised edition, 1985.
Cecchini, Riccardo, *John Huston*, 1969.
Tozzi, Romano, John Huston, *A Picture Treasury of his Films*, New
York, 1971.
Kaminsky, Stuart, *John Huston: Maker of Magic*, London, 1978.
Madsen, Axel, *John Huston*, New York, 1978.
Giannetti, Louis D., *Masters of the American Cinema*, Englewood
Cliffs, New Jersey, 1981.
Hammen, Scott, *John Huston*, Boston, 1985.
Ciment, Gilles, editor, *John Huston*, Paris, 1987.
McCarty, John, *The Films of John Huston*, Secaucus, New Jersey,
1987.
Grobel, Lawrence, *The Hustons*, New York, 1989.

On HUSTON: articles—

"Huston Issues" of *Positif* (Paris), August 1952 and January 1957.
Mage, David, "The Way John Huston Works," in *Films in Review*
(New York), October 1952.
Laurot, Edouard, "An Encounter with John Huston," in *Film Culture*
(New York), no. 8, 1956.
Archer, Eugene, "John Huston—The Hemingway Tradition in
American Film," in *Film Culture* (New York), no. 19, 1959.
"John Huston, The Bible and James Bond," in *Cahiers du Cinema in
English* (New York), no. 5, 1966.
Koningsberger, Hans, "From Book to Film—via John Huston," in
Film Quarterly (Berkeley), Spring 1969.
"Huston Issue" of *Film Comment* (New York), May/June 1973.
Bachmann, Gideon, "Watching Huston," in *Film Comment* (New
York), January/February 1976.
Jameson, R.T., "John Huston," in *Film Comment* (New York), May/
June 1980.
Drew, B., "John Huston: At 74 No Formulas," in *American Film*
(Washington, D.C.), September 1980.
Millar, G., "John Huston," in *Sight and Sound* (London), Summer
1981.
"John Huston," in *Film Dope* (London), January 1983.
Hachem, S., *"Under the Volcano,"* in *American Cinematographer*
(Los Angeles), October 1984.
Combs, Richard, "The Man who would be Ahab: The Myths and
Masks of John Huston," in *Monthly Film Bulletin* (London),
December 1985.
"Huston Issue" of *Positif* (Paris), January 1986.
Taylor, John Russell, "John Huston: The Filmmaker as Dandy," in
Films and Filming (London), August 1986.
Edgerton, G., "Revisiting the Recordings of Wars Past: Remembering the Documentary Trilogy of John Huston," in *Journal of
Popular Film and TV* (Washington, D.C.), Spring 1987.
McCarthy, T., obituary, in *Variety* (New York), 2 September 1987.
Schulz-Keil, W., and B. Walker, "Huston," in *Film Comment* (New
York), September/October 1987.
Buckley, M., obituary in *Films in Review* (New York), November
1987.
Combs, Richard, "John Huston: An Account of One Man Dead," in
Monthly Film Bulletin (London), December 1987.

John Huston

Literature/Film Quarterly (Salisbury, Maryland), vol. 17, nos. 2 and 4, 1989.
American Film (Washington, D.C.), June 1989.

On HUSTON: films—

Kronick, William, *On Location: The Night of the Iguana*, for TV, U.S., 1964.
Graef, Roger, *The Life and Times of John Huston, Esquire*, Great Britain, 1967.
Joyce, Paul, *Ride This Way Grey Horse*, Great Britain, 1970.
Huston, Danny, *The Making of the Dead*, U.S., 1989.

*   *   *

Few directors have been as interested in the relationship of film to painting as has John Huston and, perhaps, none has been given as little credit for this interest. This lack of recognition is not completely surprising. Criticism of film, despite the form's visual nature, has tended to be derived primarily from literature and not from painting or, as might be more reasonable, a combination of the traditions of literature, painting, theater, and the unique forms of film itself.

In a 1931 profile in *The American Mercury* accompanying a short story by John Huston, the future director said that he wanted to write a book on the lives of French painters. The following year, unable to or dissatisfied with work as a film writer in London, Huston moved to Paris to become a painter. He studied for a year and a half, making money by painting portraits on street corners and singing for pennies. Huston's interest in painting has continued throughout his life and he from time to time "retires" from filmmaking to concentrate on his painting.

Each of Huston's films has reflected this prime interest in the image, the moving portrait and the use of color, as well as the poetic possibilities of natural dialogue. Each film has been a moving canvas on which Huston explores his main subject: the effect of the individual ego on the group and the possibility of the individual's survival.

Huston began exploring his style of framing in his first film, *The Maltese Falcon*. Following his sketches, he set up shots like the canvases of paintings he had studied. Specifically, Huston showed an interest in characters appearing in the foreground of a shot, with their faces often covering half the screen. Frequently, too, the person whose face half fills the screen is not talking, but listening. The person reacting thus becomes more important than the one speaking or moving.

Huston's first film as a director presented situations he would return to again and again. Spade is the obsessed professional, a man who will adhere to pride and dedication, to principle unto death. Women are a threat, temptations that can only sway the hero from his professional commitment. They may be willfully trying to deceive, as with Brigid and Iva, or they may, as in later Huston films, be the unwitting cause of the protagonist's defeat or near-defeat. In *The Asphalt Jungle*, for example, the women in the film are not evil; it is the men's obsession with them that causes disaster.

Even with changes and cuts, a film like *The Red Badge of Courage* reflects Huston's thematic and visual interests. Again, there is a group with a quest that may result in death. These soldiers argue, support each other, pretend they are not frightened, brag, and some die.

In the course of the action, both the youth and the audience discover that the taking of an isolated field is not as important as the ability of the young men to face death without fear. Also, as in other Huston films, the two central figures in *The Red Badge of Courage*, the youth and Wilson, lie about their attitudes. Their friendship solidifies only when both confess that they have been afraid during the battle and have run.

Visually, Huston has continued to explore an important aspect of his style, the placement of characters in a frame so that their size and position reflect what they are saying and doing. He developed this technique with Bogart, Holt, and Walter Huston in *The Treasure of the Sierra Madre* and Audie Murphy and Bill Mauldin in *The Red Badge of Courage*.

Early in *The African Queen*, after Rosie's brother dies, there is a scene with Rosie seated on the front porch of the mission. Charlie, in the foreground, dominates the screen while Rosie, in the background, is small. As Charlie starts to take control of the situation and tell Rosie what must be done, he raises his hand to the rail and his arm covers our view of her. Charlie is in command.

Thematically, *Moulin Rouge* was a return to Huston's pessimism and exploration of futility. The director identified with Lautrec who, like Huston, was given to late hours, ironic views of himself, performing for others, sardonic wit, and a frequent bitterness toward women. Lautrec, like Huston, loved horses, and frequently painted pictures of them.

The narrative as developed by Huston and Ray Bradbury in *Moby Dick* is in keeping with the director's preoccupation with failed quests. Only one man, Ishmael, survives. All the other men of the Pequod go down in Ahab's futile attempt to destroy the whale. But Huston sees Ahab in his actions and his final gesture as a noble creature who has chosen to go down fighting.

The Roots of Heaven is yet another example of Huston's exploration of an apparently doomed quest by a group of vastly different people led by a man obsessed. In spite of the odds, the group persists in its mission and some of its members die.

As in many Huston films, the quest is not a total failure; there is the likelihood of continuation, if not success, but the price that must be paid in human lives is high.

In *The Misfits* there was again the group on a sad and fruitless quest. This time they are searching for horses. But they find far fewer than they had expected. The expedition becomes a bust and the trio of friends are at odds over a woman, Roslyn (Marilyn Monroe), who opposes the killing and capturing of the horses.

With the exception of Guido, the characters represent the least masked or disguised group in Huston's films. Perhaps it is this very element of never-penetrated disguise in Guido that upset Huston about the character and drove him to push for a motivation scene, an emotional unmasking.

As a Huston film, *Freud* has some particular interests: Huston serves as a narrator, displaying an omnipotence and almost Biblical detachment that establishes Freud as a kind of savior and messiah. The film opens with Huston's description of Freud as a kind of hero or God on a quest for mankind. "This is the story of Freud's descent into a region as black as hell, man's unconscious, and how he let in the light," Huston says in his narration. The bearded, thin look of Freud, who stands alone denounced before the tribunal of his own people, also suggests a parallel with Christ. Freud brings a message of salvation which is rejected, and he is reluctantly denounced by his chief defender, Breuer.

Of all Huston's films, *The List of Adrian Messenger* is the one that deals most literally with people in disguise. George, who describes himself as unexcused evil, hides behind a romantic or heroic mask that falls away when he is forced to face the detective, who functions very much like Freud. The detective penetrates the masks, revealing the evil, and the evil is destroyed.

Huston's touch was evident in *The Night of the Iguana* in a variety of ways. First, he again took a group of losers and put them together in an isolated location. The protagonist, Shannon, once a minister, has been reduced to guiding tourists in Mexico. At the furthest reaches of despair and far from civilization, the quest for meaning ends and the protagonist is forced to face himself. Religion is an important theme. The film opens with Richard Burton preaching a sermon to his congregation. It is a startling contrast to Father Mapple's sermon in *Moby Dick*. Shannon is lost, confused, his speech is gibberish, an almost nonsensical confession about being unable to control his appetites and emotions. The congregation turns away from him.

This choice between the practical and the fantastic is a constant theme in Huston's life and films. There is also a choice between illusion and reality, a choice Huston finds difficult to make. Religion is seen as part of the fantasy world, a dangerous fantasy that his characters must overcome if they are not to be destroyed or absorbed by it. This theme is present in *The Bible, Wise Blood*, and *Night of the Iguana*.

There are clearly constants in Huston's works—man's ability to find solace in animals, and nature, the need to challenge oneself—but his world is unpredictable, governed by a whimsical God or no God at all. Each of Huston's characters seeks a way of coming to terms with that unpredictability, establishing rules of behavior by which he can live.

The Huston character, like Cain or Adam, is often weak, and frequently his best intentions will not carry him through to success or even survival. The more a man thinks in a Huston film, the more dangerous it is for his survival, but carried away by emotion, or too much introspection, a man is doomed. Since the line between loss of control and rigidity is difficult to walk, many Huston protagonists do not survive. It takes a Sam Spade, Sergeant Allison, or Abraham, very rare men indeed, to remain alive in this director's world.

Reflections in a Golden Eye raised many questions about the sexuality inherent in many of the themes that most attracted Huston: riding horses, hunting, boxing, and militarism. The honesty with which the director handles homosexuality is characteristic of his willingness to face what he finds antithetical to his own nature. In the film, the equation of Leonora and her horse is presented as definitely sexual, and at one point Penderton actually beats the horse in a fury because he himself is impotent. Huston also includes a boxing match in the film which is not in the novel. The immorally provocative Leonora watches the match, but Penderton watches another spectator, Williams. *Reflections* becomes an almost comic labyrinth of voyeurism, with characters spying on other characters.

Huston's negative religious attitude is strong in *A Walk with Love and Death*, in which there are three encounters with the clergy. In the first, Heron is almost killed by a group of ascetic monks who demand that he renounce the memory of Claudia and "repent his knowledge of women." The young man barely escapes with his life. These religious zealots counsel a move away from the pleasure of the world and human love, a world that Huston believes in.

Huston's protagonists often represent extremes. They are either ignorant, pathetic, and doomed by their lack of self-understanding (Tully and Ernie in *Fat City*, Dobbs in *The Treasure of the Sierra Madre*, Peachy and Danny in *The Man Who Would Be King*) or intelligent, arrogant, but equally doomed by their lack of self-understanding (Penderton in *Reflections in a Golden Eye* and Ahab in *Moby Dick*). Between these extremes is the cool, intelligent protagonist who will sacrifice everything for self-understanding and independence (Sam Spade in *The Maltese Falcon*, and Freud). Huston always finds the first group pathetic, the second tragic, and the third heroic. He reserves his greatest respect for the man who retains his dignity in spite of pain and disaster.

Many of Huston's films can de divided between those involving group quests that fail and those involving a pair of potential lovers who must face a hostile world generally, Huston's films about such lovers end in the union of the couple or, at least, their survival. In that sense, *A Walk with Love and Death*, starring his own daughter, proved to be the most pessimistic of his love stories, and *Annie*, his most commercial venture, proved to be his most optimistic.

—Stuart M. Kaminsky

ICHIKAWA, Kon.

Japanese. Born Uji Yamada in Ise, Mie Prefecture, 20 November 1915. Educated at Ichioka Commercial School, Osaka. Married scriptwriter Natto Wada, 1948. Worked in animation dept. of J.O. Studios, Kyoto, from 1933; assistant director on feature-filmmaking staff, late 1930's; transferred to Tokyo when J.O. became part of Toho company, early 1940's; collaborated on scripts with wife, 1948–56; used pen name "Shitei Kuri" (after Japanese rendering of Agatha Christie), from 1957; writer and director for TV, 1958–66. Recipient: San Giorgio Prize, Venice Festival, for *Harp of Burma*, 1956.

Films as Director:

1946   *Musume Dojoji* (*A Girl at Dojo Temple*) (+ co-sc)
1947   *Toho senichi-ya* (*1001 Nights with Toho*) (responsible for some footage only)
1948   *Hana hiraku* (*A Flower Blooms*); *Sanbyaku rokujugo-ya* (*365 Nights*)
1949   *Ningen moyo* (*Human Patterns. Design of a Human Being*); *Hateshinaki jonetsu* (*Passion without End. The Endless Passion*)
1950   *Ginza Sanshiro* (*Sanshiro of Ginza*); *Netsudeichi* (*Heat and Mud. The Hot Marshland*) (+ co-sc): *Akatsuki no tsuiseki* (*Pursuit at Dawn*)
1951   *Ieraishan* (*Nightshade Flower*) (+ co-sc): *Koibito* (*The Lover*) (+ co-sc); *Mukokuseki-sha* (*The Man without a Nationality*); *Nusumareta koi* (*Stolen Love*) (+ co-sc); *Bungawan Solo* (*River Solo Flows*) (+ co-sc); *Kekkon koshinkyoku* (*Wedding March*) (+ co-sc)
1952   *Rakkii-san* (*Mr. Lucky*); *Wakai hito* (*Young People, Young Generation*) (+ co-sc); *Ashi ni sawatta onna* (*The Woman Who Touched Legs*) (+ co-sc); *Ano te kono te* (*This Way, That Way*) (+ co-sc)
1953   *Puu-san* (*Mr. Pu*) (+ co-sc); *Aoiro kakumei* (*The Blue Revolution*); *Seishun Zenigata Heiji* (*The Youth of Heiji Zenigata*) (+ co-sc); *Ai-jin* (*The Lover*)
1954   *Watashi no subete o* (*All of Myself*) (+ co-sc); *Okuman choja* (*A Billionaire*) (+ co-sc); *Josei ni kansuru juni-sho* (*Twelve Chapters on Women*)
1955   *Seishun kaidan* (*Ghost Story of Youth*); *Kokoro* (*The Heart*)
1956   **Biruma no tategoto (The Burmese Harp. Harp of Burma)**; *Shokei no heya* (*Punishment Room*); *Nihonbashi* (*Bridge of Japan*)
1957   *Manin densha* (*The Crowded Streetcar*) (+ co-sc); *Tohoku no zummu-tachi* (*The Men of Tohoku*) (+ sc); *Ana* (*The Pit. The Hole*) (+ sc)
1958   *Enjo* (*Conflagration*)
1959   *Sayonara, konnichiwa* (*Goodbye, Hello*) (+ co-sc); *Kagi* (*The Key. Odd Obsession*) (+ co-sc); **Nobi (Fires on the Plain)**; *Jokyo II: Mono o takaku uritsukeru onna* (*A Woman's Testament, Part 2: Women Who Sell Things at High Prices*)
1960   *Bonchi* (+ co-sc); *Ototo* (*Her Brother*)
1961   *Kuroijunin no onna* (*Ten Dark Women*)

1962   *Hakai* (*The Outcast. The Broken Commandment*); *Watashi wa nisai* (*I Am Two. Being Two Isn't Easy*)
1963   *Yukinojo henge* (*An Actor's Revenge. The Revenge of Yukinojo*); *Taiheiyo hitoribotchi* (*My Enemy, the Sea. Alone on the Pacific*)
1964   *Zeni no odori* (*The Money Dance. Money Talks*) (+ sc)
1965   *Tokyo Orimpikku* (*Tokyo Olympiad*) (+ co-sc)
1967   *Toppo Jijo no botan senso* (*Toppo Gigio and the Missile War*) (+ co-sc)
1969   *Kyoto* (+ sc)
1970   *Nihon to Nihonjin* (*Japan and the Japanese*) (+ sc)
1972   *Ai futatabi* (*To Love Again*)
1973   *Matatabi* (*The Wanderers*) (+ pr, co-sc); "The Fastest" episode of *Visions of Eight*
1975   *Wagahai wa neko de aru* (*I Am a Cat*)
1976   *Tsuma to onna no aida* (*Between Women and Wives*) (co-d); *Inugami-ke no ichizoku* (*The Inugami Family*) (+ co-sc)
1977   *Akuma no temari-uta* (*A Rhyme of Vengeance. The Devil's Bouncing Ball Song*) (+ sc); *Gokumonto* (*The Devil's Island. Island of Horrors*) (+ co-sc)
1978   *Jo-bachi* (*Queen Bee*) (+ co-sc)
1980   *Koto* (*Ancient City*) (+ co-sc); *Hi no tori* (*The Phoenix*) (+ co-sc)
1982   *Kofuku* (*Lonely Hearts, Happiness*) (+ co-sc)
1983   *Sasame Yuki* (*The Makioka sisters*); *Fine Snow*
1985   *Ohan*; *Biruma no tategoto* (*The Burmese Harp*)
1987   *Eiga Joyu* (*The Actress*); *Taketori Monogatari* (*Princess from the Moon*)

Other Film:

1970   *Dodes'ka-den* (Kurosawa) (pr)

Publications:

By ICHIKAWA: book—

Seijocho 271 Banchi, with Natto Wada, Tokyo, 1961.

By ICHIKAWA: articles—

Article in *Filmmakers on Filmmaking*, edited by Harry M. Geduld, Bloomington, Indiana, 1967.
"Kon Ichikawa at the Olympic Games," an interview in *American Cinematographer* (Los Angeles), November 1972.

On ICHIKAWA: books—

Anderson, Joseph, and Donald Richie, *The Japanese Film: Art and Industry*, Rutland, Vermont, 1960; revised edition, Princeton, 1982.
Mellen, Joan, *Voices from the Japanese Cinema*, New York, 1975.
Soumi, Angelo, *Kon Ichikawa*, Florence, 1975.
Mellen, Joan, *The Wave at Kenji's Door: Japan Through Its Cinema*, New York, 1976.
Bock, Audie, *Japanese Film Directors*, New York, 1978; revised edition, Tokyo, 1985.
Burch, Noël, *To the Distant Observer: Form and Meaning in the Japanese Cinema*, Berkeley, 1979.
Allyn, John. *Kon Ichikawa: A Guide to References and Resources*, Boston, 1985.

Kon Ichikawa

On ICHIKAWA: articles—

Richie, Donald, "The Several Sides of Kon Ichikawa," in *Sight and Sound* (London), Spring 1966.

Milne, Tom, "The Skull Beneath the Skin," in *Sight and Sound* (London), Autumn 1966.

Tessier, Max, "Kon Ichikawa l'entomologiste," in *Jeune Cinéma* (Paris), March 1967.

Dewey, Langdon, "Kon Ichikawa," in *International Film Guide 1970*, London, 1969.

"Ichikawa Issue" of *Cinema* (Los Angeles), no. 2, 1970.

Johnson, W., "Ichikawa and *The Wanderers*," in *Film Comment* (New York), September/October 1975.

Gillett, John, "Kon Ichikawa," in *Film Dope* (London), January 1983.

*　　　*　　　*

Kon Ichikawa is noted for a wry humor which often resembles black comedy, for his grim psychological studies, portrayals of misfits and outsiders, and for the visual beauty of his films. Noted as one of Japan's foremost cinematic stylists, he has commented, "I began as a painter and I think like one."

His early films show a perverse sense of humor as they reveal human foibles and present an objective view of corruption. In *Mr. Pu* a projector breaks down while showing scenes of an atomic explosion; in *A Billionaire*, a family dies from eating radioactive tuna, leaving only a lazy elder son and a sympathetic tax collector. In *The Key*, a group of rather selfish, despicable people are poisoned inadvertently by a senile old maid, who becomes the only survivor. The film is a study of an old man who becomes obsessed with sex to compensate for his fears of impotency. He becomes a voyeur and through the manipulation of the camera, we come to share in this activity. Slowly, however, he emerges as being sympathetic while the other characters are revealed in their true light.

Throughout his career Ichikawa has proven himself a consistent critic of Japanese society, treating such themes as the rebirth of militarism (*Mr. Pu*), the harshness and inhumanity of military feudalism (*Fires on the Plain*), the abuse of the individual within the family (*Bonchi* and/*Her Brother*), as well as familial claustrophobia and the tendency of repression to result in perversion and outbreaks of violence (*The Key*). His films usually refuse a happy ending and Ichikawa has been frequently criticized for an unabashed pessimism, bordering on nihilism.

Two of his most important films, *Harp of Burma* and *Fires on the Plain*, deal with the tragedies of war. The former concerns a soldier who adopts Buddhist robes and dedicates himself to burying the countless Japanese dead on Burma; the latter is about a group of demoralized soldiers who turn to cannibalism. A third work, *Tokyo Olympiad*, provided a new approach to sports films, giving as much attention to human emotions and spectator reactions as to athletic feats.

Ichikawa is a master of the wide screen and possesses a strong sense of composition, creating enormous depth with his use of diagonal and overhead shots. Often he utilizes black backgrounds, so as to isolate images within the frame, or a form of theatrical lighting, or he blocks out portions of the screen to alter the format and ratio.

Ichikawa remains fascinated with experimental techniques. His excellent use of the freeze frame in *Kagi* reflects his case study approach to characterization. He has also done much in the way of color experimentation. *Kagi* is bathed in blues which bleach skin tones to white, thus creating corpse-like subjects. *Her Brother* is so filtered that it resembles a black and white print with dull pinks and reds. On most of his films, Ichikawa has used cameramen Kazuo Miyagawa or Setsuo Kobayashi.

After *Tokyo Olympiad* Ichikawa encountered many studio difficulties. His projects since then include a 26-part serialization of *The Tale of Genji*, *The Wanderers*, a parody of gangster films with a nod to *Easy Rider*, plus a dozen documentaries and fiction features, among which *The Inugami Family*, a suspense thriller, proved to be the biggest box office success in Japanese film history.

—Patricia Erens

IMAI, Tadashi.

Japanese. Born in Tokyo, 8 January 1912. Educated at Tokyo Imperial University, until 1935. Married in 1934 and 1955. Assistant at J.O. Studio, Kyoto, from 1935; directed first film, *Numazu Hei-gakko*, 1939; joined Communist party, late 1940's; left Toho, helped initiate independent film production movement, 1950; "prestige director" for Toei, Daiei, and other studios, 1953 through 1960's; resumed independent production, 1969. Recipient: Mainichi Film Competition Award, for *The People's Enemy*, 1946; 5 Kinema Jumpo Awards for Best Japanese Film, 1950's. Address: 1-4-1 Yazakicho, Fuchu City, Tokyo, Japan.

Films as Director:

1939 *Numazu Hei-gakko (Numazu Military Academy)*; *Waga kyokan (Our Teacher)*
1940 *Tajiko mura (The Village of Tajiko)*; *Onna no machi (Women's Town)*; *Kakka (Your Highness)*
1941 *Kekkon no seitai (Married Life)*
1943 *Boro no kesshitai (The Suicide Troops of the Watch Tower. The Death Command of the Tower)*
1944 *Ikari no umi (Angry Sea)*
1945 *Ai to chikai (Love and Pledge)*
1946 *Minshu no teki (An Enemy of the People. The People's Enemy)*; *Jinsei tonbo-gaeri (Life Is Like a Somersault)*
1947 *Chikagai nijuyo-jikan (Twenty-four Hours of a Secret Life)*
1949 *Aoi sanmyaku (Green Mountains) parts I and II*; *Onna no kao (A Woman's Face)*
1950 *Mata au hi made (Until We Meet Again)*
1951 *Dokkoi ikiteiru (Still We Live)*
1952 *Yamabiko gakko (School of Echoes)*
1953 *Himeyuri no to (The Tower of Lilies. Himeyuri Lily Tower)*; *Nigori-e (Muddy Water)*
1955 one episode of *Aisureba koso (Because I Love)*; *Koko ni izumi ari (Here Is a Fountain)*; *Yukiko*
1956 *Mahiru no ankoku (Darkness at Noon)*
1957 *Kome (Rice)*; *Junai monogatari (The Story of Pure Love)*
1958 *Yoru no tsuzumi (The Adulteress. Night Drum)*; *Kiku to Isamu (Kiku and Isamu)*
1960 *Shiroi gake (The Cliff. White Cliff)*
1961 *Are ga minato no hikari da (That Is the Port Light)*
1962 *Nippon no obachan (Japanese Grandmothers. The Old Women of Japan)*
1963 *Bushido zankoku monogatari (Bushido: Samurai Saga. The Cruel Story of the Samurai's Way)*
1964 *Echigo tsutsuishi oyashirazu (Death in the Snow)*; *Adauchi (Revenge)*
1967 *Sato-gashi ga kazureru toki (When the Cookie Crumbles)*
1968 *Fushin no toki (The Time of Reckoning)*
1969 *Hashi no nai kawa (River without Bridges)*
1970 *Hashi no nai kawa (River without Bridges) Part II*
1971 *En to iu onna (A Woman Named En)*
1972 *Aa koe naki tomo (Ah! My Friends without Voice)*; *Kaigun tokubetsu shonen hei (Special Boy Soldiers of the Navy)*
1974 *Kobayashi Takiji (The Life of a Communist Writer)*
1976 *Ani imoto (Mon and Ino. Older Brother and Younger Sister)*; *Yoba (The Old Woman Ghost)*
1982 *Himeyuri no to (Himeyuri Lily Tower) (remake)*

Publications:

On IMAI: books—

Anderson, Joseph, and Donald Richie, *The Japanese Film*, New York, 1961; revised edition, Princeton, 1982.
Mellen, Joan, *Voices from the Japanese Cinema*, New York, 1975.
Mellen, Joan, *The Waves at Genji's Door*, New York, 1976.

On IMAI: articles—

Philippe, Pierre, "Imai: La Femme infidèle," in *Cinema* (Paris), February 1964.
Tayama, Rikiya, "Imai Tadashi," in *Image et Son* (Paris), July 1964.
Iawaski, Akira, "La Production independante," in *Cinema* (Paris), September/October 1969.

*   *   *

Despite his early Marxist commitment, Imai was forced to give up politics under the wartime military regime. Because of the regime's ideological restriction, Imai's first works were so-called "war-collaboration" films. Some of them are nonetheless valued for Western-style action sequence technique (e.g. *The Death Command of the Tower*) and for the successful depiction of the personality of an army officer (*Our Teacher*).

Imai's postwar return to Marxism surprised his audience. As early as 1946, he made a film which severely attacked the corruption of the wartime rulers, and he preached on behalf of the postwar democracy in *The People's Enemy*. Imai's real fame came with his record-breaking commercial success, *Green Mountains*, which became legendary for its reflection of the almost revolutionary excitement of the postwar period. The film depicts, in a light, humorous style, the struggle at a small town high school against the established institutions and values.

Until We Meet Again became another legendary film for its romantic, lyrical treatment of tragic wartime love. In particular, the scene of the young lovers kissing through the window glass became famous. The Red Purge at the time of the Korean War drove Imai out of the organized film industry. He then became one of the most active filmmakers, initiating the postwar leftist independent film production movement.

His successive films fall into two main genre—films analyzing social injustice and oppression from the Communist point of view, and meticulously made literary adaptations. The films of the first category outnumber the second. Imai was much influenced by Italian neorealism in his themes and semi-documentary method based on location shooting. The hardship and tribulations of the proletariat are depicted in *Still We Live* (about day-laborers), *Rice* (concerning farmers), and *That Is the Port Light* (about fishermen and the Japan-Korea problems). Social problems are treated in *School of Echoes* (concerning the progressive education movement in a poor mountain village), *Kiku and Isamu*, which deals with Japanese-black mixed-blood children, *Japanese Grandmother* (on the aged), and *River without Bridges I* and *II*, about discrimination against the outcast class. The mistaken verdict in a murder case is the subject of *Darkness at Noon* which condemns the police and the public prosecutor. *Himeyuri Lily Tower*, another commercial hit, depicts the tragic fighting on Okinawa toward the end of the war, showing the cruelty of both the Japanese and the American forces. *Night Drum, The Cruel Story of the Samurai's Way, Revenge*, and *A Woman Named En* focus on feudalism and its oppression from the viewpoint of its victims.

These films all embody an explicit and rather crude leftist point-of-view. However, Imai's talent at entertaining the audience with deft story-telling and comfortable pacing attracted popular and critical support for his work. Imai is especially skillful in powerful appeals to the audience's sentimentalism. His distinctive lyrical and humanistic style is valued and helps us to differentiate Imai from other more dogmatic leftist directors.

Imai is also appreciated for his depiction of details. This trait helped make his literary adaptations (e.g. *Muddy Water*) so successful that every ambitious actress was said to want to appear in Imai's films to obtain prizes. The collaboration of the excellent scenario writer, Yoko Mizuki, is indispensable to Imai's success.

Imai's unchanged formula of the poor being oppressed by the authorities became increasingly out-of-date through the 1960s and '70s. However, his lyricism still proved to be attractive in more recent works such as *Older Brother and Younger Sister*.

—Kyoko Hirano

IMAMURA, Shohei.

Japanese. Born in Tokyo, 1926. Educated in technical school, Tokyo, until 1945; studied occidental history at Waseda University, Tokyo, graduated 1951. Assistant director at Shochiku's Ofuna studios, 1951; moved to Nikkatsu studios, 1954; assistant to director Yuzo Kawashima, 1955–58; directed first film, *Nusumareta yokuju*, 1958; formed Imamura Productions, 1965; worked primarily for TV, from 1970; founder and teacher, Yokohama Broadcast Film Institute. Recipient: Palme d'Or, Cannes Festival, for *The Ballad of Narayama*, 1983.

Films as Director:

1958 *Nusumareta yokujo (Stolen Desire)*; *Nishi Ginza eki mae (Lights of Night. Nishi Ginza Station)* (+ sc); *Hateshinaki yokubo (Endless Desire)* (+ co-sc)
1959 *Nianchan (My Second Brother. The Diary of Sueko)* (+ co-sc)
1961 *Buta to gunkan (The Flesh Is Hot. Hogs and Warships)* (+ co-sc)
1963 *Nippon konchuki (The Insect Woman)* (+ co-sc)

1964 *Akai satsui (Unholy Desire. Intentions of Murder)* (+ co-sc)
1966 *Jinruigaku nyumon (The Pornographers: Introduction to Anthropology)* (+ co-sc, pr)
1967 *Ningen johatsu (A Man Vanishes)* (+ sc, role, pr)
1968 *Kamigami no fukaki yokubo (The Profound Desire of the Gods. Kuragejima: Tales from a Southern Island)* (+ co-pr, co-sc)
1970 *Nippon sengoshi: Madamu Omboro no seikatsu (History of Postwar Japan as Told by a Bar Hostess)* (+ co-pr, planning, role as interviewee)
1975 *Karayuki-san (Karayuki-san, the Making of a Prostitute)* (for TV) (+ co-pr, planning)
1979 **Fukushu suruwa ware ni ari (Vengeance Is Mine)**
1980 *Eijanaika (Why Not?)* (+ co-sc)
1983 *Narayama Bushi-Ko (The Ballad of Narayama)*
1987 *Zegen (The Pimp)*
1988 *Kuroi Ame (Black Rain)*

Other Films:

1951 *Bakushu (Early Summer)* (Ozu) (asst d)
1952 *Ochazuke no aji (The Flavor of Green Tea over Rice)* (Ozu) (asst d)
1953 **Tokyo monogatari (Tokyo Story)** (Ozu) (asst d)
1954 *Kuroi ushio (Black Tide)* (Yamamura) (asst d)
1955 *Tsukiwa noborinu (Moonrise)* (Tanaka) (asst d)
1956 *Fusen (The Balloon)* (Kawashima) (asst d)
1958 *Bakumatsu Taiyoden (Saheiji Finds a Way. Sun Legend of the Shogunate's Last Days)* (Kawashima) (co-sc)
1959 *Jigokuno magarikago (Turning to Hell)* (Kurahara) (co-sc)
1962 *Kyupora no aru machi (Cupola Where the Furnaces Glow)* (Uravama) (sc)
1963 *Samurai no ko (Son of a Samurai. The Young Samurai)* (Wakasugi) (co-sc)
1964 *Keirin shonin gyojoki* (Nishimira) (co-sc)
1967 *Neon taiheiki-keieigaku nyumon (Neon Jungle)* (Isomi) (co-sc)
1968 *Higashi Shinaki (East China Sea)* (Isomi) (story, co-sc)

Publications:

By IMAMURA: book—

Sayonara dake ga jinsei-da [Life Is Only Goodbye: biography of director Yuzo Kawashima], Tokyo, 1969.

By IMAMURA: articles—

"Monomaniaque de l'homme . . . ," in *Jeune Cinéma* (Paris), November 1972.
Interview with S. Hoass, in *Cinema Papers* (Melbourne), September/October 1981.
Interview with Max Tessier, in *Revue du Cinéma* (Paris), September 1983.
Interview with C. Tesson, in *Cahiers du Cinéma* (Paris), November 1987.
Interview in *Revue du Cinéma/Image et Son* (Paris), November 1989.

On IMAMURA: books—

Imamura Shohei no eiga [The Films of Shohei Imamura], Tokyo, 1971.
Mellen, Joan, *Voices from the Japanese Cinema*, New York, 1975.
Sugiyama, Heiichi, *Sekai no eiga sakka 8: Imamura Shohei* [Film Directors of the World 8: Shohei Imamura], Tokyo, 1975.
Bock, Audie, *Japanese Film Directors*, New York, 1978; revised edition, Tokyo, 1985.
Tessier, Max, editor, *Le Cinema japonais au present: 1959–1979*, Paris, 1980.
Richie, Donald, with Audie Bock, *Notes for a Study on Shohei Imamura*, Bergamo, 1987.
Piccardi, Adriano, and Angelo Signorelli, *Shohei Imamura*, Bergamo, 1987.

On IMAMURA: articles—

Yamada, Koichi, "Les Cochons et les dieux: Imamura Shohei," in *Cahiers du Cinéma* (Paris), May/June 1965.
"Dossier on Imamura," in *Positif* (Paris), April 1982.

Shohei Imamura: *The Profound Desire of the Gods*

Gillett, John, "Shohei Imamura," in *Film Dope* (London), January 1983.

Casebier, A., "Images of Irrationality in Modern Japan: The Films of Shohei Imamura," in *Film Criticism* (Edinboro, Pennsylvania), Fall 1983.

Kehr, Dave, "The Last Rising Sun," in *Film Comment* (New York), September/October 1983.

"Imamura Section" of *Positif* (Paris), May 1985.

*   *   *

Outrageous, insightful, sensuous, and great fun to watch, the films of Shohei Imamura are among the greatest glories of the postwar Japanese cinema. Yet, Imamura remains largely unknown outside of Japan. Part of the reason, to be sure, lies in the fact that Imamura has until recently worked for small studios such as Nikkatsu or on his own independently financed productions. But it may also be because Imamura's films fly so furiously in the face of what most westerners have come to expect Japanese films to be like.

After some amateur experience as a theater actor and director, Imamura joined Shochiku Studios in 1951 as an assistant director, where he worked under, among others, Yasujiro Ozu. His first important work, *My Second Brother*, an uncharacteristically gentle tale set among Korean orphans living in postwar Japan, earned him third place in the annual *Kinema Jumpo* "Best Japanese Film of the Year" poll, and from then on Imamura's place within the Japanese industry was more or less firmly established. Between 1970 and 1978, Imamura "retired" from feature filmmaking, concentrating his efforts instead on a series of remarkable television documentaries which explored little-known sides of postwar Japan. In 1978, Imamura returned to features with his greatest commercial and critical success, *Vengeance Is Mine*, a complex, absorbing study of a cold-blooded killer. In 1983, his film *The Ballad of Narayama* was awarded the Gold Palm at the Cannes Film Festival, symbolizing Imamura's belated discovery by the international film community.

Imamura has stated that he likes to make "messy films," and it is the explosive, at times anarchic quality of his work which makes him appear "uncharacteristically Japanese" when seen in the context of Ozu, Mizoguchi, or Kurosawa. Perhaps no other filmmaker anywhere has taken up Jean-Luc Godard's challenge to end the distinction between "documentary" and "fiction" films. In preparation for filming, Imamura will conduct exhaustive research on the people whose story he will tell, holding long interviews, not only to extract information, but also to become familiar with different regional vocabularies and accents (many of his films are set in remote regions of Japan). Insisting always on location shooting and direct sound, Imamura has been referred to as the "cultural anthropologist" of the Japanese cinema. Even the titles of some of his films—*The Pornographers: Introduction to Anthropology* and *The Insect Woman* (whose Japanese title literally translates to "Chronicle of a Japanese Insect")—seem to reinforce the "scientific" spirit of these works. Yet, if anything, Imamura's films argue against an overly-clinical approach to understanding Japan, as they often celebrate the irrational and instinctual aspects of Japanese culture.

Strong female protagonists are usually at the center of Imamura's films, yet it would be difficult to read these films as "women's films" in the way that critics describe works by Mizoguchi or Naruse. Rather, women in Imamura's films are always the ones more directly linked to "ur-Japan,"—a kind of primordial fantasy of Japan not only before "westernization" but before any contact with the outside world. In *The Profound Desire of the Gods*, a brother and sister on a small southern island fall in love and unconsciously attempt to recreate the myth of Izanagi and Izanami, sibling gods whose union founded the Japanese race. Incest, a subject which might usually be seen as shocking, is treated as a perfectly natural expression, becoming a crime only due to the influence of "westernized" Japanese who have come to civilize the island. Imamura's characters indulge freely and frequently in sexual activity, and sexual relations tend to act as a kind of barometer for larger, unseen social forces. The lurid, erotic spectacles in *Eijanaika*, for example, are the clearest indication of the growing frustration that finally bursts forth with the massive riots which conclude the film.

—Richard Peña

INGRAM, Rex.

Irish/American. Born Reginald Ingram Montgomery Hitchcock in Dublin, 15 January 1893. Educated at Saint Columba's College, Dublin; studied sculpture at Yale, 1911. Served in Canadian Air Force (wounded in action), 1918. Married 1) actress Doris Pawn, 1917 (divorced 1920); 2) Alice Terry, 1921. Emigrated to U.S., 1911; actor in England, 1912; assistant for Edison Co., New York, also scenario writer for Stuart Blackton and screen actor, 1913; moved to Vitagraph, 1914; hired by Fox, changed name to Rex Ingram, 1915; director for Universal, 1916; contracted by Paralta-W.W. Hodkinson Corp., 1918; joined Metro Pictures, 1920; moved to France, 1923; modernized Studios de la Victorine de Saint-Augustin, Nice, 1924; established Ingram Hamilton Syndicated Ltd. production company, London, 1928; moved to Egypt, 1934; returned to Hollywood, 1936. Recipient: honorary degree, Yale University; Légion d'honneur française. *Died in California, 1950.*

Films as Director:

1916   *The Great Problem* (Truth) (+ sc); *Broken Fetters* (*A Human Pawn*) (+ sc); *Chalice of Sorrow* (*The Fatal Promise*) (+ sc); *Black Orchids* (*The Fatal Orchids*) (+ sc)
1917   *The Reward of the Faithless* (*The Ruling Passion*) (+ sc); *The Pulse of Life* (+ sc); *The Flower of Doom* (+ sc); *Little Terror* (+ sc)
1918   *His Robe of Honor*; *Humdrum Brown*
1919   *The Day She Paid*
1920   *Under Crimson Skies* (*The Beach Comber*); *Shore Acres*; *Hearts Are Trumps*
1921   **The Four Horsemen of the Apocalypse** (+ pr); *The Conquering Power* (*Eugenie Grandet*); *Turn to the Right*
1922   *The Prisoner of Zenda*; *Trifling Women* (+ sc) (remake of *Black Orchids*); *Where the Pavement Ends* (+ sc)

1923   *Scaramouche* (+ pr)
1924   *The Arab* (*L'Arabe*) (+ sc)
1925   *Mare Nostrum* (+ co-pr)
1926   *The Magician* (+ co-pr, sc)
1927   *The Garden of Allah*
1929   *The Three Passions* (*Les Trois Passions*) (+ sc)
1931   *Baroud* (*Love in Morocco. Passion in the Desert*) (+ pr, co-sc)

Other Films:

1913   *Hard Cash* (Reid) (role, sc); *The Family's Honor* (Ridgely) (sc); *Beau Brummel* (Young) (role); *The Artist's Great Madonna* (Young) (role); *A Tudor Princess* (Dawley) (role)
1914   *Witness to the Will* (Lessey) (role); *The Necklace of Ramses* (Brabin) (role); *The Price of the Necklace* (Brabin) (role); *The Borrowed Finery* (role); *Her Great Scoop* (Costello and Gaillord) (role); *The Spirit and the Clay* (Lambart) (role); *The Southerners* (Ridgely and Collins) (role); *Eve's Daughter* (North) (role); *The Crime of Cain* (Marston) (role); *The Circus and the Boy* (Johnson) (role); *David Garrick* (Young) (role); *The Upper Hand* (Humphrey) (role); *Fine Feathers Make Fine Birds* (Humphrey) (role); *His Wedded Wife* (Humphrey) (role); *Goodbye, Summer* (Brooke) (role); *The Moonshine Maid and the Man* (Gaskill) (role)
1915   *Should a Mother Tell?* (Edwards) (sc); *The Song of Hate* (Edwards) (sc, role); *The Wonderful Adventure* (Thompson) (sc); *The Blindness of Devotion* (Edwards) (sc); *A Woman's Past* (Powell) (sc); *The Galley Slave* (Edwards) (co-sc, uncredited); *The Evil Men Do* (Costello and Gaillord) (role); *Snatched From a Burning Death* (Gaskill) (role)
1916   *The Cup of Bitterness* (sc)
1923   *Mary of the Movies* (McDermot) (role as a guest)
1925   **Greed** (von Stroheim) (co-ed 2nd cut)

Publications:

By INGRAM: articles—

Interview with L. Montanye, in *Motion Picture Classic* (Brooklyn), July 1921.
Interview with J. Robinson, in *Photoplay* (New York), August 1921.
Article in *Motion Picture Directing* by Peter Milne, New York, 1922.

On INGRAM: books—

Predal, Rene, *Rex Ingram*, Paris, 1970.
O'Leary, Liam, *Rex Ingram, Master of the Silent Cinema*, Dublin, 1980.

On INGRAM: articles—

Obituary in *New York Times*, 23 July 1950.
Geltzer, George, "Hollywood's Handsomest Director," in *Films in Review* (New York), May 1952.
O'Laoghaire, Liam, "Rex Ingram and the Nice Studios," in *Cinema Studies* (England), December 1961.
Bodeen, Dewitt, "Rex Ingram and Alice Terry," in two parts in *Films in Review* (New York), February and March 1975.
O'Leary, Liam, "Rex Ingram," in *Film Dope* (London), July 1983.

On INGRAM: film—

Graham, Dan, *The Conquering Power: Rex Ingram 1893–1950*, 1990.

        *   *   *

Due to his retirement from films in the early 1930s when sound had taken over, Ingram has tended to be overlooked and forgotten. He began his career in films in 1913, working as designer, script-writer and actor for Edison, Vitagraph and Fox, until in 1916 he directed his own story *The Great Problem* for Universal at the age of only 23. His educational background was that of an Irish country rectory and the Yale School of Fine Arts where he studied sculpture under Lee Lawrie, and developed an aesthetic sense which informed all his films.

Rex Ingram with Alice Terry

The early films he made for Universal have disappeared. His version of *La Tosca* transferred to a Mexican setting as *Chalice of Sorrow*, and *Black Orchids* remade in 1922 as *Trifling Women*, earned critical attention for the quality of the acting and their visual beauty. Cleo Madison starred in both these films. The fragment that exists of *The Reward of the Faithless* shows a realism that is reminiscent of von Stroheim who was later to acknowledge his indebtedness by allowing Ingram to do the second cutting on *Greed*. It may be noted also that greed was the theme of *The Conquering Power*. A characteristic element of Ingram's work was the use of grotesque figures like dwarfs and hunchbacks to offset the glamour of his heroes. After a period of ups and downs, he made another film for Universal in 1920, *Under Crimson Skies*, which won critical acclaim.

With *The Four Horsemen of the Apocalypse* in 1921 he achieved top status in his profession. Ordinarily, Valentino dominates discussion of this film but Ingram's work is of the highest quality, and with his team of cameraman John Seitz, and editor Grant Whytock he went on to make a dazzlingly successful series of films for Metro. His financial and artistic success gave him carte blanche and his name became a box-office draw. *The Conquering Power, The Prisoner of Zenda* and *Scaramouche* featured his wife, the beautiful and talented Alice Terry, and the latter two films introduced a new star,

Ramon Novarro, who also played with Alice Terry in the South Seas romance *Where the Pavement Ends*. Ingram made stars and knew how to get the best out of players. He was now considered the equal of Griffith, von Stroheim, and DeMille.

In 1924 the formation of Metro-Goldwyn-Mayer saw a tightening up of front office control over the creative director and Ingram sought fresh fields to conquer. He made *The Arab* with Terry and Novarro in North Africa with which he fell in love. He next moved to Nice where he founded the Rex Ingram Studios and released his masterpiece *Mare Nostrum* in 1926 for "Metro-Goldwyn". (He would never allow his arch-enemy Louis B. Mayer to have a credit.) In this Alice Terry gave her best performance as the Mata Hari-like heroine. This film as well as *The Four Horsemen* was later suppressed because of its anti-German feeling, both being authored by Blasco Ibañez.

The German-inspired *The Magician* featured Paul Wegener (the original *Golem*) and was based on a Somerset Maugham story. After *The Garden of Allah* Ingram broke with MGM in 1926. *The Three Passions*, with an industrial background, followed in 1929, and his last film *Baroud*, a sound film in which he himself played the lead, completed a distinguished career. He sold his studios in Nice where he had reigned as an uncrowned king; as the Victorine Studios they were to become an important element in French film production. Ingram retired to North Africa and later rejoined his wife Alice Terry in Hollywood. He indulged his hobbies of sculpture, writing, and travel.

Ingram was the supreme pictorialist of the screen, a great director of actors, a perfectionist whose influence was felt not least in the films of David Lean and Michael Powell. The themes of his films ranged over many locations but his careful research gave them a realism and authenticity that balanced the essential romanticism of his work.

—Liam O'Leary

IOSELIANI, Otar.

Soviet Georgian. Born 2 February 1934. Educated in music, Tbilisi Conservatory; studied graphic art; degree in mathematics, Moscow University; studied under Alexander Dovzhenko, V.G.I.K., Moscow. Directed first feature, *April*, 1961; failed to receive authorization for its distribution, abandoned film-making; returned to direct *Listopad*, 1966; Recipient: FIPRESCI Prize, Berlin Festival, for *Pastorale*, 1982.

Films as Director:

1958   *Watercolor* (short, for TV)
1959   *The Song About Flowers* (short)
1961   *April* (*Stories About Things*) (not released) (+ sc)
1964   *Cast-Iron* (+ sc) (short)
1966   *Listopad* (*When Leaves Fall. Falling Leaves*)
1972   *Zil pevcij drozd* (*There Was a Singing Blackbird. There Lived a Thrush*) (+ co-sc)
1976   *Pastoral* (*The Summer in the Country*) (+ co-sc)
1984   *Les Favoris de la Lune*

Publications:

By IOSELIANI: articles—

Interview with G. Kopaněvová, in *Film a Doba* (Prague), May 1974.
Interview with Michel Ciment, in *Positif* (Paris), May 1978.
Interview with Serge Daney and S. Toubiana, in *Cahiers du Cinéma* (Paris), November 1979.
Interview with A. Gerber, in *Film a Doba* (Prague), February 1981.
Interview with Serge Toubiana and Alain Bergala, in *Cahiers du Cinéma* (Paris), February 1985.

Otar Ioseliani: *When Leaves Fall*

On IOSELIANI: articles—

Cereteli, K., "Stat' ja iz gazety 'Zarja Vostoka'," in *Iskusstvo Kino* (Moscow), November 1973.

"Il était une fois un merle chanteur de O. Iosseliani," in *Revue Belge du Cinéma* (Brussels), vol. 13, no. 1–2, 1975/76.

Martin, Marcel, "L'Art 'Comme la vie' d'Otar Iosseliani," in *Image et Son* (Paris), September 1980.

"Ioseliani Section" of *Positif* (Paris), January 1985.

Gauthier, G., and R. Bassan, "Otar Iosseliani," in *Revue du Cinéma* (Paris), February 1985.

Navailh, F., "Otar Iosseliani," in *Cinéma* (Paris), February 1985.

Christie, Ian, "Pastoral Hide and Seek," in *Monthly Film Bulletin* (London), March 1985.

*   *   *

The Georgian cinema has a long history that goes back to the 1920s, and has known a renaissance in the 1960s with Otar Ioseliani as its most remarkable representative. Together with Tarkovsky (but in a very different way) he is the young Soviet director who has been the most uncompromising and the most consistent in his aesthetic approach. Born in 1934, he studied music at the Tbilisi Conservatory, as well as graphic art, and graduated from Moscow University in mathematics. But finally he chose cinema as his favorite field and graduated from VGIK after attending Alexander Dovzhenko's class. His first film, *April*, of which little is known, was not released. His second, *When Leaves Fall*, shows the characteristic elements of his style. Ioseliani, like many of his contemporaries, is hostile to the cinema of Eisenstein, to his intellectual montage, to the theoretical aspect of his work. In presenting Jean Vigo as his master, Ioseliani insists that he tries "to capture moments of passing life," and in doing so wants to reach the ultimate goal of art. In a way his films are close to the Czech new wave (Forman, Passer, Menzel) but the realism is counterbalanced by a more formal treatment, particularly in the use of sound and off-screen space.

His films also show a disregard for conventional ways of life. Ioseliani's nonconformity, his stubbornness, his frankness, have alienated the authorities. *When Leaves Fall* takes place in a wine factory and shows an innocent and honest young man trying to live in a bureaucratic universe. He does not wear a moustache, that Georgian symbol of bourgeois respectability.

There Was a Singing Blackbird, Ioseliani's third film, portrays the life of a musician in the Tbilisi orchestra who always arrives at the last minute to perform, being busy enjoying his life, drinking and courting girls. His behavior is an insult to an official morality based on work and duty. Ioseliani's fancifulness and sense of humor are shown at their best in this sprightly comedy that ends tragically with the hero's death. *Pastoral*, which had problems with the Moscow authorities (though the film was shown regularly in Georgia), is about a group of five musicians from the city who come to live with a peasant family. Ioseliani observes the opposition of city and country, and makes a young peasant girl the observer of his delightful conflict of manners and morals. Using many non-professionals—as in his earlier films—the director manages to show us poetically and with truthfulness the life of the Georgian people. Discarding any kind of plot, observing his characters with affection and irony, he is faithful to his anti-dogmatic stance: "Everyone is born to drink the glass of his life." Ioseliani's limited output is of a very high level indeed.

—Michel Ciment

_____

ITAMI, Juzo.

Japanese. Born in Kyoto, 1933, the son of film director Mansaku Itami. Educated at High School. Married to actress Nobuko Miyamoto, two children. Amateur boxer and commercial designer, before becoming a film actor, 1960 (sometimes as Ichizo Itami); subsequently stage actor, TV actor and director, TV chat-show host, author, translator, and keen chef; also edited magazine on psychoanalysis. Lives in Tokyo.

Films as Director and Scriptwriter:

1984   *Ososhiki (The Funeral)*
1986   *Tampopo (Dandelion)*
1987   *Marusa no onna (A Taxing Woman)*
1988   *Marusa no onna II (A Taxing Woman Returns)*
1990   *A-Ge-Man (A-Ge-Man—Tales of a Golden Geisha)* (+ pr)

Films as Actor:

1960   *Kirai Kirai Kirai (Dislike)* (Edagawa); *Nise Daigakusei (The Phoney University Student)* (Masamura); *Ototo (Her Brother)* (Ichikawa)
1961   *Kuroi junin no onna (The Ten Dark Women)* (Ichikawa)
1963   *55 Days at Peking* (Nicholas Ray)
1964   *Lord Jim* (Brooks)
1966   *Otoko no kao wa rirekisho (A Man's Face is His History)* (Kato)
1967   *Nihon Shunka ko (A Treatise on Japanese Bawdy Songs)* (Oshima)
1974   *Imoto (My Sister, My Love)* (Fujita)
1975   *Wagahai wa nwko dearu (I Am a Cat)* (Ichikawa)
1980   *Kusa Meikyu (Labyrinth in the Field)* (Terayama); *Yugure made (Until Dusk)* (Kuroki)
1983   *Sasameyuki (The Makioka Sisters)* (Ichikawa); *Kazoku gemu (The Family Game)* (Morita)

Publications:

By ITAMI: books—

Yoroppa taikutsu nikki (Diary of Boring Days in Europe), Tokyo, 1965.

Onnatachi yo! (Listen, Women)

Nippon sekenbanashi taikei (Panorama of Japanese Gossips)

Enjoy French Cooking with Me, 1987.

By ITAMI: articles—

Interview with B. Meares, in *Cinema Papers* (Melbourne), July 1985.

Interview with Tony Rayns, in *Monthly Film Bulletin* (London), April 1988.

Interview with Alan Stanbrook, in *Films and Filming* (London), April 1988.

Interview with L. Tanner, in *Films in Review* (New York), May 1988.

On ITAMI: article—

Sipe, Jeffrey, "Death and Taxes: A Profile of Juzo Itami," in *Sight and Sound* (London), Summer 1989.

*   *   *

It is probable that Itami's films convey meanings to Japanese audiences that are not readily accessible to westerners: they are pervasively concerned with rituals, customs and practices that go back through centuries, with the contemporary economic and socio-political actualities, and with the interaction between these. On the other hand, Itami is clearly aware of international cinematic practice, and his films seem made partly with an international spectatorship in mind—assumptions confirmed by the fact that he is about to make his first film in English, an adaptation of *A Taxing Woman* to American

Juzo Itami

culture. Offered here is a westerner's assessment of the films: incomplete, but nonetheless valid.

A westerner, then, would situate Itami somewhere between Buñuel and Almodóvar, *The Funeral* leaning toward the former, *Tampopo* toward the latter (the two *Taxing Woman* movies, though not at all inconsistent with these in tone and attitude, in their general irreverence and scepticism, stand somewhat apart from them). Itami has not so far achieved the extraordinary distinction of Buñuel at his best (but neither did Buñuel until he was very old, and then in only a very few films). On the other hand, if *Tampopo*, in its comic-erotic audacities and its seemingly free and inconsequential handling of narrative, evokes a heterosexual Almodóvar, the comparison works very much in Itami's favour, underlining his greater maturity, discipline and powers of self-criticism: casual *divertissement* as it may seem, *Tampopo* manifests a security of taste, tone and attitude to which Almodóvar, with his apparently uncritical faith in the sanctity of his own impulses, cannot yet lay claim.

The Funeral can be at once "placed" and done justice to by being juxtaposed with, on the one hand, Buñuel's late films, and, on the other, Altman's *A Wedding*. Superficially, it has far more in common with the latter: a satirical view of ritualized social performances and their emptiness, exposing the manifold hypocrisies they generate. Yet the complexity of attitude—the disturbing fusion of critical rigour and emotional generosity—is closer to Buñuel. *A Wedding*, among the worst films of one of the most uneven of directors, is more complicated than complex, its proliferation of characters and incident encompassed by Altman's contempt for all of it and desire to assert his superiority: the simplicity and unpleasantness of the attitude precludes any possibility of genuine disturbance. *A Funeral* analyses the traditional elaborate rites in documentary detail and precision, while undercutting the reverence they are supposed to express with a pervasive sense of absurdity: the old man whose death necessitates all this ceremony, expenditure and hypocrisy was an unlovable egoist for whom no one felt any particular affection or respect while he was alive. Yet Itami, unlike Altman, never presents his characters as merely stupid, and shows no inclination to demonstrate his superiority to them. If the tone is never *not* satirical, it is never *only* satirical. One might single out as example the disturbing interplay of conflicting responses generated by the scene where the son-in-law has sex in the bushes with his mistress while his wife (the dead man's daughter), fully aware of what is going on, quietly distracts herself on a swing. The juxtaposition, through the editing, of the seduction (treated as broad comedy) and the wife's sense of troubled hurt, in the context of death that encloses the whole action, creates a complex effect capped by the abrupt appearance of Chishu Ryu as the officiating priest, and the accumulated resonances he brings with him from so many Ozu movies. If this is not exactly the tone of *Viridiana*, we are at least not far from that of *The Discreet Charm of the Bourgeoisie*, though the comparison brings with it the reflection that Itami's film has no equivalent for the three "insert narratives" of the Buñuel and the dimension of radical pain and disturbance they introduce.

A Taxing Woman and *A Taxing Woman's Return* represent a remarkably successful attempt to appropriate a popular genre (criminal investigation) for purposes of radical social criticism. For the westerner, at least, they relate interestingly to the recent wave of feminist detective fiction centred on female investigators, of which Sara Paretsky's series of novels remains the most impressive example. There is a crucial difference between Paretsky's V.I. Warshawski and the heroine of Itami's movies: the former is a "private eye," a lone operator, the latter the leader of a government-employed team. Yet the parallel is strong: in both cases the woman becomes committed not simply to the solution of a specific "case" but to the exposure of the corruption and inherent criminality of the patriarchal-capitalist power structure. The radicalism has its limitations. The fact that the "taxing woman" (Itami's wife Nobuko Miyamoto) works for the government prohibits—for all the force of her personal crusade against corporate corruption—the raising of the key question (to what ends are taxes actually used within a capitalist state?): the films attack the corruption but are unable to challenge the system that produces it. Itami's commitment to feminism is also somewhat dubious: one suspects that it is more an incidental offshoot of his desire to work with his extremely talented wife (a brilliant comedienne who commands rapid and subtle shifts of tone) rather than being rooted in any firm theoretical basis. Despite these limitations, the films (together with their wide and international commercial success) are, like Paretsky's novels, sufficient proof that popular genres can be used to dramatize radical positions, and for once the sequel actually improves on the original: tougher, darker, with an altogether bleaker ending, its powerful and disturbing rigour was doubtless made possible by the success of its more lightweight predecessor.

—Robin Wood.

————

IVENS, Joris.

Dutch. Born Georg Henri Anton Ivens in Nijmegen, Holland, 18 November 1898. Educated at Economische Hogeschool, Rotterdam, 1916–17 and 1920–21; studied chemistry and photography at Technische Hochschule, Charlottenberg, 1922–23. Military service as lieutenant in Artillery, 1917–18. Married 1) photographer Germaine Krull, 1937 (divorced 1943); 2) Marceline Loridan. Technical director for CAPI (father's firm selling photographic equipment), also member of Filmliga film club, Amsterdam, from 1926; travelled to U.S.S.R. to meet Soviet filmmakers, 1930; made industrial documentaries in Holland, and began association with cinematographer John Fernhout (John Ferno), 1931; returned to U.S.S.R., 1932; clandestinely filmed striking Belgian miners for *Borinage*, 1933; visited New York, formed group, with Hemingway, Dos Passos, Lillian Hellman, Fredric March, and Luise Rainer, to finance films on contemporary events, 1936; filmed *Spanish Earth* during Spanish Civil War, 1937; filmed *400 Million* in China, 1938; made industrial documentaries, U.S., 1939–40; taught at University of Southern California, 1941; invited by John Grierson to direct *Alarm!* for national Film Board of Canada, 1942–42; worked on *Why We Fight* series, Hollywood, 1943–44; travelled to Sydney, Australia, to make *Indonesia Calls*, regarded as traitorous act by Dutch authorities, 1945–6; moved to Prague, 1947; taught in Lodz, Poland, 1950–51; moved to Paris, 1957; taught filmmaking in Peking, 1958; filmed in Italy and Africa, 1959–60; taught filmmaking in Cuba, 1960–61; taught in Chile, 1962–63; Ivens Archive established after retrospective at Nederlands Filmmuseum, 1964; made first of Vietnam War documentaries, 1965; made 12-part documentary, *Comment Yu-Kong déplaça les montagnes*, with Marceline Loridan and others, in China, 1971–75. Recipient: World Peace Prize, Helsinki, 1955; Palme d'Or for Best Documentary for *La Seine a rencontre Paris*, Cannes Festival, 1958; Diploma *Honoris Causa*, Royal College of Art, London, 1978. *Died of a heart attack, in Paris, 28 June 1989.*

Joris Ivens: *Misère au Borinage*

Films as Director:

1911 *De brandende straal* or *Wigwam* (*Flaming Arrow*) (+ ed, ph)
1927 *Zeedijk-Filmstudie* (*Filmstudy—Zeedijk*) (+ ed, ph)
1928 *Etudes de mouvements* (+ ed, ph); *De Brug* (*The Bridge*) (+ ed, ph)
1929 *Branding* (*The Breakers*) (co-d, ed, ph); *Regen* (*Rain*) (+ ed, ph) (sound version prepared 1932 by Helen van Dongen); *Ik-Film* ("*I*" *Film*) (co-d, ed, ph) (unfinished); *Schaatsenrijden* (*Skating. The Skaters*) (+ ed, ph) (unfinished); *Wij Bouwen* (*We Are Building*) (+ co-sc, ed, ph) [footage shot for but not used in Wij bouwen used for following films: *Heien* (*Pile Driving*) (+ co-sc, ed, ph); *Nieuwe architectur* (*New Architecture*) (+ co-sc, ed, ph); *Caissounbouw Rotterdam* (+ co-sc, ed, ph); *Zuid Limburg* (*South Limburg*) (+ co-sc, ed, ph)]
1929/30 *N.V.V. Congres* (*Congres der Vakvereeinigingen*) (+ ed, ph); *Arm Drenthe* (+ ed, ph)
1930 *De Tribune film: Breken en bouwen* (*The Tribune Film: Break and Build*) (+ ed, ph); *Timmerfabriek* (*Timber Industry*) (+ co-ph, co-ed); *Film-notities uit de Sovjet-Unie* (*News from the Soviet Union*) (+ ed); *Demonstratie van proletarische solidariteit* (*Demonstration of Proletarian Solidarity*) (+ ed)
1931 *Philips-Radio* (*Symphonie industrielle, Industrial Symphony*) (+ co-ph, co-ed); *Creosoot* (*Creosote*) (+ sc, ph, ed)
1932 *Pesn o Gerojach* (*Youth Speaks. Song of Heroes*) (+ ed)
1933 *Zuyderzee* (+ sc, co-ph)
1934 *Misère au Borinage* (*Borinage*) (co-d, co-sc, co-ed, co-ph);

Nieuwe Gronden (*New Earth*) (+ sc, co-ph, co-ed, narration)
1937 **The Spanish Earth** (+ sc, co-ph)
1939 *The Four Hundred Million* (*China's Four Hundred Million*) (co-d, sc)
1940 *Power and the Land* (+ co-sc): *New Frontiers* (unfinished)
1941 *Bip Goes to Town*; *Our Russian Front* (co-d); *Worst of Farm Disasters*
1942 *Oil for Aladdin's Lamp*
1943 *Alarme!* or *Branle-Bas de combat* (*Action Stations!*) (+ sc, ed) (released in shorter version *Corvette Port Arthur*)
1946 *Indonesia Calling* (+ sc, ed)
1949 *Pierwsze lata* (*The First Years*) (+ co-ed, produced 1947)
1951 *Pokoj zwyciezy swiat* (*Peace Will Win*) (co-d)
1952 *Naprozod mlodziezy* (*Freundschaft siegt. Friendship Triumphs*) (co-d); *Wyscig pokoju Warszawa-Berlin-Praga* (*Friedensfahrt. Peace Tour*) (+ sc)
1954 *Das Lied der Ströme* (*Song of the Rivers*) (+ co-sc)
1957 *La Seine a rencontré Paris* (+ co-sc); *Die Abenteuer des Till Ulenspiegel* (*The Adventures of Till Eulenspiegel*) (co-d)
1958 *Before Spring* (*Early Spring. Letters from China*) (+ sc, ed); *Six Hundred Million People Are With You* (+ ed)
1960 *L' Italia non e un paese povero* (*Italy is Not a Poor Country*) (+ co-sc, co-ed); *Demain à Nanguila* (*Nanguila Tomorrow*)
1961 *Carnet de viaje* (+ sc): *Pueblos en armas* (*Cuba, pueblo armado. An Armed Nation*) (+ sc)
1963 *. . . à Valparaiso* (+ sc): *El circo mas pequeño* (*Le Petit Chapiteau*)
1964 *El tren de la victoria* (*Le Train de la victoire*)

1966   *Pour le mistral* (+ co-sc); *Le Ciel, la terre* (*The Sky, the Earth*) (+ narration, appearance); *Rotterdam-Europoort* (*Rotterdam-Europort. The Flying Dutchman*)
1967   Hanoi footage in *Loin du Viêt-nam* (*Far from Vietnam*) (co-d)
1968   *Le Dix-septième parallèle* (*The Seventeenth Parallel*) (co-d, co-sc); *Aggrippès à la terre* (co-d); *Déterminés à vaincre* (co-d)
1969   *Rencontre avec le Président Ho Chi Minh* (co-d); (next 7 titles made as part of collective including Marceline Loridan, Jean-Pierre Sergent, Emmanuele Castro, Suzanne Fen, Antoine Bonfanti, Bernard Ortion, and Anne Rullier): *Le Peuple et ses fusils* (*The People and Their Guns*); *L' Armée populaire arme le peuple*; *La Guerre populaire au Laos*; *Le Peuple peut tout*; *Qui commande aux fusils*; *Le Peuple est invincible*; *Le Peuple ne peut rien sans ses fusils*
1976   *Comment Yukong déplaça les montagnes* (in 12 parts totalling 718 minutes) (co-d)
1977   *Les Kazaks—Minorité nationale—Sinking* (co-d); *Les Ouigours—Minorité nationale—Sinkiang* (co-d)
1988   *Une Histoire de vent* (co-d)

Other Films:

1929/30   *Jeugd-dag* (*Days of Youth*) (co-ed)
1931   Short film in *VVVC Journal* series (ed)
1956   *Mein Kind* (*My Child*) (Pozner and Machalz) (artistic supervisor)
1957   *Die Windrose* (*The Wind Rose*) (Bellon and others) (co-supervisor)
1972   *Grierson* (Blais) (role as interviewee)
1981   *Conversations with Willard Van Dyke* (Rothschild) (role as interviewee)

Publications:

By IVENS: books—

Lied der Ströme, with Valdimir Pozner, Berlin, 1957.
Joris Ivens, edited by W. Klaue and others, Berlin, 1963.
Autobiografie van een Filmer, Amsterdam, 1970.
The Camera and I, Berlin, 1974.
Entretiens avec Joris Ivens, with Claire Devarrieux, Paris, 1979.
Joris Ivens: ou, La Memoire d'un regard, with Robert Destanque, Paris, 1982.

By IVENS: articles—

Numerous articles in *Filmliga* (Amsterdam), 1928/32.
"Notes on Hollywood," in *New Theatre* (New York), 28 October 1936.
"Collaboration in Documentary," in *Film* (New York), 1940.
"Apprentice to Film," in *Theatre Arts* (New York), March and April 1946.
"*Borinage*—A Documentary Experience," in *Film Culture* (New York), no. 1, 1956.
"Ik-Film," in *Skoop* (Amsterdam), no. 2, 1964.
"Ivens Issue" of *Film Culture* (New York), Spring 1972.
"Entretien avec Joris Ivens and Marceline Loridan," with J. Grant and G. Frot-Coutaz, in *Cinéma* (Paris), April 1976.
"Joris Ivens Filming in China," interview with D. Bickley, in *Filmmakers Newsletter* (Ward Hill, Massachusetts), February 1977.
Interview with E. Naaijkems and others, in *Skrien* (Amsterdam), October 1977.
Interview with E. Decaux and B. Villien, in *Cinématographe* (Paris), September 1982.
"Borinage," in *Revue Belge du Cinéma* (Brussels), Winter 1983/Spring 1984.
Interview with P. van Bueren, in *Skoop* (Amsterdam), February/March 1984.
Interview with D. Shaffer, in *Cineaste* (New York), vol. 14, no. 1, 1985.

On IVENS: books—

Hemingway, Ernest, *The Spanish Earth*, Cleveland, 1938.
Zalzman, Abraham, *Joris Ivens*, Paris, 1963.
Grelier, Robert, *Joris Ivens*, Paris, 1965.
Wegner, Hans, *Joris Ivens, Dokumentarist den Wahrheit*, Berlin, 1965.

Loridan, Marceline, *Dix-septieme Parallèle, la guerre du peuple*, Paris, 1968.
Meyer, Han, *Joris Ivens, de weg naar Vietnam*, Utrecht, 1970.
Kremeier, Klaus, *Joris Ivens, ein Filmer an den Fronten der Weltrevolution*, Berlin, 1976.
Joris Ivens; 50 jaar wereldcineast, Nederlands Filmmuseum, Amsterdam, 1978.
Passek, Jean-Loup, editor, *Joris Ivens: Cinquante ans de cinéma*, Paris, 1979.
Brunel, Claude, *Joris Ivens*, Paris, 1983.
Waugh, Thomas, editor, *"Show us Life": Toward a History and Aesthetics of the Committed Documentary*, Metuchen, New Jersey, 1984.

On IVENS: articles—

Ferguson, Otis, "Guest Artist," in the *New Republic* (New York), 15 April and 13 May 1936.
Grenier, Cynthia, "Joris Ivens: Social Realist vs. Lyric Poet," in *Sight and Sound* (London), Spring 1958.
"Ivens Issue" of *Cine Cubano* (Havana), no.3, 1960.
Waugh, Thomas, "*How Yukong Moved the Mountains*: Filming the Cultural Revolution," in *Jump Cut* (Berkeley), 30 December 1976.
Sklar, Robert, "Joris Ivens—The China Close-Up," in *American Film* (Washington, D.C.), June 1978.
Hogenkamp, B., "Joris Ivens 50 jaar wereldcineast," in *Skrien* (Amsterdam), November 1978.
van Dongen, Helen, "'Ik kwam Joris Ivens tegen': 'waarom ben je bij de film gegaan?'," in *Skoop* (Amsterdam), November 1978.
Jervis, N., "The Chinese Connection: Filmmaking in the People's Republic," in *Film Library Quarterly* (New York), no.1, 1979.
Hogenkamp, B., "Joris Ivens and the Problems of the Documentary Film," in *Framework* (Norwich, England), Autumn 1979.
Waugh, Thomas, "Travel Notebook—A People in Arms: Joris Ivens' Work in Cuba," in *Jump Cut* (Berkeley), May 1980.
Waugh, Thomas, and P. Pappas, "Joris Ivens Defended," letters, in *Cineaste* (New York), Fall 1980.
"Ivens Issue" of *Avant-Scène du Cinéma* (Paris), 1 January 1981.
Waugh, Thomas, "Men cannot act in front of the camera in the presence of death," in *Cineaste* (New York), vol. 12, no. 2, 1982.
"Joris Ivens," in *Film Dope* (London), July 1983.
Revue du Cinéma/Image et Son (Paris), March 1989.
Sight and Sound (London), Autumn 1989.

On IVENS: film—

Hudon, Wieslaw, *A chacun son Borinage*, Belgium, 1978.

*   *   *

From his debut with *The Bridge* in 1928, Joris Ivens made over 50 documentary films. A staunch advocate of a socialist society, Ivens consistently attacked fascism and colonialism in his films made after 1930. His first two films, *The Bridge* and *Rain*, are rather abstract. Here Ivens's main concern is the elaboration of a varied, often breath-taking, rhythm of images. In this, he appears to be indebted to the French and German avant-garde films, notably those by Ruttmann and Man Ray.

In 1930 Ivens visited the USSR at the invitation of Pudovkin. The compelling expressiveness of Russian agit-prop films had a deep influence upon Ivens in shaping his unique and powerful style. According to Ivens, films should convey social and political insights by confronting the public directly with reality. This analytical and didactic viewpoint is already exemplified in *Komsomol*, the first film Ivens made in Russia. *Misère au Borinage* not only shows in pitiful and often violent images the miserable conditions under which the Belgian coalminers lived and worked; the film also indicates that the desperate situation of the workers follows necessarily from a specific social order. To deepen his analysis and to strengthen the urgency of his message, Ivens reconstructed a number of scenes, such as the May Day celebration. This procedure also reflects Ivens's conviction that a documentary films is an emotional presentation of facts. Ivens has said that the maker of a documentary film should be in search of truth. To attain truth, one must have solidarity with the people whose situation is depicted. Mutual confidence and understanding are essential to a good documentary film.

Ivens's techniques bear the mark of such filmmakers as Eisenstein and Pudovkin. In addition to developing specific ways of shooting and styles of montage, Ivens has always attached great importance to spoken commentary. In *Spanish Earth*, a film about the Spanish civil war, Ernest Hemingway speaks the commentary; Jacques Prévert does so in *La Seine a rencontré Paris*. Commentary plays a secondary role in the films Ivens made during the 1970s, notably in *How Yukong Moved the Mountains*. In this documentary epos about daily life in China after the cultural revolution, people tell about their own situation. Ivens's style here is descriptive, with many long sequences and with less dramatic montage.

Ivens was one of the founders in 1926 of the Dutch Film League which united a number of intellectuals and Dutch filmmakers. Their efforts to promote quality films included the publication of a review, the organization of film screenings and inviting important foreign avant-garde filmmakers to give talks. Among these were René Clair and Man Ray, while Ivens's contacts with Pudovkin and Eisenstein date to this period. Ivens's contributions to Dutch film culture are immense, although he remained a controversial figure. His manifest sympathy for the struggle of the Indonesian people against colonialism (*Indonesia Calling*) brought him into conflict with the Dutch government, and until 1956 Ivens was deprived of his Dutch passport.

His films have examined important social and political issues. From 1938 till 1945 he lived in the U.S. *Power and the Land* is about the improvements in farming brought about by the use of electricity. With *Our Russian Front* Ivens intended to urge the Americans to enter World War II and to support the Russians. The film was financed by Ivens himself and some of his New York Russian friends. He hoped to make more films of this kind, but the project titled *Letters to the President* was coolly received. It led to only one film, *A Sailor on Convoy Duty to England*, which was financed by the National Film Board of Canada. In the 1950s Ivens worked in Eastern Europe and *The First Years* shows the transformation of a capitalist society into a socialist one; the film concentrates on episodes from postwar life in Bulgaria, Czechoslovakia, and Poland.

In 1956 the Dutch Government returned Ivens's passport; he then took up residence in Paris. After that he worked in Latin America (Cuba, Chile) and even more extensively in Asia (Vietnam, Laos, and China). *Travel Notebook* is about daily life in Cuba; *An Armed People* shows how the militia of the Cuban people captures a small group of counter-revolutionaries. *Le Train de la victoire* is a report on the election campaign of Salvador Allende, later President of Chile. Ivens also taught Vietnamese filmmakers, and engagement with the cause of the Vietnamese people manifests itself in such films as *The Threatening Sky and The 17th Parallel*.

Ivens always had great influence on new technical developments in the domain of film equipment. He hailed the professionalization of the 16mm camera as a big step foward, since it enabled the camera to take part in the action. He taught at numerous film schools and advised many colleagues. In the 1950s he was an advisor to the Defa Studios (GDR) and collaborated on many films there. Together with a number of leftist French filmmakers (Jean-Luc Godard, Alain Resnais, Agnès Varda and others), Ivens made the filmic pamphlet of solidarity, *Loin du Viët-nam*.

For Ivens the documentary film provided the only possibility of surviving as an artist outside the field of commercial films. He always succeeded in financing his projects on such terms that he conserved maximum artistic freedom and full responsibility for the final product. This even holds for the two films which he made at an early stage in his career and which were commissioned by commercial firms (*Creosoot* and *Philips-Radio*).

Within his lifetime Ivens became a legend. His films comment on many events which shaped the modern world. His art, his intelligence, his sophisticated political views, and his deep sincerity account for the unique position Joris Ivens holds among documentary filmmakers.

—Dorothee Verdaasdonk

IVORY, James.

American. Born in Berkeley, California, 7 June 1928. Educated in architecture and fine arts, University of Oregon; studied filmmaking at University of Southern California, M.A. 1956. Corporal in U.S. Army Special Services, 1953–55. Founder and partner, Merchant-Ivory Productions, New York, 1961; directed first feature, also began collaboration with writer Ruth Prawer Jhabvala on *The Householder*, 1963. Recipient: Guggenheim Fellowship, 1973. Address: c/o Merchant-Ivory Productions, Ltd., 250 W. 57th St., Suite 1913-A, New York, NY 10107, U.S.A.

Films as Director:

1957   *Venice: Themes and Variations* (doc) (+ sc, ph)
1959   *The Sword and the Flute* (doc) (+ sc, ph, ed)
1963   *The Householder*
1964   *The Delhi Way* (doc) (+ sc)
1965   *Shakespeare Wallah* (+ co-sc)
1968   *The Guru* (+ co-sc)
1970   *Bombay Talkie* (+ co-sc)
1971   *Adventures of a Brown Man in Search of Civilization* (doc)
1972   *Savages* (+ pr, sc)
1974   *The Wild Party*
1975   *Autobiography of a Princess*
1977   *Roseland*
1979   *Hullabaloo over Georgie and Bonnie's Pictures; The Europeans* (+ pr, co-sc, role as man in warehouse)
1980   *Jane Austen in Manhattan*
1981   *Quartet* (+ co-sc)
1982   *Courtesans of Bombay* (doc) (+ co-sc)
1983   *Heat and Dust*
1984   *The Bostonians*
1986   **A Room with a View**
1987   *Maurice* (+ co-sc)
1989   *Slaves of New York*
1990   *Mr. and Mrs. Bridge*

Publications:

By IVORY: books—

Savages, with Ruth Prawer Jhabvala, New York, 1973.
Shakespeare Wallah: A Film, with Ruth Prawer Jhabvala, New York, 1973.
Autobiography of a Princess: Also Being the Adventures of an American Film Director in the Land of the Maharajas, New York, 1975.

By IVORY: articles—

"*Savages*," in *Sight and Sound* (London), Autumn 1971.
Interviews with Judith Trojan, in *Take One* (Montreal), January/ February 1974 and May 1975.
Interview with D. Eisenberg, in *Inter/View* (New York), January 1975.

James Ivory

Interview with P. Anderson, in *Films in Review* (New York), October 1984.

"The trouble with Olive," in *Sight and Sound* (London), Spring 1985.

"Dialogue on Film: James Ivory," in *American Film* (Washington, D.C.), January/February 1987.

Interviews in *Hollywood Reporter*, 31 March and 6 May 1989.

"Arachnophobia," in *Sight and Sound* (London), Autumn 1990.

On IVORY: book—

Pym, John, *The Wandering Company: Twenty-One Years of Merchant-Ivory Films*, London, 1983.

Martini, Emanuela, *James Ivory*, Bergamo, 1985.

On IVORY: articles—

Gillett, John, "Merchant-Ivory," in *Sight and Sound* (London), Spring 1973.

Gillett, John, "A Princess in London," in *Sight and Sound* (London), Summer 1974.

Hillgartner, D., "The Making of *Roseland*," in *Filmmakers Newsletter* (Ward Hill, Massachusetts), January 1978.

"*Quartet* Issue" of *Avant-Scène du Cinéma* (Paris), 1 October 1981.

McFarlane, Brian, "Some of James Ivory's later films," in *Cinema Papers* (Melbourne), June 1982.

Firstenberg, J.P., "A Class Act Turns Twenty-Five," in *American Film* (Washington, D.C.), September 1987.

Monthly Film Bulletin (London), November 1987.

*   *   *

The work of James Ivory was a fixture in independent filmmaking of the late 1960s and 1970s. *Roseland*, for example, Ivory's omnibus film about the habitués of a decaying New York dance palace, garnered a standing ovation at its premiere at the New York Film Festival in 1977, and received much critical attention afterward. However, it was not until *A Room with a View*, Ivory's stately adaptation of E. M. Forster's novel, that Ivory gained the full international reputation he was to enjoy throughout the late 1980s. The name-making films Ivory directed earlier in the decade—two adaptations of Forster and two of Henry James among them—linked him inextricably with the contemporary British cinema's tradition of urbane, even ultra-genteel costume-dramas.

Ivory's independence, his influential involvement with English film, and his sustained collaborative partnership with Ismail Merchant, the producer, invite a comparison with an earlier pairing in British cinema, Michael Powell and Emeric Pressburger. Both teams have found themselves attracted to material dealing with the effects of sexual repression or with the clash of differing cultures, as in, for example, *Black Narcissus* (Powell/Pressburger, 1947) or *The Europeans* (Ivory/Merchant, 1979). However, while Powell and Pressburger work with various forms of visual experimentation, employing heightened colors, frequently moving cameras, and various forms of cinematographic juxtaposition to achieve an opulent, metaphorical visual texture, Ivory's work represents a distinct retrenchment, a withdrawal from visual hyperbole, a comparative conservatism of visual style. An example of one of Ivory's few attempts at visual expressionism (a moment in his work that seems directly inspired by Powell, in fact) illustrates this point. In *The Bostonians*, Ivory attempts to express Olive Chancellor's hysteria by using stylized colors and superimposition in isolated dream sequences. Because the film's style is deeply rooted in naturalism, unlike that of Powell, the sequences look stilted and awkward, remarkably out of place in the context of the film.

The naturalism of Ivory's style often perfectly complements the director's interest in the dynamics of isolated communities: the drama troupe in *Shakespeare Wallah*, for example, or the dancers in *Roseland*, or the members of the New York downtown-punk scene in *Slaves of New York*. Ivory's films characteristically trace the formation of community around a common interest—or, more often, a common flaw or a shared loss—and his observation is enlivened by minute gestural detail and a keen sympathy for marginal characters. Such sympathy, surely, is what attracts him, for example, to Evan Connell's densely ironic but ultimately equally sympathetic accounts of quietly desperate middle-class lives in Kansas City, the novels *Mrs. Bridge* and *Mr. Bridge*; and it accounts as well for Ivory's handling of characters, for instance Charlotte Bartlett in *Room with a View*. In Forster's novel, Miss Bartlett is lampooned tirelessly, emerging as one of the novel's chief examples of English hypocrisy, of the way in which Forster conceives of high culture as the poison of the spirit (this is in spite of a half-hearted reprieve for the character in the novel's last pages). In the film, Maggie Smith's agile, witty performance makes the character far more appealing, and Ivory's treatment of the character, cutting from the lovers' final union to shots of Miss Bartlett's soundless, unbending loneliness, shows that he clearly interprets her as a fully sympathetic character of great pathos.

Ivory's two Forster adaptations, *Room with a View* and *Maurice*, may well prove to be the high-water mark of his career. These two films do more than demonstrate Ivory's often bracingly literary sensibility; not only are most of Ivory's films adaptations, but they doggedly strive for extreme "faithfulness" to their source material. In the Forster adaptations, however, this "faithfulness" co-exists with crucial shifts of emphasis that provide, simultaneously, modern interpretations—*re*-visions—of the prior texts. An example of this occurs in the scene of the murder in the square in *Room with a View*. In its use of hand-held cameras, graphic matches, and rhythmic editing that mercurially shifts the tone of the sequence from gravity to exultation, the sequence becomes one of the film's set-pieces, supplying the complexities Forster largely avoids in his comparatively laconic treatment of the scene. If Ivory's style continues to evolve, it will likely do so around this conception of adaptation as a process of *interpretation*, of *creation*.

—James Morrison

JANCSÓ, Miklós.

Hungarian. Born in Vác, Hungary, 27 September 1921. Educated in law at Kolozsvár University, Romania, doctorate 1944; Budapest Academy of Dramatic and Film Art, graduated 1950. Married director Márta Mészáros, son Miklos Jr. is cameraman. Newsreel director, early 1950's; shot documentaries in China, 1957; directed first feature, *A harangok Römába mentek*, 1958; director at "25th" theatre, Budapest, 1960's. Recipient: Hungarian Critics' Prize, for *Cantata*, 1963; Best Director Award, Cannes Festival, for *Red Psalm*, 1972; Special Prize, Cannes Festival, 1979.

Films as Director:
(of short films and documentaries):

1950   *Kezunbe vettuk a béke ugyét* (*We Took Over the Cause of Peace*) (co-d)
1951   *Szovjet mezögazdasági hüldöttsek tanításai* (*The Teachings of a Soviet Agricultural Deputation*) (co-d)
1952   *A 8. szabad Május 1* (*Ezerkilencszázötvenkettö. 1952 Május 1. The Eighth Free May Day*)
1953   *Választás elött* (*Before Election*); *Arat az Orosházi Dözsa* (*Harvest in the Cooperative "Dosza"*); *Közös útan* (*Ordinary Ways. On a Common Path*) (co-d)
1954   *Galga mentén* (*Along the Galgu River*); *Ösz Badacsonyban* (*Autumn in Badacsony*); *Éltetö Tisza-víz* (*The Health-Giving Waters of Tisza. Life-Bringing Water*); *Emberek! Ne engedjétek!* (*Comrades! Don't Put Up with It*) (co-d, co-sc); *Egy kiállitás képei* (*Pictures at an Exhibition*)
1955   *Angyalföldi fiatalok* (*Children of Angyalfold. The Youth of "The Land of Angels"*); *A Varsoí vit* (*Varsoí Világifjusági Találkozö I–III. Warsaw World Youth Meeting I–III*); *Egy délután Koppánymonostorban* (*One Afternoon in Koppanymonostor. An Afternoon in the Village*); *Emlékezz, ifjúság* (*Young People, Remember*)
1956   *Móricz Zsigmond* (*Zsigmond Moricz 1879–1942*)
1957   *A város peremén* (*In the Outskirts of the City*); *Dél-Kína tájain* (*The Landscapes of Southern China*); *Színfoltok Kínaböl* (*Colorful China. Colors of China*); *Pekingi palotái* (*Palaces of Peking*); *Kína vendégei voltunk* (*Our Visit to China*)
1958   *Derkovitz Gyula 1894–1934*; *A harangok Römába mentek* (*The Bells Have Gone to Rome*) (feature)
1959   *Halhatatlanság* (*Immortality*) (+ sc, ph); *Izotöpok a gyögyászatban* (*Isotopes in Medical Science*)
1960   first episode of *Három csillág* (*Three Stars*); *Az eladás müvészete* (*The Art of Revival. The Art of Salesmanship*) (co-d); *Szerkezettervezés* (*Construction Design*) (+ sc)
1961   *Az idö kereke* (*The Wheels of Time*) (+ sc); *Alkonyok és hajnalok* (*Twilight and Dawn*) (+ sc); *Indiántörténet* (*Indian Story*) (+ sc)
1963   *Oldás és kötés* (*Cantata*) (+ co-sc); *Hej, te eleven Fa . . .* (*Living Tree . . . An Old Folk Song*) (+ sc)

(of feature films):

1964   *Így jöttem* (*My Way Home*)

1965   *Szegénylegények* (*The Round-Up*); *Jelenlét* (*The Presence*) (short) (+ sc); *Közelrölia: a vér* (*Close-up: The Blood*) (short)
1967   **Csillagosok, katonák (The Red and the White)** (+ co-sc)
1968   *Csend és kiáltás* (*Silence and Cry*) (+ co-sc); *Vörös Május* (*Red May*) (short)
1969   *Fényes szelek* (*The Confrontation*); *Sirokkó* (*Teli sirokkó lek. Winter Wind*) (+ co-sc)
1970   *Égi bárány* (*Agnus Dei*) (+ co-sc); *La pacifista* (*The Pacifist*) (+ co-sc); *Füst* (*Smoke*) (short)
1972   **Még kér a nép (Red Psalm)**
1975   *Szerelmem, Elektra* (*Elektreia*)
1976   *Vizi privati, pubbliche virtù* (*Vices and Pleasures*)
1978   *Eletünket és vérunket: Magyar rapszödia 1* (*Hungarian Rhapsody*) (+ co-sc); *Allegro barbaro: Magyar rapszödia 2* (*Allegro barbaro*) (+ co-sc)
1981   *A zsranok szíve avagy Boccaccio Magyarországon* (*The Tyrant's Heart. Boccaccio in Hungary*) (+ co-sc)
1984   *Omega, Omega . . .*; *Muzsika* (*Music*)
1986   *L'Aube* (*Dawn*)
1987   *Szörnyek Evadja*
1989   *Jézus Krisztus Horoszkója*

Other Films:

1950   *A Maksimenko brigád* (*The Maximenko Brigade*) (Koza) (story)
1968   *A Pál utcai fiúk* (*The Boys of Paul Street*) (Fabri) (role)
1977   *Difficile morire* (Silva) (role)

Publications:

By JANCSÓ: articles—

Interview, in *The Image Maker*, edited by Ron Henderson, Richmond, Virginia, 1971.
"L'Idéologie, la technique et le rite," interview with Claude Beylie, in *Ecran* (Paris), December 1972.
"I Have Played Christ Long Enough: A Conversation with Miklos Jancso," with Gideon Bachmann, in *Film Quarterly* (Berkeley), Fall 1974.
"Entretien . . . sur *Vitam et sanguinem*," with Michel Ciment and J.-P. Jeancolas, in *Positif* (Paris), May 1979.
"A jelenlét," interview with I. Antal, in *Filmkultura* (Budapest), November/December 1981.
Interview with L. Somogyi, in *Filmkultura* (Budapest), October 1986.
Interview in *Hungarofilm Bulletin* (Budapest), no. 2, 1988.

On JANCSÓ: books—

Taylor, John, *Directors and Directions*, New York, 1975.
Petrie, Graham, *History Must Answer to Man: The Contemporary Hungarian Cinema*, London, 1978.
Marlia, Giulio, *Lo schermo liberato: il cinema di Miklos Jancso*, Florence, 1982.
Paul, David, W., editor, *Politics, Art and Commitment in the East European Cinema*, New York, 1983.

Miklós Jancsó

On JANCSÓ: articles—

"Miklós Jancsó," in *International Film Guide 1969* edited by Peter Cowie, London, 1968.

Houston, Penelope, "The Horizontal Man," in *Sight and Sound* (London), Summer 1969.

Kane, P., and others, "Lectures de Jancsó: hier et aujourd'hui," in *Cahiers du Cinéma* (Paris), March and May 1969, and April 1970.

Robinson, D., "Quite Apart from Miklos Jancso," in *Sight and Sound* (London), Spring 1970.

Czigany, Lorant, "Jancsó Country: Miklos Jancso and the Hungarian New Cinema," in *Film Quarterly* (Berkeley), Fall 1972.

Bachmann, Gideon, "Jancso Plain," in *Sight and Sound* (London), Autumn 1974.

"Jancso Issue" of *Etudes Cinématographiques* (Paris), no. 104–108, 1975.

Robinson, David, "Old Jancso Customs," in *Sight and Sound* (London), no.1, 1978/79.

Biro, Y., "Landscape During the Battle," in *Millenium* (New York), Summer/Fall 1979.

Gillett, John, "Miklos Jancso," in *Film Dope* (London), July 1983.

"Special Section" of *Filmfaust* (Frankfurt), March/April 1984.

Petrie, G., "Miklós Jancsó," in *Revue Belge du Cinéma* (Brussels), Summer 1985.

On JANCSÓ: films—

Kovács, Zsolt, *Kamerával Kosztromában* (With a Camera in Kosztroma), short, 1967.

Comolli, Jean-Louis, *Miklos Jancso*, for TV, France, 1969.

*   *   *

Internationally, Miklós Jancsó is probably the best known of the directors to emerge from the new wave Hungarian cinema of the 1960s. With his hypnotic, circling camera, the recurrent—some critics say obsessive—exploration of Hungary's past, and his evocative use of the broad plains of his countries' Puszta, Jancsó fashioned a highly individual cinema within the confines of a state operated film industry. Although a prolific director of short films during the 1950s and an equally prolific director of feature films since the early 1970s, it is for his work during the middle and late 1960s that Jancsó is best known outside his own country.

Beginning with *Igy Jöttem* (*My Way Home*), which dealt with a young Hungarian soldier caught up in the German retreat and Soviet advance during the Second World War, Jancsó discovered both a set of themes and a style which helped him to fashion his own voice. In spite of the fact that *My Way Home*, unlike most of Jancsó's films, has a hero, he often behaves in a most unheroic way as he makes his way home. Set free by the chaos of the war's end, he is fired upon both by the Russians and the Germans, finally donning a Russian uniform as a protective disguise. Although clearly focused on the individual figures of the film itself, Jancsó's movie does contain an interesting allegory of the fate of his native country as, freed from Nazi oppression, the soldier only reluctantly dons the Russian uniform.

Szegénylegények (*The Round-Up*, literally *The Hopeless*) established him as a filmmaker of international importance. The film is set in the Hungarian plain in a fort which houses a group of peasants under surveillance following the Kossuth rebellion of 1848, and focuses on the ritual quality of the games played by both sides as tormentors and informers and rebels interchange in a mysterious elliptical dance of human passions. Shot in black and white, the film also revealed a purity of style as each meticulously composed shot conveys Jancsó's preoccupation with humans dislodged from convention and pummeled by history. In spite of its scope, however, the film won praise for its analysis of the politics of terror and of the Kafka-esque state machinery through which such terror works.

Csillagosok Katonák (1967, *The Red and the White*) and *Csend és Kiáltás* (1968, *Silence and Cry*) moved into the early 20th century and are concerned with the communist revolutions of the immediate post-World War I period. *The Red and the White* was commissioned by the Soviet government to commemorate the 50th anniversary of the October revolution. The film isolates a group of Hungarian volunteers who are fighting on the side of the reds during the Russian civil war. Once again the expansive plain provides an open background against which huddle the opposing groups, both red and white. It is interesting considering the source of his commission that Jancsó refuses to choose to side with either the red or the whites but rather to present each as a mixture of compassion and understanding, barbarity and stupidity. *Silence and Cry*, operating on a smaller scale, deals with an isolated farmstead but also raises questions about people caught up in a society torn by social and political change. Here Jancsó's circling camera becomes hypnotic and his tendency to de-psychologize his characters most extreme. Jancsó explains very little in his plot, leaving the viewer to wrestle with its obscurities and ellipses.

The claustrophobic qualities of *Silence and Cry* prepared his audience for *Fényes Szelek* (*The Confrontation*), a film set in the immediate post-war world and which deals with students, both Catholic and Communist, who square off in a quadrille interweaving accusation and intimidation. Clearly the film was occasioned by the student riots and sit-ins in 1968–69 in Budapest. It pits the Marxist students as the voice of change and revolution against the conventions of the Catholic students. The plot is minimal and Jancsó's camera at its most vertiginous, hardly ever stopping in its unceasing search for the truth. The truth, of course, as it so often does, eludes us, as the confrontation finally has more to do with temporary power games than it does with ultimate reality.

In *Sirokkó* (*Winter Wind*), made in Yugoslavia as a Franco-Hungarian co-production, he returned to the use of color as in *The Confrontation* and photographed, like *Silence and Cry*, with a minimum of shots, in this case twelve. The story deals with the historical and political irony of a Croatian anarchist leader of the 1930s who is destroyed by his own forces only later to be resurrected as a hero. A favorite film of Jancsó's, and regarded by many Hungarians as his most nationalistic, *Égi Bárány* (*Agnus Dei*) is once again set in the broad Hungarian plain during the period of civil war but is far more symbolic and anticipates the new ground he would explore in his next film.

With *Még Kér a Nép* (*Red Psalm*), Jancsó returned to the Puszta and to the end of the last century during a period of peasant unrest in which a confrontation between the workers and their landowners is interrupted by the army. The subsequent action follows patterns established earlier in Jancsó's other films. But there is a difference in *Red Psalm* as the symbolic elements always present in the other films becomes foregrounded: a dead soldier is resurrected by a kiss from a young girl, the soldiers join the peasants in a Maypole dance but eventually surround the rebellious farmers and shoot them down; a girl outside the circle using a gun tied with a red ribbon guns down all of the soldiers. The mannerisms noted by a number of critics are missing here, and Jancsó seems to have found a new direction amidst old material: the symbolism of the film elevates it beyond Jancsó's usual concerns. *Red Psalm* exemplifies what is often hidden in his other films: the totality of the film, and the celebration of life in the revolution which will bring joy in the renewed possibilities for human expression and freedom.

Although Miklós Jancsó has gone on to make other films, many of them outside Hungary itself, his body of work from *My Way Home* to *Red Psalm* seem to best exemplify his unique contribution to world cinema. Like many of the other new

Hungarian filmmakers Jancsó rejected the traditions of the conservative and classic bound national cinema he inherited, turning to a more liberating and avant-garde style which allowed him not only greater artistic expression but also increased freedom from state censorship. By adopting a more modernist approach, most notably evident in his use of a minimal plot and in the dialectical tensions between the images, he has urged his audiences out of their complacency by challenging the status quo through his questioning of the uses and abuses of state power wielded in the name of the people. This has made his films truly revolutionary.

In spite of the positive critical response his films received on their initial release, their repetitiveness and obscurity have clouded their more recent reception. Having rejected the sentimental socialism of his immediate predecessors and the naive political values of the West, Jancsó has made for himself an ambiguous position between political factions, belonging to neither yet tied to both. And through it all, Miklós Jancsó has retained his independence as a maker of highly personal films, yet still committed; internationalist, yet deeply Hungarian.

—Charles L.P. Silet

JARMAN, Derek.

British. Born in Northwood, Middlesex, 31 January 1942. Educated at King's College, London, 1960–63; Slade School of Fine Art, 1963–67. First exhibition, Lisson Gallery, London, 1967. Set designer for Royal Ballet, Ballet Rambert, and English National Opera, 1968; film designer for Ken Russell on *The Devils*, 1970; began working in Super-8 film, 1971; directed first feature, *Sebastiane*, 1976; directed promo videos for The Smiths, 1986; directed video and stage show for Pet Shop Boys, 1989. Recipient: British Film Institute Award, 1990. Lives in Dungeness, Kent.

Films as Director:
(Short Super-8 Films unless stated otherwise)

1971   *Studio Bankside*; *Miss Gaby*; *A Journey to Avebury*
1972   *Garden of Luxor* (*Burning the Pyramids*); *Andrew Logan Kisses the Glitterati*; *Tarot* (*The Magician*)
1973   *The Art of Mirrors* (*Sulphur*); *Building the Pyramids*
1974   *The Devils at the Elgin* (*Reworking the Devils*); *Fire Island*; *Duggie Fields*
1975   *Ula's Fête* (*Ula's Chandelier*); *Picnic at Ray's*; *Sebastiane Wrap*
1976   *Gerald's Film*; *Sloane Square, A Room of One's Own* (*Removal Party*); *Houston Texas*; *Sebastiane* (16mm feature)
1977   *Jordan's Dance*; *Every Woman For Herself and All For Art*
1978   *Jubilee* (16mm feature)
1979   *Broken English* (short, Super-8 and 16mm); *The Tempest* (16mm feature)
1980   *In the Shadow of the Sun* (includes re-edited versions of earlier 8mm films)
1981   *TG Psychic Rally in Heaven*
1982   *Diese Machine ist mein antihumanistisches Kunstwerk*; *Pirate Tape* (*W.S. Burroughs*); *Pontormo and Punks at Santa Croce*
1983   *Waiting for. Waiting for Godot* (short, Super-8 and video); *B2 Tape/Film*; *The Dream Machine*
1984   *Catalan* (for TV); *Imagining October*
1985   *The Angelic Conversation* (Super-8 and video)
1986   *The Queen is Dead* (promo videos on Super-8); *Caravaggio* (35mm feature)

1987   "Depuis le jour" episode of *Aria* (Super-8 and 35mm); *The Last of England* (Super-8 feature)
1988   *L'Ispirazione*; *War Requiem* (35mm feature)
1990   *The Garden* (Super-8 and 16mm feature)

Other Films:

1970   *The Devils* (Russell) (designs)
1972   *Savage Messiah* (Russell) (designs)
1975   *The Bible* (Russell) (sc)
1986   *Ostia* (role)
1987   *Prick Up Your Ears* (Frears) (role)
1988   *Behind Closed Doors* (role)

Publications:

By JARMAN: books—

Dancing Ledge, edited by Shaun Allen, London, 1984.
Caravaggio, London, 1986.
Last of England, London, 1987.
War Requiem, London, 1989.

By JARMAN: articles—

Interviews in *Time Out* (London), November 1976 and 31 January 1985.
Interview in *Film Directions* (Belfast), vol. 2, no. 8, 1979.
Interviews with Michael O'Pray, in *Monthly Film Bulletin* (London), June 1984 and April 1986.
"Renaissance Man," an interview with M. Sutton, in *Stills* (London), April 1986.
Interview in *American Film* (Washington, D.C.), September 1986.
Interview in *Filmfaust* (Frankfurt), September/October 1986.
Interview with Anne-Marie Hewitt, in *Cinema Papers* (Melbourne), September 1987.
Interview with D. Heinrich, in *Cinéma* (Paris), 16 December 1987.
Interview in *City Limits* (London), 6 July 1989.
Interview in *Listener* (London), 16 August 1990.

On JARMAN: articles—

"Jarman Issue" of *Afterimage* (London), Autumn 1985.
Rayns, Tony, "Unnatural Lighting," in *American Film* (Washington, D.C.), September 1986.

*   *   *

Since making his feature debut with *Sebastiane*, Derek Jarman has been one of Britain's most original and highly controversial film-makers. Vilified by the self-appointed guardians of the nation's morals he has been hailed as a genius by others. It is Jarman's uncompromising and direct approach to cinema which has resulted in such extreme and polarised evaluations of his work. Like Ken Russell, who introduced him to film-making by inviting him to design *The Devils* and *Savage Messiah*, Jarman has consistently assaulted cosy and conservative assumptions of "good taste." The powerful and explicit treatment of homo-erotic passion in his work has generated the greatest hostility, with *Sebastiane*, one of the most erotic and uninhibited British films ever made, the target of a particularly nasty anti-homosexual campaign generated by the tabloid press.

Drawing on personal experience more than most British film-makers, Jarman's sexuality and his public school/military background have profoundly influenced his cinema. He has paid tribute to other gay artists such as *Caravaggio*, deducing his tragic love affair with Ranuccio Thomasoni from clues in his paintings, and Benjamin Britten, creating stunning images for his *War Requiem*. He has also interpreted the island in Sha-

Derek Jarman © **Andrew Hamilton Lane**

kespeare's *The Tempest* as a metaphor for homosexuality and read his sonnets as homo-erotic love poems, incorporating them into the sound track of *The Angelic Conversation*. Jarman's films also abound with militaristic images, particularly uniformed authority figures. Such images are often ambivalent, an echo of Jarman's own fraught relationship with his father, who was a wing commander in the RAF. His later work is more explicitly autobiographical. *The Last of England* for example is constructed around the presence of the artist: the fictional elements of the film integrated with sequences featuring Jarman working at home and wandering around the streets with a camera. There are also fragments of old home movie footage shot by Jarman's father and grandfather, including images of the film-maker as a child playing with his mother and sister.

Despite being regarded as subversive by many, Jarman is paradoxically a traditionalist. He is nostalgic for a world uncorrupted by the bourgeois bureaucrats and advertising executives whom he regards as controlling our culture. The motif of the garden, that very English of personal spaces, a haven to be cherished and protected, occurs time and time again, particularly in his later work such as *The Angelic Conversation*, his section for *Aria* and *The Garden*, the title of which relates to Jarman's own garden at Dungeness on the Kent coast.

Trained as a painter, Jarman's cinema betrays a diversity of aesthetic influences. In contrast to the dominant literary/theatrical tradition in British cinema, he draws heavily on painting and poetry. He has consistently experimented with narrative from the cut-up collage approach of *Jubilee* to the poetic open narrative style of his Super-8 work from *Imagining October* to *The Last of England*. Such an approach requires an active participation on the part of the audience, often forcing them to impose their own coherence and meaning on the visual and aural collage. This aesthetic eclecticism is reflected in the design of Jarman's productions which frequently eschew realism by mixing period costumes and props with modern elements, his purpose being to generate and communicate living ideas and concepts rather than attempting to excavate a dead past. In contrast to the clutter which characterises much British realist cinema, the interior designs in Jarman's films are often rather austere, drawing attention to the significance of objects.

Derek Jarman has sought to preserve his independence from the aesthetic and ideological compromises inherent in mainstream commercial cinema. This has made the task of raising finance for projects extremely difficult and he has been forced to make his films on shoestring budgets. No other major British film-maker has consistently worked with such meagre resources. The seven-year struggle to raise money for *Caravaggio* prompted Jarman to return to the Super-8 film-making of his pre-*Sebastiane* days. By the mid-1980s it was possible to make technically sophisticated experimental films by generating images on Super-8 then transferring this material to video tape for editing and post-production while maintaining the texture and quality of the Super-8 film image in the process. The results have been extremely interesting, culminating in the production of *The Last of England*, the first full-length British feature film to be made in this way. These experiments confirm Jarman's status as a genuine innovator constantly challenging orthodox approaches to film-making. His refusal to be absorbed into the mainstream ensures his integrity as an artist but has kept him on the margins of a rather conservative British film culture.

—Duncan J. Petrie

JARMUSCH, Jim.

American. Born in Akron, Ohio, 1953. Educated at Columbia University, New York, graduated 1975; New York University Graduate Film School, 1976–79, as Teaching Assistant to Nicholas Ray. With help of Ray, completed first film, *Permanent Vacation*, costing $10 000, 1980; made *New World* with 30 minutes of leftover film, 1982; added another hour's worth of film to it to make *Stranger than Paradise*, 1984; recording artist with "The Del-Byzanteens." Recipient: Golden Leopard, Locarno Festival, Best Film Award, National Society of Film Critics, and Camera d'Or for Best New Director, Cannes Festival, for *Stranger than Paradise*, 1984. Lives in the Bowery, New York.

Films as Director and Scriptwriter:

1980   *Permanent Vacation* (+ mus)
1982   *The New World* (*Stranger than Paradise, Part One*) (short)
1984   *Stranger Than Paradise*
1986   *Down By Law*; *Coffee and Cigarettes*
1989   *Mystery Train*

Other Films:

1979   *Red Italy* (Mitchel) (role)
1980   *Lightning Over Water* (*Nick's Movie*) (Wenders and Ray) (prod asst); *Underground U.S.A.* (Mitchel) (sound recordist)
1981   *Only You* (Vogel) (role); *You Are Not I* (Driver) (ph)
1982   *Burroughs* (Brookner) (sound recordist); *The State of Things* (Wenders) (featured songs by The Del-Byzanteens)
1983   *Fraulein Berlin* (Lambert) (role); *American Autobahn* (Degas) (role)
1984   *Sleepwalk* (Driver) (ph)

Publications:

By JARMUSCH: articles—

Interview (on Nicholas Ray) with F. Vega, in *Casablanca* (Madrid), February 1983.
Interview with H. Leroux and Y. Lardeau, in *Cahiers du Cinéma* (Paris), December 1984.
Interview with H. Jacobson, in *Film Comment* (New York), January/February 1985.
Interview in *American Cinematographer* (Los Angeles), March 1985.
Interview in *American Film* (Washington, D.C.), October 1986.
Interview with Jonathan Rosenbaum, in *Cahiers du Cinéma* (Paris), November 1986.
Interview with Saskia Baron, in *Stills* (London), February 1987.
"Asphalt Jungle Jim," an interview with M. Mordue, in *Cinema Papers* (Melbourne), January 1988.

On JARMUSCH: articles—

Kiolkowski, F., "Independent Film: *Stranger than Paradise*," in *On Film* (Los Angeles), Fall 1984.
Klady, J., "Jim Jarmusch," in *American Film* (Washington, D.C.), October 1986.
Stiller, Nikki, "A Sad and Beautiful Film," in *Hudson Review* (New York), vol. 40, no. 1, 1987.
Monthly Film Bulletin (London), January 1987.
Leibowitz, Flo, "Neither Hollywood nor Godard: The Strange Case of *Stranger than Paradise*," in *Persistence of Vision* (Maspeth, New York), no. 6, 1988.

*   *   *

Jim Jarmusch has risen quickly to the forefront of young, independent American filmmakers. Recognition has been his from the very beginning, with his first film, *Stranger than Paradise*, winning a Camera d'Or at the 1984 Cannes Film Festival (for

Jim Jarmusch: *Stranger Than Paradise*

best "first film") and "Best Picture" from the National Society of Film Critics. The key to Jarmusch's success is a well defined and thoughtfully conceived stylistic approach and a coherent circle of interests.

The focal point of all Jarmusch's work is the apparent contradiction that exists between the popular perception of the American Dream and what that dream actually holds for the individual who doesn't quite fit in. This contradiction is explored through the interaction of a characteristic ensemble of characters. Each of Jarmusch's films is built around a trio of characters though *Mystery Train* varies that slightly using three separate stories to explore this central theme. The characters are all decidedly off-beat, but all seem to have a vision or aspiration which echoes a popular perception of America. The central characters—Tom Waits' down and out disc-jockey in *Down By Law*, or John Lurie's small-time pimp in the same film—are forced to confront their misconceptions and misguided dreams when they are thrown together by fate with a foreigner who views this dream as an observer. In *Down By Law*, for example, the two central characters find themselves in jail with an Italian immigrant who has murdered someone for cheating at cards. The character carries a small notebook of American slang expressions from which he quotes dutifully and incorrectly. He refers to this notebook as ". . . everything I know about America." It is this kind of character situation that Jarmusch uses to scoff at an America he sees as misguided and woefully out of touch with itself.

Stylistically, Jarmusch's work echoes the work of the French "New Wave" filmmakers, in particular the Godard of films like *Breathless* and *Weekend*. Jump-cuts are frequently used to disconnect characters from sublime and rational passages of time and space. A sense of disenfranchisement is created in this way, separating characters from the continuity of space and time which surrounds them. In *Down By Law*, for example, Tom Waits sits in his cell, then lays on the floor, then lays across his bed, but what seems like "a day in the life" editing approach actually concludes with days having passed, not hours. Jarmusch also uses moving-camera a great deal, but unlike his predecessors in other traditions his fluid camera style is not functional. Camera movements in films like *Down By Law* and *Mystery Train* create a visual world that is always in transition. *Down By Law* opens with camera movement first right to left down a street in a small town, then left to right. As a result, the audience is introduced, through a visual metaphor, to the conclusion course that is central to the film's themes.

Like other young filmmakers of his generation, such as Spike Lee, Jim Jarmusch approaches the America way of life with a sense of hip cynicism. A product of contemporary American film school savvy, Jarmusch incorporates a sense of film history, style, and awareness in his filmmaking approach. The tradition which he has chosen to follow, the one which offers him the most freedom, is that established by filmmakers such as Chabrol, Godard, and Truffaut in the 1950s and 1960s.

—Rob Winning

JENNINGS, Humphrey.

British. Born Frank Humphrey Sinkler Jennings in Walberswick, Suffolk, 1907. Educated at Perse School and Pembroke College, Cambridge, until 1934. Joined General Post Office (GPO) film unit as scenic designer and editor, 1934; worked with Len Lye at Shell films, from 1936; returned to GPO film unit (became Crown Film Unit, 1940), 1938; became associated with Mass Observation movement, late 1930's; director for Wessex Films, 1949. *Died, after falling from a cliff while scouting locations for film, in Poros, Greece, 1950.*

Films as Director:

1938   *Penny Journey*
1939   *Spare Time* (+ sc); *Speaking from America*; *SS Ionian* (*Her Last Trip*); *The First Days* (*A City Prepares*) (co-d)
1940   *London Can Take It* (co-d); *Spring Offensive* (*An Unrecorded Victory*); *Welfare of the Workers* (co-d)
1941   *Heart of Britain* (*This is England*); *Words for Battle* (+ sc)
1942   **Listen to Britain** (co-d, co-sc, co-ed)
1943   **Fires Were Started** (*I Was a Fireman*) (+ sc); *The Silent Village* (+ pr, sc)
1944   *The Eighty Days* (+ pr); *The True Story of Lilli Marlene* (+ sc); *VI* (+ pr)
1945   **A Diary for Timothy** (+ sc)
1946   *A Defeated People*
1947   *The Cumberland Story* (+ sc)
1949   *Dim Little Island* (+ pr)
1950   *Family Portrait* (+ sc)

Other Films:

1934   *Post-Haste* (ed); *Pett and Pott* (Cavalcanti) (sets ed, role as grocer); *Glorious Sixth of June* (Cavalcanti) (role as telegraph boy); *The Story of the Wheel* (ed)
1935   *Locomotives* (ed)
1936   *The Birth of a Robot* (Lye) (color direction and production)

Publications:

By JENNINGS: books—

Pandaemonium 1660–1886: The Coming of the Machine as seen by Contemporary Observers, edited by Mary-Lou Jennings and Charles Madge, London, 1985.

On JENNINGS: books—

Grierson, John, *Humphrey Jennings: A Tribute*, London, 1951.
Hardy, Forsyth, *Grierson on Documentary*, revised edition, London, 1966.
Lovell, Alan, and Jim Hillier, *Studies in Documentary*, New York, 1972.
Sussex, Elizabeth, *The Rise and Fall of British Documentary: The Story of the Film Movement Founded by John Grierson*, Berkeley, California, 1975.
Hodgkinson, Anthony, and Rodney Sheratsky, *Humphrey Jennings: More than a Maker of Films*, Hanover, New Hampshire, 1982.
Jennings, Mary-Lou, editor, *Humphrey Jennings: Film-Maker/Painter/Poet*, London, 1982.
Vaughan, Dai, *Portrait of an Invisible Man: The Working Life of Stewart McAllister, Film Editor*, London, 1983.
Aldgate, Anthony, and Jeffrey Richards, *Britain Can Take It: The British Cinema in the Second World War*, Oxford, 1986.
Tomicek, Harry, *Jennings*, Vienna, 1989.

On JENNINGS: articles—

Wright, Basil, "Humphrey Jennings," in *Sight and Sound* (London), December 1950.
Lambert, Gavin, "Jennings' Britain," in *Sight and Sound* (London), May 1951.
Védrès, Nicole, "Humphrey Jennings—A Memoir," in *Sight and Sound* (London), May 1951.
Anderson, Lindsay, "Only Connect: Some Aspects of the Work of Humphrey Jennings," in *Sight and Sound* (London), April/June 1954.
Dand, Charles, "Britain's Screen Poet," in *Films in Review* (New York), February 1955.
Strick, Philip, "Great Films of the Century: *Fires Were Started*," in *Films and Filming* (London), May 1961.
Rhode, Eric, and Gabriel Pearson, "Cinema of Appearance," in *Sight and Sound* (London), Autumn 1961.
"Jennings Issue" of *Film Quarterly* (Berkeley), Winter 1961/62.
Millar, Daniel, "*Fires Were Started*," in *Sight and Sound* (London), Spring 1969.
Belmans, Jacques, "Humphrey Jennings, 1907–1950," in *Anthologie du Cinéma. Vol. VI*, Paris, 1971.
Sharatsky, R.E., "Humphrey Jennings: Artist of the British Documentary," special issue of *Film Library Quarterly* (New York), v.8, no.3–4, 1975.
Zaniello, T.A., "Humphrey Jennings' Film *Family Portrait*: The Velocity of Imagistic Change," in *Literature/Film Quarterly* (Salisbury, Maryland), no.1, 1979.
Eaton, Mick, "In the Land of the Good Image," in *Screen* (London), May/June 1982.
Robson, K.J., "Humphrey Jennings: The Legacy of Feeling," in *Quarterly Review of Film Studies* (New York), Winter 1982.
"Humphrey Jennings," in *Film Dope* (London), December 1983.
Colls, R., and P. Dood, "Representing the Nation: British Documentary Film 1930–45," in *Screen* (London), January/February 1985.
Nowell-Smith, Geoffrey, "Humphrey Jennings, Surrealist Observer," in *All Our Yesterdays*, edited by Charles Barr, London, 1986.

*   *   *

Though Jennings was (from 1934 on) part of the Grierson documentary group, he was never fully part of it. Grierson regarded him as something of a dilettante; Jennings's taste and interests were subtler and gentler than Grierson's. It wasn't until Grierson had left England to become wartime head of the National Film Board of Canada that Jennings gained creative control over the films on which he worked.

The outbreak of World War II seemed to let loose in Jennings a special poetic eloquence, and his finest work was done at the Crown Film Unit during the war years. *Listen to Britain, Fires Were Started*, and *A Diary for Timothy* are generally regarded as his masterpieces.

Jennings was part of the English intellectual aristocracy. Extremely well educated, he had done a good deal of research into English literature and cultural history. He was also a surrealist painter and poet. In his wartime films his deep-felt affection for English tradition mingles with impressionist observations of the English people under the stress of war. Rather than following the sociological line of the Griersonian documentaries of the 1930's, Jennings offered a set of cultural notations—sights and sounds, people and places—illuminated by his very special aesthetic sensibility and complete mastery of the technique of the black and white sound film. His films present an idealized English tradition in which class tensions don't appear. They record and celebrate contemporary achievement in preserving a historical heritage, along with commonplace decencies and humor in the face of an enemy threat. They also are experiments with form, of such breathtaking distinctiveness that they never really have been imitated. (Though Lindsay Anderson and other Free Cinema filmmakers would later acknowledge the importance of Jennings's work to them as inspiration, the Free Cinema films are radically different from Jennings's films in what they say about England, and are also much simpler in form.)

Listen to Britain, a short, is a unique impressionistic mosaic of images and sounds, including much music (as is usual in Jennings's work)—a sort of free-association portrait of a nation at a particular historical moment. The feature-length *Fires Were Started* carries the understated emotionality of the British war-

Humphrey Jennings (centre) directing *A Diary for Timothy*

time semi-documentary form to a kind of perfection: a very great deal about heroic effort and quiet courage is suggested through an austere yet deeply moving presentation of character and simple narrative. In *A Diary for Timothy*, which runs about forty minutes, Jennings attempted to fuse the impressionism of *Listen to Britain* with the narrativity of *Fires Were Started*. In its formal experimentation it is the most complex and intricate of all of Jennings's films.

With the Germans massed across the Channel, and bombs and then rockets being dropped on Britain, the British people needed a kind of emotional support different from the wartime psychological needs in other countries. In rising to this particular occasion Jennings became one of the few British filmmakers whose work might be called poetic. He is also one of a small international company of film artists whose propaganda for the state resulted in lasting works of art.

—Jack C. Ellis

JEWISON, Norman.

Canadian. Born in Toronto, Ontario, 21 July 1926. Educated at Malvern Collegiate Institute; Victoria College, University of Toronto, B. A., 1945; studied piano and music theory at the Royal Conservatory. Served in the Royal Canadian Navy. Married Margaret Ann Dixon, 1953, two sons, one daughter. Actor and scriptwriter in London, 1950–52; producer and director, Canadian Broadcasting Corporation, 1953–58; director for CBS, New York, won several Emmy awards, 1958–61; moved to Hollywood, 1961; after directing first feature, *40 Pounds of Trouble*, signed 7-picture contract with Universal, 1963; executive producer, *The Judy Garland Show*, for TV, 1963–64; moved to MGM for *The Cincinnati Kid*, 1965. Recipient: Golden Globe and Oscar for Best Director, for *In the Heat of the Night*, 1968; Officer, Order of Canada, 1982; Honorary LL.D, University of Western Ontario; Honored by American Civil Liberties Union, 1984. Address: 18 Glouster Street, 4th Floor, Toronto, Ontario, M4Y ILS, Canada.

Films as Director:

1962   *Forty Pounds of Trouble*
1963   *The Thrill of It All*
1964   *Send Me No Flowers*
1965   *The Art of Love*; *The Cincinnati Kid*
1966   *The Russians are Coming, the Russians are Coming* (+ pr)
1967   *In the Heat of the Night*

1968 *The Thomas Crown Affair* (+ pr)
1969 *Gaily, Gaily* (*Chicago, Chicago*) (+ pr)
1971 *Fiddler on the Roof* (+ pr)
1973 *Jesus Christ Superstar* (+ co-pr, co-sc)
1975 *Rollerball* (+ pr)
1978 *F.I.S.T.* (+ pr)
1979 *And Justice for All* (+ co-pr)
1982 *Best Friends* (+ co-pr)
1984 *A Soldier's Story* (+ co-pr)
1985 *Agnes of God* (+ co-pr)
1988 *Moonstruck* (+ co-pr)
1989 *In Country*

Other Films:

1970 *The Landlord* (Ashby) (pr)
1973 *Billy Two-Hats* (Kotcheff) (co-pr)
1980 *The Dogs of War* (Irvin) (exec pr)
1984 *Iceman* (Schepisi) (pr)

Publications:

By JEWISON: articles—

"Norman Jewison Discusses Thematic Action in *The Cincinnati Kid*," in *Cinema* (Beverly Hills), July/August 1965.
"Turning On in Salzburg," in *Action* (Los Angeles), July/August 1969.
Interview in *Directors at Work*, edited by Bernard Kantor and others, New York, 1970.
Interview with Gordon Gow, in *Films and Filming* (London), January 1971.
Interview with C. Tadros, in *Cinema Canada* (Montreal), September 1985.
Interview in *Premiere* (New York), Autumn 1987.
Interview with A. Hunter, in *Films and Filming* (London), April 1988.

On JEWISON: articles—

Carducci, M., "Norman Jewison directs *Rollerball*," in *Millimeter* (New York), March 1975.
Mariani, J., "Norman Jewison directs *And Justice for All*," in *Millimeter* (New York), October 1979.
American Film (Washington, D.C.), July 1990.

*   *   *

The very model of the modern up-market commercial director, Jewison seems cut out to make the kind of prestige pictures once handled at MGM by Clarence Brown and Victor Fleming. No theme is so trashy or threadbare that he cannot elevate it by stylish technique and apt casting into a work of merit, even on occasion art.

Early work with an ageing and cantankerous Judy Garland marked him as a man at ease with the cinema's sacred monsters; in the indifferent sex comedies of the early 1960s, he acquired equal skill with the pastels of Hollywood color and the demands of widescreen. A recognizable Jewison style was first evident in *The Cincinnati Kid*. Its elements—rich crimsons; the sheen of faces, tanned or sweating, in shadowed rooms; an edgy passion in performance—reappeared in *In the Heat of the Night* and *The Thomas Crown Affair*, novelettes redeemed by their visual flair and a sensual relish, not for sex, but for the appurtenances of power.

Not at home in the domestic or the comic, Jewison brought little to Ben Hecht's film memoir *Gaily, Gaily*, the literary ellipsis of *The Landlord* or, more recently, to comedies like *Best Friends*. Two musicals, *Fiddler on the Roof* and *Jesus Christ, Superstar*, did, however, offer an invitation to location shooting and unconventional staging which Jewison confidently accepted. Though little liked on release, the latter shows a typical imagination and sensuality applied to the subject, which Jewison relocated in contemporary Israel to spectacular effect. *Rollerball*, his sole essay in science fiction, belongs with *Thomas Crown* in its relish for high life. The strong points are not the eponymous gladiatorial game but the dark glamor of life among his future power elite.

A pattern of one step forward, two steps backward, dominates Jewison's career into the 1980s. The Israel-shot western *Billy Two Hats* was a notable miscalculation, as was the Sylvester Stallone union melodrama F.I.S.T., a program picture that needed to be an epic to survive. He was on surer ground in *And Justice for All*, a dark and sarcastic comedy/drama about the idiocy of the law, with a credible Al Pacino in command. But films like the novelettish post-Vietnam melodrama *In Country* did little to enhance his reputation. It is a cause for concern that he could never put together his projected musical remake of *Grand Hotel*, whose elements seem precisely those with which he works most surely. A taint of the high-class advertising lay-out characterises Jewison's best work, just as the style and technique of that field rescues his often banal material. Within the ambit of the glossy magazine, with its rich colours and crepuscular compositions, he seems destined to spend his career.

—John Baxter

JIREŠ, Jaromil.

Czechoslovak. Born in Bratislava, 10 December 1935. Educated at film technical school, Cmelice; the FAMU Film Faculty, Prague, graduate in photography, 1958, and direction, 1960. Married Hana Jiesová. Worked with Polyecran and the Magic Lantern, 1960–62; director of feature films, Barrandov Film Studio, from 1963; director of documentary films at Short Film Prague, from 1965; also TV director, from 1974, specialising in opera and ballet, late 1980's. Address: Na ostrohu 42, Praha 6, 160 00, Ceskoslovensko.

Films as Director:

1958 *Horečka* (*Fever*) (+ sc)
1959 *Strejda* (*Uncle*) (+ sc)
1960 *Sál ztracených kroku* (*The Hall of Lost Steps*) (+ sc, ph); *Stopy* (*Footprints*); *Polyekrán pro BVV* (*Polyecran for the Brno Industrial Fair*) (co-d)
1961 *Polyekrán pro Mezinárodní výstavu práce Turin* (*Polyecran for International Exposition of Labor Turin*) (co-d)
1962 *Houslový koncert* (*The Violin Concert*) (co-d, Magic Lantern program)
1963 *Křik* (*The Cry*) (+ co-sc)
1964 "Romance" episode of *Perličky na dně* (*Pearls in the Deep*) (+ sc)
1965 *Srub* (*The Log Cabin*) (+ sc)
1966 *Občan Karel Havlíček* (*Citizen Karel Havlíček*) (+ co-sc)
1967 *Hra na krále* (*The King Game*) (+ sc)
1968 *Zert* (*The Joke*) (+ sc); *Don Juan 68* (+ sc); *Dědáček* (*Granpa*) (+ sc)
1969 *Cesta do Prahy Vincence Moštek a Simona Pešla z Vlčnova 1.p. 1969* (*The Journey of Vincenc Moštek and Simon Pešl of Vlčnov to Prague, 1969 A.D.*) (co-d, co-sc)
1970 *Valerie a týden divu* (*Valerie and a Week of Wonders*) (+ sc)
1972 *. . . a pozdravuji vlaštovky* (*My Love to the Swallows*) (+ sc)
1973 *Kasař* (*The Safe Cracker*) (+ sc)
1974 *Lidé z metra* (*The People from the Metro*) (+ co-sc); *Leoš Janáček* (+ sc, for TV)
1975 *Il Divino Boemo* (+ sc)
1976 *Ostrov stříbrných volavek* (*The Island of Silver Herons*)
1977 *Talíře nad Velkým Malíkovem* (*Flying Saucers Over Velký Malík*) (+ sc)
1978 *Mladý muž a bílá velryba* (*The Young Man and the White Whale*) (+ sc)
1979 *Causa králík* (*The Rabbit Case*) (+ sc)

Jaromil Jires

1980 *Svět Alfonso Muchy* (*The World of Alphonse Mucha*) (+ sc);
    Útěky domu (*Escapes Home*) (+ co-sc)
1981 *Opera ve vinici* (*Opera in the Vineyard*) (+ sc)
1982 *Kouzelna Praha Rudolfa II* (*The Magic Prague of Rudolph II*)
    (+ sc); *Neúplné zatměni* (*Partial Eclipse*) (+ co-sc)
1983 *Katapult* (*Catapult*)
1984 *Prodloužený čas* (*The Prolonged Time*)
1985 *Cuckoo's Egg: Milos Forman* (doc)
1987 *Lev s bílou hřívou* (*The Lion with the White Mane*); *I Love
    NY: Sidney Lumet*; *F. Murray Abraham: Man and Actor*
1990 *Antonín Dvořák*

Publications:

By JIRES: articles—

Interview, in *The Image Maker*, edited by Ron Henderson, Richmond, Virginia, 1971.
Interview with E. Zaoralová, in *Film a Doba* (Prague), February 1981.
Interview with V. Kratochvilova, in *Film a Doba* (Prague), June 1985.
Interview with M. Storchova, in *Czechoslovak Film* (Prague), Autumn 1986.
Interview with J. Sitarova, in *Film a Doba* (Prague), April 1987.

On JIRES: books—

Janoušek, Jiří, *3¹/₂ po druhé*, Prague, 1969.
Hames, Peter, *The Czechoslovak New Wave*, Berkeley, 1985.

On JIRES: articles—

Sarris, Andrew, "Movers," in *Saturday Review* (New York), 23 December 1967.
"Jaromil Jireš," in *Film Dope* (London), December 1983.

*   *   *

Having finished his studies at the Prague Film School, Jireš entered filmmaking at the end of the 1950s with several short films, the most engaging of which was *Sál ztracených kroku* (*The Hall of Lost Steps*). In 1963 he made his debut in feature-length films with the picture *Křik* (*The Cry*), which earned him a place among the ranks of young directors striving for new content and a new film language. In his debut Jireš reacts to modern film currents, above all to the stylistics of the cinéma vérité, whose elements he utilizes, conscious, of course, of the danger that this can hold for the representation of reality and the expression of truth. The story of *The Cry* suppresses traditional dramatic structure. It consists of the fragmentary memories of the two main protagonists, a husband and wife, on the day their child is to be born. Arranging individual recollections, combining fictional segments with documentary shots, and using a hidden camera, Jireš seeks to convince the viewer of man's connection with the present, the past, and the future, and his close and immediate link with the whole world. (Jireš: "We live in a time when a person's most intimate experiences are connected with the major currents of world events.") *The Cry* was very well received and won several awards; it is the first pinnacle of Jireš's creative work.

The second pinnacle was achieved in two totally disparate pictures from the early 1970s. One film was *Valerie a týden divu* (*Valerie and a Week of Wonders*), based on a novel by the eminent modern Czech poet Viítězslav Nezval. What interested Jireš about the novel was "the juncture of reality and dream and the playful struggle between horror and humor." The other film, *. . . a pozdravuji vlaštovky* (*My Love to the Swallows*), is purely Jireš's own. The director was inspired by the life and death of the real-life character of Maruška Kudeříková, a young woman who fought against German fascism during the Second World War. Here, in a different connection, Jireš used the same method of alternating real-life elements and reminiscences, as in *The Cry*, but for a different purpose, namely, to demonstrate a person's inner strength, the source of her faith and hope.

The following years, in which Jireš made three pictures, were a period of stagnation. The fairy-tale film *Lidé z metra* (*The People from the Metro*) and *Ostrov stříbrných volavek* (*The Island of Silver Herons*), in which he returns to the days of the First World War, are equally undistinguished. Even less noteworthy is the fantastic tale *Talíře nad Velkým Malíkovem* (*Flying Saucers Over Velký Malík*).

Jireš's creative path took a new turn in 1978 with *Mladý muž a bílá velryba* (*The Young Man and the White Whale*). The film is an adaptation of Vladimír Páral's novel of the same name and deals with modern man's uneasy oscillation between a mask of cynicism and pure human feeling. Next came *Causa králík* (*The Rabbit Case*), an apparently humorous morality piece with a bitter finale on the struggle for justice against cunning and evil. The heroine of Jireš's next work, *Útěky domu* (*Escapes Home*), is a young woman who must face a conflict between her desire for self-fulfillment in a challenging profession and her duties as a wife and the mother of a family. In *Neúplné zatmění* (*Partial Eclipse*), about a little blind girl, he speculates on an emotional level about the meaning of life and the quest for human personality. All these recent films address problems of modern life in the area of the ethics of human relations.

Documentary films form an integral part of Jireš's creative work. Unlike his friends of the same generation, Jireš remained faithful to the documentary genre throughout his artistic career. This segment of his work shows great thematic breadth. We can nonetheless delineate two fundamental areas of interest for Jireš. In the 1960s his attention was drawn to the folklore of southern Moravia, where several of his short films have their setting. Jireš returned to this region and to this subject matter in a modified form in 1981 with the ballad story *Opera ve vinici* (*Opera in the Vineyard*). From the 1970s his documentary films turn more and more to the world of art, to music, painting, and architecture.

—Vladimir Opela
[translated by Robert Streit]

————

JORDAN, Neil.

Irish. Born in Sligo, 1950. Read History and Literature at University College, Dublin. Formed Irish Writers' Co-op, 1974, and had first collection of short stories, *Night in Tunisia*, published, 1976; worked as assistant on John Boorman's *Excalibur*, in fringe theatre, and as a writer, before directorial debut with *Angel*, 1982. Recipient: Guardian Prize for fiction, for *A Night in Tunisia*, 1979; Palme d'Or, Cannes Festival, and De Sica Award, Sorrento Festival, for *Mona Lisa*, 1986. Lives in Bray, near Dublin.

Films as Director:

1982 *Angel* (*Danny Boy*) (+ sc)
1984 *The Company of Wolves* (+ sc)
1986 **Mona Lisa** (+ co-sc)
1988 *High Spirits* (+ sc)
1989 *We're No Angels*

Publications:

By JORDAN: books—

A Night in Tunisia, London, 1976.
The Past, London, 1980.

Neil Jordan   © **Andrew Hamilton Lane**

Dream of the Beast, London, 1983.
Mona Lisa, with David Leland, London, 1986.
High Spirits, London, 1989.

By JORDAN: articles—

Interview with M. Open, in *Film Directions* (Belfast), volume 5, no. 17, 1982.
Interviews in *Time Out* (London), 13 October 1983 and 13 September 1984.
Interview with Paul Taylor and Steve Jenkins, in *Monthly Film Bulletin* (London), September 1984.
Interview with J. Powers, in *American Film* (Washington, D.C.), July/August 1986.
"Lines Written in Dejection," in *Producer* (London), May 1987.
Interview in *City Limits* (London), 8 December 1988.

*   *   *

The film career of Neil Jordan could be said to parallel the fortunes of the British film industry during the 1980s. He made a stunning impact with his first two films, *Angel*, arguably the most accomplished film-making debut sponsored by Channel 4, and *The Company of Wolves*, the first feature to be produced by Palace, one of the more exciting film companies to emerge in the decade. *Mona Lisa* consolidated his reputation as a distinctive and visionary film-maker. However, by the end of the decade both Jordan and the British film industry seemed to have run out of steam. In comparison with his earlier work the more overtly commercial *High Spirits* and *We're No Angels* can only be described as mediocre and sadly lacking in ideas.

At its most successful, Jordan's cinema demonstrates forcefully his ability to make the familiar seem strange and in doing so to question our assumptions about the nature of the world. All his films to some extent revolve around the idea that reality is not straightforward but, rather, complex and multi-faceted. Jordan's characters often encounter nightmare worlds which they must negotiate rather than push aside precisely because they are unacknowledged dimensions of reality. *Angel* and *Mona Lisa* are similar in structure, each dealing with individuals who become inadvertently caught up in personal nightmares which threaten to destroy them: Danny with sectarian violence and bloody revenge and George with the hellish underworld of teenage prostitution and drug addiction.

The idea of the nightmare world is given a more literal rendition in *The Company of Wolves*. Based on a short story by Angela Carter, the film is a reworking of the Little Red Riding Hood story, a bizarre and sumptuous mixture of fairy tale, gothic horror and Freudian psychoanalysis which betrays a rich variety of cinematic influences from Cocteau through Michael Powell and Hammer horror to Laughton's *Night of the Hunter*. The film explicitly challenges the spurious division between reality and fantasy by setting up two distinct worlds: the "real" world of the girl asleep in bed, suffering from the onset of her first menstrual period, and the "dream world" of Rosalean and her granny, set in a magical forest which was entirely constructed in a studio. At the end of the barrier between these two worlds is broken down, the wolves from the dream invade the sleeping girl's bedroom by smashing through a picture and the window.

It follows that symbolism is extremely important in Jordan's work. *The Company of Wolves* is rife with symbolic images relating to sexuality and procreation: the wolves, animals in the forest, the red shawl, blood, the stork, and so on. *Mona Lisa* employs such devices to explore the film's central thematic concern with innocence and corruption. Images relating to childhood, and by extension innocence—the white rabbit, the silly glasses, the old woman's shoe, the dwarves—are juxtaposed with scenes of degradation, depravity and violence. In *Angel* lost innocence is again explored this time through Danny swapping his saxophone for a gun, effectively symbolis-

ing the idea of the heavenly musician turned avenging angel. It is precisely the ambiguity of Danny—a figure who straddles the divine/demonic divide—which gives the film its power. Initially repulsed by the violence which claims the angelic deaf mute girl, Danny becomes a cold blooded killer himself in his pursuit of the perpetrators. In comparison the religious symbolism of *We're No Angels* seems rather clumsy and sentimental.

Despite being a powerful piece of cinema, there were indications in *Mona Lisa* that Jordan had begun to lose his sense of direction. The film lacks the moral ambiguity which made *Angel* so challenging. George remains a rather naïve and socially inept character, his uncomplicated and thoroughly "decent" moral code at odds with the world in which he becomes involved, a world he cannot begin to understand. But his naïvety is too overwhelming to be credible, and his social ineptitude borders on cliché. Unlike *Angel* and *The Company of Wolves*, the resolution of *Mona Lisa* is rather cozy and contrived with George returned to "normality," apparently none the worse for his traumatic experience.

Significantly, Jordan also attempted to lighten *Mona Lisa* by introducing comic elements, courtesy of the eccentric Thomas played by Robbie Coltrane. This is a strategy rather familiar in British cinema which more often than not serves to blunt a film's cutting edge. From then on the rot began to set in. *High Spirits* and *We're No Angels* demonstrate rather painfully that Jordan does not have a feel for comedy. The former relies on unimaginative stereotyping and comic cliché while the latter descends at times into messy slapstick reminiscent of Abbott and Costello or the Three Stooges. Indeed apart from the odd visual touch it is virtually impossible to recognise this as the work of the person who made *Angel* or *The Company of Wolves*. One can only hope that he will return to the kind of perceptive and innovative filmmaking which made his name.

—Duncan J. Petrie

————

JUTRA, Claude.

Canadian. Born in Montreal, 11 March 1930. Doctor of Medicine, University of Montreal, 1952. Made first films, in collaboration with Michel Brault, 1947; worked intermittently for National Film Board, 1954–66; founded Films Cassiopée to produce *A tout prendre*, 1961. Recipient: First Prize for experimental film, with Norman McLaren, Venice Festival, for *A Chairy Tale*, 1958; Best Film, Canadian Film Awards, for *A tout prendre*, 1964. *Died, after apparently committing suicide, November 1986 (body found in St. Lawrence River, near Quebec City, April 1987).*

Films as Director:

1947   *Le Dément du Lac Jean Jeune* (co-d)
1949   *Mouvement perpétuel* (co-d, sc)
1956   *Pierrot des bois* (+ sc, ed, role); *Les Jeunesses musicales* (+ sc)
1957   *A Chairy Tale* (*Il etait une chaise*) (co-d with Norman McLaren, role)
1958   *Les Mains nettes*
1959   *Anna la bonne*; *Félix Leclerc, troubadour*; *Fred Barry, comédien* (+ sc)
1961   *Le Niger—jeune république* (+ ed); *La Lutte* (*Wrestling*) (co-d, co-ph, co-ed, co-sound)
1962   *Québec-USA* (*L'Invasion pacifique. Visit to a Foreign Country*) (co-d, ed)

1963   *Les Enfants du silence* (co-d, ed, commentary); *Petit Discours de la méthode* (co-d, ed, commentary); *A tout prendre* (*Take It All*) (+ sc, ed, role)
1966   *Comment savoir* (*Knowing to Learn*); *Rouli-Roulant* (*The Devil's Toy*) (+ ph, ed, commentary)
1969   *Wow* (+ sc, co-ed); *Au coeur de la ville*
1970   *Marie-Christine*
1971   *Mon Oncle Antoine* (+ role as Fernand)
1972   *Kamouraska*
1975   *Pour le meilleur et pour le pire*
1978   *Surfacing*
1980   *By Design*
1985   *La Dame en couleurs*

Other Film:

1978   *Two Solitudes* (role)

Publications:

By JUTRA: articles—

"En courant derrière Rouch," in *Cahiers du Cinéma* (Paris), November 1960, and January and February 1961.
Interview in *Cahiers du Cinéma* (Paris), April/May 1968.
"Claude Jutra: Une Exploration dans une morale pathologique," an interview with G. Langlois, in *Cinéma* (Paris), January 1973.
"Un espèce de joie dans la création," an interview with J.-P. Tadros, in *Cinéma Québec* (Montreal), March/April 1973.
Interview with G.C. Koller and P. Wronski, in *Cinema Canada* (Montreal), November 1975.
"Jutra on the Tube," an interview with P. Kelman, in *Cinema Canada* (Montreal), March 1979.

On JUTRA: books—

Marsolais, Gilles, *Le Cinéma canadien*, Paris, 1968.
Chabot, Jean, *Cinéastes du Québec Quatre: Claude Jutra*, Montreal, 1970.
Beattie, Eleanor, *A Handbook of Canadian Film*, Toronto, 1973.
May, John R., and Michael Bird, editors, *Religion in Film*, Knoxville, Tennessee, 1982.

On JUTRA: articles—

Prédal, René, "Jeune Cinéma canadien," in *Premier Plan* (Lyons), no. 45, 1967.
Blumer, Ronald, "Dr. Claude Jutra: Filmmaker," in *McGill Medical Journal* (Montreal), December 1969.
"Les honneurs siéent bien à Claude Jutra," in *Séquences* (Montréal), July 1985.
Obituary in *Variety* (New York), 29 April 1987.
"Claude Jutra Section" of *Séquences* (Montreal), October 1987.
Billard, J.-A., obituary, in *24 Images* (Montreal), no. 36, 1986/87.

*   *   *

Claude Jutra won his first Canadian Film Award at the age of 19 for *Mouvement perpétuel*. At 21 he received his Doctor of medicine from the Université de Montréal. Two years later, in 1953, he authored the first ever teleplay to be screened on the French Radio Canada network. By the following year he was established at the National Film Board of Canada, in that era a stronghold of the Griersonian documentary approach and its technique. Jutra commuted to the Film Board, then based in Ottawa, from Montréal where he was studying theatre at the Théatre du Nouveau Monde.

After winning acclaim at the 1957 Venice Festival with *A Chairy Tale*, an animated film using the pixilation technique of his co-director, Norman McLaren, Jutra left Canada to spend four years working in France where he directed the short film of Jean Cocteau's *Anna, la bonne*, produced by François Truffaut. Jutra also spent time learning from, working with and developing a close friendship with cinéma verité pioneer, Jean Rouch.

His return to Québec in 1961 fresh from the experience and energy of the French New Wave, indubitably helped to set Jutra apart from the English Canadian filmmakers working at that time. Simultaneously, a group of French Canadian filmmakers, including Jutra's early collaborator, Michel Brault, the great Québecois proponent of cinéma verité, Pierre Perrault, and Gilles Carle, amongst others, had begun to carve out a separate aesthetic space for themselves within the Canadian film industry; an aesthetic space inextricable from their identity as Francophones living and working in Québec in the early years of what was then called the Quiet Revolution.

Jutra's independently made feature, *A tout prendre*, a cinéma directe film wherein the actors played "themselves," dealt with the relationship between Claude and Johanne, Jutra's African-Canadian girlfriend, and also touched upon the issue of homosexuality. The film both shocked and impressed the film industry of the early 1960s winning the Canadian Film Awards Best Feature Film prize for Jutra, the director, writer, co-producer and lead player.

Mon oncle Antoine, later to be voted Canada's best Film of all time, was released in 1971. Jutra's intimate, comic—poetic feature, based on the reminiscences of screenwriter Clément Perron's childhood in rural Québec, swept the Canadian Film Awards that year, winning eight prizes. The film had previously been rejected by the Cannes Festival committee, had been screened in English Canada without subtitles and suffered innumerable delays before its release.

Jutra went on to film Anne Hébert's period novel *Kamouraska*, starring Genevieve Bujold. Although the film won Best Feature and Bujold the prize for Best Actress, French and English filmmakers in Canada had come to increasing odds and the Canadian Film Awards ceremony in 1973 had been boycotted by Québecois filmmakers. Meanwhile, the National Film Board found itself unable to come to terms with the harsh and hard hitting political work of its Francophone filmmakers; films which, at this point in the history of Québec, were an interpretation and reaction to the October Crisis of 1970. Although Jutra's work was not overtly political in the same sense as his contemporaries, he too was affected by the slump in the Québecois film industry at the time and in 1975 left Montréal for Toronto where he spent the next six years working for CBC television and directing two features. It was, he claimed, "like working in a foreign country."

By the late 1970s however, Jutra recognized that his once impeccable memory had begun to slide; his mental health was at the beginning of its long decline. It was in his native Montréal, in 1984, that Jutra completed his last film, *La dame en couleur*. Work became impossible in the efforts of day-to-day survival, his affable personality and childlike energy all but submerged by what was eventually diagnosed as Alzheimer's Disease.

On November 5, 1986, after having left a note for the sister who had become his caretaker, Claude Jutra disappeared from his Montréal home. Newspaper headlines in the following months speculated as to whether Jutra had left the country or had simply retreated to a secret location outside of the city. In the spring of 1987, down the St. Lawrence river from Montréal and close to Québec City, Jutra's body was discovered. Found in a personal journal alongside which were detailed descriptions of his mental decline, Claude Jutra had written down the directions to the Jacques Cartier bridge, where he apparently took his own life at the age of 56.

—Clea H. Notar

K

KACHYŇA, Karel.

Czechoslovak. Born in Vyskov, 1 May 1924. Educated at Film Academy (FAMU), Prague, 1947–51. Associated with co-director Vojtěch Jasný, 1949–55; after working for Armed Forces Film Studio, joined Barrandov Film Studios, 1959; associated with writer Jan Procházka, late 1950's–1970. Recipient: Czech Film Critics Award, for *Smugglers of Death*, 1959.

Films as Director:

1950   *Není stále zamřečeno* (*The Clouds Will Roll Away*) (co-d, co-sc with Vojtěch Jasný, ph); *Vedeli si rady* (*They Know What to Do*) (co-d, co-sc, ph)
1951   *Za život radostný* (*For a Joyful Life*) (co-d, co-sc with Jasný)
1952   *Neobyčejná léta* (*Extraordinary Years*) (co-d, co-sc)
1953   *Lidé jednoho srdce* (*People of One Heart*) (co-d, co-sc, co-ph)
1954   *Stará čínská opera* (*Old Chinese Opera*) (co-d, co-sc, ph); *Z čínskëo zápisniku* (*From a Chinese Notebook*) (co-d, co-sc, ph)
1955   *Dnes večer všechno skonči* (*Everything Ends Tonight*) (co-d, co-sc)
1956   *Ztracená stopa* (*The Lost Track*) (+ sc); *Křivé zrcadlo* (*Crooked Mirror*) (+ sc)
1957   *Mistrovství světa leteckých modelářu* (*World Championship of Air Models*) (+ sc); *Pokušeni* (*Temptation*) (+ sc, ph)
1958   *Tenkrát o vánocich* (*That Christmas*) (+ co-sc); *Ctyřikrát o Bulharsku* (*Four Times About Bulgaria*) (+ sc); *Městomä svou tvář* (*The City Has Your Face*) (+ sc)
1959   *Král Sumavy* (*The King of the Sumava*) (+ co-sc)
1960   *Práče* (*The Slinger*) (+ co-sc)
1961   *Pouta* (*The Country Doctor. Fetters*) (+ co-sc); *Trápeni* (*Stress of Youth*) (co-sc)
1962   *Závrat* (*Vertigo*) (+ co-sc)
1963   *Nadeje* (*Hope*) (+ co-sc)
1964   *Vysoká zed* (*The High Wall*) (+ co-sc)
1965   *Ať žije republika* (*Long Live the Republic*) (+ co-sc)
1966   *Kočár do Vídně* (*Carriage to Vienna*) (+ co-sc)
1967   *Noc nevěsty* (*Night of the Bride*) (+ co-sc)
1968   *Vánoce s Alžbětou* (*Christmas with Elizabeth*) (+ co-sc)
1969   *Směšný pán* (*Funny Old Man*) (+ co-sc); *Ucho* (*The Ear*)
1970   *Už zase skáču přes kaluže* (*Jumping the Puddles Again*) (+ co-sc);
1972   *Vlak do stanice nebe* (*Train to Heaven*) (+ co-sc); *Láska* (*Love*) (+ co-sc); *Horká zima* (*Hot Winter*) (+ co-sc)
1974   *Pavlínka*; *Robinsonka* (*Robinson Girl*)
1975   *Skaredá dědina* (*The Ugly Village*); *Smrt mouchy* (*The Death of a Fly*)
1976   *Malá mořská víla* (*The Little Mermaid*) (+ co-sc)
1977   *Setkání v červenci* (*Meeting in July*)
1978   *Cekání na déšť* (*Waiting for the Rain*)
1979   *Láska mezi kapkami deště* (*Love Between the Raindrops*)
1980   *Cukrová bouda* (*Sugar Cottage. The Little Sugar House*)
1981   *Pozor vizita!* (*Watch Out, The Rounds!*)
1982   *Fandy, ó Fandy* (*Fandy, Oh Fandy*)
1983   *Sestricky* (*Nurses*)

1985   *Dobré svetlo* (*Good Light*)
1986   *Smrt krásnych srncu* (*Death of a Beautiful Dream*)
1987   *Kam pánové, kam jdete?* (*And What Now, Gentlemen?*)
1988   *Oznamuje se láskam vasim* (*Let It Be Known to All Your Loves*)
1989   *Blázni a devcátka* (*Young Girls, Crazy Guys*)
1990   *The Last Butterfly*

Other Film:

1952   *Věda jde s lidem* (*Science Goes with People*)

Publications:

By KACHYNA: articles—

Interview with E. Hepnerová, in *Film a Doba* (Prague), February 1976.
Interview in *Film a Doba* (Prague), January 1982.
Interview with L. Hofmanova, in *Film a Doba* (Prague), November 1986.

On KACHYNA: books—

Bocek, Jaroslav, *Modern Czechoslovak Film 1945–65*, Prague, 1965.
Bartoskovi, Sárka and Lubos, *Filmové profily*, Prague, 1966.
Liehm, Antonin, *Closely Watched Films*, New York, 1974.
CSF—Czechoslovak Cinema, Czechoslovak Film Institute, Prague, 1982.
Hames, Peter, *The Czechoslovak New Wave*, Berkeley, 1985.

On KACHYNA: articles—

Melounek, P., in *Film a Doba* (Prague), May 1984.

*   *   *

Karel Kachyňa is an artist with a broad range of ideas which constitute the starting point for his thinking in images. Despite their formal variety, his works bear an individual creative stamp characterized by a play of poetic images precisely tailored to the dramatic structure of the story. Like any original artist who continuously seeks new paths of self-expression, Kachyňa has brief periods which seem to be at odds with the rest of his work. These are the exceptions, the experiments, the preparations for great artistic work to come.

At first it seemed that Kachyňa's main calling would be making documentary films. He has gone beyond these; they served as a point of departure for his dramatic films. His first creative period is characterized by innovatively-conceived documentaries which not only captured the facts but also expressed the view of the filmmaker. His attempts to combine elements of fantasy, story, and style led him to the dramatic film, where he concentrated on films of wartime adventure and suspense. In so doing he did not forget what he had learned in making documentaries: to capture reality and transform it into a new artistic image in a carefully conceived story. The culmination of this period is *Král Sumavy* (*The King of the Sumava*).

Gradually other elements asserted themselves in his films: detailed psychological characterization and a precise portrayal of relationships against the backdrop of a given historical situation. Since he was never an independent writer of his own films, he was able to detach himself from the given material and consider it from a unique viewpoint. He was most interested in the contradiction-fraught relationships of people taking their first steps into adulthood, or the world of children on the verge of some kind of awakening, a discovery of life in the brief interval in which reality stimulates the world of thoughts, dreams, and memories and becomes itself only a framework for a profound catharisis of feelings: *Trápeni* (*Stress of Youth*), *Závral* (*Vertigo*), *Už zase skáču přes kaluže* (*Jumping the Puddles Again*), *Smrt mouchy* (*Death of a Fly*), and others. His films are first and foremost images interspersed with brief dialogue, where small details, objects, and nature come to life. He directs his actors, be they amateurs or professionals, in a way that enables them to live the roles they play, to create the truth of life, to shape and express their own feelings and views. His tendency to create intimate dramas, however, leads to formal refinement in which an objective view of reality is often lost.

Kachyňa has been served by several literary works which were sensitively adapted for the screen. But the foundation of his work remains the cinematic poem of feelings, for example *Pavlinka, Robinsonka*, or *Skaredá dědina* (*The Ugly Village*). "I like drawing-room stories set in an atmosphere of feelings, where the leading role is played by image, music, and often by what cannot even be expressed, that which is a part of our lives but is not concrete and cannot even be described. Apprehensions, hopes, dreams, someone's touch . . . I would always like to have these things in my films. I think they are an essential part of the truth of life. And this truth is what film is mainly about. A film will never be a work of art unless it mirrors that truth, however subtly it may strive in other ways to express the most sublime thought," said Karel Kachyňa in one conversation. And it is this credo that he strives strictly to uphold in his own films. After a lengthy period in which he focused on the world of children at the threshold of adulthood, he has turned in his more recent works to an adult milieu.

—Vacláv Merhaut

KADÁR, Ján.

Czechoslovak. Born in Budapest, 1 April 1918. Gave up law studies to study photography at Bratislava school, 1938. Prisoner in Nazi labor camp, early 1940's; after war, producer and director, Bratislava Studio of Short Films; scriptwriter and assistant director, Barrandov Studio, Prague, from 1947; began association with Elmar Klos (born in Brno, 26 January 1910), 1952; moved to U.S., 1969. Recipient: Oscar for Best Foreign Language Film, for *The Shop on Main Street*, 1965; National Artist of Czechoslovakia, 1969. *Died in Los Angeles, 1 June 1979.*

Films as Director:

1945   *Life is Rising from the Ruins*
1950   *Katka* (*Kitty*) (+ co-sc)
1952   *Unos* (*Kidnapped*) (co-d, co-sc with Elmar Klos)
1954   *Hudba z Marsu* (*Music from Mars*) (co-d, co-sc with Klos)
1957   *Tam na konečné* (*The House at the Terminus*) (co-d with Klos)

1958   *Tři přání* (*Three Wishes*) (co-d, co-sc with Klos)
1963   *Smrt si řiká Engelchen* (*Death Is Called Engelchen*) (co-d, co-sc with Klos)
1964   *Obžalovaný* (*The Accused. The Defendant*) (co-d, co-sc with Klos)
1965   **Obchod na korze (The Shop on Main Street. The Shop on the High Street)** (co-d, co-sc with Klos)
1970   *The Angel Levine*
1971   *Touha zvaná Anada* (*Adrift. Something Is Drifting on the Water*) (completed 1969) (co-d with Klos)
1975   *Lies My Father Told Me*
1978   *Freedom Road*

Other Films:

1947   *Nevité o bytě?* (*Looking for a Flat*) (sc)

Publications:

By KADÁR: articles—

"Elmar Klos and Jan Kadar," interview with Jules Cohen, in *Film Culture* (New York), Fall/Winter 1967.
Interview with Robert Haller, in *Film Heritage* (Dayton, Ohio), Spring 1973.
Interview with L. Vigo, in *Image et Son* (Paris), June 1973.

On KADÁR: books—

Bocek, Jaroslav, *Modern Czechoslovak Film 1945–1965*, Prague, 1965.
Liehm, Antonin, *Closely Watched Films*, White Plains, Prague, 1974.
Hames, Peter, *The Czechoslovak New Wave*, Berkeley, 1985.

On KADÁR: articles—

"Director," in the *New Yorker*, 12 February 1966.
"The Czech Who Bounced Back," in *Films Illustrated* (London), April 1972.
Obituary, in *New York Times*, 4 June 1979.
Moret, H., obituary in *Ecran* (Paris), 15 July 1979.
Gervais, G., obituary in *Jeune Cinéma* (Paris), July/August 1979.
Keenan, Richard C., "The Sense of an Ending: Jan Kadár's Distortion of Stephen Crane's *The Blue Hotel*," in *Literature/Film Quarterly* (Salisbury, Maryland), vol. 16, no. 4, 1988.

*   *   *

Ján Kadár is undoubtedly best known for his film *The Shop on the High Street*, made with his long time collaborator Elmar Klos. This was the first Czechoslovak film to win an Oscar, and was heralded as signalling the beginnings of the Czech film renaissance of the 1960s. In fact, Kadár made his first feature, *Katka*, in 1950, and Klos was one of those who helped to draw up the plans for the nationalisation of the film industry in that decade. This, of course, was a mixed blessing, as Kadár himself pointed out: "to innovative filmmakers this was a dream—it would liberate them from commercial pressures. Instead, there was political pressure. This was the disadvantage of subsidised art."

Katka itself ran into political difficulties. Made in Kadár's native Slovakia it was the story of a village girl who becomes a factory worker. However, as the director points out, at about this time "it had been decided that it was no longer necessary to urge people to leave their homes for industry. But above all, the film wasn't 'national' enough, it wasn't sufficiently steeped in folklore and Slovakism. And that was referred to as 'the bourgeois point of view.'" Expelled from the Slovak film industry, Kadár "became Czech" and began his partnership with Klos. Their first collaboration was *Kidnapped* which Kadár later described as "an extremely naive, dogmatic, cold-war type of film" but which was nonetheless criticised at the time for "bourgeois objectivism." Saved by the intervention of V. I. Pudovkin they went on to make *Music From Mars*, a mus-

Ján Kadár: *Lies My Father Told Me*

ical satire on bureaucracy, which gave rise to complaints that they had slandered public figures.

Their next film steered clear of trouble. This was *House at the Terminus*, which posed the question: is it right to bring children into the world in its present state? Given the country's low and falling birth rate this was more than simply a philosophical question. By avoiding explicitly "public" problems and issues and concentrating instead on the private sphere the film managed to avoid censure for drawing what is surely a rather depressing picture of Czech society. Peter Hames in *The Czechoslovak New Wave* speaks of its air of "gloomy desolation" and remarks that although "there is little overt political criticism, the implicit criticism is considerable, and the problems with which it deals take place in a social context. Hence loneliness, cynicism, personal and professional failure, compromise, wrongful imprisonment, and lack of faith are shown as generalised characteristics of a supposedly socialist society," one in which, that is, such problems have supposedly been eliminated.

Three Wishes, a modern version of the old fairy tale in which a character is granted his heart's desire, only to find that the dream turns sour, was banned until 1963 (that is, once the process of de-Stalinization had got under way). Again, the problem seems to have been that it painted a less than ideal view of society, since it shows the central character realising his wishes by exploiting the corruption and hypocrisy which he finds around him in society at large.

After this, Kadár and Klos were unable to work again for two years, but during the ensuing period of thaw they produced their most famous work, *The Shop on the High Street*. This is set in Slovakia during the period of the independent fascist state, described by one Czechoslovak critic as "a gruesomely grotesque miniature of the apocalypse of the Third Reich" and by Klos as representing "a special kind of national fascism." The story concerns an old, deaf Jewish woman and her relationship with the Slovak who is assigned to her shop as an "Aryan controller." An extremely effective picture of everyday fascism in an ordinary small community, the film may revolve around a grim and tragic theme but it is actually played largely as a gentle comedy. Kadár once claimed that his favourite directors were Chaplin, Truffaut and Fellini, and their presences can all be felt here in the quirky, offbeat humour, the mingling of the comic and tragic, and the gentle observation of its characters' failures and all-too-human shortcomings. One is also, of course, put in mind of the early works of Passer, Forman and Menzel. Like the old lady at the centre of the film

Kadár was himself Jewish, and although by his own account he himself never encountered anti-Semitism personally, *The Shop* later attracted charges of Zionism from certain quarters, particularly after Kadár's departure for the States.

With the end of the "Prague Spring" Kadár left Czechoslovakia for Vienna and from there went to America. At the time of the invasion he and Klos were working on a Czech-American co-production entitled *Adrift*, which was made in collaboration with the Hungarian writer Imre Gyöngyössy, who later went on to become a director himself. On his arrival in the States Kadár was fortunate enough to be offered the direction of *The Angel Levine* from a Bernard Malamud story. He then returned to Czechoslovakia to complete *Adrift* (a rather untypical film, clearly influenced by Resnais and Robbe-Grillet, about a girl who may or may not have been saved from drowning in the Danube), before leaving for good in 1971.

In the States and Canada (where he also found work) the Jewish theme in his films clearly came to the fore—hence *The Angel Levine, Lies My Father Told Me* and *Mendelstam's Witness*. Other works which must surely have had a strong personal resonance for the director were the TV movies *The Case Against Milligan*, which examines the theme of freedom of conscience, and *The Other Side of Hell* which looks at the plight of the sane person in an insane society. And while none of his later films attain the level of *The Shop on the High Street* they nonetheless attest to the warmth and generosity of spirit which is the hallmark of Kadár's best and most typical work.

—Julian Petley.

KAPOOR, Raj.

Indian. Born Ranbirraj Kapoor in Peshwar (now in Pakistan), 14 December 1942. Educated in Calcutta and Bombay. Married Krishna (Kapoor), three sons, two daughters. Entered film industry as clapper boy, late 1930's; assistant on Bombay Talkies, then production manager, art director, and actor, Prithvi Theatres, early 1940's; first leading role, in *Neel Kamal*, 1947; directed first film, *Aag*, 1948. Recipient: Filmfare Award for Best Director, for *My Name is Joker*, 1970. *Died, of complications from asthma attack, in New Delhi, 2 June 1988.*

Films as Director:

1948 *Aag (Fire)* (+ pr, role)
1949 *Barsaat* (+ role)
1951 ***Awara (The Vagabond)*** (+ role)
1955 *Shri 420 (Mister 420)* (+ role)
1964 *Sangam* (+ role, pr)
1970 *Mera Naam Joker (My Name is Joker)* (+ role, pr)
1974 *Bobby* (+ pr)
1978 *Satyam Shivam Sundaram* (+ pr)
1982 *Prem Rog* (+ pr)

Other Films:

1935 *Inquilab* (role)
1943 *Hamari Baat* (role); *Gowri* (role)
1946 *Valmiki* (role)
1947 *Neel Kamal* (role); *Chithod Vijay* (role); *Jail Yaatra* (role); *Dil Ki Raani* (role)

1948 *Gopinath* (role)
1949 *Andaz* (role); *Parivartan* (role); *Sunehere Din* (role)
1950 *Banwara* (role); *Banware Nayan* (role); *Dastaan* (role); *Jaan Pehchan* (role); *Pyaar* (role); *Sargam* (role)
1952 *Ambar* (role); *Anhonee* (role); *Aashiyana*; (role); *Bewafa* (role)
1953 *Dhoon* (role); *Paapi* (role); *Aah* (pr, role)
1954 *Boot Polish* (pr)
1956 *Jagte Raho* (pr, role); *Chori Chori* (role)
1957 *Ab Dilli Dur Nahin* (pr)
1958 *Sharada* (role); *Parvarish* (role); *Phir Subah Hogi* (role)
1959 *Anadi* (role); *Char Dil Char Rahen* (role); *Do Ustad* (role); *Kanhaiya* (role); *Main Nashe Me Hoon* (role)
1960 *Jis Desh Me Ganga Behti Hai (Where the Ganges Flows)* (pr, role); *Chaliya* (role); *Shriman Satyavadi* (role)
1961 *Nazraana* (role)
1962 *Aashik* (role)
1963 *Dil Hi To Hai* (role); *Ek Dil Sou Afsane* (role)
1964 *Dulha Dulhan* (role)
1966 *Teesri Kasam* (role)
1967 *Around the World* (role); *Diwana* (role)
1968 *Sapnon Ka Saudgar* (role)
1972 *Kal, Aaj Aur Kal* (pr, role)
1975 *Dhadram Karam* (pr); *Do Jasoos* (role)
1976 *Khaan Dost* (role)
1977 *Chandi Sona* (role)
1981 *Biwi O Biwi* (pr); *Abdullah* (role)
1982 *Gopichand Jasoos* (role)

Publications:

On KAPOOR: books—

Barnouw, Erik, and S. Krishnaswamy, *Indian Film*, New York, 1965.
Sarkar, Kobita, *The Indian Cinema Today*, New Delhi, 1975.
Abbas, Ahmad, *I Am Not An Island: An Experiment in Autobiography*, New Delhi, 1977.
Burra, Rani, editor, *Looking Back 1896–1960*, New Delhi, 1981.
Willemen, Paul, and Behroze Gandhy, *Indian Cinema*, London, 1982.
Ramachandran, T.M., *70 Years of Indian Cinema (1913–1983)*, Bombay, 1985.
Dissanayake, Wimal, and Malti Sahai, *Raj Kapoor's Films: Harmony of Discourses*, New Delhi, 1987.
Reuben, Bunny, *Raj Kapoor, The Fabulous Showman: An Intimate Biography*, Bombay, 1988.

On KAPOOR: articles—

"Special Issue" of *Film Français* (Paris), Spring 1953.
Tesson, C., "Le Rêve indien," in *Cahiers du Cinéma* (Paris), March 1985.
Thomas, R., "Indian Cinema: pleasures and Popularity," in *Screen* (London), May/August 1985.
Hollywood Reporter, November 1985.
Obituary in *Variety* (New York), 8 June 1988.

*   *   *

Raj Kapoor was the best-known screen personality in India. He acted major roles in over 50 films, produced more than a dozen films, and, during the course of a 35-year career directed six of the most popular films of the Hindi cinema. (*Awara, Shri 420, Sangam, Mera Nam Joker, Bobby,* and *Satyam Shivam Sundaram*). The popularity of Raj Kapoor's work derives from a paradoxical achievement: he intensified in his films both the lavishness and the social consciousness of the Hindi cinema. His films are characterized by elaborate sets, evocative music, new stars, dramatic confrontations and narrow escapes from heartbreak. At the same time he introduced into his films the themes of poverty and injustice, and the plight of individuals insisting on their own way against the massive force of social conventions. Indian audiences responded enthusiastically to Raj Kapoor's mixture of entertainment and concern; it is clear that his films articulate at some level the longings of an entire people.

Raj Kapoor in *Shri 420*

Raj Kapoor's first film *Aag* is restrained by smallness of scale; the set is modest and the fiery character of the emotional triangle in the story is rendered chiefly through high-contrast lighting. But his third and fourth films (*Awara* and *Shri 420*) disclose a fully operatic style. In *Awara*, the key court scene is played in a deep, amply lit hall; and in both *Awara* and *Shri 420*, the houses of the rich are magnificently spacious, fitted with winding stairs, high ceilings and tall, curtained windows. For music, Raj Kapoor employed the lyricist Shailendra and the composers Shankar-Jaikishen, who specialized in brightening up traditional melodies; a number of their songs for Raj Kapoor (*Awara Hun*, *Mera Joota Hai Japani*) are among the songs which run through the heads of most people in India. Raj Kapoor also delights in soaring camera movements, as over the courtroom in *Awara* and under the circus tent in *Mera Nam Joker*. The speed and freedom of the camera contributes to the audience's sense of dynamic onward progress in Raj Kapoor's films.

Raj Kapoor's films deal with important cultural experiences: *Shri 420* is concerned with the ruthlessness which confronts new migrants to the city; *Awara* with the malign influence of slum environments; *Sangam*, *Bobby* and *Satyam Shivam Sundaram* with tensions between spontaneous affection and the social protocols for intimacy; and *Mera Nam Joker* presents the loneliness of a circus clown as an archetype for people who have been uprooted. Both plot and music invite viewers to identify with the experience of unfortunate protagonists. Meanwhile the mise-en-scène directs the attention of viewers to the furnishings of rich houses (*Shri 420* and *Awara*), to the mountain spectacle of various Himalayan resorts (*Bobby*), to a spacious temple courtyard and a daringly costumed dancer (*Satyam Shivam Sundaram*) and to entire acts of the Soviet State Circus (*Mera Nam Joker*).

Since the time of Raj Kapoor's first films, filmmaking in India has moved towards greater generic variety and coherence. From the perspective of the new political films, Raj Kapoor's productions seem complacent; from the perspective of the new realist films, his work seems gaudy. Nonetheless, his work is certain to be remembered for its spectacular vitality.

—Satti Khanna

KASDAN, Lawrence.

American. Born in Miami Beach, Florida, 14 January 1949. Educated at University of Michigan, B.A., 1970, M.A. (Education), 1972. Married Meg Goldman, 1971, two sons. Advertising copywriter, Detroit, 1972–75, and Los Angeles, 1975–77; screenwriter, from 1977; directed first film, *Body Heat*, 1981. Recipient: Directors Guild of America Award, for *The Big Chill*, 1983. Address: c/o Kasdan Productions, 4117 Radford Avenue, Studio City, CA 91604.

Films as Director:

1981   *Body Heat* (+ sc)
1983   *The Big Chill* (+ exec pr, sc)
1985   *Silverado* (+ pr, co-sc)
1988   *The Accidental Tourist*
1989   *I Love You to Death*

Other Films:

1980   *The Empire Strikes Back* (co-sc)
1981   *Raiders of the Lost Ark* (co-sc); *Continental Divide*
1983   *Return of the Jedi* (co-sc)

Publications:

By KASDAN: books—

The Empire Strikes Back Notebook, edited by Diane Attias and Lindsay Smith, New York, 1980.
The Art of Return of the Jedi, with George Lucas, New York, 1983.
The Big Chill, with Barbara Benedek, New York, 1987.

By KASDAN: articles—

Interview in *Film Comment* (New York), September/October 1981.
Interview with Minty Clinch, in *Films* (London), March 1982.
"Dialogue on Film: Lawrence Kasdan," in *American Film* (Washington, D.C.), April 1982.
Interview with P.H. Broeske, in *Films in Review* (New York), April 1984.
Interview with A. Garel and others, in *Revue du Cinéma* (Paris), December 1985.
Interview in *American Film* (Washington, D.C.), January/February 1989.

On KASDAN: articles—

"Lawrence Kasdan," in *Film Dope* (London), March 1984.

*   *   *

On the basis of relatively few films, Lawrence Kasdan has had a prestigious career as screen writer and director, though one that is difficult to characterize easily. His early work is notable for toying humorously with established genres like the action-adventure serial, film noir and the Western without ever going all the way into parody. That is, he was able to convey a certain "hip" sensibility without neglecting an appeal to some viewers' nostalgia for the past and a great many more viewers' craving for good storytelling. His very 1980s approach to older movie genres worked splendidly in *Raiders of the Lost Ark* (written, not directed, under the Lucas-Spielberg aegis) and the hypersultry *Body Heat*, but was less successful in *Silverado*, a kind of postmodern Western, which lacked a consistently graspable tone and effective narrative pacing. (Though the complicated plot makes sense in outline, some of the subplots don't seem to exist in the same narrative world, like those of the struggling black family, presented heavy-handedly, and the preposterous romantic implications of the Kevin Kline-Linda Hunt relationship.)

Kasdan's less classifiable dramas have some of the same quirky humor as the genre pieces. *The Big Chill*, his most controversial film to date, was variously loved or hated for its sympathetic yet satirical portrayal of the ego crises of a spectrum of 1960s activists finding themselves in the doldrums of the early 1980s. By the standards of classical Hollywood storytelling, *The Big Chill* is pleasingly loose, though theatrical, in structure, with its assembly of former friends in close encounters during a long weekend; but it seemed to some viewers contrived and slick in comparison to the more low-key, low-budget film by John Sayles on the same subject, *The Return of the Secaucus 7*. *The Accidental Tourist*, Kasdan's first effort in

adapting a literary text, also drew mixed reactions, but this time over its success or failure in adapting a highly regarded novel, and over William Hurt's extremely subdued performance. Kasdan's 1990 effort, *I Love You to Death*, is not much like any of the earlier films, falling into a comedy subgenre involving farcically unsuccessful efforts at murder. Some viewers found the black comedy insufficiently black or comical; certainly, one finds less of the cool, sly humor of the earlier films.

Kasdan may eventually be remembered as a starmaker. *Body Heat* introduced Kathleen Turner and the sultry persona she continues to use; it offered Mickey Rourke a memorable supporting role; and it made William Hurt a new kind of leading man, with a distinctively 1980s manner, even when playing a 1940s-style victim of a femme fatale, or later in *The Big Chill* an erstwhile hippie. *The Big Chill* boosted the careers of Glenn Close, Kevin Kline and Meg Tilly, as *Silverado* did that of Kevin Costner and *The Accidental Tourist* that of Geena Davis. At the same time as promoting individual talents, Kasdan seems particularly skilled in directing ensemble acting, especially in *The Big Chill* and the more recent films. Indeed, the glimpses of eccentric family life in *The Accidental Tourist* and the joint murder efforts in *I Love You to Death* may be those films' best scenes.

Kasdan's visual style from film to film may be more difficult to characterize than his handling of dialogue and actors, though one may note consistently fluid camera movements and a determination to give each film a distinctive look and mood, while keeping a number of the same technical personnel. One remembers the blues, whites and shadows of a sweltering Florida in *Body Heat*; the autumnal glow of *The Big Chill*; the conventional but still handsome Techniscope vistas of *Silverado*; and the pale colors and vacant widescreen spaces of *The Accidental Tourist*.

Kasdan's first film may in the future still be seen as his best work of the 1980s. The derivativeness of *Body Heat*'s plot is offset by its gentle, knowing allusions to a *film noir* past, and its dialogue remains snappy, its moments of suspense are ingeniously handled, and its joy is great in its outrageously blatant atmosphere of an erotic/violent steamy Florida where only the most primitive air conditioners seem to have been invented. Whether he can continue to find a voice for himself, avoiding being labeled a genre manipulator or spokesperson for ageing baby-boomers, remains to be seen.

—Joseph Milicia

KAUL, Mani.

Indian. Born 25 December 1942 in Jodhpur, near Rajasthan. Educated at Rajasthan College, until 1963; studied under Ritwik Ghatak at Film and Television Institute (FTII) at Poona, late 1960's. With support from Indian Film Finance Corp., made first film, *Uski Roti*, 1969; first exhibition as a painter, 1975; later set up film co-op in Bombay; currently teacher at FTII, Poona.

Films as Director:

1969   *Uski Roti* (*A Day's Bread*)
1971   *Ashad Ka Ek Din* (*A Monsoon Day*)
1973   *Duvidha* (*In Two Minds*)

1980 *Satah Se Uthata Aadmi* (*Rising From the Surface*)
1984 *Dhrupad*
1986 *Mati Manas* (*The Mind of Clay*)

Publications:

By KAUL: articles—

Interview in *Film World*, September 1972.
Interview in *Cinéma* (Paris), September/October 1975.
Article in *India National Centre Quarterly*, March 1981.
Interview with C. Biarese, in *Segnocinema* (Vicenza), September 1985.

On KAUL: books—

da Cunha, Uma, editor, *The New Generation, 1960–80: An Examination of India's New Cinema*, New Delhi, 1981.
Willemen, Paul, and Behroze Ghandy, *Indian Cinema*, London, 1982.
Ramachandran, T.M., editor, *70 Years of Indian Cinema (1913–1983)*, Bombay, 1985.

On KAUL: articles—

Anand, M.S., "Mani Kaul," in *Skrien* (Amsterdam), February 1982.
Piel, J.-L., "Mani Kaul," in *Cinématographe* (Paris), April 1982.

* * *

Mani Kaul graduated from the Film and Television Institute of India in the late 1960s and he and Kumar Shahani were the first of its young directors to announce a distinctively new approach to film form and narrative. Both directors acknowledged the influence of European modernism, especially of Robert Bresson (Kaul also refers to Jancsó and Tarkovsky), but both seek to recover a tradition of indigenous aesthetics which they believe has been submerged by the colonial experience. The work of the Marxist historian, Damodar Kosambi, on ancient Indian society, was particularly important for them, as was the film-making of the Bengali director Ritwik Ghatak, who also taught the two at the Film Institute.

This project—the recovery (or rather, the re-invention) of the indigenous, but within an unparochial dialogue with the counter-cultural modernism of the west—places both directors within the tradition of a post-colonial "Third" cinema. Original as some of their work has been, their impact has been remarkably negligible. In contrast the films of their contemporary, Adoor Gopalakrishnan, have maintained a certain narrative accessibility, while fully exhibiting a modernist awareness of film's formal qualities. As a result, unlike Kaul and Shahani, Adoor has gained commercial release for his films in his native state, Kerala.

Perhaps the difference lies in the level of abstraction Kaul and Shahani work at. One aspect of this is Kaul's use of the kind of deadpan mode of dialogue delivery familiar from Bresson. This is related to the fact that *Uski Roti* (*A Day's Bread*), *Ashad Ka Ek Din* (*A Monsoon Day*), *Duvidha* (*In Two Minds*), and *Satah Se Uthata Aadmi* (*Rising From the Surface*), all come from literary sources, and the recitative mode is used to emphasise this. The voices suggest, matter-of-factly, an archaeology of the text, the way in which the filmic text is layered over the already existing literary one.

More distinctively, Kaul uses a spatially disjointed storytelling mode, whose peculiarities can be observed at the beginning of *Duvidha*, when we watch a newly married couple being taken to the husband's house on a bullock cart. The narrative space is broken up into the spaces occupied by the man and woman in the cart, and a natural space outside from which the voices of the cart drivers also filter through. At one stage the woman briefly moves into this other space, to eat some wild fruit. A system of shots tied to gendered spaces is inaugurated, and such a division is not smoothed over by continuity shots, of glance off-screen and shot-reverse-shot. Angles are not

returned to, and sometimes the distance of the camera from the character's body may be disconcertingly short. Sound is used in a minimalist way, sometimes with a repetitive, chorus-like effect. This use of sound was something which Ghatak, the mentor of the avant-garde, employed to remarkable effect in his very first film, *Nagarik* (*Citizen*, 1950), but in a much lusher, less self-conscious way.

The mode is abstract because it withholds perspective, pressing the spectator's look to the concrete detail. In *Duvidha*, the style filmically materialises sexual difference, and relates it dynamically with an idealised folk space. Discourses of female desire are opposed to male worldliness and calculation, differences which are brought in line with a series of textures: of fabric, colour, wild fruit, the off-screen voices of the bullock cart-drivers. Later in the film, stills interrupt the flow of the narration, to alienate the spectator certainly, but in a particular way; so as to underline the almost anthropological, folkloristic status of the camera in relation to the story. This is a mode which may well be Mani Kaul's characteristic way of handling his materials.

—Ravi Vasudevan

KÄUTNER, Helmut.

German. Born Düsseldorf, 1908. Educated at Munich University and at Munich Art School, studying poster design, graphics and interior design. Married actress/director Erica Balqué, 1934. Writer and director for Munich Student Cabaret, "Die vier Nachrichter," 1931–35; stage actor and director, in Germany, Austria and Switzerland, from 1936; founder, with Wolfgang Staudte and Harald Braun, of production company Camera-Filmproduktion (later Freie Filmproduktion); later director, actor, and designer for TV. *Died 1980.*

Films as Director:

1939 *Kitty und die Weltkonferenz* (+ sc, lyrics)
1940 *Frau nach Mass* (+ sc); *Kleider machen Leute* (+ sc)
1941 *Auf Wiedersehen, Franziska!* (+ co-sc)
1942 *Anuschka* (+ adapt); *Wir machen Musik* (+ sc, lyrics)
1943 *Romanze in Moll* (+ co-sc, role)
1944 *Grosse Freiheit Nr. 7* (+ co-sc, lyrics, role)
1945 *Unter den Brücken* (+ co-sc)
1947 *In jenen Tagen* (+ co-sc, role)
1948 *Der Apfel ist ab* (+ co-sc, role)
1949 *Königskinder* (+ co-sc, role)
1950 *Epilog* (*Das Geheimnis der Orplid*) (+ co-sc, role)
1951 *Weisse Schatten* (+ co-sc)
1953 *Käpt'n Bay-Bay* (+ co-sc)
1954 *Die letzte Brücke* (+ co-sc, role); *Bildnis einer Unbekannten* (+ co-sc); *Ludwig II—Glanz und Elend eines Königs*
1955 *Des Teufels General* (+ co-sc, role); *Himmel ohne Sterne* (+ sc)
1956 *Ein Mädchen aus Flandern* (+ co-sc, role); *Der Hauptmann von Köpenick* (+ co-sc, role)
1957 *Die Zürcher Verlobung* (+ co-sc, lyrics, role); *Montpi* (+ sc, role)
1958 *The Restless Years* (*The Wonderful Years*); *A Stranger in My Arms*; *Der Schinderhannes* (+ role)
1959 *Der Rest ist Schweigen* (+ co-sc, co-pr, role); *Die Gans von Sedan* (*Sans tambour ni trompette*) (+ co-sc, role)
1960 *Das Glas Wasser* (+ sc, lyrics)
1961 *Scwarzer Kies* (+ co-sc); *Der Traum von Lieschen Müller* (*Happy-End im siebten Himmel*) (+ co-sc, lyrics)

Helmut Käutner (right) with cameraman Kurt Hasse

1962   *Die Rote* (*La Rossa*) (+ sc)
1963   *Das Haus in Montevideo* (+ sc)
1964   *Lausbubengeschichten*
1970   *Die Feuerzangenbowle*

Other Films:

1932   *Kreuzer Emden* (Ralph) (role)
1939   *Schneider Wibbel* (de Kowa) (co-sc); *Salonwagen E 417*
       (Verhoeven) (co-sc); *Die Stimme aus dem Äther* (Paulsen)
       (co-sc); *Marguerite: 3—Eine Frau für Drei* (Lingen) (co-sc)
1947   *Film ohne Titel* (Jugert) (co-sc)
1951   *Nachts auf den Strassen* (Jugert) (co-sc)
1955   *Griff nach den Sternen* (Schroth) (co-sc)
1957   *Franziska* (*Auf Wiedersehen, Franziska*) (Liebeneiner) (co-sc)
1961   *Zu jung für die Liebe*? (Erica Balqué) (co-sc, role)
1972   *Versuchung in Sommerwind* (Thiele) (role)
1974   *Karl May* (Syberberg) (title role)

Publications:

By KÄUTNER: books—

Von der Filmidee zum Drehbuch, with Béla Balázs and others, 1949.
Abblenden, Munich, 1981.

On KÄUTNER: books—

Koschnitzki, Rudiger, *Filmographie Helmut Käutner*, Wiesbaden, 1978.

Gillett, John, *18 Films by Helmut Käutner*, Goethe Institute, London, 1980.

On KÄUTNER: articles—

Cahiers du Cinéma (Paris), July 1957.
Obituary in *Filme* (Paris), no. 4, 1980.
Obituary in *Screen International* (London), 19 April 1980.
Obituary in *Cinéma* (Paris), June 1980.
Gillett, John, "Helmut Käutner," in *Film Dope* (London), March 1984.

On KÄUTNER: films—

Harmsen, Henning, *Erlebte Filmgeschichte Helmut Käutner*, for German TV, 1975.
von Troschke, Harald, *Im Gespräch porträtiert: Helmut Käutner*, for German TV, 1978.

*　　*　　*

Along with Forst and Sirk, Käutner was one of the great stylists of the cinema of the Third Reich. Admittedly the competition was extremely thin but this in no way belittles the achievement of the director, whose best work stands comparison with Ophüls and is rooted in the same rich vein of Austro-German romanticism. In particular one notices the same concern with the passing of an era, an elegance bordering on dandyism, and what Louis Marcorelles has called "a subtle perfume of death and decadence." As John Gillett puts it in the catalogue produced to accompany a pioneering season of Käutner's films at

London's Goethe Institute, the work of Käutner, Ophüls and Forst "consolidated a film-making genre notable for its attention to period detail, its elaborate costuming and art direction, and for directorial styles which used the mobile camera to achieve a uniquely filmic musical structure and rhythm."

Käutner entered cinema as a scriptwriter in 1938 (although he had appeared in a small role in Louis Ralph's *Kreuzer Emden* in 1932) having studied architecture, philosophy, theatre and art history, worked in cabaret in Munich as both writer and performer from 1931 to 1935, and gone into "straight" theatre in 1936. Some of his more caustic cabaret sketches had annoyed the Nazis, and as he noted, "I was not really interested in the cinema. Politically I was left-wing and that meant that I was disinterested in the cinema which, since Hugenberg, had been moving in a right-wing, nationalistic direction. I really wanted to go on working in the theatre, and I had very clear-cut ideas about the theatre—others would have called it cabaret."

His first film, *Kitty und die Weltkonferenz*, a light, frothy comedy, evoked comparisons with Lubitsch but its favourable portrait of a British minister and slightly satirical view of relations between Italy and Germany incurred Goebbels' displeasure and the film vanished from view. His next film, an adaptation of Keller's novella *Kleider Machen Leute*, in which a humble tailor finds himself mistaken for a Russian prince, could certainly be read as, beneath its apparent retreat into Biedermeyer mannerism, an allegory about Germans' exaggerated respect for figures of power and authority and their consequent readiness to fall under the Nazi spell. However, this doesn't seem to have occurred to the authorities. The film has a lightness of touch and a feeling for fantasy that anticipates both Minnelli and Cocteau, and is distinguished by some marvellous swirling camerawork in the musical scenes. On the whole Käutner avoided contemporary subjects during his Third Reich period, an exception being *Auf Wiedersehen, Franziska* which deals with the strains in a newsreel reporter's marriage caused by his numerous absences. The authorities insisted on an upbeat, flag-waving ending quite out of key with the film's poignant, carefully nuanced atmosphere and, like Sirk in *Stutzen der Gesellschaft*, Käutner deliberately makes the whole thing stand out a mile. The film is also distinguished by a marvellous performance by Marianne Hoppe.

Käutner's masterpiece is undoubtedly *Romanze in Moll*, a highly Ophülsian adaptation of Maupassant's *Les Bijoux*. Maupassant's dark vision of life did not endear him to the literary authorities in the Reich and this film, though not banned, was condemned in some quarters as "defeatist" and "destructive of marriage and morals." Käutner himself acts in the film, playing the part of a resigned, world-weary poet, a role which, his films suggest, was close to his own in real life. As Francis Courtade and Pierre Cadars put it in their excellent *Histoire du Cinéma Nazi*, "Everything centres on the almost palpable recreation of this fin-de-siécle milieu in which a woman, condemned to death by her surroundings, suffers. Composition, framing, camera movement, editing, sound, remain, from start to finish, crystal clear. . . . Like Claude Autant-Lara, Käutner is fanatical over details. His direction of actors is magisterial. . . . The overall result is an exemplary reconstruction of the style and atmosphere of the original story, and one of the two or three most faithful adaptations of Maupassant."

In spite of his difficulties with the authorities, Käutner was entrusted with an expensive and elaborate Agfacolor project in the latter days of the Reich. This was *Grosse Freiheit Nr. 7*, a melancholy, bitter-sweet story of disappointed love set amongst the sailors' clubs and bars of the Hamburg waterfront, with clear overtones of Carné, Clair and in particular (through the presence of Hans Albers of *Blue Angel* fame) Von Stern-

berg. Apart from difficulties caused by bombing, Käutner also had to cope with Goebbels' request that the film include shots of the harbour with ships flying the Nazi flag. His response was to make copious use of artificial fog in the panoramic long shots. When the film was released Admiral Dönitz complained that the film's representation of German sailors visiting prostitutes and drinking was damaging to the reputation of Germany in general and Hamburg in particular and the film was banned.

Käutner's last Third Reich film, and one of his best, was *Unter den Brücken* which is set amongst the bargees of the River Havel and, like its predecessor, shows the clear influence of French pre-war "poetic realism": in particular there are distinct overtones of *L'Atalante*. At one time thought to be a "lost" film, *Unter den Brücken* finally turned up and revealed itself to be, in the words of the *Süddeutsche Zeitung* "a subtle depiction of a private world, half-tones full of melancholy and a quiet sublimination of the free life . . . a story told with great sensitivity which, softly but insistently, counteracts the grimness of contemporary reality with the longing for private happiness and the right to a non-regimented self-realisation."

Käutner's post-war films never reached the heights of his best work in the Third Reich, though some of them are not without interest. The main problem seems to have been a rather ill-advised turn towards social realism and "problem" subjects in films such as *In Jenen Tagen, Die Letzte Brücke, Himmel Ohne Sterne* and *Schwarzer Kies* which simply didn't suit his artistic temperament. In *Der Apfel ist Ab* and *Der Traum von Lieschen Müller* Käutner attempted to bring something of his old cabaret style into the contemporary cinema, but with mixed results. In 1957 he signed a seven-year contract with Universal in Hollywood which resulted in *The Restless Years* (*The Wonderful Years* in the UK) and *Stranger in My Arms*. In 1959 he directed a modern-day version of Hamlet entitled *Der Rest ist Schweigen*, but in the 1960s his time was increasingly taken up with more conventional literary adaptations (many of them for television), a direction already signalled in the 1950s with his productions of Zuckmayer's *Des Teufels General, Ein Mädchen aus Flandern* and *Der Hauptmann von Köpenick*. He also played the German pulp writer Karl May in Hans-Jurgen Syberberg's film of the same name, which also included several other notables from the cinema of the Third Reich, a period which it is hard not to regard as representing Käutner's finest hour. One German critic has suggested that his films of this period are "illustrative of an inner immigration which could express its opposition only secretly and in cyphers," and it may well be that the need to proceed by allusion, understatement, ambiguity and suggestion suited Käutner's remarkable talents peculiarly well.

—Julian Petley.

―――――

KAWALEROWICZ, Jerzy.

Polish. Born in Gwózda (Gwozdziec), now part of Soviet Ukraine, 19 January 1922. Educated at Film Institute, Cracow. Married actress Lucyna Winnicka. Assistant director and scriptwriter, 1946–51; co-directed first feature with Kazimierz Sumerski, 1952; head of Studia Kadr, from 1955. Recipient: Premio Evrotecnica, Venice Festival, for *Night Train*, 1959; Silver Palm, Cannes Festival, for *Mother Joan of the Angels*, 1961; Silver Bear, Berlin Festival, for *The President's Death*, 1977.

Jerzy Kawalerowicz: *Faraon*

Films as Director:

1952   *Gromada* (*The Village Mill. Commune*) (co-d)
1954   *Celuloza* (*Cellulose*) (+ co-sc); *Pod gwiazda frygijska* (*Under the Phrygian Star*) in two parts (+ co-sc)
1956   *Cién* (*The Shadow*)
1957   *Prawdziwy koniec wielkiej wojny* (*The Real End of the Great War*) (+ co-sc)
1959   *Pociag* (*Night Train. Baltic Express*) (+ co-sc)
1961   ***Matka Joanna od Aniolów (Mother Joan of the Angels)*** (+ co-sc)
1965   *Faraon* (*The Pharaoh*) (+ co-sc)
1968   *Gra* (*The Game*) (+ sc)
1970   *Maddalena*
1977   *Śmierć Prezydenta* (*Death of a President*) (+ co-sc)
1979   *Spotkanie na Atlantyku* (*Meeting on the Atlantic*) (+ co-sc)
1982   *Austeria* (+ co-sc)

Other Films:

1946   *Jutro premiera* (*Morning Premiere*) (asst d)
1947   *Zakazane piosenki* (*Forbidden Songs*) (asst d); *Ostatni etap* (*The Last Stage*) (asst d)
1948   *Stalowe serca* (*Steel Hearts*) (asst d); *Czarci źleb* (*The Devil's Pass*) (asst d)

Publications:

By KAWALEROWICZ: articles—

"Historia i forma," interview with K. Zórawski, in *Kino* (Warsaw), September 1977.

Interview with M. Dipont, in *Kino* (Warsaw), October 1980.
Interview, in *Filmowy serwis prasowy* (Warsaw), no. 2, 1983.
Interview with G. Delmas, in *Jeune Cinéma* (Paris), May/June 1987.

On KAWALEROWICZ: books—

Grzelecki, Stanislaw, *Twenty Years of Polish Cinema*, Warsaw, 1969.
Michalek, Boleslaw, *Film—sztuka w ewolucji*, Warsaw, 1975.
Kuszewski, Stanislaw, *Contemporary Polish Film*, Warsaw, 1978.

On KAWALEROWICZ: articles—

Kornatowska, M., "Jerzy Kawalerowicz czyli miłość do geometrii," in *Kino* (Warsaw), February 1978.
Modrzejewska, E., in *Kino* (Warsaw), April 1985.
"Jerzy Kawalerowicz," in *Film Dope* (London), March 1984.
Heinrich, D., "La Pologne par le coeur," in *Cinéma* (Paris), 10 February 1988.

*   *   *

It is no simple matter to give a precise characterization of this filmmaker. His work is not uniform, but full of twists and turns, strange shifts, and new experiments. The films of Jerzy Kawalerowicz are uneven; it is as though the filmmaker, after momentary triumphs and outstanding artistic achievement, would lapse into a crisis which prepared him for yet another masterpiece. His films are long in preparation. Between individual works come the lengthy pauses in which the director carefully absorbs raw material from a wide range of disciplines, in order to personally work it into film form. Only in a very few directors' works do we find such range, from the realistic film to the profound psychological drama, from the historical epic to the political drama.

Kawalerowicz has always gone his own way, and it has not been an easy path, especially when we realize that he has never turned back, never given a particular theme further development. Although he began at the same time as Wajda and Munk, he never created a work that belonged to the "Polish school of film." After his first independent film, *Celuloza* (*Cellulose*), both a realistic portrayal and a literary adaptation, he never came back to this subject or form. In his next creative period he quickly turned out several films which are unusual analytic studies of human relationships, earnest psychological examinations of lonely people marked by war (*The Real End of the Great War*), isolated while travelling on an overnight express (*Night*), or within the walls of a cloister (*Mother Joanna of the Angels*). Kawalerowicz demonstrates his creative mastery with these films. In fact, they initiated an entire trend of intimate dramas, popular with other directors several years later.

The historical epic *Faraon* (*Pharaoh*), adapted from the celebrated novel by Boleslaw Prus, is once again unusual in composition. It is a film on a grand scale, a monumental fresco, but at the same time an unusual psychological film with political and philosophical elements. In this drama of a struggle for power in ancient Egypt, the director finds room for an account of human qualities, motives, and feelings.

Emotions are the leitmotif of Kawalerowicz's work. After the grand epic *Faraon*, the filmmaker attempted a return to the intimate, psychologically-oriented film. A crisis sets in. His subsequent work fails to attain the level of his earlier pieces. There is a kind of break, a respite which will bear fruit in the later, purely political film and documentary drama *Death of a President*. The approach taken by Kawalerowicz on this film, which is the chronicle of an actual event—the assassination of President Gabriel Natutowicz in the 1930s—served as the director's credo. "When we studied the documents and the testimony and compiled the chronology of events, we ascertained that the drama of history, the drama of real events, is far more persuasive than what we ourselves could invent." Captivated by the facts, Kawalerowicz relates not only a real-life event but also a common human story that is timeless. After this film the critics expected the director to continue in this same genre, in which he had shown such mastery. But once again Kawalerowicz was experimenting with new genres and forms, though outstanding literary works and actual political or historical events, shaped into provocative dramas, remain the foundation of his creative work.

—Vacláv Merhaut

KAZAN, Elia.

American. Born Elia Kazanjoglou in Constantinople (now Istanbul), Turkey, 7 September 1909. Educated at Mayfair School; New Rochelle High School, New York; Williams College, Massachusetts, B.A. 1930; Yale Drama School, 1930–32; Married 1) Molly Day Thatcher, 1932 (died 1963), two sons, two daughters; 2) actress Barbara Loden, 1967 (died 1980), one son; 3) Frances Rudge, 1982. Moved with family to New York, 1913; actor, property manager, then director, Group Theatre, New York, from 1933; stage director, including plays by Tennessee Williams and Arthur Miller, 1935 through 1960s; co-founder, with Cheryl Crawford, Actors'

Studio, New York, 1948; appeared voluntarily before HUAC, admitting membership of Communist Party, 1934–36, and naming fellow members, 1952; began career as novelist, 1961; left Actors' Studio to direct newly-formed Lincoln Center Repertory Company, 1962–64. Recipient: many awards for theatre work; Oscar for Best Director, and Best Direction Award, New York Film Critics, for *Gentleman's Agreement*, 1947; International Prize, Venice Festival, for *Panic in the Streets*, 1950; Special Jury Prize, Venice Festival, for *A Streetcar Named Desire*, 1951; Oscar for Best Director, and Most Outstanding Directorial Achievement, Directors Guild of America, for *On the Waterfront*, 1954; Honorary doctorates from Wesleyan University, Carnegie Institute of Technology, and Williams College. Address: c/o 432 W. 44th St., New York, NY 10036, U.S.A.

Films as Director:

1937	*The People of the Cumberlands* (+ sc) (short)
1941	*It's Up to You*
1945	*A Tree Grows in Brooklyn*
1947	*The Sea of Grass*; *Boomerang*; *Gentleman's Agreement*
1949	*Pinky*
1950	*Panic in the Streets*
1952	***A Streetcar Named Desire***; *Viva Zapata!*; *Man on a Tightrope*
1954	***On the Waterfront***
1955	***East of Eden*** (+ pr)
1956	*Baby Doll* (+ pr, co-sc)
1957	*A Face in the Crowd* (+ pr)
1960	*Wild River* (+ pr)
1961	*Splendour in the Grass* (+ pr)
1964	*America, America* (+ sc, pr)
1969	*The Arrangement* (+ pr, sc)
1972	*The Visitors*
1976	*The Last Tycoon*
1978	*Acts of Love* (+ pr)
1982	*The Anatolian* (+ pr)
1989	*Beyond the Aegean*

Other Films:

1934	*Pie in the Sky* (Steiner) (short) (role)
1940	*City for Conquest* (Litvak) (role as Googie, a gangster)
1941	*Blues in the Night* (Litvak) (role as a clarinetist)

Publications:

By KAZAN: books—

America America, New York, 1961.
The Arrangement, New York, 1967.
The Assassins, New York, 1972.
The Understudy, New York, 1974.
Acts of Love, New York, 1978.
Anatolian, New York, 1982.
Elia Kazan: A Life, New York and London, 1988.

By KAZAN: articles—

"The Writer and Motion Pictures," in *Sight and Sound* (London), Summer 1957.
Interview with Jean Domarchi and André Labarthe, in *Cahiers du Cinéma* (Paris), April 1962.
Article in *Cahiers du Cinéma* (Paris), December 1963/January 1964.
Interview with S. Byron and M. Rubin, in *Movie* (London), Winter 1971/72.
Interview with G. O'Brien, in *Inter/View* (New York), March 1972.
"Visiting Kazan," interview with C. Silver and J. Zukor, in *Film Comment* (New York), Summer 1972.
"All You Need to Know, Kids," in *Action* (Los Angeles), January/February 1974.
"Hollywood Under Water," interview with C. Silver and M. Corliss, in *Film Comment* (New York), January/February 1977.

Elia Kazan (right) directing *On the Waterfront*

"Kazan Issue" of *Positif* (Paris), April 1977.

"Visite à Yilmaz Güney ou vue d'une prison turque," with O. Adanir, in *Positif* (Paris), February 1980.

"L'Homme tremblant: Conversation entre Marguerite Duras et Elia Kazan," in *Cahiers du Cinéma* (Paris), December 1980.

Interview with Tim Pulleine, in *Stills* (London), July/August 1983.

Interview with P. Le Guay, in *Cinématographe* (Paris), February 1986.

Interview in *Time Out* (London), 4 May 1988.

On KAZAN: books—

Clurman, Harold, *The Fervent Years: The Story of the Group Theatre and the Thirties*, New York, 1946.

Tailleur, Roger, *Elia Kazan*, revised edition, Paris, 1971.

Ciment, Michel, *Kazan on Kazan*, London, 1972.

Giannetti, Louis, *Masters of the American Cinema*, Englewood Cliffs, New Jersey, 1981.

Pauly, Thomas H., *An American Odyssey: Elia Kazan and American Culture*, Philadelphia, 1983.

Michaels, Lloyd, *Elia Kazan: A Guide to References and Resources*, Boston, 1985.

On KAZAN: articles—

Stevens, Virginia, "Elia Kazan: Actor and Director of Stage and Screen," in *Theatre Arts* (New York), December 1947.

Archer, Eugene, "Elia Kazan: The Genesis of a Style," in *Film Culture* (New York), vol. 2, no. 2, 1956.

Archer, Eugene, "The Theatre Goes to Hollywood," in *Films and Filming* (London), January 1957.

Neal, Patricia, "What Kazan Did for Me," in *Films and Filming* (London), October 1957.

Bean, Robin, "The Life and Times of Elia Kazan," in *Films and Filming* (London), May 1964.

Tailleur, Roger, "Elia Kazan and the House Un-American Activities Committee," in *Film Comment* (New York), Fall 1966.

"Kazan Issue" of *Movie* (London), Spring 1972.

Changas, E., "Elia Kazan's America," in *Film Comment* (New York), Summer 1972.

Kitses, Jim, "Elia Kazan: a Structural Analysis," in *Cinema* (Beverly Hills), Winter 1972/73.

Biskind, P., "The Politics of Power in *On the Waterfront*," in *Film Quarterly* (Berkeley), Autumn 1975.

"*A l'est d'Eden* Issue" of *Avant-Scène du Cinéma* (Paris), November 1975.

Kazan Section of *Positif* (Paris), April 1981.

"Kazan Issue" of *Avant-Scène du Cinéma* (Paris), 1 July 1983.

"Elia Kazan," in *Film Dope* (London), March 1984.

Michaels, Lloyd, "Elia Kazan: A Retrospective," in *Film Criticism* (Edinboro, Pennsylvania), Fall 1985.

Neve, Brian, "The Immigrant Experience on Film: Kazan's *America America*," in *Film and History* (New York), vol. 17, no. 3, 1987.

Nangle, J., "The American Museum of the Moving Image Salutes Elia Kazan," in *Films in Review* (New York), April 1987.

Georgakas, Dan, "Don't Call Him Gadget: Elia Kazan Reconsidered," in *Cineaste* (New York), vol. 16, no. 4, 1988.

Rathgeb, Douglas, "Kazan as Auteur: The Undiscovered *East of Eden*," in *Literature/Film Quarterly* (Salisbury, Maryland), vol. 16, no. 1, 1988.

McGilligan, Patrick, "Scoundrel Tome," in *Film Comment* (New York), May/June 1988.

Butler, T., "Polonsky and Kazan. HUAC and the Violation of Personality," in *Sight and Sound* (London), Autumn 1988.

*   *   *

Elia Kazan's career has spanned more than four decades of enormous change in the American film industry. Often he has been a catalyst for these changes. He became a director in Hollywood at a time when, following World War Two, the studios were interested in producing the kind of serious, mature, and socially conscious stories Kazan had been putting on the stage since his Group Theatre days. During the late 1940s and mid-1950s, initially under the influence of Italian neorealism and then the pressure of American television, he was a leading force in developing the aesthetic possibilities of location shooting (*Boomerang, Panic in the Streets, On the Waterfront*) and CinemaScope (*East of Eden, Wild River*). At the height of his success, Kazan formed his own production unit and moved back east to become a pioneer in the new era of independent, "personal" filmmaking which emerged during the 1960s and contributed to revolutionary upheavals within the old Hollywood system. As an archetypal *auteur*, he progressed from working on routine assignments to developing more personal themes, producing his own pictures, and ultimately directing his own scripts. At his peak during a decade and a half (1950-1965) of anxiety, gimmickry, and entropy in Hollywood, Kazan remained among the few American directors who continued to believe in the cinema as a medium for artistic expression and who brought forth films that consistently reflected his own creative vision.

Despite these achievements and his considerable influence on a younger generation of New York-based filmmakers including Sidney Lumet, John Cassavetes, Arthur Penn, Martin Scorsese, and even Woody Allen, Kazan's critical reputation in America currently rests at its lowest ebb. The turning point both for Kazan's own work and the critics' reception of it was almost certainly his decision to become a friendly witness before the House Un-American Activities Committee in 1952. While "naming names" cost Kazan the respect of many liberal friends and colleagues (Arthur Miller most prominent among them), it ironically ushered in the decade of his most inspired filmmaking. If Abraham Polonsky, himself blacklisted during the 1950s, is right in claiming that Kazan's post-HUAC movies have been "marked by bad conscience," perhaps he overlooks how that very quality of uncertainty may be what makes films like *On the Waterfront, East of Eden*, and *America America* so much more compelling than Kazan's previous studio work.

His apprenticeship in the Group Theater and his great success as a Broadway director had a natural influence on Kazan's films, particularly reflected in his respect for the written script, his careful blocking of scenes, and, pre-eminently, his employment of Method acting on the screen. While with the Group, which he has described as "the best thing professionally that ever happened to me," Kazan acquired from its leaders, Harold Clurman and Lee Strasberg, a fundamentally artistic attitude toward his work. Studying Marx led him to see art as an instrument of social change, and from Stanislavski he learned to seek a play's "spine" and emphasize the characters' psychological motivation. Although he developed a lyrical quality which informs many later films, Kazan generally employs the social realist mode he learned from the Group. Thus, he prefers location shooting over studio sets, relatively unfamiliar actors over stars, long shots and long takes over editing, and naturalistic forms over genre conventions. *On the Waterfront* and *Wild River*, though radically different in style, both reflect the Group's quest, in Kazan's words, "to get poetry out of the common things of life." And while one may debate the ultimate ideology of *Gentleman's Agreement, Pinky, Viva Zapata!* and *The Visitors*, one may still agree with the premise they all share, that art should illuminate society's problems and the possibility of their solution.

Above all else, however, it is Kazan's skill in directing actors that has secured his place in the history of American cinema. 21 of his performers have been nominated for Academy Awards; nine have won. He was instrumental in launching the film careers of Marlon Brando, Julie Harris, James Dean, Carroll Baker, Warren Beatty, and Lee Remick. Moreover, he elicited from such undervalued Hollywood players as Dorothy McGuire, James Dunn, Eva Marie Saint, and Natalie Wood perhaps the best performances of their careers. For all the long decline in critical appreciation, Kazan's reputation among actors has hardly wavered. The Method, which became so identified with Kazan's and Lee Strasberg's teaching at the Actors Studio, was once simplistically defined by Kazan himself as "turning psychology into behavior." An obvious example from *Boomerang* would be the suspect Waldron's gesture of covering his mouth whenever he lies to the authorities. But when Terry first chats with Edie in the park in *On the Waterfront*, unconsciously putting on one of the white gloves she has dropped as he sits in a swing, such behavior becomes not merely psychological but symbolic and poetic. Here Method acting transcends Kazan's own mundane definition.

His films have been most consistently concerned with the theme of power, expressed as either the restless yearning of the alienated or the uneasy arrangements of the strong. The struggle for power is generally manifested through wealth, sexuality, or, most often, violence. Perhaps because every Kazan film except *A Tree Grows in Brooklyn* and *The Last Tycoon* (excluding a one-punch knockout of the drunken protagonist) contains at least one violent scene, some critics have complained about the director's "horrid vulgarity" (Lindsay Anderson) and "unremitting stridency" (Robin Wood), yet even his most "overheated" work contains striking examples of restrained yet resonant interludes: the rooftop scenes of Terry and his pigeons in *On the Waterfront*, the tentative reunion of Bud and Deanie at the end of *Splendor in the Grass*, the sequence in which Stavros tells his betrothed not to trust him in *America America*. Each of these scenes could be regarded not simply as a necessary lull in the drama, but as a privileged, lyrical moment in which the ambivalence underlying Kazan's attitude toward his most pervasive themes seems to crystallize. Only then can one fully realize how Terry in the rooftop scene is both confined by the *mise-en-scène* (seen within the pigeon coop) and free on the roof to be himself; how Bud and Deanie are simultaneously reconciled and estranged; how Stavros becomes honest only when he confesses to how deeply he has been compromised.

—Lloyd Michaels

KEATON, Buster.

American. Born Joseph Francis Keaton in Piqua, Kansas, 4 October 1895. Served in U.S. Army, France, 1918. Married 1)

Natalie Talmadge, 1921 (divorced 1932), two sons; 2) Mae Scribbens, 1933 (divorced 1935); 3) Eleanor Norris, 1940. Part of parents' vaudeville act, The Three Keatons, from 1898; family act broken up, became actor for Comique Film Corp., moved to California, 1917; appeared in 15 two-reelers for Comique, 1917–19; offered own production company with Metro Pictures by Joseph Schenk, 1919, produced 19 two-reelers, 1920–23; directed ten features, 1923–28; dissolved production company, signed to MGM, 1928; announced retirement from the screen, 1933; starred in 16 comedies for Educational Pictures, 1934–39; worked intermittently as gag writer for MGM, 1937–50; appeared in 10 two-reelers for Columbia, 1939–41; on TV and in commercials, from 1949; Cinémathèque Française Keaton retrospective, 1962. *Died, of lung cancer, in Woodland Hills, California, 1 February 1966.*

Films as Director and Actor:

1920 *One Week* (co-d, co-sc with Eddie Cline); *Convict Thirteen* (co-d, co-sc with Cline); *The Scarecrow* (co-d, co-sc with Cline)

1921 *Neighbors* (co-d, co-sc with Cline); *The Haunted House* (co-d, co-sc with Cline); *Hard Luck* (co-d, co-sc with Cline) *The High Sign* (co-d, co-sc with Cline); *The Goat* (co-d, co-sc with Mal St. Clair); *The Playhouse* (co-d, co-sc with Cline); *The Boat* (co-d, co-sc with Cline)

1922 *The Paleface* (co-d, co-sc with Cline); *Cops* (co-d, co-sc with Cline); *My Wife's Relations* (co-d, co-sc with Cline); *The Blacksmith* (co-d, co-sc with Mal St. Clair); *The Frozen North* (co-d, co-sc with Cline); *Day Dreams* (co-d, co-sc with Cline); *The Electric House* (co-d, co-sc with Cline)

1923 *The Balloonatic* (co-d, co-sc with Cline); *The Love Nest* (co-d, co-sc with Cline); *The Three Ages*; *Our Hospitality* (co-d)

1924 **Sherlock Jr.** (co-d); **The Navigator** (co-d)

1925 *Seven Chances*; *Go West* (+ story)

1926 *Battling Butler*; **The General** (co-d, co-sc)

1927 *College* (no d credit)

1928 *Steamboat Bill, Jr.* (no d credit); *The Cameraman* (no d credit, pr)

1929 *Spite Marriage* (no d credit)

1938 *Life in Sometown, U.S.A.*; *Hollywood Handicap*; *Streamlined Swing*

Other Films:

1917 *The Butcher Boy* (Fatty Arbuckle comedy) (role as village pest); *A Reckless Romeo* (Arbuckle) (role as a rival); *The Rough House* (Arbuckle) (role); *His Wedding Night* (Arbuckle) (role); *Oh, Doctor!* (Arbuckle) (role); *Fatty at Coney Island* (Coney Island) (Arbuckle) (role as husband touring Coney Island with his wife); *A Country Hero* (Arbuckle) (role)

1918 *Out West* (Arbuckle) (role as a dude gambler); *The Bell Boy* (Arbuckle) (role as a village pest); *Moonshine* (Arbuckle) (role as an assistant revenue agent); *Good Night, Nurse!* (Arbuckle) (role as the doctor and a visitor); *The Cook* (Arbuckle) (role as the waiter and helper)

1919 *Back Stage* (Arbuckle) (role as a stagehand); *The Hayseed* (Arbuckle) (role as a helper)

1920 *The Garage* (Arbuckle) (role as a garage mechanic); *The Round Up* (role as an Indian); *The Saphead* (role as Bertie "the Lamb" Van Alstyne)

1922 *Screen Snapshots, No. 3* (role)

1929 *The Hollywood Revue* (role as an oriental dancer)

1930 *Free & Easy* (*Easy Go*) (role as Elmer Butts); *Doughboys* (pr, role as Elmer Stuyvesant)

1931 *Parlor, Bedroom & Bath* (pr, role as Reginald Irving); *Sidewalks of New York* (pr, role as Tine Harmon)

1932 *The Passionate Plumber* (pr, role as Elmer Tuttle); *Speak Easily* (role as Professor Timoleon Zanders Post)

1933 *What! No Beer!* (role as Elmer J. Butts)

1934 *The Gold Ghost* (role as Wally); *Allez Oop* (role as Elmer); *Le Roi des Champs Elysees* (role as Buster Garnier and Jim le Balafre)

1935 *The Invader* (*The Intruder*) (role as Leander Proudfoot); *Palookah from Paducah* (role as Jim); *One Run Elmer* (role as Elmer); *Hayseed Romance* (role as Elmer); *Tars & Stripes* (role as Elmer); *The E-Flat Man* (role as Elmer); *The Timid Young Man* (role as Elmer)

1936 *Three On a Limb* (role as Elmer); *Grand Slam Opera* (role as Elmer); *La Fiesta de Santa Barbara* (role as one of several stars); *Blue Blazes* (role as Elmer); *The Chemist* (role as Elmer); *Mixed Magic* (role as Elmer)

1937 *Jail Bait* (role as Elmer); *Ditto* (role as Elmer); *Love Nest on Wheels* (last apearance as Elmer)

1939 *The Jones Family in Hollywood* (co-sc): *The Jones Family in Quick Millions* (co-sc); *Pest from the West* (role as a traveler in Mexico); *Mooching through Georgia* (role as a Civil War veteran); *Hollywood Cavalcade* (role)

1940 *Nothing But Pleasure* (role as a vacationer); *Pardon My Berth Marks* (role as a reporter); *The Taming of the Snood* (role as an innocent accomplice); *The Spook Speaks* (role as a magician's housekeeper); *The Villain Still Pursued Her* (role); *Li'l Abner* (role as Lonesome Polecat); *His Ex Marks the Spot* (role)

1941 *So You Won't Squawk* (role); *She's Oil Mine* (role); *General Nuisance* (role)

1943 *Forever and a Day* (role as a plumber)

1944 *San Diego, I Love You* (role as a bus driver)

1945 *That's the Spirit* (role as L.M.); *That Night with You* (role)

1946 *God's Country* (role); *El Moderno Barba azul* (role as a prisoner of Mexicans who is sent to moon)

1949 *The Loveable Cheat* (role as a suitor); *In the Good Old Summertime* (role as Hickey); *You're My Everything* (role as butler)

1950 *Un Duel a mort* (role as a comic duellist); **Sunset Boulevard** (Wilder) (role as a bridge player)

1952 **Limelight** (Chaplin) (role as the piano accompanist in a musichall sketch); *L'incantevole nemica* (role in a brief sketch); *Paradise for Buster* (role)

1955 *The Misadventures of Buster Keaton* (role)

1956 *Around the World in Eighty Days* (role as a train conductor)

1960 *When Comedy was King* (role in a clip from *Cops*); *The Adventures of Huckleberry Finn* (Curtiz) (role as a lion tamer)

1963 *Thirty Years of Fun* (appearance in clips); *The Triumph of Lester Snapwell* (role as Lester); *It's a Mad, Mad, Mad, Mad World* (Kramer) (role as Jimmy the Crook)

1964 *Pajama Party* (role as an Indian chief)

1965 *Beach Blanket Bingo* (role as a would-be surfer); *Film* (role as Object/Eye); *How to Stuff a Wild Bikini* (role as Bwana); *Sergeant Deadhead* (Taurog) (role as Private Blinken); *The Rail-rodder* (role); *Buster Keaton Rides Again* (role)

1966 *The Scribe* (role); *A Funny Thing Happened on the Way to the Forum* (Lester) (role as Erronius)

1967 *Due Marines e un Generale* (*War, Italian Style*) (role as the German general)

1970 *The Great Stone Face* (role)

Publications:

By KEATON: book—

My Wonderful World of Slapstick, with Charles Samuels, New York, 1960; revised edition, 1982.

By KEATON: articles—

"Why I Never Smile," in *The Ladies Home Journal* (New York), June 1926.

Interview with Christopher Bishop, in *Film Quarterly* (Berkeley), Fall 1958.

Interview with Herbert Feinstein, in *Massachusetts Review* (Amherst), Winter 1963.

Interview with Kevin Brownlow, in *Film* (London), no. 42, 1965.

"Keaton: Still Making the Scene," interview with Rex Reed, in *New York Times*, 17 October 1965.

Buster Keaton

"Keaton at Venice," interview with John Gillett and James Blue, in *Sight and Sound* (London), Winter 1965.

Interview with Arthur Friedman, in *Film Quarterly* (Berkeley), Summer 1966.

Interview with Christopher Bishop, in *Interviews with Film Directors* edited by Andrew Sarris, New York, 1967.

"'Anything Can Happen—And Generally Did': Buster Keaton on His Silent Film Career,"' interview with George Pratt, in *Image* (Rochester), December 1974.

1920's articles reprinted in *Cahiers du Cinéma* (Paris), January 1979.

On KEATON: books—

Pantieri, José, *L'Originalissimo Buster Keaton*, Milan, 1963.

Turconi, Davide, and Francesco Savio, *Buster Keaton*, Venice, 1963.

Coursodon, Jean-Pierre, *Keaton et Compagnie: Les Burlesques américaines du "muet"*, Paris, 1964.

Oms, Marcel, *Buster Keaton*, Premier Plan No. 31, Lyons, 1964.

Blesh, Rudi, *Keaton*, New York, 1966.

Lebel, Jean-Pierre, *Buster Keaton*, New York, 1967.

Brownlow, Kevin, *The Parade's Gone By*, New York, 1968.

McCaffrey, Donald, *Four Great Comedians*, New York, 1968.

Robinson, David, *Buster Keaton*, London, 1968.

Denis, Michel, "Buster Keaton," in *Anthologie du Cinéma*, vol. 7, Paris, 1971.

Coursodon, Jean-Pierre, *Buster Keaton*, Paris, 1973.

Kerr, Walter, *The Silent Clowns*, New York, 1975.

Anobile, Richard, editor, *The Best of Buster*, New York, 1976.

Wead, George, *Buster Keaton and the Dynamics of Visual Wit*, New York, 1976.

Moews, Daniel, *Keaton: The Silent Features Close Up*, Berkeley, California, 1977.

Wead, George, and George Ellis, *The Film Career of Buster Keaton*, Boston, 1977.

Dardis, Tom, *Keaton: The Man Who Wouldn't Lie Down*, New York, 1979.

Benayoun, Robert, *The Look of Buster Keaton*, Paris, 1982; London, 1984.

Coursodon, Jean-Pierre, *Buster Keaton*, Paris, 1986.

On KEATON: articles—

Brand, Harry, "They Told Buster to Stick to It," in *Motion Picture Classic* (New York), June 1926.

Keaton, Joe, "The Cyclone Baby," in *Photoplay* (New York), May 1927.

Saalschutz, L., "Comedy," in *Close Up* (London), April 1930.

Agee, James, "Great Stone Face," in *Life* (New York), 5 September 1949.

Kerr, Walter, "Last Call for a Clown," in *Pieces at Eight*, New York, 1957.

Agee, James, "Comedy's Greatest Era," in *Agee on Film*, New York, 1958.

Dyer, Peter, "Cops, Custard—and Keaton," in *Films and Filming* (London), August 1958.

"Keaton Issue" of *Cahiers du Cinéma* (Paris), August 1958.

Bishop, Christopher, "The Great Stone Face," in *Film Quarterly* (Berkeley), Fall 1958.

Baxter, Brian, "Buster Keaton," in *Film* (London), November/December 1958.

Robinson, David, "Rediscovery: Buster," in *Sight and Sound* (London), Winter 1959.

Beylie, Claude, and others, "Rétrospective Buster Keaton," in *Cahiers du Cinéma* (Paris), April 1962.

Buñuel, Luis, "*Battling Butler [College]*," in *Luis Buñuel: An Introduction* edited by Ado Kyrou, New York, 1963.

Lorca, Federico García, "Buster Keaton Takes a Walk," in *Sight and Sound* (London), Winter 1965.

Crowther, Bosley, "Dignity in Deadpan," in *The New York Times*, 2 February 1966.

Sadoul, Georges, "Le Génie de Buster Keaton," in *Les Lettres Françaises* (Paris), 10 February 1966.

Benayoun, Robert, "Le Colosse de silence," and "Le Regard de Buster Keaton," in *Positif* (Paris), Summer 1966.

McCaffrey, Donald, "The Mutual Approval of Keaton and Lloyd," in *Cinema Journal* (Evanston), no. 6, 1967.

Rhode, Eric, "Buster Keaton," in *Encounter* (London), December 1967.

Houston, Penelope, "The Great Blank Page," in *Sight and Sound* (London), Spring 1968.

Villelaur, Anne, "Buster Keaton," in *Dossiers du Cinéma: Cinéastes I*, Paris, 1971.

Maltin, Leonard, "Buster Keaton," in *The Great Movie Shorts*, New York, 1972.

Gilliatt, Penelope, "Buster Keaton," in *Unholy Fools*, New York, 1973.

Mast, Gerald, "Keaton," in *The Comic Mind*, New York, 1973.

Sarris, Andrew, "Buster Keaton," in *The Primal Screen*, New York, 1973.

"Keaton Issue" of *Avant-Scène du Cinéma* (Paris), February 1975.

Cott, Jeremy, "The Limits of Silent Film Comedy," in *Literature/Film Quarterly* (Salisbury, Maryland), Spring 1975.

Rubinstein, E., "Observations on Keaton's *Steamboat Bill Jr.*," in *Sight and Sound* (London), Autumn 1975.

Everson, William, "Rediscovery: *Le Roi des Champs Elysees*," in *Films in Review* (New York), December 1976.

Wade, G., "The Great Locomotive Chase," in *American Film* (Washington, D.C.), July/August 1977.

Valot, J., "Discours sur le cinéma dans quelques films de Buster Keaton," in *Image et Son* (Paris), February 1980.

Gifford, Denis, "Flavour of the Month," in *Films and Filming* (London), February 1984.

"Buster Keaton," in *Film Dope* (London), March 1984.

Sight and Sound (London), Spring 1985.

Cazals, T., "Un Monde à la démesure de l'homme," in *Cahiers du Cinéma* (Paris), March 1987.

*   *   *

Buster Keaton is the only creator-star of American silent comedies who equals Chaplin as one of the artistic giants of the cinema. He is perhaps the only silent clown whose reputation is far higher today than it was in the 1920s, when he made his greatest films. Like Chaplin, Keaton came from a theatrical family and served his apprenticeship on stage in the family's vaudeville act. Unlike Chaplin, however, Keaton's childhood and family life were less troubled, more serene, lacking the darkness of Chaplin's youth that would lead to the later darkness of his films. Keaton's films were more blithely athletic and optimistic, more committed to audacious physical stunts and cinema tricks, far less interested in exploring moral paradoxes and emotional resonances. Keaton's most famous comic trademark, his "great stone face," itself reflects the commitment to a comedy of the surface, but attached to that face was one of the most resiliently able and acrobatic bodies in the history of cinema, and Keaton's comedy was based on the conflict between that imperviously dead-pan face, his tiny but almost superhuman physical instrument, and the immensity of the physical universe that surrounded them.

After an apprenticeship in the late 1910s making two-reel comedies that starred his friend Fatty Arbuckle, and after service in France in 1918, Keaton starred in a series of his own two-reel comedies beginning in 1920. Those films displayed Keaton's comic and visual inventiveness: the delight in bizarrely complicated mechanical gadgets (*The Scarecrow*, *The Haunted House*), the realization that the cinema itself was an intriguing mechanical toy (his use of split-screen in *The Playhouse* of 1921 allows Buster to play all members of the orchestra and audience, as well as all nine members of a minstrel troupe), the games with framing and composition (*The Balloonatic* is a comic disquisition on the surprises one can generate merely by entering, falling out of, or suppressing information in the frame), the breathtaking physical stunts and chases (*Daydreams*, *Cops*), and the underlying fatalism when his exuberant efforts produce ultimately disastrous results (*Cops*, *One Week*, *The Boat*).

In 1923, Keaton's producer, Joseph M. Schenck, decided to launch the comic star in a series of feature films, to replace a previously slated series of features starring Schenck's other comic star, the now scandal-ruined Fatty Arbuckle. Between 1923 and 1929, Keaton made an even dozen feature films on a regular schedule of two a year—always leaving Keaton free in the early autumn to travel East for the World Series. This regular pattern of Keaton's work—as opposed to Chaplin's lengthy laboring and devoted concentration on each individual project—reveals the way Keaton saw his film work. He was not making artistic masterpieces but knocking out everyday entertainment, like the vaudevillian playing the two-a-day. Despite the casualness of this regular routine (which would be echoed decades later by Woody Allen's regular one-a-year rhythm), many of those dozen silent features are comic masterpieces, ranking alongside the best of Chaplin's comic work.

Most of those films begin with a parodic premise—the desire to parody some serious and familiar form of stage or screen melodrama—the Civil War romance (*The General*), the mountain feud (*Our Hospitality*), the Sherlock Holmes detective story (*Sherlock, Jr.*), the Mississippi riverboat race (*Steamboat Bill, Jr.*), or the western (*Go West*). Two of the features were built around athletics (boxing in *Battling Butler* and every sport but football in *College*), and one was built around the business of motion picture photography itself (*The Cameraman*). The narrative lines of these films were thin but fast-paced, usually based on the Keaton character's desire to satisfy the demands of his highly conventional lady love. The film's narrative primarily served to allow the film to build to its extended comic sequences, which, in Keaton's films, continue to amaze with their cinematic ingenuity, their dazzling physical stunts, and their hypnotic visual rhythms. Those sequences usually forced the tiny but dexterous Keaton into combat with immense and elemental antagonists—a rockslide in *Seven Chances*; an entire ocean liner in *The Navigator*; a herd of cattle in *Go West*; a waterfall in *Our Hospitality*. Perhaps the cleverest and most astonishing of his elemental foes appears in *Sherlock, Jr.* when the enemy becomes cinema itself—or, rather, cinematic time and space. Buster, a dreaming movie projectionist, becomes imprisoned in the film he is projecting, subject to its inexplicable laws of montage, of shifting spaces and times, as opposed to the expected continuity of space and time in the natural universe. Perhaps Keaton's most satisfyingly whole film is *The General*, virtually an extended chase from start to finish, as the Keaton character chases north, in pursuit of his stolen locomotive, then races back south with it, fleeing his Union pursuers. The film combines comic narrative, the rhythms of the chase, Keaton's physical stunts, and his fondness for mechanical gadgets into what may be the greatest comic epic of the cinema.

Unlike Chaplin, Keaton's stardom and comic brilliance did not survive Hollywood's conversion to synchronized sound. It was not simply a case of a voice's failing to suit the demands of both physical comedy and the microphone. Keaton's personal life was in shreds, after a bitter divorce from Natalie Talmadge. Always a heavy social drinker, Keaton's drinking increased in direct proportion to his personal troubles. Neither a comic spirit nor an acrobatic physical instrument could survive so much alcoholic abuse. In addition, Keaton's contract had been sold by Joseph Schenck to MGM (conveniently controlled by his brother, Nicholas Schenck, head of Loew's Inc., MGM's parent company). Between 1929 and 1933, MGM assigned Keaton to a series of dreary situation comedies—in many of them as Jimmy Durante's co-star and straight man. For the next two decades, Keaton survived on cheap two-reel sound comedies and occasional public appearances, until his major role in Chaplin's *Limelight* led to a comeback. Keaton remarried, went on the wagon, and made stage, television, and film appearances in featured roles. In 1965 he played the embodiment of existential consciousness in Samuel Beckett's only film work, *Film*, followed shortly by his final screen appearance in Richard Lester's *A Funny Thing Happened on the Way to the Forum*.

—Gerald Mast

———

KHAN, Mehboob, *See* **MEHBOOB KHAN.**

———

KIEŚLOWSKI, Krzysztof.

Polish. Born in Warsaw, 27 June 1941. Studied at School of Cinema and Theatre, Lodz, graduated 1969. Worked as director of documentaries and fiction films for TV, from 1969; directed first feature for cinema, *Blizna*, 1976; vice-president of the Union of Polish Cinematographers, 1978–81; teacher at faculty of Radio and Television, University of Silesia, 1979–82; made *Dekalog*, series of short films for Polish TV, 1988–89, then gained finance to make longer versions of two episodes for cinematic release. Recipient: First Prize, Mannheim Festival, for *Personel*, 1975; FIPRESCI Prize, Moscow Festival, for *Amator*, 1979; Diploma from the Polish Ministry of Foreign Affairs, 1979; Special Jury Prize, Cannes Festival, and Oscar for Best Foreign Feature Film, for *A Short Film About Killing*, 1988.

Films as Director:
(documentary shorts unless otherwise stated)

1967   *Urzad* (*The Job*)
1968   *Zdjecie* (*The Photograph*) (for TV)
1969   *Z miasta Lodzi* (*From the City of Lodz*)
1970   *Byzem Zolnierzem* (*I Was a Soldier*); *Przed rajdem* (*Before the Rally*); *Fabryka* (*Factory*)
1971   *Gospordaze* (*Workers*) (co-d)
1972   *Miadzy Wroclawiem a Zielona Gora* (*Between Wroclaw and Zielona Gora*); *Podstawy w kopalni miedzi* (*The Degree of Hygiene and Safety in a Copper Mine*); *Robotnicy 71 nic o nas bez nas* (*Workers 71*) (co-d); *Refren* (*Refrain*)
1973   *Murarz* (*Bricklayer*); *Dziecko* (*Child*); *Pierwsza milosc* (*First Love*) (for TV); *Przeswietlenie* (*X-Ray*); *Podziamne Przjscie* (*Pedestrian Subway*) (feature for TV)
1975   *Zycioris* (*Life Story*); *Personel* (*Personnel*) (feature for TV)
1976   *Klaps* (*Slate*); *Szpital* (*Hospital*); *Spokoj* (*Stillness*) (feature for TV); *Blizna* (*The Scar*) (feature)
1977   *Nie Wiem* (*I Don't Know*); *Z punktu widzenia nocneo porteria* (*Night Porter's Point of View*)
1978   *Siedem kobiet w roznym wieku* (*Seven Women of Various Ages*)
1979   *Amator* (*Camera Buff*) (feature)
1980   *Dworzec* (*The Station*); *Gadajace Glowy* (*Talking Heads*)
1981   *Krotki dzian pracy* (*A Short Working Day*) (feature for TV)
1982   *Przypadek* (*Blind Chance*) (feature, released 1987)
1984   *Bez konca* (*No End*) (feature)
1988   *Krótki film o zabi janiu* (*A Short Film About Killing*) (feature); *Krótki film o miłósci* (*A Short Film About Love*) (feature)
1989   *Dekalog* (*Decalogue*) (10 episodes for TV)
1990   *City Life* (*Episode in Netherlands*) (feature)

Publications:

By KIEŚLOWSKI: book—

Decalogue, London, 1991.

By KIEŚLOWSKI: articles—

Interview in *Jeune Cinéma* (Paris), December 1979.
Interview with H. Samsonówska, in *Kino* (Warsaw), October 1981.
Interview with S. Magela and C. Göldenboog, in *Filmfaust* (Frankfurt), April/May 1983.
Interview with Marszalek, in *Kino* (Warsaw), August 1987.
Interview with A. Tixeront, in *Cinéma* (Paris), December 1988.
Interview in *Time Out* (London), 15 November 1989.

On KIEŚLOWSKI: articles—

"Krzysztof Kieslowski," in *International Film Guide 1981*, edited by Peter Cowie, London, 1980.
Zaoral, F., "Krzysztof Kieslowski," in *Film a Doba* (Prague), September 1985.
Kieslowski Section of *Positif* (Paris), December 1989.
Revue du Cinéma/Image et Son (Paris), January 1990.
Cavendish, Phil, "Kieslowski's *Decalogue*," in *Sight and Sound* (London), Summer 1990.

* * *

In the late 1970s, when the conflict between the State and the citizens of Poland was imminent, a new trend emerged in cinematography—the "cinema of moral unrest." All the films in this trend have one common denominator: an unusually cutting critical view of the state of the society and its morals, human relationships in the work process, public and private life. It is more than logical that Krzysztof Kieślowski belongs to this trend; he has long been concerned with the moral problems of the society, and has paid attention to them throughout his film career with increasing urgency. The direction of his artistic course was anticipated by his graduation film *From the Town of Lodz*, in which he sketched the problems of workers, and by his participation in the stormy protest meeting of young film-makers in Cracow in 1971, who warned against a total devaluation of basic human values.

A broad scale of problems can be found in the documentary films Kieślowski made between shooting feature films: disintegration of the economic structure, criticism of executive work, and the relationship of institutions and individuals. These documentaries are not a mere recording of events, phenomena, or a description of people and their behaviour, but always attempt instead to look underneath the surface. The director often uses non-traditional means. Sometimes the word dominates the image, or he may borrow the stylistics of slapstick or satire, or he interferes with the reality in front of the camera by a staged element. Kieślowski does not emphasize the aesthetic function of the image, but stresses its real and literal meaning.

His feature films have a similar orientation: he concentrates on the explication of an individual's situation in the society and politics, on the outer and inner bonds of man with the objectively existing world, and on the search for connections between the individual and the general. He often places his heroes in situations when they have to make a vital decision (in his TV films *The Staff*, and *The Calm*, and in his films for theatrical release).

The Amateur is the synthesis of his attitudes and artistic search of the 1970s, and is also one of the most significant films of the "cinema of moral unrest." In the story of a man who buys a camera to follow the growth of a newborn daughter, and who gradually, thanks to this film instrument, begins to realize his responsibility for what is happening around him, the director places a profound importance on the role of the artist in the world, on his morality, courage, and active approach to life.

Krzysztof Kieślowski ⓒ **Peter Smith**

Here Kieślowski surpasses, to a large extent, the formulaic restrictions of the "cinema of moral unrest" resulting from the outside-the-art essence of this trend. These restrictions are also eliminated in his following films. In *The Accident* (made in 1981, released in 1987) he extends his exploration of man and his actions by introducing the category of the accidental. The hero experiences three times the same events (Poland in 1981) three times, and therefore is given three destinies, but each time on a different side. Two destinies are more or less given by accident, the third one he chooses himself, but even this choice is affected by the accidental element. The transcendental factor appears in the *Without End* (a dead man intervenes in worldly events), but the film is not an exploration of supernatural phenomena so much as a ruthless revelation of the tragic period after the declaration of the state of emergency in December 1981, and a demonstration of the professed truth that private life cannot be lived in isolation from the public sphere.

Kieślowski's work has culminated in a TV cycle and two films with subjects from the Ten Commandments. *A Short Film about Killing* is based on the fifth commandment (Thou shalt not kill), while *A Short Film about Love* comes from the sixth. Both films and the TV cycle are anchored in the present and express the necessity of a moral revival, both of the individual and the society, in a world which may be determined by accidentality, but which does not deliver us from the right and duty of moral choice.

—Blažena Urgošíková

KING, Henry.

American. Born in Christianburg, Virginia, 24 January 1888. Married twice. Worked with Empire Stock Company, travelling repertory company, also in circus, vaudeville, and burlesque, early 1900's; actor and writer for Lubin Co., Philadelphia, 1912–16; actor and director, Balbao Films, Long Beach, California, from 1916; moved to American Film Company, 1918; worked mainly for Fox, 1930 through 1961. *Died in San Fernando Valley, 29 June 1982.*

Films as Director:

1915 *Who Pays?*
1916 *Little Mary Sunshine; Joy and the Dragon; Pay Dirt; The Strained Pearl*
1917 *The Mainspring; The Climber; Southern Pride; A Game of Wits; The Mate of the Sally Ann; Twin Kiddies; Told at Twilight; Sunshine and Gold*
1918 *Beauty and the Rogue; Powers That Prey; Hearts or Diamonds; Up Romance Road; The Locked Heart; Hobbs in a Hurry; The Unafraid; Souls in Pawn; The Spectre of Suspicion; The Bride's Silence*
1919 *When a Man Rides Alone; Where the West Begins; Brass Buttons; Some Liar; Sporting Chance; This Hero Stuff; Six Feet Four; A Fugitive from Matrimony; 23$^{1}/_{2}$ Hours Leave; Haunting Shadows*

1920 *The White Dove; Uncharted Channels; One Hour Before Dawn; Help Wanted—Male; Dice of Destiny*
1921 *When We Were Twenty-One; Mistress of Shenstone; Salvage; The Sting of the Lash;* **Tol'able David**
1922 *The Seventh Day; Sonny; The Bond Boy*
1923 *Fury; The White Sister*
1925 *Sackcloth and Scarlet; Any Woman; Romola*
1926 *Stella Dallas; Partners Again;* The Winning of Barbara Worth
1927 *The Magic Flame*
1928 *The Woman Disputed*
1929 *She Goes to War*
1930 *Hell Harbor; Eyes of the World; Lightnin'*
1931 *Merely Mary Ann; Over the Hill*
1932 *The Woman in Room Thirteen*
1933 *State Fair; I Love You Wednesday*
1934 *Carolina; Marie Galante*
1935 *One More Spring; Way Down East*
1936 *The Country Doctor; Ramona; Lloyd's of London*
1937 *Seventh Heaven*
1938 *In Old Chicago; Alexander's Ragtime Band*
1939 *Jesse James; Stanley and Livingstone*
1940 *Little Old New York; Maryland; Chad Hanna*
1941 *A Yank in the RAF; Remember the Day*
1942 *The Black Swan*
1943 *The Song of Bernadette*
1944 *Wilson*
1945 *A Bell for Adano*
1946 *Margie*
1947 *Captain from Castille*

Henry King: *Stella Dallas*

1948 *Deep Waters*
1949 *The Prince of Foxes*
1950 *Twelve O'Clock High; The Gunfighter*
1951 *I'd Climb the Highest Mountain; David and Bathsheba*
1952 *Wait 'til the Sun Shines, Nellie;* "The Gift of the Magi" episode of *O. Henry's Full House; The Snows of Kilimanjaro*
1953 *King of the Khyber Rifles*
1955 *Untamed; Love Is a Many-Splendored Thing*
1956 *Carousel*
1957 *The Sun Also Rises*
1958 *The Bravados*
1959 *This Earth Is Mine; Beloved Infidel*
1961 *Tender Is the Night*

Publications:

By KING: articles—

"Filmmakers as Goodwill Ambassadors," in *Films in Review* (New York), October 1958.
"Henry King: The Flying Director," interview with Richard Cherry, in *Action* (Los Angeles), July/August 1969.
"Pioneers '73," with C. Kirk, in *Action* (Los Angeles), November/December 1973.
Interview with S. Eyman, in *Focus on Film* (London), Winter 1976.
Interviews and article with J. Lacourcelles and P. Guinle, in *Ecran* (Paris), June and July 1978.
Interview with D. Badder, in *Sight and Sound* (London), Winter 1977/78.
Interview with Gene D. Phillips, in *Séquences* (Montreal), October 1983.

On KING: books—

Brownlow, Kevin, *The Parade's Gone By*, London, 1968.
Denton, Clive, and others, *The Hollywood Professionals Vol. 2: Henry King, Lewis Milestone, Sam Wood*, New York, 1974.
Coppedge, Walter, *Henry King's America*, Metuchen, New Jersey, 1986.

On KING: articles—

Shibuk, Charles, and Christopher North, "The Life and Films of Henry King," in *Films in Review* (New York), October 1958.
Mitchell, G.J., "Henry King," in *Films in Review* (New York), July 1964.
Pickard, Roy, "The Tough Race," in *Films and Filming* (London), September 1971.
Obituary, in *New York Times*, 1 July 1982.
Rabourdin, D., obituary, in *Cinéma* (Paris), September 1982.
"Henry King," in *Film Dope* (London), September 1984.
Reilly, J.P., "The Authenticity of Henry King," in *Films in Review* (New York), October 1984.

*   *   *

Henry King has been called the "pastoral poet" of American motion pictures by a small coterie of film historians, but in general his lengthy and prominent career as a director has been slighted, partly because many of his silent films remain inaccessible and partly because his interpretation of life in rural America has been overshadowed by the works of such directors as King Vidor, John Ford, and D.W. Griffith.

At their best, King's films recreated a charming and honestly sentimental America, evoking a sincere nostalgia and naturalism, and expressing an optimistic and durable view of romantic love. He presented his stories in a simple, straightforward manner, not attempting any "between-the-lines" analyses. He relied on plot and the competence of his actors to interpret his stories. Technically his films were spare and unencumbered by cinematic tricks. No technical virtuoso, he nevertheless possessed a remarkable facility for creating rustic tableaux which represented the virtues of American country life.

King came to motion pictures via acting both in theatre stock companies and, like his contemporaries John Ford and Raoul Walsh, in silent pictures. Acting led to directing, his first film of note being *23¹/₂ Hours Leave*, produced by Thomas Ince. *Tol'able David*, his interpretation of life in his native rural Virginia, brought his first real acclaim, including praise from the Russian master Pudovkin. The Lillian Gish vehicle *The White Sister* was a beautifully-conceived religious tragedy and one of the first major U.S. productions filmed abroad. His *Stella Dallas* remains the best and least maudlin version of that often-filmed tear-jerker and contains a remarkable performance by Belle Bennett.

With the arrival of sound, King signed a contract with Fox, where he would remain for the balance of his career, frequently working with the esteemed cinematographer Leon Shamroy. King proved a supreme studio craftsman and his first sound masterpiece was the memorable *State Fair*, starring the popular Will Rogers. The best of his many films for Fox relied heavily on nostalgia and Americana, and exhibited a steadfast earnestness (e.g. *In Old Chicago, Alexander's Ragtime Band, Jesse James,* and *Stanley and Livingstone*). In *Song of Bernadette* he transcended the sentimentality of the novel; *Wilson*, however, for all its nobility, was really more Darryl F. Zanuck than King and today is tedious to watch.

Twelve O'Clock High is a compelling depiction of a U.S. Air Force commander's breakdown and contains Gregory Peck's best performance, while *The Gunfighter* is a vivid, albeit offbeat Western. *I'll Climb the Highest Mountain*, a greatly underrated film, is the synthesis of all of King's love of ordinary country life and romance, and *The Snows of Kilimanjaro* is better Hemingway than most critics admit and was the author's favorite among the film adaptions of his writings.

Love Is a Many-Splendored Thing is another example of how King could make audiences believe in pure, romantic love, and *The Bravados*, an austere western, was his last good film; *Beloved Infidel* is an embarrassment and *Tender Is the Night*, which has its moments, was botched by David O. Selznick's meddling.

Before his death in 1982, King began to see a renewed interest in his work through numerous retrospectives. In 1969, the International Motion Picture Almanac listed what it deemed the "Greatest Hundred" films and six of King's works appeared on that list: *Tol'able David, The White Sister, Stella Dallas, Alexander's Ragtime Band, The Song of Bernadette,* and *Wilson*.

King's venerable career deserves more recognition than it has yet received; as Andrew Sarris has stated, King is a "subject for further research."

—Ronald Bowers

KING HU.

(Pseudonym of Hu Chin-Ch'üan; as actor known as Chin Ch'üan; name in pinyin: Hun Jinquan.) Chinese. Born in Peking, 29 April 1931. Educated at Hui-Wen Middle School, Peking; Peking National Art College. Married scriptwriter Chong Ling (separated). Moved to Hong Kong, 1949; worked in design dept., Yong Hua Film Company, as actor, and as assistant director and scriptwriter, 1950–54; set designer, Great Wall Film Company, mid-1950's; radio producer, worked for Voice of America, 1954–58; actor, scriptwriter, and director for Shaw Brothers, 1958–65; director and production manager, Union (Liangbang) Film Company, 1965–70; founded King Hu Productions, 1970. Recipient: Grand Prix, Cannes Festival, for *A Touch of Zen*, 1975.

Films as Director:

1962 *Yü T'ang Ch'un (The Story of Sue San)* (credited as exec d, disowned)
1963 *Liang Shan-po yü Chu Ying T'ai (Eternal Love)* (co-d)
1964 *Ta Ti Erh Nü (Children of the Good Earth. Sons and Daughters of the Good Earth)*
1965 *Ta Tsui Hsia (Come Drink With Me)* (+ co-sc, lyrics)
1967 *Lung Men K'o Chan (The Dragon Gate Inn)* (+ sc)
1970 *Hsia Nü (A Touch of Zen)* (+ sc, ed); "Nu" ("Anger") episode of *Hsi Nu Ai Le (Four Moods)* (+ sc)
1973 *Ying Ch'un Ko Chih Fêng Po (The Fate of Lee Khan. Trouble at Spring Inn)* (+ co-sc, pr)
1974 *Chung Lieh T'u (The Valiant Ones. Portrait of the Patriotic Heroes)* (+ sc, pr)
1978 *Shan Chung Ch'uan Chi (Legend of the Mountain)* (+ pr)
1979 *K'ung Shan Ling Yü (Raining in the Mountain)* (+ sc, pr)
1981 *Chung Shên Ta Shih (The Juvenizer)* (+ pr)
1983 episode of *Ta Lun Hui (The Wheel of Life)*
1989 *Hsiao Ao Chiang Hu (The Swordsman)* (co-d)

Other Films:

1958 *Hung Hu-Tzu (Red Beard)* (P'an Lei) (sc)
1961 *Hua T'ien-T'so (Bridenapping)* (Yen Chun) (sc)
1976 *Lung Men Fêng Yun (Dragon Gate)* (Ou-yang Chun) (sc)

Publications:

By KING HU: articles—

Interview with Michel Ciment, in *Positif* (Paris), May 1975.

On KING HU: articles—

Rayns, Tony, "Director: King Hu," in *Sight and Sound* (London), Winter 1975/76.
Elley, Derek, "King Hu," in *International Film Guide 1978*, London, 1977.
Tessier, Max, "King Hu dans les montagnes," in *Ecran* (Paris), July 1978.
Ooi, V., "Jacobean Drama and the Martial Arts Films of King Hu: A Study in Power and Corruption," in *Australian Journal of Screen Theory* (Kensington, New South Wales), no. 7, 1980.
Vos, J.-M., and others, "King Hu," in *Film en Televisie* (Brussels), January 1980.
Bady, P., and Tony Rayns, in *Positif* (Paris), July/August 1982.
Kennedy, Harlan, "Beyond Kung-Fu: Seven Hong-Kong Firecrackers," in *Film Comment* (New York), September/October 1983.
"King Hu Section" of *Cahiers du Cinéma* (Paris), September 1984.

*   *   *

King Hu is not only a master in the historical martial art film genre (known in Chinese as Wu Hsia P'ien or Wu Xia Pian), but a revolutionary of the form as well. One of the most popular genres in Chinese film history, it reached its peak in the 1970s in Hong Kong. In fact, the very first film made in China was a historical martial art film documenting Peking Opera performer T'an Hsin P'ei, who performed some fighting scenes from the opera *Ting Chun Shang* in 1906.

Influenced by Peking opera, King Hu always presents his main characters clearly and vividly in their first appearances on screens and lets the characters' interactions occur within a limited space. The presentations provide the audience with an early introduction of the main characters' backgrounds, personalities, motives and duties, giving a clear indication of where everyone fits in the moral landscape. This restricted realm creates denser and more intensive emotional developments, paving the way to a higher dramatic climax. Such structuring can be observed at the temple in *Raining in the Mountain*, and the inn in both *The Dragon Gate Inn* and *The Fate of Lee Khan*.

Most filmmakers in this genre tend to focus on fighting scenes and on displaying various styles of kungfu. In many cases the plots are constructed simply to support the fighting, which itself is given over to such elaborate special effects as to resemble more closely a supernatural force than a manifestation of human struggle. History itself loses its meaning: it simply provides an excuse for making another "historical" martial art film. This destruction of referentiality becomes all the balder when a character from the Han dynasty wears a hat from the Ming dynasty to go with his Han dynasty robe, goes into an inn that is a mess of Tang architecture and Ching furniture. As a result, the historical martial art film genre's main function is to create an imaginary and mystical world for the audience to escape to. But King Hu's work stands out with its professionalism in art direction and the director's personal philosophy in historical backgrounding.

The Ming dynasty (1386–1644 A.D.) has been King Hu's favorite historical period, reflecting as it does two major issues of the contemporary Chinese political situation. First of all, the legitimacy of the Chinese government—should it belong to the Nationalist Party, founded by Dr. Sun Yat-sen, or the Chinese Communist Party, which enjoys the support of the majority of Chinese? King Hu never gives an answer, but he surely does not hesitate to take a Han-centric viewpoint of the Ming Dynasty. In Chinese history, it is commonly perceived as an act of legitimization of authority when Chu Yuan-chang, the founding emperor of the Ming dynasty, started a revolution to overthrow the Yuan Dynasty, founded by Mongolian "invaders." Chu is a Han, the majority ethnic group of China. In *The Fate of Lee Khan*, the revolutionaries led by Chu are brave, intelligent, united, self-sacrificing and virtuous, while the Mongolians are cowardly, stupid, selfish and morally corrupted. Although it seems to be an exception that the Mongolian Lord and Princess are equally brave, smart and know the secrets of kungfu, they are cruel to their people. They even attempt to kill a traitor to Chu, who offers them secret information about Chu's military power. In the end, the Mongolian Lord, Princess and the traitor are killed by the revolutionaries.

Another parallel to contemporary times is the Ming dynasty's power struggles. The rivalries among corrupt officers, ministers and eunuchs not only deceived the emperors, but ruined the welfare of the Chinese people. Facing a chaotic era like this, King Hu's solution seems to be found in *A Touch of Zen*, which won the Grand Prix de Technique Superieur at Cannes in 1975, marking a milestone in his career. King Hu expresses the limitations of scholarly and chivalric life in the first half of *A Touch of Zen*, while in the other half he initiates the audience into a surrealistic visionary world—the realm of Zen metaphysics: a monk bleeds gold and possesses extraordinary powers that seem to stem from the sun and other natural forces.

However, one may find a different philosophy in *The Swordsman*, which he co-directed with Tsui Hark, a leading figure of the Hong Kong New Wave and director of *Peking Opera Blues*. Although the artistic disputes between Tsui Hark and King Hu caused the latter to leave in the middle of production, *The Swordsman* surprisingly ends up being a combination of several filmmakers' virtues. Stylistically, there are kungfu scenes from martial art director Chen Hsiao Tung (director of *Chinese Ghost Story*), visionary special effects from Tsui Hark and art design from King Hu, who eventually set the story in his preferred Ming Dynasty. Its pace is one of the contemporary commercial Hong Kong film, much faster than King Hu's normal work. It employs Tsui Hark's cynical view of life, showing almost none of the characters to be trustworthy: they all have their own selfish ambitions, the fact of which breaks down the easy formulation of hero and villain. King Hu's specialty, the power struggles within intensive circumstances, is still in evidence, while a rather forced romantic relationship is evidence of Chen's hand.

King Hu's metaphysical Zen and the sublimation of the spiritual are not themes in *The Swordsman*. They are replaced by the nihilism of Tsui Hark, as seen when the protagonist and his girlfriend ride without a clear direction on an uncultivated field after they both encounter some of the complexities of life. Somehow more rooted in reality, King Hu subsequently prepared a film about the Chinese railroad workers' early U.S. history following immigration in the 19th century.

—Vivian Huang

KINOSHITA, Keisuke.

Japanese. Born in Hamamatsu City, Shizuoka Prefecture, 5 December 1912. Educated at Hamamatsu Engineering School; Oriental Photography School, Tokyo, 1932–33. Military service, 1940–41. Laboratory assistant, Shochiku's Kamata studios, 1933; camera assistant under chief cinematographer for Yasujiro Shimazu, 1934–36; assistant director, Shimazu's group, 1936–42; chief assistant to director Kozaburo Yoshimura, 1939; director, from 1943; left Shochiku, began as TV director, 1964. Recipient: Kinema Jumpo Best Film of the Year, for *The Morning of the Osone Family*, 1946, *24 Eyes*, 1954, and *The Ballad of Narayama*, 1958. Address: Mamiana Mansions, #910, 44 Maniana-cho, Minato-ku, Tokyo, Japan.

Films as Director:

1943   *Hanasaku minato* (*The Blossoming Port*); *Ikite-iru Magoroku* (*The Living Magoroku*) (+ sc)
1944   *Kanko no machi* (*Jubilation Street. Cheering Town*); *Rikugun* (*The Army*)
1946   *Osone-ke no asa* (*Morning for the Osone Family*); *Waga koiseshi otome* (*The Girl I Loved*) (+ sc)
1947   *Kekkon* (*Marriage*) (+ story); *Fujicho* (*Phoenix*) (+ sc)
1948   *Onna* (*Woman*) (+ sc); *Shozo* (*The Portrait*); *Hakai* (*Apostasy*)
1949   *Ojosan kanpai* (*A Toast to the Young Miss. Here's to the Girls*); *Yotsuya kaidan, I–II* (*The Yotsuya Ghost Story, Parts I and II*); *Yabure daiko* (*Broken Drum*) (+ co-sc)
1950   *Konyaku yubiwa* (*Engagement Ring*) (+ sc)
1951   *Zemma* (*The Good Fairy*) (+ co-sc); *Karumen kokyo ni kaeru* (*Carmen Comes Home*) (+ sc); *Shonen ki* (*A Record of Youth*) (+ co-sc); *Umi no hanabi* (*Fireworks over the Sea*) (+ sc)
1952   *Karumen junjo su* (*Carmen's Pure Love*) (+ sc)
1953   *Nihon no higeki* (*A Japanese Tragedy*) (+ sc)
1954   *Onna no sono* (*The Garden of Women*) (+ sc); *Nijushi no hitomi* (*Twenty-four Eyes*) (+ sc)
1955   *Toi kumo* (*Distant Clouds*) (+ co-sc); *Nogiku no gotoki kimi nariki* (*You Were Like a Wild Chrysanthemum*) (+ sc)
1956   *Yuyake-gumo* (*Clouds at Twilight*); *Taiyo to bara* (*The Rose on His Arm*) (+ sc)
1957   *Yorokobi mo kanashimi mo ikutoshitsuki* (*Times of Joy and Sorrow, The Lighthouse*) (+ sc); *Fuzen no tomoshibi* (*A Candle in the Wind, Danger Stalks Near*) (+ sc)
1958   *Narayamabushi-ko* (*The Ballad of the Narayama*) (+ sc); *Kono ten no niji* (*The Eternal Rainbow. The Rainbow of This Sky*) (+ sc)
1959   *Kazabana* (*Snow Flurry*) (+ sc); *Sekishun-cho* (*The Bird of Springs Past*) (+ sc); *Kyo mo mata kakute arinan* (*Thus Another Day*) (+ sc)
1960   *Haru no yume* (*Spring Dreams*) (+ sc); *Fuefuki-gawa* (*The River Fuefuki*) (+ sc)
1961   *Eien no hito* (*The Bitter Spirit. Immortal Love*) (+ sc)
1962   *Kotoshi no koi* (*This Year's Love*) (+ sc); *Futari de aruita iku-haru-aki* (*The Seasons We Walked Together*) (+ sc)
1963   *Utae, wakodo-tachi* (*Sing, Young People!*); *Shito no densetsu* (*Legend of a Duel to the Death*) (+ sc)
1964   *Koge* (*The Scent of Incense*) (+ sc)
1967   *Natsukashiki fue ya taiko* (*Lovely Flute and Drum*) (+ pr, sc)
1976   *Suri Lanka no ai to wakare* (*Love and Separation in Sri Lanka*) (+ sc)
1979   *Shodo satsujin: Musukoyo* (*My Son*) (+ sc)
1983   *Kono ko o nokoshite* (*The Children of Nagasaki. These Children Survive Me*)
1986   *Yorokobi mo kanashima mo ikutoshitsuki* (*Times of Joy and Sorrow. Big Joys, Small Sorrows*)

Publications:

By KINOSHITA: article—

"Jisaku o kataru," [Keisuke Kinoshita Talks About His Films], in *Kinema Jumpo* (Tokyo), no.115, 1955.
Interview with P. Vecchi, in *Cineforum* (Bergamo), August 1984.
Interview with A. Tournès, in *Jeune Cinéma* (Paris), November–December 1986.

On KINOSHITA: books—

Anderson, Joseph, and Donald Richie, *The Japanese Film*, New York, 1961.
Mellen, Joan, *The Waves at Genji's Door*, New York, 1976.
Bock, Audie, *Japanese Film Directors*, Tokyo, 1978.
König, Regula, and Marianne Lewinsky, *Keisuke Kinoshita: Entretien, etudes, filmographie, iconographie*, Locarno, 1986.

On KINOSHITA: articles—

"Keisuke Kinoshita," in *Film Dope* (London), September 1984.
Tournès, A., "Terres inconnues du cinéma japonais," in *Jeune Cinéma* (Paris), October 1984.
Niogret, H., "Keisuke Kinoshita: Un metteur en scène de compagnie," in *Positif* (Paris), July/August 1986.
National Film Theatre Programme (London), March 1987.

*   *   *

Kinoshita's films are characteristic of the Shochiku Studio's work: healthy home drama and melodrama as conventionalized by the studio's two masters, Shimazu and Ozu. The latter two specialized in the genre of depicting everyday family life. Kinoshita gravitated towards sentimentalism and a belief in the eventual triumph of good will and sincere efforts. It was against this "planned unity" that the new generation of Shochiku directors (e.g. Oshima and his group) reacted.

Within this framework, Kinoshita is skilled in various genres. His light satiric comedies began with his first film, *The Blossoming Port*. Although ostensibly it illustrated the patriotism of two con men in a small port town, this film demonstrated Kinoshita's extraordinary talent for witty mise-en-scène and briskly-paced storytelling. His postwar comedies include *Broken Drum*, *Carmen Comes Home*, *Carmen's Pure Love* and *A Candle in the Wind*, which captured the liberated spirit of postwar democratization. *A Toast to the Young Miss* was a kind of situation comedy which became unusually successful due to its excellent cast.

The romantic melodrama became the favorite of women filmgoers. *Marriage* and *Phoenix* surprised the audience with their bold and sophisticated expression of love, helping pioneer the new social morality. *You Were Like a Wild Chrysanthemum* is a romantic, sentimental love story. They were followed by *Distant Clouds* and, years later, *Immortal Love*, *The Scent of Incense*, and *Love and Separation in Sri Lanka*.

The sentimental human drama became Kinoshita's most characteristic genre. It is typified by *24 Eyes*, which deftly appeals to the Japanese audience's sentimentality, depicting the life of a woman teacher on a small island. This was followed

Keisuke Kinoshita

by films such as *Times of Joy and Sorrow, The Seasons We Walked Together*, and *Lovely Flute and Drum*. The Shochiku Studio was proud that these films could attract "women coming with handkerchiefs to wipe away their tears."

Films of rather straightforward social criticism include *Morning for the Osone Family, Apostasy, A Japanese Tragedy, The Garden of Women, The Ballad of the Narayama*, and *Snow Flurry*. These vary from rather crude "postwar democratization" films to ones which deal with the world of folklore, struggles against the feudalistic system, and current social problems.

Kinoshita is adventurous in his technical experimentation. *Carmen Comes Home* is the first Japanese color film, and is highly successful in its use of the new technology. In its sequel, *Carmen's Pure Love*, he employs tilting compositions throughout the film, producing a wry comic atmosphere. In *A Japanese Tragedy*, newsreel footage is inserted to connect the historical background with the narrative. *You Were Like a Wild Chrysanthemum*, a film presented as an old man's memory of his youth, creates a nostalgic effect by vignetting with an oval shape and with misty images. *The Ballad of the Narayama*, except for the last outdoor sequence, takes place on a set which accentuates artificiality and theatricality, with the added effect of a peculiar use of color. Kabuki-style acting, music, and storytelling create the fable-like ambience of this film. In *The River Fuefuki*, the film is entirely tinted in colors which correspond to the sentiment of each scene (e.g. red for fighting scenes, blue for funerals, and green for peaceful village life).

After the Japanese film industry sank into a depression in the 1960s, Kinoshita successfully continued his career in TV for a long period. His skill at entertaining and his sense of experimentation have kept him popular with television audiences as well.

—Kyoko Hirano

KINUGASA, Teinosuke.

Japanese. Born Teinosuke Kogame in Mie Prefecture, 1 January 1896. Educated at Sasayama Private School. Ran away to Nagoya, began theatrical apprenticeship, 1913; stage debut, 1915; *oyama* actor (playing female roles), Nikkatsu Mukojima studio, 1918; wrote and directed first film, 1921; moved to Makino Kinema, 1922; contract director for Shochiku Company, formed Kinugasa Motion Picture League, became involved with new actors' and technicians' union, led mass walkout over plan to replace *oyama* actors with female performers, mid-20's; travelled to Russia and Germany, 1928; returned to Japan, 1929; began association with kabuki actor Hasegawa, 1935; moved to Toho Company, 1939; moved to Daiei Company, 1949, (appointed to board of directors, 1958). Recipient: Best Film, Cannes Festival, Oscar for Best Foreign Film, and Best Foreign Film, New York Film Critics, for *Gate of Hell*, 1954; Purple Ribbon Medal, Japan, for distinguished cultural service, 1958.

Films as Director:

1921   *Imoto no shi (The Death of My Sister)* (+ sc, role)
1922   *Niwa no kotori (Two Little Birds)* (+ sc); *Hibana (Spark)* (+ sc)
1923   *Hanasake jijii* (+ sc); *Jinsei o Mitsumete* (+ sc); *Onna-yo*

ayamaru nakare (+ sc); *Konjiki yasha (The Golden Demon)* (+ sc); *Ma no ike (The Spirit of the Pond)* (+ sc)

1924   *Choraku no kanata (Beyond Decay)* (+ sc); *Kanojo to unmei (She Has Lived Her Destiny)* (in two parts) (+ sc); *Kire no ame (Fog and Rain)* (+ sc); *Kishin yuri keiji* (+ sc); *Kyoren no buto (Dance Training)* (+ sc); *Mirsu (Love)* (+ sc); *Shohin (Shuto)* (+ sc); *Shohin (Shusoku)* (+ sc); *Jashumon no onna (A Woman's Heresy)* (+ sc); *Tsuma no himitsu (Secret of a Wife)*; *Koi (Love)*; *Sabishi mura (Lonely Village)*

1925   *Nichirin (The Sun)*; *Koi to bushi (Love and a Warrior)* (+ sc); *Shinju yoimachigusa*; *Tsukigata hanpeita*; *Wakaki hi no chuji*

1926   *Kurutta ippeiji (A Page of Madness)*; *Kirinji*; *Teru hi kumoru hi (Shining Sun Becomes Clouded)*; *Hikuidori (Cassowary)*; *Ojo Kichiza*; *Oni azami*; *Kinno jidai (Epoch of Loyalty)*; *Meoto boshi (Star of Married Couples)*; *Goyosen*; *Dochu sugoruku bune*; *Dochu sugoruku kago (The Palanquin)*; *Akatsuki no yushi (A Brave Soldier at Dawn)*; *Gekka no kyojin (Moonlight Madness)*

1928   ***Jujiro (Crossroads)*** (+ sc); *Benten Kozo (Gay Masquerade)*; *Keiraku hichu*; *Kaikokuki (Tales from a Country by the Sea)*; *Chokon yasha (Female Demon)*

1931   *Reimei izen (Before Dawn)* (+ sc); *Tojin okichi*
1932   *Ikinokata Shinsengumi (The Surviving Shinsengumi)* (+ sc); *Chushingura (The Loyal 47 Ronin. The Vengeance of the 47 Ronin)* (+ sc)
1933   *Tenichibo to iganosuke* (+ sc); *Futatsu doro (Two Stone Lanterns)* (+ sc); *Toina no Ginpei (Ginpei from Koina)* (+ sc)
1934   *Kutsukate tokijiro* (+ sc); *Fuyaki shinju* (+ sc); *Ippan gatana dohyoiri (A Sword and the Sumo Ring)* (+ sc); *Nagurareta kochiyama* (+ sc)
1935   *Yukinojo henge (The Revenge of Yukinojo. Yukinojo's Revenge)* (+ co-sc) (in 3 parts, part 3 released 1936); *Kurayama no ushimatsu* (+ sc)
1937   *Hito hada Kannon (The Sacred Protector)* (+ sc) (in 5 parts); *Osaka natsu no jin (The Summer Battle of Osaka)* (+ sc)
1938   *Kuroda seichuroku* (+ sc)
1940   *Hebi himesama (The Snake Princess)* (+ sc) (in two parts)
1941   *Kawanakajima kassen (The Battle of Kawanakajima)* (+ sc)
1943   *Susume dokuritsuki (Forward Flag of Independence)*
1945   *Umi no bara (Rose of the Sea)*
1946   *Aru yo no tonosama (Lord for a Night)*
1947   "Koi no sakasu (The Love Circus)" section of *Yottsu no koi no monogatari (The Story of Four Loves)*; *Joyu (Actress)* (+ co-sc)
1949   *Kobanzame (part 2)* (+ sc); *Koga yashiki (Koga Mansion)* (+ sc); *Satsujinsha no kao (The Face of a Murderer)*
1951   *Beni komori* (+ sc); *Tsuki no watari-dori (Migratory Birds Under the Moon)* (+ sc); *Meigatsu somato (Lantern Under a Full Moon)* (+ sc)
1952   *Daibutsu kaigen (Saga of the Great Buddha. The Dedication of the Great Buddha)* (+ sc); *Shurajo hibun* (+ sc) (in 2 parts)
1953   ***Jigokumon (Gate of Hell)*** (+ sc)
1954   *Yuki no yo ketto (Duel of a Snowy Night)* (+ sc); *Hana no nagadosu (End of a Prolonged Journey)* (+ sc); *Tekka bugyo* (+ sc)
1955   *Yushima no shiraume (The Romance of Yushima. White Sea of Yushima)* (+ sc); *Kawa no aru shitamachi no hanashi (It Happened in Tokyo)* (+ sc); *Bara ikutabi (A Girl Isn't Allowed to Love)* (+ sc)
1956   *Yoshinaka o meguru sannin no onna (Three Women Around Yoshinaka)* (+ sc); *Hibana (Spark)* (+ sc); *Tsukigata hanpeita* (in 2 parts) (+ sc)
1957   *Shirasagi (White Heron. The Snowy Heron)* (+ sc); *Ukifune (Floating Vessel)* (+ sc); *Naruto hicho (A Fantastic Tale of Naruto)* (+ sc)
1958   *Haru koro no hana no en (A Spring Banquet)* (+ sc); *Osaka no onna (A Woman of Osaka)* (+ sc)
1959   *Joen (Tormented Flame)* (+ sc); *Kagero ezu (Stop the Old Fox)* (+ sc)
1960   *Uta andon (The Old Lantern)* (+ sc)
1961   *Midare-gami (Dishevelled Hair)* (+ sc); *Okoto to Sasuke (Okoto and Sasuke)* (+ sc)

Teinosuke Kinugasa directing *White Heron*

1963 *Yoso* (*Priest and Empress. The Sorcerer*) (+ sc); episode of
Uso (*When Women Lie, Lies*)
1967 *Chiisana tobosha* (*The Little Runaway*) (co-d)

Other Films: (incomplete listing)

1918 *Nanairo yubi wa* (*The Seven Colored Ring*) (Oguchi) (film
acting debut)
1920 *Ikeru shikabane* (*The Living Corpse*) (Tanaka) (role)

Publications:

By KINUGASA: articles—

Interview with H. Niogret, in *Positif* (Paris), May 1973.
"Une Page folle," interview with Max Tessier, in *Ecran* (Paris), April
1975.

On KINUGASA: book—

Anderson, Joseph, and Donald Richie, *The Japanese Film: Art and
Industry*, New York, 1960; revised edition, Princeton, New Jersey,
1982.

On KINUGASA: articles—

Tessier, Max, "Yasujiro Ozu et le cinéma japonais à la fin du muet," in
Ecran (Paris), December 1979.
Tessier, Max, obituary, in *Image et Son* (Paris), April 1982.
Obituary in *Cinéma* (Paris), June 1982.
Petric, Vlad, "*A Page of Madness*: A Neglected Masterpiece of the
Silent Cinema," in *Film Criticism* (Meadville, Pennsylvania), Fall
1983.
"Teinosuke Kinugasa," in *Film Dope* (London), January 1985.
Cinema Journal (Champaign, Illinois), Autumn 1989.

* * *

Teinosuke Kinugasa made two of the most famous films ever to
come out of Japan, and was, historically, the first of his country's directors known in the West. When *Rashomon* began that
process by which we began to understand and admire Japanese
cinema, some older observers remembered *Crossroads* (1928),
which had some showings in Europe in 1929 and in New York
in 1930, under the title *The Slums of Tokyo*. On one hand this
is the Japanese equivalent of the German "street" films, and
on the other it is the oft-told local tale of a hard-working, self-
sacrificing woman who suffers on behalf of her idle younger
brother, who is, as ever, in love with a painted lady.

The pace is slow, but the film is the work of a master. As in
his earlier surrealist, experimental *A Page of Madness* (1926),
which made a late, freak appearance in the West in 1973, he
intercuts furiously, both to express mental agitation and to
move backwards and forwards in time, in a way seldom used in
Western cinema until the *Nouvelle Vague* in the 1960s.

Kinugasa's films of the 1930s confirm the impression that he
did not regard the camera as a mere recorder: we may be astonished by the number of glides, of overhead shots, of sudden
close-ups, each correctly juxtaposed against the images on
either side. It is clear that Kinugasa, along with his peers, used
this "decorative" approach rather more freely with historical
subjects: if you compare his most popular film, *The Revenge of
Yukinojo* with Ichikawa's 1963 remake, *An Actor's Revenge*,
you will find many of the shots duplicated, despite the stunning
addition of colour and wide screen. (The same actor, Kazuo
Hasegawa, appeared in both, but here under the pseudonym
Chojiro Hayashi.)

The two films are too far apart, chronologically, to make
further comparisons, but in 1947 Kinugasa directed *Actress*,
while Mizoguchi tackled the same subject, based on fact, in
The Love of Sumako the Actress. In this case Mizoguchi's version has an intensity lacking in Kinugasa's film, but that has
more subtlety.

Gate of Hell (1953) was the first Japanese colour film seen in
the West, and only one other film had preceded it, after *Rashomon*. It bowled over almost everyone who saw it: the gold,
scarlet, beige, white and green of the costumes; the mists, the
moon, the sea, the distant hills. We did not know then how
many Japanese films start this way, with an exposition of a
country torn apart by war and revolution—nor how many of
them concerned murderous and amorous intrigues concerning
feudal warlords and their courtesans. *Gate of Hell* is an exquisite picture, but it remains overshadowed by Mizoguchi's
(black-and-white) historical films of this period. It lacks their
power, tension, their breadth and their sheer craftsmanship:
but then, they are among the greatest films ever made.

It was in this decade and into the 1960s that the Japanese cinema flowered, with a series of masterpieces by Kurosawa,
Kobayashi, Ichikawa and others. Some of the older directors,
including Kinugasa, continued to make films of integrity and
skill: but many of their films look a little plodding beside those
made by the younger generation.

—David Shipman

———

KLIMOV, Elem.

Soviet. Born in Volgograd, 9 July 1933. Studied at Moscow
Higher Institute of Aviation, graduated 1957; VGIK Film
School, Moscow (under Efim Dzigan), graduated 1964. Married director Larisa Shepitko (killed in car crash, July 1979).
Worked as an engineer, from 1957, then as foreign correspondent for TV and radio before Film School; director for Mosfilm, from 1964; appointed Head of the Soviet Filmmakers'
Union, 1986. Recipient: Grand Prix, Moscow Festival, for *Idi i
smotri*, 1985.

Films as Director:

1959 *Smotritye Nyebo!* (*Look—The Sky!*) (short); *Zhenikh* (*The
Suitor*) (short)
1964 *Dobro pozhalovat, ili postoronnim vkhod vospreshchyon*
(*Welcome, or No Entry for Unauthorised Persons*)
1965 *Pokhozhdyeniya zubnovo vracha* (*Adventures of a Dentist*)
1967 *Otsy—Odinochkiye* (*Single Fathers*) (short)
1970 *Sport, Sport, Sport*
1974 *I vyso taki ya vyeryu* (*And Nonetheless I Believe*) (co-d)
1975 *Agoniya* (*Agony. Rasputin*) (shown at Moscow Festival, 1981,
released 1984)
1980 *Larisa* (short)
1981 ***Proshchanie (Farewell)***
1985 *Idi i smotri* (*Come and See*)

Publications:

By KLIMOV: book—

*Larisa: Vospmininaniya, vystuplenya, yntervoryu, kinostsenarii, sta-
tory*, compiled by Klimov, Moscow, 1987.

By KLIMOV: articles—

Interview in *Filmfaust* (Frankfurt), June/September 1983.
Interview with M. Martin and C. Zander, in *Jeune Cinéma* (Paris),
December 1983/January 1984.
Interview in *Iskusstvo Kino* (Moscow), June 1984.
Interview in *Jeune Cinéma* (Paris), November/December 1985.
"Le Cinéma non plus ne peut attendre," in *Positif* (Paris), December
1986.

Interview with L. Tanner, in *Films in Review* (New York), January 1987.

Interview in *Time Out* (London), 13 May 1987.

"Back in the USSR," in *American Film* (Washington, D.C.), March 1988.

On KLIMOV: articles—

Navailh, F., "Union Soviétique: Des Films sous le boisseau," in *Cinéma* (Paris), May 1983.

Soviet Film, no. 11, 1986 and nos. 5 and 12, 1987.

Positif (Paris), December 1986.

Le Fanu, Mark, "Elem Klimov," in *Sight and Sound* (London), Winter 1986/87.

Kitson, Claire, "Elem Klimov," in *National Film Theatre Booklet* (London), April 1987.

Christie, Ian, "Klimov," in *Sight and Sound* (London), Summer 1987.

Lewis, B., "Farewell to Agony," in *Films and Filming* (London), June 1987.

Christie, Ian, "Unauthorised Persons Enter Here," in *Monthly Film Bulletin* (London), July 1987.

*   *   *

There is a sense in which Elem Klimov can be seen as an example of the particular moment of *glasnost* and *perestroika* in the Soviet Union. His career as the author of half a dozen feature films made over some twenty years, nearly all of which were subject to bureaucratic interference which resulted in them being 'shelved' is emblematic. The script for *Agonia*, Klimov's bold and rhetorical picture of court life and politics chez the Romanovs, was written eight years before it was finally able to be shot, while its release was delayed another ten.) Only *Nonetheless I Believe*, the film Klimov completed following the death of Mikhail Romm, passed unproblematically to the screen. Klimov's appointment as First Secretary of the newly empowered Film Makers' Union likewise personifies the triumph of the creative over the merely bureaucratic to which the new policies were dedicated. It is Klimov too who in his travels to the West has acted as ambassador and spokesman for these policies.

Klimov's work falls into two very distinct phases, although it is possible to trace the persistence of certain preoccupations and techniques across his films. The early comedies, *The Adventures of a Dentist*, *Sport Sport Sport* or *Welcome, or No Entry for Unauthorised Persons* resort to irony and metaphor, weapons of the sixties thaw familiar from the Czech New Wave, potent weapons too in a period of stagnation. In *Adventures of a Dentist* the practitioner concerned discovers a method of painless tooth extraction and finds himself under attack—the reward of initiative. All three films make use of fantasy sequences, montage and framing devices of various sorts, as well as an interest in the possibilities afforded by "found footage" of various kinds, documentary and newsreel film. These effects are put to serious use in *Come and See* in which footage of Hitler and the death camps is used to "prove" film's impotence to "roll back" history. (The newsreel footage is rewound until we, and the film's protagonist, are confronted by a photograph of an infant Hitler.) Likewise in *Farewell* there is a shot of a figure capped and coated like the Lenin familiar from hagiographic portrayal, going down with his sinking ship.

In both *Farewell*, a project inherited from his wife Larissa Shepitko who died during the shooting (Klimov does not use any of her footage) and *Come and See*, Klimov furthered his explorations of alternatives to naturalism in another direction, taking cinema into the rich territory of 19th-century poetic realism as explored for instance, by the landscape artist Ivan Shishkin. As in Shishkin's canvasses, in Klimov's films the Russian landscape becomes a character in its own right. Based on a story by the "village" writer Valentin Rasputin, *Farewell*

traces the destruction of a village by the development of a hydro-electric scheme. In doing so it takes up Rasputin's Slavophilic lament for the integrity of a "lost" and idealised peasant culture. Likewise in *Come and See*, perhaps the ultimate *glasnost* film with all that word implies of bearing witness, the landscape and especially the forest, initially Eden-like and unsullied, becomes, before our eyes, despoiled and degraded.

Although explicitly commemorating Nazi genocide in Byelorussia, the film's first third or so seems to bear witness to a far more generalised sense of betrayal and desecration. It is a film of disillusionment pitched to the level of a nightmare. It also, shot for shot and character by character, acts as a riposte to a whole generation of heroic war films.

Whether or not Klimov will continue to explore this particular seam within the far more pluralistic conditions that now exist, his importance for Soviet (or perhaps more accurately Russian) cinema, lies in his recognition of the cinema's power to explore—rather than merely exploit—experience.

—Verina Glaessner

———

KLUGE, Alexander.

German. Born in Halberstadt, 14 February 1932. Educated at Charlottenburger Gymnasium, Berlin, Abitur 1949; studied law and history at Freiburg, Marburg, and Johann-Wolfgang Goethe Universität, Frankfurt (degree in law, 1953). Lawyer, novelist, and political writer, 1950's; began in films as assistant to Fritz Lang, 1958; leader and spokesman of group of German filmmakers protesting condition of German filmmaking, Oberhausen Festival, 1962; head of film division of Hochschule für Gestaltung in Ulm (known as "Institut für Filmgestaltung"), from 1962; founder, Kairos-Films, 1963. Recipient: Berliner Kuntspreis for *Lebensläufe*, 1964; Bayrischer Staatspreis für Literatur, for *Porträt einer Bewärung* and for *Schlachtbeschreibung*; Golden Lion, Venice Festival, for *Die Artisten in der Zirkus-kuppel: ratlos*, 1967; Honorary Professor, University of Frankfurt am Main, 1973; International Critics award, Cannes Festival, for *Ferdinand the Strongman*, 1976; Fontane-Preis, 1979; Grosser Breme Literatur-preis, 1979.

Films as Director:

1960 *Brutalität in Stein* (*Die Ewigkeit von gestern*) [Brutality in Stone, Yesterday Goes On for Ever] (co-d) (short)

1961 *Rennen* [Racing] (co-d) (short)

1963 *Lehrer im Wandel* [Teachers in Transformation] (co-d) (short)

1964 *Porträt einer Bewährung* [Portrait of One Who Proved His Mettle] (short)

1966 *Pokerspiel* (short); *Abschied von gestern* (*Yesterday Girl*)

1967 *Frau Blackburn, geb. 5.Jan. 1872, wird gefilmt* [Frau Blackburn, Born 5 Jan. 1872, Is Filmed] (short); *Die Artisten in der Zirkuskuppel: ratlos* (*Artistes at the Top of the Big Top—Disoriented*)

1968 *Feuerlöscher E.A.Winterstein* [Fireman E.A.Winterstein] (short)

1969 *Die unbezähmbare Leni Peickert* [The Indomitable Leni Peickert]; *Ein Arzt aus Halberstadt* [A Doctor from Halberstadt] (short)

1970 *Der grosse Verhau* [The Big Dust-up]

1971 *Wir verbauen 3 × 27 Milliarden Dollar in einen Angriffsschlachter* (*Der Angriffsschlachter*) [We'll Blow 3 × 27 Billion Dollars on a Destroyer (The Destroyer)] (short); *Willi Tobler und der Untergang der sechste Flotte* (*Willi Tobler and the Wreck of the Sixth Fleet*)

Alexander Kluge: *Abschied von gestern*

1972 *Besitzbürgerin, Jahrgang 1908* [A Woman from the Property-
owning Middle Class, Born 1908] (short)
1973 *Gelegenheitsarbeit einer Sklavin* (*Occasional Work of a Female
Slave*)
1974 *In Gefahr und grösster Not bringt der Mittelweg den Tod* (*The
Middle of the Road Is a Very Dead End*)
1975 *Der starke Ferdinand* (*Strongman Ferdinand*); *Augen aus
einem anderen Land*
1977 *Die Menschen, die die Staufer-Austellung vorbereiten* (*Die
Menschen, die das Stauferjahr vorbereiten*) [The People
Who Are Preparing the Year of the Hohenstaufens] (co-d)
(short); '*Zu böser Schlacht schleich' ich heut' Nacht so bang'*
[In Such Trepidation I Creep Off Tonight to the Evil
Battle''] (revised version of *Willi Tobler and the Wreck of
the Sixth Fleet*)
1979 *Die Patriotin* (*The Patriotic Woman*)
1980 *Der Kandidat* (co-d)
1983 *Krieg und Frieden* (co-d); *Die Macht der Gefühle*
1985 *Der Angriff der Gegenwart auf die Ubrige Zeit*
1987 *Vermischte Nachrichten*

Other Films:

1965 *Unendliche Fahrt—aber begrenzt* (Reitz) (feature) (text)
1973 *Die Reise nach Wien* (Reitz) (sc)
1978 *Deutschland im Herbst* (*Germany in Autumn*) (Schlöndorff)
(contribution)

Publications:

By KLUGE: books—

Kulturpolitik und Ausgabenkontrolle, Frankfurt, 1961.
Lebensläufe, Stuttgart, 1962; 2nd edition, Frankfurt, 1974.

Schlachtbeschreibung, Olten and Freiburg, 1964; expanded edition,
Munich, 1978.
Abschied von gestern, Frankfurt am Main, undated.
*Die Artisten in der Zirkuskuppel: ratlos. Die Ungläubige. Projekt Z.
Sprüche der Leni·Peickert*, Munich, 1968.
Der Untergang der sechsten Armee—Schlachtbeschreibung, Munich,
1969.
*Öffentlichkeit und Erfahrung. Zur Organisationsanalyse bürgerlicher
und proletarischer öffentlichkeit*, with Oskar Negt, Frankfurt, 1972.
*Filmwirtschaft in der Bundesrepublik Deutschland und in Europa.
Götterdämmerung in Raten*, with Florian Hopf and Michael Dost,
Munich, 1973.
Lernprozesse mit tödlichem Ausgang, Frankfurt, 1973.
Gelegenheitsarbeit einer Sklavin. Zur realistischen Methode, Frank-
furt, 1975.
Neue Erzählungen. Hefte 1–18 "Unheimlichkeit der Zeit", Frankfurt,
1977.
Die Patriotin, Frankfurt, 1979.
Geschichte und Eigensinn, with Oskar Negt, 1982.
Die Macht der Gefühle, Frankfurt, 1984.
Der Angriff de Gegenwart auf die übrige zeit, Frankfurt, 1985.

By KLUGE: articles—

"Medienproduktion," in *Perspektiven der kommunalen Kulturpolitik*
edited by Hoffman and Hilmar, Frankfurt, 1974.
"KINO-Gespräch mit Alexander Kluge," interview with A. Meyer, in
KINO (Berlin), May 1974.
Interview with J. Dawson, in *Film Comment* (New York), November/
December 1974.
"Film ist das natürliche Tauschverhältnis der Arbeit . . . ," interview
with B. Steinborn, in *Filmfaust* (Frankfurt), December 1977.
"Das Theater der spezialisten, Kraut und Rüben," interview with M.
Schaub, in *Cinema* (Zurich), May 1978.
"Kluge Issue" of *ZEIT Magazin*, no. 11, 9 March 1979.
"*Die Patriotin*: Entstehungsgeschichte—Inhalt," in *Filmkritik* (Mun-
ich), November 1979.
"Eine realistische Haltung müsste der Zuschauer haben, müsste ich
jaben, müsste der Film Haben," with R. Frey, in *Filmfaust* (Frank-
furt), November 1980.
Interviews with B. Steinborn in *Filmfaust* (Frankfurt), February/
March 1982 and February/March 1983.

ON KLUGE: books—

Buselmeier, M., *In Gefahr und grösster Not bringt der Mittelweg den
Tod. Zur Operativität bei Alexander Kluge*, Heidelberg, 1975.
Gregor, Ulrich, and others, *Herzog, Kluge, Straub*, Munich, 1976.
Kötz, M., and P. Höhe, *Sinnlichkeit des Zusammenhangs, Zur Film-
strategie Alexander Kluges*, Frankfurt, 1979.
Lewandowski, Rainer, *Alexander Kluge*, Munich, 1980.
Sandford, John, *The New German Cinema*, Totowa, New Jersey,
1980.
Franklin, James, *New German Cinema: From Oberhausen to Ham-
burg*, Boston, 1983.
Phillips, Klaus, *New German Filmmakers: From Oberhausen through
the 1970s*, New York, 1984.
Carp, Stefanie, *Kriegsgeschichten: Zum Werk Alexander Kluges*,
Munich, 1987.
Rentschler, Eric, *West German Filmmakers on Film: Visions and
Voices*, New York, 1988.
Elsaesser, Thomas, *New German Cinema: A History*, London, 1989.

On KLUGE: articles—

"Kluge Issue" of *Filmkritik* (Munich), December 1976.
Moeller, H.-B., and C. Springer, "Directed Change in the Young Ger-
man Film: Alexander Kluge and Artists under the Big Top: Per-
plexed," in *Wide Angle* (Athens, Ohio), v.2, no.1, 1978.
Bruck, J., "Kluge's Antagonistic Concept of Realism," in *Australian
Journal of Screen Theory* (Kensington, New South Wales), no.
13/14, 1983.
Tournès, A., "Kluge: L'intelligence du sentiment. Armer les enti-
ments," in *Jeune Cinéma* (Paris), November 1983.
"Alexander Kluge," in *Film Dope* (London), January 1985.
Hansen, M., "The Stubborn Discourse: History and Story-Telling in
the films of Alexander Kluge," in *Persistence of Vision* (Maspeth,
New York), Fall 1985.

Steinborn, B., "Der Verfuhrerische Charme der Phantasie," in *Film-faust* (Frankfurt), December 1985/January 1986.

* * *

Alexander Kluge, the chief ideologue of the new German cinema, is the author of various books in the areas of sociology, contemporary philosophy, and social theory. In 1962 he helped initiate, and was the spokesman for, the "Oberhausen Manifesto" in which "Das Opas Kino" ("grandpa's cinema") was declared dead.

At the same time Kluge published his first book, *Lebensläufe*: a collection of stories that presented a comprehensive cross-section of contemporary life along with its deeply-rooted historical causes. His method is grounded in a rich and representative mosaic of sources: fiction, public records and reports, essays, actual occurrences, news, quotations, observations, ideas, and free associations. The method is used by Kluge as a principle of construction in his best films such as *Abschied von gestern, Die Artisten . . . , In Gefahr . . . ,* and in the series of collective films: *Deutschland im Herbst, Der Kandidat,* and *Krieg und Frieden.* The theme of war, in particular the Second World War, appears in all his works.

Kluge views filmmaking as another form of writing since it essentially continues the recording of his participation in the development of society and in everyday life. His unifying creative trait could be called verbal concentration, or image concentration. His filmic activity is a living extension of his comprehensive epistemological and sociological researches, which he has published, together with Oskar Negt (associated with the "Frankfurt School" of Adorno and Horkheimer), as *Öffentlichkeit und Erfahrung* (1972) and *Geschichte und Eigensinn* (1982).

Kluge's films probe reality—not by way of the fantastic fictions of Fassbinder, or film school pictures as with Wenders—but through establishing oppositions and connections between facts, artifacts, reflections, and bits of performance. The protagonists of his feature films are mostly women who seek to grasp and come to terms with their experiences. For the sake of continuity these women are played either by Alexandra Kluge, his sister, or by Hannelore Hoger. They move through the jungle of contemporary life, watching and witnessing, suffering and fighting. The director mirrors their experiences.

As a filmmaker, Kluge is unique, but not isolated. The three collective films, which together with Volker Schlöndorff, Fassbinder, Stephan Aust, and others, he has devoted to the most pressing contemporary events, are something new and original in the history of world cinema. Without Kluge these would be inconceivable, since it is he who pulls together and organizes, aesthetically and ideologically, the fragments filmed by the others. He creates film forms and image structures to transform the various narrative modes and artistic conceptions into a new, conscious, mobilized art of cinema, free of fantasy. This cinema is not only non-traditional, but conveys a socio-historical content.

Without Kluge a new German cinema would be scarcely conceivable, since creative inspiration needs to be supported by a strong film-political foundation. It is thanks to him, above all, that film was officially promoted in the Federal Republic, and that film in Germany has been taken seriously in the last two decades. An untiring fighter for the interests of his colleagues, Kluge gets involved whenever the fate of the new German cinema is at stake.

—Maria Racheva

KOBAYASHI, Masaki.

Japanese. Born in Hokkaido, 4 February 1916. Educated in Oriental art at Waseda University, Tokyo, 1933–41. Assistant at Shochiku's Ofuna studios for 8 months, 1941; drafted into military service, served in Manchuria, 1942–44; following his refusal to be promoted above rank of private as expression of opposition to conduct of war, transferred to Ryukyu Islands, 1944, then interned in detention camp on Okinawa. Returned to Shochiku, 1946; assistant director on staff of Keisuke Kinoshita, 1947–52; directed first film, 1952; Recipient, Special Jury Prizes, Cannes Festival, for *Seppuku*, 1963, and for *Kwaidan*, 1965.

Films as Director:

1952   *Musuko no seishun (My Sons' Youth)*
1953   *Magokoro (Sincerity. Sincere Heart)*
1954   *Mittsu no ai (Three Loves)* (+ sc); *Kono hiroi sora no dokoka ni (Somewhere under the Broad Sky)*
1955   *Uruwashiki saigetsu (Beautiful Days)*
1956   *Kabe atsuki heya (The Thick-Walled Room)* (completed 1953); *Izumi (The Spring. The Fountainhead)*; *Anata kaimasu (I'll Buy You)*
1957   *Kuroi kawa (Black River)*
1959   ***Ningen no joken I (The Human Condition, Part I: No Greater Love)*** (+ co-sc); ***Ningen no joken II (The Human Condition, Part II: Road to Eternity)*** (+ co-sc)
1961   ***Ningen no joken III (The Human Condition, Part III: A Soldier's Prayer)*** (+ co-sc)
1962   *Karami-ai (The Entanglement. The Inheritance)*; ***Seppuku (Harakiri)***
1964   ***Kaidan (Kwaidan)***
1967   *Joiuchi (Rebellion)*
1968   *Nihon no seishun (The Youth of Japan. Hymn to a Tired Man)*
1971   *Inochi bo ni furo (Inn of Evil. At the Risk of My Life)*
1975   *Kaseki (Fossils)* (originally made for TV as 8-part series)
1983   *Tokyo saiban (The Tokyo Trials)* (documentary)
1985   *Shokutaku no nai ie (The Empty Table)*

Publications:

By KOBAYASHI: articles—

"Harakiri, Kobayashi, Humanism," interview with James Silke, in *Cinema* (Beverly Hills), June/July 1963.
"Cinq japonais en quête de films: Masaki Kobayashi," interview with Max Tessier, in *Ecran* (Paris), March 1972.
Interview with Joan Mellen, in *Voices from the Japanese Cinema*, New York, 1975.
Interview with A. Tournès, in *Jeune Cinéma* (Paris), April 1985.

On KOBAYASHI: books—

Bock, Audie, *Japanese Film Directors*, New York, 1978; revised edition, Tokyo, 1985.
Blouin, Claude R., *Le Chemin détourné: Essai sur Kobayashi et le cinéma Japonais*, Quebec, 1982.

On KOBAYASHI: articles—

Richie, Donald, "The Younger Talents," in *Sight and Sound* (London), Spring 1960.
Iwabuchi, M., "Kobayashi's Trilogy," in *Film Culture* (New York), Spring 1962.
Esnault, Philippe, "L'Astre japonais," in *Image et Son* (Paris), February 1969.
Kobayashi Section of *Cinéma Québec* (Montreal), February/March 1974.
Tucker, Richard, "Masaki Kobayashi," in *International Film Guide 1977*, London, 1976.
"Masaki Kobayashi," in *Film Dope* (London), January 1985.
Gillett, John, "Masaki Kobayashi: Power and Spectacle," in *National Film Theatre Booklet* (London), July 1990.

* * *

The dilemma of the dissentient—the individual who finds himself irrevocably at odds with his society—is the overriding preoccupation of Kobayashi's films, and one which stems directly from his own experience. In 1942, only months after starting his career at Shochiku studios, Kobayashi was drafted into the Imperial Japanese Army and sent to Manchuria. A reluctant conscript, he refused promotion above the rank of private, and was later made a prisoner of war. Released in 1946, he returned to filmmaking, becoming assistant to Keisuke Kinoshita, whose flair for lyrical composition clearly influenced Kobayashi's own style—though he succeeded, fortunately, in shaking off the older director's penchant for excessive sentimentality.

Initially, Kobayashi's concern with social justice, and the clash between society and the individual, expressed itself in direct treatment of specific current issues: war criminals in *Kabe atsuki heya* (*The Thick-Walled Room*)—a subject so sensitive that the film's release was delayed three years; corruption in sport in *Anata kaimasu* (*I'll Buy You*); and in *Kuroi kawa* (*Black River*) the organized crime and prostitution rampant around U. S. bases in Japan. This phase of Kobayashi's career culminated in his towering three-part, nine-hour epic, *Ningen no joken* (*The Human Condition*), a powerful and moving indictment of the systematized brutality inherent in a militaristic society.

The ordeal of the pacifist Kaji, hero of *Ningen no joken* (played by Tatsuya Nakadai, Kobayashi's favorite actor), closely parallels the director's own experiences during the war. Kaji is the archetypal Kobayashi hero, who protests, struggles, and is finally killed by an oppressive and inhumane system. His death changes nothing, and will not even be recorded; yet the mere fact of it stands as an assertion of indomitable humanity. Similarly, the heroes of Kobayashi's two finest films, *Seppuku* (*Harakiri*) and *Joiuchi* (*Rebellion*), revolt, make their stand, and die—to no apparent avail. In these films Kobayashi turned the conventions of the *jidai-geki* (period movie) genre to his own ends, using historical settings to universalize his perennial theme of the dissident individual. The masterly blend of style and content, with the unbending ritual of samurai convention perfectly matched by cool, reticent camera movement and elegantly geometric composition, marks in these two films the peak of Kobayashi's art.

By Japanese standards, Kobayashi has made few films, working slowly and painstakingly with careful attention to detail. From *Seppuku* onwards, an increasing concern with formal beauty has characterized his work, most notably in *Kaidan* (*Kwaidan*). This film, based on four of Lafcadio Hearn's ghost stories, carried for once no social message, but developed a strikingly original use of color and exquisitely stylized visual composition.

The crisis that overtook Japanese cinema in the late 1960's hit Kobayashi's career especially hard. His uncompromising seriousness of purpose, and the measured cadences of his style, held little appeal for an industry geared increasingly to flashy exploitation movies. Few of his projects came to fruition, and *Kaseki* (*Fossils*) had initially to be made for television, a medium he dislikes. He refused to watch the eight-hour TV transmission, regarding it merely as rough footage for his 213-minute cinema version.

Kaseki, in which a middle-aged businessman confronts the prospect of incurable cancer, seemed to mark a move away from Kobayashi's wider social concerns—as did the far weaker *Moeru aki* (*Glowing Autumn*). *Tokyo saiban* (*The Tokyo Trials*), though, found him back on more characteristic ground. A *tour-de-force* of editing, it used archive and newsreel footage to make compelling drama of the Allied trials of Japanese wartime leaders. And with *Shokutaku no nai ie* (*The Empty Table*), Kobayashi returned to his central preoccupation, with a principled individual (Nakadai once again) standing out against daunting social pressures. Though lacking the impact of *Ningen no joken* or *Seppuku*, it evinced his undiminished skill in exploiting the tension between outward formality and inner turmoil, and reaffirmed the austere integrity that informs all his work.

—Philip Kemp

KONCHALOVSKY, Andrei. *See* **MIKHALKOV-KONCHALOVSKY, Andrei.**

KORDA, Alexander.

Hungarian/British. Born Sándor László Kellner in Puszta Turpósztó, Hungary, 16 September 1893. Educated at schools in Kisújszállás, Mezötúr, and Budapest, until 1909. Married 1) Maria Farkas (actress Maria Corda), 1919 (divorced 1930), one son; 2) Merle Oberon, 1939 (divorced 1945); 3) Alexander Boycun, 1953. Adopted surname Korda, from journalistic pseudonym "Sursum Corda" (meaning "lift up your hearts"), from 1910; worked at Pathé studios, Paris, 1911; title writer and secretary, Pictograph films, Budapest, and founder of film journal *Pesti mozi*, 1912; directed first film, 1914; formed Corvin production company, with Miklós Pásztory, built studio near Budapest, 1917; arrested under Horthy regime, fled to Vienna, 1919; formed Corda Film Consortium, 1920 (dissolved 1922); formed Korda-Films, Berlin, 1923; with wife, contracted to First National, Hollywood, 1927; hired by Paramount French subsidiary, 1930; moved to British Paramount, London, 1931; founder, London Films, 1932; built Denham Studios, also made partner in United Artists, 1935 (sold interest, 1944); lost control of Denham Studios, 1938; formed Alexander Korda Productions, retained position as head of London Films, 1939; based in Hollywood, 1940–43; entered partnership with MGM, 1943 (dissolved 1946); reorganized London Films, bought controlling interest in British Lion (distributors), 1946; founder, British Film Academy (now British Academy of Film and Television Arts), 1947. Recipient: Knighthood, 1942. *Died in London, 23 January 1956.*

Films as Director:

1914   *A becsapott újságíró* [The Duped Journalist] (co-d); *Tutyu és Totyo* [Tutyu and Totyo] (co-d)
1915   *Lyon Lea* [Lea Lyon] (co-d); *A tiszti kardbojt* [The Officer's Swordknot] (+ sc)
1916   *Fehér éjszakák* [White Nights] or *Fedora* (+ sc); *A nagymama* [The Grandmother] (+ sc); *Mesék az írógépröl* [Tales of the Typewriter] (+ sc); *A kétszívü férfi* [The Man with Two Hearts]; *Az egymillió fontos bankó* [The One Million Pound Note] (+ sc); *Ciklámen* [Cyclamen]; *Vergödö szívek* [Struggling Hearts]; *A nevetö Szaszkia* [The Laughing Saskia]; *Mágnás Miska* [Miska the Magnate]
1917   *Szent Péter esernyöje* [St. Peter's Umbrella] (+ pr); *A gólyakalifa* [The Stork Caliph] (+ pr); *Mágia* [Magic] (+ pr); *Harrison és Barrison* [Harrison and Barrison] (+ pr)
1918   *Faun* (+ pr); *Az aranyember* [The Man with the Golden Touch] (+ pr); *Mary Ann* (+ pr)

Alexander Korda directing *An Ideal Husband*

1919 *Ave Caesar!* (+ pr); *Fehér rózsa* [White Rose] (+ pr); *Yamata*
    (+ pr); *Se ki, se be* [Neither In Nor Out] (+ pr); *A 111-es*
    [Number 111] (+ pr)
1920 *Seine Majestät das Bettelkind* (*Prinz und Bettelknabe. The
    Prince and the Pauper*)
1922 *Heeren der Meere* [Masters of the Sea]; *Eine Versunkene Welt*
    (*Die Tragödie eines Verschollenen Fürstensohnes*) [A
    Vanished World]; *Samson und Delilah* (*Samson and
    Delilah*) (+ pr)
1923 *Das unbekannte Morgen* (*The Unknown Tomorrow*) (+ pr)
1924 *Jedermanns Frau* (*Jedermanns Weib*) [Everybody's Woman]
    (+ pr); *Tragödie im Hause Habsburg* (*Das Drama von
    Mayerling*) [Tragedy in the House of Hapsburg] (+ pr)
1925 *Der Tänzer meiner Frau* (*Dancing Mad*)
1926 *Madame wünscht keine Kinder* (*Madame Wants No Children*)
1927 *Eine Dubarry von heute* (*A Modern Dubarry*); *The Stolen
    Bride*; *The Private Life of Helen of Troy*
1928 *Yellow Lily*; *Night Watch*
1929 *Love and the Devil*; *The Squall*; *Her Private Life*
1930 *Lilies of the Field*; *Women Everywhere*; *The Princess and the
    Plumber*
1931 *Die Manner um Lucie* (+ pr); *Rive Gauche* (French version of
    Die Manner um Lucie) (+ pr); *Marius*; *Zum Goldenen
    Anker* (German version of *Marius*)
1932 *Service for Ladies* (*Reserved for Ladies*) (+ pr)
1933 *Wedding Rehearsal* (+ pr); **The Private Life of Henry VIII** (+
    pr); *The Girl from Maxim's* (+ co-pr)

1934 *La Dame de Chez Maxim* (French version) (+ pr); *The Private
    Life of Don Juan* (+ pr)
1936 *Rembrandt* (+ pr)
1941 *That Hamilton Woman* (*Lady Hamilton*) (+ pr)
1945 *Perfect Strangers* (*Vacation from Marriage*) (+ pr)
1947 *An Ideal Husband* (+ pr)

Publications:

On KORDA: books—

Balcon, Michael, and others, *Twenty Years of British Films, 1925–45*,
    London, 1947.
Brunel, Adrian, *Nice Work: The Story of Thirty Years in British Film
    Production*, London, 1949.
Tabori, Paul, *Alexander Korda*, London, 1959.
Cowie, Peter, *Korda*, in *Anthologie du Cinéma* no. 6, Paris, 1965.
Nemeskurty, István, *Word and Image: A History of the Hungarian
    Cinema*, Budapest, 1968.
Kulik, Karol, *Alexander Korda: The Man Who Could Work Miracles*,
    London, 1975.
Korda, Michael, *Charmed Lives: A Family Romance*, New York,
    1979.

On KORDA: articles—

Watts, Stephen, "Alexander Korda and the International Film," in
    Cinema Quarterly, Autumn 1933.

Lejeune, C.A., "Alexander Korda: A Sketch," in *Sight and Sound* (London), Spring 1935.

Harman, Jympson, "'Alex': A Study of Korda," in *British Film Yearbook 1949–50*, London, 1949.

Price, Peter, "The Impresario Urge," in *Sight and Sound* (London), November 1950.

Campbell, Colin, "The Producer: Sir Alexander Korda," in *Sight and Sound* (London), Summer 1951.

Gilliat, Sidney, and others, "Sir Alexander Korda," in *Sight and Sound* (London), Spring 1956.

Richards, Jeffrey, "Korda's Empire: Politics and Films in *Sanders of the River, The Drum* and *The Four Feathers*," in *Australian Journal of Screen Theory* (Kensington, New South Wales), no. 5–6, 1980.

Taylor, John Russell, "Tales of the Hollywood Raj. Alexander Korda: Showman or Spy?," in *Films and Filming* (London), July 1983.

"Alexander Korda," in *Film Dope* (London), January 1985.

Street, Sarah, "Denham Studios: The Golden Jubilee of Korda's folly," in *Sight and Sound* (London), Spring 1986.

Street, Sarah, "Alexander Korda, Prudential assurance and British Film Finance in the 1930's," in *Historical Journal of Film, Radio and TV* (Abingdon, Oxon), October 1986.

On KORDA: films—

Vas, Robert, *The Golden Years of Alexander Korda*, BBC TV documentary, 1968.

*   *   *

Alexander Korda may be Britain's most controversial film figure, but there is no doubt that his name stands everywhere for the most splendid vision of cinema as it could be, if one had money and power. Both of these Korda had, although several times he was close to bankruptcy, living on pure Hungarian charm and know-how. He at least had a dream that came near reality on several occasions.

He had two younger brothers, Zoltan, who worked with him as a director, and Vincent, who was an art director; both were outstanding in their fields. Alexander worked as a journalist and film magazine editor before he directed his first film in Hungary in 1914. He had labored long in the cinematic fields of Vienna and Berlin when finally in 1926 his film production of *A Modern Dubarry* earned him a contract in Hollywood with First National, where his initial film was the extravagantly beautiful *The Private Life of Helen of Troy*, starring his wife Maria Corda as Helen. It brought him instant recognition. He directed four features starring Billie Dove (who should have played Helen of Troy for him): *The Stolen Bride, The Night Watch, The Yellow Lily*, and *Her Private Life*, a remake of Zoë Akins's play, which Corinne Griffith had filmed earlier under its stage title, *Declassé*. Korda also directed a sound feature starring Miss Griffith, *Lilies of the Field*. Alexander Korda could soon write his own ticket.

He did just that in 1931, leaving Hollywood to return to England where he set up his own production company, London Film Productions. There he was almost fully occupied with production details, and only directed eight of the many films which his company produced. It was an exciting era for an ambitious producer like Korda. His company's product was so lavish that he seemed in a fair way not only to rival Hollywood but to surpass it. His first big success was *The Private Life of Henry VIII*, starring Charles Laughton as Henry and with Merle Oberon making her debut as the unfortunate Anne Boleyn. Korda then married Miss Oberon, and started to set the stage for her stardom.

Hers was not the only career he established, for he had much to do with the film careers of Laurence Olivier, Vivian Leigh, Robert Donat, and Leslie Howard, among others. He was the power behind it all who set up financial deals for pictures that starred these actors.

While the pictures he directed, like *Rembrandt, That Hamilton Woman*, and *Vacation from Marriage* were done in exquisite taste, he was also involved in the production of such pictures as *Catherine the Great, The Scarlet Pimpernel, Elephant Boy, The Ghost Goes West, Drums, The Four Feathers, The Thief of Bagdad, The Fallen Idol*, and *The Third Man*.

Three times Korda built and rebuilt his company and the third time it was with national aid. Even after the Korda empire collapsed he was able to secure new financial alliances which allowed him to keep producing until his death in 1956. His name stood for glory and when, after 1947, his name ceased to appear as part of the film credits, the lustre surrounding a London Film Production vanished.

—DeWitt Bodeen

KOVÁCS, András.

Hungarian. Born in Kide, 20 June 1925. Educated at Academy of Theatre and Film Art, Budapest, 1946–50. Head of scenario department, Film Studios of Budapest, 1951–57; directed first film, 1960; President, Union of Hungarian Filmmakers, 1981–86. Recipient: Hungarian Critics Prize, for *Difficult People*, 1965, and for *The Stud Farm*, 1978. Address: Magyar Jakobinusok tere 2–3, 1122 Budapest, Hungary.

Films as Director:

1960   *Zápor* (*A Summer Rain*)
1961   *Pesti háztetök* (*On The Rooves of Budapest*)
1962   *Isten öszi csillaga* (*Autumn Star*)
1964   *Nehéz emberek* (*Difficult People*) (+ sc)
1965   *Két arckép* (*Two Portraits*) (doc); *Ma vagy holnap* (*Today or Tomorrow*) (doc)
1966   *Hideg napok* (*Cold Days*) (+ sc)
1968   *Falak* (*Walls*) (+ sc)
1970   *Örökösök* (*Heirs*) (doc); *Staféta* (*Relay Race*) (+ sc)
1972   *A magyar ugaron* (*Fallow Land*) (+ sc)
1975   *Bekötött szemmel* (*Blindfold*) (+ sc); *Kié a müvészet* (*People and Art*) (doc)
1976   *Labirintus* (*Labyrinth*) (+ sc)
1978   *A ménesgazda* (*The Stud Farm*) (+ sc)
1979   *Októberi vasárnap* (*A Sunday in October*) (+ sc)
1983   *Szeretök* (*An Afternoon Affair*)
1985   *A vörös grófnö* (*The Red Countess*)
1987   *Valahol Magyarországon* (*Rearguard Struggle*)

Publications:

By KOVÁCS: book—

Falak, Budapest, 1968.
Egy fiem forrasvidéke, Budapest, 1971.
Októberi vasárnap, Budapest, 1980.

By KOVÁCS: articles—

"L'opposition, les murs et le parti," in *Etudes Cinématographiques* (Paris), no. 73/74, 1969.
Interview with F. Dufour, in *Cinéma* (Paris), June 1973.
Interview with I. Zsugán, in *Filmkultura* (Budapest), September/October 1974.
"*Labirintus*," in *Filmkultura* (Budapest), March/April 1976.
"A szovjet film demokratizmusarol," in *Filmkultura* (Budapest), July/August 1979.
Interview with Ju Hanjutin, in *Iskusstvo Kino* (Moscow), September 1982.
Interviews with G. Giuricin, in *Cinema Nuovo* (Bari), June and August/October 1983.
Interviews in *Hungarofilm Bulletin* (Budapest), no. 2, 1984, and no. 3, 1987.

András Kovács

On KOVÁCS: books—

Trosin, *András Kovács*, Moscow, 1979.
Veres, J., *Kovács András*, Budapest, 1980.
Giuricin, Giuliano, *András Kovács*, Florence, 1981.

On KOVÁCS: articles—

Giuricin, G., "La dialettica marxista nel cinema di András Kovács," in *Cinema Nuovo* (Turin), September/October 1976.
"Kovács Section" of *Filmkultura* (Budapest), January/February 1983.

*   *   *

András Kovács, together with Zoltán Fábri and Miklós Jancsó, was the filmmaker who provoked discussions about a new Hungarian cinema at the beginning of the 1960s. After making many more or less conventional films in the 1950s, most of which show traces of Stalinistic aesthetics from the period of the cult of personality, these filmmakers, at the time in their thirties, tried to introduce another kind of cinema.

Thematically their films treated "difficult" subjects, controversial moments from the nations's history. They portrayed events in which heroes often turned out to be villains, and the usual interpretation of historical facts was put into question. A typical example of this trend is *Cold Days*, which dealt with the liquidation of hundreds of Bosnians by the Hungarian fascists during the Second World War.

In his subsequent films—*Walls, Relay Race*, and *Labyrinth*, Kovács treats contemporary problems of Hungarian society. These films are constructed as discussions during which a number of protagonists express in detail their arguments and points of view. Because of this approach, Kovács came to be called a "publicist with a camera," the communist conscience of the Hungarian cinema. Stylistically these works are uneven, rough, overloaded with dialogue. This is the reason why many

Hungarian and foreign critics consider him as a social, but not artistic phenomenon, as opposed to Miklós Jancsó.

In 1978 Kovács created the film *The Chief of the Horse-Farm*, which demonstrated a new aspect of his cinematic gift. The film presents the birth pains of the socialist system in Hungary in 1950, and analyzes why and how that birth took place in the midst of bloody tragedies.

This is the story of the ancient peasant Buso, who is given the task of ruling a farm where the former owners and supervisors have become the grooms. The resulting conflicts end in the death of Buso and the others, because none of them manages to understand and master the complicated situation of political fighting and intrigue. This is Kovács's best film, dealing profoundly with the first years of the new system in Hungary and illustrating processes which everyone who wishes to understand the Hungarian experience must grasp. Stylistically, it is a very beautiful, poetically narrated ballad, with masterfully lit and composed shots, and with strong acting.

With this film Kovács buried the notion that he is merely a chronicler, a polemicist, a quasi-documentary director. He proved that a beautiful, lyrical film need not lead to mythologizing, but can demythologize. Once more Kovács managed to create a masterpiece, overcoming the greatest resistance. He is what one calls an artist, engaged in the problems of reality.

—Maria Racheva

KOZINTSEV, Grigori.

Russian. Born in Kiev, 22 March 1905. Educated at gymnasium, Kiev; studied Art with Alexandra Exter, Kiev; Academy of Fine Arts, Petrograd, 1919. Scenic artist, Lenin Theatre, Kiev, 1918; sent to Petrograd by Union of Art Workers of Kiev, 1919; founder, with Leonid Trauberg and Sergei Yutkevitch, The Factory of the Eccentric Actor (FEKS), 1921; with Trauberg, made first film, 1924; with Trauberg, prepared film on life of Karl Marx (unrealized), 1939–40. Recipient: Stalin Prize for the Maxim Trilogy, 1941; Lenin Prize for *Hamlet*, 1965. *Died in Leningrad, 11 May 1973.*

Films as Director:

1924 *Pokhozdeniya Oktyabrini* [The Adventures of Octyabrina] (co-d with Leonid Trauberg, co-sc)
1925 *Michki protiv Youdenitsa* [Mishka Against Yudenitch] (co-d with Trauberg, co-sc)
1926 *Chyortovo Koleso* [The Devil's Wheel] (co-d with Trauberg); *Shinel* [The Cloak] (co-d with Trauberg)
1927 *Bratichka* [Little Brother] (co-d with Trauberg, co-sc); *S.V.D. (Soyuz Velikogo Dela)* [The Club of the Big Deed] (co-d with Trauberg)
1929 **Novyi Vavilon (The New Babylon)** (co-d with Trauberg)
1931 *Odna (Alone)* (co-d with Trauberg, co-sc)
1935 **Yunost Maksima (The Youth of Maxim)** (co-d with Trauberg, co-sc)
1937 **Vozvrashcheniye Maksima (The Return of Maxim)** (co-d with Trauberg, co-sc)
1939 **Vyborgskaya storona (The Vyborg Side)** (co-d with Trauberg, co-sc)
1945 *Prostiye Lyudi (Plain People)* (released in re-edited version 1956 which Kozintsev disowned) (co-d with Trauberg, co-sc)
1947 *Pirogov*
1953 *Belinski* (+ co-sc)

Grigori Kozintsev

1957   *Don Quixote*
1963   *Hamlet* (+ sc)
1971   **Korol Lir (King Lear)** (+ sc)

Publications:

By KOZINTSEV: books—

Shakespeare: Time and Conscience, New York, 1966.
Glubokij ekran, Moscow, 1971.
King Lear: The Space of Tragedy, Berkeley, California, 1977.

By KOZINTSEV: articles—

"Deep Screen," in *Sight and Sound* (London), Summer/Autumn 1959.
"The Hamlet Within Me," in *Films and Filming* (London), September 1962.
"Over the Parisiana," in *Sight and Sound* (London), Winter 1962/63.
"Prostrantsvo tragedii," in *Iskusstvo Kino* (Moscow), January, April, June, August, and November 1972, and January 1973.
"A Child of the Revolution," in *Cinema in Revolution* edited by Luda and Jean Schnitzer, New York, 1973.
"Gogoliada," in *Iskusstvo Kino* (Moscow), May, June and July 1974.
"Iz pisem raznyh let," in *Iskusstvo Kino* (Moscow), May 1983.

On KOZINTSEV: books—

Leyda, Jay, *Kino*, London, 1960.
Verdone, Mario, and Barthelemy Amengual, *La Feks*, Paris, 1970.
Rapisarda, Giusi, editor, *La FEKS: Kozintsev e Trauberg*, Rome, 1975.
Christie, Ian, and John Gillett, *Futurism, Formalism, FEKS: Eccentrism and Soviet Cinema 1918–36*, London, 1978.
Leaming, Barbara, *Grigori Kozintsev*, Boston, 1980.

Christie, Ian, and Richard Taylor, editors, *The Film Factory: Russian and Soviet Cinema in Documents 1896–1939*, London, 1988.

On KOZINTSEV: articles—

"A Meeting with Grigori Kozintsev," in *Film* (London), Autumn 1967.
Barteneva, Yevgeniya, "One Day with *King Lear*," in *Soviet Film* (Moscow), no. 9, 1969.
Yutkevitch, Sergei, "The Conscience of the King," in *Sight and Sound* (London), Autumn 1971.
"Director of the Year," in *International Film Guide 1972*, London, 1971.
Robinson, David, "Grigori Kozintsev, 1905–1973," in *Sight and Sound* (London), Summer 1973.
Obituaries, in *Iskusstvo Kino* (Moscow), October 1973.
Hejfic, I., and others, "G.M. Kozincev, kakim my ego znali . . . ," in *Iskusstvo Kino* (Moscow), November 1974.
Tsikounas, M., and Leonid Trauberg, "*La Nouvelle Babylone*," in *Avant-Scène du Cinéma* (Paris), 1 December 1978.
Shklovsky, V., and others, "Iz myslej o G.M. Kozinceve," in *Iskusstvo Kino* (Moscow), April 1980.
"Grigori Kozintsev," in *Film Dope* (London), January 1985.
Gerasimov, Sergei, and Iosif Heifitz, "Licnost' mastera," in *Iskusstvo Kino* (Moscow), March 1985.

*   *   *

A man of enormous enthusiasms, bursting with theories which were always intended to be put into practice as soon as possible, Kozintsev started his career at the age of 15 by giving public performances of plays in his family's sitting room in Kiev.

When he went to art school in Petrograd he met Sergei Yutkevich and the two boys joined with Leonid Trauberg to found FEKS, the Factory of the Eccentric Actor. They produced a book on *Eccentrism*, "published in Eccentropolis (formerly Petrograd)" and they produced all sorts of street theater, an amalgam of music hall, jazz, circus, and posters, meanwhile exhibiting their paintings at avant-garde shows.

Kozintsev was barely 19 when he and Trauberg brought all this flashy modernism, their love of tricks and devices, their commitment to a new society, and their boundless energy together in their first film *The Adventures of Oktyabrina*. Through their next few productions the two young directors perfected their art, learned how to control the fireworks and developed a mature style which, however, never lost its distinctive FEKS flavor.

In *The New Babylon*, a story about the Paris Commune of 1870, largely set in a fantastic department store, they reached that standard of excellence only achieved by the greatest silent films: in complete control of the medium, using Enei's brilliant art direction to the full, but peopling a gripping story with human characters only the correct degree larger than life that the medium demanded. A young composer, Shostakovich, was commissioned to write the accompanying score.

Kozintsev and Trauberg were themselves a little disappointed with their first sound film, *Alone*, a contemporary subject, although it was by no means a failure and it at least brought Shostakovich to the notice of the world at large. For the *Maxim Trilogy* they returned to a "historical-revolutionary" subject with tremendous success, building on their own experience with *New Babylon*, but completely integrating sound and dialogue rather than merely adding them to the previous recipe.

Sadly, the trilogy was really the last work of this highly successful partnership; their *Plain People*, about the wartime evacuation of a Leningrad factory to Central Asia, ran into serious official trouble and, although completed in 1945, was not released until 1956 in a version that Kozintsev refused to acknowledge.

For the rest of his independent career he remained loyal to the Leningrad studios and, perhaps because of the troubles with *Plain People*, devoted himself exclusively to historical or literary themes. After two "biopics"—*Pirogov* and *Belinski*—he turned to *Don Quixote*, which was well received at home and abroad. His *Hamlet*, with its brooding Scandinavian background, superb photography and beautifully handled acting, won even wider international acclaim as did his even more brooding and original *King Lear*. These films were not merely very accomplished interpretations of Shakespeare's plays: they were the result of Kozintsev's own "brooding," years of deep research and careful thought, electrified, however, by equally profound emotions—the final flowering, in fact, of that enthusiastic 15-year-old in Kiev.

He himself wrote to Yutkevich after *King Lear*, "I am certain that every one of us . . . in the course of his whole life, shoots a single film of *his own* . . . " This film of one's own "is made . . . in your head, through other work, on paper . . . in conversation: but it lives, breathes, somehow prolongs into old age something that began its existence in childhood!" (*Sight and Sound*, autumn 1971). And indeed *King Lear* still combines Kozintsev's original emotionalism with his commitment to a cause; it is no accident that, despite its humanistic values, the film can be analyzed in terms of dialectical materialism. His enthusiasm never deserted him. Not long before his death, after a private London showing of *King Lear*, triggered by a question about which translation of the play he had used, Kozintsev, waving his arms in excitement, his eyes flashing, his voice rising several octaves, launched himself into a passionate

eulogy and defense of the officially discredited poet, Boris Pasternak. So Kozintsev was an "eccentric actor" to the last—but, as always, with a deep concern for humanity and truth, regardless of any personal consequences.

—Robert Dunbar

KRAMER, Stanley.

American. Born Stanley Earl Kramer in New York, 29 September 1913. Educated at New York University, degree in business administration, 1933. Served in U.S. Army Signal Corps, making training films, 1943–45. Married 1) Anne Pearce, 1950, one son, one daughter; 2) Karen Sharpe, 1966, two daughters. Apprentice writer, 20th Century-Fox, 1934; senior editor, Fox, 1938; staff writer for Colombia and Republic Pictures, 1939–40; joined MGM, 1942; with Herbert Baker and Carl Foreman, formed Screen Plays Inc., 1947; formed Stanley Kramer Productions (became Stanley Kramer Co., 1950), 1949; Stanley Kramer Co. joined Colombia Pictures, 1951; formed Stanley Kramer Pictures Corp., 1954; directed first film, 1955. Recipient: Oscar for Best Director, and Best Director, New York Critics, for *The Defiant Ones*, 1958; Irving G. Thalberg Award, Academy of Motion Picture Arts and Sciences, 1961; Gallatin Medal, New York University, 1968. Address: c/o Stanley Kramer Productions, PO Box 158, Bellevue, Washington, 90889, U.S.A.

Films as Director:

1955   *Not as a Stranger* (+ pr)
1957   *The Pride and the Passion* (+ pr)
1958   *The Defiant Ones* (+ pr)
1959   *On the Beach* (+ pr)
1960   *Inherit the Wind* (+ pr)
1961   *Judgement at Nuremberg* (+ pr)
1963   *It's a Mad Mad Mad Mad World* (+ pr)
1965   *Ship of Fools* (+ pr)
1967   *Guess Who's Coming to Dinner?* (+ pr)
1969   *The Secret of Santa Vittoria* (+ pr)
1970   *RPM* (+ pr)
1971   *Bless the Beasts and Children* (+ pr)
1973   *Oklahoma Crude* (+ pr)
1976   *The Domino Principle* (+ pr)
1979   *The Runner Stumbles* (+ pr)

Other Films:

1948   *So This Is New York* (Fleischer) (pr)
1949   *Champion* (Robson) (pr); *Home of the Brave* (Robson) (pr)
1950   *The Men* (Zinnemann) (pr); *Cyrano de Bergerac* (Gordon) (pr)
1951   *Death of a Salesman* (Benedek) (pr)
1952   *My Six Convicts* (Fregonese) (pr); *The Sniper* (Dmytryk) (pr); **High Noon** (Zinnemann) (pr); *The Happy Time* (Fleischer) (pr); *The Four Poster* (Reis) (pr); *Eight Iron Men* (Dmytryk) (pr); *The Member of the Wedding* (Zinnemann) (pr)
1953   *The Juggler* (Dmytryk) (pr); *The Five Thousand Fingers of Dr. T* (Rowland) (pr)
1954   *The Wild One* (Benedek) (pr); *The Caine Mutiny* (Dmytryk) (pr)
1962   *Pressure Point* (Cornfield) (pr)

Stanley Kramer

1963 *A Child is Waiting* (Cassavetes) (pr)
1964 *Invitation to a Gunfighter* (Wilson) (pr)

Publications:

By KRAMER: articles—

"The Independent Producer," in *Films in Review* (New York), March 1951.
"Kramer on the Future," in *Films in Review* (New York), May 1953.
"Politics, Social Comment, and My Emotions," in *Films and Filming* (London), June 1960.
"Sending Myself the Message," in *Films and Filming* (London), February 1964.
"Nine Times Across the Generation Gap," in *Action* (Los Angeles), March/April 1968.
Interview, in *Directors at Work*, edited by Bernard Kantor and others, New York, 1970.
"Stanley Kramer: The Man and His Film," interview, in *American Cinematographer* (Los Angeles), November 1979.
"Dialogue on Film: Stanley Kramer," in *American Film* (Washington, D.C.), March 1987.

On KRAMER: books—

Spoto, Donald, *Stanley Kramer: Film Maker*, New York, 1978.
Houston, Penelope, "Kramer and Company," in *Sight and Sound* (London), July/September 1952.
Bogdanovich, Peter, "Dore Schary—Stanley Kramer Syndrome," in *New York Film Bulletin*, no. 12–14, 1960.
Alpert, Hollis, and Arthur Knight, "Haunting Question: Producer-Director at Work," in *Saturday Review* (New York), 2 December 1961.
Tracy, Spencer, and Montgomery Clift, "An Actor's Director," in *Films and Filming* (London), January 1962.
Cowie, Peter, "The Defiant One," in *Films and Filming* (London), March 1963.
Decter, Midge, "Movies and Messages," in *Commentary* (New York), November 1965.
Omatsu, Mary, "Guess Who Came to Lunch?," in *Take One* (Montreal), v.1, no. 9, 1968.
"A Recipe for Greatness," in *Films and Filming* (London), March 1968.
McGillivray, D., "Stanley Kramer," in *Focus on Film* (London), Autumn 1973.
"Stanley Kramer," in *Film Dope* (London), January 1985.
Luft, H.G., "Stanley Kramer," in *Films in Review* (New York), March 1985.

*   *   *

Kramer was among the first of the successful, postwar independent producers in Hollywood. His oeuvre offers testimony to the virtues of such a position in terms of control over subject-matter, while also confirming the power of the tacit constraints that limit social criticism in Hollywood. Films produced, or produced and directed by Stanley Kramer remain close to the typical styles of postwar Hollywood narrative: location realism in *The Sniper, The Juggler, On the Beach*, and *Judgment at Nuremberg*; a clean narrative trajectory, except for somewhat "preachy" scenes when characters discuss the overt issues confronting them (medical care for the psychopath in *The Sniper* and *Pressure Point*, the need to support those with legal authority in *High Noon* or *The Caine Mutiny*); and a stress on the dilemmas of particular individuals via the mechanisms of psychological realism, although Kramer's characters bear a greater than average burden of representing social types and prominent social attitudes or beliefs.

What gives Kramer's work its greatest distinction is its frequent attention to topical social issues (criminality vs. mental illness, G.I. rehabilitation, racism, campus unrest in the sixties, juvenile delinquency, the need for and limits to legitimate authority, the hazard of nuclear war, and so on), even though some of Kramer's work is only obliquely issue-related (*The*

Four Poster, Cyrano de Bergerac, It's a Mad Mad Mad Mad World, and *The 5000 Fingers of Dr. T*). When, through most of the 1950s, fewer and fewer topical, social issue films were being produced, Kramer continued to bring such fare to the screen. His films are not radical or revolutionary by any means: they tend to plead for a respect for the existing institutions of law and authority although they do point to serious structural rather than individual flaws in need of redress. They lack the idiosyncratic, more stylistically expressive sensibility of film-makers less overtly socially-conscious who nevertheless raise similar issues, such as Samuel Fuller or John Cassavetes. Even so, Kramer's films continue a long-standing Hollywood tradition of marrying topical issues to dramatic forms, a tradition in which we find many of Hollywood's more openly progressive films. In many ways, Kramer's films address the kind of issues those who were blacklisted during the 1950s hoped to address within the terms of popular culture as defined by Hollywood. (Kramer himself was not blacklisted though he was and is still regarded as a socially concerned liberal.)

In fact, Stanley Kramer's career is ripe for reinvestigation. Criticized or dismissed by the left for failing to support black-listed individuals or for not taking a sufficiently critical view of existing institutions, Kramer has also been criticized and dismissed by auteurist critics for failing to evince a personal enough stylistic signature (or the kind of fascination evoked by the romantic individualism of a Fuller or Ray). Structuralists have also overlooked his work, and so it remains a scantily studied, poorly assessed body of very significant work—as revealing of the limits of critical approaches as it may be of Kramer's own artistic or political sensibilities.

—Bill Nichols

———

KUBRICK, Stanley.

American. Born in New York, 26 July 1928. Educated in New York City public schools; attended evening classes at City College of the City University of New York, 1945. Married 1) Toba Metz, 1947 (divorced 1952); 2) dancer Ruth Sobotka, 1952, one daughter; 3) actress Suzanne Christiane Harlan, 1958, two daughters. Apprentice photographer, *Look* magazine, New York, 1946; made first film, 1950; formed Harris-Kubrick Productions, with James Harris, 1955 (dissolved 1962); worked on *One-Eyed Jacks* with Marlon Brando, 1958; planned film on Napoléon, 1969; moved to England, 1974. Recipient: Best Direction, New York Film Critics Award, and Best Written American Comedy (screenplay) Award (with Peter George and Terry Southern), Writers Guild of America, for *Dr. Strangelove*, 1964; Oscar for Special Visual Effects, for *2001*, 1968; Best Direction, New York Film Critics, for *A Clockwork Orange*, 1971; Best Direction, British Academy Award, for *Barry Lyndon*, 1975. Address: PO Box 123, Borehamwood, Hertfordshire, England.

Films as Director:

1952 *Day of the Fight* (doc) (+ pr, sc, ph, ed); *Flying Padre* (doc) (+ sc, ph)
1953 *The Seafarers* (+ ph); *Fear and Desire* (+ pr, co-sc, ph, ed)
1955 *Killer's Kiss* (+ co-pr, co-sc, ph, ed)
1956 *The Killing* (+ co-pr, sc)
1957 *Paths of Glory* (+ co-pr, co-sc)

Stanley Kubrick

1960 *Spartacus*
1962 *Lolita*
1964 **Dr. Strangelove: Or, How I Learned to Stop Worrying and Love the Bomb** (+ pr, co-sc)
1968 **2001: A Space Odyssey** (+ pr, co-sc, special effects designer)
1971 **A Clockwork Orange** (+ pr, sc)
1975 *Barry Lyndon* (+ pr, sc)
1980 *The Shining* (+ pr, co-sc)
1987 *Full Metal Jacket* (+ pr, co-sc)

Publications:

By KUBRICK: books—

Stanley Kubrick's A Clockwork Orange, New York, 1972.
Full Metal Jacket, New York and London, 1987.

By KUBRICK: articles—

"Bonjour, Monsieur Kubrick," interview with Raymond Haine, in *Cahiers du Cinéma* (Paris), July 1957.
"Words and Movies," in *Sight and Sound* (London), Winter 1961.
"How I Learned to Stop Worrying and Love the Cinema," in *Films and Filming* (London), June 1963.
"Kubrick Reveals All," in *Cinéaste* (New York), Summer 1968.
"A Talk with Stanley Kubrick," with Maurice Rapf, in *Action* (Los Angeles), January/February 1969.
"What Directors Are Saying," in *Action* (Los Angeles), January/February and November/December 1971.
"Kubrick," interview with Gene Phillips, in *Film Comment* (New York), Winter 1971/72.
Interview with Phillip Strick and Penelope Houston, in *Sight and Sound* (London), Spring 1972.
Interview with Michel Ciment, in *Positif* (Paris), June 1972.
"Something More," interview with Gordon Gow, in *Films and Filming* (London), October 1975.

On KUBRICK: books—

Austen, David, *The Cinema of Stanley Kubrick*, London, 1969.
Agel, Jerome, *The Making of Kubrick's 2001*, New York, 1970.
Kagan, Norman, *The Cinema of Stanley Kubrick*, New York, 1972.
Walker, Alexander, *Stanley Kubrick Directs*, New York, 1972.
Devries, Daniel, *The Films of Stanley Kubrick*, Grand Rapids, Michigan, 1973.
Phillips, Gene, *Stanley Kubrick: A Film Odyssey*, New York, 1977.
Ciment, Michel, *Kubrick*, Paris, 1980, revised edition 1987; London, 1983.
Kolker, Robert Philip, *A Cinema of Loneliness: Penn, Kubrick, Coppola, Scorsese, Altman*, Oxford, 1980; revised edition, 1988.
Nelson, Thomas Allen, *Kubrick: Inside a Film Artist's Maze*, Bloomington, Indiana, 1982.
Hummel, Christoph, editor, *Stanley Kubrick*, Munich, 1984.
Brunetta, Gian Piero, *Stanley Kubrick: Tempo, spazio, storia e mondi possibili*, Parma, 1985.
Coyle, Wallace, *Stanley Kubrick: A Guide to References and Resources*, Boston.

On KUBRICK: articles—

"Twenty-nine and Running: The Director with Hollywood By the Horns," in *Newsweek* (New York), 2 December 1957.
Noble, Robin, "Killers, Kisses, and *Lolita*," in *Films and Filming* (London), December 1960.
Burgess, Jackson, "The Antimilitarism of Stanley Kubrick," in *Film Quarterly* (Berkeley), Fall 1964.
"Stanley Kubrick," in *Cahiers du Cinéma* (Paris), December/January 1964/65.
Bernstein, Jeremy, "Profiles: How About a Little Game?," in the *New Yorker*, 12 November 1966.
Ciment, Michel, "L'Odyssee de Stanley Kubrick," in *Positif* (Paris), October 1968.
Houston, Penelope, "Kubrick Country," in *Saturday Review* (New York), 25 December 1971.
Deer, Harriet and Irving, "Kubrick and the Structures of Popular Culture," in *Journal of Popular Film* (Bowling Green, Ohio), Summer 1974.
Carducci, Mark, "In Search of Stanley K.," in *Millimeter* (New York), December 1975.

Feldmann, Hans, "Kubrick and His Discontents," in *Film Quarterly* (Berkeley), Fall 1976.
Moskowitz, Ken, "Clockwork Violence," in *Sight and Sound* (London), Winter 1976/77.
Kennedy, H., "Kubrick Goes Gothic," in *American Film* (Washington, D.C.), June 1980.
Brown, J., "Kubrick's Maze: The Monster and the Critics," in *Film Directions* (Belfast), no. 16, 1982.
Kinney, J.L., "Mastering the Maze," in *Quarterly Review of Film Studies* (New York), Spring 1984.
Combs, Richard, "Stanley Kubrick: To Be or Not To Be . . . Again and Again," in *Monthly Film Bulletin* (London), July 1984.
Sklar, Robert, "Stanley Kubrick et l'industrie Hollywoodienne," in *Filméchange* (Paris), no. 38, 1987.
Rafferty, T., "Remote Control," in *Sight and Sound* (London), Autumn 1987.
Lacayo, R., "Semper fi," in *Film Comment* (New York), September/October 1987.
"Kubrick Section" of *Positif* (Paris), October 1987.
Cazals, T., "L'Homme labyrinthe," in *Cahiers du Cinéma* (Paris), November 1987.
"*Full Metal Jacket* Section" of *Literature/Film Quarterly* (Salisbury, Maryland), vol. 16., no. 4, 1988.
Phillips, Gene D., "Stanley Kubrick," in *Major Film Directors of the American and British Cinema*, Cranbury, New Jersey, 1989.
French, Philip, "*A Clockwork Orange*," in *Sight and Sound* (London), Spring 1990.

* * *

Few American directors have been able to work within the studio system of the American film industry with the independence which Stanley Kubrick has achieved. By steadily building a reputation as a filmmaker of international importance, he has gained full artistic control over his films, guiding the production of each of them from the earliest stages of planning and scripting through post-production. Kubrick has been able to capitalize on the wide artistic freedom that the major studios have accorded him because he learned the business of filmmaking from the ground up.

In the early 1950s he turned out two documentary shorts for RKO; he was then able to secure financing for two low-budget features which he says today were "crucial in helping me to learn my craft," but which he would otherwise prefer to forget. He made both films almost singlehandedly, doing his own camerawork, sound, and editing, besides directing the films.

Then, in 1955, he met James Harris, an aspiring producer; together they made *The Killing*, about a group of small-time crooks who rob a race track. *The Killing* not only turned a modest profit but prompted the now legendary remark of *Time* magazine that Kubrick "has shown more imagination with dialogue and camera than Hollywood has seen since the obstreperous Orson Welles went riding out of town."

Kubrick next acquired the rights to Humphrey Cobb's 1935 novel *The Paths of Glory*, and in 1957 turned it into one of the most uncompromising anti-war films ever made. One film historian has written that Kubrick uses his camera in the film "unflinchingly, like a weapon," as it sweeps across the slopes to record the wholesale slaughter of a division.

Spartacus, a spectacle about slavery in pre-Christian Rome, Kubrick recalls as "the only film over which I did not have absolute control," because the star, Kirk Douglas, was also the movie's producer. Although *Spartacus* turned out to be one of the better spear-and-sandal epics, Kubrick vowed never to make another film unless he was assured of total artistic freedom and he never has.

Lolita, about a middle-aged man's obsessive infatuation with his pre-teen step-daughter, was the director's first comedy. "The surprising thing about *Lolita*," Pauline Kael wrote, "is how enjoyable it is. It's the first new American comedy since those great days in the 1940s when Preston

Sturges re-created comedy with verbal slapstick. *Lolita* is black slapstick and at times it's so far out that you gasp as you laugh."

For those who appreciate the dark humor of *Lolita*, it is not hard to see that it was just a short step from that film to Kubrick's masterpiece in that genre, *Dr. Strangelove: Or How I Learned to Stop Worrying and Love the Bomb*, concerning a lunatic American general's decision to launch an attack inside Russia. The theme implicit in the film is man's final capitulation to his own machines of destruction. Kubrick further examined his dark vision of man in a mechanistic age in *2001: A Space Odyssey*.

Kubrick's view of life, as it is reflected in *2001*, seems to be somewhat more optimistic than it was in his previous pictures. *2001* holds out hope for the progress of mankind through man's creative encounters with the universe. In *A Clockwork Orange*, however, the future appears to be less promising than it did in *2001*; in the earlier film Kubrick showed (in the "person" of the talking computer Hal) the machine becoming human, whereas in *A Clockwork Orange* he shows man becoming a machine through brainwashing and thought control.

Ultimately, however, the latter film only reiterates in somewhat darker terms a repeated theme in all of Kubrick's previous work: man must retain his humanity if he is to survive in a dehumanized, highly mechanized world. Moreover, *Clockwork Orange* echoes the warning of *Dr. Strangelove* and *2001* that man must strive to gain mastery over himself if he is to master the machines of his own invention.

After a trio of films set in the future, Kubrick reached back into the past and adapted Thackeray's historical novel *Barry Lyndon* to the screen in 1975. Kubrick has portrayed Barry, an eighteenth century rogue, and his times in the same critical fashion as Thackeray did before him.

The film echoes a theme which appears in much of the director's best work, that through human error the best-laid plans often go awry; and hence man is often thwarted in his efforts to achieve his goals. The central character in *Lolita* fails to possess a nymphet exclusively; the "balance of terror" between nations designed to halt the nuclear arms race in *Dr. Strangelove* does not succeed in averting global destruction; and modern technology turns against its human instigators in *Dr. Strangelove, 2001*, and *A Clockwork Orange*. In this list of films about human failure the story of Barry Lyndon easily finds a place, for its hero's lifelong schemes to become a rich nobleman in the end come to nothing. And the same can be said for the frustrated writing aspirations of the emotionally disturbed hero of Kubrick's provocative "thinking man's thriller," *The Shining*, derived from the horror novel by Stephen King.

It is clear, therefore, that Kubrick can make any source material fit comfortably into the fabric of his work as a whole, whether it be a remote and almost forgotten Thackeray novel, or a disturbing story about the Viet Nam war by a contemporary writer, as with *Full Metal Jacket*, based on the book by Gustav Hasford.

Furthermore, it is equally evident that Kubrick wants to continue to create films that will stimulate his audience to think about serious human problems, as his pictures have done from the beginning. Because of the success of his movies in the past, Kubrick can go on making films in the way he wants to, proving in the future as he has in the past, that he values the artistic freedom which he has worked so hard to win and he has used so well.

—Gene D. Phillips

—————

KULESHOV, Lev.

Soviet. Born Lev Vladimirovich Kuleshov in Tambov, Russia, 14 January 1899. Studied painting at Fine Arts School, Moscow, 1914–16. Set designer for director Evgeni Bauer, from 1916, also began experiments with editing; first theoretical article published, 1918; helped found first National Film School, 1919, teacher from 1920; made short *agitki* and forms film workshop, 1919–21; temporarily stopped filmmaking, 1933; director of State Institute of Cinematography, Moscow, from 1944. Recipient: Merited Artist of the RSFSR, 1935. *Died 29 March 1970.*

Films as Director:

1918   *Proyekt inzhenera Praita (Engineer Prite's Project)* (+ art d)
1919   *The Unfinished Love Song* (co-d, art d); Newsreels: *Vskrytiye moshchei Sergiya Radonezhskogo (The Exhumation of the Holy Remains of St. Sergius of Radonezh* (co-d); *Reviziya VTiSK v Tverskoi Gubernii (The VTiSK Inspection in the Tver Province)*; *Ural* (+ sc); *Pervoye maya 1920 v Moskve (May 1, 1920 in Moscow)*
1920   *Na krasnom fronte (On the Red Front)* (+ sc, role)
1924   *Kavkazskiye mineralniye vody (Mineral Waters of the Caucasus); Neobychainye priklucheniya Mistera Vesta v stranye bolshevikov (The Extraordinary Adventures of Mr. West in the Land of the Bolsheviks)* (+ art d)
1925   *Luch smerti (Death Ray)* (+ role)
1926   *Po zakonu (By the Law)*
1927   *Vasha znakomaya (Your Acquaintance)*
1929   *Vesyolaya kanareika (The Happy Canary)*; *Dva-Buldi-Dva (The Two Buldis)* (co-d); *(Parovoz B-1000) Locomotive No. B-1000* (unreleased)
1930   *Sorok serdets (Forty Hearts)*
1933   *Gorizont (Horizon)* (+ co-sc); *Velikii uteshitel (The Great Consoler)* (+ co-sc, art d)
1935   *Dokhunda* (unreleased)
1940   *Sibiriaki (The Siberians)*
1942   *Klyatva Timura (Timur's Oath)*; *Uchitelnitsa Kartashova (The Teacher Kartashova)* (unreleased)
1944   *My s Urala (We Are From the Urals)* (co-d)

Other Films:

1917   *Nabat (The Alarm)* (Bauer) (co-art d); *Za schastyem (For Happiness)* (Bauer) (art d, role); *Teni lyubvi (Shadows of Love)* (Gromov) (art d); *Zhizn'trekh dnei (Three Days' Life)* (Gromov) (art d); *Korol' Parizha (King of Paris)* (Bauer and Rakhmanova) (art d); *Chernaya lyubov (Black King)* (Strizhevsky) (art d, role)
1918   *Vdova (The Widow)* (Komissarzhevsky) (art d); *Miss Meri (Miss Mary)* (Tchaikovsky) (art d); *Slyakot' bulvarnaya (Boulevard Slush)* (Tchaikovsky) (art d)
1919   *Thérèse Raquin* (Tchaikovsky) (art d) (unreleased); *Son Tarasa (Taras' Dream)* (Zhelyabuzhsky) (short) (ed); *Smelchak (Daredevil)* (Narakov and Turkin) (co-ed)
1930   *Sasha* (Khokhlova) (co-sc)
1934   *Krazha zreniya (Theft of Sight)* (Obolensky) (artistic supervisor)
1940   *Sluchai v vulkane (Incident in a Volcano)* (Schneider) (directorial advisor)

Publications:

By KULESHOV: books—

Eisenstein: Potiemkine, with V. Shlovsky and E. Tisse, Moscow, 1926.
The Art of Cinema [in Russian], Moscow, 1929.
Fundamentals of Film Direction [in Russian], Moscow, 1941.
Traité de mise-en-scène. Les Premières Prises de vues, Paris, 1962.
Kuleshov on Film, edited by Ronald Levaco, Berkeley, 1974.
Lev Kuleshov. Selected Works: Fifty Years in Films, edited by E. Khokhlova, Moscow, 1987.

Lev Kuleshov: *The Great Consoler*

Sobranie sochinenii v trekh tomakh [Collected Works in Three Volumes], Moscow, 1987–89.

By KULESHOV: articles—

Interview with André Labarthe and Bertrand Tavernier, in *Cahiers du Cinéma* (Paris), May/June 1970.
"Souvenirs (1918–1920)," in *Cahiers du Cinéma* (Paris), July 1970.
"Selections from *Art of the Cinema*," in *Screen* (London), Winter 1971/72.

On KULESHOV: books—

Leyda, Jay, *Kino*, London, 1960.
Taylor, Richard, and Ian Christie, editors, *The Film Factory: Russian and Soviet Cinema in Documents, 1896–1939*, London and Cambridge, Massachusetts, 1988.

On KULESHOV: articles—

Sadoul, Georges, "Au début du cinéma soviétique était Lev Koulechov. Portrait d'un ami," in *Lettres Françaises* (Paris), 18 October 1962.
Sadoul, Georges, "Lev Koulechov grand théoreticien du cinéma," in *Le Techicien du Film* (Paris), January 1965.
Hill, Steven, "Kuleshov—Prophet Without Honor?," in *Film Culture* (New York), Spring 1967.
"Lev Kuleshov: 1899–1970," in *Afterimage* (Rochester, New York), April 1970.
Zorkaia, Neïa, "Lev Koulechov," in *Cahiers du Cinéma* (Paris), May/June 1970.

Taylor, Richard, "Lev Kuleshov, 1899–1970," in *Silent Pictures* (London), Autumn 1970.
Levaco, Ronald, "Kuleshov," in *Sight and Sound* (London), Spring 1971.
"The Classic Period of Soviet Cinema," in *Film Journal* (New York), Fall/Winter 1972.
Gromov, E., in *Iskusstvo Kino* (Moscow), September and October 1982.
Soviet Film (Moscow), no. 1, 1985.
"Lev Kuleshov," in *Film Dope* (London), March 1985.
Navailh, F., in *Cinéma* (Paris), November 1988.
Revue du Cinéma/Image et Son (Paris), February 1989.
Yampolsky, M., "Kuleshov's Experiments and the New Anthropology of the Actor," in *Inside the Film Factory: New Approaches to Russian and Soviet Cinema*, edited by Richard Taylor and Ian Christie, London and New York, 1991.

*   *   *

Kuleshov is known to Soviet film-makers quite simply as the "father of Soviet cinema." He began his career in cinema before the Revolution working with Evgeni Bauer and became one of Soviet cinema's leading film directors and theorists. Vsevolod Pudovkin, who was one of his pupils, once wrote, "We make films, Kuleshov made cinema."

It was the desire to establish a theoretical foundation for the legitimacy of cinema as an art form independent of theatre that led Kuleshov to be the first to distinguish montage as the key element specific to cinema in an article written in 1917. This idea was to be taken up and developed by various schools of Soviet film-making, above all by Eisenstein and Vertov, but the distinctive feature of Kuleshov's theory was a belief in serial montage, a brick-by-brick construction of a filmic narrative.

In the early post-Revolutionary period, when there was a desperate shortage of everything, including film stock, Kuleshov worked at the new State Film School with a small workshop of actors, refining his techniques in the so-called "films without film." Central to these was the experiment that has become known as the "Kuleshov effect," which demonstrated that the viewer's interpretation of an individual shot is determined by the context (or sequence) in which that shot is seen. The same shot could be interpreted differently in different contexts. But Kuleshov also appreciated the importance of acting and was responsible for developing the notion of the actor as *naturshchik* or "model," deriving from the Delsartian school of acting technique. By economical and stylised gestures, refined during an intensive period of rehearsal, the *naturshchik* could convey precise meanings to the audience in accordance with the director's plan. Kuleshov would produce an "action score" for every movement in his films.

These techniques were first applied on a large scale in Kuleshov's first feature film, the highly original satirical comedy *The Extraordinary Adventures of Mr West in the Land of the Bolsheviks* (1924), in which Pudovkin played one of the criminals. The apotheosis of the *naturshchik* was the role of "the Countess," played by Kuleshov's wife, the extraordinary actress, Alexandra Khokhlova. The film's technique also demonstrated one of Kuleshov's other preoccupations of the period, an obsession with the characteristic features of American cinema, which he dubbed *amerikanshchina*, "Americanism" or "Americanitis," and which included fast action, stylised gesture and, above all, rapid cutting and maximum economy. There are no *lacunae* in a Kuleshov film.

His next film, *The Death Ray*, a thriller, was popular with audiences but not with officialdom. On the other hand, *By the Law*, set in the Yukon during the Gold Rush and based on a story by Jack London, was a great critical success. But his next three films were variously regarded as failures: *Your Acquaintance, The Happy Canary* and *The Two Buldis*. The end of the 1920s was no time for experimentation: film-makers were increasingly expected to fulfil the "social command" associated with the 1st Five-Year Plan by making films that were "accessible to the millions."

After this, Kuleshov came under increasingly frequent attack from the authorities for his alleged Formalism and his apparent inability (widely shared) to produce a film on a contemporary theme. His subsequent films include at least one further masterpiece, *The Great Consoler*, which can be understood on many different, but sometimes overlapping, levels. It confronts the problem of differing layers of reality at a time when the doctrine of socialist realism was being promulgated and a single officially inspired version of reality held up as a paradigm. *The Great Consoler* was Kuleshov's first sound film, again starring Khokhlova, and still demonstrating a fascination with experimenting to push cinema to its limits. His other, later films were less distinguished, and he complained vociferously about his treatment at the hands of the authorities. Nevertheless, in 1935 he received the title of Merited Artist of the RSFSR.

Throughout his career Kuleshov was an eminent teacher: in 1939 he was made a Professor at the State Institute of Cinema, and in 1944 he became Director. His theories of cinema are expounded in Russian in his *The Art of Cinema* (1929), *The Rehearsal Method in Cinema* and *The Practice of Film Direc-*tion (both 1935) and *The Foundations of Film Direction* (1941). The importance of his role as teacher can be measured by the fact that almost all these books were published at a time when he was no longer able to make films himself.

Kuleshov's career and influence have been much underappreciated in the West. This is mainly because so much of his significance lies in his scarcely translated theoretical work, known largely by indirect repute, and in his teaching, which is almost impossible to quantify. But any Soviet film scholar asked to list the most important figures in the history of Soviet cinema will almost certainly begin with Kuleshov, whether as film-maker, theorist or teacher.

—Richard Taylor

KUROSAWA, Akira.

Japanese. Born in Tokyo, 23 March 1910. Educated at Kuroda Primary School, Edogawa; Keika High School; studied at Doshusha School of Western Painting, 1927. Married Yoko Yaguchi, 1945, one son (producer Hisao Kurosawa), one daughter. Painter, illustrator, and member, Japan Proletariat Artists' Group, from late 1920's; assistant director, P.C.L. Studios (Photo-Chemical Laboratory, later Toho Motion Picture Co.), studying in Kajiro Yamamoto's production group, from 1936; also scriptwriter, from late 1930's; directed first film, *Sugata Sanshiro*, 1943; began association with actor Toshiro Mifune on *Yoidore tenshi*, and founder, with Yamamoto and others, Motion Picture Artists Association (Eiga Gei jutsuka Kyokai), 1948; formed Kurosawa Productions, 1959; signed contract with producer Joseph E. Levine to work in U.S., 1966 (engage in several aborted projects through 1968); with directors Keisuke Kinoshita, Kon Ichikawa, and Masaki Kobayashi, formed Yonki no Kai production company, 1971. Recipient: Oscar for Best Foreign Language Film, and Grand Prix, Venice Festival, for *Rashomon*, 1951; Golden Bear Award for Best Direction and International Critics Prize, Berlin Festival, for *The Hidden Fortress*, 1959; Oscar for Best Foreign Language Film, for *Dersu Uzala*, 1976; European Film Academy Award, for "humanistic contribution to society in film production," 1978; Best Director, British Academy Award, and Palme d'Or, Cannes Festival, for *Kagemusha*, 1980; Order of Culture of Japan, 1985; British Film Institute Fellowship, 1986.

Films as Director:

1943   *Sugata Sanshiro* (*Sanshiro Sugata. Judo Saga*) (remade as same title by Shigeo Tanaka, 1955, and by Seiichiro Uchikawa, 1965, and edited by Kurosawa) (+ sc)
1944   *Ichiban utsukushiku* (*The Most Beautiful*) (+ sc)
1945   *Zoku Sugata Sanshiro* (*Sanshiro Sugata—Part 2. Judo Saga—II*) (+ sc); *Tora no o o fumu otokotachi* (*Men Who Tread on the Tiger's Tail*) (+ sc)
1946   *Asu o tsukuru hitobito* (*Those Who Make Tomorrow*); *Waga seishun ni kuinashi* (*No Regrets for Our Youth*) (+ co-sc)
1947   *Subarashiki nichiyobi* (*One Wonderful Sunday*) (+ co-sc)
1948   *Yoidore tenshi* (*Drunken Angel*) (+ co-sc)
1949   *Shizukanaru ketto* (*A Silent Duel*) (+ co-sc); *Nora inu* (*Stray Dog*) (+ co-sc)
1950   *Shubun* (*Scandal*) (+ co-sc); **Rashomon** (+ co-sc)
1951   *Hakuchi* (*The Idiot*) (+ co-sc)
1952   *Ikiru* (*To Live. Doomed*) (+ co-sc)
1954   *Shichinin no samurai* (*Seven Samurai*) (+ co-sc)

Akira Kurosawa

1955 *Ikimono no kiroku* (*Record of a Living Being, I Live in Fear.*
     What the Birds Knew) (+ co-sc)
1957 *Kumonosu-jo* (*The Throne of Blood. The Castle of the Spider's*
     Web) (+ co-sc, co-pr); *Donzoko* (*The Lower Depths*) (+
     co-sc, co-pr)
1958 *Kakushi toride no san-akunin* (*The Hidden Fortress. Three*
     Bad Men in a Hidden Fortress) (+ co-sc, co-pr)
1960 *Warui yatsu hodo yoku nemuru* (*The Worse You Are the Better*
     You Sleep. The Rose in the Mud) (+ co-sc, co-pr); *Yojimbo*
     (*The Bodyguard*) (+ co-sc)
1962 *Sanjuro* (+ co-sc)
1963 *Tengoku to jigoku* (*High and Low. Heaven and Hell. The*
     Ransom) (+ co-sc)
1965 *Akahige* (*Red Beard*) (+ co-sc)
1970 *Dodesukaden* (*Dodeskaden*) (+ co-sc, co-pr)
1975 *Dersu Uzala* (+ co-sc)
1980 **Kagemusha (The Shadow Warrior)** (+ co-sc, co-pr)
1985 **Ran**
1990 *Dreams*

Other Films:

1941 *Uma* [Horses] (Yamamoto) (co-sc)
1942 *Seishun no kiryu* [Currents of Youth] (Fushimizi) (sc);
     Tsubasa no gaika [A Triumph of Wings] (Yamamoto) (sc)
1944 *Dohyo-matsuri* [Wrestling-Ring Festival] (Marune) (sc)
1945 *Appare Isshin Tasuke* [Bravo, Tasuke Isshin!] (Saeki) (sc)
1947 *Ginrei no hate* (*To the End of the Silver Mountains*)
     (Taniguchi) (co-sc); *Hatsukoi* (*First Love*) segment of
     Yottsu no koi no monogatari (*Four Love Stories*) (Toyoda)
     (sc)
1948 *Shozo* (*The Portrait*) (Kinoshita) (sc)
1949 *Yakoman to Tetsu* (*Yakoman and Tetsu*) (Taniguchi) (sc);
     Jigoku no kifujin (*The Lady from Hell*) (Oda) (sc)
1950 *Akatsuki no dasso* (*Escape at Dawn*) (Taniguchi) (sc); *Jiruba*
     no Tetsu (*Tetsu 'Jilba'*) (Kosugi) (sc); *Tateshi danpei*
     (*Fencing Master*) (Makino) (sc)
1951 *Ai to nikushimi no kanata e* (*Beyond Love and Hate*)
     (Taniguchi) (sc); *Kedamono no yado* (*The Den of Beasts*)
     (Osone) (sc); *Ketto Kagiya no tsuji* (*The Duel at Kagiya*
     Corner) (Mori) (sc)
1957 *Tekichu odan sanbyakuri* (*Three Hundred Miles through*
     Enemy Lines) (Mori) (sc)
1960 *Sengoku guntoden* (*The Saga of the Vagabond*) (Sugie) (sc)

Publications:

By KUROSAWA: books—

Ikiru, with Shinobu Hashimoto and Hideo Oguni, edited by Donald
    Richie, New York, 1968.
Rashomon, with Shinobu Hashimoto, edited by Donald Richie, New
    York, 1969; also New Brunswick, New Jersey, 1987.
The Seven Samurai, New York, 1970.
Kurosawa Akira eiga taikei [Complete Works of Akira Kurosawa],
    edited by Takamaro Shimaji, in 12 volumes, Tokyo, 1970/72.
Something Like an Autobiography, New York, 1982.
Ran, London, 1986.

By KUROSAWA: articles—

"Waga eiga jinsei no ki," [Diary of My Movie Life], in *Kinema jumpo*
    (Tokyo), April 1963.
"Why Mifune's Beard Won't Be Red," in *Cinema* (Los Angeles), July
    1964.
"L'Empereur: entretien avec Kurosawa," with Yoshio Shirai and
    others, in *Cahiers du Cinéma* (Paris), September 1966.
Interview with Donald Richie, in *Interviews with Film Directors* edited
    by Andrew Sarris, New York, 1967.
Interview with Joan Mellen, in *Voices from the Japanese Cinema*, New
    York, 1975.
"Tokyo Stories: Kurosawa," interview with Tony Rayns, in *Sight and
    Sound* (London), Summer 1981.
Interview with E. Decaux and B. Villien, in *Cinématographe* (Paris),
    April 1982.
"Kurosawa on Kurosawa," in *American Film* (Washington, D.C.),
    April 1982.

Interview with Kyoko Hirano, in *Cineaste* (New York), May 1986.
Interview in *Time Out* (London), 9 May 1990.

On KUROSAWA: books—

Anderson, Joseph, and Donald Richie, *The Japanese Film: Art and
    Industry*, New York, 1960; revised edition, Princeton, New Jersey,
    1982.
Sato, Tadao, *Kurosawa Akira no sekai* [The World of Akira Kuro-
    sawa], Tokyo, 1968.
Richie, Donald, *The Films of Akira Kurosawa*, Berkeley, California,
    1970; revised edition, 1984.
Richie, Donald, *Japanese Cinema: Film Style and National Character*,
    New York, 1971.
Richie, Donald, editor, *Focus on Rashomon*, Englewood Cliffs, New
    Jersey, 1972.
Mesnil, Michel, *Kurosawa*, Paris, 1973.
Mellen, Joan, *The Waves at Genji's Door: Japan Through Its Cinema*,
    New York, 1976.
Bock, Audie, *Japanese Film Directors*, New York, 1978; revised edi-
    tion, Tokyo, 1978.
Erens, Patricia, *Akira Kurosawa: A Guide to References and Re-
    sources*, Boston, 1979.
Bazin, André, *The Cinema of Cruelty: From Buñuel to Hitchcock*,
    New York, 1982.
Sato, Tadao, *Currents in Japanese Cinema*, Tokyo, 1982.
Desser, David, *The Samurai Films of Akira Kurosawa*, Ann Arbor,
    Michigan, 1983.
Tassone, Aldo, *Akira Kurosawa*, Paris, 1983.
Achternbusch, Herbert, and others, *Akira Kurosawa,* Munich, 1988.

On KUROSAWA: articles—

Leyda, Jay, "The Films of Kurosawa," in *Sight and Sound* (London),
    October/December 1954.
Anderson, Lindsay, "Two Inches Off the Ground," in *Sight and
    Sound* (London), Winter 1957.
Anderson, Joseph, and Donald Richie, "Traditional Theater and the
    Film in Japan," in *Film Quarterly* (Berkeley), Fall 1958.
McVay, Douglas, "The Rebel in a Kimono," and "Samurai and Small
    Beer," in *Films and Filming* (London), July and August 1961.
"Kurosawa Issues" of *Kinema jumpo* (Tokyo), April 1963 and 5 Sep-
    tember 1964.
"Akira Kurosawa," in *Cinema* (Los Angeles), August/September
    1963.
"Kurosawa Issue" of *Études Cinématographiques* (Paris), no. 30–31,
    Spring 1964.
Akira, Iwasaki, "Kurosawa and His Work," in *Japan Quarterly* (New
    York), January/March 1965.
"Akira Kurosawa: Japan's Poet Laureate of Film," in *Film Makers on
    Film Making*, edited by Harry Geduld, Bloomington, Indiana,
    1967.
Richie, Donald, "Dostoevsky with a Japanese Camera," in *The Emer-
    gence of Film Art* edited by Lewis Jacobs, New York, 1969.
Manvell, Roger, "Akira Kurosawa's *Macbeth, The Castle of the Spid-
    er's Web*," in *Shakespeare and the Film*, London, 1971.
Tessier, Max, "Cinq japonais en quete de films: Akira Kurosawa," in
    Ecran (Paris), March 1972.
Mellen, Joan, "The Epic Cinema of Kurosawa," in *Take One* (Mon-
    treal), June 1972.
Kaminsky, Stuart, "The Samurai Film and the Western," in *The Jour-
    nal of Popular Film* (Bowling Green, Ohio), Fall 1972.
Tucker, Richard, "Kurosawa and Ichikawa: feudalist and individ-
    ualist," in *Japan: Film Image*, London, 1973.
"Kurosawa Issue" of *Kinema jumpo* (Tokyo), 7 May 1974.
Richie, Donald, "Kurosawa: A Television Script," in *1000 Eyes* (New
    York), May 1976.
Silver, Alain, "Akira Kurosawa," in *The Samurai Film*, Cranbury,
    New Jersey, 1977.
McCormick, Ruth, "Kurosawa: The Nature of Heroism," in *1000
    Eyes* (New York), April 1977.
Ray, Satyajit, "Tokyo, Kyoto et Kurosawa," in *Positif* (Paris),
    December 1979.
Mitchell, G., "Kurosawa in Winter," in *American Film* (Washington,
    D.C.), April 1982.
Dossier on *Ran*, in *Revue du Cinéma* (Paris), September 1985.
"Kurosawa Section" of *Positif* (Paris), October 1985.

Lannes-Lacroutz, M., "Le Sabra et la camélia," in *Positif* (Paris), March 1987.

Prince, S., "Zen and Selfhood: Patterns of Eastern Thought in Kurosawa's Films," in *Post Script* (Jacksonville, Florida), Winter 1988.

American Film (Washington, D. C.), April 1989.

Positif (Paris), June 1990.

On KUROSAWA: film—

Richie, Donald, *Akira Kurosawa: Film Director*, 1975.

*   *   *

Unquestionably Japan's best-known film director, Akira Kurosawa introduced his country's cinema to the world with his 1951 Venice Festival Grand Prize winner, *Rashomon*. His international reputation has broadened over the years with numerous citations, and when 20th Century-Fox distributed his 1980 Cannes Grand Prize winner, *Kagemusha*, it was the first time a Japanese film achieved world-wide circulation through a Hollywood major.

At the time *Rashomon* took the world by surprise, Kurosawa was already a well-established director in his own country. He had received his six-year assistant director's training at the Toho Studios under the redoubtable Kajiro Yamamoto, director of both low-budget comedies and wartime epics such as *The War at Sea from Hawaii to Malaya*. Yamamoto described Kurosawa as more than fully prepared to direct when he first grasped the megaphone for his own screenplay *Sanshiro Sugata* in 1943. This film, based on a best-selling novel about the founding of judo, launched lead actor Susumu Fujita as a star and director Kurosawa as a powerful new force in the film world. Despite numerous battles with wartime censors, Kurosawa managed to get approval on three more of his scripts for production before the Pacific War ended in 1945. He was already fully established with his studio and his audience as a writer-director. His films were so successful commercially that he would, until late in his career, receive a free creative hand from his producers, ever-increasing budgets and extended schedules, and never would he be subjected to a project that was not of his own initiation and his own writing.

In the pro-documentary, female emancipation atmosphere that reigned briefly under the Allied Occupation of Japan, Kurosawa created his strongest woman protagonist and produced his most explicit pro-left message in *No Regrets for Our Youth*. But internal political struggles at Toho left bitterness and creative disarray in the wake of a series of strikes, and Kurosawa's 1947 *One Wonderful Sunday* is as a result perhaps his weakest film, an innocuous and sentimental story of a young couple who are too poor to get married.

The mature Kurosawa appears in the 1948 *Drunken Angel*. Here he displays not only a full command of black-and-white filmmaking technique with his characteristic variety of pacing, lighting, and camera angles for maximum editorial effect, but his first use of sound-image counterpoints in the "Cuckoo Waltz" scene where the lively music contrasts with the dying gangster's dark mood. Here too is the full-blown appearance of the typical Kurosawan master-disciple relationship first suggested in *Sanshiro Sugata*, and here is the overriding humanitarian message despite a tragic outcome to the story. The master-disciple roles assume great depth in the blustery alcoholic doctor played by Takashi Shimura opposite the vain, hotheaded young gangster played by Toshiro Mifune, through the tension generated by Shimura's questionable worthiness as a mentor and Mifune's violent unwillingness as a pupil. These two actors would recreate similar testy relationships in numerous Kurosawa films from the late 1940s through the mid-1950s, including the noir police drama *Stray Dog*, the doctor dilemma film *Quiet Duel*, and the all-time classic *Seven Samurai*. In the 1960s Yuzo Kayama would assume the disciple role to

Mifune's master in the feudal comedy *Sanjuro* and in *Red Beard*, about humanity's struggle to modernize.

Part of Kurosawa's characteristic technique is the typical Japanese studio practice of using the same crew or "group" on each production. He consistently worked with cinematographer Asakazu Nakai and composer Fumio Hayasaka, for example. Kurosawa's group became a kind of family that extended to actors as well. Mifune and Shimura were the most prominent names of the virtual private repertory company that through lifetime studio contracts could survive protracted months of production on a Kurosawa film and fill in with more normal four-to-eight-week shoots in between. Kurosawa was thus assured of getting the performance he wanted every time.

Kurosawa's own studio contract and consistent box-office record enabled him to exercise creativity never permitted lesser talents in Japan. He was responsible for numerous technical innovations as a result. He pioneered the use of long lenses and multiple cameras in the famous final battle scenes in the driving rain and splashing mud of *Seven Samurai*. His was the first use of widescreen in Japan in the 1958 samurai entertainment classic *Hidden Fortress*. To the dismay of the leftist critics and the delight of audiences he invented realistic swordfighting and serious portrayals of violence in such extravagant confrontations as those of *Yojimbo*, which spawned the entire Clint Eastwood spaghetti western genre in Italy. Kurosawa further experimented with long lenses on the set in *Red Beard*, and accomplished breathtaking work with his first color film *Dodeskaden*, now no longer restorable. A firm believer in the importance of motion picture science, Kurosawa pioneered the use of Panavision and multi-track Dolby sound in Japan with *Kagemusha*. His only reactionary practice is his editing, which he does entirely himself on an antique Moviola, better and faster than anyone else in the world.

Western critics have most often chastised Kurosawa for using symphonic music in his films. His reply to this is to point out that he and his entire generation grew up on more Western music than native Japanese, which to a contemporary audience sounds artificially exotic. Nevertheless, he has succeeded in his films in adapting not only boleros and elements of Beethoven, but snatches of Japanese popular songs and musical instrumentation from Noh theater and folk song.

Perhaps most startling of Kurosawa's achievements in a Japanese context, however, have been his innate grasp of a story-telling technique that is not culture bound, and his flair for adapting Western classical literature to the screen. No other Japanese director would have dared to set Dostoevski's *Idiot*, Gorki's *Lower Depths*, or Shakespeare's *Macbeth* (*Throne of Blood*) and *King Lear* (*Ran*) in Japan. But he also adapted works from the Japanese Kabuki theater (*Men Who Tread on the Tiger's Tail*) and used Noh staging techniques and music in both *Throne of Blood* and *Kagemusha*. Like his counterparts and most admired models, Jean Renoir, John Ford, and Kenji Mizoguchi, Kurosawa has taken his cinematic inspirations from the full store of world film, literature, and music. And yet the completely original screenplays of his two greatest films, *Ikiru*, the story of a bureaucrat dying of cancer who at last finds purpose in life, and *Seven Samurai*, the saga of seven hungry warriors who pit their wits and lives against marauding bandits in the defense of a poor farming village, reveal that his natural story-telling ability and humanistic convictions transcend all limitations of genre, period and nationality.

—Audie Bock

LA CAVA, Gregory.

American. Born in Towanda, Pennsylvania, 10 March 1892. Educated in Rochester, New York; Art Institute of Chicago; Art Students League and National Academy of Design, New York. Married (2nd time) Grace Carland, 1941, one son. Cartoonist for American Press Association, New York, then head of animated cartoon unit, Hearst Enterprises, 1917; worked on *Mutt and Jeff* series, then *Torchy* stories for Johnny Hines, from 1921; director, from 1922, then writer and director for Paramount, from 1924 (moved to Hollywood 1929); director for First National, 1929, then Pathé, 1930; signed with 20th Century Pictures, 1933, then freelance, from 1934; hired by Mary Pickford company to direct *One Touch of Venus*, then left set after dispute, 1948. Recipient: New York Film Critics Circle Award, for *Stage Door*, 1937. *Died in 1952*.

Films as Director:

(partial list)

1917   *Der Kaptain Discovers the North Pole* ("Katzenjammer Kids" series) (co-d) (animated short)
1919   *How Could William Tell?* ("Jerry on the Job" series) (animated short)
1920   *Smokey Smokes (and) Lampoons* ("Judge Rummy Cartoons" series) (animated short); *Judge Rummy in Bear Facts* (animated short); *Kats Is Kats* ("Krazy Kat Cartoon") (animated short)
1922   *His Nibs* (5 reels); *Faint Heart* (2 reels); *A Social Error* (2 reels)
1923   *The Four Orphans* (2 reels); *The Life of Reilly* (2 reels); *The Busybody* (2 reels); *The Pill Pounder* (2 reels); *So This Is Hamlet?* (2 reels); *Helpful Hogan* (2 reels); *Wild and Wicked* (2 reels); *Beware of the Dog* (2 reels); *The Fiddling Fool* (2 reels)
1924   *The New School Teacher* (+ co-sc); *Restless Wives*
1925   *Womanhandled*
1926   *Let's Get Married*; *So's Your Old Man*; *Say It Again*
1927   *Paradise for Two* (+ pr); *Running Wild*; *Tell It to Sweeney* (+ pr); *The Gay Defender* (+ pr)
1928   *Feel My Pulse* (+ pr); *Half a Bride*
1929   *Saturday's Children*; *Big News*
1930   *His First Command* (+ co-sc)
1931   *Laugh and Get Rich* (+ sc, co-dialogue); *Smart Woman*
1932   *Symphony of Six Million*; *Age of Consent*; *The Half Naked Truth* (+ co-sc)
1933   *Gabriel over the White House*; *Bid of Roses* (+ co-dialogue); *Gallant Lady*
1934   *Affairs of Cellini*; *What Every Woman Knows* (+ pr)
1935   *Private Worlds* (+ co-sc); *She Married Her Boss*
1936   *My Man Godfrey* (+ pr, co-sc)
1937   *Stage Door*
1939   *Fifth Avenue Girl* (+ pr)
1940   *Primrose Path* (+ pr, co-sc)
1941   *Unfinished Business* (+ pr)
1942   *Lady in a Jam* (+ pr)
1947   *Living in a Big Way* (+ story, co-sc)

Publications:

On LA CAVA: articles—

Article in *Life* (New York), 15 September 1941.
Obituary in *New York Times*, 2 March 1952.
Sarris, Andrew, "Esoterica," in *Film Culture* (New York), Spring 1963.
Beylie, Claude, "Enfin, La Cava vint . . . ," in *Ecran* (Paris), May 1974.
McNiven, R., "Gregory La Cava," in *Bright Lights* (Los Angeles), no. 4, 1979.
"Gregory La Cava," in *Film Dope* (London), March 1985.

*   *   *

Although many of his individual films are periodically reviewed and reassessed by film scholars, Gregory La Cava remains today a relatively under-appreciated director of some of the best "screwball comedies" of the 1930s. Perhaps his apparent inability to transcend the screwball form or his failure with a number of straight dramas contributed to this lack of critical recognition. Yet, at his best, he imposed a vitality and sparkle on his screen comedies that overcame their often weak scripts and some occasionally pedestrian performances from his actors

The great majority of his films reflect an instinctive comic sense undoubtedly gained during his early years as a newspaper cartoonist and as an animator with Walter Lantz on such fast and furious cartoons as those in "The Katzenjammer Kids" and "Mutt and Jeff" series. He subsequently became one of the few directors capable of transferring many of these techniques of animated comedy to films involving real actors. His ability to slam a visual gag home quickly sustained such comedies as W.C. Fields's *So's Your Old Man* and *Running Wild*. Yet his real forte emerged in the sound period when the swiftly-paced sight gags were replaced by equally quick verbal repartee.

La Cava's "screwball comedies" of the 1930s were characterized by improbable plots and brilliantly foolish dialogue but also by a dichotomous social view that seemed to delight in establishing satirical contrasts between the views of themselves held by the rich and by the poor. Although treated in varying degrees in *Fifth Avenue Girl, She Married Her Boss* and *Stage Door*, La Cava's classic treatment of this subject remains *My Man Godfrey*. Made during the depths of the Depression, it juxtaposes the world of the rich and frivolous with the plight of the real victims of the economic disaster through the sharply satiric device of a scavenger hunt. When one of the hunt's objectives turns out to be "a forgotten man," in this case a hobo named Godfrey Parke (William Powell), it provides a platform for one of the Depression's victims to lash out at the upper class as being composed of frivolous "nitwits."

Gregory La Cava: Carole Lombard and William Powell in *My Man Godfrey*

However, the film seemingly pulls its punches at the end when, although one socialite, Irene Bullock (Carole Lombard) achieves some realization of the plight of the less fortunate, the hobo Godfrey turns out to be a formerly wealthy Harvard man who actually renews his fortune through his association with her, although he has been somewhat tempered by his experience with the hoboes.

La Cava, perhaps more than other directors working in the screwball genre, was able, by virtue of doing much of the writing on his scripts, to impose his philosophical imprint upon the majority of his films. While he was often required to keep a foot in both the conservative and the liberal camps, his films do not suffer. On the contrary, they maintain an objectivity that has allowed them to grow in stature with the passage of years. *My Man Godfrey*, *Stage Door* and *Gabriel Over the White House*, which is only now being recognized as a political fantasy of great merit, give overwhelming evidence that critical recognition of Gregory La Cava is considerably overdue.

—Stephen L. Hanson

LANDIS, John.

American. Born Chicago, 30 August 1950. Educated at Oakwood School, Los Angeles, until 1966; progressive education programme, U.C.L.A. Married costume designer Deborah Nadoolman, 1980, one daughter. Mailboy at 20th Century-Fox, then production assistant on *Kelly's Heroes* for MGM, 1970; dialogue coach and stuntman in Europe, 1970–72; directed first feature, *Schlock*, 1973; acquitted of manslaughter charges arising from the deaths of actor Vic Morrow and two child actors on the set of *Twilight Zone—The Movie*, 1987; retrospective of his work at Edinburgh Film Festival, 1990. Lives in Los Angeles.

Films as Director:

1973   *Schlock (The Banana Monster)* (+ sc, stuntman)
1977   *The Kentucky Fried Movie* (+ role)
1978   *National Lampoon's Animal House*
1980   *The Blues Brothers* (+ co-sc, role as Trooper La Fong)
1981   *An American Werewolf in London* (+ sc, stuntman)
1983   "Prologue" and "Back There" episodes in *Twilight Zone—The Movie* (+ co-pr); *Thriller* (+ co-pr) (music

video); *Making Michael Jackson's Thriller* (doc) (+ co-sc, pr); *Trading Places*
1985 *Into the Night* (+ story, role as Savak); *Spies Like Us*
1986 *The Three Amigos*
1987 *Amazon Women on the Moon* (co-d, + exec pr)
1988 *Coming to America*

Other Films:

1970 *Kelly's Heroes* (Hutton) (pr. asst.)
1973 *Battle for the Planet of the Apes* (Thompson)
1975 *Death Race 2000* (Bartel)
1979 *1941* (Spielberg) (role)
1982 *Eating Raoul* (Bartel) (role)
1984 *The Muppets Take Manhattan* (Oz)
1985 *Clue* (Lynn) (exec pr, story)

Publications:

By LANDIS: articles—

Interview in *Time Out* (London), 2 March 1979.
Interview in *Sight and Sound* (London), Winter 1981/82.
Interview (in 2 parts) in *Cinema* (London), Winter 1981 and no. 1, 1982.
"Dialogue on Film: John Landis," in *American Film* (Washington, D.C.), May 1982.
Interview with Jack Arnold in *Cahiers du Cinéma* (Paris), June 1982.

On LANDIS: articles—

"John Landis," in *Film Dope* (London), March 1985.
Hollywood Reporter, 1 June 1987.

*   *   *

John Landis is a filmmaker who has become more famous for scandalous production practices than for his million-dollar-grossing farces. Month after month in the mid–1980s America lived the adventures of the *Twilight Zone: The Movie* court-room drama. Landis was accused of helping fashion the deaths of actor Vic Morrow and two children in a helicopter accident. Many film fans might not remember that Landis had directed the wildly successful *National Lampoon's Animal House*, but few did not know that on 23 July 1983 a spectacular explosion on the set of *Twilight Zone: The Movie*, that Landis directed and co-produced with Steven Spielberg, knocked a helicopter out of the sky and into the path of veteran actor Morrow and the two children, Renee Chen, six, and My-Ca Lee, seven. In the end on 29 May 1987 Landis and four associates were acquitted of all charges. But the press played up the fact and most who cared knew only that the children were working illegally after dark, without the required permits or appropriate supervision.

Landis's career had been on a roll. After *National Lampoon's Animal House*, he had directed a string of blockbusters

John Landis: Dan Aykroyd and John Belushi in *The Blues Brothers*

including *Trading Places*, *War Games*, and *Coming to America*. To Hollywood's movie moguls *National Lampoon's Animal House* had been the surprise hit of 1978, finishing third in domestic grosses for the year. Landis, then only twenty-seven, was seen as having his finger on the pulse of the American moviegoing youth market. *Trading Places* finished third its year as did *Coming to America*. Landis seemed destined to forever ride on Eddie Murphy's coattails to future fame and fortune.

But amidst this success had been filmic failure as well. If *The Blues Brothers* and *An American Werewolf in London* did not match *National Lampoon's Animal House* for minting money, they did prove he could craft genre efforts aimed at the lowest common denominator of the core youth audience. The developing Landis style sought demolition derby realism in some variation of the old fashioned chase sequence: one critic calculated that there were some three hundred car wrecks in *The Blues Brothers* alone. But *Three Amigos*, starring Chevy Chase, Steve Martin and Martin Short, did not even earn back its inflated cost of production. His trio of stars were apparently trying to be modern day Ritz brothers, whose *Argentine Nights* (1940) was a direct inspiration for the weak script. Landis seemed unable to find the delicate line between broad-based comedy and wretched excess.

Landis's rise to fame and fortune was a strange one indeed, a throwback to an earlier era when few Hollywood filmmakers ever went to college: he never ventured past the tenth grade, even though his parents lived within the shadow of UCLA. Landis started in the mail room at Twentieth Century Fox, served as an assistant on *Kelly's Heroes* (1970), worked as a stunt man on spaghetti westerns in Europe, and journeyed back to Hollywood to wait for his break. It came with *Kentucky Fried Movie* (1977), a collection of sophomoric skits (filmed in 21 days) that became a cult favorite. With *National Lampoon's Animal House*, the young Landis had achieved a position thousands of film students could only dream of—the pick of his upcoming projects, producers lining up with scripts at his doorstep. But the questions remain. John Landis surely has made a mark in Hollywood of the 1980s, but his future remains in doubt.

—Douglas Gomery

LANG, Fritz.

German/American. Born in Vienna, 5 December 1890, became U.S. citizen, 1935. Studied engineering at the Technische Hochschule, Vienna. Married (2nd time), writer Thea von Harbou, 1924 (separated 1933). Cartoonist, fashion designer, and painter, in Paris, 1913; returned to Vienna, served in army, 1914–16; after discharge, worked as scriptwriter and actor, then moved to Berlin, 1918; reader and story editor for Decla, then wrote and directed first film, *Halbblut*, 1919; worked with von Harbou, from 1920; visited Hollywood, 1924; *Das Testament des Dr. Mabuse* banned by Nazis, 1933; offered post as supervisor of Nazi film productions by Goebbels, but fled Germany; after working in Paris and London, went to Hollywood, 1934; signed with Paramount, 1940; cofounder, then President, Diana Productions, 1945; quit Hollywood, citing continuing disputes with producers, 1956; directed two films in India, 1958–59, before last film, directed in Germany, 1960. Recipient: Officier d'Art et des Lettres, France. *Died in Beverly Hills, 2 August 1976.*

Films as Director:

1919   *Halbblut* (*Half Caste*) (+ sc); *Der Herr der Liebe* (*The Master of Love*) (+ role); *Hara-Kiri*; *Die Spinnen* (*The Spiders*) Part I: *Der Goldene See* (*The Golden Lake*) (+ sc)

1920   *Die Spinnen* (*The Spiders*) Part II: *Das Brillantenschiff* (*The Diamond Ship*) (+ sc); *Das Wandernde Bild* (*The Wandering Image*) (+ co-sc); *Kämpfende Herzen* (*Die Vier um die Frau. Four Around a Woman*) (+ co-sc)

1921   *Der müde Tod: Ein Deutsches Volkslied in Sechs Versen* (*The Weary Death. Between Two Worlds. Beyond the Wall. Destiny*) (+ co-sc)

1921/22   **Dr. Mabuse, der Spieler (Dr. Mabuse, the Gambler. The Fatal Passions)** in 2 parts: **Ein Bild der Zeit (Spieler aus Leidenschaft. A Picture of the Time)** and: **Inferno—Menschen der Zeit (Inferno des Verbrechens. Inferno—Men of the Time)** (+ co-sc)

1924   *Die Nibelungen* in 2 parts: **Siegfrieds Tod (Death of Siegfried)** and **Kriemhilds Rache (Kriemhild's Revenge)** (+ co-sc, uncredited)

1927   *Metropolis* (+ co-sc, uncredited)

1928   *Spione* (*Spies*) (+ pr, co-sc, uncredited)

1929   *Die Frau im Mond* (*By Rocket to the Moon. The Girl in the Moon*) (+ pr, co-sc, uncredited)

1931   **M, Mörder unter Uns (M)** (+ co-sc, uncredited)

1933   **Das Testament des Dr. Mabuse (The Testament of Dr. Mabuse. The Last Will of Dr. Mabuse)** (+ co-sc, uncredited) (German and French versions)

1934   *Liliom* (+ co-sc, uncredited)

1936   *Fury* (+ co-sc)

1937   **You Only Live Once**

1938   *You and Me* (+ pr)

1940   *The Return of Frank James*

1941   *Western Union*; **Man Hunt**; *Confirm or Deny* (co-d, uncredited)

1942   *Moontide* (co-d, uncredited)

1943   *Hangmen Also Die!* (+ pr, co-sc)

1944   *Ministry of Fear*; *The Woman in the Window*

1945   *Scarlet Street* (+ pr)

1946   *Cloak and Dagger*

1948   *Secret Beyond the Door* (+ co-pr)

1950   *House by the River*; *An American Guerrilla in the Philippines*

1952   *Rancho Notorious*; *Clash by Night*

1953   *The Blue Gardenia*; **The Big Heat**

1954   *Human Desire*

1955   *Moonfleet*

1956   *While the City Sleeps*; **Beyond a Reasonable Doubt**

1959   *Der Tiger von Eschnapur* (*The Tiger of Bengal*) and *Das Indische Grabmal* (*The Hindu Tomb*) (+ co-sc) (released in cut version as *Journey to the Lost City*)

1960   *Die Tausend Augen des Dr. Mabuse* (*The Thousand Eyes of Dr. Mabuse*) (+ pr, co-sc)

Other Films:

1917   *Die Hochzeit im Ekzentrik Klub* (*The Wedding in the Eccentric Club*) (May) (sc); *Hilde Warren und der Tod* (*Hilde Warren and Death*) (May) (sc, four roles); *Joe Debbs* (series) (sc)

1918   *Die Rache ist mein* (*Revenge Is Mine*) (Neub) (sc); *Herrin der Welt* (*Men of the World*) (May) (asst d); *Bettler GmbH* (sc)

1919   *Wolkenbau und Flimmerstern* (*Castles in the Sky and Rhinestones*) (d unknown, co-sc); *Totentanz* (*Dance of Death*) (Rippert) (sc); *Die Pest in Florenz* (*Plague in Florence*) (Rippert) (sc); *Die Frau mit den Orchiden* (*The Woman with the Orchid*) (Rippert) (sc); *Lilith und Ly* (sc)

1921   *Das Indische Grabmal* (in 2 parts: *Die Sendung des Yoghi* and *Der Tiger von Eschnapur*) (co-sc)

1963   *Le Mépris* (*Contempt*) (Godard) (role as himself)

Publications:

By LANG: articles—

"The Freedom of the Screen," 1947 (reprinted in *Hollywood Directors 1941–1976* by Richard Koszarski, New York, 1977).

Fritz Lang (center) directing *Human Desire*

"Happily Ever After," 1948 (collected in *Film Makers on Film Making* edited by Harry Geduld, Bloomington, Indiana, 1969).

"Fritz Lang Today," interview with H. Hart, in *Films in Review* (New York), June/July 1956.

"The Impact of Television on Motion Pictures," interview with G. Bachmann, in *Film Culture* (New York), December 1957.

Interview with Jean Domarchi and Jacques Rivette, in *Cahiers du Cinéma* (Paris), September 1959.

"On the Problems of Today," in *Films and Filming* (London), June 1962.

"Fritz Lang Talks About Dr. Mabuse," interview with Mark Shivas, in *Movie* (London), November 1962.

"Was bin ich, was sind wir?," in *Filmkritik* (Munich), no.7, 1963.

"La Nuit viennoise: Une Confession de Fritz Lang," edited by Gretchen Berg, in *Cahiers du Cinéma* (Paris), August 1965 and June 1966.

Interview with Axel Madsen, in *Sight and Sound* (London), Summer 1967.

"Autobiography," in *The Celluloid Muse: Hollywood Directors Speak* by Charles Higham and Joel Greenberg, London, 1969.

"Interviews," in *Dialogue on Film* (Beverly Hills), April 1974.

Interview with Gene Phillips, in *Focus on Film* (London), Spring 1975.

"Fritz Lang Gives His Last Interview," with Gene Phillips, in the *Village Voice* (New York), 16 August 1976.

On LANG: books—

Kracauer, Siegfried, *From Caliari to Hitler: A Psychological History of the German Film*, Princeton, New Jersey, 1947.

Courtade, Francis, *Fritz Lang*, Paris, 1963.

Moullet, Luc, *Fritz Lang*, Paris, 1963.

Eibel, Alfred, editor, *Fritz Lang*, Paris, 1964.

Bogdanovich, Peter, *Fritz Lang in America*, New York, 1969.

Eisner, Lotte, *The Haunted Screen: Expressionism in the German Cinema and the Influence of Max Reinhardt*, Berkeley, 1969.

Jensen, Paul, *The Cinema of Fritz Lang*, New York, 1969.

Johnston, Claire, *Fritz Lang*, London, 1969.

Grafe, Frieda, Enno Patalas, and Hans Prinzler, *Fritz Lang*, Munich 1976.

Eisner, Lotte, *Fritz Lang*, edited by David Robinson, New York, 1977.

Armour, Robert, *Fritz Lang*, Boston, 1978.

Ott, Frederick, *The Films of Fritz Lang*, Secaucus, New Jersey, 1979.

Jenkins, Stephen, editor, *Fritz Lang: The Image and the Look*, London, 1981.

Kaplan, E. Ann, *Fritz Lang: A Guide to References and Resources*, Boston, 1981.

Maibohm, Ludwig, *Fritz Lang: Seine Filme—Sein Leben*, Munich, 1981.

Dürrenmatt, Dieter, *Fritz Lang: Leben und Werk*, Basle, 1982.

Humphries, Reynold, *Fritz Lang: Cinéaste Américain*, Paris, 1982.

Humphries, Reynold, *Fritz Lang: Genre and Representation in His American Films*, Baltimore, 1988.

On LANG: articles—

Wilson, Harry, "The Genius of Fritz Lang," in *Film Quarterly* (Berkeley), Summer 1947.

Truffaut, François, "Aimer Fritz Lang," in *Cahiers du Cinéma* (Paris), January 1954.

Lambert, Gavin, "Fritz Lang's America," in *Sight and Sound* (London), Summer 1955.

Demonsablon, Phillipe, "La Hautaine Dialectique de Fritz Lang," and Michel Mourlet, "Trajectoire de Fritz Lang," in *Cahiers du Cinéma* (Paris), September 1959.

Franju, Georges, "Le Style de Fritz Lang," in *Cahiers du Cinéma* (Paris), November 1959.

Taylor, John, "The Nine Lives of Dr. Mabuse," in *Sight and Sound* (London), Winter 1961.

Sarris, Andrew, "Fritz Lang," in *Film Culture* (New York), Spring 1963.

Rhode, Eric, "Fritz Lang (The German Period, 1919–1933)," in *Tower of Babel*, London, 1966.

"Lang Issue" of *Image et Son* (Paris), April 1968.

Joannides, Paul, "Aspects of Fritz Lang," in *Cinema* (London), August 1970.

Burch, Noel, "De *Mabuse* à *M*: Le Travail de Fritz Lang," in special issue of *Revue d'esthétique* (Paris), 1973.

Appel, Alfred Jr., "Film Noir: The Director, Fritz Lang's American Nightmare," in *Film Comment* (New York), November/December 1974.

Gersch, Wolfgang, and others, "*Hangmen Also Die!*: Fritz Lang und Bertolt Brecht," in *Filmkritik* (Munich), July 1975.

Sarris, Andrew, "Fritz Lang (1890–1976) Was the Prophet of Our Paranoia," in *Village Voice* (New York), 16 August 1976.

Overby, David, "Fritz Lang, 1890–1976," in *Sight and Sound* (London), Autumn 1976.

Kuntzel, Thierry, "The Film-Work," in *Enclitic* (Minneapolis), Spring 1978.

Willis, Don, "Fritz Lang: Only Melodrama," in *Film Quarterly* (Berkeley), Winter 1979/80.

Magny, Joel, and others, "Actualité de Fritz Lang," in *Cinéma* (Paris), June 1982.

Neale, Steve, "Authors and Genres," in *Screen* (London), July/August 1982.

Duval, B., "Le crime de M. Lang. Portrait d'un Fritz en artisan de Hollywood," in *Image et Son* (Paris), November 1982.

McGivern, William P., "Roman Holiday," in *American Film* (Washington, D.C.), October 1983.

Rotondi, C.J., and E. Gerstein, "The 1984 Review. The 1927 review. Fritz Lang: The Maker of *Metropolis*," in *Films in Review* (New York), October 1984.

Lang Section of *Positif* (Paris), November 1984.

"*Der Tiger von Eschnapur* Issue" of *Avant-Scène du Cinéma* (Paris), April 1985.

"*Das indische Grabmal* Issue" of *Avant-Scène du Cinéma* (Paris), May 1985.

"Fritz Lang," in *Film Dope* (London), November 1985.

Giesen, R., "Der Trickfilm," in *Cinefex* (Riverside, California), February 1986.

Bernstein, M., "Fritz Lang, Incorporated," in *Velvet Light Trap* (Madison, Wisconsin), no. 22, 1986.

Pelinq, M., in *Jeune Cinéma* (Paris), April/May and June/July 1989.

On LANG: films—

Luft, Friedrich, and Guido Schütte, *Künstlerporträt: Fritz Lang*, for TV, Germany, 1959.

Fleischmann, Peter, *Begegnung mit Fritz Lang*, Germany, 1963.

Leiser, Erwin, *Das war die Ufa*, Germany, 1964.

Leiser, Erwin, *Zum Beispiel Fritz Lang*, for TV, Germany, 1968.

Dütsch, Werner, *Die Schweren Träume des Fritz Lang*, for TV, Germany, 1974.

* * *

Fritz Lang's career can be divided conveniently into three parts: the first German period, 1919–1933, from *Halbblut* to the second Mabuse film, *Das Testament des Dr. Mabuse*; the American period, 1936–1956, from *Fury* to *Beyond a Reasonable Doubt*; and the second German period, 1959–60, which includes the two films made in India and his last film, *Die tausend Augen des Dr. Mabuse*.

Lang's apprentice years as a scriptwriter and director were spent in the studios in Berlin where he adopted certain elements of expressionism, and was imbued with the artistic seriousness with which the Germans went about making their films. In Hollywood this seriousness would earn Lang a reputation for unnecessary perfectionism, a criticism also thrown at fellow émigrés von Stroheim and von Sternberg. Except for several films for Twentieth Century-Fox, Lang never worked long for a single studio in the United States, and he often preferred to work on underbudgeted projects which he could produce, and therefore control, himself. The rather radical dissimilarities between the two studio worlds within which Lang spent most of his creative years not surprisingly resulted in products which look quite different from one another, and it is the difference in look or image which has produced the critical confusion most often associated with an assessment of Lang's films.

One critical approach to Lang's work, most recently articulated by Gavin Lambert, argues that Lang produced very little of artistic interest after he left Germany; the *Cahiers du cinéma* auteurists argue the opposite, namely that Lang's films made in America are superior to his European films because the former were clogged with self-conscious artistry and romantic didacticism which the leanness of his American studio work eliminated. A third approach, suggested by Robin Wood and others, examines Lang's films as a whole, avoiding the German-American division by looking at characteristic thematic and visual motifs. Lang's films can be discussed as exhibiting certain distinguishing features: economy, functional precision, detachment, and as containing basic motifs such as the trap, a suppressed underworld, the revenge motive, and the abuse of power. Investigating the films from this perspective reveals a more consistent development of Lang as a creative artist and helps to minimize the superficial anomalies shaped by his career.

In spite of the narrowness of examining only half of a filmmaker's creative output, the sheer number of Lang's German movies which have received substantial critical attention as "classic" films has tended to submerge the critical attempt at breadth and comprehensiveness. Not only did these earlier films form an important intellectual center for the German film industry during the years between the wars, as Siegfried Kracauer later pointed out, but they had a wide international impact as well and were extensively reviewed in the Anglo-American press. Lang's reputation preceded him to America, and although it had little effect ultimately on his working relationship, such as it was, with the Hollywood moguls, it has affected Lang's subsequent treatment by film critics.

If Lang is a "flawed genius," as one critic has described him, it is less a wonder that he is "flawed" than that his genius had a chance to develop at all. The working conditions Lang survived after his defection would have daunted a less dedicated director. Lang, however, not only survived but flourished, producing films of undisputed quality: the four war movies, *Man Hunt, Hangmen Also Die!, Ministry of Fear*, and *Cloak and Dagger*, and the urban crime films of the 1950s, *Clash by Night, The Blue Gardenia, The Big Heat, Human Desire*, and *While the City Sleeps*.

These American films reflect a more mature director, tighter mise-en-scène, and more control as a result of Lang's American experience. The films also reveal continuity. As Robin Wood has written, the formal symmetry of his individual films is mirrored in the symmetry of his career, beginning and ending in Germany. All through his life, Lang adjusted his talent to meet the changes in his environment, and in so doing produced a body of creative work of unquestionable importance in the development of the history of cinema.

—Charles L.P. Silet

LATTUADA, Alberto.

Italian. Born in Milan, 13 November 1914. Educated in architecture. Married Carla Del Poggio, 1945 (divorced). Cofounder of avant-garde journal *Camminare*, 1933; helped found *Corrente*; with Mario Ferreri and Luigi Comencini, founder of Cineteca Italiana, Italian film archive, 1940; directed first film, 1942; opera director, from 1970. Address: Via N. Paganini, 7 Rome, Italy.

Films as Director and Co-Scriptwriter:

1942   *Giacomo l'idealista*
1945   *La freccia nel fianco*; *La nostra guerra* (documentary)
1946   *Il bandito*
1947   *Il delitto di Giovanni Episcopo* (*Flesh Will Surrender*)
1948   *Senza pietà* (*Without Pity*)
1949   *Il mulino del Po* (*The Mill on the Po*)
1950   *Luci del varietà* (*Variety Lights*) (co-d, co-pr)
1952   *Anna*; *Il cappotto* (*The Overcoat*)
1953   *La lupa* (*The She-Wolf*); "Gli italiani si voltano" episode of *Amore in città* (*Love in the City*)
1954   *La spiaggia* (*The Beach*); *Scuola elementare*
1956   *Guendalina*
1958   *La tempesta* (*Tempest*)
1960   *I dolci inganni*; *Lettere di una novizia* (*Rita*)
1961   *L'imprevisto*
1962   *Mafioso*; *La steppa*
1965   *La mandragola* (*The Love Root*)
1966   *Matchless*
1967   *Don Giovanni in Sicilia* (+ co-pr)
1968   *Fräulein Doktor*
1969   *L'amica*
1970   *Venga a prendere il caffe . . . da noi* (*Come Have Coffee With Us*)
1971   *Bianco, rosso e . . .* (*White Sister*)
1973   *Sono stato io*
1974   *Le farò da padre . . .* (*Bambina*)
1976   *Cuore di cane*; *Bruciati da cocente passione* (*Oh Serafina!*)
1978   *Cosi come sei*
1980   *La cicala*
1983   *Cristoforo Colombo* (*Christopher Columbus*)
1987   *Una spina nel cuore*

Other Films:

1935   *Il museo dell'amore* (asst d)
1936   *La danza delle lancette* (collaborator on experimental short)
1941   *Piccolo mondo antico* (Soldati) (asst d)
1942   *Si signora* (asst d, co-sc)
1958   *Un eroe dei nostri tempi* (Monicelli) (role)

Publications:

By LATTUADA: books—

Occhio quadrate, album of photos, Milan, 1941.
La tempesta, Bologna, 1958.
La steppa, Bologna, 1962.
Gli uccelli indomabili, Rome, 1970.
Cuore di cane, Bari, 1975.
A proposito di Cosi come sei, edited by Enrico Oldrini, Bologna, 1978.
Diario di un grane amatore, Milan, 1980.
Feuillets au vent, Paris, 1981.
La massa, Rome, 1982.

By LATTUADA: articles—

"We Took the Actors into the Streets," in *Films and Filming* (London), April 1959.
"Alberto Lattuada: du néoréalisme au réalisme magique," interview with A. Tournès, in *Jeune Cinéma* (Paris), December/January 1974/75.
"*Moi et le diable*: je ne puis vivre ni avec toi ni sans toi," in *Positif* (Paris), June 1978.
Interview with G. Volpi, in *Positif* (Paris), September and October 1978.
"Alberto Lattuada: une foi dans la beauté," interview with C. Depuyper and A. Cervoni, in *Cinéma* (Paris), April 1981.
Interview with L. Codelli, in *Films and Filming* (London), July 1982.

On LATTUADA: books—

De Sanctis, Filippo Mario, *Alberto Lattuada*, Parma, 1961, and Lyons, 1965.
Bruno, Edoardo, *Lattuada o la proposta ambigua*, Rome, 1968.
Broher, J.J., *Alberto Lattuada*, Brussels, 1971.

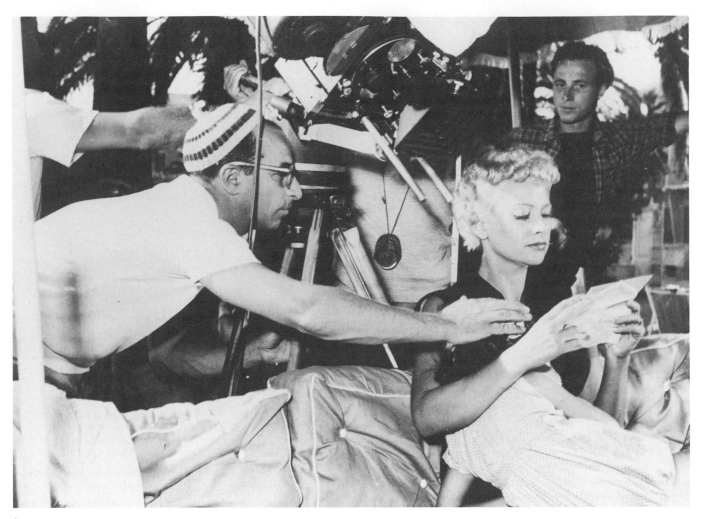

Alberto Lattuada directing Martine Carol in *La spiaggia*

Turroni, Giuseppe, *Alberto Lattuada*, Milan, 1977.
Zanellato, Angelo, *L'uomo (cattivo sorte): il cinema di Lattuada*, Padua, 1978.
Bruno, Edoardo, *Italian Directors: Alberto Lattuada*, Rome, 1981.
Camerini, Claudio, *Alberto Lattuada*, Florence, 1982.
Cosulich, Callisto, *I film di Alberto Lattuada*, Rome, 1985.

On LATTUADA: articles—

Turroni, G., "Film e figurazione: la riflessione metalinguistica," in *Filmcritica* (Rome), January 1979.
Duval, Bernard, "Lattuada: un précursor perpetuel," in *Image et Son* (Paris), July 1979.
"Alberto Lattuada," in *Film Dope* (London), November 1985.

*   *   *

One of the most consistently commercially-successful directors in Italy, Lattuada has continued to enjoy a freedom of subject matter and style despite ideological shifts and methodological changes. His main films during the neorealist period (which he claims never to have taken part in) succeeded in further establishing the Italian cinema in the international market and, unlike many of his colleagues' works, also proved popular in the domestic market. *Il bandito* and *Il mulino del Po*, for example, combined progressive ideology, realistic detail due to location shooting and attention to quotidian activities, and tight narrative structure due to an attention to editing. In fact, Lattuada's entire career has demonstrated an on-going interest in editing, which he considers more fundamental than the script, and which gives his films a strictly controlled rhythm with no wasted footage. He shoots brief scenes that, he claims, are more attractive to an audience and that can be easily manipulated at the editing stage.

Lattuada's background stressed the arts and his films display a sophisticated cultural appreciation. As a boy, he took an active interest in his father's work as musician in the orchestra of La Scala in Milan. As a young man, Lattuada worked as a film critic, wrote essays on contemporary painters, co-founded cultural magazines, and worked as an assistant director and scriptwriter. Lattuada co-scripts most of his films, as well as occasionally producing them. He also co-founded what became the Milan film archive, the Cineteca Italiana.

As a director, he has been most often called eclectic because of his openness to projects and his ability to handle a wide variety of subject matter. His major commercial successes have been *Bianco, rosso e . . .* which he wrote especially for Sophia Loren; *Matchless*, a parody of the spy genre; *Anna*, the first Italian film to gross over one billion lire in its national distribution; *La spiaggia*, a bitter satire of bourgeois realism; and *Mafioso*, starring Alberto Sordi and filmed in New York, Sicily, and Milan.

Lattuada has also filmed many adaptations of literary works, which remain faithful to the source but are never simply static re-enactments. These range from the comically grotesque *Venga a prendere . . .*, to a version of Brancati's satirical *Don Giovanni in Sicilia*, and include the horror film *Cuore di cane* taken from a Bulgakov novel; a version of a D'Annunzio novel in 1947 praised for its set design, interpretation of the text and the high quality of the acting; the spectacular big-budget *La tempesta* from two Pushkin stories; and Chekhov's metaphorical journey in *La steppa*. His 1952 version of *The Overcoat* is considered his masterpiece for its portrayal of psychological states and the excellence of Renato Rascel's performance. Lattuada is famous for his handling of actors, and has launched the career of many an actress, including Catherine Spaak, Giulietta Masina and Nastassia Kinski.

Notwithstanding the diversity of subject matter he has directed, Lattuada's main interest has been pubescent sexuality, the passage of a girl into womanhood, and the sexual relationship of a couple as the primary attraction they have for each other. Thus, his films deal with eroticism as a central theme and he chooses actresses whose physical beauty and sensuousness are immediately apparent. This theme appeared in Lattuada's work as early as his second feature and has been his main preoccupation in his films since 1974.

His films have been critically well-received in Italy, although rarely given the attention enjoyed by some of his contemporaries. In France, however, his work is highly acclaimed; *Il bandito* and *Il cappotto* received much praise at the Cannes festivals when they were shown. With a few exceptions, his more recent work is little known in Britain and the United States, although when *Come Have Coffee with Us* was released commercially in the U.S. ten years after it was made, it enjoyed a fair success at the box office and highly favorable reviews.

—Elaine Mancini

LAUNDER, Frank, and Sidney GILLIAT.

Launder. British. Born in Hitchin, Hertfordshire, 1906. Educated in Brighton. Civil servant, then actor, in Brighton; studio assistant, 1928; first collaboration with fellow writer Sidney Gilliat, 1935; with Gilliat, wrote radio serials *Crooks Tour* and *Secret Mission 609*, 1939; co-directed first film, *Millions Like Us*, 1943; formed Individual Pictures production company with Gilliat, 1944 (dissolved 1950).

Gilliat. British. Born in Edgeley, Cheshire, 1908. Educated at London University. Hired by Walter Mycroft, film critic of London Evening Standard (edited by Gilliat's father) and Scenario Chief at British International Pictures, Elstree, as studio assistant, 1928; gagman and dogsbody for director Walter Forde, 1929–30; collaborator with Frank Launder (see above), from 1935; President, Screen Writers Association, 1946; Director, British Lion, 1958–72; Chairman of Shepperton Studios, from 1961; also co-founder of TV Commercial company, Littleton Park Film Productions; wrote opera libretto for *Our Man in Havana*, 1963.

Films Directed, Produced and Written by Launder and Gilliat:

1943   *Millions Like Us* (Launder and Gilliat)
1944   *Two Thousand Women* (Launder)
1945   *The Rake's Progress* (*The Notorious Gentleman*) (Gilliat)
1946   *Green For Danger* (Gilliat); *I See a Dark Stranger* (Launder)
1947   *Captain Boycott* (Launder)
1948   *The Blue Lagoon* (Launder); *London Belongs To Me* (*Dulcimer Street*) (Gilliat)
1950   *State Secret* (*The Great Manhunt*) (Gilliat); *The Happiest Days of Your Life* (Launder)
1951   *Lady Godiva Rides Again* (Launder)
1952   *Folly To Be Wise* (Launder)
1953   *The Story of Gilbert and Sullivan* (*The Great Gilbert and Sullivan*) (Gilliat)
1954   *The Constant Husband* (Gilliat); *The Belles of St. Trinians* (Launder)
1955   *Geordie* (*Wee Geordie*) (Launder)
1956   *Fortune Is a Woman* (*She Played With Fire*) (Gilliat)
1957   *Blue Murder at St. Trinians* (Launder)
1959   *The Bridal Path* (Launder); *Left, Right and Centre* (Gilliat)
1960   *The Pure Hell of St. Trinian's* (Launder)
1961   *Only Two Can Play* (Gilliat)
1965   *Joey Boy* (Launder)
1966   *The Great St. Trinian's Train Robbery* (Launder and Gilliat)

Films Written by Launder and Gilliat:

1936   *Seven Sinners* (de Courville); *Twelve Good Men* (Ince)
1938   ***The Lady Vanishes*** (**Hitchcock**)
1939   *Inspector Hornleigh On Holiday* (Forde)
1940   *They Came By Night* (Lachman); *Night Train to Munich* (Reed)
1942   *The Young Mr. Pitt* (Reed)
1956   *The Green Man* (Day) (+pr)

Other Films—Launder:

1928   *Cocktails* (Banks) (titles)
1929   *Under the Greenwood Tree* (Lachman) (co-sc)
1930   *The Compulsory Husband* (Banks) (dialogue/dubbing); *Song of Soho* (Lachman) (co-sc); *Harmony Heaven* (Bentley) (addl dialogue); *The W Plan* (Saville) (addl dialogue); *The Middle Watch* (Walker) (co-sc); *Children of Chance* (Esway) (co-sc); *How He Lied to Her Husband* (Lewis) (sc)
1931   *Keepers of Youth* (Bentley) (sc); *Hobson's Choice* (Bentley) (co-sc); *A Gentleman of Paris* (Hill) (co-sc); *The Woman Between* (Mander) (co-sc)
1932   *After Office Hours* (Bentley) (co-sc); *The Last Coupon* (Bentley) (co-sc); *Arms and the Man* (Lewis) (co-sc, uncredited); *Josser in the Army* (Lee) (sc)
1933   *Hawleys of High St* (Bentley) (co-sc); *Facing the Music* (Hughes) (co-sc); *You Made Me Love You* (Banks) (sc); *A Southern Maid* (Hughes) (co-adapt, sc); *Happy* (Zelnik) (co-sc)
1934   *Those Were the Days* (Bentley) (co-adapt, sc)
1935   *Emil and the Detectives* (Rosmer) (co-sc); *Rolling Home* (R. Ince) (sc); *So You Won't Talk* (Beaudine) (co-sc); *Mr. What's His Name* (Ince) (co-sc); *I Give My Heart* (Varnel) (adapt/sc); *Get Off My Foot* (Beaudine) (co-sc); *The Black Mask* (Ince) (co-sc)
1936   *Where's Sally* (Woods) (co-sc); *Educated Evans* (Beaudine) (co-sc); *Windbag the Sailor* (Beaudine) (sc editor)
1937   *Good Morning Boys* (Varnel) (sc editor); *Bank Holiday* (Reed) (sc editor); *O-Kay for Sound* (Varnel) (sc editor); *Doctor Syn* (Neill) (sc editor); *Oh, Mr. Porter!* (Varnel) (story)
1938   *Owd Bob* (Stevenson) (sc editor); *Strange Boarders* (Mason) (sc editor); *Convict 99* (Varnel) (sc editor); *Alf's Button Afloat* (Varnel) (sc editor); *Hey! Hey! U.S.A.!* (Varnel) (sc editor); *Old Bones of the River* (Varnel) (sc editor)
1939   *Ask a Policeman* (Varnel) (sc editor); *A Girl Must Live* (Reed) (sc); *The Frozen Limits* (Varnel) (sc editor)
1940   *Inspector Hornleigh Goes To It* (Forde) (story)
1969   *An Elephant Called Slowly* (Hill) (sc uncredited)
1980   *Wildcats of St. Trinians* (d, sc)

Other Films—Gilliat:

1928   *Toni* (Maude) (titles); *Champagne* (Hitchcock) (titles);

Adam's Apple (Whelan) (titles); *Weekend Wives* (Lachman) (titles); *The Manxman* (Hitchcock) (research)

1929 *The Tryst* (short) (co-d); (*Would You Believe It?* (Forde) (asst d, +role)

1930 *Red Pearls* (Forde) (asst d); *You'd Be Surprised* (Forde) (asst d, +role); *The Last Hour* (Forde) (asst d); *Lord Richard in the Pantry* (Forde) (sc); *Bed's Breakfast* (Forde) (sc)

1931 *3rd Time Lucky* (Ford) (addl dialogue); *The Ghost Train* (Forde) (addl dialogue); *A Gentleman of Paris* (Hill) (sc); *The Happy Ending* (Webb) (co-sc, uncredited); *A Night in Marseilles* (*Night Shadows*) (de Courville) (sc); *Two Way Street* (King) (sc)

1932 *Lord Babs* (Forde) (addl dialogue); *Jack's the Boy* (Forde) (sc continuity); *Rome Express* (Forde) (sc); For the Love of Mike (Banks) (co-sc)

1933 *Sign Please* (Rawlins—short (sc); *Post Haste* (Cadman—short) (sc); *Facing the Music* (Hughes) (co-story); *Falling For You* (Hulbert and Stevenson) (story); *Orders Is Orders* (Forde) (co-sc); *Friday the Thirteenth* (Saville) (co-story)

1934 *Jack Ahoy!* (Forde) (co-sc); *Chu-Chin-Chow* (Forde) (co-sc); *My Heart Is Calling* (Gallone) (adapt/dialogue)

1935 *Bulldog Jack* (*Alias Bulldog Drummond*) (Forde) (co-sc); *King of the Damned* (Forde) (co-sc)

1936 *Tudor Rose* (Stevenson) (assoc pr); *Where There's a Will* (Beaudine) (sc); *The Man Who Changed His Mind* (*The Man Who Lived Again*) (Stevenson) (co-sc, assoc pr); *Strangers on a Honeymoon* (de Courville) (co-sc)

1937 *Take My Tip* (Mason) (co-sc); *A Yank at Oxford* (Conway) (story)

1938 *Strange Boarders* (Mason) (co-sc); *The Gaunt Stranger* (*The Phantom Strikes*) (Forde) (sc)

1939 *Ask a Policeman* (Varnel) (story); *Jamaica Inn* (Hitchcock) (sc)

1940 *The Girl in the News* (Reed) (sc)

1941 *The Ghost Train* (Forde) (addl dialogue); *Kipps* (*The Remarkable Mr. Kipps*) (Reed) (sc); *Mr. Proudfoot Shows a Light* (Mason—short) (story); *You're Telling Me!* (Peak—short) (sc); *From the Four Corners* (Havelock-Allan—short) (sc, uncredited)

1942 *Unpublished Story* (French) (co-sc); *Partners in Crime* (short) (co-d, sc)

1944 *Waterloo Road* (d, sc)

1957 *The Smallest Show on Earth* (Dearden) (pr)

1972 *Ooh . . . You Are Awful* (*Get Charlie Tully*) (Owen) (co-exec pr); *Endless Night* (d, sc)

Publications:

On LAUNDER AND GILLIAT: books—

Durgnat, Raymond, *A Mirror for England*, 1971.
Brown, Geoff, *Launder and Gilliat*, London, 1977.

On LAUNDER AND GILLIAT: articles—

Sight and Sound (London), Autumn 1946, December 1949, and Autumn 1958.

Films and Filming (London), July 1963.
Brown, Geoff, in *National Film Theatre Booklet* (London), November/December 1977.
Films Illustrated (London), November 1979.
"Frank Launder," in *Film Dope (London), November 1985.*

*   *   *

Launder and Gilliat's chosen specialty was intelligent entertainment with a distinctive British flavour. Each had their individual style and preferences. Launder favoured the breezy implausibilities of farce (*The Happiest Days of Your Life*, the *St. Trinian's* films), tempered with a dose of Celtic whimsy (*Geordie*, *The Bridal Path*, parts of *I See a Dark Stranger*). Gilliat leaned more towards caustic social comedy (*The Rake's progress*, *Only Two Can Play*) and rigorously detailed thrillers (*State Secret*). But they functioned admirably as a team: first as screenwriters (working in tandem from 1935); then, from 1943, as writer-producer-directors—though only on their first feature, *Millions Like Us*, did they attempt joint direction, side by side.

Both separately entered the industry in lowly capacities in 1928, and gradually worked up the ladder during the 1930s, serving in various studio script departments. As a team they earned their reputation with thrillers. *Seven Sinners*, their first collaboration, established their talent for concocting ingenious plot twists, expertly balancing comedy with suspense, and stamping even the most minor character with individuality. Subsequent films refined the formula: *The Lady Vanishes*, for instance (their script was substantially written before Hitchcock came on board as director), and *Night Train to Munich*, one of several scripts directed by Carol Reed. Both these films featured Charters and Caldicott—comic, imperturbable Englishmen, played by Basil Radford and Naunton Wayne, who bumbled obliviously round a jittery Europe, babbling about cricket scores and picking up *Mein Kampf* at a German station bookstall only after a fruitless request for *Punch*.

Charters and Caldicott make an appearance in *Millions Like Us*, laying beach mines. But this was only for old times' sake: the film belonged firmly to the women factory workers, whose hopes and problems were explored in a rich tapestry of individual plot-lines. Few other British feature films of World War Two evoke the Home Front's daily round with quite the same nose for detail or emotional pull. Gilliat's next production *Waterloo Road* slipped into melodrama at times, but still maintained a strong realistic atmosphere in its triangular drama of an AWOL soldier, the soldier's roving wife, and a muscle-flexing local spiv.

In 1944, Launder and Gilliat launched their own company, Individual Pictures. They began on a high level, working from their own original scripts. Gilliat's *The Rake's Progress* offered a biting satirical treatment of a profligate charmer (Rex Harrison, ideally cast) washed up on the rocks of the 1930s. Launder's marvellous *I See a Dark Stranger* wrapped up its far-fetched story about a naive Irish girl persuaded to spy for Germany with Hitchcockian panache. Subsequent films followed a more obviously commercial path, though Gilliat's *Green for Danger* and *State Secret* demonstrated his witty way with thriller conventions, while *The Happiest Days of Your Life*, adapted from John Dighton's popular play, displayed Launder's happy ability to keep the wildest farce on an even keel.

Artistically, the 1950s and 1960s proved less rewarding. The *St. Trinian's* series, inspired by the hideous schoolgirls featured in Ronald Searle's cartoons, began briskly enough with *The Belles of St. Trinian's*, but the formula and humour coarsened drastically as the sequels followed. The pleasant whimsy of *Geordie*—launder's tale of the amazing growth of an under-sized Scot and his exploitation by others—was no match for the barbed blarney that lit up *I See a Dark Stranger*, while Gilliat's gift for social comedy appeared stunted in *The Constant Husband* and *Left, Right and Centre*.

Much of their energies were now being spent in boardroom activities: as directors of British Lion, they nursed several films by other film-makers through the production process, including the lively prison comedy *Two-Way Stretch*. But Gilliat managed a confident return to form in *Only Two Can Play*, a lively version of Kingsley Amis's novel about a philandering Welsh librarian, fully alert to the comic drabness of provincial life.

After *Endless Night*, an elegant diversion adapted from Agatha Christie, unfairly mauled by the critics, Gilliat retired from film-making. Launder, however, unwisely returned in 1980 with *The Wildcats of St. Trinian's*—one of the few films in the team's long career which seemed out of step with audience's tastes.

—Geoff Brown

___

LEACOCK, Richard.

British. Born in the Canary Islands, 18 July 1921. Educated in England, then studied physics at Harvard University, graduated 1943. Began making documentaries in the Canaries, 1935; moved to U.S., 1938; served as combat photographer, World War II; worked on documentaries with Robert Flaherty, Louis de Rochemont, John Ferno, and Willard Van Dyke among others, from late 1940s; worked with Robert Drew of Time-Life, then formed partnership with D.A. Pennebaker, 1960s; founder then Head of Department of Film at Massachusetts Institute of Technology, from 1969.

Films as Director and Cinematographer:

1935   *Canary Bananas*
1938   *Galápagos Islands*
1944/49   *Pelileo Earthquake*
195?   *The Lonely Boat*
1954   *Toby and the Tall Corn*
1955   *How the F-100 Got Its Tail*
1958   *Bernstein in Israel*
1959   *Bernstein in Moscow*; *Coulomb's Law*; *Crystals*; *Magnet Laboratory*; *Points of Reference*
1960   *Primary* (co-d, co-ph, ed); *On the Pole* (co-d, co-ph, co-ed); *Yanqui No* (co-d, co-ph)
1961   *Petey and Johnny* (co-d, co-ph); *The Children Were Watching* (co-d, co-ph)
1962   *The Chair* (co-d, co-ph); *Kenya, South Africa* (co-d, co-ph)
1963   *Crisis* (co-d, co-ph); *Happy Mother's Day* (co-d, co-ph, co-ed)
1964   *A Stravinsky Portrait* (+ ed); *Portrait of Geza Anda* (+ ed); *Portrait of Paul Burkhard* (+ ed); *Republicans—The New Breed* (co-d, co-ph)
1965   *The Anatomy of Cindy Fink* (co-d, co-ph); *Ku Klux Klan—The Invisible Empire*
1966   *Old Age—The Wasted Years*; *Portrait of Van Cliburn* (+ ed)
1967   *Monterey Pop* (+ co-ph); *Lulu*
1968   *Who's Afraid of the Avant-Garde* (co-d, co-ph, co-ed); *Hickory Hill*
1969   *Chiefs* (+ ed)
1970   *Queen of Apollo* (+ ed)
1986   *Impressions de L'Ile des Morts* (co-d)

Other Films:

1940 *To Hear Your Banjo Play* (Van Dyke, W.) (ph)
1946 *Louisiana Story* (Flaherty) (ph, assoc pr)
1944/49 *Geography Films Series* (ph)
1950 *New Frontier* (*Years of Change*) (ph, ed)
1951 *The Lonely Night* (ph)
1952 *Head of the House* (ph)
195? *New York* (ph)
1958 *Bullfight at Málaga* (ph)
1959 *Balloon* (co-ph)
1968 *Maidstone* (co-ph)
1971 *Sweet Toronto* (co-ph); *One P.M.* (co-ph); *Keep On Rockin'* (co-ph)

Publications:

By LEACOCK: articles—

"To Far Places with Camera and Sound-Track," in *Films in Review* (New York), March 1950.
"Richard Leacock Tells How to Boost Available Light," with H. Bell, in *Popular Photography* (Boulder, Colorado), February 1956.
"The Work of Ricky Leacock: Interview," in *Film Culture* (New York), no.22–23, 1961.
"For an Uncontrolled Cinema," in *Film Culture* (New York), Summer 1961.
Interview, in *Movie* (London), April 1963.
"Ricky Leacock on *Stravinsky* Film," in *Film Culture* (New York), Fall 1966.
"On Filming the Dance," in *Filmmakers Newsletter* (Ward Hill, Massachusetts), November 1970.
"Richard Leacock,"in *Documentary Explorations* edited by G. Roy Levin, Garden City, New York, 1971.
"Remembering Frances Flaherty," in *Film Comment* (New York), November/December 1973.
"Leacock at M.I.T.," an interview with L. Marcorelles, in *Sight and Sound* (London), Spring 1974.
"(Richard) Leacock on Super 8, Video Discs and Distribution," interview with M. Sturken, in *Afterimage* (Rochester, New York), May 1979.
Interview with H. Naficy, in *Literature/Film Quarterly* (Salisbury, Maryland), vol. 10, no. 4, October 1982.

On LEACOCK: books—

Issari, M. Ali, *Cinéma Verité*, East Lansing, Michigan, 1971.
Mamber, Stephen, *Cinéma Verité in America: Studies in Uncontrolled Documentary*, Cambridge, Massachusetts, 1974.
Issari, M. Ali, and Doris A. Paul, *What is Cinéma Verité?* Metuchen, New Jersey, 1979.

On LEACOCK: articles—

Callenbach, Ernest, "Going Out to the Subject," in *Film Quarterly* (Berkeley), Spring 1961.
Bachmann, Gideon, "The Frontiers of Realist Cinema: The Work of Ricky Leacock," in *Film Culture* (New York), Summer 1961.
Mekas, Jonas, "Notes on the New American Cinema," in *Film Culture* (New York), no.24, 1962.
Blue, James, "One Man's Truth," in *Film Comment* (New York), Spring 1965.
Vanderwildt, A., "Richard Leacock Uses Super-8," in *Lumiere* (Melbourne), September 1973.
"Richard Leacock," in *Film Dope* (London), November 1985.
Barsam. R.M., "American Direct Cinema: The Re-Presentation of Reality," in *Persistence of Vision* (Maspeth, New York), Summer 1986.

*   *   *

Richard Leacock has been an important contributor to the development of the documentary film, as cinematographer, producer, director, and editor, specifically in *cinéma verité*, now often called *direct cinema*.

For direct cinema filming, the lightweight 16mm camera, handheld, synced to a quiet recorder, is essential for its mobility, and because it allows the filmmaker to intrude as little as possible into the lives of those being filmed. From the very beginning of his interest in this kind of filming, Leacock has been an active experimenter, and inventor of mobile 16mm equipment for filming events, lifestyles, ongoing problematic situations, and other varieties of live history. At Massachusetts Institute of Technology, where he heads the department of film, he has developed super-8 sync-sound equipment and related technology. As a patient, courteous and informative lecturer to hundreds of teachers in many workshops, he has demonstrated this equipment and its use for TV, shown his films, and indirectly taught many youngsters who went on to work in film, TV, and related fields.

At 14, Leacock, already an active still photographer, impressed his schoolmates in England with a 16-minute film made on his home island. An indicator, perhaps, of his later concentration on non-subjective filming, his 1935 *Canary Bananas* is still a good, straightforward silent film about what workers do on a banana plantation. Leacock's later work on such diverse subjects as the life of a traveling tent show entertainer, communism and democracy in South America, excitement about quintuplets in South Dakota, a recent portrait of the mind and work of an artist, and his opera filming attest to the breadth of his interests.

Leacock treasures his experience as photographer with poetic filmmaker/explorer Robert Flaherty on *Louisiana Story*, commissioned by Standard Oil to show preliminary steps in searching and drilling for oil, but emerging as a film poem about a boy in the bayou. From Flaherty, Leacock learned, he says, to discover with a camera. But having realized how difficult Flaherty's ponderous un-synced equipment had made direct shooting, Leacock later joined a group, led by Robert Drew of Time-Life in 1960, committed to making direct cinema films for TV.

An example of the Drew unit's work was *Primary*, an account of the campaign of Democratic Senators John F. Kennedy and Hubert Humphrey in the Wisconsin presidential primary which Leacock worked on with Donn Alan Pennebaker, Robert Drew, and Terry Filgate. Critics called this film an excellent report on the inner workings of a political campaign as well as an appealing glimpse of the personal lives of candidates and their families. But Leacock was not satisfied because the camera people could never get in to film behind-the-scenes activity such as p.r. methods.

Leacock has frequently indicated his own and other documentarists concerns about obstacles to achieving direct cinema. It is often controversial, now more than ever explorations of poverty, exploitation, disease, and war. Leacock, always critical of his own work, is concerned about distribution problems, thoughtful about the role of films in effecting social change. His attachment to creating less expensive, more manageable apparatus, to portraying art and artists, to experimenting, to letting situation and event tell their own story, and to teaching, continues as strongly as ever.

—Lillian Schiff

———

LEAN, David.

British. Born in Croydon, Surrey, 25 March 1908. Educated at Leighton Park Quaker School, Reading. Married 1) Kay Walsh, 1940 (divorced 1949); 2) Ann Todd, 1949 (divorced 1957); 3) Leila Matkar, 1960 (divorced 1978); 4) Sandra Hotz, 1981 (marriage dissolved 1985). Clapperboard boy at Lime

Grove Studios under Maurice Elvey, 1926; camera assistant, then cutting room assistant, 1928; chief editor for Gaumont-British Sound News, 1930, then for British Movietone News, from 1931; editor for British Paramount, from 1934; invited by Noel Coward to co-direct *In Which We Serve*, 1942; co-founder, with Ronald Neame and Anthony Havelock-Allan, Cineguild, 1943 (dissolved 1950); began association with producer Sam Spiegel, 1956; returned to filmmaking after 14 year absence to make *A Passage to India*, 1984. Recipient: British Film Academy Award for *The Sound Barrier*, 1952; Commander Order of the British Empire, 1953; Best Direction, New York Film Critics, 1955; Oscar for Best Director, and Best Direction, New York Film Critics, for *The Bridge on the River Kwai*, 1957; Oscars for Best Director and Best Film, for *Lawrence of Arabia*, 1962; Officier des Arts et des Lettres, France, 1968; Fellow of the British Film Institute, 1983; Fellow of the American Film Institute, 1989. *Died in London, 16 April 1991.*

Films as Director:

1942 *In Which We Serve* (co-d)
1944 *This Happy Breed* (+ co-adapt)
1945 *Blithe Spirit* (+ co-adapt); *Brief Encounter* (+ co-sc)
1946 *Great Expectations* (+ co-sc)
1948 *Oliver Twist* (+ co-sc)
1949 *The Passionate Friends* (*One Woman's Story*) (+ co-adapt)
1950 *Madeleine*
1952 *The Sound Barrier* (*Breaking the Sound Barrier*) (+ pr)
1954 *Hobson's Choice* (+ pr, co-sc)
1955 *Summer Madness* (*Summertime*) (+ co-sc)
1957 *The Bridge on the River Kwai*
1962 *Lawrence of Arabia*
1965 *Doctor Zhivago*
1970 *Ryan's Daughter*
1984 *A Passage to India*

Other Films:

1935 *Escape Me Never* (Czinner) (ed)
1936 *As You Like It* (Czinner) (ed)
1937 *Dreaming Lips* (Czinner) (ed)
1938 *Pygmalion* (Asquith and Howard) (ed)
1939 *French Without Tears* (Asquith) (ed)
1941 *Major Barbara* (Pascal) (ed)
1942 *49th Parallel* (Powell) (ed); *One of Our Aircraft Is Missing* (Powell) (ed)

Publications:

By LEAN: articles—

"*Brief Encounter*," in *The Penguin Film Review* (New York), no.4, 1947.
"David Lean on What You Can Learn from Movies," in *Popular Photography* (Boulder, Colorado), March 1958.
"Out of the Wilderness," in *Films and Filming* (London), January 1963.
Interview, in *Interviews with Film Directors* edited by Andrew Sarris, New York, 1967.
Interview with S. Ross, in *Take One* (Montreal), November 1973.
Interview with Graham Fuller and Nick Kent, in *Stills* (London), March 1985.
Interview with J.-L. Sablon, in *Revue du Cinéma* (Paris), June 1989.

On LEAN: books—

Phillips, Gene, *The Movie Makers*, Chicago, 1973.
Pratley, Gerald, *The Cinema of David Lean*, New York, 1974.
Silver, Alain, and James Ursini, *David Lean and His Films*, London, 1974.
Castelli, Louis P., and Caryn Lynn Cleeland, *David Lean: A Guide to References and Resources*, Boston, 1980.
Anderegg, Michael A., *David Lean*, Boston, 1984.

Sesti, Mario, *David Lean*, Florence, 1988.
Silverman, Stephen M., *David Lean*, London, 1989.

On LEAN: articles—

Lejeune, C.A., "The Up and Coming Team of Lean and Neame," in *New York Times*, 15 June 1947.
Holden, J., "A Study of David Lean," in *Film Journal* (New York), April 1956.
Watts, Stephen, "David Lean," in *Films in Review* (New York), April 1959.
"David Lean, Lover of Life," in *Films and Filming* (London), August 1959.
Alpert, Hollis, "The David Lean Recipe: A Whack in the Guts," in *New York Times Magazine*, 23 May 1965.
Lightman, Herb, "On Location with *Ryan's Daughter*," in *American Cinematographer* (Los Angeles), August 1968.
Kael, Pauline, "Bolt and Lean," in the *New Yorker*, 21 November 1970.
Thomas, B., "David Lean," in *Action* (Los Angeles), November/December 1973.
Pickard, Ron, "David Lean: Supreme Craftsman," in *Films in Review* (New York), May 1974.
Andrews, George, "A Cinematographic Adventure with David Lean," in *American Cinematographer* (Los Angeles), March 1979.
Kennedy, Harlan, and M. Sragow, "David Lean's Right of *Passage*," in *Film Comment* (New York), January/February 1985.
Combs, Richard, "David Lean: Riddles of the Sphinx," in *Monthly Film Bulletin* (London), April 1985.
Levine, J.P., "Passage to the Odeon: Too Lean," in *Literature/Film Quarterly* (Salisbury, Maryland), vol. 14, no. 3, 1986.
"David Lean," in *Film Dope* (London), March 1986.
McInerney, J.M., "Lean's *Zhivago*: A Re-Appraisal," in *Literature/Film Quarterly* (Salisbury, Maryland), vol. 15, no. 1, 1987.

* * *

There is a trajectory that emerges from the shape of David Lean's career, and it is a misleading one. Lean first achieved fame as a director of seemingly intimate films, closely based on plays of Noel Coward. His first directorial credit was shared with Coward, for *In Which We Serve*. In the 1960s he was responsible for extraordinarily ambitious projects, for an epic cinema of grandiose effects, difficult location shooting, and high cultural, even literary pretention. But, in fact, Lean's essential approach to the movies never changed. All of his films, no matter how small or large their dimensions, demonstrate an obsessive cultivation of craft, a fastidious concern with production detail that defines the "quality" postwar British cinema. That craft and concern are as hyperbolic in their devices as is the medium itself. Viewers surprised at the attention to detail and to composition in *Ryan's Daughter*, a work whose scope would appear to call for a more modest approach, had really not paid attention to the truly enormous dimensions of *Brief Encounter*, a film that defines, for many, intimist cinema.

Lean learned the movies during long years of apprenticeship, with particularly important experience as an editor. It is clear, even in the first films he directed with and then for Coward, that his vision is not bound to the playwright's West End proscenium. *This Happy Breed*, a lower class version of *Cavalcade*, makes full use of the modest terraced house that is the film's prime locus. The nearly palpable patterns of the mise-en-scène are animated by the highly professional acting characteristic of Lean's early films. Watching the working out of those patterns created by the relationship between camera, decor and actor is like watching choreography at the ballet, where the audience is made aware of the abstract forms of placement on the stage even as that placement is vitalized by the individual quality of the dancer. The grief of Celia Johnson and Robert Newton is first expressed by the empty room that they are about to enter, then by the way the camera's oblique backward movement respects their silence.

David Lean, 1949

It is in *Brief Encounter* that the fullness of the director's talent becomes clear. This story of chance meeting, love and renunciation is as apparently mediocre, conventional, and echoless as Flaubert's *Madame Bovary*. What could be more boringly middle-class than the romantic longing of a 19th-century French provincial housewife or the oh-so-tasteful near adultery of two "decent" Britishers? In both cases, the authorial interventions are massive. Lean conveys the film's passion through a set of disproportions, through the juxtaposition of the trite situation against the expressionistic violence of passing express trains and the wrenching departure of locals, against the decadent romanticism of the Rachmaninoff score, and most emphatically against one of the most grandiose and hyperbolic exposures of an actress in the history of film. The size of Celia Johnson's eyes finally becomes the measure of *Brief Encounter*, eyes whose scope is no less expansive than Lawrence's desert or Zhivago's tundra.

Lean's next two successes were his adaptations (with Ronald Neame) of novels of Dickens, *Great Expectations* and *Oliver Twist*. And again, intimacy on the screen becomes the moment of gigantic display. The greatness of Pip's expectations are set by the magnitude of his frightful encounter with an escaped convict who, when he emerges into the frame, reminds us all what it is like to be a small child in a world of oversized, menacing adults. A variation of this scale is in Pip's meeting with mad Miss Havisham, in all her gothic splendor.

Lean's next few films seem to have more modest ambitions, but they continue to demonstrate the director's concern with expressive placement. Of his three films with his then wife Ann Todd, *Madeleine* most fully exploits her cool blond beauty. Then there occurs a significant change in the development of his career. Lean's reputation as a "location" director with a taste for the picturesque is made by *Summertime*, an adaptation of the play *The Time of the Cuckoo*, in which the city of Venice vies with Katharine Hepburn for the viewer's attention. It is from this point that Lean must be identified as an international rather than an English director. And the international packages that result are perhaps the reasons for the widespread (and unjust) opinion that Lean is more of an executive than a creator with a personal vision.

The personality of Lean is in his compulsive drive to the perfectly composed shot, whatever the cost in time, energy and money. In this there is some affinity between the director and his heroes. The Colonel (Alec Guinness) in *The Bridge on the River Kwai* must drive his men to build a good bridge, even if it is for the enemy. Lawrence (Peter O'Toole) crosses desert after desert in his quest for a self purified through physical ordeal, and the viewers must wonder about the ordeals suffered by the filmmakers to photograph those deserts. The same wonder is elicited by the snowy trek of Dr. Zhivago (Omar Sharif) and the representation of life in early 20th-century Russia.

That perfectly composed shot is emblemized by the principal advertising image used for *Ryan's Daughter*—an umbrella floating in air, suspended over an oceanside cliff. This is a celebration of composition per se, composition that holds unlikely elements in likely array. Composition is an expressive tension, accessible to viewers as it simultaneously captures the familiar and the unfamiliar. It is the combination that makes so many viewers sensitive to *Brief Encounter*, where middle-class lives (the lives of film-goers) are filled with overwhelming passion and overwhelming style. Laura and Alex fall in love when they go to the movies.

—Charles Affron

LEDUC, Paul.

Mexican. Born in Mexico City, 11 March 1942. Educated in architecture and theatre, Universidad Nacional Autónoma de México; Institut des hautes études cinématographiques (IDHEC), Paris, 1965–66. Film critic in Mexico, early 1960s; worked for French TV, then returned to Mexico, 1967.

Films as Director:

1968 *Comunicados del comité nacional de huelga* (3 shorts)
1969 *Parto psicoprofiláctico* (doc short)
1973 *Reed: México insurgente* (*Reed: Insurgent Mexico*)
1974 *Sur, sureste 2604* (short); *El mar*
1975 *Bach y sus intérpretes*
1978 *Etnocidio: notas sobre el Mezquital*; *Estudios para un retrato (Francis Bacon)* (doc short); *Puebla hoy* (doc); *Monjas coronadas* (doc short)
1979 *Historias prohibidas de Pulgarcito*
1981 *Complot petrolero*; *La cabeza de la hidra*
1982 *Como ves?* (*Whaddya Think?*)
1984 *Frida: Naturaleza vita* (*Frida*)
1989 *Barroco* (*Baroque*)

Publications:

By LEDUC: articles—

Interview with Nelson Carro, in *Imagenes* (Mexico City), October 1979.
Interview with Enrique Pineda Barnet, in *Cine Cubano* (Havana), no. 104, 1983.
"Caminar por el continente," in *Cine Cubano* (Havana), no. 105, 1983.
Interview with Dennis West, in *Cineaste* (New York), vol. 26, no. 4, 1988.
"Nuevo cine latinoamericano: Dramaturgia y autocrítica," in *Pantalla* (Mexico City), August 1985.
Interview with Dennis West, in *Cineaste* (New York), vol. 16, no. 4, 1988.

On LEDUC: books—

Blanco, Jorge Ayala, *La búsqueda del cine mexicano*, Mexico City, 1974.
Sánchez, Alberto Ruy, *Mitologia de un cine en crisis*, Mexico City, 1981.
Mora, Carl, *Mexican Cinema: Reflections of a Society, 1896–1980*, Berkeley, 1982.
Blanco, Jorge Ayala, *La condicíon del cine mexicano*, Mexico City, 1986.
Costa, Paola, *La "aperatura" cinematográfica*, Puebla, 1988.

On LEDUC: articles—

Espinasa, José María, "El cine mexicano hoy," in *Hojas de cine*, vol. 2, Mexico City, 1988.
Bejar, Ruth, "*Frida*," in *American Historical Review*, October 1989.

*   *   *

Generally acknowledged as the most talented and socially conscious of contemporary Mexican directors, Paul Leduc has been forced to make his films on the margins of commercial cinema. Leduc began his career in a university department of film studies, an initiation increasingly prevalent among the younger generation of Mexican filmmakers. His first films were documentaries, a typical beginning for directors of the "New Latin American Cinema." Then, Leduc was able to take some advantage of a novel situation: during the reign of President Luis Echeverria (1970–76) the Mexican government actively intervened as a producer of cinema, the only time since the 1930s (e.g., *Redes*) that it has attempted to create some sort of alternative to the wretched fare provided by the country's commercial film industry. The government paid for the amplification of *Reed: Insurgent Mexico* to 35mm and co-produced *Mezquital* with the Canadian National Film Board. Since that time, however Leduc has funded his films independently, through universities and unions, and with collective efforts.

Reed: Insurgent Mexico is perhaps Leduc's most accomplished fiction film, and was the first really distinctive work of the "New Cinema" movement in Mexico. Although the film was shot on a minuscule budget in 16mm, it has an exquisite sepia tone which reproduces the ambience of antique revolutionary photographs. Deliberately undramatic, *Reed* demystified the Mexican revolution (1910–17) in a way that had not been seen since Fernando De Fuentes's masterpieces of 1933–35. One Mexican critic, Jorge Ayala Blanco, described *Reed* as "raging against, incinerating, and annihilating the spider web that had been knitted over the once-living image of the revolution, while briefly illuminating the nocturnal ruins of our temporal and cultural distance from the men who participated in that upheaval." The film is a dramatization of John Reed's famous account of the revolution, *Insurgent Mexico*, with Reed as the main protagonist. Although the film is a beautiful and important work, it doesn't really rise above the level of a vignette (perhaps too greatly influenced by the book's form), nor does it achieve the heights of De Fuentes's films.

Leduc's following works reflected his concern for actuality. *Etnocidio: notas sobre el Mezquital* is probably the best documentary on the extermination of the native peoples in Latin America, allowing the Otomi Indians of the Mezquital region in Mexico to relate their experiences with "civilization." The film is an interesting example of collaborative effort, for the "script" was written by Roger Bartra, Mexico's leading rural sociologist, who based it on his years of research in the area. *Historias prohibidas* is a flawed work that Leduc made in a collective; but it does contain a lively analysis of El Salvador's history. *Complot petrolero* is a made-for-TV thriller about an attempt by right-wing elements (including the CIA and anti-Castro Cubans) to take over the oil and uranium resources of Mexico. Actually a mini-series totaling 3 1/2 hours, it has never been shown on Mexican television, which is largely dominated by series and made-for-TV movies imported from the U.S.

Just when it appeared that Leduc was firmly settled in the aesthetic of realism, he directed a highly-expressionist, lyrical work on the painter Frida Kahlo, *Frida: Naturaleza viva*. An experimental film which keeps words, whether spoken or written, to an absolute minimum, the movie has been most controversial. And, while one must admire Leduc for risking a break with traditional cinematographic styles, the absence of dialogue reduces pivotal figures of history and culture such as Diego Rivera, León Trotsky, David Alfaro Siqueiros, André Breton, and Frida Kahlo to caricatures of themselves. Instead of using the film to develop these characters in political or personal terms, Leduc takes the easy way out, allowing them to remain at the lowest common denominator of the popular stereotypes fomented in mass culture.

In general, Mexico has proven to be a difficult context for Leduc, who appropriately describes cinema there as "a perfect disaster, composed of *churros*—vulgar, cheap, and badly-made films." Dominated by the "fastbuck" mentality typical of dependent capitalism, Mexican commercial cinema has offered few opportunities for Leduc to direct the kind of films which interest him.

—John Mraz

LEE, Spike.

American. Born Shelton Jackson Lee in Atlanta, Georgia, 1957, son of jazz musician Bill Lee. Studied at Morehouse College, Atlanta, graduated 1978; New York University Graduate Film School, studying with Martin Scorsese. Set up production company 40 Acres and a Mule; directed first feature, *She's Gotta Have It*, 1986; also directs music videos and commercials for Nike/Air Jordan.

Films as Director, Scriptwriter and Editor:

1977   *Last Hustle in Brooklyn* (Super-8 short)
1980   *The Answer* (short)
1981   *Sarah* (short)
1982   *Joe's Bed-Stuy Barbershop: We Cut Heads*
1986   *She's Gotta Have It*
1988   *School Daze*
1989   *Do the Right Thing*
1990   *Mo' Better Blues*

Publications:

By LEE: books—

Spike Lee's She's Gotta Have It: Inside Guerilla Filmmaking, New York, 1987.
Uplift the Race: The Construction of School Daze, New York, 1988.
Do the Right Thing: A Spike Lee Joint, with Lisa Jones, New York, 1989.
Mo' Better Blues, with Lisa Jones, New York, 1990.

By LEE: articles—

Interview in *New York Times*, 10 August 1986.
Interview in *Village Voice* (New York), 12 August 1986.
"Class Act," in *American Film* (Washington, D.C.), January/February 1988.
Interview with M. Glicksman, in *Film Comment* (New York), July/August 1989.
Interview with Mike Wilmington, in *Empire* (London), October 1990.

On LEE: articles—

Tate, G., "Spike Lee," in *American Film* (Washington, D.C.), September 1986.
Glicksman, M., "Lee Way," in *Film Comment* (New York), September/October 1986.
Sharkey, B., and T. Davis, "Knocking on Hollywood's Door," in *American Film* (Washington, D.C.), July/August 1989.
O'Pray, Michael, "Do Better Blues—Spike Lee," in *Monthly Film Bulletin* (London), October 1990.

*   *   *

Spike Lee is one of the few blacks to have succeeded in breaking through the Hollywood establishment to create in just a few years a notable career for himself. What makes this all the more notable is that he is not a comedian—the one role in which Hollywood has always allowed blacks to excel—but a prodigious, creative, multifaceted talent who writes, directs, edits, and acts, a filmmaker who invites comparisons with American titans like Woody Allen, John Cassavetes, and Orson Welles.

His films, which deal with different facets of the black experience, are innovative and controversial even within the black community. Spike Lee refuses to be content with presenting blacks in their "acceptable" stereotypes: noble Poitiers demonstrating simple moral righteousness are nowhere to be found. Lee's characters are three-dimensional and often vulnerable to moral criticism. His first feature film, *She's Gotta Have It*, dealt with black sexuality, unapologetically supporting the heroine's promiscuity. His second film, *School Daze*, drawing heavily upon Lee's own experiences at Morehouse

Spike Lee

College, examined the black university experience and dealt with discrimination within the black community based on relative skin colors. His third film, *Do the Right Thing*, dealt with urban racial tensions and violence. His fourth film, *Mo' Better Blues*, dealt with black jazz and its milieu.

His breakthrough feature was *She's Gotta Have It*, an independent film budgeted at $175,000 and a striking box office success: a film made by blacks for blacks which also attracted white audiences. *She's Gotta Have It* reflects the sensibilities of an already sophisticated filmmaker and harkens back to the early French New Wave in its exuberant embracing of bravura technique—intertitles, black-and-white cinematography, a sense of improvisation, characters directly addressing the camera—all wedded nevertheless to serious philosophical/sociological examination. The considerable comedy in *She's Gotta Have It* caused many critics to call Spike Lee the "black Woody Allen," a label which would increasingly reveal itself as a rather simplistic, muddle-headed approbation, particularly as Lee's career developed. (Indeed, in his work's energy, style, eclecticism, and social commitment, he more resembles Martin Scorsese, who also comes out of the N.Y.U. film school.) Even to categorize Spike Lee as a black filmmaker is to denigrate his talent, since there are today virtually no American filmmakers (except Allen) with the ambitiousness and talent to write, direct, and perform in their own films. And Lee edits as well.

Do The Right Thing, Lee's third full-length feature, is by far the director's most daring achievement so far, presenting one sweltering day which culminates in a riot in the Bedford Stuyvesant section of Brooklyn. From its first images—assailing jump cuts of a woman dancing frenetically to the rap "Fight the Power" while colored lights stylistically flash on a location ghetto block upon which Lee has constructed his set—we know we are about to witness something deeply disturbing. The film's sound design is incredibly dense and complex, and the volume alarmingly high, as the film continues to assail us with tight close-ups, extreme angles, moving camera, colored lights, distorting lenses, and individual scenes directed like high operatic arias.

Impressive, too, is the well-constructed screenplay, particularly the perceptively drawn Italian family at the center of the film who feel so besieged by the changing, predominantly black neighborhood around them. A variety of ethnic characters are drawn sympathetically, if unsentimentally; perhaps never in American cinema has a director so accurately presented the relationships among the American urban underclasses. Particularly shocking and honest is a scene in which catalogs of racial and ethnic epithets are shouted directly into the camera. The key scene in *Do the Right Thing* has the character of Mookie, played by Spike Lee, throwing a garbage can through a pizzeria window as a moral gesture which works to make the riot inevitable. The film ends with two quotations: one from Martin Luther King, Jr. eschewing violence; the other from Malcolm X, rationalizing violence in certain circumstances.

Do the Right Thing was one of the most controversial films of the last decade. Politically conservative commentators denounced the film, fearful it would incite inner-city violence. Despite widespread acclaim the film was snubbed at the Cannes Film Festival, outraging certain Cannes judges; despite the accolades of many critics' groups, the film was also largely snubbed by the Motion Picture Academy, receiving a nomination only for Spike Lee's screenplay and Danny Aiello's performance as the pizzeria owner.

Interesting, almost as an aside, is Lee's canny ability to use certain catch phrases in his films which help both to attract and delight audiences. In *She's Gotta Have It*, there was the constant refrain uttered by Spike Lee as Mars Blackmon, "Please baby, please baby, please baby, baby baby, please. . . . "; in *Do the Right Thing*, the disc jockey's "And that's the truth, Ruth." Lee's fusion of popular forms and audience-pleasing entertainment with significant cultural commentary is particularly impressive coming from a filmmaker still so young. Notable also is the director's assembly—in the style of Bergman and Chabrol and Woody Allen in their prime—of a consistent stable of very talented collaborators, including his father Bill Lee as musical composer, production designer Wynn Thomas, producer Monty Ross, and cinematographer Ernest Dickerson, among others.

—Charles Derry

LEENHARDT, Roger.

French. Born in Montpellier, 23 July 1903. Educated in literature and philosophy, the Sorbonne. Film editor, from 1933; formed production company Les Films du Compas, making documentaries with René Zuber, 1934; film critic for revue *Esprit* and other journals, from 1935; with Georges Sadoul and Alexandre Astruc, film critic for *L'Ecran français*, from 1945; founder, with Bresson and Cocteau, of *Objectif 49*, precursor of *Cahiers du cinéma*, 1949; director of TV documentaries, 1970s. Recipient: Best Documentary Film, Brussels World Film Festival, for *Naissance du cinéma*, 1947. *Died in Paris, 4 December 1985.*

Films as Director:

1934   *En Crête sans les Dieux* (co-d) (short doc); *L'Orient qui vient* (co-d) (short doc); *Rezzou* (co-d) (short doc)
1935   *Le Tapis moquette* (short doc)
1937   *R N 37* (short doc)
1938   *Revêtements routiers* (short doc); *La Course au petrole* (+ pr) (short doc)
1939   *Fêtes de France* (short doc)
1943   *Le Chant des ondes* (short doc); *A la poursuite du vent* (short doc)
1945   *Lettre de Paris* (short doc); *Le Chantier en ruines* (short doc)
1946   *Départs pour l'Allemagne* (short doc); *Naissance du cinéma* (short doc); *Le Barrage de l'Aigle* (short doc)
1948   *Côte d'Azur* (short doc); *Entrez dans la danse* (short doc)
1949   *Le Pain de Barbarie* (short doc); *Les Dernières Vacances* (+ co-sc)
1950   *L'Héritage du croissant* (short doc); *Les Hommes du Champagne* (+ pr) (short doc); *Le Métro* (short doc); *La Fugue de Mahmoud* (short doc)
1951   *Victor Hugo* (short doc)
1952   *Du charbon et des hommes* (+ pr) (short doc); *La France est un jardin* (short doc)
1954   *François Mauriac* (short doc); *Louis Capet* (short doc)
1955   *La Conquête de l'Angleterre* (short doc)
1956   *Bâtir à notre âge* (+ pr) (short doc)
1957   *Jean-Jacques Rousseau* (co-d) (short doc); *En plein Midi* (co-d) (short doc); *Paris et le désert français* (short doc)
1958   *Daumier* (short doc)
1959   *Paul Valéry* (short doc)
1960   *Entre Seine et mer* (short doc); *Le Maître de Montpellier* (short doc)
1961   *La Traversée de la France* (co-d, pr) (short doc)
1962   *Le Coeur de la France* (short doc); *L'Homme à la pipe* (short doc); *Le Rendezvous de minuit*
1963   *Des femmes et des fleurs* (short doc); *Monsieur de Voltaire* (short doc)
1964   *Demain Paris* (short doc); *Europe* (short doc); *Daguerre ou la naissance de la photographie* (short doc); *Une Fille dans la montagne* (+ co-sc) (for TV)
1965   *Corot* (short doc)
1967   *Monsieur Ingres* (short doc); *Le Beatnik et le minet* (fiction film)
1970   *Douze mois en France* (co-d, pr) (short doc)
1972   *Abraham Bosse* (short doc)
1975   *Pissarro* (short doc)
1976   *La Langue docienne* (short doc); *Var-matin* (short doc)
1977   *Anjou* (short doc)
1978   *Du plaisir à la joie* (short doc)
1980   *Manet ou le novateur malgré lui* (short doc)

Other Films:

1964   *La Femme mariée* (Godard) (appearance as "l'intelligence")
1977   *L'Homme qui aimait les femmes* (Truffaut) (silhouette)

Publications

By LEENHARDT: books—

Les Yeux ouverts: entretiens avec Jean Lacouture, Paris, 1979.
Les Dernières Vacances, screenplay, Paris, 1980.
Chroniques de Cinéma, Paris, 1986.

By LEENHARDT: articles—

Interview, in *Cahiers du Cinéma* (Paris), November 1962.
"Interview with Roger Leenhardt and Jacques Rivette," with Louis Marcorelles, in *Sight and Sound* (London), Autumn 1963.
Interview, in *Les Lettres Françaises* (Paris), 7 June 1972.
"*Les Dernières Vacances* Issue" of *Avant-Scène du Cinéma* (Paris), 1 November 1980.

On LEENHARDT: book—

Armes, Roy, *French Cinema Since 1946: Vol.I*, New York, 1970.

On LEENHARDT: articles—

Bazin, André, "Le Style c'est l'homme même," in *Revue du Cinéma* (Paris), June 1948.
Narboni, Jean, "L'oeil juste," in *Cahiers du Cinéma* (Paris), January 1986.
Beylie, Claude, "In memoriam Roger Leenhardt," in *Avant-Scène du Cinéma* (Paris), January/February 1986.
"Roger Leenhardt," in *Film Dope* (London), March 1986.

On LEENHARDT: films—

Labarthe, André-S., *Roger Leenhardt ou le dernier humaniste*, for TV, 1965.
Fayard, Claude, *Roger Leenhardt, homme du Midi*, for TV, 1979.
Réa, Robert, *Roger Leenhardt, homme de parole*, for TV, 1979.

*   *   *

Roger Leenhardt has made only two feature films, yet his reputation as a sage of the cinema is fabled and his influence on the course of French film has been great.

Leenhardt is a rare man indeed, for in no way did he decide to give himself up to a profession as cineaste. To this Renaissance man the cinema has been only one interest among many animating his life. He leaped at the opportunity to make his two feature films, and he struggled to bring a few other personal projects to the screen, projects which were for one reason or another abandoned; but he has never been tempted to become a contract director or to work as assistant on major films.

Many feel that Leenhardt, an intellectual from Montpellier, initiated modern film criticism in France. In any case his writings in *Esprit* were virtually the only serious essays on the cinema to be published in the 1930s and they had a great effect. André Bazin, for instance, was lured into studying the cinema by these essays, and continued to consider Leenhardt his inspiration, dedicating *What is Cinema?* to him.

Men of letters intrigued by the cinema, such as Gide and Sartre, found in Leenhardt a sensibility they could rely on and an expertise they could respect. As early as 1940 Leenhardt had proven his intellectual worth (in serious philosophical and political essays published in *Esprit*) and had become a serviceable filmmaker, auteur of a half-dozen shorts.

At the close of World War II he stood in an enviable position, for he was respected and experienced at a time when it appeared that the film industry was opening up to new blood. In fact it was in 1948 that he made *Les Dernières Vacances*. A charming hymn to the end of adolescence, set in the society of the grande bourgeoisie, this film also puts into play a number of the principles of film theory Leenhardt had long advocated in print. Philippe Agostini's mobile camera and Léon Barsacq's decor give the film the appearance of a quality production. But the direction is so insistently personal that it became a harbinger of the New Wave movement. Bazin wrote about it lavishly in *Esprit*. Astruc, another close friend from the St. Germain café circle, considered it to be an example of "le caméra-stylo." The whole pre-*Cahiers* community (Cocteau, Bresson, Doniol-Valcroze, etc.) hailed it. And, predictably, Leenhardt became the father figure for the New Wave. Jean-Luc Godard underlined this in 1966 when he gave Leenhardt a role in *A Married Woman* flashing "l'intelligence" as an intertitle upon his appearance.

During the humdrum 1950s Leenhardt occupied himself with short films. His *Birth of the Cinema* is a classic, and his biographical portraits of Rosseau, Mauriac, Valéry, and others stand out for their technical excellence and ingenuity as well as for their depth of understanding of their subjects. Leenhardt claims that filmmaking has been a way for him to pursue his other interests (biography, geography, art history).

At the coming of the New Wave it was only natural for Leenhardt to be given another chance at a major film; in 1961 the aid laws made it profitable for producers to risk money on new directors. Leenhardt was both new and old, a safe bet. *Le Rendezvous de minuit*, starring Lili Palmer, was a perfect New Wave idea, a film within a film. But either because it came too late in the movement (1962) or because Leenhardt's cool classicism didn't fit the passionate excesses for which that movement is known, the film found little success.

Leenhardt went back to documentaries with television an obvious market for his productions. His encyclopedic knowledge of French culture, his personal acquaintance with many of the most vibrant figures of the century (Dos Passos, Merleau-Ponty, etc.), and his technical and theoretical mastery of the medium have justified his reputation.

—Dudley Andrew

LEFEBVRE, Jean-Pierre.

Canadian. Born in Montreal, 17 August 1942. Educated in French Literature, University of Montreal. Staff writer for *Objectif* (Montreal), 1960–67; Professor of French, 1963–65; formed Cinak production company, 1969; initiated "Premières Oeuvres" section of Office National du Film, 1969–71; President of Association des Réalisateurs de Films du Quebec, 1974.

Films as Director and Scriptwriter:

1964   *L'Homoman* (short) (+ pr, ph)
1965   *Le Révolutionnaire* (+ pr)
1966   *Patricia et Jean-Baptiste* (+ pr); *Mon Oeil* (*My Eye*) (unrealized)
1967   *Il ne faut pas mourir pour ça* (*Don't Let It Kill You*) (+ pr); *Mon Amie Pierrette*
1968   *Jusqu'au coeur*
1969   *La Chambre blanche* (*House of Light*)
1970   *Un Succès commercial* (*Q-bec My Love*)
1971   *Les Maudits sauvages* (*Those Damned Savages*); *Ultimatum*
1973   *On n'engraisse pas les cochons à l'eau claire*; *Les Dernières Fiançailles* (*The Last Betrothal*)
1975   *Le Gars des vues*; *L'Amour blessé*
1977   *Le Vieux Pays ou Rimbaud est mort*
1978   *Avoir 16 ans*
1982   *Les Fleurs sauvages* (*The Wild Flowers*)
1983   *Au Rythme de mon coeur* (*To the Rhythm of My Heart*)
1984   *Le Jour "S . . ."*
1987   *Laliberté* (*Alfred Lalibereté, sculpteur*)
1988   *La Boîte à soleil* (*The Box of Sun*)

Publications:

By LEFEBVRE: book—

Parfois quand je vis (poems), Montreal, 1970.

By LEFEBVRE: articles—

"Complexes d'une technique," in *Objectif* (Montreal), March 1961.
"L'Equipe française souffre-t-elle de Roucheole?," with Jean-Claude Pilon, in *Objectif* (Montreal), August 1962.
"Les Années folles de la critique ou petite histoire des revues de cinéma au Québec," in *Objectif* (Montreal), October/November 1964.
"La Crise du language et le cinéma canadien," in *Objectif* (Montreal), April/May 1965.
"La Méche et la bombe," in *Cahiers du Cinéma* (Paris), March 1966.
"Les Paradis perdus du cinéma canadien, chapitre 1: notes en guise d'introduction à une préface éventuelle," in *Objectif* (Montreal), November/December 1966.

Interview with Michel Delahaye, in *Cahiers du Cinéma* (Paris), January 1967.
"Les Paradis perdus du cinéma canadien, chapitre 2: illustration existentielle du chapitre 1 à partir de données oniriques," in *Objectif* (Montreal), May 1967.
"Les Paradis perdus du cinéma canadien, chapitre 3: Saint Gabiaz, priez pour nous," in *Objectif* (Montreal), August/September 1967.
"Les Quatres Saisons," in *Cahiers du Cinéma* (Paris), April/May 1968.
Interview with M. Amiel, in *Cinéma* (Paris), December 1972.
Interviews with J.-P. Tadros, in *Cinéma Québec* (Montreal), December 1973/January 1974, and no. 6, 1977.
"Des lois et des cadres: La Guerre des gangs," in *Cinéma Québec* (Montreal), no. 4, 1976.
"Commission d'enquête sur le cinéma organisé," in *Cinéma Québec* (Montreal), no. 5, 1976.
Interview with René Prédal, in *Jeune Cinéma* (Paris), February 1978.
Interviews with B. Samuels and S. Barrowclough, in *Cinema Canada* (Montreal), May 1982.
"Un Métier merveilleusement périlleux," in *Copie Zéro* (Montreal), October 1984.
Interview with C. Racine, in *24 Images* (Montreal), Autumn 1984/Winter 1985.
"La leçon de l'ami Moreau," in *Copie Zéro* (Montreal), March 1986.

On LEFEBVRE: books—

Marsolais, Gilles, *Le Cinéma canadien*, Paris, 1968.
Cinéastes de Québec 3: Jean-Pierre Lefebvre, Ottawa, 1970.
Bérubé, Renald, and Yvan Patry, editors, *Jean-Pierre Lefebvre*, Montreal, 1971.
Barrowclough, Susan, editor, *Jean-Pierre Lefebvre: The Quebec Connection*, London, 1981.
Harcourt, Peter, *Jean-Pierre Lefebvre*, Ottawa, 1981.

On LEFEBVRE: articles—

Fraser, Graham, "The Gentle Revolutionary," in *Take One* (Montreal), October 1967.
Larsen, André, "Le Sens de la contestationet Jean-Pierre Lefebvre," in *Le Cinéma Québecois: Tendences et prolongements*, Cahiers Ste-Marie, 1968.
La Rochelles, Real, and Gilbert Maggi, "Political Situation of Quebec Cinema," in *Cineaste* (New York), Summer 1972.
Gauthier, G., "Sur deux films de Jean-Pierre Lefebvre," in *Image et Son* (Paris), January 1975.
Barrowclough, Susan, "The Films of Jean-Pierre Lefebvre," in *Ciné-Tracts* (Montreal), Winter 1982.
Bessette, M., "Jean Pierre Lefebvre: au rythme de son coeur," in *Copie Zero* (Montreal), October 1988.

*   *   *

There is a filmmaker who has been invited to present his work at the Cannes Film Festival Director's Fortnight more often than any other filmmaker in the world. His career began, not in film school or under the aegis of a state-funded film organization, but instead as a poet, a critic and as a student and then professor of French literature. With 18 films to his credit in a career of just over 24 years, he has barely reached the age of 50. The filmmaker is Jean Pierre Lefebvre, a French Canadian, born and educated in Montreal, Quebec, respected and lauded by Francophone film audiences and critics and yet still relatively unknown in the English language film world and in the world of commercial cinema.

In many ways Jean Pierre Lefebvre is the archetypal Francophone intellectual. His large film oeuvre is stamped with the imprint of a philosopher, a humourist, a poet, an observer and a humble yet assured commentator on the state of things. Lefebvre's films play with the idea of relationships; relationships between individuals, between individuals and their surroundings, and between individuals and the language they use—and personalize through their poetic and colloquial misuse—when communicating with their environment. He is concerned also with the relationship of the elements which make up film language, and the relationship between the individual film spectator and with what is being projected on the film screen. Lefebvre plays with sound, with words and with images, more often than not succeeding in drawing the spectator's attention to the possibilities contained within language, film language and the situation in which we confront these vehicles for communication. As the Canadian film critic Peter Harcourt has observed of Lefebvre's filmic technique, " . . . the extended takes give us time not only to experience an action but also to think about what we may be feeling."

The work of Jean Pierre Lefebvre is also indicative of an intellectual and artistic movement which is endemic to French Canadians of Quebecois origin, and in particular, to those who came of intellectual age during the 1960s. In the 1960s Quebecois culture, which had hitherto been colonized, both literally and metaphorically, by the French, the English, the church and the Americans, made its voice heard at home and on the international front through demonstrations, civil disobedience and the radical presence of the Front de Liberation du Quebec. Quebecois culture began to assert itself through its vocal and visible difference; a difference which hinged greatly on the language of the Quebecois population. What was to become the vogue 20 years later in intellectual circles involved in reading the new French philosophical and cultural criticism and in interpreting these texts within feminist, marxist, psychoanalytic and post-structuralist frameworks, was to a great extent at the core of the Quebecois intellectual's approach at this pivotal time. Jean Pierre Lefebvre himself describes the role of film in this historical situation: "At the beginning in the late 1950s and 1960s, cinema was terribly important for naming our society, for making it exist in people's mind . . . the cinema became so important because we had never seen ourselves, we were hidden to ourselves . . . above all, it was our language which was hidden, almost forbidden."

Working within the constraints of a small budget, Jean Pierre Lefebvre has constructed film works which speak of a specific political time and place just as they speak of the universal, philosophical (and humourous), personal (and sexual) condition. Lefebvre's wife and collaborator, the late Marguerite Duparc acted as editor and producer on many of Lefebvre's works as well as co-directing Cinak, the production company set up by Lefebvre in the late 1960s. In the light of Duparc's awareness of how little film funding was available from Canadian and Quebecois organizations and boards, she was known to sacrifice her own creative projects in order to ensure that monetary assistance would be concentrated on Lefebvre's own works. It was not that Lefebvre's work might be less favoured by film funding agencies but rather that the situation for fiction filmmakers in Quebec during the 1970s and 1980s was economically difficult. Outside of the National Film Board of Canada, where in the 1960s Quebecois documentary filmmakers such as Gilles Groulx, Pierre Perrault, Michel Brault and their peers found steady employment—as well as the occasional political conflict with English language Board directors—the business of making films in Quebec suffered from both the competition of American films with their high production value glossiness, and from the lack of a supportive federal and provincial legislation regarding film production, distribution and exhibition.

However, the films of Jean Pierre Lefebvre escape reductive attempts at categorization and this would not make marketing them easy. Lefebvre's work is "political" in the personal, formal and aesthetic sense and not always in the easily identifiable party political sense. His style varies with the subject matter he tackles, as he adapts the structure of his features to the nature of the narratives and the queries they pose. He often experiments with sound and image and narrative without permitting easy comparison to Godard or Bresson, two filmmakers to whose work Lefebvre's has been compared. At the same time, he stands apart from his contemporaries in the Quebecois film industry and cannot be grouped in with any particular indigenous movement. Nevertheless, the film work of Jean Pierre Lefebvre continues to attract critical and public attention for its continuing commitment to the politics and the beauty of language, of Quebecois culture and of the fine art of cinema.

—Clea H. Notar

LE GRICE, Malcolm.

British. Born in Plymouth, Devon, 15 May 1940. Studied Painting at Plymouth Art College, 1957–61; Slade School of Fine Art, 1961–64. Began working with London Film-Makers Co-op, 1967; first one-man painting and film show, Drury Lane Arts Lab, 1968; teacher at St. Martin's College, London, from 1968.

Films:

1966   *Castle 1*; *China Tea*
1967   *Little Dog for Roger* (double projection version 1968); *Yes No Maybe Maybenot*; *Talla*; *Blind White Duration*
1968   *Castle 2*; *Grass*; *Wharf*
1970   *Spot the Microdot*; *Your Lips No. 1*; *Lucky Pigs*; *Reign of the Vampire*; *Berlin Horse*; *Horror Film 1*
1971   *Love Story 1*; *Love Story 2*; *1919, A Russian Funeral*; *Your Lips 3*
1972   *Love Story 3*; *Horror Film 2*; *Newport*; *Whitchurch Down (Duration)*; *Threshold*; *Blue Field Duration*; *White Field Duration*
1973   *Pre-Production*; *Four Wall Duration*; *Gross Fog*; *Matrix and Joseph's Coat*; *After Leonardo*; *Don't Say*; *Principles of Cinematography*; *After Leslie Wheeler*; *FRPS*; *MBKS*
1974   *Screen—Entrance Exit*; *After Lumiere, L'Arroseur Arrosé*
1975   *After Manet, After Giorgione, Le Dejeuner sur l'herbe*
1977   *Blackbird Descending* (*Tense Alignment*); *Art Works 1: Academic Still Life* (*Cezanne*); *Art Works 2: Time and Motion Study*
1979   *Emily* (*Third Party Speculation*)
1983   *Finnegan's Chin*

Publications:

By LE GRICE: books—

Abstract Film and Beyond, Cambridge, Massachusetts, 1977.

By LE GRICE: articles—

"Film," in *Studio International* (Lugano), September/October 1976.
"Towards Temporal Economy," in *Screen* (London), Winter 1979/80.

On LE GRICE: book—

Gidal, Peter, *Materialist Film*, London, 1989.

On LE GRICE: articles—

Dawson, Jan, and Claire Johnston, "More British Sounds," in *Sight and Sound* (London), Summer 1970.

*   *   *

Malcolm Le Grice is a British film artist, theoretician, and educator. He may be best known in the United States for his 1977 MIT Press publication *Abstract Film and Beyond*, a complex and very sophisticated theoretical/historical comparison of American and European contemporary experimental film.

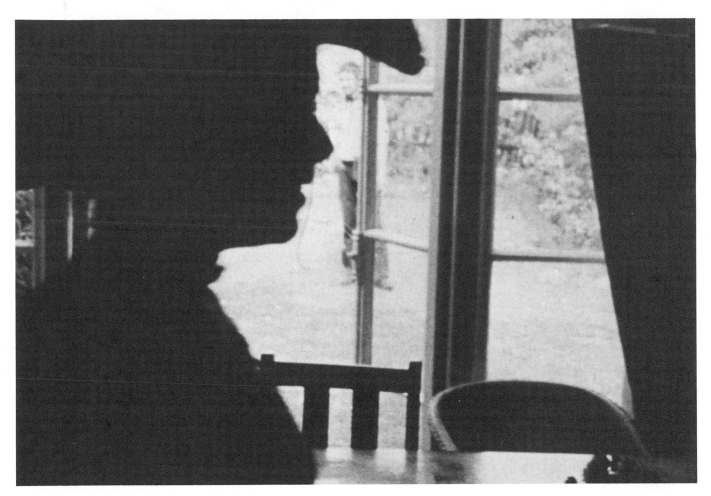

Malcolm Le Grice: *After Lumière*

However, with over 40 experimental productions to his credit, he is foremost an experimental filmmaker of international reputation.

By his own account, Le Grice's artistic career has enjoyed "three interconnected phases." All are related to his theoretical writings and insightful regard for the evolution of experimental film as a historical quest to establish cinema's distinct elements—that is, those characteristics and artistic resources which distinguish film from alternate modes such as written literature, the theater, painting, music, etc. Of all the major genres of film, experimental film seems especially qualified for this very theoretical task. Its independence of financing and controls, its attraction for technical and structural innovation, and its acollaborative construction allowing expression of a single artist's vision *sans* the filtered metamorphosis of more typical crews and companies—all this allows experimental film to reflexively examine cinema's essence for the sake of either pure or applied research goals.

During the earliest phase of his career, from 1967 to 1970, Le Grice advanced such research through concentration upon the medium's "material aspects" (such as emulsion or sprocket holes) in works like *Little Dog for Roger, Yes, No, Maybe, Maybenot* and *Berlin Horse*. During the middle phase, Le Grice concentrated upon elements of screening and projection. Indeed, multi-projection formats or the employ of pure shadows mark works like *Horror Film Two* and the four-screen *Matrix and Joseph's Coat*. Some works from this period—such as his 1972 *Pre-production*—are classified more as media-events than distributional motion-picture products.

His more recent, third phase works, such as the 1974 *After Lumière*, at once return to distributional units and to cinema's classic history. Faithful to experimental film's characteristics, Le Grice's productions are brief (though exceptions to such brevity exist, such as his 1977 work, *Blackbird Descending*, which runs over two hours). *After Lumière* is a 16-minute, single screen work that is largely a cinematic allusion to Lumière's nineteenth-century classic, *L'Arroseur arrosé*. Le Grice's strategy was to add an observing female character to Lumière's original, simple, one-shot story of a boy's trick upon a gardener with his garden hose. This character practices piano throughout the many repetitions of the core event, providing the study with a musical track that helps distinguish it from its 1895 prototype. Indeed, Le Grice's employ of such elements as sound, loop-like repetitions, editing, and subjective camera only gain their aesthetic force through implicit contradistinction to the original French film—a classic well-known to film artists and scholars throughout the world.

In *Abstract Film and Beyond*, Le Grice contends that film has evolved "towards a form which is not dependent on other areas of art for the source of its conventions." Le Grice's own film work can well be regarded as related exploration, "genuinely cinematographic in concept," beyond the confines of theater, literature, painting, and music.

—Edward S. Small

Mitchell Leisen

LEISEN, Mitchell.

American. Born in Menominee, Michigan, 6 October 1898. Educated at Art Institute of Chicago; studied architecture at Washington University, St. Louis. Costume Designer for Cecil B. De Mille, Hollywood, 1919; set dresser, then art director for De Mille and others, from 1920; director for Paramount, from 1933; TV director for *Wagon Train*, *Twilight Zone* and others, 1950s; also worked as interior designer. *Died 1972.*

Films as Director:

1933 *Tonight Is Ours* (co-d); *Eagle and the Hawk* (co-d); *Cradle Song*
1934 *Death Takes a Holiday*; *Murder at the Vanities*
1935 *Behold My Wife*; *Four Hours to Kill*; *Hands Across the Table*
1936 *Thirteen Hours by Air*; *The Big Broadcast of 1937*
1937 *Swing High, Swing Low*; *Easy Living*
1938 *The Big Broadcast of 1938*; *Artists and Models Abroad*
1939 *Midnight*
1940 *Remember the Night*; *Arise, My Love*
1941 *I Wanted Wings*; *Hold Back the Dawn*
1942 *The Lady Is Willing*; *Take a Letter, Darling*
1943 *No Time for Love*
1944 *Lady in the Dark*; *Frenchman's Creek*; *Practically Yours*
1945 *Masquerade in Mexico*; *Kitty*
1946 *To Each His Own*
1947 *Suddenly It's Spring*; *Golden Earrings*
1948 *Dream Girl*
1949 *Bride of Vengeance*; *Song of Surrender*
1950 *No Man of Her Own*; *Captain Carey, U.S.A.*
1951 *The Mating Season*; *Darling, How Could You*
1952 *Young Man with Ideas*
1953 *Tonight We Sing*
1955 *Bedevilled*
1957 *The Girl Most Likely*
1967 *Spree* (co-d) (filmed in 1963 as *Here's Las Vegas*)

Publications:

By LEISEN: articles—

"You Women Won't Like This," in *Silver Screen* (New York), May 1946.
"A Visit with Mitchell Leisen," with Leonard Maltin, in *Action* (Los Angeles), November/December 1969.
Interview with J.B. Kelley and J. Schultheiss, in *Cinema* (Beverly Hills), Spring 1973.

On LEISEN: book—

Chierechetti, David, *Hollywood Director*, New York, 1973.

On LEISEN: articles—

Sarris, Andrew, "Likable but Elusive," in *Film Culture* (New York), Spring 1963.
Greenberg, J., "Mitchell Leisen," in *Films in Review* (New York), March 1966.
Beylie, Claude, obituary in *Ecran* (Paris), January 1973.
Kelley, J.B., and J. Schultheiss, "Hollywood Contract Director: Mitchell Leisen," in *Cinema* (Beverly Hills), Spring 1973.
Adair, Gilbert, "The Magic Mountain," in *Sight and Sound* (London), Summer 1980.
Schultheiss, J., "Director Mitchell Leisen: an annotated filmography," in *Journal of Popular Film* (Washington, D.C.), Fall 1980.
"Mitchell Leisen," in *Film Dope* (London), March 1986.
Tobin, Yann, "Mitchell Leisen," in *Positif* (Paris), December 1987.

*   *   *

Costume and set designers who turn to direction are sufficiently rare for the career of Mitchell Leisen to be worthy of comment. As a soldier in the De Mille entourage of the 1920s, he responded meekly to the master's demands for decorative camera-fodder. But in his first directing job, as "associate" to Stuart Walker in *The Eagle and the Hawk*, Leisen contrived, even while displaying the lovely young Carole Lombard to striking advantage in an extravagant silver gown, to turn her scene with Fredric March into an encounter humming with passion. He was no less skillful with the languid melodrama of *Death Takes a Holiday*, where once again he worked with the talented March to create scenes that transcend the high-life setting.

Such legerdemain became a Leisen trademark. He directed much that was beneath his intelligence, but always with style, taste, and decorative flair. The musicals are lush exemplars of Paramount's up-market European approach, from the backstage peep-show of *Murder at the Vanities* through the drama-with-music of *Swing High Swing Low* to *Lady in the Dark*'s lavish Broadway pastels and psychoanalytic fantasy.

Leisen directed some of the best Billy Wilder/Charles Brackett screenplays, including the sublime comedy *Midnight*, and those curious romantic melodramas *Arise My Love* and *Hold Back the Dawn*, cultured and ironic reflections on a world of refugees, intrigue and casual passion. Also for Leisen, Preston Sturges wrote the sarcastic *Remember the Night* for MacMurray and Stanwyck, and in *Easy Living* created a superb wise-cracking parody of capitalistic excess. Both were handled by the director with flawless skill.

Perhaps in reaction against DeMille, Leisen avoided costume pictures. Those he did make are notable less for couture than performance. *Kitty* is a regency sex comedy for Paulette Goddard, and *Bride of Vengeance* a Renaissance romp for the same star, this time playing an improbable Lucrezia Borgia to John Lund's distracted Duke of Ferrara, who has invasion and intrigue to contend with in city and bedroom both.

The typus of the Hollywood gay director, Leisen seldom slipped below a self-imposed standard of visual elegance, nor rose above a stylish superficiality. As the leader of Paramount's directorial second string, he was often saddled with its less-accomplished leads. He extracted creditable work from MacMurray, Lund, Goddard, and even Betty Hutton, but was moved to greater heights by Fontaine, Milland, Boyer, and Lombard. That he is remembered by *Cahiers du cinéma* as little more than "a great couturier" and by other reference books more for the writers and performers he directed is a fate suffered by many artists of Hollywood's 1930s cinema, stronger on wit and taste than self-advertisement.

—John Baxter

———

LELOUCH, Claude.

French. Born in Paris, 30 October 1937. Married Christine Cochet (divorced), one son. Maker of short films as "cinereporter," 1956–58; served in Service-Cinéma des Armées (S.C.A.), 1958–60; founder, Les Films 13 production company, 1960; made some 250 "scopitones," 2–3 minute mini-musicals shown on a type of jukebox, 1960–62; directed first feature, 1962. Recipient: Oscar for Best Story and Screenplay, and Palme d'Or, Cannes Festival, for *Un Homme et une femme*, 1966; Grand Prix du Cinéma français, for *Vivre pour vivre*, 1967; Prix Raoul Levy, 1970. Address: 15 avenue Hoche, 75008 Paris, France.

Films as Director:

1953 *Le Mal du siècle* (+ pr, sc, ed); *USA en vrac* (+ pr, sc, ed)

Claude Lelouch

1957　*Quand le rideau se lève* (+ pr, sc, ed)
1959　*La Guerre du silence* (+ pr, sc, ed); *Les Mécaniciens de l'armée de l'air* (+ pr, sc, ed); *S.O.S. hélicoptère* (+ pr, sc, ed)
1960　*Le Propre de l'homme* (*The Right of Man*) (+ pr, sc, role as Claude); *La Femme spectacle* (*Night Women*) (+ pr, sc)
1964　*Une Fille et des fusils* (*To Be a Crook*) (+ pr, sc, ph); *Vingt-quatre heures d'amant* (+ pr, sc)
1965　*Les Grands Moments* (+ pr, sc, ph); *Jean-Paul Belmondo* (+ pr, sc); *Pour un maillot jaune* (+ pr, sc)
1966　*Un Homme et une femme* (*A Man and a Woman*) (+ co-ed, ph, sc)
1967　*Vivre pour vivre* (*Live for Life*) (+ pr, sc); episode of *Loin du Vietnam* (*Far From Vietnam*)
1968　*Treize jours en France* (*Grenoble*) (+ co-ph, pr, sc); *La Vie, l'amour, la mort* (*Life Love Death*) (+ co-sc, pr)
1969　*Un Homme qui me plaît* (*Love Is a Funny Thing*) (+ co-pr, co-sc)
1970　*Le Voyou* (*The Crook*) (+ pr, sc)
1971　*Smic Smac Smoc* (+ ph, pr, sc)
1972　*L'Aventure c'est l'aventure* (*Money Money Money*) (+ co-sc, pr); *La Bonne année* (*Happy New Year*) (+ co-pr, co-sc, ph)
1973　"The Losers" episode in *Visions of Eight* (+ co-sc, pr)
1974　*Toute une vie* (*And Now My Love*) (+ pr, sc); *Mariage* (*Marriage*) (+ co-sc, pr)
1975　*Le Chat et la souris* (*Cat and Mouse*) (+ pr, sc); *Le Bon et les méchants* (*The Good and the Bad*) (+ pr, sc)
1976　*Rendez-vous* (+ pr, sc); *Si c'était à refaire* (*If I Had to Do It All Over Again*) (+ ph, pr, sc)
1977　*Another Man, Another Chance* (+ co-pr, sc)
1978　*Robert et Robert* (+ pr, sc)
1979　*À nous deux* (*An Adventure for Two. Us Two*) (+ pr, sc)
1981　*Les Uns et les autres* (+ pr, sc)
1982　*Edith et Marcel* (+ pr, sc)
1984　*Vive la Vie!*
1985　*Partir, revenir* (*Going and Coming Back*) (+ pr, sc)
1986　*Un Homme et une femme: Vingt ans déja* (*A Man and a Woman: Twenty Years Later*)
1987　*Attention Bandits*
1988　*L'Itinéraire d'un enfant gâté*

Other Films:

1988　*Happy New Year* (Avildsen) (role)

Publications:

By LELOUCH: books—

A Man and a Woman, with Pierre Uytterhoeven, New York, 1971.
Ma vie pour un film, Paris, 1986.

By LELOUCH: articles—

"*Un homme et une femme* Issue" of *Avant-Scène du Cinéma* (Paris), December 1966.
"Claude Lelouch at the Olympic Games," an interview, in *American Cinematographer* (Los Angeles), November 1972.
Interview with J. Craven, in *Filmmakers Newsletter* (Ward Hill, Massachusetts), March 1974.
Interview with P. Lev, in *Take One* (Montreal), August 1977.
Interview with S. McMillin, in *Filmmakers Newsletter* (Ward Hill, Massachusetts), February 1978.
Interview with Tim Pulleine, in *Sight and Sound* (London), Summer 1983.
Interview with P. Carcassonne, in *Cinématographe* (Paris), May 1984.
Interview with M. Elia, in *Séquences* (Montreal), March 1989.

On LELOUCH: books—

Armes, Roy, *French Cinema Since 1946: Vol.2—The Personal Style*, New York, 1966.
Guidez, Guylaine, *Claude Lelouch*, Paris, 1972.
Ronchetti, Pierluigi, *Claude Lelouch*, Citta di Castello, Italy, 1979.
Lev, Peter, *Claude Lelouch, Film Director*, New York, 1983.
Alberti, Olympia, *Lelouch Passion*, Paris, 1987.

On LELOUCH: articles—

"Lelouch: table ronde," in *Cinéma* (Paris), May 1965.
Comolli, Jean-Louis, "Claude Lelouch, ou la bonne conscience retrouvée," in *Cahiers du Cinéma* (Paris), June 1966.
Perisset, Maurice, "Le Cas Lelouch," in *Cinéma* (Paris), May 1969.
Garel, A., "A propos de *Toute une vie* ou Lelouchiens si vous saviez," in *Image et Son* (Paris), January 1975.
Eyles, A., "*And Now My Love*," in *Focus on Film* (London), Summer 1975.
Johnston, Sheila, "The Ins and Outs of Claude Lelouch," in *Stills* (London), July/August 1983.
"Claude Lelouch," in *Film Dope* (London), March 1986.
Hunter, Allan, "A Man and a Woman: Twenty Years Later," in *Films and Filming* (London), August 1986.
Elia, M., "Claude Lelouch," in *Séquences* (Montreal), April 1987.

*　　　*　　　*

The films of Claude Lelouch may be classified under three diverse headings: romance, crime, and liberal politics. Occasionally, they focus on one specific area; more often, the categories will be combined.

A Man and a Woman is a love story simply and purely. Despite Lelouch's many commercial successes, he is most identified with this glossy, gimmicky, tremendously popular tale of script girl Anouk Aimée, a widow, and her widower counterpart, race car driver Jean-Louis Trintignant. *A Man and a Woman* became one of the most beloved romantic films of its time, a favorite of young couples. The scenario may be a soap opera, photographed on what some critics perceive as postcard-pretty locations; still, it is emotionally touching and truthful. Most significantly, there is refreshingly flexible camera work. Lelouch, who also photographed (besides co-editing the film and co-authoring the screenplay), uses his camera like a paintbrush, with total ease and freedom.

More typically, Lelouch mixes love and politics in *Live for Life*, the story of television journalist Yves Montand, whose work takes him to Vietnam and Africa; this character leaves devoted wife Annie Girardot for fashion model Candice Bergen. The filmmaker combines love and crime in *Happy New Year*, in which two robbers plan a caper and one falls for the proprietress of a nearby antique store. He blends crime and politics in *Money, Money, Money*, in which a gang of crooks realize that the changing times will allow them to gain greater profits by committing political crimes.

Lelouch has always had one eye on box office receipts, once too often selecting his subject matter with commercial potential being the sole consideration. Early in his career he directed *Night Woman*, a relatively erotic film about, as the filmmaker explains, "all the kinds of women one wouldn't like to marry," in the hope of earning a financial success. His first box office hit was *To Be a Crook*, the story of four men and a deaf-and-dumb girl who become kidnappers and murderers; highlighted are gunfights, and a striptease.

Lelouch does have political concerns: he participated (with Alain Resnais, Jean-Luc Godard, Joris Ivens, William Klein, and Agnes Varda) in the anti-war compilation film *Far From Vietnam*. And he has made quite a few delightfully clever entertainments: *Happy New Year*; *Money, Money, Money*; *Cat and Mouse*, a mystery-comedy about a police inspector's efforts to uncover a rich philanderer's killer; *The Crook* and *And Now My Love*, which utilizes comedy, music, and drama to unite lovers Marthe Keller and Andre Dussollier. Yet he will all too often repeat himself, with uninspired results. For example, *Live for Life*, the follow-up to *A Man and a Woman*, is just too frilly, a slickly photographed soap opera lacking the warmth of its predecessor. *Another Man, Another Chance* is a blatant rip-off of *A Man and a Woman*, with James Caan the widower and Genevieve Bujold the widow. Despite his many successes, Claude Lelouch ultimately cannot be ranked with the top filmmakers of his generation.

—Rob Edelman

LENI, Paul.

German. Born in Stuttgart, 8 July 1885. Painter and stage designer, and member of avant-garde movement associated with publication *Der Sturm*, Berlin, 1900s; production designer, from 1914; directed first film, 1916; also worked as scenarist and actor; hired for Universal in Hollywood by Carl Laemmle, 1927. *Died of blood poisoning, 2 September 1929.*

Films as Director:

1916 *Das Tagebuch des Dr. Hart*
1917 *Dornröschen* (+ sc)
1919 *Platonische Ehe* (+ co-prod des); *Prinz Kuckuk* (+ co-prod des)
1920 *Patience* (+ sc, prod des)
1921 *Fiesco* (*Die Verschwöhrung zu Genua*) (+ co-prod des); *Das Gespensterschiff* (+ prod des); *Hintertreppe* (*Backstairs*) (co-d, prod des); *Komödie der Leidenschaften* (+ prod des)
1924 **Das Wachsfigurenkabinett (Waxworks)** (+ prod des)
1927 *The Cat and the Canary* (in US); *The Chinese Parrot* (in US)
1928 *The Man Who Laughs* (in US)
1929 *The Last Warning* (in US)

Other Films:

1914 *Das Panzergewölbe* (May) (prod des)
1915 *Der Katzensteg* (Mack) (prod des); *Das achte Gebot* (Mack) (prod des)
1917 *Das Rätsel von Bangalor* (assoc d, co-sc)
1920 *Der weisse Pfau* (Dupont) (co-prod des, co-sc); *Die Schuld der Lavinia Morland* (May) (co-prod des, role); *Veritas Vincit* (May) (co-prod des)
1921 *Die Geier Wally* (Dupont) (prod des); *Kinder der Finsternis* (Dupont) (prod des)
1922 *Frauenopfer* (Grüne) (prod des)
1923 *Tragödie der Liebe* (May) (prod des)
1925 *Die Frau von vierzig Jahren* (Oswald) (prod des); *Der Farmer aux Texas* (May) (prod des); *Der Tänzer meiner Frau* (Korda) (prod des)
1926 *Manon Lescaut* (Robinson) (costumes); *Fiaker Nr. 13* (Kertesz) (prod des); *Wie einst im Mai* (Wolff) (prod des); *Der goldene Schmetterling* (Kertesz) (prod des)

Publications:

By LENI: articles—

"L'image comme action," in *Cinématographe* (Paris), February 1982.

On LENI: books—

Kracauer, Siegfried, *From Caligari to Hitler*, Princeton, 1947.
Eisner, Lotte, *The Haunted Screen: Expressionism in the German Cinema and the Influence of Max Reinhardt*, Berkeley, 1969.
Willett, John, *Art and Politics in the Weimar Period: The New Sobriety 1917–1933*, New York, 1978.
Bock, Hans-Michael, *Paul Leni: Grafik, Theater, Film*, Frankfurt, 1986.

Paul Leni

On LENI: articles—

Buache, Freddy, "Paul Leni 1885–1929," in *Anthologie du Cinéma*, vol.4, Paris, 1968.
"Paul Leni," in *Film Dope* (London), March 1986.

*   *   *

Siegfried Kracauer, in *From Caligari to Hitler*, calls Leni "one of the outstanding film directors of the post-World War I era," and refers to the Jack-the-Ripper episode of *Waxworks* as being "among the greatest achievements of film art." Yet Leni's name is familiar only to film scholars today.

He predates Hitchcock as a maker of thrillers; the screen cliches of trembling hands intent on murdering unsuspecting innocents, and corpses falling from opened doors, were first presented in his *The Cat and the Canary*. Excluding the films of Lon Chaney, he was the foremost practitioner of utilizing make-up to create grotesque creatures, silent-screen monsters who terrified audiences by looks alone.

Leni's death from blood poisoning at 44 denied the cinema what might have developed into a major career. Leni commenced his work in the German cinema as a painter, set designer and art director, most notably collaborating with Max Reinhardt. These concerns carry through into his own films: his sets are strikingly stylized, dreamlike, and expressionistic.

Leni's attempt to go beyond the limits of photographed reality utilizing set and costume design was never more successfully realized than in *Das Wachsfigurenkabinett* (*Waxworks*). The film, with its distorted sets and ingenious lighting, is as profound an example of surreal cinematic madness as *The Cabinet of Dr. Caligari*. Three of the best-known actors in the post-World War I German cinema starred as the wax-work villains: Emil Jannings, Conrad Veidt and Werner Krauss. Each appears in a separate episode as, respectively, Haroun-al-Raschid, Ivan the Terrible (who places hourglasses near each of his poison victims, so that they will know the exact moment of their deaths), and Jack the Ripper (a sequence that, in its dreaminess, is extremely Caligari-like). Veidt's Ivan allegedly influenced Sergei Eisenstein's conception of the character.

Like many foreign talents of the period, Leni ended up in Hollywood. As a result of his success with *Waxworks*, he was signed by Universal's Carl Laemmle. His first project was *The Cat and the Canary*, the original haunted house movie and quite unlike its successor: here, heiress Laura La Plante and her nervous cronies spend a night in an old dark house. To his credit, Leni did not sensationalize the material. The film's chills result from atmosphere, from stylized, expressionistic set design. The mansion, seen in the distance, is eerily gothic; inside are long, winding corridors and staircases. *The Cat and the Canary* is not just a chiller, in that Leni adds charming touches of humor to the scenario. Paul Leni made only four features in Hollywood. His final one, prophetically titled *The Last Warning*, was his only talkie.

—Rob Edelman

LEONE, Sergio.

Italian. Born in Rome, 3 January 1929, son of director Vincenzo Leone. Attended law school, Rome. Married Carla (Leone), 1960, three daughters. Assistant to, then 2nd unit director for, Italian filmmakers and American directors working in Italy such as LeRoy, Walsh and Wyler, 1947–56; scriptwriter, from late 1950s; directed first feature, *Il colosso di Rodi*, 1961; headed own production company, Rafran Cinematografica, 1970s. *Died, in Rome, April 1989.*

Films as Director:

1961   *Il colosso di Rodi* (*The Colossus of Rhodes*) (+ co-sc)
1964   *Per un pugno di dollari* (*A Fistful of Dollars*) (+ co-sc)
1965   *Per qualche dollaro in più* (*For a Few Dollars More*) (+ co-sc)
1966   *Il buono il brutto il cattivo* (***The Good, the Bad, and the Ugly***) (+ co-sc)
1968   *C'era una volta il West* (***Once Upon a Time in the West***) (+ co-sc)
1972   *Giù la testa* (*Duck You Sucker. Il était une fois la révolution*) (+ co-sc)
1975   *Un genio due compari e un pollo* (+ co-sc)
1984   *Once Upon a Time in America* (+ co-sc)

Other Films:

1958   *Nel segno di Roma* (*Sign of the Gladiator*) (co-sc)
1959   *Gli ultimi giorni di Pompeii* (*The Last Days of Pompeii*) (Bonnard) (co-sc, uncredited co-d)
1961   *Sodoma e Gommorra* (*Sodom and Gomorrah*) (Aldrich) (2nd unit d, co-d according to some sources)
1973   *My Name is Nobody* (story idea)
1978   *Il gatto* (pr)

Publications:

By LEONE: books—

Conversations avec Sergio Leone, edited by Noel Simsolo, Paris, 1987.

By LEONE: articles—

Interview, in *Take One* (Montreal), January/February 1972.
"Il était une fois la révolution," interview with G. Braucourt, in *Ecran* (Paris), May 1972.
"Pastalong Cassidy Always Wears Black," with Cynthia Grenier, in *Oui* (Chicago), April 1973.
Interview with M. Chion and others, in *Cahiers du Cinéma* (Paris), May 1984.
Interview with J.-P. Domecq and J.-A. Gili, in *Positif* (Paris), June 1984.
Interview with M. Corliss and E. Lomenzo, in *Film Comment* (New York), July/August 1984.
Interview with G. Graziani, in *Filmcritica* (Florence), October/November 1984.

On LEONE: books—

Lambert, Gavin, *Les Bons, les sales, les méchants et les propres de Sergio Leone*, Paris, 1976.
Frayling, Christopher, *Spaghetti Westerns: Cowboys and Europeans: From Karl May to Sergio Leone*, London, 1981.
Cèbe, Gilles, *Sergio Leone*, Paris, 1984.
De Fornari, Oreste, *Tutti i Film di Sergio Leone*, Milan, 1984.
Cumbow, Robert C., *Once Upon a Time: The Films of Sergio Leone*, Metuchen, New Jersey, 1987.
Cressard, Gilles, *Sergio Leone*, Paris, 1989.
Mininni, Francesco, *Sergio Leone*, Paris, 1989.

On LEONE: articles—

Witonski, Peter, "Meanwhile . . . Back at Cinecitta," in *Film Society Review* (New York), Fall 1965.
Sarris, Andrew, in *Village Voice* (New York), 19 and 26 September 1968.
Frayling, Christopher, "Sergio Leone," in *Cinema* (London), August 1970.
Kaminsky, Stuart, in *Take One* (Montreal), January/February 1972.
Jameson, Richard, "Something To Do With Death," in *Film Comment* (New York), March/April 1973.
Garel, A., and F. Joyeux, "Il etait une fois . . . le western: de Sergio Leone," in *Image et Son* (Paris), July 1979.

Sergio Leone

Nicholls, D., "Once Upon a Time in Italy," in *Sight and Sound* (London), Winter 1980/81.

Mitchell, T., "Leone's America," in *Sight and Sound* (London), Summer 1983.

"Sergio Leone," in *Film Dope* (London), March 1986.

Cohn, L., obituary in *Variety* (New York), 3 May 1989.

Bertolucci, Bernardo, obituary in *Film Comment* (New York), July/August 1989.

Thomson, D., "Leonesque," in *American Film* (Washington, D.C.), September 1989.

*   *   *

Not since Franz Kafka's *America* has a European artist turned himself with such intensity to the meaning of American culture and mythology. Sergio Leone's career is remarkable in its unrelenting attention to both America and American genre film. In France, Truffaut, Godard and Chabrol have used American film as a touchstone for their own vision, but Leone, an Italian, a Roman who began to learn English only after five films about the United States, devoted most of his creative life to this examination.

Leone's films are not realistic or naturalistic visions of the American nightmare or fairy tale, but comic nightmares about existence. The feeling of unreality is central to Leone's work. His is a world of magic and horror. Religion is meaningless, a sham which hides honest emotions; civilization is an extension of man's need to dominate and survive by exploiting others. The Leone world, while not womanless, is set up as one in which men face the horror of existence. In this, Leone is very like Howard Hawks: as in Hawks's films, death erases a man. A man who dies is a loser, and the measure of a man is his ability to survive, to laugh or sneer at death. This is not a bitter point in Leone films. There are few lingering deaths and very little blood. Even the death of Ramon (Gian Maria Volonte) in *Fistful of Dollars* takes place rather quickly and with far less blood than the comparable death in *Yojimbo*. A man's death is less important than how he faces it. The only thing worth preserving in Leone's world is the family—and his world of American violence is such a terrible place that few families survive. In *Fistful of Dollars*, Clint Eastwood's primary emotional reaction is to attempt to destroy the family of the woman Ramon has taken. In the later films, *The Good, the Bad, and the Ugly* and *Once Upon a Time in the West*, *Duck, You Sucker* and *Once Upon a Time in America*, family life is minimal and destroyed by self-serving evil, not out of hatred but by a cold, passionless commitment to self-interest. Leone's visual obsessions contribute to his thematic interests. Many directors could work with and develop the same themes and characters, but Leone's forte lies in the development of these themes and characters in a personal world. No director, with the possible exception of Sam Fuller, makes as extensive use of the close-up as does Leone, and Leone's close-ups often show only a portion of the face, usually the eyes of one of the main characters. It is the eyes of these men that reveal what they are feeling—if they are feeling anything.

Such characters almost never define their actions in words. Plot is of minimal interest to Leone. What is important is examination of the characters, watching how they react, what makes them tick. It appears almost as if everything is, indeed, happening randomly, as if we are watching with curiosity the responses of different types of people, trying to read meaning in the slightest flick of an eyelid. The visual impact of water dripping on Woody Strode's hat, or Jack Elam's annoyed reaction to a fly, is of greater interest to Leone than the gunfight in which the two appear in *Once Upon a Time in the West*.

The use of the pan in Leone films is also remarkable. The pan from the firing squad past the church and to the poster of the governor, behind which Rod Steiger watches in bewilderment through the eyes of the governor's image, is a prime example in *Duck, You Sucker*. The shot ties the execution to the indifferent church, to the non-seeing poster, and to Steiger's reaction in one movement.

The apparent joy and even comedy of destruction and battle in Leone films are often followed immediately by some intimate horror, some personal touch that underlines the real meaning of the horror which moments before had been amusing. The death of Dominick and his final words, "I slipped," in *Once Upon a Time in America* undercut the comedy and zest for battle. There is little dialogue; the vision of the youthful dead dominates as it does in the cave scene in *Duck, You Sucker* in which Juan's family lies massacred.

At the same time, Leone's fascination with spontaneous living, his zeal for existence in the midst of his morality films, can be seen in his handling of details. For example, food in his films is always colorful and appetizing and people eat it ravenously.

The obsession of Leone protagonists and villains, major and minor, with the attainment of wealth can be seen as growing out of a dominant strain within American genres, particularly western and gangster films. The desire for wealth and power turns men into ruthless creatures who violate land and family.

Leone's films are explorations of the mythic America he created. Unlike many directors, he did not simply repeat the same convention in a variety of ways. Each successive film takes the same characters and explores them in greater depth, and Leone's involvement with this exploration is intense.

—Stuart M. Kaminsky

LEROY, Mervyn.

American. Born in San Francisco, 15 October 1900. Attended night school, 1919–1924. Married 1) Doris Warner, 1933 (divorced), one son, one daughter; 2) Kathryn Spiegel, 1946. Newsboy, from 1910; hired to portray newsboy in film *Barbara Fritchie*, 1912; film extra and vaudeville performer (as "The Singing Newsboy," later, with Clyde Cooper, as "Leroy and Cooper: 2 Kids and a Piano") 1912–1919; through cousin Jesse Lasky, gets job in films, folding costumes, 1919; also film actor, to 1924; gag writer and comedy construction specialist for director Alfred E. Green, 1924; directed first film, *No Place to Go*, for 1st National, 1927; hired by MGM as producer and director, 1938; started own production company, 1944. Recipient: Special Oscar, for *The House I Live In*, 1945; Victoire du Cinéma français, for *Quo Vadis*, 1954; Irving Thalberg Academy Award, 1975. *Died, in Beverly Hills, 13 September 1987.*

Films as Director:

1927	*No Place to Go*
1928	*Flying Romeos*; *Harold Teen*; *Oh, Kay!*
1929	*Naughty Baby* (*Reckless Rosie*); *Hot Stuff*; *Broadway Babies* (*Broadway Daddies*); *Little Johnny Jones*
1930	*Playing Around*; *Showgirl in Hollywood*; *Numbered Men*; *Top Speed*; *Little Caesar*; *Too Young to Marry*; *Broad-Minded*; *Five Star Final* (*One Fatal Hour*); *Tonight or Never*
1932	*High Pressure*; *Heart of New York*; *Two Seconds*; *Big City Blues*; *Three on a Match*; **I Am a Fugitive from a Chain Gang**
1933	*Hard to Handle*; *Tugboat Annie*; *Elmer the Great*; **Gold Diggers of 1933**; *The World Changes*
1934	*Heat Lightning*; *Hi, Nellie!*; *Happiness Ahead*
1935	*Oil for the Lamps of China*; *Page Miss Glory*; *I Found Stella Parish*; *Sweet Adeline*

Mervyn LeRoy and writer Sally Benson with set designs for *Little Women*

1936 *Anthony Adverse*; *Three Men on a Horse*
1937 *The King and the Chorus Girl*; *They Won't Forget*
1938 *Fools for Scandal*
1940 *Waterloo Bridge*; *Escape* (+ pr)
1941 *Blossoms in the Dust* (+ pr); *Unholy Partners*; *Johnny Eager*
1942 *Random Harvest*
1944 *Madame Curie*
1945 *Thirty Seconds Over Tokyo*
1946 *Without Reservations*
1948 *Homecoming*
1949 *Little Women* (+ pr); *Any Number Can Play*
1950 *East Side, West Side*; *Quo Vadis?*
1952 *Lovely to Look At*; *Million Dollar Mermaid* (*The One-Piece Bathing Suit*)
1953 *Latin Lovers*
1954 *Rose Marie* (+ pr)
1955 *Strange Lady in Town* (+ pr); *Mister Roberts* (co-d)
1956 *The Bad Seed* (+ pr); *Toward the Unknown* (*Brink of Hell*) (+ pr)
1958 *No Time for Sergeants* (+ pr); *Home Before Dark* (+ pr)
1959 *The FBI Story* (+ pr)
1960 *Wake Me When It's Over* (+ pr)
1961 *The Devil at Four O'Clock* (+ pr); *A Majority of One* (+ pr)
1962 *Gypsy* (+ pr)
1963 *Mary, Mary* (+ pr)
1965 *Moment to Moment* (+ pr)

Other Films:

(partial list)

1920 *Double Speed* (Wood) (role as juvenile)
1922 *The Ghost Breaker* (Green) (role as a ghost)
1923 *Little Johnny Jones* (Rosson and Hines) (role as George Nelson); *Going Up* (Ingraham) (role as bellboy); *The Call of the Canyon* (Fleming) (role as Jack Rawlins)
1924 *In Hollywood with Potash and Perlmutter* (*So This is Hollywood*) (gag-writer); *Broadway After Dark* (Bell) (role as Carl Fisher); *The Chorus Lady* (Ralph Ince) (role as Duke)
1925 *Sally* (gag-writer); *The Desert Flower* (gag-writer); *The Pace That Thrills* (gag-writer); *We Moderns* (gag-writer)
1926 *Irene* (gag-writer); *Ella Cinders* (gag-writer); *It Must Be Love* (gag-writer); *Twinkletoes* (gag-writer)
1927 *Orchids and Ermines* (gag-writer)
1932 *The Dark Horse* (Green) (uncredited help)
1937 *The Great Garrick* (Whale) (pr)
1938 *Stand Up and Fight* (Van Dyke, W.S.) (pr); *Dramatic School* (pr); *At the Circus* (pr)
1939 *The Wizard of Oz* (Fleming) (pr)
1945 *The House I Live In* (pr)
1947 *Desire Me* (Cukor) (uncredited direction)
1949 *The Great Sinner* (Siodmak) (uncredited direction and editing)
1968 *The Green Berets* (Wayne and Kellogg) (assisted Wayne)

Publications:

By LEROY: books—

It Takes More Than Talent, as told to Alyce Canfield, New York, 1953.
Mervyn LeRoy: Take One, as told to Dick Kleiner, New York, 1974.

By LEROY: articles—

"The Making of Mervyn LeRoy," in *Films in Review* (New York), May 1953.
"What Directors Are Saying," in *Action* (Los Angeles), May/June 1970.
"Mervyn LeRoy Talks with William Friedkin," in *Action* (Los Angeles), November/December 1974.

On LEROY: articles—

Surtees, Robert, "The Filming of *Quo Vadis* in Italy," in *American Cinematographer* (Hollywood), October 1951.
Sarris, Andrew, "Likable, but Elusive," in *Film Culture* (New York), Spring 1963.
"Should Directors Produce?," in *Action* (Los Angeles), July/August 1968.
Campbell, Russell, "*I Am a Fugitive From a Chain Gang*," in *Velvet Light Trap* (Madison, Wisconsin), June 1971.
Kaminsky, Stuart, "*Little Caesar* and Its Role in the Gangster Film Genre," in *Journal of Popular Film* (Bowling Green, Ohio), Summer 1972.
Canham, Kingsley, "Mervyn LeRoy: Star-making, Studio Systems and Style,"in *The Hollywood Professionals* Vol.5, London, 1976.
Veillon, O.-R., "Mervyn LeRoy à la Warner," in *Cinématographe* (Paris), October 1982.
"Mervyn Le Roy revisited," in *Image et Son* (Paris), December 1982.
"Mervyn Leroy," in *Film Dope* (London), September 1986.
Obituary in *Films and Filming* (London), November 1987.

*　　　*　　　*

The career of Mervyn LeRoy, one of the most successful in the heyday of the studio system, is a reflection of that system. When at Warner Brothers, through most of the 1930s, LeRoy was a master of the style dominant at that studio, demonstrated in the fast-paced toughness of films like his *Little Caesar* and *I Am a Fugitive from a Chain Gang*. As producer-director at MGM, until the mid-1950s, he presided over lushly romantic vehicles for Greer Garson and Vivien Leigh. Prolific, versatile (at home in action films, women's films, musicals, historical spectacles), LeRoy's fluency marks him as the kind of director who validates collaborative creativity. Sensitive to the particular individuals with whom he works, and to the wide-ranging needs of the various materials he treats, LeRoy offers us an image of the Hollywood technique during the development of the classic Hollywood narrative.

This often makes it difficult to locate that which is LeRoy's specific contribution to films as dissimilar as the taut courtroom drama, *They Won't Forget* (that featured the memorable debut of Lana Turner, the "sweater girl" under personal contract to the director) and the colossal pageantry of *Quo Vadis*?, where decor completely submerges character. But if LeRoy lacks the recognizable visual and thematic coherence we notice in the works of "auteurs" (Welles, Ford, Griffith) it would be incorrect to characterize him as a director without a personal vision, or at least an affinity for specific subjects. Some of his best remembered films contain narrative configurations that display the protagonists in situations of pathetic isolation. It is as if the director's eye and the spectator's eye spied a character in a state of embarrassing vulnerability. At the end of *I Am a Fugitive*, a film about a man wrongly charged with a crime and perpetually hounded by the police, the hero confesses that he must now steal to live. Staged in a dark alley, the last words emerge from total blackness that ironically hides the speaker's face in this moment of painful revelation. (It has been said that the blackout was due to a power failure on the set. This in no

way lessens the significance of the decision to leave the scene in, as shot.) In *Random Harvest*, one of the most popular films LeRoy made at MGM, the director repeatedly finds ways to underscore the pain of the wife who "plays" at being the secretary of her husband, an amnesia victim who has forgotten her identity. Here, as in *Waterloo Bridge* where the heroine represents one thing to the audience (a prostitute) and another to the hero (his long-lost fiancée), the staging exploits this ironic brand of double identity.

In a film made at Warners in 1958, *Home Before Dark*, the dual representation of character is extended into the figure of the schizophrenic (Jean Simmons) who, wishing to be like her sister, appears in a crowded nightclub wearing an oversized gown and garishly inappropriate makeup. This sort of embarrassing exposure reaches a theatrical peak in *Gypsy* where the mother of the striptease artists does her own "turn" on the bare stage of an empty theater, stripping down to her raw ambition and envy.

—Charles Affron

LESTER, Richard.

American. Born in Philadelphia, 19 January 1932. Educated at the William Penn Charter School, Germanstown, Pennsylvania; University of Pennsylvania, Philadelphia, B.S. in Clinical Psychology, 1951. Married dancer and choreographer Deirdre Vivian Smith, 1956, two children. Music editor, assistant director, then director, CBS TV, Philadelphia, 1951–54; director and composer, ITV, London, 1955–57, then producer, 1958; director, Courtyard Films, Ltd., from 1967; also composer and musician, and, from 1960, director of TV commercials. Recipient: Palme d'Or, Cannes Festival, for *The Knack*, 1965; Gandhi Peace Prize, Berlin Festival, for *The Bed Sitting Room*, 1969. Address: c/o Twickenham Studios, St. Margarets, Middlesex, England.

Films as Director:

1959　*The Running, Jumping and Standing Still Film* (+ ph, mu, co-ed)
1962　*It's Trad, Dad* (*Ring-a-Ding Rhythm*)
1963　*The Mouse on the Moon*
1964　**A Hard Day's Night**
1965　**The Knack—and How to Get It**; *Help!*
1966　*A Funny Thing Happened On the Way to the Forum*
1967　*How I Won the War* (+ pr)
1968　*Petulia*
1969　*The Bed Sitting Room* (+ co-pr)
1974　*The Three Musketeers* (*The Queen's Diamonds*); *Juggernaut*
1975　*The Four Musketeers* (*The Revenge of Milady*); *Royal Flash*
1976　*Robin and Marian* (+ co-pr); *The Ritz*
1979　*Butch and Sundance: The Early Days*; *Cuba*
1981　*Superman II*
1983　*Superman III*
1984　*Finders Keepers*
1989　*Return of the Musketeers*

Publications:

By LESTER: articles—

"In Search of the Right Knack," in *Films and Filming* (London), July 1965.

Richard Lester

"Lunch with Lester," with George Bluestone, in *Film Quarterly* (Berkeley), Summer 1966.

"Richard Lester and the Art of Comedy," in *Film* (London), Spring 1967.

Interview with Ian Cameron and Mark Shivas, in *Movie* (London), Winter 1968/69.

"What I Learned from Commercials," in *Action* (Los Angeles), January/February 1969.

"Running, Jumping and Standing Still: An Interview with Richard Lester," with Joseph McBride, in *Sight and Sound* (London), Spring 1973.

"The Pleasure in the Terror of the Game," interview with Gordon Gow, in *Films and Filming* (London), October 1974.

"Richard Lester: Doing the Best He Can," interview with Gerald Pratley, in *Film* (London), February 1975.

"Deux Entretiens avec Richard Lester," with Michel Ciment, in *Positif* (Paris), November 1975.

Interview with J. Brosnan, in *Sight and Sound* (London), Summer 1983.

Interview with E. Vincent, in *Cinématographe* (Paris), July/August 1986.

On LESTER: books—

Rosenfeldt, Diane, *Richard Lester: A Guide to References and Resources*, Boston, 1978.

Sinyard, Neil, *The Films of Richard Lester*, London, 1985.

On LESTER: articles—

"Richard Lester," in the *New Yorker*, 28 October 1967.

Gelmis, Joseph, "Richard Lester," in *The Film Director as Superstar*, Garden City, New York, 1970.

Kantor, Bernard, and others, editors, "Richard Lester," in *Directors at Work*, New York, 1970.

McBride, Joseph, "Richard Lester," in *International Film Guide 1975*, London, 1974.

Monaco, James, "Some Late Clues to the Lester Direction," in *Film Comment* (New York), May 1974.

Armes, Roy, "The Return of Richard Lester," in *London Magazine*, December/January 1974/75.

Thomas, Bob, "Richard Lester: *Robin and Marian*," in *Action* (Los Angeles), November/December 1975.

Maillet, D., "Richard Lester," in *Cinématographe* (Paris), March 1977.

Lefèvre, R., "Richard Lester: Un odyssée en apesanteur," in *Revue du Cinéma* (Paris), February 1983.

"Richard Lester," in *Film Dope* (London), September 1986.

*   *   *

It is ironic that *A Hard Days Night*, the one film guaranteed to ensure Richard Lester his place in cinema history, should in many ways reflect his weaknesses rather than his strengths. If the film successfully captures the socio-historical phenomenon that was the Beatles at the beginning of their superstardom, it is as much due to Alun Owen's "day in the life" style script which provides the ideal complement to (and restraint on) Lester's anarchic mixture of absurd/surreal humour, accelerated motion, and cinema verité, to name but a few ingredients. Lester made a mark on cinema through his innovative utilisation of the techniques of television adverts and pop shows. His inability to entirely dispense with these methods, regardless of the subject matter to which they were applied, wrecked too many of his later projects.

The Knack stands as a supreme example of style (or styles) obliterating content. Bleached imagery, choruses of schoolboys reciting the litany of the "knack," disapproving members of the older generation talking to camera, seem randomly assembled to no apparent end. Worse is the lack of taste. Can the sight of Rita Tushingham running down a street crying "rape" to an assortment of indifferent individuals have ever seemed funny? *How I Won the War* fails along similar lines. Realistic battlefields and bloodshed clash with a ridiculous plot (soldiers sent to construct a cricket pitch on enemy territory) and characters who are peculiar rather than likeable. One does not doubt Lester's sincerity in his aim of making his audience ashamed of watching men die for their entertainment, but his lack of judgement is disconcerting. All this is a far cry from the skilfully orchestrated physical comedy of *A Funny Thing Happened on the Way to the Forum* or the opening section of *Superman III*, both free from a desire to preach.

Where Lester's major strength as a director lies is in his ability to produce personal works within the confines of an established genre, such as the swashbuckler (*The Three Musketeers/The Four Musketeers*), the western (*Butch and Sundance: The Early Days*) and fantasy (*Superman II*). If we wish to seek out underlying themes in his work these later films provide fertile ground (the mythical hero surrendering his power for human love in *Superman II*, Robin Hood attempting to regain his heroic status in a world no longer interested in heroes in *Robin and Marian*) while avoiding the collapse into uneasy self-importance or significance suffered by earlier work. Occasional lapses into heavy handedness (the priest blessing the cannons for use in a religious war while muttering to himself in Latin in *The Four Musketeers*, the overly bloody beating inflicted on the mortal Clark Kent in *Superman II*) can be discounted as minor flaws.

It is this talent for creating something original out of conventional material that gives Lester his distinction, rather than his misguided, if bold attempts at "serious" comedy (with all the accompanying cinematic tricks which ultimately produce only weariness in the viewer). Though it may seem paradoxical, Lester is a director who needs a firm foundation to work from before his imagination can be let loose.

—Daniel O'Brien

LEVINSON, Barry.

American. Born in Baltimore, Maryland, 1942. Studied Broadcast Journalism, American University, Washington, D.C. Comedy performer and writer, Los Angeles, from mid-1960s; writer for TV, including Carol Burnett Show and Marty Feldman Show, winning 3 Emmy awards, from 1970; directed first feature, *Diner*, 1982. Recipient: Oscar for Best Director, for *Rain Man*, 1988. Agent: Creative Artists Agency, 1888 Century Park East, Suite 1400, Los Angeles, CA 90067, U.S.A.

Films as Director and Scriptwriter:

1982   *Diner*
1984   *The Natural*
1985   *Young Sherlock Holmes*
1987   *Tin Men*; *Good Morning, Vietnam*
1988   *Rain Man*
1990   *Avalon*

Other Films:

1974   *Street Girls* (Miller) (co-sc, asst ph)
1976   *Silent Movie* (Brooks) (co-sc, role as Executive)
1978   *High Anxiety* (Brooks) (co-sc, role as bellhop)
1979   *. . . And Justice For All* (Jewison) (co-sc)
1980   *Inside Moves* (Donner) (co-sc)
1981   *History of the World, Part 1* (Brooks) (role as column salesman)
1982   *Best Friends* (Jewison) (co-sc)
1984   *Unfaithfully Yours* (Zieff) (co-sc)

Publications:

By LEVINSON: articles—

Interview with Stephen Farber, in *New York Times*, 18 April 1982.
Interview with R. Ward, in *American Film* (Washington, D.C.), June 1982.
Interview in *Inter/View* (New York), July 1984.
Interview in *Screen International* (London), 27 October 1984.
Interview with M. Cieutat and G. Gressard, in *Positif* (Paris), March 1989.
Interview with Alex Ward, in *New York Times Magazine*, 11 March 1990.

On LEVINSON: articles—

"Barry Levinson," in *Film Dope* (London), September 1986.

*   *   *

Although his most lucrative Oscar-winning film *Rain Man* was set in conservative Cincinnati, Los Angeles, Las Vegas, and several points in between, Barry Levinson has never forgotten his roots and is still regarded by Marylanders as the ultimate Baltimore filmmaker. *Diner*, the film that launched his directing career in 1982, was based in the Baltimore suburb of Forest Park, where he grew up. So was *Tin Men*, made five years later. And in 1989, at the age of 47, following the success of *Rain Man* and *Good Morning, Vietnam*, Levinson was back again in Baltimore, to the delight of the Maryland Film Commission, shooting *Avalon*.

It could not have been otherwise, since *Avalon* is based upon Levinson's own family immigrating to Baltimore from Russia in 1914. Baltimore is his city and his most personal films have focussed upon ordinary people he might have met there growing up during the 1940s and 1950s—the youngsters of *Diner*, the aluminum siding hucksters of *Tin Men*. Levinson has internalized the values of middle-America and has succeeded most brilliantly when filming stories about characters who live by those values.

If some of the critics were disturbed that Robert Redford's Roy Hobbs was not as seriously flawed as the original character in Bernard Malamud's *The Natural*, it is perhaps because Levinson's interpretation of the character is governed by assumptions different from Malamud's and that Levinson's orientation is decidedly more optimistic. The fidelity of Levinson's *The Natural* can be and has been challenged on pedantic grounds. The film might better be regarded not as an adaptation, but as an interpretation that will stand on its own, regardless of its source.

Barry Levinson told the *New York Times Magazine* (11 March 1990) that he does not consider himself as a writer or a "writer-director." As Alex Ward rightly suggested, however, Levinson can be considered an American *auteur* who will leave his personal imprint on any project he touches, through sentimental touches (in *The Natural* or *Tin Men*, for example), quirky casting, or inspired comedic improvisation. He has an unfailing sense of what might constitute the right touch in a given dramatic situation. "I don't like other people directing what I write," Levinson told Ward, "but I don't mind directing something somebody else wrote."

In fact, after moving to the West Coast from American University in Washington, Levinson worked for over two years as a writer for Mel Brooks on two pictures, *Silent Movie* and *High Anxiety* (also making his screen debut as an insane bellhop in the *Psycho* parody scene). While working with Brooks on *High Anxiety* he first met Mark Johnson, who later became the Executive Producer of *Diner*. At that point Levinson had already won three Emmy Awards for his network television writing with "The Tim Conway Show" and "The Carol Burnett Show."

Levinson collaborated with Valerie Curtin (whom he met at the Comedy Store in Los Angeles) on two feature film scripts, *. . . And Justice for All* (for Norman Jewison) and *Inside Moves* (for Richard Donner), before writing the script for *Diner*, his debut film as director, about young men "hanging out" in Baltimore over Christmas of 1959, one of them (Steve Guttenberg) enjoying his last days of bachelorhood before getting married. Mel Brooks told him that the script idea resembled *I vitelloni*, but Levinson had not even seen Fellini's film. Levinson told Stephen Farber of the *New York Times* (18 April 1982) that the Guttenberg character was based upon his cousin Eddie, who "loved fried bologna sandwiches" and "slept until 2:30 in the afternoon." The cast also featured Mickey Rourke and talented newcomers Kevin Bacon and Ellen Barkin. It was the lowest-budgeted "sleeper" produced by MGM that year. It started slow after being reviewed in *Rolling Stone* and *The New Yorker*, then gradually built a following and staying power. (The president for distribution at MGM/UA referred to it as "Lazarus.") Vincent Canby in the *New York Times* called it the "happiest surprise of the year to date," and Levinson was "discovered."

Levinson also collaborated with Valerie Curtin in writing *Best Friends* (starring Burt Reynolds and Goldie Hawn) and a remake of the Preston Sturges classic *Unfaithfully Yours*. The screenplay for *. . . And Justice for All* meanwhile was nominated for an Academy Award, demonstrating the quality of the Levinson-Curtin team. Levinson also directed the high-spirited fantasy *Young Sherlock Holmes*, but aside, perhaps, from *Rain Man* and *The Natural*, Levinson will best be remembered for his Baltimore pictures, drawn from his own experience and marked with his own special brand of compassionate humor and nostalgia. As a personal filmmaker he is perhaps the nearest American equivalent to François Truffaut.

—James M. Welsh

LEWIS, Jerry.

American. Born Joseph Levitch in Newark, New Jersey, 16 March 1926. Educated at Irvington High School, New Jersey, through 10th grade. Married 1) singer Patti Palmer, 1944, five sons; 2) Sandra Pitnick, 1983. Stage debut in 1931; develops comic routines and attracts Irving Kaye as manager, 1942; began working with Dean Martin at Atlantic City club, 1946; with Martin, signed by Hal Wallis for Paramount, 1948; acted in first feature, also founded production company to direct series of pastiches of Hollywood films (later Jerry Lewis Productions), 1949; Chairman of Muscular Dystrophy Association of America, raising funds from annual telethons, from 1952; started solo career, 1956; signed seven year contract with Paramount-York, 1959; after abandonment of *The Day the Clown Cried*, left films for eight years, 1972. Recipient: Commander of the Order of Arts and Letters, and Commander of the Legion of Honour, France, 1984. Address: c/o Jerry Lewis Films, Inc., 1888 Century Park East, Suite 830, Los Angeles, CA 90067, U.S.A.

Films as Director: (partial list)

1949　*Fairfax Avenue* (short pastiche of *Sunset Boulevard*); *A Spot in the Shade* (short pastiche of *A Place in the Sun*); *Watch on the Lime* (pastiche); *Come Back, Little Shicksa* (pastiche); *Son of Lifeboat* (pastiche); *The Re-Inforcer* (pastiche); *Son of Spellbound* (pastiche); *Melvin's Revenge* (pastiche); *I Should Have Stood in Bedlam* (pastiche of *From Here to Eternity*); *The Whistler* (pastiche)
1960　*The Bellboy* (+ sc, pr, role as Stanley)
1961　*The Ladies' Man* (+ sc, pr, roles as Herbert H. Heebert and his mother Mrs. Heebert); *The Errand Boy* (+ sc, role as Morty S. Tachman)
1963　**The Nutty Professor** (+ sc, roles as Julius F. Kelp and Buddy Love)
1964　*The Patsy* (+ sc, role as Stanley Belt)
1965　*The Family Jewels* (+ pr, sc, roles as Willard Woodward, Uncle James Peyton, Uncle Eddie Peyton, Uncle Julius Peyton, Uncle Shylock Peyton, Uncle Bugs Peyton)
1966　*Three on a Couch* (+ pr, + roles as Christopher Prise, Warren, Ringo Raintree, Rutherford, Heather)
1967　*The Big Mouth* (+ pr, sc, roles as Gerald Clamson, Sid Valentine)
1970　*One More Time*; *Which Way to the Front?* (+ pr, roles as Brendan Byers III, Kesselring)
1972　*The Day the Clown Cried* (+ principal actor) (not completed)
1980　*Hardly Working* (+ sc, principal actor)
1982　*Smorgasbord* (+ sc, principal actor)

Other Films:

1949　*My Friend Irma* (Marshall) (role as Seymour)
1950　*My Friend Irma Goes West* (Walker) (role as Seymour)
1951　*At War with the Army* (Walker) (role as Soldier Korwin); *That's My Boy* (Walker) (role as "Junior" Jackson)
1952　*Sailor Beware* (Walker) (role as Melvin Jones); *Jumping Jacks* (Taurog) (role as Hap Smith)
1953　*The Stooge* (Taurog) (role as Ted Rogers); *Scared Stiff* (Marshall) (role as Myron Myron Mertz); *The Caddy* (Taurog) (role as Harvey Miller)
1954　*Money from Home* (Marshall) (role as Virgil Yokum); *Living It Up* (Taurog) (role as Homer Flagg); *Three Ring Circus* (Pevney) (role as Jerry Hotchkiss)
1955　*You're Never Too Young* (Taurog) (role as Wilbur Hoolick); *Artists and Models* (Tashlin) (role as Eugene Fullstack)
1956　*Pardners* (Taurog) (role as Wade Kingsley Jr.); *Hollywood or Bust* (Tashlin) (role as Malcolm Smith)
1957　*The Delicate Delinquent* (McGuire) (role as Sidney Pythias, pr); *The Sad Sack* (Marshall) (role as Meredith T. Bixby); *The Geisha Boy* (Tashlin) (pr, role as Gilbert Wooley)

1958　*Rock-a-Bye Baby* (Tashlin) (pr, role as Clayton Poole)
1959　*Don't Give Up the Ship* (Taurog) (role as John Paul Steckley VII)
1960　*Visit to a Small Planet* (Taurog) (role as Kreton); *Cinderfella* (Tashlin) (pr, role as Fella); *Li'l Abner* (Frank) (brief appearance)
1962　*It's Only Money* (Tashlin) (role as Lester March)
1963　*It's a Mad, Mad, Mad, Mad World* (Kramer) (role as man who drives over Culpepper's hat); *Who's Minding the Store?* (Tashlin) (role as Raymond Phiffier)
1964　*The Disorderly Orderly* (Tashlin) (role as Jerome Littlefield)
1965　*Boeing Boeing* (Rich) (role as Robert Reed)
1966　*Way Way Out* (Douglas) (role as Peter Matamore)
1967　*Don't Raise the Bridge, Lower the River* (Paris), (role as George Lester)
1969　*Hook, Line and Sinker* (Marshall) (pr, role as Peter Ingersoll alias Dobbs)
1982　*The King of Comedy* (Scorsese) (role as Jerry Langford); *Slapstick* (Paul) (role)

Publications:

By LEWIS: book—

The Total Film-Maker, New York, 1971.

By LEWIS: articles—

"Mr. Lewis is a Pussycat," interview with Peter Bogdanovich, in *Esquire* (New York), November 1962.
"America's Uncle: Interview with Jerry Lewis," with Axel Madsen, in *Cahiers du Cinéma in English* (New York), no.4, 1966.
Interview, in *Directors at Work* edited by Bernard Kantor and others, New York, 1970.
"Five Happy Moments," in *Esquire* (New York), December 1970.
"Dialogue on Film: Jerry Lewis," in *American Film* (Washington, D.C.), September 1977.
Interview with D. Rabourdin, in *Cinéma* (Paris), April 1980.
Interview with Serge Daney, in *Cahiers du Cinéma* (Paris), May 1983.

On LEWIS: books—

Gehman, Richard, *That Kid—The Story of Jerry Lewis*, New York, 1964.
Maltin, Leonard, *Movie Comedy Teams*, New York, 1970.
Marx, Arthur, *Everybody Loves Somebody Sometime (Especially Himself): The Story of Dean Martin and Jerry Lewis*, New York, 1974.
Marchesini, Mauro, *Jerry Lewis: Un comico a perdere*, Verona, 1983.

On LEWIS: articles—

Farson, Daniel, "Funny Men: Dean Martin and Jerry Lewis," in *Sight and Sound* (London), July/September 1952.
Kass, Robert, "Jerry Lewis Analyzed," in *Films in Review* (New York), March 1953.
Hume, Rod, "Martin and Lewis—Are Their Critics Wrong?," in *Films and Filming* (London), March 1956.
Taylor, John, "Jerry Lewis," in *Sight and Sound* (London), Spring 1965.
Sarris, Andrew, "Editor's Eyrie," in *Cahiers du Cinema in English* (New York), no.4, 1966.
Schickel, Richard, "Jerry Lewis Retrieves a Lost Ideal," in *Life* (New York), 15 July 1966.
Camper, Fred, "Essays in Visual Style," in *Cinema* (London), no.8, 1971.
Vialle, G., and others, "Jerry Lewis," in *Image et Son* (Paris), no. 278, 1973.
Coursodon, J.-P., "Jerry Lewis's Films: No Laughing Matter?," in *Film Comment* (New York), July/August 1975.
LeBour, F., and R. DeLaroche, "Which Way to Jerry Lewis?," in *Ecran* (Paris), July 1976.
Shearer, H., "Telethon," in *Film Comment* (New York), May/June 1979.
McGilligan, P., "Recycling Jerry Lewis," in *American Film* (Washington, D.C.), September 1979.
Jerry Lewis Section of *Casablanca* (Madrid), June 1983.

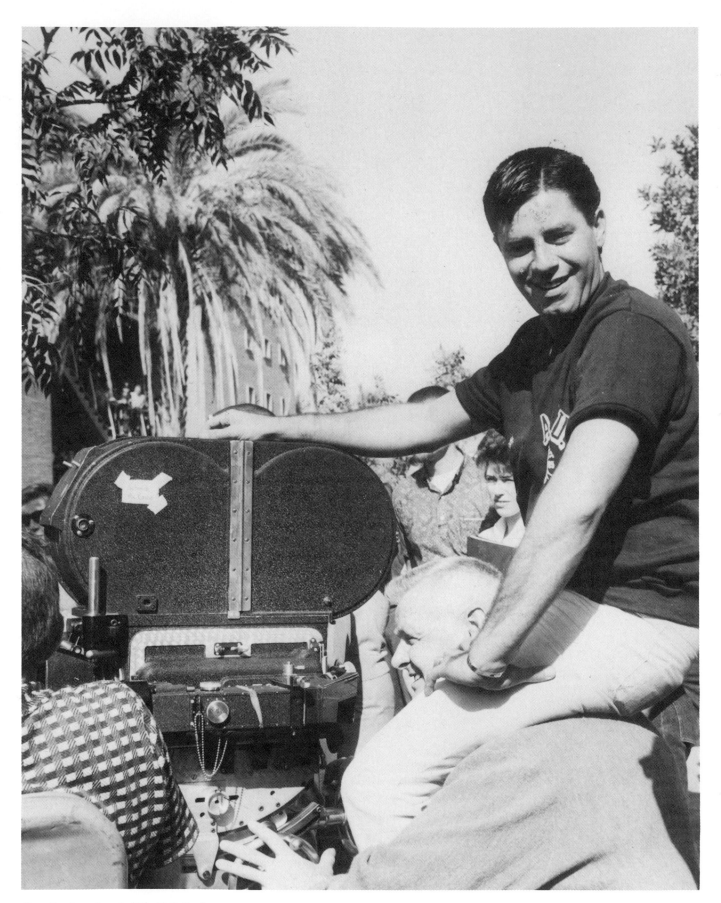

Jerry Lewis on the set of *The Nutty Professor*

Polan, Dana, "Being and Nuttiness: Jerry Lewis and the French," in *Journal of Popular Film and Television* (Washington, D.C.), Spring 1984.

Liebman, R.L., "Rabbis or Rakes, Schlemiels or Supermen? Jewish Identity in Charles Chaplin, Jerry Lewis and Woody Allen," in *Literature/Film Quarterly* (Salisbury, Maryland), vol. 12, no. 3, July 1984.

"Jerry Lewis," in *Film Dope* (London), September 1986.

Beynaud, B., "Qui a peur de Jerry Lewis? Pas nous, pas nous," in *Cahiers du Cinéma* (Paris), February 1989.

*   *   *

In France, Jerry Lewis is called "Le Roi de Crazy" and adulated as a genius by filmmakers as respectable as Alain Resnais, Jean-Luc Godard, and Claude Chabrol. In America, Jerry Lewis is still an embarrassing and unexplained paradox, often ridiculed, awaiting a persuasive critical champion. This incredible gulf can in part be explained by American access, on television talk shows and Lewis's annual muscular dystrophy telethon, to Lewis's contradictory public persona: egotistical yet insecure, insulting yet sentimental, juvenile yet adult, emotionally naked yet defensive. Were not the real Lewis apparently so hard to love, the celluloid Lewis might be loved all the more. And yet a Lewis cult thrives among American cinephiles; and certainly *The Bellboy, The Errand Boy, The Nutty Professor* and *Which Way To The Front?* appear today to be among the most interesting and ambitious American films of the 1960s.

Lewis's career can be divided into four periods: first, the partnership with singer Dean Martin which resulted in a successful nightclub act and popular series of comedies, including *My Friend Irma* and *At War with the Army*, as well as several highly-regarded films directed by former cartoonist and Lewis mentor, Frank Tashlin; second, (after professional and personal tensions fueled by Lewis's artistic ambitions irrevocably destroyed the partnership) an apprenticeship as a solo comedy star, beginning with *The Delicate Delinquent* and continuing through Tashlin's *Cinderfella*; third, the period as the self-professed "total filmmaker," inaugurated in 1960 with *The Bellboy* and followed by a decade of Lewis films directed by and starring Lewis which attracted the attention of auteurist critics in France and overwhelming box-office response in America, culminating with a string of well-publicized financial failures, including *Which Way to the Front?* and the unreleased, near-mythical *The Day the Clown Cried*, in which clown Lewis leads Jewish children to Nazi ovens; and finally, the period as valorized, if martyred auteur, exemplified by Lewis's work as an actor in Martin Scorsese's *The King of Comedy* and Lewis's sporadic, unsuccessful attempts to reestablish his own directorial career.

Lewis's appeal is significantly rooted in the American silent film tradition of the individual comedian: like Chaplin, Lewis is interested in pathos and sentiment; like Keaton, Lewis is fascinated by the comic gag which could only exist on celluloid; like Harry Langdon, Lewis exhibits, within an adult persona, childish behavior which is often disturbing and embarrassing; like Stan Laurel, whose first name Lewis adopts as an *hommage* in several of his films, Lewis is the lovable innocent often endowed with almost magical qualities. What Lewis brings uniquely to this tradition, however, is his obsession with the concept of the schizophrenic self; his typical cinema character has so many anxieties and tensions that it must take on other personalities in order to survive. Often, the schizophrenia becomes overtly autobiographical, with the innocent, gawky kid escaping his stigmatized existence by literally becoming "Jerry Lewis," beloved and successful comedian (as in *The Bellboy* and *The Errand Boy*) or romantic leading man, perhaps representing the now absent Dean Martin (as in *The Nutty Profes-*

sor). Jerry Lewis's physical presence on screen in his idiot persona emphasizes movement disorders in a way which relates provocatively to his highly publicized work for the Muscular Dystrophy Association. Schizophrenia is compounded in *The Family Jewels*: what Jean-Pierre Coursodon calls Lewis's "yearning for self-obliteration" is manifested in seven distinct personalities. Ultimately, Lewis escapes by turning himself into his cinema, as evidenced by the credits in his failed comeback film, which proudly announce: "Jerry Lewis is . . . *Hardly Working*." This element of cinematic escape and schizophrenia is especially valued by the French who politicize it as a manifestation of the human condition as influenced by American capitalism.

Much must also be said about the strong avant-garde qualities to Lewis's work: his interest in surrealism; his experimentalism and fascination with self-conscious stylistic devices; his movement away from conventional gags toward structures apparently purposely deformed; his interest in plotlessness and ellipsis; the reflexivity of his narrative; his studied use of extended silence and gibberish in a sound cinema; the ambiguous sexual subtext of his work; and finally, his use of film as personal revelation in a tradition which ultimately recalls Maya Deren and Stan Brakhage more than Chaplin and Keaton. Perhaps only Lewis's death will allow any definitive American evaluation of his substantial career.

—Charles Derry

LEWIS, Joseph H.

American. Born in New York, 6 April 1907 (other sources say 1900). Educated at De Witt Clinton High School. Served in U.S. Army Signal Corps, 1943–44. Brother of MGM editor Ben Lewis. Camera boy at MGM, 1926; editor and director of title sequences at Mascot studio (became Republic, 1935), 1930s; director, from 1937; director in charge of second units at Universal and Republic, 1940s; TV director, from late 1950s; subject of retrospective, Edinburgh Film Festival, 1980.

Films as Director:

1937   *Navy Spy* (co-d); *Courage of the West; Singing Outlaw*
1938   *The Spy Ring (International Spy); Border Wolves; Last Stand*
1939   *Two Fisted Rangers (Forestalled)*
1940   *Blazing Six Shooters (Stolen Wealth); The Man from Tumbleweeds; Texas Stagecoach (Two Roads); The Return of Wild Bill (False Evidence); Boys of the City; That Gang of Mine; Pride of the Bowery (Here We Go Again)*
1941   *Invisible Ghost; Criminals Within; Arizona Cyclone; The Mad Doctor of Market Street*
1942   *Bombs Over Burma* (+ co-sc); *The Silver Bullet; Boss of Hangtown Mesa*
1943   *Secret of a Co-ed (Silent Witness)*
1944   *Minstrel Man*
1945   *The Falcon in San Francisco; My Name is Julia Ross*
1946   *So Dark the Night*
1947   *The Swordsman*
1948   *The Return of October (Date with Destiny)*
1949   *Undercover Man; Gun Crazy (Deadly as the Female)*
1950   *A Lady Without Passport*
1952   *Retreat, Hell!; Desperate Search*
1953   *Cry of the Hunted*
1954   *The Big Combo*
1955   *Man on a Bus; A Lawless Street*

1956 *7th Cavalry*
1957 *The Halliday Brand*
1958 *Terror in a Texas Town*

Other Films:

1934 *In Old Santa Fe* (Howard) (sup ed)
1935 *Behind the Green Lights* (Cabanne) (ed); *The Miracle Rider* (Eason and Shaefer) (ed); *One Frightened Night* (Cabanne) (ed); *The Headline Woman* (*The Woman in the Case*) (Nigh) (ed); *Ladies Crave Excitement* (Grindé) (ed); *The Adventures of Rex and Rinty* (Eason and Beebe); *Harmony Lane* (Santley) (sup ed); *Streamline Express* (Fields) (ed); *Waterfront Lady* (Santley) (sup ed); *Confidential* (Cahn) (sup ed); *$1000 a Minute* (Scotto) (sup ed)
1936 *Hitch Hike Lady* (*Eventful Journey*) (Scotto) (sup ed); *The Leavenworth Case* (Collins) (sup ed); *Darkest Africa* (*Hidden City*) (Eason and Kane) (sup ed); *The House of a Thousand Candles* (Lubin) (sup ed); *Laughing Irish Eyes* (Santley) (sup ed); *The Harvester* (Santley) (sup ed); *Undersea Kingdom* (Eason and Kane) (sup ed); *The Devil on Horseback* (Wilbur) (ed)
1946 *The Jolson Story* (Green) (d production numbers)
1953 *The Naked Jungle* (Haskin) (begun by Lewis)

Publications:

By LEWIS: articles—

Interview with L. Ruhmann, and others, in *Velvet Light Trap* (Madison, Wisconsin), Summer 1983.

On LEWIS: books—

Sarris, Andrew, *The American Cinema*, New York, 1968.
Flynn, C., and T. McCarthy, *Kings of the Bs*, New York, 1975.
Shadoian, Jack, *Dreams and Dead Ends*, Cambridge, Massachusetts, 1977.
Silver, Alain, and Elizabeth Ward, *Film Noir*, New York, 1979.
Wicking, C., *The American Vein*, New York, 1979.

On LEWIS: articles—

Anderson, Lindsay, "*Gun Crazy*,"in *Sequence* (London), Autumn 1950.
Flinn, T., "*The Big Heat* and *The Big Combo*," in *Velvet Light Trap* (Madison, Wisconsin), no. 11, 1974.
Bogdanovich, Peter, Paul Schrader, and others, in *Cinema* (Los Angeles), Fall 1971.
Lewis Section of *Positif* (Paris), July/August 1975.
Lewis Sections of *Monthly Film Bulletin* (London), March and April 1980.
Pulleine, Tim, "Joseph Lewis," in *Films and Filming* (London), October 1983.
Sattin, R., "Joseph H. Lewis: Assessing an (Occasionally) Brilliant Career," in *American Classic Screen*, November/December 1983.
Kerr, Paul, "My name is Joseph H. Lewis," in *Screen* (London), July/October 1983, also January/February 1984.
Hunter, Allan, "Joseph H. Lewis at the NFT," in *Films and Filming* (London), September 1985.
Tesson, Charles, "Joseph Lewis ou la loi du genre," and "*Get Me a Gun*," in *Cahiers du Cinéma* (Paris), November 1985 and January 1986.
"Joseph H. Lewis," in *Film Dope* (London), September 1986.

*   *   *

Joseph H. Lewis simultaneously supports and confounds the critical methodology of authorship. His 41 features in 21 years provide enough examples of strong visual creativity, originality, and intelligence under the severe budgetary constraints of B film production to warrant bestowing the title "auteur." Yet, banal scripts, meager production values, and unaccomplished actors, seem to deny him the opportunity to articulate a "consistent world view," reducing Lewis to a "metteur en scene." This dichotomy between a recognizable (if inconsistent) personal style and a lack of personally revealing (or expressive) thematic content forms the core of the Lewis debate.

Lewis labored for many studios adapting to many genres,

but began his best work while at Columbia after World War II. In 1945 and 1946, he directed *My Name is Julia Ross* and *So Dark the Night*, *films noirs* which precipitated his first important critical recognition. Until 1955, with a few exceptions, he continued surveying *film noir*, directing *Undercover Man, A Lady Without Passport*, and the *noir*-influenced *Desperate Search* and *Cry of the Hunted*, culminating his fluency in the genre with two "undisputed masterpieces," *Gun Crazy* and *The Big Combo*. The critical favor awarded these films, and their eventual cult status, pushes Lewis into an intimate association with *film noir*, even though he directed many more Westerns.

His *films noir*, like his other films, were co-features or B movies slotted for the second half of a double bill. Typically based on weak scripts with witless dialogue, running under 90 minutes (many under 75), and receiving little distribution marketing, they were shot in less than 2 or 3 weeks, with miniscule budgets, on inexpensive black and white film stock, without stars or accomplished actors, using a few minimal sets or locations, and without rehearsed crowd scenes. These limitations functioned as a catalyst for his ingenuity. Improvising practical solutions to production limitations, Lewis devised a complex and unique visual style—a combination of Bresson and Ophuls—upon which his reputation and signature rest. His films emphasize images, employing low key lighting, high contrast, location shooting, long takes, camera movement, great depth of focus with dominating foreground objects, choreographed violence and sexuality, montage, off-screen action, sound manipulation, and a reduction of dialogue to a minimum. The employ of each aspect ultimately accommodates a dual purpose: economic and aesthetic.

The use of low key lighting served three practical economic purposes associated with B movie making (it cost less than high key lighting; it allowed the construction of only partial sets; it concealed meager production values) while also serving a vital aesthetic purpose (it provided a striking visual style differentiating film noir from other genres). High contrast images resulted from the use of cheap black & white film stocks, yet underscored the visual play of blinding light cutting through opaque darkness. Location shooting reduced the dependence on sets and sound stage work while evoking a gritty urban realism. The combination of exceptionally long takes, great depth of focus with dominating foreground objects, and camera movement reduced shooting schedules and post-production expenses. They also added a documentary "time" and "atmosphere" to the realism of the films. The depiction of violence and sexuality through montage, off-screen space, and sound manipulation suggested events and locations that needed neither complete performance nor extensive construction, intensified their effect on the spectator, and circumvented the Production Code. The reduction of dialogue hid the limited acting skills of his performers and returned the emphasis of his films to the visual. Examples of the combined utilization of these techniques include: the celebrated 4-minute Hampton robbery one-take and the Armour robbery sequence in *Gun Crazy*; the torture by hearing-aid, the "kissing" shot, and the climax in *The Big Combo*; the report of the girl's death in *So Dark the Night*; and Rocco's assassination in *Undercover Man*. In other words, due to economic factors, Lewis's *films noirs* represent the genre reduced to its visual essence.

Lewis's visual style stands without question. Whether or not this textual surface supports a consistent thematic content initiates a heated debate. Is he, as Richard Combs claims, "a stylistic authority operating in a vacuum," or as Richard Sattin explains, someone with visual intelligence and style who doesn't recognize the need for theme? Or is he, as Andrew Sarris states in Lewis's description under "Expressive Esoterica," a "somber personality revealed through a complex visual style?" Traditional analyses see his films betraying efforts to construct thematic coherence because their pleasure exists only as complex textual surfaces. More recent approaches can note the pleasure of his films' complex textual surfaces precisely activating the thematic concerns of *film noir* as well as inaugurating a disturbing and fascinating exploration of Existentialism.

The primacy of textual surface derived from the economic limitations of B movie making denies Lewis the luxury of psychologizing characters, character motivation, and events. Consequently, behavior finds its truest and clearest (and only) expression in action. Action is readily observable and objectively presentable as "pure" textuality. The accent on action as textual surface offers no judgement on or explanation of existence, only description. The world described is Existential, devoid of logic, justice, and order. Events happen with little explanation, meaning, or consequence. Life is only the sum of actions lived. No moral code, except self-preservation and hedonism, prevails. Human love seems elusive, banal, and empty; often only a catalyst for thrill-seeking, crime, and transient pleasures. One can do anything one wants because nothing matters—a liberating and exciting potential.

Lewis approached these Existential themes by eliding individual identity with social action. Action is identity; one expresses self and emotion through action. Survival in an evil world depends upon self-preservation and emotional detachment; one either hunts or is hunted. Love exists only as *l'amour fou*; obsessive and ultimately destructive. Family may offer temporary sanctuary, but it cannot withstand the onslaught of meaningless action. These themes find their sharpest focus in Lewis's masterpieces, *Gun Crazy* and *The Big Combo*, but appear in all his *films noirs* and his late Westerns (*A Lawless Street, The Halliday Brand*, and *Terror in a Texas Town*).

Lewis's film career ended in 1958, coinciding with the death of "classical" *film noir*. His intensification and fusing of textuality and Existentialism within the genre pushed *film noir* to its logical extreme. His work, however, influenced a budding French movement, the Nouvelle Vague (A comparison between *Gun Crazy* and its focus on *l'amour fou* and Godard's *A bout de souffle* and *Pierrot le fou* would prove an interesting study), and may even stand as the base for today's technologically driven and production design oriented action-adventure films.

—Greg S. Faller

L'HERBIER, Marcel.

French. Born in Paris, 23 April 1888. Educated at Lycée Voltaire, Sainte-Marie de Monceau; University of Paris. Served with Service Auxiliaire, 1914–17, and with Section Cinématographique de l'Armée, 1917–18. Scriptwriter, from 1917; directed first film, *Rose-France*, 1918; organized Cinégraphic production company, 1922; secretary general of Association des Auteurs de Films, 1929; co-founder, Cinémathèque Française, 1936; co-founder (1937) then President, Syndicat des Techniciens, from 1938; founder and President of Institut des Hautes Etudes Cinématographiques (IDHEC), French film school, 1943; President of Comité de Défense du Cinéma Français, 1947; producer for TV, 1952–62. Recipient: Commandeur de Légion d'Honneur et des Arts et Lettres. *Died 26 November 1979.*

Films as Director:

1918   *Phantasmes* (+ sc) (incomplete); *Rose-France* (+ sc)
1919   *Le Bercail* (+ sc); *Le Carnaval des vérités* (+ sc)
1920   *L'Homme du large* (+ sc); *Villa Destin* (+ sc)
1921   *El Dorado* (+ sc); *Prométhée . . . banquier*
1922   *Don Juan et Faust* (+ sc)
1923   *Résurrection* (+ sc) (incomplete)
1924   *L'Inhumaine* (*The New Enchantment*) (+ co-sc)
1925   ***Feu Mathias Pascal*** (***The Late Mathias Pascal***) (+ sc)
1926   *Le Vertige* (+ sc)
1927   *Le Diable au coeur* (*L'Ex-Voto*) (+ sc)
1928   *Nuits de Prince* (+ sc)
1929   ***L'Argent*** (+ sc); *L'Enfant de l'amour* (+ sc)
1930   *La Femme d'une nuit* (*La donna d'una notte*) (+ sc); *La Mystère de la chambre jaune* (+ sc)
1931   *Le Parfum de la dame en noir* (+ sc)
1933   *L'Epervier* (*Les Amoureux. Bird of Prey*) (+ sc)
1934   *Le Scandale*; *L'Aventurier* (+ sc); *Le Bonheur* (+ sc)
1935   *La Route impériale* (+ sc); *Veille d'armes* (*Sacrifice d'honneur*) (+ co-sc)
1936   *Les Hommes nouveux* (+ sc); *La Porte du large* (*The Great Temptation*) (+ sc); *Nuits de feu* (*The Living Corpse*) (+ co-sc)
1937   *La Citadelle du silence*) (*The Citadel of Silence*) (+ sc); *Forfaiture* (+ sc)
1938   *La Tragédie impériale* (*Rasputin*) (+ sc); *Adrienne Lecouvreur*; *Terre de feu*; *La Brigade sauvage* (*Savage Brigade*) (completed by J. Dreville)
1939   *Entente cordiale*; *Children's Corner* (short); *La Mode rêvée* (short) (+ sc)
1940   *La Comédie du bonheur* (+ sc)
1941   *Histoire de rire* (*Foolish Husbands*)
1942   *La Nuit fantastique*; *L'Honorable Catherine*
1943   *La Vie de Bohême*
1945   *Au petit bonheur*
1946   *L'Affaire du collier de la Reine* (*The Queen's Necklace*)
1947   *La Révoltée* (*Stolen Affections*) (+ sc)
1948   *Les Derniers Jours de Pompéi* (*The Last Days of Pompeii*) (+ co-sc)
1953   *Le Pére de mademoiselle* (co-d)
1963   *Hommage à Debussy* (short)
1967   *Le Cinéma du diable* (anthology film)

Other Films:

1917   *Le Torrent* (Hervil) (sc); *Bouclette* (*L'Ange de minuit*) (Mercanton and Hervil) (sc)
1932   *Le Martyre de l'Obèse* (Chenal) (supervisor)
1933   *La Bataille* (Farkas) (supervisor)
1938   *Terra di fuoco* (Ferroni) (Italian version of *Terre de feu*) (supervisor)
1943   *Le Loup des Malveneur* (Radot) (supervisor)
1947   *Une Grande Fille tout simple* (Manuel) (supervisor)

Publications:

By L'HERBIER: books—

Au jardin des jeux secrets, Paris, 1914.
L'Enfantement du mort, Paris, 1917.
Intelligence du cinématographe (anthology), Paris, 1947 (revised 1977).
La Tête qui tourne, Paris, 1979.

By L'HERBIER: articles—

Interview, in *Cahiers du Cinéma* (Paris), no.202, 1968.
Interview with J. Fieschi and others, in *Cinématographe* (Paris), no. 40, 1978.
"Un Cinéaste . . . ," in *Avant-Scène du Cinéma* (Paris), 1 January 1980.
Interview, in *Cinémagazine*, reprinted in *Avant-Scène du Cinéma* (Paris), 15 October 1981.

Marcel L'Herbier: *L'Inhumaine*

On L'HERBIER: books—

Jaque-Catelain présente Marcel L'Herbier, Paris, 1950.
Burch, Noël, *Marcel L'Herbier*, Paris, 1973.
Hommage à Marcel L'Herbier en cinq films de l'art muet, brochure for retrospective, Paris, 1975.
Brossard, Jean-Pierre, editor, *Marcel L'Herbier et son temps*, La Chaux-de-Fonds, Switzerland, 1980.
Canosa, Michele, *Marcel L'Herbier*, Parma, 1985.

On L'HERBIER: articles—

"The Big Screens," in *Sight and Sound* (London), Spring 1955.
Roud, Richard, "Memories of Resnais," in *Sight and Sound* (London), Summer 1969.
Blumer, R.H., "The Camera as Snowball: France 1918–1927," in *Cinema Journal* (Evanston), Spring 1970.
Article on five films of L'Herbier, in *Ecran* (Paris), no.43, 1976.
"L'Herbier Issue" of *Avant-Scène du Cinéma* (Paris), 1 June 1978.
Trosa, S., "Archeologie du cinéma," in *Cinématographe* (Paris), December 1978.
Obituary, in *New York Times*, 28 November 1979.
Fieschi, J., "Marcel L'Herbier," in *Cinématographe* (Paris), December 1979.
Obituary, in *Image et Son* (Paris), January 1980.
"Marcel L'Herbier," in *Film Dope* (London), September 1986.

*   *   *

Marcel L'Herbier was one of the most prominent members of the French 1920s avant-garde. His direct involvement with film-making extended into the 1950s and he made important contributions to the organization of the industry, to the foundation of the film school, the IDHEC, and to early television drama.

Like so many of his generation he turned to cinema after an early enthusiasm for literature and the theatre, and in his case it was Cecil B. DeMille's *The Cheat* with Sessue Hayakawa which opened his eyes to the unrealized potential of the new medium. He came to prominence in the years 1919–22 with a series of films made for Léon Gaumont's "Pax" series. Among the half-dozen films made for Gaumont, two at least stand out as artistic and commercial successes: *L'Homme du large*, a melodrama shot partly on location on the Brittany coast, where the director's interest in visual effects and symbolism is very apparent, and *El Dorado*, a Spanish drama in which L'Herbier's use of cinema to convey the mental and psychological states of characters finds perfect expression. *El Dorado* achieved a success to match that of Gance's *La Roue* the following year.

Difficulties with Gaumont over the production of the ambitious *Don Juan et Faust* led L'Herbier to set up his own company, Cinégraphic, in 1922. He was able to assist the debuts of young filmmakers such as Jaque Catelain and Claude Autant-Lara as well as produce the last film of Louis Delluc, *L'Inondation*. His own films were made largely in co-production and ranged widely in style and approach. The celebrated but controversial *L'Inhumaine*, partly financed by its star the singer Georgette Leblanc, aimed to offer a mosaic of the decorative modern art of 1925, with sets produced by four very individual designers, including Fernand Léger and Robert Mallet-Stevens. In total contrast, *Feu Matthias Pascal* was essentially an experiment with complex narrative structures, co-produced with the Albatros company which had been set up by Russian exiles and starring the great silent actor, Ivan Mosjoukine. L'Herbier's eclectic approach and love of juxtapositions are very apparent in these films, together with his immense visual refinement. After a couple of commercial works he made his silent masterpiece, an updating of Zola's *L'Argent* in 1929. Inspired by the scope of Gance's *Napoléon*, L'Herbier created a strikingly modern work marked by its opulent, oversized sets and a complex, multi-camera shooting style.

L'Herbier was in no way hostile to the coming of sound, but despite a pair of interesting adaptations of comic thrillers by Gaston Leroux, *Le Mystére de la chambre jaune* and *Le Parfum de la dame en noir*, L'Herbier was largely reduced to the role of efficient but uninspired adaptor of stage plays in the 1930s. During the occupation years L'Herbier again came to prominence with his delicately-handled dreamlike *La Nuit fantastique* but his subsequent work, which included a spectacular version of *Les Derniers Jours de Pompei* in 1948, attracted little critical favor. In more recent years, however, L'Herbier's reputation has benefitted from the revival of interest in the experimental aspects of French 1920s cinema. Though to some extent overshadowed by the towering figure of Abel Gance, L'Herbier emerges as a figure of considerable interest. In particular the work of the critic and theorist Noël Burch has emphasized the modernity of the approach to shooting and to narrative construction displayed in his ambitious *L'Argent*. There seems little doubt that French 1920s cinema offers a rich and largely unexplored area for future film studies and that L'Herbier's reputation can only benefit from fresh investigation of his varied 1920s oeuvre.

—Roy Armes

LITTIN, Miguel.

Chilean. Born in Palmilla (Colchagua), Chile, 9 August 1942. Educated at Theatre School of the University of Chile, Santiago. Married Eli Menz. TV director and producer, 1963; stage director and actor, and assistant on several films, 1964–67; founding member, Committee of the Popular Unity Filmmakers, 1969; named director of national production company Chile Films by Salvador Allende, 1970; made weekly newsreels for Chile Films, 1970–71; emigrated to Mexico following coup d'etat, 1973; member of Executive Committee of Latin American Filmmakers, 1974. Recipient: Chilean Critics Prize, for *El Chacal de Nahueltoro*, 1970.

Films as Director and Scriptwriter:

1968   *Por la tierra ajena* (*On Foreign Land*)
1969   *El chacal de Nahueltoro* (*The Jackal of Nahueltoro*)
1971   *Compañero Presidente*
1973   **La tierra prometida (The Promised Land)**
1975   *El recurso del método* (*Viva el Presidente. Reasons of State*) (co-sc)
1980   *La viuda de Montiel* (*Montiel's Widow*)
1982   *Alsino y el cóndor* (*Alsino and the Condor*)
1985   *Actas de Marusia* (*Letters from Marusia*)
1986   *Acta General de Chile* (*General Statement on Chile*)

Other Films:

1965   *Yo tenía un camarada* (*I Had a Comrade*) (Soto) (role)
1966   *Mundo mágico* (*Magic World*) (Soto) (role); *ABC do amor* (*The ABC of Love*) (role)

Publications:

By LITTIN: books—

Cine chileno: La tierra prometida, Caracas, 1974.
El Chacal de Nahueltoro: La tierra prometida, Mexico City, 1977.

By LITTIN: articles—

"Film in Chile," an interview in *Cineaste* (New York), Spring 1971.
Interview with M. Torres, in *Cine Cubano* (Havana), no. 76/77, 1972.
"Culture populaire et lutte impérialiste," an interview with J.-R. Huleu and others, in *Cahiers du Cinéma* (Paris), July/August 1974.
Interview with Marcel Martin, in *Ecran* (Paris), November 1977.
"Cine Chileno en exilio," an interview with Gastón Ancelovici, in *Contracampo* (Madrid), December 1979.
Interview with Emilia Palma, in *Cine Cubano* (Havana), no. 100, 1981.
"Lo desmesurado, el espacio real del sueño americano," in *Cine Cubano* (Havana), no. 105, 1983.
"Coming Home," in *American Film* (Washington, D.C.), January/February 1986.

On LITTIN: books—

Bolzoni, Francesco, *El cine de Allende*, Valencia, 1974.
Chanan, Michael, editor, *Chilean Cinema*, London, 1976.
García Marquéz, Gabriel, *Clandestine in Chile: The Adventures of Miguel Littin*, New York, 1987.

On LITTIN: articles—

Wilson, David, "Aspects of Latin American Political Cinema," in *Sight and Sound* (London), Summer 1972.
Burton, Julianne, "*The Promised Land*," in *Film Quarterly* (Berkeley), Fall 1975.
Scott, R., "The Arrival of the Instrument in Flesh and Blood: Deconstruction in Littin's *Promised Land*," in *Ciné-Tracts* (Montreal), Spring/Summer 1978.
Kovacs, K.S., "Miguel Littin's *Recurso del método*: the aftermath of Allende," in *Film Quarterly* (Berkeley), Spring 1980.
Le Pennec, Françoise, "Cinéma du Chili: en exil ou sur place," in *Cinéma* (Paris), February 1983.
Mouesca, J., "El cine chileno en el exilio (1973–1983)," in *Cine Cubano* (Havana), no. 109, 1984.
"Miguel Littin," in *Film Dope* (London), September 1986.

* * *

"Each of my movies corresponds to a moment in Chilean political life." From this manifesto-like stance in his earlier career, Miguel Littin's cinematic concerns have widened geographically but maintained their political orientation. Certainly it is an attitude that has earned him detractors. But it is fair to say that his best work has been provoked by the *contradictions* offered to socialist ideals by the lessons of history. Squaring this circle, or for Littin, seeing how imperialism, dictatorship, and subjugation are self-perpetuating, allows us to trace the fine line in his work between political sentimentality and genuine cinematic ingenuity.

El chacal de Nahueltoro courageously addresses the notion of ideology in the true story of an illiterate peasant who murders his common-law wife and her five children. Taking this popular personification of Evil, Littin shows the irony of a peasant who only achieves self-enlightenment at the point of judicial persecution, only becomes literate to sign his death warrant, and only becomes a good Catholic in time to die one. But the film seeks to avoid the perpetuation of bourgeois forms itself: flashbacks culminate at a point midway through the film when the crime is actually committed; the real dialogue of the peasant is used; handheld camera shots and journalistic techniques simultaneously invoke sensations of authenticity and manipulation.

The film pitched Littin into the leading ranks of Latin American directors, an achievement he followed with *La tierra prometida*. Again closely historically detailed, it tells the story of a popular revolt that is finally massacred by the army. But it moved to a larger cinematic scope, starring the peasants of the Santa Cruz region, and invoked the ambiguity of folk symbolism in an allegory of the weaknesses in Allende's Popular

Unity. Two months after it was made a similar military coup put an end to Allende's Government.

After the coup Littin went to Mexico and looked back on Chile's recent, violent history in *Actas de Marusia*. It began to document the roots of right-wing domination in an English Mining Company's exploitation of a small Chilean town at the start of the century, ending in torture, hostage-taking, and mass-murder. For some, however, it was laying it on too thick, calling it "nothing so much as a Stalinist hymn to the glories of suicidal sacrifice." Nonetheless it's ochre-toned intensity gained it an Oscar nomination as Best Foreign Film.

From here his career took a different turn. The emerging fashion for Latin American "magical realism" in European and American literary tastes saw Littin making a parallel *rapprochement* with "western" intellectual culture—the previous agent of cultural contamination. *El recurso del método*, based on a Carpentier novel, was archly thoughtful, quoting from Descartes in its portrayal of an exiled Latin American Dictator. But again it detailed his concern with the forms of ideology that condone dictatorship—here in the delusion of subjectivity: "The dictator can seem nice and understandable in his behaviour, but at the same time he reveals the extent to which he himself has been destroyed by the ideology of imperialism. . . . Therefore I didn't want to stress the individual." Mirrors, paintings and lamps refract the lighting, rendering illumination and identification uncertain: "It is a play of reflections between truths, lies, ambiguities, and from the joining of all these elements, the spectator will be able to draw a conclusion, to become aware of what a dictatorship is." *El recurso del método* struck the plangent note of the exiled Littin's own political pessimism, a note that was echoed in *La viuda de Montiel* whose literary tableaux showed the widow of a local tyrant gradually becoming aware of her previous self-delusions. In spite of Marquéz providing the story, the film failed to take off.

Taking as its subject a boy's dream of flying, *Alsino y el cóndor* did, however. It showed Littin's return to contemporary Latin American realities, in the context of Somoza's Nicaragua of 1979. Some saw its clear political sympathies as hampering it at the Academy Awards where it was nominated for Best Foreign Film. But it was clear it was a film that cinematically transcended its political objectives in a powerful, emotive vision of a country torn by civil war, seen through the eyes of a crippled child.

That innocent eye is one that Littin himself tried to capture when he surreptitiously returned to Chile after twelve years in exile to secretly film life under Pinochet. Disguised as a Uruguayan businessman, and covertly directing four film crews, the resultant four-part documentary *Acta General de Chile* is a testament to Littin's flexibility and bravado.

Littin's place in Latin American film history is ensured, for reasons that go beyond the aesthetic. Paradoxically, what has earned him posterity has often cost him aesthetically. This responsiveness to a changing political climate renders him an unpredictable director, but nonetheless bodes well for the future.

—Saul Frampton

LITVAK, Anatole.

Russian/American. Born Mikhail Anatol Litvak in Kiev, 21 May 1902, became U.S. citizen, 1940. Educated at University of Leningrad, PhD. in philosophy, 1921; State School of Theatre, 1922. Married 1) Miriam Hopkins, 1937 (divorced 1939); 2) Sophie Steur, 1949. Theatre director and assistant director, then art director, Nordkino film studios, Leningrad, from 1923; moved to Paris, then editor for G.W. Pabst at Ufa studios, Berlin, 1925; assistant to emigré director Alexander Volkoff, 1926–30; directed first film, 1930; moved to Paris, 1933; contract director at Warners in Hollywood, 1937–41; joined Special Services Film Unit, U.S. Army, 1942, working with Frank Capra; returned to Paris, 1949. Recipient: Croix de guerre; Légion d'honneur; International Prize, Venice Festival, for *The Snake Pit*, 1949. *Died in Paris, 15 December 1974.*

Films as Director:

1923 *Tatiana* (short)
1924 *Hearts and Dollars* (short)
1930 *Dolly macht Karriere*
1931 *Nie wieder Liebe* (+ co-adapt); French version *Calais-Douvres*
1932 *Coeur de Lilas* (+ sc); *Das Lied einer Nacht*; English version *Be Mine Tonight*
1933 *Cette vielle canaille* (+ co-adapt); *Sleeping Car*
1935 *L'Equipage* (+ co-sc)
1936 *Mayerling*
1937 *The Woman I Love*; *Tovarich*
1938 *The Amazing Dr. Clitterhouse*; *The Sisters*
1939 **Confessions of a Nazi Spy**
1940 *Castle on the Hudson*; *City for Conquest*; *All This and Heaven Too*
1941 *Out of the Fog*; *Blues in the Night*
1942 *This Above All*; **Why We Fight** series—No.2: **The Nazis Strike** (co-d)
1943 **Why We Fight** series—No.3: **Divide and Conquer** (co-d)
1944 **Why We Fight** series—No.7: **The Battle of Russia** (+ co-sc); No.8: **The Battle of China** (co-d)
1945 **Why We Fight** series—No.9: **War Comes to America** (+ co-sc)
1947 *The Long Night*
1948 *Sorry, Wrong Number* (+ co-pr); *The Snake Pit* (+ co-pr)
1951 *Decision Before Dawn* (+ co-pr)
1954 *Act of Love* (+ co-sc)
1955 *The Deep Blue Sea* (+ co-pr)
1956 *Anastasia*
1957 *Mayerling* (remake for TV)
1959 *The Journey* (retitled after release as *Some of Us May Die*) (+ pr)
1961 *Aimez-vous Brahms?* (*Goodbye Again*) (+ pr, appearance in nightclub scene)
1962 *Le Cocteau dans la plaie* (*Five Miles to Midnight*)
1966 *10:30 P.M. Summer* (+ pr)
1967 *The Night of the Generals*
1970 *The Lady in a Car with Glasses and a Gun* (*La Dame dans l'auto avec des lunettes et un fusil*) (+ co-pr)

Other Films:

1925 *Samii yunii pioner* [A Very Young Pioneer] (Derzhavin) (co-sc)
1927 *Casanova* (*The Loves of Casanova* (asst d to Alexander Volkoff)
1929 *Sheherazade* (*Secrets of the Orient*) (asst d to Volkoff)
1930 *Der weisse Teufel* (*The White Devil*) (asst d to Volkoff, d dialogue and musical sequences)
1932 *La Chanson d'une nuit* (French version of *Das Lied einer Nacht*) (Clouzot and Colombier) (artistic supervisor)
1947 *Meet Me at Dawn* (co-play basis)

Publications:

By LITVAK: article—

"A Cutter at Heart," an interview with Allen Eyles and Barrie Pattison, in *Films and Filming* (London), February 1967.

Anatole Litvak

On LITVAK: book—

Roddick, Nick, *A New Deal in Entertainment: Warner Brothers in the 1930s*, London, 1983.

On LITVAK: articles—

Article on production of *The Snake Pit*, in *Time* (New York), 20 December 1948.
Nolan, Jack, "Anatole Litvak," in *Films in Review* (New York), November 1967.
Obituary in *Ecran* (Paris), February 1975.
"Anatole Litvak," in *Film Dope* (London), September 1986.

*   *   *

Anatole Litvak was a minor, commercially successful director whose personal and professional life can be characterized in one word: disingenuous. He was a multi-lingual cosmopolitan who possessed an anti-establishment political consciousness. He understood the technique and potential of the film medium, for example, in his use of location shooting and realistic documentary effects as early as the 1930s; he emphasized realistic sound effects over dialogue in sound films; and he capably used camera tracking shots and pans. Yet his films were erratic in quality and uneven in content; his intelligence and talents never found a satisfying cinematic expression.

Litvak acted and directed at the State School of Theatre and probably was assistant director and/or set decorator for at least nine silent Russian films at Leningrad's Nordkino studios. He was evasive about his background and life in Russia. Little is known except that he fled to Berlin in 1925 where he was an editor on G.W. Pabst's *Die freudlose Gasse*, worked as general assistant to Russian emigré director Nicholas Alexander Bolkoff, claims to have been one of the many editors on Abel Gance's *Napoléon*, and made his directorial debut with Ufa's *Dolly macht Karriere* in 1929. Two years later he directed *Nie wieder Liebe*, which was filmed simultaneously in a French version entitled *Calais-Douvres*, with Max Ophüls as Litvak's assistant. He went to Paris to direct *Coeur de lilas* in which he used natural street sounds which he found to be "another support for a film's images, heightening their pictoral values, underscoring their visual beauty."

Paris became his home after he fled Hitler's Germany, and a favorite locale for his films—13 of his 37 pictures were set in Paris. It was also the city where he directed *Mayerling*, the internationally popular film which brought him to Hollywood.

Upon arriving in Hollywood he directed *The Woman I Love* for RKO (a re-make of *L'Equipage* which he had directed in Paris with Annabella and Charles Vanel) and which starred Miriam Hopkins whom he later married. Litvak then signed a 4-year contract with Warner Brothers and while that studio was deeply entrenched in its politically-conscious period, an atmosphere which would have seemed very well suited to his temperament, he was apparently too independent, if not overtly iconoclastic, to fit into the studio mold. For the most part his films there were sophisticated women's fare—*Tovar-*

ich, The Sisters, and *All This and Heaven Too*. One exception was the now-dated, anti-Nazi propaganda film, *Confessions of a Nazi Spy*. Here Edward G. Robinson played a FBI agent who breaks up a ring of Nazi spies in the U.S., and Litvak used newsreels of actual U.S. Nazi rallies for a docu-drama effect.

During World War II he directed or co-directed for the U.S. Army's Special Services Film Unit and was in charge of motion picture operations during the Normandy invasion. His war efforts brought him the *Légion d'honneur* and the *Croix de guerre*.

Following the war Litvak produced and directed his two best and most popular American films—*Sorry, Wrong Number* and *The Snake Pit*, a starkly realistic depiction of life in an insane asylum. Litvak then left the United States to live and work in Paris for the remainder of his career. There he produced and directed what is probably his best film—*Decision Before Dawn*, a compelling drama about German prisoners of war who returned to spy in their native Germany in an effort to defeat Nazism.

Thereafter, Litvak's films were star-studded trifles with the exception of the immensely dramatic and moving *Anastasia* which was Ingrid Bergman's return to mainstream films. The most notable of Litvak's late films was the sadistic and lurid *The Night of the Generals* starring Peter O'Toole. His last picture was a non-entity entitled *The Lady in the Car with Glasses and a Gun*.

—Ronald Bowers

———

LOACH, Ken.

British. Born Kenneth Loach in Nuneaton, Warwickshire, 17 June 1937. Read law at Oxford University. Served 2 years in the Royal Air Force. Married Lesley (Loach), 3 children. Actor with repertory company, Birmingham, then joined BBC, 1961; director of *Z Cars* for TV, 1962, then for *Wednesday Play* for TV, 1965; first collaboration with producer Tony Garnett was *Up the Junction*, 1965; with Garnett, set up Kestrel Films production company, 1969; freelance, though working mainly for Central TV, from 1970s. Recipient: TV Director of the Year Award, British TV Guild, 1965; Special Jury Prize, Cannes Festival, for *Hidden Agenda*, 1990. Lives in London.

Films as Director and Co-Scriptwriter:

1967	*Poor Cow*
1969	*Kes*
1971	*The Save the Children Fund Film* (short); *Family Life*
1979	*Black Jack*
1981	*Looks and Smiles*
1986	*Fatherland*
1990	*Hidden Agenda*
1991	*Riff Raff*

Films for TV:

1964	*Catherine*; *Profit By Their Example*; *The Whole Truth*; *The Diary of a Young Man*
1965	*Tap on the Shoulder*; *Wear a Very Big Hat*; *Three Clear Sundays*; *Up the Junction*; *The End of Arthur's Marriage*; *The Coming Out Party*
1966	*Cathy Come Home*

1967	*In Two Minds*
1968	*The Golden Vision*
1969	*The Big Flame*; *In Black and White* (not transmitted)
1971	*The Rank and File*; *After a Lifetime*
1973	*A Misfortune*
1976	*Days of Hope* (in 4 parts)
1977	*The Price of Coal*
1979	*The Gamekeeper*
1980	*Auditions*
1981	*A Question of Leadership*
1983	*The Red and the Blue*; *Questions of Leadership* (in 4 parts, not transmitted)
1984	*Which Side Are You On?*
1985	*Diverse Reports: We Should Have Won*
1989	*Split Screen: Peace in Northern Ireland*

Publications:

By LOACH: articles—

"Spreading Wings at Kestrel," an interview with P. Bream, in *Films and Filming* (London), March 1972.
Interview with M. Amiel, in *Cinéma* (Paris), December 1972.
Interview with J. O'Hara, in *Cinema Papers* (Melbourne), April 1977.
"A Fidelity to the Real," an interview with L. Quart, in *Cineaste* (New York), Fall 1980.
Interview with Julian Petley, in *Framework* (Norwich), no. 18, 1982.
Interview with Robert Brown, in *Monthly Film Bulletin* (London), January 1983.
"Voice in the Dark," an interview with Gavin Smith, in *Film Comment* (New York), March/April 1988.

On LOACH: articles—

Taylor, John, "The *Kes* Dossier," in *Sight and Sound* (London), Summer 1970.
"Tony Garnett and Ken Loach," in *Documentary Explorations: Fifteen Interviews with Filmmakers*, by G. Roy Levin, New York, 1971.
McAsh, Iain, "One More Time," in *Films Illustrated* (London), December 1978.
Petley, Julian, "Questions of Censorship," in *Stills* (London), November 1984.
Kerr, Paul, "The Complete Ken Loach," in *Stills* (London), May/June 1986.
Fatherland Section of *Jeune Cinéma* (Paris), January/February 1987.
Petley, Julian, "Ken Loach—Politics, Protest and the Past," in *Monthly Film Bulletin* (London), March 1987.
"Kenneth Loach," in *Film Dope* (London), February 1987.
Nave, B., "Portrait d'un cinéaste modeste: Ken Loach," in *Jeune Cinéma* (Paris), October/November 1987.
Grant, Steve, "Troubles Shooter," in *Time Out* (London), 2 January 1991.
Pannifer, Bill, "Agenda Bender," in *Listener* (London), 3 January 1991.

*   *   *

Ken Loach is not only Britain's most political film-maker, he is also its most censored—and the two are not entirely unconnected. Loach's career illustrates all too clearly the immense difficulties facing the radical film-maker in Britain today: the broadcasting organisations' position within the state makes them extraordinarily sensitive sites in which to tackle certain fundamental political questions (about labour relations, "national security," or Northern Ireland, for example), whilst the film industry, though less subject to political interference and self-censorship, simply finds Loach's projects too "uncommercial," thanks to its habitually poverty-stricken state. And what other film-maker, British or otherwise, has found one of his films the subject of vitriolic attacks by sections of his *own* country's press at a major international film festival—as happened at Cannes in 1990 with *Hidden Agenda*?

For all the obvious *political* differences with Grierson, Loach is the chief standard bearer of the British cinematic tradition that started with the documentary movement in the

Ken Loach directing *Family Life*

1930s. His quintessentially naturalistic approach was apparent even in his earliest works—his contributions to the seminal BBC police series *Z Cars*—but really came to the fore with *Up the Junction* and *Cathy Come Home*. In the days when television drama was still finding its way beyond the proscenium arch and out from under the blanket of middle-brow, middle class, literary-based classics, *Cathy's* portrayal of a homeless family hounded by the forces of a pitiless bureaucracy caused a sensation and led directly to the founding of the housing charity Shelter. Indeed, one critic described it as "effecting massive, visceral change in millions of viewers in a single evening." Typically, however, Loach himself has been far more circumspect, arguing that the film was *socially* as opposed to *politically* conscious, that it made people aware of a problem without giving them any indication of what they might do about it. He concludes that "Ideally I should have liked *Cathy* to lead to the nationalisation of the building industry and home ownership. Only political action can do anything in the end"—a point of view to which he has remained faithful throughout his career.

Accordingly, in *The Big Flame, The Rank and File* and the four-part series *Days of Hope* Loach turned to more directly political subjects. It is in these dramas that Loach begins his project of giving voice to the politically silenced and marginalised. As he put it, "I think it's a very important function to let people speak who are usually disqualified from speaking or who've become non-persons—activists, militants, or people who really have any developed political ideas. One after the other in different industries, there have been people who've developed very coherent political analyses, who are really just

excluded. They're vilified—called extremists and then put beyond the pale."

Such views made enemies Left, Right and Centre but, typically, Loach's critics cloaked what were basically *political* objections in apparently *aesthetic* rhetoric. In particular, Loach became dragged into the much-rehearsed argument that the "documentary-drama" form dishonestly and misleadingly blurs the line between fact and fiction and, in particular, presents the latter as the former. Loach himself dismisses such criticisms as "ludicrous" and a "smokescreen," citing the numerous uncontroversial disinterrings of Churchill, Edward VII and others and concluding that "It's an argument that's always dragged out selectively when there's a view of history, a view of events, that the Establishment doesn't agree with—it's not really the form which worries them at all. It's such an intellectual fraud that it doesn't bear serious consideration."

Loach's work, especially *Days of Hope*, was also drawn into a more serious debate which raged at one time in the pages of *Screen* about whether films with "progressive" political content can be truly "progressive" if they utilise the allegedly outworn and ideologically dubious conventions of realism. Loach's response was to accuse such critics of "not seeing the woods for the trees. The big issue which we tried to make plain to ordinary folks who aren't film critics was that the Labour leadership had betrayed them fifty years ago and were about to do so again. That's the important thing to tell people. It surprised me that critics didn't take the political point, but a rather abstruse cinematic point. . . . Even the more serious critics always avoid confronting the content of the film and deciding if they think it is truthful. They'll skirt around it by talking about realism and the Function of Film or they'll do a little paragraph while devoting all their space to some commercial film they pretend to dislike."

With the coming of the 1980s Loach began to shift increasingly into documentary proper, abandoning dramatic devices altogether. This was partly to do with the increasing difficulty, both economic and political, of making the kind of films in which he was most interested, but also related to the advent of Thatcherism in 1979. As he himself explained, "There were things we wanted to say head on and not wrapped up in fiction, things that should be said as directly as one can say them. Thatcherism just felt so urgent that I thought that doing a fictional piece for TV, which would take a year just to get commissioned and at least another year to make, was just too slow. Documentaries can tackle things head on, and you can make them faster than dramas too—though with hindsight it's just as hard, if not harder, to get them transmitted." Indeed, Loach had major problems with his analysis of the relationship between trade union leaders and the rank and file in *A Question of Leadership* and the series *Questions of Leadership*, the first of which was cut in order to include a final "balancing" discussion and broadcast in only one ITV region, while the second was never broadcast at all, following numerous legal wrangles over alleged defamation. Similarly, Loach's coal dispute film, *Which Side Are You On?*, was banned by the company (London Weekend Television) which commissioned it and finally shown on Channel 4, but only after it could be "balanced" by a programme less sympathetic to the striking miners than Loach's. It says a great deal about the system of film and television programme making in Britain that one of the country's most experienced and politically conscious directors was, and remains, unable to produce a full-scale work about one of the most momentous political events in the country's recent history.

Exactly the same could be said about Loach and Northern Ireland. Revealingly, the initial idea for what was to become *Hidden Agenda* came from David Puttnam when he was studio boss at Columbia, after two of Loach's long cherished Irish projects, one with the BBC and the other with Channel 4, had foundered. However, Loach has borne his treatment at the hands of the British establishment with remarkable fortitude. With his particular political outlook he would presumably be surprised if things were otherwise. Nor does he have an inflated view of the role of film and the film-maker. As his remarks about *Cathy* clearly testify, Loach is a great believer in the primacy of the political. And, as he himself concludes, "Filmmakers have a very soft life really, in comparison to people who have to work for a living. And so it's easy to be a radical filmmaker. The people who really are on the front line aren't filmmakers. We're in a very privileged position, very free and good wages—if you can keep working."

—Julian Petley

LORENTZ, Pare.

American. Born in Clarksburg, West Virginia, 11 December 1905. Educated at Wesleyan College; University of West Virginia. Married Eliza Meyer. Writer and film critic for *McCall's*, *Town and Country*, and Ring features, 1930s; directed first film, *The Plow That Broke the Plains*, for the U.S. Resettlement Agency, 1936; director of U.S. Film Service, 1938–40; directed shorts for RKO, 1941; made 275 navigational films for U.S. Air Force, 1941–45; chief of film section of War Department's Civil Affairs Division, 1946–47; film consultant, New York, 1960s; "saluted" by Academy of Motion Pictures Arts and Sciences, 1981.

Films as Director and Scriptwriter:

1936   *The Plow That Broke the Plains*
1937   *The River*
1940   *The Fight for Life*
1946   *Nuremberg Trials*

Other Films:

1939   *The City* (Steiner and Van Dyke) (co-sc)

Publications:

By LORENTZ: article—

"The Narration of *The River*," in *Film Comment* (New York), Spring 1965.

On LORENTZ: books—

Snyder, Robert L., *Pare Lorentz and the Documentary Film*, Norman, Oklahoma, 1968.
Barsam, Richard, *Non-Fiction Film*, New York, 1973.
MacCann, Richard Dyer, *The People's Films*, New York, 1973.
Barnouw, Erik, *Documentary—A History of the Non-Fiction Film*, New York, 1974.
Alexander, William, *Film on the Left: American Documentary Film from 1931–42*, Princeton, New Jersey, 1981.
Ellis, Jack C., *The Documentary Idea*, Englewood Cliffs, New Jersey, 1989.

On LORENTZ: articles—

Goodman, Ezra, "The American Documentary," in *Sight and Sound* (London), Autumn 1938.
White, W.L., "Pare Lorentz," in *Scribner's* (New York), January 1939.
Black, C.M., "He Serves Up America: Pare Lorentz," in *Collier's* (New York), 3 August 1940.
Van Dyke, Willard, "Letter from *The River*," in *Film Comment* (New York), Spring 1965.
"Conscience of the Thirties," in *Newsweek* (New York), 5 August 1968.
Harmetz, Aljean, "Hollywood Hails Lorentz, Documentary Pioneer," in *New York Times*, 22 October 1981.
"Pare Lorentz," in *Film Dope* (London), February 1987.

On LORENTZ: film—

"Pare Lorentz on Film," in four instalments produced by WGBH in Boston for NET network.

*   *   *

In this country it was Pare Lorentz who was in a position for leadership in relation to documentary film comparable to that of John Grierson in Britain and later in Canada. Lorentz was founding head and leader of the short-lived government program, which began in 1935, became the United States Film Service in 1938, and ended in 1940. He established American precedent for the government use of documentaries, which would be continued during World War II (by the Armed Forces and the Office of War Information) and afterwards (by the United States Information Agency, now International Communication Agency). From Lorentz's efforts five large and important films resulted, the first three of which he directed: *The Plow that Broke the Plains, The River, The Fight for Life, Power and the Land* (directed by Joris Ivens), and *The Land* (directed by Robert Flaherty).

In *The Plow that Broke the Plains* and *The River*, Lorentz developed an original, personal style of documentary that also became a national style (similarities can be seen in the films of

Pare Lorentz: *The River*

others, *The City* and *And So They Live*, for example). In his two mosaic patterns of sight (carefully composed images shot silent) and sound (symphonic music, spoken words, noises), no one element says much by itself. Together they offer a form and content that resemble epic poems. They seem close to the attitudes of American populism and are rooted in frontier tradition. The sweeping views of a big country, the free verse commentaries with their chanted litany of place names and allusions to historic events, make one think of Walt Whitman. The use of music is quite special, with composer Virgil Thomson sharing more fully than usual in the filmmaking process; a sort of operatic balance is achieved between the musical score and the other elements. (Thomson made his scores for these two films into concert suites which have become part of the standard orchestral repertoire.)

In *The Fight for Life*, Lorentz is much less sure in his control of its narrative form than he was of the poetic form of the two preceding films. He seems to have been much more comfortable with land and rivers than with people. *Fight for Life* is about the work of the Chicago Maternity Center in delivering babies among the impoverished. It is an interesting film, if curiously flawed by melodramatic excesses. It is important in its innovations and might be regarded as a prototype for the postwar Hollywood semi-documentaries; e.g. *The House on 92nd Street, Boomerang, Call Northside 777*.

In contributing two lasting masterpieces to the history of documentary—*The Plow* and, especially, *The River*—Lorentz joins a very select company, that of the artists of documentary. (Flaherty and Jennings would be other members of that company.) Some would argue that *The River* is the finest American documentary to date—aesthetically and in terms of expressing aspects of the American spirit. Lorentz's major limitations appear most sharply in the light that Grierson would cast on them.

First, Lorentz relied on the impermanent partisan support of the party in power. Lorentz had the support of President Franklin Roosevelt and the films were associated with Democratic policies. When the balance in Congress shifted to Republican in 1940, the United States Film Service was not allowed to continue. Second, even within that New Deal context Lorentz opted for a few big films sponsored by agencies related to one department (four of the five films were on agricultural subjects), rather than many smaller films from various departments that would have broadened the base of sponsorship and made for a steady flow of film communication. Third, he was creating art at public expense—making personal films à la Flaherty—with no real commitment to public service. (Lorentz disliked the term documentary and considered much of Grierson's work in England too school-teacherish; instead Lorentz was trying to create, he said, "films of merit.") Finally, Lorentz remained aloof in Washington. He made no efforts to seek sponsorship for documentary film making outside the government; he had no real connection with the New York City documentarians responsible for the nongovernmental documentaries of the 1930s (though some of them had worked with him on the government films).

On the other hand, the situation was not the same here as in Britain or Canada. If Lorentz couldn't establish a film unit, he couldn't follow through on the other things Grierson called for. The government of the United States *is* highly partisan; we don't have the centuries-old tradition of public servants working outside party as in England. (Lorentz claimed that Grierson had stolen his plan: that the National Film Board accepted by the Canadian Parliament was essentially the same as the U.S. Film Service which Congress abolished.) It is not clear that Grierson could have done any better here than Lorentz did; Grierson's criticisms tend to ignore the central differences

of government structure and tradition.

However one chooses to look at the matter, it would be generally agreed that documentary in the United States remained a non-movement of individual rivalries, competitiveness, and political differences. The closing down of the U.S. Film Service proved a great waste and inefficiency. Shortly after its demise the United States entered World War II and government film making on a vast scale had to be started from scratch. It was the Hollywood filmmakers, without documentary experience, who assumed leadership in the wartime government production. Lorentz spent the war making films as guides to navigation for the U.S. Air Corps. Subsequent to his film on the Nuremberg war-crimes trials he made no more films, working instead mainly as a "film consultant."

—Jack C. Ellis

———

LOSEY, Joseph.

American. Born in La Crosse, Wisconsin, 14 January 1909. Educated at Dartmouth College, New Hampshire, B.A., 1929; Harvard University, M.A. in English Literature, 1930. Stage director, New York, 1932–34; attended Eisenstein film classes, Moscow, 1935; staged Living Newspaper productions and other plays for Federal Theater Project, New York, 1947; hired by Dory Schary for RKO, 1948; blacklisted, moved to London, 1951; began collaboration with writer Harold Pinter and actor Dirk Bogarde, 1963; directed *Boris Godunov*, Paris, Opera, 1980. Recipient: Chevalier de l'Ordre des Arts et des Lettres, 1957; International Critics Award, Cannes Festival, for *Accident*, 1967; Palme d'Or, Cannes Festival, for *The Go-Between*, 1971; Honorary Doctorate, Dartmouth College, 1973. *Died in London, 22 June 1984.*

Films as Director:

1939 *Pete Roleum and His Cousins* (short) (+ p, sc)
1941 *A Child Went Forth* (short) (+ co-p, sc); *Youth Gets a Break* (short) (+ sc)
1945 *A Gun in His Hand* (short)
1949 *The Boy with Green Hair*
1950 *The Lawless*
1951 *The Prowler*; *M*; *The Big Night* (+ co-sc)
1952 *Stranger on the Prowl* (*Encounter*) (d as "Andrea Forzano")
1954 *The Sleeping Tiger* (d as "Victor Hanbury")
1955 *A Man on the Beach*
1956 *The Intimate Stranger* (*Finger of Guilt*) (d as "Joseph Walton")
1957 *Time Without Pity*
1958 *The Gypsy and the Gentleman*
1959 *Blind Date* (*Chance Meeting*)
1960 *The Criminal* (*The Concrete Jungle*)
1962 *Eve*
1963 *The Damned* (*These Are the Damned*); **The Servant** (+ co-p)
1964 *King and Country* (+ co-p)
1966 *Modesty Blaise*
1967 **Accident** (+ co-p)
1968 *Boom!*; *Secret Ceremony*
1970 *Figures in a Landscape*; *The Go-Between*
1972 *The Assassination of Trotsky* (+ co-p)
1973 *A Doll's House*
1975 *Galileo* (+ co-sc); *The Romantic Englishwoman*
1977 *Mr. Klein*
1979 *Don Giovanni*

Joseph Losey

1982 *The Trout*
1985 *Steaming*

Publications:

By LOSEY: books—

Losey on Losey, edited by Tom Milne, New York, 1968.
Le Livre de Losey: entretiens avec le cinéaste, edited by Michel Ciment, Paris 1979; as *Conversations with Losey*, London, 1985.

By LOSEY: articles—

"A Mirror to Life," in *Films and Filming* (London), June 1959.
"Entretiens," in *Cahiers du Cinéma* (Paris), September 1960.
Interview with Penelope Houston and John Gillett, in *Sight and Sound* (London), Autumn 1961.
"The Monkey on My Back," in *Films and Filming* (London), October 1963.
"Speak, Think, Stand Up," in *Film Culture* (New York), Fall/Winter 1970.
"Losey and Trotsky," interview with Tony Rayns, in *Take One* (Montreal), March 1973.
Interview with Gene Phillips, in *Séquences* (Montreal), April 1973.
"Something More," interview with Gordon Gow, in *Films and Filming* (London), October 1975.
"The Reluctant Exile," interview with Richard Roud, in *Sight and Sound* (London), no. 3, 1979.
"Dialogue on Film: Joseph Losey," in *American Film* (Washington, D.C.), November 1980.
Interview with Michel Ciment, in *Positif* (Paris), October 1982.
"Screenwriters, Critics and Ambiguity," an interview with J. Weiss, in *Cineaste* (New York), vol. 13, no. 1, 1983.
Interview with Allen Eyles, in *Stills* (London), May 1985.

On LOSEY: books—

Leahy, James, *The Cinema of Joseph Losey*, New York, 1967.
Ledieu, Christian, *Joseph Losey*, Paris, 1970.
Hirsch, Foster, *Joseph Losey*, Boston, 1980.

On LOSEY: articles—

"Losey Issue" of *Cahiers du Cinéma* (Paris), September 1960.
Jacob, Gilles, "Joseph Losey, or The Camera Calls," in *Sight and Sound* (London), Spring 1966.
Ross, T.J., "Notes on an Early Losey," in *Film Culture* (New York), Spring 1966.
Durgnat, Raymond, "Puritan Maids," in *Films and Filming* (London), April and May 1966.
Phillips, Gene, "The Critical Camera of Joseph Losey," in *Cinema* (Beverly Hills), Spring 1968.
Strick, Philip, "The Mice in the Milk," in *Sight and Sound* (London), Spring 1969.
Gow, Gordon, "Weapons," in *Films and Filming* (London), October 1971.
Combs, Richard, "Losey, Galileo, and the Romantic Englishwoman," in *Sight and Sound* (London), Summer 1975.
Legrand, G., "Pro-positions à propos de Losey," in *Positif* (Paris), October 1976.
Phillips, Gene, "The Blacklisting Era: Three Cases," in *America* (New York), 18 December 1976.
Houston, B., and Marcia Kinder, "The Losey-Pinter Collaboration," in *Film Quarterly* (Berkeley), Fall 1978.
McCarthy, T., obituary, in *Variety* (New York), 27 June 1984.
Amiel, M., obituary, in *Cinéma* (Paris), September 1984.
Roud, Richard, "Remembering Losey," in *Sight and Sound* (London), Winter 1984/85.
Elsaesser, Thomas, "Joseph Losey: Time Lost and Found," in *Monthly Film Bulletin* (London), June 1985.
Losey Section of *Positif* (Paris), July/August 1985.
"Joseph Losey," in *Film Dope* (London), February 1987.

* * *

Joseph Losey's career spanned five decades and included work in both theater and film. Latterly an American expatriate living in Europe, the early years of his life as a director were spent in the very different milieus of New Deal political theater projects and the paranoia of the Hollywood studio system during the McCarthy era. He was blacklisted in 1951 and left America for England where he continued making films, at first under a variety of pseudonyms. His work is both controversial and critically acclaimed, and Losey has long been recognized as a director with a distinctive and highly personal cinematic style.

Although Losey rarely wrote his own screenplays, preferring instead to work closely with other authors, there are nevertheless several distinct thematic concerns which recur throughout his work. It is his emphasis on human interaction and the complexity of interior thought and emotion that makes a Losey film an intellectual challenge, and his interest has always lain with detailed character studies rather than with so-called "action" pictures. Losey's domain is interior action and his depiction of the physical world centers on those events which are an outgrowth or reflection of his characters inner lives. From *The Boy with Green Hair* to *The Trout*, his films focused on individuals and their relationships to themselves, to those around them, and to their society as a whole.

One of Losey's frequent subjects is the intruder who enters a pre-existing situation and irrevocably alters its patterns. In his earlier films, this situation often takes the form of a community reacting with violence to an individual its members perceive as a threat. The "boy with green hair" is ostracized and finally forced to shave his head by the inhabitants of the town in which he lives; the young Mexican-American in *The Lawless* becomes the object of a vicious manhunt after a racially motivated fight; and the child-murderer in Losey's 1951 version of *M* inspires a lynch mob mentality in the community he has been terrorizing. In each of these cases, the social outsider who, for good or evil, does not confirm to the standards of the community, evokes a response of mass rage and suspicion. And as the members of the group forsake their individuality and rational behavior in favor of mob rule, they also forfeit any hope of future self-deception regarding their own capacity for unthinking brutality.

In Losey's later films, the scope of the "intruder" theme is often narrowed to explore the effect of a newcomer on the relationship of a husband and wife. *The Sleeping Tiger, Eve, Accident, The Romantic Englishwoman,* and *The Trout* all feature married couples whose lives are disrupted and whose relationships are shattered or redefined by the arrival of a third figure. In each of these films, either the husband or the wife is strongly attracted to the outsider. In *The Sleeping Tiger, Eve,* and *The Trout,* this attraction leads to tragedy and death for one of the partners, while the couples in *Accident* and *The Romantic Englishwoman* are forced to confront a serious rift in a seemingly untroubled relationship. A further level of conflict is added by the fact that the intruder in all of the films is either of a different social class (*The Sleeping Tiger, Eve, The Trout*) or a different nationality (*Accident, The Romantic Englishwoman*) than the couple, representing not only a sexual threat but a threat to the bourgeois status quo as well.

This underlying theme of class conflict is one which runs throughout Losey's work, emerging as an essential part of the framework of films as different as *The Lawless, The Servant,* and *The Go-Between.* Losey's consistent use of film as a means of social criticism has its roots in his theatrical work of the 1930s and his association with Bertolt Brecht. The two collaborated on the 1947 staging of Brecht's *Galileo Galilei,* starring Charles Laughton—a play which 27 years later Losey would bring to the screen—and Brecht's influence on Losey's own career is enormous. In addition to his interest in utilizing film as an expression of social and political opinions, Losey has adapted many of Brecht's theatrical devices to the medium as well. The sense of distance and reserve in Brechtian theatre is a keynote to Losey's filmic style, and Brecht's use of a heightened dramatic reality is also present in Losey's work. The characters in a Losey film are very much of the "real" world, but their depiction is never achieved through a documentary-style approach. We are always aware that it is a drama that is unfolding, as Losey makes use of carefully chosen music on the soundtrack or photography that borders on expressionism or deliberately evokes an atmosphere of memory to comment on the characters and their state of mind. It is this approach to the intellect rather than the emotions of the viewer that ties Losey's work so closely to Brecht.

Losey's films are also an examination of illusion and reality, with the true nature of people or events often bearing little resemblance to their outer appearances. The friendly community that gives way to mob violence, the "happy" marriage that unravels when one thread is plucked; these images of actual vs. surface reality abound in Losey's work. One aspect of this theme manifests itself in Losey's fascination with characters who discover themselves through a relationship which poses a potential threat to their position in society. Tyvian, in *Eve,* can only acknowledge through his affair with a high-class prostitute that his fame as a writer is actually the result of plagiarism, while Marian, in *The Go-Between,* finds her true sexual nature, which her class and breeding urge her to repress, in her affair with a local farmer.

Several of Losey's films carry this theme a step further, offering characters who find their own sense of self-identity becoming inextricably bound up in someone else. In *The Servant,* the complex, enigmatic relationship between Tony and his manservant, Barrett, becomes both a class struggle and a battle of wills as the idle young aristocrat slowly loses control of his life to the ambitious Barrett. This is an idea Losey pursues in both *Secret Ceremony* and *Mr. Klein.* In the former, a wealthy, unbalanced young girl draws a prostitute into a destructive fantasy in which the two are mother and daughter, and

the prostitute finds her initial desire for money becoming a desperate need to believe the fantasy. Alain Delon in *Mr. Klein* portrays a man in occupied France who becomes obsessed with finding a hunted Jew who shares his name. At the film's conclusion, he boards a train bound for the death camps rather than abandon his search, in effect becoming the other *Mr. Klein.* Losey emphasizes his characters' identity confusion cinematically, frequently showing them reflected in mirrors, their images fragmented, prism-like, or only partially revealed.

Losey's choice of subject led to his successful collaboration with playwright Harold Pinter on *The Servant, Accident,* and *The Go-Between,* and Losey once hoped to film Pinter's screenplay of Proust's *Remembrance of Things Past.* Their parallel dramatic interests served both men well, and their work together is among the finest in their careers. Yet if Losey found his most nearly perfect voice in Pinter's screenplays, his films with a wide variety of other writers have still resulted in a body of work remarkably consistent in theme and purpose. His absorbing, sometimes difficult films represent a unique and uncompromising approach to cinema, and guarantee Losey's place among the world's most intriguing directors.

—Janet E. Lorenz

LUBITSCH, Ernst.

German/American. Born in Berlin, 28 January 1892, became U.S. citizen, 1936. Educated at the Sophien Gymnasium. Married 1) Irni (Helene) Kraus, 1922 (divorced 1930); 2) Sania Bezencenet (Vivian Gaye), 1935 (divorced 1943), one daughter. Taken into Max Reinhardt Theater Company, 1911; actor, writer, then director of short films, from 1913; member of Adolph Zukor's Europäischen Film-Allianz (Efa), 1921; joined Warner Brothers, Hollywood, 1923; began association with Paramount, 1928; began collaboration with writer Ernest Vajda, 1930; Head of Production at Paramount, 1935 (relieved of post after a year); left Paramount for 3-year contract with 20th Century-Fox, 1938; suffered massive heart attack, 1943. Recipient: Special Academy Award (for accomplishments in the industry), 1947. *Died in Hollywood, 29 November 1947.*

Films as Director:

1914   *Fräulein Seifenschaum* (+ role); *Blindkuh* (+ role); *Aufs Eis geführt* (+ role)

1915   *Zucker und Zimt* (co-d, co-sc, role)

1916   *Wo ist mein Schatz?* (+ role); *Schuhpalast Pinkus* (+ role as Sally Pinkus); *Der gemischte Frauenchor* (+ role); *Der G.m.b.H. Tenor* (+ role); *Der Kraftmeier* (+ role); *Leutnant auf Befehl* (+ role); *Das schönste Geschenk* (+ role); *Seine neue Nase* (+ role)

1917   *Wenn vier dasselbe Tun* (+ co-sc, role); *Der Blusenkönig* (+ role); *Ossis Tagebuch*

1918   *Prinz Sami* (+ role); *Ein fideles Gefängnis; Der Fall Rosentopf* (+ role); *Der Rodelkavalier* (+ co-sc); *Die Augen der Mumie Mâ; Das Mädel vom Ballett; Carmen*

1919   *Meine Frau, die Filmschauspielerin; Meyer aus Berlin* (+ role as apprentice); *Das Schwabemädle; Die Austernprinzessin; Rausch; Madame DuBarry; Der lustige Ehemann* (+ sc); *Die Puppe* (+ co-sc)

1920   *Ich möchte kein Mann sein!* (+ co-sc); *Kohlhiesels Töchter* (+ co-sc); *Romeo und Julia im Schnee* (+ co-sc); *Sumurun* (+ co-sc); *Anna Boleyn*

1921   *Die Bergkatze* (+ co-sc)

Ernst Lubitsch

1922   *Das Weib des Pharao*
1923   *Die Flamme*; *Rosita*
1924   *The Marriage Circle*; *Three Women*; *Forbidden Paradise* (+ co-sc)
1925   *Kiss Me Again* (+ pr); *Lady Windermere's Fan* (+ pr)
1926   *So This Is Paris* (+ pr)
1927   *The Student Prince in Old Heidelberg* (+ pr)
1928   *The Patriot* (+ pr)
1929   *Eternal Love* (+ pr); **The Love Parade** (+ pr)
1930   *Paramount on Parade* (anthology film); *Monte Carlo* (+ pr)
1931   *The Smiling Lieutenant* (+ pr)
1932   *The Man I Killed* (*Broken Lullaby*) (+ pr); *One Hour with You* (+ pr); **Trouble in Paradise** (+ pr); *If I Had a Million* (anthology film)
1933   *Design for Living* (+ pr)
1934   *The Merry Widow* (+ pr)
1936   *Desire* (co-d, pr)
1937   *Angel* (+ pr)
1938   *Bluebeard's Eighth Wife* (+ pr)
1939   **Ninotchka** (+ pr)
1940   *The Shop Around the Corner* (+ pr)
1941   *That Uncertain Feeling* (+ co-pr)
1942   **To Be or Not to Be** (co-source, co-pr)
1943   *Heaven Can Wait* (+ pr)
1946   *Cluny Brown* (+ pr)
1948   *That Lady in Ermine* (co-d)

Other Films:

1913   *Meyer auf der Alm* (role as Meyer)
1914   *Die Firma Heiratet* (Wilhelm) (role as Moritz Abramowski); *Der Stolz der Firma* (Wilhelm) (role as Siegmund Lachmann); *Fräulein Piccolo* (Hofer) (role); *Arme Marie* (Mack) (role); *Bedingung—Kein Anhang!* (Rye) (role); *Die Ideale Gattin* (role); *Meyer als Soldat* (role as Meyer)
1915   *Robert und Bertram* (Mack) (role); *Wie Ich Ermordert Wurde* (Ralph) (role); *Der Schwarze Moritz* (Taufstein and Berg) (role); *Doktor Satansohn* (Edel) (role as Dr. Satansohn); *Hans Trutz im Schlaraffenland* (Wegener) (role as Devil)

Publications:

By LUBITSCH: articles—

"American Cinematographers Superior Artists," in *American Cinematographer* (Los Angeles), December 1923.
"Concerning Cinematography . . . as Told to William Stull," in *American Cinematographer* (Los Angeles), November 1929.
"Lubitsch's Analysis of Pictures Minimizes Director's Importance," in *Variety* (New York), 1 March 1932.
"Hollywood Still Leads . . . Says Ernst Lubitsch," interview with Barney Hutchinson, in *American Cinematographer* (Los Angeles), March 1933.
"A Tribute to Lubitsch, with a Letter in Which Lubitsch Appraises His Own Career," in *Films in Review* (New York), August/September 1951.
Letter to Herman Weinberg (10 July 1947), in *Film Culture* (New York), Summer 1962.

On LUBITSCH: books—

Verdone, Mario, *Ernst Lubitsch*, Lyon, 1964.
Baxter, John, *The Hollywood Exiles*, New York, 1976.
Poague, Leland, *The Cinema of Ernst Lubitsch: The Hollywood Films*, London, 1977.
Weinberg, Herman, *The Lubitsch Touch: A Critical Study*, 3rd revised edition, New York, 1977.
Carringer, R., and B. Sabath, *Ernst Lubitsch: A Guide to References and Resources*, Boston, 1978.
Paul, William, *Ernst Lubitsch's American Comedy*, New York, 1983.
Prinzler, Hans Helmut and Enno Patalas, editors, *Lubitsch*, Munich, 1984.
Cahiers du Cinéma/Cinématheque Française: Ernst Lubitsch, Paris, 1985.

Petrie, Graham, *Hollywood Destinies: European Directors in Hollywood 1922–31*, London, 1985.
Bourget, Eithne, and Jean-Loup, *Lubitsch: ou, La Satire Romanesque*, Paris, 1987.
Nacache, Jacqueline, *Lubitsch*, Paris, 1987.

On LUBITSCH: articles—

Merrick, Mollie, "Twenty-five Years of the 'Lubitsch Touch' in Hollywood," in *American Cinematographer* (Los Angeles), July 1947.
"E. Lubitsch Dead: Film Producer, 55," in *New York Times*, 1 December 1947.
"Ernst Lubitsch: A Symposium," in *Screen Writer*, January 1948.
Wollenberg, H.H., "Two Masters: Ernst Lubitsch and Sergei M. Eisenstein," in *Sight and Sound* (London), Spring 1948.
Lubitsch section of *Revue du Cinéma* (Paris), September 1948.
"The Films of Ernst Lubitsch," special issue of *Film Journal* (Australia), June 1959.
"A Tribute to Lubitsch (1892–1947)," in *Action!* (Los Angeles), November/December 1967.
Eisenschitz, Bernard, "Lubitsch (1892–1947)," in *Anthologie du Cinéma* vol. 3, Paris, 1968.
Lubitsch Section of *Cahiers du Cinéma* (Paris), February 1968.
Eisner, Lotte, "Lubitsch and the Costume Film," chapter 4 in *The Haunted Screen*, Berkeley, 1969.
Weinberg, Herman, "Ernst Lubitsch: A Parallel to George Feydeau," in *Film Comment* (New York), Spring 1970.
Sarris, Andrew, "Lubitsch in the Thirties," in *Film Comment* (New York), Winter 1971/72 and Summer 1972.
Mast, Gerald, "The 'Lubitsch Touch' and the Lubitsch Brain," in *The Comic Mind: Comedy and the Movies*, Indianapolis, Indiana, 1973; revised edition, 1979.
McBride, J., "The Importance of Being Ernst," in *Film Heritage* (New York), Summer 1973.
Schwartz, N., "Lubitsch's Widow: The Meaning of a Waltz," in *Film Comment* (New York), March/April 1975.
Horak, Jan-Christopher, "The Pre-Hollywood Lubitsch," in *Image* (Rochester, New York), December 1975.
Whittemore, Don, and Philip Cecchettini, "Ernst Lubitsch," in *Passport to Hollywood: Film Immigrants: Anthology*, New York, 1976.
Baxter, John, "The Continental Touch," in *American Film* (Washington, D.C.), September 1976.
Bond, Kirk, "Ernst Lubitsch," in *Film Culture* (New York), no.63–64, 1977.
Gillett, John, "Munich's Cleaned Pictures," in *Sight and Sound* (London), Winter 1977/78.
Truffaut, François, "Lubitsch Was a Prince," in *American Film* (Washington, D.C.), May 1978.
McVay, D., "Lubitsch: The American Silent Films," in *Focus on Film* (London), April 1979.
Traubner, R., "Lubitsch Returns to Berlin," in *Films in Review* (New York), October 1984.
Lubitsch Section of *Cinéma* (Paris), April 1985.
Lubitsch Sections of *Positif* (Paris), June and July/August 1986.
"Ernst Lubitsch," in *Film Dope* (London), February 1987.
Nave, B., "Aimer Lubitsch," in *Jeune Cinéma* (Paris), May/June 1987.

*   *   *

Ernst Lubitsch's varied career is often broken down into periods to emphasize the spectrum of his talents—from an actor in Max Reinhardt's Berlin Theater company to Head of Production at Paramount. Each of these periods could well provide enough material for a sizeable book. It is probably most covenient to divide Lubitsch's output into 3 phases: his German films between 1913 and 1922; his Hollywood films from 1923 to 1934; and his Hollywood productions from 1935 till his death in 1947.

During the first half of Lubitsch's filmmaking decade in Germany he completed about 19 shorts. They were predominantly ethnic slapsticks in which he played a "Dummkopf" character by the name of Meyer. Only three of these one- to five-reelers still exist. He directed 18 more films during his last five years in Germany, almost equally divided between comedies, some of which anticipate the concerns of his Hollywood works, and epic costume dramas. Pola Negri starred in most of these historical spectacles and the strength of her performances together with the quality of Lubitsch's productions brought them both international acclaim. Their *Madame Dubarry* (retitled *Passion* in the U.S.) was not only one of the films responsible for breaking the American blockade on imported German films after World War I, but it also began the "invasion" of Hollywood by German talent.

Lubitsch came to Hollywood at Mary Pickford's invitation. He had hoped to direct her in *Faust*, but they finally agreed upon *Rosita*, a costume romance very similar to those he had done in Germany. After joining Warner Brothers, he directed five films that firmly established his thematic interests. The films were small in scale, dealt openly with sexual and psychological relationships in and out of marriage, refrained from offering conventional moral judgments, and demystified women. As Molly Haskell and Marjorie Rosen point out, Lubitsch created complex female characters who were aggressive, unsentimental, and able to express their sexual desires without suffering the usual pains of banishment or death. Even though Lubitsch provided a new and healthy perspective on sex and increased America's understanding of woman's role in society, he did so only in a superficial way. His women ultimately affirmed the status quo. The most frequently cited film from this initial burst of creativity, *The Marriage Circle*, also exhibits the basic narrative motif found in most of Lubitsch's work—the third person catalyst. An essentially solid relationship is temporarily threatened by a sexual rival. The possibility of infidelity serves as the occasion for the original partners to reassess their relationship. They acquire a new self-awareness and understand the responsibilities they have towards each other. The lovers are left more intimately bound than before. This premise was consistently reworked until *The Merry Widow* in 1934.

The late 1920s were years of turmoil as every studio tried to adapt to sound recording. Lubitsch, apparently, wasn't troubled at all; he considered the sound booths nothing more than an inconvenience, something readily overcome. Seven of his ten films from 1929 to 1934 were musicals, but not of the proscenium-bound "all-singing, all-dancing" variety. Musicals were produced with such prolific abandon during this time (what better way to exploit the new technology?) that the public began avoiding them. Film histories tend to view the period from 1930 to 1933 as a musical void, yet it was the precise time that Lubitsch was making significant contributions to the genre. As Arthur Knight notes, "He was the first to be concerned with the 'natural' introduction of songs into the development of a musical-comedy plot." Starting with *The Love Parade*, Lubitsch eliminated the staginess that was characteristic of most musicals by employing a moving camera, clever editing, and the judicial use of integrated musical performance, and in doing so constructed a seminal film musical format.

In 1932 Lubitsch directed his first non-musical sound comedy, *Trouble in Paradise*. Most critics consider this film to be, if not his best, then at least the complete embodiment of everything that has been associated with Lubitsch: sparkling dialogue, interesting plots, witty and sophisticated characters, and an air of urbanity, all part of the well-known "Lubitsch Touch." What constitutes the "Lubitsch Touch" is open to continual debate, the majority of the definitions being couched in poetic terms of idolization. Andrew Sarris comments that the "Lubitsch Touch" is a counterpoint of poignant sadness during a film's gayest moments. Leland A. Poague sees Lubitsch's style as being gracefully charming and fluid, with an " . . . ingenious ability to suggest more than he showed. . . . "

Observations like this last one earned Lubitsch the unfortunate moniker of "director of doors," since a number of his jokes relied on what unseen activity was being implied behind a closed door.

Regardless of which romantic description one chooses, the "Lubitsch Touch" can be most concretely seen as deriving from a standard narrative device of the silent film: interrupting the dramatic interchange by focusing on objects or small details that make a witty comment on or surprising revelation about the main action. Whatever the explanation, Lubitsch's style was exceptionally popular with critics and audiences alike. Ten years after arriving in the United States he had directed 18 features, parts of two anthologies, and was recognized as one of Hollywood's top directors.

Lubitsch's final phase began when he was appointed head of production at Paramount in 1935, a position that lasted only one year. Accustomed to pouring all his energies into one project at a time, he was ineffective juggling numerous projects simultaneously. Accused of being out of step with the times, Lubitsch up-dated his themes in his first political satire, *Ninotchka*, today probably his most famous film. He continued using parody and satire in his blackest comedy, *To Be or Not to Be*, a film well liked by his contemporaries, and today receiving much reinvestigation. If Lubitsch's greatest talent was his ability to make us laugh at the most serious events and anxieties, to use comedy to make us more aware of ourselves, then *To Be or Not to Be* might be considered the consummate work of his career.

Lubitsch, whom Gerald Mast terms the greatest technician in American cinema after Griffith, completed only two more films. At his funeral in 1947, Mervyn LeRoy presented a fitting eulogy: " . . . he advanced the techniques of screen comedy as no one else has ever done. Suddenly the pratfall and the double-take were left behind and the sources of deep inner laughter were tapped."

—Greg S. Faller

LUCAS, George.

American. Born in Modesto, California, 14 May 1944. Attended Modesto Junior College; University of Southern California Film School, graduated 1966. Six-month internship at Warner Bros. spent as assistant to Francis Ford Coppola, 1967–68; co-founder, with Coppola, American Zoetrope, Northern California, 1969; directed first feature, *THX-1138*, 1971; established special effects company, Industrial Light and Magic, at San Rafael, California, 1976; formed production company Lucasfilm, Ltd., 1979; founded post production company Sprocket Systems, 1980; built Skywalker Ranch, then executive producer for Disneyland's 3-D music space adventure, *Captain EO*, 1980s. Recipient: New York Film Critics Award for Best Screenwriting (with Gloria Katz and Willard Huyck), 1973. Address: c/o Lucasfilm, Ltd., P.O. Box 2009, San Rafael, California 94912, U.S.A.

Films as Director and Scriptwriter:

(short student films)

1964–66   *Look at Life*; *Freiheit*; *1.42.08*; *Herbie*; *Anyone Lived in a Pretty How Town*; *6.18.67*; *The Emperor*; *THX 1138: 4 EB*
1968   *Filmmaker* (doc)

(feature films)
1970   *THX 1138*

1973   *American Graffiti* (co-sc)
1977   *Star Wars*

Films as Executive Producer:

1979   *More American Graffiti* (Norton) (+ story)
1980   *The Empire Strikes Back* (Kershner) (+ story)
1981   *Raiders of the Lost Ark* (Spielberg) (+ story)
1983   *Return of the Jedi* (Marquand) (+ co-sc, story)
1984   *Indiana Jones and the Temple of Doom* (Spielberg) (+ story)
1985   *Mishima* (Schrader)
1986   *Howard the Duck* (Huyck); *Labyrinth* (Henson)
1988   *Willow* (Howard); *Tucker: The Man and His Dream* (Coppola)
1989   *Indiana Jones and the Last Crusade* (Spielberg) (+ story)

Publications:

By LUCAS: book—

American Graffiti: A Screenplay, with Gloria Katz and Willard Stuyck, New York, 1973.

By LUCAS: articles—

"*THX-1138*," in *American Cinematographer* (Los Angeles), October 1971.
"The Filming of *American Graffiti*," an interview with L. Sturhahn, in *Filmmakers Newsletter* (Ward Hill, Massachusetts), March 1974.
Interview with S. Zito, in *American Film* (Washington, D.C.), April 1977.
Interview with Robert Benayoun and Michel Ciment, in *Positif* (Paris), September 1977.
Interview with Audie Bock, in *Take One* (Montreal), no. 6, 1979.
Interview with M. Tuchman and A. Thompson, in *Film Comment* (New York), July/August 1981.

On LUCAS: books—

Weinberg, Larry, *Star Wars: The Making of the Movie*, New York, 1980.
Pollock, Dale, *Skywalking: The Life and Films of George Lucas*, New York, 1983.
Smith, Thomas G., *Industrial Light and Magic: The Art of Special Effects*, New York, 1986.

On LUCAS: articles—

Farber, Steven, "George Lucas: The Stinky Kid Hits the Big Time," in *Film Quarterly* (Berkeley), Spring 1974.
"Behind the Scenes of *Star Wars*," in *American Cinematographer* (Los Angeles), July 1977.
Fairchild, B.H., Jr., "Songs of Innocence and Experience: The Blakean Vision of George Lucas," in *Literature/Film Quarterly* (Salisbury, Maryland), no. 2, 1979.
Pye, Michael, and Lynda Myles, "The Man Who Made *Star Wars*," in *Atlantic Monthly* (Greenwich, Connecticut), March 1979.
Harmetz, A., "Burden of Dreams: George Lucas," in *American Film* (Washington, D.C.), June 1983.
Garsault, A., "Les paradoxes de George Lucas," in *Positif* (Paris), September 1983.
Schembri, J., "Robert Watts: Spielberg, Lucas and the Temple of Doom," in *Cinema Papers* (Melbourne), October/November 1984.
"George Lucas," in *Film Dope* (London), February 1987.
Star Wars Section of *Variety* (New York), 3 June 1987.
Kearney, J., and J. Greenberg, "The Road Warrior," in *American Film* (Washington, D.C.), June 1988.

*   *   *

In whatever capacity George Lucas works—director, writer, producer—the films in which he is involved are a mixture of the familiar and the fantastic. Thematically, Lucas's work is often familiar, but the presentation of the material usually carries his unique mark. His earliest commercial science fiction film, *THX 1138*, is not very different in plot from previous stories of futuristic totalitarian societies in which humans are subordinate to technology. What is distinctive about the film is its visual impact. The extreme close-ups, bleak sets, and crowds of "properly sedated" shaven-headed people moving mechanically through hallways effectively produce the physical environment of this cold, well-ordered society. The endless whiteness of the vast detention center without bars could not be more oppressive.

Although not a special effects film, *American Graffiti*, Lucas's second feature, does show his attention to detail and his interest in archetypal themes. Within the 24-hour period of the film, the hero potential is brought forth from within the main characters, either through courageous action or the making of courageous decisions. The film captures America on the verge of transition from the 1950s to the brave new world of the 1960s. Lucas does this visually by recreating the 1950s on screen down to the smallest detail, but he also communicates through his characters the feeling that their lives will never be the same again.

The combination of convention, archetype, and fantasy comes together fully in Lucas's subsequent films—the *Star Wars* and *Indiana Jones* series. On one level the *Star Wars* trilogy is a fairy tale set in outerspace, as suggested in the opening title: "A long time ago in a galaxy far, far away. . . . " The basic plot conventions of the fairy tale are present: a princess in distress, a powerful evil ruler, and courageous knights. The trilogy is also a tale of the emergence of the hero within and the quest by which individuals realize their true selves, for the princess is really a Shaman, the evil ruler a self divided in need of healing, and the knights latent heroes who do not realize themselves as such at the beginning of the tale.

Scenes, especially from *Star Wars* and *The Empire Strikes Back*, look and sound like *Flash Gordon* episodes. Members of the Empire—the Emperor, Darth Vadar, the storm troopers—are an easily identifiable evil in their dark, drab clothing and cloaked or helmeted faces. Their movements are accompanied by a menacing, martial film score of the type that ushered Ming the Merciless on screen. Another reference that associates the Empire with a great evil is that the storm troopers in several scenes resemble the rows of assembled storm troopers on review in *Triumph of the Will*. In contrast to these images of darkness, the rebel forces and their habitats are colorful and full of life.

The *Star Wars* trilogy is also very much science fiction. The special effects developed to realize Lucas's futuristic vision brought about technological advances in motion picture photography. The workshop formed for the production of *Star Wars*, Industrial Light and Magic, continues on as an independent special effects production company. While working on *Star Wars*, John Dykstra developed the Dykstraflex camera for which he received an Academy Award. The camera was used in conjunction with a computer to achieve the accuracy necessary in photographing multiple exposure visual effects. Another advancement in motion control photography was developed for *The Empire Strikes Back*, Brian Edlund's Empireflex camera.

Lucas and Steven Spielberg then set out to make a film based on the romantic action/adventure movies of the 1940s. The successful result was *Raiders of the Lost Ark*. Indiana Jones, based on the rough-edged, worldly-wise screen heroes of those earlier adventure films, is set to such mythic tasks as the quest for the Ark of the Covenant and the quest for the Holy Grail. Jones's enemies on these quests (which occur in the first and the last films of the series), the Nazis, are representatives of the dark side of this universe and carry legendary status of their own. As in the *Star Wars* trilogy, the main characters, includ-

George Lucas

ing the extraordinary Indiana, face challenges that will bring forth qualities and strengths they had not yet realized. The dialogue in *Indiana Jones and the Last Crusade* especially emphasizes the theme of the hero within. At one point the senior Jones tells Indiana that "The search for the cup of Christ is the search for the divine in all of us"; later in the film Indiana is challenged to look within himself by the enemy as he is told, "It's time to ask yourself what you believe."

The films contain references to genre conventions and to earlier films. Also familiar in Lucas's films are the archetypal figures from myths and legends. At the same time, the films are fantastic and unfamiliar, filled with stunning visuals and exotic settings produced by innovative special effects.

—Marie Saeli

LUMET, Sidney.

American. Born in Philadelphia, 25 June 1924. Educated at Professional Children's school, New York; Columbia University extension school. Served in Signal Corps, U.S. Army, 1942–46. Married 1) Rita Gam (divorced); 2) Gloria Vanderbilt, 1956 (divorced 1963); 3) Gail Jones, 1963 (divorced 1978); 4) Mary Gimbel, 1980, two daughters. Acting debut in Yiddish Theatre production, New York, 1928; Broadway debut in *Dead End*, 1935; film actor, from 1939; stage director, off-Broadway, from 1947; assistant director, then director, for TV, from 1950. Recipient: Directors Guild Awards, for *Twelve Angry Men*, 1957, and *Long Day's Journey into Night*, 1962. Address: c/o LAH Film Corporation, 1775 Broadway, New York, NY 10019, U.S.A.

Films as Director:

1957   ***Twelve Angry Men***
1958   *Stage Struck*
1959   *That Kind of Woman*
1960   *The Fugitive Kind*
1962   *A View from the Bridge*; *Long Day's Journey Into Night*
1964   *Fail Safe*
1965   *Pawnbroker*; *Up from the Beach*; *The Hill*
1966   *The Group* (+ pr)
1967   *The Deadly Affair* (+ pr)
1968   *Bye Bye Braverman* (+ pr); *The Seagull* (+ pr)
1969   *Blood Kin* (doc) (co-d, co-pr)
1970   *King: A Filmed Record . . . Montgomery to Memphis* (doc) (co-d, co-pr); *The Appointment*; *The Last of the Mobile Hot Shots*
1971   *The Anderson Tapes*
1972   *Child's Play*
1973   *The Offense*; *Serpico*
1974   *Lovin' Molly*; *Murder on the Orient Express*
1975   *Dog Day Afternoon*
1977   *Equus*; *Network*
1978   *The Wiz*
1980   *Just Tell Me What You Want* (+ pr)
1981   *Prince of the City*
1982   *Deathtrap*; *The Verdict*
1983   *Daniel*
1984   *Garbo Talks*
1986   *Power*; *The Morning After*
1988   *Running on Empty*
1989   *Family Business*
1990   *Q & A*

Other Films:

1939   *One Third of a Nation* (Murphy) (role as Joey Rogers)
1940   *Journey to Jerusalem* (role as youthful Jesus)

Publications:

By LUMET: articles—

Interview with Peter Bogdanovich, in *Film Quarterly* (Berkeley), Winter 1960.
"Sidney Lumet," in *Cahiers du Cinéma* (Paris), December 1963/January 1964.
"Keep Them on the Hook," in *Films and Filming* (London), October 1964.
Interview with Luciano Dale, in *Film Quarterly* (Berkeley), Fall 1971.
"Sidney Lumet on the Director," in *Movie People: At Work in the Business*, edited by Fred Baker, New York, 1972.
Interview with Susan Merrill, in *Films in Review* (New York), November 1973.
Interviews with Gordon Gow, in *Films and Filming* (London), May 1975 and May 1978.
Interview with Dan Yakir, in *Film Comment* (New York), December 1978.
Interview with Michel Ciment and O. Eyquem, in *Positif* (Paris), February 1982.
"Delivering *Daniel*," an interview with Richard Combs, in *Monthly Film Bulletin* (London), January 1984.
Interview with K.M. Chanko, in *Films in Review* (New York), October 1984.
Interview with M. Burke, in *Stills* (London), February 1987.
"Sidney Lumet: Lion on the Left," an interview with G. Smith, in *Film Comment* (New York), July/August 1988.

Sidney Lumet (center) directing *The Deadly Affair*

On LUMET: books—

Bowles, Stephen, *Sidney Lumet: A Guide to References and Resources*, Boston, 1979.
De Santi, Gualtiero, *Sidney Lumet*, Florence, 1988.

On LUMET: articles—

Petrie, Graham, "The Films of Sidney Lumet: Adaptation as Art," in *Film Quarterly* (Berkeley), Winter 1967/68.
Rayns, Tony, "Across the Board," in *Sight and Sound* (London), Summer 1974.
Sidney Lumet Section of *Cinématographe* (Paris), January 1982.
Chase, D., "Sidney Lumet Shoots *The Verdict*," in *Millimeter* (New York), December 1982.
Shewey, D., "Sidney Lumet: the Reluctant Auteur," in *American Film* (Washington, D.C.), December 1982.
"TV to Film: A History, a Map and a Family Tree," in *Monthly Film Bulletin* (London), February 1983.
"Sidney Lumet," in *Film Dope* (London), June 1987.

* * *

Although Sidney Lumet has applied his talents to a variety of genres (drama, comedy, satire, caper, romance, and even a musical), he has proven himself most comfortable and effective as a director of serious psychodramas and was most vulnerable when attempting light entertainments. His Academy Award nominations, for example, have all been for character studies of men in crisis, from his first film, *Twelve Angry Men*, to *The Verdict*.

Lumet was, literally, a child of the drama. At the age of four he was appearing in productions of the highly popular and acclaimed Yiddish theatre in New York. He continued to act for the next two decades but increasingly gravitated toward directing. At 26 he was offered a position as an assistant director with CBS television. Along with John Frankenheimer, Robert Mulligan, Martin Ritt, Delbert Mann, George Roy Hill, Franklin Schaffner, and others, Lumet quickly won recognition as a competent and reliable director in a medium where many faltered under the pressures of producing live programs. It was in this environment that Lumet learned many of the skills that would serve him so well in his subsequent career in films: working closely with performers, rapid preparation for production, and working within tight schedules and budgets.

Because the quality of many of the television dramas was so

impressive, several of them were adapted as motion pictures. Reginald Rose's *Twelve Angry Men* brought Lumet to the cinema. Although Lumet did not direct the television production, his expertise made him the ideal director for this low budget film venture. *Twelve Angry Men* was an auspicious beginning for Lumet. It was a critical and commercial success, and, established Lumet as a director skilled at adapting theatrical properties to motion pictures. Fully half of Lumet's complement of films have originated in the theater. Another precedent set by *Twelve Angry Men* was Lumet's career-long disdain for Hollywood.

Lumet prefers to work in contemporary urban settings, especially New York. Within this context, Lumet is consistently attracted to situations in which crime provides the occasion for a group of characters to come together. Typically these characters are caught in a vortex of events they can neither understand nor control but which they must work to resolve. *Twelve Angry Men* explores the interaction of a group of jurors debating the innocence or guilt of a man being tried for murder; *The Hill* concerns a rough group of military men who have been sentenced to prison; *The Deadly Affair* involves espionage in Britain; *The Anderson Tapes* revolves around the robbery of a luxury apartment building; *Child's Play*, about murder at a boy's school, conveys an almost supernatural atmosphere of menace; *Murder on the Orient Express, Dog Day Afternoon*, and *The Verdict* all involve attempts to find the solution to a crime, while *Serpico* and *Prince of the City* are probing examinations of men who have rejected graft practices as police officers.

Lumet's protagonists tend to be isolated, unexceptional men who oppose a group or institution. Whether the protagonist is a member of a jury or party to a bungled robbery, he follows his instincts and intuition in an effort to find solutions. Lumet's most important criterion is not whether the actions of these men are right or wrong but whether the actions are genuine. If these actions are justified by the individual's conscience, this gives his heroes uncommon strength and courage to endure the pressures, abuses, and injustices of others. Frank Serpico, for example, is the quintessential Lumet hero in his defiance of peer group authority and the assertion of his own code of moral values.

Nearly all the characters in Lumet's gallery are driven by obsessions or passions that range from the pursuit of justice, honesty, and truth to the clutches of jealousy, memory, or guilt. It is not so much the object of their fixations but the obsessive condition itself that intrigues Lumet. In films like *The Fugitive Kind, A View from the Bridge, Long Day's Journey into Night, The Pawnbroker, The Seagull, The Appointment, The Offense, Lovin' Molly, Network, Just Tell Me What You Want*, and many of the others, the protagonists, as a result of their complex fixations, are lonely, often disillusioned individuals. Consequently, most of Lumet's central characters are not likable or pleasant and sometimes, not admirable figures. And, typically, their fixations result in tragic or unhappy consequences.

Lumet's fortunes have been up and down at the box office. One explanation seems to be his own fixation with uncompromising studies of men in crisis. His most intense characters present a grim vision of idealists broken by realities. From Val in *A View from the Bridge* and Sol Nazerman in *The Pawnbroker* to Danny Ciello in *Prince of the City*, Lumet's introspective characters seek to penetrate the deepest regions of the psyche.

—Stephen E. Bowles

LUMIÈRE, Louis.

French. Born in Besançon, 5 October 1864. Educated at l'école de la Martinière, Besançon, degree 1880; Conservatoire de Lyon, 1880–81. Chemist and inventor, son of an industrialist specialising in photographic chemistry and the making of emulsions; after seeing Edison Kinetoscope demonstrated in Paris, developed with brother Auguste Lumière (1862–1954) the "Cinématographe Lumière," incorporating invention of claw driven by eccentric gear for advancing film, 1894; projected first film, showing workers leaving the Lumière factory, 1895 (projects first program for a paying audience at Grand Café, Boulevard des Capucines, Paris, 28 December 1895); Société du Cinématographe Lumière formed, 1896; projected film onto 16 by 21 foot screen at Paris Exposition, 1900; company ceased film production, 1905; subsequently invented and manufactured photographic equipment; worked on stereo projection method, from 1921; première of "cinéma en relief" in Paris, 1936. *Died in Bandol, France, 6 June 1948.*

Films as Director:

1896–1900 Directed about 60 films and produced about 2000, mostly documentary
1894 or 95 *La Sortie des usines* (version no. 1)
1895   *La Sortie des usines* (version no. 2); **L'Arroseur arrosé** (*Le Jardinier*); *Forgerons; Pompiers; Attaque du feu; Le Repas de bébé* (*Le Déjeuner de bébé. Le Gouter de bébé*); *Pêche aux poissons rouges; La Voltige; Débarquement* (*Arrivée des congressistes à Neuville-sur-Saône*); *Discussion de M. Janssen et de M. Lagrange; Saut à la couverture* (*Brimade dans une caserne*); *Lyon, place des Cordeliers; Lyon, place Bellecour; Récréation à la Martinière; Charcuterie mécanique; Le Maréchalferrant; Lancement d'un navire à La Ciotat; Baignade en mer; Ateliers de La Ciotat; Barque sortant du port* (*La Sortie du port*); *Arrivée d'un train à La Ciotat; Partie d'écarté; Assiettes tournantes; Chapeaux à transformations* (*Trewey: Under the Hat*); *Photographe; Démolition d'un mur* (*Le Mur*); *Querelle enfantine; Aquarium; Bocal aux poissons-rouges; Partie de tric-trac; Le Dejeuner du chat; Départ en voiture; Enfants aux jouets; Course en sac; Discussion*
1896–97 *Barque en mer; Baignade en mer, Arrivée d'un bateau à vapeur; Concours de boules; Premiers pas de Bébé; Embarquement pour le promenade; Retour d'une promenade en mer; Marché; Enfant et chien; Petit frère et petite soeur; Douche après le bain; Ronde enfantine; Enfants au bord de la mer; Bains en mer; Touristes revenant d'une excursion; Scènes d'enfants; Laveuses; Repas en famille; Bal d'enfants; Leçon de bicyclette; Menuisiers; Radeau avec baigneurs; Le Goûter de bébé*
1900   *Inauguration de l'Exposition universelle; La Tour Eiffel; Le Pont d' Iéna; Danses espagnoles* and other films shown on large screen at Paris Exposition 1900
1936   *Arrivée d'un train en gare de La Ciotat* and other films presented in "cinéma en relief" program.

Publications:

By LUMIÈRE: books—

Cinématographe Auguste et Louis Lumière: Catalogue des Vues, first through seventh lists, Lyon, France 1897–98
Catalogue des vues pour cinématographe, Lyon, 1907.

By LUMIÈRE: articles—

"Lumière—The Last Interview," with Georges Sadoul, in *Sight and Sound* (London), Summer 1948.
"Bellecour—Monplaisir," with H. Bitomsky, in *Filmkritik* (Munich), August 1978.

Louis Lumière: poster for *L'Arroseur arrosé*

On LUMIÈRE: books—

Kubnick, Henri, *Les Frères Lumière*, Paris, 1938.
Bessy, Maurice, and Lo Duca, *Louis Lumière, inventeur*, Paris, 1948.
Leroy, Paul, *Au seuil de paradis des images avec Louis Lumière*, Paris, 1948.
Sadoul, Georges, *Histoire générale du cinéma* vols. 1 and 2, Paris, 1949.
Pernot, Victor, *A Paris, il y a soixante ans, naissait le cinéma*, Paris, 1955.
Mitry, Jean, *Filmographie Universelle* vol.2, Paris, 1964.
Sadoul, Georges, *Louis Lumière*, Paris, 1964.
Chardère, Bernard, and others, *Les Lumières*, Paris, 1985.
Rittaud-Hutinet, *Le Cinéma des origines: frères Lumière et leur opérateurs*, Seyssel, 1985.
Sauvage, Leo, *L'Affaire Lumière*, Paris, 1985.
Redi, Riccardo, editor, *Lumière*, Rome, 1986.
André, Jacques and Marie, *Uns Saison Lumière à Montpelier*, Perpignan, 1987.

On LUMIÈRE: articles—

Browne, Mallory, "Artisan in Light," in the *Christian Science Monitor Magazine* (Boston), 7 August 1935.
"Lumiere Jubilee," in *Time* (New York), 18 November 1935.
Deutelbaum, M., "Structural Patterning in the Lumière Films," in *Wide Angle* (Athens, Ohio), no. 1, 1979.
Decaux, E., "Lieux du cinéma: lettre du Chateau Lumière," in *Cinématographe* (Paris), January 1979.
Vaughan, Dai, "Let There Be Lumière," in *Sight and Sound* (London), Spring 1981.

Dubois, P., "Le gros plan primitif," in *Revue Belge du Cinéma* (Brussels), Winter 1984/85.
Rinieri, D., "Lumière fut," in *Cinématographe* (Paris), September 1985.
"Louis Lumière: 8 Films de la soirée du Grand café," in *Avant-Scène du Cinéma* (Paris), November 1984.
Masson, André, "Lumière!," in *Positif* (Paris), January 1986.
Chardère, B., and others, "Les Droits des films Lumière," in *Filmèchange* (Paris), Autumn 1986.
Gorki, Maxim, and P. Delpeut, in *Versus* (Nijmegen), no. 2, 1988.
Chardère, B., "Les sorties des usines Lumière. Jamais deux sans trois," in *Positif* (Paris), June 1989.

*   *   *

Few directors since Louis Lumière have enjoyed such total control over their films. As inventor of the *cinématographe*, the first camera-cum-projector, he determined not only the subjects but also the aesthetics of early cinema. A scientist devoted to the plastic arts, Lumière initially specialised in outdoor photography. This experience, coupled with an appreciation of framing, perspective, and light values in a composition, informed his pioneering films.

To promote the *cinématographe*, he made demonstration shorts which, because of the camera's limited spool capacity, lasted less than a minute. If art refines itself through constraint, Lumière's films are excellent models. He overcame the *cinématographe's* technical limitations to achieve tightly structured views of contemporary life, both public and private.

Though Lumière's role in establishing the cinema has been dutifully recorded together with the audience's thrilled disbelief at his moving images, his contribution to film practice deserves more recognition. His first film, *La Sortie des usines*, pictures employees leaving his photographic factory. Framed by the open gates, they disperse before the camera set at a medium close-up distance, and with the closure of the gates the sequence ends. The film does not result from a casual pointing of the camera at the chosen subject: all has been pre-planned, from the placing of the hidden camera to the squaring of the action's duration with the available footage.

Over the next two years or so, Lumière experimented with diverse subjects and filming techniques. His themes reflect an unquestioning confidence in the permanence of contemporary political and social structures. Whether recording aspects of city life or the calmer pleasures of the seaside, the work of the artisan, fireman or soldier, more personal family subjects or rehearsed comic episodes, his films imply a well-ordered, contented society where individuals cheerfully perform their allotted roles. Images of social deprivation or discontent are noticeably absent.

Scenes featuring family or friends are often filmed in medium close-up, with the single framing here reinforcing the intimacy and denying a world outside. Immaculate children, invariably in white, are shown feeding (*Repas de bébé*), learning to walk (*Premiers pas de bébé*), playing with toys (*Enfants aux jouets*), arguing (*Querelle enfantine*), dancing (*Bal d'enfants*), or delightfully trying to catch goldfish (*Pêche aux poissons rouges*). In *Concert*, Madame Lumière plays a violin, while card games involve family friends (*Partie d'écarté* and *Partie de tric-trac*). A cat lapping milk (*Déjeûner du chat*) is filmed in close-up and in *Aquarium* the fish tank fills the frame to create the illusion of underwater photography.

In films such as *Place des Cordeliers* and *Place Bellecour* the atmosphere of public squares alive with horse-drawn carriages and bustling crowds is captured, while in films such as *Baignade en mer* the novelties of sea-bathing are recorded. Other films prefigure newsreels by documenting particular events. The first of these, *Débarquement*, records photographers arriving for their Conference and was projected the next day. Similar events include a street sack race (*Course en sac*), the demolition of a wall (*Démolition d'un mur*) the launching of a ship (*Lancement d'un navire à La Ciotat*) and various arrivals or departures such as *Touristes revenant d'une excursion*, or *Arrivée d'un bateau à vapeur*. An early triumph was *Barque sortant du port*, where glistening waves and a sudden swell rocking the boat impressed themselves on a public familiar only with static images. Sequences capturing movement were an immediate attraction.

Lumière's most celebrated arrival subject was the train entering La Ciotat station (*Arrivée d'un train à la Ciotat*). Here the dramatic resources of depth of field are exploited, with the platform and the track forming strong diagonals reaching into the distance. The train, first pictured in longshot, thrusts itself towards the camera to create a dynamic close-up. So powerful was the illusion of the train's immanence that the first audiences reportedly feared for their safety. The creative use of perspective was also fundamental to the depiction of ploughing in *Labourage* and to the sack race in *Course en sac*.

Documentaries concerning artisans or the military reveal a studied composition. The camera is positioned to make actions comprehensible, whether in terms of shoeing horses (*Maréchal-ferrant*), shaping iron bars (*Forgerons*) or horsemanship (*Voltige*). Cooperation with the fire service produced a more substantial documentary. Recognising the dramatic potential of his subject, Lumière portrayed a full scale fire practice in four linked films: *Sortie de la Pompe*; *Mise en Batterie*; *Attaque du feu*; and *Sauvetage*.

Comic sketches required careful preparation. In *L'Arroseur arrosé* a young prankster soaks an unsuspecting gardener by interrupting, then releasing, the water supply to a hose. All is tightly organized in time and space to meet the limitations of the fixed camera. In *Photographe* the innocent subject is again drenched, while in *Charcuterie mécanique* (which ridicules American mechanisation long before Tati's postman in *Jour de fête*) a pig is converted into sausages which then magically transform themselves into a pig again. Although Lumière renounced filmmaking, he extended his influence through trained operators, such as Promio, Mesguish and Doublier. His impact on early cinema is evident in the way others, notably Méliès, imitated his subjects. His abiding presence in French film culture is witnessed in various homages: in *Les Mistons* Truffaut affectionately alludes to *L'Arroseur arrosé* while in *Les Carabiniers* Godard parodies *L'Arrivée d'un train à la Ciotat* and *Le Repas de bébé*.

—R F. Cousins

LYNCH, David.

American. Born Missoula, Montana, 1946. Educated at High School in Alexandria, Virginia; Pennsylvania Academy of Fine Art, Philadelphia; American Film Institute Centre for Advanced Studies, studying under Frank Daniel, 1970. Married 1) 1967 (divorced), daughter writer/director Jennifer Lynch; 2) Mary Fisk, 1977 (separated), one son. Spent 5 years making *Eraserhead*, Los Angeles, 1971–76; worked as paperboy and shed-builder, late 1970s; invited by Mel Brooks to direct *The Elephant Man*, 1980; with Mark Frost, made *Twin Peaks* for Video (two-hour version) and as TV series, 1989. Recipient: National Society of Film Critics Awards for Best Film and Best Director, for *Blue Velvet*, 1986; Palme d'Or, Cannes Festival, for *Wild at Heart*, 1990.

Films as Director and Scriptwriter:

1968	*The Alphabet* (short)
1970	*The Grandmother* (short)
1978	*Eraserhead*
1980	*Elephant Man* (co-sc)
1984	*Dune*
1986	**Blue Velvet**
1988	episode in *Les Français vus par . . .*
1990	*Wild at Heart*

Publications:

By LYNCH: articles—

Interview with Serge Daney and Charles Tesson, in *Cahiers du Cinéma* (Paris), April 1981.
Interview with D. Chute, in *Film Comment* (New York), September/October 1986.
Interview with K. Jaehne and L. Bouzereau, in *Cineaste* (New York), vol. 15, no. 3, 1987.
Interview with A. Caron and M. Girard, in *Séquences* (Montreal), February 1987.
Interview with D. Marsh and A. Missler, in *Cinema Papers* (Melbourne), March 1987.
Interview with Jane Root, in *Monthly Film Bulletin* (London), April 1987.

David Lynch

On LYNCH: articles—

Hinson, H., "Dreamscapes," in *American Film* (Washington, D.C.), December 1984.

David Lynch Section of *Revue du Cinéma* (Paris), February 1987.

Combs, Richard, "Crude Thoughts and Fierce Forces," in *Monthly Film Bulletin* (London), April 1987.

French, Sean, "The Heart of the Cavern," in *Sight and Sound* (London), Spring 1987.

"David Lynch," in *Film Dope* (London), June 1987.

McDonagh, M., "The Enigma of David Lynch," in *Persistence of Vision* (Maspeth, New York), Summer 1988.

Gehr, R., "The Angriest Painter in the World," in *American Film* (Washington, D.C.), April 1989.

Woodward, Robert B., "Wild at Heart . . . weird on top," in *Empire* (London), September 1990.

*   *   *

The undoubted perversity that runs throughout the works of David Lynch extends to his repeated and unexpected career turns, coming off the semi-underground *Eraserhead* to make the semi-respectable *The Elephant Man*, with a distinguished British cast, then bouncing into a Dino de Laurentiis mega-budget science fiction fiasco, *Dune*, creeping back with the seductive and elusive small town mystery of *Blue Velvet*, capping that by transferring his uncompromising vision of lurking sexual violence to American network television in *Twin Peaks*, and alienating the viewers of that bizarre soap with the rambling, intermittently stupefying, road movie, *Wild at Heart*. Although there are recognisable Lynchian elements, with both *Eraserhead* and *Blue Velvet*—his two most commercially and critically successful movies—leaking images and ideas into the pairs of movies that followed them up, Lynch has proved surprisingly difficult to pin down. Given one Lynch movie, it has been—until the slightly too self-plagiaristic *Wild at Heart*—almost impossible to predict the next step. A painter and animator—his first films are Svankmajer-style shorts *The Grandmother* and *Alphabet*—Lynch came into the film industry through the backdoor, converting his thesis movie into *Eraserhead* on a shooting schedule that stretched over some years and required the eternal soliciting of money from friends, like Sissy Spacek, who had gone on to do well.

Eraserhead is one of the rare cult movies that deserves its cult reputation, although it's a hard movie to sit still for a second time around. Set in a monochrome fantasy world that suggests the slums of Oz, it follows a pompadoured drudge Henry (John Nance) through his awful life in a decaying apartment building, with occasional bursts of light relief from the fungus-cheeked songstress behind the radiator, and winds up with two extraordinarily bizarre and horrid fantasy sequences, one in which Henry's head falls off and is mined for indiarubber to be used in pencil erasers, and the other in which he cuts apart his skinned foetus of a mutant child and is deluged with a literal tide of excrement. Without really being profound, the film manages to worm its way into the hearts of the college crowd, cannily appealing—in one of Lynch's trademarks—to intellectuals who relish the multiple allusions and evasive "meanings" of the film, and to horror movie fans who just like to go along with the extreme imagery. With *The Elephant Man*, also in black and white and laden with the steamy industrial imagery of *Eraserhead*, Lynch, cued perhaps by the poignance of John Hurt's under-the-rubber performance and the presence of the sort of cast (Anthony Hopkins, John Gielgud, Freddie Jones, Michael Elphick) one would expect from some BBC-TV Masterpiece Theatre serial, opts for a more humanist approach, mellowing the sheer nastiness of the first film. In the finale, as the mutant John Merrick attends a lovingly recreated Victorian magic show, Lynch even pays hommage to the gentle magician whose *The Man With the Indiarubber Head* might be cited as a precursor to *Eraserhead*, Georges Méliès.

Dune is a folly by anyone's standards, and the re-cut television version—which Lynch opted to sign with the Director's Guild pseudonym Allan Smithee—is no help in sorting out the multiple plot confusions of Frank Herbert's pretentious and unfilmable science fiction epic. Hoping for a fusion of *Star Wars* and *Lawrence of Arabia*, De Laurentiis, who stuck by Lynch throughout the troubled $40,000,000 production, wound up with a turgid mess, overloaded with talented performers in nothing roles, that only spottily seems to have engaged Lynch's interest, mostly when there are monsters on screen or when Kenneth McMillan is campily overdoing his perverse and evil Emperor act. *Dune* landed Lynch in the doldrums, and his comeback movie, also for the forgiving De Laurentiis, was very carefully crafted to evoke the virtues and cult commercial appeal of *Eraserhead* without seeming a throwback. Drawing on *Shadow of a Doubt*, Lynch made a small town mystery that deigns to work on a plot level, and then shot it through with his own cruel insights into the teeming, insectoid nightmare that exists beneath the red, white and blue prettiness of the setting, coaxing sinister meaning out of resonant pop songs like "Blue Velvet" and "In Dreams," and establishing the core of a repertory company—Kyle MacLachlan of *Dune*, Isabella Rossellini, Laura Dern—who would recur in his next projects. *Blue Velvet*, far more than the muddy *Dune*, established Lynch as a master of colour in addition to his black and white skills, and also, through his handling of human monster Dennis Hopper's abuse of Rossellini, as a chronicler of extreme emotions, often combining sex and violence in one disturbing, yet undeniably appealing package.

Twin Peaks, a series Lynch devised and for which he directed the pilot film, is a strange offshoot of *Blue Velvet*, set in a similar town and with MacLachlan again the odd investigator of a crime the nature of which is hard to define. Although it lacks the explicit tone of the earlier film, in which Dennis Hopper is given to basic outbursts like "baby wants to fuck!," *Twin Peaks* is also insidiously fascinating, using the labyrinthine plot convolutions of the typical soap opera—among other things, the show is a lineal descendant of *Peyton Place*—in addition to the puzzle-solving twists of the murder mystery to probe under the surface of a folksy America of junk food and picket fences. As a reaction to the eerie restraint of *Twin Peaks, Wild at Heart* is an undisciplined, half-satisfactory movie, a road film which evokes Elvis in Nicolas Cage's subtly overwrought performance and straggles along towards its *Wizard of Oz* finale, passing by the highpoints of Lynch's career (featuring players and jokes from all his earlier movies) as it plays out its couple-on-the-run storyline in a surprisingly straightforward and aboveboard manner. With Willem Dafoe's dirty-teeth monster replacing Dennis Hopper's gas-sniffing gangster, *Wild at Heart* echoes the violent and sexual excesses of *Blue Velvet*, including one exploding head stunt out of *The Evil Dead* and many Heavy Metal-scored heavy-duty sex scenes, but suffers perhaps from its relative predictability.

Both a genuine artist and a cunning commercial survivor, Lynch stands, with maybe David Cronenberg, as the Best Hope for cinema in the 1990s.

—Kim Newman

MACKENDRICK, Alexander.

Scottish. Born in Boston, 1912. Educated at Glasgow School of Art. Commercial artist, animator of advertising films, also worked in Holland with George Pal, 1930s; made short propaganda films for Ministry of Information, World War II; later head of documentary and newsreel dept. of Psychological Warfare Branch, Rome; joined Ealing Studios as scriptwriter, 1946; directed first feature, *Whisky Galore*, 1946; signed contract with Hecht-Lancaster (Harold Hecht and Burt Lancaster) to make *Sweet Smell of Success* in U.S., 1956; Dean, Film Dept. of California Institute of the Arts, Valencia, from 1969; resigned Deanship, continued to teach at CalArts, from 1978.

Films as Director:

1949   *Whisky Galore (Tight Little Island)* (+ co-sc)
1951   ***The Man in the White Suit*** (+ co-sc)
1952   *Mandy (The Story of Mandy. Crash of Silence)*
1954   *The Maggie (High and Dry)* (+ story)
1955   *The Ladykillers*
1957   ***Sweet Smell of Success***
1963   *Sammy Going South (A Boy Ten Feet Tall)*
1965   *A High Wind in Jamaica*
1967   *Oh Dad, Poor Dad, Mamma's Hung You in the Closet and I'm Feelin' So Sad* (Quine) (d add'l scenes); *Don't Make Waves*

Other Films:

1950   ***The Blue Lamp*** (Dearden) (add'l dialogue)

Publications:

By MACKENDRICK: article—

Interview with Bernard Cohn, in *Positif* (Paris), February 1968.

On MACKENDRICK: books—

Balcon, Michael, *A Lifetime of Films*, London, 1969.
Barr, Charles, *Ealing Studios*, London, 1977.
Perry, George, *Forever Ealing*, London, 1981.
Kemp, Philip, *Lethal Innocence: The Cinema of Alexander Mackendrick*, London, 1991.

On MACKENDRICK articles—

Cutts, John, "Mackendrick Finds the Sweet Smell of Success," in *Films and Filming* (London), June 1957.
"Alexander Mackendrick," in *Films and Filming* (London), January 1963.
Sarris, Andrew, "Oddities and One-Shots," in *Film Culture* (New York), Spring 1963.
"Mackendrick Issue" of *Dialogue on Film* (Washington, D.C.), no. 2, 1972.
Barr, Charles, "'Projecting Britain and the British Character': Ealing Studios," in *Screen* (London), Summer 1974.

Goldstone, P., "Focus on Education: The Mackendrick Legacy," in *American Film* (Washington, D.C.), March 1979.
"Alexander Mackendrick," in *Film Dope* (London), June 1987.
Kemp, Philip, "Mackendrick Land," in *Sight and Sound* (London), Winter 1988/89.

*   *   *

In 1955 Alexander Mackendrick made *The Ladykillers*, the last of his four Ealing comedies. Two years later, in Hollywood, came his brilliantly acid study of corruption and betrayal, *Sweet Smell of Success*. At first glance, the gulf is prodigious. Yet on closer examination, it narrows considerably: the apparent contrast between the two films becomes little more than a matter of surface tone. For behind the comedies that Mackendrick made for Ealing can be detected a mordant humor, a pessimism, and even an instinct for cruelty which sets them apart from the gentle sentimentality of their stablemates (Hamer's *Kind Hearts and Coronets* always excepted). The mainstream of Ealing comedy, even including such classics as *Passport to Pimlico* and *The Lavender Hill Mob*, presents (as Charles Barr has pointed out) "a whimsical daydream of how things might be." There is little of that daydream about Mackendrick's films; at times—as in *The Ladykillers*—they edge closer to surrealist nightmare.

In *Whisky Galore* the English outsider, Captain Waggett, is subjected by the islanders to continual humiliation, unalleviated even in their triumph by the slightest friendly gesture. Similarly Marshall, the American tycoon in *The Maggie*, is abused, exploited, and physically assaulted by the Scots he encounters. Both workers and bosses, in *The Man in the White Suit*, turn violently upon Sidney Stratton, the idealistic inventor; and *The Ladykillers* culminates in a whole string of brutal murders. Not that this blackness detracts in the least from the effectiveness of the comedy. Rather, it lends the films a biting edge which makes them all the funnier, and may well explain why they have dated far less than most other Ealing movies.

A constant theme of Mackendrick's films is the clash between innocence and experience. Innocence connotes integrity, but also blindness to the interests of others; experience brings shrewdness, but also corruption. Generally, innocence is defeated, but not always: in *The Ladykillers* it is serenely innocent Mrs. Wilberforce who survives—as does Susan Hunsecker in *Sweet Smell of Success*, albeit at a price. Children feature prominently in Mackendrick's films—*Mandy, Sammy Going South, The Maggie*—and often embody the principle of innocence, though again not always. In *A High Wind in Jamaica*, against all audience expectations, it is the pirates, not the children they capture, who prove to be the innocents, and who suffer death for it. As so often with Mackendrick's characters, they are doomed by their lack of perception; trapped, like the deaf heroine of *Mandy*, in a private world, they see only what they expect to see.

Mackendrick established a reputation as an exacting and

Alexander Mackendrick directing Tony Curtis in *The Sweet Smell of Success*

perfectionist director, bringing to his films a visual acuteness and a flair for complex fluid composition to support the tight dramatic structure. After *Sweet Smell of Success*, though the quality of his work is generally considered to have declined, and he has made no films since 1967. A planned project on *Mary Queen of Scots* (intriguingly outlined by Mackendrick as "a sophisticated French lady landed in Boot Hill") never materialised. From 1969 to 1978 he headed an outstanding film department at the California Institute of the Arts; but the withdrawal of such a subtle and individual director from active filmmaking is greatly to be regretted.

—Philip Kemp

MAKAVEJEV, Dusan.

Yugoslavian. Born in Belgrade, 13 October 1932. Educated in Psychology at Belgrade University, graduated 1955; studied direction at the Academy for Theatre, Radio, Film and Television, Belgrade. Married Bojana Marijan, 1964. Experimental filmmaker for Kino-Club, 1955–58; joined Zagreb Films, 1958; military service, 1959–60; worked for Avala films, 1961; went to U.S. on Ford Foundation Grant, 1968; worked in U.S., since 1974.

Films as Director:

(shorts and documentaries):
1953 *Jatagan Mala* (+ sc)
1955 *Pečat* (*The Seal*) (+ sc)
1957 *Antonijevo razbijeno ogledalo* (*Anthony's Broken Mirror*) (+ sc)
1958 *Spomenicima ne treba verovati* (*Don't Believe in Monuments*) (+ sc); *Slikovnica pčelara* (*Beekeeper's Scrapbook*) (+ sc); *Prokleti praznik* (*Damned Holiday*) (+ sc); *Boje sanjaju* (*Colors are Dreaming*) (+ sc)
1959 *Sto je radnički savjet?* (*What is a Workers' Council?*)
1961 *Eci, pec, pec* (*One Potato, Two Potato . . .*) (+ sc); *Pedagoška bajka* (*Educational Fairy Tale*) (+ sc); *Osmjeh 61* (*Smile 61*) (+ sc)
1962 *Parada* (*Parade*) (+ sc); *Dole plotovi* (*Down with the Fences*) (+ sc); *Ljepotica 62* (*Miss Yugoslavia 62*) (+ sc); *Film o knjizi A.B.C.* (*Film about the Book*) (+ sc)
1964 *Nova igračka* (*New Toy*) (+ sc); *Nova domaća zivotinja* (*New Domestic Animal*) (+ sc)

(feature films):

1966 *Covek nije tica* (*Man Is Not a Bird*) (+ sc)
1967 *Ljubavni Slučaj, tragedija sluzbenice PTT* (*Love Affair. Switchboard Operator. An Affair of the Heart*) (+ sc)

1968 *Nevinost bez zaštite* (*Innocence Unprotected*) (+ sc)
1971 **W.R.: Misterije organizma** (**W.R.: Mysteries of the Organism**) (+
   sc)
1974 *Sweet Movie* (+ co-sc)
1981 *Montenegro* (*Or Pigs and Pearls*) (+ sc)
1985 *The Coca Cola Kid*
1988 *For a Night of Love*
1989 *Manifesto*

Publications:

By MAKAVEJEV: books—

A Kiss for Komradess Slogan, 1964.
Nevinost bez zaštite [Innocence Unprotected], Zagreb, 1968.
WR: Mysteries of the Organism, New York, 1972.

By MAKAVEJEV: articles—

"Fight Power with Spontaneity and Humor: An Interview with Dusan Makavejev," with Robert Sutton and others, in *Film Quarterly* (Berkeley), Winter 1971/72.
Interview with R. Colacielo, in *Interview* (New York), February 1972.
Interview with G. Braucourt, in *Ecran* (Paris), September/October 1972.
"Let's Put the Life Back in Political Life," interview with C.B. Thompson, in *Cinéaste* (New York), v.6, no.2, 1974.
Interview with Robert Benayoun and Michel Ciment, in *Positif* (Paris), June 1974.
Interview with Edgardo Cozarinsky and Carlos Clarens, in *Film Comment* (New York), May/June 1975.
"Film Censorship in Yugoslavia," in *Film Comment* (New York), July/August 1975.
Interview with F. La Polla, in *Cineforum* (Bergamo), June/July 1986.

On MAKAVEJEV: book—

Taylor, John, *Directors and Directions*, New York, 1975.

On MAKAVEJEV: articles—

Wood, Robin, "Dušan Makavejev," in *Second Wave*, New York, 1970.
Oppenheim, O., "Makavejev in Montreal," in *Sight and Sound* (London), Spring 1970.
"Makavejev and the Mysteries of the Organism," in *Film* (London), Autumn 1971.
Robinson, David, "Joie de Vivre at the Barricades: The Films of Dušan Makavejev," in *Sight and Sound* (London), Autumn 1971.
MacBean, J.R., "Sex and Politics," in *Film Quarterly* (Berkeley), Spring 1972.
Vogel, Amos, "Makavejev: Toward the Edge of the Real . . . and Over," in *Film Comment* (New York), November/December 1973.
"Dušan Makavejev," in *Fifty Major Filmmakers* edited by Peter Cowie, South Brunswick, New Jersey, 1974.
"Sweet Movie," in *Avant-Scène du Cinéma* (Paris), October 1974.
Schaub, M., "Unbeschützte und verlorene Unschuld, Dusan Makavejevs Spekulationen," in *Cinema* (Zurich), v.21, no.2, 1975.
Perlmutter, R., "The Cinema of the Grotesque," in *Georgia Review* (Athens, Ohio), no.1, 1979.
Cavell, Stanley, "On Makavejev on Bergman," in *Critical Inquiry* (Chicago), no.2, 1979.
"Dusan Makavejev," in *Film Dope* (London), December 1987.

*   *   *

Before making his first feature film, *Man Is Not a Bird*, Makavejev had developed his filmmaking skills and formulated his chief thematic and formal concerns by producing a number of 35mm experimental shorts and documentaries. His second feature, *Love Affair*, furthered Makavejev's reputation and situated him within a growing community of Eastern European filmmakers committed to exploring the potential of the film medium by opening it up to new subject matter and experimenting with non-conventional narrative forms. *Love Affair* deals with the romance between a Hungarian-born switchboard operator, Isabella, and Ahmed, an Arab sanitation engineer, the breakdown of the relationship, Isabella's death,

and Ahmed's arrest for her murder. However, this straightforward plot is only the skeleton which supports the rest of the film. Influenced by Eisenstein and Godard, Makavejev builds an elaborate, Brechtian amalgam of documentary-like examinations of rat extermination, interviews with a sexologist and criminologist, actual stock footage of the destruction of church spires during the October Revolution, as well as almost quaint digressions on how mattress stuffing is combed and how strudel is made. Makavejev questions the nature of sexual relationships in a changing, post-revolutionary, but still puritanical society by juxtaposing ostensibly unrelated images. For example, the razing of the church spires is intercut with and comments on Isabella's seduction of Ahmed and the destruction of his archaic sexual inhibitions.

Innocence Unprotected also manifests Makavejev's interest in the dialectics of montage, the ability to create new ideas by juxtaposing incongruous or contradictory images. In this film, Makavejev rescues a little bit of "unprotected innocence" from oblivion by incorporating the original *Innocence Unprotected*, the first Serbian "all-talking" feature into a new cinematic context. This 1940s romance-adventure—filmed by a well known local strongman-daredevil during the Nazi Occupation, censored by the occupation government, and ironically later denounced as being Nazi-inspired—is intercut with interviews Makavejev conducted with members of the original production crew as well as newsreel footage from the period of the occupation. Moreover, Makavejev hand-tints portions of the original film to contribute to the critical distance created by the archaic quality of the footage. Perhaps more than any of his other films, *Innocence Unprotected* shows Makavejev's loving interest in traditional Yugoslavian folk culture and humor.

WR—Mysteries of the Organism deals with the sexuality of politics and the politics of sexuality. A radical condemnation of both the sterility of Stalinism and the superficial commercialism of Western capitalism, *WR* is certainly a document of its time—of Yugoslavia attempting to follow its "other road" to socialism while America fights in Vietnam and Moscow invades Czechoslovakia. Makavejev looks to Wilhelm Reich (the 'WR' of the title) for enlightenment. Reich was, early in his career, one of the first to recognize the profound interconnections between socio-political structure and the individual psyche. His radical sexual ideas alienated the psychoanalytic profession and his unorthodox medical theories and practices eventually led to his imprisonment in the U.S.

Although elaborate cross-cutting blends the two sections of the film, roughly the first half of *WR* is devoted to a documentary study of Wilhelm Reich's life in the U.S. Interviews with Reich's therapists, Reich's relatives, even people who knew him casually including his barber, are intercut with an examination of American sexual mores circa 1970 via interviews with Jackie Curtis, Barbara Dobson, one of the editors of *Screw* magazine, and others. The second half of the film is primarily a fictional narrative set in Belgrade, which concerns the love affair between a young female admirer of Reich (Milena) and a rather priggish and prudish Soviet ice skater named Vladimir Ilyich. Freed of his inhibitions by Milena's persistence, Vladimir makes love to her and then, unable to deal with his sexuality, decapitates her with his ice skate. However, after death, Milena's severed head continues to speak. Vladimir sings a song with a lyric written by a Soviet citizen critical of his government. *WR* ends with a photo of the smiling Reich—a sign of hope, a contradictory indication of the possibility for change and new beginnings.

WR was never released in Yugoslavia, and Makavejev made his two subsequent films, *Sweet Movie* and *Montenegro*, in the U.S. and Europe. Like *WR, Sweet Movie* has two parts. In the first a beauty contestant, Miss World, is wedded to and violated by Mr. Kapital and, after other humiliations, ends up in Otto Muehl's radical therapy commune. Miss World is taken in and nurtured by actual commune members who engage in various types of infantile regressions (including carrying their shit displayed on dinner plates) as therapy. The second part of the film is an allegorical commentary on the East. A ship, with a figurehead of Karl Marx, sails about under the command of Anna Planeta, who seduces and murders young men and boys, while providing for their rebirth out of a hold filled with white sugar and corpses.

Montenegro continues this development of allegory in favor of Makavejev's earlier documentary interests. Marilyn, an American-born Swedish housewife, is lured into a world peopled by earthy and sexually active Yugoslavian immigrants, who run a club called Zanzibar as an almost anarchistic communal venture. Like the heroes and heroines of Makavejev's earlier films, Marilyn cannot deal with her newly acquired sexual freedom, and she, like Ahmed, Vladimir Ilyich, and Anna Planeta, kills her lovers. *Montenegro's* linear plot contrasts sharply with the convoluted narrative structure and elaborate montage techniques characteristic of Makavejev's earlier works.

While being accused of making needlessly ambiguous films with scenes of gratuitous violence and sexuality, Makavejev has consistently explored the interrelationship of sexual life and socioeconomic structure while experimenting with narrative forms that challenge traditional notions of Hollywood filmmaking.

—Gina Marchetti

Terrence Malick (right) with Martin Sheen

MALICK, Terrence.

American. Born in Waco, Texas, 30 November 1943. Educated at Harvard University, B.A., 1966; Oxford University on Rhodes Scholarship; Center for Advanced Film Studies, American Film Institute, 1969. Journalist for *Newsweek, Life*, and the *New Yorker*, late 1960s; lecturer in philosophy, Massachusetts Institute of Technology, 1968; directed first feature, *Badlands*, 1973. Recipient: Best Director Awards, National Society of Film Critics, and New York Film Critics, 1978, and Cannes Festival, 1979, for *Days of Heaven*. Lives in Paris. Office: c/o Evarts Ziegler Associates, Inc., 9255 W. Sunset Boulevard, Los Angeles, CA 90069, U.S.A.

Films as Director and Screenwriter:

1973   *Badlands* (+ pr)
1978   ***Days of Heaven***

Other Films:

1969   *Lanton Mills* (short) (sc)
1972   *Pocket Money* (Rosenberg) (sc)
1974   *The Gravy Train* (Starrett?) (co-sc, under pseudonym David Whitney)
1982   *Deadhead Miles* (Zimmerman) (co-sc) (filmed 1970)

Publications:

By MALICK: articles—

"The Filming of *Badlands*," an interview with G.R. Cook, in *Filmmakers Newsletter* (Ward Hill, Massachusetts), June 1974.

"Malick on *Badlands*," an interview with B. Walker, in *Sight and Sound* (London), Spring 1975.
Interview with Michel Ciment, in *Positif* (Paris), June 1975.

On MALICK: articles—

Johnson, William, "*Badlands*," in *Film Quarterly* (Berkeley), Spring 1974.
Fox, Terry Curtis, "The Last Ray of Light," in *Film Comment* (New York), September/October 1978.
Hodenfield, Chris, "Terrence Malick: *Days of Heaven*'s Image Maker," in *Rolling Stone* (New York), 16 November 1978.
Combs, Richard, "The Eyes of Texas," in *Sight and Sound* (London), Spring 1979.
Maraval, P., "Dossier: Hollywood '79: Terrence Malick," in *Cinématographe* (Paris), March 1979.
Donough, P., "West of Eden: Terrence Malick's *Days of Heaven*," in *Post Script* (Jacksonville, Florida), Fall 1985.
"Terrence Malick," in *Film Dope* (London), December 1987.

*   *   *

Though he has directed only two feature films, Terrence Malick has received the kind of critical attention normally reserved for more experienced and prolific filmmakers. His career reflects a commitment to quality instead of quantity—an unusual and not always profitable gamble in the film industry.

In 1972, Malick wrote the screenplay for *Pocket Money* which starred Paul Newman and Lee Marvin, a film memorable more for character study than story. The following year, Malick made his first feature, *Badlands*. The film was an amazing debut. Based loosely on the sensational Starkweather-Furgate murder spree, *Badlands* concerns Kit Carruthers, a 25-year old James Dean look-alike, and Holly Sargis, his 15-year-old girlfriend. After murdering Holly's father, they begin a flight across the northeastern United States, killing five others along the way.

This disturbing and beautiful film is narrated by Holly (Sissy Spacek) who unemotionally describes the couple's actions and feelings. Her partner in crime, Kit (Martin Sheen), is a likeable, unpredictable, and romantic killer who is so confident of his place in American history as a celebrity that he marks the spot where he is arrested, and gives away his possessions as souvenirs to police officers.

Days of Heaven, Malick's long-awaited second feature, was released five years later. The film was critically acclaimed in the United States, and Malick was named best director at the Cannes Film Festival. *Days of Heaven* is a homage to silent films (the director even includes a glimpse of Chaplin's work) with stunning visual images, and little dialogue. Moving very slowly at first, the film's pace gradually accelerates as the tension heightens. Its plot and style elaborate on that of *Badlands*: the flight of two lovers following a murder, and the use of unemotional narration, and off-beat characterizations.

Malick now lives in Paris, and as critics wait for his next endeavor, some wonder how the director will remain profitable to any studio with his lapses between projects, his aversion to interviews, and his refusal to help in the marketing of his films. Paramount, however, is confident of Malick's value, and has continued to send the director scripts plus a yearly stipend.

—Alexa Foreman

MALLE, Louis.

French. Born in Thumeries, France, 30 October 1932. Educated at Collège des Carmes; Institut d'Études Politiques at the Sorbonne, Paris, 1951–53; Institut des Hautes Études Cinématographiques (IDHEC), 1953–54. Married 1) Anne-Marie Deschodt (divorced 1967); 2) actress Candice Bergen, 1980, three children. Assistant and cameraman to Jacques Cousteau, 1954–55; assistant to Robert Bresson on *Un Condamné à mort s'est échappé*, 1956; cameraman on Tati's *Mon Oncle*, 1957; directed first film, 1958; reported from Algeria, Vietnam and Thailand for French Television, 1962–64; moved to India, 1968; moved to the U.S., 1976; returned to France to make *Au revoir les enfants*, 1987. Recipient: Palme d'Or, Cannes Festival, 1956, and Oscar for Best Documentary, 1957, for *The Silent World*; Prix Louis-Delluc for *Ascenseur pour l'échafaud*, 1958; special jury prize, Venice Festival, for *Les Amants*, 1958; special jury prize, Venice Festival, for *Le Feu follet*, 1963; Prix Raoul Levy and Prix Méliès for *Lacombe, Lucien*, 1974; Golden Lion, Venice Festival, and Prix Louis Delluc, for *Au revoir les enfants*, 1987. Manager: c/o Gelfand, Rennert & Feldman, 489 Fifth Avenue, New York, NY 10017, U.S.A. Office: N.E.F., 92 Avenue des Champs Elysees, 75008 Paris, France.

Films as Director:

1956   *Le Monde du silence* (*The Silent World*) (co-d, ph)
1958   *Ascenseur pour l'échafaud* (*Elevator to the Gallows. Frantic*) (+ pr, co-sc); *Les Amants* (*The Lovers*) (+ pr, co-sc)
1960   *Zazie dans le Métro* (*Zazie*) (+ pr, co-sc)
1962   *Vie privée* (*A Very Private Affair*) (+ pr, co-sc)
1963   *Le Feu follet* (*The Fire Within. A Time to Live, a Time to Die*) (+ pr, sc)
1965   *Viva Maria* (+ co-pr, co-sc)
1967   *Le Voleur* (*The Thief of Paris*) (+ pr, co-sc)

1968   "William Wilson" episode of *Histoires extraordinaires* (*Spirits of the Dead*) (+ pr, sc)
1969   *Calcutta* (+ pr, sc); *L'Inde fantôme* (*Phantom India*) (+ pr, sc) (6 hour feature presentation of TV documentary)
1971   ***Le Souffle au coeur*** (***Murmur of the Heart***) (+ pr, sc)
1972   *Humain trop humain* (+ pr, sc)
1973   *Lacombe, Lucien* (+ pr, co-sc)
1975   *Black Moon* (+ pr, co-sc)
1978   *La Petite* (+ pr, sc); *Pretty Baby* (+ pr, co-story)
1980   *Atlantic City* (+ pr, sc)
1981   *My Dinner with Andre* (+ pr, sc)
1984   *Crackers* (+ pr, sc)
1985   *Alamo Bay* (+ pr, sc); *God's Country* (+ pr, sc)
1986   *And the Pursuit of Happiness* (+ pr, sc)
1987   ***Au Revoir les enfants*** (***Goodbye, Children***) (+ pr, sc)
1990   *Milou en Mai* (+ pr, sc)

Other Films:

1969   *La Fiancée du pirate* (Kaplan) (role)

Publications:

By MALLE: books—

Lacombe, Lucien, with Patrick Modiano, New York, 1975.
Louis Malle par Louis Malle, with S. Kant, Paris, 1978.
Au revoir les enfants, Paris, 1989.
Milou en mai, with Jean-Claude Carrière, Paris, 1990.

By MALLE: articles—

"Avec *Pickpocket*, Bresson a trouvé," in *Arts* (Paris), 3 January 1960.
"*Les Amants*," (text) in *L'Avant-Scène du Cinéma* (Paris), 15 March 1961.
"*Le Feu follet*," (text) in *L'Avant-Scène du Cinéma* (Paris), 15 October 1963.
"Louis Malle: Murmuring From the Heart," with N. Pasquariello, in *Inter/View* (New York), July 1972.
"Phantom India," with E.L. Rodrigues, in *Film Heritage* (New York), Fall 1973.
"Louis Malle on *Lacombe Lucien*," in *Film Comment* (New York), September/October 1974.
"Like Acid," interview with Gordon Gow, in *Films and Filming* (London), December 1975.
"From *The Lovers* to *Pretty Baby*," interview with Dan Yakir, in *Film Quarterly* (Berkeley), Summer 1978.
"Creating a Reality That Doesn't Exist," interview with A. Horton, in *Literature/Film Quarterly* (Salisbury, Maryland), no.2, 1979.
Interview with P. Carcassonne and J. Fieschi, in *Cinématographe* (Paris), March/April 1981.
Interview in *Post Script* (Jacksonville, Florida), Autumn 1982 and Winter 1983.
Interview with Robert Benayoun, and others, in *Positif* (Paris), October 1987.
"Dialogue on Film: Louis Malle," in *American Film* (Washington, D.C.), April 1989.

On MALLE: books—

Chapier, Henri, *Louis Malle*, Paris, 1964.

On MALLE: articles—

Strick, P., "Louis Malle," in *Film* (London), Spring 1963.
Ledieu, Christian, "Louis Malle détruit son passé à chaque nouveau film," in *Arts* (Paris), 9 October 1963.
Gow, Gordon, "Louis Malle's France," in *Films and Filming* (London), August 1964.
Price, James, "Night and Solitude: The Cinema of Louis Malle," in *London Magazine*, September 1964.
"Director of the Year," in *International Film Guide*, London, 1965.
Lej, Russell, "Louis Malle," in the *New Left Review* (New York), March/April 1965.
McVay, D., "Louis Malle," in *Focus on Film* (London), Summer 1974.
"Black Moon," in *Avant-Scène du Cinéma* (Paris), December 1975.

Louis Malle

Rollet, R.T., and others, "The Documentary Films of Louis Malle," in special Malle issue of *Film Library Quarterly* (New York), v.9, no.4, 1977.

Chemasi, A., "*Pretty Baby*: Love in Storyville," in *American Film* (Washington, D.C.), November 1977.

"Louis Malle," in *Film Dope* (London), December 1987.

"*Au revoir les enfants* Issue" of *Avant-Scène du Cinéma* (Paris), July 1988.

Prédal, René, "L'oeuvre de Louis Malle, ou les étapes d'une évolution personnelle," in *Jeune Cinéma* (Paris), September/October 1988.

Roud, Richard, "Malle x 4," in *Sight and Sound* (London), Spring 1989.

* * *

In the scramble for space and fame that became the *nouvelle vague*, Louis Malle began with more hard experience than Godard, Truffaut, or Chabrol, and showed in *Ascenseur pour l'échafaud* that his instincts for themes and collaborators were faultless. Henri Decaë's low-light photography and Malle's use of Jeanne Moreau established him as emblematic of the new French cinema. But the *Cahiers* trio with their publicist background made artistic hay while Malle persisted in a more intimate voyage of discovery with his lovely star. As the cresting new wave battered at the restrictions of conventional narrative technique, Malle created a personal style, sexual and emotional, which was to sustain him while flashier colleagues failed. Of the new wave survivors, he is the most old-fashioned, the most erotic, and, arguably, the most widely successful.

Re-viewing reveals *Ascenseur* as clumsy and improbable, a failure redeemed only by the Moreau and Maurice Ronet performances. A flair for coaxing the unexpected from his stars had often saved Malle from the consequences of too-reverent respect for production values, a penchant for burnished low-lit interiors being his most galling stylistic weakness. But playing Bardot against type in *Vie privée* as a parody of the harried star, and with Moreau, as one of a pair of comic Western trollops (in *Viva Maria*), showed the irony that was to make his name.

Thereafter he became a gleeful chronicler of the polymorphously perverse. Moreau's hand falling eloquently open on the sheet in *Les Amants* as she accepts the joy of cunnilingus is precisely echoed in her genuflection to fellate a yoked George Hamilton in *Viva Maria*. Incest in *Souffle au coeur*, child prostitution in *Pretty Baby*, and, in particular, the erotic and sadomasochistic overtones of Nazism in *Lacombe, Lucien* found in Malle a skillful, committed and sensual celebrant.

The Indian documentaries of 1969 belong more to the literature of the mid-life crisis than to film history. *Black Moon* likewise explores an arid emotional *couloir*. Malle returned to his richest sources with the US-based films of the late 1970s and after. *Pretty Baby, Atlantic City, My Dinner with Andre* and *Alamo Bay* delight in overturning the stones under which closed communities seethe in moist darkness. The ostensible source material of the first, Bellocq's New Orleans brothel photographs, receives short shrift in favour of a lingering interest in the pre-pubescent Brooke Shields. *Atlantic City* relishes the delights of post-climacteric potency, giving Burt Lancaster one of his richest roles as the fading ex-strong-arm man, dubbed "Numb Nuts" by his derisive colleagues, who seizes a last chance for sexual passion and effective action as the friend and protector of Susan Sarandon's ambitious night-club croupier.

My Dinner with Andre focuses with equal originality on the social eroticism of urban intellectuals. A globe-trotting theatrical voluptuary reviews his thespian conquests to the grudging admiration of his stay-at-home colleague. An account of theatrical high-jinks in a Polish wood with Jerzy Grotowski and friends becomes in Andre Gregory's fruity re-telling, and with Malle's lingering attention, something very like an orgy. Again, production values intrude on, even dominate the action; mirrors, table settings, the intrusive old waiter and even the food itself provide a rich, decorated background that adds considerably to the sense of occasion. Malle sends his audiences out of the cinema conscious of having taken part in an event as filling as a five-course meal.

Given this general richness, it may be by contrast that certain of his quieter, less vivid works shine. *Zazie dans le Métro*, his fevered version of Queneau's farce, marked his first break with the stable pattern of the new wave, and, compared with Godard's *Une Femme est une femme*, shows Malle as the more skillful of the two at remaking the genre film. The terse *Le Feu follet*, a vehicle for Maurice Ronet, adapted from F. Scott Fitzgerald's *Babylon Revisited*, showed Malle moving towards what had become by then the standard "new" French film, characterized by the work of the so-called "Left Bank" group of Resnais, Varda, Rivette, and Rohmer. But again Malle found in the character a plump, opulent self-regard that turned *Le Feu follet*, despite its black and white cinematography and solemn style, into a celebration of self-pity, Ronet at one point caressing the gun with which he proposes to put an end to his life. Like the relish with which Belmondo's gentleman thief in *Le Voleur* savours the objects he steals, Malle's love of physicality, of weight and color and texture, seems so deeply rooted as to be almost religious. (And Malle did, after all, work as assistant to Bresson on *Un Condamné à mort s'est échappé*.) Sensual and perverse, Malle is an unlikely artist to have sprung from the reconstructed film-buffs of the *nouvelle vague*. It is with his early mentors—Bresson, Cousteau, Tati—that he seems, artistically and spiritually, to belong, rather than with Melville, spiritual hero of the *Cahiers* group, and there is a strong flavour of essentially French autobiographical soul searching in his *Au revoir les enfants* and *Milou en mai*. If Truffaut turned into the René Clair of the new French cinema, Malle may yet become its Max Ophüls.

—John Baxter

MAMOULIAN, Rouben.

American. Born in Tiflis, Caucasia, Russia, 8 October 1897, became U.S. citizen in 1930. Educated at Lycée Montaigne, Paris; gymnasium in Tiflis; University of Moscow; Vakhtangov Studio Theatre, Moscow. Married Azadia Newman, 1945. Stage director in London, from 1920; production director of Eastman Theater, Rochester, New York, 1923–26; directed *Porgy* on Broadway, 1927; signed to Paramount, directed first film, 1929; stage director, especially of musicals, through the 1940s. Recipient: Best Direction, New York Film Critics, for *The Gay Desperado*, 1936; Award of Excellence, Armenian American Bicentennial Celebration, 1976. *Died, in Los Angeles, 4 December 1987.*

Films as Director:

1929	*Applause*
1931	*City Streets*
1932	*Dr. Jekyll and Mr. Hyde* (+ pr); *Love Me Tonight* (+ pr)
1933	*Song of Songs* (+ pr); *Queen Christina*
1934	*We Live Again*
1935	*Becky Sharp*
1936	*The Gay Desperado*
1937	*High, Wide and Handsome*
1939	*Golden Boy*
1940	*The Mark of Zorro*
1941	*Blood and Sand*
1942	*Rings on Her Fingers*
1948	*Summer Holiday*
1957	*Silk Stockings*

Publications:

By MAMOULIAN: books—

Abigail, New York, 1964.
Hamlet Revised and Interpreted, New York, 1965.
Rouben Mamoulian: Style is the Man, edited by James Silke, Washington, D.C., 1971.

By MAMOULIAN: articles—

"Some Problems in the Direction of Color Pictures," in *International Photographer*, July 1935, also in *Positif* (Paris), September 1986.
"Controlling Color for Dramatic Effect," in *American Cinematographer* (Los Angeles), June 1941; also in *Hollywood Directors 1941–1976*, edited by Richard Koszarski, Oxford, 1977.
"Bernhardt versus Duse," in *Theatre Arts* (New York), September 1957.
"Painting the Leaves Black," an interview with David Robinson, in *Sight and Sound* (London), Summer 1961.
Interview with Jean Douchet and Bertrand Tavernier, in *Positif* (Paris), no. 64–65, 1965.
Article in *Interviews with Film Directors*, by Andrew Sarris, Indianapolis, 1967.
Interview in *The Celluloid Muse*, edited by Charles Higham and Joel Greenberg, London, 1969.
"*Dr. Jekyll and Mr. Hyde*," an interview with T.R. Atkins, in *Film Journal* (New York), January/March 1973.
"Bulletin Board: Mamoulian on Griffith," in *Action* (Los Angeles), September/October 1975.
Interview with J.A. Gallagher and M.A. Amoruco, in *Velvet Light Trap* (Madison, Wisconsin), no. 19, 1982.
Interview with H.A. Hargrave, in *Literature/Film Quarterly* (Salisbury, Maryland), vol. 10, no. 4, October 1982.
"Dialogue on Film: Rouben Mamoulian," in *American Film* (Washington, D.C.), January/February 1983.

On MAMOULIAN: books—

Milne, Tom, *Rouben Mamoulian*, London, 1969.
Prinzler, Hans Helmut, and Antje Goldau, *Rouben Mamoulian: Eine Dokumentation*, Berlin, 1987.

On MAMOULIAN: articles—

Horgan, P., "Rouben Mamoulian: The Start of a Career," in *Film's in Review* (New York), August/September 1973.
McCarthy, T., obituary, in *Variety* (New York), 9 December 1987.
Hanke, K., "Rouben Mamoulian," in *Films in Review* (New York), August/September 1988.

*   *   *

Rouben Mamoulian

Rouben Mamoulian is certainly one of the finest directors in American film history. While not considered strictly an *auteur* with a unifying theme running through his films, the importance of his movies on an individual basis is significant. Mamoulian did not have a large output, having completed only 16 assignments in his 20-year career in motion pictures, principally because he was also very active in the theater. His most famous stage successes were the highly innovative productions of Richard Rodgers and Oscar Hammerstein II's musicals *Oklahoma!* and *Carousel* in the mid-1940s.

His first film, *Applause*, was a poignant story of a third-rate vaudevillian played by the popular singer Helen Morgan. The first film to utilize two sound tracks instead of one to produce a better quality sound, *Applause* was also noteworthy for its innovative use of a moving camera.

Mamoulian's third film, *Dr. Jekyll and Mr. Hyde*, is still regarded by most historians as the definitive film version of the Robert Louis Stevenson novella, as well as being one of the best horror films of all time. Yet it would be doing the film a disservice to call it "just" a horror movie. The use of light and shadows, the depth of emotion expressed by the main character, and the evocation of the evil hidden in all men make it a classic. For the time it was a very sensual film. Miriam Hopkins as Ivy Pearson is not just a girl from the lower strata of society as the character was in other versions. In Mamoulian's film she is deliberately sensual. Fredric March, in a truly magnificent performance, is troubled by his desire for Ivy long before he turns into Hyde, which is especially evident in the erotic dream sequence. What Mamoulian was able to do in this film is show the simultaneous existence of good and evil in Jekyll before it erupted into the drug-induced schizophrenic manifestation of Mr. Hyde.

Becky Sharp, although not particularly noteworthy for its dramatic style, is today remembered as being the first film in the three strip Technicolor process. Unusually for a director more closely associated with the stage than film, Mamoulian tried to learn and perfect virtually all of the techniques of filmmaking, and he could be accomplished in almost any genre: horror, musical, swashbuckler, or historical drama. Perhaps the only genre at which he was not successful was light comedy. His only real comedy, *Rings on Her Fingers*, was entertaining, but did not live up to the standards which he set in his other films. The three previous films, *Golden Boy*, *The Mark of Zorro*, and *Blood and Sand*, were all very successful films which are still applauded by critics and audiences alike.

Mamoulian's last film, *Silk Stockings*, was a very popular adaption of the musical play derived from *Ninotchka*, with a lively score by Cole Porter. The combination of Cyd Charisse and Fred Astaire in the lead roles was naturally responsible for a great part of the movie's success, and Mamoulian's direction and staging allowed their talents to be shown to their best advantage. *Silk Stockings* has a variety of delightful "specialty" numbers which do not detract from the main action, notably "Stereophonic Sound," besides some charming character roles played by Peter Lorre, Jules Munshin, and George Tobias.

Rouben Mamoulian was one of the most talented, creative filmmakers of all time, and while his films are few, virtually every one is a tribute to his genius.

—Patricia King Hanson

MANKIEWICZ, Joseph L.

Born Joseph Leo Mankiewicz in Wilkes-Barre, Pennsylvania, 11 February 1909. Educated at Stuyvesant High School, New York; Columbia University, B.A., 1928. Married 1) Elizabeth Young, 1934 (divorced 1937), one son; 2) Rosa Stradner, 1939 (died 1958), two sons; 3) Rosemary Matthews, 1962, one daughter. Reporter for Chicago Tribune, and stringer for *Variety* in Berlin, 1928; with help of brother Herman, became junior writer at Paramount, 1929; writer for MGM, 1933, then producer, from 1935; contract taken over by Twentieth Century-Fox, 1943; directed *La Bohème* for Metropolitan Opera, New York, 1952; formed Figaro Inc., independent production company, 1953. Recipient: Oscars for Best Director and Best Screenplay, for *A Letter to Three Wives*, 1949, and for Best Director and Best Screenplay, for *All about Eve*, 1950. Address: RFD 1, Box 121, Bedford, New York, 10506, U.S.A.

Films as Director:

1946	*Dragonwyck* (+ sc); *Somewhere in the Night* (+ co-sc)
1947	*The Late George Apley*; *The Ghost and Mrs. Muir*
1948	*Escape*
1949	*A Letter to Three Wives* (+ sc); *House of Strangers* (+ co-sc, uncredited)
1950	*No Way Out* (+ co-sc); **All About Eve** (+ sc)
1951	*People Will Talk* (+ sc)
1952	*Five Fingers* (+ dialogue, uncredited)
1953	*Julius Caesar* (+ sc)
1954	*The Barefoot Contessa* (+ sc)
1955	*Guys and Dolls* (+ sc)
1958	*The Quiet American* (+ sc)
1959	*Suddenly, Last Summer*
1963	*Cleopatra* (+ co-sc)
1967	*The Honey Pot* (+ co-p, sc)
1970	*There Was a Crooked Man . . .* (+ pr)
1972	*Sleuth*

Other Films:

1929	*Fast Company* (Sutherland) (sc, dialogue)
1930	*Slightly Scarlet* (co-sc); *The Social Lion* (Sutherland) (sc, adaptation and dialogue); *Only Saps Work* (Gardner and Knopf) (sc, dialogue)
1931	*The Gang Buster* (Sutherland) (sc, dialogue); *Finn and Hattie* (Taurog) (sc, dialogue); *June Moon* (Sutherland) (co-sc); *Skippy* (Taurog) (co-sc); *Newly Rich* (*Forbidden Adventure*) (co-sc); *Sooky* (Taurog) (co-sc)
1932	*This Reckless Age* (sc); *Sky Bride* (co-sc); *Million Dollar Legs* (Cline) (co-sc); "Rollo and the Roadhogs" and "The Three Marines" sketches of *If I Had a Million* (sc)
1933	*Diplomaniacs* (co-sc); *Emergency Call* (co-sc); *Too Much Harmony* (Sutherland) (sc); *Alice in Wonderland* (McLeod) (co-sc)
1934	*Manhattan Melodrama* (Van Dyke, W.S.) (co-sc); *Our Daily Bread* (Vidor) (sc, dialogue); *Forsaking All Others* (Van Dyke, W.S.) (pr)
1935	*I Live My Life* (Van Dyke, W.S.) (sc)
1936	*Three Godfathers* (pr); **Fury** (Lang) (pr, co-story, uncredited); *The Gorgeous Hussy* (Brown) (pr); *Love on the Run* (Van Dyke, W.S.) (pr)
1937	*The Bride Wore Red* (Arzner) (pr); *Double Wedding* (pr)
1938	*Mannequin* (Borzage) (pr); *Three Comrades* (Borzage) (pr); *The Shopworn Angel* (pr); *The Shining Hour* (Borzage) (pr); *A Christmas Carol* (pr)
1939	*The Adventures of Huckleberry Finn* (*Huckleberry Finn*) (pr)
1940	*Strange Cargo* (Borzage) (pr); **The Philadelphia Story** (Cukor) (pr)
1941	*The Wild Man of Borneo* (pr); *The Feminine Touch* (Van Dyke, W.S.) (pr)

Joseph L. Mankiewicz

1942   *Woman of the Year* (Stevens) (pr); *Cairo* (Van Dyke, W.S.)
       (pr); *Reunion in France* (pr)
1944   *The Keys of the Kingdom* (Stahl) (pr, co-sc)

Publications:

By MANKIEWICZ: books—

More About ALL ABOUT EVE, with Gary Carey, New York, 1972.

By MANKIEWICZ: articles—

"Putting on the Style," in *Films and Filming* (London), January 1960.
"Measure for Measure: Interview with Joseph L. Mankiewicz," with
    Jacques Bontemps and Richard Overstreet, in *Cahiers du Cinema in
    English* (New York), February 1967.
"Auteur de films! Auteur de films!," in *Positif* (Paris), September
    1973.
Interview with Michel Ciment, in *Positif* (Paris), September 1973.
Interview with A. Charbonnier and D. Rabourdin, in *Cinéma* (Paris),
    June 1981.
Interview with David Shipman, in *Films and Filming* (London),
    November 1982.

On MANKIEWICZ: books—

Taylor, John, *Joseph L. Mankiewicz: An Index to His Work*, London,
    1960.
Brodsky, Jack, and Nathan Weiss, *The Cleopatra Papers: A Private
    Correspondence*, New York, 1963.
Geist, Kenneth, *Pictures Will Talk*, New York, 1978.
Dick, Bernard F., *Joseph L. Mankiewicz*, Boston, 1983.
La Polla, Franco, *L'Insospettabile Joseph Leo Mankiewicz*, Venice,
    1987.

On MANKIEWICZ: articles—

Nugent, Frank, "All About Joe," in *Collier's* (New York), 24 March
    1951.
Reid, John, "Cleo's Joe," in *Films and Filming* (London), August and
    September 1963.
Göw, Gordon, "Cocking a Snook," in *Films and Filming* (London),
    November 1970.
Springer, John, "The Films of Joseph Mankiewicz," in *Films in Review*
    (New York), March 1971.
Segond, J., "More About Joseph L. Mankiewicz," in *Positif* (Paris),
    September 1973.
Geist, K., "Mankiewicz: The Thinking Man's Director," in *American
    Film* (Washington, D.C.), April 1978.
Tesson, Charles, "All about Mankiewicz," in *Cahiers du Cinéma*
    (Paris), October 1980.
Charbonnier, A., "Dossier-auteur (II): Joseph L. Mankiewicz—le
    temps et la parole," in *Cinéma* (Paris), July/August 1981.
Farber, S., and M. Green, "Family Plots," in *Film Comment* (New
    York), July/August 1984.
Buckley, M., and J. Nangle, "The Regency Salutes the Brothers Man-
    kiewicz," in *Films in Review* (New York), October and November
    1984.
"Joseph L. Mankiewicz," in *Film Dope* (London), December 1987.

          *   *   *

Few of his contemporaries experimented so radically with narrative form. In *The Barefoot Contessa*, Mankiewicz (who
wrote most of the films he directed) let a half-dozen voice-over
narrators tell the Contessa's story, included flashbacks within
flashbacks, and even showed one event twice (the slapping
scene in the restaurant) from two different points of view. Multiple narrators tell the story in *All About Eve*, too, and in the
non-narrated framing story for that film, Mankiewicz uses slow
motion to make it seem as if the elapsed time between the
beginning of the film and the end is only a few seconds. For
much of the film, *The Quiet American* also has a narrator, and
he seems almost totally omniscient. Apparently, he looks back
at events with a firm understanding of their development and
of the motivation of the people involved. But in the end, we
find out that the narrator was wrong about practically every-

thing, and so gave us an inaccurate account of things. *A Letter
to Three Wives* is made up, primarily, of several lengthy flashbacks, and hallucinogenic flashback sequences provide the
payoff to the story in Mankiewicz's adaption of the Tennessee
Williams play, *Suddenly Last Summer*.

    Mankiewicz's films, then, stand out in part because of the
way they tell their stories. But there are also thematic motifs
that turn up again and again, and one of the most important is
the impact of the dead upon the living. Frequently, a dead character is more important in a Mankiewicz film than any living
one. *The Late George Apley*, of course, concerns someone
who has already died. Understanding a mother's dead son is
the key for the psychiatrist in *Suddenly Last Summer*. In *The
Ghost and Mrs. Muir*, it is the presence of the non-corporeal
sea captain that makes the film so entertaining. *The Barefoot
Contessa* opens with the Contessa's funeral, and then various
mourners tell us what they know about the woman who has just
been buried. And, of course, a famous funeral scene forms the
centerpiece of another Mankiewicz film; Mark Antony's oration in *Julius Caesar*.

    It is Antony's stirring performance as a eulogist that turns his
countrymen against Brutus. Indeed, Mankiewicz's films deal
constantly with the notion of effective and highly theatrical
performance. *All About Eve*, for instance, is all about performing, since it concerns people who work on the Broadway
stage. The barefoot contessa goes from cabaret dancer to Hollywood star. In *The Honey Pot*, an aging man pretends to be
dying, to see how it affects his mistress. And in *Sleuth*, one
marvels at the number of disguises worn by one man in his
attempt to gain revenge on another.

    Perhaps because he began as a screenwriter, Mankiewicz
has often been thought of as a scenarist first and a director only
second. But not only is he an eloquent scriptwriter, he is also
an elegant visual stylist whose talents as a director far exceed
his reputation. He is one of the few major American directors
who was more appreciated during the early years of his career
than during the later stages. He won consecutive Best Director
Academy Awards in 1949 and 1950 (for *A Letter to Three
Wives* and *All About Eve*), but after the 1963 disaster *Cleopatra*, Mankiewicz's standing as a filmmaker declined rapidly.

—Eric Smoodin

MANN, Anthony.

American. Born Anton or Emil Bundsmann in Point Loma or
San Diego, California, 1907. Educated in New York City public schools. Married 1) Mildred Kenyon, 1931 (divorced 1956),
one son, one daughter; 2) Sarita Montiel, 1957 (marriage annulled 1963); 3) Anna (Mann), one son. Began work in theatre following father's death, 1923; Production Manager for Theater Guild, New York, from late 1920s, then director, 1933;
director for Federal Theater Project, New York, 1936–38;
talent scout for David Selznick, and casting director, Hollywood, 1938; assistant director at Paramount, 1939; signed to
Republic Pictures, 1943, to R.K.O., 1945, then to MGM,
1949; withdrew from *Spartacus* after quarrelling with Kirk
Douglas, 1960. *Died, during shooting of last film, in Germany,
29 April 1967.*

Anthony Mann directing *The Man from Laramie*

Films as Director:

1942 *Dr. Broadway; Moonlight in Havana*
1943 *Nobody's Darling*
1944 *My Best Gal; Strangers in the Night*
1945 *The Great Flamarion; Two O'Clock Courage; Sing Your Way Home*
1946 *Strange Impersonation; The Bamboo Blonde*
1947 *Desperate; Railroaded*
1948 *T-Men* (+ co-sc, uncredited); *Raw Deal; He Walked by Night* (co-d, uncredited)
1949 *Reign of Terror (The Black Book); Border Incident*
1950 *Side Street; Devil's Doorway; The Furies; Winchester '73*
1951 *The Tall Target*
1952 *Bend of the River*
1953 *The Naked Spur; Thunder Bay*
1954 *The Glenn Miller Story*
1955 *The Far Country; Strategic Air Command; The Man from Laramie; The Last Frontier*
1956 *Serenade*
1957 *Men in War; The Tin Star*
1958 *God's Little Acre; Man of the West*
1961 *Cimarron; El Cid*
1964 *The Fall of the Roman Empire*
1965 *The Heroes of Telemark*
1968 *A Dandy in Aspic* (co-d)

Publications:

By MANN: articles—

Interview, in *Cahiers du Cinéma* (Paris), March 1957.
"Now You See It: Landscape and Anthony Mann," interview with J.H. Fenwick and Jonathan Green-Armytage, in *Sight and Sound* (London), Autumn 1965.
"A Lesson in Cinema," interview with Jean-Claude Missiaen, in *Cahiers du Cinema in English* (New York), December 1967.
Interview with Christopher Wicking and Barrie Pattison, in *Screen* (London), July/October 1969.
"Empire Demolition," in *Hollywood Directors 1941–1976* edited by Richard Koszarski, New York, 1977.

On MANN: books—

Missiaen, Jean-Claude, *Anthony Mann*, Paris, 1964.
Kitses, Jim, *Horizons West*, Bloomington, Indiana, 1970.
Wright, Will, *Sixguns and Society*, Berkeley, California, 1975.
Basinger, Jeanine, *Anthony Mann*, Boston, 1979.

On MANN: articles—

Reid, J.H., "Mann and His Environment," in *Films and Filming* (London), January 1962.
Reid, J.H., "Tension at Twilight," in *Films and Filming* (London), February 1962.
Wagner, Jean, "Anthony Mann," in *Anthologie du Cinéma* vol. 4, Paris, 1968.
Handzo, Stephen, "Through the Devil's Doorway: The Early Westerns of Anthony Mann," in *Bright Lights* (Los Angeles), Summer 1976.
Smith, Robert, "Mann in the Dark," in *Bright Lights* (Los Angeles), Fall 1976.
Special Mann double issue of *Movietone News* (Seattle), Fall 1978.
Miller, Don, "Eagle-Lion: The Violent Years," in *Focus on Film* (London), November 1978.
Willeman, Paul, "Anthony Mann—Looking at the Male," in *Framework* (Norwich, England), Summer 1981.
Pulleine, Tim, "History, drama, Abstraction: Mann's Route to Madrid," and "Mann's Route to Madrid, Part II," in *Monthly Film Bulletin* (London), March and April 1982.
"Anthony Mann," in *Film Dope* (London), December 1987.

*   *   *

Though he incidentally directed films in various genres (the musical, the war movie, the spy drama), Anthony Mann's career falls into three clearly marked phases: the early period of low-budget, B-feature films noir; the central, most cele-brated period of westerns, mostly with James Stewart; and his involvement in the epic (with Samuel Bronston as producer). All three periods produced distinguished work (in particular, *El Cid* has strong claims to be considered the finest of all the 1950s–'60s wide screen historical epics, and the first half of *The Fall of the Roman Empire* matches it) but it is the body of work from the middle period in which Mann's achievement is most consistent and on which his reputation largely depends.

The first of the Stewart westerns, *Winchester 73*, contains most of the major components Mann was to develop in the series that followed. There is the characteristic use of landscape, never for the superficial beauty or mere pictorial effect that is a cliché of the genre, nor to ennoble the human figures through monumental grandeur and harmonious man-in-nature compositions, as in the classical westerns of Ford. In Mann, the function of landscape is primarily dramatic, and nature is felt as inhospitable, indifferent or hostile. If there is a mountain, it will have to be climbed, arduously and painfully; barren rocks provide a favourite location for a shoot-out, offering partial cover but also the continued danger of the ricochet. The preferred narrative structure of the films is the journey, and its stages are often marked by a symbolic progression in landscape, from fertile valley to bare rock or snow-covered peak, corresponding to a stripping-away of the trappings of civilization and civilized behavior: *Bend of the River* represents the most systematic treatment of this prior to *Man of the West*. *Winchester 73* also establishes the Mann hero ("protagonist" might be a better word): neurotic, obsessive, driven, usually motivated by a desire for revenge that reduces him emotionally and morally to a brutalized condition scarcely superior to that of the villain. Hero and villain, indeed, become mirror reflections of one another: in *Winchester 73* they are actually brothers (one has murdered the father, the other seeks revenge); in *Bend of the River*, both are ex-gunfighters, Stewart bearing the mark around his neck of the hangman's noose from which, at the beginning of the film, he saves Arthur Kennedy. Violence in Mann's westerns is never glorified: it is invariably represented as ugly, disturbing and painful (emotionally as much as physically), and this is true as much when it is inflicted by the heroes as by the villains.

Mann's supreme achievement is certainly *Man of the West*, the culmination of the Stewart series despite the fact that the Stewart role is taken over by Gary Cooper. It remains one of the great American films and one of the great films *about* America. It carries to their fullest development all the components described above, offering a magnificently complete realization of their significance. Cooper plays Link Jones (the "link" between the old West and the new), a reformed outlaw stranded in the wilderness while on a mission to hire a teacher for the first school in the new township of Good Hope, sucked back into involvement with his old gang of "brother," "cousins," and monstrous adoptive father Dock Tobin (Lee J. Cobb), forced into more and more excessive violence, as he destroys his doubles in order finally to detach himself, drained and compromised, from his own roots.

—Robin Wood

————

MARKER, Chris.

French. Born Christian François Bouche-Villeneuve in Neuilly sur Seine, 29 July 1921. During World War II, resistance fighter, then joined American army. Novelist, poet,

Chris Marker: *Le Mystère Koumiko*

playwright and journalist, from late 1940s; formed SLON film cooperative (Société pour le Lancement des Oeuvres Nouvelles), 1967. Recipient: Golden Bear, Berlin Festival, for *Description d'un combat*, 1961; International Critics Prize, Cannes Festival, for *Le Joli Mai*, 1963.

Films as Director:

1952   *Olympia 52* (+ sc, co-ph)
1953   *Les Statues meurent aussi* (co-d, co-sc)
1956   *Dimanche à Pekin* (+ sc, ph)
1958   *Lettre de Sibérie* (*Letter from Siberia*) (+ sc)
1960   *Description d'un combat* (+ sc); *Les Astronautes* (co-d, sc)
1961   *Cuba Si!* (+ sc, ph)
1963   **Le Joli Mai** (+ sc)
1964   *La Jetée* (completed 1962) (+ sc)
1965   *Le Mystère Koumiko* (*The Koumiko Mystery*) (+ sc)
1966   *Si j'avais quatre dromadaires* (+ sc)
1968   *La Sixième Face du Pentagone* (collaboration with Francois Reichenbach) (+ sc)
1969   *A bientôt j'espère* (+ sc)
1970   *La Bataille des dix millions* (*Cuba: Battle of the Ten Million*) (+ sc); *Les Mots ont un sens* (+ sc)
1973   *Le Train en marche* (+ sc)
1977   *Le Fond de l'air est rouge* (in 2 parts) (+ sc)
1983   *Sans soleil*
1985   *A.K.*

Other Films:

1957   *Le Mystère de l'atelier* (commentary, collaborator on production)
1967   *Loin du Vietnam* (*Far from Vietnam*) (Resnais) (pr, ed)
1970   *L'Aveu* (*The Confession*) (Costa-Gavras) (asst ph)
1973   *Kashima Paradise* (commentary)
1975/76   **La batalla de Chile** (**The Battle of Chile**) (Guzmá) (co-pr)
1976   *La Spirale* (contributor)

Publications:

By MARKER: books—

Le Coeur net, Lausanne, 1950.
Giraudoux par lui-même, Paris, 1952.
Coreennes, photographs, Paris, 1962.
Commentaires, Paris, 1962.

By MARKER: articles—

"Kashima Paradise," interview with G. Braucourt and Max Tessier, in *Ecran* (Paris), November 1974.

On MARKER: articles—

Cameron, Ian, "I Am Writing to You from a Far Country . . . ," in *Movie* (London), October 1962.
Graham, Peter, "Cinéma Vérité in France," in *Film Quarterly* (Berkeley), Summer 1964.
Jacob, Gilles, "Chris Marker and the Mutants," in *Sight and Sound* (London), Autumn 1966.

Roud, Richard, "SLON," in *Sight and Sound* (London), Spring 1973.

Valade, P., "Un Programme Chris Marker," in *Jeune Cinéma* (Paris), February 1975.

"Si j'avais quatre dromadaires. La Solitude du chanteur de fond," in *Avant-Scène du Cinéma* (Paris), March 1975.

Roud, Richard, "The Left Bank Revisited," in *Sight and Sound* (London), Summer 1977.

Hennebelle, Guy, "Le Fond de l'air est rouge," in *Ecran* (Paris), December 1977.

Gaggi, S., "Marker and Resnais: Myth and Reality," in *Literature/Film Quarterly* (Salisbury, Maryland), no.1, 1979.

Van Wert, W.F., "Chris Marker: the SLON Films," in *Film Quarterly* (Berkeley), no.3, 1979.

Rafferty, T., "Marker Changes Trains," in *Sight and Sound* (London), Autumn 1984.

Durgnat, Raymond, "Resnais & Co.: Back to the Avant-Garde," in *Monthly Film Bulletin* (London), May 1987.

* * *

Marker's principal distinction may be to have developed a form of personal essay within the documentary mode. Aside from his work little is known about him; he is elusive bordering on mysterious. Born in a suburb of Paris, he has allowed a legend to grow up about his birth in a "far-off country." Marker is not his name; it is one of half-a-dozen aliases he has used. He chose "Marker," it is thought, in reference to the Magic Marker pen.

He began his career as a writer (publishing poems, a novel, and various essays and translations) and journalist (whose travels took him all over the world). He is the writer of all his films and cinematographer on many of them. Their verbal and visual wit almost conceal the philosophical speculation and erudition they contain. Their commentaries are a kind of stream of consciousness; their poetry is about himself as well as about the subjects—his reactions to what he and we are seeing and hearing.

Marker is the foreign correspondent and inquiring reporter. He is especially interested in transitional societies, in "Life in the process of becoming history," as he has put it. His films are not only set in specific places, they are about the cultures of those places. Though he has tended to work in socialist countries more than most Western filmmakers, he is also fascinated by Japan. Concerned with leftist issues, he remains a member of the intellectual Left, politically committed but not doctrinaire. "Involved objectivity" is his own phrase for his approach.

In *Le Joli Mai* for example, Marker interviews Parisians about their ambitions, their political views, their understanding of the society they live in. His sample is a cross section—a streetcorner clothing salesman, a clerk, a house painter, a black student, a young couple wanting to get married, an Algerian worker—with a substantial working-class representation. The interviewees find that work offers no satisfaction. Its goal is money; what happiness money will bring is by no means certain. Marker insists to one interviewee who opts for material success that his view of life is "a trifle limited." "No interest in other things?" Marker asks.

This exchange is characteristic. Marker's tone is frequently ironical and implicitly judgmental. He engages in argument with the interviewees and makes known his disappointment in some of their answers. The interviews assume the form of a dialectic.

In the second half of *Le Joli Mai* Marker breaks away from individuals and interviews altogether. Instead he deals with news events—a police charge which crushed eight people to death in the Métro, the half-million mourners at their funeral, violent responses to the acquittal of General Salan (former commander-in-chief of French forces in Algeria), massive rail-road and Renault strikes—intercut with nightclub revelry. The events refer back to those interviewed in the first half who felt themselves "unfree" to alter or even to question the social system.

The Koumiko Mystery, set amidst the 1964 Tokyo Olympics, begins but never stays with them for long. Its real subject is a young Japanese woman named Kumiko Moroaka, her city (Tokyo), her country, and the Far East as a whole. If, in a sense, Kumiko is protagonist, there is also an antagonist of sorts. The Western world and its influences are seen again and again in images on television screens, in the tastes evident in department store windows. Part of the film is photographed directly off black-and-white television screens. In this way the concerns and attitudes of the larger world are isolated. The rest of the film, which is in color, is wholly personal.

Marker is always willing to impose his own shaping intelligence and imagination on his material. His films are most valuable for what he perceives and understands about what he is observing, and for their whimsical juggling of forms, their tweaking of conventions and expectations, and their idiosyncratic style.

—Jack C. Ellis

MARKOPOULOS, Gregory.

American. Born in Toledo, Ohio, 12 March 1928. Educated at University of Southern California. Completed first experimental films, 1948; lecturer on film at University of Athens, Greece, 1954–55; worked on *Serenity*, 1955–60; writer on film, from early 1960s.

Films as Director:

1947   *Du sang de la volupté et de la mort* (trilogy comprising *Psyche, Lysis*, and *Charmides*)
1948   *The Dead Ones*
1949   *Flowers of Asphalt*
1950   *Swain*
1951   *Arbres aux champignons*
1953   *Eldora*
1955/61   *Serenity*
1963   *Twice a Man*
1965   *The Death of Hemingway*
1966   *Galaxie; Through a Lens Brightly: Mark Turbyfill; Ming Green*
1967   *Himself as Herself; Eros, O Basileus; The Iliac Passion; Bliss; The Divine Damnation; Gammelion*
1968   *Mysteries*
1969   *Index Hans Richter*
1970   *Genius*
1971   *Doldertal 7; Hagiographia; 35 Boulevard General Koenig*

Publications:

By MARKOPOULOS: books—

Quest for Serenity, New York, 1965.
A Bibliography Containing the Marvelous Distortions of My Films as Reviewed in Books, Programs, Periodicals and Newspapers during 33 Years: 1945–1978, St. Moritz, 1978.

By MARKOPOULOS: articles—

"On *Serenity*," in *Film Culture* (New York), Summer 1961.
"Toward a New Narrative Form in Motion Pictures," in *Film Comment* (New York), Fall 1963.

Interview with Robert Brown, in *Film Culture* (New York), Spring 1964.

"Random Notes During a Two-Week Lecture Tour of the United States," in *Film Culture* (New York), Fall 1964.

"The Driving Rhythm," in *Film Culture* (New York), Spring 1966.

"From 'Fanshawe' to 'Swain'," in *Film Culture* (New York), Summer 1966.

"'Galaxie' (Production and Critical Notes)," in *Film Culture* (New York), Fall 1966.

"The Film-Maker as Physician of the Future," in *Film Culture* (New York), Spring 1967.

"Gregory Markopoulos: Free Association—Rough Transcription for Paper on Levels of Creative Consciousness," interview with David Brooks, in *Film Culture* (New York), Summer 1967.

"Correspondences of Smells and Visuals," in *Film Culture* (New York), Autumn 1967.

"Index to the Work of Gregory Markopoulos, Years 1967/70," with Jonas Mekas, in *Film Culture* (New York), Spring 1971.

"The Adamantine Bridge," in *Film Culture* (New York), Spring 1972.

On MARKOPOULOS: book—

Sitney, P. Adams, *Visionary Film: The American Avant-Garde 1943–1978*, New York, 1979.

On MARKOPOULOS: articles—

Filmwise 3 & 4: Gregory Markopoulos, Spring 1963.
Kelman, K., "Portrait of the Young Man as Artist: From the Notebook of Robert Beavers," in *Film Culture* (New York), no. 67/69, 1979.

*　　*　　*

Gregory J. Markopoulos made his first film (a version of *A Christmas Carol*) in 1940 with a borrowed 8mm silent movie camera. By the time he left the University of Southern California in 1947, he completed a trilogy titled *Du sang de la volupté et de la mort* (comprising *Psyche*, *Lysis*, and *Charmides*). His first 35mm film was *The Dead Ones* in 1948. With these beginnings, Markopoulos became one of the best-known avant-gardists of the post-World War II period, although his output in the 1950s was limited to four films—*Flowers of Asphalt*, *Arbres aux champignons*, *Eldora*, and *Serenity*.

Elements of homoeroticism pervade many of the Markopoulos experiments and they are as audacious and outrageous as the works of Adolfas and Jonas Mekas. In his trilogy, a battering ram becomes a phallic symbol. When the film was shown to a class at New York University in 1951, it caused Henry Hart, then the far-right editor of *Films in Review* magazine, to berate professor George Amberg for allowing it to be shown. Hart described some of the images included in the films—"a male nipple, a painted and coiffeured male head, a buttock . . . and quite a few suggestions that abnormal perceptions and moods are desirable." Markopoulos soon became a much talked-about and controversial filmmaker.

The first Markopoulos film of the 1960s was *Serenity*, a dramatic film about the Greco-Turkish War of 1921–22, shot in Greece and released in 1962. This was followed by *Twice a Man*, a recreation of the Greek myths of Hippolytus, Phaedra, and Asclepius dealing openly for the first time (for Markopoulos) with male homosexuality.

Galaxie consisted of 30 three-minute 16mm silent clips of his friends (Parker Tyler, Jonas Mekas. W.H. Auden, Allen Ginsberg, Shirley Clarke, Maurice Sendak, Susan Sontag, and Gian Carlo Menotti, among others) with an electronic "clang" ending each segment as the only sound on the film. Markopoulos's subsequent films are in 16mm.

Single-frame editing and superimpositions were used in *Himself as Herself*, a strange film about a half man/half woman shot in and around Boston and released in 1967. In March of that year, *Eros, O Basileus* appeared, consisting of nine sequences involving a young man representing Eros. *The Marko-*

poulos Passion, a dramatic movie filmed over a three-year period, was finally released in 1968 as *The Iliac Passion*, a version of the Prometheus legend set in New York City.

Until 1981, he resided in St. Moritz, and there published a 1978 folio entitled *A Bibliography Containing the Marvelous Distortions of My Films as Reviewed in Books, Programs, Periodicals and Newspapers during Thirty-Three Years: 1945–1978*. He has been a leader in the avant-garde film movement for nearly 40 years.

—James L. Limbacher

———

MAURO, Humberto.

Brazilian. Born in Volta Grande, Minas Gerais, 30 April 1897. Educated in engineering. Began filmmaking at Cataguases, small town near birthplace, and participated in founding of production company Sul América Filme (later Brasil Filme S.A.), 1925; received top prize of Rio de Janeiro film publication *Cinearte* for *Thesouro perdido*, 1927; hired by *Cinearte* publisher Adhemar Gonzaga to direct for his Cinedia Studios, Rio, 1930; made short fiction films and documentaries for *Instituto Nacional de Cinema Educativo* (INCE), from 1937.

Films as Director: (partial list)

1925 *Valadão, o cratera* (*Valadao the Disaster*) (+ sc, ph)
1926 *Na primavera da vida* (*In the Springtime of Life*) (+ sc)
1927 *Thesouro perdido* (*Tesouro perdido. Lost Treasure*) (+ sc)
1928 *Brasa dormida* (*Sleeping Ember. Extinguished Cinders*) (+ sc)
1929 *Sangue Mineiro* (*Minas Blood. Blood of Minas*) (+ sc)
1930 *Labios sem beijos* (*Lips without Kisses*) (+ sc)
1932 *Ganga bruta* (*Rough Diamond*) (+ sc)
1934 *Favela dos meus amores* (*Favela of My Loves*) (+ sc); *Cidade mulher*
1937 *O descobrimento do Brasil* (+ sc)
1939 *Um apólogo* (shorts for Instituto Nacional de Cinema Educativo) (+ sc)
1940 *Argila* (*Clay*); *Bandeirantes* (short for Instituto Nacional de Cinema Educativo) (+ sc)
1942 *O despertar da redentora* (short for Instituto Nacional de Cinema Educativo) (+ sc)
1944 *O segredo das Asas* (medium-length film) (+ pr, sc)
1945/56 "Brasilianas" series (includes *Manhã na Roça* and *Engenhos e usinas*) (shorts for Instituto Nacional de Cinema Educativo) (+ sc)
1952 *O canto da saudade* (*The Song of Sadness*) (+ pr, sc)
1956 *Meus oito anos* (shorts for Instituto Nacional de Cinema Educativo) (+ sc)
1964 *A velha a Fiar* (short for Instituto Nacional de Cinema Educativo) (+ sc)

Publications:

On MAURO: articles—

Article, in *Filme Cultura* (Rio de Janeiro), October/November 1967.
Paranagua, P.A., "Cannes 82: homenaje a dos maestros del cine latinoamericano," in *Contracampo* (Madrid), August/September 1982.
Gomes, P.E.S., "Mauro et deux autres grands," in *Positif* (Paris), April 1987.

*　　*　　*

One of the greatest of all Latin American filmmakers, Humberto Mauro was a fascinating, deeply original talent whose best work exhibited a lyrical integration of characters and envi-

Humberto Mauro

ronment reminiscent of Dovzhenko. Trained as an engineer, Mauro was living in Cataguases—a small city in the state of Minas Gerais, north of Rio, which produced an impressive number of important writers and artists in that era—when friends encouraged him to make a short documentary, *Valadão, o cratera*, in 1925. After another amateur experience, on the fiction feature *In the Springtime of Life*, Mauro attempted his first professional production with *Lost Treasure*, an exciting adventure story clearly influenced by the American westerns Mauro would continue to love all his life. *Lost Treasure* received some small circulation around Brazil, and in 1927 was awarded *Cinearte* magazine's "Best Brazilian Film of the Year," the first such award ever given. His next film, *Sleeping Ember*, also made in Cataguases, was one of his very finest; here Mauro demonstrated his extraordinary talent for eliciting sensitive, nuanced performances from non-professional actors, a feature of many of his best works.

Lost Treasure and *Sleeping Ember* brought Mauro to the attention of Adhemar Gonzaga and Carmen Santos, two film enthusiasts who had plans to found a professional film studio in Rio. In 1930, Mauro moved to Rio, where he became the principal director at Gonzaga's fledgling Cinedia Studios in the early 1930s. Curiously, he continued to make silent films, even though the first Brazilian talkie, Luiz de Barro's *The End of the Hicks*, premiered in 1929. Mauro's final silent feature, *Rough Diamond*—released with a musical soundtrack—is unques-

tionably his masterpiece. After murdering his wife on their honeymoon night—he had discovered that she wasn't a virgin—a man attempts to piece together again his life and his relations with women. Some of the film's blatantly Freudian symbolism seems too contrived, and the plot's resolution isn't totally satisfying, but these shortcomings are more than made up for by the film's many exquisite passages.

After a few more studio films, notably the now-lost *Favela of My Loves*, Mauro began working as filmmaker-in-residence for the National Institute of Educational Cinema, a newly-founded branch of the Ministry of Education. For the next 30 years, Mauro would continue to work for this agency, producing well over 100 documentaries on a variety of subjects. During this period, he occasionally did return to work on features—*Clay*, with Carmen Santos, in 1940, and the tender pastoral romance, *The Song of Sadness*, in 1952.

Unlike other Brazilian directors, Mario Peixoto for instance, Mauro was able, happily, to cope with the seemingly insurmountable difficulties of working in a film industry as beleaguered as that of Brazil. Mauro's greatest strength lay in his sensitivity for the people and places of his native state of Minas Gerais; curiously, by concentrating on mostly regional ways of life and themes, Mauro created the single body of film work of any universal significance before the explosion of Cinema Novo in the early 1960s. That generation of filmmakers—Glauber Rocha, Nelson Pereira dos Santos, Joaquim Pedro—lionized Mauro, and saw him as the spiritual grandfather of their movement to create a truly Brazilian cinema.

—Richard Peña

MAYSLES, Albert and David.

American. Albert born in Brookline, Massachusetts, 26 November 1926; David Paul born in Brookline, 10 January 1932. Albert attended Brookline High School; Syracuse University, New York, degree in psychology; Boston University, M.A. in psychology. David attended Brookline High School; Boston University, degree in psychology. During World War II, Albert served in U.S. Army Tank Corps, David served in the Army at Headquarters, Military Intelligence school, Oberammergau, Germany. David married Judy (Maysles), one son, one daughter. Albert taught psychology at Boston University, from late 1940s, then travelled to Russia to make first film, 1955; David worked as production assistant on *Bus Stop* and *The Prince and the Showgirl*, 1956; they make first film together, 1957; David worked as reporter on *Adventures on the New Frontier* for TV, late 1950s-early 1960s; Albert worked as cameraman for Richard Leacock, 1960; formed production company together and made first film, 1962; Albert worked as cameraman on one section of Godard's *Paris vu par*, and the brothers received Guggenheim Fellowship in experimental film, 1965; continued making full-length documentaries and industrial and corporate promotional films together, from 1970. *David died, in New York, 3 January 1987.*

Films as Directors:

1955 *Psychiatry in Russia* (Albert only)
1957 *Youth in Poland*
1960 ***Primary*** (Albert only, co-d)
1962 *Showman*

1964   *What's Happening: The Beatles in the USA*
1965   *Meet Marlon Brando*
1966   *With Love From Truman*
1969   *Salesman* (co-d)
1970   *Gimme Shelter* (co-d)
1972   *Christo's Valley Curtain* (co-d)
1975   *Grey Gardens* (co-d)
1977   *Running Fence*
1984   *Islands*
1986   *Vladimir Horowitz, the Last Romantic*

Publications:

By the MAYSLES: articles—

Interview, in *Movie* (London), April 1963.
Interview with Bob Sitton, in *Film Library Quarterly* (New York), Summer 1969.
"Albert and David Maysles," in *Documentary Explorations* edited by G. Roy Levin, Garden City, New York, 1971.
Interview with R.P. Kolker, in *Sight and Sound* (London), Autumn 1971.
"*Gimme Shelter*: Production Notes," in *Filmmakers Newsletter* (Ward Hill, Massachusetts), December 1971.
"Financing the Independent Non-fiction Film," interview, in *Millimeter* (New York), June 1978.
"'Truthful Witness': An Interview with Albert Maysles," with H. Naficy, in *Quarterly Review of Film Studies* (Pleasantville, New York), Spring 1981.

On the MAYSLES: books—

Issari, M. Ali, *Cinema Verité*, Ann Arbor, Michigan, 1971.
Issari, M. Ali, and Doris A. Paul, *What is Cinema Verité*, Metuchen, New Jersey, 1979.

On the MAYSLES: articles—

Heleff, Maxine, "The Maysles Brothers and Direct Cinema," in *Film Comment* (New York), no.2, 1964.
Blue, James, "Thoughts on Cinéma Vérité and a Discussion with the Maysles Brothers," in *Film Comment* (New York), no. 4, 1964.
"Maysles Brothers," in *Film Culture* (New York), Fall 1966.
Steele, Robert, "*Meet Marlon Brando*," in *Film Heritage* (Dayton, Ohio), Fall 1966.
Rosenthal, Alan, "*Salesman*," in *The New Documentary in Action: A Casebook in Film Making*, Berkeley, California, 1971.
Sadkin, David, "*Gimme Shelter*: A Corkscrew or a Cathedral?," in *Film News* (New York), December 1971.
Safier, A.M., "Shooting Hidden Camera/Real People Spots," in *Millimeter* (New York), April 1979.
Robson, K.J., "The Crystal Formation: Narrative Structure in *Grey Gardens*," in *Cinema Journal* (Chicago), Winter 1983.
Barsam, R.M., "American Direct Cinema: The Re-Presentation of Reality," in *Persistence of Vision* (Maspeth, New York), Summer 1986.
Obituary in *Variety* (New York), 7 January 1987.

*   *   *

Shooting unobtrusively in sync sound with no instructions to the subject, the Maysles brothers made films in what they preferred to call "direct cinema." Albert, gifted photographer and director of all their projects, carried the lightweight, silent camera that he perfected on his shoulder, its accessories built in and ready for adjustment. Maysles characters, who occasionally talk to the filmmakers on screen, seem astonishingly unaware that strangers and apparatus are in the room.

David, the soundman, carried a sensitive directional mike and a Nagra recorder unattached to the camera. He was often involved in the editing and as producer had final say. During the shooting a story might become apparent, or a dominant character may surface. These elements may become clear only as the editors examine and cut the vast amounts of footage to be structured that they receive in the dailies.

In 1962, after Albert's brief experience in documentary film-making and David's in Hollywood feature films, they formed a partnership committed to direct cinema. Commercials and industrial filmmaking supported their preferred activity from time to time.

The company's production of two feature documentaries, distributed by them commercially, *Salesman*, a study of four bible salesmen, and *Grey Gardens*, an essay on two eccentric women, fed the constant discussions between documentarists and critics about whether objectivity is at all possible in documentaries. Both films were charged with dishonesty, exploitation, and tastelessness, but from other quarters received praise for the Maysles' sensitivity, rapport with their subjects, and choice of situations that viewers could identify with.

The Maysles answered the criticism and described their philosophy and working methods at screenings of their films, in articles and in letters to editors. Their instinct took them, they said, to situations related to closeness between human beings, also pointing out that they could not do films about people they dislike. They looked on their work as discovery of how people really are, first spending time with them to get acquainted, then filming their lives as lived. All their subjects agreed to the project beforehand, and several have spoken of their satisfaction with the finished film and their good relationship with Albert and David whom they trust.

The Maysles did not deny that their choices affected their creation in some way; much footage, for example must be discarded. They emphasized that nothing was staged and that structure eventually emerges from the material. In their own work they saw a relationship to Truman Capote's concepts and methods for his "non-fiction novel": discarding preconceptions about their subjects, while concentrating on learning about them and understanding their motivations and feelings.

Albert and David Maysles have an important place in the history of the documentary for many reasons. They produced a large, varied, evocative body of work in their chosen style, as very active members of their own small company. Despite some severe criticism of their work, they are admired, and probably envied for qualities that Americans value. Directly influential or not on documentaries today, their work is certainly part of the flow of films that aim to show the truth about contemporary problems. While many other filmmakers' reports and studies embrace large communities, or even whole countries, Maysles productions are about individuals and their concerns which often illuminate larger aspects of society as well as its general attitudes toward non-traditional behavior.

—Lillian Schiff

———

MAZURSKY, Paul.

American. Born Irwin Mazursky in Brooklyn, New York, 25 April 1930. Educated Brooklyn College, degree 1951; studied acting with Paul Mann, Curt Conway, and Lee Strasberg. Married Betsy Purdey, 1953, two daughters. Night-club comedian, actor, and director, off-Broadway, from 1954; joined Second City in Los Angeles, 1959; writer, with Larry Tucker, for *The Danny Kaye Show* for TV, 1964–67; co-creator of *The Monkees* for TV, 1965; directed first film, *Bob and Carol and Ted and Alice*, 1969. Address: c/o Telecote Productions, Inc., 280 South Beverly Drive, Suite 311, Beverly Hills, CA 90212, U.S.A.

Paul Mazursky

Films as Director:

1969 *Bob and Carol and Ted and Alice* (+ co-sc)
1970 *Alex in Wonderland* (+ co-sc, role as Hal Stern)
1973 *Blume in Love* (+ sc, pr, role as Hellman)
1974 *Harry and Tonto* (+ co-sc, pr)
1976 *Next Stop Greenwich Village* (+ sc, co-pr)
1978 *An Unmarried Woman* (+ sc, co-pr, role as Hal)
1980 *Willie and Phil* (+ sc)
1982 *The Tempest* (+ sc)
1984 *Moscow on the Hudson* (+ co-sc, pr, role)
1986 *Down and Out in Beverly Hills* (+ co-sc, pr, role)
1988 *Moon Over Parador* (+ co-sc, pr, role)
1989 *Enemies, a Love Story* (+ co-sc, pr, role)
1990 *Scenes From a Mall* (+ co-sc, pr, role)

Other Films:

1951 *Fear and Desire* (Kubrick) (role)
1955 *Blackboard Jungle* (Brooks) (role as Emmanuel Stoken)
1966 *Deathwatch* (Morrow) (role as petty thief)
1976 *A Star is Born* (Pierson) (role as John Norman's manager)
1979 *A Man, a Woman, and a Bank* (Black) (role)
1985 *Into the Night* (Landis) (role)
1988 *Punchline* (Seltzer) (role); *Scenes From the Class Struggle in Beverly Hills* (Bartel) (role)

Publications:

By MAZURSKY: book—

The Tempest: A Screenplay, with Leon Capetanos, New York, 1982.

By MAZURSKY: articles—

"Paul Mazursky Seminar," in *Dialogue on Film* (Washington, D.C.), November 1974.
Interview with N. Pasquariello, in *Millimeter* (New York), vol. 3, no. 5, 1975.
Interview with Max Tessier, in *Ecran* (Paris), July 1976.
Interview with Terry Fox, in *Film Comment* (New York), March/April 1978.
Interview with R. Appelbaum, in *Films and Filming* (London), August 1978.
Interview with James Monaco, in *American Film* (Washington, D.C.), July/August 1980.
Interview with M. Tuchman, in *Film Comment* (New York), January/February 1986.

On MAZURSKY: articles—

Burgess, John, in *Film Society Review* (New York), May 1970.
Cocks, J., "Portrait of the Artisan," in *Time* (New York), 18 January 1971.
Corliss, Richard, "Paul Mazursky: The Horace with the Heart of Gold," in *Film Comment* (New York), March/April 1975.
Jacobs, Diane, "Paul Mazursky," in *Hollywood Renaissance*, New York, 1977.
Fieschi, J., "Dossier: Hollywood 79: Paul Mazursky," in *Cinématographe* (Paris), March 1979.
Mascuch, P., "Directors Series: Paul Mazursky," in *Films in Review* (New York), November 1980.
Siegel, J.E., "Bourgeois Blues," in *American Film* (Washington, D.C.), May 1984.
Silvester, Christopher, "You Look Like a Nice Boy to Me, He Said," in *20/20* (London), April 1990.

*   *   *

It is no small irony that Paul Mazursky's best film is one he wrote (with Larry Tucker), but was not given the chance to direct. *I Love You Alice B. Toklas*, like most of Mazursky's work, stages a humorous, if somewhat predictable, encounter between deadening forms of everyday life (especially the monotonous regularity of heterosexual monogamy) and the bewildering, if attractive otherness of nonconformity. Directed by Hy Averback (at the insistence of star Peter Sellers, who would not work with a novice), this film records the fall of its main character, seduced by free love and marijuana brownies, into a late 1960s California underworld of unlimited self-indulgence, social honesty, and brotherly tolerance. Recovering his desire for a comfortable working life and marriage to the right girl, the Sellers character almost decides to go straight, but refuses at the very end to choose between the extremes his culture offers, the discontents of which have been equally and mercilessly exposed.

The commercial and critical success of *Alice* gave Mazursky an entree into New Hollywood directing. Unlike the film school whiz-kids (Coppola, Scorsese, Lucas, Spielberg, and company) who came into prominence at this same time, Mazursky had spent many years in show business, developing not only an acting career (which he has continued, if in a more limited way, after turning to directing) but a fair reputation as a writer (among other credits he wrote, with Tucker, the pilot episode of *The Monkees*). Like the more famous talents of the Hollywood Renaissance, however, Mazursky has manifested an abiding interest not only in a critical social realism, but also in the European art film, which, through imitation and *hommage*, he has attempted to domesticate for the general American audience. His cinema, at the same time, favors the writer and the actor; not interested in or capable of an individual, arresting visual style, his films are based on literate scripts and afford excellent opportunities for affecting performance. And yet, unlike *Alice*, they usually retreat from the harsh conclusions which their initially penetrating analyses of contemporary life should require.

Bob and Carol and Ted and Alice, for example, offers an upwardly-mobile California couple whose lives, following what appears to be a marathon Essalen encounter session, find a new direction. Taking the message of absolute honesty and non-stop self-expression to heart, they resolutely transform their social selves, experimenting with free love and attempting to loosen up their best friends, a more traditional couple who use up their energy in self-defeating games and manipulations. The foursome, now mixed, eventually winds up in a luxurious resort bed together, but are unable, presumably because of a residual conservatism, to consummate their contemplated new relationship. The film, however, offers this ideological dead-end as a triumph, as a happy ending whose import is hardly clear. Traditional marriage, with its jealousies and lies, has been mercilessly satirized, but open marriage, Mazursky seems to suggest, does not suit basic human needs. And yet Mazursky's relentless tenderness toward his characters, a sentimentality that surfaces as his desire to make the spectator identify with their predicament, blunts this critique by focussing attention on a relief-filled retreat from choice (the irony that the characters are set free to enjoy themselves in Las Vegas is not underlined).

Bob and Carol made a good deal of money during its initial release in 1969, perhaps because it dared to deal with some of the conflicts of the developing sexual revolution; it has not worn well. Most of Mazursky's subsequent films re-stage the same dramatic and ideological conflicts with mixed results. *Harry and Tonto* begins by challenging notions of ageing, but winds up confirming a whole range of social stereotypes: despite an occasional bitter note, the film exudes a warm, accepting humanism that trivializes its criticism of socially acceptable self-indulgence and mindless role-playing (the main character finds his niche as a lovably cantankerous septuagenarian who likes cats). *An Unmarried Woman* cuts its richly pampered Upper East Side heroine adrift from her cheating husband only to enmesh her in a suitably vague conventional fantasy—having to choose between wonderful sex and a bohemian lifestyle with a handsome artist, on the one hand, and the self-fulfilling exploration of the world of work (whose details are deliberately left rather vague), on the other. *Alex in Wonderland* strikes an autobiographical note with its portrait of a director, naturally enamored of Fellini, in search of a powerful theme for his next project. Compared to Woody Allen's similar *hommage* (*Stardust Memories*), the film lacks biting humor and fails to find interesting reflexes for Fellini's modernist technique and intellectual seriousness. *Willie and Phil* cannot create American equivalents for Truffaut's cinema of interpersonal conflict and triumph, while *Down and Out in Beverly Hills*, based on a classic Renoir study of the venality and selfishness that cut across class lines, becomes an unintentional comedy of integration, constructing a cinematic world that sentimentalizes the inauthentic, the mindless, and the hypocritical. Like its director, the film's main character has his heart in the right place and is a reasonable success in his chosen field, even if he is unable to master the madness of the world around him without romanticizing its foibles and absurdities.

—R. Barton Palmer

McCAREY, Leo.

American. Born in Los Angeles, 3 October 1898. Educated at Los Angeles High School; University of Southern California Law school. Married Stella Martin, 1920, one daughter. Lawyer in San Francisco and Los Angeles, 1916–17; 3rd assistant to Tod Browning, then script supervisor, at Universal, 1918–19; supervisor and director of about 300 comedy shorts for Hal Roach studios, 1923–28; gagman for Our Gang series, 1923–24; teamed Stan Laurel and Oliver Hardy, 1927; signed with Fox Studios, 1930; signed with Paramount, 1933; formed Rainbow Productions with Bing Crosby and others, 1946. Recipient: Oscar for Best Direction for *The Awful Truth*, 1937; Oscars for Best Direction and Best Original Story for *Going My Way*, 1944. Died 5 July 1969.

Films as Director:

1921 *Society Secrets* (+ pr)
1924 *Publicity Pays* (+ co-sc); *Young Oldfield* (+ co-sc); *Stolen Goods* (+ co-sc); *Jeffries Jr.* (+ co-sc); *Why Husbands Go Mad* (+ co-sc); *A Ten Minutes Egg* (+ co-sc); *Seeing Nellie Home* (+ co-sc); *Sweet Daddy* (+ co-sc); *Why Men Work* (+ co-sc); *Outdoor Pajamas* (+ co-sc); *Sittin' Pretty* (+ co-sc); *Too Many Mamas* (+ co-sc); *Bungalow Boobs* (+ co-sc); *Accidental Accidents* (+ co-sc); *All Wet* (+ co-sc); *The Poor Fish* (+ co-sc); *The Royal Razz* (+ co-sc)
1925 *Hello Baby* (+ co-sc); *Fighting Fluid* (+ co-sc); *The Family Entrance* (+ co-sc); *Plain and Fancy Girls* (+ co-sc); *Should Husbands Be Watched?* (+ co-sc); *Hard Boiled* (+ co-sc); *Is Marriage the Bunk?* (+ co-sc); *Bad Boy* (+ co-sc); *Big Red Riding Hood* (+ co-sc); *Looking For Sally* (+ co-sc); *What Price Goofy?* (+ co-sc); *Isn't Life Terrible?* (+ co-sc); *Innocent Husbands* (+ co-sc); *No Father to Guide Him* (+ co-sc); *The Caretaker's Daughter* (+ co-sc); *The Uneasy Three* (+ co-sc); *His Wooden Wedding* (+ co-sc)
1926 *Charley My Boy* (+ co-sc); *Mama Behave* (+ co-sc); *Dog Shy* (+ co-sc); *Mum's the Word* (+ co-sc); *Long Live the King* (+ co-sc); *Mighty Like a Moose* (+ co-sc); *Crazy Like a Fox* (+ co-sc); *Bromo and Juliet* (+ co-sc); *Tell 'em Nothing* (+ co-sc); *Be Your Age* (+ co-sc)
1928 *We Faw Down* (*We Slip Up*); *Should Married Men Go Home?* (+ co-sc, supervisor); *Two Tars* (+ story, supervisor); *Should Women Drive?* (+ co-sc); *A Pair of Tights* (+ co-sc); *Blow By Blow* (+ co-sc); *The Boy Friend* (+ co-sc); *Came the Dawn* (+ co-sc); *Do Gentlemen Snore?* (+ co-sc); *Dumb Daddies* (+ co-sc); *Going Ga-ga* (+ co-sc); *Pass the Gravy* (+ co-sc); *Tell It to the Judge* (+ co-sc); *That Night* (+ co-sc)
1929 *Liberty* (+ co-sc); *Wrong Again* (+ co-sc); *Dad's Day* (+ co-sc); *Freed 'em and Weep* (+ co-sc); *Hurdy Gurdy* (+ co-sc); *Madame Q* (+ co-sc); *Sky Boy* (+ co-sc); *The Unkissed Man* (+ co-sc); *When Money Comes* (+ co-sc); *Why is Plumber* (+ co-sc)
1929 *The Sophomore* (+ co-sc); *Red Hot Rhythm* (+ co-sc)
1930 *Wild Company*; *Part Time Wife* (+ co-sc)
1931 *Indiscreet*
1932 *The Kid from Spain*
1933 **Duck Soup**
1934 *Six of a Kind*; *Belle of the Nineties* (*It Ain't No Sin*); *Ruggles of Red Gap*
1935 *The Milky Way*
1937 *Make Way for Tomorrow* (*The Years Are So Long. When the Wind Blows*) (+ pr); *The Awful Truth*
1938 *Love Affair*
1940 *My Favorite Wife* (+ co-sc)
1942 *Once Upon a Honeymoon* (+ pr)
1944 *Going My Way* (+ pr, story)
1945 *The Bells of Saint Mary's* (+ pr, story)
1948 *Good Sam* (+ pr, co-story)
1952 *My Son John* (+ pr, story, co-sc)
1957 *An Affair to Remember* (+ co-sc)
1958 *Rally 'round the Flag, Boys!* (+ pr, co-sc)
1961 *Satan Never Sleeps* (*China Story*) (+ pr, co-sc)

Other Films:

1927 *Second Hundred Years* (story)
1938 *The Cowboy and the Lady* (co-story)

Publications:

By McCAREY: articles—

"What Makes a Box Office Hit?," in *Cinema* (Los Angeles), June 1947.

On McCAREY: books—

Gehring, Wes, *Leo McCarey and the Comic Anti-Hero in American Film*, New York, 1980.
Poague, Leland, *Wilder and McCarey*, New York, 1980.

On McCAREY: articles—

Carroll, Sidney, "Everything Happens to McCarey," in *Esquire* (New York), May 1943.
Leo McCarey Section of *Cahiers du Cinéma* (Paris), February 1965.
Crosby, Bing, and David Butler, "Remembering Leo McCarey," in *Action* (Los Angeles), September/October 1969.
Smith, H. Allen, "A Session with McCarey," in *Variety* (New York), January 1970.
Lloyd, P., "Some Affairs to Remember: The Style of Leo McCarey," in *Monogram* (London), no. 4, 1972.
Lourcelles, Jacques, "Leo McCarey," in *Anthologie du Cinéma*, vol. 7, Paris, 1973.
Richards, Jeffrey, "Great Moments: Leo McCarey," in *Focus on Film* (London), Spring 1973.
Silver, C., "Leo McCarey: From Marx to McCarthy," in *Film Comment* (New York), September/October 1973.
Morris, George, "McCarey and McCarthy," in *Film Comment* (New York), January/February 1976.
Gehring, Wes, "Leo McCarey: The Man Behind Laurel and Hardy," in *Films in Review* (New York), November 1979.
Everson, William K., and others (letters), "McCarey/Laurel and Hardy," in *Films in Review* (New York), February 1980; also letter from Wes Gehring, April 1980.
Shipman, David, "Directors of the Decade," in *Films and Filming* (London), April 1983.

Leo McCarey

Bourget, J.-L., "Rally Once Again: Leo McCarey à la télévision," in *Positif* (Paris), April 1985.

"Leo McCarey," in *Film Dope* (London), June 1987.

* * *

McCarey has always presented *auteur* criticism with one of its greatest challenges and one that has never been convincingly met. The failure to do so should be seen as casting doubt on the validity of *auteurism* (in its cruder and simpler forms) rather than on the value of the McCarey oeuvre. He worked consistently (and apparently quite uncomplainingly) within the dominant codes of shooting and editing that comprise the anonymous "classical Hollywood" style; the films that bear his name as director, ranging from *Duck Soup* to *The Bells of St. Mary's*, from Laurel and Hardy shorts to *My Son John*, from *The Awful Truth* to *Make Way for Tomorrow* (made the same year!), resist reduction to a coherent thematic interpretation. Yet his name is on some of the best—and best-loved—Hollywood films (as well as on some that embarrass many of even his most fervent defenders).

In fact, it might be argued that McCarey's work validates a more sophisticated and circumspect *auteur* approach: not the author as divinely inspired individual creative genius, but the author as the animating presence in a project within which multiple determinants—collaborative, generic, ideological—complexly interact. The only adequate approach to a McCarey film would involve the systematic analysis of that interaction. A few notes can be offered, however, towards defining the "animating presence."

McCarey's formative years as an artist were spent working with the great clowns of the late silent/early sound period: Harold Lloyd, Mae West, W.C. Fields, the Marx Brothers and (especially) Laurel and Hardy, for whom he was "supervising manager" for many years, personally directing two of their greatest shorts (*Liberty* and *Wrong Again*). His subsequent career spans (with equal success) the entire range of American comedy from screwball (*The Awful Truth*) to romantic (*An Affair to Remember*). The director's congenial characteristic seems to have been a commitment to a spontaneous, individualist anarchy which he never entirely abandoned, accompanied by a consistent scepticism about institutions and restrictive forms of social organization, a scepticism which produces friction and contradiction even within the most seemingly innocuous, conservative projects. *Going My Way* and *The Bells of St. Mary's* are usually rejected outright by the intelligentsia as merely pious and sentimental, but their presentation of Catholicism is neither simple, straightforward, nor uncritical, and it is easy to mistake for sentimentality, in contexts where you expect to find it anyway (such as Hollywood movies about singing priests), qualities such as tenderness and generosity. The celebration of individualism is of course a mainspring of American ideology, yet, pushed far enough in certain directions, it can expose contradictions *within* that ideology: its oppressive response to many forms of individuality, for example.

Make Way for Tomorrow (which, understandably, remained McCarey's favorite among his own films) is exemplary in this respect. Taking as its starting point an apparently reformable social problem (with Lee Grant's *Tell Me a Riddle* it is one of the only important Hollywood films about the aged), and opening with an unassailably respectable Biblical text ("Honor thy father and thy mother"), it proceeds to elaborate what amounts to a systematic radical analysis of the constraints, oppression and divisiveness produced by capitalist culture, lending itself to a thoroughgoing Marxist reading that would certainly have surprised its director. Typically, the film (merely very good for its first three-quarters) suddenly takes off into greatness at the moment when Victor Moore asks the ultimate anarchic question "Why not?", and proceeds to repudiate his family in favour of rediscovering the original relationship with his wife before they become absorbed into the norms of democratic-capitalist domesticity. The process is only completed when, in one of the Hollywood cinema's most poignant and subversive moments, he "unmarries" them as they say their last farewell at the train station: "It's been a pleasure knowing you, Miss Breckenridge."

—Robin Wood

McLEOD, Norman Z.

American. Born Norman Zenos McLeod in Grayling, Michigan, 20 September 1898. Educated in Natural Science, University of Washington, B.S., M.S. Combat pilot in Royal Canadian Air Force, World War I. Married Evelyn Ward. Gagman and writer for Al Christie Comedies, 1919–27; assistant director on Wellman's *Wings*, 1927; director for Fox Film Company, 1928; director mainly for Paramount, 1930–36; director for MGM, United Artists, and RKO, 1937–46; director mainly for RKO and Paramount, after 1947; TV director, late 1950s; suffered stroke, 1962. *Died 27 January 1964.*

Films as Director:

1928 *Taking a Chance*
1930 *Along Came Youth* (co-d)
1931 *Finn and Hattie* (co-d, co-sc); *Monkey Business*; *Touchdown*
1932 *The Miracle Man*; *Horse Feathers*; "The Forger" episode of *If I Had a Million*
1933 *A Lady's Profession*; *Mama Loves Papa*; *Alice in Wonderland* (+ co-sc)
1934 *A Melody in Spring*; *Many Happy Returns*; *It's a Gift*
1935 *Redheads on Parade*; *Here Comes Cookie*; *Coronado*
1936 *Early to Bed*; *Pennies from Heaven*
1937 *Mind Your Own Business*; *Topper*
1938 *Merrily We Live*; *There Goes My Heart*
1939 *Topper Takes a Trip*; *Remember?* (+ co-sc)
1940 *Little Men*
1941 *The Trial of Mary Dugan*; *Lady Be Good*
1942 *Jackass Mail*; *Panama Hattie*
1943 *The Powers Girl* (*Hello Beautiful*); *Swing Shift Maisie* (*The Girl in Overalls*)
1946 *The Kid from Brooklyn*
1947 *The Secret Life of Walter Mitty*; *Road to Rio*
1948 *Isn't It Romantic?*; *The Paleface*
1950 *Let's Dance*
1951 *My Favorite Spy*
1953 *Never Wave at a WAC* (*The Private Wore Skirts. The Newest Profession*)
1954 *Casanova's Big Night*
1957 *Public Pigeon No. 1*
1959 *Alias Jesse James*

Other Films:

1931 *Skippy* (Taurog) (co-sc); *Sooky* (Taurog) (co-sc)

Publications:

On McLEOD: articles—

Articles, in *Lion's Roar* (Los Angeles), 1942 and 1943.

tablish any kind of an editing style, but it did allow the comedy of a scene to play out to its full extent.

Many of the gags in McLeod's films are based on the use of comic props. For example, in *Monkey Business* Harpo works in perfect harmony with the puppets from a Punch and Judy show (at no time is there any indication of a puppeteer). In *It's a Gift*, W.C. Fields's sleep on the back porch is interrupted by a coconut that insists on banging its way down every inch of three flights of stairs. In these (and other) examples, inanimate objects seem to take on a life of their own and exhibit comic characteristics.

On a few occasions the gags in McLeod's films are based on self-reflexive humor. For example, when in *Horse Feathers* Groucho is forced to sit through one of Chico's piano recitals, Groucho gets up and tells the audience, "I *have* to stay here, but there's no reason why you folks shouldn't go out in the lobby until this thing blows over." At the end of *Casanova's Big Night*, Bob Hope is about to be beheaded by the executioner's axe when the scene is interrupted by a freeze frame. What follows is Bob Hope's version of a happy ending where he triumphs and wins the girl. The audience is left to decide which ending they prefer.

—Linda J. Obalil

Norman Z. McLeod

Crichton, K., "Gamble with Music," in *Collier's* (New York), 23 March 1946.
Obituary, in *New York Times*, 28 January 1964.
"Norman Z. McLeod," in *Film Dope* (London), December 1987.

*   *   *

The film career of Norman Z. McLeod is unusual in that he worked exclusively within the field of comedy. Several of his films have been recognized as classics of the genre, including *It's a Gift, Topper*, and *The Secret Life of Walter Mitty*. His films were generally box-office successes, which in turn led to his directing more comedies.

McLeod specialized in working with comic personalities, including the Marx Brothers, W.C. Fields, Red Skelton, Danny Kaye, and Bob Hope. His directing style was very unobtrusive (almost to the point of being non-existent), which allowed these comic personalities to shine through. He was known as a quiet director since, by his own admission, he could easily be out-talked by people like Bob Hope or Danny Kaye. Much of McLeod's instruction came in the form of sketches and little caricatures. He felt that it was easier to show the kinds of physical reactions he wanted by drawing comic postures for his actors.

Most of McLeod's films are short on plot; they are mainly comprised of a series of gags and routines only loosely tied together. For example, underneath *The Secret Life of Walter Mitty* lies a spy story which exists only as a framework for Danny Kaye's daydreaming sequences. *The Paleface* is a western vehicle to support the comic antics of Bob Hope. The Marx Brothers tear their way through an ocean liner in *Monkey Business* to no particular end. Such unmemorable stories allow the performers to dominate the films.

Most of the comedians who worked in Norman McLeod's films came from a vaudeville or stage background, and McLeod photographed them as if they were still on the stage. The framing was often full or three-quarter figure and the camera rarely moved. Most of the scenes in McLeod's films were done as long continuous takes. This technique did little to es-

MEHBOOB KHAN.

Indian. Born Mehboob Khan Ramzan Khan in Bilmora, in the Gandevi Taluka of Baroda State, India, 1909. Married 1925, one son. Extra at Imperial Film Studio, Bombay, from 1927; actor of "bit" parts for subsidiary, Sagar Movietone, from 1931; directed first film, for Sagar Film Co., 1935; established Mehboob Productions, 1943; built Mehboob Studios, 1952. *Died of a heart attack, on hearing of Nehru's death, 27 May 1964.*

Films as Director:

1935   *Judgement of Allah (Alhilal)* (+ sc)
1936   *Deccan Queen*; *Manmohan*
1937   *Jagirdar*
1938   *Hum Tum Aur Woh (We Three)*; *Watan*
1939   *Ek Hi Rasta (The Only Way)*
1940   *Alibaba*; *Aurat (Woman)*
1941   *Bahen (Sister)*
1942   *Roti (Bread)*
1943   *Najma* (+ pr); *Taqdeer* (+ pr)
1945   *Humayun* (+ pr)
1946   *Anmol Ghadi (Priceless Watch)* (+ pr)
1947   *Elan* (+ pr)
1948   *Anokhi Ada (A Special Charm)* (+ pr)
1949   *Andaz (Style)* (+ pr)
1952   *Aan (Pride)* (+ pr)
1954   *Amar* (+ pr)
1957   **Bharat Mata (Mother India)** (+ pr)
1962   *Son of India* (+ pr)

Other Films:

1927   *Alibaba and Forty Thieves* (Misra) (role as thief)
1929   *Maurya Patan (Fall of Mauryas)* (Choudhury) (role)
1930   *Mewad No Mawali (Rogues of Rajasthan)* (Vakil) (role)
1931   *Dilawar* (Torney) (role); *Abul Hasan* (Ghosh) (role)

Mehboob Khan

1932   *Romantic Prince* (*Meri Jaan*) (Ghosh)
1933   *Premi Pagal* (*Mad Cap*) (Mir) (role); *Bulbule Baghdad*
       (Vakil) (role)
1934   *Grihalaxmi* (Badami) (role); *Nautch Girl* (*Dancing Girl*)
       (Desai) (role); *Sati Anjana* (Rathod) (role)
1956   *Awaz* (Sarhady) (pr); *Paisa Hi Paisa* (Mehrish) (pr)

Publications:

On MEHBOOB: books—

Barnouw, Erik, and S. Krishnaswany, *Indian Film*, New York, 1965.
Willemen, Paul, and Behroze Ghandy, *Indian Cinema*, London, 1982.
Pfleiderer, Beatrice, and Lothar Lutze, *The Hindi Film: Agent and Re-Agent of Cultural Change*, New Delhi, 1985.
Ramachandran, T.M., *70 Years of Indian Cinema* (*1913–1983*), Bombay, 1985.

On MEHBOOB: articles—

Film Quarterly (Berkeley), Autumn 1960.
Ray, Satyajit, "Under Western Eyes," in *Sight and Sound* (London), Autumn 1982.
Tesson, Charles, "Le rêve indien," in *Cahiers du Cinéma* (Paris), March 1985.
Thomas, R., "Indian Cinema: Pleasures and Popularity," in *Screen* (London), May/August 1985.

*   *   *

The urbane director K.A. Abbas once referred to Mehboob as the "great rustic" of the Hindi cinema. And, indeed, a certain mythology developed around Mehboob, that of the man with popular roots. This image owed much to stories about his origins (the small town boy who worked his way up through the Bombay studios), and to certain films which dwelt on the tra-vails of the poor and the destitute, such as *Aurat* (*Woman*) and *Roti* (*Bread*).

In fact Mehboob's output as director was very varied. After he founded his own company, Mehboob Productions, in 1943, he made historical works (*Humayun*) and fantasy spectaculars (*Aan/Pride*). Even films such as *Anmol Ghadi* (*Priceless Watch*) and *Anokhi Ada* (*A Special Charm*) which appeared to address the class divide, were variations of the triangular love story, the favoured convention of the Hindi cinema.

In these films social representation becomes incidental to the basic plot because the narrative spaces of a simple rural life or of urban destitution are constructed in an idealised rather than in a realistic way. The lighting style of such scenes show them as composed of smooth studio surfaces, and there is an indifference to the more squalid details of characterisation. The emphasis lies in the fullness of melodramatic sentiments—of loss and of romantic longing—which occasion the use of lushly orchestrated songs. All this is a pleasurable closing off of the cinema and its audience from social references, a tendency in Mehboob's work best represented by his venture into the swashbuckling colour film, *Aan*.

Elements of this romantic mode are observable even in Mehboob's "social" films. In *Aurat* and its later colour version, *Mother India*, rural life is often conveyed as a series of spectacularly choreographed scenes of harvesting, festivals, and the romantic engagement of its characters. *Andaz* (*Style*), on the other hand, invites the audience to soak in the luxuries of the modern, upper-class settings in which its characters live.

In this sense, Mehboob was not simply a popularly rooted "rustic" artist, but engaged in creations of high artifice and escapism. However, these elements were often integrated with quite powerful constructions of meaning. *Aurat*, for example, achieves an almost anthropological view of gender roles. This is accomplished not by the accuracy of its observations about rural life, but by using the grim struggles of rural life as a way of drawing out the role performed by Indian women. This provides the basis for the film's main interest, the melodrama of the unrelieved suffering of a woman (Sardar Akhtar) on behalf of her sons (Surendra and Yakub). The subsequent version of this film, *Mother India*, is an interesting contrast. The focus is still on the suffering of the mother (Nargis); but this capacity to suffer is transformed into a distinctly mythical power which moves beyond her immediate family to inspire the whole village community. In both films the woman is the bearer of a patriarchal inheritance for her son, but *Mother India* may have represented a new, mythicised role model for women, one whose power often co-exists uneasily with its conservative functions.

Perhaps most interesting is *Andaz*, a drama, at least implicitly, of illicit desire. The story is about Nina (Nargis) who, while faithful to her absent fiancé (Raj Kapoor), relates vivaciously to an attractive young man (Dilip Kumar). The heroine is shown to be a naive innocent who cannot perceive that relaxed social relations between men and women can lead to misunderstanding, and this generates the tragic events that follow. And yet, moving beyond, or perhaps deeper into, its own fascination with the settings and mores of its upper class characters, the narration introduces an interesting, fantastical ambiguity. Nina's denials that she is attracted to a man other than her husband are put into doubt for the audience through scenes depicting the hallucinations and dreams that assail the heroine. In this way the "rustic" Mehboob was surprisingly well equipped to convey certain strikingly modern problems of sexuality and desire.

—Ravi Vasudevan

MEKAS, Jonas.

Lithuanian. Born in Semeniskiai, 24 December 1922. Educated at Gymnasium, Birzai, Lithuania, graduated 1942; studied philosophy and literature, Johannes Gutenberg University, Mainz, and University of Tübingen. Married Hollis Melton, 1974, children: Oona and Sebastian. During German occupation, taken, with brother Adolfas, to forced labor camp near Hamburg, 1944; they escaped, 1945; in displaced persons camps, 1945–49; while studying in Germany, edited Lithuanian emigré literary magazine *Zvilgsniai* (Glimpses), and wrote collections of short stories and poetry; moved to New York, 1949; worked in factories and shops in various capacities, through 1950s; founded *Film Culture* magazine, 1955, remains Editor-in-Chief; began "Movie Journal" column for *Village Voice*, 1958; shot first film, *Guns of the Trees*, and helped organize New American Cinema Group, 1960; organized The Film-Makers' Cooperative, 1961; organized the Film-Makers' Cinematheque, arrested and charged with showing obscene film (Jack Smith's *Flaming Creatures*), given 6-month suspended sentence, 1964; co-founder, with P. Adams Sitney, then acting director, Anthology Film Archives, 1970; Recipient: Documentary Award, Venice festival, for *The Brig*, 1965. Address: c/o Anthology Film Archives, 32 Second Avenue, New York, NY 10003, U.S.A.

Films as Director:

1961   *Guns of the Trees*
1963   *Film Magazine of the Arts*
1964   *The Brig*; *Award Presentation to Andy Warhol*
1966   *Report from Millbrook*; *Hare Krishna*; *Notes on the Circus*; *Cassis*
1968   *Walden* (*Diaries, Notes, and Sketches*)
1969   *Time & Fortune Vietnam Newsreel*
1972   *Reminiscences of a Journey to Lithuania*
1976   *Lost, Lost, Lost*
1978   *In Between*
1980   *Paradise Not Yet Lost, or Oona's Fifth Year*
1981   *Notes for Jerome*
1986   *He Stands in the Desert Counting the Seconds of His Life*

Publications:

By MEKAS: articles—

Mekas founded *Film Culture* magazine 1955, contributes regularly and remains its Editor-in-Chief
Weekly column "Movie Journal," in *The Village Voice* (New York), since 1958.
Statement, in *Film Comment* (New York), Winter 1964.
Interview with B.L. Kevles, in *Film Culture* (New York), Fall 1965.
Interview with Gerald Barrett, in *Literature/Film Quarterly* (Salisbury, Maryland), Spring 1973.
Interview with Antonin Liehm, in *Thousand Eyes* (New York), October 1976.

On MEKAS: articles—

Harrington, Stephanie, "Pornography is Undefined at Film-Critic Mekas' Trial," in *The Village Voice* (New York), 18 June 1964.
Levy, Alan, "Voice of the Underground Cinema," in *The New York Times Magazine*, 19 September 1965.
Simon, Bill, "New Forms in Film," in *Artforum* (New York), October 1972.
Tompkins, Calvin, "Profile: All Pockets Open," in the *New Yorker*, 6 January 1973.
Goldstein, R., "Give It Away on 2nd Avenue," in *The Village Voice* (New York), 29 January 1979.
MacDonald, S., "Lost lost lost over *Lost lost lost*," in *Cinema Journal* (Champaign, Illinois), Winter 1986.

*   *   *

Jonas Mekas

Born in Lithuania in 1922, Jonas Mekas was a poet and resistance worker against both the German and Soviet occupations during the Second World War. After some years in a German camp for displaced persons, he and his brother, Adolfas, also a filmmaker, emigrated to New York where they later founded the journal *Film Culture*. Initially hostile to the American avant-garde, Mekas became its champion and spokesman in the 1960s. Throughout that decade he exerted great influence through *Film Culture*, his "Movie Journal" column in the *Village Voice* and his founding of the Film-makers Cooperative (in 1962) to distribute independent films, and the Film-makers Cinematheque (founded in 1963) as a New York showcase.

His first film, *Guns of the Trees*, a 35mm feature, describes aspects of Beat culture in New York through the lives of four fictional characters. It reflects his hopes, at that time, for the establishment of a feature length narrative cinema on the model of the French and Polish "New Waves." By the time he made *The Brig* with his brother, directly filming Ken Brown's stage play in the Living Theatre Production as if it were a documentary, he had already shifted his energies to his on-going cinematic diary. The diary had actually begun in the mid-1950s when he reached the United States, but it took the liberating inspiration of Stan Brakhage and Marie Menken for Mekas to acknowledge that his artistic talent was focused outside of the feature film tradition he had been espousing.

The first installment of his *Diaries, Notes, and Sketches*, the nearly three-hour-long *Walden*, records his life, with numerous portraits of his friends and colleagues in the mid-1960s. Its techniques are characteristic of the filmmaker's mature work:

staccato, single-frame flashes, composed directly in the camera, are counterpointed to longer sketches of weddings, trips to the circus, meetings. Printed intertitles often occur. Long passages have musical accompaniment. The filmmaker repeatedly breaks in on the soundtrack to offer private reflections and aphorisms.

In 1976 he released *Lost, Lost, Lost*, another three hour section of the megadiary. This time, he went back to his initial experiments with the camera, in a more conventional and leisurely style, to document the aspirations and frustrations of his life as an exile dreaming of the re-establishment of an independent Lithuanian republic. Bits of this material had already appeared in his masterly and moving *Reminiscences of a Journey to Lithuania*, a three-part film made with the help of German television. The middle section of that film describes the emotional reunion of both brothers with their mother, then almost 90 years old, when they returned home for their first visit since the war. The film opens with a summary of Mekas's initial experiences in America and ends with a recognition of the impossibility of recovering the past, as he joins a group of his friends, mostly artists, in Vienna.

That elegiac tone is sustained and refined in *Notes for Jerome*, the record of his visits to the estate of Jerome Hill, in Cassis, France, in the late 1960s, and edited after Hill's death in 1972. Mekas married Hollis Melton in 1974. Their first child Oona was born the next year. *Paradise Not Yet Lost*: or *Oona's Fifth Year* deals with his family life, but continues the theme of lost childhood which permeates Mekas's vision. It is filmed in the style of *Walden* as is *In Between* which records the years between *Lost, Lost, Lost* and *Walden*.

—P. Adams Sitney

MÉLIÈS, Georges.

French. Born in Paris, 8 December 1861. Educated at the Lycée Imperial, Vanves, 1868–70; Lycée Louis-le-Grand, Paris, 1871–80; Married 1) Eugénie Genin, 1885, children: Georgette and André; 2) Fanny Manieux (born Charlotte-Stéphanie Faës, stage name Jahanne D'Arcy), 1925. Introduced to illusionism by English conjuror John Maskelyne, 1884; bought Théâtre Robert-Houdin, Paris, began to present performance of magic and illusionism, and began association with technician Eugène Calmels, 1888; attended première of Cinematographe Lumière, 1895; bought Animatographe projector in London, developed camera with Lucien Reulos, built first studio at Montreuil, began shooting first film *Partie des cartes*, "Star Film Company" begun, 1896; transformed theatre into cinema, 1897; brother Gaston Méliès opens Star Film branch in New York, 1903; 2nd Montreuil studio built, 1905; studio closes temporarily due to American competition, 1909; returned to stage as magician, 1910 (last performance 1920); Méliès retrospective, Paris, after "rediscovery" by Leon Druhot, 1929; given an apartment at Chateau d'Orly by the Mutuelle du Cinéma, 1932. Recipient: Legion of Honour, 1933. *Died, in Paris, 21 January 1938.*

Films as Director, Producer, Scenarist, Art Director and Actor:

1896 (78 films, 2 extant): *Une Nuit terrible (A Terrible Night)*; *Escamotage d'une dame chez Robert-Houdin (The Vanishing Lady)*

1897 (52 films, 4 extant): *Entre Calais et Douvres (Between Calais and Dover)*; *L'Auberge ensorcelée (The Bewitched Inn)*; *Après le bal (After the Ball)*; *Danse au sérail (Dancing in a Harem)*; *Combat naval en Grèce*

1898 (30 films, 8 extant): *Visite sous-marine du Maine (Divers at Work on the Wreck of the Maine)*; *Panorama pris d'un train en marche (Panorama from Top of a Moving Train)*; *Le Magicien*; *Illusions fantasmagoriques (The Famous Box Trick)*; *La Lune à un mètre (The Astronomer's Dream)*; *Un Homme de tête (The Four Troublesome Heads)*; *La Tentation de Saint-Antoine (The Temptation of Saint Anthony)*; *Salle à manger fantastique (A Dinner Under Difficulties*

1899 (34 films, 4 extant): *Cléopâtre (Robbing Cleopatra's Tomb)*; *L'Impressioniste fin de siècle (An Up-To-Date Conjurer)*; *Le Portrait mystérieux (A Mysterious Portrait)*; *L'Affaire Dreyfus (The Dreyfus Affair)*

1900 (33 films, 7 extant): *Les Miracles de Brahmane (The Miracles of Brahmin)*; *L'Exposition de 1900 (Paris Exposition, 1900)*; *L'Homme orchestre (The One-Man Band)*; *Le Rêve de Noël (The Christmas Dream)*; *Gens qui pleurent et gens qui rient (Crying and Laughing)*; *Nouvelles Luttes extravagantes (The Wrestling Sextette)*; *Le Malade hydrophobe (The Man with Wheels in His Head)*

1901 (29 films, 4 extant): *Le Brahmane et le papillon (The Brahmin and the Butterfly)*; *Dislocations mystérieuses (Extraordinary Illusions)*; *Le Charlatan (Painless Dentistry*; *Barbe-Bleue (Blue Beard)*

1902 (23 films, 5 extant): *L'Homme à la tête de caoutchouc (The Man with the Rubber Head. India Rubber Head)*; *Eruption volcanique à la Martinique (The Eruption of Mount Pelée)*; **Le Voyage dans la lune (A Trip to the Moon)**; *Le Sacré d'Édouard VII (The Coronation of Edward VII)*; *Les Trésors de Satan (The Treasures of Satan)*

1903 (29 films, 28 extant): *La Corbeille enchantée (The Enchanted Basket)*; *La Guirlande merveilleuse (The Marvellous Wreath)*; *Les Filles du Diable (Beelzebub's Daughters)*; *Un Malheur n'arrive jamais seul (Misfortune Never Comes Alone)*; *Le Cake-walk infernal (The Infernal Cake Walk)*; *La Boîte à malice (The Mysterious Box)*; *Le Puits fantastique (The Enchanted Well)*; *L'Auberge du bon repos (The Inn Where No Man Rests)*; *La Statue animée (The Drawing Lesson)*; *La Flamme merveilleuse (The Mystical Flame)*; *Le Sorcier (The Witch's Revenge)*; *L'Oracle de Delphes (The Oracle of Delphi)*; *Le Portrait spirite (A Spiritualist Photographer)*; *Le Mélomane (The Melomaniac)*; *Le Monstre (The Monster)*; *Le Royaume des Fées (The Kingdom of the Fairies)*; *Le Chaudron infernal (The Infernal Cauldron)*; *Le Revenant (The Apparition)*; *Le Tonnerre de Jupiter (Jupiter's Thunderbolts*; *La Parapluie fantastique (Ten Ladies in One Umbrella)*; *Tom Tight et Dum Dum (Jack Jaggs and Dum Dum)*; *Bob Kick, l'enfant terrible (Bob Kick the Mischievous Kid)*; *Illusions funambulesques (Extraordinary Illusions)*; *L'Enchanteur Alcofrisbas (Alcofrisbas, the Master Magician)*; *Jack et Jim*; *La Lanterne magique (The Magic Lantern)*; *La Rêve du maître de ballet (The Ballet Master's Dream)*; *Faust aux enfers (The Damnation of Faust)*

1904 (35 films, 19 extant): *Le Bourreau turc (The Terrible Turkish Executioner)*; *Au Clair de la lune ou Pierrot malheureux (A Moonlight Serenade, or The Miser Punished)*; *Un Bonne Farce avec ma tête (Tit for Tat)*; *Le Coffre enchanté (The Bewitched Trunk)*; *Les Apparitions fugitives (Fugitive Apparitions)*; *Le Roi du maquillage (Untamable Whiskers)*; *La Rêve d'horloger (The Clockmaker's Dream)*; *Les Transmutations imperceptibles (The Imperceptible Transformations)*; *Un Miracle sous l'inquisition (A Miracle Under the Inquisition)*; *Benvenutto Cellini ou une curieuse évasion (Benvenuto Cellini, or a Curious Evasion)*; *La Damnation du Docteur Faust (Faust and Marguerite)*; *Le Thaumaturge chinois (Tchin-Chao, the Chinese Conjurer)*; *Le Merveilleux éventail vivant (The Wonderful Living Fan)*; *Sorcellerie culinaire (The Cook in Trouble)*; *La Sirène (The Mermaid)*; *Le Rosier miraculeux (The Wonderful Rose*

Georges Méliès (left) with Carl Laemmle, 1935

Tree); *Le Voyage à travers l'impossible* (*The Impossible Voyage*); *Le Juif errant* (*The Wandering Jew*); *La Cascade de Feu* (*The Firefall*)

1905 (22 films, 11 extant): *Les Cartes vivants* (*The Living Playing Cards*); *Le Diable noir* (*The Black Imp*); *Le Menuet lilliputien* (*The Lilliputian Minuet*); *Le Bacquet de Mesmer* (*A Mesmerian Experiment*); *Le Palais des mille et une nuits* (*The Palace of the Arabian Nights*); *La Compositeur toqué* (*A Crazy Composer*); *La Chaise à porteurs enchantée* (*The Enchanted Sedan Chair*); *Le Raid Paris-Monte Carlo en deux heures* (*An Adventurous Automobile Trip*); *Un Feu d'artifice improvisé* (*Unexpected Fireworks*); *La Légende de Rip van Winkle* (*Rip's Dream*); *Le Tripot clandestin* (*The Scheming Gambler's Paradise*)

1906 (18 films, 10 extant): *Une Chute de cinq étages* (*A Mix-up in the Galley*); *La Cardeuse de Matelas* (*The Tramp and the Mattress-Makers*); *Les Affiches en goguette* (*The Hilarious Posters*); *Histoire d'un crime* (*A Desperate Crime*); *L'Anarchie chez Guignol* (*Punch and Judy*); *L'Hôtel des voyageurs de commerce* (*A Roadside Inn*); *Les Bulles de savon animées* (*Soap Bubbles*); *Les 400 Farces du Diable* (*The Merry Frolics of Satan*); *L'Alchimiste Prarafaragamus ou la Cornue infernale* (*The Mysterious Retort*); *La Fée caraboose ou le Poignard fatal* (*The Witch*)

1907 (19 films, 7 extant): *La Douche d'eau bouillanie* (*Rogue's Tricks*); *Le Mariage de Victorine* (*How Bridget's Lover Escaped*); *Le Tunnel sous la manche ou Le Cauchemar franco-anglais* (*Tunnelling the English Channel*); *L'Eclipse du soleil en pleine lune* (*The Eclipse, or the Courtship of the Sun and the Moon*); *Pauvre John ou Les Aventures d'un buveur de whiskey* (*Sight-Seeing Through Whiskey*); *La Colle universelle* (*Good Glue Sticks*); *Ali Barbouyou et Ali Bouf à l'huile* (*Delirium in a Studio*)

1908 (68 films, 21 extant): *Le Tambourin fantastique* (*The Knight of the Black Art*); *Il y a un dieu pour les ivrognes* (*The Good Luck of a Souse*); *La Génie de feu* (*The Genii of Fire*); *Why the Actor Was Late*; *Le Rêve d'un fumeur d'opium* (*The Dream of an Opium Fiend*); *La Photographie electrique à distance* (*Long Distance Wireless Photography*); *Salon de coiffure* (*In the Barber Shop*); *Le Nouveau Seigneur du village* (*The New Lord of the Village*); *Sideshow Wrestlers*; *Lulli ou le violon brisé* (*The Broken Violin*); *The Woes of Roller Skates*; *Le Fakir de Singapoure* (*The Indian Sorcerer*); *The Mischances of a Photographer*; *His First Job*; *French Cops Learning English*; *A Tricky Painter's Fate*; *Au patys des jouets* (*Grandmother's Story*); *Buncoed Stage Johnnie*; *Not Guilty*; *Hallucinations pharmaceutiques* (*Pharmaceutical Hallucinations*); *La Bonne Bergère et la méchante princesse* (*The Good Shepherdess and the Evil Princess*)

1909 (9 films, none extant)

1910 (13 films, 3 extant): *Hydrothérapie fantastique* (*The Doctor's Secret*); *Le Locataire diabolique* (*The Diabolic Tenant*); *Les Illusions fantaisistes* (*Whimsical Illusions*)

1911 (2 films, 1 extant): *Les Hallucinations du Baron Münchausen* (*Baron Münchausen's Dream*)

1912 (4 films, 3 extant): *À la conquête du Pôle* (*The Conquest of the Pole*); *Cendrillon ou la pantoufle mystérieuse* (*Cinderella or the Glass Slipper*); *Le Chevalier des neiges* (*The Knight of the Snows*)

Publications:

By MÉLIÈS: articles—

"En marge de l'histoire du cinématographe," in *Ciné Journal* (Paris), August 1926.

"Les Phénomènes du spiritisme," in *Journal de l'Association Française des artistes prestidigitateurs* (Paris), July/August 1936.

"The Silver Lining," in *Sight and Sound* (London), Spring 1938.

"A Letter from Georges Méliès to Merritt Crawford, Esq.," in *Film Culture* (New York), no. 70–71, 1983.

"*Le Livre magique* and *Le Voyage dans la lune*," in *Avant-Scène du Cinéma* (Paris), November 1984.

On MÉLIÈS: books—

Warwick Film Catalogue, London, 1901.

Star Film Catalogue, New York-Paris, 1905.

Ford, Charles, *Georges Méliès*, Brussells, 1959.

Bessy, Maurice, and Lo Duca, *Georges Méliès, Mage*, Paris, 1961.

Exposition commémorative du Centenaire de Georges Méliès, exhibition catalogue, Paris, 1961.

Sadoul, Georges, *Georges Méliès*, Paris, 1961.

Deslandes, Jacques, *Le Boulevard du cinéma à l'époque de Georges Méliès*, Paris, 1963.

Kyrou, Ado, *De Méliès a l'expressionisme, le surréalisme au cinéma*, Paris, 1963.

Malthête-Méliès, Madeleine, *Georges Méliès, créateur du spectacle cinématographique, 1861–1938*, Paris, 1966.

Malthête-Méliès, Madeleine, *Méliès, l'enchanteur*, Paris, 1973.

Hammond, Paul, *Marvellous Méliès*, New York, 1975.

Brakhage, Stan, *Film Biographies*, Berkeley, California, 1977.

Frazer, John, *Artificially Arranged Scenes: The Films of Georges Méliès*, Boston, 1979.

Usai, Paolo Cherci, *Georges Méliès*, Florence, 1983.

Jenn, Pierre, *Georges Méliès cinéaste: Le montage cinématographique chez Georges Méliès*, Paris, 1984.

Malthête-Méliès, Madeleine, *Méliès et la naissance du spectacle cinématographique*, Paris, 1984.

Sadoul, Georges, *Lumière et Méliès*, Paris, 1984.

Langlois, Henri, and others, *Méliès: Un homme d'illusions*, Paris, 1986.

Redi, Riccardo, editor, *Verso il Centenario: Méliès*, Rome, 1987.

Crawford, Merritt, and John Mulholland, *Georges Méliès, Film Pioneer*, New York, not dated.

On MÉLIÈS: articles—

Cavalcanti, Alberto, "Father of the Fantasy Film," in *The Listener* (London), 2 June 1938.

Sadoul, Georges, "An Index to the Creative Work of Georges Méliès," in *Sight and Sound* (London), no.11, 1947.

Eisner, Lotte, "Tribute to Mme Méliès," in *Film* (London), January/February 1957.

Stephenson, Ralph, "Commemorating Méliès," in *Sight and Sound* (London), Autumn 1961.

Stephenson, Ralph, "A Film a Day," in *Films and Filming* (London), December 1961.

Bessy, Maurice, "Méliès," in *Anthologie du Cinéma* vol.2, Paris, 1967.

"An Interview with Madeleine Méliès," in *Film Culture* (New York), Winter/Spring 1970.

Franju, Georges, "Le Classicisme de Méliès et Zecca," in *Cinéma* (Paris), January 1971.

Hammond, Paul, "A Georges Méliès Scrapbook," in *Cinéma* (Beverly Hills), Summer 1971.

Kovacs, Katherine, "Georges Méliès and La Féerie," in *Cinema Journal* (Evanston, Illinois), Fall 1976.

Franju, Georges, "A propos du 'Grand Méliès'," in *Positif* (Paris), December/January 1977/78.

Barnouw, Eric, "The Magician and the Movies," in *American Film* (Washington, D.C.), April 1978.

McInroy, P., "The American Méliès," in *Sight and Sound* (London), no.4, 1979.

Haleff, M., "André Méliès Interviewed," in *Film Culture* (New York), no.67–69, 1979.

Bezombes, R., "Les Burlesque de Méliès," in *Cinématographe* (Paris), April 1979.

Questerbert, M.-C., "Revoir Méliès: Méliès et la proliferation," and interview with Albert Levy, in *Cahiers du Cinéma* (Paris), April 1979.

Courant, G., "Point d'histoire: Méliès: la fin d'un mythe?," in *Cinéma* (Paris), May 1979.

Quevrain, M.A.M., "L'Idéologie de Méliès et son epoque," in *Cinéma* (Paris), September 1979.

Veillon, O.-R., "Portrait de l'artiste en magicien," in *Cinématographe* (Paris), January 1981.

Williams, L., "Film Body: An Implantation of Perversions," in *Ciné-Tracts* (Montreal), Winter 1981.

Hammond, P., "Georges, this is Charles," in *Afterimage* (London), no.8–9, Spring 1981.

"*Le Grand Méliès,*" in *Avant-Scène du Cinéma* (Paris), April 1984.

Dubois, P., "Le gros plan primitif," in *Revue Belge du Cinéma* (Brussels), Winter 1984/85.

Masson, André, "Le Cinéma des incomparables: sur Georges Méliès," in *Positif* (Paris), April 1985.

Gaudreault, André, "Theatricality, Narrativity and Trickality: Reevaluating the Cinema of Georges Méliès," in *Journal of Popular Film and Television* (Washington, D.C.), Fall 1987.

Barnes, John, "Méliès: An NFA discovery," in *Sight and Sound* (London), Spring 1989.

On MÉLIÈS: films—

Cavalcanti, Alberto, *Film and Reality*, 1943.
Franju, Georges, *Le Grand Méliès*, 1952.
Malthête-Méliès, Madeleine, *Georges Méliès*, 1969.
Montgomery, Patrick, *Georges Méliès: Cinema Magician*, 1977.

* * *

Georges Méliès, prestidigitator and master illusionist in the Parisian theatre of the late 19th century, turned to the cinema and made some 500 films of every kind fashionable at the time between 1896 and 1912. Of these less than 90 survive, though working drawings (Méliès was a prolific and considerable graphic artist) remain to supplement his work.

Born in Paris in 1861, Méliès as a youth habitually attended the Théâtre Robert-Houdin, a first-floor establishment with 200 seats and a stage carefully devised to present Jean-Eugène Robert-Houdin's technically advanced forms of conjuring and illusion. He was also influenced by visits to Maskelyne and Cooke's Egyptian Hall in London, where for a while his father, a wealthy bootmaker, sent him to work. Maskelyne presented spectacular dramatic shows involving illusion of the kind Méliès was himself to develop when, in 1888, selling his share in his late father's business to his brothers, he was able to buy the Théâtre Robert-Houdin and take over as showman illusionist. In addition, he exhibited lantern-slide shows with an illusion of movement achieved by continuities of superimposition. After seeing the celebrated Cinématographe Lumière in Paris in December 1895, Méliès could not rest until he had obtained equipment for himself. He acquired his first motion picture apparatus in 1896 from R.W. Paul in London, and presented his first film show at the Robert-Houdin on 4 April 1896, using Edison's kinetoscope loops; his own initial ventures into filmmaking—moving snap-shots much like Lumière's—were exhibited in the fall.

In his first year Méliès made 78 films, all but one running about one minute; the exception, *The Devil's Castle*, was a vampire film playing three minutes. Within a year, by March 1897, he had constructed a glass studio in the garden of his house in Montreuil, near Paris, its equipment modelled on that for the stage in the Théâtre Robert-Houdin, which he then turned over, in part at least, to screening programs made up exclusively of films. With his staff he built the sets, designed and made the costumes, photographed and processed the films, using cameras made mainly by Gaumont, Lumière, and Pathé. He sold the prints outright to fairground and music-hall showmen, initially in France and England. He worked at a furious pace, being a tough employer of both artists and technicians. At first he used non-professional players, often performing himself.

Although he was to try his hand at every kind of film, his more lasting reputation was for burlesque, magical pantomime, and stage-derived illusion, but like other producers he made money out of the bogus newsreel reconstruction, theatrical melodrama, adaptions from literary sources, historical costume drama, and even so-called "stag" films (mild strip-tease) and advertising films. Among his staged newsreels were films that purported to be coverage of the Greco-Turkish war (1897), and American involvement in Cuba and the Philippines (1898). He even reconstructed *The Eruption of Mount Pelée* on Martinique in 1902, using models, and *The Coronation of Edward VII* before that event, which in any case was postponed.

It is well-known that Méliès was an exponent of trick photography, inspired, according to Georges Sadoul, the French film historian, by the publication in 1897 of Albert Allis Hopkins's *Magic, Stage Illusions and Scientific Diversions, Including Trick Photography*, though his most reliable biographer, Paul Hammond, claims Méliès would have been familiar with such devices long before. His standard techniques included duplex photography (through which a single man could appear as himself and a double in a single frame) and spirit (ghost) photography using multiple images. These techniques enabled him to make films projecting stage illusions like *The Vanishing Lady* and *The Astronomer's Dream*—dream films are recurrent in his catalogue—and *The Four Troublesome Heads*, in which a magician repeatedly removes his head. Méliès was to specialize in comic dismemberment of heads and limbs.

By the turn of the century he was handling historical subjects—*Joan of Arc* and even a pro-Dreyfus film of 13 minutes, *The Dreyfus Affair*; literary adaptions, such as *The Damnation of Faust*; and coverage (backed by phonograph recordings) of the comedian-singer Paulus in a series of films, using for the first time electric arc-lights. He even made *Christ Walking on the Water* as well as simple travel or view films, including panoramas of Paris for the 1900 World Fair. He also reproduced in modern form the past glories of celebrated ghost and skeleton exhibitions, such as *Pepper's Ghost* of London in 1862 and Robertson's *Fantasmagorie* of Paris in 1794. His mildly pornographic "stag" films included *After the Ball* and *The Bridegroom's Dilemma*, in which the actress Jahanne d'Arcy (Méliès's mistress, to become much later, in 1925, his second wife) appeared.

Most of Méliès's more celebrated films depended on illusion, comic burlesque, and pantomime, such as *The Man with the Rubber Head*—in which Méliès's own head is seen expanding to giant size and exploding; the delightfully absurd *A Trip to the Moon*—with acrobats playing the Selenites and hand-waving dancing girls sitting on stars; *The Melomaniac*, in which Méliès conjures with numerous images of his own head, creating out of them musical notes; the space-travelling burlesque, *The Impossible Voyage* (length 24 minutes); the pantomimic *The Merry Frolics of Satan*, with its animated, skeleton puppet horse; a 91-minute version of *Hamlet*; *The Conquest of the Pole*, with its man-eating Giant of the Snows, a vast marionette; and *Cinderella and the Glass Slipper*, produced in association with Pathé and cut by his order from 54 to 33 minutes.

Until around 1909 Méliès remained a largely successful filmmaker. In 1900 he had been elected president of the International Convention of Cinematograph Editors (a position he held until 1912), and in 1904 he became president of the Chambre Syndicale de la Prestidigitation. There were agencies for his Star Film company in Berlin, Barcelona, London, and New York. Some of his films were available at double or treble cost in hand-tinted color prints. But the introduction of the practice of renting films, advocated by Pathé and other well-financed producers, was finally to defeat Méliès. He began to turn his attention back to theatrical presentation, producing pantomimes in Paris. However, his brother Gaston, based now in America, began to produce live-action films for Star, including Westerns in Texas and California, even for a while employing Francis Ford, John Ford's older brother, and later in 1912 touring the South Seas and Far East to make travelogues. (Gaston was to die of food poisoning in Algeria in 1914.) Georges Méliès ceased filmmaking in 1912, his kind of work outdated and unwanted, and by 1914, now a widower in his sixties, he was forced to rent his properties or see them taken over for war purposes, though one of his studios was converted into a vaudeville theater and run from 1917 to 1923 by his daughter, Georgette. Méliès gave his last show in the Théâtre Robert-Houdin in 1920, by which time he was deeply in debt. Many of his negatives and prints were destroyed for scrap.

As an artist of stage and screen, Méliès was at once illusionist and pantomimist; in his films, human beings became comic creatures with fantastic costumes and make-up, liable to disintegrate or metamorphose into anything. Méliès world was one of ceaseless change, a product partly of fairground magic and of costume tableaux vivants. Chaplin described him as an "alchemist of light." His sets, often beautifully painted in trompe-l'oeil with deceptive perspective, were essentially theatrical. His remarkable drawings, many happily preserved, show what a magnificent cartoon animator he could have become with his Protean imagination for the grotesque and the marvellous. As it was, adopting the cinema in the very year of its birth, he endowed it with the work of his highly individualist imagination, an imagination unlike that of any other filmmaker of his time. The best study of him in English is that by Paul Hammond, *Marvellous Méliès*.

—Roger Manvell

———

MELVILLE, Jean-Pierre.

French. Born Jean-Pierre Grumbach in Paris, 20 October 1917. Educated at the Lycées Condorcet and Charlemagne, Paris, and Michelet, Vanves. Began military service, 1937; evacuated to England after Dunkirk, then served with Free French Forces in North Africa and Italy. Founder, O.G.C. (Organisation générale cinématographique) as production company, 1945; built own studio, Paris, 1949 (destroyed by fire, 1967). Recipient: Prix René-Jeanne for *Le cercle rouge*, 1970; Chevalier de la Légion d'honneur; Chevalier des Arts et des Lettres. *Died, in Paris, 2 August 1973.*

Films as Director:

1946   *Vingt quatre heures de la vie d'un clown* (+ sc, pr)
1948   *Le Silence de la mer* (+ pr, sc)
1950   *Les Enfants terribles* (+ co-sc, pr, art d)
1953   *Quand tu liras cette lettre* (+ sc)
1956   *Bob le flambeur* (+ pr, co-art d, sc)
1959   *Deux hommes dans Manhattan* (+ pr, sc, role as Moreau)
1963   *Léon Morin, prêtre* (+ sc); *Le Doulos* (+ sc); *L'Aîné des Ferchaux* (+ sc)
1966   *Le Deuxième Souffle* (+ sc)
1967   *Le Samourai* (+ sc)
1969   *L'Armée des ombres* (+ sc)
1972   *Le Cercle rouge* (+ sc); *Un Flic* (+ sc)

Other Films:

1948   *Les Dames du Bois de Boulogne* (Bresson) (role)
1949   *Orphée* (Cocteau) (role as hotel director)
1957   *Un Amour de poche* (role as police commissioner)
1960   *A bout de souffle* (Godard) (role as the writer Parvulesco)
1962   *Landru* (Chabrol) (role as Georges Mandel)

Publications:

By MELVILLE: articles—

Interview with Claude Beylie and Bertrand Tavernier, in *Cahiers du Cinéma* (Paris), October 1961.
"Finding the Truth Without Faith," in *Films and Filming* (London), March 1962.
"*Léon Morin, prêtre*: Découpage intégrale," in *Avant-Scène du Cinéma* (Paris), no.10
Interview with Eric Brietbart, in *Film Culture* (New York), Winter 1964/65.
"*Le Doulos*: Découpage intégrale," in *Avant-Scène du Cinéma* (Paris), no.24
Interview with Michel Dancourt, in *Arts* (Paris), 25 April 1966.
"A Samurai in Paris," interview with Rui Nogueira and François Truchaud, in *Sight and Sound* (London), Summer 1968.
"Apres Un Flic, Jean-Pierre Melville a-t-il besoin d'un deuxième souffle?," interview with R. Elbhar, in *Séquences* (Montreal), April 1973.
Interview with F. Guérif, in *Cahiers du Cinématheque* (Paris), Spring/Summer 1978.

On MELVILLE: books—

Wagner, Jean, *Jean-Pierre Melville*, Paris, 1964.
Armes, Roy, *French Cinema Since 1946: Vol.2—The Personal Style*, New York, 1966.
Nogueira, Rui, *Melville on Melville*, London, 1971.
McArthur, Colin, *Underworld U.S.A.*, London, 1972.
Nogueira, Rui, *Le Cinéma selon Melville*, Paris, 1973.
Zimmer, Jacques, and Chantal de Béchade, *Jean-Pierre Melville*, Paris, 1983.

On MELVILLE: articles—

Chabrol, Claude, "Saluer Melville?," in *Cahiers du Cinéma* (Paris), October 1956.
Beylie, Claude, "Melville le flambeur," in *Cinéma* (Paris), no.40, 1959.
Domarchi, Jean, "Plaisir à Melville," in *Cahiers du Cinéma* (Paris), December 1959.
Ledieu, Christian, "Jean-Pierre Melville," in *Études Cinématographiques* (Paris), no.6 and 7, 1960.
Porcile, François, "Melville ou l'amour du cinéma," in *Cinéma-texte* (Paris), January 1963.
Austen, David, "All Guns and Gangsters," in *Films and Filming* (London), June 1970.
Beylie, Claude, "Quand tu liras cette lettre . . . ," in *Ecran* (Paris), September/October 1973.
Renaud, T., "Il fut quand même Melville . . . ," in *Cinéma* (Paris), September/October 1973.
"L'Armée des ombres," in *Image et Son* (Paris), no.331 bis, 1978.
Schlöndorff, Volker, "A Parisian-American in Paris," in *The Village Voice* (New York), 6 July 1982.

*   *   *

The career of Jean-Pierre Melville is one of the most independent in modern French cinema. The tone was set with his first feature film, *Le Silence de la mer*, made quite outside the confines of the French film industry. Without union recognition or even the rights to the novel by Vercors which he was adapting, Melville proceeded to make a film which, in its counterpointing of images and a spoken text, sets the pattern for a whole area of French literary filmmaking, extending from Bresson and Resnais down to Duras in the 1980s. *Les Enfants terribles*, made in close collaboration with Jean Cocteau, was an equally interesting amalgam of literature and film, but more influential was *Bob le flambeur*, a first variation on gangster film themes which emerged as a striking study of loyalty and betrayal. But by the time that the New Wave directors were drawing from *Bob le flambeur* a set of stylistic lessons which were to be crucial to their own breakthrough—economical location shooting, use of natural light, improvisatory approaches and use of character actors in place of stars—Melville himself had moved

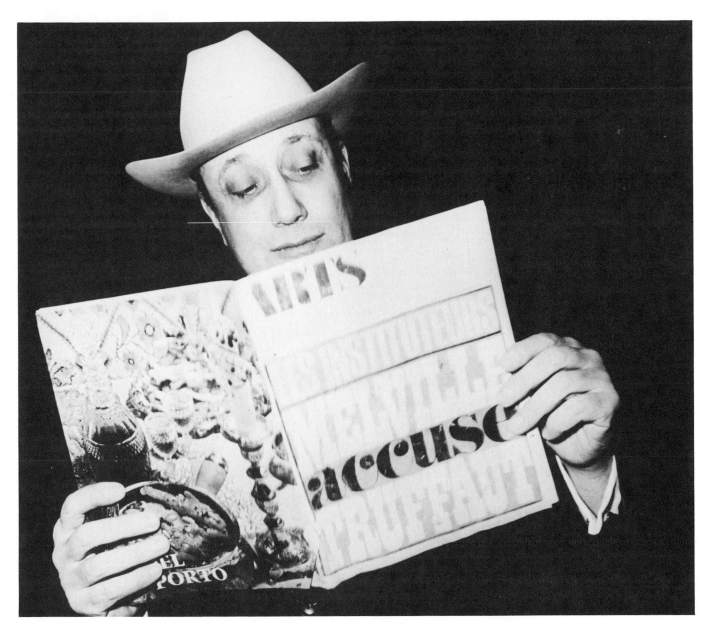

Jean-Pierre Melville

in quite a different direction. *Léon Morin, prêtre* marks Melville's decision to leave this directly personal world of low-budget filmmaking for a mature style of solidly commercial genre filmmaking, using major stars and tightly wrought scripts to capture a wide audience.

This style is perfectly embodied in the trio of mid-1960s gangster films which constitute the core of Melville's achievement in cinema. Melville's concern with the film as a narrative spectacle is totally vindicated in these films, each of which is built around a star performance: Jean-Paul Belmondo in *Le Doulos*, Lino Ventura in *Le Deuxième Souffle* and Alain Delon in *Le Samourai*. Drawing on his 1930s viewing and his adolescent reading of American thrillers, Melville manipulates the whole mythology of the gangster film, casting aside all pretence of offering a social study. His criminals are idealized figures, their appearance stylized with emphasis on the belted raincoat, soft hat, and ever present handgun. Their behavior oddly blends violence and ritualized politeness, and lifts them out from their settings. Melville has no interest in the realistic portrayal of life as it is and disregards both psychological depth and accuracy of location and costume. He uses his stars to portray timeless, tragic figures caught up in ambiguous conflicts and patterns of deceit, relying on the actor's personality and certainty of gesture to fill the intentional void.

Le Samourai is a perfect distillation of the cinematic myth of the gangster, and remains Melville's masterpiece. Subsequent attempts to widen his range by transposing his characters into the world of Occupation and Resistance in *L'Armée des ombres*, or combining his particular gift for atmosphere with a *Rififi*-style presentation of the mechanics of a robbery in *Le Cercle rouge*, produced interesting but flawed works. Melville's frustration and dissatisfaction is reflected in his last work, *Un Flic*, which completes the passage towards abstraction begun in the mid-1960s and offers a derisory world lacking even the human warmth of loyalty and friendship which the director had earlier celebrated. In retrospect, it seems likely that Melville's reputation will rest largely on his ability, almost unique in French cinema, to contain deeply-felt

Jiří Menzel: *Postrizny*

personal attitudes within the tight confines of commercial genre production. Certainly his thrillers are unequalled in European cinema.

—Roy Armes

MENZEL, Jiri.

Czechoslovak. Born in Prague, 23 February 1938. Educated at Film Academy (FAMU), Prague, 1957–62. Assistant director on Věra Chýtilová's *Something Different*, 1963; director at Barrandov Studios, from 1965; also stage director for Drama Club and Semafor Theatre, Prague, from 1967. Recipient: Oscar for Best Foreign Film, for *Closely Watched Trains*, 1967; Grand Prize, Karlovy Vary Festival, for *Capricious Summer*, 1968. Address: Solidarita E/31, 100 00 Praha 10, Czechoslovakia.

Films as Director:

1965   *Zločin v dívčí škole* (*Crime at a Girls' School*) (+ co-sc); *Smrt pana Baltisbergra* (*The Death of Mr. Baltisberger*) (+ co-sc)
1966   ***Ostře sledované vlaky*** (***Closely Watched Trains***) (+ co-sc, role as the doctor)
1968   *Rozmarné léto* (*Capricious Summer*) (+ co-sc, role as the magician Arnoštek); *Zločin v šantánu* (*Crime in a Night Club*) (+ co-sc)
1969   *Skřivánci na niti* (*Larks on a String*) (+ co-sc)
1975   *Kdo hledá zlaté dno* (*Who Seeks the Gold Bottom*)
1977   *Na samotě u lesa* (*Seclusion Near a Forest*) (+ co-sc)
1979   *Báječni muži s klikou* (*Magicians of the Silver Screen*) (+ co-sc, role as the director)
1980   *Postřižny* (*Short Cut, Cutting It Short*) (+ co-sc)
1983   *Slavnosti sněženek*
1985   *Prague*; *Vesnicko ma strediskova* (*My Sweet Little Village*)
1989   *Koneč starych casu* (*The End of the Good Old Days*)

Other Films: (incomplete listing)

1964   *Courage for Every Day* (role as guest in a pub); *If One Thousand Clarinets* (role as soldier Schulze); *A Place in a Crowd* (role as a secretary of the SCM); *The Defendant* (role as the young defense lawyer)
1965   *Wandering* (role as Dohnal); *Nobody Shall Be Laughing* (role as a bicyclist)
1967   *Dita Saxová* (role as the shy suitor)
1977   *The Apple Game* (Chytilova) (role as the doctor)

Publications:

By MENZEL: book—

Closely Watched Trains, script, with Bohumil Hrabal, New York, 1977.

By MENZEL: articles—

"O režii a herectvi, o filmu a dicadle—Rozhovor s Jiřim Menzelem," interview with K. Pošová, in *Film a Doba* (Prague), December 1977.
Interview with A. Tournès, in *Jeune Cinéma* (Paris), May/June 1987.
Interview with M. Buruiana and J. Beaulieu, in *Séquences* (Montreal), September 1988.

On MENZEL: books—

Skvorecký, Josef, *All the Bright Young Men and Women*, Toronto, 1971.
Liehm, Antonin, *Closely Watched Films*, White Plains, New York, 1974.
Stoil, Michael, *Cinema Beyond the Danube*, Metuchen, New Jersey, 1974.
Liehm, Mira and Antonin, *The Most Important Art*, Berkeley, 1977.

Skvorecký, Josef, *Jiří Menzel and the History of the Closely Watched Trains*, Boulder, Colorado, 1982.
Hames, Peter, *The Czechoslovak New Wave*, Berkeley, 1985.

On MENZEL: articles—

Liehm, A.J., "Zádný strach o Jiřího Menzela" [Never Fear for Jiří Menzel], in *Film a Doba* (Prague), no.1, 1967.
Kolodny, Irving, "The Man Who Made *Closely Watched Trains*," in *Action* (Los Angeles), May/June 1968.
Crick, P., "Three East European Directors," in *Screen* (London), March/April 1970.

*   *   *

Menzel's chief claim to a firm place in the history of the Czech cinema to date is his masterpiece, *Closely Watched Trains*. He received an Oscar for it in 1967, and the film was the biggest box office success of all the works of the New Wave in Czechoslovakia. Banned from the industry after the Soviet invasion of 1968, Menzel eventually saved his career by recanting and publicly dissociating himself from his pre-invasion films, including *Closely Watched Trains*. However, even in his humiliation he scored one important point against the establishment: he refused to return his Oscar to Hollywood as the authorities had demanded (he was supposed to explain that he "did not accept awards from Zionists") and merely made a repentance movie, *Who Seeks the Gold Bottom*, a social realist formula story about workers building a huge dam.

Like Milos Forman, Menzel was influenced by Czech novelists rather than by western filmmakers, and for a considerable time worked under the tutelage of his teacher from the Film Academy, Otakar Vávra, and his admired older colleague Věra Chytilová. Except for *Crime in a Night Club*, which was based on an original idea by novelist Josef Skvorecký, his pre-invasion films are adaptions of novels and short stories by Czech authors, either modern classics (*Capricious Summer* from a novella by Vladislav Vančura), or his contemporaries (Bohumil Hrabal's *Closely Watched Trains*, *The Death of Mr. Baltisberger*, and *Larks on a String*, and Skvorecký's *Crime at a Girls' School*). Except for *Capricious Summer*, all these films were banned, *Larks on a String* even before release. After three hesitant efforts following his recantation, all developed from original ideas, Menzel found his old self in another adaption of Hrabal, *Short Cut*. An even less subliminal anti-establishment message is contained in *The Snowdrop Festival*, whose hero sacrifices his life for a pot of tripe soup. His recent, very amusing comedy *My Sweet Little Village*, and another adaptation of Vančura, *The End of Old Times*, though largely apolitical, show him as the supreme craftsman of contemporary Czech cinema.

Except in his black comedies (*Crime at a Girls' School*, *Crime in a Night Club*), Menzel is essentially a realist whose method could, perhaps, be described by the theories of André Bazin: he reveals rather than describes reality. There is very little of the formalist elements of movie making, and if, occasionally, there are some (e.g. the opening montage in *Closely Watched Trains*), they are used mainly for comic effect. Menzel even dropped the achronological structure of the novella from which he made *Closely Watched Trains*, and replaced it with linear narrative. However, there is inventive use of subtle symbolism (e.g. the clocks and their chiming in *Closely Watched Trains*), excellent work with actors, both professional and non-professional, and superb editing. The trend towards subtle symbolism culminates in *Short Cut*, a Rabelaisian tribute to *elan vital*, which, however, hides a caustic, encoded comment on "goulash socialism," on the Marxist refutation of Freud (the commanding image of the pretty girl sitting on a high chimney), and on various smaller malpractices of "Realsozialismus" such as jamming foreign broadcasts. The nearly subliminal nature of such satirical stabs apparent also in *The Snowdrop Festival* is a nut too hard for the censors to crack.

Unlike his mentor Chytilová's crude defensive moral statements, the messages of Menzel's pre-1968 works (and of *Short Cut* and *The Snowdrop Festival*) are—in the light of establishment philosophy—extremely provocative. In a way, his entire *oeuvre* is one continuous eulogy of sex—a subject at best tolerated by Marxist aestheticians in Czechoslovakia. The shock value of *Closely Watched Trains* is the combination of commendable resistance heroism with an embarrassing sexual problem: an anathema in socialist realism. Similarly, the "crime" in *Crime at a Girls' School* turns out to be not murder but loss of virginity, and the "philosophical" ruminations of the three elderly Don Juans in *Capricious Summer* concentrate on a young artiste. The main theme of *Short Cut*—characterized by the phallic symbolism of the chimney which dominates the small central Bohemian Sodom—is simply the joy of sex. Considering that sex has always been the most dangerous enemy of puritanical revolutions, Menzel's message is clear. It is a much less acceptable one than the moralizing of Chytilová, whose eccentric form and merciless vision, on the other hand, stand against everything the government watchdogs would like to see. The two artists, taken together, represent the two basic headaches any repressive aesthetic necessarily faces—the objectionable form, and the objectionable content. The survival of Menzel and Chytilová in a national cinema so full of victims demonstrates that, with perseverance, intelligence, cunning, and good luck, art can occasionally triumph over censorship.

—Josef Skvorecký

MÉSZÁROS, Márta.

Hungarian. Born in Budapest, 19 September 1931. Educated at VGIK (Film School), Moscow, 1957. Married 1), divorced 1959; 2) director Miklós Jancsó (divorced); 3) actor Jan Nowicki. Emigrated with family to U.S.S.R., 1936; returned to Hungary, 1946; worked at the newsreel studio, Budapest, 1954; worked for the Alexandru Sahia documentary studio, Bucharest, Romania, 1957–59; made science popularization shorts and documentary shorts, Budapest, 1959–68; joined Mafilm Group 4, mid-1960s; directed first feature, 1968.

Films as Director:

(short films in Hungary):

1954 *Ujra mosolyognak* (*Smiling Again*)
1955 *Albertfalvai történet* (*A History of Albertfalva*); *Tul a Kálvin-téren* (*Beyond the Square*); *Mindennapi történetek* (*Everyday Stories*)
1956 *Országutak vándora* (*Wandering on Highways*)

(short films in Romania):

1957 *Sa zimbeasca toti copiii*
1958 *Femeile zilelor noastre*; *Popas in tabara de vara*
1959 *Schimbul de miine*

(short films in Hungary):

1959 *Az élet megy tovább* (*Life Goes On*)
1960 *Az eladás müvészete* (*Salesmanship*); *Riport egy TSZ-elnökröl* (*Report on the Chairman of a Farmers' Co-Operative*); *Rajtunk is mulik* (*It Depends on Us Too . . .*)

1961 *Szivdobogás* (*Heartbeat*); *Vásárhelyi szinek* (*Colors of Vásárhely*); *Danulon gyártás* (*Danulon Production*); *A szár és a gyökér fejlödése* (*The Development of the Stalk and the Root*)
1962 *Tornyai János* (*János Tornyai*); *Gyermekek, könyvek* (*Children, Books*); *Kamaszváros* (*A Town in the Awkward Age*); *Nagyüzemi tojástermelés* (*Mass Production of Eggs*); *A labda varása* (*The Spell of the Ball*)
1963 *1963.julius 27.szombat* (*Saturday, July 27, 1963*); *Munka vagy hivatás?* (*Work or Profession?*); *Szeretet* (*Care and Affection*)
1964 *Festök városa—Szentendre* (*Szentendre—Town of Painters*); *Bóbita* (*Blow-Ball*); *Kiáltó* (*Proclamation*)
1965 *15 perc 15 évről* (*Fifteen Minutes on Fifteen Years*)
1966 *Borsós Miklós* (*Miklós Borsós*); *Harangok városa—Veszprém* (*Veszprém—Town of Bells*)

(feature films):

1968 *Eltávozott nap* (*The Girl*) (+ sc); *Mészáros László emlékére* (*In Memoriam László Mészáros*) (short); *A "holdudvar"* (*Binding Sentiments*) (+ sc)
1970 *Szép lányok, ne sirjatok* (*Don't Cry, Pretty Girls*)
1971 *A lörinci fonóban* (*At the Lörinc Spinnery*) (short)
1973 *Szabad lélegzet* (*Riddance, Free Breathing*) (+ sc)
1975 *Örökbefogadás* (*Adoption*) (+ co-sc)
1976 *Kilenc hónap* (*Nine Months*)
1977 *Ök ketten* (*The Two of Them*)
1978 *Olyan, mint otthon* (*Just Like at Home*)
1979 *Utközben* (*En cours de route*)
1980 *Örökseg* (*The Heiresses*)
1981 *Anya és leánya* (*Mother and Daughter*) (+ co-sc)
1982 *Nema Kiáltás* (*Silent Cry*) (+ sc); *Napló gyermekeimnek* (*Diary For My Children*)
1983 *Délibábok országa* (*The Land of Mirages*)
1987 *Napló szerelmeimnek* (*Diary for My Loves*) (+ sc)
1988 *Piroska és a farkas* (*Bye-Bye Red Riding Hood*)
1989 *Utinapló* (docu)
1990 *Napló apámnak, anyámnak* (*Diary For My Father and My Mother*)

Publications:

By MÉSZÁROS: articles—

Interviews in *Filmkultura* (Budapest), November/December 1972 and March/April 1977.
Interview in *Hungarofilm Bulletin* (Budapest), no. 2, 1977.
Interview with T. Giraud and D. Villain, in *Cahiers du Cinéma* (Paris), January 1978.
Interview with C. Clouzot and others, in *Ecran* (Paris), 15 January 1979.
Interview with L. Bonneville, in *Séquences* (Montreal), September 1988.

On MÉSZÁROS: articles—

Elley, Derek, "Hiding It Under a Bushel: Breaking Free," in *Films and Filming* (London), February 1974.
Elley, Derek, "Márta Mészáros," in *International Film Guide 1979*, London, 1978.
Martineau, B.H., "The Films of Marta Mészáros or, the Importance of Being Banal," in *Film Quarterly* (Berkeley), Fall 1980.
"Hungarian Film Section" of *Filmfaust* (Frankfurt), January/February 1984.
"Diary for My Loves," in *Hungarofilm Bulletin* (Budapest), no. 2, 1987.

* * *

Márta Mészáros is the sole contemporary woman filmmaker consistently making films both critically and commercially successful for an international audience. Her eight feature films made from 1968 to 1979 are concerned with the social oppression, economic constraints, and emotional challenges faced by Hungarian women. Mészáros explains: "I tell banal, common-

Márta Mészáros

place stories, and then in them the leads are women—I portray things from a woman's angle."

Trained in filmmaking on a scholarship at Moscow's film school, she worked at the Newsreel Studios in Budapest, made four short films at the Bucharest Documentary Studios, married a Romanian citizen in 1957, and was divorced in 1959. She returned to Budapest where she made more than 30 documentaries before attempting a feature. Mészáros's documentaries deal with subjects as diverse as science (*Mass Production of Eggs*), a Hungarian hero (*Saturday, July 27th 1963*), orphans (*Care and Affection*), and artists (*Szentendre—Town of Painters*, which she considers her best documentary.)

In the mid-1960s Mészáros joined Mafilm Group 4 where she met Miklós Jancsó whom she later married. She wrote and directed her first feature, *The Girl*, in 1968. A hopeless mood pervades this story of the quest by an orphan girl for her biological parents who had abandoned her. The girl leaves her textile factory job to comfort her mother, who introduces her as her niece to her husband and relatives. The girl meets a man whom she believes is her father. The man neither confirms nor denies this. The girl returns home, attends a factory dance where she meets a young man interested in her. As with most Mészáros features the film is open-ended, lacking a conventional plot. Dialogue is sparse. Derek Elley asserts that *The Girl* is a model to which Mészáros adheres in her subsequent features; her visual compositions are "carefully composed, rarely showy," and "characterisation never remains static."

In *Binding Sentiments* the conflicts between an aging mother and her son's fiancée are delineated with understated solemnity and subtle humor. A semi-musical, *Don't Cry, Pretty Girls*, lightheartedly captures the romance between a rural girl and a city musician in a hostel and youth camp setting. Mészáros's short, *Woman in the Spinnery*, studies the working status and conditions of the factory worker that are also the subject of her feature *Riddance*. In this generation gap tale, a pair of lovers must deceive the young man's parents who object to his love for a girl who was raised in a children's home with no family. *Riddance* urges assertiveness and truth to oneself, and shows little sympathy for the older generation.

A fortyish woman wants a child from her unmarried lover in *Adoption*. She meets a teenager raised by the state who wants to marry her boyfriend. The relationship which develops between these two women and the man in their lives becomes the subject of Mészáros's most illuminating work.

A factory woman with one child has an affair with an engineer in *Nine Months*. The conflicts in their relationship are never resolved; they cannot agree on the terms and conditions of a life together; neither can surrender enough self to form a partnership. The woman leaves him to bear her second child

Interview with P. Broeske, in *Films in Review* (New York), October 1982.
Interview with Tony Crawley, in *Starburst* (London), no. 51, 1983.
Interview with T. Ryan, in *Cinema Papers* (Melbourne), January 1988.

On MILLER: book—

Mathews, Sue, *35mm Dreams*, Ringwood, Victoria, 1984.

On MILLER: articles—

Samuels, B., "Dr. George Miller: Mephisto in a Polka-Dot Tie," in *Cinema Canada* (Toronto), February 1983.
George Miller Section of *Positif* (Paris), December 1985.

*   *   *

Along with contemporaries Peter Weir, Bruce Beresford, and Gillian Armstrong, George Miller helped to bring the Australian film to international forefront by the mid-1980s with his brilliant trilogy of *Mad Max, Mad Max 2*, [*The Road Warrior* in the United States], and *Mad Max: Beyond Thunderdome*. In a desolate Australian space, sometime in the future, the police have their hands full trying to keep the roads safe from suicidal, maniacal gangs. Cop Mel Gibson quits, but then seeks revenge when his wife and child are murdered. *Mad Max* was almost lost when it was released in the late 1970's, but with the success of the sequel, the style and bleak outlook were seen to represent a *tour de force* of genre filmmaking. We have little doubt what will happen; but the way the story unspools is what attracted audiences around the world. George Miller Made "Mad Max" and made fellow countryman Mel Gibson an international star.

The greatness of the *Mad Max* films come the images of burnt out men and women in a post-apocalyptic world of desolate highways. Characters are dressed in what was left after the "end of the world," including football uniform parts from American-style teams, and other assorted bits and pieces of clothing. Miller seems to have patterned his hero after a Japanese samurai, but more insight can be gained by comparing these three films with the westerns of Sergio Leone, such as *Once Upon a Time in the West*. The director's inventions make mundane stories into something altogether new and fresh.

For audiences the trilogy was *Dirty Harry* thrown into a desert of madness. Miller's style of directing has been called mathematical in nature, building a movie in the same manner prescribed by the early Sergei Eisenstein, and utilized by the mature Hitchcock. Many argued that Miller, an Australian, outdid Steven Spielberg, the Hollywood wunderkind. And in the early 1980s "Mad Max" became a pop cult craze.

With the third instalment Miller moved into mainstream Hollywood. Thus while it had the usual cast of unknown character actors and actresses placed in the sweeping, endless desert of the Australian outback, Tina Turner was cast as the ruler of Bartertown, a primitive community in the bleak futuristic post-Atomic world. Mel Gibson, again as Max, battled to the death in the Roman style arena of Thunderdome. Miller proved he could continue the Mad Max appeal even though his partner of the first two, Byron Kennedy, died in 1983.

And although Miller was chosen by Spielberg for a segment of *Twilight Zone: The Movie*, he continued to work in Australia, on mini-series such as "The Dismissal." In the late 1980s Miller changed courses, and directed the hit *The Witches of Eastwick* for Warner Bros. With Jack Nicholson and Cher, *The Witches of Eastwick* offered a lively, colorful fantasy set a New England town. This was a popular film, far from the visceral violence of *Mad Max*. For *Twilight Zone: The Movie* Miller's segment, "Nightmare at 20,000 Feet," was the ultimate white-knucklers' airplane paranoid fantasy, with a computer technician staring out the window seeing a gremlin sabotaging the engines. John Lithgow turned in a bravura performance in a role originally played by William Shatner. The Miller segment, of the four, was the one most often praised in a movie now most associated with the grim tragedy of the filming of the John Landis episode.

Miller took a strange path to directorial success. But once one sees and analyzes the *Mad Max* trilogy, it makes sense. After graduating in medicine from the University of New South Wales in 1970, this "self-confessed movie freak" spent eighteen months in the Emergency Room of a large city hospital dealing with auto accident victims. Perhaps this is where he developed his strange view of the world.

Finally, no portrait of the talented Miller, with much of his creative future still ahead of him, should end without noting that this George Miller is *not* the same "George Miller," also an Australian, who made a reputation as the director of *The Man From Snowy River* (1982).

—Douglas Gomery

MINNELLI, Vincente.

American. Born in Chicago, 28 February 1910. Educated at the Art Institute of Chicago, mid-1920s. Married 1) Judy Garland, 1945 (divorce 1951), daughter Liza; 2) Georgette Magnani, 1954 (divorced 1958), one daughter; 3) Denise Giganti, 1961 (divorced 1971); 4) Lee M. Anderson, 1982. Child actor, Minnelli Brothers Dramatic Tent Show, 1913–1918; billboard painter, then window dresser, Marshall Field's department store, Chicago, 1929; assistant stage manager and costume designer, Balaban and Katz theatre chain, Chicago, then set and costume designer, Paramount Theater, New York, 1931–33; art director, Radio City Music Hall, New York, 1934; director of ballets and musicals for the stage, then signed as producer/director, Paramount Pictures, Hollywood, 1936; bought out contract after eight months and returned to New York as theatre director; joined MGM under auspices of Arthur Freed, 1940; directed sequences in *Babes on Broadway* (1941) and *Panama Hattie* (1942); directed first feature, *Cabin in the Sky*, 1942; returned to stage directing with *Mata Hari*, 1967, closed after 2-week run. Recipient: Oscar for Best Director for *Gigi*, 1958; Order of Arts and Letters, France, for contribution to French culture. *Died, in Beverly Hills, California, 25 July 1986.*

Films as Director:

1942	*Cabin in the Sky*
1943	*I Dood It (By Hook or By Crook)*
1944	**Meet Me in St. Louis**
1945	*The Clock (Under the Clock)*; *Yolanda and the Thief*
1946	*Ziegfeld Follies* (co-d); *Undercurrent*
1947	*Till the Clouds Roll By* (Whorf) (Judy Garland sequences only)
1948	*The Pirate*
1949	*Madame Bovary*
1950	*Father of the Bride*
1951	**An American in Paris**; *Father's Little Dividend*
1952	*Lovely to Look At* (LeRoy) (fashion show sequence only)
1953	"Mademoiselle" episode of *The Story of Three Loves*; *The Bad and the Beautiful*; **The Band Wagon**
1954	*The Long, Long Trailer*; *Brigadoon*
1955	*The Cobweb*; *Kismet*
1956	*Lust for Life*; *Tea and Sympathy*

Vincente Minnelli

1957 *Designing Woman*; *The Seventh Sin* (Neame; replaced Neame as director, refused credit)
1958 *Gigi*; *The Reluctant Debutante*
1959 *Some Came Running*
1960 *Home from the Hill*; *Bells Are Ringing*
1962 *The Four Horsemen of the Apocalypse*; *Two Weeks in Another Town*
1963 *The Courtship of Eddie's Father*
1964 *Goodbye Charlie*
1965 *The Sandpiper*
1970 *On a Clear Day You Can See Forever*
1976 *A Matter of Time*

Publications:

By MINNELLI: book—

I Remember It Well, with Hector Arce, New York, 1974.

By MINNELLI: articles—

Interview with Charles Bitsch and Jean Domarchi, in *Cahiers du Cinéma* (Paris), August/September 1957.
"So We Changed It," in *Films and Filming* (London), November 1958.
"The Rise and Fall of the Musical," in *Films and Filming* (London), January 1962.
"Rencontre avec Vincente Minnelli," with Jean Domarchi and Jean Douchet, in *Cahiers du Cinéma* (Paris), February 1962.

"On the Relationship of Style to Content in *The Sandpiper*," in *Cinema* (Los Angeles), July/August 1965.
Interview, in *The Celluloid Muse: Hollywood Directors Speak* edited by Charles Higham and Joel Greenberg, London, 1969.
"Vincente Minnelli and Gigi," interview with Digby Diehl, in *Action* (Los Angeles), September/October 1972.
"The Nostalgia Express," interview with Gideon Bachmann, in *Film Comment* (New York), November/December 1976.
"Two Weeks in Another Town," interview with P. Lehman and others, in *Wide Angle* (Athens, Ohio), no. 1, 1979.

On MINNELLI: books—

Truchaud, Francois, *Vincente Minnelli*, Paris, 1966.
Knox, Donald, *The Magic Factory: How M-G-M Made "An American in Paris"*, New York, 1973.
Delameter, J., *Dance in the Hollywood Musical*, Ann Arbor, Michigan, 1981.
Guerif, François, *Vincente Minnelli*, Paris, 1984.
Brion, Patrick, and others, *Vincente Minnelli*, Paris, 1985.
Harvey, Stephen, *Directed by Vincente Minnelli*, New York, 1989.
Lang, Robert, *American Film Melodrama: Griffith, Vidor, Minnelli*, Princeton, New Jersey, 1989.

On MINNELLI: articles—

Harcourt-Smith, Simon, "Vincente Minnelli," in *Sight and Sound* (London), January/March 1952.

Johnson, Albert, "The Films of Vincente Minnelli," in *Film Quarterly* (Berkeley), Winter 1958 and Spring 1959.

McVay, Douglas, "The Magic of Minnelli," in *Films and Filming* (London), June 1959.

Shivas, Mark, "Minnelli's Method," in *Movie* (London), June 1962.

Mayersberg, Paul, "The Testament of V. Minnelli," in *Movie* (London), October 1962.

Torok, Jean-Paul, and Jacques Quincey, "V.M. ou Le Peintre de la vie rêvée," in *Positif* (Paris), March 1963.

"Minnelli Issue" of *Movie* (London), June 1963.

Galling, Dennis, "V.M. is One of the Few Hollywood Directors Who Has an Art Sense," in *Films in Review* (New York), March 1964.

Nowell-Smith, G., "Minnelli and Melodrama," in *Australian Journal of Screen Theory* (Kensington, New South Wales), no.3, 1977.

McVay, D., "Minnelli and *The Pirate*," in *Velvet Light Trap* (Madison), Spring 1978.

Simsolo, Noël, "Sur quelques films de Minnelli," in *Image et Son* (Paris), October 1981.

Telotte, J.P., "Self and Society: Vincente Minnelli and Musical Formula," in *Journal of Popular Film* (Washington, D.C.), Winter 1982.

McCarthy, T., obituary in *Variety* (New York), 30 July 1986.

Harvey, S., obituary in *Film Comment* (New York), September/October 1986.

Taylor, John Russell, "Tribute to Minnelli," in *Films and Filming* (London), October 1986.

Gourget, J.L., "L'oeuvre de Vincente Minnelli," in *Positif* (Paris), December 1986.

Thomas, Nick, "Vincente Minnelli," in *Annual Obituary 1986*, London and Chicago, 1989.

* * *

Between 1942 and 1962, Vincente Minnelli directed 29 films and parts of several others at Metro-Goldywn-Mayer, eventually becoming the studio's longest-tenured director. Brought to Hollywood following a tremendously successful career as a Broadway set designer and director of musicals, he was immediately placed at the helm of MGM's biggest musical productions, beginning with the all-black *Cabin in the Sky*. Over the next decade-and-a-half, he gained a reputation as the premiere director at work in the genre, based on a remarkable series of productions including *Meet Me in St. Louis, The Pirate, An American in Paris*, and *The Band Wagon*, and culminating with a Best Director's Oscar for *Gigi*. Yet Minnelli's career was by no means restricted to musicals. During the same period he also directed a series of successful comedies and melodramas with flair and stylistic elegance.

If anything, Minnelli's accomplishments as a stylist, which were recognized from the beginning of his Hollywood career, worked against his being taken seriously as a director-auteur. By the late 1950s he had been dubbed (by critic Albert Johnson) "the master of the decorative image," which seemed, at the time, the highest compliment which might be paid a director of musicals. Indeed, Minnelli's films are impeccably crafted—filled with lushly stylized sets, clever, graceful performances, a partiality for long tales, and a fluid mobile camera suited to the filming of dance, mounting and preserving performance spatially, even as the camera involves the audience in the choreographed movement. Yet it also informs the non-musical sequences of Minnelli's films with the same kind of liberal sensibility associated with contemporaries like Otto Preminger and Nicholas Ray, one that allows both the characters and the eyes of the audience a certain freedom of movement within a nearly seamless time and space. An accompanying theatricality (resulting from a tendency to shoot scenes from a fourth-wall position) blends with Minnelli's specifically cinematic flourishes in a clever realization of the themes of art and artificiality, themes which run throughout his films.

Stylization and artifice are necessarily addressed by musical films in general, and Minnelli's films do so with great verve—most thoroughly in the baroque otherworldliness of *Yolanda and the Thief*; most brilliantly in the interplay of character and actor, stage and screen in *The Band Wagon*. But an equal concern with levels of unreality informs most of his films, most obviously perhaps in the Pirandellian meditation on Hollywood, *The Bad and the Beautiful*, and its bizarre, Cinecitta-made quasi-sequel, *Two Weeks in Another Town*. This exploration surely reaches a kind of limit in Minnelli's last film, *A Matter of Time*, where the story of an aspiring actress, played by Liza Minnelli, becomes an examination of his own daughter's talents and persona (haunted by the ghost of Judy Garland), making the film into the director's own *Vertigo*, a fitting conclusion to a career devoted to the interplay of various levels of fantasy.

Filmic fantasy is almost always present in Minnelli's films, even when they address the most mundane human problems in basically realistic settings. Virtually every Minnelli film contains a fantasy sequence, which is to say a moment in which the narrative recedes in order to allow a free play of symbols on an almost exclusively formal level. In the musicals, this is invariably an extended "ballet"—most memorably, the 20-minute number which concludes *An American in Paris*; but perhaps most powerfully, Judy Garland's erotic fantasy of Gene Kelly as "Mack the Black" in *The Pirate*. In *Meet Me in St. Louis*, the burst of pure style occurs in the non-musical, and surprisingly horrific Halloween sequence. In the comedy *Father of the Bride*, it is a tour-de-force dream sequence in which all of Spencer Tracy's fatherly anxieties are unleashed. The position is filled by a hallucinatory chase through a carnival in *Some Came Running*, by fantastic visions of the title figures in *The Four Horsemen of the Apocalypse*, and by mad car rides in both *The Bad and the Beautiful* and *Two Weeks in Another Town*. Such extra-narrative sequences serve to condense and resolve plot elements on a visual/emotional plane, providing the only escape routes from the exigencies of a world which Minnelli otherwise depicts as emotionally frustrating, overly complex, and terribly delicate.

Indeed, Andrew Sarris quite rightly noted that "Minnelli had an unusual, sombre outlook for musical comedy," a fact which seems responsible for lending most of his films an unexpected depth. Certainly one of the factors responsible for the continued interest in *Meet Me in St. Louis* is the overt morbidity of its nostalgic tone. Yet Minnelli's troubled perspective is probably most evident in the existential isolation of his characters, and in the humanistic, yet stoic attitude he adopts in treating equally their petty jealousies and their moral fears. A genuinely pained sense of the virtual impossibility of meaningful human contact informs the machinations of such stylized melodramas as *Some Came Running, Home from the Hill*, and *The Four Horsemen*. And the tenuousness of love and power is nowhere more artfully rendered than in his generic masterpiece, *The Cobweb*, where an argument over drapes for the rec room of a mental hospital reveals a network of neuroses, amongst the staff and their families, as deep-seated as the disorders of the patients.

At worst, Minnelli has been cited as the epitome of Hollywood's "middlebrow" aspirations toward making art accessible to the mass audience. At best, he was championed by the British critics at *Movie* during the early 1960s as one of Hollywood's consummate auteurs. For one such critic, V.F. Perkins, Minnelli's films provided some of the best examples of classical narrative style, which naturalized meaning through understated flourishes of mise-en-scène. It is certainly this capacity which enabled Minnelli to employ a 40-foot trailer as an effortless metaphor for the marriage of newlyweds Lucille Ball and Desi Arnaz (*The Long, Long Trailer*), to critique the manipulations of parental love by consumer culture in terms of an increasingly overblown wedding (*Father of the Bride*), and to displace a child's incapacity to deal with his mother's death onto his horror at the discovery of his dead goldfish (*The Courtship of Eddie's Father*).

We must certainly categorize Minnelli as something more than a decorative artist, for the stylistic devices of his films are informed with a remarkably resilient intelligence. And even if we are finally to conclude that, throughout his work, there is a dominance of style over theme, it ultimately serves only to confirm his contribution to the refinement of those techniques by which Hollywood translates meanings into style and presents both as entertainment.

—Ed Lowry

MIZOGUCHI, Kenji.

Japanese. Born in Tokyo, 16 May 1898. Educated at Aohashi Western painting Research Institute, Tokyo, enrolled 1914. Apprentice to textile designer, 1913; newspaper illustrator, Kobe, 1916; assistant director to Osamu Wakayama, 1922; directed first film, 1923; began association with art director Hiroshi Mizutani on *Gio matsuri*, 1933; began collaboration with writer Yoshikata Yoda on *Naniwa ereji*, 1936; member of Cabinet Film Committee, from 1940; elected President of Japanese directors association, 1949; signed to Daiei company, 1952. Recipient: International Prize, Venice Festival, for *The Life of Oharu*, 1952. Died, of leukemia, in Kyoto, 24 August 1956.

Films as Director:

1923   *Ai ni yomigaeru hi* (*The Resurrection of Love*); *Furusato* (*Hometown*) (+ sc); *Seishun no yumeji* (*The Dream Path of Youth*) (+ sc); *Joen no chimata* (*City of Desire*) (+ sc); *Haizan no uta wa kanashi* (*Failure's Song is Sad*) (+ sc); *813* (*813: The Adventures of Arsene Lupin*); *Kiri no minato* (*Foggy Harbor*); *Chi to rei* (*Blood and Soul*) (+ sc); *Yoru* (*The Night*) (+ sc); *Haikyo no naka* (*In the Ruins*)

1924   *Toge no uta* (*The Song of the Mountain Pass*) (+ sc); *Kanashiki hakuchi* (*The Sad Idiot*) (+ story); *Gendai no joo* (*The Queen of Modern Times*); *Josei wa tsuyoshi* (*Women Are Strong*); *Jinkyo* (*This Dusty World*); *Shichimencho no yukue* (*Turkeys in a Row*); *Samidare zoshi* (*A Chronicle of May Rain*); *Musen fusen* (*No Money, No Fight*); *Kanraku no onna* (*A Woman of Pleasure*) (+ story); *Akatsuki no shi* (*Death at Dawn*)

1925   *Kyohubadan no joo* (*Queen of the Circus*); *Gakuso o idete* (*Out of College*) (+ sc); *Shirayuri wa nageku* (*The White Lily Laments*); *Daichi wa hohoemu* (*The Earth Smiles*); *Akai yuhi ni terasarete* (*Shining in the Red Sunset*); *Furusato no uta* (*The Song of Home*); *Ningen* (*The Human Being*); *Gaijo no suketchi* (*Street Sketches*)

1926   *Nogi Taisho to Kuma-san* (*General Nogi and Kuma-san*); *Doka o* (*The Copper Coin King*) (+ story); *Kaminingyo haru no sayaki* (*A Paper Doll's Whisper of Spring*); *Shin ono ga tsumi* (*My Fault, New Version*); *Kyoren no onna shisho* (*The Passion of a Woman Teacher*); *Kaikoku danji* (*The Boy of the Sea*); *Kane* (*Money*) (+ story)

1927   *Ko-on* (*The Imperial Grace*); *Jihi shincho* (*The Cuckoo*)

1928   *Hito no issho* (*A Man's Life*)

1929   *Nihombashi* (+ sc); *Tokyo koshinkyoku* (*Tokyo March*); *Asahi wa kagayaku* (*The Morning Sun Shines*); *Tokai kokyogaku* (*Metropolitan Symphony*)

1930   *Furusato* (*Home Town*); *Tojin okichi* (*Mistress of a Foreigner*)

1931   *Shikamo karera wa yuku* (*And Yet They Go*)

1932   *Toki no ujigami* (*The Man of the Moment*); *Mammo Kenkoku no Reimei* (*The Dawn of Manchukuo and Mongolia*)

Kenji Mizoguchi

1933   *Taki no Shiraito* (*Taki no Shiraito, the Water Magician*); *Gion matsuri* (*Gion Festival*) (+ sc); *Jimpuren* (*The Jimpu Group*) (+ sc)

1934   *Aizo toge* (*The Mountain Pass of Love and Hate*); *Orizuru osen* (*The Downfall of Osen*)

1935   *Maria no Oyuki* (*Oyuki the Madonna*); *Gubijinso* (*Poppy*)

1936   **Naniwa ereji** (**Osaka Elegy**) (+ story); **Gion no shimai** (**Sisters of the Gion**) (+ story)

1937   *Aienkyo* (*The Straits of Love and Hate*)

1938   *Aa furusato* (*Ah, My Home Town*); *Roei no uta* (*The Song of the Camp*)

1939   *Zangiku monogatari* (*The Story of the Last Chrysanthemum*)

1944   *Danjuro sandai* (*Three Generations of Danjuro*); *Miyamoto Musashi* (*Musashi Miyamoto*)

1945   *Meito Bijomaru* (*The Famous Sword Bijomaru*); *Hisshoka* (*Victory Song*) (co-d)

1946   *Josei no shori* (*The Victory of Women*); *Utamaro o meguru gonin no onna* (*Utamaro and His Five Women*)

1947   *Joyu Sumako no koi* (*The Love of Sumako the Actress*)

1948   *Yoru no onnatachi* (*Women of the Night*)

1949   *Waga koi wa moenu* (*My Love Burns*)

1950   *Yuki Fujin ezu* (*A Picture of Madame Yuki*)

1951   *Oyu-sama* (*Miss Oyu*); *Musashino Fujin* (*Lady Musashino*)

1952   **Saikaku ichidai onna** (**The Life of Oharu**)

1953   **Ugetsu monogatari** (**Ugetsu**); *Gion bayashi* (*Gion Festival Music*)

1954   **Sansho dayu** (**Sansho the Bailiff**); *Uwasa no onna* (*The Woman of the Rumor*); **Chikamatsu monogatari** (**A Story from Chikamatsu. Crucified Lovers**)

1955   *Yokihi* (*The Princess Yang Kwei-fei*); *Shin Heike monogatari* (*New Tales of the Taira Clan*)

1956   *Akasen chitai* (*Street of Shame*)

Publications:

By MIZOGUCHI: articles—

Texts, in *Cahiers du Cinéma* (Paris), May 1959.
"Kenji Mizoguchi," in *Positif* (Paris), November 1980.
"Table ronde avec Kenji Mizoguchi" in *Positif* (Paris), December 1980 and January 1981.

On MIZOGUCHI: books—

Anderson, Joseph, and Donald Richie, *The Japanese Film: Art and Industry*, New York, 1960.
Ve-Ho, *Kenji Mizoguchi*, Paris, 1963.
Mesnil, Michel, *Mizoguchi Kenji*, Paris, 1965.
Iwazaki, Akira, "Mizoguchi," in *Anthologie du Cinéma* vol. 3, Paris, 1968.
Yoda, Yoshikata, *Mizoguchi Kenji no hito to geijutsu* [Kenji Mizoguchi: The Man and His Art], Tokyo, 1970.
Mesnil, Michel, editor, *Kenji Mizoguchi*, Paris, 1971.
Mellen, Joan, *Voices from the Japanese Cinema*, New York, 1975.
Mellen, Joan, *The Waves at Genji's Door: Japan Through Its Cinema*, New York, 1976.
Bock, Audie, *Japanese Film Directors*, New York, 1978; revised edition, Tokyo, 1985.
Freiberg, Freda, *Women in Mizoguchi Films*, Melbourne, 1981.
Serceau, Daniel, *Mizoguchi: De la revolte aux songes*, Paris, 1983.
Andrew, Dudley, *Film in the Aura of Art*, Princeton, New Jersey, 1984.
McDonald, Keiko, *Mizoguchi*, Boston, 1984.

On MIZOGUCHI: articles—

Mizoguchi issue of *Cinéma* (Paris), no.6, 1955.
Anderson, Joseph, and Donald Richie, "Kenji Mizoguchi," in *Sight and Sound* (London), Autumn 1955.
Rivette, Jacques, "Mizoguchi vu d'ici," in *Cahiers du Cinéma* (Paris), no.81, 1958.
Godard, Jean-Luc, "L'Art de Kenji Mizoguchi," in *Art* (Paris), no.656, 1958.
Mizoguchi issue of *L'Ecran* (Paris), February/March 1958.
Mizoguchi issue of *Cahiers du Cinéma* (Paris), March 1958.
"Dossier Mizoguchi," in *Cahiers du Cinéma* (Paris), August/September 1964.
"The Density of Mizoguchi's Scripts," in interview with Yoshikata Yoda, in *Cinema* (Los Angeles), Spring 1971.
Wood, Robin, "Mizoguchi: The Ghost Princess and the Seaweed Catcher," in *Film Comment* (New York), March/April 1973.
"Les Contes de la lune vague après la pluie," special Mizoguchi issue of *Avant-Scène du Cinéma* (Paris), 1 January 1977.
Cohen, R., "Mizoguchi and Modernism," in *Sight and Sound* (London), Spring 1978.
Legrand, G., and others, special Mizoguchi section, in *Positif* (Paris), November 1978.
Sato, Tadao, and Dudley Andrew, "On Kenji Mizoguchi," in *Film Criticism* (Edinboro, Pennsylvania), Spring 1980.
Andrew, Dudley, "Kenji Mizoguchi: La Passion de la identification," in *Positif* (Paris), January 1981.
Leach, J., "Mizoguchi and Ideology," in *Film Criticism* (Edinboro, Pennsylvania), Fall 1983.

*   *   *

By any standard Kenji Mizoguchi must be considered among the world's greatest directors. Known in the West for the final half-dozen films which crowned his career, Mizoguchi considered himself a popular as well as a serious artist. Having made 85 films is evidence of that popularity and makes him, like John Ford, one of the few directorial geniuses to play a key role in a major film industry. In fact, Mizoguchi once headed the vast union governing all production personnel in Japan, and was awarded more than once the industry's most coveted citations. But it is as a meticulous, passionate artist that Mizoguchi will be remembered. His temperament drove him to astounding lengths of research, rehearsal, and execution. Decade after decade he refined his approach while energizing the industry with both his consistency and his innovations.

Mizoguchi's obsessive concern with ill-treated women, and his maniacal pursuit of a lofty notion of art, stem from his upbringing. His obstinate father, unsuccessful in business, refused to send his older son beyond primary school. With the help of his sister, a onetime geisha who had become the mistress of a wealthy nobleman, Mizoguchi managed to enroll in a western-style art school. For a short time he did layout work and wrote reviews for a newspaper, but his real education came through the countless books he read and the theater he attended almost daily. In 1920 he presented himself as an actor at Nikkatsu studio, where a number of his friends worked. He moved quickly into scriptwriting, then became an assistant director, and finally a director. Between 1922 and 1935, he made 55 films, mostly melodramas, detective stories, and adaptations. Only six of these are known to exist today.

Though these lost films might show the influences on his development of other Japanese films, of German expressionism, and of American dramatic filmmaking (not to mention Japanese theatrical style and western painting and fiction), Mizoguchi himself dismissed his early efforts, claiming that his first real achievement as an artist came in 1936. Working for the first time with scriptwriter Yoshikata Yoda, who would be his collaborator on nearly all his subsequent films, he produced *Osaka Elegy* and *Sisters of the Gion*, stories of exploited women in contemporary Japan. Funded by Daiichi, a tiny independent company he helped set up to by-pass big-studio strictures, these films were poorly distributed and had trouble with the censors on account of their dark realism and touchy subject. While effectively bankrupting Daiichi, these films caused a sensation among the critics and further secured Mizoguchi's reputation as a powerful, if renegade, force in the industry.

Acknowledged by the wartime culture as Japan's chief director, Mizoguchi busied himself during the war mainly with historical dramas which were ostensibly non-political, and thus acceptable to the wartime government. Under the Allied occupation Mizoguchi was encouraged to make films about women, in both modern and historical settings, as part of America's effort to democratize Japanese society. With Yoda as scriptwriter and with actress Kinuyo Tanaka as star, the next years were busy but debilitating for Mizoguchi. He was beginning to be considered old-fashioned in technique even if his subjects were volatile. Ironically it was the West which resuscitated this most oriental director. With his critical and box-office reputation on the decline, Mizoguchi decided to invest everything in *The Life of Oharu*, a classic seventeenth-century Japanese picaresque story, and in 1951 he finally secured sufficient financing to produce it himself. Expensive, long, and complex, *Oharu* was not a particular success in Japan, but it gained an international reputation for Mizoguchi when it won the grand prize at Venice. Daiei Films, a young company aimed at the export market recently opened for Japanese films, then gave Mizoguchi virtual carte blanche, under which he was able to create his final string of masterpieces, beginning with his most famous film *Ugetsu*.

Mizoguchi's fanatic attention to detail, his insistence on multiple rewritings of Yoda's scripts, and his calculated tyranny over actors are legendary, as he sought perfection demanded by few other film artists. He saw his later films as the culmination of many years work, his style evolving from one in which a set of tableaux were photographed from an imperial distance and then cut together (one scene/one shot) to one in which the camera moves between two moments of balance, beginning with the movements of a character, then coming to rest at its own proper point.

It was this later style which hypnotized the French critics and through them the West in general. The most striking oppositions in his themes and dramas (innocence vs. guilt, good vs. bad) unroll like a seamless scroll until in the final camera flourish one feels the achievement of a majestic, stoic contemplation of life.

More recently Mizoguchi's early films have come under scrutiny, both for their radical stylistic innovations such as the shared flashbacks of the 1935 *Downfall of Osen*, and for the radical political position which they virtually shriek (the final close-ups of *Sisters of the Gion* and *Osaka Elegy*). When charges of mysticism are levelled at Mizoguchi, it is good to recall that his final film, *Street of Shame*, certainly helped bring about the ban on prostitution in Japan in 1957.

A profound influence on the New Wave directors, Mizoguchi continues to fascinate those in the forefront of the art (Godard, Straub, Rivette). Complete retrospectives of his 31 extant films in Venice, London, and New York resulted in voluminous publications about Mizoguchi in the 1980s. A passionate but contemplative artist, struggling with issues crucial to cinema and society, Mizoguchi will continue to reward anyone who looks closely at his films. His awesome talent, self-discipline, and productivity guarantee this.

—Dudley Andrew

MOLANDER, Gustaf.

Swedish. Born in Helsingfors (now Helsinki), Finland, 18 November 1888. Educated at Royal Dramatic Theatre, Stockholm. Married to Karin (Molander), 1910–18. Member of Swedish National Theatre Company, Helsingfors, directed by father, 1910–11; stage actor in Stockholm, 1913–26; began writing film scripts for Mauritz Stiller, 1917; directed first film, 1920; director for Svensk Filmindustri, from 1923; introduced Ingrid Bergman, 1935. *Died, in Stockholm, 20 June 1973.*

Films as Director:

1920   *Bodakunden* (*King of Boda*) (+ sc)
1922   *Thomas Graals myndling* (*Thomas Graal's Ward*) (+ sc); *Pärlorna* (*The Amateur Film*) (+ sc)
1924   *33.333* (+ sc); *Polis Paulus påskasmäll* (*Constable Paulus's Easter Bomb*) (+ sc)
1925   *Ingmarsarvet* (*The Ingmar Inheritance*) (+ co-sc)
1926   *Till Österland* (*To the Orient*) (+ co-sc); *Hon den enda* (*She's the Only One*; *Hans engelska fru* (*His English Wife*)
1927   *Förseglade löppar* (*Sealed Lips*)
1928   *Parisiskor* (*Women of Paris*); *Synd* (*Sin*)
1929   *Hjärtats triumf* (*Triumph of the Heart*)
1930   *Charlotte Löwenskjöld* (Charlotte Löwensköld); *Fridas visor* (*Frida's Songs*)
1931   *Från yttersta skären*; *En natt* (*One Night*)
1932   *Svarta rosor* (*Black Roses*); *Kärlek och kassabrist* (*Love and Deficit*) (+ co-sc); *Vi som går köksvägen* (*We Go Through the Kitchen*) (+ co-sc)
1933   *Kära släkten* (*Dear Relatives*) (+ co-sc)
1934   *En stilla flirt* (*A Quiet Affair*) (+ co-sc); *Fasters miljoner* (*My Aunt's Millions*); *Ungkarlspappan* (*Bachelor Father*) (+ co-sc)
1935   *Under falsk flagg* (*Under False Colors*) (+ co-sc); *Swedenhielms* (+ co-sc); *Bröllöpsresan* (*The Honeymoon Trip*) (+ co-sc)
1936   *På solsidan* (*On the Sunny Side*) (remade for TV 1966); *Intermezzo* (+ co-sc); *Familjens hemlighet* (*The Family Secret*)
1937   *Sara lär sig folkvett* (*Sara Learns Manners*); *Dollar* (+ co-sc)
1938   *En kvinnas ansikte* (*A Woman's Face*) (+ co-sc); *En enda natt* (*One Single Night*) (+ co-sc); *Ombyte förnöjer* (+ co-sc)

1939   *Emilie Högqvist* (+ co-sc)
1940   *En, men ett lejon* (*One But a Lion*); *Den ljusnande framtid* (*Bright Prospects*) (+ co-sc)
1941   *I natt eller aldrig* (*Tonight or Never*); *Striden går vidare* (*The Fight Goes On*) (+ co-sc)
1942   *Jacobs stege* (*Jacob's Ladder*); *Rid i natt* (*Ride Tonight!*) (+ sc)
1943   *Det brinner en eld* (*There Burned a Flame*); *Älskling, jag ger mig* (*Darling I Surrender*); *Ordet* (*The Word*)
1944   *Den osynliga muren* (*The Invisible Wall*); *Kejsaren av Portugallien* (*The Emperor of Portugal*) (+ co-sc)
1945   *Galgamannen* (*Mandragora*) (+ co-sc)
1946   *Det är min modell* (*It's My Model*)
1947   *Kvinna utan ansikte* (*Woman without a Face*)
1948   *Nu börjar livet* (*Life Begins Now*) (+ sc); *Eva* (+ co-sc)
1949   *Kärleken segrar* (*Love Will Conquer*)
1950   *Kvartetten som sprängdes* (*The Quartet That Split Up*)
1951   *Fästmö uthyres* (*Fiancée for Hire*); *Frånskild* (*Divorced*)
1952   *Trots* (*Defiance*) (+ sc); *Kärlek* (*Love*) (+ co-sc)
1953   *Glasberget* (*Unmarried*) (+ co-sc)
1954   *Herr Arnes pengar* (*Sir Arne's Treasure*) (+ co-sc) (remake)
1955   *Enhörningen* (*The Unicorn*) (+ co-sc)
1957   *Sången om den eldröda blommon* (*Song of the Scarlet Flower*) (remake)
1967   "*Smycket* (*The Necklace*)" episode of *Stimulantia* (shot 1965)

Other Films:

1917   *Terje Vigen* (Sjöstrom) (co-sc); *Thomas Graals bästa film* (*Thomas Graal's Best Film*) (Stiller) (co-sc)
1918   *Thomas Graals bästa born* (*Thomas Graal's First Child*) (Stiller) (sc); *Sängen om den eldröda blommon* (*Song of the Scarlet Flower*) (Stiller) (sc)
1919   **Herr Arnes pengar** (**Sir Arne's Treasure**) (Stiller) (sc)
1923   *Mälarpirater* (*Pirates on Lake Mälar*) (sc)

*   *   *

Gustav Molander was a screenwriter/director whose work remains largely unknown outside his native Sweden. Although his career spanned nearly 50 years and resulted in over 60 feature films, he is best remembered as the man who "discovered" Ingrid Bergman and who wrote and directed *Intermezzo*, the film which brought that remarkably beautiful and talented actress to the attention of producer David O. Selznick.

Molander was a cultivated man whose career was mostly devoted to making elegant comedies and romantic dramas. Along with Victor Seastrom and Mauritz Stiller, he was one of the noted directors of Sweden's "golden age of cinema"—1913–1924—and although not as artistically creative as those two masters, he was a respected journeyman director. Further unlike Seastrom and Stiller, he chose not to emigrate to Hollywood, refusing Selznick's invitation in 1937.

In 1917 he had written the screenplay for Seastrom's milestone, *Terje Vigen*, about the English blockade of Norway during the Napoleonic wars. He also wrote the scripts for three important films directed by Mauritz Stiller—*Thomas Graal's Best Film*; *Thomas Graal's Best Child*, and the sophisticated sex comedy, *Erotikon*. These three films starred Karin Molander, Molander's vivacious wife, who later married Lars Hanson. Molander began directing with *King of Boda*, and very often wrote his own screenplays. He was also the director of the Royal Dramatic Theatre and it was he who, in the spring of 1923, suggested the young Greta Gustaffsson—later Garbo—for Stiller's *Gösta Berlings Saga*.

Following the decline of Sweden's "golden age," much of Molander's creativity was directed toward launching the career of Ingrid Bergman. He directed her first screen test, encouraged her, directed her in seven films, most notably *Intermezzo*, which he wrote especially for her. Years later he would modestly state: "The truth is nobody discovered her.

Gustaf Molander: Ingrid Bergman in *Intermezzo*

Nobody launched her. She discovered herself." His first film with the young actress was the intelligent romantic comedy, *Swedenhielms*, about a wealthy girl who is engaged to the son of a brilliant but impoverished scientist, played by the great Gosta Ekman. *On the Sunny Side* was a charming, lightweight comedy co-starring Bergman and Lars Hanson. *Intermezzo*, again with Hanson, followed, after which Bergman went to Hollywood to film the U.S. version of that romantic classic about the love between a beautiful young pianist and a famous, married violinist. That film made an international star of Ingrid Bergman but she did return to her native Sweden to star in three more films directed by Molander. *Dollar* was a sophisticated farce with Bergman playing an actress; *A Woman's Face* the dramatic story of a facially-scarred criminal, was later remade with Joan Crawford; and *En enda natt* was another elegant film which dealt with illegitimacy and extra-marital sex.

During World War II, Molander directed several anti-Nazi dramas, and the ambitious religious allegory, *The World*, remade by Carl Dreyer in 1955. Molander also helped launch the career of another young Swedish actress from the Royal Dramatic Theatre, Signe Hasso. Molander's post-World War II career consisted mostly of rather pedestrian filmic renderings of plays and novels which relied heavily on dialogue, such as the turgid remaking of *Sir Arne's Treasure*. Molander's version of that popular novel by Selma Lagerlof bore little comparison to Stiller's masterful 1919 production. Two exceptions to

this stagnant period in Molander's career were *Eva* and *Divorce*, both derived from scripts by Ingmar Bergman.

After *Song of the Scarlet Flower*, Molander retired, but interrupted his retirement in 1964 to direct Ingrid Bergman one last time in *Stimulantia*, a four-episode film released in 1967. The Molander segment was entitled "The Necklace" and was based on Guy de Maupassant's short story. Upon completion of that film a reporter asked, "And what are your plans for the future?" Molander replied, "The graveyard." Molander died in 1973, and while little-known outside Sweden, his lengthy career spanned the history of Swedish cinema.

—Ronald Bowers

MONICELLI, Mario.

Italian. Born in Viareggio, Tuscany, 16 May 1915. Studied history and philosophy at Universities of Pisa and Milan. Won prize at Venice Festival for 16mm film *I ragazzi dela via Paal*, 1935; worked as assistant director to Gustav Machaty, Pietro Germi, Mario Camerini, Mario Bonnard, and others, from 1936; army service, 1940–43; scriptwriter, from 1944; began directing and scriptwriting team with Steno (Stefano Vanzina), 1949; directed first solo feature, *Proibito*, 1953. Recipient: Best Direction, Berlin Festival, for *Fathers and Sons*, 1957; Golden Lion, Venice Festival, for *The Great War*, 1959; Best Director, Berlin Festival, for *Caro Michele*, 1976, and *Il Marchese del Grillo*, 1982. Address: Via del Babuino, 135, Rome, Italy.

Films as Director and Co-Scriptwriter:

1935   *I ragazzi della via Paal* (d only); *Il cuore rivelatore* (short) (d only)
1949   *Al diavolo la celebrità* (co-d with Steno)
1950   *Totò cerca casa* (co-d with Steno); *Vita da cani* (co-d with Steno); *È arrivato il cavaliere* (co-d with Steno)
1951   *Guardie e ladri* (*Cops and Robbers*) (co-d with Steno)
1952   *Totò e i re di Roma* (co-d with Steno)
1953   *Totò e le donne* (co-d with Steno); *Le infideli* (co-d with Steno)
1954   *Proibito*
1955   *Totò e Carolina* (shot in 1953); *Un eroe dei nostri tempi*
1956   *Donatella*
1957   *Padri e figli* (*Fathers and Sons*); *Il medico e lo stregone*
1958   *I soliti ignoti* (*Big Deal on Madonna Street*)
1959   *La grande guerra* (*The Great War*)
1960   *Risate di gioia* (*The Passionate Thief*)
1962   "Renzo e Luciana" episode of *Boccaccio '70*
1963   *I compagni* (*The Organizer*)
1964   "Gente moderne (Modern People)" episode of *Alta infidelità* (*High Infidelity*)
1965   *Casanova '70*; *L'armata Brancaleone*
1966   "Fata Armenia (Queen Armenia)" episode of *Le Fate* (*The Queens*)
1968   *La ragazza con la pistola* (*Girl with a Gun*); "La bambinaia" episode of *Capriccio all'italiana*
1969   *To, è morta la nonna!*
1970   "Il frigorifero" episode of *Le coppie*; *Brancaleone alle Crociate* (*Brancaleone alla crusada*)
1971   *La mortadella* (*Lady Liberty*)
1973   *Vogliamo di colonnelli*
1974   *Romanzo popolare*
1975   *Amici miei* (*My Friends*) (co-d, took over from Pietro Germi)
1976   *Caro Michele*; one episode of *Signore e signori, buonanotte*; one episode of *La Goduria*
1977   *Un borghese piccolo piccolo*; *I nuovi mostri* (co-d)
1978   *Viaggio con Anita* (*Travels with Anita*)
1979   *Temporale Rosy*
1981   *Camera d'albergo*
1982   *Amici miei, atto 2*; *Il Marchese del Grillo*
1984   *Bertoldo, Bertoldini e Cacasenno*
1985   *Le due vite di Marttia Pascal*
1986   *Speriamo che sia femmina* (*Let's Hope It's a Girl*)
1987   *I Picari* (*The Picaros*)

Other Films: (partial list)

1946   *Aquila Nera* (*The Black Eagle*) (Freda) (sc)
1947   *I miserabili* (in 2 parts: *La caccia all'uomo* and *Tempesta su Parigi*) (Freda) (sc); *Gioventù perduta* (*Lost Youth*) (Germi) (asst d, sc)
1948   *Il cavaliere misterioso* (Freda) (sc)
1949   *Il Conte Ugolino* (*Il cavaliere di ferro*) (Freda) (sc); *In nome della legge* (*Mafia*) (Germi) (sc)
1951   *Il tradimento* (Freda) (co-sc)
1961   *A cavallo della tigre* (Comencini) (co-sc)

Publications:

By MONICELLI: books—

La grande guerra, edited by Franco Calderoni, Bologna, 1959.
Boccaccio '70, edited by Carlo di Carlo and Gaio Fratini, Bologna, 1962.
I compagni, edited by Pio Baldelli, Bologna, 1963.
L'arte della commedia, Bari, 1986.

By MONICELLI: articles—

Interview with A. Tassone, in *Image et Son* (Paris), February 1974.
"Pietro Germi, mon ami," in *Ecran* (Paris), September 1976.
Interview with L. Dahan and B. Villien, in *Cinématographe* (Paris), June 1977.
"À la recherche de la comédie italienne," interview with L. de La Fuente and D. Rabourdin, in *Cinéma* (Paris), February 1978.
Interview with J.-L. Comolli and F. Gere, in *Cahiers du Cinéma* (Paris), March 1979.
Interview with L. Codelli, in *Positif* (Paris), June 1986.
Interview with M. Buruiana, in *24 Images* (Montreal), Spring 1987.

*   *   *

The cinema quickly attracted Mario Monicelli who, at the age of 21, co-directed a short 16mm film with A. Mondadori, called *I ragazzi della Via Paal*. However, Monicelli underwent a long apprenticeship as assistant director and/or scriptwriter before he was able to debut as a director in 1949. Even then his first eight features were co-directed with Steno (Stefano Vanzina). They were modest comedies usually serving as vehicles for the talents of the famous comedian, Totò. Monicelli's first significant film came with *Un eroe dei nostri tempi* starring Alberto Sordi. Although its production values were quite modest, its ironic description of a common man, typical of his time and society, who refuses any responsibility, insists on never taking a stand, and lives in conformism and fear, was quite well-drawn and insightful. From then on, Monicelli has concentrated on using popular genres to investigate the social positions and internal dilemmas of common people, in his features and his frequent collaborations on episode films, a popular Italian form since 1954. Monicelli enjoys collaboration, having worked closely with the scriptwriters Age and Scarpelli. Also, he directed *Amici miei* in honor of his friend, fellow filmmaker Pietro Germi, who conceived the idea but was too ill to realize the project.

One of Monicelli's best-known films, in Italy and abroad (it is one of the few Italian films that has always been available from distributors in the U.S., at least in 16mm) is *Big Deal on Madonna Street*. It is a comedy about a group of totally inept thieves (including Renato Salvatori and Marcello Mastroianni), led by master thief Totò (in one of his most subtle performances) who bungle a robbery and return home empty-handed. It also remains Monicelli's personal favorite because it appeared on the screen exactly as he imagined it.

Despite the fact that Monicelli is regarded as a director of comedies, some of his finest works have used comic elements in highly dramatic situations. Two outstanding examples in this regard are *La grande guerra* and *I compagni*. The first won a Golden Lion at Venice although, in pre-production, it caused a controversy among government and military officials who considered it unpatriotic and harmful to the country's morale. It expresses the point-of-view of two common soldiers (Alberto Sordi and Vittorio Gassman) and their experiences through four years in the First World War. These soldiers, despite the enormous significance of the situations in which they find themselves, remain ignorant and naive, the source of the film's comedy. Despite having chosen Sordi and Gassman, Monicelli wanted to play down the impact of the star system and concentrate on collective protagonists, which he succeeded in doing.

I compagni tells the story of a strike in Turin at the turn of the century. Even though the strike fails, it is shown to be a necessary experience for the workers' maturation and understanding of the forces that control them. Again, although it has an all-star cast including Mastroianni, Salvatori, Annie Girardot, and Bernard Blier, Monicelli wanted a collective protagonist and a portrait of a group of people.

On the other hand, *Un borghese piccolo piccolo* (which received a fair distribution in the United States) is predominantly a bitter portrait of the petit-bourgeois world in all its grotesque and melodramatic manifestations. However, it is also a comedy and not without sympathy for the protagonist, a living fossil who is overly protective of his son and suspicious and afraid of everything else. The main role offered Sordi a complex character to interpret which gave full range to his talents. In its ambiguity of tone, the film contains all the traits of Italian comedy, but has gone beyond the formula, approaching tragedy.

—Elaine Mancini

MULLIGAN, Robert.

American. Born in the Bronx, New York, 23 August 1925. Educated in theological seminary; studied radio communications, Fordham University, New York. Marine radio operator, World War II. Worked in editorial dept. of *The New York Times*, late 1940s; began working in TV as messenger for CBS, then TV director on *Suspense, TV Playhouse, Playhouse 90*, and others, mid-1950s; directed first feature film, *Fear Strikes Out*, 1957; founded Pakula-Mulligan Productions with Alan J. Pakula, 1962 (dissolved 1969).

Films as Director:

1957 *Fear Strikes Out*
1960 *The Rat Race*
1961 *The Great Imposter*; *Come September*
1962 *The Spiral Road*
1963 *Love With a Proper Stranger*
1965 *Baby the Rain Must Fall*
1966 *Inside Daisy Clover*
1967 *Up the Down Staircase*
1968 *The Stalking Moon*
1971 *The Pursuit of Happiness*; *Summer of '42*
1972 *The Other* (+ pr)
1975 *The Nickel Ride* (+ pr)
1978 *Blood Brothers*
1979 *Same Time, Next Year* (+ co-pr)
1982 *Kiss Me Goodbye* (+ co-pr)
1988 *Clara's Heart* (+ co-pr)

Publications:

By MULLIGAN: articles—

Interview with Michel Ciment, in *Positif* (Paris), January 1973.
Interview with J.-A. Gili, in *Ecran* (Paris), October 1974.
"Time for Thought," an interview with R. Appelbaum, in *Films and Filming* (London), January 1975.

On MULLIGAN: book—

Belton, John, *Cinema Stylists*, Metuchen, New Jersey, 1983.

On MULLIGAN: articles—

Godfrey, Lionel, "Flawed Genius: The Work of Robert Mulligan," in *Films and Filming* (London), January 1967.
Taylor, John, "Inside Robert Mulligan," in *Sight and Sound* (London), Autumn 1971.
Falonga, M., "Mysterious Islands: *Summer of '42*," in *Film Heritage* (New York), Fall 1972.
"TV to Film: A History, a Map and a Family Tree," in *Monthly Film Bulletin* (London), February 1983.

*   *   *

In an era in which consistent visual style seems perhaps too uniformly held as the prerequisite of the valorized auteur, one can all too easily understand why Robert Mulligan's work has failed to evince any passionate critical interest. His films all look so different; for instance, *To Kill a Mockingbird*, with its black-and-white measured pictorialism; *Up the Down Staircase*, photographed on location with a documentary graininess; *The Other*, with its heightened Gothic expressionism rather conventional to the horror genre, if not to Mulligan's previous work; and *The Summer of '42*, with a pastel prettiness which suffuses each image with the nostalgia of memory. If some would claim this visual eclecticism reflects the lack of a strong personality, others could claim that Mulligan has too much respect for his material to impose arbitrarily upon it some monolithic consistency and instead brings to his subjects the sensibility of a somewhat self-effacing Hollywood craftsman. Yet there are certainly some sequences in Mulligan's work which spring vividly to mind: the silent, final seduction in *The Summer of '42*; the almost surreal walk home by a child dressed as a ham in *To Kill a Mockingbird*; the high school dance in *Up the Down Staircase*; the climactic camera movement in *The Other*, from Niles to that empty space where Holland, were he not imaginary, would be sitting.

Even Mulligan's two biggest critical successes, *To Kill a Mockingbird* and *The Summer of '42*, both examples of the kind of respectable Hollywood filmmaking which garners Academy Award nominations, have not yet been greeted by any significant critical cult. And yet, if Mulligan's good taste has been steadfastly held against him, it must be noted that his films, albeit generally ignored, hold up remarkably well. Mulligan has a strong sense of narrative; and all his films are imbued with human values and a profound compassion which make for compelling audience identification with Mulligan's characteristic protagonists. Mulligan's tendency is to work in less familiar movie genres (such as Hollywood exposé, the family drama, the teacher film, the cinematic *Bildungsroman*), but to avoid—through sincerity and human insight—that emphasis on the purely formal which sometimes makes genre works "go dead" for their audiences upon repeated viewings. Perhaps it is American mistrust of male emotional expression which contributes to Mulligan's facile dismissal by many; certainly it appears that those critics who attacked as sentimental *The Summer of '42*, Mulligan's tasteful and bittersweet paean to lost virginity, failed to assess negatively those same qualities in so many of the French New Wave films, especially, for instance, the Antoine Doinel cycle by François Truffaut, which were instead praised for their lyrical and compassionate exploration of human interaction. Is nostalgia somehow more acceptable when it is French?

An eventual re-evaluation of Robert Mulligan as a significant, if minor artist, may eventually materialize, especially if the consistency of his thematic motifs is more extensively examined. Certainly Mulligan seems especially interested in the deviant, the outsider, the loner: the mentally unbalanced Jimmy Peirsall in *Fear Strikes Out*; the enlightened attorney whose values put him in conflict with a bigoted community in *To Kill a Mockingbird*; the ex-convict trying to accustom himself to life outside the penitentiary in *Baby the Rain Must Fall*; the character of Ferdinand Demara, based on real life, who, in *The Great Imposter*, succeeds by the sheer force of his skillful impersonations in insinuating himself into a variety of environments in which he would otherwise never be accepted; the students in *Up the Down Staircase* who, psychologically stunted and economically deprived, may—even with a committed teacher's help—never fit into mainstream society. Like Truffaut, Mulligan has an extraordinary insight into the world of the child or adolescent and the secret rituals of that world.

Robert Mulligan

Mulligan's children never display that innocence conventionally associated with children, instead participating in often traumatic ceremonies of passage. One thinks of the child through whose eyes the innate racism of small-town America is seen in *To Kill a Mockingbird*; the precocious child-star in *Inside Daisy Clover*; the lost and often already jaded students in *Up the Down Staircase*; the pubescent adolescents who learn about sex and morality in *The Summer of '42*; and the irrevocably evil child, Niles, and his twin, Holland, in *The Other*.

Some final note too must be made of the consistently fine performances elicited by Mulligan from his players: Anthony Perkins in *Fear Strikes Out*, Gregory Peck and Mary Badham in *To Kill a Mockingbird*, Sandy Dennis in *Up the Down Staircase*, Jennifer O'Neil in *The Summer of '42*, Richard Gere in *Blood Brothers*, and all the children and adolescents who populate Mulligan's world.

—Charles Derry

MUNK, Andrzej.

Polish. Born in Cracow, 16 October 1921. Educated in engineering and law, 1946–48; State Cinema School, Lodz, degree 1950. Married Joanna Prochnik. Labourer, also active in resistance, World War II; general secretary of Z.N.M.S., organization of socialist students, late 1940s; director at documentary film studio, Warsaw, 1950–55; teacher at State Film School, Lodz, from 1957. *Died, in auto accident, 20 September 1961.*

Films as Director:

1949   *Kongres kombatantów* [Congress of Fighters] (co-d)
1950   *Sztuka młodych* [Art of Youth] (co-d, sc); *Zaczęło się w Hiszpanii* [It Began in Spain] (+ ed)
1951   *Kierunek Nowa Huta* [Direction: Nowa Huta]; *Nauka bliżej życia* [Science Closer to Life] (+ co-ph)
1952   *Bajka w Ursusie* [The Tale of Ursus] or *Poemat symfoniczny "Bajka" Stanisława Moniuszki* [The Symphonic Poem "Fable" of Stanislas Moniuszko]; *Pamiętniki chłopów* [Diaries of the Peasants] (+ sc)
1953   *Kolejarskie słowo* [A Railwayman's Word] (+ sc)
1954   *Gwiazdy muszą płonąć* [The Stars Must Shine] (co-d, co-sc)
1955   *Niedzielny poranek* (*Sunday Morning. Un Dimanche Matin. Ein Sonntagmorgen in Warschau*) (+ sc); *Błękitny krzyż* (*Men of the Blue Cross. Les Hommes de la croix bleue. Die Männer vom blauen Kreuz*) (+ sc)
1956   *Człowiek na torze* (*Man on the Track. Un Homme sur la voie. Der Mann auf den Schienen*) (+ co-sc)
1957   **Eroica** (**Eroica—Polen 44**)
1958   *Spacerek staromiejski* (*A Walk in the Old City of Warsaw*) (+ sc)
1959   *Kronika jubileuszowa* or *Polska kronika filmowa nr 52 A–B* (+ sc)
1960   *Zezowate szczęście* (*Bad Luck. De la veine a revendre. Das schielende Glück*) (+ role as bureaucrat)
1963   *Pasażerka* (*The Passenger. La Passagère. Die Passagierin*) (+ co-sc) (film assembled posthumously by Witold Lesiewicz)

Publications:

By MUNK: articles—

"Expérience du cinéma polonais," interview with P.-L. Thirard, in *Les Lettres Françaises* (Paris), no. 790, 1959.
"National Character and the Individual," in *Films and Filming* (London), vol.8, no.2, 1961.

"Naszych twórców ączy jedna cecha—poważne podejście do tematu i poważne traktowanie odbiorcy," [That which unites our filmmakers is a serious attitude toward the subject and the public] in *Ekran* (Warsaw), no.22, 1961.
"Le dernier entretien avec . . . ," in *Cinéma* (Paris), no.71, 1962.

On MUNK: books—

Haudiquet, Philippe, *Nouveaux cinéastes polonais*, Premier Plan no.27, Lyon, 1963.
Andrzej Munk, collective work, Warsaw, 1964.
Historia Filmu Polskiego IV, Warsaw, 1981.

On MUNK: articles—

Sadoul, Georges, "Andrzej Munk," in *Les Lettres Françaises* (Paris), no. 894, 1961.
Haudiquet, Philippe, "Andrzej Munk," in *Image et Son* (Paris), January 1964.
Special Munk issue of *Études Cinématographiques* (Paris), no.45, 1965.
Brzozowski, Andrzej, "Munk et *La Passàgere*," in *Cahiers du Cinéma* (Paris), no. 163, 1965.
Plazewsky, Jerzy, "Andrzej Munk," in *Anthologie du cinéma* vol. 3, Paris, 1968.
Amette, Jacques-Pierre, "Andrzej Munk," in *Dossiers du cinéma*, Cinéastes 1, Paris, 1971.
Profile on Munk, in *Illuzjon* (Warsaw), no. 3, 1986.

*   *   *

Andrzej Munk is one of the creators of the so-called Polish school of filmmaking and one of the most important Polish film directors. He belongs to the skeptical generation of directors who spent their early youth in the difficult years of the Second World War and embarked on filmmaking in the 1950s with no rosy illusions but with a sense of responsibility for themselves, their actions, and the time in which they lived, a time which shaped them but was also transformed by them. Their common trait is their critical view of the present and the recent events in their people's history (the defeat of Poland in September 1939, the Warsaw Uprising of 1944, the postwar disputes and struggles over the fate of Poland, and the years marked by the cult of personality). In comparison with others in his generation and members of the "school," Munk stands out as a perceptive analyst and rationalist with a sober and searching view of people and events, a view which is only seldom presented metaphorically. Andrzej Munk adopted this view at the outset of his film career in the Documentary Film Studio, where he made several short pictures. Some of these were attributable to the prevailing schematic conception of socialist realism, but three of them (*Kolejarskie słowo, Gwiazdy muszą płonąć, Niedzielny poranek*) already show the rudiments of Munk's later approach to the dramatic film. Munk termed these films dramatic reportage, for they combine the authenticity of reality with certain dramatic elements. This step is further developed in Munk's first long film, *Błękitny krzyż*, about a successful action by the mountain service to rescue wounded partisans from territory still occupied by German units. The result, however, did not match the potential. Alongside successful sequences were others which shattered the unity of the work; dramatic sequences clashed with the paradocumentary parts.

Munk resolved this contradiction in his very next film, *Człowiek na torze*, which is the first manifestation of Munk's style based on rational reflection and analysis. Through a system of successive returns to the past, the director analyzes individual situations in the human fate of a railway worker who faces a conflict between his own sense of responsibility and the demands of society; the director's purpose is then to combine these forces in a synthesis that reveals the truth that is sought. His next two films, *Eroica* and *Zezowate szczęście*—both films are key works in the Polish film school—reveal another salient

Andrzej Munk

feature of Munk's artistic personality; added to his critical insight are irony, sarcasm, and, in the context of the Polish filmmaking of the time, a unique sense of comic exaggeration in exposing the function of certain national myths. In the tragic-grotesque stylization of *Eroica* he criticizes the superficiality of the prevalent conception of heroism (Wajda does the same thing in a tragic key), while in the film *Zezowate szczęście* he engages in a polemic with the simplistic depiction of the hero in contemporary Polish films by making his hero a man who constantly adapts to various changes in the social situation.

Munk's last major work is *Pasażerka*, produced only after his death in a reworking by Witold Lesiewicz. It returns once again to the Second World War, to the horrible environment of a concentration camp, and confronts this period with postwar recollections. Despite the cogency of the Lesiewicz reconstruction, in which already completed film clips alternate with stills from the unfinished sequences, it is impossible to make a safe guess as to where Munk's future path would have taken him. He was unmistakably tending toward a certain change in his artistic methods. But his work is closed. It is not extensive—a few short pictures, five dramatic films, one of them unfinished. Nevertheless, right up to the present time, his work, by the strength of its artistic appeal, has exercised an influence on the following generation of young filmmakers and viewers. It continues to attract them with its individual, unifying style, whose components are a perfect composition of shots, meaningful camera movement, eloquent montage, sober action, laconic dialogue, and counterpoint of image and sound; it is a style that serves precisely what Munk wished to communicate to the viewer.

—B. Urgošíková

MURNAU, F.W.

German. Born Friedrich Wilhelm Plumpe in Bielefeld, Germany, 28 December 1888. Educated in philology, University of Berlin; art history and literature, University of Heidelberg. Served in German army, from 1914; transferred to air force, interned in Switzerland following crash landing, 1917. Attended Max Reinhardt theater school, 1908, later joined company; founder, with other Reinhardt school colleagues, Murnau Veidt Filmgesellschaft, 1919; invited by William Fox to Hollywood, 1926; returned to Germany, 1927; sailed to Tahiti with Robert Flaherty to prepare *Tabu*, 1929. *Died, in auto accident, California, 11 March 1931.*

Films as Director:

1919   *Der Knabe in Blau* (*Der Todessmaragd. The Boy in Blue*)
1920   *Satanas*; *Sehnsucht* (*Bajazzo*); *Der Bucklige und die Tanzerin* [The Hunchback and the Dancer]; *Der Januskopf* (*Schrecken. Janus-Faced*); *Abend . . . Nacht . . . Morgen*
1921   *Der Gang in die Nacht*; *Schloss Vogelöd* (*Haunted Castle*); ***Nosferatu—Eine Symphonie des Grauens* (*Nosferatu the Vampire*)**
1922   *Marizza, genannt die Schmuggler-Madonna*; *Der Brennende Acker* (*Burning Soil*); *Phantom*
1923   *Die Austreibung* (*Driven from Home*)
1924   *Die Finanzen des Grossherzogs* (*The Grand Duke's Finances*); ***Der Letzte Mann* (*The Last Laugh*)**
1926   *Tartüff*; *Faust*
1927   ***Sunrise* (*Sunrise: A Song of Two Humans*)**
1928   *Four Devils*

1930   *Die zwolfte Stunde—Eine Nacht des Grauens* (*Nosferatu the Vampire*) (*Nosferatu* adapted for sound); *Our Daily Bread*
1931   ***Tabu*** (+ co-pr, co-sc)

Publications:

By MURNAU: book—

Sunrise (*Sonnenaufgang*), *Ein Drehbuch von Carl Mayer mit handschriftlichen Bemerkungen von Friedrich Wilhelm Murnau*, German Institute for Film Studies, Wiesbaden, 1971.

By MURNAU: articles—

"The Ideal Picture Needs No Titles," in *Theatre Magazine* (New York), January 1928.
"Étoile du Sud," in *La Revue du Cinéma* (Paris), May 1931.
"Turia, an Original Story," and "*Tabu* (*Tabou*), a Story of the South Sea," with Robert Flaherty, in *Film Culture* (New York), no.20, 1959.

On MURNAU: books—

Jameux, Charles, *Murnau*, Paris, 1965.
Domarchi, Jean, "Murnau," in *Anthologie du cinéma* vol.1, Paris, 1966.
Kracauer, Siegfried, *From Caligari to Hitler*, New York, 1966.
Eisner, Lotte, *The Haunted Screen*, Berkeley, California, 1969.
Eisner, Lotte, *Murnau*, Berkeley, California, 1973.
Petrie, Graham, *Hollywood Destinies: European Directors in America 1922–1931*, London, 1985.
Berg-Ganschow, Uta, and others, editors, *F.W. Murnau 1888–1988*, Bielefeld, 1988.

On MURNAU: articles—

Josephson, Matthew, "F.W. Murnau—The German Genius of the Films," in *Motion Picture Classic* (New York), October 1926.
Astruc, Alexandre, "Le Feu et la glace," in *Cahiers du Cinéma* (Paris), December 1952; in *Cahiers du Cinéma in English* (New York), January 1966.
Wood, Robin, "*Tabu*," in *Film Culture* (New York), Summer 1971.
Dorr, J., "The Griffith Tradition," in *Film Comment* (New York), March/April 1974.
"L'Aurore," special Murnau issue of *Avant-Scène du Cinéma* (Paris), June 1974.
"Per una ri-lettura critica di F.W. Murnau," special Murnau issue of *Filmcritica* (Rome), July 1974.
Audibert, L., "Dossier: Le Pont traversé," in *Cinématographe* (Paris), January 1977.
Latil Le Dantec, M., "De Murnau à Rohmer: les pièges de la beauté," in 2 parts, in *Cinématographe* (Paris), January and February 1977.
Special Murnau issue of *Avant-Scène du Cinéma* (Paris), July/September 1977.
Mitry, Jean, and others, "Griffith, Murnau et les historiens," in *Avant-Scène du Cinéma* (Paris), 15 March 1978.
Gehler, F., "F.W. Murnau, Hollywood and die Südsee," in *Film und Fernsehen* (Berlin), May 1981.
Cardullo, B., "*Der letzte Mann* Gets the Last Laugh: F.W. Murnau's Comic Vision," in *Post Script* (Jacksonville, Florida), Fall 1981.
Murnau Section of *Casablanca* (Madrid), October 1981.
Elsaesser, Thomas, "Secret Affinities," in *Sight and Sound* (London), Winter 1988/89.

*   *   *

Murnau was studying with Max Reinhardt when the First World War began. He was called up for military service, and after achieving his lieutenancy, he was transferred to the air service, where he served as a combat pilot; but his plane was forced down in Switzerland, where he was interned for the duration. Through the German Embassy, however, he managed to direct several independent stage productions, and he began his lifelong dedication to the motion picture, compiling propaganda film materials and editing them, which made it possible for him to enter the reborn film industry after peace as a full-fledged director.

His first feature film as director was in 1919, *The Boy in Blue*,

F.W. Murnau (left) with cameraman Charles Rosher

and he made 21 full-length features from that year until 1926, when Fox Studios brought him to Hollywood. Unfortunately, most of the pictures he made in his native country no longer exist except in fragmentary form. They are tempting to read about, especially items like *Janus-Faced*, a study of a Jekyll and Hyde personality, which he made in 1920 with Conrad Veidt and Bela Lugosi. Critics found it more artistic than the John Barrymore version of the story made at about the same time in Paramount's New York studios.

Extant today in a complete version is *Nosferatu*, which was subtitled "a symphony of horror." It was a more faithful version of Bram Stoker's *Dracula* than any made thereafter, and the film is still available, starring the incredibly gaunt and frightening Max Schreck as the vampire.

The next film of Murnau's that is still viewable is *The Last Laugh*, which starred Emil Jannings. At the time of its release, it was noted as being a picture without subtitles, told almost completely in pantomine. Its real innovation was the moving camera, which Murnau used brilliantly. The camera went everywhere; it was never static. Audiences watched spellbound as the camera moved upstairs and down, indoors and out, although it was in this case only the simple story of a proud commissionaire reduced in his old age to menial work as a lavatory attendant. The camera records, nevertheless, a very real

world in an impressionistic way. In fact, Murnau, because of his skill with the moving camera, was generally known as the Great Impressionist, for he gave a superb impression of actual reality.

That title fits him even more aptly in his next two features, both of which also starred Emil Jannings. They are *Tartuffe*, a screen adaption of Moliere's black comedy, in which Lil Dagover and Werner Krauss were also featured. It is topped by what must be the most definitive film version of Goethe's *Faust*, starring Jannings as Mephistopheles, with the handsome Swedish favorite, Gosta Ekman, in the title role; Camilla Horn as Marguerite; the great Parisian star, Yvette Guilbert, as Marthe; and a young William Dieterle as Valentine. Again, the camera not only moved, it soared, especially in the sequence where Faust is shown the world which will be his if he sells his soul to the devil. Murnau was a master of light and shadow, and his work is always brilliantly choreographed as it moves from lightness to the dark.

It came as no surprise when in 1926 Murnau was invited to Hollywood, where the red carpet at Fox was unrolled for him. He was allowed to bring his cameraman, writers, and other craftsmen to work with him, and his initial feature was to be called *Sunrise*, subtitled "a song of two human beings." The two stars were to be Janet Gaynor and George O'Brien playing a young farm couple who make their first trip to the big city, which was constructed on the Fox lot, so that Murnau and his camera could follow them everywhere indoors and out of doors and onto a moving streetcar. Again, the story was very simple, adapted from a Hermann Suderman novel, *A Trip to Tilsit*, and simply proved that real love will always be triumphant.

Sunrise was highly praised by all critics, and was one of three pictures which brought Janet Gaynor an Academy Award as Best Actress in the 1927–28 year. Quite naturally, awards also went to cinematographers Charles Rosher and Karl Struss and to interior decorator Harry Oliver, while *Sunrise* was given a special award for its Artistic Quality of Production, a category never again specified.

For all that, *Sunrise* was not a box-office success, and the studio moved in to supervise Murnau closely on his next two productions. *Four Devils* was a circus story of four young aerialists, which gave Murnau's camera a chance to fly with them from one performing trapeze to another. All prints of *Four Devils* are unfortunately lost, which is a fate common to most of the last great silent films. Murnau began shooting on his final film at Fox, called *Our Daily Bread*, with Charles Farrell and Mary Duncan, but he was not allowed to finish the picture. The overwhelming popularity of the talking screen was allowed to flaw it, for the only version of it now shown is called *City Girl*, and is only effective when it is recognizably silent and all Murnau. As a part-talkie, it is crude and not at all Murnau.

Murnau then allied himself with Robert Flaherty, and the two men journeyed to the South Seas to make *Tabu*. Flaherty, however, withdrew, and *Tabu* is pure Murnau; some praise it as his greatest film. Murnau returned to California and was on the eve of signing at Paramount, which treated directors like Mamoulian, Lubitsch, and von Sternberg very kindly in their talking debuts. Unfortunately, Murnau lost his life in a motor accident on the Pacific Coast highway. He was only 42, and after the success of *Tabu*, a new fame might have been his.

—DeWitt Bodeen

N

NARUSE, Mikio.

Japanese. Born in Tokyo, 1905. Educated in Tokyo technical school, 1918–20. Married 1) actress Sachiko Chiba, 1937 (separated 1942), one child; 2). Prop man for Shochiku film company at Tokyo Kamata studios, 1920; assistant to director Yoshinobu Ikeda, 1921–28; comedy writer under pen name "Chihan Miki"; joined staff of Heinosuke Gosho, 1929; directed first film (now lost), 1930; left Shochiku, joined P.C.L. studios (later Toho Company), 1934; left Toho to freelance, 1945. *Died 1969.*

Films as Director:

1930   *Chambara fufu (Mr. and Mrs. Swordplay); Junjo (Pure Love); Fukeiki jidai (Hard Times)* (+ story); *Ai wa chikara da (Love Is Strength); Oshikiri shinkonki (A Record of Shameless Newlyweds)* (+ story)

1931   *Nee kofun shicha iya yo (Now Don't Get Excited); Nikai no himei (Screams from the Second Floor)* (+ sc); *Koshiben gambare (Flunky, Work Hard!)* (+ sc); *Uwaki wa kisha ni notte (Fickleness Gets on the Train)* (+ sc); *Hige no chikara (The Strength of a Moustache)* (+ sc); *Tonari no yane no shita (Under the Neighbors' Roof)*

1932   *Onna wa tamoto o goyojin (Ladies, Be Careful of Your Sleeves)* (+ sc); *Aozora ni naku (Crying to the Blue Sky); Eraku nare (Be Great!)* (+ sc); *Mushibameru haru (Motheaten Spring); Chokoreito garu (Chocolate Girl); Nasanu naka (Not Blood Relations)*

1933   *Kimi to wakarete (Apart from You)* (+ sc); *Yogoto no yume (Every Night Dreams)* (+ story); *Boku no marumage (A Man with a Married Woman's Hairdo); Sobo (Two Eyes)*

1934   *Kagirinaki hodo (Street Without End)*

1935   *Otome-gokoro sannin shimai (Three Sisters with Maiden Hearts)* (+ sc); *Joyu to shijin (The Actress and the Poet); Tsuma yo bara no yo ni (Wife! Be Like a Rose)* (+ sc); *Sakasu gonin-gumi (Five Men in the Circus; Uwasa no musume (The Girl in the Rumor)* (+ sc)

1936   *Tochuken Kumoemon (Kumoemon Tochuken)* (+ sc); *Kimi to iku michi (The Road I Travel with You)* (+ sc); *Asa no namikimichi (Morning's Tree-lined Street)* (+ sc)

1937   *Nyonin aishu (A Woman's Sorrows)* (+ co-sc); *Nadare (Avalanche)* (+ sc); *Kafuku I, II (Learn from Experience, Parts I, II)*

1938   *Tsuruhachi tsurujiro (Tsuruhachi and Tsurujiro)·*(+ sc)

1939   *Hataraku ikka (The Whole Family Works)* (+ sc); *Magokoro (Sincerity)* (+ sc)

1940   *Tabi yakusha (Traveling Actors)* (+ sc)

1941   *Natsukashi no kao (A Face from the Past* (+ sc); *Shanhai no tsuki (Shanghai Moon); Kideko no shasho-san (Hideko the Bus Conductor)* (+ sc)

1942   *Haha wa shinazu (Mother Never Dies)*

1943   *Uta andon (The Song Lantern)*

1944   *Tanoshiki kana jinsei (This Happy Life)* (+ co-sc); *Shibaido (The Way of Drama)*

1945   *Shori no hi made (Until Victory Day); Sanjusangendo toshiya monogatari (A Tale of Archery at the Sanjusangendo)*

1946   *Urashima Taro no koei (The Descendants of Taro Urashima); Ore mo omae mo (Both You and I)* (+ sc)

1947   *Yottsu no koi no monogatari, II: Wakare mo tanoshi (Four Love Stories, Part II: Even Parting Is Enjoyable); Haru no mezame (Spring Awakens)* (+ co-sc)

1949   *Furyo shojo (Delinquent Girl)* (+ sc); *Ishinaka sensei gyojoki (Conduct Report on Professor Ishinaka); Ikari no machi (The Angry Street)* (+ co-sc); *Shiroi yaju (White Beast)* (+ co-sc); *Bara gassen (The Battle of Roses)*

1951   *Ginza gesho (Ginza Cosmetics); Maihime (Dancing Girl); Meshi (Repast)*

1952   *Okuni to Gohei (Okuni and Gohei); Okasan (Mother); Inazuma (Lightning)*

1953   *Fufu (Husband and Wife); Tsuma (Wife); Ani imoto (Older Brother, Younger Sister)*

1954   *Yama no oto (Sound of the Mountain); Bangiku (Late Chrysanthemums)*

1955   *Ukigumo (Floating Clouds); Kuchizuke, III: Onna doshi (The Kiss, Part III: Women's Ways)*

1956   *Shu-u (Sudden Rain); Tsuma no kokoro (A Wife's Heart); Nagareru (Flowing)*

1957   *Arakure (Untamed)*

1958   *Anzukko* (+ co-sc); *Iwashigumo (Herringbone Clouds)*

1959   *Kotan no kuchibue (Whistling in Kotan. A Whistle in My Heart)*

1960   *Onna ga kaidan o agaru toki (When a Woman Ascends the Stairs); Musume tsuma haha (Daughters, Wives and a Mother); Yoru no nagare (Evening Stream)* (co-d); *Aki tachinu (The Approach of Autumn)*

1961   *Tsuma toshite onna toshite (As a Wife, as a Woman. The Other Woman)*

1962   *Onna no za (Woman's Status); Horoki (A Wanderer's Notebook. Lonely Lane)*

1963   *Onna no rekishi (A Woman's Story)*

1964   *Midareru (Yearning)*

1966   *Onna no naka ni iru tanin (The Stranger Within a Woman. The Thin Line); Hikinige (Hit and Run. Moment of Terror)*

1967   *Midaregumo (Scattered Clouds. Two in the Shadow)*

Publications:

On NARUSE: books—

Bock, Audie, *Japanese Film Directors*, Tokyo, 1978.
Burch, Noel, *To the Distant Observer*, London, 1979.
Ritchie, Donald, *The Japanese Movie*, revised edition, Tokyo, 1982.
Sato, Tadao, *Currents in Japanese Cinema: Essays*, translated by Gregory Barrett, Tokyo, 1982.
Bock, Audie, *Mikio Naruse: un maître du cinéma japonais*, Locarno, 1983.

On NARUSE: articles—

Bock, Audie, "Mikio Naruse," in *Film Criticism* (Meadville, Pennsylvania), no.55, 1979.
Interim, L., "Mikio Naruse le quatrième grand," in *Cahiers du Cinéma* (Paris), February 1983.
Niogret, H., "Mikio Naruse et l'agencement des émotions," in *Positif* (Paris), January 1984.

Tessier, Max, and Y. Mizuki, "Mikio Naruse," in *Revue du Cinéma* (Paris), February 1984.

Lopate, P., "A Taste for Naruse," in *Film Quarterly* (Berkeley), Summer 1986.

*   *   *

Mikio Naruse belongs in the second echelon of Japanese directors of his generation, along with Gosho, Ozu and Kinoshita—that is, behind Mizoguchi, Kurosawa, Ichikawa and Kobayashi, who broke out beyond the bounds of the conventions of the Japanese cinema, whereas the others were mostly content to work within it. This is not to say that all of them did not tackle contemporary as well as historical subjects. And certainly Gosho, Ozu, Kinoshita and Naruse were no less accomplished technically, though it might be noted that the last two did not respond to the challenge of the wide screen as excitingly as Kurosawa and Kobayashi.

The homogeneity of Japanese cinema and the concomitant audience acceptance of remake after remake (at least while Naruse was working) enables us to categorise these directors: Naruse's domestic comedies share themes and situations with those of Gosho and Kinoshita, and his domestic dramas are not unlike those of middle-period Ozu, after he had lost the freshness and urgency of his early work, before he had atrophied. But Naruse, although most of his (lost) silent films were simple slapsticks, was not later prolific in comedy. He was, however, occasionally drawn out into greater subjects, particularly towards the end of his career, and in rising to the occasion his career parallels that of Gosho, for both their filmographies contain some unexpected masterpieces. Most comments on Naruse emphasise that he was a pessimist because of his orphaned childhood, but most Japanese films tend to examine the shackles—rather than the joys—of family life or life in the geisha-house. His best films are suffused with a melancholy, with a desire for what might-have-been, which becomes, as art, warming and enlightening—and despairing rather than depressing.

It is true, however, that the few of his silent films that survive are chiefly tragedies of a not particularly high order. *Apart From You* (1933) and *Every Night Dreams* (1933) make it clear that the meek shall not inherit the earth. Naruse wrote the screenplay of the first, in which an adolescent geisha is determined that her younger sister will not follow her into that way of life; and he provided the story of the second, in which a barmaid is confronted with her useless husband, who had walked out on her some years previously. The men are weak but dangerous; the women are strong but compromised. Both are simple films, but *Street Without End* (1934) is of a richness and complexity rare for the period, despite the limitations of soap opera, imposed by the newspaper serial on which it was based. It is one of the earliest surviving examples of showcasing the talents of a particular local star—usually female, as in this case, permitting audiences to sympathise to the ultimate with her difficulties. Naruse brings truth to this tale which, shot on an amazing number of urban locations, has as an underlying theme the survival of feudalism in modern city life.

For his first sound film Naruse adapted a novel by Yasunari Kawabata, *Three Sisters With Maiden Hearts* (1935), and it is no better constructed than those of Ozu and Mizoguchi at this point, with flashbacks within flashbacks to complicate matters, but with an imaginative use of sound. *Wife! Be Like a Rose* (1935) concerns a girl's renewed relationship with her father, who had left his self-centred wife to live happily in the country with another woman. This is Naruse's 25th film, one of the few to survive from this period, and an elegant, subtle domestic drama with more humour than hitherto. This was a transitional film for him, rejecting melodrama entirely, as he did again in *Tsuruhachi and Tsurujiro* (1938), which details the destructive

Mikio Naruse

relationship of a man-woman shamizen team, while *The Whole Family Works* (1939) makes Western domestic dramas of the period look horrendously melodramatic.

Indeed Naruse's pictures over the next few years cannot escape a charge of monotony. The martial subjects demanded by the authorities during the War did not interest him, nor, it would seem, did those taken on during the Occupation, after he had left Toho. With *Repast* (1951), the story of a failing marriage, he began a series of domestic dramas which were to constitute a compassionate body of work, more sustained than either Ozu or Gosho, also concentrating on *shomin-geki*. *Repast* was based on a novel by Fumiko Hayashi, and he was to turn to her work again for four more of his best movies, *Lightning* (1952), *Late Chrysanthemums* (1954), *Floating Clouds* (1955) and the autobiographical *Lonely Lane* (1962). Hayashi was somewhat more optimistic than Naruse, but he finds in her work that life must go on, if imperfectly, and then asks why. The unanswerable questions, particularly in his studies of married life, bring him close to Bergman—though Bergman was considerably less interested in the banality of everyday existence.

It is interesting to compare Naruse's version of the novel by Saisei Muroo, *Older Brother Younger Sister* (1953) with those made in 1936 by Sotoji Kimura and in 1976 by Tadashi Imai. Each is of its period and each presents the riverside neighbourhood vividly, but Naruse's film is by far the best, infused with an intensity and a sensitivity that the others lack. As his peers accepted the challenge presented in the 1950s by the international reception of the Japanese cinema, so did he, but the relatively minor *Mother* (1952) was the only one of his films then seen in the West. *Floating Clouds*, from Hayashi's novel about life in the immediate postwar period, is perhaps his richest and most compelling film, an example of a director at his most confident working on completely congenial material.

Perhaps an equally successful achievement is *Flowing* (1956), a haunting study of the disillusionments which come to ageing geishas. Unlike his contemporaries, Naruse had not seemed interested in geishas or prostitutes, except as an escape from poverty. His marital dramas looked away from sex, which he seemed to think was more a preoccupation for the young, while many of his women look yearningly at other women, only because they might be preferable to men. Towards the end of his career he was to widen his range, perhaps in response to Ozu's restriction of his own. He took to colour and the wide screen with *Herringbone Clouds* (1958), one of his rare rural dramas, about the break-up of feudal family rules under the pressure of modern times. Thereafter he worked chiefly in monochrome and wide screen, more rewardingly than some of his colleagues, for whom mere prettiness was enough. Some of them were content to turn out tear-jerkers with very popular stars, but while Naruse continued to work with his preferred actress, Hideko Takemine, he did so with a rigour which others could well have emulated. In *When a Woman Ascends the Stairs* (1960) she has a tough time managing a bar in the Ginza, not least because of amorous complications, and in *Yearning* (1964), again widowed, she is running a small grocer's shop in the face of the new competition, thrusting supermarkets. As films, both are schematic (as can happen with ageing directors), but in *Yearning* a passion develops when Takemine refuses to submit to the romantic and sexual demands of her brother-in-law. As he pursues her to a small spa town, Naruse brings to the fore his mastery of the medium (locations, photography, acting, editing), delving into the mysteries and mixed motives of his two protagonists. In the telling a good film has become a great one.

He made only three more films, and the last two, *Hit and Run* (1966) and *Scattered Clouds* (1967), were both thrillers, set among people much more affluent than we had been accustomed to from this director. It is exhilarating to see them, not only for the supremacy of what was for him a new form but because, like all great film-makers, he could surprise his admirers.

—David Shipman

NEGULESCO, Jean.

Romanian. Born in Craiova, 29 February 1900. Educated at Lyceul Carol; studied painting at Academie Julian, Paris, early 1920s. Married Ruth (Dusty) Anderson, 1946. Lived in Paris, attempted to study art, 1914–15; hospital orderly, Romania, following outbreak of war; worked in Art Theatre, Craiova, Romania, 1925–26; exhibited paintings in U.S.A., 1929 (some sources say 1927); assisted in 2nd unit direction on Borzage's *Farewell to Arms*, 1932, continued 2nd unit work at Paramount and Universal, through 1930s; assistant to producer Benjamin Glazer, from 1933; collaborator on scripts, from 1937; director for Warners, from 1944; signed with 20th Century-Fox, 1948; shot *The Heroes* in Iran, 1969; returned to help establish Iranian film industry, early 1970s.

Films as Director:

1940/44　approximately 50 1- and 2-reel films released under Warner Brothers "Melody Masters" series

1941	*Singapore Woman* (co-d, though received d credit)
1944	*The Mask of Dimitrios*; *The Conspirators*
1946	*Three Strangers*; *Nobody Lives Forever*; *Humoresque*
1947	*Deep Valley*
1948	*Johnny Belinda*; *Road House*
1949	*The Forbidden Street*
1950	*Under My Skin*; *Three Came Home*; *The Mudlark*
1951	*Take Care of My Little Girl*
1952	*Phone Call from a Stranger*; *Lydia Bailey*; *Lure of the Wilderness*; "The Last Leaf" episode of *O.Henry's Full House*
1953	*Titanic*; *Scandal at Scourie*; *How to Marry a Millionaire*
1954	*Three Coins in the Fountain*; *A Woman's World*
1955	*Daddy Long Legs*; *The Rain of Ranchipur*
1957	*Boy on a Dolphin*
1958	*The Gift of Love*; *A Certain Smile*
1959	*Count Your Blessings*; *The Best of Everything*
1962	*Jessica*
1964	*The Pleasure Seekers*
1970	*Hello Goodbye*; *The Heroes* (*The Invincible Six*)

Other Films:

1937	*Expensive Husbands* (Connolly) (co-sc); *Fight for Your Lady* (Stoloff) (co-sc)
1938	*Beloved Brat* (Lubin) (story); *Swiss Miss* (Blystone) (co-sc)
1939	*Rio* (Brahm) (story)

Publications:

By NEGULESCO: book—

Things I Did . . . and Things I Think I Did, New York, 1984.

By NEGULESCO: article—

Interview in *The Celluloid Muse*, edited by Charles Higham and Joel Greenberg, London, 1969.

On NEGULESCO: articles—

"Director-Artist," in *Life* (New York), 19 June 1944.
Campion, J., "Jean Negulesco," in *Films in Review* (New York), April 1973; see also R. Braff, August/September 1973.

*　　　*　　　*

Jean Negulesco is a good example of a director whose modest talents were dissipated by the studio system. He was a painter-turned-director who at Warner Brothers during the 1940s exhibited a painter's vision and an ability to handle actors and plot intricacies. Warner Brothers was an autocratic studio which held a tight rein on its directors, a disciplined atmosphere which Negulesco apparently needed. When he moved to the more lenient milieu of 20th Century-Fox in the 1950s, his career immediately descended into one of making sentimental divertissements enhanced only occasionally by exceptional imagery.

It was Negulesco's art work that brought him to Hollywood where he worked on the second unit of Frank Borzage's *A Farewell to Arms* and was hired as assistant to Benjamin Glazer, producer of *The Story of Temple Drake*, after Negulesco had created some sketches depicting Miriam Hopkins's rape scene which were deemed capable of passing the censors for that film version of William Faulkner's controversial *Sanctuary*. He was then hired to direct short subjects at Warner Brothers—mostly ballet and musical shorts—and almost made his feature film debut as the director of *The Maltese Falcon*, but when that assignment was handed to its screenwriter John Huston, Negulesco went on to direct part of a B-picture called *Singapore*. More short subjects followed until he finally got his chance to direct with *The Mask of Dimitrios*, based on Eric Ambler's novel, *The Coffin of Dimitrios*.

That film was a clever and intricate story of a master criminal which teamed Sidney Greenstreet and Peter Lorre and in which, says Negulesco, "I established a sombre, low-key mood that I followed in a number of subsequent films. I learned that

Jean Negulesco

the public loves to share the actor's situation, to be a vicarious part of the action. It's curious that when you see the actors moving and talking in semi-darkness it's always more exciting than seeing them plainly, because you identify with them more."

Negulesco used Greenstreet and Lorre successfully again in *The Conspirators* and in *Three Strangers*, after which he used his exceptional painter's eye, with remarkable results, directing the popular *Humoresque*, a superior woman's picture. Joan Crawford was at her best as the wealthy, sophisticated patron of violinist John Garfield, and Ernest Haller's black and white photography complemented Negulesco's artistic vision.

Johnny Belinda is Negulesco's best film and here too his visual sensibility was evident as he superbly captured the everyday life in a small Nova Scotia town. Jack Warner objected to *Johnny Belinda* as being too preachy and offbeat—it was the story of a deaf mute girl (Jane Wyman) who is raped then murders her rapist—and he shelved the picture and fired Negulesco. By the time it had received 12 Oscar nominations, including one for Best Director, Negulesco had been hired by 20th Century-Fox.

In comparing the two studios, Negulesco described Warners as "a very tough training ground, with schedules which you couldn't exceed by so much as a day"; but, he says, "Fox was much more relaxed."

Unfortunately, despite the apparently comfortable atmosphere, Negulesco's tenure at Fox was one of steady decline. He made the modestly respectable *Three Came Home*, *The Mudlark*, and *Phone Call From a Stranger*, and the above average *Titanic*. But increasingly Negulesco sank from making gripping melodramas to frothy, shallow entertainments which were little more than colorful travelogues in CinemaScope, such as *How to Marry a Millionaire*, which did have a few good Marilyn Monroe moments, and the sugary sudser *Three Coins in the Fountain*. *The Best of Everything* was patent soap opera, and after directing the miniscule *Hello-Goodbye*, Negulesco retired.

—Ronald Bowers

NEILAN, Marshall.

(Known as "Mickey" Neilan.) American. Born in San Bernadino, California, 11 April 1891. Educated one year, Harvard Military Academy, Los Angeles. Married 1) Gertrude Bambrick, 1913 (divorced 1921), one son; 2) Blanche Sweet, 1922 (divorced 1929). Messenger boy for California Fruit Growers Assn., blacksmith's helper, employee of Santa Fe Railway, and boy actor for Belasco Stock Company, Los Angeles, and Barney Bernard Stock Company, San Francisco, 1902–1908; salesman for Simplex Motor Car Co., Los Angeles, and chauffeur to entrepreneur Oliver Morosco, 1908; sometime driver for D.W. Griffith at Biograph, 1909–10 and 1911; began acting at Kalem Studios, Santa Monica, 1911; joined Allan Dwan's company, American (Flying A); hired by Griffith at Biograph, 1913; signed as director for Kalem, also acts for Dwan, 1914; wrote for and starred opposite Mary Pickford, 1915; directed first feature, *The Cycle of Fate*, at Selig Chicago studios, 1916; hired by Samuel Goldwyn as Blanche Sweet's director at Lasky Company, 1917; directed series of Mary Pickford films 1917–18; began directing for First National, 1920; contracted to Goldwyn Company, 1922–24; did some writing and 2nd Unit directing, worked briefly as agent, 1930s; filed for bankruptcy, 1933 (and 1937); on payroll of 20th Century-Fox as writer, World War II. *Died, in Hollywood, 27 October 1958.*

Films as Director (Features):

1916	*The Cycle of Fate*; *The Prince Chap*; *Country That God Forgot*
1917	*Those Without Sin*; *The Bottle Imp*; *Tides of Barnegat*; *The Girl at Home*; *Silent Partner*; *Freckles*; *The Jaguar's Claws*; *Rebecca of Sunnybrook Farm*; *The Little Princess*
1918	*Stella Maris*; *Amarilly of Clothes-Line Alley*; *M'liss*; *Hit-the-Trail Holliday*; *Heart of the Wilds*; *Out of a Clear Sky*
1919	*3 Men and a Girl*; *Daddy-Long-Legs*; *The Unpardonable Sin*; *In Old Kentucky*
1920	*Her Kingdom of Dreams*; *The River's End*; *Don't ever Marry* (co-d); *Go and Get It*; *Dinty* (co-d)
1921	*Bob Hampton of Placer*; *Bits of life* (co-d); *The Lotus Eater*
1922	*Penrod* (co-d); *Fools First*; *Minnie* (co-d); *Stranger's Banquet*
1923	*Eternal Three* (co-d); *The Rendezvous*
1924	*Dorothy Vernon of Haddon Hall*; *Tess of the D'Urbervilles*
1925	*Sporting Venus*; *The Great Love*
1926	*Mike*; *The Skyrocket*; *Wild Oats Lane*; *Diplomacy*; *Everybody's Acting*
1927	*Venus of Venice*; *Her Wild Oats*
1928	*3-Ring Marriage*; *Take Me Home*; *Taxi 13*; *His Last Haul*
1929	*Black Waters*; *The Awful Truth*; *Tanned Legs*; *The Vagabond Lover*
1930	*Sweethearts on Parade*
1934	*Chloe*; *Social Register*; *The Lemon Drop Kid*
1935	*This is the Life*
1937	*Sing While You're Able*; *Swing It, Professor*

Other Films:

From 1911 Numerous supporting then leading roles through late teens
1956   *A Face in the Crowd* (Kazan) (role as Senator Fuller)

Publications:

By NEILAN: articles—

Interviews in *Motion Picture Classic* (Brooklyn), April/May 1920 and December 1921.

On NEILAN: books—

Milne, Peter, *Motion Picture Directing: The Facts and Theories of the Newest Art*, New York, 1922.
Spears, Jack, *Hollywood: The Golden Era*, New York, 1971.

On NEILAN: articles—

Cohn, A.A., "Director 'Mickey'," in *Photoplay* (New York), September 1917.
St. Johns, Adela, in *Photoplay* (New York), March 1923.
Obituary in *New York Times*, 28 October 1958.
Obituary in *Time* (New York), 10 November 1958.
Gribbel, J., "Marshall Neilan," in *Films in Review* (New York), March 1960.
Spears, Jack, "Marshall Neilan," in *Films in Review* (New York), November 1962.
Lewis, K., "Blanche Sweet and Marshall Neilan," in *Films in Review* (New York), June/July 1981.

*   *   *

In the late 1910s, Marshall Neilan was hailed as the "youngest director genius of the industry." Yet, by the coming of sound he was reduced to directing "B" features, and at the age of 46 he was unemployable. His was an extraordinary career, begun out of a zest for the excitement which film directing offered and ended through a drinking problem and a failure to work within the studio system. During the height of his career, Marshall Neilan could afford to insult the studio bosses—he inscribed one photograph with the words, "May you never miss the love that Louis B. Mayer does"—but when his drinking and his volatile temper got the better of him, the industry was happy to forget Neilan's successes and assign him to the depths of ignominy which are reserved for those unable to come to terms with the studio system.

From leading man to the likes of Blanche Sweet (whom he was to marry), Marguerite Clark, Mary Pickford, and Ruth Roland—and Neilan was a handsome leading man—he became one of Hollywood's most talented directors, equally at home with the comedy of *Daddy-Long-Legs*, the pathos of *Stella Maris* and the militaristic propaganda of *The Unpardonable Sin*. Neilan was particularly at ease directing Mary Pickford (whom he directed in seven features), who later said, "I can truthfully say that no director, not even the great D.W. Griffith or Cecil DeMille, could wring the performance from me that Mickey did." As Jack Spears has written, Marshall Neilan was "the boy wonder of Hollywood," a director who could do no wrong as far as the stars, the public or the critics were concerned. All of his films seemed destined to be automatic box-office successes, and all displayed Neilan's remarkable understanding of lighting and emotional audience involvement. Despite his quick temper and apparent private lack of decency (particularly after the ever more frequent bouts of drinking), Neilan was able to come to the set and produce a film of exquisite tenderness and charm.

Through the 1920s Marshall Neilan was able to keep a hold on the medium, directing such major achievements as *Dorothy Vernon of Haddon Hall* and *Tess of the D'Urbervilles*, but the coming of sound found Neilan not only at a low personal ebb (following a divorce from Blanche Sweet), but also apprehensive about the future. He simply destroyed his own career (although *Social Register* illustrates that Neilan could produce a competent and pleasurable little picture), and it was depressing to see this once-great director reduced to playing a small role in Elia Kazan's 1956 *A Face in the Crowd*.

—Anthony Slide

NEMEC, Jan.

Czechoslovakian. Born in Prague, 12 July 1936. Educated at Film Faculty, Academy of Music and Arts (FAMU), Prague, 1955–60. Married 1) Ester Krumbachová (divorced); 2) Marta Kubisová. While at film academy, assistant to directors Vaclav Krska and Martin Frič; co-scripted 2 features, also 5 shorts and 5 mini-musicals for TV, with then wife, 1964–66; after *Martyrs of Love*, blacklisted by Barrandov Studios for political reasons, 1966; filmed entry of Soviet forces into Prague, footage broadcast around the world (later used in both U.S. and Soviet propaganda films), 1968; made only film following Soviet invasion, a short documentary about intensive care unit, Prague, 1972; able to leave Czechoslovakia, worked with Veronika Schamoni in Germany, 1974, then moved to U.S.A. Address: 21607 Rambla Vista, Malibu, California, 90265, U.S.A.

Films as Director:

1960   *Sousto* (*The Loaf. A Loaf of Bread. A Bite to Eat. The Morsel*)
1963   *The Memory of Our Day*
1964   *Demanty noci* (*Diamonds of the Night*) (+ co-sc); "Pdvodnici (The Liars, Impostors)" segment of *Perličky na dně* (*Pearls of the Deep*)

1966   *O slavnosti a hostech* (*The Party and the Guests*. **Report on the Party and the Guests**) (+ co-sc)
1967   *Mučedníci lásky* (*Martyrs of Love*) (+ co-sc); *Mother and Son* (short) (+ co-sc)
1968   *Oratorio for Prague* (*Oratorium for Prague*) (documentary) (+ co-sc)
1972   *Between Three and Five Minutes* (documentary short) (+ co-sc)
1975   *Le Décolleté dans le dos* (+ co-sc); *Metamorphosis* (short) (+ co-sc); *The Czech Connection* (+ co-sc)

Publications:

On NEMEC:

Books:

Skvorecký, Josef, *All the Bright Young Men and Women*, Toronto, 1971.

Liehm, Antonin, *Closely Watched Films*, White Plains, New York, 1974.

Stoil, Michael, *Cinema Beyond the Danube*, Metuchen, New Jersey, 1974.

Liehm, Mira and Antonin, *The Most Important Art*, Berkeley, 1977.

Habova, Milada, and Jitka Vysekalova, editors, *Czechoslovak Cinema*, Prague, 1982.

Hames, Peter, *The Czechoslovak New Wave*, Berkeley, 1982.

*   *   *

Nemec's Czech filmography includes three shorts, three features and a segment of a compilation work. All three features were co-scripted by his then wife, Ester Krumbachová. He reached international fame with the 1968 screening of *The Party and the Guests* at the New York Film Festival, which followed a two-year struggle to screen the film within Czechoslovakia. After completing *The Martyrs of Love* in 1966, Nemec was blacklisted by Barrandov Studios for political reasons and was unable to work in Czechoslovakia. He emigrated to the West in 1974, settling first in Paris, then in Germany, and finally in the United States, but he was unable to re-establish his film career despite the fact that he was one of the foremost talents of the Czech New Wave.

Thematically all of Nemec's films deal with obstacles to human freedom and the ways which men and women cope with these limitations. He has stated, "In *Diamonds of the Night* man is not free as a result of that most external of pressures called war. In *The Party and the Guests*, it is a lack of freedom that people bring on themselves by being willing to enter into any sort of collaborative relationship. In *Martyrs of Love*, it is a matter of a lack of freedom or opportunity to act out one's own folly, one's own madness, or dreams of love and human happiness." Within the context, Nemec is most concerned with the psychological effects of these restrictions.

Stylistically Nemec developed a highly metaphoric cinema utilizing several experimental techniques. He calls this style "dream realism." His works function as political and psychological parables. His first feature *Diamonds of the Night*, based on a novel by Holocaust survivor Arnost Lustig, follows two Jewish boys who jump from a Nazi transport on its way to the concentration camps. As the boys wander through the forest looking for food, time shifts back and forth. There are memories of war-torn Prague, distorted visions of elongated trams, and menacing looks of strangers. The boys hallucinate about falling trees and swarming ants. Eventually they are arrested by the Home Guard, composed of old men more concerned with drinking and singing than with the boys. The film ends ambiguously with the fate of the two still an open question. Jaroslav Kučera's hand-held camera creates tension as the boys scamper like animals or stare subjectively into the impassive faces of their captors.

The Party and the Guests begins with a summer picnic. Sud-

Jan Nemec: *O Slavnosti a hostech*

denly a group of men appear, forcing the picnickers to obey new rules. Next they are feted at an elaborate banquet. Only one man is unwilling to participate in the festivities. At the end, accompanied by a menacing dog, the group set out to capture the non-conformist. Here again are the themes of impersonal group control, conformity, man's indifferences, and the casual use of violence, and Nemec again creates a surreal world where the extraordinary takes on the look of everyday events.

Nemec's last major work, *Martyrs of Love*, is composed of three comic stories about young men in pursuit of romance. Their inability to achieve their goal ultimately turns comedy into sadness. In creating the dream-like world of the film, Nemec used only minimal dialogue. The images are accompanied by a jazzy score, reflecting the passion for American music among young Czechs during the 1960s.

Nemec's short works deal with the same themes developed in his features. His graduation film *The Loaf of Bread*, portrays a group of prisoners who steal a loaf of bread from their Nazi captors. Here Nemec depicts human beings under stress. As he has commented, "I am concerned with man's reactions to the drastic situation in which, through no fault of his own, he may find himself." *Mother and Son*, made in Holland in 1967, deals with the death of a sadistic soldier, who has beaten and executed prisoners. When young boys try to desecrate his grave, his old mother staunchly protects it. The film ironically concludes with the title, "Love between one human being and another is the only important thing in life."

Nemec's contribution to *Pearls from the Deep* is an episode entitled "The Poseurs." Here two senile patients at a private clinic ramble on about their former achievements, despite their failing memories. Nemec's shots of the mortuary, the place where they will ultimately reside, provide a sad and chilling commentary on all human life. Nemec's remaining works are *Metamorphosis*, an adaptation of the Kafka story filmed in Germany in 1957, and *The Czech Connection*, made the same year.

—Patricia Erens

NIBLO, Fred.

American. Born Federico Nobile in York, Nebraska, 6 January 1874. Married Josephine Cohan (died 1916); one son; 2) actress Enid Bennett, 1917, three children. Vaudeville performer, blackface monologuist, through 1907; shot travelogues on round-the-world cruise, 1907; company manager and actor for George M. Cohan and Sam Harris; took American repertory company to Australia, 1912–15; directed film for Australian theatrical company J.C. Williamson, 1915;

Fred Niblo with his wife Enid Bennett

joined Ince company, Hollywood, 1918; co-founder, Academy of Motion Picture Arts and Sciences, 1928. *Died, in New Orleans, 11 November 1948.*

Films as Director:

1915 *Get-Rich-Quick Wallingford* (+ role)
1918 *Coals of Fire*; *The Marriage Ring*; *When Do We Eat?*; *A Desert Wooing*; *Fuss and Feathers*
1919 *Happy Though Married*; *The Haunted Bedroom*; *Partners Three*; *The Virtuous Thief*; *Stepping Out*; *What Every Woman Learns*
1920 *The Woman in the Suitcase*; *The False Road*; *Her Husband's Friend*; *Dangerous Hours*; *Sex*; *Hairpins*; *The Mark of Zorro*
1921 *Silk Hosiery*; *Mother o' Mine*; *Greater than Love*; *The Three Musketeers*
1922 *The Woman He Married*; *Rose o' the Sea*; *Blood and Sand*
1923 *The Famous Mrs. Fair*; *Strangers of the Night* (+ co-pr)
1924 *Thy Name Is Woman*; *The Red Lily* (+ story)
1926 **Ben-Hur**; *The Temptress*
1927 *Camille* (+ pr); *The Devil Dancer* (+ pr)
1928 *The Enemy* (+ pr); *Two Lovers* (+ pr); *The Mysterious Lady*; *Dream of Love*
1930 *Redemption* (+ pr); *Way Out West*
1931 *Donovan's Kid*; *The Big Gamble*
1932 *Two White Arms*; *Diamond Cut Diamond* (co-d); *Blame the Woman*

Other Films:

1915 *Officer 666* (role)
1930 *Free and Easy* (Sedgwick) (role)
1940 *Ellery Queen, Master Detective* (Bellamy) (role); *I'm Still Alive* (role)
1941 *Life with Henry* (Reed) (role)
1944 *Four Jills in a Jeep* (Seiter) (co-sc)

Publications:

By NIBLO: articles—

Interview with M. Cheatham, in *Motion Picture Classic* (Brooklyn), July 1920.
"Sketch," with K. McGaffey, in *Motion Picture Classic* (Brooklyn), October 1921.
"The Filming of *Ben Hur*," interview with R. Wharton, in *Classic Film/Video Images* (Indiana, Pennsylvania), Winter 1978.

On NIBLO: book—

Brownlow, Kevin, *The Parade's Gone By*, New York, 1968.

On NIBLO: articles—

Obituary, in *The New York Times*, 12 November 1948.
Obituary, in *Variety* (New York), 12 November 1948.
Route, W.D., "Buried Directors," in *Focus* (Chicago), Spring 1972.

*   *   *

Fred Niblo directed some of the most legendary stars of the 1920s, in some of that decade's biggest films: *Blood and Sand* (with Valentino); *The Mark of Zorro* and *The Three Musketeers* (Fairbanks); and *Ben Hur*. He guided Garbo through *The Temptress* (replacing her mentor, Mauritz Stiller) and *The Mysterious Lady*. He worked with Lillian Gish, Ronald Colman and Conrad Nagel, Lionel Barrymore, Vilma Banky and Norma Talmadge.

Valentino, Fairbanks, and Garbo first come to mind at the mention of their films with Niblo. The other actors' best work was done elsewhere, for other more rightfully distinguished filmmakers. Niblo's one distinction is his credit on *Ben Hur*, the cinema's first real super-spectacle. *Ben Hur* is the *Cleopatra* of its day, a boondoggle that ran way over budget and took two years to complete. It was begun by the Goldwyn Company, and passed along when Goldwyn, Loew's Metro, and Louis B. Mayer joined together to form Metro-Goldwyn Mayer. *Ben Hur* was initially shot on location in Italy. The dissatisfied studio ordered a revised script. Ramon Novarro replaced George Walsh in the title role and Niblo, the choice of Mayer and Irving Thalberg, took over for Charles Brabin. The Coliseum was rebuilt several blocks from the MGM lot; inside the studio, Roman galleys floated inside a large tank. Eventually, the budget climbed to $3-million—perhaps even higher—with over one million feet of film shot.

Niblo not so much directed as coordinated *Ben Hur*, and the result was all effect and no drama. Sometimes the film is confusing, and even tiring, yet it is also at its best thrilling. The image of Navarro and Francis X. Bushman (as Messala) racing their chariots remains one of the best-recalled of the silent era. This sequence is supposed to have influenced the staging of the same one in William Wyler's far superior remake.

Ultimately, Niblo's career is more a case of luck than any inherent talent or aesthetic vision. In 1917, he married Enid Bennett, who worked for Thomas Ince; the following year, he began making films for Ince. Later, Niblo was hired by Mayer, who liked him and brought him along to MGM. Niblo's career as an A-film director did not last many years past *Ben Hur*. He made only a handful of films during the 1930s, even working in Britain before retiring in 1941. In his later years, he took small roles in films—he had commenced his career as an actor, in vaudeville, on tour and Broadway—and was employed as a radio commentator and master of ceremonies.

Before *Don Juan*, *The Jazz Singer*, and the demise of silent movies, Niblo made some intriguing prognostications. He foresaw the advent of sound, declaring that motion picture music would be synchronized by radio to replace the live piano; subtitles would be synchronized and broadcast in the same way, in the actual voices of the actors. He predicted the wide use of color cinematography, and three-dimensional screens to prevent distortion, and theaters specializing in children's films.

While Niblo may be at best called a decent technician, he was far more adept with a crystal ball than in a director's chair.

—Rob Edelman

NICHOLS, Mike.

American. Born Michael Igor Peschkowsky in Berlin, 6 November 1931; became U.S. citizen, 1944. Educated at University of Chicago, 1950–53; studied acting with Lee Strasberg, 1954. Married 1) Patricia Scott, 1957 (divorced), one daughter; 2) Margot Callas, 1974 (divorced); 3) Annabel (Nichols), two children. Member of Compass Players improvisational theatre group, Chicago, 1955–57; Partnership with Elaine May, 1957–61; director on Broadway, from 1963; produced *The Family* for TV, 1976. Recipient: 5 Tony Awards; Oscar for Best Direction, for *The Graduate*, 1968. Office: c/o Marvin B. Meyer, Rosenfeld, Meyer and Sussman, 9601 Wilshire Blvd., Beverly Hills, CA 90210, U.S.A.

Films as Director:

1966	*Who's Afraid of Virginia Woolf?*
1967	***The Graduate***
1970	*Catch-22*
1971	*Carnal Knowledge* (+ pr)
1973	*The Day of the Dolphin*
1975	*The Fortune* (+ co-pr)
1983	*Silkwood*
1986	*Heartburn* (+ pr)
1988	*Biloxi Blues*; *Working Girl*
1990	*Postcards from the Edge*

Publications:

By NICHOLS: articles—

Interview with Barry Davy, in *Films and Filming* (London), November 1968.
Interview with Lillian Hellman, in *New York Times*, 9 August 1970.
Interview in *The Film Director as Superstar*, by Joseph Gelmis, New York, 1971.
Interview with D. Kennedy, in *Listener* (London), 16 March 1989.
Interview with Richard Combs, in *Sight and Sound* (London), Spring 1989.

On NICHOLS: books—

Kiley, Frederick, and Walter McDonald, editors, *A "Catch-22" Casebook*, New York, 1973.
Schuth, H. Wayne, *Mike Nichols*, Boston, 1978.

On NICHOLS: articles—

Rice, Robert, "A Tilted Insight," in *New Yorker*, 15 April 1961.
Bart, Peter, "Mike Nichols, Moviemaniac," in *New York Times*, 1 July 1967.
Lightman, Herb, "On Location with *Carnal Knowledge*," in *American Cinematographer* (Los Angeles), January 1971.
Brown, John, "Pictures of Innocence," in *Sight and Sound* (London), Spring 1972.
Rich, Frank, "The Misfortune of Mike Nichols: Notes on the Making of a Bad Film," in *New York Times*, 11 July 1975.
Sarris, Andrew, "After *The Graduate*," in *American Film* (Washington, D.C.), July/August 1978.
Fieschi, J., "Hollywood 79: Mike Nichols," in *Cinématographe* (Paris), March 1979.
Combs, Richard, "Mike Nichols: Comedy in Four Unnatural Acts," in *Monthly Film Bulletin* (London), May 1989.

* * *

The films of Mike Nichols are guided by an eye and ear of a satirist whose professional gifts emerge from a style of liberal, improvisational comedy that originated in a Chicago theater club and developed into a performing partnership with Elaine May in the late 1950s and early 1960s. In clubs and recordings, on radio, television and Broadway, Nichols and May routines gnawed hilariously close to the bone. Aimed at literate, self-aware audiences, their skits (anticipating key elements of Nichols's films) gleefully anatomized men and women dueling in post-Freudian combat, by turns straying from the marriage bond and clinging to it for dear life.

Before directing *Who's Afraid of Virginia Woolf?* for the screen in 1966, Nichols earned a reputation as a skillful Broad-

Mike Nichols

way director with particular flair for devising innovative stage business and eliciting unusually polished performances from his casts. That sure theatrical sense, honed by his subsequent direction of Broadway plays by writers as diverse as Neil Simon, Anton Chekhov, Lillian Hellman, David Rabe, and Tom Stoppard, combines in his best films with the sardonic attitude toward American life underlying even the gentlest of his collaborations with Elaine May.

Nichols's major films begin as comedies and evolve into mordant, generically ambiguous dissections of the American psyche. Their central characters exist in isolation from the landscapes they inhabit, manufacturing illusions to shield themselves against reality (George and Martha in *Virginia Woolf*, Sandy and Jonathan in *Carnal Knowledge*) or fleeing with mounting desperation societies whose values they alone perceive as neurotic (Benjamin in *The Graduate*) or murderous (Yossarian in *Catch-22*).

Martha and George, Edward Albee's Strindbergian couple, flail at each other on their New England campus and reveal a tormented relationship that concludes with a glimmer of hope but seems nevertheless to imply the futility of monogamy, a view reenforced by *Carnal Knowledge* and *The Graduate*. Until he dates Elaine Robinson, Ben Braddock is segregated by script and camera from the company of friends: in a packed airplane, on the Berkeley campus teeming with students, surrounded by his parents' partying guests, Ben is alone. His detachment, italicized by numerous shots within the film, permits him to function as the funnel for *The Graduate's* social satire. In this respect he is Nichols's surrogate but the director complicates the viewer's empathetic response to Ben by scrutinizing him rather as an experimenting scientist scrutinizes a mouse darting about a maze, especially as he scampers in frantic pursuit of Elaine.

In Dustin Hoffman's memorable screen debut, Ben became the moralistic spokesman for a generation that mistrusted anyone over thirty and vowed never to go into plastics. But like other Nichols heroes Ben is himself more than a little crazy, the inevitable child of a Southern California lifestyle that leads him to anticipate instant gratification. Nichols, moreover, intentionally undermines the comic resolution toward which the film has been heading through ambivalent shots of Ben and Elaine on their departing bus, implicating them in mutual recognition of a colossal mistake. At film's end, Ben Braddock still has considerable cause to be "worried about [his] future."

For Yossarian, worrying about the future means literally staying alive. To survive a catch-22 universe he must behave like a lunatic but the more bizarrely he acts the more sanely is he regarded according to the military chop-logic that drives him toward madness. In *Catch-22* time is fractured (in Buck Henry's screenplay) to retain the basic storytelling method of Joseph Heller's novel. Flashbacks occur within flashbacks. Conversations are inaudible (as in the opening scene), incidents only partially revealed (as in the first Snowden se-

quences), to be played later in the film with deleted elements restored.

Fond of foreground shooting, long takes and distorting close-ups to intensify the sense of his characters' entrapment, Nichols also frequently employs overlapping sound and a spare, modernistic mise-en-scène (the latter at times reminiscent of Antonioni) to convey an aura of disorientation and sterility. In the underpraised and misunderstood *Carnal Knowledge*, Nichols uses whiteouts (also prominent in *Catch-22*) and Bergmanesque talking heads as structural and thematic devices to increase the viewer's alienation from the two central characters and to ridicule notions of male sexual fantasy at the core of the film. Visually and textually (in Jules Feiffer's original screenplay) Jonathan and Sandy are the most isolated and self-deluded of Nichols's characters.

Things are seldom what they initially seem in this director's work. Like Nick and Honey, misled by George and Martha's pretense of hospitality in *Who's Afraid of Virginia Woolf?*, the viewer is easily duped by a deceptively comic tone, enticing visual stylization, and innovative storytelling technique into misreading the bleak vision that the films usually harbor. Even *The Fortune*, a farce in the screwball tradition, hinges on the attempted murder by the film's two heroes of its heroine, whose fate hangs in the balance at the final fadeout.

Nichols directs literate, intelligent scripts that pull few punches in their delineations of sexual subjects (*Virginia Woolf, The Graduate, Carnal Knowledge*) and political ones (*Catch-22, Day of the Dolphin, Silkwood*). The same production designer (Richard Sylbert) and editor (Sam O'Steen) worked on the six films from *Virginia Woolf* to *The Fortune*, contributing substantially to a developing visual style and pace. While *The Graduate* continues to be regarded as an American classic, Nichols is sometimes undervalued for his film work because he prefers the New York theater and because his contributions to his pictures are periodically credited to their writers' screenplays (Buck Henry, Jules Feiffer) or their theatrical and literary sources (Edward Albee, Joseph Heller, Charles Webb). But Nichols is very much the auteur who works intimately with his collaborators on all aspects of his films, principally the writing.

The films uphold Nichols's original reputation as a gifted director of actors: Hoffman in *The Graduate*, Elizabeth Taylor and Richard Burton in *Who's Afraid of Virginia Woolf?*, Jack Nicholson, Ann-Margret, and Art Garfunkel in *Carnal Knowledge*, Alan Arkin in *Catch-22*, Meryl Streep in *Silkwood*. They also reveal, even in their intermittent self-indulgence, a director of prodigious versatility and insight.

—Mark W. Estrin

OLCOTT, Sidney.

American. Born John Sidney Alcott in Toronto, 20 January 1874. Married actress Valerie Grant. Actor in New York, from early 1890s; actor in short films for American Mutoscope and Biograph, then assistant at Biograph, 1904–06; director for newly-formed Kalem company, New Jersey, from 1907; Kalem moved to Jacksonville, Florida, 1908; directed first American film shot on location outside U.S.A., in Ireland, 1910; also shot in England, Germany, North Africa and Palestine; resigned from Kalem and formed independent company, G.G. Feature Players with actress and scenarist Gene Gauntier in Jacksonville, 1912; produced series of films in Ireland, 1914; signed with Famous Players, 1915. *Died in Hollywood, 16 December 1949.*

Films as Director:
(also edited early films and acted in many of them)

1907   *The Sleigh Bells* (+ sc); *Ben Hur* (+ sc); *The Scarlet Letter* (+ sc)

1908   *Washington at Valley Forge* (+ sc); *A Florida Feud* (*Florida Crackers*) (+ sc); *Dr. Jekyll and Mr. Hyde* (+ sc); *The Wooing of Miles Standish* (+ sc)

1909   *The Escape from Andersonville* (+ sc); *The Factory Girl* (+ sc); *The Tomboy* (+ sc); *The Queen of the Quarry* (+ sc); *Out of Work* (+ sc); *The Pay Car* (+ sc); *Hiram's Bride* (+ sc); *The Conspirators* (+ sc); *The Winning Boat* (+ sc); *The Mystery of the Sleeper Trunk* (+ sc); *The Hand Organ Man* (+ sc); *The Girl Scout* (+ sc); *The Cattle Thieves* (+ sc); *The Man and the Girl* (+ sc); *A Brother's Wrong* (+ sc); *Dora* (+ sc); *The Governor's Daughter* (+ sc); *The Rally Round the Flag* (+ sc); *The Geisha Who Saved Japan* (+ sc); *The Law of the Mountains* (+ sc); *Her Indian Hero* (+ sc); *The Cardboard Baby* (+ sc)

1910   *The Lad from Old Ireland* (+ sc); *The Feud* (+ sc); *Further Adventures of the Girl Spy* (+ sc); *The Priest of Wilderness* (+ sc); *Hannah Dusten* (+ sc); *The Sacred Turquoise of the Zuni* (+ sc); *The Forager* (+ sc); *The Bravest Girl in the South* (+ sc); *The Love Romance of the Girl Spy* (+ sc); *The Aigrette Hunter* (*The Egret Hunt*) (+ sc); *The Stranger* (+ sc); *The Seminole Halfbreed* (+ sc); *Her Soldier Sweetheart* (+ sc); *The Canadian Moonshiners* (+ sc); *For a Woman's Honor* (+ sc); *Up the Thames to Westminster* (doc) (+ sc); *The Little Spreewald Maiden* (+ sc); *The Indian Mother* (+ sc); *Seth's Temptation* (+ sc); *A Romance of Old Erin* (+ sc); *The Girl Spy Before Vicksburg* (+ sc)

1911   *Rory O'Moore* (+ sc); *Arrah-na-Pogue* (+ sc); *The Colleen Bawn* (+ sc); *You Remember Ellen?* (+ sc); *The Sister* (+ sc); *Grandmother's War Story* (+ sc); *The Irish Honeymoon* (+ sc); *Her Chum's Brother* (+ sc); *In Old Florida* (+ sc); *The Carnival* (+ sc); *Tangled Lives* (+ sc); *To the Aid of Stonewall Jackson* (+ sc); *The Little Soldier of '64* (+ sc); *The Seminole's Vengeance* (+ sc); *Hunted Through the Everglades* (+ sc); *When the Dead Return* (+ sc); *The*

Fishermaid of Bally David (+ sc); *Sailor Jack's Reformation* (+ sc); *Little Sister* (+ sc); *The Fiddle's Requiem* (+ sc); *In Blossom Time* (+ sc)

1912   *From the Manger to the Cross* (+ sc); *An Irish Girl's Love* (+ sc); *Missionaries in Darkest Africa* (doc) (+ sc); *Driving Home the Cows* (+ sc); *The O'Kalems' Visit to Killarney* (doc) (+ sc); *His Mother* (+ sc); *The Vagabonds* (+ sc); *The Kalemites Visit Gibralter* (doc) (+ sc); *The Fighting Dervishes* (+ sc); *Egypt* (doc) (+ sc); *Captured by Bedouins* (+ sc); *Tragedy of the Desert* (+ sc); *Egypt the Mysterious* (doc) (+ sc); *Making Photoplays in Egypt* (doc) (+ sc); *An Arabian Tragedy* (+ sc); *Winning a Widow* (+ sc); *A Prisoner of the Harem* (+ sc); *Egyptian Sports* (doc) (+ sc); *Easter Celebration at Jerusalem* (doc) (+ sc); *Palestine* (doc); *From Jerusalem to the Dead Sea* (doc) (+ sc); *Ancient Temples of Egypt* (doc) (+ sc); *A Day in Jerusalem* (doc) (+ sc); *Along the River Nile* (doc) (+ sc); *The Kerry Gow* (+ sc); *The Major from Ireland* (+ sc); *Conway the Kerry Dancer* (+ sc); *Ireland the Oppressed* (+ sc); *The Shaughraun* (+ sc)

1913   *The Wives of Jamestown* (+ sc); *Lady Peggy's Escape* (+ sc); *A Daughter of the Confederacy* (+ sc); *The Mystery of Pine Tree Camp* (+ sc); *In the Power of the Ku-Klux-Klan* (+ sc); *The Little Rebel* (+ sc)

1914   *When Men Would Kill*; *The Eye of the Government*; *Come Back to Erin*; *The Brute*; *A Mother of Men*; *Tricking the Government*; *The Moth and the Flame*

1915   *The Melting Plot*; *The Irish in America*; *All for Old Ireland*; *Bold Emmett*; *Ireland's Martyr* (+ sc); *Nan o' the Backwoods* (+ sc); *The Ghost of the Twisted Oaks*; *The Taint*; *Madame Butterfly*; *Seven Sisters*

1916   *The Innocent Lie*; *Poor Little Peppina*; *The Daughter of MacGregor*; *My Lady Incog*; *Jean o' the Heather*

1918   *The Belgian*

1919   *A Marriage for Convenience*

1920   *Scratch My Back*

1921   *The Right Way* (+ pr); *Pardon My French*; *God's Country and the Law*

1922   *Timothy's Quest*

1923   *The Green Goddess*; *Little Old New York*

1924   *Monsieur Beaucaire*; *The Humming Bird*; *The Only Woman*

1925   *The Charmer*; *Not So Long Ago*; *Salome of the Tenements*; *The Best People*

1926   *Ranson's Folly*; *The White Black Sheep*; *The Amateur Gentleman*

1927   *The Claw*

Publications:
By OLCOTT: article—

"Blazing a Trail in the Movies," an interview with P. Gaddis, in *Photoplay* (New York), September 1914.

On OLCOTT: articles—

Obituary, in the *New York Times*, 18 December 1949.
Obituary, in *Time* (New York), 26 December 1949.

Conluain, Proinsias, "Ireland's First Films," in *Sight and Sound* (London), October/December 1953.

Mitchell, George, "Sidney Olcott," in *Films in Review* (New York), April 1954 (also letter from G. Geltzer, May 1954, and Mitchell reply June/July 1954).

*   *   *

A pioneer in location shooting, Olcott was the first director of the Kalem Company and a filmmaker of taste and refinement whose work continued successfully into the 1920s. From being newspaper boy and touring actor he moved to the Biograph Company of New York, departing from this organization with Frank Marion to direct for Kalem their first film *The Sleigh Bells*. His production of the first *Ben Hur* led to the first check on film piracy when the film was declared in breach of copyright and Kalem had to pay heavy indemnities. Olcott continued to direct many films in the New York and Florida Kalem studios, often acting in his films and using the scripting and acting talents of Miss Gene Gauntier. With her and George Hollister, the cameraman, he visited the land of his fathers in 1910, making his first Irish film, *The Lad From Old Ireland*. The plot was stereotypical: Irish peasant boy makes good in America and returns in time to save his boyhood sweetheart from eviction. But Olcott was observing the Irish at first hand and he returned to Beaufort, Killarney, to the home of Annie O'Sullivan which became his headquarters for four summers to come. He filmed patriotic dramas which led to conflict with the British authorities in Ireland and indeed he was denounced on another level from the local pulpit as the director of "these painted actors desecrating the homes of our ancestors." He filmed the popular dramas of Dion Boucicault, *The Colleen Bawn, Arrah-na-Pogue,* and *The Shaughraun.* With his company of players he also travelled to Egypt and Palestine where his *From the Manger to the Cross* was filmed. The depiction of sacred figures of the New Testament led to violent controversy, one Irish newspaper denouncing it as "American simony at its worst." After he and Miss Gauntier left Kalem they returned again to Killarney in 1913, and in 1914 Olcott returned with his wife, Valentine Grant. The outbreak of war put an end to his plans for building a film studio in Killarney.

His *The Belgian* was much admired and touched directly on the war. Before this, however, he directed Mary Pickford in two films. *Madame Butterfly* did not run smoothly and star clashed with director on interpretation. Olcott demanded oriental restraint while Pickford wanted girlish high spirits. The presence of Marshall Neilan as Pinkerton did not make for harmony either. One recalls that Miss Pickford also clashed with Lubitsch in a similar matter. *Poor Little Peppina,* which followed, found a more docile Pickford. Olcott's recognized talent as a director brought him the opportunity to direct many of Hollywood's leading players of the 1920s, notably George Arliss (*The Green Goddess*), Marion Davies (*Little Old New York*), Valentino (*Monsieur Beaucaire*), Gloria Swanson, Pola Negri and Richard Barthelmess. Relying less on star appeal, he made some other films which revealed his own talents such as *Scratch My Back, Timothy's Quest,* and *The Right Way.* In 1927 he directed his last film *The Claw.* A plan to film in England came to nothing as Olcott refused to direct a subject he considered to glorify crime.

He lived on to 1949 and died at the home of his old-time friend, Robert Vignola, with whom he lived after the death of his wife. He was a great-hearted man, demanding in his pursuit of perfection, hypnotic in his control of actors, and tasteful in his film presentations.

—Liam O'Leary

OLIVEIRA, Manoel de.

Portuguese. Born Manoel Cândido Pinto de Oliveira in Oporto, 10 December 1908. Married Maria Isabel Carvalhais, 1940, four children. Athlete and racing car driver, 1920–27; directed first film, 1929, then returned to sporting activities, 1930s; directed first feature, *Aniki-Bóbó,* 1941; unable to make films, worked in agriculture, 1943–1971; full-time filmmaker, from 1972.

Films as Director:

1931   *Douro, faina fluvial* (*Hard Labor on the River Douro*) (short) (+ pr, sc, ed)
1939   *Miramar praia das rosas* (short) (+ pr, sc, ed); *Ja se fabricam automovels em Portugal* (short) (+ pr, sc, ed)
1940   *Famalicão* (short) (+ pr, sc, ed)
1942   *Aniki-Bóbó* (+ sc)
1956   *O pintor e a cidade* (*The Painter and the Town*) (+ pr, sc, ed, ph)
1959   *O pão* (*Bread*) (+ ed, ph, sc)
1960   *O coracão* (*The Heart*) (short) (+ sc)
1963   *Acto da primavera* (*The Passion of Jesus*) (+ pr, ed, ph, sc); *A caça* (*The Hunt*) (+ ph, ed, sc)
1965   *As pinturas de meu irmão Júlio* (*Pictures of My Brother Julio*) (short) (+ pr, ph, ed)
1972   *O passado e o presente* (*Past and Present*) (+ co-pr, ed)
1975   *Benilde ou a Virgem Mãe* (*Benilde: Virgin and Mother*) (+ ed)
1978   *Amor de perdicão* (**Doomed Love**) (+ sc)
1981   *Francisca*
1982   *Memórias e confissoes* (*Memories and Confessions*) (to be released only after de Oliveira's death)
1983   *Lisboa Cultural* (*Cultural Lisbon*)
1984   *Nice à propos de Jean Vigo*
1985   *O Sapato de cetim* (*Le Soulier de satin. The Satin Slipper*) (+ sc)
1986   *O Meu Caso—Repeticoes* (*Mon Cas*) (+ sc)
1988   *Os Canibais* (*The Cannibals*); *A Bandeira Nacional* (*The National Flag*) (doc short)
1990   *Não ou a Vã Glória de Mandar* (*Non or the Vain Glory of Command*) (+ sc, ed)

Other Films:

1933   *A Canção de Lisboa* (Telmo) (role)

Publications:

By OLIVEIRA: book—

Aniki-Bóbó, Porto, 1963.

By OLIVEIRA: articles—

"O cinema e o capital," in *Movimento* (Lisbon), October 1933.
Interview with Paulo Rocha, in *Critica* (Lisbon), March 1972.
Interview with João Botelho and Cabral Martins, in *M* (Lisbon), August/September 1975.
"A propos de Benilde ou a Virgem-Mãe," in *Image et Son* (Paris), February 1977.
"Los Paisajes pintados," an interview with F. Llináa and S. Zunzunegui, in *Contracampo* (Madrid), January 1981.
Interview with Richard Peña, in *Journal of Film and Video* (Carbondale, Illinois), Summer 1983.
Interview with Charles Tesson and others, in *Cahiers du Cinéma* (Paris), January 1986.

On OLIVEIRA: books—

Manoel de Oliveira, Ciné-Club of Estremoz, 1955.
Manoel de Oliveira, with "Diálogo com Manoel de Oliveira," Cinemateca Portuguesa, Lisbon, 1981.

França, J.A., L. Pina, and A. Costa, *Introdução à obra de Manoel de Oliveira*, Lisbon, 1982.

Passek, Jean-Loup, *Le cinéma portugais*, Paris, 1982.

Lardeau, Yann, *Manoel de Oliveira*, Paris, 1988.

On OLIVEIRA: articles—

Demeure, Jacques, "Manoel de Oliveira," in *Positif* (Paris), no. 25–26, 1957.

Biette, J.C., "Notes sur l'oeuvre de Manoel de Oliveira," in *Cahiers du Cinéma* (Paris), February 1966.

Daney, Serge, "Notes sur les films de Manuel de Oliveira," in *Cahiers du Cinéma* (Paris), May 1977.

Magny, J., "Dossier-auteur Manoel de Oliveira," in *Cinéma* (Paris), March 1980.

Gillett, John, "Manoel de Oliveira," in *Sight and Sound* (London), Summer 1981.

Fonseca, M.S., "Manoel de Oliveira, o cinema e a crueldade," in *Expresso* (Lisbon), October 1981.

Lehmann, I., "Die Tetralogie der 'amours frustrés.' Zu Manoel de Oliveiras Filmen über Liebe und Tod," in *Frauen und Film* (Berlin), February 1982.

*   *   *

Simultaneously rugged and tender, the tortured work of Manoel de Oliveira, in which a personal vision is transformed into a unique expression of Portuguese culture, finds its only counterpart in that of Carl Th. Dreyer. The radical aesthetic and ethical programs of both filmmakers met with incomprehension; in both, one finds a tragic fusion of profane desire and an aspiration toward the sacred.

No man is a prophet in his own country; Oliveira, an artist of magnitude disproportionate to such a diminutive nation, confirms this aphorism. He found no favor under the Salazar regime, being condemned by its pettiness to silence and inactivity. Persecution did not cease with the death of the dictator. Oliveira continued to be charged with "not being natural" and was accused of the sin of "elitism." This is the reason there are so many films that Oliveira *did not* make. Only relatively late in his career did international acclaim force a measure of national recognition.

The first phase of Oliveira's work, what he calls "the stage of the people," is dominated by an intense dialogue between documentary and fiction. From the very beginning Oliveira had refused to subjugate himself to the "genres" and "schools." An unmistakable movement toward fiction, toward the autonomy of the cinema vis à vis *the real*, can be seen in his documentaries from *Douro* to *Pinturas*. In registering its images, Oliveira's camera approaches quotidien reality as a stage. Through montage, the world can be fixed, cut, and reproduced as a series of fragments.

The second phase begins in 1972 and is characterized by a more complete expression of the impulse towards fiction. There is a concomitant change of objectives: the "stage of the people" is replaced by the "stage of the bourgeoisie." This phase comprises four films, from *O Passado e o presente* to *Francisca*, known as the "Tetralogy of Frustrated Loves." Alluringly romantic, possessed in particular by the love of perdition as expressed in the Portuguese literature of the time, these films attain an aesthetic refinement unsurpassed in European cinema.

In the 1930s Oliveira belonged to the cinematic vanguard. From 1940 to 1963 this cinematic craftsman anticipated many of the innovative aesthetic experiments of later filmmakers—from Italian neorealism to the cinema of Straub—without reducing his work to mere formalism. With the "Tetralogy," a risky and original project makes its appearance: the destruction of the narrative grammar which relies on the shot/countershot, and the destruction of psychological correspondences through the creation, in these films, of a "point

of view belonging to no one." Refusing to identify itself with either the characters or the spectator, the camera alters spatial relationships in an effort not exactly to neutralize itself, but to situate itself in a space without a subject in order to fix faces and voices. "Voices" because, being films adapted from literary works, they resolutely assume the literary nature of the *text*, to which long and fixed shots or the repetition of such shots confer a temporality without parallel in the history of the cinema. The obsessive use of the studio is also underscored, reenforcing a sense of enclosure and restriction. A similar emphasis is placed on the style or *representation* which situates actors and objects on the same level; their function is simply to be present.

Linking this formal experimentation with undeniably vigorous fiction, *Francisca* is Oliveira's masterpiece. In *Francisca*, a grandiose synthesis of literary, musical, and pictorial materials, a tellurian identification is revealed which is the origin of desire, fear, guilt, and perdition—the principle themes of Oliveira. After all, such an identification echoes an entire culture which, at its best, transcends a tormented pessimism and bitter irony, though it retains only the consolation of melancholy. This culture is Portuguese and Oliveira is its filmmaker.

—Manuel Dos Santos Fonseca

OLMI, Ermanno.

Italian. Born in Bergamo, 24 July 1931. Attended Accadémia d'Arte Drammatica, Milan. Married Loredana Detto, three children. Worked for electric company, Edisonvolta S.p.A., Milan, from 1949; director and supervisor of over 40 shorts and documentaries for, or sponsored by, Edisonvolta, 1952–61; directed first feature, semi-documentary *Il tempo si è fermato*, 1959; formed production company "22 December S.p.A." with Tullio Kezich and others, 1961; TV director, from 1964.

Films as Director:

1953   *La digi sul ghiaccio* (short/doc) (+ spvr)
1954   *La pattuglia di passo San Giacomo* (short/doc) (+ spvr)
1955   *Società Ovesticino-Dinamo* (short/doc) (+ spvr); *Cantiere d'inverno* (short/doc) (+ spvr); *La mia valle* (short/doc) (+ spvr); *L'onda* (short/doc) (+ spvr); *Buongiorno natura* (short/doc) (+ spvr)
1956   *Michelino la B* (short/doc) (+ spvr); *Construzione meccaniche riva* (short/doc) (+ spvr)
1958   *Tre fili fino a Milano* (short/doc) (+ spvr); *Giochi di Colonia* (short/doc) (+ spvr); *Venezia città minore* (short/doc) (+ spvr)
1959   *Il tempo si è fermato* (*Time Has Stopped. Time Stood Still*) (+ sc, spvr)
1960   *Il grande paese d'Acciaio* (short/doc) (+ spvr)
1961   *Le grand barrage* (short/doc) (+ spvr); *Un metro lungo cinque* (short/doc) (+ spvr); *Il posto* (**The Sound of Trumpets. The Job**) (+ sc)
1963   *I fidanzati* (*The Fiancés. The Engagement*) (+ pr, sc)
1965   *. . . e venne un uomo* (*A Man Called John. And There Came a Man*) (+ co-sc)
1968   *Un certo giorno* (*One Fine Day* (+ sc, ed)
1969   *I recuperanti* (*The Scavengers*) (+ co-sc, ph) (for TV); *Un certo giorno* (*One Fine Day*) (+ sc)
1971   *Durante l'estate* (*During the Summer. In the Summertime*) (+ co-sc, ph, ed) (for TV)
1974   *La circostanza* (*The Circumstance* (+ pr, sc, ph, ed) (for TV)

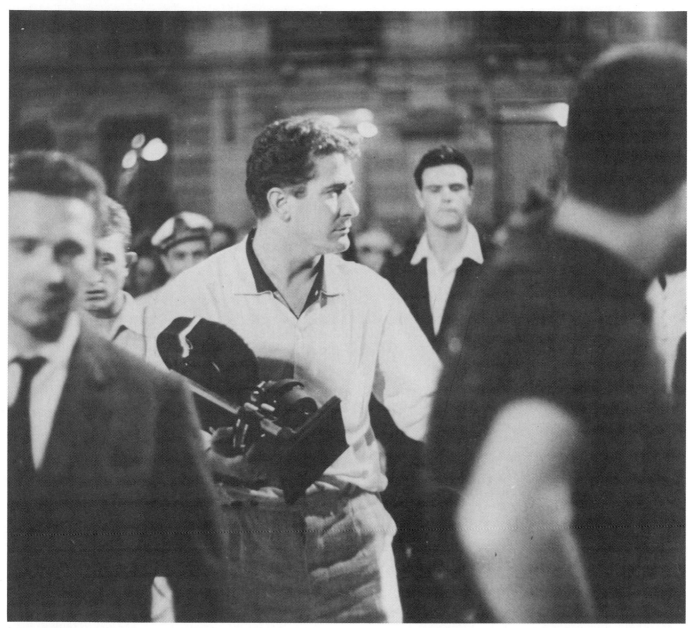

Ermanno Olmi

1978   *L'albero degli zoccoli* (**The Tree of the Wooden Clogs**) (+ sc, ph, ed)
1983   *Cammina, cammina* (*Keep Walking*)
1984   *Milano '83* (doc)
1987   *Lunga Vita alla Signora* (*Long Live the Lady!*) (+ sc, co-ph)
1988   *La leggenda del santo bevitore* (*The Legend of the Holy Drinker*)

Other Films:

1955   *La tesatura meccanica della linea a 220.000 volt* (short/doc) (spvr); *San Massenza* (*Cimego*) (short/doc) (spvr)
1956   *Pantano d'avio* (short/doc) (spvr); *Peru—Istituto de Verano* (short/doc) (spvr); *Fertilizzanti complessi* (short/doc) (spvr)
1957   *Fibre e civilta* (short/doc) (spvr); *Progresso in agricoltura* (short/doc) (spvr); *Campi sperimentali* (short/doc) (spvr)
1958   *Colonie Sicedison* (short/doc) (spvr); *Bariri* (short/doc) (spvr); *Il frumento* (short/doc) (spvr)

1959   *El frayle* (short/doc) (spvr); *Fertiluzzanti produtti dalla Societa del Gruppo Edison* (short/doc) (spvr); *Cavo olio fludio 220.000 volt* (short/doc) (spvr); *Auto chiese* (short/doc) (spvr); *Natura e chimica* (short/doc) (spvr)
1961   *Il pomodoro* (short/doc) (spvr); *Il sacco in Plypac* (short/doc) (spvr); *Po: forza 50.000* (short/doc) (pr)
1962   *Una storia milanese* (E. Visconti) (role)

Publications:

By OLMI: articles—

Interview with Gideon Bachmann, in *Nation* (New York), 25 May 1964.
"Ermanno Olmi, A Conversation with John Francis Lane," in *Sight and Sound* (London), Summer 1970.
Interview with A. Tassone, in *Cinéma* (Paris), January 1976.
Interview with M. Devillers and others, in *Cinématographe* (Paris), no. 40, 1978.

Interview with J.-A. Gili and L. Codelli, in *Positif* (Paris), November 1983.
Interview with Don Ranvaud, in *Monthly Film Bulletin* (London), October 1988.

On OLMI: books—

Samuels, Charles Thomas, *Encountering Directors*, New York, 1972.
Dillon, Jeanne, *Ermanno Olmi*, Florence, 1986.
Tabanelli, Giorgio, *Ermanno Olmi: nascita del documentario poetica*, Rome, 1987.

On OLMI: articles—

Lane, J.F., "The Triumph of Italy's Realism," in *Films and Filming* (London), December 1961.
Solomos, G.P., "Ermanno Olmi," in *Film Culture* (New York), Spring 1962.
Kauffman, Stanley, "A Fine Italian Hand," in the *New Republic* (New York), 15 February 1964.
Houston, Penelope, "The Organisation Man," in *Sight and Sound* (London), Spring 1964.
Walsh, M., "Ermanno Olmi," in *Monogram* (London), Summer 1971.
Gervais, M., "Ermanno Olmi: Humanism in the Cinema," in *Sight and Sound* (London), Autumn 1978.
Special section on *L'Albero degli zoccoli*, in *Positif* (Paris), September 1978.
Elley, Derek, "Ermanno Olmi," in *International Film Guide 1981*, London, 1980.
De Santi, G., "Il tradimento e la vendetta dei chierici," in *Cineforum* (Bergamo), January/February 1984.
Kennedy, Harlan, "Searching for the Star Child," in *Film Comment* (New York), September/October 1984.
Kieffer, A., "A la recherche d'Olmi," in *Jeune Cinéma* (Paris), February/March 1988.
Keates, J., "Inn the cascina," in *Sight and Sound* (London), Winter 1988/89.

*   *   *

Olmi, born in Bergamo in 1931, is the Italian filmmaker most committed to and identified with a regional heritage. His films are distinctly Lombardian; for the most part they describe life in Milan, the provincial capital (for example *Il posto, Un certo giorno, Durante l'estate* and *La circonstanza*). He has also filmed in the Lombardian Alps (*Il tempo si è fermato*), and his native Bergamo (*L'albero degli zoccoli*), but even when he ventures to Sicily, it is to make a film of a Milanese worker temporarily assigned to the south who longs for home (*I fidanzati*), and when he makes a semi-documentary biography (. . . *e venne un uomo*), it is of the Lombardian Pope, John XXIII.

Furthermore, his work bears affinities to the central literary figure of the Lombardian tradition, Alessandro Manzoni, whose great historical novel, *I promessi sposi*, is variously reflected in at least three of Olmi's films: most directly in *I findanzati*, whose very title recasts the 1827 novel, but also in the idealization of a great ecclesiastic (. . . *e venne un uomo*), and in the vivid recreation of a past century (*L'albero degli zoccoli*), which portrays peasant life in the late 19th century rather than Manzoni's 17th. The most significant Manzonian characteristic of Olmi's cinema is its Catholicism: of all the major Italian filmmakers he has the least problematic relationship with the Church. He embodies the spirit of the "opening to the Left" which has characterized both religious and parliamentary politics in Italy since the early 1960s. For the most part, his films center upon an individual worker caught between employment and an individual quest to assert dignity through labor. Quite often this tension carries over from work to the conjugal or preconjugal love life of the protagonist.

Like Pasolini, Rosi, and Bertolucci, Olmi is a filmmaker nurtured by post-war neorealism. Like his great precursors, Rossellini, De Sica, and Visconti, he has worked extensively with amateur actors, chosen simplified naturalistic settings, eschewed elaborate artifices or lighting, and employed an ascetic camera style. What mobility his camera has comes largely from his extensive use of the zoom lens. In contrast, however, to the first generation of neorealists, he has a high tolerance for abstraction and ambiguity in his story telling. Dramatic and emotional moments are consistently understated. Instead of a mobile camera, he has relied heavily upon montage (especially in the intercutting of scenes between Milan and Sicily in *I fidanzati*) and even more on the overlapping of sounds. In fact, Olmi's meticulous attention to sound, his isolation and manipulation of auditory details, tends to transform his realistically photographed scenes into psychologically-inflected domains of space and time.

—P. Adams Sitney

OPHULS, Marcel.

French/American. Born in Frankfurt-am-Main, Germany, 1 November 1927, son of director Max, became citizen of France, 1938, and of the U.S.A., 1950. Educated at Hollywood High School, graduated 1945; Occidental College; University of California at Berkeley; studied philosophy, the Sorbonne. Married Regina Ackermann, 1956, three daughters. Moved to France, 1932, and to Hollywood, 1941; served with Occupation forces in Japan, performed with theater unit, Tokyo, 1946; 3rd assistant director, using name "Marcel Wall," Paris, from 1951; radio and TV story editor for Sudwestfunk, Baden-Baden, West Germany, also director for radio, stage and TV, 1956–59; returned to Paris, 1960; TV journalist and director of *Zoom*, TV news magazine, 1966–68; directed first major documentary, *Munich, or Peace in Our Time*, 1967; senior story editor at NDR TV, Hamburg, 1968–71; Senior Visiting Fellow, Council of the Humanities, Princeton University, 1973–74; staff producer at CBS-News, then ABC News, 1975–78; returned to Europe, 1979; Secretary General, French Filmmakers' Society, and on Board of Directors, Societé des gens de lettres. Recipient: Prix de Dinard, Prix Georges Sadoul, British Film Academy Award, National Society of Film Critics Special Award, and Special Citation, New York Film Critics, for *The Sorrow and the Pity*, 1971; Oscar for Best Documentary, for *Hotel Terminus*, 1988.

Films as Director:

1960 *Matisse, or The Talent for Happiness* (+ sc)
1961 German episode of *L'Amour à vingt ans* (*Love at Twenty*) (+ sc)
1963 *Peau de banane* (*Banana Skin*) (+ co-sc)
1964 *Feu à volonté* (*Faites vos jeux. Fire at Will*) (+ co-sc)
1966 *Till Eulenspiegel* (co-d, co-sc, quit during filming) (in 2 parts, for German TV)
1967 *Munich, ou La Paix pour cent ans* (*Munich, or Peace in Our Time*) (for French TV) (+ sc)
1969 *Le Chagrin et la pitié* (*The Sorrow and the Pity*) (for TV, in 2 parts, 4.5 hours long) (+ sc)
1970 *Clavigo* (for TV); *The Harvest of My Lai* (for TV) (+ sc)
1971 *America Revisited* (for TV, in 2 parts) (+ sc); *Zwei ganze tage* (*Two Whole Days*) (for TV)
1972 *A Sense of Loss* (+ sc)
1976 *The Memory of Justice* (+ sc)
1988 *Hotel Terminus: Klaus Barbie, His Life and Times*
1990 *November Days: Voices and Choices* (for TV)

Marcel Ophuls

Other Films:

(partial list)
1953   *Moulin Rouge* (Huston) (asst d)
1954   *Un Acte d'amour* (*Act of Love*) (Litvak) (asst d); *Marianne de
       ma jeunesse* (Duvivier) (asst d)
1955   *Lola Montès* (Max Ophüls) (asst d)

Publications:

By OPHULS: articles—

"*The Sorrow and the Pity, A Sense of Loss*, a Discussion with Marcel
    Ophuls," with B.J. Demby, in *Filmmakers Newsletter* (Ward Hill,
    Massachusetts), December 1972.
"Why Should I Give You Political Solutions?," an interview in *Film
    Critic* (New York), November/December 1973.
"Politics and Autobiography," an interview with D. Yergin, in *Sight
    and Sound* (London), Winter 1973/74.
"Marcel Ophuls Tells Us We Cannot Afford to Forget," an interview
    with Terry Fox, in the *Village Voice* (New York), 11 October 1976.
"*Memory of Justice*," an interview with P. Lehman and others, in *Wide
    Angle* (Athens, Ohio), vol .2, no. 2, 1978.
"A War Over Justice," an interview with F. Manchel, in *Literature/
    Film Quarterly* (Salisbury, Maryland), Winter 1978.
Article about Max Ophüls, in *Positif* (Paris), July/August 1980.
"Changing the Rules of the Game," in *American Film* (Washington,
    D.C.), May 1984.
"Joy to the World!," an interview with Michel Ciment, in *American
    Film* (Washington, D.C.), September 1988.
Interview with F. Strauss, in *Cahiers du Cinéma* (Paris), September
    1988.
Interview with Graham Fuller, in *Listener* (London), 10 November
    1988.

On OPHULS: articles—

"Jean-Pierre Melville Talks to Rui Nogueira About *Le Chagrin et la
    pitié*," in *Sight and Sound* (London), Winter 1971/72.
"La Chagrin et la pitié," special Ophuls issue of *Avant-Scène du
    Cinéma* (Paris), July/September 1972.

* * *

Marcel Ophuls' 1974 film, *A Memory of Justice*, which examines War Crimes by juxtaposing the Nuremburg Trials with the
conflict in Vietnam, managed to please neither the critic Pauline Kael ("I feel a pang of guilt, because I think it's a very bad
film—chaotic and plodding, and with an excess of self-
consciousness which at times Ophuls seems to mistake for
art") nor David Puttnam, one of its British producers, who
claimed that the work was far too "personal" and who apparently urged Ophuls to be more "fascist" in his approach.
Ophuls was not inclined to be seduced by Radical Chic: he
refused to make glib parallels between Auschwitz and the My
Lai massacre, and thus enraged his backers. The film was over-
long (Ophuls had been contracted to make a 4 hour 30 minute
documentary and had come up with 4 hours 38 minutes), over-
budget, and featured pubic hair in a sauna sequence which had
the BBC, the project's co-sponsor, throwing up its arms in horror. Puttnam elbowed Ophuls off the production after a stormy
meeting in the Ritz Bar and called in another director, Lutz
Becker, to recut the footage. The film was "rescued" by an
intrepid production assistant who stole a scratch print and
smuggled it over to America, where it was watched in darkened Manhattan viewing rooms by Mike Nichols, Lillian
Hellman, Susan Sontag and other New York cultural luminaries. A wealthy backer bought back the negative. The movie
was premiered in its intended form, acclaimed as a masterpiece
by same, and savaged by Kael.

Ophuls is so closely associated with polemical documentaries that court controversy and split the critics that it seems surprising his first feature was made in France, under the aegis of
François Truffaut, starred Jeanne Moreau and Jean-Paul Belmondo, and had a title no more contentious than *Banana Skin*.
One forgets that the filmmaker spent his school days at Hollywood High. Ophuls claims the two directors who really
influenced him were his father, Max, and Truffaut. His
grounding was in fiction. He worked for his father on *Lola
Montès*, was on the crew of Huston's *Moulin Rouge*, and spent
a three year apprenticeship in the 1950s on 2nd Features. He
has always taken a determinedly personal approach toward
documentary and is full of disdain for filmmakers who use it as
a smokescreen behind which to hide their own lack of creative
ability. *Hotel Terminus*, his 1988 investigation into the Klaus
Barbie affair, was, he claims, structured along the lines of TV's
Columbo, with Ophuls the interviewer casting himself as the
detective in the dirty raincoat.

If his follow-up to *Banana Skin, Feu a Volonte* (1964) had
not been such a failure, it is quite conceivable that he would
have turned into a filmmaker along the lines of Chabrol and
Rivette. As it was, he was lured away (or fled) into the world of
TV journalism, working for "60 Minutes" in Germany and
learning about reportage and interview technique. *The Sorrow
and the Pity*, the film which made his name, was originally intended for French TV and only by accident found a new lease
of life in the Art Houses when French broadcasters refused to
show it.

As a documentary maker, Ophuls examines how the past is
mediated and constructed by the present: he is interested in the
past as fiction, not as actuality, in the "process of recollection,
in things like choice, selective memory, rationalization." He
does not try to maintain the charade of impartiality: he is an
egotist who inserts himself, his character and feelings, into the

films he makes. He is polite in his anger, willing to shake Barbie's hand or to listen to Albert Speer's side of the story. Often, the most startling information he garners is the incidental, the discursive: Klaus Barbie was kind to animals and was much liked by cats. Always with an eye on a profit, the Nazi tried to charge journalists for interviews when he was waiting to be extradited from Bolivia. Hannah Arendt's old cliche about the banality of evil finds new currency in Ophuls' work. Like Claud Lanzmann, he is loath to allow us the easy convenience of forgetting.

His photography is often ramshackle and his work has been accused of lacking structure. He is nonetheless a consummate editor, who believes that films are made in the cutting room. He tends not to use commentary or voice-over but to allow his interviewees to tell their myriad different stories in their own voices. However, he is not above using editing to make his point and to caricature the opinions he disagrees with. In his film about sectarian violence in Belfast, *A Sense of Loss*, for example, he manages to make a whole galaxy of Protestant grotesques while his representations of Catholics are generally favourable. He is a quixotic director who will continue to infuriate critics by intruding into his documentaries when they feel he should be behind the camera, paring his fingernails. A great admirer of the comedies of Ernst Lubitsch, in particular *To Be Or Not To Be*, Ophuls has lectured on Hollywood comedy at Princeton University and probably feels somewhat burdened by his reputation as the maker of grave, earnest and very long films which go down well with the liberal intellectuals of Greenwich Village. (Woody Allen queues to see the *Sorrow and the Pity* in *Annie Hall*.) It seems to have eluded his critics that he too has a sense of humour.

—G.C. Macnab

OPHÜLS, Max.

Born Max Oppenheimer in Saarbrucken, Germany, 6 May 1902, became French citizen, 1938. Married actress Hilde Wall in 1926, one son, director Marcel Ophuls. Acting debut, 1919; began as stage director, 1924; began working at Burgtheater, Vienna, 1926; dialogue director to Anatole Litvak at UFA, 1929; directed first film, 1930; with family, left Germany, 1932; directed in France, Italy and Holland, 1933–40; worked in Switzerland, 1940, then moved to Hollywood, 1941; "rediscovered" by Preston Sturges, 1944; returned to France, 1949; directed for German radio, mid-1950s. *Died in Hamburg, 26 March 1957.*

Films as Director:

1930 *Dann schon lieber Lebertran* (+ co-adaptation)
1932 *Die verliebte Firma*; *Die verkaufte Braut* (*The Bartered Bride*)
1933 *Die lachende Erben* (produced 1931); *Liebelei*; *Une Histoire d'amour* (French version of *Liebelei*)
1934 *On a volé un homme*; *La Signora di tutti* (+ co-sc)
1935 *Divine* (+ co-sc)
1936 *Komedie om Geld* (+ co-sc); *Ave Maria* (short); *La Valse brillante* (short); *La Tendre Ennemie* (*The Tender Enemy*) (+ co-sc)
1937 *Yoshiwara* (+ co-sc)
1938 *Werther* (*Le Roman de Werther*) (+ co-adaptation)
1940 *Sans lendemain*; *De Mayerling à Sarajevo* (*Mayerling to Sarajevo*); *L'Ecole des femmes* (unfinished)

1946 *Vendetta* (co-d, uncredited)
1947 *The Exile*
1948 ***Letter from an Unknown Woman***
1949 *Caught*; *The Reckless Moment*
1950 ***La Ronde*** (+ co-sc)
1952 *Le Plaisir* (*House of Pleasure*) (+ co-sc)
1953 ***Madame de . . .*** (***The Earrings of Madame De***) (+ co-sc)
1955 ***Lola Montès*** (***The Sins of Lola Montes***) (+ co-sc)

Publications:

By OPHÜLS: books—

Novelle by Goethe, radio adaptation, Frankfurt am Main, 1956.
Max Ophüls par Max Ophüls, Paris, 1963.

By OPHÜLS: articles—

"Hollywood, petite île . . . ," in *Cahiers du Cinéma* (Paris), December 1955.
"Le Dernier Jour de tournage," in *Cahiers du Cinéma* (Paris), May 1956.
Interview with Jacques Rivette and François Truffaut, in *Cahiers du Cinéma* (Paris), June 1957.
"Les Infortunes d'un scenario," and "Mon experience," in *Cahiers du Cinéma* (Paris), March 1958.
"*La Ronde*: Scenario et adaptation," with Jacques Natanson, in *Avant-Scène du Cinéma* (Paris), April 1963.
"Memory and Max Ophüls," in *Interviews with Film Directors* edited by Andrew Sarris, New York, 1967.
"*Lola Montès*: Scenario et adaptation," with Jacques Natanson, in *Avant-Scène du Cinéma* (Paris), January 1969.
Interview with Robert Aldrich, in *The Celluloid Muse* edited by Charles Higham and Joel Greenberg, Chicago, 1971.
"Interview with Ophüls (1950)," with Francis Koval, in *Masterworks of the French Cinema* edited by John Weightman, New York, 1974.
"*Madame de . . .* Issue" of *Avant Scène du Cinéma* (Paris), no. 351, 1986.

On OPHÜLS: books—

Roud, Richard, *Max Ophüls: An Index*, London, 1958.
Annenkov, Georges, *Max Ophüls*, Paris, 1962.
Beylie, Claude, *Max Ophüls*, Paris, 1963; revised edition, 1984.
Willemen, Paul, editor, *Ophüls*, London, 1978.
Williams, Alan, *Max Ophüls and the Cinema of Desire*, New York, 1980.
Guérin, William, *Max Ophüls*, Paris, 1988.
Asper, Helmut G., and others, *Max Ophüls*, Munich, 1989.

On OPHÜLS: articles—

Truffaut, François, "Une Certaine Tendence du cinéma français," in *Cahiers du Cinéma* (Paris), January 1954.
Archer, Eugene, "Ophüls and the Romantic Tradition," in *Yale French Studies* (New Haven), no. 17, 1956.
Tributes to Ophüls, in *Sight and Sound* (London), Summer 1957.
"Ophüls Issue" of *Cahiers du Cinéma* (Paris), March 1958.
Beylie, Claude, "Max Ophüls," in *Anthologie du Cinéma* (Paris), June 1965.
"Max Ophüls," in *Retrospektive* [1] edited by Peter Schumann, Berlin, 1966.
Williams, Forrest, "The Mastery of Movement," in *Film Comment* (New York), Winter 1969.
Koch, Howard, "Script to Screen with Max Ophüls," in *Film Comment* (New York), Winter 1970/71.
"Ophüls Issue" of *Film Comment* (New York), Summer 1971.
Camper, Fred, "Distance and Style: The Visual Rhetoric of Max Ophüls," in *Monogram* (London), no. 5, 1974.
"Ophuls Issues" of *Filmkritik* (Munich), November and December 1977.
Special Ophüls section, in *Positif* (Paris), July/August 1980.
"Ophüls Issue," of *Movie* (London), Summer 1982.
Koch, G., "Die Schnitzler-Verfilmungen von Max Ophüls," in *Frauen und Film* (Berlin), October 1982.
Houseman, John, "Houseman, Ray and Ophüls," in *Sight and Sound* (London), Autumn 1986.

Max Ophüls

Amiel, V., "Ophüls les yeuxs fermés," in *Positif* (Paris), December 1986.

Morrison, James, "Ophüls and Authorship: A Reading of *The Reckless Moment*," in *Film Criticism* (Edinboro, Pennsylvania), vol. 11, no. 3, 1987.

Doane, Mary Ann, "The Abstraction of a Lady: *La Signora di tutti*," in *Cinema Journal* (Champaign, Illinois), vol. 28, no. 1, 1988.

* * *

Ophüls's work falls neatly into three periods, marked by geographical locations and diverse production conditions, yet linked by common thematic concerns and stylistic/formal procedures: the pre-Second World War European period (during which he made films in four countries and four languages); the four Hollywood films of the late 1940s (to which one might add the remarkable Howard Hughes-produced *Vendetta*, on which he worked extensively in its early pre-production phases and which bears many identifiable Ophülsian traces, both thematic and stylistic); the four films made in France in the 1950s on which Ophüls's current reputation chiefly rests, and in which certain stylistic traits (notably the long take with elaborately mobile camera) are carried to their logical culmination.

Critical estimation of Ophüls has soared during the past 20 years; prior to that, the prevailing attitude was disparaging (or at best condescending), and the reasons for this now seem highly significant, reflecting far more on the limitations of the critics than of the films. The general consensus was that Ophüls's work had distinctive qualities (indeed, this would be difficult to deny), but was overly preoccupied with "style" (regarded as a kind of spurious, slightly decadent ornamentation) and given over to trivial or frivolous subjects quite alien to the "social" concerns considered to characterize "serious" cinema. In those days, the oppression of women within the patriarchal order was not identified as a "social concern"—especially within the overwhelmingly male-dominated field of film criticism. Two developments have contributed to the revaluation of Ophüls: the growth of *auteur* criticism in the 1960s and of feminist awareness, and I shall consider his work in relation to these phenomena.

1. *Ophüls and auteurism*. One of the first aims of auteur criticism was to dethrone the "subject" as the prime guarantee of a film's quality, in favor of style, mise-en-scène, the discernible presence of a defined directorial "voice": in Andrew Sarris's terms, the "how" was given supremacy over the "what." "Subject," in fact, was effectively redefined as what the auteur's mise-en-scène created. Ophüls was a perfect rallying-point for such a reformulation of critical theory. For a start, he offered one of the most highly developed and unmistakable styles in world cinema, consistent through all changes of time and place (though inevitably modified in the last two Hollywood melodramas, *Caught* and *The Reckless Moment*): elaborate tracking-and-craning camera movements, ornate décor, the glitter of glass and mirrors, objects intervening in the foreground of the image between characters and camera: a style that can be read as in itself implying a meaning, a metaphysic of entrapment in movement, time and destiny. Further, this style could be seen as developing, steadily gaining in assurance and definition, through the various changes in cultural background and circumstances of production—from, say, *Liebelei* through *Letter from an Unknown Woman* to *Madame de.* . . . Ophüls could be claimed (with partial justice) as a major creative artist whose personal vision transcended the most extreme changes of time and place.

The stylistic consistency was underlined by an equally striking thematic consistency. For example, the same three films mentioned above, though adapted from works by fairly reputable literary figures (respectively, Arthur Schnitzler, Stefan Zweig, Louise de Vilmorin), all reveal strong affinities in narrative/thematic structure: all are centered on romantic love, which is at once celebrated and regarded with a certain irony; all move towards a climactic duel in which the male lover is destroyed by an avenging patriarch, an offended husband; in all three, patriarchal authority is embodied in military figures. Finally, style and theme were perceived as bound together by a complicated set of visual motifs recurring from period to period. The eponymous protagonist of Ophüls's last film, *Lola Montès*, declares "For me, life is movement"; throughout his work, key scenes take place in vehicles of travel, places of transition: carriages, trains, staircases, and railway stations figure prominently in many of the films. Even a superficially atypical work like *The Reckless Moment* (set in modern California rather than the preferred "Vienna, 1900" or its equivalent) contains crucial scenes on the staircase, in moving cars, on a ferry, at a bus station. Above all, the dance was recognized as a central Ophülsian motif, acquiring complex significance from film to film: the romantic/ironic waltz scene if *Letter from an Unknown Woman*, the fluid yet circumscribed dances of *Madame de* . . . , the hectic and claustrophobic *palais de danse* of *Le Plaisir*, the constricted modern dance floor of *Caught*, the moment in *De Mayerling à Sarajevo* where the lovers are *prevented* from attending the ball: reminders that "life is movement" is not the simple proposition it may at first appear.

There is no doubt that the development of *auteur* theory enormously encouraged and extended the appreciation of Ophüls's work. In its pure form (the celebration of the individual artist), however, auteurism tends towards a dangerous imbalance in the evaluation of specific films: a tendency, for example, to prefer the "typical" but slight *La Ronde* (perhaps the film that most nearly corresponds to the "primitive" account of Ophüls) to a masterpiece like *The Reckless Moment*, in which Ophüls's engagement with the structural and thematic materials of the Hollywood melodrama results in an amazingly rich and radical investigation of ideological assumptions.

2. *Ophüls and Feminism*. Nearly all of Ophüls's films are centered on a female consciousness. Before the 1960s this tended merely to confirm the diagnosis of them as decorative, sentimental, and essentially frivolous: the social concerns with which "serious" cinema should be engaged were those which could be resolved within the patriarchal order, and more fundamental social concerns that threatened to undermine the order itself simply could not be recognized. The films belong, of course, to a period long before the eruption of what we now know as radical feminism; they do not (and could not be expected to) explicitly engage with a feminist politics, and they are certainly not free of a tendency to mythologize women. In retrospect, however, from the standpoint of the feminist theory and consciousness that evolved in the 1970s, they assume a quite extraordinary significance: an incomparably comprehensive, sensitive, and perceptive analysis of the position of women (subject to oppression) within patriarchal society. The films repeatedly present and examine the options traditionally available to women within our culture—marriage, prostitution (in both the literal and the looser sense), romantic love—and the relationship between those options. *Letter from an Unknown Woman*, for example, dramatizes marriage (Lisa's to von Stauffer, her mother's to the "military tailor") and prostitution ("modelling") as opposite cultural poles, then goes on to show that they really amount to the same thing: in both cases, the women are selling themselves (this opposition/parallel is brilliantly developed through the three episodes of *Le Plaisir*). Essentially, *Letter from an Unknown Woman* is an enquiry into the validity of romantic love as the only possible means of transcending this illusory dichotomy. Clearly, Ophüls is emotionally committed to Lisa and her vision; the extraordinary complexity and intelligence of the film lies in its

simultaneous acknowledgement that romantic love can only exist as narcissistic fantasy and is ultimately both destructive and self-destructive.

Far from being incompatible, the auteurist and feminist approaches to Ophüls demand to be synthesized. The identification with a female consciousness and the female predicament is the supreme characteristic of the Ophülsian thematic; at the same time, the Ophüls style—the commitment to grace, beauty, sensitivity—amounts to a celebration of what our culture defines as "femininity," combined with the force of authority, the drive, the organizational (directorial) abilities construed as masculine. In short, the supreme achievement of Ophüls's work is its concrete and convincing embodiment of the collapsibility of our culture's barriers of sexual difference.

—Robin Wood

OSHIMA, Nagisa.

Japanese. Born in Kyoto, 31 March 1932. Educated in political history at Kyoto University, graduated 1954. Student leader, involved in left-wing activities, early 1950s; assistant director at Shochiku Ofuna Studios, from 1954; film critic and editor-in-chief of film magazine *Eiga hihyo*, from 1956; directed first film, 1959; left Shochiku after *Night and Fog in Japan* pulled from circulation, founded production company Sozosha, 1961 (dissolved 1973); made TV documentaries, early 1960s; created Oshima productions, 1975; acquitted on obscenity charge relating to *Realm of the Senses*, 1976.

Films as Director:

1959   *Ai to kibo no machi* (*A Town of Love and Hope*) (+ sc); *Asu no taiyo* (short)
1960   *Seishun zankoku monogatari* (*Cruel Story of Youth. Naked Youth, a Story of Cruelty*) (+ sc); *Taiyo no hakaba* (*The Sun's Burial*) (+ co-sc); *Nihon no yoru to kiri* (*Night and Fog in Japan*) (+ co-sc)
1961   *Shiiku* (*The Catch*)
1962   *Amakusa shiro tokisada* (*Shiro Tokisada from Amakusa. The Rebel*) (+ co-sc)
1964   *Chiisana boken ryoko* (*Small Adventure. A Child's First Adventure*) (+ co-sc); *Watashi wa Bellet* (collective direction, advertising film)
1965   *Etsuraku* (*Pleasures of the Flesh*) (+ sc); *Yunbogi no nikki* (*The Diary of Yunbogi*) (+ pr, sc, ph) (short)
1966   *Hakuchu no torima* (*Violence at Noon*)
1967   *Ninja bugeicho* (*Band of Ninja*) (+ co-pr, co-sc); *Nihon shunka-ko* (*A Treatise on Japanese Bawdy Song. Sing a Song of Sex*)) (+ co-pr, co-sc); *Muri-shinju: Nihon no natsu* (*Japanese Summer: Double Suicide*) (+ co-sc)
1968   *Koshikei* (*Death by Hanging*) (+ co-pr, co-sc); *Kaettekita yopparai* (*Three Resurrected Drunkards. A Sinner in Paradise*) (+ co-sc)
1969   *Shinjuku dorobo nikki* (*Diary of a Shinjuku Thief*) (+ co-sc): *Shonen* (*Boy*)
1970   *Tokyo senso sengo hiwa* (*He Died After the War. The Man Who Left His Will on Film*) (+ co-sc)
1971   *Gishiki* (*The Ceremony*) (+ co-sc)
1972   *Natsu no imoto* (*Summer Sister*) (+ co-sc)
1976   *Ai no corrida* (*In the Realm of the Senses. Empire of the Senses*) (+ sc)
1978   *Ai no borei* (*Empire of Passion. The Phantom of Love*) (+ co-pr, sc)
1983   *Merry Christmas Mr. Lawrence*
1986   *Max, Mon Amour* (+ co-sc)

Other Films:

1956   *Shinkei gyogun* (sc) (unproduced but published)
1959   *Tsukimiso* (Iwaki) (sc); *Donto okoze* (Nomura) (co-sc); *Jusan nichi no kinyobi* (unproduced) (sc)
1969   *Yoiyami semareba* (Jissoji) (sc)

Publications:

By OSHIMA: books—

Sengo eiga: Hakai to sozo [Postwar Film: Destruction and Creation], Tokyo, 1963.
Taikenteki sengo eizo ron [A Theory of the Postwar Image Based on Personal Experience], Tokyo, 1975.
Écrits (1956–1978): Dissolution et jaillissement, translated by Jean-Paul Le Pape, Paris, 1980.

By OSHIMA: articles—

"Situation et sujet du cinéma japonais (1)," in *Positif* (Paris), October 1972.
"Je suis constamment concerné par le temps où je vis . . . ," an interview with Noel Simsolo, in *Cinéma* (Paris), November 1972.
Interview with R. McCormick, in *Cineaste* (New York), vol. 6, no. 2, 1974.
"Oshima Uncensored," an interview with M. de la F. McKendry, in *Interview* (New York), November 1976.
"Ecrits," in *Positif* (Paris), May 1978 and November 1979.
"L'Empire de la passion," an interview with Max Tessier, in *Ecran* (Paris), September 1978.
"Currents in Japanese Cinema: Nagisa Oshima, Sachiko Hidari," with S. Hoass, in *Cinema Papers* (Melbourne), September/October 1979.
Interview with P. Lehman, in *Wide Angle* (Athens, Ohio), vol. 4, no. 2, 1980.
"Tokyo Stories: Oshima," an interview with Tony Rayns, in *Sight and Sound* (London), Summer 1981.
Interview with Pascal Bonitzer and others, in *Cahiers du Cinéma* (Paris), June/July 1983.
Interview with Nick Roddick, in *Stills* (London), July/August 1983.
"Oshima and Bowie: Culture Shock," an interview with Tadao Sato, in *American Film* (Washington, D.C.), September 1983.
"Campaigner in the World of the Absurd," an interview with S. Suga, in *Framework* (Norwich), no. 26–27, 1985.

On OSHIMA: books—

Sato, Tadao, *Oshima Nagisa no sekai* [The World of Nagisa Oshima], Tokyo, 1973.
Bock, Audie, *Japanese Film Directors*, New York, 1978; revised edition, Tokyo, 1985.
Tessier, Max, editor, *Le Cinéma Japonais au présent: 1959–1979*, Paris, 1980.
Sato, Tadao, *Currents in Japanese Cinema*, Tokyo, 1982.
Magrelli, Enrico, and Emanuela Martini, *Il Rito, il rivolta: Il cinema di Nagisa Oshima*, Rome, 1984.
Polan, Dana B., *The Political Language of Film and the Avant-Garde*, Ann Arbor, Michigan, 1985.
Danvers, Louis, and Charles Tatum, *Nagisa Oshima*, Paris, 1986.

On OSHIMA: articles—

Cameron, Ian, "Nagisa Oshima," in *Movie* (London), Winter 1969/70.
"Director of the Year," in *International Film Guide 1971*, London, 1970.
"La Cérémonie," special issue of *Avant-Scène du Cinéma* (Paris), May 1973.
McCormick, R., "Ritual, the Family and the State: a Critique of Nagisa Oshima's The Ceremony," in *Cineaste* (New York), vol. 6, no. 2, 1974.
Dawson, J., "Nagisa Oshima: Forms and Feelings Under the Rising Sun," in *Cinema Papers* (Melbourne), September/October 1976.
McCormick, R., "In the Realm of the Senses," in *Cineaste* (New York), Winter 1976/77.

Nagisa Oshima

High, P.B., "Oshima: A Vita Sexualis on Film," in *Wide Angle* (Athens, Ohio), vol. 2, no. 4, 1978.
Hughes, J., "Oshima in Paris: Reaching for the Flame," in *Take One* (Montreal), September 1978.
Polan, Dana, "Politics as Process in Three Films by Nagisa Oshima," in *Film Criticism* (Edinboro, Pennsylvania), Fall 1983.
Lehman, P., "The Mysterious Orient, the Crystal Clear Orient," and M. Turim, "Oshima's Tales of Youth and Politics," in *Journal of Film and Video* (Boston), Winter 1987.
"Oshima Issue" of *Wide Angle* (Athens, Ohio), vol. 9, no. 2, 1987.

* * *

Oshima Nagisa, the Godard of the East, spent much of the 1980s engaged in international co-productions. He directed *Merry Christmas, Mr Lawrence* in 1983 for Jeremy Thomas, who was later to produce *The Last Emperor* for Bertolucci, and he combined with Luis Buñuel's old scriptwriter, Jean-Claude Carrière, for a Ionesco-like anatomy of bourgeois mores, in which Charlotte Rampling has an affair with an ape, *Max, Mon Amour*.

These European excursions seem a world apart from the early work of the former student activist and leader of the Japanese New Wave of the late 1950s. Back in those days, Oshima was telling cruel stories of youth, using the ingredients of American teenage exploitation movies, namely sex and violence, to make a trenchant critique of post-war Japanese society. Railing against the US-Japan Security Pact, and despairing of the old left communists' ability to make a meaningful intervention as the country experienced its "economic miracle," Oshima mobilized deliquency and nihilism. Unlike the French *nouvelle vague*, who tended merely to aestheticize the exploits of their young petty criminals and misfits, the Antoine Doinels and Jean Paul Belmondos, and who took until 1968 to become obstreperously political, Oshima was engaged from the outset.

He learned his craft as an assistant-director at the Shochiku Studios, where he directed his first features. However, the controversy surrounding his fourth film, *Night and Fog in Japan*, (the title was deliberately designed to echo Resnais's "gas chamber" documentary), pushed him toward working as an independent. A despairing indictment of the disunity of the Japanese left—the old left were felt to have betrayed the new—*Night and Fog* is as notable for its formal characteristics as for its topical content. For a start, it contains only 43 shots. (Compare this to his 1966 work, *Violence at Noon*, which is a masterpiece of frenetic cutting, boasting over 2000 shots in its 90 odd minutes, and you realize that Oshima is a formalist jackdaw, ready to experiment in whatever way he thinks fit.) And it was made in CinemaScope. Oshima, like Godard in *A bout de souffle*, has a penchant for hand-held camera shots. These, though, are rather more jarring when used in 70 mm than in 16 mm.

Cast out on his own when Shochiku withdrew *Night and Fog*

only three days after its release, Oshima remained active in both film and television throughout the 1960s. His first independent movie, *The Catch*, set the tone for much that was to follow. It tells the story of a black American POW, held hostage by a small village. While waiting for the military police to remove their "catch," the villagers make the man a scapegoat for all their own problems, eventually murdering him.

In its concern with racism and brutality, whether institutional or practiced by private individuals, *The Catch* anticipates Oshima's most famous film of the 1960s, and the one that finally brought his work to the attention of the west. Shown out of competition at Cannes, *Death By Hanging* is as gruesome a film about capital punishment as one could ever wish to see. Based, like many of this director's works on a "true story," of a young Korean sentenced to death for the brutal murder and rape of a Japanese high school girl, the film operates on several levels, both formally and thematically. Japanese racism toward Koreans—for so long the untouchables of Japanese society—the mindless bureaucracy involved in state licensed murder, and good old adolescent existential angst are amongst its narrative components. As Noel Burch has observed, the film's style is constantly shifting: it starts as drama-documentary, shot in sober black and white, but it later develops into a self-reflexive avant-garde text in which the audience is addressed directly. It uses theatrical masquerade, paying homage to the tradition of Japanese kabuki theatre. Its early "classical realism" is utterly usurped. The Korean fails to die when he is hanged. The officials—wardens, priests, police—must recreate his crime for him because he has lost his memory. In their bid to remind him of his guilt, they actually repeat his murder.

Jean Genet, the French vagabond thief and writer, is Oshima's constant inspiration. With its emphasis on crime, sexuality and role playing, *Death By Hanging* is akin to Genet's *The Balcony*. Oshima borrowed a Genet title for his *Diary of a Shinjuku Thief*, and his rather more whimsical *Three Resurrected Drunkards*, an exemplary modernist text that literally starts again half way through (at the 1983 Edinburgh Film Festival there was a minor riot from patrons certain that the projectionist was accidentally replaying the opening reel) looks at the question of Korean immigration in terms of costume and identity. (Three Korean immigrants steal the clothes of three drunken Japanese youths. The three Japanese, with nothing to wear and no money, become "honorary" Koreans and are appropriately persecuted.)

It is perhaps unfortunate that Oshima's best known film remains *In The Realm of the Senses*, a work customarily shown in late-night double-bills with *Last Tango in Paris* and, like the Brando vehicle, generally esteemed as the perfect marriage between art and pornography. Another "true story," this time of the notorious case of Abe Sada, who strangled and castrated her lover, Kichizo, and was arrested with his genitals in her pocket, it marks Oshima's most intimate meshing of the political with the sexual. Politics constitute the film's structuring absence. It is 1936, the high point of Japanese militarism; the two lovers' retreat into the realm of the senses must always be seen against this historical backcloth. The links between political and sexual repression are obvious, but it seems somewhat glib to view this innately tragic story as being about a straightforward liberation of female sexuality, a sort of "geisha's revenge." A familiar male response to the movie, as to Bataille's novel *The Story of Eye*, is to welcome it as a scathing critique of the male gaze: instead of being a film about a couple making love, it is transmogrified, becoming a film about what it means to be a spectator of a film about a couple making love. And, of course, it sells out every time it shows.

What now for Oshima? *Max, Mon Amour* was not best received. (It took three years for it to be released in Britain.) Will he ever again be able to recapture the delinquent energy of his youth. . . ?

—G.C. Macnab

OTTINGER, Ulrike.

German. Born in 1942. Studied as an artist, Paris, 1960s. Made first film, *Laokoon und Soehne*, 1972, and began collaboration with actor and costume designer Tabea Blumenschein; first feature-length film, *Madame X—Eine absolute Herrscherin*, 1977. Recipient: Special Jury Prize, Florence Festival, 1984; German Film Critics Prize, for *China—Die Kunste—Der Alltag*, 1986.

Films as Director, Scriptwriter, Producer and Cinematographer:

1972   *Laokoon und Soehne* (*Lacoon and Sons*)
1975   *Die Betoenung der blauen Matrosen* (*The Bewitchment of Drunken Sailors*)
1977   *Madame X—Eine absolute Herrscherin* (*Madame X—An Absolute Ruler*)
1979   *Bildnis einer Trinkerin—aller jamais retour* (*Portrait of a Female Alcoholic—Ticket of No Return*)
1981   *Freak Orlando: Kleines Welttheter in fuenf Episoden* (*Freak Orlando: Small Theatre of the World in Five Episodes*)
1984   *Dorian Gray im Spiegel der Boulevardpresse* (*Dorian Gray in the Mirror of the Popular Press*)
1985   *China—Die Künste—Der Alltag* (*China—The Arts—Everyday Life*)
1988   *Johanna d'Arc of Mongolia*

Publications:

By OTTINGER: articles—

Interview with R. Frey, in *Filmfaust* (Frankfurt), December 1981/January 1982.
Interview with Erica Carter in *Screen Education* (London), no. 41, 1982.

On OTTINGER: articles—

Lennsen, C., and others, "German Film Women," in *Jump Cut* (Berkeley), February 1984.
Perlmutter, Ruth, in *Film Criticism* (Edinboro, Pennsylvania), Winter 1984/85.
Kuhn, Annette, and Patricia White, "Encounter Between Two Cultures, *Madame X of the China Seas*," in *Screen* (London), Autumn 1987.
Knight, Julia, "Ulrike Ottinger," in *The Women's Companion to International Film*, edited by Annette Kuhn, London, 1990.

*   *   *

Ulrike Ottinger's training in fine art is displayed in her style of associative visual-musical collage. Her work is concerned with an exploration of image/sound relation, rather than with narrative structure. A major objective of her cinema is the renegotiation of a visual pleasure for the female and lesbian spectator.

Ottinger's episodic narratives are conveyed through beautiful and stylized tableaux that are underscored with a highly manipulated sound track. She prefers post-synchronization to direct recording and uses a great deal of music, along with unusual and heightened noises, in order to broaden the associ-

Ulrike Ottinger: *Madame X – Eine Absolute Herrscherin*

ative possibilities. From the outset, unlike many contemporary feminist filmmakers, she rejected a realist treatment of women's issues. Instead, Ottinger (in a manner reminiscent of Werner Schroeter) deploys exaggeration, artifice and parody. She juxtaposes art and cliché and deploys "ironic 'quotes' of films and images."

When Ottinger's early films were screened in independent cinemas, the anti-realist stance of her allegorical fables were out-of-sync with the issue-centred approach of the Women's Movement in the 1970s. *Madame X—Eine absolute Herrscherin*, her first television co-production, got a more general audience than her previous films and provoked mostly hostile responses. The film is a parodic feminist reworking of the pirate film genre. A group of women sail off on the Chinese junk Orlando to find adventure, but having broken with a male dominated society, they only reproduce amongst themselves the same destructive rituals of domination and submission. Monika Treut, another lesbian filmmaker, pointed out, however, that *Madame X* does not represent female power, or its absence, but that the film simulates reality by employing and parodying the signs and symbols of power. In the contemporary context of post-modernist debates, Ottinger's aesthetics have become familiar enough strategies in other media, and therefore they are now better understood.

Bildnis einer Trinkerin is not as the title suggests a social problem film, for here alcoholism merely becomes a metaphor for alienation. The film aims to represent female desire, and parodies the conventions of woman as spectacle in order to block male voyeurism. However, the ensuing violent debate amongst feminists demonstrated the problem of an endeavour where artistic references clearly pre-figure the general awareness of the Women's Movement.

Freak Orlando relates the mythology of the social outcast through the ages. Orlando, a symbolic figure who undergoes several transformations in sexual and historical identity, encounters compassion only from other freaks, and persecution, misunderstanding and cruelty from everyone else. The final episode depicts a contest for the ugliest person. It is, however, won by the so-called "normal" person who happens to be present. Ottinger shows that to identify a freak is a matter of perspective. "The absolute outsider is the average citizen, the conformist. Conformity is just another form of deformation."

With the documentary *China—Die Künste—Der Alltag*, Ottinger's recurring theme of exoticism in her own culture is extended to engage with the "real" exotica of Chinese art and society. As a Westerner she approaches the subject of a foreign culture by keeping her camera at a respectful distance, refraining from the use of penetrating zooms. She lets the images and sounds speak for themselves without imposing a commentary. In contrast to her controversial fiction films, this documentary was unanimously acclaimed by the critics.

In *Johanna d'Arc of Mongolia* Western and Oriental culture are opposed. Four female protagonists have become travelling companions on the Trans-Siberian/Trans-Mongolian-Express when they are hijacked by a mysterious Mongolian princess. In their captivity each woman reacts differently in encountering a culture which is alien to herself. Whereas the first part is highly stylised, that is, the interior of the compartments functions like a stage and the scenic view is provided on painted backdrops, the second part is shot on location and the emphasis is on real time.

Although Ottinger's films still do not attract wide audiences, they nevertheless have become a focus for film theorists interested in the possibilities for non-patriarchal forms of representation. Ottinger's insistence on mythologising and aestheticising women's experience has retrospectively been validated by many critics as a more fruitful approach than a feminism which focuses on subject matter.

—Ulrike Sieglohr

———

OZU, Yasujiro.

Japanese. Born in Tokyo, 12 December 1903. Educated at the Uji-Yamada (now Ise) Middle School, Matsuzaka, graduated 1921. Teacher, 1922–23; after introduction from uncle, began as assistant cameraman at Shochiku Motion Picture Co., 1923; assistant director, 1926; directed first film, 1927; military service in China, 1937–39; made propaganda films in Singapore, 1943; interned for 6 months as British POW, 1945. *Died in Kamakura, 12 December 1963.*

Films as Director:

1927   *Zange no yaiba* (*The Sword of Penitence*)
1928   *Wakodo no yume* (*The Dreams of Youth*) (+ sc); *Nyobo funshitsu* (*Wife Lost*); *Kabocha* (*Pumpkin*); *Hikkoshi fufu* (*A Couple on the Move*); *Nikutai bi* (*Body Beautiful*) (+ co-sc)
1929   *Takara no yama* (*Treasure Mountain*) (+ story); *Wakaki hi* (*Days of Youth*) (+ co-sc); *Wasei kenka tomodachi* (*Fighting Friends, Japanese Style*); *Daigaku wa deta keredo* (*I Graduated, But . . .*); *Kaisha-in seikatsu* (*The Life of an Office Worker*); *Tokkan kozo* (*A Straightforward Boy*) (+ co-story)
1930   *Kekkon-gaku nyumon* (*An Introduction to Marriage*); *Hogaraka ni ayume* (*Walk Cheerfully*); *Rakudai wa shita keredo* (*I Flunked, But . . .*) (+ story); *Sono yo no tsuma* (*That Night's Wife*); *Erogami no onryo* (*The Revengeful Spirit of Eros*); *Ashi ni sawatta koun* (*Lost Luck*); *Ojosan* (*Young Miss*)
1931   *Shukujo to hige* (*The Lady and the Beard*); *Bijin aishu* (*Beauty's Sorrows*); *Tokyo no gassho* (*Tokyo Chorus*)
1932   *Haru wa gofujin kara* (*Spring Comes from the Ladies*) (+ story); *Umarete wa mita keredo* (*I Was Born, But . . .*) (+ story); *Seishun no yume ima izuko* (*Where Now Are the Dreams of Youth?*); *Mata au hi made* (*Until the Day We Meet Again*)
1933   *Tokyo no onna* (*A Tokyo Woman*) (+ story); *Hijosen no onna* (*Dragnet Girl*) (+ story); *Dekigokoro* (*Passing Fancy*) (+ story)
1934   *Haha o kowazu-ya* (*A Mother Should Be Loved*); *Ukigusa monogatari* (*A Story of Floating Weeds*)
1935   *Hakoiri musume* (*An Innocent Maid*); *Tokyo no yado*
1936   *Daigaku yoi toko* (*College Is a Nice Place*) (+ story); *Hitori musuko* (*The Only Son*) (+ story)
1937   *Shukujo wa nani o wasuretaka* (*What Did the Lady Forget?*) (+ co-story)

1941   *Toda-ke no kyodai* (*The Brothers and Sisters of the Toda Family*) (+ co-sc)
1942   *Chichi ariki* (*There Was a Father*) (+ co-sc)
1947   *Nagaya no shinshi roku* (*The Record of a Tenement Gentleman*) (+ co-sc)
1948   *Kaze no naka no mendori* (*A Hen in the Wind*) (+ co-sc)
1949   ***Banshun*** (***Late Spring***) (+ co-sc with Kogo Noda)
1950   *Munekata shimai* (*The Munekata Sisters*) (+ co-sc with Kogo Noda)
1951   *Bakushu* (*Early Summer*) (+ co-sc with Kogo Noda)
1952   *Ochazuke no aji* (*The Flavor of Green Tea over Rice*) (+ co-sc with Kogo Noda)
1953   ***Tokyo monogatari*** (***Tokyo Story***) (+ co-sc with Kogo Noda)
1956   *Soshun* (*Early Spring*) (+ co-sc with Kogo Noda)
1957   *Tokyo boshoku* (*Twilight in Tokyo*) (+ co-sc with Kogo Noda)
1958   ***Higanbana*** (***Equinox Flower***) (+ co-sc with Kogo Noda)
1959   *Ohayo* (+ co-sc with Kogo Noda); ***Ukigusa*** (***Floating Weeds***) (+ co-sc with Kogo Noda)
1960   *Akibiyori* (*Late Autumn*) (+ co-sc with Kogo Noda)
1961   *Kohayagawa-ke no aki* (*The End of Summer*) (+ co-sc with Kogo Noda)
1962   ***Samma no aji*** (***An Autumn Afternoon***) (+ co-sc with Kogo Noda)

Publications:

On OZU: books—

Anderson, Joseph, and Donald Richie, *The Japanese Film: Art and Industry*, New York, 1960.
Richie, Donald, *Five Pictures of Yasujiro Ozu*, Tokyo, 1962.
Richie, Donald, *Japanese Cinema: Film Style & National Character*, New York, 1971.
Sato, Tadao, *Ozu Yasujiro no Geijutsu* [The Art of Yasujiro Ozu], Tokyo, 1971.
Satomi, Jun, and others, editors, *Ozu Yasujiro—Hito to Shigoto* [Yasujiro Ozu: the Man and His Work], Tokyo, 1972.
Schrader, Paul, *Transcendental Style in Film: Ozu, Bresson, Dreyer*, Berkeley, California, 1972.
Burch, Noël, *Theory of Film Practice*, New York, 1973.
Tessier, Max, "Yasujiro Ozu," in *Anthologie du cinéma* vol. 7, Paris, 1973.
Richie, Donald, *Ozu*, Berkeley, California, 1974.
Schrader, Leonard, and Haruji Nakamura, editors, *Masters of Japanese Film*, Tokyo, 1975.
Bock, Audie, *Japanese Film Directors*, New York, 1978; revised edition, Tokyo, 1985.
Burch, Noël, *To the Distant Observer*, Berkeley, 1979.
Tessier, Max, editor, *Le Cinéma japonais au présent: 1959–79*, Paris, 1980.
Sato, Tadao, *Currents in Japanese Cinema*, Tokyo, 1982.
Bordwell, David, *Ozu and the Poetics of Cinema*, Princeton, New Jersey, 1988.

On OZU: articles—

"Ozu Issues" of *Kinema Jumpo* (Tokyo), June 1958 and February 1964.
Ryu, Chishu, "Yasujiro Ozu," in *Sight and Sound* (London), Spring 1964.
Iwasaki, Akira, "Ozu," in *Film* (London), Summer 1965.
"Ozu Spectrum," in *Cinema* (Beverly Hills), Summer 1970.
Rosenbaum, Jonathan, "Ozu," in *Film Comment* (New York), Summer 1972.
Zeaman, Marvin, "The Zen Artistry of Yasujiro Ozu: The Serene Poet of Japanese Cinema," in *Film Journal* (New York), Fall/Winter 1972.
Branigan, Edward, "The Space of *Equinox Flower*," in *Screen* (London), Summer 1976.
Thompson, Kristin, and David Bordwell, "Space and Narrative in the Films of Ozu," in *Screen* (London), Summer 1976.
Thompson, Kristin, "Notes on the Spatial System of Ozu's Early Films," in *Wide Angle* (Athens, Ohio), vol. 1, no. 4, 1977.
Bergala, Alain, "L'Homme qui se lève," in *Cahiers du Cinéma* (Paris), May 1980.

Yasujiro Ozu

"Le Cinéma toujours recommencé de Yasujiro Ozu," special section, in *Cinéma* (Paris), January 1981.

Bock, Audie, "Ozu Reconsidered," in *Film Criticism* (Edinboro, Pennsylvania), Fall 1983.

Berta, R., "A la recherche du regard," in *Cahiers du Cinéma* (Paris), December 1985.

Geist, Kathe, "Narrative Style in Ozu's Silent Films," in *Film Quarterly* (Berkeley), Winter 1986/87.

Lehman, P., "The Mysterious Orient, the Crystal Clear Orient . . .," in *Journal of Film and Video* (Boston), Winter 1987.

*   *   *

Throughout his career, Yasujiro Ozu worked in the mainstream film industry. Obedient to his role, loyal to his studio (the mighty Shochiku), he often compared himself to the tofu salesman, offering nourishing but supremely ordinary wares. For some critics, his greatness inheres in his resulting closeness to the everyday realities of Japanese life. Yet since his death another critical perspective has emerged. This modest conservative has come to be recognized as one of the most formally intriguing filmmakers in the world, extending the genre he worked within and developing a rich and unique cinematic style.

Ozu started his career within a well-established genre system, and he quickly proved himself versatile, handling college comedies, wistful tales of office workers, even gangster films. By 1936, however, he had started to specialize. The "home drama," a Shochiku speciality, focused on the trials and joys of middle-class or working-class life—raising children, finding a job, marrying off sons and daughters, settling marital disputes, making grandparents comfortable. It was this genre in which Ozu created his most famous films and to which he is said to have paid tribute on his deathbed: "After all, Mr. President, the home drama."

Ozu enriched this genre in several ways. He strengthened the pathos of family crisis by suggesting that many of them arose from causes beyond the control of the individual. In the 1930s works, this often leads to strong criticism of social forces like industrialization, bureaucratization, and Japanese "paternalistic" capitalism. In later films, causes of domestic strife tend to be assigned to a mystical super-nature. This "metaphysical" slant ennobles the characters' tribulations by placing even the most trivial action in a grand scheme. The melancholy resignation that is so pronounced in *Tokyo Story* and *An Autumn Afternoon* constitutes a recognition of a cycle of nature that society can never control.

To some extent, the grandiose implications of this process are qualified by a homely virtue: comedy. Few Ozu films wholly lack humor, and many involve outrageous sight gags. As a genre, the home drama invited a light touch, but Ozu proved able to extend it into fresh regions. There is often an unabashed vulgarity, running to jokes about eating, bodily functions, and sex. Even the generally sombre *Autumn Afternoon* can spare time for a gag about an elderly man run ragged by the sexual demands of a young wife. *Ohayo* is based upon equating talk, especially polite vacuities, with farting. Ozu risks breathtaking shifts in tone: in *Passing Fancy*, after a tearful scene at a boy's sickbed, the father pettishly says that he wishes his son had died. The boy responds that the father was singly looking forward to a good meal at the funeral.

Ozu also developed many narrative tendencies of the home drama. He exploited the family-plus-friends-and-neighbors cast by creating strict parallels among characters. If family A has a son of a certain type, family B will have a daughter of that type, or a son of a different sort. The father may encounter a younger or older man, whom he sees as representing himself at another point in his life. The extended-family format allows Ozu to create dizzying permutations of comparisons. The sense is again of a vast cycle of life in which an individual occupies many positions at different times.

Ozu has one of the most distinctive visual styles in the cinema. Although critics have commonly attributed this to the influence of other directors or to traditions of Japanese art, these are insufficient to account for the rigor and precision of Ozu's technique. No other Japanese director exhibits Ozu's particular style, and the connections to Japanese aesthetics are general and often tenuous. (Ozu once remarked: "Whenever Westerners don't understand something, they simply think it's Zen.") There is, however, substantial evidence that Ozu built his unique style out of deliberate imitation of and action against Western cinema (especially the work of Chaplin and Lubitsch).

Ozu limited his use of certain technical variables, such as camera movement and variety of camera position. This can seem a wilful asceticism, but it is perhaps best considered a ground-clearing that let him concentrate on exploring minute stylistic possibilities. For instance, it is commonly claimed that every Ozu shot places the camera about three feet off the ground, but this is false. What Ozu keeps constant is the perceived *ratio* of camera height to the subject. This permits a narrow but nuanced range of camera positions, making every subject occupy the same sector of each shot. Similarly, most of Ozu's films employ camera movements, but these are also systematized to a rare degree. Far from being an ascetic director, Ozu is quite virtuosic, but within self-imposed limits. His style reveals vast possibilities within a narrow compass.

Ozu's compositions rely on the fixed camera-subject relation, adopting angles that stand at multiples of 45 degrees. He employs sharp perspective depth; the view down a corridor or street is common. Ozu enjoyed playing with the positions of objects within the frame, often rearranging props from shot to shot for the sake of minute shifts. In the color films, a shot will be enhanced by a fleck of bright and deep color, often red; this accent will migrate around the film, returning as an abstract motif in scene after scene.

Ozu's use of editing is no less idiosyncratic. In opposition to the 180-degree space of Hollywood cinema, Ozu employed a 360-degree approach to filming a scene. This "circular" shooting space yields a series of what Western cinema would consider incorrect matches of action and eyelines. While such devices crop up in the work of other Japanese filmmakers, only Ozu used them so rigorously—to undermine our understanding of the total space, to liken characters, and to create abstract graphic patterns. Ozu's shots of objects or empty locales extend the concept of the Western "cutaway": he will use them not for narrative information but for symbolic purposes or for temporal prolongation. Since Ozu early abjured the use of fades and dissolves, cutaways often stand in for such punctuations. And because of the unusually precise compositions and cutting, Ozu is able to create a sheerly graphic play with the screen surface, "matching" contours and regions of one shot with those of the next.

Ozu's work remains significant not only for its extraordinary richness and emotional power but also because it suggests the extent to which a filmmaker working in popular mass-production filmmaking can cultivate a highly individual approach to film form and style.

—David Bordwell

PABST, G.W.

Austrian. Born Georg Wilhelm Pabst in Raudnitz, Bohemia, 27 August 1885. Educated in engineering at technical school, Vienna, and at Academy of Decorative Arts, Vienna, 1904–06. Married Gertrude (Pabst), one son. Actor, from 1906; travelled to U.S.A. with German language troupe, 1910; returned to Europe, interned as prisoner-of-war, Brest, 1914–18; directed season of expressionist theatre in Prague, 1919; artistic director, Neuen Wiener Bühne, also joined Carl Froelich's film production company, 1920; directed first film, 1923; formed Volksverband für Filmkunst (Popular Association for Film Art) with Heinrich Mann, Erwin Piscator and Karl Freund, 1928; studied sound film techniques in London, 1929; moved to Hollywood, 1933, returned to France, 1935; planned to emigrate to U.S.A. on outbreak of war, but illness forced him to remain in Austria; formed Pabst-Kiba Filmproduktion in Vienna, 1949; worked in Italy, 1950–53. Recipient: Légion d'honneur, 1931; Best Director, Venice Festival, for *Der Prozess*, 1948. *Died in Vienna, 29 May 1967.*

Films as Director:

1923   *Der Schatz* (*The Treasure*) (+ co-sc)
1924   *Gräfin Donelli* (*Countess Donelli*)
1925   *Die freudlose Gasse* (*The Joyless Street*); *Geheimnesse einer Seele* (*Secrets of a Soul*)
1926   *Man spielt nicht mit der Liebe* (*One Does Not Play with Love*)
1927   *Die Liebe der Jeanne Ney* (*The Love of Jeanne Ney*)
1928   *Abwege* (*Begierde*) [Crisis (Desire)]; **Die Büchse der Pandora (Pandora's Box)**
1929   *Die weisse Hölle vom Pitz-Palu* (*The White Hell of Pitz-Palu*) (co-d); *Das Tagebuch einer Verlorenen* (*Diary of a Lost Girl*) (+ pr)
1930   *Westfront 1918*; *Skandal um Eva* (*Scandalous Eva*)
1931   **Die Dreigroschenoper (The Threepenny Opera)**; **Kameradschaft (Comradeship)**
1932   *L'Atlantide* (*Die Herrin von Atlantis*)
1933   *Don Quichotte*; *Du haut en bas* (*High and Low*)
1934   *A Modern Hero*
1936   *Mademoiselle Docteur* (*Salonique, nid d'espions*)
1938   *Le Drame de Shanghai*
1939   *Jeunes Filles en détresse*
1941   *Komödianten* (+ co-sc)
1943   *Paracelsus* (+ co-sc)
1944   *Der Fall Molander* (unfinished and believed destroyed)
1947   *Der Prozess* (*The Trial*)
1949   *Geheimnisvolle Tiefen* (+ pr)
1952   *La Voce del silenzio*
1953   *Cose da pazzi*
1954   *Das Bekenntnis der Ina Kahr*
1955   *Der Letzte Akt* (*The Last Ten Days. Ten Days to Die*); *Es geschah am 20 Juli* (*Jackboot Mutiny*)
1956   *Rosen für Bettina*; *Durch die Walder, durch die Auen*

Other Films:

1921   *Im Banne der Kralle* (Frohlich) (role)

Publications:

By PABST: book—

Classic Film Scripts: Pandora's Box (*Lulu*), translated by Christopher Holme, New York, 1971.

By PABST: articles—

"Censor the Censor!," an interview with Beatrix Moore, in *Sight and Sound* (London), Winter 1938/39.
"Le Réalisme est un passage," in *Revue du Cinéma* (Paris), October 1948.
"Über zwei meiner Filme," in *Filmkunst* (Vienna), 1960.
"*The Threepenny Opera*," edited by Roger Manvell, in *Masterpieces of the German Cinema*, New York, 1973.

On PABST: books—

Kracauer, Siegfried, *From Caligari to Hitler*, Princeton, New Jersey, 1947.
Joseph, Rudolph, editor, *Der Regisseur: G.W. Pabst*, Munich, 1963.
,Buache, Freddy, *G.W. Pabst*, Premier Plan No. 39, Lyons, 1965.
Amengual, Barthélémy, *Georg Wilhelm Pabst*, Paris, 1966.
Aubry, Yves, and Jacques Pétat, "G.W. Pabst," in *Anthologie du Cinéma* vol. 4, Paris, 1968.
Eisner, Lotte, *The Haunted Screen*, Berkeley, 1969.
Hull, David, *Film in the Third Reich*, Berkeley, 1969.
Atwell, Lee, *G.W. Pabst*, Boston, 1977.
Brooks, Louise, *Lulu in Hollywood*, New York, 1981.

On PABST: articles—

Bryher, "G.W. Pabst: A Survey," in *Close Up* (London), December 1927.
Moore, John, "Pabst, Dovjenko: A Comparison," in *Close Up* (London), September 1932.
Potamkin, Harry, "Pabst and the Social Film," in *Hound & Horn* (New York), January–March 1933.
Rotha, Paul, "Pabst, Pudovkin and the Producers," in *Sight and Sound* (London), Summer 1933.
Bachmann, Gideon, editor, "Six Talks on G.W. Pabst," in *Cinemages* (New York), no. 3, 1955.
"Pabst Issue" of *Filmkunst* (Vienna), no. 18, 1955.
Card, James, "The Intense Isolation of Louise Brooks," in *Sight and Sound* (London), Summer 1958.
Stanbrook, Alan, "Brecht et le cinéma," in *Cahiers du Cinéma* (Paris), December 1960.
Luft, Herbert, "G.W. Pabst," in *Films in Review* (New York), February 1964.
Brooks, Louise, "Pabst and Lulu," in *Sight and Sound* (London), Summer 1965.
Rotha, Paul, "Thoughts on Pabst," in *Films and Filming* (London), February 1967.
Eisner, Lotte, "Meeting with Pabst," in *Sight and Sound* (London), Autumn 1967.

G.W. Pabst directing *La Voce del silenzo*

Stuart, John, "Working with Pabst," in *Silent Picture* (London), Autumn 1970.

"*Loulou* Issue" of *Avant-Scène du Cinéma* (Paris), 1 December 1980.

Petat, J., "Pabst, aujourd'hui?—une réévaluation nécessaire," in *Cinéma* (Paris), April 1981.

Elsaesser, Thomas, "Lulu and the Meter Man," in *Screen* (London), July/October 1983.

Horak, J.-C., "G.W. Pabst in Hollywood, or Every Modern Hero Deserves a Mother," in *Film History* (Philadelphia), vol. 1, no. 1, 1987.

*   *   *

Bryher, writing in *Close Up* in 1927, noted that "it is the thought and feeling that line gesture that interest Mr. Pabst. And he has what few have, a consciousness of Europe. He sees psychologically and because of this, because in a flash he knows the sub-conscious impulse or hunger that prompted an apparently trivial action, his intense realism becomes, through its truth, poetry."

Pabst was enmeshed in the happenings of his time, which ultimately engulfed him. He is the chronicler of the churning maelstrom of social dreams and living neuroses, and it is this perception of his time which raises him above many of his contemporary filmmakers.

Like other German directors, he drifted to the cinema through acting and scripting. His first film, *Der Schatz*, dealt with a search for hidden treasure and the passions it aroused. Expressionist in feeling and design, it echoed the current trend in German films, but in *Die freudlose Gasse* he brought clinical observation to the tragedy of his hungry postwar Europe. For Pabst the cinema and life grew closer together. In directing the young Greta Garbo and the more experienced Asta Nielsen, Pabst was beginning his gallery of portraits of women to whom he would add Brigitte Helm, Louise Brooks and Henny Porten.

Geheimnisse einer Seele carried Pabst's interest in the subconscious further, dealing with a Freudian subject of the dream and using all the potential virtues of the camera to illuminate the problems of his central character, played by Werner Krauss. *Die Liebe der Jeanne Ney*, based on a melodramatic story by Ilya Ehrenburg, reflected the upheavals and revolutionary ideas of the day. It also incorporated a love story that ranged from the Crimea to Paris. Through his sensitive awareness of character and environment Pabst raised the film to great heights of cinema. His individual style of linking image to create a smoothly flowing pattern induced a rhythm which carried the spectator into the very heart of the matter.

Two films have a special significance. *Die Büchse der Pandora* and *Das Tagebuch einer Verlorenen* featured the American actress Louise Brooks, in whom Pabst found an ideal interpreter for his analysis of feminine sensuality.

Between the high spots of his career there were such films as *Grafin Donelli* which brought more credit to its star, Henny Porten, than to Pabst. *Man spielt nicht mit der Liebe* featured Krauss and Lily Damita in a youth and age romance. *Abwege*, a more congenial subject of a sexually frustrated woman, gave Pabst the opportunity to direct the beautiful and intelligent

Brigitte Helm. His collaboration with Dr. Arnold Fanck on *Die weisse Hölle vom Pitz-Palu* resulted in the best of the mountain films, aided by Leni Riefenstahl and a team of virtuoso cameramen, Angst, Schneeberger and Allgeier.

The coming of sound was a challenge met by Pabst. Not only did he enlarge the scope of filmmaking techniques, but he extended the range of his social commitments in his choice of subject matter. Hans Casparius, his distinguished stills cameraman and friend, has stressed the wonderful teamwork involved in a Pabst film. There were no divisions of labor; all were totally involved. *Westfront 1918*, *Die Dreigroschenoper* and *Kameradschaft* were made in this manner when Pabst began to make sound films. Vajda the writer, Fritz Arno Wagner the cameraman (who had filmed *Jeanne Ney*) and Ernö Metzner, another old colleague, worked out the mise-en-scène with Pabst, assuring the smooth, fluid process of cinema. With Pabst the cinema was still a wonder of movement and penetrating observation. The technical devices used to ensure this have been described by the designer Metzner.

Westfront 1918 was an uncompromising anti-war film which made *All Quiet on the Western Front* look contrived and artificial. Brecht's *Die Dreigroschenoper*, modified by Pabst, is still a stinging satire on the pretensions of capitalist society. *Kameradschaft*, a moving plea for international cooperation, shatters the boundaries that tend to isolate people. All these films were studio-made and technically stupendous, but the heart and human warmth were given to them by G.W. Pabst.

Germany was now in the grip of growing Nazi domination. Pabst looked elsewhere to escape from that Germany of which he had once been so much a part. *L'Atlantide* was based on the Pierre Benoit novel of adventure in the Sahara, the former success of Jacques Feyder and now featuring Brigitte Helm as the mysterious Antinea. *Don Quixote* with Chaliapin did not fulfil its promise. *A Modern Hero*, made in Hollywood for Warner Brothers, had little of Pabst in it. On his return to France he handled with some competence *Mademoiselle Docteur*, *Le Drame de Shanghai*, and *Jeunes Filles en détresse*.

In 1941 circumstances compelled him to return to his estate in Austria. He was trapped, and if he was to make films, it had to be for the Nazi regime. *Komödianten* was a story of a troupe of players who succeed in establishing the first National Theatre at Weimar. Its leading player was Pabst's old friend Henny Porten, who gave an excellent performance. The film won an award at the then Fascist-controlled Venice Biennale. *Paracelsus*, again an historical film, showed Pabst had lost none of his power. For his somewhat reluctant collaboration with the Nazis, Pabst has been savagely attacked, but it is hard to believe that any sympathy could have ever existed from the man who made *Kameradschaft* for the narrow chauvinists who ruled his country.

After the war Pabst made *Der Prozess*, dealing with Jewish pogroms in 19th-century Hungary. It was a fine film. After some work in Italy he made *Der letze Akt* dealing with the last days of Hitler, and *Es geschah am 20 Juli* about the generals' plot against Hitler. Both were films of distinction.

Pabst died in Vienna in 1967, having been a chronic invalid for the last ten years of his life. As Jean Renoir said of him in 1963: "He knows how to create a strange world, whose elements are borrowed from daily life. Beyond this precious gift, he knows how, better than anyone else, to direct actors. His characters emerge like his own children, created from fragments of his own heart and mind."

—Liam O'Leary

PAGNOL, Marcel.

French. Born in Aubagne, near Marseilles, 25 (or 28) February 1895. Educated at Lycée Thiers, Marseilles; University of Montpellier, degree in letters. Served with French Infantry, 1914–17, and in 1940. Married Jacqueline Bouvier, 1945, two sons. Founded literary magazine *Fortunio*, 1911; teacher of English, from 1912; appointed professor at Lycée Condorcet, Paris, 1922; resigned teaching position after success of play *Marius*, 1929; created film company and founded magazine *Les Cahiers du film*, 1931; opened studio at Marseilles, 1933; directed first film, 1934; President of Society of French Dramatic Authors and Composers, 1944–46. Recipient: member, Academie française, 1947. Officer of the Légion d'honneur. *Died 18 April 1974.*

Films as Director:

1934 *Le Gendre de Monsieur Poirier* (+ pr, sc); *Jofroi* (+ pr, sc); *L'Article 330* (+ pr, sc); *Angèle* (+ pr, sc)
1935 *Merlusse* (+ pr, sc); *Cigalon* (+ pr, sc)
1936 *Topaze* (2nd version) (+ pr, sc); *César* (+ pr, sc)
1937 *Regain* (+ pr, sc)
1938 *Le Schpountz* (+ pr, sc); *La Femme du boulanger* (+ pr, sc)
1940 *La Fille du puisatier* (+ pr, sc)
1945 *Naïs* (+ pr, sc)
1948 *La Belle Meunière* (+ pr, sc)
1951 *Topaze* (3rd version) (+ pr, sc)
1952 *Manon des sources* (+ pr, sc)
1954 *Les Lettres de mon moulin* (+ pr, sc)
1967 *Le Curé de Cucugnan* (for TV) (+ pr, sc)

Other Films:

1931 *Marius* (Korda) (sc)
1932 *Fanny* (Allégret) (co-pr, sc)
1933 *Topaze* (Gasnier) (original play) (sc); *Un Direct au coeur* (Lion) (co-author of original play, sc); *L'Agonie des aigles* (Richebé) (co-pr, sc)
1934 *Tartarin de Tarascon* (Bernard) (sc)
1939 *Monsieur Brotonneau* (Esway) (pr, sc)
1950 *Le Rosier de Madame Husson* (Boyer) (sc)
1953 *Carnaval* (Verneuil) (pr, sc)
1962 *La Dame aux camélias* (Gir) (sc)
1986 *Jean de Florette* (Berri) (original story); *Manon des sources* (Berri) (original story)

Publications:

(related to cinema)

By PAGNOL: books—

Les Sermons de Pagnol, edited by Robert Morel, Paris, 1968.
Confidences, Paris, 1981.
Inédits, edited by J. and F. Pagnol, Paris, 1986.

By PAGNOL: articles—

"Je n'ai pas changé de métier," an interview with Michel Gorel, in *Cinémonde* (Paris), 17 August 1933.
"Cinématurgie de Paris," in *Les Cahiers du Film* (Paris), 16 December 1933, 15 January 1934, and 1 March 1934; collected in *Cahiers du Cinéma* (Paris), no. 173.
"Il n'y a rien de plus bête que la technique," an interview with Maurice Bessy, in *Cinémonde* (Paris), 6 October 1938.
"Mon ami Rene Clair," in *Cinémonde* (Paris), 23 April 1946.
"Adieu à Raimu," in *L'Ecran Française* (Paris), 3 October 1951.
Interview with J.-A. Fieschi and others, in *Cahiers du Cinéma* (Paris), December 1965.
Interview with Claude Beylie and Guy Braucourt, in *Cinéma* (Paris), March 1969.

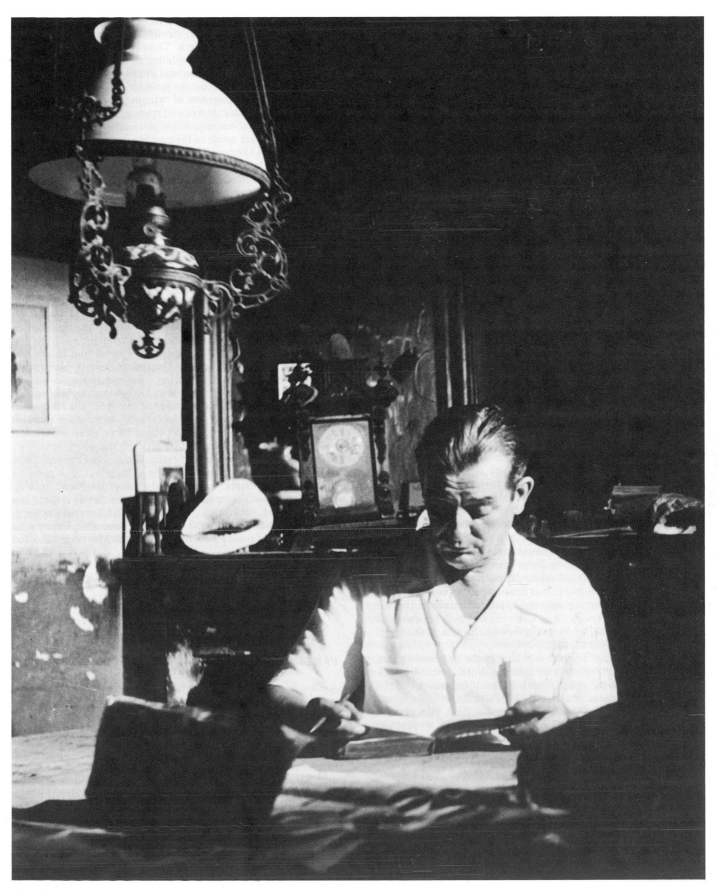

Marcel Pagnol

withered as his three subsequent features fared poorly at the box office.

Those three films, *Law and Disorder, Crime and Passion*, and *The Silver Bears*, are all flawed works, but not necessarily artistic failures. Each a curious satire on aspects of modern corruption, their commercial failure seems to have stemmed from the unresolved nature of their plots. Choosing to focus on the motivations and mysteries of the highly individualized misfits who are his central characters, Passer has generally neglected narrative clarity, matching unresolved plots to unfulfilled characters. In *Law and Disorder*, an examination of urban violence, a group of citizens takes the law into its own hands by forming an auxiliary police force which turns out to be as corrupt as both the legal and criminal forces it wishes to combat.

While these films work as character studies and display Passer's technical skill, the shifts between laughter and pain are often so unsettlingly subtle as to leave the spectator unsure of the director's moral position. All three films seem more interesting and their ideas clearer in light of *Cutter's Way*, his meditation on political and financial power, personal responsibility and the mysteries of friendship.

In this adaptation of Newton Thornburg's novel, Passer depicted his most successfully eccentric character—Alex Cutter—a multiple amputee and Vietnam vet whose anarchic behavior is a result of his need to find a focus for his rage. In this devastatingly grim examination of the Vietnam nightmare which is masked by our insistent belief in the American dream, Passer unearths misconceptions of heroism and success, finding a corrupt mentality behind each while refusing to point the finger of blame in any particular direction. Alex Cutter's condition is a result of his having bought the dream; his revenge is the desire to bring down a powerful man, a synecdoche for the system which caused his martyrdom. The hauntingly unresolved nature of the film's ending is an achievement missing from Passer's earlier American films. The spectator here is forced to supply both the meaning and the outcome of the final action.

Cutter's Way was not only a personal achievement for Passer but became the film which demonstrated the viability of UA Classics, a subsidiary of the parent company which, in post-*Heaven's Gate* hysteria, had abandoned the film on its initial release. With special handling, *Cutter's Way* became a *cause célèbre*, a minor financial success, and the hope of many for the recognition Passer deserved. Unfortunately, since then he has directed only two films: *Creator*, a love story of an eccentric professor and a much younger free spirit; and *Haunted Summer*, his first period piece, about a meeting between Byron and Shelley in June 1816. Both, unfortunately, were box-office failures, but another major film from this gifted director remains a much-awaited event.

—Doug Tomlinson

PASTRONE, Giovanni.

(Also known as Piero Fosco.) Italian. Born at Montechario d'Asti, 11 September 1883. Administrative assistant, Carlo Rossi & Company, Turin, 1905; company reorganized as Itala Film, becomes adminstrative director, 1907; director, from 1910; production supervisor of Itala, from 1914; left film industry, worked on medical research, early 1920s. *Died in Turin, 27 June 1959.*

Films as Director:

1910	*Agnese Visconti* (+ pr); *La caduta di Troia* (+ pr)
1912	*Padre* (co-d, pr)
1914	**Cabiria** (+ pr)
1915	*Il fuoco* (+ pr); *Maciste* (+ pr)
1916	*Maciste alpino* (co-d, pr); *Tigre reale* (+ pr)
1919	*Hedda Gabler* (+ pr)
1923	*Povere bimbe* (+ pr)

Publications:

On PASTRONE: books—

Margadonna, Ettore, *Cinema ieri ed oggi*, Milan, 1932.
Palmieri, Eugenio, *Vecchio cinema italiano*, Venice, 1940.
Prolo, Maria, *Storia del cinema muto italiano*, Milan, 1951.
Usai, Paola Cherchi, editor, *Giovanni Pastrone: gli anni d'oro del cinema a Torino*, Turin, 1986.

On PASTRONE: articles—

Caudana, Mino, "Vita laboriosa e geniale di Giovanni Pastrone," in *Film* (Rome), 25 February and 4 March 1939.
"Omaggio a Pastrone" issue of *Centrofilm* (Turin), no. 12, 1961.
Verdone, Mario, "Pastrone, ultimo incontro," in *Bianco e Nero* (Rome), June 1961.
Special Pastrone and Griffith issue of *Bianco e Nero* (Rome), May/August 1975.

*   *   *

The firm Carlo Rossi and Company (of Turin) began in 1907 to manufacture films and apparatus, drawing their personnel from the Pathé Company of Paris. When Rossi left the Company, Sciamengo and Giovanni Pastrone took over what was by then Itala Films, and Pastrone soon proved himself an active and inspired manager. André Deed, the French comedian, was acquired in 1908 and proved a goldmine with his role of Cretinetti. Another valuable addition to the Company was Segundo de Chomon, the Spanish cameraman and a master of special effects. His first film for Itala was the sensational thriller *Tigris* in 1912. In the meantime Pastrone's ambitions led him into direction, and in 1910 he made *Agnese Visconti* and the sensational *Caduta del Troia*, which reached American cinemas in spite of an embargo on foreign films. His film *Padre* introduced the famous actor Ermete Zacconi to the screen. In 1913 Pastrone conceived a vast project set in the time of the Punic Wars when Scipio conquered Carthage. With a showman's instinct Pastrone approached d'Annunzio, and secured the approval and prestige of the great man's name for a tidy sum. Pastrone, under the name Piero Fosco, directed the film *Cabiria* with a script duly credited to the famous author, D'Annunzio. With dynamic thoroughness Pastrone did his homework. The period behavior, architecture and costumes were patiently researched. Vast structures were built. Shooting took six months, ranging from the Itala studios in Turin to Tunisia, Sicily and the Val de Lanzo where Hannibal is reputed to have crossed the Alps. Not only was the film spectacular but, artistically, it broke new ground. The striking camerawork by de Chomon made use of travelling shots with remarkable skill, and the effects of the eruption of Mount Etna and the naval battle of Syracuse were awe-inspiring. The character of the strong man Maciste became a legend of the cinema. Later, Pastrone directed this ex-dock laborer in a further adventure, *Maciste*, and in the same year, he directed Pina Menichelli and Febo Mari in *Il Fuoco*, the love story of a young painter and a wealthy woman. The film's erotic atmosphere caused it to be banned and there were clerical demonstrations against the film.

In 1916 he again directed Menichelli in work by Verga, *Tigre*

Giovanni Pastrone: *Cabiria*

reale, and in 1919 he directed his former star of *Cabiria*, Itala Almirante Manzini, in *Hedda Gabler*. Before he retired at about that time he made several more films with his creation, Maciste. He abandoned the cinema to pursue researches in therapeutic medicine.

—Liam O'Leary

PEARSON, George.

British. Born in London, 1875. Producer/director for British Pathé, from 1913; joined G.B. Samuelson, 1914; joined Gaumont, 1915; formed Welsh Pearson Company with partner T.A. Welsh, 1918; went to U.S. to supervise first Anglo-American co-production, *Journey's End*, 1929; producer, director and writer for newly formed Colonial Film Unit, 1940; retired, 1955. Recipient: Order of the British Empire. *Died 6 February 1973.*

Films as Director:

1913 *Fair Sussex* (doc); *In Dickens Land* (doc); *Rambles Through Hopland* (doc); *Lynmouth* (doc); *Where History Has Been Written* (doc); *Kentish Industries* (doc); *Wonderful Nights of Peter Kinema* (series of shorts); *A Lighter Burden* (short); *Mr. Henpeck's Dilemma* (short); *The Fool*; *Sentence of Death*; *Heroes of the Mine*

1914 *A Fishergirl's Folly* (short); *The Live Wire*; *A Study in Scarlet*; *Christmas Day in the Workhouse* (short); *A Son of France* (short); *Incidents in the Great European War*; *The Cause of the Great European War*; *The Life of Lord Roberts VC*

1915 *Buttons* (short); *For the Empire* (short); *A Cinema Girl's Romance*; *The True Story of the Lyons Mail*; *John Halifax Gentleman*; *Ultus the Man from the Dead*

1916 *Ultus and the Grey Lady*; *Ultus and the Secret of the Night*; *Sally Bishop*

1917 *Ultus and the Three Button Mystery*; *The Man Who Made the Army* (doc); *Canadian Officers in the Making* (doc)

1918 *The Better 'ole*; *The Kiddies in the Ruins*

1919 *Hughie at the Victory Derby* (short)

1920 *Garryowen*; *Nothing Else Matters*

1921 *Mary find the Gold*; *Squibs*

1922 *Mord Em'ly*; *The Wee MacGregor's Sweetheart*; *Squib Wins the Calcutta Sweep*

1923 *Love Life and Laughter*; *Squibs M.P.*; *Squibs' Honeymoon*

1924 *Reveille*

1925 *Satan's Sister*

1926 *The Little People*; *Blinkeyes*

1927 *Huntingtower*

1928 *Love's Option*

1929 *Auld Lang Syne*

1931 *East Lynne on the Western Front*

George Pearson

1932 *The Third String*
1933 *A Shot in the Dark*; *The Pointing Finger*
1934 *River Wolves*; *Four Masked Men*; *Whispering Tongues*; *Open All Night*
1935 *Ace of Spades*; *That's My Uncle*; *Gentleman's Agreement*; *Once a Thief*; *Jubilee Window*; *Checkmate*
1936 *The Secret Voice*; *Wednesday Luck*; *Murder by Rope*
1937 *The Fatal Hour*; *Midnight at Madame Tussaud's*
1938 *Souvenirs* (short); *Old Soldiers* (short); *Mother of Men* (short)
1940 *Land of Water* (doc); *Take Cover* (doc); *Rural School* (doc); *A British Family in Peace and War* (doc)
1941 *British Youth* (doc); *An African in London* (doc)

Other Films:

1912 *Peg Woffington* (sc)
1919 *Pallard the Punter* (sc); *Angel Esquire* (sc)
1930 *Journey's End* (Whale) (supervising pr)
1932 *The Good Companions* (Saville) (assoc pr)
1936 *Shipmates o' Mine* (sc)
1937 *Command Performance* (sc)
1938 *Follow Your Star* (sc)

Publications:

By PEARSON: book—

Flashback: An Autobiography of a British Film Maker, London, 1957.

By PEARSON: article—

"Lambeth Wall to Leicester Square," in *Sight and Sound* (London), Winter 1938/39.

On PEARSON: books—

Low, Rachael, *History of the British Film, 1914–18*, London, 1950
Low, Rachael, *History of the British Film, 1918–29*, London, 1971.

On PEARSON: articles—

"Pearson Issue" of *Silent Picture* (London), Spring 1969.
Slide, Anthony, "Tribute to George Pearson," in *International Film Guide 1974*, London, 1973.
Peet, S., "George Pearson: 1875–1973," in *Sight and Sound* (London), Spring 1973.
Slide, Anthony, "*Journey's End*," letter, in *Films in Review* (New York), March 1975.

* * *

George Pearson was a quiet, scholarly man, as far removed from the public image of a film director as it was possible to be. He had been a schoolmaster, and did not enter a film studio until he was 36 years old, but once Pearson decided he wanted to be a director he quickly became one of the best of the British silent cinema. Pearson never ceased expressing his admiration for D.W. Griffith, and he modeled his directorial style after the master, using the cinema to arouse an audience through emotion rather than technical virtuosity.

The director's first films offered little out of the ordinary for British silent shorts until 1914 when he was given the opportunity to direct *A Study in Scarlet*, the first major adaptation of a Sherlock Holmes story. *A Study in Scarlet* is also noteworthy for its ambitious use of locations, with the Cheddar Gorge standing in for the Rocky Mountains and the Southport Sands for the Salt Lake desert. With the "Ultus" series, produced between 1915 and 1917, George Pearson showed a grasp of the mystery film genre which led to a comparison with France's Louis Feuillade.

In 1918, George Pearson formed his own company in partnership with Tommy Welsh, and produced and directed *The Better 'ole*, based on the cartoons of Bruce Bairnsfather. The film was perhaps the first to treat the First World War in the comic terms of the participating soldiers, and was widely reviewed and released in the United States, one of the first British features to receive international recognition. With *Nothing Else Matters*, George Pearson discovered Betty Balfour, who quickly became the British silent cinema's most popular star. She worked with Pearson on more than half-a-dozen films, notably the "Squibs" series which told of the comic adventures of a cockney flower seller and *Reveille*, a moving study of the after-effects of the First World War on a group of working-class Londoners.

With the coming of sound, George Pearson's career took a downward plunge, and he was kept busy in the 1930s directing a series of low-budget, quota-quickie films, which display little evidence of Pearson's earlier talent. With the Second World War, Pearson was back in demand in his old profession as a teacher with the Colonial Film Unit, educating young filmmakers from the emerging nations. Pearson's value to the British film industry as an instructor should not be overlooked, for many technicians learned their craft with him, notably Thorold Dickinson and Alberto Cavalcanti, who were associated with Pearson on *The Little People*. It was Thorold Dickinson who noted, "Between Cecil Hepworth and Alfred Hitchcock, George Pearson was the outstanding personality in British silent cinema."

—Anthony Slide

PECKINPAH, Sam.

American. Born David Samuel Peckinpah in Fresno, California, 21 February 1925. Educated at Fresno State College, B.A. in Drama 1949; University of Southern California, M.A. 1950. Married 1) Marie Selland, 1947, four children; 2) Begonia Palacios, 1964 (divorced), one child; 3) Joie Gould, 1972 (divorced). Enlisted in Marine Corps, 1943; director/producer in residence, Huntington Park Civic Theatre, California, 1950–51; propman and stagehand, KLAC-TV, Los Angeles, then assistant editor at CBS, 1951–53; assistant to Don Siegel, from 1954; writer for TV, including "Gunsmoke" and "The Rifleman," late 1950s; worked on scripts at Walt Disney Productions, 1963. *Died, of a heart attack, 28 December 1984.*

Films as Director:

1961 *The Deadly Companions* (*Trigger Happy*)
1962 **Ride the High Country** (**Guns in the Afternoon**) (+ co-sc, uncredited)
1965 *Major Dundee* (+ co-sc)
1966 *Noon Wine* (+ sc)
1969 **The Wild Bunch** (+ co-sc)
1970 *The Ballad of Cable Hogue*
1971 *Straw Dogs* (+ co-sc)
1972 *Junior Bonner*; *The Getaway*
1973 *Pat Garrett and Billy the Kid*
1974 *Bring Me the Head of Alfredo Garcia* (+ co-sc)
1975 *The Killer Elite*
1977 *Cross of Iron*
1978 *Convoy*
1983 *The Osterman Weekend*

Other Films:

1956 **Invasion of the Body Snatchers** (Siegel) (role as Charlie the meter reader)

Sam Peckinpah

1978　*China 9 Liberty 37* (Hellmann) (role)
1980　*Il Visitatore* (Paradise) (role)

Publications:

By PECKINPAH: articles—

"A Conversation with Sam Peckinpah," with Ernest Callenbach, in *Film Quarterly* (Berkeley), Winter 1963/64.
"Peckinpah's Return," an interview with Stephen Farber, in *Film Quarterly* (Berkeley), Fall 1969.
"Talking with Peckinpah," with Richard Whitehall, in *Sight and Sound* (London), Autumn 1969.
"Playboy Interview: Sam Peckinpah," with William Murray, in *Playboy* (Chicago), August 1972.

"Don Siegel and Me," in *Don Siegel: Director* by Stuart Kaminsky, New York, 1974.
"Mort Sahl Called Me a 1939 American," in *Film Heritage* (New York), Summer 1976.

On PECKINPAH: books—

Kitses, Jim, *Horizons West*, Bloomington, Indiana, 1970.
Evans, Max, *Sam Peckinpah: Master of Violence*, Vermilion, South Dakota, 1972.
Wurlitzer, Rudolph, *Pat Garrett and Billy the Kid*, New York, 1973.
Caprara, Valerio, *Peckinpah*, Bologna, 1976.
Butler, T., *Crucified Heroes: The Films of Sam Peckinpah*, London, 1979.
McKinney, Doug, *Sam Peckinpah*, Boston, 1979.
Seydor, Paul, *Peckinpah: The Western Films*, Urbana, Illinois, 1980.
Simmons, Garner, *Peckinpah: A Portrait in Montage*, Austin, Texas, 1982.
Arnols, Frank, and Ulrich von Berg, *Sam Peckinpah: Eine Outlaw in Hollywood*, Frankfurt, 1987.
Buscombe, Ed, editor, *The BFI Companion to the Western*, London, 1989.

On PECKINPAH: articles—

McArthur, Colin, "Sam Peckinpah's West," in *Sight and Sound* (London), Autumn 1967.
Sassone, Rich, "The Ballad of Sam Peckinpah," in *Filmmakers Newsletter* (Ward Hill, Massachusetts), March 1969.
Blum, William, "Toward a Cinema of Cruelty," in *Cinema Journal* (Evanston, Illinois), Spring 1970.
Reisner, Joel, and Bruce Kane, "Sam Peckinpah," in *Action* (Los Angeles), June 1970.
Shaffer, Lawrence, "*The Wild Bunch* versus *Straw Dogs*," in *Sight and Sound* (London), Summer 1972.
Andrews, Nigel, "Sam Peckinpah: The Survivor and the Individual," in *Sight and Sound* (London), Spring 1973.
Madsen, A., "Peckinpah in Mexico," in *Sight and Sound* (London), Spring 1974.
Macklin, Anthony, editor, special Peckinpah issue of *Film Heritage* (New York), Winter 1974/75.
Miller, Mark, "In Defense of Sam Peckinpah," in *Film Quarterly* (Berkeley), Spring 1975.
Pettit, Arthur, "Nightmare and Nostalgia: The Cinema West of Sam Peckinpah," in *Western Humanities Review* (Salt Lake City), Spring 1975.
Kael, Pauline, "Notes on the Nihilist Poetry of Sam Peckinpah," in the *New Yorker*, 12 January 1976.
Humphries, R., "The Function of Mexico in Peckinpah's Films," in *Jump Cut* (Berkeley), August 1978.
Fuller, Sam, "A Privilege to Work in Films: Sam Peckinpah Among Friends," in *Movietone News* (Seattle), February 1979.
Jameson, R.T., and others, "Midsection: Sam Peckinpah," in *Film Comment* (New York), January/February 1981.
McCarthy, T., obituary, in *Variety* (New York), 2 January 1985.
Murphy, K., "No Bleeding Heart," in *Film Comment* (New York), March/April 1985.
Bryson, J., "Sam Peckinpah," in *American Film* (Washington, D.C.), April 1985.
Engel, L.W., "Sam Peckinpah's Heroes: Natty Bumppo and the Myth of the Rugged Individual Still Reign," in *Literature/Film Quarterly* (Salisbury, Maryland), January 1988.
Roth, Paul A., "Virtue and Violence in Peckinpah's *The Wild Bunch*," in *Post Script* (Jacksonville, Florida), vol. 7, no. 2, 1988.
Sharrett, Christopher, "Peckinpah the Radical: *The Wild Bunch* Reconsidered," in *CineAction!* (Toronto), no. 13–14, 1988.

*　　　*　　　*

It is as a director of westerns that Sam Peckinpah remains best known. This is not without justice. His non-western movies often lack the sense of complexity and resonance that he brings to western settings. He was adept at exploiting this richest of genres for his own purposes, explaining its ambiguities, pushing its values to uncomfortable limits. *Ride the High Country, Major Dundee,* and *The Wild Bunch* are the work of a filmmaker of high ambitions and rare talents. They convey a sense of important questions posed, yet finally left open and unanswered. At their best they have a visionary edge unparalleled in American cinema.

His non-westerns lose the additional dimensions that the genre brings, as in, for example, *Straw Dogs*. A polished and didactic parable about a besieged liberal academic who is forced by the relentless logic of events into extremes of violence, it is somehow too complete, its answers too pat, to reach beyond its own claustrophobic world. Though its drama is entirely compelling, it lacks the referential framework that carries Peckinpah's westerns far beyond the realm of tautly-directed action. Compared to *The Wild Bunch*, it is a one-dimensional film.

Nevertheless, *Straw Dogs* is immediately recognizable as a Peckinpah movie. If a distinctive style and common themes are the marks of an *auteur*, then Peckinpah's right to that label is indisputable. His concern with the horrors and the virtues of the male group was constant, as was his refusal to accept conventional movie morality. "My father says there's only Right and Wrong, Good and Evil, with nothing in between. But it's not that simple, is it?" asks Elsa in *Ride the High Country*. Judd's reply could almost be Peckinpah's: "No. It should be, but it isn't".

In traditional westerns, of course, right and wrong are clearly distinguishable. The westerner, as Robert Warshow has characterised him, is the man with a code. In Peckinpah's westerns, as in some of his other movies such as *Cross of Iron*, it is the code itself that is rendered problematic. Peckinpah explores the ethic rather than taking it for granted, plays off its elements one against the other, uses his characters as emblems of those internal conflicts. He presents a world whose moral certainty is collapsing, leaving behind doomed variations on assertive individualism. In some modern westerns that theme has been treated as elegy; in Peckinpah it veers nearer to tragedy. His is a harsh world, softened only rarely in movies like *The Ballad of Cable Hogue* and *Junior Bonner*.

His richest achievements remain the two monumental epics of the 1960s, *Major Dundee* and *The Wild Bunch*. In both, though *Major Dundee* was butchered by its producers both before and after shooting, there is ample evidence of Peckinpah's ability to marshall original cinematic means in the service of a morally and aesthetically complex vision. It has become commonplace to associate Peckinpah with the rise of explicit violence in modern cinema, and it is true that few directors have rendered violence with such horrific immediacy. But his cinema is far more than that, his reflections upon familiar western themes technically sophisticated, elaborately constructed, and, at their best, genuinely profound.

—Andrew Tudor

PENN, Arthur.

American. Born in Philadelphia, 27 September 1922. Educated at Black Mountain College, North Carolina, 1947–48; studied at Universities of Perugia and Florence, 1949–50; trained for the stage with Michael Chekhov. Married actress Peggy Maurer, 1955, two children. Enlisted in Army, 1943; joined Soldiers Show Company, Paris, 1945; assistant director on *The Colgate Comedy Hour*, 1951–52; TV director, from 1953, working on *Gulf Playhouse: 1st Person* (NBC), *Philco Television Playhouse* (NBC), and *Playhouse 90* (CBS), from 1953; directed first feature, *The Left-Handed Gun*, 1958; director on Broadway, from 1958. Address: c/o 2 West 67th Street, New York, NY 10023, U.S.A.

Films as Director:

1958 *The Left-Handed Gun*
1962 *The Miracle Worker*
1965 *Mickey One* (+ pr)
1966 *The Chase*
1967 **Bonnie and Clyde**
1969 *Alice's Restaurant* (+ co-sc)
1970 *Little Big Man* (+ pr)
1973 "*The Highest*" in *Visions of 8*
1975 *Night Moves*
1976 *The Missouri Breaks*
1981 *Four Friends*
1985 *Target*
1987 *Dead of Winter*
1989 *Penn and Teller Get Killed*

Publications:

By PENN: articles—

"Rencontre avec Arthur Penn," with André Labarthe and others, in *Cahiers du Cinéma* (Paris), October 1965.
"*Bonnie and Clyde*: Private Morality and Public Violence," in *Take One* (Montreal), vol. 1, no. 6, 1967.
Interview with Michael Lindsay, in *Cinema* (Beverly Hills), vol. 5, no.3, 1969.
Interview in *The Director's Event* by Eric Sherman and Martin Rubin, New York, 1970.
"Metaphor," an interview with Gordon Gow, in *Films and Filming* (London), July 1971.
"Arthur Penn at the Olympic Games," an interview in *American Cinematographer* (Los Angeles), November 1972.
"Night Moves," an interview with T. Gallagher, in *Sight and Sound* (London), Spring 1975.
"Arthur Penn ou l'anti-genre," an interview with Claire Clouzot, in *Ecran* (Paris), December 1976.
Interview with R. Seidman and N. Leiber, in *American Film* (Washington, D.C.), December 1981.
Interview with A. Leroux, in *24 Images* (Montreal), June 1983.
Interview with Richard Combs, in *Monthly Film Bulletin* (London), August 1986.

On PENN: books—

Wood, Robin, *Arthur Penn*, New York, 1969.
Marchesini, Mauro, and Gaetano Stucchi, *Cinque Film di Arthur Penn*, Turin, 1972.
Cawelti, John, editor, *Focus on Bonnie and Clyde*, Englewood Cliffs, New Jersey, 1973.
Carlini, Fabio, *Arthur Penn*, Milan, 1977.
Kolker, Robert Phillip, *A Cinema of Loneliness: Penn, Kubrick, Coppola, Scorsese, Altman*, Oxford, 1980; revised edition, 1988.
Zuker, Joel S., *Arthur Penn: A Guide to References and Resources*, Boston, 1980.
Giannetti, Louis D., *Masters of the American Cinema*, Englewood Cliffs, New Jersey, 1981.
Haustrate, Gaston, *Arthur Penn*, Paris, 1986.
Vernaglione, Paolo, *Arthur Penn*, Florence, 1988.

On PENN: articles—

Hillier, Jim, "Arthur Penn," in *Screen* (London), January/February 1969.
Gelmis, Joseph, "Arthur Penn," in *The Film Director as Superstar* (same author), New York, 1970.
Wood, Robin, "Arthur Penn in Canada," in *Movie* (London), Winter 1970/71.
Margulies, Lee, "Filming the Olympics," in *Action* (Los Angeles), November/December 1972.

"*Le Gaucher* Issue" of *Avant-Scène du Cinéma* (Paris), November 1973.

Byron, Stuart, and Terry Curtis Fox, "What *Is* a Western?," in *Film Comment* (New York), July/August 1976.

Butler, T., "Arthur Penn: The Flight from Identity," in *Movie* (London), Winter 1978/79.

Penn Section of *Casablanca* (Madrid), March 1982.

"TV to Film: A History, a Map and a Family Tree," in *Monthly Film Bulletin* (London), February 1983.

Gallagher, J., and J. Hanc, "Penn's Westerns," in *Films in Review* (New York), August/September 1983.

Camy, G., "Arthur Penn: Un regard sévère sur les U.S.A. des années 60–70," in *Jeune Cinéma* (Paris), April 1985.

* * *

Arthur Penn has often been classed—along with Robert Altman, Bob Rafelson and Francis Coppola—among the more "European" American directors. Stylistically, this is true enough. Penn's films, especially after *Bonnie and Clyde*, tend to be technically experimental, and episodic in structure; their narrative line is elliptical, undermining audience expectations with abrupt shifts in mood and rhythm. Such features can be traced to the influence of the French New Wave, in particular the early films of François Truffaut and Jean-Luc Godard, which Penn greatly admired.

In terms of his thematic preoccupations, though, few directors are more utterly American. Repeatedly, throughout his work, Penn has been concerned to question and re-assess the myths of his country. His films reveal a passionate, ironic, intense involvement with the American experience, and can be seen as an illuminating chart of the country's moral condition over the past 30 years. *Mickey One* is dark with the unfocused guilt and paranoia of the McCarthyite hangover, while the stunned horror of the Kennedy assassination reverberates through *The Chase*. The exhilaration, and the fatal flaws, of the 1960s anti-authoritarian revolt are reflected in *Bonnie and Clyde* and *Alice's Restaurant*. *Little Big Man* reworks the trauma of Vietnam, while *Night Moves* is steeped in the disillusioned malaise that pervaded the Watergate era.

As a focus for his perspective on America, Penn often chooses an outsider group and its relationship with mainstream society. The Indians in *Little Big Man*, the Barrow Gang in *Bonnie and Clyde*, the rustlers in *The Missouri Breaks*, the hippies in *Alice's Restaurant*, the outlaws in *The Left-Handed Gun*, are all sympathetically presented as attractive and vital figures, preferable in many ways to the conventional society which rejects them. But ultimately they suffer defeat, being infected by the flawed values of that same society. "A society," Penn has commented, "has its mirror in its outcasts."

An exceptionally intense, immediate physicality distinguishes Penn's work. Pain, in his films, unmistakably *hurts*, and tactile sensations are vividly communicated. Often, characters are conveyed primarily through their bodily actions: how they move, walk, hold themselves or use their hands. Violence is a recurrent feature of his films—notably in *The Chase, Bonnie and Clyde*, and *The Missouri Breaks*—but it is seldom gratuitously introduced, and represents, in Penn's view, a deeply rooted element in the American character which has to be acknowledged.

Penn's reputation as a director was established by *Bonnie and Clyde*, one of the most significant and influential films of its decade. But since 1970 he has made only five films, none of which did well at the box-office. *Night Moves* and *The Missouri Breaks*, both poorly received on initial release, now rank among his most subtle and intriguing movies, and *Four Friends*, though uneven, remains constantly stimulating with its oblique, elliptical narrative structure.

In the last ten years, though, Penn seems to have lost his way. Neither *Target*, an unremarkable spy thriller, nor *Dead of Winter*, a reworking of Joseph H Lewis's cult B-movie *My Name is Julia Ross*, offered material worthy of his distinctive talents. "It's not that I've drifted away from film," he told Richard Combs in 1986. "I'm very drawn to film, but I'm not sure that film is drawn to me." Given the range, vitality and sheer creative unpredictability of his earlier work, it's to be hoped that the estrangement is only temporary.

—Philip Kemp

PEREIRA DOS SANTOS, Nelson.

Brazilian. Born in São Paolo, 1928. Educated in law; studied at IDHEC, Paris. Journalist, editor at *Jornal do Brasil*, late 1940s; directed first feature, *Rio, quarenta graus*, 1955; teacher of cinema, University of Brasilia, from 1956; collaborated on short films with I. Rozemberg and J. Manzon, 1958–60; director of Dept. of Cinematographic Art, Federal University of Nitéroi, from 1968; participated in founding of filmmakers' cooperative, late 1970s; also editor and co-director of film revue *Luz e Açao*.

Films as Director and Scriptwriter:

1950 *Juventude* (short); *Atividades politicas em Sao Paolo* (short)
1955 *Rio, quarenta graus* (*Rio, 40 Degrees*)
1957 *Rio, zona norte* (*Rio, zone nord*)
1958 *Soldados do fogo* (short)
1960 part of a documentary on Karl Gass made in East Germany
1961 *Mandacaru vermelho* (+ co-pr, role)
1962 *O Bôca de Ouro*; *Ballet do Brasil* (short)
1963 *Vidas secas* (*Barren Lives*); *Um môco de 74 anos* (short)
1964 *O Rio de Machado de Assis* (short)
1965 *Fala Brasilia*
1966 *Cruzada ABC*
1967 *El justiciero* (*Le Justicier*) (+ co-pr)
1968 *Fome de amor* (*Soif d'amour*); *Abastecimento, nova política* (short)
1969 *Azyllo muito louco* (*L'Alieniste*) (co-d)
1971 ***Como é gostoso o meu francês* (*How Tasty Was My Little Frenchman*) (+ co-pr)**
1972 *Quem e beta* (*Pas de violence entre nous*)
1974 *O Amuleta de Ogum* (*The Amulet of Ogum*)
1977 *Tenda dos milagres* (*Tent of Miracles*)
1980 *Na estrada da vida* (*On the Highway of Life*)
1984 *Memorias do carcere* (*Memories of Jail*)
1986 *Jubiaba*

Other Films:

1951 *O scai* (Nanni) (asst d)
1952 *Agulha no palheiro* (Viany) (asst d)
1953 *Balança mas nao caid* (Vanderlei) (asst d)
1958 *O grande momento* (Santos) (pr)
1962 *Barravento* (Rocha) (ed); *Pedreira de São Diogo* (Hirszman) (ed)

Publications:

By PEREIRA DOS SANTOS: articles—

Interview with Leo Murray, in *Cahiers du Cinéma* (Paris), March 1966.

Interview with Fedéric de Cárdenas and Max Tessier, in *Etudes Ciné-matographiques* (Paris), no. 93–96, 1972.

Interview with J. Frenais, in *Cinéma* (Paris), October 1976.

Interview with A. Lima, in *Filme Cultura* (Rio de Janeiro), February 1979.

Interview with Agustin Mahieu, in *Cine Libre* (Madrid), no. 6, 1983.

Interview with Richard Peña, in *Framework* (Norwich), no. 29, 1985.

Interview with Robert Stam, and others, in *Cineaste* (New York), vol. 14, no. 2, 1985.

"Manifesto por un cinema popular," in *Hojas de cine*, by Marcelo Beraba, Mexico City, 1986.

On PEREIRA DOS SANTOS: books—

Rocha, Glauber, *Revisao critica do cinema brasiliero*, Rio de Janeiro, 1963.

Frías, Isaac Léon, *Los años de la conmoción*, Mexico City, 1979.

Johnson, Randal, and Robert Stam, editors, *Brazilian Cinema*, Rutherford, New Jersey, 1982.

Johnson, Randal, *Cinema Novo x 5*, Austin, Texas, 1984.

Burton, Julianne, editor, *Cinema and Social Change in Latin America*, Austin, Texas, 1986.

On PEREIRA DOS SANTOS: articles—

Lefèvre, Raymond, "*Vidas secas*," in *Cinéma* (Paris), November 1965.

Monteiro, José, "Nelson Pereira dos Santos," in *Filme Cultura* (Rio de Janeiro), September/October 1970.

Kinder, Marsha, "*Tent of Miracles*," in *Film Quarterly* (Berkeley), Summer 1978.

"Dossier criticos: *Barre Pesada*," in *Filme Cultura* (Rio de Janeiro), February 1979.

Xavier, I., and others, "Cerimonia da purificaçao," in *Filme Cultura* (Rio de Janeiro), April/August 1984.

Paranagua, P.-A., "Nelson Pereira dos Santos: Trajectoire d'un dépouillement," in *Positif* (Paris), December 1985.

Peña, Richard, "After *Barren Lives*: The Legacy of Cinema Novo," in *Reviewing Histories*, edited by Coco Fusco, Buffalo, New York, 1987.

Mraz, John, "What's Popular in the New Latin American Cinema?," in *Studies in Latin American Popular Culture*, no. 7, 1988.

*   *   *

Considered to be the "mentor" and "conscience" of *Cinema Novo* (New Cinema)—the movement that fundamentally transformed the theory and practice of film in Brazil and Latin America—Nelson Pereira dos Santos encapsulates many of its ideals in his works. The most important of these is the reaction against the domination of Brazilian screens by foreign films and imported cinematic models, for *Cinema Novo* is the result of efforts by directors such as Pereira, Glauber Rocha, and Carlos Diegues to make a genuinely "popular cinema." This concept has been used in a variety of ways, but to Pereira it represents a combination of commercial success and a concern with national identity. Thus, though he criticized early *Cinema Novo* works because they were inaccessible to the general public, he also feels that marketability is not the only criteria by which to judge what is "popular." For Pereira, films must also affirm the principles of Brazilian popular culture, which he sees as dramatically different from "superficial, elitist cultural forms that follow antiquated, colonized models."

The first film to embody the principles of *Cinema Novo* was *Rio, 40 Degrees*, which Pereira dos Santos made in 1955. Greatly influenced by Italian neo-realism, *Rio* was made in the streets of that city and outside studios, and was immersed in Brazil's reality. The story-line presents the poles of Brazilian society, contrasting the lives of the upper and the lower classes through the device of following the activities of five peanut vendors who leave their slum houses to sell their wares in different parts of Rio. Aside from the thematic focus on everyday life, Pereira considers the film's innovative approach to be reflected in the structure of production. The work was made with an absolute minimum of technical resources (a camera and some lights); the crew was composed of friends who did whatever was required of them, rather than technicians who worked only in their speciality; and the film was shot on location, in the places where the stories take place. However, in spite of such low-budget strategies, *Rio* was still expensive enough to sink Pereira so deeply in debt that he was unable to make another feature for four years.

When Pereira did return to feature production, it was to make another "classic" of *Cinema Novo, Barren Lives*. During 1957 and 1958, the filmmaker had been directing documentaries in the Brazilian northeast, where he was greatly struck by the extreme drought conditions typical of that region. At the time, there was much debate about Brazil's agrarian problems, and Pereira participated in that discussion by adapting Graciliano Ramos' book, *Vidas secas*, to the screen. Pereira's experience in making documentaries there served him well, for he was aware that the usual camera filters transformed the arid countryside into an exotic garden. He worked closely with Luiz Carlos Barreto, one of the finest Brazilian cameramen, to produce an austere photography, achieved through high-contrast film shot without filters, which reflected the reality of the area. Pereira further struggled against the sentimentalized and picturesque vision so often rendered of such regions by creating a sound-track in which harsh noises punctuate the narrative.

History is an important source of national identity, and Pereira has directed two historical films of uncommon power and beauty: *How Tasty was my Little Frenchman* and *Prison Memories*. *My Little Frenchman* was made at a time when government censorship made it difficult to produce films on contemporary problems; as Pereira noted: "The government financed historical films, but it wanted the history to be within official parameters—the hero, the father of the country, all those things we have been told since elementary school." This was a seemingly impossible task, but one that Pereira turned to his own uses by making a work that subverted "Official History" by focusing on the Indian perspective of the "discovery" of America and through incorporating contradictions between the images shown and the discourses of government officials in the film. With *Prison Memories*, Pereira returned to Graciliano Ramos for inspiration. Freely adapting the novel in which Ramos described his experiences as a political prisoner during the 1930s, Pereira turned the jail into a metaphor for "the prison of social and political relations which oppress the Brazilian people." In his contemporary and historical cinema, Nelson Pereira dos Santos has explored the depths of Brazilian reality as well as the heights to which that nation's culture is capable of raising it.

—John Mraz

———

PERIES, Lester James.

Sri Lankan. Born in Colombo, Ceylon (now Sri Lanka), 5 April 1919. Educated at Catholic priests' college until 1938. Married director and editor Sumitra Gunawardana. Worked in theatre and on radio, during World War II; sent to London by parents, 1946; returned to Ceylon and joined Government Film Unit, 1952; with cameraman William Blake and editor Titus De Silva (Titus Thotawatte), quit Film Unit to make first Sinhalese language feature shot on location, *Rekava*, 1955.

Films as Director:

1949 *Soliloquy* (short)
1950 *Farewell to Childhood* (short); *A Sinhalese Dance* (short)
1954 *Conquest in the Dry Zone* (short)
1955 *Be Safe or Be Sorry* (short)
1956 *Rekava* (*The Line of Destiny. The Line of Life*) (+ pr, sc)
1960 *Sandesaya* (*The Message*) (+ co-sc)
1961 *Too Many Too Soon* (short)
1962 *Home from the Sea* (short)
1964 *Forward into the Future* (short); *Gamperaliya* (*Changes in the Village*)
1966 *Delovak Athara* (*Between Two Worlds*) (+ co-sc)
1967 *Ran Salu* (*The Yellow Robe*)
1968 *Golu Hadawatha* (*Silence of the Heart*)
1969 *Steel* (short); *Akkara Paha* (*Five Acres of Land*)
1970 *Forty Leagues from Paradise*; *Nidhanaya* (*The Treasure*)
1971 *Kandy Perahera* (*The Procession of Kandy*) (short)
1972 *Desa Nisa* (*The Eyes*)
1973 *The God King*
1976 *Madol Duwa* (*Enchanted Island*)
1978 *Ahasin Polawatha* (*White Flowers for the Dead*)
1979 *Pinhamy* (short); *Veera Puran Appu* (*Rebellion*)
1980 *Baddegama* (*Village in the Jungle*) (+ co-sc)
1982 *Kaliyugaya* (*The Time of Kali*)
1983 *Yuganthayo* (*End of an Era*)

Publications:

By PERIES: articles—

"A Filmmaker in Ceylon," in *Sight and Sound* (London), Autumn 1957.
Interview with M. Sibra, in *Cinéma* (Paris), December 1976.
Interview with A.J. Gunawardana, in *Sight and Sound* (London), Summer 1977.
"A la découverte de Lester James Peries au Festival de La Rochelle," an interview and article with I. Jordan and J.-P. Hautin, in *Positif* (Paris), October 1980; (also November 1980).

On PERIES: book—

Coorey, Philip, *The Lonely Artist*, Colombo, Ceylon (Sri Lanka), 1970.

On PERIES: articles—

Gunawardana, A.J., "A Personal Cinema," in *The Drama Review* (New York), Spring 1971.
Gauthier, G., "Lester James Peries: cinéaste de Sri Lanka," in *Image et Son* (Paris), March 1981.
Elley, Derek, "Lester James Peries," in *International Film Guide 1983*, London, 1982.
Robinson, D., "Bombay/Colombo/Calcutta," in *Sight and Sound* (London), Summer 1985.

*   *   *

The film industry of Sri Lanka (formerly Ceylon), like those of many small countries, suffers from the proximity of a similar but much larger and more prolific industry which dominates both the home market, and potential export markets. For Sri Lankan filmmakers and their audience, film means Indian film, in particular the fantasy-formula movies so beloved of South Indian (Tamil) cinema. Home production has tended to rehash these movies in a Sinhalese version. When Lester James Peries broke away from the Government Film Unit, which largely made documentaries, with the aim of making "films that truly reflected the life of the people of this country . . . valid in terms of cinema as it is generally accepted in other countries," he initiated a revolution in the Sinhalese industry simply, as Philip Coorey remarks in his authoritative study of Peries, *The Lonely Artist*, by "making his films in the way he thought best."

Lester James Peries

"The way he thought best" took Peries out of the studio-bound industry, with its painted backcloths and equally painted actors, into a world of real locations and real people. His first film, *Rekava* (*The Line of Destiny*), was a commercial failure, though critically well-received abroad. As yet, Sri Lankan audiences were not prepared to accept a realistic view of themselves, instead preferring fantasies. But the barrier had been broken, and despite this setback, Peries and his associates persisted, encouraging others to break with the tradition.

In his subsequent films, Peries has endeavoured "to explore human relationships as truly as I can, even if that truth be unpalatable, to do so with sympathy and compassion"—thus producing films with both local relevance, and universal significance. Such works as *Gamperaliya* (*Changes in the Village*), *Nidhanaya* (*The Treasure*), and *Baddegama* (*Village in the Jungle*) are characterized by warmth, visual lyricism, and a powerful narrative instinct which occasionally (by western standards) verges on melodrama.

With some justification, critics have accused Peries of making films which are too slow, too uncommitted. His preoccupation is with the internal conflict of his characters, rather than with the external situations which have precipitated their angst. His is a contemplative cinema—in Coorey's words, "he eavesdrops on the inner and exterior life of his characters." Peries may not specifically condemn social conditions, or make political exposés of the corrupt influences in Sri Lankan society, but by concentrating on the lives of his characters he subtly shows how Sri Lanka, and to some extent every society, imposes on people through superstition, caste and/or class systems, and social mores, a way of life which can lead to much unhappiness, gross stupidity, and a general waste of human potential. A more serious charge against Peries might be that his films show a tendency towards the sentimental. The slow, lyrical style of his work can lead to a softness of approach, where a harder edge might give better dramatic results. However, such attempts at a more dynamic style of cinema as *The God King* (a co-production with Great Britain) have been less than convincing—although still fascinating.

In his compassionate portrayal of his people. Lester James Peries has earned a place beside Satyajit Ray, Flaherty, Renoir,—and Ozu, in the pantheon of humanist filmmakers. But his most distinctive achievement has been the creation, virtually single-handed, of a truly Sri Lankan cinema.

—Theresa FitzGerald

PERRAULT, Pierre.

Canadian. Born in Montreal, 29 June 1927. Educated in classical studies, Collège de Montréal and Collège Grasset, then at Collège Sainte-Marie; studied law, Universities of Montreal, Paris and Toronto. Married Yolande Simard, 1951, two children. Practiced law in Montreal, 1954–56; scriptwriter for Société Radio-Canada, from 1956; directed *Au pays de Neufve-France* for TV, 1959–60; directed (with Michel Brault), first feature, *Pour la suite du monde*, 1963.

Films as Director:

1963   *Pour la suite du monde* (co-d)
1967   *Le Règne du jour*
1969   *Les Voitures d'eau*; *Le Beau Plaisir*
1970   *Un Pays sans bon sens*; *L'Acadie, L'Acadie!* (co-d)
1976   *Le Retour à la terre*; *Un Royaume vous attend*; *Le Goût de la farine*
1977   *C'était un Québécois en Bretagne, madame!*
1979   *Le Pays de la terre sans arbre*; *Gens d'Abitibi*
1982   *La Bête lumineuse*
1983   *Les Voiles bas et en travers*
1986   *Grande allure*

Publications:

By PERRAULT: books

Portulan (poems), Montreal, 1961.
Ballades du temps précieux (poems), Montreal, 1963.
Toutes Isles (stories), Montreal, 1963.
Au coeur de la rose (play), Montreal, 1964.
Le Règne du jour Montreal, 1968.
Les Voitures d'eau, Montreal, 1969.
En désespoir de cause (poems), Montreal, 1971.
Un Pays sans bon sens, Montreal, 1972.
Chouennes (poems), Montreal, 1975.
Discours sur la condition sauvage et québécoise, Montreal, 1977.
Gélivures (poems), Montreal, 1977.
La Bête lumineuse, Montreal, 1982.
Caméramages, Paris, 1983.

By PERRAULT: articles—

"Discours sur la parole," in *Culture Vivante* (Quebec), no. 1, 1966; also in *Cahiers du Cinéma* (Paris), no. 191, 1967.
"La Parole est à Perrault," an interview with M. Basset, in *Cahiers de la Cinémathèque* (Paris), Spring 1972.
"La Femme dans le cinéma québécoise," with G. Gauthier, in *Image et Son* (Paris), January 1973.

"Pierre Perrault et Bernard Gosselin: le gout de la parole québécoise," an interview with P. Demers, in *Cinéma Québec* (Montreal), no. 5, 1976.
Interview with J. Bouthillier Lévesque, in *Positif* (Paris), October 1977.

On PERRAULT: articles—

"Perrault Issue" of *Image et Son* (Paris), January 1972.
La Rochelle, R., and G. Maggi, "The Political Situation of Quebec Cinema," in *Cineaste* (New York), Summer 1972.
Martin, M., and P. Staran, "Trois Aspects du cinéma québécois," in *Ecran* (Paris), April 1977.
Ohlin, P., "The Film as Word (Perrault)," in *Ciné-Tracts* (Montreal), Spring/Summer 1978.
Dansereau, F., and others, "Faut-il bruler le cinéma quebecois?; le leçon du direct," in *Image et Son* (Paris), February 1979.
Clandfield, D., "Le Film ethnographique comme métaculture: la contribution de Pierre Perrault," in *Copie Zéro* (Montreal), October 1981.
Pevere, Geoff, "Aching to Speak: Power and Language in Pierre Perrault's *La Bête Lumineuse*," in *CineAction!* (Toronto), no. 8, 1987.

*   *   *

Canadian Pierre Perrault, along with Americans Richard Leacock and Frederick Wiseman, and France's Jean Rouch, has been the most exemplary practioner of cinema-verité, or candid-eye camera, which revolutionized cinema in the 1960s and introduced new ways of looking at reality. Living in Quebec, he has suffered from a relative isolation so that his important work is not well known outside France or his own country. Colleague Jean Rouch defines his originality well when he states that "it is Bresson's camera coming out of Dziga Vertov's brain and falling on Flaherty's heart: it is *Man of Aran* with direct sound, *Farrebique* with a travelling camera."

The work of Pierre Perrault can be considered an ethnological investigation of the Canadian French community. It could have been achieved only by a man with wide cultural interests. Born in 1927 in Montreal, Perrault has been a lawyer, an athlete, a poet, and a playwright. He also worked on the radio, which explains his great interest in the spoken word (he did 300 broadcasts on the subject of popular traditions). His first documentary work, (13 thirty-minute films for TV in 1959–1960), traditional in style, concerns the Northern side of the Saint Lawrence River and prefigures his major work, the trilogy *Pour la suite du monde, Le Règne du jour*, and *Les Voitures d'eau*. These films center on the Ile aux Coudres (an island which is a microcosm of the French Canadian community), the conflicts of generations, and their search for an identity. With the major contribution of cameraman Michel Brault (who co-directed *Pour la suite du monde* and later *L'Acadie, l'Acadie*), Perrault has made his camera a participant in the life of his people while also attempting to catch their true selves in concrete action. For *Pour la suite du monde*, he asked the islanders to resume sea-hog fishing 38 years after it had been abandoned. Like Flaherty he lived with the community before starting to shoot and asked them to collaborate on the film, thus making it possible for them to express their worries and their passions, going beyond surface realism toward their fantasies and even a collective unconscious.

The development of cinema techniques, particularly light-weight camera equipment and extremely faithful sound recording, have allowed a remarkable flexibility to the film shape, and made possible the recording of people as they see themselves and not as an outsider would see them. The importance of speech (the French Canadians' fight for their autonomy is based on a defense of their language) is paramount in Perrault's work, but we also witness *physically* the problems faced by the islanders. In *Pour la suite du monde*, we see the shaping of a human community through a collective project; in *Le*

Règne du jour, the burial of French culture as a model to follow; in *Les Voitures d'eau* the necessity to adapt an ancient technique of building boats to a more modern usage. Later Perrault's films become much more politicized, even violent. *Un Pays sans bon sens* is a new affirmation of the Quebec identity on the occasion of a trip to French Brittany, and *L'Acadie, l'Acadie* tells of the student fights at Moncton University.

In the 1970s Perrault pursued his investigation of ethnic communities, particularly in a cycle of four films centered on the Abitibi region (*Un Royaume vous attend, Le Retour à la terre, C'était un Québecois en Bretagne, madame!, Gens d'Abitibi*). *La Bête lumineuse*, a totally new experience, is about a hunting party which is given a mythological dimension, very much like Faulkner in his short story *The Bear*. The chase of an animal which we never see and will never be captured becomes a truculent saga where the members of the group reveal themselves through speech and behavior. Faithful to his methods, Perrault adds one more fascinating chapter to his human comedy.

—Michel Ciment

PETRI, Elio.

Italian. Born Eraclio Petri in Rome, 29 January 1929. Educated in literature, University of Rome. Film critic for Communist daily *L'Unita*, 1950s; scriptwriter and assistant director, through 1950s; directed first feature, 1961. Recipient: Oscar for Best Foreign-Language Film, for *Investigation of a Citizen Above Suspicion*, 1970; Best Film (*ex aequo*), Cannes Festival, for *The Working Class Goes to Paradise*, 1972. Died 1982.

Films as Director:

1954 *Nasce un campione* (short) (+ co-sc)
1957 *I sette Contadini* (short) (+ co-sc)
1961 *L'assassino* (*The Lady Killer of Rome*) (+ co-sc)
1962 *I giorni contati* (+ co-sc)
1963 *Il maestro di Vigevano*
1964 "Peccato nel pomeriggio (Sin in the Afternoon)" episode of *Alta infedelta* (*High Infidelity*)
1965 *La decima vittima* (*The Tenth Victim*) (+ co-sc)
1967 *A ciascuno il suo* (*We Still Kill the Old Way*) (+ co-sc)
1968 *Un tranquillo posto di campagna* (*A Quiet Place in the Country*) (+ co-sc)
1970 *Indagine su un cittadino al di sopra di ogni sospietto* (*Investigation of a Citizen Above Suspicion*) (+ co-sc); "Documenti su Giuseppe Pinelli" episode of *Ipotesi* (+ co-sc)
1971 *La classe operaia va in paradiso* (*The Working Class Goes to Heaven. Lulu the Tool*) (+ co-sc)
1973 *La proprietà non è piú un furto* (+ co-sc)
1976 *Todo modo* (+ co-sc)
1978 *Le mani sporche* (for TV) (+ sc)
1979 *Le buone notizie* (+ co-sc)

Other Films:

1952 *Roma ore undici* (*Rome Eleven O'Clock*) (De Santis) (co-sc)
1953 *Un marito per Anna Zaccheo* (*A Husband for Anna*) (De Santis) (co-sc)
1954 *Giorni d'amore* (*Days of Love*) (De Santis) (co-sc)

Elio Petri

1956 *Uomini e lupi* (*Men and Wolves*) (De Santis) (co-sc)
1957 *L'Uomo senza domenica* (De Santis) (co-sc)
1958 *Cesta duga godinu dana* (*La strada lunga un anno*) (De Santis) (co-sc)
1960 *La Garçonnière* (De Santis) (co-sc)

Publications:

By PETRI: books—

L'assassino, Milan, undated.
Roma ora undici, Rome and Milan, 1956.
Indagine su un cittadino al di sopra ogni sospetto, with Ugo Pirro, Rome, 1970.

By PETRI: articles—

Interview with G. Haustrate, in *Cinéma* (Paris), July/August 1972.
"Cinema Is Not for an Elite but for the Masses," an interview with Joan Mellen, in *Cinéaste* (New York), vol. 6, no. 1, 1973.
"*Todo modo*," an interview with J.A. Gili, in *Ecran* (Paris), January 1977.
"L'Enfer selon Petri: bonnes nouvelles," an interview with A. Tournès and A. Tassone, in *Jeune Cinéma* (Paris), September/October 1980.

On PETRI: books—

Gili, Jean, *Elio Petri*, Nice, 1974.
Michalczyk, John J., *The Italian Political Filmmakers*, Cranbury, New Jersey, 1986.

On PETRI: articles—

MacBean, James, in *Film Quarterly* (Berkeley), Spring 1972 and Spring 1973.

Alemanno, R., "Da Rosi a Petri todo modo dentro il contesto," in *Cinema Nuovo* (Bari), July/August 1976.

Roy, J., obituary, in *Cinéma* (Paris), January 1983.

Savioli, A., "I trent'anni di Elio Petri," in *Bianco e Nero* (Rome), October/December 1983.

Elio Petri Section of *Jeune Cinéma* (Paris), December 1983/January 1984.

*   *   *

In his brief career, Elio Petri became renowned as one of the major political filmmakers of the 1960s and 1970s. He was also among the directors who achieved an international stature for the Italian cinema for the third time in its history. From his first feature, an original variation on the police thriller, he maintained a consistently high quality of style and poignant subject matter. Even with the bitterness, grotesqueness and complexity of his films, many of them achieved a huge commercial success.

The Tenth Victim, for example, a stylized science-fiction collage of Americanisms which concentrates on the voracious rapport between a man (Marcello Mastroianni) and a woman (Ursula Andress), plays repeatedly on American television. *Investigation of a Citizen Above Suspicion* (which won the Oscar for best foreign film) and *The Working Class Goes to Heaven* have enjoyed continued success with contemporary audiences through repertory screenings and 16mm distribution. With *Investigation*, Petri wanted to make a film against the police and the mechanisms that guaranteed immunity to the servants of power, yet intended no precise political references. His claim was that the state manifests itself through the police. Like his earlier film, *A ciascuno il suo*, it opens with a murder committed by a police official (Gian Maria Volonté) but, because of his position and manipulation of the system, it remains a crime without punishment. The film brilliantly studies the psychopathology of power whereas, with his other enormous success, *The Working Class . . .*, Petri wanted to return to what he considered was the real basis of Italian neorealism—a popular hero. Filmed in a factory whose director was serving a prison sentence, it investigates the reasons why a worker is driven to strike. Again the protagonist was played by Volonté (whose name in the film, Massa, means "the masses"). Although he is a highly individualized character, Petri continually stresses that his actions, thoughts, goals, and even his sexuality, are determined by society and its rules.

Two common themes running throughout Petri's work have been the alienation of modern man and investigations of the socio-political relationships between an individual and his/her society. Petri usually employs a highly stylistic form which he often describes as expressionist. This is most obvious, for example, in *Todo modo*, aptly described as a celebration of death. Quite grotesque, the film was not well received in Italy where, despite its extreme stylization, it was read as a precise analogy of the ruling political party.

Petri began his film career as a scriptwriter, most notably for Giuseppe De Santis's *Rome Eleven O'Clock*: Petri often stated that De Santis was his only mentor and, like him, Petri directed relatively few films, carefully chosen for content and precisely planned in style and detail. Filmmaking was, in his opinion, the most powerful tool with which a culture could understand itself. Thus, he is considered not an artisan, but an auteur, a filmmaker who closely identified the filmmaking process with personal, social, moral and political duties.

—Elaine Mancini

PHALKE, Dadasaheb.

Indian. Born Dhundiraj Govind Phalke in Trymbakeshwar, near Nasik, 30 April 1870. Studied drawing at J.J. School of Arts, Bombay; art studies at Kalabhavan, Baroda. Married 1) 1885 (died 1900); 2) Saraswatabai (Phalke), daughter Mandakini. Portrait photographer and scene painter, from 1900; draughtsman and photographer, Government of India's Archaelogical Department, 1903; opened Phalke Engraving and Printing Works, 1905; left business, saw *Life of Christ* in Bombay, inspired to make films, 1910; made short film, *Growth of a Pea Plant*, 1911; suffered temporary blindness; travelled to London to buy filmmaking equipment, met Cecil Hepworth, 1912; returned to build studio in Bombay, then made first feature film and first Indian film, *Raja Harishchandra*, released April 1913; "Phalke's Films" incorporated into the Hindustan Film Company, 1917; daughter played role of boy Krishna in *Kaliya Mardan*, 1918; retired to Benares, 1919; recalled to direct, 1922; attempted to set up business selling enamel boards, 1933; recalled for last film as director, *Gangavataran*, 1934 (completed 1936). *Died in Nasik, 16 February 1944.*

Films as Director, Scriptwriter, Producer, and Cinematographer:

(partial list: Phalke made approximately 100 feature films and 22 shorts)

1911   *Growth of a Pea Plant* (short)
1913   *Raja Harishchandra*
1914   *Mohini Bhasmasur*; *Pithache Panje* (short); *Savitri Stayavan*
1914/15 *Soulagna Rasa*; *Mr. Sleepy's Good Luck*; *Agkadyanchi Mouj* (anim); *Animated Coins* (anim); *Vichitra Shilpa* (*Inanimate Animated*) (anim); *Sinhasta Parvani*; *Kartiki Purnima Festival*; *Ganesh Utsava*; *Glass Works* (doc); *Talegaon* (doc); *Bird's Eye View of Budh Gaya* (doc); *Rock-Cut Temples of Ellora* (doc); *How Films Are Made* (short); *Prof. Kelpha's Magic* (+ role)
1916/17 *Raja Harishchandra* (new version); *Lanka Dahan*
1918   *Shree Krishna Janma*; *Kaliya Mardan*
1923   *Sati Mahananda*
1932   *Setu Bandhan*
1937   *Gangavataran*
1965   *Raja Harishchandra: D.G. Phalke (1870–1944): The First Indian Film Director* (compiled by Prof. Satish Bahadur)

Publications:

By PHALKE: articles—

Four articles in *Navyug* (Bombay), September 1983.
Interview reprinted in *Close Up* (India), July 1968.

On PHALKE: books—

Barnouw, Erik, and S. Krishnasway, *Indian Film*, New York, 1965.
Ramachandran, T.M., *70 Years of Indian Cinema (1913–1983)*, Bombay, 1985.

On PHALKE: articles—

Close Up (India), January/March 1979.
Cinema Vision, January 1980.
Rajadhyaksha, A., "Neo-traditionalism," in *Framework* (Norwich), no. 32–33, 1986.

*   *   *

In 1912, Dadasaheb Phalke made *Raja Harishchandra*, conventionally considered India's first feature film. Between 1912 and 1917, despite problems relating to finance and the import of equipment because of the war, Phalke and Co., as this director's concern was called, managed to remain in production.

And so Phalke's grand-sounding claim, that he started the Indian film industry, is actually quite a reasonable one.

Phalke brought an impressive string of qualifications to the cinema: painter, printer, engraver, photographer, drama teacher and magician. The last distinction is particularly notable. He explained that his decision to make Hindu mythological films was due not only to to the religious-mindedness of his audiences, but also because such subjects allowed him "to bring in mystery and miracles." The mythological was especially suited to fulfil the early fascination with the cinema as magical toy: hence the extensive use of dissolves and superimpositions to herald miraculous happenings in the handful of Phalke's films that have survived.

The Phalke biography is instructive for the insights it provides about media history. A well-known early story is that Phalke's immersion in intense viewing and experimentation led to ill health and temporary blindness. There is a revelatory, metaphorical aspect to the loss and recovery of sight in a man who declared that he would bring images of revered Indian deities to the screen, just as Christ's had been in the West. Earlier, as photographer and printer Phalke had been involved in the mass production of the famous religious paintings of Raja Ravi Varma. Phalke's work therefore wove into the early history of cultural self-representation through new media technologies, a period intimately related to the creation of a mass market in indigenous imagery and identity.

Equally important was his relationship with the theatre. At the time Phalke's first films were released in Bombay, it was said that the cinema was displacing traditional entertainments, such as the theatre and circus, because of its astounding popularity. When Phalke took his films to Poona in 1913, they were screened at a theatre which normally exhibited performances of *Tamasha*, a western Indian dramatic form. But theatre left its mark on the new entertainment. In *Raja Harischandra*, the priest as comic character, a staple of the western Indian stage, was used. And it was because of the development of the theatrical tradition that Phalke was able get the women performers he sought for his female roles—even prostitutes had refused to associate themselves with films. A lay-off in a theatrical company briefly secured for him the services of Durgabhai Gokhale and her daughter, Kamalabhai, the first women actresses of the Indian cinema.

For financial reasons, Phalke and Co. merged with the Hindustan Film Company in 1918, and except for the period 1919–22, Phalke continued to work with this company till 1932, when it was wound up. In his working life as director, which spanned the ages of 42 to 64, Phalke made some 122 feature films and shorts, concluding his career with *Gangavataran*, the only one planned as a talkie. Thereafter he conceived of various schemes, such as setting up a production unit for short films for the Prabhat company, but nothing came of these ideas, and the last years of his life were spent in relative obscurity.

—Ravi Vasudevan

PIALAT, Maurice.

French. Born in Puy de Dôme, 31 August 1925. Studied Art at Ecole des Arts Décoratifs and Ecole des Beaux Arts, Paris. Exhibited work at salons, 1945–47; actor and assistant stage director to Michel Vitold, from 1955; worked in TV, made films, from 1960; directed first feature, 1967. Recipient: Jean Vigo Prize, for *L'Enfance nue*, 1967; Prix Louis Delluc, and César for Best Film, for *A Nos Amours*, 1983; Palme d'Or, Cannes Festival, for *Sous le Soleil de Satan*, 1987.

Films as Director:

1960   *L'Amour existe* (short)
1961   *Janine* (for TV)
1962   *Maitre Galip* (for TV)
1967   *L'Enfance nue* (+ sc)
1971   *La Maison des bois* (for TV) (+ role)
1972   *Nous ne vieillirons pas ensemble* (+ sc, pr)
1974   *La Gueule ouverte* (+ sc, pr)
1979   *Passe ton bac d'abord*
1979   *Loulou*
1983   *A Nos Amours* (*To Our Loves*)
1985   *Police* (+ co-sc)
1987   *Sous le soleil de Satan* (*Under Satan's Sun*) (+ co-sc)

Other Film:

1969   *Que la bete meure* (Chabrol) (role)

Publications:

By PIALAT: book—

Nous ne vieillirons pas ensemble, Paris, 1972.

By PIALAT: articles—

Interview in *Image et Son* (Paris), March 1972.
Interviews in *Positif* (Paris), May 1974 and October 1980.
Interviews in *Cahiers du Cinéma* (Paris), October 1979 and December 1983.
Interview with E. Carrère and M. Sineux, in *Positif* (Paris), January 1984.
Interview with Michel Ciment and others, in *Positif* (Paris), October 1985.
Interview with Serge Toubiana and Alain Philippon, in *Cahiers du Cinéma* (Paris), September 1987.

On PIALAT: articles—

Bonitzer, Pascal, "Le rayonnement Pialat," in *Cahiers du Cinéma* (Paris), May 1981.
Dossier on Pialat, in *Cinématographe* (Paris), November 1983.
Pialat Section of *Cahiers du Cinéma* (Paris), December 1983.
Gras, P., "Maurice Pialat," in *Revue du Cinéma* (Paris), September 1985.
Vincendeau, Ginette, "Pialat le terrible," in *Monthly Film Bulletin* (London), March 1986.
Martin, Marcel, and G. Lenne, "Le Silence de Dieu. Critiques dans l'auditorium: perplexes," in *Revue du Cinéma* (Paris), September 1987.

*   *   *

Described by Alain Bergala in *Cahiers du cinéma* as "Renoir's true heir today," Maurice Pialat is squarely in the tradition of French *auteur* cinema. Like Renoir, Feyder and Grémillon in the 1930s, and Godard, Resnais, Varda and a few others after the war, Pialat is an artisan who works both within and against the French film industry. He has often acknowledged his "debt" to Renoir, as well as to Pagnol, in terms of both working methods and a certain conception of realism. However, unlike the benign humanism of these two predecessors, Pialat's work is marked by harshness, violence and conflict, both on and off screen.

From his first feature (*L'Enfance nue*, on deprived childhood), Pialat's films have shown an almost ethnographic con-

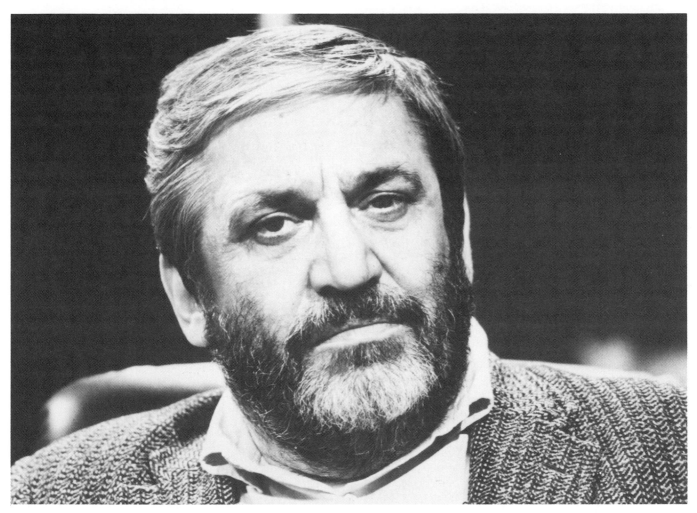

Maurice Pialat

cern with unglamorous areas of French society: difficult adolescents (*Passe ton bac d'abord*), semi-hooligans (*Loulou*), the bitter breakdown of a couple (*Nous ne vieillirons pas ensemble*) and cancer (*La Gueule ouverte*), combining a quasi *cinéma-vérité* approach with the reworking of deeply personal matters. Although Pialat has claimed to be "fed up with realism," and even though he has made forays into genre films with *Police* and *Sous le soleil de Satan*, his cinema is still within a realistic idiom, fusing the New Wave (and neo-realist) concern with location shooting and contemporary setting with the "intimate" realism of the central European cinema of the 1960s. His films draw on basic realist strategies such as the use of non-professional or little-known actors (sometimes alongside stars like Gérard Depardieu, and on occasion—Renoir-style—the charismatic Pialat himself), the frequent recourse to improvisation and colloquial language, hand-held camerawork, long takes, and shooting without a finished script. If these strategies traditionally produce a sense of immediacy and authenticity, they often combine, in Pialat's films, with a rare violence.

Pialat has earned a reputation as a "difficult" director. To some extent, this is an inherent part of the myth of *auteur* cinema which stresses the romantic pains of creation. Yet Pialat's career is littered with well-publicized working and personal conflicts: with actors Gérard Depardieu (*Loulou*) and Sophie Marceau (*Police*), with scriptwriter Catherine Breillat over *Police*, and with technicians on many occasions. But part of his method consists precisely of inscribing his own personal relationships within the fabric of his films, as epitomised in *A nos amours* by the Pialat/Bonnaire couple (on several professional and personal levels).

"*Pialat le terrible*," as he was dubbed by a French paper, sometimes makes headlines, and occasionally the courtrooms. This would be mere gossip if it didn't echo the very subject matter of his films. In the same way as Sam Fuller defined cinema as "a battleground," Pialat's filmmaking might be described as belonging to the boxing ring. He has repeatedly stated his preference for situations where people have rows, where they clash, where "there is trouble," and this is borne out by all his films, where conflict is the preferred element, a type of conflict which moreover assumes a great physicality. In Pialat's cinema, contact is more likely to be made through violence than through tenderness, particularly within the family, where the boxing ring overlaps with the Oedipal stage. This is true both thematically (families and couples tearing each other apart), and in the way Pialat's films address their spectators. A predominance of indoor scenes shot in claustrophobic medium close-ups, and the deliberate inclusion of "flawed" episodes, of moments of rupture or tension in the films, are ways of capturing "the truth" of characters or situations, sometimes with little regard for narrative continuity. Pialat doesn't pull his punches and his cinema, in the words of editor Yann Dedet, "tends more towards emotion than comprehension."

If Pialat's films, in their bleak examination of some of the least palatable aspects of contemporary French society and personal emotions, make for difficult viewing, their reward lies in an emotional and documentary power rare in French cinema today.

—Ginette Vincendeau

PICK, Lupu.

(also known as "Lupu-Pick.") Romanian. Born in Iasi (Jassy), 2 January 1886. Married Edith Pasca. Actor in Romania, 1914; emigrated to Germany, acted in Hamburg and Berlin, 1915; founded production company Rex Filmgesellschaft, 1917; directed first film, 1918; elected President of DACHO (German actors' union), 1930. *Died in Berlin, 9 March 1931.*

Films as Director:

1918   *Der Weltspiegel; Die Liebe des van Royk; Die Rothenburger; Die tolle Heirat von Laló; Mister Wu*

1919   *Der Seelenverkäufer; Herr über Leben und Tod; Kitsch; Marionetten der Leidenschaft; Mein Wille ist Gesetz; Tötet nicht mehr!; Misericordia* (+ pr)
1920   *Der Dummkopf (The Idiot)* (+ role); *Niemand weiss es*
1921   *Aus den Erinnerungen eines Frauenarztes* Part 2; *Grausige Nächte; Scherben (Shattered)*
1922   *Zum Paradies der Damen*
1923   *Sylvester (New Year's Eve); Der verbotene Weg* (+ role)
1924   *La Péniche tragique*
1925   *Das Haus der Lüge*
1926   *Das Panzergewölbe (Armored Vault)* (+ co-sc)
1928   *Eine Nacht in London (A Night in London)* (+ pr)
1929   *Napoléon a Sainte-Hélène (Napoleon auf St. Helena)*
1931   *Les Quatres Vagabonds; Gassenhauer*

Other Films:

1915   *Schlemihl* (Oswald) (role); *Hoffmanns Erzählungen* (Oswald) (role); *Die Pagode* (Mr. Wu) (role)
1916   *Nächte des Grauens* (Robison) (role); *Homunculus* series (role)
1917   *Die Fremde* (role)
1917/18   *Es werde Licht* (3 episodes) (role)
1922   *Fliehende Schatten* (Lamprecht) (co-sc, role)
1923   *Stadt in Sicht* (role)
1926   *Alte Herzen, neue Zeiten* (role)
1928   *Spione* (Lang) (role)

Lupu Pick: *Scherben*

Publications:

On PICK: books—

Kracauer, Siegfried, *From Caligari to Hitler: A Psychological History of the German Film*, Princeton, New Jersey, 1947.
Borde, Raymond, Freddy Bauche, François Courtade, and Marcel Tariol, *Le Cinéma réaliste allemand*, Paris, 1959.
Eisner, Lotte, *The Haunted Screen: Expressionism in the German Cinema and the Influence of Max Reinhardt*, translated by Robert Greaves, Berkeley and Los Angeles, 1969.
Manvell, Roger, and Heinrich Fraenkel, *The German Cinema*, New York, 1971.

*　　　*　　　*

Lupu Pick, a pioneer of the German *Kammerspielfilm* that led the way from expressionism to the new realism of the late 1920s, came to the cinema from the Berlin stage where he worked as an actor under Piscator and Reinhardt. His first films as a director were segments of an adventure series for popular actor Bernd Aldor.

Two films that Pick created with scriptwriter Carl Mayer, *Scherben* and *Sylvester*, are the basis of his reputation. *Scherben* was the first German experiment in filmmaking without intertitles. Pick and Mayer adapted the name of Reinhardt's smallest stage—which had come to represent the intimacy and concentration of the plays staged there—in the subtitle of their first film together; *Scherben, ein deutsches Filmkammerspiel*. Critics often attribute the success of *Scherben* and *Sylvester* to Mayer. Indeed, Mayer wrote many of the films usually counted as *kammerspielfilme*, working with Murnau, Jessner and Gerlack. But, undeniably, Pick contributed his unique interpretation of Mayer's scripts.

Scherben uses a single intertitle and is distinguished by the extended use of a moving camera, especially in long tracking shots along railway ties. This movement contrasts sharply with the stationary plot, the slow movement of the actors and the long held, still shots. At times masks seem to be used in response to the expressionist punctuation Mayer used in his scripts. Diagonal slash masks isolate an image just as Mayer's one word sentences are set off by exclamation marks.

Pick was concerned to created a new, non-expressionist style, concentrating on naturalistic detail rather than on abstraction. Perhaps it was this enthusiasm for naturalism which led Pick to linger over the process of mechanical tasks and everyday events. Yet his work remains tied to the Expressionist movement. The actors, especially his wife Edith Posca and Werner Krauss, operated within the range of theatrical Expressionist style. Shot at Pick's own Rex Studios in Berlin, *Scherben* is to a great extent manufactured in the studio, although its intent and its effect involve a realist illusion.

Unlike filmmakers truly caught up in Expressionism, Pick was concerned with portraying individual psychology. In his attempts to construct a drama without language he developed a system of irises and dissolves that is quite different from the psychological editing style then developing in Hollywood. Rather than cut to a reaction, Pick often masked the frame, isolating a single character. At other times he would compose a shot so that an object, framed in relation to a character, could represent a thought.

Perhaps it can be said that the style Pick developed had little influence on subsequent filmmaking, but nevertheless, it was a bold experiment in film narrative in its time.

Originally Pick and Mayer had planned a trilogy including *Scherben, Sylvester* and *Der letze Mann*, but a disagreement over the character of the doorman in the third film led to Pick's leaving the project.

The films Pick made after his collaboration with Mayer are

not remembered by many. He continued to work as an actor both on stage and in films. His best known role is that of Dr. Matsumoto in Lang's *Spione*. Pick made a single sound film, *Gassenhauer*, reportedly an experiment in asynchronous sound.

—Ann Harris

————

POLANSKI, Roman.

Polish. Born in Paris, 18 August 1933. Educated at Krakow Liceum Sztuk Plastycznych (art school), 1950–53; State Film School, Lodz, 1954–59. Married 1) actress Barbara Kwiatkowska, 1959 (divorced 1961); 2) actress Sharon Tate, 1968 (died 1969); 3) actress Emmanuelle Seigner, 1989. Returned to Poland, 1936; actor on radio and in theatre, from 1945, in films from 1951; joined filmmaking group KAMERA as assistant to Andrzej Munk, 1959; directed first feature, *Knife in the Water*, 1962, denounced by Polish Communist Party chief Gomulka, funding for subsequent films denied, moved to Paris, 1963; moved to London, 1964, then Los Angeles, 1968; wife Sharon Tate and 3 friends murdered in Bel Air, California, home by members of Charles Manson cult, 1969; opera director, from 1974; convicted by his own plea of unlawful sexual intercourse in California, 1977; committed to a diagnostic facility, Department of Correction; upon completion of study, returned to Paris; also stage actor and director. Recipient: Silver Bear, Berlin Film Festival, for *Repulsion*, 1965; Golden Bear, Berlin Festival, for *Cul-de-Sac*, 1966; César Award, for *Tess*, 1980. Lives in Paris.

Films as Director and Scriptwriter:

1955/7　*Rower* (*The Bike*) (short)
1957/8　*Morderstwo* (*The Crime*) (short)
1958　*Rozbijemy zabawe* (*Break Up the Dance*) (short); *Dwaj ludzie z szasa* (*2 Men and a Wardrobe*) (short) (+ role)
1959　*Gdy spadaja anioly* (*When Angels Fall*)) (short) (+ role as old woman)
1961　*Le Gros et le maigre* (*The Fat Man and the Thin Man*) (short) (co-sc, + role as servant)
1962　*Ssaki* (*Mammals*) (short) (co-sc, + role); *Nóz w wodzie* (***Knife in the Water***) (co-sc)
1963　"La Rivière de diamants" ("A River of Diamonds") episode of *Les Plus Belles Escroqueries du monde* (*The Most Beautiful Swindles in the World*) (co-sc)
1964　***Repulsion*** (co-sc)
1965　*Cul-de-sac* (co-sc)
1967　*The Fearless Vampire Killers* (*Pardon Me, But Your Teeth Are in My Neck. Dance of the Vampires*) (co-sc, + role as Alfred)
1968　***Rosemary's Baby***
1972　*Macbeth* (co-sc)
1973　*What?* (*Che?. Diary of Forbidden Dreams*) (co-sc, + role as Mosquito)
1974　***Chinatown*** (d only, + role as man with knife)
1976　*Le Locataire* (*The Tenant*) (co-sc, + role as Trelkovsky)
1979　*Tess* (co-sc)
1985　*Pirates* (co-sc)
1988　*Frantic* (co-sc)

Other Films:

1953　*Trzy opowiesci* (*Three Stories*) (Nalecki, Poleska, Petelski) (role as Maly)

Roman Polanski

1954 *Pokolenie* (*A Generation*) (Wajda) (role as Mundek)
1955 *Zaczárowany rower* (*The Enchanted Bicycle*) (Sternfeld) (role as Adas)
1956 *Koniec wojny* (*End of the Night*) (Dziedzina, Komorowski, Uszycka) (role as Maly)
1957 *Wraki* (*Wrecks*) (Petelski) (role)
1958 *Zadzwoncie do mojej zony* (*Phone My Wife*) (Mach) (role)
1959 *Lotna* (Wajda) (role as bandsman)
1960 *Niewinni czarodzieje* (*Innocent Sorcerors*) (Wajda) (role as Dudzio); *Ostroznie yeti* (*The Abominable Snowman*) (Czekalski) (role); *Do Widzenia do Jutra* (*See You Tomorrow*) (Morgenstern) (role as Romek); *Zezowate szczescie* (*Bad Luck*) (Munk) (role)
1964 *Do You Like Women?* (Léon) (co-sc)
1968 *The Woman Opposite* (Simon) (co-sc)
1969 *A Day at the Beach* (Hessera) (pr); *The Magic Christian* (McGrath) (role)
1972 *Weekend of a Champion* (Simon) (pr, role as interviewer)
1974 *Blood for Dracula* (Morrissey) (role as a villager)

Publications:

By POLANSKI: books—

What?, New York, 1973.
3 Films, London, 1975.
Roman, London, 1984.

Polanski par Polanski, edited by Pierre-André Boutang, Paris, 1986.

By POLANSKI: articles—

Interview with Gretchen Weinberg, in *Sight and Sound* (London), Winter 1963/64.
"Landscape of a Mind: Interview with Roman Polanski" with Michel Delahaye and Jean-André Fieschi, in *Cahiers du Cinema in English* (New York), February 1966.
Interview with Michel Delahaye and Jean Narboni, in *Cahiers du Cinéma* (Paris), January 1968.
"Polanski in New York," an interview with Harrison Engle, in *Film Comment* (New York), Fall 1968.
Interview with Joel Reisner and Bruce Kane, in *Cinema* (Los Angeles), vol. 5, no. 2, 1969.
"Satisfaction: A Most Unpleasant Feeling," an interview with Gordon Gow, in *Films and Filming* (London), April 1969.
Interview, in *The Film Director as Superstar* by Joseph Gelmis, Garden City, New York, 1970.
"Playboy Interview: Roman Polanski," with Larry DuBois, in *Playboy* (Chicago), December 1971.
"Andy Warhol Tapes Roman Polanski," in *Inter/View* (New York), November 1973.
"Dialogue on Film: Roman Polanski," in *American Film* (Washington, D.C.), August 1974.
"Roman Polanski on Acting," with D. Brandes, in *Cinema Papers* (Melbourne), January 1977.
"*Tess*," an interview with Serge Daney and others, in *Cahiers du Cinéma* (Paris), December 1979.

Interview with P. Pawlikowski and L. Kolodziejczyk, in *Stills* (London), April/May 1984.

Interview with O. Darmon, in *Cinématographe* (Paris), May 1986.

On POLANSKI: books—

Butler, Ivan, *The Cinema of Roman Polanski*, New York, 1970.

Kane, Pascal, *Roman Polanski*, Paris, 1970.

Belmans, Jacques, *Roman Polanski*, Paris, 1971.

Bisplinghoff, Gretchen, and Virginia Wexman, *Roman Polanski: a Guide to References and Resources*, Boston, 1979.

Kiernan, Thomas, *The Roman Polanski Story*, New York, 1980.

Leaming, Barbara, *Polanski: The Filmmaker as Voyeur: A Biography*, New York, 1981; as *Polanski: His Life and Films*, London, 1982.

Paul, David W., *Politics, Art, and Commitment in the Eastern European Cinema*, New York, 1983.

Dokumentation: Polanski und Skolimowski: Das Absurde im Film, Zurich, 1985.

Wexman, Virginia Wright, *Roman Polanski*, Boston, 1985.

Jacobsen, Wolfgang, and others, *Roman Polanski*, Munich, 1986.

Avron, Dominique, *Roman Polanski*, Paris, 1987.

On POLANSKI: articles—

Haudiquet, Philippe, "Roman Polanski," in *Image et Son* (Paris), February/March 1964.

Brach, Gérard, "Polanski via Brach," in *Cinéma* (Paris), no. 93, 1965.

McArthur, Colin, "Polanski," in *Sight and Sound* (London), Winter 1968.

McCarty, John, "The Polanski Puzzle," in *Take One* (Montreal), May/June 1969.

Tynan, Kenneth, "Polish Imposition," in *Esquire* (New York), September 1971.

"Le Bal des vampires," special Polanski issue of *Avant-Scène du Cinéma* (Paris), January 1975.

Leach, J., "Notes on Polanski's Cinema of Cruelty," in *Wide Angle* (Athens, Ohio), vol. 2, no. 1, 1978.

Kennedy, H., "*Tess*: Polanski in Hardy Country," in *American Film* (Washington, D.C.), October 1979.

"L'Univers de Roman Polanski," special section, in *Cinéma* (Paris), February 1980.

Sinyard, Neil, "Roman Polanski," in *Cinema Papers* (Melbourne), November/December 1981.

Polanski Section of *Kino* (Warsaw), July 1986.

Polanski Section of *Positif* (Paris), May 1988.

Sutton, M., "Polanski in Profile," in *Films and Filming* (London), September 1988.

*   *   *

As a student at the Polish State Film School and later as a director working under government sponsorship, Roman Polanski learned to make films with few resources. Using only a few trained actors (there are but three characters in his first feature) and a hand-held camera (due to the unavailabililty of sophisticated equipment) Polanski managed to create several films which contributed to the international reputation of the burgeoning Polish cinema. These same limitations contributed to the development of a visual style which was well suited to the director's perspective on modern life: one which emphasized the sort of precarious, unstable world suggested by a hand-held camera, and the sense of isolation or removal from a larger society which follows the use of only small groupings of characters. In fact, Polanski's work might be seen as an attempt to map out the precise relationship between the contemporary world's instability and tendency to violence and the individual's increasing inability to overcome his isolation and locate some realm of meaning or value beyond himself.

What makes this concern with the individual and his psyche especially remarkable is Polanski's cultural background. As a product of a socialist state and its official film school at Lodz, he was expected to use his filmmaking skills to advance the appropriate social consciousness and ideology sanctioned by the government. However, Polanski's first feature, *Knife in the Water*, drew the ire of the Communist Pary and was denounced at the Party Congress in 1964 for showing the negative aspects of Polish life. Although less an ideological statement than an examination of the various ways in which individual desires and powers determine our lives, *Knife in the Water* and the response it received seem to have precipitated Polanski's subsequent development into a truly international filmmaker. In a career that has taken him to France, England, Italy, and the United States in search of opportunities to write, direct, and act, he has consistently shown more interest in holding up a mirror to the individual impulses, unconscious urges, and the personal psychoses of human life than in dissecting the different social and political forces he has observed.

The various landscapes and geographies of Polanski's films certainly seem designed to enhance this focus, for they pointedly remove his characters from most of the normal structures of social life as well as from other people. The boat at sea in *Knife in the Water*, the oppressive flat and adjoining convent in *Repulsion*, the isolated castle and flooded causeway of *Cul-de-sac*, the prison-like apartments of *Rosemary's Baby* and *The Tenant*, and the empty fields and deserted manor house in *Tess* form a geography of isolation that is often symbolically transformed into a geography of the mind, haunted by doubts, fears, desires, or even madness. The very titles of films like *Cul-de-sac* and *Chinatown* are especially telling in this regard, for they point to the essential strangeness and isolation of Polanski's locales, as well as to the sense of alienation and entrapment which consequently afflicts his characters. Brought to such strange and oppressive environments by the conditions of their culture (*Chinatown*), their own misunderstood urges (*Repulsion*), or some inexplicable fate (*Macbeth*), Polanski's protagonists struggle to make the unnatural seem natural, to turn entrapment into an abode, although the result is typically tragic, as in the case of *Macbeth*, or absurd, as in *Cul-de-sac*.

Such situations have prompted numerous comparisons, especially of Polanski's early films, to the absurdist dramas of Samuel Beckett. As in many of Beckett's plays, language and its inadequacy play a significant role in Polanski's works, usually forming a commentary on the absence or failure of communication in modern society. The dramatic use of silence in *Knife in the Water* actually "speaks" more eloquently than much of the film's dialogue of the tensions and desires which drive its characters and operate just beneath the personalities they try to project. In the conversational clichés and banality which mark much of the dialogue in *Cul-de-sac*, we can discern how language often serves to cloak rather than communicate meaning. The problem, as the director most clearly shows in *Chinatown*, is that language often simply proves inadequate for capturing and conveying the complex and enigmatic nature of the human situation. Detective Jake Gittes's consternation when Evelyn Mulwray tries to explain that the girl he has been seeking is both her daughter and her sister—the result of an incestuous affair with her father—points out this linguistic inadequacy for communicating the most discomfiting truths. It is a point driven home at the film's end when, after Mrs. Mulwray is killed, Gittes is advised not to try to "say anything." His inabililty to articulate the horrors he has witnessed ultimately translates into the symptomatic lapse into silence also exhibited by the protagonists of *The Tenant* and *Tess*, as they find themselves increasingly bewildered by the powerful driving forces of their own psyches and the worlds they inhabit.

Prompting this tendency to silence, and often cloaked by a proclivity for a banal language, is a disturbing force of violence which all of Polanski's films seek to analyze—and for which they have frequently been criticized. Certainly, his own life has brought him all too close to this most disturbing impulse, for when he was only eight years old Polanski and his parents were interned in a German concentration camp where his mother died. In 1969 his wife Sharon Tate and several friends were brutally murdered by Charles Manson's followers. The cataclysmic violence in the decidedly bloody adaptation of *Macbeth*, which closely followed his wife's death, can be traced through all of the director's features, as Polanski has repeatedly tried to depict the various ways in which violence erupts from the human personality, and to confront in this specter the problem of evil in the world. The basic event of *Rosemary's Baby*, Rosemary's bearing the offspring of the devil, a baby whom she fears yet, because of the natural love of a mother for her own child, nurtures, might be seen as a paradigm of Polanski's vision of evil and its operation in our world. Typically, it is the innocent or unsuspecting individual, even one with the best of intentions, who unwittingly gives birth to and spreads the very evil or violence he most fears. The protagonist of *The Fearless Vampire Killers*, for example, sets about destroying the local vampire and saving his beloved from its unnatural hold. In the process, however, he himself becomes a vampire's prey and, as a concluding voice-over solemnly intones, assists in spreading this curse throughout the world.

It is a somber conclusion for a comedy, but a telling indication of the complex tone and perspective which mark Polanski's films. He is able to assume an ironic, even highly comic attitude towards the ultimate and, as he sees it, inevitable human problem—an abiding violence and evil nurtured even as we individually struggle against these forces. The absurdist stance of Polanski's short films, especially *Two Men and a Wardrobe* and *The Fat and the Lean*, represents one logical response to this paradox. That his narratives have grown richer, more complicated, and also more discomfiting in their examination of this situation attests to Polanski's ultimate commitment to understanding the human predicament and to rendering articulate that which seems to defy articulation. From his own isolated position—as a man effectively without a country—Polanski tries to confront the problems of isolation, violence, and evil, and to speak of them for an audience prone to their sway.

—J.P. Telotte

POLLACK, Sydney.

American. Born in Lafayette, Indiana, 1 July 1934. Educated at South Bend Central High School; studied with Sanford Meisner, Neighborhood Playhouse, New York. Married Claire Griswold, 1958, three children. Actor on Broadway and for TV, also acting instructor, from 1955; served in U.S. Army, 1957–59; TV director in Los Angeles, from 1960; directed first film, 1965; also produced his own films, from 1975. Recipient: Emmy Award for *The Game*, 1966; Oscars for Best Film and Best Direction, for *Out of Africa*, 1986. Address: c/o Mirage Enterprises, 100 Universal Plaza, Building 414, Universal City, CA 91608, U.S.A.

Films as Director:

1965	*The Slender Thread*
1966	*This Property Is Condemned*
1968	*The Swimmer* (Perry) (d one sequence only); *The Scalphunters*
1969	*Castle Keep*; *They Shoot Horses, Don't They?*

1972	*Jeremiah Johnson*
1973	*The Way We Were*
1975	*Three Days of the Condor*; *The Yakuza* (*Brotherhood of the Yakuza*) (+ pr)
1976	*Bobby Deerfield* (+ pr)
1979	*The Electric Horseman*
1981	*Absence of Malice* (+ pr)
1982	*Tootsie* (+ co-pr, role as George Fields)
1985	*Out of Africa* (+ pr)
1990	*Havana* (+ co-pr)

Other Films:

1961	*The Young Savages* (Frankenheimer) (dialogue coach)
1962	*War Hunt* (Sanders) (role as Sergeant Van Horn)
1963	*Il gattopardo* (***The Leopard***) (Visconti) (supervisor of dubbed American version)
1973	*Scarecrow* (Schatzberg) (pr)
1980	*Honeysuckle Rose* (Schatzberg) (exec pr)
1984	*Songwriter* (Rudolph) (pr); *Sanford Meisner—The Theater's Best Kept Secret* (doc) (exec pr)
1988	*Bright Lights, Big City* (Bridges) (pr)
1990	*Presumed Innocent* (Pakula) (pr); *White Palace* (Mandoki) (exec pr)

Publications:

By POLLACK: book—

Out of Africa: The Shooting Script, with Kurt Luedke, New York, 1987.

By POLLACK: articles—

Interview with G. Langlois, in *Cinéma* (Paris), July/August 1972.
"Nos Plus Belles Années," an interview with Max Tessier, in *Ecran* (Paris), April 1974.
Interview with L. Salvato, in *Millimeter* (New York), June 1975.
"Sydney Pollack: The Way We Are," an interview with Patricia Erens, in *Film Comment* (New York), September/October 1975.
"Dialogue on Film: Sydney Pollack," in *American Film* (Washington, D.C.), April 1978.
"Sydney Pollack, An Actor's Director," an interview with P. Childs, in *Millimeter* (New York), December 1979.
Interview with P. Carcassonne and J. Fieschi, in *Cinématographe* (Paris), March/April 1981.
Interview with T. Ryan and S. Murray, in *Cinema Papers* (Melbourne), May–June 1983.
Interview in *Post Script* (Jacksonville, Florida), Fall 1983.
Interview with J.-A. Gili and M. Henry, in *Positif* (Paris), April 1986.
"Dialogue on Film: Sydney Pollack," in *American Film* (Washington, D.C.), December 1986.

On POLLACK: books—

Gili, Jean A., *Sydney Pollack*, Nice, 1971.
Taylor, William R. *Sydney Pollack*, Boston, 1981.

On POLLACK articles—

Madsen, Axel, "Pollack's Hollywood History," in *Sight and Sound* (London), Summer 1973.
Massuyeau, M., "Dossier: Hollywood 79: Sidney Pollack," in *Cinématographe* (Paris), March 1979.
"*Le Cavalier électrique* Issue" of *Avant-Scène du Cinéma* (Paris), 15 June 1980.
Camy, G., "Sydney Pollack: Souvenirs d'Amérique," in *Jeune Cinéma* (Paris), May/June 1986.

*   *   *

Sydney Pollack is especially noted for his ability to elicit fine performances from his actors and actresses and has worked with leading Hollywood stars, including Robert Redford (who has appeared in five Pollack films), Jane Fonda, Barbra Strei-

Sydney Pollack directing Robert Redford in *The Electric Horseman*

sand, Dustin Hoffman, Paul Newman and Burt Lancaster, among others.

Though Pollack has treated a cross-section of Hollywood genres, the majority of his films divide into male-action dramas and female melodramas. Among the former are *The Scalphunters, Castle Keep, Jeremiah Johnson, Three Days of the Condor*, and *The Yakuza*. Among the latter are *The Slender Thread, This Property is Condemned, The Way We Were*, and *Bobby Deerfield*.

The typical Pollack hero is a loner whose past interferes with his ability to function in the present. Throughout the course of the narrative, the hero comes to trust another individual and exchanges his isolation for a new relationship. For the most part, Pollack's heroines are intelligent women, often with careers, who possess moral strength, although in several cases they are victims of emotional weakness. Pollack is fond of portraying the attraction of opposites. The central issue in all of Pollack's work focuses on the conflict between cultural antagonists. This can be racial as in *The Slender Thread, The Scalphunters* or *Jeremiah Johnson* (black vs. white; white vs. Indian), religious as in *The Way We Were* (Protestant vs. Jew), geographic as in *This Property is Condemned* and *The Electric Horseman* (city vs. town), nationalistic as in *Castle Keep* (Europe vs. America; East vs. West) or based on gender differences as in *Tootsie* (feminine vs. masculine).

Pollack's films do not possess a readily identifiable visual style. However, his works are generally noteworthy for their total visual effect, and he frequently utilizes the helicopter shot. Structurally the plots possess a circular form, often ending where they began. Visually this is echoed in the circular dance floor of *They Shoot Horses, Don't They?*, but is also apparent in *Jeremiah Johnson* and *The Way We Were*.

Along with Sidney Lumet, Pollack is one of Hollywood's foremost liberals. His work highlights social and political issues, exposing organized exploitation rather than individual villainy. Most prominent among the issues treated are racial discrimination (*The Scalphunters*), the destructiveness of war (*Castle Keep*), the Depression (*They Shoot Horses, Don't They?*), Hollywood blacklisting (*The Way We Were*), CIA activities (*Three Days of the Condor*), commercial exploitation (*The Electric Horseman*), media exploitation (*Absence of Malice*), and feminism (*Tootsie*). Although Pollack has often been attacked for using these themes as background, rather than delving deeply into their subtleties, the French critics, among others, hold his work in high esteem.

—Patricia Erens

POLONSKY, Abraham.

American. Born in New York City, 5 December 1910. Educated at City College of New York; Columbia University, law degree. Lawyer with Manhattan firm, then quit to write; signed with Paramount, late 1930s; served in Europe with O.S.S. (Office of Strategic Studies), World War II; moved to Enterprise Productions, 1947; directed first feature, 1948; spent year in France, 1949; signed with 20th Century-Fox, 1950; called to testify before House Un-American Activities Committee, invoked 5th Amendment, 1951; blacklisted until 1968. Also novelist.

Films as Director and Scriptwriter:

1948   *Force of Evil*
1970   *Tell Them Willie Boy Is Here*
1971   *Romance of a Horsethief*

Other Films:

1947   *Golden Earrings* (Leisen) (sc); *Body and Soul* (Rossen) (sc)
1951   *I Can Get It For You Wholesale* (Gordon) (sc)
1968   *Madigan* (Siegel) (sc)
1979   *Avalanche Express* (Robson) (sc)

Publications:

By POLONSKY: articles—

"Abraham Polonsky and *Force of Evil*," an interview with William Pechter, in *Film Quarterly* (Berkeley), Spring 1962.
Interview in *Interviews with Film Directors*, by Andrew Sarris, New York, 1967.
Interview with William Pechter, in *Film Quarterly* (Berkeley), Winter 1968/69.
Interview with Jim Cook and Kingsley Canham, in *Screen* (London), Summer 1970.
"How the Blacklist Worked," in *Film Culture* (New York), Fall/Winter 1970.
"Making Movies," in *Sight and Sound* (London), Spring 1971.
"Nuits blanches pendant la liste noir: Extrait de journal," in *Positif* (Paris), December/January 1977/78.

On POLONSKY: articles—

Canham, Kingsley, "Polonsky," in *Film* (London), Spring 1970.
Butler, T., "Polonsky and Kazan. HUAC and the Violation of Personality," in *Sight and Sound* (London), Autumn 1988.
Neve, Brian, "Fellow Traveller," in *Sight and Sound* (London), Spring 1990.

*   *   *

Abraham Lincoln Polonsky's filmography is quite thin: his second film as director, *Tell Them Willie Boy Is Here*, was released 21 years after his first, *Force of Evil*. "I was a left-winger," he told *Look* magazine in 1970. "I supported the Soviet Union. In the middle 1940s, we'd have meetings at my house to raise money for strikers and radical newspapers." For these crimes—and, equally, for the less than superficially patriotic qualities of his protagonists—a promising, perhaps even major, directorial career was squelched in its infancy by the insidious Hollywood blacklist.

A discussion of Polonsky would be incomplete without noting his collaborations with John Garfield, the American cinema's original anti-hero. Polonsky scripted *Body and Soul*, one of the best boxing films of all time, and both authored and directed *Force of Evil*, a "B film" ignored in its time, but now a cult classic highly regarded for its use of blank verse dialogue.

Garfield stars in *Force of Evil* as a lawyer immersed in the numbers racket. When his brother, a small-time gambler, is murdered by his gangster boss, he hunts the hood down and turns himself in to the police. In *Body and Soul*, the actor portrays a poor boy with a hard, knockout punch who rises in the fight game while alienating his family, friends, and the girl he loves. In the end he reforms, defying the mob by refusing to throw a fight. "What are you gonna do, kill me?" he chides the chief thug, "Everybody dies." With that, he walks off into the night with his girl. The final cut of *Body and Soul* is as much Polonsky's as it is director Robert Rossen's. Polonsky claimed to have prevented Rossen from altering the film's finale.

Both of Polonsky's protagonists become casualties of their desire for success. They seek out the all-American dream, but are corrupted in the process. They can only attain status by throwing fights, aligning themselves with lawbreakers. Fame and money, fancy hotels and snazzy suits, come not by hard work and honesty but by cheating, throwing the fight, fixing the books—the real American way.

Polonsky, and Garfield, were blacklisted as much for the tone of their films as their politics. Polonsky's heroes are cocky, cynical loner-losers, estranged from society's mainstream, who break the rules and cause others extreme sorrow—not the moral, honest, often comic book caricatures of American manhood that dominated Hollywood cinema. In addition, Polonsky created a character in *Body and Soul*, a washed-up boxer (lovingly played by Canada Lee) who was one of the earliest portraits of a black man as a human being with emotions and feelings, a man exploited. *Body and Soul* and *Force of Evil* played the nation's moviehouses in 1947 and 1948, when anything less than a positive vision of America was automatically suspect.

Polonsky's plight is particularly sad. His passport was revoked, and he could not escape to find work abroad. Years after others who had been blacklisted, had returned to the good graces of the cinema establishment, he toiled in obscurity writing television shows and perhaps dozens of film scripts—some Academy Award winners—under assumed names. His first post-blacklist directorial credit, *Willie Boy*, is a spiritual cousin of his earlier work. It is the tale of a noncomformist Paiute Indian (Robert Blake, who played Garfield as a child in *Humoresque*), victimized by an insensitive society after he kills in self-defense. The parallels between Polonsky and his character's fate are clear.

Before the blacklist, Polonsky had hoped to film Thomas Mann's novella, *Mario and the Magician*; in 1971, he was again planning this project, among others. None was ever completed. But most significantly, the films that he might have made between 1948 and 1969—the prime years of his creative life—can now only be imagined.

—Rob Edelman

PONTECORVO, Gillo.

Italian. Born Gilberto Pontecorvo in Pisa, 19 November 1919. Studied chemistry, University of Pisa. Journalist, and partisan fighter, Milan, (commanded 3rd Brigade), World War II; Youth Secretary, Italian Communist party, 1946; Paris correspondent for Italian journals, late 1940s; began in films as assistant to Yves Allegret on *Les Miracles n'ont lieu qu'une fois*, 1951; made ten shorts, 1953–55; left Communist Party following invasion of Hungary, 1956. Recipient: Golden Lion, Venice Festival, for *The Battle of Algiers*, 1966.

Gillo Pontecorvo directing *Kapò*

Films as Director:

1955 "Giovanna" episode of *Die Windrose*
1957 *La grande strada azzurra* (*La lunga strada azzurra. The Long Blue Road*) (+ co-sc)
1960 *Kapò* (+ co-sc)
1966 **La battaglia di Algeri** (**The Battle of Algiers**) (+ co-sc, co-mus)
1969 *Queimada* (*Burn!*)
1979 *Ogro* (*Operation Ogro*)
1988 *The Devil's Bishop*

Other Films:

1946 *Il sole sorge ancora* (Vergano) (role as partisan)

Publications:

By PONTECORVO: articles—

Interview with Guy Hennebelle, in *Cinéma* (Paris), December 1965.
"*The Battle of Algiers*: An Adventure in Filmmaking," in *American Cinematographer* (Los Angeles), April 1967.
Interview with Joan Mellen, in *Film Quarterly* (Berkeley), Fall 1972.
"Using the Contradictions of the System," an interview with H. Kalishman, in *Cineaste* (New York), vol. 6, no. 2, 1974.
Interview with C. Lucas, in *Cineaste* (New York), Fall 1980.

On PONTECORVO: book—

Mellen, Joan, *Filmguide to "The Battle of Algiers"*, Bloomington, Indiana, 1973.
Solinas, Franco, *Gillo Pontecorvo's "The Battle of Algiers": A Film Written by Franco Solinas*, New York, 1973.
Michalczyk, John J., *The Italian Political Filmmakers*, Cranbury, New Jersey, 1986.

On PONTECORVO: articles—

Wilson, David, "Politics and Pontecorvo," in *Sight and Sound* (London), Fall 1970.

*   *   *

Gillo Pontecorvo is concerned with the oppressed, those kept down by the unjust and cruel use of power—and who will eventually rebel against the oppressor. "I've always wanted to look at man during the hardest moments of his life," the filmmaker has stated. An examination of his filmography indicates that he has been true to his goals and ideals.

Kapo, for example, is the story of a young Jewish girl and her attempt to survive in a Nazi concentration camp. But Pontecorvo's masterpiece is *The Battle of Algiers*, a meticulous recreation of the historical events surrounding the successful rebellion against the French by Algeria between 1954 and 1962. Shot in authentic locales with both actors and nonprofessionals in a cinéma-vérité style, Pontecorvo's black-and-white images seem like newsreels rather than staged sequences; the viewer can easily forget that the film is not a documentary. Additionally, the villains (chiefly, the French Colonel Mathieu, played by Jean Martin) are not sadistic, one-dimensional imperialists, thugs and goons who abuse the rights of those they have colonized. While Mathieu is far from benevolent, he is believable and sympathetic, as much the victim of an exploitive society as the Algerians; the colonel even admits that the Algerians are destined to win—this is a lesson of history—and his job is just to temporarily put off the inevitable.

The same is true for the most visible tyrant in *Burn!*, Sir William Walker (Marlon Brando), a confused, self-destructive British adventurer who betrays the slaves who revolt on a Portuguese-controlled, sugar-producing Caribbean island in the mid 19th century. Both Walker and Mathieu are depicted as human beings—with misguided values, perhaps, but human

beings nonetheless. However, while *The Battle of Algiers* is a near-flawless film, the scenario of *Burn!* is muddled in that Walker's motives are never really clear. Both films are potent politically in that the imperialists are not caricatured, yet at the same time it is clear that Pontecorvo sides with the Algerians and the slaves. At the beginning of *The Battle of Algiers*, for example, a tortured Algerian is held up by French paratroopers. Despite all that follows, this sequence is in and of itself a political statement, one that sets the tone for all that follows.

Pontecorvo is a Marxist: in 1941, at the age of 22, he became a member of the Italian Communist Party. His initial film, the "Giovanna" episode from *Die Windrose*, is a women's rights movie shot in East Germany. And, in *The Battle of Algiers*, he deals specifically with partisans of the Algerian National Liberation Front who, via their actions, increase the political awareness of their fellow citizens. Here Pontecorvo illustrates how a group of individuals can unite into a political force and defeat a common enemy. This is achieved by violent means: if freedom is to be earned, suffering and physical force and even the deaths of innocent people may be necessary. Gillo Pontecorvo is a filmmaker whose art is scrupulously true to his politics.

—Rob Edelman

———

PORTER, Edwin S.

American. Born Edwin Stratton Porter in Connellsville, Pennsylvania, 21 April 1869. Left school at 14, worked as sign painter, theater cashier and stagehand; served in U.S. Navy, assisted in development of gunnery range finder, 1893–96; worked for Raff & Gammon, marketers of Edison Vitascope, helped arrange first New York screening of motion pictures, 1896; invented and manufactured projector, 1898; business ruined by fire, rejoined Edison Company, 1900; director and cameraman, then supervisor of production at Edison studio, New York City; quit Edison, founded Defender Pictures, 1909; organized Rex Film Company, 1910; sold interest in Rex, founded, with Adolph Zukor, "Famous Players in Famous Plays" company, 1912; director general and treasurer, supervisor and director at Famous Players until 1915; became President of Precision Machine Corp., manufacturer of Simplex projector, which he helped develop, from 1915. *Died 30 April 1941.*

Films as Director:

(partial list, also frequently sc, ph and ed)
1899 *The America's Cup Race*
1900 *Why Mrs. Jones Got a Divorce*; *Animated Luncheon*; *An Artist's Dream*; *The Mystic Swing*; *Ching Lin Foo Outdone*; *Faust and Marguerite*; *The Clown and the Alchemist*; *A Wringing Good Joke*; *The Enchanted Drawing*
1901 *Terrible Teddy the Grizzly King*; *Love in a Hammock*; *A Day at the Circus*; *What Demoralized the Barber Shop*; *The Finish of Bridget McKeen*; *Happy Hooligan Surprised*; *Martyred Presidents*; *Love by the Light of the Moon*; *Circular Panorama of the Electric Tower*; *Panorama of the Esplanade by Night*; *The Mysterious Cafe*
1902 *Uncle Josh at the Moving Picture Show*; *Charleston Chain Gang*; *Burlesque Suicide*; *Rock of Ages*; *Jack and the Beanstalk*; *Happy Hooligan Turns Burglar*; *Capture of the Biddle Brothers*; *Fun in a Bakery Shop*
1903 *The Life of an American Fireman*; *The Still Alarm*; *Arabian Jewish Dance*; *Razzle Dazzle*; *Seashore Frolics*; *Scenes in an*

Edwin S. Porter: *The Great Train Robbery*

Orphans' Asylum; The Gay Shoe Clerk; The Baby Review; The Animated Poster; The Office Boy's Revenge; Uncle Tom's Cabin; **The Great Train Robbery**; The Messenger Boy's Mistake; Casey and His Neighbor's Goat

1904 The Ex-Convict; Cohen's Advertising Scheme; European Rest Cure; Capture of Yegg Bank Burglars; City Hall to Harlem in Fifteen Seconds via the Subway Route; Casey's Frightful Dream; The Cop Fools the Sergeant; Elephant Shooting the Chutes at Luna Park

1905 The Kleptomaniac; Stolen by Gypsies; How Jones Lost His Roll; The Little Train Robbery; The White Caps; Seven Ages; The Life of an American Policeman

1906 The Dream of a Rarebit Fiend; The Life of a Cowboy; Three American Beauties; Kathleen Mavourneen

1907 Daniel Boone; Lost in the Alps; The Midnight Ride of Paul Revere; Laughing Gas; Rescued from an Eagle's Nest; The Teddy Bears

1908 Nero and the Burning of Rome; The Painter's Revenge; The Merry Widow Waltz Craze; The Gentleman Burglar; Honesty Is the Best Policy; Love Will Find a Way; Skinny's Finish; The Face on the Barroom Floor; The Boston Tea Party; Romance of a War Nurse; A Voice from the Dead; Saved by Love; She; Lord Feathertop; The Angel Child; Miss Sherlock Holmes; An Unexpected Santa Claus

1909 The Adventures of an Old Flirt; A Midnight Supper; Love Is Blind; A Cry from the Wilderness; Hard to Beat; On the Western Frontier; Fuss and Feathers; Pony Express; Toys of Fate; The Iconoclast; Hansel and Gretel; The Strike; Capital versus Labor

1910 All on Account of a Laundry Mark; Russia—the Land of Oppression; Too Many Girls; Almost a Hero; The Toymaker on the Brink and the Devil

1911 By the Light of the Moon; On the Brink; The White Red Man; Sherlock Holmes Jr.; Lost Illusions

1912 A Sane Asylum; Eyes That See Not; The Final Pardon; Taming Mrs. Shrew

1913 The Prisoner of Zenda (co-d); His Neighbor's Wife; The Count of Monte Cristo (co-d); In the Bishop's Carriage (co-d); A Good Little Devil (co-d)

1914 Hearts Adrift; Tess of the Storm Country; Such a Little Queen (co-d)

1915 The Eternal City (co-d); Zaza (co-d); Sold (co-d); The Prince and the Pauper (co-d); Bella Donna (co-d)

1916 Lydia Gilmore (co-d)

Publications:

By PORTER: articles—

Statement, in *Filmmakers on Filmmaking* edited by Harry Geduld, Bloomington, Indiana, 1967.

On PORTER: books—

Balshofer, Fred, and Arthur Miller, *One Reel a Week*, Berkeley, 1967.
Pratt, George, *Spellbound in Darkness*, Greenwich, Connecticut, 1973.

Salt, Barry, *Film Style and Technology: History and Analysis*, London, 1983.

Burch, Noël, *Life to Those Shadows*, Berkeley, 1990.

Elsaesser, Thomas, and Adam Barker, editors, *Early Cinema: Space-Frame-Narrative*, London, 1990.

On PORTER: articles—

Sadoul, Georges, "English Influences on the Work of Edwin S. Porter," in *Hollywood Quarterly*, Fall 1947.

Spears, Jack, "Edwin S. Porter," in *Films in Review* (New York), June/July 1970.

Burch, Noël, "Porter, or Ambivalence," in *Screen* (London), Winter 1978/79.

Schulberg, Budd, letter, in *Variety* (New York), 9 May 1979.

Gaudreault, André, "Detours in Film Narrative: The Development of Cross-Cutting," in *Cinema Journal* (Evanston), Fall 1979.

Musser, Charles, "Early Cinema of Edwin Porter," in *Cinema Journal* (Evanston), Fall 1979.

Ranvaud, Don, "After the Great Train Robbery . . . ," in *Monthly Film Bulletin* (London), December 1983.

Pearson, R., "The Filmmaker as Scholar and Entertainer: An Interview with Charles Musser," in *Cineaste* (New York), vol. 8, no. 3, 1984.

On PORTER: film—

Musser, Charles, *Before the Nickelodeon*, U.S., 1984.

*   *   *

In the annals of film history, Edwin S. Porter is often credited as the first American film director. Although this may not be true in the literal sense, it is not unjustified to give Porter this title. Porter was first and foremost an engineer, an inventor, and a cameraman. In the early days of filmmaking, "cameraman" was synonymous with "director," and Porter found himself handling both jobs. He was also his own editor and discovered new ways of creating a narrative. While most early motion pictures were composed of a single shot showing only one continuous action from beginning to end, Porter began to combine and juxtapose his filmed images, creating new meanings as one scene "psychologically" led into another. Porter became one of the first American can directors to tell a story in his films.

Porter acknowledged an influence in his filmmaking from Georges Méliès, the French filmmaker whose "trick films" were extremely popular in the United States. Being a designer of motion picture cameras, Porter was able to study and discover the secrets to many of Méliès's "tricks." Most importantly, Porter was struck by the fact that these films told a story. However, while Méliès's films told a straightforward, linear narrative, Porter expanded this idea with the use of cross-narrative (parallel action) to depict two simultaneous events or points of view.

Porter's first film of major importance was *The Life of an American Fireman*, made in 1902 or early 1903. This film was largely composed of stock shots from earlier Edison Company films. Racing fire engines were a popular subject for early filmmakers and Porter had much footage at his disposal. To complement these stock shots, Porter filmed additional footage, showing a mother and child trapped in a burning building. By editing these scenes together Porter created the story of the mother and child's rescue by the firefighters. Porter intercut the scenes of mother and child with stock footage of the racing fire engines, thereby creating a dramatic tension—will the firefighters rescue the two victims from the burning building in time? While this technique of storytelling may seem blasé by today's standards, it was innovative and exciting to 1903 audiences.

Porter continued to develop his film editing techniques in his best known and most popular film, *The Great Train Robbery*.

On its most simplistic level, the film is a story of crime, pursuit, and capture. But it is perhaps the first great American chase film, a form still popular today. Again Porter edited his film using cross-cutting to show events that were supposedly occurring at the same time: the bandits begin their escape while the posse organizes a pursuit. *The Great Train Robbery* was an enormously popular film at a time when nickelodeons were just opening across the country and the film did a great deal of repeat business.

Surprisingly, after *The Great Train Robbery*, Porter did little else to advance the art of filmmaking. In 1912, he formed the Famous Players Film Co. with Adolf Zukor and David Frohman, acting as director-general of the company. However, his films of this period (such as *The Count of Monte Cristo* and *The Prisoner of Zenda*) contain none of the energy of his earlier films. In fact, they took several steps backward technically, being photographed in a very stagey, single point-of-view manner. Apparently, Porter was never really interested in directing films. He soon sold his shares in Famous Players and became more involved in designing motion picture cameras and projectors, including the Simplex. However, Porter's one important contribution to filmmaking—a freer style of editing—was a turning point in the development of film as a narrative art form.

—Linda J. Obalil

POWELL, Michael, and Emeric PRESSBURGER.

Powell. British. Born Michael Latham Powell at Bekesbourne, near Canterbury, Kent, 30 September 1905. Married 1) Frances Reidy, 1943 (died 1983), two sons; 2) editor Thelma Schoonmaker, 1984. Worked in various capacities on films of Rex Ingram, Léonce Perret, Alfred Hitchcock, Lupu Pick, from 1922; director, from 1931; (Senior Director in Residence, Zoetrope Studios, 1981). **Pressburger.** Hungarian/British. Born Imre Pressburger in Miskolc, Hungary, 5 December 1902. Studied at Universities of Prague and Stuttgart. Contract writer for UFA, Berlin, 1930, later in France, and, from 1935, in England, for Alexander Korda's London Films.

Powell and Pressburger began collaboration, on *The Spy in Black*, 1939; formed "The Archers," as producing, directing and writing team, 1942 (disbanded 1956); also set up Vega Productions Ltd.; Recipients: (joint) British Film Institute Special Award, 1978; Fellowship, BAFTA, 1981; Fellowship, British Film Institute, 1983; (Powell) honorary doctorate, University of East Anglia, 1978; Golden lion, Venice Festival, 1982. *Pressburger died, in Suffolk, 5 February 1988. Powell died, in Gloucestershire, 19 February 1990.*

Films by Powell and Pressburger:

(Powell as director, Pressburger as scriptwriter)

1939 *The Spy in Black* (*U-Boat*)
1940 *Contraband* (*Blackout*)
1941 *49th Parallel* (*The Invaders*)
1942 *One of Our Aircraft Is Missing*
1972 *The Boy Who Turned Yellow*

(produced, directed and scripted by "The Archers")

1943 ***The Life and Death of Colonel Blimp***; *The Volunteer*
1944 *A Canterbury Tale*

Michael Powell (left) and Emeric Pressburger during the making of *A Canterbury Tale*

1945 *I Know Where I'm Going*
1946 **A Matter of Life and Death** (*Stairway to Heaven*)
1947 **Black Narcissus**
1948 **The Red Shoes**
1949 *The Small Back Room* (*Hour of Glory*)
1950 *Gone to Earth* (*The Wild Heart*); *The Elusive Pimpernel* (*The Fighting Pimpernel*)
1951 *The Tales of Hoffman*
1955 *Oh! Rosalinda* (*Fledermaus '55*)
1956 *The Battle of the River Plate* (*Pursuit of the Graf Spee*); *Ill Met By Moonlight* (*Intelligence Service. Night Ambush*)

Other Films Directed by Powell:

1931 *Two Crowded Hours; My Friend the King; Rynox; The Rasp; The Star Reporter*
1932 *Hotel Splendide; C.O.D.; His Lordship; Born Lucky*
1933 *The Fire-Raisers* (+ co-sc)
1934 *The Night of the Party; Red Ensign* (+ co-sc); *Something Always Happens; The Girl in the Crowd*
1935 *Lazybones; The Love Test; The Phantom Light; The Price of a Song; Someday*
1936 *The Man Behind the Mask; Crown Versus Stevens; Her Last Affair; The Brown Wallet*
1937 *Edge of the World* (+ sc)
1939 *The Lion Has Wings* (co-d)
1940 *The Thief of Bagdad* (co-d)
1941 *An Airman's Letter to His Mother* (short)
1955 *The Sorceror's Apprentice* (short)
1956 *Luna de miel* (*Honeymoon*) (+ pr)
1960 **Peeping Tom** (+ pr, role)
1961 *Queen's Guards* (+ pr)
1964 *Bluebeard's Castle*
1966 *They're a Weird Mob* (+ pr)
1968 *Sebastian* (Greene) (co-pr only)
1969 *Age of Consent* (+ pr)
1974 *Trikimia* (*The Tempest*) (+ pr, sc)
1978 *Return of the Edge of the World* (doc for TV) (+ pr)

Other Films Written By Pressburger:

1953 *Twice Upon a Time* (+ d, pr)
1957 *Miracle in Soho* (Amyes) (+ pr)

Publications:

By POWELL: book—

A Waiting Game, London, 1975.
The Red Shoes (with Pressburger), London, 1978.
A Life in Movies: An Autobiography, London, 1986.
Edge of the World, London, 1990.

By PRESSBURGER: books—

Killing a Mouse on Sunday, London, 1961
The Glass Pearls, London, 1966.
The Red Shoes (with Powell), London, 1978.

By POWELL and PRESSBURGER: articles—

"Michael Powell: The Expense of Naturalism," an interview with R. Collins and Ian Christie, in *Monogram* (London), no. 3, 1972.
Powell interview with R. Lefèvre and R. Lacourbe, in *Cinéma* (Paris), December 1976.
"Powell and Pressburger: The War Years," an interview with D.J. Badder, in *Sight and Sound* (London), no. 1, 1979.
"Michael Powell," an interview with Oliver Assayas, in *Cahiers du Cinéma* (Paris), March 1981.
"Michael Powell's Guilty Pleasures," in *Film Comment* (New York), July/August 1981.
Powell interview with T. Williams, in *Films and Filming* (London), November 1981.

Powell, Michael, "Leo Marks and Mark Lewis," in *Cinématographe* (Paris), December 1983.
"Powell's Life," an interview with Allan Hunter, in *Films and Filming* (London), October 1986.
Powell, Michael, "Dance, Girl, Dance," in *American Film* (Washington, D.C.), vol. 12, no. 5, 1987.

On POWELL and PRESSBURGER: books—

Durgnat, Raymond, *A Mirror for England: British Movies from Austerity to Affluence*, London, 1970.
Gough-Yates, Kevin, *Michael Powell*, London, 1971.
Armes, Roy, *A Critical History of British Cinema*, London, 1978.
Christie, Ian, editor, *Powell, Pressburger, and Others*, London, 1978.
Cosandey, Roland, editor, *Retrospective: Powell and Pressburger*, Locarno, 1982.
Gottler, Fritz, and others, *Living Cinema: Powell and Pressburger*, Munich, 1982.
Christie, Ian, *Arrows of Desire: The Films of Michael Powell and Emeric Pressburger*, London, 1985.
Martini, Emanuela, editor, *Powell and Pressburger*, Bergamo, 1986.
Murphy, Robert, *Realism and Tinsel: British Cinema and Society 1939–48*, London, 1989.

On POWELL and PRESSBURGER: articles—

Green, O.O., "Michael Powell," in *Movie* (London), Autumn 1965.
Gough-Yates, Kevin, "Private Madness and Public Lunacy," in *Films and Filming* (London), February 1972.
Everson, William K., "A Meeting of Two Great Visual Stylists," in *Films in Review* (New York), November 1977.
Taylor, John Russell, "Michael Powell—Myths and Supermen," in *Sight and Sound* (London), Autumn 1978.
Andrews, Nigel, and Harlan Kennedy," Peerless Powell," in *Film Comment* (New York), May/June 1979.
Everson, William K., "Michael Powell," in *Films in Review* (New York), August/September 1980.
Thompson, D., "The Films of Michael Powell: A Romantic Sensibility," in *American Film* (Washington, D.C.), November 1980.
"*Question de vie ou de mort* Issue" of *Avant-Scène du Cinéma* (Paris), 15 December 1980.
Durgnat, Raymond, "Aiming at the Archers," in *Positif* (Paris), February 1981.
McVay, D., "Cinema of Enchantment: The Films of Michael Powell," and "Michael Powell, Three Neglected Films," *Films and Filming* (London), December 1981 and January 1982.
Christie, Ian, "Alienation Effects: Emeric Pressburger and British Cinema," and "Powell and Pressburger: Putting Back the Pieces," in *Monthly Film Bulletin* (London), October and December 1984.
Brennan, M., "Powell and Pressburger at the NFT," in *Film and Filming* (London), October 1985.
Baron, Saskia, "The Archer at 80," in *Cinema Papers* (Melbourne), July 1986.
Boyd-Bowman, S., "Heavy Breathing in Shropshire," in *Screen* (London), November/December 1986.
McCarthy, T., obituary of Pressburger, in *Variety* (New York), 10 February 1988.
Bergan, Ronald, "Emeric Pressburger," in *Film and Filming* (London), April 1988.
Cardiff, Jack, "Michael Powell," in *Films and TV Technician* (London), April 1990.
Millar, Gavin, "Cox's Orange Pippin," in *Sight and Sound* (London), Summer 1990.

On POWELL and PRESSBURGER: film—

Millar, Gavin, *The Archers*, for "Arena," BBC TV, 1981.

*   *   *

Between the years 1942 and 1957, English director Michael Powell and his Hungarian partner, Emeric Pressburger, formed one of the most remarkable partnerships in cinema. Under the collaborative pseudonym "The Archers," the two created a series of highly visual and imaginative treatments of romantic and supernatural themes that have defied easy categorization by film historians. Although both were listed jointly as director, screenwriter, and frequently as producer, and the extent of each one's participation on any given film is difficult to measure, it is probably most accurate to credit Powell with the actual visualization of the films, while Pressburger functioned primarily as a writer. The latter, in fact, had no background as a director before joining Powell and had drifted through the Austrian, German, and French film industries as a screenwriter before coming to England in 1936.

Many of the gothic, highly expressionistic characteristics of the films produced by the partnership seem to trace their origins to Powell's apprenticeship at Rex Ingram's studio in Nice in the 1920s. There he performed various roles on at least three of the visionary director's silent productions, *Mare Nostrum* (1926), *The Magician* (1926) and *The Garden of Allah* (1927). Working on these films and subsequently on his own features in the 1930s, Powell developed a penchant for expressionism that manifested itself in several rather unique ways. The most fundamental of these was in his use of the fantasy genre, as illustrated by *A Matter of Life and Death* with its problematic juxtaposition of psychiatry and mysticism. Another was in an almost philosophical sadism which permeated his later films, such as *Peeping Tom*, with a camera that impales its photographic subjects on bayonet-like legs. The mechanical camera itself, in fact, represents still another Powell motif: the use of machines and technology to create or heighten certain aspects of fantasy. For example, the camera obscura in *A Matter of Life and Death* and the German warship in the *Pursuit of the Graf Spee* (which is revealed through a slow camera scan along its eerie structure, causing it to turn into a metallic killer fish) effectively tie machines into each film's set of symbolic motifs. In doing so, a technological mythology is created in which these objects take on near-demonic proportions.

Finally, the use of color, which most critics cite as a trademark of the Powell-Pressburger partnership, is shaped into an expressionistic mode. Powell chose his hues from a broad visual palette, and brushed them onto the screen with a calculated extravagance that became integrated into the themes of the film as a whole. In the better films, the visual and technological aspects complement each other in a pattern of symbolism. The mechanical staircase which descends from the celestial vortex in *A Matter of Life and Death*, for example, blends technology and fantasy as no other image has. Similarly, when the camera replaces the young pilot's eye in the same film and the pink and violet lining of an eyelid descends over it, the effect is extravagant, even a bit bizarre, but it effectively serves notice that the viewer is closing his eyes to external reality and entering another world. The audience is left to decide whether that world is supernatural or psychological.

This world has been most palatable in popular Powell-Pressburger fantasies like *The Red Shoes*, a ballet film used as an allegory for the artist's unremitting dedication to his art; or *The Tales of Hoffman* in which the moody eccentricities of style have been kept in bounds by the built-in circumscriptions of the fantasy genre. However, at least one critic has noted a strange morbidity in *The Red Shoes* derived from the directors' use of certain pecularities of color, a criticism that has been magnified when some of Powell's and Pressburger's fantastic techniques occur in more realistic films. Their appearance usually upsets normal audience expectations when occurring in otherwise veracious contexts. *Black Narcissus* and Powell's *Peeping Tom* both created some problems for critics by going to extremes in the exaggeration of otherwise plausible storylines.

Thematically, Powell and Pressburger operate in a limbo somewhere between romance and realism. The former, characterized by technical effects, camera angles and movements, and the innovative use of color, often intrudes in the merest of details in fundamentally naturalistic films. In the eyes of some, this weakens the artistic commitment to realism. On the other hand, the psychological insights embodied in serious fantasies like *A Matter of Life and Death* are too often dismissed as simply entertainment. Most of the Powell-Pressburger efforts are, in fact, attempts at fundamental reconciliations between modern ideas and the irrational, between science and savagery, or between religion and eroticism. This dichotomy usually occurs in one character's mind, as in Peter Carter's in *A Matter of Life and Death*, or in that of the sex-obsessed nun in *Black Narcissus*, and hinges upon a second character, as in *A Matter's* Dr. Frank Reeves, who effects a degree of movement between the two sides of the dichotomy, particularly through his own death.

Although such mergings of reality and fantasy met with approval by the moviegoing public, Powell and Pressburger were less successful with the British film establishment. In a sense they were alienated from it through their exercise of a decidedly non-British flamboyance. To some degree, the Clive Candy character in *The Life and Death of Colonel Blimp* embodies the British film community during the period after the war. Powell and Pressburger's visual and thematic extravagances of style conflicted with the self-consciousness of the film industry's strivings for a rigid postwar realism not to be embellished by colorful and expressionistic ventures.

The team broke up in 1957 after *Ill Met by Moonlight*, and although Pressburger made some films by himself they were not well received. Powell, though, continued in the vein established by his collaboration with the Hungarian director. *Luna de Miel* and *The Queen's Guards* pursue all of the philosophical concerns of his earlier efforts while *Peeping Tom*, which is now regarded as his masterpiece, indicates a certain morbid refinement of his thematic interests. Unfortunately, it was perhaps ahead of its time—a problem that plagued the director and his collaborator for most of their careers.

—Stephen L. Hanson

PREMINGER, Otto.

American. Born in Vienna, 5 December 1905, became U.S. citizen, 1943. Educated at University of Vienna, LL.D, 1926. Married 1) Marion Deutsch (stage name Marion Mill), 1932 (divorced); 2) Mary Gardner, 1951 (divorced 1959); 3) Hope (Preminger), 1960, two children; also one son by Gypsy Rose Lee. Actor with Max Reinhardt company, 1924; joined Theater in der Josefstadt, 1928 (succeeding Reinhardt as director, 1933); invited to Hollywood by Joseph Schenck, 1935; contract with Fox broken, moved to New York, 1937; director on Broadway, 1938–41 (and later); returned to Hollywood as actor, 1942; signed 7-year contract with Fox, 1945; independent producer, from early 1950s. *Died of cancer, in New York City, 23 April 1986.*

Films as Director:

1931 *Die grosse Liebe*
1936 *Under Your Spell*
1937 *Danger, Love at Work*
1943 *Margin for Error* (+ role as Nazi consul Rudolf Forster)
1944 *In the Meantime, Darling* (+ pr); *Laura* (+ pr)
1945 *Royal Scandal*; *Fallen Angel* (+ pr)
1946 *Centennial Summer* (+ pr)

Otto Preminger

.1947 *Forever Amber*; *Daisy Kenyon* (+ pr)
1948 *That Lady in Ermine*
1949 *The Fan* (*Lady Windermere's Fan*) (+ pr); *Whirlpool* (+ pr)
1950 *Where the Sidewalk Ends* (+ pr); *The Thirteenth Letter* (+ pr)
1952 *Angel Face*
1953 *The Moon is Blue* (+ co-pr)
1954 *River of No Return*; *Carmen Jones* (+ pr)
1955 *The Man with the Golden Arm* (+ pr); *The Court Martial of Billy Mitchell* (*One Man Mutiny*)
1957 *Saint Joan* (+ pr); *Bonjour Tristesse* (+ pr)
1959 *Porgy and Bess*; **Anatomy of a Murder** (+ pr)
1960 *Exodus* (+ pr)
1962 *Advise and Consent* (+ pr)
1963 *The Cardinal* (+ pr)
1964 *In Harm's Way* (+ pr)
1965 *Bunny Lake is Missing* (+ pr)
1966 *Hurry Sundown* (+ pr)
1968 *Skidoo* (+ pr)
1970 *Tell Me That You Love Me, Junie Moon* (+ pr)
1971 *Such Good Friends* (+ pr)
1975 *Rosebud* (+ pr)
1980 *The Human Factor* (+ pr)

Other Films:

1942 *The Pied Piper* (role); *They Got Me Covered* (role)
1945 *Where Do We Go from Here* (role)
1953 *Stalag 17* (Wilder) (role as camp commandant)
1981 *Unsere Leichen Leben Noch* (Von Prauheim) (role)

Publications:

By PREMINGER: book—

Preminger: An Autobiography, Garden City, New York, 1977.

By PREMINGER: articles—

"Recontre avec Otto Preminger," with Jacques Rivette, in *Cahiers du Cinéma* (Paris), December 1953.
"Movie Critic Versus Movie Director," with Bosley Crowther, in *Esquire* (New York), October 1958.
"Your Taste, My Taste . . . and the Censors," in *Films and Filming* (London), November 1959.
Interview with Jacques Doniol-Valcroze and Eric Rohmer, in *Cahiers du Cinéma* (Paris), July 1961.
"Sex and Censorship in Literature and the Arts," with Norman Mailer and others, in *Playboy* (Chicago), July 1961.
"*The Cardinal* and I," in *Films and Filming* (London), November 1963.
Interview with Ian Cameron and others, in *Movie* (London), Summer 1965.
Interview in *Interviews with Film Directors* edited by Andrew Sarris, New York, 1967.
"Otto Preminger auteur de force," an interview with D. Lyons, in *Inter/View* (New York), July 1972.
Interview with Gene Phillips, in *Focus on Film* (London), August 1979.
"Cult and Controversy," an interview with Gordon Gow, in *Films and Filming* (London), November 1979.

On PREMINGER: books—

Preminger, Marion Mill, *All I Want is Everything*, New York, 1957.
Lourcelles, Jacques, *Otto Preminger*, Paris, 1965.
Pratley, Gerald, *The Cinema of Otto Preminger*, New York, 1971.
Frischauer, Willi, *Behind the Scenes of Otto Preminger*, London, 1973.

On PREMINGER: articles—

Gehman, Richard, "Otto Preminger," in *Theater Arts* (New York), January 1961.
"Preminger Issue" of *Présence du Cinéma* (Paris), February 1962.
"Preminger Issue" of *Movie* (London), September 1962.
"Preminger Issues" of *Interciné* (Toulouse), no. 1, and no. 2, 1963.

"Preminger Issue" of *Movie* (London), no. 4, 1963.
Sarris, Andrew, "Preminger's Two Periods—Studio and Solo," in *Film Comment* (New York), Summer 1965.
Ross, Lillian, "Profiles: Anatomy of a Commercial Interruption," in the *New Yorker*, 19 February 1966.
Bogdanovich, Peter, "Otto Preminger," in *On Film*, 1970.
Borok, B., "*Laura*: The Story Behind the Picture," in *Thousand Eyes* (New York), November 1976.
Lacourcelles, J., "*Laura* Issue" of *Avant-Scène du Cinéma* (Paris), July/September 1978.
Wegner, H., "From Expressionism to Film Noir: Otto Preminger's *Where the Sidewalk Ends*," in *Journal of Popular Film* (Washington, D.C.), Summer 1983.
McCarthy, T., obituary, in *Variety* (New York), 30 April 1986.
Luft, H.G., in *Films in Review* (New York), August/September 1986.
Lippe, Richard, "At the Margins of *Film Noir*: Preminger's *Angel Face*," in *CineAction!* (Toronto), no. 13–14, 1988.
Sarris, Andrew, "Otto Preminger," in *American Film* (Washington, D.C.), June 1989.

* * *

The public persona of Austrian-born Otto Preminger has epitomized for many the typical Hollywood movie director: an accented, autocratic, European-born disciplinarian, terrorizing his actors, bullying his subordinates, and spending millions of dollars to ensure that his films be produced properly, although economically. Before the *Cahiers du Cinéma* critics began to praise Preminger, it may have been this public persona, more than anything else, which impeded an appreciation of Preminger's extraordinarily subtle style or thematic consistencies.

Preminger's career can be divided into two periods. Throughout the first period, Preminger worked as a studio director for Twentieth-Century Fox, where he had several well-publicized conflicts with Darryl F. Zanuck and found it difficult to conform to the studio demands or to collaborate without retaining overall artistic control. His evocative and romantic mystery *Laura* was his breakthrough film. Among the eclectic assignments he directed at Fox, the most interesting include a series of films noir in the late 1940s: *Whirlpool, Where the Sidewalk Ends, The Thirteenth Letter*, and *Angel Face*.

Throughout the second and far more interesting period of Preminger's career, Preminger worked as one of the first notable independent producer-directors, in the process successfully undermining the studio system in various ways. He fought against institutional censorship by releasing several films without the Motion Picture Association seal (for example, *The Moon is Blue*); he explored controversial subjects the studios might have been hesitant to touch (such as criticism of the War Department in *The Court-Martial of Billy Mitchell* or homosexuality in *Advise and Consent*); he championed the independent producers movement by exploiting the Paramount Divorcement Decree and aggressively marketing and arranging exhibition for his films; he incorporated fresh and authentic backgrounds by promoting location shooting away from Hollywood; he worked diligently to discover new performers (such as Jean Seberg) and to develop properties (such as *Carmen Jones* and *Hurry Sundown*) which would allow the casting of Hollywood's under-used black performers; he even helped to break the studio blacklist by hiring and publicly crediting Dalton Trumbo as screenwriter on *Exodus*.

Preminger's tastes have always been as eclectic as the disparate sources from which his films have been adapted. Throughout the 1950s and 1960s, however, Preminger's films grew in pretention, displaying considerable interest in monolithic institutions (the military in *The Court Martial of Billy Mitchell* and *In Harms's Way*; the Senate in *Advise and Consent*; the Catholic Church in *The Cardinal*; the medical profession in *Such Good Friends*) as well as examining social and political problems (drug addiction in *The Man with the Golden Arm*; Jewish repatriation in *Exodus*; racial prejudice in *Hurry, Sundown*; political terrorism in *Rosebud*). A consistent archetype in Preminger's films is the quest for truth; indeed, the director's recurring image is the courtroom. What has especially fascinated Preminger's admirers is the subtlety of his mise-en-scène; his most typical effort is a widescreen film with long takes, no pyrotechnical montage, few reaction shots, fluid and simple camera movements, and careful yet unselfconscious compositions. Preminger's style, though apparently invisible, is one which forces the audience to examine, to discern, to arrive at some ultimate position. Several critics have written persuasively on the ambiguity associated with Preminger's apparent objectivity, including Andrew Sarris, who has characterized Preminger as a "director who sees all problems and issues as a single-take two-shot, the stylistic expression of the eternal conflict, not between right and wrong, but between the right-wrong on one side and the right-wrong on the other, a representation of the right-wrong in all of us as our share of the human condition." If Preminger's formula floundered in the 1970s and 1980s, an era in which the American cinema seemed dominated by mainstream genre works and overt escapism, one cannot help but feel nostalgia and profound respect for Preminger's serious subjects and artistry. Indeed, his series of films beginning with *Bonjour, Tristesse* in 1957 and continuing through *Porgy and Bess, Anatomy of a Murder, Exodus, Advise and Consent, The Cardinal, In Harm's Way, Bunny Lake Is Missing*, and *Hurry, Sundown* in 1966, constitute one of the longest strings of ambitious, provocative films in American cinema.

—Charles Derry

PROTAZANOV, Yakov.

Russian. Born Yakov Alexandrovitch Protazanov in Moscow, 4 February 1881. Educated in commercial school, Moscow. Film actor, from 1905; translator, then writer of scenarios and director, Gloria studios, from 1909; moved to Ermoliev company, began collaboration with actor Ivan Mozhukhin, 1915; Ermoliev studios moved to Yalta, 1918, then to Istanbul and Marseilles, 1919–20; moved to Paris, worked in France and Germany, 1920–22; returned to Russia, joined Mezhrabpom-Rus Studio, Moscow, 1923. Recipient: Merited Artist of the RSFSR, 1935. *Died in Moscow, 8 August 1945.*

Films as Director:

1909   *The Fountains of Bakhisarai*
1911   *Pesnya katorzhanina (The Prisoner's Song)* (+ sc)
1912   *Anfisa; Ukhod velikovo startza (Departure of a Grand Old Man)* (co-d)
1913   *Razbitaya vaza (The Shattered Vase)* (+ sc); *Klyuchi shchastya (Keys to Happiness)* (co-d); *Kak khoroshi, Kak svezhi byli rozi (How Fine, How Fresh the Roses Were)* (+ sc)
1915   *Petersburgskiye trushchobi (Petersburg Slums)* (co-d, co-sc); *Voina i mir (War and Peace)* (co-d, co-sc); *Plebei (Plebeian)* (+ sc); *Nikolai Stavrogin* (+ sc)
1916   *Pikovaya dama (The Queen of Spades)*; *Zhenshchina s kinzhalom (Woman with a Dagger)*; *Grekh (Sin)* (co-d)
1917   *Prokuror (Public Prosecutor)*; *Andrei Kozhukhov* (+ sc); *Ne nado krovi (Blood Need Not Be Spilled)* (+ sc); *Prokliatiye millioni (Cursed Millions)*; *Satana likuyushchii (Satan Triumphant)*

1918   *Otets Sergii (Father Sergius)*
1919   *Taina koroloevy (The Queen's Secret)* (+ sc)
1920/23   *L'Angoissante aventure*; *L'Amour et la loi (Love and Law)*; *Pour une nuit d'amour*; *Justice d'Abord*; *Le Sens de la mort*; *L'Ombre du péché*; *Der Liebes Pielgerfahrt*
1924   *Aelita*
1925   *Yevo prizyv (Broken Chains. His Call)*; *Zakroichik iz Torzhka (Tailor from Torzhok)*
1926   *Protsess o tryokh millyonakh (The Three Million Case)* (+ co-sc)
1927   *Sorok pervyi (The 41st)*
1928   *Byelyi orel (The White Eagle)* (+ co-sc); *Dondiego i Pelaguya (Don Diego and Pelagea)*
1929   *Chiny i liudi (Ranks and People)* (+ co-sc); *The Man From the Restaurant*
1930   *Prazdnik svyatovo Iorgena (The Feast of St Jorgen)* (+ sc)
1931   *Tommy* (+ sc)
1934   *Marionetki (Marionettes)*
1937   *Bespridannitsa (Without Dowry)* (+ co-sc)
1938   *Pupils of the Seventh Grade*
1941   *Salavat Yulayev*
1943   *Nasreddin v Bukhare (Nasreddin in Bukhara)*

Publications:

On PROTAZANOV: books—

Yakov Protazanov, Moscow, 1957.
Leyda, Jay, Kino, *A History of the Russian and Soviet Film*, London, 1960.
Lebedev, Nikolai, *Il cinema muto sovietico*, Turin, 1962.
Robinson, David, and others, editors, *Silent Witnesses*, London, 1989.

On PROTAZANOV: articles—

Alisova, N., "Priobžčenie k poesii," in *Iskusstvo Kino* (Moscow), April 1973.
Raizman, Yuli, and others, "Protazanov," in *Soviet Film* (Moscow), no. 6, 1981.
Vajsfel'd, I., and others, "Effect Protazanova," in *Iskusstvo Kino* (Moscow), August 1981.
Tumanova, N., "Zabytaja stat'ja Jakova Protazanova," in *Iskusstvo Kino* (Moscow), July 1984.
Robinson, David, "Evgeni Bauer and the Cinema of Nikolai II," in *Sight and Sound* (London), Winter 1989/90.

*   *   *

As a pioneer of the Czarist Cinema, as a director who filmed in Moscow, Yalta, Paris and Berlin, and as one who worked under various social systems and managed to survive, Yakov Protazanov has a unique place in the story of the Russian Cinema.

Originally intended for a commercial career, he fell under the spell of films and began his apprenticeship with Gloria Films in Moscow, later to become Thiemann and Reinhardt. The cinema in Russia had been socially acceptable from the beginning and enjoyed the patronage of Imperial circles. From script-writing and acting Protazanov moved into directing and in 1911 made *Pesnya katorzhanina (The Prisoner's Song)* with Vladimir Shaternikov, an actor he was to use many times. The following year Andreyev scripted for him an adaptation of his play *Anfisa*. The same year he made *Ukhod velikovo startza (The Departure of a Grand Old Man)*, thereby antagonising Countess Tolstoy who objected to the depiction of her husband as played by Shaternikov. The film was banned in consequence. A happier venture was *Klyuchishchastya (Keys to Happiness)* by a popular novelist, A Verbitskaya. The wide appeal of this film made it the greatest box-office success throughout Russia.

By the time of the World War of 1914–18 Protazanov had directed some forty films covering a wide range of material

Yakov Protazanov

stoy's story of the spiritual struggles of a young officer of the Imperial Court who gives up a life of pleasure to become a monk was a *tour de force* for Mozhukin. The actor's transition from youth to age, the authenticity of the settings and the cohesion of the film help to make it one of the great classics of the Cinema.

On a very different level was *Taina koroloevy* (*The Queen's Secret*) based on a novel by Elinor Glynn, again with Mozhukin. This was filmed in Moscow and Yalta for with the coming of the Revolution many film artists fled to the south. Ermoliev transferred his studio to Yalta bringing all his equipment, technicians and artists with him. Here Protazanov made three films. But political unrest soon made work impossible and Ermoliev with all his people embarked on a British ship at Odessa which took them to Constantinople where Protazanov continued with the direction of the film *L'Angoissante Aventure* from a script by Mozhukin. This ambulatory film went on from Constantinople to Marseilles and Paris where Ermoliev's production continued at Méliès old studio at Monteuil. In spite of the circumstances under which it was made *L'Angoissante Aventure* was a quite ingenious comedy exploiting the diverse talents of Mozhukin and ranged from comedy to tragedy but was resolved by the typically Russian device of being a dream. Protazanov's *Justice d'Abord* was a remake of *Prokuror* but he broke away from Ermoliev and his company and adapted novels by Zola and Paul Bourget before going to Berlin where he made *Liebes Pilgerfahrt*. Invited back to Russia to make a film of *Taras Bulba* he directed instead *Aelita* for Mezhrabpom-Russ. This fantasy in which life on Mars is compared with contemporary Russia featured extraordinary sets by Alexandra Exter of the Kamerny Theatre. *Yevo prizyv* (*His Call*), the following year, could be called a propaganda film with a human face and showed that Protazanov was still his own man. *Protsess o tryoch millyonakh* (*The Three Million Case*) of 1926 and subsequent films like *Sorok Pervyi* (*The 41st*), *Byelyi orel* (*The White Eagle*), *Dondiego i Pelaguya* (a satiric comment on bureaucracy), *Chiny i Liudi* (*Ranks and People*, a compendium of three Chekhov stories), *Prazdnik svyatovo Iorgena* (*The Feast of St Jorgen*, a satirical anti-relgious film), all established him as holding his own with the new young school of Russian film directors.

In *Sorok pervyi* (*The Forty First*), a story of the fighting in Turkestan, a young girl partisan is torn between love and duty and has to kill a young White officer, the only man she ever loved. Set in a memorable landscape of sandy desert the film develops with a powerful impact. *Tommy* was Protazanov's first sound film in 1931. It tells of a British soldier's reaction to a group of partisans.

Recipient of official honours, Protazanov continued to be regarded as an outstanding creative artist and many of his films were set in far-flung locations in outlying Soviet Republics. When the centre of Soviet film production noved to Alma Ata in the Urals during the German invasion of Russia in World War Two, Protazanov moved with it. However his last film *Nazreddin ve Bukhare* (*Nazreddin in Bukhara* was filmed on location in Uzbekistan and was a delightful comedy with Meyerhold's great actor Lev Sverdlin in the title role giving a performance reminiscent of Fairbanks' *Thief of Bagdad*. When Protazanov died in 1945 he was working on a script based on a play by Ostrovsky. He was a great man of the Cinema, a prolific creator of films and a great human being.

—Liam O'Leary.

from the perfervid, morbid and even decadent themes so popular in Russia at the time, to historical spectacles and films based on the literary heritage of his country. In *Kak khoroshi, kak svezhi byli rosi* (*How Fine, How Fresh the Roses Were*) of 1913 he was inspired by Turgenev and had Shaternikov again, playing Lev Tolstoy.

After his experiences as a soldier Protazanov joined the Ermoliev Company as did his former colleague Vladimir Gardin. In 1915 they shared the direction of an elaborate *Voina i mir* (*War and Peace*), and a serial *Petersburgskiye trushchobi* (*Petersburg slums*), while Protazanov directed a version of Strindberg's *Froken Julie* under the title *Plebei* (*Plebian*) In these three films the lead was taken by Olga Preobrazhenskaya, herself to become a director of distinction in later years.

Ermoliev's greatest actor was Ivan Mozhukin, whose knowledge and interest in the whole field of cinema transcended his interpretive skills. Protazanov directed him in *Nicolai Stavrogin* (based on Dostoievsky) in 1915 and the following year in *Pikovaya dama* (*The Queen of Spades*). It was a milestone in Mozhukin's career. The script, incidentally, was written by a young Fedor Otsep. Other important films with Mozhukin were *Prokuror* (*Public Prosecutor*), *Satana likuyushchii* (*Satan Triumphant*), *Andrei Kozhukov* and above all *Otets Sergii* (*Father Sergius*). This is undoubtedly his masterpiece. Tol-

PUDOVKIN, Vsevolod.

Russian. Born Vsevolod Illarionovitch Pudovkin in Penza, 16 February 1893. Educated in physics and chemistry, Moscow University; entered State Cinema School, 1920. Married actress and journalist Anna Zemtsova, 1923. Enlisted in artillery, 1914; wounded and taken prisoner, 1915; escaped and returned to Moscow, 1918; worked as writer and chemist, 1919–20; worked on agit films, 1920–21; student at Lev Kuleshov's studio, from 1922; quit State Cinema Institute to join Kuleshov's Experimental Laboratory, 1923; began collaboration with cinematographer Anatoly Golovnia and scriptwriter Nathan Zarkhi, 1925; with Alexandrov signed Eisenstein's "Manifesto on Audio-Visual Counterpoint," 1928; travelled to England and Holland, 1929; joined Communist Party, 1932; after car accident, taught theoretic studies at V.G.I.K., 1935; joined Mosfilm sudios, 1938. Recipient: Order of Lenin, 1935. *Died in Riga, 30 June 1953.*

Films as Director:

1921   *Golod . . . golod . . . golod (Hunger . . . Hunger . . . Hunger)* (co-d, co-sc, role)
1925   *Shakhmatnaya goryachka (Chess Fever)* (co-d)
1926   *Mekhanikha golovnovo mozga (Mechanics of the Brain)* (+ sc); *Mat (Mother)*
1927   **Konyets Sankt-Peterburga (The End of St. Petersburg)**
1928   **Potomok Chingis-khan (The Heir to Genghis-Khan. Storm Over Asia)**
1932   *Prostoi sluchai (A Simple Case)* (revised version of *Otchen kharacho dziviosta* [*Life's Very Good*]; first screened in 1930)
1933   *Dezertir (Deserter)*
1938   *Pobeda (Victory)* (co-d)
1939   *Minin i Pozharsky* (co-d)
1940   *Kino za XX liet (Twenty Years of Cinema)* (co-d, co-ed)
1941   *Suvorov* (co-d); *Pir v Girmunka (Feast at Zhirmunka)* (co-d) (for "Fighting Film Album")
1942   *Ubitzi vykhodyat na dorogu (Murderers Are on Their Way)* (co-d, co-sc)
1943   *Vo imya rodini (In the Name of the Fatherland)* (co-d)
1946   *Amiral Nakhimov (Admiral Nakhimov)*
1948   *Tri vstrechi (Three Encounters)* (co-d)
1950   *Yukovsky* (co-d)
1953   *Vozvrachenia Vassilya Bortnikov (The Return of Vasili Bortnikov)*

Other Films:

1920   *V dni borbi (In the Days of Struggle)* (role)
1921   *Serp i molot (Sickle and Hammer)* (asst d, role)
1923   *Slesar i kantzler (Locksmith and Chancellor)* (co-sc)
1924   **Neobychainye priklucheniya Mistera Vesta v stranye bolshevikov (Extraordinary Adventures of Mr. West in the Land of the Bolsheviks)** (Kuleshov) (co-sc, asst, role as the 'Count')
1925   *Luch smerti (The Death Ray)* (Kuleshov) (design, role); *Kirpitchiki (Little Bricks)* (role)
1928   *Zhivoi trup (A Living Corpse)* (role as Feodor Protassov)
1929   *Vessiolaia kanareika (The Cheerful Canary)* (role as the illusionist); **Novyi vavilon (The New Babylon)** (Kozintsev and Trauberg) (role as shop assistant)
1944   **Ivan Grozny (Ivan the Terrible)** (Eisenstein) (role as Nikolai the fanatic)

Publications:

By PUDOVKIN: books—

Film Technique, translated by Ivor Montagu, London, 1933.
Film-Acting, translated by Ivor Montagu, London, 1935.
Film Technique and Film Acting, New York, 1949.
Textes choisis, Moscow, 1955.
Sobranie sochinenii v trekh tomakh, Moscow, 1974.

By PUDOVKIN: articles—

"Scénario et mise en scène," in *Revue du Cinéma* (Paris), 1 September 1930.
"Poudovkine parle du montage," with René Lévy, in *Revue du Cinéma* (Paris), 1 December 1931.
"A Conversation with V.I. Pudovkin," with Marie Seton, in *Sight and Sound* (London), Spring 1933.
"The Global Film," in *Hollywood Quarterly*, July 1947.
"Two Conversations with Pudovkin," with C.H. Waddington, in *Sight and Sound* (London), Winter 1948/49.
"Stanislavsky's System in the Cinema," in *Sight and Sound* (London), January/March 1953.

On PUDOVKIN: books—

Bryher, Winifred, *Film Problems of Soviet Russia*, London, 1929.
Yezuitov, N., *Poudovkine, "Pouti Tvortchestva," "Les Voies de la création"*, Moscow, 1937.
Mariamov, A., *Vsevolod Pudovkin*, Moscow, 1952.
Leyda, Jay, *Kino: A History of the Russian and Soviet Film*, London, 1960.
Schnitzer, Luda and Jean, *Vsevolod Poudovkine*, Paris, 1966.
Amengual, Barthélemy, *V.I. Poudovkine*, Premier Plan, Lyon, 1968.
Dart, Peter, *Pudovkin's Films and Film Theory*, New York, 1974.
Marshall, Herbert, *Masters of the Soviet Cinema: Crippled Creative Biographies*, London, 1983.
Masi, Stefano, *Vsevolod I. Pudovkin*, Florence, 1985.
Taylor, Richard, and Ian Christie, editors, *The Film Factory: Russian and Soviet Cinema in Documents 1896–1939*, London, 1988.

On PUDOVKIN: articles—

Potamkin, Harry, "Pudovkin and the Revolutionary Film," in *Hound and Horn* (New York), April/June 1933.
Rotha, Paul, "Pabst, Pudovkin and the Producers," in *Sight and Sound* (London), Summer 1933.
Leyda, Jay, "Index to the Creative work of Vsevolod Pudovkin," in *Sight and Sound* (London), November 1948.
Sadoul, Georges, "Un Humaniste et un lyrique," in *Les Lettres Françaises* (Paris), 9 July 1953.
"Pudovkin Issue" of *Cahiers du Cinéma* (Paris), August/September 1953.
Weinberg, Herman, "Vsevolod Pudovkin," in *Films in Review* (New York), August/September 1953.
Wright, Basil, "V.I. Pudovkin: 1893–1953," in *Sight and Sound* (London), October/December 1953.
Herring, Robert, "Film Image—Pudovkin," in *Cinemage* (New York), May 1955.
Bizet, Jacques-André, "Les Théories du langage et de l'expression filmiques selon Poudovkine," in *Le Cinéma Pratique* (Paris), September/October and November/December 1966 and March 1967.
"Pudovkin Issue" of *Iskusstvo Kino* (Moscow), February 1973.
Hudlin, E., "Film Language: Pudovkin and Eisenstein and Russian Formalism," in *Journal of Aesthetic Education* (Urbana, Illinois), no. 2, 1979.
Burns, P.E., "Linkage: Pudovkin's Classics Revisited," in *Journal of Popular Film and Television* (Washington, D.C.), Summer 1981.
Pudovkin Section of *Iskusstvo Kino* (Moscow), February 1983.
Kepley, Vance, Jr., "Pudovkin and the Classical Hollywood tradition," in *Wide Angle* (Athens, Ohio), vol. 7, no. 3, 1985.
Jurenev, R., "Neskol'ko povsednevnyh vstrec," in *Iskusstvo Kino* (Moscow), August 1985.
Hogenkamp, Bert, "De russen komen! Poedowkin, Eisenstein en Wertow in Nederland," in *Skrien* (Amsterdam), November/December 1985.

*   *   *

Vsevolod Illarionovitch Pudovkin's major contribution to the cinema is as a theorist. He was fascinated by the efforts of his teacher, the filmmaker Lev Kuleshov, in exploring the effects of montage, and, in his own work, often created highly emotional moments by rapidly intercutting shots of diverse con-

Vsevolod Pudovkin

Bob Rafelson with Jack Nicholson on the set of *Five Easy Pieces*

hotels, Her gesture (and in Rafelson's uncommitted world we daren't ask for more) of defiance is directed against what has been the female share of the American Dream: the male has traditionally taken for himself the power that comes of wealth and left woman the illusion called "glamor." Another symbol is the blowing up of an old hotel; it collapses in a heap like the dream of enterpreneurship the protagonist momentarily shares with his brother.

Rafelson has failed to gain critical approval because he does not soften brutal political deconstruction with dazzling techniques. He devotes his attention not only to the straightforward expression of his themes but to getting brilliant acting out of his casts. He forces them to explore the darker sides of their characters—each a microcosm of society.

—Rodney Farnsworth

RAINER, Yvonne.

American. Born in San Francisco, 1934. Modern dancer, then choreographer, New York, from 1957; co-founder of Judson Dance Theater, 1962; presented choreographic work in U.S. and Europe, 1962–75; began to integrate slides and short films into dance performances, 1968; completed first feature-length film, *Lives of Performers*, 1972; teacher at New School for Social Research, New York, California Institute of the Arts, Valencia, and elsewhere. Recipient: Maya Deren Award, American Film Institute, 1988; Guggenheim Fellowship, 1989. Address: 72 Franklin St., New York, NY 10013, U.S.A.

Films:

1967 *Volleyball (Foot Film)* (short)
1968 *Hand Movie* (short); *Rhode Island Red* (short); *Trio Film* (short)
1969 *Line*
1972 *Lives of Performers*
1974 *Film About a Woman Who . . .*
1976 *Kristina Talking Pictures*
1980 *Journeys from Berlin/1971*
1985 *The Man Who Envied Women*
1990 *Privilege*

Publications:

By RAINER: books—

Work 1961–73, New York, 1974.
The Films of Yvonne Rainer, by Rainer and others, Bloomington, Indiana, 1989.

By RAINER: articles—

"A Quasi Survey of Some 'Minimalist' Tendencies in the Quantitatively Minimal Dance Activity Midst the Plethora, or An Analysis of *Trio A*," in *Minimal Art*, edited by Gregory Battcock, New York, 1968.
Interview in *Monthly Film Bulletin* (London), May 1977.
"More Kicking and Screaming from the Narrative Front/Backwater," in *Wide Angle* (Athens, Ohio), vol. 7, no. 1/2, 1985.
Interview with Mitch Rosenbaum, in *Persistence of Vision* (Maspeth, New York), Summer 1988.

On RAINER: articles—

Koch, Stephen, "Performance: A Conversation," in *Artforum* (New York), December 1972.
Borden, Lizzie, "Trisha Brown and Yvonne Rainer," in *Artforum* (New York), June 1973.
Michelson, Annette, "Yvonne Rainer: The Dancer and the Dance," and "Yvonne Rainer: *Lives of Performers*," in *Artforum* (New York), January and February 1974.
"Yvonne Rainer: An Introduction, in *Camera Obscura* (Berkeley), Fall 1976.
Rosenbaum, Jonathan, "The Ambiguities of Yvonne Rainer," in *American Film* (Washington, D.C.), March 1980.
Rich, B.R., "Yvonne Rainer," in *Frauen und Film* (Berlin), October 1984.
Vincendeau, Ginette, and B. Reynaud, "Impossible Projections," in *Screen* (London), Autumn 1987.
Cook, Pam, "Love and Catastrophe—Yvonne Rainer," in *Monthly Film Bulletin* (London), August 1987.
White, Barbara, "Destiny with the Incommensurable: A Reading of Yvonne Rainer's *The Man Who Envied Women*," in *New Orleans Review*, vol. 15, no. 3, 1988.

* * *

Although Yvonne Rainer made her first feature-length film in 1972, she had already been prominent in the New York avant-garde art scene for nearly a decade. She moved to New York from San Francisco in 1957 to study acting, but started taking dance lessons and soon committed herself to dance. By the mid-1960s, she emerged as an influential dancer and choreographer, initially drawing the attention of critics and audiences through her work with the Judson Dance Theater.

Rainer saw a problem inherent in dance as an art form, namely its involvement with "narcissism, virtuosity and display." Her alternative conception was of the performance as a kind of work or task, as opposed to an exhibition, carried out by "neutral 'doers'" rather than performers. Thus the minimalist dance that she pioneered, which depended on ordinary movements, departed radically from the dramatic, emotive forms of both its classical and modern dance precursors.

Rainer was not long content with merely stripping dance of its artifice and conventions. She became interested in psychology and sexuality, in the everyday emotions that people share, and grew dissatisfied with abstract dance, which she found too limited to express her new concerns. To communicate more personal and emotional content, Rainer began experimenting with combining movements with other media, such as recorded and spoken texts, slides, film stills, and music, creating a performance collage. Language and narrative became increasingly important components of her performance.

Rainer's first films, shorts made to be part of these performances in the late 1960s, were "... filmed choreographic exercises," as she wrote in 1971, "that were meant to be viewed with one's peripheral vision ... not to be taken seriously." Her interest in the narrative potential of film and the director's dominance of the medium drew Rainer further into filmmaking.

Her first two feature films, *Lives of Performers*, and *Film About a Woman Who ...*, both with cinematographer Babette Mangolte, originated as performance pieces. In these and in her two other films, *Kristina Talking Pictures* and *Journeys from Berlin/1971*, Rainer interweaves the real and the fictional, the personal and the political, the concrete and the abstract. She preserves the collagist methods of her performances, juxtaposing personal recollections, previous works, historical documents, and original dialogue and narration, her soundtracks often having the same richness, and the same disjunction, as the visual portions of her films.

Like Brecht, Rainer believes that an audience should contemplate what they see; they should participate in the creative process of the film rather than simply receive it passively. Thus, instead of systematically telling a story, she apposes and layers narrative elements to create meaning. The discontinuity, ambiguity, and even contradiction that often result keep Rainer's audience at a distance, so they can examine the feminist, psychological, political, or purely emotional issues she addresses. Consistent with her dance and performance, Rainer's films are theoretical, even intellectual, not dramatic, sentimental, or emotional, despite her subject matter, which is often controversial and emotion-laden.

—Jessica Wolff

———

RAY, Nicholas.

American. Born Raymond Nicholas Kienzle in Galesville, Wisconsin, 7 August 1911. Educated in architecture and theater, University of Chicago. Married 1) Jean Evans, 1930 (divorced); 2) Gloria Grahame, 1948 (divorced 1952); 3) dancer Betty Schwab (divorced); 4) Susan (Ray), four children. Director, Frank Lloyd Wright's Taliesin Playhouse, early 1930s; in Theater of Action, 1935–37; joined John Houseman's Phoenix Theater, accident results in loss of sight in right eye, 1938; named War Information Radio Program Director by Houseman, 1942; director on Broadway, 1943; assistant to Elia Kazan in Hollywood, 1944; directed first film, *They Live By Night*), 1948; walked off set of *55 Days at Peking*, moved to Paris, 1962; teacher of filmmaking at State University of New York, Binghamton, 1971–73. *Died in New York, 16 June 1979.*

Films as Director:

1948   *They Live By Night* (first release in Britain as *The Twisted Road*, U.S. release 1949); *A Woman's Secret*
1949   *Knock on Any Door*
1950   *In a Lonely Place*; *Born to Be Bad*
1951   *The Flying Leathernecks*
1952   *On Dangerous Ground*; *The Lusty Men*
1954   *Johnny Guitar*
1955   *Run for Cover*; *Rebel Without a Cause* (+ story)
1956   *Hot Blood*; *Bigger than Life*
1957   *The True Story of Jesse James*; *Bitter Victory* (+ co-sc)
1958   *Wind Across the Everglades*; *Party Girl*
1959   *The Savage Innocents* (+ sc)
1961   *King of Kings*
1963   *Fifty-five Days at Peking* (co-d)
1975   *You Can't Go Home Again* (+ sc, unfinished)
1981   *Lightning over Water* (*Nick's Movie*) (co-d, role as himself)

Other Films:

1977   *Der Amerikanische Freund* (*The American Friend*) (Wenders) (role)
1979   *Hair* (Forman) (role)

Publications:

By RAY: articles—

"Portrait de l'acteur en jeune homme," in *Cahiers du Cinéma* (Paris), no. 66, 1956.
"Story into Script," in *Sight and Sound* (London), Autumn 1956.
Interview with Charles Bitsch, in *Cahiers du Cinéma* (Paris), November 1958.
"Conversation with Nicholas Ray and Joseph Losey," with Penelope Houston, in *Sight and Sound* (London), Autumn 1961.
Interview with Jean Douchet and Jacques Joly, in *Cahiers du Cinéma* (Paris), January 1962.
Interview with Adriano Aprà and others, in *Movie* (London), May 1963.
Interview in *Interviews with Film Directors* edited by Andrew Sarris, New York, 1967.
"Nicholas Ray Today," an interview with J. Greenberg, in *Filmmakers Newsletter* (Ward Hill, Massachusetts), January 1973.
"Nicholas Ray: Rebel!," an interview with M. Goodwin and N. Wise, in *Take One* (Montreal), January 1977.
"On Directing," in *Sight and Sound* (London), Autumn 1990.

On RAY: books—

McArthur, Colin, *Underworld U.S.A.*, London, 1972.
Kreidl, John, *Nicholas Ray*, Boston, 1977.
Masi, Stefano, *Nicholas Ray*, Florence, 1983.
Allan, Blaine, *Nicholas Ray: A Guide to References and Resources*, Boston, 1984.
Hillier, Jim, editor, *Cahiers du Cinéma 1: Neo-realism, Hollywood, New Wave*, London, 1985.
Erice, Victor, and Jos Oliver, *Nicholas Ray y su tiempo*, Madrid, 1986.
Giuliani, Pierre, *Nicholas Ray*, Paris, 1987.
Wagner, Jean, *Nicholas Ray*, Paris, 1987.

On RAY: articles—

Archer, Eugene, "Generation Without a Cause," in *Film Culture* (New York), vol. 2, no. 1, 1956.
Perkins, Victor, "The Cinema of Nicholas Ray," in *Movie Reader* edited by Ian Cameron, New York, 1972.
Wood, Robin, "Film Favorites," in *Film Comment* (New York), September/October 1972.
Rosenbaum, Jonathan, "Circle of Pain: The Cinema of Nicholas Ray," in *Sight and Sound* (London), Autumn 1973.
"*Johnny Guitar* Issue" of *Avant-Scène du Cinéma* (Paris), March 1974.
Biskind, Peter, "Rebel Without a Cause: Nicholas Ray in the Fifties," in *Film Quarterly* (Berkeley), Fall 1974.
Lederer, Joseph, "Film as Experience: Nicholas Ray—The Director Turns Teacher," in *American Film* (Washington, D.C.), November 1975.
Cocks, J., "Director in Aspic," in *Take One* (Montreal), January 1977.
Thomson, D., "In a Lonely Place," in *Sight and Sound* (London), no. 4, 1979.
Obituary, in *The New York Times*, 18 June 1979.
Beylie, Claude, obituary, in *Ecran* (Paris), 15 September 1979.
Farrell, T., and others, "Nicholas Ray: The Last Movies," in *Sight and Sound* (London), Spring 1981.
Rosenbaum, Jonathan, "Looking for Nicholas Ray," in *American Film* (Washington, D.C.), December 1981.
Eisenschitz, B., "Nicholas Ray, téléaste," in *Cahiers du Cinéma* (Paris), January 1985.
Houseman, John, "Houseman, Ray and Ophüls," in *Sight and Sound* (London), Autumn 1986.

*   *   *

"The cinema is Nicholas Ray." Godard's magisterial statement has come in for a good deal of ridicule, not by any means entirely undeserved. Yet it contains a core of truth, especially if taken in reverse. Nicholas Ray is cinema—in that his films work entirely (and perhaps only) as *movies*, arrangements of space and movement charged with dramatic tension. Few directors demonstrate more clearly that a film is something beyond the sum of its parts. Consider only the more literary components—dialogue, plot, characterisation—and a film like *Party Girl* is patently trash. But on the screen the visual turbulence of Ray's shooting style, the fractured intensity of his editing, fuse the elements into a valid emotional whole. The flaws are still apparent, but have become incidental.

Nor is Ray's cinematic style in any way extraneous, imposed upon his subjects. The nervous tension within the frame also informs his characters, vulnerable violent outsiders, at odds with society and with themselves. The typical Ray hero is a loner, at once contemptuous of the complacent normal world and tormented with a longing to be reaccepted into it—to become (like Bowie and Keechie, the young lovers of *They Live by Night*) "like real people". James Dean in *Rebel Without a Cause*, Robert Ryan in *On Dangerous Ground*, Robert Mitchum in *The Lusty Men*, all start by rejecting the constraints of the nuclear family, only to find themselves impelled to recreate it in substitute form, as though trying to fill an unacknowledged void. In one achingly elegiac scene in *The Lusty Men* we see Mitchum prowling around the tumbledown shack that was his childhood home, "looking for something I thought I'd lost."

Ray's grounding in architecture (he studied at Taliesin with Frank Lloyd Wright) reveals itself in an exceptionally acute sense of space, often deployed as an extension of states of mind. In his films the geometry of locations, and especially interiors, serves as a psychological terrain in which conflict can be played out, and tension expressed, in terms of spatial areas (upstairs and downstairs, for example, or the courtyards and levels of an apartment complex) pitted against each other. Ray also credited Wright with instilling in him "a love of the horizontal line"—and hence of the CinemaScope screen, for which he felt intuitive affinity. Unlike many of his contemporaries, who found it awkward and inhibiting, Ray avidly explores the format's potential, sometimes combining it with lateral tracking shots to convey lyrical movement, at others angling his camera to create urgent diagonals, suggesting characters straining against the constrictions of the frame.

Equally idiosyncratic is his expressionist use of colour, taken at times to heights of delirium that risk toppling into the ridiculous. In *Johnny Guitar*, perhaps the most flamboyantly baroque Western ever made, Joan Crawford is colour-coded red, white or black according to which aspect of her character—whore, victim or gunslinger—is uppermost in a given scene. And the contrast, in *Bigger Than Life*, between the hero's respectable job as a schoolteacher and his déclassé moonlighting for a taxi firm is signalled by an abrupt cut from the muted grey-browns of the school to a screenful of gaudy yellow cabs, hitting our eyes with a visual slap.

Nearly all Ray's finest films were made in the 1950s, their agonized romanticism cutting across the grain of that decade's brittle optimism. "The poet of American disenchantment" (in David Thomson's phrase), Ray views social conventions as a trap, from which violence or madness may be the only escape. In *Bigger Than Life* James Mason's smalltown teacher, frustrated by his low social status, gains from a nerve drug the feelings of power and superiority he aspires to. Under its influence the metamorphoses into a hideous parody of the dominant father-figure enjoined by society. Similarly—but working from the opposite perspective—*In a Lonely Place* subverts Bogart's tough-guy persona, revealing the anguish and insecurity that underlie it and, as V F Perkins puts it, making "violence the index of the character's weakness rather than strength".

"I'm a stranger here myself." Ray often quoted Sterling Hayden's line from *Johnny Guitar* as his personal motto—and his career, as he himself was well aware, disconcertingly mirrors the fate of his own riven, alienated heroes. Unappreciated

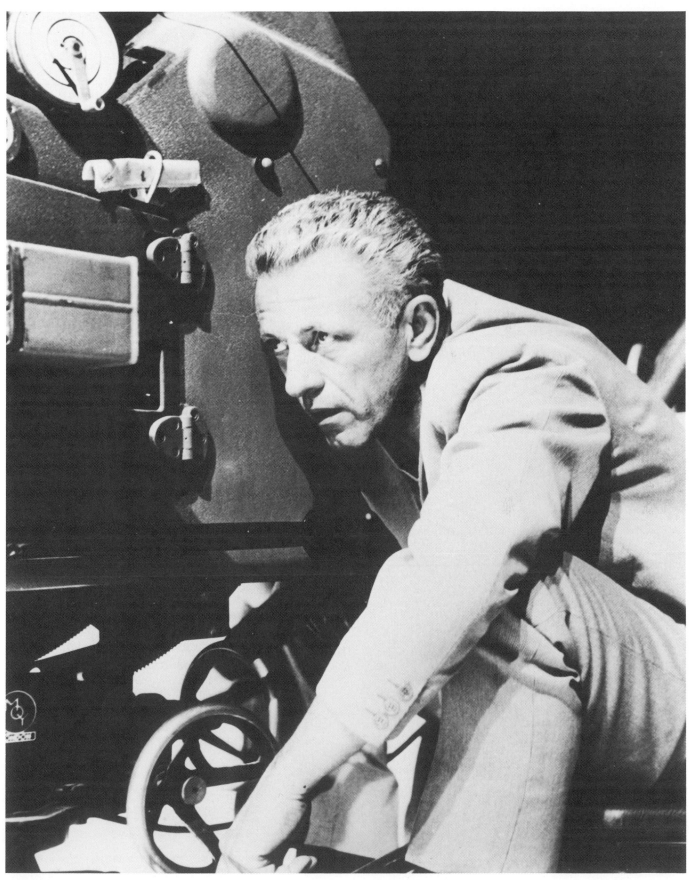

Nicholas Ray

(or so he felt) in America, and increasingly irked by the constraints of the studio system, he nonetheless produced all his best work there. In Europe, where he was hailed as one of the world's greatest directors, his craft deserted him: after two ill-starred epics, the last sixteen years of his life trickled away in a mess of incoherent footage and abortive projects. Victim of his own legend, Ray finally took self-identification with his protagonists to its ultimate tortured conclusion—collaborating, in *Lightning Over Water*, in the filming of his own disintegration and death.

—Philip Kemp

RAY, Satyajit.

Indian. Born in Calcutta, 2 May 1921. Educated Ballygunj Government School; Presidency College, Calcutta; University of Santiniketan, 1940–42. Married Bijoya Das, 1949. Commercial artist for D.J. Keymer advertising agency, Calcutta, 1943; co-founder, Calcutta Film Society, 1947; met Jean Renoir making *The River*, 1950; completed first film, *Pather Panchali*, 1955; composed own music, from *Teen Kanya* on, 1961; made first film in Hindi (as opposed to Bengali), *The Chess Players*, 1977; editor and illustrator for children's magazine *Sandesh*, 1980s. Recipient: Silver Bear for Best Direction, Berlin Festival, for *Mahanagar*, 1964, and *Charulata*, 1965; Special Award of Honour, Berlin Festival, 1966. Address: Flat 8, 1/1 Bishop Lefroy Road, Calcutta 20, India.

Satyajit Ray

Films as Director and Scriptwriter:

1955   *Pather Panchali* (*Father Panchali*)
1956   *Aparajito* (*The Unvanquished*)
1957   *Parash Pathar* (*The Philosopher's Stone*)
1958   *Jalsaghar* (*The Music Room*)
1959   *Apur Sansar* (*The World of Apu*)
1960   *Devi* (*The Goddess*) (also as composer of music)
1961   *Teen Kanya* (*Two Daughters*); *Rabindranath Tagore* (doc)
1962   *Abhijan* (*Expedition*); *Kanchanjanga*
1963   *Mahanagar* (*The Big City*)
1964   *Charulata* (*The Lonely Wife*)
1965   *Kapurush-o-Mahapurush* (*The Coward and the Saint*); *Two* (short)
1966   *Nayak* (*The Hero*)
1967   *Chiriakhana* (*The Zoo*)
1969   *Goopy Gyne Bagha Byne* (*The Adventures of Goopy and Bagha*)
1970   *Pratidwandi* (*The Adversary*); *Aranyer Din Ratri* (*Days and Nights in the Forest*)
1971   *Seemabaddha*; *Sikkim* (doc)
1972   *The Inner Eye* (doc)
1973   *Asani Sanket* (*Distant Thunder*)
1974   *Sonar Kella* (*The Golden Fortress*)
1975   *Jana Aranya* (*The Middleman*)
1976   *Bala* (doc)
1977   *Shatranj Ke Khilari* (*The Chess Players*)
1978   *Joi Baba Felunath* (*The Elephant God*)
1979   *Heerak Rajar Deshe* (*The Kingdom of Diamonds*)
1981   *Sadgati* (*Deliverance*) (for TV); *Pikoo* (short)
1984   *Ghare Bahire* (*The Home and the World*)
1989   *Ganashatru* (*An Enemy of the People*)
1990   *Shakha Proshakha* (*Branches of the Tree*)

Publications:

By RAY: books—

Our Films, Their Films, New Delhi, 1977.
The Chess Players and Other Screenplays, London, 1989.

By RAY: articles—

"A Long Time on the Little Road," in *Sight and Sound* (London), Spring 1957.
"Satyajit Ray on Himself," in *Cinema* (Beverly Hills), July/August 1965.
"From Film to Film," in *Cahiers du Cinéma in English* (New York), no. 3, 1966
Interview in *Film Makers on Filmmaking* by Harry M. Geduld, Bloomington, Indiana, 1967.
Interview in *Interviews with Film Directors* edited by Andrew Sarris, New York, 1967.
Interview with J. Blue, in *Film Comment* (New York), Summer 1968.
"Conversation with Satyajit Ray," with F. Isaksson, in *Sight and Sound* (London), Summer 1970.
"Ray's New Trilogy," an interview with C.B. Thomsen, in *Sight and Sound* (London), Winter 1972/73.
"Dialogue on Film: Satyajit Ray," in *American Film* (Washington, D.C.), July/August 1978.
Interview with Michel Ciment, in *Positif* (Paris), May 1979.
Interview with U. Gupta, in *Cineaste* (New York), vol. 12, no. 1, 1982.
"Under Western Eyes," in *Sight and Sound* (London), Autumn 1982.
"Bridging the Home and the World," an interview with A. Robinson, in *Monthly Film Bulletin* (London), September 1984.
Interview with Charles Tesson, in *Cahiers du Cinéma* (Paris), July/August 1987.
Interview with Derek Malcolm, in *Sight and Sound* (London), Spring 1989.

On RAY: books—

Seton, Marie, *Portrait of a Director*, Bloomington, Indiana, 1970.
Wood, Robin, *The Apu Trilogy*, New York, 1971.
Taylor, John Russell, *Directors and Directions: Cinema for '70s*, New York, 1975.

Rangoonwalla, Firoze, *Satyajit Ray's Art*, Shahdara, Delhi, 1980.
Satyajit Ray: An Anthology, edited by Chidananda Das Gupta, New Delhi, 1981.
Willemen, Paul, and Behroze Gandhy, *Indian Cinema*, London, 1982.
Armes, Roy, *Third World Filmmaking and the West*, Berkeley, 1987.
Nyce, Ben, *Satyajit Ray: A Study of His Films*, New York, 1988.
Robinson, Andrew, *Satyajit Ray: The Inner Eye*, London, 1989.

On RAY: articles—

Gray, H., "The Growing Edge: Satyajit Ray," in *Film Quarterly* (Berkeley, California), Winter 1958.
Rhode, Eric, "Satyajit Ray: A Study," in *Sight and Sound* (London), Summer 1961.
Stanbrook, Alan, "The World of Ray," in *Films and Filming* (London), November 1965.
Hrusa, B., "Satyajit Ray: Genius Behind the Man," in *Film* (London), Winter 1966.
Glushanok, Paul, "On Ray," in *Cineaste* (New York), Summer 1967.
Malik, A., "Satyajit Ray and the Alien," in *Sight and Sound* (London), Winter 1967/68.
Mehta, V., "Profiles," in the *New Yorker*, 21 March 1970.
Thomsen, Christian Braad, "Ray's New Trilogy," in *Sight and Sound* (London), Winter 1972/73.
Dutta, K., "Cinema in India: An Interview with Satyajit Ray's Cinematographers," in *Filmmakers Newsletter* (Ward Hill, Massachusetts), January 1975.
Hughes, J., "A Voyage in India: Satyajit Ray," in *Film Comment* (New York), September/October 1976.
"*Pather Panchali* Issue" of *Avant-Scène du Cinéma* (Paris), 1 February 1980.
Armes, Roy, "Satyajit Ray: Astride Two Cultures," in *Films and Filming* (London), August 1982.
Robinson, A., "Satyajit Ray at Work," in *American Cinematographer* (Los Angeles), September 1983.
Ray, B., "Ray off set," in *Sight and Sound* (London), Winter 1983/84.
Das Gupta, Chidananda, and Andrew Robinson, "A Passage from India," in *American Film* (Washington, D.C.), in *American Film* (Washington, D.C.), October 1985.
Robinson, Andrew, "The Music Room," in *Sight and Sound* (London), Autumn 1989.

*   *   *

From the beginning of his career as a filmmaker, Ray has been interested in finding ways to reveal the mind and thoughts of his characters. Because the range of his sympathy is wide, he has been accused of softening the presence of evil in his cinematic world. But a director who aims to represent the currents and cross-currents of feeling within people is likely to disclose to viewers the humanness even in reprehensible figures. In any case, from the first films of his early period, Ray devises strategies for rendering inner lives; he simplifies the surface action of the film so that the viewer's attention travels to (1) the reaction of people to one another, or to their environments, (2) the mood expressed by natural scenery or objects, and (3) music as a clue to the state of mind of a character. In the *Apu Trilogy* the camera often stays with one of two characters after the other character exits the frame to see their silent response. Or else, after some significant event in the narrative, Ray presents correlatives of that event in the natural world. When the impoverished wife in *Pather Panchali* receives a postcard bearing happy news from her husband, the scene dissolves to water skates dancing on a pond. As for music, in his films Ray commissioned compositions from India's best classical musicians—Ravi Shankar, Vilayat Khan, Ali Akbar Khan—but since *Teen Kanya* has been composing his own music and has progressed towards quieter indication through music of the emotional experience of his characters.

Ray's work can be divided into three periods on the basis of his cinematic practice: the early period, 1955–66, from *Pather Panchali* through *Nayak*; the middle period, 1969–1977, from *Googy Gyne Bagha Byne* through *Shatranj Ke Khilari*; and the recent period, from *Joy Baba Felunath* and through *Sadgati* and *Ghare Bahire*. The early period is characterized by thoroughgoing realism: the mise-en-scène are rendered in deep focus; long takes and slow camera movements prevail. The editing is subtle, following shifts of narrative interest and cutting on action in the Hollywood style. Ray's emphasis in the early period on capturing reality is obvious in *Kanchanjangha*, in which 100 minutes in the lives of characters are rendered in 100 minutes of film time. *The Apu Trilogy, Parash Pather, Jalsaghar*, and *Devi* all exemplify what Ray had learned from Hollywood's studio era, from Renoir's mise-en-scène and from the use of classical music in Indian cinema. *Charulata* affords the archetypical example of Ray's early style, with the decor, the music, the long takes, the activation of various planes of depth within a composition and the reaction shots all contributing significantly to a representation of the lonely wife's inner conflicts. The power of Ray's early films comes from his ability to suggest deep feeling by arranging the surface elements of his films unemphatically.

Ray's middle period is characterized by increasing complexity of style; to his skills at understatement Ray adds a sharp use of montage. The difference in effect between an early film and a middle film becomes apparent if one compares the early *Mahanagar* with the middle *Jana Aranya*, both films pertaining to life in Calcutta. In *Mahanagar*, the protagonist chooses to resign her job in order to protest the unjust dismissal of a colleague. The film affirms the rightness of her decision. In the closing sequence, the protagonist looks up at the tall towers of Calcutta and says to her husband so that we believe her, "What a big city! Full of jobs! There must be something somewhere for one of us!" Ten years later, in *Jana Aranya*, it is clear that there are no jobs and that there is precious little room to worry about niceties of justice and injustice. The darkness running under the pleasant facade of many of the middle films seems to derive from the turn in Indian politics after the death of Nehru. Within Bengal, many ardent young people joined a Maoist movement to destroy existing institutions, and more were themselves destroyed by a ruthless police force. Across India, politicians abandoned Nehru's commitment to a socialist democracy in favor of a scramble for personal power. In *Seemabaddha* or *Aranyer Din Ratri* Ray's editing is sharp but not startling. In *Shatranj Ke Khilari*, on the other hand, Ray's irony is barely restrained: he cuts from the blue haze of a Nawab's music room to a gambling scene in the city. In harsh daylight, commoners lay bets on fighting rams, as intent on their gambling as the Nawab was on his music.

Audiences in India who have responded warmly to Ray's early films have sometimes been troubled by the complexity of his middle films. A film like *Shatranj Ke Khilari* was expected by many viewers to reconstruct the splendors of Moghul India as the early *Jalsaghar* had reconstructed the sensitivity of Bengali feudal landlords and *Charulata* the decency of upper class Victorian Bengal. What the audience found instead was a stern examination of the sources of Indian decadence. According to Ray, the British seemed less to blame for their role than the Indians who demeaned themselves by colluding with the British or by ignoring the public good and plunging into private pleasures. Ray's point of view in *Shatranj* was not popular with distributors and so his first Hindi film was denied fair exhibition in many cities in India.

Ray's more recent style, most evident in the short features *Pikoo* and *Sadgati*, pays less attention than earlier to building a stable geography and a firm time scheme. The exposition of characters and situations is swift: the effect is of great concision. In *Pikoo*, a young boy is sent outside to sketch flowers so that his mother and her lover can pursue their affair indoors. The lover has brought along a drawing pad and colored pens to divert the boy. The boy has twelve colored pens in his packet with which he must represent on paper the wealth of colors in nature. In a key scene (lasting ten seconds) the boy looks at a flower, then down at his packet for a matching color. Through that action of the boy's looking to match the world with his means, Ray suggests the striving in his own work to render the depth and range of human experience.

In focussing on inner lives and on human relations as the ground of social and political systems, Ray continues the humanist tradition of Rabindranath Tagore. Ray studied at Santiniketan, the university founded by Tagore, and was close to the poet during his last years. Ray has acknowledged his debt in a lyrical documentary about Tagore, and through the Tagore stories on which he has based his films, *Teen Kanya*, *Charulata*, and the recent *Ghare Bahire*. As the poet Tagore was his example, Ray has become an example to important younger filmmakers (such as Shyam Benegal, M.S. Sathyu, G. Aravindan), who have learned from him how to reveal in small domestic situations the working of larger political and cultural forces.

—Satti Khanna

REED, Carol.

British. Born in Putney, London, 30 December 1906, son of actor Herbert Beerbohn Tree. Educated at King's School, Canterbury. Married 1) Diana Wynyard (divorced); 2) actress Penelope Ward, two sons. Actor on London stage, from 1924; dramatic advisor to author Edgar Wallace, 1927; stage director, from 1929; dialogue director for Associated Talking Pictures, 1932; directed first feature, 1933; served in British Army Film Unit, World War II; began collaboration with writer Graham Greene, 1946. Recipient: Best British Film Award, British Film Academy, for *Odd Man Out*, 1947; Best British Film Award, British Film Academy, and Best Direction, New York Film Critics, for *The Fallen Idol*, 1948; Best British Film Award, British Film Academy, and Quarterly Award, Directors Guild of America, for *The Third Man*, 1949; Knighted, 1952; Oscar for Best Director, for *Oliver!*, 1968. *Died in London, 1976.*

Films as Director:

1933   *Midshipman Easy (Men of the Sea)*
1936   *Laburnum Grove*; *Talk of the Devil* (+ story)
1937   *Who's Your Lady Friend?*
1938   *Bank Holiday (Three on a Week-End)*; *Penny Paradise*
1939   *Climbing High*; *A Girl Must Live*; *The Stars Look Down*
1940   *Night Train to Munich (Night Train)*; *The Girl in the News*
1941   *Kipps (The Remarkable Mr. Kipps)*; *A Letter from Home* (short documentary)
1942   *The Young Mr. Pitt*; *The New Lot*
1944   *The Way Ahead*
1945   *The True Glory* (collaboration with Garson Kanin)
1947   **Odd Man Out**
1948   *The Fallen Idol*
1949   **The Third Man**
1951   *Outcast of the Islands*
1953   *The Man Between*
1955   *A Kid for Two Farthings*
1956   *Trapeze*
1958   *The Key*
1960   *Our Man in Havana*

1963   *The Running Man* (+ pr)
1965   *The Agony and the Ecstasy* (+ pr)
1968   *Oliver!*
1970   *Flap*
1972   *Follow Me (The Public Eye)*

Other Film:

1937   *No Parking* (Raymond) (story)

Publications:

By REED: article—

Interview in *Encountering Directors*, by Charles Samuels, New York, 1972.

On REED: books—

Greene, Graham, *The Third Man*, London and New York, 1968; as *The Third Man: A Film by Graham Greene and Carol Reed*, New York, 1984.
Phillips, Gene D., *Graham Greene: The Films of His Fiction*, New York, 1974.
DeFelice, James, *Filmguide to Odd Man Out*, Bloomington, Indiana, 1975.
Armes, Roy, *A Critical History of the British Cinema*, London, 1978.
Moss, Robert F., *The Films of Carol Reed*, New York, 1987.
Phillips, Gene D., *Major Film Directors of the American and British Cinema*, Cranbury, New Jersey, 1989.
Wapshott, Nicholas, *The Man Between: A Biography of Carol Reed*, London, 1990.

On REED: articles—

Goodman, E., "Carol Reed," in *Theatre Arts* (New York), May 1947.
Wright, Basil, "The Director: Carol Reed," in *Sight and Sound* (London), Summer 1951.
De La Roche, Catherine, "A Man with No Message," in *Films and Filming* (London), December 1954.
Sarris, Andrew, "Carol Reed in the Context of His Time," in 2 parts, in *Film Culture* (New York), no. 10, 1956 and no. 11, 1957.
Sarris, Andrew, "First of the Realists," and "The Stylist Goes to Hollywood," in *Films and Filming* (London), September and October 1957.
Fawcett, Marion, "Sir Carol Reed," in *Films in Review* (New York), March 1959.
Voigt, M., "Pictures of Innocence: Sir Carol Reed," in *Focus on Film* (London), Spring 1974.
Obituary, in *Cinéma* (Paris), June 1976.
Phillips, Gene D., "Carol Reed," in *Films in Review* (New York), August/September 1982.
Kemp. Philip, "Fallen Idol," in *Sight and Sound* (London), Spring 1988.
Lefèvre, Raymond, and Claude Beylie, "Carol Reed, un cinéaste au carrefour des influences," in *Avant-Scène du Cinéma* (Paris), March 1989.
Driver, Paul, "A *Third Man* Cento," in *Sight and Sound* (London), Winter 1989/90.

*   *   *

Carol Reed came to films from the theater where he worked as an assistant to Edgar Wallace. He served his apprenticeship in the film industry first as a dialogue director, and then graduated to becoming a director in his own right by making a series of low-budget second features.

Reed's early films, such as *Midshipman Easy*, are not remarkable; but then few British films before World War II were. In the 1920s and 1930s British distributors were more interested in importing films from abroad, especially from America, than in encouraging film production at home. As a result British films were, with rare exceptions, bargain-basement imitations of Hollywood movies. In 1938, however,

Carol Reed

the British government stipulated that producers must allocate sufficient funds for the making of domestic films in order to allow an adequate amount of time for preproduction preparation, shooting, and the final shaping of each picture. Directors like Carol Reed took advantage of this increased support of British production to produce films which, though still modestly made by Hollywood standards, demonstrated the artistry of which British filmmakers were capable. By the late 1930s, then, Reed had graduated to making films of considerable substance, like *Night Train to Munich*.

"For the first time," Arthur Knight has written, "there were English pictures which spoke of the British character, British institutions—even social problems such as unemployment and nationalization—with unexpected frankness and awareness." An outstanding example of this new trend in British film making was Reed's *The Stars Look Down*, an uncompromising picture of life in a mining community, which brought the director serious critical attention on both sides of the Atlantic.

Reed went on to work on some of the best documentaries to come out of the war, such as the Academy Award-winning *The True Glory*, as well as to direct the documentary-like theatrical feature, *The Way Ahead*, an unvarnished depiction of army life. The experience which Reed gained in making wartime documentaries not only influenced his direction of *The Way Ahead*, but also was reflected in his post-war cinematic style, enabling him to develop further in films like *Odd Man Out* the strong sense of realism which had first appeared in *The Stars Look Down*. The documentary approach that Reed used to tell the story of *Odd Man Out*, which concerns a group of anti-British insurgents in Northern Ireland, was one to which audiences were ready to respond. Wartime films, both documentary and fictional, had conditioned moviegoers in Britain and elsewhere to expect a greater degree of realism in post-war cinema, and Reed provided it.

The more enterprising British producers believed that films should be made to appeal primarily to the home market rather than to the elusive American market, and it was precisely films such as Carol Reed was creating in the post-war years, films which were wholly British in character and situation, which were the first such movies to win wide popularity in the United States. Among these, of course, was *Odd Man Out*, the first film which Reed both produced and directed, a factor which guaranteed him a greater degree of creative freedom than he had enjoyed before the war.

For the first time, too, the theme that was to appear so often in his work was perceptible in *Odd Man Out*. In depicting for us in this and other films a hunted, lonely hero caught in the middle of a crisis usually not of his own making, Reed implies that man can achieve maturity and self-mastery only by accepting the challenges that life puts in his way and by struggling with them as best he can.

The Fallen Idol was the first of a trio of masterful films which he made in collaboration with novelist-screenwriter Graham Greene, one of the most significant creative associations between a writer and a director in the history of film. The team followed *The Fallen Idol* with *The Third Man*, which dealt with the black market in post-war Vienna, and, a decade later, *Our Man in Havana*. Commenting on his collaboration with the director, Greene has written that the success of these films was due to Reed, "the only director I know with that particular warmth of human sympathy, the extraordinary feeling for the right face for the right part, the exactitude of cutting, and not the least important, the power of sympathizing with an author's worries and an ability to guide him."

Because most of the films which Reed directed in the next decade or so were not comparable to the post-war films mentioned above, it was thought that he had passed his peak for

good. *Oliver!* in fact proved that Reed was back in top form. In her *New Yorker* review of the film, Pauline Kael paid Reed a tribute that sums up his entire career in the cinema: "I applaud the commercial heroism of a director who can steer a huge production and keep his sanity and perspective and decent human feelings as beautifully intact as they are in *Oliver!*."

A genuinely self-effacing man, Reed was never impressed by the awards and honors that he garnered throughout his career (he was knighted in 1952). Summarizing his own approach to filmmaking some time before his death at sixty-nine in 1976, he said simply, "I give the public what *I* like, and hope they will like it too." More often than not, he was right.

—Gene D. Phillips

————

REEVES, Michael.

British. Born in London, 1944. Educated at Radley College. Worked as dialogue director in Los Angeles, 1962; returned to Britain, worked as runner for Irwin Allen, and as assistant director for TV, 1963–65; took over direction of *Castle of the Living Dead*, in Italy, 1964; directed first feature, *The Revenge of the Blood Beast*, in 18 days, 1965; formed production partnership with Pat Curtis. *Died of drugs overdose (a verdict of "accidental death"), in London, February 1969.*

Films as Director:

1964   *Castle of the Living Dead* (d some sequences only)
1965   *The Revenge of the Blood Beast* (*Sister of Satan*)
1967   *The Sorcerers* (+ co-sc)
1968   **Witchfinder General (The Conqueror Worm)** (+ co-sc)

Publications:

By REEVES: article—

Letter, in *Listener* (London), 30 May 1968.

On REEVES: books—

Pirie, David, *A Heritage of Horror: The English Gothic Cinema 1946–72*, London, 1973.
Newman, Kim, *Nightmare Movies: A Critical History of the Horror Film from 1968*, London, 1988.

On REEVES: articles—

Taylor, John Russell, "Horror, and Something More," in the *Times* (London, 11 May 1968.
Bennett, Alan, in *Listener* (London), 16 May 1968.
Milne, Tom, in *Monthly Film Bulletin* (London), July 1968.
Wood, Robin, "In Memoriam Michael Reeves," in *Movie* (London), no. 17, 1969.
Paul, William, "Michael Reeves Revisited," in *Village Voice* (New York), 26 August 1971.
Starburst (London), June 1982.

*   *   *

Michael Reeves completed only three films, and yet by the time of his death—of a drug overdose at the age of 26—he had already emerged as a significant figure in the horror genre.

Reeves's choosing to specialise in horror must be seen in part as pragmatic: in the 1960s, horror was one of the most consistently popular of genres in Europe (where Reeves made his directorial debut with the Italian *Revenge of the Bloodbeast*) and Britain, and it provided greater opportunities for young filmmakers than some of the more reputable areas of cinema. But in the power of horror to disturb and provoke Reeves also found the ideal vehicle for his distinctive and somewhat unnerving vision of the world.

In formal terms Reeves's work is characterised by a restless cutting from moments of realistically presented violence to moments of relative calm (with the latter often associated with nature, especially in *Witchfinder General* which demonstrates a keen awareness of the visual possibilities of the English landscape). The sense of conflict thereby set up stylistically is reproduced within the films' narratives. In these a battle is obsessively staged and restaged between forces standing for youth and modernity and other forces representing age and tradition, with this conflict leading inevitably to mutual destruction. (This has obvious significance in the late 1960s, as that decade's youth culture, and the idealism associated with it, began to disintegrate.) For examples of this, one needs only to look at the apocalyptic conclusions of Reeves's final two films. In *The Sorcerers*, both the aged Monserrat couple and the young man they have been controlling telepathically are burned to death while in *Witchfinder General*, the director's most accomplished work, the Witchfinder is hacked to pieces and his axe-wielding assailant, the film's notional hero, loses his sanity. Even in the less successful *Revenge of the Bloodbeast*, made when Reeves was a mere 21 years old, one finds this young/old conflict sketched in a rudimentary form as Vardella, a hideously aged witch, disrupts the lives of a modern couple.

Viewed in this way, in terms of their ostensible content, Reeves's films—expertly made as they might be—could possibly be dismissed as the precocious fantasies of a morbid mind. However, such a criticism does not fully engage with the complexities of Reeves's treatment and understanding of violence. For him, it is essentially a social phenomenon. He repeatedly shows it as emerging from a repressive social order, an order which systematically maims its inhabitants, both physically and mentally. His revealing of the callous selfishness lurking behind the hedonistic values of 1960s youth in *The Sorcerers* and the brutalising Civil War setting for *Witchfinder General* need to be seen in this light.

Because of this insight, Reeves is able to treat all of his characters—even monstrous figures such as Estelle Monserrat in *The Sorcerers* and Matthew Hopkins in *Witchfinder General*—with considerable sympathy, presenting them as three-dimensional individuals capable of suffering pain as well as inflicting it. Moreover, he understands and shows without prejudice the desires and fears that motivate their actions: in Estelle's case, these take the form of a yearning for the physical sensations of the youth revolution from which she and her husband have been cruelly excluded, while Matthew Hopkins is driven by an inner conflict between a fanatical misogyny and a thwarted romanticism (with this suggested mainly through Vincent Price's subtle performance, surely one of his best).

Reeves's "humanization" of evil is both the most shocking and the most compelling thing about his work. Watching his films can be an uncomfortable experience, but the disquiet they generate is an integral part of their project. This is because Reeves refuses to construct a position for his audience from which it can safely judge and moralise over the drama. Instead, through his sympathetic portrayal of his characters' plights, Reeves seeks to implicate us in the horrifying acts of violence they will eventually commit. Such an approach requires the utmost skill and sensitivity if it is not to degenerate into a voyeuristic prurience. It is to Reeves's lasting credit that in an all-too-short filmmaking career he successfully negotiated and

to a certain extent claimed as his own this most difficult of cinematic terrains.

—Peter Hutchings

REISZ, Karel.

Czechoslovakian/British. Born in Ostrava, Czechoslovakia, 21 July 1926. Educated at Leighton Park School, Reading, England, 1938–44; Emmanuel College, Cambridge, 1945–47. Married 1) Julia Coppard (divorced); 2) Betsy Blair, 1963, three sons. Arrived in England as refugee from Nazi threat, 1938; joined Czechoslovakian wing of R.A.F., 1944–45; teacher in London grammar school, 1947–49; film critic for *Sequence* and *Sight and Sound*, from 1950; programme director for National Film Theatre, London, 1952–55; "officer of commercials" for Ford Motor Co. in England, 1956–57; directed first feature, 1960. Address: c/o Film Contrasts, 2 Lower James Street, London W1, England.

Films as Director:

1956   *Momma Don't Allow* (co-d)
1959   *We Are the Lambeth Boys* (doc)
1960   ***Saturday Night and Sunday Morning***
1964   *Night Must Fall* (+ co-pr)
1966   *Morgan, a Suitable Case for Treatment* (*Morgan!*)
1968   *Isadora* (*The Loves of Isadora*)
1974   *The Gambler*
1978   *Who'll Stop the Rain* (*Dog Soldiers*)
1981   *The French Lieutenant's Woman*
1985   *Sweet Dreams*
1989   *Everybody Wins*

Other Films:

1957   *Every Day Except Christmas* (Anderson) (co-pr)
1963   ***This Sporting Life*** (Anderson) (pr)

Publications:

By REISZ: book—

The Technique of Film Editing, revised by Gavin Miller, London, 1968.

By REISZ: articles—

"Hollywood's Anti-Red Boomerang," in *Sight and Sound* (London), January/March 1953.
"Stroheim in London," in *Sight and Sound* (London), April/June 1954.
"Experiment at Brussels," in *Sight and Sound* (London), Summer 1958.
"Karel Reisz and Experimenters: An Exchange of Correspondence," in *Films and Filming* (London), December 1961.
"How to Get into Films—By the People Who Got in Themselves," in *Films and Filming* (London), July 1963.
"Desert Island Films," in *Films and Filming* (London), August 1963.
Interview with Gene D. Phillips, in *Cinema* (Los Angeles), Summer 1968.
"Outsiders," an interview with Gordon Gow, in *Films and Filming* (London), January 1979.
"Karel Reisz: permanence d'un personnage: le mal adapté," an interview with J. Grissolange, in *Jeune Cinéma* (Paris), October 1979.
Interview with B. Gilbert, in *Stills* (London), Winter 1982.

Karel Reisz

On REISZ: books—

Barsam, Richard, *Non-Fiction Film*, New York, 1973.
Walker, Alexander, *Hollywood U.K.: The British Film Industry in the 60's*, New York, 1974.
Leyda, Jay, editor, *Voices of Film Experience*, New York, 1977.
Armes, Roy, *A Critical History of the British Cinema*, New York, 1978.
Gaston, Georg, *Karel Reisz*, Boston, 1980.

On REISZ: articles—

Lambert, Gavin, "Free Cinema," in *Sight and Sound* (London), Spring 1956.
Hoggart, Richard, "*We Are the Lambeth Boys*," in *Sight and Sound* (London), Summer/Autumn 1959.
"Karel Reisz: Free Czech," in *Films and Filming* (London), February 1961.
Zito, Stephen, "*Dog Soldiers*: Novel into Film," in *American Film* (Washington, D.C.), September 1977.
"Reisz Issue" of *Positif* (Paris), November 1978.
Kennedy, H., "Minute Reisz: Six Earlier Films," in *Film Comment* (New York), September/October 1981.
Armes, Roy, "Karel Reisz," in *International Film Guide* edited by Peter Cowie, London, 1982.
"*Saturday Night and Sunday Morning* Issue" of *Avant-Scène du Cinéma* (Paris), 15 October 1982.

*   *   *

Karel Reisz came to filmmaking from the world of academia and scholarship. He had taught in an English grammar school, written film criticism, co-edited with Lindsay Anderson the last issue of the slightly snooty magazine *Sequence*, and written a theoretical textbook still in use today on *The Technique of Film Editing* (without having spent one working day in the industry). With such a background, it was obvious he would have preconceived notions about filmmaking, but they were notions without regard to established filmmaking practices. Reisz wanted to improve the British film industry (also the critical aim of *Sequence*) and had his first chance with two documentary shorts, *Momma Don't Allow* (co-directed with Tony Richardson) and *We Are the Lambeth Boys*. In these films, Reisz depicted contemporary Britain from a working-class viewpoint, and when they were first screened at London's National Film Theatre, they were presented along with films from Lindsay Anderson and others—as "British Free Cinema." In fact, these films were to herald a new wave in British filmmaking, which reached its zenith with Reisz's first feature, *Saturday Night and Sunday Morning*.

Jack Clayton's *Room at the Top* paved the way for *Saturday Night and Sunday Morning*, a study of a tough, young machinist, played by Albert Finney, who takes out his frustrations with his work and his life through sex and alcohol. He is the quintessential British rebel, the English answer to James Dean, who takes his revenge on society by impregnating his boss's wife. It is an uninhibited, fresh and frank look at British working-class existence, and it brought critical fame to Karel Reisz.

The only problem was that Reisz seemed temporarily unable to follow up on that first success. (Reisz's output is pathetically small: a sign perhaps not so much of a careful director as a director with whom producers feel uneasy.) Next, Reisz directed Albert Finney again in *Night Must Fall*, which had worked as a classic melodrama in the 1930s but had little relevance to the 1960s. The unconventionality of *Morgan* also seemed strained, and even a little pretentious (a claim that can easily be made against Reisz's outdated study of a Vietnam vet, *Who'll Stop the Rain?*). It was not until *Isadora* that Reisz began to demonstrate a new side to his work, a romantic side, perhaps born of his Czech background (he did not come to Britain until he was twelve).

Both *Isadora* and the director's more recent success, *The French Lieutenant's Woman*, showed that Reisz had discovered how to successfully blend romanticism and the realism of his first films. In *Isadora* it is perhaps a little more subtly accomplished than in *The French Lieutenant's Woman*, where the two elements fight against each other for existence.

As to his directorial techniques, Reisz appears to be very willing to listen to others. He is quoted as saying, "For me the great thing about a film is to allow everyone to make their contribution and to keep the process fluid. The process of adaptation is a free process and the process of rehearsal is a free process and the process of shooting is a free process." Free process, free cinema, and a healthy freedom in his choice of subjects have marked Reisz's career to date.

—Anthony Slide

———

RENOIR, Jean.

French/American. Born in Paris, 15 September 1894, son of painter Auguste Renoir, became citizen of United States (naturalized) in 1946, retained French citizenship. Educated at Collége de Sainte-Croix, Neuilly-sur-Seine, 1902; Ecole Sainte-Marie de Monceau, 1903; Ecole Massina, Nice, until 1912; University of Aix-en-Provence, degree in mathematics and philosophy, 1913. Married 1) Andrée Madeleine Heuschling ("Dédée," took name Catherine Hessling following 1924 appearance in *Catherine*), 1920 (divorced 1930); 2) Dido Freire, 1944, one son. Served in French cavalry, 1914–15; transferred to French Flying Corps, 1916, demobilized 1918; worked as potter and ceramicist, 1920–23; directed first film, *La Fille de l'eau*, 1924; joined Service Cinématographique de l'Armée, *La Règle du jeu* banned by French government as demoralizing, 1939; Robert Flaherty arranged Renoir's passage to U.S., 1940; signed with 20th Century-Fox, 1941; signed with Universal, then terminated contract, 1942; re-established residence in Paris, retained home in Beverly Hills, 1951; active as theatre, through 1950s; Compagnie Jean Renoir formed with Anna de Saint Phalle, 1958; taught theatre at University of California, Berkeley, 1960. Recipient: Prix Louis Delluc, for *Les Bas-Fonds*, 1936; Chevalier de la Légion d'honneur, 1936; International Jury Cup, Venice Biennale, for *La Grande Illusion*, 1937; New York Critics Award, for *Swamp Water*, 1941; Best Film, Venice Festival, for *The Southerner*, 1946; Grand Prix de l'Academie du Cinéma for *French Cancan*, 1956; Prix Charles Blanc, Academie Française, for *Renoir*, biography of father, 1963; Honorary Doctorate in Fine Arts, University of California, Berkeley, 1963; Fellow of the American Academy of Arts and Sciences, 1964. Osella d'Oro, Venice Festival, 1968; Honorary Doctorate of Fine Arts, Royal College of Art, London, 1971; Special Oscar for Career Accomplishment, 1975. *Died in Beverly Hills, 12 February 1979.*

Films as Director:

1925 *La Fille de l'eau* (+ pr)
1926 *Nana* (+ pr, adaptation)
1927 *Catherine (Une vie sans joie. Backbiters)* (co-d, co-pr, sc, role as sub-prefect); *Sur un air de Charleston (Charleston-Parade)* (+ pr, ed); *Marquitta* (+ pr, adaptation)
1928 *La Petite Marchande d'allumettes (The Little Match Girl)* (co-d, co-pr, sc)

Jean Renoir

1928 *Tire au flanc* (+ co-sc); *Le Tournoi dans la cité* (*Le Tournoi*) (+ adaptation)
1929 *Le Bled*
1931 *On purge bébé* (+ co-sc); *La Chienne* (+ co-sc)
1932 *La Nuit du carrefour* (*Night at the Crossroads*) (+ sc); **Boudu sauvée des eaux** (**Boudu Saved from Drowning**) (+ co-sc)
1933 *Chotard et cie* (+ co-sc)
1934 *Madame Bovary* (+ sc)
1935 *Toni* (*Les Amours de Toni*) (+ co-sc)
1936 *Le Crime de Monsieur Lange* (*The Crime of Monsieur Lange*) (+ co-sc); *La Vie est à nous* (*The People of France*) (co-d, co-sc); *Les Bas-Fonds* (*Underworld, The Lower Depths*) (+ adaptation)
1937 *La Grande Illusion* (*Grand Illusion*) (+ co-sc)
1938 *La Marseillaise* (+ co-sc); **La Bête humaine** (**The Human Beast. Judas Was a Woman**) (+ co-sc)
1939 **La Règle du jeu** (**Rules of the Game**) (+ co-sc, role as Octave)
1941 *La Tosca* (*The Story of Tosca*) (co-d, co-sc); *Swamp Water*
1943 *This Land is Mine* (+ co-p, co-sc)
1944 *Salute to France* (*Salut à France*) (co-d, co-sc)
1945 **The Southerner** (+ sc)
1946 **Une Partie de campagne** (**A Day in the Country**) (+ sc) (filmed in 1936); *The Diary of a Chambermaid* (+ co-sc)
1947 *The Woman on the Beach* (+ co-sc)
1951 *The River* (+ co-sc)
1953 *Le Carrosse d'or* (**The Golden Coach**) (+ co-sc)
1955 *French Cancan* (*Only the French Can*) (+ sc)
1956 *Elena et les hommes* (*Paris Does Strange Things*) (+ sc)
1959 *Le Testament du Docteur Cordelier* (*The Testament of Dr. Cordelier. Experiment in Evil* (+ sc); *Le Déjeuner sur l'herbe* (*Picnic on the Grass*) (+ sc)
1962 *Le Caporal épinglé* (*The Elusive Corporal. The Vanishing Corporal*) (co-d, co-sc)
1970 *Le Petit Théâtre de Jean Renoir* (*The Little Theatre of Jean Renoir*) (+ sc)

Other Films:

1927 *Le Petit Chaperon rouge* (Cavalcanti) (co-sc, role as the Wolf)
1930 *Die Jagd nach dem Gluck* (Gliese) (role as Robert)
1937 **The Spanish Earth** (Ivens) (wrote commentary and narration for French version)
1971 *The Christian Licorice Store* (Frawley) (role as himself)

Publications:

By RENOIR: books—

This Land is Mine, in *Twenty Best Film Plays*, edited by Gassner and Nichols, New York, 1943.
The Southerner, in *Best Film Plays—1945*, edited by Gassner and Nichols, New York, 1946.
Renoir: Souvenirs de mon père, Paris, 1948; as *Renoir, My Father*, New York, 1958.
Orvet, Paris, 1955.
The Notebooks of Captain George, Boston, 1966.
La Grande Illusion, London, 1968; Paris, 1974.
Rules of the Game, New York, 1970.
Ecrits 1926–1971, edited by Claude Gauteur, Paris, 1974.
My Life and My Films, New York, 1974.
Jean Renoir: Essays, Conversations, Reviews, edited by Penelope Gilliatt, New York, 1975.
Oeuvres de cinéma inédités, edited by Claude Gauteur, Paris, 1981.
Lettres d'Amérique, edited by Dido Renoir and Alexander Sesonske, Paris, 1984.
Renoir on Renoir: Interviews, Essays and Remarks, Cambridge, 1989.

By RENOIR: articles—

"Jean Renoir à Hollywood," an interview with Paul Gilson, in *L'Ecran Française* (Paris), 15 August 1945.
Interview with Jacques Rivette and François Truffaut, in *Cahiers du Cinema* (Paris), April 1954; reprinted in part as "Renoir in America," in *Sight and Sound* (London), Autumn 1954.

"*Paris-Provence*: Inspiration pour un film," in *Cahiers du Cinéma* (Paris), May 1954.
"Enquête sur la censure et l'éroticisme: le public a horreur de ça," in *Cahiers du Cinéma* (Paris), December 1954.
"*French Cancan*," in *Cahiers du Cinéma* (Paris), May 1955.
"Nouvel entretien avec Jean Renoir," with Jacques Rivette and François Truffaut, in *Cahiers du Cinéma* (Paris), Christmas 1957; also in *La Politique des auteurs* by André Bazin and others, Paris, 1972.
"*Le Testament du Docteur Cordelier*," in *L'Avant-Scène du Cinéma* (Paris), July 1961.
"Jean Renoir: propos rompus," an interview with Jean-Louis Noames, in *Cahiers du Cinéma* (Paris), May 1964.
"*La Grande Illusion*," in *L'Avant-Scène du Cinéma* (Paris), January 1965.
"*La Règle du jeu*," in *L'Avant-Scène du Cinéma* (Paris), October 1965.
"Renoir at 72," an interview with Axel Madsen, in *Cinema* (Los Angeles), Spring 1966,
"The Situation of the Serious Filmmaker," in *Film Makers on Film Making* edited by Harry Geduld, Bloomington, Indiana, 1967.
"My Next Films," an interview with Michel Delahaye and Jean-André Fieschi, in *Cahiers du Cinema in English* (New York), March 1967.
Interview with Rui Nogueira and François Truchaud, in *Sight and Sound* (London), Spring 1968.
"C'est la révolution! (Crème de beauté)," in *Cahiers du Cinéma* (Paris), May 1968.
"Conversation with Jean Renoir," with Louis Marcorelles, in *Interviews with Film Directors* edited by Andrew Sarris, New York, 1969.
Interview with James Silke, in *The Essential Cinema* edited by P. Adams Sitney, New York, 1975.
Articles and interview, in special Renoir issue of *Positif* (Paris), September 1975.
"*La Chienne*," in *L'Avant-Scène du Cinéma* (Paris), October 1975.

On RENOIR: books—

Davay, Paul, *Jean Renoir*, Brussels, 1957.
Cauliez, Armand-Jean, *Jean Renoir*, Paris, 1962.
Analyses des films de Jean Renoir, Institut des Hautes Etudes Cinématographiques, Paris, 1966.
Bennett, Susan, *Study Unit 8: Jean Renoir*, London, 1967.
Poulle, François, *Renoir 1938 ou Jean Renoir pour rien. Enquête sur un cinéaste*, Paris, 1969.
Leprohon, Pierre, *Jean Renoir*, New York, 1971.
Braudy, Leo, *Jean Renoir: The World of his Films*, New York, 1972; 2nd edition, 1989.
Bazin, André, *Jean Renoir*, edited by François Truffaut, Paris, 1973.
Mast, Gerald, *Filmguide to The Rules of the Game*, Bloomington, Indiana, 1973.
Durgnat, Raymond, *Jean Renoir*, Berkeley, California, 1974.
Beylie, Claude, *Jean Renoir: le spectacle, la vie*, Paris, 1975.
Faulkner, Christopher, *Jean Renoir: A Guide to References and Resources*, Boston, 1979.
Sesonske, Alexander, *Jean Renoir: The French Films 1924–1939*, Cambridge, Massachusetts, 1980.
Serceau, Daniel, *Jean Renoir*, Paris, 1985.
Bertin, Celia, *Jean Renoir*, Paris, 1986.
Faulkner, Christopher, *The Social Cinema of Jean Renoir*, Princeton, New Jersey, 1986.
Vincendeau, Ginette, and Keith Reader, *La Vie est a Nous: French Cinema of the Popular Front 1935–1938*, London, 1986.
Viry-Babel, Roger, *Jean Renoir: Le Jeu et la Règle*, Paris, 1986.
Beylie, Claude, and Maurice Bessy, *Jean Renoir*, Paris, 1989.

On RENOIR: articles—

"Renoir Issue" of *Cahiers du Cinéma* (Paris), January 1952.
Brunius, Jacques, "Jean Renoir," in *En marge du cinéma français* (same author), Paris, 1954.
"Renoir Issue" of *Cahiers du Cinéma* (Paris), Christmas 1957.
Rohmer, Eric, "Jeunesse de Jean Renoir," in *Cahiers du Cinéma* (Paris), December 1959.
Belanger, Jean, "Why Renoir Favors Multiple Camera, Long Sustained Take Technique," in *American Cinematographer* (Los Angeles), March 1960.
Dyer, Peter, "Renoir and Realism," in *Sight and Sound* (London), Summer 1960.

Alain Resnais directing Delphine Seyrig in *L'Année dernière à Marienbad*

Monaco, James, *Alain Resnais: The Role of Imagination*, New York, 1978.

Benayoun, Robert, *Alain Resnais: Arpenteur de l'imaginaire*, Paris, 1980; revised edition, 1986.

Sweet, Freddy, *The Film Narratives of Alain Resnais*, Ann Arbor, Michigan, 1981.

Vergerio, Flavio, *I film di Alain Resnais*, Rome, 1984.

Roob, Jean-Daniel, *Alain Resnais: Qui êtes-vous?*, Lyons, 1986.

Oms, Marcel, *Alain Resnais*, Paris, 1988.

Riambau, Esteve, *La ciencie y la ficcion: El cine de Alain Resnais*, Barcelona, 1988.

Thomas, François, *L'Atelier de Alain Resnais*, Paris, 1989.

On RESNAIS: articles—

Bazin, André, "Alain Resnais," in *Qu'est-ce que le cinéma*

Marcorelles, Louis, "Rebel with a Camera," in *Sight and Sound* (London), Winter 1960.

"*Nuit et brouillard* Issue" of *Avant-Scène du Cinéma* (Paris), February 1961.

Kael, Pauline, "Fantasies of the Art House Audience," in *Sight and Sound* (London), Winter 1961/62.

Taylor, John Russell, "Alain Resnais" in *Cinema Eye, Cinema Ear*, New York, 1964.

Stanbrook, Alan, "The Time and Space of Alain Resnais," in *Films and Filming* (London), January 1964.

"*Guernica* Issue" of *Avant-Scène du Cinéma* (Paris), June 1964.

"*Toute la mémoire du monde* Issue" of *Avant-Scène du Cinéma* (Paris), October 1965.

"Resnais Issue" of *L'Avant-Scène du Cinéma* (Paris), Summer 1966.

Roud, Richard, "Memories of Resnais," in *Sight and Sound* (London), Summer 1969.

Armes, Roy, "Resnais and Reality," in *Films and Filming* (London), May 1970.

Harcourt, Peter, "Memory is Kept Alive with Dream," in *Film Comment* (New York), November/December 1973.

Harcourt, Peter, "Toward a Certainty of Doubt," in *Film Comment* (New York), January/February 1974.

"Resnais Issue" of *Cinéma* (Paris), July/August 1980.

Rosenbaum, Jonathan, "In Search of the American Uncle," in *American Film* (Washington, D.C.), May 1981.

Dossier on Resnais, in *Cinématographe* (Paris), April 1982.

Brown, R., "Everyone Has His Reasons," in *Monthly Film Bulletin* (London), May 1984.

Parra, D., "Alain Resnais, cinéaste de la limpidité," in *Revue du Cinéma* (Paris), September 1984.

Moses, John W., "Vision Denied in *Night and Fog* and *Hiroshima Mon Amour*," in *Literature/Film Quarterly* (Salisbury, Maryland), vol. 15, no.3, 1987.

"*Mélo* Issue" of *Avant-Scène du Cinéma* (Paris), April 1987.

Durgnat, Raymond, "Resnais & Co.: Back to the Avant-Garde," in *Monthly Film Bulletin* (London), May 1987.

Forbes, Jill, "Resnais in the 80s," in *Sight and Sound* (London), Summer 1987.

Tomasulo, Frank P., "The Intentionality of Consciousness: Subjectivity in Resnais's *Last Year at Marienbad*," in *Post Script* (Jacksonville, Florida), vol. 7, no. 2, 1988.

Prédal, René, "L'oeuvre de Alain Resnais: Regard du cinéaste et place du spectateur," in *Jeune Cinéma* (Paris), April/May 1989.

*   *   *

Alain Resnais is a prominent figure in the modernist narrative film tradition. His emergence as a feature director of international repute is affiliated with the eruption of the French New Wave in the late 1950s. This association was signaled by the fact that his first feature *Hiroshima mon amour* premiered at the Cannes Film Festival at the same time as François Truffaut's *Les 400 coups*. However, Resnais had less to do with the group of directors emerging from the context of the *Cahiers du cinéma* than he did with the so-called Left Bank group, including Jean Cayrol, Marguerite Duras, Chris Marker, and Alain Robbe-Grillet. This group provided an intellectual and creative context of shared interest. In the course of his film career Resnais frequently collaborated with members of this group.

Marker worked with him on several short films in the 1950s; Cayrol wrote the narration for *Nuit et brouillard* and the script for *Muriel*; Duras scripted *Hiroshima mon amour*; and Robbe-Grillet wrote *L'Année dernière à Marienbad*. All of these people are known as writers and/or filmmakers in their own right; their association with Resnais is indicative of his talent for fruitful creative collaboration.

Resnais began making films as a youth in 8 and 16mm. In the early 1940s he studied acting and filmmaking, and after the war made a number of 16mm films including a series about artists. His first film in 35mm was the 1948 short, *Van Gogh*, which won a number of international awards. It was produced by Pierre Braunberger, an active supporter of new talent, who continued to finance his work in the short film format through the 1950s. From 1948–58 Resnais made eight short films, of which *Nuit et brouillard* is probably the best known. The film deals with German concentration camps, juxtaposing past and present, exploring the nature of memory and history. To some extent the film's reputation and sustained interest is due to its subject matter. However, many of the film's formal strategies and thematic concerns are characteristic of Resnais's work more generally. In particular, the relationship between past and present, and the function of memory as the mechanism of traversing temporal distance, are persistent preoccupations of Resnais's films. Other films from this period similarly reveal familiar themes and traits of Resnais's subsequent work. *Toute la memoire du monde* is a documentary about the Bibliothèque Nationale in Paris. It presents the building, with its processes of cataloguing and preserving all sorts of printed material, as both a monument of cultural memory and as a monstrous, alien being. The film almost succeeds in transforming the documentary film into a branch of science fiction. Indeed Resnais has always been interested in science fiction, the fantastic, and pulp adventure stories. If this interest is most overtly expressed in the narrative of *Je t'aime, je t'aime* (in which a human serves as a guinea pig for scientists experimenting with time travel), it also emerges in the play of fantasy/imagination/reality pervading his work, and in many of his unachieved projects (including a remake of *Fantômas* and *The Adventure of Harry Dickson*).

Through editing and an emphasis on formal repetition, Resnais uses the medium to construct the conjunctions of past and present, fantasy and reality, insisting on the convergence of what are usually considered distinct domains of experience. In *Hiroshima mon amour* the quivering hand of the woman's sleeping Japanese lover in the film's present is directly followed by an almost identical image of her nearly-dead German lover during World War II. Tracking shots through the streets of Hiroshima merge with similar shots of Nevers, where the woman lived during the war. In *Stavisky*, the cutting between events in 1933 and a 1934 investigation of those events presents numerous, often conflicting versions of the same thing; one is finally convinced, above all else, of the indeterminacy and contingency of major historical events. The central character in *Providence* is an aged writer who spends a troubled night weaving stories about his family, conjoining memory and fantasy, past, present, and future, in an unstable mix.

The past's insistent invasion of the present is expressed in many different ways in Resnais's films. In *Nuit et brouillard*, where the death camps are both present structures and repressed institutions, it is a question of social memory and history; it is an individual and cultural phenomenon in *Hiroshima mon amour*, as a French woman simultaneously confronts her experiences in occupied France and the Japanese experience of the atomic bomb; it is construed in terms of science fiction in *Je t'aime, je t'aime* when the hero is trapped in a broken time-machine and continuously relives moments from his past; and is a profoundly ambiguous mixture of an individual's real and imagined past in *L'Année dernière à Marienbad* (often considered Resnais's most avant-garde film) as X pursues A with insistence, recalling their love affair and promises of the previous year, in spite of A's denials. In all of these films, as well as Resnais's other work, the past is fraught with uncertainty, anxiety, even terror. If it is more comfortable to ignore, it inevitably erupts in the present through the workings of the psyche, memory traces, or in the form of documentation and artifacts.

Resnais's filmic output has been relatively small. He nonetheless stands as a significant figure in modernist cinema. His strategies of fragmented point-of-view and multiple temporality, as well as his use of the medium to convey past/present and fantasy/imagination/reality as equivocal and equivalent modes of experience have amplified our understanding of film's capacity for expression.

—M.B. White

RICHARDSON, Tony.

British. Born Cecil Antonio Richardson in Shipley, West Yorkshire, 5 June 1928. Educated at Wadham College, Oxford University, degree in English 1952. Married actress Vanessa Redgrave, 1962 (divorced 1967), daughters actresses Natasha and Joely. President of Oxford University Drama Society, 1949–51; producer and director for BBC TV, 1953; formed English Stage Company with George Devine, 1955; began collaboration with writer John Osborne on first production of *Look Back in Anger* at the Royal Court Theatre, London, 1956; with Osborne, formed Woodfall Productions, 1958; directed first feature, *Look Back in Anger*, 1959; continues to work as stage director; director for TV, including *Penalty Phase* (1986), *Shadow on the Sun* (1988), and *Phantom of the Opera* (1990). Recipient: Oscar for Best Direction, and New York Film Critics Award for Best Direction, for *Tom Jones*, 1963. Address: c/o Woodfall Film Productions, 1478 North Kings Road, Los Angeles, CA 90069, U.S.A.

Films as Director:

1955 *Momma Don't Allow* (co-d)
1959 *Look Back in Anger*
1960 *The Entertainer*
1961 *Sanctuary*; *A Taste of Honey* (+ pr, co-sc)
1962 *The Loneliness of the Long Distance Runner* (+ pr)
1963 *Tom Jones* (+ pr)
1965 *The Loved One*; *Mademoiselle*
1967 *The Sailor from Gibraltar* (+ co-sc)
1968 *Red and Blue*; *The Charge of the Light Brigade*
1969 *Laughter in the Dark* (*La Chambre obscure*); *Hamlet*
1970 *Ned Kelly* (+ co-sc)
1973 *A Delicate Balance*; *Dead Cert*
1977 *Joseph Andrews* (+ co-sc)
1978 *Death in Canaan*
1982 *The Border*
1984 *Hotel New Hampshire* (+ sc)
1985 *Turning a Blind Eye* (doc)
1990 *Blue Sky*

Other Films

1960 *Saturday Night and Sunday Morning* (Reisz) (pr)
1964 *Girl with Green Eyes* (Davis) (exec pr)

Publications:

By RICHARDSON: articles—

"The Films of Luis Buñuel," in *Sight and Sound* (London), January/March 1954.
"The Metteur-en-Scène," in *Sight and Sound* (London), October/December 1954.
"The Method and Why: An Account of the Actor's Studio," in *Sight and Sound* (London), Winter 1956/57.
"The Man Behind an Angry-Young-Man," in *Films and Filming* (London), February 1959.
"Tony Richardson: An Interview in Los Angeles," with Colin Young, in *Film Quarterly* (Berkeley), Summer 1960.
"The Two Worlds of Cinema: Interview," in *Films and Filming* (London), June 1961.
Article, in *Film Makers on Film-making* edited by Harry M. Geduld, Bloomington, Indiana, 1967.
"Within the Cocoon," an interview with Gordon Gow, in *Films and Filming* (London), June 1977.

On RICHARDSON: books

Villelaur, Anne, *Tony Richardson, Dossiers du Cinema*, Cineastes I, Paris, 1971.
Lovell, Alan, and Jim Hillier, *Studies in Documentary*, New York, 1972.
Walker, Alexander, *Hollywood, England: The British Film Industry in the 60s*, London, 1975.
Hill, John, *Sex, Class and Realism: British Cinema 1956–63*, London, 1986.

On RICHARDSON: articles—

Houston, Penelope, "Two New Directors," in *Sight and Sound* (London), Winter 1958/59.
"Director," in the *New Yorker*, 12 October 1963.
Moller, David, "Britain's Busiest Angry Young Man," in *Film Comment* (New York), Winter 1964.
Lellis, George, "Recent Richardson," in *Sight and Sound* (London), Summer 1969.
Villelaur, Anne, "Tony Richardson," in *Dossiers du Cinéma 1*, Paris, 1971.
Gomez, Joseph, "*The Entertainer*: From Play to Film," in *Film Heritage* (Dayton, Ohio), Spring 1973.
Broeske, P., "The Company of Birds," in *Stills* (London), October 1984.

*   *   *

Tony Richardson belongs to that generation of British film directors which includes Lindsay Anderson and Karel Reisz, all of them university-trained middle-class artists who were sympathetic to the conditions of the working classes and determined to use cinema as a means of personal expression, in line with the goals of the "Free Cinema" movement. After Oxford, he enrolled in a directors' training program at the British Broadcasting Corporation before turning to theatre and founding, with George Devine, the English Stage Company in 1955 at London's Royal Court Theatre, a company that was to include writers Harold Pinter and John Osborne. Among Richardson's Royal Court productions were *Look Back in Anger*, *A Taste of Honey*, and *The Entertainer*, dramatic vehicles that he would later transform into cinema.

Also in 1955, working with Karel Reisz, Richardson co-directed his first short film, *Momma Don't Allow*, funded by a grant from the British Film Institute and one of the original productions of the "Free Cinema" movement. Richardson's realistic treatment of the works of John Osborne (*Look Back in Anger*), Shelagh Delaney (*A Taste of Honey*), and Alan Sillitoe (*Loneliness of the Long-Distance Runner*) would infuse British cinema with the "kitchen sink" realism Richardson had helped to encourage in the British theatre. Indeed, Richardson's link with the "Angry Young Men" of the theatre was firmly established before he and John Osborne founded their

Tony Richardson directing *A Taste of Honey*

film production unit, Woodfall, in 1958 for the making of *Look Back In Anger*.

Richardson's strongest talent has been to adapt literary and dramatic works to the screen. In 1961 he turned to Hollywood, where he directed an adaptation of Faulkner's *Sanctuary*, which he later described as arguably his worst film. His most popular success, however, was *Tom Jones*, his brilliant adaptation and abridgement of Henry Fielding's often rambling eighteenth-century novel, which in other hands would not have been a very promising film project but which, under Richardson's direction, won four Academy Awards in 1963. In 1977 Richardson tried to repeat his earlier success by adapting Fielding's other great comic novel, *Joseph Andrews*, to the screen, but, though the story was effectively shaped by Richardson and the casting was splendid the film was not the overwhelming commercial success that *Tom Jones* had been. Nonetheless, Vincent Canby singled out *Joseph Andrews* as "the year's most cheerful movie . . . and probably the most neglected movie of the decade."

Other adaptations and literary collaborations included *The Loved One* (Evelyn Waugh), *Mademoiselle* (Jean Genet), *The Sailor from Gibralter* (Marguerite Duras), *Laughter in the Dark* (Nabokov), and *A Delicate Balance* (Albee). Perhaps Richardson's most enduring dramatic adaptation, however, is his rendering of *Hamlet*, filmed in 1969, remarkable for the eccentric but effective performance by Nicol Williamson as Hamlet, which it captures for posterity, and also for Anthony Hopkins's sinister Claudius. Filmed at the Roundhouse Theatre in London where it was originally produced, it is a bril-

liant exercise in filmed theatre in the way it keeps the actors at the forefront of the action, allowing them to dominate the play as they would do on stage. Richardson has defined cinema as a director's medium, but his *Hamlet* effectively treats it as an actor's medium, as perhaps no other filmed production has done.

Other Richardson films seem to place a premium upon individualism, as witnessed by his treatment of the legendary Australian outlaw, *Ned Kelly* (starring Mick Jagger, a project Karel Reisz had first undertaken with Albert Finney.) This concern for the individual can also be discerned ten years later in *The Border*, a film Richardson completed for Universal Pictures in 1982, starring Jack Nicholson as a guard on the Mexican-American border, a loner who fights for human values against a corrupt constabulary establishment. Unfortunately *The Border*, which turned out to be a caricatured and flawed melodrama, did not reflect the director's intentions in its released form, since Universal Studios apparently wanted—and got—"a much more up-beat ending where Nicholson emerges as a hero." That a talented director of considerable vision, intelligence, and accomplishment should experience such an impasse is a sorry commentary and a measure of an apparently declining career. Nonetheless, Richardson migrated to the Hollywood Hills by choice and claims to prefer California to his native England. He continues to work; whether he can regain success by Hollywood standards remains to be seen.

—James M. Welsh

RICHTER, Hans.

German. Born in Berlin, 1888. Educated at Berlin Academy for Fine Arts, 1908; Weimar Academy of Art, 1909. Collaborator on *Aktion* journal, from 1915; military service, 1915–16; joined Dada group in Zurich, 1916; with Viking Eggeling returned to Germany, 1918–19; experimental focus shifts completely to film, 1920; publisher of art magazine, *G*, 1923–26; emigrated to U.S., 1940; Director of Film Institute, City College of New York, 1942. *Died in Locarno, 1976.*

Films as Director:

1921–24   *Rhythmus 21* (+ graphic artist, ph) (original title: *Film ist Rhythmus*)
1923–24   *Rhythmus 23* (+ graphic artist)
1925   *Rhythmus 25* (+ graphic artist)
1926   *Filmstudie* (+ graphic artist, co-ph)
1927–28   *Inflation* (+ graphic artist, sc); *Vormittagsspuk* (*Ghosts Before Breakfast*) (co-d and graphic work, co-story, role)
1928–29   *Rennsymphonie* (*Race Symphony*) (+ sc); *Zweigroschenzauber* (*Two-Penny Magic*) (+ sc); *Alles dreht sich, alles bewegt sich* (*Everything Turns, Everything Revolves*) (+ co-sc); *Forty Years of Experiment* Part 1 (comprised of experimental films and film fragments by Richter from 1921–30) (+ sc)
1944–47   *Dreams That Money Can Buy* (+ sc)
1954–57   *8 x 8* (+ sc)
1956–61   *Dadascope* (+ sc)
1963   *Alexander Calder* (+ sc)

Publications:

By RICHTER: books—

Filmgegner von heute—Filmfreunde von morgen, Berlin, 1929 (reprinted Zurich, 1968).
Hans Richter by Hans Richter, edited by Cleve Gray, London, 1971.
Der Kampf um den Film, Munich and Vienna, 1976.
The Struggle for the Cinema: Towards a Socially Responsible Cinema, edited by Jürgen Romhild, Aldershot, Hampshire, 1986.

By RICHTER: articles—

"The Avant-Garde Film Seen From Within," in *Hollywood Quarterly*, Fall 1949.
"Thirty Years of Experimental Films," an interview with Herman Weinberg, in *Films in Review* (New York), December 1951.
"Eight Free Improvisations on the Game of Chess," in *Film Culture* (New York), January 1955.
"*8 x 8*: A Sequence from Hans Richter's Latest Experimental Film," in *Film Culture* (New York), Winter 1955.
"Hans Richter on the Nature of Film Poetry," an interview with Jonas Mekas, in *Film Culture* (New York), no. 11, 1957.
"From Interviews with Hans Richter During the Last Ten Years," in *Film Culture* (New York), no. 31, 1963/64.
"Learning from Film History," in *Filmmakers Newsletter* (Ward Hill, Massachusetts), November 1973.

On RICHTER: books—

Joray, Marcel, editor, *Hans Richter*, Neuchâtel, 1965.
O'Konor, Louise, *Viking Eggeling, 1880–1925, Artist and Filmmaker: Life and Work*, Stockholm, 1971.
Russett, Robert, and Cecile Starr, *Experimental Animation*, New York, 1976.

On RICHTER: articles—

Young, Vernon, "Painter and Cinematographer Hans Richter: A Retrospective of Four Decades," in *Arts Magazine* (New York), September 1959.
Gray, C., "Portrait: Hans Richter," in *Art in America* (New York), January 1968.
Codroico, R., and L. Pezzolato, "Richter e l'uomo visibile," in *Cinema Nuovo* (Turin), July/August 1972.
Bassan, H., and M. Roudevitch, "Se souvenir de Hans Richter," in *Ecran* (Paris), May 1977.

*   *   *

Like many other filmmakers of the European avant-garde, Richter was initially a painter, influenced by such movements as futurism and cubism, and like his colleague Viking Eggeling, Richter came to extend his theoretical concerns beyond the limitations of paint and canvas to, first, abstract scrolls and then to film. Today he is highly regarded as a very early influence upon that major genre of production generally termed "experimental film," through his published theoretical writings (such as *Universelle Sprache*, with Viking Eggeling) and about a dozen films realized over four decades. Perhaps his most famous and most influential film was his first, *Rhythmus 21*.

Typical of experimental production, *Rhythmus 21* is a brief, acollaborative work, realized outside the financial and organizational constraints of the film industry. It is a silent, black and white film, running less than two minutes, an animated exploration of simple cut-out paper squares of various sizes and shades. The film's aesthetic force draws upon structures and strategies common to non-representational painting or graphic design. Part of the film's value comes from its explicit remove from theatrical or fictive prototypes, which dominated cinema in the 1920s as fully as today. Certainly *Rhythmus 21*'s value is as much predicated upon the later influence of its non-narrative structure (especially in international experimental film) as upon the lively dynamics of its simple yet stunning metamorphoses of shapes and tonalities. Richter went on to construct a number of companion pieces (e.g. *Rhythmus 23*). Later his film work took on more representational elements, as in his 1926 *Film Study* which employed animated suns, clouds, eyes, etc., with a somewhat surrealistic exchange of imagery. This embrace of film's representational resources grew more pronounced for Richter and, by 1930, he had largely ceased his concern with animated records of graphic materials. *Vormittagsspuk* (*Ghosts before Breakfast*) is a zany Dada story dependent upon shots of real objects and people. *Alles dreht sich, alles bewegt sich* (*All Revolves, All Moves*) embodies a somewhat documentary examination of a fairground. Still, such works clearly fall under the classification of the experimental genre, in part due to their fascination with a phenomenology of mental imagery—dream, fantasy, and reverie. This same concern also marks Richter's post-war production, such as the still surreal yet somewhat Jungian *Dreams that Money Can Buy*.

Richter's experimental film production occurred during an extraordinarily long career. As recently as the 1960s he was still realizing new pieces, such as *Dadascope*. Yet his influence and importance to film historians and experimental filmmakers probably centers upon his early abstract, animated work. *Rhythmus 21* remains one of the best-known and most influential products of the European avant-garde.

—Edward S. Small

———

RIEFENSTAHL, Leni.

German. Born Helene Berta Amalie Riefenstahl in Berlin, 22 August 1902. Attended Russian Ballet School, Berlin. Married Peter Jacob, 1944 (divorced 1946). Dancer, from 1920;

Hans Richter (bottom left) directing *Dreams That Money Can Buy*

Leni Riefenstahl

appeared in "mountain films" directed by Arnold Franck, from 1936; established own production company, Riefenstahl Films, 1931; first film, *Das blaue Licht*, released, 1932; appointed "film expert to the National Socialist Party" by Hitler, 1933; detained in various prison camps by Allied Forces on charges of pro-Nazi activity, 1945–48; charges dismissed by Berlin court, allowed to work in film industry again, 1952; suffered serious auto accident while working in Africa, 1956; commissioned by *The Times* (London), to photograph the Munich Olympics, 1972; honored at Telluride Film Festival, Colorado (festival picketed by anti-Nazi groups), 1974. Recipient: Exposition Internationale des Arts et des Techniques, Paris, Diplôme de Grand Prix, for *Triumph des Willens*, 1937; Polar Prize, Sweden, for *Olympia*, 1938. Lives in Munich.

Films as Director:

1932   *Das blaue Licht* (*The Blue Light*) (+ co-sc, role as Junta)
1933   *Sieg des Glaubens* (*Victory of the Faith*)
1935   ***Triumph des Willens*** (***Triumph of the Will***) (+ pr, ed); *Tag der Freiheit: unsere Wermacht* (+ ed)
1938   ***Olympia*** (***Olympische Spiele 1936***) (+ sc, co-ph, ed)
1944   *Tiefland* (*Lowland*) (+ sc, ed, role as Marta) (released 1954)

Other Films:

1926   *Der heilige Berg* (Fanck) (role as Diotima)
1927   *Der grosse Sprung* (Fanck) (role)
1929   *Das Schiscksal derer von Hapsburg* (Raffé) (role); *Die weisses Hölle vom Piz Palü* (Fanck) (role)
1930   *Stürme über dem Montblanc* (Fanck) (role)
1931   *Der weiss Rausch* (Fanck) (role)
1933   *S.O.S. Eisberg* (Fanck) (role)

Publications:

By RIEFENSTAHL: books—

Kampf in Schnee und Eis, Leipzig, 1933.
Hinter den Kulissen des Reichsparteitagsfilms, Munich, 1935 (uncredited ghost writer Ernst Jaeger)
Schönheit im Olympischen Kampf, Berlin, 1937.
The Last of the Nuba, New York, 1974.
Jardins du corail, Paris, 1978.
Memoiren, Munich, 1987.

By RIEFENSTAHL: articles—

"An Interview with a Legend," with Gordon Hitchens, in *Film Comment* (New York), Winter 1965.
Interview with Michel Delahaye, in *Interviews with Film Directors* edited by Andrew Sarris, New York, 1967.
"A Reply to Paul Rotha," with Kevin Brownlow, in *Film* (London), Spring 1967.
"Statement on Sarris-Gessner Quarrel about Olympia," in *Film Comment* (New York), Fall 1967.
Interview with Herman Weigel, in *Filmkritik* (Munich), August 1972.
"Why I Am Filming *Penthesilea*," in *Film Culture* (New York), Spring 1973.

On RIEFENSTAHL: books—

Cadars, Pierre, and Francis Courtade, *Histoire du cinema Nazi*, Paris, 1972.
Fanck, Arnold, *Er furte Regie mit Gletschern, Sturmen, Lawinen*, Munich, 1973.
Hull, David Stewart, *Film in the Third Reich*, New York, 1973.
Leiser, Erwin, *Nazi Cinema*, London, 1974.
Barsam, Richard, *Filmguide to "Triumph of the Will"*, Bloomington, Indiana, 1975.
Infield, Glenn, *Leni Riefenstahl, the Fallen Film Goddess*, New York, 1976.

Ford, Charles, *Leni Riefenstahl*, Paris, 1978.
Hinton, David, *The Films of Leni Riefenstahl*, Metuchen, New Jersey, 1978.
Infield, G.B., *Leni Riefenstahl et le troisieme Reich*, Paris, 1978.
Berg-Pan, Renata, *Leni Riefenstahl*, Boston, 1980.
Heck-Rabi, Louise, *Women Filmmakers: A Critical Reception*, Metuchen, New Jersey, 1984.
Graham, Cooper C., *Leni Riefenstahl and Olympia*, Metuchen, New Jersey, 1986.

On RIEFENSTAHL: articles—

"The Case of Leni Riefenstahl," in *Sight and Sound* (London), Spring 1960.
Gunston, David, "Leni Riefenstahl," in *Film Quarterly* (Berkeley), Fall 1960.
Berson, Arnold, "The Truth about Leni," in *Films and Filming* (London), April 1965.
Gregor, Ulrich, "A Comeback for Leni Riefenstahl," in *Film Comment* (New York), Winter 1965.
Brownlow, Kevin, "Leni Riefenstahl," in *Film* (London), Winter 1966.
Rotha, Paul, "I Deplore . . . ," in *Film* (London), Spring 1967.
Corliss, Richard, "Leni Riefenstahl—A Bibliography," in *Film Heritage* (Dayton, Ohio), Fall 1969.
Richards, J., "Leni Riefenstahl: Style and Structure," in *Silent Pictures* (London), Autumn 1970.
Alpert, Hollis, "The Lively Ghost of Leni," in the *Saturday Review* (New York), 25 March 1972.
"Riefenstahl Issue" of *Film Culture* (New York), Spring 1973.
Barsam, R.M., "Leni Riefenstahl: Artifice and Truth in a World Apart," in *Film Comment* (New York), November/December 1973.
Sontag, Susan, "Fascinating Fascism," in the *New York Review of Books*, 6 February 1975.
Sokal, Harry R., "Über Nacht Antisemitin geworden?," in *Der Spiegel* (Germany), no. 46, 1976.
"Zur Riefenstahl-Renaissance," special issue of *Frauen und Film* (Berlin), December 1977.
Fraser, J., "An Ambassador for Nazi Germany," in *Films* (London), April 1982.
Horton, W.J., "Capturing the Olympics," in *American Cinematographer* (Los Angeles), July 1984.
Loiperdinger, M., and D. Culbert, "Leni Riefenstahl, the SA, and the Nazi Party Rally Films, Nuremberg 1933–1934: *Sieg des Glaubens* and *Triumph des Willens*," in *Historical Journal of Film, Radio and TV* (Abingdon, Oxon), vol. 8, no. 1, 1988.

*   *   *

The years 1932 to 1945 define the major filmmaking efforts of Leni Riefenstahl. Because she remained a German citizen making films in Hitler's Third Reich, two at the Fuhrer's request, she and her films were viewed as pro-Nazi. Riefenstahl claims she took no political position and committed no crimes. In 1948, a German court ruled that she was a follower of, not active in, the Nazi Party. Another court in 1952 reconfirmed her innocence of war crimes. But she is destined to remain a politically controversial filmmaker who made two films rated as masterpieces.

She began to learn filmmaking while acting in the mountain films of Arnold Fanck, her mentor. She made a mountain film of her own, *The Blue Light*, using smoke bombs to create "fog." She used a red and green filter on the camera lens over her cameraman's objections, to obtain a novel magical effect. This film is Leni's own favorite. She says it is the story of her own life. Hitler admired *The Blue Light*. He asked her to photograph the Nazi Party Congress in Nuremburg. She agreed to make *Victory of the Faith*, which was not publicly viewed. Hitler then asked her to film the 1934 Nazi Party rally.

Triumph of the Will, an extraordinary work, shows Hitler arriving by plane to attend the rally. He proceeds through the crowded streets of Nuremburg, addresses speeches to civilians and uniformed troops, and reviews a five-hour parade. The question is: Did Riefenstahl make *Triumph* as pro-Nazi propaganda or not? "Cinematically dazzling and ideologically vicious," is R.M. Barsam's judgment. According to Barsam, three basic critical views of *Triumph* exist: (1) those who cannot appreciate the film at all, (2) those who can appreciate and understand the film, and (3) those who appreciate it in spite of the politics in the film.

Triumph premiered March 29, 1935, was declared a masterpiece, and subsequently earned three awards. *Triumph* poses questions of staging. Was the rally staged so that it could be filmed? Did the filming process shape the rally, give it meaning? Riefenstahl's next film, *Olympia*, posed the question of financing. Did Nazi officialdom pay for the film to be made? Riefenstahl claims the film was made independently of any government support. Others differ.

The improvisatory techniques Riefenstahl used to make *Triumph* were improved and elaborated to make *Olympia*. She and her crew worked 16-hour days, seven days a week. *Olympia* opens as *Triumph* does, with aerial scenes. Filmed in two parts, the peak of Olympia I is Jesse Owens's running feat. The peak of Olympia II is the diving scenes. In an interview with Gordon Hitchens in 1964, Riefenstahl revealed her guidelines for making *Olympia*. She decided to make two films instead of one because "the form must excite the content and give it shape. . . . The law of film is architecture, balance. If the image is weak, strengthen the sound, and vice-versa; the total impact on the viewer should be 100%." The secret of *Olympia*'s success, she affirmed, was its sound, all laboratory-made. Riefenstahl edited the film for a year and a half. It premiered April 20, 1938, and was declared a masterpiece, being awarded four prizes.

Riefenstahl's career after the beginning of World War II is comprised of a dozen unfinished film projects. She began *Penthesilea* in 1939, *Van Gogh* in 1943, and *Tiefland* in 1944, releasing it in 1954. Riefenstahl acted the role of a Spanish girl in it while co-directing with G.W. Pabst this drama of peasant-landowner conflicts. Visiting Africa in 1956, she filmed *Black Cargo*, documenting the slave trade, but her film was ruined by incorrect laboratory procedures. In the 1960s, she lived with and photographed the Mesakin Nuba tribe in Africa.

—Louise Heck-Rabi

RISI, Dino.

Italian. Born in Milan, 23 December 1917. Educated in medicine, specializing in psychiatry. Assistant to Mario Soldati and Alberto Lattuada, early 1940s; emigrated to Switzerland, studied filmmaking with Jacques Feyder, 1944; after liberation, returned to Milan as documentary maker and film critic, from 1946; with support of producer Carlo Ponti, directed first feature, *Vacanze col gangster*, 1952.

Films as Director:

1946   *I bersaglieri della signora* (doc short); *Barboni* (doc short); *Verso la vita* (doc short)
1947   *Pescatorella* (doc short); *Strade di Napoli* (doc short); *Tigullio minore* (doc short); *Cortili* (doc short)
1948   *Costumi e bellezze d'Italia* (doc short); *Cuore rivelatore* (doc short); *1848* (doc short); *La fabbrica del Duomo* (doc short); *Segantini, il pittore della montagna* (doc short)
1949   *La città dei traffici* (doc short); *Caccia in brughiera* (doc short); *La montagna di luce* (doc short); *Vince il sistema* (doc short); *Terra ladina* (doc short); *Il siero della verità*; *Seduta spiritica*
1950   *L'isola bianca* (doc short); *Il grido della città* (doc short); *Buio in sala* (doc short); *Fuga in città* (doc short)
1952   *Vacanze col gangster* (*Vacation with a Gangster*) (+ co-sc, story)
1953   *Il viale della speranza* (*Hope Avenue* (+ co-sc); "Paradiso per 4 ore (Paradise for Four Hours)" episode of *Amore in città* (*Love in the City*) (+ co-sc)
1955   *Il segno di Venere* (*The Sign of Venus*) (+ co-sc); *Pane, amore e . . .* (*Scandal in Sorrento*) (+ co-sc)
1956   *Poveri ma belli* (*Poor but Beautiful*) (+ co-sc)
1957   *La nonna Sabella* (*Grandmother Sabella*) (+ co-sc); *Belle ma povere* (*Beautiful but Poor, Irresistible*) (+ co-sc)
1958   *Venezia, la luna e tu* (*I due gondolieri, Venice, the Moon, and You*) (+ co-sc); *Poveri milionaire* (*Poor Millionaires*) (+ co-sc)
1959   *Il vedovo* (*The Widower*) (+ co-sc); *Il mattatore* (*Love and Larceny*)
1960   *Un amore a Roma* (*Love in Rome*); *A porte chiuse* (*Behind Closed Doors*) (+ co-sc)
1961   *Una vita difficile* (*A Difficult Life*)
1962   *La marcia su Roma* (*The March to Rome*); *Il sorpasso* (*The Easy Life. The Overtaking*) (+ co-sc)
1963   *Il successo* (*The Success*) (co-d with Morassi, uncredited); *I mostri* (*The Monsters. Opiate '67. Fifteen from Rome*) (+ co-sc); *Il giovedì* (*Thursday*) (+ co-sc)
1964   *Il gaucho* (*The Gaucho*); "La telefonata (The Telephone Call)" episode of *Le bambole* (*The Dolls*)
1965   "Una giornata decisiva (A Decisive Day)" episode of *I complessi* (*The Complexes*) (+ co-sc); *L'ombrellone* (*The Parasol. Weekend Italian Style*) (+ co-sc)
1966   "Il marito di Attilia (or) Nei secoli fedele (Attilia's Husband or Forever Faithful)" episode of *I nostri mariti* (*Our Husbands*); *Operazione San Gennaro* (*Operation San Gennaro. Treasure of San Gennaro*) (+ co-sc)
1967   *Il tigre* (*The Tiger and the Pussycat*) (+ co-sc); *Il profeta* (*The Prophet. Mr. Kinky*) (+ co-sc)
1968   *Straziami ma di baci saziami* (*Tear Me But Satiate Me with Your Kisses*) (+ co-sc)
1969   *Vedo nudo* (*I See Everybody Naked*) (+ co-sc); *Il giovane normale* (*The Normal Young Man*) (+ co-sc)
1970   *La moglie del prete* (*The Priest's Wife*) (+ co-sc)
1971   *Noi donne siamo fatte così* (*Women: So We Are Made*) (+ co-sc)
1972   *In nome del popolo italiano* (*In the Name of the Italian People*)
1973   *Mordi e fuggi* (*Bite and Run*) (+ co-sc); *Sesso matto* (*Mad Sex. How Funny Can Sex Be?*) (+ co-sc)
1974   *Profumo di donna* (*Scent of a Woman*) (+ co-sc)
1975   *Telefoni bianchi* (*White Telephones. The Career of a Chambermaid*) (+ co-sc)
1976   *Anima persa* (*Lost Soul*) (+ co-sc)
1977   *La stanza del vescovo* (*The Bishop's Room*) (+ co-sc); *I nuovi mostri* (*The New Monsters. Viva Italia*) (co-d)
1978   *Primo amore* (*First Love*) (+ co-sc)
1979   *Caro Papa* (*Dear Father*) (+ co-sc)
1980   *Sunday Lovers* (co-d); *Sono fotogenico* (*I Am Photogenic*) (+ co-sc)
1981   *Fantasmo d'amore* (*Ghost of Love*) (+ co-sc)
1982   *Sesso e violentieri* (*Sex and Violence*) (+ co-sc)
1984   *Le Bon Roi Dagobert* (*Dagobert*); *E la vita continua*
1985   *Scemo di guerra*
1987   *Teresa*; *Il commissario Lo Gatto* (*Inspector Lo Gatto*)
1990   *Tolgo il disturbo*; *Come un bambino*

Other Films:

1941   *Piccolo mondo antico* (Soldati) (asst d)
1942   *Giacomo l'idealista* (Lattuada) (asst d)
1951   *Anna* (Lattuada) (co-sc); *Totò e i re di Roma* (Steno and Monicelli) (co-sc)

Dino Risi on the set of *La moglie del prete*

1952   *Gli eroi della domenica* (Camerini) (co-sc)
1956   *Montecarlo* (Taylor) (co-sc)

Publications:

By RISI: articles—

Interviews with L. Codelli, in *Positif* (Paris), September 1972,
     November 1974, and October 1975.
"Sous le rire, des choses graves . . . ," interview with J.-A. Gili, in
     Ecran (Paris), November 1974.
Interview with A. Tassone, in *Cinéma* (Paris), January 1976.
"Le Cinema: Dessins," in *Positif* (Paris), December/January 1977/78.
Interview with D. Fasoli, in *Filmcritica* (Florence), May 1982.

On RISI: books—

Vigano, A., *Dino Risi*, Milan, 1977.

On RISI: articles—

Garel, A., "Sur quatre films de Dino Risi," in *Image et Son* (Paris),
     November 1974.
"Parfum de femme," in *Avant-Scène du Cinéma* (Paris), December
     1975.
"Une Vie difficile Issue" of *Avant-Scène du Cinéma* (Paris), 15 Febru-
     ary 1977.
Codelli, L., and A. Vigano, "Minimaximes," special section, in *Positif*
     (Paris), June 1978.
Turroni, G., "Film e figurazione: la riflessione metalinguistica," in
     Filmcritica (Rome), January 1979.
Codelli, Lorenzo, "Dino Risi," in *International Film Guide 1983*, Lon-
     don, 1982.

* * *

No other genre of Italian filmmaking has proliferated as
successfully as the Italian comedy, a mixture of sexual farce,
romantic comedy, and biting social satire. Dino Risi is one of
the prime movers in this field. Brother of the poet and documentary filmmaker, Nelo Risi, he began work as a journalist
before studying filmmaking with Jacques Feyder and becoming a screenwriter. Between 1946 and 1949 he directed 13
shorts and documentaries. Although Risi worked on important neorealist films (as assistant to Alberto Lattuada), his real
interests were always determined by an unswerving belief that
cinema meant entertainment and enjoyment for the ticket
buyer. Undoubtedly, he was one of the youthful forces who
helped steer the industry away from the provocative criticism
of the neorealist film and toward the superficial but expertly-
devised comedies in which it would become mired by the late
1950s. Moving out of the catastrophic postwar period and into
the surefooted capitalism of the "economic miracle," Italian
audiences sought out more of the lighter fare, putting Risi in
the mainstream of surefire profit-makers.

Generally adhering to simplicity of story line and concentrating on a representation of the "little man," the unexceptional character finding himself in a frustrating,
misapprehending world, Risi's work often suggests the
influence of neorealist dramaturgy. In "Paradiso per quattro
ore," an episode in *Amore in città*, Risi's camera has all the
scrutinizing inquisitiveness of direct cinema, and his capacity
to draw characters deftly and economically rivals that of Fellini. By means of such characterizations, he sets up a group of
satirical situations at a teenage dance which abjure any need
for larger narrative structures. Couples are physically mis-
matched or too well-matched; "Gregory Peck," the local teenage sheik, enters and takes command of the field with feigned
suavity; a mother checks out each boy who asks her daughter
to dance, approving only the best-dressed. This brief episode is
the first of a series of particularly Risian character studies, films
composed of a quick succession of effective vignettes illustrat-

ing the defects and eccentricities of the Italian male, often starring the well-balanced, polished acting duet of Vittorio
Gassman and Ugo Tognazzi, who alternately played friends
and adversaries and who brought a sense of personal tragedy to
their work as well, in *I mostri*, *Vedo nudo*, *Sesso matto*, and *I
nuovi mostri*.

In 1955 he made *Pane, amore, e . . .* , taking over from
Comencini the popular series about the adventures of a *bersaglieri* marshall played by Vittorio De Sica and helping with it to
launch the career of Sophia Loren. This was followed by *Poveri ma belli* and *Belle ma povere*, the story of two young "spivs"
who court each other's sisters.

Seven films later, in 1961, Risi's satire assumed a serious
edge and jettisoned much farcical frivolity. In *Una vita difficile*
he takes stock of Italy's politico-economic transition in the
story of a former partisan working as a left-wing journalist
(Alberto Sordi) who finds himself set upon by government,
family, and colleagues alike. *La marcia su Roma* is a wry look
at Mussolini's famous march to power, depicting the cowardice
and selfishness of the King who made it easy for Mussolini.
Tognazzi plays an incorruptible magistrate who destroys evidence that would acquit the dishonest industrialist (Gassman)
in *In nome del popolo italiano*. Several films, including *Il gaucho* and *Telefoni bianchi* reflect Risi's desire to turn the satirical weapon of film on the film industry itself.

The high calibre of the director's projects can often be attributed to excellence in the script stage due to the work of writers like Ennio Flaiano, Age and Scarpelli, Bernadino
Zapponi, and Ettore Scola.

—Joel Kanoff

RITT, Martin.

American. Born in New York City, 2 March 1902. Educated
at Dewitt Clinton High School, New York City; attended Elon
College, North Carolina; St. John's University, Brooklyn.
Member, Elia Kazan's Group Theater, 1937–42; served in
U.S. Army Air Force, 1942–46; stage director, New York
City, from 1946; director and actor, live productions for CBS
TV, 1948–51; blacklisted by TV industry when a Syracuse
grocer charged him with donating money to Communist
China, 1951; taught acting at Actor's Studio, directed stage
plays, 1951–56; directed first film, *Edge of the City*, 1957. *Died
of cardiac disease, in Santa Monica, California, 8 December
1990.*

Films as Director:

1957   *Edge of the City (A Man Is Ten Feet Tall)*; *No Down Payment*
1958   *The Long Hot Summer*
1959   *The Sound and the Fury*; *The Black Orchid*
1960   *Jovanka e le altri (Five Branded Women)*
1961   *Paris Blues*
1962   *Adventures of a Young Man (Hemingway's Adventures of a
         Young Man)*
1963   *Hud* (+ co-pr)
1964   *The Outrage*
1966   *The Spy Who Came in from the Cold* (+ pr)
1967   *Hombre* (+ co-pr)
1968   *The Brotherhood*
1970   *The Molly Maguires* (+ co-pr); *The Great White Hope*
1971   *Sounder*

Martin Ritt

1972 *Pete 'n' Tillie*
1974 *Conrack* (+ co-pr)
1976 *The Front* (+ pr)
1978 *Casey's Shadow*
1979 *Norma Rae*
1981 *Back Roads*
1983 *Cross Creek*
1985 *Slugger's Wife*
1986 *Murphy's Romance*
1987 *Nuts*
1989 *Stanley and Iris* (*Letters. Union Street*)

Other Films:

1944 *Winged Victory* (Cukor) (role as Gleason)
1975 *Der Richter und sein Henker* (*End of the Game*) (Schell) (role)

Publications:

By RITT: articles—

"It's the Freedom That Counts," in *Films and Filming* (London), May 1961.
"Martin Ritt—Conversation," in *Action* (Los Angeles), March/April 1971.
"The Making of *Conrack*," an interview with B.J. Demby, in *Filmmakers Newsletter* (Ward Hill, Massachusetts), April 1974.
"Paranoia Paradise," an interview with A. Stuart, in *Films and Filming* (London), March 1977.
Interview with D. Chase, in *Millimeter* (New York), June 1979.
"Portrait of a Director: The Completely Candid Martin Ritt," an interview with D.S. Reiss, in *Filmmakers Monthly* (Ward Hill, Massachusetts), April 1981.
"Dialogue on Film: Martin Ritt," in *American Film* (Washington, D.C.), November 1983.
Interview with P. McGilligan, in *Film Comment* (New York), January/February 1986.

On RITT: book—

Whitaker, Sheila, *The Films of Martin Ritt*, London, 1972.

On RITT: articles—

Young, Colin, "The Hollywood War of Independence," in *Film Quarterly* (Berkeley), Spring 1959.
"Personality of the Month," in *Films and Filming* (London), April 1960.
Lightman, Herb, "The Photography of *Hud*," in *Action* (Los Angeles), July 1963.
McVay, Douglas, "The Best and Worst of Martin Ritt," in *Films and Filming* (London), December 1964.
Field, Sydney, "*Outrage*: A Print Documentary on Hollywood Film-Making," in *Film Quarterly* (Berkeley), Spring 1965.
Farber, Stephen, "*Hombre* and *Welcome to Hard Times*," in *Film Quarterly* (Berkeley), Fall 1967.
Cook, B., "Norma Rae's Big Daddy," in *American Film* (Washington, D.C.), April 1980.
Trainor, Richard, "Blacklist," in *Sight and Sound* (London), Summer 1988.

*　　*　　*

As his roots in the Group Theater would indicate, Martin Ritt was a man with a social conscience. He had himself known misfortune: he was blacklisted during the McCarthy hypocrisy of the 1950s and, in *The Front*, he poignantly attacks that odious practice. Often, the characters in his films are underdogs, victims of racism or sexism or capitalism who live lives of quiet dignity while struggling and occasionally triumphing over adversity.

Most refreshingly, Ritt's films are inhabited by odd couplings, characters from diverse backgrounds who unite for a common good while in the process expanding their own aware-

ness. In *Norma Rae*, for example, Southern cotton mill worker Sally Field and New York Jewish labor organizer Ron Leibman form a curious coalition as they unionize a factory. In a hilarious sequence, which symbolizes the cinema of Martin Ritt, Field joins the Lower East Side and Dixie when she petulantly utters the Yiddish word *kvetch* while complaining to Leibman. (The director also deals with the hardships of overworked, underpaid employees in *The Molly Maguires*, set in the Pennsylvania coal mines of the 1870s.)

Blacks and whites have regularly aligned themselves in Ritt films, from easy-going, hard-working railroad yard worker Sidney Poitier befriending confused army deserter John Cassavetes in *Edge of the City* to schoolteacher Jon Voight educating underprivileged black children in *Conrack*. In all of these, the black characters exist within a white society, their identities irrevocably related to whites. The exception is *Sounder*, released after Hollywood had discovered that black audiences do indeed attend movies; it was produced at a point in time when blacks on movie screens were able to exist solely within a black culture. *Sounder* pointedly details the struggles of a black family to overcome adversity and prejudice. Despite spending his youth in New York City, Ritt has set many of his films in the South: *Sounder, Conrack, Norma Rae, The Long Hot Summer, The Sound and the Fury*—the latter two based on William Faulkner stories.

While Ritt's films are all solidly crafted, they are in no way visually distinctive: Ritt cannot be called a great visual stylist, and is thus not ranked in the pantheon of his era's filmmakers.

—Rob Edelman

RIVETTE, Jacques.

French. Born Jacques Pierre Louis Rivette in Rouen, 1 March 1928. Educated at Lycée Corneille, Rouen. Moved to Paris, began writing for *Gazette du cinéma*, 1950; writer on *Cahiers du cinéma*, from 1952; worked on films in various capacities, 1952–56; directed first film in 35mm, *Le Coup de berger*, 1956, co-scripted with Chabrol, and featuring Godard and Truffaut in small roles; first feature, *Paris nous appartient*, released 1961; editor-in-chief, *Cahiers du cinéma*, 1963–65; director for French TV, from late 1960s. Lives in Paris.

Films as Director:

1950 *Aux Quatre Coins*; *Le Quadrille*
1952 *Le Divertissement*
1956 *Le Coup de berger* (+ co-sc)
1961 *Paris nous appartient* (*Paris Belongs to Us*) (+ role as party guest)
1966 *La Religieuse* (*Suzanne Simonin, la religieuse de Denis Diderot. The Nun*) (+ co-sc); *Jean Renoir, le patron* (for TV)
1968 *L'Amour fou* (+ co-sc)
1971 *Out 1: noli me tangere* (for TV, never released)
1974 *Out 1: ombre* (+ co-sc); *Céline et Julie vont en bateau* (*Céline and Julie Go Boating*) (+ co-sc)
1976 *Duelle* (*Twilight*) (+ co-sc); *Noroît* (*Northwest*) (+ co-sc)
1979 *Merry-Go-Round* (+ co-sc) (released 1983)
1981 *Le Pont du Nord* (*North Bridge*); *Paris s'en va*
1984 *L'Amour par terre*
1985 *Hurlevent* (*Wuthering Heights*)
1989 *La Bande des quatre*
1990 *Belle noiseuse* (+ sc)

Jacques Rivette: *Céline et Julie vont en bateau*

Other Films:

1955 *French Cancan* (Renoir) (asst); *Une Visite* (Truffaut) (ph)
1960 *Chronique d'un été* (***Chronicle of a Summer***) (Morin and
       Rouch) (role as Marilu's Boyfriend)

Publications:

By RIVETTE: articles—

Regular contributor to *Cahiers du Cinéma* (Paris), 1952–69, and to
Arts (Paris), 1950s.
Interviews in *Sight and Sound* (London), Autumn 1963 and Autumn
1974.
Interview in *Les Lettres Françaises* (Paris), April 1966.
Interview in *Cahiers du Cinéma* (Paris), September 1968.
Interview in *Film Comment* (New York), September/October 1974.
Interview in *Film Quarterly* (Berkeley), Winter 1974/75.
Interview with S. Daney and J. Narboni, in *Cahiers du Cinéma* (Paris),
May 1981.
Interview with P. Carcassonne and others, in *Cinématographe* (Paris),
March 1982.

On RIVETTE: books—

Armes, Roy, *French Cinema Since 1946: Vol 2—The Personal Style*,
New York, 1966.
Monaco, James, *The New Wave*, New York, 1976.
Rosenbaum, Jonathan, editor, *Rivette: Texts and Interviews*, London,
1977.

On RIVETTE: articles—

Burch, Noël, "Qu'est-ce que la Nouvelle Vague?," in *Film Quarterly*
(Berkeley), Winter 1959.

Tyler, Parker, "The Lady Called A: or, If Jules and Jim Had Only
Lived at Marienbad," in *Film Culture* (New York), Summer 1962.
Stein, E., "Suzanne Simonin, Diderot's Nun," in *Sight and Sound*
(London), Summer 1966.
Lloyd, P., "Jacques Rivette and *L'Amour Fou*," in *Monogram* (London), Summer 1971.
"Rivette Issue" of *Cinéma* (Paris), March 1975.
Bassan, Raphaël, "Sur l'oeuvre de Jacques Rivette," in *Image et Son*
(Paris), October 1981.
Chevrie, M., "Jacques Rivette, la ligne et l'aventure," in *Cahiers du
Cinéma* (Paris), October 1984.
Blanchet, C., "Jacques Rivette: Une poétique du complot," in
Cinéma (Paris), November 1984.
Magny, Joel, and others, "Côte cour, côte jardin," in *Cahiers du
Cinéma* (Paris), February 1989.

*   *   *

In the days when the young lions of the New Wave were busy
railing against "Le Cinéma du papa" in magazine articles and
attending all-night screenings of Frank Tashlin and Jerry Lewis
movies at La Cinémathèque, Jacques Rivette was quite the
keenest cinephile of them all. He made a short as early as 1950,
worked as an assistant director for Becker and Renoir, and
wrote endless essays for *Gazette du cinéma* and *Cahiers du
cinéma*, which he would later edit. If his films seem academic
and acutely self-reflexive, we must remember that he is somebody who has spent an eternity theorizing about cinema.
    Rivette's first feature, *Paris nous appartient*, clocks in at a
mere 140 minutes, and takes as its theme the abortive attempt
of a group of French actors to mount a production of Sha-

kespeare's *Pericles*. Rivette's fascination with the play-within-the-film, a leitmotif of his work, is given an initial, and not entirely successful, airing here. The film seems stage-bound, literary and rather earnest, something which Rivette himself would later acknowledge: "I am very unhappy about the dialogue, which I find atrocious."

After his second feature, *La Religieuse*, was briefly banned on account of its perceived anti-clericalism (but nonetheless made money), Rivette decided to abandon completely conventional narrative cinema. Unlike Godard, who never managed to fully overcome the cult of personality (even *Tout Va Bien* and his other post-68 collaborations with Gorin are inevitably treated as the great Jean-Luc's personal statements), Rivette easily evolved a kind of collective cinema, where the director's role was on a par with the actor's. He gave the actor the task of improvising his/her dialogue and character and let the narrative stumble into being. A haphazard and risky working method, Rivette found this infinitely preferable to rigidly conforming to a pre-conceived script. Rivette's films are rarely polished and finished. Their subject matter is often rehearsal: they explore the process of creation, rather than the finished artefact itself. *L'Amour fou*, an account of a company's attempts to produce Racine's *Andromaque* while the director and his actress-wife have a break-up, stops short of opening night.

In his monumental work, *Out*, which lasts a full thirteen hours but has only ever seen the commercial light of day as a four-hour shadow, *Ombre*, of itself, Rivette takes his theory of Direct Cinema as far as it will go. Wanting to make a film "which, instead of being predicated on a central character presented as the conscience, reflecting everything that happens in the action, would be about a collective," the director assembled a large cast of actor/characters, amongst them Juliet Berto and Jean-Pierre Leaud. The film opens as a documentary. Only very gradually does Rivette allow a fictional narrative to emerge through the interaction of the cast. He describes *Out* as being "like a game . . . a crossword."

Rivette commissioned Roland Barthes to write for *Cahiers du cinéma*. Not only does he share Barthes' well chronicled suspicion of authors, for Rivette is also a fervent "intertextualist": his films abound in references to other books, to other films. *The Hunting of the Snark*, Aeschylus and Balzac, Shakespeare and Edgar Allen Poe are all liable to be thrown into the melting pot. He mixes 16mm and 35 mm film stock in *L'Amour fou*, where he actually depicts a TV crew filming the same rehearsals that he is filming: a case of Chinese boxes, perhaps, that goes some way to explaining his unpopularity with certain British critics. Harold Hobson in the *Sunday Times* described the director's 1974 film, *Céline et Julie vont en bateau*, as a "ghastly exhibition of incompetent pretentiousness" while David Robinson suggested that *L'Amour par terre* offered the director's "now accustomed fey and onanistic silliness." It should be noted that both the films attacked offer strong parts for women. Rivette, more than most of his New Wave contemporaries, has provided opportunities for actresses. He is hardly the most prolific director and the length of his films has often counted against him. Nonetheless, his clinical, self-reflexive essays in film form, the sophisticated games he continues to play within the "house of fiction," reveal him as a cinematic purist whose commitment to the celluloid muse has hardly diminished since the heady days of the 1950s.

—G.C. Macnab

ROCHA, Glauber.

Brazilian. Born in Vitoria da Conquista, Bahia, Brazil, 14 March 1938. Studied law, 1959–61. Founder, "Lemanja-Filmes" production company, 1957; directed first feature, *Barravento*, 1962; went into exile, 1970; directed in Italy, France and Spain, early 1970s; returned to Brazil, 1976. *Died in Rio de Janeiro, 22 August 1981.*

Films as Director:

1957 *Um dia na rampa* (short) (co-d)
1958 *O patio* (short); *A cruz na praça* (short)
1962 *Barravento* (*The Turning Wind*) (+ co-sc)
1964 *Deus e o diablo na terra do sol* (*Black God, White Devil*) (+ co-pr, sc)
1965 *Amazonas Amazonas* (doc) (+ sc); *Maranhão 66* (doc) (+ sc)
1967 *Terra em transe* (*Land in Anguish*) (+ sc)
1968 *Cancer* (+ sc) (completed in Cuba, 1973–4)
1969 **Antônio das Mortes (*O dragão da maldade contra o santo querreiro*)** (+ co-pr, sc, art d)
1970 *Der leone have sept cabecas* (*The Lion Has Seven Heads*) (+ co-sc, co-ed); *Cabezas cortadas* (*Severed Heads*) (+ sc)
1975 *Claro* (+ sc)
1978 *Di* (doc short)
1979 *Jorjamado no cinema* (doc short)
1980 *A idade da terra* (*The Age of the Earth*) (+ sc)

Other Films:

1965 *A grande feira* (d of pr); *Menino de engenho* (pr)
1966 *A grande cidade* (co-pr)

Publications:

By ROCHA: books—

Revisao critica do cinema brasiliero, Rio de Janeiro, 1962.
Revoluçao do cinema novo, Rio de Janeiro, 1981.
Riverao Sussuarana, Rio de Janeiro, 1981.
O seculo do cinema, Rio de Janeiro, 1983.

By ROCHA: articles—

"Un cinéma en transe," in *Image et Son* (Paris), January 1968.
Interview with M. Delahaye and others, in *Cahiers du Cinéma* (Paris), July 1969.
"Cinema Novo vs. Cultural Colonialism: An Interview with Glauber Rocha," in *Cineaste* (New York), Summer 1970.
Interview with Gordon Hitchens, in *Film Quarterly* (Berkeley), Fall 1970.
"Beginning at Zero: Notes on Cinema and Society," in *The Drama Review* (Cambridge, Massachusetts), Winter 1970.
Interview in *Afterimage* (London), no. 3, 1971.
"Lumière, magie, action," in *Positif* (Paris), December 1974.
Interviews in *Los años de la conmoción*, by Isaac Léon Frías, Mexico City, 1979.
"Humberto Mauro and the Historical Position of Brazilian Cinema," and "Hunger vs Profit Aesthetic," in *Framework* (Norwich), Autumn 1979.
"The History of Cinema Novo," in *Framework* (Norwich), Summer 1980.
"Epistolario: Cartas de Glauber Rocha," in *Cine Cubano* (Havana), no. 101, 1982.
"The Aesthetics of Hunger" and "Down With Populism," in *25 Years of the New Latin American Cinema*, edited by Michael Chanan, London, 1983.
"*Deus e o diablo na terra do sol*," in *Filme Cultura* (Rio de Janeiro), January/April 1984.
"Cinema Novo and the Dialectics of Popular Culture," an interview in *Cinema and Social Change in Latin America*, by Julianne Burton, Austin, Texas, 1986.

"Revisión crítica del cine brasileño," "No al populismo," and "Estética de la violencia," in *Hojas de cine: Testimonios y documentos del Nuevo Cine Latinoamericano*, Mexico City, 1986.

On ROCHA: books—

Gerber, Raquel, editor, *Glauber Rocha*, Rio de Janeiro, 1977.
Johnson, Randal, and Robert Stam, *Brazilian Cinema*, New Brunswick, New Jersey, 1982.
Hollyman, Burnes, *Glauber Rocha and the Cinema Novo in Brazil: A Study of His Critical Writings and Films*, New York, 1983.
Johnson, Randal, *Cinema Novo X 5*, Austin, Texas, 1984.
Armes, Roy, *Third World Filmmaking and the West*, Berkeley, 1987.
Pierre, Sylvie, *Glauber Rocha*, Paris, 1987.
King, John, *Magical Reels: A History of Cinema in Latin America*, London, 1990.

On ROCHA: articles—

Callenbach, Ernest, "Comparative Anatomy of Folk Myth Films: *Robin Hood* and *Antonio das Mortes*," in *Film Quarterly* (Berkeley), Winter 1969/70.
"Rocha Issue" of *Etudes Cinématographiques* (Paris), no. 97–99, 1973.
Gardies, R., "Structural Analysis of a Textual System: Presentation of a Method," in *Screen* (London), Spring 1974.
Cinema Novo Section of *Jump Cut* (Chicago), June 1976.
Van Wert, W.F., "Ideology in the Third World Cinema: A Study of Ousmane Sembene and Glauber Rocha," in *Quarterly Review of Film Studies* (Pleasantville, New York), no., 2, 1979.
Bruce, Graham, "Music in Glauber Rocha's Films," in *Jump Cut* (Berkeley), May 1980.
Armes, Roy, "The Incoherence of Underdevelopment," in *Films and Filming* (London), November 1981.
Rocha Section of *Cahiers du Cinéma* (Paris), November 1981.
Rocha Sections of *Cine Cubano* (Havana), nos. 100 and 101, 1982.
Rocha Section of *Film Cultura* (Rio de Janeiro), August/October 1982.
Paranagua, P., "Luis Buñuel et Glauber Rocha," in *Positif* (Paris), October 1983.
Burton, Julianne, "Modernist form in *Land in Anguish* and *Memories of Underdevelopment*," in *Post Script* (Jacksonville, Florida), Winter 1984.
Gomes, P.E. Sallès, "Glauber Rocha," in *Positif* (Paris), April 1987.

*   *   *

"A camera in your hand and an idea in your head" was how Glauber Rocha described the minimalist conditions in which the filmmakers of Brazil's *Cinema Novo* (New Cinema) began. Though the origins of *Cinema Novo* can be traced to Nelson Pereira dos Santos's movie, *Rio 40 Degrees* (1955), the "official" starting point for the movement which redefined Brazilian and Latin American film is 1962, when Rocha directed *Barravento*. Rocha was *Cinema Novo*'s principle theorist and most flamboyant practitioner, developing many of its key concepts and realizing them on the screen. The most important element in Rocha's theory is his recurrent insistence on discovering a filmic language which is Brazilian and Latin American, ending the practice endemic to neo-colonies of aping Hollywood and European cinema. This new idiom was to arise out of working directly within the reality of Latin America; thus, in one of his best-known essays, he argued that its core was an aesthetic of hunger and violence: "Hunger is the essence of our society . . . and hunger's most noble cultural manifestation is violence." Rocha was looking for a popular, but not a populist, form of expression, and he felt that this would lead to new acting styles, different ways of using music and color, and innovative forms of montage.

If the base of Rocha's cinema was the traditional culture of Brazil, modern influences were also important. One of these was the Cuban revolution, which offered the example of radical social transformation in Latin America, and had made possible the birth of a truly Cuban cinematography. Another was the New Wave in France, from whence sprang the concept of the director as "auteur" which so influenced Rocha, and whose adherents had pioneered the path he traveled from critic to filmmaker. However, Rocha clearly distinguished between the psychologistic cinema of Europe, which expressed the existential anguish of the developed world, and the epic cinema which he believed more appropriate to articulating the social and economic crises of Latin America. As he pithily polemicized: "We're not interested in neurotics' problems, we're interested in the problems faced by those who are lucid."

After some short films, and relatively extensive experience as a critic, Rocha burst onto the international cinematic scene with *Barravento*. Although in later years he was to express dissatisfaction with the film, even disclaiming authorship because he had taken it over from another director half-way through the shooting, at the time he called it the "first great denunciation realized in Brazilian cinema." Filmed in a neo-realist style which was characteristic of many *Cinema Novo* directors—though this was the only instance in which Rocha employed this form—the movie focused on the harsh living conditions of a fishing village. If the work's realism is at odds with Rocha's later theatricality, the film nonetheless contains many of the elements found throughout his oeuvre. For example, the narrative leaps and the fighting which is choreographed as dancing presage the reflexivity of films that will follow. Also present is the dialectic of the traditional and the modern; for, while Rocha criticizes the mysticism that is part of the fishing people's underdevelopment, he also shows how their popular culture provides them with a defense against the ravages of capitalism.

The films that came after *Barravento* are extravagant and operatic, expressive of Rocha's search for a cinematic tropicalism equivalent to the magic realism of Latin American writers such as Gabriel García Márquez and Alejo Carpentier. One of the unique formal elements in Rocha's work is the combination of this tropicalism with the self-reflexivity of the New Wave through such strategies as the placing of a film within a film in *Land in Anguish* and the use of highly stylized violence in *Antonio das Mortes*. In both of these films he also pricks the audience's critical sense through making the perspective of the works larger than that of their central protagonist, thus cutting back against the very identification that he simultaneously foments in the films. This sort of systematic contradiction is characteristic of Rocha's efforts to realize a dialectical form, and is perhaps most evident in the counter-point he consistently established between image and sound.

Rocha's concern with thematic dialectics is most apparent in his explorations in Brazilian popular culture, which he perceives as representing both a permanent rebellion against oppression and the evasion of social problems. His interest in resolving this contradiction and turning popular culture and myth into a progressive force is portrayed in *Black God, White Devil* and *Antonio das Mortes* through the conflict between the *cangaceiros*, the social bandits of the Brazilian north-east, and Antonio, the killer hired to eradicate the law-breakers but who ends up embodying their social ideals. That it is popular, and not populist, culture which offers the only possibility for national liberation is made explicit by Rocha in *Land in Anguish*, where he contrasts traditional values to those of liberal populism, which is shown to lead inevitably to co-option by the bourgeoisie. Rocha's efforts to form a genuinely Brazilian cinema, founded on authentic themes and expressed through an idiom peculiar to Latin America, led him to make beautiful and moving films which continue to speak for his ideals.

—John Mraz

ROEG, Nicolas.

British. Born Nicolas Jack Roeg in London, 15 August 1928. Educated at Mercers School. Married 1) Susan Rennie Stephens; 2) actress Theresa Russell. Junior at Marylebone Studio, dubbing French films and making tea, from 1947; hired at MGM's Borehamwood Studios as part of camera crew on *The Miniver Story*, 1950; camera operator, from 1958; directed first feature (with Donald Cammell), *Performance*, 1970. Address: c/o Hatton and Baker, 18 Jermyn Street, London SW1Y 6HN.

Films as Director:

1970   *Performance* (co-d, + ph)
1971   ***Walkabout*** (+ ph)
1973   ***Don't Look Now***
1976   *The Man Who Fell to Earth*
1980   *Bad Timing*
1982   *Eureka*
1985   *Insignificance*
1986   *Castaway*
1987   episode in *Aria*
1988   *Track 29*
1989   *The Witches*; *Sweet Bird of Youth* (for TV)
1990   *Cold Heaven*

Other Films:

(as camera operator)

1958   *A Woman Possessed* (Max Varnel); *Moment of Indiscretion* (Max Varnel); *The Man Inside* (Gilling)
1959   *The Great Van Robbery* (Max Varnel); *Passport to Shame* (Rakoff); *The Child and the Killer* (Max Varnel)
1960   *The Trials of Oscar Wilde* (Hughes); *Jazz Boat* (Hughes)
1961   *The Sundowners* (Zinnemann); *Information Received* (Lynn)
1962   *Lawrence of Arabia* (Lean) (2nd unit ph); *Dr. Crippen* (Lynn) (as lighting cameraman)
1963   *The Caretaker* (Donner); *Just For Fun* (Flemyng); *Nothing But the Best* (Donner)
1964   ***The Masque of the Red Death*** (Corman); *The System* (*The Girl Getters*) (Winner); *Every Day's a Holiday* (Hill); *Victim Five* (*Code Seven, Victim Five*) (Lynn)
1965   *Judith* (Mann) (2nd unit ph)
1966   *A Funny Thing Happened on the Way to the Forum* (Lester); *Farenheit 451* (Truffaut)
1967   *Far from the Madding Crowd* (Schlesinger); *Casino Royale* (Huston et al) (some sections only)
1968   *Petulia* (Lester)

Publications:

By ROEG: articles—

Interview with Gordon Gow, in *Films and Filming* (London), January 1972.
"*Don't Look Now*," an interview with Tom Milne and Penelope Houston, in *Sight and Sound* (London), Winter 1973/74, also Winter 1974/75.
"Nick Roeg . . . and the Man Who Fell to Earth," with John Lifflander and Stephan Shroyer, in *Inter/View* (New York), March 1976.
"Roegian Thought Patterns," an interview with J. Padroff, in *Films* (London), September 1981.
Interview with Harlan Kennedy, in *Film Comment* (New York), March/April 1983.
Interview with Richard Combs, in *Sight and Sound* (London), Winter 1984/85.
Interview with Nick Roddick, in *Cinema Papers* (Melbourne), September 1985.

On ROEG: books—

Feineman, Neil, *Nicolas Roeg*, Boston, 1978.
Houston, Beverle, and Marsha Kinder, *Self and Cinema: A Transformalist Perspective*, Pleasantville, New York, 1980.
Walker, John, *The Once and Future Film: British Cinema in the '70s and '80s*, London, 1983.
Lanza, Joseph, *Fragile Geometry: The Films, Philosophy, and Misadventures of Nicolas Roeg*, New York, 1989.

On ROEG: articles—

Kleinhans, Chuck, "Nicolas Roeg: Permutations without Profundity," in *Jump Cut* (Chicago), September/October 1974.
Mayersberg, Paul, "Story so far . . . *The Man Who Fell to Earth*," in *Sight and Sound* (London), Autumn 1975.
Kolker, Robert, "The Open Texts of Nicolas Roeg," in *Sight and Sound* (London), Spring 1977.
Kennedy, H., "The Illusions of Nicholas Roeg," in *American Film* (Washington, D.C.), January/February 1980.
Cros, Jean-Louis, and Raymond Lefevre, "Pour rehabiliter Nicholas Roeg," in *Image et Son* (Paris), June 1981.
Gomez, J., "Another Look at Nicholas Roeg," in *Film Criticism* (Edinboro, Pennsylvania), Fall 1981.
Pursell, M., "From Gold Nugget to Ice Crystal: The Diagenetic Structure of Roeg's *Eureka*," in *Literature/Film Quarterly* (Salisbury, Maryland), vol. 11, no. 4, October 1983.
Barker, Adam, "What the Detective Saw, or A Case of Mistaken Identity," in *Monthly Film Bulletin* (London), July 1988.

*   *   *

Nicolas Roeg is a visual trickster who plays havoc with conventional screen narratives. Choosing an oblique storytelling formula, he riddles his plots with ambiguous characters, blurred genres, distorted chronologies and open-ended themes to invite warring interpretations.

Even the most facile Roeg synopsis betrays alienation and incongruity, with characters getting caught in bewildering and hostile situations. His first effort *Performance* (with co-director Donald Cammell) offers a dark look at the last days of a pursued gangster (James Fox) who undergoes a psychosexual identity change while hiding out with a has-been rock star (Mick Jagger). This psychedelic cornucopia of androgynous sex, violence and Borges allusions blessed and cursed Roeg with the lingering label "cult director."

We had already been warned of Roeg's charming peculiarities during his cinematographer days. Such notable films as *Far from the Madding Crowd* and *Fahrenheit 451* had an odd, even anachronistic look that sometimes ran contrary to the story proper. In fact, the latter film barely resembles Truffaut at all and looks more Roegish with its dreamy color schemes and chilly atmospherics.

Even his relatively tame second feature *Walkabout* has narrative trap doors. Jarring cross-cuts, sensuous photography and Edward Bond's enigmatic script are more satisfying to mystics than humanists. James Vance Marshall's novel is much more clear in its tale of two Australian children (Jenny Agutter and Lucien John) who get lost in the outback and are saved by an aborigine (David Gumpilil). Roeg's version is a more complex and fatalistic expose of people from separate cultures who have no hope of connecting.

Roeg flaunts a talent for shattering a relatively simple story into heady fragments with his adaptation of Daphne du Maurier's *Don't Look Now*. The tragedy of a couple (Julie Christie and Donald Sutherland) haunted in Venice by a psychic (Hilary Mason) claiming to communicate with their drowned daughter turns into something more than just a proto-Hitchcock thriller. As in most Roegian journeys, we emerge from *Don't Look Now* more discombobulated than we were at the start. Is the psychic a fraud? Is there foul play among the Venetian authorities? Could the occult implications be just a

Nicolas Roeg with Theresa Russell

ruse? Roeg operates on a logic that is more visceral than intellectual. Instead of outright clues, we get recurrent shapes, sounds, colors and gestures that belie a hidden order linking people and events.

Of all Roeg's work, *The Man Who Fell to Earth* is the most accomplished and de-centered. A space alien (David Bowie) arrives on Earth, starts a multi-million dollar enterprise and is later captured by a government-corporate collusion. What threatens to be another trite sci-fi plot becomes, in Roeg's hands, a visually stunning mental conundrum. All the continuity gaffes plaguing many an outer-space movie are here intentionally exacerbated to the point where we doubt that the "visitor" is really an alien at all. We see events mostly through the alien's abstruse viewpoint as days, months, years, even decades transpire sporadically and inconsistently. The story is a sleight-of-hand distraction that forces our attention more onto the transitory mood of loneliness and dissociation.

Unlike a purely experimental director who would flout story-lines altogether, Roeg retains the bare bones of old genres only to disfigure them. His controversial *Bad Timing* could easily have been an updated "Inner Sanctum" spin-off with its pathological lovers (Art Garfunkel and Theresa Russell) and the voyeuristic detective (Harvey Keitel) snooping for foul play. But the film unfolds with vignettes that tell us one thing and show another. Time and motive—the staples of mysteries—are so deviously jumbled that we can only resign ourselves to the Roeg motto that "nothing is what it seems."

Roeg's under-appreciated and least-seen *Eureka* starts out as an adventure about a Yukon prospector (Gene Hackman) who finds gold and becomes one of the world's richest men. But soon the story splinters into soap opera, romance, murder mystery and even splatter film—a tortuous, visionary, frustrating and ultimately mad epic.

Since *Eureka*, Roeg has been more skittish about re-entering the labyrinth. Films like *Insignificance* (about a night when the prototypes of Albert Einstein, Marilyn Monroe, Joe DiMaggio and Joe McCarthy meet) and *Castaway* (based on Lucy Irvine's ordeal with a lover on a deserted island) have shades of the older Roeg films but lack his gift for reckless lust. The "Twilight Zone" teasers reemerge somewhat in *Track 29*, where he teams with absurdist scriptwriter Dennis Potter in a tale about a woman beleaguered by a man her own age who claims to be her illegitimate son. Once more, Roeg treats us to another story about frustrated love and the fragile border between "reality" and hallucination.

—Joseph Lanza

ROHMER, Eric.

French, Born Jean-Marie Maurice Scherer in Tulle, 4 April 1920. Literature teacher at lycée, Nancy, 1942–50; film critic, from 1948; founder, with Godard and Rivette, *La Gazette du cinéma*, Paris, 1950; editor-in-chief of *Cahiers du cinéma*, 1957–63; directed first feature, *Le Signe du lion*, 1959; made the "Six contes moraux" (6 Moral Tales), 1962–73; with *La Femme de l'aviator*, began new series, "Comédies et proverbes," 1980. Recipient: Prix Max Ophüls, for *My Night at Maud's*, 1970; Prix Louis Delluc, and Prix Méliès, for *Claire's Knee*, 1971; Special Jury Prize, Cannes Festival, for *The Marquise of O . . .*, 1976; Officier des Arts et des Lettres. Office: 26 av. Pierre-1er-de-Serbie, 75116 Paris, France.

Films as Director and Scriptwriter:

1950   *Journal d'un scélérat*
1951   *Présentation ou Charlotte et son steak* (*Charlotte and Her Steak*)
1952   *Les Petites Filles modèles* (co-d) (unfinished)
1954   *Bérénice*
1956   *La Sonate à Kreutzer* (*The Kreutzer Sonata*)
1958   *Véronique et son cancre*
1959   *Le Signe du lion* (*Sign of the Lion. The Sign of Leo*)
1963   *La Boulangerie de Monceau* (first of the "Contes moraux"; following five films identified by "CM" and number assigned by Rohmer); *La Carrière de Suzanne* (*Suzanne's Profession*) (CM no. 2)
1964   *Nadja à Paris*
1964–69   Films for educational television: *Les Cabinets de physique au XVIIIème siècle*; *Les Métamorphoses du paysage industriel*; *Perceval*; *Don Quichotte*; *Edgar Poë*; *Pascal*; *La Bruyère*; *Mallarmé*; *La Béton dans la ville*; *Les Contemplations*; *Hugo architecte*; *Louis Lumière*
1965   Films for television series "Cinéastes de notre temps": *Carl Dreyer, Le Celluloid et la marbre*; "Place de l'étoile" episode of *Paris vu Par . . .* (*Six in Paris*)
1966   *Une Étudiante d'aujourd'hui*
1967   *La Collectionneuse* (CM no. 4) (+ sc); *Fermière à Montfaucon*
1969   *Ma Nuit chez Maud* (*My Night at Maud's*) (CM no. 3)
1970   *Le Genou de Claire* (*Claire's Knee*) (CM no. 5)
1972   *L'Amour l'après-midi* (*Chloe in the Afternoon*) (CM no. 6)
1976   *La Marquise d'O . . .* (*The Marquise of O . . .*)
1978   *Perceval le Gaullois*
1980   *La Femme de l'aviator* (*The Aviator's Wife*)
1982   *Le Beau Mariage* (*The Perfect Marriage*)
1983   *Loup y es-tu?* (*Wolf, Are You There?*); *Pauline à la plage* (*Pauline at the Beach*)
1984   *Les Nuits de la pleine lune* (*Full Moon in Paris*)
1986   *Le Rayon vert* (*The Green Ray*)
1987   *L'Ami de mon amie* (*My Girlfriend's Boyfriend*); *Quatre Aventures de Reinette et Mirabelle* (*Four Adventures of Reinette and Mirabelle*)
1989   *Conte de printemps* (*A Tale of Springtime*)

Publications:

By ROHMER: books—

Hitchcock, with Claude Chabrol, Paris, 1957.
Six contes moraux, Paris, 1974.
The Marquise of O, New York, 1985.
Le Gout de la beauté, edited by Jean Narboni, Paris, 1989.
A Taste for Beauty, Cambridge, 1990.

By ROHMER: articles—

Interview with Graham Petrie, in *Film Quarterly* (Berkeley), Summer 1971.
"Eric Rohmer Talks About Chloe," in *Inter/View* (New York), November 1972.

"Programme Eric Rohmer," an article and interview with Claude Beylie, in *Ecran* (Paris), April 1974.
"*La Marquise d'O . . .*," in *Avant-Scène du Cinéma* (Paris), October 1976.
"Rohmer's Perceval," an interview with G. Adair, in *Sight and Sound* (London), Autumn 1978.
"Rehearsing the Middle Ages," an interview with N. Tesich-Savage, in *Film Comment* (New York), September/October 1978.
"Un Allegorie policière," with Claude Chabrol, in *Avant-Scène du Cinéma* (Paris), June 1980.
Interview with Pascal Bonitzer and Serge Daney, in *Cahiers du Cinéma* (Paris), May 1981.
"Comedies and Proverbs," an interview with F. Ziolkowski, in *Wide Angle* (Athens, Ohio), vol. 5, no. 1, 1982.
"Eric Rohmer on Film Scripts and Film Plans," an interview with R. Hammond and J.-P. Pagliano, in *Literature/Film Quarterly* (Salisbury, Maryland), vol. 10, no. 4, October 1982.
Interview with A. Carbonnier and Joel Magny, in *Cinéma* (Paris), January 1984.
Interview with H. Niogret, and others, in *Positif* (Paris), November 1986.
Interview with Alain Philippon, in *Cahiers du Cinéma* (Paris), February 1987.

On ROHMER: books—

Mellen, Joan, *Women and Sexuality in the New Film*, New York, 1973.
Angeli, G., *Eric Rohmer*, Milan, 1979.
Estève, Michel, *Eric Rohmer 2*, Paris, 1986.
Magny, Joel, *Eric Rohmer*, Paris, 1986.
Crisp, C.G., *Realist and Moralist*, Bloomington, Indiana, 1988.

On ROHMER: articles—

"Eric Rohmer," in *Film* (London), Spring 1968.
Clarens, Carlos, "L'Amour Sage," in *Sight and Sound* (London), Winter 1969/70.
"Director of the Year," in *International Film Guide 1972*, London, 1971.
Nogueira, Rui, "Eric Rohmer: Choice and Chance," in *Sight and Sound* (London), Summer 1971.
Mellen, Joan, "The Moral Psychology of Rohmer's Tales," in *Cinema* (Beverly Hills), Fall 1971.
Amiel, M., and others, "Dossier-auteur: Eric Rohmer à la recherche de l'absolu," in *Cinéma* (Paris), February 1979.
Fieschi, J., and others, "Dossier: le cinéma d'Eric Rohmer," in *Cinématographe* (Paris), February 1979.
"*Pauline à la plage* Issue" of *Avant-Scène du Cinéma* (Paris), no. 310, 1983.
Borchardt, E., "Eric Rohmer's *Marquise of O* and the Theory of the German Novella," in *Literature/Film Quarterly* (Salisbury, Maryland), vol. 12, no. 2, April 1984.
Bergala, Alain, and Alain Philippon, "Eric Rohmer, la Grace et la Rigeur," in *Cahiers du Cinéma* (Paris), October 1984.
"Rohmer Issue" of *Avant-Scène du Cinéma* (Paris), January 1985.
"*Le Rayon Vert* Issue" of *Avant-Scène du Cinéma* (Paris), December 1986.
Pym, John, "Silly Girls," in *Sight and Sound* (London), Winter 1986/87.
Elia, M., "Les jeux de la liberté et du hasard dans les films d'Eric Rohmer," in *Séquences* (Montreal), August 1987.
Aumont, Jacques, "L'extraordinaire et le solide," in *Avant-Scène du Cinéma* (Paris), December 1987.
Mayne, Richard, "Still Waving, Not Drowning," in *Sight and Sound* (London), Summer 1990.
"Eric Rohmer: The Enlightenment's Last Gleaming," in *Monthly Film Bulletin* (London), July 1990.

*   *   *

By virtue of a tenure shared at *Cahiers du cinéma* during the 1950s and early 1960s, Eric Rohmer is usually classified with Truffaut, Godard, Chabrol, and Rivette as a member of the French New Wave. Yet, except for three early shorts made with Godard, Rohmer's films seem to share more with the traditional values of such directors as Renoir and Bresson than with the youthful flamboyance of his contemporaries. Much of

Eric Rohmer: *Ma Nuit chez Maud*

this divergence is owed to an accident of birth. Born Maurice Scherer at Tulle in 1920, Rohmer was at least ten years older than any of the other critic/filmmakers in the *Cahiers* group. By the time he arrived in Paris in 1948, he was an established teacher of literature at the lycée in Nancy and had published a novel, *Elizabeth* (1946), under the pseudonym Gilbert Cordier. When he joined the *Cahiers* staff in 1951 Rohmer had already spent three years as a film critic with such prestigious journals as *La Revue du cinéma* and Sartre's *Les Temps modernes*. Thus Rohmer's aesthetic preferences were more or less determined before he began writing for *Cahiers*.

Still the move proved decisive. At *Cahiers* he encountered an environment in which film critics and filmmaking were thought of as merely two aspects of the same activity. Consequently, the critics who wrote for *Cahiers* never doubted that they would become film directors. As it turned out, Rohmer was one of the first to realize this ambition. In 1951 he wrote and directed a short 16mm film called *Charlotte and Her Steak* in which Godard as the sole performer plays a young man who tries to seduce a pair of offscreen women. Two of his next three films were experiments in literary adaption. These inaugurated

his long association with Barbet Schroeder who produced or co-produced all of Rohmer's subsequent film projects.

In 1958 filmmaking within the *Cahiers* group was bustling. Rivette, Truffaut, and Chabrol were all shooting features. Rohmer, too, began shooting his first feature, *Sign of the Lion*. The result, however, would not be greeted with the same enthusiasm that was bestowed on Godard and Truffaut. Rohmer has always maintained that his films are not meant for a mass audience but rather for that small group of viewers who appreciate the less spectacular qualities of the film medium. Unfortunately, *Sign of the Lion* failed to find even this elite audience. And while Truffaut's *The 400 Blows* and Godard's *Breathless* were establishing the *Cahiers* group as a legitimate film force, it was not until 1963 that Rohmer was able to secure funding for a film of any length. That same year he ended his association with *Cahiers du cinéma*. The journal had for some time been moving away from the aesthetic policies of Bazin and towards a more leftist variety of criticism. Rohmer had always been viewed as something of a reactionary and was voted down as co-director. He chose to leave the magazine and devote his entire career to making films. At just this moment

Barbet Schroeder was able to find money for a short 16mm film.

While writing the scenario for *Suzanne's Profession* Rohmer conceived the master plan for a series of fictional films, each a variation on a single theme: a young man, on the verge of committing himself to one woman, by chance meets a second woman whose charms cause him to question his initial choice. His entire way of thinking, willing, desiring, that is to say, the very fabric of his moral life starts to unwind. The young man eventually cleaves to his original choice, his ideal woman against whom he measures all his other moral decisions, but the meeting with the second woman or, as is the case in *Claire's Knee*, a trinity of women, creates a breathing space for the young man, a parenthesis in his life for taking stock. The vacillations of the young man, who often functions as the film's narrator, comprise the major action of the six films known as the moral tales.

Rohmer recognizes the irony in his use of cinema, a medium which relies on objective, exterior images, to stage his interior moral dramas. But by effecting minute changes in the exterior landscape he expresses subtle alterations in his protagonist's interior drama. This explains why Rohmer pays such scrupulous attention to rendering surface detail. Each film in the Six Moral Tales was shot on the very location and at the exact time of year in which the story is set. Rohmer was forced to postpone the shooting of *My Night at Maud's* for an entire year so that Jean-Louis Trintignant would be available during the Christmas season, the moment when the fiction was scripted to begin. The painter, Daniel, in *La Collectioneuse* is played by Daniel Pommereulle, a painter in real life. The Marxist historian and the priest who preaches the sermon at the end of *My Night at Maud's* are, in real life, historian and priest. The female novelist of *Claire's Knee* is a novelist and the married couple of *Chloe in the Afternoon* are man and wife. Such attention to detail allowed Rohmer to realize an advance in the art of cinematic adaption with his next two films, *The Marquise of O* and *Perceval*.

As he entered the 1980s, Rohmer completed two films of a new series of moral tales which he calls "Parables." In contrast to the Six Moral Tales, the Parables are not played out on the interior landscape of a single character but rather engage an entire social milieu. In *The Aviator's Wife* a young postal clerk trails his mistress around Paris to spy on her affair with another man. During his peregrinations, he meets a young female student, loses track of his mistress, then decides he prefers the company of the young student only to discover her in the arms of another man. *The Perfect Marriage* chronicles the attempts of a young Parisian woman to persuade the man whom she had decided will make her a perfect husband that she will, in turn, make him the perfect wife. She discovers, too late, that he has been engaged to another woman all along.

Emerging from the crucible of the French New Wave, Rohmer has forged a style that combines the best qualities of Bresson and Renoir with distinctive traits of the Hollywood masters. And though he was never as flamboyant as Godard or Truffaut, Rohmer's appeal has proved much hardier. The international success that met *My Night at Maud's* and *The Marquise of O* has built a following that awaits the new set of moral dilemmas limned by each further installment of the Parables with eagerness and reverence.

—Dennis Nastav

ROMERO, George A.

American. Born in the Bronx, New York, 1940. Studied art, design and theater at Carnegie-Mellon Institute, Pittsburgh. Maker of short 8mm films, from 1954; actor/director in Pittsburgh, 1960s; directed first feature, 1968; established "Latent Image" to produce commercial/industrial films, early 1970s; worked extensively as TV director, 1970s; began collaboration with make-up artist Tom Savini on *Martin*, 1977; began association with writer Stephen King on *Creepshow*, 1982; executive producer, *Tales From the Dark Side*, for TV, 1983. Lives in Pittsburgh, Pennsylvania, U.S.A.

Films as Director:

1954/6 *The Man from the Meteor* (short); *Gorilla* (short); *Earthbottom* (short)
1958 *Curly* (short); *Slant* (short)
1960/62 *Expostulations* (short)
1968 *Night of the Living Dead* (*Night of the Flesh Eaters*) (+ co-sc, ph, ed)
1972 *There's Always Vanilla* (*The Affair*) (+ ph)
1973 *Hungry Wives* (*Jack's Wife. Season of the Witch*) (+ sc, ph, ed); *The Crazies* (*Code Name: Trixie*) (+ sc, ed)
1977 *Martin* (+ sc, ed)
1978 *Zombies* (*Dawn of the Dead*) (+ sc, co-ed, role as TV director)
1981 *Knightriders* (+ sc, co-ed)
1982 *Creepshow* (+ co-ed)
1985 *Day of the Dead* (+ sc)
1988 *Monkey Shines* (+ sc)
1990 *Due occhi diabolici* (+ sc); *Dark Half* (+ sc, pr)

Other Films:

1987 *Creepshow 2* (Gornick) (sc)
1990 *Night of the Living Dead* (Savini) (sc); *Tales from the Dark Side—The Movie* (Harrison) (sc)

Publications:

By ROMERO: books—

Martin (novelization, with Susanna Sparrow), New York, 1977.
Dawn of the Dead (novelization, with Susanna Sparrow), New York, 1979.

By ROMERO: articles—

"Filming *Night of the Living Dead*," an interview with A.B. Block, in *Filmmakers Newsletter* (Ward Hill, Massachusetts), January 1972.
"George Romero from *Night of the Living Dead* to *The Crazies*," in *Inter/View* (New York), April 1973.
Interview with D. Chase, in *Millimeter* (New York), October 1979.
"The McDonaldization of America," an interview with J. Hanners and H. Kloman, in *Film Criticism* (Edinboro, Pennsylvania), Fall 1982.

On ROMERO: books—

McCarty, John, *Splatter Movies: Breaking the Last Taboo*, New York, 1981.
Hoberman, Jay, and Jonathan Rosenbaum, *Midnight Movies*, New York, 1983.
Wood, Robin, *Hollywood From Vietnam to Reagan*, New York, 1986.
Gagne, Paul R., *"The Zombies That Ate Pittsburgh": The Films of George A. Romero*, New York, 1987.
Newman, Kim, *Nightmare Movies: A Critical History of the Horror Film From 1968*, London, 1988.

On ROMERO: articles—

McCollough, P., "A Pittsburgh Horror Story," in *Take One* (Montreal), November 1974.

George A. Romero

Stewart, Robert M., "George Romero: Spawn of EC," in *Monthly Film Bulletin* (London), February 1980.

Vernieri, J., "A Day with the Dead," in *Film Comment* (New York), May/June 1985.

"Twilight's Last Gleaming: George A. Romero," in *Monthly Film Bulletin* (London), February 1990.

* * *

Between 1968 and 1979, Romero produced a body of work comparable in distinction to that of Larry Cohen in the same period: both are centered in the horror genre, both extremely uneven, but achieve in certain instances an impressive intensity and concentration. Above all, both are rooted in (and appear significantly dependent upon) the disturbances in American society during that period.

Romero's first film, *Night of the Living Dead*, is a landmark in the evolution of the American horror film. It proved decisively that significant and commercially successful work in that genre could be produced outside Hollywood, on a low budget, independent of major studios. Thematically, it drew together the twin attitudes that underlie and motivate what must now be regarded as the golden age of horror film: general disillusionment with authority/government (this is the period of Vietnam), and specific disillusionment with the institution whereby authority/domination structures are transmitted, the patriarchal nuclear family. The film opens with a brother and sister driving to a remote country graveyard over which flies the American flag; they are reluctantly honoring a dead father neither of them cares about, on behalf of an invalid mother. They bicker, brother taunts sister in a repetition of childhood behavior patterns, sister responds with bitterness and helpless frustration; the first zombie lurches forward to attack sister and kill brother, the emanation of family tensions and the embodiment of the "living dead" that is the legacy of the American past. The film follows through from this premise with exemplary rigor, paralleling the zombies and the authorities as equally mindless and destructive, flouting all generic expectations (the young couple, traditionally the guarantee of the perpetuation of the family, are killed and devoured, the hero is mistaken for a zombie and casually shot down by the sheriff's posse), tracing the progress of the nuclear family's self-destruction, as zombie-daughter kills and eats her parents and "dead" brother leads the final assault on his sister.

The sequel, *Dawn of the Dead*, is even more remarkable, and among the few outstanding American films of the 1970s. Here the zombies are associated with entrapment in consumer-capitalism, from whose structures and characteristic relationship patterns the surviving humans must learn to extricate themselves or succumb to the "living dead." The heroine, Fran, ultimately rejects marriage (clearly depicted as an institution for the oppression of women); her lover—a traditional male needing the support of a subordinated woman for the confirmation of his identity—becomes a zombie. The ending of the film centers on two emblems of male authority: the surviving male surrenders his rifle to the zombies while Fran (cast earlier as helpless and dependent) flies the helicopter for their escape. The two have become mutually supportive but no future love-relationship is suggested. Fran is pregnant. They fly off to an uncertain destination and a precarious future, in which new male/female relationships must be constructed.

Romero's achievement so far is centered on those two films, though around them are grouped several related early works which are more distinguished than their neglect suggests. *The Crazies* takes up concerns from *Night of the Living Dead* and tentatively anticipates the more forward-looking potential of *Dawn of the Dead*; *Jack's Wife* and *Martin* are a closely linked pair of minor works concerned with their eponymous protagonists' striving for identity and dignity in a debased, materialistic world that offers them no recognition or autonomy, and their flight into roles (witch, vampire respectively) that offer false prestige and worse entrapment.

Since *Dawn of the Dead* Romero's career seems to have lost its sense of direction. Its powerful radical impulse, rooted in the Vietnam/Watergate syndrome of disillusionment, protest and subversion, did not sustain itself into the Reagan era. One may feel some sympathy (though little admiration) for the attempt in *Knight Riders* to convey liberal attitudes (and, regrettably, liberal platitudes) to the youth audience, but the film remains essentially a remake of *Alice's Restaurant*, ten years too late and with all the complexities ironed out. Nothing, however, had prepared one for *Creep Show*, a five-part anthology film made in collaboration with Stephen King, virtually indistinguishable from the British Amicus horror films of the 1970s: the same pointlessness, the same moral squalor: nasty people doing nasty things to other nasty people.

—Robin Wood

ROOS, Jørgen.

Danish. Born in Gilleleje, 14 August 1922. Married Naomi Silberstein, 1957. Cameraman, 1939–47; founder, Copenhagen film club with painter Albert Mertz; scriptwriter, director and cameraman on documentaries, from 1947; co-founder, the Association of Danish Film Directors, 1956. Recipient: Silver Bear, Berlin Festival, for *Knud*, 1966. Address: Ved Amagerport 5, DK-2300 Copenhagen S, Denmark.

Films as Director:

(documentaries unless indicated)

1942 *Flugten* (*The Flight*) (co-d with Albert Mertz)
1943 *Kaerlighed paa Rulleskøjter* (co-d with Mertz); *Hjertetyven* (*Thief of Hearts*) (co-d with Mertz)
1944 *Richard Mortensens bevaegelige Maleri*; *Historien om en Mand* (*Story of a Man*) (co-d with Mertz) (unfinished)
1947 *Paa Besøg hos Kong Tingeling* (co-d with Mertz); *Goddag Dyr!* (co-d with Mertz); *Isen brydes* (co-d); *Johannes V. Jensen*; *Opus 1*; *Reflexfilm*
1948 *Mikkel*
1949 *Paris på to måder*; *Jean Cocteau*; *Tristan Tzara, dadaismens fader*; *Det definitive afslag på anmodningen om et kys* (co-d)
1950 *Spiste horisonter* (co-d); *Johannes Jørgensen i Assisi*; *Shakespeare og Kronborg* (*Hamlet's Castle*)
1951 *Historien om et slot, J.F. Willumsen*
1952 *Den strømlinjede gris*; *Slum*; *Feriebørn*
1953 *Lyset i natten*; *Spaedbarnet*; *The Newborn* (*Goddag børn*); *Skyldig—ikke skyldig*
1954 *Kalkmalerier*; *Inge bliver voksen*; *Avisen*; *Martin Andersen Nexos sidste rejse*; *Johannes Jørgensen i Svendborg*
1955 *Mit livs eventyr* (*My Life Story*)
1956 *Sølv*
1957 *Ellehammer*; *Johannes Larsen*
1958 *Magie du diamant* (*Magic of the Diamond*); *6-dagesløbet* (*The Six Days*) (feature)
1959 *Friluft* (*Pure Air*)
1960 *En by ved navn København* (*A City Called Copenhagen*); *Danish Design*; *Staphylokok-faren*
1961 *Føroyar Faerøerne*; *Hamburg*
1962 *Vi haenger i en tråd*
1963 *Oslo*
1965 *Støj*
1966 *Carl Th. Dreyer*; *Knud*; *Sisimiut*

Jørgen Roos

1967	*En fangerfamilie i Thuledistriktet; 17 minutter Grønland; Grønlandske dialektoptagelser og trommedanse fra Thuledistriktet; Et år med Henry*
1968	*Ultima Thule*
1969	*Det er tilladt at vaere åndssvag*
1970	*Kaláliuvit (Er du grønlaender)*
1971	*Andersens hemmelighed*
1972	*Huse til mennesker; Udflytterne; To maend i ødemarken; Ulrik fortaeller en historie*
1974	*I den store pyramide; J. Th. Arnfred*
1975	*Andersen hos fotografen*
1977	*14 dage i jernalderen; Monarki og demokrati*
1978	*Carl Nielsen 1865–1931*
1979	*Nuuk 250 år*
1980	*Slaedepatruljen Sirius; Grønland*
1982	*Knud Rasmussens mindeekspedition til Kap Seddon*
1984	*Lille Cirkus; De unge gamle*
1985	*Harald Sæverud—1 en alder af 88 år*
1988	*Chr. IV—Tegselver icke mig*
1989	*Den levende virkelighed; Victor Brockdorff—en portrætskitse*

Other Film:

1971	*Er i bange (Are You Afraid)* (Carlsen) (ph)

*   *   *

Jørgen Roos is the unrivalled master of the Danish documentary film, having worked for more than 40 years in this field. He has won international recognition and has received prizes at international short film festivals. Only once has he tried to direct a feature film.

He started out as a cameraman, taught by his brother, Karl Roos, and Theodor Christensen, the pioneer of the documentary film in Denmark. Karl Roos and Theodor Christensen were both active filmmakers, and also eminent film theoreticians. Christensen was influenced by the British documentary movement and considered himself a committed documentary filmmaker. Jørgen Roos was inspired by those two and he acquired a wide knowledge of the theory and the history of cinema. After having worked as a cameraman, he made his first experimental film in 1942 with the painter Albert Mertz, and this couple created the most interesting and original Danish avant-garde films of the 1940s. Since 1952 Jørgen Roos has made numerous documentaries for governmental institutions and private companies. Besides these commissioned films he has worked on projects of his own, and in recent years he has had his own production company.

To the commissioned film Jørgen Roos has brought a fresh and unconventional approach, and his way of solving the official tasks is often witty, surprising, and keen. His films are always one-man projects. He writes his own scripts, directs, and is often cameraman. And he is always the editor, because it is in the cutting room that he gives his films their definitive and personal form. Jørgen Roos is superior in the short form: his editing is rhythmical, and his films have a fascinating, fast-moving drive. He likes to tease, to find unusual points of view, and he has an eye for the curious. His brilliant technique however, can lead him into the superficial.

In 1955 he made one of his best films, *Mit livs eventyr*, about Hans Andersen. In this film he brought the iconographic technique to perfection, and he used it in later films. One of his most popular and widely known films is *A City Called Copenhagen* from 1960, an untraditional and ironic tourist film. Jørgen Roos was asked to make similar city portraits of Hamburg and Oslo, and has portrayed Danish personalities such as Nobel laureate Johannes V. Jensen, Carl Th. Dreyer, Greenland explorer Knud Rasmussen, and composer Carl Nielsen. In the last 20 or so years Jørgen Roos has shown a special inter-

est in Greenland. He has lost his heart to this exceptional country and he has explored both the old and the new Greenland in many films. The cool and detached view, which was characteristic of Jørgen Roos's films, has been replaced by a deep-felt commitment to the land which he, more than anyone else, has brought to the screen.

—Ib Monty

———

ROSI, Francesco.

Italian. Born in Naples, 15 November 1922. Educated in law, Naples University. Military service, 1942. Radio journalist in Naples, early 1940s; worked in theatre as actor, stage designer, and assistant director, Rome, from 1946; assistant director and script collaborator, through 1956, also dubbing director for Italian versions of foreign films; directed first film, *La sfida*, 1957. Recipient: Special Jury Prize, Venice Festival, for *La sfida*, 1958; Silver Bear for Best Direction, Berlin Festival, for *Salvatore Giuliano*, 1963; Golden Lion, Venice Festival, for *Le mani sulla città*, 1963.

Films as Director and Co-Scriptwriter:

1958	*La sfida (The Challenge)*
1959	*I magliari*
1961	**Salvatore Giuliano**
1963	*Le mani sulla città (Hands Over the City)*
1965	*Il momento della verità (The Moment of Truth)* (co-d)
1967	*C'era una volta (More than a Miracle)*
1970	*Uomini contro*
1972	*Il caso Mattei (The Mattei Affair)*
1973	*A proposito Lucky Luciano (Lucky Luciano)*
1976	*Cadaveri eccelenti (Illustrious Corpses)*
1979	*Cristo si è fermato a Eboli (Christ Stopped at Eboli)*
1981	*Tre fratelli (Three Brothers)*
1984	*Carmen (Bizet's Carmen)*
1988	*Cronaca di una morte annunciata (Chronicle of a Death Foretold)*
1990	*Dimenticare Palermo*

Other Films:

1947	**La terra trema** (Visconti) (asst d)
1949	*La domenica d'agosto* (Emmer) (asst d)
1950	*Tormento* (Matarazzo) (asst d)
1951	*I figli di nessuno* (Matarazzo) (asst d); *Parigi e sempre parigi* (Emmer) (asst d, co-sc); *Bellissima* (Visconti) (asst, co-sc)
1952	*Camicie Rosse* (supervised post-production after director Goffredo Alessandri abandoned project); *I vinti* (Antonioni) (asst d); *Processo alla città* (Zampa) (sc)
1954	*Carosello Napoletano* (Giannini) (asst d); *Proibito* (Monicelli) (asst d); *Senso* (Visconti) (asst d)
1955	*Racconti Romani* (Franciolini) (co-sc)
1956	*Il bigamo* (Emmer) (asst d, co-sc)

Publications:

By ROSI: articles—

Interview with Gideon Bachmann, in *Film Quarterly* (Berkeley), Spring 1965.
"Moments of truth," an interview with John Lane, in *Films and Filming* (London), September 1970.

Interviews with Michel Ciment, in *Positif* (Paris), January 1974 and February 1979.
Interview with Gary Crowdus, in *Cineaste* (New York), vol. 7, no. 1, 1975.
Interviews in *Sight and Sound* (London), Summer 1976 and Winter 1981/82.
"Un Débat d'idées, de mentalités," de moralités," in *Avant-Scéne du Cinéma* (Paris), May 1976.
"Sono lo psicologo del film e non del personaggio," an interview with F. Durazzo Baker, in *Cinema Nuovo*, (Bari), October 1979.
"Personalizing Political Issues," an interview with Gary Crowdus, in *Cineaste* (New York), vol. 12, no. 2, 1982.
Interview with M. Kimmel, in *Films in Review* (New York), May 1982.
"Chronicle of a Film Foretold," an interview with Michel Ciment, in *Sight and Sound* (London), Winter 1986/87.
Interview with Michel Ciment, in *Positif* (Paris), March 1990.

On ROSI: books—

Michalczyk, John J., *The Italian Political Filmmakers*, Cranbury, New Jersey, 1986.
Ciment, Michel, editor, *Le Dossier Rosi*, Paris, 1987.

On ROSI: articles—

Lane, John, "A Neapolitan Eisenstein," in *Films and Filming* (London), August 1963.
Rosi Section of *Image et Son* (Paris), June/July 1976.
Alemanno, R., "Da Rosi a Petri todo modo dentro il contesto," in *Cinema Nuovo* (Bari), July/August 1976.
Rosi Section of *Thousand Eyes* (New York), November 1976.
Rosi Section of *Positif* (Paris), May 1980.
"Francesco Rosi Issue" of *Cinéma* (Zurich), vol. 28, no. 2, 1982.
"*Tre fratelli* Issue" of *Avant-Scène du Cinéma* (Paris), 1 June 1982.
Ciment, Michel, "Rosi in a New Key," in *American Film* (Washington, D.C.), September 1984.
Lennon, Peter, "A 'Cinema Fanatic' with a Social Conscience," in *Listener* (London), 14 May 1987.
Rosi Sections of *Positif* (Paris), May and June 1987.

* * *

The films of Francesco Rosi stand as an urgent riposte to any proposal of aesthetic puritanism as a *sine qua non* of engaged filmmaking. From *Salvatore Giuliano* to *Illustrious Corpses* and *Chronicle of a Death Foretold*, he uses a mobilisation of the aesthetic potential of the cinema not to decorate his tales of corruption, complicity and death, but to illuminate and interrogate the reverberations these events cause. If one quality were to be isolated as especially distinctive and characteristic it would have to be the sense of intellectual passion, of direction propelled by an impassioned sense of inquiry. This can be true in a quite literal way in *Salvatore Giuliano* in which any "suspense" accruing to Giuliano's death is put aside in favour of a search for another kind of knowledge, and *The Mattei Affair*, in which the soundtrack amasses evidence which is presented virtually in opposition to the images before us, or, in a more metaphoric sense, *Christ Stopped at Eboli* represents an inquiry into the social conditions of the South of Italy.

Rosi traces the evolution of his style to his early experience as an assistant on Rosselini's *Terra Trema*, where he learnt the value of immediacy, improvisation and the use of non-professional performers. It was a mode of filmmaking that suited the working through of concerns found within a particular current in Italian thought, which finds expression in the paintings and writings of Carlo Levi and the writing of Leonardo Sciascia, both of whom are concerned with the problem of the South and both of whose work Rosi has adapted for the screen. It is a current that also finds political expression in the work of Antonio Gamsci. Rosi's films are perhaps above all the films of an industrialising Italy, the Italy of Fiat, that exists dialectically with that of the peasant South.

Throughout his work there is an abiding interest in the social conditions in which individuals live their lives and their expression at the public or civic level, licit or illicit. Concern with organised crime and its social roots—though free from any taint of sociologizing—appears as a major thread through films as diverse as *Salvatore Giuliano*, *Hands Over the City*, *The Mattei Affair*, *Lucky Luciano* and *Chronicle of a Death Foretold*. Although Rosi uses the appurtenances of the thriller or the gangster film (in *Lucky Luciano*, for instance) his interests, as Michel Ciment has pointed out, are not at all with whodunnit but with what the crime reveals about the social context of individual lives. *Lucky Luciano* for example, is not (unlike *The Godfather*) in the business of creating monsters but of creating a way of understanding the men who are thus mythologised. It is a tribute to Rosi's virtuosity and commitment that the trajectory he describes is not a whit less exciting.

He may examine the mesh of the individual and his context from the point-of-view of the public sphere (*Illustrious Corpses*) or the private (*Three Brothers* or *Christ Stopped at Eboli*). The issue might be the ruthless mechanics of market forces in *Hands Over the City*, or the process whereby the Mafia is set in place in *The Mattei Affair*. If his most recent films may be less wholly satisfying than, say, the urgent definitiveness of *Hands Over the City* or as rigorously aesthetic as *Illustrious Corpses*, they still reveal a rare and vital intellectual committment to cinema as a platform for debate and testimony.

—Verina Glaessner

ROSSELLINI, Roberto.

Italian. Born in Rome, 8 May 1906. Married 1) Marcella de Marquis (marriage annulled), two children; 2) actress Ingrid Bergman, 1950 (divorced), three children, including actress Isabella; 3) screenwriter Somali Das Gupta (divorced), one son. Worked on films, in dubbing and sound effects, then as editor, from 1934; directed first feature, *La Nave bianca*, 1940; technical director in official film industry, while simultaneously shooting documentary footage of Italian resistance fighters, 1940–45; accepted offer from Howard Hughes to make films for RKO with Ingrid Bergman in Hollywood, 1946; apparently fell out of public favour over scandal surrounding relationships with Bergman and later Das Gupta; TV director of documentaries, 1960s. *Died 4 June 1977.*

Films as Director:

1936 *Daphne* (+ sc)
1938 *Prelude à l'apres-midi d'une faune* (+ sc)
1939 *Fantasia sottomarina* (+ sc); *Il tacchino prepotente* (+ sc); *La vispa Teresa* (+ sc)
1941 *Il Ruscello di Ripasottile* (+ sc); *La nave bianca* (+ co-sc)
1942 *Un pilota ritorna* (+ co-sc); *I tre aquilotta* (uncredited collaboration)
1943 *L'uomo della croce* (+ co-sc); *L'invasore* (+ supervised production, sc); *Desiderio* (+ co-sc) (confiscated by police and finished by Marcello Pagliero in 1946)
1945 *Roma, città aperta* (*Rome, Open City*) (+ co-sc)
1946 *Paisà* (*Paisan*) (+ co-sc, pr)
1947 *Germania, anno zero* (*Germany, Year Zero*) (+ co-sc)
1948 *L'amore* (*Woman, Ways of Love* (+ sc); *Il miracolo* (*The Miracle*) (+ co-sc); *La macchina ammazzacattivi* (+ co-sc, pr)
1949 *Stromboli, terra di dio* (*Stromboli*) (+ co-sc, pr)

1950 *Francesco—giullare di Dio* (*Flowers of St. Francis*) (+ co-sc)
1952 "L'Invidia" episode of *I sette peccati capitali* (*The Seven Deadly Sins*) (+ co-sc); *Europa '51* (*The Greatest Love*) (+ co-sc)
1953 *Dov'è la libertà* (+ co-sc); *Viaggio in Italia* (**Voyage to Italy. Strangers. The Lonely Woman**) (+ co-sc); "Ingrid Bergman" episode of *Siamo donne*
1954 "Napoli '43" episode of *Amori di mezzo secolo* (+ sc); *Giovanna d'Arco al rogo* (*Joan of Arc at the Stake*) (+ sc); *Die Angst* (*Le Paura. Fear*); *Orient Express* (+ sc, production supervision)
1958 *L'India vista da Rossellini* (ten episodes) (+ sc, pr); *India* (+ co-sc)
1959 *Il Generale della Rovere* (+ co-sc)
1960 *Era notte a Roma* (+ co-sc); *Viva l'Italia* (+ co-sc)
1961 *Vanina Vanini* (*The Betrayer*) (+ co-sc); *Torino nei centi'anni*; *Benito Mussolini* (*Blood on the Balcony*) (+ sc, production supervision)
1962 *Anima nera* (+ sc); "Illibatezza" episode of *Rogopag* (+ sc)
1966 *La Prise de pouvoir par Louis XIV* (*The Rise of Louis XIV*)
1967 *Idea di un'isola* (+ pr, sc)
1968 *Atti degli apostoli* (co-d, co-sc, ed)
1970 *Socrate* (*Socrates*) (+ co-sc, ed)
1972 *Agostino di Ippona*
1975 *Blaise Pascal*; *Anno uno*
1978 *Il Messia* (*The Messiah*) (+ co-sc)

Other Films:

1938 *Luciano Serra, pilota* (sc)
1963 *Le carabiniere* (co-sc)
1964 *L'eta del ferro* (sc, pr)
1967 *La lotta dell'uomo per la sua sopravvivenza* (sc, pr)

Publications:

By ROSSELLINI: books—

Era notte a Roma, with others, Bologna, 1961.
Le Cinéma révélé, edited by Alain Bergala, Paris, 1984.
Il mio metodo: Scritti e intervisti, edited by Adriano Apra, Venice, 1987.
Quasi un autobiografie, Milan, 1987.

By ROSSELLINI: articles—

"*Paisà*: Sixth Sketch," with others, in *Bianco e Nero* (Rome), October 1947.
Interview with Francis Koval, in *Sight and Sound* (London), February 1951.
"Coloquio sul neo-realismo," with Mario Verdone, in *Bianco e Nero* (Rome), February 1952.
Interview with Maurice Schèrer and François Truffaut, in *Cahiers du Cinéma* (Paris), July 1954.
"Dix ans de cinéma," in *Cahiers du Cinéma* (Paris), August/September and November 1955, and January 1956.
"Cinema and Television: Interview," with André Bazin, in *Sight and Sound* (London), Winter 1958/59.
"Censure et culture," in *Cinéma* (Paris), October 1961.
"Conversazione sulla cultura e sul cinema," in *Filmcritica* (Rome), March 1963.
"Intervista con Roberto Rossellini," with Adriano Aprá and Maurizio Ponzi, in *Filmcritica* (Rome), April/May 1965.
Interview with Jean Collet and Claude-Jean Philippe, in *Cahiers du Cinéma* (Paris), September 1966.
"Conversazione con Roberto Rossellini," with Michele Mancin, Renato Tomasino, and Lello Maiello, in *Filmcritica* (Rome), August 1968.
"La decisione di Isa," in *Bianco e Nero* (Rome), January/March 1985.

On ROSSELLINI: books—

Hovald, Patrice, *Roberto Rossellini*, Paris, 1958.
Steele, Joseph Henry, *Ingrid Bergman: An Intimate Portrait*, New York, 1959.

Mida, Massimo, *Roberto Rossellini*, Parma, 1961.
Verdone, Mario, *Roberto Rossellini*, Paris, 1963.
Guarner, José Luis, *Roberto Rossellini*, translated by Elizabeth Cameron, New York, 1970.
Baldelli, Pio, *Roberto Rossellini*, Rome, 1972.
Menon, Gianni, *Dibattio su Rossellini*, Rome, 1972.
Rondolino, Gianni, *Roberto Rossellini*, Florence, 1974.
Ranvaud, Don, *Roberto Rossellini*, London, 1981.
Cahiers du Cinéma 1, The 1950s: Neo-Realism, Hollywood, New Wave, edited by Jim Hillier, London, 1985.
Serceau, Michel, *Roberto Rossellini*, Paris, 1986.
Aprà, Adriano, *Rosselliniana*, Rome, 1987.
Brunette, Peter, *Roberto Rossellini*, Oxford, 1987.
Gansera, Rainer, and others, *Roberto Rossellini*, Munich, 1987.
Rossi, Patrizio, *Roberto Rossellini: A Guide to References and Resources*, Boston, 1988.
Bergala, Alain, and Jean Narboni, editors, *Roberto Rossellini*, Paris, 1990.

On ROSSELLINI: articles—

Venturi, Lauro, "Roberto Rossellini," in *Hollywood Quarterly*, Fall 1949.
Harcourt-Smith, Simon, "The Stature of Rossellini," in *Sight and Sound* (London), April 1950.
Truffaut, François, "Rossellini," in *Arts* (Paris), January 1955.
Rivette, Jacques, "Lettre sur Rossellini," in *Cahiers du Cinéma* (Paris), May 1955.
Fieschi, Jean-André, "Dov'e Rossellini?," in *Cahiers du Cinéma* (Paris), May 1962.
Sarris, Andrew, "Rossellini Rediscovered," in *Film Culture* (New York), no. 32, 1964.
Casty, Alan, "The Achievement of Roberto Rossellini," in *Film Comment* (New York), Fall 1964.
Aprà, Adriano, "Le nouvel âge de Rossellini," in *Cahiers du Cinéma* (Paris), August 1965.
"*Roma, città aperta* Issue" of *Avant-Scène du Cinéma* (Paris), 1971.
MacBean, J.R., "Rossellini's Materialist Mise-en-Scene," in *Film Quarterly* (Berkeley), Winter 1971/72.
"Rossellini Issue" of *Screen* (London), Winter 1973/74.
Norman, L., "Rossellini's Case Histories for Moral Education," in *Film Quarterly* (Berkeley), Summer 1974.
Wood, Robin, "Rossellini," in *Film Comment* (New York), July/August 1974.
"Rossellini Issue" of *Filmcritica* (Rome), May/June 1976.
Walsh, M., "*Rome, Open City: The Rise to Power of Louis XIV*. Re-evaluating Rossellini," in *Jump Cut* (Chicago), no. 15, 1977.
Hughes, J., "In Memoriam: Roberto Rossellini," in *Film Comment* (New York), July/August 1977.
Lawton, H., "Rossellini's Didactic Cinema," in *Sight and Sound* (London), Autumn 1978.
Ranvaud, Don, "Documentary and Dullness: Rossellini According to the British Critic," in *Monthly Film Bulletin* (London), February 1981.
Brunette, Peter, "Rossellini and Cinematic Realism," in *Cinema Journal* (Champaign, Illinois), Fall 1985.
"*Viaggio in Italia* Issue" of *Avant-Scène du Cinéma* (Paris), June 1987.
Tournès, A., "Rossellini: Le courage d'être humblement un homme," in *Jeune Cinéma* (Paris), January/February 1988.
Gallagher, Tag, "Rossellini, Neo-Realism, and Croce," in *Film History* (Philadelphia), vol. 2, no. 1, 1988.
Truffaut, François, and others, "Roberto Rossellini," in *Cahiers du Cinéma* (Paris), July/August 1988.

* * *

Roberto Rossellini has been so closely identified with the rise of the postwar Italian style of filmmaking known as neo-realism that it would be a simple matter to neatly pigeonhole him as merely a practitioner of that technique and nothing more. So influential has that movement been that the achievement embodied in just three of his films, *Roma, città aperta*, *Paisà*, and *Germania, anno zero*, would be enough to secure the director a major place in film history. However, to simply

Roberto Rossellini (left) on the set of *Era notte a Roma*

label Rossellini a neorealist is to drastically undervalue his contribution to the thematic aspects of his art.

At its most basic level, his dominant concern appears to be a preoccupation with the importance of the individual within various aspects of the social context that emerged from the ashes of World War II. In his early films, which a number of historians have simplistically termed fascist, his concern for the individual was not balanced by an awareness of their social context. Thus, a film like his first feature, *La nave bianca*, while portraying its sailors and hospital personnel as sensitive and caring, ignores their ideological and political milieu. It is *Roma, città aperta*, despite its carry-over of the director's penchant for melodrama, that is properly considered Rossellini's "rite of passage" into the midst of the complex social issues confronting the individual in post-war Europe. The crude conditions under which it was shot, its authentic appearance, and certain other naturalistic touches lent it an air of newsreel-like veracity, but its raw power was derived almost entirely from the individuals that Rossellini placed within this atmospheric context. With the exception of Anna Magnani and Aldo Fabrizi, the cast was made up of non-professionals who were so convincing that the effect upon viewers was electric. Many were certain that what they were viewing must have been filmed as it was actually occurring.

Despite legends about Rossellini's neo-realistic style having arisen out of the scarcities and adverse shooting conditions immediately after the war, the director had undoubtedly begun to conceive the style as early as his aborted *Desiderio* of 1943, a small-scale forerunner of neo-realism which Rossellini dropped in mid-shooting. Certainly, he continued the style in *Paisà* and *Germania anno zero*, the remaining parts of his war trilogy. In both of these, he delineates the debilitating effects of war's aftermath on the psyche of modern man. The latter film was a particularly powerful statement on the effect of Nazi ideology on the mind of a young boy, simultaneously criticizing the failure of traditional social institutions like the church to counter fascism's corrupting influence.

The Rossellini films of the 1950s shed many of the director's neo-realistic trappings and in doing so he shifted his emphasis somewhat to the spiritual aspects of man, revealing the instability of life and of human relationships. *Stromboli, Europa '51, Voyage to Italy*, and *La paura* reflect a quest for a transcendent truth akin to the secular saintliness achieved by the priest in *Open City*. In the 1950s films, however, his style floated unobtrusively between involvement and contemplation. This is particularly obvious in his films with Ingrid Bergman but best exemplified by *Voyage to Italy* with its leisurely-paced questioning of the very meaning of life. Every character in the film is ultimately in search of his soul. What little action there is has relatively little importance since most of the character development is an out-growth of spiritual aspirations rather than a reaction to events. In this sense, its structure resembled the kind of neo-realism practiced by De Sica in *Umberto D*, without its excessively emotional overtones and yet reaffirming Rossellini's concern for his fellow men and for Italy. At the same time, through his restriction of incident, he shapes the viewer's empathy for his characters by allowing the viewer to participate in the film only to the extent of being companion to the various characters. The audience is free to intellectually wander away from the story, which it undoubtedly does, only to find its involvement in the character's spiritual development unchanged since its sympathy is not based upon the physical actions of a plot.

Such an intertwining of empathetic involvement of sorts with a contemplative detachment carried over into Rossellini's historical films of the 1960s and 1970s. His deliberately obtrusive use of zoom lenses created in the viewer of such films as *Viva l'Italia* and *Agostino di Ippona* a delicate distancing and a constant but subtle awareness that the director's point of view was inescapable. Such managing of the viewers' consciousness of the historical medium turns his characters into identifiable human beings who, though involving our senses and our emotions, can still be scrutinized from a relatively detached vantage point.

This, then, is the seeming contradiction central to Rossellini's entire body of work. As most precisely exemplified in his early, pure neo-realistic films, his camera is relentlessly fixed on the physical aspects of the world around us. Yet, as defined by his later works which both retain and modify much of this

temporal focus, the director is also trying to capture within the same lens an unseen and spiritual landscape. Thus, the one constant within all of his films must inevitably remain his concern for fundamental human values and aspirations, whether they are viewed with the anger and immediacy of a *Roma, città aperta* or the detachment of a *Viaggio in Italia*.

—Stephen L. Hanson

ROSSEN, Robert.

American. Born Robert Rosen in New York City, 16 March 1908. Attended New York University. Married Sue Siegal, 1954, three children. Staged plays for Washington Square Players, later the Theater Guild, 1920s; actor, stage manager, and director in New York City, 1930–35; writer under contract to Mervyn LeRoy and Warner Bros., 1936–45; member of Communist Party in Hollywood, 1937–45; directed first fea-

Robert Rossen

ture, *Johnny O'Clock*, 1947; subpoenaed by House Un-American Activities Committee (HUAC), hearing suspended after arrest of Hollywood 10, 1947; produced first film, 1949; blacklisted after refusing to cooperate when called again to testify before HUAC, 1951–53; allowed to work again after naming names, 1953. Recipient: Best Direction, New York Film Critics, for *The Hustler*, 1961. *Died 18 February 1966.*

Films as Director:

1947   *Johnny O'Clock* (+ sc); *Body and Soul*
1949   **All the King's Men** (+ sc, pr)
1951   *The Brave Bulls* (+ pr)
1955   *Mambo* (+ co-sc)
1956   *Alexander the Great* (+ sc, pr)
1957   *Island in the Sun*
1959   *They Came to Cordura* (+ co-sc)
1961   *The Hustler* (+ co-sc, pr)
1964   *Lilith* (+ co-sc, pr)

Other Films:

1937   *Marked Woman* (Bacon) (co-sc); *They Won't Forget* (LeRoy) (co-sc)
1938   *Racket Busters* (co-sc)
1939   *Dust Be My Destiny* (sc); *The Roaring Twenties* (Walsh) (co-sc)
1940   *A Child is Born* (Bacon) (sc)
1941   *Blues in the Night* (Litvak) (sc); *The Sea Wolf* (Curtiz) (sc); *Out of the Fog* (Litvak) (co-sc)
1943   *Edge of Darkness* (Milestone) (sc)
1946   *A Walk in the Sun* (Milestone) (sc); *The Strange Love of Martha Ivers* (Milestone) (sc)
1947   *Desert Fury* (sc)
1949   *The Undercover Man* (pr)

Publications:

By ROSSEN: articles—

"The Face of Independence," in *Films and Filming (London), August 1962.*
"Lessons Learned in Combat: Interview," with Jean-Louis Noames, in *Cahiers du Cinéma in English* (New York), January 1967.

On ROSSEN: books—

Hearings Before the Committee on Un-American Activities, House of Representatives, 1953 Volume, Washington, D.C., 1953.
Casty, Alan, *The Films of Robert Rossen*, New York, 1969.

On ROSSEN: articles—

"Rossen Issue" of *Films in Review* (New York), June/July 1962.
Cohen, Saul, "Robert Rossen and the Filming of *Lilith*," in *Film Comment* (New York), Spring 1965.
Casty, Alan, "The Films of Robert Rossen," in *Film Quarterly* (Berkeley), Winter 1966/67.
"Rossen Issue" of *Cahiers du Cinéma in English* (New York), January 1967.
Casty, Alan, "Robert Rossen," in *Cinema* (Beverly Hills), Fall 1968.
Dark, C. "Reflections of Robert Rossen," in *Cinema* (London), August 1970.
Wald, M., "Robert Rossen," in *Films in Review* (New York), August/September 1972.
Neve, Brian, "The Screenwriter and the Social Problem Film, 1936–38: The Case of Robert Rossen at Warner Brothers," in *Film and History* (Newark, New Jersey), February 1984.
Combs, Richard, "The Beginner's Rossen," in *Monthly Film Bulletin* (London), January 1986.
Nolletti, Arthur, "The Fissure in the Spider Web: A Reading of Rossen's *Lilith*," in *Film Criticism* (Meadville, Pennsylvania), vol. 11, no. 1/2, 1987.

*   *   *

Robert Rossen died as he was beginning to regain a prominent position in the cinema, his premature death leaving us with a final film which pointed to a new, deepening devotion to the pictorialization of deteriorating psychological states.

As a contract writer for Warner Bros. in the late 1930s and early 1940s, Rossen had worked on many excellent scripts which showed a strong sympathy for individuals destroyed by or battling the system. His first produced screenplay, *Marked Woman*, a little-known and highly underrated Bette Davis vehicle, deserves serious attention for its study of prostitution racketeering and the empowerment of women to overthrow corruption. His fifth film, *The Roaring Twenties*, is a thoughtful study of the obsessive drive for power and money amidst the harshness of the post-World War I period and the beginnings of the Great Depression. While his early scripts occasionally displayed an idealism which bordered on naiveté, Rossen deserves credit for his commitment to the depiction of economic and social injustice.

According to Alan Casty in his book *The Films of Robert Rossen*, Rossen was invited to direct his own screenplay for *Johnny O'Clock*, a tale of murder among gamblers, at the insistence of the film's star, Dick Powell. Rossen followed this poorly-received directorial debut with two of his most critically and financially successful films: *Body and Soul* and *All the King's Men*, two male-centered studies of corruption and the drive for success, the first in the boxing ring, the second in the political arena. The success of *Body and Soul* (from a screenplay by Abraham Polonsky) allowed Rossen the financial stability to set up his own company with a financing and releasing contract through Columbia Pictures. As a result, he wrote, directed, and produced *All the King's Men*, which was awarded the Best Picture Oscar in 1949.

The unfortunate result of these back-to-back successes seems to have been a problem of directorial ego: production accounts of the later films detail Rossen's inability to openly accept collaboration. This paranoia was exacerbated by his deepening involvement with the HUAC proceedings. Despite a 1953 reprieve after naming names, he was unable to revive his Hollywood career. He seemed a particularly unlikely candidate to direct his next three films, the Ponti-DeLaurentiis melodrama *Mambo*, the historical epic *Alexander the Great*, and the interracial problem drama, *Island in the Sun*. The last of his 1950s films, *They Came to Cordura*, is an interesting film which should have succeeded. Its failure so obsessed Rossen he spent many years unsuccessfully trying to re-edit it for re-release.

His final films, *The Hustler* and *Lilith*, show a return to form, due in great part to the atmospheric cinematography of Eugene Schufftan. Rossen, firmly entrenched in the theatrical values of content through script and performance, had previously worked with strong cinematographers (especially James Wong Howe and Burnett Guffey), but had worked from the conviction that content was the prime area of concern. As he told *Cahiers du cinéma*, "Technique is nothing compared to content." In *The Hustler*, a moody film about winners and losers set in the world of professional pool-playing, the studied script was strongly enhanced by Schufftan's predominantly claustrophobic framings. Schufftan, long a respected European cameraman (best known for his work on Lang's *Metropolis* and Carné's *Quai des brumes*), had been enthusiastically recommended to Rossen by Jack Garfein who had brought Schufftan back to America for his *Something Wild*.

Schufftan's working posture was one of giving the director what he asked for and production notes from the set of *The Hustler* indicate he gave Rossen what he wanted, meanwhile achieving affects one feels were beyond Rossen's vision. There was no denying Schufftan's influence in the film's success (it won him an Oscar), and Rossen wisely invited him to work on his next film.

Lilith, an oblique and elliptical film in which a psychiatric worker ends up seeking help, signalled an advance in Rossen's cinematic sensibility. While several of the purely visual passages border on being overly symbolic, one feels that Rossen was beginning to admit the communicative power of the visual. Less idealistic and with less affirmative endings, these last two films showed a deeper sense of social realism, with Rossen striving to portray the effect of the psychological rather than social environment on his characters. His last, unrealized, project would have allowed him to portray both the social and psychological problems of people living in the vicinity of Cape Canaveral (Cape Kennedy) and allowed him a further opportunity to break away from his tradition of dialogue-bound character studies.

—Doug Tomlinson

ROTHA, Paul.

British. Born Paul Thompson in London, 3 June 1907. Educated at Highgate School; Slade School of Fine Art, London, 1923–25. Married 1) Margaret Louise Lee, 1930 (divorced 1939); 2) Margot Rose Perkins, 1943; 3) actress Constance Smith. Painter, designer, book illustrator, 1925; art critic, *Connoisseur*, 1927–28; property man, 1928, then assistant designer, British International Pictures Ltd.; author and film historian, from 1930; producer, Empire Marketing Board, 1932; directed first film, *Contact*, 1932; director of productions, Strand Films, 1936–38; Rockefeller Foundation Fellow, 1937–38; set up Associated Realist Film Productions, and founded, *Documentary News Letter*, 1939; managing director, Paul Rotha Productions Ltd., 1941–76; made 100 documentaries for British Ministry of Information, World War II; Head of Documentary Film Department, BBC, 1953–55; lecturer on documentary films, U.S.A., 1953–54; member of board, Isotype Institute, from 1959; Simon Senior Research Fellow, University of Manchester, 1967–68. Recipient: Gold Medals, Venice Festival, 1934, Brussels festival, 1935, and Leipzig Festival, 1962; British Film Academy Awards for *The World is Rich*, 1947, and *World Without End*, 1953; Fellow, British Film Institute, 1951; Honorary Member (posthumous), ACTT, 1984. *Died 7 March 1984.*

Films as Director and Scriptwriter:
(documentary unless indicated)

1932   *Contact*
1933   *The Rising Tide* (reissued as *Great Cargoes*, 1935); *Shipyard*
1935   *Death on the Road*; *Face of Britain*
1936   *The Future's in the Air*; *Cover to Cover*; *The Way to the Sea*; *Peace of Britain*
1937   *Statue Parade*; *Today We Live*; *Here is the Land*
1939   *New Worlds for Old*; *Roads Across Britain* (co-d with Sidney Cole)
1940   *The Fourth Estate* (not shown until 1964); *Mr. Borland Thinks Again*
1943   *World of Plenty*
1944   *Soviet Village*
1945   *Total War in Britain*; *Land of Promise*
1946   *A City Speaks*
1947   *The World is Rich*

1950   *No Resting Place* (feature)
1953   *World Without End* (co-d with Basil Wright)
1953/55   *Hope for the Hungry*; *The Waiting People*; *No Other Way*; *The Wealth of Waters*; *The Virus Story*
1958   *Cat and Mouse* (feature)
1959   *Cradle of Genius*
1961   *Das Leben von Adolf Hitler* (*The Life of Adolf Hitler*)
1962   *De Overval* (*The Silent Raid*) (feature)

Publications:

By ROTHA: books—

The Film Till Now: A Survey of the Cinema, London, 1930; 2nd edition, with Richard Griffith, 1949; 3rd edition, 1960; 4th edition, 1967.
Celluloid: The Film Today, London, 1931.
Documentary Film: The Use of the Film Medium to Interpret Creatively and in Social Terms the Life of the People as it Exists in Reality, London, 1936; 2nd edition, 1939; 3rd edition, 1952.
Movie Parade, London, 1936; as *Movie Parade: 1888–1949: A Pictorial Survey of World Cinema*, with Roger Manvell, 1950.
World of Plenty: The Book of the Film, with Eric Mowbray, London, 1945.
Eisenstein, 1898–1948, with others, London, 1948.
Portrait of a Flying Yorkshireman: Letters from Eric Knight to Paul Rotha (editor), London, 1952.
Television in the Making (editor), London, 1956.
Rotha on the Film, London, 1958.
The Innocent Eye, with others, London, 1963.
Documentary Diary: An Informal History of the British Documentary Film 1928–1939, London, 1973.
Richard Winnington: Film Criticism and Caricature, London, 1975.
Robert J. Flaherty: A Biography, edited by Jay Ruby, Philadelphia, 1983.

By ROTHA: articles—

"The Lament," in *Sight and Sound* (London), Autumn 1938.
Documentary News Letter (London), 1939–1946.
"Television and the Future of Documentary," in *Quarterly Review of Film, Radio and TV* (New York), Summer 1955.
"The Critical Issue," with others, in *Sight and Sound* (London), August 1958.
Films and Filming (London), July 1966 to May 1967 (monthly column).
Letter in *Film and TV Technician* (London), February 1983 (reply, July 1983).

On ROTHA: books—

Wright, Basil, *The Long View*, London, 1974.
Sussex, Elizabeth, *The Rise and Fall of British Documentary: The Story of the Film Movement Founded By John Grierson*, Berkeley, 1975.
Morris, Paul, editor, *Paul Rotha*, London, 1982.
Ellis, Jack C., *The Documentary Idea*, Englewood Cliffs, New Jersey, 1989.

On ROTHA: articles—

"Rotha and the World," in *Quarterly Review of Film, Radio and TV* (New York), Fall 1955.
Film Forum (London), January 1963.
Hollywood Reporter, 23 June 1978.
"British Cinema: Paul Rotha," in *National Film Theatre Booklet* (London), August 1979.
Powell, Dilys, obituary, in *Film and TV Technician* (London), April 1984.
Obituary in *Revue du Cinéma* (Paris), May 1984.
Anstey, Edgar, "Paul Rotha and Thorold Dickinson," in *Sight and Sound* (London), Summer 1984.
"Paul Rotha," in *Annual Obituary 1985*, London and Chicago, 1985.

*   *   *

Rotha's position in the British documentary movement has

Paul Rotha

always been somewhat equivocal. Unlike other members of the group, he served only briefly in the government units Grierson assembled in the 1930s. Before that he had trained as a painter and designer, and *The Film Till Now*—the first aesthetic history of film in English, perhaps in any language—had already been published. After six months at the Empire Marketing Board Film Unit he continued in documentary as an independent producer, his ability to obtain private sponsorship unusual for those early years when documentary was just becoming a recognized mode.

Rotha's films were frequently innovative and experimental, with his creative impulse more akin to conceptual art than to personal expression, often mixing forms and styles. Though original in their combinations, their aspects derived from precedents that attracted Rotha. *Shipyard*, for example, takes a hard look at the cycles of work followed by unemployment that characterized the British shipbuilding industry. In this respect it makes one think of Joris Ivens's *Borinage*, about the miserable conditions in the mining region of Belgium. But it also contains extended passages of visual artistry of the giant ship in stages of construction—silhouettes of the hull frame and the like—that seem to stem from the "city symphonies" of early documentary, or perhaps from Ivens's *The Bridge* (1928).

World of Plenty (1943) and its sequel, *The World is Rich*

(1947), seem equally original and yet, as Rotha acknowledged, their inspiration came from the sort of Depression theater called "The Living Newspaper" he had seen while on a trip to the U.S.A. in the late 1930s to spread the documentary gospel. They are intelligent, imaginative, and finally a bit too clever, the rhetorical devices attracting as much attention as the argument itself. *World Without End* is unusual in coupling footage about the work of UNESCO shot by Basil Wright in Thailand with that of Rotha in Mexico, an undertaking reminiscent of D. W. Griffith's monumental *Intolerance*. But somehow it evokes no real, or anyway deep, sympathy for the peoples and their problems.

Of his three fiction features, the first, *No Resting Place*, is clearly in the semi-documentary tradition which Harry Watt had carried from the wartime Crown Film Unit over to commercial features. It is about the lives of itinerant tinkers, shot on location in Ireland, using non-actors as well as little-known professionals.

His compilation, *The Life of Adolf Hitler*, again skillful and intelligent, follows a vein much mined by American and British television. (Rotha was head of BBC-TV documentary during 1953–55.) Specifically it recalls "The Twisted Cross" (1956) of NBC's *Project XX* series.

Along with his filmmaking Rotha wrote constantly: his

Films as Director and Scriptwriter:

1960 *La maleta* (unfinished)
1967 *El tango del viudo* (unfinished)
1968 *Los tres triste tigres* (*Tres Tristes Tigres. Three Sad Tigers*)
1969 *Militarismo y tortura* (doc short); *La cate naria* (unfinished)
1970 *Que hacer?* (co-d)
1971 *La colonia penal* (*The Penal Colony*); *Ahor te vamos a llamar hermano* (*Now We Will Call You Brother*) (short); *Nadie dijo nada* (*Nobody Said Nothing*); *Mapuches* (doc short)
1972 *Los minuteros* (*The Minute Hands. The Street Photographer*) (short)
1973 *La expropriación* (*The Expropriation*) (completed in Germany); *Nueva canción Chilena* (*New Chilean Song*) (short); *El realismo socialista* (*Socialist Realism*); *Palomilla brava* (*Bad Girl*); *Palomita blanca* [Little White Dove] (co-d, unfinished due to coup); *Abastecimiento* (*Supply*) (short)
1974 *Diálogo de exilados* (*Dialogue of Exiles*)
1975 *El cuerpo repartido y el mundo al revez* (*Mensch verstreut und Welt verkehrt. The Scattered Body and the World Turned Upside Down*)
1976 *Sotelo* (doc short)
1977 *Colloque de chiens* (*Dog's Language*) (short); *La Vocation suspendue* (*The Suspended Vocation*)
1978 *L'Hypothèse du tableau volé* (*The Hypothesis of a Stolen Painting*); *Les Divisions de la nature* (short)
1979 *De Grands Evènements et des gens ordinaires* (*Of Great Events and Ordinary People*); *Petit Manuel d'histoire de France* (*Short History of France*); *Images du débat* (*Images of Debate*); *Jeux* (*Games*); *Rue des archives 79*
1980 *Le Jeu de l'oie* (*Snakes and Ladders*) (short); *La Ville nouvelle* (*The New Town*) (short); *L'Or gris* (*Grey Gold*); *Teletests* (short); *Pages d'un catalogue* (*Pages from a Catalogue*) (short); *Fahlstrom* (short)
1981 *Le Territoire* (*The Territory*); *Le Borgne* (serial); *Het dak van de walvis* (*On Top of the Whale. The Whale's Roof*)
1982 *Les Trois Couronnes du Matelot* (*The Sailor's Three Crowns*); *Classification des plantes* (short); *Les Ombres chinoise* (*Chinese Shadows*) (short); *Querelle de jardins* (*The War of the Gardens*) (short)
1983 *Bérénice*; *La Ville des pirates* (*City of Pirates*); *Point de fuite*; *Voyage autour d'une main* (short); *Le retour d'un amateur de bibliothèque* (short, for TV); *La présence réelle* (*The Real Presence*)
1985 *L'Éveillé du pont de l'Alma*; *Les Destins de Manoel* (*Manuel's Destinies*); *Dans un miroir* (*In a Mirror*); *Richard III*
1986 *Mammame*; *Régime sans pain*; *L'Ile au trésor* (*Treasure Island*)
1987 *Memoire des apparences*; *Vie est un songe*; *La chouette aveugle*
1988 *Brise-Glace* (*Icebreaker*) (co-d)
1989 *Allegory*
1990 *The Golden Boat* (+ sc)

Publications:

By RUIZ: articles—

"Chili: le cinema de l'unité populaire," an interview with H. Ehrmann, in *Ecran* (Paris), February 1974.
"Notes sur *La Vocation suspendue*," in *Positif* (Paris), December/January 1977/78.
"Les Relations d'objets au cinéma," in *Cahiers du Cinéma* (Paris), April 1978.
Interview with Don Ranvaud, in *Framework* (Norwich, England), Spring 1979.
"Filters, Exile and Cunning: Problems of Time, Space and Perception," an interview with Ian Christie, in *Monthly Film Bulletin* (London), December 1984.
Interview with Alain Philippon, in *Cahiers du Cinéma* (Paris), May 1985.
Interview with D. Ehrenstein, in *Film Quarterly* (Berkeley), Fall 1986.

On RUIZ: books—

Buci-Glucksmann, Christine, and Fabrice Revault d'Allonnes, *Raoul Ruiz*, Paris, 1987.
King, John, *Magical Reels: A History of Cinema in Latin America*, London, 1990.

On RUIZ: articles—

Pick, Zuzana, "Le Cinéma chilien sous le signe de l'Unité Populaire (1970–1973)," in *Positif* (Paris), January 1974.
Roud, Richard, "Turning Points: Ruiz & Truffaut," in *Sight and Sound* (London), Summer 1978.
"Exile and Cunning: Raul Ruiz," special section, in *Afterimage* (Rochester, New York), no. 10, 1981.
"Raul Ruiz Issue" of *Cahiers du Cinéma* (Paris), March 1983.
Raul Ruiz Section of *Positif* (Paris), December 1983.
Mouesca, J., "El cine chileño en el exilio (1973–1983)," in *Cine Cubano* (Havana), no. 109, 1984.
Raul Ruiz Section of *Casablanca* (Madrid), January 1984.
Adair, Gilbert, "Raúl: Sheheruizade, or 1001 Films," in *Sight and Sound* (London), Summer 1984.
Rosenbaum, Jonathan, "Beating the Labyrinth," in *Monthly Film Bulletin* (London), January 1985.
Christie, Ian, "Raul Ruiz and the House of Culture," in *Sight and Sound* (London), Spring 1987.

*   *   *

A prodigious storyteller, Raul Ruiz is also a prolific manufacturer of moving images. This Chilean filmmaker, now living in exile in Paris, has molded his films by a deeply personal concern with representation and discourse. His innovative and experimental work thus defies any attempt at classification.

The cinema of Ruiz is a cinema of ideas. He has unmasked ideological stereotypes (*Three Sad Tigers, Nobody Said Nothing*, and *Dialogue of Exiles*), has exposed the contradictions of despotic institutions (*The Suspended Vocation*), and unveiled his own tortured world (*The One-Eyed Man*) torn between his cultural origins and the false cosmopolitanism of forced exile (*The Whale's Roof*). His mise-en-scéne is preoccupied with representation (*The Hypothesis of a Stolen Painting* and *The Divisions of Nature*) and the fragmentation of reality (*The Sailor's Three Crowns*). His narrative is imbued with an intense research into performance and the ambiguity of the spoken language. His storylines never appear to enjoy a privileged position within the overall narrative of his films (*The Expropriation*). The voice-over narration (*The War of the Gardens*), the commentary (*The Divisions of Nature*) or even the dialogue (*The Penal Colony*), by detaching themselves from the image track, acquire an independent life or serve to lure the spectator into the wilful contradictions that Ruiz wants to explore. The spoken language, saturated with Chilean slang, often makes his films incomprehensible for non-Chilean spectators. In France Ruiz has found an audience for whom simulations of Cartesian logic are the playful components of a fictional labyrinth.

Few filmmakers have taken better advantage of commissioned work. His video essays and documentary films for television and the Centre Beaubourg are original experiments with technology and narrative which inform the strategies of his feature work. A didactic comparison of French- and English-style gardens is displaced in favour of a playful suspense story (*The War of the Gardens*). A commissioned film on Beaubourg's cartography exhibition becomes a diabolic snakes-and-ladders game (*Snakes and Ladders*). Ruiz has a passionate affair with technology. Working with innovative directors of photography—Diego Bonancina in Chile, Sacha Vierny and Henri Alekan in France—he has brought back the magic of French poetic realism to explore a world of manipulation, impotence, and violence. He favors lighting, filters, and mirrors to deform filmic reality into a kaleidoscopic maze that traps his performers (*Snakes and Ladders*) and turns familiarity into fantastic exoticism (*The Territory*). Ruiz's originality stems from personal paradox. He is an exiled filmmaker in search of a territory, mastering a new language while stubbornly upholding his roots and confined in a culture he recognizes as having colonized his own.

Ruiz's contribution to Chilean cinema has been openly acknowledged since *Three Sad Tigers* in 1969. His innovative approach to film, his independence and his critical stance on political reductionism have often set him apart from the mainstream. A name rarely mentioned in discussions on the new Latin American cinema, Ruiz retrospectives in Madrid, Edinburgh, London, Rotterdam, and Paris have finally brought him public recognition. After years of relative obscurity, critical acclaim has earned him a leading position within the French avant-grade. Chilean cinema in exile has found in Ruiz a respected and vital representative. A total filmmaker, for whom theater, music, literature, and visual arts are familiar territory, Ruiz successfully combines intellectual inquiry with Latin American hedonism.

—Zuzana Mirjam Pick

————

RUSSELL, Ken.

British. Born Henry Kenneth Alfred Russell in Southampton, England, 3 July 1927. Educated Pangbourne Nautical College, 1941–44. Married Shirley Ann Kingdom, 1957, three children. Served in merchant navy, 1945, and in Royal Air Force, 1946–49; dancer with Ny Norsk ballet, 1950; actor with Garrick players, from 1951; documentary maker for the BBC's *Monitor*, from 1959; directed first feature, *French Dressing*, 1963; TV director for *Omnibus*, from 1966, and for *South Bank Show*, from 1983. Lives in the Lake District, England.

Films as Director:

1957 *Amelia and the Angel* (amateur short)
1958 *Peep Show* (amateur short); *Lourdes* (amateur short)
1959 *Poet's London* (for TV); *Gordon Jacob* (for TV); *Guitar Craze* (for TV); *Variations on a Mechanical Theme* (for TV); untitled film on Robert McBryde and Robert Colquhoun (for TV); *Portrait of a Goon* (for TV)
1960 *Marie Rambert Remembers* (for TV); *Architecture of Entertainment* (for TV); *Cranks at Work* (for TV); *The Miners' Picnic* (for TV); *Shelagh Delaney's Salford* (for TV); *A House in Bayswater* (for TV); *The Light Fantastic* (for TV)
1961 *Old Battersea House* (for TV); *Portrait of a Soviet Composer* (for TV); *London Moods* (for TV); *Antonio Gaudi* (for TV)
1962 *Pop Goes the Easel* (for TV); *Preservation Man* (for TV); *Mr. Chesher's Traction Engines* (for TV); *Lotte Lenya Sings Kurt Weill* (co-d) (for TV); *Elgar* (for TV)
1963 *French Dressing*; *Watch the Birdie* (for TV)
1964 *Lonely Shore* (for TV); *Bartok* (for TV); *The Dotty World of James Lloyd* (for TV); *Diary of a Nobody* (for TV)
1965 *The Debussy Film* (for TV); *Always on Sunday* (for TV)
1966 *Don't Shoot the Composer* (for TV); *Isadora Duncan, The Biggest Dancer in the World* (for TV)
1967 *Billion Dollar Brain*; *Dante's Inferno* (for TV)
1968 *Song of Summer* (for TV)
1969 *Women in Love*
1970 *The Music Lovers* (+ pr); *The Dance of the Seven Veils* (for TV)
1971 *The Devils* (+ sc, co-pr); *The Boy Friend* (+ pr, sc)

1972 *Savage Messiah* (+ pr)
1974 *Mahler* (+ sc); *Tommy* (+ co-pr, sc)
1975 *Lisztomania* (+ sc)
1977 *Valentino* (+ co-sc)
1978 *Clouds of Glory, Parts I and II* (for TV)
1980 *Altered States*
1983 *Ken Russell's View of the Planets* (for TV)
1984 *Crimes of Passion*; *Elgar* (for TV); *Vaughan Williams* (for TV)
1986 *Gothic*
1987 episode in *Aria*
1988 *Salome's Last Dance*; *The Lair of the White Worm*; *Ken Russell's ABC of British Music* (for TV)
1989 *The Rainbow*; *Ken Russell—A British Picture* (for TV)
1990 *Strange Affliction of Anton Bruckner* (for TV)
1991 *Whore*

Other Films:

1991 *The Russia House* (Schepisi) (role)

Publications:

By RUSSELL: book—

An Appalling Talent: Ken Russell, with John Baxter, London, 1973.
A British Picture: An Autobiography, London, 1989.

By RUSSELL: articles—

"Shock Treatment: Interview," with Gordon Gow, in *Films and Filming* (London), July 1970.
Interview with Gene D. Phillips, in *Film Comment* (New York), Fall 1970.
"Ken Russell Writes on Raising Kane," in *Films and Filming* (London), May 1972.
"Savage Saviour: Interview," with Peter Buckley, in *Films and Filming* (London), October 1972.
"Ideas for Films," in *Film* (London), January/February 1973.
"Ken Russell," with B. Wiener and C. Hemphill, in *Inter/View* (New York), March 1975.
"Fact, Fantasy, and the Films of Ken Russell," with Gene Phillips, in *Journal of Popular Film* (Bowling Green, Ohio), vol. 5, no. 3–4, 1976.
"With Ken Russell on the Set of *Valentino*," with Herb Lightman, in *American Cinematographer* (Los Angeles), November 1977.
Interview with R. Gentry, in *Post Script* (Jacksonville, Florida), Spring/Summer 1983.
"Something Wilde," an interview with D. Nicholson, in *Films and Filming* (London), July 1988.

On RUSSELL: books—

Wilson, Colin, *Ken Russell: A Director in Search of a Hero*, London, 1974.
Atkins, Thomas, *Ken Russell*, New York, 1976.
Gomez, Joseph, *Ken Russell: The Adaptor as Creator*, London, 1976.
Rosenfeldt, Diane, *Ken Russell: A Guide to Reference Sources*, Boston, 1978.
Phillips, Gene D., *Ken Russell*, Boston, 1979.
Hanke, Ken, *Ken Russell's Films*, Metuchen, New Jersey, 1984.
Phillips, Gene D., *Major Film Directors of the American and British Cinema*, Cranbury, New Jersey, 1989.

On RUSSELL: articles—

Dempsey, Michael, "The World of Ken Russell," in *Film Quarterly* (Berkeley), Spring 1972.
Fisher, Jack, "Three Paintings of Sex: The Films of Ken Russell," in *Films Journal* (New York), September 1972.
Kolker, Robert, "Ken Russell's Biopics: Grander and Gaudier," in *Film Comment* (New York), May/June 1973.
Farber, Stephen, "Russellmania," in *Film Comment* (New York), November/December 1975.

Ken Russell

Gomez, Joseph, "*Mahler* and the Methods of Ken Russell's Films on Composers," in *Velvet Light Trap* (Madison, Wisconsin), Winter 1975.

Gilliatt, Penelope, "Genius, Genia, Genium, Ho Hum," in the *New Yorker*, 26 April 1976.

Dempsey, Michael, "Ken Russell, Again," in *Film Quarterly* (Berkeley), Winter 1977/78.

Yacowar, M., "Ken Russell's *Rabelais*," in *Literature/Film Quarterly* (Salisbury, Maryland), vol. 8, no. 1, 1980.

Jaehne, Karen, "Wormomania: Ken Russell's Best Laid Planaria," in *Film Criticism* (Meadville, Pennsylvania), vol. 24, no. 6, 1988.

* * *

British director Ken Russell was 42 when his film of D.H. Lawrence's *Women in Love* placed him in the ranks of movie directors of international stature. For more than a decade before that, however, British television viewers had been treated to a succession of his skilled TV biographies of great artists like Frederick Delius (*Song of Summer*) and Isadora Duncan. Russell has always gravitated toward the past in choosing subjects for filming because, as he says, "topics of the moment pass and change. Besides, we can be more dispassionate and therefore more truthful in dealing with the past. And to see the past from the vantage point of the present is to be able to judge the effect of the past on the present."

His first TV documentaries, like that on Edward Elgar, correspond to what he calls "the accepted textbook idea of what a documentary should be; you were supposed to extol the great artists and their work. Later I turned to showing how great artists transcended their personal problems and weakness in creating great art." But this more realistic approach, exemplified in his telefilm about Richard Strauss (*Dance of the Seven Veils*) and his feature film, *The Music Lovers*, about Tchaikovsky, upset some of the members of the audience for both his TV and theatrical films.

As he advanced from the small screen to the large in continuing to turn out what has come to be called his biopics, he has almost singlehandedly revolutionized the whole concept of the conventional film biography—to the point where the genre will never be quite the same again. One need only recall the heavily romanticized Hollywood screen biographies on subjects like Cole Porter to grasp how Russell's biopics have come to grips with the problems of an artist's life in relation to his work in a way that makes for much more challenging and entertaining films than the sugar-coated Hollywood screen biographies.

In addition to experimenting with the nature of biographical films, Russell has at the same time been seeking by trial and error to discover in all of his films, biopics or not, to what extent a motion picture can be cut loose from the moorings of conventional storytelling; and his mind-bending science fiction thriller *Altered States* is an excellent example of this experimentation. If these experiments in narrative technique account for occasional lapses in narrative logic, as in *Lisztomania*, his biopic about Franz Liszt, they also account for the intricate and arresting blend of past and present, fact and fantasy, that characterize his best work.

Among his outstanding films must surely be numbered his screen adaptations of Lawrence's two companion novels, *Women in Love* (1969) and *The Rainbow* (1989), which focus on the personal lives of two sisters, as they struggle to carve out their destinies in the modern world. The two films, taken together, represent Russell's finest achievement in the cinema.

Although Russell has often been looked upon as a maverick who makes films that are perhaps more subjective and personal than many directors working today, it is worth noting he is the only British director in history ever to have three films playing first-run engagements in London simultaneously: *The*

Music Lovers, *The Devils*, and *The Boy Friend*. Indeed, this provocative and fascinating director has already assured himself a place in the history of world cinema.

—Gene D. Phillips

RUTTMANN, Walter.

German. Born in Frankfurt am Main, 28 December 1887. Educated at Goethe-Gymnasium, Abitur 1905; architectural studies in Zurich, from 1907; studied painting in Munich, 1909. Served as artillery lieutenant on Eastern Front, World War I; suffered nervous breakdown, sent to sanatorium until 1917; began filmmaking, 1919; moved to Berlin, 1923; worked with Lotte Reiniger and Carl Koch on *The Adventures of Prince Achmed*, 1925–26; worked with G.W. Pabst and Abel Gance in Paris, 1929–31. *Died in Berlin, 15 July 1941.*

Films as Director:

1921   *Opus I*
1920–23   *Opus II, III, IV*
1923   "Der Falkentraum (Dream of Hawks)" sequence in **Die Nibelungen** part 1 (Lang)
1924   Abstract Alps dream sequence for *Lebende Buddhas* (Wegener)
1925–26   *Opus V*
1926–27   **Berlin, die Sinfonie der Grossstadt (Berlin, Symphony of a Great City)**
1928   "Tönende Welle" episode for *Das weisse Stadion* (Fanck)
1929   *Melodie der Welt (World Melody)*; *Des Haares und der Liebe Wellen* (short fiction film)
1930   *Weekend (Wochenende)*
1931   *In der Nacht (In the Night)*; *Feind im Blut* (documentary)
1932–33   *Acciaio*
1933   *Blut und Boden*
1934   Short film incorporated into *Altgermanische Bauernkultur*; *Metall des Himmels*; Prologue to **Triumph des Willens (Triumph of the Will)** (Riefenstahl)
1935   *Kleiner Film einer grossen Stadt—Die Stadt Düsseldorf am Rhein*; *Stadt Stuttgart, 100. Cannstatter Volksfest*; *Stuttgart, die Grossstadt zwischen Wald und Reben*
1936   *Schiff in Not*
1937   *Mannesmann*
1938   *Henkel, ein deutsches Werk in seiner Arbeit*; *Weltstrasse See—Welthafen Hamburg*; *Im Dienste der Menschheit*
1940   *Deutsche Waffenschmiede (Waffenkammern Deutschland)*; *Deutsche Panzer*; *Aberglaube*
1941   *Ein Film gegen die Volkskrankheit Krebs—jeder Achte . . .*

Other Films:

1923–26   *Die Abenteuer des Prinzen Achmed (The Adventures of Prince Achmed)* (Reiniger) (collaborated on making abstract, moving backgrounds)

Publications:

On RUTTMANN: books—

Kracauer, Siegfried, *A Psychological History of the German Film*, Princeton, New Jersey, 1974.

Russett, Robert, and Cecile Starr, *Experimental Animation*, New York, 1976.

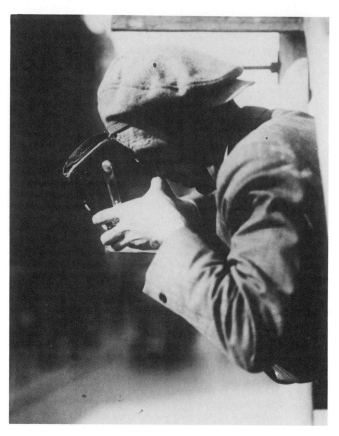

Walter Ruttmann

Film as Film: Formal Experiment in Film, 1910–1975, exhibition catalog, London, 1979.

On RUTTMANN: articles—

Falkenberg, Paul, "Sound Montage: A Propos de Ruttmann," in *Film Culture* (New York), no. 22–23, 1961.
Cowie, Peter, "*Berlin*," in *Films and Filming* (London), August 1961.
"Walter Ruttmann," in *Travelling* (Lausanne), Summer 1979.
Fulks, Barry A., "Walter Ruttmann, the Avant-Garde Film, and Nazi Modernism," in *Film and History* (Newark, New Jersey), May 1984.
Brandt, H.-J., "Walter Ruttmann: Vom Expressionismus zum Faschismus," (3 parts) in *Filmfaust* (Frankfurt), October/November 1985, December 1985/January 1986, and February/March 1986.

* * *

Walter Ruttmann is often associated with the films of others: he created the "Dream of the Hawks" sequence in Fritz Lang's *Die Nibelungen*, and directed several sequences in Paul Wegener's *Lebende Buddhas*; later on, he assisted in the editing of Leni Riefenstahl's *Olympia*. Easily his own most influential work is *Berlin, Symphony of a Great City*, one of the outstanding abstract documentaries of the 1920s.

Berlin is a visual essay on an average working day in the city, from dawn to the dead of night. The quiet, seemingly abandoned metropolis comes alive with a train on its way through the suburbs, workers on their way to factories, the wheels of industry set in motion, everyday occurrences in cafes and on streets. Night approaches, and Berlin becomes lit up like a birthday cake. Boys flirt with girls, chorus girls dance, an orchestra performs Beethoven. Lovers seek out privacy in a hotel. And it will all begin again with the sunrise.

Berlin is indeed a symphony, with Ruttmann stressing the movement of people and machinery in what amounts to a visual tapestry. The key is in the editing: for example, shots of people walking on a street are followed by those of cows' legs. Ruttmann makes no social commentary, as rich and poor, man and animal, exist side by side. His sole interest is the imagery, the creation of visual poetry—even when he contrasts poor children and the food in a restaurant. His use of montage was influenced by the Russian, Dziga Vertov. Yet while Vertov's newsreels depicted the progress of a post-Revolutionary Soviet society, the life in Berlin could just as well be the life in Brussels or Amsterdam or Paris. Ruttmann is concerned with the details of daily reality edited together to form a unified whole, but he never comments or editorializes on the lives of his subjects.

The filmmaker, who appropriately began his career as an abstract painter, preceded *Berlin* with a series of experimental "Opus" films. Siegfried Kracauer describes his *Opus I* as "a dynamic display of spots vaguely recalling X-ray photographs." Additionally, Ruttmann realized that the advent of sound in motion pictures was inevitable, and attempted to attune his images to the soundtracks that he felt would ultimately outweigh the visuals in importance. In *World Melody*, made after *Berlin*, music and sound effects are orchestrated to relate to the images; *In der Nacht* is a union of imagery and Schumann's music.

Because Ruttmann did not exhibit a social conscience in his early work, it is perhaps not surprising that, by the end of his life, he had been co-opted as a propagandist. An artist whose work was initially apolitical, Ruttmann neither protested nor went into exile with the advent of National Socialism. Instead, he conformed. His last documentaries were odes to Nazism, to Germany's military might.

—Rob Edelman

SANJINÉS, Jorge.

Bolivian. Born in La Paz, Bolivia, 31 July 1936. Studied film-making and philosophy at Catholic University in Santiago, Chile, late 1950s. Made first film, *Sueños y realidades*, with Oscar Soria, in Bolivia, 1961; named head of Bolivian Film Institute, 1965; left Bolivia following coup led by Hugo Banzer, 1972; returned to Bolivia, 1979.

Films as Director:

1961	*Sueños y realidades* (co-d)
1963	*Revolución*; *Una día Paulino* (co-d)
1965	*Aysa*
1966	*Ukamau*
1969	***Yawar mallku (Blood of the Condor)***
1971	*El coraje del pueblo*
1974	*El enemigo principal*
1976	*Fuera de aquí*
1983	*Las banderas del amanecer* (co-d)

Publications:

By SANJINÉS: articles—

"Cinema and Revolution," an interview in *Cineaste* (New York), Winter 1970/71.

"*Ukamau* and *Yawar Mallku*: An Interview with Jorge Sanjinés," in *Afterimage* (London), Summer 1971.

"Sobre *Fuera de Aquí!*," and "Llamado del Grupo *Ukamau*," in *Cine Cubano* (Havana), no. 93, 1980.

"El Cine revolucionario en Bolivia," in *Cine Cubano* (Havana), no. 99, 1981.

"Faire du cinéma un instrument de liberation," an interview with G. Gervais, in *Jeune Cinéma* (Paris), March 1982.

"Nuestro principal destinatario," in *Cine Cubano* (Cuba), no. 105, 1983.

"Revolutionary Cinema: The Bolivian Experience," in *Cinema and Social Change in Latin America: Conversations with Filmmakers*, edited by Julianne Burton, Austin, Texas, 1986.

On SANJINÉS: books—

Gisbert, Carlos D. Mesa, and others, *Cine Boliviano: Del realizador al critico*, La Paz, 1979.

Gisbert, Carlos D. Mesa, *La aventura del cine boliviano 1952–85*, La Paz, 1985.

Armes, Roy, *Third World Filmmaking and the West*, Berkeley, 1987.

On SANJINÉS: articles—

Wilson, David, "Aspects of Latin American Political Cinema," in *Sight and Sound* (London), Summer 1972.

Campbell, Leon G., and Carlos Cortes, "Film as Revolutionary Weapon: A Jorge Sanjinés Retrospective," in *History Teacher*, May 1979.

Ledgard, M., "Jorge Sanjinés: El cine urgente," in *Hablemos de Cine* (Lima), June 1981.

West, Dennis, "Film and Revolution in the Andes," in *New Scholar* (San Diego), vol. 8, no. 1/2, 1982.

West, Dennis, "Alternative Cinema in Latin America," in *Roads to Freedom: The Struggle Against Dependence in the Developing World*, edited by Edwin G. Clausen and Jack Bermingham, Brookfield, Vermont, 1989.

*   *   *

The Bolivian Jorge Sanjinés has become internationally recognized as a leading filmmaker in spite of the fact that his country has few significant filmmaking traditions or production facilities. Working outside of a film-industry context, Sanjinés has doggedly overcome formidable obstacles, including economic ones. For instance, to finance the fiction feature *Yawar mallku* Sanjinés and other members of his Ukamau production group sold personal belongings and accepted contributions. After finishing *Yawar mallku*, members of the Ukamau collective toured the Bolivian highlands with a 16 mm print and portable projection equipment in an effort to reach the film's intended audience—the Indian peasantry.

Sanjinés is a militant filmmaker whose primary goal is to bring a revolutionary Marxist political agenda to peasant and working-class audiences. His principal films respond to a militant Marxist aesthetic by examining oppressed collective protagonists (e.g. an Andean peasant community) in their historical situations, by educating viewers to an understanding of those situations, and by inspiring audiences to transform the political and socioeconomic status quo in order to build a higher stage of society. The depiction of oppression in these films has in some cases been based on documented historical events.

Sanjinés' works offer a defense of the Andean Indian way of life and expose and attack the Indians' enemies. *Yawar mallku* denounces a Progress Corps (read Peace Corps) pediatrics clinic that sterilizes unsuspecting Andean women, while in the documentary reconstruction *El coraje del pueblo*, Bolivian government and military officials responsible for the massacres of Indian miners are specifically identified. The fiction feature *El enemigo principal* illustrates the exploitation and brutality suffered by indigenous peasants at the hands of powerful landowners and links the power of the landowners to U.S. imperialism. The mise-en-scène of these films reflects Sanjinés' defense of the Indian way of life. For instance, in *El enemigo principal* the Inca heritage of the modern Andean Indian pervades the mise-en-scène: the predominance of Quechua dialogue, the centuries-old custom of chewing coca leaves, the trapezoidal niches and doors characterizing Inca masonry, the ancient agricultural ritual, the everyday work of spinning and weaving.

The structural, narrative, and stylistic approaches used by Sanjinés have evolved in accordance with his basic goal of optimum communication with his peasant and working-class audiences. When exhibiting *Yawar mallku* to Indians in remote

Carlos Saura: *Carmen*

areas, Sanjinés drew on an Inca oral tradition; and before showing the film he first had a narrator introduce the story and the characters to the cinematically unsophisticated audiences. Later, in *El enemigo principal*, Sanjinés built a narrator into the film itself: a well-known Indian peasant leader periodically appears to speak, in Quechua, directly to viewers in order to introduce the characters and events which will follow. From peasant reaction to his early films, Sanjinés found that unsophisticated viewers were shocked when a close shot follows an establishing shot. Therefore, in *El enemigo principal* outdoor group scenes appear initially in long shot; and then the camera slowly zooms in, much as a spectator would approach. Although *Yawar mallku* involved an Indian community in the filming, Sanjinés later sought from indigenous groups an even more active collective participation in an effort to make films "from the people, to the people." In *El coraje del pueblo*, survivors of the army's 1967 massacre of miners actively participated in the filmmaking by recreating their own activities before and during the bloodbath.

Since the appearance of *Yawar mallku*, Sanjinés has been a well-known and controversial figure in Bolivia; but he has at times been banished from his native country by right-wing regimes because of his highly political filmmaking activities. International critical opinion considers Sanjinés one of the leading Latin American militant filmmakers because of his oft demonstrated ability to make aesthetically and politically significant feature films—both documentaries and fiction features—in spite of extremely limited technical and financial resources.

SAURA, Carlos.

Spanish. Born in Huesca, 4 January 1932. Studied filmmaking at Instituto de Investigaciones y Experiencas Cinematográficos (IIEC), Madrid, 1952–57. Professional photographer, 1950–53; teacher at IIEC, from 1957, left for political reasons, 1964; directed first feature, *Los golfos*, 1960. Recipient: Silver Bear, Berlin Festival, for *La caza*, 1966, and *Peppermint frappé*, 1968; Special Jury Award, Cannes Festival, for *La prima Angelica*, 1974, and *Cria cuervos*, 1976; Golden Bear, Berlin Festival, for *Hurry, Hurry*, 1981.

Films as Director and Scriptwriter:

1957 *La tarde del domingo (Sunday Afternoon)* (short)
1958 *Cuenca* (short)
1960 *Los golfos (The Hooligans)* (+ role)
1964 *Llanto por un bandido (Lament for a Bandit)*
1966 *La caza (The Hunt. The Chase)*
1967 *Peppermint frappé*
1968 *Stress es tres, tres (Stress is Three, Three)*
1969 *La madriguera (The Honeycomb. The Net)*
1970 *El jardín de las delicias (The Garden of Delights)*
1973 *Ana y los lobos (Ana and the Wolves)*
1974 *La prima Angélica (Cousin Angelica)*
1976 *Cria cuervos (Raise Ravens)*
1977 *Elisa, vida mía (Elisa, My Love)*
1978 *Los ojos vendados (Blindfold)*
1979 *Mamá cumple cien años (Mama Turns a Hundred)*
1980 *Deprisa, deprisa (Hurry, Hurry)*
1981 *Dulces horas (Sweet Hours)*; *Bodas de sangre (Blood Wedding)*
1982 *Antonieta*
1983 *Carmen*
1984 *Los zancos (The Stilts)*
1985 *El amor brujo (Love the Magician)*
1987 *El dorado*
1989 *La noche oscura (The Dark Night)*
1990 *Ay! Carmela*

Publications:

By SAURA: articles—

Interviews with E. Brasó, in *Positif* (Paris), May and October 1974.
Interview with G. Braucourt, in *Thousand Eyes* (New York), October 1976.
Interview with M. Capdenac and others, in *Ecran* (Paris), July 1977.
"El cumpleaños de Saura," interview with J.L. Guerin, in *Cinema 2002* (Madrid), January 1980.
"Carlos Saura: bodas de prisa," interview with M. Pereira, in *Cine Cubano* (Havana), no.99, 1981.
Interview with Nick Roddick in *Stills* (London), September/October 1983.

On SAURA: books—

Brasó, Enrique, *Carlos Saura*, Madrid, 1974.
Gubern, Roman, *Homenaje a Carlos Saura*, Huelva, 1979.
Arnold, Frank, and others, *Carlos Saura*, Munich, 1981.
Oms, Marcel, *Carlos Saura*, Paris, 1981.
Eichenlaub, Hans M., *Carlos Saura*, Freiburg, 1984.
Hopewell, John, *Out of the Past: Spanish Cinema After Franco*, London, 1986.
Higginbotham, Virginia, *Spanish Film Under Franco*, Austin, Texas, 1988.
Vidal, Agustin Sanchez, *El cine de Carlos Saura*, Zaragoza, 1988.

On SAURA: articles—

"*Anne et des loups* Issue" of *Avant-Scène du Cinéma* (Paris), November 1974.
"*Cria cuervos* Issue" of *Avant-Scène du Cinéma* (Paris), 15 October 1978.
Kinder, Marcia, "Carlos Saura: The Political Development of Individual Consciousness," in *Film Quarterly* (Berkeley), no.3, 1979.
Kovács, Katherine, "Loss and Recuperation in *The Garden of Delights*," in *Cine-Tracts* (Montreal), Summer/Fall 1981.
Tate, S., "Carlos Saura, Spain and *Mama Turns One Hundred*," in *Cinema Papers* (Melbourne), April 1982.
Bartholomew, G., "The Development of Carlos Saura," in *Journal of Film and Video* (Carbondale, Illinois), Summer 1983.
D'Lugo, M., : "Carlos Saura: Constructive Imagination in Post-Franco Cinema," and A. Insdorf, "*Soñar con tus ojos*: Carlos Saura's Melodic Cinema," in *Quarterly Review of Film Studies* (New York), Spring 1983.
Hernandez, V., "Lectura e interpretacion, el contexto y la referencia en el cine de Carlos Saura," in *Contracampo* (Madrid), Winter 1984.
Hopewell, John, "Mr. Carlosawa," in *Sight and Sound* (London), Autumn 1986.
D'Lugo, Marvin, "Historical Reflexivity: Carlos Saura's Anti-*Carmen*," in *Wide Angle* (Baltimore, Maryland), vol. 9, no. 3, 1987.

*   *   *

Over the past three decades, Carlos Saura has attained international stature while exploring quintessentially Spanish themes. Saura was one of the first Spanish filmmakers to deal with the Spanish Civil War and its aftermath. In several films, he explored the impact of the war years and of the postwar period on the men and women of his generation, those who were born in the 1930s and who suffered emotional and psychological damage that affected them well into their adult years. In a number of movies, we witness the efforts of Saura's adult protagonists to resurrect their past memories in order to come to terms with them once and for all. In the course of their recollections, we see the negative effects not only of the war, but also of the repressive system of education and of the confining family structures that were consolidated by the triumph of Franco in the postwar period.

Until Franco's death in 1975, it was not possible to express this viewpoint openly. Films were censored first at the script stage and again upon completion. Nothing controversial was allowed. Even in the 1960s, during a period of liberalization when some experimentation was allowed and the New Spanish Cinema movement was born, Saura and the other young directors associated with this movement walked a delicate and difficult line trying to convey their ideas while avoiding the hurdles imposed by the censor.

It was in this atmosphere that Saura developed his cinematic style and method of working. In order to deal with taboo subjects, he (and the other young directors of that time) resorted to tactics of allusion, association, and allegory. In one of Saura's first movies, *The Hunt*, a hunting party arranged by four former comrades-in-arms under Franco is used to represent the legacy of the Civil War and the moral bankruptcy it has engendered. In other movies, Saura destroys the chronological sequence of events in order to show the impact of the past and its continued importance in explaining the present. Actions and events taking place in the present often recall or evoke corresponding past moments and Saura's protagonists come to exist in several temporal dimensions simultaneously. We participate in their memories as well as in their dreams and visions as Saura creates a fluid movement from present to past and in and out of dreams. What is original about these shifts in time and in perspective is that Saura dispenses with the dissolves and soft-focus shots usually used to effectuate a time change in films. In his movies present and past, reality and fantasy are deliberately fused together. Dream figures seem to be as palpable and as concrete as any of the "real" actors on screen. The audience learns to distinguish them through a series of narrative clues and through changes in clothing and in the actors' voices and facial expressions.

This method places substantial demands upon the actors with whom Saura works closely. He has often used the same actors in several movies. Saura has also worked with the same producer and crew for most of his career. There is a great deal of continuity from one of his movies to the next. Sometimes images or sequences from one movie recur in later ones. As Saura himself has said, "Every film is a consequence of the film before."

Every film is also a consequence of the particular political and social climate prevailing in Spain. With the death of Franco and the subsequent abolition of film censorship and restoration of democratic rule, Saura moved away from the complex, nonlinear narrative forms he had cultivated under Franco and began to make simpler, almost documentary-like movies. One of them, which dealt with juvenile delinquents in Madrid, was shot with nonprofessional actors from the slums of the capital (*De prisa, de prisa*). Two others are filmed versions of flamenco ballets that are based upon well-known literary works (*Bodas de sangre* and *Carmen*). In these as in other movies which contain references to Spanish plays, poems, and paintings, Saura affirms his ties to Spanish cultural traditions and shows their relevance to the Spain of today.

—Katherine Singer Kovács

SAUTET, Claude.

French. Born in Montrouge, Paris, 23 February 1924. Educated at Ecole des Arts Decoratif, entered IDHEC, 1948. Music critic for newspaper *Combat*, late 1940s; assistant director to Pierre Montazel, Gut Lefranc, Georges Franju and Jacques Becker, 1950s; also TV producer; directed first feature, *Classe tous risques*, 1960.

Films as Director and Scriptwriter:

1951   *Nous n'irons plus au bois* (short)
1956   *Bonjour sourire* (d only)
1960   *Classe tous risques* (The Big Risk)
1965   *L'Arme à gauche* (Guns for the Dictator)
1970   *Les Choses de la vie* (The Things of Life)
1971   *Max et les ferrailleurs*
1972   *César et Rosalie* (Cesar and Rosalie)
1974   *Vincent, François, Paul . . . et les autres*
1976   *Mado*
1978   *Une Histoire simple*
1980   *Un Mauvais Fils* (A Bad Son)
1983   *Garçon*
1988   *Quelques Jours avec moi*

Other Films:

(incomplete listing)

1954   *Touchez pas au Grisbi* (Grisbi)
1959   *Les Yeux sans visages* (**Eyes Without a Face**) (Franju) (asst d)

Publications:

By SAUTET: articles—

Interviews with Claude Beylie, in *Ecran* (Paris), December 1972 and November 1974.
"Claude Sautet, c'est la vitalité," with François Truffaut, in *Avant-Scène du Cinéma* (Paris), December 1974.
Interviews with Michel Ciment and others, in *Positif* (Paris), December 1976 and January 1979.
"Romy Schneider: une actrice qui depasse le quotidien," in *Avant-Scène du Cinéma* (Paris), 15 March 1979.
Interview with G. Legrand and I. Jordan in *Positif* (Paris), December 1983.

On SAUTET: book—

Korkmaz, Joseph, *Le Cinéma de Claude Sautet*, Paris, 1985.

On SAUTET: articles—

Sineux, M., "Entretien avec Philippe Sarde sur Claude Sautet et quelques autres," in *Positif* (Paris), January 1979.
"Claude Sautet Issue" of *Avant-Scène du Cinéma* (Paris), January 1984.

*   *   *

The career of Claude Sautet was slow in getting under way but by the 1970s he had virtually become the French cinema's official chronicler of bourgeois life. He had made his directing debut with a solidly constructed thriller, *Classe tous risques*, in 1960, but a second film, *L'Arme à gauche*, did not follow until 1965 and was markedly less successful. Despite numerous scriptwriting assignments, his directing career did not really get under way until he completed *Les Choses de la vie* in 1969. This set the pattern for a decade of filmmaking. The core of any Sautet film is a fairly banal emotional problem—a man caught between two women in *Les Choses de la vie* or a married woman confronted with a former lover in *César et Rosalie*. Around this situation Sautet weaves a rich pattern of bourgeois life: concerns with home and family, with money and possessions, give these films their particular tone. This is a cinema of warm, convincingly depicted characters for whom Sautet clearly has great affection and more than a touch of complicity. Problems and motivations are always explicitly set out, for this is a style of psychological realism in which the individual, not the social, forms the focus of attention. The director's style is a sober, classical one, built on the model of Hollywood narrative traditions: action, movement, vitality. Though his style can encompass such set pieces as the boxing match in *Vincent, Francois, Paul . . . et les autres*, Sautet is more concerned with

Claude Sautet directing Romy Schneider in *Les Choses de la vie*

the unfolding of a strong and involving narrative line. A key feature of all his work are the confrontation scenes which offer such excellent opportunities for the talented stars and solid character players who people his films.

Sautet's films since the mid-1970s—*Mado, Une Histoire simple*, and *Une Mauvais Fils*—are all characterized by a total assurance and a mastery of the medium. This mastery, however, is exercised within very precise limits, not in terms of the subject matter, which widens to take in the problems of affluence, women's independence, and juvenile delinquency, but in the manner in which such issues of the moment are approached. Sautet's classicism of form and ability to communicate directly with his audience is not accompanied by the resonances of social criticism which characterize the best North American cinema. Seeking to move his audience rather than enlighten it, Sautet uses powerful actors cast to type in carefully constructed roles, but any probing of the essential contradictions is avoided by a style of direction which keeps rigidly to the surface of life, the given patterns of bourgeois social behaviour. His approach is therefore condemned to a certain schematism, particularly in the handling of dialogue scenes, but his work gets its sense of vitality from the vigor with which the group scenes—the meals and excursions—and the typical locations of café or railway station are handled. Sautet offers a facsimile of life, a reflection of current problems or issues, but contained within a form calculated not to trouble the spectator after he has left the cinema. This conformism

may seem limiting to the contemporary critic, but it will offer future generations a rare insight into the manner in which the French middle classes liked to see themselves in the 1970s.

—Roy Armes

SAVILLE, Victor.

British/American. Born Victor Salberg in Birmingham, England, 25 September 1897, became U.S. citizen, 1950. Educated at King Edward VI Grammar School, Birmingham. Married Phoebe Vera Teller, 1920, two children. Wounded at Battle of Loos, 1915, and invalided out of the Army, 1916; manager of small cinema in Coventry, then joined Features and Newsreels Dept. of Pathé Frères, London, 1917; formed Victory Motion Pictures with Michael Balcon, 1919; producer for Gaumont, 1926–27; founder, independent production company Burlington Film Co., and directed first film, *The Arcadians*, 1927; director for Michael Balcon, 1930–35; formed Victor Saville Productions, Ltd., 1936; Signed contract with MGM, 1937, worked in Hollywood, from 1939; joined Columbia, made *Tonight and Every Night*, then rejoined

Victor Saville

MGM, 1943; formed Parklane Productions, 1952; returned to London, 1960. *Died in London, 8 May 1979.*

Films as Director:

1927	*The Arcadians* (+ pr)
1928	*Tesha (Woman in the Night)*
1929	*Kitty*; *Woman to Woman*
1930	*The W Plan*; *A Warm Corner*
1931	*The Sport of Kings*; *Michael & Mary*; *Sunshine Susie (The Office Girl)*
1932	*The Faithful Heart*; *Love on Wheels*
1933	*The Good Companions*; *I Was a Spy*; *Friday the Thirteenth*
1934	*Evergreen*; *Evensong*; *The Iron Duke*
1935	*The Dictator (The Loves of a Dictator)*; *Me and Marlborough*; *First a Girl*
1936	*It's Love Again*
1937	*Dark Journey* (+ pr); *Storm in a Teacup* (co-d, pr)
1938	*South Riding* (+ pr)
1943	*Forever and a Day* (co-d)
1945	*Tonight and Every Night* (+ pr)
1946	*The Green Years*
1947	*Green Dolphin Street*; *If Winter Comes*
1949	*The Conspirator*
1950	*Kim*
1951	*Calling Bulldog Drummond*
1952	*Twenty-four Hours of a Woman's Life (Affair in Monte Carlo)*
1954	*The Long Wait*
1955	*The Silver Chalice*

Other Films:

1923	*Woman to Woman* (Cutts) (co-pr with Michael Balcon); *The White Shadow* (Cutts) (co-pr with Balcon)
1924	*The Prudes Fall* (Cutts) (co-pr with Balcon)
1926	*Mademoiselle from Armentieres* (Elvey) (pr)
1927	*Roses of Picardy* (Elvey) (pr); *The Glad Eye* (Elvey) (pr); *The Flight Commander* (Elvey) (pr)
1931	*Hindle Wakes* (Elvey) (pr)
1937	*Action for Slander* (Whelan) (pr)
1938	*The Citadel* (Vidor) (pr)
1939	*Goodbye, Mr. Chips* (Wood) (pr); *Earl of Chicago* (Thorpe) (pr)
1940	*The Mortal Storm* (Borzage) (pr); *Bitter Sweet* (Van Dyke) (pr)
1941	*A Woman's Face* (Cukor) (pr); *Dr. Jekyll and Mr. Hyde* (Fleming) (pr); *Smilin' Through* (Borzage) (pr); *The Chocolate Soldier* (Del Ruth) (pr)
1942	*White Cargo* (Thorpe) (pr); *Keeper of the Flame* (Cukor) (pr)
1943	*Above Suspicion* (Thorpe) (pr)
1953	*I, the Jury* (Essex) (pr)
1955	*Kiss Me Deadly* (Aldrich) (exec pr)
1961	*The Greengage Summer* (Gilbert) (pr)
1962	*Mix Me a Person* (Norman) (exec pr)

Publications:

On SAVILLE: books—

Balcon, Michael, *A Lifetime of Films*, London, 1969.
Rollins, Cyril, *Victor Saville*, London, 1972.
Perry, George, *The Great British Picture Show*, London, 1974.
Armes, Roy, *A Critical History of the British Cinema*, London, 1978.

On SAVILLE: articles—

Obituary, in the *New York Times*, 10 May 1979.
Obituary, in *Variety* (New York), 16 May 1979.

*　　　*　　　*

A former film salesman who became a producer in partnership with Michael Balcon—both men were born in Birmingham—Victor Saville began his directorial career in the late 1920s in England, and during the next decade became firmly established as one of that country's more stylish filmmakers. Unlike his contemporaries in the British film industry, Saville never made films that were particularly English in content or style; his manner of directing was quite definitely borrowed from Hollywood and he understood the need for glamor and sophistication in order to appeal to the international film market.

One of Victor Saville's earliest films, *Tesha* (released in the U.S. as *Woman in the Night*) is notable for its mature subject matter, a married woman who has a child by her husband's best friend. *Kitty* is a curiosity as one of Britain's first talkies, with the sound sequences shot at the Paramount Astoria Studios on Long Island. However, it was in the 1930s that Victor Saville hit his stride as a director, with a series of romantic comedies featuring Jessie Matthews—*The Good Companions, Friday the Thirteenth, Evergreen, First a Girl*, and *It's Love Again*—and a brilliant First World War spy melodrama, *I Was a Spy*, which made an international star of Madeleine Carroll.

MGM recognized Victor Saville's internationality by selecting him to produce its first two prestigious British productions, *The Citadel*, and *Goodbye, Mr. Chips*. These films led to Saville's coming to the United States, where he produced (but did not direct) a string of quality films, notably *Bitter Sweet, Dr. Jekyll and Mr. Hyde, Smilin' Through*, and *Keeper of the Flame*. As with all of Saville's American films, they were solid, slightly dull, but always well-made entertainment pictures. The same may be said of the U.S. features which Saville directed, particularly *Green Dolphin Street* and *Kim*, which are heavy on production values and light on any originality in direction.

Victor Saville once remarked that films must "bounce off the times we live in," a philosophy which his early work upholds. If his later films have any linking continuity it is that they were derived from popular literary works. One project which never saw the light of day, however, was Victor Saville's planned production of Agatha Christie's long-running play, *The Mousetrap*, which he had hoped to produce with Tyrone Power starring under the direction of Billy Wilder.

—Anthony Slide

————

SAYLES, John.

American. Born John Thomas Sayles in Schenectady, New York, 28 September 1950. Attended Williams College, Williamstown, Massachusetts, B.S. in psychology, 1972. First novel published, 1975; writer for Roger Corman's New World Pictures, from 1977; first film as director, *The Return of the Secaucus Seven*, 1980; directed own plays *New Hope for the Dead* and *Turnbuckle*, Off-Off-Broadway, 1981; writer and director for TV, from 1980; director of promo videos for Bruce Springsteen, including "Born in the U.S.A.," and "I'm on Fire." Address: c/o Red Dog Films, Inc., 306 W. 38th Street, New York, NY 10018, U.S.A. Lives in Hoboken, New Jersey.

Films as Director and Scriptwriter:

1980	*The Return of the Secaucus Seven* (+ ed, role as Howie)
1981	*Lianna* (+ ed, role as Jerry)
1983	*Baby, It's You*
1984	*The Brother from Another Planet* (+ ed, role as bounty hunter)

John Sayles

1987   *Matewan* (+ role as preacher)
1988   *Eight Men Out* (+ role as Ring Lardner)

Other Films:

1978   *Piranha* (Dante) (sc)
1979   *The Lady in Red* (*Kiss Me and Die. Guns, Sin, and Bathtub
          Gin*) (Teague) (sc)
1980   *Battle Beyond the Stars* (Murakami) (sc); *The Howling*
          (Dante) (co-sc); *Alligator* (Teague) (sc)
1982   *The Challenge* (Frankenheimer) (co-sc)
1984   *Hard Choices* (King) (role as Don)
1985   *The Clan of the Cave Bear* (Chapman)
1987   *Wild Thing* (Reid) (sc); *Something Wild* (Demme) (role as
          motorcycle cop)
1989   *Breaking In* (Forsyth) (sc)

Publications:

By SAYLES: articles—

The Pride of the Bimbos, New York, 1975.
Union Dues, New York, 1977.
The Anarchists' Convention, New York, 1979.
Thinking in Pictures: The Making of the Movie "Matewan", New
    York, 1987.

By SAYLES: articles—

Interview with T. Crawley, in *Monthly Film Bulletin* (London),
    December 1982.

Interview with D. Popkin in *Cineaste* (New York), vol. 13, no. 1, 1983.
Interview with Paul Kerr in *Monthly Film Bulletin* (London), January
    1984.
Interview with Richard Laermer in *Films in Review* (New York),
    February 1985.
"Dialogue on Film: John Sayles," in *American Film* (Washington
    D.C.), May 1986.
Interview with Pat Aufderheide in *Cineaste* (New York), vol. 15, no. 4,
    1987.
"Color Bars," in *American Film* (Los Angeles), vol. 13, no. 6, April
    1988.

On SAYLES: articles—

Levine, H., "Features for Under a Million: John Sayles," in *Millimeter*
    (New York), February 1982.
Osborne, David, "John Sayles: from Hoboken to Hollywood—and
    Back," in *American Film* (Washington, D.C.), October 1982.
Milligan, P., "Sayles Management," in *Film Directions* (London),
    Summer 1984.
Valen, M., "John Sayles," in *Films and Filming* (London), September
    1984.
Fishbein, Leslie, "John Sayles' *Matewan*: Violence and Nostalgia," in
    Film and History (Newark, New Jersey), vol. 18, no. 3, 1988.
Isaacs, Neil D., "John Sayles and the Fictional Origin of *Matewan*," in
    Literature/Film Quarterly (Salibury, Maryland), vol. 16, no. 4, 1988.
Lardner, Ring, Jr., "Foul Ball," in *American Film* (Los Angeles), vol.
    13, no. 9, 1988.
Wilson, David, "Of Anarchists and Alligators" in *Monthly Film Bull-
    etin* (London), June 1989.

*   *   *

No other American director has so successfully straddled both Hollywood and independent film-making as John Sayles. While his fellow-independents have tended to restrict themselves either in terms of audience (Jim Jarmusch, Henry Jaglom) or creative scope (Woody Allen), Sayles has continued to make highly individual, idiosyncratic films of increasingly ambitious range, aimed firmly at a mainstream audience, without compromising his own subversive outlook.

Even before launching out as a director, Sayles had established his reputation both as a novelist and as a provider of witty, literate scripts for genre movies—*Alligator*, *The Howling*, *The Lady in Red*—into whose conventions he deftly introduced sharp touches of political allegory. His own films, though, have steered clear of generic formulae, remaining (in subject-matter as in treatment) fresh and quirkily unpredictable. The first of them, *The Return of the Secaucus Seven*, observed the reunion of a bunch of ex-1960s radicals with an affection, and a relaxed humour, that Kasdan's glossier treatment in *The Big Chill* never quite matched. "There was a realism there," Roger Corman noted, "which more money might have obscured." The film picked up several awards, and rapidly became a cult favourite.

Secaucus, for all its small-scale subject and slightly shaggy charm, established the priorities of all Sayles's work to date: in his own words, "the acting, and believing in the characters and caring about them." His films, situated (as Pat Aufderheide put it) "at the intersection of culture and politics," favour ensemble playing over star performances, communication over sensation, and the exploration of character and ideas over pictorial values or technical bravura. "I don't regard anything I do as art. That's a foreign world to me. I regard it as a conversation. Very often in a conversation, you tell a story to illustrate something you think or feel."

Even so, Sayles's work has developed steadily in terms of visual as well as dramatic complexity. His early films, such as *Secaucus* and *Lianna*, a sympathetic account of a married woman awakening to her lesbian nature, were criticised in some quarters for their static camerawork. Sayles, while readily conceding his lack of technical experience, pointed out that "Fluid camera work takes money. Unless it's an action movie, why cut away from good actors?" More recently, however, with *Matewan* and *Eight Men Out*, he has adopted a more sophisticated and even elegant shooting style, though never to the detriment of the story. In *Matewan*, scenes of nocturnal wood-smoky encampments in the Appalachian foothills, moodily shot by Haskell Wexler in dark grainy tones, recall classic elements of late Ford—*Wagonmaster*, say, or *The Horse Soldiers*.

Not that Sayles (unlike his "movie brat" near-contemporaries) is interested in strewing his pictures with allusive film-buff references. "I want people to leave the theater thinking about their own lives, not about other movies." His work draws its resonance from his social concerns, from his sense of character as a product of historical and cultural influences, from his acute ear for dialogue and his insight into the political process. The mismatched young couple of *Baby It's You* are no less constrained by the pressures of their class and environment (smalltown 1960s New Jersey) than the West Virginian miners of *Matewan* or the baseball professionals of *Eight Men Out*. Sayles's hope is that we, as viewers, will extrapolate from what we see, grasping its relevance to our own situation. "If storytelling has a positive function, it's to put us in touch with other people's lives, to help us connect and draw strength or knowledge from people we'll never meet, to help us see beyond our own experience."

Sayles's sympathy for his characters can on occasion verge on sentimentality, as in *The Brother from Another Planet*, his least satisfactory though perhaps most likeable film. (Or, more damagingly, in his atypically emollient script for Bill Forsyth's *Breaking In*.) His attitude to the movie industry, though, displays a clear-eyed realism, and an integrity which has so far resisted the lure—and the attendant compromises—of Hollywood mega-budgets. In his most recent work as a director, Sayles has extended and deepened his personal vision of his country's history. If he can sustain the balancing act, funding his own staunchly independent work with lucrative scripting for other people's movies, he looks set to become one of the most original and incisive cinematic interpreters of the American myth.

—Philip Kemp

SCHAFFNER, Franklin J.

American. Born in Tokyo, 30 May 1920. Educated at Franklin and Marshal College; studied law at Columbia University. Served in U.S. Navy, 1942–46. Married Helen Jean Gilchrist, 1948, two daughters. Assistant director, *March of Time* series, late 1940s; television director for CBS, 1949–62, work included *Studio One*, *Ford Theater*, and *Playhouse 90*; with Worthington Miner, George Roy Hill and Fielder Cook formed "Unit Four" production company, 1955; directed *Advise and Consent* on Broadway, 1961; signed 3-picture contract with 20th Century-Fox and directed first feature, *A Summer World* (incomplete), 1961; TV counselor to President Kennedy, 1961–63; president, Gilchrist Productions, 1962–68; president, Franklin Schaffner Productions, from 1969; president, Directors Guild of America, 1987–89. Recipient: 3 Emmy Awards; Oscar for Best Director, and Directors Guild Award, for *Patton*, 1970. *Died, of cancer, in Santa Monica, California, 2 July 1989.*

Films as Director:

1961   *A Summer World* (incomplete)
1963   *The Stripper (Woman of Summer)*
1964   *The Best Man*
1965   *The War Lord*
1967   *The Double Man* (+ role)
1968   *Planet of the Apes*
1970   *Patton (Patton—Lust for Glory. Patton: A Salute to a Rebel)*
1971   *Nicholas and Alexandra* (+ pr)
1973   *Papillon* (+ co-pr)
1977   *Islands in the Stream*
1978   *The Boys from Brazil*
1981   *Sphinx* (+ exec pr)
1982   *Yes, Giorgio*
1987   *Lionheart*
1989   *Welcome Home*

Publications:

By SCHAFFNER: book—

Worthing Miner: Interviewed by Franklin J. Schaffner, Metuchen, New Jersey, 1985.

By SCHAFFNER: articles—

Interview with Gerald Pratley, in *Cineaste* (New York), Summer 1969.
Interview with R. Feiden, in *Inter/View* (New York), March 1972.
"Chronicler of Power," an interview with Kathe Geist, in *Film Comment* (New York), September/October 1972.
Interview with R. Appelbaum, in *Films and Filming* (London), February 1979.
Interview with D. Castelli, in *Films Illustrated* (London), May 1979.

Franklin J. Schaffner: Steve McQueen and Dustin Hoffman in *Papillon*

On SCHAFFNER: book—

Kim, Erwin, *Franklin J. Schaffner*, Metuchen, New Jersey, 1986.

On SCHAFFNER: articles—

Wilson, David, "Franklin Schaffner," in *Sight and Sound* (London), Spring 1966.

Sarris, Andrew, "Director of the Month—Franklin Schaffner: The Panoply of Power," in *Show* (Hollywood), April 1970.

Lightman, Herb, "On Location with *Islands in the Stream*," in *American Cinematographer* (Los Angeles), November 1976.

"Franklin J. Schaffner," in *Kosmorama* (Copenhagen), Autumn 1977.

Cook, B., "The War Between the Writers and the Directors: Part II: The Directors," in *American Film* (Washington, D.C.), June 1979.

"TV to Film: a History, a Map and a Family Tree," in *Monthly Film Bulletin* (London), February 1983.

Obituary, in *Variety* (New York), 5 July 1989.

*   *   *

Franklin J. Schaffner has often been referred to as an "actors' director." A former actor himself, he spent over a decade directing television drama before making his first film. This experience proved invaluable when he arrived in Hollywood. All his films starred well-established professionals such as Fonda, Heston, Brynner, Scott, Hoffman, Peck, and Olivier.

His first film, *The Stripper*, was based on William Inge's play *A Loss of Roses*. Producer Jerry Wald died while it was being made, and after completion the film was taken out of Franklin's hands and re-edited. As a result the character of the "stripper," played by Joanne Woodward, was sadly lacking in contrast. Schaffner's experience working on political television programs stood him in very good stead when he directed his second film, *The Best Man*, a story of two contenders for the Presidential nomination at a political convention in Los Angeles. Set mainly in hotel rooms and corridors, it could have become very static. But Schaffner accepted the challenge and turned out a compelling drama.

After the intimacy of *The Best Man* came the vastness of *The War Lord*. A medieval costume picture was a complete change for Schaffner, but he succeeded in capturing the visual splendor of the outdoor sequences—particularly the first few minutes—and the excitement and gusto of the battle scenes. Although an "action" film, it had a literate script—and once again it was cut by the studio. *The Double Man* was an average spy drama, but not a great film. His first big financial success was *Planet of the Apes*, in which he had to produce realistic performances from actors in monkey suits. Handled by another director it could easily have been turned into a farce, but Schaffner's craftsmanship made it a science fiction satire.

In 1970 he directed George C. Scott in the role of General Patton. 27 years earlier Schaffner himself had taken part in the landings in Sicily under Patton. The film was shot in 70mm, but he insisted on cutting it in 35mm so as to avoid being influenced by the scope of 70mm. Scott's performance was widely praised, but he refused an Academy Award. (Schaffner accepted his!).

It was his interest in history that first attracted Schaffner to *Nicholas and Alexandra*. Here he told what was basically an intimate story of two people, but two people surrounded by the overflowing retinue of the court and the boundless expanse of the countryside. Schaffner used the contrast to great effect, and the film was nominated for an Oscar.

Papillon is the only film which Schaffner directed in sequence, and this was not by choice. Dalton Trumbo was rewriting the script as the film was being shot, often just managing to keep up with the production. This was the second time that Schaffner had worked with cinematographer Fred Koenekamp, and they were teamed again for his next feature, *Islands in the Stream*. This time he faced the problem of space and isolation, having to fill the large screen for a long time with just

one man. He also found it necessary to use two cameras for some of the action sequences, something which he never did if it could be avoided. Several studios turned down *The Boys from Brazil* because it was impossible to cast, but Schaffner thought it would work if he cast against type. So Gregory Peck, always known as a "good guy," played Mengele—the German doctor intent on producing clones of Hitler. Olivier, who had earlier played the German in *Marathon Man*, was the Jewish doctor trying to track down the Nazi. In the early 1980s Schaffner made *Sphinx*, an adventure story set amongst the pyramids, and *Yes, Giorgio*, his first "musical," with Luciano Pavarotti.

Schaffner has a reputation for getting the best out of his actors and coping well with intimate dramas. Yet he has also achieved success with large-scale epics and has been compared with David Lean because of the beauty of his compositions and the breadth of his dramatic power. He revels in films about men struggling to achieve a certain goal. A craftsman, he does his homework and prepares each scene before arriving on the set. He knows what he wants.

—Colin Williams

SCHEPISI, Fred.

Australian. Born Frederic Alan Schepisi in Melbourne, Victoria, 26 December 1939. Briefly attended seminary school. Married 1) Joan Ford, 1960, four children; 2) casting director Rhonda Finlayson, 1973, two children. Worked in advertising, from 1956; television production manager, Daton Advisory Service, Melbourne, 1961–64; manager of Cinesound Productions, Victoria, 1964, then managing director of newly-formed The Film House, Melbourne, making advertising shorts and documentaries, 1964–66 (chairman, from 1979); first feature, *The Devil's Playground*, won six Australian Oscars, 1976; moved to U.S.A., 1979; returned to Australia to make *A Cry in the Dark*, 1988; Governor of the Australian Film Institute. Agent: c/o Sam Cohn, International Creative Management, 40 W. 57th Street, New York, NY 10019, U.S.A.

Films as Director:

1970	*The Party* (short)
1973	"The Priest" episode of *Libido*
1976	*The Devil's Playground* (+ sc, pr)
1978	***The Chant of Jimmie Blacksmith*** (+ sc, pr)
1981	*Barbarosa*
1984	*Iceman*
1985	*Plenty*
1987	*Roxanne*
1988	*A Cry in the Dark* (*Guilty By Suspicion. Evil Angels*)
1990	*The Russia House*

Publications:

By SCHEPISI: articles—

Interview in *Cinema Papers* (Melbourne), January 1978.

"Le sauvage qui n'avait pas été enfant," an interview with V. Amiel and others in *Positif* (Paris), February 1983.

Interview with M. Magill in *Films in Review* (New York), January 1984.

Interview with B. Lewis in *Films and Filming* (London), December 1985.

Interview in *Screen International* (London), 4 January 1986.

Fred Schepisi

"Dialogue on Film: Fred Schepisi," in *American Film* (Washington D.C.), July/August 1987.

"The Making of *Evil Angels*," an interview with P. Hawker in *Cinema Papers* (Melbourne), November 1988.

On SCHEPISI: books—

Tulloch, John, *Australian Cinema: Industry, Narrative and Meaning*, Sydney and London, 1982.

Hall, Sandra, *The New Australian Cinema in Review*, Adelaide, 1985.

Moran, Albert, and Tom O'Regan, editors, *An Australian Film Reader*, Sydney, 1985.

Mathews, Sue, *35mm Dreams: Conversations with Five Directors About the Australian Film Revival*, Ringwood, Australia, 1987.

McFarlane, Brian, *Australian Cinema 1970–85*, London, 1987.

On SCHEPISI: articles—

Bromby, Robin, "Test for Australia," in *Sight and Sound* (London), Spring 1979.

Stratton, D., "Man of Plenty," in *Cinema Papers* (Melbourne), March 1986.

*   *   *

More than any other director of the Australian new wave, Fred Schepisi reflects, in his deal-making expertise, his emphasis on production values, even in his choice of New York as an adoptive base, the values of his home city, Melbourne, traditionally Australia's capital of political conservatism, old money, the church and the law.

Schepisi's first two features assaulted Australia's endemic provincialism. *The Devil's Playground*, a story of sexual repression and dead belief set in a Catholic seminary, is based on Schepisi's 18 adolescent months in a monastery. (The theme was rehearsed in *The Priest*, his episode of the sketch film *Libido*, written by lapsed Catholic novelist Thomas Keneally.) The film's gloomy, sensual elegance is typical of Schepisi's later work, but his adolescent hero's moral and religious doubts are dealt with sketchily, Schepisi preferring to emphasise the celibate staff's problems with sex and drink, especially in a memorable scene of priest Arthur Dignam spying on naked girls at a public swimming pool.

The Chant of Jimmie Blacksmith, again based on Thomas Keneally, is a period drama from the true story of 19th-century renegade aboriginal Jimmie Governor, who revolted against the white dehumanisation of his race. Schepisi's use of landscape echoes the westerns of Anthony Mann, underlining the similarities between his film and Hollywood's pro-Indian dramas like *Broken Arrow* and *Tell Them Willie Boy is Here*. In a film that, like Schepisi's later *A Cry in the Dark*, mixes, sometimes uneasily, social protest with widescreen melodrama, an inexperienced Tommy Lewis rampages bloodily but unconvincingly across rural Australia as the ill-used part-aboriginal driven to massacre by corruption in law, religion and the state.

A highly successful producer of TV commercials and documentaries, the pragmatic Schepisi conformed more comfortably than most Australian directors to Hollywood. Though his first American production, the revenge western *Barbarosa*, has all the earmarks of a test piece, he extracted good performances from an ageing Gilbert Roland, and the project's co-producers, Willie Nelson and a famously aggressive Gary Busey ("I am the first director he hasn't destroyed," Schepisi said proudly.) Schepisi proved equally decisive in *Ice Man*, a piece of Green s-f in which John Lone's defrosted Neanderthal beguiles technocrat Tim Hutton with earth magic and Ice Age mythology.

Schepisi's first hit was an adaptation of David Hare's play *Plenty*. As the ex-Resistance heroine who finds only disillusion in Britain's post-war affluence, Meryl Streep replaced Kate Nelligan, who created the role on stage. The casting turned *Plenty* into a star vehicle, winning international success at the cost of Hare's more precise political arguments, though Schepisi, as impatient as only an Australian can be with the British, manipulates Sir John Gielgud, Charles Dance and especially Ian McKellen in waspish parodies of Imperial privilege.

Confirmed now as a technician able to tame any project or performer, Schepisi made *Roxanne*, a comedy version of Rostand's *Cyrano de Bergerac*, reset in the Pacific northwest as a vehicle for comic Steve Martin. In the wake of its enormous success, he returned to Australia to film *A Cry in the Dark* (*Evil Angels*), the sensational true story of a young mother's trial and imprisonment for infanticide. Lindy Chamberlain insisted a wild dog had stolen her baby Azaria from one of Australia's most famous desert tourist sites, Ayers Rock, but the lack of a body, taken with Lindy's own unusual religious affiliations—she was a Seventh Day Adventist—fuelled rumours that the child had been sacrificed in some arcane rite. She was freed only after investigators decisively discredited the forensic evidence.

In a typical calculated risk, Schepisi cast Meryl Streep as Lindy and used the film to reprise *The Chant of Jimmie Blacksmith*. Australia itself becomes the villain, and Chamberlain another victim, like Blacksmith and the boy of *The Devil's Playground*, of national bigotry and ignorance. *A Cry in the Dark* depicts Australia's press as vulgar and meretricious, and its police as malicious and bumbling. Far from resenting either the imported star or the national slur, Australians greeted the film with enthusiasm, and the Streep name guaranteed a modest international success. Schepisi debated further Australian-based projects, but with the local industry's financial base crumbling in the financial freeze of the late 1980s, he returned to New York (though much of the film was shot on location in Moscow) for the latest in a string of high-budget international projects, John Le Carre's *The Russia House*.

—John Baxter.

SCHLESINGER, John.

British. Born John Richard Schlesinger in London, 16 February 1926. Educated at Uppingham School and Balliol College, Oxford, 1945–50. Maker of short films, from 1948; actor with Colchester Repertory Company then Ngaio Marsh's Touring Company, 1950–52; directed 24 short documentaries for BBC TV series *Tonight* and *Monitor*, 1956–61; directed first feature, *A Kind of Loving*, 1962; associate director, National Theatre, London, from 1973; opera director, 1980s; also director for TV, work includes *Separate Tables*, 1982, and *An Englishman Abroad*, 1983. Recipient: Best Direction, New York Film Critics, for *Darling*, 1965; Oscar for Best Director, Best Direction Award, British Film Academy, and Directors Award, Directors Guild of America, for *Midnight Cowboy*, 1969; Best Direction Award, British Film Academy, for *Sunday, Bloody Sunday*, 1970; Commander of the British Empire, 1970; British Film and TV Academy Award, for *An Englishman Abroad*, 1983. Agent: c/o Duncan Heath, 162 Wardour Street, London W1, England.

Films as Director:

1961	*Terminus* (doc) (+ sc)
1962	*A Kind of Loving*
1963	*Billy Liar*
1965	*Darling* (+ sc)
1967	*Far from the Madding Crowd*
1969	*Midnight Cowboy* (+ co-pr)
1971	*Sunday, Bloody Sunday*
1972	"Olympic Marathon" section of *Visions of Eight*
1975	*The Day of the Locust*
1976	*Marathon Man*
1979	*Yanks*
1980	*Honky Tonk Freeway*
1981	*Privileged* (consultant d only)
1985	*The Falcon and the Snowman* (+ pr)
1987	*The Believers* (+ pr)
1988	*First and Last*; *Madame Sousatzka*
1990	*Pacific Heights*

Other Films:

1953	*Single-Handed* (*Sailor of the King*) (Boulting) (role)
1955	*The Divided Heart* (Crichton) (role as ticket collector)
1956	*The Last Man to Hang?* (Fisher) (role as Dr. Goldfinger)
1957	*The Battle of the River Plate* (*Pursuit of the Graf Spee*) (Powell and Pressburger) (role); *Brothers in Law* (Boulting) (role)
1986	*Fifty Years of Action!* (appearance as himself)

Publications:

By SCHLESINGER: articles—

"How to Get Into Films by the People Who Got in Themselves," in *Films and Filming* (London), July 1963.
"John Schlesinger," in *Directors in Action* edited by Bob Thomas, Indianapolis, 1968.
Interview with David Spiers, in *Screen* (London), Summer 1970.
Interview with Valerie Wade, in *Interview* (New York), July 1974.
Interview with Gene D. Phillips, in *Film Comment* (New York), May/June 1975.
"Dialogue on Film: John Schlesinger," with James Powers, in *American Film* (Washington, D.C.), December 1979.
"Treason to Believe," interview with Graham Fuller in *Stills* (London), April 1985.
"Dialogue on Film: John Schlesinger," in *American Film* (Washington D.C.), November 1987.
Interview with L. Farrah in *Films and Filming* (London), May 1988.

On SCHLESINGER: books—

Perry, George, *The Great British Picture Show*, London, 1974.
Walker, Alexander, *Hollywood UK: The British Film Industry in the Sixties*, London, 1974.
Sherman, Eric, *Directing the Film: Film Directors on their Art*, Boston, 1976.
Brooker, Nancy J., *John Schlesinger: A Guide to References and Resources*, Boston, 1978.
Phillips, Gene D., *John Schlesinger*, Boston, 1981.
Salizzato, Claver, *John Schlesinger*, Florence, 1986.

John Schlesinger

Phillips, Gene D., *Major Film Directors of the American and British Cinema*, Cranbury, New Jersey, 1989.

On SCHLESINGER: articles—

Phillips, Gene D., "John Schlesinger, Social Realist," in *Film Comment* (New York), Winter 1969.

Hall, William, "John Schlesinger, Award Winner," in *Action* (Los Angeles), July/August 1970.

"John Schlesinger at the Olympic Games," in *American Cinematographer* (Hollywood), November 1972.

Rand, Kenn, "Behind the Scenes of *Day of the Locust*," in *American Cinematographer* (Hollywood), June 1975.

Phillips, Gene D., "Exile in Hollywood: John Schlesinger," in *Literature/Film Quarterly* (Salisbury, Maryland), Spring 1977.

Phillips, Gene D., "On *Yanks* and Other Films," in *Focus on Film* (London), Fall 1978.

Fuller, Graham, "An Englishman Abroad," in *Cinema Papers* (Melbourne), July 1985.

*   *   *

John Schlesinger began his professional career by making short documentaries for the BBC. His first major venture in the cinema was a documentary for British Transport called *Terminus*, about 24 hours at Waterloo Station, which won him an award at the Venice Film Festival. Schlesinger's documentaries attracted the attention of producer Joseph Janni; together they formed a creative association which has included several of Schlesinger's British films, beginning with *A Kind of Loving*, which won the Grand Prize at the Berlin Film Festival.

Schlesinger began directing feature films in Britain at the point when the cycle of low-budget, high-quality movies on social themes (called "Kitchen Sink" dramas) was in full swing. Because these films were made outside the large studio system, Schlesinger got used to developing his own film projects. He has continued to do so while directing films in Hollywood, where he has worked with increasing regularity in recent years, starting with his first American film, *Midnight Cowboy*.

"I like the cross-fertilization that comes from making films in both England and America," he explains. "Although I am English and I do like to work in England, I have gotten used to regarding myself more and more as mid-Atlantic." As a matter of fact, foreign directors like Lang and Hitchcock and Schlesinger, precisely because they are not native Americans, are sometimes able to view American life with a vigilant, perceptive eye for the kind of telling details which home-grown directors might easily overlook or simply take for granted. Indeed, reviews of *Midnight Cowboy* by and large noted how accurately the British-born Schlesinger had caught the authentic atmosphere of not only New York City, but also of Miami Beach and the Texas Panhandle, as surely as he had captured the atmosphere of a factory town in his native England in *A Kind of Loving*.

"Any film that is seriously made will reflect the attitudes and problems of society at large," he says, and consequently possess the potential to appeal to an international audience, as many of his films have. "But it is inevitable that a director's own attitudes will creep into his films. For my part I try in my movies to communicate to the filmgoer a better understanding of other human beings by exploring the hazards of entering into a mutual relationship with another human being, which is the most difficult thing on earth to do, because it involves a voyage of discovery for both parties." Hence his prime concern as a director with examining complex human relationships from a variety of angles—ranging from the social outcasts of *Midnight Cowboy* to members of the jet set in *Darling*.

Among the standout films of his later career are *The Falcon and the Snowman*, the true story of two young Americans who betrayed their country to the Russians; and *Madame Sousatzka*, about a dedicated, demanding London piano teacher, whose exacting standards threaten to drive her most promising pupil away. In sum, John Schlesinger is a member of the growing international community of filmmakers who are trying to speak to an equally international audience. That is the way the world cinema is headed, and directors like Schlesinger are helping to lead it there.

—Gene D. Phillips

—————

SCHLÖNDORFF, Volker.

German. Born in Wiesbaden, 31 March 1939. Educated at Lycée Henri IV, Paris; studied political science and economics; studied film directing at IDHEC, Paris. Married filmmaker Margarethe von Trotta, 1969. Assistant to various French directors, 1960–64; returned to Germany, 1965; formed Hallelujah-Film with Peter Fleischmann, went into partnership with German TV stations, 1969; formed Bioskop-Film with Reinhard Hauff, 1973; opera director, from 1974. Recipient: FIPRESCT Prize, Cannes Festival, for *Young Törless*, 1966; Oscar for Best Foreign-Language Film, and Best Film, Cannes Festival (*ex aequo*), for *The Tin Drum*, 1979.

Films as Director:

1960　*Wen kümmert's . . . (Who Cares . . .)* (short, unreleased)
1966　*Der junge Törless (Young Törless)* (+ sc)
1967　*Mord und Totschlag (A Degree of Murder)* (+ co-sc)
1969　*Michael Kohlhaas—Der Rebell (Michael Kohlhaas—The Rebel)* (+ co-sc)
1970　*Baal* (for TV) (+ sc); *Ein unheimlicher Moment (An Uneasy Moment)* (short; originally episode of uncompleted feature *Paukenspieler*, filmed 1967); *Der plötzlicher Reichtum der armen Leute von Kombach (The Sudden Fortune of the Poor People of Kombach)* (+ co-sc)
1971　*Die Moral der Ruth Halbfass (The Moral of Ruth Halbfass)* (+ co-sc); *Strohfeuer (A Free Woman, Strawfire. Summer Lightning)* (+ co-sc)
1974　*Übernachtung in Tirol (Overnight Stay in the Tyrol)* (for TV) (+ co-sc)
1975　*Georginas Grunde (Georgina's Reasons)* (for TV); **Die verlorene Ehre der Katharina Blum (The Lost Honor of Katharina Blum)** (co-d, co-sc)
1976　*Der Fangschuss (Coup de grâce)*
1977　*Nur zum Spass—Nur zum Spiel. Kaleidoskop Valeska Gert (Only for Fun—Only for Play. Kaleidoscope Valeska Gert)* (doc) (+ sc)
1978　*Deutschland im Herbst (Germany in Autumn)* (co-d)
1979　*Der Blechtrommel (The Tin Drum)* (+ co-sc)
1980　*Der Kandidat (The Candidate)* (doc) (+ co-sc)
1981　*Die Fälschung (The Forgery)* (+ sc); *Circle of Deceit*
1983　*Krieg und Frieden (War and Peace)* (doc)
1984　*Swann in Love (Un Amour de Swann)*
1985　*Death of a Salesman*
1987　*Vermischte Nachrichten (Odds and Ends)* (co-d)
1990　*The Handmaid's Tale*
1991　*Last Call from Passenger Faber* (+ sc)

Publications:

By SCHLÖNDORFF: books—

Die Blechtrommel als Film, Frankfurt, 1979.

By SCHLÖNDORFF: articles—

"Volker Schloendorff: The Rebel," interview with Rui Nogueira and Nicoletta Zalaffi, in *Film* (London), Summer 1969.
"Feu de paille," interview with M. Martin, in *Ecran* (Paris), February 1973.
"Melville und der Befreiungskampf in Baltikum," interview with H. Wiedemann, in *Film und Ton* (Munich), December 1976.
"*Die Blechtrommel*," in *Film und Ton* (Munich), June 1979.
"The Tin Drum: Volker Schlöndorff's 'Dream of Childhood', interview with J. Hughes, in *Film Quarterly* (Berkeley), Spring 1981.
"The Limits of Journalism," an interview with A. Auster and L. Quart in *Cineaste* (New York), vol. 12, no. 2, 1982.
Interview with B. Steinborn in *Filmfaust* (Frankfurt), February/March 1983.

On SCHLÖNDORFF: books—

Lewandowski, Rainer, *Die Filme von Volker Schlöndorff*, Hildesheim, 1981.
Franklin, James, *New German Cinema: From Oberhausen to Hamburg*, Boston, 1983.
Phillips, Klaus, editor, *New German Filmmakers: From Oberhausen through the 1970s*, New York, 1984.
Elsaesser, Thomas, *New German Cinema: A History*, London, 1989.

On SCHLÖNDORFF: articles—

"*Le Coup de grâce* Issue" of *Avant-Scène du Cinéma* (Paris), 1 February 1977.
Eichenlaub, H.M., "Den deutschen Film international machen: Volker Schlöndorff und *Die Blechtrommel*," in *Cinema* (Zurich), no.2, 1979.
Holloway, Ronald, "Volker Schlöndorff," in *International Film Guide 1982*, London, 1981.
Rickey, C., "The War Lovers," in *American Film* (Washington D.C.), January/February 1982.
"*Un Amour de Swann* Issue" of *Avant-Scène du Cinéma* (Paris), no. 321/322, 1984.

On SCHLÖNDORFF: film—

Private Conversation (doc about the making of *Death of a Salesman*), directed by Christian Blackwood, 1985.

*　　　*　　　*

In discussions of the New German Cinema, Volker Schlöndorff's name generally comes up only after the mention of Fassbinder, Herzog, Wenders, and perhaps Straub, Syberberg, or von Trotta. Though his work certainly merits consideration alongside that of any of his countrymen, there are several reasons why he has stood apart from them.

As a teenager, Schlöndorff moved to France to study, earning academic honors and a university degree in economics and political science. He enrolled at IDHEC with an interest in film directing but chose instead to pursue an active apprenticeship within the French film industry. Eventually he served as assistant director to Jean-Pierre Melville, Alain Resnais, and Louis Malle. Schlöndorff then returned to Germany and scored an immediate triumph with his first feature, *Young Törless*. Like his mentor Louis Malle, then, he ushered in his country's new wave of film artists, but also like that of Malle, Schlöndorff's eclectic range of projects has defied easy categorization, causing his work to seem less personal than that of almost any other German filmmaker's. His decade in France also set Schlöndorff apart in other ways, not the least of which was his thorough professional training there that instilled in him an appreciation for the highly-crafted, polished filmmaking that marks his style. (The quality of the photography in his work—both black and white and in color, and whether by Sven Nykvist, Franz Rath, or Igor Luther—has been consistently exceptional.) While most of his contemporaries declared their antipathy toward the look and production methods of the declining German film industry of the 1960s, Schlöndorff endeavored successfully to make larger-scaled features.

Volker Schlöndorff

Toward this end he helped form and continues to operate two production companies—Hallelujah-Film and Bioskop-Film—and has regularly obtained financing from German television and a variety of international producers. Yet he has met shooting schedules of just three weeks, and his wide career includes shorts, documentaries, and television films (one is a production of Brecht's *Baal* with Fassbinder in the title role). In the mid-1970s he even turned to directing opera: Janáček's *Katya Kabanova* and a work by Hans Werner Henze.

Intellectual, literate, and fluent in several languages, he has chiefly been attracted to the adaption of literary works—a practice which attracts mixed critical reactions and which has yielded mixed results: *Young Törless*, from Robert Musil, remains one of his best films, and there is much to praise in *The Tin Drum*, the New German Cinema's foremost commercial success, which Günter Grass helped to adapt from his novel. Despite strengths in each, Kleist's *Michael Kohlhaas* and Marguerite Yourcenar's *Coup de grace* turned out unevenly for quite different reasons. The admirable *Lost Honor of Katharina Blum* comes from a Heinrich Böll story; the problematic *Circle of Deceit* from the novel by Nicolas Born.

Among "original" projects, on the other hand, are *A Degree of Murder*, a failure by all accounts; the fine *A Free Woman*; and the excellent *Sudden Wealth of the Poor People of Kombach*.

Despite the variety of his subjects, Schlöndorff is almost invariably drawn to material that allows him expression as social critic. All the films cited above share this characteristic. Some of his projects have been courageously political: *Katharina Blum* is an undisguised attack on Germany's powerful right-wing, scandal-mongering press, which serves large-scale social repression. As notable are his leading contributions to three collaborative documentaries: *Germany in Autumn*, a response to the authoritarian climate in the country in the wake of the Baader-Meinhof affair; *The Candidate*, shot during the election campaign and examining the career of ultra-conservative Christian Social Unionist Franz Josef Strauss; and *War and Peace*, an agit-prop film essay on the deployment of new American nuclear missiles in the Federal Republic.

Schlöndorff's major theme is the temptation toward moral and political equivocation within an ambiguous or malignant social order, and his films are wryly or skeptically realistic about any hoped-for solutions, even courting controversy. *A Free Woman* chastens unbridled feminist idealism; *Circle of Deceit* (made prior to the Israeli invasion of Lebanon) refuses to take sides in the Lebanese conflict.

Margarethe von Trotta, to whom he is married, has performed in a number of Schlöndorff's films and is a frequent collaborator on his scripts; interestingly, her own work as director is characterized not only by a polish equal to Schlöndorff's and similar political inspiration but also by a compelling intelligence and power of evocation.

—Herbert Reynolds

SCHOEDSACK, Ernest B.

American. Born Ernest Beaumont Schoedsack in Council Bluffs, Iowa, 8 June 1893. Married actress Ruth Rose, 1926, one son. Worked with engineering road gangs in San Francisco area, then secured job as cameraman for Mack Sennett through brother Felix (G.F.) Schoedsack, early 1910s; served in photographic dept. of U.S. Signal Corps. in France, 1916, then captain in Red Cross photographic unit; freelance newsreel cameraman, Europe, then returned to U.S., 1922; collaborated with Merian C. Cooper and newspaper correspondent Marguerite Harrison on first film, *Grass*, 1925; suffered severe eye injury while testing photographic equipment for U.S. Air Force, World War II. *Died 23 December 1979.*

Films as Director:

1925   *Grass* (doc) (co-d, co-pr, co-sc, co-ph)
1927   *Chang* (doc) (co-d, co-pr)
1929   *The Four Feathers* (co-d, co-pr)
1931   *Rango* (+ pr)
1932   *The Most Dangerous Game* (*The Hounds of Zaroff*) (co-d, co-pr)
1933   *King Kong* (co-d, co-pr); *Son of Kong*; *Blind Adventure*
1934   *Long Lost Father*
1935   *The Last Days of Pompeii*
1937   *Trouble in Morocco*; *Outlaws of the Orient*
1940   *Dr. Cyclops*
1949   *Mighty Joe Young*
1952   *This Is Cinerama* (d prologue only, uncredited)

Publications:

By SCHOEDSACK: articles—

"*Grass*: the making of an epic," in *American Cinematographer* (Hollywood), February 1983.

On SCHOEDSACK: books—

Goldner, Orville, and George Turner, *The Making of King Kong*, Cranbury, New Jersey, 1975.
Gottesman, Ronald, and Harry Geduld, editors, *The Girl in the Hairy Paw*, New York, 1976.

On SCHOEDSACK: articles—

Boone, Andrew R., "Prehistoric Monsters Roar and Hiss for the Sound Film," in *Popular Science Monthly* (New York), 1933.
"The Making of the Original *King Kong*," in *American Cinematographer* (Los Angeles), January 1977.
"RKO: They Also Served," in *Monthly Film Bulletin* (London), December 1979.
Goimard, J., "Cooper et Schoedsack: une longue collaboration," in *Avant-Scène du Cinéma* (Paris), November 1982.

*   *   *

Ernest B. Schoedsack: poster for *King Kong*

Ernest B. Schoedsack's initial fame as a filmmaker came from his work in the documentary mode, directing "natural dramas" as he and his partner Merian C. Cooper called their films. Schoedsack's spirit for adventure in these pictures can be traced to the kind of life he himself led. He began his film career simply enough as a cameraman with the Mack Sennett Keystone Studios. When World War I broke out Schoedsack enlisted with the photographic section of the Signal Corps. He was stationed in France where he gained a great deal of film experience as a newsreel cameraman. With the signing of the Armistice, Schoedsack decided to remain in Europe and aid the Poles in their battle against the Russians. While in Poland Schoedsack continued to make newsreels. However, this occupation was mainly a cover to disguise the fact that he was smuggling supplies and Poles out of Russian-occupied territory.

It was in Poland that Schoedsack met his future partner Merian C. Cooper. Like Schoedsack, Cooper was an American who wanted to help the Polish people in their struggle for freedom. Cooper's exploits during the Russian-Polish conflict resulted in his being imprisoned by the Russians as a spy. Fortunately he managed to escape before he could be executed. The true-life adventures of both Cooper and Schoedsack make it easy to see why these two sought out the most distant, difficult, and dangerous locations they could find for their films.

Their first motion picture collaboration, titled *Grass*, concerned the yearly migration of the Bakhtiari tribes in Persia as they crossed over the Zardeh Kuh mountain range to find grazing land for their sheep and cattle. Although the trip was long and treacherous, Cooper and Schoedsack made the journey with the tribesmen, filming every step of the way. Back home *Grass* was an extremely successful film, and along with *Nanook of the North*, helped to set the style for documentary travelogues.

Their next project together, *Chang*, was a documentary film set in China, but with a more centralized story line than *Grass*. This film dealt with one man's efforts to protect his family from the dangers of nature. In order to help dramatize the story, some events in the film were staged. For example, the climactic elephant stampede toward the end of the film was directed at a mock village so that no lives would be endangered. However, audiences in America were none the wiser, and *Chang* played to large crowds on Broadway.

With each successive film Cooper and Schoedsack moved more and more toward fiction, although their films still retained a documentary look. For example, their next film, *The Four Feathers*, had background scenes filmed in Africa, while the principal actors were filmed on a Hollywood stage. Eventually Cooper and Schoedsack moved their filmmaking partnership entirely to Hollywood and away from real locations. However, they continued to make films in the documentary style, as shown by their most famous film of all, *King Kong*.

As a work of fiction, *King Kong* is a fantasy version of Cooper and Schoedsack's ultimate documentary adventure—a journey to a faraway uncharted island in search of the "Eighth Wonder of the World." The film was the box-office surprise of 1933 and it is still popular today.

After *King Kong* Schoedsack directed little of note. He directed two more giant ape pictures, *Son of Kong* and *Mighty Joe Young*. An accident during World War II left Schoedsack partially blinded. However, his documentary films by themselves have earned Schoedsack an important place in the tradition of non-fiction filmmaking.

—Linda J. Obalil

SCHORM, Evald.

Czechoslovakian. Born in Prague, 15 December 1931. Educated at FAMU Film Faculty, Prague, 1957–62. Married Blanka Schormová, one son. Construction worker, 1949–56; assistant director to Zdenek Podskalsky, 1961; began making documentaries at Short Film, Prague, from 1962; senior lecturer at FAMU Film Faculty, 1962–71; TV director, from 1963; director for theatre and opera, from 1967. *Died in Prague, 14 December 1988.*

Films as Director:

1959   *Kdo své nebe neunese* (*Too Much to Carry*) (short); *Blok 15* (*Block 15*) (+ co-sc)
1961   "Kostelník" [Sexton] shot in *Zurnál FAMU* (*The FAMU Newsreel*); *Jan Konstantin* (+ sc, ed); *Turista* (*The Tourist*) (+ co-sc)
1962   *Země zemi* (*Country to Country*) (+ sc); *Helsinky 62* (*Helsinki 62*) (+ sc); *Stromy a lidé* (*Trees and People*) (+ sc)
1963   *Komorní harmonie* (*Chamber Harmony*) (for TV) (+ sc); *Železničáři* (*Railwaymen*) (+ sc); *Žit svuj život* (*To Live One's Life*) (+ sc)

1964   *Proč?* (*Why?*) (+ sc); *Každý den odvahu* (*Every Day Courage, Courage for, Every Day*); "Dum radosti" [House of Pleasure] episode of *Perličky na dně* (*Pearls in the Deep*)
1965   *Zrcadlení* (*Reflection*) (+ co-sc); *Odkaz* (*Heritage*) (+ sc); *Sukovo trio* (*Suk's Trio*) (for TV) (+ sc)
1966   *Zalm* (*The Psalm*) (+ co-sc); *Návrat ztraceného syna* (*The Return of the Prodigal Son*) (+ co-sc); *Gramo von Balet* (for TV) (+ co-sc); *Pět holek na krku* (*Five Girls to Cope With*)
1967   *Král a žena* (*The King and the Woman*) (for TV)
1968   *Carmen nejen podle Bizeta* (*Carmen, Not According to Bizet*) (+ co-sc); "Chlebové střevíčky" [Shoes Made of Bread] episode of *Pražské noci* (*Prague Nights*) (+ co-sc); *Fařařuv konec* (*The Priest's End*) (+ co-sc)
1969   *Rozhovory* (*Dialogues*) (for TV) (+ co-sc); *Den sedmý, osmá noc* (*Seventh Day, Eighth Night*) (+ co-sc)
1970   *Psi a lidé* (*Dogs and People*); *Koncert pro studenty* (*Concert for Students*) (for TV); *Z mého života* (*From My Life*) (for TV); *Lítost* (*Regret*) (for TV); *Sestry* (*Sisters*) (for TV) (+ sc)
1971   *Lepší pán* (*A Well-To-Do Gentleman*) (for TV)
1972   *Úklady a láska* (*Intrigue and Love*) (for TV)
1974   *Laska v barvách karnevalu* (*Love in Mardi Gras Colors*) (co-d, Magic Lantern program)
1976   *Etuda o zkoušce* (*An Essay on Rehearsing*) (+ sc)
1977   *Kouzelný cirkus* (*The Magic Circus*) (co-d, co-sc, Magic Lantern program)
1978   *Sněhová královna* (*The Snow Queen*) (Magic Lantern program)
1980   *Noční zkouška* (*The Night Rehearsal*) (Magic Lantern program)
1988   *Vlastně se nic nestalo*

Other Films:

1961   *Spadla s měsíce* (*She Fell from the Moon*) (asst d)
1966   **O slavnosti a hostech (*A Report on the Party and the Guests*)** (Němec) (role as husband); *Hotel pro cizince* (*Hotel for Strangers*) (Máša) (role as chaplain)
1968   *Zert* (*The Joke*) (Jireš) (role as Kostka)
1969   *Bludiště moci* (*The Labyrinth of Power*) (for TV) (Weigl) (role as form)
1974   *Bástyasétány 74* (*Bastion Promenade 74*) (Gazdag) (role as Master Rudolf)
1978   *Město mé naděje* (*The Town of My Hope*) (collaborator)
1980   *Útěky domu* (*Escapes Home*) (Jireš) (role as (Jílek)
1987   *Krajina Shábytkem* (Smyczek) (role)

Publications:

By SCHORM: articles—

Interview in *Film a Doba* (Prague), no. 2, 1966.
Interview with Claude Sembain, in *Image et Son* (Paris), no. 221, 1968.

On SCHORM: books—

Janoušek, Jiří, *3½ po druhé*, Prague, 1969.
Liehm, Mira and Antonin, *The Most Important Art: East European Film after 1945*, Berkeley, 1977.
Bernard, Jan, *Evald Schorm*, Prague, 1979.
Habova, Milada, and Jitka Vysekalova, editors, *Czechoslovak Cinema*, Prague, 1982.
Hames, Peter, *The Czechoslovak New Wave*, Berkeley, 1985.

*   *   *

It was a noteworthy class that studied directing together at the Prague FAMU under the leadership of Otakar Vávra—Věra Chytilová, Jiří Menzel, Jan Schmidt, Evald Schorm. Each of these individuals had a personal but emphatic influence on the development of Czech cinema. Evald Schorm finished his studies with the short film *Turista* (*The Tourist*), in which he attempts to depict the inner world of a worker who has failed both in his work and in his personal life. Upon receiving his certification, Schorm went off to Krátký film Praha and made,

Evald Schorm

in rapid succession, *Helsinky 62* , a report on the Eighth World Youth Festival; *Země zemi* (*Country to Country*), which saw the beginning of years of collaboration with cameraman Jan Spáta and composer Ivan Klusák; *Zit svuj život* (*To Live One's Life*), an attempt at a portrait of the modern Czech photographer Josef Sudek; and the film *Proč* (*Why?*), in which he tries to portray the conflict between the stated wishes of society and the facts of life, to expose the tension between appearance and substance. In the documentary inquiry *Zrcadleni* (*Reflection*), produced later, Schorm is interested in man at the boundary between life and death, his view on questions of the meaning of life, values, the way one lives, and one's attitude toward death.

He made his full-length debut in 1964 with *Každý den odvahu* (*Courage for Every Day*). In this film he captures the inner crisis of a man who had devoted a piece of his life to false ideals, a man at the turning point between youth and maturity, and his disillusionment. Then came *Návrat ztraceného syna* (*The Return of the Prodigal Son*), the drama of a neurotic trying to find himself, his lost inner values and confidence. His next film *Pět holek na krku* (*Five Girls to Cope With*) portrays the hopes and anxieties of a young girl growing up without friendships, sympathy and love during the period when a person's character is being molded. The film is an analysis of the mechanism of envy, malice and hostility and its effect on the human soul. The farce *Farářuv konec* (*The End of a Priest*), which deals with a bogus priest, and the parable *Psi a lidé*

(*Dogs and People*) mark the end of Schorm's work in fictional feature films.

In the 1970's Schorm collaborated in film only rarely. His major creative domain became opera and theater directing. His directing of Shakespeare, Dostoevsky, Brecht and Hrabal confirmed his standing as one of the most important Czech theatrical directors of our time.

Schorm's film oeuvre has met with varying critical responses both in Czechoslovakia and abroad. His documents are a meditation on a theme provided by real life, documentaristic essays that strive for a more profound, philosophical expression of reality. His works inquire into the meaning of man's world and life and examine man's relationship to society and to history. Schorm is a sensitive diagnostician of social life; his approach is characterized by emotional subtlety, integrity, and humility. He persistently and repeatedly pursues the meaning of things, the essence, and the truth about man and his world. Perhaps it is this creative type that best embodies the words of the writer Karel Capek: " . . . passionately and patiently you demand better vision and better hearing, clearer understanding and greater love. You create so you can recognize in your work the form and the perfection of things. Your service to things is a divine service."

—Vladimír Opěla

————

SCHRADER, Paul.

American. Born in Grand Rapids, Michigan, 22 July 1946. Educated in Ministry of Christian Reformed religion at Calvin College, Grand Rapids, Michigan, graduated 1968; took summer classes in film at Columbia University, New York; University of California at Los Angeles Film School, M.A., 1970. Married actress Mary Beth Hurt, 1983, one daughter. Moved to Los Angeles, 1968; writer for *Los Angeles Free Press*, then became editor of *Cinema* magazine; first script to be filmed, *The Yakuza*, 1974; directed first feature, *Blue Collar*, 1977. Agent: Jeff Berg, International Creative Management, 8899 Beverly Blvd., Los Angeles, CA 90048, U.S.A.

Films as Director and Scriptwriter:

1977   *Blue Collar*
1978   *Hardcore*
1979   *American Gigolo*
1981   *Cat People*
1985   *Mishima: A Life in Four Chapters*
1987   *Light of Day*
1988   *Patty Hearst*
1990   *The Comfort of Strangers*

Other Films:

1974   *The Yakuza* (Pollack) (co-sc)
1976   *Taxi Driver* (Scorsese) (sc); *Obsession* (De Palma) (co-sc)
1977   *Rolling Thunder* (Flynn) (sc); **Close Encounters of the Third Kind** (Spielberg) (co-sc, uncredited)
1978   *Old Boyfriends* (Tewkesbury) (co-sc, exec pr)
1980   **Raging Bull** (Scorsese) (co-sc)
1986   *The Mosquito Coast* (Weir) (sc)
1988   *The Last Temptation of Christ* (Scorsese) (sc)
1990   *Investigation* (Schatzberg) (sc)

Publications:

By SCHRADER: books—

Transcendental Style in Film: Ozu, Bresson, Dreyer, Berkeley, 1972.
Schrader on Schrader, edited by Kevin Jackson, London, 1989.

By SCHRADER: articles—

Editor of *Cinema* (Beverly Hills), early 1970s.
"Robert Bresson, Possibly," in *Film Comment* (New York), September/October 1977.
Interview with Gary Crowdus and D. Georgakas, in *Cineaste* (New York), Winter 1977/78.
"Paul Schrader's Guilty Pleasures," in *Film Comment* (New York), January/February 1979.
Interview with M.P. Carducci, in *Millimeter* (New York), February 1979.
Interview with Mitch Tuchmann, in *Film Comment* (New York), March/April 1980.
"Truth with the Power of Fiction," interview with Tim Pulleine in *Sight and Sound* (London), Autumn 1984.
Interview with Michel Ciment in *Positif* (Paris), June 1985.
"The Japanese Way of Death," an interview with David Thomson in *Stills* (London), June/July 1985.
Interview with Allan Hunter in *Films and Filming* (London), November 1985.
Interview with Karen Jaehne in *Film Quarterly* (Berkeley), Spring 1986.
Interview with Glenn Rechler in *Cineaste* (New York), vol. 17, no. 1, 1989.
"Dialogue on Film: Paul Schrader," in *American Film* (Los Angeles), July/August 1989.

On SCHRADER: articles—

Toubiana, Serge, and L. Bloch-Morhange, "Trajectoire de Paul Schrader," in *Cahiers du Cinéma* (Paris), November 1978.
Cuel, F., "Dossier: Hollywood 79: Paul Schrader," in *Cinématographe* (Paris), March 1979.
Wells, J., "*American Gigolo* and Other Matters," in *Film Comment* (New York), March/April 1980.
Sinyard, Neil, "Guilty Pleasures: the Films of Paul Schrader," in *Cinema Papers* (Melbourne), December 1982.
Eisen, K., "The Young Misogynists of American Cinema," in *Cineaste* (New York), vol 13, no. 1, 1983.
Gehr, Richard, "Citizen Paul," in *American Film* (Los Angeles), vol. 13, no. 10, 1988.
Fraser, Peter, "*American Gigolo* and Transcendental Style," in *Literature/Film Quarterly* (Salisbury, Maryland), vol. 16, no. 2, 1988.
Combs, Richard, "Patty Hearst and Paul Schrader: A Life and a Career in 14 Stations," in *Sight and Sound* (London), Summer 1989.

*   *   *

While it is doubtless fanciful and recherche to read Schrader's movies as unmediated reflections of his own life and feelings, it is nonetheless true that the director/screenwriter's "religious fascination with the redeeming hero" echoes his extreme fascination with himself. The incredible urge that his characters have to confess, (Schrader frequently resorts to voice-over, to interior monologue), exemplified by Travis Bickle's mutterings in *Taxi Driver*, Christ's musings on the cross during his *Last Temptation*, and Patty Hearst's thoughts about her abduction, suggest that his films are firmly rooted in self-analysis. The recent book, *Schrader on Schrader*, and the filmmaker's enthusiasm for the bio-pic (*Mishima, Patty Hearst*) a genre that had been more or less moribund since the time of Paul Muni, testify that he does indeed share the Calvinist urge to account for everything, to make his art out of the introspective inventory of his, or somebody else's life.

Appropriately, for a confirmed fan of the films of Bresson, the image of the condemned man/woman attempting to escape his/her fate is a leitmotif in his work. He seems obsessed with prison metaphors, with images of captivity. In *Patty Hearst*, Natasha Richardson is locked up in a cupboard. In *Cat People*, Nastassia Kinski ends up behind bars, in a zoo—a human captive in a panther's body. Richard Gere, in *American Gigolo*, is "framed" (he is "framed" for a murder he did not commit and "framed" as the object of the gaze—the camera seems to love him), and the last time we see him, he is reaching out for Lauren Hutton but is separated from her by the glass panel in the prison interview booth. Christ, predictably, ends up on the cross: he too is trapped. A last, sad image of *Raging Bull* is of Jake La Motta (Robert De Niro) banging his head against his cell wall. Schrader's work abounds in figures cabined, cribbed, confined. Travis Bickle, that emissary from 1970's America, is a prisoner in the city, a prisoner in his own body, a prisoner behind the wheel of his taxi, a slave to pornography and junk food, and he is trying, in his mildly psychotic way, to free Jodie Foster's child prostitute, who is similarly trapped. Season Hubley in *Hardcore* is whisked away from a Calvinist Convention, kidnapped by a snuff movie producer and needs an Ahab/John Wayne figure (George C. Scott) from the suburbs, to rescue her, to try and reincarcerate her within the family. Even Schrader's Venice in *The Comfort of Strangers*, studio-built and full of interminable dark corridors, seems more like San Quentin than a beautiful European city on water.

An American of Dutch/German extraction, Schrader had a strict religious upbringing in Grand Rapids, Michigan. He didn't watch as much TV as he should have done, and when it came to the cinema, he was cruelly deprived: incredibly, he saw his first film, *The Absent-Minded Professor*, when he was seventeen. Then came the revelation of *Wild in the Country*, a

Paul Schrader

lurid Elvis Presley vehicle which gave him his vision on the Road to Damascus: he was captured by the celluloid muse. This Calvinist background combined with his early career as film historian/critic (he was a Pauline Kael protege, a "Paulette" as he describes it: it was Kael's influence which got him onto the film course at UCLA) make him among the more academically inclined of mainstream Hollywood filmmakers. Few of his contemporaries have been Fellows of the American Film Institute or have written ineffably unfathomable monographs on Transcendental Style in the movies of Ozu, Bresson and Dreyer. He straddles two mutually exclusive cultures, traditions, discourses. As Dr Jekyll, he is the film scholar and expert in European and Japanese Cinema. As Mr. Hyde, he is the hack Hollywood director and screenwriter. It is a tension which he seems to enjoy. Is he the artist locked up in a commercial catacomb or is he the popular filmmaker, hampered by his own notions of art? Or is he, perhaps, just plain religious freak and show-off: ". . . the reason I put that Bressonian ending onto *American Gigolo* was a kind of outrageous perversity, saying I can make this fashion-conscious, hip Hollywood movie and at the end claim it's really pure; and in *Cat People* I can make this horror movie and say it was about Dante and Beatrice."

Sometimes he seems too clever by half. Kael, attacking *Patty Hearst*, suggested he lacked a basic instinct for moviemaking: "he doesn't reach an audience's emotions." This is probably unfair. His own scripts have a relentless narrative drive, generally toward some kind of Judgement Day (witness his work with Scorsese): when he is directing another writer's scenario, he can lose that obsessive will to destruction, salvation, damnation. Both *Patty Hearst* and *The Comfort of Strangers*—though it must be taxing for any director to try to animate a Pinter script—lack the momentum, the frenetic desire to tell a story of the films which he wrote himself.

Apparently, he worked with Spielberg on early drafts of *Close Encounters*, but Spielberg elbowed him off the project because Schrader didn't share his Capra-like love of the common man and wanted to make the protagonist a crusading religious fruitcake *à la* Travis Bickle. Whatever one's reservations about Schrader's evangelism, his tedious self-obsession, he is undoubtedly one of Hollywood's most formally arresting filmmakers. He pays enormous attention to set design. (He has worked frequently with Scarfiotti, Bertolucci's designer on *The Conformist*.) He seems equally at home with the lush, magical opulence of New Orleans in *Cat People*, with the sober, almost drama-doc look of *Patty Hearst*, with the glossy, superficial LA, all hotels, restaurants and expensive apartments, of *American Gigolo*, or with the stagey, elaborate sets on *Mishima*. Edgy, prowling tracks (the opening shot of *The Comfort of Strangers* is a virtuoso effort in camera peripeteia to rival the first few minutes of Welles' *Touch of Evil*), a predilection for high angle shots (humans as bugs) and his discerning use of music (he has worked with Philip Glass and Giorgio Moroder amongst others) show him as a filmmaker with a consummate love of his craft.

Yet he thrives on controversy. He was sacked from his job as film critic for the *LA Free Press* because he gave a debunking review to *Easy Rider*. *American Gigolo* was attacked as being homophobic. *Mishima* provoked an outcry in Japan. *The Last Temptation of Christ* brought the moral majority out on the picket line. Apparently a student radical in the 1960s, Schrader caricatures the Symbionese Liberation Army, Patty Hearst's abductors, as idiotic mouthers of revolutionary platitudes. His films seem to abound in right-wing visionaries (Travis Bickle, George C. Scott in *Hardcore*, Mishima, Christopher Walken in *The Comfort of Strangers*) and, while he doesn't straightforwardly endorse their viewpoints, he respects their right to be individuals and their struggle for redemption, a struggle which invariably leaves onlookers dead and dying in the crusading hero's wake. Social historians of American culture and politics in the 1970s and 1980s will find rich pickings in the Schrader *oeuvre*.

—G.C. Macnab

SCHROETER, Werner.

German. Born in Georgenthal, Thuringia, 7 April 1945. Educated in Bielefeld and Heidelberg, and Naples; studied psychology at Mannheim; left Munich Television and Film Academy after a few weeks. Worked as journalist, then began making 8mm films, 1967; director for TV, from 1970; first film to get theatrical release, *The Kingdom of Naples*, 1978; also director for opera and theatre, and actor in several films. Recipient: Golden Bear, Berlin Festival, for *Palermo or Wolfsburg*, 1980.

Films as Director:

1967   *Verona* (*Zwei Katzen*) (short)
1968   *Callas Walking Lucia* (short); *Callas Text mit Doppelbeleuchtung* (short); *Maria Callas Porträt* (short); *Mona Lisa* (short); *Maria Callas singt 1957 Rezitativ und Arie der Elvira aus Ernani 1844 von Giuseppe Verdi* (short); *La morte d'Isotta*; *Himmel Hoch* (short); *Paula—"je reviens"*; *Grotesk—Burlesk—Pittoresk* (co-d with Rosa von Praunheim); *Faces* (short); *Aggressionen* (short); *Neurasia*; *Argila*; *Virginia's Death* (short)
1969   *Eika Katappa*; *Nicaragua*
1970   *Der Bomber-pilot* (for TV); *Anglia*
1971   *Salome* (for TV); *Macbeth* (for TV); *Funkausstellung 1971—Hitparade* (for TV)
1972   *Der Tod der Maria Malibran* (*The Death of Maria Malibran*) (for TV)
1973   *Willow Springs* (for TV)
1974   *Der Schwarze Engel* (*The Black Angel*) (for TV)
1975   *Johannas Traum* (short)
1976   *Flocons d'or* (*Goldflocken. Goldflakes*)
1978   *Regno di Napoli* (*Neapolitanische Geschwister. Kingdom of Naples*)
1980   *Palermo oder Wolfsburg* (*Palermo or Wolfsburg*); *Weisse Reisse* (*White Journey*); *Die Generalprobe* (*La Répétition générale. The Dress Rehearsal*)
1982   *Der Tag der Idioten* (*Day of Idiots*); *Das Liebeskonzil* (*Lovers' Council*)
1983   *Der lachende Stern* (*The Smiling Star*)
1985   *De l'Argentine* (*About Argentina*); *Der Rosenkönig* (*Rose King*); *A la recherche du soleil* (for TV)
1991   *Malina*

Publications:

By SCHROETER: book—

Liebeskonzil. Filmbuch, with Oskjar Panizza and Antonio Salines, Munich, 1982.

By SCHROETER: articles—

Interview with Gérard Courant and Jean-Claude Moireau, in *Cahiers du Cinéma* (Paris), January 1980.
Interview with Alain Carbonnier and Noël Simsolo in *Cinéma* (Paris), March 1984.

On SCHROETER: books—

Schmid, Eva, and Frank Scurla, editors, *Werner Schroeter. Filme 1968–70*, Bochum, 1971.
Jansen, Peter W., and Wolfram Schütte, editors, *Werner Schroeter*, Munich, 1980.
Courant, Gérard, editor, *Werner Schroeter*, Paris, 1982.
Elsaesser, Thomas, *New German Cinema: A History*, London, 1989

On SCHROETER: articles—

Wenders, Wim, "Filme von Werner Schroeter," in *Filmkritik* (Munich), May 1969; reprinted in *Emotion Pictures: Reflections on the Cinema*, London, 1990.
Grafe, Frieda, "Schauplatz für Sprache: Neurasia," in *Filmkritik* (Munich), no. 3, 1970.
Greenberg, Alan, "Notes on Some European Directors," in *American Film* (Washington, D.C.), vol. 3, no. 1, 1977.
Corrigan, Timothy, "Werner Schroeter's Operatic Cinema," in *Discourse* (Berkeley), Spring 1981.
Indiana, Gary, "Scattered Pictures: The Movies of Werner Schroeter," in *Art Forum* (New York), March 1982.
Kuhlbrodt, Dietrich, "Werner Schroeter," in *CineGraph. Lexikon zum deutschsprachigen Film*, edited by Hans-Michael Bock, Munich, 1984.
Bassan, R., and M. Martin, "Werner Schroeter," in *Revue du Cinéma* (Paris), February 1984.
Corrigan, Timothy, "On the Edge of History: The Radiant Spectacle of Werner Schroeter," in *Film Quarterly* (Berkeley), Summer 1984.

*   *   *

Werner Schroeter's hyper-melodramatic films tend to provoke either intense admiration or outraged hostility. He is one of the most controversial filmmakers associated with the New German Cinema. His emotionally charged, performance-inspired cinema draws on and radically reinterprets 19th-century Italian *bel canto* Opera and the music of German Romanticism. Schroeter's central figure is always the outsider—the homosexual, the mad person, the foreigner—and his major theme is the yearning for self-realization through passionate love and artistic creativity.

Schroeter's concept of cinema relies on intense stylization, deploying manneristic prolonged gestures. The characters are framed in sumptuous tableaux compositions and a highly manipulated soundtrack underscores the visuals. Images, music and sound are non-synchronized in the early films: the performers mime exaggeratedly to the lyrics or spoken words on the soundtrack. The songs, arias and literary citations (mostly from Lautréamont) give rise to stories which repeat distilled moments of desire, loss and death. Schroeter is not interested in reproducing an illusion of reality with psychologically motivated actions, but in creating visions for a psychic reality. He wants to break with conventional viewing habits, hence fragmentation, non synchronization, extended duration and deliberately over-the-top acting. At its best, this approach to cinema simultaneously involves the spectator through the music, whilst distancing through anti-naturalist conventions (although they should not be confused with Brechtian distanciation techniques). Schroeter's cinema of excess and artifice occupies a transitional space between the avant-garde and art cinema, neither quite abstract nor quite narrative.

Music, central in all of Schroeter's films, is more important for the content than the mood: the music comments, but also contradicts at times. Juxtaposing classical with popular music is a major characteristic of Schroeter's cinema. For example, he puts Maria Callas, the opera diva, side by side with Caterina Valente, the German popular singer. This blurs the hierarchical distinction between "high" and "low" culture, between art and kitsch. Yet Schroeter has been accused of elitism—of making films for "culture vultures"—since the complex system of citing from pop, opera and literature demands a high degree of cultural literacy from the spectator. Moreover, with Schroeter one can never be quite certain whether he parodies or celebrates.

Over the years, and thanks to major retrospectives in London, Paris and New York, Schroeter has gained an international cult following. Though his cinema is marginal in terms of general audience appeal, Schroeter has been a seminal presence in the New German Cinema of the 1970s. Fassbinder, Herzog and Wenders have acknowledged him as a decisive influence on their work. And with Syberberg the impact is so apparent that Fassbinder even accused him of plagiarism.

Eika Katappa, a radical appropriation of famous 19th-century opera scenes, won the Josef von Sternberg prize (as "the most idiosyncratic film") in 1969 at the Mannheim Film Festival and provided Schroeter with a major breakthrough. As a consequence he got taken up by television, and during the 1970s his films were produced almost exclusively by a small experimental television department. It is rather ironic that Schroeter's "total cinema" (owing more to the spectacle than to the narrative arts) found a home in television.

Der Tod der Maria Malibran, sublime and bizarre, is considered by many, (including Michel Foucault and Schroeter himself) as one of his best films, but it is also the most difficult. The historical figure of the singer Maria Malibran provides merely a starting point for a dense network of references and allusions, encompassing Goethe, Lautréamont, Elvis Presley and Janis Joplin. With *Regno di Napoli* Schroeter had shifted towards art cinema and it became his first commercial release. It was received with an unusual consensus of critical acclaim. Many who had regarded Schroeter as a filmmaker of fantastic fables, were surprised subsequently at his politically hardhitting documentaries. *The Laughing Star* is an extraordinary collage documentary on Marcos's corrupt regime and *Zum Beispiel Argentinien* denounces Galtieri's dictatorship.

Schroeter's gay sensibility is expressed as an aesthetic approach that could be described as "high camp." His conception has frequently been compared to and contrasted with (not always favourably) Rosa von Praunheim's much more militant stance. Schroeter insists on the romantic version of homosexuality. In most of his films we get the gay historical subtext, rather than thematic treatment. *Der Rosenkönig*, an excessive and entrancing hallucinatory fable of oedipal and homosexual passion, is his most explicit gay film. It was be also be his last fiction film for six years. Only in 1990 did he begin shooting his new film, *Malina*. It should be noted also that in the 1980s Schroeter became much more widely known as a theatre and opera director, staging a range of productions in Germany and in other countries. Some are highly acclaimed, but all are controversial, even more so than his films.

—Ulrike Sieglohr

SCOLA, Ettore.

Italian. Born in Trevico, Avellino, 10 May 1931. Educated in law, University of Rome. Scriptwriter on films with Ruggero Maccari, from 1953; directed first film, *Se permette parliamo di donne*, 1964. Recipient: César Award, for *C'eravamo tanto amati*, 1975; Best Director, Cannes Festival, for *Brutti, sporchi e cattivi*, 1976; Special Jury Prize, Cannes Festival, for *Una giornata particolari*, 1977.

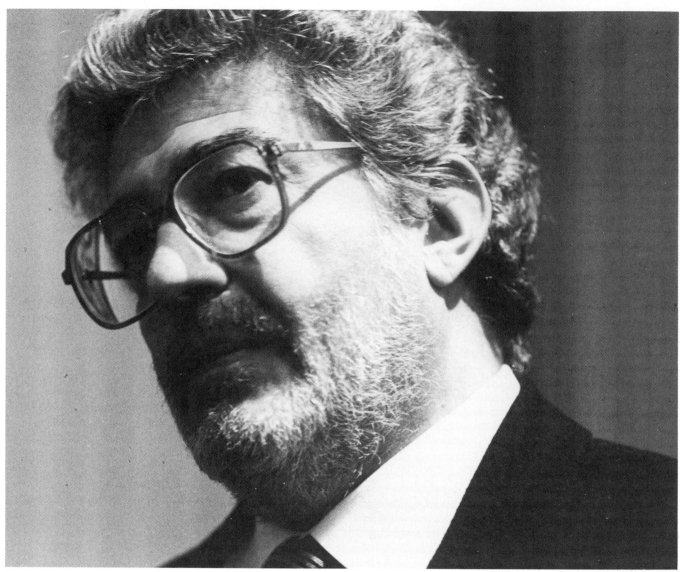

Ettore Scola ©Peter Smith

Films as Director:

1964 *Se permette parliamo di donne (Let's Talk About Women)* (+ co-sc); *La congiuntura* (+ co-sc)
1965 "Il vittimista" episode of *Thrilling* (+ co-sc)
1966 *L'arcidiavolo (Il diavolo innamorato. The Devil in Love)* (+ co-sc)
1968 *Il commissario Pepe* (+ co-sc); *Riusciranno i nostri eroi a trovare il loro amico misteriosamente scomparso in Africa?* (+ co-sc)
1970 *Dramma della gelosia—Tutti i particolari in cronaca (The Pizza Triangle. A Drama of Jealousy (and Other Things))* (+ co-sc)
1971 *Permette? Rocco Papaleo (Rocco Papaleo)* (+ co-sc)
1972 *La piú bella serata della mia vita* (+ co-sc)
1973 *Trevico-Torino . . . Viaggio nel Fiat Nam* (+ co-sc)
1974 *C'eravamo tanto amati (We All Loved Each Other So Much)* (+ co-sc)
1976 *Brutti, sporchi e cattivi (Down and Dirty)* (+ co-sc); one episode of *Signori e signore, buonanotte* (+ co-sc)
1977 *Una giornata particolare (A Special Day)* (+ co-sc); one episode of *I nuovi mostri (The New Monsters. Viva Italia!)* (+ co-sc)
1979 *Che si dice a Roma* (+ co-sc)
1980 *La terrazza* (+ co-sc)
1981 *Passione d'amore* (+ co-sc)
1982 *Il mondo nuovo* (+ co-sc); *La Nuit de Varennes* (+ co-sc)
1984 *Le Bal* (+ co-sc)
1985 *Maccheroni (Macaroni)*
1987 *Famiglia (The Family)*
1989 *Splendor (The Last Movie)*
1990 *Che ora e*
1991 *Viaggio di Capitan Fracassa*

Other Films:

1954 *Un americano a Roma* (Steno) (co-sc with Ruggero Maccari); *Due notti con Cleopatra (Two Nights with Cleopatra)* (co-sc with Maccari); *Una Parigina a Roma* (co-sc with Maccari)
1956 *Lo scapolo* (Pietrangeli) (co-sc with Maccari)
1958 *Nata di marzo* (co-sc with Maccari)
1960 *Il mattatore (Love and Larceny)* (co-sc with Maccari); *Adua e le compagne (Love à la Carte)* (co-sc with Maccari); *Fantasmi a Roma (Ghosts of Rome)* (co-sc with Maccari); "La storia di un soldato (The Soldier)" episode of *L'amore difficile (Erotica. Of Wayward Love)* (Manfredi) (co-sc with Maccari)
1962 *Anni ruggenti (Roaring Years)* (Zampa) (co-sc with Maccari); *Il sorpasso (The Easy Life)* (Risi) (co-sc with Maccari)

1963 *I mostri* (*The Monsters. Opiate '67. Fifteen from Rome*) (Risi) (co-sc with Maccari); *La visita* (co-sc with Maccari)
1964 *Il gaucho* (*The Gaucho*) (Risi) (co-sc); *Alta infedeltà* (*High Infidelity*) (co-sc); *Il magnifico cornuto* (*The Magnificent Cuckold*) (co-sc)
1965 *Io la conoscevo bene* (Pietrangeli) (co-sc); *Made in Italy* (Loy) (co-sc)
1966 *Follie d'estate* (co-sc)
1967 *Le dolci signore* (*Anyone Can Play*) (Zampa) (co-sc)
1971 *Noi donne siamo fatte così* (*Women: So We Are Made*) (Risi) (co-sc)
1988 *Vacanza* (Guillot) (pr); *Mitico Gianluca* (Lazotti) (pr); *O samba* (Constantin) (pr)

Publications:

By SCOLA: articles—

"Se permettete parliamo di Scola," with J.A. Gili, in *Ecran* (Paris), November 1976.
Interview with Aldo Tassone, in *Image et Son* (Paris), November 1977.
Interview with A. Cornand and others in *Revue du Cinéma* (Paris), February 1984.
"Monsieur le President ovvero un modo meno nevrotico di stare a Cannes," in *Bianco e Nero* (Rome), July/September 1988.

On SCOLA: books—

De Santi, Pier Marco, and Rossano Vittori, *I film di Ettore Scola*, Rome, 1987.
Ellero, Roberto, *Ettore Scola*, Florence, 1988.

On SCOLA: articles—

"Nous nous sommes tant aimés," dossier in *Image et Son* (Paris), no.331bis, 1978.
"*Macaroni* Issue" of *Avant-Scène du Cinéma* (Paris), April 1986.

*   *   *

Before directing his own first feature in 1964 Ettore Scola was a writer and illustrator for satirical magazines, a writer for radio, and for movies, mainly comedy, directed by Nanni Loy, Antonio Pietrangeli, and Dino Risi, among others. His scripts have contributed to the fame of such Italian mainstays as Vittorio Gassman, Ugo Tognazzi, and Alberto Sordi.

Gassman speaks of Scola as "meticulous," delving "deeper into the psychology of characters"; Sophia Loren sees him as "continuing the tradition of De Sica and Rossellini . . . sensitive, intelligent," having "a lot of patience with actors" and "a great eye for detail." Stefania Sandrelli says he "understands women better than anybody."

Scola's scripts and feature films confirm these actors' opinions as well as the variety of his subject matter and the intellectuality and humor of his approach. His work has progressed from a particularly Italian kind of comedy—bungling incompetents muddling through desperate situations, war's grotesqueries, life's ironies—to studies of Italians dealing with their history and social environment.

C'eravamo tanto amati, a tribute to Vittorio De Sica, is not only about the difficult and frustrating post-World War II years of three men with class and personal differences who had been close when they fought in the Resistance. It is also a complex survey of 30 years of Italian cinema and its relationship to Italian history, photographed in various appropriate cinema styles. *La terrazza* also examines the Italy-cinema relationship as well as the mores of Italian intellectuals, now middle-aged, no longer creative, and disappointed in their lives and professions.

In *Una giornata particolare* Scola accomplished a skillful integration of plot, theme, setting, acting and photography, demonstrating oppression in a super-organized society without depicting the usual overt violence of the genre. The fluid camera examines the facade and interiors of a workers' dwelling. It

is May 6, 1938; the Italian dictator is welcoming the German one to Rome. Family talk conveys the excitement and devotion to the Duce's program; the radio blares fascist self-confidence. Two marginal members of this society, a woman and an anti-fascist homosexual, meet by chance and share their humanity for a few hours.

Camera work, details of costume and milieu are integrated into Scola's cinema of ideas unobtrusively. (But see *Brutti, sporchi e cattivi*, literally "dirty, nasty, and bad," for the unavoidably disgusting appearance of everyone and everything in a community far below subsistence level, while *Riusciranno*, set in modern Angola and filmed on location, features an Italian bourgeois's leftover 19th-century concept of a safari costume.)

In *La Nuit de Varennes* the French Revolution is happening, but there are no starving peasants center stage, and the King who is trying to flee the country does not appear. The film is an essay of thoughts and opinions, fears and worries of mostly upper class people, about monarchy and a changing world. Indeed, examining the past to interpret the present continues to be a Scola theme.

—Lillian Schiff

———

SCORSESE, Martin.

American. Born in Flushing, New York City, 17 November 1942. Educated at Cardinal Hayes High School, Bronx, 1956–60; New York University, B.A., 1964, M.A., 1966. Married 1) Laraine Brennan, 1965 (divorced), one daughter; 2) Julia Cameron (divorced), one daughter; 3) Isabella Rossellini, 1979 (divorced 1983); 4) Barbara DeFina, 1985. Film Instructor, NYU, 1968–70; directed TV commercials in England, and first feature, *Who's That Knocking at My Door*, 1968; directed *Boxcar Bertha* for producer Roger Corman, 1972; directed *The Act* on Broadway, 1977; director for TV of "Mirror, Mirror" for *Amazing Stories*, 1985; directed promo video for Michael Jackson's "Bad," 1987. Recipient: Best Director, National Society of Film Critics, for *Taxi Driver*, 1976; Best Director, National Society of Film Critics, for *Raging Bull*, 1980; Best Director, Cannes festival, for *The Color of Money*, 1986. Addresses: Office: United Artists, 10202 W. Washington Boulevard, Culver City, CA 90230; Agent: c/o Harry Ufland Ufland-Roth Productions, Lions Gate Studio, 1861 S. Bundy Drive, Los Angeles, CA 90025, U.S.A.

Films as Director:

1963 *What's a Nice Girl Like You Doing in a Place Like This?* (short) (+ sc)
1964 *It's Not Just You, Murray* (short) (+ co-sc)
1967 *The Big Shave* (short) (+ sc)
1968 *Who's That Knocking at My Door?* (+ sc, role as gangster)
1970 *Street Scenes* (doc)
1972 *Boxcar Bertha* (+ role as client of bordello)
1973 *Mean Streets* (+ co-sc, role as Shorty the Hit Man)
1974 *Italian-American* (doc) (+ co-sc)
1975 *Alice Doesn't Live Here Anymore* (+ role as customer at Mel and Ruby's)
1976 *Taxi Driver* (+ role as passenger)
1977 *New York, New York*
1978 *The Last Waltz* (doc)
1979 *American Boy* (doc) (+ sc)

Martin Scorsese

1980 *Raging Bull*
1983 *The King of Comedy* (+ role as assistant)
1985 *After Hours* (+ role as disco patron)
1986 *The Color of Money*
1988 *The Last Temptation of Christ*
1989 "Life Lessons" episode in *New York Stories*
1990 *Goodfellas* (+ sc); *Schindler's List*; *Man in Milan* (doc)
1991 *Cape Fear*

Other Films:

1965 *Bring on the Dancing Girls* (sc)
1967 *I Call First* (sc)
1970 *Woodstock* (ed, asst d)
1976 *Cannonball* (Bartel) (role)
1979 *Hollywood's Wild Angel* (Blackwood) (role); *Medicine Ball Caravan* (assoc pr, post prod spvr)
1981 *Triple Play* (role)
1982 *Bonjour Mr. Lewis* (Benayoun) (role)
1990 *Dreams* (Kurosawa) (role); *The Grifters* (Frears) (pr); *Fear No Evil* (Winkler) (role); *The Crew* (Antonioni) (exec pr); *Mad Dog and Glory* (McNaughton) (exec pr)

Publications:

By SCORSESE: books—

Scorsese on Scorsese, edited by Ian Christie and David Thompson, London, 1989.
Goodfellas, with Nicholas Pileggi, London, 1990.

By SCORSESE: articles—

"The Filming of *Mean Streets*," an interview with A.C. Bobrow, in *Filmmakers Newsletter* (Ward Hill, Massachusetts), January 1974.
Interview with M. Carducci, in *Millimeter* (New York), vol. 3, no. 5, 1975.
Interview with M. Rosen, in *Film Comment* (New York), March/April 1975.
Martin Scorsese Seminar, in *Dialogue on Film* (Washington, D.C.), April 1975.
"Scorsese on *Taxi Driver* and Herrmann," with C. Amata, in *Focus on Film* (London), Summer/Autumn 1976.
Interview with Jonathan Kaplan, in *Film Comment* (New York), July/August 1977.
Interview with Richard Combs and Louise Sweet, in *Sight and Sound* (London), Winter 1977/78.
"Martin Scorsese's Guilty Pleasures," in *Film Comment* (New York), September/October 1978.
Interview with Paul Schrader in *Cahiers du Cinéma* (Paris), April 1982.
Interview with B. Krohn in *Cahiers du Cinéma* (Paris), May 1986.
"Body and Blood," an interview with Richard Corliss, in *Film Criticism* (Meadville, Pennsylvania), vol. 24, no. 5, 1988.
Interview with Chris Hodenfield in *American Film* (Los Angeles), March 1989.

On SCORSESE: books—

Kolker, Robert Phillip, *A Cinema of Loneliness: Penn, Kubrick, Coppola, Scorsese, Altman*, Oxford, 1980; revised edition, 1988.
Bliss, Michael, *Martin Scorsese and Michael Cimino*, Metuchen, New Jersey, 1986.
Arnold, Frank, and others, *Martin Scorsese*, Munich, 1986.
Cietat, Michel, *Martin Scorsese*, Paris, 1986.
Domecq, Jean-Philippe, *Martin Scorsese: Un Rêve Italo-Américain*, Renens, Switzerland, 1986.
Weiss, Ulli, *Das Neue Hollywood: Francis Ford Coppola, Steven Spielberg, Martin Scorsese*, Munich, 1986.
Wood, Robin, *Hollywood from Vietnam to Reagan*, New York, 1986.
Weiss, Marian, *Martin Scorsese: A Guide to References and Resources*, Boston, 1987.

On SCORSESE: articles—

Gardner, P. "Martin Scorsese," in *Action* (Los Angeles), May/June 1975.

Scorsese Section of *Positif* (Paris), April 1980.
"Martin Scorsese vu par Michael Powell," in *Positif* (Paris), April 1981.
Rickey, C., "Marty," in *American Film* (Washington D.C.), November 1982.
Rafferty, T., "Martin Scorsese's Still Life," in *Sight and Sound* (London), Summer 1983.
Braudy, Leo, "The Sacraments of Genre: Coppola, De Palma, Scorsese," in *Film Quarterly* (Berkeley), Spring 1986.
Bruce, B., "Martin Scorsese: Five Films," in *Movie* (London), Winter 1986.
"Scorsese Issue" of *Film Comment* (New York), September/October 1988.
Jenkins, Steve, "From the Pit of Hell," in *Monthly Film Bulletin* (London), December 1988.

*　　*　　*

At present, with regard to the Hollywood cinema of the last fifteen years, two directors appear to stand head-and-shoulders above the rest, and it is possible to make large claims for their work on both formal and thematic grounds: Scorsese and Cimino. The work of each is strongly rooted in the American and Hollywood past, yet is at the same time audacious and innovative. Cimino's work can be read as at once the culmination of the Ford/Hawks tradition and a radical re-thinking of its premises; Scorsese's involves an equally drastic re-thinking of the Hollywood genres, either combining them in such a way as to foreground their contradictions (western and horror film in *Taxi Driver*) or disconcertingly reversing the expectations they traditionally arouse (the musical in *New York, New York*, the boxing movie and "biopic" in *Raging Bull*). Both directors have further disconcerted audiences and critics alike 'in their radical deviations from the principles of classical narrative: hence *Heaven's Gate* is received by the American critical establishment with blank incomprehension and self-defensive ridicule, while Scorsese has been accused (by Andrew Sarris, among others) of lacking a sense of structure. Hollywood films are not expected to be innovative, difficult, and challenging, and must suffer the consequences of authentic originality (as opposed to the latest in fashionable *chic* that often passes for it).

The Cimino/Scorsese parallel ends at this shared tension between tradition and innovation. While *Heaven's Gate* can be read as the answer to (and equal of) *Birth of a Nation*, Scorsese has never ventured into the vast fresco of American epic, preferring to explore relatively small, limited subjects (with the exception of *The Last Temptation of Christ*), the wider significance of the films arising from the implications those subjects are made to reveal. He starts always from the concrete and specific—a character, a relationship: the vicissitudes in the careers and love-life of two musicians (*New York, New York*); the violent public and private life of a famous boxer (*Raging Bull*); the crazy aspirations of an obsessed nonentity (*King of Comedy*). In each case, the subject is remorselessly followed through to a point where it reveals and dramatizes the fundamental ideological tensions of our culture.

His early works are divided between self-confessedly personal works related to his own Italian-American background (*Who's That Knocking at my Door?*, *Mean Streets*) and genre movies (*Boxcar Bertha*, *Alice Doesn't Live Here Anymore*). The distinction was never absolute, and the later films effectively collapse it, tending to take as their starting point not only a specific character but a specific star: Robert De Niro. The Scorsese/De Niro relationship has proved one of the most fruitful director/star collaborations in the history of the cinema; its ramifications are extremely complex. De Niro's star image is central to this, poised as it is on the borderline between "star" and "actor"—the charismatic personality, the self-effacing impersonator of diverse characters. It is this ambiguity in the De Niro star persona that makes possible the ambiguity in the actor/director relationship: the degree to which Scorsese identifies with the characters De Niro plays, versus the degree to which he distances himself from them. It is this tension (communicated very directly to the spectator) between identification and repudiation that gives the films their uniquely disturbing quality.

Indeed, Scorsese is perhaps the only Hollywood director of consequence who has succeeded in sustaining the radical critique of American culture that developed in the 1970s through the Reagan era of retrenchment and recuperation. Scorsese probes the tensions within and between individuals until they reveal their fundamental, cultural nature. Few films have chronicled so painfully and abrasively as *New York, New York* the impossibility of successful heterosexual relations within a culture built upon sexual inequality. The conflicts arising out of the man's constant need for self-assertion and domination and the woman's bewildered alterations between rebellion and complexity are—owing to the peculiarities of the director/star/ character/spectator relationship—simultaneously experienced and analysed.

Raging Bull goes much further in penetrating to the root causes of masculine aggression and violence, linking socially approved violence in the ring to socially disapproved violence outside it, violence against men to violence against women. It carries to its extreme that reversal of generic expectations so characteristic of Scorsese's work: a boxing melodrama/success story, it is the ultimate anti-*Rocky*; a filmed biography of a person still living, it flouts every unwritten rule of veneration for the protagonist, celebration of his achievements, triumph after tribulation, etc. Ostensibly an account of the life of Jake LaMotta, it amounts to a veritable case history of a paranoiac, and can perhaps only be fully understood through Freud. Most directly relevant to the film is Freud's assertion that every case of paranoia, without exception, has its roots in a repressed homosexual impulse; that the primary homosexual love-objects are likely to be father and brothers; that there are four "principle forms" of paranoia, each of which amounts to a *denial* of homosexual attraction (see the analysis of the Schreber case and its postscript). *Raging Bull* exemplifies all of this with startling (if perhaps largely inadvertent) thoroughness: all four of the "principle forms" are enacted in Scorsese's presentation of LaMotta, especially significant being the paranoid's projection of his repressed desires for men on to the woman he ostensibly loves. The film becomes nothing less than a statement about the disastrous consequences, for men and women alike, of the repression of bisexuality in our culture.

King of Comedy may seem at first sight a slighter work than its two predecessors, but its implications are no less radical and subversive: it is one of the most complete statements about the emotional and spiritual bankruptcy of patriarchal capitalism today that the cinema has given us. The symbolic Father (once incarnated in figures of mythic force, like Abraham Lincoln) is here revealed in his essential emptiness, loneliness, and inadequacy. The "children" (De Niro and Sandra Bernhard) behave in exemplary Oedipal fashion: he wants to *be* the father, she wants to screw the father. The film moves to twin climaxes. First, the father must be reduced to total impotence (to the point of actual immobility) in order to be loved; then Bernhard can croon to him "You're gonna love me/like nobody's loved me," and remove her clothes. Meanwhile, DeNiro tapes his TV act which (exclusively concerned with childhood, his parents, self-depreciation) culminates in a joke about throwing up over his father's new shoes, the shoes he is (metaphorically) now standing in. We see ambivalence towards the father, the hatred-in-rivalry of "brother" and "sister", the son's need for paternal recognition (albeit in fantasy)

before he can announce himself to the woman he (very dubiously) loves; and the irrelevance of the mother (a mere, intermittently intrusive, off-screen voice) to any "serious"—i.e. Oedipal patriarchal—concerns. Thus *King of Comedy* constitutes one of the most rigorous assaults we have on the structures of the patriarchal nuclear family and the impossible desires, fantasies, frustrations, and violence those structures generate: an assault, that is, on the fundamental premises of our culture.

—Robin Wood

SCOTT, Ridley.

English. Born in South Shields, County Durham, 1939. Studied at West Hartlepool College of Art and at the Royal College of Art, London. Married, three children. Set designer, then director for BBC TV, including episodes of *Z-Cars*, and *The Informer*, 1966/67; set up production company Ridley Scott Associates, directed more than 2000 commercials, from 1967; directed first feature, *The Duellists*, 1977. Recipient: Special Jury Prize, Cannes Festival, for *The Duellists*, 1977.

Films as Director:

1977   *The Duellists*
1979   *Alien*
1982   ***Blade Runner***
1985   *Legend*
1987   *Someone to Watch Over Me*
1989   *Black Rain*

Publications:

By SCOTT: articles—

"Ridley Scott cinéaste du décor," interview with O. Assayas and S. LePéron in *Cahiers du Cinéma* (Paris), September 1982.
"Designer Genes," an interview with Harlan Kennedy in *Films* (London), September 1982.
Interview with Hubert Niogret in *Positif* (Paris), September 1985.
Interview with Sheila Johnston in *Films and Filming* (London), November 1985.
Interview with Raphael Bassan and Raymond Lefevre in *Revue du Cinéma* (Paris), February 1986.
Interview with M. Buckley in *Films in Review* (New York), January 1987.

On SCOTT: articles—

"*Blade Runner* Issue" of *Cinefex* (Riverside, California), July 1982.
"*Blade Runner* Issues" of *Starburst* (London), September/November 1982.
Kellner, Douglas, Flo Leibowitz, and Michael Ryan, "*Blade Runner*: A Diagnostic Critique," in *Jump Cut* (Chicago), no. 29, 1983.
Caron, A., "Les archétypes chez Ridley Scott," in *Jeune Cinéma* (Paris), March 1983.
Durgnat, Raymond, "Art for Film's Sake," in *American Film* (Washington, D.C.), May 1983.
Milmo, Sean, "Ridley Scott Makes the Details Count," in *Advertising Age* (Chicago), 21 June 1984.
Doll, Susan, and Greg Faller, "*Blade Runner* and Genre: Film Noir and Science Fiction," in *Literature/Film Quarterly* (Salisbury, Maryland), no. 2, 1986.
Rosen, Barbara, "How the Man Who Made *Alien* Invaded Madison Avenue," in *Business Week* (New York), 24 March 1986.
Davis, Brian, "Ridley Scott: He Revolutionized TV Ads," in *Adweek* (Chicago), 2 October 1989.

*   *   *

Ridley Scott

Ridley Scott has enjoyed more critical acclaim and financial success as a director of television commercials than he has as a feature filmmaker. Ironically, the very element that has made him an award-winning director of commercials—his emphasis on visual design to convey the message—has often been at the core of the criticism aimed at his films.

Though Scott began his career directing popular TV programs for the BBC, he found that his meticulous attention to detail in terms of set design and props was more suited to making commercials. Scott honed his craft and style on hundreds of ad spots for British television during the 1970s, as did future film directors Alan Parker, Hugh Hudson, Adrian Lyne, and Tony Scott (Ridley's brother). In 1979, Scott became a fixture in the American television marketplace with a captivating commercial for Chanel No. 5 entitled "Share the Fantasy." Still innovative in this arena, Scott continues to spark controversy with his "pocket versions of feature films"—his term for commercials.

Scott approaches his feature films with the same emphasis on mise-en-scène that distinguishes his commercials, prompting some critics to refer to him as a visual stylist. Scott assumes control over the visual elements of his films as much as possible rather than turn the set design completely over to the art director or the photography over to the cinematographer. Because his first feature, *The Duellists*, was shot in France, Scott was able to serve as his own cinematographer for that film—a luxury not allowed on many subsequent films due to union rules.

Hallmarks of Scott's style include a detailed, almost crowded set design that is as prominent in the frame as the actors, a fascination with the tonalities of light, a penchant for foggy atmospheres backlit for maximum effect, and a reliance on long lenses, which tend to flatten the perspective. While these techniques are visually stunning in themselves, they are often tied directly to plot and character in Scott's films.

Of all Scott's films, *Blade Runner* and *Legend* make the fullest use of set design to enhance the theme. In *Blade Runner*, the polluted, dank metropolis teems with hordes of lower-class merchants and pedestrians, who inhabit the streets at all hours. Except for huge, garish neon billboards, fog and darkness pervade the city, suggesting that urban centers in the future will have no daylight hours. This pessimistic view is in sharp contrast to the sterile, brightly lit sets found in conventional science-fiction films. Inherent in the set design is a critique of our society, which has allowed its environment to be destroyed. The overwrought set design also complements the feverish attempts by a group of androids to find the secret to longer life. *Blade Runner* influenced the genre with its dystopian depiction of the future, though the cluttered set design and low-key lighting were used earlier by Scott in the science-fiction thriller *Alien*.

Legend, a fairy tale complete with elves, goblins, and unicorns, employs a simple theme of good and evil, which is reinforced through images of light and darkness. The magical unicorns, for example, have coats of the purest white; an innocent, virginal character is costumed in flowing, white gowns; sunbeams pour over glades of white flowers; and light shimmers across silver streams as the unicorns gallop through the forest. In contrast, a character called Darkness (actually the Devil) looks magnificently evil in an array of blood reds and wine colors; the sinister Darkness resides in the dark, dismal bowels of the Earth, where no light is allowed to enter; and a corrupted world is symbolized by a charred forest devoid of flowers and leaves and black clouds that cover the sky. The forest set was constructed entirely inside the studio and is reminiscent of those huge indoor sets created for Fritz Lang's *Siegfried*.

In *Black Rain*, Scott once again reinforced the film's theme through its mise-en-scène, though here he made extensive use of actual locations instead of relying so much on studio sets. *Black Rain* follows the story of two New York detectives tracking a killer through the underworld of Osaka, Japan. The two characters are frequently depicted against the backdrop of Osaka's ornate neon signs and ultramodern architecture. Shot through a telephoto lens and lit from behind, the characters seem crushed against the huge set design, which serves as a metaphor for their struggle to penetrate the culture in order to track their man.

Though Scott has forged a style that is recognizably his own, his approach to filmmaking has a precedent in German Expressionist filmmaking. The Expressionists were among the first to use the elements of mise-en-scène (set design, lighting, props, costuming) to suggest traits of character or enhance meaning. Similarly, Scott's techniques are stunning yet highly artificial, a trait often criticized by American reviewers who too often value plot and character over visual style, and realism over symbolism.

—Susan Doll

SEIDELMAN, Susan.

American. Born in 1953. Educated in Philadelphia; studied design and film at Drexel University; New York University Graduate School of Film and TV, 1974–77. Directed first feature, *Smithereens*, 1982. Lives in Greenwich Village, New York.

Films as Director:

1976/77 *And You Act Like One, Too* (short); *Deficit* (short); *Yours Truly, Andrea G. Stern* (short)
1982 *Smithereens* (+ pr, story)
1985 ***Desperately Seeking Susan***
1987 *Making Mr. Right* (+ exec pr)
1989 *Cookie* (+ sc)
1990 *She-Devil* (+ pr)

Publications:

By SEIDELMAN: articles—

Interview with Richard Patterson in *American Cinematographer* (Los Angeles), May 1983.

Interview with Dan Yakir in *Film Comment* (New York), May/June 1985.
Interview with P. Golden in *Films in Review* (New York), June/July 1985.
"Céline and Julie, Susan and Susan," interview with Jane Root in *Stills* (London), October 1985.

On SEIDELMAN: articles—

Hachem, S., "Susan Seidelman," in *Millimeter* (New York), August 1983.
Rickey, C., "Where the Girls Are," in *American Film* (Washington D.C.), January/February 1984.
Jaehne, Karen, "In Search of Susan," in *Stills* (London), May 1985.
Stacey, Jackie, "Desperately Seeking Difference," in *Screen* (London), Winter 1987.
Cook, Pam, "Good Girl/Bad Girl—Susan Seidelman," in *Monthly Film Bulletin* (London), May 1990.

* * *

After graduating from NYU film school, where she made two award-winning shorts, and emerging into the New York arts scene in a period of punk-inspired creativity, Seidelman directed *Smithereens*, a low-budget feature (she paid the crew in subway tokens), and the first ever American independent selected for competition at Cannes. The story of an itinerant punk girl drifting through new-wave New York, the film establishes Seidelman's distinctive concerns and influences; her art school background, fascination with pop culture and kitsch Americana, a love of New York, and an off-beat sense of humour, Lodging her in a hip independent tradition, both this and her second film, *Desperately Seeking Susan*, attained cult status alongside films like Jonathan Demme's *Something Wild* and Albert Brooks's *Lost in America*. However, Seidelman's female voice distinguishes her films from these. Women's experiences form the core of her narratives, and she appropriates all those pleasures that patriarchal culture derides as "feminine," validating them as a context for narrative, plot and visual style.

In the ground-breaking and highly popular *Susan*, stylish and streetwise popstar Madonna was perfectly cast in the title role. She undoubtedly added to the film's success, attracting a youth audience to complement the more sophisticated adults at whom the film was originally targetted. Even apart from its star, *Susan* holds its own pleasures. A sumptuous female buddy movie/screwball caper, it delighted feminist audiences so long deprived of the most fundamental of cinematic pleasures—fantasy, desire and fun.

Moving away from New York, *Making Mr Right* unfolds in a kitschly surreal Miami, where a successful career woman discovers that she can only find true love with a robot. Her boring boyfriend is ultimately sent off on a space programme while she keeps the automaton for herself. This is obviously no conventional heterosexual coupling, and, as he literally comes to pieces each time they make love, the "happy ending" is somewhat ambiguous. It is perhaps the prevalence here of Seidelman's blacker side, and an ambivalent, less celebratory relationship with kitsch Americana that made *Mr Right* less of a commercial success than *Susan*.

Seidelman's films had by now become instantly recognisable, to the point, some might argue, of following a formula of style and "whackiness" above all else. Without exception, they feature popular music, strong screwball-inspired heroines, close female friendships, and shifting identities (through fashion, dressing-up and disguise). Committed to unconventional and theoretically risky casting decisions, (using unknowns, or rising stars like Madonna and Emily Lloyd, or even by casting Meryl Streep in her first comedy role), and using predominantly female production teams, Seidelman's films are always

Susan Seidelman   ©**Orion Pictures Corp.**

quirky. Quirkiness, however, doesn't guarantee a good film, as Seidelman's later work sadly testifies.

Cookie, a mafia caper about a rebellious daughter's relationship with her gangster father, attempts to recapture too much of the kinetic energy that propelled *Susan*, and is pale, tired and embarrassingly derivative. Critics praised the performances and the visual style, but tellingly panned the plot and the script. Seidelman began her career as an artist. She is not, and never has been, a writer. So, while *Cookie* has the pace and feel of Seidelman's earlier successes, it ultimately fails.

After two relative failures, Seidelman was still able to make *The Life and Loves of a She-Devil*, based on Fay Weldon's darkly feminist novel, and starring Meryl Streep and Roseanne Barr. Scripted by Nora Ephron, writer of *When Harry met Sally*, 1989's phenomenally popular romantic comedy, the film's credentials are immaculate. However, the "girls just want to have fun" feeling that illuminates and inspires her early films begins now to wear somewhat thin. Weldon's premise—that a woman's transgression entails her own destruction—translates poorly into Seidelman's chirpy story. Both texts lose out, giving way to a sense of loss and wasted chances.

It would be easy to conclude that Seidelman is a victim of her own success, that she should have remained in the independent sector, where she seemed best to flourish. It is too simple, however, to hem in women film-makers in this way. Seidelman could never return to low budget independents, because she has become more of a rarity, a (still) bankable, (still) popular woman director. Even if she fails ever again to recapture the originality and exhilaration of her early work, her legacy is already a valuable and exciting one.

—Samantha Cook

SEMBENE, Ousmane.

Senegalese. Born at Ziguinchor, Senegal, 8 January 1923. Worked as mechanic, 1937–38; joined Free French Forces fighting in Africa, 1942, demobilized at Marseilles, 1946; returned to Senegal, 1948, then moved to France, 1948; docker in Marseilles, and Secretary General of black workers organization in France; published first novel, *Le Docker noir*, 1956; returned to Senegal, 1960; studied cinema in Moscow, under Sergei Gerasimov and Mark Donskoi, 1962; made first film, *L'Empire Sonrai*, 1963.

Films as Director and Scriptwriter:

1963   *Songhays* (*L'Empire Sonrai*) (documentary, unreleased)
        Borom Sarret

Ousmane Sembene

1964   *Niaye*
1966   **La Noire de . . . (The Black Girl from . . .)**
1968   *Mandabi* (*The Money Order*)
1970   *Tauw* (*Taw*)
1971   *Emitai*
1974   **Xala (Impotence)**
1977   *Ceddo* (*The People*)
1987   *Camp de Thiaroye*

Other Films:

1983   *Camera d'Afrique* (Boughedir) (role)

Publications:

By SEMBENE: books—

Le Docker noir, Paris, 1956.
O pays, mon beau peuple, Paris, 1957.
Les Bouts de bois de Dieu, Paris, 1960.
Voltaïque, Paris, 1962.
L'Harmattan, Paris, 1964.
Vehi Ciosane ou blanche genèse suivi de *Mandat*, Paris, 1965.
Xala, Paris, 1973; Westport, Connecticut, 1976.
Le Dernier de l'Empire, Paris, 1981.

By SEMBENE: articles—

Interview with Guy Hennebelle, in *Jeune Cinéma* (Paris), November 1968.
"Film-makers have a great responsibility to our people," interview with H.D. Weaver, Jr., in *Cineaste* (New York), v.6, no.1, 1973.
Interview with G.M. Perry, in *Film Quarterly* (Berkeley), Spring 1973.
"Ousmane Sembene, Carthage et le cinéma africain," and "Problématique du cinéaste africain: l'artiste et la révolution," interviews with T. Cheriaa, in *Cinéma Québec* (Montreal), August 1974.
Interview with C. Bosseno, in *Image et Son* (Paris), September 1979.
Interview with A. Tournès in *Jeune Cinéma* (Paris), November/December 1988.

On SEMBENE: books—

Vieyra, Paulin Soumanou, *Ousmane Sembene, cinéaste. Première période 1962–71*, Paris, 1972.
Vieyra, Paulin Soumanou, *Le Cinéma africain: des origines à 1973*, Paris 1975.
Martin, Angela, editor, *African Films: The Context of Production*, London, 1982.
Moore, Carried Dailey, *Evolution of an African Artist: Social Realism in the Work of Ousmane Sembene*, Ann Arbor, Michigan, 1984.
Pfaff, Françoise, *The Cinema of Ousmane Sembene*, Westport, Connecticut, 1984.
Armes, Roy, *Third World Filmmaking and the West*, Berkeley, 1987.

Downing, John D.H., editor, *Film and Politics in the Third World*, New York, 1987.
Pfaff, Françoise, *25 Black African Filmmakers: A Critical Study*, Westport, Connecticut, 1988.

On SEMBENE: articles—

Ghali, N., "Ousmane Sembene," in *Cinématographe* (Paris), April 1976.
Van Wert, William, "Ideology in the Third World Cinema: A Study of Ousmane Sembene and Glauber Rocha," in *Quarterly Review of Film Studies* (Pleasantville, New York), Spring 1979.
Armes, Roy, "Ousmane Sembene: Questions of Change," in *Ciné Tracts* (Montreal), Summer-Fall 1981.
Landy, M., and others "Ousmane Sembene's Films," in *Jump Cut* (Berkeley), July, 1982.
Landy, M., "Political Allegory and 'Engaged Cinema': Sembene's *Xala*," in *Cinema Journal* (Champaign, Illinois), Spring 1984.
Turvey, G., "*Xala* and the Curse of Neo-Colonialism," in *Screen* (London), May/August 1985.

*　　*　　*

Ousmane Sembene is one of the most important literary figures of sub-Saharan Africa and, at the same time, its premier filmmaker. Born in 1923 in Senegal, he received little formal education. His first literary work, autobiographical in nature, dates from 1956 and he has as its backdrop the port city of Marseilles where he worked as a docker. Sembene came to the film by necessity: painfully aware that he could not reach his largely pre-literate compatriots by means of a written art form, he studied film in Moscow in 1961 and began to work in this medium shortly thereafter. It is interesting and important to note that four of his films are based on texts, written by Sembene, which first appeared as novels or short stories. Between 1963 and 1977 he produced eight films while publishing three works of fiction. Following *Borom Sarret* and *Niaye*, Sembene made *La Noire de . . .*, the first feature-length film to come out of sub-Saharan Africa: it received several awards. While technically flawed, it is still a powerful piece which deals with the issue of neocolonialism in post-independence Africa, a common theme in Sembene's work. His next film, *Mandabi* (*The Money Order*), marked an important breakthrough for Sembene: it is his first film in color, but, more importantly, it is the first work to use an African language—in this case Wolof, rather than French—and this allowed him to reach his primary audience in an even more direct manner than previously possible. His use of African languages continues with the creation of *Emitai*, which is made in Diola. It is noteworthy that this is the first full-length film by Sembene which is not an adaption from a written text.

The conditions of filmmaking in Africa are difficult and the lack of trained personnel and financial support have discouraged many African artists from working in this medium. Sembene has managed to overcome these problems and has even made a virtue of certain necessities: his almost exclusive reliance on non-professional actors and actresses, including those playing leading roles, is an example of this. He is able to increase both the general force of the film—the audience can more easily identify with them than with "stars"—and testify to his belief in the common man and the collective heroism of the masses.

Sembene's films are not innovative in a technical sense and their power and critical success come rather from the compelling portraits of Third World men and women struggling against forces, both internal and external, which would threaten dignity and, in fact, very existence. Sembene clearly sees himself as a Marxist-Leninist and sees art as necessarily both functional and politically committed. But this does not mean that he is a mere propagandist and, in fact, his art transcends narrow definition. His art is clearly African at base, despite his extensive contacts with the West: the filmmaker is the descendant of the traditional *griot*, recording the history of his society, criticizing its faults, finding strength in its people in the face of the denigration of African society and culture inherent in all forms of colonialism.

—Curtis Schade

SEN, Mrinal.

Indian. Born in East Bengal (now Bangladesh), 4 May 1923. Studied physics in Calcutta. Freelance journalist and medical representative in Uttar Pradesh; involved with Indian People's Theatre Association, sponsored by Communist Party of India, 1943–47; directed first film, *Raat Bhore*, 1956. Recipient: Silver Bear, Berlin Festival, for *Akaler Sandhane*, 1981.

Films as Director:
(in Bengali unless indicated)

1956 *Raat Bhore* (*The Dawn. Night's End*)
1959 *Neel Akasher Neechey* (*Under the Blue Sky*)
1960 *Baishey Shravana* (*The Wedding Day*)
1961 *Punnascha* (*Over Again*)
1962 *Abasheshey* (*And at Last*)
1964 *Pratinidhi* (*The Representative. Two Plus One*)
1965 *Akash Kusum* (*Up in the Clouds*)
1967 *Matira Manisha* (*Two Brothers*) (+ co-sc, in Bengali); *Moving Perspectives* (doc)
1969 *Bhuvan Shome* (*Mr. Shome*) (+ pr, sc, in Hindi)
1970 *Ichhapuran* (*The Wish-Fulfillment*) (+ sc, in Bengali, also Hindi version)
1971 *Interview*
1972 *Calcutta 71* (+ sc); *Ek Adhuri Kahani* (*An Unfinished Story*)
1973 *Padatik* (*The Guerilla Fighter*)
1974 *Chorus*
1976 *Mrigaya* (*The Royal Hunt*) (+ co-sc, in Hindi)
1977 *Oka Oorie Katha* (*The Outsiders*) (+ co-sc, in Telugu)
1978 *Parashuram* (*The Man with the Axe*)
1979 *Ek Din Pratidin* (*And Quiet Rolls the Dawn*)
1980 *Akaler Sandhane* (*In Search of Famine*)
1981 *Chalachitra* (*The Kaleidoscope*)
1982 *Kharij* (*The Case Is Closed*)
1983 *Khandahar* (*The Ruins*)
1985 *Tasveer Apni Apni*
1986 *Genesis*
1989 *Ek din achanak* (+ sc)
1990 *Calcutta, My El Dorado* (doc) (+ pr)

Publications:

By SEN: books—

In Search of Famine, Calcutta, 1983; London, 1990.
The Ruins (*Khandahar*), Calcutta, 1984.

By SEN: articles—

"Introducing Mrinal Sen," interview with U. Gupta, in *Jump Cut* (Berkeley), no.12/13, 1976.
"Mrinal Sen: cineasta de los humildes," interview with M. Pereira, in *Cine Cubano* (Havana), no.99, 1981.
Interview with S.S. Chakravarty in *Ciné-Tracts* (Montreal), 1981.
Interview with Michel Ciment in *Positif* (Paris), January 1982.
"New Visions in Indian Cinema," an interview with U. Gupta in *Cineaste* (New York), vol. 11, no. 4, winter 1982.

On SEN: books—

da Cunha, Uma, editor, *The New Generation 1960–1980: An Examination of India's New Cinema*, New Delhi, 1981.

Willemen, Paul, and Behroze Gandhy, *Indian Cinema*, London, 1982.
Hauff, Reinhard, *Hauff on Sen: Ten Days in Calcutta: A Portrait of Mrinal Sen*, Calcutta, 1987.

On SEN: articles—

Williams, Forrest, "The Art Film in India: Report on Mrinal Sen," in *Film Culture* (New York), Winter/Spring 1970.
"Mrinal Sen," in *International Film Guide 1982*, edited by Peter Cowie, London, 1981.
Malcolm, D., "Guerrilla Fighter," in *Sight and Sound* (London), Autumn 1981.
Vreeswijk, L., and others, "Sen dossier," special section, in *Skrien* (Amsterdam), October 1981.
Bassan, Raphael, "Mrinal Sen," in *Revue du Cinéma* (Paris), March 1985.
Roddick, Nick, "Original Sen," in *Cinema Papers* (Melbourne), July 1986.

On SEN: film—

Hauff, Reinhard, *Ten Days in Calcutta: A Portrait of Mrinal Sen*, 1987.

*   *   *

Mrinal Sen's work is distinguished by the attention he pays to the lives of the underprivileged in India. The style of his films varies considerably, and even within individual films his achievement is uneven, but the body of his work adds up to an important attempt in India at making political films, films which point to prevailing injustices and urge people to change society. Sen is India's pre-eminent activist filmmaker.

Sen's early films testify to the influences of the Italian neorealists and of Satayajit Ray's first films. Sen filmed people at the ragged edge of society, using natural locations and employing non-professional actors. Nothing in his films touched up the drabness of poor villages. Unlike Ray, however, Sen's attitude had less humanism in it than political urgency. In a strong film like *Baishey Shravana*, Sen suggests that a bourgeois mentality makes bad conditions worse by interposing the claims of respectability on matters of survival.

Although Sen established a reputation in Bengal with *Baishey Shravana*, he came to be known throughout India for the comic *Bhuvan Shome*, made in Hindi in 1969. The film describes a railway official's encounter with the wife of a ticket collector under fire for accepting bribes. The prudish railway official (played in restrained slapstick by Utpal Dutt) is charmed by a country girl while on holiday in Gujarat and only later discovers that the girl is married to the offending ticket collector. The film is shot among sand dunes and sugarcane fields and reveals Sen's skill at sustaining a simple narrative. To some critics, *Bhuvan Shome* remains Sen's best film, an example of his little-used talents as a confectioner of cinema.

Conditions of near civil war in Calcutta in the late 1960s led to three films known as the Calcutta trilogy—*Interview, Calcutta 71* and *Padatik*. In these films, Sen moved away from the surface realism of his previous work to allegorical characters and symbolic utterance. Sen returned to conventional narrative with the Hindi film *Mrigaya* in 1976 and has continued since then to present stories about marginal people, framing the story so that the viewer is led to discover his or her own complicity with oppression. *Akaler Sandhane* describes the adventure of a film crew out to film a story about the Bengal famine of 1943. The villages in which the crew works are no more prosperous in 1980 than they were 40 years ago; an afternoon's shopping for the film team cleans out the village vegetable market. *Akaler Sandhane* is intensively effective in the film-within-film, when actors recreate the dire poverty of a disabled peasant's household. The wife has sold herself to the landlord in order to bring home a potful of rice. Sen cuts from a chilling night scene of the lame husband beating his wife to the crowd of onlookers; it is an open question whether the dis-sipation of intensity which follows this distancing serves a necessary political purpose.

Communist critics generally favor Sen's work; liberal critics point to characteristic weakness of structure. But Sen's caring and energy are never contested. In film after film he probes the fate of those people [tribals (*Mrigaya*), outcastes (*Oka Oorie Katha*), pavement dwellers (*Parashuram*), working women (*Ek Din Pratidin*), servants (*Kharij*)] who are treated as if they were sub-human. Sen's more recent films affect a subdued tone and, unlike the Calcutta trilogy, trust the audience to draw its own moral from the films. Outside of India, too, critics discern a new phase of maturity in Sen's work.

—Satti Khanna

———

SENNETT, Mack.

Canadian. Born Mikall (Michael) Sinnott in Danville, Quebec, 17 January 1880. Burlesque performer and chorus boy on Broadway, 1902–08; actor in Biograph films, 1908–10; director of Biograph shorts, from 1910, moved to Hollywood; formed Keystone Production Company with Charles Bauman and Adam Kessel, 1912; Keystone absorbed into Triangle Film Corporation with Thomas Ince's and D.W. Griffith's production companies, 1915; Formed production company Mack Sennett Comedies following collapse of Triangle, 1917, though films released by Paramount; associated with Pathé, 1923–28, and with Educational Films, 1929–32, also returned to directing; producer and director of shorts for Paramount, from 1932, and experimented with early color process called "Natural Color"; returned to Educational Films, 1935, then retired to Canada; held nominal position at 20th Century-Fox, from 1939. Recipient: Special Oscar for contributions to screen comedy, 1937. *Died 1960.*

Films as Director:

1910   *The Lucky Toothache* (+ sc, role); *The Masher* (+ sc, role)
1911   *Comrades* (+ role); *Priscilla's April Fool Joke; Cured; Priscilla and the Umbrella; Cupid's Joke; Misplaced Jealousy; The Country Lovers; The Manicure Lady* (+ role); *Curiosity; A Dutch Gold Mine* (+ role); *Dave's Love Affair; Their Fates Sealed; Bearded Youth; The Delayed Proposal; Stubbs' New Servants; The Wonderful Eye; The Jealous Husband; The Ghost; Jinks Joins the Temperance Club; Mr. Peck Goes Calling; The Beautiful Voice; That Dare Devil* (+ role); *An Interrupted Game; The Diving Girl; $500,000 Reward* (+ role); *The Baron; The Villain Foiled; The Village Hero* (+ role); *The Lucky Horseshoe; A Convenient Burglar; When Wifey Holds the Purse Strings; Too Many Burglars; Mr. Bragg, A Fugitive; Trailing the Counterfeit* (+ role); *Josh's Suicide; Through His Wife's Picture; The Inventor's Secret; A Victim of Circumstances; Their First Divorce Case* (+ role); *Dooley Scheme; Won Through a Medium; Resourceful Lovers; Her Mother Interferes; Why He Gave Up; Abe Gets Even With Father; Taking His Medicine; Her Pet; Caught with the Goods* (+ role); *A Mix-up in Raincoats; The Joke on the Joker; Who Got the Reward; Brave and Bold; Did Mother Get Her Wash; With a Kodak; Pants and Pansies; A Near-Tragedy; Lily's Lovers; The Fatal Chocolate* (+ role); *Got a Match; A Message from the Moon; Priscilla's Capture; A Spanish Dilemma* (+ role); *The Engagement Ring; A Voice from the Deep; Hot Stuff; Oh, Those Eyes; Those Hicksville Boys;*

Their First Kidnapping Case (+ role); *Help, Help; The Brave Hunter; Won by a Fish; The Leading Man; The Fickle Spaniard; When the Fire Bells Rang; The Furs; A Close Call; Helen's Marriage; Tomboy Bessie; Algy, the Watchman; Katchem Kate; Neighbors; A Dash through the Clouds; The New Baby; Trying to Fool; One Round O'Brien; The Speed Demon; His Own Fault; The Would Be Shriner* (+ role); *Willie Becomes an Artist; The Tourists; What the Doctor Ordered; An Interrupted Elopement; The Tragedy of a Dress Suit; Mr. Grouch at the Seashore; Through Dumb Luck*

1912 *Cohen Collects a Debt (Cohen at Coney Island)* (+ pr); *The Water Nymph* (+ pr); *Riley and Schultz* (+ pr); *The New Neighbor* (+ pr); *The Beating He Needed* (+ pr); *Pedro's Dilemma* (+ pr, role); *Stolen Glory* (+ pr, role); *The Ambitious Butler* (+ pr, role); *The Flirting Husband* (+ pr); *The Grocery Clerk's Romance* (+ pr); *At Coney Island* (+ pr, role); *Mabel's Lovers* (+ pr); *At It Again* (+ pr, role); *The Deacon's Troubles* (+ pr); *A Temperamental Husband* (+ pr); *The Rivals* (+ pr, role); *Mr. Fix It* (+ pr, role); *A Desperate Lover* (+ pr); *A Bear Escape* (+ pr, role); *Pat's Day Off* (+ pr, role); *Brown's Seance* (+ pr); *A Family Mixup* (+ pr, role); *Useful Sheep* (+ pr); *Hoffmeyer's Legacy* (+ pr); *The Drummer's Vacation* (+ pr); *The Duel* (+ pr, role); *Mabel's Strategem* (+ pr)

1913 *Saving Mabel's Dad* (+ pr); *A Double Wedding* (+ pr); *The Cure That Failed* (+ pr); *How Hiram Won Out* (+ pr); *For Lizzie's Sake* (+ pr); *Sir Thomas Lipton Out West* (+ pr); *The Mistaken Masher* (+ pr, role); *The Deacon Outwitted* (+ pr); *The Elite Ball* (+ pr); *Just Brown's Luck* (+ pr); *The Battle of Who Run* (+ pr, role); *The Jealous Waiter* (+ pr); *The Stolen Purse* (+ pr, role); *Mabel's Heroes* (+ pr, role); *Her Birthday Present* (+ pr); *Heinze's Resurrection* (+ pr); *A Landlord's Troubled* (+ pr); *Forced Bravery* (+ pr); *The Professor's Daughter* (+ pr); *A Tangled Affair* (+ pr); *A Red Hot Romance* (+ pr); *A Doctored Affair* (+ pr); *The Sleuth's Last Stand* (+ pr, role); *A Deaf Burglar* (+ pr); *The Sleuths at the Floral Parade* (+ pr, role); *A Rural Third Degree* (+ pr); *A Strong Revenge* (+ pr, role); *The Two Widows* (+ pr); *Foiling Fickle Father* (+ pr); *Love and Pain* (+ pr); *The Man Next Door* (+ pr); *A Wife Wanted* (+ pr); *The Rube and the Baron* (+ pr, role); *Jenny's Pearls* (+ pr); *The Chief's Predicament* (+ pr); *At Twelve O'Clock* (+ pr); *Her New Beau* (+ pr, role); *On His Wedding Day* (+ pr); *The Land Salesman* (+ pr); *Hide and Seek* (+ pr); *Those Good Old Days* (+ pr); *A Game of Poker* (+ pr); *Father's Choice* (+ pr); *A Life in the Balance* (+ pr); *Murphy's I.O.U.* (+ pr); *A Dollar Did It* (+ pr); *Cupid in the Dental Parlor* (+ pr); *A Fishy Affair* (+ pr); *The Bangville Police* (+ pr); *The New Conductor* (+ pr); *His Chum, the Baron* (+ pr); *That Ragtime Band* (+ pr); *Algie on the Force* (+ pr); *His Ups and Downs* (+ pr); *The Darktown Belle* (+ pr); *A Little Hero* (+ pr); *Mabel's Awful Mistake* (+ pr, role); *The Foreman and the Jury* (+ pr); *The Gangster* (+ pr); *Barney Oldfield's Race for a Life* (+ pr, role); *Passions—He Had Three* (+ pr); *Help! Help! Hydrophobia!* (+ pr); *The Hansom Driver* (+ pr, role); *The Speed Queen* (+ pr); *The Waiter's Picnic* (+ pr); *The Tale of the Black Eye* (+ pr); *Out and In* (+ pr); *A Bandit* (+ pr); *Peeping Pete* (+ pr); *His Crooked Career* (+ pr, role); *For Love of Mabel* (+ pr); *Safe in Jail* (+ pr); *The Telltale Light* (+ pr); *Love and Rubbish* (+ pr); *A Noise from the Deep* (+ pr); *The Peddler* (+ pr); *Love and Courage* (+ pr); *Professor Bean's Removal* (+ pr); *Cohen's Outing* (+ pr); *The Firebugs* (+ pr); *Baby Day* (+ pr); *Mabel's New Hero* (+ pr); *Mabel's Dramatic Career* (+ pr, role); *The Gypsy Queen* (+ pr); *Willie Minds the Dog* (+ pr); *When Dreams Come True* (+ pr); *Mother's Boy* (+ pr); *The Bowling Match* (+ pr); *The Speed Kings* (+ pr); *Love Sickness at Sea* (+ pr, role); *A Muddy Romance* (+ pr); *Cohen Saves the Flag* (+ pr); *Zuzu the Band Leader* (+ pr)

1914 *In the Clutches of the Gang* (+ pr); *Mabel's Strange Predicament* (co-d, pr); *Love and Gasoline* (+ pr); *Mack at it Again* (+ pr, role); *Mabel at the Wheel* (+ pr, role); *The Knockout* (+ pr); *A New York Girl* (+ pr, role); *His*

Talented Wife (+ pr, role); *Tillie's Punctured Romance* (+ pr, feature); *The Fatal Mallet* (co-d with Chaplin, pr, role)

1915 *Hearts and Planets* (+ pr, role); *The Little Teacher* (+ pr, role); *My Valet* (+ pr, role); *A Favorite Fool* (+ pr); *Stolen Magic* (+ pr, role)

1921 *Oh, Mabel Behave* (co-d, pr, role)

1927 *A Finished Actor* (co-d, pr)

1928 *The Lion's Roar* (+ sc, pr)

1929 *The Bride's Relation* (+ pr); *The Old Barn* (+ pr); *Whirls and Girls* (+ pr); *Broadway Blues* (+ pr); *The Bee's Buzz* (+ pr); *Girl Crazy* (+ pr); *The Barber's Daughter* (+ pr); *Jazz Mamas* (+ pr); *The New Bankroll* (+ pr); *The Constable (The Constabule)* (+ pr); *Midnight Daddies* (+ pr); *The Lunkhead* (+ pr); *The Golfers* (+ pr); *A Hollywood Star* (+ pr)

1930 *Scotch* (+ pr); *Sugar Plum Papa* (+ pr); *Bulls and Bears* (+ pr); *Match Play* (+ pr); *Honeymoon Zeppelin* (+ pr); *Fat Wives for Thin* (+ pr); *Campus Crushes* (+ pr); *The Chumps* (+ pr); *Goodbye Legs* (+ pr); *Average Husband* (+ pr); *Vacation Loves* (+ pr); *The Bluffer* (+ pr); *Grandma's Girl* (+ pr); *Divorced Sweethearts* (+ pr); *Racket Cheers* (+ pr); *Rough Idea of Love* (+ pr)

1931 *A Poor Fish* (+ pr); *Dance Hall Marge* (+ pr); *The Chiseler* (+ pr); *Ghost Parade* (+ pr); *Hollywood Happenings* (+ pr); *Hold 'er Sheriff* (+ pr); *Monkey Business in America* (+ pr); *Movie-Town* (+ pr, role); *The Albany Bunch* (+ pr); *I Surrender Dear* (+ pr); *Speed* (+ pr); *One More Chance* (+ pr)

1932 *Hypnotized* (+ pr, sc)

1935 *Ye Olde Saw Mill* (+ pr, sc); *Flicker Fever* (+ pr); *Just Another Murder* (+ sc, pr); *The Timid Young Man* (+ pr); *Way Up Thar* (+ pr)

Other Films:
(incomplete list)

1908 *Baked at the Altar* (Griffith) (role); *Father Gets in the Game* (Griffith) (role); *The Song of the Shirt* (Griffith) (role); *Mr. Jones at the Ball* (Griffith) (role)

1909 *Mr. Jones Has a Card Party* (Griffith) (role); *The Curtain Pole* (Griffith) (role); *The Politician's Love Story* (Griffith) (role); *The Lonely Villa* (Griffith) (role); *The Way of a Man* (Griffith) (role); *The Slave* (Griffith) (role); *Pippa Passes* (Griffith) (role); *The Gibson Goddess* (Griffith) (role); *Nursing a Viper* (Griffith) (role)

1910 *The Dancing Girl of Butte* (Griffith) (role); *All on Account of the Milk* (Griffith) (role); *The Englishman and the Girl* (Griffith) (role); *The Newlyweds* (Griffith) (role); *An Affair of Hearts* (Griffith) (role); *Never Again!* (Griffith) (role); *The Call to Arms* (Griffith) (role); *An Arcadian Maid* (Griffith) (role)

1911 *The Italian Barber* (Griffith) (role); *Paradise Lost* (Griffith) (role); *The White Rose of the Wilds* (Griffith) (role); *The Last Drop of Water* (Griffith) (role)

1912 *The Brave Hunter* (role)

1913 *Their First Execution* (pr); *Hubby's Job* (pr); *Betwixt Love and Fire* (pr); *Toplitsky and Company* (pr); *Feeding Time* (pr); *Largest Boat Ever Launched Sidewalks* (pr); *Rastus and the Game-Cock* (pr); *Get Rich Quick* (pr); *Just Kids* (pr); *A Game of Pool* (pr); *The Latest in Life Saving* (pr); *A Chip Off the Old Block* (pr); *The Kelp Industry* (pr); *Fatty's Day Off* (pr); *Los Angeles Harbour* (pr); *The New Baby* (pr); *What Father Saw* (pr); *The Faithful Taxicab* (pr); *Billy Dodges Bills* (pr); *Across the Alley* (pr); *The Abalone Industry* (pr); *Schnitz the Tailor* (pr); *Their Husbands* (pr); *A Healthy Neighborhood* (pr); *Two Old Tars* (pr); *A Quiet Little Wedding* (pr); *The Janitor* (pr); *The Making of an Automobile Tire* (pr); *Fatty at San Diego* (pr); *A Small Town Act* (pr); *The Milk We Drink* (pr); *Wine* (pr); *Our Children* (pr); *Fatty Joins the Force* (pr); *The Woman Haters* (pr); *The Rogues' Gallery* (pr); *The San Francisco Celebration* (pr); *A Ride for a Bride* (pr); *The Horse Thief* (pr); *The Gusher* (pr); *Fatty's Flirtation* (pr); *Protecting San Francisco from Fire* (pr); *His Sister's Kids* (pr); *A Bad Game*

Mack Sennett

(pr); *Some Nerve* (pr); *The Champion* (pr); *He Would A Hunting Go* (pr);

1914 *A Misplaced Foot* (pr); *A Glimpse of Los Angeles* (pr); *Love and Dynamite* (pr); *Mabel's Stormy Love Affair* (pr); *The Under Sheriff* (pr); *A Flirt's Mistake* (pr); *How Motion Pictures Are Made* (pr); *Too Many Brides* (pr); *Won in a Closet* (pr): *Rebecca's Wedding Day* (pr); *Little Billy Triumphs* (pr); *Mabel's Bare Escape* (pr); *Making A Living* (pr); *Little Billy's Strategy* (pr); *Kid Auto Races at Venice* (pr); *Olives and their Oil* (pr); *A Robust Romeo* (pr); *Raffles* (pr); *Gentleman Burglar* (pr); *A Thief Catcher* (pr); *Twixt Love and Fire* (pr); *Little Billy's City Cousin* (pr); *Between Showers* (pr); *A Film Johnnie* (pr); *Tango Tangles* (pr); *His Favorite Pastime* (pr); *A Rural Demon* (pr); *The Race (How Villains Are Made)* (pr); *Across the Hall* (pr); *Cruel, Cruel Love* (pr); *Barnyard Flirtations* (pr); *A Back Yard Theater* (pr); *Chicken Chaser* (pr); *The Star Boarder* (pr); *Fatal High* (pr); *The Passing of Izzy* (pr); *A Bathing Beauty (A Bathhouse Beauty)* (pr); *Twenty Minutes of Love* (pr); *Where Hazel Met the Villain* (pr); *Bowery Boys* (pr); *Caught in a Cabaret* (pr); *When Villains Wait* (pr); *Caught in the Rain* (pr); *A Busy Day* (pr); *The Morning Papers* (pr); *A Suspended Ordeal* (pr); *Finnegan's Bomb* (pr); *Mabel's Nerve* (pr); *The Water Dog* (pr); *When Reuben Fooled the Bandits* (pr); *Acres of Alfalfa* (pr); *Our Large Birds* (pr); *The Fatal Flirtation* (pr); *The Alarm* (pr); *The Fatal Mallet* (pr); *Her Friend the Bandit* (pr); *Our Country Cousin* (pr); *Mabel's Busy Day* (pr); *A Gambling Rube* (pr); *A Missing Bride* (pr); *Mabel's Married Life* (pr); *The Eavesdropper* (pr); *Fatty and the Heiress* (pr); *Caught in Tights* (pr); *Fatty's Finish* (pr); *Love and Bullets* (pr); *Row-Boat Romance* (pr); *Laughing Gas* (pr); *Love and Salt Water* (pr); *World's Oldest Living Thing* (pr); *Mabel's New Job* (pr); *The Sky Pirate* (pr); *The Fatal Sweet Tooth* (pr); *Those Happy Days* (pr); *The Great Toe Mystery* (pr); *Soldiers of Misfortune* (pr); *The Property Man* (pr, role); *A Coat's Tale* (pr); *The Face on the Barroom Floor* (pr); *Recreation* (pr); *The Yosemite* (pr); *Such a Cook* (pr); *That Minstrel Man* (pr); *Those Country Kids* (pr); *Caught in a Flue* (pr); *Fatty's Gift* (pr); *The Masquerader* (pr); *Her Last Chance* (pr); *His New Profession* (pr); *The Baggage Smasher* (pr); *A Brand New Hero* (pr); *The Rounders* (pr); *Mabel's Latest Prank* (pr); *Mabel's Blunder* (pr); *All at Sea* (pr); *Bombs and Bangs* (pr); *Lover's Luck* (pr); *He Loved the Ladies* (pr); *The New Janitor* (pr); *Fatty's Debut* (pr); *Hard Cider* (pr); *Killing Hearts* (pr); *Fatty Again* (pr); *Their Ups and Downs* (pr); *Hello Mabel* (pr); *Those Love Pangs* (pr); *The Anglers* (pr); *The High Spots on Broadway* (pr); *Zipp, the Dodger* (pr); *Dash, Love and Splash* (pr); *Santa Catalina Islands* (pr); *The Love Thief* (pr); *Stout Heart But Weak Knees* (pr); *Shot in the Excitement* (pr); *Doug and Dynamite* (pr); *Gentlemen of Nerve* (pr); *Lovers' Post Office* (pr); *Curses! They Remarked* (pr); *His Musical Career* (pr); *His Trysting Place* (pr); *An Incompetent Hero* (pr); *How Heroes Are Made* (pr); *Fatty's Jonah Day* (pr); *The Noise of Bombs* (pr); *Fatty's Wine Party* (pr); *His Taking Ways* (pr); *The Sea Nymphs* (pr); *His Halted Career* (pr); *Among the Mourners* (pr); *Leading Lizzie Astray* (pr); *Shotguns That Kick* (pr); *Getting Acquainted* (pr); *Other People's Business* (pr); *His Prehistoric Past* (pr); *The Plumber* (pr); *Ambrose's First Falsehood* (pr); *Fatty's Magic Pants* (pr); *Hogan's Annual Spree* (pr); *A Colored Girl's Love* (pr); *Wild West Love* (pr); *Fatty and Minnie-He-Haw* (pr); *His Second Childhood* (pr); *Gussle the Golfer* (pr); *Hogan's Wild Oats* (pr); *A Steel Rolling Mill* (pr); *The Knockout* (Chaplin) (role)

1915 *A Dark Lover's Play* (pr); *Hushing the Scandal* (pr); *His Winning Punch* (pr); *U.S. Army in San Francisco* (pr); *Giddy, Gay and Ticklish* (pr); *Only A Farmer's Daughter* (pr); *Rum and Wall Paper* (pr); *Mabel's and Fatty's Wash Day* (pr); *Hash House Mashers* (pr); *Love, Speed, and Thrills* (pr); *Mabel and Fatty's Simple Life* (pr); *Hogan's Messy Job* (pr); *Fatty and Mabel at the San Diego Exposition* (pr); *Colored Villainy* (pr); *Mabel, Fatty and the Law* (pr); *Peanuts and Bullets* (pr); *The Home Breakers* (pr); *Fatty's*

New Role (pr); *Hogan the Porter* (pr); *Caught in the Park* (pr); *A Bird's a Bird* (pr); *Hogan's Romance Upset* (pr); *Hogan's Aristocratic Dream* (pr); *Ye Olden Grafter* (pr); *A Glimpse of the San Diego Exposition* (pr); *A Lucky Leap* (pr); *That Springtime Fellow* (pr); *Hogan Out West* (pr); *Ambrose's Sour Grapes* (pr); *Wilful Ambrose* (pr); *Fatty's Reckless Fling* (pr); *From Patches to Plenty* (pr); *Fatty's Chance Acquaintance* (pr); *Love in Armor* (pr); *Beating Hearts and Carpets* (pr); *That Little Band of Gold* (pr); *Ambrose's Little Hatchet* (pr); *Fatty's Faithful Fido* (pr); *A One Night Stand* (pr); *Ambrose's Fury* (pr); *Gussie's Day of Rest* (pr); *When Love Took Wings* (pr); *Ambrose's Lofty Perch* (pr); *Droppington's Devilish Dream* (pr); *The Rent Jumpers* (pr); *Droppington's Family Tree* (pr); *The Beauty Bunglers* (pr); *Do-Re-Mi-Fa* (pr); *Ambrose's Nasty Temper* (pr); *Fatty and Mabel Viewing the World's Fair at San Francisco* (pr); *Love, Loot and Crash* (pr); *Gussie Rivals Jonah* (pr); *Their Social Splash* (pr); *A Bear Affair* (pr); *Mabel's Wilful Way* (pr); *Gussie's Backward Way* (pr); *A Human Hound's Triumph* (pr); *Our Dare Devil Chief* (pr); *Crossed Love and Swords* (pr); *Miss Fatty's Seaside Lover* (pr); *He Wouldn't Stay Down* (pr); *For Better—But Worse* (pr); *A Versatile Villain* (pr); *Those College Girls* (pr); *Mabel Lost and Won* (pr); *Those Bitter Sweets* (pr); *The Cannon Ball* (pr); *A Home Breaking Hound* (pr); *Foiled by Fido* (pr); *Court House Crooks* (pr); *When Ambrose Dared Walrus* (pr); *Dirty Work in a Laundry* (pr); *Fido's Tin-Type Tangle* (pr); *A Lover's Lost Control* (pr); *A Rascal of Wolfish Ways* (pr); *The Battle of Ambrose and Walrus* (pr); *Only a Messenger Boy* (pr); *Caught in the Act* (pr); *His Luckless Love* (pr); *Viewing Sherman Institute for Indians at Riverside* (pr); *Wished on Mabel* (pr); *Gussie's Wayward Path* (pr); *Settled at the Seaside* (pr); *Gussie Tied to Trouble* (pr); *A Hash House Fraud* (pr); *Merely a Married Man* (pr); *A Game Old Knight* (pr); *Her Painted Hero* (pr); *Saved by Wireless* (pr); *Fickle Fatty's Fall* (pr); *His Father's Footsteps* (pr); *The Best of Enemies* (pr); *A Janitor's Wife's Temptation* (pr); *A Village Scandal* (pr); *The Great Vacuum Robbery* (pr); *Crooked to the End* (pr); *Fatty and the Broadway Stars* (pr, role); *A Submarine Pirate* (pr); *The Hunt* (pr)

1916 *The Worst of Friends* (pr); *Dizzy Heights and Daring Hearts* (pr); *The Great Pearl Tangle* (pr); *Fatty and Mabel Adrift* (pr); *Because He Loved Her* (pr); *A Modern Enoch Arden* (pr); *Perils of the Park* (pr); *A Movie Star* (pr); *His Hereafter* (pr); *He Did and He Didn't (Love and Lobsters)* (pr); *Love Will Conquer* (pr); *His Pride and Shame* (pr); *Fido's Fate* (pr); *Better Late Than Never* (pr); *Bright Lights* (pr); *Cinders of Love* (pr); *Wife and Auto Troubles* (pr); *The Judge* (pr); *A Village Vampire* (pr); *The Village Blacksmith* (pr); *A Love Riot* (pr); *Gipsy Joe* (pr); *By Stork Delivery* (pr); *An Oily Scoundrel* (pr); *A Bathhouse Blunder* (pr); *His Wife's Mistake* (pr); *His Bread and Butter* (pr); *His Last Laugh* (pr); *Bucking Society* (pr); *The Other Man* (pr); *The Snow Cure* (pr); *A Dash Of Courage* (pr); *The Lion and the Girl* (pr); *His Bitter Pill* (pr); *Her Marble Heart* (pr); *Bathtub Perils* (pr); *The Moonshiners* (pr); *Hearts and Sparks* (pr); *His Wild Oats* (pr); *Ambrose's Cup of Woe* (pr); *The Waiter's Ball* (pr); *The Surf Girl* (pr); *A Social Club* (pr); *Vampire Ambrose* (pr); *The Winning Punch* (pr); *His Lying Heart* (pr); *She Loved a Sailor* (pr); *His Auto Ruination* (pr); *Ambrose's Rapid Rise* (pr); *His Busted Trust* (pr); *Tugboat Romeos* (pr); *Sunshine* (pr); *Her Feathered Nest* (pr); *No One to Guide Him* (pr); *Her First Beau* (pr); *His First False Step* (pr); *The Houseboat* (pr); *The Fire Chief* (pr); *Love on Skates* (pr); *His Alibi* (pr); *Love Comet* (pr); *A la Cabaret* (pr); *Haystacks and Steeples* (pr); *A Scoundrel's Toll* (pr); *The Three Slims* (pr); *The Girl Guardian* (pr); *Wings and Wheels* (pr); *Safety First Ambrose* (pr); *Maid Mad* (pr); *The Twins* (pr); *Piles of Perils* (pr); *A Cream Puff Romance* (pr); *The Danger Girl* (pr); *Bombs* (pr); *His Last Scent* (pr); *The Manicurist* (pr)

1917 *The Nick of Time Baby* (pr); *Stars and Bars* (pr); *Maggie's First False Step* (pr); *Villa of the Movies* (pr); *Dodging His*

Doom (pr); *Her Circus Knight* (pr); *Her Fame and Shames* (pr); *Pinched in the Finish* (pr); *Her Nature Dance* (pr); *Teddy at the Throttle* (pr); *Secrets of a Beauty Parlor* (pr); *A Maiden's Trust* (pr); *His Naughty Thought* (pr); *Her Torpedoed Love* (pr); *A Royal Rogue* (pr); *Oriental Love* (pr); *Cactus Nell* (pr); *The Betrayal of Maggie* (pr); *Skidding Hearts* (pr); *The Dog Catcher's Love* (pr); *Whose Baby* (pr); *Dangers of a Bride* (pr); *A Clever Dummy* (pr); *She Needed a Doctor* (pr); *Thirst* (pr); *His Uncle Dudley* (pr); *Lost a Cook* (pr); *The Pawnbroker's Heart* (pr); *Two Crooks* (pr); *A Shanghaied Jonah* (pr); *His Precious Life* (pr); *Hula Hula Land* (pr); *The Late Lamented* (pr); *The Sultan's Wife* (pr); *A Bedroom Blunder* (pr); *Roping Her Romeo* (pr); *The Pullman Bride* (pr); *Are Waitresses Safe* (pr); *An International Sneak* (pr); *That Night* (pr); *Taming Target Center* (pr)

1918   *The Kitchen Lady* (pr); *His Hidden Purpose* (pr); *Watch Your Neighbors* (pr); *It Pays to Exercise* (pr); *Sheriff Nell's Tussle* (pr); *Those Athletic Girls* (pr); *Friend Husband* (pr); *Saucy Madeline* (pr); *His Smothered Love* (pr); *The Battle Royal* (pr); *Love Loops the Loop* (pr); *Two Tough Tenderfeet* (pr); *Her Screen Idol* (pr); *Ladies First* (pr); *Her Blighted Love* (pr); *She Loved Him Plenty* (pr); *The Summer Girls* (pr); *Mickey* (pr); *His Wife's Friend* (pr); *Sleuths* (pr); *Beware the Boarders* (pr); *Whose Little Wife Are You* (pr); *Her First Mistake* (pr); *Hide and Seek Detectives* (pr); *The Village Chestnut* (pr)

1919   *Cupid's Day Off* (pr); *Never Too Old* (pr); *Rip & Stitch, Tailors* (pr); *East Lynne with Variations* (pr); *The Village Smithy* (pr); *Reilly's Wash Day* (pr); *The Foolish Age* (pr); *The Little Widow* (pr); *When Love is Blind* (pr); *Love's False Faces* (pr); *Hearts and Flowers* (pr); *No Mother to guide Him* (pr); *Trying to Get Along* (pr); *Among Those Present* (pr); *Yankee Doodle in Berlin* (pr); *Why Beaches Are Popular* (pr); *Treating 'em Rough* (pr); *A Lady's Tailor* (pr); *Uncle Tom Without the Cabin* (pr); *The Dentist* (pr); *Back to the Kitchen* (pr); *Up in Alf's Place* (pr); *Salome vs. Shenandoah* (pr); *His Last False Step* (pr); *The Speak Easy* (pr)

1920   *The Star Boarder* (pr); *Ten Dollars or Ten Days* (pr); *Gee Whiz* (pr); *The Gingham Girl* (pr); *Down on the Farm* (pr); *Fresh from the City* (pr); *Let 'er Go* (pr); *By Golly* (pr); *You Wouldn't Believe It* (pr); *Married Life* (pr); *The Quack Doctor* (pr); *Great Scott* (pr); *Don't Weaken* (pr); *It's a Boy* (pr); *Young Man's Fancy* (pr); *His Youthful Fancy* (pr); *My Goodness* (pr); *Movie Fans* (pr); *Fickle Fancy* (pr); *Love, Honor, and Behave* (pr); *A Fireside Brewer* (*Home Brew*) (pr); *Bungalow Troubles* (pr)

1921   *Dabbling in Art* (pr); *An Unhappy Finish* (pr); *On a Summer's Day* (pr); *A Small Town Idol* (pr, sc); *Wedding Bells Out of Tune* (pr); *Officer Cupid* (pr); *Away from the Steerage* (*Astray from the Steerage*) (pr); *Sweetheart Days* (pr); *Home Talent* (pr, sc); *She Sighed by the Seaside* (pr); *Hard Knocks and Love Taps* (pr); *Made in the Kitchen* (pr); *Call a Cop* (pr); *Love's Outcast* (pr); *Molly O* (pr, sc)

1922   *By Heck* (pr); *Be Reasonable* (pr); *Bright Eyes* (pr); *The Duck Hunter* (pr); *On Patrol* (pr); *Step Forward* (pr); *Gymnasium Jim* (pr); *The Crossroads of New York* (pr, sc); *Oh Daddy!* (pr); *Home-Made Movies* (pr); *Ma and Pa* (pr); *Bow Wow* (pr); *Love and Doughnuts* (pr); *When Summer Comes* (pr)

1923   *Suzanna* (pr); *The Shriek of Araby* (pr, sc); *Where is My Wandering Boy This Evening* (pr); *Nip and Tuck* (pr); *Pitfalls of a Big City* (pr); *Skylarking* (pr); *Down to the Sea in Shoes* (pr); *The Extra Girl* (pr, co-sc); *Asleep at the Switch* (pr); *One Cylinder Love* (pr); *The Dare-Devil* (pr); *Flip Flops* (pr); *Inbad the Sailor* (pr)

1924   *Ten Dollars or Ten Days* (remake, pr); *One Spooky Night* (pr); *Picking Peaches* (pr); *The Half-Back of Notre Dame* (pr); *Smile Please* (pr); *Scarem Much* (pr); *Shanghaied Ladies* (pr); *The Hollywood Kid* (pr); *Flickering Youth* (pr); *Black Oxfords* (pr); *The Cat's Meow* (pr); *Yukon Jake* (pr); *The Lion and the Souse* (pr); *His New Mama* (pr); *Romeo and Juliet* (pr); *Wall Street Blues* (pr); *The First Hundred Years* (pr); *East of the Water Plug* (pr, sc); *Lizzies of the Field* (pr); *The Luck of the Foolish* (pr); *Three Foolish Wives* (pr); *Little Robinson Corkscrew* (pr); *The Hansom Cabman* (*Be Careful*) (pr); *Riders of the Purple Cows* (pr); *The Reel Virginian* (*The West Virginian*) (pr); *Galloping Bungalows* (pr); *All Night Long* (pr); *Love's Sweet Piffle* (pr); *The Cannon Ball Express* (pr); *Feet of Mud* (pr); *Off His Trolley* (pr); *Bull and Sand* (pr); *Watch Out* (pr); *Over Here* (pr); *The Lady Barber* (pr); *North of 57* (pr); *Love's Intrigue* (pr); *The Stunt Man* (pr)

1925   *The Sea Squaw* (pr); *The Plumber* (pr); *The Wild Goose Chaser* (pr); *Honeymoon Hardships* (pr); *Boobs in the Woods* (pr); *The Beloved Bozo* (pr); *Water Wagons* (pr); *His Marriage Wow* (pr); *The Raspberry Romance* (pr); *Bashful Jim* (pr); *Giddap* (pr); *Plain Clothes* (pr); *Breaking the Ice* (pr); *The Marriage Circus* (pr); *The Lion's Whiskers* (pr); *Remember When* (pr); *He Who Gets Smacked* (pr); *Skinners in Silk* (pr); *Good Morning, Nurse!* (pr); *Super-Hooper-Dyne Lizzies* (pr); *Don't Tell Dad* (pr); *Isn't Love Cuckoo* (pr); *Sneezing Breezes* (pr); *Cupid's Boots* (pr); *Tee for Two* (pr); *The Iron Nag* (pr); *Lucky Stars* (pr); *Cold Turkey* (pr); *Butter Fingers* (pr); *There He Goes* (pr); *Hurry, Doctor* (pr); *A Rainy Knight* (pr); *Love and Kisses* (pr); *Over There-Abouts* (pr); *Good Morning, Madam* (pr); *A Sweet Pickle* (pr); *Dangerous Curves Behind* (pr); *The Soapsuds Lady* (pr); *Take Your Time* (pr); *The Window Dummy* (pr); *From Rags to Britches* (pr); *Hotsy Toty* (pr)

1926   *The Gosh-Darn Mortgage* (pr); *Wide Open Faces* (pr); *Hot Cakes for Two* (pr); *Whispering Whiskers* (pr); *Saturday Afternoon* (pr); *Funnymooners* (pr); *Trimmed in Gold* (pr); *Gooseland* (pr); *Circus Today* (pr); *Meet My Girl* (pr); *Spanking Breezes* (pr); *Wandering Willies* (pr); *Hooked at the Altar* (pr); *A Love Sundae* (pr); *Soldier Man* (pr); *The Ghost of Folly* (pr); *Fight Night* (pr); *Hayfoot, Strawfoot* (pr); *A Yankee Doodle Dude* (pr); *Muscle-Bound Music* (pr); *Oh, Uncle!* (pr); *Puppy Lovetime* (pr); *Ice Cold Cocos* (pr); *A Dinner Jest* (pr); *A Sea Dog's Tale* (pr); *Baby's Pets* (pr); *A Bachelor Butt-in* (pr); *Smith's Baby* (pr); *Alice Be Good* (pr); *When a Man's a Prince* (pr); *Smith's Vacation* (pr); *Hubby's Quiet Little Game* (pr); *Her Actor Friend* (pr); *Hoboken to Hollywood* (pr); *The Prodigal Bridegroom* (pr); *The Perils of Petersboro* (pr); *Smith's Landlord* (pr); *Love's Last Laugh* (pr); *Smith's Visitor* (pr); *Should Husbands Marry* (pr); *Masked Mamas* (pr); *A Harem Knight* (pr); *Smith's Uncle* (pr); *Hesitating Houses* (pr); *The Divorce Dodger* (pr); *A Blonde's Revenge* (pr); *Flirty Four-Flushers* (pr); *Smith's Picnic* (pr)

1927   *Kitty from Killarney* (pr); *Smith's Pets* (pr); *Should Sleepwalkers Marry* (pr); *Pass the Dumpling* (pr); *A Hollywood Hero* (pr); *Smith's Customer* (pr); *Peaches and Plumbers* (pr); *Plumber's Daughter* (pr); *A Small Town Princess* (pr); *A Dozen Socks* (pr); *The Jolly Jilter* (pr); *Smith's Surprise* (pr); *Smith's New Home* (pr); *Broke in China* (pr); *Smith's Kindergarten* (pr); *Crazy to Act* (pr); *Smith Fishing Trip* (pr); *His First Flame* (pr); *Pride of Pickeville* (pr); *Cured in the Excitement* (pr); *Catalina, Here I Come* (pr); *The Pest of Friends* (pr); *Love's Languid Lure* (pr); *College Kiddo* (pr); *Smith's Candy Shop* (pr); *The Golf Nut* (pr); *Smith's Pony* (pr); *A Gold Digger of Weepah* (pr); *Smith's Cook* (pr); *Daddy Boy* (pr); *For Sale a Bungalow* (pr); *Smith's Cousin* (pr); *The Bull Fighter* (pr); *Fiddlesticks* (pr); *Smith's Modiste Shop* (pr); *The Girl from Everywhere* (pr); *Love in a Police Station* (pr); *Hold that Pose* (pr)

1928   *Smith's Holiday* (pr); *Run, Girl, Run* (pr); *The Beach Club* (pr); *Love at First Sight* (pr); *Smith's Army Life* (pr); *The Best Man* (pr); *The Swan Princess* (pr); *Smith's Farm Days* (pr); *The Bicycle Flirt* (pr); *The Girl From Nowhere* (pr); *His Unlucky Night* (pr); *Smith's Restaurant* (pr); *The Good-bye Kiss* (pr); *The Chicken* (pr); *Taxi for Two* (pr); *Caught in the Kitchen* (pr); *A Dumb Waiter* (pr); *The Campus Carmen* (pr); *Motor Boat Mamas* (pr); *The Bargain Hunt* (pr); *Smith's Catalina Rowboat Race* (*Catalina Rowboat Race*) (pr); *A Taxi Scandal* (pr); *Hubby's Latest Alibi* (pr); *A Jim Jam Janitor* (pr); *The Campus Vamp* (pr); *Hubby's*

Week-end Trip (pr); *The Burglar* (pr); *Taxi Beauties* (pr); *His New Stenographer* (pr)

1929 *Clunked on the Corner* (pr); *Baby's Birthday* (pr); *Uncle Tom* (pr); *Calling Hubby's Bluff* (pr); *Taxi Spooks* (pr); *Button My Back* (pr); *Ladies Must Eat* (pr); *Foolish Husbands* (pr); *Matchmaking Mamas* (pr); *The Rodeo* (pr); *Pink Pajamas* (pr); *The Night Watchman's Mistake* (pr); *The New Aunt* (pr); *Taxi Dolls* (pr); *Don't Get Jealous* (pr); *Caught in a Taxi* (pr); *A Close Shave* (pr); *The Big Palooka* (pr); *Motoring Mamas* (pr); *Clancy at the Bat* (pr); *The New Half-Back* (pr); *Uppercut O'Brien* (pr)

1930 *He Trumped Her Ace* (pr); *Radio Kisses* (pr); *Hello Television* (pr); *Take Your Medicine* (pr); *Don't Bite Your Dentist* (pr); *Strange Birds* (pr); *A Hollywood Theme Song* (pr)

1931 *No, No, Lady* (pr); *One Yard to Go* (pr); *The College Vamp* (remake, pr); *The Bride's Mistake* (pr); *The Dog Doctor* (pr); *Just a Bear (It's a Bear)* (pr); *Ex-Sweeties* (pr); *In Conference* (pr); *The Cowcatcher's Daughter* (pr); *Slide, Speedy, Slide* (pr); *Fainting Lover* (pr); *Too Many Husbands* (pr); *The Cannonball* (pr); *The Trail of the Swordfish* (pr); *Poker Windows* (pr); *The World Flier* (pr); *Who's Who in the Zoo* (pr); *Taxi Troubles* (pr); *The Great Pie Mystery* (pr); *Wrestling Swordfish* (pr); *All American Kickback* (pr); *Half Holiday* (pr); *The Pottsville Palooka* (pr)

1932 *Playgrounds of the Mammals* (pr); *Dream House* (pr); *The Girl in the Tonneau* (pr); *Shopping with Wife* (pr); *Lady! Please!* (pr); *Heavens! My Husband!* (pr); *The Billboard Girl* (pr); *The Flirty Sleepwalker* (pr); *Speed in the Gay Nineties* (pr); *Man-Eating Sharks* (pr); *Listening In* (pr); *The Spot in the Rug* (pr); *Divorce a la Mode* (pr); *The Boudoir Brothers* (pr); *Freaks of the Deep* (pr); *The Candid Camera* (pr); *Sea Going Birds* (pr); *Hatta Marri* (pr); *Alaska Love* (pr); *For the Love of Ludwig* (pr); *Neighbor Trouble* (pr); *His Royal Shyness* (pr); *Young Onions* (pr); *The Giddy Age* (pr); *Lighthouse Love* (pr); *Hawkins and Watkins* (pr); *The Singing Plumber* (pr); *Courting Trouble* (pr); *False Impressions* (pr); *Bring Back 'em Sober* (pr); *A Hollywood Double* (pr); *The Dentist* (pr); *Doubling in the Quickies* (pr); *The Lion and the House* (pr); *Human Fish* (pr)

1933 *Blue of the Night* (pr); *The Wrestlers (A Wrestler's Bride)* (pr); *Don't Play Bridge with Your Wife* (pr); *The Singing Boxer* (pr); *Too Many Highballs* (pr); *Easy on the Eyes* (pr); *A Fatal Glass of Beer* (pr); *Caliente Love* (pr); *Sing, Bing, Sing* (pr); *The Plumber and the Lady* (pr); *Sweet Cookie* (pr); *The Pharmacist* (pr); *Uncle Jake* (pr); *Dream Stuff* (pr); *Roadhouse Queen* (pr); *See You Tonight* (pr); *Daddy Knows Best* (pr); *Knockout Kisses* (pr); *Husband's Reunion* (pr); *The Big Fibber* (pr); *The Barber Shop* (pr)

1939 *Hollywood Cavalcade* (role)
1949 *Down Memory Lane* (role)

Publications:

By SENNETT: book—

Mack Sennett: King of Comedy, as Told to Cameron Shipp, New York, 1954.

By SENNETT: article—

Interview with T. Dreiser, in *Photoplay* (New York), August 1928.

On SENNETT: books—

Lejeune, C.A., *Mack Sennett*, London, 1931.
Fowler, Gene, *Father Goose: the Story of Mack Sennett*, New York, 1934.
Chevallier, Jacques, *Le Cinéma burlesque américain, 1912–30*, Paris, 1964.
Turconi, David, *Mack Sennett*, Paris, 1966.
Geduld, Harry M., editor, *Film Makers on Filmmaking*, Bloomington, Indiana, 1967.
Lahue, Kalton C., *Dreams for Sale: The Rise and Fall of the Triangle Film Corporation*, New York, 1971.
Lahue, Kalton C., *Mack Sennett's Keystone: The Man, the Myth, and the Comedies*, South Brunswick, New Jersey, 1971.
Pratt, George C., *Spellbound in Darkness*, Greenwich, Connecticut, 1973.
Mast, Gerald, *The Comic Mind: Comedy and the Movies*, Chicago, 1974; revised edition, 1979.

On SENNETT: articles—

Carr, H.C., "Mack Sennett—Laugh Tester," in *Photoplay* (New York), May 1915.
Carr, H., "The Secret of Making Film Comedies," in *Motion Picture Classic* (Brooklyn), October 1925.
Manners, D., "Defense of Low-Brow Comedy," in *Motion Picture Classic* (Brooklyn), October 1930.
Agee, James, "Comedy's Greatest Era," in *Life* (New York), 5 September 1949.
Knight, Arthur, "Era of Great Comedians," in the *Saturday Review* (New York), 18 December 1954.
Dyer, Peter John, "Cops, Custard, and Keaton," in *Films and Filming* (London), August 1958.
"Sennett Issue" of *Cinéma* (Paris), August/September 1960.
"Sennett Issue" of *Image et Son* (Paris), April 1964.
Durgnat, Raymond, "The World of Comedy: Breaking the Laugh Barrier," in *Films and Filming* (London), October 1965.
Giroux, Robert, "Mack Sennett," in *Films in Review* (New York), December 1968.
Hoffner, J.R., "King of Keystone," in *Classic Film Collector* (Indiana, Pennsylvania), Summer 1971.
Bodeen, Dewitt, "All the Sad Young Bathing Beauties," in *Focus on Film* (London), Autumn 1974.
"Mack Sennett Section" of *Cinema Nuovo* (Bari), April 1984.
Stempel, T., "The Sennett Screenplays," in *Sight and Sound* (London), Winter 1985/86.

*   *   *

Mack Sennett was the outstanding pioneer and primitive of American silent comedy. Although Sennett's name is most commonly associated with the Keystone Company, which he founded in 1912, Sennett's film career began four years earlier with the Biograph Company, the pioneering film company where D.W. Griffith established the principles of film narrative and rhetoric. Sennett and Griffith were colleagues and contemporaries, and Sennett served as actor, writer, and assistant under Griffith in 1908 and 1909, then, beginning in 1910, as director of his own films under Griffith's supervision. Sennett became associated with comic roles and comic films from the beginning under Griffith. In his first major role for Griffith, *The Curtain Pole* in 1908, Sennett played a comically drunk Frenchman who visits chaos upon all he meets in a desperate race through town to replace a broken curtain rod. Already that film contains those traits that would become associated with the mature Sennett style: the breathless chase; the reduction of human beings to venal stereotypes; the reduction of human society and its physical surroundings to chaotic rubble; and playing games with the cinema mechanism itself, through accelerated motion (by undercranking) and reverse motion. In other roles for Griffith, Sennett consistently played the comic rube or dumb servant—roles that took advantage of Sennett's shambling bulk and oafish facial expressions.

According to legend, Sennett founded the Keystone Company when he conned his bookies, Adam Kessel and Charles Bauman, to go double or nothing on his gambling debts and stake him to a film company. Kessel and Bauman, however, had been out of the bookmaking business and in the movie-making business for at least five years as owners of Thomas Ince's flourishing New York Motion Picture Company. Between late 1912 and early 1914, Sennett assembled a troupe of the finest of raucous physical comedians and burlesque clowns in the film business. From Biograph he brought the pretty Mabel Normand, who was also an extremely agile and athletic physical comedienne, and the loony Ford Sterling, with his big-gesturing burlesque of villainy and lechery. Among the other physical comedians he found in those years were the burly Mack Swain, the tiny Chester Conklin, the round Fatty Arbuckle, and the cross-eyed Ben Turpin. He also found such future comic stars as Charles Chaplin, Harold Lloyd, and Harry Langdon, as well as the future director of sound comedies, Frank Capra. Perhaps more important than any artistic contribution was Sennett's managerial ability to spot comic talent and give it the opportunity to display itself.

At the root of Sennett's comic style was the brash, the vulgar, and the burlesque. His films parodied the serious film and stage hits of the day, always turning the serious romance or melodrama into outrageous nonsense. There were no serious moral, psychological, or social issues in Sennett films, simply raucous burlesque of social or emotional material. His short comedies were exuberantly impolite, often making public jokes out of ethnic, sexual, or racial stereotypes. Among the characters around whom he built film series were the German Meyer and Heinie, the Jewish Cohen, and the black Rastus. Many of these films were so brashly vulgar in their stereotypic humor that they cannot be shown in public today. As indicators of social attitudes of the 1910s, these films seem to suggest that the still largely immigrant American society of that time was more willing to make and respond to jokes openly based on ethnic and sexist stereotypes than they are today in an era of greater sensitivity to the potential harm of these stereotypes. In defense of Sennett's making sport of ethnic types, it must be said that the method and spirit was consistent with his films' refusal to take any social or psychological matters seriously.

Sennett's Keystone films were extremely improvisational; a typical formula was to take a camera, a bucket of whitewash, and four clowns (two male, two female) out to a park and make a movie. Sennett's aesthetic was not so much an art that conceals art but an art that derides art. His many Keystone films reveal the same contempt for orderly, careful, well-crafted art that one can see in the Marx Brothers' Paramount films or W.C. Fields's Universal films two decades later. The one conscious artistic tool which Sennett exploited was speed, speed, speed—keeping the actors, and the action, and the gags, and the machines, and the camera in perpetual speeding motion. The typical Keystone title might be something like *Love, Speed, and Thrills* or *Love, Loot, and Crash*. Among other Sennett inventions were the Keystone Kops, a burlesque of attempts at social order, and the Bathing Beauties, a burlesque of attempts at pornographic sexuality. Sennett served his apprenticeship in the American burlesque theater, and he brought to the Keystone films that same kind of entertainment which took place at the intersection of vulgar lunacy and comic pornography. His most memorable films include a series of domestic films starring Mabel Normand, married either to Fatty Arbuckle or Charlie Chaplin, a series of films pairing the beefy Mack Swain and the diminutive Chester Conklin, a series featuring Ben Turpin as a cross-eyed burlesque of romantic movie stars, a series built around remarkably athletic automobiles and rampaging jungle beasts starring Billy Bevan, and a series of short films featuring the pixieish childclown, Harry Langdon. Sennett also produced and personally directed the first comic feature film produced in America (or anywhere else), *Tillie's Punctured Romance*, starring Chaplin, Normand, and stage comedienne Marie Dressler in her first film role.

Sennett ceased to direct films after 1914, becoming the producer and overseer of every comic film made by his company for the next two decades. Although the Keystone company had folded by the late 1910s, Sennett's immensely long filmography is a testament to the sheer number of comic films he produced,

well into the sound era. Sennett's real importance to film history, however, derives from that crucial historical moment between 1912 and 1915, a period when a comic assumption, the evolution of film technique, and a collection of talented physical clowns all came together under Sennett's stewardship to create a unique, memorable and unduplicatable type of comedy that has assumed its place, not only in the history of cinema, but in the much longer history of comedy itself.

—Gerald Mast

SHAHINE, Youssef. *See* CHAHINE, Youssef.

SHINDO, Kaneto.

Japanese. Born in Hiroshima Prefecture, 28 April 1912. Married 1) 1939 (died 1940); 2) (divorced late 1940s); 3) actress Nobuko Otowa. Joined art section of Shinko-Kinema Tokyo Studio, 1928; moved to scenario department, 1939; moved to Koa Film, from 1942 (absorbed by Shochiku-Ofuna Studio, 1943); with director Kosaburo Yoshimura, left Shochiku to form independent production company Kindai Eiga Kyokai with producer Hisao Itoya, director Tengo Yamada, and actor Taiji Tonoyama, 1950; directed first film, 1951; became president of Japanese Association of Scenario Writers, 1972. Recipient: Grand Prix, Moscow Festival, for *Naked Island*, 1960; Asahi Prize, Japan, for activities in independent film production, 1975. Address: 4-8-6 Zushi, Zushi-City, Kanagawa, Japan.

Films as Director:

1951 *Aisai monogatari (Story of My Loving Wife)* (+ sc)
1952 *Nadare (Avalanche)* (+ sc); *Genbakuno-ko (Children of the Atomic Bomb)* (+ sc)
1953 *Shukuzu (Epitome)* (+ sc); *A Life of a Woman* (+ sc)
1954 *Dobu (Gutter)* (+ co-sc)
1955 *Ookami (Wolves)* (+ sc)
1956 *Gin-Shinju (Silver Double Suicide)* (+ sc); *Ruri no kishi (Bank of Departure* (+ sc); *Joyu (An Actress)* (+ sc)
1957 *Umi no yarodomo (Guys of the Sea)* (+ sc)
1958 *Kanashimi wa onna dakeni (Sorrow Is Only for Women)* (+ sc)
1959 *Dai go fukuryu-maru* (+ co-sc); *Hanayome san wa sekai-ichi (The World's Best Bride)* (+ sc); *Rakugaki kokuban (Graffiti Blackboard)* (+ sc)
1960 ***Hadaka no shima (Naked Island. The Island)*** (+ sc)
1962 *Ningen (Human Being)* (+ sc)
1963 *Haha (Mother)* (+ sc)
1964 *Onibaba* (+ sc)
1965 *Akuto (A Scoundrel)* (+ sc)
1966 *Honno (Instinct)* (+ sc); *Totsuseki iseki (Monument of Totsuseki)* (+ sc); *Tateshina no shiki (Four Seasons of Tateshina)* (+ sc)
1967 *Sei no kigen (Origin of Sex)* (+ sc)
1968 *Yabu no naka no kuroneko (A Black Cat in the Bush)* (+ sc); *Tsuyomushi onna (&) yawamushi otoko (Strong Woman and Weak Man)* (+ sc)
1969 *Kagero (Heat Haze)* (+ co-sc)

1970 *Shokkaku* (*Tentacles*) (+ sc); *Hadaka no jukyu-sai* (*Naked Nineteen-year-old*) (+ co-sc)
1972 *Kanawa* (*Iron Ring*) (+ sc); *Sanka* (*A Paean*) (+ sc)
1973 *Kokoro* (*Heart*) (+ sc)
1974 *Waga michi* (*My Way*) (+ sc)
1975 *Aru eiga-kantoku no shogai: Mizoguchi Kenji no kiroku* (*Life of a Film Director: Record of Kenji Mizoguchi*) (doc) (+ sc)
1977 *Chikuzan hitori-tabi* (*Life of Chikuzan*) (+ sc)
1982 *Hokusai manga* (*Hokusai, Ukiyoe Master*) (+ sc)
1984 *Chiheisen* (*The Horizon*)

Other Films:
(partial list: has written over 200 scripts)

1939 *Nanshin josei* (*South Advancing Women*) (Ochiai) (sc)
1946 *Machiboke no onna* (*Woman Who Is Waiting*) (Makino) (sc); *Josei no shori* (*The Victory of Women*) (Mizoguchi) (sc)
1947 *Anjo-ke no butokai* (*The Ball of the Anjo Family*) (Yoshimura) (sc)
1948 *Yuwaku* (*Seduction*) (Yoshimura) (sc); *Waga shogai no kagayakeru hi* (*My Life's Bright Day*) (Yoshimura) (sc)
1949 *Waga koi wa moenu* (*My Love Burns*) (Mizoguchi) (co-sc); *Shitto* (*Jealousy*) (Yoshimura) (sc); *Mori no Ishimatsu* (*Ishimatsu of Mori*) (Yoshimura) (sc); *Ojosan kanpai* (*Toast to a Young Miss*) (Kinoshita) (sc)
1951 *Itsuwareru seiso* (*Deceiving Costume*) (Yoshimura) (sc); *Genji monogatari* (*Tale of Genji*) (Yoshimura) (sc)
1955 *Bijo to kairyu* (*The Beauty and the Dragon*) (Yoshimura) (sc)
1958 *Hadaka no taiyo* (*Naked Sun*) (Ieki) (sc); *Yoru no tsuzumi* (*Night Drum*) (Imai) (co-sc)
1963 *Shitoyakana kemono* (*Soft Beast*) (Kawashima) (sc)
1964 *Kizudarake no sanga* (*Mountains and Rivers with Scars*) (Yamamoto) (sc)
1967 *Hanaoko Seishu no tsuma* (*Seishu Hanaoka's Wife*) (Masumura) (sc)
1972 *Gunki hatameku shitani* (*Under the Military Flag*) (Fukasaku) (sc)

Publications:

On SHINDO: books—

Mellen, Joan, *Voices from the Japanese Cinema*, New York, 1975.
Mellen, Joan, *The Waves at Genji's Door*, New York, 1976.
Anderson, Joseph, and Donald Richie, *The Japanese Film*, expanded edition, Princeton, 1982.

*   *   *

Shindo began his career in film as a scenario writer. An episode portraying his study of scenario writing, under the perfectionist director Kenji Mizoguchi, is included in his own first film as a director, *Story of My Loving Wife*. The rigorous influence of his mentor on Shindo's style is seen both in his scenarios and his direction. Such persistent influence, by one director on another, on mise-en-scène, and writing, is rarely found in the work of other filmmakers.

Shindo became a very successful scenario writer mainly for Kosaburo Yoshimura's films at Shochiku. However, after this team was subjected to commercial pressure from the studio, they left to produce their own films, establishing Kindai Eiga Kyokai, or the Society of Modern Film. Thus, they have been able to pursue their own interests and concerns in choosing subjects and styles.

Shindo, a Hiroshima native, frequently deals with the effects of the atomic bomb. He traced Hiroshima's aftermath in *Children of the Atomic Bomb* based on the compositions of Hiroshima children. This subject could be treated only after the American Occupation ended. *Mother* focuses on a surviving woman's decision to become a mother after much mental and physical trauma. *Instinct* deals with a middle-aged survivor whose sexual potency is revived by the love of a woman. *Dai go*

fukuryu-maru is about the tragedy of the fishermen heavily exposed to nuclear fallout after American testing in the South Pacific. Shindo condemns nuclear weapons for causing such misery to innocent people, but also strongly affirms the survivor's will to live.

Shindo's best-known film internationally, *Naked Island*, is experimental in not using any dialogue but only music. It also uses local people except for a professional actor and actress who play a couple living on a small island. We are impressed with the hardship of their farming life as well as with the beauty of their natural surroundings throughout the cycle of the seasons. The joy, sorrow, anger, and desperation of the hardworking couple is silently but powerfully expressed in a semi-documentary manner.

The peaceful atmosphere of this film is in contrast to many of Shindo's more obsessive works, such as *Epitome, Gutter, Sorrow Is Only for Women, Onibaba,* and *A Scoundrel*. These convey a claustrophobic intensity by using only a few small settings for the action, with much close-up camera work.

In 1975, Shindo expressed his life-long homage to his mentor, Mizoguchi, in a unique documentary: *The Life of A Film Director: Record of Kenji Mizoguchi*. In this film, he brought together many interesting and honest accounts of Mizoguchi by interviewing people who had worked for this master. These personal recollections, along with sequences from Mizoguchi's films, are a testimony to the greatness of Mizoguchi's art, and to his intriguing personality.

Like Mizoguchi, Shindo creates many strong female figures who, by virtue of their love and the power of their will, try to "save" their male counterparts. While Mizoguchi's women seem to rely more on their generous compassion to sustain their men, Shindo's women tend to inspire and motivate their men by their own energy and power. In much the same way, Shindo's own energy and perseverance have supported his artistic vision through four decades of independent filmmaking.

—Kyoko Hirano

———

SHINODA, Masahiro.

Japanese. Born in Gifu Prefecture, 9 March 1931. Studied drama and literature at Waseda University, Tokyo, graduated 1952. Married actress Shima Iwashita. Assistant director at Shochiku-Ofuna Studios, from 1953; began as director of "youth" films, 1960; left Shochiku, 1965; directed first film for independent production company Hyogen-sha [Expression Company], *Clouds at Sunset*, 1967. Address: 1-11-13, Kitasenzoku, Ota-Ku, Tokyo, Japan.

Films as Director:

1960 *Koi no katamichi kippu* (*One Way Ticket to Love*) (+ sc); *Kawaita mizuumi* (*Dry Lake. Youth in Fury*)
1961 *Yuhi ni akai ore no kao* (*My Face Red in the Sunset. Killers on Parade*); *Waga koi no tabiji* (*Epitaph to My Love*) (+ co-sc); *Shamisen to otobai* (*Love Old and New*)
1962 *Watakushi-tachi no kekkon* (*Our Marriage*) (+ co-sc); *Yama no sanka: moyuru wakamono-tachi* (*Glory on the Summit: Burning Youth*); *Namida o shishi no tategami ni* (*Tears on the Lion's Mane*) (+ co-sc)
1963 *Kawaita hana* (*Pale Flower*) (+ co-sc)
1964 *Ansatsu* (*Assassination*)

Masahiro Shinoda

1965   *Utsukushisa to kanashimi to* (*With Beauty and Sorrow*); *Ibun sarutobi sasuke* (*Samurai Spy. Sarutobi*)
1966   *Shokei no shima* (*Punishment Island. Captive's Island*)
1967   *Akanegumo* (*Clouds at Sunset*)
1969   *Shinju ten no Amijima* (*Double Suicide*)
1970   *Buraikan* (*The Scandalous Adventures of Buraikan*)
1971   *Chinmoku* (*Silence*)
1972   *Sapporo Orimpikku* (*Sapporo Winter Olympic Games*)
1973   *Kaseki no mori* (*The Petrified Forest*)
1974   *Himiko*
1975   *Sakura no mori no mankai no shita* (*Under the Cherry Blossoms*) (+ co-sc)
1976   *Nihon-maru* (*Nihon-maru Ship*) (documentary); *Sadono kuni ondeko-za* (*Sado's Ondeko-za*) (documentary)
1977   *Hanare goze Orin* (*The Ballad of Orin*) (+ co-sc)
1979   *Yashagaike* (*Demon Pond*)
1980   *Aku Ryoto* (*Devil's Island*)
1984   *Setouchi Shonen Yakyudan* (*MacArthur's Children*)
1986   *Yari no Gonza* (*Gonza, the Spearman*)
1989   *Maihime* (*Die Tänzerin. The Dancer*)
1990   *Shonnenjidai* (*Takeshi*)

Publications:

By SHINODA: articles—

Shinoda interview in *American Film* (New York), May 1985.
"*MacArthur's Children*," an interview with R. Silberman and K. Hirano in *Cineaste* (New York), vol. 14, no. 3, 1986.

On SHINODA: books—

Sekai no eiga sakka 10: Shinoda Masahiro, Yoshida Yoshishige [Film Directors of the World 10: Masahiro Shinoda and Yoshishige Yoshida], Tokyo, 1971.
Richie, Donald, *Japanese Cinema: Film Style and National Character*, New York, 1971.
Mellen, Joan, *Voices from the Japanese Cinema*, New York, 1975.

Mellen, Joan, *The Waves at Genji's Door*, New York, 1976.
Bock, Audie, *Japanese Film Directors*, Tokyo, 1978; revised edition, Tokyo, 1985.

*   *   *

After his debut with *One Way Ticket to Love* in 1960, Shinoda (along with Oshima and Yoshida) was termed a "Japanese Nouvelle Vague" director. However, Shinoda's devotion to sensual modernism contrasted with Oshima's direct expression of his political concerns. Shinoda's early films center on the fickle and frivolous entertainment world, petty gangsters, or confused student terrorists, ornamented by pop-art settings and a sensibility which may be largely attributed to his scenario writer, poet Shuji Terayama.

Being an intellectual and ideologue, Shinoda analyzes the fates of his marginal but likable characters with a critical eye on the social and political milieu. Even his work on Shochiku Studio home drama and melodrama projects show his critical views of the social structure.

His indulgent aestheticism, which appears in his films as incomparable sensuality, has been connected with images of death and destruction (*Assassination, With Beauty and Sorrow, Clouds at Sunset, Double Suicide, The Ballad of Orin*) and of degradation (*Silence, The Petrified Forest, Under the Cherry Blossoms*). This stance again contrasts with that of Oshima, whose sexual and political outlook ultimately affirms the value of life and survival. Shinoda's fundamental pessimism, represented by the image of falling cherry blossoms in his films, is rooted in the ephemerality of life.

The stylistic aspect of Shinoda's work originated in his long interest in the Japanese traditional theater. *Double Suicide* received the highest acclaim for his bold art direction (elaborate calligraphy on the set was done by his cousin, Toko Shinoda), ambitious experimentation as in his use of men dressed in black (recalling traditional Japanese puppeteers) appearing to lead the characters to their destinies, and the double roles of the contrasting and competing heroines, the prostitute and the wife. This black-and-white film presents a most imaginative adaptation of Bunraku, the Japanese puppet play. *The Scandalous Adventures of Buraikan* is an elaborate and colorful adaptation of Kabuki drama, playful in spirit. *Himiko* recalls the origin of Japanese theater in the primordial Japanese tribe's rituals, making use of avant-garde dancers. The two leading female roles in *Demon Pond* are played by the popular young Kabuki actor, Tamasaburo Bando.

Another unique aspect of Shinoda's work is his interest in sports. As an ex-athlete, he was well qualified for the assignment of making the official documentary, *Sapporo Winter Olympic Games*, and a documentary on runners, *Sado's Ondeko-za*. In these films, he succeeds in conveying in a beautiful visual manner the emotions of athletes in lonely competition.

Shinoda has also played an important role as the head of an independent film production firm, Hyogen-sha or Expressive Company, since he left Shochiku in 1965. Thus he has pursued his own concerns in choices of subjects and methods of expression, mostly through the adaption of traditional and modern Japanese literary works. He has developed many talented collaborators—actress Shima Iwashita (to whom he is married), music composer Toru Takemitsu, art directors Jusho Toda and Kiyoshi Awazu, and poet Taeko Tomioka, working as his scenario writer.

—Kyoko Hirano

Esther Shub: *The Fall of the Romanov Dynasty*

SHUB, Esther.

Soviet Ukrainian. Born Esfir Ilyianichna Shub in Chernigovsky district, Ukraine, 3 March 1894. Studied literature, Moscow; Institute for Women's Higher Education, Moscow. Administrator with Theatre Dept. of Narkompros (People's Commissariat of Education), collaborated on stage work with Meyerhold and Mayakovsky; joined film company Goskino, re-editing imported films for Soviet distribution and producing compilation and documentary films, 1922; directed first "compilation film," *The Fall of the Romanov Dynasty*, 1927; taught montage for Eisenstein class at VGIK (film school), 1933–35; left Goskino to become chief editor of *Novosti Dnya* (*The News of the Day*) for Central Studio for Documentary Film, Moscow, 1942. Recipient: Honored Artist of the Republic, 1935. *Died in Moscow, 21 September 1959.*

Films as Director:

1927 *Padenye dinastii romanovykh* (*The Fall of the Romanov Dynasty*) (+ sc, ed); *Veliky put'* (*The Great Road*) (+ sc, ed)
1928 *Rossiya Nikolaya II i Lev Tolstoi* (*The Russia of Nicholas II and Lev Tolstoy*) (+ sc, ed)
1930 *Segodnya* (*Today*) (+ sc, ed)
1932 *K-SH-E* (*Komsomol—Leader of Electrification. Komsomol—The Guide to Electrification*) (+ sc, ed)

1934 *Moskva stroit metro* (*Moscow Builds the Subway. The Metro By Night*) (+ sc, ed)
1937 *Strana Sovietov* (*Land of the Soviets*) (+ sc, ed)
1939 *Ispaniya* (*Spain*) (+ sc, ed)
1940 *Kino za XX liet* (*20 let sovetskogo kino. Twenty Years of Cinema*) (co-d, co-ed, sc)
1941 *Fashizm budet razbit* (*Fascism Will Be Destroyed. The Face of the Enemy*) (+ sc, ed)
1942 *Strana rodnaya* (*The Native Country*) (+ sc, ed)
1946 *Po tu storonu Araksa* (*Across the Araks*) (+ sc, ed); *Sud v Smolenske* (*The Trial in Smolensk*) (+ sc, ed)

Other Films:

1922–25 Edited 200 foreign fiction films and 10 Soviet films, final one being (*The Skotinins*) (Roshal)
1926 *Krylya kholopa* (*Wings of a Serf*) (ed)

Publications:

By SHUB: books—

Krupnyn planom [In the Close-Up], Moscow, 1959.
Zhizn moya—kinematogra [My Life—Cinema], Moscow, 1972.

By SHUB: articles—

"Road from the Past," in *Sovietskoye Kino* (Moscow), November/December 1934.
"Kuleshov, Eisenstein, and the Others: Part 1: On Kuleshov," interview with S.P. Hill, in *Film Journal* (New York), Fall/Winter 1972.

On SHUB: books—

Leyda, Jay, *Kino: A History of the Russian and Soviet Film*, New York, 1973.
Waugh, Thomas, editor, *"Show Us Life": Toward a History and Aesthetics of the Committed Documentary*, Metuchen, New Jersey, 1984.
Taylor, Richard, and Ian Christie, editors, *The Film Factory: Russian and Soviet Cinema in Documents 1896–1939*, London, 1988.

On SHUB: articles—

Halter, R., "Esther Schub—ihre Bedeutung für die Entwicklung des Dokumentarfilms," in *Frauen und Film* (Berlin), October 1976.
Petric, Vlada, "Esther Shub: Cinema Is My Life," in *Quarterly Review of Film Studies* (Pleasantville, New York), Fall 1978.

* * *

In Russia, as directors traditionally do their own editing, famous film editors are rare. A great exception to this rule was Esther Shub. After gaining her reputation and experience in the early 1920s, re-editing foreign productions and then working on a dozen Soviet features, she became, largely on her own initiative, a pioneer of the "compilation film," producing work that has seldom since been equalled. She brought to this genre far more than her speed, industry and flair: she brought a positive genius for using all sorts of ill-considered oddments of old footage as a painter uses his palette and as if it had all been especially shot for her. For her first two brilliant compilations, *The Fall of the Romanov Dynasty*, and *The Great Road*, about the first decade of the revolution (both released in 1927), she scavenged everywhere, with indefatigable determination, old newsreels, amateur footage shot by the imperial family and their friends, official footage from a pair of official imperial cinematographers, cellars, vaults and closets of wartime cameramen, even managing to purchase valuable material from the United States. All of this was against the original reluctance of her studios to go ahead with these projects, and they refused to recognize her rights as author when she had finished the films.

Originally planning, as her third work, a film biography of Tolstoy, even Shub failed to dig out more than a few hundred feet of material. Undaunted she wove this with great effect into other early fragments and came out with *The Russia of Nicholas II and Lev Tolstoy*.

With the advent of sound Shub made an abrupt change in her methods. For *K-SH-E* (*Komsomol—Leader of Electrification*) she created her own version of the Communist Hero—young, passionate and dedicated, complete with high-necked Russian blouse and leather jerkin. She forsook her cutting table to become a sort of investigative journalist, deliberately turning her back on archive material, sweeping generalizations and bravura montage, forging instead a new, original style of ultra-realism, pre-dating by 30 years many of the practices and theories of cinema verité. 40 years later a Soviet film historian was to chide her for "indulging herself with a contemporary enthusiasm for the future of sound film and with the peculiar cult for film-apparatus." This was because she opened the film in a sound studio full of every kind of cinematic machinery with what she termed a "parade of film techniques," and occasionally cut back to this theme throughout the production. She purposely included shots in which people looked into the lens, screwed up their eyes at the arc-lamps, stumbled and stuttered in front of cameras and microphones visible in the scenes, and, in general, tried to augment reality by reminding the audience that the crew and camera were actually *there* instead of pretending that they were part of some all-seeing, omnipotent but unobtrusive eye.

Another important Shub film was *Spain*, a history of the Spanish Civil War, once more an "editor's film," which she put together from newsreels and the frontline camerawork of Roman Karmen and Boris Makaseyev, with a commentary by Vsevolod Vishnevski, who also collaborated on the script. In the following year Pudovkin collaborated on her compilation *Twenty Years of Cinema*, a history of the Soviet industry. She continued her documentary work through the war years and into the late 1940s.

Although as a woman and an editor she perhaps suffered some bureaucratic indifference and obstruction ("they only join pieces of film together"), Shub was an influential filmmaker who deserves at least a niche in the Soviet Film pantheon alongside such other originals (in both senses) as Pudovkin and Eisenstein, who certainly appreciated her work.

—Robert Dunbar

———

SIEGEL, Don.

American. Born in Chicago, 26 October 1912. Educated at Jesus College, Cambridge University, England; Royal Academy of Dramatic Art, London. Married 1) actress Viveca Lindfors, 1948 (divorced 1953), one son; 2) Doe Avedon, 1957, four children; 3) Carol Rydall. Actor with the Contemporary Theater, Los Angeles, 1930; joined Warner Bros. as film librarian, 1934, later assistant editor, then joined insert department; set up montage department at Warners, 1939; 2nd unit director for Michael Curtiz, Raoul Walsh and others, 1940–45; directed first film, *Star in the Night*, 1945, and first feature, *The Verdict*, 1946; worked for Howard Hughes at RKO, 1948–51; producer and director for TV, from 1961; executive producer for *Trial and Error*, for TV, 1988. Recipient: Oscars for Best Short Subject, for *Star in the Night*, and for Best Documentary, for *Hitler Lives?*, 1946. Address: c/o Flekmann, Carswell, Cohen & Company, 9171 Wilshire Boulevard, Suite 530, Beverly Hills, CA 90210, U.S.A.

Films as Director:

1945	*Star in the Night*; *Hitler Lives?*
1946	*The Verdict*
1949	*Night Unto Night*; *The Big Steal*
1952	*No Time For Flowers*; *Duel at Silver Creek*
1953	*Count the Hours* (*Every Minute Counts*); *China Venture*
1954	*Riot in Cell Block 11*; *Private Hell 36*
1955	*An Annapolis Story* (*The Blue and the Gold*)
1956	**Invasion of the Body Snatchers**; *Crime in the Streets*
1957	*Spanish Affair*; *Baby Face Nelson*
1958	*The Gun Runners*; *The Line-Up*
1959	*Edge of Eternity* (+ co-pr, role as man at the pool); *Hound Dog Man*
1960	*Flaming Star*
1962	*Hell is for Heroes*
1964	*The Killers* (+ pr, role as short-order cook in diner); *The Hanged Man*
1967	*Stranger on the Run*
1968	*Madigan*
1969	*Coogan's Bluff* (+ pr, role as man in elevator); *Death of a Gunfighter* (uncredited co-d)
1970	*Two Mules for Sister Sara*
1971	*The Beguiled* (+ pr); **Dirty Harry** (+ pr)
1973	*Charley Varrick* (+ pr, role as Murph)
1974	*The Black Windmill* (+ pr)
1976	*The Shootist*
1977	*Telefon*

Don Siegel

1979 *Escape from Alcatraz* (+ pr, role as doctor)
1980 *Rough Cut*
1982 *Jinxed!*

Other Films:

1940 *City for Conquest* (Litvak) (montage d)
1941 *Blues in the Night* (Litvak) (montage d)
1942 ***Casablanca*** (Curtiz) (art d)
1943 *Edge of Darkness* (Milestone) (set d); *Mission to Moscow* (Curtiz) (art d); *Northern Pursuit* (Walsh) (special effects d)
1944 *The Adventures of Mark Twain* (Rapper) (ph)
1971 ***Play Misty For Me*** (Eastwood) (role as Marty the bartender)
1978 *Invasion of the Body Snatchers* (Kaufman) (cab driver)
1985 *Into the Night* (Landis) (role as embarrassed man)

Publications:

By SIEGEL: articles—

Interview with Peter Bogdanovich, in *Movie* (London), Spring 1968.

"The Anti-Heroes," in *Films and Filming* (London), January 1969.
"Conversation with Donald Siegel," with Leonard Maltin, in *Action* (Los Angeles), July/August 1971.
Interview with Sam Fuller, in *Interview* (New York), May 1972.
Interview with Stuart Kaminsky, in *Take One* (Montreal), June 1972.
"Stimulation," interview with Gordon Gow, in *Films and Filming* (London), November 1973.
"The Man Who Paid His Dues," interview with B. Drew, in *American Film* (Washington, D.C.), December/January 1977/78.

On SIEGEL: books—

McArthur, Colin, *Underworld, U.S.A.*, London, 1972.
Kaminsky, Stuart M., *Don Siegel: Director*, New York, 1974.
Kaminsky, Stuart M., *American Film Genres*, Dayton, Ohio, 1974; revised edition, Chicago, 1983.
Belton, John, *Cinema Stylists*, Metuchen, New Jersey, 1983.
Vaccino, Roberto, *Donald Siegel*, Florence, 1985.

On SIEGEL: articles—

Austen, David, "Out for the Kill," in *Films and Filming* (London), May 1968.

Mundy, Robert, "Don Siegel: Time and Motion, Attitudes and Genre," in *Cinema* (London), February 1970.

Kael, Pauline, "Saint Cop," in the *New Yorker*, 15 January 1972.

Gregory, Charles T., "The Pod Society Vs. the Rugged Individualist," in *Journal of Popular Film* (Bowling Green, Ohio), Winter 1972.

Pirie, D., "Siegel's Bluff," in *Sight and Sound* (London), Autumn 1973.

Kass, Judith M., "Don Siegel," in *The Hollywood Professionals*, Vol.4, London, 1975.

Allombert, Guy, "Donald Siegel: cinéaste de la violence et du anti-héros," in *Image et Son* (Paris), May 1976.

Chase, A., "The Strange Romance of 'Dirty Harry' Callahan and Ann Mary Deacon," in *Velvet Light Trap* (Madison), Winter 1977.

Combs, R., "Less Is More: Don Siegel from the Block to the Rock," in *Sight and Sound* (London), Spring 1980.

Combs, Richard, "Count the Hours: the Real Don Siegel," in *Monthly Film Bulletin* (London), February 1984.

*   *   *

Siegel's virtues—tightly constructed narratives and explosive action sequences—have been apparent from the very beginning. Even his B pictures have an enviable ability to pin audiences to their seats through the sheer force and pace of the events they portray. Unlike some action movie specialists, however, Siegel rarely allows the action to overcome the characterization. The continuing fascination of *Riot in Cell Block 11*, for instance, stems as much from its central character's tensions as from the violent and eventful story. Dunn is a paradigmatic Siegel protagonist, caught between a violent inclination and the strategic need for restraint. Such incipient personal instability animates many Siegel films, finding material expression in the hunts and confrontations which structure their narratives. His people react to an unpleasant world with actions rather than words, often destroying themselves in the process. They rarely survive with dignity.

Siegel's singular distinction, however, lies in his refusal to strike conventional moral postures in relation to this depressing and often sordid material. Though one cannot fail to be involved in and excited by his action-packed stories, there is always a clear sense that he remains outside of them as something of a detached observer. In the 1950s that seeming "objectivity" gave him a minor critical reputation as a socially conscious and "liberal" director, though this was a liberalism by implication rather than a direct and paraded commitment. In retrospect the 1950s movies seem best described as individualistic, antagonistic to unthinking social conformity, rather than liberally sentimental after the fashion of "socially concerned" Hollywood movies of the period. These films are generalized warnings, not exercises in breast-beating. Their spirit is that of Kevin McCarthy's cry to his unheeding fellows in Siegel's original ending to *Invasion of the Body Snatchers* (United Artists added an epilogue): "You're next!"

In the 1960s and 1970s Siegel's reputation and his budgets grew. He struck out in new directions with such films as *Two Mules for Sister Sara* and *The Beguiled*, though his major concerns remained with action and with his emotionally crippled "heroes." The three cop movies (*Madigan, Coogan's Bluff*, and *Dirty Harry*) are representative, the latter especially encouraging the critical charge that Siegel had become a law-and-order ideologue. Its "wall-to-wall carpet of violence" (Siegel's description) easily lent itself to a "tough cop against the world" reading. Yet, just as his earlier films cannot be reduced to simple liberal formulae, so the later movies are far more complex than much criticism has suggested. A colleague remarks of Madigan: "For him everything's either right or wrong—there's nothing in between." In exploring his characters' doomed attempts to live by such absolutes Siegel refuses to make their mistake. And though he does not presume to judge them, that does not mean that he approves of their ac-

tions. As the less frenetic films like *The Shootist* and *Escape from Alcatraz* make clear, his appreciation of character and morality is far more subtle than that.

More than any other action director of his generation Siegel has avoided the genre's potential for reductive simplification. He has combined entertainment with perception, skilled filmmaking economy with nicely delineated characters, and overall moral detachment with sympathy for his hard-pressed protagonists. His movie world may often seem uncongenial, but its creator has never appeared callous or unconcerned. His films have achieved much deserved commercial success; his skill and subtlety have deserved rather more in the way of critical attention.

—Andrew Tudor

———————

SILVER, Joan Micklin.

American. Born Omaha, Nebraska, 1935. Studied at Sarah Lawrence College, New York, B.A., 1956. Married Raphael D. Silver, three daughters. Freelance writer for an educational film company, New York, from 1967; directed first feature, *Hester Street*, 1974; directed *Chilly Scenes of Winter* for United Artists, 1979, studio changed the title and the ending, but released in its original form in 1982; director for stage and TV, 1980s. Address: c/o Midwest Films, 600 Madison Avenue, New York, NY 10022, U.S.A.

Films as Director:

1972	*Immigrant Experience: The Long Long Journey* (short)
1974	*Hester Street* (+ sc)
1977	*Between the Lines*
1979	*Chilly Scenes of Winter* (*Head Over Heels*) (+ sc)
1985	*Finnegan, Begin Again* (for TV)
1988	*Crossing Delancey*
1990	*Loverboy*

Publications:

By SILVER: articles—

Interview in *Image et Son* (Paris), November 1975.

"Dialogue on Film: Joan Micklin Silver," in *American Film* (Los Angeles), May 1989.

Interview with Graham Fuller in the *Independent* (London), 7 April 1989.

On SILVER: books—

Cohen, Sarah Blacher, *From Hester Street to Hollywood: The Jewish-American Stage and Screen*, Bloomington, Indiana, 1983.

Squire, Jason, E., *The Movie Business Book*, Englewood Cliffs, New Jersey, 1983.

Wood, Robin, *Hollywood from Vietnam to Reagan*, New York, 1986.

*   *   *

Undoubtedly, the impact of the feminist movement during the 1960s and early 1970s was instrumental in making it possible for women to establish themselves as directors by the latter half of the 1970s and Joan Micklin Silver was one of the first to do so. Silver's films aren't explicitly feminist in content but she consistently displays an awareness of and sensitivity to women's identities and concerns.

As in her initial effort, *Hester Street*, Silver's films have tended to be intimate character studies centred on a hetero-

Joan Micklin Silver

sexual relationship (or, as in *Between the Lines*, a set of relationships) that is in a transitional process. In several of the
films, Silver, while not minimizing her significance, decentres
the film's female protagonist: in *Finnegan Begin Again* the
Robert Preston character dominates the narrative, but the two
most striking examples are the films featuring John Heard, *Between the Lines* and *Chilly Scenes of Winter*. In both films,
Heard plays a character with similar characteristics: a tendency
to be possessive about the woman he professes to love and a
casting of the relationship in the terms of romantic love. In
Chilly Scenes of Winter, Heard imbues the film with his consciousness. His fantasy regarding a meeting with the Mary
Beth Hurt character is visualized and he frequently directly addresses the viewer, providing access to his mental and/or emotional responses to a specific situation. By the film's
conclusion, Heard has relinquished his romantic passion but
not without undergoing a considerable psychic and emotional
strain. While Hurt rejects Heard and his overwhelming
demands, she appears, on the other hand, to have no clearly
formed idea of what she either wants or needs from a love relationship. Interestingly, the film doesn't imply that Hurt's
uncertainty is a negative condition—she is just beginning to
discover that she can explore the range of sexual and/or romantic involvements available to a contemporary woman.

In *Chilly Scenes of Winter*, the most complex and disturbing
of her films, Silver indicates that from Hurt's point of view
romantic love is oppressive and destructive; in *Crossing Delancey*, Silver employs a woman, the Amy Irving character, to investigate what could be called a romantic "perception" about
possible relationships. Irving rejects the Peter Riegert character before she gets to know him on the grounds that the conditions of their meeting and his profession preclude the
possibility of a romance between them. To an extent, Irving's
rejection is motivated by her desire to distance herself from her
Jewish ghetto origins. Most often, in Silver's films, a character's attitude to his or her origins, profession, etc., is shown to
be a contributing factor in the shaping of the romantic fantasy.

In the Heard films, the character is frustrated by (*Between the
Lines*) or indifferent to (*Chilly Scenes of Winter*) his professional life. In *Crossing Delancey*, it isn't until Irving can distinguish between her notion of the romantic and Riegert as he
actually is that a romance between the two can develop.

With *Lover Boy*, Silver addresses another aspect of the
thematic: a young man, played by Patrick Dempsey, learns
gradually through his experiences as the paid lover of a number
of frustrated married women that sexual desire, pleasure and
fulfilment are enriched by having a romantic attitude towards
intimate relationships (in courting women, Dempsey's musical
tastes move from heavy metal to Fred Astaire). In her films,
there is a continual probing of what the romantic means—the
various dimensions of the concept and its possible significance
to both of the sexes. As a concept, the romantic isn't gender
specific and, potentially, it can be either negative or positive in
application.

In *Hollywood From Vietnam to Reagan*, Robin Wood
argues that *Chilly Scenes of Winter*, to be fully appreciated,
needs to be read in relation to the generic expectations it in
part fulfils but also undermines. Wood's contention that the
film belongs to the classical Hollywood tradition of the light
comedy is well-taken; essentially, the same can be said of both
Crossing Delancey, which is a reworking of the classical
romantic comedy, and *Lover Boy* which has its antecedents in
the 1930s screwball comedy. (Similarly, Silver's graceful but
unobtrusive mise-en-scène is a reflection of the classical filmmaking tradition.) In making this claim, it is important to indicate that the films aren't evoking these classical genres for
nostalgic purposes; instead, the films, while utilizing the structural strengths and comic potentials of the generic formulas,
are offering a contemporary vision of the tensions under-
pinning heterosexual relations and predominantly respond to
these tensions in a progressive manner. From this perspective,
Silver's films can be compared to Woody Allen's light romantic
comedies. (*Annie Hall, Manhattan, Broadway Danny Rose*)
though of the two directors, Silver is much less sentimental and
precious about her characters, and particularly so in regard to
the films' male protagonists.

In the last fifteen years, Silver has produced a small but personal and distinguished body of work. She remains an underrated filmmaker; in part, this may be due to the fact that her
films aren't big budget projects or star vehicles. (Consistently,
her films are conceived as ensemble pieces and contain beautifully judged performances.) It may also be due to the fact that
the tone of Silver's films tends to be decidedly off-beat: although the films are clearly "serious" about the complexities of
heterosexual relations, Silver infuses the films with a slightly
absurdist humour. On the one hand, this may produce a distancing effect that alienates the viewer but, on the other, it
allows the viewer to take a more contemplative attitude
towards her depiction of the often aching pleasures involved in
love relationships.

—Richard Lippe

SIODMAK, Robert.

American/German. Born in Memphis, Tennessee, 8 August
1900. Educated at University of Marburg, Germany. Actor
with German repertory companies, 1920–21; bank worker,
1921–23; titler for imported American films, 1925; editor for
Herbert Nossen and Seymour Nebenzal, 1926–28; hired by

Robert Siodmak

Erich Pommer to scout for writers for UFA, 1928; directed first feature, 1930; following attack by Goebbels on film *Brennende Geheimnis*, moved, with brother Curt, to Paris, 1933; moved to Hollywood, 1940, signed 2-year contract with Paramount, then moved to Universal under 7-year contract; after filming *The Crimson Pirate* in England and Spain, remained in Europe, from 1952; began working for Arthur Brauner's CCC Company, 1934. *Died in 1973.*

Films as Director:

1929   *Menschen am Sonntag* (*People on Sunday*) (doc) (co-d)
1930   *Abschied* (*So sind die Menschen*)
1931   *Der Mann der seinen Mörder sucht* (*Looking for His Murderer*); *Voruntersuchung* (*Inquest*)
1932   *Stürme der Leidenschaft* (*The Tempest. Storm of Passion*); *Quick* (*Quick—König der Clowns*)
1933   *Brennendes Geheimnis* (*The Burning Secret*) (+ pr); *Le Sexe faible*
1934   *La Crise est finie* (*The Slump Is Over*)
1936   *La Vie parisienne*; *Mister Flow* (*Compliments of Mr. Flow*)
1937   *Cargaison blanche* (*Le Chemin de Rio. French White Cargo, Traffic in Souls. Woman Racket*)
1938   *Mollenard* (*Hatred*); *Ultimatum* (co-d; completed for Robert Wiene)
1939   *Pièges* (*Personal Column*)
1941   *West Point Widow*
1942   *Fly by Night*; *The Night Before the Divorce*; *My Heart Belongs to Daddy*
1943   *Someone to Remember*; *Son of Dracula*
1944   *Phantom Lady*; *Cobra Woman*; *Christmas Holiday*
1945   *The Suspect*; *Uncle Harry* (*The Strange Affair of Uncle Harry. The Zero Murder Case*); *The Spiral Staircase*
1946   **The Killers**; *The Dark Mirror*
1947   *Time Out of Mind* (+ pr)
1948   *Cry of the City*
1949   *Criss Cross*; *The Great Sinner*
1950   *Thelma Jordan*; *Deported*
1951   *The Whistle at Eaton Falls*
1952   *The Crimson Pirate*
1954   *Le Grand Jeu* (*Flesh and Woman*)
1955   *Die Ratten*
1956   *Mein Vater der Schauspieler*
1957   *Nachts wann der Teufel kam* (*The Devil Strikes at Night*)
1959   *Dorothea Angermann*; *The Rough and the Smooth* (*Portrait of a Sinner*)
1960   *Katya* (*Un Jeune Fille un seul amour. Magnificent Sinner*); *Mein Schulefreund*
1962   *L'Affaire Nina B* (*The Nina B Affair*); *Tunnel 28* (*Escape from East Berlin*)
1964   *Der Schut*
1965   *Der Schatz der Azteken*; *Die Pyramide des Sonnengottes*
1968   *Custer of the West* (*A Good Day for Fighting*)
1968/69   *Der Kampf um Rom* (in 2 parts)

Other Films:

1936   *Le Grand Refrain* (*Symphonie d'amour*) (Mirande) (supervisor)
1945   *Conflict* (Bernhardt) (co-story)

Publications:

By SIODMAK: articles—

"Hoodlums: The Myth and the Reality," with Richard Wilson, in *Films and Filming* (London), June 1959.

On SIODMAK: books—

McArthur, Colin, *Underworld U.S.A.*. London, 1972.
Dumont, Hervé, *Robert Siodmak: Le maître du Film Noir*, Lausanne, 1981.

On SIODMAK: articles—

Marshman, D., "Mister Siodmak," in *Life* (New York), August 1947.
Taylor, John, "Encounter with Siodmak," in *Sight and Sound* (London), Summer/Autumn 1959.
Nolan, Jack, "Robert Siodmak," in *Films in Review* (New York), April 1969.
Flinn, Tom, "Three Faces of Film Noir," in *Velvet Light Trap* (Madison, Wisconsin), Summer 1972.
Beylie, Claude, "Robert Siodmak l'éclectique," in *Ecran* (Paris), May 1973.
"Robert Siodmak," in *Monthly Film Bulletin* (London), June 1978.
Masson, André "Des genres creux, du clinquant, du simili," in *Positif* (Paris), September 1982.
Telotte, J.P., "Siodmak's Phantom Women and Noir Narrative," in *Film Criticism* (Meadville, Pennsylvania), Spring 1987.

*   *   *

Robert Siodmak is an example of the UFA-influenced German directors who moved to Hollywood when war threatened Europe. Less well known than his compatriots Billy Wilder and Fritz Lang, Siodmak demonstrated his cinematic skills early in his career with his innovative movie *Menschen am Sonntag*, which featured a non-professional cast, hand-held camera shots, stop motion photography, and the sort of flashbacks that later became associated with his work in America.

Siodmak carried with him to Hollywood the traditions and skills of his German film heritage, and became a major influence in American *film noir* of the 1940s. Deep shadows, claustrophobic compositions, elegant camera movements, and meticulously created settings on a grand scale mark the UFA origins of his work. Such themes as the treachery of love and the prevalence of the murderous impulse in ordinary people recur in his American films. The use of the flashback is a dominant narrative device, reflecting his fatalistic approach to story and character. *The Killers* (1946 version) presents a narrative that includes multiple flashbacks, each one of which is a part of the total story and all of which must be accumulated to understand the opening sequence of the film. This opening, based directly on Ernest Hemingway's famous short story, is a masterful example of film story-telling.

A typical Siodmak film of his *noir* period is *Phantom Lady*, a mini-masterpiece of mood and character, creating intense paranoia through lighting and setting. Two key sequences demonstrate Siodmak's method. In the first, the heroine follows a man into the subway, a simple action that sets off feelings of danger and tension in viewers, feelings that grow entirely out of sound, light, cutting, and camera movement. In the second, one of the most famous sequences in *film noir*, Siodmak uses jazz music and cutting to build up a narrative meaning that is implicitly sexual as the leading lady urges a drummer to a faster and faster beat.

Siodmak's work is frequently discussed in comparison with that of Alfred Hitchcock, partly because they shared a producer, Joan Harrison, for a period of time. Harrison produced two Siodmak films for Universal, *The Suspect* and *Uncle Harry*. In both films a seemingly ordinary and/or innocent man is drawn into a tangled web of murder, while retaining the audience's sympathy. *Criss Cross*, arguably Siodmak's best *noir*, ably demonstrates his ability to create depth of characterization through music, mood, and action, particularly in a scene in which Burt Lancaster watches his ex-wife, Yvonne DeCarlo, dance with another man. His fatal obsession with his wife and the victim/victimizer nature of their relationship is capably demonstrated through purely visual means.

In later years, Siodmak turned to such action films as *The Crimson Pirate* and *Custer of the West*, the former a celebrated romp, and one of the first truly tongue-in-cheek anti-genre films of its period. Although Siodmak's films were successful both critically and commercially in their day, he has never achieved the recognition which the visual quality of his work should have earned. An innovative and cinematic director, he explored the criminal or psychotic impulses in his characters through the ambience of his elegant mise-en-scène. The control of all cinematic tools at his command—camera angle, lighting, composition, movement, and design—was used to establish effectively a world of fate, passion, obsession, and compulsion. Although his reputation has been elevated in the past decade or so, his name deserves to be better known.

—Jeanine Basinger

SIRK, Douglas

German/American. Born Claus Detlev Sierk in Skagen, Denmark, 26 April 1900. Studied law, philosophy, and art history in Copenhagen, Munich, Jena and Hamburg, until 1922. Dramaturg for Deutsches Schauspiele, Hamburg, 1921; director for Chemnitz "Kleinez Theater," 1922; artistic director, Bremen Schauspielhaus, 1923–29; director of Altes Theater, Leipzig, 1929–36; directed first film, as Detlef Sierck, for UFA, 1935; head of Leipzig drama school, 1936; left Germany, worked on scripts in Austria and France (notably Renoir's *Partie de campagne*, 1937; signed for Warners in Hollywood, 1939, but inactive, 1940–41; contract as writer for Columbia, 1942; director for Universal, from 1950; returned to Europe, 1959; active in theatre in Munich and Hamburg, 1960s. *Died of cancer, in Lugano, Switzerland, 14 January 1987.*

Films as Director:

(as Detlef Sierck)

1935 *It Was een April* (Dutch version); *April, April* (German version); *Das Madchen vom Moorhof*; *Stutzen der Gesellschaft*
1936 *Schlussakkord* (Final Accord) (+ co-sc); *Das Hofkonzert* (+ co-sc); *La Chanson du souvenir* (Song of Remembrance) (co-d) (French version of *Das Hofkonzert*)
1937 *Zu neuen Ufern* (To New Shores. Paramatta. Bagne de femmes) (+ co-sc); *La Habanera*
1939 *Boefje* (+ co-sc)

(directed as Douglas Sirk):

1943 *Hitler's Madman*
1944 *Summer Storm* (+ co-sc)
1946 *A Scandal in Paris*
1947 *Lured*
1948 *Sleep My Love*
1949 *Slightly French*; *Shockproof*
1950 *Mystery Submarine*
1951 *The First Legion* (+ co-pr); *Thunder on the Hill*; *The Lady Pays Off*; *Weekend with Father*
1952 *No Room for the Groom*; *Has Anybody Seen My Gal?*; *Meet Me at the Fair*; *Take Me to Town*
1953 *All I Desire*; *Taza, Son of Cochise*
1954 *Magnificent Obsession*; *Sign of the Pagan*; *Captain Lightfoot*
1955 **All That Heaven Allows**; *There's Always Tomorrow*
1956 *Never Say Goodbye* (Hopper) (d uncredited, completed film); **Written on the Wind**
1957 *Battle Hymn*; *Interlude*; *The Tarnished Angels*
1958 *A Time to Love and a Time to Die*
1959 *Imitation of Life*

(for Munich Film School)

1975 *Talk to Me Like the Rain*
1977 *Sylvesternacht*
1979 *Bourbon Street Blues*

Other Films:

1937 *Liebling der Matrosen* (Hinrich) (co-sc as Detlef Sierck)
1938 *Dreiklang* (Hinrich) (story as Detlef Sierck)
1939 *Accordfinal* (Bay) (supervision, uncredited); *Sehnsucht nach Afrika* (Zoch) (role)
1986 *My Life for Zarah Leander* (Blackwood) (doc) (role)

Publications:

By SIRK: articles—

Interview with Serge Daney and Jean-Louis Noames, in *Cahiers du Cinema* (Paris), April 1967.
"Douglas Sirk," with interview with D. Rabourdin and others, in *Cinema* (Paris), October 1978.
Interview with M. Henry and Y. Tobin in *Positif* (Paris), September 1982.

On SIRK: books—

Halliday, Jon, *Sirk on Sirk*, New York, 1972.
Edinburgh Film Festival 1972: Douglas Sirk, Edinburgh, 1972.
Bourget, Jean-Loup, *Douglas Sirk*, Paris, 1984.
Gledhill, Christine, editor, *Home Is Where the Heart Is: Studies in Melodrama and the Woman's Film*, London, 1987.
Laüfer, Elisabeth, *Skeptiker des Lichts: Douglas Sirk und seine Filme*, Frankfurt, 1987.
Sirk in Germany, Goethe Institute, London, 1988.
Mulvey, Laura, *Visual and Other Pleasures*, London, 1989.

On SIRK: articles—

Comolli, Jean-Louis, "L'Aveugle et le miroir, ou l'impossible cinema de Douglas Sirk," in *Cahiers du Cinema* (Paris), April 1967.
"Sirk Issue" of *Screen* (London), Summer 1971.
Bourget, E., and J.-L. Bourget, "Sur Douglas Sirk," in three parts, in *Positif* (Paris), April and September 1972.
Willemen, P., "Towards an Analysis of the Sirkian System," in *Screen* (London), Winter 1972/73.
"Fassbinder on Sirk," in *Film Comment* (New York), November/December 1975.
McCourt, J., "Douglas Sirk: Melo Maestro," in *Film Comment* (New York), November/December 1975.
Stern, M., "Patterns of Power and Potency, Repression and Violence," in *Velvet Light Trap* (Madison), Fall 1976.
Degenfelder, P., "Sirk's The Tarnished Angels: 'Pylon' Recreated," in *Literature/Film Quarterly* (Salisbury, Maryland), Summer 1977.
Mulvey, Laura, "Notes on Sirk and Melodrama," in *Movie* (London), Winter 1977/78.
Honickel, T., "Idol der Munchner Filmstudenten: Douglas Sirk wieder in der HFF," in *Film und Ton* (Munich), February 1979.
Pulleine, T., "Stahl into Sirk," in *Monthly Film Bulletin* (London), November 1981.
"Douglas Sirk Issue" of *Positif* (Paris), September 1982.
Feuer, Jane, "Melodrama, Serial Form and Television Today," in *Screen* (London), January/February 1984.
Bourget, J.-L, "Vers de nouveaux rivages. Les débuts américains de Douglas Sirk," in *Positif* (Paris), July/August 1984.
Heung, Marina, "'What's the Matter with Sara Jane?': Daughters and Mothers in *Imitation of Life*," in *Cinema Journal* (Champaign, Illinois), vol. 26, no. 3, 1987.
Obituary in *Variety* (New York), 21 January 1987.
Bourget, J.-L., "Rêverie; sur les sources scandinaves de Sirk," in *Positif* (Paris), September 1987.
Petley, Julian, "Sirk in Germany," in *Sight and Sound* (London), Winter 1987/1988.
Hunter, Ross, "Magnificent Obsessions," in *American Film* (Los Angeles), April 1988.
Klinger, Barbara, "Much Ado About Excess: Genre, Mise-en-Scène and the Woman in *Written on the Wind*," in *Wide Angle* (Baltimore), vol. 11, no. 4, 1989.

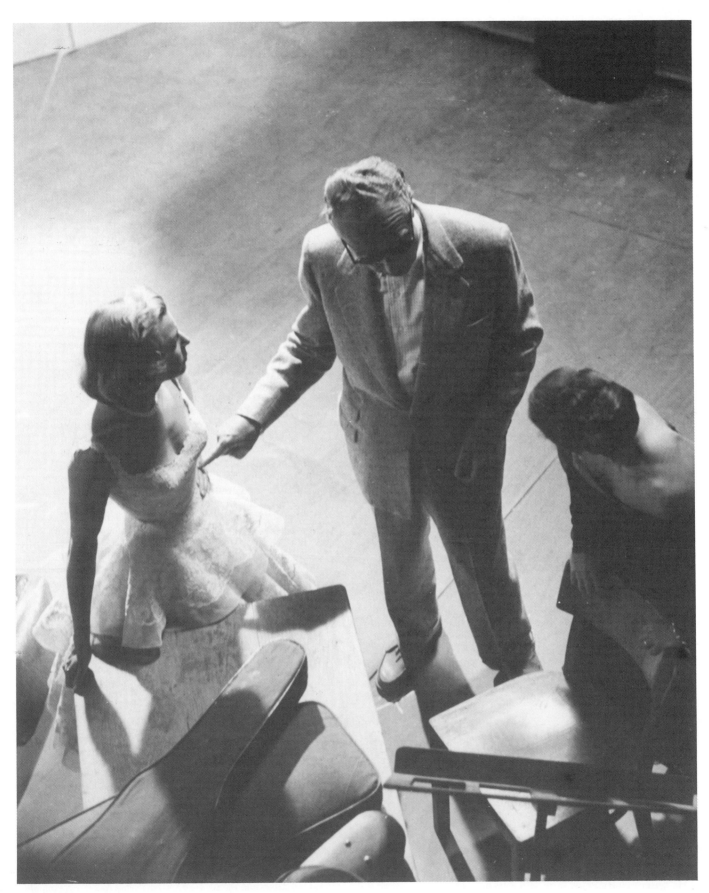

Douglas Sirk directing *Interlude*

Douglas Sirk's critical reputation has almost completely reversed from the time when he was a popular studio director at Universal in the 1950s. He was regarded by contemporary critics as a lightweight director of soap operas who showcased the talents of Universal name stars such as Rock Hudson and Lana Turner. His films often were labelled "women's pictures," with all of the pejorative connotations that term suggested. After his last film, *Imitation of Life*, Sirk retired to Germany, leaving behind a body of work which was seldom discussed, but which was frequently revived on television late shows.

Standard works of film criticism either totally ignored or briefly mentioned him with words such as "not a creative film maker" (quoted from his brief entry in Georges Sadoul's *Dictionary of Film Makers*). In the early 1970s, however, a few American critics began to re-evaluate his works. The most important innovators in Sirk criticism in this period were Jon Halliday whose lengthy interview in book form, *Sirk on Sirk* has become a standard work, and Andrew Sarris, whose program notes on the director's films were compiled into the booklet *Douglas Sirk—The Complete American Period*. From the time of these two works, it became more and more appropriate to speak of Sirk in terms of "genius" and "greatness." By 1979, Sirk was even honored by BBC Television with a "Sirk Season" during which the now loyal following was treated to a weekly installment from the Sirk *oeuvre* as it now fashionably could be called.

Critics today see in Sirk's films more than melodrama with glossy photography and upper-middle-class houses. The word "expressionist" is frequently used to describe his technique, indicating not only the style of Sirk's work in the United States, but also his background in films within the framework of German expressionism in the 1920s and early 1930s. Sirk, who was born in Denmark, but emigrated to Germany in the teens, began work in the theater, then switched to films in the mid-1930s. Known for his "leftist" leanings, Sirk left Germany with the rise of Nazism, and eventually came to the United States in the early 1940s. The first part of his American career was characterized by low budget films which have gone into oblivion. His first well-known film was *Sleep My Love*, a variation on the *Gaslight* theme starring Don Ameche and Claudette Colbert. Soon he began directing films which starred several of the "hot" new Universal stars, among them Hudson and John Gavin, as well as many of the now middle-aged *grandes dames* of the 1930s and 1940s, such as Barbara Stanwyck, Lana Turner, and Jane Wyman. Although today he is known primarily for his dramas, Sirk did make a few lighter pieces, among them *Has Anybody Seen My Gal?*, a musical comedy set in the 1920s, and remembered by movie buffs as one of the first James Dean movies.

Many critics consider *Written on the Wind* to be his best film. It was also the one which was best received upon its initial release. All of Sirk's movies deal with relationships which are complicated, and often at a dead-end. In *Written on the Wind*, despite their wealth and attractiveness, the main characters are unhappy. They have little to interest them and seek outlets for their repressed sexuality. One of the four main characters, Kyle Hadley (Robert Stack), has always lived in the shadow of his more virile friend Mitch Wayne (Rock Hudson). He hopes to forget his own feelings of inadequacy by drinking and carousing, but his activities only reinforce his problems. Sexuality, either in its manifestation or repression, is a strongly recurrent theme in all of Sirk's works, but perhaps no where is it more blatantly dramatized than in *Written on the Wind*, where sex is the core of everyone's problems. Mitch is the only truly potent figure in the film, and thus he is the pivotal figure. Hudson's role as Mitch is very similar to that of Ron Kirby in *All That Heaven Allows*. Ron and Mitch both exhibit a strong sense of sexuality that either attracts or repels the other characters and initiates their action.

Kyle's feelings of sexual inadequacy and jealousy of Mitch are interrelated; Mitch is the manly son Kyle's father always wanted and the virile lover his wife Lucy (Lauren Bacall) loves. Kyle admires Mitch, yet hates him at the same time. Similarly, Carey Scott in *All That Heaven Allows* desires the earthy gardener Ron, yet she is shocked at her own sexuality, an apparent rejection of the conventions of her staid upper-middle-class milieu. In *There's Always Tomorrow*, Clifford Groves (Fred MacMurray) is faced with a similar situation. He seeks sexual and psychological freedom from his stifling family with Norma Vail (Barbara Stanwyck), yet his responsibilities and sense of morality prevent him from finding the freedom he seeks.

It is an ironic key to Sirk's popular acclaim now that exactly the same stars whose presence seemed to confirm his films as being "programmers" and "women's pictures" have ultimately added a deeper dimension to his works. By using popular stars of the 1930s through 1950s—stars who often peopled lightweight comedies and unregenerate melodramas, Sirk has revealed another dimension of American society. His films often present situations in which the so-called "happy endings" of earlier films are played out to their ultimate (and often more realistic) outcomes by familiar faces. For example, in *There's Always Tomorrow*, Clifford and his wife Marion (Joan Bennett) might very well have been the prototypes for the main characters of a typical 1930s comedy in which "boy gets girl" in the last reel. Yet, in looking at them after almost 20 years of marriage, their lives are shallow. The happy ending of a youthful love has not sustained itself. Similarly, in *All That Heaven Allows*, the attractive middle-aged widow of a "wonderful man" has few things in life to make her happy. Whereas she was once a supposedly happy housewife, the loving spouse of a pillar of the community, her own identity has been suppressed to the point that his death means social ostracism. These two examples epitomize the cynicism of Sirk's view of what was traditionally perceived as the American dream. Most of Sirk's films depict families in which a house, cars, and affluence are present, but in which sexual and emotional fulfillment are not. Many of Sirk's films end on a decidedly unhappy note; the ones that do end optimistically for the main characters are those in which traditions are shattered and the strict societal standards of the time are rejected.

—Patricia King Hanson

SJÖBERG, Alf.

Swedish. Born in Stockholm, 21 June 1903. Educated at Royal Dramatic Theater. Stage actor, from 1925; stage director, from 1927 (chief director, Royal Dramatic Theater, from 1930); directed first film, *Den starkaste*, 1929; returned to filmmaking, 1940. Recipient: Best Film (*ex aequo*), Cannes Festival, for *Fröken Julie*, 1951. *Died in Stockholm, 17 April 1980.*

Films as Director:

1929   *Den starkaste* (*The Strongest*) (+ story)
1940   *Med livet som insats* (*They Staked Their Lives*) (+ co-sc); *Den blomstertid* (*Blossom Time*) (+ sc)

Alf Sjöberg

1941   *Hem från Babylon* (*Home from Babylon*) (+ co-sc)
1942   *Himlaspelet* (*The Road to Heaven*) (+ co-sc)
1944   *Hets* (*Torment*); *Kungajakt* (*The Royal Hunt*)
1945   *Resan bort* (*Journey Out*) (+ sc)
1946   *Iris och lö jtnantsh järta* (*Iris and the Lieutenant*) (+ sc)
1949   *Bara en mor* (*Only a Mother*) (+ co-sc)
1951   ***Fröken Julie*** (***Miss Julie***) (+ sc)
1953   *Barabbas* (+ co-sc)
1954   *Karin Mansdotter* (+ sc)
1955   *Vildfåglar* (*Wild Birds*) (+ co-sc)
1956   *Sista paret ut* (*Last Pair Out*)
1960   *Domaren* (*The Judge*) (+ co-sc)
1966   *On* (*The Island*)
1969   *Fadern* (*The Father*)

Publications:

By SJÖBERG: articles—

Interview in *Chaplin* (Stockholm), December 1965.
"Ingmar Bergman's Schooldays," an interview with Peter Cowie in *Monthly Film Bulletin* (London), April 1983.

On SJÖBERG: books—

Cowie, Peter, *Swedish Cinema*, New York, 1966.
Lundin, Gunnar, *Filmregi Alf Sjöberg*, Lund, 1979.

On SJÖBERG: articles—

Chaplin (Stockholm), no. 7, 1969.
Obituary, in *Variety* (New York), 30 April 1980.
"Bergman on Sjöberg," in *National Film Theatre Booklet* (London), September 1982.
Werner, Gosta, "Alf Sjoberg som filmskapare," in *Chaplin* (Stockholm), vol. 25, no. 3, 1983.

*   *   *

Along with Sjöström, Stiller and Bergman, Sjöberg must be counted as one of the most significant directors of the Swedish cinema, and indeed as the most important in that long period between the departure of Sjöström and Stiller for Hollywood and the establishment of Bergman as a mature talent. However, it is hard not to agree with the judgement of Peter Cowie when he states that "he is hampered by a want of thematic drive, for he is not preoccupied, like Bergman, with a personal vision. He has not created a world to which one returns with an immediate feeling of recognition and empathy. Each of his films is a solitary achievement, illuminating for a moment the universe of Strindberg, Lagerkvist and others with a cinematic expertise that rarely falters. . . . If one concludes that Sjöberg's most successful accomplishments are founded on the inspiration of others . . . , it is not to deny his impeccable craftsmanship, his uncanny grasp of historical period, and his gift for describing his characters compellingly within their environment."

After studying with Greta Garbo at Stockholm's famous Dramatic Theatre School, Sjöberg rapidly made a name for himself as a theatre director, becoming Chief Director at the Stockholm Theatre by 1930. In the late 1920s he encountered the films of Eisenstein and Pabst but the chief influence on his early films would appear to be the fatalism and melancholy of French "poetic realism" of the 1930s. However, in his first film, *The Strongest*, an epic tale of the seal hunters of Arctic Norway, the influences would appear to be an intriguing blend of Jack London, Robert Flaherty, the Sjöström of *The Outlaw and His Wife* and, in the remarkably fluidly edited bear-hunt that climaxes the film, Eisenstein. However, all this was too much for a cinema industry preoccupied with feeble studio comedies and light dramas and Sjöberg was unable to make another film for ten years. Instead he confined his experiments in mise-en-scène to the theatre.

In *They Stake Their Lives*, a sombre story of the underground in an unidentified Baltic totalitarian state, and *The Royal Hunt*, which deals with Russian attempts to overthrow Gustav III of Sweden in the late 18th century, there are clear references to the Nazi threat; in more general terms these films deal with the theme of power and domination which is one of the threads which runs through the director's work. More important, however, is *The Road to Heaven*, a film very much in the Sjöström/Lagerlöf tradition that is generally regarded as one of the finest of the period 1920–1950 and an important milestone in the revival of the Swedish cinema at this time. A sort of Swedish Pilgrim's Progress, it draws heavily on the same kind of Swedish peasant art which influenced *The Seventh Seal*, though it is both more nationalistic and more specifically and directly Christian in inspiration than that work. However, as Forsyth Hardy has pointed out, "it helped to give spiritual structure to the revival of the Swedish cinema."

Frenzy signalled a new departure both for Swedish cinema in general and Sjöberg's work in particular, as well as the arrival of a powerful new talent in the form of its scriptwriter—Ingmar Bergman. In its story of a tyrannical schoolmaster (aptly nicknamed Caligula) who torments one of his students beyond endurance, Sjöberg clearly found a subject close to his heart, one which went beyond the obvious theme of youthful ardour vs. oppressive, reactionary middle and old age and allowed him to explore power relationships (with all their distinctly sexual ramifications) in a more general way. Sjöberg creates a remarkably claustrophobic and sombre atmosphere to match Bergman's agonised screenplay—there are few sets, less still exterior shots, and the harsh, louring lighting at times recalls the German silent cinema. One of the themes explored in *Frenzy* is the destructive effect of outdated class divisions, and the evils of class society are also very much to the fore in *Only a Mother* which is set among the "stataren," rural communities where farm labourers and their families were forced to endure almost serf-like conditions. The social dimension of Sjöberg's work at this time is a reminder that Sweden had recently introduced the full apparatus of a welfare state. At the same time the director is still much preoccupied with formal matters, experimenting here with deep focus, huge close-ups, and sharply angled interior shots.

Sjöberg's best known film is probably *Miss Julie* which transforms Strindberg's by then rather outdated condemnation of the class system into a study of power relationships between the sexes. Here the sado-masochistic element comes right to the fore, which earned the film a rather risqué reputation in Anglo-Saxon countries. As well as modifying the original quite considerably Sjöberg also experimented with rapid transitions between past and present, often without the aid of cuts, and the film also contains a rare example of the flash-forward. Like *Iris and the Lieutenant* and *Only a Mother*, *Miss Julie* is also an indictment of the position of women under a stern patriarchal order. Strindberg was also the inspiration behind *Karin Mansdotter*, parts of which were based on his play *Erik XIV*. Beginning with a bizarre (and rather out of place) parody of cinematic costume drama the film is beautifully shot, mostly on location in some of Sweden's most spectacular castles, by Sven Nykvist.

In his later work Sjöberg returned to contemporary Swedish society. The struggle between the sexes is continued in *Wild Birds* and the Bergman-scripted *The Last Pair Out*, while the director's concern with social injustice is evident in *The Judge*, an indictment of dubious legal goings-on, and *The Island* in which the central character urges his apathetic fellow islanders to fight government plans to take away their land and turn it into a gunnery range. However, it has to be admitted that Sjöberg's later work does not show him at his best; characters too often come across as mere puppets, there are too many wordy passages, and Sjöberg often seems unable to sustain any consistency of mood or refrain from exaggerated melodramatics. However, his dramatically resonant use of settings, and the way in which he controls his characters' movements within them, remain interesting, reminding one that Sjöberg, at his best, has been compared to Emile Zola.

—Julian Petley.

SJÖSTRÖM, Victor.

(also known as Victor Seastrom) Swedish. Born Victor David Sjöström in Silbodal, Sweden, 20 September 1879. Attended High School in Uppsala, Sweden. Married 1) Sascha St. Jagoff, 1900 (died 1916); 2) Lili Bech, 1916; 3) actress Edith Erastoff, 1922 (died 1945), two children. Lived in Brooklyn, New York, from 1880; returned to Sweden to live with aunt, 1887; stage actor and director in Sweden and Finland, from 1896; formed own theater company, 1911; film director for Svenska Biograf film studio, Stockholm, from 1912; director for MGM, Hollywood, from 1923, name "Americanized" to "Seastrom"; returned to Sweden as actor, 1930; artistic director, Svensk Filmindustri, 1943–49. *Died in Stockholm, 3 January 1960.*

Films as Director:

1912   *Trädgårrdsmaästaren (The Gardener)* (+ role); *Ett Hemligt giftermaål (A Secret Marriage)*; *En sommarsaga (A Summer Tale)*
1913   *Lö jen och tårar (Ridicule and Tears)*; *Blodets röst (Voice of the Blood)* (+ sc, role) (released 1923); *Lady Marions sommarflirt (Lady Marion's Summer Flirt)*; *Äktenskapsbrydån (The Marriage Agency)* (+ sc); *Livets konflikter (Conflicts of Life)* (co-d, role); *Ingeborg Holm* (+ sc); *Halvblod (Half Breed)*; *Miraklet*; *På livets ödesvägar (On the Roads of Fate)*
1914   *Prästen (The Priest)*; *Det var i Maj (It Was in May)* (+ sc); *Kärlek starkare än hat (Love Stronger Than Hatred)*; *Dömen icke (Do Not Judge)*; *Bra flicka reder sig själv (A Clever Girl Takes Care of Herself)* (+ sc); *Gatans barn (Children of the Street)*; *Högfjällets dotter (Daughter of the Mountains)* (+ sc); *Hjärtan som mötas (Meeting Hearts)*
1915   *Strejken (Strike)* (+ sc, role); *En av de många (One of the Many)* (+ sc); *Sonad oskuld (Expiated Innocence)* (+ co-sc); *Skomakare bliv vid din läst (Cobbler Stay at Your Bench)* (+ sc)
1916   *Lankshövdingens dottrar (The Governor's Daughters)* (+ sc); *Rösen på Tistelön (Havsgammar. The Rose of Thistle Island. Sea Eagle)*; *I. Prövningens stund (Hour of the Trial)* (+ sc, role); *Skepp som motas (Meeting Ships)*; *Hon segrade (She Conquered)* (+ sc, role); *Therese* (+ co-sc)
1917   *Dödskyssen (Kiss of Death)* (+ co-sc, role); *Terje Vigen (A Man There Was)* (+ co-sc, role)
1918   *Berg-Ejvind och hans hustru (The Outlaw and His Wife)* (+ co-sc, role); *Tösen från stormyrtorpet (The Lass from the Stormy Croft)* (+ co-sc)
1919   *Ingmarsönerna, Parts I and II (Sons of Ingmar)* (+ sc, role); *Hans nåds testamente (The Will of His Grace)*
1920   *Klostret I Sendomir (The Monastery of Sendomir)* (+ sc); *Karin Ingmarsdotter (Karin, Daughter of Ingmar)* (+ co-sc, role); *Mästerman (Master Samuel)* (+ role)
1921   *Körkarlen (The Phantom Chariot.* **Thy Soul Shall Bear Witness***)* (+ sc, role as David Holm)

1922   *Vem dömer (Love's Crucible)* (+ co-sc); *Det omringgade huset (The Surrounded House)* (+ co-sc, role)
1923   *Eld ombord (The Tragic Ship)* (+ role)
1924   *Name the Man*; *He Who Gets Slapped*
1925   *Confessions of a Queen*; *The Tower of Lies*
1927   *The Scarlet Letter*
1928   *The Divine Woman*; **The Wind**; *Masks of the Devil*
1930   *A Lady to Love*
1931   *Markurells I Wadköping* (+ role)
1937   *Under the Red Robe*

Other Films:

1912   *Vampyren* (Stiller) (role as Lt. Roberts); *De svarta maskerna* (Stiller) (role as the Lieutenant); *I livets vår* (Garbagni) (role)
1913   *Nar karlekan dodar* (Stiller) (role as the painter); *Barnet* (Stiller) (role as medical student)
1914   *För sin kädleks skull* (Stiller) (role as Borgen); *Högfjällets dotter* (Stiller) (role); *Guldspindeln* (Magnusen) (role); *Thomas Graals bästa film* (Stiller) (role as Thomas Graal); *Thomas Graals bästa barn* (Stiller) (role as Thomas Graal)
1934   *Synnove Solbakken* (T. Ibsen) (role)
1935   *Valborgsmaässoafton* (Edgren) (role)
1937   *John Ericsson* (role)
1939   *Gubben Kommer* (Lindberg) (role); *Mot nya tider* (Wallen) (role)
1941   *Striden går vidare* (Molander) (role)
1943   *Det brinner en eld* (Molander) (role); *Ordet* (Molander) (role)
1944   *Kejsaren av Portugalien* (Molander) (role)
1947   *Rallare* (Mattson) (role)
1940s   *Farlig vår* (Mattson) (role)
1950   *Till Glädje* (Bergman) (role); *Kvartetten som sprängdes* (Molander) (role)
1952   *Hård klang* (Mattson) (role)
1955   *Nattens väv* (Mattson) (role)
1957   *Smultronstället* (**Wild Strawberries**) (Bergman) (role as Professor)

Publications:

On SJÖSTRÖM: books—

Idestam-Almquist, Bengt, *Den Svenska Filmens Drama: Sjöström och Stiller*, Stockholm, 1938.
Hardy, Forsyth, *Scandinavian Film*, London, 1951.
Lauritzen, Einar, *Swedish Film*, New York, 1962.
Jeanne, Reńe, and Charles Ford, *Sjöström et l'ecole suédois*, Paris, 1963.
Cowie, Peter, *Swedish Cinema*, London, 1966.
Pensel, Hans, *Seastrom and Stiller in Hollywood*, New York, 1969.
Petrie, Graham, *Hollywood Destinies: European Directors in Hollywood 1922–31*, London, 1985.
Forslund, Bengt, *Victor Sjöström: His Life and His Work*, New York, 1988.

On SJÖSTRÖM: articles—

Vaughn, Dai, "Victor Sjöström and D.W. Griffith," in *Film* (London), January/February 1958.
"Bergman on Victor Sjöström," in *Sight and Sound* (London), Spring 1960.
Turner, Charles L., "Victor Sjöström," in *Films in Review* (New York), May and June 1960.
Wood, Robin, "Essays on the Swedish Cinema (Part 2)," in *Lumiere* (Melbourne), April/May 1974.
Gillett, John, "Swedish Retrospect," in *Sight and Sound* (London), Summer 1974.
Milne, Tom, "Lost and Found," in *Sight and Sound* (London), Autumn 1975.
Beylie, Claude, and M. Martin, "Sjöström, Stiller et L'Amérique," in *Ecran* (Paris), September 1978.
Torbacke, J., "Vem såg Victor Sjöström mästerverk?," in *Chaplin* (Stockholm), v.22, no.6, 1980.

Victor Sjöström (left)

"Victor Sjostrom Issue" of *Avant-Scene du Cinéma* (Paris), July/ August 1984.

Niogret, H., "Notes sur quelques films de Victor Sjostrom," in *Positif* (Paris), September 1987.

Viviani, C., "Trois films américains pour connaître Victor Sjöström," in *Positif* (Paris), June 1989.

*   *   *

With a career in film that in many ways paralleled that of his close friend Mauritz Stiller, Victor Sjöström entered the Swedish film industry at virtually the same time (1912), primarily as an actor, only to become almost immediately, like Stiller, a film director. However, whereas Stiller had spent his youth in Finland, Sjöström had spent six formative years as a child in America's Brooklyn; later, back in Sweden and after an unhappy childhood, his training for the theater had born fruit and he had become a well-established actor before entering the film industry at the age of 32: "The thing that brought me into filmmaking was a youthful desire for adventure and a curiosity to try this new medium," he once said in interview. The first films in which he appeared in 1912 were Stiller's *The Black Masks* and *Vampyren*.

Although Sjöström proved excellent as an actor in comedy, his innate seriousness of outlook was reflected in the films he directed. He developed a deep response to nature, to the spectacular northern landscape, the expanses of ice, snow, trees, and mountains in all their (to him as to other Scandinavians) mystical force. One of his earliest films was *Ingeborn Holm*, which exposed the cruelties of the forced labor system to which the children of paupers were still subjected. This film was produced partially outdoors; Sjöström's pantheistic response to nature was developed in *Terje Vigen*, his adaptation of Ibsen's ballad poem with its narrative set in the period of the Napoleonic confrontation with Britain. Sjöström himself played Terje, the bitter Norwegian sailor who had been imprisoned for a while by the British for attempting to break through their blockade at sea in order to bring food through to the starving people, including his wife and son, in his village. He fails, and they die in consequence. Terje's obsessive desire for vengeance is later purged as a result of his response to his British captor's child, whom he rescues in a storm.

Sjöström became a prolific director. He completed approaching 30 films between 1912 and 1918, the year he directed *The Outlaw and His Wife*, of which the French critic and filmmaker, Louis Delluc, wrote in 1921, "Here without doubt is the most beautiful film in the world. Victor Sjöström has directed it with a dignity that is beyond words . . . it is the first love duet heard in the cinema. A duet that is entire life. Is it a drama? . . . . I don't know. . . . People love each other and live. That is all." In this film a rich widow abandons her estate to live in the mountains with her outlaw lover until, hounded by her pursuers, they die together in the snow. It is typical of the Swedish film that winter, after the symbolic summer of love, should become the synonym for Death. Sjöström's intense feeling for nature expanded still further in his first adaptation of a novel by Selma Lagerlöf who, as a writer in the grand tradition, became one of the primary inspirers of the Swedish cinema of this period. This adaptation was from *The Lass from the Stormy Croft*, with its magnificent rustic setting which seems at once to transcend and embody the exigencies of human passion—the frustration of the poor peasant girl with her illegitimate child and the troubles that afflict the son of a landowner (played by Lars Hanson in his first important film role), who tries to befriend her. As Carl Dreyer, who in the same year made *The Parson's Widow* in Sweden, commented, "Selma Lagerlöf's predilection for dreams and supernatural events appealed to Sjöström's own somewhat sombre artistic mind."

Sjöström's most famous film before his departure for Hollywood in 1923 was *The Phantom Chariot* (also known as *Thy Soul Shall Bear Witness*), also based on a novel by Selma Lagerlöf. The legend had it that the phantom chariot came once each year, on New Year's Eve, St. Sylvester's Night, to carry away the souls of sinners. In the film the central character is David Holm, a violent and brutalized man who is brought to relive his evil past on St. Sylvester's Night, especially the ill-treatment he had given his wife, until his conscience is awakened. As Holm recalls his wicked deeds in flashback he is haunted by the approach of the chariot, and is saved just in time through reunion with his wife, whose imminent suicide he prevents. Holm is played brilliantly by Sjöström himself, while Julius Jaenzen's multi-exposure camerawork emphasizes the distinction between body and soul in visuals that surpass virtually all that had been achieved in cinematography by 1920.

When, in the postwar era, Swedish films, with their comparatively heavy themes, began to prove less popular as exports, Sjöström, like Stiller, left for America on the invitation of Louis B. Mayer at MGM. He was to remain in Hollywood six years, and direct nine films under the name of Victor Seastrom. Of these *The Scarlet Letter*, with Lillian Gish as Hester Prynne and Lars Hanson as the priest, and *The Wind*, also with Lillian Gish and Lars Hanson, are the more significant, the latter ranking now as a masterpiece of the silent cinema. Lillian Gish has said of Sjöström that "his direction was a great education for me . . . the Swedish school of acting is one of repression." In *The Wind* she plays a sensitive girl from Kentucky forced into marriage with a coarse cattleman from Texas, a repellent marriage which, along with the harsh Texan environment, finally drives her nearly insane and impels her to kill a male intruder in self-defense. The film, shot in the Mojave region, suffered some re-editing by the studio, and the imposition of a sound track. Sjöström's single attempt to recreate Sweden in America was *The Tower of Lies* (with Lon Chaney and Norma Shearer), an adaptation of Selma Lagerlöf's novel, *The Emperor of Portugal*, which at least one American reviewer praised for, "its preservation of the simplicity of treatment in *Thy Soul Shall Bear Witness*."

Sjöström returned to Sweden in 1928 and directed one good sound film, *Markurells i Wadköping*, in which he starred as a grim man, much like Terje Vigen, who is finally purged of his desire for revenge. Apart from directing a lame period romance in England, *Under the Red Robe*, with Raymond Massey and Conrad Veidt, Sjöström concentrated on his career as an actor, giving at the age of 78 a great performance as the aged professor in Bergman's *Wild Strawberries*.

—Roger Manvell

SKOLIMOWSKI, Jerzy.

Polish. Born in Warsaw, 5 May 1938. Educated in literature and history at Warsaw University, diploma 1959; State Film School Lodz, 1960–64. Published first collection of poetry, *Quelque part près de soi*, 1959; directed first feature (as film student), *Rysopis*, 1964; *Rece de gory* banned by Polish authorities, left Poland, 1967. Recipient: Best Screenplay, Cannes Festival, for *Moonlighting*, 1982.

Films as Director:

1960   *Oko wykol* (*L'Oeil Torve*) (short) (+ sc); *Hamles* (*Le Petit Hamlet*) (short) (+ sc); *Erotyk* (*L'Érotique*) (short) (+ sc)

Jerzy Skolimowski

1961   *Boks* (*Boxing*) (short) (+ sc); *Piednadze albo zycie* (*La Bourse ou la vie*) (short) (+ sc); *Akt* (short) (+ sc)
1964   *Rysopis* (*Identification Marks: None*) (+ sc, pr, art d, ed, role as Andrzej Leszczyc)
1965   *Walkower* (*Walkover*) (+ sc, co-ed, role as Andrzej Leszczyc)
1966   *Bariera* (*Barrier*) (+ sc)
1967   *Le Départ* (+ co-sc); *Rece do gory* (*Hands Up!*) (+ sc, co-art d, role as Andrzej Leszczyc)
1968   *Dialog* (*Dialogue*) (+ sc, art d)
1970   *The Adventures of Gerard* (+ co-sc); *Deep End* (+ co-sc)
1971   *King, Queen, Knave* (+ co-sc)
1978   *The Shout* (+ co-sc)
1982   *Moonlighting* (+ sc, co-pr)
1984   *Success is the Best Revenge*
1985   *The Lightship*
1989   *Torrents of Spring* (+ sc)
1991   *Ferdydurke* (+ sc)

Other Films:

1959   *Niewinni czardodzieje* (*Innocent Sorcerers*) (Wajda) (co-sc)
1960   *Noz w wodzie* (**Knife in the Water**) (Polanski) (co-sc); *Przy Jaciel* (*A Friend*) (co-sc)
1981   *Falschung* (Schlöndorff) (role)
1985   *White Knights* (Hackford) (role)

Publications:

By SKOLIMOWSKI: books—

Quelque part près de soi, 1958.
La Hache et le ciel, 1959.

By SKOLIMOWSKI: articles—

"Passages and Levels: Interview with Jerzy Skolimowski," with Michel Delahaye, in *Cahiers du Cinema in English* (New York), December 1967.
"'An Accusation That I Throw in the Face of My Generation'—A Conversation with the Young Polish Director, Jerzy Skolimowski," in *Film Comment* (New York), Fall 1968.
"Jerzy Skolimowski: A Conversation," with Peter Blum, in *Film Culture* (New York), Fall 1968.
Interview with Michel Ciment and Bernard Cohn, in *Positif* (Paris), February 1972.
"Skolimowski's Cricket Match," interview with Philip Strick, in *Sight and Sound* (London), Summer 1978.
"Jerzy Skolimowski," an interview with P. Carcassonne and others, in *Cinématographe* (Paris), June 1978.
Interview with K.L. Geist in *Films in Review* (New York), vol. 33, no.9, November 1982.
Interview with Dan Yakir in *Film Comment* (New York), November/December 1982.
Interviews in *Cahiers du Cinéma* (Paris), January 1983 and Summer 1984.
Interview with E. Carrière and Michel Ciment in *Positif* (Paris), February 1986.
"*Under Western Eyes*: Skolimowski's Conradian Progress," interview with Richard Combs in *Monthly Film Bulletin* (London), May 1986.

On SKOLIMOWSKI: books—

Borin, Fabrizio, *Jerzy Skolimowski*, Florence, 1987.

On SKOLIMOWSKI: articles—

Toeplitz, Krzysztof-Teodor, "Jerzy Skolimowski: Portrait of a Debutant Director," in *Film Quarterly* (Berkeley), Fall 1967.
Thomsen, Christian, "Skolimowski," in *Sight and Sound* (London), Summer 1968.
Bean, Robin, "Adventures of Yurek," in *Films and Filming* (London), December 1968.
"Director of the Year," in *International Film Guide 1970*, London, 1969.
Lefèvre, R., "Jerzy Skolimowski ou la poésie du dérisoire," in *Cinéma* (Paris), September/October 1973.

Powers, J., "*Under Western Eyes*," in *American Film* (Washington D.C.), December 1986.

*   *   *

Together with Roman Polanski, Jerzy Skolimowski is the most remarkable representative of the second generation of the Polish new wave. Younger than Wajda, Munk, or Kawalerowicz, these two did not share the hope for a new society after World War II and are more skeptical, to the point sometimes of cynicism. With Polanski, Skolimowski wrote *Knife in the Water*, which deals precisely with the relationship between two generations, after having also collaborated on the script of Wajda's *Innocent Sorcerers*, one of the director's rare attempts at portraying Poland's youth. A student in ethnography, a poet, an actor, and a boxer, Skolimowski went to the Lodz film school (1960–1964) and graduated with a diploma work that brought world attention to his talent. That film, *Rysopis* (*Identification Marks: None*), and its totally controlled sequel *Walkover*, reveal an astonishing flexible style which follows a central character, Andrzej Leszczyc, played by Skolimowski himself. Without resorting to a subjective camera, the director nevertheless makes us see reality through his hero, refusing dramatic plot twists, and filming very much like a jazz musician—all rhythm and improvisation. *Rysopis* tells of the few hours before being called up for military service, and *Walkover* of the time preceding a boxing match. A limited number of shots (39 and 29 respectively!) gives an extraordinary sense of fluidity, of life caught in its most subtle shifts. *Bariera* is a much more literary and symbolic work. It offers the same themes and milieu (young people, often students), although with a dreamlike atmosphere, a somnambulistic quality which will reappear later in Skolimowski's work, but more successfully integrated into its realistic surface. "Our cynical and indifferent generation still possesses romantic aspirations," says one of the characters. And this sums up well the filmmaker's ambivalent attitude towards life.

If *Bariera* was, according to Skolimowski, influenced by Godard's *Pierrot le fou*, his next film, *Le Départ*, shot in Belgium, borrowed two actors, Jean-Pierre Léaud and Catherine Duport, from the French director's *Masculin féminin*. It deals with a young hairdresser who dreams of becoming a rally driver, and his relationship with a girl. The same sensitive portrait of youth will be found again in a more accomplished work, *Deep End*, a brilliant portrayal of a London swimming bath attendant and his tragic love affair. Skolimowski's very titles (*Walkover, Barrier, Departure, Hands Up, Deep End*) suggest the relationship to sports, movement and physical effort that characterizes his nervous and dynamic style. *Hands Up*, banned for fifteen years by the Polish authorities because of its bleak symbolic portrayal of a group of people shut up inside a railway carriage, prompted Skolimowski to work in the West though he has always returned regularly to his home country. But the difficulties linked to an international career appeared quickly with the failure of *The Adventures of Gerard*, a spoof on Conan Doyle's Napoleonic novel, and the more evident one of *King, Queen, Knave*, shot in Munich from Nabokov's novel.

However, Skolimowski came back to the forefront of European filmmaking with *The Shout* and *Moonlighting*. The former, adapted from a Robert Graves short story, has a sense of the absurd which verges on creating a surrealistic atmosphere—a classic component of Polish culture. This film about a triangular relationship between a kind of sorcerer, the woman he is in love with, and her husband, is an intense, haunting piece of work. *Moonlighting*, arguably Skolimowski's best film to date, was written and shot within a few months and looks deceptively simple. The tale of four Polish workers, sent from Warsaw to refurbish the house a rich Pole has bought in London, reveals, little by little, layers of meaning, contacts between East and West, and repression in Poland. The nightmare emerges slowly from a close scrutiny of reality, confirming that Skolimowski's materialism and lucidity do not contradict but rather refine his unique poetic sensibility.

—Michel Ciment

SNOW, Michael.

Canadian. Born Michael James Aleck Snow in Toronto, Ontario, 10 December 1929. Educated at Upper Canada College, Toronto, 1946–51; Ontario College of Art, Toronto, 1951–55. Married filmmaker Joyce Wieland, 1959. Independent artist, musician, filmmaker and photographer, Toronto, from 1955; worked at Graphic Films, Toronto, and directed first film, animated short *A to Z*, 1955–56; moved to New York City, 1962; worked in several media, began concentrating on film, from mid-1960s; represented Canada at Venice Biennale with films and other art works, 1970; Professor of Advanced Film Studies, Yale University, 1970; returned to Toronto, 1971; Visiting Artist, Nova Scotia College of Art & Design, Halifax, 1970, 1974, and Ontario College of Art, 1973, 1974, 1976. Recipient: Guggenheim Fellowship, 1972; LL.D., Brock University, St. Catherine's, Ontario, 1975; Order of Canada, 1981; Independent Experimental Film Award, Los Angeles, Film Critics Association, 1983. Address: c/o The Isaacs Gallery, 179 John Street, Toronto, Ontario M5T 1X3, Canada.

Films:

1956   *A to Z* (short)
1964   *New York Eye and Ear Control* (*A Walking Woman Work*)
1965   *Short Shave*
1966/67   ***Wavelength***
1967   *Standard Time*
1968/69 ←→ (*Back and Forth*); *One Second in Montreal*; *Dripping Water* (with Joyce Wieland)
1970   *Side Seat Paintings Slides Sound Film*
1970/71   *La Region centrale* (*The Central Region*)
1972/76   *Breakfast* (*Table Top Dolly*)
1974   *Two Sides to Every Story* (2-screen)
1972/74   *Rameau's Nephew by Diderot* (*Thanx to Dennis Young*) by *Wilma Schoen*
1982   *Presents*; *This is it*
1983   *So is This*
1989   *Seated Figures*

Other Films:

1988   *I Will Not Take Any More Boring Art* (MacGillivray) (doc) (role)

Publications:

By SNOW: books—

Michael Snow: A Survey, exhibition catalogue, Art Gallery of Toronto, 1970.
Cover to Cover, Nova Scotia, 1976.

By SNOW: articles—

"Letter from Michael Snow," in *Film Culture* (New York), no.46, 1967.

"Conversation with Michael Snow," with Jonas Mekas and P. Adams Sitney, in *Film Culture* (New York), Autumn 1967.
"Michael Snow on 'La Region Centrale'," in *Film Culture* (New York), Spring 1971.
"Passage," in *Artforum* (New York), September 1971.
"The Life and Times of Michael Snow," interview with J. Medjuck, in *Take One* (Montreal), April 1972.
"Snow's Sinema Soufflé," with interview, with A. Ibranyi-Kiss, in *Cinema Canada* (Montreal), May/June 1975.
"Michael Snow in San Francisco," interview with P. Adams Sitney and others, in *Cinemanews* (San Francisco), no.2/4, 1979.
Interview with Jonas Mekas and P. Adams Sitney, in *Cahiers du Cinéma* (Paris), January 1979.
"The 'Presents' of Michael Snow," an interview with Jonathan Rosenbaum, in *Film Comment* (New York), May/June 1981.
Interview with F. Ziolkowski in *On Film* (Los Angeles), Spring 1984.
Interview with P. Lehman in *Wide Angle* (Baltimore, Maryland), vol. 7, nos. 1/2, 1985.

On SNOW: books—

Hanhardt, John, and others, *A History of the American Avant-Garde*, New York, 1976.

On SNOW: articles—

Michelson, Annette, "Toward Snow," in *Artforum* (New York), June 1971.
Mekas, Jonas, "A Note on Michael Snow, Written in a Minnesota Snowstorm," in *Take One* (Montreal), April 1972.
Skoller, Donald, "Aspects of Cinematic Consciousness . . . ," in *Film Comment* (New York), September/October 1972.
Simon, Bill, "New Forms in Film," in *Artforum* (New York), October 1972.
Marcorelles, L., and T. Raneri, "Snow Storms Italy," in *Cinema Canada* (Montreal), February/March 1973.
Hayum, A., "A Casing Shelved," in *Film Culture* (New York), Spring 1973.
Heath, S., "Narrative Space," in *Screen* (London), no.3, 1976.
Cornwell, R., "Hitting on 'A Lot of Near Mrs.'," in *Film Reader* (Evanston, Illinois), no.3, 1978.
Bloch, L., "Digne (À propos de Michael Snow)," in *Cahiers du Cinéma* (Paris), July/August 1978.
Michelson, A., "About Snow," in *October* (Cambridge, Massachusetts), Spring 1979.
Elder, R. B., "'/All Things in Their Times'," in *Ciné-Tracts* (Montreal), Summer/Fall 1982.
"Michael Snow Issue" of *Afterimage* (London), Winter 1982/83.

*   *   *

After studies at the Ontario College of Art, Snow simultaneously pursued careers as a jazz musician and an artist, making sculpture, paintings, and photography. He began to make films while working for a commercial film company in Canada, but his first important film, *New York Eye and Ear Control*, was made in New York, as an extension of his attempt to represent a graphic image (his "Walking Woman" outline) in a wide range of media. The film is notable for its use of a powerful jazz soundtrack.

In *Wavelength*, he built the entire film around the exploration of the illusionary properties of the zoom lens. That set the program for his most ambitious cinematic works, several of which examine the range of possibilities inherent in a given technique. In ←→, the entire film consists of panning movements, first horizontally, then vertically, and finally a superimposed recapitulation for both. *One Second in Montreal* brought the film composed wholly of stills to a new intensity of stasis, testing the possibilities of perceptual distinctions when shots are held unusually long, but for varying lengths of time.

The Central Region employs a specially built, remote-controlled equitorial mount to perform intricate movements, sweeping the entire, desolate landscape of the zone of northern Canada where it was set up, to present the visible world as if it were the inside of a great sphere. This three-hour-long film without human presence develops the tensions between cinematic time, as emphasized by the unequivocally mechanical camera gyrations, and the natural cycle of the solar day.

Rameau's Nephew by Diderot (Thanx to Dennis Young) by Wilma Schoen takes on an encyclopedic range of topics related to picture and sound, with a Duchampian "study" of language most prominent. For 285 minutes, in apparently 24 distinct sections, the film explores the human body as a source of sound. The inherent independence of picture and sound in all films becomes the justification for the invention of a series of totally improbable environments born of the disembodiment of sound: someone plays a sink, a voice roves around a room filled with people, a male/female urinating context is grotesquely simplified, a chair guffaws wildly; a piano moans out an orgasm, and so on. Like all of Snow's major films, this, his longest, takes a technical fact as the generating force for a wholly cinematic presentation of space.

In *Presents* he directs his attention to editing. The results are somewhat less impressive than his earlier films, perhaps because of the enormity of this theme and the weight of original editing strategies by other filmmakers. After a hilarious parody of his own ←→, in which the stage rocks back and forth rather than the camera, he enters an extended series of very short takes, each glimpsing a different place. Then, with *This is it* he made a film of nothing but words. The film speaks to us one word at a time, about its own structure and aspirations, often lying outrageously.

Snow has also published a narrative, self-reflexive book of photographs, *Cover to Cover*, and has issued records of his own compositions, in jazz and concrete music.

—P. Adams Sitney

SOLANAS, Fernando E., and Octavia GETINO.

Argentinian. Solanas born in Buenos Aires, 1936; Getino born in Spain, moved to Argentina, 1952. Solanas studied law, theater, and musical composition. Getino active as writer, also made short documentary *Trasmallos*, early 1960s; Solanas worked in advertising, early 1960s; both enter Cine Liberación group, making underground films, 1966; Perón returned to power, Getino accepted post on national film board, 1973; following military coup against Perón, Solanas moved to Paris, Getino moved to Peru, working for TV, 1976; Getino moved to Mexico as member of Film Dept. of the Universidad Autónoma de México, 1982. Recipient: Solanas, Best Director Award, Cannes Festival, for *Sur*, 1988.

Films as Directors:

1968 *La hora de los hornos (The Hour of the Furnaces)* (Solanas d, co-sc, co-ph, ed, mus; Getino co-sc, sound)
1971 *Perón: actualización politica y doctrinaria para la toma del poder; Perón: La revolución justicialista* (both films made as part of Grupo de Cine Liberación)
1973 *El familiar* (Getino only)
1976 *Los hijos de Fierro* (Solanas only)
1978 *La familia Pichilin* (Getino only) (not yet released)
1979 *La mirada de los otros (Régard des autres)* (doc) (Solanas only)
1986 *Tangos—el exilio de Gardel (Tangos—l'exil de Gardel)* (Solanas only)
1988 *Sur* (Solanas only)

Publications:

By SOLANAS AND GETINO: books—

Cine, cultura y descolonización, Mexico City, 1973.
Getino, Octavio, *Notas sobre cine argentino y latinoamericano*, Mexico City, 1984.

By SOLANAS AND GETINO: articles—

"Cinema as a Gun," an interview with Solanas by Gianni Volpi and others, in *Cineaste* (New York), Fall 1969.
"Fernando Solanas: An Interview," in *Film Quarterly* (Berkeley), Fall 1970.
Getino, Octavio, and Fernando Solanas, "Towards a Third Cinema," in *Cineaste* (New York), Winter 1971.
Solanas, Fernando, and others, "Situation et perspectives du cinéma d'Amérique Latine," in *Positif* (Paris), June 1972.
"Dar espacio a la expresión popular," Solanas interview in *Cine Cubano* (Havana), no. 86/88, 1973.
"Argentina: Fernando Solanas," an interview with Don Ranvaud, in *Framework* (Norwich), Spring 1979.
Solanas, Fernando, and others, "Round Table: The Cinema: Art Form or Political Weapon," in *Framework* (Norwich), Autumn 1979.
"Godard on Solanas/Solanas on Godard," in *Reviewing Histories*, edited by Coco Fusco, Buffalo, New York, 1987.
"The Tango of Esthetics and Politics," interview with Solanas by Coco Fusco in *Cineaste* (New York), vol. 16, nos. 1/2, 1987/1988.
"De *La hora de los hornos* a *Sur*: Entrevista con Fernando Solanas," with Luis Gastelum, in *Dicine* (Mexico City), September 1989.

On SOLANAS AND GETINO: books—

Pick, Zuzana Mirjam, *Latin American Filmmakers and the Third Cinema*, Ottawa, 1978.
King, John, and Nissa Torrents, editors, *The Garden of Forking Paths: Argentine Cinema*, London, 1988.
Pines, Jim, and Paul Willemen, editors, *Questions of Third Cinema*, London, 1989.
King, John, *Magical Reels: A History of Cinema in Latin America*, London, 1990.

On SOLANAS AND GETINO: articles—

Matthews, John, " . . . And After?: A Response to Solanas and Getino," in *Afterimage* (London), Summer 1971.
Wilson, David, "Aspects of Latin American Political Cinema," in *Sight and Sound* (London), Summer 1972.
Burton, Julianne, "The Camera as 'Gun': Two Decades of Culture and Resistance in Latin America," in *Latin American Perspectives*, Winter 1978.
Hennebelle, Guy, "Le Réalisme magique et les élans du coeur," in *Ecran* (Paris), 15 March 1979.
Stam, Robert, "*Hour of the Furnaces* and the Two Avant-Gardes," in *Millennium* (New York), Fall/Winter 1980/81.
"Solanas Issue" of *Avant-Scène du Cinéma* (Paris), January/February 1989.

*   *   *

Originators of the pivotal "third cinema" concept, Solanas and Getino demonstrated its practice in the only really important film they were to make—the influential *La hora de los hornos*. "Third cinema" was the product of a very specific context: the world-wide insurrections during the late 1960s. While U.S. students were burning banks in protest against the Vietnam war, Argentina moved close to genuine social revolution for the first time in its history. Solanas and Getino participated in that movement as cineastes, but they made it clear that their concern was with social change, not film art, in their first declaration as the Cine Liberacion Group: "Our commitment as cineastes in a dependent country is not with universal culture or art or abstract man; before anything else it is with the liberation of our country and the Latin American peoples."

As intellectuals and artists in a neo-colonial situation, Solanas and Getino were greatly influenced by the "Third Worldism" of the period, frequently citing ideologists from the African (Frantz Fanon) and Asian (Mao Tse-Tung) struggles. They contrasted "third cinema" to the "first cinema" of the Hollywood industry and to the auteurist "second cinema" in various ways, distinguishing it first of all for its ideological commitment to anti-imperialism and the struggle for socialism. Against the consumerism provoked by the hermetic narrative structures of Hollywood, they proposed a cinema which would require active audience participation. Thus, a film was important as a "detonator" or a "pretext" for assembling a group, not as an experience that was born and died on the screen. Likening themselves to guerillas who open paths with machete blows, they perceived cinema as a provisional tool: "Our time is one of hypothesis rather than thesis, a time of works in process—unfinished, unordered, violent works made with the camera in one hand and a rock in the other."

The most realized description of "third cinema" can be found near the end of their often-reprinted essay, "Towards a Third Cinema." There they summarize it in the following manner: "The third cinema above all counters the film industry of a cinema of characters with one of themes, that of individuals with that of masses, that of the author with that of the operative group, one of neocolonial misinformation with one of information, one of escape with one that recaptures the truth, that of passivity with that of aggressions. To an institutionalized cinema, it counterposes a guerilla cinema; to movies as shows, it opposes a film act . . . to a cinema made for the old kind of human being, it proposes a *cinema fit for a new kind of human being, for what each one of us has the possibility of becoming.*"

Given their concern to produce a cinema of information rather than one of fantasies to be consumed, the obvious path led to the documentary. However, they conceived of the documentary as "not fundamentally one which illustrates, documents, or passively establishes a situation; rather it attempts to intervene in the situation as an element providing thrust or rectification . . . it provides discovery through transformation." *La Hora de los hornos* may be a bit too didactic at times, but it was certainly more "revolutionary" than the documentaries they were to make as the official cineastes they became on the return of Juan Perón, the urban populist who was President of Argentina (1946–55 and 1973–74).

Because of the timeliness of *La Hora de los hornos* and due to the extensive publication of Solanas' and Getino's theoretical writings and interviews, they have received attention which may be disproportionate to that given to other Latin American cineastes of greater achievement, most notably the Cubans. Nonetheless, the French film critic Guy Hennebelle argued that "third cinema" is the concept that seems to be "most viable" as a counterpoint to traditional film study, stating, "According to this perspective, a veritable 'counter-history' of the seventh art is yet to be written." In both their writings and their cinematic practice, Solanas and Getino have provided an alternative and a clearly articulated challenge to bourgeois cinema.

—John Mraz

SOLAS, Humberto.

Cuban. Born in Havana, December 1942. Studied architecture, 1957. Involved in insurrectionary movement against Batista government, 1957–59; member of Instituto Cubano de Arte e Industria Cinematografico (ICAIC), from 1959; directed first film in collaboration with Hector Veitia, under supervision of Joris Ivens, 1961; Licenciatura in History, University of Havana, 1978.

Films as Director:

1961   *Casablanca*
1962   *Minerva traduce el mar* (co-d)
1963   *Variaciones*; *El retrato*
1964   *El acoso*
1965   *La acusation*; *Manuela*
1968   **Lucia**
1972   *Un dia de Noviembre*
1974   *Simparele*
1975   *Cantata de Chile*
1977   *Nacer en Leningrado* (short)
1978   *Wilfredo Lam*
1982   *Cecilia Valdés*
1983   *Amada*
1986   *Un hombre de exito* (*A Successful Man*)

Publications:

By SOLAS: articles—

Interview with Pastor Vega, in *Cine Cubano* (Havana), no. 42/44, 1967.
Interviews with Gerardo Chijona, in *Ecran* (Paris), January 1977, and in *Cine Cubano* (Havana), March 1978.
Interview with Julianne Burton and Marta Alvear, in *Jump Cut* (Chicago), December 1978.
Interview with J. King, in *Framework* (Norwich), Spring 1979.
"Reflexiones," in *Cine Cubano* (Havana), no. 102, 1982.
"Alrededor de una dramaturgia cinematográfica latinoamericano," in *Cine Cubano* (Havana), no. 105, 1983.
Interview in *Cine Cubano* (Havana), no. 116, 1986.
Interview with P.L. Thirard and P.A. Paranagua in *Positif* (Paris), December 1988.

On SOLAS: books—

Nelson, L., *Cuba: The Measure of a Revolution*, Minneapolis, 1972.
Myerson, Michael, *Memories of Underdevelopment: The Revolutionary Films of Cuba*, New York, 1973.
Chanan, Michael, *The Cuban Image*, London, 1985.
Burton, Julianne, editor, *Cinema and Social Change in Latin America: Conversations with Filmmakers*, Austin, Texas, 1986.

On SOLAS: articles—

Sutherland, Elizabeth, "Cinema of Revolution—Ninety Miles From Home," in *Film Quarterly* (Berkeley), Winter 1961/62.
Adler, Renata, in the *New York Times*, 10, 11 and 12 February 1969.
Engel, Andi, "Solidarity and Violence," in *Sight and Sound* (London), Autumn 1969.
Biskind, P., "*Lucia*: Struggles With History," in *Jump Cut* (Chicago), July/August 1974.
Mraz, John, "*Lucia*: History and Film in Revolutionary Cuba," in *Film and History* (Newark, New Jersey), February 1975.
Kovacs, Steven, "*Lucia*: Style and Meaning in Revolutionary Film," in *Monthly Review* (New York), June 1975.
"Solas Issue" of *Jump Cut* (Chicago), December 1978.

*   *   *

Perhaps the foremost practitioner of the historical genre for which Cuban cinema has achieved international acclaim, Humberto Solas is a member of the first generation of directors to mature under the revolution. Of humble origins, Solas became an urban guerrilla at 14 and later left school altogether because, "It was a very unstable time to try to study. Either Batista (dictator of Cuba) closed down the university, or we

Humberto Solas

did." Prior to the triumph of the revolution, being a filmmaker "seemed like an unrealizable dream," but Solas financed a short film out of his savings and was invited to join the Cuban Film Institute (ICAIC) soon after its founding in 1959. Although it is customary for Cuban directors to serve an extensive apprenticeship in documentaries, Solas directed several early fiction shorts as well. He considers his imitating of European film styles in these works to be typical of feelings of cultural inferiority and alienation in the underdeveloped world, and affirms: "Neither me, nor my generation, nor my country can be seen in any of these films."

Historical subjects proved to be Solas's avenue to Cuban and Latin American reality. He believes that the importance attached to historical films in Cuba derives from the fact that "Our history had been filtered through a bourgeois lens. We lack a coherent, lucid, and dignified appreciation of our national past." *Manuela*, a medium-length film on the guerrilla war in the mountains, was the first of Solas's works to embody "more genuinely Cuban forms of expression." His continuing search for national (and Latin American) cinematic idioms and themes led him to direct his masterpiece to date, *Lucía*, at age 26. Focusing on three periods of Cuban history through the characters of representative women, Solás used three different film styles to portray forms of experience and cognition during these epochs. In his later films, Solas interpretively analyzed

the history of Haiti (*Simparele*), Chile (*Cantata de Chile*), and slavery in Cuba (*Cecilia Valdés*). These works are marked by an exciting blend of music, dance, documentary footage, primitive painting, and the re-enactment of historical events in an operatic style.

Solas considers his films "historical melodramas," in which a Marxist perspective provides a materialistic explanation for events and personal psychology. He contrasts this to common melodrama and its "particular world of valorative abstractions" which determine events, but lack the power to explain them. For example, although the travails suffered by the heroines of *Lucía* are experienced personally, they are depicted as deriving specifically from the colonial and neo-colonial situation of Cuba (and vestigial machismo), rather than from any "eternal passions" which have no relationship to concrete historical circumstances.

For Solas, historical cinema is always a dialogue about the present, and he has often chosen women as a central metaphor in his films because, as a dominated group, they feel more deeply and reflect more immediately the contradictions of society—for example, the maintenance of archaic forms such as *machismo* in a revolutionary situation. As Solas states: "The sad masquerade of limited, archetyped, and suffocating human relations in defense of private property is most transparent in the case of the women—half of humanity. The pathetic carnival of economic exploitation begins there." To Solas, the past is only present insofar as it continues to condition (for both good and bad) the lives of people today. It is about this past/present that Humberto Solas has made and continues to make beautiful and moving cinema.

—John Mraz

SPIELBERG, Steven.

American. Born in Cincinnati, Ohio, 18 December 1947. Educated California State College at Long Beach, BA in English, 1970. Married 1) actress Amy Irving (divorced) one son. Won amateur film contest with 40-minute film *Escape to Nowhere*, 1960; on strength of film *Amblin'*, became TV director for Universal, late 1960s; TV work included episodes of *Marcus Welby, M.D., Columbo* and *Night Gallery*, and TV films, including *Duel*, then given theatrical release; directed first feature, *The Sugarland Express*, 1974; formed own production company, *Amblin Productions*; Address: c/o Amblin Productions, Burbank Studios, 4000 Warner Blvd., Burbank, CA 91522, U.S.A.

Films as Director, Scriptwriter and Producer:

1971　*Duel* (for TV)
1974　*The Sugarland Express*
1975　**Jaws**
1977　**Close Encounters of the Third Kind** (2nd version released 1980)
1979　*1941*
1981　**Raiders of the Lost Ark**
1982　**E.T.—The Extraterrestrial**
1983　episode of *The Twilight Zone—The Movie*
1984　*Indiana Jones and the Temple of Doom*
1986　**The Color Purple**
1987　*Empire of the Sun*
1989　*Indiana Jones and the Last Crusade*
1990　*Always*

Steven Spielberg

Other Films:

1973   *Ace Eli and Rodger of the Skies* (Erman) (story)
1978   *I Want to Hold Your Hand* (Zemeckis) (pr)
1980   *Used Cars* (Zemeckis); *The Blues Brothers* (Landis) (role)
1982   *Poltergeist* (Hooper) (pr)
1984   *Gremlins* (Dante)
1985   *Back to the Future* (Zemeckis) (exec pr); *Young Sherlock Holmes* (Levinson) (exec pr)
1986   *The Money Pit* (Benjamin) (exec pr)
1988   *Who Framed Roger Rabbit?* (Zemeckis) exec pr)
1989   *An American Tail 2* (Nibbelink) (pr)
1990   *Schindler's List* (Scorsese) (pr)
1991   *Cape Fear* (Scorsese) (exec pr)

Publications:

By SPIELBERG: book—

The Sugarland Express—Spielberg, Barwood and Robbins, Zsigmond, edited by Rochelle Reed, Washington, D.C., 1974.

By SPIELBERG: articles—

Steven Spielberg Seminar, in *Dialogue on Film* (Washington, D.C.), July 1974.
"From Television to Features," interview with M. Stettin, in *Millimeter* (New York), March 1975.

"Close Encounter of the Third Kind: Director Steve Spielberg," with C. Austin, in *Filmmakers Newsletter* (Ward Hill, Massachusetts), December 1977.
"The Unsung Heroes or Credit Where Credit is Due," in *American Cinematographer* (Los Angeles), January 1978.
Interview with Mitch Tuchman, in *Film Comment* (New York), January/February 1978.
"Directing *1941*," in *American Cinematographer* (Los Angeles), December 1979.
"Of Narrow Misses and Close Calls," in *American Cinematographer* (Los Angeles), November 1981.
Interview with T. McCarthy in *Film Comment* (New York), May/June 1982.
"Dialogue on Film: Steven Spielberg," in *American Film* (Los Angeles), June 1988.

On SPIELBERG: books—

Pye, Michael, and Lynda Myles, *The Movie Brats: How the Film Generation Took Over Hollywood*, London, 1979.
Kolker, Robert Phillip, *A Cinema of Loneliness: Penn, Kubrick, Scorsese, Spielberg, Altman*, Oxford, 1980; revised edition, 1988.
Crawley, Tony, *The Steven Spielberg Story*, London, 1983.
Goldau, Ant je, and Hans Helmut Prinzler, *Spielberg: Film als Spielzeug*, Berlin, 1985.
Mott, Donald R., and Cheryl McAllister Saunders, *Steven Spielberg*, Boston, 1986.

Smith, Thomas G., *Industrial Light and Magic: The Art of Special Effects*, London, 1986.

Weiss, Ulli, *Das Neue Hollywood: Francis Ford Coppola, Steven Spielberg, Martin Scorsese*, Munich, 1986.

Godard, Jean-Pierre, *Spielberg*, Paris, 1987.

Sinyard, Neil, *The Films of Steven Spielberg*, London, 1987.

On SPIELBERG: articles—

Eyles, A., "Steven Spielberg," in *Focus on Film* (London), Winter 1972.

Cumbow, R.C., "The Great American Eating Machine," in *Movietone News* (Seattle), 11 October 1976.

Cook, B., "Close Encounters with Steven Spielberg," in *American Film* (Washington, D.C.), November 1977.

Jameson, R.T., "Style vs. 'Style'," in *Film Comment* (New York), March/April 1980.

Geng, Veronica, "Spielberg's Express," in *Film Comment* (New York), July/August 1981.

Auty, Chris, "The Complete Spielberg?," in *Sight and Sound* (London), Autumn 1982.

Turner, G.E., "Steven Spielberg and *E.T.—the Extra-Terrestrial*," in *American Cinématographer* (Los Angeles), January 1983.

McGillivray, D., "The Movie Brats: Steven Spielberg," in *Films and Filming* (London), May 1984.

Smetak, J.R., "Summer at the Movies, Steven Spielberg: Gore, Guts and PG-13," in *Journal of Film and Popular Television* (Washington D.C.), Spring 1986.

Britton, Andrew, "Blissing Out: The Politics of Reaganite Entertainment," in *Movie* (London), Winter 1986.

Combs, Richard, "Master Steven's Search for the Sun," in *Listener* (London), February 1988.

*   *   *

Perhaps any discussion of Steven Spielberg must inevitably begin with the consideration that as of 1991, Spielberg remains the most commercially successful director the world has yet seen—an incredible, if mind-boggling proposition which, in another time, might have immediately made the director's films ineligible for serious critical consideration. Yet the fact that Spielberg's combined films have grossed well over one billion dollars attests to their power in connecting to the mass audience and offers the analyst an immediate conundrum which may take a more distanced generation of critics and filmgoers to answer fully: What does Spielberg know? And why has so much of his work invited such audience approval?

Spielberg has worked in a variety of genres: the television film *Duel* is a thriller; *Jaws* is a horror film; *1941* is a crazy comedy; *Close Encounters of the Third Kind* is a science-fiction film; *Raiders of the Lost Ark* is an adventure film patterned after film serials of the early fifties; *E.T.—The Extraterrestrial* is a fantasy/family film combining elements from *The Wizard of Oz*, *Lassie*, and *Peter Pan*; *The Color Purple* is a social drama; *Empire of the Sun* is an expansive war-time epic. And yet virtually all of Spielberg's films are united by the same distinctive vision: a vision imbued with a sense of wonder which celebrates the magic and mystery that imagination can reveal as an alternative to the humdrum and the everyday. The artistic consistency within Spielberg's work is demonstrated further by his narratives, which are structurally similar. In the typical Spielberg film, an Everyman protagonist has his conception of the world enlarged (often traumatically) as he comes face to face with some extraordinary and generally non-human antagonist who is often hidden from the rest of the world and/or the audience until the narrative's end. In *Duel*, a California businessman named Mann finds himself pitted against the monstrous truck whose driver's face is never shown; in *Jaws*, the water-shy sheriff must face an almost mythological shark whose jaws are not clearly shown until the final reel; in *Close Encounters*, a suburban father responds to the extrasensory messages sent by outer-space creatures who are not revealed

until the last sequence of the film; in *Raiders of the Lost Ark*, Indiana Jones quests for the Lost Ark which does not let forth its Pandora's Box of horrors until summoned up by those who would attempt to profit from it; and, of course, in *E.T.*, a small boy whose life is already steeped in imagination keeps secret his adoption of a playful extra-terrestrial (although one could easily argue that the non-human antagonist here is not really the sensitive E.T., but the masked and terrifying government agents who, quietly working behind the scenes throughout the narrative, finally invade the suburban house and crystallize the protagonist's most horrific fears). Structural analysis even reveals that *Poltergeist*, the Spielberg-produced Tobe Hooper-directed film which relates to Spielberg's career in the same way the Howard Hawks-produced Christian Nyby-directed *The Thing* related to Hawks's career, is indeed a continuation of the Spielberg canon. In *Poltergeist*, a typical American family ultimately discovers that the antagonists responsible for the mysterious goings-on in their suburban home are the otherworldly ghosts and skeletons not shown until the end of the film when the narrative also reveals the villainy of the real estate developer who had so cavalierly disposed of the remains from an inconveniently located cemetery.

Technically proficient and dazzling, Spielberg's films are voracious in their synthesis of the popular culture icons which have formed the director's sensibilities: Hitchcock movies, John Wayne, comic books, *Bambi*, suburban homes, fast food, the space program, television. His vision is that of the child-artist—the innocent and profound imagination that can summon up primeval dread from the deep as well as transcendent wonder from the sky. If Spielberg's films are sometimes attacked for a certain lack of interest in social issues or "adult concerns," they may be defended on the grounds that his films—unlike so many of the "special effects" action films of the 1970s and 1980s—derive from a sensibility which is sincerely felt. A more subtle attack on Spielberg would hold that his interest in objects and mechanical effects (as in *1941* and *Raiders of the Lost Ark*), though provocative, may not always be in perfect balance with his interest in sentiment and human values. Spielberg himself acknowledges his debt to Walt Disney, whose theme "When You Wish Upon a Star," a paean to faith and imagination, dictates the spirit of several Spielberg films. And yet certainly if intellectual and persuasive critical constructions be sought to justify our enjoyment of Spielberg's cinema, they can easily be found in the kind of mythic, Jungian criticism which analyzes his very popular work as a kind of direct line to the collective unconscious. *Jaws*, for instance, is related to the primal fear of being eaten as well as to the archetypal initiation rite; *Close Encounters* is constructed according to the archetypal form of the quest and its attendant religious structures of revelation and salvation; and of course *E.T.* has already been widely analyzed as a re-telling of the Christ story—complete with a sacred heart, a ritual death, a resurrection brought about by faith, and an eventual ascension into heaven as E.T. returns home.

If Spielberg is especially notable in any other way, it is perhaps that he represents the most successful example of what has been called the film school generation which is increasingly populating the new Hollywood: a generation which has been primarily brought up on television and film, rather than literature, and for whom film seems apparently to have replaced life as a repository of significant experience. And yet if the old Hollywood's studio system is dead, it has been partially replaced by a solid, if informal matrix of friendships and alliances: between Spielberg and a fraternity that includes George Lucas, Francis Ford Coppola, Lawrence Kasdan, John Milius, Bob Zemeckis, Robert Gale, Hal Barwood, Matthew Robbins, Melissa Mathison, and Harrison Ford. Worthy of note as well, in regard to the community in which Spielberg finds himself, is the fact that Hollywood, though consistently accused of a preference for box-office appeal over critical acclaim, has nevertheless refused—despite Spielberg's popular and critical success—to valorize publicly Spielberg's work. The Academy of Motion Picture Arts and Sciences has consistently chosen to pass over Spielberg's films and direction—in 1975 bypassing *Jaws* in favor of *One Flew Over the Cuckoo's Nest* and Milos Forman; in 1977, bypassing *Close Encounters* for *Annie Hall* and Woody Allen; in 1981 bypassing *Raiders of the Lost Ark* for *Chariots of Fire* and Warren Beatty (as director of *Reds*); in 1982 bypassing *E.T.* for *Ghandi* and Richard Attenborough; and in 1985 bypassing *The Color Purple* for *Out of Africa* and Sydney Pollack.

More than requiring an explanatory footnote in film history texts, these "slights" make it increasingly clear that the industry has come to hold Spielberg responsible for the juvenilization of the American cinema in the late 1970s and 1980s. The overwhelming number of Spielberg imitators, many producing films under Spielberg's own auspices, have largely contributed commercially successful hackwork. There is irony, too, in that it was in the Spielberg production of *The Twilight Zone* movie (directed by John Landis), that two children and actor Vic Morrow should have been killed in a clearly avoidable accident in which the children's employment violated child-labor law. *The Color Purple*, although conforming to Spielberg's typical pattern of the hidden antagonist, backed off from an explicit representation of Celie's lesbianism, turning her instead into a cute E.T.-like creature. Thus the confrontation of the hidden antagonist (Celie's true nature) becomes a kind of missing climax in a film which many critics ridiculed. *Always*, a remake of *A Guy Named Joe* in which Spielberg tried to portray adult relationships within a fantasy context which included ghostly spirits, was both a critical and financial failure.

A variety of open questions remain: If the Coppolas and Scorseses attempted to remake Hollywood to their own vision of a freer, more European, artistic sensibility, should Spielberg now be held responsible for a betrayal of their earlier victories? Is there a point at which Spielberg, in his insistence on avoiding adult themes and his continuing refuge in nostalgia, remakes, and sequels, must take responsibility for an incredibly pernicious influence which has almost taken on a life of its own and which has demonstrably prevented non-Spielberg varieties of film from being produced? As America in the 1990s moves slowly away from the Reagan era, will Spielberg find new materials and adult themes, or will he seek continuing refuge in tried and true formulas? And will those formulas continue to work? And finally, will Spielberg manage to successfully mediate his apparent dual interests—being a modern day mogul in the style of Walt Disney or Cecil B. De Mille as well as being a respected artist whose work requires no apology?

—Charles Derry

STAHL, John M.

American. Born in New York City, 21 January 1886. Educated in New York City public schools. Married Roxana Wray, 1932. Actor on stage and later in films, from 1901; hired by Vitagraph Studio, Brooklyn, as director, 1914; moved to Hollywood, worked for Louis B. Mayer in independent pro-

ductions then at MGM, 1917; vice-president and directorial producer, Tiffany-Stahl Studios, 1928; sold interest in studio and joined Universal, 1930. *Died 12 January 1950.*

Films as Director:

(incomplete listing prior to 1918):

1914 *The Boy and the Law*
1917 *The Lincoln Cycle* (14-reeler distributed in 6 chapters including *My Mother, My Father, My Self, The Call to Arms*)
1918 *Scandal Mongers*; *Wives of Men* (+ sc); *Suspicion*
1919 *Her Code of Honor*; *A Woman Under Oath*
1920 *Greater Than Love*; *Women Men Forget*; *The Woman in His House*; *Sowing the Wind*; *The Child Thou Gavest Me* (+ pr)
1922 *The Song of Life*; *One Clear Call* (+ pr); *Suspicious Wives*
1923 *The Wanters* (+ pr); *The Dangerous Age* (+ pr)
1924 *Why Men Leave Home*; *Husbands and Lovers* (+ pr)
1925 *Fine Clothes*
1926 *Memory Lane* (+ pr, co-sc); *The Gay Deceiver*
1927 *Lovers?* (+ pr); *In Old Kentucky* (+ pr)
1930 *A Lady Surrenders*
1931 *Seed*; *Strictly Dishonorable*
1932 *Back Street*
1933 *Only Yesterday*
1934 *Imitation of Life*
1935 *Magnificent Obsession*
1937 *Parnell*
1938 *Letter of Introduction* (+ pr)
1939 *When Tomorrow Comes* (+ pr)
1941 *Our Wife*
1942 *The Immortal Sergeant*
1943 *Holy Matrimony*
1944 *The Eve of St. Mark*; *The Keys of the Kingdom*
1946 *Leave Her to Heaven*
1947 *Forever Amber* (replaced by Otto Preminger); *The Foxes of Harrow*
1948 *The Walls of Jericho*
1949 *Father Was a Fullback*; *Oh, You Beautiful Doll*

Publications:

By STAHL: article—

"Oh, the Good Old Days," in *The Hollywood Reporter*, 16 May 1932.

On STAHL: books—

Glèdhill, Christine, editor, *Home is Where the Heart Is: Studies in Melodrama and the Woman's Film*, London, 1987.

On STAHL: articles—

Obituary, in *The New York Times*, 14 January 1950.
Sarris, Andrew, "Esoterica," in *Film Culture* (New York), Spring 1963.
Morris, G., "John M. Stahl: The Man Who Understood Women," in *Film Comment* (New York), May/June 1977.
Pulleine, Tim, "Stahl into Sirk," in *Monthly Film Bulletin* (London), November 1981.
Renov, Michael, "*Leave Her to Heaven*: The Double Bind of Post-War Women," in *Journal of the University Film and Video Association*, Winter 1983.

*   *   *

John Stahl was a key figure in the development of the Hollywood "women's melodrama" during the 1930s and 1940s, and quite possibly in the 1910s and 1920s as well. Although he began directing in 1914, and apparently made as many films before sound as after, only two of his silents (*Her Code of Honor* and *Suspicious Wives*) seem to have survived. Yet this is hardly the only reason that the ultimate critical and historical significance of his work remains to be established. More pertinent is the critical disrepute of the "tearjerker" genre in which

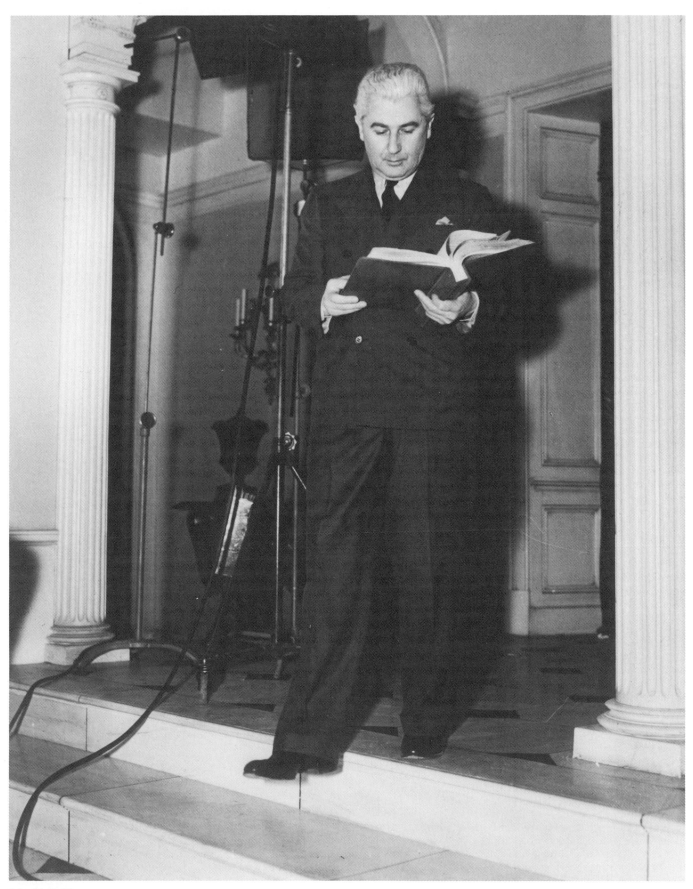

John M. Stahl

he worked almost exclusively—a genre which had to await the discovery of Douglas Sirk's melodramas and the reworking of the form by R.W. Fassbinder to attract serious critical attention.

Comparisons between Sirk's baroquely aestheticized and Stahl's straightforwardly unadorned treatments of equally improbable plots is somewhat useful, and virtually inevitable, given that Sirk remade three of Stahl's classic 1930s "weepies": *Imitation of Life* (1934/1959), *Magnificent Obsession* (1935/1954), and *When Tomorrow Comes* (1939), which became *Interlude* (1957). In a genre focusing on the problems presented by the social/sexual order for the individual (most frequently, the bourgeois female), Sirk tended to abstract dramatic conflicts in the direction of Brecht, while Stahl chose to emphasize the effects of social rigidities through the emotions of his characters.

Stahl's career seemed to flourish most at Universal in the 1930s with the highly accomplished *Back Street, Only Yesterday*, and the three films Sirk remade, all of which present emotionally similar heroines buffeted by twists of fate which wreak havoc on their socially-determined modes of behavior. In his version of Fannie Hurst's *Back Street* (remade in 1941 and 1961), Stahl encourages sympathy with Irene Dunne, an independent working woman who gives up everything to be "kept" in isolation by the respectable married man she loves. Audacious contradictions emerge from the very simplicity with which Stahl presents outrageous plot twists. Dunne meets the "kept woman" next door to her back street apartment, for example, only when the woman literally catches on fire and must be rescued. Recognizing a sister in shame, Dunne counsels the injured woman against allowing herself to be exploited by the man she loves; yet what seems to be a dawning moment of self-awareness on the part of our heroine is instantly obscured by a romantic haze when her own lover walks through the door in the middle of her diatribe. Similarly powerful contradictions abound in *Imitation of Life* (based on another Hurst novel), where best friends Claudette Colbert and Louise Beavers find themselves incapable, despite their best intentions, of breaking the social conventions which keep the black woman subservient to the white, even when the former is responsible for the latter's wealth and success.

Given material such as Fannie Hurst, the "inspirational" message of Lloyd C. Douglas's *Magnificent Obsession*, and the hopelessly romantic *Only Yesterday* (virtually remade as Max Ophüls's *Letter from an Unknown Woman*), and considering the period during which Stahl worked, the point of reference seems not to be Sirk so much as Stahl's better-appreciated contemporary Frank Borzage. It is Borzage's unrelenting romanticism which is usually assumed to characterize the "weepies" of the 1920s and 1930s; yet Stahl's work offers another perspective. While he clearly encourages emotional identification with his heroines, Stahl seems more interested in exposing their romantic illusions than in relishing them. In fact, his meditative restraint in such situations has prompted George Morris to suggest that "it is Carl Th. Dreyer whom Stahl resembles more than directors like Sirk or Borzage." Yet ultimately, Stahl's visual style seems largely dependent upon studio and cinematographer, a fact most clearly demonstrated by *Leave Her to Heaven*, a preposterously plotted drama of a psychotically duplicitous woman shot in Technicolor by Leon Shamroy on the modernesque sets of 20th Century-Fox, where the director's mise-en-scène emerges as florid and baroque as Sirk in his heyday—and a full decade earlier.

It seems that Stahl's films represent something of a missing link between Borzage's romanticism and Sirk's distancation. Certainly, an examination of his work expands an understanding of the variety of Hollywood's strategies in personalizing overtly ideological questions of sex, status, and money. In fact, if film scholars are serious about studying the melodrama in any depth, then the films of John Stahl remain a top and current priority.

—Ed Lowry

————

STAUDTE, Wolfgang.

German. Born in Saarbrücken, 9 October 1906. Educated as engineer. Stage actor for Max Reinhardt and Erwin Piscator, until 1933; film actor, from 1931; writer and director of advertising films and shorts, 1930s; directed first feature, *Akrobat schö-ö-ön*, for Tobis Film, also co-founder, with Harald Braun and Helmut Kaütner, "Freie Film-Produktion-GmbH," 1943; worked for DEFA Studios, East Germany, 1945; worked in West Germany, from 1953; TV director, from 1970s. Recipient: Silver Lion, Venice Festival, for *Ciske de Rat*, 1955. *Died of heart failure, in Zigarski, 19 January 1984.*

Films as Director:

1943 *Akrobat schö-ö-ön* (+ sc)
1944 *Ich hab' von Dir geträumt*
1945 *Frau über Bord*
1946 *Die Mörder sind unter uns* (*The Murderers Are Among Us*) (+ sc)
1948 *Die seltsamen Abenteuer des Herrn Fridolin B.* (+ sc)
1949 *Rotation* (+ co-sc); *Schicksal aus zweiter Hand* (+ sc); *Der Untertan* (*The Submissive*) (+ co-sc)
1953 *Die Geschichte des kleinen Muck* (*The Story of Little Mook*) (+ co-sc)
1954 *Leuchtfeuer* (+ co-sc)
1955 *Ciske—Ein Kind braucht Liebe* (*Ciske—A Child Wants Love*) (+ sc)
1957 *Rose Bernd*
1958 *Kanonen-Serenade* (*The Muzzle*) (+ co-sc); *Madeleine und der Legionär*; *Der Maulkorb*
1959 *Rosen für den Staatsanwalt* (*Roses for the Prosecutor*) (+ story)
1960 *Kirmes* (*Kermes*) (+ sc); *Der letzte Zeuge* (*The Last Witness*)
1962 *Die glücklichen Jahre der Thorwalds* (co-d)
1963 *Die Dreigroschenoper* (*The Threepenny Opera*)
1964 *Herrenpartie* (*Me's Outing*); *Das Lamm* (*The Lamb*)
1966 *Ganovenehre* (*Hoodlum's Honor*)
1968 *Heimlichkeiten* (+ sc)
1970 *Die Herren mit der weissen Weste* (*Those Gentlemen Who Have a Clean Sheet*)
1971 *Fluchtweg St. Pauli—Grossalarm für die Davidswache*
1972 *Verrat ist kein Gesselschaftsspiel* (for TV); *Marya Sklodowska-Curie. Ein Mädchen, das die Welt verändert* (for TV)
1973 *Nerze Nachts am Strassenrand* (for TV); *The Seawolf*
1974 *Ein herrliches Dasein*
1976 *Zwei Erfahrungen Reicher* (for TV)
1978 *Des Verschollene Inka-Gold* (for TV); *Zwischengleis* (*Memories*)

Other Films:

1931 *Gassenhauer* (Pick) (role)
1945 *Der Mann, dem man den Namen stahl* (co-sc)
1949 *Das Beil von Wandsbek* (co-sc)
1950 *Geheimnis des blauen Zimmers* (role); *Tannenberg* (role); *Der Choral von Leuthen* (role); *Heimkehr ins Glück* (role); *Pechmarie* (role); *Die Bande von Hoheneck* (role);

Wolfgang Staudte

Schwarzer Jäger Johanna (role); *Stärker als Paragraphen* (role); *Gleisdreieck* (role); *Susanne im Bade* (role); *Am seidenen Faden* (role); *Lauter Lügen* (role); *Pour le mérite* (role); *Mordsache Holm* (role); *Spiel im Sommerwind* (role); *Das Gewehr über* (role); *Die fremde Frau* (role); *Drei Unteroffiziere* (role); *Brand im Ozean* (role); *Legion Condor* (role); *Blutsbrüderschaft* (role); *Aus erster Ehe* (role); *Jud Süss* (role); *Jungens* (role); *Friedemann Bach* (role); *. . . reitet für Deutschland* (role); *Das grosse Spiel* (role)

Publications:

By STAUDTE: article—

"Aber wenn geschlagen wird im diesem Land . . . ," interview, in *Film und Fernsehen* (Berlin), no.5, 1979.

On STAUDTE: articles—

Bachmann, J., "Wolfgang Staudte," in *Film* (London), Summer 1963.
"Kurt Maetzig, Wolfgang Staudte," in *Information* (Wiesbaden), no.3–6, 1976.
Karkosch, K., "Wolfgang Staudte," in *Film und Ton* (Munich), March 1976.

*   *   *

Wolfgang Staudte is one of the few important German directors of the postwar years. *Die Mörder sind unter uns*, the first German postwar film, remains today among the director's best works. A surgeon, Hans Mertens, returns home from the war, becomes an alcoholic, and lives hopelessly among the ruins. His girlfriend Susanne has survived a concentration camp and attempts to help him overcome his apathy. The apathy is quickly dispelled by the appearance of an industrialist, formerly a Nazi, whose outlook remains unchanged and who, just as before, uses deceptive phrases to justify the new situation.

This contemporary material was realized by Staudte in a thoroughly realistic style with expressionistic strokes, in a manner that suggests analogies with Rossellini's *Paisà*. An English critic identified the director as a successor to Lang and Pabst. The phrase "The murderers are among us" became a symbolic expression for the spirit of the time, in which progressive German intellectuals sought every means to reckon with the fascist past. It was not by chance that the film was made in the Soviet sector of Berlin and produced by the newly-founded DEFA studios. Staudte's efforts to interest cultural officials in the western zones in his project met with no success. This was also the case with *Rotation* and *Der Untertan*, a satiric version of Heinrich Mann's novel of the same title, set in an actual embassy.

Staudte was a political artist because, as he said, he was a political person. He had perfect command of a variety of means of expression and narrative forms, and used a rich palette of symbolic images in realistically-structured filmic space. His films often led to comparisons with René Clément and Rossellini. Only his own country—the media and public as well as the authorities—could not accept him and systematically and conclusively thwarted him. In the beginning he was repeatedly labelled a communist because of his association with DEFA and was urged to make West German films. In 1951 he decided to do this, and so began an unhappy period for him which consisted in attempting "to improve the world with the money of people who already find the world to be just fine." He was regularly reproached with fouling his own nest, and was reluctantly reduced to making entertainment films. In its headlong rush toward economic development, West German society wanted to see neither fundamental analysis of the Nazi past, nor pessimistic mistrust directed against the new, American-oriented NRD-model.

Years of harassment by the press and cultural authorities went by with Staudte working away, often in vain, writing unengaging comedies. He nevertheless made a few masterpieces: *Rosen für den Staatsanwalt*, *Kirmes*, and *Herrenpartie*. These films are united by Staudte's conviction that the present and the past are bound together and that man today remains inseparable from yesterday. The most imposing of these films is *Herrenpartie*: it confronts two worlds—that of today's German bourgeoisie, which would gladly bury Nazi memories, and that of a village of Yugoslavian widows who, despite everything, are better able to behave humanely than the Germans.

Wolfgang Staudte ended up making TV detective stories. His case demonstrates that the new German cinema has worthy predecessors who nevertheless remain unappreciated even by their colleagues.

—Maria Racheva

————

Sternberg, Josef von. *See* **von Sternberg, Josef.**

————

STEVENS, George.

American. Born George Cooper Stevens in Oakland, California, 18 December 1904. Married 1) Joan (Stevens) (divorced), one son; 2). Actor and stage manager for father's theatrical company, 1920–21; moved to Hollywood, 1921, worked as assistant and 2nd cameraman, then cameraman; joined Hal Roach as cameraman for Laurel and Hardy shorts, 1927; director of two-reel shorts for Roach, from 1930, and for RKO and Universal, from 1932; directed first feature, *The Cohens and Kellys in Trouble*, 1933; also producer, from 1938; joined U.S. Army Signal Corps, became head of Special Motion Pictures Unit assigned to photograph activities of 6th Army, 1943; Unit awarded citation from General Eisenhower, 1945. Recipient: Oscars for Best Director, for *A Place in the Sun*, 1951, and *Giant*, 1956; Irving G. Thalberg Award, Academy of Motion Picture Arts and Sciences, 1953. *Died in Paris, 9 March 1975.*

Films as Director:

1930   *Ladies Past*
1931   *Call a Cop!*; *High Gear*; *The Kick-Off*; *Mama Loves Papa*
1932   *The Finishing Touch*; *Boys Will Be Boys*; *Family Troubles*
1933   *Should Crooners Marry*; *Hunting Trouble*; *Rock-a-bye Cowboy*; *Room Mates*; *A Divorce Courtship*; *Flirting in the Park*; *Quiet Please*; *Grin and Bear It*; *The Cohens and the Kellys in Trouble*
1934   *Bridal Bail*; *Ocean Swells*; *Bachelor Bait*; *Kentucky Kernels*
1935   *Laddie*; *The Nitwits*; *Alice Adams*; *Annie Oakley*
1936   *Swing Time*
1937   *Quality Street*; *A Damsel in Distress*
1938   *Vivacious Lady* (+ pr)
1939   *Gunga Din* (+ pr)
1940   *Vigil in the Night* (+ pr)
1941   *Penny Serenade* (+ pr)
1942   *Woman of the Year*; *The Talk of the Town* (+ pr)
1943   *The More the Merrier* (+ pr)
1948   *I Remember Mama* (+ co-pr)
1951   **A Place in the Sun** (+ pr)

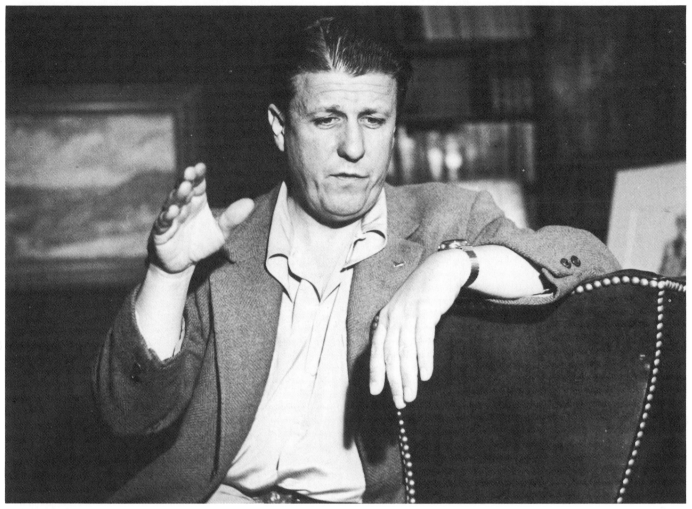

George Stevens

1952 *Something to Live For* (+ pr)
1953 ***Shane*** (+ pr)
1956 ***Giant*** (co-pr)
1959 *The Diary of Anne Frank* (+ pr)
1965 *The Greatest Story Ever Told* (+ pr)
1970 *The Only Game in Town*

Other Films:
(partial list)

1924 *The White Sheep* (cameraman); *The Battling Oriole*
       (cameraman)
1925 *Black Cyclone* (cameraman)
1926 *The Devil Horse* (cameraman); *The Desert's Toll*
       (cameraman); *Putting Pants on Philip* (cameraman)
1927 *No Man's Law* (cameraman); *The Valley of Hell*
       (cameraman); *Lightning* (cameraman); *The Battle of the
       Century* (cameraman)
1928 *Leave 'em Laughing* (cameraman); *Two Tars* (McCarey)
       (cameraman); *Unaccustomed as We Are* (cameraman)
1929 *Big Business* (cameraman)

Publications:

By STEVENS: articles—

Interview, in *Cinema* (Beverly Hills), December/January 1965.
"George Stevens: Shorts to Features: Interview," with Leonard Maltin, in *Action* (Los Angeles), November/December 1970.

On STEVENS: books—

Richie, Donald, *George Stevens: An American Romantic*, New York,
   1970.
Phillips, Gene D., *The Movie Makers: Artists in the Industry*, Chicago,
   1973.
Petri, Bruce, *A Theory of American Film: The Films and Techniques of
   George Stevens*, New York, 1987.

On STEVENS: articles—

"Best Director in Hollywood," in *Time* (New York), 16 February
   1942.
Houston, Penelope, "*Shane* and George Stevens," in *Sight and Sound*
   (London), Fall 1953.
Cecil, N., "George Stevens: Letter," in *Films in Review* (New York),
   February 1954.
Archer, E., "George Stevens and the American Dream," in *Film Cul-
   ture* (New York), no.1, 1957.
Luft, Herbert, "George Stevens," in *Films in Review* (New York),
   November 1958.
Stasey, Joanne, "Hollywood Romantic," in *Films and Filming* (Lon-
   don), July 1959.
Silke, J.R., "The Costumes of George Stevens," in *Cinema* (Beverly
   Hills), November/December 1963.
Bartlett, N., "Sentiment and Humanism," in *Film* (London), Spring
   1964.
"Stevens Issue" of *Cinema* (Beverly Hills), December/January
   1964/65.

McVay, D., "Greatest Stevens," in *Films and Filming* (London), April 1965.

Stanbrook, Alan, "The Return of Shane," in *Films and Filming* (London), May 1966.

Beresford, Bruce, "George Stevens," in *Film* (London), Summer 1970.

"Stevens Issue" of *Dialogue on Film* (Washington, D.C.), no.1, 1972.

Obituary, in *Action* (Los Angeles), March/April 1975.

Beylie, Claude, obituary, in *Ecran* (Paris), May 1975.

"Stevens Issue" of *Dialogue on Film* (Washington, D.C.), May/June 1975.

"A George Stevens Album," in *Action* (Los Angeles), May/June 1975.

Petri, Bruce, "George Stevens: The Wartime Comedies," in *Film Comment* (New York), July/August 1975.

McGilligan, P., and J. McBride, "George Stevens: A Piece of the Rock," in *Bright Lights* (Los Angeles), no.4, 1979.

Adair, Gilbert, "Directors of the Decade: Forties," *Films and Filming* (London), June 1983.

Combs, Richard, "Slow Burner," in *Listener* (London), 12 February 1987.

* * *

Katharine Hepburn had originally been responsible for bringing George Stevens to the attention of those in the front office. He had directed a great many two-reelers for Hal Roach, and was just entering films as a director of features when Hepburn met him, liked him, and asked that he be assigned as director to her next film, *Alice Adams*. It was a giant step forward for Stevens, but *Alice Adams*, from the Booth Tarkington novel, was a project right up his alley.

Two years later Stevens directed Hepburn again in a charming version of Barrie's play, *Quality Street*, and then in 1941 Hepburn again got him over to MGM to direct her and Spencer Tracy in *Woman of the Year*, the first film they did together.

In the first half of his film career Stevens directed a Barbara Stanwyck feature, *Annie Oakley*, one of the best Astaire-Rogers dancing romances, *Swing Time*, and a delightful Ginger Rogers feature, *Vivacious Lady*. Astaire was never more debonair than in the adaption of Wodehouse's novel, *A Damsel in Distress*, with George Burns and Gracie Allen. Stevens then really hit his stride as director of *Gunga Din*, a Kiplingesque glorification of romantic derring-do, with Cary Grant, Victor McLaglen, and Douglas Fairbanks Jr. Two romances, *Vigil in the Night*, starring Carole Lombard, and *Penny Serenade*, co-starring Irene Dunne with Cary Grant, added to his reputation as an ideal director for romance, especially the weepy sort. His final feature before departing for wartime Europe was one of his best, a very funny comedy of the wartime housing situation in the national capital, *The More The Merrier*.

After the war, Stevens decided that he would like to produce and direct something that glorified America's past, preferably a comedy. Fortunately, Stevens had been named by Irene Dunne as one of those she would like to work for as the projected star of *I Remember Mama*.

The film was in production for six months, and went far over schedule and budget. Stevens was a perfectionist, and determined not to be caught short of any piece of film he needed when making his first cut. He shot a master scene fully, with moving camera, and then he shot and kept shooting the same scene from every conceivable angle. For a montage sequence involving Sir Cedric Hardwicke, Stevens spent nearly ten days shooting footage of Sir Cedric reading aloud while the family listened. He overshot, and it was expensive, but the end result was as near perfect as any movie could be. Because of an excessive negative cost ($3,068,000), *I Remember Mama* did not realize the profit it might have earned, although it played five continuous weeks at Radio Music City Hall, where it premiered, gathering rave notices and honors for all concerned.

Stevens had proved that he was back in form and at the top. He moved over to Paramount, where he made two of his best pictures—*A Place in the Sun*, from Theodore Dreiser's American classic, and *An American Tragedy*, with three perfectly-cast players, Montgomery Clift, Elizabeth Taylor, and Shelly Winters. He was the producer-director of one of the most remarkable westerns ever filmed, *Shane*. Told through the eyes of a young boy, the film has a disarming innocence in spite of its violence.

Stevens moved over to Warner Bros. to film Edna Ferber's novel about Texas, *Giant*, with Elizabeth Taylor, Rock Hudson, and James Dean. It was Dean's final credit, for he was killed in an auto crash directly after the shooting of his scenes was finished. Steven's last three features, *The Diary of Anne Frank*, *The Greatest Story Ever Told*, and *The Only Game in Town*, were released by 20th Century-Fox. The last one, the best of the three, was virtually sloughed off in its release. When asked what the story was about, Stevens replied, "It's about an aging hooker and a losing gambler, if you think the world is ready for that." He had become embittered. The climate had changed in Hollywood, and it was difficult to get a first-class release for a picture made with the kind of extravagance Stevens was accustomed to.

—De Witt Bodeen

STEVENSON, Robert.

British/American. Born Buxton, Derbyshire, 1905, became U.S. citizen, 1940. Educated at Shrewsbury School; St. John's College, Cambridge University, degree in Mechanical Sciences, 1926. Married actress Anna Lee, 1933 (divorced 1944). Editor of *Granta* magazine, 1927; scriptwriter, Gaumont British and Gainsborough Studios, from 1929; directed first film, *Happy Ever After*, for UFA in Germany, 1932; signed by David O. Selznick, moved to Hollywood, 1939; served as motion picture producer with U.S. War Dept., from 1942, Major in U.S. Army reserve, 1946–53; director for RKO, late 1940s and early 1950s; director for Walt Disney Productions, 1956–77; also producer, writer and director for TV, from 1950s. *Died in Santa Barbara, California, 30 April 1986.*

Films as Director:

1932 *Happy Ever After* (co-d)
1933 *Falling For You* (co-d)
1936 *Jack of All Trades* (co-d); *Tudor Rose* (*Nine Days a Queen*); *The Man Who Changed His Mind* (*The Man Who Lived Again*)
1937 *King Solomon's Mines*; *Non-Stop New York*
1938 *Owd Bob* (*To the Victor*)
1939 *The Ware Case*; *A Young Man's Fancy*; *Return to Yesterday*
1940 *Tom Brown's Schooldays*
1941 *Back Street*
1942 *Joan of Paris*
1944 *Forever and a Day* (co-d); *Jane Eyre*
1947 *Dishonoured Lady*
1948 *To the Ends of the Earth*
1949 *I Married a Communist* (*The Woman on Pier 13*)
1950 *Walk Softly, Stranger*
1951 *My Forbidden Past*
1952 *The Las Vegas Story*
1957 *Johnny Tremain*; *Old Yeller*
1959 *Darby O'Gill and the Little People*

Robert Stevenson directing Anna Lee and Cedric Hardwicke in *King Solomon's Mines*

1960 Kidnapped; The Absent-Minded Professor
1962 In Search of the Castaways
1963 Son of Flubber
1964 The Misadventures of Merlin Jones; Mary Poppins
1965 The Monkey's Uncle; That Darn Cat
1967 The Gnome Mobile
1968 Blackbeard's Ghost
1969 The Love Bug
1971 Bedknobs and Broomsticks
1974 Herbie Rides Again; The Island at the Top of the World
1975 One of Our Dinosaurs is Missing
1976 The Shaggy D.A.

Publications:

By STEVENSON: book—

Darkness in the Land, London, 1938.

By STEVENSON: articles—

Interviews in Film Weekly (London), 6 August 1938 and 8 April 1939.
Interview in American Film (Washington, D.C.), March 1978.

On STEVENSON: books—

Maltin, Leonard, The Disney Films, New York, 1973; revised edition, 1984.
Holliss, Richard, and Brian Sibley, The Disney Studio Story, London, 1988.

On STEVENSON: articles—

Films in Review (New York), August–September 1969.
Films Illustrated (London), March 1975.
"British Cinema: Robert Stevenson," in National Film Theatre Booklet (London), January 1979.
Obituary in Variety (New York), 7 May 1986.

* * *

A poll in the trade magazine Variety in 1977, the year he retired from film-making at the age of 72, named Robert Stevenson as "the most commercially successful director in the history of films". Though by now surpassed, this accolade reflected a long career at the Walt Disney studios where he directed such huge international successes as Mary Poppins and The Love Bug, aimed squarely at the family audience. Yet such prominence came only after a series of almost separate careers.

The British film industry that Robert Stevenson joined in the late 1920s was still far from respectable, and had become notorious for its cheap, low-quality "quota quickies," films produced in response to the 1927 Cinematograph Act. Yet Stevenson, with his first-class degree in mechanical sciences from Cambridge University, was one of a new breed of well educated, bright young men, introduced into the industry by the more far-sighted producers of the day, whose diverse talents were to enhance greatly the standing of British cinema. Some went into the documentary field, encouraged by John Grierson, but Stevenson, along with others like Carol Reed and Anthony Asquith, chose to enter the mainstream of feature-film production. In 1929 he started as a scriptwriter for Gainsborough-Gaumont-British, then under the control of Michael Balcon, later the head of Ealing Studios.

By 1932 Stevenson had directed his first film, Happy Ever After, an amiable star vehicle for the popular comic pairing of Jack Hulbert and Cicely Courtneidge, a typical product of the studio. In 1936 he wrote and directed Tudor Rose, an historical costume drama in the style of Alexander Korda's internationally successful The Private Life of Henry VIII. It won him critical as well as popular acclaim and he enhanced his reputation with several other noteworthy films in the late 1930s, including an ambitious version of King Solomon's Mines with Paul Robeson. By 1939 he was named by fellow director Anthony Asquith, in an article in Film Weekly, as one of a new breed of

directors who were developing a discernibly British style. Ironically, it was at this point that Stevenson, now the leading director at Gaumont-British after the departure of Alfred Hitchcock to America, also chose to go, along with his actress wife, Anna Lee, to Hollywood.

There was some resentment in England towards those filmmakers who remained in the United States after the outbreak of World War II, although interestingly, two of Stevenson's best films from this period (when he was under contract to David O. Selznick) were adaptations of classic English novels; Tom Brown's Schooldays, starring Freddie Bartholomew, and an atmospheric version of Jane Eyre, co-directed by Orson Welles. In 1940, however, Stevenson had become an American citizen, and as well as making documentary films for the US War Department, served in the US Army, remaining a major in the US Reserve for several years after the war. He continued making films throughout this period, including To the Ends of the Earth, a fine thriller, made for RKO in 1948 and featuring the dimly-lit sets and complicated plot twists characteristic of American cinema of the time. His next film, however, I Married a Communist, was more characteristic of the anti-Red paranoia of its producer Howard Hughes, and proved a disaster at the box office. After only three more films, Stevenson left RKO in 1952 to start a career as a writer and director for the new medium of television. He directed over 100 productions for American TV, including Playhouse of the Stars, General Electric Theater, and Alfred Hitchcock Presents (an ironic reunion with his former colleague at Gaumont-British) before accepting, at the age of 51, an unexpected offer from Walt Disney. As he later recalled, "I was hired for six weeks, and stayed for 20 years."

It was a period of Stevenson's career that was as successful as it was (initially, at least) unlikely. He had shown himself to be a versatile and technically adept director, but was as surprised as anyone by his phenomenal career at the Disney studios, where he directed no less than eleven major box-office hits, including The Absent-Minded Professor, The Love Bug, Mary Poppins, Bedknobs and Broomsticks, and One of Our Dinosaurs Is Missing. These films were all enjoyable, live-action comic fantasies, deliberately broad in their appeal, typically combining frenzied action, eccentric characters and impressive special effects, often blending animation and film. The success of these well-made films owed much to Stevenson's old-fashioned insistence on the importance of a good story, and his skill as a craftsman in deftly pacing the narrative. He also possessed an instinctive awareness of what made an audience laugh, revealing a consistently popular touch rare enough in Hollywood, let alone for an Englishman of his upper-middle-class background.

Apart from an Academy Award nomination for Mary Poppins in 1964 (which won five Oscars and brought the studio over $30 million), he retained a low profile outside the industry, while remaining hugely respected within it. Of his work, he once said, "When I'm directing a picture, what I have in mind is a happy audience, enjoying it in a movie house." Such a deceptively simple statement reflects his modest and unpretentious approach but belies the skill with which Robert Stevenson was able to keep audiences happy.

—Nicholas Thomas

STILLER, Mauritz.

Swedish/Russian. Born Mosche Stiller in Helsinki, Finland, 17 July 1883, became citizen of Sweden, 1921. Actor in Finland, from 1899; moved to Sweden to avoid Russian military draft, worked as actor in Sweden, from 1904; manager of avant-garde theatre Lilla Teatern, Stockholm, 1911; hired as film director (also writer and actor) for newly-formed Svenska Biograf film studio, Stockholm, 1912; began collaboration with Greta Gustafsson (Greta Garbo), 1923; moved to Hollywood under contract to MGM, 1925; fired by MGM before completing a film, hired by Erich Pommer at Paramount to direct *Hotel Imperial*, then returned to Sweden, 1927. *Died 8 November 1928.*

Films as Director:

1912   *Mor och dotter (Mother and Daughter)* (+ sc, role as Count Raoul de Saligny); *När svärmor regerar (When the Mother-in-Law Reigns)* (+ sc, role as the pastor); *Vampyren (Vampire)* (+ sc); *Barnet (The Child)*; *De svarta makerna (The Black Masks)* (+ co-sc); *Den tryanniske fästmannen (The Tyrannical Fiancée)* (+ sc, role as Elias Petterson)

1913   *När kärleken dödar (When Love Kills)* (+ co-sc); *När larmhlockan ljuder (When the Alarm Bell Rings)*; *Den okända (The Unknown Woman)* (+ sc); *Bröderna (Brothers)* (+ co-sc); *Den moderna suffragetten (The Suffragette)* (+ sc); *Pålivets ödesväger (The Smugglers)*; *Mannekägen (The Model)* (+ sc); *För sin kärleks skull (The Stockbroker)* (+ sc); *Gränsfolken (The Border Feud)*; *Livets konflikter (Conflicts of Life)* (+ sc); *Kammarjunkaren (Gentleman of the Room)* (+ sc)

1914   *Lekkamraterna (The Playmates)* (+ sc); *Stormfågeln (The Stormy Petrel)*; *Det röda tornet (The Master)* (+ co-sc); *Skottet (The Shot)*; *När konstnärer älska (When Artists Love)*

1915   *Hans hustrus förflutna (His Wife's Past)*; *Hämnaren (The Avenger)*; *Madame de Thèbes (The Son of Destiny)*; *Mästertjuven (The Son of Fate)*; *Hans bröllopsnatt (His Wedding Night)*; *Minlotsen (The Mine Pilot)*; *Dolken (The Dagger)* (+ co-sc); *Lyckonälen (The Motorcar Apaches)* (+ co-sc)

1916   *Balettprimadonnan (Anjuta, the Dancer)*; *Kärlek och journalistik (Love and Journalism)*; *Kampen om hans hjärta (The Struggle for His Heart)*; *Vingarne (The Wings)* (+ co-sc)

1917   *Thomas Graals bästa film (Thomas Graal's Best Picture)*; *Alexander den Store (Alexander the Great)* (+ sc)

1918   *Thomas Graals bästa barn (Thomas Graal's First Child)* (+ co-sc); *Sången om den eldröda blomman (Song of the Scarlet Flower. The Flame of Life)*

1919   *Fiskebyn (The Fishing Village)*; **Herr Arnes Pengar (Sir Arne's Treasure)** (+ co-sc)

1920   **Erotikon (Bonds That Chafe)** (+ co-sc); *Johan* (+ sc)

1921   *De Landsflyktige (The Exiles)* (+ co-sc)

1922   *Gunnar Hedes saga (Gunnar Hede's Saga. The Old Mansion)* (+ sc)

1923   **Gösta Berlings saga (The Story of Gösta Berling. The Atonement of Gösta Berling)** (+ co-sc)

1926   *The Temptress* (finished by Fred Niblo) (+ sc)

1927   *Hotel Imperial* (+ co-sc); *The Woman on Trial*; *Barbed Wire* (finished by Rowland Lee) (+ sc)

1928   *The Street of Sin* (finished by Ludvig Berger) (+ sc)

Publications:

On STILLER: books—

Idestam-Almquist, Bengt, *Den Svenska Filmens Drama: Sjöström och Stiller*, Stockholm, 1938.

Hardy, Forsyth, *Scandinavian Film*, London, 1951.

Waldekranz, Rune, *Swedish Cinema*, Stockholm, 1959.

Lauritzen, Einar, *Swedish Film*, New York, 1962.

Mauritz Stiller

Cowie, Peter, *Swedish Cinema*, London, 1966.

Pensel, Hans, *Seastrom and Stiller in Hollywood*, New York, 1969.

Werner, Gösta, *Mauritz Stiller och hans filmer*, Stockholm, 1969.

Petrie, Graham, *Hollywood Destinies: European Directors in Hollywood 1922–31*, London, 1985.

On STILLER: articles—

Idestam-Almquist, Bengt, "Stiller, a Pioneer of the Cinema," in *Biografbladet* (Stockholm), Fall 1950.

Idestam-Almquist, Bengt, "The Man Who Found Garbo," in *Films and Filming* (London), August 1956.

Sjöström, Victor, "As I Remember Him," in *Film Comment* (New York), Summer 1970.

Wood, Robin, "Essays on the Swedish Cinema (Part 2)," in *Lumiere* (Melbourne), April/May 1974.

Gillett, John, "Swedish Retrospect," in *Sight and Sound* (London), Summer 1974.

Robertson, J., "Mauritz Stiller," in *Monthly Film Bulletin* (London), December 1977.

Beylie, Claude, and M. Martin, "Sjöström, Stiller et l'Amérique," in *Ecran* (Paris), September 1978.

Sopocy, M., "Oltre il realisimo. 'Griffithiana'," in *Quarterly Review of Film Studies* (New York), September 1986.

*   *   *

Like the other two distinguished pioneers of the early Swedish cinema, Sjöström and Sjöberg, Mauritz Stiller had an essentially theatrical background. But it must be remembered he was reared in Finland of Russian-Jewish stock, did not emigrate to Sweden until he was 27, and remained there only 15 years before going to Hollywood. He responded, relatively late, to the Swedish cultural tradition, so heavily influenced by the country's extreme northern climate and landscape, and by the fatalistic, puritanical literary and dramatic aura exerted most notably by the Swedish dramatist Strindberg and the Nobel prize-winning novelist Selma Lagerlöf, whose works inspired by tradition and legend, *Herr Arne's Treasure, Gunnar Hede's Saga*, and *Gösta Berlings Saga*, were all to be adapted by Stiller for the silent screen.

After establishing himself as a talented stage actor, Stiller's work on film began in 1912. He proved at once a meticulous craftsman, with a strong visual instinct and a polished sense of timing and rhythm; his early work showed how much he had learned technically from the considerable number of D.W. Griffith's short narrative films shown in Sweden. For example, *The Black Masks*, made in 1912, is noted by Forsyth Hardy as having, "over a hundred scenes, a constantly changing combination of interiors and exteriors, close-ups and panoramic shots." Stiller even made in 1913 a film based on the activities of Mrs. Pankhurst, *Den moderna suffragetten*, reflecting his reputation in the theater for avant-garde subjects.

He was to prove adept at comedy, as his films *Love and Journalism, Thomas Graal's Best Film*—one of the earliest films about filmmaking—and *Thomas Graal's First Child* reveal, with their skirmishing and coquetry that characterize the relationship of the sexes. Stiller insisted however on restraint in acting style; he was an autocratic perfectionist, and Emil Jannings, Germany's leading actor, termed him "the Stanislavski of the cinema." The second of these films had a complex structure, full of flashbacks and daydreams; the director Victor Sjöström starred in all three, as well as in other of Stiller's films and in certain of the earliest Stiller appeared himself. The climax to his career in the production of elegant and graceful comedies of sex manners was *Erotikon*; though better known, because of its alluring title, than its predecessors, it is somewhat less accomplished. Elaborately staged and full of sexual by-play—the wife of a preoccupied professor has two lovers in hot pursuit, a young sculptor and an elderly baron—it includes a specially commissioned ballet performed by the opera in Stockholm. These sophisticated silent films rank alongside the early comedies of Lubitsch, whose work in this genre in Germany in fact succeeded them. Lubitsch readily acknowledged his debt to Stiller. Again like Lubitsch (with whose career Stiller's can best be compared at this stage), Stiller was also to work on epic-style, historical subjects. He took over the adaptation of Selma Lagerlöf's novel, *Sir Arne's Treasure* from Sjöström, its original director. This was essentially an 18th-century story of escape and pursuit—three Scottish mercenaries in the service of King John III are imprisoned for conspiracy. They abscond in the depths of winter, undertaking a desperate journey overland to flee the country. In the process they become increasingly violent and menacing until they come on Arne's mansion. They steal his treasure, burn his house, slaughter its inhabitants except for an orphan girl, Elsalill, who survives the massacre, a haunted figure half-attracted to the leader of the Scottish renegades, but eventually betraying him and dying in the final confrontation in which the Scots are recaptured. The long, snake-like column of black-robed women moving over the icy waste in the girl's funeral procession is Stiller's concluding panoramic scene; one of the best-known spectacular shots in early cinema, it still appears in most history books. The film illustrates grandly the response of the early Swedish filmmakers to the menacing magnificence of the northern winter landscape.

After completing *Erotikon* and a Finnish subject, *Johan*—a dark and satiric study of the triangular relationship of husband, wife, and the visitant, stranger-lover, set in the desolate expanse of the countryside, with a climax worthy of Griffith as the guilty couple, chased by the husband, ride the rapids in a small boat—Stiller crowned his career in Sweden with his two further adaptations from Lagerlöf: *Gunnar Hedes Saga* and *Gösta Berlings Saga*. In the former—in every way an outstanding film of its period, in its immixture of dream and actuality—the hero, Nils (Einar Hansson), a violinist, is inspired to emulate his father, who made a fortune by driving a vast herd of reindeer south from the Arctic circle. Nils's adventure in realizing this dream only leads to severe injury resulting in amnesia; back home in the forests of the south he experiences hallucinations from which the girl who loves him finally liberates him. The film's duality is striking: the realism of the trek with the reindeer involving panoramic shots of the great herds and brilliant tracking shots of the catastrophic stampede which leads to Nils's accident, is in marked contrast to the twilit world of his hallucinations.

Gösta Berling's Saga, on the other hand, though famous for its revelation of the star quality of the young drama student, Greta Garbo, and its melodramatic story of the defrocked priest (Lars Hanson) fatally in love with Garbo's Italian girl, is clumsy in structure compared with *Gunnar Hede's Saga*, and was later destructively cut for export to half its original length of four hours.

Stiller travelled in 1925 to America at the invitation of Louis B. Mayer of MGM on the strength of his reputation as a sophisticated European director, but mostly (it would seem) because he was Garbo's Svengali-like and obsessive mentor. He very soon fell out with Mayer who endured him because he wanted Garbo as a contract player. All but mesmerized by Stiller, Garbo insisted he direct her in *The Temptress*; the inevitable difficulties arose and he was withdrawn from the film. His best film in America was made at Paramount, *Hotel Imperial* starring Pola Negri; it concerned a wartime love affair between a hotel servant and an Austrian officer and was notable for its spectacular, composite hotel set over which the camera played suspended from an overhead rail. After finishing a second film with Negri, *The Woman on Trial*, Stiller never managed to complete another film; the respiratory illness that was undermining his health forced him to part from Garbo and return to Sweden, where he died in 1928 at the age of 45.

—Roger Manvell

STONE, Oliver.

American. Born in New York City, 1946. Studied at Yale University, dropped out, 1965; studied filmmaking under Martin Scorsese, New York University, B.F.A., 1971. Married 1) Majwa Sarkis, 1971 (divorced 1977); 2) Elizabeth Burkit Cox, 1981. Teacher at Free Pacific Institute, Cholon, Vietnam, 1965; joined U.S. Merchant Marine, 1966; volunteered for 25th Infantry Division, U.S. Army, 1967, awarded Bronze Star for Valor, and the Purple Heart with Oak Leaf Cluster; directed first film, *Seizure*, 1974. Recipient: Oscar for Best Screenplay Adaptation, and Writers Guild Award, for *Midnight Express*, 1979; Directors Guild of America Award, Oscar for Best Director, and Golden Globe Award for Best Director, for *Platoon*, 1987 and also for *Born on the Fourth of July*, 1989. Address: c/o 9025 Wilshire Boulevard, Suite 301, Beverly Hills, CA 90211, U.S.A.

Films as Director and Scriptwriter:

1974   *Seizure*

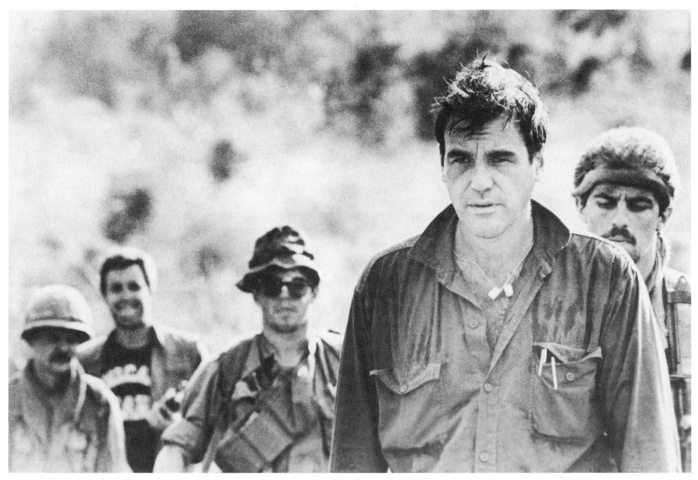

Oliver Stone on the set of *Platoon*

1981	*The Hand*
1986	***Salvador*** (+ pr, co-sc); *Platoon*
1987	*Wall Street* (co-sc)
1988	*Talk Radio* (co-sc)
1989	*Born on the Fourth of July* (co-sc)
1991	*The Doors* (co-sc); *Evita*

Other Films:

1978	*Midnight Express* (Parker) (sc)
1982	*Conan the Barbarian* (Milius) (co-sc)
1983	*Scarface* (De Palma) (sc)
1985	*Year of the Dragon* (Cimino) (sc)
1986	*8 Million Ways to Die* (Ashby) (co-sc)

Publications:

By STONE: books—

Platoon and Salvador: The Screenplays, with Richard Boyle, Cranbury, New Jersey, 1987.

By STONE: articles—

Interview with Nigel Floyd in *Monthly Film Bulletin* (London), January 1987.
Interview with Pat McGilligan in *Film Comment* (New York), January/February 1987.
Interview with M. Burke in *Stills* (London), 29 February 1987.
Interview with Louise Tanner in *Films in Review* (New York), March 1987.
Interview with M. Sineux and Michel Ciment in *Positif* (Paris), April 1987.

Interview with Alexander Cockburn in *American Film* (Washington D.C.), December 1987.
Interview with Gary Crowdus in *Cineaste* (New York), vol. 16, no. 3, 1988.
Interview with M. Tessier and others in *Revue du Cinéma* (Paris), April 1989.

On STONE: articles—

Sklar, Robert, and others, "*Platoon* on Inspection: A Critical Symposium," in *Cineaste* (New York), vol. 15, no. 4, 1987.
Boozer, Jack, Jr., "*Wall Street*: The Commodification of Perception," in *Journal of Popular Film and Television* (Washington, D.C.), vol. 17, no. 3, 1989.
Corliss, Richard, "Who Cares?," in *Film Criticism* (Meadville, Pennsylvania), vol. 25, no. 1, 1989.
Jones, G., "Trash Talk: Oliver Stone's *Talk Radio*," in *Enclitic* (Los Angeles), vol. 11, no. 2, 1989.
Wrathall, J., "Greeks, Trojans and Cubans—Oliver Stone," in *Monthly Film Bulletin* (London), October 1989.

*   *   *

Anyone attempting, with any degree of success, both artistic and commercial, to make overtly political movies that sustain a left-wing position within the Hollywood cinema of the 1980s deserves at least our respectful attention. In fact, his work dramatizes, in a particularly extreme and urgent form, the quandary of the American left-wing intellectual.

Platoon and *Wall Street* provide a useful starting-point, as they share the same basic structure. A young man (Charlie Sheen, in both films) has to choose in terms of values between the Good Father (Willem Dafoe, Martin Sheen) and the Bad

Father (Tom Berenger, Michael Douglas); he learns to choose the Good Father and destroy the Bad. The opposition is very similar in both cases: the Good Father is a liberal with a conscience, aware of the impossibility of changing or radically affecting the general situation but committed to the preservation of his personal integrity; the Bad Father has no conscience, and no integrity to preserve, and this, combined with a total ruthlessness, is what equips him to survive (until the dénouement) and makes him an insidiously seductive figure. The Bad Father is completely adapted to a system that the Good Father can protest against but do nothing to change. The young man can exact a kind of individual justice by destroying the Bad Father, but the system remains intact.

Platoon and *Wall Street* do not represent Stone's work at its best: their targets are a bit too obvious, the characteristic rage comes too easily, tinged with self-righteousness, so that the alienating aspects of his manner—the heavy stylistic rhetoric, the emotional bludgeoning—are felt at their most obtrusive. But the two films encapsulate the quandary—one might say the *blockage*—that is treated more complexly elsewhere: what does one fight for within a system one perceives as totally corrupt but in which the only alternative to capitulation is impotence?

The fashionable buzz-phrase "structuring absence" becomes resonant when applied to Stone's films: in the most literal sense, his work so far is structured precisely on the absence of an available political alternative, which could only be a commitment to what is most deeply and hysterically tabu in American culture, a form of Marxist socialism. There is a curious paradox here which Americans seem reluctant to notice: Lincoln's famous formula, supposedly one of the foundations of American political ideology, "Government of the people, by the people and for the people," could only be realized in a system dubbed, above all else, "un-American" (American capitalism, as Stone sees very clearly, is government *by* the rich and powerful *for* the rich and powerful). In both *Salvador* and *Born on the Fourth of July* the protagonist declares, at a key point in the development, "I am an American, I love America," and we must assume he is speaking for Stone. But we must ask, *which* America does he love, since the American actuality is presented in both films as unambiguously and uniformly hateful? What is being appealed to here is clearly a *myth* of America, but the films seem, implicitly and with profound unease, to recognize that the myth cannot possibly be realized, that capitalism *must* take the forms it has historically taken. Hence the sense one takes from the films of a just but impotent rage: without the availability of the alternative there is no way out.

This is nowhere clearer than in *Salvador*, one of Stone's strongest, least flawed works and a gesture of great courage within its social-political context. While in American capitalist democracy it is still possible to make a film like *Salvador* (the equivalent in Stalinist Russia would have been unthinkable), it is not possible for the film to go further than it does, to take the necessary, logical step. Impotent rage is permissible, the promotion of a constructive alternative is not. Stone's films can be acceptable, even popular, even canonized by Academy Awards precisely because their ultimate effect, beyond the rage is to suggest that things *can't* be changed (as indeed they can't, while one remains within the system). *Salvador* offers a lucid and cogent analysis of the political situation, a vivid dramatization of historical events (the death of Romero, the rape and murder of the visiting Nicaraguan nuns), and an outspoken denunciation of American intervention. Neither does it chicken out at the end: the final scene, where the protagonist at last gets his lover and her two children over the border into the "land of the free," to have them abruptly and brutally sent back by American security officers, is as chilling as anything that modern Hollywood cinema has to offer. But the film's attitude to the concept of a specifically *socialist* revolution (as opposed to a vague notion of people "fighting for their freedom") is thoroughly cagy and equivocal. Nothing is done to demystify the habitual American conflation of socialism and Marxism with Stalinism.

All the film can say is that the threat of a general "Communist" takeover is either imaginary or grossly exaggerated (if it weren't, presumably the horrors we are shown would all be justified or at least pardonable), that the Salvadoreans, like good Americans, just want their liberty, and that America, in its own interests, has betrayed its founding principles by intervening on the wrong side.

Born on the Fourth of July recapitulates the earlier film's force, rage and outspokenness, and also its impasse. It seems to me to be weakened, however, by its final construction of its protagonist as a redeemer-hero. Ron Kovic, by the end of the film, in realizing (with whatever irony) his mother's dream that he would one day speak before thousands of people saying wonderful things, at once regains his full personal integrity and sense of self-worth and offers an apparent political escape by revealing the "truth." But recent history has shown many times that the revelation of truth can be very readily mythified and absorbed into the system (the Oscar awards and nominations for Stone's movies represent an exact equivalent).

Talk Radio received no such accolades and seems generally regarded as a minor, marginal work. On the contrary, it is arguably Stone's most completely successful film to date and absolutely central to his work, to the point of being confessional. It has been taken as more an Eric Bogosian movie than a Stone movie. We can credit Stone with firmer personal integrity and higher ambitions than are evidenced by Barry Champlain (Bogosian's character), but, that allowance made, Stone has found here the perfect "objective correlative" for his own position, his own quandary. Champlain's rage, toppling over into hysteria, parallels the tone of much of Stone's work and identifies one of its sources, the frustration of grasping that no one really listens, no one understands, no one *wants* to understand; the sense of addressing a people kept in a state of mystification so complete, by a system so powerful and pervasive, that no formal brainwashing could improve on it (this "reading" of the American public is resumed in *Born on the Fourth of July*). The film is indeed revelatory, and very impressive in its honesty and nakedness.

—Robin Wood.

STORCK, Henri.

Belgian. Born in Ostend, 5 September 1907. Married photographer Virginia Lierens. Began making films in 8mm, 1927; organized cine-club in Ostend, made first "reportages," 1928; assistant in France to Pierre Billon, Jean Croillon, and Jean Vigo, 1931; with Joris Ivens, made *Borinage*, 1933; began making films about art and folklore, 1936; directed first Belgian-international co-production, *Le Banquet des fraudeurs*, 1951; president (for 15 years), Association Belge des Auteurs de Films et Auteurs de Television, and co-founder, Royal Film Archive of Belgium.

Henri Storck

Films as Director:

1927–28   amateur films on Ostend
1929–30   *Pour vos beaux yeux*; *Images d'Ostende*
1930   *Une Pêche au hareng*; *Le Service de sauvetage sur la côte belge*; *Les Fêtes du centenaire*; *Trains de plaisir*; *Tentative de films abstraits*; *La Mort de Vénus*; *Suzanne au bain*; *Ostende, reine des plages*
1931   *Une Idylle à la plage*
1932   *Travaux du tunnel sous l'Escaut*; *Histoire du soldat inconnu*; *Sur les bords de la caméra*
1933   *Trois Vies une corde*; *Misère au Borinage* (co-d, co-ph)
1934   *Création d'ulcères artificiels chez le chien*; *La Production sélective du réseau à soixante-dix*
1935   *Electrification de la ligne Bruxelles-Anvers*; *L'Île de Pâques*; *Le Trois-Mâts*; *Cap du sud*; *L'Industrie de la tapisserie et du meuble sculpté*; *Le Coton*
1936   *Les Carillons*; *Les Jeux de l'été et de la mer*; *Sur les routes de l'ete*; *Regards sur la Belgique ancienne*
1937   *La Belgique nouvelle*; *Un ennemi public*; *Les Maisons de la misère*
1938   *Comme une lettre à la poste*; *La Roue de la fortune*; *Terre de Flandre*; *Vacances*; *Le Patron est mort*
1939   *Voor Recht en Vrijheid te Kortrijk*
1940   *La Foire internationale de Bruxelles*
1942–44   *Symphonie paysanne* (co-d, ph)
1944   *Le Monde de Paul Delvaux* (+ ph)
1947   *La Joie de revivre*
1947–48   *Rubens*
1949   *Au carrefour de la vie*
1950   *Carnavals*
1951   *Le Banquet des fraudeurs* (feature)
1952   *La Fenêtre ouverte*
1953   *Herman Teirlinck*
1954   *Les Belges et la mer*; *Les Portes de la maison*; *Le Tour du monde en bateau-stop*
1955   *Le Trésor d'Ostende*
1956   *Décembre, mois des enfants*
1957   *Couleur de feu*
1957–60   *Les Seigneurs de la forêt*
1960   *Les Gestes du silence*
1961   *Les Dieux du feu*; *L'Énergie et vous*
1962   *Variation sur le geste*; *Le Bonheur d'être aimée* (+ co-pr, co-sc); *Les Malheurs de la guerre*
1963   *Plastiques*
1964   *Matières nouvelles*
1965   *Le Musée vivant*
1966   *Jeudi on chantera comme dimanche*
1968   *Forêt secrète d'Afrique*
1969–70   *Paul Delvaux ou les femmes défendues* (+ ed)
1969–72   *Fêtes de Belgiques*
1974–75   *Fifres et tambours d'Entre-Sambre-et-Meuse*; *Les Marcheurs de Sainte Rolende*; *Les Joyeux Tromblons*
1975   *Les Marcheurs de Sainte Rolende*
1985   *Permeke*

Other Film:

1975   **Jeanne Dielman, 23, Quai du commerce, 1080 Bruxelles** (Akerman) (role as 1st caller)

Publications:

By STORCK: articles—

Interview, in *Documentary Explorations* by G. Roy Levin, New York, 1972.
Interview with Bert Hogenkamp, in *Skrien* (Amsterdam), July/August 1977.
Interview with J. -P. Everaerts in *Film en Televisie* (Brussels), September 1987.
Interviews with A. Tournès in *Jeune Cinéma* (Paris), May/June and July/August 1988.

On STORCK: articles—

Blakeston, Oswell, "The Romantic Cinema of Henri Storck," in *Architectural Review* (New York), May 1931.
Bassan, R., "Storck le touche-à-tout," in *Ecran* (Paris), September 1977.
Grelier, R., "Henri Storck," in *Image et Son* (Paris), September 1977.
Davay, P., "Henri Storck à l'honneur," in *Amis du Film et de la Télévision* (Brussels), January 1979.
"Storck Issue" of *Revue Belge du Cinéma* (Brussels), August 1979.
De Bongnie, J., "Storck vu par un jeune Hudon," in *Amis du Film et de la Télévision* (Brussels), November 1979.
"Storck Section" of *Revue Belge du Cinéma* (Brussels), Winter/Spring 1983/84.

*   *   *

After growing up in the seaside town of Ostend, Henri Storck naturally chose the beach and the sea, with the surrounding sand dunes, as background and subject for many of his early films. He became friendly with Ostend's resident and visiting artists, and they all apparently absorbed creative strength from the solid tradition of Flemish paintings as well as physical stamina from the invigorating North Sea air. Primarily a documentarist, Storck's prolific output of over 70 films does include a couple of fiction films: *Une Idylle à la plage*, a short film about adolescent love, and a feature film with a thriller framework, *Le Banquet des fraudeurs*. Storck has described the work of his mentor, Charles DeKeukeleire, another Belgian film pioneer, as having " . . . lyrical expression, faithfulness to authentic reality, and a sense of rhythm in editing." These words are just as applicable to Storck's own *oeuvre*. *Borinage*, a film about a coal miners' strike in the Borinage—a district southwest of Brussels—is a powerful revelation of the miners' living conditions. The film cinematically echoes the feelings that Van Gogh expressed in his drawings of an earlier period. *Borinage* is full of strong, intense images. A daring project, made in collaboration with Joris Ivens, the film had to be shot covertly in order to evade the police. Banned from public showing in Belgium and Holland at the time it was released, *Borinage* became a time-tested classic and an inspiration to the "Grierson boys" in England. *Symphonie paysanne*, made in a completely different style, depicted the passage of the seasons on a Belgian farm. This pastoral eulogy again demonstrated Storck's ability to express his humane sensibility in a cinematic manner. After the war, Storck immensely enhanced a developing genre—films analyzing the visual arts. *Rubens* (made in collaboration with Paul Haesaerts) and the *World of Paul Delvaux* are outstanding examples which were immediately recognized as *tours de force*. *The Open Window* and *The Sorrows of the War* were also worthy contributions to this category. A later film about Delvaux, *Paul Devaux or the Forbidden Women* was, to Storck's great amusement, promoted on Times Square as a pornographic film. In his films about art, Storck was particularly innovative in his use of camera movement to display the details of the art works, and in some films used animated lines to demonstrate their structures of composition. Henri Storck's humanistic vision is revealed by his films and crosses all national and cultural boundaries.

—Robert Edmonds

STRAUB, Jean-Marie, and Danièle HUILLET.

French, German. Jean-Marie Straub born in Metz, 8 January 1933. Straub studied literature, Universities of Strasbourg and Nancy, 1950–54. Straub moved to Paris and began collaboration with Huillet, 1954; Straub assistant to French directors Abel Gance, Jean Renoir, Jacques Rivette, Robert Bresson, and Alexandre Astruc, 1954–58; Straub left France to avoid military service in Algerian conflict, 1958 (amnestied 1971); Straub and Huillet moved to Munich, 1959; moved to Italy, 1969.

Films as Directors:

1963   *Machorka-Muff* (Straub: d, co-ed, co-sound; Huillet: sc, co-ed, co-sound)
1965   *Nicht versöhnt oder Es hilft nur Gewalt, wo Gewalt herrscht* (*Es hilft nicht, wo Gewalt herrscht. Not Reconciled*) (Straub: d, co-ed, co-ph; Huillet: sc, co-ed, co-ph)
1968   *Chronik der Anna Magdalena Bach* (***Chronicle of Anna Magdalena Bach***) (Straub: d; Huillet: sc); *Der Bräutigam, die Komödiantin und der Zuhälter* (*The Bridegroom, the Comedienne and the Pimp*) (Straub: d, co-ed; Huillet: sc, co-ed)
1969   *Othon* (*Les Yeux ne veulent pas en tout temps se fermer ou Peut-être qu'un jour Rome se permettra de choisir à son tour. Die Augen wollen sich nicht zu jeder Zeit schliessen oder Vielleicht eines Tages wird Rom sich erlauben, seinerseits zu wählen. Eyes Do Not Want to Close at All Times or Perhaps One Day Rome Will Permit Herself to Choose in Her Turn, Othon*) (co-d, co-ed; Huillet + sc, Straub + role under pseudonym Jubarithe Semaran); *Einleitung zu Arnold Schoenberg Begleit Musik zu einer Lichtspielscene* (*Introduction to Arnold Schoenberg's Accompaniment for a Cinematographic Scene*) (+ co-pr, co-ed; Huillet + sc) (for TV)
1972   *Geschichtsunterricht* (*History Lessons*) (+ co-pr, co-ed; Huillet + sc)

1975   *Moses und Aron* (*Moses and Aaron*) (+ co-ed; Huillet + sc)
1976   *Fortini/Cani* (*I cani del Sinai*) (+ co-ed; Huillet + sc)
1977   *Toute révolution est un coup de dés* (*Every Revolution Is a Throw of the Dice*) (Huillet + sc)
1979   *Della nube alla resistenza* (*From the Cloud to the Resistance*) (Huillet + sc)
1983   *Trop tot, trop tard* (*Too Early, Too Late*)
1985   *Klassenverhältnisse* (*Class Relations*)
1987   *Tod des Empedokles*
1989   *Schwarze Sunde*; *Cézanne*

Other Films: Straub:

1954   *La Tour des Nesle* (Gance) (asst d)
1955   *French Cancan* (Renoir) (asst d)
1956   *Eléna et les hommes* (Renoir) (asst d); *Le Coup de Berger* (Rivette) (asst d); ***Un Condamné à mort s'est échappé*** (Bresson) (asst d)
1958   *Une Vie* (Astruc) (asst d)

Publications:

By STRAUB AND HUILLET: books—

Klassenverhältnisse, edited by Wolfram Schütte, Frankfurt, 1984.

By STRAUB AND HUILLET: articles—

"Frustration of Violence," in *Cahiers du Cinema in English* (New York), January 1967.
"*Moses und Aron* as an Object of Marxist Reflection," interview with J. Rogers, in *Jump Cut* (Chicago), no.12–13, 1976.
"Decoupage di Fortini/Cani," in *Filmcritica* (Rome), November/December 1976.
Interview with R. Gansera, in *Filmkritik* (Munich), September 1978.
Interview with Serge Daney and J. Narboni, in *Cahiers du Cinéma* (Paris), November 1979.

On STRAUB AND HUILLET: books—

Roud, Richard, *Jean-Marie Straub*, London, 1971.
Walsh, Martin, *The Brechtian Aspect of Radical Cinema*, London, 1981.
Franklin, James, *New German Cinema: From Oberhausen to Hamburg*, Boston, 1983.
Phillips, Klaus, *New German Filmmakers: From Oberhausen through the 1970s*, New York, 1984.
Rosetti, Riccardo, editor, *Straub-Huillet Film*, Rome, 1984.
Elsaesser, Thomas, *New German Cinema: A History*, London, 1989.

On STRAUB AND HUILLET: articles—

Baxter, B., "Jean-Marie Struab," in *Film* (London), Spring 1969.
Engel, Andi, "Jean-Marie Straub," in *Second Wave*, New York, 1970.
Walsh, M., "Political Formations in the Cinema of Jean-Marie Straub," in *Jump Cut* (Chicago), November/December 1974.
"*Moses und Aron* Issue" of *Cahiers du Cinéma* (Paris), October/November 1975.
"Straub and Huillet Issue" of *Enthusiasm* (London), December 1975.
Bonitzer, P., "J.-M.S. et J.-L.G.," in *Cahiers du Cinéma* (Paris), February 1976.
Dermody, S., "Straub/Huillet: The Politics of Film Practice," in *Cinema Papers* (Melbourne), September/October 1976.
"Danièle Huillet Jean-Marie Straub's *Fortini/Cani*," special issue of *Filmkritik* (Munich), January 1977.
Simsolo, Noel, "Jean-Marie Straub et Danièle Huillet," in *Cinéma* (Paris), March 1977.
Bennett, E., "The Films of Straub Are Not 'Theoretical'," in *Afterimage* (Rochester), Summer 1978.
Rosenbaum, Jonathan, "Jean-Luc, Chantal, Danielle, Jean-Marie and the Others," in *American Film* (Washington, D.C.), February 1979.
Daney, Serge, "Le Plan Straubien," in *Cahiers du Cinéma* (Paris), November 1979.
Petley, Julian, "Straub/Huillet's *Empedocles*," in *Sight and Sound* (London) Summer 1990.

*   *   *

Jean-Marie Straub and Danièle Huillet: *Moses und Aron*

The films of Jean-Marie Straub and Danièle Huillet are best understood in the context of contemporary developments in radical, materialist cinema. They offer what many people see as a genuine alternative to both dominant narrative cinema and conventional art movies. Their work is formally austere and demands attentive, intellectual participation from audiences. However, it must be acknowledged that many people find their films nearly impenetrable and absolutely boring. This is explained in part by the fact that the films do not rely on standard narrative construction or conventional characters. While the films of Straub and Huillet are by no means "abstract" it is nearly impossible to (re)construct a unified, imaginary, referential "world" through them.

In a sense their work might be explained in terms of strategies of displeasure, a wilful refusal to captivate audiences with a coherent fictional world, in favor of promoting a distanciated, intellectual interaction between viewer and film. Because of this insistence on critical distance, audiences must work with the film in a dialectical process of meaning construction. (In fact, Straub is notoriously critical of "lazy" viewers who are unwilling to engage in this activity.)

Straub and Huillet's films directly address the nature of cinematic signification and its political implications. This includes breaking away from conventional assumptions and practices of dominant narrative cinema. Their films exploit all channels of the medium—music, sounds, words, and images—as equivalent carriers of meaning, rather than privileging the "visual"

or relegating music and sound effects to the task of support material. Thus, there are times when extremely long, static shots accompany lengthy, complex verbal passages (a singularly "uncinematic" practice according to conventional canons of film aesthetics). Sequences may be developed along the lines of montage construction, juxtaposing graphic material, verbal material, and moving images. Both of these strategies are used in *Introduction to Schoenberg's "Accompaniment for a Cinematographic Scene"*; and the starting point for this short film was a piece of music written by the composer. The major texts, read on-screen (though interrupted at intervals by black frames), are a letter from Schoenberg to Kandinsky explaining his reasons for not participating in the Bauhaus, and a text by Brecht elaborating the relationship between fascism and capitalism. The readings of these texts take up most of the film, which includes Straub and Huillet as on-camera narrators "placing" the texts, and concludes with a montage sequence. The political aspect of the film derives not only from the logical argument advanced, the Brecht analysis standing as a critique of Schoenberg's "liberal" position, but also from the film's rejection of documentary norms. At the same time it has been pointed out that Schoenberg's music stands in relation to classical rules of harmonic composition as Straub and Huillet films stand in relation to the conventions of dominant cinema.

The incorporation of musical works and verbal texts, as both a source for and signifying material within their films, is an important aspect of their work. The figure of Bertolt Brecht is perhaps the most pervasive presence in Straub and Huillet's films. His writing is included in *Introduction to Schoenberg* and provided the source for *History Lessons*. More crucially, the strategies of deconstruction and distanciation in their films derive from principles advanced in Brechtian theory. These include concepts of alienation and anti-illusionism elaborated in Brecht's theory of epic theater. Straub and Huillet have developed these ideas in the context of their films and their persistent concern with the politics of cinematic expression.

—M.B. White

Stroheim, Erich von. *See* von Stroheim, Erich.

STURGES, John.

American. Born in Oak Park, Illinois, 3 January 1911. Educated at Marin Junior College, California. Worked in blueprint dept., RKO-Radio Pictures, 1932; assistant to designer Robert Edmond Jones on first Technicolor films, and as production assistant to David O. Selznick; worked in RKO cutting rooms, from 1935; served in Army Air Corps, directed about 45 documentaries, 1942–45; signed as director for Columbia, and directed first feature, 1946; joined MGM, 1949; began working on independent productions, 1960; co-founder The Mirisch Company. Recipient: Outstanding Directorial Achievement, Directors Guild of America, for *Bad Day at Black Rock*, 1955. Address: c/o The Alpha Corp., 13063 Ventura Blvd., Suite 202, North Hollywood, CA 91604, U.S.A.

Films as Director:

1946   *The Man Who Dared*; *Shadowed*
1947   *Alias Mr. Twilight*; *For the Love of Rusty*; *Keeper of the Bees*
1948   *Best Man Wins*; *The Sign of the Ram*
1949   *The Walking Hills*
1950   *Mystery Street*; *The Capture*; *The Magnificent Yankee*; *Right Cross*
1951   *Kind Lady*; *The People Against O'Hara*; *It's a Big Country* (co-d)
1952   *The Girl in White*
1953   *Jeopardy*; *Fast Company*; *Escape from Fort Bravo*
1954   **Bad Day at Black Rock**
1955   *Underwater*; *The Scarlet Coat*
1956   *Backlash*
1957   *Gunfight at the O.K. Corral*
1958   *The Old Man and the Sea* (took over direction from Fred Zinnemann); *The Law and Jake Wade*
1959   *Last Train from Gun Hill*; *Never So Few*
1960   *The Magnificent Seven*
1961   *By Love Possessed*
1962   *Sergeants Three*; *A Girl Named Tamiko*
1963   *The Great Escape*
1965   *The Satan Bug*; *The Hallelujah Trail*
1967   *The Hour of the Gun*
1968   *Ice Station Zebra*
1969   *Marooned*
1972   *Joe Kidd*
1973   *Valdez il mezzosangue* (*Chino. The Valdez Horses*)
1974   *McQ*
1976   *The Eagle Has Landed*

Publications:

By STURGES: articles—

"How the West Was Lost!," in *Films and Filming* (London), December 1962.

On STURGES: articles—

Anderson, Joseph, "When the Twain Meet: *Seven Samurai* vs. *The Magnificent Seven*," in *Film Quarterly* (Berkeley), Spring 1962.
Cherry, Richard, "Capsule of John Sturges," in *Action* (Los Angeles), November/December 1969.
Jones, D., "The Merit of Flying Lead," in *Films and Filming* (London), February 1974.
Jones, D., "The Power of the Gun," in *Films and Filming* (London), February 1974.

*   *   *

John Sturges has had a long and varied career in film. In the thirties he was an editor and then a producer. After working on documentaries during the war, he began directing in 1946. Popular film critics either pass over his work or they demean it. Andrew Sarris regards him as a mislabeled "expert technician," whose career is anything but "meaningful." Sturges has had success at the box office with some of the many action films he has done. *Gunfight at the OK Corral, The Magnificent Seven*, and *The Great Escape* were all major winners with audiences.

Sturges's films frequently deal with a group of men working towards a specific goal. In *The Great Escape* this theme is emphasized as each of the characters tries to escape from a German P.O.W. camp unsuccessfully. Only when they work together as a unit can success be achieved. While the goals are usually attained, the attempt is often costly. In several of the films, the group is decimated by the end of the mission. In *Marooned* only two of the astronauts survive and *The Magnificent Seven* is reduced to three by the end of the battle.

Sturges's work does not exclude women but the women are usually shown only as fringe characters. They are identified by the men they are associated with and react to what the men do or say. This is particularly clear in *Marooned*. In one sequence, each astronaut's wife is allowed a moment to talk to her husband via a television hook-up and say good-bye as the astronauts are trapped in their capsule in outer space.

Sturges holds a respected position in the film industry. His successes at the box office have helped him to gain that respect, but he also has an excellent eye for casting. His films have begun and furthered the careers of many actors. Steve McQueen's progress toward stardom can be traced in his films with Sturges—*Never So Few, The Magnificent Seven*, and *The Great Escape*. James Coburn, Charles Bronson, Ernest Borgnine, and Lee Marvin received career boosts from their roles in Sturges's films. Unlike Andrew Sarris, Hollywood appreciated Sturges's handling of wide-screen formats in his films of the 1950s. It is thought that he was one of the first directors to develop the wide screen as a technique rather than use it as a gimmick. It is also very clear from Sturges's films that Hollywood has felt confident in giving Sturges a project with a large cast and big budget. He capably handles large-scale projects, is able to deal with star egos (he has directed "rat pack" films with Frank Sinatra) and produces commercial successes. Hollywood could not ask for more.

—Ray Narducy

John Sturges

STURGES, Preston.

American. Born Edmund P. Biden in Chicago, 29 August 1898; adopted by mother's second husband, Solomon Sturges. Educated in Chicago (Coulter School); Lycée Janson, Paris; Ecole des Roches, France; Villa Lausanne, Switzerland; and in Berlin and Dresden. Married 1) Estelle Mudge (divorced 1928); 2) Eleanor Post Hutton, 1932 (annulled 1932); 3) Louise Sergeant Tervis (divorced); 4) actress Anna Nagle (known professionally as Sandy Mellen), three sons. Managed mother's cosmetic shop in Deauville, then New York, early 1910s; runner for Wall Street brokerage firm, 1914; enlisted in Air Corps, attended School of Military Aeronautics, Austin, Texas, 1917; returned to cosmetic business in New York, invented kissproof lipstick, 1919; turned business over to mother, worked in various jobs and as inventor; playwright, from 1927; *The Guinea Pig* ran 16 weeks on Broadway, 1929; scriptwriter from 1930, moved to Hollywood, 1932; directed own screenplays, from 1940; also manager of Sturges Engineering Company, producing diesel engines; began association with Howard Hughes, 1944; moved to Paris, 1949. Recipient: Oscar for Best Original Screenplay, for *The Great McGinty*, 1940; Laurel Award for Achievement (posthumously), Writers Guild of America, 1974. *Died at the Algonquin Hotel, New York, 6 August 1959.*

Films as Director and Scriptwriter:

1940   *The Great McGinty*; *Christmas in July*
1941   **The Lady Eve**; **Sullivan's Travels**
1942   **The Palm Beach Story**
1944   *Hail the Conquering Hero*; **The Miracle of Morgan's Creek**; *The Great Moment*
1947   *Mad Wednesday* (+ pr)
1948   *Unfaithfully Yours* (+ pr)
1949   *The Beautiful Blonde from Bashful Bend* (+ pr)
1951   *Vendetta* (co-d with Ferrer, uncredited)
1957   *Les Carnets du Major Thompson* (*The French, They Are a Funny Race*)

Other Films:

1930   *The Big Pond* (Henley) (co-sc, co-dialogue); *Fast and Loose* (Newmeyer) (sc, dialogue)
1931   *Strictly Dishonorable* (Stahl) (sc, play basis)
1933   *The Power and the Glory* (Howard) (sc); *Child of Manhattan* (Buzzell) (sc, play basis)
1934   *Thirty Day Princess* (Gering) (co-sc); *We Live Again* (Mamoulian) (co-sc); *Imitation of Life* (Stahl) (co-sc, uncredited)
1935   *The Good Fairy* (Wyler) (sc); *Diamond Jim* (Sutherland) (co-sc)
1936   *Next Time We Love* (Edward Griffith) (co-sc, uncredited); *One Rainy Afternoon* (Lee) (lyrics for "Secret Rendezvous")
1937   *Hotel Haywire* (Archainbaud) (sc); *Easy Living* (Leisen) (sc)
1938   *Port of Seven Seas* (Whale) (sc); *If I Were King* (Lloyd) (sc)
1940   *Remember the Night* (Leisen) (sc)
1947   *I'll Be Yours* (Seiter) (screenplay basis)
1951   *Strictly Dishonorable* (Frank and Panama) (play basis)
1956   *The Birds and the Bees* (Taurog) (screenplay basis)
1958   *Rock-a-bye Baby* (Tashlin) (screenplay basis); *Paris Holiday* (Oswald) (role as Serge Vitry)

Publications:

By STURGES: books—

5 *Screenplays by Preston Sturges*, edited by Brian Henderson, Berkeley, 1985.

Preston Sturges by Preston Sturges, edited by Sandy Sturges, New York, 1990.

By STURGES: articles—

"Conversation with Preston Sturges," with Gordon Gow, in *Sight and Sound* (London), Spring 1956.
Interview, in *Interviews with Film Directors* edited by Andrew Sarris, New York, 1967.

On STURGES: books—

Cywinski, Ray, *Satires and Sideshows: The Films and Career of Preston Sturges*, Ann Arbor, Michigan, 1981.
Gordon, James R., *Comic Structures in the Films of Preston Sturges*, Ann Arbor, Michigan, 1981.
Curtis, James, *Between Flops: A Biography of Preston Sturges*, New York, 1982.
Cywinski, Ray, *Preston Sturges: A Guide to References and Resources*, Boston, 1984.
Dickos, Andrew, *Intrepid Laughter: Preston Sturges and the Movies*, Metuchen, New Jersey, 1985.
Spoto, Donald, *Madcap: The Life of Preston Sturges*, Boston, 1990.

On STURGES: articles—

Ericsson, Peter, "Preston Sturges," in *Sequence* (London), Summer 1948.
Kracauer, Siegfried, "Preston Sturges or Laughter Betrayed," in *Films in Review* (New York), February 1950.
King, Nel, and G.W. Stonier, "Preston Sturges," in *Sight and Sound* (London), Summer/Autumn 1959.
Farber, Manny, and W.S. Poster, "Preston Sturges: Success in the Movies," and Eric Jonsson, "Preston Sturges and the Theory of Decline," in *Film Culture* (New York), no.26, 1962.
Houston, Penelope, "Preston Sturges," in *Sight and Sound* (London), Summer 1965.
Budd, Michael, "Notes on Preston Sturges and America," in *Film Society Review* (New York), January 1968.
Sarris, Andrew, "Preston Sturges in the Thirties," in *Film Comment* (New York), Winter 1970/71.
Corliss, Richard, "Preston Sturges," in *Cinema* (Beverly Hills), Spring 1972.
Rubenstein, E., "The Home Fires: Aspects of Sturges's Wartime Comedy," in *Quarterly Review of Film Studies* (New York), Spring 1982.
Rebello, S., and J. Curtis, "King of Comedy: the Rise of Preston Sturges," in *American Film* (Washington D.C.), May 1982.
Rubinstein, E., "The End of Screwball Comedy: *The Lady Eve* and *The Palm . . . ,*" in *Post Script* (Jacksonville, Florida), Spring–Summer 1982.
"Preston Sturges Issue" of *Positif* (Paris), July/August 1984.
Schickel, Richard, "Preston Sturges: Alien Dreamer," in *Film Comment* (New York), November/December 1985.
Henderson, B., "Sturges at Work," in *Film Quarterly* (Berkeley), Winter 1985/1986.
Brown, Geoff, "Preston Sturges Inventor," in *Sight and Sound* (London), Autumn 1986.
Sarris, Andrew, "Comedies With Bite," in *American Film* (Washington D.C.), October 1986.
Shokoff, James, "A Knockenlocker by Any Other Word: The Democratic Comedy of Preston Sturges," in *Post Script* (Jacksonville, Florida), vol. 8, no. 1, 1988.

*   *   *

As a screenwriter, Sturges stands out for his narrative inventiveness. All of the amazing coincidences and obvious repetitions in such comedies as *Easy Living* and *The Good Fairy* show Sturges's mastery of the standard narrative form, and also his ability to exaggerate it, and to shape it to his own needs. And in *The Power and the Glory* (an early model for *Citizen Kane*), Sturges pioneered the use of voice-over narration to advance a story.

Along with John Huston, Sturges was one of the first of the sound-era screenwriters to become a director, and those films that he made from his own screenplays take even further the

Preston Sturges

narrative experiments he began as a writer in the 1930s. He continued making comedies, but often he combined them with elements that more properly belonged to social dramas in the Warner Brothers tradition, even though Sturges himself worked primarily for Paramount. *The Great McGinty*, for instance, deals with big-city political corruption. *Christmas in July*, despite its happy end, analyzes an American dream perverted by dishonesty and commercial hype. And *Sullivan's Travels*, even as it mixes aspects of *It Happened One Night* and *I Am a Fugitive From a Chain Gang*, examines the uses of comedy in a society burdened by poverty and social injustice.

With *The Palm Beach Story* and *The Lady Eve*, Sturges goes from combining genres to parodying the standard narrative form. Traditionally, in the classical narrative, elements repeat from scene to scene, but with slight differences each time. The story, then, becomes a series of episodes that are similar, but not obviously so. *The Palm Beach Story*, however (although we cannot be sure of this until the end), deals with two sets of twins, one pair male and the other female, and Sturges takes full advantage of a practically infinite number of possibilities for doubling and repetition.

In *The Lady Eve*, there are no twins to call our attention to how Sturges exaggerates the typical narrative. But the central female character, Jean, changes her identity and becomes Eve Harrington, an English aristocrat, so she can double-cross the man who jilted her when he found out she made her living as a con artist. So in this film, too, Sturges provides us with some obvious doubling. In fact, *The Lady Eve* divides neatly into two very similar parts: the shipboard romance of Charles and Jean, and then the romance, on land, of Charles and Jean-as-Eve. In this second half, the film virtually turns into a screwball comedy version of *Vertigo*. Charles falls in love with a woman who looks exactly like another woman he had loved and lost, and who, indeed, really is that woman.

The Lady Eve is most interesting in the way that it stands narrative convention on its head. Charles Pike, a wealthy ale heir, looks for snakes on the Amazon, but as soon as he leaves the jungle and heads back to civilization, the hunter becomes the hunted. This inversion itself is hardly remarkable, either in literature or the cinema. What does stand out as unusual is that the predators are all women. Pike boards a luxury liner steaming back to the United States, and every unmarried woman on board decides to end the voyage engaged to him, to have "caught" him just as Charles had been trying to capture reptiles. Certainly, there are few films from this period with such active, aggressive female characters.

Sturges works out the notion of feminine entrapment not only in his script but also through his visual style. On board, Jean plots to get Charles, and Sturges shows us her predatory skill by letting her capture Pike's image. In the dining room, Jean watches as various women attempt to attract Pike's attention. She does not want him to see her staring, so she turns away from Pike's table and holds a mirror to her face, as if she were giving a quick re-arrangement to her makeup. But instead she uses the mirror to watch Charles. Sturges cuts to a close-up of the mirror, and so we share Jean's point of view. As spectators, we are used to an appreciative male gaze, and to a woman as the subject of that gaze. But here, once again, Sturges reverses our expectations. It is Jean who plays the voyeur and, as an added show of her strength, it is Jean who apparently controls the images, since she holds the mirror, and it is she who captures an unknowing Charles within the frame of a looking-glass.

Sturges's most interesting achievement may be his 1948 film, *Unfaithfully Yours*. Here, he shows the same event three times. While fairly common in literature, this sort of narrative construction is extremely rare in the cinema. But even in liter-

ature, the repeated event almost always comes to us from the points of view of different characters. In Sturges's films, we see the event the first and second time through the eyes of the same man: an orchestra conductor plots revenge on his wife, whom he suspects of infidelity, and he imagines two different ways of getting it. Then, the next repetition, rather than being imaginary, is actual. We watch as the conductor attempts to murder his wife. So, since the conductor acts once again as the main character, even this last repetition comes to us from his point of view. The film stands out, then, as a remarkable case study of the thoughts and actions of a single character, and as one more of Sturges's experiments in narrative repetition.

During the early and mid-1940s, critics hailed Sturges as a comic genius. But after *Unfaithfully Yours*, over the last eleven years of his life, Sturges made only two more films. Upon leaving Paramount, he set out to make films for Howard Hughes, but the attempt was an ill-fated one, and Sturges's standing in the critical community declined rapidly. For several years, though, a reevaluation has been underway. Sturges's sophisticated handling of sexual relations (which the heiress in *The Palm Beach Story* refers to as "Topic A") make his films seem remarkably contemporary. And there can be no doubting Sturges's screenwriting abilities. But only recently have critics come to appreciate Sturges's consummate skills as a filmmaker.

—Eric Smoodin

SUCKSDORFF, Arne.

Swedish. Born in Stockholm, 3 February 1917. Studied painting with Otto Skold and photography with Rudolf Klein-Rogge, Reimannschule, Berlin. Married 1) Astrid Bergman; 2). First two films attracted attention of Svensk Filmindustri, who produced next 11 shorts, from 1940; directed first feature, 1953; moved to Brazil, taught at film school, Rio de Janeiro. Recipient: Oscar for Best Short Subject, for *Symphony of a City*, 1948; Prize for Superior Technique, Cannes Festival, for *The Great Adventure*, 1954.

Films as Director:

1939   *En Augustirapsodi* (*An August Rhapsody*) (short)
1940   *Din tillvaros land* (*This Land Is Full of Life. Your Own Land*) (short)
1941   *En Sommersaga* (*A Summer's Tale*) (short)
1943   *Vinden från väster* (*Wind from the West*) (short); *Sarvtid* (*Reindeer People*) (short)
1944   *Trut!* (*Gull!*) (short)
1945   *Gryning* (*Dawn*) (short); *Skugger över snön* (*Shadows on the Snow*) (short)
1947   *Människor i stad* (*Symphony of a City. Rhythm of a City*) (short); *Den drömda dalen* (*Soria-Moria. Tale of the Fjords. The Dream Valley*) (short) (+ ph)
1948   *Uppbrott* (*The Open Road*) (short) (+ ph, ed); *En kluven värld* (*A Divided World*) (short) (+ sc)
1950   *Strandhugg* (*Going Ashore*) (short) (+ sc); *Ett horn i norr* (*The Living Stream*) (short)
1951   *Indisk by* (*Indian Village*) (short) (+ pr); *Vinden och floden* (*The Wind and the River*) (short) (+ ph)
1953   *Det stora äventyret* (*The Great Adventure*)
1957   *En djungelsaga* (*The Flute and the Arrow*)
1961   *Pojken i trädet* (*The Boy in the Tree*)
1965   *Mitt hem är Copacabana* (*My Home Is Copacabana*)
1971   Antarctic animal sequences in *Forbush and the Penguins*

Arne Sucksdorff: *Det stora äventyret*

Publications:

By SUCKSDORFF: article—

Interview and article, in *Cinema* (Beverly Hills), July/August 1965.

On SUCKSDORFF: book—

Sundgren, Nils, *The New Swedish Cinema*, Stockholm, 1970.

On SUCKSDORFF: articles—

Hardy, Forsyth, "The Films of Arne Sucksdorff," in *Sight and Sound* (London), Summer 1948.

Knight, Arthur, "Producer-Director-Writer-Photographer Emerges as a New Talent Through a Series of Short Subjects," in *The New York Times*, 21 November 1948.

Ericsson, Peter, "Arne Sucksdorff," in *Sequence* (London), Spring 1949.

Ulrichsen, E., "Arne Sucksdorff," in *Films in Review* (New York), October 1953.

De La Roche, Catherine, "Arne Sucksdorff's Adventures," in *Sight and Sound* (London), October/December 1953.

De La Roche, Catherine, "Film-Maker on His Own," in *Sight and Sound* (London), November 1954.

"Arne Sucksdorff," in *Image* (Rochester, New York), May 1955.

* * *

Swedish filmmaker Arne Sucksdorff is what the French film critics call an *auteur*, or author of his work. He wrote, shot, edited, and/or supervised his films, and they bear the stamp of his personality. His films, taken as a whole, have similar themes and style, and they reflect his personal vision.

Sucksdorff, as a young man, studied both biology and art. After working with still photography, he combined his knowledge and love of nature with filmmaking. Working primarily in the documentary and semi-documentary traditions in the 1940s and 1950s, he used the images and sounds of reality and shaped them as would a poet. His films are often set in the country, and his characters are often wild animals and children (non-actors). He prefers black and white to color. Unlike Walt Disney's "true life adventures," where nature is often seen as comforting and even fun, and unlike Robert Flaherty's romantic films where outdoor life is presented as it should be, Sucksdorff shows how things are. "This is life," says Sucksdorff, "and whether we like it or not, this is the way life goes on." The spider web is almost a signature in a Sucksdorff film. It is at once beautiful and dangerous. A shadowy forest may hide a beautiful deer or a hungry bear. Animals chase and kill each other for survival. They prey upon each other. But life has its beautiful moments, too, and it is, as in the title of his most famous film, the great adventure.

Sucksdorff had considerable technical skill. Each frame of film is beautifully composed, from an extreme close-up of a gull's eye to an extreme long shot of an island cliff. Sucksdorff often used great depth-of-field and high-contrast lighting (the moon on a snowy lake) in order to create a poetic, yet realistic, mood. He also took great care in capturing foreground and background action for a sense of excitement. He spent months in the wilderness waiting for birds on the wing, rabbits washing their faces, and lynxes stalking their prey. He made much use of natural sounds, music, and narration with little, if any, dialogue. He then spent months in the cutting room on even his short films in order to present his vision. His technical skill, however, was never used to show off, but to help us see the natural world in new ways.

Svensk Filmindustri sponsored many of his early films, which often cost as much as a feature. His most famous short film is *Symphony of a City*, where people in Stockholm (rather than animals in the wilderness) are seen, sometimes through the eyes of a child. The fishing nets look like spider webs. There is beauty in the docks and a cathedral, but also disquiet in crowds, traffic, and the precarious angles of faces.

His most personal statement is the feature length *The Great Adventure*, produced by his own company and filmed in central Sweden. The adventure of the title is life, and Sucksdorff presents it (as he does in many other films) through the eyes of young animals and children (his son and his son's friend). In the film, a fox must care for her young; two boys save an otter from a hunter and care for it. In spring, the young foxes are grown and the otter needs to be free. Although there is sorrow as the otter leaves for the wilderness, there is joy in seeing the cranes fly free overhead. Soon the boys will also be grown in the great adventure of life.

Sucksdorff went on to make *The Flute and the Arrow*, about the ancient Muria tribe in Central India. Surprisingly, he then made a dramatic fiction feature, *The Boy in the Tree*, and was shaken when it was unsuccessful.

He left Sweden and spent some years as a teacher of film in Rio de Janeiro. Several of his students became the leading directors of the Brazilian Cinema Novo. Sucksdorff's film *My Home is Copacabana* is about children in Rio and their gift for survival.

Sucksdorff's films of the 1940s and 1950s are the most critically acclaimed. Since many were made on his own and distributed in 16mm through the non-theatrical film industry to schools and libraries, his films live primarily in the classroom rather than on television or in theatres. But what more appropriate place for films that show " . . . the way life goes on."

—H. Wayne Schuth

SYBERBERG, Hans-Jurgen.

German. Born in Nossendorf, Pomerania, 8 December 1935. Educated in literature and art history, Munich. Lived in East Germany until early 1950s; made 8mm films of Bertolt Brecht's Berliner Ensemble at work, 1950s (blown up for release on 35mm, 1970); made 185 current affairs and documentary shorts for Bavarian Television, 1963–66; formed own production company, 1965; made five feature-length "character portraits" on Fritz Kortner and others, 1965–69; directed first feature, *Scarabea*, 1968; made "German Trilogy," 1972–77.

Films as Director:

1965   *Fünfter Akt, siebte Szene. Fritz Kortner probt Kabale und Liebe* (*Act Five, Scene Seven. Fritz Kortner Rehearses*

Kabale und Liebe) (doc); *Romy. Anatomie eines Gesichts* (*Romy. Anatomy of a Face*) (doc)

1966   *Fritz Kortner spricht Monologe für eine Schallplatte* (*Fritz Kortner Recites Monologues for a Record*) (doc); *Fritz Kortner spricht Shylock* (*Fritz Kortner Recites Shylock*) (short; extract from *Fritz Kortner spricht Monologe . . .*); *Fritz Kortner spricht Faust* (*Fritz Kortner Recites Faust*) (short; extract from *Fritz Kortner spricht Monologe . . .*); *Wilhelm von Kobell* (short, doc)

1967   *Die Grafen Pocci—Einige Kapitel zur Geschichte einer Familie* (*The Counts of Pocci—Some Chapters Towards the History of a Family*) (doc); *Konrad Albert Pocci, der Fussballgraf vom Ammerland—Das vorläufig letzte Kapitel einer Chronik der Familie Pocci* (*Konrad Albert Pocci, the Football Count from the Ammerland—Provisionally the Last Chapter of a Chronicle of the Pocci Family*) (extract from the preceding title)

1968   *Scarabea—Wieviel Erde braucht der Mensch?* (*Scarabea—How Much Land Does a Man Need?*)

1969   *Sex-Business—Made in Passing* (doc)

1970   *San Domingo; Nach Meinem letzten Umzug* (*After My Last Move*); *Puntila* and *Faust* (shorts; extracts from the preceding title)

1972   *Ludwig—Requiem für einen jungfräulichen König* (*Ludwig—Requiem for a Virgin King*); *Theodor Hierneis oder: Wie man ehem. Hofkoch wird* (*Ludwig's Cook*)

1974   *Karl May*

1975   *Winifred Wagner und die Geschichte des Hauses Wahnfried von 1914–1975* (*The Confessions of Winifred Wagner*)

1977   **Hitler. Ein Film aus Deutschland** (**Hitler, a Film from Germany. Our Hitler**) (in 4 parts: 1. **Hitler ein Film aus Deutschland** (**Der Graal**), 2. **Ein deutscher Traum**, 3. **Das Ende eines Wintermärchens**, 4. **Wir Kinder der Hölle**)

1983   *Parsifal*

1985   *Nacht*

Publications:

By SYBERBERG: books—

Le Film, musique de l'avenir, Paris, 1975.
Syberberg Filmbuch, Munich, 1976.
Hitler, ein Film aus Deutschland, Reinbek bei Hamburg, 1978.
Die Freudlose Gesellschaft: Notizen aus dem Letzten Jahr, Munich, 1981.
Parsifal, ein Filmessay, Munich, 1982.
Der Wald Steht Schwarz und Schweiger, Neue Notizen aus Deutschland, Zurich, 1984.

By SYBERBERG: articles—

Interview with A. Tournès, in *Jeune Cinéma* (Paris), December/January 1972/73.
"Forms of Address," interview and article with Tony Rayns, in *Sight and Sound* (London), Winter 1974/75.
Interview with M. Martin, in *Ecran* (Paris), July 1978.
"Form ist Moral: 'Holocaust' Indiz der grössten Krise unserer intellektuellen Existenz," in *Medium* (Frankfurt), April 1979.
Interview with B. Erkkila in *Literature/Film Quarterly* (Salisbury, Maryland), October 1982.
Interview with I. Schroth in *Filmfaust* (Frankfurt), October/November 1985.
"Sustaining Romanticism in a Postmodernist Cinema," an interview with Christopher Sharrett in *Cineaste* (New York), vol. 15, no. 3., 1987.

On SYBERBERG: books—

Franklin, James, *New German Cinema: From Oberhausen to Hamburg*, Boston, 1983.
Phillips, Klaus, editor, *New German Filmmakers: From Oberhausen through the 1970s*, New York, 1984.
Rentschler, Eric, editor, *West German Filmmakers on Film: Visions and Voices*, New York, 1988.
Elsaesser, Thomas, *New German Cinema: A History*, London, 1989.

On SYBERBERG: articles—

Pym, John, "Syberberg and the Tempter of Democracy," in *Sight and Sound* (London), Autumn 1977.

Sauvaget, D., "Syberberg: dramaturgie, anti-naturaliste et germanitude," in *Image et Son* (Paris), January 1979.

"Syberberg Issue" of *Revue Belge du Cinéma* (Brussels), Spring 1983.

*   *   *

The films of Hans-Jürgen Syberberg are at times annoying, confusing, overlong—but also ambitious and compelling. In no way is he ever conventional or commercial: critics and audiences have alternately labelled his work brilliant and boring, absorbing and pretentious, and his films today are still rarely screened. Stylistically, it is difficult to link him with any other filmmaker or cinema tradition. In this regard he is an original, the most controversial of all the New German filmmakers and at the vanguard of the resurgence of experimental filmmaking in his homeland.

Not unlike his contemporary, Rainer Werner Fassbinder, Syberberg's most characteristic films examine recent German history: a documentary about Richard Wagner's daughter-in-law, a close friend of Hitler (*The Confessions of Winifred Wagner*); his trilogy covering 100 years of Germany past (*Ludwig II: Requiem for a Virgin King, Karl May*, and, most famously, *Hitler, A Film From Germany*, also known as *Our Hitler*). These last are linked in their depictions of Germans as hypocrites, liars, egocentrics, and in the final part he presents the rise of the Third Reich as an outgrowth of German romanticism. Even more significantly, Syberberg is concerned with the cinema's relationship to that history. *Our Hitler*, seven hours and nine minutes long, in four parts and 22 specific chapters, is at once a fictional movie, documentary, three-ring circus (the "greatest show on earth"), and a filmed theatrical marathon. The Führer is presented with some semblance of reality, via Hans Schubert's performance. But he is also caricatured, in the form of various identities and disguises: in one sequence alone, several actors play him as a house painter, Chaplin's Great Dictator, the Frankenstein monster, Parsifal (Syberberg subsequently filmed the Wagner opera), and a joker. Hitler too becomes an object, a ventriloquist's doll, and a stuffed dog. In all, twelve different actors play the role, and there are 120 dummy Führers. The result: Syberberg's Hitler is both a fascist dictator who could have risen to power at any point in time, in any number of political climates (though the filmmaker in no way excuses his homeland for allowing Hitler to exist, let alone thrive), and a monstrous movie mogul, whose *Intolerance* would be the Holocaust.

Syberberg unites fictional narrative and documentary footage in a style that is at once cinematic and theatrical, mystical and magical. His films might easily be performed live (*Our Hitler* is set on a stage), but the material is so varied that the presence of the camera is necessary to thoroughly translate the action. The fact that his staging has been captured on celluloid allows him total control of what the viewer sees at each performance. Additionally, the filmmaker is perceptibly aware of how the everyday events that make up history are ultimately comprehended by the public via the manner in which they are presented in the media. History is understood more by catchwords and generalities than facts. As a result, in this age of mass media, real events can easily become distorted and trivialized. Syberberg demonstrates this in *Our Hitler* by presenting the Führer in so many disguises that the viewer is often desensitized to the reality that was this mass murderer.

"Aesthetics are connected with morals," Syberberg says. "Something like *Holocaust* is immoral because it's a bad film. Bad art can't do good things." And, also, "My three sins are that I believe Hitler came out of us, that he is one of us; that I am not interested in money, except to work with; and that I love Germany." *Our Hitler*, and his other films, clearly reflect these preferences.

—Rob Edelman

SZABÓ, Istvan.

Hungarian. Born in Budapest, 18 February 1938. Educated at Academy of Theatre and Film Art, Budapest, graduated 1961. Directed two shorts for Béla Balázs Studio, 1961–63; directed first feature, *Almodozások kora*, 1964. Recipient: Silver Bear, Berlin Festival, for *Confidence*, 1980; Oscar for Best Foreign Film, and Best Screenplay Award and FIPRESCI Prize, Cannes Festival, for *Mephisto*, 1982.

Films as Director:

1961   *Koncert (Concert)* (short) (+ sc): *Variációk egy témára (Variations on a Theme)* (short) (+ sc)
1963   *Te (You . . .)* (short) (+ sc)
1964   *Álmodozások kora (The Age of Daydreaming)* (+ sc)
1966   *Apa (Father)* (+ sc)
1967   *Kegyelet (Piety)* (short) (+ sc)
1970   *Szerelmesfilm (Love Film)* (+ sc)
1971   *Budapest, amiért szeretem (Budapest, Why I Love It)* (series of shorts: *Alom a házröl (Dream About a House)*, *Duna—halak—madarak (The Danube—Fishes—Birds)*, *Egy tukor (A Mirror)*, *Léanyportre (A Portrait of a Girl)*, *Tér (A Square)*, *Hajnal (Dawn)*, *Alkony (Twilight)* (+ sc)
1973   *Tüzoltó utca 25 (25 Fireman's Street)* (+ sc)
1974   *Ösbemutató (Premiere)* (+ sc)
1976   *Budapesti mesék (Budapest Tales)* (+ sc)
1977   *Várostérkép (City Map)* (short) (+ sc)
1979   *Bizalom (Confidence)* (+ sc); *Der grüne Vogel (The Green Bird)* (+ sc)
1981   ***Mephisto*** (+ sc)
1984   *Bali*
1985   *Redl Ezredes (Colonel Redl)*
1988   *Hanussen*
1990   *Meeting Venus*

Publications:

By SZABÓ: articles—

Interview with Yvette Biro, in *Cahiers du Cinéma* (Paris), July 1966.

"Hungarian Director Szabo Discusses His Film Father," with Robert Siton, in *Film Comment* (New York), Fall 1968.

"Conversation with István Szabó," in *Hungarofilm Bulletin* (Budapest), no. 5, 1976.

"Mit adhat a magyar film a világnak?," interview, in *Filmkultura* (Budapest), January/February 1978.

"The Past Still Plays a Major Role," interview, in *Hungarofilm Bulletin* (Budapest), no.2, 1979.

"Dreams and Nightmares," interview with L. Rubenstein in *Cineaste* (New York), vol.12, no. 2, 1982.

"*Mephisto*: Istvan Szabo and 'the Gestapo of Suspicion'," interview with J.W. Hughes in *Film Quarterly* (Berkeley), Summer 1982.

"I'd Like to Tell a Story," in *Hungarofilm Bulletin* (Budapest), vol. 2, no. 84, 1984.

Interview with Karen Jaehne in *Stills* (London), December 1985/January 1986.

On SZABÓ: book—

Petrie, Graham, *History Must Answer to Man: The Contemporary Hungarian Cinema*, London, 1978.

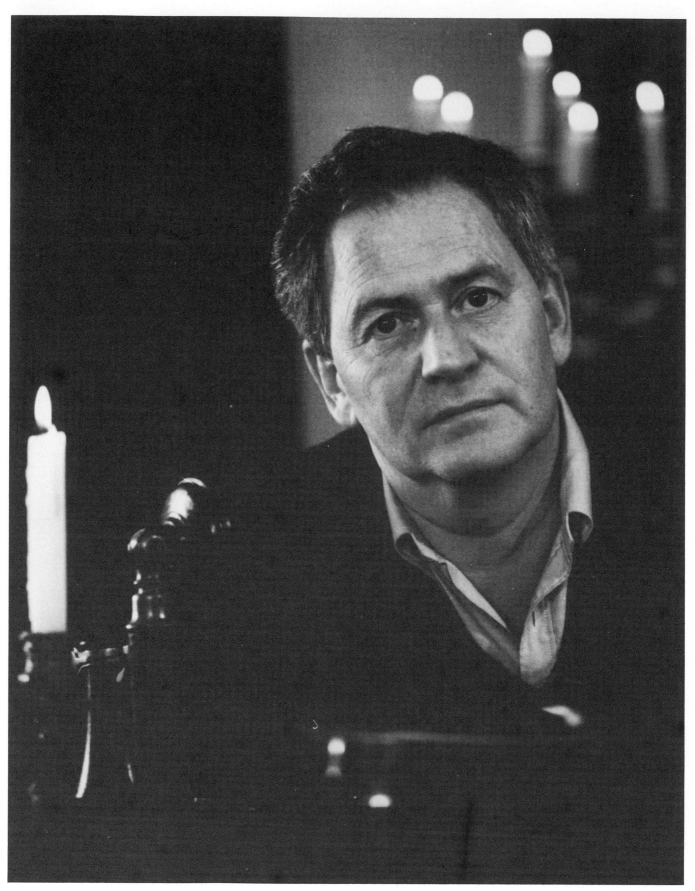

Istvan Szabo

On SZABÓ: articles—

Jaehne, Karen, "Istvan Szabo: Dreams of Memories," in *Film Quarterly* (Berkeley), Fall 1978.
Hirsch, T., "Filmek családfája," in *Filmkultura* (Budapest), March/April 1981.
"*Colonel Redl* Issue" of *Avant-Scène du Cinéma* (Paris), March 1986.
Christensen, Peter G., "Collaboration in Istvan Szabo's *Mephisto*," in *Film Criticism* (Meadville, Pennsylvania), vol. 12, no. 3, 1988.

*   *   *

Szabó's films are noted for the fact that he works with a rich spectrum of possibilities and decisions, which only in their totality attain the poetic quality that becomes the viewer's primary experience after they have been looked at together. István Szabó reacts like a sensitive membrane to everything that has happened around him in the past or is just happening. At the same time he builds solely from motives that brand a film reel with the mark of an individual personality, even when he strives for seemingly objective symbols, for example, a streetcar—that constantly recurring, tangibly real and yet poetically long logogram for his individual and very special world." Such were the words of the noted Hungarian historian and film theoretician Josef Marx as he considered the work of director István Szabó. They underscore the essential characteristic of Szabó's work, its inventiveness, which in his films takes on general forms in the broadest sense.

From his first feature film *Álmodozások kora*, which, together with Gaal's *Sordásban*, was the most expressive confession of an artistic generation and became a model for other artists, his entire work has built up an unprecedented picture of contemporary life and its activities. In his earliest period Szabó's starting point was his own experience, which he transformed into artistic images. At the same time he carefully absorbed everything that was happening around him, made observations, and attempted to discern the essence of modern people, and to come to an understanding of their concerns, endeavors, and aspirations. His films examine young engineers at the start of their careers; the personal ideals of a young man on the threshold of maturity; the changing relationship of two people, framed within a quarter-century of Hungarian history; the dreams and locked-up memories of people living together in an old apartment building; the story of an ordinary city streetcar with an allegorical resemblance to our contemporaries; the love and distrust between a pair of completely different people in a charged wartime atmosphere; and a deep probe into the character of a young actor whose talents are displayed and subordinated by the totalitarian power of nascent German fascism.

All of these films are linked by the setting off of intimate confession against historical reality. In the images of Szabó's films—full of poetry and the symbolism of dreamlike conceptions, the small dramas of ordinary people, their disappointments, successes, loves, enthusiasms, moments of anxiety and ardor, joy and pain—the history of post-war Hungary passes by in contrapuntal details. István Szabó creates auteur films (except for his last) in which the shaping of the theme and the screenplay are just as important as the direction, so that the resulting works bears a unique stamp. The heroes of his films are not only people, but also cities, streets, houses, parks—his native Budapest, which is the point of intersection of human fates. Under Szabó's creative eye the city awakens, stirs, arises, wounded after the tumult of the war, and lives with its heroes.

Only recently has István Szabó deviated from the rule of auteur films (the model for his film *Mephisto* was a novel by Klaus Mann). This detracted nothing from the importance of the work, which won an Oscar, among other awards. Even in this film the director left his imprint and managed to develop it into a picture of personal tragedy painted into a fresco of historical events. At the same time, it shows that the creative process is a tireless search for pathways. Only a responsible approach to history and the way it is shaped can help the artist to complete understanding of today's world.

"To awaken an interest in the people I want to tell about; to capture their essence so that a viewer can identify with them; to broaden people's understanding and sympathy—and my own as well: That's what I'd like to do . . . ," István Szabó once said in an interview. His films are an affirmation of this credo.

—Vacláv Merhaut

T

TANNER, Alain.

Swiss. Born in Geneva, 6 December 1929. Educated in economic sciences, Calvin College, Geneva. Shipping clerk, early 1950s; moved to London, worked at British Film Institute, 1955; assistant producer for the BBC, 1958; returned to Switzerland, 1960; co-founder, Association Suisse des Réalisateurs, early 1960s; director for Swiss French TV, 1964–69; began collaboration with writer John Berger on *Une Ville à Chandigarh*, 1966; co-founder, Groupe 5, 1968. Recipient: Experimental Film Prize, Venice Festival, for *Nice Time*, 1957; Best Screenplay (with Berger), National Society of Film Critics, for *Jonah Who Will Be 25 in the Year 2000*, 1976; Special Jury Prize, Cannes Festival, for *Les Années lumière*, 1981.

Films as Director:

1957   *Nice Time* (short) (co-d)
1959   *Ramuz, passage d'un poète* (short)
1962   *L'Ecole* (sponsored film)
1964   *Les Apprentis* (doc feature)
1966   *Une Ville à Chandigarh*
1969   *Charles, mort ou vif* (*Charles, Dead or Alive*)
1971   *Le Salamandre* (*The Salamander*)
1973   *Le Retour d'Afrique*
1974   *Le Milieu du monde* (*The Middle of the World*)
1976   *Jonah qui aura 25 ans en l'année 2000* (*Jonah Who Will Be 25 in the Year 2000*)
1978   *Messidor*
1981   *Les Années lumière* (*Light Years Away*)
1983   *Dans la ville blanche* (*In the White City*)
1985   *No Man's Land*
1986   *François Simon—La présence*
1987   *Flamme dans mon coeur* (*A Flame in My Heart*); *Vallée Fantôme*
1989   *Femme de Rose Hill*

Publications:

By TANNER: book—

Jonah Who Will Be 25 in the Year 2000, with John Berger, Berkeley, 1983.

By TANNER: articles—

Interview with Michel Delahaye and others in *Cahiers du Cinéma* (Paris), June 1969.
Interview with L. Bonnard, in *Positif* (Paris), February 1972.
"*Le Milieu du monde*," an interview with Noel Simsolo and Guy Braucourt, in *Ecran* (Paris), October 1974.
"Irony is a Double-Edged Weapon," an interview with L. Rubinstein, in *Cineaste* (New York), vol. 6, no. 4, 1975.
"Keeping Hope for Radical Change Alive," an interview with L. Rubinstein, in *Cineaste* (New York), Winter 1976/77.
"Alain Tanner: After Jonah," an interview with M. Tarantino, in *Sight and Sound* (London), no.1, 1978/79.

Interview with Jill Forbes in *Films and Filming* (London), February 1982.
Interview with Martyn Auty in *Monthly Film Bulletin* (London), November 1983.
Interview with J. Chevallier and Y. Alion in *Revue du Cinéma* (Paris), September 1985.
Interview with F. Sabouraud and S. Toubiana in *Cahiers du Cinéma* (Paris), October 1987.

On TANNER: books—

Leach, Jim, *A Possible Cinema: The Films of Alain Tanner*, Metuchen, New Jersey, 1984.
Dimitriu, Christian, *Alain Tanner*, Paris, 1985.

On TANNER: articles—

"Tanner Issue" of *Cinema* (Zurich), vol. 20, no. 1, 1974.
Tarantino, M., "Tanner and Berger: the Voice Off-Screen," in *Film Quarterly* (Berkeley), Winter 1979/80.
Harrild, A.E., "Tanner-Jonah-Ideology," in *Film Directions* (Belfast), vol. 3, no. 11, 1980.
"The Screenwriter as Collaborator," interview of John Berger, in *Cineaste* (New York), Summer 1980.
"*Les Années lumière* Issue" of *Avant-Scène du Cinéma* (Paris), 15 June 1981.
Pulleine, Tim, "Tanner's White City," in *Sight and Sound* (London), Winter 1983/1984.
Buache, Freddy, "Alain Tanner," in *Revue Belge du Cinéma* (Brussels), Winter 1985.

*   *   *

Alain Tanner's involvement with film began while attending Geneva's Calvin College where he and Claude Goretta formed Geneva's first film society. Here Tanner developed an admiration for the ethnographic documentaries of Jean Rouch and fellow Swiss Henry Brandt, an influence that continued throughout his career. After a brief stint with the Swiss merchant marine, Tanner spent a year in London as an apprentice at the BFI, where, with Goretta, he completed an experimental documentary, *Nice Time*, chronicling the night life of Piccadilly Circus. While in London he participated in the Free Cinema Movement, along with Karel Reisz, Tony Richardson, and Lindsay Anderson. Through Anderson, Tanner made the acquaintance of novelist and art critic, John Berger, who would later write the scenarios for *Le Salamandre*, *Middle of the World*, *Jonah Who Will Be 25 in the Year 2000*, and *Le Retour d'Afrique*.

Upon returning to Switzerland in 1960, he completed some 40 documentaries for television. Among these were: *Les Apprentis*, concerning the lives of teenagers (using the methods of Rouch's direct cinema); *Une Ville à Chandigarh*, on the architecture designed by Le Corbusier for the Punjab capital (the narration for this film was assembled by John Berger); and newsreel coverage of the events of May 1968 in Paris. This last provided the ammunition for Tanner (once again with Goretta) to form Groupe 5, a collective of Swiss filmmakers.

Alain Tanner   ©**Peter Smith**

They proposed an idea to Swiss TV for the funding of full-length narrative features to be shot in 16mm and then blown-up to 35mm for release. The plan enabled Tanner to make his first feature, *Charles, Dead or Alive*, which won first prize at Locarno in 1969. The film tells of a middle-aged industrialist who, on the eve of receiving an award as the foremost business personality of the year, discovers his disaffection for the institution-laden society in which he finds himself. Following an innate sense of anarchism that Tanner posits as universal, he attempts to reject this lifestyle. His retreat into madness is blocked by his family and friends who compel him, out of duty, to resume his responsibilities. All Tanner's films follow a similar scenario: individuals or a group become alienated from society; rejecting it, they try to forge a new society answerable to themselves alone, only to be defeated by the relentless pressures of traditional society's institutions, whose commerce they never cease to require. This theme receives its fullest and most moving expression in *Jonah*. . . . Here the failure of the collective and the survivors of 1968, who come together at Marguerite's farm outside Geneva, is not viewed as a defeat so much as one generation's attempt to keep the hope of radical social change alive by passing on the fruits of its mistakes, that is, its education or its lore, to the succeeding generation.

Tanner's style is a blend of documentary and fable. He uses techniques such as one scene/one shot, a staple of cinéma-vérité documentary, to portray a fable or folk-story. This tension between fact and fiction, documentary and fable, receives its most exacting treatment in *Le Salamandre*. Rosemonde's indomitable rebellious vitality repeatedly defeats the efforts of the two journalists to harness it in a pliable narrative form. After *Jonah* . . . , Tanner introduces a darker vision in *Messidor, Light Years Away*, and *Dans la ville blanche*. The possibility of escaping society by returning to nature is explored and shown to be equally provisional. The tyranny of physical need is portrayed as being just as oppressive and compromising as that of the social world.

—Dennis Nastav

———

TARKOVSKY, Andrei.

Soviet Russian. Born in Moscow, 4 April 1932. Educated at Institute of Oriental Languages, graduated 1954; All-Union State Cinematography Institute (VGIK), graduated 1960. Married 1), two children; 2), one son. Geological prospector in Siberia, 1954–56; on diploma work *The Steamroller and the Violin*, began collaboration with cameraman Yadim Yusov and Vyacheslav Ovchinnikov, 1960; directed opera *Boris Godunov* at Covent Garden, 1983; made last film, *The Sacrifice*, in Sweden, 1986. Recipient: Lion of St. Mark for Best Film, Venice Festival, for *Ivan's Childhood*, 1962; International Critics Award, Cannes Festival, for *Andrei Rublev*, 1969; Special Jury Prize, Cannes Festival, for *Solaris*, 1972; Merited Artistic Worker of the RSFSR, 1974; Grand Prix, Cannes Festival, for *The Sacrifice*, 1986. *Died of cancer, in Paris, 29 December 1986.*

Films as Director:

1959 *There Will Be No Leave Today* (short)
1960 *Katok i skripka* (*The Steamroller and the Violin*) (+ co-sc)

1962 *Ivanovo detstvo* (*Ivan's Childhood*)
1969 ***Andrei Rublev*** (+ co-sc)
1971 *Solyaris* (*Solaris*) (+ co-sc)
1975 *Zerkalo* (*The Mirror*) (+ co-sc)
1979 *Stalker*
1983 *Nostalghia* (*Nostalgia*)
1986 ***Offret*** (***The Sacrifice***)

Publications:

By TARKOVSKY: book—

Andrei Rublev, Paris, 1970.
Sculpting in Time: Reflections on the Cinema, London, 1986; revised edition, 1989.

By TARKOVSKY: articles—

Interview with O. Surkova in *Iskusstvo Kino* (Moscow), July 1977.
"Against Interpretation," an interview with Ian Christie, in *Framework* (Norwich), Spring 1981.
"Tarkovsky in Italy," an interview with T. Mitchell in *Sight and Sound* (London), Winter 1982/83.
Interview with J. Hoberman in *American Film* (Washington D.C.), November 1983.

On TARKOVSKY: books—

Liehm, Mira and Antonín, *The Most Important Art: Eastern European Film After 1945*, Berkeley, 1977.
Borin, Fabrizio, *Andrej Tarkovsky*, Venice, 1987.
Jacobsen, Wolfgang, and others, *Andrej Tarkovskij*, Munich, 1987.
Le Fanu, Mark, *The Cinema of Andrei Tarkovsky*, London, 1987.
Gauthier, Guy, *Andrei Tarkovsky*, Paris, 1988.
Turovskaya, Maya, *Tarkovsky: Cinema as Poetry*, London, 1989.

On TARKOVSKY: articles—

Montagu, Ivor, "Man and Experience: Tarkovski's World," in *Sight and Sound* (London), Spring 1973.
Ward, M., "The Idea That Torments and Exhausts," in *Stills* (London), Spring 1981.
Strick, Philip, "Tarkovsky's Translations," in *Sight and Sound* (London), Summer 1981.
Dempsey, M. "Lost Harmony—Tarkovsky's *The Mirror* and *The Stalker*," in *Film Quarterly* (Berkeley), Fall 1981.
"Tarkovsky Issue" of *Positif* (Paris), October 1981.
Zak, M., in *Iskusstvo Kino* (Moscow), September 1982.
Ratschewa. M., "The Messianic Power of Pictures: The Films of Andrei Tarkovsky," in *Cineaste* (New York), vol. 13, no. 1, 1983.
Mitchell, T., "Andrei Tarkovsky and *Nostalghi*," in *Film Criticism* (Meadville, Pennysylvania), Spring 1984.
Tarkovsky Section of *Positif* (Paris), October 1984.
Green, P., "The Nostalgia of *The Stalker*," in *Sight and Sound* (London), Winter 1984/1985.
Tarkovsky Sections of *Positif* (Paris), May and June 1986.
Tarkovsky Section of *Cahiers du Cinéma* (Paris), July/August 1986.
Obituary in *Variety* (New York), 31 December 1986.
Christie, Ian, "Raising the Shroud," in *Monthly Film Bulletin* (London), February 1987.
Green, Peter, obituary in *Sight and Sound* (London), Spring 1987.
Kennedy, Harlan, "Tarkovsky, a Thought in Nine Parts," in *Film Comment* (New York), May/June 1987.
Leszczylowski, Michal, "A Year with Andrei," in *Sight and Sound* (London), Autumn 1987.
Tarkovsky Section of *Positif* (Paris), February 1988.
Strick, Philip, "Releasing the Balloon, Raising the Bell," in *Monthly Film Bulletin* (London), February 1991.

On TARKOVSKY: film—

Leszczylowski, Michal, *Directed by Andrei Tarkovsky*, 1986.

* * *

"Tarkovsky is the greatest of them all. He moves with such naturalness in the room of dreams. He doesn't explain. What should he explain anyhow?" Thus Ingmar Bergman, in his autobiography *The Magic Lantern*, bows down before the Russian director while hinting at what makes Tarkovsky's work so

Andrei Tarkovsky

awkward to critics: it can verge on the inscrutable. Too opaque to yield concrete meaning, it offers itself as sacral art, demanding a rapt, and even religious, response from its audiences. In the 1979 film, *Stalker*, there is a place called the Zone where all "desires come true." Rather like the land of Oz, this mysterious outland promises to reveal the secret of things to any intrepid travellers who prospect it to its core. But there are no cowardly lions or tin men to ease the journey, no yellow brick road to follow. The Zone is an austere realm, typical Tarkovsky territory, whose bleak landscapes are populated by characters laden with a peculiarly Russian gloom.

Watching Tarkovsky's films, his "sculptures in time," spectators can find themselves on a journey every bit as arduous as that undertaken by the pilgrims who headed toward the Zone. The son of a poet, the director treated film as a medium in which he could express himself in the first person. His six years at the Moscow State Film School, during which he received a thorough grounding in film technique from such Soviet luminaries as Mikhail Romm, did nothing to disabuse him of the notion that cinema was a "high art." He felt he could tap the same vein of poetic intimacy that his father sought in lyric verse: the necessary intrusion of camera crews and actors, and the logistical problems of exhibition and distribution, worried him not a jot. Although all his films are self-reflexive, he does not draw attention to the camera for radical Brechtian reasons. He is not laying bare the device, emphasizing the formal qualities of his work because he wants to draw a link between the images that appear on the screen and the money and labour that facilitate their appearance. He is not trying to subvert bourgeois narrative codes. He is not even assaulting the tenets of Socialist Realism, a doctrine he found every bit as unappealing as Western mass culture aimed at the "consumer," (although his ex-partner, Konchalovsky, ended up in Hollywood directing Sylvester Stallone vehicles). What his constant use of tracking shots, slow motion and never ending pans, indeed his entire visual rhetoric seems to emphasize, is that he is moulding the images. He is a virtuoso, and he wants us to be aware of the fact.

Tarkovsky's first two feature length projects, *Ivan's Childhood* and *Andrei Rublev*, mark a curious collision between the personal and the political. On one level, the former is a propaganda piece, telling yet again the great Soviet story of the defeat of the Nazi scourge during World War II. But Tarkovsky destabilizes the film with dream sequences. The "big questions" that are ostensibly being addressed turn out to be peripheral: the director is more concerned with the poetic rekindling of childhood than with a triumphal narrative of Russian resilience. Similarly, *Rublev*, an epic, three-hour bio-pic of a medieval icon painter, in spite of the specificity and grandeur of its locations, is a rigorous account of the role of the artist in society, as applicable to the 1960s as to the 1300s.

As if to display his versatility, Tarkovsky skipped genres, moving from the distant past to the distant future for his third feature, *Solaris*, a rather ponderous sci-fi movie, taken from a novel by the Polish writer, Stanislaw Lem. The harsh, Kubrick-like spaceship interiors suit the director far less well than his customary wet and muddy landscapes. The musings on love and immortality engaged in by the cosmonauts as they hover above a sea of liquid gas—for a filmmaker with such a flair for images, Tarkovsky resorts with surprising frequency to portentuous dialogue—weigh the story down. Again, it is on an intimate level, that of a man trying to come to terms with the death of his wife, that *Solaris* works.

Mirror is quintessential Tarkovsky, ravishing to look at, full of classical music and so narratively dense as to be almost unfathomable on a first viewing. There are only 200 or so shots in it, and it is a film that fell into shape, almost by accident, late in the editing stage, but it is Tarkovsky's richest and most resonant work. The narrative flits between the present and the past, between the "adult" mentality of the narrator, and the memory of his childhood; the wide open spaces of the countryside where Tarkovsky spent his earliest years are contrasted with the constricting rooms of city apartments. Poems by the director's father, Arseny, appear on the soundtrack. Complementing these, Tarkovsky is at his most elemental: the wind rustling the trees, fire and water are constant motifs. He went to enormous lengths to recreate the landscape of his infancy, planting buckwheat a year before shooting started, and constructing, from memory and old photographs, the bungalow where he had lived. There is a humour and warmth in *Mirror* sometimes absent in his work as a whole. (This may have something to do with the fact that it is his only film to have a woman protagonist. Margarita Terekova, who ranks with Anatoli Solonitzine as Tarkovsky's favourite actor, plays both the narrator's wife and his mother.) Generally, Tarkovsky terrain is desolate, ravaged by war, or threatened with catastrophe as in *The Sacrifice*, but here the forests and rivers and fields are nurturing and colourful. Accused by the authorities of being narratively obscure, Tarkovsky testified that he received many letters from viewers who had seen their own childhoods miraculously crystallize as they watched the film.

Nostalgia, his first film in exile after his defection to the West, shot in Italy, showed the Russian pining for his homeland. He wouldn't live to see it again.

The Sacrifice is a typically saturnine final testament from a filmmaker overly aware of his own reputation. Tarkovsky believed that "modern mass culture, aimed at the consumer . . . is crippling people's souls." A self-conscious exercise in spiritual plumbing, his last work before his premature death from cancer in 1987 is weighed down by its own gravitas. Shot by Sven Nykvist, using natural light for the interior scenes and full of intricate pans, it has the formal beauty that one has come to associate with the director, but its endless and wordy metaphysical surmising stops it from tugging at memory and emotion in the way of the best of his work, most notably *Mirror*.

—G.C. Macnab

———

TASHLIN, Frank.

American. Born in Weehawken, New Jersey, 19 February 1913. Educated in public school, Astoria, Long Island. Married Mary Costa. Errand boy for Max Fleischer, 1928; worked on *Aesop's Fables* cartoons at RKO, from 1930, became animator; sold cartoons to magazines under pseudonym "Tish-Tash," until 1936; moved to Hollywood, worked at Vitaphone Corp. om *Merrie Melodies* and *Looney Tunes*, 1933; comic strip *Van Boring* syndicated, 1934–36; gagman at Hal Roach Studios, 1935, then director and scriptwriter for *Looney Tunes*; story director at Disney studios for *Mickey Mouse* and *Donald Duck* series, 1939–40; executive producer, Columbia's Screen Gems Cartoon Studios, 1941; returned to *Merrie Melodies* and *Looney Tunes*, 1942, also directed first *Private Snafu* cartoon for Frank Capra's Army Signal Corps Unit; first non-animated film credit as co-scriptwriter for *Delightfully Dangerous*, 1944; gag writer at Paramount, 1945; writer for Eddie Bracken's CBS radio shows, 1946; took over direction of *The Lemon Drop Kid* at request of Bob Hope, 1950; writer, producer and director for TV, from 1952. *Died in Hollywood, 5 May 1972.*

Frank Tashlin

Films as Director:

1950 *The Lemon Drop Kid* (co-d, uncredited, + co-sc)
1951 *The First Time* (+ co-sc); *Son of Paleface* (+ co-sc)
1953 *Marry Me Again* (+ sc); *Susan Slept Here* (+ co-sc uncredited)
1955 *Artists and Models* (+ co-sc); *The Lieutenant Wore Skirts* (+ co-sc)
1956 *Hollywood or Bust* (+ co-sc uncredited); *The Girl Can't Help It* (+ pr, co-sc)
1957 *Will Success Spoil Rock Hunter?* (+ sc, pr)
1958 *Rock-a-Bye Baby* (+ sc); *The Geisha Boy* (+ sc)
1959 *Say One for Me* (+ co-sc uncredited, pr)
1960 *Cinderfella* (+ sc)
1962 *Bachelor Flat* (+ co-sc)
1963 *It's Only Money* (+ co-sc); *The Man from The Diner's Club*; *Who's Minding the Store?* (+ co-sc)
1964 *The Disorderly Orderly* (+ sc)
1965 *The Alphabet Murders*
1966 *The Glass Bottom Boat*; *Caprice* (+ co-sc)
1968 *The Private Navy of Sergeant O'Farrell* (+ sc)

Other Films:

1944 *Delightfully Dangerous* (Lubin) (sc)
1947 *Variety Girl* (Marshall) (co-sc); *The Paleface* (McLeod) (co-sc); *The Fuller Brush Man* (*That Mad Mr Jones*) (Simon) (co-sc)
1948 *One Touch of Venus* (Seiter) (co-sc); *Love Happy* (Miller) (co-sc)
1949 *Miss Grant Takes Richmond* (*Innocence Is Bliss*) (Bacon) (co-sc); *Kill the Umpire* (Bacon) (sc); *The Good Humor Man* (Bacon) (sc)
1950 *The Fuller Brush Girl* (*The Affairs of Sally*) (Bacon) (sc)
1956 *The Scarlet Hour* (Curtiz) (co-sc)

Publications:

By TASHLIN: articles—

"Frank Tashlin—An Interview and an Appreciation," with Peter Bogdanovich, in *Film Culture* (New York), no. 26, 1962.

On TASHLIN: book—

Schneider, Steve, *That's All Folks!: The Art of Warner Bros. Animation*, New York, 1988.

On TASHLIN: articles—

Benayoun, Robert, and others, articles, in *Positif* (Paris), no. 29
Boussinot, Roger, "Frank Tashlin," in *Cinéma* (Paris), no. 49, 1960.
Cameron, Ian, "Frank Tashlin and the New World," in *Movie* (London), February 1963.
Bogdanovich, Peter, "Tashlin's Cartoons," in *Movie* (London), Winter 1968/69.
Bogdanovich, Peter, "Frank Tashlin," in *The New York Times*, 28 May 1972.
Beylie, Claude, "La Fin d'un amuseur," in *Ecran* (Paris), July/August 1972.
Grisolia, M., "Frank Tashlin ou la poétique de l'objet," in *Cinéma* (Paris), July/August 1972.
Cohen, M.S., "Looney Tunes and Merrie Melodies," in *Velvet Light Trap* (Madison), Autumn 1975.

*   *   *

Frank Tashlin had achieved recognition as a children's writer when he entered the film industry to work in the animation units at Disney and Warner. Both of these early careers would have decisive import for the major films that Tashlin would direct in the 1950s. This early experience allowed Tashlin to see everyday life as a visually surreal experience, as a kind of cartoon itself, and gave him a faith in the potential for natural experience to act as a resistance to the increased mechanization of everyday life. Tashlin's films of the 1950s are great displays of cinematic technique, particularly as it developed in a TV-fearing Hollywood: wide-screen, radiant color, frenetic editing, and a deliberate recognition of film as film. Tashlin's films often resemble live versions of the Warners cartoons. Jerry Lewis, who acted in many of Tashlin's films, seemed perfect for such a visual universe with his reversions to a primal animality, his deformations of physicality, and his sheer irrationality.

Tashlin's films are also concerned with the ways the modern world is becoming more and more artificial; the films are often filled with icons of the new mass culture (rock and roll, comic books, television, muscle men, Jayne Mansfield, Hollywood) and are quite explicit about the ways such icons are mechanically produced within a consumer society. For example, in *Will Success Spoil Rock Hunter?*, the successful romance of Rita Marlow (Jayne Mansfield) will cause other women to engage in dangerous bust-expanding exercises to the point of nervous exhaustion. Yet the very critique of mass culture by an artist working in a commercial industry creates the central contradiction of Tashlin's cinema: if the danger of modern life is its increasing threat of mechanization, then what is the critical potential of an art based on mechanization? Significantly, Tashlin's films can be viewed as a critique of the ostentatious vulgarity of the new plastic age while they simultaneously seem to revel in creating ever better and more spectacular displays of sheer technique to call attention to that age. For example, *The Girl Can't Help It* chronicles the making of a non-talent (Jayne Mansfield) into a star, viewing the process with a certain cynicism, but at the same time participating in that process. These films are vehicles for Mansfield as Mansfield, and are thus somewhat biographical.

As with Lewis, serious treatment of Tashlin began in France (especially in the pages of *Positif*, which has always had an attraction to the comic film as an investigator of the Absurd). Anglo-American criticism tended to dismiss Tashlin (for example, Sarris in *American Cinema* called him "vulgar"). In such a context, Claire Johnston and Paul Willemen's *Frank Tashlin* has the force of a breakthrough, providing translations from French journals, and analyses of the cinematic and ideological implications of Tashlin's work.

—Dana B. Polan

————

TATI, Jacques.

French. Born Jacques Tatischeff in Le Pecq, France, 9 October 1908. Educated at Lycée de St.-Germain-en-Laye; also attended a college of arts and engineering, 1924. Married Micheline Winter, 1944; children: Sophie and Pierre. Rugby player with Racing Club de Paris, 1925–30; worked as pantomimist/impressionist, from 1930; recorded one of his stage routines, "Oscar, champion de tennis," on film, 1932; toured European music halls and circuses, from 1935; served in French Army, 1939–45; directed himself in short film, *L'Ecole des facteurs*, 1946; directed and starred in first feature, *Jour de fête*, 1949; offered American TV series of 15 minute programs, refused, 1950s; made *Parade* for Swedish TV, 1973. Recipient: Best Scenario, Venice Festival, for *Jour de fête*, 1949; Max Linder Prize (France) for *L'Ecole des facteurs*, 1949; Prix Louis Delluc, for *Les Vacances de M. Hulot*, 1953; Special Prize, Cannes Festival, for *Mon Oncle*, 1958; Grand Prix National des Arts et des Lettres, 1979; Commandeur des Arts et des Lettres. *Died 5 November 1982.*

Films as Director:

1947   *L'Ecole des facteurs* (+ sc, role)
1949   *Jour de fête* (+ co-sc, role as François the postman)
1953   **Les Vacances de Monsieur Hulot (Mr. Hulot's Holiday)** (+ co-sc, role as M. Hulot)
1958   *Mon Oncle* (+ co-sc, role as M. Hulot)
1967   **Playtime** (+ sc, role as M. Hulot)
1971   *Trafic* (*Traffic*) (+ co-sc, role as M. Hulot)
1973   *Parade* (+ sc, role as M. Loyal)

Other Films:

1932   *Oscar, champion de tennis* (sc, role)
1934   *On demande une brute* (Barrois) (co-sc, role)
1935   *Gai Dimanche* (Berry) (co-sc, role)
1936   *Soigne ton gauche* (Clément) (role)
1938   *Retour à la terre* (pr, sc, role)
1945   *Sylvie et le fantôme* (Autant-Lara) (role as ghost)
1946   *Le Diable au corps* (Autant-Lara) (role as soldier)

Publications:

By TATI: articles—

"Tati Speaks," with Harold Woodside, in *Take One* (Montreal), no. 6, 1969.
Interview with E. Burcksen in *Cinématographe* (Paris), May 1977.
Interview with M. Makeieff in *Cinématographe* (Paris), January 1985.

On TATI: books—

Sadoul, Georges, *The French Film*, London, 1953.
Bazin, André, *Qu'est ce-que le cinéma*, London, 1958.
Carrière, Jean-Claude, *Monsieur Hulot's Holiday*, New York, 1959.
Cauliez, Armand, *Jacques Tati*, Paris, 1968.

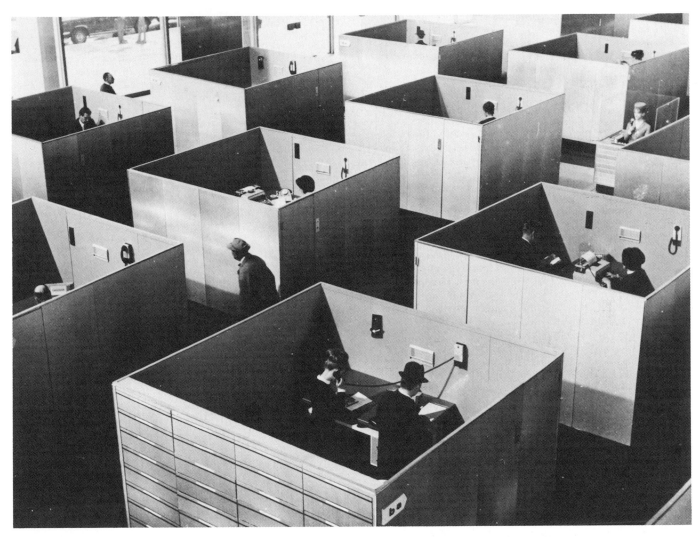

Jacques Tati: *Playtime*

Mast, Gerald, *The Comic Mind*, New York, 1973; revised edition, Chicago, 1979.

Kerr, Walter, *The Silent Clowns*, New York, 1975.

Gilliatt, Penelope, *Jacques Tati*, London, 1976.

Maddock, Brent, *The Films of Jacques Tati*, Metuchen, New Jersey, 1977.

Fischer, Lucy, *Jacques Tati: A Guide to References and Resources*, Boston, 1983.

Harding, James, *Jacques Tati: Frame by Frame*, London, 1984.

Chion, Michel, *Jacques Tati*, Paris, 1987.

Dondey, Marc, *Tati*, Paris, 1989.

On TATI: articles—

"Mr. Hulot," in the *New Yorker*, 17 July 1954.

Mayer, A.C., "The Art of Jacques Tati," in *Quarterly of Film, Radio, and Television* (Berkeley), Fall 1955.

Simon, John, "Hulot: or The Common Man as Observer and Critic," in the *Yale French Review* (New Haven, Connecticut), no. 23, 1959.

Houston, Penelope, "Conscience and Comedy," in *Sight and Sound* (London), Summer/Autumn 1959.

Marcabru, Pierre, "Jacques Tati contre l'ironie française," in *Arts* (Paris), 8 March 1961.

Armes Roy, "The Comic Art of Jacques Tati," in *Screen* (London), February 1970.

Dale, R.C., "Playtime and Traffic, Two New Tati's," in *Film Quarterly* (Berkeley), no. 2, 1972–73.

Rosenbaum, Jonathan, "Tati's Democracy," in *Film Comment* (New York), May/June 1973.

Thompson, K., "Parameters of the Open Film: Les Vacances de Monsieur Hulot," in *Wide Angle* (Athens, Ohio), vol. 1, no. 4, 1977.

"Tati Issue" of *Cahiers du Cinéma* (Paris), September 1979.

Schefer, J.-L., "Monsieur Tati," in *Cahiers du Cinéma* (Paris), December 1982.

Fischer, Lucy, "*Jour de fête*: Americans in Paris," in *Film Criticism* (Meadville, Pennsylvania), Winter 1983.

"Jacques Tati Issue" of *Cinéma* (Paris), January 1983.

Rosenbaum, Jonathan, "The Death of Hulot," in *Sight and Sound* (London), Spring 1983.

Carriére. J.-C. "Comedie à la Française," in *American Film* (New York), December 1985.

Thompson, Kristin, "*Parade*, a Review of an Unreleased Film," in *Velvet Light Trap* (Madison, Wisconsin), no. 22, 1986.

* * *

Jacques Tati's father was disappointed that his son didn't enter the family business, the restoration and framing of old paintings. He shouldn't have been, for in Jacques Tati's films, the art of framing—of selecting borders and playing on the limits of the image—achieved new expressive heights. Instead of old paintings, Tati restored the art of visual comedy, bringing out a new density and brilliance of detail, a new clarity of composition. He is one of the handful of film artists—the others would include Griffith, Eisenstein, Murnau, Bresson—who can be said to have transformed the medium at its most basic level, to have found a new way of seeing.

After a short career as a rugby player, Tati entered the French music hall circuit of the early 1930s; his act consisted of pantomine parodies of the sports stars of the era. Several of his routines were filmed as shorts in the 1930s (and he appeared as a supporting actor in two films by Claude Autant-Lara), but he did not return to direction until after the war, with the 1947 short *L'Ecole des facteurs*. Two years later, the short was expanded into a feature, *Jour de fête*. Here Tati plays a village postman who, struck by the "modern, efficient" methods he sees in a short film on the American postal system, decides to streamline his own operations. The satiric theme that runs through all of Tati's work—the coldness of modern technology—is already well developed, but more importantly, so is his visual style. Many of the gags in *Jour de fête* depend on the use of framelines and foreground objects to obscure the comic event—not to punch home the gag, but to hide it and purify it, to force the spectator to intuit, and sometimes invent, the joke for himself. Tati took four years to make his next film, *Les Vacances de Monsieur Hulot* (*Mr. Hulot's Holiday*), which introduced the character he was to play for the rest of his career—a gently eccentric Frenchman, whose tall, reedy figure was perpetually bent forward as if by the weight of the pipe he always kept clamped in his mouth. The warmth of the characterization, plus the radiant inventiveness of the sight gags, made *Mr. Hulot* an international success, yet the film already suggests Tati's dissatisfaction with the traditional idea of the comic star. Hulot is not a comedian, in the sense of being the source and focus of the humor; he is, rather, an attitude, a signpost, a perspective that reveals the humor in the world around him.

Mon Oncle is a transitional film: though Hulot had abdicated his star status, he is still singled out among the characters—prominent, but strangely marginal. With *Playtime*, released after nine years of expensive, painstaking production, Tati's intentions become clear. Hulot was now merely one figure among many, weaving in and out of the action much like the Mackintosh Man in Joyce's *Ulysses*. And just as Tati the actor refuses to use his character to guide the audience through the film, so does Tati the director refuse to use close-ups, emphatic camera angles, or montage to guide the audience to the humor in the images. *Playtime* is composed almost entirely of long-shot tableaux that leave the viewer free to wander through the frame, picking up the gags that may be occurring in the foreground, the background, or off to one side. The film returns an innocence of vision to the spectator; no value judgements or hierarchies of interest have been made for us. We are given a clear field, left to respond freely to an environment that has not been polluted with prejudices.

But audiences, used to being told what to see, found the freedom of *Playtime* oppressive. The film (released in several versions, from a 70mm stereo cut that ran over three hours to an absurdly truncated American version of 93 minutes) was a commercial failure, and plunged Tati deep into personal debt. His last theatrical film, the 1971 *Traffic*, would have seemed a masterpiece from anyone else, but for Tati it was clearly a protective return to a more traditional style. Tati's final project, a 60-minute television film titled *Parade*, has never been shown in America. Five films in 25 years is not an impressive record in a medium where stature is often measured by prolificity, but *Playtime* alone is a lifetime's achievement—a film that liberates and revitalizes the act of looking at the world.

—Dave Kehr

TAVERNIER, Bertrand.

French. Born in Lyons, 25 April 1941. Studied law for one year. Married writer Colo O'Hagan (separated), two children. Film critic for *Positif* and *Cahiers du Cinema*, Paris, early 1960s; press agent for producer Georges de Beauregard, 1962; freelance press agent, associated with Pierre Rissient, 1965; directed first film, *L'Horloger de St. Paul*, 1974. Recipient: Prix Louis Delluc, for *L'Horloger de St. Paul*, 1974; Cesar Awards for Best Director and Best Original Screenplay (with Jean Aurenche), for *Que la fête commence*, 1975.

Films as Director and Co-Scriptwriter:

1964 "Une Chance explosive" episode of *La Chance et l'amour*
1965 "Le Baiser de Judas" episode of *Les Baisers*
1974 *L'Horloger de Saint-Paul* (*The Clockmaker*)
1975 *Que la fête commence* (*Let Joy Reign Supreme*)
1976 *Le Juge et l'assassin* (*The Judge and the Assassin*)
1977 *Des enfants gâtés* (*Spoiled Children*)
1979 *Femmes Fatales*
1980 *La Mort en direct* (*Death Watch*)
1981 *Une Semaine de vacances* (*A Week's Vacation*)
1982 *Coup de torchon* (*Clean Slate*); *Philippe Soupault et le surréalisme*) (doc)
1983 *Mississippi Blues* (*Pays d'Octobre*) (co-d)
1984 *Un Dimanche à la campagne* (*A Sunday in the Country*)
1986 *'Round Midnight* (***Autour de minuit***)
1987 *Le Passion Béatrice*
1988 *Lyon, le regard intérieur* (doc for TV)
1989 *La Vie et rien d'autre* (*Life and Nothing But*)
1990 *Daddy Nostalgie* (*These Foolish Things*)

Other Films:

1967 *Coplan ouverte le feu à Mexico* (Freda) (sc)
1968 *Capitaine Singrid* (Leduc) (sc)
1977 *Le Question* (Heynemann) (pr)
1979 *Rue du pied de Grue* (Grandjouan) (pr); *Le Mors aux dents* (Heynemann) (pr)

Publications:

By TAVERNIER: book—

30 ans de cinéma américaine, with Jean-Pierre Coursodon, Paris.

By TAVERNIER: articles—

"Il n'y a pas de genre à proscrire ou à conseiller . . . ," an interview with D. Rabourdin, in *Cinéma* (Paris), May 1975.
"Les Rapports de la justice avec la folie et l'histoire," in *Avant-Scène du Cinéma* (Paris), June 1976.
"Notes éparses," in *Positif* (Paris), December/January 1977/78.
"Blending the Personal with the Political," an interview with L. Quart and L. Rubinstein, in *Cineaste* (New York), Summer 1978.
"Cleaning the Slate," an interview with I.F. McAsh, in *Films* (London), August 1982.
Interviews in *Films in Review* (New York), March and April 1983.
Interview with Michel Ciment and others in *Positif* (Paris), May 1984.
Interview with Dan Yakir in *Film Comment* (New York), September/October 1984.
"*Round Midnight*," an interview with Jean-Pierre Coursodon, in *Cineaste* (New York), vol. 15, no. 2, 1986.
Interview with Michael Dempsey in *Film Quarterly* (Berkeley), Spring 1987.

On TAVERNIER: books—

Bion, Danièle, *Bertrand Tavernier: cinéaste de l'émotion*, Renens, 1984.
Mereghetti, Paolo, editor, *Bertrand Tavernier*, Venice, 1986.
Douin, Jean-Luc, *Tavernier*, Paris, 1988.

Bertrand Tavernier (right) directing Michel Piccoli and Christine Pascal in *Des enfants gâtés*

On TAVERNIER: articles—

"*L'Horloger de Saint-Paul* Issue" of *Avant-Scène du Cinéma* (Paris), May 1974.
Auty, M., "Tavernier in Scotland," in *Sight and Sound* (London), Winter 1976/77.
Hennebelle, G., and others, "Le Cinéma de Bertrand Tavernier," in *Ecran* (Paris), September and October 1977.
Magretta, W.R. and J., "Bertrand Tavernier: The Constraints of Convention," in *Film Quarterly* (Berkeley), Summer 1978.
"Bertrand Tavernier Dossier" in *Revue du Cinéma* (Paris), April 1984.
Ciment, Michel, "Sunday in the Country With Bertrand," in *American Film* (Washington D.C.), October 1984.

*   *   *

It is significant that Bertrand Tavernier's films have been paid little attention by the more important contemporary film critics/theorists: his work is resolutely "realist" and realism is under attack. Realism has frequently been a cover for the reproduction and reinforcement of dominant ideological assumptions, and to this extent that attack is salutary. Yet Tavernier's cinema demonstrates effectively that the blanket rejection of realism rests on very unstable foundations. Realism has been seen as the bourgeoisie's way of talking to itself. It does not necessarily follow that its only motive for talking to itself is the desire for reassurance; nor need we assume that the only position Realist fiction constructs for the reader/viewer is one of helpless passivity (Tavernier's films clearly postulate an alert audience ready to reflect and analyze critically).

Tavernier's three films, *Death Watch, Coup de torchon*, and *A Week's Vacation*, if they do not unambiguously answer the attacks on realism, strongly attest to the inadequacy of their formulation. For a start, the films' range of form, tone and address provides a useful reminder of the potential for variety that the term "classical realist text" tends to obliterate. To place beside the strictly realist *A Week's Vacation*, on the one hand the futurist fantasy of *Death Watch*, and on the other the scathing, all-encompassing caricatural satire and irony of *Coup de torchon*, is to illustrate not merely a range of subject-matter but a range of strategy. Each film constructs for the viewer a quite distinct relationship to the action and to the protagonist, analyzable in terms of varying degrees of identification and detachment which may also shift *within* each film. Nor should the description of *A Week's Vacation* as "strictly realist" be taken to suggest some kind of simulated cinéma-vérité: the film's stylistic poise and lucid articulation, its continual play between looking *with* the protagonist and looking *at* her, consistently encourage an analytical distance.

Through all his films, certainly, the bourgeoisie "talks to itself," but the voice that articulates is never reassuring, and bourgeois institutions and assumptions are everywhere rendered visible and opened to question. Revolutionary positions are allowed a voice and are listened to respectfully. This was clear from Tavernier's first film, *The Clockmaker*, among the screen's most intelligent uses of Simenon, in which the original project is effectively transformed by introducing the political issues that Simenon totally represses, and by changing the crime from a meaningless, quasi-existentialist *acte gratuit* to a gesture of radical protest. But Tavernier's protagonists are always bourgeois: troubled, questioning, caught up in social institutions but not necessarily rendered impotent by them, capable of growth and awareness. The films, while basically committed to a well-left-of-center liberalism, are sufficiently open, intelligent and disturbed to be readily accessible to more radical positions than they are willing actually to adopt.

Despite the difference in mode of address, the three films share common thematic concerns (most obviously, the fear of conformism and dehumanization, the impulse towards protest and revolt, the difficulties of effectively realizing such a protest in action). They also have in common a desire to engage, more or less explicitly, with interrelated social, political and aesthetic issues. The caustic analysis of the imperialist mentality and the kind of personal rebellion it provokes (itself corrupt, brutalized and ultimately futile) in *Coup de torchon* is the most obvious instance of direct political engagement. *Death Watch*, within its science fiction format, is fascinatingly involved with contemporary inquiries into the construction of narrative and the objectification of women. Its protagonist (Harvey Keitel) attempts to create a narrative around an unsuspecting woman (Romy Schneider) by means of the miniature television camera surgically implanted behind his eyes. The implicit feminist concern here becomes the structuring principle of *A Week's Vacation*. Without explicitly raising feminist issues, the film's theme is the focusing of a contemporary bourgeois female consciousness, the consciousness of an intelligent and sensitive woman whose identity is not defined by her relationship with men, who is actively engaged with social problems (she is a schoolteacher), and whose fears (of loneliness, old age, death) are consistently presented in relation to contemporary social realities rather than simplistically defined in terms of "the human condition."

We should not celebrate the resurgence of "bourgeois realism" in Tavernier's films (and they do not stand alone) without qualification or misgivings. Certainly, one regrets the failure of contemporary cinema substantially to follow up the radical experimentation with narrative that characterized the most interesting European films of the 1960s and 1970s. Nonetheless, Tavernier's work testifies to the continuing vitality and validity of a tradition many theorists have rejected as moribund.

—Robin Wood

TAVIANI, Paolo and Vittorio.

Italian. Paolo born in San Miniato, Pisa, 8 November 1931; Vittorio born in San Miniato, Pisa, 20 September 1929. Educated at University of Pisa, Paolo in liberal arts, Vittorio in law. With Valentino Orsini ran cine-club at Pisa, 1950; with Cesare Zavattini directed short on Nazi massacre at San Miniato; together and in collaboration with Orsini, made series of short documentaries, 1954–59; worked with Joris Ivens, Roberto Rossellini, and others, early 1960s; with Orsini, directed first feature, *A Man for Burning*, 1962. Recipients: Best Film and International Critics prize, Cannes Festival, for *Padre padrone*, 1977; Special Jury Prize, Cannes

Festival, for *La notte di San Lorenzo*, 1982; Best Director Award (shared), National Society of Film Critics, for *The Night of the Shooting Stars*, 1983.

Films as Directors:
(documentary shorts, sometimes in collaboration with Valentino Orsini):

1954   *San Miniato, luglio '44*
1955   *Voltera, comune medievale*
1955–59   *Curtatone e Montanara; Carlo Pisacane; Ville della Brianza; Lavatori della pietra; Pittori in città; I Pazzi della domenica; Moravia; Carbunara*
1960   episode of *L'Italia non è un paesa povero*

(features):

1962   *Un uomo da bruciare (A Man for Burning)* (co-d, co-sc)
1963   *I fuorilegge del matrimonio* (co-d, co-sc)
1967   *Sovversivi* (+ sc, + Vittorio in role)
1969   *Sotto il segno dello scorpione (Under the Sign of Scorpio)* (+ sc)
1971   *San Michele aveva un gallo* (+ sc)
1974   *Allonsanfan* (+ sc)
1977   *Padre padrone (Father Master)* (+ sc)
1979   *Il prato (The Meadow)* (+ sc)
1982   *La notte di San Lorenzo* (+ sc)
1983   *The Night of the Shooting Stars* (+ sc)
1984   **Kaos**
1986   *Good Morning Babilonia (Good Morning Babylon)*
1990   *Il Sole anche di notte (The Night Sun)*

Publications:

By the TAVIANIS: books—

San Michele aveva un gallo/Allonsafan, Cappelli, 1974.
Good Morning Babylon, with Tonino Guerra, London, 1987.

By the TAVIANIS: articles—

Interview with G. Mingrone and others in *Filmcritica* (Rome), January 1972.
"Très longue rencontre avec Paolo et Vittorio Taviani," with J.-A. Gili, in *Ecran* (Paris), July/August 1975.
"The Brothers Taviani," an interview with V. Glaessner, in *Cinema Papers* (Melbourne), January 1978.
Interview with Gary Crowdus in *Cineaste* (New York), vol. 12, no. 3, 1983.
"Vittorio Taviani: an interview," with P. Brunette, in *Film Quarterly* (Berkeley), Spring 1983.
Interview with F. Accialini and L. Coluccelli in *Cineforum* (Bergamo), January 1985.
Interview with Robert Katz in *American Film* (Washington D.C.), June 1987.

On the TAVIANIS: books—

Ferrucci, Riccardo, editor, *La bottega Taviani: un viaggio nel cinema di San Miniato a Hollywood*, Florence, 1987.
De Santi, Pier Marco, *I film di Paolo e Vittorio Taviani*, Rome, 1988.

On the TAVIANIS: articles—

Aristarco, Guido, "Dall'utile attraverso il vero verso il bello," in *Cinema Nuovo* (Turin), September/October 1974.
Zambetti, S., editor, "Speciale Taviani," in *Cineforum* (Bergamo), October 1974.
Mitchell, T., "Towards Utopia, By Way of Research, Detachment, and Involvement," in *Sight and Sound* (London), no. 3, 1979.
Ranvaud, Don, "A Tuscan Romance," in *Monthly Film Bulletin* (London), December 1982.
Yakir, Dan, "The Tavianis," in *Film Comment* (New York), March/April 1983.

*   *   *

Since the early 1960s, when they realized that fiction feature films were going to be their main interest, Paolo and Vittorio

Paolo and Vittorio Taviani: *Padre padrone*

Taviani have written scenarios and scripts, designed settings, developed a filmmaking style and philosophy, directed a dozen features, and patiently explained their methods and concepts to many interviewers and audiences in Italy and abroad.

Although influenced to some extent by neorealism—*e.g.*, the films of Rossellini and De Santis characterized by on-location settings, natural lighting, authentic environmental sounds, non-professional actors, and an emphasis on "the people" as protagonists—the Tavianis want reviewers to see their films as invented and staged, as interpretations of history rather than as documentaries. They draw upon their early interests and background—as youngsters they saw musicals and concerts but not movies—using artistic and technical means and methods similar to those of theater and opera. Their films in which music is part of plot and theme reveal an inventory of flutes, accordions, record players, radios, human singing voices, folktunes, opera and oratorio (mostly Italian but also German), and even "The Battle Hymn of the Republic."

The photography in their films takes the eye back to the horizon, or across a huge field, far along a road or deep into the front of a church or schoolroom. Even casual viewers must realize the frequent alternation of intense close-ups and long shots that never cease to remind one of locale.

Thoughts and dreams are often given visual expression. A picture of a girl and her brother studying on a couch follows her interior monologue about missing the long yellow couch in her living room (*La notte di San Lorenzo*). A prisoner in solitary for 10 years creates a world of sound and sight expressed on the screen (*San Michele aveva un gallo*).

With theatrical form and technique as framework for their political cinema, and complex, individualistic characters as protagonists, the Tavianis are as concerned with corruption, abuse of power, poverty and suffering as were the neorealists and their successors. Struck by the autobiography of Gavino Ledda which became their well-received *Padre Padrone*, they investigate the abuse of power by a father, compelled by tradition and his own need to survive, to keep his son a slave. Amazingly, the illiterate, virtually mute shepherd boy whom a quirk of fate (army service) rescues from lifetime isolation, becomes a professor of linguistics through curiosity, will and energy. In *Un uomo da Bruciare* Salvatore, who wants to help Sicilian peasants break the Mafia's hold, is complex, intellectual, and egotistical.

Other themes and topics in Taviani films are divorce, revolution as an ongoing effort interrupted by interludes of other activity, the changing ways of dealing with power and corruption, resistance in war, fascism, and the necessity of communal action for accomplishment. The Tavianis use the past to illuminate the present, show the suffering of opposing sides, and stress the major role of heritage and environment. Their characters ask questions about their lives that lead to positive solutions, and sometimes to failure. The two directors believe that utopia is possible, eventually.

—Lillian Schiff

TORRE NILSSON, Leopoldo.

Argentinian. Born in Buenos Aires, 5 May 1924, son of filmmaker Leopoldo Torres Rios. Married writer Beatriz Guido. Assistant to father, from 1939; with father, directed first feature, 1949; began working with Guido, 1957; founder of production company Producciones Angel, 1959; signed contract with Columbia to make *El ojo de la cerradura*, 1964. Recipient: International Critics Prize, Cannes Festival, for *Hands in the Trap*, 1961. *Died 8 September 1978*.

Films as Director:

1947 *El muro (The Wall)* (short)
1950 *El crimen de Oribe (Oribe's Crime)* (co-d)
1953 *El hijo del crack (Son of the "Star")* (co-d); *La Tigra (The Tigress)*
1954 *Días de odio (Days of Hate)*
1955 *Para vestir (The Spinsters)*
1956 *El protegido (The Protégé)*; *Graciela*
1957 *La casa del ángel (End of Innocence. The House of the Angel)* (+ co-sc with Beatriz Guido, based on Guido novel); *Precursores de la pintura argentina* (short) (Guido:sc); *Los arboles de Buenos-Aires* (short) (Guido:sc)
1958 *El secuestrador (The Kidnapper)* (Guido:sc)
1959 *La cáida (The Fall)* (+ co-sc with Guido); *Fin de fiesta (The Party Is Over, The Blood Feast)* (Guido:sc)
1960 *Un guapo del 900* (+ co-pr)
1961 *La mano en la trampa (The Hand in the Trap)* (Guido:sc); *Piel de verano (Summer Skin)* (+ pr, Guido:sc)
1962 *Setenta veces siete (The Female: 70 Times 7)* (Guido:sc); *Homenaje a la hora de la siesta (Homage at Siesta Time)* (Guido:sc); *La terraza (The Terrace)* (Guido:sc)
1964 *El ojo de la cerradura (The Eavesdropper)* (Guido:sc)
1965 *Once Upon a Tractor* (for United Nations) (Guido:sc)
1966 *La chica del lunes (Monday's Child)* (Guido:sc); *Los traidores de San Angel (The Traitors of San Angel)* (Guido:sc); *Cavar un foso (To Dig a Pit)* (Guido:sc)
1968 *Martin Fierro* (Guido:sc)
1969 *El santo de la espada (The Knight of the Sword)* (Guido:sc)
1970 *Güemes—La terra en armas* (Guido:sc)
1972 *La maffia (The Mafia)* (Guido:sc)
1973 *Los siete locos (The Seven Madmen)* (Guido:sc)
1974 *Boquitas pintadas (Painted Lips)* (Guido:sc)
1975 *Diario de la guerra del cerdo (La guerra del cerdo. Diary of the Pig War)* (Guido:sc); *El pibe cabeza* (Guido:sc)
1976 *Piedra libre* (Guido:sc)

Other Films:

1975 *Los gauchos judíos (Jewish Gauchos)* (co-pr)

Publications:

By TORRE NILSSON: book—

Entre sajones y el arrabal, edited by Jorge Alvarez, Buenos Aires, 1967.

By TORRE NILSSON: articles—

Interview in *Cuadernos de cine* (Buenos Aires), October 1954.
Interview with Hector Grossi in *Mundo Argentino* (Buenos Aires), February 1957.
Interview in *Tiempo de cine* (Buenos Aires), October 1960.
"How to Make a New Wave," in *Films and Filming* (London), November 1962.
Interview with I. León Frías and R. Bedoya in *Hablemos de Cine* (Lima), April 1979.

On TORRE NILSSON: books—

Martin, Jorge Abel, *Los films de Leopoldo Torre Nilsson*, Buenos Aires, 1980.
Barnard, Tim, *Argentine Cinema*, Toronto, 1986.
King, John, and Nissa Torrents, editors, *Argentine Cinema: The Garden of Forking Paths*, London, 1988.

On TORRE NILSSON: articles—

Trajtenberg, Mario, "Torre-Nilsson and His Double," in *Film Quarterly* (Berkeley), Fall 1961.
Di Nubila, Domingo, "An Argentine Partnership," in *Films and Filming* (London), September 1961.
Botsford, Keith, "Leopoldo Torre-Nilsson: The Underside of the Coin," in *Show* (Hollywood), November 1962.
"Director of the Year," in *International Film Guide 1967*, London, 1966.
Cozarinsky, E., "Torre-Nilsson Remembered," in *Sight and Sound* (London), no. 1, 1978–79.
Mahieu, A., "Revisión Crítica del cine Argentino," in *Cine Cubana* (Havana), vol. 104, 1984.

* * *

Leopoldo Torre Nilsson's international reputation is based on a handful of films made in the late 1950s and at the very beginning of the 1960s, but his career as a director spanned three decades and through his father, the director Leopoldo Torre Rios, he had direct links with the pioneering days of Argentine cinema. Born in Buenos Aires of part Spanish-Catholic, part Swedish-Protestant ancestry, he began his involvement with cinema at the age of fifteen, when he became his father's assistant. In all, he worked as assistant director on sixteen of his father's films and scripted ten features in the 1940s, before making his directing debut with a short film, *El Muro*, in 1947. His feature debut, with *El Crimen de Oribe*, the first of two films co-directed with his father, already shows some signs of his future concerns: literary adaptation (here from a short story by Adolfo Bioy Casares) and stylistic experiment. The same is true of his first solo feature, *Dias de Odio*, adapted from a story by Jorge Luis Borges, "Emma Zunz."

Torre Nilsson himself regarded his first five films as an independent director as apprentice efforts, and certainly they achieved little commercial success in Argentina. He reached maturity as a director and far wider international audiences in 1957, when he began his collaboration with the novelist Beatriz Guido, whom he subsequently married. Complementary personalities, they proved a highly successful team, with Guido creating a claustrophobic world and sets of characters ideally suited to her husband's virtuoso camerawork and concern with symbolic detail. Three highly successful films starring the young Elsa Daniel exemplify the qualities of the pair. *The House of the Angel* contained an acid picture of upper middle-class life in Buenos Aires in the 1920s (a combination of puritanical religion and political corruption) but its central theme is the destruction of virginal innocence, with the adolescent heroine bound for ever to the man who has half-seduced, half-raped her on the eve of a duel. Subsequently the director evoked with great force and conviction the enclosed, Cocteau-esque world of *The Fall* which combined the sexual tensions of a young girl with the amorality of four wild children whose

Leopoldo Torre Nilsson: *La mano en la trampa*

governess she becomes. In 1961 Torre Nilsson adapted two further novels by his wife, both of which depicted a young woman at odds with her elders and caught in a trap of her own devising. In *The Hand in the Trap*, one of the director's most successful works, Elsa Daniel uncovers the secret of her aunt's withdrawal from the world and arranges a confrontation with the man who jilted her. But the cost of this curiosity is high, since she herself falls victim to the same seducer and realises that she will live out her aunt's story all over again. *Summer Skin*, which shows the director at his brilliant visual best, is a further tale of lost innocence with Graciela Borges playing a girl who sells herself as "companion" to her dying cousin. The film has an open-air setting of beach and summer resort, but like the previous films portrays a morally corrupt society.

Even at this period of his greatest acclaim, Torre Nilsson achieved comparatively little success with films outside this narrow range, such as his study of poverty, *The Kidnapper* or his films on history and politics, *The Party is Over* and *A Tough Guy of 1900*. Torre Nilsson's subsequent attempts to widen the scope of his filmmaking had a mixed reception. Films in which he tried to combine his literary and historical concerns with the requirements of local commercial formulas received little international attention, but within Argentina his constant struggle to maintain an independent voice made him an important figure. He managed to continue working through the difficult years of censorship until two years before his death, when his last feature, *Piedra libre* (1976) was banned. But his reputation rests essentially on the handful of stylish depictions of corruption and loss of innocence which made such an impact on the art cinema and international festival circuits of the years around 1960.

—Roy Armes

———

TOURNEUR, Jacques.

American/French. Born in Paris, 12 November 1904, son of director Maurice Tourneur; became U.S. citizen, 1919. Educated at Hollywood High School. Married actress Christianne (died). Moved to U.S. with family, 1914; office boy at MGM, 1924, later actor; script clerk for father's last 6 American films; moved to Paris, edited father's films, 1928; directed first film, in France, 1931; 2nd unit director for MGM, Hollywood, 1935; directed shorts, then B features, from 1939; director for producer Val Lewton at RKO, from 1942; TV director, from late 1950s. *Died in Bergerac, 19 December 1977.*

Films as Director:

1931   *Un vieux garçon*; *Tout ça ne vaut pas l'amour*
1933   *La Fusée*; *Toto*; *Pour être aimée*

Jacques Tourneur on the set of *Canyon Passage*

1934   *Les Filles de la concierge*
1939   *They All Came Out*; *Nick Carter, Master Detective*
1940   *Phantom Raiders*
1941   *Doctors Don't Tell*
1942   ***Cat People***
1943   *I Walked with a Zombie*; *The Leopard Man*
1944   *Days of Glory*; *Experiment Perilous*
1946   *Canyon Passage*
1947   ***Out of the Past*** (***Build My Gallows High***)
1948   *Berlin Express*
1949   *Easy Living*
1950   *The Flame and the Arrow*; *Stars in My Crown*
1951   *Circle of Danger*; *Anne of the Indies*
1952   *Way of a Gaucho*
1953   *Appointment in Honduras*
1955   *Stranger on Horseback*; *Wichita*
1956   *Great Day in the Morning*
1957   *Nightfall*; *Night of the Demon* (*Curse of the Demon*)
1958   *The Fearmakers*
1959   *Timbuktu*; *La battaglia di Maratona* (*The Battle of Marathon*);
        Frontier Rangers (originally for TV)
1963   *The Comedy of Terrors*
1965   *War Gods of the Deep* (*City Under the Sea*)

Other Films:

1923   *Scaramouche* (Ingram) (role)
1927   *The Fair Co-ed* (Wood) (role); *Love* (Goulding) (role)
1929   *The Trail of '98* (Brown) (role)

Publications:

By TOURNEUR: articles—

"Taste without Clichés," in *Films and Filming* (London), November
   1956.
Interview with Patrick Brion and Jean-Louis Comolli in *Cahiers du
   Cinéma* (Paris), August 1966.
Interview in *The Celluloid Muse* edited by Charles Higham and Joel
   Greenberg, London, 1969.

On TOURNEUR: books—

Siegel, Joel, *Val Lewton: The Reality of Terror*, London, 1972.
Henry, Michel, *Jacques Tourneur, Dossiers du Cinéma*, Paris, 1974.
Selby, Spencer, *Dark City: The Film Noir*, London, 1990.

On TOURNEUR: articles—

Sarris, Andrew, "Esoterica," in *Film Culture* (New York), Spring
   1963.
Noames, Jean-Louis, "Trois Tourneur," in *Cahiers du Cinéma*
   (Paris), May 1964.
Tavernier, Bertrand, "Propos de Tourneur," in *Positif* (Paris),
   November 1971.
Wood, Robin, "The Shadow Worlds of Jacques Tourneur," in *Film
   Comment* (New York), Summer 1972.
Henry, M., "Le Jardin aux sentiers qui bifurquent (Sur Jacques Tour-
   neur)," in *Positif* (Paris), April 1973.
McCarty, John, "The Parallel Worlds of Jacques Tourneur," in *Cine-
   fantastique* (Oak Park, Illinois), Summer 1973.
Passek, J.L., "Jacques Tourneur," in *Cinéma* (Paris), February 1978.
Turner, G., "*Out of the Past*," in *American Cinematographer* (Los
   Angeles), March 1984.

*   *   *

The first director Val Lewton hired for his RKO unit was Jacques Tourneur, and the first picture made by that unit was *Cat
People*, an original screenplay by DeWitt Bodeen.

When Tourneur's father, Maurice, returned to Paris to continue his directing career abroad, Jacques had gone with him,
working as assistant director and editor for his father. In 1933,
he made a few directorial solos in the French language and
then returned to Hollywood, where he became an assistant
director at MGM. It was at this time that he first met Val Lew-

ton, and the two young men worked as special unit directors
for Jack Conway on *A Tale of Two Cities*; it was Lewton and
Tourneur who staged the storming of the Bastille sequence for
that film.

Tourneur remained at MGM, directing over 20 short subjects, and Lewton eventually went on to become David O.
Selznick's story editor. When Lewton left Selznick to head his
own production unit at RKO, he had already made up his mind
that Tourneur would direct his first production, *Cat People*.
Tourneur came to RKO, where he served as director for Lewton's first three films—*Cat People*, *I Walked With a Zombie*,
and *The Leopard Man*. The front office held his work in such
esteem that he was given the "A" treatment—solo direction of
a high budget film, *Days of Glory*, Gregory Peck's first starring
film. It was not held against him that *Days of Glory* bombed.
Tourneur had gone immediately into another high budget picture at RKO—*Experiment Perilous*, starring Hedy Lamarr
with Paul Lukas and George Brent. Under Tourneur's skillful
direction, it became a suspenseful mood period film, certainly
one of his and Hedy Lamarr's best.

Tourneur stayed on at RKO to direct Robert Mitchum in
one of his finest, *Out of the Past* (aka *Build My Gallows High*),
as well as an excellent melodrama, *Berlin Express*, starring
Merle Oberon and Robert Ryan with Paul Lukas. It was filmed
partially in Berlin, the first Hollywood picture to be made in
Germany since the end of the war.

Tourneur then directed three excellent westerns for his
friend, Joel McCrea—*Stars in My Crown*, *Stranger on Horseback*, and *Wichita* with McCreas as Wyatt Earp. He had
directed *The Flame and the Arrow* starring Burt Lancaster; and
then another western at RKO, *Great Day in the Morning* with
Robert Stack and Virginia Mayo. He went back to make
another horror picture in England, *Night of the Demon*, with
Dana Andrews, which is rated as highly as those he made for
Lewton.

Television direction occupied the greater part of his time for
the next decade, but he retired in 1966, and returned to his
native country, where he died in Bergerac on December 19,
1977. The best pictures which he directed were those of suspense and genuine terror, though he also did well with those
that had a great deal of action. He resisted, wisely, scenes with
long patches of dialogue, always frowning and saying "It
sounds so corny."

—DeWitt Bodeen

———

TOURNEUR, Maurice.

French/American. Born Maurice Thomas in Paris, 2 February
1876; became U.S. citizen, 1921. Educated at Lycée Condorcet. Married Fernande Petit (stage name Van Doren), 1904
(separated 1927), son Jacques Tourneur. Illustrator and
graphic and interior designer, from 1894; assistant to Auguste
Rodin and Puvis de Chavannes; military service in Artillery,
late 1890s; actor, then stage director, from 1900; actor, then
director for Eclair films, from 1912; moved to U.S., 1914; production head of Paragon studio, 1915; contracted to Jesse
Lasky for 3 Olga Petrova vehicles, 1917; formed own production company, 1918; moved to California, contracted to
Paramount, formed Associated Producers Inc. with Thomas
Ince and others (failed 1921), 1919; moved to Universal, 1920;
quit direction of *The Mysterious Island*, returned to France,
1926; son Jacques edited films, from 1930. *Died 1961.*

Films as Director:

1912 *Le Friquet* (+ sc); *Jean la poudre* (+ sc); *Le Système du Docteur Goudron et du Professeur Plume*; *Figures de cire*

1913 *Le Dernier Pardon* (+ sc); *Le Puits mitoyen*; *Le Camée*; *Sœurette* (+ sc); *Le Corso rouge*; *Mademoiselle 100 millions*; *Les Gaites de l'escadron* (+ sc); *La Dame de Montsoreau* (+ sc)

1914 *Monsieur Lecocq* (+ sc); *Rouletabille I: Le Mystère de la chambre jaune* (+ sc); *Rouletabille II: La Dernière Incarnation de Larson* (+ sc); *Mother* (+ sc); *The Man of the Hour* (+ sc); *The Wishing Ring* (+ sc); *The Pit*

1915 *Alias Jimmy Valentine* (+ sc); *The Cub*; *Trilby* (+ sc); *The Ivory Snuff Box* (+ sc); *A Butterfly on the Wheel*; *Human Driftwood*

1916 *The Pawn of Fate*; *The Hand of Peril* (+ sc); *The Closed Road* (+ sc); *The Rail Rider*; *The Velvet Paw*

1917 *A Girl's Folly*; *The Whip*; *The Undying Flame*; *Exile*; *The Law of the Land* (+ sc); *The Pride of the Clan*; *The Poor Little Rich Girl*; *Barbary Sheep*; *The Rise of Jennie Cushing*

1918 *Rose of the World*; *A Doll's House*; *The Blue Bird*; *Prunella*; *Woman*; *Sporting Life*

1919 *The White Heather*; *The Life Line*; *Victory*; *The Broken Butterfly* (+ co-sc)

1920 *My Lady's Garter*; *The County Fair*; *Treasure Island*; *The White Circle*; *Deep Waters*; *The Last of the Mohicans*

1921 *The Bait*; *The Foolish Matrons*

1922 *Lorna Doone*

1923 *While Paris Sleeps* (made in 1920); *The Christian*; *The Isle of Lost Ships*; *The Brass Bottle*; *Jealous Husbands*

1924 *Torment* (+ co-sc); *The White Moth*

1925 *Never the Twain Shall Meet*; *Sporting Life* (+ sc) (remake); *Clothes Make the Pirate*

1926 *Aloma of the South Seas*; *Old Loves and New*; *The Mysterious Island* (co-d, sc)

1927 *L'Equipage* (+ co-sc)

1929 *Das Schiff der verlorene Menschen* (*Le Navire des hommes perdus*)

1930 *Accusée, levez-vous*

1931 *Maison de danses*; *Partir . . .* or *Partir!*

1932 *Au nom de la loi*; *Les Gaites de la escadron* (+ co-sc); *L'Idoire* (+ co-sc)

1933 *Les Deux Orphelines* (+ co-sc); *L'Homme mysterieux* (*Obsession*)

1934 *Le Voleur*

1935 *Justin de Marseille*

1936 *Konigsmark*; *Samson*; *Avec le sourire*

1938 *Le Patriote*; *Katia*

1940 *Volpone*

1941 *Péchés de jeunesse*; *Mam'zelle Bonaparte*

1942 *La Main du diable*

1943 *Le Val d'enfer*; *Cecile est morte*

1947 *Après l'amour*

1948 *L'Impasse des deux anges*

Other Films:

1920 *The Great Redeemer* (Brown) (supervisor)

Publications:

By TOURNEUR: articles—

"Stylization in Motion Picture Direction," in *Motion Picture* (New York), September 1918.

Interview with M.S. Cheatham in *Motion Picture Classic* (Brooklyn), February 1920.

Article in *Film Comment* (New York), July/August 1976, reprinted from *Shadowland*, May 1920.

On TOURNEUR: articles—

Haskins, H., "Work of Maurice Tourneur," in *Motion Picture Classic* (Brooklyn), September 1918.

Geltzer, George, "Maurice Tourneur," in *Films in Review* (New York), April 1961.

Sight and Sound (London), Autumn 1961 (also notes and corrections, Winter 1961).

Beylie, Claude, "Tombeau de Tourneur," in *Cahiers du Cinéma* (Paris), January 1962.

Koszarski, Richard, "Maurice Tourneur: The First of the Visual Stylists," in *Film Comment* (New York), March/April 1973.

Deslandes, J., "Maurice Tourneur—films parlants 1930/1948," in *Avant-Scène du Cinéma* (Paris), 15 June 1977.

Brownlow, Kevin, letter, in *American Classic Screen* (Shawnee Mission, Kansas), Fall 1979.

Tourneur Section of *Griffithiana* (Pordenone), 1988.

* * *

Maurice Tourneur is one of the greatest pictorialists of the cinema, deriving his aesthetic from his early associations with Rodin and Puvis de Chavannes. Having worked for André Antoine as an actor and producer, he joined the Eclair Film Company in 1912 and travelled to their American Studios at Fort Lee, New Jersey, in 1914. Here he directed films based on successful stage plays. In *The Wishing Ring* it is possible to see the charm and visual beauty he brought to his work. His team consisted of John van der Broek, the cameraman who later tragically drowned during one of Tourneur's productions, Ben Carré, the art director, and Clarence Brown, his editor who would later achieve fame as Garbo's favorite director.

Tourneur was most literate in his pronouncements on the cinema, individualistic and iconoclastic at times. He saw the cinema in perspective and would not concede it a status equal to the other arts. He stated, "to speak of the future development of the art of the cinema is futile. It cannot be. It costs a great deal of money to produce a motion picture. The only way the financial backer can get his money back, to say nothing of a profit, is to appeal to the great masses. And the thing that satisfies millions cannot be good. As Ibsen once wrote, it is the minority which is always right." In practice, however, his own work belied this statement. To everything he did he brought a sense of beauty and great responsibility to his audiences.

He directed Clara Kimball Young in *Trilby*, Mary Pickford in *Pride of the Clan* and *Poor Little Rich Girl*, the latter a very successful film. He made three films with Olga Petrova. In 1918 five memorable films came from his hand: Elsie Ferguson appeared in his *The Doll's House*; two other stage plays, *The Bluebird* by Maeterlinck and *Prunella* by Granville Barker, gave Tourneur full scope for his visual style; *Woman* a film of episodes, dealt with Adam and Eve, Claudius and Messalina, Heloise and Abelard, a Breton fisherman and a mermaid and a Civil War story; and, *Sporting Life* was significant for its absence of stars and its depiction of a fog-ridden London, anticipating Griffith's *Broken Blossoms* of the following year.

For Paramount, in 1919, he made Joseph Conrad's *Victory*, and in 1920, a delightful *Treasure Island* with Shirley Mason (as Jim Hawkins) and Lon Chaney, who also starred in *While Paris Sleeps*. For Associated Producers he made *The Last of the Mohicans*, which many consider to be his masterpiece although Clarence Brown took over direction when Tourneur fell ill during production.

Tourneur believed in location shooting and many of his films took him to far-off places. He shot in Puerto Rico, Big Bear Lake and the Marquesas.

His remaining Hollywood films included *Lorna Doone*, *The Christian*, *The Isle of Lost Ships*, *The Brass Bottle*, *The White Moth*, *Never the Twain Shall Meet* and *Aloma of The South Seas*. During the production of *The Mysterious Island* for M.G.M., Tourneur resented the interference of his work by a producer, walked off the set, and returned to France. He continued to work in films in Europe, his first being *L'Equipage*. In 1929 he made *Das Schiff der Verlorene* in Germany with Marlene Dietrich. This was his last silent film, but he accepted the

Maurice Tourneur

coming of sound and, before his death in 1961, he had made over 20 sound films. The most important of these were *Les Deux Orphelines*, the delightful *Katia* with Danielle Darieux, *Volpone* with Harry Baur and Louis Jouvet, *La Main du diable* from a story by Gerard de Nerval and featuring Pierre Fresnay, and his last film *L'Impasse des deux anges*.

Tourneur was a man who had no illusions about working in films. He realized the limitations of Hollywood and the films he was given to direct. However, he brought his considerable talent as a designer to bear on his work, and did not hesitate to experiment. He stylized his sets, and was influenced by new movements in the theater, but he also used the effects of Nature to heighten his dramas. His awareness of the potentialities of the camera was profound, giving strength to his images.

—Liam O'Leary

TROTTA, Margarethe von. *See* **VON TROTTA, Margarethe.**

TRUFFAUT, François.

French. Born in Paris, 6 February 1932. Educated at Lycée Rollin, Paris. Married Madeleine Morgenstern, 1957 (divorced), two daughters. Founded own cine-club in Paris, lack of funds caused closing, was jailed for inability to pay debts, released with help of André Bazin, 1947; with Godard, Rivette and Chabrol, member of Ciné-club du Quartier Latin, 1949; enlisted in Army, but deserted on eve of departure for Indochina, 1951, later released for "instability of character"; briefly employed by the Service Cinématographique of the Ministry of Agriculture, 1953; writer on film for *Cahiers du cinéma*, then *Arts*, from 1953, including seminal article, "Une Certain Tendance du cinéma français," in 1954; with Rivette and Resnais, made short 16mm film, 1955; assistant to Roberto Rossellini, 1956–58; directed first feature, *Les Quatre Cents Coups*, and wrote script for Godard's *A bout de souffle*, 1959; published *Le Cinéma selon Hitchcock*, 1966; instigated shutting down of 1968 Cannes Festival in wake of May uprisings. Recipient: Best Director, Cannes Festival, for *Les Quatres Cents Coup*, 1959; Prix Louis Delluc, and Best Director, National Society of Film Critics, for *Stolen Kisses*, 1969; Oscar for Best Foreign-Language Film, Best Director, National Society of Film Critics, Best Direction, New York Film Critics, and British Academy Award for Best Direction, for *Day for Night*, 1973. *Died of cancer, in Paris, 21 October 1984.*

Films as Director:

1955   *Une Visite* (+ sc, co-ed)
1957   *Les Mistons* (+ co-sc)
1958   *Une Histoire d'eau*
1959   **Les Quatre Cents Coups (The Four Hundred Blows)** (+ sc)
1960   **Tirez sur le pianist (Shoot the Piano Player)** (+ co-sc)
1961   **Jules et Jim (Jules and Jim)** (+ co-sc)
1962   "Antoine et Colette" episode of *L'Amour a vingt ans* (*Love at Twenty*) (+ sc, role)
1964   *La Peau douce* (*The Soft Skin*) (+ co-sc)
1966   *Fahrenheit 451* (+ co-sc)

1967   *La Mariée était en noir* (*The Bride Wore Black*) (+ co-sc)
1968   *Baisers volés* (*Stolen Kisses*) (+ co-sc)
1969   *La Sirène du Mississippi* (*Mississippi Mermaid*) (+ sc); *L'Enfant sauvage* (*The Wild Child*) (+ co-sc, role as Dr. Jean Itard)
1970   *Domicile conjugal* (*Bed and Board*) (+ co-sc)
1971   *Les Deux Anglaises et le continent* (*Two English Girls*) (+ co-sc)
1972   *Une Belle Fille comme moi* (*Such a Gorgeous Kid Like Me*) (+ co-sc)
1973   *La Nuit américaine* (*Day for Night*) (+ co-sc, role as Ferrand)
1975   *L'Histoire d'Adèle H.* (*The Story of Adele H.*) (+ co-sc)
1976   *L'Argent de poche* (*Small Change*) (+ co-sc)
1977   *L'Homme qui aimait les femmes* (*The Man Who Loved Women*) (+ co-sc)
1978   *La Chambre verte* (*The Green Room*) (+ co-sc, role as Julien Davenne)
1979   *L'Amour en fuite* (*Love on the Run*) (+ co-sc)
1980   *Le Dernier Metro* (*The Last Metro*) (+ sc)
1981   *La Femme d'à côté* (*The Woman Next Door*)
1984   *Vivement dimanche!* (*Finally Sunday*)

Other Films:

1977   **Close Encounters of the Third Kind** (Spielberg) (role as French scientist)

Publications:

By TRUFFAUT: books—

Les Quatre Cent Coups, with Marcel Moussy, Paris, 1959; as *The Four Hundred Blows: A Film by François Truffaut*, New York, 1969.
Le Cinéma selon Hitchcock, Paris, 1967; as *Hitchcock*, New York; revised edition, 1985.
Ce n'est qu'un début, Paris, 1968.
Jules et Jim, New York, 1968.
The Adventures of Antoine Doinel: Four Autobiographical Screenplays, New York, 1971.
La Nuit américaine et le journal de tournage de Farenheit 451, Paris, 1974.
Day for Night, New York, 1975.
Les Films de ma vie, Paris, 1975; as *The Films in My Life*, New York, 1978.
The Wild Child, New York, 1975.
Small Change, New York, 1976.
The Story of Adele H., New York, 1976.
L'Homme qui aimait les femmes, Paris, 1977.
The Last Metro, New Brunswick, New Jersey, 1985.
Truffaut par Truffaut, edited by Dominique Rabourdin, Paris, 1985; as *Truffaut on Truffaut*, New York, 1987.
Le Plaisir des yeux, Paris, 1987.
François Truffaut: correspondence, edited by Gilles Jacob and Claude de Givray, Renens, 1988; as *François Truffaut: Letters*, translated by Gilbert Adair, London, 1990.
La petite voleuse, with Claude de Givray, Paris, 1989.

By TRUFFAUT: articles—

"Une Certain Tendance du cinéma français," in *Cahiers du Cinéma* (Paris), January 1954.
"Renoir in America," with J. Rivette, in *Sight and Sound* (London), July/September 1954.
"La Crise d'ambition du cinéma français," in *Arts* (Paris), 30 March 1955.
Interview of Rossellini, with Maurice Scherer, in *Film Culture* (New York), March/April 1955.
"On the Death of André Bazin," in *Cahiers du Cinéma* (Paris), January 1959.
"On Film: Truffaut Interview," in the *New Yorker*, 20 February 1960.
"Les Mistons," in *Avant-Scène du Cinéma* (Paris), no. 4, 1961.
"Histoire d'eau," in *Avant-Scène du Cinéma* (Paris), no. 7, 1961.
"Jules et Jim," in *Avant-Scène du Cinéma* (Paris), June 1962.
"Sex and Life," in *Films and Filming* (London), July 1962.
"Vivre sa vie," in *Avant-Scène du Cinéma* (Paris), October 1962.

François Truffaut directing *Jules et Jim*

"Sur le cinéma américaine," in *Cahiers du Cinéma* (Paris), December 1963 and January 1964.

"Skeleton Keys," in *Film Culture* (New York), Spring 1964.

"*La Peau douce*," in *Avant-Scène du Cinéma* (Paris), May 1965.

"*Farenheit 451*," (working notes by Truffaut), in *Cahiers du Cinéma* (Paris), February/July 1966.

"Jean-Luc Godard," in *Les Lettres Françaises* (Paris), 16 March 1967.

"Georges Sadoul," in *Les Lettres Françaises* (Paris), 18 October 1967.

"Ernst Lubitsch," in *Cahiers du Cinéma* (Paris), February 1968.

"Francoise Dorlèac," in *Cahiers du Cinéma* (Paris), April/May 1968.

"Is Truffaut the Happiest Man on Earth? Yes," in *Esquire* (New York), August 1970.

"*L'Enfant Sauvage*," in *Avant-Scène du Cinéma* (Paris), October 1970.

"Intensification," an interview with Gordon Gow, in *Films and Filming* (London), July 1972.

"The Lesson of Ingmar Bergman," in *Take One* (Montreal), July 1973.

"A Portrait of Francois Truffaut," an interview with S. Mallow, in *Filmmakers Newsletter* (Ward Hill, Massachusetts), December 1973.

Interview with Charles Higham in *Action* (Los Angeles), January/February 1974.

"Adèle H.," an interview with Gilbert Adair, in *Sight and Sound* (London), Summer 1975.

"François Truffaut: The Romantic Bachelor," with Melanie Adler, in *Andy Warhol's Inter/View* (New York), March 1976.

"Dialogue on Film: Interview with Truffaut," in *American Film* (Washington, D.C.), May 1976.

"Kid Stuff: François Truffaut on *Small Change*," with J. McBride and T. McCarthy, in *Film Comment* (New York), September/October 1976.

"Truffaut, Part V," an interview in the *New Yorker*, 18 October 1976.

"François Truffaut: Feminist Filmmaker?," with Annette Insdorf, in *Take One* (Montreal), January 1978.

"Truffaut: Twenty Years After," an interview with D. Allen, in *Sight and Sound* (London), no. 4, 1979.

"My Friend Hitchcock," in *American Film* (Washington, D.C.), March 1979.

Interview with A. Gillain in *Wide Angle* (Athens, Ohio), vol. 4, no. 4, 1981.

Interview with Marcel Ophuls in *American Film* (New York), May 1985.

On TRUFFAUT: books—

Petrie, Graham, *The Cinema of François Truffaut*, New York, 1970.

Crisp, C.G., and Michael Walker, *François Truffaut*, New York, 1971.

Fanne, Dominique, *L'Univers de François Truffaut*, Paris, 1972.

Allen, Don, *Finally Truffaut*, London, 1973; revised edition, 1985.

Monaco, James, *The New Wave: Truffaut, Godard, Chabrol, Rohmer, Rivette*, New York, 1976.

Collet, Jean, *Le Cinéma de François Truffaut*, Paris, 1977; revised edition, 1985.

Insdorf, Annette, *François Truffaut*, Boston, 1978

Walz, Eugene P., *François Truffaut: A Guide to References and Resources*, Boston, 1982.

Winkler, Willi, *Die Film von François Truffaut*, Munich, 1984.

Bergala, Alain, and others, *Le Roman de François Truffaut*, Paris, 1985.

De Fornari, Oreste, *I filme di François Truffaut*, Rome, 1986.

Dalmais, Hervé, *Truffaut*, Paris, 1987.

Ciment, Gilles, and others, *Les 400 Couples de François Truffaut*, Paris, 1988.

Guerif, François, *François Truffaut*, Paris, 1988.

Cahoreau, Gilles, *François Truffaut, 1932–84*, Paris, 1989.

Insdorff, Annette, *François Truffaut: le cinéma est-il magique?*, Paris, 1989.

Merrick, Hélène, *François Truffaut*, Paris, 1989.

On TRUFFAUT: articles—

Sadoul, Georges, "Notes on a New Generation," in *Sight and Sound* (London), October 1959.

Burch, Noël, "Qu'est-ce que la Nouvelle Vague?," in *Film Quarterly* (Berkeley), Winter 1959.

Farber, Manny, "White Elephant Art vs. Termite Art," in *Film Culture* (New York), Winter 1962/63.

Shatnoff, Judith, "François Truffaut—The Anarchist Imagination," in *Film Quarterly* (Berkeley), Spring 1963.

Taylor, Stephen, "After the Nouvelle Vague," in *Film Quarterly* (Berkeley), Spring 1965.

Klein, Michael, "The Literary Sophistication of François Truffaut," in *Film Comment* (New York), Summer 1965.

Braudy, Leo, "Hitchcock, Truffaut, and the Irresponsible Audience," in *Film Quarterly* (Berkeley), Summer 1968.

Wood, Robin, "Chabrol and Truffaut," in *Movie* (London), Winter 1969/70.

Bordwell, David, "A Man Can Serve Two Masters," in *Film Comment* (New York), Spring 1971.

Beylie, Claude, and others, "Le Continent, Truffaut et le deux anglaises," in *Ecran* (Paris), January 1972.

Jebb, Julian, "Truffaut: The Educated Heart," in *Sight and Sound* (London), Summer 1972.

Houston, Beverle, and Marsha Kinder, "Truffaut's Gorgeous Killers," in *Film Quarterly* (Berkeley), Winter 1973/74.

Lefanu, Mark, "The Cinema of Irony: Chabrol, Truffaut in the 1970s," in *Monogram* (London), no. 5, 1974.

Martin, Marcel, "Vingt ans après: une certain constante du cinéma français," in *Ecran* (Paris), January 1974.

Coffey, B., "Art and Film in François Truffaut's *Jules and Jim* and *Two English Girls*," in *Film Heritage* (New York), Spring 1974.

Hess, J., "La Politique des auteurs: Part 2: Truffaut's Manifesto," in *Jump Cut* (Chicago), July/August 1974.

Thomas, P., "The Sorcerer's Apprentice: Bazin and Truffaut on Renoir," in *Sight and Sound* (London), Winter 1974/75.

Carcassonne, P., "Truffaut le narrateur," in *Cinématographe* (Paris), November 1977.

"*La Chambre vert* Issue" of *Avant-Scène du Cinéma* (Paris), 1 November 1978.

Tintner, A.R., "Truffaut's *La Chambre vert*," in *Literature/Film Quarterly* (Salisbury, Maryland), vol. 8, no. 2, 1980.

"*Le Dernier Metro* Issue" of *Avant-Scène du Cinéma* (Paris), March 1983.

Turner, D., "Made in USA: The American Child in Truffaut's *400 Blows*," in *Literature/Film Quarterly* (Salisbury, Maryland), April 1984.

Obituary in *Cahiers du Cinéma* (Paris), November 1984.

"Truffaut Issue" of *Cinéma* (Paris), December 1984.

"Truffaut Issue" of *Cinématographe* (Paris), December 1984.

Truffaut Section of *Wide Angle* (Baltimore, Maryland), vol. 7, nos. 1/2, 1985.

Jameson, R. T., and others, in *Film Comment* (New York), January/February 1985.

Dixon, W., "François Truffaut: A Life in Film," in *Films in Review* (New York), June/July and August/September 1985.

"*Tirez sur le pianiste* and *Vivement dimanche!* Issue" of *Avant-Scène du Cinéma* (Paris), July/August 1987.

Moullet, Luc, "La balance et le lien," in *Cahiers du Cinéma* (Paris), July/August 1988.

Allen, Don, "Truffaut's *Miller's Tale*," in *Sight and Sound* (London), Spring 1989.

*   *   *

François Truffaut was one of five young French film critics, writing for André Bazin's *Cahiers du cinéma* in the early 1950s, who became the leading French filmmakers of their generation. It was Truffaut who first formulated the *politique des auteurs*, a view of film history and film art that defended those directors who were "true men of the cinema"—Renoir, Vigo, Tati in France; Hawks, Ford, Welles in America—rather than those more literary, script-oriented film directors and writers associated with the French "tradition of quality." Truffaut's original term and distinctions were subsequently borrowed and translated by later generations of Anglo-American film critics, including Andrew Sarris, Robin Wood, V.F. Perkins, and Dave Kehr. When Truffaut made his first feature in 1959, *Les Quatre Cent Coups*, he put his ideas of cinema spontaneity into practice with the study of an adolescent, Antoine Doinel, who breaks free from the constrictions of French society to face an uncertain but open future. Since that debut, Truffaut's career has been dominated by an exploration of the Doinel character's future (five films) and by the actor (Jean-Pierre Léaud) whom Truffaut discovered to play Antoine. In Truffaut's 25 years of making films, the director, the Doinel character, and Léaud all grew up together.

The rebellious teenager of *Les Quatre Cent Coups* becomes a tentative, shy, sexually clumsy suitor in the "Antoine et Colette" episode of *Love at Twenty*. In *Baisers volés*, Antoine is older but not much wiser at either love or money making. In *Domicile conjugal* Antoine has married but is still on the run toward something else—the exotic lure of other sexual adventures. And in *L'Amour en fuite*, Antoine is still running (running became the essential metaphor for the Doinel character's existence, beginning with the lengthy running sequence that concludes *Les Quatre Cent Coups*). Although Antoine is now divorced, the novel which he has finally completed has made his literary reputation. That novel, it turns out, is his life itself, the entire Doinel saga as filmed by Truffaut, and Truffaut fills his films with film clips that are both visual and mental recollections of the entire Doinel cycle. Traffaut deliberately collapses the distinction between written fiction and filmed fiction, between the real life of humans and the fictional life of characters. The collapse seems warranted by the personal and professional connections between Truffaut the director, Doinel the character, and Léaud the actor.

Many of Truffaut's non-Doinel films are style pieces that similarly explore the boundaries between art and life, film and fiction. The main character of *Tirez sur le pianist* tries to turn himself into a fictional character, as does Catherine in *Jules et Jim*. Both find it difficult to maintain the consistency of fictional characters when faced with the demanding exigencies of real life. *La Mariée etait en noir* was Truffaut's elegy to Hitchcock, a deliberate style piece in the Hitchcock manner, while *Fahrenheit 451*, his adaption of Ray Bradbury's novel, explores the lack of freedom in a society in which books—especially works of fiction—are burned. Adele H in *L'Histoire d'Adele H*, attempts to convert her passion into a book, her diary, but life can neither requite nor equal her passion, driving her to madness and a total withdrawal from life into the fantasy of her romantic fiction. In *L'Homme qui aimait les femmes*, an incurable womanizer translates his desire into a successful novel, but the existence of that work in no way diffuses, alleviates, or sublimates the desire that vivified it. *The Green Room* is Truffaut's homage to fiction and the novelist's craft—a careful, stylish adaption of a Henry James story. Given his conscious commitment to film and fiction, it was not surprising that Truffaut devoted one of his films to the subject of filmmaking itself. *La Nuit américaine* is one of the most loving and revealing films about the business of making films, an exuberant illustration of the ways in which films use artifice to capture and convey the illusion of life. This film, in which Truffaut himself plays a film director, is a comically energetic defense of the joys and pains of filmmaking, in deliberate response to the more tortured visions of Fellini's 8$^{1}/_{2}$ or Bergman's *Persona*.

Those Truffaut films not concerned with the subject of art are frequently about education. *L'Enfant sauvage* explores the beneficial power and effects of civilization on the savage passions of a child who grew up in the forest, apparently raised by beasts. Truffaut again plays a major role in the film (dedicated to Jean-Pierre Léaud), the patient scientist who effects the boy's conversion from savagery to humanity. Like the director he played in *La Nuit américaine*, Truffaut is the wise and dedicated patriarch, responsible for the well-being of a much larger enterprise. *L'Argent de poche* examines the child's life at school and the child's relationships both to adults and other children. As opposed to the imprisoning restrictions which confined children in the world of *Les Quarte Cent Coups*, the now adult Truffaut realizes that adults—parents and teachers—treat children with far more care, love, and devotion than the children (like the younger, rebellious Truffaut himself) are able to see.

Unlike his friend and contemporary, Jean-Luc Godard, Truffaut remained consistently committed to his highly formal themes of art and life, film and fiction, youth and education, art and education, rather than venturing into radical political critiques of film forms and film imagery. Truffaut seems to state his position in *Le Dernier Métro*, his most political film, examining a theater troupe in Nazified Paris. The film director seems to confess that, like those actors in that period, he can only continue to make art the way he knows how, that his commitment to formal artistic excellence will eventually serve the political purposes that powerful art always serves, and that for him to betray his own artistic powers for political, programmatic purposes would perhaps lead to his making bad art and bad political statements. In this rededication to artistic form, Truffaut is probably restating his affinity with the Jean Renoir he wrote about for *Cahiers du cinéma*. Renoir, like Truffaut, progressed from making more rebellious black-and-white films in his youth to more accepting color films in his maturity; Renoir, like Truffaut, played major roles in several of his own films; Renoir, like Truffaut, believed that conflicting human choices could not be condemned according to facile moral or political formulae; and Renoir, like Truffaut, saw the creation of art (and film art) as a genuinely humane and meaningful response to the potentially chaotic disorder of formless reality. Renoir, however, lived much longer than Truffaut, who died of cancer in 1984 at the height of his powers.

—Gerald Mast

U

ULMER, Edgar.

Austrian. Born Edgar Georg Ulmer in Vienna, 17 September 1904. Studied architecture at Academy of Arts and Sciences, Vienna; studied stage design at Burgteater, Vienna. Married Shirley Castle, one daughter. Designer for Decla-Bioscope film company, 1918; designer for Max Reinhardt, Vienna, 1919–22; designer for Universal in New York, 1923; returned to Germany as assistant to Murnau, 1924; returned to U.S., art director and production assistant at Universal, from 1925; co-directed first film, with Robert Siodmak, 1929; art director at MGM and stage designer for Philadelphia Grand Opera Co., 1930–33; made public health documentaries for minority groups, New York, mid-1930s; director and writer for Producers' Releasing Corporation (PRC), Hollywood, 1942–46; worked in U.S., Mexico, Italy, Germany and Spain, through 1950s. *Died in Woodland Hills, California, 30 September 1972.*

Films as Director:
(claimed to have directed 128 films; following titles are reported in current filmographies):

1929   *Menschen am Sonntag (People on Sunday)* (co-d, co-sc)
1933   *Damaged Lives* (+ co-sc); *Mr. Broadway*
1934   *The Black Cat* (+ co-sc); *Thunder over Texas* (d as 'John Warner')
1937   *Green Fields* (co-d)
1938   *Natalka Poltavka* (+ sc, assoc pr); *The Singing Blacksmith* (+ pr); *Zaporosch Sa Dunayem* (*Cossacks in Exile. The Cossacks Across the Danube*)
1939   *Die Tlatsche* (*The Light Ahead*) [original title: *Fishe da Krin*] (+ pr); *Moon Over Harlem*; *Americaner Schadchen* (*The Marriage Broker. American Matchmaker*); *Let My People Live*
1940   *Cloud in the Sky*
1941   *Another to Conquer*
1942   *Tomorrow We Live*
1943   *My Son, the Hero* (+ co-sc); *Girls in Chains* (+ story); *Isle of Forgotten Sins* (+ story); *Jive Junction*
1944   *Bluebeard*
1945   *Strange Illusion* (*Out of the Night*); *Club Havana*; *Detour*
1946   *The Wife of Monte Cristo* (+ co-sc); *Her Sister's Secret*; *The Strange Woman*
1947   *Carnegie Hall*
1948   *Ruthless*
1949   *I pirati de Capri* (*Pirates of Capri*)
1951   *St. Benny the Dip*; *The Man from Planet X*
1952   *Babes in Bagdad*
1955   *Naked Dawn*; *Murder Is My Beat* (*Dynamite Anchorage*)
1957   *The Daughter of Dr. Jekyll*; *The Perjurer*
1960   *Hannibal*; *The Amazing Transparent Man*; *Beyond the Time Barrier*; *L'Atlantide* (*Antinea. L'amante della città Sepolta*; *Journey Beneath the Desert*) (co-d)
1964   *Sette contro la morte* (*Neunzing Nächte und ein Tag*)
1965   *The Cavern*

Other Films:

1927   *Sunrise* (Murnau) (asst prod des)
1934   *Little Man, What Now?* (set design)
1942   *Prisoner of Japan* (story)
1943   *Corregidor* (co-sc); *Danger! Women at Work* (co-story)

Publications:

By ULMER: articles—

Interview in *Cahiers du Cinéma* (Paris), August 1961.
Interview with Peter Bogdanovich in *Film Culture* (New York), no. 58/60, 1974.

On ULMER: books—

Belton, John, *The Hollywood Professionals Vol. 3*, New York, 1974.
McCarthy, Todd, and Charles Flynn, editors, *Kings of the B's: Working Within the Hollywood System*, New York, 1975.
Belton, John, *Cinema Stylists*, Metuchen, New Jersey, 1983.

On ULMER: articles—

Moullet, Luc, "Edgar G. Ulmer," in *Cahiers du Cinéma* (Paris), April 1956.
Sarris, Andrew, "Esoterica," in *Film Culture* (New York), Spring 1963.
Belton, John, "Prisoners of Paranoia," in *Velvet Light Trap* (Madison, Wisconsin), Summer 1972; reprinted Winter 1977.
Beylie, Claude, "Edgar G. Ulmer, dandy de grand chemin," in *Ecran* (Paris), December 1972.
"*Le Chat Noir* Issue" of *Avant-Scène du Cinéma* (Paris), 1982.
Jenkins, Steve, "Ulmer and PRC: a Detour down Poverty Row," in *Monthly Film Bulletin* (London), July 1982.
Krohn, B., "King of the B's," in *Film Comment* (New York), July/August 1983.
Mandell, P., "Edgar Ulmer and *The Black Cat*," in *American Cinematographer* (Los Angeles), October 1984.
Prédal, René, "L'usine aux maléfices," in *Avant-Scène du Cinéma* (Paris), March 1985.

*   *   *

The films of Edgar G. Ulmer have generally been classified as "B" pictures. However, it might be more appropriate to reclassify some of these films as "Z" pictures. On an average, Ulmer's pictures were filmed on a six-day shooting schedule with budgets as small as $20,000. He often worked without a decent script, adequate sets, or convincing actors. But these hardships did not prevent Ulmer from creating an individual style within his films.

Part of the look of Ulmer's films was, naturally, a result of their small budgets. The cast was kept to a minimum., the sets were few and simple, and stock footage helped to keep costs down (even when they didn't quite match the rest of the film). The length of the scripts was also kept to a minimum. Most of Ulmer's films ran only 60 to 70 minutes and it was not uncommon for his pictures to open upon characters who were not formally introduced. Ulmer often plunged his audience into the

Edgar Ulmer (left) with Bela Lugosi

middle of the action, which would add to their suspense as the story finally did unfold.

It is a common element of Ulmer's films for the characters to find themselves in strange and distant surroundings. This plight is especially true for the title character of *The Man from Planet X*. This curious being is stranded on earth (which from his point of view is an alien world) and is at the mercy of the strangers around him. In another example, the Allisons, a young couple on their honeymoon in *The Black Cat*, find themselves trapped in the futuristic home of the bizarre Mr. Poelzig. They are held against their will with all avenues of escape blocked off. Many of Ulmer's characters find that they are prisoners. Some of them are innocent, but many times they live in prisons of their own making.

Another theme that is prevalent in Ulmer's films is fate. His characters rarely have control over their own destiny, an idea verbalized by Al Roberts in *Detour* who says, "whichever way you turn, Fate sticks out its foot to trip you." In *The Amazing Transparent Man*, a scientist who has been forced to work against his will on experiments with nuclear material, explains

that he "didn't do anything by choice." The Allisons in *The Black Cat* have no control over their destiny, either—their fate will be determined by the outcome of a game of chess. In most cases the characters in Ulmer's films find themselves swept away in a series of circumstances that they are unable to stop.

The critical recognition of Ulmer's work has been a fairly recent "discovery." Initial reviews of Ulmer's films (and not all of his films received reviews) were far from complimentary. Part of the reason for their dismissal may have been their exploitative nature. Titles like *Girls in Chains* and *Babes in Bagdad* could conceivably have some difficulty in finding a respectable niche in the film world. However, taken as a whole, the work of Edgar Ulmer reveals a personal vision that is, at the very least, different and distinctive from the mainstream of film directors.

—Linda Obalil

VADIM, Roger.

French. Born Roger Vadim Plemiannikov in Paris, 26 January 1928. Educated in political science; studied acting with Charles Dullin. Married 1) Brigitte Bardot, 1952 (divorced); 2) Annette Stroyberg, 1958 (divorced), one child; child by Catherine Deneuve; 3) Jane Fonda, 1967 (divorced); 4) Catherine Schneider, 1975 (divorced), one child. Stage actor, 1944–47; assistant to Marc Allégret on *Juliette*, 1953, and others; journalist for *Paris-Match* and TV director, early 1950s; directed first film, *Et . . . Dieu créa la femme*, 1956. Address: 24–29 Beverly Avenue, Santa Monica, CA 90405, U.S.A.

Films as Director:

1956   *Et . . . Dieu créa la femme (And . . . God Created Woman)* (+ co-sc)
1957   *Sait-on jamais? (No Sun in Venice)* (+ sc)
1958   *Les Bijoutiers du clair de lune (Heaven Fell That Night. The Night That Heaven Fell)* (+ co-sc)
1959   *Les Liaisons dangereuses* (+ co-sc)
1960   *Et mourir de plaisir (Blood and Roses)* (+ co-sc)
1961   *La Bride sur le cou (Please, Not Now!)* (co-d, uncredited, co-sc)
1962   "L'Orgueil (Pride)" episode of *Les Sept Pechées capitaux (Seven Deadly Sins)* (+ co-sc); *Le Repos du guerrier (Warrior's Rest. Love on a Pillow)* (+ co-sc)
1963   *Le Vice et la vertu (Vice and Virtue)* (+ co-sc, pr); *Château en Suède (Nutty Naughty Chateau)* (+ co-sc)
1964   *La Ronde (Circle of Love)* (+ co-sc, co-adapt)
1966   *La Curée (The Game Is Over)* (+ co-sc, pr)
1968   "Metzengerstein" episode of *Histoires extraordinaires (Spirits of the Dead)* (+ co-sc); *Barbarella* (+ co-sc)
1971   *Pretty Maids All in a Row*
1972   *Hellé* (+ story)
1973   *Don Juan 1973 ou si Don Juan était une femme (Ms. Don Juan, Don Juan, or If Don Juan Were a Woman)* (+ co-sc)
1974   *La Jeune Fille assassinée (Charlotte)* (+ pr, sc, role)
1976   *Une Femme fidèle* (+ co-sc)
1979   *Night Games*
1980   *The Hot Touch*
1981   *Art of Deceit*
1983   *Surprise Party*
1983   *Come Back*
1987   *Et Dieu créa la femme (And God Created Woman)*

Publications:

By VADIM: books—

Les Liaisons dangereuses, with Roger Vailland and Claude Brulé, New York, 1962.
Memoirs of the Devil, New York, 1976.
The Hungry Angel, New York, 1984.

Bardot, Deneuve and Fonda: The Memoirs of Roger Vadim, London, 1986.

By VADIM: articles—

"Pretty Maids," in *Playboy* (Chicago), April 1971.
"Meeting the Gallic Svengali," an interview with M. Rosen, in *Millimeter* (New York), October 1975.
"So Who Created Vadim?," an interview with Marc Mancini, in *Film Criticism* (Meadville, Pennsylvania), vol. 24, no. 2, 1988.

On VADIM: books—

Carpozi, George Jr., *The Brigitte Bardot Story*, New York, 1961.
de Beauvoir, Simone, *Brigitte Bardot and the Lolita Syndrome*, London, 1961.
Frydland, Maurice, *Roger Vadim*, Paris, 1963.

On VADIM: articles—

Mardore, Michel, "Roger Vadim," in *Premier Plan* (Lyon), October 1959.
Burch, Noël, "Qu'est-ce que la Nouvelle Vague?," in *Film Quarterly* (Berkeley), Winter 1959.
Billard, G., "Ban on Vadim," in *Films and Filming* (London), November 1959.
Maben, A., "Vadim and Zola," in *Films and Filming* (London), October 1966.

*   *   *

With *Et . . . Dieu créa la femme* Roger Vadim created the commercial climate which made the *nouvelle vague* possible. Despite this, his reputation as director has always lagged behind that as a connoisseur of the beautiful women who inhabit his films. His relationships with Brigitte Bardot, Annette Stroyberg, Catherine Deneuve, Jane Fonda and others established him, in English-speaking countries at least, as the archetypal "French" director. The American retitling of *Le Repos du guerrier* as *Love on a Pillow*, and *Chateau en Suède* as *Nutty, Naughty Chateau* glumly emphasizes his raffish image.

Vadim claims in his fanciful autobiography that a prostitute provided by producer Raoul Levy to relieve the tedium of screenwriting furnished him with rationale for Bardot's character in *Et . . . Dieu créa la femme*—unselfishness. "If she's not interested in money, people won't think she's a whore." This motive recurs in Vadim's work, where generous, warmhearted and sensual women lavish their favors on indifferent, often evil love objects. Fulfilment comes only with death. In *La Jeune Fille assassiné*, Vadim even makes death in the throes of orgasm the sole ambition of his heroine, and his first American film, *Pretty Maids All in a Row*, casts Rock Hudson as an improbable mass-murdering psychiatrist in a girls' college.

For an artist with a single subject, Vadim has proved remarkably imaginative. *Sait-on jamais* exploits Venice with style, the Modern Jazz Quartet's chiming score harmonizing precisely with Vadim's romantic thriller. His lesbian vampire

Roger Vadim

melodrama, *Et mourir de plaisir*, is among the lushest of horror films, enlivened by a clever use of color and a surrealist dream sequence which reminds one that he knew Cocteau and acted in *La Testament d'Orphée*. Jane Fonda never looked more beautiful than in the incest drama *La Curée*, and in *Barbarella* he turned Jean-Claude Forest's comic strip into something between Grand Guignol and an erotic *tableau vivant*. Even his lamentable American re-make of *Et . . . Dieu créa la femme* transformed Rebecca de Mornay from rural tart into temptress.

He is at his best in the high style, where the material encourages grand gestures. Bardot in *Le Repos du guerrier* standing like the Winged Victory in a ruined church, face turned into a torrent of wind; Stroyberg in an 18th-century white gown gliding through the cypresses of Hadrian's Villa to Jean Prodromides's score of harp and pizzicati strings in *Et mourir de plaisir*—these are images that briefly transcend the novelettish material from which they spring.

—John Baxter

VANDERBEEK, Stan.

American. Born in New York City, 1927. Studied painting. Married, two children. Began making collage-films, early 1960s; built dome-studio ("The Movie-Drome") in Stony Point, New York, mid-1960s; University lecturer and teacher, from mid-1960s; worked at Bell Telephone Laboratory, Murray Hill, New Jersey on experiments in computer graphics, late 1960s. Recipient: First Prize in Animation, Bergamo Festival, for *Mankinda*, 1960. *Died 19 September 1984.*

Films as Director:

1957 *What Who How*; *Mankinda*; *Astral Man*
1957–58 *One and Yet*
1958 *Ala Mode*; *Wheeeeels No.1*; *Visioniii*
1959 *Wheeeeels No. 2*; *Dance of the Looney Spoons*; *Science Friction*; *Achoo Mr. Keroochev*; *Street Meat* (documentary, not completed)
1960 *Skullduggery*; *Blacks and Whites in Days and Nights*
1961 *Snapshots of the City*
1961–62 *Misc. Happenings* (documentaries of Claus Oldenberg happenings); *Summit*

1964   *Breathdeath*; *Phenomenon No.1*
1965   *The Human Face Is a Monument*; *Variations No.5*; *Feedback*
1966   *Poem Field No.2*
1967   *See, Saw, Seems*; *Poem Field No.1*; *Man and His World*; *Panels for the Walls of the World*; *Poem Field No.5*; *Free Fall*; *Spherical Space No.1*; *The History of Motion in Motion*; *T.V. Interview*; *Poem Field No.7*
1968   *Newsreel of Dreams No.1*; *Vanderbeekiana*; *Oh*; *Super-Imposition*; *Will*
1968–70   *Found Film No.1*
1969   *Newsreel of Dreams No.2*
1970   *Film Form No.1*; *Film Form No.2*; *Transforms*
1972   *Symmetricks*; *Videospace*; *Who Ho Ray No.1*; *You Do, I Do, We Do*
1973   *Computer Generation*
1977   *Color Fields*
1978   *Euclidean Illusions*
1980   *Mirrored Reason*; *Plato's Cave Inn*; *Dreaming*
1981   *After Laughter*

Publications:

By VANDERBEEK: articles—

"On *Science Friction*," in *Film Culture* (New York), Summer 1961.
"The Cinema Delimina: Films from the Underground," in *Film Quarterly* (Berkeley), Summer 1961.
"If the Actor is the Audience," in *Film Culture* (New York), Spring 1962.
"Antidotes for Poisoned Movies," in *Film Culture* (New York), Summer 1962.
"Simple Syllogism," in *Film Culture* (New York), no. 29, 1963.
"Interview: Chapter One," in *Film Culture* (New York), no. 35, 1964/65.
"Compound Entendre," in *Film: A Montage of Theories*, edited by Richard MacCann, New York, 1966.
"*Culture: Intercom* and Expanded Cinema," in *Film Culture* (New York), Spring 1966.
"Re: Vision," in *American Scholar* (Washington, D.C.), Spring 1966.
"Disposable Art—Synthetic Media—and Artificial Intelligence," in *Take One* (Montreal), January/February 1969.
"Re Computerized Graphics," in *Film Culture* (New York), no. 48–49, 1970.
"Media (W)rap-around: Or a Man with No Close," in *Filmmakers Newsletter* (Ward Hill, Massachusetts), March 1971.
"Social-Imagistics: What the Future May Hold," in *American Film Institute Report*, Washington, D.C., May 1973.
"Animation Retrospective," in *Film Comment* (New York), September/October 1977.

On VANDERBEEK: book—

Hanhardt, John, and others, *A History of the American Avant-Garde*, exhibition catalogue, The American Federation of Arts, New York, 1976.

On VANDERBEEK: articles—

Christgau, Robert, "Vanderbeek: Master of Animation," in *Popular Photography* (Boulder, Colorado), September 1965.
Manica, A., and W. Van Dyke, "Four Artists as Filmmakers," in *Art in America* (New York), January 1967.
"New Talent: the Computer," in *Art in America* (New York), January 1970.
Weiss, M.W., "VanDerBeek to students: take a high risk," in *Journal of the University Film Association* (Carbondale), Spring 1982.
"Stan Vanderbeek Obituary" in *Film Comment* (New York), January/February 1985.

*   *   *

Typical to a great number of experimental filmmakers, Stan Vanderbeek studied painting before actually beginning his film production. Indeed his earliest films are animated collage pieces which embody his background in graphics (e.g. *Breathdeath*).

Vanderbeek's career spanned about a third of a century, a

period of almost constant creativity with extraordinary amalgamations of media. As such, it is a difficult career to summarize, especially in light of the fact that no definitive list of his truly countless productions seems to exist. Vanderbeek appeared to exude creations at a rate that escaped even his own cataloguing.

Soon after his early animation work, he was to focus upon a unique multi-projection apparatus of his own design. This "Movie-Drome" (at Stony Point, New York) provided the presentation of a number of "Vortex-Concerts," prototypes for a satellite-interconnected "Culture Intercom" that might allow better (and quicker) international communication. At the same time, he continued experiments with dance films, paintings, polaroid photography, architecture, 195-degree cinematography, and intermedia events.

However, Vanderbeek's more recent explorations of computer generated images and video graphics not only provide a clear contemporary perspective for his career, but moreover signalled a technostructural metamorphosis which marks the ongoing evolution of that major genre generally known as the "experimental film." Experimental filmmakers of Vanderbeek's prestige and prominence have, at times, found the fortune of industry support. In the late 1960s, Vanderbeek came to collaborate with computer specialist like Ken Knowlton of New Jersey's Bell Telephone Laboratories. The result was a number of cathode-ray-tube mosaics called *Poem Fields*. Today these early exercises with computer graphic possibilities still retain aesthetic power as transparent tapestries in electronic metamorphosis. Typically brief, non-narrative and abstract, the various *Poem Fields* often reveal subtle, stunning *mandala* patterns, strikingly similar to classic Asian meditative devices with their symmetrical concentricity.

Vanderbeek's final projects retain his address of electronically constructed imagery. Some of his work (e.g. *Color Fields*) employs the same painterly interest in abstraction which characterized *Poem Fields*. Others (e.g. *Mirrored Reason*, made in video and released in film) are more representational and narrative. Still others (e.g. *After Laughter*) recall the rapidly paced irony that marked Vanderbeek's earliest animation like *Breathdeath*.

This noteworthy quantity, quality, and extraordinary technological diversity of output resulted in exceptional institutional support for Vanderbeek throughout the years. He was artist-in-residence at USC, Colgate, WGBH-TV, and NASA. His work has been presented on CBS, ABC, and such CATV showcases as "Night Flight." His performances outside the United States took him to such cities as Berlin, Vienna, Tokyo, Paris, and Toronto; he has been a U.S.I.A. speaker in nations like Israel, Iran, Turkey, Greece, and England. His grants and awards are equally numerous and prestigious, and his academic recognition provided Vanderbeek not only with guest lectures and screenings throughout the United States, but faculty appointments at such schools as Columbia, Washington, and M.I.T.

—Edward S. Small

VAN DYKE, Willard.

American. Born Willard Ames Van Dyke in Denver, Colorado, 5 December 1906. Educated at University of California. Married 1) Mary Gray Barnett, 1938 (divorced 1950),

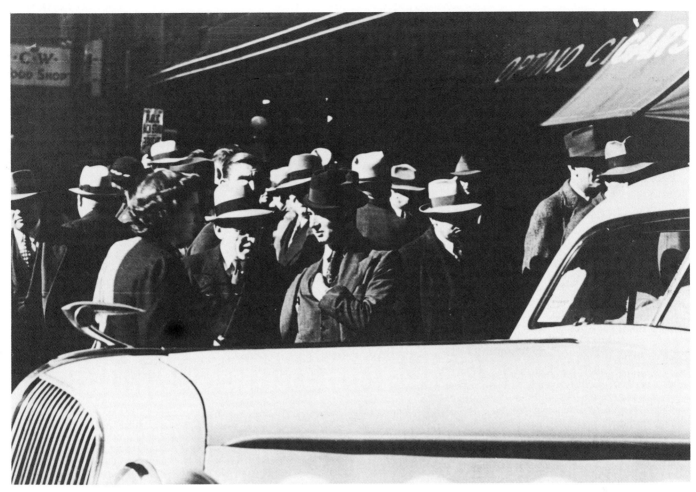

Willard Van Dyke: *The City*

two children; 2) Margaret Barbara Murray Millikin, 1950, two children. Photographer on WPA Art Project in San Francisco, 1934; photographer for *Harper's Bazaar*, 1935; cameraman on Pare Lorentz's *The River*, 1936–37; directed first film (with Ralph Steiner), *The City*, 1939; producer for Office of War Information's Motion Picture Bureau, 1941–45; made films for variety of sponsors and for TV, 1946–65; director of film department, Museum of Modern Art, New York, 1965–73; vice-president, International Federation of Film Archives. *Died in Jackson, Tennessee, 23 January 1986.*

Films as Director:

1939   *The City* (co-d, co-pr, co-ph)
1940   *Valley Town* (+ co-sc); *The Children Must Learn* (+ sc); *Sarah Lawrence*; *To Hear Your Banjo Play*; *Tall Tales*
1942   *The Bridge*
1943   *Oswego*; *Steeltown*
1944   *Pacific Northwest* (+ co-ph)
1945   *San Francisco*
1946   *Journey into Medicine*
1947   *The Photographer*
1948   *Terribly Talented*
1949   *This Charming Couple*; *Mount Vernon*
1950   *Years of Change*
1952   *New York University*
1953   *Working and Playing to Health*; *There is a Season*
1954   *Recollections of Boyhood: An Interview with Joseph Welch*; *Cabos Blancos*; *Excursion House*; *Toby and the Tall Corn*

1957   *Life of the Molds*
1958   *Skyscraper* (co-d); *Tiger Hunt in Assam*; *Mountains of the Moon*
1959   *Land of White Alice*; *The Procession*
1960   *Ireland, the Tear and the Smile*; *Sweden*
1962   *So That Men Are Free*; *Search ino Darkness*
1963   *Depressed Area*
1964   *Rice*; *Frontiers of News*
1965   *Pop Buell, Hoosier Farmer in Laos*; *Taming the Mekong*; *The Farmer: Feast or Famine* (co-d); *Frontline Cameras 1935–1965*
1968   *Shape of Things to Come*

Other Films:

1937   *The River* (Lorentz) (ph)

Publications:

By VAN DYKE: articles—

"The Interpretive Camera in Documentary," in *Hollywood Quarterly*, July 1946.
"The American Documentary—Limitations and Possibilities: An Interview with Willard Van Dyke," with Edouard De Laurot and Jonas Mekas, in *Film Culture* (New York), no. 3, 1956.
"Thirty Years of Social Inquiry: An Interview with Willard Van Dyke," with Harrison Engle, in *Film Comment* (New York), Spring 1965.
Interview with B.L. Kevles in *Film Culture* (New York), Fall 1965.
"The Role of the Museum of Modern Art in Motion Pictures," in *Film Library Quarterly* (New York), Winter 1967–68.

"Willard Van Dyke," in *Documentary Explorations* edited by G. Roy Levin, Garden City, New York, 1971.

"Glancing Backward . . . Without Nostalgia," with Lora Hays, in *Film Library Quarterly* (New York), Summer 1971.

Hitchens, Gordon, "Conversations with Willard Van Dyke," in *Cineaste* (Montreal), vol. 13, no. 1., 1983.

On VAN DYKE: articles—

"Director on Location," in the *Saturday Review* (New York), 10 September 1949.

Zuckerman, Art, "Focus on Willard Van Dyke," in *Popular Photography* (Boulder, Colorado), April 1965.

Obituary in *Variety* (New York), 29 January 1986.

Lamont, A., Obituary in *Film Comment* (New York), March/April 1986.

On VAN DYKE: film—

Rothschild, Amalie R., *Conversations with Willard Van Dyke*, 1981.

* * *

During the 1930s and 1940s, an American documentary tradition was established by a group of filmmakers concerned with then-current issues and crises: the Depression-era Dust Bowl (in Pare Lorentz's *The Plow That Broke the Plains*); the destruction of the Mississippi River basin (Lorentz's *The River*); the advantages of electricity in the rural Midwest (Joris Iven's *Power and the Land*); and the construction of oil rigs in the Louisiana swamp (Flaherty's *Louisiana Story*). One of the seminal filmmakers of this period was Willard Van Dyke, who photographed *The River*, and, with Ralph Steiner, made *The City*, a plea for the necessity of city planning.

The City, produced by the American Institute of Planners for screening at the New York World's Fair, is as revelant today as it was in 1939. The focus is on the need for, and development of, model cities with a stress on human and social considerations. Communities must be livable; they must be by, of, and for people. Van Dyke and Steiner trace the development of modern urban America, with an emphasis on the manner in which city planners had erred in judgment; at the finale, they present an ideal planned community. There is a minimum of narration: scenes of New York City tenements and subways—and, specifically, a sequence in which a man attempts to cross a street in traffic—are ample proof of the filmmakers' argument. While the film's strength remains its visuals, at the same time the soundtrack music (by Aaron Copland) poignantly expresses emotion. As with Virgil Thomson's score for *The River* and Marc Blitzstein's for Van Dyke's next documentary, *Valley Town*, the music is as meaningful as the images or words in communicating ideas and feelings. The New York *Herald-Tribune* reported, weeks after the film's premiere, "Already several thousand persons have seen *The City*, many of whom had never before seen a documentary film, and it may be predicted that its cordial reception by critics and public alike will benefit greatly the already widening beginnings of the documentary form in this country."

In *Valley Town*, a stylized examination of the results of automation on the people in a Pennsylvania steel town, Van Dyke had his narrator serve as the town's mayor, who discusses the problems of his municipality. Rarely were any of his later films as trenchant as his first two. He shot documentaries for a variety of sources, including the Office of War Information (during World War II), the U.S. State Department, the Ford Motor Company, the United Church of Christ, and the television shows *Omnibus*, *High Adventure* and *Twentieth Century*. Van Dyke's subjects ranged from the folk music of Pete Seeger, Josh White and Burl Ives (*To Hear Your Banjo Play*, *Tall Tales*) to the establishment of the United Nations (*San Francisco*); recreational therapy in a mental hospital (*Working and Playing to Health*) to life in India (*Tiger Hunt in Assam*), Africa (*Mountains of the Moon*) and Appalachia (*Depressed Area, U.S.A.*).

However, Willard Van Dyke's most typical subject matter relates to the social implications of change, whether again examining the lives of steelworkers (in *Steeltown*), or auto workers (*There Is a Season*), or farmers in Puerto Rican cooperatives (*Cabos Blancos*), or Protestant clergymen (*The Procession*). All have their roots in *The City* and *Valley Town*.

—Rob Edelman

VAN DYKE, W.S.

American. Born Woodbridge Strong Van Dyke II in San Diego, California, 21 March 1889 (known by childhood name "Woody"). Debut as child actor, 1892; besides theatrical activities, worked as miner, electrician, music hall performer and mercenary in Mexico, 1903–15; left theater, became assistant director for Essanay Studios, Chicago, 1915; assistant to D.W. Griffith, 1916; assistant to James Young at Paramount, directed first film, 1917; signed by Thalberg for MGM, 1926; mobilized as Marine Corps officer, 1941. *Died 4 February 1943.*

Films as Director:

1917   *Her Good Name* (+ sc); *Clouds*; *Mother's Ordeal* (+ sc); *The Land of Long Shadows* (+ sc); *The Range Boss* (+ sc): *The Open Places* (+ sc); *The Men of the Desert* (+ sc); *Our Little Nell* (+ sc); *The Gift o' Gab* (+ sc); *Sadie Goes to Heaven* (+ sc)

1919   *Lady of the Dugouts* (+ co-sc)

1920   *Daredevil Jack* (+ co-sc); *The Hawk's Trail* (+ co-sc)

1921   *Double Adventure* (+ co-sc): *The Fortieth Door* (unfinished); *The Avenging Arrow* (co-d, co-sc)

1922   *White Eagle* (co-d, co-sc); *Ruth of the Range* (d: Warde; Van Dyke directed action scenes); *The Milky Way*; *According to Hoyle*; *Forget Me Not*; *The Boss of Camp Four*

1923   *The Girl Next Door* (*You Are in Danger*); *The Destroying Angel*; *The Miracle Makers*; *Half-a-Dollar Bill*

1924   *Loving Lies*; *The Battling Fool*; *The Beautiful Sinner*; *Winner Takes All*; *Gold Heels*

1925   *The Chicago Fire* (*Barriers Burned Away*); *Ranger of the Big Pines*; *The Trail Rider*; *Hearts and Spurs*; *The Timber Wolf*; *The Desert's Price*

1926   *The Gentle Cyclone*; *Eyes of the Totem*; *The Heart of the Yukon* (+ co-sc)

(for Metro-Goldwyn-Mayer):

1926   *War Paint* (*Rider of the Plains*); *Winners of the Wilderness*

1927   *Under the Black Eagle*; *California*; *Foreign Devils*; *The Adventurer* (*The Gallant Gringo*) (d: Tourjanski; Van Dyke finished film); *Spoilers of the West*; *Wyoming* (+ co-sc)

1928   *White Shadows in the South Seas* (co-d)

1929   *The Pagan*

1931   *Trader Horn* (+ co-dialogue); *Guilty Hands*; *Never the Twain Shall Meet*; *The Cuban Love Song* (*Rumba*)

1932   *Tarzan the Ape Man*; *Night Court* (*Justice for Sale*)

1933   *Penthouse*; *The Prizefighter and the Lady* (*Every Woman's Man*) (+ co-pr); *Eskimo* (*Mala the Magnificent*) (+ co-sc)

1934   *Laughing Boy*; *Manhattan Melodrama*; **The Thin Man**; *Hide Out*; *The Painted Veil* (d: Boleslawski; Van Dyke finished film); *Forsaking All Others*

1935   *Naughty Marietta*; *I Live My Life*; *A Tale of Two Cities* (co-d; Van Dyke replaced Jack Conway); *Rose Marie*

W.S. Van Dyke

1936   *His Brother's Wife* (*Lady of the Tropics*) (+ pr); *San Francisco* (+ co-pr); *The Devil Is a Sissy* (*The Devil Takes the Count*); *Love on the Run*; *After the Thin Man* (*Nick, Gentleman Detective*)

1937   *Personal Property* (*Man in Possession*); *They Gave Him a Gun*; *The Prisoner of Zenda* (Cromwell and Cukor; Van Dyke directed action scenes); *Rosalie*

1938   *Marie Antoinette* (Julien Duvivier directed Revolution scenes); *Sweethearts*; *Stand Up and Fight*

1939   *It's a Wonderful World*; *Andy Hardy Gets Spring Fever*; *Another Thin Man*; *I Take This Woman* (film begun in 1938 by von Sternberg, then Borzage as *New York Cinderella*)

1940   *I Love You Again*; *Bitter Sweet*

1941   *Rage in Heaven*; *The Feminine Touch*; *Shadow of the Thin Man*; *Dr. Kildare's Victory* (*The Doctor and the Debutante*); *I Married an Angel*; *Cairo*; *Journey for Margaret*

1943   *Dragon Seed* (completed by Jack Conway and Harold Bucquet)

Other Films:

1915   *The Raven* (asst d); *A Daughter of the City* (Windom) (sc)

1916   *The Little Girl Next Door* (Windom) (sc); *The Little Shepherd of Bargain Row* (Barthelet) (sc); *Orphan Joyce* (Berthelet) (sc); *The Chaperon* (Berthelet) (co-sc); *The Discard* (Windom) (sc); *The Return of Eve* (Berthelet) (co-sc); *The Primitive Strain* (Berthelet) (sc); *Intolerance* (Griffith) (asst d); *Oliver Twist* (Young) (asst d); *Sins of the Parents* (Nichols) (sc)

1927   *Riders of the Dark* (Grinde) (sc)

Publications:

By VAN DYKE: book—

Horning into Africa, Los Angeles, 1931.

By VAN DYKE: articles—

"From Horse Opera to Epic," in *Cue* (New York), 16 March 1935.
"The Motion Picture and the Next War," in *Hollywood Reporter*, 8 June 1936.
"Rx for a Thin Man," in *Stage* (New York), January 1937.

On VAN DYKE: books—

Cannom, Robert, *Van Dyke and the Mythical City of Hollywood*, Culver City, California, 1948.
Crowther, Bosley, *The Lion's Share: The M-G-M Story*, New York, 1957.
Thomas, Bob, *Thalberg, Life and Legend*, New York, 1969.

On VAN DYKE: articles—

Johnston, Alva, "Van Dyke—Lord Fauntleroy in Hollywood," in *New Yorker*, 28 September 1935.
Penfield, Cornelia, "Hollywood Helmsmen: W.S. Van Dyke and Frank Capra," in *Stage* (New York), 13 April 1936.
Riggan, Byron, "Damn the Crocodiles, Keep the Camera Rolling!," in *American Heritage* (New York), June 1968.
Selander, Lesley, "Up From Assistant Director," in *Action* (Los Angeles), January/February 1971.
Dumont, Hervé, "Woody S. Van Dyke et l'âge d'or d'Hollywood," in *Travelling* (Lausanne), no. 37, 1973.
Dumont, Hervé, "W.S. Van Dyke (1889–1943)," in *Anthologie du Cinéma* (Paris), July/September 1975.

*   *   *

The one thing that best characterizes the style of W.S. Van Dyke is exemplified by his famous nickname, "One Take" Van Dyke. Known for the speed and economy such an epithet indicates, Van Dyke was the unofficial "house director" at Metro-Goldwyn-Mayer for most of his career. Because he died before the collapse of the studio system, he did not face the economic constraints many former MGM directors, accustomed to lavish budgets, were forced to deal with during the 1950s. Based on his record for swift and skillful set-ups, and his experience directing series films which involved a recurring set of characters, he presumably would not only have survived the collapse of the studios, but might also have become one of the biggest names in television. As it is, his career stands as a tribute to the studio system and what it could turn out in as little as three weeks. His films not only pleased those who saw them upon initial release, but they continue to delight new audiences today with their careless charm.

Van Dyke is not an artist. His work is sometimes downright sloppy, with poorly matched cuts and an improvisational quality that is more desperate than deliberate. However, he was a confident craftman, and his best films are pure fun. Whether he worked with a typical Metro big budget (as in *Marie Antoinette*) or found himself with less money and time (the *Thin Man* films), he stressed story and character, and getting the job done without sacrificing too much of the Metro gloss. He became a favorite with studio bosses, and directed some of MGM's most successful series film, among them the first Johnny Weismuller/Maureen O'Sullivan Tarzan film, *Tarzan the Ape Man*, and the first Nelson Eddy/Jeanette MacDonald pairing, *Naughty Marietta*. He also directed an Andy Hardy, a Dr. Kildare, and several others in the Eddy/MacDonald series. He is generally given credit for the idea of casting William Powell and Myrna Loy as Nick and Nora Charles in the first *Thin Man* movie, which he directed along with several others in the series.

Van Dyke's first movie (circa 1917) taught him the out-in-the-field improvisational filmmaking of the silent era. When he became a contract director at MGM, he was able to use these skills, as in his 1926 costume film, *Winners of the Wilderness*, one of Joan Crawford's first starring vehicles. It is an effective combination of location shooting, action sequences, and lavish costume drama built around a beautiful female star. Such movies as *White Shadows of the South Seas, Trader Horn*, and *Eskimo* continued his penchant for out-of-door filming, and for the fresh, open quality such movie-making required.

The interesting thing about Van Dyke's career is that, given the restrictions of working at MGM during the 1930s, he never lost his breezy, off-hand approach to films. Although he seemed willing to assume any assignment, and his overall work does not add up to a personal cinema, he was adept at directing the great female stars that MGM had under contract during those years. He was able to make significant contributions to their personae by seeing in them qualities that were the opposite of those that had originally brought them stardom. For instance, instead of restricting Myrna Loy to roles as an exotic, Oriental beauty, he suggested her for the lead in a modern comedy, helping her to reveal her "good pal" side in order to play the perfect wife of *The Thin Man*. The serious side of Jean Harlow (whose intelligence he respected) and the comic side of Joan Crawford were explored in *Personal Property* and *Love on the Run* respectively. Norma Shearer's experience as a silent film actress was allowed to flower in the final scenes of *Marie Antoinette*, as he saw her as being more than just a glamorous clothes horse. He also helped turn the unlikely combination of Nelson Eddy and Jeanette MacDonald into one of the most successful screen teams in the history of musical films.

Van Dyke is more or less a forgotten director today. Yet his films are revived regularly, and as Andrew Sarris correctly perceived in *American Cinema*, "he made more good movies than his reputation for carelessness and haste would indicate." Van Dyke made entertainment films, not art, but he is a perfect example of a man who could survive in the studio system.

—Jeanine Basinger

VARDA, Agnès.

Belgian. Born in Brussels, 30 May 1928. Educated in literature and psychology at the Sorbonne, Paris; studied art history at the Ecole du Louvre; studied photography at night school. Married director Jacques Demy, two children. Stage photographer for Theatre Festival of Avignon, then for Theatre National Populaire, Paris, Jean Vilar; directed first film, 1954; accompanied Chris Marker to China as advisor for *Dimanche à Pekin*, 1955; directed two shorts in U.S., 1968; founded production company Ciné-Tamaris, 1977. Recipient: Prix Méliès for *Cléo de 5 à 7*, 1961; Prix Louis Delluc and Special Award, Berlin Festival, for *Le Bonheur*, 1966.

Films as Director:

1954   *La Pointe courte* (+ pr, sc)
1957   *O saisons, o châteaux* (documentary short)
1958   *L'Opéra-Mouffe* (short); *Du côté de la Côte* (short)
1961   **Cléo de cinq à sept** (+ sc)
1963   *Salut les Cubains* (*Salute to Cuba*) (+ text) (short documentary)
1965   *Le Bonheur* (+ sc)
1966   *Les Créatures*
1967   *Uncle Yanco*; episode of *Loin du Vietnam* (*Far From Vietnam*)
1968   *Black Panthers* (*Huey*) (documentary)
1969   *Lion's Love* (+ pr)
1970   *Nausicaa* (for TV)
1975   *Daguerrotypes* (+ pr); *Réponses de femmes* (8mm)
1977   *L'Une chante l'autre pas* (*One Sings the Other Doesn't*)
1980   *Mur Murs* (*Wall Walls. Mural Murals*) (+ pr)
1981   *Documenteur: An Emotion Picture* (+ pr)
1983   *Ulysse*
1984   *Les Dites cariatides*; *Sept P., Cuis., S. de B., . . . a saisir*
1986   *Vagabonde* (*Sans Toit ni loi. Vagabond*)
1988   *Kung Fu Master* (*Don't Say It*); *Jane B. par Agnès V.* (doc)

Other Films:

1971   **Last Tango in Paris** (Bertolucci) (co-dialogue)
1978   *Lady Oscar* (Demy) (pr)

Publications:

By VARDA: articles—

"*Cleo de cinq à sept*: Script Extract," in *Films and Filming* (London), December 1962.
"Pasolini—Varda—Allio—Sarris—Michelson," in *Film Culture* (New York), Fall 1966.
"*Le Bonheur*," in *Cinema* (Beverly Hills), December 1966.
"The Underground River," an interview with Gordon Gow, in *Films and Filming* (London), March 1970.
"Mother of the New Wave," an interview with J. Levitin, in *Women and Film* (Santa Monica), vol. 1, no. 5–6, 1974.
"*L'Une chante, l'autre pas*," an interview with J. Narboni and others, in *Cahiers du Cinéma* (Paris), May 1977.
"One Sings, the Other Doesn't," an interview with R. McCormick, in *Cineaste* (New York), Winter 1977/78.
"Un cinéma plus 'partageable': Agnès Varda," an interview with A. Tournés, in *Jeune Cinéma* (Paris), February 1982.
Interview with J. Sabine in *Cinema Papers* (Melbourne), October 1982.
"Un jour sous le soleil," in *Monthly Film Bulletin* (London), December 1985.
Interview with Rob Edelman in *Cineaste* (New York), vol. 15, no. 1, 1986.
Interview with Barbara Quart in *Film Quarterly* (Berkeley), Winter 1986/1987.
Interview with F. Audé in *Positif* (Paris), March 1988.

On VARDA: books—

Armes, Roy, *French Cinema Since 1946: Vol.2—The Personal Style*, New York, 1966.
Flitterman-Lewis, Sandy, *To Desire Differently: Feminism and the French Cinema*, Urbana, Illinois, 1990.

On VARDA: articles—

Strick, Philip, "Agnès Varda," in *Film* (London), Spring 1963.
Pyros, J., "Notes on Women Directors," in *Take One* (Montreal), November/December 1970.
Roud, Richard, "The Left Bank Revisited," in *Sight and Sound* (London), Summer 1977.
Beylie, Claude, "Les Chardons ardents d'Agnès Varda," in *Ecran* (Paris), 15 April 1979.
Ranvaud, Don, "Travellers Tales," in *Monthly Film Bulletin* (London), May 1986.
Durgnat, Raymond, "Resnais & Co.: Back to the Avant-Garde," in *Monthly Film Bulletin* (London), May 1987.
Prédal, René, "Agnès Varda, une certaine idée de la marginalité," in *Jeune Cinéma* (Paris), October/November 1987.
Forbes, Jill, "Agnès Varda—The Gaze of the Medusa?," in *Sight and Sound* (London), Spring 1989.

*   *   *

Agnès Varda's startlingly individualistic films have earned her the title "grandmother of the New Wave" of French filmmaking. Her statement that a filmmaker must exercise as much freedom as a novelist became a mandate for New Wave directors, especially Chris Marker and Alain Resnais. Varda's first film, *La Pointe courte*, edited by Resnais, is regarded, as Georges Sadoul affirms, as "the first film of the French *nouvelle vuage*. Its interplay between conscience, emotions, and the real world make it a direct antecedent of *Hiroshima, mon amour*."

The use of doubling, and twin story lines; the personification of objects; the artistic determination of cinematic composition, color, texture, form, and time; and the correlation of individual subjectivity to societal objectivity to depict socio-political issues are denominators of Varda's films, which she writes, produces, and directs.

After *La Pointe courte* Varda made three documentaries in 1957–8. The best of these was *L'Opéra-Mouffe*, portraying the Mouffetard district of Paris. Segments of the film are prefaced by handwritten intertitles, a literary element Varda is fond of using. In 1961–2, Varda began but did not complete two film projects: *La Cocotte d'azur* and *Melangite*. Her next film, *Cléo de cinq à sept*, records the time a pop singer waits for results of her exam for cancer. Varda used physical time in *Cleo*: events happening at the same tempo as they would in actual life. The film is divided into chapters, using Tarot cards which symbolize fate. Varda next photographed 4,000 still photos of Castro's revolution-in-progress, resulting in *Salute to Cuba*.

Le Bonheur is considered Varda's most stunning and controversial achievement. Critics were puzzled and pleased. Of her first color film, Varda says it was "essentially a pursuit of the palette . . . Psychology takes first place." A young carpenter lives with his wife and children. Then he takes a mistress; when his wife drowns, his mistress takes her place. The film was commended for its superb visual beauties, the use of narrative in *le nouveau roman* literary pattern, and its tonal contrasts and spatial configurations. Critics continue to debate the film's theme.

Elsa is an essay portraying authors Elsa Triolet and her husband Louis Aragon. *Les Créatures* uses a black and white with red color scheme in a fantasy-thriller utilizing an inside-outside plot that mingles real and unreal events. As in *La Pointe courte*, a young couple retreat to a rural locale. The pregnant wife is mute, due to an accident. Her husband is writing a

Agnès Varda

book. He meets a recluse who operates a machine forcing people to behave as his or her subconscious would dictate. The wife gives birth, regaining her speech.

Visiting the United States, Varda and her husband Jacques Demy each made a film. Varda honored her *Uncle Janco* in the film so named. *The Black Panthers* (or *Huey*) followed. Both documentaries were shown at the London Film Festival in 1968. She next directed a segment of the anti-war short, *Far From Vietnam*.

Using an American setting and an English-speaking cast, including the co-authors of the musical *Hair*, Varda made *Lions Love* in Hollywood. This jigsaw-puzzle work includes a fake suicide, and images of a TV set reporting Robert Kennedy's assassination. G. Roy Levin declared that it was hard to distinguish between the actual and the invented film realities. *Nausicaa* dealt with Greeks living in France. Made for television, it was not shown, Varda says, because it was against military-ruled Greece.

In 1971, Varda helped write the script for *Last Tango in Paris*. Varda's involvement in the women's movement began about 1972; a film dealing with feminist issues, *Réponses de femmes*, has yet to be shown. Made for German television, *Daguerreotypes* has no cast. Varda filmed the residents and shops of the Rue Daguerre, a tribute to L.J.M. Daguerre.

In 1977, Varda made *One Sings, the Other Doesn't* and established her own company, Ciné-Tamaris, to finance it. This "family" of workers created the film. Chronicling the friendship of two women over 15 years, it earned mixed reviews, some referring to it as feminist propaganda or as sentimental syrup. But Varda, narrating the film and writing the song lyrics, does not impose her views. In *One Sings*, she wanted to portray the happiness of being a woman, she says. Today, with over three decades of filmmaking experience, Varda's reputation as a filmmaker dazzles and endures.

—Louise Heck-Rabi

VASILIEV, Sergei and Georgi.

Soviet. Georgi Nikolaievitch Vasiliev born in Vologda, 25 November 1899; Sergei Dmitrievitch Vasiliev born in Moscow, 4 December 1900. (Though not related, they came to be known as the Vasiliev brothers because of a shared surname and because they worked together.) Georgi educated at technical institute, Warsaw, and theatre course in Moscow, 1922–23; Sergei educated in filmmaking, Moscow. Sergei took part in storming of Winter Palace, 1917, then served in Red Army; Georgi served with Red Army, 1918–22; Sergei joined Sevzapkino as film editor, 1923; Georgi film editor for Goskino, from 1924; Goskino and Sevzapkino merged, the "brothers" began working together, 1928; Sergei became administrator at Lenfilm Studios, 1944; Sergei directed *The Heroes of Shipka*, 1954; Council of Ministers of the RSFSR created a prize for artistic achievement named for the Vasiliev brothers, 1965. Recipients: Order of Lenin, 1935; Georgi named Artist of Merit of the RSFSR, 1940; State Prizes for *Chapayev*, 1940, and *The Defense of Tsaritsyn*, 1942; Order of the Red Star for *The Front*, 1944; Sergei named People's Artist of the USSR, 1948, and Best Director, Cannes Festival, for *The Heroes of Shipka*, 1955. *Georgi Vasiliev died 8 June 1946. Sergei Vasiliev died 16 December 1959.*

Films as Directors:

1928   *Podvig vo idach* (*An Exploit on the Ice. The Ice-Breaker Krassnin*)
1930   *The Sleeping Beauty* (*The Woman of the Sleeping Forest*) (+ co-sc)
1932   *A Personal Affair* (*A Personal Matter*)
1934   **Chapayev** (+ sc)
1937   *Volochayevskiye dni* (*The Days of Volochayev. Far East. Intervention in the Far East*) (+ sc)
1942   *Oborona Tsaritsina* (*The Defense of Tsaritsyn*) (+ sc)
1943   *Front* (+ sc)
1954   *Geroite na Shipka* (*The Heroes of Shipka*) (Sergei d only)
1958   *Oktiabr' dni* (*October Days, The Days of October*) (Sergei d only; co-sc)

Publications:

By the VASILIEVS: books—

Chapayev, Moscow, 1936.
Tchapaïev, La Défense de Tsaritsyne, Les Jours de Volotchaïev, in *Scénarios choisis du cinéma soviétique* vol. 2, Paris, 1951.

On the VASILIEVS: book

Leyda, Jay, *Kino: A History of the Russian and Soviet Film*, London, 1960.

On the VASILIEVS: articles—

Schmulévitch, Eric, "Les Frères Vasiliev," in *Avant-Scène du Cinéma* (Paris), 1 and 15 January 1977.
Pisarevsky, D., "Brat'ja Vasil'evy: put' i metod," in *Iskusstvo Kino* (Moscow), November 1980.
Shlovsky, Viktor, and others, "*Chapayev*—50," in *Iskusstvo Kino* (Moscow), November 1984.

*   *   *

The Vasiliev "Brothers" were not related, but met when Goskino and Sevzapkino, where Georgi and Sergei respectively were editors, merged. They used the nickname on their first credits and collaborated until Georgi's death. Their evolution faithfully followed the successive stages of Soviet cinema: a documentary compilation, an avant-garde Bolshevik exercise, the patriotic epics of Socialist Realism. But *Chapayev* eclipsed everything, prompting Georgi's rueful reference to an old proverb, "We wet-nursed an elephant and had to feed it all our lives."

The post-Revolutionary scarcity of resources favoured editors, or rather re-editors, who adapted foreign films to Russian tastes and Communist ideology. Shlovski particularly admired Georgi's taking the last frame of a man yawning, and multiple-printing it to look like an agonised convulsion, with the clinching title, "Death by heart-attack."

Their first feature assembled documentary footage from the Russian expeditions sent to rescue an Italian airship in the Arctic. A scientific documentary (lost, title unknown) on rabbit-rearing charmed spectators by featuring a rabbit as presenter. Their first "artistic" film, *The Sleeping Beauty*, struck a blow for the Bolshevik formalists against "realist" directors surviving from the Tsarist cinema. A Tsarist troupe performs that ballet in a theatre, from whose boxes Red Guards hurl pamphlets; the effete and obsolete gestures on stage contrast with virile actions in the auditorium. Perhaps the film failed with audiences, perhaps formalism failed with the bureaucrats, or both, but their next film, *A Personal Affair*, was strenuously realist, subordinating montage to scenario, actors, and "someone to love and someone to hate". Despite alcoholism and sabotage by reactionaries, a man melts a church-bell into a ship's propeller, thus glorifying the tasks of the Reconstruction Era.

Chapayev revisited the Civil War, but to emphasise the continuing struggle, and Party hegemony over every social sphere.

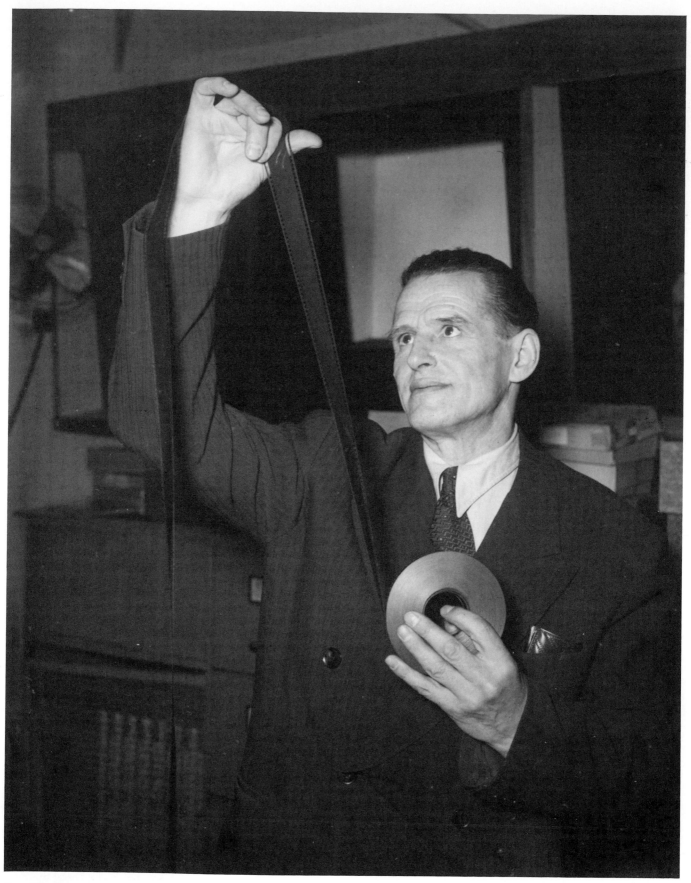

Sergei Vasiliev

Chapayev (B. Babotchkine, typecast foreverafter), a dashing, brave but old-fashioned army commander, becomes increasingly dependent, as he should, on Red Army shells (industrialisation), and on the spiritual and even tactical wisdom of the ever-present Commissar (L. Kmit). As homogenous, even monolithic, as its epico-heroic aspects may seem, it integrated the Vasilievs' hitherto separate aesthetics (and sound, of which the Vasilievs, like Eisenstein, were initially suspicious, accepting its use in "montage" counterpoint to the image but denouncing any "tautology" with the image, lest it lead to "filmed theatre"). The story combined a factual basis, a highly personalised hero, a careful (though not intricate) dramatic structure, and a nimbus of epic and legendary feeling. Monumental graphics, dynamic camera-angles, bold montage, and spare but imaginative sound endowed bodies, huts, fields, fences with a power and grandeur matching Dovzhenko's. Enormously popular, it conclusively demonstrated the compatibility of formalist, realist, and dramatic qualities, and still repays the closest possible study.

The Vasilievs' subsequent films, though well prized at Film Festivals, were scantily shown in the West. Vast military frescos, with some topical point, they stressed different aspects of leader-mass relationships. The 1937 film The Days of Volochayev describes the Civil War campaign against the Japanese, who were then probing Manchuria. It conspicuously lacks any central figure or issue, possibly to encourage general vigilance and suspicion. Stalingrad, besieged through 1942–3, was previously called Tsaritsyn, and in the Vasiliev film The Defense of Tsaritsyn Stalin masterminds its defence in the Civil War. The Vasilievs called The Front a "chamber play", based on a theatre piece which criticized Red Army Generalship during the first Nazi onslaught (to exculpate Stalin, of course). The 1954 film The Heroes of Shipka, in colour, celebrated Russian support for Bulgaria against the Turks in 1877/8, thus exalting the presence of the Red Army throughout Eastern Europe. Friendly critics praised its diversity of precisely-etched character-cameos. October Days celebrated the 30th anniversary of the 1917 Army mutinies, taking its cue from the account thereof in John Reed's Ten Days That Shook the World. More "chronicle" than "history," it concentrates on the movements of the masses, and some vigorously articulated battle-scenes; by now Kruschev had denounced "the cult of personality," and continuing uncertainties about de-Stalinisation could explain the relative obnubilation of leader-mass relations (Lenin is everywhere, Stalin fitfully useful). Friendly critics praised its giving life to dry-as-dust historical phrases.

The one Vasiliev project to seem not entirely militant was a filmed opera, Tchaikovski's The Queen of Spades, begun but soon abandoned in 1943/4. Sergei's administrative activities included Deanship of the Faculty of Cinema at the Unified University of Art Workers. From 1955 he was simultaneously Director of Lenfilm Studios and Secretary of the Leningrad Branch of the Cineastes' trade union.

—Raymond Durgnat

————

VERTOV, Dziga.

Russian. Born Denis Arkadievitch Kaufman in Byalistok, Poland (then annexed to Russia), 2 January 1896. Educated at the music academy in Byalistok, Poland, 1912–15; also attended medical school in St. Petersburg/Petrograd, 1916–17. Married Elizoveta Svilova. Set up a lab for the study of sound, while student, 1915–17; adopted pseudonym "Dziga Vertov" (translates as "spinning top"), and became editor and writer for newsreel section of Moscow Cinema Committee, 1917; directed first personal film and published Kinoks-Revolution Manifesto, 1919; organized film activities on government agit-steamboats and agit-trains, 1921; began developing theory of "Kino-Glaz" (Kino-Eye), 1922; worked on Kino-Pravda and Goskinokalender newsreel series, 1922–25; directed newsreel series Novostidnia, from 1947. Died 1954.

Films as Director:

1918–19   Kino-Nedelia (Weekly Reels) series no. 1–43 (co-d; according to Sadoul, he did not take part in the production of nos. 38–42)
1919   Godovshchina revoliutsiya (Anniversary of the Revolution) (+ ed); Protsess Mironova (The Trial of Mironov); Vskrytie moschei Sergeia Radonezhskogo (Exhumation of the Remains of Sergius of Radonezh)
1920   Boi pod Tsaritsinom (Battle for Tsaritsin) (+ ed); Vserusski starets Kalinin (All Russian Elder Kalinin); Instruktorii Parokhod 'Krasnaia Zvezda' (Instructional Steamer 'Red Star')
1921   Agitpoezd VTsIK (The VTIK Train. Agit-Train of the Central Committee)
1922   Istoriia grazhdenskoi voini (History of the Civil War) (+ ed); Protsess Eserov (Trial of the Social Revolutionaries); Univermag (Department Store)
1922–23   Kino-Pravda (Cinema-Truth. Film-Truth) series, nos. 1–23
1923–25   Goskinokalender series nos. 1–53; Sevodiva (Today)
1924   Sovetskie igrushki (Soviet Toys); Iumoreski (Humoresques); Daesh vozkukh (Give Us Air); Khronika-molniya (Newsreel-Lightning); Kino-glaz (Kino-Eye)
1925   Zagranichnii pokhod sudov Baltiiskogo flota kreisere 'Aurora' i uchebnogo sudna 'Komsomolts', August 8, 1925; (The Seventh Anniversary of the Red Army)
1926   Shagai, Soviet! (Stride, Soviet!); Shestaya chast' mira (A Sixth of the World)
1928   Odinnadtsatii (The Eleventh Year)
1929   Chelovek s kinoapparatom (The Man With a Movie Camera)
1931   Entuziazm: Simfoniia Donbassa (Enthusiasm: Symphony of the Don Basin)
1934   Tri pensi o Lenine (Three Songs of Lenin)
1937   Kolibel'naya (Lullaby) (+ narration); Pamyati Sergo Ordzhonikidze (In Memory of Sergo Ordzhonikidze); Sergo Ordzhonikidze (co-d)
1938   Slava Sovetskim Geroiniam (Famous Soviet Heroes); Tri geroini (Three Heroines) (+ co-sc)
1941   Krov' za krov', smert' za smert': slodeianiya Nemetsko-Fashistkih zakhvatchikov na territorii C.C.C.P. me ne zabudem (Blood for Blood, Death for Death); Soiuzkinozhurnal No. 77; Soiuzkinozhurnal No. 87
1943   Tebe, Front: Kazakhstan Front (For You at the Front: The Kazakhstan Front)
1944   V gorakh Ala-Tau (In the Mountains of Ala-Tau); Kliatva molodikh (Youth's Oath. The Oath of Youth)
1944–54   Novosti dnia series (contributed various issues through 1954)

Publications:

By VERTOV: books—

Statii, dnevniki, zamysly, edited by S. Drobashenko, Moscow, 1966.
Dsiga Wertow: aus den Tagebüchern, edited by Peter Konlechner and Peter Kubelka, Vienna, 1967.
Articles, Journaux, Projets, edited and translated by Sylviane and Andrée Robel, Paris, 1972.
Kino-Eye: The Writings of Dziga Vertov, edited by Annette Michelson, Berkeley, 1984.

By VERTOV: articles—

"Iz rabochikh tetradei Dziga Vertov," in Iskusstvo Kino (Moscow), no. 4, 1957.

"Vespominaiia o s'emkakh V.I. Lenin," in *Iz Istorii Kino* (Moscow), no. 2, 1959.

"Manuscrit sans titre," translated by J. Aumont, in *Cahiers du Cinéma* (Paris), May/June 1970.

"Doklad na pervoi vsesoyuznoi . . . ," in *Iz Istorii Kino* (Moscow), no. 8, 1971.

Various articles in *Film Comment* (New York), Spring 1972.

"From the Notebooks of Dziga Vertov," translated by Marco Carynnyk, in *Artforum* (New York), March 1972.

"Dak rodilsja i rasvivalsfa *Kinoglaz*," in *Iskusstvo Kino* (Moscow), February 1986.

On VERTOV: books—

Bryher, Winnifred, *Film Problems of Soviet Russia*, Terrutent, Switzerland, 1929.

Lozowick, Louis, Joseph Freeman, and Joshua Kunitz, *Voices of October: Art and Literature in Soviet Russia*, New York, 1930.

Marshall, Herbert, *Soviet Cinema*, London, 1945.

Dickinson, Thorold, and Catherine De La Roche, *Soviet Cinema*, London, 1948.

Eisenstein, Sergei, *Film Form*, edited and translated by Jay Leyda, New York, 1949.

Pudovkin, V.I., G. Alexandrov and I. Piryev, *Soviet Films: Principle Stages of Development*, Bombay, India, 1951.

Babitsky, Paul, and John Rimberg, *The Soviet Film Industry*, New York, 1955.

Abramov, N.P., *Dziga Vertov*, Moscow, 1962; Lyons, 1965.

Borokov, V., *Dziga Vertov*, Moscow, 1967.

Geduld, Harry, editor, *Film Makers on Filmmaking*, Bloomington, Indiana, 1967.

Issari, M. Ali, *Cinéma Vérité*, East Lansing, Michigan, 1971.

Sadoul, Georges, *Dziga Vertov*, Paris, 1971.

Barnouw, Erik, *Documentary: A History of the Non-Fiction Film*, New York, 1974.

Kuleshov, Lev, *Kuleshov on Film*, translated and edited by Ronald Levaco, Berkeley, California, 1974.

Feldman, Seth, *Evolution of Style in the Early Work of Dziga Vertov*, New York, 1977.

Feldman, Seth R., *Dziga Vertov: A Guide to References and Resources*, Boston, 1979.

Marshall, Herbert, *Masters of the Soviet Cinema: Crippled Creative Biographies*, London, 1983.

Waugh, Thomas, editor, *"Show Us Life": Toward a History and Aesthetics of the Committed Documentary*, Metuchen, New Jersey, 1984.

Petric, Vlad, *Constructivism in Film: The Man with the Movie Camera: A Cinematic Analysis*, Cambridge, 1987.

On VERTOV: articles—

Lenauer, Jean, "Vertov, His Work and His Future," in *Close-Up* (London), December 1929.

Hughes, Pennethorne, "Vertov ad Absurdum," in *Close-Up* (London), September 1932.

Koster, Simon, "Dziga Vertov," in *Experimental Cinema* (New York), no. 5, 1934.

Vaughan, Dai, "The Man with the Movie Camera," in *Films and Filming* (London), November 1960.

Sadoul, Georges, "Actualité de Dziga Vertov," in *Cahiers du Cinéma* (Paris), June 1963.

Weinberg, Herman G., "The Man With the Movie Camera," in *Film Comment* (New York), Fall 1966.

Abramov, Nikolai, "Dziga Vertov, Poet and Writer of the Cinema," in *Soviet Film* (Moscow), no. 11, 1968.

Rotha, Paul, and Richard Griffith, in *Documentary Film*, New York, 1968.

Giercke, Christopher, "Dziga Vertov," in *Afterimage* (Rochester), April 1970.

Brik, Osip, "The So-Called 'Formal Method'," translated by Richard Sherwood, in *Screen* (London), Winter 1971/72.

Bordwell, David, "Dziga Vertov: An Introduction," in *Film Comment* (New York), Spring 1972.

Michelson, Annette, "The Man with the Movie Camera: From Magician to Entomologist," in *Artforum* (New York), March 1972.

Enzensberger, Marsha, "Dziga Vertov," in *Screen* (London), Winter 1972/73.

Feldman, Seth, "Cinema Weekly and Cinema Truth: Dziga Vertov and the Leninist Proportion," in *Sight and Sound* (London), Winter 1973/74.

Brik, Osip, "Mayakovsky and the Literary Movements of 1917–30," translated by Diana Matias, in *Screen* (London), Autumn 1974.

Mayne, J., "Kino-truth and Kino-praxis: Vertov's *Man with a Movie Camera*," in *Ciné-Tracts* (Montreal), Summer 1977.

Denkin, H., "Linguistic Models in Early Soviet Cinema," in *Cinema Journal* (Evanston), Fall 1977.

Fischer, L., "Enthusiasm: from Kino-eye to Radio-eye," in *Film Quarterly* (Berkeley), Winter 1977/78.

"Dziga Vertov," in *Travelling* (Lausanne), Summer 1979.

Rouch, Jean, "Five Faces of Vertov," in *Framework* (Norwich, England), Autumn 1979.

"Vertov Issue" of *October* (Cambridge, Massachusetts), Winter 1979.

Petric, Vlad, "The Difficult Years of Dziga Vertov: Excerpts from his Diaries," in *Quarterly Review of Film Studies* (New York), Winter 1982.

Tesson, C., "L'homme sans limites," in *Cahiers du Cinéma* (Paris), July–August 1987.

*   *   *

Dziga Vertov, pioneer Soviet documentarist, was born Denis Arkadievitch Kaufman. He and two younger brothers, Mikhail and Boris, were sons of a librarian in the Polish city of Byalistok, which at the time was within the Tsarist empire. When World War I broke out, the parents took the family to what seemed the comparative safety of Petrograd—St. Petersburg renamed to expunge the Germanic link. When the Bolshevik revolution began, Denis, who was twenty-one, and Mikhail, who was nineteen, became involved. Denis volunteered to the cinema committee and became a newsreel worker. Soon he was editing footage of revolutionary upheaval and the struggles against American, British, French, and Japanese intervention forces. His hastily assembled reels went out as war reports and morale boosters. He was now Dziga Vertov; a name suggesting a spinning top, and perhaps meant to convey perpetual motion. The newsreel, titled *Kino-Nedelia* (Film Weekly), continued until the end of the hostilities in 1920. Vertov used selected footage for the multi-reel *Godovshchina revoliutsiva* (Anniversary of the Civil War) and other compilations.

He now hoped to launch a more ambitious series of film reports on the building of a new society, but a period of frustration followed. A New Economic Policy, introduced as a temporary measure, permitted limited private enterprise to stimulate the prostrate economy. Cinemas could import foreign features, and were soon filled with old American, German, French and English films. Vertov, outraged, turned polemicist, a writer of fiery manifestos. Addressing the film world, he wrote: "'Art' works of pre-revolutionary days surround you like icons and still command your prayerful emotions. Foreign lands abet you in your confusion, sending into the new Russia the living corpses of movie dramas garbed in splendid technological dressing." He tended to look on these films, and even on fiction films in general, as dangerous corrupting influences, another "opium of the people." He urged producers to "come to life."

His vitriol won Vertov enemies in the film world, but he also had support in high places. Early in 1922 Lenin is said to have told his Commissar of Education, Anatoli Lunacharsky, "Of all the arts, for us film is the most important." Lenin emphasized newsreels and proclaimed a "Leninist film-proportion": along with fiction, film programs should include material reflecting "Soviet reality." All this enabled Vertov to launch, in May 1922, the famous *Kino-Pravda* (Film Truth), which continued as an official monthly release until 1925. His wife Elizoveta Svilova became film editor. Mikhail Kaufman, giving up a planned law career, became chief cameraman.

Dziga Vertov

The *Kino-Pravda* group scorned prepared scenarios. Vertov outlined ideas but left wide latitude to Mikhail and other cameramen. Sallying forth with cameras, they caught moments when a Moscow trolley line, long defunct in torn-up streets, was finally put back into action. Army tanks, used as tractors, were seen leveling an area for an airport. A children's hospital was trying to save war-starved waifs. A travelling film team was seen arriving in a town, unpacking gear, and preparing an outdoor showing—of *Kino-Pravda*. The reels were always composed of "fragments of actuality" but Vertov also put emphasis on their provocative juxtaposition. Superimpositions, split screens, slowed or speeded motion could play a part in this. If the fragments were "truths," the manipulations were to bring out other "truths"—relationships and meanings.

For a time the *Kino-Pravda* releases were virtually the only item in cinema programs that touched the historic movement, and they therefore gained wide impact. Footage was from time to time reused, with new footage, in feature documentaries. Among the most successful was *Shestaya chast' mira* (One Sixth of the World), in which Vertov made impressive use of subtitles. Short, intermittent subtitles formed a continuing apostrophe addressing the people of the Soviet Union. "You in the small villages . . . You in the tundra . . . You on the ocean." Having established, via footage and words, a vast geographic dispersion, the catalog turned to nationalities: "You Uzbeks . . . You Kalmiks." Then it addressed occupations, age groups, sexes. The continuing sentence went on for minutes, then ended with: "You are the owners of one sixth of the world." The incantation style, reminiscent of Walt Whit-

man—much admired by Vertov—continued throughout the film, projecting the destiny foreseen for the "owners." To men and women with only a dim awareness of the scope and resources of their land, the film must indeed have been a prideful pageant.

Vertov's career gradually became clouded, especially in the Stalin years. His aversion to detailed scenarios, which he said were inapplicable to reportage documentaries, marked him as "antiplanning." He agreed to write "analyses" of what he had in mind, but his proposals were often rejected. Articulated social doctrine was increasingly mandatory; experiments in form were decried. Ironically, Vertov remains best known for one of his most experimental films, *Chelovek s kinoapparatom* (Man with a Movie Camera). Featuring Mikhail in action, and intended to demonstrate the role of the cameraman in showing "Soviet reality," it also became an anthology of film devices and tricks. Eisenstein, usually a Vertov supporter, criticized it for "unmotivated camera mischief" and even "formalism."

During the following years Vertov and Kaufman worked in the Ukraine studios, apparently a reflection of disfavor in Moscow. But in the Ukraine Vertov created one of the most inventive of early sound films, *Entuziazm: Simfoniia Donbassa* (Enthusiasm: Symphony of the Don Basin), a virtuoso exploration of the possibilities of nonsynchronous sound. Another such exploration was the moving *Tri pesni O Lenine* (Three Songs About Lenin), utilizing the precious fragments of Lenin footage. But Vertov had lost standing. In his final years he was again a newsreel worker, arriving and leaving the job on schedule, no longer writing manifestos.

His ideas were, however, echoed in later years in cinéma vérité, the movement of the 1960s named after Vertov's *Kino-Pravda*. The 1960s and 1970s saw an international revival of interest in Vertov. It included rehabilitation in the Soviet Union, with retrospectives of his films, biographical works, and publication of selections from Vertov's journals, manifestos, and other writings.

—Erik Barnouw

VIDOR, Charles.

Hungarian/American. Born in Budapest, 27 July 1900. Educated at Universities of Budapest and Berlin. Married 1) actress Karen Morley, 1932 (divorced 1943), one son; 2) Mrs. Doris Warner Leroy, 1945, two sons. Infantry lieutenant, World War I; assistant cutter and assistant director at UFA studios, Berlin, early 1920s; moved to U.S., 1924, worked as opera singer and as longshoreman; moved to Hollywood, late 1920s, assistant director, editor and scriptwriter; directed first feature, for MGM, 1932; after dispute with Harry Cohn at Columbia, returned to MGM, 1949; formed Aurora productions, 1956. *Died of heart attack, in Vienna, 4 June 1959.*

Charles Vidor with Irene Dunne

Films as Director:

1931	*The Bridge* (short)
1932	*The Mask of Fu Manchu* (co-d, uncredited)
1933	*Sensation Hunters*
1934	*Double Door*
1935	*Strangers All*; *The Arizonian*; *His Family Tree*
1936	*Muss 'em Up*
1937	*A Doctor's Diary*; *The Great Gambini*; *She's No Lady*
1939	*Romance of the Redwoods*; *Blind Alley*; *Those High Grey Walls*
1940	*My Son, My Son!*; *The Lady in Question*
1941	*Ladies in Retirement*; *New York Town*
1942	*The Tuttles of Tahiti*
1943	*The Desperadoes*
1944	*Cover Girl*; *Together Again*
1945	*A Song to Remember*; *Over Twenty-one*
1946	**Gilda**
1948	*The Loves of Carmen* (+ pr)
1952	*It's a Big Country* (co-d); *Hans Christian Andersen*
1953	*Thunder in the East*
1954	*Rhapsody*
1955	*Love Me or Leave Me*
1956	*The Swan*
1957	*The Joker Is Wild*
1958	*A Farewell to Arms*
1960	*Song without End* (completed by George Cukor)

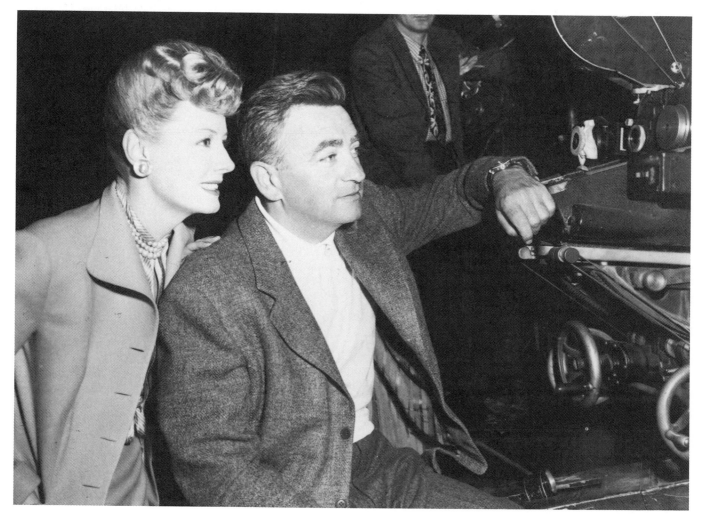

Publications:

On VIDOR: articles—

Pryor, Thomas, "Vidor Graph," in *The New York Times*, 5 November 1944.

Gray, Martin, "No Swansong for Director Charles Vidor," in *Films and Filming* (London), June 1956.

Obituary in *The New York Times*, 5 June 1959.

Doane, M.A., "*Gilda*: Epistemology as Striptease," in *Camera Obscura* (Berkeley), Fall 1983.

* * *

Charles Vidor's filmography is as unremarkable as it is varied: an average musical (*Cover Girl*) enhanced by the charm of Gene Kelly, the presence of Rita Hayworth, and the comedy of Phil Silvers and Eve Arden; Grace Kelly's final screen credit (*The Swan*); a cute comedy of a middle-aged man in the military (*Over 21*); a turgid Alan Ladd adventure (*Thunder in the East*); a fine gothic melodrama (*Ladies in Retirement*); a solid Randolph Scott western (*The Desperadoes*); a campy Boris Karloff vehicle (*The Mask of Fu Manchu*, co-directed with Charles Brabin); a clumsy Hemingway remake (*A Farewell to Arms*); and programmers for various studios during the 1930s.

A majority of his credits are romances and musicals, and he also specialized in cinematizing the lives of the famous. Vidor's two show-business biographies mix entertainers and mobsters: *The Joker Is Wild*, the life of the nightclub performer Joe E. Lewis, featuring one of Frank Sinatra's better performances; *Love Me or Leave Me*, with Doris Day good as Ruth Etting and James Cagney great as "The Gimp." He also chronicled the lives of *Hans Christian Andersen*, Fredric Chopin (*A Song to Remember*) and Franz Liszt (*Song without End*, completed by George Cukor on his death). Other films also have classical settings or origins: *Rhapsody* (wealthy Elizabeth Taylor torn between pianist John Ericson and violinist Vittorio Gassman); *The Loves of Carmen* (again with Hayworth, but without Bizet's music).

Vidor's one fascinating—and very atypical—credit is *Gilda*, starring Hayworth, his favorite actress. It is exceptionally erotic for 1946, highlighted by Rita's energetic nightclub dance in which she peels off her long white gloves. *Blind Alley* is another noteworthy film, one of Hollywood's initial features which seriously deals with psychology: mobster Chester Morris is analyzed by his hostage, psychiatrist Ralph Bellamy.

Vidor occasionally elicits above-average performances from his stars, and many of his films are enjoyable. But they cannot compare with similar films by other filmmakers, and his actors—with the exception of Hayworth in *Gilda*—give their most characteristic performances elsewhere. *Cover Girl*, by no means a classic musical, is far from Gene Kelly's cinematic zenith. *The Swan* is more of a footnote to Grace Kelly's career. *Ladies in Retirement* is no *Wuthering Heights* or *Rebecca*. *Rhapsody*, next to *Intermezzo*, is hokum. His classical biographies are not as grotesque as those of Ken Russell, but this is certainly no recommendation. None of his biographies rank with the best in the genre. Charles Vidor is, at best, an entertainer whose films are enhanced by the talents of those in his casts. He cannot truly be considered an artist.

—Rob Edelman

VIDOR, King.

American. Born King Wallis Vidor in Galveston, Texas, 8 February 1894. Attended Peacock Military Academy, San Antonio, Texas. Married 1) actress Florence Arto, 1915 (divorced 1924), one daughter; 2) actress Eleanor Boardman, 1926 (divorced 1932); 3) Elizabeth Hall, 1932 (died 1973). Ticket-taker and part-time projectionist in Galveston's first movie house, 1909–10; amateur newsreel photographer, 1910–15; drove to Hollywood in Model T, financed trip by shooting footage for Ford's advertising newsreel, 1915; worked at various jobs in film industry, then directed first feature, *The Turn in the Road*, 1919; hired by 1st National, built studio called Vidor Village, 1920 (shut down, 1922); director for Goldwyn Studios, 1923, later absorbed by MGM; taught graduate course in cinema, University of California, Los Angeles, 1960s. Recipient: Best Direction, Venice Festival, for *Wedding Night*, 1935; Special Prize, Edinburgh Festival, 1964; Honorary Oscar, 1978. *Died of heart failure, in California, 1 November 1982.*

Films as Director:

1919	*The Turn in the Road* (+ sc); *Better Times* (+ sc); *The Other Half* (+ sc); *Poor Relations* (+ sc)
1920	*The Jack Knife Man* (+ pr, co-sc); *The Family Honor* (+ co-pr);
1921	*The Sky Pilot*; *Love Never Dies* (+ co-pr)
1922	*Conquering the Woman* (+ pr); *Woman, Wake Up* (+ pr); *The Real Adventure* (+ pr); *Dusk to Dawn* (+ pr)
1923	*Peg-O-My-Heart*; *The Woman of Bronze*; *Three Wise Fools* (+ co-sc)
1924	*Wild Oranges* (+ co-sc); *Happiness*; *Wine of Youth*; *His Hour*
1925	*Wife of the Centaur*; *Proud Flesh*; **The Big Parade**
1926	*La Bohème* (+ pr); *Bardelys, The Magnificent* (+ pr)
1928	**The Crowd** (+ co-sc); *The Patsy*; *Show People*
1929	**Hallelujah**
1930	*Not So Dumb*; *Billy the Kid*
1931	*Street Scene*; *The Champ*
1932	*Bird of Paradise*; *Cynara*
1933	*Stranger's Return*
1934	*Our Daily Bread* (+ pr, co-sc)
1935	*Wedding Night*; *So Red the Rose*
1936	*The Texas Rangers* (+ pr, co-sc)
1937	*Stella Dallas*
1938	*The Citadel* (+ pr)
1940	*Northwest Passage* (+ pr); *Comrade X* (+ pr)
1941	*H.M. Pulham, Esq.* (+ pr, co-sc)
1944	*American Romance* (+ pr, co-sc)
1946	**Duel in the Sun**
1949	*The Fountainhead*; *Beyond the Forest*
1951	*Lightning Strikes Twice*
1952	*Ruby Gentry* (+ co-pr)
1955	*Man Without a Star*
1956	*War and Peace* (+ co-sc)
1959	*Solomon and Sheba*

Publications:

By VIDOR: books—

A Tree is a Tree, New York, 1953; reprinted 1977.

King Vidor on Filmmaking, New York, 1972.

King Vidor, an interview by Nancy Dowd and David Shepard, Metuchen, New Jersey, 1988.

By VIDOR: articles—

"Easy Steps to Success," in *Motion Picture Classic* (New York), August 1919.

"Credo," in *Variety* (New York), January 1920.

Interview with M. Cheatham in *Motion Picture Classic* (New York), June 1928.

"The Story Conference," in *Films in Review* (New York), June/July 1952.

"Lillian Gish in Opera," in *Films and Filming* (London), January 1955.

"The End of an Era," in *Films and Filming* (London), March 1955.

King Vidor

"Me . . . and My Spectacle," in *Films and Filming* (London), October 1959.
Interview with V.F. Perkins and Mark Shivas in *Movie* (London), July/August 1963.
"King Vidor at N.Y.U.," an interview in *Cineaste* (New York), Spring 1968.
"War, Wheat and Steel," an interview with J. Greenburg, in *Sight and Sound* (London), Autumn 1968.
"King Vidor," an interview with D. Lyons and G. O'Brien, in *Inter/View* (New York), October 1972.
"King Vidor on D.W. Griffith's Influence," an interview with A. Nash, in *Films in Review* (New York), November 1975.

On VIDOR: books—

Brownlow, Kevin, *The Parade's Gone By . . .* , New York, 1968.
Higham, Charles, and Joel Greenberg, editors, *The Celluloid Muse: Hollywood Directors Speak*, London, 1969.
Baxter, John, *King Vidor*, New York, 1976.
Comuzio, Ermanno, *King Vidor*, Florence, 1986.
Durgnat, Raymond, and Scott Simmon, *King Vidor—American*, Berkeley, 1988.
Lang, Robert, *American Film Melodrama: Griffith, Vidor, Minnelli*, Princeton, New Jersey, 1989.
Mulvey, Laura, *Visual and Other Pleasures*, London, 1989.

On VIDOR: articles—

Harrington, C., "King Vidor's Hollywood Progress," in *Sight and Sound* (London), April/June 1953.
Brownlow, Kevin, "King Vidor," in *Film* (London), Winter 1962.
Sarris, Andrew, "Second Line," in *Film Culture* (New York), Spring 1963.
"The Directors Choose the Best Films," in *Cinema* (Beverly Hills), August/September 1963.

Mitchell, G.J., "King Vidor," in *Films in Review* (New York), March 1964.
Higham, C., "King Vidor," in *Film Heritage* (Dayton, Ohio), Summer 1966.
"King Vidor at NYU: Discussion," in *Cineaste* (New York), Spring 1968.
Barr, C., "King Vidor," in *Brighton* (London), March 1970.
Luft, H.G., "A Career that Spans Half a Century," in *Film Journal* (New York), Summer 1971.
Higham, C., "Long Live Vidor, A Hollywood King," in *The New York Times*, 3 September 1972.
Durgnat, Raymond, "King Vidor," in two parts, in *Film Comment* (New York), July/August and September/October 1973.
"Vidor Issues" of *Positif* (Paris), September and November 1974.
"*Notre pain quotidien* Issue" of *Avant-Scène du Cinéma* (Paris), 1 May 1977.
Dover, B., "Tribute to King Vidor," in *Films in Review* (New York), June/July 1978.
Lang, J., "Hommage à King Vidor," in *Cinéma* (Paris), November 1981.
Carbonner, A., "King Vidor ou l'ambivalence du désir," in *Cinéma* (Paris) December 1982.
Luft, H.G., "King Vidor," in *Films in Review* (New York), December 1982.
Allen, W., "King Vidor and *The Crowd*," in *Stills* (London), Winter 1982.
Eyman, S., "Remembering King Vidor," in *Films and Filming* (London), January 1983.
Kirkpatrick, S.D., "Hollywood Whodunit," in *American Film* (Washington D.C.), June 1986.
Gillett, John, and Richard Combs, "King Vidor—Worth Overdoing!" in *National Film Theatre Booklet* (London), May 1991.

* * *

King Vidor began work in Hollywood as a company clerk for Universal, submitting original scripts under the pseudonym Charles K. Wallis. (Universal employees weren't allowed to submit original work to the studio.) Vidor eventually confessed his wrongdoing and was fired as a clerk, only to be rehired as a comedy writer. Within days, he lost this job as well when Universal discontinued comedy production.

Vidor next work as the director of a series of short dramatic films detailing the reform work of Salt Lake City Judge Willis Brown, a Father Flanagan-type. Vidor tried to parlay this experience into a job as a feature director with a major studio but was unsuccessful. He did manage, however, to find financial backing from nine doctors for his first feature, a picture with a Christian Science theme titled *The Turn in the Road*. Vidor spent the next year working on three more features for the newly-christened Brentwood Company, including the comedy *Better Times*, starring his own discovery Zasu Pitts.

In 1920, Vidor accepted an offer from First National and a check for $75,000. He persuaded his father to sell his business in order that he might build and manage "Vidor Village," a small studio which mirrored similar projects by Chaplin, Sennett, Griffith Ince, and other. Vidor directed eight pictures at Vidor Village, but was forced to close down in 1922. The following year, he was hire by Louis B. Mayer at Metro to direct aging stage star Laurette Taylor in *Peg-O-My-Heart*. Soon after, he went to work for Samuel Goldwyn, attracted by Goldwyn's artistic and literary aspirations. In 1924, Vidor returned to Metro with the merger that resulted in MGM. He would continue to work there for the next 20 years, initially entrusted with molding the careers of rising stars, John Gilbert, and Eleanor Boardman, soon to be Vidor's second wife.

The Big Parade changed Vidor's status from contract director to courted screen artist. Produced by Irving Thalberg, the film grew from a minor studio production into one of MGM's two biggest hits of 1926, grossing 18 million. *The Big Parade* satisfied Vidor's desire to make a picture with lasting value and extended exhibition. It was the first of three films he wanted to make on the topics of "wheat, steel, and war." Vidor went on to direct Gilbert, and the studio's new acquisition Lillian Gish, in *La Bohème*.

Encouraged by the popularity of German films of the period and their concern with urban life, Vidor made *The Crowd*, "*The Big Parade* of peace." It starred unknown actor James Murray, whose life would end in and alcoholic suicide, and who inspired one of Vidor's projects, and unproduced picture titled *The Actor*. Like *The Big Parade*, *The Crowd* presented the reactions of an everyman, this time to the anonymity of the city and the rigors of urban survival. Vidor's silent career continued with two of Marion Davies's comedies *The Patsy* and *Show People*, and extended into "talkies" with a third comedy, *Not So Dumb*. Though only moderately successful, Vidor became a favorite in William Randolph Hearst's entourage.

Vidor was in Europe when the industry announced its conversion to sound. He quickly returned to propose *Hallelujah*, with an all-black cast. Although considered a politically-astute director for Hollywood, the film exposes Vidor's political shortcomings in its paternalistic attitude toward blacks. With similar political naiveté, Vidor's next great film, the pseudo-socialist agricultural drama *Our Daily Bread*, was derived from a *Reader's Digest* article.

By this point in his career, Vidor's thematics were fairly intact. Informing most of his lasting work is the struggle of Man against Destiny and Nature. In his great silent pictures, *The Big Parade* and *The Crowd*, the hero wanders through an anonymous and malevolent environment, war-torn Europe and the Amercan City, respectively. In his later sound films, *The Citadel*, *Northwest Passage*, *Duel in the Sun*,, and *The Fountainhead* various forms of industry operate as a vehicle of Man's battle to subdue Nature. Unlike the optimism in Ford's and Capra's films, Vidor's follow a Job-like pattern, in which victory comes, if at all, with a great deal of personal sacrifice. Underlying all of Vidor's great work are the biblical resonances of a Christian Scientist, where Nature is ultimately independent from and disinterested in Man, who always remains subordinate in the struggle against its forces.

Following *Our Daily Bread*, Vidor continued to alternate between films that explored this personal thematic and projects seemingly less suited to his interests. In more than 50 features, Vidor worked for several producers, directing *Wedding Night* and *Stella Dallas* for Samuel Goldwyn, *The Citadel*, *Northwest Passage*, and *Comrade X* for MGM, *Bird of Paradise*, where he met his third wife Elizabeth Hill, and *Duel in the Sun* for David O. Selznick, *The Fountainhead*, *Beyond the Forest*, and *Lightning Strikes Twice* for Warner Brothers, and late in his career, *War and Peace* for Dino De Laurentiis. Vidor exercised more control on his films after *Our Daily Bread*, often serving as producer, but his projects continued to fluctuate between intense metaphysical drama and light-weight comedy and romance.

In the 1950s Vidor's only notable film was *Ruby Gentry*, and his filmmaking career ended on a less-than-praiseworthy note with *Solomon and Sheba*. In the 1960s he made two short documentaries, *Truth and Illusion*, and *Metaphor*, about his friend Andrew Wyeth. Vidor wrote a highly praised autobiography in 1953, *A Tree is a Tree*, and in 1979, received an honorary Oscar, following his nomination as a director five times. In the last years of his life, he was honored in his hometwon of Galveston with an annual King Vidor film festival.

—Michael Selig

VIGO, Jean.

French. Born in Paris, 26 April 1905, son of anarchist Miguel Alemreyda (Eugène Bonaventure de Vigo). Attended a number of schools, including the Boys School of St. Cloud, until 1917; following death of father, attended boarding school in Nimes, under the name Jean Sales. Married Elizabeth Lozinska, 1929, child: Luce. Father found dead under mysterious circumstances in jail cell, 1917; mother confined to a hospital, 1923; experienced health problems, entered clinic in Montpellier, then moved to Nice because of his tuberculosis, 1929; directed first film *A propos de Nice*, 1930, then returned to live in Paris, 1932; *Zéro de conduite* removed from circulation by censors because it is considered "anti-France"; became seriously ill with leukemia, 1933. *Died 5 October 1934.*

Film as Director:

1930   *À propos de Nice*
1931   *Taris (Taris roi de l'eau. Jean Taris champion de natation)*
1933   *Zéro de conduite*
1934   *L'Atalante*

Publications:

By VIGO: books—

The Complete Jean Vigo, London, 1983.
Oeuvres de cinéma: Films, scénarios, projets de films, texts sur le cinéma, edited by Pierre Lherminier, Paris, 1985.

By VIGO: articles—

"Towards a Social Cinema," in *Millenium* (New York), Winter 1977/78.

On VIGO: books—

Kyrou, Ado, *Amour, érotisme et cinéma*, Paris, 1957.
Salès-Gomès, P.E., *Jean Vigo*, Paris, 1957; Los Angeles, 1971.
Agel, Henri, *Miroirs de L'insolite dans le cinéma français*, Paris, 1958.
Pornon, Charles, *Le Rêve et le fantastique dans le cinéma français*, Paris, 1959.
Buache, Freddy, and others, editors, *Hommage à Jean Vigo*, Lausanne 1962.
Lherminier, Pierre, *Jean Vigo*, Paria, 1967.
Lovell, Alan, *Anarchist Cinema*, London, 1967.
Martin, Marcel, *Jean Vigo, Anthologie du Cinéma* vol. 2, Paris, 1967.
Smith, John, *Jean Vigo*, New York, 1971.
Simon, William G., *The Films of Jean Vigo*, Ann Arbor, Michigan, 1981.
Andrew, Dudley, *Film in the Aura of Art*, Princeton, New Jersey, 12984.

On VIGO: articles—

Cavalcanti, Alberto, "Jean Vigo," in *Cinema Quarterly* (Edinburgh), Winter 1935.
Kracauer, Siegfried, "Jean Vigo," in *Hollywood Quarterly*, April 1947.
Weinberg, Herman G., "The Films of Jean Vigo," in *Cinema* (Beverly Hills), July 1947.
Agee, James, "Life and Work of Jean Vigo," in *Nation* (New York), 12 July 1947.
Zilzer, G., "Remembrances of Jean Vigo," in *Hollywood Quarterly*, Winter 1947/48.
"Vigo Issue" of *Ciné-Club* (Paris), February 1949.
"Vigo Issue" of *Positif* (Lyon), no. 7, 1953.
De Laurot, Edouard, and Jonas Mekas, "An Interview with Boris Kaufman," in *Film Culture* (New York), Summer 1955.
Sallès-Gomès, P.E., "Le Mort de Jean Vigo," in *Cahiers du Cinéma* (Paris), August/September 1955.
Ashton, D.S., "Portrait of Vigo," in *Film* (London), December 1955.
Tranchant, François, "Dossier Jean Vigo," in *Image et Son* (Paris), October 1958.

Jean Vigo

"Vigo Issue" of *Premier Plan* (Lyon), no. 19, 1961.

Chevassu, François, "Jean Vigo," in *Image et Son* (Paris), February 1961.

Ellerby, John, "The Anarchism of Jean Vigo," in *Anarchy 6* (London), August 1961.

"Vigo Issue" of *Études Cinématographiques* (Paris), no. 1–52, 1966.

Mills, B., "Anarchy, Surrealism, and Optimism in *Zéro de conduite*," in *Cinema* (London), no. 8, 1971.

Teush, B., "The Playground of Jean Vigo," in *Film Heritage* (New York), Fall 1973.

Baldwin, D., *L'Atalante* and the Maturing of Jean Vigo," in *Film Quarterly* (Berkeley), Fall 1985.

Wood, Robin, "*L'Atalante*: The Limits of Liberation," in *CineAction!* (Toronto), no. 10, 1987.

Painlevé, J., "Sur un point de détail curieux à l'usage exclusif de vigolâtres érudits," in *Jeune Cinéma* (Paris), October/November 1989.

Thompson, David J., "*L'Atalante*," in *Sight and Sound* (London), Summer 1990.

*   *   *

It is difficult to think of another director who made so few films and yet had such a profound influence on other filmmakers. Jean Vigo's *À propos de Nice*, his first film, is his contribution to the French Surrealist movement. The film itself is a direct descendant of Vertov's *Man with a Movie Camera*. Certainly, his films make political statements similar to Vertov's. Vertov's documentary celebrates a people's revolution, while Vigo's chastizes the bourgeois vacationers in a French resort town. Even more importantly, both films revel in the pyrotech-nics of the camera and the editing room. They are filled with dizzying movement, fast cutting, and the juxtaposition, from frame to frame, of objects that normally have little relation to each other. In yet another link between the two directors, Vertov's brother, Boris Kaufman, photographed *À propos de Nice*, as well as Vigo's other three films.

À propos de Nice provides a look at a reality beyond the prosaic, common variety that so many films give us. The movie attempts nothing less than the restructuring of our perception of the world by presenting it to us not so much through a seamless, logical narrative, but rather through a fast-paced collection of only tangentially related shots.

After *À propos de Nice*, Vigo began combining his brand of surrealism with the poetic realism that would later be so important to a generation of French directors, such as Jean Renoir and Marcel Carné. For his second film, he made another documentary, *Taris*, about France's champion swimmer. Here Vigo takes his camera underwater as Taris clowns at the bottom of a pool and blows at the lens. *Taris* certainly has some striking images, but it is only eleven minutes long. Indeed, if Vigo had died in 1931, after finishing *Taris*, instead of in 1934 (and given the constantly precarious state of his health, this would not have been at all unlikely), he would have been remembered, if at all, as a director who had shown great potential, yet who could hardly be considered a major talent.

However, Vigo's third film, *Zéro de conduite*, stands out as one of the cinema's most influential works. Along with films such as Sagan's *Mädchen in Uniform* and Wyler's *These Three*, it forms one of the more interesting and least studied genres of the 1930s—the children's boarding school film. Although it is Vigo's first fiction film, it continues the work he began with *À propos de Nice*. That first movie good-naturedly condemns the bourgeoisie, showing the rich as absolutely useless, their primary sin being banality rather than greed or cruelty. In *Zéro de conduite*, teachers, and not tourists, are the representatives of the bourgeoisie. But like the Nice vacationers, they are not so much malicious as they are simply inadequate, instructing their schoolboys in nothing important, and prizing the school's suffocating regulations above all else. Vigo lets the schoolboys rebel against this sort of mindless monotony, having them engage in an apocalyptic pillow fight, and then allowing them to bombard their teachers with fruit during a stately school ceremony. The film's anarchic spirit led to its being banned in France until 1945. But during the 1950s, it became one of the inspirations for the French New Wave directors. In subject matter, it somewhat resembles Truffaut's *400 Blows*. But it is the film's style—the mixture of classical Hollywood visuals with the dreamlike illogic of slow motion, fast action, and quick cutting—that particularly influenced a new generation of filmmakers.

Vigo's last film, *L'Atalante*, is his masterpiece. It is a love story that takes place on a barge, with Vigo once again combining surrealism with poetic realism. The settings are naturalistic and the characters lower-class, and so bring to mind Renoir's poetic realist films, for instance *Toni* and *Les Bas-Fonds*. There is also an emphasis on the imagination and on the near-sacredness of banal objects that places the film strongly in the tradition of such Surrealist classics as *Un Chien andalou*. After Juliette leaves Jean, the barge captain, Jean jumps into the river, and sees his wife's image everywhere around him. The underwater sequence not only makes the viewer think of *Taris*, but also makes us aware that we are sharing Jean's obsession with him. This dreamy visualization of a character's thoughts brings to mind the priority that the Surrealists gave to all mental processes. The Surrealists prized, too, some of the more mundane aspects of everyday life, and Vigo's film is full of ordinary objects that take on (for Juliette) a magical status.

They are only puppets, or fans, or gramophones piled in a heap in the room of Père Jules, Jean's old assistant, but Juliette has spent her entire life in a small town, and for her, these trinkets represent the mysteries of faraway places. They take on a special status, the banal being raised to the level of the exotic.

Despite the movie's links to two film movements, *L'Atalante* defies categorization. It is a masterpiece of mood and characterization, and along with *Zéro de conduite*, it guarantees Vigo's status as a great director. But he was not granted that status by the critical community until years after his death. Because of the vagaries of film exhibition and censorship, Vigo was little known while he was making films, receiving nowhere near the acclaim given to his contemporaries Jean Renoir and René Clair.

—Eric Smoodin

VISCONTI, Luchino.

Italian. Born Count Don Luchino Visconti di Modrone in Milan, 2 November 1906. Educated at private schools in Milan and Como; also attended boarding school of the Calasanzian Order, 1924–36. Served in Reggimento Savoia Cavalleria, 1926–28. Stage actor and set designer, 1928–29; moved to Paris, assistant to Jean Renoir, 1936–37; returned to Italy to assist Renoir on *La Tosca*, 1939; directed first film, *Ossessione*, 1942; directed first play, Cocteau's *Parenti terrible*, Rome, 1945; directed first opera, *La vestale*, Milan, 1954; also ballet director, 1956–57. Recipient: International Prize, Venice Festival, for *La terra trema*, 1948; 25th Anniversary Award, Cannes Festival, 1971. *Died 17 March 1976.*

Films as Director:

1942 *Ossessione* (+ co-sc)
1947 *La terra trema* (+ sc)
1951 *Bellissima* (+ co-sc); *Appunti su un fatto di cronaca* (2nd in series *Documento mensile*)
1953 "We, the Women" episode of *Siamo donne* (+ co-sc)
1954 *Senso* (+ co-sc)
1957 *Le notti bianche* (*White Nights*) (+ co-sc)
1960 *Rocco e i suoi fratelli* (*Rocco and His Brothers*) (+ co-sc)
1962 "Il lavoro (The Job)" episode of *Boccaccio '70* (+ co-sc)
1963 *Il gattopardo* (*The Leopard*) (+ co-sc)
1965 *Vaghe stelle dell'orsa* (*Of A Thousand Delights. Sandra*) (+ co-sc)
1967 "Le strega bruciata viva" episode of *Le streghe*; *Lo straniero* (*L'Etranger*) (+ co-sc)
1969 *La caduta degli dei* (*The Damned. Götterdämmerung*) (+ co-sc)
1970 *Alla ricerca di Tadzio*
1971 *Morte a Venezia* (*Death in Venice*) (+ pr, co-sc)
1973 *Ludwig* (+ co-sc)
1974 *Gruppo di famiglia in un interno* (+ co-sc)
1976 *L'innocente* (*The Innocent*) (+ co-sc)

Other Films:

1936 *Les Bas-fonds* (Renoir) (asst d)
1937 *Une Partie de campagne* (Renoir) (asst d) (released 1946)
1940 *La Tosca* (Renoir) (asst d)
1945 *Giorni di gloria* (De Santis) (asst d)

Publications:

By VISCONTI: books—

Senso, Bologna, 1955.
Le notti bianche, Bologna, 1957.
Rocco e i suoi fratelli, Bologna, 1961.
Il gattopardo, Bologna, 1963.
Vaghe stelle dell'orsa (*Sandra*), Bologna, 1965.
Three Screenplays, New York, 1970.
Morte a Venezia, Bologna, 1971.
Il mio teatro, in 2 volumes, Bologna, 1979.

By VISCONTI: articles—

"Il cinéma antropomorfico," in *Cinema* (Rome), 25 September 1943.
"*La terra trema*," in *Bianco e Nero* (Rome), March 1951.
"*Marcia nuziale*," in *Cinema Nuovo* (Turin), 1 May 1953.
Interview with Jacques Doniol-Valcroze and Jean Domarchi in *Cahiers du Cinéma* (Paris), March 1959.
"The Miracle That Gave Men Crumbs," in *Films and Filming* (London), January 1961.
"Drama of Non-Existence," in *Cahiers du Cinema in English* (New York), no. 2, 1966.
"Violence et passion," special Visconti issue of *Avant-Scène du Cinéma* (Paris), June 1975.
Interview with Peter Brunette in *Sight and Sound* (London), Winter 1986/87.

On VISCONTI: books—

Pellizzari, Lorenzo, *Luchino Visconti*, Milan, 1960.
Baldelli, Pio, *I film di Luchino Visconti*, Manduria, Italy, 1965.
Guillaume, Yves, *Visconti*, Paris, 1966.
Nowell-Smith, Geoffrey, *Luchino Visconti*, New York, 1968.
Ferrero, Adelio, editor, *Visconti: il cinema*, Modena, 1977.
Tornabuoni, Lietta, editor, *Album Visconti*, foreward by Michelangelo Antonioni, Milan, 1978.
Stirling, Monica, *A Screen of Time: A Study of Luchino Visconti*, New York, 1979.
Rondolini: *Luchino Visconti*, Turin, 1981.
Servadio, Gaia, *Luchino Visconti: A Biography*, London, 1981.
Bencivenni, Alessandro, *Luchino Visconti*, Florence, 1982.
Tonetti, Claretta, *Luchino Visconti*, Boston, 1983.
Ishaghpour, Youssef, *Luchino Visconti: Le sens de l'image*, Paris, 1984.
Sanzio, Alain, and Paul-Louis Thirard, *Luchino Visconti: Cinéaste*, Paris, 1984.
De Giusti, Luciano, *I film di Luchino Visconti*, Rome, 1985.
Mancini, Elaine, *Luchino Visconti: A Guide to References and Resources*, Boston, 1986.
Villien, Bruno, *Visconti*, Paris, 1986.
Schifano, Laurence, *Luchino Visconti: Les feux de la passion*, Paris, 1987; as *Luchino Visconti: The Flames of Passion*, London, 1990.

On VISCONTI: articles—

Renzi, Renzo, "Mitologia e contemplasione in Visconti, Ford e Eisenstein," in *Bianco e Nero* (Rome), February 1949.
Demonsablon, Philippe, "Notes sur Visconti," in *Cahiers du Cinéma* (Paris), March 1954.
Lane, John Francis, "The Hurricane Visconti," in *Films and Filming* (London), December 1954.
Castello, Giulio, "Luchino Visconti," in *Sight and Sound* (London), Spring 1956.
Lane, John Francis, "Visconti—The Last Decadent," in *Films and Filming* (London), July 1956.
Dyer, Peter John, "The Vision of Visconti," in *Film* (London), March/April 1957.
Poggi, Gianfranco, "Luchino Visconti and the Italian Cinema," in *Film Quarterly* (Berkeley), Spring 1960.
"Visconti Issue" of *Premier Plan* (Paris), May 1961.
"Visconti Issue" of *Etudes Cinématographiques* (Paris), no. 26–27, 1963.
Elsaesser, Thomas, "Luchino Visconti," in *Brighton* (London), February 1970.
"Visconti Issue" of *Cinema* (Rome), April 1970.

Luchino Visconti

Aristarco, Guido, "The Earth Still Trembles," in *Films and Filming* (London), January 1971.

Korte, Walter, "Marxism and Formalism in the Films of Luchino Visconti," in *Cinema Journal* (Evanston, Illinois), Fall 1971.

Cabourg, J., "Luchino Visconti, 1906–1976," in *Avant-Scène du Cinéma* (Paris), 1 and 15 March 1977.

Sarris, Andrew, "Luchino Visconti's Legacy," in *The Village Voice* (New York), 15 January 1979.

Rosi, Francesco, "En travaillant avec Visconti: sur le tournage de *La Terra trema*," in *Positif* (Paris), February 1979.

Lyons, D., "Visconti's Magnificient Obsessions," in *Film Comment* (New York), March/April 1979.

Graham, A., "The Phantom Self," in *Film Criticism* (New York), Fall 1984.

Aristarco, Guido, "Luchino Visconti: Critic or Poet of Decadence?," in *Film Criticism* (Meadville, Pennsylvania), Spring 1988.

*　　*　　*

The films of Luchino Visconti are among the most stylistically and intellectually influential of postwar Italian cinema. Born a scion of ancient nobility, Visconti integrated the most heterogeneous elements of aristocratic sensibilty and taste with a committed Marxist political consciousness, backed by a firm knowledge of Italian class structure. Stylistically, his career follows a trajectory from a uniquely cinematic realism to an operatic theatricalism, from the simple quotidian eloquence of modeled actuality to the heightened effect of lavishly appointed historical melodramas. His career fuses these interests into a mode of expression uniquely Viscontian, prescribing a potent, double-headed realism. Visconti turned out films steadily but rather slowly form 1942 to 1976. His obsessive care with narrative and filmic materials is apparent in the majority of his films.

Whether or not we choose to view the wartime *Ossessione* as a precursor or a determinant of neorealism or merely as a continuation of elements already present in Fascist period cinema, it is clear that the film remarkably applies a realist mise-en-scène to the formulaic constraints of the genre film. With major emendations, the film is, following a then-contemporary interest in American fiction of the 1930s, a treatment (the second and best) of James M. Cain's *The Postman Always Rings Twice*. In it the director begins to explore the potential of a long-take style, undoubtedly influenced by Jean Renoir for whom Visconti had worked as assistant. Having met with the disapproval of the Fascist censors for its depiction of the shabbiness and desperation of Italian provincial life, *Ossessione* was banned from exhibition.

For *La terra trema*, Visconti further developed those documentary-like attributes of story and style generally associated with neorealism. Taken from Verga's late 19th-century verist masterpiece *I malavoglia*, the film was shot entirely on location in Sicily and employs the people of the locale, speaking in their native dialect, as actors. Through them, Visconti explores the problems of class exploitation and the tragedy of family dissolution under economic pressure. Again, a mature long-shot/long-take style is coupled with diverse, extensive camera movements and well-planned actor movements to enhance the sense of a world faithfully captured in the multiplicity of its activities. The extant film was to have become the first episode of a trilogy on peasant life, but the other two parts were never filmed.

Rocco e i suoi fratelli however, made over a dozen years later, continues the story of this Sicilian family or at least one very much like it. Newly arrived in Milan from the South, the Parandis must deal with the economic realities of their poverty as well as survive the sexual rivalries threatening the solidarity of their family unit. The film is episodic in nature, affording time to each brother's story (in the original version), but special attention is given to Rocco, the forebearing and protective brother who strives at all costs to keep the group together, and Simone, the physically powerful and crudely brutal one, who is unable to control his personal fears, insecurities, and moral weakness. Unable to find other work, they both drift into prize fighting, viewed here as class exploitation. Jealousy over a prostitute, Nadia, causes Simone to turn his fists against his brother, then to murder the woman, but Rocco impelled by strong traditional ties would still act to save Simone from the police. Finally, the latter is betrayed to the law by Ciro, the fourth youngest and a factory worker who has managed to transfer some of his familial loyalty to a social plane and the labor union. Coming full circle from *La terra trema*, Luca, the youngest dreams of a day when he will be able to return to the Southern place of his birth. *Rocco* is perhaps Visconti's greatest contribution to modern tragedy, crafted along the lines of Arthur Miller and Tennessee Williams (whose plays he directed in Italy). The Viscontian tragedy is saturated with melodramatic intensity, a stylization incurring more than a suggestion of decadent sexuality and misogyny. There is, as in other Visconti works, a rather ambiguous intimation of homosexuality (here between Simone and his manager.)

By *Senso* Visconti had achieved the maturity of style that would characterize his subsequent work. With encompassing camera movements—like the opening shot moving from the stage of an opera house across the audience, taking in each tier of seats where the protest against the Austrians will soon erupt—and with a melodramatic rendering of historical fact, Visconti begins to mix cinematic realism with compositional elegance and lavish romanticism. Against the colorful background of the Risorgimento, he paints the betrayal by an Austrian lieutenant of his aristocratic Italian mistress who, in order to save him, has compromised the partisans. The love story parallels the approaching betrayal of the revolution by the bourgeois political powers. Like Gramsci who often returned to the contradictions of the Risorgimento as a key to the social problems of the modern Italian state, Visconti explores that period once more in *Il gattopardo* from the Lampedusa novel. An aristocratic Sicilian family undergoes transformation as a result of intermarriage with the middle-class at the same time that the Mezzogiorno is undergoing unification with the North. The bourgeoisie, now ready and able to take over from the dying aristocracy, usurps Garibaldi's revolution; in this period of *transformismo*, the revolutionary process will be assimilated into the dominant political structure and defused.

Still another film that focuses on the family unit as a barometer of history and changing society is *La caduta degli dei*. This treatment of a German munitions industry family (much like Krupp) and its decline into betrayal and murder in the interests of personal gain and the Nazi state intensifies and brings up-to-date an examination of the social questions of the last mentioned films. Here again a meticulous, mobile camera technique sets forth and stylistically typifies a decadent, death-surfeited culture.

Vaghe stelle dell'orsa removes the critique of the family from the social to the psychoanalytic plane. While death or absence of the father and the presence of an uprising surrogate is a thematic consideration in several Visconti films, he here explores it in conjunction with Freudian theory in this deliberate yet entirely transmuted re-telling of the Elektra myth. We are never completely aware of the extent of the relationship between Sandra and her brother, and the possibility of past incest remains distinct. Both despise Gilardini, their stepfather, whom they accuse of having seduced their mother and having denounced their father, a Jew, to the Fascists. Sandra's love for and sense of solidarity with her brother follows upon a racial solidarity with her father and race, but Gianni's love, on the other hand, is underpinned by a desire for his mother, transferred to Sandra. Nevertheless, dramatic confrontation propels the dialectical investigations of the individual's position with respect to the social even in this, Visconti's most densely psychoanalytic film.

Three films marking a further removal from social themes and observation of the individual, all literary adaptations, are generally felt to be his weakest: *Le notte bianche* from Dostoevski's *White Nights* sets a rather fanciful tale of a lonely man's hopes to win over a despairing woman's love against a decor that refutes, in its obvious, studio-bound staginess, Visconti's concern with realism and material verisimilitude. The clear inadequacy of this Livornian setting, dominated by a footbridge upon which the two meet and the unusually claustrophobic spatiality that results, locate the world of individual romance severed from large social and historical concerns in an inert, artificial perspective that borders on the hallucinatory. He achieves similar results with location shooting in *Lo straniero*, where—despite alterations of the original Camus—he perfectly captures the difficult tensions and tone of individual alienation by utilizing the telephoto lens pervasively. Rather than provide a suitable Viscontian dramatic space rendered in depth, it reduces Mersault to the status of a Kafkaesque insect-man observed under a microscope. Finally, *Morte a Venezia* based on Thomas Mann, among Visconti's most formally beautiful productions is one of his least critically successful. The baroque elaboration of mise-en-scène and camera work does not rise above self-pity and self-indulgence, and is cut off from social context irretrievably.

—Joel Kanoff

VOLKOV, Alexander.

(also spelt Volkoff.) Russian. Born in Moscow, 1885. Singer in the Imperial Opera of Moscow until called to serve in Russo-Japanese War, 1903; after meeting film producer Paul Thieman, worked as actor, writer, director, and distributor, from 1906; appointed head of Tiflis (Tblisi) Studios, 1913; wounded in action, 1914; joined Ermoliev's company, Moscow, 1916; moved with the company to France, 1920; company absorbed into Albatros films, 1922; worked in France, Germany, Switzerland, and Italy, until 1941. *Died, in Rome, 1942.*

Films as Director:

1913	*The Prisoner of the Caucasus* (+ role)
1916	*Zelyonyi pauk* (*The Green Spider*)
1922–23	*La Maison du mystère* (serial)
1924	*Kean* (*Kean ou Désordre et Génie*)
1925	*Les Ombres qui passent*
1927	*Casanova* (*Prince of Adventurers*)
1928	*Geheimnisse des Orients* (*Secrets of the East*)
1931	*Der Weisse Teufel* (*The White Devil*)
1933	*Mille et deuxième nuit*
1934	*Volga Volga*; *Enfany du carnaval*
1936	*Stenka Rasin*
1941	*Amore Imperiale*

(Other Films as Director: Dates Unknown)

La Marquée des anciens plaisirs; *Pourquoi le violon pleurait-il?*; *Le Piedestal brise*; *L'Arène de la vengeance*; *Vavocka*; *Lui: Sny mimoletnye*; *Sny Bezrabotnye sniatsia lis' raz*; *Belle Comme la mort*; *Le Fuyard*; *Ismael Bey*; *Femme ou mère*; *L'Araignée verte*; *Le Coeur de mal*; *Au sommet de la gloire*; *Le Père serge*; *Le Chemin de la croix est coupable*; *La Pocharde*; *Sergeant X*

Other Films:

1913	*Razbitaya vaza* (*The Shattered Vase*) (Protazanov) (role); *Klyuchi shchastya* (*Keys to Happiness*) (Gardin and Protazanov) (role); *Portret Doriana Greya* (*Portrait of Dorian Gray*) (Meyerhold) (sc)
1918	*Otets Sergii* (*Father Sergius*) (Protazanov) (sc)
1924	*Unfinished Fresco* (role)
1927	*Napoleon* (Gance) (d some scenes)

Publications:

On VOLKOV: books—

Leyda, Jay, *Kino*, London, 1960.
Tsivian, Yuri, and others, *Silent Witnesses: Russian Film 1909–1918*, London and Pordenone, 1989.

*   *   *

Unlike in America, the status of the newest art stood very high in Russia and received recognition and encouragement from Imperial circles. Thus the people who entered films came from the arts and the professions such as the law, engineering or the theatre.

Alexander Volkov came from a cultured aristocratic family devoted to music and the arts generally. Young Alexander devoted himself to painting and his portrait of the Empress Theodorovna won an award at the Paris Exposition of 1900. Possessing a fine baritone voice he entered the Imperial Opera of Moscow but became involved in the Russo-Japanese war. On demobilisation he returned to his world of the arts and, meeting the pioneer film producer Paul Thiemann, he came interested in the Cinema. As scriptwriter, actor and film distributor he learned every branch of the profession. As a film distributor he was familiar with the then popular films of Nordisk, Svenska and Vitagraph. He even doubled for the great Danish actor Valdemar Psilander in films. Thiemann and Reinhardt were now among the leading film producers and Volkov was appointed head of their Tiflis Studios where he was in charge from 1913 to the Great War. As director, scriptwriter and producer he distinguished himself. He directed and played in *The Prisoner of the Caucasus* and generally raised the standard of subject matter of his films abandoning the sensationalism of the crime stories and concentrating on the great Russian writers as well as on writers of quality from abroad.

Wounded at the Front in 1914 his life was in danger but he survived and in 1916 he joined Ermoliev's Company. Here he was to work with a distinguished team of actors and technicians who were to be his close collaborators in the years to come. Notably he formed a friendship with the actor Ivan Mozhukin and wrote the script for *Otets Sergeii* (*Father Sergius*), one of the masterpieces of the Czarist cinema. The teamwork of the Ermoliev group was very important and accounts for the high standard of their work. Superb designers like Lochakov, and cameramen like Mundviller and Bourgassov lent their talents to the films that came from this studio. Volkov played many roles in this group as director, scriptwriter and actor.

With the coming of the Revolution in 1917 and the unrest and violence in Moscow Ermoliev moved all his production to the South, setting in Yalta for a short time until he brought all his key personnel to France via Constantinople and Marseilles. Amongst the little company of actors, directors, cameramen and designers was Volkov. They arrived in Paris in August 1920 and set up in Méliès' old studio in Montreuil on the out-

Alexander Volkov: *Casablanca*

skirts of the city. Here their work flourished and not only did they make films of outstanding quality but exerted a profound influence on the French Cinema. Eventually the company was kept going by the formation of Albatros Films by Alexander Kamenka, a producer of talent and imagination.

Volkov now became closely associated with the work of Ivan Mozhukin, with whom he was to achieve his greatest success. The serial *La Maison du mystère* of 1922–23 attracted attention for the intelligent and diverse acting abilities of Mozhukin. It was a story of love and hatred with the villain being played by the talented Charles Vanel. The team of Lochakov, the designer, and the cameramen Toporkov, Bourgassov and Mundviller ensured the technical brilliance of the film. This team was to continue to play a large part in the subsequent Volkov-Mozhukin productions. Volkov collaborated in Mozhukin's own bravura *Le Brasier Ardent* and was to make his greatest film in 1924, *Kean ou Désordre et Génie*, based on Alexandre Dumas's life of the great English actor, Edmund Kean. It was a film for actors and about actors and was Mozhukin's greatest showpiece. Its sensitive creation of the British Regency period, its superb performance by Mozhukin and its innovative editing contributed to a major French film. The next year *Les Ombres qui passent*, a story of a naive young man entrapped by a scheming adventuress, displayed Mozhukin's flair for comedy very much in the Chaplin tradition. The final film in the group was the spectacular *Casanova* supervised by Noël Bloch, who was associated with such grand-scale productions as *Michel Strogoff* and *Napoleon* (Volkov had assisted Gance on *Napoleon* in filming several great scenes.) Volkov handled a large canvas with its eye-catching scene of the Carnival of Venice and its snowy Russian landscapes and the resplendent glory of Catherine the Great's court. His tasteful control of this huge production managed to keep a marvellous balance between the amusing antics of Mozhukin and the pictorially magnificent background. The film got world distribution by Universal Films, but unfortunately there was some censorship and even the title was changed to *Prince of Adventurers* and the name of Casanova changed to Roberto Ferrara.

By this time the talents of the Albatros Company were beginning to drift to other spheres of activity. Volkov's next production was the oriental extravaganza *Geheimnisse des Orients* (*Secrets of the East*), based on the Arabian Nights and featuring the comedian Nicolai Koline, whom Volkov had directed many times in the past. Again he gathered the old talents together to make a film visually stunning. One more film for the UFA company in Berlin in 1931, *Der Weisse Teufel* (*The White Devil*), based on Tolstoy's *Hadschi Murad* was made silent but issued with sound accompaniment. It was spectacular and visually beautiful. Mozhukin as the Cossack chief was again supported by an international cast. It was to be his last big role for with the coming of sound his foreign accent limited his possibilities and he fell on hard times. Volkov returned to France, his later films there being pale shadows of his former work. He returned to Germany to remake *Volga Volga* in 1934 which had been previously done as a silent film by his confrère Tourjansky. His last film *Amore Imperiale* was filmed in Rome where he died in 1942.

He was a great man of the Cinema to which he brought a cultured mind, a sense of visual beauty, a deep knowledge of the skills and mechanics of films and a wide experience of life and people.

—Liam O'Leary

VON STERNBERG, Josef.

Austrian. Born Jonas Sternberg in Vienna, 19 May 1894. Educated briefly at Jamaica High School, Queens, New York, returned to Vienna to finish education. Married 1) Riza Royce, 1926 (divorced 1930); 2) Jeanne Annette McBride, 1943, two children. Film patcher for World Film Co. in Fort Lee, New Jersey, 1911; joined U.S. Army Signal Corps to make training films, 1917; scenarist and assistant for several directors, 1918–24; attached "von" to his name at suggestion of actor Elliot Dexter, 1924; directed first film *The Salvation Hunters*, then signed 8-picture contract with MGM (terminated after two abortive projects), 1925; directed *The Sea Gull* for Charlie Chaplin, Chaplin did not release it, 1926; director for Paramount, 1926–35; began collaboration with Marlene Dietrich on *Der blaue Engel*, made for UFA in Berlin, 1930; attempted to direct *I, Claudius* for Alexander Korda in England, 1937 (not completed); made documentary *The Town* for U.S. Office of War Information, 1941; taught class in film direction, University of Southern California, 1947. Recipient: George Eastman House Medal of Honor, 1957; Honorary Member, Akademie der Künste, Berlin, 1960. *Died 22 December 1969.*

Films as Director:

1925   *The Salvation Hunters* (+ pr, sc); *The Exquisite Sinner* (+ co-sc) (remade by Phil Rosen); *The Masked Bride* (remade by Christy Cabanne)
1926   *The Sea Gull* (*Woman of the Sea*) (+ sc)
1927   *Children of Divorce* (d add'l scenes only); **Underworld**
1928   *The Last Command* (+ sc); *The Drag Net*; *The Docks of New York*
1929   *The Case of Lena Smith*; *Thunderbolt*
1930   **Der blaue Engel** (**The Blue Angel**); *Morocco*
1931   *Dishonored*; *An American Tragedy*
1932   **Shanghai Express**; *Blonde Venus* (+ co-sc); *I Take This Woman*
1934   **The Scarlet Empress**
1935   **The Devil is a Woman** (+ co-ph); *Crime and Punishment*
1936   *The King Steps Out*
1939   *Sergeant Madden*; *New York Cinderella* (remade by Frank Borzage and W.S. Van Dyke)
1941   *The Shanghai Gesture* (+ co-sc)
1943–44   *The Town*
1946   **Duel in the Sun** (d several scenes only)
1951   *Macao* (re-shot almost entirely by Nicholas Ray)
1953   *Anatahan* (*The Saga of Anatahan*) (+ sc, ph)

1957   *Jet Pilot* (completed 1950)

Other Films:

(partial list)

1919   *The Mystery of the Yellow Room* (asst d); *By Divine Right* (asst d, sc, ph); *Vanity's Price* (asst d)

Publications:

By VON STERNBERG: books—

Daughters of Vienna, free adaptation of stories by Karl Adolph, Vienna, 1922.
Dokumentation, eine Darstellung, Mannheim, Germany, 1966.
Fun in a Chinese Laundry, New York, 1965
The Blue Angel (screenplay), New York, 1968.

By VON STERNBERG: articles—

Interview in *Motion Picture Classic* (New York), May 1931.
"On Life and Film," in *Films in Review* (New York), October 1952.

Josef von Sternberg

"More Light," in *Sight and Sound* (London), Autumn 1955.
"Acting in Film and Theater," in *Film Culture* (New York), Winter 1955.
Interview with D. Freppel and B. Tavernier in *Cinéma* (Paris), March 1961.
"A Taste for Celluloid," in *Films and Filming* (London), July 1963.
"The von Sternberg Principle," in *Esquire* (New York), October 1963.
"Sternberg at 70," with John Pankake, in *Films in Review* (New York), May 1964.
Interview with Peter Bogdanovich in *Movie* (London), Summer 1965.
Interview with F.A. Macklin in *Film Heritage* (Dayton, Ohio), Winter 1965–66.
"*L'Ange bleu*," in *Avant-Scène du Cinéma* (Paris), March 1966.
Interview with Kevin Brownlow in *Film* (London), Spring 1966.

On VON STERNBERG: books—

Harrington, Curtis, *An Index to the Films of Josef von Sternberg*, London, 1949.
Sarris, Andrew, *The Films of Josef von Sternberg*, New York, 1966.
Walker, Alexander, *The Celluloid Sacrifice*, New York, 1967.
Weinberg, Herman G., *Josef von Sternberg: A Critical Study*, New York, 1967.
Anthologie du cinéma Vol. 6, Paris, 1971.
Baxter, John, *The Cinema of Josef von Sternberg*, New York, 1971.
Mérigeau, Pascal, *Josef Von Sternberg*, Paris, 1983.
Studlar, Gaylyn, *In the Realm of Pleasure: Von Sternberg, Dietrich and the Masochistic Aesthetic*, Urbana, Illinois, 1988.
Zucker, Carole, *The Idea of the Image: Josef von Sternberg's Dietrich Films*, Cranbury, New Jersey, 1988.

On VON STERNBERG: articles—

Pringle, Henry, "Profile of Josef von Sternberg," in the *New Yorker*, 28 March 1931.
Harrington, Curtis, "Josef von Sternberg," in *Cahiers du Cinéma* (Paris), October/November 1951.
Labarthe, André, "Un metteur en scène baudelairien," in *Cahiers du Cinéma* (Paris), April 1956.
Weinberg, Herman G., "The Lost Films, Part 1," in *Sight and Sound* (London), August 1962.
Smith, Jack, "A Belated Appreciation of von Sternberg," in *Film Culture* (New York), Winter 1963/64.
Green, O.O., "Six Films of Josef von Sternberg," in *Movie* (London), no. 13, 1965.
Weinberg, Herman G., "Sternberg and Stroheim—Letter," in *Sight and Sound* (London), Winter 1965/66.
Kyrou, Ado, "Sternberg, avant, pendant, après Marlene," in *Positif* (Paris), May 1966.
Camper, Fred, "Essays on Film Style," in *Cinema* (London), no. 8, 1971.
Flinn, T., "Joe, Where Are You?," in *Velvet Light Trap* (Madison, Wisconsin), Fall 1972.
Rheuban, Joyce, "Josef von Sternberg: The Scientist and the Vamp," in *Sight and Sound* (London), Autumn 1973.
Gow, Gordon, "Alchemy: Dietrich + Sternberg," in *Films and Filming* (London), June 1974.
Wood, Robin, "Sternberg's Empress: The Play of Light and Shade," in *Film Comment* (New York), March/April 1975.
Willis, D., "Sternberg: The Context of Passion," in *Sight and Sound* (London), Spring 1978.
Articles from *Ciné-Magazine* reprinted in *Avant-Scène du Ciné* (Paris), 15 March 1980.
Luft, Herbert, "Josef von Sternberg," in *Films in Review* (New York), January 1981.
Magny, Joel, "Josef von Sternberg: la lumière du désir," in *Cinéma* (Paris), December 1982.
Von Sternberg Section of *Skrien* (Amsterdam), April/May 1985.
Baxter, Peter, "*Blonde Venus*: Memory, Legend and Desire," and Florence Jacobowitz, "Power and the Masquerade: *The Devil is a Woman*," in *CineAction!* (Toronto), no. 8, 1987.

On VON STERNBERG: film:

Duncalf, Bill, director, *The Epic That Never Was—"I, Claudius"*, for BBC-TV, London, 1966.

*   *   *

There is a sense in which Jonas Sternberg never grew up. In his personality, the twin urges of the disturbed adolescent towards self-advertisement and self-effacement fuse with a brilliant visual imagination to create an artistic vision unparalleled in the cinema. But Sternberg lacked the cultivation of Murnau, the sophistication of his mentor von Stroheim, the humanity of Griffith or the ruthlessness of Chaplin. His imagination remained immature, and his personality malicious, obsessive. His films reflect a schoolboy's fascination with sensuality and heroics. That they are sublime visual adventures from an artist who contributed substantially to the sum of cinema technique is one paradox to add to the stock that make up his career.

Much of Sternberg's public utterance, and in particular his autobiography, was calculated to confuse; the disguise of his real Christian name under the diminutive "Jo" is typical. Despite his claims to have done so, he did not "write" all his films, though he did re-write the work of some skilled collaborators, notably Jules Furthman and Ben Hecht. While his eye for art and design was highly developed he never designed sets, merely "improved" them with props, veils, nets, posters, scribbles, but above all with light. Of this last he was a natural master, the only director of his day to earn membership of the American Society of Cinematographers. Given a set, a face, a camera and some lights, he could create a mobile portrait breath-taking in its beauty.

Marlene Dietrich was his greatest model. He dressed her like a doll, in feathers and sequins, in a gorilla suit, in a tuxedo, in a succession of gowns by Paramount's master of couture, Travis Banton. She submitted to his every demand with the skill and complaisance of a great courtesan. No other actress provided him with such malleable material. With Betty Compson, Gene Tierney and Akemi Negishi he fitfully achieved the same "spiritual power," as he called the mood of yearning melancholy which was his ideal, but the effect never equalled that of the seven Dietrich melodramas.

Sternberg was born too early for the movies. The studio system constrained his fractious temperament; the formula picture stifled his urge to primp and polish. He battled with MGM, who offered him a lucrative contract after the success of his von Stroheim-esque expressionist drama *The Salvation Hunters*, fell out with Chaplin, producer of the still-suppressed *Woman of the Sea*, and fought constantly with Paramount until Ernst Lubitsch, acting studio head, "liquidated" him for his intransigence; the later suppression of his last Paramount film, *The Devil Is a Woman*, in a political dispute with Spain merely served to increase Sternberg's alienation.

For the rest of his career, Sternberg wandered from studio to studio, country to country, lacking always the facilities he needed to achieve his best work. Even Korda's lavish *I Claudius*, dogged by disaster and finally terminated in a cost-cutting exercise, shows in its surviving footage only occasional flashes of Sternbergian brilliance. By World War II, he had already achieved his best work, though he was able to live for another 30 years.

Sternberg alarmed a studio establishment whose executives thought in terms of social and sexual stereotypes, formula plotting, stock happy endings; whose narrative ideal was a *Saturday Evening Post* novelette. No storyteller, he derided plot; "the best source for a film is an anecdote," he said. From a single coincidence and a handful of characters, edifices of visual poetry could be constructed. His films leap years in the telling to follow a moral decline or growth of an obsession.

The most important film of his life was one he never made. After the humiliation of the war years, when he produced only the propaganda short *The Town*, and the nadir of his career, as close-up advisor to King Vidor on *Duel in the Sun*, he wrote *The Seven Bad Years*, a script that would, he said, "demonstrate the adult insistence to follow the pattern inflicted on a child in its first seven helpless years, from which a man could extricate himself were he to realize that an irresponsible child was leading him into trouble." He was never to make this work of self-analysis, nor any film which reflected a mature understanding of his contradictory personality.

Sternberg's theories of cinema were not especially profound, deriving largely from the work of Reinhardt, but they represented a quantum jump in an industry where questions of lighting and design were dealt with by experts who jealously guarded this prerogative. In planning his films not around dialogue but around the performers' "dramatic encounter with light," in insisting that the "dead space" between the camera and subject be filled and enlivened, and above all in seeing every story in terms, not of star quality, but "spiritual power," he established a concept of personal cinema which presaged the *politique des auteurs* and the Movie Brat generation.

In retrospect, his contentious personality, the self-conscious affecting of uniforms and costumes on the set, the epigrammatic style of communicating with performers which drove many of them to frenzy, all reveal themselves as reactions against the banality of his chosen profession. Sternberg was asked late in life if he had a hobby. "Yes. Chinese philately." Why that? "I wanted," he replied in the familiar weary, uninflected voice, "a subject I could not exhaust."

—John Baxter

VON STROHEIM, Erich.

Austrian. Born Erich Oswald Stroheim in Vienna, 22 September 1885; became U.S. citizen, 1926. According to von Stroheim he attended Mariahilfe Military Academy, though several biographers doubt this; he did serve briefly in the Austro-Hungarian Army. Married 1) Margaret Knox, 1914 (died 1915); 2) May Jones, 1916 (divorced 1918), one son; 3) Valerie Germonprez, 1918 (separated), one son. Moved to America and worked as salesman, railroad worker, short story writer and travel agent, 1909–14; actor, assistant and military adviser for D.W. Griffith, 1914–15; assistant director, military adviser and set designer for director John Emerson, 1915–17; became known as "The Man You Love to Hate" after role as Prussian officer in *For France*, 1917; directed *Blind Husbands* for Carl Laemmle at Universal, 1918 (terminated contract with Universal, 1922); directed *Greed* for Goldwyn Co., his version cut to 10 reels by studio, 1924; moved to France, 1945. *Died 12 May 1957.*

Films as Director:

1918 *Blind Husbands* (+ sc, art d, role as Lieutenant von Steuben)
1919 *The Devil's Passkey* (+ sc, art d)
1921 *Foolish Wives* (+ sc, co-art d, co-costume, role as Count Wladislas Serge Karamazin)
1922 *Merry-Go-Round* (+ sc, co-art d, co-costume) (completed by Rupert Julian)
1924 *Greed* (+ sc, co-art d)
1925 *The Merry Widow* (+ sc, co-art d, co-costume)
1927 *The Wedding March* (+ sc, co-art d, co-costume, role as Prince Nicki)
1928 *The Honeymoon* (+ sc, role as Prince Nicki—part 2 of *The Wedding March* and not released in U.S.); *Queen Kelly* (+ sc, co-art d) (completed by others)

1933 *Walking Down Broadway* (+ sc) (mostly reshot by Alfred Werker and Edwin Burke and released as *Hello Sister*)

Other Films:

1914 *Captain McLean* (Conway) (role)
1915 *Old Heidelberg* (Emerson) (asst d, military advisor, role as Lutz); *Ghosts* (Emerson) (role); *The Birth of a Nation* (Griffith) (role)
1916 *Intolerance* (Griffith) (asst d, role as second Pharisee); *The Social Secretary* (Emerson) (asst d, role as a reporter); *Macbeth* (Emerson) (asst d, role); *Less Than the Dust* (Emerson) (asst d, role); *His Picture in the Papers* (Emerson) (asst d, role as the traitor)
1917 *Panthea* (Dwan) (asst d, role as Russian policeman); *Sylvia of the Secret Service* (Fitzmaurice) (asst d, role); *In Again—Out Again* (Emerson) (asst d, art d, role as Russian officer); *For France* (Ruggles) (role as Prussian officer)
1918 *Hearts of the World* (Griffith) (asst d, military advisor, role as German officer); *The Unbeliever* (Crosland) (role as German officer); *The Hun Within* (Cabanne) (role as German officer)
1927 *The Tempest* (sc)
1929 *The Great Gabbo* (Cruze) (role as Gabbo)
1930 *Three Faces East* (del Ruth) (role)
1931 *Friends and Lovers* (Schertzinger) (role)
1932 *The Lost Squadron* (Archimbaud and Sloane) (role); *As You Desire Me* (Fitzmaurice) (role)
1934 *Crimson Romance* (Howard) (military advisor, role as German pilot); *Fugitive Road* (sc/co-sc, military advisor)
1935 *The Crime of Dr. Crespi* (Auer) (role as Dr. Crespi); *Anna Karenina* (Brown) (military advisor)
1936 *Devil Doll* (Browning) (sc/co-sc); *San Francisco* (Van Dyke) (sc/co-sc); *Marthe Richard* (Bernard) (role as German officer)
1937 *Between Two Women* (sc/co-sc); *La Grande Illusion* (Renoir) (role as von Rauffenstein); *Mademoiselle Docteur* (Gréville) (role as Col. Mathesius); *L'Alibi* (Chenal) (role as Winkler)
1938 *Les Pirates du rail* (Christian-Jaque) (role as Tschou-Kin); *L'Affaire Lafarge* (Chenal) (role as Denis); *Les Disparus de Saint-Agil* (Christian-Jaque) (role as German professor); *Ultimatum* (Wiene and Siodmak) (role as Général Simovic); *Gibraltar* (*It Happened in Gibraltar*) (Ozep) (role as Marson); *Derrière la façade* (Lacombe) (role as Eric)
1939 *Menaces* (Gréville) (role as Hoffman); *Rappel immédiat* (Mathot) (role as Stanley Wells); *Pièges* (Siodmak) (role as Pears); *Tempête sur Paris* (Bernard-Deschamps) (role as Kohrlick); *La Révolte des vivants* (Pottier) (role as Emile Lasser); *Macao l'enfer* (Delannoy) (role as Knall); *Paris—New York* (Heymann and Mirande) (role)
1940 *I Was an Adventuress* (Ratoff) (role); *So Ends Our Night* (Cromwell) (role)
1943 *Five Graves to Cairo* (Wilder) (role as Field Marshall Rommel); *The North Star* (Milestone) (role as German medic)
1944 *The Lady and the Monster* (Sherman) (role); *Storm over Lisbon* (Sherman) (role)
1945 *The Great Flamarion* (Mann) (role as Flamarion); *Scotland Yard Investigation* (Blair) (role); *The Mask of Dijon* (Landers) (role as Dijon)
1946 *On ne meurt pas comme ça* (Boyer) (role as Eric von Berg)
1947 *La Danse de mort* (Cravenne) (co-adapt, co-dialogue, role as Edgar)
1948 *Le Signal rouge* (Neubach) (role)
1949 *Portrait d'un assassin* (Bernard-Roland) (role)
1950 *Sunset Boulevard* (Wilder) (role as Max)
1952 *Minuit, quai de Bercy* (Stengel) (role); *Alraune* (*La Mandragore*) (Rabenalt) (role)
1953 *L'Envers du paradis* (Gréville) (role as O'Hara); *Alerte au sud* (Devaivre) (role)
1954 *Napoléon* (Guitry) (role as Beethoven)
1955 *Série noire* (Foucaud) (role); *La Madone des sleepings* (Diamant-Berger) (role)

Erich von Stroheim

Publications:

By VON STROHEIM: books—

Paprika, New York, 1935.
Les Feux de la Saint-Jean: Veronica (Part 1), Givors, France, 1951.
Les Feux de la Saint-Jean: Constanzia (Part 2), Givors, France, 1954, reissued 1967.
Poto-Poto, Paris, 1956.
Greed (full screenplay), Cinémathèque Royale de Belgique, Brussels, 1958.

By VON STROHEIM: articles—

Interviews in *Motion Picture* (New York), August 1920, October 1921, May 1922, September 1923, and April 1927.
"Charges Against Him and His Reply," with C. Belfrage, in *Motion Picture Classic* (Brooklyn), June 1930.
"My Own Story," in *Film Weekly* (London), April/May 1935.
"Stroheim in London," with Karel Reisz, in *Sight and Sound* (London), April/June 1954.
"Erich von Stroheim," in *Interviews with Film Directors*, edited by Andrew Sarris, New York, 1967.
"*Citizen Kane*," in *Positif* (Paris), March 1968 (reprinted from 1941).
"*Les Rapaces (Greed)*," (scenario), in *Avant-Scène du Cinéma* (Paris), September 1968.

On VON STROHEIM: books—

Atasceva, P., and V. Korolevitch, *Erich von Stroheim*, Moscow, 1927.
Drinkwater, John, *The Life and Adventures of Carl Laemmle*, New York, 1931.
Fronval, Georges, *Erich von Stroheim, sa vie, ses films*, Paris, 1939.
Noble, Peter, *Hollywood Scapegoat: The Biography of Erich von Stroheim*, London, 1951.
Bergut, Bob, *Erich von Stroheim*, Paris, 1960.
Barna, Jan, *Erich von Stroheim*, Vienna, 1966.
Gobeil, Charlotte, editor, *Hommage à Erich von Stroheim*, Ottawa, 1966.
Ciment, Michel, *Erich von Stroheim*, Paris, 1967.
Brownlow, Kevin, *The Parade's Gone By . . .*, New York, 1968.
Finler, Joel, *Stroheim*, Berkeley, 1968.
Curtiss, Thomas Quinn, *Erich von Stroheim*, Paris, 1969.
Buache, Freddy, *Erich von Stroheim*, Paris, 1972.
Pratt, George C., *Spellbound in Darkness*, Greenwich, Connecticut, 1973.
Weinberg, Herman G., *Stroheim: A Pictorial Record of His Nine Films*, New York, 1975.
Bazin, André, *The Cinema of Cruelty: From Buñuel to Hitchcock*, New York, 1982.
Koszarski, Richard, *The Man You Loved to Hate: Erich von Stroheim and Hollywood*, New York, 1983.
Bessy, Maurice, *Erich von Stroheim*, Paris, 1984.

On VON STROHEIM: articles—

Yost, Robert, "Gosh, How They Hate Him!," in *Photoplay* (New York), December 1919.
Weinberg, Herman G., "Erich von Stroheim," in *Film Art* (London), Spring 1937.
"Tribute to Stroheim," in *Film Quarterly* (London), Spring 1947.
"Von Stroheim Issue" of *Ciné-club* (Paris), April 1949.
Schwerin, Jules, "The Resurgence of von Stroheim," in *Films in Review* (New York), April 1950.
Lambert, Gavin, "Stroheim Revisited: The Missing Third in American Cinema," in *Sight and Sound* (London), April/June 1955.
Eisner, Lotte, "Notes sur le style de Stroheim," in *Cahiers du Cinéma* (Paris), January 1957.
"Von Stroheim Issue" of *Cinéma* (Paris), February 1957.
Everson, William K., "The Career of Erich von Stroheim," in *Films in Review* (New York), August/September 1957.
"Von Stroheim Issue" of *Film Culture* (New York), April 1958.
Marion, Denis, "Stroheim, the Legend and the Fact," in *Sight and Sound* (London), Winter 1961/62.
Weinberg, Herman G., "The Legion of Lost Films," in *Sight and Sound* (London), Autumn 1962.

Weinberg, Herman G., "Sternberg and Stroheim," in *Sight and Sound* (London), Winter 1965/66.
"Von Stroheim Issue" of *Etudes Cinématographiques* (Paris), no. 48/50, 1966.
Gilliatt, Penelope, "The Scabrous Poet from the Estate Belonging to No One," in the *New Yorker*, 3 June 1972.
"Von Stroheim Issue" of *Cinema* (Zurich), December 1973.
Rosenbaum, Jonathan, "Second Thoughts on Stroheim," in *Film Comment* (New York), May/June 1974.
Koszarski, Richard, and William K. Everson, "Stroheim's Last 'Lost' Film: The Making and Remaking of *Walking Down Broadway*," in *Film Comment* (New York), May/June 1975.
Brownlow, Kevin, "The Merry Widow Affair," in *American Film* (Washington D.C.), July/August 1981.
Wilder, Billy, "Stroheim, l'homme que vous aimerez," in *Positif* (Paris), July/August 1983.
Grindon, Leger, "From Word to Image: Displacement and Meaning in *Greed*," in *Journal of Film and Video* (Boston), vol. 41, no. 4, 1989.

*   *   *

Erich von Stroheim had two complementary careers in cinema, that of actor-director, primarily during the silent period, and that of distinguished character actor when his career as a director was frustrated through inability to bring his genius to terms with the American film industry.

After edging his way into the industry in the humblest capacities, his lengthy experience as bit player and assistant to Griffith paid off. His acceptance during the pioneer period of American cinema as Prussian "military adviser," and his bullet-headed physical resemblance to the traditional monocled image of the tight-uniformed Hun officer, enabled him to create a more established acting career and star in his own films, and with his first personal film, *Blind Husbands*, he became the prime creator in Hollywood of witty, risqué, European-like sex-triangle comedy-dramas. His initial successes in the early 1920s were characterized by subtle acting touches, and a marked sophistication of subject that impressed American audiences of the period as essentially European and fascinatingly decadent. *Blind Husbands* was followed by other films in the same genre, the 12-reel *The Devil's Pass Key* and the critically successful *Foolish Wives*. In all three, women spectators could easily identify with the common character of the lonely wife, whose seduction by attractively wicked Germanic officers and gentlemen (usually played by Stroheim, now publicized as "the man you love to hate") provided the essential thrill. Stroheim also cunningly included beautiful but excitingly unprincipled women characters in both *The Devil's Pass Key* and *Foolish Wives*, played by Maude George and Mae Busch. Details of bathing, dressing, and the ministration of servants in the preparation of masters or mistresses in boudoir or dressing room were recurrent, and the Stroheim scene always included elaborate banquets, receptions, and social ceremonies.

Stroheim's losing battle with the film industry began in his clashes with Irving Thalberg at Universal. His obsessive perfectionism over points of detail in setting and costume had pushed the budget for *Foolish Wives* to the million dollar mark. Though the publicists boasted of Stroheim's extravagance, the front office preferred hard profits to such self-indulgent expenditure. Thalberg also refused Stroheim's demands that his films should be of any length he determined, and *Foolish Wives* (intended to be in two parts) was finally taken out of his hands and cut from 18–20 to some 12–14 reels. Although a critical success, the film lost money.

Foolish Wives was Stroheim's most discussed film before *Greed*. In it he played a bogus aristocratic officer, in reality a swindler and multi-seducer. His brilliant, sardonic acting "touches" brought a similar psychological verisimilitude to this grimly satiric comedy of manners as Lubitsch was to establish in his *Kammerspielfilme* (intimate films). He also specialized in decor, photographic composition and lighting. Unforgettable is the latticed light and shadow in the sequence when the seducer in full uniform visits the counterfeiter's underworld den with hope of ravishing the old man's mentally defective daughter.

Greed, Stroheim's most important film, was based meticulously on Norris's Zolaesque novel, *McTeague*. Stroheim's masterpiece, it was eventually mutilated by the studio because of its unwieldy length; under protest by Stroheim it was reduced from 42 reels to 24 (between 5 and 6 hours), and then finally cut to 10 reels by the studio. Stroheim's stress on the ugly and bizarre in human nature emerged in his psychologically naturalistic study of avarice and degradation in the mis-matched couple—McTeague, the impulsive, primitive (but bird-loving) lowerclass dentist, and Trina, the pathologically avaricious spinster member of a German-Swiss immigrant family and winner of a $5,000 lottery. After their marriage, Trina hoards her money as their circumstances decline to the point where the husband becomes drunk and brutal, and the wife mad. After he murders her, and becomes a fugitive, McTeague ends in the isolated wastes of Death Valley, handcuffed to Marcus, his former friend whom he has killed. Using the streets of San Francisco and the house where the actual murder that had inspired Norris had taken place, Stroheim anticipated Rossellini in his use of such locations. But his insistence on achieving an incongruous and stylized realism, starting with McTeague's courtship of Trina sitting on a sewerpipe and culminating in the macabre sequence in Death Valley goes beyond that straight neorealism of the future. Joel W. Finler, in his book *Stroheim*, analyzes the wholesale cutting in the 10-reel version, exposing the grave losses that render the action and motivation of the film unclear. But the superb performances of Zasu Pitts and Gibson Gowland compensate, and the grotesque Sieppe family provide a macabre background, enhanced by Stroheim's constant reminder of San Francisco's "mean streets." The film was held to be his masterpiece by many, but also condemned as a "vile epic of the sewer."

Stroheim was to work as director on only five more films: the Ruritanian *Merry Widow* (adapted from the operetta), *The Wedding March* (in two parts, and again severely cut), the erotic *Queen Kelly* (directed for Gloria Swanson, but never completed by Stroheim, though released by Swanson with her own additions), and the sound films *Walking Down Broadway* (*Hello, Sister* reworked and never released in Stroheim's original version), and *The Emperor's Candlesticks* on which it appears he collaborated only in direction. The silent films portray the same degenerate Imperial Viennese society Stroheim favored, half romantic, half grotesque fantasy, and are once again presented with Stroheim's meticulous attention to detail in decor and characterization. *The Wedding March* (in spite of studio intervention) is the high point in Stroheim's career as a director after *Greed*. Subsequently he remained content to star or appear in films made by others, some 50 appearances between 1929 and 1955, most notably Renoir's *La Grande Illusion* and Wilder's *Five Graves to Cairo* and *Sunset Boulevard*, in which his past as a director is almost ghoulishly recalled.

—Roger Manvell

VON TROTTA, Margarethe.

German. Born in Berlin, 21 February, 1942. Educated at Universities of Munich and Paris; studied acting in Munich. Married director Volker Schlöndorff. Actress in theatres in Dinkelsbül, Stuttgart, and Frankfurt, 1960s; works only in TV and film, from 1969; directed first film, *Die verlorene Ehre der Katharina Blum*, 1975. Recipient: Golden Lion, Venice Festival, for *Die bleierne Zeit*, 1981.

Films as Director:

1975   *Die verlorene Ehre der Katharina Blum* (*The Lost Honor of Katharina Blum*) (co-d, co-sc)
1977   *Das zweite Erwachen der Christa Klages* (*The Second Awakening of Christa Klages*) (+ sc)
1979   *Schwestern oder Die Balance des Glücks* (*Sisters, or The Balance of Happiness*) (+ sc)
1981   *Die bleierne Zeit* (*Leaden Times. Marianne and Julianne. The German Sisters*) (+ sc)
1983   *Heller Wahn* (*Sheer Madness*) (+ sc)
1986   *Rosa Luxemburg*
1987   episode of *Felix*
1988   *Paura e amore* (*Three Sisters. Love and Fear*)
1990   *Die Rückkehr* (*Return. L'Africana*)

Other Films:

1968   *Schräge Vögel* (Ehmck) (role)
1969   *Brandstifter* (Lemke) (role); *Götter der Pest* (Fassbinder) (role as Margarethe)
1970   *Baal* (Schlöndorff) (role as Sophie); *Der amerikanische Soldat* (Fassbinder) (role as maid)
1971   *Der plötzliche Reichtum der armen Leute von Kombach* (Schlöndorff) (co-sc, role as Heinrich's woman); *Die Moral der Ruth Halbfass* (Schlöndorff) (role as Doris Vogelsang)
1972   *Strohfeuer* (Schlöndorff) (role as Elisabeth, co-sc)
1973   *Desaster* (Hauff) (role); *Übernachtung in Tirol* (Schlöndorff) (role as Katja)
1974   *Invitation à la chasse* (Chabrol) (for TV) (role as Paulette); *Georgina's Gründe* (Schlöndorff) (for TV) (role as Kate Theory)
1975   *Das andechser Gefühl* (Achternbusch) (role as film actress)
1976   *Der Fangschuss* (Schlöndorff) (co-sc, role as Sophie von Reval)
1984   *Blaubart* (*Bluebeard*) (Zanussi) (role); *Unerreichbare Nahe* (Hirtz) (sc)

Publications:

By VON TROTTA: books—

Die bleierne Zeit, Frankfurt, 1981.
Heller Wahn, Frankfurt, 1983.
Rosa Luxemburg, with Christiane Ensslin, Frankfurt, 1986.

By VON TROTTA: articles—

"*Die verlorene Ehre der Katharina Blum*," in *Film and Fernsehen* (Berlin), no. 8, 1976.
"Gespräch zwischen Margarethe von Trotta und Christel Buschmann," in *Frauen und Film* (Berlin), June 1976.
"Frauen haben anderes zu sagen . . . ," an interview with U. Schirmeyer-Klein, in *Film und Fernsehen* (Berlin), no. 4, 1979.
Interview with Sheila Johnston in *Stills* (London), May/June 1986.
Interview with Karen Jaehne and Lenny Rubenstein in *Cineaste* (New York), vol. 15, no. 4, 1987.

On VON TROTTA: books—

Franklin, James, *New German Cinema: From Oberhausen to Hamburg*, Boston, 1983.
Phillips, Klaus, editor, *New German Filmmakers: From Oberhausen through the 1970s*, New York, 1984.

Margarethe von Trotta

Todd, Janet, editor, *Women and Film: Women and Literature*, New York, 1988.

Elsaesser, Thomas, *New German Cinema: A History*, London, 1989.

On VON TROTTA: articles—

"*Le Coup de grâce* Issue" of *Avant-Scène du Cinéma* (Paris), 1 February 1977.

Elsaesser, Thomas, "Mother Courage and Divided Daughter," in *Monthly Film Bulletin* (London), July 1983.

Dossier on von Trotta, in *Revue du Cinéma* (Paris), November 1983.

Moeller, H.B., "West German Women's Cinema: The case of Margarethe von Trotta," in *Film Criticism* (Meadville, Pennsylvania), Winter 1984/85; reprinted Fall-Winter 1986/87.

Linville, Susan, and Kent Casper, "The Ambiguity of Margarethe von Trotta's *Sheer Madness*," in *Film Criticism* (Meadville, Pennsylvania), vol. 12, no. 1, 1987.

Donough, Martin, "Margarethe von Trotta: Gynemegoguery and the Dilemmas of a Filmmaker," in *Literature/Film Quarterly* (Salisbury, Maryland), vol. 17, no. 3, 1989.

*   *   *

An important aspect of Margarethe von Trotta's filmmaking which affects not only the content but also the representation of that content, is her emphasis on women and the relationships that can develop between them. For example, von Trotta chose as the central theme in two of her films, *Sisters or the Balance of Happiness* and *Marianne and Juliane*, one of the most intense and complex relationships that can exist between two women, that of sisters. Whether von Trotta is dealing with overtly political themes as in *The Second Awakening of Christa Klages* (based on the true story of a woman who robs a bank in order to subsidize a daycare center) and *Marianne and Juliane* (based on the experiences of Christine Ensslin and her "terrorist" sister) or with the lives of ordinary women as in *Sisters or the Balance of Happiness* or *Sheer Madness*, von Trotta shows that the relationships between women are political. By paying close attention to these relationships von Trotta brings into question the social and political systems which either sustain them or do not allow them to exist.

Although the essence of von Trotta's films is political and critical of the status quo, their structures are quite conventional. Her films are expensively made and highly subsidized by the film production company Bioskop, which was started by her husband. Volker Schlöndorff, and Reinhard Hauff, both filmmakers. Von Trotta joined the company when she started making her own films. She did not go through the complicated system of incentives and grants available to independent filmmakers in Germany. Rather, she began working for Schlöndorff as an actress and then as a scriptwriter, and finally on her own as a director and co-owner in the production company which subsidizes their films.

Von Trotta has been criticized by some feminists for working too closely within the system and for creating characters and structures which are too conventional to be of any political value. Other critics find that a feminist aesthetic can be found in her choice of themes. For although von Trotta uses conventional women characters she does not represent them in traditional fashion. Nor does she describe them with stereotyped, sexist clichés, rather she allows her characters to develop on screen through gestures, glances and nuances. Great importance is given to the psychological and subconscious delineation of her characters by von Trotta's constant attention to dreams, visions, flashbacks and personal obsessions. In this way, her work can be seen as inspired by the films of Bresson and Bergman, filmmakers who also use the film medium to portray psychological depth.

"The unconscious and subconscious behavior of the characters is more important to me than what they do," says von Trotta. For this reason, von Trotta spends a great deal of time with her actors and actresses to be sure that they really understand the emotions and motivations of the characters which they portray. This aspect of her filmmaking caused her to separate her work from that of her husband, Volker Schlöndorff. During their joint direction of *The Lost Honor of Katharina Blum*, it became apparent that Schlöndorff's manner of directing, which focused on action shots, did not mix with her own predilections for exploring the internal motivation of the characters. Her films are often criticized for paying too much attention to the psychological, and thus becoming too personal and inaccessible.

Von Trotta has caused much controversy within the feminist movement and outside of it. Nevertheless, her films have won several awards not only in her native Germany but also internationally, drawing large, diverse audiences. Her importance cannot be minimized. Although she employs the commonly used and accepted structures of popular filmmakers, her message is quite different. Her main characters are women and her films treat them seriously and innovatively. Such treatment of women within a traditional form has in the past been undervalued or ignored. Her presentation of women has opened up possibilities for the development of the image of women on screen and in turn the development of film itself.

Von Trotta's choice of conventional structures and characters indicates that change can happen anywhere there is uneasiness brewing under the surface of people's lives.

—Gretchen Elsner-Sommer

WAJDA, Andrzej.

Polish. Born in Suwałki, Poland, 6 March 1926. Educated at the Fine Arts Academy, Kraków, 1945–48; High School of Cinematography, Lodz, 1950–52. Served in the A.K. (Home Army) of the Polish government in exile, from 1942. Assistant to director Aleksandr Ford, 1953, then directed first feature, *Pokolenie*, 1955; directed first play, 1959; made first film outside Poland, *Sibirska Ledi Magbet* for Avala Films, Belgrade, 1962; directed *Pilatus und andere* for West German TV, 1972; following imposition of martial law, concentrated on theatrical projects in Poland and film productions outside Poland; government dissolved Wajda's Studio X film production group, 1983. Recipient: Palme d'Or, Cannes Festival, for *Man of Iron*, 1981.

Films as Director and Scriptwriter:

1950   *Kiedy ty śpisz* [While You Sleep]; *Zły chłopiec* [The Bad Boy]
1951   *Ceramika Itžecka* [The Pottery of Ilzecka]
1955   *Pokolenie* (A Generation); *Ide ku słońcu* (*Idę do słońca*) [I Walk to the Sun]
1957   ***Kanał (They Loved Life)*** [Sewer]
1958   ***Popiół i diament* (*Ashes and Diamonds*)**
1959   *Lotna*
1960   *Niewinni czarodzieje* (*Innocent Sorcerers*)
1961   *Samson*
1972   *Sibirska Ledi Magbet* (*Lady Macbeth of Mtsensk. Fury is a Woman*) [Siberian Lady Macbeth]; "Warszawa" episode of *L'Amour à Vingt Ans*
1965   *Popioły* (*Ashes*)
1967   *Bramy raju* (*Gates to Paradise. The Gates of Heaven. The Holy Apes*)
1968   *Wszystko na sprzedaż* (*Everything for Sale*); *Przekładaniec* [Roly-Poly]
1969   *Polowanie na muchy* (*Hunting Flies*); *Makbet* (*Macbeth*) (for Polish TV)
1970   *Krajobraz po bitwie* (*Landscape After the Battle*); *Brzezina* [The Birchwood]
1972   *Pilatus und andere—ein Film für Karfreitag* (*Pilate and Others*); *Wesele* (*The Wedding*)
1974   *Ziemia obiecana* (*Promised Land*) (also as series on Polish TV)
1976   *Smuga cienia* (*The Shadow Line*)
1977   ***Człowiek z marmuru* (*Man of Marble*)**; *Bez znieczulenia* (*Without Anesthetic*)
1978   *Zaproszenie do wnętrza* (*Invitation to the Inside*) (doc)
1979   *Dyrygent* (*The Conductor*); *Panny z Wilka* (*The Girls from Wilko*)
1981   *Człowiek z żelaza* (*Man of Iron*)
1982   *Danton*
1983   *Land of Promise*
1985   *A Love in Germany*
1986   *Kronika wypadkow milosnych* (*Chronicle of a Love Affair*)
1987   *Les Possédés* (*The Possessed*)
1990   *Korczak*

Publications:

By WAJDA: books—

Un Cinéma nommé désir, Paris, 1986.
Double Vision: My Life in Film, New York, 1989; London, 1990.

By WAJDA: articles—

"Destroying the Commonplace," in *Films and Filming* (London), November 1961.
"Andrzej Wajda Speaking," in *Kino* (Warsaw), no. 1, 1968.
"Living in Hope," an interview with Gordon Gow, in *Films and Filming* (London), February 1973.
"Filmer les noces," in *Positif* (Paris), February 1974.
Interview with K.K. Przybylska in *Literature/Film Quarterly* (Salisbury, Maryland), Winter 1977.
"Between the Permissible and the Impermissible," an interview with D. Bickley and L. Rubinstein, in *Cineaste* (New York), Winter 1980/81.
"Wajda August '81," an interview and article by G. Moszcz, in *Sight and Sound* (London), Winter 1982.
Interview with Gideon Bachmann in *Film Quarterly* (Berkeley), Winter 1982/83.
Interview with Marcel Ophuls in *American Film* (Washington D.C.), October 1983.
Interview with Dan Yakir in *Film Comment* (New York), November/December 1984.
Interview with K. Farrington and L. Rubenstein in *Cineaste* (New York), vol. 14, no. 2, 1985.
Interview with W. Wertenstein in *Sight and Sound* (London), Summer 1985.

On WAJDA: books—

McArthur, Colin, editor, *Andrzej Wajda: Polish Cinema*, London, 1970.
Michalek, Bolesław, *The Cinema of Andrzej Wajda*, translated by Edward Rothert, London, 1973.
Douin, Jean-Luc, *Wajda*, Paris, 1981.
Paul, David W., editor, *Politics, Art and Commitment in the Eastern European Cinema*, New York, 1983.
Karpinski, Maciej, *The Theatre of Andrzej Wajda*, Cambridge, 1989.

On WAJDA: articles—

Szydlowski, Roman, "The Tragedy of a Generation," in *Film* (Poland), no. 46, 1958.
Michalek, Bolesław, "Polish Notes," in *Sight and Sound* (London), Winter 1958/59.
Higham, Charles, "Grasping the Nettle: The Films of Andrzej Wajda," in *Hudson Review* (Nutley, New Jersey), Autumn 1965.
"Wajda Issue" of *Etudes Cinématographiques* (Paris), no. 69–72, 1968.
Austen, David, "A Wajda Generation," in *Films and Filming* (London), July 1968.
Toeplitz, K., "Wajda Redivivus," in *Film Quarterly* (Berkeley), Winter 1969/70.
Cowie, Peter, "Wajda Redux," in *Sight and Sound* (London), Winter 1979/80.
"Wajda Issue" of *Avant-Scène du Cinéma* (Paris), 1 January 1980.

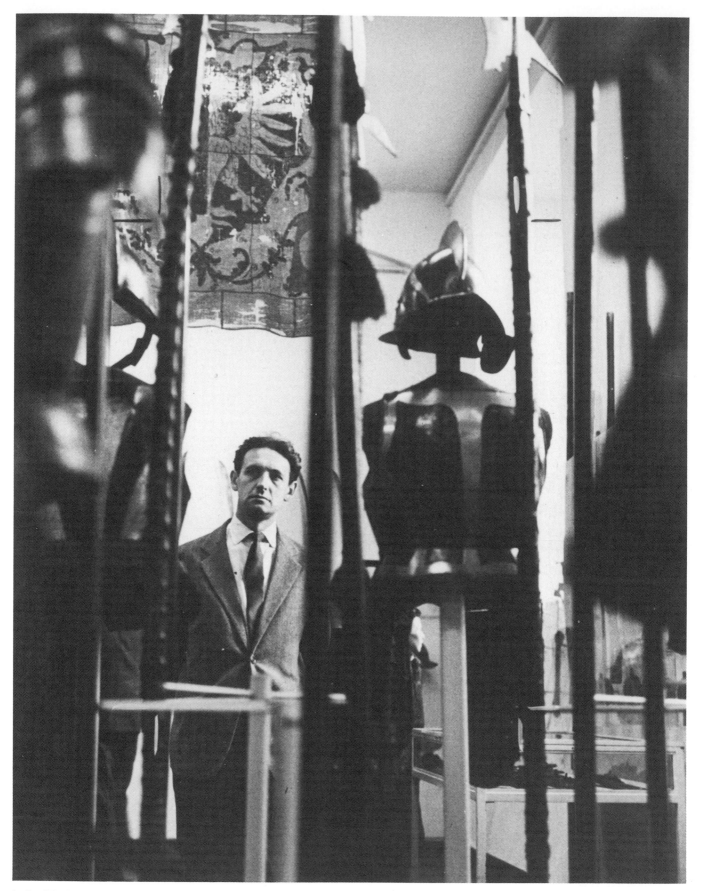

Andrzej Wajda

Aufderheide, Pat, and others "Solidarity and the Polish Cinema," in *Cineaste* (New York), vol. 13, no. 3, 1984.

*   *   *

The history of Polish film is as old as the history of filmmaking in most European countries. For entire decades, however, its range was limited to Polish territory and a Polish audience. Only after the Second World War, at the end of the 1950s, did the phenomenon known as the "Polish school of filmmaking" make itself felt as a part of world cinema. The phenomenon went hand in hand with the appearance of a new generation of film artists who, despite differences in their artistic proclivities, have a number of traits in common. They are approximately the same age, having been born in the 1920s. They spent their early youth in the shadow of the fascist occupation, and shared more or less similar postwar experiences. This is also the first generation of cinematically accomplished artists with a complete grasp of both the theoretical and practical sides of filmmaking.

Their debut was conditioned by the social climate, which was characterized by a desire to eliminate the negative aspects of postwar development labelled as the cult of personality. The basic theme of their work was the effort to come to grips with the painful experience of the war, the resistance to the occupation, and the struggle to put a new face on Polish society and the recent past. Temporal distance allowed them to take a sober look at all these experiences without schematic depictions, without illusions, and without pathetic ceremony. They wanted to know the truth about those years, in which the foundations of their contemporary life were formed, and express it in the specific destinies of the individuals who lived, fought, and died in those crucial moments of history. And one of the most important traits uniting all the members of the "school" was the attempt to debunk the myths and legends about those times and the people who shaped them.

The most prominent representative of the Polish school is Andrzej Wajda. In the span of a few short years he made three films, *Pokolenie*, *Kanał*, and *Popiół i diament*, which form a kind of loose trilogy and can be considered among the points of departure for the emergence of popular Poland. *Pokolenie* tells of a group of young men and women fighting in occupied Warsaw; *Kanał* is a tragic story of the 1944 Warsaw Uprising; *Popiół i diament* takes place at the watershed between war and peace. Crystallized in these three films are the fundamental themes of Wajda's work, themes characteristic of some other adherents of the "school" as well. In these films we also see the formation of Wajda's own artistic stamp, his creative method, which consists of an emotional approach to history, a romantic conception of human fate, a rich visual sense, and dense expression that is elaborate to the point of being baroque. In his debut *Pokolenie* he renounces the dramatic aspect of the battle against the occupation and concentrates on the inner world of people for whom discovering the truth about their stuggle was the same as discovering the truth about love. In *Kanał* he expresses disagreement with a myth long ago rooted in the consciousness of the Polish people and propounded in portrayals of the Warsaw Uprising—that the greatest meaning of life is death on the barricades. In the film *Popiół i diament* we hear for the first time in clear tones the theme of the Pole at the crossroads of history and the tragedy of his choice. Wajda expresses this theme not in abstract constructions but in a concrete reality with concrete heroes.

Wajda returns to the war experience several times. *Lotna*, in which the historical action precedes the above-mentioned trilogy, takes place in the tragic September of 1939, when Poland was overrun. Here Wajda continues to take a critical view of national tradition. Bitterness and derision toward the romanti-

cization of the Polish struggle are blended here with sober judgment, and also with understanding for the world and for the people playing out the last tragicomic act on the historical stage. In the film *Samson*, the hero, a Jewish youth, throws off his lifelong passivity and by this action steps into the struggle. Finally, there is the 1970 film *Krajobraz po bitwie*, which, however, differs sharply from Wajda's early films. The director himself characterized this difference in the following way: "It's not I who am drawing back [from the war]. It's the war. It and I are growing old together, and therefore it is more and more difficult for me to discover anything in it that was close to me."

Krajobraz po bitwie has apparently become Wajda's definitive farewell to the war. This does not mean, however, that the fundamental principles of the artistic method found in his early films have disappeared from his work, in spite of the fact that his work has developed in the most diverse directions over the course of over thirty years. The basic principles remain and, with time, develop, differentiate, and join with other motifs brought by personal and artistic experience. Some of the early motifs can be found in other contexts. Man's dramatic attitude towards history, the Pole at the crossroads of history and his tragic choice—these we can find in the film *Popióły*, in the image of the fate of Poland in the period of the Napoleonic Wars, when a new society was taking shape in the oppressive atmosphere of a defeated country divided up among three victorious powers. People living in a time of great changes are the main heroes of *Ziemia obiecana*, which portrays the precipitous, drastic, and ineluctable course of the transition from feudalism to the capitalist order. A man's situation at dramatic historical moments is also the subject of several of his later films (*Człowiek z marmuru*, *Człowiek żelaza*, *Danton*), which have met with more controversy than the preceding works.

Wajda's work reveals many forms and many layers. Over time, historical films alternate with films on contemporary subjects; films with a broad social sweep alternate with films that concentrate on intimate human experiences. Wajda is conscious of these alternations. From history he returns to contemporaneity, so as not to lose contact with the times and with his audience. After a series of war films, he made the picture *Niewinni czarodzieje*, whose young heroes search for meaning in their lives. In the film *Wszystko na sprzedaż*, following the tragic death of his friend, the actor Zbigniew Cybulski, he became absorbed in the traces a person leaves behind in the memories and hearts of friends; at the same time he told of the problems of artistic searching and creation. Wajda's attitudes on these questions are revealed again in the next film *Polowanie na muchy*, and even more emphatically in *Dyrygent*, where they are linked to the motif of faithfulness to one's work and to oneself, to one's ideals and convictions. The motif links *Dyrygent* with *Popiół i diament*. Another theme of *Dyrygent*—the inseparability of one's personal, private life from one's work life and the mutual influence of the two—is the basic problem treated in *Bez znieczulenia*. In Wajda there are many such examples of the migration of themes and motifs from one film to another. They affirm the unity of his work despite the fact that alongside great and powerful works there are lesser and weaker films. Such, for example, is Wajda's sole attempt in the genre of comedy, *Polowanie na muchy*, or the adaptation of Joseph Conrad's novel *Heart of Darkness*, which underwent a cinematic transformation. Another unifying element in Wajda's oeuvre is his faithfulness to literary and artistic sources. A significant portion of his films come from literature, while the pictorial aspect finds its inspiration in the romantic artistic tradition. In addition to such broad historical frescoes as *Popióły* or *Ziemia obiecana*, these include, for example, Stanisaw Wyspianski's drama of 1901, *Wesele*, important for its grasp of

Poland at a bleak point in the country's history. Wajda translated it to the screen in all the breadth of its meaning, with an accent on the impossibility of mutual understanding between disparate cultural milieus. The director also selected from the literary heritage works that would allow him to address man's existential questions, attitudes towards life and death. This theme resonates most fully in adaptations of two works by the writer Jarosaw Iwaszkiewicz, *Brzezina* and *Panny z Wilka*, in which the heroes are found not in history but in life, where they are threatened not by war but by old age, illness, and death, and where they must struggle only with themselves. To address such existential tension he also developed a transcription of Mikhail Bulgakov's prose work *The Master and Margarita*, filmed for television in the German Democratic Republic under the title *Pilatus und andere–ein Film für Karfreitag*.

Wajda's oeuvre, encompassing artistic triumphs and failures, forms a unified but incomplete whole. The affinity among his films is determined by a choice of themes which enables him to depict great historical syntheses, metaphors, and symbols. He is constantly drawn to those moments in the destinies of individuals and groups that are crossroads of events with tragic consequences. In his films the main motifs of human existence are interwoven—death and life, love, defeat and the tragic dilemma of having to choose, the impossibility of realizing great aspirations. All these motifs are subordinated to history, even a feeling as subjective as love.

Wajda's films have not been, and are not, uniformly received by audiences or critics. They have always provoked discussions in which enthusiasm has confronted condemnation and agreement has confronted disagreement and even hostility; despite some failures, however, Wajda's films have never been met with indifference.

—Blažena Urgošiková

WALSH, Raoul.

American. Born in New York City, 11 March 1887 (some sources say 1892). Educated Public School 93, New York; attended Seton Hall College. Married 1) Miriam Cooper, 1916 (divorced 1927); 2) Mary Edna Simpson, 1941. Sailed to Cuba on uncle's trading ship, 1903; horse wrangler in Mexico, 1903–4; worked in variety of jobs in U.S., including surgeon's assistant and undertaker, 1904–10; cowboy actor in films for Pathé Studio, New Jersey, then for Biograph, from 1910; actor and assistant to D.W Griffith, then director at Biograph, Hollywood, from 1912; director for William Fox, from 1916; lost eye in auto accident, 1928; introduced John Wayne as feature actor in *The Big Trail*, 1930; director for various studios, then retired to ranch, 1964. *Died in California, 31 December 1980.*

Films as Director:

1912   *The Life of General Villa* (co-d, role as Young Villa); *Outlaw's Revenge*

1913   *The Double Knot* (+ pr, sc, role); *The Mystery of the Hindu Image* (+ pr, sc); *The Gunman* (+ pr, sc; credit contested)

1914   *The Final Verdict* (+ pr, sc, role); *The Bowery*

1915   *The Regeneration* (+ co-sc); *Carmen* (+ pr, sc); *The Death Dice* (+ pr, sc; credit contested); *His Return* (+ pr); *The Greaser* (+ pr, sc, role); *The Fencing Master* (+ pr, sc); *A Man for All That* (+ pr, sc, role); *11:30 P.M.* (+ pr, sc); *The Buried Hand* (+ pr, sc); *The Celestial Code* (+ pr, sc); *A*

   Bad Man and Others (+ pr, sc); *Home from the Sea*; *The Lone Cowboy* (+ co-sc)

1916   *Blue Blood and Red* (+ pr, sc); *The Serpent* (+ pr, sc); *Pillars of Society*

1917   *The Honor System*; *The Silent Lie*; *The Innocent Sinner* (+ sc); *Betrayed* (+ sc); *The Conqueror* (+ sc); *This is the Life*

1918   *Pride of New York* (+ sc); *The Woman and the Law* (+ sc); *The Prussian Cur* (+ sc); *On the Jump* (+ sc); *I'll Say So*

1919   *Should a Husband Forgive* (+ sc); *Evangeline* (+ sc); *Every Mother's Son* (+ sc)

1920   *The Strongest* (+ sc); *The Deep Purple*; *From Now On*

1921   *The Oath* (+ pr, sc); *Serenade* (+ pr)

1923   *Lost and Found on a South Sea Island* (*Passions of the Sea*); *Kindred of the Dust* (+ pr, sc)

1924   *The Thief of Bagdad*

1925   *East of Suez* (+ pr); *The Spaniard* (+ co-pr); *The Wanderer* (+ co-pr)

1926   *The Lucky Lady* (+ co-pr); *The Lady of the Harem*; *What Price Glory*

1927   *The Monkey Talks* (+ pr); *The Loves of Carmen* (+ sc)

1928   *Sadie Thompson* (*Rain*) (+ co-sc, role); *The Red Dance*; *Me Gangster* (+ co-sc)

1929   *In Old Arizona* (co-d); *The Cock-eyed World* (+ co-sc); *Hot for Paris* (+ co-sc)

1930   *The Big Trail*

1931   *The Man Who Came Back*; *Women of all Nations*; *The Yellow Ticket*

1932   *Wild Girl*; *Me and My Gal*

1933   *Sailor's Luck*; *The Bowery*; *Going Hollywood*

1935   *Under Pressure*; *Baby Face Harrington*; *Every Night at Night*

1936   *Klondike Annie*; *Big Brown Eyes* (+ co-sc); *Spendthrift*

1937   *O.H.M.S.* (*You're in the Army Now*); *When Thief Meets Thief*; *Artists and Models*; *Hitting a New High*

1938   *College Swing*

1939   *St. Louis Blues*; **The Roaring Twenties**

1940   *The Dark Command* (+ pr); *They Drive by Night*

1941   **High Sierra**; *The Strawberry Blonde*; *Manpower*; *They Died With Their Boots On*

1942   *Desperate Journey*; *Gentleman Jim*

1943   *Background to Danger*; *Northern Pursuit*

1944   *Uncertain Glory*; *San Antonio* (uncredited co-d); *Salty O'Rourke*; *The Horn Blows at Midnight*

1946   *The Man I Love*

1947   *Pursued*; *Cheyenne*; *Stallion Road* (uncredited co-d)

1948   *Silver River*; *Fighter Squadron*; *One Sunday Afternoon*

1949   *Colorado Territory*; **White Heat**

1950   *The Enforcer* (uncredited co-d); *Montana* (uncredited co-d)

1951   *Along the Great Divide*; *Captain Horation Hornblower*; *Distant Drums*

1952   *The World in his Arms*; *The Lawless Breed*; *Blackbeard the Pirate*

1953   *Sea Devils*; *A Lion in the Streets*; *Gun Fury*

1954   *Saskatchewan*

1955   *Battle Cry*; *The Tall Men*

1956   *The Revolt of Mamie Stover*; *The King and Four Queens*

1957   *Band of Angels*

1958   *The Naked and the Dead*; *The Sheriff of Fractured Jaw*

1959   *A Private's Affair*

1960   *Esther and the King* (+ pr, sc)

1961   *Marines, Let's Go* (+ pr, sc)

1964   *A Distant Trumpet*

Other Films:

1910   *The Banker's Daughter* (Griffith) (role as bank clerk); *A Mother's Love* (role as young man); *Paul Revere's Ride* (Emile Cocteau) (role as Paul Revere)

1915   **Birth of a Nation** (Griffith) (role as John Wilkes Booth)

Publications:

By WALSH: books—

Each Man in His Time, New York, 1974.
Un Demi-siècle à Hollywood, Paris, 1976.

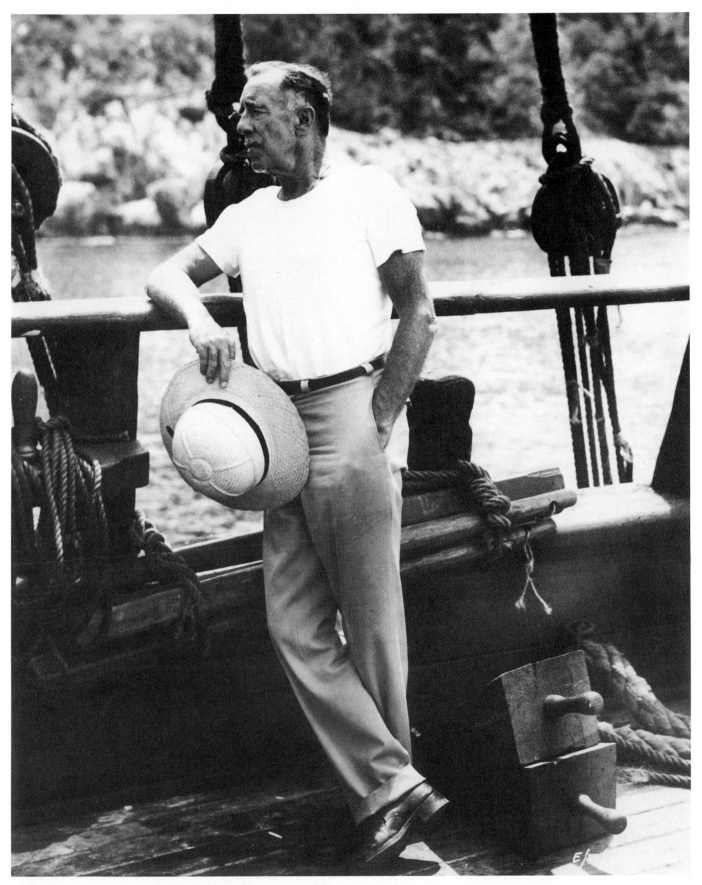

Raoul Walsh

By WALSH: articles—

Interview with Jean-Louis Noames in *Cahiers du Cinéma* (Paris), April 1964.
Interview with Guy Braucourt in *Ecran* (Paris), September/October 1972.
"Can You Ride the Horse?," an interview with J. Childs, in *Sight and Sound* (London), Winter 1972/73.
"Raoul Walsh Talks About D.W. Griffith," with P. Montgomery, in *Film Heritage* (New York), Spring 1975.
"Raoul Walsh Remembers Warners," an interview with P. McGilligan and others, in *Velvet Light Trap* (Madison), Autumn 1975.

On WALSH: books—

Brownlow, Kevin, *The Parade's Gone By . . .*, New York, 1968.
Marmin, Michael, *Raoul Walsh*, Paris, 1970.
Canham, Kingsley, *The Hollywood Professionals*, New York, 1973.
Hardy, Phil, editor, *Raoul Walsh*, Edinburgh, 1974.
Comizio, Ermanno, *Raoul Walsh*, Florence, 1982.
Giluiani, Pierre, *Raoul Walsh*, Paris, 1986.

On WALSH: articles—

"Walsh Issue" of *Présence du Cinéma* (Paris), May 1962.
"Walsh Issue" of *Cahiers du Cinéma* (Paris), April 1964.
Dienstfrey, Harris, "Hitch Your Genre to a Star," in *Film Culture* (New York), Fall 1964.
Brownlow, Kevin, "Raoul Walsh," in *Film* (London), Autumn 1967.
Lloyd, R., "Raoul Walsh," in *Brighton* (London), November, December, and January 1970.
Conley, W., "Raoul Walsh—His Silent Films," in *Silent Picture* (London), Winter 1970/71.
Fox, J., "Action All the Way," "Going Hollywood," and "Hollow Victories," in *Films and Filming* (London), June, July and August 1973.
Farber, Manny, "Raoul Walsh: 'He Used to Be a Big Shot'," in *Sight and Sound* (London), Winter 1974/75.
McNiven, R., "The Western Landscape of Raoul Walsh," in *Velvet Light Trap* (Madison), Autumn 1975.
Cocchi, J., and others, "Raoul Walsh filmographie: l'oeuvre 'parlante' 1929/1961," in *Avant-Scène du Cinéma* (Paris), April 1976.
Halliday, J., "Trying to Remember an Afternoon with Raoul Walsh," in *Framework* (Norwich, England), Spring 1981.
McNiven, R., "Raoul Walsh: 1887–1981," in *Film Comment* (New York), July/August 1981.
Bodeen, De Witt, "Raoul Walsh," in *Films in Review* (New York), April 1981.
Gallagher, John, "Raoul Walsh," in *Films in Review* (New York), October 1987.

*   *   *

Raoul Walsh's extraordinary career spanned the history of the American motion picture industry from its emergence, through its glory years in the 1930s and 1940s, and into the television era. Like his colleagues Alan Dwan, King Vidor, John Ford, and Henry King, whose careers also covered 50 years, Walsh continuously turned out popular fare, even several extraordinary hits. Movie fans have long appreciated the work of this director's director. But only when auteurists began to closely examine his films was Walsh "discovered," first by the French (in the 1960s), and then by American and British critics (in the 1970s). To these critics Walsh's action films come to represent a unified view, put forth by means of a simple, straightforward technique. Raoul Walsh is now accepted as an example of a master Hollywood craftsman who worked with a naive skill, and an animal energy, both frustrated and buoyed by the studio system.

Unfortunately, this view neglects Walsh's important place in the silent cinema. Raoul Walsh began his career with an industry still centered in and around New York City, the director's birth place. He started as an actor in Pathé westerns filmed in New Jersey, and then journeyed to California to be with D.W. Griffith's Fine Arts production company. Walsh apprenticed with Griffith as an actor, appearing in his most famous role as John Wilkes Booth in *Birth of a Nation*.

Walsh then turned to directing, first for the fledgling Fox Film Company. For the next five years (interrupted by World War I service experience) Walsh would master the craft of filmmaking, absorbing lessons which would last him more than forty years. His apprenticeship led to major assignments, and his greatest financial successes came in the 1920s. Douglas Fairbanks's *The Thief of Bagdad* was directed by Walsh at the height of that famous star's career.

Walsh took advantage of this acclaim by moving for a time to the top studio of that era, Paramount, and then signed a lucrative long-term contract with Fox. At that point Fox began expanding into a major studio. Walsh contributed to that success with hits like *What Price Glory?* and *The Cockeyed World*. The introduction of new sound-on-film technology, through its Movietone Newsreels, helped Fox's ascent. Consequently, when Fox was about to convert to all-sound features, corporate chieftains turned to Walsh to direct *In Old Arizona*, in 1929. (It was on location for that film that Walsh lost his eye.) Through its experience with newsreel shooting, only Fox at the time could film and record quality sound on location. Walsh's next film used the 70mm "Grandeur" process on a western, *The Big Trail*. The film did well but could not save the company from succumbing to the Great Depression.

Walsh's career stagnated during the 1930s. He and Fox never achieved the heights of the late 1920s. When Darryl F. Zanuck came aboard with the Twentieth Century merger in 1935, Walsh moved on, freelancing until he signed with Warners in 1939. For slightly more than a decade, Walsh functioned as a contract director at Warners, turning out two or three films a year. Walsh never established the degree of control he had over the silent film projects, but he seemed to thrive in the restrictive Warners environment. Walsh's first three films at Warners fit into that studio's mode of crime melodramas: *The Roaring Twenties*, *They Drive By Night*, and *High Sierra*. The Roaring Twenties was not a classic gangster film, like Warners' *Little Caesar* and *Public Enemy*, but a realistic portrait of the socio-economic environment in the United States after World War I. *High Sierra* looked ahead to the film noir of the 1940s. In that film the gangster became a sympathetic character trapped by forces he did not understand. During the World War II era Walsh turned to war films with a textbook example of what a war action film ought to be. Walsh continued making crime melodrama and war films in the late 1940s and early 1950s. *Battle Cry*, *The Naked and the Dead*, and *Marines, Let's Go* proved that he could adapt to changing taste within familiar genres.

Arguably Walsh's best film of the post-war era was *White Heat* made for Warners in 1949. The James Cagney character is portrayed against type: we see the gangster hiding and running, trying to escape his past and his social, economic, and psychological background. *White Heat* was the apex of Walsh's work at Warners, at once fitting into an accepted mode, and transcending the formula. *White Heat* has come to symbolize the tough Raoul Walsh action film. Certainly that same sort of style can also be seen in his westerns at Warners, *They Died With Their Boots On*, *Pursued*, and the remake of *High Sierra*, *Colorado Territory*. But there are other sides of the Walsh oeuvre, usually overlooked by critics, or at most awkwardly positioned among the action films. *The Strawberry Blonde* is a warm, affectionate, turn-of-the-century tale of small town America. *Gentleman Jim* of 1942 also swims in sentimentality. This action director certainly had a soft touch when required. Indeed, when closely examined, Walsh had the ability to adapt to many different themes and points of view.

The 1950s seemed to have passed Walsh by. Freed from the

confines of the rigid studio system Walsh's output became less interesting. But a survivor he was, completing his final feature, a cavalry film for Warners in 1964, *A Distant Trumpet*, at age 72 or 77 depending on which biographical reports one believes. By then Raoul Walsh had truly become a Hollywood legend, having reached two career peaks in a more than fifty-year career. To carefully examine the career of Raoul Walsh is to study the history of the American film in toto, for the two are nearly the same length and inexorably interwined.

—Douglas Gomery

————

WALTERS, Charles.

American. Born in Pasadena, California, 17 November 1911. Educated at the University of Southern California. Broadway debut as actor and dancer in *New Faces*, 1934; began choreographing on Broadway with *Sing Out the News*, 1938; first film appearance, 1942; began as choreographer on *DuBarry Was a Lady*, 1943; shot and staged "Brazilian Boogie" number, in *Broadway Rhythm*, 1944; directed first feature, *Good News*, for Arthur Freed, 1947. *Died in Malibu, California, 13 August 1982.*

Films as Director:

1942   *Spreadin' the Jam* (short)
1947   *Good News*
1948   *Easter Parade*
1949   *The Barkleys of Broadway*
1950   *Summer Stock* (*If You Feel Like Singing*) (+ choreo)
1951   *Three Guys Named Mike*; *Texas Carnival*
1952   *The Belle of New York*
1953   *Lili* (+ choreo, role); *Dangerous When Wet*; *Torch Song* (+ choreo, role); *Easy to Love*
1955   *The Glass Slipper*; *The Tender Trap*
1956   *Don't Go Near the Water*
1957   *High Society* (+ choreo)
1959   *Ask Any Girl*
1960   *Please Don't Eat the Daisies*
1961   *Two Loves* (*Spinster*)
1962   *Billy Rose's Jumbo*
1964   *The Unsinkable Molly Brown*
1966   *Walk, Don't Run*

Other Films:

1942   *Seven Days Leave* (Whelan) (choreo, role/dancer)
1943   *DuBarry Was a Lady* (Del Ruth) (choreo); *Presenting Lily Mars* (Taurog) (co-choreo, role/dancer); *Best Foot Forward* (Buzzell) (choreo); *Girl Crazy* (Taurog) (choreo, role/dancer)
1944   *Broadway Rhythm* (Del Ruth) (co-choreo); *Three Men in White* (Goldbeck) (choreo); ***Meet Me in St. Louis*** (Minnelli) (choreo)
1945   *Thrill of a Romance* (Thorpe) (choreo); *Her Highness and the Bellboy* (Thorpe) (choreo); *Weekend at the Waldorf* (Leonard) (choreo); *The Harvey Girls* (Sidney) (choreo); *Abbott & Costello in Hollywood* (Simon) (choreo)
1946   *Ziegfeld Follies* (Minnelli and others) (choreo Judy Garland's "An Interview" sequence)
1962   *Summer Holiday* (Yates) (choreo)

Publications:

By WALTERS: articles—

"On the Bright Side," an interview with John Cutts, in *Films and Filming* (London), August 1970.
Interview with P. Sauvage in *Positif* (Paris), November/December 1972.

On WALTERS: books—

Feuer, Jane, *The Hollywood Musical*, London, 1982.
Altman, Rick, *The American Film Musical*, Bloomington, Indiana, 1989.

On WALTERS: articles—

Sarris, Andrew, "Likable but Elusive," in *Film Culture* (New York), Spring 1963.
"Walters Issue" of *Positif* (Paris), November/December 1972.
McVay, D., "Charles Walters," in *Focus on Film* (London), no. 27, 1977.
Obituary in *Variety* (New York), 25 August 1982.
Obtiuary in *Films and Filming* (London), October 1982.

*   *   *

Before going to Hollywood Charles Walters spent about eight years on Broadway. For the most part he was a dancer, then in 1938 he choreographed his first show. A few years later Robert Altman introduced him to MGM and he began to stage routines for the screen. He worked with Gene Kelly on a number for *Du Barry Was A Lady*, then began staging musical numbers for some of Metro's leading ladies such as June Allyson, Gloria De Haven, Lucille Ball, and Judy Garland. Judy became a great friend and he worked on a number of her films, sometimes dancing with her. His first effort at directing was Lena Horne's "Brazilian Boogie" number in *Broadway Rhythm*. The following year he directed a short film called *Spreadin' the Jam*, but it was not until 1947 that he made his first feature, *Good News*.

As a dancer, movement was very much on his mind. As a director he moved not only the performers but also the camera, making full use of tracking shots, pans, and crane shots. The studio was impressed with the result and gave him *Easter Parade* with Astaire and Garland. The budget was twice that of his first film, and notable for the "Couple of Swells" number—which Walters danced with her when she did her memorable show at the Palace a few years later. *The Barkleys of Broadway* should have starred Astaire and Garland again, but Judy was ill and Ginger Rogers returned to the screen in her stead. These first three films were made under his original contract as a choreographer, and at the same fee. But by now he had proved himself, and was recognized as a director of musicals ready to follow into the footsteps of those other MGM stalwarts Stanley Donen and Vincente Minnelli. *Summer Stock* began with the pleasantly relaxed number "If You Feel Like Singing," as the camera moved through the window into the shower, and followed Judy into the dressing-room. But the rest of the filming was far from relaxed as Walters had to cope with Judy's nerves and weight problems. The final song, "Get Happy," was staged by Walters after the film was finished because they needed a good number for the climax, and Judy's loss of weight was quite noticable.

In 1951 he directed his first straight picture, *Three Guys Named Mike*, a passable romantic comedy. His least favourite film, *The Belle of New York*, was followed by his favorite, *Lili*. In this light, whimsical piece he drew a charming performance from Leslie Caron and received an Oscar nomination. *Dangerous When Wet* was one of three films he made with Esther Williams. Walters staged the lively opening number with each character taking up the song, and "Ain't Nature Grand," with Charlotte Greenwood showing great vitality in her high kicks.

Charles Walters

In the dramatic musical *Torch Song* Walters was the first to direct Joan Crawford in a color film. He got to know her well, and put a lot of the real Joan Crawford into the character of Jenny. His careful handling of Frank Sinatra in *The Tender Trap* was most opportune. After a string of dramatic roles, this film confirmed Sinatra's talent as a comedy actor. In 1957 he was reunited with Sinatra for what is arguably his best film, *High Society*. Every number in this film is significant, yet they are all completely different. One of the high spots was Crosby and Sinatra's "Well, Did You Evah," which Walters himself had introduced years before with Betty Grable. It took place in two rooms and was shot without a single cut. In the early 1960s he made *The Unsinkable Molly Brown* and *Billy Rose's Jumbo*, the latter being by far the better of the two.

Walters was a sincere director whose musicals had a style of their own. He was equally at home with a field full of dancers as he was with soloist or a group on a bandstand. He not only moved his cameras and his performers, but staged many numbers on moving vehicles—a car, a carriage, a coach, a trolley, a boat, and even a tractor. His use of color and his sudden cuts produced striking effects, and the energy and, spirit of his work contributed a great deal to the Hollywood musical.

—Colin Williams

WARHOL, Andy.

American. Born Andrew Warhola in McKeesport, Pennsylvania, 6 August 1928. Studied at Carnegie Institute of Technology, Pittsburgh, B.F.A., 1949. Illustrator for *Glamour Magazine* (New York), 1949–50; commercial artist, New York, 1950–57; independent artist, New York, 1957 until his death in 1987; first silk-screen paintings, 1962; began making films, mainly with member of his "Factory," Paul Morrissey, 1963; shot by former "Factory" regular Valerie Solanas, 1968; editor, *Inter/View* magazine, New York; made promo video for "Hello Again" by The Cars, 1984. Recipient: 6th Film Culture Award, New York, 1964; Award, Los Angeles Film Festival, 1964. *Died of cardiac arrest following routine gall bladder operation in New York, 22 February 1987.*

Films as Director and Producer:

1963   *Tarzan and Jane Regained . . . Sort Of*; *Sleep*; *Kiss*; *Andy Warhol Films Jack Smith Filming Normal Love*; *Dance Movie (Roller Skate)*; *Salome and Delilah*; *Haircut*; *Blow Job*
1964   *Empire*; *Batman Dracula*; *The End of Dawn*; *Naomi and Rufus Kiss*; *Henry Geldzahler*; *The Lester Persky Story (Soap Opera)*; *Couch*; *Shoulder*; *Mario Banana*; *Harlot*; *Taylor Mead's Ass*
1965   *Thirteen Most Beautiful Women*; *Thirteen Most Beautiful Boys*; *Fifty Fantastics*; *Fifty Personalities*; *Ivy and John*; *Screen Test I*; *Screen Test II*; *The Life of Juanita Castro*; *Drunk*; *Suicide*; *Horse*; *Vinyl*; *Bitch*; *Poor Little Rich Girl*; *Face*; *Restaurant*; *Afternoon*; *Prison*; *Space*; *Outer and Inner Space*; *Camp*; *Paul Swan*; *Hedy (Hedy the Shoplifter or The Fourteen Year Old Girl)*; *The Closet*; *Lupe*; *More Milk, Evette*
1966   *Kitchen*; *My Hustler*; *Bufferin (Gerard Malanga Reads Poetry)*; *Eating Too Fast*; *The Velvet Underground*; **Chelsea Girls**
1967   ***** (*Four Stars*); [parts of ****: *International Velvet*; *Alan and Dickin*; *Imitation of Christ*; *Coutroom*; *Gerard Has His*

Hair Removed with Nair; *Katrina Dead*; *Sausalito*; *Alan and Apple*; *Group One*; *Sunset Beach on Long Island*; *High Ashbury*; *Tiger Morse*]; *I, a Man*; *Bike Boy*; *Nude Restaurant*; *The Loves of Ondine*
1968   *Lonesome Cowboys*; *Blue Movie (Fuck)*; *Flesh* (d Morrissey, pr Warhol)
1970   *Trash* (d Morrissey, pr Warhol)
1972   *Women in Revolt* (co-d with Morrissey); *Heat* (d Morrissey, pr Warhol)
1973   *L'Amour* (co-d, pr, co-sc with Morrissey)
1974   *Andy Warhol's Frankenstein* (d Morrissey, pr Warhol); *Andy Warhol's Dracula* (d Morrissey, pr Warhol)
1977   *Andy Warhol's Bad* (d Morrissey, pr Warhol)

Publications:

By WARHOL: books—

Blue Movie, script, New York, 1970.
The Philosophy of Andy Warhol (From A to B and Back Again), New York, 1975.
The Andy Warhol Diaries, edited by Pat Hackett, New York, 1989.

By WARHOL: articles—

Interview with David Ehrenstein in *Film Culture* (New York), Spring 1966.
"Nothing to Lose," an interview with Gretchen Berg, in *Cahiers du Cinema in English* (New York), May 1967.
Numerous interviews conducted by Warhol in *Inter/View* (New York)
Interview with Warhol in *The Film Director as Superstar* by Joseph Gelmis, Garden City, New York, 1970.
Interview with Tony Rayns in *Cinema* (London), August 1970.
Interview with Ralph Pomeroy in *Afterimage* (Rochester), Autumn 1970.

On WARHOL: books—

Coplans, John, *Andy Warhol*, New York, 1970.
Crone, Rainer, *Andy Warhol*, New York, 1970.
Gidal, Peter, *Andy Warhol*, New York, 1970.
Wilcox, John, *The Autobiography and Sex Life of Andy Warhol*, New York, 1971.
Koch, Stephen, *Stargazer: Andy Warhol's World and His Films*, New York, 1973; revised edition, 1985.
Smith, Patrick S., *Andy Warhol's Art and Films*, Ann Arbor, Michigan, 1986.
Bourdon, David, *Warhol*, 1989.
Finkelstein, Nat, *Warhol: The Factory Years 1964–67*, London, 1989.
Gidal, Peter, *Materialist Film*, London, 1989.
Guiles, Fred Lawrence, *Loner at the Ball: The Life of Andy Warhol*, New York, 1989.
James, David E., *Allegories of Cinema: American Film in the Sixties*, Princeton, New Jersey, 1989.
O'Pray, Michael, *Andy Warhol: Film Factory*, London, 1989.

On WARHOL: articles—

Stoller, James, "Beyond Cinema: Notes on Some Films by Andy Warhol," in *Film Quarterly* (Berkeley), Fall 1966.
Tyler, Parker, "Dragtime and Drugtime: or Film à la Warhol," in *Evergreen Review* (New York), April 1967.
"Warhol," in *Film Culture* (New York), Summer 1967.
Lugg, Andrew, "On Andy Warhol," in *Cineaste* (New York), Winter 1967/68 and Spring 1968.
Rayns, Tony, "Andy Warhol's Films Inc.: Communication in Action," in *Cinema* (London), August 1970.
Heflin, Lee, "Notes on Seeing the Films of Andy Warhol," in *Afterimage* (Rochester), Autumn 1970.
Bourdon, David, "Warhol as Filmmaker," in *Art in America* (New York), May/June 1971.
Cipnic, D.J., "Andy Warhol: Iconographer," in *Sight and Sound* (London), Summer 1972.
Larson, R., "A Retrospective Look at the Films of D.W. Griffith and Andy Warhol," in *Film Journal* (New York), Fall/Winter 1972.
James, David E., "The Producer as Author," in *Wide Angle* (Baltimore, Maryland), vol. 7, no. 3, 1985.
Cohn, L., obituary in *Variety* (New York), 25 February 1987.

Andy Warhol

By the time he screened his first films in 1963, Andy Warhol was well on his way to becoming the most famous "pop" artist in the world, and his variations on the theme of Campbell's soup cans had already assumed archetypal significance for art in the age of mechanical reproduction. Given Warhol's penchant for the automatic and mass-produced, his movement from sculpture, canvas, and silk-screen into cinema seemed logical; and his films were as passive, as intentionally "empty," as significant of the artist's absence as his previous work or as the image he projected of himself. One of his earliest films, *Kiss*, was no more nor less than a series of people kissing in closeup, each scene running the 3-minute length of a 16mm daylight reel, complete with flash frames at both ends. But it was his 1963 film *Sleep*, a 6-hour movie comprised of variously framed shots of a naked sleeping man, which made Warhol a star on the burgeoning New York underground film scene. As though to dispel any doubts that his message was the medium, Warhol followed *Sleep* with *Empire*, an 8-hour stationary view of the Empire State Building, creating a kind of cinematic limit case for the Bazinian integrity of the shot; a film of such conceptual significance that if it did not exist it would have to be invented; yet a film which was equally unwatchable (even Warhol refused to sit through it).

During the period 1963 to 1967, Warhol made some 55 films, ranging in length from 4 minutes (*Mario Banana*, 1964) to 25 hours (****, 1967). All were informed by the passive, mechanical aesthetic of simply turning on the camera to record what was in front of it. Generally, what was recorded were the antics of Warhol's E. 47th Street "factory" coterie—a host of friends, artists, junkies, transvestities, rock singers, hustlers, fugitives, and hangers-on. Ad-libbing, "camping," being themselves (and often more than themselves) before the unblinking eye of Warhol's camera, they became "superstars"—underground celebrities epitomizing Warhol's consumer-democratic ideal of fifteen minutes' fame for everyone.

Despite Warhol's cultivated image as the "tycoon of passivity," his films display a cool, but very dry wit. *Blow Job*, for example, consisted of thirty minutes of a closeup of the expressionless face of a man being fellated outside the frame—a coyly humorous presentation of a forbidden act in an image perversely composed as a denial of pleasure (for the actor and the audience). *Mario Banana* simply presented the spectacle of transvestite Mario Montez eating bananas while in drag. *Harlot*, Warhol's first sound film, featured Mario (again eating bananas) sitting next to a woman in an evening dress, with the entirety of the virtually inaudible dialogue coming from three men positioned off-screen.

In the course of his films, Warhol seemed to be retracing the history of the cinema, from silence to sound to color (*Chelsea Girls*); from a fascination with the camera's "documentary" capabilities (*Empire*) to attempts at narrative by 1965. *Vinyl*, an adaption of Anthony Burgess's *A Clockwork Orange*, involved a single high-angle camera position tightly framing a group of mostly uninvolved factory types, with protagonist Gerard Malanga sitting in a chair, reading his lines off a script on the floor, and being tortured with dripping candle wax and a "popper" overdose. When the camera accidently fell over in the middle of the proceedings, it was quickly returned to its original position without a break in the action. *My Hustler* offered a modicum of story, audible dialogue, and two shots—one of them a repetitive pan from a gay man talking to friends on the deck of a Fire Island beach house to his hired male prostitute sunning himself on the beach. The second shot, which fails to reveal the outcome of a wager made in the first section, shows the hustler and another man taking showers and grooming themselves in a crowded bathroom (a scene which made the pages of *Life* magazine for its brief male nudity).

It was *Chelsea Girls*, however, which provided Warhol's break-through to national and international exposure. A 3-hour film in black-and-white and color, shown on two screens at once, it featured almost all the resident "superstars" in scenes supposedly taking place in various rooms of New York's Chelsea Hotel. After *Chelsea Girls'* financial success, subsequent Warhol films like *I, A Man*, *Bike Boy*, *Nude Restaurant*, and *Lonesome Cowboys* became a bit more technically astute and conventionally feature-length; and the scenes taking place in front of the camera, while maintaining their bizarre, directionless, ad-libbed quality, became more sensational in their presentation of nudity and sex. Warhol's last hurrah, *Lonesome Cowboys* was actually shot in Arizona, featuring a number of "superstars" dressing in western garb, posing and walking through a nearly non-existent story amongst western movie sets. It was the last film Warhol completed before he was seriously wounded in an assassination attempt by marginal factory character Valerie Solanas.

Warhol's shooting marked the beginning of a period of reclusiveness for the artist. Subsequent "Warhol" films were the product of cohort and collaborator Paul Morrissey, who has been credited with the increasing commercialism of the 1967 films (not to mention the decline of the factory "scene"). While Warhol lay in the hospital recovering from gunshot wounds, Morrissey completed a film on his own entitled *Flesh*—a series of episodes basically recounting a day in the life of Joe Dallesandro (who appears nude more often than not), featuring Warhol-like performances and camera work, but adding a discernible story line and even character motivations. From 1970 to 1974, Morrissey's films under Warhol's name quickly became not only more commercial, but more technically accomplished and traditionally plotted as well. After *Trash*, a kind of watershed film featuring Joe and Holly Woodlawn in a narrative comedy about some marginal New York junkies and low-lifes, Morrissey even began to tone down the nudity. *Women in Revolt* was virtually a full-fledged melodrama, but with three transvestites playing the women of the title. *Heat*, shot in Los Angeles, had Dallesandro and New York cult actress/screen personality Sylvia Miles playing out a sleazy remake of *Sunset Boulevard*. *L'Amour* took the whole Morrissey coterie to Paris.

Morrissey's big step into mainstream filmmaking came with the 1974 production of *Andy Warhol's Frankenstein*, a preposterously gory, tongue-in-cheek horror rendered in perfectly seamless, classical Hollywood style, and in a highly accomplished 3-D process. As outrageous as it was in its surrealistically bloody excess, and for all its "high-camp" attitude, the film bore almost no resemblance to the films of Andy Warhol; nor did Morrissey's *Blood for Dracula*, made at the same time, with virtually the same cast, but without 3-D. Since that time, Morrissey has pursued a career apart from Warhol's name, as an independent commercial filmmaker.

—Ed Lowry

WATERS, John.

Born Baltimore, Maryland, 1945. Educated at High School, Baltimore; claims to have been thrown out of film school. Made first short film with 8mm camera, 1964; directed first feature, *Mondo Trasho* (financed for $2000 by father), and began collaboration with Divine, 1969; arrested on eve of premiere of *Mondo Trasho* and charged with "conspiracy to commit indecent exposure,"; directed first ever scratch and sniff movie, *Polyester*, 1981; teacher at Baltimore Prison, 1980s. Lives in Baltimore.

Films as Director:

1964	*Hag in a Leather Jacket* (short)
1966	*Roman Candles* (3 shorts)
1968	*Eat Your Makeup* (short)
1969	*Mondo Trasho*
1970	*Multiple Maniacs*
1972	*Pink Flamingoes*
1974	*Female Trouble*
1977	*Desperate Living*
1981	*Polyester*
1988	*Hairspray*
1990	*Cry Baby*

Publications:

By WATERS: books—

Shock Value, New York, 1981.
Crackpot: The Obsessions of John Waters, New York, 1986.
Trash Trio: The Screenplays: Pink Flamingoes; *Desperate Living*; *Flamingoes Forever*, New York, 1988.

By WATERS: articles—

Interview in *Film Comment* (New York), June 1981.
"John Waters' Guilty Pleasures," in *Film Comment* (New York), July/August 1983.
Interview with Karen Jaehne in *Stills* (London), November/December 1983.
"Blackboard Jungle," in *American Film* (New York), April 1985.
"How Not to Make a Movie," in *American Film* (Washington D.C.), July/August 1986 and "Hard Travelling," November 1986.
Interview in *Inter/View* (New York), December 1986.
Interview in *A Critical Cinema: Interviews with Independent Filmmakers*, by Scott MacDonald, Berkeley, 1988.

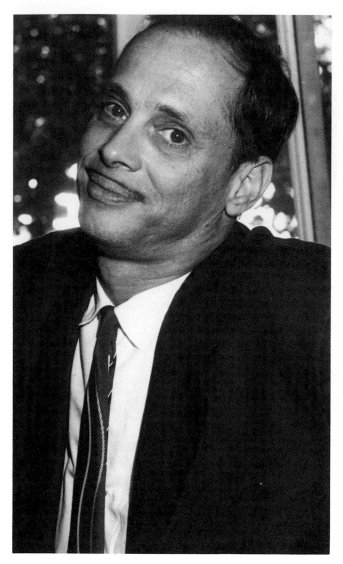

John Waters

Interview with Jonathan Ross in *Time Out* (London), 22 June 1988.
"*The National Enquirer*," in *Time Out* (London), 21 September 1988.
"John Waters: From Sleaze to Tease," an interview with K. Bail, in *Cinema Papers* (Melbourne), November 1988.
Interview with Robert Seidenberg in *Empire* (London), August 1990.

On WATERS: books—

Hoberman, Jim, and Jonathan Rosenbaum, editors, *Midnight Movies*, New York, 1983

On WATERS: articles—

Spratt, M., "John Waters: Good Bad Taste," in *Cinema Papers* (Melbourne), March 1983.

*   *   *

One of the major surprises of *Hairspray* is that, in addition to being quite charmingly benign, it exhibits a technical competence, even flair, totally unsuggested by Waters' earlier works. Between his 17-minute home movie *Hag in a Black Leather Jacket* and his semi-overground scratch 'n' sniff feature *Polyester*, the Baltimore-based Waters' films improve only insofar as increasing, though still minuscule, budgets allow for such luxuries as colour, synchronised sound and camera set-ups. His best-known early works, *Pink Flamingoes*, *Female Trou-*

ble and *Desperate Living* manage to combine the conceptually outrageous with all the technical skills of the average home movie or hardcore porno quickie. Financing his first films through shop-lifting and surrounding his habitual star—300 lb transvestite Divine—with various comically depraved and/or hideous friends who are at once funnier, grosser and more extreme than Warhol's factory folk, Waters created in *Mondo Trasho* and *Multiple Maniacs* a self-contained world of the defiantly sick, where beauty and ugliness, good and bad and restraint and excess are juggled to a surprisingly moral, endearing effect. His scatological obsessions are less Swiftian than preadolescent, and he always seems to view his movies as ratty fairytales in the Saki or Disney manner, often poking fun at the very idea of something being offensive even while going as far as is possible on screen.

Pink Flamingoes is Waters' disposable masterpiece, in which Divine and entourage—including the horrifying Edy Massey—battle with a group of more uptight degenerates—including the talented Mink Stole, who has stuck with Waters throughout his career—for the title of "World's Filthiest Person." Waters simply uses the premise as an excuse for getting as much depravity on screen as possible, winding up with an unforgettable punchline as Divine outgrosses everyone by cheerfully eating dogshit. The rest of the picture matches the tone of this classic moment, with a DIY artificial insemination, a musical rectum, a half-naked egg-sucking grandmother, a touch of hardcore gay sex, a hokey cannibal orgy that satirises *Night of the Living Dead*, plentiful ranting ("filth is my politics, filth is my life," claims Divine), bad-taste Manson jokes and a sexual act that involves killing chickens to add to the gross-out count. Typical of the film's trashiness and compounding of illegality with the distasteful is the idea of Divine shoplifting a hunk of frozen meat by slipping it into her panties and then serving it to her family for dinner, claiming that it has been "warmed in her own oven." Nevertheless, much of the funniest stuff in the movie is deadpanned, as when Divine's loyal son staunchly reacts to an insult to his mother with "Mama, nobody sends you a turd and expects to live."

Waters has claimed that "I pride myself in the fact that my work has no socially redeeming value," but underneath it all he is an All-American Boy seeing how far he can go before his parents send him up to his room, and his essays—collected in *Shock Value* and *Crackpot*—reveal that he is a witty moralist. At worst, his films are merely tedious, but at best they are life-affirming in the way that Tom Lehrer's gleefully sick songs can be. *Pink Flamingoes*, no matter how difficult it might be to sit through, is a one-of-a-kind movie, disarming and necessary in the way that *Wavelength* and *The Act of Seeing With One's Own Eyes* are, but it proved an almost impossible act to follow. *Female Trouble* and *Desperate Living* are more of the same, with Divine leading a glamorous life of crime in the former and dying beautifully in the electric chair and Mink Stole running away to join a community of murderous lesbian outcasts in the latter, only not as effectively offensive. Both films have their moments, both of humour (Divine strangling a hare krishna) and sickness (Susan Lowe reversing her sex change by snipping off her new penis with a pair of scissors), but they don't have the demented charm of *Pink Flamingoes*. *Polyester*, a nervous step towards the mainstream with less overt violence and one name actor (Tab Hunter), is a half-hearted picture, turning its back on sex and violence because Waters justifiably felt that other movies (*Ilsa, She-Wolf of the SS*, *Thundercrack!*, *Cafe Flesh*, *Appointment With Agony*) had gone further than he would care to, but finding little in its left over soap-opera plot worth guying, although it has a priceless joke about a Drive-In cinema advertising "three great Marguerite Duras hits." It was also becoming notable that Waters' mainly amateur casts had never been quite up to the demands of his acid, cleverly-turned dialogue, and that Divine—as disastrously revealed in *Lust in the Dust*—was incapable of turning a drag act into an acting performance worth building a film around.

So, after six years of relative inaction—teaching film courses in prisons and writing amusing essays for *Film Comment* and *National Lampoon*—Waters returned with *Hairspray*, a spoof teen movie which retained Divine, albeit in a digestible secondary role, and a fascination with 1960s pop ephemera from the early movies (pirated pop had always been used on Waters' soundtracks, and the plot of *Female Trouble* revolves around cha-cha heels), but which otherwise seems more like the sort of well-observed period picture one might have expected from Baltimore's other resident local auteur, Barry Levinson. Like *Diner* and *Tin Men*, *Hairspray* is about a specific phenomenon of the place and period, in this case a television dance show. Waters doesn't take his subject seriously, and enjoys the opportunity to guy more conventional nostalgia movies, but also shows that he has developed a grasp of the needs of real movie-making, including a flair for staging musical numbers that was carried over into *Cry-Baby*, a parody of 1950s juvenile delinquent movies that is very much in the vein of—and, indeed, is slightly overshadowed by—*Hairspray*. The death of Divine forced Waters to cast an actress, Susan Tyrrell, in his role in *Cry-Baby*, with effective results, and his period musicals are further distinguished by his clever and fruitful use of *kitsch* casting—Pia Zadora, Deborah Harry, Troy Donahue, Patty Hearst, Traci Lords, Iggy Pop, Sonny Bono—to replace the bizarre hangers-on who used to populate his movies. *Hairspray* and *Cry-Baby* may be less repulsive than *Pink Flamingoes*, but much of the curiously innocent heart of the earlier film is carried over, along with the major contribution of art director Vincent Periano, as is Waters' love of overheated B-movie melodrama. Currently, he runs the risk of exhausting his musical mode as definitively as he did his filth theme, but he remains an engaging, disarming and surprising talent.

—Kim Newman

WATKINS, Peter.

British. Born in Norbiton, Surrey, 29 October 1935. Educated at Christ College, Brecknockshire; studied acting at Royal Academy of Dramatic Arts, London. Served with East Surrey Regiment. Assistant producer of TV shorts and commercials for London ad agency, late 1950s; awards for amateur 16mm films led to job as assistant editor, producer and director of documentaries for the BBC, 1961; *The War Game* banned by BBC, 1965, subsequently shown theatrically; directed first fiction feature, *Privilege*, 1967; moved to Sweden, 1968, then worked in U.S., 1969–71; film biography of August Strindberg, commissioned by Swedish Film Institute, abandoned due to financial disagreements, 1981. Address: c/o Swedish Film Institute, Film House, Box 271 26, 102 52 Stockholm, Sweden.

Films as Director:

1956   *The Web* (amateur)
1958   *The Field of Red* (amateur)
1959   *Diary of an Unknown Soldier* (amateur)
1961   *The Forgotten Faces* (amateur)
1962   *Dust Fever* (amateur, unfinished)
1964   *Culloden*
1966   *The War Game*
1967   *Privilege*
1969   *Gladiatorerna* (*The Gladiators. The Peace Game*)
1971   *Punishment Park*
1974   *Edvard Munch* (released in U.S. 1976)
1975   *70-Talets Människor* (*The Seventies People*); *Fällen* (*The Trap*)
1977   *Aftenlandet* (*Evening Land*)
1987   *The Journey* (doc)

Publications:

By WATKINS: book—

The War Game, New York, 1967.

By WATKINS: articles—

Blue, James, and Michael Gill, "Peter Watkins Discusses His Suppressed Nuclear Film *The War Game*," in *Film Comment* (New York), Fall 1965.
"Left, Right, Wrong," in *Films and Filming* (London), March 1970.
"Peter Watkins Talks About the Suppression of His Work within Britain," in *Films and Filming* (London), February 1971.
"*Punishment Park* and Dissent in the West," in *Literature/Film Quarterly* (Salisbury, Maryland), no. 4, 1976.
"*Edvard Munch*: A Director's Statement," in *Literature/Film Quarterly* (Salisbury, Maryland), Winter 1977.
Interview with S. MacDonald in *Journal of the University Film Association* (Carbondale, Illinois), Summer 1982.

On WATKINS: books—

Welsh, James M., *Peter Watkins: A Guide to References and Resources*, Boston, 1986.

On WATKINS: articles—

Kawin, B.F., "Peter Watkins: Cameraman at World's End," in *Journal of Popular Film* (Washington), Summer 1973.
Gomez, Joseph A., "Peter Watkins' *Edvard Munch*," in *Film Quarterly* (Berkeley), Winter 1976/77.
Cunningham, Stuart, "Tense, Address, Tendenz: Questions of the Work of Peter Watkins," in *Quarterly Review of Film Studies* (Pleasantville, New York), Fall 1980.
Welsh, James M., "The Dystopian Cinema of Peter Watkins," in *Film Criticism* (Edinboro, Pennsylvania), Fall 1982.
Welsh, James M., "The Modern Apocalypse: *The War Game*," in *Journal of Popular Film and Television* (Bowling Green, Ohio), Spring 1983.
McDonald, J., and G. Kenny, "Peter Watkins: a Stormy Relationship with Film," in *Filmnews* (Sydney), January/February 1983.
"Peter Watkins Issue" of *Literature/Film Quarterly* (Salisbury, Maryland), October 1983.
Nolley, Ken, "Narrative Innovation in *Edvard Munch*," in *Literature/Film Quarterly* (Salisbury, Maryland), vol. 15, no. 2, 1987.
Nolley, Ken, "Making *The Journey* with Peter Watkins," in *CineAction!* (Toronto), no. 12, 1988.

*   *   *

From his early amateur days to his most recent unfinished projects, Peter Watkins has attempted to make uniquely personal films which delineate disturbing social and political dimensions. Like George Orwell, he is preoccupied with the growth of a repressive world order, the suppression of individual freedoms, and the dangerous spread of a soothing conformity. Beyond these obvious thematic concerns in his work, Watkins has also made significant contributions to the area of film as art. Almost all of his films push beyond the traditions of conventional cinema. Over the years he has developed a particular style of "documentary reconstruction" which often blends realistic and expressionistic structure to the point that his editing techniques have become a stylistic hallmark, and, since *Punishment Park*, he has managed to create sound montages equal in complexity to his visual arrangements. Finally, Watkins, in his films, in various essays, and on numerous world-wide lecture tours, has offered perceptive analysis and stinging criticism of the dangers of the media in today's world.

As early as *The Forgotten Faces*, Watkins subverted the deep-seated cinematic conventions that actors do not see the camera and that the camera always knows what will happen next and therefore is accurately focused and properly framed. On the basis of this amateur film reconstruction of the 1956 Hungarian uprising (which was actually filmed in the back streets of Canterbury), Watkins was hired by the BBC, where he further developed his techniques of reconstruction (the use of amateur actors, extensive cross-cutting, a distinctive interview method, etc.) in *Culloden* and *The War Game*. Part of the impact of the latter film, which chillingly depicts the possible effects of a nuclear attack on Great Britain, derives from what Watkins calls the film's "block structure." This structure juxtaposes the strategies of the present with the supposed "fantasy" of the future, but Watkins cleverly reverses the usual presentation of fantasy and reality. The future in Watkins's films becomes the "reality" and is graphically depicted via newsreel-like techniques. The "fantasy" element of present-day opinions about the aftermath of a nuclear attack is reinforced by the artificiality of the presentation of authority figures and by the use of printed captions and quotations.

Although *The War Game* won an Academy Award for the Best Documentay of 1966, the BBC imposed a world-wide ban on the screening of the film on television. After the suppression of *The War Game*, Watkins resigned from the BBC, and, after making *Privilege*, left England because he felt that he could no longer make films there. During this period of exile, which has lasted to the present, he made films in Sweden, Norway, Denmark, and the United States.

The most controversial of these works is *Punishment Park*, a metaphorical depiction in documentary style of the polarization of political attitudes in the U.S. during the war in Vietnam. Through experiments with improvisation and a further development of his interview style in order to elicit direct emotional response from his audience, Watkins hoped to create a film that would serve as a catalyst for the viewer to seek "a new and more meaningful solution to the present human dilemma posed within Western Society."

The intense hostility to this film in the United States has almost been matched by the hostility of Scandinavian critics to *The 70s People* and *Evening Land*, but a majority of film critics on both sides of the Atlantic seem to agree that Watkins's crowning achievement is *Edvard Munch*. This epic yet paradoxically personal work manages to provide a unique balance between the actuality of Munch's statements and the improvisations of non-professional actors expressing their own feelings and concerns. As such, the film functions on multiple levels—it delineates Munch's own fears and anxieties, provides penetrating insight into the nature of his artistic creation, captures accurately the historical nuances of that era in which he lived, and finally allows the viewers to perceive, in this intricate amalgam, problems of contemporary society which touch them directly.

Unfortunately, Peter Watkins still remains very much the outsider whose work is usually either viciously attacked ("offensive," "hysterical," and "paranoid") or simply ignored. His role in film history, however, is significant, and as Raymond Durgnat rightly notes "Watkins is as crucial as John Grierson in the development of documentary."

—Joseph A. Gomez

WATT, Harry.

Scottish. Born in Edinburgh, 18 October 1906. Educated at Edinburgh University. Joined Empire Marketing Board (EMB) under John Grierson, 1931 or 1932; joined General Post Office (GPO) film unit after EMB film unit is transferred to GPO, also directed first film, 1934; after outbreak of war, GPO film unit incorporated into newly-formed Ministry of Information, 1939; also worked for Army Film Unit, 1939–42; joined Ealing Studios, 1942; directed films in Australia, 1945–48, and in West Africa, 1951–53; producer for Granada TV, England, 1955; rejoined Ealing Studios, 1956; wrote autobiography, *Don't Look at the Camera*, 1974. Died 2 April 1987.

Films as Director:

1934	*BBC: Droitwich* (co-d); *6:30 Collection* (co-d)
1936	*Night Mail* (co-d); *The Saving of Bill Blewitt* (+ sc)
1937	*Big Money* (co-d)
1938	*North Sea*; *Health in Industry*
1939	*The First Days* (co-d)
1940	*Squadron 992*; *London Can Take It* (co-d); *The Front Line*; *Britain at Bay*
1941	*Target for Tonight* (+ sc); *Christmas Under Fire*
1942	*Dover Revisited*; *21 Miles*
1943	*Nine Men* (+ sc)
1944	*Fiddlers Three* (+ sc)
1946	*The Overlanders* (+ sc)
1949	*Eureka Stockade* (*Massacre Hill*) (+ sc)
1951	*Where No Vultures Fly* (*Ivory Hunter*)
1954	*West of Zanzibar* (+ co-sc)
1958	*People Like Maria*
1959	*The Siege of Pinchgut* (+ co-sc)
1962	*Den Hvide Hingst*
1963	*Messenger of the Mountains*

Other Films:

1937 *Four Barriers* (co-pr)

Publications:

By WATT: books—

Don't Look at the Camera, New York, 1974.

On WATT: books—

Lovell, Alan, and Jim Hillier, *Studies in Documentary*, New York, 1972.
Sussex, Elizabeth, *The Rise and Fall of British Documentary: The Story of the Film Movement Founded by John Grierson*, Berkeley, California, 1975.
Vaughan, Dai, *Portrait of an Invisible Man: The Working Life of Stewart McAllister, Film Editor*, London, 1983.
Ellis, Jack C., *The Documentary Idea*, Englewood Cliffs, New Jersey, 1989.
Swann, Paul, *The British Documentary Film Movement 1926–46*, Cambridge, 1989.

On WATT: articles—

Flaherty, Robert, article on *North Sea*, in *Sight and Sound* (London), Summer 1938.
Lacey, Bradner, article on *Where No Vultures Fly*, in *Films in Review* (New York), June/July 1952.
"Personality of the Month," in *Films and Filming* (London), June 1959.
Vaughan, Dai, article on *The Siege of Pinchgut*, in *Films and Filming* (London), October 1959.
Obituary in *Variety* (New York), 8 April 1987.

* * *

Harry Watt directing Elisabeth Welch and Sonny Hale in *Fiddlers Three*

Watt was a member of the Grierson documentary group who, during World War II, moved over into feature film directing, carrying his documentary heritage with him. He was one of the two most talented directors to come out of British documentary of the 1930s; Humphrey Jennings being the other. Whereas Jennings was the poet, Watt was the story teller.

He early demonstrated his flair for narrative, for characterization, and for humor—an ability rare among documentary filmmakers. It first became evident in *Night Mail*. Though the creative origins of that film seem to be genuinely collective, it was unquestionably Watt who drew the engaging performances—the naturalness, the bits of banter and occasional tension—from the cast of mailmen. Next, *The Saving of Bill Blewitt* offered a comic anecdote concocted by Watt about a Cornwall fisherman and the Post Office Savings Bank. In *North Sea*, which followed, Watt's attraction to the dramatic is given full reign. Though a short like the others, the situation—of a disabled fishing trawler awash in high seas, loved ones waiting at home, efforts to aid the stricken ship—has all of the ingredients for a feature. *Squadron 992* continued Watt's feeling for narrative, humor, and excitement into the beginning of the war.

But it was *Target for Tonight* that emerged as Watt's major contribution: it became the prototype for the British wartime semi-documentary feature. This form involved a real situation, though it might be composite and representative rather than actual; in this case it was a typical British bombing raid into Germany. The nonactors, here RAF airmen, were given some characterization and dialogue. The exposition, conflict, climax, and denouement follow narrative/dramatic convention. (The bomber on which the film concentrates is hit with flack and the main question becomes whether its crew will return safely.) The semi-documentary was, in other words, half fact and half fiction.

As one can infer from his charming autobiography, *Don't Look at the Camera*, Watt had always thought that filmmaking was really the making of fiction feature films for the theaters. Since the semi-documentary form was picked up and developed by the commercial studios as well as by the government Crown Film Unit, when Watt moved over to Ealing Studios in 1942 he continued along the semi-documentary lines he had begun. Of his features made for Ealing, *The Overlanders* is the most successful, certainly in critical and probably in commercial terms as well. It was shot in Australia and chonicles a cattle drive across the awesome Outback occasioned by the fear of Japanese invasion after Japan's entry into World War II. Though actors play the roles, it is a recreation of an actual occurrence. Watt once said of himself as a filmmaker: "I am a dramatic reporter."

—Jack C. Ellis

WEBER, Lois.

American. Born in Allegheny City, Pennsylvania, 1882. Married Phillips Smalley, 1906, (divorced 1922). Touring concert pianist, then Church Home Missionary in Pittsburgh, 1890s; actress in touring melodrama *Why Girls Leave Home* for company managed by future husband Smalley, 1905; writer and director (then actor) for Gaumont Talking Pictures, from 1908; teamed up with Smalley, moved to Reliance, then Rex, working for Edwin S. Porter; the Smalleys (as they were known) took over Rex, a member of the Universal conglomerate, following Porter's departure, 1912; joined Hobart Bosworth's company, 1914; Universal funded private studio for Weber at 4634 Sunset Boulevard, 1915; founded own studio, 1917; signed contract with Famous Players-Lasky for $50 000 per picture and a percentage of profits, 1920; dropped by company after three unprofitable films, 1921, subsequently lost company, divorced husband and suffered nervous collapse; briefly resumed directing, late 1920s; script-doctor for Universal, 1930s. *Died in Hollywood, 13 November 1939.*

Films as Director:
(partial list—directed between 200 and 400 films)

1912   *The Troubadour's Triumph*
1913   *The Eyes of God*; *The Jew's Christmas* (co-d, sc, role); *The Female of the Species* (+ role)
1914   *The Merchant of Venice* (co-d, role as Portia); *Traitor*; *Like Most Wives*; *Hypocrites!* (+ sc); *False Colors* (co-d, co-sc, role); *It's No Laughing Matter* (+ sc); *A Fool and His Money* (+ role); *Behind the Veil* (co-d, sc, role)
1915   *Sunshine Molly* (co-d, role, sc); *Scandal* (co-d, sc, role)
1916   *Discontent* (short); *Hop, the Devil's Brew* (co-d, sc, role); *Where Are My Children?* (co-d, sc); *The French Downstairs*; *Alone in the World* (short); *The People vs. John Doe* (+ role); *The Rock of Riches* (short); *John Needham's Double*; *Saving the Family Name* (co-d, role); *Shoes*; *The Dumb Girl of Portici* (co-d); *The Flirt* (co-d)
1917   *The Hand That Rocks the Cradle* (co-d, pr, role); *Even As You and I*; *The Mysterious Mrs. M*; *The Price of a Good Time*; *The Man Who Dared God*; *There's No Place Like Home*; *For Husbands Only* (+ pr)
1918   *The Doctor and the Woman*; *Borrowed Clothes*
1919   *When a Girl Loves*; *Mary Regan*; *Midnight Romance* (+ sc); *Scandal Mongers*; *Home*; *Forbidden*
1921   *Too Wise Wives* (+ pr, sc); *What's Worth While?* (+ pr); *To Please One Woman* (+ sc); *The Blot* (+ pr, sc); *What Do Men Want?* (+ pr, sc)
1923   *A Chapter in Her Life* (+ co-sc)
1926   *The Marriage Clause* (+ sc)
1927   *Sensation Seekers* (+ sc); *The Angel of Broadway*
1934   *White Heat*

Other Films:

1915   *A Cigarette, That's All* (sc)

Publications:

By WEBER: article—

Interview with Aline Carter in *Motion Picture Magazine* (New York), March 1921.

On WEBER: book—

Heck-Rabi, Louise, *Women Filmmakers: A Critical Reception*, Metuchen, New Jersey, 1984.

On WEBER: articles—

Pyros, J., "Notes on Women Directors," in *Take One* (Montreal), November/December 1970.

Koszarski, Richard, "The Years Have Not Been Kind to Lois Weber," in *Women and the Cinema*, edited by Karyn Kay and Gerald Peary, New York, 1977.
"Lois Weber—whose role is it anyway?." in *Monthly Film Bulletin* (London), May 1982.
Ostria, V., "Lois Weber, cette inconnue," in *Cahiers du Cinéma* (Paris), April 1985.
"Lois Weber Issue" of *Film History* (Philadelphia), vol. 1, no. 4, 1987.

*   *   *

Lois Weber was a unique silent film director. Not only was she a woman and certainly the most important female director the American film industry has known, but, unlike many of her colleagues up to the present, her work was regarded in its day as equal to, if not a little better than that of most male directors. She was a committed filmmaker in an era when commitment was virtually unknown, a filmmaker who was not afraid to make features with subject matter in which she devoutly believed, subjects as varied as Christian Science (*Jewel* and *A Chapter in Her Life*) or birth control (*Where Are My Children*). *Hypocrites* was an indictment of hypocrisy and corruption in big business, politics, and religion, while *The People vs. John Doe* opposed capital punishment. At the same time, Lois Weber was quite capable of handling with ease a major spectacular feature, such as the historical drama, *The Dumb Girl of Portici*, which introduced Anna Pavlova to the screen.

During the teens, Lois Weber was under contract to Universal where she appears to have been given total freedom as to the subject matter of her films, all of which where among the studio's biggest moneymakers and highly regarded by the critics of the day. (The Weber films, however, did run into censorship problems and the director was the subject of a vicious attack in a 1918 issue of *Theatre Magazine* over the "indecent and suggestive" nature of her titles.) Eventually the director felt the urge to move on to independent production, and during 1920 and 1921 she released a series of highly personal intimate dramas dealing with married life and the types of problems which beset ordinary people. None of these films was particularly well received by the critics, who unanimously declared them dull, while the public displayed an equal lack of enthusiasm. Nonetheless, features such as *Too Wise Wives* and *The Blot* demonstrate Weber at her directorial best. In the former she presents a study of two married couples. Not very much happens, but in her characterizations and attention to detail (something for which Weber was always noted), the director is as contemporary as a Robert Altman or an Ingmar Bergman. *The Blot* is concerned with "genteel poverty" and is marked by the underplaying of its principals—Claire Windsor and Louis Calhern—and an enigmatic ending which leaves the viewer uninformed as to the characters' future, an ending unlike any in the entire history of the American silent film. These films, as with virtually all of the director's work, were also written by Lois Weber.

Through the end of her independent productions in 1921, Lois Weber worked in association with her husband Phillips Smalley, who usually received credit as associate or advisory director. After the two were divorced, Lois Weber's career went to pieces. She directed one or two minor program features together with one talkie, but none equalled her work from the teens and early twenties. She was a liberated filmmaker who seemed lost without companionship both at home and in the studio of a husband. Her career and life is in many ways as enigmatic as the ending of *The Blot*.

—Anthony Slide

Lois Weber (center)

WEIR, Peter.

Australian. Born Peter Lindsay Weir in Sydney, 8 August 1944. Educated in Arts/Law course at Sydney University. Married Wendy Stiles, 1966, two children. Worked for family real estate business, then joined TV Station ATN 7, Sydney, 1967; assistant cameraman and production assistant, Commonwealth Film Unit (now Film Australia), 1969; signed multi-film contract with Warner bros., 1980. Recipient: Grand Prix, Australian Film Institute, for *Homesdale*, 1971; Neville Wran Award for excellence in filmmaking, 1988.

Films as Director and Scriptwriter:

1967   *Count Vim's Last Exercise* (short)
1968   *The Life and Times of the Reverend Buck Shotte* (short)
1970   "Michael" episode of *Three to Go*
1971   *Homesdale* (short)
1972   *Incredible Floridas* (short)
1973   *Whatever Happened to Green Valley?* (short)
1974   *The Cars That Ate Paris* (*The Cars That Ate People*)
1975   *Picnic at Hanging Rock* (d only)
1977   **The Last Wave**
1978   *The Plumber* (for TV)
1981   *Gallipoli*
1982   *The Year of Living Dangerously*
1985   **Witness** (d only)
1986   *The Mosquito Coast* (d only)
1989   *Dead Poets' Society*
1990   *Green Card* (+ pr)

Publications:

By WEIR: articles—

Interview with D. Castell in *Films Illustrated* (London), November 1976.
Interviews with H. Béhar in *Image et Son* (Paris), January and February 1978.
Interview with P. Childs in *Millimeter* (New York), March 1979.
Interview with Brian McFarlane and T. Ryan in *Cinema Papers* (Melbourne), September/October 1981.
Interview with Michael Dempsey in *Film Quarterly* (Berkeley), Summer 1982.
Interview with M. Bygrave in *Stills* (London), May 1985.
"Dialogue on Film: Peter Weir," in *American Film* (Washington D.C.), March 1986.
Interview with Patrick McGilligan in *Film Comment* (New York), November/December 1986.
Interview with C. Viviani and others in *Positif* (Paris), April 1987.
Interview in *Cinema Papers* (Melbourne), August 1990.

On WEIR: books—

Tulloch, John, *Australian Cinema: Industry, Narrative, and Meaning*, Sydney, 1982.

Peter Weir: *Picnic at Hanging Rock*

Peeters, Theo, *Peter Weir and His Films: A Critical Biography*, Melbourne, 1983.

Mathews, Sue, *35mm Dreams: Conversations with Five Directors About the Australian Film Revival*, Ringwood, Victoria, 1984.

Hall, Sandra, *Critical Business: The New Australian Cinema in Review*, Adelaide, 1985.

Moran, Albert, and Tom O'Regan, editors, *An Australian Film Reader*, Sydney, 1985.

McFarlane, Brian, *Australian Cinema 1970–1985*, London, 1987.

On WEIR: articles—

Nicholls, R., "Peter Weir," in *Lumière* (Melbourne), March 1973.

Brennan, R., "Peter Weir," in *Cinema Papers* (Melbourne), January 1974.

McFarlane, Brian, "The Films of Peter Weir," in *Cinema Papers* (Melbourne), April/May 1980.

Magill, M., "Peter Weir," in *Films in Review* (New York), October 1981.

Poulle, F., "Bienvenu au héros conradien," in *Jeune Cinéma* (Paris), October 1983.

Sesti, M., "Peter Weir e il vuoto della ragione," in *Bianco e Nero* (Rome), October/December 1985.

Film Quarterly (Berkeley), Winter 1990/91.

*   *   *

If, as Yugoslav director Dusan Makavajev contends, "Australia is Switzerland, but it wants to be Texas," then it's to the Swiss side that Peter Weir belongs. Even his apprentice shorts show international concerns and a fantasy alien to Australia's documentary-based cinema. *Incredible Floridas* is a *hommage* to Rimbaud, *Michael* a vision of a future Australia gripped by revolution, while the macabre *Homesdale* evokes evil in the unlikely setting of an isolated retirement home.

Weir dropped out of university to travel to Europe, an experience that profoundly affected him: "It struck me very strongly that I was a European, that this was where we had come from and where I belonged." An ancient sculpture found on a Tunisian beach prompted *The Last Wave*, and he conceived *The Cars That Ate Paris* when a French autoroute detour triggered the idea of a tiny village where, he surmised, anything might happen—including local hoodlums customising cars into killing machines.

The absurdist vision of *The Cars That Ate Paris* puzzled Australian audiences but interested Hollywood. Roger Corman gave the film a small US release while also borrowing some its concepts for Bartel's *Death Race 2000*. Universal acclaim, however, greeted *Picnic at Hanging Rock*, a Victorian fantasy, drowsy, cryptic and sensual. Weir filmed Joan Lindsay's novel with such skill that most audiences believe the disappearance of three schoolgirls on a rocky monolith on St. Valentine's Day, 1900 to be based on fact.

Weir chose Richard Chamberlain to star in *The Last Wave* as a lawyer uncovering aboriginal cults which foretell the world's end in a new Flood, but Australian audiences greeted the film's obscure theme and American star with suspicion. In reaction, Weir made *The Plumber*, a TV feature recognizable as his work only in the faintly surrealistic premise of an unsummoned tradesman invading a baffled housewife's cosy suburban environment.

With *Gallipoli*, which he calls his "graduation film," Weir shook off his reputation both as an occult specialist and a director of essentially local concerns. Though set against Australia's first military adventure, the disastrous 1916 Dardenelles campaign, its scale, style and outlook, all broadly international, won *Gallipoli* mass American release, and both director and star Mel Gibson were given Hollywood contracts.

Weir's first fully-funded studio project, *The Year of Living Dangerously*, marked him as an artist capable of handling both big stars and bigger emergencies. When threats of violence from Muslim extremists drove the production out of Manila, he recreated Djakarta in Sydney suburbia. The film turned Mel Gibson into an international romantic lead, and also remade another career when Weir, unsatisfied with the actor playing dwarf Chinese cameraman Billy Kwan, recast the role with Linda Hunt, who delivered an Oscar-winning performance.

When plans to film *The Mosquito Coast* with Jack Nicholson collapsed, Weir stepped at short notice into a thriller with Harrison Ford as a city cop finding affinities with the Amish religious fundamentalists who hide him. *Witness*, an unexpected hit, decisively freed Ford from his Indiana Jones image, and the revived *The Mosquito Coast* starred not Nicholson but Ford as Paul Theroux's dizzy technocrat dragging his family to South America in a doomed celebration of American mechanical genius. The film's relative failure in no way harmed Weir's reputation as a director who could change careers and remake images, and Robin Williams entrusted him with his first major dramatic role in *Dead Poets Society* as the 1950s schoolteacher bucking a version of McCarthyism. Its critical and financial success powered Weir into *Green Card*, his first original screenplay about an emigre musician marrying an American girl to get a work permit. The story attracted Gérard Depardieu, anxious to penetrate the English-language market. "I have the impression of having discovered a brother," the actor said, "Like with Truffaut . . . "—evidence that Weir, while mastering Hollywood, has not lost touch with his early European concerns.

—John Baxter.

———

WEISS, Jiri.

Czechoslovakian. Born in Prague, 29 March 1913. Educated in law, Charles University, Prague. Advertising writer, also made first film, 1935; director for Barrandov Studios, Prague, 1936; following Nazi invasion, escaped to London, 1939; worked with British Documentarists for Crown Film Unit, World War II; returned to Prague, 1945; teacher at film school, West Berlin, 1963; at Venice Festival at time of Soviet invasion of Czechoslovakia, sought political asylum in Italy, 1968. Recipient: Artist of Merit, Czechoslovakia.

Films as Director:

1935   *People in the Sun*
1936   *Give Us Wings*
1937   *Song of a Sad Country*
1938   *Journey from the Shadows*
1939   *The Rape of Czechoslovakia*
1941   *Eternal Prague*
1943   *Before the Raid*
1945   *Věrni zustaneme* (*Interim Balance*) (+ sc)
1947   *Uloupená hranice* (*The Stolen Frontier*) (+ co-sc)
1948   *Dravci* (*Wild Beasts. Beast of Prey*) (+ co-sc); *Ves v pohraniči* (*The Village on the Frontier*)
1949   *Píseň o sletu I, II* (*Song of the Meet, I and II. High Flies the Hawk, I and II*)
1950   *Vstanou noví bojovníci* (*New Warriors Will Arise*); *Poslední výstřel* (*The Last Shot*)
1953   *Muj přítel Fabián* (*My Friend Fabian. My Friend the Gypsy*) (+ co-sc)
1954   *Punt'a a čtyřlístek* (*Punta and the Four-Leaf Clover. Doggy and the Four*) (+ co-sc)

Jiří Weiss

1956 *Hra o život (Life at Stake. Life Was at Stake)* (+ co-sc)
1957 *Vlčí jáma (Wolf Trap)* (+ co-sc)
1959 *Taková láska (Appassionata. That Kind of Love)* (+ co-sc)
1960 *Romeo, Julie a tma (Romeo, Juliet and the Darkness. Sweet Light in the Dark Window)* (+ co-sc)
1962 *Zbabělec (Coward)* (+ co-sc)
1963 *Zlaté kapradí (The Golden Fern)* (+ co-sc)
1965 *Třicet jedna ve stínu (Ninety in the Shade)* (+ co-sc)
1966 *Vražda po našem (Murder Czech Style)* (+ co-sc)
1968 *Prípad pro Selwyn (Justice for Selwyn)* (for Czech TV)
1990 *Martha und Ich* (+ sc)

Publications:

By WEISS: articles—

"Czech Cinema Has Arrived," in *Films and Filming* (London), March 1959.
"Mixing It," in *Films and Filming* (London), June 1965.
Interview in *Closely Watched Films* by Antonin Liehm, White Plains, New York, 1974.

On WEISS: books—

Boček, Jaroslav, *Modern Czechoslovak Film*, Prague, 1965.
Pitera, Zbigniew, *Leksykon rezyserow filmowych*, Warsaw, 1978.
Liehm, Mira, and Antonín, *The Most Important Art: East European Film after 1945*, Berkeley, 1977.
Habova, Milada, and Jitka Vysekalova, editors, *Czechoslovak Cinema*, Prague, 1982.

* * *

Jiří Weiss is one of the most significant and certainly most interesting Czech directors of the last 50 years. He studied at Jura and had worked as a journalist before making his first film in 1934, a documentary which received a prize at Venice that year. Until the outbreak of war he continued to work on documentaries.

In 1939 Weiss fled the Nazis to England, befriended an English documentarist and made several films including *Before the Raid*. Later, as a film specialist, he took part in the battles of the Czech exile army. He returned to his homeland in 1945. His first theatrical film, *Uloupená hranice*, dealt with the Munich accord of 1938, shortly before the fascist occupation of his country. A subsequent film, *Vstanou noví bojovníci*, depicted the establishment of the worker's movement in Czechoslovakia, and brought the director not only official recognition at home but also attention abroad. Afterward Weiss made films dealing with contemporary problems and people's everyday life. In the 1953 *My Friend Fabian* he described how the gypsies adjusted, with many difficulties, to a new life in socialist Czechoslovakia. *Hra o život* appeared in 1956, a critical film about the destruction of a bourgeois family in the period of the German occupation. *Taková láska*, a dramatic psychological work, displayed the director's ability to develop richly human characterization.

Vlčí jama impressed further through the deep psychological treatment of the characters and the careful attention to cultural surroundings by which he delineated the *zeitgeist*, the atmosphere and the milieu of the petit bourgeoisie prior to World War I. An honorable mayor of a small city, who feels a devotion for his ageing wife, nevertheless falls in love with a young girl who lives in the same house.

This film revealed the full range of Jiří Weiss's style. It is based in a solid critical realism, rooted in the epic novels of the 19th century. This approach sets out fully-realized and many-sided human figures within an accurately-described milieu. The cinema of Weiss draws on Czech cultural tradition, and at the same time strives toward broader European dimensions. In this way his works attain to a certain cosmopolitanism.

On the one hand, Weiss was strongly influenced by neorealism as were all the other filmmakers of his generation. Although not so pathetically inclined as, for example, Andrzej Wajda, Weiss showed in his masterpiece *Romeo, Julie a tma* the influences of the neorealist aesthetic, especially in the case of the theme, again broadly European, of the tragic fate of two young lovers in Prague in 1942. The Jewish schoolgirl Hanna is hidden by young Pavel, a tender love develops, and is cut short by Hanna's death. Weiss had created a tragic and poetic work, without filmic innovation, but nevertheless a serious, noble film.

In the 1960s Weiss made *Zlaté kapradí*, *Trícet jedna ve stínu*, and *Vražda po našem*, which attained a high standard in terms of craft, but broke no new ground formally or thematically. Living since 1968 in the West, he has made the occasional film for television.

—Maria Racheva

WELLES, Orson.

American. Born in Kenosha, Wisconsin, 6 May 1916. Educated at Todd School in Woodstock, Illinois, 1926–31. Married 1) Virginia Nicholson, 1934 (divorced 1939), one son; 2) Rita Hayworth, 1943 (divorced 1947), one daughter; 3) Paola Mori, 1955, one daughter. Actor and director at the Gate Theatre, Dublin, 1931–34; debut on Broadway with Katherine Cornell's road company, also co-directed first film, 1934; collaborated with John Houseman for the Phoenix Theatre Group, 1935, later producer and director for Federal Theater Project; co-founder, with Houseman, Mercury Theatre Group, 1937; moved into radio with "Mercury Theatre on the Air," 1938, including famous dramatization of H.G. Wells's *War of the Worlds*, Halloween, 1938; given contract by RKO, 1939; directed feature debut, *Citizen Kane*, 1941; began documentary *It's All True*, 1942, then Welles and his staff were removed from RKO; directed *The Lady from Shanghai* for Columbia Studios, 1947; directed *Macbeth* for Republic Pictures, 1948; moved to Europe, 1949; completed only one more film in U.S., *Touch of Evil*, 1958; appeared in advertisements, and continued to act, from 1960s. Recipient: 20th Anniversary Tribute, Cannes Festival, 1966; Honorary Oscar, for "Superlative artistry and versatility in the creation of motion pictures," 1970; Life Achievement Award, American Film Institute, 1975; Fellowship of the British Film Institute, 1983. *Died in Hollywood, 10 October 1985.*

Films as Director:

1934 *The Hearts of Age* (16mm short) (co-d)
1938 *Too Much Johnson* (+ co-pr, sc) (unedited, not shown publicly, destroyed in 1970 fire)
1941 *Citizen Kane* (+ pr, co-sc, role as Charles Foster Kane)
1942 *The Magnificent Ambersons* (+ pr, sc); *It's All True* (+ pr, co-sc) (not completed and never shown)
1943 *Journey into Fear* (co-d, uncredited, pr, co-sc, role as Colonel Haki)
1946 *The Stranger* (+ co-sc, uncredited, role as Franz Kindler alias Professor Charles Rankin)
1948 *The Lady from Shanghai* (+ sc, role as Michael O'Hara) (produced in 1946); *Macbeth* (+ pr, sc, co-costumes, role as Macbeth)
1952 *Othello* (+ pr, sc, role as Othello and narration)
1955 *Mr. Arkadin (Confidential Report)* (+ sc, art d, costumes, role as Gregory Arkadin and narration); *Don Quixote* (+ co-pr, sc, asst ph, role as himself and narration) (not completed)

Orson Welles

1958 *Touch of Evil* (+ sc, role as Hank Quinlan)
1962 *Le Procès* (*The Trial*) (+ sc, role as Hastler and narration)
1966 *Chimes at Midnight* (Falstaff) (+ sc, costumes, role as Sir John Falstaff)
1968 *The Immortal Story* (+ sc, role as Mr. Clay)
1970 *The Deep* (+ sc, role as Russ Brewer)
1972 *The Other Side of the Wind* (+ sc) (filming begun in 1972, uncompleted)
1975 *F for Fake* (+ sc)

Other Films:

1937 *The Spanish Earth* (Ivens) (original narration)
1940 *Swiss Family Robinson* (Ludwig) (off-screen narration)
1943 *Jane Eyre* (R. Stevenson) (role as Edward Rochester)
1944 *Follow the Boys* (Sutherland) (revue appearance with Marlene Dietrich)
1945 *Tomorrow is Forever* (Pichel) (role as John McDonald)
1946 *Duel in the Sun* (Vidor) (off-screen narration)
1947 *Black Magic* (Ratoff) (role as Cagliostro)
1948 *Prince of Foxes* (role as Cesare Borgia)
1949 *The Third Man* (Reed) (role as Harry Lime)
1950 *The Black Rose* (Hathaway) (role as General Bayan)
1951 *Return to Glennascaul* (Edwards) (role as himself)
1953 *Trent's Last Case* (Wilcox) (role as Sigsbee Manderson); *Si Versailles m'était conté* (Guitry) (role as Benjamin Franklin); *L'uomo, la bestia e la virtu* (Steno) (role as the beast)
1954 *Napoléon* (Guitry) (role as Hudson Lowe); "Lord Mountdrago" segment of *Three Cases of Murder* (O'Ferrall) (role as Lord Mountdrago)
1955 *Trouble in the Glen* (Wilcox) (role as Samin Cejador y Mengues); *Out of Darkness* (documentary) (narrator)
1956 *Moby Dick* (Huston) (role as Father Mapple)
1957 *Pay the Devil* (Arnold) (role as Virgil Renckler); *The Long Hot Summer* (Ritt) (role as Will Varner)
1958 *The Roots of Heaven* (Huston) (role as Cy Sedgwick); *Les Seigneurs de la forêt* (Sielman and Brandt) (off-screen narration); *The Vikings* (Fleischer) (narration)
1959 *David e Golia* (Pottier and Baldi) (role as Saul); *Compulsion* (Fleischer) (role as Jonathan Wilk); *Ferry to Hong Kong* (Gilbert) (role as Captain Hart); *High Journey* (Baylis) (off-screen narration); *South Sea Adventure* (Dudley) (off-screen narration)
1960 *Austerlitz* (Gance) (role as Fulton); *Crack in the Mirror* (Fleischer) (role as Hagolin/Lamorcière); *I tartari* (Thorpe) (role as Barundai)
1961 *Lafayette* (Dréville) (role as Benjamin Franklin); *King of Kings* (Ray) (off-screen narration); *Désordre* (short) (role)
1962 *Der grosse Atlantik* (documentary) (narrator)
1963 *The V.I.P.s* (Asquith) (role as Max Buda); *Rogopag* (Pasolini) (role as the film director)
1964 *L'Echiquier de Dieu* (*La Fabuleuse Aventure de Marco Polo*) (de la Patellière) (role as Ackermann); *The Finest Hours* (Baylis) (narrator)
1965 *The Island of Treasure* (J. Franco) (role); *A King's Story* (Booth) (narrator)
1966 *Is Paris Burning?* (Clément) (role); *A Man for All Seasons* (Zinnemann) (role as Cardinal Wolsey)
1967 *Casino royale* (Huston and others) (role); *The Sailor from Gibralter* (Richardson) (role); *I'll Never Forget Whatshisname* (Winner) (role)
1968 *Oedipus the King* (Saville) (role as Tiresias); *Kampf um Rom* (role as Emperor Justinian); *The Southern Star* (Hayers) (role)
1969 *Tepepa* (role); *Barbed Water* (documentary) (narrator); *Una su 13* (role); *Michael the Brave* (role); *House of Cards* (Guillermin) (role)
1970 *Catch-22* (Nichols) (role as General Dweedle); *Battle of Neretva* (Bulajia) (role); *Start the Revolution without Me* (Yorkin) (narrator); *The Kremlin Letter* (Huston) (role); *Waterloo* (Bondarchuk) (role as King Louis XVIII)

1971 *Directed by John Ford* (Bogdanovich) (narrator); *Sentinels of Silence* (narrator); *A Safe Place* (Jaglom) (role)
1972 *La Decade prodigieuse* (role); *Malpertius* (role); *I racconti di Canterbury* (Pasolini) (role); *Treasure Island* (Hough) (role as Long John Silver); *Get to Know Your Rabbit* (De Palma) (role)
1973 *Necromancy* (Gordon) (role)
1975 *Bugs Bunny Superstar* (Jones) (narrator)
1976 *Challenge of Greatness* (documentary) (narrator); *Voyage of the Damned* (Rosenberg) (role)
1977 *It Happened One Christmas* (Thomas) (for TV) (role)
1979 *The Late Great Planet Earth* (on-camera narrator); *The Muppet Movie* (Frawley) (role as J.P. Morgan); *Tesla* (role as Yug)
1981 *Butterfly* (Cimber) (role as the judge); *The Man Who Saw Tomorrow* (Guenette) (role)
1984 *Where is Parsifal?* (Helman) (role); *Almonds and Raisins* (Karel) (narrator)
1985 *Genocide* (Schwartzman) (narrator)
1987 *Someone to Love* (Jaglom) (role)

Publications:

By WELLES: books—

Everybody's Shakespeare, New York, 1933; revised as *The Mercury Shakespeare*, 1939.
The Trial (script), New York, 1970.
The Films of Orson Welles, by Charles Higham, Berkeley, 1970.
Citizen Kane, script, in *The Citizen Kane Book* by Pauline Kael, New York, 1971.
This Is Orson Welles, with Peter Bogdanovich, New York, 1972.
Touch of Evil, edited by Terry Comito, New Brunswick, New Jersey, 1985.
The Big Brass Ring: An Original Screenplay, with Oja Kodar, Santa Barbara, California, 1987.
Chimes at Midnight, New Brunswick, New Jersey, 1988.

By WELLES: articles—

Preface to *He That Plays the King* by Kenneth Tynan, New York, 1950.
Interview with Francis Koval in *Sight and Sound* (London), December 1950.
"The Third Audience," in *Sight and Sound* (London), January/March 1954.
"For a Universal Cinema," in *Film Culture* (New York), January 1955.
Interviews with André Bazin and Charles Bitsch in *Cahiers du Cinéma* (Paris), June and September 1958.
"Conversation at Oxford," with Derrick Griggs, in *Sight and Sound* (London), Spring 1960.
"Citizen Kane," in *Avant-Scène du Cinéma* (Paris), January 1962.
"Le Procès," in *Avant-Scène du Cinéma* (Paris), February 1963.
Interview with Everett Sloane in *Film* (London), no. 37, 1965.
"A Trip to Don Quixoteland: Conversations with Orson Welles," with Juan Cobos and others, in *Cahiers du Cinema in English* (New York), June 1966.
Interview with Kenneth Tynan in *Playboy* (Chicago), March 1967.
"First Person Singular," with Joseph McBride, in *Sight and Sound* (London), Winter 1971/72.
"Heart of Darkness," in *Film Comment* (New York), November/December 1972.

On WELLES: books—

Fowler, Roy A., *Orson Welles, A First Biography*, London, 1946.
Bazin, André, *Orson Welles*, Paris, 1950.
MacLiammóir, Micheál, *Put Money in Thy Purse*, London, 1952.
Noble, Peter, *The Fabulous Orson Welles*, London, 1956.
Bogdanovich, Peter, *The Cinema of Orson Welles*, New York, 1961.
Cowie, Peter, *The Cinema of Orson Welles*, London, 1965.
Bessy, Maurice, *Orson Welles*, New York, 1971.
Higham, Charles, *The Films of Orson Welles*, Berkeley, 1971.
Kael, Pauline, *The Citizen Kane Book*, New York, 1971.
Houseman, John, *Run Through: A Memoir*, New York, 1972.
McBride, Joseph, *Orson Welles*, London, 1972.
Bazin, André, *Orson Welles: A Critical View*, translated by Jonathan Rosenbaum, New York, 1978.

Naremore, J., *The Magic World of Orson Welles*, New York, 1978.

Valentinetti, Claudio M., *Orson Welles*, Florence, 1981.

Bergala, Alain, and Jean Narboni, editors, *Orson Welles*, Paris, 1982.

Andrew, Dudley, *Film in the Aura of Art*, Princeton, New Jersey, 1984.

Carringer, Robert L., *The Making of Citizen Kane*, Los Angeles, 1985.

Higham, Charles, *Orson Welles: The Rise and Fall of an American Genius*, New York, 1985.

Leaming, Barbara, *Orson Welles: A Biography*, New York, 1985.

Parra, Danièle, and Jacques Zimmer, *Orson Welles*, Paris, 1985.

Taylor, John Russell, *Orson Welles: A Celebration*, London, 1986.

Brady, Frank, *Citizen Welles: A Biography of Orson Welles*, New York, 1989.

Wood, Bret, *Orson Welles: A Bio-Bibliography*, Westport, Connecticut, 1990.

On WELLES: articles—

Cocteau, Jean, profile of Welles, in *Cinémonde* (Paris), 6 March 1950.

MacLiammóir, Micheál, "Orson Welles," in *Sight and Sound* (London), July/September 1954.

"L'Oeuvre d'Orson Welles," in *Cahiers du Cinéma* (Paris), September 1958.

Gerasimov, Sergei, "All is Not Welles," in *Films and Filming* (London), September 1959.

Stanbrook, Alan, "The Heroes of Welles," in *Film* (London), no. 28, 1961.

"Welles Issue" of *Image et Son* (Paris), no.139, 1961.

Weinberg, Herman G., "The Legion of Lost Films," in *Sight and Sound* (London), Autumn 1962.

Tyler, Parker, "Orson Welles and the Big Experimental Film Cult," in *Film Culture* (New York), Summer 1963.

Pechter, William, "Trials," in *Sight and Sound* (London), Winter 1963/64.

Johnson, William, "Orson Welles: Of Time and Loss," in *Film Quarterly* (Berkeley), Fall 1967.

Daney, Serge, "Welles in Power," in *Cahiers du Cinema in English* (New York), September 1967.

"Special Report: Orson Welles," in *Action* (Los Angeles), May/June 1969.

McBride, Joseph, "Welles Before Kane," in *Film Quarterly* (Berkeley), Spring 1970.

Wilson, Richard, "It's Not Quite All True," in *Sight and Sound* (London), Autumn 1970.

Henderson, Brian, "The Long Take," in *Film Comment* (New York), Summer 1971.

Prokosch, Mike, "Orson Welles," in *Film Comment* (New York), Summer 1971.

Goldfarb, Phyllis, "Orson Welles' Use of Sound," in *Take One* (Montreal), July/August 1971.

Coulouris, George, and Bernard Herrmann, "'The *Citizen Kane* Book'," in *Sight and Sound* (London), Spring 1972.

Cohen, H., "The Heart of Darkness in Citizen Kane," in *Cinema Journal* (Evanston), Fall 1972.

Goldfarb, Phyllis, "Heston on Welles," in *Take One* (Montreal), October 1972.

Hale, N., "Welles and the Logic of Death," in *Film Heritage* (New York), Fall 1974.

Gow, Gordon, "A Touch of Orson," in *Films and Filming* (London), December 1974.

"Hollywood Salutes its 'Maverick' Genius Orson Welles," special issue of *American Cinematographer* (Los Angeles), April 1975.

Brady, Frank, "The Lost Film of Orson Welles," in *American Film* (Washington, D.C.), November 1978.

McBride, Joseph, "All's Welles," in *Film Comment* (New York), November/December 1978.

Poague, Lee, "The Great God Orson: Chabrol's 'Ten Days' Wonder," in *Film Criticism* (Edinboro, Pennsylvania), no. 3, 1979.

Neale, Steve, "Re-viewing Welles," in *Screen* (London), May/June 1982.

Houston, Beverle, "Power and Dis-integration in the Films of Orson Welles," in *Film Quarterly* (Berkeley), Summer 1982.

McLean, A.M, "Orson Welles and Shakespeare: History and Consciousness in *Chimes at Midnight*," in *Literature/Film Quarterly* (Salisbury, Maryland), no. 3, 1983.

Beja, M., "Where You Can't Get at Him: Orson Welles and the Attempt to Escape From Father," in *Literature/Film Quarterly* (Salisbury, Maryland), January 1985.

Strick, Philip, "Orson Welles," in *Films and Filming* (London), July 1985.

McCarthy, Todd, obituary in *Variety* (London), 16th October 1985.

Kauffmann, Stanley, obituary in *New Republic* (New York), 11 November 1985.

Stubbs, J.C., "The Evolution of Orson Welles's *Touch of Evil* from Novel to Film," in *Cinema Journal* (Champaign, Illinois), Winter 1985.

Orson Welles Sections of *Cahiers du Cinéma* (Paris), November and December 1985.

Wood, Michael, "The Magnificent Orson," in *American Film* (New York), December 1985.

Maxfield, J., "A Man Like Ourselves," in *Literature/Film Quarterly* (Salisbury, Maryland), no. 3, 1986.

Harper, W.R., "Polanski v Welles on *Macbeth*: Character or Fat?," in *Literature/Film Quarterly* (Salisbury, Maryland), no. 4, 1986.

"Welles Issue" of *Avant-Scène du Cinéma* (Paris), January/February 1986.

Kehr, Dave, obituary in *Film Comment* (New York), January/February 1986.

Rosenbaum, Jonathan, "The Invisible Orson Welles," in *Sight and Sound* (London), Summer 1986.

Bates, Robin, "Fiery Speech in a World of Shadows: Rosebud's Impact on Early Audiences," in *Cinema Journal* (Champaign, Illinois), vol. 26, no. 2, 1987.

Sartre, Jean-Paul, "Citizen Kane," in *Post Script* (Jacksonville, Florida), vol. 7, no. 1, 1987.

Anderegg, Michael, "Every Third Word a Lie: Rhetoric and History in Orson Welles' *Chimes at Midnight*," in *Film Quarterly* (Berkeley), Spring 1987.

Rodman, Howard A., "The Last Days of Orson Welles," in *American Film* (Washington D.C.), June 1987.

France, Richard, "Orson Welles' First Film," in *Films in Review* (New York), August/September 1987.

Bywater, William, "The Desire for Embodiment in Orson Welles's *Citizen Kane*," in *Post Script* (Jacksonville, Florida), vol. 7, no. 2, 1988.

Jewell, Richard B., "Orson Welles, George Schaefer and *It's All True*," in *Film History* (Philadelphia), vol. 2, no. 4, 1988.

Kalinak, Kathryn, "The Text of Music: A Study of *The Magnificent Ambersons*," in *Cinema Journal* (Champaign, Illinois), vol. 27, no. 4, 1988.

Perlmutter, Ruth, "Working with Welles: an Interview with Henry Jaglom," in *Film Quarterly* (Berkeley), Spring 1988.

Stainton, A., "*Don Quixote*: Orson Welles' Secret," in *Sight and Sound* (London), Autumn 1988.

White, Armond, "Wishing Welles," in *Film Comment* (New York), October 1988.

"Orson Welles Issue" of *Persistence of Vision* (Maspeth, New York), no. 7, 1989.

Vidal, Gore, "Remembering Orson Welles," in *New York Review of Books*, 1 June 1989.

* * *

References to Orson Welles as one of America's most influential directors and *Citizen Kane* as one of the great American films have become a simplistic way to encapsulate Welles's unique contribution to cinema. It is a contribution which seems obvious but is difficult to adequately summarize without examining his complex career.

Welles began as an actor in Ireland at Dublin's famous Gate Theater, bluffing his way into the theater's acting troupe by claiming to be well-known on the Broadway stage. He began directing plays in New York, and worked with John Houseman in various theatrical groups. For the Federal Theater Project, they attempted to stage Marc Blitzstein's leftist, pro-labor *The Cradle Will Rock*, but government agents blocked the opening night's production. Performers and audience moved to another theater in one of Broadway's most famous episodes.

The incident led to Houseman being fired and Welles's resignation from the Project. Houseman and Welles formed the Mercury Theatre Group with a manifesto written by Houseman declaring their intentions to foster new talent, experiment with new types of plays, and to appeal to the same audiences that frequented the Federal Theater plays. Welles's work on the New York stage was generally leftist in its political orientation, and inspired by the expressionist theater of the 1920s, prefiguring the look of his films.

Welles and his Mercury Theater Group expanded into radio as the Mercury Theater on the Air. In contrast to most theater-oriented shows on radio, which consisted merely of plays read aloud, the Mercury group adapted their works in a more natural, personal manner: most of the plays were narrated in the first person. Shrewd imitations of news announcements and technical breakdowns heightened the realism of his 1938 Halloween *War of the Worlds* broadcast to such a degree that the show has become famous for the panic it caused as Americans thought New Jersey was actually being invaded by Martians. This event itself has become a pop culture legend, shrouded in exaggeration and half-truths.

RKO studios hired Welles in 1939 hoping he could repeat the success on film for them that he had enjoyed on stage and in radio. Welles, according to most sources, accepted the job because his Mercury Theater needed money to produce an elaborate production called *5 Kings*, an anthology of several of Shakespeare's plays. Whatever the reason, his contract with RKO began an erratic and rocky relationship with the Hollywood industry that would, time and again, end in bitter disappointment for Welles, leading finally to his self-imposed exile in Europe.

The film on which Welles enjoyed the most creative freedom was his first and most famous, *Citizen Kane*. At the time the film created a controversy over both its subject matter and style. Loosely based on the life of newspaper magnate William Randolph Hearst, the film supposedly upset Hearst to such a degree that he attempted to stop the production, and then the distribution and exhibition. In the end, his anger was manifested in the scathing reviews critics gave the film in all his newspapers. The film's innovative structure consisting of flashbacks from the differing points-of-view of the various characters, in addition to other formal devices so different from the classic Hollywood cinema, also contributed to *Kane's* financial failure and commercial down-fall, though critics other than those on Hearst's papers generally gave the film positive reviews. Other controversies surrounding the film include that over the correct scriptwriting credit. Originally Welles claimed solo credit for writing the film, but the Writer's Guild forced him to acknowledge Herman Mankiewicz as co-author. Each writer's *exact* contributions remain unknown, but the controversy was revived during the early 1970s by critic Pauline Kael, who attempted to prove that Mankiewicz was most responsible for the script. Whatever the case, the argument becomes unimportant and even ludicrous given the unique direction which shapes the material, and which is undeniably Welles's.

Due to the failure of *Kane*, Welles was supervised quite closely on his next film, *The Magnificent Ambersons*. After shooting was completed, Welles went to South America to begin work on a documentary, *It's All True*, designed to help dispel Nazi propaganda in Latin America. He took a rough cut of *Ambersons* with him, hoping to coordinate cutting with editor Robert Wise. However, a sneak preview of Welles's *Ambersons* proved disastrous and the studio cut his 140-minute-plus version to 88 minutes, adding a "happy ending." The film was a critical and commercial failure, and the entire Mercury staff was removed from the RKO lot.

Welles spent the remainder of his Hollywood career sparring with various producers or studios over the completed versions of his films and his uncredited direction on films in which he starred. For example, *Journey Into Fear* was begun by Welles but finished by Norman Foster, though Welles claims he made contributions and suggestions throughout. *Jane Eyre*, which made Welles a popular star, was directed by Robert Stevenson, but the gothic overtones, the mise-en-scène, and other stylistic devices, suggest a Wellesian contribution. With *The Stranger*, directed for Sam Spiegel, he adhered closely to the script and a preplanned editing schedule, evidently to prove that he could turn out a Hollywood product on time and on budget. However, Welles refers to *The Stranger* as "the worst of my films," and several Welles scholars agree. He directed one of his best films, *The Lady from Shanghai*, for Harry Cohn of Columbia. The film, a loose, confusing, noirish tale of double-crosses and corrupted innocence, starred Welles's wife at the time, Rita Hayworth. Cohn was supposedly already dissatisfied with their marriage, because he felt it would reduce Hayworth's box-office value, but was furious with what Welles did to her image in *Shanghai*. The film, shot mostly on location, was made under stressful circumstances with Welles often re-writing during the shooting. It was edited several times, and finally released two years after its completion, but failed commercially and critically. His final Hollywood project, a version of *Macbeth* for Republic Studios, was also considered a commercial flop.

Disenchanted with Hollywood, Welles left for Europe where he began the practice of acting in other directors' films in order to finance his own projects. His portrayal of Harry Lime in Carol Reed's *The Third Man* is considered his finest work from this period, and Welles continued to create villainous antagonists who are often more interesting, complex, or exciting than the protagonists of the films. In the roles of Col. Haki in *Journey Into Fear*, Will Varner in Martin Ritt's *The Long Hot Summer*, Quinlan in *Touch of Evil*, and in *Mr. Arkadin*, Welles created a sinister persona for which he has become as famous as for his direction of *Citizen Kane*. His last roles were often caricatures of that persona, as in Marlo Thomas's *It Happened One Christmas*, or parodies as in *The Muppet Movie*.

Welles's European ventures include his *Othello*, shot over a period of years between acting assignments, often under chaotic circumstances. The difficulties of the film's production are often described as though they were the madcap adventures of a roguish artist, but in reality it must have been an extreme hardship to assemble and reassemble the cast over the course of the film's shooting. At one point, he "borrowed" equipment under cover of night from the set of Henry King's *The Black Rose* (in which Welles was starring) to quickly shoot a few scenes. Welles later obtained enough financial backing to make *Mr. Arkadin*, a *Kane*-like story of a powerful man who made his fortune as a white slaver, and also *Chimes at Midnight*. He returned to America in the late 1950s to direct *Touch of Evil*, starring Charlton Heston. Originally approached only to star in the film, Welles mistakenly thought he was also to direct. Heston intervened and insisted he be allowed to do so. Welles immediately threw out the original script, rewriting it without reading the book upon which the script was based, *Badge of Evil*. Welles's last works include *The Immortal Story*, a one-hour film made for French television, and *F for Fake*, a strange combination of documentary footage shot by another director, some Welles footage from earlier ventures, and Welles's own narration.

Welles's outsider status in connection with the American film industry is an interesting part of cinema history in itself, but his importance as a director is due to the innovations he has introduced through his films and the influence they have had on filmmaking and film theory. Considering the turbulent relationship Welles experienced with Hollywood and the circumstances under which his films were made in Europe, it is surprising there is any thematic and stylistic consistency in his work at all.

The central character in many of his films is often a powerful, egotistical man who lives outside or above the law and society. Kane, Arkadin, and Mr. Clay (*The Immortal Story*) are enabled to do so by their wealth and position; Quinlan (*Touch of Evil*) by his job as a law enforcer, which allows him to commit injustices to suit his own purposes. Even George Minafer (*Ambersons*) becomes an outsider as a modern, industrialized society supercedes his aristocratic, 19th-century way of life. These characters are never innocent, but seem to be haunted by an innocence they have lost. *Kane's* "Rosebud," the emblem of childhood that he clings to, is the classic example, but this theme can also be found in *Mr. Arkadin* where Arkadin is desperate to keep his daughter from discovering his sordid past. Many parallels between the two films have been drawn including the fact that the title characters are both wealthy and powerful men whose past lives are being investigated by a stranger. Interestingly, just as Kane whispers "rosebud" on his deathbed, Arkadin speaks his daughter's name at the moment of his death. Quinlan, in *Touch of Evil*, is confronted with his memories and his past when he runs into Tanya, now a prostitute in a whorehouse. The ornaments and mementoes in her room (some of them from Welles's personal collection), seem to jog his memory of a time when he was not a corrupt law official. In *Shanghai*, it is interesting to note that Welles does not portray the egotist, Bannister, but instead the "innocent" Michael O'Hara, who is soiled by his dealings with Bannister's wife. That the corrupt antagonist is doomed is often indicated by a prologue or introductory sequence which foreshadows his destruction—the newsreel sequence in *Kane*; the opening montage of *Ambersons* which condenses 18 years of George Minafer's life into 10 minutes to hint that George will get his "comeuppance" in the end; the opening funeral scene of *Othello*; and the detailing of Mr. Clay's sordid past in *The Immortal Story*. The themes of lost innocence and inescapable fate often shroud Welles's films with a sense of melancholy, which serves to make these characters worthy of sympathy.

Much has been made of Welles's use of deep-focus photography, particularly in *Kane* and *Ambersons*. Though a directorial presence is often suggested in the cinema through the use of editing, with Welles it is through mise-en-scène, particularly in these two films. Many Welles scholars discuss the ambiguous nature of long-shot/deep-focus photography, where the viewer is allowed to sift through the details of a scene and make some of his own choices about what is important to the narrative, plot development, and so on. However, Welles's arrangement of actors in specific patterns, his practice of shooting from unusual angles, and use of wide-angle lenses which distort the figures closest to them, are all intended to convey meaning. For example, the exaggerated perspective of the scene where Thatcher gives young Charles Kane a sled makes Thatcher appear to tower over the boy, visually suggesting his unnatural and menacing hold on him (at least from young Kane's point of view).

Welles also employed rather complex sound tracks in *Kane* and *Ambersons*, perhaps a result of his radio experience. The party sequence of *Ambersons*, for example, makes use of overlapping dialogue, as the camera tracks along the ballroom, as though one were passing by, catching bits of conversation.

His visual style becomes less outrageous and he is less concerned with effects as his career continues. There seems to be an increasing concentration on the acting, particularly in the Shakespeare films. Welles had a lifelong interest in Sha-

kespeare and his plays, and is well known for his unique handling and interpretations of the material. *Macbeth*, for example, was greatly simplified, with much dialogue omitted and scenes shifted around. A primitive feel is reflected by badly synchronized sound, and much of the impact of the spoken word is lost. *Othello*, shot in Italy and Morocco, makes use of outdoor locations in contrast to the staginess of *Macbeth*. Again, Welles was quite free with interpretation: Iago's motives, for example, are suggested to be the result of sexual impotency. His most successful adaptation of Shakespeare is *Chimes at Midnight*, an interpretation of the Falstaff story with parts taken from *Henry IV*, parts one and two, *Henry V, Merry Wives of Windsor*, and *Richard II*. In *Chimes*, Falstaff, as with many of Welles's central characters, is imprisoned by the past. Like George Minafer, he straddles two ages, one medieval and the other modern. Falstaff is destroyed not only by the ageing process but also by the problems of being forced into a new world, as are Minafer and perhaps Kane. Again Welles is quite individualistic in his presentation of the material, making Falstaff a true friend to the king and an innocent, almost child-like, victim of a new order.

In the years before he died, Welles became known for his appearances in television commercials and on talk shows, playing the part of the celebrity to its maximum. His last role was as a narrator on an innovative episode of the television detective series *Moonlighting*, starring Bruce Willis and Cybill Shepherd. It is unfortunate that his latter-day persona as a *bon vivant* often overshadows his contributions to the cinema.

—Susan Doll

WELLMAN, William.

American. Born William Augustus Wellman in Brookline, Massachusetts, 29 February 1896. Attended Newton High School, Newton Highlands, Massachusetts, 1910–14. Married 1) Helene Chadwick, 1918 (divorced 1920); 3 other marriages 1920–33; 5) Dorothy Coonan, 1933, seven children. Professional ice hockey player for minor league team, 1914; joined volunteer ambulance corps destined for France, 1917, then joined French Foreign Legion, where he learnt to fly planes; when U.S. entered war, became part of Lafayette Flying Corps, an arm of the Lafayette Escadrille; film actor, U.S., from 1919; messenger for Goldwyn Pictures, then directed first film, 1920; director for 20th Century-Fox, 1923; signed by Paramount, 1927; Recipient: Oscar for *Wings*, 1927; Oscar for Best Writing (Original Story) for *A Star is Born* (shared with Robert Carson), 1937. *Died 9 December 1975.*

Films as Director:

1920   *The Twins from Suffering Creek*
1923   *The Man Who Won; 2nd Hand Love; Big Dan; Cupid's Fireman*
1924   *The Vagabond Trail; Not a Drum Was Heard; The Circus Cowboy*
1925   *When Husbands Flirt*
1926   *The Boob; The Cat's Pajamas; You Never Know Women*
1927   *Wings*
1928   *The Legion of the Condemned; Ladies of the Mob; Beggars of Life*
1929   *Chinatown Nights; The Man I Love; Woman Trap*
1930   *Dangerous Paradise; Young Eagles; Maybe It's Love*

William Wellman

1931   *Other Men's Women*; **The Public Enemy**; *Night Nurse*; *Star Witness*; *Safe in Hell*
1932   *The Hatchet Man*; *So Big*; *Love is a Racket*; *The Purchase Price*; *The Conquerors*
1933   *Frisco Jenny*; *Central Airport*; *Lily Turner*; *Midnight Mary*; *Heroes for Sale*; *Wild Boys of the Road*; *College Coach*
1934   *Looking for Trouble*; *Stingaree*; *The President Vanishes*
1935   *The Call of the Wild*
1936   *The Robin Hood of Eldorado* (+ co-sc); *Small Town Girl*
1937   *A Star is Born* (+ co-sc); *Nothing Sacred*
1938   *Men with Wings* (+ pr)
1939   *Beau Geste* (+ pr); *The Light That Failed* (+ pr)
1941   *Reaching for the Sun* (+ pr)
1942   *Roxie Hart*; *The Great Man's Lady* (+ pr); *Thunder Birds*
1943   **The Ox-Bow Incident**; *The Lady of Burlesque*
1944   *Buffalo Bill*
1945   *This Man's Navy*; *The Story of G.I. Joe*
1946   *Gallant Journey* (+ pr, co-sc)
1947   *Magic Town*
1948   *Iron Curtain*
1949   *Yellow Sky*; *Battleground*
1950   *The Next Voice You Hear*
1951   *Across the Wide Missouri*
1952   *Westward the Women*; *It's a Big Country* (co-d); *My Man and I*
1953   *Island in the Sky*
1954   *The High and the Mighty*; *Track of the Cat*
1955   *Blood Alley*
1958   *Darby's Rangers*; *Lafayette Escadrille* (+ pr, co-sc)

Other Film:

1919   *Knickerbocker Buckaroo* (Parker) (role)

Publications:

By WELLMAN: book—

A Short Time for Insanity: An Autobiography, New York, 1974.

By WELLMAN: articles—

"Director's Notebook—Why Teach Cinema?," in *Cinema Progress* (Los Angeles), June/July 1939.
Interview in *Cinema* (Beverly Hills), July 1966.

On WELLMAN: books—

Brownlow, Kevin, *The Parade's Gone By . . .*, New York, 1968.
Thompson, Frank T., *William A. Wellman*, Metuchen, New Jersey, 1983.

On WELLMAN: articles—

Pringle, H.F., "Screwball Bill," in *Collier's* (New York), 26 February 1938.
Griffith, Richard, "Wyler, Wellman, and Huston," in *Films in Review* (New York), February 1950.
Sarris, Andrew, "Fallen Idols," in *Film Culture* (New York), Spring 1963.
Brownlow, Kevin, "William Wellman," in *Film* (London), Winter 1965/66.
Smith, J.M., "The Essential Wellman," in *Brighton* (London), January 1970.
Wellman, William, Jr., "William Wellman: Director Rebel," in *Action* (Los Angeles), March/April 1970.
Brooks, Louise, "On Location with Billy Wellman," in *Film Culture* (New York), Spring 1972.
Fox, J., "A Man's World," in *Films and Filming* (London), March 1973.
Eyman, S., and Allen Eyles, "'Wild Bill' William A. Wellman," in *Focus on Film* (London), no. 29, 1978.
Langlois, Gerard, "William Wellman 1896–1975," in *Avant-Scène du Cinéma* (Paris), 1 March 1978.
Gallagher, John, "William Wellman," in *Films in Review* (New York), May, June/July and October 1982.

*　　　*　　　*

William Wellman's critical reputation is, in many respects still in a state of flux long after re-evaluations and recent screenings of his major films should have established some consensus of opinion regarding his place in the pantheon of film directors. While there is some tentative agreement that he is, if nothing else, a competent journeyman director capable of producing entertaining male-dominated action films, other opinions reflect a wide range of artistic evaluations ranging from comparisons to D.W. Griffith to outright condemnations of his films as clumsy and uninspired. His own preferred niche, as is indicated by his flamboyant personality and his predilection for browbeating and intimidating his performers, would probably be in the same general class with highly masculine filmmakers like Howard Hawks, John Ford, and Raoul Walsh. While those three enjoy a distinct *auteur* status, a similiar designation for Wellman is not so easily arrived at since much of his early work for Warner Bros. in the late 1930s is, at first glance, not easily distinguishable from the rest of the studio's output of sociological problem films and exposés of organized crime. In addition, his later films do not stand comparison, in many scholars' opinions, to treatments of similiar themes (often employing the same actors and locales) by both Ford and Hawks.

It might be argued, however, that Wellman actually developed what has come to be regarded as the Warner Bros. style to a degree greater than that of the studio's other directors. His 1931 *Public Enemy*, for example, stands above most of the other gangster films of the era in its creative blend of highly vivid images and in the subtle manner in which it created a heightened impression of violence and brutality by giving only hints of it on the screen. Exhibiting similar subtlety, Wellman's depiction of a gangster, beginning with his childhood, graphically alluded to the sociological roots of organized crime. While many of his more typical treatments of men in adversity, like 1927's Academy Award-winning *Wings*, were sometimes artificial, everything worked in *Public Enemy*.

In his later films like *The Ox-Bow Incident*, *The Story of G.I. Joe*, and *Battleground*, the interactions of men in various groupings are shaped in such a way as to determine the direction and thematic force of each story. In others, like *Track of the Cat*, the emphasis shifts instead to one individual and his battle with forces of nature beyond his control. Yet in all cases, the issue is one of survival, a concept that manifests itself in some manner in all of Wellman's films. It is overt and recognizable in war dramas like *Battleground* or in a disaster film like *The High and the Mighty*, but it is reflected at least as much in the psychological tensions of *Public Enemy* as it is in the violence. It becomes even more abstract in a complex picture like *Track of the Cat* when the issue concerns the family unit and the insecurity of its internal relationships. In the more heavy-handed propaganda films, *The Iron Curtain and Blood Alley*, the theme centers on the threat to democratic forms of government, and finally, in the *Ox-Bow Incident*, the issue is the very fragility of society itself in the hands of a mob.

Wellman's supporters feel that these concerns arise from the latent cynicism of a disappointed romantic but are expressed by an instinctive artist with a keen awareness of the intellectual force of images conveyed with the raw power of many of those in *Public Enemy*. Yet it is the inconsistency of these images and a corresponding lack of inspiration in his work overall that clouds his stature as an *auteur* of the first rank. While, ultimately, it is true Wellman's films cannot be easily separated from the man behind them, his best works are those that sprang from his emotional and psychological experiences. His lesser ones have been overshadowed by the cult of his personality and are best remembered for the behind-the-scenes fistfights, parties, and wild stunts, all detracting from the production. Perhaps he never got the chance to make the one film that would thematically support all of the seemingly irreconcilable aspects of his personality and allow him to create an indisputable masterpiece to firmly establish him as a director of the first magnitude.

—Stephen L. Hanson

WENDERS, Wim.

German. Born Wilhelm Wenders in Düsseldorf, 14 August 1945. Educated in medicine and philosophy; studied at Hochschule für Fernsehen und Film, Munich, 1967–70. Film critic in Munich for *Süddeutsche Zeitung* and *Filmkritik*, late 1960s; professional filmmaker, from 1971. Recipient: Golden Lion, Venice Festival, for *The State of Things*, 1982; Best Director, Cannes Festival, for *Wings of Desire*, 1987. Agent: c/o Gary Salt, The Paul Kohner Agency, 9169 Sunset Blvd., Los Angeles, CA 90069, U.S.A.

Films as Director:

1967 *Schauplätze* (*Locations*) (short); *Same Player Shoots Again* (short)
1968 *Silver City* (short); *Victor I* (short)
1969 *Alabama–2000 Light Years* (short); *Drei amerikanische LPs* (*Three American LPs*) (short)
1970 *Polizeifilm* (*Police Film*) (short); *Summer in the City* (*Dedicated to the Kinks*) (diploma film)
1971 *Die Angst des Tormanns beim Elfmeter* (*The Goalie's Anxiety at the Penalty Kick*)
1972 *Der scharlachrote Buchstabe* (*The Scarlet Letter*)
1973 *Alice in den Städten* (*Alice in the Cities*)
1974 *Aus der Familie der Panzerechsen* [From the Family of the Crocodilia] (short, for TV); *Die Insel* [The Island] (short, for TV); *Falsche Bewegung* (*Wrong Movement*)
1976 **Im Lauf der Zeit** (*Kings of the Road. In the Course of Time*)
1977 **Der amerikanische Freund** (**The American Friend**)
1981 *Lightning Over Water* (*Nick's Film*)
1982 *Hammett*; *Der Stand der Dinge* (*The State of Things*)
1984 **Paris, Texas**; *Room 666* (doc)
1985 *Tokyo-Ga* (doc)
1987 *Der Himmel über Berlin* (*Wings of Desire*)
1989 *Aufzeichnungen zu Kleidern und Städten* (*Notebook on Cities and Clothes*) (doc)

Other Films:

1985 *I Played it For You* (Blakley) (role)
1987 *Helsinki Napoli: All Night Long* (Mika Kaurismaki); *Yer Demir, Gok Bakir* (Livaneli) (pr)
1990 *Isabelle Eberhardt* (Pringle) (pr)

Publications:

By WENDERS: books—

The Film by Wim Wenders: Kings of the Road (*In the Course of Time*), with Fritz Müller-Scherz, Munich, 1976.
Nick's Film—Lightning Over Water, with Chris Sievernich, Frankfurt, 1981.
Paris, Texas, with Sam Shepard, Berlin, 1984.
Written in the West: Photographien aus dem amerikanische Western, Munich, 1987.
Emotion Pictures: Reflections on the Cinema, London, 1989.

By WENDERS: articles—

"*Alice in den Städten*," an interview with W.-E. Bühler and P.B. Kleiser, in *Filmkritik* (Munich), March 1974.
"Wim Wenders über *Im Lauf der Zeit*," an interview with H. Wiedemann and F. Müller-Scherz, in *Film und Ton* (Munich), May 1976.
"Wenders on Kings of the Road," in *Monthly Film Bulletin* (London), July 1977.
"King of the Road," an interview with Carlos Clarens, in *Film Comment* (New York), September/October 1977.
"Filming Highsmith," an interview with Jan Dawson, in *Sight and Sound* (London), Winter 1977/78.
Interview with P. Lehman and others in *Wide Angle* (Athens, Ohio), vol. 2, no. 4, 1978.
Interview with Serge Daney in *Cahiers du Cinéma* (Paris), December 1980 and June 1982.
Interview with Richard Combs in *Monthly Film Bulletin* (London), March 1983.
Interview with John Gallagher in *Films in Review* (New York), June/July 1983.
Interview with Michel Ciment and Hubert Niogret in *Positif* (Paris), September 1984.
Interview with K. Dieckman in *Film Quarterly* (Berkeley), Winter 1984/85.
Interview with Coco Fusco in *Cineaste* (New York), vol. 16, no. 4, 1988.
Interview with Robert Seidenberg in *American Film* (Los Angeles), vol. 13, no. 8, 1988.
Interview with L. Antoccia in *Films and Filming* (London), August 1988.

On WENDERS: books—

Geist, Kathe, *The Cinema of Wim Wenders 1967–77*, Ann Arbor, Michigan, 1981.
Johnston, Sheila, *Wim Wenders*, London, 1981.
Buchka, Peter, *Augen Kann man nicht Kaufen: Wim Wenders und seine Filme*, Munich, 1983.
Franklin, James, *New German Cinema from Oberhausen to Hamburg*, Boston, 1983.
Grob, Norbert, *Die Formen des filmische Blicks: Wenders: Die fruhen Filmwe*, Munich, 1984.
Phillips, Klaus, editor, *New German Filmmakers: From Oberhausen through the 1970s*, New York, 1984.
Devillers, Jean-Pierre, *Berlin, L.A., Berlin: Wim Wenders*, Paris, 1985.
Geist, Kathe, *The Cinema of Wim Wenders: From Paris, France, to Paris, Texas*, Ann Arbor, Michigan, 1988.
Rentschler, Eric, editor, *West German Filmmakers on Film: Visions and Voices*, New York, 1988.
Boujut, Michel, *Wim Wenders: Un Voyage dans ses films*, Paris, 1989.
Elsaesser, Thomas, *New German Cinema: A History*, London, 1989.
Estève, Michel, *Wim Wenders*, Paris, 1989.
Joyce, Paul, *Motion and Emotion: The Films of Wim Wenders*, London, 1989.
Künzel, Uwe, *Wim Wenders: Ein Filmbuch*, 3rd edition, Freiburg, 1989.

On WENDERS: articles—

Rayns, Tony, "Forms of Address," in *Sight and Sound* (London), Winter 1974/75.
Ghali, N., "Dossier-auteur: Wim Wenders," in *Cinéma* (Paris), December 1976.
Covino, M., "Wim Wenders: A Worldwide Homesickness," in *Film Quarterly* (Berkeley), Winter 1977/78.
Stamelman, P., "Wenders at Warners," in *Sight and Sound* (London), Autumn 1978.
Corrigan, Timothy J., "The Realist Gesture in the Films of Wim Wenders: Hollywood and the New German Cinema," in *Quarterly Review of Film Studies* (Pleasantville, New York), Spring 1980.
"Wenders Issue" of *Caméra/Stylo* (Paris), January 1981.
"*Alice dans les villes* Issue" of *Avant-Scène du Cinéma* (Paris), 1 May 1981.
Bishop, R., and T. Ryan, "Wim Wenders. An American Saga," in *Cinema Papers* (Melbourne), August 1984.
Wim Wenders Section of *Cinéma* (Paris), September 1984.

Wim Wenders

Wim Wenders Section of *Positif* (Paris), September 1984.

Ranvaud, Don, "*Paris, Texas* to Sydney," and John Pym, "The Road from Wuppertal," in *Sight and Sound* (London), Autumn 1984.

Combs, Richard, "Ich Bin Ein Englander or Show Me the Way to Go Home," in *Monthly Film Bulletin* (London), May 1985.

Corrigan, Timothy, "Cinematic Snuff: German Friends and Narrative Murders," in *Cinema Journal* (Champaign, Illinois), Winter 1985.

Geist, Kathe, "Filmmaking as Research: Wim Wenders' *The State of Things*," in *Post Script* (Jacksonville, Florida), Winter 1986.

Snyder, Stephen, "Wim Wenders: The Hunger Artist in America," in *Post Script* (Jacksonville, Florida), Winter 1987.

American Friends Section of *Literature/Film Quarterly* (Salisbury, Maryland), vol. 16, no. 3, 1988.

Paneth, Ira, "Wim and His Wings," in *Film Quarterly* (Berkeley), vol. 42, no. 1, 1988.

Green, Peter, "Germans Abroad," in *Sight and Sound* (London), Spring 1988.

*   *   *

Of the three young German filmmakers who achieved the greatest international fame in the 1970s as the vanguard of a German New Wave, Wim Wenders had perhaps a less radical though no less distinctive film style than his compatriots R.W. Fassbinder and Werner Herzog. Though critics typically cite American influences upon Wenders' "road trilogy" of the mid-1970s, there is a greater affinity with the modernist tradition of the European "art film" exemplified by the Antonioni of *L'avventura* and *Red Desert*—dramas of alienation in which restless, unrooted individuals wander through haunted, sterile, but bleakly beautiful landscapes within a free-floating narrative structure. True, the *ennui* in these films shades into *angst* and American Beat gestures, and the alienation has strong roots in the spiritual yearning, the love of loneliness and wandering, of German Romanticism. Romanticism seems too to be at the root of Wenders' conception of himself (well articulated in numerous interviews) as an artist: one who evolves spiritually with each work, or reaches dead ends (as he has called *The State of Things*) from which he must break out; and who sees each new work as an adventure, not to be mapped out too much in advance.

A crucial observation about Wenders' art is found in cinematographer Ed Lachman's remark that "light and landscape are actors" in his films. Wenders' characters are typically revealed against urban or rural landscapes, upon which the camera frequently lingers as the actors pass from the frame. Most of the films take place predominantly out-of-doors (the studio sets of *Hammett* making that film all the more of an anomaly), or offer striking views from high-rise windows and moving vehicles. The urban views most often suggest sterility but have a certain grandeur, sharing with his views of desert (*Paris, Texas*) or sea (*The State of Things*) that vastness the Romantics called "sublime." The climactic scene in the peep-show booth in *Paris, Texas* is all the more powerful and inventive in the context of the epic vistas of the rest of the film. And the urban scene finally becomes the central "actor" in *Wings of Desire/Himmel über Berlin*, indeed a "Symphony of a Great City," in which the Wall is no barrier to the gliding camera or the angelic inhabitants.

Wenders' films are dialectical: they structure contrasts not as simple polarities but as rich ongoing dialogue, and the later films seem to be in dialogue with the earlier ones. Among the central concerns from film to film are American versus European culture, the creation of mood versus tight narrative, a sense of "home" versus rootless "freedom," and even black-and-white versus color photography.

Wenders' ambivalent fascination with America has been a favorite topic for critics. None of his films is without interest in this regard, but *Alice in the Cities* is the first to be shot partially in America—a world of boardwalks, motels, neon and skyscrapers, though still not so different from the urban, industrial Europe of the second half; it is also his first feature to make extensive use of American music, including the Chuck Berry concert in Wuppertal. *The American Friend* is a dizzying vortex of allusiveness, with its gangsters and cowboys, iconographic presences of Nicholas Ray and Dennis Hopper, miniature Statue of Liberty in Paris, Ripley's digs in Hamburg, hints of an allegory of the American film industry in Germany (the pornographers seducing the hapless framemaker), and a narrative derived from a novel by an expatriate American and strongly echoing *Strangers on a Train*. Wenders' "American period" from *Hammett* through *Paris, Texas* is of course of central interest here, with a whimsically mystical and lyrical embracing of humanity and the particulars of physical life that recalls Walt Whitman. Wenders still calls his production company "Road Movies" (in English).

The mid-1970s films may owe much to the American "road movie" of a few years earlier (themselves echoing Kerouac's *On the Road*), but the classical Hollywood cinema is defined by its tight narrative structures, and Wenders can be felt to be wrestling with such a structure in *The American Friend*. He has said of *Paris, Texas*, in a *Film Quarterly* interview, "For once I was making a movie that wasn't meandering all over the place. That's what Sam [Shepard] brought to this movie of mine as an American writer: forward movement, which is very American in a way." Still, *Paris, Texas* is very unlike a classical Hollywood film, though the problematic *Hammett*, ironically enough, *is* like one; and the later *Wings of Desire* is much more a fantasia than a classical symphony of a great city. (*Tokyo-Ga* too meanders through a great city rather than being a tight documentary on Yasujiro Ozu.)

Also explored dialectically are the concepts of home and homelessness, omni-present concerns in Wenders' films. *Alice in the Cities* and *Kings of the Road* could have as epigraph a Barbara Stanwyck line from *Clash by Night* quoted by Wenders in a piece on Fritz Lang: "Home is where you get when you run out of places." *The State of Things* is perhaps Wenders' most bleak portrayal of homelessness, while *Paris, Texas* expresses the greatest yearning for home. *Wings of Desire* features an angel wishing he could "come home like Philip Marlowe and feed the cat"; an acrobat who has always felt "alone" and unattached, but now, in love, can feel "loneliness," which means "I am finally whole"; and a conclusion in which the former angel muses, "I found Home . . . instead of forever hovering above"—presumably like Wenders' camera. Obviously the issues of home/homelessness shade into the other prominent Wenders theme of aloneness versus tentative human bonds, explored especially in terms of adult-child friendships, unstable male bondings, and in *Wings*, the angelic/mortal possibilities of adult heterosexual love.

Wenders once claimed, with some relish of paradox, or perhaps recollection of *The Wizard of Oz*, that black-and-white was suited to realism, color to fantasy. Hence those tales of murder *The Goalie's Anxiety* and *The American Friend* were in color, and the "road trilogy" not, with *Kings of the Road* declaring itself "a Wim Wenders film in black/white." He further declared himself incapable of making a documentary in color—though he was soon to make more than one. Once again *Wings of Desire* seems a synthesis of previous concerns, if not a downright reversal, with the angels seeing the spiritual essence of things in black-and-white but humans perceiving the particularities of mortal life in color. Such inconsistency (or rather willingness to change perspective) in a minor matter may be taken as representative of the exploratory nature of Wenders' film work as a whole.

—Joseph Milicia

WERTMÜLLER, Lina.

Italian. Born Arcangela Felice Assunta Wertmüller von Elgg Spanol von Braueich in Rome, 14 August 1928. Attended several Catholic schools; Academy of Theatre, Rome, 1947–51. Married artist Enrico Job, 1968. Joined Maria Signorelli's puppet troupe, 1951–52; actress, stage manager, set designer, publicist, and writer for theatre, radio and TV, from 1952; assistant to Fellini on 8½, 1962; directed first feature, *I basilischi*, 1963; first film to be given U.S. release, *Film d'amore e d'anarchia*, 1973; hired by Warner Bros. to direct 4 films, contract terminated after financial failure of first film.

Films as Director and Scriptwriter:

1963   *I basilischi* (*The Lizards*)
1965   *Questa volta parliamo di uomini* (*Now Let's Talk About Men. This Time Let's Talk About Men*)
1967   *Non stuzzicate la zanzara* (*Don't Tease the Mosquito*)

1972   *Mimi metallurgio ferito nell'onore* (*The Seduction of Mimi. Mimi the Metalworker. Wounded in Honour*)
1973   ***Film d'amore e d'anarchia, ovvero stamattina alle 10 in Via dei fiori nella nota casa di tolleranza* (*Film of Love and Anarchy, or This Morning at Ten in the Via dei fiori at the Well-Known House of Tolerance*)**
1974   *Tutto a posto e niente in ordine* (*Everything's in Order but Nothing Works. All Screwed Up*); *Travolti da un insolito destino nell'azzurro mare d'agosto* (*Swept Away by a Strange Destiny on an Azure August Sea*)
1976   *Pasqualino settebellezze* (*Pasqualino Seven Beauties. Seven Beauties*)
1978   *The End of the World in Our Usual Bed in a Night Full of Rain*; *Shimmy lagarno tarantelle e vino*
1979   *Revenge*
1980   *Blood Feud*
1981   *E una Domenica sera di novembre* (for TV)
1983   *Scherzo del destinoin aqquato dietro l'angelo come un brigante di strada* (*A Joke of Destiny, Lying in Wait Around the Corner Like a Street Bandit*)
1984   *Sotto, Sotto*
1985   *Un complicato intrigo di Donne, Vicoli e delitti*
1986   *Camorra*; *Notte d'estate, con profilo Greco, occhi amandorla e odore di basilico* (*Summer Night With a Greek Profile, Almond Coloured Eyes and the Scent of Basil*)
1989   *In una notte di chiaro luna* (+ sc); *Decimo clandestino*
1990   *Saturday, Sunday, Monday* (+ sc)

Other Films:

1963   *Otto e mezzo* (*8½*) (Fellini) (asst d)
1966   *Rita la zanzara* (*Rita the Mosquito*) (d musical numbers only, sc)

Publications:

By WERTMÜLLER: books—

The Screenplays of Lina Wertmüller, New York, 1977.
The Head of Alvise, London, 1983.

By WERTMÜLLER: articles—

Interview in *Woman and Film* (Santa Monica), no. 5–6, 1974.
Interview in *Inter/View* (New York), March 1975.
"Look, Gideon—Gideon Bachmann Talks with Lina Wertmüller," in *Film Quarterly* (Berkeley), Spring 1977.
"Lina Sweeps in," an interview with G. Ott, in *Cinema Canada* (Montreal), March 1978.
Interview with C. J. Rotondi in *Film in Review* (New York), November 1984.
Interview with B. Steinborn in *Filmfaust* (Frankfurt), April/May 1986.

On WERTMÜLLER: books—

Michalczyk, John J., *The Italian Political Filmmakers*, Cranbury, New Jersey, 1986.
Dokumentation: Lina Wertmüller/Martin Scorsese, Zurich, 1986.
Bruno, Giuliana, and Maria Nadotti, *Off Screen: Women and Film in Italy*, London, 1988.
Jacobsen, Wolfgang, and others, *Lina Wertmüller*, Munich, 1988.

On WERTMÜLLER: articles—

Durgnat, Raymond, in *Films and Filming* (London), October 1964.
Biskind, Peter, "Lina Wertmüller: The Politics of Private Life," in *Film Quarterly* (Berkeley), Winter 1974/75.
Willis, Ellen, "Is Lina Wertmuller Just One of the Boys?," in *Rolling Stone* (New York), 25 March 1976.
Quacinella, L., "How Left is Lina?," in *Cineaste* (New York), Fall 1976.
Jacobs, Diane, "Lina Wertmüller," in *International Film Guide 1978*, London, 1977.
Tutt, Ralph, "*Seven Beauties* and the Beast: Bettelheim, Wertmüller, and the Uses of Enchantment," in *Literature/Film Quarterly* (Salisbury, Maryland), vol. 17, no. 3, 1989.

*   *   *

Lina Wertmüller directing *The End of the World . . .*

By the mid-1970s, Lina Wertmüller had directed a series of features which brought her international fame. In recent years, though, her critical reputation has been tarnished: her detractors have dubbed her a reactionary, labelling her films as grotesque and self-absorbed, with little love for people; meanwhile, her champions call her a feminist and socialist, a defender of the downtrodden, an idealistic anarchist who realizes anarchy is impractical but still cherishes the notion of total individual freedom. Upon examining her films, one may decide that most of her characters are caricatures, or may consider them as sympathetic human beings. It all depends on the interpretation.

Wertmüller's films most characteristically focus on the eternal battle of the sexes, fought in the setting of a class war via noisy screaming matches and comical seductions. Her most typical features may be found in the midsection of her filmography, from *The Seduction of Mimi* through *Swept Away. . . .* These are all uneven: for every inspired sequence—most notably, in *The Seduction of Mimi*, Giancarlo Giannini's antics between the sheets with a ridiculously obese woman—there are long stretches of repetitious ax-grinding on sex, love, anarchy, fascism, and the class struggle. All but *All Screwed Up* star Giannini, Wertmüller's favorite actor. His characters think they are suave, lusty studs, but are really just stubborn and stupid, in constant trouble both politically and sexually. An example: in *Love and Anarchy*, set in 1932, he plays an anarchist, riding in a brothel, who falls for a prostitute while planning to assassinate Mussolini. Wertmüller's women on the other hand, are not politically aware and are uninterested in struggling for self-sufficiency.

Seven Beauties, filled with stunning images, is a searing drama about survival in a surreal, insane world. Its reputation has suffered primarily because Wertmüller's more recent features have been misfires: *The End of the World in Our Usual Bed in a Night Full of Rain*, her first English language effort, an overly verbose marital boxing match pitting journalist/communist Giannini and photographer/feminist Candice Bergen; and *Revenge*, also known as *Blood Feud*, the overdone tale of a radical lawyer (Marcello Mastroianni) and a gangster (Giannini) who both love widow Sophia Loren during the early years of Fascist rule in Italy.

—Rob Edelman

———

WHALE, James.

British. Born in Dudley, England, 22 July 1889 (some sources state 1896). Cartoonist for *The Bystander*, from 1910; held in prisoner-of-war camp, World War I; actor and set designer for Birmingham Repertory Theatre, 1917–25; actor on London stage, from 1925; directed *Journey's End* on London stage, 1929; moved to Hollywood to direct film version, 1930; director for Universal, mostly of horror films, 1931–41; retired from film to pursue painting, 1941; attempted comeback *Hello Out There* failed, 1949; occasional stage director, from 1949. *Died 30 May 1957.*

Films as Director:

1930   *Journey's End*
1931   *Waterloo Bridge*; **Frankenstein**
1932   *The Impatient Maiden*; **The Old Dark House**
1933   *The Kiss Before the Mirror*; *The Invisible Man*
1934   *By Candlelight*; *One More River*
1935   **The Bride of Frankenstein**; *Remember Last Night*
1936   *Showboat*
1937   *The Road Back*; *The Great Garrick*
1938   *The Port of Seven Seas*; *Sinners in Paradise*; *Wives Under Suspicion*
1939   *The Man in the Iron Mask*
1940   *Green Hell*
1941   *They Dare Not Love*

Publications:

On WHALE: books—

Clarens, Carlos, *An Illustrated History of the Horror Film*, New York, 1968.
Baxter, John, *Hollywood in the Thirties*, New York, 1970.
Butler, Ivan, *Horror in the Cinema*, 2nd revised edition, New York, 1970.
Anobile, Richard, *James Whale's "Frankenstein"*, New York, 1974.
Everson, William, *Classics of the Horror Film*, Secaucus, New Jersey, 1974.
Tropp, Martin, *Mary Shelley's Monster: The Story of Frankenstein*, Boston, 1976.
Derry, Charles, *Dark Dreams: A Psychological History of the Modern Horror Film*, New York, 1977.
Ellis, Reed, *Journey into Darkness: The Art of James Whale's Horror Films*, New York, 1980.
Curtis, James, *James Whale*, Metuchen, New Jersey, 1983.

On WHALE: articles—

Obituary in the *New York Times*, 30 May 1957.
Edwards, Roy, "Movie Gothick: A Tribute to James Whale," in *Sight and Sound* (London), Autumn 1957.
Durgnat, Raymond, "The Subconscious: From Pleasure Castle to Libido Motel," in *Films and Filming* (London), January 1962.
Fink, Robert, and William Thomaier, "James Whale," in *Films in Review* (New York), May 1962.
Jensen, Paul, "James Whale," in *Film Comment* (New York), Spring 1971.
Milne, Tom, "One Man Crazy: James Whale," in *Sight and Sound* (London), Summer 1973.

James Whale (right) on the set of *Impatient Maiden*

Evans, Walter, "Monster Movies: A Sexual Theory," in *Journal of Popular Film* (Bowling Green, Ohio), Fall 1973.

Evans, Walter, "Monster Movies and Rites of Initiation," in *Journal of Popular Film* (Bowling Green, Ohio), Spring 1975.

White, D.L., "The Poetics of Horror: More than Meets the Eye," in *Film Genre: Theory and Criticism* edited by Barry Grant, Metuchen, New Jersey, 1977.

Clarens, Carlos, and Mary Corliss, "Designed for Film: The Hollywood Art Director," in *Film Comment* (New York), May/June 1978.

Taylor, John Russell, "Tales of the Hollywood Raj," in *Films and Filming* (London), June 1983.

Mank, G., "Mae Clarke Remembers James Whale," in *Films in Review* (New York), May 1985.

*   *   *

Although he is primarily remembered as the director of the cult horror films *Frankenstein*, *The Old Dark House*, *The Invisible Man*, and *The Bride of Frankenstein*, James Whale contributed much more to the cinema with his handling of such stylish and elegant productions as *Waterloo Bridge* and *One More River*, which had little critical impact when they were first released and are, unfortunately, largely unknown today.

A quite, introspective man, James Whale's background was the stage, notably the original London and New York productions of R.C. Sheriff's pacifist play *Journey's End*. Aside from some work assisting Howard Hughes with the direction of *Hell's Angels* (work which is both negligible and best forgotten), James Whale made his directorial debut with *Journey's End*, a film which illustrates many of the qualities which were to mark Whale's later work: close attention to acting and dialogue, a striving for authenticity in settings and a thoughtful use of camera (here somewhat hampered by the limits imposed on early talkies).

From 1930 through 1937, while Whale was under contract to Universal and under the patronage of studio production head Carl Laemmle, Jr., the director was able to turn out a group of literate and accomplished features. Among his varied productions was the First World War melodrama *Waterloo Bridge*, later remade in a gaudy Hollywood fashion by Mervyn LeRoy, but in this version noteworthy for its honest approach to its leading character's prostitution and a stunning performance by Mae Clarke (a favorite Whale actress). Both *The Invisible Man* and *The Bride of Frankenstein*, are influenced by the director's earlier *Frankenstein*, but both contain an element of black humor which lifts them above the common horror film genre. *The Kiss Before the Mirror* and *By Candlelight* possess an intangible charm, while *One More River* is simply one of Hollywood's best depictions of upper-class British life, memorable for the ensemble playing of its cast, headed by Diana Wynyard, and the one-liners from Mrs. Patrick Campbell. *Show Boat* demonstrates that Whale could handle a musical as easily as a romantic drama and is, without question, the finest screen version of the Jerome Kern-Oscar Hammerstein hit. All of Whale's Universal features were well received, with the exception of his last, *The Road Back*, based on an Erich Maria Remarque novel, intended as a sequel to *All Quiet on the Western Front*. *The Road Back* today appears badly constructed, a problem created in part by the studio's interference with the production out of concern that the German government might find the film unacceptable.

Whale's final films after leaving Universal are uniformly without interest, and contemporary response to them was lukewarm at best. The director simply grew tired of the hassles of filmmaking and retired. It has been suggested that Whale's homosexuality may have been unacceptable in Hollywood and helped to end his career, but he was a very private man who kept his personal life to himself, and it seems unlikely that his sexual preference created any problem for him or his employees; certainly Whale's homosexuality is not evident from his films, unless it be in the casting of the delightfully "camp" Ernest Thesiger in *The Old Dark House* and *The Bride of Frankenstein*.

—Anthony Slide

———————

WIELAND, Joyce.

Canadian. Born in Toronto, 1931. Educated at Central Technical Vocational High School, Toronto. Married artist Michael Snow, 1957. Independent artist and commercial artist, Toronto, 1950s; animator for Jim McKay and George Dunning's Graphic Films, 1955–56; with Snow moved to New York City, 1963; formed company Corrective film, 1964; moved back to Toronto, 1971; worked on funding, producing and directing *The Far Shore*, 1971–76; continues working as visual artist; retrospective of art and films at Art Gallery of Ontario, 1987. Address: 497 Queen Street East, Toronto, Ontario M5A 1V1, Canada.

Films as Director

1958	*Tea in the Garden* (co-d)
1959	*A Salt in the Park* (co-d)
1963	*Larry's Recent Behaviour*
1964	*Peggy's Blue Skylight*; *Patriotism* (Parts 1 and 2)
1964/65	*Watersark*
1965	*Barbara's Blindness* (co-d)
1967/68	*Sailboat*; *1933*; *Hand-tinting*
1968	*Catfood*; *Rat Life and Diet in North America*
1968/69	*La Raison avant la passion* (*Reason over Passion*)
1969	*Dripping Water* (co-d with Michael Snow)
1972	*Pierre Vallières*; *Birds at Sunrise*
1973	*Solidarity*
1976	*The Far Shore*
1984	*A & B in Ontario* (co-d with Hollis Frampton)
1985	*Birds at Sunrise*; *Wendy and Joyce* (incomplete)

Other Films:

1967	*Sky Socialist* (Jacobs) (role); **Wavelength** (Snow) (role); *Standard Time* (Snow) (role)
1972	*Knocturne* (George and Mike Kuchar) (role); "*Rameau's Nephew" by Diderot* (*Thanx to Dennis Young*) *by Wilma Schoen* (Snow) (role)

Publications:

By WIELAND: book—

True Patriot Love/Veritable Amour patriotique, with interview by Pierre Théberge, Ottawa, 1971.

By WIELAND: articles—

"North America's Second All-Woman Film Crew," in *Take One* (Montreal), December 1967.

"Jigs and Reels," in *Form and Structure in Recent Film*, edited by Dennis Wheeler, Vancouver Art Gallery, 1972.

"Kay Armatage Interviews Joyce Wieland," in *Take One* (Montreal), February 1972.

Interview with Lauren Rabinovitz in *Afterimage* (Rochester, New York), May 1981.

On WIELAND: articles—

Farber, Manny, "Joyce Wieland," in *Artforum* (New York), February 1970.

Sitney, P. Adams, "There Is Only One Joyce," in *ArtsCanada* (Toronto), April 1970.

McPherson, Hugo, "Wieland: An Epiphany of North," in *ArtsCanada* (Toronto), August/September 1971.

Cornwell, Regina, "*True Patriot Love*: The Films of Joyce Wieland," in *Artforum* (New York), September 1971.

Martineau, B.H., "The Far Shore: A Film About Violence, A Peaceful Film About Violence," in *Cinema Canada* (Montreal), April 1976.

Delaney, Marshall, "Wielandism: A Personal Style in Full Bloom," in *Canadian Film Reader* edited by Feldman and Nelson, Ontario, 1977.

Martineau, B.H., "Ragged History and Contemporary Scatterings," in *Cinema Canada* (Montreal), January/February 1981.

Rabinovitz, Lauren, "The Development of Feminist Strategies in the Experimental Films of Joyce Wieland," in *Film Reader* (Evanston), no. 5, 1982.

McCarty, L.M., "The Experimental Films of Joyce Wieland," in *Cine-Tracts* (Montreal), Summer/Fall 1982.

Rabinovitz, "The Films of Joyce Wieland," in *Joyce Wieland*, 1987.

Scott, Jay, "Full Circle," and Susan M. Crean, "Notes from the Language of Emotion," in *Canadian Art*, Spring 1987.

O'Pray, Michael, "Joyce Wieland: In Search of the Far Shore," in *Art Monthly* (London), March 1988.

On WIELAND: films—

Steed, Judy, director, *A Film About Joyce Wieland*, Canada, 1972.
Armatage, Kay, *Artist on Fire*, Canada, 1972.

*   *   *

Joyce Wieland achieved her reputation as one of a group of experimental filmmakers who contributed to the creation of an avant-garde film style in the middle and late 1960s. Wieland's films formally investigate the limitations and shared properties of several media while they developed increasingly pointed themes regarding Canadian nationalism and feminism.

When Toronto developed into a leading Canadian art center in the late 1950s and 1960s, Wieland became the only woman who achieved artistic prominence among the new group of Canadian painters influenced by Abstract Expressionism and Pop Art. Concerned about being even closer to the most recent developments among vanguard artists, Wieland and Snow moved to New York City in 1963. Although they remained expatriates until 1971, Wieland continued to exhibit her work throughout Canada and established a reputation during the next decade as the country's leading woman artist.

In New York City, Wieland became friendly with many members of the "underground" film community, a group whose bohemian behavior and outrageously styled home movies were gaining increased notoriety. Influenced by underground filmmakers Harry Smith, Ken Jacobs, and George Kuchar, Wieland began making short, personal films, and her movies were soon included in the group's regular Greenwich Village screenings.

The cinematic style that evolved out of several underground filmmakers' works became known by the late 1960s as "structural film." These films addressed the nature of the film viewing experience itself and created self-reflexive statements about such basic materials of filmmaking as projected light, celluloid, and the camera apparatus. Structural filmmaking paralleled painterly developments in minimal art and received international recognition as the new radical forefront of avant-garde film. Wieland's films, often grouped and discussed with those by such other structural filmmakers as Snow, Jacobs, Hollis Frampton, and Ernie Gehr, played at museums, film festivals, and colleges in Europe and North America.

In 1969, Wieland directed a feature-length movie that wedded the highly conceptual and experimental concerns of structural film with her own political feelings regarding Canada. The result, *Reason Over Passion* is an experimental documentary film about the country of Canada, Canadian culture and identity. Following the film's release, Wieland expressed and developed the same themes in an art show entitled "True Patriot Love" at the National Gallery of Canada in 1971. The show's Pop Art styled quilts, embroideries, and knittings served as patriotic banners for nationalism and feminism.

Because of the direction her work was taking, and because of her increased involvement in Canadian artists' political groups and causes, Wieland returned in 1971 to Toronto. There she completed two additional short structural documentaries. *Pierre Vallières* is about a French-Canadian revolutionary and the problems between French and English Canada. *Solidarity* is about a labor stike at an Ontario factory whose workers were mostly women. At the same time, Wieland co-wrote, co-produced, and directed a theatrical feature-length film. *The Far Shore* is a romantic melodrama that tells the story of a French Canadian woman whose failing marriage to a stuffy Toronto bourgeois results in her liberating affair with a Canadian painter. The film was not commercially successful but has subsequently been featured at film festivals, colleges, and museums in North America and Europe. After the completion of *The Far Shore*, Wieland returned primarily to drawing, painting, and printmaking and has since produced several series of new works. In 1987, the Art Gallery of Ontario hosted a retrospective of her art and films. It was the museum's first such honoring a living woman artist.

—Lauren Rabinovitz

————————

WIENE, Robert.

German. Born in Dresden, 1881. Actor, writer and director, Lessing-Theater, Berlin, until 1913; offered film directing debut by producer Kolowrat, 1913; collaborated with Walter Turszinsky on several comic films, 1915; directed a number of Henny Porten films, 1916; worked in Austria, 1924–26; left Nazi Germany, 1934. *Died in Paris, 17 July 1938.*

Films as Director:

1912   *Die Waffen der Jugend* (d: Wiene or Friedrich Müller, + sc)
1915   *Frau Eva* (*Arme Eva*) (+ co-sc): *Die Konservanbraut*; *Der springende Hirsch* (*Die Diebe von Günsterburg*) (co-d?)
1916   *Der Sekretär der Königen* (+ sc); *Der Liebesbrief der Königin* (+ sc); *Das wandernde Licht*; *Die Räuberbraut*; *Der Mann Spiegel* (+ sc)
1917   *Der standhafte Benjamin* (+ sc): *Das Leben—ein Traum* (+ co-sc)
1918   *Der Umweg zur Ehe* (d: Wiene or Fritz Freisler, + co-sc); *Die Millionärin* (alternate title of preceding?)
1919   *Die verführte Heilige* (+ sc); *Ein gefährliches Spiel* (+ sc); *Um das Lächeln einer Frau* (alternate title for preceding?)
1920   *Die Drei Tänze der Mary Wilford* (+ co-sc); **Das Kabinett des Dr. Caligari** (**The Cabinet of Dr. Caligari**); *Genuine*; *Die Nacht der Konigin Isabeau* (+ sc)
1921   *Die Rache einer Frau*; *Das Spiel mit den Feuer* (+ co-sc)
1922   *Die höllische Macht*
1923   *Raskolnikow* (*Schuld und Sühne*) (+ sc): *Der Puppenmacher von Kiang-Ning*; *I.N.R.I.* (*Ein Film der Menschlichkeit*) (+ sc)

Robert Wiene: *Orlacs Hände*

1924   *Orlacs Hände; Pension Groonen*
1925   *Der Leibgardist (Der Gardeoffizier); Der Rosenkavalier (+ co-sc): Die Königin vom Moulin-Rouge*
1927   *Die Geliebte; Die berühmte Frau; Le Tombeau sous L'Arc de Triomphe*
1928   *Die Frau auf der Folter; Die grosse Abenteuerin; Leontines Ehemänner; Unfug der Liebe*
1930   *Der Andere* (French version: *Le Procureur Hallers*)
1931   *Der Liebesexpress (Acht Tage Gluck)* (French version: *Huit Jours de bonheur*); *Panik in Chicago*
1933   *Polizeiakte 909 (Der Fall Tokeramo)* (+ sc)
1934   *Eine Nacht in Venedig* (+ sc)
1938   *Ultimatum* (completed by Robert Siodmak)

Other Films:

1915   *Fräulein Barbier* (Albes) (co-sc); *Arme Marie* (Zeyn and Mack) (sc); *Flucht der Schönheit (Seine schöne Mama)* (Rector, i.e. Zeiske) (co-sc); *Die büssende Magdalena* (Albes) (co-sc); *Lottekens Feldzug* (Ziener) (co-sc); *Der Schirm mit dem Schwan* (Froelich) (sc)
1916   *Gelöste Ketten* (Biebrach) (sc)
1917   *Frank Hansens Glück* (Larsen) (sc); *Die Prinzessin von Neutralien* (Biebach) (sc)

1918   *Die Heimkehr des Odysseus* (Biebrach) (sc); *Das Geschlecht derer von Rinwall* (Biebrach) (sc); *Opfer der Gesellschaft* (Grunwald) (sc); *Die Dame, der Teufel und die Probiermamsell* (Biebrach) (sc): *Am Tor des Lebens (Am Tor des Todes)* (Conrad Wiene) (sc)
1919   *Satanas* (Murnau) (artistic spvr); *Ihr Sport* (Biebrach) (sc); *Die lebende Tote* (Biebrach) (sc)
1920   *Das Blut der Ahnen* (Gerhardt) (co-sc); *Die Jagd nach dem Tode* and *Die verbotene Stadt* (Gerhardt in 2 parts) (co-sc); *Die Abenteuer des Dr. Kircheisen* (Biebrach) (sc)
1923   *Die Macht der Finsternis* (Conrad Wiene) (sc)
1924   ***Das Wachsfigurenkabinett*** (***Waxworks***) (Leni) (artistic spvr)
1928   *Heut Spielt der Strauss (Der Walzerkönig)* (Conrad Wiene) (sc)
1936   *The Robber Symphony* (Feher) (artistic supervision)

Publications:

By WIENE: book—

The Cabinet of Dr. Caligari, New York, 1972.

On WIENE: books—

Kracauer, Siegfried, *From Caligari to Hitler: A Psychological History of the German Film*, Princeton, New Jersey, 1947.
Eisner, Lotte, *The Haunted Screen*, Berkeley, 1969.
Manvell, Roger, and Heinrich Fraenkel, *The German Cinema*, New York, 1971.

Laqueur, Walter, *Weimar: A Cultural History 1918–1933*, New York, 1974.

Barton, John D., *German Expressionist Film*, Boston, 1982.

On WIENE: article—

Mayer, Carl, "*Le Cabinet du Docteur Caligari*," in *Avant-Scène du Cinéma* (Paris), July/September 1975.

*   *   *

Robert Wiene's name will ever be associated with his most famous film although there are critics who would minimize his responsibility for this masterpiece of the cinema. His work is uneven and often blatantly commercial but in spite of this many of his films show some originality of theme and distinguished performances by actors who worked under him.

Das Kabinett des Dr. Caligari, originally intended for Fritz Lang, put Wiene's name on the map. It is the most important of the expressionist films and today its power seems undiminished and its daring timeless. It ran continuously in Paris for seven years, thereby creating a record, and at the Brussels World's Fair of 1958 it was chosen by 117 film historians from 26 countries as one of the top twelve most important films of all time.

In *Genuine* Wiene failed to repeat his success in the same genre although the film was also scripted by the talented Carl Mayer. In 1923 three films show an interesting range of subject matter. I.N.R.I. dealt with the death of Christ and was mounted on a grand scale, with the cream of German acting in the leading roles, and with settings by the promising young Hungarian designer, Ernö Metzner. *Der Puppenmacher von Kiang-Ning* a tragic-comedy with a script by Carl Mayer, and *Raskolnikow* with fantastic sets by the Russian designer Andreiv completed an interesting trilogy. The latter used emigrée actors in an adaptation of Dostoievsky's *Crime and Punishment*.

From 1924 to 1926 Wiene worked in Austria where he made other distinguished films—*Orlacs Hände*, a horror film with Conrad Viedt as a sensitive musician who has the hands of a murderer grafted on to him, and *Der Rosenkavalier* a film adaptation of the Strauss opera, co-scripted by Hugo von Hoffmanstahl and with a special score arranged by the composer, who personally conducted the orchestra when it had its premiere at the Dresden State Opera House and at the Tivoli Cinema in London. The leading roles were taken by the French stars Huguette Duflos and Jacque Catelain.

Wiene returned to Germany but his later work showed no special qualities and consisted of lightweight comedies with artists like Lily Damita, Dina Gralla, and Maria Jacobini. He directed Mady Christians and Andre Roanne in a French production *La Duchesee de Les Folies*. Of his sound films the Johann Strauss operetta *Eine Nacht in Venedig* merits attention. He died in Paris in 1938 while directing Erich von Stroheim and Dita Parlo in *Ultimatum* which was completed by Robert Siodmak. In 1935 he had supervised in England *The Robber Symphony* directed by his former actor from *Caligari*, Friedrich Feher.

While he covered a wide range of material in his films he never developed a personal style. His merit lay in encouraging many diverse talents and often securing outstanding contributions from them. He controlled his productions, in most cases writing the scripts himself. He lived in a great period of cinema which he served in his fashion.

—Liam O'Leary

———

WILCOX, Herbert.

British. Born in Cork, Ireland, 19 April 1891. Educated in Brighton, England. Married actress Anna Neagle, 1943. Worked on newspaper, until 1914; served as pilot with Royal Flying Corps, World War I; secretary and director of Astra Films, 1919; with Graham Cutts founded Graham Wilcox Productions, 1920; began as producer with *The Wonderful Story*, 1922; organized British and Dominion Productions, 1929; began making films with Anna Neagle, 1932; chairman and managing director, Imperator Film Productions, Ltd., 1937; signed agreement with RKO-Radio for distribution of his films, 1938; director in Hollywood for RKO, from 1940; returned to England, 1942; signed contract with 20th Century-Fox for series of pictures, 1945; forced into bankruptcy, 1964. *Died in London*, 15 May 1977.

Films as Director:

1922	*Whispering*
1923	*Chu-Chin-Chow*
1924	*Southern Love*; *Decameron Nights*
1926	*The Only Way*
1927	*Tip Toes*; *London*; *Mumsie*; *Nell Gwynne*
1928	*The Scarlet Pimpernel*; *Madame Pompadour*
1929	*The Woman in White*; *The Rosary*; *The Bondman*
1930	*The Loves of Robert Burns*; *Mountains of Mourne*
1931	*The Blue Danube*; *The Chance of a Night Time*
1932	*The Little Damozel*; *Carnival*; *Goodnight Vienna*; *The Flag Lieutenant*; *The Love Contract*; *The King's Cup*
1933	*Bitter Sweet*
1934	*The Queen's Affair*
1935	*Nell Gwynne*
1936	*Peg of Old Drury*; *Fame*; *Limelight*
1937	*The Three Maxims*; *Millions*; *This'll Make You Whistle*; *London Melody*; *Victoria the Great*
1938	*Sixty Glorious Years*
1939	*Nurse Edith Cavell*
1940	*No No Nanette*; *Irene*
1941	*Sunny*
1942	*They Flew Alone*
1943	*The Yellow Canary*; *Forever and a Day* (co-d)
1945	*I Live in Grosvenor Square*
1946	*Piccadilly Incident*
1947	*The Courtneys of Curzon Street*
1948	*Spring in Park Lane*
1949	*Elizabeth of Ladymead*; *Maytime in Mayfair*
1950	*Odette*
1951	*The Lady with a Lamp*; *Into the Blue*; *Derby Day*
1952	*Trent's Last Case*
1953	*Laughing Anne*
1954	*Lilacs in the Spring*; *Trouble in the Glen*
1955	*King's Rhapsody*
1956	*My Teenage Daughter*
1957	*These Dangerous Years*
1958	*The Man Who Wouldn't Talk*; *Wonderful Things*
1959	*The Lady Is a Square*; *The Heart of a Man*

Other Films:

1922	*The Wonderful Story* (Cutts) (pr); *Flames of Passion* (Cutts) (pr)
1923	*Paddy-the-Next-Best-Thing* (Cutts) (pr)
1932	*Thark* (pr); *The Flag Lieutenant* (Edwards) (pr); *The Love Contract* (Selpin) (pr)
1933	*Say It with Music* (Raymond) (pr)
1934	*Sorrell and Son* (Raymond) (pr)
1935	*Brewster's Millions* (Freeland) (pr)
1937	*The Gang Show* (Goulding) (pr); *The Rat* (Goulding) (pr); *Our Fighting Navy* (Walker) (pr); *The Frog* (Raymond) (pr)

Herbert Wilcox

1938   *Sunset in Vienna* (Walker) (pr); *Blondes for Danger*
      (Raymond) (pr)
1957   *Yang-tse Incident* (Anderson) (pr)

Publications:

By WILCOX: book—

25,000 Sunsets: The Autobiography of Herbert Wilcox, London, 1967.

On WILCOX: books—

Neagle, Anna, *It's Been Fun*, London, 1949.
Neagle, Anna, *There's Always Tomorrow*, London, 1974.
Armes, Roy, *A Critical History of the British Cinema*, London, 1978.

On WILCOX: article—

Passek, Jean-Loup, "Herbert Wilcox," in *Cinéma* (Paris), August/
  September 1977.

*   *   *

In the opening chapter of his autobiography, Herbert Wilcox
wrote, "I was born starry-eyed on 19 April, with Aries at its
zenith, and I've lived with stars in my eyes ever since." In fact,
Wilcox had only one star in his eyes through most of his career,
and that star was his wife Anna Neagle, who was featured in
virtually every film that Wilcox made from 1932 onwards. They
were a team, whose charms helped override some of their basic

deficiencies as director and actress. What is apparent from the
films, as Nöel Coward noted in his diary, was "the unimpaired
'niceness' of both of them." Herbert Wilcox was an affable,
easy-going director, with an eye to the box office, who thought
he could transform Anna Neagle into any character from history: Nell Gwynne, Queen Victoria (in *Victoria the Great* and
Sixty Glorious Years), Nurse Edith Cavell, Amy Johnson (in
They Flew Alone), French spy Odette, or Florence Nightingale
(in *The Lady with the Lamp*). Sometimes he succeeded.

A film salesman turned producer in the early 1920s, Herbert
Wilcox's silent career was notable for his realization that it was
stars who brought commercial fame, and as Britain had so few
film stars it was necessary to import them from the States. To
this end he brought over Mae Marsh, Dorothy Gish, Blanche
Sweet, and even Will Rogers. Those early films were light and
frothy affairs, but Wilcox began to take himself seriously with
The Only Way (featuring Sir John Martin Harvey in his famous
stage version of Dicken's *A Tale of Two Cities*), and *Dawn*,
with Sybil Thorndike as Edith Cavell. Both were surprisingly
well-made, but Wilcox professed a strong dislike for realism
and insisted that entertainment must always be the chief component in his productions. In the 1930s, therefore, he made
musicals with Jack Buchanan and Anna Neagle, until struck by
a sense of patriotism (and perhaps a desire to prove that Miss

Neagle could act) which led to two features dealing with the life of Queen Victoria and a remake of *Dawn* (*Nurse Edith Cavell*), obviously intended as anti-German propaganda.

The success of the Wilcox-Neagle films in the United States led to a RKO contract in Hollywood, and more "entertainment" through remakes of *Irene*, *No No Nanette*, and *Sunny*. Returning to a Britain governed by socialists. Herbert Wilcox embarked on another series of films, billed as being filled with "Music, Gaiety, Laughter and Romance," this time concerned with upper-middle-class Londoners of Park Lane and Curzon Street, living in a world far removed from the reality of rationing and postwar austerity.

It was not until the 1950s that Herbert Wilcox began to lose his grip on the audience. He tried unsuccessfully to turn Errol Flynn into an Ivor Novello matinee idol with *Lilacs in the Spring* and *King's Rhapsody*. Anna Neagle was forced to come to grips with teenage rebellion and rock-and-roll in *My Teenage Daughter*, *These Dangerous Years*, and *The Lady Is a Square*. Audiences were not interested. In 1964 Wilcox was declared bankrupt, and his last years were spent in futile attempts to obtain funding for film projects which would once again glorify England, as he had done in the 1930s.

For almost half a century, Herbert Wilcox was Britain's most successful producer/director, and while it is perhaps easy to sneer at many of his films, one should not overlook his understanding of the audience, and the professionalism and care which are obvious in all of his features (qualities lacking from the works of many of his English contemporaries).

—Anthony Slide

WILDER, Billy.

Born Samuel Wilder in Sucha, Austria (now part of Poland), 22 June 1906, became U.S. citizen, 1934. Journalist in Vienna, then in Berlin, from 1926; collaborated with Robert and Kurt Siodmak, Edgar Ulmer, Fred Zinnemann and Eugen Schüfftan on *Menschen am Sonntag*, 1929; scriptwriter, mainly for UFA studios, 1929–33; moved to Paris, co-directed *Mauvaise graine*, first directorial effort, then moved to Hollywood, 1933; hired by script department at Columbia, then 20th Century-Fox; hired by Paramount, began collaboration with Charles Brackett on *Bluebeard's 8th Wife*, 1937; directed first American film, *The Major and the Minor*, 1942; served in U.S. Army as Colonel in Psychological Warfare Division of the Occupational Government, Berlin, 1945; began making films as independent producer/director with *The Seven Year Itch*, 1955; began collaboration with writer I.A.L. Diamond on *Love in the Afternoon*, 1957; directed *The Front Page* for Universal, 1974. Recipient: Oscars for Best Direction and Best Screenplay (with Charles Brackett), and Best Direction Award, New York Film Critics, for *The Lost Weekend*, 1945; Oscar for Best Story and Screenplay (with Charles Brackett), for *Sunset Boulevard*, 1950; Oscars for Best Direction and Best Screenplay (with I.A.L. Diamond), Best Direction Award and Best Writing Award (with Diamond), New York Film Critics, for *The Apartment*, 1960. Address: c/o Equitable Investment Corporation, P.O. Box 93877, Hollywood, CA 90093, U.S.A.

Films as Director:

1933   *Mauvaise graine* (co-d)

1942   *The Major and the Minor* (+ co-sc)
1943   *Five Graves to Cairo* (+ co-sc)
1944   **Double Indemnity** (+ co-sc)
1945   **The Lost Weekend** (+ co-sc)
1948   *The Emperor Waltz* (+ co-sc); *Foreign Affair* (+ co-sc)
1950   **Sunset Boulevard** (+ co-sc)
1951   *Ace in the Hole* (*The Big Carnival*) (+ co-pr, co-sc)
1953   *Stalag 17* (+ pr, co-sc)
1954   *Sabrina* (+ pr, co-sc)
1955   *The Seven Year Itch* (+ co-pr, co-sc)
1957   *The Spirit of St. Louis* (+ co-sc); *Love in the Afternoon* (+ co-sc, pr)
1958   *Witness for the Prosecution* (+ co-sc)
1959   **Some Like It Hot** (+ co-sc, pr)
1960   **The Apartment** (+ co-sc, pr)
1961   *One, Two, Three* (+ co-sc, pr)
1963   *Irma La Douce* (+ co-sc, pr)
1964   *Kiss Me, Stupid* (+ co-sc, pr)
1966   *The Fortune Cookie* (+ co-sc, pr)
1970   *The Private Life of Sherlock Holmes* (+ co-sc, pr)
1972   *Avanti!* (+ co-sc, pr)
1974   *The Front Page* (+ co-sc)
1978   *Fedora* (+ co-pr, co-sc)
1981   *Buddy Buddy* (+ co-sc)

Other Films:
(in Germany):

1929   *Menschen am Sonntag* (*People on Sunday*) (Siodmak) (co-sc); *Der Teufelsreporter* (co-sc)
1930   *Seitensprünge* (story)
1931   *Ihre Hoheit befiehlt* (co-sc); *Der falsche Ehemann* (co-sc); *Emil und die Detektive* (*Emil and the Detectives*) (sc); *Der Mann der seinen Mörder sucht* (*Looking for his Murderer*) (Siodmak) (co-sc)
1932   *Es war einmal ein Walzer* (co-sc); *Ein blonder Traum* (co-sc); *Scampolo, ein Kind der Strasse* (co-sc); *Das Blaue von Himmel* (co-sc)
1933   *Madame wünscht keine Kinder* (co-sc); *Was Frauen träumen* (co-sc)

(in the United States):

1933   *Adorable* (Dieterle) (co-story, based on *Ihre Hoheit befiehlt*)
1934   *Music in the Air* (co-sc); *One Exciting Adventure* (co-story)
1935   *Lottery Lover* (co-sc)
1937   *Champagne Waltz* (Sutherland) (co-story)
1938   *Bluebeard's Eighth Wife* (Lubitsch) (co-sc)
1939   *Midnight* (Leisen) (co-sc); *What a Life* (co-sc); **Ninotchka** (Lubitsch) (co-sc)
1940   *Arise My Love* (Leisen) (co-sc)
1941   *Hold Back the Dawn* (Leisen) (co-sc); *Ball of Fire* (Hawks) (co-sc)

Publications:

By WILDER: articles—

"Wilder in Paris," with John Gillett, in *Sight and Sound* (London), Winter 1956.
"One Head is Better than Two," in *Films and Filming* (London), February 1957.
"The Old Dependables," with Colin Young, in *Film Quarterly* (Berkeley), Fall 1959.
Interview with Jean Domarchi and Jean Douchet in *Cahiers du Cinéma* (Paris), August 1962.
"Meet Whiplash Wilder," with Charles Higham, in *Sight and Sound* (London), Winter 1967.
Interview with Robert Mundy and Michael Wallington in *Cinema* (London), October 1969.
"Billy Wilder: Broadcast to Kuala Lampur," with Vanessa Brown, in *Action* (Los Angeles), November/December 1970.
Interview with Michael Ciment in *Positif* (Paris), January 1974.
"In the Picture: *The Front Page*," with Joseph McBride, in *Sight and Sound* (London), Autumn 1974.

Billy Wilder

Interview with Gene Phillips in *Film/Literature Quarterly* (Salisbury, Maryland), Winter 1975.

"Wilder Bewildered," an interview with Gilbert Adair, in *Sight and Sound* (London), Winter 1976/77.

"Going for Extra Innings," an interview with J. McBride and T. McCarthy, in *Film Comment* (New York), January/February 1979.

Interview with C. Columbus in *American Film* (Washington D.C.), March 1986.

On WILDER: books—

Madsen, Axel, *Billy Wilder*, Bloomington, Indiana, 1969.

Wood, Tom, *The Bright Side of Billy Wilder, Primarily*, New York, 1970.

Corliss, Richard, *Talking Pictures: Screenwriters in the American Cinema*, New York, 1975.

Seidman, Steve, *The Film Career of Billy Wilder*, Boston, 1977.

Zolotow, Maurice, *Billy Wilder in Hollywood*, New York, 1977.

Dick, Bernard F., *Billy Wilder*, Boston, 1980.

Giannetti, Louis, *Masters of the American Cinema*, Englewood Cliffs, New Jersey, 1981.

Jacob, Jerome, *Billy Wilder*, Paris, 1988.

Seidl, Claudius, *Billy Wilder: Seine Filme, sein Leben*, Munich, 1988.

On WILDER: articles—

Lightman, Herb, "Old Master, New Tricks," in *American Cinematographer* (Los Angeles), September 1950.

McVay, Douglas, "The Eye of the Cynic," in *Films and Filming* (London), January 1960.

Higham, Charles, "Cast a Cold Eye: The Films of Billy Wilder," in *Sight and Sound* (London), Spring 1963.

Sarris, Andrew, "Fallen Idols," in *Film Culture* (New York), Spring 1963.

"The Films of Billy Wilder," in *Film Comment* (New York), Summer 1965.

Mundy, Robert, "Wilder Reappraised," in *Cinema* (London), October 1969.

McBride, Joseph, and Michael Wilmington, "The Private Life of Billy Wilder," in *Film Quarterly* (Berkeley), Summer 1970.

Ciment, Michel, "Sept Réflexions sur Billy Wilder," in *Positif* (Paris), May 1971.

Farber, Stephen, "The Films of Billy Wilder," in *Film Comment* (New York), Winter 1971.

Onosko, Tom, "Billy Wilder," in *Velvet Light Trap* (Madison, Wisconsin), Winter 1971.

"Dialogue on Film: Billy Wilder and I.A.L. Diamond," in *American Film* (Washington, D.C.), July/August 1976.

Sarris, Andrew, "Billy Wilder: Closet Romanticist," in *Film Comment* (New York), July/August 1976.

"*Fedora* Issue" of *Avant-Scène du Cinéma* (Paris), 15 November 1978.

Poague, Lee, "Some Versions of Billy Wilder," in *Cinemonkey* (Portland), no. 1, 1979.

Morris, G., "The Private Films of Billy Wilder," in *Film Comment* (New York), January/February 1979.

Allen, T., "Bracketting Wilder," in *Film Comment* (New York), May/June 1982.

"Billy Wilder Issue" of *Filmcritica* (Florence), November/December 1982.

"Dossier Billy Wilder," in *Positif* (Paris), July/August 1983.

Billy Wilder Section of *Positif* (Paris), September 1983.

Gallagher, Brian, "Sexual Warfare and Homoeroticism in Billy Wilder's *Double Indemnity*," in *Literature/Film Quarterly* (Salisbury, Maryland), vol. 15, no. 4, 1987.

Willett, R., "Billy Wilder's *A Foreign Affair* (1945–1948): 'the Trials and Tribulations of Berlin'," in *Historical Journal of Film, Radio and Television* (Abingdon, Oxon), March 1987.

* * *

During the course of his directorial career, Billy Wilder succeeded in offending just about everybody. He offended the public, who shunned several of his movies as decisively as they flocked to others; he offended the press with *Ace in the Hole*, the US Congress with *A Foreign Affair*, the Hollywood establishment with *Sunset Boulevard* ("This Wilder should be horsewhipped!" fumed Louis B Mayer), and religious leaders with *Kiss Me, Stupid*; he offended the critics, both those who found him too cynical and those who found him not cynical enough. And he himself, in the end, seems to have taken offence at the lukewarm reception of his last two films, and retired into morose silence.

Still, if Wilder gave offence, it was never less than intentional. "Bad taste," the tweaking or flouting of social taboos, is a key tactic throughout his work. His first film as director, *The Major and the Minor*, hints slyly at paedophilia, and several other Wilder movies toy with offbeat sexual permutations: transvestism in *Some Like It Hot*, spouseswapping in *Kiss Me, Stupid*, an ageing woman buying herself a young man in *Sunset Boulevard*, the reverse in *Love in the Afternoon*. Even when depicting straightforward romantic love, as in *The Emperor Waltz*, Wilder can't resist counterpointing it with the eager ruttings of a pair of dogs.

He also relishes emphasising the more squalid of human motives. *Stalag 17* mocks prison-camp mythology by making a mercenary fixer the only hero on offer, and *Double Indemnity* replays *The Postman Always Rings Twice* with greed replacing honest lust. In *The Apartment* Jack Lemmon avidly demeans himself to achieve professional advancement (symbolised by the key to a lavatory door), and virtually everybody in *Ace in the Hole*, perhaps the most acerbic film ever made in Hollywood, furthers personal ends at the expense of a poor dupe dying trapped in an underground crevice. Wilder presents a disillusioned world, one (as Joan Didion put it) "seen at dawn through a hangover, a world of cheap *double entendres* and stale smoke . . . the true country of despair."

Themes of impersonation and deception, especially emotional deception, pervade Wilder's work. People disguise themselves as others, or feign passions they don't feel, to gain some ulterior end. Frequently, though—all too frequently, perhaps—the counterfeit turns genuine, masquerade love conveniently developing into the real thing. For all his much-flaunted cynicism, Wilder often seems to lose the courage of his own disenchantment, resorting to unconvincing changes of heart to bring about a slick last-reel resolution. Some critics have seen this as blatant opportunism. "Billy Wilder," Andrew Sarris remarked, "is too cynical to believe even his own cynicism." Others have detected a sentimental undertow, one which surfaces in the unexpectedly mellow, almost benign late films like *Avanti!* and *The Private Life of Sherlock Holmes*.

But although, by comparison with a true moral subversive like Buñuel, Wilder can seem shallow and even facile, the best of his work retains a wit and astringent bite that sets it refreshingly off from the pieties of the Hollywood mainstream. When it comes to black comedy, he ranks at least the equal of his mentor, Lubitsch, whose audacity in wringing laughs out of concentration camps (*To Be or Not To Be*) is matched by Wilder's in pivoting *Some Like It Hot* around the St Valentine's Day Massacre.

The consistency of Wilder's sardonic vision allows him to operate with assurance across genre boundaries. *Sunset Boulevard*—"full of exactness, cleverness, mastery and pleasure, a gnawing, haunting and ruthless film with a dank smell of corrosive delusion hanging over it," wrote Axel Madsen—has yet to be surpassed among Hollywood-on-Hollywood movies. In its cold fatality, *Double Indemnity* qualifies as archetypal *noir*, yet the same sense of characters trapped helplessly in the rat-runs of their own nature underlies both the erotic farce of *The Seven Year Itch* and the autumnal melancholy of *Sherlock Holmes*. Acclamation, though, falls beyond Wilder's scope: his Lindbergh film, *The Spirit of St Louis*, is respectful, impersonal and dull.

By his own admission, Wilder became a director only to protect his scripts, and his shooting style is essentially functional. But though short on intricate camerawork and stunning compositions, his films are by no means visually drab. Several of them contain scenes that lodge indelibly in the mind: Swanson as the deranged Norma Desmond, regally descending her final staircase; Jack Lemmon dwarfed by the monstrous perspectives of a vast open-plan office; Ray Milland (*The Lost Weekend*) trudging the parched length of Third Avenue in search of an open pawn-shop; Lemmon again, tangoing deliriously with Joe E Brown, in full drag with a rose between his teeth. No film-maker capable of creating images as potent—and as cinematic—as these can readily be written off.

—Philip Kemp

WISE, Robert.

American. Born in Winchester, Indiana, 19 September 1914. Studied journalism at Franklin College. Hired as assistant editor at RKO where brother was employed, 1933; editor, from 1939; took over direction of *The Curse of the Cat People*, 1944; independent producer for Mirisch Corporation, 1959, and for Fox, 1963. Recipient: Oscar for Best Direction (with Jerome Robbins), for *West Side Story*, 1961; Oscar for Best Direction, and Directors Award, Directors Guild of America, for *The Sound of Music*, 1965; Irving G. Thalberg Memorial Academy Award, 1966. Address: c/o Robert Wise Productions, Sunset Gower Studios, 1438 North Gower St., Suite 562, Hollywood, CA 90028, U.S.A.

Films as Director:

1944   *The Curse of the Cat People* (co-d); *Mademoiselle Fifi*
1945   *The Body Snatchers*
1946   *A Game of Death*; *Criminal Court*
1947   *Born to Kill*
1948   *Mystery in Mexico*; *Blood on the Moon*
1949   *The Set-Up*
1950   *Three Secrets*; *Two Flags West*
1951   *The House on Telegraph Hill*; *The Day the Earth Stood Still*
1952   *Destination Gobi*; *Something for the Birds*
1953   *The Desert Rats*; *So Big*
1954   *Executive Suite*
1955   *Helen of Troy*; *Tribute to a Bad Man*
1956   *Somebody Up There Likes Me*
1957   *This Could Be the Night*; *Until They Sail*
1958   *Run Silent, Run Deep*; *I Want to Live*
1959   *Odds Against Tomorrow* (+ pr)
1961   *West Side Story* (co-d)
1962   *Two For the Seesaw*
1963   *The Haunting* (+ pr)
1965   *The Sound of Music* (+ pr)
1966   *The Sand Pebbles* (+ pr)
1968   *Star!*
1970   *The Andromeda Strain* (+ pr)
1971   *Two People* (+ pr)
1975   *The Hindenburg*
1977   *Audrey Rose*
1979   *Star Trek: The Motion Picture*
1987   *I, Zorba*
1989   *Rooftops*

Other Films:
(partial list)

1940   *Dance, Girl, Dance* (Arzner) (ed)

1941   *Citizen Kane* (Welles) (ed)
1942   *The Magnificent Ambersons* (Welles) (ed)

Publications:

By WISE: articles—

Interview in *Directors at Work*, edited by Bernard Kantor and others, New York, 1970.
"Impressions of Russia," in *Action* (Los Angeles), July/August 1971.
"Robert Wise at RKO," an interview with Ruy Nogueira, in *Focus on Film* (London), Winter 1972.
"Robert Wise at Fox," an interview with Ruy Nogueira, in *Focus on Film* (London), Spring 1973.
"Robert Wise Continued," with Ruy Nogueira and Allen Eyles, in *Focus on Film* (London), Autumn 1973.
"Robert Wise to Date," an interview with Ruy Nogueira, in *Focus on Film* (London), Autumn 1974.
"The Production of *The Hindenburg*," in *American Cinematographer* (Los Angeles), January 1976.
"Robert Wise Talks About 'The New Hollywood'," in *American Cinematographer* (Los Angeles), July 1976.
"*Audrey Rose*: In Search of a Soul," an interview with R. Appelbaum, in *Films and Filming* (London), November 1977.
"Time and Again," an interview in *Monthly Film Bulletin* (London), November 1979.
"An AFI Seminar with Robert Wise and Milton Krasner ASC," in *American Cinematographer* (Los Angeles), March 1980.

On WISE: book—

Grivel, Danièle, and Roland Lacourbe, *Robert Wise*, Paris, 1985.

On WISE: articles—

Stark, Samuel, "Robert Wise," in *Films in Review* (New York), January 1963.
"Wise Issue" of *Dialogue on Film* (Washington, D.C.), vol. 2, no. 1, 1972.
Stamelman, P., "Robert Wise and *The Hindenburg*," in *Millimeter* (New York), November 1975.
Guérif, F., "Nous avons gagné ce soir," in *Avant-Scène du Cinéma* (Paris), 1 March 1980.

* * *

In the early 1940s there were two young men in the editorial department at RKO who worked as editors on Val Lewton pictures: Robert Wise and Mark Robson. The latter was promoted to a full directorship of Lewton's *Seventh Victim*, a moody script by DeWitt Bodeen and Charles O'Neal, about a cult of devil worshippers in modern Manhattan.

Meanwhile, Robson's immediate superior in the editorial department, Robert Wise, got his first directorial opportunity when the front office was displeased with Gunther von Fritsch, who was halfway through *Curse of the Cat People*, and was dismissed because he was behind schedule, a cardinal sin in the days of the studios. It was natural that Robert Wise, being the editor of *Curse of the Cat People*, should take over and complete the film, for only he knew the continuity of what had already been shot. Wise did so admirable a job that Lewton immediately got him assigned to his unit as full director for *Mademoiselle Fifi* with Simone Simon and *The Body Snatcher* with Boris Karloff.

Wise had edited two Orson Welles films for RKO—two that became classics, *Citizen Kane* and *The Magnificent Ambersons*. After now being made a full director, he diligently went into an acting class because he felt that actors had a special knowledge and language of their own; it was the ideal way of seeing film from the actor's point of view. It paid off almost immediately; he got an assignment as director for *The Set-Up*, a realistic picture of the prize ring that made a top star of Robert Ryan and a top director as well of Wise. *The Set-Up* won him the Critics Prize at the Cannes Film Festival.

Robert Wise

In 1950 he was at Warner Bros., where he directed a distinguished mood film, *Three Secrets*, and went on to direct a remake of Edna Ferber's *So Big* with Jane Wyman, and *The Desert Rats* at 20th Century-Fox with Richard Burton. *Executive Suite* at MGM raised his status a notch higher, as did *Tribute to a Bad Man* with James Cagney. *Somebody Up There Likes Me* was an excellent prize ring picture starring Paul Newman, while *Run Silent, Run Deep* was a splendid submarine thriller for Gable and Lancaster. *I Want to Live* at long last won Susan Hayward an Academy Award as Best Actress for 1958. A couple of years later Wise shared an Academy Award as Best Director with Jerome Robbins for *West Side Story*.

He returned to the mood horror film to make one of the most memorable of all time, *The Haunting*, which he also produced. He was director/producer again for *The Sound of Music*, a top box office winner which won him once more the Academy's Oscar as Best Director, while *The Sand Pebbles*, with the late Steve McQueen, also earned him admiration.

—DeWitt Bodeen

WISEMAN, Frederick.

American. Born in Boston, 1 January 1930. Educated Williams College; Yale Law School; Harvard University. Served in U.S. Army, 1954–56. Practiced law in Paris, and began experimental filmmaking, 1956–58; taught at Boston University Law School, 1958–61; bought rights to *The Cool World* by Warren Miller, and produced documentary version directed by Shirley Clarke; directed first film, *Titicut Follies*, 1966; received foundation grant to do *High School*, 1967; directed 3 films funded in part by PBS and WNET Channel 13 in New York, 1968–71; contracted to make documentaries for WNET, 1971–81; continued to make films for PBS, through 1980s; also theatre director, late 1980s. Recipient: Emmy Award for Best Documentary Direction for *Hospital*, 1970.

Films as Director, Producer and Editor:

1967   *Titicut Follies*
1968   *High School*
1969   *Law and Order*
1970   *Hospital*
1971   *Basic Training*
1972   *Essene*
1973   *Juvenile Court*
1974   *Primate*
1975   *Welfare*; *Meat*
1977   *Canal Zone*
1979   *Sinai Field Mission*
1980   *Manoeuvre*
1981   *Model*
1982   *Seraphita's Diary* (+ sc)
1983   *The Store*
1985   *Racetrack*
1986   *Deaf*; *Blind*; *Multi-Handicapped*; *Adjustment and Work*
1988   *Missile*
1989   *Near Death*
1990   *Central Park*

Other Films:

1964   *The Cool World* (Clarke) (pr)
1968   *The Thomas Crown Affair* (Jewison) (sc, uncredited)

Publications:

By WISEMAN: articles—

"The Talk of the Town: New Producer," in the *New Yorker*, 14 September 1963.
Interview with Janet Handelman in *Film Library Quarterly* (New York), Summer 1970.
Interview with Ira Halberstadt in *Filmmaker's Newsletter* (Ward Hill, Massachusetts), February 1974.
"Vérités et mensonges du cinéma américain," an interview with M. Martin and others, in *Ecran* (Paris), September 1976.
"Wiseman on Polemic," an interview with A.T. Sutherland, in *Sight and Sound* (London), Spring 1978.

On WISEMAN: books—

Issari, M. Ali, *Cinema Verité*, Ann Arbor, Michigan, 1971.
Maynard, Richard A., *The Celluloid Curriculum: How to Use Movies in the Classroom*, New York, 1971.
Barsam, Richard, *Nonfiction Film: A Critical History*, New York, 1973.
Atkins, Thomas, editor, *Frederick Wiseman*, New York, 1976.
Ellsworth, Liz, *Frederick Wiseman: A Guide to References and Resources*, Boston, 1979.
Nichols, Bill, *Ideology and the Image: Social Representation in the Cinema and Other Media*, Bloomington, Indiana, 1981.
Benson, Thomas W., and Carolyn Anderson, *The Films of Frederick Wiseman*, Carbondale, Illinois, 1989.

On WISEMAN: articles—

Dowd, Nancy, "Popular Conventions," in *Film Quarterly* (Berkeley), Spring 1969.
Schickel, Richard, "A Verité View of High School," in *Life* (New York), 12 September 1969.
Denby, David, "Documentary America," in *Atlantic Monthly* (Greenwich, Connecticut), March 1970.
Mamber, Stephen, "The New Documentaries of Frederick Wiseman," in *Cinema* (Beverly Hills), Summer 1970.
Williams, Donald, "Frederick Wiseman," in *Film Quarterly* (Berkeley), Fall 1970.
"Frederick Wiseman," in *Documentary Explorations* edited by G. Roy Levin, New York, 1971.
Atkins, Thomas, "Frederick Wiseman Documents the Dilemmas of Our Institutions," in *Film News* (New York), October 1971.
"Frederick Wiseman," in *Cinema Verité in America: Studies in Uncontrolled Documentary* by Stephen Mamber, Cambridge, Massachusetts, 1974.
Atkins, Thomas, "American Institutions: The Films of Frederick Wiseman," in *Sight and Sound* (London), Autumn 1974.
Tuch, R., "Frederick Wiseman's Cinema of Alienation," in *Film Library Quarterly* (New York), vol. 11, no. 3, 1978.
Nichols, Bill, "Fred Wiseman's Documentaries: Theory and Structure," in *Film Quarterly* (Berkeley), Spring 1978.
Le Peron, S., "Fred Wiseman," in *Cahiers du Cinéma* (Paris), September 1979.
Armstrong, D., "Wiseman's *Model* and the Documentary Project: Toward a Radical Film Practice," in *Film Quarterly* (Berkeley), Winter 1983/84.
Barsam, R.M., "American Direct Cinema: the Re-presentation of Reality," in *Persistence of Vision* (Maspeth, New York), Summer 1986.

*   *   *

Wiseman's documentaries are comprehensively anti-traditional. They feature no commentary and no music; their sound-tracks carry no more than the sounds Wiseman's recorder encounters; they are long, in some cases over three hours; and they are monochrome. Like the Drew/Leacock "direct cinema" filmmakers, Wiseman uses lightweight equipment and high-speed film to explore worlds previously inaccessible. In direct cinema the aim was to achieve more honest reportage. Wiseman's insight, however, has been to recognize that there is no pure documentary, and that all filmmaking is a process of imposing order on the filmed materials.

applied." What emerges is a powerful vision of people trapped by the ramifications of their own social institutions.

Some critics, while recognising Wiseman's undoubted skill and intelligence, attack him for not propagandizing more overtly. They argue that when he shows us police violence (*Law and Order*), army indoctrination (*Basic Training*), collapsing welfare services (*Welfare*), or animal experiments (*Primate*) he should be more willing to apportion blame and make his commitments clear. Wiseman avoids the easy taking of sides for he is committed to the view that our institutions overrun us in more complex ways than we might imagine. By forcing us to piece together the jigsaw that he offers, he ensures that we understand more profoundly how it is that our institutions can go so terribly wrong. To do that at all is a remarkable achievement. To do it so uncompromisingly over so many years is quite unique.

In 1982 Wiseman turned to "fiction," though *Seraphita's Diary* is hardly orthodox and it is an intelligible extension of his interests. His abiding influence, however, remains in being the most sophisticated documentarist of modern cinema, with *Welfare* his most compelling achievement.

—Andrew Tudor

Frederick Wiseman

For this reason he prefers to call his films "reality fictions." Though he shoots in direct cinema fashion (operating the sound system, usually in tandem with cameraman William Brayne), the crucial stage is the imposition of structure during editing. As much as 40 hours of film may be reduced to one hour of finished product, an activity he has linked to that of a writer structuring a book. This does not mean that Wiseman's films "tell a story" in any conventional sense. The pattern and meaning of Wiseman's movies seem to slowly emerge from events as if somehow contained within them. Only after seeing the film do the pieces fall into place, their significance becoming clear as part of the whole system of relations that forms the movie. Thus, to take a simple example, the opening shots of the school building in *High School* make it look like a factory, yet it is only at the end when the school's principal reads out a letter from a former pupil in Vietnam that the significance of the image becomes clear. The soldier is, he says, "only a body doing a job," and the school a factory for producing just such expendable bodies.

Wiseman is not an open polemicist; his films do not appear didactic. But as we are taken from one social encounter to the next, as we are caught up in the leisurely rhythms of public ritual, we steadily become aware of the theme uniting all the films. In exploring American institutions, at home and abroad, Wiseman shows us social order rendered precarious. As he puts it, he demonstrates that "there is a gap between formal and actual practice, between the rules and the way they are

WOOD, Sam.

American. Born Samuel Grosvenor Wood in Philadelphia, 10 July 1884. Educated at Stanton School, Philadelphia. Married Clara Roush, two daughters. Headed west in gold rush, settled in Reno, 1900; real estate broker, Los Angeles, 1904; film acting debut in *A Gentleman of Leisure* for Famous Players Company, 1908; assistant to Cecil B. De Mille, 1914, then director, from 1916; director for Paramount, from 1919; director for newly-formed MGM, 1926–39; directed final scenes of *Gone With the Wind*, 1939; named president of Motion Picture Alliance for the Preservation of American Ideals, 1944; testified before House Un-American Activities Committee, 1947. *Died 22 September 1949.*

Films as Director:

1920 *Double Speed*; *Excuse My Dust*; *What's Your Hurry?*; *Sick Abed*; *The Dancing Fool*; *City Sparrow*; *Peck's Bad Boy* (+ sc)
1921 *Her First Elopement*; *The Snob*; *Her Beloved Villain*; *The Great Moment*; *Under the Lash*; *Don't Tell Everything*
1922 *Impossible Mrs. Bellew*; *Her Husband's Trademark*; *Beyond the Rocks*
1923 *My American Wife*; *Prodigal Daughters*; *Her Gilded Cage*; *Bluebeard's Eighth Wife*; *His Children's Children*
1924 *Bluff*; *The Female*; *The Next Corner*; *The Mine with the Iron Door*
1925 *The Re-Creation of Brian Kent*
1926 *Fascinating Youth*; *One Minute to Play*
1927 *The Fair Co-ed*; *Rookies*; *A Racing Romeo*
1928 *Telling the World*; *The Latest from Paris*
1929 *It's a Great Life*; *So This Is College*
1930 *Way for a Sailor*; *The Richest Man in the World*; *Sins of the Children*; *The Girl Said No*; *They Learned About Women* (co-d); *Paid*
1931 *A Tailor Made Man*; *New Adventures of Get-Rich-Quick Wallingford*
1932 *Prosperity*; *Huddle*
1933 *Hold Your Man* (+ pr); *The Barbarian*; *Christopher Bean*

Sam Wood

1934 *Stamboul Quest*
1935 *A Night at the Opera*; *Let 'em Have It*
1936 *Whip Saw*; *The Unguarded Hour*
1937 *Navy Blue and Gold*; *Madame X*; *A Day at the Races* (+ co-pr)
1938 *Stablemates*; *Lord Jeff* (+ co-pr)
1939 *Goodbye, Mr. Chips*
1940 *Raffles*; *Our Town*; *Kitty Royle*; *Rangers of Fortune*
1941 *King's Row*; *The Devil and Miss Jones*
1942 *The Pride of the Yankees*
1943 *For Whom the Bell Tolls* (+ pr)
1944 *Casanova Brown*
1945 *Guest Wife*; *Saratoga Trunk*
1946 *Heartbeat*
1947 *Ivy* (+ co-pr)
1948 *Command Decision*
1949 *The Stratton Story*; *Ambush*

Other Films:

1939 *Gone with the Wind* (Fleming: d final scenes)
1944 *Address Unknown* (pr)

Publications:

On WOOD: books—

Kaufman, George S., and others, *A Night at the Opera*, New York, 1972.
Pirosh, Robert, and others, *A Day at the Races*, New York, 1972.
Denton, Clive, and others, *The Hollywood Professionals—Vol.2*, New York, 1974.

On WOOD: articles—

Obituary in the *New York Times*, 23 September 1949.
"Sam Wood," in *Contracampo* (Madrid), October/November 1980.

*   *   *

Samuel Grosvenor Wood was one of the more prolific directors in Hollywood history. Working continously at his craft from 1916 to 1949, he created an average of nearly three films per year. His most noted motion pictures came during the last fifteen years of his career: *A Night at the Opera*, *A Day at the Races*, *Goodbye Mr. Chips*, *Kitty Foyle*, *King's Row*, and *For Whom the Bell Tolls*. Wood also worked on, uncredited, *Gone With the Wind*. Yet in all these films Sam Wood seemed unable to develop an identifiable personal style. He knew the Hollywood system, created clean crisp narratives, but never transcended the system to create complex films as did his contemporaries, John Ford and Howard Hawks.

In 1908, at age 23, Sam Wood established his career as a Los Angeles real estate agent. But through a chance meeting, he did try acting in motion pictures, and gradually worked his way up to substantial roles for the Famous Players Company. In 1914 he became an assistant to Cecil B. De Mille; in 1916 he was promoted to director. Sam Wood directed films for Famous Players (later Paramount) until 1926. Then he signed on with the newly formed Metro-Goldwyn-Mayer Company. He remained with MGM through the studio's salad days of the 1930s. But after his experience with *Gone With the Wind*, Wood struck out on his own. During the 1940s he worked for RKO, Paramount, Warner Bros., MGM, and independent producers Sol Lesser and Sam Goldwyn.

Sam Wood's directorial career seems to be divided into two parts. Until 1935 he was a traditional contract director at two of Hollywood's more important studios: Paramount and MGM. He directed many noted stars (Wallace Reid, Gloria Swanson, Jackie Coogan, Norma Shearer, Robert Montgomery, John Gilbert, Ramon Novarro, Clark Gable, Jean Harlow, and Marie Dressler), and earned a reputation as a solid, dependable director, one who brought films in on time. Sam Wood rose to the top echelon of Hollywood's contract directors through his association with Irving Thalberg and the Marx Brothers. *A Night at the Opera* became one the of the major revenue generators of the 1935–36 movie season. From then on Sam Wood was able to pick and choose his projects. By 1939 he was considered a "money director," only taking on projects with million dollar budgets. From 1939 on his films consistently finished among the top box office draws of the year. He was nominated for the Academy Award for best director in 1939 (*Goodbye Mr. Chips*), 1940 (*Kitty Foyle*), and 1942 (*King's Row*), but never won.

However Sam Wood is more often in film history books for his part in organizing the anti-Communist group, the Motion Picture Alliance for the Preservation of American Ideals. Named president in 1944, Wood carried out a campaign to purge the film industry of left-wing sympathizers. Along with Walt Disney, Gary Cooper, King Vidor, and others, Wood used the Alliance to attack proponents of progressive politics. Indeed, on the morning of his fatal heart attack he was quarreling with Columbia Pictures about the necessity of expelling a screenwriter. In his will Wood specified no heir could inherit anything unless he (or she) swore that they "are not now, nor ever have been, a Communist." Sam Wood, a former supporter of Franklin Roosevelt, died amidst front page debate concerning Hollywood's witchhunt, and thus is now remembered more for his right-wing politics than his nearly one hundred films.

—Douglas Gomery

————

WRIGHT, Basil.

British. Born Basil Charles Wright in London, 12 June 1907. Educated at Sherborne School and at Corpus Christi College, Cambridge. Joined Empire Marketing Board (EMB) film unit as assistant under John Grierson, 1930; directed first film, 1931; transferred with Grierson to General Post Office (GPO) film unit after EMB film unit dissolved, 1934; formed Realist Film Unit with John Taylor, and joined Film Centre, 1937; began making films for Ministry of Information after GPO film unit is absorbed by them, 1940; adviser on information technique and policy in Canada, World War II; producer in charge of Crown Film Unit, 1945, later worked at UNESCO under Sir Julian Huxley and John Grierson; formed own production company, International Realist, 1946; lectured on filmmaking at University of California, 1960s; wrote critical history of film, *The Long View*, 1974. *Died in London, 14 October 1987.*

Films as Director:

1931 *The Country Comes to Town* (+ co-ph, sc)
1932 *O'er Hill and Dale* (+ ph, sc); *Gibraltar* (+ ph, sc)
1933 *Windmill in Barbados* (+ ph, sc); *Liner Cruising South* (+ ph, sc); *Cargo from Jamaica* (+ ph)
1934 *Song of Ceylon* (+ ph, co-sc, ed)
1936 *Night Mail* (co-d, co-sc, co-ed)
1937 *Children at School* (+ co-pr)
1938 *The Face of Scotland* (+ sc)
1940 *Harvest Help*
1945 *This Was Japan*
1948 *Bernard Miles on Gun Dogs* (+ pr, sc)
1950 *Waters of Time* (co-d)

1953 *World Without End* (co-d)
1955 *Stained Glass at Fairford* (+ pr)
1958 *The Immortal Land* (+ co-pr)
1959 *Greek Sculpture* (co-d)
1960 *A Place for Gold* (+ pr)

Other Films:

1934 *Pett and Pott* (asst d)
1937 *The Smoke Menace* (asst pr)
1939 *The Londoners* (co-pr)
1945 *A Diary for Timothy* (Jennings) (pr)

Publications:

By WRIGHT: books—

The Use of Film, London, 1948.
The Long View, London, 1974.

By WRIGHT: articles—

"The Documentary Dilemma," in *Hollywood Quarterly*, Summer 1951.
Article on *World Without End*, in *Sight and Sound* (London), Summer 1953.
"Basil Wright on the Big Screen," in *Film* (London), December 1955.
"Which Way is Ahead?," in *Film* (London), November/December 1957.
"Basil Wright and *Song of Ceylon*," an interview with Cecile Starr, in *Filmmakers Newsletter* (Ward Hill, Massachusetts), November 1975.
"Basil Wright on Art, Anthropology and the Documentary," with S. Thomas, in *Quarterly Review of Film Studies* (Pleasantville, New York), Fall 1979.
Interview with P. Mareth and A. Bloom in *Film and History* (Newark, New Jersey), December 1980.

On WRIGHT: books—

Hardy, Forsyth, *Grierson on Documentary*, revised edition, London, 1966.
Levin, G. Roy, *Documentary Explorations*, Garden City, New York, 1972.
Lovell, Alan, and Jim Hillier, *Studies in Documentary*, New York, 1972.
Sussex, Elizabeth, *The Rise and Fall of British Documentary: The Story of the Film Movement Founded by John Grierson*, Berkeley, California, 1975.
Hardy, Forsyth, *John Grierson: A Documentary Biography*, London, 1979.
Ellis, Jack C., *The Documentary Idea*, Englewood Cliffs, New Jersey, 1989.
Swann, Paul, *The British Documentary Film Movement 1926–46*, Cambridge, 1989.

On WRIGHT: articles—

Rotha, Paul, article on *World Without End*, in *Sight and Sound* (London), Summer 1953.
Hardy, Forsyth, article on *World Without End*, in *Sight and Sound* (London), January/March 1954.
Gillett, John, article on *Stained Glass at Fairford*, in *Sight and Sound* (London), Winter 1956/57.
Gay, Ken, article on *The Immortal Land*, in *Films and Filming* (London), December 1958.
Cavender, Kenneth, article on *The Immortal Land*, in *Sight and Sound* (London), Winter 1958/59.
Barrot, O., "Basil Wright," in *Cinéma d'aujourd'hui* (Paris), February/March 1977.
Obituary in *Variety* (New York), 21 October 1987.
Obituary by Elizabeth Sussex in *Sight and Sound* (London), Winter 1987/1988.

*   *   *

Of the young men hired by Grierson at the Empire Marketing Board, at the beginning of British documentary, Wright was the first. He came from a wealthy liberal family and, like many of the others, had recently completed his education at Cambridge University. Wright became one of Grierson's most loyal colleagues, remaining in touch and being involved with him on various projects over many years.

His apprenticeship consisted of editing together bits of stock footage for what were called "poster films." In the first films that he directed Wright's special talent for poetic observation became evident; for example, *O'er Hill and Dale*, and *Cargo from Jamaica*. It achieved its fullest expression in *Song of Ceylon*, which is not only Wright's masterpiece but one of the few British documentaries of the 1930s with the kind of aesthetic value to have kept it in active circulation ever since. *Song of Ceylon* is untypical of early British documentary not only in its extraordinary formal experimentation, but in its subject (an exotic foreign culture) and theme (admiration for the religious spirit of that culture and sadness and perhaps anger at the impact of Western commerce on it). Though a number of people played important roles in its creation (Grierson as producer, Walter Leigh as composer, Cavalcanti as sound editor), *Song of Ceylon* is very much Wright's film, including most of its marvelous cinematography.

Wright shares directorial credit for *Night Mail* with Harry Watt. The original script seems largely to have been Wright's and the completed film contains some of the poetic touches one associates with him working at his best. But the strong narrative line and deft bits of characterization and humor seem much more in the directorial style Watt was developing.

In his work which followed, Wright moved into an obvious imitation of the American *March of Times* series, which was greatly admired by Grierson and other British documentarians. *Children at School*, one of a program of shorts sponsored by the British Commercial Gas Association, was an example. Though competent in technique and hard-hitting as exposé, in its impersonality it might have been directed by any number of other documentarians. It represents Wright's deep and genuine social concern arrived at intellectually rather than the emotional core of his being out of which his most personal and best work came.

In the 1951 *Waters of Time* he returned to the poetic; but by then what earlier would have been gentle reflectiveness seems to have become slack. It was made after the Grierson tradition had become diffused. *World Without End*, which had both some poetry and some force, was the last of the films with which Wright was involved that are concerned clearly with the Griersonian main line. A big and ambitious film, it was made on behalf of UNESCO in collaboration with Paul Rotha, another veteran of the early Grierson group. Rotha shot in Mexico and Wright in Thailand, with their material being intercut. Ultimately the film says that the world has grown together and that a low water level in a Mexican lake and a terrible tropical disease are of concern to us all, a very Griersonian idea.

—Jack C. Ellis

————

WYLER, William.

American. Born Willy Wyler in Mulhouse (Mülhausen), Alsace-Lorraine, 1 July 1902, became U.S. citizen, 1928. Married 1) Margaret Sullavan, 1934 (divorced 1936); 2) Margaret Tallichet, 1938, four children. Travelled to America at invitation of cousin Carl Laemmle, 1920; worked in publicity depart-

Basil Wright

William Wyler

ment for Universal in New York, then transferred to Universal City, Hollywood, 1921; assistant director at Universal, from 1924; directed first film, *Crook Buster*, 1925, and first feature, *Lazy Lightning*, 1926; signed contract with Samuel Goldwyn, 1936; served as Major in U.S. Army Air Corps, 1942–45; helped to found Committee for the First Amendment to counteract Hollywood investigations by House Un-American Activities Committee, 1947; "Hommage à William Wyler" organized by Henri Langlois at the Cinémathèque française, 1966; retired from directing, 1972. Recipient: Oscar for Best Direction, for *Mrs. Miniver*, 1942; Oscar for Best Direction and New York Film Critics Award for Best Direction, for *The Best Years of Our Lives*, 1946; Oscar for Best Direction, for *Ben Hur*, 1959; Irving G. Thalberg Award, 1965; American Film Institute Lifetime Achievement Award, 1976. *Died 29 July 1981.*

Films as Director:

1925   *Crook Buster*
1926   *The Gunless Bad Man*; *Ridin' for Love*; *Fire Barrier*; *Don't Shoot*; *The Pinnacle Rider*; *Martin of the Mounted*; *Lazy Lightning*; *Stolen Ranch*
1927   *Two Fister*; *Kelly Gets His Man*; *Tenderfoot Courage*; *The Silent Partner*; *Galloping Justice*; *The Haunted Homestead*; *The Lone Star*; *The Ore Riders*; *The Home Trail*; *Gun Justice*; *Phantom Outlaw*; *Square Shooter*; *The Horse Trader*; *Daze in the West*; *Blazing Days*; *Hard Fists*; *The Border Cavalier*; *Straight Shootin'*; *Desert Dust*
1928   *Thunder Riders*; *Anybody Here Seen Kelly*
1929   *The Shakedown*; *The Love Trap*
1930   *Hell's Heroes*; *The Storm*
1931   *A House Divided*
1932   *Tom Brown of Culver*
1933   *Her First Mate*; *Counselor at Law*
1934   *Glamour*; *The Gay Deception*
1936   *These Three*; *Dodsworth*; *Come and Get It*
1937   *Dead End*
1938   *Jezebel*
1939   *Wuthering Heights*
1940   *The Westerner*; *The Letter*
1941   **The Little Foxes**
1942   **Mrs. Miniver**
1944   *Memphis Belle*
1946   **The Best Years of Our Lives**
1947   *Thunder-Bolt*
1949   *The Heiress*
1951   *Detective Story*
1952   *Carrie*
1953   *Roman Holiday*
1955   *The Desperate Hours*
1956   *Friendly Persuasion*
1958   *The Big Country*
1959   *Ben-Hur*
1962   *The Children's Hour*
1965   *The Collector*
1966   *How to Steal a Million*
1968   *Funny Girl*
1970   *The Liberation of L.B. Jones*

Publications:

By WYLER: articles—

"William Wyler: Director with a Passion and a Craft," with Hermine Isaacs, in *Theater Arts* (New York), February 1947.
"Interview at Cannes," in *Cinema* (Beverly Hills), July/August 1965.
Interview with Charles Higham in *Action* (Los Angeles), September/October 1973.
"Wyler on Wyler," with Alan Cartnel, in *Inter/View* (New York), March 1974.
"Dialogue on Film," in *American Film* (Washington, D.C.), April 1976.

"No Magic Wand," in *Hollywood Directors: 1941–76* edited by Richard Koszarski, New York, 1977.
Interview with P. Carcassonne and J. Fieschi in *Cinématographe* (Paris), March/April 1981.
Lecture excerpts in *Films and Filming* (London), October 1981.

On WYLER: books—

Drinkwater, John, *The Life and Adventures of Carl Laemmle*, New York, 1930.
Griffith, Richard, *Samuel Goldwyn: The Producer and His Films*, New York, 1956.
Reisz, Karel, editor, *William Wyler, an Index*, London, 1958.
Madsen, Axel, *William Wyler*, New York, 1973.
Kolodiazhnaia, V., *Uil'iam Uailer*, Moscow, 1975.
Anderegg, Michael A., *William Wyler*, Boston, 1979.
Kern, Sharon, *William Wyler: A Guide to References and Resources*, Boston, 1984.
Fink, Guido, *William Wyler*, Florence, 1989.

On WYLER: articles—

Griffith, Richard, "Wyler, Wellman, and Huston," in *Films in Review* (New York), February 1950.
Reisz, Karel, "The Later Films of William Wyler," in *Sequence* (London), no. 13, 1951.
"Personality of the Month," in *Films and Filming* (London), July 1957.
Heston, Charlton, "The Questions No One Asks About Willy," in *Films and Filming* (London), August 1958.
Reid, John Howard, "A Little Larger Than Life," in *Films and Filming* (London), February 1960.
Reid, John Howard, "A Comparison of Size," in *Films and Filming* (London), March 1960.
Sarris, Andrew, "Fallen Idols," in *Film Culture* (New York), Spring 1963.
Brownlow, Kevin, "The Early Days of William Wyler," in *Film* (London), Autumn 1963.
Heston, Charlton, "Working with William Wyler," in *Action* (Los Angeles), January/February 1967.
Hanson, Curtis, "William Wyler," in *Cinema* (Beverly Hills), Summer 1967.
Carey, Gary, "The Lady and the Director: Bette Davis and William Wyler," in *Film Comment* (New York), Fall 1970.
Doeckel, Ken, "William Wyler," in *Films in Review* (New York), October 1971.
Higham, Charles, "William Wyler," in *Action* (Los Angeles), September/October 1973.
Phillips, Gene, "William Wyler," in *Focus on Film* (London), Spring 1976.
Heston, Charlton, "The *Ben-Hur* Journal," in *American Film* (Washington, D.C.), April 1976.
Swindell, Larry, "A Life in Film," in *American Film* (Washington, D.C.), April 1976.
Renaud, T., "William Wyler: 'L'Homme qui ne fit pas jamais un mauvais film'," in *Cinéma* (Paris), September 1981.

On WYLER: film—

Directed by William Wyler (Slesin), 1986.

*   *   *

William Wyler's career is an excellent argument for nepotism. Wyler went to work for "Uncle" Carl Laemmle, the head of Universal, and learned the movie business as assistant director and then director of programmers, mainly westerns. One of his first important features, *A House Divided*, demonstrates many of the qualities that mark his films through the next decades. A transparent imitation of Eugene O'Neill's *Desire under the Elms*, it contains evidence of the staging strategies that identify Wyler's distinctive mise-en-scène. The film's premise holds particular appeal for a director who sees drama in claustrophobic interiors, the actors held in expressive tension by their shifting spatial relationships to each other, the decor, and the camera. In *A House Divided* Wyler extracts that tension from the dynamics implicit in the film's principal set, the downstairs room that confines the crippled father (Walter Huston), the stairs leading to the landing between the rooms of the son (Kent Douglass) and the young step-mother (Helen Chandler). The stairway configuration is favored by Wyler for the opportunity it gives him to stack the agents of the drama and to fill the frame both vertically and in depth. When he later collaborates with cinematographer Gregg Toland, the potential of that depth and height is enhanced through the varying degrees of hard and soft focus. (Many critics, who are certainly unfamiliar with Wyler's early work, have unjustly credited Toland for the staging in depth that characterizes the partnership.)

The implications of focus in Wyler's stylistics go far beyond lighting procedures, lenses, even staging itself. Focus directs the viewer's attention to varieties of information within the field, whatever its shape or extent. Focus gives simultaneous access to discordant planes, characters, objects that challenge us to achieve a full, fluctuating reading of phenomena. André Bazin, in his important essay on Wyler in the French edition of *What Is Cinema?*, speaks of the director's "democratic" vision, his way of taking in the wholeness of a field in the unbroken time and space of the "*plan-séquence*," a shot whose duration and complexity of staging goes far beyond the measure of the conventional shot. Bazin opposes this to the analytic montage of Soviet editing. In doing so he perhaps underestimates the kind of control that Wyler's deep field staging exerts upon the viewer, but he does suggest the richness of the visual text in Wyler's major films.

Counselor At Law is a significant test of Wyler's staging. The Broadway origins of the property are not disguised; they are made into a virtue. The movement through the law firm's outer office, reception room and private spaces reflects a fluidity that is a function of the camera's mobility and a challenge to the fixed frame of the proscenium. Wyler's *tour de force* rivals that of the film's star, John Barrymore. Director and actor animate the attorney's personal and professional activities in a hectic, ongoing present, sweeping freely through the sharply delineated (and therefore sharply perceived) vectors of the cinematic/theatrical space.

Wyler's meticulousness and Samuel Goldwyn's insistence on quality productions resulted in the series of films, often adaptations of prestigious plays, that most fully represent the director's method. In *Dodsworth*, the erosion of a marriage is captured in the opening of the bedroom door that separates husband and wife; the staircase of *These Three* delimit the public and private spaces of a film about rumor and intimacy; the

elaborate street set of *Dead End* is examined from a dizzying variety of camera angles that create a geometry of urban life; the intensity of *The Little Foxes* is sustained through the focal distances that chart the shape of family ties and hatreds. After the war, the partnership of Wyler and Toland is crowned by *The Best Years of Our Lives*, a film whose subject (the situation of returning servicemen) is particularly pertinent, and whose structure and staging are the most personal in the director's canon.

In his tireless search for the perfect shot, Wyler was known as the scourge of performers, pushing them through countless retakes and repetitions of the same gesture. Since performance in his films is *not* pieced together in the editing room but is developed in complex blockings and shots of long duration, Wyler required a high degree of concentration on the part of the actors. Laurence Olivier, who was disdainful of the medium prior to his work in *Wuthering Heights*, credits Wyler for having revealed to him the possibilities of the movies. But it is Bette Davis who defines the place of the star actor in a Wyler film. The three she did with Wyler demonstrate how her particular energies both organize the highly controlled mise-en-scène and are contained within it. For *Jezebel* she won her second Academy Award. In *The Letter*, an exercise in directorial tyranny over the placement of seemingly every element in its highly charged frames, the viewer senses a total correspondence between the focus exercised by director and performer.

During the last decades of Wyler's career many of the director's gifts that flourished in contexts of extreme dramatic tension and the exigencies of studio shooting were dissipated in excessively grandiose properties and "locations." There were, however, exceptions. Wyler's presence is strongly felt in the narrow staircase of *The Heiress* and the dingy station house of *Detective Story*. He even manages to make the final shootout of *The Big Country* adhere to the narrowest of gulches, thereby reducing the dimensions of the title to his familiar focal points. But the epic scope of *Ben Hur* and the ego of Barbra Streisand (in *Funny Girl*) escape the compact economies of the director's boxed-in stackings and plane juxtapositions. Only in *The Collector*, a film that seems to define enclosure (a woman is kept prisoner in a cellar for most of its duration) does Wyler find a congenial property. In it he proves again that the real expanse of cinema is measured by its frames.

—Charles Affron

XIE JIN.

Chinese. Born Shaoxing (province of Zhejiang), China, 1923. Studied at School of Dramatic art, Jiang'an, 1946–48. Assistant to directors Wu Renzhi, 1948, and Zheng Xiaoqui, 1949; directed first film, *A Crisis*, 1954.

Films as Director:

1954   *A Crisis*; *A Wave of Unrest*; *Rendezvous at Orchard Bridge*
1955   *Spring in the Land of Waters*
1957   *Woman Basketball Player Number Five*
1958   episodes of *Small Leaders of the "Big Leap"* and *Small Stories of a Big Storm*; *Huang Baomei*
1960   *The Women's Red Army Detachment*
1962   *Big Li, Young Li, and Old Li*
1964   **Wutai Jiemei (Two Stage Sisters)**
1972   *The Door*
1975   *Chunmiao*
1976   *The Bay of Rocks*
1977   *Youth*
1980   *Ah, Cradle*
1981   *The Legend of Tianyun Mountain*
1982   *The Herdsman*
1983   *Qiu Jin*
1984   *Garlands at the Foot of the Mountain*
1987   *Hibiscus Town*
1989   *The Last Aristocrats*

Other Films:

1948   *The Silent Wife* (Wu Renzhi) (asst d)
1949   *The Martyr of the Garden of the Pear Trees* (Zheng Xiaoqiu) (asst d)
1953   *The Feather Letter* (Shi Hui) (asst d)

Publications:

On XIE JIN: books—

Leyda, Jay, *Dianying: An Account of Films and the Film Audience in China*, Cambridge, Massachusetts, 1972.
Lösel, Jörg, *Die Politische Funktion des Spielfilms in der Volksrepublic China Zwischen 1949 and 1965*, Munich, 1980.
Rayns, Tony, and Scott Meek, *Electric Shadows: 45 Years of Chinese Cinema*, London, 1980.
Bergeron, Regis, *Le Cinéma chinois 1949–1983*, 3 vols., Paris, 1983–84.
Jenkins, Alan, and Cathy Grant, *A Teaching Guide to the Films of the People's Republic of China*, Oxford, 1984.
Berry, Chris, editor, *Perspectives on Chinese Cinema*, New York, 1985; revised edition, 1991.
Quiquemelle, Marie-Claire, and Jean-Loup Passek, editors, *Le Cinéma chinois*, Paris, 1985.
Armes, Roy, *Third World Filmmaking and the West*, Berkeley, 1987.

Clark, Paul, *Chinese Cinema: Culture and Politics Since 1949*, Cambridge, 1987.
Semsel, George Stephen, editor, *Chinese Film: The State of the Art in the People's Republic*, New York, 1987.

On XIE JIN: articles—

Jin Xie Section of *Positif* (Paris), March 1985.
Manceau, J.-L., "Portrait de Xie Jin dans le panorama chinois," in *Cinéma* (Paris), 5 March 1986.
Rayns, Tony, "Let a hundred flowers . . . ," in *Monthly Film Bulletin* (London), July 1988.

*　　　*　　　*

Because of the length of his career, his ability to dramatize popular political sentiments, and his commitment to the melodrama as a vehicle for the expression of his aesthetic vision, Chinese filmmaker Xie Jin has been compared to Douglas Sirk and Frank Capra. Since his career spans over four decades with contributions to every stage of the development of filmmaking from the earliest days of the post-Revolutionary period, Xie Jin must be counted as one of the most significant filmmaking veterans still making features today in the People's Republic of China. He has not become a mere "fossil" tolerated by an industry grateful for his contributions in the 1950s and early 1960s. Rather, Xie continues to be controversial and exceptionally popular with Chinese audiences both inside and outside of China.

Trained in the theatre, Xie came to the Shanghai studios in the early 1950s and was soon promoted from assistant to full director. His name rather rapidly became associated with the political melodramas he is still known for today. His 1957 film *Woman Basketball Player Number Five*, for example, helped to establish his reputation as a "woman's director." Unlike the maligned "woman's film" genre in Hollywood, melodramas featuring strong female leads became the favored vehicle for the dramatic examination of the role the Revolution was playing in reshaping both men's and women's lifestyles and attitudes toward gender in the People's Republic. Blending Soviet socialist realism with the aesthetic directives of Mao and the popularity of classical Hollywood tear-jerkers, Xie was creating a peculiarly Chinese political aesthetic. This aesthetic can still be appreciated today for the ways in which it stretched beyond the modes of representation usually reserved for women at that time in both Asian and Western film cultures.

Before the onset of the Cultural Revolution in the mid-1960s, Xie Jin perfected his revolutionary woman's films in *The Women's Red Army Detachment* and *Two Stage Sisters*. Although *The Women's Red Army Detachment* won the first 100 Flower Award (the PRC equivalent of the Oscar still coveted today), *Two Stage Sisters* was doomed by a storm of criticism unleased by the Cultural Revolution. *Two Stage Sisters* features the story of the relationship between two Shaox-

Xie Jin: poster for *Two Stage Sisters*

ing opera performers from their beginnings as itinerant entertainers in the feudal countryside of 1930s China through success in Shanghai during the Japanese occupation, eventual separation, and reunion during the post-Revolutionary period. Changes in the style of the operas presented in the film (e.g., folk opera, Western-influenced critical realist operas, Mao's favored "revolutionary romanticism" in opera form) also parallel broader social and political changes. Although probably the pinnacle of his career and the most complete flowering of his political aesthetic, *Two Stage Sisters* was only fully appreciated after the Cultural Revolution ended.

During the Cultural Revolution, Xie suffered much the same fate as most of his generation. At times under house arrest, he was still enlisted to help direct Jiang Qing's "model opera" films during that period. These films, in fact, are aesthetically and politically at odds with his earlier work.

After the Cultural Revolution, Xie Jin went back to making political melodramas featuring female protagonists. *The Legend of Tianyun Mountain*, in fact, was one of the first films made after the Cultural Revolution to condemn not only its political excesses but also the strains the Anti-Rightist Campaign of the 1950s had placed on Chinese society. He has continued in this socially critical vein with *The Herdsman* and *Hibiscus Town* (both dealing with the Cultural Revolution), while also making patriotic dramas like *Qiu Jin* (based on the life of the well-known Qing Dynasty female revolutionist) and *Garlands at the Foot of the Mountain* (on the recent Sino-Vietnamese war). Xie's most recent film, *The Last Aristocrats*, deals with the lives of four young Chinese women living abroad and was partially shot in the United States.

Ironically, even though Xie Jin has devoted virtually his entire life's work to films about politically active, modern Chinese heroines, he is most often criticized today for his supposed "feudal" depiction of women as "good" wives and mothers. He has also been condemned for his "old-fashioned" style of filmmaking. However, while some younger filmmakers tend to disregard audience tastes, hoping for an art house following in Europe and the United States, Xie Jin, despite his critics, has continued to please Chinese audiences

—Gina Marchetti

XIAOXIAN, Hou. *See* **HOU HSIAO-HSIEN.**

YATES, Peter.

British. Born in Aldershot, Surrey, 24 July 1929. Educated at Charterhouse school; studied acting at Royal Academy of Dramatic Art, London. Married Virginia Pope, 1960, three children. Actor, stage manager and director with repertory companies, early 1950s; managed racing car drivers for two years, worked with Stirling Moss and Peter Collins; began editing documentaries and dubbing foreign films, 1957; assistant director, from 1959, also stage and TV director; directed first feature, *Summer Holiday*, 1962; moved to U.S., 1967. Address: c/o Tempest Productions, Inc., 1775 Broadway, Suite 621, New York, NY 10019, U.S.A.

Films as Director:

1962 *Summer Holiday*
1964 *One Way Pendulum*
1967 *Robbery* (+ co-sc)
1968 *Bullitt*
1969 *John and Mary*
1971 *Murphy's War*
1972 *The Hot Rock* (*How to Steal a Diamond in Four Uneasy Lessons*)
1973 *The Friends of Eddie Coyle*
1974 *For Pete's Sake*
1976 *Mother, Jugs & Speed* (+ co-pr)
1977 *The Deep*
1979 *Breaking Away* (+ pr)
1980 *Eyewitness* (+ pr)
1982 *Krull*
1984 *The Dresser* (+ pr)
1985 *Eleni*
1987 *Suspect*
1988 *The House on Carroll Street* (*Jigsaw*)
1989 *An Innocent Man*

Other Films:

1960 *The Entertainer* (Richardson) (asst d); *Sons and Lovers* (Cardiff) (asst d)
1961 *A Taste of Honey* (Richardson) (asst d); *The Roman Spring of Mrs. Stone* (Quintero) (asst d); *The Guns of Navarone* (Thompson) (asst d)

Publications:

By YATES: articles—

Interview with Gordon Gow in *Films and Filming* (London), April 1971.
"The Making of *Friends of Eddie Coyle*," an interview with A.C. Bobrow, in *Filmmakers Newsletter* (Ward Hill, Massachusetts), October 1973.

"Making *The Deep*," in *Filmmakers Newsletter* (Ward Hill, Massachusetts), May 1977.
"*Breaking Away* to *Eyewitness*: The Success of the Ensemble Director," in *Millimeter* (New York), December 1980.
Interview with B. Drew in *American Film* (Washington D.C.), March 1981.
"Dialogue on Film: Peter Yates," in *American Film* (Washington D.C.), April 1984.
Interview with A. Sibley in *Films and Filming* (London), June 1988.

On YATES: articles—

Cowie, Peter, "Peter Yates," in *International Film Guide 1981*, London, 1980.
"Peter Yates Dossier" in *Revue du Cinéma* (Paris), May 1984.

*   *   *

Not since Alfred Hitchcock has a British director so successfully assimilated to American movie-making as Peter Yates. It seems an unexpected destiny for someone whose first film was a vehicle for so anodynely British a figure as Cliff Richard. But Yates has always been a thoroughgoing professional, ready to take on unpromising material and make an accomplished, impersonal job of it—especially if by doing so he can gain the money and reputation needed to make the kind of films he really wants.

A chance combination of circumstances gave him his breakthrough. His third British film, *Robbery*, otherwise a drably downbeat account of the Great Train Robbery, included a car chase filmed with exceptional pace and flair. This sequence attracted the attention of Steve McQueen, who invited Yates to direct his next film. Yates, sharing the actor's enthusiasm for fast cars (he was once racing manager for Stirling Moss), readily agreed. So did the studio, who wanted to sink McQueen, and reckoned an unknown British director a sure guarantee of disaster. Instead, *Bullitt* proved a massive box-office success, thanks largely to the brilliantly handled San Francisco car chase sequence, and became highly influential. For some years no crime movie was thought complete without careening hubcaps, and Yates's reputation was made.

On the strength of *Bullitt*, he directed *John and Mary*, a quietly humorous conversation piece with Dustin Hoffman and Mia Farrow. One of Yates's own favorite films, it was a total flop at the box-office. "I'd much prefer to develop simplicities and nuances than decide which lamppost a car is going to hit," Yates remarked, but bowed to financial necessity. Since then, his recurrent aim has been to reconcile his bankable skills as virtuoso action director with his predilection for low-key social realism—either by using one to finance the other, or by attempting, from time to time, to combine the two in the same film.

Hot Rock came close to it, mixing pleasingly offbeat comedy with some spectacular helicopter sequences; although other attempts to blend humor with action—*Murphy's War*, *For*

Peter Yates

Pete's Sake, Mother, Jugs and Speed—fell flat. But in the dourly atmospheric *The Friends of Eddie Coyle* Yates displayed a rare feel for locale (in this case a bleak and wintry Boston), as well as eliciting one of Robert Mitchum's finest performances. Despite critical acclaim, it attracted meagre audiences.

Yates redeemed himself in the eyes of the studio accountants with the sub-aqueous hokum of *The Deep*, a thumping commercial success which ensured him the backing for *Breaking Away*. Engagingly scripted by Steve Tesich, and filmed around the scriptwriter's home town of Bloomington, Indiana, this is probably Yates's best movie to date, offering a fresh and unaccustomed view of class-ridden middle America, and climaxing in an exhilarating bicycle race. *Eyewitness*, a thriller also scripted by Tesich, again proved quirky and consistently diverting, though sometimes to the detriment of the suspense.

Since then, though, Yates has relapsed into formula, relying on sheer proficiency to carry off the undemanding sci-fantasy

of *Krull*, the staginess of *The Dresser* and the paranoid-thriller routines of *Suspect*. *Eleni* reunited him with Tesich, but with disappointing results—overblown melodrama, with pasteboard villains—while the scrupulously recreated period atmosphere of *The House on Carroll Street* was wasted on inept plotting.

The lineal descendant, in professional terms, of such skilled studio workhorses as Walsh or Curtiz, Peter Yates seems capable of making a respectable job of whatever comes to hand. It takes the stimulus of an exceptional script, as with *Breaking Away* or *Eddie Coyle*, to bring out his more individual qualities—and in recent years, such scripts seem to have become sadly rare.

—Philip Kemp

YOSHIMURA, Kozabura.

(also known as Kimisaburo Yoshimura). Japanese. Born in Shiga Prefecture, 9 September 1911. Educated at Nihon High School, Tokyo, graduated 1929. Married Tomoko Oouchi, 1940. Assistant director to Yasujiro Shimazu at Shochiku-Kamata Studio, 1929; drafted into military, 1932; after return from service, directed first film, *Sneaking*, 1934; assistant director to Shimazu, Heinosuke Gosho, Dhiro Toyota and Mikio Naruse, 1934–39; moved to newly established Shochiku-Ofuna studios, 1936; resumed directing, 1939; served in machine gun unit, then as information officer on general staff, 1944; repatriated, spent year in prison and repatriation camp, 1945; began collaboration with scriptwriter Kaneto Shindo, 1947; founded independent production company Kindai Eiga Kyokai (Society of Modern Film), with Shindo, producer Hisao Itoya, director Tengo Yamada and actor Taiji Tonoyama, 1950; contracted by Daiei Studio, 1956; TV director, 1960. Recipient: Eiga Seikai-sha New director's Prize, for *Danryo*, 1939; Kinema Jumpo Number One Film, *Anjo-ke no bukokai*, 1947; Mainichi Director's Prize for *Itsureru seiso*, 1951; Shiju-Hosho Decoration, Japanese Government, 1976. Address: 4-3-37 Zushi, Zushi City, Kanagawa, Japan.

Films as Directors:

1934 *Nukiashi sashiashi (Sneaking)*
1939 *Onna koso ie o momore (Women Defend the Home!. Women Should Stay at Home)*; *Yokina uramachi (Cheerful Alley. Gay Back Alley)*; *Asu no odoriko (Dancers of Tomorrow)*; *Gonin no kyodai (Five Brothers and Sisters)*; *Danryu (Warm Current)*
1940 *Nishizumi sanshacho den (The Story of Tank Commander Nishizumi)*
1941 *Hana (Flower)*
1942 *Kancho mada shinazu (The Spy Has Not Yet Died)* (+ story); *Minami ni kaze (South Wind)*; *Zoko minami no kaze (South Wind: Sequel)*
1943 *Laisen no zenya (The Night Before the War Begins)*; *Tekki kushu (Enemy Air Attack)*
1944 *Kessen (A Decisive Battle)*
1947 *Zo o kutta renchu (The Fellows Who Ate the Elephant)*; *Anjo-ke no butokai (The Ball of the Anjo Family)*
1948 *Yuwaku (Temptation. Seduction)*; *Waga shogai no kagayakeru hi (The Bright Day of My Life)*
1949 *Shitto (Jealousy)*; *Mori no Ishimatsu (Ishimatsu of the Forest. Ishimatsu of Mori)*; *Mahiru no enbukyoku (Waltz at Noon)*
1950 *Shunsetsu (Spring Snow)*; *Senka no hate (The Height of Battle. The End of Battle Fire)*
1951 *Itsuwareru seiso (Deceiving Costume)*; *Jiyu gakko (Free School)*; *Genji monogatari (A Tale of Genji)*
1952 *Nishijin no shimai (Sisters of Nishijin)*; *Boryoku (Violence)*
1953 *Senba-zuru (A Thousand Cranes)*; *Yokubo (Desire)*; *Yoake mae (Before the Dawn)*
1954 *Ashizuri misaki (Cape Ashizuri)*; *Wakai hitotachi (Young People)*
1955 *"Hanauri musume (The Flower Girl, The Girl Who Sells Flowers)"* episode of *Aisureba koso (If You Love Me. Because I Love)*; *Ginza no onna (Women of the Ginza)*; *Bijo to kairyu (The Beauty and the Dragon)*
1956 *Totsugu hi (Day of Marriage. The Day to Wed)*; *Yoru no kawa (Night River. Undercurrent)*; *Yonjuhassai no teiko (48-Year-Old Rebel. Protest at 48 Years Old)*
1957 *Osaka monogatari (An Osaka Story)*; *Yoru no cho (Night Butterfly)*; *Chijo (On the Earth)*
1958 *Hitotsubu no mugi (One Grain of Barley)*; *Yoru no sugao (The Naked Face of Night)*
1959 *Denwa wa yugata ni naru (Telephone Rings in the Evening)*; *Kizoku no kaidan (Aristocrat's Stairs)*
1960 *"Koi o wasureta onna (A Woman's Testament, The Woman Who Forgot Love)"* episode of *Jokei (Women's Scroll)*; *Onna no saka (Woman's Descent)*
1961 *Konki (Marriage Time)*; *Onna no kunsho (Woman's Decoration)*
1962 *Kazoku no jijo (A Night to Remember. Family's Situation)*; *Sono yo wa wasurenai (I Won't Forget That Night)*
1963 *"Shayo nigo (Company's Business)"* episode of *Echizen take ningyo (Bamboo Doll of Echizen)*
1966 *Kokoro no sanmyaku (The Heart of the Mountains)*
1967 *Daraku suru onna (A Fallen Woman)*
1968 *Nemureru bijo (Sleeping Beauty. The House of the Sleeping Virgins)*; *Atsui yoru (A Hot Night)*
1971 *Amai himitsu (Sweet Secret)*
1973 *Konketsuji Rika (Rika, the Mixed-Blood Girl)*; *Hamagure no komoriuta (Lullaby of Hamagure)*
1974 *Ranru no hata (Ragged Flag)*

Publications:

By YOSHIMURA: book—

Eiga no gijutsu to mikata [Film Technique and How to Look at Films], 1952.

On YOSHIMURA: books—

Mellen, Joan, *Voices from the Japanese Cinema*, New York, 1975.
Mellen, Joan, *The Waves at Genji's Door*, New York, 1976.
Anderson, Joseph, and Donald Richie, *The Japanese Film*, expanded edition, Princeton, 1982.

*   *   *

Although Kozaburo Yoshimura's early work followed the drama and comedy conventions of the Shochiku Studio productions of the 1930s, he gradually proved himself an ambitious artist who broke away from these conventions through his varied selections of themes and subjects, and his bold exploration of styles. His technical maturity has been consistent over the years and through all genres, from the melodramatic *Warm Current* which first brought Yoshimura recognition, through the wartime production *The Story of Tank Commander Nishizumi* which successfully portrayed the decent, human side of the war hero with exciting action scenes, to the patriotic spy film *The Night Before the War Begins* which stylistically resembles an American suspense film.

The postwar liberation allowed him to employ more freely his favorite American film styles and techniques. Typical of this period is *The Ball of the Anjo Family*, which surprised the Japanese postwar audience not only with its fresh techniques, but also with its striking theme of the contrasts between the falling and emerging social classes of the time.

The challenges of the varied subjects of his subsequent films confirmed his energy and versatility, as in *The Bright Day of My Life*, which illustrated a flamingly passionate love unusual to Japanese films, between a couple who had belonged to opposing political groups before the war. *Ishimatsu of Mori* is regarded as one of the first successful postwar period films. From the familiar legend, Yoshimura made a satirical comedy which alludes critically to the contemporary gangster's mentality. *Deceiving Costume*, a postwar adaption of Mizogushi's prewar masterpiece, *Sisters of the Gion*, demonstrated a similar emotional intensity and powerful social criticism through its story of the life of geisha sisters. *The Beauty and the Dragon* is a new adaptation of a popular Kabuki play, made with the assistance of the innovative theater troupe, Zenshin-za.

Scenario writer Kaneto Shindo's collaboration with Yoshimura was indispensable to Yoshimura's success, from *The Ball of the Anjo Family* to *The Day to Wed*, during which time they produced 22 films together. When in 1950 Shochiku Studio subjected the pair to commercial pressures, they decided to establish an independent production company, Kindai Eiga

Kyokai or Society of Modern Film. It enabled the two to pursue their artistic experimentation and thus produce many masterpieces which attracted critical attention.

Yoshimura became well known for literary adaptations—*A Tale of Genji, A Thousand Cranes, Before the Dawn, Sleeping Beauty,* and *Cape Ashizuri*—as well as for light comedy—*Free School,* about contemporary social life, *Desire, Young People,* and *One Grain of Barley,* among others. Particularly noteworthy is a series of films on the life of contemporary women using many of Daiei Studio's prime actresses, *Night River, Night Butterfly, Naked Face of Night,* and others. He has continued his independent efforts, notably with *Heart of the Mountains* and *Ragged Flag,* which powerfully depicts the life of a pioneering opponent of pollution in Japan in the early years of this century.

Yoshimura has consistently shown excellent story-developing skill which has won popular support for his films. His best films often contain social criticism, but at the same time do not preach, relying instead on the depiction of heightened emotions among the characters to successfully appeal to the audience.

—Kyoko Hirano

Z

ZANUSSI, Krzyszstof.

Polish. Born in Warsaw, 17 June 1939. Educated in physics, Warsaw, 1955–59; faculty of philosophy, University of Cracow, 1959–62; directing course, State Film school, Lodz, graduated 1966. Director, from 1966; appointed to faculty of Lodz film school, and named vice-president of Association of Polish Filmmakers, 1973; chosen by Pope John Paul II to make his film biography *From a Far Country*, 1980; during suppression of Solidarity movement, directed mainly in Western Europe, 1980s. Recipient: Best Film, Polish film critics, for *The Structure of Crystals*, 1970; State Award, Polish Minister of Culture and Arts, 1973.

Films as Director:

1958   *Droga do nieba* (*The Way to the Skies*) (amateur film in collaboration with Wincenty Ronisz)
1966   *Smierc prowincjala* (*The Death of a Provincial*) (short, diploma film); *Przemysl*; *Maria Dabrowska*
1967   *Komputery* (*Computers*)
1968   *Twarza w twarz* (*Face to Face*) (+ co-sc) (for TV); *Krzysztof Penderecki* (for TV)
1969   *Zaliczenie* (*An Examination. Pass Mark*) (+ co-sc) (for TV); *Struktura krsztalu* (*The Structure of Crystals*) (+ co-sc)
1970   *Gory o zmierzchu* (*Mountains at Dusk*) (for TV); *Zycie rodzinne* (*Family Life*) (+ sc)
1971   *Rola* (*Die Rolle*) (+ sc) (for West German TV); *Za sciana* (*Behind the Wall*) (+ co-sc) (for TV)
1972   *Hipoteza* (*Hypothesis*) (+ sc) (for TV)
1973   *Illuminacja* (*Illumination*) (+ sc)
1974   *The Catamount Killing*
1975   *Milosierdzie platne z gory* (*Nachtdienst. Night Duty*) (for TV); *Bilans kwartalny* (*A Woman's Decision*) (+ sc)
1976   *Barwy ochronne* (*Camouflage*) (+ sc)
1977   *Anatomie stunde* (*Lekcja anatomii. Anatomy Lesson*) (for TV); *Haus der Frauen* (*House of Women*); *Penderecki, Lutoslawa*; *Brigitte Horney*
1978   *Spirala* (*Spiral*) (+ sc)
1979   *Wagen in der Nacht* (*Ways in the Night. Paths into the Night*) (+ sc)
1980   *Constans* (*The Constant Factor*)
1981   *Kontract* (*The Contract*); *From a Far Country*; *Versuchung* (for TV)
1982   *Uerreichbare* (*Imperative*)
1984   *Blaubart*; *Rok spokojnego slonca*
1985   *Le Pouvoir du mal* (*Paradigme*)
1986   *The Year of the Quiet Sun*
1987   *Wherever We Are*
1989   *Stan Posiadania* (+ sc)
1990   *Touch*
1991   *Last Dance*; *Wittold Lutoslawski* (doc)

Other Film:

1978   *Amator* (*Camera Bluff*) (Kieślowski) (role as himself)

Publications:

By ZANUSSI: articles—

"The Ethics of Being Krzysztof Zanussi," an interview with S. Murray, in *Cinema Papers* (Melbourne), September/October 1976.
"Opcja przekorna: za świadomościa," an interview with T. Krzemień, in *Kino* (Warsaw), February 1977.
"L'Oeuvre de Zanussi: le refus de la compromission," an interview with René Prédal, in *Jeune Cinéma* (Paris), November 1980.
"The Workings of a Pure Heart," an interview with Jiri Weiss, in *Cineaste* (New York), vol. 11, no. 2, 1981.
Interview with P. Pawlikowski in *Stills* (London), Winter 1982.
Interview with T. Sobolewski in *Kino* (Warsaw), June 1988.

On ZANUSSI: books—

Paul, David W., editor, *Politics, Art and Commitment in the Eastern European Cinema*, New York, 1983.
Estève, Michel, *Krzysztof Zanussi*, Paris, 1987.

On ZANUSSI: articles—

Hopfinger, M., "Zanussiego ćwiczenia z życia," in *Kino* (Warsaw), January 1973.
Boleslaw, M., "The Cinema of Krzysztof Zanussi," in *Film Quarterly* (Berkeley), Spring 1973.
"Krzysztof Zanussi," in *International Film Guide 1976*, London, 1975.
Tassone, A., and others, special Zanussi section of *Positif* (Paris), December 1979.
Martin, Marcel, and others, "Les Constantes de Krzysztof Zanussi," special section of *Image et Son* (Paris), September 1980.
Cowie, Peter, "Made in Poland: The Metaphysical Cinema of Krzysztof Zanussi," in *Film Comment* (New York), September/October 1980.
Paul, David, and S. Glover, "The Difficulty of Moral Choice: Zanussi's *Contract* and *The Constant Factor*," in *Film Quarterly* (Berkeley), Winter 1983/84.

*　　　*　　　*

The cinema of Krzysztof Zanussi explores a continuum of conflict ranging from the individual and interpersonal to the larger social order. He explores the relationship of the individual's conscience to society's norms of morality. Appearing as himself in Krzysztof Kieslowski's *Camera Buff*, Zanussi says that he feels an obligation to question why the corrupt manipulators are the survivors. His is a provocative, cerebral cinema, objectifying its characters through both attention to detail and cool observation of the stages of conflict. During this process Zanussi demands the intellectual participation of his audience, and ultimately its response. The spectator should attain the level of self-awareness that his protagonists reach.

Zanussi has worked chiefly under a system of government subsidy in his native Poland. He has headed one of the three Polish film units. Yet while West German television has pro-

Krzysztof Zanussi

duced many of his recent, non-Polish films, they are still subject to Polish government approval. His films have therefore occupied a space between individual self-expression and government tolerance. Prior self-censorship has been a factor in both his message and the discourse which conveys it. No clear separation exists between the private world of Zanussi the artist-intellectual and the public realm in which he operates.

Three major types of conflicts permeate the films. The first is between determinism and free will (often clouded by chance). He elaborates this as the bridgeable gap between empiricism (rational analysis) and Catholicism (grace) in, for example, *Illumination*, *The Constant Factor*, and *Imperative*. Zanussi's background in physics and philosophy strongly influences these films. Conflict between the individual and the corruption of (contemporary Polish) society occurs in *Camouflage*, *The Constant Factor*, and *Contract*. Zanussi masks the conflict in *Ways in the Night*, which presents the dilemma of an intelligent, sensitive young German officer who must uphold the policies of the National Socialists. The third major opposition is between the individual's self-awareness and the invisible (yet pervasive) pressures of the immediate social milieu; this is strongest in *Spiral* and *The Contract*.

From a Far Country, his biography of the Polish Pope John Paul II, is an important key to understanding Zanussi's world view. In this film no separation exists between the actions of the individual and the larger network of social forces in which he moves. The dichotomy of free will and determinism underlies the entire project.

Although Zanussi sets his films in a precise historical context, he does explore some of the issues that have been universally debated by artists and intellectuals for many centuries. What distinguishes him as a filmmaker is his particular deployment of the technology of the cinema as a vehicle for his thematic concerns. His orchestration is meticulous. *Spiral* exemplifies the plight of the solitary individual living disharmoniously with himself and those around him. Zanussi follows the tortured protagonist with a jerky handheld camera through the maze of rooms and characters in a ski resort. In *Family Life* an individual in conflict with his family must resolve his dilemma, which will otherwise haunt him in his interaction with the larger social order. He introduces the protagonist through a carefully plotted series of zooms, pans, and tilts, contextualizing the different spheres of conflict. In *Contract* Zanussi adds both an aural and a visual dimension to the conflict between the son and his family. The handheld camera follows his attempt to burn down the family home. Zanussi intercuts this obsessive behavior with the repetitive sound of bells from a sleigh which carries his family. At the end of *The Constant Factor*, a stone falls in slow motion from where the protagonist, who has fallen from occupational grace because of his incorruptibility, is cleaning windows. It strikes a child playing below; chance plays a hand in a universe beyond the individual's control. Zanussi then cuts to the majestic, desolate mountains, as if to say there is no rational method for solving the existential dilemma.

In all of his films these moments of cinematic self-consciousness alternate with long takes of intellectual debate and questioning. During these probing conversations Zanussi is least obtrusive in the application of cinematic techniques. The irony is that during these verbal conflicts, the ideological imprint of the director is most overt.

—Howard Feinstein

ZEFFIRELLI, Franco.

Italian. Born Gianfranco Corsi in Florence, 12 February 1923. Studied architecture at University of Florence, and at Accademia di Belle Arti, Florence. Theatre director, from 1945; designer for opera, from 1946; made only acting appearance in Zampa's *Angelina*, 1947; assistant director to Visconti, for films and theatre, from 1948; opera director, from 1953; directed first film, 1957; made *Jesus of Nazareth* for TV, 1977. Address: c/o Via due Macelli 31, Rome, Italy.

Films as Director:

1957 *Camping* (+ co-sc)
1966 *The Taming of the Shrew* (+ co-sc)
1968 *Romeo and Juliet* (+ co-sc)
1972 *Fratelli sole sorella luna* (*Brother Sun, Sister Moon*) (+ co-sc)
1977 *Gesu di Nazareth* (*Jesus of Nazareth*) (for TV) (+ co-sc)
1979 *The Champ*
1981 *Endless Love*
1982 *La Traviata*; *La Bohème* (for TV)
1983 *Strasphere* (doc)
1986 *Otello* (*Othello*)
1988 *Il Giovane Toscanini* (*Young Toscanini*)
1990 *Hamlet* (+ co-sc)

Other Films:

1947 *Angelina* (Zampa) (role)
1948 *La terra trema* (Visconti) (asst d)
1951 *Bellissima* (Visconti) (asst d)
1954 *Senso* (Visconti) (asst d)

Publications:

By ZEFFIRELLI: books—

Zeffirelli: The Autobiography of Franco Zeffirelli, London, 1986.

By ZEFFIRELLI: articles—

"Versatility," an interview with Gordon Gow, in *Films and Filming* (London), April 1973.
Interview with B.J. Demby in *Filmmakers Newsletter* (Ward Hill, Massachusetts), September 1973.
"Knowing, Feeling, Understanding, then Expression," an interview with A. Stuart, in *Films and Filming* (London), August 1979.
"A Dialogue with Franco Zeffirelli," in *American Cinematographer* (Los Angeles), October 1981.
"Une aventure esaltante mais risquée," an interview with J.-M. Brèque, in *Avant-Scène du Cinéma* (Paris), July/August 1988.
Interview with Steve Grant in *Time Out* (London), 17 April 1991.

On ZEFFIRELLI: articles—

Lane, John, "*The Taming of the Shrew*," in *Films and Filming* (London), October 1966.
Chase, D., "*The Champ*: Round Two," in *American Film* (Washington, D.C.), July/August 1978.
Pursell, M., "Artifice and Authenticity in Zeffirelli's *Romeo and Juliet*," in *Literature/Film Quarterly* (Salisbury, Maryland), October 1986.

*   *   *

Franco Zeffirelli imbues his theater, opera and film productions with a dazzling array of baroque imagery, visual pyrotechnics, sumptuous sets and costumes, and overt eroticism. Of his major motion pictures, nearly all are adaptions of classical derivation set in another era. To many his films are hollow, banal, and superfluous romantic exercises, but Zeffirelli defends his love of the past and tradition by saying: "We have no guarantee for the present or the future. Therefore the only choice is to go back to the past and respect traditions. I have

Franco Zeffirelli

been a pioneer in this line of thinking, and the results have proven me right . . . The reason I am box-office everywhere is that I am an enlightened conservative continuing the discourse of our grandfathers and fathers, renovating texts but never betraying them.''

After studying architecture at the University of Florence, Zeffirelli took up acting. Luchino Visconti saw him in a production of Jean Cocteau's *Les Parents terribles* and hired him to act in two stage productions—*Eurydice* by Jean Anouilh and *Crime and Punishment* by Dostoevsky. Zeffirelli also involved himself in designing sets and costumes for Visconti's stage presentations and appeared in the film *L'onorevole Angelina*, directed by Luigi Zampa and starring Anna Magnani. As a result of that film he was offered a seven-year acting contract at RKO-Radio by screenwriter Helen Deutsch but turned it down to become Visconti's assistant on three films—*La terra trema, Bellissima*, and *Senso*.

His natural talent at set and costumes design and his love of opera provided an obvious segue into staging opera productions. These productions gained a reputation for opulence and for the focusing of attention on the lead female singers. Zeffirelli says he ''adores fun, fantasy and women,'' and he emphasized these elements in his operas. His most famous and successful association in opera was with the volatile Maria Callas for whom he staged productions of *La Traviata, Lucia de Lammermoor, Norma*, and *Tosca*.

His lengthy apprenticeship in the various theatrical arts earned Zeffirelli a reputation as a Renaissance man of sorts. He turned to feature film directing in 1967 bringing his romanticized traditionalism to *The Taming of the Shrew* starring Elizabeth Taylor and Richard Burton. While unarguably a bowdlerization of Shakespeare, its slapstick and boisterous merriment was engaging.

Romeo and Juliet was another matter entirely. Here the very heart of Shakespeare was replaced with Romeo and Juliet as flower children. It was an unabashed combination of theatricality, nude love scenes, and a Mercutio which Zeffirelli describes as ''a self-portrait of Shakespeare himself as a homosexual.'' The film was tremendously popular with the young movie-going audience and received Academy Awards for cinematography and costume design.

Fratello sole sorella lune (*Brother Sun Sister Moon*) was also aimed at the young, this time the Jesus freaks, but this outrageous portrait of St. Francis of Assisi was a complete flop.

Zeffirelli's 1978 Easter television presentation, *Jesus of Nazareth*, employed a star-studded cast and surprised many serious critics with its sensitivity and restraint. This was not the case, however, with his syrupy diminishing of *The Champ*, a sentimental classic which should never have been updated.

Zeffirelli disavows the explicitly erotic *Endless Love*, a vehicle for Brooke Shields, which, he says, was a beautiful story of the tragedy of two families in its original three-hour-version. He labels the truncated version ''trash'' and vowed to finish trying to capture the young audience. Appropriately, his next picture was the opulent and admirably cinematic presentation of *La Traviata*. For his *Hamlet*, however, he courted controversy by the casting of heartthrob Mel Gibson in the title role.

Zeffirelli defends his extravagant approach to filmmaking by saying, ''I am a flag-bearer of the crusade against boredom, bad taste and stupidity in the theater,'' but he is still the target of critical barbs such as those from the *Time* magazine reviewer who stated he was ''a director in need of a director.''

—Ronald Bowers

ZEMECKIS, Robert.

American. Born in Chicago, Illinois, 14 May 1951. Attended Northern Illinois University; University of Southern California School of Cinema, graduated 1973. Married Mary Ellen Trainor. Following graduation, with Bob Gale, asked to develop material for Steven Spielberg and John Milius; also worked as cutter of advertisements, 1970s; directed first feature, *I Wanna Hold Your Hand*, 1978; also writer for TV. Recipient: Oscar for Best Student Film, for *Field of Honor*, 1973. Agent: Jack Rapke, Creative Artists Agency, 1888 Century Park E., Suite 1400, Los Angeles, CA 90067, U.S.A.

Films as Director:

1973   *Field of Honor* (short) (+ sc)
1978   *I Wanna Hold Your Hand* (+ co-sc)
1980   *Used Cars* (+ co-sc)
1984   *Romancing the Stone*
1985   *Back to the Future* (+ co-sc)
1988   *Who Framed Roger Rabbit?*
1989   *Back to the Future II*
1990   *Back to the Future III*

Other Film:

1979   *1941* (Spielberg) (co-sc)

Publications:

By ZEMECKIS: articles—

Interview in *Filmmakers Newsletter* (Ward Hill, Massachusetts), June 1978.
Interview with A. Crystal in *Films and Filming* (London), December 1985.
Interview with A. Garel in *Revue du Cinéma* (Paris), November 1985.
''Back With a Future,'' an interview with Mark Horowitz, in *American Film* (Los Angeles), July/August 1988.
Interview in *Time Out* (London), 23 November 1988.

*   *   *

Will Robert Zemeckis ''out-Spielberg'' Spielberg? As it stands now Zemeckis is close to beating his closest mentor at his own game. Still, there has been a catch to all this: Zemeckis's work has been much celebrated for its dazzling technological inventiveness, and then pretty much left at that. While his films, especially recently, are technically impressive, they are also more than that. *Who Framed Roger Rabbit* does indeed blend animation with live action brilliantly, but that observation does not exhaust the film. Zemeckis, in all his work, also displays narratives that work out conflicts arising from a complex dual structure, a fondness for injecting his films with both a serious moral undertone and black comedy, and a carefully controlled kinetic sense that works both to hold these movies together and to keep them extraodinarily dynamic.

All Zemeckis's films present narratives in which different worlds are at odds at each other, starting with his celebrated short ''Field of Honor.'' Continuing the line, *I Wanna Hold Your Hand* contrasts the frustrating glimpses that the Beatle-crazed protagonists get of the group with the satisfying television representation of them on the Sullivan show. Zemeckis repeatedly returns to this narrative tension as characters' lives interact with highly mediated visions in *Used Cars* (politics clashes with and merges with advertising), *Romancing the Stone* (Kathleen Turner's onscreen adventures contrast with her romance novel ideals), and *Roger Rabbit* (humans interact uneasily with 'toons). In the *Back to the Future* trilogy, the pre-

Robert Zemeckis: *Back to the Future*

sent, 1985 suburban California, matches up against both the past and the future. Zemeckis's characters generally find the less mediated, more "real" world to be lacking but ultimately acceptable. For instance, in *Romancing the Stone* Michael Douglas does not meet Kathleen Turner's expectations for Jess, her ideal man, but she pines for him anyway, and in the end goes to him. Only *Roger Rabbit* suggests that some sort of happy compromise is possible as both types of characters walk off together toward 'Toontown at closure, though a case could be made for *Future III*, which combines the vistas of Ford with the optimism of Hawks.

These films also ponder serious questions in an entertaining way. *Used Cars*, as it explores the commercialization of American politics, itself can be seen as an extended form of the joke often told in reference to Nixon: "Would you buy a used car from this man?" Even more directly, the *Future* films, and to a lesser extent *Roger Rabbit*, overtly address questions concerning the impact that the present has on the future and some revolving around our responsibilities to history. While bringing up such questions so directly in genre film is fairly rare, the unsystematic treatment such issues get here is not. Christopher Lloyd in the *Future* trilogy illustrates this cavalier treatment well. When faced with a question of how he could risk the spacetime continuum so blithely, he responds, "Oh, what the hell." Also, while he repeatedly stresses the risks to the universe occasioned by his inventions, he always fixes his time machine "one last time" and even fashions an entirely new one at the end of *Future III*.

Zemeckis combines this interest in moral questions with an almost Buñuelian sense of humor. His use of black comedy is evident most obviously in *Used Cars*, which, among other things, uses a corpse as a comedy prop. *Romancing the Stone* contains this exchange: "Have they found her husband's body yet?" "Just the one piece." Further, the dark vision of 1985 in *Future II* is there at the edges of the other films in the trilogy. The porno theaters and winos that sprout in the middle film are present in the other installments in smaller numbers, often used for comedic effect, as when the same homeless person reappears again and again at different times. Even in *Roger Rabbit* some representations of the victims of World War II can be seen in the Terminal Bar.

Zemeckis makes use of a consistent spatial design to keep these disparate elements together. His spaces often take on readily discernible circular shapes. Chases are almost always chases *around* things: around the New Deal Used Car Lot, around the kitchen during the "Something's Cookin'" segment of *Roger Rabbit*, around the courthouse square in the *Future* films. Fights also usually move around objects: around a broken stick in *Romancing the Stone*, around a 'toon mallet in *Roger Rabbit*, around Biff's speeding car in *Future II*. These broad movements are mirrored by characters and objects in a number of other ways, especially by Roger Rabbit after taking a drink, by Biff getting punched, and by the looping take-offs of the flying time machines. On a different level this kinetic concern mirrors the circular narrative elements mentioned above, as the characters explore other worlds and typically settle for the one with which they started. Zemeckis blends these elements to form extremely vital, extremely satisfying wholes.

—Mark Walker

ZETTERLING, Mai.

Swedish. Born in Västeras, 24 May 1925. Educated at Royal Dramatic Theatre School, Stockholm, 1942–45. Married 1) actor Tutte Lemkow (divorced), two children; 2) writer David Hughes (divorced). Stage debut and film debut, 1941; in company of Royal Dramatic Theatre, Stockholm, 1945–47; began collaborating on TV documentaries with husband Hughes, 1960s; directed episode of *Mistress of Suspense* for TV, 1990. Recipient: Golden Lion, Venice Festival, for *The War Game*, 1963. Lives in France.

Films as Director:

1960   *The Polite Invasion* (short, for BBC TV)
1961   *Lords of Little Egypt* (short, for BBC TV); *The War Game* (short) (+ pr)
1962   *The Prosperity Race* (short, for BBC TV)
1963   *The Do-It-Yourself Democracy* (short, for BBC TV)
1964   *Alskande par* (Loving Couples) (co-d with David Hughes)
1966   *Nattlek* (Night Games) (co-d with Hughes)
1967   *Doktor Glas* (co-d with Hughes)
1968   *Flickorna* (*The Girls*) (co-d with Hughes)
1971   *Vincent the Dutchman* (co-d with Hughes, pr) (documentary)
1973   "The Strongest" episode of *Visions of Eight* (co-d with Hughes)
1976   *We har manje namn* (*We Have Many Names*) (+ ed, role)
1977   *Stockholm* (+ role) (for Canadian TV)
1978   *The Rain's Hat* (+ ed) (for TV)
1982   *Love* (for TV)
1983   *Scrubbers*
1986   *Amorosa*
1990   *Sunday Pursuit*

Other Films:

1941   *Lasse-Maja* (Olsson) (role)
1943   *Jag drapte* (Molander) (role)
1944   *Hets* (*Torment. Frenzy*) (Sjöberg) (role); *Prins Gustaf* (Bauman) (role)
1946   *Iris och Lojtnantshjarta* (*Iris and the Lieutenant*) (Sjöberg) (role); *Frieda* (Relph) (role); *Driver dagg faller Regn* (*Sunshine Follows Rain*) (role)
1948   *Musik i morker* (Bergman) (role); *Nu borjar livet* (Molander) (role); *Quartet* (Smart and others) (role); *The Bad Lord Byron* (MacDonald) (role); *Hildegard* (role)
1949   *Portrait from Life* (*The Girl in the Painting*) (Fisher) (role); *The Romantic Age* (Gréville) (role); *The Lost People* (Knowless) (role)
1950   *Blackmailed* (Marc Allégret) (role); *The Ringer* (Hamilton) (role)
1952   *The Tall Headlines* (*The Frightened Bride*) (Young) (role)
1953   *The Desperate Moment* (Bennett) (role); *Knock on Wood* (Frank and Panama) (role)
1954   *Prize of Gold* (Robson) (role); *Dance Little Lady* (Guest) (role)
1956   "Ett dockhem (A Doll's House)" episode of *Giftas* (Henriksson) (role); *Abandon Ship* (*Seven Waves Away*) (Sale) (role)
1957   *The Truth About Women* (Box) (role)
1958   *Lek pa regnbagen* (Kjellgren) (role)
1959   *Jet Storm* (Endfield); *Faces in the Dark* (Eady) (role)
1960   *Piccadilly Third Stop* (Rilla) (role); *Offbeat* (Owen) (role)
1961   *Only Two Can Play* (Gilliat) (role)
1962   *The Main Attraction* (Petrie) (role); *The Man Who Finally Died* (Lawrence) (role)
1963   *The Bay of St. Michel* (Ainsworth) (role)
1965   *The Vine Bridge* (Nykvist) (role)
1988   *Calling the Shots* (doc) (Cole) (appearance)
1989   *The Witches* (Roeg) (role)
1990   *Hidden Agenda* (Loach) (role)

Publications:

By ZETTERLING: books—

Bird of Passage, New York, 1976.
All Those Tomorrows, London, 1985.

By ZETTERLING: articles—

"Some Notes on Acting," in *Sight and Sound* (London), October/December 1951.
"Mai Zetterling at the Olympic Games," an interview in *American Cinematographer* (Los Angeles), November 1972.

On ZETTERLING: books—

Bjorkman, Stig, *Film in Sweden, the New Directors*, London, 1979.
Heck-Rabi, Louise, *Women Filmmakers: A Critical Reception*, Metuchen, New Jersey, 1984.

On ZETTERLING: articles—

"Meeting with Mai Zetterling," in *Cahiers du Cinéma in English* (New York), December 1966.
Pyros, J., "Notes on Women Directors," in *Take One* (Montreal), November/December 1970.
McGregor, C., "Mai is Behind the Camera Now," in *The New York Times*, 30 April 1972.
Elley, Derek, "Hiding it Under a Bushel: Free Fall," in *Films and Filming* (London), April 1974.

*   *   *

Mai Zetterling's career as a filmmaker stemmed from her disillusionment with acting. Trained at Stockholm's Royal Dramatic Theater, Zetterling debuted on stage and screen in 1941. She considered the film *Torment* her best acting achievement. She worked in British theatre, enacting roles from Chekhov, Anouilh, and Ibsen plays, and in British films. After one part in a Hollywood film, *Knock on Wood* with Danny Kaye, she spurned contract offers and returned home.

With her husband, David Hughes, she made several documentaries in the 1960s dealing with political issues. Zetterling's feature films depict the social status and psyche of women, reflecting her feminist concerns. The uncompromising honesty of perception and technical virtuosity in her films correspond to the pervasive and dominant themes of loneliness and obsession. Zetterling says: "I want very strongly to do things I believe in. I can't do jobs for the money. I just can't do it."

In 1960, Roger Moorfoot of the BBC financed her idea for a film on the immigration of Swedes to Lapland, *The Polite Invasion*. Three more followed: *The Lords of Little Egypt* depicted the gypsies at Saintes-Maries-de-la-Mer; her view of Swedish affluence in *The Prosperity Race* was not appreciated in Stockholm; and *Do-It-Yourself Democracy* commented on Icelandic society and government. Her first independent effort was the 15-minute anti-war film *The War Game*, in which two boys tussle for possession of a toy gun.

Her first feature film, *Loving Couples* was based on the fifth volume of Swedish author Agnes von Krusenstjerna's seven-volume novel, *The Misses von Pahlen*. Zetterling wrote the script in one year, with sketches of each shot to indicate camera positions. In it, three expectant mothers in a Stockholm hospital recall their lives in the moment of, and then beyond, the births of their babies. Critic Derek Elley suggests that Zetterling developed her theories and themes of film in *Loving Couples*, and rarely deviated from them in later works. She employs elaborate time lines as well as flashbacks, which she uses often and well, intertwining them one within another. Her films peak emotionally in scenes of parties and social gatherings. Her films are cohesive compositions, with a literary base, filmed in the stark contrasts of black to white, with a range of grays intervening. Zetterling's scenes of sexual behavior are integral to her themes of loneliness and obsession. *Loving Couples* exemplifies these characteristics.

Mai Zetterling: *Night Games*

Night Games, derived from Zetterling's novel with the same title, was banned from the Venice Film Festival. The critics who saw it were angered by the Marxist and Freudian elements in it; shocked by scenes of vomiting, masturbation, and childbirth. Based on Hjalmar Soderberg's 1905 novel, her next film, *Doktor Glas*, records the haunted love of a young physician for a pastor's wife. Even though the wife does not respond to the physician's erotic overtures, he administers a lethal drug to the pastor. It is Zetterling's grimmest study of loneliness, as Derek Elley observes, and her most pessimistic film, told in one extended flashback, "a far cry from *Night Games*."

She returned to a strongly feminist story in *Flickorna* and, as in *Loving Couples*, it contains three female roles of equal weight. In *Flickorna* three actresses perform *Lysistrata* on tour, acting out the views of the play in their private lives. Some critics reacted negatively, finding it self-indulgent, a mix of Greek comedy and soap opera, with heavy symbolism and confusing time structures. Other critics liked the various forms of humor effectively employed, and the arresting imagery.

In 1971, Zetterling filmed a documentary in color about Vincent Van Gogh. Titled *Vincent the Dutchman*, it was shown on American and British television. David Wolper then asked her to film any phase of the 1972 Olympics she chose; she filmed the weightlifting sequence, "The Strongest," for *Visions of Eight*.

In the 1970s, Zetterling published three novels, pursuing creative directions other than filmmaking. She also continued making documentaries (one on Stan Smith, tennis champion, one dealing with Stockholm, another on marriage customs) along with a seven-hour adaptation for French television of Simone de Beauvoir's *The Second Sex*. Zetterling reasserts that whatever she films, "It will be something I believe in."

—Louise Heck-Rabi

ZINNEMANN, Fred.

Austrian/American. Born in Vienna, 29 April 1907. Educated in law, University of Vienna, degree 1927; studied one year at the Ecole Technique de Photographie et Cinématographie, Paris. Married Renée Bartlett, 1936, one son. Assistant cameraman in Paris and Berlin, then with Billy Wilder, Eugen Schüfftan and Robert Siodmak, made *Menschen am Sonntag*, 1928; moved to Hollywood, became assistant cameraman and cutter for Berthold Viertel, 1929; worked with Robert Flaherty on unrealized documentary project, Berlin, 1931; worked in Mexico with Paul Strand on *Los Redes*, 1934–35; hired by MGM to direct short subjects, 1937; directed first feature, 1942; vice-president, Directors Guild of America, 1961–64. Recipient: Oscars for Best Short Subject, for *That Mothers Might Live*, 1938, and *Benjy*, 1951; Best Direction, New York Film Critics, for *High Noon*, 1952; Oscar for Best Director, and Director Award, Directors Guild of America, for *From Here to Eternity*, 1953; Best Direction, New York Film Critics, for *The Nun's Story*, 1959; Oscar for Best Director, Best Direction, New York Film Critics, and Director Award, Directors Guild of America, for *A Man for All Seasons*, 1966; D.W. Griffith Award, 1971; Order of Arts and Letters, France, 1982.

Films as Director:

1934/35   *Los Redes* (*The Wave*)

1938   *A Friend Indeed* (short for MGM); *The Story of Dr. Carver* (short for MGM); *That Mothers Might Live* (short for MGM); *Tracking the Sleeping Death* (short for MGM); *They Live Again* (short for MGM)
1939   *Weather Wizards* (short for MGM); *While America Sleeps* (short for MGM); *Help Wanted!* (short for MGM); *One Against the World* (short for MGM); *The Ash Can Fleet* (short for MGM); *Forgotten Victory* (short for MGM)
1940   *The Old South* (short for MGM); *Stuffie* (short for MGM); *The Way in the Wilderness* (short for MGM); *The Great Meddler* (short for MGM)
1941   *Forbidden Passage* (short for MGM); *Your Last Act* (short for MGM)
1942   *The Lady or the Tiger?* (short for MGM); *The Kid Glove Killer*; *Eyes in the Night*
1944   *The Seventh Cross*
1945   *Little Mr. Jim*
1946   *My Brother Talks to Horses*
1947   *The Search*
1948   *Act of Violence*
1950   *The Men*
1951   *Teresa*; *Benjy* (short)
1952   **High Noon**; *The Member of the Wedding*
1953   **From Here to Eternity**
1955   *Oklahoma*
1957   *A Hatful of Rain*
1958   *The Nun's Story*
1960   *The Sundowners* (+ pr)
1963   *Behold a Pale Horse* (+ pr)
1966   *A Man for All Seasons* (+ pr)
1973   *The Day of the Jackal* (+ pr)
1977   *Julia* (+ pr)
1982   *Five Days One Summer* (+ pr); re-edited version released 1988.

Other Films:

1927   *La Marche des machines* (Deslaw) (asst cameraman)
1929   *Ich Küsse Ihre Hand, Madame* (Land) (asst cameraman); *Sprengbagger 1010* (Achaz-Duisberg) (asst cameraman); *Menschen am Sonntag* (*People on Sunday*) (Siodmak) (asst cameraman)
1930   *Man Trouble* (asst d to Berthold Viertel); *All Quiet on the Western Front* (Milestone) (bit role)
1931   *The Spy* (asst d to Viertel)
1932   *The Wiser Sex* (asst d to Viertel); *The Man from Yesterday* (asst d to Viertel); *The Kid from Spain* (asst to Busby Berkeley)
1989   *Stand Under the Dark Clock* (doc) (Walker) (role)

Publications:

By ZINNEMANN: book—

Fred Zinnemann: My Life in the Movies, New York, 1990.

By ZINNEMANN: articles—

"Different Perspective," in *Sight and Sound* (London), Autumn 1948.
"Choreography of a Gunfight," in *Sight and Sound* (London), July/September 1952.
"The Impact of Television on Motion Pictures," an interview with Gideon Bachmann, in *Film Culture* (New York), no. 2, 1957.
"A Conflict of Conscience," in *Films and Filming* (London), December 1959.
Interview with John Russell Taylor in *Sight and Sound* (London), Winter 1960/61.
"A Discussion: Personal Creation in Hollywood: Can It Be Done?," in *Film Quarterly* (Berkeley), Spring 1962.
"Zinnemann—True or False?," in *Cinema* (Beverly Hills), February/March 1964.
"Revelations," in *Films and Filming* (London), September 1964.
"Zinnemann Talks Back," an interview in *Cinema* (Beverly Hills), October/November 1964.
"Montgomery Clift," in *Sight and Sound* (London), Autumn 1966.
"Some Questions Answered," in *Action* (Los Angeles), May/June 1967.

Fred Zinnemann

Interview with Gene D. Phillips in *Focus on Film* (London), Spring 1973.

"Fred Zinnemann and *Julia*," an interview with Cecile Starr, in *Filmmakers Newsletter* (Ward Hill, Massachusetts), November 1977.

"Individualism Against Machinery," an interview with Gordon Gow, in *Films and Filming* (London), February 1978.

Interview with M. Buckley in *Films in Review* (New York), January 1983.

"Dialogue on Film: Fred Zinnemann," in *American Film* (Washington D.C.), January/February 1986.

"*From Here to Eternity*," in *Sight and Sound* (London), Winter 1987/1988.

On ZINNEMANN: books—

Griffith, Richard, *Fred Zinnemann*, New York, 1958.

Foreman, Carl, *High Noon*, New York, 1971.

Phillips, Gene D., *The Movie Makers: Artists in an Industry*, Chicago, 1973.

On ZINNEMANN: articles—

Knight, Arthur, "Fred Zinnemann," in *Films in Review* (New York), January 1951.

Hart, Henry, "Zinnemann on the Verge," in *Films in Review* (New York), February 1953.

Schickel, Richard, "Fred Zinnemann: Quiet Man on the Set," in *Show* (Hollywood), August 1964.

Stanbrook, Alan, "A Man for All Movies: The Films of Fred Zinnemann," in *Films and Filming* (London), June 1967.

Adler, D., "Zinnemann's Fate," in *Show* (Hollywood), May 1970.

"*High Noon*," in *Values in Conflict*, edited by Richard Maynard, New York, 1974.

* * *

In 1928 Fred Zinnemann worked as assistant to cinematographer Eugene Schüfftan on Robert Siodmak's *Menschen am Sonntag* (*People on Sunday*), along with Edgar Ulmer and Billy Wilder, who wrote the scenario for this semi-documentary silent feature made in the tradition of Flaherty and Vertov. Having been strongly influenced by realistic filmmaking, particularly the work of Erich von Stroheim, King Vidor, and Robert Flaherty, Zinnemann immigrated to the United States in 1930 and worked with Berthold Viertel, Flaherty ("probably the greatest single influence on my work as a filmmaker," he later stated), and the New York photographer-documentarist Paul Strand on *Los Redes*, the first of a proposed series intended to document everyday Mexican life. *Los Redes* told the story of the struggle of impoverished fishermen to organize themselves against economic exploitation. The film was shot in Vera Cruz, and Zinnemann was responsible for directing the actors.

Zinnemann's documentary training and background developed his style as a "social realist" in a number of early pictures (several shorts he directed, for example, in MGM's *Crime Does Not Pay* and *The Passing Parade* series) during the years 1937–1942. His medical short *That Mother Might Live*, won an Academy Award and enabled Zinnemann to direct feature films. His first feature at MGM was a thriller, *The Kid Glove Killer*, with Van Heflin and Marsha Hunt. *The Seventh Cross* was adapted from Anna Segher's anti-fascist World War II novel. Starring Spencer Tracy, the film was notable for its atmosphere and documentary style. *The Search*, shot on location in Europe in 1948, with Montgomery Clift, gave a realistic portrayal of children who had been displaced by the turmoil of World War II and was a critical as well as a commercial success. *The Men* was the first of a three-picture contract Zinnemann signed with Stanley Kramer and dealt with the problem of paraplegic war veterans, marking Marlon Brando's debut as a film actor. Zinnemann filmed *The Men* on location at the Birmingham Veteran's Hospital and used a number of patients there as actors.

Zinnemann's next film for Kramer, *High Noon*, was significant because of the way Zinnemann's realistic style turned the genre of the Western upside down. It featured Gary Cooper in an Oscar-winning performance as Will Kane, a retired marshal who has taken a Quaker bride (Grace Kelly), but whose marriage is complicated by the anticipated return of paroled desperado Frank Miller, expected on the noon train. Zinnemann treated his "hero" as an ordinary man beset with doubts and fears in an existential struggle to protect himself and the community of Haddleyville, a town that proves to be undeserving of his heroism and bravery. Zinnemann created a tense drama by coordinating screen time to approximate real time, which is extended only when the fateful train arrives, bearing its dangerous passenger. Working against the stylized and mythic traditions that had come to dominate the genre, *High Noon* established the trend of the "psychological" western and represents one of Zinnemann's finest accomplishments.

Zinnemann's last Kramer picture was *The Member of the Wedding*, a Carson McCullers novel that had been adapted to a popular Broadway production by McCullers herself. The film utilized the same cast that had made the stage production successful (Julie Harris, Brandon de Wilde, and Ethel Waters) but created cinematically an effective atmosphere of entrapment. *Member of the Wedding* is a model of effective theatrical adaption. Zinnemann went on to adapt the 1955 movie version of the Rodgers and Hammerstein classic *Oklahoma!*, removing the exclamation point, as one wit noted, in a spacious and lyrical, but also rather perfunctory effort.

In 1953 Zinnemann moved to Columbia Pictures to direct the adaption of the popular James Jones novel *From Here to Eternity*, a huge popular success starring Montgomery Clift, Frank Sinatra, and Ernest Borgnine, that won Zinnemann an Academy Award for Best Director. Zinnemann's approach effectively utilized newsreel footage of the Japanese attack on Pearl Harbor and his realistic style both tightened and dramatized the narrative. *A Hatful of Rain* applied Zinnemann's documentary approach to the problem of drug addiction in New York. *The Nun's Story* (with Audrey Hepburn and Peter Finch) has been linked to *A Man For All Seasons* in that both reflect conflicts of conscience, a recurring motif in Zinnemann's films. *A Man for All Seasons*, adapted from Robert Bolt's play, won Paul Scofield an Academy Award for his portrayal of St. Thomas More.

Among Zinnemann's political films are *Behold a Pale Horse*, starring Gregory Peck and set during the Spanish Civil War, a picture that also incorporated newsreel authenticity, and *The Day of the Jackal*, a story about an assassin's attempt on the life of Charles de Gaulle, shot on location "like a newsreel." A later and in many ways impressive political film involving a conflict of conscience was Zinnemann's *Julia*, adapted by Alvin Sargent from Lillian Hellman's *Pentimento*, concerning Hellman's love affair with the writer Dashiell Hammett (Jason Robards) and her long-standing friendship with the mysterious Julia (Vanessa Redgrave), the daughter of a wealthy family who becomes a socialist-intellectual politicized by events in Germany under the Nazi regime. *Julia* is a perfect Zinnemann vehicle, impressive in its authenticity and historical reconstruction, and also psychologically tense, particularly in the way Zinnemann films Hellman's suspense-laden journey from Paris to Moscow via Berlin. It demonstrates the director's sense of psychological realism and his apparent determination to make worthwhile pictures that are nevertheless highly entertaining.

—James M. Welsh

NOTES ON ADVISERS AND CONTRIBUTORS

AFFRON, Charles. Essayist. Professor of French, New York University, since 1965. Author of *Star Acting: Gish, Garbo, Davis*, 1977; *Cinema and Sentiment*, 1982; *Divine Garbo*, 1985; and *Fellini's 8½*, 1987. General Editor of Rutgers Films in Print Series. **Essays:** Capra; Goulding; Lean; LeRoy; Wyler.

AFFRON, Mirella, Jona. Essayist. Professor, Program in Cinema Studies since 1985, and Dean of Humanities and Social Sciences since 1987, College of Staten Island, City University of New York. Former Member of the Executive Council, Society for Cinema Studies. **Essay:** Castellani.

AMBROGIO, Anthony. Essayist. Formerly Film and Composition Instructor, Wayne State University, Detroit. Contributor to *Film Criticism* and *Pukka Afflatus*. **Essay:** Dante.

ANDERSON, Joseph. Adviser. Manager for Operations, WGBH, Boston, and President, Mass Comm/Masu Komi media consultants. Author, with Donald Richie, of *The Japanese Film: Art and Industry*, 1959, 1982.

ANDREW, Dudley. Adviser and Essayist. Angelo Bertocci Professor of Critical Studies and Director of the Institute for Cinema and Culture at the University of Iowa (joined faculty in 1969). Author of *Major Film Theories*, 1976; *André Bazin*, 1978; *Kenji Mizoguchi: A Guide to References and Resources* (co-author), 1981; *Concepts in Film Theory*, 1984; and *Film in the Aura of Art*, 1984. **Essays:** Allégret; Astruc; Becker; Cayatte; Christian-Jaque; Clément; Clouzot; Delannoy; Duvivier; Grémillon; Leenhardt; Mizoguchi.

ARMES, Roy. Adviser and Essayist. Reader in Film and Television at the Middlesex Polytechnic, London. Author of *French Cinema since 1946*, 1966, 1970; *The Cinema of Alain Resnais*, 1968; *French Film*, 1970; *Patterns of Realism*, 1972, 1983; *Film and Reality*, 1974; *The Ambiguous Image*, 1976; *A Critical History of British Cinema*, 1978; *The Films of Alain Robbe-Grillet*, 1981; *French Cinema*, 1985; *Third World Filmmaking and the West*, 1987; *On Video*, 1988; *Studies in Arab and African Film*, 1991. **Essays:** Allio; Benegal; Carné; Chahine; Cocteau; Delluc; Dickinson; Epstein; Feuillade; Gance; Gerima; Güney; Hondo; L'Herbier; Melville; Sautet; Torre Nilsson.

ARROYO, José. Essayist. Lecturer in Communications, Simon Fraser University, Vancouver. **Essays:** Almodóvar; Babenco.

BARDASKY, Dimitar. Adviser. With the Short Films Department, Bulgarian Cinematography, Sofia, since 1982. With the Programming and Publications Department, Bulgarian National Film Archive, Sofia, 1978–81. Contributor to and editor of the biographical section, *In the World of Cinema*, 3 volumes, 1982–83.

BARNOUW, Erik. Adviser. Professor Emeritus of Dramatic Arts, Columbia University, New York City, since 1973 (joined faculty, 1946; organized and chaired the film division of the School of Arts). Head, Writers Guild of America, 1957–59. Film and Television Specialist, 1977, and Chief of the Motion Picture, Broadcasting and Recorded Sound Division, 1978–81, Library of Congress, Washington, D.C. Author of *Indian Film*, with S. Krishnaswamy, 1963, 1980; *Documentary: A History of the Non-Fiction Film*, 1974, 1983; *Tube of Plenty: The Evolution of American Television*, 1975; *The Sponsor: Notes on a Modern Potentate*, 1978; and *The Magician and the Cinema*, 1981. Editor in Chief, *International Encyclopaedia of Communications*, 1989.

BASINGER, Jeanine. Essayist. Professor of Film, Wesleyan University, Middletown, Connecticut, since 1969. Trustee, American Film Institute, National Center for Film and Video Preservation. Member of Advisory Board, Foundation for Independent Video and Film. Author of *Working with Kazan*, 1973; *Shirley Temple*, 1975; *Gene Kelly*, 1976; *Lana Turner*, 1977; *Anthony Mann: A Critical Analysis*, 1979; *The World War II Combat Book: Anatomy of a Genre*, 1986; *The "It's a Wonderful Life" Book*, 1986; and numerous articles. **Essays:** De Toth; Fleming; Ruggles; Siodmak; W.S. Van Dyke.

BAXTER, John. Essayist. Novelist, screenwriter, TV producer and film historian. Visiting Lecturer, Hollins College, Virginia,

1974–75; Broadcaster with B.B.C. Radio and Television, 1976–91. Author of six novels, two anthologies of science fiction (editor), various screenplays for documentary films and features, and works of film criticism: *Hollywood in the Thirties*, 1968; *The Australian Cinema*, 1970; *Science Fiction in the Cinema*, 1970; *The Gangster Film*, 1970; *The Cinema of Josef von Sternberg*, 1971; *The Cinema of John Ford*, 1971; *Hollywood in the Sixties*, 1972; *Sixty Years of Hollywood*, 1973; *An Appalling Talent: Ken Russell*, 1973; *Stunt*, 1974; *The Hollywood Exiles*, 1976; *King Vidor*, 1976; with Brian Norris, *The Video Handbook*, 1982; *Filmstruck*, 1989. **Essays:** Bogdanovich; Richard Brooks; Ford; Frankenheimer; Jewison; Leisen; Malle; Schepisi; Vadim; von Sternberg; Weir.

BOCK, Audie. Essayist. Freelance author and lecturer. Visiting lecturer at Harvard, Yale, University of California and others, 1975–83; assistant producer of the international version of Kurosawa's *Kagemusha*, 1980. Author of *Japanese Film Directors*, 1978, 1985, and *Mikio Naruse: un maître du cinéma japonais*, 1983; translator of *Something Like an Autobiography* by Kurosawa, 1982. **Essay:** Kurosawa.

BODEEN, DeWitt. Adviser and Essayist. Screenwriter and film critic. Author of screenplays for *Cat People*, 1942; *Seventh Victim*, 1943; *Curse of the Cat People*, 1944; *The Yellow Canary*, 1944; *The Enchanted Cottage*, 1945; *Night Song*, 1947; *I Remember Mama*, 1948; *Mrs. Mike*, 1959; *Billy Budd*, 1962; also numerous teleplays, 1950–68. Also author of *Ladies of the Footlights*; *The Films of Cecil B. De Mille*; *Chevalier*; *From Hollywood*; *More from Hollywood*; *13 Castle Walk* (novel); editor of *Who Wrote the Movie and What Else Did He Write?* Died 1988. **Essays:** Borzage; Brown; Cromwell; Guitry; Korda; Murnau; Stevens; Jacques Tourneur; Wise.

BORDWELL, David. Essayist. Professor of Film, University of Wisconsin, Madison, since 1973. Author of *Filmguide to La Passion de Jeanne d'Arc*, 1973; *Film Art: An Introduction*, with Kristin Thompson, 1979; *French Impressionist Cinema*, 1980; *The Films of Carl-Theodor Dreyer*, 1981; *The Classical Hollywood Cinema: Film Style and Mode of Production to 1960*, with Janet Staiger and Kristin Thompson, 1984; *Narration in the Fiction Film*, 1985; *Ozu and the Poetics of Cinema*, 1988; and *Making Meaning: Inference and Rhetoric in the Interpretation of Cinema*, 1990. **Essay:** Ozu.

BOWERS, Ronald. Essayist. Financial Editor, E.F. Hutton and Company, since 1982. Editor, *Films in Review*, 1979–81. Author of *The MGM Stock Company*, with James Robert Parish, 1973; and *The Selznick Players*, 1976. **Essays:** Dwan; King; Litvak; Molander; Negulesco; Zeffirelli.

BOWLES, Stephen E. Essayist. Associate Professor of Film, University of Miami, since 1976. Author of *An Approach to Film Study*, 1974; *Index to Critical Reviews from British and American Film Periodicals 1930–71*, 3 volumes, 1974–75; *Sidney Lumet: A Guide to References and Resources*, 1979; and *Index to Critical Film Reviews: Supplement 1, 1971–76*, 1983. **Essay:** Lumet.

BRITO, Rui Santana. Adviser. Film Historian, Cinemateca Portuguesa, Lisbon.

BROWN, Geoff. Essayist. Chief Film Critic of *The Times*, London. Author of *Launder and Gilliat*, 1977; *Walter Forde*, 1977; *Der Produzent: Michael Balcon und der englische Film*, 1981; and *The Common Touch: The Films of John Baxter*, 1989. **Essays:** Baxter; Launder and Gilliat.

BURGOYNE, Robert. Adviser and Essayist. Associate Professor of English, Wayne State University, Detroit. Editor of *Enclitic*, and contributor to *Cinema Journal*, *Film Quarterly*, and *October*. Author of *Bertolucci's 1990: A Narrative and Historical Analysis*; and *Key Terms in Film Semiotics*, 1991. **Essay:** Bertolucci.

BURTON, Julianne. Essayist. Associate Professor, Merrill College and the Board of Studies in Literature, University of California at Santa Cruz, since 1982 (Assistant Professor, 1974–82). Author of more than 40 publications on the Latin American Cinema. **Essay:** Birri.

CAMPER, Fred. Essayist. Independent filmmaker and writer and lecturer on film since 1965. Has taught at various American colleges and universities. **Essays:** Baillie; Cohen; Frampton.

CIMENT, Michel. Adviser and Essayist. Associate Professor in American Studies, University of Paris. Member of the Editorial Board of *Positif.* Author of *Erich von Stroheim,* 1967; *Kazan by Kazan,* 1973; *Le Dossier Rosi,* 1976; *Le Livre de Losey,* 1979; *Kubrick,* 1980; *Les Conquérants d'un nouveau monde,* 1981; *Elia Kazan: An Outsider,* 1982; *All about Mankiewicz,* 1983; *Boorman,* 1985; *Francesco Rosi: Chronique d'un film annoncé,* 1987; and *Passport pour Hollywood,* 1987. **Essays:** Angelopoulos; Brocka; Comencini; Guerra; Ioseliani; Mikhalkov-Konchalovsky; Panfilov; Perrault; Skolimowski.

CONLEY, Tom. Essayist. Professor of French and Comparative Literature, University of Minnesota. Former editor, *Enclitic,* and contributor to *Theater Journal, MLN, Hors Cadre, Revue des Lettres Modernes,* and *Littérature.* **Essays:** Delvaux; Renoir.

COOK, David. Adviser. Professor and Director of Film Studies, Emory University, since 1985. Author of *A History of Narrative Film,* 1981, 2nd ed., 1990.

COOK, Samantha. Essayist. Freelance editor, researcher and writer, London. **Essays:** Bemberg; Seidelman.

COUSINS, R.F. Essayist. Lecturer in French, University of Birmingham. Author of *Zola's Thérèsa Raquin,* 1991, and contributor to *University Vision* and *Literature/Film Quarterly.* Executive Member of British Universities Film and Video Council. **Essays:** Beineix; Lumière; Claude Miller.

D'ARPINO, Tony. Essayist. Freelance writer. Author of *The Tree Worshipper,* 1983, and *Untitled Zodial,* 1984. **Essay:** Pasolini.

DERRY, Charles. Essayist. Head of Motion Picture Studies, Wright State University, Dayton, Ohio, since 1978. Author of *Dark Dreams: A Psychological History of the Modern Horror Film,* 1978; *The Film Book Bibliography 1940–1975* (co-author), 1980; and *The Suspense Thriller: Films in the Shadow of Alfred Hitchcock,* 1988. **Essays:** Altman; Chabrol; Lee; Jerry Lewis; Mulligan; Preminger; Spielberg.

DIXON, Wheeler Winston. Essayist. Director, Film Studies Program, University of Nebraska, Lincoln. Filmmaker and author of *The 'B' Directors: A Biographical Directory,* 1985; *The Cinematic Vision of F. Scott Fitzgerald,* 1986; and *Terence Fisher: The Critical Reception,* 1991. **Essay:** Frears.

DOLL, Susan M. Essayist. Instructor in Film at Oakton Community College and at the School of the Art Institute of Chicago. Author of *Marilyn: Her Life and Legend,* 1990; and *The Films of Elvis Presley,* 1991. **Essays:** Scott; Welles.

DUNBAR, Robert. Adviser and Essayist. Freelance film critic and historian; held various visiting professorships and lectureships, from 1975. Worked for Gainsborough and Gaumont-British Studios, 1933–38, 1948–49; Director of Public and Cultural Relations, British Embassy, Moscow, 1944–47; General Manager, Imperadio Pictures, 1949–51; independent producer of feature films and documentaries, 1952–63; Chairman, London School of Film Technique, 1963–74. Died 1988. **Essays:** Gerasimov; Kozintsev; Shub.

DURGNAT, Raymond. Essayist. Visiting Professor of Film, Wright State University, Dayton, Ohio. Author of numerous publications on film, including *Durgnat on Film,* 1975; *King Vidor— American,* 1988; and *Michael Powell and the English Genius,* 1991. **Essays:** Boultings; Clayton; Vasilievs.

EDELMAN, Rob. Essayist. Lecturer and freelance writer, New York. Director of programming, Home Film Festival. Formerly coordinator of National Film programs, American Film Institute. Contributing editor, *Leonard Maltin's TV Movies,* and contributor to *New York Times, Variety, American Film, Cineaste* and other periodicals. **Essays:** Blier; Broca; Costa-Gavras; Cruze; Dassin; Donskoi; Dovz-

henko; Ferreri; Garnett; Lelouch; Leni; Micheaux; Niblo; Polonsky; Pontecorvo; Pudovkin; Ritt; Ruttmann; Syberberg; Willard Van Dyke; Charles Vidor; Wertmüller.

EDMONDS, Robert. Essayist. Professor-at-Large, Columbia College, Chicago, since 1975. Author of *About Documentary: Anthropology on Film,* 1974; and *The Sights and Sounds of Cinema and Television,* 1982. Editor of the English translation of *The Aesthetics and Psychology of the Cinema* by Jean Mitry, 1976. **Essay:** Storck.

ELLIS, Jack C. Adviser and Essayist. Professor of Film and Former Chair of the Department of Radio/Television/Film at Northwestern University, Evanston, Illinois. Also taught at UCLA, New York University, and the University of Texas at Austin. Author of *A History of Film,* 1979, 3rd edition 1990; *John Grierson: A Guide to References and Resources,* 1986; and *The Documentary Idea,* 1989. Founding member and Past President of Society for Cinema Studies, editor of its journal, *Cinema Journal,* 1976–82. **Essays:** Cavalcanti; Grierson; Jennings; Lorentz; Marker; Rotha; Rouch; Watt; Wright.

ELSNER-SOMMER, Gretchen. Essayist. Film critic and director of Foreign Images distribution company. Formerly Associate Editor of *Jump Cut.* **Essay:** von Trotta.

ERENS, Patricia. Essayist. Associate Professor, Rosary College, River Forest, Illinois, since 1977. Author of *Akira Kurosawa: A Guide to References and Resources,* 1979, and *The Jew in American Cinema,* 1984; editor of *Sexual Stratagems: The World of Women in Film,* 1979. **Essays:** Hani; Ichikawa; Němec; Pollack.

ESTRIN, Mark W. Essayist. Professor of English and Director of Film Studies, Rhode Island College, Providence, since 1966. Author of *Lillian Hellman: Plays, Films, Memoirs,* 1980, and contributor to *Literature/Film Quarterly, Modern Drama,* and *Journal of Narrative Technique.* **Essays:** Allen; Nichols.

EVERSON, William K. Adviser. Film critic/historian. Teaches at New York University, the New School for Social Research, and the School of Visual Arts, New York City. Author of numerous books, including *The Art of W.C. Fields; Classics of the Horror Film;* and *The Western.*

FALK, Quentin. Essayist. Founding editor of *Flicks* magazine, and regular contributor to national newspapers. Formerly editor of *Screen International,* London, and author of books on Graham Greene, Anthony Hopkins, the Rank Organisation, and Albert Finney. **Essay:** Parker.

FALLER, Greg S. Adviser and Essayist. Associate Professor in Film, Towson State University, Baltimore, since 1986. Taught at Northwestern University 1984–6. Assistant/Associate Editor of The International Dictionary of Films and Filmmakers, first edition, vols. 3, 4 and 5; and of *Journal of Film and Video,* 1985–87. Editor of *Film Reader 6,* 1985. **Essays:** Donen; Fosse; Joseph H. Lewis; Lubitsch.

FARNSWORTH, Rodney. Essayist. Assistant Professor of English, Indiana University-Purdue University, Fort Wayne. **Essays:** Herzog; Rafelson.

FEINSTEIN, Howard. Essayist. Film editor, *The Village Voice,* New York. **Essay:** Zanussi.

FELPERIN, Leslie. Essayist. Graduate Student in film at University of Kent at Canterbury. **Essay:** Armstrong.

FERRARI, Lilie. Essayist. Writer and researcher. London. **Essay:** Arzner.

FITZGERALD, Theresa. Essayist. Managing Director and Writer-Producer-Director, Camden Productions Ltd., London, since 1982. Secretary, London Screenwriters Workshop, since 1983. **Essays:** Dearden; Peries.

FONSECA, M.S. Essayist. Researcher, Programming Department, Cinemateca Portuguesa, since 1981. Film critic for *Expresso* newspaper, Lisbon, and author of *Panorama do Cinema Dinamarqués*, 1983, and *Cinema Novo Potugués*, 1985, among others. **Essay:** Oliveira.

FOREMAN, Alexa. Essayist. Account executive, Video Duplications, Atlanta, since 1986. Formerly Theatre manager, American Film Institute. Author of *Women in Motion*, 1983. **Essay:** Malick.

FRAMPTON, Saul. Essayist. Graduate student at the University of Oxford, and contributor to *Time Out* and *20/20*. **Essays:** Davies; Greenaway; Littin.

GIANNETTI, Louis D. Adviser. Member of the faculty, Case-Western Reserve University, Cleveland. Author of articles and books on the cinema, including *Masters of the American Cinema*, 1981.

GILLETT, John. Adviser and Essayist. Programme Researcher, National Film Theatre, London. Contributor to *Monthly Film Bulletin*, *Sight and Sound*, and *Film Dope*. **Essay:** Blasetti.

GLAESSNER, Verina. Essayist. Film critic, London. Contributor to *The Economist*, *Monthly Film Bulletin* and *The Guardian*. **Essays:** Chen Kaige; Klimov; Rosi.

GOMERY, Douglas. Adviser and Essayist. Professor, Department of Radio/Television/Film, University of Maryland, and Senior Researcher, Media Studies Project, Woodrow Wilson Center for International Scholars, Washington, D.C. Author of *High Sierra: Screenplay and Analysis*, 1979; *Film History: Theory and Practice* (co-author), 1985; *The Hollywood Studio System*, 1986; *The Will Hays Papers*, 1987; *American Media* (co-author), 1989; and *Movie History: A Survey*, 1991. **Essays:** Bacon; Benton; Curtiz; Landis; George Miller; Walsh; Wood.

GOMEZ, Joseph A. Essayist. Lecturer in Film Studies, North Carolina State University. Contributor to *Literature/Film Quarterly*. **Essay:** Watkins.

HANSON, Patricia King. Essayist. Executive Editor, American Film Institute, Los Angeles, since 1983. Film critic, *Screen International*, since 1986. Associate Editor, Salem Press, 1978–83. Editor of *American Film Institute Catalog of Feature Films 1911–1920* and *1931–40*. Co-editor of *Film Review Index*, vols. I and II, 1986–87, and of *Source Book for the Performing Arts*, 1988. **Essays:** Daves; Mamoulian; Sirk.

HANSON, Steve. Essayist. Humanities Biographer, University of Southern California, Los Angeles, since 1969. Film critic. *Screen International*, since 1986. Associate Editor, Salem Press, 1978–83. Co-editor of *Film Review Index*, vols. I and II, 1986–87, and of *Sourcebook for the Performing Arts*, 1988. **Essays:** Fellini; Germi; La Cava; Milestone; Powell and Pressburger; Rossellini; Wellman.

HARRIS, Ann. Essayist. Doctoral student in Cinema Studies, New York University. **Essay:** Pick.

HECK-RABI, Louise. Essayist. Freelance writer, author of *Women Filmmakers: A Critical Reception*, 1984, and producer and co-writer of *Video Slow Reader*, 1991. **Essays:** Deren; Guy; Mészáros; Riefenstahl; Varda; Zetterling.

HIRANO, Kyoko. Essayist. Film program Coordinator, Japan Society, New York, since 1986. Editor, *Cinéma Gras*, Tokyo, 1977–79, and contributor to *Cineaste* and *Theater Craft*. **Essays:** Gosho; Imai; Kinoshita; Shindo; Shinoda; Yoshimura.

HOLDSTEIN, Deborah. Essayist. Assistant Professor of English, Illinois Institute of Technology, Chicago, since 1980. **Essay:** Pakula.

HUANG, Vivian. Essayist. Film critic for *Centre Daily News*, New York, and contributor to *Cinevue*, *The New Asian American Times*, *Transpacific* and other periodicals. **Essays:** Hou Hsiao-Hsien; King Hu.

HUTCHINGS, Peter. Essayist. Lecturer in Film Studies in the department of Historical and Critical Studies at Newcastle Polytechnic. **Essays:** Fisher; Reeves.

KAMINSKY, Stuart M. Essayist. Professor of Film, Northwestern University, Evanston, Illinois. Author of *Don Siegel, Director*, 1973; *Clint Eastwood*, 1974; *American Film Genres*, 1977; *John Huston, Maker of Magic*, 1978; *Coop: The Life and Legend of Gary Cooper*, 1980; *Basic Filmmaking* (c-author), 1981; *American Television Genres*, 1985; and *Writing for Television*, 1988. Editor of *Ingmar Bergman: Essays in Criticism*, 1975. Also a novelist: works include *Murder on the Yellow Brick Road*, 1978; *He Done Her Wrong*, 1983; *A Cold, Red Sunrise*, 1988; and *Buried Caesars*, 1989. **Essays:** Mel Brooks; Hathaway; Huston; Leone.

KANOFF, Joel. Essayist. Lecturer in the Visual Arts, Princeton University, New Jersey, since 1983. **Essays:** De Sica; Visconti.

KAPLAN, E. Ann. Adviser. Director, The Humanities Institute, SUNY, Stony Brook, and Professor of Film and English. Author of *Women in Film Noir*; *Fritz Lang: A Guide to References and Resources*; and *Rocking Around the Clock: Music Television, Postmodernism and Consumer Culture*.

KATZ, Ephraim. Adviser. Filmmaker, writer and critic. Has written, directed and produced documentary, educational and industrial films. Author of *The Film Encyclopaedia*, 1979.

KEHR, Dave. Adviser and Essayist. Film Critic, *Chicago Tribune*, since 1986. **Essays:** Edwards; Tati.

KEMP, Philip. Adviser and Essayist. Freelance writer and film historian, contributor to *Sight and Sound* and *World Film Directors*. Author of *Lethal Innocence: The Cinema of Alexander Mackendrick*, 1991, and of forthcoming biography of Michael Balcon. **Essays:** Clair; Crichton; Hamer; Kobayashi; Mackendrick; Penn; Ray; Sayles; Wilder; Yates.

KHANNA, Satti. Adviser and Essayist. Research Associate, Center for South and Southeast Asia Studies, University of California, Berkeley, since 1976. Author of *Indian Cinema and Indian Life*, 1980. **Essays:** Kapoor; Satyajit Ray; Roy; Sen.

KOVACS, Katherine Singer. Essayist. Formerly Assistant Professor, Department of Comparative Literature, University of Southern California, Los Angeles, editor of *Humanities in Society* and member of the executive committee, *Quarterly Review of Film Studies*. Died 1989. **Essays:** Bardem; García Berlanga; Saura.

LANZA, Joseph. Essayist. Freelance writer. Author of *Fragile Geometry: The Films, Philosophy and Misadventures of Nicolas Roeg*, 1989. Contributor to *Kirkus Reviews*, *Performing Arts Journal*, *ReSearch* and *Forum*. **Essay:** Roeg.

LIMBACHER, James L. Essayist. Audio-Visual Librarian, Dearborn, Michigan Department of Libraries, 1955–83, National President, American Federation of Film Societies, 1962–65, and Educational Film Library Association, 1966–70; host of the TV series *Shadows on the Wall* and *The Screening Room*. Author of *Four Aspects of the Film*, 1968; *Film Music: From Violins to Video*, 1974; *Haven't I Seen You Somewhere Before?*, 1979; *Sexuality in World Cinema*, 1983; and *Feature Films on 8mm, 16mm and Video*, 7 editions. **Essay:** Markopoulos.

LIPPE, Richard. Essayist. Lecturer in Film at Atkinsonn College, York University, Ontario. On the Editorial Board of *CineAction!*. **Essay:** Silver.

LOCKHART, Kimball. Essayist. Member of the faculty, Department of Romance Studies, Cornell University, Ithaca, New York. Founding editor, *Enclitic*, 1977–80, and member of editorial board, *Diacritics*, since 1978. **Essay:** Antonioni.

LORENZ, Janet E. Essayist. Associate Editor and Film Critic, *Z Channel Magazine*, since 1984. Assistant Supervisor, University of Southern California Cinema Research Library, Los Angeles,

1979–82, and film critic, *SelecTV Magazine*, 1980–84. **Essay:** Losey.

LOWRY, Ed. Essayist. Formerly Assistant Professor of Film Studies, Southern Illinois University, Carbondale. Contributor to various film periodicals. Died 1987. **Essays:** Aldrich; Anger; Minnelli; Stahl; Warhol.

MacCANN, Richard Dyer. Adviser. Professor of Film, University of Iowa, Iowa City, from 1970 (Emeritus professor since 1986). Editor, *Cinema Journal*, 1967–76. Author of *Hollywood in Transition*, 1962; *The People's Films: A Political History of U.S. Government Motion Pictures*, 1973; *The First Tycoons*, 1987; and *The First Film Makers*, 1989. Editor of *Film and Society*, 1964; *Film: A Montage of Theories*, 1966; *The New Film Index*, 1975; and *Cinema Examined*, 1982.

MACNAB, G.C. Essayist. Freelance writer, researcher, and filmmaker, London. Author of the forthcoming *J. Arthur Rank and the British Film Industry*. **Essays:** De Antonio; Marcel Ophuls; Oshima; Rivette; Rudolph; Schrader; Tarkovsky.

MANCINI, Elaine. Essayist. Has taught film at the College of Staten Island, and at St. John's University, New York. Author of *The Films of Luchino Visconti: A Reference Guide*, and the forthcoming *The Struggles of the Italian Film Industry During Fascism*. **Essays:** De Santis; Gallone; Lattuada; Monicelli; Petri; Risi.

MANVELL, Roger. Essayist. Formerly Professor of Film, Boston University. Director, British Film Academy, London, 1947–59, and a Governor and Head of Department of Film History, London Film School, until 1974; Bingham Professor of the Humanities, University of Louisville, 1973. Editor, *Penguin Film Review*, 1946–49, and the Pelican annual *Cinema*, 1950–52; Associate Editor, *New Humanist*, 1968–75, and Director, Rationalist Press, London, from 1966; Editor-in-Chief, *International Encyclopaedia of Film*, 1972. Author of *Film*, 1944; *The Animated Film*, 1954; *The Film and the Public*, 1955; *On the Air*, 1955; *The Technique of Film Music*, 1957, 1976; *The Technique of Film Animation*, with John Halas, 1959; *The Living Screen*, 1961; *Design in Motion*, with John Halas, 1962; *What is a Film?*, 1965; *New Cinema in Europe*, 1966; *This Age of Communication*, 1967; *New Cinema in the U.S.A.*, 1968; *New Cinema in Britain*, 1969; *Art in Movement*, 1970; *The German Cinema*, with Heinrich Fraenkel, 1971; *Shakespeare and the Film*, 1971; *Films and the Second World War*, 1975; *Love Goddesses of the Movies*, 1975; *Theatre and Film*, 1979; *Art and Animation: Halas and Batchelor, 1940–1980*, 1980; *Ingmar Bergman*, 1980; *Images of Madness: The Portrayal of Insanity in the Feature Film*, with Michael Fleming, 1985; also novels, biographies of theatrical personalities and of personalities of the Third Reich. Died 1987. **Essays:** Bergman; Méliès; Sjöström; Stiller; von Stroheim.

MARCHETTI, Gina. Essayist. Assistant Professor, University of Maryland, College Park, since 1986. Research Editor for *Asian Cinema* and a staff editor on *Jump Cut*. Contributor to *Current Research in Film*, *Afterimage*, and *Journal of Film and Video*. **Essays:** Makavajev; Xie Jin.

MAST, Gerald. Adviser and Essayist. Formerly professor of English and General Studies in the Humanities, University of Chicago. Member of the faculty, Richmond College, New York, 1967–78. Author of *A Short History of the Movies*, 1971, 3rd edition 1981; *The Comic Mind: Comedy and the Movies*, 1974, 1979; *Film/Cinema/Movie: A Theory of Experience*, 1977, 1982; and *Howard Hawks, Storyteller*, 1982. Editor of *Film Theory and Criticism: Introductory Readings*, with Marshall Cohen, 1974, 1979; and *Movies in Our Midst: Documents in the Cultural History of Film in Ameica*, 1982. Died 1987. **Essays:** Chaplin; Hawks; Keaton; Sennett; Truffaut.

MERHAUT, Václav. Essayist. Film historian and member of staff, Film Archives of Czechoslovakia, Prague. Author of *Actors and Actresses of the Italian Cinema*. **Essays:** Cacoyannis; Donner; Gaál; Kachyňa; Kawalerowicz; Szabó.

MERRITT, Russell. Essayist. Professor, University of Wisconsin, Madison. **Essay:** Griffith.

MICHAELS, Lloyd. Essayist. Professor of English, Allegheny

College, Meadville, Pennsylvania. Editor of *Film Criticism* since 1977. Author of *Elia Kazan: A Guide to References and Resources*, 1985. **Essay:** Kazan.

MILICIA, Joseph. Essayist. Has taught at Colgate University, Stevens Institute, Northwestern University, and the University of Wisconsin at Sheboygan. **Essays:** Kasdan; Wenders.

MILLER, Norman. Essayist. Journalist and author, London. Author of forthcoming *Toontown: Cartoons, Comedy and Creativity*, and contributor to a variety of periodicals. **Essays:** Demme; Gilliam.

MONTY, Ib. Adviser and Essayist. Director of Det Danske Filmmuseum, Copenhagen, since 1960. Literary and Film critic for the newspaper *Morgenavisen Jyllands-Posten*, since 1958. Editor-in-Chief of the film periodical *Kosmorama*, 1960–67. Author of *Leonardo da Vinci*, 1953; editor, with Morten Piil, *Se-det-er film I-iii* (anthology of articles on film), 1964–66, and *TV Broadcasts on Films and Filmmakers*, 1972. **Essays:** Blom; Christensen; Dreyer; Gad; Henning-Jensen; Holger-Madsen; Roos.

MORRISON, James E. Essayist. Lecturer in the English Department, North Carolina State University, Raleigh. Contributor to *New Orleans Review*, *Centennial Review* and *Film Criticism*. **Essay:** Ivory.

MRAZ, John. Adviser and Essayist. Researcher, Center for the Study of Contemporary History, University of Puebla, Mexico, since 1984. Distinguished Visiting Professor, Art and Latin American Studies, University of Connecticut, 1990. Visiting Professor, History, University of California, Santa Cruz, 1988. Coordinator of Graphic History, Center for the Historical Study of the Mexican Labor Movement. 1981–83. Contributor to *Jump Cut*. **Essays:** Alvarez; De Fuentes; Diaz; Diegues; Fernández; Manuel Octavio Gómez; Sara Gómez; Leduc; Pereira dos Santos; Rocha; Solanas and Getino; Solas.

MURPHY, William T. Essayist. Chief, Motion Picture, Sound and Video Branch, National Archives, Washington, D.C., since 1976. Author of *Robert Flaherty: A Guide to References and Resources*, 1978. **Essay:** Flaherty.

NARDUCY, Ray. Essayist. Film critic and historian, Chicago. **Essays:** Ashby; George Roy Hill; John Sturges.

NASTAV, Dennis. Essayist. Critic and documentary filmmaker. **Essays:** Pagnol; Rohmer; Tanner.

NEWMAN, Kim. Essayist. Freelance writer and broadcaster. Author of *Nightmare Movies*, 1988, and *Wild West Movies*, 1990. Contributor to *Sight and Sound*, *Empire*, *New Musical Express*, and other periodicals, and Film Critic for *Box Office* on Channel 4, London. Also a writer of fiction. **Essays:** Carpenter; Craven; Cronenberg; Hughes; Lynch; Waters.

NICHOLS, Bill. Essayist. Professor and head, Department of Film Studies, Queen's University, Kingston, Ontario, since 1976. Author of *Ideology and the Image*, 1981, and *Newsreel: Documentary Filmmaking on the American Left*, 1981; editor of *Movies and Methods*, 1976. **Essays:** Dmytryk; Stanley Kramer.

NOTAR, Clea H. Essayist. Freelance writer and lecturer. Contributor to *Cinema Canada* and other periodicals, and broadcaster for the Canadian Broadcasting Corporation. **Essays:** Jutra; Lefebvre.

OBALIL, Linda J. Essayist. Assistant, Special Effects Unit, Dreamscape, Bruce Cohn Curtis Productions/Bella Productions, since 1983. **Essays:** McLeod; Porter; Schoedsack; Ulmer.

O'BRIEN, Daniel. Essayist. Freelance writer and critic, London. **Essay:** Lester.

O'KANE, John. Essayist. Film critic and historian, Minneapolis. **Essay:** Fassbinder.

O'LEARY, Liam. Adviser and Essayist. Film Viewer, Radio Telefis Eireann, Dublin, 1966–86. Director, Liam O'Leary Film Archives, Dublin, since 1976. Producer, Abbey Theatre, 1944. Director of the Film History Cycle at the National Film Theatre, London, and Acquisitions Officer, National Film Archive, London, 1953–66; Co-founder, 1936, and Honorary Secretary, 1936–44, Irish Film Society. Director of the films, *Our Country*, 1948; *Mr. Careless*, 1950; and *Portrait of Dublin*, 1951. Author of *Invitation to the Film*, 1945; *The Silent Cinema*, 1965; and *Rex Ingram, Master of the Silent Cinema*, 1980. **Essays:** Dieterle; Dupont; Feyder; Ingram; Olcott; Pabst; Paradzhanov; Pastrone; Protazanov; Maurice Tourneur; Volkov; Wiene.

OPELA, Vladimir. Essayist. Film historian, Czechoslovakian Film Archives, Prague. **Essays:** Frič; Jireš; Schorm.

PALMER. R. Barton. Essayist. Professor of English, Georgia State University, since 1973. Editor of *Studies in the Literary Imagination*. **Essay:** Mazursky.

PEÑA, Richard. Adviser and Essayist. Director, New York Film Festival. Formerly Director, Film Centre at the School of the Art Institute of Chicago. **Essays:** Bellochio; Imamura; Mauro.

PETLEY, Julian. Essayist. Lecturer in Communications at Brunel University. Contributor to *Sight and Sound, Monthly Film Bulletin* and *Broadcast*. **Essays:** Heifitz; Kadár; Käutner; Loach; Sjöberg.

PETRIE, Duncan J. Essayist. Research Officer at the British Film Institute, London. Author of *Creativity and Constraint in the British Film Industry*, 1991. **Essays:** Forsyth; Jarman; Jordan.

PHILLIPS, Gene D., S.J. Essayist. Professor of English, Loyola University, Chicago (joined faculty 1970). Contributing Editor, *Literatures/Film Quarterly*, since 1977. Author of several books, including *Hemingway and Film*, 1980; *John Schlesinger*, 1981; *George Cukor*, 1982; *Alfred Hitchcock*, 1984; *Fiction, Film, and F. Scott Fitzgerald*, 1986; *Fiction, Film, and Faulkner*, 1988; and *Major Directors of the American and British Cinema*, 1989. **Essays:** Coppola; Cukor; Kubrick; Reed; Russell; Schlesinger.

PICK, Zuzana Mirjam. Essayist. Assistant Professor, Film Studies Department, Carleton University, Ottawa, since 1976. Editor of *Latin American Filmmakers and the Third Cinema*, 1978. **Essay:** Ruiz.

POLAN, Dana B. Essayist. Professor of English, University of Pittsburgh. **Essays:** Fuller; Tashlin.

PORTON, Richard. Essayist. Graduate student in Film Studies, New York University. **Essay:** Goretta.

RABINOVITZ, Lauren. Adviser and Essayist. Associate Professor of American Studies and Communication Studies, University of Iowa, since 1986. **Essays:** Clarke; Wieland.

RACHEVA, Maria. Adviser and Essayist. Selector of films for the International Film Festival, Munich, since 1983. Teacher of Film History, High School for Cinema, Sofia, Bulgaria, 1974–81. Editor of the cultural review *Westermanns Monatschefte*, Munich, 1981–82. Author of *Presentday Bulgarian Cinema*, 1970; *Andrzej Wajda*, with Klaus Eder, 1980; and *Kino: For and Against*, 1986. **Essays:** Kluge; Kovács; Staudte; Weiss.

REYNOLDS, Herbert. Essayist. Historian and Project Coordinator, Museum of Modern Art Department of Film, New York City, since 1981. Consultant, American Federation of Arts Film Program, since 1982. **Essay:** Schlöndorff.

RUBINSTEIN, E. Essayist. Formerly coordinator of the Program in Cinema Studies, College of Staten Island, City University of New York. Author of *Filmguide to "The General"*, 1973. Died 1988. **Essay:** Buñuel.

SAELI, Marie. Essayist. Instructor in English and Lecturer in Film Theory, Triton College, River Grove, Illinois, since 1983. **Essays:** Anderson; Friedkin; Lucas.

SCHADE, W. Curtis. Essayist. Director for Admissions, Westover School, Connecticut. **Essay:** Sembene.

SCHIFF, Lillian. Essayist. Freelance film critic and consultant, New York. Author of *Getting Started in Filmmaking*, 1978. **Essays:** Akerman; Leacock; Maysles; Scola; Tavianis.

SCHUTH, H. Wayne. Essayist. Professor of Drama and Communications, University of New Orleans. Author of *Mike Nichols*, 1978. Member of the Board of Directors, University Film and Video Association, 1983–85. **Essay:** Sucksdorff.

SELIG, Michael. Essayist. Assistant Professor, University of Vermont, since 1983. Contributor to *Film Reader, Jump Cut*, and *Journal of Popular Film and Television*. **Essay:** King Vidor.

SHIPMAN, David. Essayist. Film historian and critic, London. Author of *The Great Movie Stars: The Golden Years*, 1970, 3rd ed., 1989; *The Great Movie Stars: The International Years*, 1972, 3rd ed., 1989; *Brando*, 1974; *The Story of Cinema: From the Beginnings to Gone With The Wind*, 1982; *The Good Film and Video Guide*, 1984, 1986; *The Story of Cinema: From Citizen Kane to the Present Day*, 1984; *A Pictorial History of Science Fiction Films*, 1985; *Caught in the Act: Sex and Eroticism in the Cinema*, 1985; *Movie Talk: Who Said What about Whom in the Movies*, 1988; *Marlon Brando*, 1989; *The Great Movie Stars: The Independent Years*, 1991. **Essays:** Bauer; Camerini; Kinugasa; Naruse.

SIEGLOHR, Ulrike. Essayist. Graduate student, University of East Anglia, and Film Lecturer. **Essays:** Ottinger; Schroeter.

SILET, Charles L.P. Essayist. Professor of English, Iowa State University, Ames. Author of *Lindsay Anderson: A Guide to References and Resources*, 1979, and co-editor of *The Pretend Indians: Images of American Indians in the Movies*, 1980. Contributor to *Quarterly Review of Film, Film Heritage, Journal of Popular Film*, and *Magill's Cinema Annual*. **Essays:** Beresford; Jancsó; Lang.

SIMMON, Scott. Essayist. Film Programmer, Mary Pickford Theatre, Library of Congress, Washington, D.C., since 1983. Contributor to *Film Comment, Journal of popular Film and Video*, and *Literature/Film Quarterly*, and co-author of *King Vidor—American*, 1989. **Essay:** Boetticher.

SITNEY, P. Adams. Adviser and Essayist. Lecturer, Princeton University. Formerly Director of Library and Publications at Anthology Film Archives. Author of *Film Culture Reader; Essential Cinema; The Avant-Garde Film*; and *Visionary Film*. **Essays:** Brakhage; Bresson; Mekas; Olmi; Snow.

SKVORECKÝ, Josef. Essayist. Professor of English and Film, University of Toronto, Canada, since 1969. Member, Central Committee, Czechoslovakian Film and Television Artists Union, 1967–68. Author of *All the Bright Young Men and Women: A Personal History of the Czech Cinema*, 1972; *Jiri Menzel and the History of 'Closely Watched Trains'*, 1982. Also a novelist: works include: *Miss Silver's Past*, 1975; *The Bass Saxophone*, 1977; *The Engineer of Human Souls*, 1984; and *The Miracle Game*, 1990. **Essays:** Chytilová; Forman; Menzel.

SLIDE, Anthony. Adviser and Essayist. Freelance writer. Associate Film Archivist, American Film Institute, 1972–75; Resident Film Historian, Academy of Motion Picture Arts and Sciences, 1975–80. Author of *Early American Cinema*, 1970; *The Griffith Actresses*, 1973; *The Films of D.W. Griffith*, with Edward Wagenknecht, 1975; *The Idols of Silence*, 1976; *The Big V: A History of the Vitagraph Company*, 1976; *Early Woman Directors*, 1977; *Aspects of American Film History Prior to 1920*, 1978; *Films on Film History*, 1979; *The Kindergarten of the Movies: A History of the Fine Arts Company*, 1980; *Fifty Great American Silent Films 1912–1920*, with Edward Wagenknecht, 1980; *The Vaudevillians*, 1981; *A Collector's Guide to Movie Memoribilia*, 1983; *Fifty Classic British Films 1932–1982*, 1985; *The American Film Industry: A Historical Dictionary*, 1986; and *The International Film Industry: A Historical Dictionary*, 1989. Editor of *Selected Film Criticism 1896–1950*, 7 volumes, and the Scarecrow Press

Filmmakers Series. **Essays:** Blackton; Brenon; Browning; Fejös; Florey; Hepworth; Howard; Neilan; Pearson; Reisz; Saville; Weber; Whale; Wilcox.

SMALL, Edward S. Essayist. Director of Film Studies, University of Missouri, Columbia, since 1983. Executive Vice-President, University Film and Video Association, 1983–86. **Essays:** Emshwiller; Le Grice; Vanderbeek.

SMOODIN, Eric. Essayist. Lecturer, Department of Literature, American University, Washington, D.C. Contributor to *Film Studies Annual* and *Journal of the University Film* and *Video Association*. **Essays:** De Mille; Mankiewicz; Preston Sturges; Vigo.

STARR, Cecile. Essayist. Freelance writer, lecturer and filmmaker. Film critic, *The Saturday Review*, New York, 1949–59. Author of *Discovering the Movies*, 1972, and, with Robert Russett, *Experimental Animation*, 1976. **Essay:** Dulac.

TABERY, Karel . Essayist. Film researcher and historian, France. Historian/Archivist, Czechoslovakian Film Archives, Prague, 1974–82. **Essay:** Fábri.

TAYLOR, Richard. Essayist. Senior Lecturer in Politics and Russian Studies at the University College of Swansea. Author of *The Politics of Soviet Cinema, 1917–29*, 1979; *Film Propaganda: Soviet Russia and Nazi Germany*, 1979; *The Film Factory: Russian and Soviet Cinema in Documents, 1896–1939* (co-editor), 1988; and editor of English-language edition of Eisenstein's *Selected Works*, 1988 onwards. **Essays:** Barnet; Eisenstein; Kuleshov.

TELOTTE, J.P. Essayist. Associate Professor of English, Georgia Institute of Technology. Author of *Dreams of Darkness: Fantasy and the Films of Val Lewton*, and *Voices in the Dark: The Narrative Patterns of Film Noir*. Member of the Editorial Board, *Film Criticism* and *Literature/Film Quarterly*, and co-editor, *Post Script*. **Essay:** Polanski.

THOMAS, Nicholas. Essayist. Editor of the *International Dictionary of Films and Filmmakers*. **Essays:** Asquith; Stevenson.

THORPE, Frances. Adviser. Formerly Librarian, British Film Institute, London, and editor of *International Directory of Film and TV Documentation Centres*.

TOMLINSON, Doug. Essayist. Associate Professor of Film Studies, Montclair State College, New Jersey. Principal researcher for *Voices of Film Experience*, edited by Jay Leyda, 1977, and editor of *Actors on Acting for the Screen*, 1989. **Essays:** Berkeley; Bolognini; Passer; Rossen.

TUDOR, Andrew. Essayist. Head of the Department of Sociology, University of York. Author of *Theories of Film: Image and Influence*, and *Monsters and Mad Scientists*. **Essays:** Boorman; Walter Hill; Peckinpah; Siegel; Wiseman.

URGOŠÍKOVÁ, Blažena. Essayist. Film historian, Czechoslovakian Film Archives, Prague. Author of *History of Science Fiction Films*. **Essays:** Kieślowski; Munk; Wajda.

VASUDEVAN, Ravi. Adviser and Essayist. Graduate Student at the University of East Anglia. Formerly Film Critic of *The Sunday Observer*, Delhi. **Essays:** Dutt; Kaul; Mehboob Khan; Phalke.

VERDAASDONK, Dorothee. Essayist. Lecturer in Film and Television, Utrecht University, since 1982. Secretary, Department of Film, Dutch National Arts Council, 1975–82. Author of *The First Wave*, 1983; editor of *Bert Haanstra*, 1983. **Essays:** Haanstra; Ivens.

VINCENDEAU, Ginette. Essayist. Lecturer in Film Studies at the University of Warwick. Co-editor of *French Film: Texts and Contexts*, 1989. **Essay:** Pialat.

WALKER, Mark. Essayist. Teacher and freelance writer, Maryland. Author of *Writing for Television*, 1988, and the forthcoming *Vietnam Veteran Films*. **Essays:** Badham; Zemeckis.

WEINBERG, Herman. Essayist. Teacher of Film History, City College, New York. Columnist, *Films in Review*. Author of *Josef von Sternberg: A Critical Study*; *The Lubitsch Touch*; *Saint Cinema*; *The Complete "Greed"*; *The Complete "Wedding March"*; *Stroheim: A Pictorial Record of His Nine Films*; and others. **Essay:** D'Arrast.

WELSH, James M. Essayist. Associate Professor of English, Salisbury State University. Editor, *Literature/Film Quarterly*. Author of *His Majesty the American: The Films of Douglas Fairbanks Sr.*, 1977; *Abel Gance*, 1978; *Peter Watkins: A Guide to References and Resources*, 1986; and the forthcoming *Abel Gance and the Seventh Art*. **Essays:** Levinson; Richardson; Zinnemann.

WEST, Dennis. Essayist. Associate Professor, University of Idaho, Moscow, since 1981. Director, Indiana University Film Studies Program, 1976–77. Contributor on Latin American and Spanish cinema to *Latin American Research Review*, *Cineaste*, and *New Scholar*, and others. **Essays:** Gutiérrez Alea; Guzmán; Hermosillo; Sanjinés.

WHITE, M.B. Essayist. Assistant Professor, Department of Radio/TV/Film, Northwestern University, Evanston, Illinois. Contributor to *Enclitic* and other periodicals. **Essays:** Autant-Lara; Duras; Resnais; Straub and Huillet.

WILLIAMS, Colin. Essayist. Researcher and writer, London. **Essay:** Walters.

WINE, Bill. Essayist. Assistant Professor of Communications, LaSalle College, Philadelphia, since 1981. Film, Theatre and Television Critic, *Camden Courier-Post*, 1974–81. **Essay:** Cassavetes.

WINNING, Rob. Essayist. Author and film scholar, Pittsburgh. **Essay:** Jarmusch.

WOLFF, Jessica R. Essayist. Freelance researcher, writer and editor, New York City. **Essay:** Rainer.

WOOD, Robin. Adviser and Essayist. Professor of Film Study, Department of Fine Arts, Atkinson College, York University, Toronto, 1977–90. Member of the Film Studies Department, Queen's University, Kingston, Ontario, 1969–72, and University of Warwick, England, 1973–77. Author of *Hitchcock's Films*, 1965; *Howard Hawks*, 1977; *Arthur Penn*, 1968; *Ingmar Bergman*, 1969; *Antonioni* (co-author), 1970; *Claude Chabrol* (co-author), 1971; *The Apu Trilogy of Satyajit Ray*, 1971; *Personal Views: Explorations in Film*, 1976; *The American Nightmare; Essays on the Horror Film (co-author)*, 1979; *Hollywood from Vietnam to Reagan*, 1985; and *Hitchcock's Films Revisited*, 1989. Took early retirement to devote himself to fiction, 1990. Novels: *That Last and Fatal Time*, 1990; *I Remember . . .*, 1991.